You're *looking* at
The Good
Pub Guide.

2013

The Good Pub Guide 2013

Edited by Alisdair Aird and Fiona Stapley

Managing Editor: Karen Fick
Associate Editor: Patrick Stapley
Editorial Assistance: Fiona Wright

EBURY PRESS
LONDON

Please send reports on pubs to:

The Good Pub Guide
FREEPOST TN1569, Wadhurst, East Sussex, TN5 7BR

or **feedback@goodguides.com**

or visit our website: **www.thegoodpubguide.co.uk**

If you would like to advertise in the next edition of *The Good Pub Guide*, please email **goodpubguide@tbs-ltd.co.uk**

10 9 8 7 6 5 4 3 2 1

Published in 2012 by Ebury Press, an imprint of Ebury Publishing

A Random House Group Company

Text © Random House Group Ltd 2012
Maps © PerroGraphics 2012

Alisdair Aird and Fiona Stapley have asserted their right to be identified as the authors of this Work in accordance with the Copyright, Designs and Patents Act 1988

The Random House Group Limited Reg. No. 954009

Addresses for companies within the Random House Group can be found at www.randomhouse.co.uk

A CIP catalogue record for this book is available from the British Library

The Random House Group Limited supports The Forest Stewardship Council (FSC®), the leading international forest certification organisation. Our books carrying the FSC label are printed on FSC® certified paper. FSC is the only forest certification scheme endorsed by the leading environmental organisations, including Greenpeace. Our paper procurement policy can be found at www.randomhouse. co.uk/environment

To buy books by your favourite authors and register for offers visit www. randomhouse.co.uk

Typeset from authors' files by Jerry Goldie Graphic Design
Project manager and copy editor Ruth Jarvis
Proofreader John Pym

Printed and bound by CPI Group (UK) Ltd, Croydon, CR0 4YY

ISBN 9780091948719

Cover design by Two Associates
Cover photographs reproduced by kind permission of the pubs:
Front: Rose & Crown, Trent, Dorset; *Spine:* Olde Coach House, Ashby St Ledgers, Northants; *Back top left:* The Queens Head, Kirkby la Thorpe, Lincs; *Back top right:* Barbury Inn, Swindon, Wilts; *Back bottom left:* Shurlock Inn, Shurlock Row, Berks; *Back bottom right:* Inn on the Green, Ingham, Lincs

Contents

Introduction

At last the pub tide is turning. Since 2008, things have been pretty grim for most pubs, with many closing – even some top food pubs. But this year we have seen clear signs of a turnaround. Most strikingly, the mood among the publicans themselves is changing. Each year, we speak to many hundreds of landlords and landladies. This year, for the first time since the early 2000s, most have been more upbeat – even if still keeping their fingers crossed.

It's us, the customers, who are fuelling this more optimistic mood. Good pubs are no longer short of good customers – as they certainly were a couple of years ago. And what has kept us coming, in these tough economic times, is **sheer value**.

Knowing how vital it now is to give us value, publicans have been pulling out all the stops. Despite their own rising costs, they have done all they can to hold down prices. While it is true that the price of a good pub meal has on average crept up a little, this 1% increase is less than half the general rate of price inflation. What's more, about half of our pubs have kept the price of their most popular dishes at, or even below, last year's prices. **Over one in four have actually cut the price this year.** This is obviously great news.

All sorts of enterprising schemes have helped to please customers. **Special deals** on price, quite rare a few years ago, are now common: two- or three-course set menus, bargain steak, curry or fish and chips nights, two-for-the-price-of-one offers, early-bird menus. A few years ago, Sunday was the pub chef's day off. Now, Sunday lunch is many a pub's busiest mealtime. Then there are wine or beer tasting evenings with guest speakers, theme nights, food festivals celebrating local seasonal specialities from asparagus to lobster, and so on.

Even with all these deals, landlords and landladies have told us that in their determination to keep prices down they have had to absorb cost increases personally – in effect taking a cut in their own pay. But they certainly haven't scrimped on staff pay, and this has shown in what we'd say are **higher standards of service**. We have had fewer complaints from readers about service this year than we can ever remember in the *Guide*'s history. What's more, in our anonymous inspections of pubs, we have this year found unfailingly good service, always with a good welcome. This is a first for us.

The Plus Pubs

A great many pubs are now more than just pubs. We call these the Plus Pubs, the places that go the extra mile, adding something you wouldn't normally expect from a pub.

At the most basic level, this means being **open when customers find it useful**, and not just at lunchtime and in the evening.

Now, more than half of all good pubs stay open all day every day, and another quarter stay open all day for part of the week, usually weekends. A quarter serve some sort of food all day, at least on some days. But with all of these, 'all day' means from when they open – more than one in three 'all day' pubs in fact don't open their doors before midday.

Pubs that do open earlier are a boon to anyone hoping for a morning coffee. About one in three good pubs open at 11. And the real heroes are those few pubs – only about one in 15 – which open before then, with a growing number of these serving breakfasts.

Many pubs have now cottoned on to the way people like dropping in for tea in the afternoon. Pubs which now make something of a speciality of **cream teas** are the Egerton Arms at Chelford (Cheshire), Pandora near Mylor Bridge (Cornwall), Cricketers at Clavering (Essex), Kilcot Inn, Kilcot, and Feathered Nest at Nether Westcote (Gloucestershire), Hurdles near Droxford (Hampshire), and Angel in Stoke-by-Nayland (Suffolk).

This year our readers' favourite pub 'find' has been the combination of **pub plus shop** – farm shop, delicatessen, or village stores. The big sellers have been the pubs' own jams, chutneys and sometimes bread, and a few pubs also sell their own ready-made meals. Some favourite examples are the Swan at Inkpen (Berkshire), Eagle & Child at Bispham Green (Lancashire), Jolly Farmers at Buckland (Surrey), Fleece at Addingham and Kings Arms at Sandhutton (Yorkshire), and Bunch of Grapes in Pontypridd (Wales).

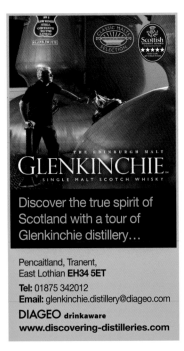
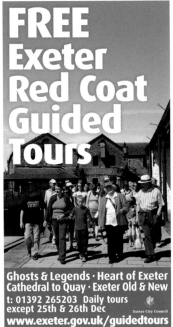

The year of the dog

Dogs in pubs have never had it so good. The great majority of good pubs welcome dogs – by our count, more than eight out of ten, usually in the bar. But one in five are happy to allow dogs in any part of the pub, and that includes many of the very foodiest pubs. Four out of ten pubs with bedrooms let people staying bring their dogs, too. Quite a few pubs go out of their way to welcome dogs particularly warmly. Bowls of water are now the general rule, but a lot of pubs add biscuits or other treats – a few even do menus for dogs. We'd single out the Red Lion at East Chisenbury (Wiltshire) who make their own special treats, the Albion in Chester (Cheshire) which often has a sausage or two for hopeful mutts, and the Beckford Arms at Fonthill Gifford (also in Wiltshire) who keep bones for visiting dogs, and even have a dog bath out in the garden.

We are celebrating in early 2013 by bringing out a new edition of our *Good Guide to Dog Friendly Pubs, Hotels and B&Bs.*

A new venture is the pub **cooking class** or demonstration, as offered at the Bell in Walberswick (Suffolk), Fleece at Addingham and Durham Ox at Crayke (Yorkshire), and Bunch of Grapes in Pontypridd (Wales).

With more and more **cycle trails** bringing people to pubs on two wheels, some pubs now make special efforts to welcome cyclists. A prime example is the Kilcot Inn (Gloucestershire), owned by Weston's, the cider people, with its spanking new cycle shed.

The best pub group

The doyen of the smaller independent pub groups is unquestionably Brunning & Price, which has more than two dozen pubs with consistently high standards of food, drink and service, and which can be relied on for individual décor in buildings of real character. They are certainly the standard-setters.

Several smaller and often newer groups are now making their own mark, with great pubs that tick all the right boxes. These are the ones which have made the deepest impression on us this year: Ainscoughs up in the North West, Cheshire Cat mostly in Cheshire, Flying Kiwi in Norfolk, Individual Inns mainly in Yorkshire, Provenance Inns also in Yorkshire, Salisbury Pubs mainly in Buckinghamshire, Ribble Valley mainly in Lancashire and Thurlby Group in Lincolnshire. Almost invariably, each of these depends for its success on a small team built around the vision and vigour of one or two individuals.

It's a great achievement that Brunning & Price, with considerably more pubs than any of these smaller groups, still preserves the individuality and all-round merit of their pubs. Brunning & Price takes the award of **Pub Group of the Year 2013**.

Value in your glass?

In England, the North/South divide is stark: in Surrey and London, the price of a pint of beer is typically around £3.50, but in the Midlands and the North pints average under £3. Head to Staffordshire for exceptional beer bargains – our pubs there charged an average of only £2.56 for a pint.

Wherever you are, **pubs which brew their own beer** offer big savings. In our survey, the two dozen own-brew pubs charged an average of £2.64 a pint – saving nearly 50p compared with the overall national average of £3.11.

The top ten own-brew pubs, each outstanding in its way, are the Driftwood Spars at Trevaunance Cove (Cornwall), Hawkshead Beer Hall at Staveley and Watermill at Ings (Cumbria), Church Inn at Uppermill (Lancashire), Grainstore in Oakham (Leicestershire and Rutland), Keelman in Newburn (Northumbria), Mill Green at Edwardstone (Suffolk), New Inn at Cropton (Yorkshire), and Old Inn at Gairloch and Fox & Hounds in Houston (Scotland). A great favourite with readers, and doing so well that it is having to expand its brewhouse, moving it across the river, the Watermill at Ings is **Own Brew Pub of the Year 2013**.

The Watermill and the Grainstore both have a great range of other breweries' ales, too. Another pub which brews its own, the Fat Cat in Norwich (Norfolk), also has a fantastic choice of guest beers. These would certainly be in any top ten choice of beer pubs. Our own list would add the Bhurtpore at Aston and Mill in Chester (Cheshire), Old Spot in Dursley (Gloucestershire), Malt Shovel in Northampton (Northamptonshire), Crown at Churchill (Somerset), Fat Cat in Ipswich (Suffolk), and Nags Head in Malvern (Worcestershire). With dozens of bottled beers from around the world, interesting imported lager, and a staggering changing choice of well over two dozen ales from handpumps or tapped from the cask, Colin Keatley's Fat Cat in Norwich is **Beer Pub of the Year 2013**.

All these pubs show off the richness of the variety of beers brewed in the UK – there are now literally hundreds of brewers, from one-man operations turning out a barrel or two a week through regional favourites to the international giants. It was over 20 years ago down in Devon that we first came across a nicely named new beer called Otter – and can still remember that first taste. With a well balanced range of several varieties, all brewed using water from their own spring, it has become quite widely available. For its quality, its price is attractive, generally 10p or 15p a pint less than the usual, and has been held steadier than most. About one in 25 of good pubs – and a far higher proportion in the West Country – now stock Otter as their lowest-price beer. Otter is **Brewery of the Year 2013**.

With a largely Scottish editorial team, we make no apology for our special interest in whisky. Luckily, a great many pubs share that interest. For example, Brunning & Price pubs usually have around 80 different whiskies – their Old Orchard in Harefield (Outer London) and Pant-yr-Ochain in Gresford (Wales) have perhaps the best choice. For a top ten list we'd add to these two the Bhurtpore at Aston and Old Harkers Arms in Chester (Cheshire), Nobody Inn at Doddiscombsleigh

(Devon), Red Lion in Weymouth (Dorset), Sandpiper in Leyburn (Yorkshire), and Bon Accord in Glasgow, Fox & Hounds in Houston, Stein Inn and Sligachan Hotel both on Skye (Scotland). Yes, that does add up to one over the ten – easily done with whisky! The Sligachan Hotel, with a different whisky for nearly every day of the year, is **Whisky Pub of the Year 2013**.

If a pub doesn't have a very large number of wine-drinking customers, it makes sense for it to have just a small choice by the glass – to avoid tired wines in bottles that have been left open too long. Quite a lot of good pubs take that line, but choose the wines with care so as to give a decent if not necessarily adventurous choice. Even better for wine lovers are the pubs with landlords and landladies who take real pleasure in offering an unusual range of wines by the glass, and manage to make sure that they are kept fresh. Our top ten wine pubs all have an extraordinary range, in which even the most jaded wine buffs will find something to surprise them: the Old Bridge in Huntingdon (Cambridgeshire), Harris Arms at Portgate (Devon), Bell in Horndon-on-the-Hill (Essex), Yew Tree at Clifford's Mesne and Wheatsheaf in Northleach (Gloucestershire), Queens Head at Corton Denham and Woods in Dulverton (Somerset), Crown at Stoke-by-Nayland (Suffolk), Vine Tree at Norton (Wiltshire), and Inn at West End (Surrey). For the third year running Patrick Groves's Woods at Dulverton walks away with the top award of **Wine Pub of the Year 2013**; what an amazing pub that is for the wine lover.

Pubs with real heart in town and country

Quite a number of Britain's best pubs are places that seem in a time warp, unchanged for decades, and often run by the same family for generations. These are not places for everyone, and can seem a bit on the stark side to anyone expecting plush banquettes and fancy meals. But they are an absolute delight for people who want real character, with no pretentions. Our top ten unspoilt pubs are the Barley Mow at Kirk Ireton (Derbyshire), Rugglestone near Widecombe (Devon), Digby Tap in Sherborne and Square & Compass at Worth Matravers (Dorset), Viper at Mill Green (Essex), Harrow at Steep (Hampshire), Carpenters Arms at Walterstone (Herefordshire), Crown at Churchill and Rose & Crown, Huish Episcopi (Somerset), and Swan at Birlingham (Worcestershire). Full of individuality, the cottagey Crown at Churchill is **Unspoilt Pub of the Year 2013**.

Don't be surprised at the fact that in several of those pubs the lavatories are outside. What has surprised us this year is the very high standard of some outside lavatories: instead of the cobwebs, spiders and less mentionable features that used to be the norm, you can now find the smartest décor and fittings. Two memorable examples are the Tram at Eardisley (Herefordshire) and Red Lion in Alnmouth (Northumbria): the gents' at the Tram at Eardisley earns it the title of **Outside Loo of the Year 2013**.

In towns and cities, pubs often strike a casual visitor as rather impersonal. But there are plenty of good town pubs that show the

personal touch of a really committed landlord or landlady, and that
are often interesting buildings, too. This year's top ten town pubs
are the Old Harkers Arms in Chester (Cheshire), Old Spot in Dursley
(Gloucestershire), Wykeham Arms in Winchester (Hampshire), Tobie
Norris in Stamford (Lincolnshire), Old Joint Stock in Birmingham
and Bear in Stratford-upon-Avon (Warwickshire and West Midlands
chapter), Castle in Bradford-on-Avon and Weymouth Arms in
Warminster (Wiltshire), Olde Mitre in Central London and Café Royal
in Edinburgh (Scotland). The civilised Wykeham Arms in Winchester,
a short and attractive stroll from this rich city's cathedral, is **Town
Pub of the Year 2013**.

More than half this *Guide*'s top pubs could probably be called
'country pubs'. We have combed through these to select ten
which truly embody old-fashioned country values, with open fires,
heart-warming food and drink, a properly rustic atmosphere, and
attractive rural surroundings with plenty of walks nearby. Our top
ten country pubs are the Pot Kiln at Frilsham (Berkshire), White
Horse at Hedgerley (Buckinghamshire), Kirkstile Inn at Loweswater
(Cumbria), Brace of Pheasants at Plush (Dorset), Sun at Bentworth
and Royal Oak at Fritham (Hampshire), Chase at Upper Colwall
(Herefordshire), Golden Cross at Ardens Grafton (Warwickshire),
Malet Arms at Newton Tony (Wiltshire), and Harp at Old Radnor
(Wales). The quaint thatched Royal Oak at Fritham, part of a working
New Forest farm, is **Country Pub of the Year 2013**.

More soul than most hotels

At least four out of ten good pubs now have bedrooms – a great
increase over the last decade. Most of these hold our Stay Award,
which shows that we ourselves (staying anonymously) and/or our
readers have enjoyed staying in them, and found them good value
for their price range. Our top ten inns are the Old Coastguard in
Mousehole (Cornwall), Sea Trout at Staverton (Devon), Feathered
Nest at Nether Westcote (Gloucestershire), Inn at Whitewell
(Lancashire), Olive Branch at Clipsham (Leicestershire and Rutland),
Royal Oak at Luxborough (Somerset), Durham Ox at Crayke and
Blue Lion at East Witton (Yorkshire) and Bear in Crickhowell and
Griffin at Felinfach (Wales). The Griffin at Felinfach, faultlessly run
yet comfortably informal – with eggs from their own hens for your
breakfast – is **Inn of the Year 2013**.

Value is vital

Dishes which this year have caught pub chefs' imagination – and
cash-strapped customers' attention – are ones where that little
extra touch turns something relatively ordinary and inexpensive
into something special. The humble burger has had a makeover –
based on well hung minced steak from rare breeds, with double- or
even triple-cooked chips, all sorts of enterprising topping, and the
chef's own relishes and chutneys. In winter virtually every good pub
now has some kind of game dish, usually local, from rabbit terrine
through venison carpaccio to the now immensely popular game pie.

Endlessly imaginative sausage variations with all manner of different mashes and gravies can now be found everywhere from the simplest taverns to the smartest dining pubs.

Our top ten value pubs, all with a good choice of interesting dishes for under £10, are the Eight Bells in Long Crendon (Buckinghamshire), Carpenters Arms at Great Wilbraham (Cambridgeshire), Drake Manor at Buckland Monachorum (Devon), Anchor in Oldbury-on-Severn (Gloucestershire), Yew Tree at Lower Wield (Hampshire), Horse & Jockey at Stanford in the Vale (Oxfordshire), Bell at Middleton and Lord Nelson in Southwold (Suffolk), Marneys in Esher (Surrey), and Six Bells at Chiddingly (Sussex). The Anchor in Oldbury-on-Severn is **Value Pub of the Year 2013**.

Moving up into the pub stratosphere – the top dining pubs which outclass most restaurants – prices are of course higher, often much higher. But here too value counts more than ever. When the quality matches the price, everyone goes home happy.

The top pub chefs go to extraordinary lengths to get the best local seasonal produce, usually from small producers. Some shoot their own game or catch their own fish, others now rear their own animals, keep their own hens, and grow some of their own vegetables and fruit. Many make absolutely everything from scratch themselves – not just baking their own bread but smoking fish and meat, making cheese and ice-cream, and so forth.

Our top ten dining pubs are the Cock at Hemingford Grey

(Cambridgeshire), Gate at Yanwath (Cumbria), Purefoy Arms at Preston Candover (Hampshire), Stagg at Titley (Herefordshire), Olive Branch at Clipsham (Leicestershire and Rutland), Rose & Crown at Romaldkirk (Northumbria), Wheatsheaf at Combe Hay (Somerset), Beckford Arms at Fonthill Gifford (Wiltshire), Crown at Roecliffe (Yorkshire) and Griffin at Felinfach (Wales). Bouncing back from a devastating fire in 2010, and now better than ever, the Beckford Arms at Fonthill Gifford is **Dining Pub of the Year 2013**.

Pub of the year

With a bumper crop of **252 new entries** this year – the most ever – we have found some absolute corkers. They range right across the board, from the warm-hearted simplicity of the Crown at Catton (Northumbria) or picture-book country charm of the unpretentious Swan at Birlingham (Worcestershire) through the mildly eccentric and very relaxing Lord Nelson in Oakham (Leicestershire and Rutland) to the smartly civilised Feathered Nest at Nether Westcote (Gloucestershire) or Wheatsheaf at Combe Hay (Somerset). Other particular favourite finds have been the Gloucester Old Spot at Combe Hill (Gloucestershire), Tram at Eardisley (Herefordshire) and Chase at Upper Colwall (Herefordshire). The Chase at Upper Colwall, perched on the Malvern Hills with a lovely view to the west, and warmly snug inside, is **Newcomer of the Year 2013**.

Extra-special commitment and care for both their pubs and their customers make some landlords and landladies the absolute aristocrats of the pub world: Mike Norris of the Red Lion at Chenies (Buckinghamshire), Peter and Angela Gatling of the Merry Harriers at Clayhidon and Carole and George Cowie of the New Inn in Coleford (Devon), Jeremy Lee of the New Inn in Cerne Abbas (Dorset), Simon and Sally Jackson of the Horse & Groom at Upper Oddington (Gloucestershire), Marie Holmes of the Sun at Bentworth and Tim Gray of the Yew Tree at Lower Wield (Hampshire), Norman and Janet Whittall of the Three Horseshoes at Little Cowarne (Herefordshire), David and Trish McManus of the Hare Arms at Stow Bardolph (Norfolk), Derek Geneen of the Fox at Broughton Gifford (Wiltshire), and the Key family of the Nags Head in Usk (Wales). Peter and Angela Gatling of the Merry Harriers are **Licensees of the Year 2013**.

All of which brings us to Britain's very best pubs. This year, the top ten pubs, all getting rave reviews from our army of reader-reporters, are the Cock at Hemingford Grey (Cambridgeshire), Masons Arms at Cartmel Fell and Watermill at Ings (Cumbria), Merry Harriers at Clayhidon (Devon), Kings Head at Bledington (Gloucestershire), Olive Branch at Clipsham (Leicestershire and Rutland), Crown in Southwold (Suffolk), Running Horses at Mickleham (Surrey), Potting Shed at Crudwell (Wiltshire) and Blue Lion at East Witton (Yorkshire). The Cock at Hemingford Grey, combining a really good proper bar with its excellent restaurant side – and a charming peaceful garden for summer – is **Pub of the Year 2013**.

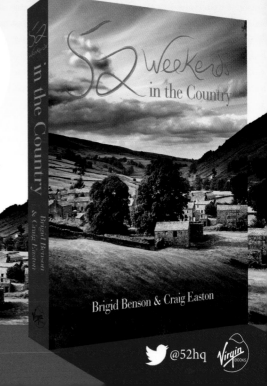

The Good Pub Guide Awards 2013

Beer Pub of the Year

Fat Cat, Norwich (Norfolk)

Knowledgeable landlord Colin Keatley keeps up to 30 quickly changing real ales – including their own brews – on handpump or tapped from the cask, plus imported draught beers and over 50 bottled beers from around the world.

Own Brew Pub of the Year

Watermill, Ings (Cumbria).

Hard-working, hands-on landlord Brian Coulthwaite's eight Watermill own brews are so popular that the brewery is having to expand; they also keep up to 11 guests from other breweries, too, as well as lots of bottled beers, farm cider and 40 malt whiskies.

Brewery of the Year

Otter Brewery in Devon, run by the McCaig family for 23 years, uses water from its own springs and produces five beers plus a winter seasonal one. From small beginnings, it's now one of the West Country's most successful breweries – and a big plus is that they manage to keep the price of a pint below many other real ale choices in a high proportion of our Main Entry pubs.

Wine Pub of the Year

Woods, Dulverton (Somerset)

Our winner of this Award for the third year running. Patrick Groves, the charming landlord, will open any of the 400 wines on his extraordinary list to serve just a glass. He also keeps an unlisted collection of around 500 well aged, New World wines which he will happily chat about. It's an amazing pub for a wine lover.

Whisky Pub of the Year

Sligachan Hotel, Sligachan, Isle of Skye (Scotland)

With an exceptional list of 350 whiskies, which make an impressive display behind the counter, the Sligachan, in the village of the same name on the Isle of Skye, is our outright winner. That's a whisky for almost every day of the year!

Pub Group of the Year

Our winner is unquestionably **Brunning & Price**, which runs more than two dozen places in buildings of real character. They manage to preserve individuality in each of their pubs and you can be sure of consistently high standards of food, drink and service in every single one of them.

Unspoilt Pub of the Year

Crown, Churchill (Somerset)

This cottagey place is a delight for those wanting real character with no pretensions. Ten real ales and straightforward lunchtime food with no noise from background music just add to the enjoyment.

Town Pub of the Year

Wykeham Arms, Winchester (Hampshire)

Civilised and warmly welcoming to visitors as well as their loyal regulars, this inn has bustling rooms filled with interesting collections, good food and drinks, and comfortable bedrooms; the cathedral is just a stroll away.

Country Pub of the Year

Royal Oak, Fritham (Hampshire)

Part of a working New Forest farm with pigs and ponies out on the green. Roaring log fires, friendly locals, antique furniture on oak flooring, a fine choice of real ales and simple lunchtime food ensure plenty of happy customers at all times.

Inn of the Year

Griffin, Felinfach (Wales)

A lovely place to stay, with comfortable and tastefully decorated bedrooms and hearty breakfasts that include eggs from their own hens and home-made jams and marmalade. Stylish but relaxed bar and dining rooms and first class food and drink.

Value Pub of the Year

Anchor, Oldbury-on-Severn (Gloucestershire)

Enjoyable and friendly with plenty to look at in the bustling bars, the Anchor serves a good number of interesting main dishes for under £10 – plus a very fairly priced two- or three-course set menu (not Sunday).

Dining Pub of the Year

Beckford Arms, Fonthill Gifford (Wiltshire)

An elegant old coaching inn on the edge of lovely rolling parkland that serves unfailingly excellent and imaginative food using first class ingredients – as well as a fine range of drinks including winter mulled wine and cider and cocktails using home-grown ingredients.

Newcomer of the Year

Chase, Upper Colwall (Herefordshire)

Perched on the Malvern Hills with a lovely view to the west and good surrounding walks, the Chase is chatty and companionable with an interesting variety of furnishings and décor, tasty food and half a dozen beers, and helpful staff.

Licensees of the Year

Merry Harriers, Clayhidon (Devon)

Peter and Angela Gatling are the aristocrats of the pub world and show real commitment to both their customers and their pub. You can be sure of a genuine welcome no matter how busy they are – and sure, too, of a good meal (using some home-grown produce and their own eggs) and a fine pint of ale.

Pub of the Year

Cock, Hemingford Grey (Cambridgeshire)

Combining a traditional bar and a top class restaurant, the Cock offers the best for all its customers. There are interesting beers (and an August beer festival), lots of wines by the glass, delicious food, fresh flowers and candles and helpful, courteous service. An outright winner.

Outside Loo of the Year

Tram, Eardisley (Herefordshire)

What is a good pub?

The Main Entries in this *Guide* have been through a two-stage sifting process. First of all, some 2,000 regular correspondents keep in touch with us about the pubs they visit, and double that number report occasionally. We also get a flow of reports sent to us at feedback@thegoodpubguide.co.uk or via our website, www.thegoodpubguide.com. This keeps us up to date about pubs included in previous editions: it's their alarm signals that warn us when a pub's standards have dropped (after a change of management, say), and it's their continuing approval that reassures us about keeping a pub as a full entry for another year.

New Entries

Particularly important are the reports we receive on pubs we don't know at all. It's from these new discoveries that we make up a shortlist, to be considered for possible inclusion as new Main Entries. The more people that report favourably on a new pub, the more likely it is to win a place on this shortlist, especially if

some of the reporters belong to our hardcore of about 600 trusted correspondents whose judgement we have learned to rely on. These are people who have each given us detailed comments on dozens of pubs, and shown that (when we ourselves know some of those pubs too) their judgement is closely in line with our own.

This brings us to the acid test. Each pub, before inclusion as a full entry, is inspected anonymously by one or both of the two editors. They have to find some special quality that would make strangers enjoy visiting it. What often marks the pub out for special attention is good value food (and that might mean anything from a well made sandwich, with good fresh ingredients at a low price, to imaginative cooking outclassing most restaurants in the area). The drinks may be out of the ordinary – maybe several hundred whiskies, remarkable wine lists, interesting ciders, a wide range of well kept real ales (perhaps even brewed by the pub itself), or bottled beers from all over the world. Perhaps there's a special appeal about it as a place to stay, with good bedrooms and obliging service. Maybe it's the building itself (from centuries-old parts of monasteries to extravagant Victorian gin-palaces), or its surroundings (lovely countryside, attractive waterside,

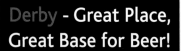

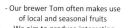
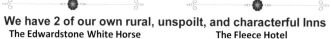
extensive well kept garden), or what's in it (charming furnishings, extraordinary collections of bric-a-brac).

Above all, though, what makes a good pub is its atmosphere. You should be able to feel at home there, and feel not just that *you're* glad you've come but that *they're* glad you've come. A good landlord or landlady makes a huge difference here – they can make or break a pub.

It follows from this that a great many ordinary locals, perfectly good in their own right, don't earn a place in the *Guide*. What makes them attractive to their regular customers (an almost clubby chumminess) may even make strangers feel rather out of place.

Another important point is that there isn't necessarily any link between charm and luxury. A basic unspoilt village tavern, with hard seats and a flagstone floor, may be worth travelling miles to find, while a deluxe pub-restaurant may not be worth crossing the street for.

Those pubs featured with Main Entries do pay a fee, which helps to cover the *Guide*'s research and production costs. But no pub can gain an entry simply by paying a fee. Only pubs that have been inspected anonymously, and approved as meeting our very high standards, are invited to join.

THE PHEASANT

Country Pub with Rooms

Real ales including our own pheasant bitter made with smoked hops

Freshly prepared seasonal food, salad leaves, fruit and vegetables grown in our 1 acre garden

Smoked fish a specialty with our own smokery on site and selection of smoked produce to purchase at the bar.

5 luxurious rooms with views of the surrounding countryside

CONTACT US:

Phone: 01787 461196
Email: info@thepheasant.net
Website: thepheasant.net
The Pheasant, Church Street, Gestingthorpe, Essex, CO9 3AU

Using the *Guide*

The Counties

England has been split alphabetically into counties. Each chapter starts by picking out the pubs that are currently doing best in the area, or are especially attractive for one reason or another.

The county boundaries we use are those of the administrative counties (not the old traditional counties, which were changed back in 1976). We have left the new unitary authorities within the counties that they formed part of until their creation in the most recent local government reorganisation. Metropolitan areas have been included in the counties around them – for example, Merseyside in Lancashire. And occasionally we have grouped counties together – for example, Rutland with Leicestershire, and Durham with Northumberland to make Northumbria. If in doubt, check the Contents page.

Scotland, Wales and London have each been covered in single chapters. Pubs are listed alphabetically (except in London, which is split into Central, East, North, South and West), under the name of the town or village where they are. If the village is so small that you might not find it on a road map, we've listed it under the name of the nearest sizeable village or town. The maps use the same town and village names, and additionally include a few big cities that don't have any listed pubs – for orientation.

We list pubs in their true county, not their postal county. Just once or twice, when the village itself is in one county but the pub is just over the border in the next-door county, we have used the village county, not the pub one.

Stars ★

Really outstanding pubs are awarded a star, and in a few cases two: these are the aristocrats among pubs. The stars do NOT signify extra luxury or especially good food – in fact some of the pubs that appeal most distinctively and strongly are decidedly basic in terms of food and surroundings. The detailed description of each pub shows what its particular appeal is, and this is what the stars refer to.

Food Award ⓦ

Pubs where food is quite outstanding.

Stay Award ⇌

Pubs that are good as places to stay at (obviously you can't expect the same level of luxury at £60 a head as you'd get for £100 a head). Pubs with bedrooms are marked on the maps as a square.

Wine Award ♀

Pubs serving particularly enjoyable wines by the glass – often a good range.

Beer Award 🍺
Pubs where the quality of the beer is quite exceptional, or pubs that keep a particularly interesting range of beers in good condition.

Value Award £
This distinguishes pubs that offer really good value food. In all the award-winning pubs, you will find an interesting choice at under £10.

Recommenders
At the end of each Main Entry we include the names of readers who have recently recommended that pub (unless they've asked us not to).

Important note: the description of the pub and the comments on it are our own and not the recommenders'.

Also Worth a Visit
The Also Worth a Visit section at the end of each county chapter includes brief descriptions of pubs that have been recommended by readers in the year before the *Guide* goes to print and that we feel are worthy of inclusion – many of them, indeed, as good in their way as the featured pubs (these are picked out by a star). We have inspected and approved nearly half of these ourselves. All the others are recommended by our reader-reporters. The descriptions of these other pubs, written by us, usually reflect the experience of several different people.

The pubs in Also Worth a Visit may become featured entries in future editions. So do please help us know which are hot prospects for our inspection programme (and which are not!), by reporting on them. There are report forms at the back of the Guide, or you can email us at feedback@goodguides.com, or write to us at The Good Pub Guide, FREEPOST TN1569, Wadhurst, East Sussex, TN5 7BR.

Locating Pubs

To help readers who use digital mapping systems we include a **postcode** for every pub. Pubs outside London are given a British Grid four-figure **map reference**. Where a pub is exceptionally difficult to find, we include a six-figure reference in the directions. The Map number (main entries only) refers to the maps at the back of our *Guide*.

Motorway Pubs

If a pub is within four or five miles of a motorway junction we give special directions for finding it from the motorway. The Special Interest Lists at the end of the book include a list of these pubs, motorway by motorway.

Prices and Other Factual Details

The *Guide* went to press during the summer of 2012, after each pub was sent a checking sheet to get up-to-date food, drink and bedroom prices and other factual information. By the summer of 2013 prices

are bound to have increased, but if you find a significantly different price please let us know.

Breweries or independent chains to which pubs are 'tied' are named at the beginning of the italic-print rubric after each Main Entry. That generally means the pub has to get most if not all of its drinks from that brewery or chain. If the brewery is not an independent one but just part of a combine, we name the combine in brackets. When the pub is tied, we have spelled out whether the landlord is a tenant, has the pub on a lease, or is a manager. Tenants and leaseholders of breweries generally have considerably greater freedom to do things their own way, and in particular are allowed to buy drinks including a beer from sources other than their tied brewery.

Free houses are pubs not tied to a brewery. In theory they can shop around but in practice many free houses have loans from the big brewers, on terms that bind them to sell those breweries' beers. So don't be too surprised to find that so-called free houses may be stocking a range of beers restricted to those from a single brewery.

Real ale is used by us to mean beer that has been maturing naturally in its cask. We do not count as real ale beer that has been pasteurised or filtered to remove its natural yeasts.

Oct-May ~ Bedrooms: £60B/£80B ~ www.thefrogatskirmett.co.uk *Recommended by Paul Humphreys, Colin and Louise English, Brian and Anna Marsden, John and Sharon Hancock, Susan Loppert, Jane Caplan, Maureen and Keith Gimson, D J and P M Taylor*

WENDOVER
Village Gate

SP8609 Map 2

Aylesbury Road (B4009); HP22 6BA

Well run country pub with plenty of outside seating, friendly bar and several dining rooms, real ales and well liked food

In warm weather there's plenty of outside seating around this neatly kept cream-painted brick dining pub: grey high-backed wicker or modern metal chairs and picnic-sets on a roped-off decked area covered by a giant parasol, on terracing, on a raised decked area and on gravel – and there are far-reaching country views at the back. Inside, the interconnected rooms have contemporary paintwork and furnishings and the atmosphere is easy-going and friendly. The bar has red leather tub chairs around log tables with polished tops in front of the woodburning stove in its brick fireplace, chunky leather stools and a mix of dining chairs around various tables, and animal prints on the walls above the half-panelling. High leather bar chairs sit against the modern bar counter with its unusual metal decoration, and they keep Fullers London Pride with guests like Greene King IPA and St Austell Tribute on handpump. The other rooms are laid out for eating with high-backed plush, wooden or leather dining chairs around a mix of tables on oak boarding (some carpeting and stone tiling, too); one of the rooms has rafters and beams in a very high ceiling and long swagged curtains.

As well as offering morning coffee and cakes and pizzas and sharing boards (available all day), the popular food might include smoked haddock fishcakes in coconut breadcrumbs, fresh mouli and carrot salad and sweet chilli sauce, caramelised onion, stilton and thyme tartlet with tomato vinaigrette, moules marinière with rustic garlic toast, steak burger with cheddar, bacon or chorizo and tomato jam, garlic and thyme spatchcock baby chicken with red lentils, spring greens and crispy pancetta, daily specials like whole lemon sole with mussels in a creamy white wine sauce and serrano-wrapped pork chop with raisin and apple mash and jus, and puddings such as Baileys chocolate pot and apple, raisin and cinnamon crumble; they also offer a good value two-course OAP lunch and Thursday is steak night. *Benchmark main dish: slow-roast pork belly with dauphinoise potatoes, apple compote and cider jus £12.95. Two-course evening meal £19.50.*

Free house ~ Licensee John Johnston ~ Real ale ~ Bar food (12-3, 6-10; 12-8 Sun) ~ Restaurant ~ (01296) 623884 ~ Children welcome ~ Dogs allowed in bar ~ Occasional live bands ~ Open 12-11.30(midnight Fri and Sat); 12-10.30 Sun ~ www.villagegatewendover.com *Recommended by Mrs Margo Finlay, Jörg Kasprowski*

WOOBURN COMMON
Chequers ♀ 🛏

SU9187 Map 2

From A4094 N of Maidenhead at junction with A4155 Marlow road keep on A4094 for another 0.75 miles, then at roundabout turn off right towards Wooburn Common and into Kiln Lane; if you find yourself in Honey Hill, Hedsor, turn left into Kiln Lane at the top of the hill; OS Sheet 175 map reference 910870; HP10 0JQ

Busy and friendly hotel with a bustling bar, four real ales, bar and more elaborate food and refurbished restaurant; comfortable bedrooms

The same friendly family has run this 17th-c former coaching inn for over 35 years and despite much emphasis being placed on the bustling hotel side, its heart is still the main bar, which continues to thrive as a welcoming local. It feels nicely pubby with low beams, standing timbers and alcoves, characterful rickety furniture and comfortably lived-in sofas on bare boards, a bright log-effect gas fire, pictures, plates, a two-man saw and tankards. In contrast, the bar to the left, with its dark brown leather sofas at low tables on wooden floors, feels plain and modern; the restaurant has been recently refurbished. They keep Greene King Old Speckled Hen, Rebellion Smuggler, XT4 from the new XT Brewing Company and a changing guest on handpump, have a good sizeable wine list (with a dozen by the glass) and a fair range of malt whiskies and brandies; background music. The spacious garden, set away from the road, has seats around cast-iron tables, and summer barbecues.

As well as sandwiches and bar snacks like home-made burger with bacon and cheese, chicken curry, cumberland sausage with onion gravy and beer-battered haddock, the enterprising food might include tea-smoked duck with sweetcorn custard, baby chard and pomegranate dressing, scallops with black pudding, squash and cashews, honey-roast root vegetable pithivier with chestnut cappuccino, sea bream fillet with crab cake and chive butter, and puddings such as banoffi mousse, caramelised banana and toffee sauce and dark chocolate brownie with honeycomb ice-cream; they also have two- and three-course set menus. *Benchmark main dish: wild boar, pheasant and venison sausages with squash purée and rosemary jus £14.95. Two-course evening meal £24.50.*

Free house ~ Licensee Peter Roehrig ~ Real ale ~ Bar food (12-2.30, 6-9.30; all day weekends) ~ Restaurant ~ (01628) 529575 ~ Children welcome ~ Dogs allowed in bar ~ Open 11am-midnight(11pm Sun) ~ Bedrooms: $99.50B/$107.50B ~ www.chequers-inn.com *Recommended by Peter and Giff Bennett, D and M T Ayres-Regan*

Also Worth a Visit in Buckinghamshire

Besides the fully inspected pubs, you might like to try these pubs that have been recommended to us and described by readers. Do tell us what you think of them: feedback@goodguides.com

ASKETT SP8105

⋆**Three Crowns** (01844) 347166
W off A4010 into Letter Box Lane; HP27 9LT Handsome, well run pub in small hamlet among the Chiltern Hills; main emphasis on the particularly good interesting food, but also real ales from herringbone brick counter, good wine list, two contemporary-styled beamed dining rooms with mix of high-backed pale wood or black leather chairs around dark wood tables, light flooring, minimal décor; some picnic-sets outside under parasols, pretty front flower beds and baskets. *(Mel Smith, Peter and Jan Humphreys)*

ASTON CLINTON SP8712

Oak (01296) 630466
Green End Street; HP22 5EU Cosy and attractive part-thatched pub, friendly and welcoming, with well kept Fullers ales and an interesting guest, good inexpensive food cooked to order (all day Sat, not Sun evening), beams and inglenook log fire; garden with plenty of room for kids, open all day. *(Brian and Barbara Brown, Sean Hayward)*

AYLESBURY SP8213

Bell (01296) 388080
Market Square; HP20 1TX New well run Wetherspoons, linked beamed rooms; children welcome, open all day. *(Tim and Ann Newell)*

AYLESBURY SP7510

Bottle & Glass (01296) 748488
A418 2 miles beyond Stone towards Thame; HP17 8TY Rambling thatched dining pub completely renovated after 2003 fire, nice modern layout and décor, enjoyable food (all day weekends) from sandwiches and sharing plates up, well kept beer and plenty of wines by the glass, friendly efficient staff; children welcome, disabled facilities, terrace tables, open all day. *(Joyce and Norman Bailey)*

AYLESBURY SP8113
⋆Kings Head (01296) 718812
Kings Head Passage (off Bourbon Street), also entrance off Temple Street; no nearby parking except for disabled; HP20 2RW Handsome town centre-pub owned by National Trust, some beautiful early Tudor windows and stunning 15th-c stained glass in former Great Hall and three timeless carefully restored rooms – stripped boards, cream walls with little decoration, upholstered sofas and armchairs, high-backed cushioned settles and some simple modern furniture, all nicely low key but civilised, Chiltern ales and guests kept well, enjoyable bar food (not Sun-Tues evenings), friendly helpful service; disabled facilities, teak seats in atmospheric medieval cobbled courtyard shared with arts and crafts shop, open all day. *(Clive and Fran Dutson, Paul Humphreys, Tim and Ann Newell, Doug Kennedy)*

BEACONSFIELD SU9490
Royal Saracens (01494) 674119
A mile from M40 junction 2; London End (A40); HP9 2JH Striking timbered façade (former coaching inn) and well updated open-plan interior, comfortable chairs around light wood tables, massive beams and timbers in one corner, log fires, welcoming efficient young staff, wide choice of enjoyable food including shared dishes and fixed-price weekday menu (busy weekends when best to book), well kept ales such as Fullers London Pride and Sharps Doom Bar, quite a few wines by the glass, large back restaurant; attractive sheltered courtyard. *(Neil Hardwick)*

BENNETT END SU7897
⋆Three Horseshoes (01494) 483273
Horseshoe Road; from Radnage on unclassified road towards Princes Risborough, left into Bennett End Road, then right into Horseshoe Road; HP14 4EB Nicely converted country pub in lovely quiet spot – seemingly off the beaten track but close to M40; Rebellion IPA and a guest, several wines by the glass, good choice of food including some traditional options (not cheap and service charge added), smartly uniformed staff, flagstoned softly lit snug bar with log fire in raised fireplace, original brickwork and bread oven, two further sitting areas, one with long winged settle, the other enclosed by standing timbers, stone-floor dining room with big windows overlooking garden, red telephone box half submerged in duck pond, unspoilt valley beyond; children welcome till 9pm, dogs in bar, six bedrooms, closed Sun evening, Mon lunchtime. *(Simon and Mandy King, Tracey and Stephen Groves, Brian and Anna Marsden, Anthony Lord, Roy Hoing)*

BLEDLOW RIDGE SU7997
Boot (01494) 481499
Chinnor Road; HP14 4AW Welcoming community-owned village local, enjoyable pubby food from sandwiches up, well kept ales such as Banks's, Fullers and Rebellion, good service. *(D and M T Ayres-Regan)*

BOURNE END SU8987
Bounty (01628) 520056
Cock Marsh, actually across the river along the Cookham towpath, but shortest walk – still about 0.25 miles – is from Bourne End, over the railway bridge; SL8 5RG Welcoming take-us-as-you-find-us pub tucked away in outstanding setting on the bank of the Thames accessible only by foot or boat; bar counter made from a boat, collection of flags, well kept Rebellion ales, basic standard food including children's meals, back dining area, bar billiards; background music inside and out; dogs and muddy walkers welcome, picnic-sets with parasols on front terrace, play area to right, open all day in summer (may be boat trips), closed winter weekdays. *(N R White)*

BRILL SP6514
⋆Pheasant (01844) 239370
Windmill Street; off B4011 Bicester– Long Crendon; HP18 9TG More or less open-plan with some beams, chatty bar with smart chairs by counter, leather tub chairs in front of woodburner, Vale Best Bitter and a guest, well liked food, dining areas with high-backed leather or dark wooden chairs, attractively framed prints, books on shelves; background music; children welcome, dogs in bar, seats on decked area and in garden, fine views over post windmill (one of the oldest in working order), comfortable bedrooms, good breakfast, open all day. *(Bruce and Sharon Eden)*

BUCKINGHAM SP6933
Villiers (01280) 822444
Castle Street; MK18 1BS Pub part of this large comfortable hotel with own courtyard entrance, big inglenook log fire, panelling and stripped masonry in flagstoned bar, good food and usually three real ales, friendly attentive staff, more formal lounges and restaurant; no dogs; children welcome till 9pm, terrace, tables, open all day. *(George Atkinson)*

BURROUGHS GROVE SU8589
Three Horseshoes (01628) 483109
Wycombe Road (back Road Marlow–High Wycombe); SL7 3RA Former coaching inn with up to six Rebellion ales, wide choice of food including good Sun roast, comfortable traditional furnishings on several levels, log fires; children and dogs welcome, big garden, good walks nearby, open all day Fri, Sat. *(Jonathan Holloway, Andy and Jill Kassube)*

BUTLERS CROSS   SP8407
Russell Arms (01296) 622618
Off A4010 S of Aylesbury, at Nash Lee roundabout; or off A413 in Wendover, passing station; Chalkshire Road; HP17 0TS Civilised pub with wide choice of good food in beamed and flagstoned bar and separate modern light and roomy restaurant, real ales, two open fires; small sheltered garden, well placed for Chilterns walks. *(Sean Hayward)*

CADSDEN   SP8204
Plough (01844) 343302
Cadsden Road; HP27 0NB Extended former coaching inn with airy open-plan bar/dining area, well spaced tables on flagstones, exposed brick and some faux beams, very popular with families and Chilterns ramblers, good choice of real ales and of hearty home-made food (not Sun evening), cherry pie festival (first Sun in Aug), friendly efficient service; lots of tables in delightful quiet front and back garden, pretty spot on Ridgeway path, bedrooms, open all day weekends. *(C Galloway, Charles Gysin, N R White, Roy Hoing)*

CHALFONT ST GILES   SU9895
✶Ivy House (01494) 872184
A413 S; HP8 4RS Old brick and flint beamed coaching inn tied to Fullers, their ales, good food including some interesting choices, decent wines by the glass, espresso coffee, friendly young staff, comfortable fireside armchairs in carefully lit and elegantly cosy L-shaped tiled bar, lighter flagstoned dining extension; dogs allowed in bar, pleasant terrace and sloping garden (some traffic noise), five bedrooms. *(Jonathan Holloway, Bratzz, Mrs S Watkins)*

CHALFONT ST GILES   SU9893
White Hart (01494) 872441
Three Households, Main Street; HP8 4LP Spacious and airy with emphasis on the enjoyable food from interesting sandwiches up including fixed-price menu (Mon-Thurs), good service, well kept Greene King ales, lots of wines by the glass, smart modern furnishings in bar and bare-boards dining room, newspapers; soft background music; children welcome, picnic-sets on sheltered back terrace and in garden beyond, 11 refurbished bedrooms, open all day. *(Rev R P Tickle)*

CHESHAM   SP9604
Black Horse (01494) 784656
Vale Road, N off A416 in Chesham; HP5 3NS Neatly extended popular black-beamed country pub, good choice of enjoyable food including OAP lunch Weds and Thurs, well kept ales such as Sharps, decent wines, good service, inglenook log fire; dogs welcome, picnic-sets out in front and on back grass, open all day Sat, Sun till 6pm. *(Roy Hoing, D and M T Ayres-Regan)*

CHESHAM   SP9501
Queens Head (01494) 778690
Church Street; HP5 1JD Popular, well run Fullers corner pub, two traditional beamed bars with scrubbed tables and log fires, their ales and a guest kept well, good authentic thai food plus lunchtime bar snacks, restaurant, friendly staff and chatty locals; sports TV; children welcome, tables in small courtyard popular with smokers, next to little River Chess, open all day. *(Brian Glozier, Chris Hall, N R White)*

CHICHELEY   SP9045
Chester Arms (01234) 391214
Quite handy for M1 junction 14; MK16 9JE Pretty roadside dining pub under new management since 2011, well liked food including fresh fish, Greene King IPA, good service, cosy low-beamed rooms off semi-circular bar, log fire, back dining room down steps; tables out in front and in small garden behind. *(Michael Sargent)*

COLESHILL   SU9495
Red Lion 01494 727020
Village Road; HP7 0LH Small popular local with welcoming long-serving landlord, generous good value pubby food (not Sun evening) from sandwiches up, Vale and guest beers, two open fires, thriving darts and dominoes teams; TV for racing, games machine; front and back gardens, good walks, open all day weekends. *(Roy Hoing, Mrs S Watkins)*

COLNBROOK   TQ0277
Ostrich (01753) 682628
1.25 miles from M4 junction 5 via A4/B3378, then 'village only' road; High Street; SL3 0JZ Spectacular timbered Elizabethan building (with even longer gruesome history) given contemporary makeover, comfortable sofas on stripped wood and a startling red plastic and stainless steel bar counter, blazing log fires, well kept changing ales, good choice of wines by the glass including champagne, enjoyable food from pub favourites up, efficient friendly service, attractive restaurant; soft background music, comedy and live music nights upstairs; children welcome, open all day Sun. *(Peter Eyles, Ian Phillips, Hunter and Christine Wright)*

With the iPhone Good Pub Guide App, you can use the iPhone's camera to send us pictures of pubs you visit – outside or inside.

CUDDINGTON   SP7311
★Crown (01844) 292222
*Spurt Street; off A418 Thame–Aylesbury;
HP18 0BB* Convivial thatched cottage with
good chatty mix of customers, comfortable
pubby furnishings including cushioned
settles in two low-beamed linked rooms,
big inglenook log fire, well kept Fullers
ales and maybe a guest, around 20 wines
by the glass, good if a little pricey food (not
Sun evening), competent friendly service,
carpeted two-room back area with dark red
walls and country-kitchen chairs around nice
mix of tables; children welcome; neat side
terrace with modern garden furniture and
planters, picnic-sets in front. *(Ian Kennedy,
Doug Kennedy, Chris Glasson, Roy Hoing, Jim
Lyon and others)*

DINTON   SP7610
Seven Stars (01296) 749000
*Signed off A418 Aylesbury–Thame, near
Gibraltar turn-off; Stars Lane;
HP17 8UL* Pretty 17th-c community-owned
pub with new french landlady (previously
at the Crown in Cuddington), inglenook
bar, beamed lounge and refurbished dining
room, well kept ales such as Black Sheep,
Fullers and Timothy Taylors, plenty of wines
by the glass, enjoyable home-made food
from pub staples up, friendly service; tables
in sheltered garden with terrace, pleasant
village, open all day weekends. *(Garth
Rodgers, Doug Kennedy, Dick O'Driscoll)*

DORNEY   SU9279
Palmer Arms (01628) 666612
*2.7 miles from M4 junction 7, via
B3026; Village Road; SL4 6QW*
Modernised extended dining pub in attractive
conservation village, popular all-day food
from pub favourites up, lots of wines by the
glass, Greene King ales, open fires, daily
papers, civilised front bar, back dining room;
background music; children welcome, dogs
in certain areas, disabled facilities, terrace
overlooking mediterranean-feel garden,
enclosed play area, good riverside walks
nearby, open all day. *(Susan and John Douglas,
Roy and Jean Russell, C and R Bromage)*

DORNEY   SU9279
Pineapple (01628) 662353
*Lake End Road; 2.4 miles from M4 J7;
left on A4 then left on B3026; SL4 6QS*
Nicely old-fashioned pub, shiny low Anaglypta
ceilings, black-panelled dados, leather chairs
around sturdy country tables (one very long,
another in big bow window), woodburner
and pretty little fireplace, china pineapples
and other decorations on shelves in one of
three cottagey carpeted linked rooms on left,
Black Sheep Bitter, Fullers London Pride
and Marstons Pedigree, up to 1,000 varieties
of sandwiches in five different fresh breads;
background music, games machine; children
and dogs welcome, rustic seats on roadside

verandah, round picnic-sets in garden, fairy-
lit decking under oak tree, some motorway
noise, open all day. *(Anon)*

EASINGTON   SP6810
★Mole & Chicken (01844) 208387
*From B4011 in Long Crendon follow
Chearsley, Waddesdon signpost
into Carters Lane opposite indian
restaurant, then turn left into Chilton
Road; HP18 9EY* Calls itself a restaurant-
with-rooms; opened up beamed interior,
cream-cushioned chairs and high-backed
leather dining chairs at oak and pine tables,
flagstones or tiles, dark leather sofas, fabric
swatches hung as wall decorations, winter
log fires, modern food including set menu
choices, real ales such as Hook Norton and
Vale; background music and occasional jazz
evenings; children welcome, dogs in bar area,
attractive raised terrace with country views,
comfortable bedrooms. *(Karen Eliot, JJW,
CMW, Dennis and Doreen Haward)*

FLACKWELL HEATH   SU8889
Crooked Billet (01628) 521216
Off A404; Sheepridge Lane; SL7 3SG
Cosily old-fashioned 16th-c pub with lovely
views (beyond road) from suntrap front
garden, low beams, good choice of reasonably
priced food, eating area spread pleasantly
through alcoves, friendly service, well kept
Brakspears, good open fire. *(Roy Hoing)*

FRIETH   SU7990
Prince Albert (01494) 881683
Off B482 SW of High Wycombe; RG9 6PY
Friendly cottagey Chilterns local with low
black beams and joists, high-backed settles,
big black stove in inglenook and log fire
in larger area on right, decent lunchtime
food from sandwiches up (also Fri and Sat
evenings), well kept Brakspears and maybe
a guest; children and dogs welcome, nicely
planted informal side garden with views
of woods and fields, good walks, open all
day. *(Ross Balaam, the Didler)*

GREAT HAMPDEN   SP8401
★Hampden Arms (01494) 488255
W off A4128; HP16 9RQ Friendly village
pub opposite cricket pitch, good mix of locals
and visitors, comfortably furnished front
and back rooms (back one more rustic with
big woodburner). Adnams, Hook Norton
and a guest from Vale, several wines by the
glass and maybe Addlestone's cider from
small corner bar, good pubby food, cheerful
efficient service; children and dogs welcome,
seats in tree-sheltered garden, good
Hampden Common walks. *(Paul Humphreys,
Ross Balaam, Roy Hoing, Brian Patterson)*

GREAT KINGSHILL   SU8798
★Red Lion (01494) 711262
A4128 N of High Wycombe; HP15 6EB
Carefully refurbished pub with contemporary
décor, interesting, popular brasserie-style

food, local beers, good wine list, plenty of space in 'lobby' plus cosy little flagstoned bar with brown leather sofas and tub armchairs, log fire, spacious candlelit dining room on left, relaxed atmosphere; well behaved children welcome. *(Anon)*

GREAT MISSENDEN   SP8901
★Cross Keys   (01494) 865373
High Street; HP16 0AU Relaxed and friendly village pub, unspoilt beamed bar divided by standing timbers, traditional furnishings including high-backed settle, log-effect gas fire in huge fireplace, well kept Fullers ales and often an unusual guest, decent food from sandwiches to Sun roasts, cheerful helpful staff, spacious beamed restaurant; children and dogs welcome, back terrace with picnic-sets, open all day. *(Michael and Deborah Ethier, Tracey and Stephen Groves, Paul Humphreys, Mel Smith)*

HAMBLEDEN   SU7886
★Stag & Huntsman   (01491) 571227
Off A4155 Henley–Marlow; RG9 6RP Major refurbishment at this handsome brick-and-flint pub as we went to press – news please.

HAWRIDGE   SP9505
★Rose & Crown   (01494) 758386
Signed from A416 N of Chesham; The Vale; HP5 2UG Roomy open-plan pub dating from 18th c, enjoyable home-made traditional food (not Sun evening, Mon) from snacks up, well kept local beers, good cider and perry, big log fire, peaceful country views from upper restaurant area; children and dogs welcome, pretty hanging baskets, broad terrace with lawn dropping down beyond, play area, open all day Thurs-Sun, closed Mon lunchtime. *(Paul Humphreys, Taff Thomas)*

HAWRIDGE COMMON   SP9406
★Full Moon   (01494) 758959
Hawridge Common; left fork off A416 N of Chesham, follow for 3.5 miles towards Cholesbury; HP5 2UH 18th-c pub with low-beamed little bar, ancient flagstones and chequered floor tiles, built-in floor-to-ceiling oak settles, hunting prints and inglenook fireplace, Adnams, Bass, Fullers London Pride, Timothy Taylors Landlord and a guest, several wines by the glass, popular bar food from sandwiches up; background music; seats in pleasant garden or on heated covered terrace with views over fields and windmill beyond, paddock for hitching horses, walks on common. *(Susan and John Douglas, John Branston, Peter and Giff Bennett, Taff Thomas, Mel Smith, Roy Hoing and others)*

ICKFORD   SP6407
Rising Sun   (01844) 339238
E of Thame; Worminghall Road; HP18 9JD Pretty thatched local with cosy low- beamed bar, friendly staff and regulars, four real ales including Adnams Broadside

and Black Sheep, simple reasonably priced home-made food. *(Dick and Madeleine Brown, David Lamb)*

IVINGHOE   SP9416
Rose & Crown   01296 668472
Vicarage Lane, off B489 opposite church; LU7 9EQ Modernised 17th-c pub with enjoyable fairly straightforward food at sensible prices, well kept changing ales such as Adnams and Butcombe, excellent choice of wines by the glass; children and dogs welcome, small secluded sun-trap terrace, pleasant village. *(Sally Donaldson)*

LACEY GREEN   SP8200
Black Horse   (01844) 345195
Main Road; HP27 0QU Friendly mix of customers in this little beamed country local, popular good value home-made food (not Sun evening, Mon), four real ales, good choice of wines by the glass, big open fire; sports TV; picnic-sets in garden with play area, closed Mon lunchtime, open all day Thurs-Sun. *(D and M T Ayres-Regan, Mel Smith)*

LACEY GREEN   SP8201
Pink & Lily   (01494) 488308
A4010 High Wycombe–Princes Risborough, follow Loosley sign, then Gt Hampden, Great Missenden one; HP27 0RJ This well liked pub with its Rupert Brooke connections closed as we went to press – news please. *(Edward Mirzoeff, Brian and Anna Marsden, Mel Smith, the Didler, Roy Hoing)*

LACEY GREEN   SP8100
Whip   (01844) 344060
Pink Road; HP27 0PG Cheery and attractive hilltop local welcoming walkers, mix of simple traditional furnishings in smallish front bar and larger downstairs dining area, usual food from sandwiches up, good choice of interesting well kept/priced ales including local Chiltern, Oct beer festival with jazz, friendly helpful service; fruit machine, TV; tables in sheltered garden looking up to windmill, open all day. *(Brian and Anna Marsden, N R White)*

LANE END   SU8091
Grouse & Ale   (01494) 882299
High Street; HP14 3JG Welcoming beamed pub with good food from standards up, helpful friendly staff, great range of wines by the glass including champagne, well kept changing ales, comfortable bar and smartly laid out restaurant with flowers on tables, newspapers, log fires; soft background music; children welcome (toys provided), seats outside. *(Catriona Coleman-Seed, Martin and Karen Wake)*

LAVENDON   SP9153
Green Man   (01234) 712611
A428 Bedford–Northampton; MK46 4HA Handsome 17th-c thatched pub in pretty

village, friendly attentive staff, good value reliable food from soup and sandwiches up, may be offers, Greene King ales and good choice of wines by the glass, nice coffee, roomy and relaxed open-plan wood-floored area with two raised sections, beams, lots of stripped stone and open woodburner, big carpeted evening/weekend restaurant; background music; children welcome, heated front terrace and large back garden, open all day. *(George Atkinson)*

LITTLE HORWOOD SP7930
Shoulder of Mutton

(01296) 713703 *Church Street; back road a mile S of A421 Buckingham–Bletchley; MK17 0PF* Partly thatched and timbered 15th-c village pub under welcoming new management, good choice of food made by landlady (can also cook your own on a hot stone), well kept Wells & Youngs and two guests, rambling beamed bar, woodburner in huge inglenook, french windows to decked area and pleasant garden, some live music; children and dogs welcome, closed Mon lunchtime, open all day weekends. *(Anon)*

LITTLE KINGSHILL SU8999
Full Moon (01494) 862397

Hare Lane; HP16 0EE Picturesque brick and flint village pub with good choice of popular well presented food, well kept Adnams, Fullers London Pride, Wells & Youngs and a guest, friendly efficient staff, traditional beamed and quarry-tiled bar with open fire, bigger dining room, live music first and third Mon of month; children and dogs welcome, round picnic-sets out at front, lawned garden with swings, good walks. *(Roy Hoing, LM)*

LITTLE MARLOW SU8788
✴Kings Head (01628) 484407

Church Road; A4155 about 2 miles E of Marlow; SL7 3RZ Long, flower-covered pub with open-plan bar, low beams, captain's chairs and other traditional seating around dark wooden tables, cricketing memorabilia, log fire, half a dozen well kept ales such as Adnams Broadside and Wychwood Hobgoblin, enjoyable blackboard food from sandwiches up, good friendly service, gingham-clothed tables in attractive dining room; big walled garden with modern terrace furniture. *(Paul Humphreys, D and M T Ayres-Regan, Roy Hoing, Ross Balaam and others)*

LITTLE MISSENDEN SU9298
✴Red Lion (01494) 862876

Off A413 Amersham–Great Missenden; HP7 0QZ Unchanging pretty 15th-c cottage with long-serving landlord, small black-beamed bar, plain seats around elm pub tables, piano squashed into big inglenook beside black kitchen range packed with copper pots, kettles and rack of old guns, little country dining room with pheasant décor, well kept Greene King IPA, Marstons Pedigree and Wadworths 6X, fair-priced wines, good coffee, enjoyable inexpensive pubby food and good friendly service, live music Tues and Sat; children welcome, dogs in bar (there's a friendly pub dog), picnic-sets out in front and on grass behind wall, back garden with little bridge over River Misbourne, some fancy waterfowl, stables farm shop, open all day Fri, Sat. *(Susan and John Douglas, LM, Michael and Deborah Ethier, Roy Hoing, John Taylor, Mrs Margo Finlay, Jörg Kasprowski and others)*

LITTLEWORTH COMMON SP9386
Blackwood Arms (01753) 645672

3 miles S of M40 junction 2; Common Lane, OS Sheet 165 map ref 937864; SL1 8PP Small brick pub in lovely spot on edge of beech woods with good walks, sturdy mix of furniture on bare boards, roaring log fire, enjoyable home-made food (not Sun evening), well kept Brakspears and guests, friendly staff; children, dogs and muddy boots welcome, good garden with paved area, closed Mon, otherwise open all day (Sun till 9.30pm). *(Eva Drewett)*

LONG CRENDON SP6908
Churchill Arms (01844) 208344

B4011 NW of Thame; HP18 9AF Comfortable village pub, long and low, with good value food in bar and thai restaurant, well kept ales, central log fire, buoyant local atmosphere; children welcome, pleasant garden overlooking cricket field. *(Doug Kennedy)*

LUDGERSHALL SP6617
✴Bull & Butcher (01844) 238094

Off A41 Aylesbury–Bicester; bear left to The Green; HP18 9NZ Nicely old-fashioned country pub facing village green, bar with low beams in ochre ceiling, wall bench and simple pub furniture on dark tiles or flagstones, inglenook log fire, back dining room, decent bar food, ales such as Wells & Youngs Eagle, aunt sally and domino teams, quiz (second Sun of month); children welcome, picnic-sets on pleasant front terrace, play area, closed Mon. *(David Lamb)*

MAIDS MORETON SP7035
Wheatsheaf 01280 815433

Main Street, just off A413 Towcester–Buckingham; MK18 1QR Attractive 17th-c thatched and low-beamed local under cheerful chatty landlord, quickly served pubby food including bargain OAP lunch

---

Places with gardens or terraces usually let children sit there – we note in the text the very few exceptions that don't.

(Tues), ales such as Oxfordshire, Silverstone and Tring, old settles, pictures and bric-a-brac, two working inglenooks, conservatory restaurant with woodburner; seats on front terrace, hatch service for pleasant quiet enclosed garden behind, open all day Sat, closed Sun evening and Mon. *(David Lamb, George Atkinson)*

MARLOW SU8586
✶Two Brewers (01628) 484140
St Peter Street, first right off Station Road from double roundabout; SL7 1NQ Interesting layout with low beams, shiny black woodwork and nice mix of furniture on bare boards, nautical pictures and brassware, Brakspears, Fullers London Pride and Rebellion, several wines by glass, well liked food (all day Sat, not Sun evening), River View room and Cellar are set for dining; children welcome, dogs in bar, cheerfully painted picnic-sets out at front with glimpse of the Thames, more seats in sheltered back courtyard, open all day. *(Anon)*

MARLOW BOTTOM SU8588
Three Horseshoes (01628) 483109
Signed from Handy Cross roundabout, off M40 junction 4; SL7 3RA Much-extended beamed pub tied to nearby Rebellion, usually their full range kept well, brewery photographs, knowledgeable helpful staff, extensive choice of popular blackboard food (not Sun evening), good value wines by the glass; back garden, open all day Fri-Sat. *(Susan and John Douglas, David Lamb)*

MARSWORTH SP9114
Red Lion (01296) 668366
Vicarage Road; off B489 Dunstable–Aylesbury;; HP23 4LU Low-beamed partly thatched 18th-c pub close to impressive flight of locks on Grand Union Canal, main quarry-tiled bar with pews and open fire, front snug, steps up to lounge and dining area, Fullers London Pride with guests like Rebellion and Vale, pubby food, games room with bar billiards, darts and juke box; children and dogs welcome, picnic-sets in small sheltered back garden with heated smokers' gazebo, more seats at front facing quiet lane. *(Susan and John Douglas, Roy Hoing, John Wooll)*

MEDMENHAM SU8084
Dog & Badger (01491) 571362
Bockmer (A4155); SL7 2HE Spacious low-beamed pub under new landlord, nice décor with good mix of old furniture on polished boards, open fire, enjoyable food in bar and restaurant; children welcome, terrace tables. *(Paul Humphreys)*

NEWTON BLOSSOMVILLE SP9251
Old Mill (01234) 881863
4 miles from M1 junction 14; off A428 at Turvey – Clifton Road; MK43 8AN Stone-built beamed village inn – rebuilt in the 1980s after fire and cleanly refurbished by present licensees; three linked areas on two levels, good fairly priced traditional food (not Sun evening), Black Sheep and a couple of guests, seven wines by the glass; children welcome, dogs in bar, courtyard seating, five well equipped bedrooms, open all day weekends. *(Michael Sargent, Peter Wiser)*

NORTH MARSTON SP7722
Pilgrim (01296) 670969
MK18 3PD Pub/restaurant owned by local consortium, beams and log fires, enjoyable locally sourced food including set menu choices (children's helpings available), Sharps, Vale and a guest beer, helpful chatty staff, events including live music and Tues quiz; garden tables, interesting village church nearby, open all day weekends. *(Anon)*

OAKLEY SP6312
✶Chandos Arms (01844) 238296
The Turnpike; brown sign to pub off B4011 Thame–Bicester; HP18 9QB Friendly 16th-c thatched village local with warmly inclusive atmosphere, two smallish rooms, one for locals and one for diners, low black beams some stripped stone, padded country kitchen chairs on patterned carpet, inglenook housing big basket of books, Courage Best, Greene King IPA and Sharps Doom Bar, sensibly priced pubby food (not Mon, Tues lunchtime), helpful service, darts; games machine, maybe quiet radio, TV; picnic-sets on terrace and aunt sally, open all day. *(Andy and Maureen Pickering, David Lamb)*

OLNEY SP8851
Bull (01234) 711470
Market Place/High Street; MK46 4EA Former 18th-c coaching inn smartened up by present licensees, sofas and other seats in three smallish front rooms, big airy eating area on right, popular food (not Sun evening) from bar snacks up including mussels done in six ways and interesting vegetarian choices, pleasant efficient service, well kept Wells & Youngs and guests (Aug bank holiday beer festival), good coffee, open and log-effect gas fires; children welcome, seats in courtyard and big back garden (no dogs) with climbing frame; start of the famous Shrove Tuesday pancake race; open all day from 10am. *(George Atkinson, D P and M A Miles)*

OLNEY SP8851
✶Swan (01234) 711111
High Street S; MK46 4AA Friendly beamed and timbered linked rooms, wide choice of enjoyable sensibly priced food (not Mon) from sandwiches up, well kept ales such as Shepherd Neame and Wadworths 6X, good choice of wines by the glass, quick helpful service, daily papers, attractive flowers, rather close-set pine tables, log fires, small back bistro dining room (booking advised for this); back courtyard tables, some cover. *(Michael Sargent)*

OVING SP7821

⋆**Black Boy** (01296) 641258

Off A413 N of Aylesbury; HP22 4HN
Extended 16th-c timbered pub near church,
low heavy beams, log fire in enormous
inglenook, steps up to snug stripped-stone
area, well kept ales such as Batemans,
Brakspears and Rebellion, lots of wines
by the glass, enjoyable pubby bar food and
more elaborate restaurant menu, modern
dining room with good-sized pine tables
and picture windows, friendly attentive
service; background music; children and
dogs welcome, tables on spacious sloping
lawns and nice terrace (music here on Sun in
summer), expansive Vale of Aylesbury views,
closed Sun evening, Mon. *(Malcolm Ward,
Robert Turnham)*

PENN SU9193
Crown (01494) 812640

*B474 Beaconsfield–High Wycombe;
HP10 8NY* Dining pub doing well under
current licensees, good fairly priced food
served by friendly staff, linked areas around
low-ceilinged medieval core; tables in split-
level garden, opposite 14th-c church on high
ridge with distant views. *(John Branston)*

PENN STREET SU9295

⋆**Hit or Miss** (01494) 713109

*Off A404 SW of Amersham, keep on
towards Winchmore Hill; HP7 0PX*
Traditional pub with friendly licensees,
heavily-beamed main bar with leather
sofas and armchairs on parquet flooring,
horsebrasses, open fire, two carpeted rooms
with interesting cricket and chair-making
memorabilia, more sofas, wheelback and
other dining chairs around pine tables,
Badger ales (summer beer festivals),
interesting if not cheap food; background
music; children welcome, dogs in bar, picnic-
sets on terrace over-looking pub's cricket
pitch, open all day. *(LM, Tracey and Stephen
Groves)*

PENN STREET SU9295
Squirrel (01494) 711291

*Off A404 SW of Amersham, opposite the
Common; HP7 0PX* Family-friendly sister
pub to nearby Hit or Miss, open-plan bar with
flagstones, log fire, comfortable sofas as well
as tables and chairs, good value home-made
traditional food from baguettes up (not Sun
evening), good children's meals, well kept
Black Sheep, Brains and two guests, free
coffee refills, bric-a-brac and cricketing
memorabilia, darts; big garden with good play
area and village cricket view, lovely walks,
open all day weekends (till 8pm Sun), closed
Mon lunchtime. *(Tracey and Stephen Groves,
Susan and John Douglas)*

PRINCES RISBOROUGH SP8104
Red Lion (01844) 344476

*Whiteleaf, off A4010; OS Sheet 165 map
reference 817043; HP27 0LL* Simple
comfortably worn-in village pub with
welcoming landlady, good generous food at
reasonable prices (freshly cooked so can take
a while), well kept Greene King and Sharps
Doom Bar, log fire, traditional games; garden
tables, charming village, good Chilterns
walks. *(Brian and Anna Marsden, David Lamb)*

SEER GREEN
Jolly Cricketers (01494) 676308

*Chalfont Road, opposite the church;
HP9 2YG* Refurbished 19th-c red-brick
dining pub; restaurant with good original
modern cooking featuring fresh fish and
game (best to book weekends, no food Sun
evening, Mon), blackboard choice in bar,
four well kept local ales, lots of wines by the
glass, cricketing odds and ends, woodburner,
live jazz and beer festivals; children and dogs
welcome, covered seating area at back, good
walks, closed Mon lunchtime, otherwise open
all day. *(Ann Gray, Kevin Thomas, Nina Randall)*

SHERINGTON SP8946
White Hart (01908) 611953

Off A509; Gun Lane; MK16 9PE
Changing ales such as Courage, Hopping
Mad and Wells & Youngs, helpful landlord
and friendly staff, good pub food (not Sun
evening) from sandwiches and tapas up,
log fires in bar and snug, contemporary
flagstoned dining room; children and dogs
welcome, picnic-sets in garden with terrace,
pretty hanging baskets, four bedrooms in
adjacent building. *(Gerry and
Rosemary Dobson)*

ST LEONARDS SP9107
White Lion (01494) 758387

*Jenkins Lane, by Buckland Common; off
A4011 Wendover–Tring; HP23 6NW*
Unspoilt little open-plan pub, highest in
the Chilterns, with old black beams and
inglenook, ales such as Batemans, Greene
King and Tring, has had good value pub
food but up for sale and under caretaker
management as we went to press; children
and dogs welcome, sheltered garden, good
walks. *(Susan and John Douglas, David Lamb,
Ross Balaam)*

STOKE GOLDINGTON SP8348

⋆**Lamb** (01908) 551233

*High Street (B526 Newport Pagnell–
Northampton); MK16 8NR* Chatty village
pub with friendly helpful licensees, up to
four interesting changing ales, Weston's farm
cider, good range of wines and soft drinks,
good generous home-made food

We say if we know a pub allows dogs.

(all day Sat, not Sun evening) from baguettes to bargain Sun roasts, lounge with log fire and sheep decorations, two small pleasant dining rooms, table skittles in public bar; may be soft background music, TV; children and dogs welcome, terrace and sheltered garden behind with play equipment, open all day weekends. *(JJW, CMW)*

STOKE MANDEVILLE   SP8310
⋆**Woolpack** (01296) 615970
Risborough Road (A4010 S of Aylesbury); HP22 5UP Boldy decorated thatched pub with contemporary and stylish bar rooms, high-backed black or beige leather dining chairs on rugs or stone flooring, cushioned wall seats, open fire, Brakspears, Purity and Timothy Taylors Landlord, several wines by the glass and interesting food; well behaved children allowed (not Fri or Sat evenings), seats in back garden and on the heated front terrace, open all day. *(Mel Smith)*

STONE   SP7912
Bugle Horn (01296) 747594
Oxford Road, Hartwell (A418 SW of Aylesbury); HP17 8QP Long 17th-c stone-built Vintage Inn (former farmhouse), comfortable linked rooms with mix of furniture, usual choice of reasonably priced food all day including fixed price menu till 5pm, three real ales and lots of wines by the glass, log fires, conservatory; children welcome, attractive terrace, lovely trees in big garden with pastures beyond. *(Phil and Jane Hodson, Tony Halford)*

SWANBOURNE   SP8027
Betsy Wynne (01296) 720825
Mursley Road; MK17 0SH Popular new pub (part of the Swanbourne Estate) built in traditional timbered style, enjoyable freshly cooked food from landlord/chef using estate and other local produce, good choice of real ales, welcoming efficient staff, spacious layout with plenty of exposed oak beams including raftered dining room, wood or terracotta-tiled floors, woodburner in central brick fireplace; children and dogs welcome, tables on terrace and lawn, play house and old tractor, open all day. *(Brian Glozier)*

THE LEE   SP8904
⋆**Cock & Rabbit** (01494) 837540
Back roads 2.5 miles N of Great Missenden, E of A413; HP16 9LZ Stylish place run for over 25 years by same friendly italian family, although much emphasis

on the good italian cooking they do keep Flowers and a guest ale and are happy to provide lunchtime baps, carefully decorated plush-seated lounge, cosy dining room and larger restaurant; seats outside on verandah, terraces and lawn. *(Paul Humphreys, Roy Hoing)*

THE LEE   SP8904
⋆**Old Swan** (01494) 837239
Swan Bottom, back road 0.75 miles N of The Lee; HP16 9NU Welcoming tucked-away 16th-c dining pub, three attractively furnished linked rooms, low beams and flagstones, cooking-range log fire in inglenook, good choice of enjoyable food, well kept Chiltern, attentive service; big back garden with play area, good walks. *(Toby Boyle, Paul Humphreys)*

TURVILLE   SU7691
⋆**Bull & Butcher** (01491) 638283
Valley road off A4155 Henley–Marlow at Mill End, past Hambleden and Skirmett; RG9 6QU Black and white pub in pretty village (famous as film and TV setting), two traditional low-beamed rooms with inglenooks, wall settles in tiled-floor bar, deep well incorporated into glass-topped table, Brakspears ales in good condition and decent wines by the glass, enjoyable food, friendly new management; background and some live music; children and dogs welcome, seats by fruit trees in attractive garden, good walks, open all day. *(John Wooll, John Saville, Jim and Frances Gowers)*

WEEDON   SP8118
Five Elms (01296) 641439
Stockaway; HP22 4NL Cottagey thatched two-bar pub, low beams and log fires, good food cooked by landlord, Tring and a guest ale, good choice of wines by the glass, old photographs and prints, separate dining room; a few picnic-sets out in front, pretty village, closed Sun evening. *(Martin Warne)*

WENDOVER   SP8607
Firecrest (01296) 628041
London Road (A413 about 2 miles S); HP22 6QG Popular roadside Vintage Inn, enjoyable choice of good value food all day including specials, neat helpful staff, three mainstream ales and several wines by the glass, civilised eating areas, old fireplace, pictures on stripped brickwork; background music, children welcome, picnic-sets in small back garden, disabled parking. *(Jeremy King, Ross Balaam)*

WEST WYCOMBE   SU8394

George & Dragon (01494) 464414

*High Street; A40 W of High Wycombe;
HP14 3AB* Popular rambling hotel bar in
preserved Tudor village, massive beams and
sloping walls, dim lighting, big log fire, four
ales including Rebellion, fairly priced food
from sandwiches and baguettes up, good
friendly staff, small family dining room;
dogs welcome, grassed area with picnic-sets
and fenced play area, character bedrooms
(magnificent oak staircase), handy for West
Wycombe Park, open all day weekends.
*(Paul Humphreys, Edward Mirzoeff, Mel Smith,
Dr A Y Drummond, C and R Bromage and others)*

WESTON UNDERWOOD   SP8650

Cowpers Oak (01234) 711382

*Signed off A509 in Olney; High St;
MK46 5JS* Wisteria-clad beamed pub
brightened-up under new owners, enjoyable
country cooking (all day weekends), Greene
King IPA, Hook Norton, Hopping Mad,
Marstons Pedigree and Woodfordes Wherry,
nice mix of old-fashioned furnishings,
painted panelling and some stripped stone,
two open fires, back restaurant; background
music; children and dogs welcome, small
suntrap front terrace, more tables on back
decking and in big orchard garden, fenced
play area, pretty thatched village, open all
day weekends. *(George Atkinson)*

WING   SP8822

Queens Head (01296) 688268

High Street; LU7 0NS Welcoming recently
refurbished 16th-c pub, good freshly cooked
food in bar and restaurant including set
deals, well kept Courage Directors, Wells &
Youngs and a guest, decent wines, afternoon
tea with home-made scones, log fires;
children welcome, disabled facilities, sunny
terrace and garden with marquee, open all
day. *(Peter Kirby, Trevor Brown, David and
Diane Young, John Wooll)*

Cambridgeshire

Good new entries here this year are the Willow Tree in Bourn (easy-going atmosphere, super food), Punter in Cambridge (inventive food, interesting furnishings), John Barleycorn at Duxford (thatched and pretty, plenty of character), Crown in Elton (splendid food cooked by chef/owner), Three Tuns at Fen Drayton (charming hands-on landlady, very fair prices), Axe & Compass in Hemingford Abbots (a thriving village pub), Pheasant in Keyston (civilised and with imaginative food), Hole in the Wall at Little Wilbraham (creative young chef offering exciting food), Anchor at Sutton Gault (excellent food in restaurant-style place) and White Hart in Ufford (friendly old pub, interesting memorabilia, huge garden). Other pubs our readers are enjoying at the moment are the Free Press in Cambridge (six real ales, honest food), Carpenters Arms at Great Wilbraham (courteous licensees, good food and wines), Blue Bell in Helpston (charming hands-on landlord, fair value food), Cock at Hemingford Grey (top class pub with excellent food), Red Lion in Hinxton (enthusiastic, hard-working landlord, happy atmosphere), Old Bridge Hotel in Huntingdon (marvellous little bar in smart hotel), and Bell in Stilton (well run and friendly old coaching inn). With consistent praise not just for the fantastic food but for the atmosphere and first class service, too, our Cambridgeshire Dining Pub 2013 title goes to the Cock at Hemingford Grey.

 BALSHAM TL5850 Map 5

Black Bull

Village signposted off A11 SW of Newmarket, and off A1307 in Linton; High Street; CB21 4DJ

Pretty thatched pub with bedroom extension – a good all-rounder

This thatched 17th-c inn has a good mix of both locals and visitors all welcomed by the friendly landlord. The beamed bar spreads around a central servery where they keep Adnams Bitter, Greene King IPA, Woodfordes Wherry and a guest beer like Nethergate Augustinian on handpump, and a good choice of wines by the glass. Dividers and standing timbers break up the space, which has an open fire, floorboards, low black beams in the front part and seating that includes small leatherette-seated dining chairs. A restaurant extension with pitched rafters and timbered ochre walls was being refurbished as we went to press. The front terrace has teak tables and chairs by a long pleasantly old-fashioned verandah and there are more seats in a small sheltered back garden. Bedrooms are in a neat single-storey extension. This pub is under the same good ownership as the Red Lion at Hinxton.

Using local produce and including bread rolls and ice-cream made on the premises, the well liked food might include sandwiches and filled ciabattas, duck liver parfait with cranberry and orange chutney, salmon and dill fishcakes with a spring onion and cucumber chilli dip, ham and free-range eggs, steak and kidney pie, pumpkin and spinach tagliatelle, braised lamb shank with rosemary jus and roast garlic mash, and puddings such as passion fruit parfait and warm chocolate fondant with salted caramel, Cointreau ice-cream and orange foam. *Benchmark main dish: steak in ale pie £12.00. Two-course evening meal £20.00.*

Free house ~ Licensee Alex Clarke ~ Real ale ~ Bar food (12-2(2.30 Fri-Sun), 6.30 (7 Sun)-9(9.30 Fri and Sat) ~ Restaurant ~ (01223) 893844 ~ Well behaved children welcome ~ Dogs welcome ~ Jazz singer first Sat of month ~ Open 11-3.30, 6-11.30; 8.30am-11.30pm Sat; 8.30am-4.30, 7-10.30 Sun ~ Bedrooms: £79B/£99B ~ www.blackbull-balsham.co.uk *Recommended by Mrs Margo Finlay, Jörg Kasprowski, M and GR*

BOURN
Willow Tree 🍽 🍷

TL3256   Map 5

High Street, just off B1046 W of Cambridge; CB23 2SQ

Light and airy dining pub with versatile choice of good up-to-date food, stylish garden

The cut-glass chandeliers, sprinkling of Louis XVI repro chairs and settees in velvet and gilt, and a profusion of silver-plate candlesticks give a slightly misleading first impression: this is quite a relaxed and informal place, with friendly considerate staff. In fact, there's a great mix of seating in various styles, and of tables – what these do often have in common are stripped tops and painted lower parts. The uncluttered décor is mostly fresh cream, with one area papered to look like shelves of books. They have a good range of wines by the glass, and Black Sheep, Brains Rev James and Woodfordes Wherry on handpump. A back deck has rather smart chairs and tables beneath an extendable canopy, and beyond the car park a huge weeping willow serves as the "pole" for a round tent in purple canvas, with teak tables and chairs, and matching purple deck chairs on the grass by fruit trees.

Inventive cooking taking care with ingredients runs from tapas, summer finger food for the garden and good fresh pizzas as well as scallop and crab lasagne, confit duck with beetroot jelly and potato crisps, cavolo nero and artichoke risotto, beef burger with cheese, bacon and caramelised onions, corn-fed chicken breast with potato and parsnip rösti and a red wine sauce, venison pie, paupiette of whiting with parma ham and spinach with mussels, tomatoes and potatoes, and pork loin wellington with confit potato and mustard and apple jelly. *Benchmark main dish: beer-battered fresh haddock and chips £10.00. Two-course evening meal £20.30.*

Punch ~ Lease Shaina Galvin ~ Real ale ~ Bar food (12-3, 5.30-9.30; 12-8 Sun) ~ (01954) 719775 ~ Children welcome ~ Live jazz twice monthly ~ Open 11-11; 12-10 Sun ~ www.thewillowtreebourn.com *Recommended by John Saville*

CAMBRIDGE
Free Press 🍺 £

TL4558 Map 5

Prospect Row; CB1 1DU

Quiet and unspoilt with interesting local décor, up to six real ales and good value food

Away from the tourist trail in a pretty little back street, this is just the place for a quiet pint by the warm log fire, with no noisy mobile phones, background music or games machines to disturb the peace. In a nod to the building's history as home to a local newspaper, the walls of the characterful bare-boarded rooms are hung with old newspaper pages and printing memorabilia, as well as old printing trays that local customers are encouraged to top up with little items. Greene King IPA, Abbot and Mild and regularly changing guests such as Brains Milkwood, Titanic 1912 and York Guzzler on handpump, 25 malt whiskies, a dozen wines by the glass, and lots of rums, gins and vodkas; assorted board games. There are seats in the sheltered and paved suntrap garden and perhaps summer morris men. Wheelchair access.

Fairly priced, enjoyable food includes lunchtime sandwiches, an antipasti plate, a platter of pubby snacks like local pork pies, sausage rolls and so forth with pickles, gammon with bubble and squeak and an egg, sausages of the day, rabbit stew with black pudding, venison steak with cumberland sauce and roasted root vegetables, and puddings such as chocolate fondant with salt-caramel ice-cream and seasonal crumble with vanilla custard; they also offer a very good value three-course set lunch (Monday-Wednesday). *Benchmark main dish: pie of the week £8.95. Two-course evening meal £12.50.*

Greene King ~ Lease Craig Bickley ~ Real ale ~ Bar food (12-2(2.30 Sat and Sun), 6(7 Sun)-9) ~ (01223) 368337 ~ Children welcome ~ Dogs welcome ~ Open 12-2.30, 6-11; 12-11 Fri and Sat; 12-3, 7-10.30 Sun ~ www.freepresspub.com *Recommended by Ralph Holland, John Wooll, Barry and Anne, Chris and Angela Buckell, Clive and Fran Dutson, David and Gill Carrington, John Honnor*

CAMBRIDGE
Punter

TL4459 Map 5

Pound Hill, on corner of A1303 ring road; CB3 0AE

Good enterprising food in relaxed surroundings with interesting furniture and decoration

Paintings, antique prints, and a pleasing mix of seating on the old dark boards – pews, elderly dining chairs, Lloyd Loom easy chairs – give these rambling and informal linked rooms quite a bit of character. One prized corner is down a few steps, behind a wooden railing. The scrubbed tables all have candles in bottles or a variety of candlesticks, and the staff are quick and friendly. They have Adnams Bitter and Broadside on handpump, and decent wines by the glass; maybe unobtrusive background music. The flagstoned former coachyard has tables and picnic-table sets, and beyond is a raftered barn bar, similar in style, with more pictures on its papered walls, a large rug on dark flagstones and a big-screen TV. This is sister pub to the Punter in Oxford.

Using seasonal game, as much local and rare-breed produce as possible and making their own bread, the highly thought of food might include a lunchtime special or two such as fishcakes with tartare sauce and wild garlic frittata, as well as scallops with black pudding, cauliflower purée and caper raisin butter, blue cheese with chicory, pear and walnut, saffron risotto with spring onion and crispy shallot rings, beef burger with cheese, whole plaice with chips and salsa verde, half a roast guinea fowl with truffled pommes purée, kale and pickled mushrooms, and duck leg with asian slaw and peanut dressing. *Benchmark main dish: pork belly and cheek with apple purée £15.00. Two-course evening meal £19.50.*

Punch ~ Lease Paul Fox ~ Real ale ~ Bar food (all day) ~ Restaurant ~ (01223) 3633221 ~ Children welcome ~ Dogs welcome ~ Open 12-12(11.30 Sun) ~ www.thepuntercambridge.com *Recommended by Colin Woodward, Clive and Fran Dutson*

DUXFORD
TL4746   Map 5
John Barleycorn 🛏

Handy for M11 junction 10; right at first roundabout, then left at main village junction; CB2 4PP

Pretty pub with friendly staff, attractive beamed interior, real ales and good wines, enjoyable food, and seats on terrace and in garden; bedrooms in converted barn

This is a charming thatched village pub with friendly, helpful staff, hops on heavy beams, and standing timbers and brick pillars creating alcoves and different drinking and dining areas: nice old floor tiles, log fires, all manner of seating from rustic blue-painted cushioned settles through white-painted and plain wooden dining chairs to some rather fine antique farmhouse chairs, quite a mix of wooden tables, and lots to look at including china plates, copper pans, old clocks, a butterchurn, a large stuffed fish and plenty of pictures on the blue or pale yellow walls. Greene King Abbot and IPA and a couple of changing guest beers on handpump, and a large wine list; background music. There are blue-painted picnic-sets beside pretty hanging baskets on the front terrace and more picnic-sets among flowering tubs and shrubs in the back garden. This is a comfortable place to stay. The pub was used by the young airmen of Douglas Bader's Duxford Wing during the Second World War. The Air Museum is close by.

 Enjoyable bar food includes lunchtime sandwiches, seared scallops wrapped in parma ham on pea risotto with white onion marmalade, grilled goats cheese with chicory, pecan, apple, radishes and cranberry dressing, bangers and mash with red wine jus, a burger with bacon and cheese, a pie of the day, butternut squash and spinach parcel with a bean cassoulet, chicken with cajun spices and sour cream dressing, slow-cooked lamb shoulder with mint-scented lamb jus, daily specials, and puddings. *Benchmark main dish: beer-battered fish of the day £10.95. Two-course evening meal £18.75.*

Greene King ~ Tenant Nicholas Kersey ~ Real ale ~ Bar food (12-2.30, 6-9.30; 12-8.30 Sun) ~ (01223) 832699 ~ Children welcome ~ Open 11-11(10.30 Sun) ~ Bedrooms: £69.50B/£89.50B ~ www.johnbarleycorn.co.uk *Recommended by John Pritchard, Colin Welborn, Mrs Margo Finlay, Jörg Kasprowski, Dave Braisted, Rghmsmith*

ELSWORTH
TL3163   Map 5
George & Dragon

Off A14 NW of Cambridge, via Boxworth, or off A428; CB3 8JQ

Popular dining pub with quite a choice of enjoyable food served by efficient staff, three real ales and several wines by the glass

It's best to book in advance to be sure of a table as this very well run and neatly kept dining pub is always busy. There's a civilised but friendly atmosphere and the pleasant panelled main bar, decorated with a fishy theme, opens on the left to a slightly elevated dining area with comfortable tables and a good woodburning stove. The garden room has tables overlooking attractive terraces and on the right is a more formal restaurant. Greene King IPA and Old Speckled Hen and a guest beer on handpump and decent wines served by courteous, attentive staff. The Rose at Stapleford (see the Also Worth a Visit section) is under the same ownership.

As well as lunchtime sandwiches, filled baguettes and wraps, the popular food might include devilled mushrooms on toast, chicken liver pâté with plum and apple chutney, hot potted crab with chilli, wild mushroom stroganoff, various omelettes, pork and stilton sausage and mash with caramelised onion gravy, steak in ale pie, their famous home-cooked ham and eggs, calves liver and bacon, and salmon and spinach en croûte with lobster sauce; they also have special evening offers – a changing three-course meal deal on Mondays, fish and chip suppers on Wednesdays and scottish steaks on Fridays. *Benchmark main dish: haddock mornay £14.00. Two-course evening meal £19.00.*

Free house ~ Licensees Paul and Karen Beer ~ Real ale ~ Bar food (12-2, 6-9.30; all day Sun) ~ Restaurant ~ (01954) 267236 ~ Children welcome ~ Dogs allowed in bar ~ Open 12-3, 6-11; 12-10.30 Sun ~ www.georgeanddragon-elsworth.co.uk
Recommended by Michael and Jenny Back, John Pritchard, Mrs Jane Kingsbury, Dr A J and Mrs Tompsett, David and Sue Atkinson

ELTON   TL0894   Map 5
Crown 🍴 🍷 🛏

Off B671 S of Wansford (A1/A47), and village signposted off A605 Peterborough–Oundle; Duck Street; PE8 6RQ

Lovely thatched inn in charming village, interesting food, several real ales, well chosen wines, and a friendly atmosphere; stylish bedrooms

Our readers feel this lovely thatched stone inn is really rather special and enjoy their visits very much; if you stay overnight, the breakfasts are especially good. The layout is most attractive and the softly lit beamed bar, which will have been refurbished by the time the *Guide* is published, has an open fire in the stone fireplace, good pictures and pubby ornaments on pastel walls, and cushioned settles and chunky farmhouse furniture on the tartan carpet. The beamed main dining area has fresh flowers and candles and similar tables and chairs on stripped boards; a more formal, circular, conservatory-style restaurant is open at weekends. Golden Crown (brewed for them by Tydd Steam), Greene King IPA and a guest beer like Oakham JHB or Slaters Top Totty on handpump, well chosen wines by the glass and farm cider. There are tables outside on the front terrace. Elton Mill and Lock are a short walk away.

Cooked by the owner/chef, the splendid food might include sandwiches and baguettes, omelettes, home-cooked ham glazed with mustard and sugar topped with a fried duck egg, rare-breed sausages with streaky bacon, mash and caramelised onion gravy, wild mushroom and parmesan tart with a mushroom cream sauce, pork cassoulet, duck breast with a port sauce and dauphinoise potatoes, scallops with bacon, black pudding and colcannon with a sherry jus, and puddings like warm fig and frangipane tart with mascarpone cream and lemon curd sponge with vanilla custard. *Benchmark main dish: steak in ale pie £11.95. Two-course evening meal £20.00.*

Free house ~ Licensee Marcus Lamb ~ Real ale ~ Bar food (12-2(3 Sun), 6.30-9; not Sun evening, not Mon lunchtime) ~ Restaurant ~ (01832) 280232 ~ Children welcome ~ Dogs allowed in bar ~ Open 12-11 (Mon 5-11); closed Mon lunchtime ~ Bedrooms: £55B/£75B ~ www.thecrowninn.org *Recommended by Ian and Helen Stafford, Michael Doswell, Howard and Margaret Buchanan, R L Borthwick*

FEN DRAYTON
Three Tuns £

TL3468 Map 5

Off A14 NW of Cambridge at Fenstanton; High Street; CB4 5SJ

Welcoming landlady in charming old pub, traditional furnishings in bar and dining room, real ales, tasty food and seats in garden

It's thought that this well preserved ancient thatched building, in a particularly delightful village, may once have housed the guildhall, and the heavy-set moulded Tudor beams and timbers certainly give the impression of solidity and timelessness. The rooms are more or less open plan with an open fire in the relaxed and friendly bar and a mix of burgundy cushioned stools, nice old dining chairs and settles. The dining room has framed prints of the pub on the walls and wooden dining chairs and tables on the red-patterned carpet. Greene King IPA and Morlands Old Speckled Hen and guests like Brains Milkwood and J W Lees Bitter on handpump and 16 wines by the glass; friendly service. A well tended lawn at the back has seats and tables, a covered dining area, and a play area for children.

 Cooked by the landlady's brother and using free-range eggs and local produce, the reasonably priced, well liked food might include lunchtime sandwiches, chicken liver terrine with home-made red onion marmalade, scallops with braised chicory, fennel and butter bean purée, sharing platters, home-baked ham with egg or pineapple, chargrilled vegetables with mozzarella, a good, hot chilli con carne, shredded duck salad, cajun chicken, beer-battered fish with home-made tartare sauce, steaks, and puddings. *Benchmark main dish: pie of the day £8.95. Two-course evening meal £14.75.*

Greene King ~ Tenant Sam Fuller ~ Real ale ~ Bar food (12-2, 6-9(9.30 Fri/Sat); not Sun evening) ~ (01954) 230242 ~ Children welcome ~ Dogs allowed in bar ~ Open 10.30-2.30, 6-11; 12-3, 6-11 Sat; 12-3 Sun; closed Sun evening ~ www.the3tuns.co.uk *Recommended by Chris Smith, Barry and Anne, Dave Braisted*

GREAT WILBRAHAM
Carpenters Arms 🍴 ♀ 🍺

TL5558 Map 5

Off A14 or A11 SW of Newmarket, following The Wilbrahams signposts; High Street; CB21 5JD

Inviting village pub with traditional bar, good food here and in back restaurant; nice garden

Since Mr and Mrs Hurley re-opened this pub, we've had nothing but warm, enthusiastic reports from our readers. It's an extremely likeable place and there's a properly pubby low-ceilinged village bar on the right with Brandon Rusty Bucket, Cambridge Moonshine CB1 and Greene King IPA on handpump, a carefully chosen wine list (strong on the Roussillon region), bar billiards, a sturdy settle by the big inglenook with its woodburning stove, copper pots and iron tools, and cushioned pews and simple seats around the solid pub tables on the floor tiles. Service is spot on: thoughtful, helpful and cheerful. On the left, a small, cosy dining area has another big stone fireplace and overflowing bookshelves and this leads through to a sitting area with comfortable sofas and plenty of magazines; the light and airy extended main dining room has country kitchen chairs around chunky tables. A huge honeysuckle swathes the tree in the pretty back courtyard; further on, an attractive homely garden, with fruit and vegetables, has round picnic-sets shaded by tall trees.

Using home-grown salad ingredients and vegetables and other top quality local and seasonal produce, the enjoyable food might include sandwiches, chicken, venison liver and brandy terrine with home-made chutney, sausages and mash with onion gravy, vegetable strudel with ale sauce, chicken, mushroom, bacon and spinach pasta bake, salmon steak with saffron sauce, a daube of beef, spiced duck breast with pork, sausage and bean cassoulet, and puddings like crème catalane with a caramelised sugar topping and upside-down apple cake; their two-course lunch menu is good value. *Benchmark main dish: beef in Guinness pie £9.95. Two-course evening meal £22.50.*

Freehouse ~ Licensees Rick and Heather Hurley ~ Real ale ~ Bar food (12-2.30(3 Sun), 7-9; not Tues and Sun evenings) ~ Restaurant ~ (01223) 882093 ~ Children welcome ~ Open 11.30-3, 6.30-11(midnight Sat); 11.30-3 Sun; closed Sun evening, Tues ~ www.carpentersarmsgastropub.co.uk *Recommended by M and GR, Jacki Grant, Edward Mirzoeff*

HELPSTON   TF1205   Map 5
Blue Bell 🍺 £
Woodgate; off B1443; PE6 7ED

Bustling pub with friendly landlord and cheerful staff, frequently changing beers and good value, tasty food

There's always a cheerful, happy atmosphere in this exceptionally (and deservedly) popular pub and the professional, hands-on landlord and his helpful staff make all their customers feel genuinely welcomed. The lounge, parlour and snug have comfortable cushioned chairs and settles, plenty of pictures, ornaments, mementoes and cartwheels, displays, and a homely atmosphere. The dining extension is light and airy with a sloping glass roof. Grainstore John Clare (exclusive to this pub) and quickly changing guests such as Adnams Sole Star, Greene King Ruddles Best Bitter, Shepherd Neame Bishops Finger and a changing guest beer on handpump, nine wines by the glass and summer scrumpy cider. They may have marmalade and jam for sale; background music, cribbage and TV. A sheltered and heated terrace has café-style chairs and tables, an awning and pretty hanging baskets; wheelchair access. The poet John Clare lived in the cottage next door, which is open to the public.

Fairly priced and generously served, the good traditional food includes sandwiches, crispy garlic mushrooms, lasagne, home-cooked ham and eggs, stilton and vegetable crumble, chicken filled with bacon and chervil pâté wrapped in serrano ham in a creamy mushroom sauce, specials such as liver and bacon hotpot, pheasant pie and sweet and sour chicken, and puddings like chocolate gateau and mincemeat crumble and custard. *Benchmark main dish: steak in ale pie £8.95. Two-course evening meal £13.70.*

Free house ~ Licensee Aubrey Sinclair Ball ~ Real ale ~ Bar food (12-2(3 Sun), 6.30-9; not Sun evening or Mon) ~ Restaurant ~ (01733) 252394 ~ Children welcome away from bar ~ Dogs allowed in bar ~ Open 11.30-2.30, 5(6 Sat)-11(midnight Sat); 12-6 Sun; closed Sun evening *Recommended by Michael and Jenny Back, Mike Proctor*

HEMINGFORD ABBOTS TL2870 Map 5
Axe & Compass £
High Street; village signposted off A14 W of Cambridge; PE28 9AH

Thriving proper village community pub, popular too for good value food made with own-grown produce

The central island servery has Greene King IPA, Sharps Doom Bar and Thwaites Wainwright on handpump, and 13 wines by the glass. Various linked rooms around it have mainly traditional pub furnishings on tiled floors, with cheery pictures and an inglenook fireplace in one red-walled room, heavy black Tudor beams and local photographs in another, and a well lit pool table and TV on the left. Around the back are an old leather sofa and comfortable library chairs by shelves of books and a dresser with the pub's own chutneys and jams for sale; darts, pool, TV and board games. Leading off is a long dining room decorated with biggish prints, and the garden between the pretty thatched pub and the tall-spired church has swings, a play area and a chicken run. Good disabled facilities.

 You can tell they take the freshness of their food seriously here by the vegetable beds and the well used herb table by the kitchen door. As well as hot or cold sandwiches, there might be poached egg, bacon and black pudding salad, home-made crab cakes with sweet chilli sauce, a vegetarian dish of the day, home-made beef burger with cheese, creamy tarragon chicken, a pie of the day, baked plaice with a parmesan crust, daily specials, and puddings like apple tarte tatin and sticky toffee pudding. *Benchmark main dish: beer-battered fish and chips £10.00. Two-course evening meal £14.25.*

Enterprise ~ Lease Nigel Colverson ~ Real ale ~ Bar food (12-2.30(3 weekends), 6-9; not Sun evening) ~ (01480) 463605 ~ Children allowed in bar until 5pm and in dining area after that ~ Dogs allowed in bar ~ Occasional live music ~ Open 12(10 weekends)-11(10 Sun) ~ Bedrooms: /£70S ~ www.axeandcompass.co.uk *Recommended by Lyn Thorne, Mrs Margo Finlay, Jörg Kasprowski*

HEMINGFORD GREY TL2970 Map 5
Cock 🍴 ⚲ 🍷
Village signposted off A14 eastbound, and (via A1096 St Ives road) westbound; High Street; PE28 9BJ
Cambridgeshire Dining Pub of the Year

Imaginative food in pretty pub, extensive wine list, four interesting beers, a bustling atmosphere, and smart restaurant

'After each visit, we start planning the next one', one of our enthusiastic readers tells us. And this well run, pretty pub is just the sort of place that customers do return to again and again as it cleverly manages to appeal to both drinkers and diners. The bar rooms have dark or white-painted beams, lots of contemporary pale yellow and cream paintwork, artwork here and there, fresh flowers and church candles, and throughout a really attractive mix of old wooden dining chairs, settles and tables. They've sensibly kept the traditional public bar on the

---

Post Office address codings confusingly give the impression that some pubs are in Cambridgeshire, when they're really in Bedfordshire, Lincolnshire, Norfolk or Northamptonshire (which is where we list them).

left for drinkers only: an open woodburning stove on the raised hearth, bar stools, wall seats and a carver, steps that lead down to more seating, Brewsters Hophead, Great Oakley Wagtail and Welland Valley Mild and Tydd Steam Barn Ale on handpump, 17 wines by the glass and local farm cider; they hold a beer festival every August Bank Holiday weekend. In marked contrast, the stylishly simple spotless restaurant on the right – you must book to be sure of a table – is set for dining with flowers on each table, pale wooden floorboards and another woodburning stove. There are seats and tables among stone troughs and flowers in the neat garden and lovely hanging baskets.

Using fresh, seasonal produce, the delicious food might include lunchtime sandwiches, pork and game terrine with carrot jam, duck parcel with sweet and sour cucumber, pea, goats cheese and red onion tagliatelle, home-made sausages with a choice of four sauces, shoulder of lamb with parsnip dauphinoise, poached leeks and gravy, venison, orange and juniper faggot with braised red cabbage and thyme mash, fish specials like seared scallops with celeriac purée and roasted chorizo, grey mullet with braised puy lentils, savoy cabbage and salsa verde and halibut steak with roasted garlic and parsley purée, and puddings such as malted crème brûlée with shortbread and chocolate tart with chocolate sauce; they also offer a popular two- and three-course set lunch menu (not weekends). *Benchmark main dish: bass and crayfish salad with salsa verde £16.75. Two-course evening meal £18.75.*

Free house ~ Licensees Oliver Thain and Richard Bradley ~ Real ale ~ Bar food (12-2.30, 6.30(6 Fri and Sat)-9(8.30 Sun)) ~ Restaurant ~ (01480) 463609 ~ Children allowed in bar lunchtime only; must be over 5 in evening restaurant ~ Dogs allowed in bar ~ Open 11.30-3, 6-11; 12-4, 6.30-10.30 Sun ~ www.thecockhemingford.co.uk
Recommended by Rob and Catherine Dunster, Gordon and Margaret Ormondroyd, John Pritchard, Don and Carole Wellings, Malcolm and Barbara Southwell, R Anderson, Derek Thomas, Michael Sargent, Pat and Stewart Gordon, Barry and Anne, Howard and Margaret Buchanan, M Mossman, Derek and Sylvia Stephenson

HINXTON
TL4945 Map 5

Red Lion 🍴 ☿ ⇦

2 miles off M11 junction 9 northbound; take first exit off A11, A1301 N, then left turn into village – High Street; a little further from junction 10, via A505 E and A1301 S; CB10 1QY

16th-c pub, handy for the Imperial War Museum at Duxford, with friendly staff, interesting bar food, real ales and a big landscaped garden; comfortable bedrooms

A new terrace for both drinkers and diners has been added just outside the porch door of this extended pink-washed old inn – there's a huge parasol for sunny days. The low-beamed bar has oak chairs and tables on wooden floorboards, two leather chesterfield sofas, an open fire in the dark green fireplace, an old wall clock and a relaxed, friendly atmosphere. Adnams Bitter, Greene King IPA, Woodfordes Wherry and a guest such as Brandon Rusty Bucket on handpump, 12 wines by the glass (they have regular wine tastings), a dozen malt whiskies and first-class service. An informal dining area has high-backed settles, and the smart dry-pegged oak-raftered restaurant is decorated with various pictures and assorted clocks. The neatly kept big garden has a pleasant terrace with teak tables and chairs, picnic-sets on grass, a dovecote and views of the village church. The bedrooms are in a separate flint and brick building. They also own the Black Bull in Balsham just up the road.

🍴 Using local, seasonal produce and including own-make rolls and ice-cream, the impressive food might include sandwiches and filled baguettes, confit duck and chicken terrine with red onion jam, home-cured gavadlax with dill potato salad and sweet mustard dressing, pumpkin and salsify risotto with jerusalem artichoke and walnut salad, sweet and sour crispy pork belly, steak in ale pudding, grilled haddock with a mustard madeira velouté and a poached egg, best end of lamb with turnip, leek and potato gratin, courgette purée and rosemary jus, and puddings such as berry panna cotta with raspberry coulis and berry sorbet and banana parfait with caramelised bananas and butterscotch sauce. *Benchmark main dish: steak in ale pie £12.00. Two-course evening meal £21.00.*

Free house ~ Licensee Alex Clarke ~ Real ale ~ Bar food (12-2(2.30 Fri and Sun), 6.30 (7 Sun)-9.30(9 Sun); all day Sat (restricted 2.30-6.30) ~ Restaurant ~ (01799) 530601 ~ Well behaved children welcome ~ Dogs allowed in bar ~ Open 11-11; 12-4, 7-10.30 Sun ~ Bedrooms: £90B/£135S(£115B) ~ www.redlionhinxton.co.uk *Recommended by Phil and Jane Hodson, Edward Mirzoeff, Gerry and Rosemary Dobson, KC*

HUNTINGDON
Old Bridge Hotel 🍴 ♟ 🛏️

TL2471 Map 5

1 High Street; ring road just off B1044 entering from easternmost A14 slip road; PE29 3TQ

Georgian hotel with smartly pubby bar, splendid range of drinks, first-class service and excellent food; lovely bedrooms

This is an attractive 18th-c hotel tucked away in a good spot by the River Great Ouse with its own landing stage and seats and tables on the waterside terrace. And while the hotel side clearly dominates, there's a wide mix of customers who very much enjoy the traditional pubby bar. This has a log fire, comfortable sofas and low wooden tables on polished floorboards and Adnams Bitter and City of Cambridge Hobson's Choice on handpump; service is first class. They also have an exceptional wine list (up to 30 by the glass in the bar) and a wine shop where you can taste a selection of the wines before you buy them. You can eat in the big airy Terrace (an indoor room, but with beautifully painted verdant murals suggesting the open air) or in the slightly more formal panelled restaurant. There are seats on the terrace by the Great Ouse. This is a very nice place to stay and some bedrooms overlook the river.

🍴 Enticing, imaginative food includes all-day sandwiches and light meals as well as crab, fennel, radicchio and pomegranate salad, ham hock and foie gras terrine with piccalilli, pork and leek sausages with white onion and mustard sauce, fillet of cod with chips, mushy peas and tartare sauce, poached and roasted ballotine of rabbit with pasta, braised lettuce, crisp pancetta and a light mustard and tarragon sauce, bass, braised fennel with orange and thyme and a shellfish sauce, and puddings such as chocolate mousse with crème fraîche sorbet and kumquats and orange crème caramel with prunes steeped in Armagnac; they also have a set two- and three-course lunchtime menu (offered as an evening alternative only on Sunday). *Benchmark main dish: pork and leek sausages with mash and white onion and mustard sauce £10.95. Two-course evening meal £22.50.*

Huntsbridge ~ Licensee John Hoskins ~ Real ale ~ Bar food (12-2.15, 6.30-10; snacks all day) ~ Restaurant ~ (01480) 424300 ~ Children welcome ~ Dogs welcome ~ Open 11-11 ~ Bedrooms: £99B/£150B ~ www.huntsbridge.com *Recommended by Martin and Pauline Jennings, R Anderson, Michael Sargent, Kay and Alistair Butler*

KEYSTON

TL0475   Map 5

Pheasant 🍴 ⚟

Just off A14 SE of Thrapston; brown sign to pub down village loop road, off B663; PE28 0RE

Good civilised country dining pub with appealing décor and attractive, well kept garden

The main bar has pitched rafters high above, dating no doubt from its long-gone days as the village smithy, with lower dark beams in side areas. The serving area has dark flagstones, with hop bines above the handpumps for Adnams Southwold and Broadside and Nene Valley ESB, a tempting array of wines by the glass, and padded stools along the leather-quilted counter. Nearby are armchairs, a chesterfield, quite a throne of a seat carved in 17th-c style, other comfortable seats around low tables, and a log fire in a lofty fireplace. The rest of the pub is mostly red-carpeted, with dining chairs around a variety of polished tables and large sporting prints – even hunting-scene wallpaper in one part. Lighted candles and tea-lights throughout, and the attentive attitude of neat friendly staff, add to the feeling of well-being. The attractively planted and well kept garden behind has tables on its lawn and terrace; from the picnic-table sets out in front of the pretty thatched building you may see the neighbours' hens pottering about by the very quiet village lane.

 Cooked by the landlord, the first class, imaginative food might include flash-fried squid with cannellini beans, shallot purée and confit garlic, carpaccio of venison with parsley root purée, chicory, walnuts and truffle oil, pork and leek sausages with white onion and mustard sauce, cod fillet with tartare sauce and pease pudding, jerusalem artichoke ravioli with braised leek, chestnuts, thyme and parmesan, veal meatballs with linguine, corn-fed chicken with lemon gnocchi and cavalo nero, bass with cime di rapa and crab and cockle chowder, calves liver with black pudding, potato rösti , spinach, rhubarb and pancetta, and puddings such as chocolate nemesis with crème fraîche and steamed orange pudding with custard. *Benchmark main dish: braised pork cheek with marjoram gnocchi, butternut squash, spring greens and parmesan £13.95. Two-course evening meal £22.00.*

Free house ~ Licensee Simon Cadge ~ Real ale ~ Bar food (12-2, 7-9.30; not Sun evening or Mon) ~ (01832) 710241 ~ Children welcome ~ Dogs welcome ~ Open 12-3, 6-11; closed Sun evening and all day Mon ~ www.thepheasant-keyston.co.uk
Recommended by George Atkinson, Michael and Jenny Back, Michael Sargent

KIMBOLTON

TL0967   Map 5

New Sun 🍴 ⚟

High Street; PE28 0HA

Interesting bars and rooms, tapas menu plus other good food, and a pleasant back garden

Neatly kept and always busy with a good mix of customers, this is an interesting town pub with reliably enjoyable food and a genuine welcome from the friendly, efficient staff. The cosiest room is perhaps the low-beamed front lounge with a couple of comfortable armchairs and a sofa beside the log fire, standing timbers and exposed brickwork, and books on shelves. This leads into a narrower locals' bar with Wells & Youngs Bombardier and Eagle and a weekly changing guest on handpump, and 15 wines by the glass (including champagne and pudding wines); background music, board games, piano and quiz machine. The traditionally furnished dining room opens off here. The airy conservatory with high-backed leather dining chairs has doors leading to the terrace where there are smart seats and tables under giant umbrellas. Do note that some of the nearby parking spaces have a 30-minute limit. This high street is lovely.

As well as lunchtime sandwiches, the highly thought of food might include popular tapas, black pudding fritters with bacon and a poached egg, king prawn stir-fry with chilli dip, various ploughman's, home-cooked ham and a free-range egg, wild mushroom and truffle oil risotto, chargrilled chicken with chorizo cassoulet, salmon with a leek and bacon rösti and pink peppercorn sauce, beef stroganoff, and puddings like Malteser cheesecake and crème brûlée with spiced apple compote and a stem ginger biscuit. *Benchmark main dish: steak and kidney pudding £10.00. Two-course evening meal £19.00.*

Charles Wells ~ Lease Stephen and Elaine Rogers ~ Real ale ~ Bar food (12-2.15(2.30 Sun), 7-9.30; not Sun or Mon evenings) ~ Restaurant ~ (01480) 860052 ~ Children welcome ~ Dogs allowed in bar ~ Open 11.30-11(10.30 Sun); 11.30-2.30, 5-11 Mon-Thurs in winter ~ www.newsuninn.co.uk *Recommended by John Cook, Simon Watkins, Ryta Lyndley*

LITTLE WILBRAHAM   TL5458 Map 5
Hole in the Wall

High Street; A1303 Newmarket Road to Stow cum Quy off A14, then left at The Wilbrahams signpost, then right at Little Wilbrahams signpost; CB1 5JY

Charming pub with great food – quite a find

Of course, much emphasis is placed on the imaginative food in this friendly country pub but there is a proper bar with real ales and the welcome is as warm for those dropping in for a pint and chat as it is for those dining. The carpeted ochre-walled bar on the right is cosy for a robust no-nonsense pub lunch, with logs burning in the big brick fireplace, 15th-c beams and timbers, snug little window seats and other mixed seating around scrubbed kitchen tables. For more of an occasion, either the similar middle room (with another fire in its open range) or the rather plusher main dining room (yet another fire here) are the places to head for. Local ales include beer from the new Fellowes Brewery, there might be Brandon Rusty Bucket, Potton Shannon IPA and Woodfordes Sundew on handpump, 10 wines by the glass, and unusual soft drinks such as pomegranate and elderflower pressé; helpful service. The neat side garden has good teak furniture and a little verandah. It's a very quiet hamlet, with an interesting walk to nearby unspoilt Little Wilbraham Fen.

Inventive and very good, the food includes ham hock and parsley terrine with piccalilli, roasted bone marrow with pickled shallots, garlic and goats cheese tartlet with a beetroot and orange salad, slow-cooked pork belly with red cabbage and black pudding mash, rump of lamb with cheese and ale croquettes and an asparagus and pea purée, bass with tomato and mussel sauce, artichoke, rocket and pesto new potatoes, daily specials, and puddings. *Benchmark main dish: duck breast with potato terrine, pickled cucumber and spiced caramel £16.00. Two-course evening meal £23.00.*

Free house ~ Licensee Alex Rushmer ~ Real ale ~ Bar food (12-2, 7-9) ~ Restaurant ~ (01223) 812282 ~ Well behaved children welcome ~ Dogs allowed in bar ~ Open 11.30-3, 6.30-11; 12-3 Sun; closed Sun evening, all day Mon; two weeks Jan ~ www.holeinthewallcambridge.co.uk *Recommended by M and GR, J F M and M West, Mrs D Crew*

STILTON

Bell ♀ ⇔

TL1689 Map 5

High Street; village signposted from A1 S of Peterborough; PE7 3RA

Fine coaching inn with several civilised rooms including a residents' bar, bar food using the famous cheese, and seats in the very pretty courtyard; bedrooms

On the Great North Road between London and York, this is a lovely example of a 17th-c coaching inn. The left-hand side is a civilised hotel but the two neatly kept right-hand bars (which have the most character) are where our readers tend to head. There are bow windows, sturdy upright wooden seats on flagstone floors as well as plush button-back built-in banquettes and a good big log fire in one handsome stone fireplace; one bar has a large cheese press. The partly stripped walls have big prints of sailing and winter coaching scenes and there's a giant pair of blacksmith's bellows hanging in the middle of the front bar. Digfield Fool's Nook, Greene King IPA and Old Speckled Hen, Oakham Bishops Farewell and a guest like Crouch Vale Best Bitter on handpump, a dozen malt whiskies and 20 wines by the glass. Other rooms include a residents' bar, a bistro and a restaurant. Through the fine coach arch is a very pretty sheltered courtyard with tables and a well that dates back to Roman times.

 Using the famous cheese in many of their dishes, the good, popular food includes sandwiches, leek, potato and stilton soup, stilton pâté with apple and pomegranate chutney, seared pigeon breast with spiced apple purée, parma ham and juniper jus, sausages of the day with parsley mash and fried onions, home-made burger topped with stilton, garlic and herb gnocchi with walnut pesto, beef in ale stew with stilton and herb dumplings, beer-battered haddock with tartare sauce, bass fillet with lemon herb risotto and vegetable crisps, and puddings like Baileys crème brûlée and lemon and mixed berry eton mess. *Benchmark main dish: braised shoulder of lamb with mint parmentier potatoes and red wine jus £13.95. Two-course evening meal £20.00.*

Free house ~ Licensee Liam McGivern ~ Real ale ~ Bar food (12-2(2.30 Sat), 6-9.30; all day Sun) ~ Restaurant ~ (01733) 241066 ~ Children allowed away from bar areas ~ Open 12-2.30(3 Sat), 6-11(midnight Sat); 12-10.30 Sun ~ Bedrooms: £73.50B/£100.50B ~ www.thebellstilton.co.uk *Recommended by Jeff and Wendy Williams, Simon Collett-Jones, Steve Cocking, Barry and Anne, Mike and Mary Carter, J F M and M West*

SUTTON GAULT

Anchor ⑪ ♀ ⇔

TL4279 Map 5

Bury Lane off High Street (B1381); CB6 2BD

Tucked-away inn with charming candlelit rooms, good modern food, real ale and thoughtful wine list; bedrooms

There's no doubt that most customers are here to enjoy the excellent food and space for drinkers only can be limited on Friday and Saturday evenings and Sunday lunchtime – but at other times you can pop in for a pint of City of Cambridge Hobson's Choice or Humpty Dumpty Nord Atlantic tapped from the cask or one of the dozen wines by the glass. The four heavily timbered rooms are stylishly simple with two log fires, antique settles and wooden dining chairs around well spaced scrubbed pine tables with candles on gently undulating old floors, and good lithographs and big prints on the walls. Service is helpful and friendly. There are seats outside and you can walk along the high embankment; the bird-watching is said to be good.

┃¶┃ Impressive food might include game croquette with oriental salad and sweet and sour quince dipping sauce, queen scallops in chilli and red pepper butter with baby samphire, butternut squash stuffed with courgette and leek risotto, fillet of whiting with gremolata, couscous and chicory and cucumber salad, pork tenderloin wrapped in parma ham on caramelised onion mash with madeira gravy, duck breast with potato rösti and sautéed leeks in a soy sauce, sesame and honey dressing, and puddings like rhubarb and stem ginger crumble with brown bread ice-cream and sticky toffee pudding with salted caramel ice-cream and dark chocolate amaretto mousse; they also offer a two- and three-course set lunch menu. *Benchmark main dish: Denham Eestate venison with red cabbage marmalade and port jus £17.00. Two-course evening meal £20.45.*

Free house ~ Licensees Carlene Bunten and Adam Pickup ~ Real ale ~ Bar food (12-2, 7-9(6.30-9.30 Sat evening; 12-2.30, 6.30-9 Sun)) ~ Restaurant ~ (01353) 778537 ~ Children welcome ~ Open 12-2, 7(6.30 Sat)-9(9.30 Sat); 12-2.30, 6.30-9 Sun ~ Bedrooms: £59.50S(£89.50B)/£99S(£115B) ~ www.anchor-inn-restaurant.co.uk
Recommended by John Saville, Mrs Margo Finlay, Jörg Kasprowski, M and GR, Alan and Jill Bull, Dave Braisted, F and M Pryor, Mr and Mrs P R Thomas

THRIPLOW   TL4346   Map 5

Green Man ¶ £

3 miles from M11 junction 10; A505 towards Royston, then first right; Lower Street; SG8 7RJ

Comfortable and cheery with pubby food and changing ales

Run by a friendly, hands-on landlady, this is a cheerful village pub with honest home-cooked food and well kept beer. There are always plenty of customers and it's all comfortably laid out with modern tables and attractive high-backed dining chairs and pews; there are beer mats on the ceiling and champagne bottles on high shelves. Two arches lead through to a restaurant on the left. The regularly changing real ales might include Oakham Citra, Slaters Premium, Titanic Anchor Bitter and Woodfordes Wherry on handpump. There are tables in the pleasant garden and the vivid blue paintwork makes an excellent backdrop for the floral displays.

┃¶┃ Well liked bar food includes filled baguettes, warm potato and chorizo salad, omelettes, sausages with whole-grain mustard mash and onion gravy, goats cheese and red pepper pasta, salmon and prawn risotto, chicken, bacon, melted cheese and whole-grain mustard sauce, beer-battered cod and chips, and puddings like melting chocolate fondant and apple crumble. *Benchmark main dish: slow-roasted pork belly with apple mash and cider gravy £12.00. Two-course evening meal £14.50.*

Free house ~ Licensee Mary Lindgren ~ Real ale ~ Bar food (not Sun evening or Mon) ~ (01763) 208855 ~ Children welcome ~ Dogs allowed in bar ~ Open 12-3, 7-11; closed Sun evening, all day Mon ~ www.greenmanthriplow.co.uk *Recommended by Simon Watkins, LM, Andy Lickfold, Phil and Jane Hodson*

Bedroom prices normally include full english breakfast, VAT and any inclusive service charge that we know of. Prices before the '/' are for single rooms, after for two people in double or twin (B includes a private bath, S a private shower). If there is no '/', the prices are only for twin or double rooms (as far as we know there are no singles).

UFFORD
White Hart ⌂

TF0904 Map 5

Main Street; S on to Ufford Road off B1443 at Bainton, then right; PE9 3BH

Friendly village pub with lots of interest in bar and restaurants, real ales, interesting food and extensive garden; bedrooms

This is a friendly 17th-c stone pub in a pretty village with three acres of gardens at the back; as well as a sunken dining area with plenty of chairs and tables and picnic-sets on the grass, there are steps and various quiet corners and lovely flowers and shrubs. Inside, the bar has an easy-going, chatty atmosphere, railway memorabilia, farm tools and chamber pots, high-backed settles and a leather sofa by the woodburning stove, exposed stone walls, and stools against the counter where they serve Adnams Bitter, Black Sheep, Grainstore Ten Fifty and Oakham JHB on handpump and quite a few wines by the glass. There's also a beamed restaurant and a light and airy little Orangery. Four of the comfortable bedrooms are in the pub itself with two more in a converted cart shed.

As well as filled baguettes, the well liked food might include omelettes using free-range eggs, linguine with king prawns, mussels and calamari in a creamy tomato and basil sauce, pithivier of brown mushrooms, spinach and caramelised onions with a beetroot and balsamic dressing, beer-battered haddock and chips, a pie of the day, corn-fed chicken with a white bean and chorizo cassoulet and a roasted garlic and rosemary dressing, lamb chump with fondant potato and a honey and lime jus, and puddings like rich chocolate torte with hazelnut praline and morello cherry frozen yoghurt and sticky toffee pudding with butterscotch sauce and toffee ice-cream. *Benchmark main dish: tallington pot-roasted lamb £16.95. Two-course evening meal £21.50.*

Free house ~ Licensee Sue Olver ~ Real ale ~ Bar food (12-2.30, 6-9; 12-6 Sun) ~ Restaurant ~ (01780) 740250 ~ Children welcome ~ Dogs allowed in bar ~ Open 12-11(9 Sun) ~ Bedrooms: /£100S ~ www.whitehartufford.co.uk *Recommended by Jeff and Wendy Williams, Bruce and Sharon Eden, Phil and Jane Hodson, F and M Pryor*

Also Worth a Visit in Cambridgeshire

Besides the fully inspected pubs, you might like to try these pubs that have been recommended to us and described by readers. Do tell us what you think of them: feedback@goodguides.com

ABINGTON PIGOTTS TL3044
Pig & Abbot (01763) 853515
High Street; SG8 0SD Spotless Queen Anne local with two small traditional bars and restaurant, good choice of enjoyable well priced food, friendly attentive staff, well kept Adnams, Fullers London Pride and guests, log fires, quiz night second Weds of month; back terrace, pretty village with good walks, open all day weekends. *(Steve Nye, David Harris)*

ARRINGTON TL3250
✳ **Hardwicke Arms** (01223) 208802
Ermine Way (A1198); SG8 0AH Handsome 18th-c coaching inn with 13th-c origins and 1792 work by Sir John Soane; enjoyable food from sandwiches and pub favourites up including good value Sun roasts, Greene King IPA and two or three interesting guests, good friendly service, dark-panelled dining room, huge central fireplace, daily papers; background music; 12 bedrooms, handy for Wimpole Hall, open all day. *(Margaret Haworth)*

BABRAHAM TL5150
George (01223) 833800
High Street; just off A1307; CB22 3AG Beamed and timbered dining pub, good well presented food from sandwiches and pub favourites to lots of fresh fish, Greene King ales and a guest, bar area with comfortable seating, refurbished dining room, efficient service; children welcome, tables in garden with heated terrace, nice setting on quiet road, open all day Fri-Sun. *(Jeremy Hebblethwaite)*

BARNACK TF0704
Millstone (01780) 740296
Off B1443 SE of Stamford; Millstone Lane; PE9 3ET Stone-built Everards pub under new management, timbered bar with clean contemporary feel, wood-effect gas fires, cosy snug area, their ales and two guests, real cider, a dozen wines by the glass, traditional home-made food (not Sun evening, Mon), Sun quiz; background music; children and dogs welcome, sheltered back courtyard, pretty village near Burghley House, good walks nearby, closed Mon. *(Anon)*

BARRINGTON TL3849
Royal Oak (01223) 870791
Turn off A10 about 3.7 miles SW of M11 junction 11, in Foxton; West Green; CB22 7RZ Rambling thatched Tudor pub with tables out overlooking classic village green, heavy low beams and timbers, mixed furnishings, beers from Adnams, Potton and Wells & Youngs, Aspall's cider, enjoyable food from pub favourites up, good friendly service, airy dining conservatory; background music; children welcome. *(Chris Smith, Kay and Alistair Butler, Rghmsmith)*

BOXWORTH TL3464
Golden Ball (01954) 267397
High Street; CB3 8LY Attractive partly thatched building with comfortably contemporary open-plan bar, three-part restaurant in original core, friendly helpful staff, enjoyable food from baguettes up, well kept Wells & Youngs ales; children welcome, nice garden and heated terrace, pastures behind, 11 quiet bedrooms in adjacent block, open all day. *(Simon Watkins, R Anderson)*

BRANDON CREEK TL6091
✶Ship (01353) 676228
A10 Ely–Downham Market; PE38 0PP Lovely spot on Norfolk border at confluence of Great and Little Ouse, plenty of tables out by the moorings; welcoming helpful staff, good choice of enjoyable pub food including specials, Adnams and up to four guests, spacious tastefully modernised bar with massive stone masonry in sunken former forge area, big log fire one end, woodburner the other, interesting old photographs and prints, restaurant; children and dogs welcome , open all day weekends, closed Mon in winter. *(Marion and Bill Cross)*

BUCKDEN TL1967
✶George (01480) 812300
High Street; PE19 5XA Handsome and stylish Georgian-faced hotel with bustling informal bar, fine fan beamwork, leather and chrome chairs, log fire, Adnams Best and a changing guest from chrome-topped counter, lots of wines including champagne by the glass, good choice of teas and coffees, friendly well trained staff, good modern food in popular brasserie with smart cream dining chairs around carefully polished tables; background music; children and dogs welcome, tables under large parasols on pretty sheltered terrace with box hedging, charming bedrooms, open all day. *(Ryta Lyndley, Barry and Anne, David and Ruth Shillitoe, Michael Sargent, George Atkinson)*

BUCKDEN TL1967
✶Lion (01480) 810313
High Street; PE19 5XA Partly 15th-c coaching inn, black beams and big inglenook log fire in airy and civilised bow-windowed entrance bar with plush bucket seats, wing armchairs and sofas, good food from lunchtime sandwiches up, fine choice of wines, Adnams Bitter and a guest, prompt friendly staff, panelled back restaurant beyond latticed window partition; children welcome, back courtyard, 14 bedrooms, open all day. *(Anon)*

CAMBRIDGE TL4558
Anchor (01223) 353554
Silver Street; CB3 9EL Well laid out if touristy pub in beautiful riverside position by a punting station, fine river views from upper bar and suntrap terrace, well kept Greene King ales, decent fairly priced pubby lunches, evening baguettes, popular Sun roast, good friendly service; children in eating areas, wheelchair access, open all day. *(John Wooll)*

CAMBRIDGE TL4558
Burleigh Arms (01223) 301547
Newmarket Road; CB5 8EG Two bars, enjoyable reasonably priced food, prompt service, five ales including Black Sheep, good wines by the glass. *(Ralph Holland, David and Gill Carrington)*

CAMBRIDGE TL4658
✶Cambridge Blue (01223) 471680
85 Gwydir Street; CB1 2LG Smashing little backstreet local, knowledgeable landlord and a dozen interesting ales (some tapped from the cask – Feb/Jun festivals), bottled beers, traditional bar food, small, attractive conservatory and two simply decorated peaceful rooms with lots of breweriana, bare-boards-style furnishings, board games; can get busy weekends; children and dogs welcome, seats in surprisingly rural-feeling back garden, open all day. *(Ralph Holland, John Saville, LM, Pete Coxon)*

CAMBRIDGE TL4459
Castle (01223) 353194
Castle Street; CB3 0AJ Full Adnams beer range and several interesting guests in big airy bare-boards bar, several pleasantly simple rooms, wide range of good value quick pubby food from sandwiches up, friendly staff, peaceful upstairs (downstairs can be louder, with background music – live jazz Sun night); picnic-sets in good walled

back courtyard. *(Ralph Holland, R Anderson, Pete Coxon)*

CAMBRIDGE TL4657
Devonshire Arms (01223) 316610
Devonshire Road; CB1 2BH Popular, light and airy Milton-tied pub with two linked bars, their ales plus guests, Crone's cider, great choice of bottled beers, well chosen wines and a dozen malts, enjoyable low-priced food from sandwiches and snacks up, cheerful chatty staff and locals, creaky wood floors, mix of furniture including long narrow refectory tables, architectural prints and steam engine pictures, woodburner in back bar; disabled access. *(Chris and Angela Buckell, Phil Randall)*

CAMBRIDGE TL4458
★ Eagle (01223) 505020
Bene't Street; CB2 3QN Go for the original architectural features (once the city's most important coaching inn); rambling rooms with two medieval mullioned windows and remains of two possibly medieval wall paintings, two fireplaces dating to around 1600, lovely worn wooden floors and plenty of pine panelling, dark red ceiling left unpainted since World War II to preserve signatures of British and American airmen made with Zippo lighters, candle smoke and lipstick, Greene King and two guests; children welcome, heavy wooden seats in attractive cobbled and galleried courtyard, open all day and can get very busy. *(Chris and Angela Buckell, Barry Collett, Phil and Jane Hodson, George Atkinson, Stuart Gideon, Mrs Catherine Simmonds, Pete Coxon and others)*

CAMBRIDGE TL4558
Elm Tree (01223) 363005
Orchard Street; CB1 1JT Traditional one-bar backstreet drinkers' pub, ten well kept ales including Wells & Youngs, good range of continental bottled beers, local ciders/perries usually poured from the barrel, friendly knowledgeable staff, nice unspoilt interior with breweriana, basic lunchtime snacks; some outside tables at side. *(Chris and Angela Buckell, David and Gill Carrington, Rob Jones)*

CAMBRIDGE TL4559
Fort St George (01223) 354327
Midsummer Common; CB4 1HA Picturesque old pub (reached by foot only) in charming waterside position overlooking ducks, swans, punts and boathouses; extended around old-fashioned Tudor core, good value bar food including traditional Sun lunch, well kept Greene King ales, decent wines, cheery chatty staff, oars on beams, historic boating photographs, stuffed fish and bric-a-brac; children welcome, wheelchair access via side door, lots of tables outside. *(John Cook, Chris and Angela Buckell, John Wooll)*

CAMBRIDGE TL4457
Granta (01223) 505016
Newnham Terrace; CB3 9EX Early 19th-c pub with balcony and heated terrace taking full advantage of view over millpond, ducks and weeping-willow meadow, inexpensive pub food from sandwiches up, Greene King ales and a guest, helpful attentive service, nice lively atmosphere; children welcome, punt hire. *(Frank Dowsland, John Wooll)*

CAMBRIDGE TL4657
★ Kingston Arms (01223) 319414
Kingston Street; CB1 2NU Well kept interesting changing ales from a dozen or so handpumps, good fresh lunchtime food including bargains, companionably big plain tables and basic seating, thriving chatty largely studenty atmosphere, good choice of wines by the glass, friendly service, no music or children inside; small pretty back yard – torch-lit, heated and partly covered, open all day Fri-Sun. *(Ralph Holland)*

CAMBRIDGE TL4557
Live & Let Live (01223) 460261
Mawson Road; CB1 2EA Popular backstreet alehouse, friendly and relaxed, with well kept Nethergate Umbel Magna and seven changing guests, lots of bottled belgians, local cider and fine selection of rums, good value bar food, heavily timbered brickwork rooms with sturdy varnished pine tables on bare boards, country bric-a-brac and some steam railway and brewery memorabilia, gas lighting (not always lit), cribbage and dominoes; children and dogs welcome, disabled access. *(Ralph Holland, Revd R P Tickle)*

CAMBRIDGE TL4458
Mitre (01223) 358403
Bridge Street, opposite St Johns College; CB2 1UF Welcoming M&B pub close to the river, rambling bar on several levels, bargain food all day including speciality fish and chips and nice pies, good friendly service, several well kept mainly mainstream ales, farm cider, well priced wines by the glass; background music; disabled access. *(Chris and Angela Buckell, Paul Spring, John Saville)*

CAMBRIDGE TL4559
★ Old Spring (01223) 357228
Ferry Path; car park on Chesterton Road; CB4 1HB Extended Victorian pub, roomy and airy, with smartly old-fashioned scrubbed-wood décor, bare boards, lots of old pictures, enjoyable well priced home-made food including enterprising dishes and Sun roasts, efficient welcoming service, well kept Greene King IPA, Abbot and three guests, good coffee and choice of wines by the glass, two log fires, long back conservatory; background music, no under-21s evenings, dogs outside only; disabled facilities, large heated well planted terrace, open all day.

(J Cameron, Raith Overhill, Chris and Angela Buckell, P and D Carpenter)

CAMBRIDGE TL4459
Pickerel (01223) 355068
Magdalene Street; CB3 0AF Nicely old-fashioned multi-roomed coaching inn, popular with locals and students (can get crowded evenings), bars front and back, low beams and some dark panelling, well kept Theakstons, Woodfordes and three quickly changing guests, good choice of wines by the glass, good value food till 8pm, friendly staff; wheelchair access with help, heated courtyard, open all day (till 1am Fri, Sat). *(Chris and Angela Buckell)*

CASTLE CAMPS TL6343
Cock (01799) 584207
High Street; CB21 4SN Run by friendly couple, beers such as Cottage, Fullers, Greene King and Woodfordes, good selection of wines, enjoyable good value food cooked by landlord (not Mon); dogs welcome. *(Michael Fearnley, Adele Summers, Alan Black)*

CASTOR TL1298
★ Prince of Wales Feathers
(01733) 380222 *Off A47; PE5 7AL* Friendly stone-built local with well kept local Castor, Woodfordes and interesting guests, farm cider and perry, landlady does good value food (not weekend evenings) including Sun roasts, side dining area; Sky TV, games machines, pool (free Thurs), Sat live music, Sun quiz; children and dogs welcome (they have a friendly setter), attractive front terrace, back one with shelters, open all day, till late weekends. *(Ian and Helen Stafford)*

CLAYHITHE TL5064
★ Bridge Hotel (01223) 860622
Clayhithe Road; CB25 9HZ Popular Chef & Brewer with good choice of enjoyable reasonably priced food, plenty of tables inside and out, friendly chatty staff, small bar area, well kept ales, beams and timbers; picturesque spot by River Cam with pretty waterside garden, moorings. *(Phil and Jane Hodson)*

CONINGTON TL3266
White Swan (01954) 267251
Signed off A14 (was A604) Cambridge–Huntingdon; Elsworth Road; CB23 4LN Attractive quietly placed 18th-c country local, well kept Greene King and guests, enjoyable home-made food (not Sun evening), friendly staff, traditional bar with tiled floor and open fire; children welcome, good big front garden with paved terrace and play area on lawn. *(Chantel Oakman)*

CROYDON TL3149
★ Queen Adelaide (01223) 208278
Off A1198 or B1042; High Street; SG8 0DN Spreading open-plan carpeted local with wide range of enjoyable food including Mon-Weds OAP lunches, friendly

prompt service, ales such as Greene King and Potton, several wines by the glass, lots of spirits, big low-beamed main area with standing timbers dividing off part with sofas, banquettes and stools, pool in games area, conservatory extension, daily papers; background music (even in gents' – a shrine to Marilyn Monroe), TV, machines; children welcome (play area on lawn), heated terrace with smokers' shelter, bedrooms, open all day Fri-Sun. *(David Harris, Simon Watkins, P and D Carpenter)*

ELSWORTH TL3163
Poacher (01954) 268167
Brockley Road; CB23 4JS Welcoming 17th-c thatched and beamed local, ales such as Shepherd Neame, Woodfordes and Wychwood, good value fresh food; children and dogs welcome, tables in back garden, good walks, open all day. *(Dennis and Doreen Haward)*

ELTISLEY TL2759
Eltisley (01480) 880308
Signed off A428; The Green; PE19 6TG Attractive dining areas including stylish barn room, flagstoned bar with beams, timbering, some zinc-topped cast-iron tables and big log fire, good interesting carefully sourced food, friendly service, Wells & Youngs ales and guests, good choice of wines by the glass; background music and live jazz (first Sun of month); children welcome, dogs in bar, nice garden behind, six good value bedrooms, closed Sun evening, Mon. *(Eithne Dandy, D C Poulton, Michael Sargent, Dave Braisted)*

ELY TL5479
★ Cutter (01353) 662713
Annesdale, off Station Road (or walk S along Riverside Walk from Maltings); CB7 4BN Beautifully placed contemporary riverside pub with carpeted dining bar and smart restaurant, enjoyable promptly served food from sandwiches up including good value Sun roasts, well kept Shepherd Neame and Sharps Doom Bar from boat-shaped bar, nice wines by the glass, decent coffee, good views from window seats and front terrace. *(John Saville, Rita Scarratt, Barry Collett, Lawrence Pearse, Pete Coxon)*

ELY TL5480
Lamb (01353) 663574
Brook Street (Lynn Road); CB7 4EJ Good choice of fairly standard locally sourced food in popular hotel's panelled lounge bar, including Sun roasts and OAP deals Mon, friendly welcoming staff, good choice of wines by the glass, Greene King ales; close to cathedral, clean comfortable bedrooms, good breakfast. *(Pete Coxon, Sue and Mike Todd)*

ELY TL5380
West End House (01353) 662907
West End, off Cambridge Road; CB6 3AY Popular old corner local with beams, some

stripped brickwork and open fires, mixed furniture including leather armchairs, pews and plush banquettes, assorted pictures and pub bric-a-brac, well kept Adnams, Shepherd Neame and two guests, lunchtime sandwiches and light snacks (no food evenings or Sun); no dogs; children welcome, courtyard garden with pergola, open all day Fri, Sat. *(Andy Wilkinson)*

FOWLMERE   TL4245
★ **Chequers** (01763) 208369
B1368; SG8 7SR Civilised 16th-c coaching inn with two comfortable downstairs rooms, long cushioned wall seats, dining chairs around dark tables, open log fire, good imaginative modern food, real ales and several wines by the glass, smart upstairs beamed and timbered dining room with interesting moulded plasterwork above one fireplace, spacious conservatory (children here only); terrace and garden with lots of tables under parasols. *(M R D Foot, Roy Hoing)*

GODMANCHESTER   TL2470
Exhibition (01480) 459134
London Road; PE29 2HZ Big flagstones and traditional furnishings, enjoyable well priced food, well kept Greene King IPA, decent choice of wines by the glass; picnic-sets on back lawn (a couple in front, too), open all day. *(John Saville)*

GRANTCHESTER   TL4355
★ **Blue Ball** (01223) 840679
Broadway; CB3 9NQ Particularly well kept Adnams and a guest ale in character bare-boards village local, said to be the area's oldest, proper hands-on landlord, good log fire, cards and traditional games including shut the box and ring the bull, lots of books; dogs welcome, tables on small terrace with lovely views to Grantchester Meadows, nice village. *(Stuart Gideon, Mrs Catherine Simmonds)*

GRANTCHESTER   TL4355
Green Man (01223) 844669
High Street; CB3 9NF Friendly pub with heavy beams, mix of old tables and chairs on bare boards, leather sofa and armchairs, log fire, well cooked food (all day weekends) from traditional to more sophisticated dishes, good range of changing local ales tapped from the cask, separate dining room with linen napkins, Sun night jazz; children welcome, dogs in bar, disabled facilities, tables in big back garden with own bar, Granchester Meadows views, open all day. *(Mrs Margo Finlay, Jörg Kasprowski, Simon Watkins)*

GRANTCHESTER   TL4355
Red Lion (01223) 840121
High Street; CB3 9NF Comfortable and spacious thatched pub, wide choice of enjoyable food including plenty of fish dishes and bargain weekday specials, children's

menu, good friendly service, Greene King ales, four modernised open areas with beams, timbers and panelling; background music; sheltered terrace and good-sized lawn, play area, easy walk to river, open all day. *(Rod Weston, John Saville)*

GREAT CHISHILL   TL4239
★ **Pheasant** (01763) 838535
Follow Heydon signpost from B1039 in village; SG8 8SR Popular split-level flagstoned pub with beams, timbering, open fires and some elaborately carved (though modern) seats and settles, good freshly made food (not Sun evening) using local produce, welcoming friendly staff, two or three ales including one for the pub from Nethergate, good choice of wines by the glass, small dining room (best to book), darts, cribbage, dominoes; no under-14s inside; dogs allowed, charming secluded back garden with small play area, open all day weekends. *(Oliver Thain, Paul Elkington, R Anderson, Mrs Margo Finlay, Jörg Kasprowski)*

GREAT SHELFORD   TL4652
Square & Compasses
(01766) 810250 *High Street; CB22 5EH* Small well kept village local with friendly welcoming staff, popular reasonably priced food, Greene King ales. *(Phil and Jane Hodson)*

HARDWICK   TL3758
Blue Lion (01954) 210328
Signed off A428 (was A45) W of Cambridge; Main Street; CB23 7QU Attractive old pub smartened up under current licensees, beams and timbers, leather armchairs by copper-canopied inglenook, good food from landlord/chef in bar and extended dining area with conservatory, friendly young uniformed staff, Greene King IPA and guest ales; pretty roadside front garden, handy for Wimpole Way walkers, open all day. *(Phil and Jane Hodson, Simon Humphrey, John Saville, M and GR)*

HARSTON   TL4251
Queens Head (01223) 870693
Royston Road (A10, near M11 junction 11); CB22 7NH Greene King pub doing well under current management, enjoyable well priced pubby food including OAP lunch deals, good friendly service, charity quiz (second Sat of month); children welcome, garden tables, open all day Fri and Sun, closed Sun evening. *(Sidney and Jean Gould, R C Vincent, David Morris, Phil and Jane Hodson)*

HEYDON   TL4339
★ **King William IV** (01763) 838773
Off A505 W of M11 junction 10; SG8 8PW Rambling dimly lit rooms with fascinating rustic jumble (ploughshares, yokes, iron tools, cowbells and so forth) along with copperware and china in nooks and

crannies, log fire, Fullers, Greene King and Timothy Taylors Landlord, good varied choice of well presented food including proper home-made pies, helpful staff; background music; children welcome, dogs in bar area, teak furniture on heated terrace and in pretty garden, open all day weekends. *(Mrs Margo Finlay, Jörg Kasprowski, John Wooll, Howard and Margaret Buchanan)*

HISTON   TL4363
⋆ **Red Lion** (01223) 564437
High Street, off Station Road; 3.7 miles from M11 junction 1; signposted off A14 E via B1049; CB4 9JD A shrine to real ale; ceiling joists in L-shaped main bar packed with hundreds of beer mats and pump clips among hop bines and whisky-water jugs, fine collection of old brewery advertisements and rack of real ale campaign literature, impressive choice of draught and bottled beers along with a farm cider and a perry, spring and early autumn festivals, limited lunchtime food (nothing on Sun), cheerful efficient service, comfortable brocaded wall seats, matching mate's chairs and pubby tables, log fires, nice antique one-arm bandit, bar on left with darts, TV and huge collection of beer bottles; no credit cards; well behaved children allowed in one part only, picnic-sets in neat garden, play area, limited parking, open all day. *(Phil and Jane Hodson, Stuart Gideon, Mrs Catherine Simmonds, Kevin McPheat)*

HOLYWELL   TL3370
Old Ferry Boat (01480) 463227
Signed off A1123; PE27 4TG Welcoming partly thatched Greene King pub in lovely peaceful setting, low beams, open fires and interesting side areas, window seats overlooking Great Ouse, well kept beer and good coffee, food from snacks up (they may ask for a credit card if you run a tab); quiet background music, machines; children welcome, plenty of tables and cocktail parasols on front terrace and riverside lawn, moorings, seven bedrooms, open all day weekends. *(Anon)*

HORSEHEATH   TL6147
Old Red Lion (01223) 892909
Linton Road; CB21 4QF Neatly kept Greene King pub, good value food, efficient staff; 12 cabin bedrooms. *(Simon Watkins)*

HUNTINGDON   TL2371
⋆ **George** (01480) 432444
George Street; PE29 3AB Relaxed, friendly and comfortable hotel lounge bar, generous reasonably priced sandwiches and bar and brasserie meals, Greene King IPA and Abbot, several wines by the glass, good coffee (or tea and pastries); background music; magnificent galleried central courtyard, comfortable bedrooms. *(Anon)*

LITTLE SHELFORD   TL4551
Navigator (01223) 843901
2.5 miles from M11 junction 11: A10 towards Royston, then left at Hauxton, The Shelfords signpost; CB2 5ES Attractive 16th-c village local with beams, pine panelling, pews and a hot-coal fire, good authentic thai food (not Sat lunchtime, offers Mon-Weds), Greene King and a guest ale, Aspall's cider, decent wines, quick obliging service; children welcome, some picnic-sets outside. *(Nathan Ward)*

LONGSTOWE   TL3154
Red House (01954) 718480
Old North Road; A1198 Royston–Huntingdon, S of village; CB3 7UT Creeper-covered pub with dark red décor and sporting theme, quarry-tiled bar with big log fire, lower part with chintzy easy chairs and sofas, well kept ales such as Church End, Potton and local Lord Conrad, several wines by the glass, straightforward home-made food; background music; children and dogs welcome, garden with picnic-sets and farmland views, good walks, open all day Sun. *(Simon Watkins)*

MADINGLEY   TL3960
⋆ **Three Horseshoes** (01954) 210221
High Street; off A1303 W of Cambridge; CB23 8AB Civilised thatched restauranty pub – most customers come here for the imaginative if not cheap italian food; there is, though, a small pleasantly relaxed bar, with simple wooden furniture on bare boards and open fire (can be a bit of a crush at peak times), Adnams and Jennings Cumberland, outstanding wine list with 23 by the glass, efficient friendly service, pretty dining conservatory; children welcome, picnic-sets under parasols in sunny garden. *(Tony Middis, Tom and Ruth Rees, Gordon and Margaret Ormondroyd, Mike and Hilary Doupe, Ian Willis)*

NEEDINGWORTH   TL3571
⋆ **Pike & Eel** (01480) 463336
Pub signed from A1123; Overcote Road; PE27 4TW Peacefully located riverside hotel with spacious lawns and small marina; plush bar opening into room with easy chairs, sofas and big open fire, civilised eating area (also separate smart restaurant) in light and airy glass-walled block overlooking water, boats and swans, good food and service, Adnams Broadside, Black Sheep and Greene King IPA, good coffee and wines; background music; children welcome, 12 clean simple bedrooms, good breakfast. *(Simon Watkins)*

NEWTON   TL4349
⋆ **Queens Head** (01223) 870436
2.5 miles from M11 J11; A10 towards Royston, then left on to B1368; CB22 7PG Lovely traditional unchanging pub run by same welcoming family for many

years, lots of loyal customers, peaceful bow-windowed main bar with crooked beams in low ceiling, bare wooden benches and seats built into cream walls, curved high-backed settle, paintings, big log fire, Adnams ales tapped from the cask, farm cider, hearty simple food, small carpeted saloon, pubby games including table skittles, shove-ha' penny and nine men's morris; no credit cards; children on best behaviour allowed in games room only, dogs welcome, seats out in front by vine trellis. *(Prof James Stevens Curl, Simon Watkins, Kay and Alistair Butler, R Anderson, Sarah Flynn)*

OFFORD D'ARCY   TL2166
Horseshoe (01480) 810293
High Street; PE19 5RH Extended former 17th-c farmhouse, emphasis on enjoyable food from sandwiches and pub favourites to local game, popular Sun lunch (must book), friendly unhurried service, changing real ales, two bars and restaurant, beams and log fires; children welcome, garden with play area, open all day Sun. *(Phil and Jane Hodson, P and D Carpenter)*

PAMPISFORD   TL4948
★ Chequers (01223) 833220
2.6 miles from M11 junction 10: A505 E, then village and pub signed off; Town Lane; CB22 4ER Traditional neatly-kept old pub with friendly licensees, low beams and comfortable old-fashioned furnishings, booth seating on pale ceramic tiles in cream-walled main area, low step down to bare-boards part with dark pink walls, Greene King IPA, Timothy Taylors Landlord, and Woodfordes Wherry, enjoyable fairly priced food including Sun carvery; TV; children and dogs welcome (their collie is called Snoopy), picnic-sets in prettily planted simple garden lit by black streetlamps, open all day (till 4pm Sun). *(Roger M Hancock, D and M T Ayres-Regan, Peter and Giff Bennett, Charles Gysin, Roy Hoing and others)*

PETERBOROUGH   TL1899
★ Brewery Tap (01733) 358500
Opposite Queensgate car park; PE1 2AA Striking conversion of old labour exchange with own-brewed Oakham beers and up to eight guests, well liked good value thai food, easy-going relaxed feel in open-plan contemporary interior with expanse of light wood and stone floors (vast glass wall divides bar and brewery), blue-painted iron pillars supporting mezzanine, stylish lighting, long curved light wood counter backed by impressive display of bottles, comfortable downstairs area, regular live bands and comedy nights; background music, big-screen sports TV, machines, gets packed evenings; children welcome during food hours only, dogs allowed in bar, same owners as Charters, open all day. *(P Dawn, Mike and Sue Loseby, Ian and Helen Stafford, John Honnor)*

PETERBOROUGH   TL1998
★ Charters (01733) 315700
Town Bridge, S side; PE1 1FP Remarkable conversion of dutch grain barge moored on River Nene; a dozen real ales including Oakham, good value pan-asian food, sizeable timbered bar on lower deck, restaurant above, lots of wooden tables and pews, regular beer festivals, live bands (Fri and Sat after 10.30pm); background music, games machines; children welcome till 9pm, dogs in bar, huge riverside garden (gets packed in fine weather), open all day. *(Steve Nye, P Dawn, Andy and Jill Kassube)*

PETERBOROUGH   TL1898
Drapers Arms (01733) 847570
Cowgate; PE1 1LZ Roomy open-plan Wetherspoons in sympathetically converted draper's, fine ale range, bargain food all day; can get very busy Fri, Sat evenings; children welcome, open all day from 9am. *(Ian and Helen Stafford)*

REACH   TL5666
★ Dyke's End (01638) 743816
From B1102 follow signpost to Swaffham Prior and Upware; village signposted; CB5 0JD New owners for this 17th-c farmhouse; simply decorated bar with kitchen chairs and heavy pine tables on dark boards, panelled section on left with smarter dining tables and step down to carpeted part with servery, have had own-brewed Devils Dyke beers plus guests, food has been good; picnic-sets on front grass, attractive spot next to church and village green, may close Mon lunchtime. *(Bruce M Drew, M and GR)*

ST IVES   TL3171
Oliver Cromwell (01480) 465601
Wellington Street; PE27 5AZ Friendly traditional two-bar pub, well priced lunchtime food (not Sun) including good homely dishes such as steak and kidney pudding, half a dozen well kept changing ales; pleasant garden with café-style furniture on terrace, open all day. *(Susan and Jeremy Arthern)*

ST IVES   TL3171
White Hart (01480) 46327
Sheep Market; PE27 5AH Welcoming old town-centre pub, family run with good helpings of sensibly priced food, well kept ales, teas and coffee, warm friendly atmosphere; dogs allowed in comfortable bar area, attractive courtyard, bedrooms. *(Robert Turnham, James and Carole Findlay)*

ST NEOTS   TL1859
★ Chequers (01480) 472116
St Mary's Street (B1043 S of centre); PE19 2TA Friendly 16th-c village pub with small carpeted beamed bar, appealing mix of furniture including an unusual rocking chair, log fire in big inglenook, changing real

ales and good choice of food, attractive back restaurant (children allowed here) with rugs on brick floor; background music; tables on terrace and in sheltered garden behind, closed Sun evening, Mon. *(John Watson)*

ST NEOTS   TL1761
Eaton Oak (01480) 219555

A1; PE19 7DB Under same ownership as the George & Dragon at Elsworth and Rose at Stapleford; wide choice of enjoyable food including fresh fish and good value set menus, Wells & Youngs ales, good friendly service, spacious dining area, conservatory; disabled access throughout, tables outside under parasols, nine bedrooms, open all day (breakfast for non-residents). *(Michael and Jenny Back and others)*

STAPLEFORD   TL4651
✶ **Rose** (01223) 843349

London Road; M11 J11; CB22 5DG Comfortable sister pub to George & Dragon at Elsworth and Eaton Oak at St Neots, emphasis on dining and can get very busy, wide choice of well cooked reasonably priced food (10% NHS discount), pleasant uniformed staff, well kept Adnams, St Austell Tribute and Woodfordes Wherry, small low-ceilinged lounge with inglenook woodburner, roomy split-level dining area; faint background music; picnic-sets on back grass. *(Phil and Jane Hodson, Michael and Jenny Back)*

STOW CUM QUY   TL5260
White Swan (01223) 811821

Off A14 E of Cambridge, via B1102; CB25 9AB Cosy beamed village local under new licensees, four well kept ales such as Adnams and Oakham JHB, Weston's cider, enjoyable food from snacks and pubby choices up, big fireplace, restaurant; children and dogs welcome, terrace picnic-sets, handy for Anglesey Abbey (NT). *(Phil and Jane Hodson, M and GR)*

STRETHAM   TL5072
Lazy Otter (01353) 649780

Elford Closes, off A10 S of Stretham roundabout; CB6 3LU Big rambling family pub on Great Ouse, good views from waterside conservatory and sizeable garden with play area, popular reasonably priced food served quickly, good choice of wines, a beer brewed for the pub plus Greene King IPA and guests, clean and nicely furnished, warm fire; background music; moorings, open all day. *(R C Vincent)*

WANSFORD   TL0799
Paper Mills (01780) 782328

London Road; PE8 6JB Attractively refurbished old stone pub with friendly buzzy atmosphere, Fullers London Pride

and a couple of guests, good wine selection, enjoyable popular food served by well trained young staff, beamed and flagstoned bar with fireplaces either side, conservatory; children and dogs welcome, tables in nicely tended garden. *(Clive Flynn, Maurice and Janet Thorpe, Phil and Jane Hodson, Sam and Christine Kilburn, G Jennings)*

WARESLEY   TL2454
Duncombe Arms (01767) 650265

Eltisley Road (B1040, 5 miles S of A428); SG19 3BS Comfortable and welcoming old pub under newish licensees, long main bar with fire at one end, enjoyable traditional food and well kept Greene King ales, friendly service, back room and restaurant; occasional live music; picnic-sets in small shrub-sheltered garden. *(D C Poulton, Simon Watkins, Roger Fox)*

WHITTLESFORD   TL4648
Bees in the Wall (01223) 834289

North Road; handy for M11 junction 10; CB2 4NZ Comfortably worn-in split-level timbered lounge with flowers on polished tables and country prints, small tiled public bar with old wall settles, darts, decent good value food (not Sun or Mon evenings) from sandwiches up, well kept Fullers London Pride, Timothy Taylors Landlord and a guest beer, open fires; may be background classical music, games machine, no dogs; picnic-sets in big paddock-style garden with terrace, bees' nest visible in wall, handy for Duxford air museum, open all day weekends. *(Chris Smith)*

WICKEN   TL5670
Maids Head (01353) 720727

High Street; CB7 5XR Old thatched dining pub with good food (not Sun evening) from bar snacks up, friendly informal atmosphere, up to four local ales, fairly priced house wines, unpretentious bar with pool and darts, restaurant (children welcome here), two open fires, events including quiz night (last Sun of month); dogs allowed in bar, tables outside, village-green setting, handy for Wicken Fen nature reserve (NT), open all day weekends (till 1am Sat). *(Rita Scarratt, David Edge, Keith and Margaret Evans, David Brown, Jamie and Sue May)*

WOODDITTON   TL6558
Three Blackbirds (01638) 731100

Signed off B1063 at Cheveley; CB8 9SQ Sympathetically restored two-bar thatched pub, low 17th-c beams, mix of old country furniture on bare boards, pictures and knick-knacks, open fires, some enterprising food together with pub favourites and lunchtime sandwiches, Adnams, Timothy Taylors and changing local guests, restaurant; children welcome, garden, closed Sun evening and Mon (except bank hols). *(Anon)*

There are report forms at the back of the book.

Cheshire

Brunning & Price started life in this part of the world and have an impressive number of pubs here, a testament to the success of their great formula – all those we feature offer a great range of drinks and good meals but we'd particularly pick out the Grosvenor Arms in Aldford (their flagship), Dysart Arms in Bunbury (embracing and homely and Cheshire Dining Pub of the Year), Old Harkers Arms in Chester (bustling warehouse conversion), Sutton Hall in Macclesfield (splendid old manor house) and Old Hall in Sandbach (an even more magnificent restoration). Most Brunning & Price pubs stock a great range of beers, but so do many other pubs in this county, particularly the Bhurtpore in Aston (gets right down to business), the Mill in Chester (useful modern hotel), the Yew Tree at Spurstow (top notch all-rounder with entertaining décor), Bears Paw at Warmingham (also enjoyable food, and new this year). Other new pubs this year include the Bulls Head at Mobberley (warmly welcoming), Swettenham Arms in Swettenham (happily back in after a break), Little Manor at Thelwall (handsome Brunning & Price restoration) and Dusty Miller at Wrenbury (canalside place with good food and also a reinstatement).

 ALDFORD   SJ4259   Map 7

Grosvenor Arms ★

B5130 Chester–Wrexham; CH3 6HJ

Spacious place with buoyantly chatty atmosphere, impressive range of drinks, wide-ranging imaginative menu, good service; lovely big terrace and gardens

One of the most consistent pubs in the Guide, this flagship in the Brunning & Price chain has had terrific reports from the first day of its inclusion. It retains plenty of individuality and its friendly staff engender a welcoming atmosphere. Spacious cream-painted areas are sectioned by big knocked-through arches with a variety of wood, quarry tile, flagstone and black and white tiled floor finishes – some richly coloured turkish rugs look well against these natural materials. Good solid pieces of traditional furniture, plenty of interesting pictures and attractive lighting keep it all intimate enough. A handsomely boarded panelled room has tall bookshelves lining one wall; good selection of board games. Lovely on summer evenings, the airy terracotta-floored conservatory has lots of gigantic low-hanging flowering baskets and chunky pale wood garden furniture. It opens out to a large, elegant suntrap terrace, and a neat lawn with picnic-sets, young trees and an old tractor. Attentive staff dispense a wide range of drinks from a fine-looking bar counter, including 20 wines by the glass and over 80 whiskies, distinctive soft drinks such as peach and elderflower cordial and Willington Fruit Farm pressed apple juice, as well as half a dozen real ales including Brunning & Price Original (brewed for them by Phoenix) and Weetwood Eastgate, with guests from brewers such as Derby, Moorhouses and Spitting Feathers.

Food here is very good with the well balanced changing menu including something to please most tastes. As well as sandwiches, there might be pork and chorizo meatballs in tomato sauce, crab spring roll and pineapple salsa, warm pigeon breast with hazelnut and apple salad, smoked salmon, broccoli and courgette linguine with lemon and dill cream sauce, malaysian chicken with coconut rice and coriander beans, confit duck leg with white bean and pancetta cassoulet, aubergine, spinach and lentil moussaka with feta and pepper salad, and puddings such as chocolate and hazelnut pavlova with ice-cream, cream and chocolate sauce and apple crumble. *Benchmark main dish: kedgeree £8.85. Two-course evening meal £18.20.*

Brunning & Price ~ Manager Tracey Owen ~ Real ale ~ Bar food (12-9.30(10 Fri, Sat; 9 Sun)) ~ (01244) 620228 ~ Children welcome ~ Dogs allowed in bar ~ Open 11.30-11; 12-10.30 Sun ~ www.grosvenorarms-aldford.co.uk *Recommended by Clive Watkin, Phil and Gill Wass, John Andrew, W K Wood*

ASTBURY   SJ8461   Map 7??

Egerton Arms £ 🛏

Village signposted off A34 S of Congleton; CW12 4RQ

Cheery village pub with straightforward bar food, large garden, and nice bedrooms

The kindly family that have run his homely old place for some years now and their long-serving staff, offer a good natured welcome to all. Part 16th-c farmhouse, its pubby cream-painted rooms are decorated with the odd piece of armour, shelves of books and, quite a few mementoes of the Sandow Brothers (one of whom was the landlady's father) who performed as 'the World's Strongest Youths'. In summer, dried flowers replace the fire in the big fireplace; background music, games machine, TV. Four Robinsons ales are on handpump, in addition to winter alcoholic warmers, about a dozen wines by the glass and a range of malt whiskies. Well placed tables outside enjoy pleasant views of the church, and a play area has a wooden fort; handy for Little Moreton Hall (National Trust).

As well as sandwiches, bar food might include starters such as jalapeno peppers stuffed with cream cheese and breaded butterfly king prawns, and main courses such as steak and kidney pudding, stilton burger, four daily roasts, chicken jalfrezi and vegetable balti, and puddings such as syrup sponge pudding and Mars Bar sundae with chocolate sauce. *Benchmark main dish: battered cod £10.95. Two-course evening meal £15.55.*

We say if we know a pub has background music.

Robinsons ~ Tenants Alan and Grace Smith ~ Real ale ~ Bar food (11.30-2, 6-9; 12-8 Sun) ~ Restaurant ~ (01260) 273946 ~ Children welcome ~ Open 11.30-11(10.30 Sun) ~ Bedrooms: £50S/£70B ~ www.egertonarms.com *Recommended by Brian and Janet Ainscough, Christopher Mobbs, Brian and Anna Marsden, Mike Proctor, Dave Webster, Sue Holland*

ASTON
THE GOOD PUB GUIDE
Bhurtpore ★ ♀ 🍺 £
SJ6146 Map 7

Off A530 SW of Nantwich; in village follow Wrenbury signpost; CW5 8DQ

Fantastic range of drinks (especially real ales) and tasty curries in a warm-hearted pub with some unusual artefacts; big garden

With the terrific range of drinks at this lovingly run place, including 11 real ales, it's no surprise that tables reserved for drinkers in the comfortable public bar are put to good use. They tell us they run through over 1,000 superbly kept real ales a year, sourced from an enterprising range of brewers from around the UK such as All Gates, Brecon, Derby, Foxfield, Hobsons, Pennine, Rowton, Salopian, Tatton and Wapping. They also stock dozens of unusual bottled beers and fruit beers, a great many bottled ciders and perries, over 100 different whiskies, carefully selected soft drinks and wines from a good list; summer beer festival. The pub is named to commemorate the siege of Bhurtpore (a town in India) during which local landowner Sir Stapleton Cotton (later Viscount Combermere) was commander in chief of the British force. The connection with India also explains some of the quirky artefacts in the carpeted lounge bar – look out for the turbaned figure in sunglasses behind the counter; also good local period photographs and some attractive furniture; board games, pool, TV and games machine. Cheery staff usually cope well with the busy weekends.

🍴 The enjoyably varied menu includes sandwiches, breaded brie, onion bhajis, smoked haddock with cheese and leek sauce, several curries, steak, goats cheese puff pastry tart, chicken and bacon salad, lamb shoulder braised in mint and sherry sauce, battered haddock, grilled duck breast on braised red cabbage with mulled red wine sauce, sirloin steak, and puddings such as warm chocolate fudge cake and waffle with honeycomb ice-cream and toffee sauce. *Benchmark main dish: steak, kidney and ale pie £10.50. Two-course evening meal £16.00.*

Free house ~ Licensee Simon George ~ Real ale ~ Bar food (12-2, 7-9.30; 12-9.30 Sat (9 Sun)) ~ Restaurant ~ (01270) 780917 ~ Children welcome till 8.30pm ~ Dogs allowed in bar ~ Open 12-2.30, 6.30-11.30; 12-midnight Fri, Sat; 12-11 Sun ~ www.bhurtpore.co.uk *Recommended by Mike Proctor, Dave Webster, Sue Holland, Gill and Keith Croxton, Dennis Jones, the Didler*

BICKLEY MOSS
THE GOOD PUB GUIDE
Cholmondeley Arms ♀
SJ5550 Map 7

Cholmondeley; A49 5.5 miles N of Whitchurch; the owners would like us to list them under Cholmondeley village, but as this is rarely marked on maps we have mentioned the nearest village, which appears more often; SY14 8HN

Imaginatively converted high-ceilinged schoolhouse with decent range of real ales and wines, well presented food and a sizeable garden

Recent refurbishments have brought a quirkily baronial feel to the interior of this former schoolhouse, with its lofty ceilings, stripped brick walls and massive stag's head by the cosy fire, though its high gothic windows, huge old radiators and various old school paraphernalia (look out for hockey sticks, tennis rackets and trunks), are all testament to its former identity. Plenty of attention to detail in the shape of fresh flowers and church candles. Warmly coloured rugs on bare boards, big mirrors, armchairs by the fire and a comfy mix of dining chairs keep it all feeling friendly and well cared for; background music. Their impressive range of 87 gins look well with the attractively carved dark wood counter, and their Cholmondeley Best and Teachers Tipple (both Weetwood beers) and three guests from brewers such as Coach House, Dunham Massey and Salopian are usefully described on little boards propped up in front of the taps. There is plenty of seating outside on the sizeable lawn, which drifts off into open countryside, and more in front overlooking the quiet road. The pub is handily placed for Cholmondeley Castle Gardens.

Bar food includes fried scallops with crispy ham and minted pea purée, devilled lambs kidneys on toast, smoked salmon fishcakes with bloody mary dressed salad, sausage and mash with shallot gravy, battered haddock, smoked pork belly with candied walnut salad and apple crisps, baked cod with brown shrimps and lemon butter and a spicy sausage and butternut hash cake, duck leg with lentil hot pot with prunes and root vegetables, well hung steaks, and puddings such as spotted dick and rhubarb crumble. *Benchmark main dish: steak and kidney pie £11.95. Two-course evening meal £18.80.*

Free house ~ Licensee Steven Davies ~ Real ale ~ Bar food (12-9.30(9.45 Sat, 8.45 Sun)) ~ (01829) 720300 ~ Children under 10 till 7pm in pub, 9pm in garden ~ Dogs welcome ~ quiz monthly ~ Open 12-11(11.30 Sat, 10.30 Sun) ~ Bedrooms: £80B/£110B ~ www.cholmondeleyarms.co.uk *Recommended by R L Borthwick, P J and R D Greaves, Peter Harrison, Mike Proctor*

BUNBURY SJ5658 Map 7

Dysart Arms

Bowes Gate Road; village signposted off A51 NW of Nantwich; and from A49 S of Tarporley – coming in this way on northernmost village access road, bear left in village centre; CW6 9PH

Cheshire Dining Pub of the Year

Civilised chatty dining pub attractively filled with good furniture in thoughtfully laid-out rooms; very enjoyable food, lovely garden with pretty views

---

A steady flow of enthusiastic reader reports confirm that this village pub is on terrific form. Although opened up and gently refurbished, its rooms retain a cosy cottagey feel and have an easy-going sociable atmosphere – there is a genuinely friendly welcome here. Neatly kept, they ramble gently around the pleasantly lit central bar. Cream walls keep it all light, clean and airy, with deep venetian red ceilings adding cosiness, and each room (some with good winter fires) is nicely furnished with an appealing variety of well spaced sturdy wooden tables and chairs, a couple of tall filled bookcases and just the right amount of carefully chosen bric-a-brac, properly lit pictures and plants. Flooring ranges from red and black tiles to stripped boards and some carpet. Service is efficient and friendly. Phoenix Brunning & Price Original, Timothy Taylors Landlord and three guests such as Adnams, Caledonian Deuchars IPA and Fullers London Pride are on handpump alongside a good selection of 17 wines by the glass from a list of about 70 bottles, and just over 20 malts. Sturdy wooden tables on the terrace and picnic-sets on the lawn in the neatly kept slightly elevated garden are lovely in summer, with views of the splendid church at the end of this pretty village, and the distant Peckforton Hills beyond.

🍴 From a changing menu, food is tasty, just imaginative enough, attractively presented and fairly priced. As well as sandwiches, there might be venison carpaccio, black pudding and chorizo salad, baked brie with pear chutney, crispy duck salad, smoked haddock and salmon fishcakes, pine nut crusted hake fillet with roast garlic mash and red wine sauce, battered haddock, spiced chick pea and red lentil fritter with roast onion, courgette and marsala sauce, and puddings such as lemon meringue pie with raspberry and basil compote and dark chocolate and orange brownie with boozy cherries. *Benchmark main dish: pheasant wrapped in bacon £12.95. Two-course evening meal £18.10.*

Brunning & Price ~ Manager Greg Williams ~ Real ale ~ Bar food (12-9.30(9 Sun)) ~ Restaurant ~ (01829) 260183 ~ Children welcome ~ Dogs allowed in bar ~ Open 11.30-11; 12-10.30 Sun ~ www.dysartarms-bunbury.co.uk *Recommended by Clive Watkin, Dave Webster, Sue Holland, Mark Delap, David Jackman, Mrs P Abell*

BURLEYDAM
Combermere Arms 🍴 🍺
SJ6042 Map 7

A525 Whitchurch–Audlem; SY13 4AT

Roomy and attractive beamed pub successfully combining a good drinking side with imaginative all-day food

The attractive but understated interior of this popular 18th-c place has been cleverly opened up to give a light and roomy feel, though its many different areas do still seem intimate. Décor and furnishings take in a laid-back mix of wooden chairs at dark wood tables, rugs on wood (some old and some new oak) and stone floors, prints hung frame to frame on cream walls, deep red ceilings, panelling and open fires. Friendly staff extend an equally nice welcome to drinkers and diners, with both aspects of the business seeming to do well. Alongside Black Sheep, Phoenix Brunning & Price Original and Weetwood Cheshire Cat, three or four guests might be from brewers such as McMullen and Stonehouse. They also stock around 60 whiskies and a dozen wines by the glass from an extensive list; a few board games. Outside there are good solid wood tables in a pretty, well tended garden; more reports please.

🍴 As well as interesting sandwiches and ploughman's, the enjoyable daily-changing menu might include garlic mushrooms on toasted brioche, crab and prawn spring roll with mango, red onion and coriander salsa, charcuterie board, crab linguine, rump steak sandwich, braised lamb shoulder, confit duck with black cherry salad, roast pork belly with five spices, asian vegetables and noodles, bouillabaisse, sausage and mash, and puddings such as chocolate and hazelnut cheesecake and steamed lemon marmalade sponge. *Benchmark main dish: venison steak £17.95. Two-course evening meal £18.30.*

Brunning & Price ~ Manager Lisa Hares ~ Real ale ~ Bar food (12-9.30; 12-10 Thurs-Sat; 12-9 Sun) ~ (01948) 871223 ~ Children welcome ~ Dogs allowed in bar ~ Open 11.30-11(10.30 Sun) ~ www.combermerearms-burleydam.co.uk *Recommended by Mr and Mrs M Stratton, Paul and Gail Betteley*

BURWARDSLEY
Pheasant ★ ♀
SJ5256 Map 7

Higher Burwardsley; signposted from Tattenhall (which itself is signposted off A41 S of Chester) and from Harthill (reached by turning off A534 Nantwich–Holt at the Copper Mine); follow pub's signpost on up hill from Post Office; OS Sheet 117 map reference 523566; CH3 9PF

Fantastic views and enjoyable food at this fresh conversion of an old heavily beamed inn; open all day

Nice hardwood furniture on the terrace and some of the tables in the bar benefit from the stunning views right across the Cheshire plains offered by the idyllic elevated position of this 17th-c sandstone and half-timbered pub – on a clear day the telescope sees as far as the cathedrals in Liverpool. Divided into separate areas and almost circling the bar, the attractive low beamed interior is quite airy and modern-feeling in parts, with comfy leather armchairs and some nice old chairs spread spaciously on its wooden floors and a log fire in a huge see-through fireplace. Drinks include local Weetwood Best and Eastgate, a local farm cider and apple juice; quiet background music, daily newspapers and large screen TV for sporting events. This is a great stop if you are walking the scenic Sandstone Trail along the Peckforton Hills.

As well as interesting sandwiches (till 6pm), the menu includes truffled mushroom and cognac soup, warm salad of poached pear and goats cheese, deli boards, caesar salad, cottage pie, chicken and ham pie, battered haddock, and puddings such as lemon posset with shortbread and warm chocolate brownie with chocolate sauce. *Benchmark main dish: battered haddock £11.95. Two-course evening meal £17.50.*

Free house ~ Licensee Andrew Nelson ~ Real ale ~ Bar food (12-3, 6-9.30 Mon, 12-9.30 Tues-Thurs, 12-10 Fri, Sat, 12-8.30 Sun) ~ Restaurant ~ (01829) 770434 ~ Children welcome ~ Dogs welcome ~ Open 11-11 ~ Bedrooms: £65B/£85B ~ www.thepheasantinn.co.uk *Recommended by Gerry and Rosemary Dobson, Pat and Graham Williamson, Bruce and Sharon Eden, Dave Webster, Sue Holland, Jonny Kershaw, Dr Kevan Tucker, Mrs P Abell*

CHELFORD   SJ8175 Map 7

Egerton Arms

A537 Macclesfield–Knutsford; SK11 9BB

Well organised and welcoming, with something for everyone; food all day

This big rambling place is nicely broken up, with dark beams, an appealingly varied mix of tables and chairs, including some attractive wicker dining chairs, carved settles and a wooden porter's chair by a grandfather clock. At one end a few steps take you down into a super little raftered games area, with tempting squishy sofas and antique farm animal prints on stripped-brick walls, as well as pool, darts, games machines and sports TV; background music. Staff are cheerful and helpful, making for a good relaxed atmosphere, and Copper Dragon Golden Pippin, Wells & Youngs Bombardier and five guests from brewers such as Mobberley, Redwillow and Tatton are served from handpumps on the long counter. An outside deck has canopied picnic-sets, with more on the grass by a toddlers' play area. There's a warm welcome for both dogs and children.

Besides sandwiches, good value cream teas and bargain moules frites on Wednesday nights, enjoyable quickly served food here includes bruschetta, brandy and herb pâté with red onion marmalade, chicken caesar salad, ploughman's, pizzas, gammon and egg, glazed pork belly with dijon mustard sauce, curry of the day, sweet potato, chick pea and aubergine saag, and puddings such as treacle sponge and profiteroles. *Benchmark main dish: salmon with lobster bisque and basil mash £11.95. Two-course evening meal £15.30.*

Free house ~ Licensees Jeremy and Anne Hague ~ Real ale ~ Bar food (12-9) ~ (01625) 861366 ~ Children welcome ~ Dogs allowed in bar ~ Open 12-11(10.30 Sun) ~ www.chelfordegertonarms.co.uk *Recommended by John Wooll*

CHESTER
Albion ★ 🍺 £

SJ4066 Map 7

Albion Street; CH1 1RQ

Strongly traditional pub with comfortable Edwardian décor and captivating World War I memorabilia; pubby food and good drinks

Most unusually, this peaceful Victorian pub is an officially listed site of four war memorials to soldiers from the Cheshire Regiment and its homely interior is entirely dedicated to the Great War of 1914-18. It's been run by the same friendly sincere licensees for over 40 years and there's something inimitably genuine about its lovely old-fashioned atmosphere. Throughout its tranquil rooms you'll find an absorbing collection of World War I memorabilia, from big engravings of men leaving for war and similarly moving prints of wounded veterans, to flags, advertisements and so on. The post-Edwardian décor is appealingly muted, with dark floral William Morris wallpaper (designed on the first day of World War I), a cast-iron fireplace, appropriate lamps, leatherette and hoop-backed chairs and cast-iron-framed tables. You might even be lucky enough to hear the vintage 1928 Steck pianola being played; there's an attractive side dining room, too. Service is friendly, though groups of race-goers are discouraged (opening times may be limited during meets), and they don't like people rushing in just before closing time. A good range of drinks includes Adnams and a couple of guests from brewers such as Hook Norton and Titanic on handpump, new world wines, fresh orange juice, organic bottled cider and fruit juice, over 25 malt whiskies and a good selection of rums and gins. Dog owners can request a water bowl and cold sausage for their pets. Bedrooms are small but comfortable and furnished in keeping with the pub's style (free parking for residents and a bottle of house wine if dining).

🍴 Even the trench rations (helpings are so generous they don't offer starters) are in period: boiled gammon and pease pudding with parsley sauce, corned beef hash with picked red cabbage, liver, bacon and onions with cider sauce, haggis, tatties and vegetables and filled staffordshire oatcakes; food service stops promptly. *Benchmark main dish: boiled gammon and parsley sauce £9.90.*

Punch ~ Lease Michael Edward Mercer ~ Real ale ~ Bar food (12-2(2.30 Sat), 5-8(6-8.30 Sat)) ~ Restaurant ~ No credit cards ~ (01244) 340345 ~ Dogs allowed in bar ~ Open 12-3, 5(6 Sat)-11; closed Sun evening ~ Bedrooms: £70B/£85B ~ www.albioninnchester.co.uk *Recommended by Mike and Eleanor Anderson, Roger and Anne Newbury, Paul Humphreys, the Didler, Trevor Graveson*

CHESTER
Mill 🍺 £

SJ4166 Map 7

Milton Street; CH1 3NF

Big hotel with huge range of real ales, good value food and cheery service in sizeable bar

Converted from an old mill, this modern hotel, which straddles either side of the Shropshire Union Canal, with a glassed-in bridge connecting its two halves, stocks a surprisingly impressive range of a dozen real ales – much enjoyed, we're told, by visiting businessmen.

Weetwood Best and Mill Premium (brewed for them by Coach House) are on all the time, with guests from brewers such as Marstons, RCH and Whim; also a dozen wines by the glass, two farm ciders and 25 malt whiskies. The very neatly kept bar has stripped light wood flooring throughout, marble-topped tables, some exposed brickwork and supporting pillars, and local photographs on cream-papered walls. One comfortable area is reminiscent of a bar on a cruise liner. Service here is very friendly and you'll find a real mix of customers; quiet background music and unobtrusively placed big-screen sports TV. Readers say the bedrooms are comfortable and make a handy base for exploring the city.

Very reasonably priced pubby food includes sandwiches and baguettes, salads, steak and ale pie, lamb burger, sausages and mash, vegetarian or chicken curry, and puddings such as chocolate brownie torte and fruit jelly terrine. *Benchmark main dish: fish and chips £7.50. Two-course evening meal £10.20.*

Free house ~ Licensees Gary and Gordon Vickers ~ Real ale ~ Bar food (11.30-11; 12-10 Sun) ~ Restaurant ~ (01244) 350035 ~ Children welcome ~ Open 9am-midnight ~ Bedrooms: £73B/£95B ~ www.millhotel.com *Recommended by Joe Green, Dave Webster, Sue Holland, Ian Malone*

CHESTER SJ4166 Map 7
Old Harkers Arms ♀ ◀

Russell Street, down steps off City Road where it crosses canal – under Mike Melody Antiques; CH3 5AL

Well run spacious canalside building with lively atmosphere, great range of drinks (including lots of changing real ales), and good tasty food

The striking industrial interior of this high-ceilinged early Victorian warehouse is divided into user-friendly spaces by brick pillars. Cheery staff spread a happy bustle, attractive lamps add cosiness and the mixed dark wood furniture is set out in intimate groups on stripped-wood floors. Walls are covered with old prints hung frame to frame, there's a wall of bookshelves above a leather banquette at one end and the Shropshire Union Canal flows just metres away from the tall windows that run the length of the main bar; selection of board games. You'll find a very wide range of drinks taking in around nine real ales on handpump including Phoenix Brunning & Price, Flowers Original and Weetwood Cheshire Cat, and half a dozen regularly changing guests from brewers such as Brimstage, Bradfield, Northumberland, Salopian and Titanic, over 100 malt whiskies, 50 well described wines (around half of them available by the glass), eight or so farmhouse ciders and local apple juice.

As well as a good range of interesting sandwiches, nicely presented bar food might include tomato and olive soup, lamb samosa with mint yoghurt, smoked salmon and spiced avocado mousse with onion salsa, beef and baby onion pudding with bacon mash, pork and leek sausages with mustard mash, fried hake with chorizo and white bean cassoulet, roast sweet potato, red pepper, artichoke and feta wellington, and puddings such as bread and butter pudding with apricot sauce and syrup sponge pudding. *Benchmark main dish: battered haddock £12.25. Two-course evening meal £18.00.*

Brunning & Price ~ Manager Paul Jeffery ~ Real ale ~ Bar food (12-9.30) ~ (01244) 344525 ~ Children over 10 welcome ~ Dogs allowed in bar ~ Open 11.30-11; 11.30-10.30 Sun ~ www.harkersarms-chester.co.uk *Recommended by Bruce and Sharon Eden, Roger and*

Anne Newbury, Dave Webster, Sue Holland, Dr Kevan Tucker, Paul Humphreys, the Didler, Trevor Graveson, Andy and Jill Kassube

COTEBROOK
SJ5765   Map 7

Fox & Barrel 🍴 🍷

A49 NE of Tarporley; CW6 9DZ

Attractive building with stylishly airy décor, an enterprising menu and good wines

There is a gentle elegance to this warmly welcoming place, which has been subtly refurbished to make the most of the building's nice old character. Much enjoyed by readers, it's run with attention to detail and appeals to drinkers and diners alike. The tiled bar is dominated by a big log fireplace and has stools along its counter. A bigger uncluttered dining area has attractive rugs and an eclectic mix of period tables on polished oak floorboards, with extensive wall panelling hung with framed old prints. The terrace and in the garden have plentiful seating, old fruit trees and a tractor. Real ales include Caledonian Deuchars IPA, Weetwood Eastgate and a couple of guests from brewers such as Beartown and Tatton; good array of wines, with about 20 by the glass.

 The changing menu is very tempting. As well as sandwiches and ploughman's it might include white onion soup, oxtail risotto and horseradish mascarpone, rabbit, ham hock and black pudding terrine with pickled vegetables, warm moroccan lamb salad with coriander yoghurt, crispy pork belly with chorizo, glazed apple and smoked paprika sauce, duck breast with butternut squash risotto and duck spring roll, aubergine, spinach and lentil moussaka, grilled plaice with caper butter, and puddings such as lemon curd and raspberry millefeuille and chocolate and macadamia nut sponge pudding. *Benchmark main dish: battered haddock and mushy peas £12.45. Two-course evening meal £19.50.*

Free house ~ Licensee Gary Kidd ~ Real ale ~ Bar food (12-9.30(9 Sun)) ~ (01829) 760529 ~ Children welcome but no pushchairs ~ Dogs allowed in bar ~ Open 12-11(10.30 Sun) ~ www.foxandbarrel.co.uk *Recommended by Hilary Forrest, David A Hammond, Bruce and Sharon Eden, Andy and Jill Kassube*

EATON
SJ8765   Map 7

Plough 🛏

A536 Congleton–Macclesfield; CW12 2NH

Neat and cosy village pub with up to four interesting beers, bar food, views from big attractive garden; good bedrooms

The carefully converted bar at this tidy red-brick 17th-c pub is friendly and welcoming with a fairly traditional feel. It has plenty of beams and exposed brickwork, a couple of snug little alcoves, comfortable armchairs and cushioned wooden wall seats on red patterned carpets, long red curtains, leaded windows and a big stone fireplace. Service is friendly and attentive; readers have been given highchairs and there's a little table with crayons and paper for children. Beers include Flowers Original and PGA and Storm Desert Storm plus a couple of guests from brewers such as Cottage and Hydes, and a decent wine list offers ten by the glass; background music and occasional TV. Moved here piece by piece from its original home in Wales, the heavily raftered barn at the back makes a striking restaurant. You get good views of the fringes of the Peak District from the big tree-filled garden, which has picnic-sets on the lawn and a covered decked terrace with heaters. The appealingly designed bedrooms are in a converted stable block. Dogs are only allowed in the pub outside food service times.

🍴 It's advisable to book if you are eating. Food includes lunchtime sandwiches, as well as mussels, tapas for two, steak and kidney pie, thai green curry, frittata, well hung aberdeen angus steaks, lambs liver and bacon, grilled blue marlin, and puddings such as cheesecake and bread and butter pudding. *Benchmark main dish: battered haddock £9.95. Two-course evening meal £17.90.*

Free house ~ Licensee Mujdat Karatas ~ Real ale ~ Bar food (12-2.30, 6-9.30; 12-9.30(7.30 Sun) Fri, Sat) ~ Restaurant ~ (01260) 280207 ~ Children welcome ~ Dogs allowed in bedrooms ~ Open 12-11(12 Sat; 10.30 Sun) ~ Bedrooms: £60B/£75B ~ www.theploughinnateaton.co.uk *Recommended by Rob and Catherine Dunster, Mike Proctor*

KETTLESHULME
Swan ◧
SJ9879 Map 7

B5470 Macclesfield–Chapel-en-le-Frith, a mile W of Whaley Bridge; SK23 7QU

Charming 16th-c cottagey pub with enjoyable food (especially fish), good beer and an attractive garden

D o tell us about your meal at this pretty white wisteria-clad cottage – we certainly think the food is good and with just a little more feedback we'd feel confident in giving a Food Award. The interior, under its heavy stone roof, is snug and cosy, with latticed windows, very low dark beams hung with big copper jugs and kettles, timbered walls, antique coaching and other prints and maps, ancient oak settles on the turkish carpet and log fires. They have well kept Marstons on handpump with a couple of guest beers such as Abbeydale Moonshine and Marble Lagonda IPA; service is polite and efficient. The front terrace has teak tables, a second two-level terrace has further tables and steamer benches under parasols, and there's a sizeable streamside garden.

🍴 As well as popular fresh fish dishes, there are plenty of other options including a fine Sunday lunch and good value bar snacks from sandwiches up. The daily changing menu might include cream of chorizo and stilton soup, dressed crab, grilled langoustines, peppered lambs kidneys with peppercorn and brandy cream, seafood risotto, bouillabaisse, gurnard fillet baked with tapenade, linguine with basil pesto, cream, parmesan and pine nuts, greek rabbit stew, braised pork belly served over garlic shredded greens with star anise and honey sauce, and puddings such as steamed lemon curd sponge and chocolate brownie. *Benchmark main dish: fish and chips £11.50. Two-course evening meal £20.50.*

Free house ~ Licensee Robert Cloughley ~ Real ale ~ Bar food (12-2, 6-8.30 Tues; 12-9 Weds, Sat; 12-7 Thurs, Fri; 12-4 Sun; not Mon) ~ (01663) 732943 ~ Children welcome ~ Dogs welcome ~ Open 12-11; closed Mon lunchtime ~ www.verynicepubs.co.uk/swankettleshulme *Recommended by Phil and Helen Holt*

LANGLEY
Hanging Gate ♀
SJ9569 Map 7

Meg Lane, Higher Sutton; follow Langley signpost from A54 beside Fourways Motel, and that road passes the pub; from Macclesfield, heading S from centre on A523 turn left into Byrons Lane at Langley, Wincle signpost; in Sutton (0.5 miles after going under canal bridge, ie before Langley) fork right at Church House Inn, following Wildboarclough signpost, then 2 miles later turn sharp right at steep hairpin bend; OS Sheet 118 map reference 952696; SK11 0NG

Remotely set old place with fires in traditional cosy rooms, lovely views from airy extension and terrace

First licensed in 1621, this low-beamed drovers' pub has an interesting history. The landlady tells us that prisoners were led from here to the gallows outside (hence the pub's name) with the last hanging taking place here in 1958. It's tucked on to the side of a hill high up in the Peak District with stunning panoramic views from its terrace, traditional pub rooms and airy glass-doored dining room over a patchwork of valley pastures to distant moors – on a clear day you can see Liverpool's Anglican Cathedral and Snowdonia. Still in their original layout, the three cosy little low-beamed rooms are simply furnished. The tiny snug bar, at its pubbiest at lunchtime, has a welcoming log fire in a big brick fireplace, just one single table, plain chairs and cushioned wall seats and a few old pub pictures and seasonal photographs on its creamy walls. The second room, with just a section of bar counter in the corner, has five tables, and there's a third appealing little oak-beamed blue room. Beers served include well kept Hydes Original and a Hydes seasonal beer with a couple of guests such as Charles Wells Bombardier on handpump; also quite a few malt whiskies and ten wines by the glass; background music, board games, dominoes, books. It can get busy so it's best to book a table in advance at weekends. Walkers are made to feel welcome with tap water and there's a dog bowl outside and free camping if you eat at the pub.

As well as good sandwiches and ploughman's made with home-baked bread, tasty enjoyable bar food might include pear, smoked trout and parmesan salad, black pudding, home-made burger with stilton, ham, pâté and cheese platter, rabbit, ham and leek pie, lamb hotpot, chargrilled vegetable tart with grilled goats cheese, thai green curry, fish and chips, roast wild boar with plums, well hung rib-eye steak, and puddings such as bread and butter pudding. *Benchmark main dish: fish and chips £12.95. Two-course evening meal £19.00.*

Hydes ~ Tenants Ian and Luda Rottenbury ~ Real ale ~ Bar food (12-2(3 Sat, Sun); 6-9) ~ Restaurant ~ (01260) 252238 ~ Children in lounge bar and restaurant till 7pm ~ Dogs welcome ~ Open 11-3, 6-11; 11-11 Sat; 10-10 Sun ~ www.thehanginggateincheshire.co.uk
Recommended by Mr & Mrs N Hall, Dr John and Mrs Shirley Minns, Bob Broadhurst, N R White, the Didler, Rob and Catherine Dunster, Stuart Paulley

MACCLESFIELD   SJ9271   Map 7

Sutton Hall ⊕ ☜

Leaving Macclesfield southwards on A523, turn left into Byrons Lane signposted Langley, Wincle, then just before canal viaduct fork right into Bullocks Lane; OS Sheet 118 map reference 925715; SK11 0HE

Historic building set in attractive grounds; fine range of drinks and good food

The gardens of this rather splendid 16th-c manor house are particularly lovely, with spaciously laid out tables, some on their own little terraces, sloping lawns and fine mature trees. The original hall that forms the heart of the building is beautifully impressive, particularly in its entrance space. Quite a series of delightful bar and dining areas, some divided by tall oak timbers, are warm and cosy with plenty of character, antique oak panelling, warmly coloured rugs on broad flagstones, board and tiled floors, lots of frame-to-frame pictures and a raised open fire – all very Brunning & Price. The atmosphere has just enough formality, with bubbly staff and an enjoyable mix of customers from dog walkers up keeping it nicely relaxed. A good range of drinks includes Flowers Original, Phoenix Brunning & Price, Wincle Lord Lucan and a couple of guests from brewers such as Rebellion and Titanic and well over a dozen wines by the glass from an extensive list.

Particularly enjoyable and fairly priced food includes imaginative sandwiches, potted smoked mackerel and crayfish with apple and fennel salad, seared scallops with sweetcorn and tarragon purée, duck, pistachio and apricot terrine, moroccan spiced pepper with giant couscous, aubergine and okra salad, battered haddock, sausage and mash, braised lamb shoulder with redcurrant gravy, honey roast duck breast with juniper gravy, coley wrapped in parma ham with ratatouille, and puddings such as toffee apple sponge pudding with rhubarb and custard ice-cream and blueberry and mascarpone cheesecake. *Benchmark main dish: steak burger £11.75. Two-course evening meal £19.25.*

Brunning & Price ~ Manager Syd Foster ~ Real ale ~ Bar food (12-10(9.30 Sun)) ~ (01260) 253211 ~ Children welcome ~ Dogs allowed in bar ~ Open 11.30-11; 12-10.30 Sun ~ www.suttonhall.co.uk *Recommended by Andy and Claire Barker, Dave Webster, Sue Holland, Brian and Anna Marsden, Dennis Jones, Hugo Buckley, Rob and Catherine Dunster, Pat and Tony Martin*

MARTON
Davenport Arms ⚓ £

J8568   Map 7

A34 N of Congleton; SK11 9HF

Handsome pub with welcoming bar, comfortable restaurant, good food and drink, and good-sized sheltered garden

One of Cheshire's bigger gooseberry shows is held at this former 18th-c farmhouse on the first Saturday in August. There is a good traditional feel to its two linked front bar rooms, and a third room leading off on the left, with their woodburning stove, ticking clock, comfortably cushioned wall settles, wing armchairs and other hand-picked furnishings on the patterned carpet, old prints on the cream walls, and colourful jugs hanging from sturdy beams. You can eat in any of these rooms (or just have a drink or coffee), and there are more formal pleasantly light and airy dining areas behind; background music. They have well kept Courage Directors, Theakstons Black Bull and a couple of guests from brewers such as Beartown and Storm on handpump, and staff are friendly and helpful. Outside is a terrace with metal garden furniture, a fairy-lit arbour, and a timber shelter, well spaced picnic-sets and a set of swings in the garden beyond, and a substantial separate play area. The 14th-c timbered church just opposite is well worth a look, and they take caravans but you must book.

As well as filled wraps and baguettes, bar food includes thai duck spring rolls with coriander and chilli dip, grilled marinated sardines on toasted caramelised onion and tomato foccacia with tomato and garlic sauce, mushrooms topped with ratatouille and brie, braised shoulder of lamb, roast pheasant with cream cider sauce, fried cajun salmon fillet with sweet potato rösti, grilled tomatoes and chive crème fraîche, pie of the day, and home-made burgers. *Benchmark main dish: fish and chips £12.50. Two-course evening meal £18.10.*

Free house ~ Licensees Ron Dalton and Sara Griffith ~ Real ale ~ Bar food (12-2.30, 6-9; 12-9 Sat; 12-8 Sun; not Mon) ~ Restaurant ~ (01260) 224269 ~ Children welcome ~ Quiz Thurs ~ Open 12-3, 6-11; 12-11 Fri; 12-midnight Sat, Sun; closed Mon lunchtime ~ www.thedavenportarms.co.uk *Recommended by John Wooll, David Heath*

MOBBERLEY

Bulls Head

Mill Lane; WA16 7HX

SJ7879 Map 7

Terrific all-rounder just over six miles from the M6

There's nothing overblown about the recent refurbishments here. It's been kept nice and pubby with just a touch of modernity, and a good villagey welcome. There's plenty of room round the counter (three Weetwood beers and three guests from brewers such as local Merlin and local Mobberley with useful tasting notes) for a chat, and dogs are particularly welcome – one reader counted three water bowls, and the friendly staff dispense doggie biscuits from a huge jar. Its several rooms, lively with the sound of happy customers, are furnished quite traditionally with an unpretentious mix of wooden tables and chairs on characterful old tiling. Black and pale grey walls contrast well with warming red lampshades, pink stripped-brick walls and pale stripped-timber detailing.

A good solid menu with quite a few pubby dishes includes bar nibbles, sharing platters, chicken livers with port wine sauce on toast, fried cod on cannellini beans, lamb shank with redcurrants, battered haddock, goats cheese hash with spiced apple sauce, sausage and mash, roast chicken breast with mushroom sauce, pork chops with apple and cider sauce and cheddar, well hung steaks, and puddings such as chocolate brownie with chocolate sauce, lemon tart and toffee apple oat crumble. *Benchmark main dish: steak and ale pie £11.95. Two-course evening meal £18.80.*

Free house ~ Licensees Jenny and Shane Boushell ~ Real ale ~ Bar food (12-9(9.45 Sat, 8.45 Sun)) ~ (01565) 873395 ~ Children over ten till 7pm in pub, till 9pm in garden ~ Dogs allowed in bar ~ quiz monthly, jazz alternate Sundays ~ Open 12-11(11.30 Sat, 10.30 Sun) ~ www.thebullsheadpub.com *Recommended by Tim Cross, Gavin McLaughlin, Paul Allott, Jane Taylor and David Dutton*

MOBBERLEY

Plough & Flail ♀

Off B5085 Knutsford–Alderley Edge; at E end of village turn into Moss Lane, then left into Paddock Hill Lane (look out for small green signs to pub); WA16 7DB

SJ8179 Map 7

Extensive family dining pub, comfortable and well run, with enjoyable food, and plenty of outside tables

Tucked away down narrow lanes this spacious place is well laid out and feels gently up-to-date. The softly lit main area around the bar has plain cream walls and bare panelled dado, chunky cushioned dining chairs around sturdy stripped tables, low rustic beams and flagstones. Near the entrance, a handsomely floored side area has low sofas with scatter cushions, and sports TV. At the far end is a smaller, comfortable, light and airy dining room, and a further conservatory dining room. They have a good choice of wines by the glass, and Boddingtons and Lees Best and Governors on handpump; attentive cheerful service; well reproduced nostalgic background music. There are lots of teak tables out on heated flagstoned terraces and picnic-sets on neat lawns around the car park; robust play area.

Besides pubby favourites such as burgers and steaks, there might be chicken liver parfait, pancetta and leek tart, baked goats cheese on toasted brioche, salmon fillet with plaice and seared scallops, braised pork with apple and cider jus, mushroom, goats cheese and spinach lasagne, and puddings such as apple and rhubarb crumble, cheesecake and chocolate brownie with cookie dough ice-cream. *Benchmark main dish: fish and chips £11.95. Two-course evening meal £20.00.*

Lees ~ Manager Jose Lourenco ~ Real ale ~ Bar food (12-2.30, 6-9.30(10 Fri, Sat); 12-8 Sun) ~ Restaurant ~ (01565) 873537 ~ Children welcome ~ Open 12-11(10.30 Sun) *Recommended by W K Wood*

 ### NETHER ALDERLEY   SJ8576   Map 7
Wizard
B5087 Macclesfield Road, opposite Artists Lane; SK10 4UB

Bustling dining pub on National Trust land with interesting food, real ales, a friendly welcome and relaxed atmosphere

This well run dining pub (most customers are here to enjoy the particularly good food) is just a few minutes from lovely walks along Alderley Edge, a dramatic red sandstone escarpment with fine views, and there are seats and tables in the pub's sizeable back garden that are just right for a relaxing lunch afterwards. Inside, the various rooms are connected by open doorways and are cleverly done up in a mix of modern rustic and traditional styles: beams and open fires, a happy mix of antique dining chairs (some prettily cushioned) and settles around all sorts of tables, rugs on pale wooden floorboards, prints and paintings on contemporary paintwork and decorative items ranging from a grandfather clock to staffordshire dogs and modern lampshades; lovely fresh flowers and plants dotted about. Thwaites Wainwright and a guest from Storm on handpump, and several wines by the glass all served by friendly, helpful staff.

Using locally sourced produce, the highly thought of food might include chicken skewers with beansprout salad, salmon fishcake with lemon butter sauce and poached egg, seared scallops with black pudding, crispy pork belly and parsnip purée, fish platter, sausage with parsley mash and braised shallot jus, mushroom, chicken and pea risotto, thai green chicken curry, fish pie, duck breast with madeira jus, and puddings such as white chocolate and raspberry crème brûlée, apple and rhubarb turnover with cinnamon custard and chocolate brownie with chocolate sauce. *Benchmark main dish: fish and chips £11.50. Two-course evening meal £20.00.*

Free house ~ Licensee Dominic Gottelier ~ Real ale ~ Bar food (12-2, 7-9; 12-10 Sat, 12-8 Sun) ~ (01625) 584000 ~ Children welcome ~ Dogs welcome ~ Open 12-2, 5.30-11; 12-11 Sat; 12-10 Sun ~ www.ainscoughs.co.uk *Recommended by Richard Gibbs, Brian and Anna Marsden, Andrew Williams*

PEOVER HEATH   SJ7973   Map 7
Dog
Off A50 N of Holmes Chapel at the Whipping Stocks, keep on past Parkgate into Wellbank Lane; OS Sheet 118 map reference 794735; note that this village is called Peover Heath on the OS map and shown under that name on many road maps, but the pub is often listed under Over Peover instead; WA16 8UP

Homely pub with interesting range of beers and generously served food; bedrooms

Gently old fashioned and comfortably cottagey, the neatly kept bar here has tied-back floral curtains at little windows, a curved cushioned banquette built into a bay window and mostly traditional dark wheelbacks arranged on a patterned carpet. A coal fire, copper pieces and pot plants add to the homely feel. A genuine local atmosphere is kept up by areas that are set aside for drinkers. Hydes (very good value at £2.30 a pint) and two beers from Weetwood are on handpump. They also have a good range of malt whiskies and wines by the glass; games room with darts, pool, a games machine, dominoes, board games and TV, background music. Friendly efficient staff cope well when it's busy. There are picnic-sets beneath colourful hanging baskets on the peaceful lane, and more out in a pretty back garden. It's a pleasant walk from here to the Jodrell Bank Centre and Arboretum.

Bar food might include king prawn piri piri, fried chicken strips with hoisin sauce, cod and parsley fishcakes with dill and lemon mayonnaise, grilled salmon with caper, lemon and thyme sauce, steak and mushroom pie, leek, stilton and mushroom pancakes, and puddings such as strawberry pavlova and sticky toffee pudding. *Benchmark main dish: cod and chips £11.50. Two-course evening meal £17.00.*

Free house ~ Licensee Steven Wrigley ~ Real ale ~ Bar food (12-2.30, 6-9; 12-9 Sat;12-8.30 Sun) ~ Restaurant ~ (01625) 861421 ~ Children welcome ~ Dogs allowed in bar ~ Live music last Fri in month ~ Open 11.30-3, 4.30-11; 11.30-midnight Sat, Sun ~ Bedrooms: £60B/£80B ~ www.thedoginnatpeover.co.uk *Recommended by Dr D J and Mrs S C Walker, Brian and Janet Ainscough, Brian and Anna Marsden*

SANDBACH
Old Hall ♈ ◖

SJ7560   Map 7

1.2 miles from M6 junction 17: A534 into town, then right into High Street; CW11 1AL

Stunning mid-17th-c hall house with impressive original features, plenty of drinking and dining space, six real ales and imaginative food

This magnificent Grade I-listed manor house – a masterpiece of timbering and fine carved gable-ends – was a challenging two-year restoration project completed by Brunning & Price in 2011. There are many lovely original architectural features, particularly in the room to the left of the entrance hall which is much as it has been for centuries, with a Jacobean fireplace, oak panelling and priest's hole. This leads into the Oak Room, divided by standing timbers into two dining rooms – heavy beams, oak flooring and reclaimed panelling. Other rooms in the original building have more hefty beams and oak boards, three open fires and a woodburning stove; the cosy snugs are carpeted. The newly built Garden Room is big and bright, with reclaimed quarry tiling and exposed A-frame oak timbering, and opens on to a suntrap back terrace with teak tables and chairs among flowering tubs. Throughout, the walls are covered with countless interesting prints, there's an appealing mix of antique dining chairs and tables of all sizes, and plenty of rugs, bookcases and plants. From the handsome bar counter they serve Phoenix Brunning & Price, Redwillow Feckless, Three Tuns XXX

Stars after the name of a pub show exceptional character and appeal.
They don't mean extra comfort. And they are nothing to do with food quality,
for which there's a separate knife-and-fork symbol. Even quite a basic pub
can win stars, if it's individual enough.

and three guests from brewers such as Oakham, Storm and Titanic on handpump, 15 good wines by the glass and 40 malt whiskies. There are picnic-sets in front of the building by rose bushes and clipped box hedging.

🍴 From the changing menu, enjoyable food includes sandwiches, roast tomato soup, thai-style potted salmon with oriental vegetable salad, venison faggot with deep fried salsify and pea purée, fried scallops with crispy pork belly and pickled fennel and apple salad, battered haddock, lentil and cashew nut roast with mushroom sauce, lemon sole with lemon and caper butter, pork fillet with blue cheese, black pudding boulangère and port and red grape sauce, roast red pepper, aubergine, courgette and ricotta lasagne, and puddings such as lemon tart with raspberry sorbet, bread and butter pudding with apricot sauce and warm pecan pie. *Benchmark main dish: braised shoulder of lamb with rosemary gravy £16.95. Two-course evening meal £19.00.*

Brunning & Price ~ Manager Chris Button ~ Real ale ~ Bar food (12-10(9 Sun)) ~ (01270) 758170 ~ Children welcome ~ Dogs allowed in bar ~ Open 11.30-11; 12-10.30 Sun ~ www.oldhall-sandbach.co.uk *Recommended by Richard Gibbs, Sandra McGechan, Brenda, Susan and Nigel Brookes, Dave Webster, Sue Holland*

SPURSTOW

Yew Tree ★ 🍽 � ⬛

SJ5657   Map 7

Off A49 S of Tarporley; follow Bunbury 1, Haughton 2 signpost into Long Lane; CW6 9RD

Great place, a top-notch all-rounder with a good deal of individuality and plenty of bounce

The décor at this thriving place is genuinely individual and entertaining. Giant Timorous Beasties' bees are papered on to the bar ceiling and a stag's head looms proudly out of the wall above a log fire. Nicely simple pale grey, off-white and cream surfaces explode into striking bold wallpaper; there's a magnified hunting print and surprisingly angled bright tartans. The island bar has half a dozen well kept and sensibly priced ales such as Acorn Barnsley Gold, Merlins Gold, Redwillow Wreckless, Stonehouse Station, Weetwood Eastgate and Woods Shropshire Lass on handpump, a beer of the month, a local cider, over two dozen malts and a good range of wines by the glass from an interesting bin ends list of about 50. The informal service is quick even when they are busy. A more dining-oriented area shares the same feeling of relaxed bonhomie (our favourite table there was snugged into a stable-stall style alcove of stripped wood). A terrace outside has teak tables, with more on the grass.

🍴 Using many ingredients from a local farm, the quickly changing menu might include tempura vegetables with sweet chilli dipping sauce, black pudding hash cake with apple rösti and poached egg, salt and pepper squid with sweet chilli jam, oxtail and kidney pie, fish stew, butternut squash and spinach open lasagne, battered haddock, chicken ballotine with red wine jus, trio of pork, and puddings such as hot cinnamon doughnuts with apple compote and custard and whisky and raspberry cranachan. *Benchmark main dish: fish pie £11.50. Two-course evening meal £19.20.*

Free house ~ Licensees Jon and Lindsay Cox ~ Real ale ~ Bar food (12-2.30, 6-9.30 (10 Fri); 12-10 Sat; 12-8 Sun) ~ (01829) 260274 ~ Children welcome ~ Dogs welcome ~ Open 12-11; 11-10.30 Sun ~ www.theyewtreebunbury.com *Recommended by Alun Jones, Edward Leetham, R T and J C Moggridge*

 SWETTENHAM   SJ7967   Map 7

Swettenham Arms

Off A54 Congleton–Holmes Chapel or A535 Chelford–Holmes Chapel;
CW12 2LF

Big old country pub in lovely setting with shining brasses, four real ales, enjoyable food and early-bird menu.

Beware of your Sat Nav when seeking out this spacious country pub – it may direct you to the middle of the local ford. Said to be as old as the interesting village church (which dates in part from the 13th c), the three communicating areas of this former nunnery are still nicely traditional, with dark heavy beams, individual furnishings, a polished copper bar, three welcoming open fires and plenty of shiny brasses, a sweep of fitted turkish carpet, a variety of old prints – military, hunting, old ships, reproduction Old Masters and so forth. Friendly efficient staff serve four beers from brewers such as Hydes, Sharps, Thwaites and Timothy Taylor; background music. Outside behind, there are tables on a lawn that merges into a lovely sunflower and lavender meadow; handy for Quinta Arboretum.

 Good popular bar food is prepared using produce from their garden, bees and hens. Dishes might include sandwiches, goats cheese on roast beetroot, puy lentil and green bean salad, scallops with cauliflower purée, pickled cauliflower and crisp pancetta, charcuterie, venison sausage with roast parsnip and red onion jus, battered cod, pheasant breast with leek and pancetta mousse, mushroom and roast butternut risotto and cauliflower cheese, and puddings such as hot mango and coconut soufflé with mango sauce, chocolate brownie and orange bread and butter pudding, and an English cheeseboard. They offer a good value early-bird evening menu. *Benchmark main dish: steak, mushroom and ale pudding £12.75. Two-course evening meal £20.50.*

Free house ~ Licensees Jim and Frances Cunningham ~ Real ale ~ Bar food (12-2.30, 5-9.30; 12-9.30 Sat, Sun) ~ No credit cards ~ (01477) 571284 ~ Children welcome ~ Dogs allowed in bar ~ Open 11.30-11 ~ www.swettenhamarms.co.uk *Recommended by Malcolm and Pauline Pellatt, Brian and Anna Marsden, Mike and Wena Stevenson*

TARPORLEY   SJ5562   Map 7

Rising Sun £

High Street; village signposted off A51 Nantwich–Chester; CW6 0DX

Friendly, bustling and quaint, with pubby food

The low-ceilinged characterful interior of this charmingly friendly and down-to-earth old place is prettily furnished with eye-catching old seats and tables, including creaky 19th-c mahogany and oak settles. An attractively blacked iron kitchen range nestles next to gleaming old cupboard doors, and sporting and other old-fashioned prints decorate the simple cream walls. It's been in the same family for over 25 years. Accommodating staff serve Robinsons Dizzy Blonde, Unicorn and a seasonal ale from handpumps. There are one or two seats and a TV for sporting events in a tiny side bar; background music.

A good range of reasonably priced bar food includes sandwiches, starters such as spicy chicken wings, smoked fish platter, main courses such as steak and mushroom pie, chicken kiev, spinach pancake, oriental chicken, seafood lasagne and beef bourguignon, and puddings such as profiteroles and eton mess cheesecake. *Benchmark main dish: fish and chips £8.55. Two-course evening meal £13.95.*

Robinsons ~ Tenant Alec Robertson ~ Real ale ~ Bar food (11.30-2, 5-9.30; 12-9 Sat, Sun) ~ No credit cards ~ (01829) 732423 ~ Children welcome ~ Open 11.30-3.30, 5.30-11; 11.30-11 Sat; 12-10.30 Sun ~ www.therisingsuntarporley.co.uk *Recommended by P J and R D Greaves, Don Bryan, the Didler*

THELWALL
Little Manor ♀

SJ6587   Map 7

Bell Lane; WA4 2SX

Recently restored manor house with plenty of character in the beamed rooms, lots to look at, well kept ales and interesting bistro-style food; seats outside

After an extensive six-month renovation, this handsome place – originally built in the 17th-c for the Percival family – has been opened by Brunning & Price. A great deal of character has been carefully preserved in the nooks and crannies of the six beamed rooms, all linked by open doorways and standing timbers. Flooring ranges from rugs on wood through carpeting to some fine old black and white tiles. There are leather armchairs by open fires (the carved wooden one is lovely), all manner of antique dining chairs around small, large, circular or square tables, and lighting from lamps, standard lamps and metal chandeliers. As well as fresh flowers and house plants, the décor includes hundreds of interesting prints and photographs covering the walls, books on shelves and lots of old glass and stone bottles on windowsills and mantelpieces. Drinks include Coach House Cromwell, Phoenix Brunning and Price, Wincle Sir Philip and three guests from brewers such as Beartown, Merlin and Salopian, about 15 wines by the glass and around 60 whiskies. Helpful young staff. In fine weather you can sit at the chunky teak chairs and tables on the terrace; some are under a gazebo.

Good, bistro-style food includes celeriac and rosemary soup, seared spiced lamb with aubergine, halloumi and tzatziki, duck liver parfait with plum chutney and toasted brioche, fried scallops with crisp pork belly, pickled fennel and apple salad, fish pie, roast hake with tomato, chorizo, butter beans and watercress sauce, duck, orange and pistachio salad, braised rabbit with tarragon dumpling, steak and kidney pudding, roast red pepper, spinach and gorgonzola lasagne with chicory, apple and grape salad, and puddings such as pecan pie with lime sorbet, meringue with lemon curd cream, passion fruit sauce and raspberry compote and black forest cheesecake. *Benchmark main dish: haddock and chips £11.95. Two-course evening meal £20.20.*

Brunning & Price ~ Manager Andrew Cloverly ~ Real ale ~ Bar food (12-10(9.30 Sun)) ~ (01925) 261703 ~ Children welcome ~ Dogs allowed in bar ~ Open 10.30-11(10.30 Sun) ~ www.littlemanor-thelwall.co.uk *Recommended by Richard Gibbs*

A very few pubs try to make you leave a credit card at the bar, as a sort of deposit if you order food. They are not entitled to do this. The credit card firms and banks which issue them warn you not to let them out of your sight. If someone behind the counter used your card fraudulently, the card company or bank could in theory hold you liable, because of your negligence in letting a stranger hang on to your card. Suggest instead that if they feel the need for security, they 'swipe' your card and give it back to you. And do name and shame the pub to us.

WARMINGHAM
SJ7161   Map 7

Bears Paw

School Lane; CW11 3QN

Nicely maintained place with enjoyable food, half a dozen real ales and well equipped bedrooms

Although completely refurbished, this extensive Victorian inn has plenty of individual character. A maze of rooms work their way into one another, with stripped wood flooring and dado keeping it all informal. You'll find plenty of cosy places to sit – we particularly liked the two little sitting rooms with their panelling, fashionable wallpaper, bookshelves and slouchy leather furniture with plumped up cushions comfortably arranged by magnificent fireplaces with woodburners. An eclectic mix of old wooden tables, with some nice old carved chairs, is well spaced throughout the dining areas, with lofty windows keeping things light and airy and big pot plants adding freshness. There are stools at the long bar counter where cheerful and efficient staff serve half a dozen real ales from Beartown, Weetwood and a guest brewer such as Moorhouses, and a dozen wines by the glass. There are tables in a small front garden by the car park.

Readers are very complimentary of the food from a changing menu that might include baked mushrooms with blue cheese, seared smoked mackerel on a warm bean, potato and pickled beetroot salad, seared scallops with minted pea purée and crispy prosciutto, leek and smoked haddock risotto, steak burger, roast chicken breast with roast mediterranean vegetables, bass with crab croquettes, spaghetti vegetables and orange cream sauce, pork steak with carrot and cumin purée and creamed leeks, and puddings such as chocolate mousse with brandy snap biscuit and baked banoffi cheesecake. *Benchmark main dish: beer battered cod £12.00. Two-course evening meal £19.25.*

Free house ~ Licensee Andrew Nelson ~ Real ale ~ Bar food (12-9.30 Mon-Thurs; 12-10(9 Sun) Fri, Sat) ~ (01270) 526317 ~ Children welcome ~ Dogs allowed in bar and bedrooms ~ Open 12-11(10.30 Sun) ~ Bedrooms: £95B/£105B ~ www.thebearspaw.co.uk
Recommended by Rachel Hine, Andrew Williams, William and Ann Reid

WRENBURY
SJ5947   Map 7

Dusty Miller

Cholmondeley Road; village signed from A530 Nantwich–Whitchurch; CW5 8HG

Generous food and views of busy canal from bars and terrace of big mill conversion

The atmosphere at this well converted 19th-c corn mill is low-key restauranty, with some emphasis on the generously served food, though drinkers are welcome. The very spacious modern-feeling main bar is comfortably furnished with a mixture of seats (including tapestried banquettes, oak settles and wheelback chairs) around rustic tables. Further in, a quarry-tiled area by the bar counter has an oak settle and refectory table. Friendly staff serve four well kept Robinsons beers on handpump and a farm cider; eclectic background music. Tables by a series of tall glazed arches and picnic-sets among rose bushes on a gravel terrace are great vantage points for the comings and goings of craft along the Shropshire Union Canal, which runs immediately outside, and passes beneath a weighted drawbridge with its old lift hoist still visible under the rafters.

🍴 As well as soup and sandwiches, the monthly changing menu might include smoked salmon, fennel and orange salad, king scallops with pea purée and pea shoots, steak, mushroom and ale pie, cod fillet with vegetable broth and grilled lemon, duck breast with beetroot and apple crisps and red wine gravy, battered haddock, shallot, fig and goats cheese tatin, rack of lamb with caper sauce vièrge, and puddings such as lemon posset, amaretto cheesecake with mint syrup and treacle sponge with honeycomb ice-cream. *Benchmark main dish: smoked haddock and crayfish risotto with poached egg £10.95. Two-course evening meal £18.00.*

Robinsons ~ Tenant Neil Clarke ~ Real ale ~ Bar food (12-3, 6-9(10 Fri); 12-10(8 Sun) Sat) ~ (01270) 780537 ~ Children welcome ~ Dogs allowed in bar ~ Open 11.30-11; 12-10.30 Sun; closed Mon in winter ~ www.dustymiller-wrenbury.co.uk
Recommended by Rebecca Patel

Also Worth a Visit in Cheshire

Besides the fully inspected pubs, you might like to try these pubs that have been recommended to us and described by readers. Do tell us what you think of them: feedback@goodguides.com

ALPRAHAM   SJ5759
Travellers Rest (01829) 260523
A51 Nantwich–Chester; CW6 9JA
Unspoilt four-room country local in same friendly family for three generations, well kept Tetleys, Weetwood and a guest, low prices, leatherette, wicker and Formica, some flock wallpaper, fine old brewery mirrors, darts and dominoes, back bowling green; no machines, background music or food (apart from crisps/nuts), closed weekday lunchtimes. *(Dave Webster, Sue Holland, the Didler)*

ANDERTON   SJ6475
Stanley Arms (01606) 75059
Just NW of Northwich; Old Road; CW9 6AG Busy friendly local by Trent & Mersey Canal overlooking amazing restored Anderton boat lift, wide choice of good value, well presented pubby food from sandwiches up, well kept Black Sheep, Greene King and John Smiths, nice family dining area; dogs welcome, tables on decked terrace, overnight mooring. *(Ben Williams)*

AUDLEM   SJ6543
Shroppie Fly (01270) 811772
Shropshire Street; CW3 0DX Popular three-room former warehouse by Locks 12/13 of Shropshire Union Canal, friendly helpful staff, good range of real ales and plenty of wines by the glass, well liked food from sandwiches and wraps up, bar made from original barge, canal memorabilia, mainly modern furnishings, central fire, pool in public bar; background music – live Sat; children and dogs welcome, waterside terrace, open all day. *(Mike and Wena Stevenson)*

BARBRIDGE   SJ6156
Barbridge Inn (01270) 528443
Just off A51 N of Nantwich; CW5 6AY Open-plan family dining pub by lively marina at junction of Shropshire Union and Middlewich canals, enjoyable well cooked food served by friendly staff, conservatory; no dogs inside; play area in riverside garden. *(Anon)*

BARTHOMLEY   SJ7752
✳**White Lion** (01270) 882242
M6 junction 16, B5078 N towards Alsager, then Barthomley signed on left; CW2 5PG Charming, unspoilt 17th-c thatched tavern with wide mix of customers, good value straightforward tasty food (lunchtime only), five real ales, friendly timeless main bar with latticed windows, heavy low beams, moulded black panelling, prints on walls and blazing open fire, steps up to room with another fire, more panelling and a high-backed winged settle; children allowed away from bar, dogs welcome, seats out on cobbles overlooking attractive village and early 15th-c red sandstone church, open all day. *(Edward Leetham, Dave Webster, Sue Holland, the Didler, David Jackman, Mike Horgan, Di Wright, Mike Proctor and others)*

BARTON   SJ4454
✳**Cock o' Barton** (01829) 782277
Barton Road (A534 E of Farndon); SY14 7HU Stylish and witty contemporary décor and furnishings in spreading bright and open skylit bar, good enterprising up-to-date food, good choice of wines by the glass, Moorhouses Pride of Pendle and Stonehouse Station, plenty of neat courteous staff; unobtrusive background music; children welcome, tables in sunken heated inner courtyard with canopies and modern water

feature, picnic-sets on back lawn, open all day, closed Mon. *(Jonny Kershaw, Tony Husband, Bradley Beazley)*

BELL O' TH' HILL   SJ5245
Blue Bell   (01948) 662172
Just off A41 N of Whitchurch; SY13 4QS Heavily beamed partly 14th-c country pub with friendly licensees and chatty locals, three or four well kept ales, traditional food from sandwiches up, two cosy attractive rooms; children and dogs welcome, pleasant garden, small caravan site next door, closed Mon. *(MLR)*

BICKERTON   SJ5254
Bickerton Poacher   (01829) 720226
A534 E of junction with A41; SY14 8BE Rambling 17th-c poacher-themed pub, linked beamed rooms with open fires, glass-covered well, copper-mining memorabilia and talkative parrot, good choice of enjoyable reasonably priced food including carvery (Sat evening, Sun), cheerful attentive staff, Caledonian Deuchars IPA, Theakstons Old Peculier and a beer badged for the pub, decent selection of wines, skittle alley; sheltered partly covered courtyard, play area, bedrooms, adjoining campsite.
(Edward Leetham)

BOLLINGTON   SJ9377
Church House   (01625) 574014
Church Street; SK10 5PY Welcoming village pub with good value home-made food including OAP menu, frequently changing ales, roaring fire, separate dining room; good local walks. *(Dr D J and Mrs S C Walker)*

BOLLINGTON   SJ9377
Holly Bush   (01625) 573073
Palmerston Street; SK10 5PW Three-room pub with panelling and traditional décor, good food from spanish chef including tapas, well kept Robinsons ales. *(Anne and Steve Thompson)*

BOLLINGTON   SJ9477
Poachers   (01625) 572086
Mill Lane; SK10 5BU Stone-built village local prettily set in good walking area, comfortable and welcoming, with five well kept ales such as Storm and Weetwood, good pubby food including bargain lunches, daily newspapers; sunny back garden, closed Mon lunchtime. *(Brian and Anna Marsden)*

BOLLINGTON   SJ9377
Vale   (01625) 575147
Adlington Road; SK10 5JT Friendly tap for Bollington Brewery in three converted 19th-c cottages, their full range and a couple

of local guests (tasters offered), good range of freshly made food, efficient knowledgeable young staff, interesting photos, newspapers and books, roaring fire; picnic-sets at back overlooking cricket pitch, near Middlewood Way and Macclesfield Canal, open all day Fri-Sun. *(Malcolm and Pauline Pelliatt, the Didler, Mike and Wena Stevenson)*

BRERETON GREEN   SJ7764
Bears Head   (01477) 544732
Handy for M6 junction 17; set back off A50 S of Holmes Chapel; CW11 1RS Beautiful 17th-c black and white timbered Vintage Inn, welcoming and civilised linked rooms with low beams, old-fashioned furniture, flagstones, bare boards and log fires, enjoyable well prepared food, ales such as Adnams, Greene King and Sharps Doom Bar; 25 bedrooms in modern block, open all day. *(Dr D J and Mrs S C Walker)*

BURTONWOOD   SJ5692
Fiddle i'th' Bag   (01925) 225442
3 miles from M62 junction 9, signposted from A49 towards Newton-le-Willows; WA5 4BT Eccentric place (not to everyone's taste) crammed with bric-a-brac and memorabilia, three changing ales, friendly staff; open all day weekends. *(Stuart Travis)*

CHESTER   SJ4065
★Bear & Billet   (01244) 351002
Lower Bridge Street; CH1 1RU Handsome 17th-c timbered Okells pub with four changing guest ales, belgian and american imports and nice range of wines by the glass, reasonably priced home-made pubby food, interesting features and some attractive furnishings in friendly and comfortable open-plan bar with fire, sitting and dining rooms upstairs; sports TVs; pleasant courtyard, open all day. *(Paul Humphreys, the Didler)*

CHESTER   SJ4065
Brewery Tap   (01244) 340999
Lower Bridge Street; CH1 1RU Tap for Spitting Feathers Brewery in interesting Jacobean building with 18th-c brick façade, steps up to lofty bar (former great hall) serving their well kept ales plus mainly local guests, real cider, hearty home-made food all day using local suppliers. *(Dave Webster, Sue Holland)*

CHESTER   SJ4066
Olde Boot   (01244) 314540
Eastgate Row N; CH1 1LQ Good value in lovely 17th-c Rows building, heavy beams, dark woodwork, oak flooring, flagstones, some exposed Tudor wattle and daub, old kitchen

---

Post Office address codings give the impression that some pubs are in Cheshire, when they're really in Derbyshire (and therefore included in this book under that chapter) or in Greater Manchester (see the Lancashire chapter).

range in lounge beyond, old-fashioned settles and oak panelling in upper area popular with families, standard food, bargain Sam Smiths OBB kept well, good cheerful service, bustling atmosphere; background music. *(the Didler)*

CHESTER   SJ4066
Pied Bull (01244) 325829
Upper Northgate Street; CH1 2HQ Old beamed and panelled coaching inn with roomy open-plan carpeted bar, own-brewed Bull Hit ale along with Adnams Broadside and four guests, enjoyable reasonably priced food all day from sandwiches and baked potatoes up, friendly staff and locals, imposing stone fireplace with tapestry above, divided inner dining area; background music, games machines; children welcome, handsome Jacobean stairs to 13 bedrooms, open all day. *(Trevor Graveson)*

CHESTER   SJ4066
Telfords Warehouse
(01244) 390090 *Tower Wharf, behind Northgate Street near railway; CH1 4EZ* Well kept interesting ales in large converted canal building, generous fresh up-to-date food including good sandwich menu, efficient staff, bare brick and boards, high pitched ceiling, big wall of windows overlooking water, massive iron winding gear in bar, some old enamel signs, steps to heavy-beamed area with sofas, artwork and restaurant; late-night live music, bouncers on door; tables out by water, open all day. *(Andy and Jill Kassube, the Didler)*

CHESTER   SJ4066
Thomas Harrison
Nicholas Street; CH1 2NX New Brunning & Price pub (expected to open Oct 2012) – news please.

CHRISTLETON   SJ4465
Cheshire Cat (01244) 332200
Whitchurch Road; CH3 6AE Large canalside Vintage Inn in restored early 19th-c building, popular good value food all day including weekday lunch deal, well kept ales and attentive cheerful service; garden, 14 bedrooms, open all day. *(Alan and Eve Harding, Steven Hunter)*

CHRISTLETON   SJ4565
Plough (01244) 336096
Plough Lane; CH3 7PT Popular 18th-c country local with three linked areas, ales such as Caledonian Deuchars IPA and Theakstons, enjoyable home-made local food (not Sun), friendly staff; garden with play area, good setting. *(Alan Hardy, the Didler)*

CHURCH LAWTON   SJ8255
Red Bull (01782) 782600
Congleton Road S (A34), by Trent & Mersey Canal; ST7 3AJ Welcoming

three-room pub by Trent & Mersey Canal, good value home-made food, well kept Robinsons and guest ales, beams and open fire, old photographs of canal barges, upstairs restaurant; outside grassy area by lock, walkers welcome (on Cheshire Ring path). *(Dr D J and Mrs S C Walker)*

CHURCH MINSHULL   SJ6660
Badger (01270) 522607
B5074 Winsford–Nantwich; handy for Shropshire Union Canal, Middlewich branch; CW5 6DY Recently refurbished dining pub in pretty village next to church, enjoyable food, Black Sheep, M&B Mild and Timothy Taylors Landlord, interesting range of wines, bar and spacious lounge leading to new back conservatory; five bedrooms. *(Edward Leetham, John and Hazel Sarkanen, Bob Scott)*

COMBERBACH   SJ6477
⋆ Spinner & Bergamot
(01606) 891307 *Warrington Road; CW9 6AY* Comfortable 18th-c beamed village pub (named after two racehorses) with two-room carpeted lounge, good home-made bar and restaurant food (12-7.30pm Sun) including fresh fish, service pleasant but can be slow at busy times, well kept Robinsons ales, good wines, log fires, hunting prints, toby jugs and brasses, some Manchester United memorabilia, daily papers, pitched-ceiling timber dining extension, simple tiled-floor public bar; unobtrusive background music; dogs welcome, picnic-sets on sloping lawn, lots of flowers, small verandah, bowling green, open all day. *(Mike Moss, Edward Leetham, Mike and Wena Stevenson)*

CONGLETON   SJ8663
Beartown Tap (01260) 270990
Willow Street (A54); CW12 1RL Friendly tap for nearby Beartown Brewery, their interesting beers well priced and perhaps a guest microbrew, farm cider, bottled belgians, bare boards in down-to-earth bar and two light airy rooms off, no food; upstairs lavatories; open all day Fri-Sun, from 4pm other days. *(the Didler)*

CONGLETON   SJ8659
Horseshoe (01260) 272205
Fence Lane, Newbold Astbury, between A34 and A527 S; CW12 3NL Former farmhouse in peaceful countryside, three small carpeted rooms with decorative plates, copper and brass and other knick-knacks (some on delft shelves), mix of seating including plush banquettes and iron-base tables, log fire, well kept Robinsons ales, popular good value home-made food, friendly staff and locals; no dogs; children welcome, rustic garden furniture, adventure play area with tractor, good walks. *(Dr D J and Mrs S C Walker)*

CREWE   SJ7055
Borough Arms (01270) 254999
Earle Street; CW1 2BG Own microbrewery
and lots of changing guest ales, friendly staff
and regulars, two small rooms off central
bar and downstairs lounge; occasional sports
TV; picnic-sets on back terrace and lawn,
closed weekday lunchtimes, open all day
weekends. *(Anon)*

DISLEY   SJ9784
Rams Head (01663) 767909
A6; SK12 2AE Large M&B dining pub doing
enjoyable food all day including fixed-price
menu and children's meals, well kept Black
Sheep, Thwaites Wainwright and a guest,
good choice of wines by the glass, prompt
friendly service, unusual gothic-arched
interior, lots of different areas, some with
open fires; big enclosed garden behind, open
all day. *(Gerry and Rosemary Dobson)*

FADDILEY   SJ5852
⋆ Thatch (01270) 524223
A534 Wrexham–Nantwich; CW5 8JE
Attractive, thatched, low-beamed and
timbered dining pub carefully extended
from medieval core, open fires, raised
room to right of bar, back barn-style dining
room (children allowed here), well kept
ales such as Salopian and Weetwood, good
choice of enjoyable popular food (booking
advised weekends), friendly helpful service,
relaxing atmosphere; soft background
music; charming country garden with play
area, landlords listed on outside plaque,
open all day weekends, closed Mon and
Tues lunchtimes. *(R L Borthwick, M J
Winterton)*

FRODSHAM   SJ5177
Netherton Hall (01928) 732342
A56 towards Helsby; WA6 6UL Large
converted town-edge farmhouse with
emphasis on good food, competent service,
Lees and two guest ales, good choice of wines
by the glass; nice setting, open all day.
(Gill and Keith Croxton)

GAWSWORTH   SJ8869
⋆ Harrington Arms (01260) 223325
Church Lane; SK11 9RJ Rustic 17th-c
farm pub with four rooms, Robinsons Hatters
Mild, Unicorn and two guests from fine
carved oak counter, traditional food plus a
few specials; children and dogs welcome,
sunny benches on small front cobbled
terrace, more seats in back garden.
(the Didler)

GRAPPENHALL   SJ6386
⋆ Parr Arms (01925) 267393
*Near M6 junction 20 – A50 towards
Warrington, left after 1.5 miles;
Church Lane; WA4 3EP* Charming
solidly traditional black-beamed pub in
picture-postcard setting with picnic-sets
out on cobbles by church, more tables on
canopied back deck, well kept Robinsons
ales, friendly personal service, decent food
from sandwiches up, daily papers, central
bar serving lounge and smaller public bar
(both comfortable), open fire; open all day
Fri-Sun. *(Anon)*

HENBURY   SJ8873
Cock (01625) 425659
Chelford Road; SK10 3LH Well kept
Robinsons ales, short menu of enjoyable
fairly simple food, friendly staff.
(Ben Williams)

LACH DENNIS   SJ7072
⋆ Duke of Portland (01606) 46264
*Holmes Chapel Road (B5082, off A556
SE of Northwich); CW9 7SY*
Stylish dining pub with carefully prepared
imaginative food (all day Fri, Sat and till 8pm
Sun), friendly young staff, beige, grey and
cream décor with comfortable leather sofas,
square leather pouffes and chunky low
tables, Brakspear Oxford Gold, Jennings
Cocker Hoop, Marstons Pedigree, Ringwood
Best and a guest from handsomely carved
counter, interesting changing choice of wines
by the glass, daily papers, bare-boards main
dining room with lofty ceiling, sturdy
balustrades and big pictures; background
music, jazz last Thurs of month; children
welcome, dogs in bar, picnic-sets and modern
planters on neat terrace, lovely country
views. *(Ran, Ian Mayland, Mrs P Abell,
Steve Whalley)*

LANGLEY   SJ9471
⋆ Leather's Smithy (01260) 252313
*Off A523 S of Macclesfield, OS Sheet 118
map reference 952715; SK11 0NE*
Isolated stone-built pub up in fine walking
country next to reservoir, well kept
Theakstons, Wells & Youngs Bombardier
and two guests, lots of whiskies, enjoyable
generous food from sandwiches and bloomers
to blackboard specials, good welcoming
service, beams and log fire, flagstoned
bar, carpeted dining areas, interesting
local prints and photographs; unobtrusive
background music, no dogs; picnic-sets in
garden behind and on grass opposite, open

If a service charge is mentioned prominently on a menu or accommodation terms,
you must pay it if service was satisfactory. If service is really bad you are legally
entitled to refuse to pay some or all of the service charge as compensation for not
getting the service you might reasonably have expected.

all day weekends. *(Brian and Anna Marsden, Dr D J and Mrs S C Walker)*

LITTLE BOLLINGTON SJ7387
Swan With Two Nicks
(0161) 9282914 *2 miles from M56 junction 7 – A56 towards Lymm, then first right at Stamford Arms into Park Lane; use A556 to get back on to M56 westbound; WA14 4TJ* Extended village pub full of beams, brass, copper and bric-a-brac, some antique settles, log fire, welcoming helpful service, good choice of enjoyable food from filling baguettes up including popular Sun lunch (best to book), several good local ales, decent wines and coffee; children and dogs welcome, tables outside, attractive hamlet by Dunham Massey (NT) deer park, walks by Bridgewater Canal, open all day. *(Anon)*

LITTLE LEIGH SJ6076
Holly Bush (01606) 853196
A49 just S of A533; CW8 4QY Ancient timbered and thatched pub, spotlessly clean, with good value fairly simple food, helpful staff, ales such as Black Sheep and Wells & Youngs, restaurant; children welcome, courtyard tables and garden with play area, 14 bedrooms in converted back barn, open all day weekends. *(Christopher Mobbs)*

LOWER PEOVER SJ7474
★ Bells of Peover (01565) 722269
Just off B5081; The Cobbles; WA16 9PZ Lovely old refurbished building in charming spot, panelling, beams, open fires and antiques, three well kept Robinsons ales, good food from sandwiches up, dining room; background music, children till 8pm, disabled facilities, terrace tables, big side lawn with trees, rose pergolas and little stream, on quiet cobbled lane with fine black and white 14th-c church, open all day. *(Donna Somerset)*

LOWER WHITLEY SJ6178
Chetwode Arms (01925) 730203
Just off A49, handy for M56 junction 10; Street Lane; WA4 4EN Rambling low-beamed dining pub, good food with austrian influences including set meals, also steaks cooked on a hot stone, welcoming efficient service, solid furnishings all clean and polished, small front bar with warm open fire, ales such as Adnams, good wines by the glass; children allowed, immaculate bowling green, closed weekday lunchtimes in winter, best to check other times. *(Roger and Gillian Holmes)*

LYMM SJ7087
Barn Owl (01925) 752020
Agden Wharf, Warrington Lane (just off B5159 E); WA13 0SW Comfortably extended popular pub in nice setting by Bridgewater Canal, enjoyable choice of good value food all day including OAP deals,

Marstons and guest beers, decent wines by the glass, friendly atmosphere, pleasant efficient service even when busy; disabled facilities, may be canal trips, moorings, open all day. *(Ben Williams, Mike and Wena Stevenson)*

LYMM SJ6886
Church Green (01925) 752068
Higher Lane; WA13 0AP Chef/landlord doing good seasonal food (some quite pricey) in refurbished bar and restaurant, Caledonian Deuchars IPA and Greene King Old Speckled Hen; background music; children welcome, disabled facilities, heated side terrace, open all day. *(W K Wood)*

MACCLESFIELD SJ9272
Railway View (01625) 423657
Byrons Lane (off A523); SK11 7JW Pair of 1700 knocked-through cottages, attractive snug corners, up to eight well kept changing ales (cheaper Mon evening), good value food, friendly service, remarkably shaped gents'; back terrace overlooking railway, open all day weekends. *(the Didler)*

MACCLESFIELD SJ9173
Waters Green Tavern (01625) 422653
Waters Green, opposite station; SK11 6LH Seven quickly changing and interesting largely northern ales in roomy L-shaped open-plan local, good value home-made lunchtime food (not Sun), friendly staff and locals, back pool room. *(David Crook, the Didler)*

MARBURY SJ5645
Swan (01948) 665447
NNE of Whitchurch; OS Sheet 117 map reference 562457; SY13 4LS White-painted 18th-c pub opposite small green, good range of food from standards up, three real ales including Caledonian Deuchars IPA and local Woodlands, roomy partly panelled lounge with upholstered banquettes and copper-canopied log fire, cottagey dining room with inglenook; background and occasional live music; children and dogs welcome, picnic-sets in big back garden, attractive village with lakeside church, not far from Llangollen Canal (Bridges 23/24). *(Anon)*

MIDDLEWICH SJ7066
Big Lock (01606) 833489
Webbs Lane; CW10 9DN Sizeable 19th-c canalside pub on two floors, good value food including deals, mainstream ales; tables out by the water, good for boat watching. *(Ben Williams)*

MOBBERLEY SJ7879
Roebuck (01565) 873322
Mill Lane; down hill from sharp bend on B5085 at E edge of 30mph limit; WA16 7HX Closed as we went to press – news please.

NANTWICH ☆ **Black Lion** (01270) 628711
SJ6452

Welsh Row; CW5 5ED Old black and white building smartened up but keeping beams, timbered brickwork and open fire, good food from short interesting menu, three Weetwood ales and three regularly changing guests, upstairs rooms with old wooden tables and sumptuous leather sofas on undulating floors; open all day. *(Edward Leetham, Dave Webster, Sue Holland)*

NANTWICH **Globe** (01270) 623374
SJ6551

Audlem Road; CW5 7EA Full range of well kept Woodlands ales and a guest, ten wines by the glass, good regularly changing food all day using local produce, lunchtime deals, friendly helpful staff, comfortable open-plan layout keeping distinct areas, local artwork, newspapers and magazines, occasional live music; garden tables. *(Dave Webster, Sue Holland)*

NANTWICH **Vine** (01270) 624172
SJ6552

Hospital Street; CW5 5RP Dates from 17th c, sympathetically modernised and stretching far back with old prints, books and dimly lit quiet corners, well kept Hydes and a guest, friendly staff and locals, lunchtime sandwiches, wraps, baked potatoes and simple hot dishes, raised seating areas; unobtrusive background music and TV; children welcome, small outside area behind, open all day. *(Edward Leetham)*

NESTON ☆ **Harp** (0151) 336 6980
SJ2976

Quayside, SW of Little Neston; keep on along track at end of Marshlands Road; CH64 0TB Tucked-away two-room country local, well kept Holts and up to five interesting guests, some good malt whiskies, good value unfussy home-made lunchtime food (not weekends), woodburner in pretty fireplace, pale quarry tiles and simple furnishings, hatch servery in one room; children (in lounge) and dogs welcome, garden behind, picnic-sets up on front grassy bank facing Dee marshes and Wales, glorious sunsets with wild calls of wading birds, open all day. *(Andy and Jill Kassube, Don Bryan, MLR)*

OLLERTON ☆ **Dun Cow** (01565) 633093
SJ7776

Chelford Road; outskirts of Knutsford towards Macclesfield; WA16 8RH Attractive well run Robinsons country pub,

emphasis on good food but room for drinkers too, modern décor, cosy alcoves, two fine log fires, dominoes; children welcome, good disabled access, seats in nice outside area, open all day Sat, closed Sun evening, Mon. *(David Heath, P J and R D Greaves, Andrew Jackson)*

PARKGATE **Boathouse** (0151) 336 4187
SJ2778

Village signed off A540; CH64 6RN Popular black and white timbered pub with attractively refurbished linked rooms, wide choice of good food from snacks up including fresh fish, cheerful attentive staff, well kept changing ales such as local Brimstage, several wines by the glass and nice coffee, big conservatory with great views to Wales over silted Dee estuary (RSPB reserve), may be egrets and kestrels. *(Pat and Tony Hinkins, Clive Watkin, John and Verna Aspinall)*

PLUMLEY **Golden Pheasant**
SJ7275

(01565) 722261 *Plumley Moor Lane (off A556 by The Smoker); WA16 9RX* Civilised well extended pub with good locally sourced food including Sun carvery, Lees ales, comfortable lounge areas, roomy restaurant and conservatory, friendly efficient staff; children welcome, spacious gardens with play area, bowling green, bedrooms. *(Malcolm and Pauline Pellatt)*

PLUMLEY ☆ **Smoker** (01565) 722338
SJ7075

2.5 miles from M6 junction 19: A556 towards Northwich and Chester; WA16 0TY Neatly kept 400-year-old thatched coaching inn popular with older people, three spotless lounges with dark panelling, deep sofas and other comfortable seats, open fires in impressive period fireplaces, reasonably priced bar food (all day Sun), five Robinsons beers and a good choice of wines and whiskies, slick service; background music; children welcome away from bar, sizeable garden with roses and play area. *(Clive Watkin, Gordon and Margaret Ormondroyd, Lesley and Peter Barrett, Andy Dolan)*

PRESTBURY ☆ **Legh Arms** (01625) 829130
SJ8976

A538, village centre; SK10 4DG Smart beamed hotel with divided up bar and lounge areas, Robinsons ales, decent wines, bar food (all day weekends) and more elaborate restaurant choices, soft furnishings, ladder-back chairs around solid dark tables, brocaded bucket seats, stylish french prints

---

We mention bottled beers and spirits only if there is something unusual about them – imported belgian real ales, say, or dozens of malt whiskies; so do please let us know about them in your reports.

and italian engravings, staffordshire dogs on mantelpiece, cosy panelled back area with comfy narrow offshoot, coal fire, daily papers; background music; children and dogs welcome, seats on heated terrace, bedrooms, open all day. *(Anon)*

STOAK   SJ4273
Bunbury Arms (01244) 301665
Little Stanney Lane; a mile from M53 junction 10, A5117 W then first left; CH2 4HW Big but cosy beamed lounge with antique furniture, pictures and books, small snug, wide choice of enjoyable food (all day Sun) from sandwiches to interesting specials including fresh fish, good changing ales, extensive wine list, open fires, board games; can get busy; garden tables (some motorway noise), short walk for Shropshire Canal users from Bridge 136 or 138, handy for Cheshire Oaks shopping outlet, open all day.
(Janet McClure)

WESTON   SJ7352
White Lion (01270) 587011
Not far from M6 junction 16, via A500; CW2 5NA Black and white timbered 17th-c inn under new management, low-beamed main room divided by gnarled black oak standing timbers, fine 18th-c style settles as well as more modern seating, two side rooms, efficient friendly service, enjoyable food with some interesting twists, three well kept ales including Salopian Shropshire Gold, dominoes team; background music; children in eating areas, lovely garden with bowling green, 17 bedrooms, open all day.
(Michelle Dawkin)

WHITELEY GREEN   SJ9278
Windmill (01625) 574222
Off A523 NW of Bollington; Hole House Lane; SK10 5SJ Modernised and extended open-plan pub with heavy-beamed core, three real ales including local Storm, over a dozen wines by the glass, enjoyable well presented food (all day weekends) using local ingredients, efficient friendly staff, light wood furniture along with leather sofas and armchairs on stone or wood-strip floors; background music (may be live Fri evening); children welcome, plenty of tables in big attractive garden, open all day Fri-Sun. *(Anon)*

WILLINGTON   SJ5367
✸ Boot (01829) 751375
Boothsdale, off A54 at Kelsall; CW6 0NH Attractive hillside dining pub in row of converted cottages, views over Cheshire plain to Wales, popular food from pub staples to daily specials (they may ask to keep a credit card while you run a tab), Greene King and local Weetwood ales, decent wines and 30 malt whiskies, friendly staff, small opened-up unpretentiously furnished rooms, lots of original features, woodburner, extension with french windows overlooking garden, pub cats, dog and donkey; well behaved children welcome (no pushchairs), picnic-sets in front on raised suntrap terrace, open all day. *(Brian and Anna Marsden, Grahame and Myra Williams)*

WILMSLOW   SJ8282
Honey Bee (01625) 526511
Altrincham Road, Styal; SK9 4LT Large red-brick Vintage Inn with linked rooms around central bar, ales such as Black sheep, Sharps Doom Bar and Thwaites Wainwright, good choice of enjoyable food including popular Sun roasts, open fires; children welcome, terrace and garden seating, open all day. *(John Wooll)*

WINCLE   SJ9665
✸ Ship (01260) 227217
Village signposted off A54 Congleton–Buxton; SK11 0QE 16th-c stone-built country pub under good friendly licensees, bare-boards bar leading to carpeted dining room, old stables area with flagstones, beams, woodburner and open fire, very good fresh food from daily-changing varied menu, up to five well kept Lees ales, a dozen wines by the glass, quick attentive service; children and dogs welcome, tables in small well kept side garden, good Dane Valley walks.
(Al M, Bob and Linda Richardson)

Cornwall

Pubs new to the Guide this year or back in these pages after a break include the Trengilly Wartha at Constantine (tucked away and a fine place to stay), Old Quay at Devoran (friendly, light and airy with good food), Plume of Feathers in Mitchell (former coaching inn with comfortable bedrooms), Old Coastguard in Mousehole (idyllic position, super food and lovely bedrooms), Pandora at Mylor Bridge (only a severe fire took this special place out of the Guide for a year), Blue at Porthtowan (easy-going bar by stunning beach), Cornish Arms in St Merryn (under Rick Stein's umbrella), New Inn on Tresco (a few minutes from the famous gardens) and Old Wainhouse at Wainhouse Corner (sister pub to the Bush at Morwenstow). Much enjoyed by our readers this year are the Blisland Inn (honest little local with eight ales), Gurnards Head Hotel (sister pub to the Old Coastguard mentioned above), Globe in Lostwithiel (always busy and friendly, with popular food), Victoria at Perranuthnoe (plenty of customers and bustling atmosphere), Blue Peter in Polperro (charming licensees in honest local) and Driftwood Spars near Trevaunance Cove (hands-on landlady, own-brewed beers and close to an attractive cove). Doing really well since its re-opening, our Cornwall Dining Pub 2013 is the Old Coastguard in Mousehole.

 BLISLAND   SX1073   Map 1

Blisland Inn 🍺 £

Village signposted off A30 and B3266 NE of Bodmin; PL30 4JF

Village local by the green with fine choice of real ales, beer-related memorabilia, pubby food and seats outside

The friendly licensees run this extremely popular local as an old-fashioned, traditional place with a fine collection of beers and honest home cooking. Every inch of the beams and ceiling is covered with beer badges or a particularly wide-ranging collection of mugs, and the walls are similarly filled with beer-related posters and the like. Tapped from the cask or on handpump, the ales include two brewed for the pub by Sharps – Blisland Special and Bulldog – as well as five or six quickly changing guests; also farm cider, fruit wines and real apple juice; good service. The carpeted lounge has a number of barometers on the walls, toby jugs on the beams and a few standing timbers, and the family room has pool, table skittles, euchre, cribbage and dominoes; background music. Plenty of picnic-sets outside. The popular Camel Trail cycle path is close by – though the hill up to Blisland is pretty steep. As with many pubs in this area, it's hard to approach without negotiating several single-track roads.

 Straightforward pubby food includes filled lunchtime baps (the crab is very good), popular sausage or ham with egg and chips, rabbit or steak in ale pies, and daily specials. *Benchmark main dish: smoked salmon and prawn platter £9.95. Two-course evening meal £16.00.*

Free house ~ Licensees Gary and Margaret Marshall ~ Real ale ~ Bar food (12-2, 6.30-9) ~ (01208) 850739 ~ Children in family room only ~ Dogs welcome ~ Open 11.30-11.30(midnight Sat); 12-10.30 Sun *Recommended by Mike Proctor, R K Phillips, Peter Salmon, the Didler, John and Bernadette Elliott*

 BOSCASTLE   SX0991   Map 1
Cobweb
B3263, just E of harbour; PL35 0HE

Heavy beams, flagstones, lots of old jugs and bottles, a cheerful atmosphere, several real ales and friendly staff

You can be sure of a warm welcome in this tall stone pub, close to the tiny steeply cut harbour and pretty village of Boscastle. There are plenty of interesting things to look at: the two bars have heavy beams hung with hundreds of bottles and jugs and lots of pictures of bygone years. There's quite a mix of seats (from settles and carved chairs to more pubby furniture) and cosy log fires. They keep four real ales such as St Austell Tribute, Sharps Doom Bar, Tintagel Harbour Special and a guest on handpump, and a local cider and, especially at peak times, there's a cheerful, bustling atmosphere; games machine, darts and pool. The restaurant is upstairs. There are picnic-sets and benches outside – some under cover. They have a self-catering apartment for rent.

 Traditional bar food includes sandwiches and filled baguettes, pasties, chicken liver pâté with black cherry compote, burgers, broccoli bake, ham or sausages with egg, lasagne, lamb curry, beef stew, chicken in a smoked bacon and white wine sauce, a mixed grill, and puddings. *Benchmark main dish: steak in ale pie £9.50. Two-course evening meal £14.50.*

Free house ~ Licensees Ivor and Adrian Bright ~ Real ale ~ Bar food (11.30-2.30, 6-9.30) ~ Restaurant ~ (01840) 250278 ~ Children welcome ~ Dogs welcome ~ Live music Sat evenings and some Sun afternoons ~ Open 10.30am(11 Sun)-11pm ~ www.cobwebinn.co.uk *Recommended by Peter and Judy Frost, the Didler, John and Sharon Hancock, Lee and Liz Potter*

CADGWITH   SW7214   Map 1
Cadgwith Cove Inn
Down very narrow lane off A3083 S of Helston; no nearby parking; TR12 7JX

Fine walks in either direction from old-fashioned inn at the bottom of fishing cove; bedrooms

At the bottom of a pretty village, this bustling local is just the place for a drink or a meal after enjoying one of the excellent cliff walks in either direction. The two snugly dark front rooms have plain pub furnishings on their mainly parquet floors, a log fire in one stripped stone end wall, lots of local photographs including some of gig races, cases of naval hat ribands and of fancy knot-work and a couple of compass binnacles. Some of the dark beams are decked out with ships' shields and others have spliced blue rope hand-holds. Otter Bitter, Sharps Doom Bar and Skinners Betty Stogs on handpump. A back bar has a huge and colourful fish mural; background music. There are green painted picnic-sets on the good-sized front terrace, some under a fairy-lit awning, looking down to the fish sheds by the bay. The bedrooms overlook the sea; guests are served house-made jams and marmalades for breakfast. While it's best to park at the top of the village and meander down through the thatched cottages, it's quite a steep hike back up again.

Traditional food might include sandwiches, crab pâté, popular pasty or beer-battered fish with chips, chicken curry, and daily specials. *Benchmark main dish: beer-battered fish and chips £10.50. Two-course evening meal £17.95.*

Punch ~ Lease David and Lynda Trivett ~ Real ale ~ Bar food (12-2, 7-9) ~ (01326) 290513 ~ Well behaved children welcome away from main bar ~ Dogs welcome ~ Open 12-11 (10.30 Sun); 12-3, 7-11 in winter; closed Mon and Weds Dec and Jan ~ Bedrooms: £45.25(£56.25S)/£60.50(£82.50S) ~ www.cadgwithcoveinn.com *Recommended by Peter Meister, Dr A McCormick, David and Sue Atkinson*

CONSTANTINE
Trengilly Wartha ♀ ⇌

SW7328   Map 1

Nancenoy; A3083 S of Helston, signposted Gweek near RNAS Culdrose, then fork right after Gweek; OS Sheet 204 map reference 731282; TR11 5RP

Well run inn surrounded by big gardens with a friendly welcome for all, popular food and drink and an informal atmosphere; bedrooms

Run by courteous, helpful licensees and just the place to relax after a walk (there are lots all around), this bustling inn is enjoyed by our readers and their families. The long low-beamed main bar has a sociable feel (especially in the evening when the locals drop in), a wide mix of tables and chairs, a woodburning stove, cricketing team photos on the walls, two ales from a choice of Dartmoor Legend, Otter Amber, Potton No Ale and Skinners Betty Stogs on handpump, up to 20 wines by the glass, and 60 malt whiskies. Leading off the bar is the conservatory family room and there's also a cosy bistro. The six acres of gardens are well worth a wander and offer plenty of seats and picnic-sets under large parasols. The cottagey bedrooms are comfortable and the breakfasts are good.

Enjoyable food might include lunchtime sandwiches, smoked mackerel pâté with home-made chutney, beetroot salad with goats cheese and walnuts, sausages of the day with onion gravy and mustard mash, home-made thai pork burger with chilli mayonnaise, pine nut and spinach risotto, chicken breast with a wild mushroom cream sauce on pasta, halibut with leek and wholegrain mustard sauce, lamb shank with creamy mash, guinea fowl with roast aubergine and walnut sauce, and puddings. *Benchmark main dish: local mussels in white wine and cream £11.80. Two-course evening meal £20.00.*

Free house ~ Licensees Will and Lisa Lea ~ Real ale ~ Bar food (12-2.15, 6-9.30) ~ Restaurant ~ (01326) 340332 ~ Children welcome away from bar area ~ Dogs allowed in bar and bedrooms ~ Folk night every other Weds ~ Open 11-3.15, 6-midnight ~ Bedrooms: £60B/£90B ~ www.trengilly.co.uk *Recommended by Chris and Angela Buckell, Walter and Susan Rinaldi-Butcher, Evelyn and Derek Walter, Geoff and Linda Payne, J R Simmons, Guy Vowles, David and Sharon Collison, Ron and Sheila Corbett*

CRAFTHOLE   SX3654 Map 1

Finnygook ♀

B3247, off A374 Torpoint road; PL11 3BQ

Carefully renovated former coaching inn with interesting furniture and décor, enjoyable food, real ales and friendly service; bedrooms

Finny was a notorious local smuggler who 'shopped' his comrades – they were then transported to Australia and Finny was subsequently murdered; his 'gook' still haunts the area. Nowadays this 15th-c former coaching inn is civilised and friendly, and the bar has beams and joists, a central log fire that warms both sides of the room, and long wall pews with attractive cushions and carved cushioned dining chairs around various wooden tables on the stripped floorboards. There are also a couple of high wooden tables and chairs near the bar counter, big bowls of lilies, black and white local photographs, big warship and other prints on the walls, and, in one large window, an old compass. St Austell Tribute, Sharps Doom Bar and a guest beer on handpump and a decent choice of wines by the glass. The carefully lit dining room on the other side of the building has all manner of dining chairs and tables, rugs on floorboards, an unusual log-effect gas fire in a big glass cabinet, church candles and plants, black and white photographs of local people, houses and beaches, and some vinyl records on the walls; there's a library at one end. Through the hop-hung windows are fine views across the Lynher and Tamar rivers. This is under the same ownership as the Turtley Corn Mill at Avonwick in Devon.

 Good bistro-style bar food includes sandwiches, chicken caesar salad with anchovies, duck liver pâté with red onion marmalade and toasted brioche, bubble and squeak cake with mushrooms, poached egg and creamy leek sauce, sausages of the day with onion gravy, gammon and free-range eggs, chinese roast belly pork with crisp vegetables, steak and Guinness pie, smoked haddock and chive fishcakes, seafood risotto, and puddings like sticky toffee pudding with sticky toffee sauce and melting chocolate fondant; they also offer two- and three-course set lunches (not Mon or Sun). *Benchmark main dish: beer-battered fish and chips £11.95. Two-course evening meal £18.50.*

Free house ~ Licensee David Colton ~ Real ale ~ Bar food (12-2.30, 6-9; all day weekends) ~ Restaurant ~ (01503) 230338 ~ Children welcome ~ Dogs allowed in bar and bedrooms ~ Open 11-3, 6-11 (may open all day in summer; phone first); 11-11 Fri and Sat; 12-10.30 Sun ~ Bedrooms: £55B/£75B ~ www.finnygook.co.uk *Recommended by Colin and Maggie Fancourt, Dr D J and Mrs S C Walker, Olly Padbury, Evelyn and Derek Walter, R T and J C Moggridge*

DEVORAN   SW7938 Map 1

Old Quay

Devoran from new Carnon Cross roundabout A39 Truro–Falmouth, left on old road, right at mini-roundabout; TR3 6NE

Light and airy bar rooms in friendly pub just up the hill from the creek; four real ales, good wines by the glass, imaginative food, helpful staff and an informal atmosphere; seats outside

As this lovely pub is just up the hill from Devoran Quay, you can arrive by boat – provided the tide is right. And for walkers, cyclists and even horse riders, it's just 50 metres from the Portreath to Devoran Minteral Tramway coast to coast path. Inside, the roomy bar has an interesting 'woodburner' set half way up one wall, a cushioned window

seat, wall settles and a few bar stools around just three tables on the
stripped boards, and bar chairs by the counter (much favoured by the
friendly and chatty locals) where Bass, Otter Bitter, Sharps Doom Bar
and Skinners Betty Stogs are kept on handpump and good wines served
by the glass by cheerful, helpful staff; you can buy their own jams and
chutneys. Off to the left is an airy room with black and white yacht
photographs on the white walls and built-in cushioned wall seating, plush
stools and a couple of big tables on the dark slate floor. To the other
side of the bar is another light room with more settles and farmhouse
chairs, attractive blue and white striped cushions dotted about and more
sailing photographs. As well as some benches at the front that look down
through the trees to the water, there's a series of snug little back terraces
with picnic-sets and chairs and tables. Nearby parking is limited unless
you arrive early.

As well as lunchtime sandwiches (gourmet ones and panini too) and dishes for
smaller appetites, the good, interesting food includes local mussels in white
wine and garlic, fish and crab cakes with home-made chilli jam, home-roasted
ham with duck eggs, a trio of local sausages with onion gravy, nut roast with root
vegetable gravy, chicken ballotine with bubble and squeak and a creamy white wine
sauce, pork belly with crispy leeks, braised red cabbage and red wine sauce, and
puddings such as hot chocolate fondant with orange ice-cream and coffee, praline
and profiterole cheesecake. *Benchmark main dish: local fish pie £10.00. Two-
course evening meal £20.45.*

~ Licensee John and Hannah Calland ~ Real ale ~ Bar food (12-3, 6-9) ~ Restaurant
~ (01872) 863142 ~ Children welcome ~ Dogs allowed in bar ~ Open 10am(11 in
winter)-11pm ~ Bedrooms: £45/£75 ~ www.theoldquayinn.co.uk *Recommended by Samuel
Partridge, H Jones, Chris and Angela Buckell, Dan Thompson, Linda Pelham*

GURNARDS HEAD
Gurnards Head Hotel 🍴 🍷 🛏

SW4337 Map 1

B3306 Zennor–St Just; TR26 3DE

**Interesting, well run inn close to the sea, with real ales, lots of wines
by the glass and very good inventive food; comfortable bedrooms and
fine surrounding walks**

'Deserves all its accolades and more,' says one of our readers with
enthusiasm, and many others agree with him. In a wonderful
position just 500 metres from the Atlantic, this is an informal dining
pub with a friendly welcome for all, imaginative food and comfortable
bedrooms that have views of the rugged moors or of the sea. The bar
rooms are decorated in bold, strong colours, there are paintings by local
artists, open fires and a happy mix of wooden dining chairs and tables
on stripped boards. Skinners Betty Stogs, St Austell Tribute and a
changing guest beer on handpump, 20 wines by the glass or carafe and
a couple of ciders; background music, darts and board games. Seats in
the large garden behind and glorious walks all around in the outstanding
bleak National Trust scenery – both inland and along the cliffy coast.
This is under the same ownership as the civilised Griffin at Felinfach
(see our Wales chapter) and their new Old Coastguard in Mousehole,
also in Cornwall.

Excellent modern dishes from sensibly short seasonal menus that use the best
local produce might include mussels with white wine, garlic and parlsey, crab
salad with pickled cucumber and dill, merguez sausages with puy lentils, broccoli
and salsa verde, braised leeks, mousseline potatoes, wild mushrooms and truffle
butter, cod with gnocchi, cockle vinaigrette and sorrel, confit duck with sauté

potatoes and grain mustard, braised beef cheek with beetroot and cumin, and puddings like lemon posset with shortbread and vanilla rice pudding with poached pear; the two- and three-course set lunch menu is popular. *Benchmark main dish: cod, sprouting broccoli, gnocchi, cockle vinaigrette and sorrel £16.50. Two-course evening meal £22.75.*

Free house ~ Licensees Charles and Edmund Inkin ~ Real ale ~ Bar food (12.30(12 Sun and summer)-2.30, 6.30(6 summer)-9) ~ Restaurant ~ (01736) 796928 ~ Children welcome ~ Dogs welcome ~ traditional cornish singing Mon evening ~ Open 10am-midnight; closed 9-12 Jan ~ Bedrooms: £82.50S/£97.50S(£167.50B) ~ www.gurnardshead.co.uk *Recommended by Laura Rosser, Robin Sykes, R T and J C Moggridge, John and Sharon Hancock, Mike and Sue Loseby, Stephen Shepherd, Robert Wivell, Bruce and Sharon Eden, Paul Holmes, M A Borthwick, Di and Mike Gillam, Richard Tilbrook, Andrea Rampley*

HELSTON   SW6522 Map 1
Halzephron ♀ 🛏

Gunwalloe, village about 4 miles S but not marked on many road maps; look for brown sign on A3083 alongside perimeter fence of RNAS Culdrose; TR12 7QB

Bustling pub in lovely spot with tasty bar food, local beers and bedrooms; good nearby walks

After enjoying one of the unspoilt surrounding walks and the fine views of Mount's Bay, this bustling, inn is just the place to head for. The neatly kept bar rooms have an informal, friendly atmosphere, comfortable seating, copper on the walls and mantelpiece, a warm winter fire in the woodburning stove and Sharps Doom Bar and Skinners Betty Stogs on handpump; also, nine wines by the glass and 40 malt whiskies. The dining room seats up to 30 people; darts and board games. Picnic-sets outside look across National Trust fields and countryside. Gunwalloe fishing cove is a 300-metre walk and Church Cove with its sandy beach is a mile away – as is the church of St Winwaloe (built into the dunes on the seashore).

Popular food (best to book a table at peak times) includes lunchtime sandwiches, chicken liver pâté with apple and sultana chutney, anise and cinnamon-spiced crispy pork belly on cauliflower purée and red wine syrup, local sausages on caramelised apple mash and onion gravy, vegetable and pearl barley stew, a casserole of the day, lemon and salt bass with mangetout and chilli oil, and confit duck leg on garlic-crushed potatoes and rosemary jus. *Benchmark main dish: local fish chowder £6.95. Two-course evening meal £18.45.*

Free house ~ Licensee Angela Thomas ~ Real ale ~ Bar food (12-2, 7-9) ~ Restaurant ~ (01326) 240406 ~ Children in family room ~ Dogs allowed in bar ~ Open 11-3, 6(6.30 in winter)-11; 12-3.30, 6-10.30 Sun ~ Bedrooms: £52S/£94S ~ www.halzephron-inn.co.uk *Recommended by Ian and Rose Lock, Peter and Judy Frost, Barry Collett, Bryan and Helen Lee, David and Sue Smith, Stephen and Jean Curtis*

LANLIVERY   SX0759 Map 1
Crown  🛏

Signposted off A390 Lostwithiel–St Austell (tricky to find from other directions); PL30 5BT

Chatty atmosphere in nice old pub, traditional rooms and well liked food and drink; the Eden Project is close by; bedrooms

Just ten minutes from the Eden Project, this ancient place has some real character and our readers enjoy staying here very much. The main bar has a warming log fire in the huge fireplace, traditional settles on big flagstones, some cushioned farmhouse chairs, a mix of wooden chairs and tables, and Penpont Cornish Arvor, Sharps Doom Bar, Skinners Betty Stogs and a changing guest beer on handpump, a dozen wines by the glass, several malt whiskies and summer farm cider. A couple of other rooms are similarly furnished (including a dining conservatory) and there's another open fire; darts and board games. There's a huge lit-up well with a glass top by the porch and plenty of picnic-sets in the quiet garden, which is particularly pretty in summer.

Well liked bar food includes lunchtime sandwiches and proper pasties, chicken liver pâté with red onion marmalade, moules marinière, beer-battered fish and chips with home-made tartare sauce, crab and prawn tagliatelle with a creamy wine and dill sauce, pea and mushroom risotto, stew with home-made herb dumplings, and pork belly with sage and onion mash and an apple and brandy sauce. *Benchmark main dish: fish pie £12.95. Two-course evening meal £19.60.*

Wagtail Inns ~ Licensee Graham Hill ~ Real ale ~ Bar food (12-2.30, 6-9 (may offer shorter menu summer afternoons)) ~ Restaurant ~ (01208) 872707 ~ Children welcome but must be away from bar ~ Dogs allowed in bar and bedrooms ~ Open 11-11; 12-10.30 Sun ~ Bedrooms: /£89.95S ~ www.wagtailinns.com *Recommended by M Mossman, Nick Lawless, Paul Rampton, Julie Harding, Norman and Sarah Keeping, Steven Green*

LOSTWITHIEL
Globe ♀ ◐

SX1059   Map 1

North Street (close to medieval bridge); PL22 0EG

Unpretentious bar in traditional local, interesting food and drinks and friendly staff; suntrap back courtyard with outside heaters

With many loyal returning customers, this well run town pub always has a cheerful, bustling feel and warmly welcoming staff. The unassuming bar is long and somewhat narrow with a good mix of pubby tables and seats, customers' photographs on pale green boarding at one end, nice, more or less local prints (for sale) on canary-yellow walls above a coal-effect stove at the snug inner end and a small red-walled front alcove. The ornately carved bar counter, with comfortable chrome and leatherette stools, dispenses Brains Bread of Heaven, Sharps Doom Bar, Skinners Betty Stogs and a changing guest on handpump, plus 11 reasonably priced wines by the glass, 20 malt whiskies and two local ciders; background music, darts, board games and TV. The sheltered back courtyard is not large but has some attractive and unusual plants, and is a real suntrap (with an extendable overhead awning and outside heaters). You can park in several of the nearby streets of the town car park (which is free). The 13th-c church is worth a look and the ancient river bridge, a few yards away, is lovely.

A good choice of enjoyable food might include sandwiches, moules marinière, pork and chicken liver pâté, brie and redcurrant tart, venison sausages with onion gravy, chilli con carne, thai chicken curry, specials like rabbit and bacon pie, a trio of fish, pork fillet in a mushroom and stilton sauce and beef in Guinness with horseradish dumplings, and puddings such as banoffi pie and raspberry cheesecake. *Benchmark main dish: steak and brie basket £10.95. Two-course evening meal £17.00.*

Free house ~ Licensee William Erwin ~ Real ale ~ Bar food (12-2, 6.30-9) ~ Restaurant ~ (01208) 872501 ~ Children welcome but no pushchairs in restaurant ~ Dogs allowed in bar ~ Live music Fri evening ~ Open 12-2.30, 6(5 Fri)-11(midnight Fri and Sat) ~

Bedrooms: /£70B ~ www.globeinn.com *Recommended by R K Phillips, Peter Salmon, Alan Bowker, Dr and Mrs M W A Haward, Michelle, Graham Oddey, John Wooll, R T and J C Moggridge, B and M Kendall*

MITCHELL   SW8554   Map 1

Plume of Feathers ⌨

Off A30 Bodmin–Redruth, by A3076 junction; take southwards road then first right; TR8 5AX

Contemporary décor in several rooms, friendly welcome, enjoyable food, real ales and seats outside; comfortable bedrooms

Our readers enjoy staying in the comfortable bedrooms here and the breakfasts are good and generous. It's a 16th-c former coaching inn with several linked bar and dining rooms: appealing and contemporary décor, painting by local artists on the Farrow & Ball pastel-coloured walls, stripped old beams and standing timbers, painted wooden dados, farmhouse dining chairs and tables, and two open fires. Sharps Doom Bar, Skinners Betty Stogs and St Austell Tribute on handpump and several wines by the glass; background music. The sizeable light and airy conservatory is pretty impressive with its high rafters, pale wooden chairs and tables on carpet, and living trees. Outside, the well planted garden areas have plenty of picnic-sets under parasols.

Using their own eggs and some own-grown produce, the enjoyable food might include sandwiches, smoked trout pâté with horseradish dressing, fishcake with citrus aioli, local mussels with chorizo, chilli and tomato sauce, chargrilled beef burger with smoked cheddar, bacon and barbecue relish, squash and braised leek linguine with chilli oil, local fish and seafood chowder, chicken breast wrapped in parma ham stuffed with yarg and basil with onion sauce and lemon crushed potatoes, and puddings such as white chocolate and raspberry sponge with chocolate sauce and pear and almond pithivier with pear syrup and honeycomb ice-cream; steak night is Wednesday. *Benchmark main dish: fish pie £11.00. Two-course evening meal £18.50.*

Free house ~ Licensee Paul Partridge ~ Real ale ~ Bar food (12-10) ~ Restaurant ~ (01872) 510387/511125 ~ Children welcome but must be away from bar ~ Dogs allowed in bar and bedrooms ~ Open 8am-11pm ~ Bedrooms: £70S/£100S ~ www.theplume.info
Recommended by Mike Proctor, Barry and Anne, Gerry and Rosemary Dobson, R J Herd, Bernard Stradling, Katherine Bright, Ron and Sheila Corbett

MORWENSTOW   SS2015   Map 1

Bush ⌨

Signed off A39 N of Kilkhampton; Crosstown; EX23 9SR

Friendly, ancient pub in fine spot, character bar, dining huts with ocean views, real ales, carefully sourced produce for well liked food, and seats outside; bedrooms with lovely views

This 13th-c pub is only ten minutes from Vicarage Cliff, one of the grandest parts of the Cornish coast (with 120-metre precipices) and also just off the South West Coast Path. The bar has some proper character with old built-in settles, flagstones, a woodburning stove in the big stone fireplace, horse tack, lots of brass and copper knick-knacks. St Austell HSD and Tribute and Skinners Betty Stogs on handpump, several wines by the glass (including an award-winning local sparkling wine) and farm cider; darts, TV and background music. Other rooms are set for dining with pale wooden dining chairs and tables, pictures on

creamy yellow walls, beams and fresh flowers; the dining room has big
windows overlooking the picnic-sets on the grass outside and there are
now a couple of heated dining huts overlooking the ocean. As well as
bedrooms, they offer self-catering, too. This was once a monastic rest
house on a pilgrim route between Wales and Spain.

Usefully served all day and using beef from their own farm and other local
produce, the food includes sandwiches, soup, creamy garlic and herb
mushrooms, aubergine, red pepper, cashew and coconut curry, home-made burger
with home-made chips, pork in ale casserole with mustard mash, home-made
fishcake, and puddings such as warm chocolate brownie with chocolate sauce and
lemon and sherry syllabub with home-made shortbread. *Benchmark main dish:
beer-battered local fish with pea purée £10.50. Two-course evening meal £17.50.*

Free house ~ Licensees Rob and Edwina Tape ~ Real ale ~ Bar food (all day) ~
Restaurant ~ (01288) 331242 ~ Children welcome ~ Dogs allowed in bar and bedrooms
~ Live folk music every two weeks ~ Open 11-11 ~ Bedrooms: $47.50S/$85S ~
www.bushinn-morwenstow.co.uk *Recommended by R K Phillips, Lois Dyer, the Didler, Mike and
Sue Loseby, Peter Thornton, M and GR, Ryta Lyndley, J D O Carter*

 MOUSEHOLE   SW4726   Map 1
Old Coastguard ♀ 🛏
The Parade (edge of village, Newlyn coast Road); TR19 6PR
Cornwall Dining Pub of the Year

**Stunning position for carefully refurbished inn, a civilised, friendly
atmosphere, character furnishings, a good choice of wines and first
rate food; bedrooms with sea views**

With a delightful garden that leads down to rock pools and on the
edge of an old fishing village, this inn has been carefully refurbished
by the brothers of the Gurnards Head (also Cornwall) and the Griffin at
Felinfach in Wales, both much loved by our readers. We have high hopes
for this, too. Throughout, the walls are painted in their trademark bold
colours and hung with paintings of local scenes and sailing boats, the
floors are stripped boards and the atmosphere is one of informal but
civilised comfort. The Upper Deck houses the bar and the restaurant
and there's a nice mix of antique dining chairs around tables of oak and
distressed pine, lamps on big barrel tables and chairs to either side of the
log fire, topped by its vast bressumer beam. St Austell and Skinners beers
on handpump, a good choice of wine in two glass sizes, by carafe and
bottle. The Lower Deck has glass windows that run the whole length of
the building and several deep sofas and armchairs and shelves of books
and games. There are seats on the terrace overlooking Mount's Bay and
St Clement's Island and tropical palms and dracaenas in the garden. Most
of the bedrooms overlook the water; they don't charge for dogs staying
overnight and offer them free biscuits.

As well as own-make bread, jams and marmalades and lots of local fresh fish,
the brasserie-style food might include crab salad, brown crab mayonnaise and
pink grapefruit, Newlyn smoked salmon with beetroot risotto, caramelised onion,
potato and blue cheese tart, cod with parsley sauce, duck confit with puy lentils
and a herb dressing, chicken with braised leeks, wild mushrooms and roasting
juices, skate wing with mussel velouté, beef onglet with vegetable herb broth and
horseradish, and puddings like sticky toffee pudding with butterscotch sauce
and poached pear with chocolate sauce; they also offer two- and three-course set
lunches. *Benchmark main dish: daily fresh fish £11.00. Two-course evening
meal £18.00.*

Free house ~ Licensees Charles and Edmund Inkin ~ Real ale ~ Bar food (12-2.30,
6-9.30(9 in winter)) ~ (01736) 731222 ~ Children welcome ~ Dogs welcome ~ Open
7am-midnight ~ Bedrooms: $70S/$110S ~ www.oldcoastguardhotel.co.uk
Recommended by Richard Gibbs

MYLOR BRIDGE   SW8137 Map 1
Pandora ♀

*Restronguet Passage: from A39 in Penryn, take turning signposted Mylor
Church, Mylor Bridge, Flushing and go straight through Mylor Bridge following
Restronguet Passage signs; or from A39 further N, at or near Perranarworthal, take
turning signposted Mylor, Restronguet, then follow Restronguet Weir signs, but turn
left down hill at Restronguet Passage sign; TR11 5ST*

**Beautifully placed waterside inn with seats on long floating pontoon,
lots of atmosphere in beamed and flagstoned rooms, and some sort of
food all day**

After a dreadful fire and a year of careful restoration, this lovely
medieval thatched pub is open again. It's in an idyllic waterside
position – best enjoyed from the picnic-sets in front or on the long
floating jetty – and many customers do arrive by boat. Inside, several
rambling, interconnecting rooms have low wooden ceilings (mind your
head on some of the beams), beautifully polished big flagstones, cosy
alcoves with leatherette benches built into the walls, old race posters,
model boats in glass cabinets, and three large log fires in high hearths (to
protect them against tidal floods). St Austell HSD, Proper Job, Trelawny
and Tribute on handpump and a dozen wines by the glass. Upstairs,
there's now a new dining room with exposed oak vaults and dark tables
and chairs on pale oak flooring. The inn gets very crowded and parking is
extremely difficult at peak times; wheelchair access.

Using produce from local farmers and fishermen, the food might include
sandwiches and filled baked potatoes, mussels with garlic, white wine and
cream, wild mushroom and chicken liver pâté with crostini, chicken caesar or
asian noodle salad, beef burger with horseradish coleslaw and chips, millefeuille
of roasted vegetables with a tomato coulis, sausages on spring onion mash with
caramelised red onion gravy, daily specials, and puddings like ginger and orange
cheesecake with rhubarb compote and warm chocolate brownie with clotted cream;
cream teas every afternoon. *Benchmark main dish: beer-battered fish and chips
£11.00. Two-course evening meal £19.00.*

St Austell ~ Tenant John Milan ~ Real ale ~ Bar food (12-9(9.30 Fri and Sat)) ~
Restaurant ~ (01326) 372678 ~ Children welcome away from bar area ~ Dogs allowed
in bar ~ Open 10.30am-11pm ~ www.pandorainn.co.uk *Recommended by Chris and Angela
Buckell, B J Harding, Graham Oddey, Christopher Turner, the Didler, Terry and Nickie Williams,
David Crook, Andrea Rampley*

PENZANCE   SW4730 Map 1
Turks Head

*At top of main street, by big domed building (Lloyds TSB), turn left down
Chapel Street; TR18 4AF*

**Cheerfully run pub with a good, bustling atmosphere and decent
food and beer**

You can be sure of a friendly welcome from the landlord and his staff
in this bustling town pub – and there's always a good mix of both
locals and visitors. The bar has old flat irons, jugs and so forth hanging

from the beams, pottery above the wood-effect panelling, wall seats and tables and a couple of elbow-rests around central pillars; background music. Sharps Doom Bar, Skinners Betty Stogs and a changing guest beer on handpump and several wines by the glass. The suntrap back garden has big urns of flowers. There has been a Turks Head here for over 700 years – though most of the original building was destroyed by a Spanish raiding party in the 16th century.

🍴 Tasty bar food includes lunchtime sandwiches and panini, chicken liver and orange terrine with date chutney, various omelettes, pork and leek sausages, honey and mustard ham with eggs, butternut squash, spinach and sweet potato curry, local fish and chips, specials such as chicken stuffed with garlic and tarragon butter wrapped in ham with a chive velouté, and puddings like lemon tart with raspberry coulis and sticky toffee pudding with butternut squash. *Benchmark main dish: fish pie £10.95. Two-course evening meal £16.50.*

Punch ~ Lease Jonathan and Helen Gibbard ~ Real ale ~ Bar food (12-2, 7-9) ~ Restaurant ~ (01736) 363093 ~ Children welcome ~ Dogs welcome ~ Open 11-11 (midnight Sat); 12-11 Sun ~ www.turksheadpenzance.co.uk *Recommended by P Dawn, R T and J C Moggridge, Alan Johnson, Trevor Graveson, David Crook*

PERRANUTHNOE
SW5329 Map 1

Victoria 🍴

Signed off A394 Penzance–Helston; TR20 9NP

Carefully furnished inn close to Mount's Bay beaches, friendly welcome, local beers, interesting fresh food and seats in pretty garden; bedrooms

'Not to be missed if you are in this part of Cornwall,' says one of our enthusiastic readers about this well run and friendly pub – and many others agree with him. There's a good bustling atmosphere and a cheerful mix of both regulars and visitors in the L-shaped bar, as well as various cosy corners, exposed joists, a woodburning stove, an attractive mix of dining chairs around wooden tables on the oak flooring, china plates, all sorts of artwork on the walls and fresh flowers. The restaurant is separate. Sharps Doom Bar and Skinners Betty Stogs on handpump and several wines by the glass; background music. The pub labrador is called Bailey. The pretty tiered garden has white metal furniture under green parasols and the beaches of Mount's Bay are a couple of minutes' stroll away. The bedrooms are light and airy (we'd love to hear from readers who have stayed here) and they have a cottage to rent in nearby St Hilary.

🍴 Extremely good, well presented food might include lunchtime sandwiches, local crab with wild garlic, new potato, aioli and herb salad, pork and peppercorn pâté with pickled vegetable salad and onion and rosemary toast, chickpea, lentil and potato curry with crispy cauliflower and a pineapple and lime pickle, chicken breast with savoy cabbage and bacon, parsley and onion stuffing and rosemary sauce, local rib-eye steak with proper chips, and puddings like rhubarb pavlova and lemon ice-cream and valrhona chocolate and espresso marquise with sea salt and caramel sauce and coffee ice-cream. *Benchmark main dish: slow-cooked local pork with black pudding, turnip and potato dauphinoise and apple sauce £14.95. Two-course evening meal £21.00.*

Pubfolio ~ Lease Anna and Stewart Eddy ~ Real ale ~ Bar food (12-2(3 Sun), 6.30-9; not Sun evening or winter Mon) ~ Restaurant ~ (01736) 710309 ~ Children welcome ~ Dogs allowed in bar ~ Open 12-2.30(3.30 Sun), 5.30-midnight; closed Sun evening, winter Mon, one week in Jan ~ Bedrooms: £50S/£75S ~ www.victoriainn-penzance.co.uk

Recommended by Roger and Donna Huggins, A J Ward, Jon B, S Chaudhuri, Robert Wivell, Paul and Claudia Dickinson, Terry and Nickie Williams, Bruce and Sharon Eden, Paul Holmes, Evelyn and Derek Walter

PERRANWELL
SW7739   Map 1
Royal Oak ♀
Village signposted off A393 Redruth–Falmouth and A39 Falmouth–Truro; TR3 7PX

Welcoming and relaxed with helpful, friendly landlord, well presented food, real ales and thoughtfully selected wines

This is a splendid little pub with a friendly hands-on landlord and a cheerful, welcoming atmosphere. The roomy, carpeted bar has a gently upmarket but relaxed atmosphere, horsebrasses and pewter and china mugs on its black beams and joists, plates and country pictures on the cream-painted stone walls and cosy wall and other seats around candlelit tables. It rambles around beyond a big stone fireplace (with a winter log fire) into a snug little nook of a room behind, with just a couple more tables. Sharps Doom Bar and IPA and Skinners Betty Stogs on handpump, as well as good wines by the glass and farm cider.

 Listed on wooden boards in the shape of an oak tree, the good, interesting food includes lunchtime sandwiches, moules marinière, game terrine with chutney, a pie of the day, brie and red onion marmalade wellington, scrumpy chicken, summer crab, lobster and scallops and puddings such as eton mess and popular vanilla cheesecake; they also hold regular themed evenings. *Benchmark main dish: beer-battered cod and chips £11.75. Two-course evening meal £20.00.*

Free house ~ Licensee Richard Rudland ~ Real ale ~ Bar food (12-2.30, 6.30-9.30) ~ Restaurant ~ (01872) 863175 ~ Children welcome ~ Dogs allowed in bar ~ Open 11-3, 6-11; 12-4, 6-11 Sun *Recommended by Gene and Tony Freemantle, A J Ward, Stephen Shepherd, Jim Banwell, Chris and Angela Buckell*

PHILLEIGH
SW8739   Map 1
Roseland
Between A3078 and B3289, NE of St Mawes just E of King Harry Ferry; TR2 5NB

Bustling pub with real ales, a wide mix of customers and well liked food

As this pretty pub is so close to the King Harry Ferry and Trelissick Gardens there are plenty of visitors at peak times, so it's best to book a table in advance. The two bar rooms (one with flagstones and the other carpeted) have wheelback chairs and built-in red cushioned seats, open fires, old photographs and some giant beetles and butterflies in glass cases. The tiny lower area is liked by regulars and there's a popular back restaurant, too. Skinners Betty Stogs and Sharps Doom Bar (and maybe their own beer in summer) on handpump and several decent wines by the glass. There are seats on a pretty paved front courtyard.

Bar food includes lunchtime sandwiches, scallops with bacon, venison pâté, tempura vegetables with sweet and sour sauce, corn-fed chicken with spinach, wild mushrooms and a tarragon cream, local fish such as whole lemon sole, gurnard with a herb and saffron risotto and bream and bass with bean cassoulet, and puddings like apple and berry crumble and glazed lemon tart with raspberry sauce. *Benchmark main dish: liver and bacon £11.95. Two-course evening meal £19.00.*

Punch ~ Tenant Philip Heslip ~ Real ale ~ Bar food (12-2.30, 6(6.30 winter)-9.30) ~ Restaurant ~ (01872) 580254 ~ Children welcome ~ Dogs allowed in bar ~ Open 11-3, 5 (6 summer)-11 (all day school summer holidays) ~ www.roselandinn.co.uk *Recommended by John and Jackie Chalcraft, Chris and Angela Buckell, R K Phillips, Trevor Swindells, Peter Thornton*

POLKERRIS
Rashleigh ◀
SX0952 Map 1

Signposted off A3082 Fowey–St Austell; PL24 2TL

Lovely beach-side spot, heaters on sizeable sun terrace, five real ales and quite a choice of food

As the big front terrace has heaters and an awning, you can make the best of this pub's lovely position even in cool weather. There's a splendid beach with a restored jetty only a few steps away and views towards the far side of St Austell and Mevagissey bays. The bar is cosy and the front part has comfortably cushioned seats, Black Sheep, Otter Bitter, Timothy Taylors Landlord and a couple of guests like St Austell HSD and Skinners Betty Stogs on handpump, several wines by the glass, two farm ciders and organic soft drinks. The more basic back area has local photographs on brown panelling and a winter log fire, and all the tables in the restaurant have a sea view. There's plenty of parking either in the pub's own car park or the large village one. The local section of the Cornish Coastal Path is renowned for its striking scenery.

As well as growing their own herbs they use only local produce for their food, which might include sandwiches, ham hock terrine with home-made piccalilli, pork and leek burgers, steak in ale pie, broccoli and blue cheese pasta, fillet of bass with home-made tartare sauce, daily specials such as slow-cooked pork belly with a cider and mustard jus and salmon fillet with stir-fried vegetables, and puddings like mixed berry crumble and key lime pie. *Benchmark main dish: beer-battered fish and chips £9.50. Two-course evening meal £.*

Free house ~ Licensees Jon and Samantha Spode ~ Real ale ~ Bar food (12-3, 6-9; cream teas and snacks during the afternoon) ~ Restaurant ~ (01726) 813991 ~ Children welcome ~ Dogs allowed in bar ~ Open 11-11; may close at 10pm in winter ~ www.therashleighinnpolkerris.co.uk *Recommended by Trevor Swindells, B and M Kendall, Anthony Wallace, the Didler*

POLPERRO
Blue Peter
SX2050 Map 1

Quay Road; PL13 2QZ

Friendly pub overlooking pretty harbour, with fishing paraphernalia, and paintings by local artists

Now opening at 8.30am for breakfast (which could be anything from a full english to crab omelette), this busy harbourside pub is as reliably well run and friendly as ever – and there's always a good mix of locals and visitors. The cosy low-beamed bar has a chatty, relaxed atmosphere, St Austell Tribute Sharps Doom Bar, and guests like Bays Gold and Otter Ale on handpump, and traditional furnishings that include a small winged settle and a polished pew on the wooden floor, fishing regalia, photographs and pictures by local artists, lots of candles and a solid wood bar counter. One window seat looks down on the harbour and another past rocks to the sea. Families must use the upstairs room; background music. There are a few seats outside on the terrace and more in an upstairs amphitheatre-style area. The pub is quite small, so it does get crowded at peak times. They have a cash machine (there's no bank in the village).

 Winning an award for their healthy meal options and using carefully sourced produce, the well liked bar food might include lunchtime sandwiches, filled baguettes and wraps, a good fish and shellfish soup, chicken liver pâté with red onion chutney, broccoli and stilton linguine, omelettes, beef in ale pie, goan curry, corned beef hash, and specials like scallops in butter, garlic and bacon and a cajun-style jambalaya. *Benchmark main dish: tempura-battered fish and chips with tartare sauce and mushy peas £9.95. Two-course evening meal £15.40.*

Free house ~ Licensees Steve and Caroline Steadman ~ Real ale ~ Bar food (12-2.30, 6.30-8.30; food all day peak season) ~ (01503) 272743 ~ Children in upstairs family room only ~ Dogs welcome ~ Live music weekends ~ Open 10.30(11.30 Sun)-11.30 ~ www.thebluepeter.co.uk *Recommended by Edward Mirzoeff, Graham Oddey, Laura Rosser, Ryta Lyndley, the Didler, Richard Tilbrook*

PORT ISAAC

SX0080 Map 1

Port Gaverne Inn 🛏

Port Gaverne signposted from Port Isaac and from B3314 E of Pendoggett; PL29 3SQ

Lively bar with plenty of chatty locals in a busy small hotel near the sea well located for cliff walks; bedrooms

There's a clever balancing act here between the hotel side and the bustling bar and always a cheerful mix of customers. It's a popular 17th-c inn and the bar has a relaxed atmosphere, low beams, flagstones as well as carpeting, some exposed stone and a big log fire; the lounge has some interesting old local photographs. You can eat in the bar or the 'Captain's Cabin' – a little room where everything is shrunk to scale (old oak chest, model sailing ship, even the prints on the white stone walls). St Austell Tribute, Sharps Doom Bar and Cornish Coaster and maybe a guest beer such as Fullers London Pride on handpump, a decent choice of wines and several whiskies; cribbage and dominoes. There are seats in the terraced garden and splendid clifftop walks all around.

 Bar food includes sandwiches, crab soup, smoked mackerel pâté, vegetarian pasta, ham and eggs, smoked haddock, mozzarella and spring onion fishcakes, beer-battered fish of the day, and evening choices like chicken with a honey and lemon sauce and grilled dover sole with herb butter. *Benchmark main dish: fish of the day £9.50. Two-course evening meal £16.50.*

Free house ~ Licensee Graham Sylvester ~ Real ale ~ Bar food (12-2(2.30 weekends), 6.30-9) ~ Restaurant ~ (01208) 880244 ~ Children welcome ~ Dogs welcome ~ Open 11-11; 12-10.30 Sun ~ Bedrooms: £75B/£120B ~ www.port-gaverne-hotel.co.uk *Recommended by Peter and Judy Frost, Christopher Turner, Clifford Blakemore, Mr and Mrs M Stratton, John and Bernadette Elliott, R T and J C Moggridge, Barry and Anne*

PORTHTOWAN

SW6948 Map 1

Blue

Beach Road, East Cliff; car park (fee in season) advised; TR4 8AW

Informal, busy bar right by wonderful beach with modern food and drinks; lively staff and customers

Of course, this is not a traditional pub. It's a cheerful bar right by a fantastic beach which makes it incredibly popular with customers of all ages – and their dogs. The atmosphere is easy and informal and huge picture windows look across the terrace to the huge expanse of sand and sea. The front bays have built-in pine seats and the rest of the large room has chrome and wicker chairs around plain wooden tables on the stripped wood floor, quite a few chrome and wooden bar stools and plenty of standing space around the bar itself; powder blue-painted walls, ceiling fans, some big ferny plants and fairly quiet background music; pool table. St Austell Tribute on handpump, several wines by the glass, cocktails and shots, and giant cups of coffee, all served by perky, helpful young staff.

Good modern bar food using local, seasonal produce includes sandwiches and ploughman's, nachos with beef, cheese and sour cream, beer-battered fish of the day with minted pea purée and tartare sauce, popular stone-baked pizzas, specials like local mussels with white wine, cream and garlic, spinach risotto topped with goats cheese, home-made fishcakes with aioli and bass with rosemary and thyme potatoes and caper cream sauce, and puddings such as warm chocolate fondant and waffle with clotted cream vanilla ice-cream and maple syrup. *Benchmark main dish: burger with mushroom and blue cheese sauce £10.00. Two-course evening meal £16.75.*

Free house ~ Licensees Tara Roberts and Luke Morris ~ Real ale ~ Bar food (12-9 though menu reduced between 3-6) ~ (01209) 890329 ~ Children welcome ~ Dogs welcome ~ Accoustic music Sat evening ~ Open 10am-11pm(10pm Sun) ~ www.blue-bar.co.uk *Recommended by David Crook, David and Sue Smith*

ST MERRYN   SW8874   Map 1

Cornish Arms

Churchtown (B3276 towards Padstow); PL28 8ND

Busy roadside pub, liked by locals and holiday makers, with bar and dining rooms, real ales, good food, friendly service and seats outside

Part of the Rick Stein stable (but under tenancy from St Austell), this bustling roadside pub naturally places strong emphasis on the good food, but also remains a local with darts and euchre teams; it gets pretty busy in summer so arrive early to be sure of a table. The main door leads into a sizeable, informal area with a pool table, plenty of cushioned wall seating and a shelf of paperbacks, and to the left of this is a light and airy dining room overlooking the terrace. There's an unusual modern, upright woodburner with tightly packed logs to each side, photographs of the sea and of past games teams, and pale wooden dining chairs around tables on the quarry tiles. You can walk from here through to two more linked rooms with ceiling joists; the first with an open fire in a stone fireplace, some black and white photographs and pubby furniture on huge flagstones and then on to the end room with more cushioned wall seating and contemporary seats and tables on parquet flooring. St Austell Proper Job, Trelawny and Tribute on handpump, friendly service, background music and TV. In summer, the window boxes are pretty and there are picnic-sets on a side terrace and more on grass.

As well as daily specials and sandwiches, the popular food might include piri piri prawns, pork terrine with beetroot chutney, summer crab salad, pork and garlic sausages with onion gravy, a good burger with chilli relish, gammon and a duck egg, mussels and chips, and puddings like treacle tart and sunken chocolate cake. They hold a curry night on Fridays and steak evenings on Saturdays. *Benchmark main dish: mussels and chips £12.00. Two-course evening meal £16.00.*

St Austell ~ Tenant Luke Taylor ~ Real ale ~ Bar food (12-2, 6-9) ~ Restaurant ~ (01841) 532700 ~ Children welcome ~ Dogs welcome ~ live music winter Fri evenings ~ Open 11.30-11 ~ www.rickstein.com/The-Cornish-Arms.html *Recommended by Peter and Judy Frost, Phil and Gill Wass*

TRESCO

SV8815   Map 1

New Inn 🍺 🛏

New Grimsby; Isles of Scilly; TR24 0QG

Attractive inn with plenty of space, real ales and enjoyable food, friendly staff and seats on sunny terrace; bedrooms

Handy for the ferries and the quay, this is a well run inn with a cheerful mix of both visitors and locals. There's a main bar room and a light, airy dining extension: comfortable old sofas, banquettes, planked partition seating and farmhouse chairs and tables, a few standing timbers, boat pictures, a large model sailing boat, a collection of old telescopes and plates on the delft shelf. The Pavilion extension has cheerful yellow walls and plenty of seats and tables on the blue wooden floors and looks over the flower-filled terrace with its teak furniture, huge umbrellas and views of the sea. Ales of Scilly Scuppered and Harbour, and Skinners Betty Stogs and Tresco Tipple on handpump, 13 good wines by the glass, quite a choice of spirits and coffees; background music, board games, darts and pool. The famous gardens are close by.

Good food includes sandwiches (all day until 5pm), duck terrine with apple chutney and toasted sourdough, mushrooms in a black pepper cream sauce in puff pastry, fish and chips with mushy peas and tartare sauce, gorgonzola risotto, mussels in a garlic, white wine and cream sauce with fries, rump of lamb with a bubble and squeak potato cake and lamb gravy, chicken kiev, and puddings such as lemon meringue tart with raspberry coulis and clotted cream and crème caramel. *Benchmark main dish: home-made beef burger with gruyère and bacon £11.00. Two-course evening meal £19.00.*

Free house ~ Licensee Robin Lawson ~ Real ale ~ Bar food (12-2, 7-9) ~ (01720) 423006 ~ Children welcome ~ Dogs allowed in bar ~ Live music regularly (not winter) ~ Open 11-11; 12-10.30 Sun; 11-2.30, 6-11 in in winter ~ Bedrooms: £100B/£200B ~ www.tresco.co.uk *Recommended by Mike Proctor, R T and J C Moggridge, R J Herd, Bernard Stradling, Michael Sargent*

TREVAUNANCE COVE

SW7251   Map 1

Driftwood Spars 🍺 🛏

Off B3285 in St Agnes; Quay Road; TR5 0RT

Friendly old inn, plenty of history, own-brew beers and wide range of other drinks, popular food, and beach nearby; attractive bedrooms

Surrounded by fine coastal walks and just up the lane from a dramatic cove and beach, this former tin-mining warehouse is particularly well run by the hard-working landlady and deservedly popular with a wide mix of customers. The bustling bars are timbered with massive ships' spars – the masts of great sailing ships, many of which were wrecked along this coast – and there are dark wooden farmhouse and tub chairs and settles around a mix of tables, padded bar stools by the counter, old ship prints and lots of nautical and wreck memorabilia, and woodburning stoves; there's said to be an old smugglers' tunnel leading from behind the bar, up through the cliff. They keep seven real ales on handpump including their own Driftwood Lous Brew and a changing guest or two from Driftwood such as Bawden Rock or Alfies Revenge, Brains SA, St Austell Dartmoor Best, Sharps Doom Bar or Skinners Betty Stogs. Also, 30 malt whiskies, 11 rums and several wines by the glass. The modern dining room overlooks the cove; service is friendly and helpful. The summer hanging baskets are pretty and there are seats in the garden. Many of their attractive bedrooms overlook the coast.

 Good, seasonally changing bar food might include sandwiches, soup, chicken liver parfait with shallot chutney, gourmet burger with emmenthal and roasted onion chutney, pasta with a fricassée of mushrooms, thai green chicken curry, beef bourguignon, specials like monkfish wrapped in parma ham with anchovy butter, and puddings such as earl grey panna cotta and saffron bread and butter pudding with vanilla bean ice-cream. *Benchmark main dish: beer-battered fish and chips £9.95. Two-course evening meal £15.00.*

Own brew ~ Licensee Louise Treseder ~ Real ale ~ Bar food (12-2.30, 6.30-9) ~ Restaurant ~ (01872) 552428 ~ Children welcome away from bar ~ Dogs allowed in bar and bedrooms ~ Live music Sat evenings ~ Open 11-11(1am Sat) ~ Bedrooms: £50S(£64B)/£86S ~ www.driftwoodspars.com *Recommended by Kev and Gaye Griffiths, Peter Salmon, Stanley and Annie Matthews, Alan Bowker, David Uren, Christopher Turner, the Didler, Michael and Maggie Betton, David and Sharon Collison*

WAINHOUSE CORNER
Old Wainhouse

SX1895   Map 1

A39; EX23 0BA

Usefully open and serving food all day, this is a cheerful pub with friendly staff, plenty of seating space, a good mix of customers, real ales and good food

It's handy that this cream-painted and black-shuttered place is open all day as it is the only pub on a 20-mile stretch of the A39 and also close to the South West Coastal Path – and food is served non-stop from 10am (11am in winter). There's a good mix of customers and an easy-going, cheerful atmosphere, and the main bar has a nice built-in settle, stripped rustic farmhouse chairs and dining chairs around a mix of tables on enormous old flagstones, a large woodburner with stone bottles on the mantelpiece above it, and beams hung with scythes, saws, a horse collar and other tack, spiles, copper pans and brass plates; do note the lovely photograph of a man driving a pig across a bridge. Leading off from here is a simpler room with similar furniture, a pool table, a flatscreen TV; background music. The main dining room to left of the main door has elegant high-backed dining chairs around pale wooden tables, another woodburner and more horse tack. Sharps Cornish and Doom Bar on handpump and friendly service. Outside, there's a grass area to one side of the building with picnic-sets.

 Being a farming family from the area, they take great care to use local meat, game and fish, and the enjoyable food includes chicken liver parfait with onion jam, spiced aubergine bruschetta with a soft boiled egg and chive oil, home-made burger with relish and their own chips, red wine and blue cheese risotto with spiced walnuts, beer-battered pollock with home-made tartare sauce, turkey and mushroom pie, venison bourguignon, and puddings like chocolate brownie with chocolate sauce and apple and cherry crumble with clotted cream; they also offer cream teas and take-away pizzas. *Benchmark main dish: beer-battered fish and chips £10.00. Two-course evening meal £18.00.*

Enterprise ~ Lease Peter Owen ~ Real ale ~ Bar food (10am(11am winter)-9pm) ~ Restaurant ~ (01840) 230711 ~ Children welcome ~ Dogs welcome ~ Open 10am-midnight ~ Bedrooms: £45S/£90S ~ www.oldwainhouseinn.co.uk *Recommended by Reg Fowle, Helen Rickwood*

Also Worth a Visit in Cornwall

Besides the fully inspected pubs, you might like to try these pubs that have been recommended to us and described by readers. Do tell us what you think of them: feedback@goodguides.com

---

ALTARNUN   SX2280
Kings Head (01566) 86241
Five Lanes; PL15 7RX Old stone-built beamed roadside pub, Greene King Abbot, Skinners Betty Stogs and a couple of guests, real ciders, reasonably priced pubby food from sandwiches and baguettes up including good Sun carvery, carpeted lounge with big log fire, slate floor restaurant and public bar with another fire; darts, pool and TV; children and dogs welcome, picnic-sets on front terrace and in garden behind, four bedrooms, open all day. *(Frank Willy)*

ALTARNUN   SX2083
✶ Rising Sun (01566) 86636
NW; village signed off A39 just W of A395 junction; PL15 7SN Tucked-away 16th-c pub with traditionally furnished L-shaped main bar, low beams, slate flagstones, coal fires, good choice of food including excellent local seafood, Penpont and Skinners ales, farm cider; background music; dogs and well behaved children allowed in bar but not in restaurant, seats on suntrap terrace and in garden, pétanque, camping field, beautiful church in nice village, open all day weekends. *(the Didler, John and Bernadette Elliott)*

ANGARRACK   SW5838
Angarrack Inn (01736) 752380
Steamers Hill; TR27 5JB Small village pub below railway viaduct, decent food (good crayfish cocktail), a couple of real ales, nice atmosphere. *(Stephen Shepherd)*

ASHTON   SW6028
Lion & Lamb (01736) 763227
Fore Street (A394 Helston–Penzance); TR13 9RW Welcoming place with several well kept ales and interesting food; seats outside, handy for SW Coastal Path. *(John and Jackie Chalcraft)*

BODINNICK   SX1352
Old Ferry (01726) 870237
Across the water from Fowey; coming by road, to avoid the ferry queue turn left as you go down the hill – car park on left before pub; PL23 1LX Up for sale but has been an old-fashioned family-run inn just up from the river with nice views from terrace, dining room and some bedrooms; three simple bars with nautical memorabilia, half model ships mounted on walls, old photographs, back family room hewn into the rock, Sharps Own and maybe Coaster, poor recent reports on food and service; dogs welcome in bar, good circular walks, lane by pub in front of ferry slipway is extremely steep and parking limited, open all day. *(Nick Lawless, Dave Webster, Sue Holland, Christopher Turner, Dr A McCormick, B and M Kendall)*

BODMIN   SX0667
Bodmin Jail (01208) 76292
Berrycoombe Road; PL31 2NR Jail museum's refurbished bar, four real ales, enjoyable generous food from lunchtime sandwiches up, good service; children and dogs welcome, can be visited without a tour of the jail, open all day. *(JJW, CMW, Jennifer Banks)*

BODMIN   SX0467
Borough Arms (01208) 73118
Dunmere (A389 NW); PL31 2RD Roomy 19th-c roadside pub with good value food including daily carvery (all day Sun), St Austell and Bass, cheerful staff, partly panelled stripped-stone walls, lots of railway photographs and posters, open fire, side family room and separate dining room; background music, quiz machine; dogs allowed in bar, picnic-sets out among shady apple trees, play area, on Camel Trail, open all day. *(Norman and Sarah Keeping)*

BOSCASTLE   SX0990
✶ Napoleon (01840) 250204
High Street, top of village; PL35 0BD Welcoming 16th-c thick-walled white cottage at top of steep quaint village (fine views halfway up); slate floors and cosy rooms on different levels including small evening bistro, oak beams and log fires, interesting Napoleon prints and lots of knick-knacks, good food from daily-changing menu, well kept St Austell tapped from the cask, decent wines and coffee, traditional games; background music – live Fri, sing-along Tues; children and dogs welcome, small covered terrace and large sheltered garden, open all day. *(Stanley and Annie Matthews, Christopher Turner, the Didler, Clifford Blakemore, Wilburoo, David Crook)*

BOSCASTLE SX0991
Wellington (01840) 250202
Harbour; PL35 0AQ Old hotel's long carpeted beamed bar, good food from snacks up, ales such as Skinners and St Austell kept well, upstairs balcony area, roaring log fire; children welcome, big secluded garden, comfortable bedrooms, good breakfast. (*David Crook*)

BOTALLACK SW3632
⋆ Queens Arms (01736) 788318
B3306; TR19 7QG Friendly old pub with good home-made food including local seafood, meat sourced within 3 miles, well kept Sharps and Skinners ales, good service, log fire in unusual granite inglenook, dark wood furniture, tin mining and other old local photographs on stripped-stone walls, family extension; dogs welcome, tables out in front and pleasant back garden, wonderful cliff top walks nearby, lodge accommodation, open all day. (*Kirsty Wilson, Terry and Nickie Williams, J D O Carter, David and Sue Smith, Richard Tilbrook*)

BOTUSFLEMING SX4061
Rising Sun (01752) 842792
Off A388 near Saltash; PL12 6NJ Convivial low-ceilinged rural local, lively games bar, smaller quieter stripped-stone room with two good coal fires, well kept changing ales; picnic-sets in garden looking over quiet valley to church, has been closed Mon-Thurs lunchtimes, open all day weekends. (*Phil and Sally Gorton, the Didler*)

BREAGE SW6128
⋆ Queens Arms (01326) 573485
3 miles W of Helston just off A394; TR13 9PD Friendly chatty pub with L-shaped bar and smallish restaurant, seven well kept ales including Cornish Chough, Sharps and Skinners, farm cider, decent wines by the glass, good well priced food from baguettes with cornish brie and cranberry to seafood and steaks, warming coal fires, plush banquettes, brass-topped tables, daily papers, games area with pool; background music; children and dogs welcome, some picnic-sets outside, covered smokers' area, two bedrooms, medieval wall paintings in church opposite, open all day Sun. (*Dennis Jenkin, Andy Beveridge*)

BUDE SS2006
Brendon Arms (01288) 354542
Falcon Terrace; EX23 8SD Popular pub (particularly in summer) near canal, two big friendly pubby bars, back family room, well kept ales such as St Austell and Sharps, decent wines by the glass, enjoyable food from doorstep sandwiches up, bargain OAP lunch Tues, nice coffee, hot spicy apple juice, good cheery service; juke box, sports TV, pool and darts; children welcome, dogs in public bar, disabled access, picnic-sets

on front grass, heated smokers' shelter, bedrooms and holiday apartments, good walks nearby. (*Michael Tack, Ryta Lyndley, Dennis Jenkin*)

CALLINGTON SX3569
Bulls Head (01579) 383387
Fore Street; PL17 7AQ Ancient unspoilt local with relaxed friendly atmosphere, handsome black timbering and stonework, well kept St Austell Tribute; erratic opening times. (*Giles and Annie Francis*)

CALSTOCK SX4368
⋆ Tamar (01822) 832487
The Quay; PL18 9QA Cheerful local dating from the 17th c, just opposite the Tamar with its imposing viaduct, dark stripped stone, flagstones, tiles and bare boards, pool room with woodburner, more modern fairy-lit back dining room, good generous straightforward food, summer cream teas, well kept ales such as Otter and Sharps Doom Bar, good service and reasonable prices, darts, some live music; children (away from bar) and well behaved dogs welcome, nicely furnished terrace, heated smokers' shelter, hilly walk or ferry to Cotehele (NT). (*Phil and Sally Gorton, Giles and Annie Francis*)

CAWSAND SX4350
⋆ Cross Keys (01752) 822706
The Square; PL10 1PF Slate-floored traditional local with lots of matchboxes, banknotes and postcards, some cask tables, steps up to carpeted dining room with nautical décor, enjoyable generous food especially seafood (worth booking in season), reasonable prices, changing ales, flexible helpful service; pool, may be background music, no nearby parking; children and dogs welcome, seats outside, pleasant bedrooms. (*Dr D J and Mrs S C Walker*)

CHAPEL AMBLE SW9975
Maltsters Arms (01208) 812473
Off A39 NE of Wadebridge; PL27 6EU More busy country restaurant than pub and they like you to book, good food and thriving atmosphere, drinkers confined to bar counter or modern back extension (if not used by diners), St Austell Tribute and Sharps Doom Bar served very cold; contemporary styling with splendid fire, beams, painted half-panelling, stripped stone and partly carpeted flagstones, light wood furniture; picnic-sets out in sheltered sunny corner. (*Fiona Loram, David Hoult*)

CHARLESTOWN SX0351
Harbourside Inn (01726) 67955
Part of Pier House Hotel; PL25 3NJ Glass-fronted warehouse conversion alongside hotel, great spot looking over classic little harbour and its historic sailing ships, up to seven ales inc Sharps Doom Bar, enjoyable pubby food, friendly efficient service, live music Sat night; sports TVs; pool; interesting

film-set conservation village with shipwreck museum, good walks, parking away from pub. *(Reg Fowle, Helen Rickwood)*

CHARLESTOWN SX0351
Rashleigh Arms (01726) 73635
Quay Road; PL25 3NX Modernised early 19th-c pub with nautical touches, public bar, lounge and dining area, well kept St Austell ales and two guests, good wine choice and coffee, enjoyable competitively priced food all day including popular Sun carvery, friendly obliging service; background music (live on Fri), free wi-fi; children welcome, dogs in bar, disabled facilities, front terrace and garden with picnic-sets, eight bedrooms (some with sea views), open all day. *(Robert Watt)*

CRACKINGTON HAVEN SX1496
✶ Coombe Barton (01840) 230345
Off A39 Bude–Camelford; EX23 0JG Much-extended old inn in beautiful setting overlooking splendid sandy bay, modernised pubby bar with plenty of room for summer crowds, neat welcoming young staff, wide range of simple bar food including local fish, popular carvery Sun lunchtime, Sharps and St Austell, good wine choice, lots of local pictures, surfboard hanging from plank ceiling, big plain family room, restaurant; darts, pool, fruit machines, background music, TV; dogs allowed in bar, side terrace with plenty of tables, fine cliff walks, roomy bedrooms, good breakfast, open all day in season. *(Dr A McCormick, Mick and Moira Brummell)*

CREMYLL SX4553
✶ Edgcumbe Arms (01752) 822294
End of B3247; PL10 1HX Super setting by Plymouth foot-ferry, good Tamar views, picnic-sets out by water; attractive layout and décor, with slate floors, big settles, comfortably old-fashioned furnishings including fireside sofas, old pictures and china, well kept St Austell ales, cheerful staff, reasonably priced food from doorstep sandwiches up, weekend carvery, good family room/games area; pay car park some way off; children in eating area, dogs allowed in one bar (most tables here too low to eat at), bedrooms, open all day. *(Peter Salmon, Dr D J and Mrs S C Walker)*

CRIPPLES EASE SW5037
Balnoon (01736) 797572
Balnoon; N, right off B3311 after 1.2 miles; TR26 3JB Modern inn with good selection of real ales and good carvery (Sun lunch, summer evenings, Fri-Sun evenings in winter); children welcome, terrace tables, bedrooms. *(J A Snell)*

CROWS NEST SX2669
✶ Crows Nest (01579) 345930
Signed off B3264 N of Liskeard; OS Sheet 201 map reference 263692;

PL14 5JQ Old-fashioned 17th-c pub with enjoyable food from chef/landlord, well kept St Austell ales and a guest like Dartmoor, decent wines by the glass, prompt friendly service, attractive furnishings under bowed beams, big log fire, chatty locals; children welcome, picnic-sets on terrace by quiet lane, handy for Bodmin Moor walks. *(Peter Salmon, Dr and Mrs M W A Haward, John and Bernadette Elliott)*

EDMONTON SW9672
✶ Quarryman (01208) 816444
Off A39 just W of Wadebridge bypass; PL27 7JA Welcoming three-room beamed bar, part of a small holiday courtyard complex; some good individual cooking besides generous pubby lunchtime food including nice baguettes, salads and fish and chips, good curry night (first Tues of month), quick friendly service, Sharps (summer only), Skinners and a couple of guest beers, good choice of wines by the glass, interesting decorations including old sporting memorabilia, cribbage and dominoes, no mobiles; well behaved dogs and children welcome, disabled facilities, courtyard with picnic-sets, open all day. *(Dr and Mrs M W A Haward, the Didler)*

EGLOSHAYLE SX0071
Earl of St Vincent (01208) 814807
Off A389, just outside Wadebridge; PL27 6HT Pretty dining pub with 200 working antique clocks, also golfing memorabilia, art deco ornaments and rich furnishings, good food from sandwiches to steaks, St Austell ales and good cornish cider; background music; well behaved children allowed lunchtime, lovely garden. *(the Didler)*

FALMOUTH SW8033
Boathouse (01326) 315425
Trevethan Hill/Webber Hill; TR11 2AG Interesting two-level nautical-themed local with buoyant atmosphere, lots of woodwork, log fire, good choice of beers and of food, friendly staff; background music; children welcome, tables outside, upper deck with awning and great harbour views. *(Steve Watkins)*

FALMOUTH SW8132
✶ Chain Locker (01326) 311085
Custom House Quay; TR11 3HH Busy place in fine spot by inner harbour with window tables and lots outside, well kept Sharps and Skinners ales, good value generous food from sandwiches and baguettes to fresh local fish and interesting vegetarian choices (they also cater for smaller appetites), cheery young staff, bare boards and masses of nautical bric-a-brac, darts alley; games machine, background music; well behaved children and dogs welcome, self-catering accommodation, open all day. *(David Crook, David and Sue Smith)*

FALMOUTH   SW8032
✶ Seven Stars (01326) 312111
The Moor (centre); TR11 3QA Quirky
17th-c local, unchanging and unsmart (not
to everyone's taste), with long-serving
and entertaining vicar-landlord, friendly
atmosphere and chatty regulars, no gimmicks,
machines or mobile phones, half a dozen
well kept ales tapped from the cask, home-
made rolls, big key-ring collection, quiet
back snug; corridor hatch serving roadside
courtyard. *(Dennis Jones, the Didler, Ted George)*

FOWEY   SX1251
Galleon (01726) 833014
*Fore Street; from centre follow Car
Ferry signs; PL23 1AQ* Superb spot by
harbour and estuary, good ale range inc local
microbrews, good generous straightforward
food, reasonable prices, nice choice of wines,
fast friendly service, fresh modern nautical
décor, lots of solid pine, dining areas off, jazz
Sun lunchtime; pool, big screen TV, evenings
can get loud with young people; children
welcome, disabled facilities, attractive
extended waterside terrace and sheltered
courtyard with covered heated area, estuary-
view bedrooms. *(Dave Webster, Sue Holland,
David Crook)*

FOWEY   SX1251
✶ King of Prussia (01726) 832450
Town Quay; PL23 1AT Handsome quayside
building with good welcoming service in
roomy neat upstairs bar, bay windows looking
over harbour to Polruan, enjoyable pubby
food including good crab sandwiches and
carve your own Sun roasts, St Austell ales
kept well, sensibly priced wines, side family
restaurant; background music, pool; seats
outside, six pleasant bedrooms, open all day
in summer. *(Edward Mirzoeff, Alan Johnson,
Nick Lawless)*

FOWEY   SX1251
Lugger (01726) 833435
Fore Street; PL23 1AH Centrally
placed St Austell pub with unpretentious
bar and small back dining area, good
mix of locals and visitors (can get busy),
enjoyable food including local fish; children
welcome, pavement tables, open all day in
summer. *(Nick Lawless)*

FOWEY   SX1251
Safe Harbour (01726) 833379
Lostwithiel Street; PL23 1BP Redecorated
19th-c former coaching inn set away from
main tourist area, lounge/dining area and
regulars' bar, good value locally sourced
home-made food, well kept St Austell
ales, welcoming landlord, old local prints,
upstairs overflow dining room; pool, darts,
games machine; heated side terrace, seven
bedrooms, self-catering apartment, open all
day till midnight. *(Dave Webster, Sue Holland,
Nick Lawless)*

FOWEY   SX1251
✶ Ship (01726) 832230
Trafalgar Square; PL23 1AZ Bustling
local with friendly staff, good choice of well
priced generous food from sandwiches up
inc fine local seafood, well kept St Austell
ales, coal fire and banquettes in tidy bar
with lots of yachting prints and nauticalia,
newspapers, steps up to family dining room
with big stained-glass window, pool/darts
room; background music, small sports TV;
dogs allowed, comfortably old-fashioned
bedrooms, some oak-panelled. *(Nick Lawless,
Ted George)*

GOLANT   SX1254
✶ Fishermans Arms (01726) 832453
Fore Street (B3269); PL23 1LN Bustling
partly flagstoned small waterside local with
lovely views across River Fowey from front bar
and terrace, good value generous home-made
food including nice crab sandwiches and
seafood, efficient friendly service, well kept
cornish ales, good wines by the glass, log fire,
interesting pictures; dogs welcome, pleasant
garden, closed Sun afternoon. *(Nick Lawless,
Stuart Paulley, the Didler)*

GORRAN CHURCHTOWN   SW9942
Barley Sheaf (01726) 843330
*Follow Gorran Haven signs from
Mevagissey; PL26 6HN* Old village pub
extensively refurbished by present owner,
good well priced food, Sharps Doom Bar and
guests, friendly staff, some live music; dogs
welcome, garden. *(Julian Able, Bill Shelton)*

GRAMPOUND   SW9348
Dolphin (01726) 882435
A390 Street Austell–Truro; TR2 4RR
White-painted St Austell pub, their ales
kept well and decent wines, food from good
baguettes up, friendly helpful staff, two-level
bar with comfortable atmosphere, black
beams and some panelling, polished wood
or carpeted floors, pubby furniture with
a few high-backed settles, pictures of old
Grampound, log fire; children welcome, dogs
in bar, wheelchair access from car park,
beer garden, smokery opposite, handy for
Trewithen Gardens. *(Dennis Jenkin, Chris and
Angela Buckell)*

GULVAL   SW4831
Coldstreamer (01736) 362072
*Centre of village by drinking fountain;
TR18 3BB* Under welcoming newish owners,
good imaginative sensibly priced food using
local produce, friendly helpful service, wide
choice of wines and several well kept local
ales, bar with woodburner, old photographs
and traditional games, updated restaurant
with modern pine furniture on wood
floor; quiet pleasant village very handy for
Trengwainton Gardens and Scillies heliport,
comfortably refurbished bedrooms, open all
day. *(Mrs B H Adams, John and Jackie Chalcraft)*

GUNNISLAKE
SX4371
Rising Sun (01822) 832201
*Calstock Road, just S of village; PL18
9BX* Attractive 17th-c two-room pub,
beams, stripped stone, panelling and
flagstones, lovely fireplaces, cheerful
service, six real ales, enjoyable food (not
Mon), may be weekend live music; pleasant
valley views from terraced garden, open all
day. *(Les Last)*

GWEEK
SW7026
Gweek Inn (01326) 221502
*Back roads E of Helston; TR12
6TU* Cheerful family chain pub, large
comfortable open-plan bar with low beams,
brasses, lots of motoring trophies (enthusiast
licensees) and woodburner in big stone
fireplace, well kept St Austell and Skinners,
decent wines, enjoyable food including
good sandwiches (may try to keep your
credit card while you eat), bright and roomy
back restaurant, live music Fri; tables on
grass (safe for children), summer kiosk
with all-day snacks, short walk from seal
sanctuary. *(Clifford Blakemore)*

HARROWBARROW
SX4069
Cross House (01579) 350482
*Off A390 E of Callington; School Road
– over towards Metherell; PL17 8BQ*
Substantial stone building, spreading
carpeted bar with some booth seating,
cushioned wall seats and stools around pub
tables, enjoyable home-made food, well kept
St Austell ales, friendly smiling service, open
fire and woodburner, darts area, restaurant;
children and dogs welcome, disabled
facilities, plenty of picnic-sets on good-sized
lawn, play area. *(Dennis Jenkin)*

HELSTON
SW6527
✶ Blue Anchor (01326) 562821
Coinagehall Street; TR13 8EL Many
(not all) love this 15th-c no-nonsense,
highly individual, thatched local; quaint
rooms off corridor, flagstones, stripped
stone, low beams and well worn furniture,
traditional games, family room, limited
bargain lunchtime food (perhaps best time
for a visit), ancient back brewhouse still
producing distinctive and very strong Spingo
IPA, Middle and seasonals like Bragget
with honey and herbs; seats out behind,
bedrooms, open all day. *(Giles and Annie
Francis, the Didler)*

HOLYWELL
SW7658
St Pirans (01637) 830205
Holywell Road; TR8 5PP Great location
backing on to dunes and popular with
holidaymakers, some recent refurbishment,
friendly helpful staff, well kept ales including
St Austell, decent wines, enjoyable pub
food with blackboard specials; children
and dogs welcome, tables on large back
terrace. *(Dennis Jenkin)*

KINGSAND
SX4350
Devonport
The Cleave; PL10 1NF Character pub with
lovely bay views from front bar, changing real
ales and enjoyable bar food, friendly service,
scrubbed floorboards and Victorian décor,
lots of ship photographs and bric-a-brac,
mix of cast-iron-framed pub furniture with
window seats and pine settles, log fire, back
snug; tables out by sea wall, good value
bedrooms. *(Suzy Miller)*

LANNER
SW7339
✶ Fox & Hounds (01209) 820251
Comford; A393/B3298; TR16 6AX
Cosily comfortable rambling low-beamed pub
under welcoming licensees, fresh food from
good sandwiches up, well kept St Austell ales
tapped from the cask, decent wines, friendly
helpful service, warm fires, high-backed
settles and cottagey chairs on flagstones,
stripped stone and dark panelling, newspapers
and books, pub games; background music;
children welcome in dining room, dogs in
bar, disabled facilities, great floral displays
in front, picnic-sets in neat back garden with
pond and play area, open all day weekends.
(R K Phillips, Dennis Jenkin)

LELANT
SW5436
✶ Old Quay House (01736) 753988
*Griggs Quay, Lelant Saltings; A3047/
B3301 S of village; TR27 6JG* Large
modern pub in marvellous spot by bird
sanctuary estuary, welcoming and neatly kept
with good value food, real ales such as Bass,
St Austell Tribute and Sharps Doom Bar, good
service, dining area off well divided open-
plan bar, children allowed upstairs; garden
with views over saltings, decent motel-type
bedrooms, open all day in summer.
(Alan Johnson)

LERRYN
SX1356
✶ Ship (01208) 872374
*Signed off A390 in Lostwithiel; Fore
Street; PL22 0PT* Lovely spot especially
when tide's in, well kept local ales, farm cider,
good wines (inc country ones) and whiskies,
imaginative sensibly priced food as well as
more traditional things, huge woodburner,
attractive adults-only dining conservatory
(booked quickly evenings and weekends),
games room with pool; children welcome,
dogs on leads, picnic-sets and pretty play
area outside, near famous stepping-stones
and three well signed waterside walks,
decent bedrooms in adjoining building
and self-catering cottages, open all day
weekends. *(Nick Lawless, B and
M Kendall, Evelyn and Derek Walter)*

LIZARD
SW7012
Top House (01326) 290974
A3083; TR12 7NQ Neat clean pub under
newish ownership, good local food (some
quite pricey) from sandwiches and snacks up

including fresh fish, children's meals and cream teas, well kept ales such as St Austell Tribute and Skinners Betty Stogs, lots of good local sea pictures, fine shipwreck relics and serpentine craftwork (note the handpumps), good log fire, friendly staff; sheltered terrace, interesting nearby serpentine shop, eight bedrooms in adjoining building (three with sea views), open all day summer, all day weekends in winter. *(Clifford Blakemore, Andy Beveridge)*

LIZARD SW7012
Witchball (01362) 290662
Lighthouse Road; TR12 7NJ Good food including fresh local fish and seafood (booking advised), ales such as Choughs, St Austell and Skinners, cornish cider, helpful friendly staff; children and dogs welcome, terrace tables, open all day. *(Clifford Blakemore)*

LOOE SX2553
Olde Salutation (01503) 262784
Fore Street, East Looe; PL13 1AE Good welcoming local bustle in big squareish slightly sloping beamed and tiled bar, reasonably priced food from notable crab sandwiches to wholesome specials and Sun roasts, fast friendly service, well kept Sharps Doom Bar, red leatherette seats and neat tables, blazing fire in nice old-fashioned fireplace, lots of local fishing photographs, side snug with olde-worlde harbour mural, step down to simple family room; may be background music, forget about parking; handy for coast path, open all day. *(Dr D J and Mrs S C Walker)*

LUDGVAN SW5033
⋆ White Hart (01736) 740574
Off A30 Penzance–Hayle at Crowlas; TR20 8EY Appealing old village pub, friendly and welcoming, with well kept Sharps, Skinners and a changing guest tapped from the cask, own cider and premium range of spirits, enjoyable blackboard food from pub standards up including good value Sun lunch, small unspoilt beamed rooms with wood and stone floors, nooks and crannies, woodburners, quiz first Weds of month; dogs welcome, beer garden and little decked area at back, interesting church next door, two refurbished bedrooms, open all day in summer. *(the Didler, John and Jackie Chalcraft, Mick and Moira Brummell, Bruce and Sharon Eden)*

MALPAS SW8442
⋆ Heron (01872) 272773
Trenhaile Terrace, off A39 S of Truro; TR1 1SL Idyllically placed creekside pub with seats on heated terrace, light and airy long narrow bar with areas leading off, flagstones and wood flooring, blue and white décor, modern yacht and heron paintings on wood-planked walls, brass nautical items, stuffed heron in cabinet, gas-effect coal fires,

St Austell beers, food from lunchtime snacks up; background music, parking difficult in high season; children welcome, open all day in summer. *(Sarah Flynn)*

MARAZION SW5130
Godolphin Arms (01736) 710202
West End; TR17 0EN Former coaching inn with great views across beach and Mount's Bay towards St Michael's Mount, traditional food including good crab sandwiches and popular carvery on Sunday, St Austell and Sharps ales, helpful friendly staff, upper lounge bar and dining area, informal lower bar with pool table, sports TV and live music (Fri); children and dogs welcome, decked beach-side terrace, ten bedrooms, most with sea view, good breakfast, open all day. *(Roger and Donna Huggins, Christopher Turner)*

MARHAMCHURCH SS2203
Bullers Arms (01288) 361277
Old Orchard Close; EX23 0HB Oak beams and settles in pleasant rambling L-shaped bar, well prepared food from extensive menu, Sun carvery, up to five well kept local ales (takeaway cartons available), wide choice of wines by the glass, friendly efficient staff, darts in flagstoned back part, restaurant, some live music inc late summer Bude Jazz Festival; children and dogs welcome; picnic-sets in sizeable garden, a mile's walk to the sea, bedrooms, open all day in summer. *(JJW, CMW, the Head family)*

MAWNAN SMITH SW7728
⋆ Red Lion (01326) 250026
W of Falmouth, off former B3291 Penryn–Gweek; The Square; TR11 5EP Old thatched and beamed pub, popular and chatty, with cosy series of dimly lit lived-in rooms including the raftered bar, open-view kitchen doing wide choice of good food from interesting menu especially seafood (should book summer evenings), quick friendly service, lots of wines by the glass, real ales such as Sharps Doom Bar kept well, good coffee, daily papers, fresh flowers, woodburner in huge stone fireplace, dark woodwork, country and marine pictures, plates and bric-a-brac; background music, TV; children (away from bar) and dogs welcome, disabled access, picnic-sets outside, handy for Glendurgan (NT) and Trebah Gardens, open all day. *(Clifford Blakemore, Chris and Angela Buckell, Richard and Liz Thorne)*

MEVAGISSEY SX0144
⋆ Fountain (01726) 842320
Cliff Street, down alley by Post Office; PL26 6QH Popular low-beamed fishermen's pub, slate floor, some stripped stone, good coal fire, old local pictures, St Austell ales, enjoyable food at reasonable prices, back locals' bar with glass-topped cellar, upstairs restaurant; pretty frontage with picnic-sets, bedrooms, open all day in summer. *(R K Phillips, the Didler, Trevor Graveson, Ian Phillips)*

MEVAGISSEY SX0144
✳ **Ship** (01726) 843324
Fore Street, near harbour; PL26 6UQ
16th-c pub with interesting alcove areas in
big open-plan bar, low beams and flagstones,
nice nautical décor, woodburner, cheery
uniformed staff, wide range of fairly priced
pubby food including good fresh fish, small
helpings available, full St Austell range
kept well, back pool table; games machines,
background and occasional live music; dogs
allowed, children welcome in two front
rooms, comfortable bedrooms, open all day in
summer. *(Stanley and Annie Matthews,
George Atkinson)*

MINIONS SX2671
Cheesewring (01579) 362321
Overlooking the Hurlers; PL14 5LE
Popular well run village pub useful for
Bodmin Moor walks, well kept ales including
Sharps Doom Bar and Special, good choice
of reasonably priced home-made food, lots of
brass and ornaments, chatty locals.
(Anthony Wallace, M A Borthwick)

MITHIAN SW7450
✳ **Miners Arms** (01872) 552375
Off B3285 E of Street Agnes; TR5 0QF
Cosy stone-built pub with traditional small
rooms and passages, pubby furnishings,
fine old wall painting of Elizabeth I in
squint-walled, irregular beam and plank
ceilinged back bar, open fires, popular good
value food, Sharps and Skinners ales kept
well, friendly helpful staff, board games;
background music; children welcome, dogs in
some rooms, seats on back terrace, in garden
and on sheltered front cobbled forecourt,
open all day. *(Barry and Anne, John and Jackie
Chalcraft, Barrie and Mary Crees, David and
Sharon Collison, Dennis Jenkin)*

MOUSEHOLE SW4626
✳ **Ship** (01736) 731234
Harbourside; TR19 6QX Bustling
harbourside local with opened-up dimly lit
main bar, black beams, flagstones, open fire,
panelling, built-in wooden wall benches
and stools around low tables, sailors' fancy
ropework, darts, well kept St Austell ales,
pubby food inc good local fish; background
music, TV, games machine, upstairs
lavatories; children and dogs welcome, lovely
village (best to park at top and walk down),
elaborate Christmas harbour lights worth a
visit, bedrooms, open all day. *(Mike Proctor,
John and Sharon Hancock)*

MULLION SW6719
Old Inn (01326) 240240
*Near church – not down in the cove;
TR12 7HN* Thatched and beamed pub
with central servery doing generous good
value food (all day July, Aug) from doorstep
sandwiches to pies and evening steaks,
well kept ales and decent wines (plenty by

the glass), linked eating areas with lots of
brasses, plates, clocks, nautical items and
old wreck pictures, big inglenook fireplace;
children welcome, picnic-sets on terrace
and in garden, good bedrooms, open all day
weekends and in Aug. *(Ian and Rose Lock,
David and Sue Smith)*

MULLION COVE SW6618
Mullion Cove Hotel (01326) 240328
End of road of Cove Road; TR12 7EP
Imposing Victorian cliff-top hotel overlooking
sea and harbour, friendly and hospitable,
with good food in bistro bar, ales such as
Sharps Doom Bar, more formal and expensive
sea-view restaurant; children welcome, 30
bedrooms, useful coastal path stop.
(Clifford Blakemore)

MYLOR BRIDGE SW8036
Lemon Arms (01326) 373666
Lemon Hill; TR11 5NA Popular and
friendly traditional village pub, opened-up
bar area with stripped stone walls and
panelling, well kept St Austell ales, enjoyable
sensibly priced food; children and dogs
welcome, wheelchair access with help, back
terrace, good coastal walks. *(Jim Banwell)*

NEWLYN SW4629
Tolcarne (01736) 363074
Tolcarne Place; TR18 5PR Traditional
17th-c quayside pub, cosy and lived in with
open fire, local fishing photos, wide choice of
good value home-made food including good
seafood, friendly staff and locals, well kept
Sharps and Skinners; terrace (harbour wall
cuts off view), good parking. *(M and GR, Rod
and Chris Pring, Richard Tilbrook)*

NEWQUAY SW8061
Fort (01637) 875700
Fore Street; TR7 1HA Massive recently
built pub in magnificent setting high
above surfing beach and small harbour,
decent standard food all day from
sandwiches, hot baguettes and baked
potatoes up, open-plan areas well divided
by balustrades and surviving fragments of
former harbourmaster's house, good solid
furnishings from country kitchen to button-
back settees, soft lighting and one panelled
area, friendly service, St Austell ales,
games part with two well lit pool tables,
excellent indoor children's play area; great
views from long glass-walled side section
and from sizeable garden with terrace and
play areas, bedrooms, open all day.
(Alan Johnson)

NEWQUAY SW8061
Lewinnick Lodge (01637) 878117
*Pentire headland, off Pentire Road;
TR7 1NX* Modern flint-walled bar/
restaurant built into the bluff above the
sea, big picture windows for the terrific
views, light and airy bar with wicker seating,
spreading dining areas with contemporary

furnishings on light oak flooring, bistro-style food, three or four well kept ales, several wines by the glass, good service and pleasant relaxed atmosphere even when busy; modern seats and tables on terraces making the most of stunning Atlantic views; under the same management as the Plume of Feathers, Mitchell. *(Anon)*

PADSTOW   SW9175
⁕ **Golden Lion** (01841) 532797
Lanadwell Street; PL28 8AN Old inn dating from the 14th c, cheerful black-beamed locals' bar, high-raftered back lounge with plush banquettes, three well kept ales such as Sharps Doom Bar, reasonably priced simple bar lunches including good crab sandwiches, evening steaks and fresh fish, friendly staff, coal fire and woodburner; pool in family area, background music, sports TV; dogs welcome, colourful floral displays at front, terrace tables, three bedrooms, open all day. *(Sally and John Quinlan, Dennis Jones, the Didler)*

PADSTOW   SW9275
Old Custom House (01841) 532359
South Quay; PL28 8BL Large, bright and airy open-plan seaside bar, comfortable and well divided, with rustic décor and cosy corners, beams, exposed brickwork and bare boards, raised section, big family area and conservatory, good food choice from baguettes up, four local ales including St Austell, efficient friendly service, adjoining fish restaurant; background and live music, TV, machines, pool; good spot by harbour, attractive sea-view bedrooms, open all day. *(Dennis Jones)*

PADSTOW   SW9175
Shipwrights (01841) 532451
North Quay; aka the Blue Lobster; PL28 8AF Long narrow quayside building with open-plan low-ceilinged bar, stripped brick, lots of wood, flagstones, lobster pots and nets, popular food served promptly by friendly staff, further upstairs eating area; background music, TV, machines, busy with young people in evenings; dogs welcome, a few tables out by water, more in back suntrap garden. *(Eddie Edwards, Dennis Jones, Robert Watt)*

PAUL   SW4627
⁕ **Kings Arms** (01736) 7311224
Mousehole Lane, opposite church; TR19 6TZ Beamed local with cosy bustling atmosphere, enjoyable sensibly priced food from sandwiches up, well kept St Austell ales, local artwork, darts, live music including bluegrass on Tues evening; children welcome, dogs in one bar, five bedrooms, open all day in summer. *(Mike Proctor, Stuart Turner)*

PELYNT   SX2054
⁕ **Jubilee** (01503) 220312
B3359 NW of Looe; PL13 2JZ Popular early 17th-c beamed inn with wide range of locally sourced home-made food (best to book in season) from good sandwiches up including Sun roasts, well kept St Austell ales, good wines by the glass, friendly helpful staff, interesting Queen Victoria mementoes (pub renamed 1897 to celebrate her diamond jubilee), some handsome antique furnishings, log fire in big stone fireplace, separate bar with darts, pool and games machine; sparkling lavatories; children and dogs welcome, disabled facilities, large terrace, 11 comfortable bedrooms, open all day weekends. *(Dudley and Moira Cockroft, Stanley and Annie Matthews, Dennis Jenkin and others)*

PENDOGGETT   SX0279
Cornish Arms (01208) 880263
B3314; PL30 3HH Picturesque old coaching inn with traditional oak settles on front bar's polished slate floor, fine prints, above-average food from good sandwiches up, also good authentic thai food, Sharps Doom Bar and a couple of guests, decent wines by the glass, friendly helpful staff, comfortably spaced tables in small dining room, proper back locals' bar with woodburner and games; provision for children, dogs welcome in bars, disabled access, terrace with distant sea view, bedrooms, open all day. *(Chris Macey, Dennis Jenkin)*

PENELEWEY   SW8140
Punch Bowl & Ladle
(01872) 862237 *B3289; TR3 6QY*
Thatched dining pub with several room areas, generous sensibly priced home-made food from good sandwiches to local steaks, children's menu, OAP lunch on Mon, efficient helpful service, St Austell ales, good wine choice, big settees and rustic bric-a-brac; background music; children and dogs welcome, small side terrace, handy for Trelissick Gardens, open all day. *(R K Phillips)*

PENTEWAN   SX0147
Ship (01726) 842855
Just off B3273 Street Austell–Mevagissey; West End; PL26 6BX Big 17th-c beamed pub opposite tiny village's harbour, comfortable and clean with bar, snug and lounge/dining area, lots of dark tables and open fire, up to four St Austell ales, draught perry, good reasonably priced fresh food including plenty of fish, helpful staff; background music – occasional live; children and dogs welcome, views from tables outside, near good sandy beach and big caravan park, open all day summer, all day weekends winter. *(Colin Woodward)*

Every entry includes a postcode for use in SatNav devices.

PENZANCE SW4730
Admiral Benbow (01736) 363448
Chapel Street; TR18 4AF Well run rambling pub, full of life and atmosphere and packed with interesting nautical gear, friendly staff, good value above-average food including local fish, real ales such as Sharps, Skinners and St Austell, cosy corners, fire, downstairs restaurant in captain's cabin style, upper floor with pool, pleasant view from back room; children welcome, open all day in summer. *(P Dawn, John and Sharon Hancock, John and Gloria Isaacs, David Crook)*

PENZANCE SW4729
✱ **Dolphin** (01736) 364106
Barbican; Newlyn road, opposite harbour after swing-bridge; TR18 4EF
Part old-fashioned pub and part bistro, good value food especially fresh fish (landlady's husband is a fisherman), St Austell ales, good wines by the glass, friendly helpful service, roomy bar, great fireplace, dining area a few steps down, cosy family room; big pool room with juke box etc, no obvious nearby parking; pavement picnic-sets, open all day. *(P Dawn, Roger and Donna Huggins, Christopher Turner)*

PENZANCE SW4730
Navy (01736) 333232
Queen Street; TR18 4DE Historic house in nice setting near the seafront, proper bar and interesting unfussy interior, good changing food with an emphasis on fish, local ales and decent choice of wines, pleasant service. *(Martin and Anne Muers)*

PERRANARWORTHAL SW7738
✱ **Norway** (01872) 864241
A39 Truro–Penryn; TR3 7NU Large pub under newish licensees, helpful friendly service, good choice of generous well presented food using local produce including vegetarian options, OAP lunch Tues, all-day Sun carvery, good selection of St Austell ales and of wines by the glass, half a dozen linked areas, beams and open fires, old-style wooden seating and big tables on slate flagstones, revamped restaurant, Mon night quiz; children welcome, tables outside, four new bedrooms, open all day. *(Peter Salmon, Chris and Angela Buckell, Mick and Moira Brummell)*

PERRANPORTH SW7554
Watering Hole (01872) 572888
The Beach; TR6 0JL Busy holiday bar (not a pub) right on miles of golden sand, popular food from baguettes and pubby standards to steaks and good Sun carvery, real ales such as Sharps Doom Bar, quick service; lively band nights, sports TV; great sunset views from picnic-sets outside, summer barbecues. *(David Crook)*

PILLATON SX3664
✱ **Weary Friar** (01579) 350238
Off Callington–Landrake back road; PL12 6QS Tucked-away welcoming 12th-c pub, good food in bar and restaurant served by friendly helpful staff, well kept Dartmoor and Sharps, farm cider, knocked-together carpeted rooms, dark beams, copper and brass, log fires in stone fireplaces; no dogs inside; children welcome, tables outside, church next door (Tues evening bell-ringing), comfortable bedrooms. *(J F Stackhouse, Ted George, Jackie Cranmer)*

POLMEAR SX0853
Ship (01726) 812540
A3082 Par–Fowey; PL24 2AR Flower-decked 18th-c pub with chatty locals and welcoming staff, enjoyable straightforward food including evening carvery, well kept Fullers London Pride, Sharps Doom Bar and a guest from rowing-boat counter, roomy bar with lots of hanging whisky-water jugs and big stove; background and live music, TV, cash machine; children and dogs welcome, two garden areas (one with summer bandstand), camping and self-catering cabin, open all day. *(Liz and Brian Barnard)*

PORT ISAAC SW9980
✱ **Golden Lion** (01208) 880336
Fore Street; PL29 3RB Bustling local atmosphere in simply furnished old rooms, open fire in back one, window seats and three balcony tables looking down on rocky harbour and lifeboat slip far below, straightforward decent food inc generous baguettes and good fish range, St Austell ales, darts, dominoes, cribbage; background music, games machine; children in eating areas, dramatic cliff walks, open all day. *(the Didler, David Hoult)*

PORTHLEVEN SW6325
Atlantic (01326) 562439
Peverell Terrace; TR13 9DZ Friendly buzzy pub in great setting up above harbour, good value tasty food, real ales including Skinners and St Austell, big open-plan lounge with well spaced seating and cosier alcoves, good log fire in granite fireplace, dining room with amazing trompe l'oeil murals; lovely bay views from front terrace, open all day. *(Geoff and Linda Payne)*

PORTHLEVEN SW6225
Harbour Inn (01326) 573876
Commercial Road; TR13 9JB Large neatly kept pub/hotel in outstanding harbourside setting, well organised friendly service, expansive lounge and bar with impressive dining area off, big public bar with panelling and leather seating, well kept St Austell ales, comprehensive wine list, good range of pubby food, lunchtime carvery Wed and Sun; quiet background music, Thurs quiz; picnic-sets on big quayside terrace, well equipped bedrooms, some with harbour view, good breakfast. *(Stanley and Annie Matthews, Tony and Gill Powell, John and Gloria Isaacs, David Crook)*

PORTHLEVEN   SW6225
⭐ **Ship** (01326) 564204
*Mount Pleasant Road (harbour) off
B3304; TR13 9JS* Friendly fishermen's
pub built into cliffs, fine harbour views
(interestingly floodlit at night) from seats
on terrace and in knocked-through bar, well
kept Courage Best, St Austell Tribute and
Sharps Doom Bar, honest bar food like good
crab sandwiches and home-made pies (may
ask to hold a credit card if you eat outside),
good service, log fires in big stone fireplaces,
some genuine individuality, family room
(converted from old smithy) with huge fire,
candlelit dining room also looking over sea;
background music, games machine; dogs
welcome in bar, open all day.
*(Clifford Blakemore, Roger and Donna Huggins,
Christopher Turner, Alan Johnson, Geoff and
Linda Payne and others)*

PORTLOE   SW9339
⭐ **Ship** (01872) 501356
At top of village; TR2 5RA Bright unspoilt
L-shaped local, popular generous food inc
fresh fish (good if pricey crab sandwiches),
well kept St Austell ales, Healey's cider/
perry, good choice of wines, friendly
welcoming service, interesting nautical
and local memorabilia and photographs,
amazing beer bottle collection; background
music; children and dogs welcome, disabled
access to main bar (road very steep though),
smokers' gazebo, sheltered and attractive
streamside picnic-sets over road, pretty
fishing village with lovely cove and coast
path above, bedrooms, open all day Fri-Sun
in summer. *(Lawrence Pearse, Chris and Angela
Buckell, Trevor Swindells, Barry Collett, Dr A
McCormick and others)*

PORTSCATHO   SW8735
Plume of Feathers (01872) 580321
The Square; TR2 5HW Cheerful largely
stripped-stone pub in pretty fishing village,
well kept St Austell and other ales, Healey's
cider, pubby food from sandwiches and
huge ploughman's up, bargain fish night
Fri, sea-related bric-a-brac in comfortable
linked room areas, small side locals' bar (can
be lively in the evening), restaurant; very
popular with summer visitors, warm local
atmosphere out of season; background music;
children, dogs and boots welcome, disabled
access, lovely coast walks, open all day in
summer (other times if busy). *(Chris and
Angela Buckell, Clifford Blakemore)*

PRAZE AN BEEBLE   SW6335
St Aubyn Arms (01209) 831425
The Square; TR14 0JR Welcoming
refurbished pub with two bars and
contemporary restaurant, well kept Otter,
St Austell and Skinners, enjoyable food

with emphasis on local steaks, Tues quiz;
background music; children and dogs
welcome, picnic-sets in large attractive
garden. *(Ernie Williams, David and Sue Smith)*

ROSUDGEON   SW5529
Falmouth Packet (01736) 762240
A394; TR20 9QE Nice place with quite
a history, bare-stone walls and open fires,
enjoyable good value food using organic
local produce, well kept Penzance and
Tater-Du, friendly landlord and good
service, conservatory; garden, self-catering
cottage. *(John and Jackie Chalcraft)*

RUAN LANIHORNE   SW8942
⭐ **Kings Head** (01872) 501263
*Village signed off A3078 St Mawes Road;
TR2 5NX* Country pub in quiet hamlet,
relaxed small bar with log fire, Skinners
and a guest, maybe farm cider, well liked
food especially local fish, friendly helpful
service, two dining areas, lots of china cups
hanging from ceiling joists, plenty of copper
and brass, hunting prints, cabinet filled
with old glass bottles, separate restaurant;
background music; well behaved children
allowed in dining areas only, dogs in bar,
terrace across road and nice lower beer
garden, interesting nearby church and walks
along Fal estuary, closed winter Sun evening,
Mon. *(R K Phillips, M Mossman, R and S Bentley,
Canon Michael Bourdeaux, Jeremy Whitehorn
and others)*

SLADESBRIDGE   SX0171
Slades House (01208) 812729
PL27 6JB Neatly kept and friendly, with
decent pub food and well kept Sharps Doom
Bar, good quick service even when busy;
children welcome. *(Tony and Gill Powell)*

ST AGNES   SW7250
Railway Inn (01872) 552310
Vicarage Road, via B3277; TR5 0TJ
Friendly low-ceilinged village local with
five well kept ales including Greene King
Abbot, Sharps Doom Bar and a guest
like local Hogswood, coal fire; sports TV;
children welcome in eating area, terrace
tables. *(Anon)*

ST DOMINICK   SX4067
⭐ **Who'd Have Thought It**
(01579) 350214 *Off A388 S of
Callington; PL12 6TG* Large, comfortable
and welcoming country pub under mother
and daughter (chef) management,
wide choice of good food from generous
sandwiches to blackboard specials, well kept
St Austell ales, decent wines, superb Tamar
views especially from conservatory, cosily
plush lounge areas with open fires; dogs
allowed in public bar, garden tables, handy
for Cotehele (NT). *(Jacquie Jones, Ted George)*

You can send reports directly to us at feedback@goodguides.com

ST GERMANS   SX3557
Eliot Arms (01503) 232733
Fore Street; PL12 5NR Stone-built slate-roofed pub with two bars and a restaurant, reasonably priced home-made food, St Austell ales; pool, darts and sports TV; picnic-sets out in front walled area with flowers and hanging baskets, four bedrooms. *(Dr D J and Mrs S C Walker)*

ST IVES   SW5140
Lifeboat (01736) 794123
Wharf Road; TR26 1LF Thriving family-friendly beamed quayside pub, wide choice of good value food all day, three St Austell ales, friendly helpful staff, well spaced harbour-view tables and cosier corners, nautical theme including lifeboat pictures; sports TV; good disabled access and facilities, open all day. *(George Atkinson)*

ST IVES   SW5441
Pedn Olva (01736) 796222
The Warren; TR26 2EA Hotel not pub, but has well kept reasonably priced St Austell ales in its roomy bar, panoramic views of sea and Porthminster beach, especially from tables on rooftop terrace, all-day bar food and separate restaurant; comfortable bedrooms. *(Alan Johnson)*

ST IVES   SW5441
Queens (01736) 796468
TR26 1RR Georgian inn with friendly relaxed atmosphere, bare-boards bar with open fire, scrubbed pine tables, tartan banquettes and some comfy leather armchairs, wall of barometers, good sensibly priced food, St Austell ales; children welcome, eight bedrooms. *(David White, Zoe Freeman)*

ST IVES   SW5140
★ Sloop (01736) 796584
The Wharf; TR26 1LP Busy low-beamed, panelled and flagstoned harbourside pub with bright St Ives School pictures and attractive portrait drawings in front bar, booth seating in back bar, good value food from sandwiches and interesting baguettes to lots of fresh local fish, quick friendly service even though busy, Greene King and Sharps, good coffee; background music, TV; children in eating area, a few beach-view seats out on cobbles, open all day (breakfast from 9am), handy for Tate Gallery. *(P Dawn, Stanley and Annie Matthews, Alan Johnson, the Didler, Bruce and Sharon Eden, Roger and Donna Huggins and others)*

ST IVES   SW5140
Union (01736) 796486
Fore Street; TR26 1AB Popular friendly low-beamed local, roomy but cosy, with good value food from sandwiches to local fish, well kept Sharps Doom Bar, decent wines, coffee, small hot fire, leather sofas on carpet, dark woodwork and masses of ship photographs; background music; dogs welcome. *(David Crook, George Atkinson, Alan Johnson)*

ST JUST IN PENWITH   SW3731
Kings Arms (01736) 788545
Market Square; TR19 7HF Welcoming place with three separate areas, granite walls and beamed and boarded ceilings, open fires, well kept St Austell ales, home-made food (not Sun evening) from short menu; live music Sun, Weds quiz night; children and dogs welcome, tables out in front. *(Richard Stanfield, Robin Sykes, Alan Johnson, the Didler, Neil Alford)*

ST JUST IN PENWITH   SW3731
★ Star (01736) 788767
Fore Street; TR19 7LL Relaxed and informal low-beamed two-room local, friendly landlord, five well kept St Austell ales, no food (bring your own lunchtime sandwiches or pasties), dimly lit main bar with dark walls covered in flags and photographs, coal fire, sleepy pub cat, darts and euchre, nostalgic juke box, live celtic music Mon evening, open mike Thurs; tables in attractive back yard with smokers' shelter, open all day. *(Alan Johnson, Patrick McLoughlin, the Didler, Terry and Nickie Williams)*

ST KEW   SX0276
St Kew Inn (01208) 841259
Village signposted from A39 NE of Wadebridge; PL30 3HB Grand-looking 15th-c pub with neat beamed bar, stone walls, winged high-backed settles and more traditional furniture on tartan carpeting, all sorts of jugs dotted about, woodburner in stone fireplace, three dining areas, St Austell beers (tapped from the cask in summer), new menu following change of chef, no evening meals on Sun in winter, live music every other Fri; children (away from bar) and dogs welcome, pretty flowering tubs and baskets outside, picnic-sets in garden over the road, open all day in summer. *(Graham Oddey, Phil and Gill Wass, the Didler, David Hoult, Paul and Penny Dawson, Barry and Anne and others)*

ST MAWES   SW8433
Idle Rocks (01326) 270771
Tredenham Road (harbour edge); TR2 5AN Comfortable, old-fashioned waterfront hotel with lovely sea views, Skinners Betty Stogs and decent wines by the glass (at a price), enjoyable lunchtime food in two-tier restaurant looking on to terrace and harbour (more formal in evening but still relaxed), also nice snacks in pleasant small bar area and separate lounge, daily papers, friendly helpful young staff; well behaved dogs (but no small children) allowed on sun terrace over harbour, smallish bedrooms overlooking the water are the best bet. *(Dennis Jenkin, R and S Bentley)*

ST MAWES   SW8433
Rising Sun (01326) 270233
The Square; TR2 5DJ Light and airy, with relaxed bar on right with end woodburner, sea-view bow window opposite, rugs on stripped wood, a few dining tables, sizeable carpeted left-hand bar with dark wood furniture, standard food, St Austell ales, good wines by the glass, friendly staff, wood-floored conservatory; background music; awkward wheelchair access, sunny terrace with picnic-sets just across road from harbour wall, bedrooms. *(Stanley and Annie Matthews, R and S Bentley)*

ST MAWES   SW8433
Victory (01326) 270324
Victory Hill; TR2 5DQ Still up for sale but carrying on as usual; locals' bare-boards bar on left, carpeted dining area on right with partitions, upstairs room with balcony, well kept Sharps and perhaps Cornish Shag (brewed at sister pub, the Roseland in Philleigh), good pubby food inc local fish, log fires, welcoming attentive staff, plain wooden seating, board games; background music, no wheelchair access ; one or two picnic-sets outside, two good value bedrooms, open all day. *(Barry Collett, Geoff and Linda Payne, M J Winterton)*

ST MAWGAN   SW8765
★ Falcon (01637) 860225
NE of Newquay, off B3276 or A3059; TR8 4EP Attractive old wisteria-clad stone inn, log-fire bar with antique coaching prints and falcon pictures, St Austell ales kept well, pubby food, good friendly service, compact stone-floored dining room, darts; children welcome, front cobbled courtyard and peaceful back garden with wishing well (they ask to keep a credit card if you eat outside), pretty village, four bedrooms, open all day in summer. *(Eddie Edwards)*

ST TUDY   SX0676
Tudy Inn (01208) 850656
Off A391 near Wadebridge; PL30 3NN Fully refurbished 16th-c village pub under new welcoming landlord, good home-cooked food at reasonable prices, well kept cornish beers from small breweries, good service, warm log fire. *(Dr and Mrs M P Bracy)*

STITHIANS   SW7640
Cornish Arms (01872) 863445
Frogpool, which is not shown on many roadmaps but is NE of A393 – ie opposite side to Stithians itself; TR4 8RP Unspoilt 18th-c village pub under brother and sister team (he cooks), long beamed bar with fires either end, cosy snug, good value wholesome food, local ales and ciders; pool, euchre, piped radio; well behaved children and dogs welcome, closed Mon lunchtime. *(John Marsh)*

STITHIANS   SW7037
Golden Lion (01209) 860332
Stithians Lake, Menherion; TR16 6NW Welcoming pub with good food from open sandwiches up, St Austell ales, oak-beams and granite walls, candlelit tables, conservatory; large well maintained garden and lakeside terrace, campsite. *(David and Sue Smith)*

STRATTON   SS2306
Tree (01288) 352038
Just E of Bude; Fore Street; EX23 9DA Rambling softly lit 16th-c beamed local with interesting old furniture and colourful décor, log fire and woodburner, well kept ales including Sharps Doom Bar, home-made food using local supplies, Sun carvery, character Elizabethan-style restaurant with old paintings; big-screen sports TV, machines, pool, darts; children welcome in back bar, seats alongside unusual old dovecote in ancient coachyard with post office, six bedrooms, open all day Fri-Sun. *(Ryta Lyndley)*

TIDEFORD   SX3459
Rod & Line (01752) 851323
Church Road; PL12 5HW Small old-fashioned local set back from road up steps, friendly lively atmosphere, Greene King Abbot and St Austell Tribute, lots of fish from local market including good crab, angling theme with rods etc, low-bowed ceiling, settles, good log fire; children and dogs welcome, tables outside. *(Ian Phillips, Dr D J and Mrs S C Walker, Julian Distin, Andrea Rampley)*

TREBARWITH   SX0585
Port William (01840) 770230
Trebarwith Strand; PL34 0HB Lovely seaside setting with glorious views and sunsets, waterside picnic-sets across road and on covered terrace, fishing nets, fish tanks and maritime memorabilia inside, gallery with local artwork, well kept St Austell ales, farm cider, enjoyable pub food (may be a wait for a table at busy times); pool and other games, background music; children in eating area, eight well equipped comfortable bedrooms, open all day. *(Mr and Mrs E Hughes)*

TREBURLEY   SX3477
Springer Spaniel (01579) 370424
A388 Callington–Launceston; PL15 9NS Relaxed place popular with locals, clean décor with high-backed settle by woodburner,

---

Half pints: by law, a pub should not charge more for half a pint than half the price of a full pint, unless it shows that half-pint price on its price list.

farmhouse chairs and other seats, further cosy room with big solid teak tables, attractive restaurant up some steps, good locally sourced food (not particularly cheap), well kept Sharps and Skinners, good wine choice; dogs welcome in bar, children in eating areas, covered terrace. *(Jacquie Jones, Giles and Annie Francis)*

TREEN SW3923

⋆ **Logan Rock** (01736) 810495

Just off B3315 Penzance–Land's End; TR19 6LG Low-beamed traditional bar with well kept St Austell ales, enjoyable generous home-made food from sandwiches and good home-made pasties up, inglenook fire, small back snug with excellent cricket memorabilia – welcoming landlady eminent in county's cricket association, family room (no under-14s in bar); dogs welcome, pretty split-level garden behind with covered area, good coast walks, open all day in season and can get very busy. *(Clifford Blakemore, the Didler, Dennis Jenkin, David Crook, Di and Mike Gillam)*

TREGADILLETT SX2983

⋆ **Eliot Arms** (01566) 772051

Village signposted off A30 at junction with A395, W end of Launceston bypass; PL15 7EU Creeper-covered with series of small rooms, interesting collections inc 72 antique clocks, 400 snuffs, hundreds of horsebrasses, barometers, old prints and shelves of books/china, fine mix of furniture on Delabole slate from high-backed settles and chaises longues to more modern seats, open fires, well kept Courage and Sharps, decent good value food, friendly service; background music, games machine and darts; children and dogs welcome, seats out front and back, lovely hanging baskets and tubs, bedrooms, open all day. *(Giles and Annie Francis, Suedinley, Jacquie Jones, the Didler, John and Bernadette Elliott)*

TREGONY SW9244

Kings Arms (01872) 530202

Fore Street (B3287); TR2 5RW Light and airy 16th-c coaching inn, long traditional main bar and two beamed and panelled front dining areas, St Austell ales, Healey's cider/ perry, nice wines, good-quality reasonably priced pub food using local produce, tea and coffee, welcoming prompt service and chatty landlord, two fireplaces, one with huge cornish range, pubby furniture on carpet or flagstones, old team photographs, back games room; children welcome, disabled access, tables in pleasant suntrap garden, charming village. *(Chris and Angela Buckell)*

TRELEIGH SW7043

Treleigh Arms (01209) 315095

Near Redruth, A3047; TR16 4AY Refurbished hospitable place with good food and well kept beers such as Bass. *(Mick and Moira Brummell, John and Jackie Chalcraft)*

TRURO SW8244

Old Ale House (01872) 271122

Quay Street; TR1 2HD Town-centre pub now owned by Skinners, their ales and guests, some tapped from casks behind bar, several wines by the glass including country ones, bargain food from open kitchen, dimly-lit beamed bar with engaging mix of furnishings, some interesting 1920s bric-a-brac, beer mats, daily papers, upstairs room with table football; juke box; children allowed away from bar, open all day. *(the Didler, David Crook, B and M Kendall)*

TRURO SW8244

Try Dower (01872) 265840

Lemon Quay; TR1 2LW Busy Wetherspoons in former newspaper offices on the quay, up to eight real ales at bargain prices, their usual meal deals, efficient service, pastel décor, sofas, family tables and quiet areas; TV news; good market outside on Weds and Sat. *(David Crook)*

TRURO SW8244

White Hart (01872) 277294

New Bridge Street (aka Crab & Ale House); TR1 2AA Compact old city-centre pub with nautical theme, friendly landlord and locals, well kept ales including St Austell Tribute and Sharps Doom Bar, good helpings of reasonably priced pub food. *(Stanley and Annie Matthews, John and Sarah Perry)*

TYWARDREATH SX0854

New Inn (01726) 813901

Off A3082; Fore Street; PL24 2QP Timeless 18th-c local, friendly and relaxed, with Bass tapped from the cask and St Austell ales on handpump, caring friendly landlord, back games/children's room with juke box, open fires; large secluded garden behind, nice village setting, bedrooms, open all day. *(the Didler)*

VERYAN SW9139

New Inn (01872) 501362

Village signed off A3078; TR2 5QA Comfortable and homely one-bar beamed local thriving under present landlord, straightforward good value food from sandwiches up (can get busy evenings so worth booking), St Austell ales, Healey's cider, good wines, friendly attentive service, inglenook woodburner, polished brass and old pictures; background music, nearby parking unlikely in summer; dogs and well behaved children welcome, wheelchair access with help, secluded beer garden behind, bedrooms, interesting partly thatched village not far from nice beach. *(Lawrence Pearse, Chris and Angela Buckell, R K Phillips, the Didler)*

WATERGATE BAY SW8464

Beach Hut (01637) 860877

B3276 coast road N of Newquay; TR8 4AA Great views from bustling modern beach bar with good mix of customers of all ages, surfing photographs on planked walls, cushioned wicker and cane armchairs around green and orange tables, weathered stripped-wood floor, unusual sloping bleached-board ceiling, big windows and doors opening to glass-fronted deck looking across sand to the sea, simpler end room, decent wines by the glass, possibly real ale, lots of coffees and teas, good modern food served by friendly young staff; background music; dogs welcome in bar, open 8.30am-11pm, 10.30am-5pm in winter. *(Eddie Edwards, Christopher Turner)*

WATERGATE BAY   SW8464
Phoenix (01637) 860353
Trevarrian Hill; TR8 4AB Popular surfers' haunt with great coast and sunset views from open balcony, bar/restaurant upstairs with enjoyable food including interesting fish dishes, downstairs bistro bar, good friendly service, well kept St Austell Tribute, Sharps Doom Bar and Skinners Betty Stogs, decent wines, sensible prices; live music, TV and pool; well behaved children and dogs welcome, disabled facilities, plenty of outside seating, open all day weekends. *(Eddie Edwards)*

WENDRON   SW6731
New Inn (01326) 572683
B3297; TR13 0EA Friendly little 18th-c granite-built village pub, well kept changing ales, enjoyable good value food from landlady including popular Sun lunch; children and dogs welcome. *(Ken and Tammy Lewis)*

WIDEMOUTH   SS1902
⋆ Bay View (01288) 361273
Village signposted (with Bude Coastal Route) off A39 N of Pounstock; Marine Drive; EX23 0AW Sizeable hotel with wonderful views of Widemouth Bay, several spreading areas with rugs on stripped-wood floors or flagstones, comfortable leather sofas, low chunky tables, log-effect gas fires, relaxed atmosphere, Sharps Doom Bar, Skinners Betty Stogs and a beer named for them, straightforward food (all day Sun), separate restaurant; children and dogs welcome, front terrace and picnic-sets on grass, play area and maybe bouncy castle, bedrooms (front ones with best views), open all day. *(the Didler)*

ZELAH   SW8151
Hawkins Arms (01872) 540339
A30; TR4 9HU Homely 18th-c stone-built beamed local, well kept Bays and guests such

as Skinners, decent good value food, friendly landlord and staff, copper and brass in bar and dining room, woodburner; children and dogs welcome, four bedrooms, back and side terraces. *(Mike and Kathryn Budd)*

ZENNOR   SW4538
⋆ Tinners Arms (01736) 796927
B3306 W of St Ives; TR26 3BY Friendly welcome and enjoyable honest food including enjoyable ploughman's with three cornish cheeses and home-baked bread, long unspoilt bar with flagstones, granite, stripped pine and real fires each end, back dining room, well kept ales such as St Austell, Sharps Doom Bar and Wadworths 6X from casks behind counter, farm cider, sensibly priced wines, decent coffee, quick service even when busy, friendly mix of locals and visitors; muddy walkers welcome, tables in small suntrap courtyard, lovely peaceful windswept setting by church near coast path. *(Mike Proctor, M and GR, Chris and Libby Allen, Mr and Mrs E Hughes, Peter and Judy Frost, P J and R D Greaves and others)*

ISLES OF SCILLY

ST AGNES   SV8808
⋆ Turks Head (01720) 422434
The Quay; TR22 0PL One of the UK's most beautifully placed pubs, idyllic sea and island views from garden terrace, can get very busy on fine days, good food from pasties to popular fresh seafood (best to get there early), well kept ales and cider, friendly licensees and good cheerful service; children and dogs welcome, closed in the winter, otherwise open all day. *(Tony and Jill Radnor, Nigel Morton, Bob and Margaret Holder, Michael Sargent)*

ST MARY'S   SV9010
⋆ Atlantic Inn (01720) 422323
The Strand; next to but independent from Atlantic Hotel; TR21 0HY Spreading and hospitable dark bar with well kept St Austell ales, good range of food including daily specials, sea-view restaurant, low beams, hanging boat and other nauticalia, mix of locals and tourists – busy evenings, quieter on sunny lunchtimes; darts, pool, games machines, piped and live music; nice raised verandah with wide views over harbour, good bedrooms in adjacent hotel. *(G M Hollington, Nigel Morton, Bob and Margaret Holder)*

Please keep sending us reports. We rely on readers for news of new discoveries, and particularly for news of changes – however slight – at the fully described pubs: feedback@goodguides.com, or (no stamp needed) The Good Pub Guide, FREEPOST TN1569, Wadhurst, E Sussex TN5 7BR.

Cumbria

A smashing number of new entries for Cumbria this year include the Wheatsheaf in Beetham (newly refurbished, friendly licensees), Cross Keys in Carleton (sister pub to Highland Drove, Great Salkeld), Sun in Coniston (hotel with eight real ales in proper bar), Punch Bowl in Crosthwaite (delicious food, lovely bedrooms, stylish surroundings), Drunken Duck near Hawkshead (own-brewed beers, charming bar), Plough in Lupton (carefully refurbished, interesting modern food, comfortable bedrooms), Greyhound at Shap (honest place, eight real ales, good pubby food), Beer Hall at Hawkshead Brewery in Staveley (showcase for the brewery, interesting tapas), and Langstrath at Stonethwaite (warmly friendly, good beers, lovely spot). Pubs that have received particularly warm praise from our readers are the Masons Arms, Cartmel Fell (idyllic spot, exceedingly popular), George & Dragon at Clifton (fantastic modern cooking using own-bred animals), Highland Drove in Great Salkeld (top class all-rounder), Watermill at Ings (16 beers including own-brew, hands on landlord), Kirkstile Inn at Loweswater (own-brewed ales, super little inn), Tower Bank Arms at Near Sawrey (backs on to Beatrix Potter's farm), Eagle & Child in Staveley (brilliant base for the area), Derby Arms in Witherslack (part of the Ainscough's stable) and Gate Inn at Yanwath (exceptional all-rounder). Many of these pubs offer excellent food in civilised surroundings but our Dining Pub for Cumbria 2013 is the extremely popular and well run Gate Inn at Yanwath.

AMBLESIDE

NY3704   Map 9

Golden Rule

Smithy Brow; follow Kirkstone Pass signpost from A591 on N side of town; LA22 9AS

Simple town local with a cosy, relaxed atmosphere and real ales

All customers – including walkers and their dogs – are made welcome in this no-frills town local; nothing changes at all, which is just the way the regulars like it. The bar area has built-in wall seats around cast-iron framed tables (one with a local map set into its top), horsebrasses on black beams, assorted pictures on the walls, a welcoming winter fire and a relaxed atmosphere. Robinsons Cumbria Way, Dark Mild, Dizzy Blonde, Double Hop, Enigma and Hartleys XB on handpump. A brass measuring rule hangs above the bar (hence the pub's name). There's also a back room with TV (not much used), a left-hand room with darts and a games machine and a further room, down a couple of steps on the right, with lots of seating. The backyard has benches and a covered heated area, and the window boxes are especially colourful. There's no car park.

There might be scotch eggs and pies but they tend to run out fast so don't assume you'll be able to get something to eat.

Robinsons ~ Tenant John Lockley ~ Real ale ~ No credit cards ~ (015394) 32257 ~ Children welcome away from bar and must leave by 9pm ~ Dogs welcome ~ Open 11-midnight ~ www.goldenrule-ambleside.co.uk *Recommended by John Prescott, G Jennings*

BASSENTHWAITE LAKE

NY1930   Map 9

Pheasant ★ ⑪ ♀ ⇦

Follow Pheasant Inn sign at N end of dual carriageway stretch of A66 by Bassenthwaite Lake; CA13 9YE

Charming, old-fashioned bar in smart hotel with enjoyable bar food and a fine range of drinks; comfortable bedrooms

The little bar in this civilised and rather smart hotel is such a surprise for first-time visitors – given that it is properly pubby and nicely old-fashioned and much frequented by chatty locals. There are mellow polished walls, cushioned oak settles, rush-seat chairs and library seats, hunting prints and photographs, and Coniston Bluebird, Cumberland Corby Ale and Hawkshead Red on handpump served by friendly, knowledgeable staff; also, a dozen good wines by the glass, over 50 malt whiskies and several gins and vodkas. There's a front bistro, a formal back restaurant overlooking the garden and several comfortable lounges with log fires, beautiful flower arrangements, fine parquet flooring, antiques and plants. There are seats in the garden, attractive woodland surroundings and plenty of walks in all directions.

You can only eat in the bar at lunchtime; in the evening the bistro serves the same menu. The interesting food might include sandwiches, chicken and duck liver pâté with cumberland sauce, twice-baked cheddar soufflé with red onion jam and mustard cream, wild mushroom and ham hock risotto with a poached egg, cumberland and venison sausage duo with red wine and mushroom sauce, a pie of the day, coq au vin, beer-battered haddock with mushy peas, and puddings such as dark chocolate brownie and sticky toffee pudding. *Benchmark main dish: braised beef £14.00. Two-course evening meal £21.00.*

Free house ~ Licensee Matthew Wylie ~ Real ale ~ Bar food (12-2, 6-9) ~ Restaurant ~ (017687) 76234 ~ Children over 8 only ~ Dogs allowed in bar and bedrooms ~

Open 11-2.30, 5.30-10.30(11 Sat); 12-2.30, 6-10.30 Sun ~ Bedrooms: £95B/£170B ~
www.the-pheasant.co.uk *Recommended by J F M and M West, Howard Bowen, Jane and Alan
Bush, Jeremy and Ruth Preston-Hoar, Martin and Sue Day, Pat and Stewart Gordon*

BEETHAM
SD4979   Map 7
Wheatsheaf
Village (and inn) signed off A6 S of Milnthorpe; LA7 7AL

**Old coaching inn with handsome timbered cornerpiece, lots of beams,
interesting food and quite a choice of drinks**

In a quiet village and opposite a pretty 14th-c church, this is a striking
old coaching inn with friendly licensees. It's been refurbished this
year in traditional style throughout with a mix of high-backed wooden,
leather and fabric-covered dining chairs around an attractive mix of
dark wooden tables on tartan carpeting with pictures and photographs
of locals scenes in gold frames on cream-painted walls, burgundy-
patterned silk curtains and chandeliers. There's an opened-up front
lounge bar with lots of exposed beams and joists, a main bar (behind on
the right) with an open fire, two upstairs dining rooms and a residents'
lounge. Cross Bay Nightfall, Tirril Queen Jean and a guest beer on
handpump, several wines by the glass and quite a few malt whiskies.
Plenty of surrounding walks.

Popular food includes sandwiches, chicken liver pâté with chutney,
smoked haddock and spring onion fishcakes with tartare sauce, cheese,
ham and egg, potato and onion pie, cumberland sausages with colcannon mash
and shallot gravy, chicken breast with peas, bacon, potatoes and a white wine
sauce, steak and mushroom stroganoff, and puddings like eton mess and warm
chocolate fudge cake with chantilly cream; they also have an early bird menu
(Monday-Thursday). *Benchmark main dish: fish pie £12.50. Two-course evening
meal £18.00.*

Free house ~ Licensees Mr and Mrs Skelton ~ Real ale ~ Bar food (9-9) ~ Restaurant
~ (015395) 62123 ~ Children welcome ~ Dogs allowed in bar ~ Open 11-11; 12-10.30
Sun ~ Bedrooms: £55B/£75B ~ www.wheatsheafbeetham.com *Recommended by Barbara
Hemingway, Simon Le Fort, Francesca Salvini, Ray and Winifred Halliday*

BOWLAND BRIDGE
SD4189   Map 9
Hare & Hounds 🍴 🍷 🛏
Signed from A5074; LA11 6NN

**17th-c inn in quiet spot with a friendly, cheerful landlady, real ales,
popular food, and fine views; comfortable bedrooms**

Just three miles from Lake Windermere, this attractive 17th-c coaching
inn is in a quiet hamlet in the Winster Valley. There's a little bar with
a log fire, daily papers to read and high chairs by the wooden counter
where they serve Hare of the Dog (brewed especially for them by
Tirril) and guests such as Cumberland Corby Blonde and Ulverston
Flying Elephants on handpump, a farm cider from half a mile away, and
ten wines by the glass. Leading off here, other rooms are appealingly
furnished with a happy mix of interesting dining chairs around all sorts
of tables on the black slate or old pine-boarded floors, lots of hunting
prints on painted or stripped-stone walls, a candlelit moroccan-style
lantern in a fireplace with neatly stacked logs to one side, and a relaxed
atmosphere; background music and board games. The collie is called
Murphy. There are teak tables and chairs under parasols on the front

terrace, with more seats in the spacious side garden and fine valley views. The bedrooms are comfortable and the breakfasts are first class.

 Using the local farm for all their meat and local, seasonal game, the very good food includes cold and hot lunchtime sandwiches, potted crab in lemon and chilli, garlic rösti topped with their own-cured ham, poached egg and wholegrain mustard cream sauce, smoked haddock bake in a dill and prawn cream sauce topped with a herb and smoked cheddar crust, layer-spiced aubergine in a spicy tomato sauce with goats cheese, specials such as pork ribs in honey, garlic and lemon, lamb and mint burger with garlic and parsley mayonnaise and duck breast on a rocket, walnut and crispy air-dried ham salad with damson chutney, and puddings like vanilla crème brûlée with damson and plum sorbet and chocolate terrine with raspberry coulis; they also offer a two-course weekday set lunch menu. *Benchmark main dish: beef in ale pie £11.50. Two-course evening meal £18.50.*

Free house ~ Licensee Kerry Parsons ~ Real ale ~ Bar food (12-2, 6-9; all day weekends) ~ (015395) 68333 ~ Children welcome ~ Dogs allowed in bar and bedrooms ~ Live music during May bank holiday beer festival ~ Open 12-11(10.30 Sun) ~ Bedrooms: /£85S ~ www.hareandhoundsbowlandbridge.co.uk *Recommended by Paul Slater, John and Sylvia Harrop, V and E A Bolton, Michael Doswell, Martin Hickes, Mr and Mrs P R Thomas, Patricia White*

BROUGHTON MILLS   SD2190   Map 9
Blacksmiths Arms 🍴
Off A593 N of Broughton-in-Furness; LA20 6AX

Friendly little pub with imaginative food, local beers and open fires; fine surrounding walks

Tucked away in a little hamlet in peaceful countryside, this bustling pub is just the place to relax after a day on the fells. The four little bars, with warm log fires, have a relaxed, friendly atmosphere and are simply but attractively decorated with straightforward chairs and tables on ancient slate floors. Barngates Cracker Ale, Cumberland Corby Blonde and Hawkshead Bitter on handpump, nine wines by the glass and summer farm cider; darts, board games and dominoes. The hanging baskets and tubs of flowers in front of the building are very pretty in summer and there are seats and tables under parasols on the back terrace.

Consistently good food includes lunchtime sandwiches, rabbit and ham hock terrine with home-made onion bread and pumpkin chutney, honey-roast ham with a poached egg and home-made chips, cumberland sausage with grain mustard mash, black pudding and an oxtail and red wine sauce, goats cheese and courgette tart with an apple, radish and watercress salad, beer-battered hake fillet with crushed minted peas and tartare sauce, slow-braised venison, mushroom and red wine pie with pickled red cabbage and puddings like berry crème brûlée with honey and pistachio biscotti and sticky toffee pudding with warm butterscotch sauce. *Benchmark main dish: slow-cooked lamb shoulder £13.95. Two-course evening meal £19.50.*

Free house ~ Licensees Mike and Sophie Lane ~ Real ale ~ Bar food (12-2, 6-9; not Mon evening) ~ (01229) 716824 ~ Children welcome ~ Dogs welcome ~ Open 12-11(5-11 Mon); 12-10.30 Sun; 12-2.30, 5-11 Tues-Fri in winter; closed Mon lunchtime ~ www.theblacksmithsarms.co.uk *Recommended by Tina and David Woods-Taylor, JES, Rosemary and Mike Fielder, Miss J F Reay*

The knife-and-fork award 🍴 distinguishes pubs where the food
is of exceptional quality.

CARLETON

NY5329   Map 9

Cross Keys ◀

A686, off A66 roundabout at Penrith; CA11 8TP

Busy, welcoming pub with several connected seating areas, real ales and popular food

A lways bustling and friendly, this well run pub has a healthy mix of both drinkers and diners – and the atmosphere is relaxed and informal. The beamed main bar has pubby tables and chairs on the light wooden floorboards, modern metal wall lights and pictures on the bare stone walls, and Theakstons Black Bull, Tirril 1823 and a changing guest on handpump. Steps lead down to a small area with high bar stools around a high drinking table and then upstairs to the restaurant – a light, airy room with big windows, large wrought-iron candelabras hanging from the vaulted ceiling, pale solid wooden tables and chairs, and doors to a verandah. At the far end of the main bar, there's yet another couple of small connected bar rooms with darts, games machine, pool, juke box and dominoes; TV and background music. There are fell views from the garden. This is under the same ownership as the Highland Drove in Great Salkeld.

Well liked food includes lunchtime sandwiches, chicken liver pâté with onion and apricot chutney, twice-baked cheese soufflé with provençale sauce and a parmesan tuile, chargrilled vegetable or seafood platters, home-made beef burger with tomato relish, vegetable and goats cheese filo parcel with sweet potato gratin, beer-battered haddock, roast chicken breast with a chicken and ham pie and herb mash, lambs liver with bacon, onion gravy and mash, and puddings like sticky toffee pudding with butterscotch sauce and passion fruit crème brûlée with home-made shortbread. *Benchmark main dish: steak in ale pie £9.75. Two-course evening meal £15.00.*

Free house ~ Licensee Paul Newton ~ Real ale ~ Bar food (12-2.30, 6(5.30 Fri and Sat)-9(8.30 Sun)) ~ Restaurant ~ (01768) 865588 ~ Children welcome ~ Dogs allowed in bar ~ Open 12-3, 5-midnight; midday-1am(midnight Sun) Sat ~ www.kyloes.co.uk
Recommended by Richard J Holloway, Phil Bryant, Rosemary and Mike Fielder

CARTMEL FELL

SD4189   Map 9

Masons Arms ⊕ ♉ ◀

Strawberry Bank, a few miles S of Windermere between A592 and A5074; perhaps the simplest way of finding the pub is to go uphill W from Bowland Bridge (which is signposted off A5074) towards Newby Bridge and keep right then left at the staggered crossroads – it's then on your right, below Gummer's How; OS Sheet 97 map reference 413895; LA11 6NW

Stunning views, beamed bar with plenty of character, interesting food and real ales plus many foreign bottled beers; self-catering cottages and apartments

I n a lovely spot, this well run pub has been a favourite with our readers for many years. The main bar has plenty of character, with low black beams in the bowed ceiling and country chairs and plain wooden tables on polished flagstones. A small lounge has oak tables and settles to match its fine Jacobean panelling, there's a plain little room beyond the serving counter with pictures and a fire in an open range, a family room with the atmosphere of an old parlour and an upstairs dining room; background music, board games and TV. Cumbrian Legendary Loweswater Gold, Hawkshead Bitter, Thwaites Wainwright and a guest beer on handpump, quite a few foreign bottled beers, 12 wines by the glass and ten malt whiskies; service is friendly and helpful. Rustic benches and tables on the heated terrace take in the stunning views down over the Winster Valley to the woods below Whitbarrow Scar. The stylish and comfortable self-catering cottages and apartments also have fine views.

Particularly good, often inventive food might include lunchtime sandwiches (the soup and sandwich deal is popular), home-potted shrimps and crayfish, sticky ribs, beef and smoky bacon burger with melting blue cheese and cajun spiced coleslaw, puff pastry tart topped with confit onions and smoked brie, battered fresh haddock and chips, daily specials like corn-fed chicken breast stuffed with mozzarella in a pink peppercorn sauce and monkfish in a creamy curry, mussel and vegetable sauce with tempura green beans, and puddings such as clotted cream baked cheesecake with Drambuie-soaked soft fruits and dark chocolate and Cointreau mousse with an orange and almond tuile. *Benchmark main dish: lamb with black pudding mash and a rich red wine, rosemary and thyme braising gravy £18.95. Two-course evening meal £19.00.*

Individual Inns ~ Managers John and Diane Taylor ~ Real ale ~ Bar food (12-2.30, 6-9; all day weekends) ~ Restaurant ~ (015395) 68486 ~ Children welcome ~ Dogs allowed in bedrooms ~ Open 11.30-11; 12-10.30 Sun ~ www.strawberrybank.com
Recommended by Tina and David Woods-Taylor, Andy and Jill Kassube, John and Hilary Penny, M G Hames, Mr and Mrs P R Thomas, Val Leonard, Karen Eliot, Christian Mole, Peter Armstrong

CLIFTON
NY5326   Map 9
George & Dragon 🍴 🍷 🛏
A6; near M6 junction 40; CA10 2ER

18th-c former coaching inn with attractive bars and sizeable restaurant, local ales, well chosen wines, imaginative food, and seats outside; smart bedrooms

The friendly welcome, relaxed atmosphere and first-class food continue to draw customers into this carefully restored 18th-c coaching inn. There's a relaxed reception room with leather chairs around a low table in front of an open fire, bright rugs on flagstones, a table in a private nook to one side of the reception desk (just right for a group of six) and a comfortable bed for Porter, the patterdale terrier. Through some wrought-iron gates is the main bar area with more cheerful rugs on flagstones, assorted wooden farmhouse chairs and tables, grey panelling topped with yellow-painted walls, photographs of the Lowther Estate and of the family with hunting dogs, various sheep and fell pictures and some high bar stools by the panelled bar counter. Cumberland Corby Blonde, Hawkshead Bitter and Hesket Newmarket High Pike Dark Amber Bitter on handpump, a dozen wines by the glass from a well chosen list, and home-made soft drinks. A further room with another open fire is similarly furnished. The sizeable restaurant to the left of the entrance is made up of four open-plan rooms: plenty of old pews and church chairs around tables set for dining, a woodburning stove, and a contemporary open kitchen. Outside, there are tables on the decoratively paved front entrance, with more in a high-walled enclosed courtyard, and a herb garden.

Using rare-breed beef and pigs, vegetables and fruit and roe and red deer – all from the Lowther Estate of which this pub is part – the inventive food might include lunchtime sandwiches, twice-baked cheese soufflé, home oak-smoked pheasant with celeriac rémoulade, local honey home-roast ham with free-range egg, shorthorn burger with hand-cut chips, leek and mascarpone risotto with toasted almonds, specials such as venison carpaccio, monkfish with saffron potatoes and cucumber and saddle of lamb, and puddings like a crumble of the day and seville orange hot chocolate fondant. *Benchmark main dish: local sausages with mash and onion gravy £11.95. Two-course evening meal £19.45*

Free house ~ Licensee Paul McKinnon ~ Real ale ~ Bar food (12-2.30, 6-9) ~ Restaurant ~ (01768) 865381 ~ Children welcome ~ Dogs allowed in bar and bedrooms ~ Open 12-midnight ~ Bedrooms: £75S/£95S ~ www.georgeanddragonclifton.co.uk
Recommended by Mr and Mrs Ian King, Richard J Holloway, V and E A Bolton, David Heath, Rosemary and Mike Fielder, Malcolm and Jo Hart, Richard Chinn, Chris Pease

---

 CONISTON   SD3098   Map 9

Sun

Signed left off A593 at the bridge; LA21 8HQ

Lovely position for extended old pub with a lively bar, plenty of dining space, real ales, well liked food and seats outside; comfortable bedrooms

This 16th-c pub is in a spectacular position surrounded by dramatic bare fells, and seats and tables on the terrace and in the big tree-sheltered garden make the most of the lovely views. The heart of the place is the cheerful bar which has a good mix of customers (and their dogs), exposed stone walls, beams and timbers, flagstones and a Victorian-style range. Also, cask seats, old settles and cast-iron-framed tables and quite a few Donald Campbell photographs (this was his HQ during his final attempt on the world water speed record). Eight real ales from breweries such as Barngates, Black Sheep, Coniston, Copper Dragon, Cumbrian Legendary, Hawkshead, Keswick, and Yates on handpump, eight wines by the glass, two farm ciders and 20 malt whiskies. Above the bar is a new room, open to the ceiling, with extra seating for families and larger groups and there's a sizeable side lounge that leads into the dining conservatory; pool, darts and TV. A front terrace has more tables and chairs. The bedrooms are quiet and comfortable and the views are pretty special.

Good food includes sandwiches, lime and cracked pepper crumbed scallops with home-made tartare sauce, mushrooms and peppers or smoked salmon with free-range local eggs, cumberland sausage with an onion and red wine gravy, lasagne, organic chicken with leeks and cheese and a pastry top, twice-baked goats cheese with home-made chips, fish pie, and puddings like sticky toffee pudding with butterscotch sauce and warm cherry yoghurt cake. *Benchmark main dish: local beer-battered haddock with home-made chips £12.95. Two-course evening meal £18.50.*

Free house ~ Licensee Alan Piper ~ Real ale ~ Bar food (12-2.30, 5.30-8.30) ~ Restaurant ~ (015394) 41248 ~ Children in eating area of bar and restaurant ~ Dogs allowed in bar ~ Open 11am-midnight ~ Bedrooms: £40S/£80S(£90B) ~ www.thesunconiston.com *Recommended by K Skuse, Dr Kevan Tucker, Ben Dobson*

CROSTHWAITE   SD4491   Map 9

Punch Bowl

Village signed off A5074 SE of Windermere; LA8 8HR

Smart dining pub with a proper bar and several other elegant rooms, real ales, a fine wine list, imaginative food and friendly staff; seats on terrace overlooking the valley; lovely bedrooms

As well as being a lovely place to stay with stylish and comfortable bedrooms and excellent food, this civilised dining pub has a proper bar with real ales and locals do pop in for a pint and a chat. This public bar is raftered and hop-hung with a couple of eye-catching rugs on flagstones, bar stools by the slate-topped counter, Barngates Westmorland Gold, Coniston Bluebird and Hawkshead Bitter on handpump, 22 wines by the glass and around a dozen malt whiskies; friendly, helpful staff. To the right are two linked carpeted and beamed rooms with well spaced country pine furniture of varying sizes, including a big refectory table, and walls painted in restrained neutral tones with an attractive assortment of prints; winter log fire, woodburning stove, lots of fresh flowers and daily papers. On the left, the wooden-floored restaurant area (also light, airy and attractive) has comfortable high-backed leather dining chairs. Throughout, the pub feels relaxing and nicely uncluttered. There are some tables on a terrace stepped into the hillside overlooking the lovely Lyth Valley. This is sister pub to the Plough at Lupton.

Using carefully sourced local produce, the inventive food might include queenie scallops with garlic, gruyère and parsley, beetroot three ways, walnut, goats cheese, raspberry and truffle vinaigrette, rump of lamb with boulangère potatoes, peas, broad beans and mint jelly, loin of cod with leek, bacon and mussel chowder and sweetcorn purée, home-made potato gnocchi, wild mushrooms, rosemary, lemon and white truffle oil, pork tenderloin with black pudding, potato scallops, and local damson purée, and puddings such as chocolate mousse, raspberry sorbet, popping candy and elderflower foam and treacle tart with vanilla jelly and clotted cream ice-cream. *Benchmark main dish: pork tenderloin with black pudding, cabbage and damson purée £15.95. Two-course evening meal £22.00.*

Free house ~ Licensees Richard Rose and co-owner ~ Real ale ~ Bar food (12-9) ~ Restaurant ~ (015395) 68237 ~ Children welcome ~ Dogs allowed in bar ~ Open 11-11 ~ Bedrooms: £94B/£140B ~ www.the-punchbowl.co.uk *Recommended by Hugh Roberts, Michael Doswell*

ELTERWATER   NY3204 Map 9

Britannia

Off B5343; LA22 9HP

Extremely popular inn surrounded by wonderful walks and scenery; up to six real ales and well liked food; bedrooms

In such a beautiful part of the Lake District, close to the central lakes and with tracks over the fells, it's not surprising that this well run place is so popular with walkers. The atmosphere is old-fashioned and the little front bar has beams and a couple of window seats that look across to Elterwater itself through the trees. The small back bar is traditionally furnished: thick slate walls, winter coal fires, oak benches, settles, windsor chairs and a big old rocking chair. Coniston Bluebird, Hawkshead Red, Hesket Newmarket Catbells Pale Ale, Jennings Bitter, Thwaites Wainwright and a guest from Coniston named for the pub on handpump, and 15 malt whiskies. The lounge is comfortable and there's a hall and dining room. Plenty of seats outside, and summer morris and step garland dancers.

Generously served and popular (you must book in advance or you might be disappointed), the food might include lunchtime sandwiches, cumberland pâté, shrimps in lemon and chervil butter, beef burger with chips and red onion marmalade, cumberland sausage and mash with onion gravy, beer-battered fresh haddock with chips and home-made tartare sauce, mushroom stroganoff, specials like pheasant breast stuffed with venison and cranberry wrapped in parma ham with sweet potato mash and red wine gravy and salmon and king prawn gratin, and puddings such as white chocolate crème brûlée and sticky toffee pudding. *Benchmark main dish: steak in ale pie £13.50. Two-course evening meal £18.25.*

Free house ~ Licensee Andrew Parker ~ Real ale ~ Bar food (12-2, 6-9; afternoon snacks 2-5) ~ Restaurant ~ (015394) 37210 ~ Children welcome ~ Dogs allowed in bar and bedrooms ~ Open 10.30-11 ~ Bedrooms: £70S/£95S ~ www.britinn.co.uk
Recommended by Ewan and Moira McCall, Tina and David Woods-Taylor, G Jennings, Julia and Richard Tredgett, Richard Scrase, Mr and Mrs Richard Osborne, Steve and Sue Griffiths, Dr Kevan Tucker, Christian Mole

GREAT SALKELD   NY5536   Map 10
Highland Drove 🍴
B6412, off A686 NE of Penrith; CA11 9NA

Bustling place with a cheerful mix of customers, good food in several dining areas, fair choice of drinks and fine views from the upstairs verandah; bedrooms

'This well-run place provides every element of the perfect village pub,' one of our readers tells us – and many others agree. The hard-working, hands-on landlord is always there to greet his customers and everything is spotlessly kept. The chatty main bar has sandstone flooring, stone walls, cushioned wheelback chairs around a mix of tables and an open fire in a raised stone fireplace. The downstairs eating area has more cushioned dining chairs around wooden tables on the pale wooden floorboards, stone walls and ceiling joists and a two-way fire in a raised stone fireplace that separates this room from the coffee lounge with its comfortable leather chairs and sofas. There's also an upstairs restaurant. Best to book to be sure of a table. Theakstons Black Bull, John Smiths and a guest beer on handpump, several wines by the glass and 30 malt whiskies; background music, juke box, darts, pool and dominoes. The lovely views over the Eden Valley and the Pennines are best enjoyed from seats on the upstairs verandah. There are more seats on the back terrace. This is under the same ownership as the Cross Keys in Carleton.

As well as lunchtime filled ciabattas (not Sunday or Monday), the highly enjoyable food might include potted brown shrimps with walnut bread, black pudding wontons with beansprouts, spring onion, red pepper and sesame seed salad and a spicy sweet chilli dip, a charcuterie or fish platter to share, beer-battered haddock with mushy peas and tartare sauce, home-made beef burger with cheese and spicy tomato relish, gammon with fried egg and pineapple, lamb shank with a mint oil and spring onion dressing, three-way pork (fillet, belly and cumberland sausage) with apple sauce, black pudding mash and a grain mustard and honey sauce, and puddings like chocolate bread and butter pudding with crème anglaise and lemon tart with raspberry coulis and fresh raspberries. *Benchmark main dish: barbary duck breast with balsamic cherries, shi-itake mushrooms and pak choi on mixed pepper jasmine rice £14.95. Two-course evening meal £19.00.*

Free house ~ Licensees Donald and Paul Newton ~ Real ale ~ Bar food (12-2, 6(5.30 Fri and Sat)-9(8.30 Sun); not Mon lunchtime) ~ Restaurant ~ (01768) 898349 ~ Children welcome ~ Dogs allowed in bar ~ Open 12-3, 6-11; 12-midnight Sat; closed Mon lunchtime ~ Bedrooms: £42.50S/£75S ~ www.kyloes.co.uk *Recommended by Richard J Holloway, Richard and Stephanie Foskett, Rosemary and Mike Fielder, John and Hazel Hayward, Dave Braisted*

HAWKSHEAD
NY3501   Map 9

Drunken Duck 🍴 🍷 ◀ 🛏

Barngates; the hamlet is signposted from B5286 Hawkshead–Ambleside, opposite the Outgate Inn; or it may be quicker to take the first right from B5286, after the wooded caravan site; OS Sheet 90 map reference 350013; LA22 0NG

Small, stylish bar, several restaurant areas, own-brewed beers and bar meals as well as innovative restaurant choices; lovely bedrooms, stunning views

This is a civilised dining pub with beautifully appointed bedrooms but at lunchtime there's much more of an informal, pubby feel and it's extremely popular for lunch, before or after a walk. The small, smart bar has leather bar stools by the slate-topped counter, leather club chairs, beams and oak floorboards, photographs, coaching prints and hunting pictures on the walls, and horsebrasses and some kentish hop bines as decoration. From their Barngates brewery, there might be Cat Nap, Cracker, Red Bull Terrier, Tag Lag and Westmorland Gold on handpump as well as 17 wines by the glass from a fine list, 18 malt whiskies and belgian and german draught beers. The three restaurant areas are elegant. Outside, wooden tables and benches on grass opposite the building offer spectacular views across the fells, and there are thousands of spring and summer bulbs.

From the lunch menu (up until 4pm), the good bar food includes sandwiches (which you can take away as well; hearty ones like shoulder of pork and stuffing are popular), ploughman's, soup, blue cheese soufflé, poached pear and walnut salad, duck leg, cherries and beer, lemon thyme chicken with root vegetable and mushroom broth and sirloin steak with béarnaise sauce, with more pricey evening choices such as lamb breast, cockles, samphire, tomato and tarragon, pigeon, radish and apple with dandelion and burdock jus, tomato, rocket and mozzarella gnocchi, red wine-braised ox cheek bourguignon, bass with peas, baby onions and gem lettuce, beef fillet with crushed artichokes, braised shallots and smoked bone marrow and puddings like chocolate delice, salted caramel and praline ice-cream and baked Alaska with pistachio, rhubarb and ginger. *Benchmark main dish: braised shoulder of lamb and shepherd's pie with home-roasted vegetables £17.50. Two-course evening meal £22.00.*

Own brew ~ Licensee Steph Barton ~ Real ale ~ Bar food (12-4, 6.30-9) ~ Restaurant ~ (015394) 36347 ~ Children welcome ~ Dogs allowed in bar ~ Open 11.30-11; 12-10.30 Sun ~ Bedrooms: £71.25B/£95B ~ www.drunkenduckinn.co.uk *Recommended by Marianne and Peter Stevens, Tina and David Woods-Taylor, Yvonne Corry, Mr and Mrs Richard Osborne, Mike and Sue Loseby, Michael Doswell, Angela Horsley, Christian Mole*

INGS
SD4498   Map 9

Watermill ◀

Just off A591 E of Windermere; LA8 9PY

Busy, cleverly converted pub with fantastic range of real ales including own brews, and well liked food; bedrooms

The own-brewed beers here are so popular that a larger brewery is to be built just across the river; they also hope to add another eight bedrooms. It's a particularly well run place with a friendly, hard-working, hands-on landlord who genuinely loves his pub and his customers – and it shows. The building has plenty of character and is cleverly converted from a wood mill and joiner's shop and the bars have a lively atmosphere, a happy mix of chairs, padded benches and solid oak tables, bar counters made from old church wood, open fires, and interesting photographs and amusing cartoons by a local artist. The spacious lounge bar, in much the same traditional style as the other rooms, has rocking chairs and a big open fire. Their own-brewed beers include Watermill A Bit'er Ruff, Wruff Justice and Wruff Night, Blackbeard, Collie Wobbles, Dogth Vadar, Isle of Dogs and Winters Tail, and they keep up to 11 other beers on handpump: Blackbeck Belle, Coniston Bluebird, Cumbrian Legendary Grasmoor Dark Ale, Hawkshead Bitter, Hop Back Summer Lightning, Keswick Thirst Ascent, Kirkby Lonsdale Tiffin Gold, Theakstons Old Peculier and Ulverston Another Fine Mess. Also, scrumpy cider, a huge choice of foreign bottled beers and 40 malt whiskies; darts and board games. Seats in the gardens and lots to do nearby. Dogs may get free biscuits and water. Our readers enjoy staying here in the comfortable bedrooms (some are bigger than others).

Using their own-reared beef, the popular food includes lunchtime sandwiches and french bread pizzas, garlic mushrooms, pork, chicken liver and brandy pâté with home-made cumberland sauce, chilli and coriander burger, mediterranean pasta bake, cumberland sausage with beer and onion gravy, chicken in a rosemary, mustard, black pepper and cream sauce, beer-battered haddock and chips, gammon with pineapple and a free-range egg, daily specials, and puddings such as chocolate Guinness cake and eton mess. *Benchmark main dish: steak in ale pie £10.75. Two-course evening meal £15.00.*

Own brew ~ Licensee Brian Coulthwaite ~ Real ale ~ Bar food (12-9) ~ (01539) 821309 ~ Children welcome ~ Dogs allowed in bar and bedrooms ~ Storytelling first Tues evening of the month ~ Open 11.30-11(10.30 Sun) ~ Bedrooms: £43S/£79S ~ www.lakelandpub.co.uk *Recommended by V and E A Bolton, Mr and Mrs Ian King, Jane Speed, Paul Hartley, Martin Smith, Rosemary and Mike Fielder, Andy and Jill Kassube, Adam Brownhill, Mr and Mrs Maurice Thompson, Colin Woodward, Mike and Sue Loseby, the Didler, Lee and Liz Potter, Dennis Jones, Karen Eliot, Mike Proctor, David Bedford, Paul Goldman, Ian and Jane Irving*

LANGDALE   NY2806   Map 9
Old Dungeon Ghyll 🍺 £
B5343; LA22 9JY

Straightforward place in lovely position with real ales fine walks and bags of atmosphere; bedrooms

Full of character and atmosphere, this traditional hotel pub is a real fell-walkers' and climbers' haven and the setting is pretty dramatic, right at the heart of the Great Langdale Valley. The feel of the place is basic but cosy and there's no need to remove boots or muddy trousers – you can sit on seats in old cattle stalls by the big, warming fire and enjoy the choice of six real ales on handpump: Dent Bitter, Jennings Cumberland, Theakston Old Peculier, Thwaites Lancaster Bomber and Yates Best Bitter; also, around 20 malt whiskies. It can get lively on a Saturday night (there's a popular National Trust campsite opposite).

Decent helpings of traditional food include lunchtime sandwiches, soup with home-made bread, a changing pâté, cumberland sausage with apple sauce and onion gravy, a pie of the day, vegetable goulash, beer-battered fish, and half a roasted chicken. *Benchmark main dish: cumberland sausage £9.95. Two-course evening meal £15.00.*

Free house ~ Licensee Neil Walmsley ~ Real ale ~ Bar food (12-2, 6-9) ~ Restaurant ~ (015394) 37272 ~ Children welcome ~ Dogs allowed in bar ~ Open 11-11(10.30 Sun) ~ Bedrooms: £58S/£116S ~ www.odg.co.uk *Recommended by Mr and Mrs Maurice Thompson, the Didler, David Bedford*

LEVENS
Strickland Arms ♀ ◀

4 miles from M6 junction 36, via A590; just off A590, by Sizergh Castle gates; LA8 8DZ

Friendly, open-plan pub with much-enjoyed food, local ales and a fine setting; seats outside

Overlooking the entrance to Sizergh Castle, this well run and extremely popular pub is a civilised place for a drink or a meal. It's largely open plan with a light and airy feel, and the bar on the right has oriental rugs on the flagstones, a log fire, Cumbrian Legendary Langdale and Loweswater Gold and four quickly changing guest beers on handpump, several malt whiskies and nine wines by the glass. On the left are polished boards and another log fire, and throughout there's a nice mix of sturdy country furniture, candles on tables, hunting scenes and other old prints on the walls, heavy fabric for the curtains and some staffordshire china ornaments; it's best to book ahead if you want to eat downstairs but there is a further dining room upstairs. Background music and board games. The flagstoned front terrace has plenty of seats. The castle, a lovely partly medieval house with beautiful gardens, is open in the afternoon (not Friday or Saturday) from April to October. It has disabled access and facilities.

 Using estate beef and other local produce, the high quality food includes filled baguettes, mushroom and lancashire blue cheese tartlet, salmon mousse, home-made burger with sweet chilli sauce, steak, mushroom and red wine pie, lamb hotpot, sweet-cured pork loin steak with black pudding and a free-range egg, specials such as haggis with a tomato kashmiri chutney, vegetable risotto and pheasant stuffed with venison and cranberries in a tomato sauce, and puddings like sticky toffee pudding with butterscotch sauce and mixed berry eton mess. *Benchmark main dish: beer-battered fish and chips £11.50. Two-course evening meal £17.35.*

Free house ~ Licensee Martin Ainscough ~ Real ale ~ Bar food (12-2, 7-9) ~ Restaurant ~ (015395) 61010 ~ Children welcome ~ Dogs welcome ~ Open 12-11(10.30 Sun); 12-2, 5-11 in winter ~ www.thestricklandarms.com *Recommended by V and E A Bolton, Mrs M B Gregg, David A Hammond, Dr and Mrs R G J Telfer, Malcolm and Pauline Pellatt, Dr Kevan Tucker, Mr and Mrs Maurice Thompson, Jack Clark, David and Sue Atkinson, John and Sylvia Harrop, Mr and Mrs P R Thomas, David Hartley, John and Sarah Perry, Ray and Winifred Halliday*

LITTLE LANGDALE
Three Shires ◀ ⇌

From A593 3 miles W of Ambleside take small road signposted The Langdales, Wrynose Pass; then bear left at first fork; LA22 9NZ

Fine valley views from seats on the terrace, local ales, quite a choice of food and comfortable bedrooms

This is a lovely spot with views over the valley from seats on the terrace to the partly wooded hills below; there are more seats on a neat lawn behind the car park, backed by a small oak wood, and award-winning summer hanging baskets. The comfortably extended back bar has a mix of green Lakeland stone and homely red patterned wallpaper (which works rather well), stripped timbers and a beam and joist stripped ceiling, antique oak carved settles, country kitchen chairs and stools on its big dark slate flagstones and Lakeland photographs. Coniston Old Man, Hawkshead Bitter, Jennings Cumberland, and a guest beer on handpump, over 50 malt whiskies and a decent wine list. The front restaurant has chunky leather dining chairs around solid tables on the wood flooring, fresh flowers and wine bottle prints on the dark red walls; a snug leads off here; darts, TV and board games. The three shires are the historical counties of Cumberland, Westmorland and Lancashire, which meet at the top of the nearby Wrynose Pass.

As well as lunchtime sandwiches, the food might include deep-fried black pudding fritter with herb and apple mash and rich onion gravy, smoked venison loin with balsamic vinegar, leek and mushroom risotto, cumberland sausage with red wine gravy, lamb rump with a port and redcurrant sauce and sweet potato and rosemary mash, cod with a lemon and dill cream sauce, and puddings like white chocolate crème brûlée with raspberry ripple ice-cream and sticky toffee pudding with butterscotch sauce and banoffi ice-cream. *Benchmark main dish: beef in ale pie £13.50. Two-course evening meal £20.50.*

Free house ~ Licensee Ian Stephenson ~ Real ale ~ Bar food (12-2, 6-9) ~ Restaurant ~ (015394) 37215 ~ Children welcome ~ Dogs allowed in bar ~ Open 11-10.30(11 Sat) ~ Bedrooms: /£114S ~ www.threeshiresinn.co.uk *Recommended by Ewan and Moira McCall, Tina and David Woods-Taylor, Barry Collett, Ann Balmforth, Hugh Roberts*

LOWESWATER   NY1421   Map 9

Kirkstile Inn 🍺 🛏

From B5289 follow signs to Loweswater Lake; OS Sheet 89 map reference 140210; CA13 0RU

Well run, popular inn in lovely spot with busy bar, own-brewed beers, good food and friendly welcome; bedrooms

'This remains exemplary both as a pub and a place to stay,' say a group of our trusted readers – and many others agree with them. The bustling main bar is nearly always (deservedly) packed out so you must book in advance to be sure of a table. There are low-beams and carpeting, a friendly atmosphere, comfortably cushioned small settles and pews, partly stripped stone walls, and a roaring log fire; board games and a slate shove-ha'penny board. As well as their own-brewed Cumbrian Legendary Esthwaite Bitter, Langdale and Loweswater Gold, they keep a guest like Watermill Collie Wobbles on handpump; nine wines by the glass and ten malt whiskies. The stunning views of the surrounding peaks can be enjoyed from picnic-sets on the lawn, from the very attractive covered verandah in front of the building and from the bow windows in one of the rooms off the bar. There are marvellous surrounding walks of all levels, and maybe red squirrels in the garden; dogs are allowed in the bar lunchtime only.

At lunchtime, the well liked food includes sandwiches and wraps, omelettes, lamb stew with black pudding, spinach, feta, ricotta and roasted vegetable lasagne and steak in ale pie, with evening extras such as rabbit, duck and pheasant terrine with pear chutney, game pudding, slow-cooked lamb shoulder with red wine and rosemary sauce, lemon and cajun salmon fillet with a parsley and white wine cream, and puddings like chocolate and kendal mint cake mousse and honey-blossom panna cotta with a fruit compote. *Benchmark main dish: steak in ale pie £9.25. Two-course evening meal £16.45.*

Own brew ~ Licensee Roger Humphreys ~ Real ale ~ Bar food (12-2, 6-9; sandwiches and soup 2-4.30) ~ Restaurant ~ (01900) 85219 ~ Children welcome ~ Dogs allowed in bar and bedrooms ~ Open 11(12 Sun)-11 ~ Bedrooms: £63.50B/£99B ~ www.kirkstile.com *Recommended by John Wooll, Peter Smith and Judith Brown, Richard and Tanya Smith, Mike and Sue Loseby, the Didler, Margaret Dickinson, John and Sylvia Harrop, Tim Maddison, Pat and Stewart Gordon, Simon Collett-Jones*

LUPTON

SO5581 Map 7

Plough ⊕ ♀ ⇔

A65, near M6 junction 36; LA6 1PJ

Stylish open-plan inn with sofas and antique furniture, woodburning stoves, daily papers, real ales and top class food; well equipped, comfortable bedrooms

Handy for the M6 and surrounded by fine walking country, this carefully refurbished 18th-c inn is sister pub to the Punch Bowl at Crosthwaite. There are spreading open-plan bar rooms with beams, hunting prints and Punch cartoons on the contemporary grey paintwork, rugs on wooden floors, a nice mix of antique dining chairs and tables, comfortable leather sofas and armchairs in front of a large woodburning stove with impressive log piles to each side, and fresh flowers and daily papers; background music. High bar stools sit beside the granite-topped counter and neatly dressed, friendly staff serve Coniston Bluebird, Hawkshead Bitter, Jennings Cumberland and Kirkby Lonsdale Monumental on handpump. There are rustic wooden tables and chairs under parasols behind a white picket fence, with more in the back garden. The bedrooms are lovely and the breakfasts very good.

Usefully served all day, the interesting modern food might include sandwiches, salt and pepper squid with soy and sesame dressing, ham hock terrine with home-made piccalilli, pea and fresh mint risotto with parmesan, roasted cod with baby beetroot, beetroot purée and horseradish mash, salmon fillet with cucumber ribbons and a cucumber beurre blanc, chicken wrapped in parma ham with peas french style, pork tenderloin with black pudding, apple mash and calvados reduction, veal escalope with parmentier potatoes and rocket and basil salad, and puddings like warm chocolate brownie with vanilla ice-cream and bread and butter pudding with poached apricots and apricot syrup. *Benchmark main dish: dry-aged sirloin steak with twice-cooked chips, home-made onion rings and blue cheese butter £19.95. Two-course evening meal £18.00.*

Free house ~ Licensees Richard Rose and co-owner ~ Real ale ~ Bar food (12-9) ~ Restaurant ~ (015395) 67700 ~ Children welcome ~ Dogs allowed in bar and bedrooms ~ Open 11-11 ~ Bedrooms: /£115B ~ www.theploughatlupton.co.uk *Recommended by Dr Kevan Tucker, Christopher Mobbs, David Heath, Pat and Graham Williamson, Canon Graham Bettridge, K H Frostick, Michael Doswell, Karen Eliot, W K Wood*

MUNGRISDALE

NY3630 Map 10

Mill Inn

Off A66 Penrith–Keswick, a mile W of A5091 Ullswater turn-off; CA11 0XR

Bustling pub in fine setting with marvellous surrounding walks, real ales, home-cooked bar food and seats in garden; bedrooms

If you stay at this friendly 17th-c Lakeland inn, you can make the most of the fantastic surrounding walks; it's a striking spot with the Glenderamakin river flowing below and the Blencathra Fell above, and there are seats in the garden by the water. Inside, there's an open log fire in the stone fireplace, and the neatly kept bar has a wooden counter with an old millstone built into it, traditional dark wooden furnishings, hunting pictures on the walls, and Robinsons Cumbria Way, Dizzy Blonde, Hartleys XB and a guest beer on handpump; there's also a separate dining room. Darts, pool in winter and dominoes.

🍴 Tasty bar food includes lunchtime sandwiches, crab cakes with seafood dressing, cumberland sausages with onion gravy, a changing vegetarian dish, steak and kidney pie, pork belly with cumberland sauce, chicken breast in pesto sauce, salmon with a creamy mushroom sauce, and puddings like blackcurrant cheesecake and sticky toffee pudding. *Benchmark main dish: slow-cooked lamb shoulder with a port, redcurrant and rosemary sauce £13.95. Two-course evening meal £20.00.*

Robinsons ~ Tenant Andrew Teasdale ~ Real ale ~ Bar food (all day) ~ Restaurant ~ (017687) 79632 ~ Children welcome ~ Dogs allowed in bar and bedrooms ~ Open 10am-1am(midnight Sun) ~ Bedrooms: $47.50S/$75S ~ www.the-millinn.co.uk *Recommended by James Morrell, J Buckby, John and Angie Millar*

 NEAR SAWREY   SD3795   Map 9

Tower Bank Arms

B5285 towards the Windermere ferry; LA22 0LF

Backing on to Beatrix Potter's farm, with well kept real ales, tasty bar food and a friendly welcome; nice bedrooms

Run by a genuinely friendly landlord and his welcoming staff, this enjoyable little inn is deservedly busy – it's best to book a table in advance during school holidays. Our readers have again this year enjoyed staying overnight, and the breakfasts are particularly good. The low-beamed main bar has plenty of rustic charm, seats on the rough slate floor, game and fowl pictures, a grandfather clock, a log fire and fresh flowers; there's also a separate restaurant. Barngates Cracker Ale and Pride of Westmorland, Cumbrian Legendary Loweswater Gold, Hawkshead Bitter and Brodies Prime on handpump, several wines by the glass, ten malt whiskies and Weston's organic perry; board games. There are pleasant views of the wooded Claife Heights from seats in the newly extended garden. Many illustrations in the Beatrix Potter books can be traced back to their origins in this village – including the pub, which features in *The Tale of Jemima Puddleduck.*

🍴 Using locally sourced produce, the popular food includes lunchtime sandwiches, chicken pâté with cumberland sauce, moules marinière, beer-battered haddock, vegetable wellington, cumberland sausage with onion gravy, salmon fillet with a lemon and dill sauce, slow-braised lamb with a mint and rosemary jus, and puddings such as sticky toffee pudding and meringue with cream and warm berries. *Benchmark main dish: beef in ale stew £11.25. Two-course evening meal £17.25.*

Free house ~ Licensee Anthony Hutton ~ Real ale ~ Bar food (12-2, 6-9(8 Sun), winter Mon-Thurs and bank hols) ~ Restaurant ~ (015394) 36334 ~ Children welcome ~ Dogs allowed in bar and bedrooms ~ Open 11-11; 12-10.30 Sun; 11.30-2.30, 5-11(10.30 Sun) in winter ~ Bedrooms: /£93S ~ www.towerbankarms.com *Recommended by Margaret Dickinson, Jayne Inman, Dave Braisted, David and Ruth Hollands, Christian Mole, G Jennings*

 RAVENSTONEDALE   NY7203   Map 10

Black Swan

Just off A685 SW of Kirkby Stephen; CA17 4NG

Bustling hotel with thriving bar, several real ales, enjoyable food, and good surrounding walks; comfortable bedrooms

Although this is a smart, family-run Victorian hotel, there's a thriving bar with a good mix of customers and a fine choice of real ales. It's U-shaped, with plenty of original period features, stripped-stone walls, plush bar stools, a comfortable green button-back banquette, various dining chairs and stools around a mix of tables, and fresh flowers. Black Sheep Ale and Bitter, John Smiths, and a couple of changing guests such as Cumberland Corby Ale and Thwaites Nutty Black on handpump, eight wines by the glass, more than 20 malt whiskies and a good choice of fruit juices and pressés; background music, TV, darts, board games, and newspapers and magazines. Service is genuinely friendly and helpful. There are picnic-sets in the tree-sheltered streamside garden across the road and lots of good walks from the door (they have leaflets describing the routes). This is an enjoyable place to stay with comfortable bedrooms; they also run the village store with outside café seating.

Using seasonal, local produce, the highly thought of food might include sandwiches, ham hock, pistachio and lentil terrine with chutney, warm poached egg and black pudding salad, beer-battered haddock, leek and blue cheese pancake, chicken with onion and potato rösti and a honey and grain mustard sauce, goan fish curry, braised lamb shank with a three-herb sauce, specials like chicken livers in brandy sauce and grilled salmon with toasted almonds and lemon zest butter, and puddings. *Benchmark main dish: beef, stilton and green peppercorn pie £11.95. Two-course evening meal £17.20.*

Free house ~ Licensees Louise and Alan Dinnes ~ Real ale ~ Bar food (12-2, 6-9 but some sort of food all day) ~ Restaurant ~ (015396) 23204 ~ Children welcome ~ Dogs allowed in bar and bedrooms ~ Open 11am-midnight(1am Sat) ~ Bedrooms: £50B/£75B ~ www.blackswanhotel.com *Recommended by Dr Kevan Tucker, Andy and Jill Kassube, C Cooper, Mr and Mrs M Wall, David Hunt, Michael Doswell*

SHAP   NY5614 Map 9
Greyhound
A6, S end, handy for M6 junction 39; CA10 3PW

Friendly and relaxed former coaching inn with straightforward furnishings in bar and dining rooms, a fine choice of up to eight real ales and honest food; bedrooms

Handy for the M6 and usefully open all day, this stone-built former coaching inn has fine views of the Lake District fells. It's an honest place and popular with locals, walkers and families. The large open-plan bar has a relaxed atmosphere, seats ranging from armchairs and a sofa to straightforward dining and tables on the patterned red carpet, an open fire, a few standing timbers and beams, horsebrasses here and there, and a flat-screen TV. The fine choice of up to eight real ales served by friendly staff includes Black Sheep, Cumberland Corby Ale and Corby Blonde, Dent Premium Bitter, Elland Best Bitter, Hawkshead Cumbrian Five Hop, Jennings Cumberland and Timothy Taylors Landlord on handpump; background music, games machine, darts, pool and daily papers. The dining rooms are traditional with red-plush cushioned, high-backed dining chairs and pubby tables and an open fire. There are picnic-sets on the flagstoned back terrace. The bedrooms are comfortable and the breakfasts are hearty.

Good, popular food includes tasty, filled malted baps, mixed roasted meat hash with a free-range egg, cumberland sausage with onion gravy, vegetarian or meaty lasagne, beer-battered haddock with mushy peas and specials like pot-roast loin of pork with bubble and squeak, sweet potato and parsnip cassoulet with garlic bread, and chicken breast stuffed with forcemeat, wrapped in bacon with a red wine and mushroom sauce. *Benchmark main dish: steak in ale pie £10.50. Two-course evening meal £16.95.*

Enterprise ~ Tenant Rob Furber ~ Real ale ~ Bar food (12-2(2.30 Sun), 6-9) ~
Restaurant ~ (01931) 716474 ~ Children welcome ~ Dogs allowed in bar and bedrooms
~ Open 7.30am-midnight; 8am-1am Sun and Sat ~ Bedrooms: £45S/£85S ~
www.greyhoundshap.co.uk *Recommended by Christine and Neil Townend*

STAVELEY   SD4798   Map 10

Beer Hall at
Hawkshead Brewery

Staveley Mill Yard, Back Lane; LA8 9LR

**Hawkshead Brewery showcase in glass-fronted building on two levels
serving their whole range, huge choice of bottled beers, knowledgeable
staff, brewery memorabilia, interesting food and brewery tours**

This spacious, modern glass-fronted building is the showcase for the
full range of real ales from the Hawkshead Brewery: Bitter, Lakeland
Gold and Lager, Pure Brewed Organic Stout, Red, Triple X Brodie's
Prime, Windermere Pale and seasonal beers on 14 handpumps; they
also keep an extensive choice of bottled beers and whiskies with an
emphasis on independent producers – all served by friendly, interested
staff. The main bar is on two levels with the lower level dominated by the
stainless steel fermenting vessels. There are high-backed chairs around
light wooden tables, benches beside long tables, nice dark leather sofas
around low tables (all on new oak floorboards) and a couple of walls
almost entirely covered with artistic photos of barley and hops and the
brewing process; darts. You can buy T-shirts, branded glasses and mini
casks and polypins and there are brewery tours; they have regular beer
festivals, too. Parking can be tricky at peak times.

As well as constantly changing tapas to complement your beer, such as a warm
scotch egg and piccalilli, potted Flookburgh shrimps, bitter-battered plaice
goujons and yorkshire pudding filled with braised beef in stout, there might be
rabbit or shepherd's pie, macaroni cheese with leeks and truffle, confit duck leg
with a butter bean and toulouse sausage casserole and puddings like bread and
butter pudding with dark chocolate sauce and real rum ice-cream and sticky toffee
pudding with caramel sauce. *Benchmark main dish: brewers lunch (a platter of
meats and pickles) £12.00.*

Hawkshead Brewery ~ Licensee Alex Brodie ~ Real ale ~ Bar food (12-3; 12-7(6 Sun)
Fri and Sat) ~ (01539) 822644 ~ Children welcome away from bar ~ Dogs welcome ~
Open 12-5(6 Tues-Thurs); 12-11 Fri and Sat; 12-8 Sun ~ www.hawksheadbrewery.co.uk
Recommended by the Didler

STAVELEY   SD4797   Map 9

Eagle & Child

Kendal Road; just off A591 Windermere–Kendal; LA8 9LP

**Welcoming inn with warming log fires, a good range of local beers and
enjoyable food; bedrooms**

'This is just what a pub should be,' says one reader enthusiastically,
and many others agree. It's a warmly welcoming little place in a
lovely spot and makes a perfect base for exploring the area – it's on the
Dales Way. There's a log fire under an impressive mantelbeam, a friendly,
bustling atmosphere, and a roughly L-shaped flagstoned main area
with plenty of separate parts to sit in, furnished with pews, banquettes,
bow-window seats and high-backed dining chairs around polished dark

tables. Also, police truncheons and walking sticks, some nice photographs and interesting prints, a few farm tools, a delft shelf of bric-a-brac and another log fire. The five real ales on handpump come from breweries such as Coniston, Cumbrian Legendary, Hawkshead and Yates, and they keep several wines by the glass, 30 malt whiskies and farm cider; background music, darts and board games. An upstairs barn-themed dining room (with its own bar for functions) doubles as a breakfast room. There are picnic-sets under cocktail parasols in a sheltered garden by the River Kent, with more on a good-sized back terrace and a second garden behind.

Fair value, generous helpings of tasty home-made food include sandwiches, soup, thai-style fishcakes with chilli and basil soy dip, vegetable and bean pie, chicken wrapped in smoked bacon with a barbecue sauce and cheese topping, cumberland sausage with caramelised onion gravy, a daily-changing fish dish, lambs liver with onions and mushrooms, slow-braised lamb and black pudding hotpot, and puddings such as apple crumble and sticky ginger pudding. *Benchmark main dish: beef in ale pie £9.95. Two-course evening meal £15.00.*

Free house ~ Licensees Richard and Denise Coleman ~ Real ale ~ Bar food (12-2.30, 6-9) ~ Restaurant ~ (01539) 821320 ~ Children welcome ~ Dogs allowed in bar ~ Open 11-11 ~ Bedrooms: $50S/$70S ~ www.eaglechildinn.co.uk *Recommended by Joe Green, Dr Kevan Tucker, John and Helen Rushton, Steve and Sue Griffiths, the Didler, Margaret Dickinson, David and Katharine Cooke, David Bedford, John and Sylvia Harrop*

STONETHWAITE   NY2513   Map 9

Langstrath 🍴 🛏

Off B5289 S of Derwentwater; CA12 5XG

Civilised little place in lovely spot, traditional food with a modern twist, four real ales, good wines and malt whiskies, and seats outside; bedrooms

A warm haven on a cold, wet day, this is a civilised little inn with friendly licensees. The neat and simple bar (at its pubbiest at lunchtime) has a welcoming log fire in a big stone fireplace, new rustic tables, plain chairs and cushioned wall seats, and walking cartoons and attractive Lakeland mountain photographs on its textured white walls. Four real ales on handpump from breweries like Black Sheep, Hawkshead, Hesket Newmarket and Jennings and 25 malt whiskies; background music and board games. The small room on the left (actually the original cottage, built around 1590) is a residents' lounge; the restaurant has fine views. Outside, a big sycamore shelters several picnic-sets with views up to Eagle Crag. There are fine surrounding walks as the pub is in a lovely spot in the heart of Borrowdale and en route for the Cumbrian Way and the Coast to Coast Walk.

Usefully serving some kind of food all day: there might be lunchtime filled baguettes, soup, potted brown shrimps, cheese soufflé with pear and walnuts, sirloin burger with spicy tomato relish, gammon with free-range eggs, cumberland sausage with wholegrain mustard mash, nettle jelly and rich onion gravy, cheese-topped roasted red pepper, onion and potato haggarty, free-range corn-fed chicken on bubble and squeak with crispy pancetta and a parsley and mustard cream sauce, fresh fish dish of the day, and puddings such as sticky toffee pudding with butterscotch sauce and vanilla crème brûlée with seasonal fruit compote. *Benchmark main dish: slow-roast leg of lamb with red wine gravy £16.95. Two-course evening meal £20.25.*

Free house ~ Licensees Guy and Jacqui Frazer-Hollins ~ Real ale ~ Bar food (12-2.30 (snacks 2.30-4), 6-9; not Mon or Dec and Jan) ~ Restaurant ~ (017687) 77239 ~

Children over 10 in restaurant but only before 7.30pm ~ Dogs allowed in bedrooms ~
Open 12-10.30; closed Mon; Dec and Jan (except New Year); best to phone for Feb hours
~ Bedrooms: £110S(£117B) ~ www.thelangstrath.com *Recommended by Peter Smith and
Judith Brown, Mr and Mrs Maurice Thompson, Mike Proctor, Martin and Sue Day*

TALKIN
NY5457 Map 10
Blacksmiths Arms ♀ ⇌
Village signposted from B6413 S of Brampton; CA8 1LE

**Neatly kept and welcoming with tasty bar food, several real ales and
good surrounding walks; bedrooms**

This early 18th-c blacksmith's, now a pub with several neatly kept,
traditionally furnished rooms, is attractively set on a village green and
has plenty of walks right from the door or just a short drive away. You
can be sure of a warm welcome from the licensees and their. The warm
lounge on the right has a log fire, upholstered banquettes and wheelback
chairs around dark wooden tables on the patterned red carpeting, and
country prints and other pictures on the walls. The restaurant is to the
left and there's a long lounge opposite the bar with another room up
a couple of steps at the back. Black Sheep Bitter, Cumberland Corby
Ale, Geltsdale Brampton Bitter and Yates Bitter on handpump, 20 wines
by the glass and 35 malt whiskies; background music, darts and board
games. There are a couple of picnic-sets outside the front door with more
in the back garden. This is a quiet and comfortable place to stay.

Reliably good food includes lunchtime sandwiches, filled baked potatoes and
burgers as well as smoked haddock and spring onion fishcakes, spinach and
ricotta cannelloni, steak and kidney pie, cumberland sausages, chicken with a pork,
herb and garlic stuffing with a creamy mushroom sauce, and specials like haggis
topped with a cream and whisky sauce, duck breast in a port and plum sauce, and
liver, bacon and onion casserole. *Benchmark main dish: beer-battered haddock
£8.95. Two-course evening meal £15.70.*

Free house ~ Licensees Donald and Anne Jackson ~ Real ale ~ Bar food (12-2, 6-9) ~
Restaurant ~ (016977) 3452 ~ Children welcome ~ Dogs allowed in bar ~ Open 12-3,
6-11; 12-12 Sat; 12-4, 6-11 Sun ~ Bedrooms: £50S/£70S ~ www.blacksmithstalkin.co.uk
Recommended by Dr Peter D Smart, David and Katharine Cooke

THRELKELD
NY3225 Map 9
Horse & Farrier £
A66 Penrith–Keswick; CA12 4SQ

**Well run and friendly 17th-c fell-foot dining pub with good food and
drinks; bedrooms**

A happy mix of locals and tourists can be found in this attractive 17th-c
inn, enjoying the real ales and hearty food. The neat, mainly carpeted
bar has sturdy farmhouse and other nice tables, seats from comfortably
padded ones to pubby chairs and from stools to bigger housekeeper's
chairs and wall settles, country pictures on its white walls, one or two
stripped beams and some flagstones; several open fires. Jennings Bitter,
Cumberland, Mild and Sneck Lifter on handpump and several wines by
the glass; friendly, efficient service. The partly stripped-stone restaurant is
smart and more formal, with quite close-set tables. There are a few picnic-
sets outside. If you plan to stay, the rooms in the inn itself are the best
bet. The views towards Helvellyn range are stunning and there are walks
straight from the door. Good disabled access and facilities.

🍴 Food on the bar menu which is served at both lunchtime and in the evening is good value and popular: sandwiches, a curry of the day, steak and kidney pie, bean and celery chilli and lasagne. They also offer more elaborate (and pricier) dishes such as duck liver pâté with fresh beetroot chutney, Morecambe Bay scallops on black pudding with an orange and tarragon dressing, a duo of sausages with spices and ale, butterbean and chive mash and onion gravy, chicken stuffed with gruyère, wrapped in bacon with a mushroom, basil, garlic and white wine cream sauce, slow-roast pork belly with an apple, sage and spring onion sauce, and puddings; breakfasts to non-residents and afternoon tea. *Benchmark main dish: battered fish and chips with mushy peas £8.75. Two-course evening meal £19.00.*

Jennings (Marstons) ~ Lease Ian Court ~ Real ale ~ Bar food (12-9) ~ Restaurant ~ (017687) 79688 ~ Children welcome ~ Dogs allowed in bar and bedrooms ~ Open 7.30am-midnight ~ Bedrooms: £50B/£80B ~ www.horseandfarrier.com *Recommended by James Morrell, Phil Bryant, Tina and David Woods-Taylor, Adele Summers, Alan Black, Mike Proctor, Martin and Sue Day*

TIRRIL   NY5026   Map 10
Queens Head
B5320, not far from M6 junction 40; CA10 2JF

18th-c Lakeland pub with several bars, real ales, speciality pies and seats outside; bedrooms

Just a couple of miles from Ullswater, this bustling inn dates from 1719. The oldest parts of the main bar have low beams, black panelling, original flagstones and floorboards, and there are nice little tables and chairs on either side of the inglenook fireplace (always lit in winter). Another bar to the right of the door has pews and chairs around sizeable tables on the wooden floor and candles in the fireplace, and the back locals' bar has heavy beams and a pool table; there are two dining rooms as well. Robinsons Cumbria Way, Dizzy Blonde, Unicorn and a guest beer on handpump and several wines by the glass. At the front of the building are some picnic-sets, with modern chairs and tables under covering on the back terrace. They also run the village shop. The pub is very close to a number of interesting places such as Dalemain House at Dacre.

🍴 As well as lunchtime sandwiches and popular pies made by their sister company, the Pie Mill, the bar food might include black pudding and haggis stack with beetroot chutney and a poached egg, fresh cod goujons with tartare sauce, cumberland sausage with mash and gravy, a curry of the day, mediterranean vegetable lasagne, gammon with eggs or pineapple, beef goulash, chicken breast with a mushroom, tarragon, white wine and cream sauce, specials like pheasant stuffed with venison and cranberry, wrapped in bacon with a red wine and rosemary reduction, and baked fresh cod topped with Morecambe Bay shrimps on spring onion mash, and puddings such as lemon cheesecake and sticky toffee pudding. *Benchmark main dish: home-made pies £9.95. Two-course evening meal £17.25.*

Robinsons ~ Tenants Margaret and Jim Hodge ~ Bar food (12-2.30, 5.30-8.30) ~ Restaurant ~ (01768) 863219 ~ Children welcome ~ Dogs allowed in bar and bedrooms ~ Open 12(though they open at 10 for coffee)-11; 12-10.30 Sun ~ Bedrooms: /£75B ~ www.queensheadinn.co.uk *Recommended by Richard Gibbs*

Bedroom prices normally include full english breakfast, VAT and any inclusive service charge that we know of. Prices before the '/' are for single rooms, after for two people in double or twin (B includes a private bath, S a private shower). If there is no '/', the prices are only for twin or double rooms (as far as we know there are no singles).

TORVER
SD2894 Map 10

Church House ♀
A593/A5084 S of Coniston; LA21 8AZ

Rambling coaching inn with bustling bar, interesting food, five real ales and seats in a neat garden with fine views; bedrooms

This is a rambling 14th-c former coaching house in a quiet village with splendid hill views from seats in the big garden. Inside, the bar has a pubby atmosphere, heavy beams, built-in wall seats and stools around plain tables on the slate flooring, a fine log fire in a sizeable stone fireplace, Lakeland bric-a-brac and a bar made from polished wooden barrels. Barngates Tag Lag, Coniston Bluebird, Copper Dragon Golden Pippin, Cumbrian Legendary Loweswater Gold and Hawkshead Windermere Pale on handpump, several wines by the glass and quite a few malt whiskies; friendly staff. There's also a comfortable lounge and a separate yellow-walled dining room; the jack russell terrier, Molly, loves catching beer mats. As well as bedrooms, they have hard standing for six caravans. The inn is just a short walk from Coniston Lake and in the shadow of Coniston Old Man.

 Often interesting, the food, which uses local produce, might include sandwiches, chicken liver parfait with red onion marmalade, maple-glazed pancetta and toasted brioche, seared scallops and crispy pork belly with a celeriac and apple purée, red wine and star anise dressing and spring onion oil, vegetarian moussaka, beer-battered haddock, sausages and mash, steak in ale pudding, fish pie, and puddings such as rhubarb trifle with home-made gingerbread and clotted cream ice-cream and crème brûlée. *Benchmark main dish: lamb and tattie hotpot £13.75. Two-course evening meal £21.00.*

Enterprise ~ Lease Mike and Mandy Beaty ~ Real ale ~ Bar food (12-3, 6-9) ~ Restaurant ~ (015394) 41282 ~ Children welcome ~ Dogs allowed in bar and bedrooms ~ Open 12-12 ~ Bedrooms: £50S/£75S ~ www.churchhouseinntorver.com
Recommended by JCW, Jon Quirk, Chris and Anne Thompson

TROUTBECK
NY4103 Map 9

Queens Head ♨ ♀ ◧ ⛵
A592 N of Windermere; LA23 1PW

Civilised inn with several rambling rooms, interesting food, quite a few real ales and friendly staff; comfortable bedrooms

You can be sure of a genuinely warm welcome from the helpful staff in this extended, rather smart former coaching inn. The big rambling, original U-shaped bar has an attractive mix of cushioned settles and mate's chairs around some sizeable tables, beams and flagstones and a log fire in the raised stone fireplace with horse harness and so forth on either side of it; there's also a coal fire, country pictures, stuffed pheasants in a big glass case and a stag's head. A massive Elizabethan four-poster bed is the basis of the finely carved counter from which they serve Robinsons Cumbrian Way, Dizzy Blonde, Hartleys XB, Old Tom and Unicorn on handpump and eight wines by the glass; background music. Other dining rooms are decorated similarly to the main bar, with oak beams and stone walls, settles along big tables, trumpets, cornets and saxophones on the walls and lots of scatter cushions; one has an open fire. Seats outside have a fine view over the Troutbeck Valley to Applethwaite Moors. The highly thought of bedrooms are in the inn itself or in the carefully transformed barn opposite.

🍴 As well as filled baguettes (until 6pm), the imaginative food includes smooth duck liver parfait and confit leg terrine with onion marmalade, home-potted crab and shrimp with lime and chilli crème fraîche on roasted red pepper blinis, sausages of the day with bubble and squeak and roasted shallot sauce, steamed lamb and cockle suet pudding, creamy fish pie, butternut squash and chestnut salad with a toasted goats cheese slice, and puddings such as sugar-glazed baked orange-scented rice pudding with toasted pistachio shortbread and a taste of apple (Appletiser jelly, granny smith sorbet, mini crumble and custard and a baked apple and cinnamon bavarois). *Benchmark main dish: venison shank with a juniper and red wine sauce and sweet and sour red cabbage £16.95. Two-course evening meal £22.90.*

Robinsons ~ Lease Ian and Anette Dutton ~ Real ale ~ Bar food (12-9(10 Fri-Sun)) ~ Restaurant ~ (015394) 32174 ~ Children welcome ~ Dogs allowed in bar and bedrooms ~ Open 10am-midnight ~ Bedrooms: £75B/£120B ~ www.queensheadtroutbeck.co.uk
Recommended by Martin Smith, Hugh Roberts, Adrian Johnson, Lesley and Peter Barrett

ULVERSTON   SD3177   Map 7
Bay Horse 🍷 🛏

Canal Foot signposted off A590 and then you wend your way past the huge Glaxo factory; LA12 9EL

Civilised waterside hotel with lunchtime bar food, three real ales and a fine choice of wines; smart bedrooms

With commanding views of both the Cumbria and Lancashire fells and on the edge of the Leven Estuary, this civilised hotel is at its most informal at lunchtime. The bar has a relaxed atmosphere despite its smart furnishings: attractive wooden armchairs, some pale green plush built-in wall banquettes, glossy hardwood traditional tables, blue plates on a delft shelf, a huge stone horse's head, and black beams and props with lots of horsebrasses. Magazines are dotted about, there's an open fire in the handsomely marbled grey slate fireplace and background music with decent sound quality; board games. Jennings Cocker Hoop and Cumberland and a guest beer on handpump, 16 wines by the glass (including champagne and prosecco) from a carefully chosen and interesting wine list and several malt whiskies. The conservatory restaurant has lovely views over Morecambe Bay (as do the bedrooms) and there are some seats out on the terrace.

🍴 Lunchtime bar food (they only serve evening food in the restaurant at 7.30-8 but will serve in the bar if all restaurant tables are taken) might include interesting hot or cold sandwiches, field mushroom, leeks and sage baked on a bed of fried breadcrumbs, chicken liver pâté with cranberry purée, broccoli, sweetcorn and blue cheese lasagne, fresh crab and salmon fishcakes with a herb cream sauce, their own corned beef with white pudding mash, chilli con carne, pork medallions with apples, calvados and cream, lamb shank with orange, ginger and red wine, and puddings such as dark chocolate crème brûlée with home-made biscuits and brown sugar meringues with strawberries and cream. *Benchmark main dish: crab and salmon fishcakes in white wine and fresh herb cream sauce £19.50. Two-course evening meal £27.00.*

Free house ~ Licensee Robert Lyons ~ Real ale ~ Bar food (12-2(3 Tues-Fri, 4 weekends), 7-9) ~ Restaurant ~ (01229) 583972 ~ Children welcome but must be over 9 in bedrooms or in evening ~ Dogs allowed in bar and bedrooms ~ Open 11-11; 12-10.30 Sun ~ Bedrooms: £80B/£100B ~ www.thebayhorsehotel.co.uk *Recommended by V and E A Bolton, Peter Salmon, John and Sylvia Harrop, W K Wood*

WITHERSLACK
SD4482 Map 10

Derby Arms 🍴 ◗ 🛏

Just off A590; LA11 6RH

Busy country inn with six real ales, good wines, enjoyable food and a friendly welcome; reasonably priced bedrooms

With friendly, courteous staff and a relaxed atmosphere, this is a well run all-rounder – our readers enjoy staying in the comfortable bedrooms, there are six real ales to choose from and the food is particularly good. The main bar has lots of sporting prints on pale grey walls, elegant old dining chairs and tables on large rugs over floorboards, some hops above the bar counter, and an open fire. A larger room to the right is similarly furnished (with the addition of some cushioned pews), and has lots of political cartoons and local castle prints, a cumbrian scene above another open fire and alcoves in the back wall full of nice bristol blue glass, ornate plates and staffordshire dogs and figurines; the large windows lighten up the rooms, helped by evening candles in brass candlesticks. There are two further rooms – one with dark red walls, a red velvet sofa, more sporting prints and a handsome mirror over the fireplace. Hardknott Confusion, Hawkshead Bitter and Windermere Pale Ale, Loweswater Gold, Thwaites Wainwright and a beer named for the pub brewed for them by Cumbrian Legendary on handpump, 11 wines by the glass, and 22 malt whiskies. The inn is handy for Levens Hall with its topiary garden and for Sizergh Castle.

 As well as sandwiches (the sandwich and soup deal is great value), the highly thought of food might include their own potted shellfish, duck and chicken liver pâté with damson chutney and organic bread, button mushroom and chive risotto with pine nuts and parmesan, cumberland sausage with rich onion gravy, braised organic beef (from their own herd) in ale pie with lancashire blue cheese pastry, gammon with fresh pineapple and a free-range egg, fell-bred rump steak with peppercorn sauce, and puddings like apple and cinnamon strudel with vanilla custard and white chocolate panna cotta with dark chocolate shavings with mango sorbet and ginger shortbread. *Benchmark main dish: beer-battered fish and chips £12.75. Two-course evening meal £19.50.*

Free house ~ Licensee Adam Thorpe ~ Real ale ~ Bar food (12-2, 6-9; all day weekends) ~ Restaurant ~ (015395) 52207 ~ Children welcome ~ Dogs welcome ~ Open 11-11; 12-10.30 Sun ~ Bedrooms: £55S/£65S ~ www.thederbyarms.co.uk *Recommended by Jack Clark, Michael Doswell, David Heath*

YANWATH
NY5128 Map 9

Gate Inn 🍴 🍷

2.25 miles from M6 junction 40; A66 towards Brough, then right on A6, right on B5320, then follow village signpost; CA10 2LF

Cumbria Dining Pub of the Year

Emphasis on imaginative food but with local beers and thoughtful wines, a pubby atmosphere and a warm welcome from the helpful staff

Once again, we've had nothing but praise for this civilised and immaculately kept 17th-c dining pub. There's a cosy bar of charming antiquity with country pine and dark wood furniture, lots of brasses on the beams, church candles on all the tables and a good log fire in the attractive stone inglenook. Friendly, courteous staff serve Barngates Tag Lag, Hesket Newmarket Doris's 90th Birthday Ale and Tirril Old Faithful on handpump and around a dozen good wines by the glass, 12 malt whiskies and Weston's Old Rosie cider. Two restaurant areas have oak floors, panelled oak walls and heavy beams; background music. There are seats on the terrace and in the garden. They have a self-catering cottage to let and the pub is handy for Ullswater.

🍽 Using top quality local produce, free-range and organic where possible, the excellent food at lunchtime includes sandwiches, scottish mussels in white wine, garlic, and cream, cumberland sausage and their own black pudding with cumberland gravy, venison burger with garlic mayonnaise, gherkin and red onion, leek, blue cheese and walnut risotto and beer-battered fish and chips; evening choices such as scottish salmon ceviche, pigeon and fig terrine with pickled walnut and watercress, monkfish and tiger prawn red thai curry, roasted goose breast with sweet potato purée and bramble sauce, and puddings like sticky date pudding with toffee sauce and orange panna cotta with candied mandarins. *Benchmark main dish: stuffed loin of saddleback pork with home-made black pudding and cider cream sauce £15.95. Two-course evening meal £25.00.*

Free house ~ Licensee Matt Edwards ~ Real ale ~ Bar food (12-2.30, 6-9) ~ Restaurant ~ (01768) 862386 ~ Children welcome ~ Dogs allowed in bar ~ Open 12-11 ~ www.yanwathgate.com *Recommended by Richard J Holloway, V and E A Bolton, Terry Davis, Michael and Maggie Betton, Gordon and Margaret Ormondroyd, Rosemary and Mike Fielder, Dave Snowden, Andy Orton, Pat and Stewart Gordon, Dr and Mrs T E Hothersall, Graham and Elizabeth Hargreaves, Rayand Winifred Halliday, Catherine Pritchard*

Also Worth a Visit in Cumbria

Besides the fully inspected pubs, you might like to try these pubs that have been recommended to us and described by readers. Do tell us what you think of them: feedback@goodguides.com

AMBLESIDE　　　　NY4008
★**Kirkstone Pass Inn**　(01539) 433624
A592 N of Troutbeck; LA22 9LQ Lakeland's highest pub, in grand scenery, hiker-friendly décor of flagstones, stripped stone and dark beams and furniture, lots of old photographs and bric-a-brac, open fires, good value food all day from 9.30am, changing ales such as Hesket Newmarket Kirkstone Pass and Tirril Old Faithful, hot drinks, daily papers, games and books; soft background music, they may try to keep your credit card while you eat; well behaved children and dogs welcome, tables outside with incredible views to Windermere, camping field next door, three bedrooms, open all day. *(Robin Constable)*

AMBLESIDE　　　　NY3704
Royal Oak　(01539) 433382
Market Place; LA22 Two-room beamed local with five real ales and enjoyable food, friendly staff; dogs welcome, courtyard tables. *(Anon)*

AMBLESIDE　　　　NY3704
Unicorn　(015394) 33216
North Road; LA22 9DT Bustling backstreet beamed local with plenty of atmosphere, good staff, well kept Robinsons and enjoyable bar food, coal fire; regular live music; dogs welcome in bar, six good value bedrooms (two sharing bath), good breakfast. *(Anon)*

AMBLESIDE　　　　NY3703
★**Wateredge Inn**　(015394) 32332
Borrans Road; LA22 0EP Lovely spot with sizeable garden running down to edge of Windermere (own moorings), lots of tables here, same splendid view through big windows in much-modernised bar (originally two 17th-c cottages), prompt cheerful staff, ales from Barngates, Theakstons, Tirril and local Watermill, several wines by the glass, wide choice of enjoyable food till 8.30pm, cosy beamed area down steps with fireside sofa; background music, can get very busy; children welcome, dogs in bar, 22 comfortable bedrooms, open all day. *(Margaret and Jeff Graham)*

APPLEBY　　　　NY6819
★**Royal Oak**　(01768) 351463
B6542/Bongate; CA16 6UN Attractive old beamed and timbered coaching inn, popular bar food (all day Sun), well kept ales such as Black Sheep, Hawkshead and Jennings, friendly efficient young staff, log fire in panelled bar, armchair lounge with carved settle, traditional snug, nicely refurbished dining room; background music; children and dogs welcome, terrace tables, good-sized bedrooms, good breakfast, open all day. *(Ivan and Margaret Scott, Claes Mauroy)*

ARMATHWAITE   NY5046

Dukes Head   (016974) 72226

*Off A6 S of Carlisle; right at T junction;
CA4 9PB* Traditional Eden Valley inn under
new management; good food using fresh local
ingredients, beers such as Black Sheep and
Lancaster Gold, cheerful helpful service,
comfortable old-fashioned lounge with settles
and little armchairs around oak and mahogany
tables, antique hunting and other prints, brass
and copper powder-flasks above open fire,
public bar with table skittles and TV; children
and dogs have been welcome, seats on heated
area outside, more on back lawn, bedrooms,
open all day. *(Michael Doswell)*

ARMATHWAITE   NY5045

★ Fox & Pheasant   (01697) 472400

*E of village, over bridge; CA4
9PY* Friendly licensees and locals in
attractive spotless brick inn with lovely River
Eden views, well kept Robinsons ales, decent
wines by the glass, sensibly short choice of
good fresh reasonably priced food, inglenook
log fire in main beamed and flagstoned
bar, another in second bar, charming small
dining room; picnic-sets outside, comfortable
bedrooms. *(Brad Oud)*

ASKHAM   NY5123

Queens Head   (01931) 712225

*Lower Green; off A6 or B5320 S of
Penrith; CA10 2PF* Traditional 17th-c
beamed pub under enthusiastic newish
licensees, enjoyable good value food all day
including gluten-free choices, well kept beers,
open fires; tables out at front and in pleasant
garden, four bedrooms. *(Colin and Sue
Wilkinson, Rosemary and Mike Fielder)*

BAMPTON   NY5118

Mardale   (01931) 713244

*Village signposted off A6 in Shap; in
Bampton turn left over bridge by Post
Office; CA10 2RQ* Pretty village pub with
several opened-up rooms decorated in
contemporary style, chunky modern country
tables and chairs on big flagstones, a few
rugs, one or two big Lakeland prints and some
rustic bygones, log fire and woodburner, four
local ales including one brewed for the pub,
fairly traditional food; well behaved children
and dogs welcome, good walks from the door,
four bedrooms, open all day. *(Pam and John
Smith, David and Katharine Cooke)*

BASSENTHWAITE   NY2332

★ Sun   (017687) 76439

Off A591 N of Keswick; CA12 4QP White-
rendered slate house in charming village with
rambling bar, low 17th-c black oak beams,
two good stone fireplaces with big winter
log fires and built-in wall seats, plush stools

around heavy wooden tables, Jennings ales
and a guest, well liked food, cosy dining
room; children (till 9pm if eating) and dogs
welcome, seats under parasols on terrace
with fine views of the fells and Skiddaw,
convenient for osprey viewing at Dodd Wood,
open all day weekends, closed weekday
lunchtimes. *(Howard Bowen, Andy and
Alice Jordan)*

BOOT   NY1701

★ Boot Inn   (01946) 723224

*aka Burnmoor; signed just off the
Wrynose/Hardknott Pass road;
CA19 1TG* Comfortable beamed pub with
ever-burning fire, Black Sheep, Jennings and
a guest ale (summer beer festival), decent
wines and malt whiskies, good friendly staff,
realistically priced home-made local food
from sandwiches up, restaurant and dining
conservatory; games room with pool and TV;
children and dogs welcome, sheltered front
lawn with play area, lovely surroundings and
walks, nine bedrooms, open all day. *(Mike
and Eleanor Anderson)*

BOOT   NY1701

★ Brook House   (01946) 723288

*handy for Eskdale railway terminus;
CA19 1TG* Good views and walks, friendly
family service, wide choice of good sensibly
priced country cooking including some
interesting dishes and unusual sandwiches,
great whisky selection (around 160), well
kept ales such as Barngates, Cumbrian and
Hesket Newmarket, Weston's farm cider,
decent wines, relaxed and comfortable
raftered bar with woodburner and stuffed
animals, smaller plush snug, peaceful
separate restaurant; children and dogs
welcome, tables on flagstoned terrace, seven
good value bedrooms, good breakfast (for
nearby campers too), mountain weather
reports, excellent drying room, open all
day. *(Kay and Alistair Butler, Pam and John
Smith, Mike and Eleanor Anderson, the Didler,
David Uren, David Bedford and others)*

BOOT   NY1901

Woolpack   (019467) 23230

*Bleabeck, mid-way between Boot
and Hardknott Pass; CA19 1TH* Last
pub before the notorious Hardknott
Pass; refurbished and welcoming, main
walkers' bar with big woodburner, snug
and restaurant, enjoyable home-made
locally sourced food all day, up to eight
well kept ales including Woolpackers (still
brewed for the pub by previous landlord),
Thatcher's cider, good choice of malts, June
beer festival; children and dogs welcome,
mountain-view garden, play area, seven
bedrooms. *(Peter and Jackie Barnett, Mike and
Eleanor Anderson)*

If we know a pub has an outdoor play area for children, we mention it.

BOUTH   SD3285

★ **White Hart** (01229) 861229

*Village signed off A590 near
Haverthwaite; LA12 8JB* Cheerful
bustling old inn with Lakeland feel, six
changing ales, 25 malt whiskies, popular
generously served food (all day Sun)
using local beef and lamb, good friendly
service, sloping ceilings and floors, old
local photographs, farm tools, stuffed
animals, collection of long-stemmed clay
pipes, two woodburners; background music;
children welcome, no dogs at mealtimes),
seats outside, fine surrounding walks, five
comfortable bedrooms, open all day. *(Peter
Smith and Judith Brown, Lucien Perring)*

**BOWNESS-ON-
WINDERMERE**   SD4096

Albert (01539) 443241

Queens Square; LA23 3BY Refurbished
Robinsons inn keeping traditional feel, their
ales and guests kept well, good choice of food
all day; children welcome, terrace tables,
six comfortable bedrooms. *(John and Helen
Rushton, Dr E Scarth and Miss A Pocock)*

**BOWNESS-ON-
WINDERMERE**   SD4096

★ **Hole in t' Wall** (015394) 43488

Lowside; LA23 3DH Bustling unchanging
pub – the town's oldest and packed in high
season; split-level rooms, beams, stripped
stone and flagstones, country knick-knacks
and old pictures, fine log fire under vast slate
mantelpiece, upper room with attractive
plasterwork, Robinsons ales, decent pub food
(not Sun evening), friendly staff; background
music; children welcome, sheltered picnic-
sets in small flagstoned and heated front
courtyard, open all day. *(Dr Kevan Tucker,
John and Helen Rushton, Kurt Woods, Dennis
Jones, David Bedford)*

**BOWNESS-ON-
WINDERMERE**   SD4096

Royal Oak (015394) 43970

Brantfell Road; LA23 3EG Handy for
steamer pier, four interconnecting rooms,
lots of bric-a-brac, open fire, well kept ales
such as Coniston, Everards, Greene King
and Jennings, generous reasonably priced
food from baguettes to specials, friendly
efficient service; pool, darts and juke box;
children welcome, tables out in front,
bedrooms. *(Dennis Jones)*

BRAITHWAITE   NY2323

Royal Oak (017687) 78533

B5292 at top of village; CA12 5SY
Bustling local atmosphere, four well kept
Jennings ales, reasonable choice of food
including children's helpings, prompt

helpful service, well worn-in flagstoned bar;
background music, Sky TV; dogs welcome
except mealtimes, open all day. *(John and
Angie Millar)*

BRIGSTEER   SD4889

★ **Wheatsheaf** (01539) 568254

Off Brigsteer Brow; LA8 8AN Attractive
relaxed dining pub with good well priced
food from interesting sandwiches (nice
breads baked here) to local trout, steaks
and game, stylishly simple contemporary
décor, cheerful attentive staff, real ale
such as Langdale, good choice of wines
by the glass, sofas and dining tables in
entrance bar, further two-room dining area;
background music; picnic-sets on pretty little
terrace across quiet lane, attractive village,
bedrooms. *(Anon)*

**BROUGHTON-IN-
FURNESS**   SD2187

Manor Arms (01229) 716286

The Square; LA20 6HY Fine choice of
interesting well priced changing ales in this
open-plan drinkers' pub on quiet sloping
square, flagstones and nice bow-window seat
in well worn front bar, coal fire in big stone
fireplace, chiming clocks, old photographs,
limited food (rolls and soup), two pool tables;
stairs down to lavatories; children allowed,
bedrooms, open all day. *(David and Sue Smith)*

BUTTERMERE   NY1716

Fish (017687) 70253

B5289 SE of Buttermere; CA13 9XA
Spacious, light and airy former coaching
inn on NT property between Buttermere
and Crummock Water, fine views, Jennings
ales and guests, wide range of good
value food, friendly helpful staff; suntrap
terrace attracting greedy sparrows and
finches, popular with walkers and anglers,
bedrooms. *(John Wooll, Simon Collett-Jones)*

CARLISLE   NY4056

Kings Head (01228) 533797

Pedestrianised Fisher Street; CA3 8RF
Heavy beams, lots of old local prints,
drawings and black and white photographs,
friendly bustling atmosphere, generous
bargain pub lunches, Yates and two or three
guests, raised dining area; background music,
TV; no children or dogs; interesting historical
plaque outside, partly covered courtyard,
open all day. *(Robert Turnham, Barbarrick, Meg
and Colin Hamilton, the Didler)*

CARTMEL   SD3778

Cavendish Arms (01539) 536240

*Cavendish Street, off main Square;
LA11 6QA* Former coaching inn with
simply furnished open-plan beamed bar,
log fire, three or four ales including one

It's very helpful if you let us know up-to-date food prices when you report on pubs.

brewed for them by Cumberland, several wines by the glass, friendly helpful staff, good range of enjoyable local food (all day) from lunchtime sandwiches up, restaurant; children welcome, dogs in bar, tables out in front and behind by stream, nice village with notable priory church, good walks, ten bedrooms – three more above their shop in the square. *(Mrs F H Banaclough, Pat and Stewart Gordon)*

CARTMEL   SD3778
Kings Arms (01539) 536220
The Square; LA11 6QB Refurbished 18th-c timbered pub in ancient village with seats facing lovely square – fine medieval stone gatehouse nearby; well kept ales such as Hawkshead, enjoyable reasonably priced food, friendly staff, weekend live music; sports TV; dogs welcome in bar, open all day (till 1am Fri, Sat). *(Peter Wiser)*

CARTMEL   SD3778
Royal Oak (015395) 36259
The Square; LA11 6QB Low-beamed flagstoned local with cosy nooks and big log fire, ornaments and brasses, enjoyable good value bar food including specials, well kept Coniston Bluebird, Timothy Taylors Landlord and two changing local guests (Aug beer festival), decent wines, welcoming helpful staff; background music and sports TV, autographed sporting memorabilia in gents'; dogs welcome, nice big riverside garden with summer bar, four bedrooms, open all day. *(Ben Williams, Phil Hollowood, Adrian Johnson)*

CASTERTON   SD6379
★ **Pheasant** (015242) 71230
A683; LA6 2RX Traditional 18th-c inn with neat beamed rooms, straightforward pubby furniture, coal-effect gas fire, Dent and Theakstons, several malt whiskies, restaurant; background music; children welcome, some roadside seats under parasols, more in pleasant garden, near church with pre-Raphaelite stained glass and paintings, ten bedrooms. *(Mr and Mrs Ian King)*

CASTLE CARROCK   NY5455
Duke of Cumberland
(01228) 670341 *Geltsdale Road; CA8 9LU* Popular cleanly refurbished village-green pub with friendly family owners, upholstered wall benches and mix of pubby furniture on slate floor, coal fire, compact dining area with old farmhouse tables and chairs, well kept Geltsdale, enjoyable good value pub food; children welcome, open all day. *(Dr Kevan Tucker, David and Katharine Cooke)*

CHAPEL STILE   NY3205
Wainwrights (015394) 38088
B5343; LA22 9JH White-rendered former farmhouse, half a dozen real ales and plenty

of wines by the glass, enjoyable quickly served pubby food from good sandwiches up, friendly service, roomy new-feeling bar welcoming walkers and dogs, slate floor and fire, other spreading carpeted areas with beams, some half-panelling, cushioned settles and mix of dining chairs around wooden tables, old kitchen range; background music, TV and games machines; children welcome, terrace picnic-sets, fine views, open all day. *(Ewan and Moira McCall, Mr and Mrs Maurice Thompson, Dr Kevan Tucker, Jane and Alan Bush, G Jennings)*

COCKERMOUTH   NY1230
★ **1761** (01900) 829282
Market Place; CA13 9NH Handsome old building with shop-front windows, ales such as Barngates, Dent, Hesket Newmarket and Thwaites, good choice of foreign beers and of wines by the glass, fair-priced interesting light snacks, two woodburners (one in back family room with some ancient stripped brick), slate flagstones by counter on left, bare boards on right, polychrome tiles of a former corridor floor dividing the two, comfortably cushioned window seats and a couple of high-backed settles, big Lakeland landscape photographs, traditional pub games; background music; dogs allowed in bar, back courtyard below lawn sloping up to church, open from 3pm. *(Pam and John Smith)*

COCKERMOUTH   NY1230
★ **Bitter End** (01900) 828993
Kirkgate, by cinema; CA13 9PJ Liked for its eight own-brewed ales and lots of bottled beers in three interesting bars – each with a different atmosphere from quietly chatty to sporty (décor reflecting this with unusual pictures of old Cockermouth to up-to-date sporting memorabilia), also framed beer mats, various bottles, jugs and books, log fire, good choice of traditional food; background music; no dogs; children welcome, public car park round the back, open all day Sat in summer. *(J Chilver, the Didler)*

COCKERMOUTH   NY1230
Trout (01900) 823591 *Crown Street; CA13 0EJ* Busy extensively refurbished hotel, welcoming helpful staff, good imaginative food, well kept local ales including Jennings, good choice of wines by the glass; gardens down to river, 49 bedrooms. *(Dr and Mrs Leach, Pat and Stewart Gordon)*

CONISTON   SD3097
Black Bull (01539) 441335/41668
Yewdale Road (A593); LA21 8DU Own-brewed Coniston beers remain a draw to this bustling old inn; back area (liked by walkers and their dogs) with slate flagstones, carpeted front part more comfortable with open fire and Donald Campbell memorabilia, bar food served

all day (not particularly cheap), residents' lounge with 'big toe' of Old Man of Coniston (large piece of stone in the wall), restaurant; they ask to keep a credit card if you run a tab; children welcome, plenty of seats in former coachyard, bedrooms, open all day from 8am (parking not easy at peak times). *(Rob and Catherine Dunster, Dr Kevan Tucker, Mike Lee, David Bedford)*

CROOK   SD4695
⋆ **Sun** (01539) 821351

B5284 Kendal–Bowness; LA8 8LA Good bustling atmosphere in low-beamed bar with two dining areas off, good generous traditional food (all day weekends), reasonable prices, prompt cheerful service, well kept Coniston and Theakstons, good value wines, roaring log fire. *(Martin Smith, Hugh Roberts)*

CUMWHITTON   NY5052
Pheasant (01228) 560102

Off B6413 Brampton–Kirkoswald; CA8 9EX Old creeper-clad stone pub run by welcoming mother and daughter, popular for its enjoyable home-made food including daily specials, but also flagstoned bar with wooden seats, darts and pool, good choice of wines, well kept Geltsdale ales including one for the pub; no dogs; children welcome, picnic-sets in small garden, closed lunchtimes and all day Mon. *(Kirsty Haridas, Ken Marshall)*

DACRE   NY4526
Horse & Farrier (017684) 86541

Between A66 and A592 SW of Penrith; CA11 0HL Pleasant 18th-c village pub with well priced home-made food (not Sun evening) from sandwiches up, well kept Jennings, unsmart front room with big old-fashioned range and nice beam-and-plank ceiling, more modern dining extension down steps on the left, darts and dominoes; children and dogs welcome, post office, pretty village, closed Mon lunchtime. *(Comus and Sarah Elliott)*

DENT   SD7086
George & Dragon (01539) 625256

Main Street; LA10 5QL Two-bar corner pub owned by Dent with seven of their well kept beers (including a real lager) and Weston's cider, some dark panelling, partitioned tables and open fire, food from light meals up, prompt friendly service, comfortable back restaurant, games room with pool; sports TV; children, walkers and dogs welcome, ten bedrooms, lovely village, open all day. *(Dr Kevan Tucker, J C Burgis, David Heath)*

DOCKRAY   NY3921
Royal (01768) 482356

A5091, off A66 or A592 W of Penrith; CA11 0JY Former coaching inn with bright open-plan bar including walkers' part with stripped settles on flagstones, Black Sheep,

Jennings and a guest, good food here from sandwiches up or in more formal restaurant, friendly attentive service; background music; children welcome, dogs in bar, picnic-sets in large peaceful garden, great setting, ten comfortable bedrooms, open all day. *(James Morrell, Comus and Sarah Elliott, Graham and Elizabeth Hargreaves)*

ENNERDALE BRIDGE   NY0716
Fox & Hounds (01946) 861373

High Street; CA23 3AR Popular community-owned pub, smart and clean with flowers on tables, good choice of beers including Black Sheep, Jennings and Loweswater, reasonably priced home-made food. *(Mr and Mrs C R Little)*

ESKDALE GREEN   NY1200
⋆ **Bower House** (01946) 723244

0.5 mile W of Eskdale Green; CA19 1TD Civilised old-fashioned stone-built inn extended around beamed and alcoved core, good fires, well kept local ales, good choice of interesting food in bar and biggish restaurant, friendly relaxed atmosphere; nicely tended sheltered garden by cricket field, charming spot with great walks, bedrooms, open all day. *(Tina and David Woods-Taylor, Paul J Robinshaw)*

FAUGH   NY5054
String of Horses (01228) 670297

S of village, on left as you go down hill; CA8 9EG Welcoming 17th-c coaching inn with cosy communicating beamed rooms, log fires, panelling and some interesting carved furniture, tasty well prepared food, Theakstons Bitter and another ale, restaurant; children welcome, sheltered terrace, comfortable bedrooms, good breakfast, closed Mon. *(Les and Sandra Brown)*

FOXFIELD   SD2085
⋆ **Prince of Wales** (01229) 716238

Opposite station; LA20 6BX Cheery bare-boards pub with half a dozen good changing ales including bargain beers brewed here and at their associated Tigertops Brewery, bottled imports, farm cider, enjoyable home-made food including lots of unusual pasties, hot coal fire, bar billiards and other pub games, daily papers and beer-related reading matter; children very welcome (games for them), four reasonably priced bedrooms, open all day Fri-Sun, from mid-afternoon Wed, Thurs, closed Mon, Tues. *(Clifford Walker)*

GOSFORTH   NY0703
Gosforth Hall (019467) 25322

Off A595 and unclassified road to Wasdale; CA20 1AZ Friendly well run Jacobean inn with interesting history, beamed carpeted bar (popular with locals) with fine plaster coat-of-arms above woodburner, lounge/reception area with huge fireplace, ales such as Hawkshead, Keswick and Yates, enjoyable home-made food including good range of pies, restaurant; TV; nice back garden with boules,13 bedrooms, self-catering lodge, good breakfast. *(Pam and John Smith, David and Katharine Cooke)*

GREAT URSWICK   SD2674
General Burgoyne (01229) 586394
Church Road; LA12 0SZ Flagstoned early 17th-c village pub overlooking small tarn, four cosy rambling rooms with beams and log fires (look for the skull in a cupboard), three Robinsons ales, some creative cooking from landlord/chef along with pub favourites, dining conservatory; children and dogs welcome, picnic-sets out at front, closed Mon and Tues lunchtimes, otherwise open all day. *(Genevieve Horsted)*

GREYSTOKE   NY4430
Boot & Shoe (01768) 483343
By village green, off B5288; CA11 0TP Cosy two-bar pub by green in pretty 'Tarzan' village; low ceilings, exposed brickwork and dark wood, good generous reasonably priced food including popular theme nights, well kept Black Sheep and local microbrews, bustling friendly atmosphere; sports TV; on national cycle route, bedrooms. *(D A Warren)*

HAVERTHWAITE   SD3284
Anglers Arms (01539) 531216
Just off A590; LA12 8AJ Busy split-level lived-in pub with good choice of real ales, friendly helpful staff, good generous fresh food from sandwiches to steaks, fair prices, sports memorabilia, separate upstairs dining room, lower area with pool; handy for steam railway. *(Dennis Jones)*

HAWKSHEAD   SD3598
Queens Head (015394) 36271
Main Street; LA22 0NS Timbered pub in charming village, low-ceilinged bar with heavy bowed black beams, red plush wall seats and stools around hefty traditional tables, decorative plates on panelled walls, open fire, snug little room off, several eating areas, well kept Robinsons ales and a guest, good wine and whisky choice, enjoyable bar food and more elaborate evening meals, friendly staff; background music, TV, darts; children welcome, seats outside, pretty window boxes, 13 bedrooms, open all day. *(Lesley and Peter Barrett)*

HESKET NEWMARKET   NY3438
⁎**Old Crown** (016974) 78288
Village signed off B5299 in Caldbeck; CA7 8JG Straightforward cooperative-owned local in attractive village, own good Hesket Newmarket beers (can book brewery tours); small friendly bar with bric-a-brac,

mountaineering kit and pictures, log fire, dining room and garden room, well presented good value pub food, folk night first Sun of month; juke box, pool and board games; children and dogs welcome, closed Mon-Thurs lunchtimes (open Weds and Thurs lunchtimes in school holidays). *(John and Anne Mackinnon, Howard Bowen, Dr Kevan Tucker)*

KENDAL   SD5192
Riflemans Arms (01539) 723224
Greenside; LA9 4LD Village-green setting on edge of town, welcoming locals and staff, Tetleys and three guests, Thurs folk night; children and dogs welcome, closed weekday lunchtimes, open all day weekends. *(Hugh Roberts)*

KESWICK   NY2623
⁎**Dog & Gun** (01768) 773463
Lake Road; off top end of Market Square; CA12 5BT Unpretentious town pub liked by locals and their dogs (menu for them), homely bar with low beams and timbers, partly slate, part wood, part carpeted flooring, fine collection of striking mountain photographs, brass and brewery artefacts, half a dozen well kept ales, reasonably priced pubby food all day including signature goulash in two sizes, log fires; children welcome if eating before 9pm. *(Mike and Sue Loseby, Dr Kevan Tucker, Mike Proctor, S Chaudhuri)*

KESWICK   NY2624
Pheasant (017687) 72219
Crosthwaite Road (A66, a mile out); CA12 5PP Small friendly beamed local with enjoyable food and well kept Jennings ales, good service, log fire, dining room; children welcome if eating, bedrooms, near ancient church of St Kentigern. *(Martin and Sue Day)*

KIRKBY LONSDALE   SD6178
Orange Tree (01524) 271716
Fairbank; LA6 2BD Family-run inn acting as tap for Kirkby Lonsdale brewery, well kept guest beers too and good choice of wines, beams, sporting pictures, old range, enjoyable food in back dining room; pool, darts, background music; children and dogs welcome, comfortable bedrooms (some next door). *(the Didler, Andy and Jill Kassube)*

KIRKBY LONSDALE   SD6178
⁎**Sun** (015242) 71965
Market Street (B6254); LA6 2AU Cheerful busy 17th-c inn striking good balance between pub and restaurant; unusual-looking building with upper floors supported by three sturdy pillars above pavement, attractive rambling beamed bar

---

with flagstones and stripped-oak boards, pews, armchairs and cosy window seats, big landscapes and country pictures on cream walls, two log fires, comfortable back lounge and modern dining room, good contemporary food (booking advised), well kept Kirkby Lonsdale, Timothy Taylors and Thwaites, good service; background music; children and dogs welcome, nice bedrooms, no car park, open all day from 9am, closed Mon till 3pm. *(Chris and Meredith Owen, Karen Eliot, Jane and Alan Bush, John and Verna Aspinall, Mrs Debbie Tether and others)*

LANGDALE   NY2906
Stickle Barn (015394) 37356
By car park for Stickle Ghyll; LA22 9JU Lovely views from this roomy and busy walkers'/climbers' bar (boots welcome), three or four changing ales such as Barngates, generous good value pub food (packed lunches available), quick friendly service, mountaineering photographs, woodburner; background music (live Sat), TV, games machines; big terrace with inner verandah, bunkhouse, open all day. *(Jane and Alan Bush)*

LEVENS   SD4885
Hare & Hounds (01539) 560408
Off A590; LA8 8PN Welcoming smartened-up village pub handy for Sizergh Castle, well kept ales including Black Sheep, friendly efficient service, good home-made pub food, partly panelled low-beamed lounge bar, front tap room with coal fire, pool room down steps, restaurant; children welcome, good views from terrace.
(Mr and Mrs Richard Osborne)

LORTON   NY1526
☆ Wheatsheaf (01900) 85199
B5289 Buttermere–Cockermouth; CA13 9UW Friendly local atmosphere in neatly furnished bar with two log fires, affable hard-working landlord, Jennings and regular changing guests, several good value wines, popular home-made food (all day Sun) from sandwiches to fresh fish (Thurs, Fri evening), smallish restaurant (best to book), good service, live music Sat; children welcome, dogs on leads, tables out behind, campsite, open all day weekends, closed Mon lunchtime and weekday lunchtimes in winter. *(Julian Cox, Chris and Anne Thompson, Mr and Mrs M Wall, Pat and Stewart Gordon, Simon Collett-Jones)*

MELMERBY   NY6137
Shepherds (01768) 881741
A686 Penrith–Alston; CA10 1HF Friendly family-run split-level country pub,

comfortable heavy-beamed dining room off flagstoned bar, spacious end room with sofa and leather chairs by woodburner, good choice of popular straightforward tasty food, well kept local ales such as Tirril, several wines by the glass, darts; children and dogs welcome, terrace tables, open all day in summer. *(Kevin and Rose Lemin, Marcus Byron)*

NETHER WASDALE   NY1204
☆ Strands (01946) 726237
SW of Wast Water; CA20 1ET Lovely spot below the remote high fells around Wast Water, brews its own Strands ales (lots of varieties), popular good value food, good-sized well cared-for high-beamed main bar with woodburner and relaxed friendly atmosphere, smaller public bar with pool, separate dining room, pleasant staff; background music may obtrude; children and dogs welcome, neat garden with terrace and belvedere, 14 bedrooms, open all day.
(Pam and John Smith)

OUTGATE   SD3599
Outgate Inn (015394) 36413
B5286 Hawkshead–Ambleside; LA22 0NQ Country pub with three neatly modernised rooms, black beams, pubby furniture on red patterned carpet, fairly priced home-made food including separate gluten-free menu, three well kept Robinsons ales, friendly staff, cheerful log fire; picnic-sets out at front and in back area, three comfortable bedrooms, good walks, open all day. *(Lesley and Peter Barrett)*

PENRUDDOCK   NY4227
☆ Herdwick (017684) 83007
Off A66 Penrith–Keswick; CA11 0QU Attractively cottagey and sympathetically renovated 18th-c inn, warm welcoming atmosphere, well kept Jennings and summer guests from unusual curved bar, decent wines, friendly efficient service, enjoyable sensibly priced food from lunchtime sandwiches up, good open fire, stripped stone and white paintwork, nice dining room with upper gallery, games room with pool and darts; children in eating areas, five good value bedrooms, open all day weekends. *(Phil Bryant, Dr and Mrs S G Barber, Mr and Mrs Maurice Thompson)*

ROSTHWAITE   NY2514
Scafell (0176 87) 77208
B5289 S of Keswick; CA12 5XB Hotel's big plain slate-floored back bar useful for walkers, weather forecast board, six well kept ales, blazing log fire, enjoyable reasonably priced food from sandwiches up, afternoon teas, also appealing cocktail bar/sun lounge

---

Stars before the name of a pub show exceptional character and appeal.
They don't mean extra comfort. Even a quite basic pub can win a star,
if it's individual enough.

and dining room, friendly helpful staff; background music, pool; children and dogs welcome, tables out overlooking beck, 23 bedrooms, open all day weekends. *(Mr and Mrs Maurice Thompson, Dr Kevan Tucker, Mike Proctor)*

RYDAL   NY3606
Glen Rothay Hotel (015394) 34500
A591 Ambleside–Grasmere; LA22 9LR Attractive small 17th-c hotel with enjoyable pubby food from sandwiches up in back bar, well kept changing local ales, helpful friendly staff, banquettes and stools, lots of badger pictures, fireside armchairs in beamed lounge bar, restaurant; walkers and dogs welcome, tables in pretty garden, boats for residents on nearby Rydal Water, eight comfortable bedrooms. *(Andy and Jill Kassube, Mr and Mrs Maurice Thompson)*

SANDFORD   NY7316
⋆ Sandford Arms (017683) 51121
Village and pub signposted just off A66 W of Brough; CA16 6NR Neat former 18th-c farmhouse in peaceful village, enjoyable food (all day weekends Apr-Oct) from chef/landlord, L-shaped carpeted main bar with stripped beams and stonework, collection of Royal Doulton character jugs and some Dickens ware, ales from Black Sheep, Lancaster and Tirril, comfortable raised and balustraded eating area, more formal dining room and second flagstoned bar, log fire; background music; children and dogs welcome, seats in front garden and covered courtyard, bedrooms, closed Tues. *(C J Beresford-Jones, M and GR)*

SANTON BRIDGE   NY1101
⋆ Bridge Inn (01946) 726221
Off A595 at Holmrook or Gosforth; CA19 1UX Charming riverside spot with fell views, beamed and timbered bar bustling with locals, log fire, some booths around stripped-pine tables, Jennings and guest ales, enjoyable traditional food including Sun carvery, family dining room, italian-style bistro, friendly helpful staff, small reception hall with log fire and daily papers; background music, games machine; dogs welcome in bar, seats outside by quiet road, plenty of walks, 16 bedrooms, open all day. *(Susan and Nigel Brookes)*

SATTERTHWAITE   SD3392
⋆ Eagles Head (01229) 860237
S edge of village; LA12 8LN Pretty and prettily placed on the edge of beautiful Grizedale Forest, low black beams, comfortable traditional furnishings, big log fire, lots of local photographs and maps, welcoming and obliging landlord, good fairly priced generous pubby food (not Mon), wider evening choice, well kept local ales including Barngates and one brewed for the pub; children welcome, picnic-sets in attractive tree-shaded courtyard garden with

pergola, comfortable bedrooms, open all day summer weekends, closed Mon and Tues lunchtimes. *(Anon)*

SEATHWAITE   SD2295
⋆ Newfield Inn (01229) 716208
Duddon Valley, near Ulpha (ie not Seathwaite in Borrowdale); LA20 6ED Genuinely friendly 16th-c cottage despite weekend and holiday popularity; local atmosphere in slate-floored bar, wooden tables and chairs, interesting pictures, Jennings and quickly changing guests, straightforward food all day, comfortable side room, games room; no credit cards; children and dogs welcome, tables in nice garden with hill views, play area, good walks, self-catering flats, open all day. *(Anon)*

SEDBERGH   SD6592
Dalesman (01539) 621183
Main Street; LA10 5BN Three busy linked modernised rooms, good interesting freshly made food from sandwiches and stone-baked pizzas up, four well kept changing ales, stripped stone and beams, central woodburner; background music; children welcome, tables out in front, bedrooms, open all day. *(John and Helen Rushton, Danny Savage)*

SEDBERGH   SD6592
⋆ Red Lion (015396) 20433
Finkle Street (A683); LA10 5BZ Cheerful beamed local, down to earth and comfortable, with good value generous food (meat from next-door butcher), well kept Jennings, good coal fire; sports TV, can get very busy weekends, no dogs. *(John and Helen Rushton)*

TROUTBECK   NY4103
Mortal Man (015394) 33193
A592 N of Windermere; Upper Road; LA23 1PL Refurbished beamed and partly panelled bar with cosy room off, log fires, Black Sheep, Coniston, Timothy Taylors Landlord and a beer for them by Hawkshead, several wines by the glass, generally well liked food in bar and picture-window restaurant, young willing staff; children and dogs welcome, great views from sunny garden, lovely village, bedrooms, open all day. *(Ian and Rose Lock, Mr and Mrs Richard Osborne, David and Katharine Cooke)*

TROUTBECK   NY4028
Sportsman (01768) 483231
B5288, just off A66 – the 'other' Troutbeck, near Penrith; CA11 0SG Small welcoming bar and large dining area with great views, enjoyable standard food, well kept Jennings ales and an interesting guest, good wine choice; children welcome, pretty back terrace overlooking valley, open all day. *(E Clark, William Brown)*

TROUTBECK   NY4103
Sun   (015394) 43274
A591 N of Windermere; LA23 1HH
Well refurbished hotel with enjoyable
reasonably priced fresh food including
lunchtime sandwiches, Hawkshead and
Jennings ales, friendly service; 12 bedrooms,
open all day Fri-Sun, from 3pm Mon-Thurs
(all day in school holidays). *(V and E A Bolton)*

ULDALE   NY2436
Snooty Fox   (016973) 71479
*Village signed off B5299 W of Caldbeck;
CA7 1HA* Comfortable well run two-bar
village inn, good-quality food (not Weds)
using local ingredients, up to four well kept
changing ales, friendly attentive staff, fox
hunting memorabilia; dogs welcome, nice
location, three bedrooms, closed lunchtimes
apart from Sun in summer. *(Dr Nigel Bowles,
Dr Ric Fordham)*

⋆ ULVERSTON   SD2878
Farmers Arms   (01229) 584469
Market Place; LA12 7BA Convivial
attractively modernised town pub, front
bar with comfortable sofas, contemporary
wicker chairs and original fireplace, daily
newspapers, quickly changing real ales
and a dozen wines by the glass, interesting
fairly priced food, second bar leading to
big raftered dining area (children here

only); unobtrusive background music; seats
on attractive heated front terrace, lots of
colourful tubs and hanging baskets, Thurs
market day (pub busy then), three cottages
to rent, open all day from 9am. *(Anon)*

WETHERAL   NY4654
Wheatsheaf   (01228) 560686
Handy for M6 junctions 42/43; CA4 8HD
Reopened under enthusiastic new licensee,
good local beers, enjoyable food including
burger menu; dogs welcome, pretty
village. *(David Heath)*

WINSTER   SD4193
⋆ Brown Horse   (015394) 43443
A5074 S of Windermere; LA23 3NR
Welcoming bustling bar with beams,
pubby furniture, some half-panelling and
woodburner, own-brew Winster Valley Best
and Old School plus changing guests, several
wines by the glass, ten malt whiskies, good
food using own estate-reared produce, smart
(but relaxed) restaurant with candles and
flowers; darts and board games; children
welcome, dogs in bar, sturdy furniture on
front terrace and in side garden with views of
Winster Valley, bedrooms, open all day. *(Tina
and David Woods-Taylor, JCW, Brian and Janet
Ainscough, Jane and Alan Bush, Peter Smith and
Judith Brown, Walter and Susan Rinaldi-Butcher
and others)*

Derbyshire

Many pubs here are nicely unspoilt, on the whole escaping the worst ravages of refurbishment. The key to the success of the simplest of these places lies in the genuinely warm welcome extended by the licensees. With this in mind, we'd particularly pick out the Barley Mow at Kirk Ireton (good range of beers from smaller brewers), Flying Childers at Stanton in Peak (simple but special), both back in the *Guide* after a break, and John Thompson at Ingleby (cosy with own-brewed beers). More elaborate food is to be found at the Devonshire Arms in Beeley (a great all rounder) and Plough at Hathersage (beautifully kept interior and Derbyshire Dining Pub of the Year). Other pubs doing well include the Barrel at Bretton (said to be the highest pub in the county), Church Inn at Chelmorton (good value pubby food) and Cheshire Cheese at Hope (good value food too). The other pubs we're happy to welcome back into the Guide this year are the Old Poets Corner at Ashover (ten real ales and own-brewed beers), Olde Gate at Brassington (lovely old interior and good, fairly priced food), Eyre Arms at Hassop (neatly traditional), Ladybower Inn at Ladybower Reservoir (great location and traditional), Bulls Head at Monyash (unpretentious local) and Lathkil at Over Haddon (super Peak views).

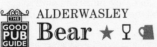

ALDERWASLEY   SK3153   Map 7

Bear ★ ♀ ◀

Left off A6 at Ambergate on to Holly Lane (turns into Jackass Lane) then right at end (staggered cross roads); DE56 2RD

Unspoilt country inn with beamed cottagey rooms, good range of real ales and a peaceful garden; bedrooms

This characterful tavern has lovely dark low-beamed rooms with warming open fires and a cheerful miscellany of antique furniture including high-backed settles and locally made antique oak chairs with derbyshire motifs. One little room is filled right to its built-in wall seats by a single vast table. Other décor includes staffordshire china ornaments, old paintings and engravings. There's no obvious front door – you get in through the plain back entrance by the car park, and as it can get busy you may need to book. Bass, Derby Blue Bear, Hartington IPA, Thornbridge Jaipur and Timothy Taylors Landlord are on handpump alongside a guest or two, and they do several wines by the glass from a decent list, as well as malt whiskies. Well spaced picnic-sets out in a lovely garden have wonderful country views. Please call before you visit to check opening times.

🍴 As well as sandwiches and home-made crusty rolls (afternoons only), bar food might include prawn cocktail, chicken liver pâté, beer-battered mushrooms stuffed with stilton and garlic with tomato sauce, steak and potato pie, pork fillet with mustard and cider sauce, lasagne, battered haddock, salmon spaghetti, brie and red onion tart, and steaks. *Benchmark main dish: steak and ale pie £10.95. Two-course evening meal £18.00.*

Free house ~ Licensee Pete Buller ~ Real ale ~ Bar food (12-3, 6-9; 12-9 Fri-Sun) ~ Restaurant ~ (01629) 822585 ~ Children welcome ~ Dogs allowed in bar ~ Open 12-11(10.30 Sun) ~ Bedrooms: /£75B ~ www.bear-hotel.com *Recommended by Simon Le Fort, Peter F Marshall, Terry Davis, David and Sue Atkinson, the Didler, Lindsay White, Stephen Shepherd, David Heath, Brian and Jacky Wilson*

ASHOVER
SK3462   Map 7
Old Poets Corner 🍺 £ 🛏
Butts Road (B6036, off A632 Matlock–Chesterfield); S45 0EW

A fine range of interesting real ales and ciders in characterful village pub with enthusiastic owners; hearty, reasonably priced food

Readers are full of praise for this individual and delightfully laid-back pub. With its cosy lived-in feel, the relaxed and informal bar is welcoming, with two roaring fires and atmospheric lighting, a mix of chairs and pews with well worn cushions, a pile of board games by a piano, lots of knick-knacks and hops around the counter. A small room opening off the bar has another fireplace, a stack of newspapers and vintage comics, and french doors leading to a tiny balcony with a couple of tables; background music. They serve an impressive range of drinks, including ten real ales, four of which come from their own microbrewery (you can do a brewery tour) and guests from mainly local brewers such as Dancing Duck, Hilden, Kelham Island, Mordue and Oakham, a terrific choice of eight farm ciders, a good choice of perries, a dozen fruit wines, 20 malt whiskies and belgian beers. They also hold regular beer festivals. The landlord is very keen on music and holds acoustic, folk and blues sessions (see below). Posters around the walls advertise forthcoming events, which might include quiz nights, poetry evenings and morris dancers. The bedrooms are attractive, and they have a holiday cottage for up to eight people.

🍴 Good honest bar food, very reasonably priced and served in generous helpings, includes filled baguettes, pies (a few available all day), whitebait, battered king prawns with chilli dip, a selection of home-made sausages (you can buy them to take away, too), chilli, beef stew, battered haddock, liver and onions, devilled kidneys, leek and mushroom crumble, salads, ham, egg and chips, daily specials such as mussels, pigeon breast with poached duck egg, wild mushroom risotto, and puddings such as bakewell tart, spotted dick and treacle sponge. On Sundays they do a good value lunchtime carvery, and they serve curries in the evening. *Benchmark main dish: meat and potato pie £7.50. Two-course evening meal £13.20.*

Own brew ~ Licensees Kim and Jackie Beresford ~ Real ale ~ Bar food (12-2(3 Sat), 6.30-9(5-9.30 Fri, Sat); 12-4, 7-9 Sun) ~ Restaurant ~ (01246) 590888 ~ Children welcome away from bar until 9pm ~ Dogs allowed in bar and bedrooms ~ Open mike Tues, quiz Weds, live bands some Fri, 50s/60s singalong Sun ~ Open 12-11.30 ~ Bedrooms: £55S/£70S ~ www.oldpoets.co.uk. *Recommended by Mike Proctor, Terry Davis, Mr and Mrs M Stratton, the Didler, Dennis Jones, David Heath, George Atkinson, Steve Short*

BEELEY   SK2667 Map 7
Devonshire Arms ⊕ ♟ 🍺 🛏

B6012, off A6 Matlock–Bakewell; DE4 2NR

Contemporary twist to lovely old interior; local beers, good wine list, interesting carefully sourced food; attractive comfortable bedrooms

You can walk to Chatsworth House from this handsome stone-built village inn, which is in an attractive Peak District village on the fringes of the Chatsworth Estate. Converted from cottages back in 1747, it became a coaching inn, with Charles Dickens as a frequent visitor. Though now offering a more formal dining experience (you might not feel completely at ease in walking gear), there is a nod to pubbyness at lunchtime (when they don't take bookings) and they keep up to six changing real ales, most likely including Brass Monkey, Buxton Blonde and Kinder Sunset, Peak Ales Chatsworth Gold, Thornbridge Jaipur and Whim Hartington, several wines by the glass from a well chosen list and a good range of malt whiskies, as well as local mineral water. Contemporary colours contrast with the attractive traditional interior: between black beams, flagstones, stripped stone, traditional settles and cheerful log fires, you'll find bright candy-coloured modern furnishings, prints and floral arrangements. Note that although dogs are permitted to stay in the stylishly comfortable bedrooms they are not allowed in the bar.

🍴 Sourcing what ingredients they can from the Chatsworth Estate, the imaginative food (with restaurant prices) is cooked to order so there might be a wait at busy times. The short but well balanced changing menu could include rabbit and mushroom tortellini, parsnip and blue cheese muffin with crispy poached egg, warm scallop and cockle salad, battered haddock, leek and mushroom tart, roast partridge, seasonal spit-roasted game (anything from woodcock to venison), and puddings such as lemon tart and chocolate and almond cake with praline sauce. *Benchmark main dish: sausage and mash £11.50. Two-course evening meal £22.00.*

Free house ~ Licensee Alan Hill ~ Real ale ~ Bar food (12-3, 6-9.30) ~ Restaurant ~ (01629) 733259 ~ Children welcome ~ Dogs allowed in bedrooms ~ Open 12-11 ~ Bedrooms: £134B/£155B ~ www.devonshirebeeley.co.uk *Recommended by Ann and Colin Hunt, Sue Dinley, Richard Cole, Richard and Mary Bailey, David Heath, Mr and Mrs D Hammond, Derek and Sylvia Stephenson*

BRASSINGTON   SK2354 Map 7
Olde Gate ★

Village signed off B5056 and B5035 NE of Ashbourne; DE4 4HJ

Lovely old interior, candlelit at night, country garden

The charming interior of this unspoilt listed building (just a few minutes' drive from Carsington Water) is full of attractive old architectural features, from mullioned windows to a Georgian panelled room. Fine old furnishings include an ancient wall clock, rush-seated chairs and antique settles, among them a lovely ancient example in black solid oak. Log fires blaze away, gleaming copper pots sit on a 17th-c kitchen range, pewter mugs hang from a beam, and a side shelf boasts a collection of embossed Doulton stoneware flagons. To the left of a small hatch-served lobby, a cosy beamed room has stripped panelled settles, scrubbed-top tables and a blazing fire under a huge mantelbeam. Marstons Pedigree and two guests from the Marstons stable of brewers such as Jennings and Ringwood are on handpump, and they keep a good selection of malt whiskies; cribbage, dominoes, cards, and maybe Sunday evening boules in summer. A very inviting garden has a good number of tables looking out to idyllic silvery-walled pastures and there are some benches in the small front yard. Please ring to check opening times.

Food here is fairly priced. As well as filled baguettes (not Sunday) the lunchtime menu includes warm chorizo and bacon on leaves, warm goats cheese on pea and walnut salad, sausage and mash, fried chicken breast with tarragon sauce and battered cod and curry, and in the evening there might be bass with herb and lemon sauce, duck breast with orange and Cointreau, trout (caught by a customer), oxtail, rack of pork with whisky sauce, and puddings such as lemon crunch, apple and rhubarb crumble and white chocolate and raspberry brioche pudding. *Benchmark main dish: steak and Guinness pie £8.95. Two-course evening meal £17.70.*

Marstons ~ Lease Peter Scragg ~ Real ale ~ Bar food (12-2(2.30 Sun), 6.30-8.45 Tues-Sat; not Sun evening) ~ (01629) 540448 ~ Children welcome ~ Dogs allowed in bar ~ Open 12-2.15(3 Sun), 6-11; 12-3, 6-10 Sun; closed Mon (except bank holidays), Tues lunchtime, Sun evening in winter ~ www.oldgateinnbrassington.co.uk *Recommended by Peter F Marshall, Robin Constable, Helene Grygar, the Didler, George Atkinson, JJW, CMW*

BRETTON
Barrel

SK2078 Map 7

Signposted from Foolow, which itself is signposted from A623 just E of junction with B6465 to Bakewell; can also be reached from either the B6049 at Great Hucklow, or the B6001 via Abney, from Leadmill just S of Hathersage; S32 5QD

Remote dining pub with traditional décor and friendly staff

This magnificently situated stone-roofed turnpike inn dates back to 1597. Being the highest pub in Derbyshire (so we're told), at the top of Bretton Clough, it enjoys glorious sweeping views over five counties – seats out on the front terrace by the road and a courtyard garden are nicely sheltered from the inevitable breeze at this height. Inside, stubs of massive knocked-through stone walls divide it into several areas. The cosy dark oak-beamed bar is charmingly traditional with its gleaming copper and brass, warming fire, patterned carpet, low doorways and stools lined up at the counter, which has Marstons Pedigree and EPA and Wychwood Hobgoblin on handpump, and tankards hanging above. Everything here is kept spick and span and the friendly staff are smartly dressed; background radio.

Sourced locally where possible, bar food might include starters such as black pudding fritters, country pork and herb terrine, arbroath smokie fishcake or beetroot and goats cheese tart, main courses such as steak and ale pie, beer-battered haddock, lambs liver with onions, fisherman's crumble, pot roast grouse and pheasant casserole. Lunchtime snacks include derbyshire oatcakes with various toppings, soda bread sandwiches, omelettes, burgers, ploughmans and salads, with puddings such as sticky toffee, bread and butter and bakewell puddings; Sunday roasts. *Benchmark main dish: steak and ale pie £11.50. Two-course evening meal £19.25.*

Free house ~ Licensee Philip Cone ~ Real ale ~ Bar food (12-2, 6-9; 12-9 Sun) ~ (01433) 630856 ~ Well behaved children welcome ~ Dogs allowed in bar ~ Open 11-11; 11-3, 6-11 Mon-Fri Oct-March ~ Bedrooms: £50S/£85B ~ www.thebarrelinn.co.uk *Recommended by Ann and Tony Bennett-Hughes, Ann and Colin Hunt, David Heath, Peter F Marshall, Hilary Forrest*

CHELMORTON   SK1170 Map 7
Church Inn ■ £

Village signposted off A5270, between A6 and A515 SE of Buxton; keep on up through village towards church; SK17 9SL

Convivial traditional inn beautifully set in High Peak walking country – good value

This welcoming pub is in a quiet spot at the end of a road up to the moors. It's opposite a largely 18th-c church and prettily tucked into woodland with fine views over the village and hills beyond from good teak tables on its two-level terrace. The warm can-do hospitable greeting from the licensees and staff really sets a friendly atmosphere in the chatty low-ceilinged tiled bar. It has a warming fire and is traditionally furnished with cushioned built-in benches and simple chairs around polished cast-iron framed tables – one or two still with their squeaky sewing treadles. Shelves of books, Tiffany-style lamps and house plants in the curtained windows, atmospheric Dales photographs and prints, and a coal-effect stove in the stripped-stone end wall all add a cosy feel. Adnams, Marstons Bitter and Pedigree and a couple of guests from brewers such as Buxton and Thornbridge might be served from handpump; darts in a tiled-floor games area on the left; TV, background music and board games.

Sensibly priced food includes sandwiches, chicken goujons, creamy garlic mushrooms, black pudding fritter with spiced fruit chutney, steak and kidney puff pastry pie, chicken balti, stuffed vegetable crêpe with cheese and tomato sauce, beef braised in Guinness, and bass fillet with tomato and basil sauce. *Benchmark main dish: rabbit pie £11.75. Two-course evening meal £14.20.*

Free house ~ Licensees Julie and Justin Satur ~ Real ale ~ Bar food (12-2.30, 6-8.30; 12-9 Fri-Sun) ~ (01298) 85319 ~ Children welcome ~ Dogs allowed in bar ~ Open 12-3, 6-midnight; 12-midnight Fri-Sun ~ Bedrooms: £50S/£75S ~ www.thechurchinn.co.uk *Recommended by Peter F Marshall, Edward Leetham, Mike Proctor, Pat and Stewart Gordon, Barry Collett, J and E Dakin, David and Sue Atkinson*

FENNY BENTLEY   SK1750 Map 7
Coach & Horses £

A515 N of Ashbourne; DE6 1LB

Cosy former coaching inn with pretty country furnishings, roaring open fires and food all day

The homely interior of this popular 17th-c coaching inn is quite traditional, with a welcoming atmosphere and a good mix of customers. It has all the trappings you'd expect of a country pub, from roaring winter fires on exposed brick hearths to black beams hung with horsebrasses, wagon-wheels and pewter mugs, and hand-made pine furniture that includes wall settles with floral-print cushions on flagstone

Post Office address codings confusingly give the impression that a few pubs are in Derbyshire, when they're really in Cheshire (which is where we list them).

floors. There's also a conservatory dining room. Marstons Pedigree and a guest such as Derby Hop Till You Drop are on handpump, and the landlord is knowledgeable about malt whiskies – he stocks just under two dozen; quiet background music. There are views across fields from tables in the side garden by an elder tree, and modern tables and chairs under cocktail parasols on the front roadside terrace. The pub is within a few minutes' walk of the popular Tissington Trail (which follows a former railway line) and is best joined at the nearby picture-book village of Tissington.

As well as lunchtime and afternoon sandwiches, reasonably priced tasty bar food might include crayfish tail and prawn cocktail, potato shells filled with bacon and black pudding in black pepper sauce, chicken korma, salmon fillet with cream, wine and crabmeat sauce, roast duck with port and berry sauce, three cheese puff pastry tart with ratatouille, lamb casserole with dumplings, and daily specials such as haddock on cheesy mash with leek butter and game casserole with herb dumpling. *Benchmark main dish: barnsley lamb chop £12.55. Two-course evening meal £16.00.*

Free house ~ Licensees John and Matthew Dawson ~ Real ale ~ Bar food (12-9) ~ No credit cards ~ (01335) 350246 ~ Children welcome ~ Open 11-11; 12-10.30 Sun *Recommended by Neil Ingoe, John Wooll, Jon Porter, the Didler, Ken and Barbara Turner, Tony W Dickinson, Mrs P M Chapman*

GREAT LONGSTONE
SK1971 Map 7
Crispin £
Main Street; DE45 1TZ

Spotless traditional pub with emphasis on good value pubby food; good drinks choice, too

You can be sure of a good homely welcome and cheerful service at this well established family-run pub in the heart of the Peak District. Décor throughout is thoroughly traditional, running from some brass or copper implements, decorative plates, a collage of regulars' snapshots and horsebrasses on the beams in the red ceiling to cushioned built-in wall benches and upholstered chairs and stools around polished tables on red carpet, and a fire. A corner area is snugly partioned off, and on the right is a separate, more formal dining room; darts, board games and maybe faint background music. Welcoming staff serve a good choice of wines and whiskies as well five Robinsons beers on handpump. There are picnic-sets out in front, set well back above the quiet lane (one under a heated canopy), and more in the recently redesigned garden.

Using eggs from their own hens, the good value food might include sandwiches, hot baguettes, creamy garlic and stilton mushrooms, seafood medley with tartare sauce, ham hock braised with cider and apples, battered haddock with mushy peas, roast parsnip with chestnut stuffing and marsala gravy, tortellini with stilton and rocket pesto, and puddings such as apple and winter berry crumble and gooseberry and elderflower fool. *Benchmark main dish: venison pie with port and stilton and suet crust £11.95. Two-course evening meal £16.75.*

Robinsons ~ Tenant Paul Rowlinson ~ Real ale ~ Bar food (12-2.30, 6-9) ~ Restaurant ~ (01629) 640237 ~ Children welcome ~ Dogs welcome ~ Open 12-3, 6-midnight; 12-midnight Sat; 12-11 Sun ~ www.thecrispin.co.uk *Recommended by Peter F Marshall, Derek and Sylvia Stephenson, Brian and Jacky Wilson*

HASSOP
SK2272 Map 7
Eyre Arms
B6001 N of Bakewell; DE45 1NS

Comfortable, neatly kept pub, with pretty views from the garden

The metre-thick walls of this 17th-c former coaching inn are completely swathed in vines, and in autumn, when they turn a vibrant orange, the building appears to glow. Inside it's snug and cosy with cheery log fires warming the low-ceilinged oak beamed rooms. Traditional furnishings include cushioned oak settles, comfortable plush chairs, a long-case clock, old pictures and lots of brass and copper. The small public bar has an unusual collection of teapots, as well as Black Sheep, Chatsworth Gold and Peak Ales Swift Nick on handpump, and several wines by the glass; piped classical music, darts. The dining room is dominated by a painting of the Eyre coat of arms above the stone fireplace. The delightful garden, with its gurgling fountain, looks straight out into fine Peak District countryside.

 As well as lunchtime sandwiches and ploughman's, bar food might include broccoli and cheddar soup, pheasant terrine with plum chutney, onion bhaji, thai-style crab cakes, venison pie, lasagne, scampi, mushroom stroganoff, braised pheasant, rabbit pie, and steaks. *Benchmark main dish: steak and kidney pie £10.95. Two-course evening meal £17.00.*

Free house ~ Licensees Nick and Lynne Smith ~ Real ale ~ Bar food (12-2, 6.30-9; 12-3, 6-9 Sat, Sun) ~ (01629) 640390 ~ Children welcome ~ Dogs allowed in bar ~ Open 11-3, 6.30-11; 11-11 Sat; 11-10.30 Sun; closed Mon evening ~ www.eyrearms.com
Recommended by Ann and Tony Bennett-Hughes, Mrs B Billington, J and E Dakin

HATHERSAGE
SK2380 Map 7
Plough 🍴 ♟ 🛏
Leadmill; B6001 towards Bakewell, OS Sheet 110 map reference 235805; S32 1BA
Derbyshire Dining Pub of the Year

Welcoming dining pub usefully placed for exploring the Peak District, with good food, beer and wine, waterside garden, and bedrooms

Readers tell us they have have felt very welcome and really enjoyed the food at this immaculately kept 16th-c inn. Still fairly traditional, the neat and tidy interior has rows of dark wood tables (with cruets giving away the emphasis on dining) and a long banquette running almost the length of one wall on bright tartan and oriental patterned carpets. There's a big log fire and a woodburning stove, decorative plates are displayed on terracotta walls and pewter tankards hang from a dark beam; quiet background music. They've a good wine list (with nearly two dozen by the glass), 25 malt whiskies, and Adnams, Black Sheep and Timothy Taylors on handpump. One of the most appealing aspects is the 9-acre grounds in a lovely spot on the banks of the River Derwent. – the pretty garden slopes right down to the water and there's a lovely suntrap courtyard.

 Bar food includes galantine of rabbit and pigeon with cranberry and chestnut relish, whitebait with lime and coriander mayonnaise, smoked haddock with potato terrine and lemon and caper jus, red mullet in seafood batter with black bean sauce, breast of duck with sweet pickled red cabbage and juniper sauce, spiced aubergine and cherry tomatoes in pastry with tomato coulis and rib of beef for two, and puddings such as passion fruit crème brûlée. *Benchmark main dish: battered cod £14.00. Two-course evening meal £24.00.*

Free house ~ Licensees Bob, Cynthia and Elliott Emery ~ Real ale ~ Bar food (11.30-9.30, 12-8.30 Sun) ~ Restaurant ~ (01433) 650319 ~ Children welcome ~ Dogs welcome ~ Open 11-11; 12-10.30 Sun ~ Bedrooms: £70B/£95B ~ www.theploughinn-hathersage.co.uk *Recommended by Karen Eliot, Ann and Colin Hunt, Mr and Mrs M Hargrave, John Branston, Richard Cole, Colin and Pat Honey*

HAYFIELD SK0388 Map 7
Lantern Pike £

Glossop Road (A624 N) at Little Hayfield, just N of Hayfield; SK22 2NG

Friendly retreat from the surrounding moors of Kinder Scout, with reasonably priced food; bedrooms

Lying as it does within the bounds of the Peak District National Park, this simple place is a handy stop if you are in the area and need a break from the windswept moors. The traditional red plush bar proudly displays photos of the original *Coronation Street* cast, many of whom were regulars here, along with Tony Warren, one of its earlier script writers, and Arthur Lowe of *Dad's Army* fame. It's quite possible that the interior hasn't changed much since those days. You'll find a warm fire, brass platters in numbers, china and toby jugs, fresh flowers on the tables and a counter lined with red plush stools (Castle Rock Harvest Pale, Timothy Taylors Landlord and Whim Hartington IPA on handpump); TV and background music. Tables on a stone-walled terrace look over a big-windowed weaver's house towards Lantern Pike. Dogs may be allowed in at the licensees' discretion and if clean.

 Served in generous helpings, good value bar food might include haddock fishcake, chicken and brandy pâté, asparagus mousse, braised lamb shank, fried red snapper with chilli and lime butter, vegetable stilton bake, stuffed peppers, pork in stilton, and chicken curry. *Benchmark main dish: steak and ale pie £9.95. Two-course evening meal £14.70.*

Enterprise ~ Lease Stella and Tom Cunliffe ~ Real ale ~ Bar food (12-2.30, 5-8.30(8 Mon); 12-8.30 Sat(8 Sun) ~ Restaurant ~ (01663) 747590 ~ Children welcome ~ Open 12-3, 5-11; 12-11 Sat, Sun; closed Mon lunchtime ~ Bedrooms: £50B/£60B ~ www.lanternpikeinn.co.uk *Recommended by Dean Johnson, Dennis Jones, David and Sue Atkinson*

HOPE SK1783 Map 7
Cheshire Cheese £

Off A6187, towards Edale; S33 6ZF

Cosy multi-level stone pub with good real ales in attractive Peak District village; bedrooms

There's plenty of traditional atmosphere in the two snug oak-beamed rooms at this popular honey-coloured 16th-c inn. Arranged on different levels, they are cosy with warming fires, red carpets or stone floors, traditional dark wood furnishings and gleaming brasses. It's a well liked place and often fills to capacity with locals as well as tourists, all welcomed equally by the friendly barman and staff. Bradfield Farmers Blonde, Kelham Island Easy Rider, Peak Ales Swift Nick and two guests such as Bradfield Farmers Brown Cow and Peak Ales Chatsworth Gold are on handpump and they've a dozen malts. There's a glorious range of local walks near here, taking in the summits of Lose Hill and Win Hill, or the cave district of the Castleton area, and the village of Hope itself is worth a stroll; parking is limited.

 Bar food includes lunchtime snacks such as sandwiches, baked potatoes and salads, as well as a whitebait, spinach and ricotta ravioli, tapas selection, filled yorkshire puddings, steak and ale pie, wild boar casserole, potato, leek and stilton crumble, gammon and egg, lambs liver and onion gravy, and puddings such as bakewell tart, lemon sponge and chocolate fudge cake. *Benchmark main dish: beer-battered haddock £9.95. Two-course evening meal £15.00.*

Enterprise ~ Lease Laura Offless ~ Real ale ~ Bar food (12-2(3 Sat, 4 Sun), 6-9) ~ Restaurant ~ (01433) 620381 ~ Children welcome ~ Dogs allowed in bar ~ Open 12-3, 6-11; 12-11 Sat, 12-6 Sun; closed Sun evening, Mon ~ Bedrooms: £45B/£70B ~ www.cheshirecheeseinn.co.uk *Recommended by Ann and Colin Hunt, Peter F Marshall, the Didler, Stuart and Jasmine Kelly, Malcolm and Pauline Pellatt*

INGLEBY   SK3427 Map 7

John Thompson

NW of Melbourne; turn off A514 at Swarkestone Bridge or in Stanton by Bridge; can also be reached from Ticknall (or from Repton on B5008); DE73 7HW

Own-brew pub that strikes the right balance between attentive service, roomy comfort and good value lunchtime food

Friendly staff serve the two beers that are brewed at the back of this relaxed and unchanging pubby place, alongside a guest such as Timothy Taylors Landlord. Simple but comfortable and immaculately kept, the big modernised lounge has ceiling joists, some old oak settles, button-back leather seats, sturdy oak tables, antique prints and paintings and a log-effect gas fire; background music. A couple of smaller, cosier rooms open off; piano, games machine, board games, darts, TV, and pool in the conservatory. There are lots of tables by flower beds on the neat lawns, or you can sit on the partly covered terrace, surrounded by pretty countryside and near the River Trent. Breakfast is left in your fridge if you stay in one of their self-catering detached chalet lodges. The pub takes its name from the licensee's father.

 The short lunchtime menu includes sandwiches, baked potatoes, hot beef sandwich, three cheese and broccoli pasta bake and salads, with puddings such as fruit crumble and Mrs Thompson's famous bread and butter pudding – a speciality of the pub for the past 40 years. *Benchmark main dish: roast beef carvery £7.45.*

Own brew ~ Licensee Nick Thompson ~ Real ale ~ Bar food (12-2) ~ Restaurant ~ (01332) 862469 ~ Children welcome in main bar till 6pm, in conservatory till 9pm ~ Dogs welcome ~ Open 11-2.30, 6-11; 11-11 Sat; 12-10.30 Sun; closed Mon lunchtime except bank hols ~ www.johnthompsoninn.com *Recommended by Theo, Anne and Jane Gaskin, the Didler, Andy Dolan, David Eberlin, Ian and Jane Irving*

KIRK IRETON   SK2650 Map 7

Barley Mow

Village signed off B5023 S of Wirksworth; DE6 3JP

Character-laden welcoming old inn that focuses on real ale and conversation; bedrooms

'A gem of a place', this marvellously unaltered Jacobean house, with its very kindly landlady (she's been here over 30 years), friendly

locals and pub dogs, is a gently relaxing place to sit and quietly chat.
An inn since around 1800, it evokes how some grander rural pubs might
have looked a century or so ago. The small main bar has a relaxed a
relaxed, pubby feel, with antique settles on the tiled floor or built into
the panelling, a roaring coal fire, four slate-topped tables and shuttered
mullioned windows. Another room has built-in cushioned pews on oak
parquet and a small woodburning stove, and a third has more pews, a
tiled floor, low beams and big landscape prints. In casks behind a modest
wooden counter are five well kept, often local, changing real ales mostly
from smaller brewers such as Abbeydale, Blue Monkey, Cottage, Storm
and Whim; french wines and farm cider too. There's a good-sized garden,
a couple of benches out in front and a shop in what used to be the
stable. This hilltop village is very pretty and is within walking distance of
Carsington Water. Bedrooms are comfortable and readers enjoy the good
breakfasts served in the stone-flagged kitchen.

> **‖¶** Very inexpensive lunchtime filled rolls are the only food; the decent evening
> meals (no choice) are reserved for those staying here; good breakfasts.

Free house ~ Licensee Mary Short ~ Real ale ~ Bar food (lunchtime sandwiches only)
~ No credit cards ~ (01335) 370306 ~ Dogs allowed in bar and bedrooms ~ Open 11-2,
7-11(10.30 Sun) ~ Bedrooms: £45S/£65B *Recommended by Joyce James, the Didler, Jamie
and Sue May, Tich Critchlow, Josh Greaves*

LADYBOWER RESERVOIR   SK1986   Map 7
Ladybower Inn ◀
A57 Sheffield–Glossop, just E of junction with A6013; S33 0AX

**All-day food in comfortable proper pub nestling above reservoir in
good walking country; good value bedrooms**

The attractive location of this friendly place can draw the crowds
at weekends and during the holidays. Traditional furnishings in its
various carpeted areas are understated and homely, taking in peach
cottagey wallpaper and curtains, little pictures, cast iron fireplaces,
wall banquettes and captain's and country kitchen chairs and the like;
the most relaxed place to eat is down at the end on the right, with
leather-padded traditional dining chairs around heavier tables, Lancaster
bomber pictures recalling the Dambusters' practice runs on the reservoir,
and a coal-effect fire. Staff are friendly and enthusiastic; unobtrusive
background music and darts. Drinks include Acorn Barnsley, Bradfield
Farmers Blonde and Greene King Ruddles County, and a couple of guests
such as Black Sheep and Sharps Doom Bar, and decent wines by the
glass. Staying in the annexe bedrooms, we were not disturbed by traffic
noise – but the road is busy, so crossing from the car park opposite needs
care, and picnic-sets out in front could be quieter.

> **‖¶** As well as sandwiches, the very generous home cooking, using local farm
> supplies and pheasant from the landlord's farm, trout from the reservoir and
> plenty of seasonal vegetables, might include warm pigeon salad with butternut and
> sage, smoked haddock fishcake with parsley sauce, fried scallops with cauliflower
> and vanilla purée and crispy proscuitto, pork fillet on mustard mash with black
> pudding sausage, roast onion and cider jus, spiced cauliflower, lentil and potato filo
> parcel with cucumber raita, filo wrapped salmon stuffed with crab with lime crème

---

The ◀ symbol shows pubs which keep their beer unusually well, have a
particularly good range or brew their own.

fraîche and sweet chilli dressing, roast lamb shank with mini cottage pie and red wine jus, and scampi. *Benchmark main dish: beef and ale pie £10.50. Two-course evening meal £17.30.*

Free house ~ Licensee Deborah Wilde ~ Real ale ~ Bar food (12-9) ~ (01433) 651241 ~ Children welcome ~ Open 10-11 ~ Bedrooms: £42.50S/£85S ~ www.ladybower-inn.co.uk
Recommended by Ann and Colin Hunt, Mike Proctor

MONYASH
Bulls Head
SK1566   Map 7

B5055 W of Bakewell; DE45 1JH

Unpretentious local with tasty home cooking

This rambling multi roomed stone pub extends a genuinely friendly welcome to visitors and locals alike. Its high-ceilinged rooms are gently unassuming, with a good log fire, straightforward traditional furnishings including plush stools lined along the bar, horse pictures and a shelf of china. A small back bar room has darts, board games and pool, and the newly decorated more cottagey feeling restaurant is cosy with leather high backed dining chairs on heated stone floors; quiet background music. Blacksheep and a couple of guests such as Bradfield Farmers Blonde are on handpump. A gate from the pub's garden leads into an entertaining village play area, and this is fine walking country.

Served in generous helpings, bar food includes sandwiches, whitebait, prawn cocktail, steak and kidney pie, quiche, chicken curry, leek and mushroom crumble, crispy pork belly, trout topped with almonds, scampi, filled baked potatoes, and mixed grill. *Benchmark main dish: yorkshire pudding filled with beef cooked in Guinness £10.50. Two-course evening meal £16.60.*

Free house ~ Licensee Sharon Barber ~ Real ale ~ Bar food (12-9; 12-2, 5.30-9 weekdays in winter) ~ Restaurant ~ (01629) 812372 ~ Children welcome ~ Dogs allowed in bar ~ Open 12-2.30, 5-11; 12-11 Fri-Sun ~ www.thebullsheadmonyash.co.uk   *Recommended by David and Sue Atkinson, Dennis Jones, Mrs P Bishop*

OVER HADDON
Lathkil
SK2066   Map 7

Village and inn signposted from B5055 just SW of Bakewell; DE45 1JE

Traditional pub well placed for Lathkill Dale with super views, good range of beers and decent food

After serving thirty years at the helm of this much-liked inn, the landlord has retired and handed the reins to his daughter Alice – we hope it continues in the same family for as long again. In an ideal position for walks along one of the most enchantingly secret dales in the Peak District (muddy boots must be left in the lobby), it has fine views from its windows and walled garden. The airy room on the right as you go in has a nice fire in the attractively carved fireplace, old-fashioned settles with upholstered cushions and chairs, black beams, a delft shelf of blue and white plates, original prints and photographs, and big windows. On the left, the sunny spacious dining area doubles as an evening restaurant. They keep Everards Tiger and Whim Hartington and three guests from brewers such as Buxton, Peak and Wincle on handpump, a reasonable range of wines (including mulled wine) and a decent selection of malt whiskies; background music, TV and board games.

🍴 Lunch, which is served buffet-style, includes simple filled rolls, cold salads, steak and kidney pie, creamy fish pie, courgette and aubergine moussaka and lamb tagine. In the evening dishes include crab cakes, pâté with apple and ale chutney, king prawns in filo pastry, breaded scampi, chicken breast stuffed with stilton and leeks in a stilton sauce, and puddings such as Mars Bar banoffi pie and date and ginger fudge pudding. *Benchmark main dish: venison and blackberry casserole £10.50. Two-course evening meal £17.00.*

Free house ~ Licensee Alice Grigor-Taylor ~ Real ale ~ Bar food (12-2(2.30 Sat, Sun), 6-8(7-8.30, Fri, Sat)) ~ Restaurant ~ (01629) 812501 ~ No children under 10 in bar ~ Dogs allowed in bar and bedrooms ~ Open 11-11; 12-10.30 Sun ~ Bedrooms: £50B/£75S(£95B) ~ www.lathkil.co.uk *Recommended by Peter F Marshall, R L Borthwick, Dennis Jones, Brian and Anna Marsden, Mrs P Bishop*

 PILSLEY SK2371 Map 7

Devonshire Arms ♀ 🍺 🛏️

Village signposted off A619 W of Baslow, and pub just below B6048; High Street; DE45 1UL

Simple yet stylish country inn, good all round; nice place to stay

Here you'll find a gentle contemporary slant to what is essentially a civilised and traditional small country inn, with a relaxed and chatty atmosphere. The flagstoned bar has four well kept ales from local brewers such as Bakewell, Peak, Thornbridge and Whim on handpump, and a good choice of wines by the glass. Several fairly compact, mainly carpeted areas open off, each with a distinct character: stripped stone here, soft grey paintwork there, rather sumptuous crimson and gold wallpaper in one part, soft heather curtains and big modern paintings, log fires in stone fireplaces, comfortable seating in leather or fabric, and thick new wooden table-tops on either sturdy modern metal columns or old cast-iron bases – at least one still with its old sewing-machine treadle. Service is polite and efficient. There are some tables outside. The pub is on the Chatsworth Estate and their renowned farm shop at the top of the lane.

🍴 Using plentry of produce from the Estate, the enjoyable traditional food tends to take centre stage here. As well as open sandwiches, the menu might include smoked salmon, dill and horseradish tartlets, butternut and beetroot risotto stuffed pepper, smooth game pâté with blueberry centre, cajun chicken, minted lamb hotpot with rosemary dumplings, faggots and mash, gammon, egg and chips, and puddings such as dark and white chocolate tart and jam sponge. *Benchmark main dish: steak and kidney pie £12.50. Two-course evening meal £17.50.*

Free house ~ Licensee Alan Hill ~ Real ale ~ Bar food (12-2.30, 5-9) ~ (01246) 583258 ~ Children welcome ~ Open 11-11(10 Sun) ~ Bedrooms: /£99B ~ www.devonshirepilsley.co.uk *Recommended by Peter F Marshall, Derek and Sylvia Stephenson*

 STANTON IN PEAK SK2364 Map 7

Flying Childers 🍺 £

Village signposted from B6056 S of Bakewell; Main Road; DE4 2LW

Top-notch beer and inexpensive simple bar lunches in warm-hearted unspoilt pub – a delight

Besides his regular Wells & Youngs Bombardier, the friendly landlord at this homely village pub (named after an unbeatable racehorse of the early 18th c) keeps a couple of constantly changing guests from brewers such as Abbeydale and Storm. The room to enjoy them best in is the snug little right-hand bar, virtually built for chat, with its dark beam-and-plank ceiling, dark wall settles, single pew, plain tables, a hot coal and log fire, a few team photographs, and dominoes and cribbage; background music. There's a bigger equally unpretentious bar on the right. A well tended garden at the back has picnic-sets and there are a couple more out in front; this beautiful steep stone village overlooks a rich green valley, and there are good walks in most directions.

 Prepared by the landlady – as friendly as her husband – lunchtime bar food includes soup, filled cobs, toasties and casseroles. They sell home-made produce in their little porch shop and sometimes use produce from their allotment. *Benchmark main dish: bowl of casserole and bread £4.80.*

Free house ~ Licensees Stuart and Mandy Redfern ~ Real ale ~ Bar food (lunchtimes only) ~ No credit cards ~ (01629) 636333 ~ Children welcome ~ Dogs welcome ~ Open 12-2(3 Sat, Sun), 7-11; closed Mon, Tues lunchtime ~ www.flyingchilders.com
Recommended by Mike Proctor, the Didler, Brian and Anna Marsden, Ann and Colin Hunt

WOOLLEY MOOR SK3661 Map 7
White Horse ♀
Badger Lane, off B6014 Matlock–Clay Cross; DE55 6FG

Attractive old dining pub with good food, pretty countryside

This immaculately kept place is in a charming rural spot with Ogston Reservoir just a couple of minutes' drive away. The sloping garden has a boules pitch, picnic-sets and a children's play area with a wooden train, boat, climbing frame and swings. Inside, it's functional and uncluttered, with tidily arranged rows of furniture (including a leather sofa) on new stone floors or wooden boards, boldy patterned curtains and blinds, little to distract on the cream walls and uniform lamps on window sills. There's a buoyantly chatty feel to the tap room, with Peak Ales Bakewell Best and Chatsworth Gold and a guest such as Copper Dragon Golden Pippin on handpump, a dozen wines by the glass from the newly built brick counter; conservatory; background music.

Good bar food includes potted ham hock with poached egg on toast, cod and salmon thai fishcakes, battered cod, sausage and mash, ploughman's, lambs liver with black pudding, blue cheese and pear tart, steak and ale casserole, duck breast with redcurrant jus, chicken breast with white wine and leek sauce, scampi in lemonade batter, fried bass with prawn and lemon risotto, and puddings such as honey and hazelnut parfait and bread and butter pudding; they also do a good value set menu Monday to Thursday. *Benchmark main dish: pork belly with smoked bacon sauce £13.95. Two-course evening meal £22.70.*

Free house ~ Licensees David and Melanie Boulby ~ Real ale ~ Bar food (12-1.45 (2.30 Sun), 6-8.45) ~ Restaurant ~ (01246) 590319 ~ Children welcome ~ Open 12-3, 5.30-11; 12-3 Sun; closed Sun evening, first three weeks of Jan ~ www.thewhitehorsewoolleymoor.co.uk *Recommended by Peter F Marshall, Ian Phillips, Peter Robson*

> The price we give for a two-course evening meal in the featured entries
> is the mean (average of cheapest and most expensive) price of a starter
> and a main course – no drinks.

Also Worth a Visit in Derbyshire

Besides the fully inspected pubs, you might like to try these pubs that have been recommended to us and described by readers. Do tell us what you think of them: feedback@goodguides.com

ASHBOURNE SK1846
Horns (01335) 347387
Victoria Square; DE6 1GG Attractive 18th-c pub with bay window overlooking steep cobbled street, enjoyable home-made food, well kept Marstons Pedigree and a couple of guests, friendly staff, rooms on different levels, open fire; seats outside. *(David and Sue Atkinson)*

ASHFORD IN THE WATER SK1969
✶ **Bulls Head** (01629) 812931
Off A6 NW of Bakewell; Church Street (B6465, off A6020); DE45 1QB Traditional village inn dating from the 16th c and run by same welcoming family for 50 years, cosy two-room beamed and carpeted bar with fires, one or two character gothic seats, spindleback and wheelback chairs around cast-iron-framed tables, local photographs and country prints on cream walls, daily papers, Robinsons ales and gently imaginative food (not Thurs evening in winter), friendly efficient service; background jazz; children welcome in some areas, dogs in bar, overshoes for walkers, hardwood tables and benches in front and in good-sized garden behind with boules and Jenga. *(P J and R D Greaves, Sue Tucker, Derek and Sylvia Stephenson)*

BAKEWELL SK2168
Castle Inn (01629) 812103
Bridge Street; DE45 1DU Bay-windowed Georgian-fronted 17th-c pub, well kept Greene King ales and good choice of sensibly priced food, three candlelit rooms with two open fires, flagstones, stripped stone and lots of pictures; dogs welcome, tables outside, four bedrooms. *(David Carr, Derek and Sylvia Stephenson)*

BASLOW SK2572
Wheatsheaf (01246) 582240
Nether End; DE45 1SR Marstons pub with good choice of food all day including specials board, their ales kept well, good service; children's play area, bedrooms. *(Derek and Sylvia Stephenson)*

BELPER SK3547
Cross Keys (01773) 599191
Market Place; DE56 1FZ Friendly pub with well kept Bass, Batemans (including a house beer) and one or two guests, straightforward food, coal fire and bar billiards in lounge, pool and TV in bar, regular beer festivals; open all day Sat, from 5pm other days. *(the Didler)*

BELPER SK3549
Fishermans Rest (01773) 825518
Broadholme Lane; DE56 2JF Four-square gritstone Marstons pub with their well kept ales (more choice in summer), enjoyable reasonably priced hearty food including warming casseroles and hotpots, friendly attentive service, L-shaped lounge bar, restaurant, pleasant relaxed atmosphere (can be quiet weekday lunchtimes); children and dogs welcome, sunny garden with play area, nice surroundings. *(Richard and Jean Green)*

BIRCHOVER SK2362
Druid (01629) 650302
Off B5056; Main Street; DE4 2BL Updated 17h-c pub with stone-floor bar area, dining room either side and upstairs restaurant with grand piano, good varied food including some unusual choices, friendly willing service, a couple of own-badged beers brewed by Titanic plus guests; children welcome, dogs in bar, tables out in front on two levels, good area for walks, Nine Ladies stone circle nearby, open all day in summer. *(Trevor and Sylvia Millum, Derek and Sylvia Stephenson, Brian and Anna Marsden, Nick Simms)*

BIRCHOVER SK2362
Red Lion (01629) 650363
Main Street; DE4 2BN Nicely traditional village pub run by same welcoming family for 50 years, cosy two-room beamed and carpeted bar with fires, one or two character gothic seats, spindleback and wheelback chairs around cast-iron-framed tables, local photographs and country prints on cream walls, Robinsons Unicorn and Old Stockport, good gently imaginative food (not Thurs evening in winter), friendly efficient service, daily papers; background jazz; children welcome in some areas, dogs in bar, tables and benches out at front, good-sized garden behind with boules. *(the Didler, Nick Simms)*

BONSALL SK2758
✶ **Barley Mow** (01629) 825685
Off A5012 W of Cromford; The Dale; DE4 2AY Basic one-room stone-built local, friendly colourful atmosphere, beams, character furnishings and coal fire, pictures and bric-a-brac, well kept Greene King, Whim and guests, decent straightforward food, live music Fri and Sat including UFO-enthusiast landlord playing his accordion; short walk out to lavatories; dogs welcome, nice little front terrace, events such as hen racing and marrow dressing, walks organised

from the pub, open all day weekends, closed Mon. *(Reg Fowle, Helen Rickwood, the Didler)*

BRACKENFIELD   SK3658
Plough (01629) 534437
A615 Matlock–Alfreton, about a mile NW of Wessington; DE55 6DD Much-modernised, oak-beamed, stone-built 16th-c former farmhouse in lovely setting, tidy and welcoming three-level bar, cheerful log-effect gas fire, well kept ales including interesting local brews, plenty of wines by the glass, good value enjoyable fresh food (not Sun evening) plus two-course lunchtime deal (Mon-Sat), appealing lower-level restaurant extension; large neatly kept gardens with terrace, open all day. *(Steve Godfrey, Ian Phillips)*

BUXTON   SK1266
✶**Bull i' th' Thorn** (01298) 83348
Ashbourne Road (A515), 6 miles S of Buxton, near Flagg and Hurdlow; SK17 9QQ Fascinating medieval hall doubling as straightforward roadside dining pub, handsome panelling, old flagstones and big log fire, armour, longcase clocks and all sorts of antique features, decent choice of enjoyable good value food all day including vegetarian options, Sun carvery, well kept Robinsons ales, jovial landlord, plain games room and family room; dogs welcome, terrace and big lawn, rare breeds farm behind, good walks, bedrooms, big breakfast, camping, open all day from 9.30am, may be closed Mon. *(Gene and Kitty Rankin, the Didler, Barry Collett)*

BUXTON   SK0573
✶**Old Sun** (01298) 23452
High Street; SK17 6HA Charming old building with several cosy and interesting traditional linked areas, well kept Marstons-related ales, good choice of wines by the glass, bargain home-made food from good sandwiches up, low beams, bare boards or tiles, soft lighting, old local photographs, open fire; background music and some live acoustic evenings, Sun quiz, no dogs; children till 7pm, roadside garden, open all day. *(Ann and Tony Bennett-Hughes, the Didler, Barry Collett, Ann and Colin Hunt)*

CALVER   SK2374
Derwentwater Arms (01433) 639211
In centre, bear left from Main Street into Folds Head; Low Side; S32 3XQ Largely bright and modern inside, big windows looking down from village-centre knoll, friendly hard-working licensees, good fairly priced food from varied menu (best to book), well kept Theakstons and guests; children and dogs welcome, terraces on slopes below (disabled access), boules, open all day Sun. *(Robert Dudgeon, Bruce and Sharon Eden)*

CASTLETON   SK1582
✶**Bulls Head** (01433) 620256
Cross Street (A6187); S33 8WH Imposing building spreading through several attractive

linked areas, handsome panelling and pictures, appealing mix of comfortable seating including sofas and easy chairs, heavy drapes, good reasonably priced food from ciabattas up, helpful friendly service, well kept Robinsons ales, coal fires; fairly unobtrusive background music, may be live jazz; some roadside picnic-sets, five bedrooms. *(David Heath)*

CASTLETON   SK1482
✶**Castle Hotel** (01433) 620578
High Street/Castle Street; S33 8WG Roomy and welcoming Vintage Inn with usual good choice of well priced food all day from sizeable sandwiches up, good selection of real ales and of wines by the glass, decent coffee, friendly efficient staff even at busy times, log fires, stripped-stone walls, beams and some ancient flagstones; background music; children welcome, heated terrace, comfortable bedrooms and good breakfast, open all day. *(Gene and Kitty Rankin, M G Hart, B M Eldridge, David Heath)*

CASTLETON   SK1482
✶**George** (01433) 620238
Castle Street; S33 8WG Busy but relaxed old pub with flagstoned bar and restaurant, well kept ales such as Courage and Wells & Youngs, good choice of malts, enjoyable home-made food at reasonable prices, decent coffee, friendly staff, ancient beams and stripped stone, copper and brass, log fires; children and dogs welcome, tables out at front and back, castle views, good walks, bedrooms, open all day. *(Ann and Colin Hunt, Roger and Pauline Pearce, David Heath)*

CASTLETON   SK1583
Olde Cheshire Cheese
(01433) 620330 *How Lane; S33 8WJ* 17th-c inn with two linked beamed and carpeted areas, cosy and spotless, with well kept ales such as Acorn, Bradfield and Peak, good range of enjoyable reasonably priced food all day, good house wine, quick friendly service, two gas woodburners, lots of photographs, toby jugs and brassware, back dining room; background music, TV, and they may swipe your credit card before running a tab; children welcome in restaurant, dogs in bar, ten bedrooms. *(David and Gill Carrington, Gene and Kitty Rankin, David Heath, David M Smith)*

CASTLETON   SK1582
✶**Olde Nags Head** (01433) 620248
Cross Street (A6187); S33 8WH Small solidly built refurbished hotel dating from the 17th c, interesting antique oak furniture and coal fire in civilised beamed and flagstoned bar with nice pictures, well kept Black Sheep, Timothy Taylors and guests, nice coffee, helpful staff, good locally sourced food in bars and bistro; attractive village, comfortable bedrooms, good breakfast choice, open all day. *(Mike Proctor, Ann and Colin Hunt, David Heath)*

CHESTERFIELD
Chesterfield Arms (01246) 236634
SK3871

Newbold Road (B6051); S41 7PH
Carefully restored and doing well under
beer-enthusiast landlord, ten changing ales
including Everards and Leatherbritches, six
ciders and good choice of wines, enjoyable
straightforward home-made food (Thurs
curry night), open fire, oak panelling and
stripped wood/flagstoned floors, weekend
back barn room, beer festivals, some live
music; outside tables on decking, open all
day. *(the Didler, Christian Yapp)*

CHESTERFIELD
Rose & Crown (01246) 563750
SK3670

Old Road (A619); S40 2QT Owned by
Brampton Brewery with their full range plus
Everards and two changing guests, Weston's
cider, enjoyable home-made food, spacious
traditional refurbishment with leather
banquettes, panelling, carpet or wood floors,
cast-iron Victorian fireplace, cosy snug area,
Tues quiz; tables outside; open all day.
(the Didler)

CHESTERFIELD
Rutland 07835 816163
SK3871

Stephenson Place; S40 1XL
Uncomplicated pub next to crooked-spire
church, welcoming and thriving, with eight
well kept ales and Weston's cider, low-priced
pub food all day from sandwiches up, friendly
polite service even when very busy, open
fires, assorted wooden furniture on bare
boards, old photographs, darts; background
music – live Thurs night, TV; children
welcome. *(the Didler, Alan Johnson, Roxanne
Chamberlain)*

CHINLEY
★ Old Hall (01663) 750529
SK0382

Whitehough; SK23 6EJ Impressive 16th-c
stone-built inn with well kept Marstons
and five changing local ales including
Thornbridge (beer festivals), bottled
belgians, real ciders in summer, efficient
enthusiastic young staff, good choice of
enjoyable well priced home-made food (all
day Sun till 7.30) including set lunch deal,
several refurbished rooms with warming
fires, minstrels gallery restaurant, some live
music; dogs welcome, garden picnic-sets,
good bedrooms, open all day. *(Annette and
John Derbyshire, Malcolm and Pauline Pellatt,
Frank Blanchard)*

CODNOR
Poet & Castle (01773) 744150
SK4249

Alfreton Road; DE5 9QY Friendly pub
with well kept Ashover ales and interesting
guests, farm cider and fruit wines, simple
wholesome food (not Mon) including popular
Sun lunch, good service, comfortable low-
ceilinged bar/lounge, upstairs restaurant,
music nights; open all day. *(the Didler, Derek
and Sylvia Stephenson)*

COMBS
★ Beehive (01298) 812758
SK0378

*Village signposted off B5470 W of
Chapel-en-le-Frith; SK23 9UT* Roomy,
neat and comfortable, with emphasis on
good freshly made food (all day Sun) from
baguettes to steaks and interesting specials,
also very good value weekday set menu,
well kept ales such as Copper Dragon and
Courage Directors, good choice of wines by
the glass, friendly service, log fire, heavy
beams and copperware; background music,
TV, Tues quiz; plenty of tables out in front,
by lovely valley tucked away from main road,
good walks, one-bed holiday cottage next
door, open all day. *(Rita and Keith Pollard,
Brian and Anna Marsden)*

CRICH
Cliff (01773) 852444
SK3454

Cromford Road, Town End; DE4 5DP
Traditional little two-room pub with well
kept local ales and reliable straightforward
food (not Mon), welcoming landlady and
friendly regulars, open fire; children and
dogs welcome, great views and walks, handy
for National Tramway Museum, open all day
weekends, from 5pm weekdays. *(the Didler)*

CROWDECOTE
Packhorse (01298) 83618
SK1065

B5055 W of Bakewell; SK17 0DB Small
three-room 16th-c pub in lovely setting,
welcoming landlord and staff, good
reasonably priced food from fairly extensive
menu, four well kept ales, split-level interior
with brick or carpeted floors, stripped-stone
walls, two woodburners, pool room; tables
out behind, beautiful views, popular walking
route. *(Dennis Jones, Brian and Jacky Wilson)*

DERBY
★ Abbey Inn (01332) 558297
SK3538

Darley Street, Darley Abbey; DE22 1DX
A treasure, former abbey gatehouse opposite
Derwent-side park (pleasant riverside
walk from centre), massive 15th-c or older
stonework remnants, brick floor, studded
oak doors, coal fire in big stone inglenook,
stone spiral stair to upper bar (open Sun
afternoon) with oak rafters and tapestries,
bargain Sam Smiths and lunchtime bar food,
pleasant service; the lavatories with their
beams, stonework and tiles are worth a look
too; background music; children welcome,
open all day weekends. *(the Didler)*

DERBY
Alexandra (01332) 293993
SK3635

Siddals Road; DE1 2QE Imposing
Victorian pub under enthusiastic couple,
two simple rooms, good heavy traditional
furnishings on bare boards or carpet,
breweriana and railway prints/memorabilia,
Castle Rock ales and quickly changing
guests, lots of continental bottled beers and
more on tap, snack food such as pork pies

and rolls; background music; children and dogs welcome, nicely planted backyard, four updated bedrooms, open all day. *(the Didler)*

DERBY   SK3535
Babington Arms *(01332) 383647*

Babington Lane; DE1 1TA Large well run open-plan Wetherspoons with up to 18 real ales, good welcoming service, usual well priced food, comfortable seating with steps up to relaxed back area; attractive verandah, open all day from 7am for breakfast. *(the Didler)*

DERBY   SK3635
★ Brunswick *(01332) 290677*

Railway Terrace; close to Derby Midland Station; DE1 2RU One of Britain's oldest railwaymen's pubs with fantastic range of 16 ales tapped from casks or on handpump (seven from own microbrewery), cheap traditional lunchtime food (not Sun), welcoming high-ceilinged panelled bar with whisky-water jugs, another room with little old-fashioned prints and high-backed wall settle by coal fire, chatty family parlour, wall displays showing history and restoration of building, interesting old train photographs, darts, jazz Thurs evening upstairs; TV, games machines, no credit cards; dogs welcome, two outdoor seating areas, open all day. *(the Didler, Ian and Helen Stafford, John Honnor)*

DERBY   SK3534
Falstaff *(01332) 342902*

Silver Hill Road, off Normanton Road; DE23 6UJ Basic unsmart local, aka the Folly, brewing its own good value ales, guest beers too, left-hand bar with games, coal fire in quieter lounge, some brewery memorabilia; open all day. *(the Didler)*

DERBY   SK3436
Mr Grundys Tavern *(01332) 349959*

Georgian House; Ashbourne Road; DE22 3AD Hotel bar serving own Mr Grundys ales (brewed here) and plenty of guests, two inviting dimly lit rooms, coal fires, panelling, old bench seating, superb collection of hats, a wall of classic film star pictures, lots of breweriana and an old red telephone box, decent food (not Sun evening); garden picnic-sets, 18 bedrooms, open all day. *(the Didler)*

DERBY   SK3536
Old Silk Mill *(01332) 369748*

Full Street; DE1 3AF Refurbished keeping traditional feel, cosy inside with two open fires, nine changing ales from main bar including a house beer from Blue Monkey,

second hop-adorned bar (open Thurs-Fri evenings, Sat, Sun lunchtime) with usually four cask-tapped beers, friendly service, regular live music; open all day. *(the Didler)*

DERBY   SK3536
Olde Dolphin *(01332) 267711*

Queen Street; DE1 3DL Quaint 16th-c timber-framed pub just below cathedral, four small dark unpretentious rooms including appealing snug, big bowed black beams, shiny panelling, opaque leaded windows, lantern lights and coal fires, half a dozen predominantly mainstream ales (good July beer festival), cheap simple food all day, upstairs steak bar (not always open); no under-14s inside; sizeable outside area for drinkers/smokers, open all day. *(the Didler)*

DERBY   SK3335
Rowditch *(01332) 343123*

Uttoxeter New Road (A516); DE22 3LL Popular character local with own microbrewery, well kept Marstons Pedigree and guests too, country wines, friendly landlord, attractive small snug on right, coal fire, pianist third Sat of month; no children or dogs; pleasant back garden, closed weekday lunchtimes. *(Malc Newton, the Didler)*

DERBY   SK3536
★ Smithfield *(01332) 370429*

Meadow Road; DE1 2BH Friendly bow-fronted local, well kept Bass, Durham, Oakham, Phoenix, Whim and guests, hearty bar lunches, back lounge with traditional settles, old prints, curios and breweriana, coal fires, daily papers; background music, good games room (children welcome here), quiz and band nights; riverside terrace with weekend barbecues, open all day. *(the Didler)*

DERBY   SK3436
★ Standing Order *(01332) 207591*

Irongate; DE1 3GL Spacious Wetherspoons in grand and lofty-domed former bank, main part with large island bar, booths down each side, handsome plasterwork, pseudo-classical torsos, high portraits of mainly local notables; good range of ales including some unusual ones, standard popular food all day, reasonable prices, newspapers; good disabled facilities. *(the Didler, Dave Braisted)*

DRONFIELD   SK3479
Coach & Horses *(01246) 413269*

Sheffield Road (B6057); S18 2GD Well managed comfortable pub next to Sheffield FC ground, up to five Thornbridge ales, home-made food, some live music; open all day, closed Mon lunchtime. *(the Didler)*

Please keep sending us reports. We rely on readers for news of new discoveries, and particularly for news of changes – however slight – at the fully described pubs: feedback@goodguides.com, or (no stamp needed) The Good Pub Guide, FREEPOST TN1569, Wadhurst, E Sussex TN5 7BR.

EARL STERNDALE   SK0966
★ Quiet Woman (01298) 83211
*Village signed off B5053 S of Buxton;
SK17 0BU* Old-fashioned unchanging
country local in lovely Peak District
countryside, simple beamed interior with
plain furniture on quarry tiles, china
ornaments and coal fire, well kept Marstons
Pedigree and guests, own-label bottled beers
(available in gift packs), good pork pies,
family room with pool, skittles and darts;
picnic-sets out in front along with budgies,
hens, turkeys, ducks and donkeys, you can buy
free-range eggs, local poetry books and even
hay, good hikes across nearby Dove Valley
towards Longnor and Hollinsclough, small
campsite next-door, caravan for hire. *(Ann
and Tony Bennett-Hughes, the Didler, Dennis Jones)*

EDALE   SK1285
Old Nags Head (01433) 670291
*Off A625 E of Chapel-en-le-Frith;
Grindsbrook Booth; S33 7ZD* Relaxed
well used traditional pub at start of Pennine
Way, good friendly staff coping well, generous
pubby food, good local ales, log fire, flagstoned
area for booted walkers, airy back family
room with board games; TV, can get very busy
weekends; front terrace and garden, open all
day, closed Mon and Tues lunchtimes out of
season. *(Ann and Colin Hunt)*

ELMTON   SK5073
Elm Tree (01909) 721261
Off B6417 S of Clowne; S80 4LS Softly
lit and popular country pub with good
unpretentious bar food all day including set
menu deal, children's menu, up to seven well
kept ales including Black Sheep, wide choice
of wines, quick friendly service, stripped
stone and panelling, back barn restaurant
(Fri and Sat evenings and for good Sun
lunch); children welcome, garden tables, play
area. *(Derek and Sylvia Stephenson, Rob and
Catherine Dunster)*

ELTON   SK2260
★ Duke of York (01629) 650367
*Village signed off B5056 W of Matlock;
Main Street; DE4 2BW* Unspoilt local kept
spotless by very long-serving amiable landlady,
bargain Adnams and Marstons, lovely little
quarry-tiled back tap room with coal fire in
massive fireplace, glazed bar and hatch to
flagstoned corridor, nice prints and more fires
in the two front rooms – one like a private
parlour with piano and big table, the other
with pool, darts, dominoes, friendly chatty
locals; outside lavatories; in charming village,
open 8.30pm-11pm and Sun lunchtime.
(the Didler)

FOOLOW   SK1976
★ Bulls Head (01433) 630873
*Village signposted off A623 Baslow–
Tideswell; S32 5QR* Friendly pub by green
in pretty upland village, simply furnished

flagstoned bar with interesting collection
of photographs including risqué Edwardian
ones, Adnams, Black Sheep, Peak and a
guest, over two dozen malts, good food with
more elaborate evening choices, step down
to former stables with high ceiling joists,
stripped stone and woodburner, sedate partly
panelled dining room with plates on delft
shelves; background music (live Fri evening),
quiz Thurs; children welcome and dogs
(resident westies are Holly and Jack), side
picnic-sets with nice views, paths from here
out over rolling pasture enclosed by dry-stone
walls, three bedrooms, closed Mon. *(Ann
and Tony Bennett-Hughes, Beth Woodhouse, Peter
F Marshall, Michael Butler, Ann and Colin Hunt,
Roger and Diana Morgan and others)*

FROGGATT EDGE   SK2476
★ Chequers (01433) 630231
A625, off A623 N of Bakewell; S32 3ZJ
Smart well run dining pub with good food (all
day weekends) including nice sandwiches,
solid country furnishings in civilised and
cosily attractive dining bar with woodburner,
antique prints and longcase clock, good
choice of wines by the glass, three well kept
changing ales, friendly staff; unobtrusive
background music; children welcome,
peaceful back garden with Froggatt Edge just
up through the woods behind, comfortable
clean bedrooms (quarry lorries use the road
from 6am weekdays), very good breakfast,
open all day weekends. *(Dennis Jones, W K
Wood, G Jennings)*

FROGGATT EDGE   SK2577
Grouse (01433) 630423
*Longshaw, off B6054 NE of Froggatt;
S11 7TZ* Nicely old-fashioned with proper
landlady, plush front bar, log fire and wooden
benches in back bar, big dining room,
enjoyable honest home-made food from nice
sandwiches to blackboard specials, well
kept Banks's, Caledonian Deuchars IPA,
Greene King Abbot and Marstons Pedigree,
friendly prompt service, handsome views;
dogs welcome, verandah and terrace,
good moorland walking country, open all
day. *(Robert Dudgeon, Geoff Schrecker)*

GLOSSOP   SK0294
Globe (01457) 852417
High Street W; SK13 8HJ Own microbrews
including a good rich porter, local guest ales,
bottled beers and farm cider, bargain food
including good vegetarian dishes, friendly
licensees, comfortable relaxed atmosphere,
old fittings and photographs, Sat live music
upstairs (busy then), Mon folk music,
occasional beer festivals; walled back garden,
closed lunchtime and Tues, open till early
hours and all day Sun. *(the Didler)*

GLOSSOP   SK0394
Star (01457) 853072
Howard Street; SK13 7DD Unpretentious
alehouse opposite station with Black Sheep

and six well priced changing ales, farm cider, friendly helpful staff, no food (you can bring your own), interesting layout including flagstoned tap room with hatch service, old local photographs; background music; bedrooms, open all day from 2pm (4pm Mon and Tues, noon Sun). *(the Didler)*

HARDWICK HALL   SK4663
Hardwick Inn   (01246) 850245
Quite handy for M1, junction 29; Doe Lea; S44 5QJ Golden stone building dating from the 15th c at the south gate of Hardwick Park, several busy linked rooms including proper bar, open fires, fine range of some 220 malt whiskies and plenty of wines by the glass, well kept Black Sheep, Theakstons, Wells & Youngs and an ale brewed for the pub by Brampton, popular well priced bar food served all day, carvery restaurant, long-serving landlord and efficient friendly staff; unobtrusive background music; children allowed, pleasant back garden, more tables out in front, open all day. *(Terry Davis, Derek and Sylvia Stephenson)*

HARTINGTON   SK1260
Charles Cotton   (01298) 84229
Market Place; SK17 0AL Popular four-square stone-built hotel in attractive village centre, large comfortable carpeted bar with open fire, simple dining room off, tearoom too, good straightforward generous home-made food all day, five ales including local Whim, bottled beers and real cider, good wines, cafetière coffee, friendly helpful service; nostalgic background music; dogs welcome in bar, bedrooms, open all day. *(Dennis Jones)*

HARTINGTON   SK1260
Devonshire Arms   (01298) 84232
Market Place; SK17 0AL Traditional unpretentious two-bar pub in attractive village, welcoming landlord, ales including Marstons Pedigree, generous home-made food, log fires; may be background music; children and dogs welcome, tables out in front facing duck pond, more in small garden, good walks, open all day weekends (food all day then too). *(Alan Johnson, Dennis Jones)*

HATHERSAGE   SK2381
★ ## Scotsmans Pack   (01433) 650253
School Lane, off A6187; S32 1BZ Cosy relaxed inn equally popular with drinkers and diners; area on left with fireplace, lots of brasses and stuffed animal heads, elsewhere plenty of dark panelling, hanging tankards, plates on delft shelving and other knick-knacks, Jennings, Marstons and guests under light blanket pressure, well liked food (all day Fri-Sun in summer) from pubby standards to more elaborate blackboard specials, pleasant staff, board games and darts; background music, games machine, TV; children welcome, pleasant terrace by trout stream, bedrooms, open all day

(closed weekday lunchtimes in winter). *(Ann and Colin Hunt, Peter F Marshall, Alan Bowker and others)*

HAYFIELD   SK0387
★ ## Royal   (01663) 742721
Market Street; SK22 2EP 18th-c stone-built hotel in former vicarage, separate pubby areas with open fires, well kept Hydes and six interesting guests (beer festival first weekend Oct), straightforward homely food including weekday deals, good friendly service, dark oak panelling, brasses, house plants, daily papers; background music; children and dogs welcome, seats on sunny front terrace, spotless bedrooms, good breakfast, open all day. *(the Didler)*

HAYFIELD   SK0486
★ ## Sportsman   (01663) 741565
Off A624 Chapel-en-le-Frith–Buxton; Kinder Road, up past the Royal, off Market Street; SK22 2LE Wide choice of enjoyable good value food in roomy and neatly kept traditional inn, good friendly staff, well kept Thwaites, decent wines, lots of malt whiskies, two coal fires; children and dogs welcome, lovely location (handy for Kinder Scout walks), bedrooms. *(Mike Proctor, Tonker, Jim Collins)*

HEAGE   SK3750
Black Boy   (01773) 856799
Old Road (B6013); DE56 2BN Smart village pub/restaurant with welcoming licensees, popular food in bar and upstairs dining area including speciality fish, a house beer brewed by Marstons and well kept regularly changing guests, open fire; no dogs; small outside seating area, children welcome, open all day. *(Michael Mellers)*

HEANOR   SK4445
Queens Head   (01773) 768015
Breach Road, Marlpool; DE75 7NJ Five-room Victorian alehouse with traditional clean interior, tiled floors, cast-iron tables, padded stools around old barrel tables, two open fires and woodburner, up to 20 well kept beers including Castle Rock, Oakham and Thornbridge (many served from cellar where customers welcome), 28 ciders, half a dozen perries, good range of wines and spirits too, some snacky food (can bring your own), daily papers; children and dogs welcome, back terrace with open-fronted log-fire room, beer garden, open all day. *(the Didler)*

HEATH   SK4467
Elm Tree   (01246) 850490
Just off M1 junction 29; A6175 towards Clay Cross, then first right; S44 5SE Popular roadside pub with half-panelled lounge/dining areas, good well priced blackboard food (all day weekends) including generous Sun carvery, three well kept Jennings ales and a guest, wide choice of wines, good helpful service,

mix of traditional wooden furniture and leather armchairs on wood and stone floors, woodburner in stone fireplace, darts in smallish bar; soft background music; children and dogs welcome, some picnic-sets out at front, attractive garden with play area and lovely views to Bolsover and beyond (but traffic noise). *(Robert Thornberry, Krish Kumar, C A Hall)*

HOGNASTON   SK2350
★ Red Lion (01335) 370396
Off B5035 Ashbourne–Wirksworth; DE6 1PR Traditional 17th-c inn with open-plan beamed bar, three fires, attractive mix of old tables, curved settles and other seats on ancient flagstones, friendly licensees, good well presented home-made food from shortish menu in bar and conservatory restaurant, nice wines by the glass, Marstons Pedigree and guests; background music; picnic-sets in field behind, boules, handy for Carsington Water, three good bedrooms, big breakfast. *(Trevor and Sylvia Millum, John Beeken, Derek and Sylvia Stephenson)*

HOLBROOK   SK3645
★ Dead Poets (01332) 780301
Chapel Street; village signed off A6 S of Belper; DE56 0TQ Reassuringly pubby and unchanging drinkers' local with nine real ales (some served from jugs), farm cider, country wines, filled cobs and good value weekday bar food, simple cottagey décor with beams, stripped-stone walls and broad flagstones, high-backed settles forming booths, big log fire, plenty of tucked-away corners, woodburner in snug, children allowed in back conservatory till 8pm; background music, no credit cards; dogs welcome, seats in heated verandah room, more in yard, open all day Fri-Sun. *(the Didler)*

HOLYMOORSIDE   SK3369
Lamb (01246) 566167
Loads Road, just off Holymoor Road; S42 7EU Small spotless village pub with half a dozen particularly well kept ales such as Black Sheep, Daleside Blonde, Fullers London Pride, Timothy Taylors Landlord and Theakstons, charming comfortable lounge, coal fire in cosy bar, friendly locals, pub games; tables outside, leafy spot, closed weekday lunchtimes. *(the Didler)*

HORSLEY WOODHOUSE   SK3944
Old Oak (01332) 881299
Main Street (A609 Belper–Ilkeston); DE7 6AW Busy roadside local linked to nearby Bottle Brook and Leadmill microbreweries, their ales and weekend back bar with another half-dozen well priced guests tapped from the cask, farm ciders,

good basic snacks, beamed rooms with blazing coal fires, chatty friendly atmosphere, occasional live music; children and dogs welcome, hatch to covered courtyard tables, nice views, closed weekday lunchtimes, open all day weekends. *(the Didler)*

HURDLOW   SK1265
Royal Oak (01298) 83288
Monyash–Longnor Road, just off A515 S of Buxton; SK17 9QJ Relaxed country atmosphere in old beamed pub, wide choice of nicely presented local food (all day) at fair prices, friendly helpful service, Marstons Pedigree, Whim Hartington and guests, good wine choice, small bar, split-level lounge/dining room and steps up to another dining area, coal fires; children and dogs welcome, on Tissington Trail, overnight stabling, self-catering barn with bunk bedrooms, campsite. *(Beth Garrard, Ivan Neary, Brian and Jacky Wilson)*

ILKESTON   SK4742
Dewdrop (0115) 932 9684
Station Street, Ilkeston Junction, off A6096; DE7 5TE Large Victorian corner local in old industrial area, not strong on bar comfort but popular for its half-dozen good ales including Castle Rock, Nottingham and Oakham, simple bar snacks, back lounge with fire and piano, connecting lobby to front public bar with pool, darts and TV, some Barnes Wallis memorabilia; sheltered outside seating at back, bedrooms, walks by former Nottingham Canal, open all day. *(Yvonne and Rob Warhurst, the Didler)*

ILKESTON   SK4742
Good Old Days (0115) 8751103
Station Road; DE7 5LJ Welcoming half-timbered one-room pub with downstairs family room, good choice of well kept interesting ales, simple food, darts, dominoes and pool; background music, TV; dogs welcome, tables in canalside garden, own moorings, open all day Fri-Sun, from 5pm other days. *(Dave Wildey, the Didler)*

ILKESTON   SK4641
Spanish Bar (0115) 9308666
South Street; DE7 5QJ Busy café-bar with well kept and well priced changing ales, bottled belgians, friendly efficient staff, evening overspill room with woodburner, Tues quiz night, popular Sun lunchtime card games with free nibbles; small garden, skittle alley, open all day. *(the Didler)*

LADYBOWER RESERVOIR   SK2084
★ Yorkshire Bridge (01433) 651361
A6013 N of Bamford; S33 0AZ Pleasant hotel in useful stopping point in dramatic

---

If you report on a pub that's not a featured entry, please tell us any lunchtimes or evenings when it doesn't serve bar food.

Upper Derwent Valley; one plush area with patterned carpets, floral wallpaper and staffordshire dogs and toby jugs above big stone fireplace, another extensive lighter area with second fire, good big black and white photographs and lots of polished brass and decorative plates, bridge room (yet another fire) and garden room with valley views, five well kept mainly local ales, good range of food (all day Sun) including vegetarian and children's choices, friendly staff; background music; disabled facilities, spotless bedrooms, open all day. *(Mike Proctor, Hilary Forrest, Simon Pyle, Barry Collett)*

LITTLE LONGSTONE   SK1971
Packhorse   (01629) 640471
Off A6 NW of Bakewell via Monsal Dale; DE45 1NN Three comfortable linked beamed rooms, pine tables on flagstones, well kept Thornbridge and usually Theakstons Bitter, good choice of wines by the glass, popular good value substantial food (Sat breakfast from 8.30am), coal fires; hikers welcome (on Monsal Trail), terrace in steep little back garden. *(Peter Waller)*

LITTON   SK1675
Red Lion   (01298) 871458
Village signposted off A623, between B6465 and B6049 junctions; also signposted off B6049; SK17 8QU Convivial all-rounder with cheerful landlady, two homely linked front rooms with low beams, panelling and log fires, bigger stripped-stone back room, Abbeydale, Oakwell and guests kept well, decent wines and malt whiskies, enjoyable fairly priced food, good service, darts, shove-ha'penny and bagatelle; evening background music, can get very busy; children over 6 welcome, dogs in bar, outdoor seating on village green, well-dressing carnival (usually last week in June) when locals create a picture from petals, moss and other natural materials, open all day (midnight Fri, Sat). *(Ann and Tony Bennett-Hughes, Peter F Marshall, Mike Proctor, Gene and Kitty Rankin, the Didler and others)*

LULLINGTON   SK2513
⋆ Colvile Arms   (01827) 373212
Off A444 S of Burton; Main Street; DE12 8EG Popular neatly preserved 18th-c village pub with high-backed settles in simple panelled bar, cosy comfortable beamed lounge, pleasant atmosphere and friendly staff, four well kept ales including Bass, Marstons Pedigree and a mild, enjoyable good value food; may be background music; picnic-sets on small sheltered back lawn overlooking bowling green, closed weekday lunchtimes. *(the Didler)*

MAKENEY   SK3544
⋆ Holly Bush   (01332) 841729
From A6 heading N after Duffield, take first right after crossing River Derwent, then first left; DE56 0RX Down-to-earth two-bar village pub (former farmhouse) with three blazing coal fires (one in old-fashioned range by snug's curved high-backed settle), flagstones, beams, black panelling and tiled floors, lots of brewing advertisements, half a dozen or so well kept changing ales (some brought from cellar in jugs), real cider, cheap food including rolls and pork pies, may be local cheeses for sale, games lobby with hatch service (children allowed here), regular beer festivals; picnic-sets outside, dogs welcome, open all day Fri-Sun. *(the Didler)*

MARSTON MONTGOMERY   SK1338
Crown   (01889) 591430
On corner of Thurvaston Road and Barway; DE6 2FF Welcoming beamed pub with friendly landlord and staff, at least three changing ales, good food from sandwiches to steaks, leather sofas and armchairs on tiled floor, woodburner in brick fireplace, restaurant; terrace tables, nice village, seven comfortable bedrooms, open all day weekends. *(Mrs C D Westwood, Derek King)*

MATLOCK   SK2960
Thorn Tree   (01629) 582923
Jackson Road, Matlock Bank; DE4 3JQ Superb valley views to Riber Castle from this homely 19th-c stone-built local, good choice of well kept beers, simple well cooked food including their locally renowned pies, friendly staff and regulars. *(Paul, Ian and Helen Stafford)*

MILFORD   SK3545
William IV   (01332) 840842
Milford Bridge; DE56 0RR Friendly and relaxing stone-built riverside pub, long room with low beams, bare boards, quarry tiles, old settles and a blazing coal fire, well kept Bass, Marstons Pedigree, Timothy Taylors Landlord and guests, simple food; bedrooms, closed lunchtime weekdays, open all day weekends. *(the Didler)*

MILLERS DALE   SK1473
⋆ Anglers Rest   (01298) 871323
Just down Litton Lane; pub is PH on OS Sheet 119, map reference 142734; SK17 8SN Spotless ivy-clad pub in lovely quiet riverside setting on Monsal Trail, two bars and dining room, log fires, good simple home-made food (Thurs pie night), well kept changing ales, cheery helpful service, reasonable prices, darts, pool and muddy walkers in public bar; children welcome, wonderful gorge views and river walks. *(Terry Davis, Dennis Jones, Peter F Marshall, Derek and Sylvia Stephenson, John Griffiths)*

MONSAL HEAD   SK1871
Monsal Head Hotel   (01629) 640250
B6465; DE45 1NL Popular inn in outstanding hilltop location, cosy stables bar with stripped timber horse-stalls, harness and brassware, cushioned oak

pews on flagstones, big open fire, ales such as Bradfield, Buxton and Wincle, german bottled beers, several wines by the glass, locally sourced food from lunchtime sandwiches up (they may ask to keep your credit card while you eat); children (over 3), well behaved dogs and muddy walkers welcome, big garden, stunning views of Monsal Dale with its huge viaduct, seven bedrooms, open all day till midnight. *(Mike Proctor, Ann and Colin Hunt, Andy and Jill Kassube, Mr and Mrs D J Nash, Dennis Jones)*

NEW MILLS
SJ9886

Fox (0161) 427 1634

Brookbottom; OS Sheet 109 map reference 985864; SK22 3AY Tucked-away unmodernised country local at end of single-track road, a nice summer family outing, friendly long-serving landlord, particularly well kept Robinsons, good value basic food (not Tues evening) including good sandwiches, log fire, darts and pool; lots of tables outside, good walking area, open all day Fri-Sun. *(Ann and Tony Bennett-Hughes, the Didler, David Hoult)*

OAKERTHORPE
SK3856

Amber (01773) 831152

Furnace; DE55 7LL Charming old-fashioned village local with friendly landlady, straightforward food, well kept Abbeydale, Fullers London Pride, Timothy Taylors Landlord and guests, blazing winter fires, lots of antiques including piano, well worn seating; good views from the back terrace, walks. *(the Didler)*

OCKBROOK
SK4236

Royal Oak (01332) 662378

Off B6096 just outside Spondon; Green Lane; DE72 3SE Quiet 18th-c village local run by same friendly family for half a century, bargain honest food (not Sat or Sun evenings) from good lunchtime cobs to steaks, Sun lunch and OAP meals, well kept Bass and interesting guest beers, good soft drinks' choice, tile-floor tap room, carpeted snug, inner bar with Victorian prints, larger and lighter side room, nice old settle in entrance corridor, open fires, darts and dominoes; children welcome, sheltered cottage garden and cobbled front courtyard, separate play area. *(the Didler, MP)*

PARWICH
SK1854

⋆**Sycamore** (01335) 390212

By church; DE6 1QL Chatty old country pub well run by cheerful welcoming young landlady, generous wholesome food lunchtimes and most Weds-Sat evenings, Robinsons ales, good log fire in neat traditional back bar, pool in small front hatch-served games room, another room serving as proper village shop; tables in front courtyard, picnic-sets on neat side grass, good walks. *(Brian and Anna Marsden)*

PENTRICH
SK3852

⋆**Dog** (01773) 513360

Main Road (B6016 N of Ripley); DE5 3RE Extended pub popular for its enjoyable all-day food, well kept ales from carved church-look counter, nice wines by the glass, woodburner, pubby bar furniture, smarter modern dining area beyond part with leather sofas etc; background music; well behaved children allowed if eating, extensive garden behind, nice views, good walks. *(the Didler)*

REPTON
SK3026

Bulls Head (01283) 704422

High Street; DE65 6GF Well reworked beamed pub with interesting mix of old and new furniture on bare boards or flagstones, woodburners, good food including wood-fired pizzas, four well kept usually local, ales, good choice of wines and decent coffee, upstairs restaurant; children welcome till 9pm, dogs away from dining areas, garden with sizeable terrace, attractive village, open all day. *(Stephen Shepherd)*

RIPLEY
SK3950

Talbot Taphouse (01773) 742626

Butterley Hill; DE5 3LT Full range of local Amber ales and changing guests kept well by knowledgeable landlord, farm ciders and bottled beers too, long narrow panelled room with new bar counter, comfy chairs, brick fireplace; friendly staff; open all day weekends, from 5pm other days. *(the Didler)*

ROWARTH
SK0189

Little Mill (01663) 743178

Signed well locally; off A626 in Marple Bridge at Mellor sign, sharp left at Rowarth sign; SK22 1EB Beautifully tucked-away 18th-c pub with welcoming landlord, well kept Banks's, Marstons and guests, good value generous food all-day (till 7pm Sun) including weekend carvery, roomy open-plan bar and upstairs restaurant, big log fire, unusual features like working waterwheel and vintage Pullman-carriage bedrooms; background music (live Fri evenings); children and dogs welcome, disabled access, verandah with terrace below, pretty garden dell across stream, good play area, open all day. *(John Fiander, Dennis Jones, Brian and Anna Marsden)*

ROWSLEY
SK2565

Grouse & Claret (01629) 733233

A6 Bakewell–Matlock; DE4 2EB Attractive family dining pub in old stone building, spacious, clean and comfortable, with welcoming licensees and friendly staff, enjoyable low-priced food (all day weekends) from sandwiches up, well kept Jennings Cumberland and Marstons Pedigree, decent wines, open fires, tap room popular with walkers; tables outside, play area, good value bedrooms, campsite, open all day. *(Derek and*

Sylvia Stephenson, David Carr, Ann and Colin Hunt, Mr and Mrs D Hammond)

ROWSLEY SK2565
⋆ **Peacock** (01629) 733518
Bakewell Road; DE4 2EB Civilised small 17th-c country hotel with comfortable chairs and sofas and a few antiques in spacious uncluttered lounge, interesting stone-floored inner bar, restful colours, enjoyable if not cheap food from lunchtime sandwiches to restaurant meals, Greene King IPA and a local guest, good wines, beautifully served coffee; attractive riverside gardens, trout fishing, good bedrooms. *(George Atkinson)*

SHARDLOW SK4430
⋆ **Malt Shovel** (01332) 799763
3.5 miles from M1 junction 24, via A6 towards Derby; The Wharf; DE72 2HG Busy old-world beamed pub in 18th-c former maltings, interesting odd-angled layout with cosy corners, Marstons-related ales, bargain home-made food (not Sat evening) from baguettes up, quick friendly service, good central open fire, black panelling, farm tools and bric-a-brac; lots of terrace tables by Trent & Mersey Canal, pretty hanging baskets. *(the Didler, Alistair Forsyth)*

SHARDLOW SK4429
Old Crown (01332) 792392
Off A50 just W of M1 junction 24; Cavendish Bridge, E of village; DE72 2HL Good value pub with great range of Marstons-related ales and guests all kept well, nice choice of malt whiskies, pubby food (not Fri or Sun evenings) from sandwiches and baguettes up, beams with masses of jugs and mugs, walls covered with other bric-a-brac and breweriana, big inglenook; children and dogs welcome, simple bedrooms, good breakfast, open all day. *(the Didler)*

SHELDON SK1768
⋆ **Cock & Pullet** (01629) 814292
Village signed off A6 just W of Ashford; DE45 1QS Charming no-frills village pub with friendly courteous licensees and plenty of locals; low beams, exposed stonework, flagstones and open fire, cheerfully mismatching furnishings, 30 clocks, various representations of poultry (some stuffed), well kept Hartington, Timothy Taylors and a guest, good inexpensive traditional food from shortish menu, pool and TV in plainer public bar; quiet background music, no credit cards; children and dogs welcome, seats and water feature on pleasant back terrace, pretty village just off Limestone Way and popular all year with walkers, clean bedrooms, open all day. *(Peter F Marshall, Jean and Douglas Troup, Roy and Lindsey Fentiman, Sara Fulton, Roger Baker and others)*

SHIRLEY SK2141
Saracens Head (01335) 360330
Church Lane; DE6 3AS Nicely modernised late 18th-c dining pub in attractive village; good range of interesting well presented food from pubby things to more expensive restaurant dishes, four Greene King ales, speciality coffees, simple country-style dining furniture, two pretty little working art nouveau fireplaces; background music; children welcome, dogs in bar area, picnic-sets under parasols on front and back terraces, self-catering cottage, open all day Sun. *(Anon)*

SMISBY SK3419
Smisby Arms (01530) 412677
Nelsons Square; LE65 2UA Ancient low-beamed village local with popular range of good reasonably priced food, friendly efficient service, well kept Marstons Pedigree and a changing guest, decent coffee, bright little dining extension down steps; no dogs; children welcome, a few tables out in front. *(Roger and Anne Newbury, Brian and Jacky Wilson)*

SOUTH WINGFIELD SK3755
Old Yew Tree (01773) 833763
B5035 W of Alfreton; Manor Road; DE55 7NH Atmospheric village pub, friendly and well run, with good choice of changing ales and modestly priced home-made food (all day weekends), good value wines, log fire, panelling, kettles and pans hanging from beams, separate restaurant area, folk night (first Weds of month), Sun quiz; children welcome, closed Mon lunchtime. *(John and Susan Miln, A J Liles)*

SPONDON SK3935
⋆ **Malt Shovel** (01332) 674203
Off A6096 on edge of Derby, via Church Hill into Potter Street; DE21 7LH Homely traditional pub with several well kept mainly Marstons-related ales in tiny bar or from hatch in tiled corridor, various other little rooms, old-fashioned décor and a huge inglenook, decent inexpensive bar lunches, friendly helpful staff, steps down to big games bar with darts and pool; lots of picnic-sets, some under cover, in large back garden with good play area, open all day Fri-Sun. *(the Didler)*

STRETTON EN LE FIELD SK2913
Cricketts (01283) 760359
Burton Road; DE12 8AP Stylishly modernised 19th-c pub with enjoyable good value food including some interesting specials, Sun carvery, good friendly service; children welcome, garden with play area, open all day. *(Deryn Mitchell, Elizabeth Devey Smith)*

SUTTON CUM DUCKMANTON SK4371
Arkwright Arms (01246) 232053
A632 Bolsover–Chesterfield; S44 5JG Friendly mock-Tudor pub with bar, pool room (dogs allowed here) and dining room, all with

real fires, good choice of well priced food all day (not Sun evening), up 16 changing ales including Low Raw, ten real ciders and four perries (beer/cider festivals Easter/Aug bank holidays); TV, games machine; no children in bar, picnic-sets out at front, new side terrace, attractive hanging baskets, garden play equipment. *(JJW, CMW, Ian Prince, Ian Stanway)*

TICKNALL SK3523
⋆**Wheel** (01332) 864488

Main Street (A514); DE73 7JZ Stylish contemporary décor in bar and restaurant, enjoyable interesting home-made food (all day weekends), friendly staff, well kept Marstons Pedigree and a guest; children welcome, nice outside area with café tables on raised deck, near entrance to Calke Abbey. *(Anon)*

TINTWISTLE SK0297
Bulls Head (01457) 853365

Old Road (off A628, N side); SK13 1JY Low-beamed Tudor pub tucked away in pretty stone-built village, good home-made food served by friendly staff, well kept ales such as Howard Town and Timothy Taylors, big log fire, plenty of character and furnishings to suit its age; children, dogs and walking groups welcome, handy for Woodhead Pass. *(Anon)*

WARDLOW SK1875
⋆**Three Stags Heads** (01298) 872268

Wardlow Mires; A623/B6465; SK17 8RW Basic farm pub of great individuality, flagstoned floors (often muddied by boots and dogs in winter), old country furniture, heating from cast-iron kitchen ranges, old photographs, plain-talking landlord and locals in favourite corners, well kept Abbeydale ales including Black Lurcher (brewed for the pub at a hefty 8% ABV), lots of bottled beers, hearty seasonal food on hardy home-made plates (licensees are potters), may be free roast chestnuts, perhaps folk music; no credit cards; children and dogs welcome, hill views from front terrace, closed lunchtimes, open all day weekends. *(Ann and Tony Bennett-Hughes, Mike Proctor, Dennis Jones, the Didler)*

WHITTINGTON MOOR SK3873
⋆**Derby Tup** (01246) 454316

Sheffield Road; B6057 just S of A61 roundabout; S41 8LS Spotless no-frills Castle Rock local with up to a dozen well kept interesting ales from long line of gleaming handpumps, farm cider and irish whiskeys too, pleasant service, simple furniture, coal fire and lots of standing room as well as two small side rooms (children allowed here), daily papers, good value basic

bar lunches (not Mon); can get very busy weekend evenings; dogs welcome, open all day at least Fri-Sun. *(the Didler, Jeremy King, Peter F Marshall)*

WINSTER SK2460
⋆**Bowling Green** (01629) 650219

East Bank, by NT Market House; DE4 2DS Traditional old stone pub with good chatty atmosphere, character landlord and welcoming staff, enjoyable reasonably priced food, at least three well kept changing local ales, good selection of whiskies, end log fire, dining area and family conservatory, quiz nights and singalongs; nice village, good walks, closed Mon, Tues and lunchtimes Weds to Fri, open all day Sun. *(Trevor and Sylvia Millum, Reg Fowle, Helen Rickwood)*

WINSTER SK2360
Miners Standard (01629) 650279

Bank Top (B5056 above village); DE4 2DR Simply furnished 17th-c stone local, relaxed at lunchtime, livelier in the evening, well kept ales such as Black Sheep, Flowers IPA and Marstons Pedigree, good value generous pubby food including huge pies, big woodburner, lead-mining photographs and minerals, lots of brass, backwards clock, ancient well, snug and restaurant; background music; children allowed away from bar, attractive view from garden, campsite next door, interesting stone-built village below, open all day weekends. *(Trevor and Sylvia Millum, Reg Fowle, Helen Rickwood, David Heath, Dennis Jones)*

YEAVELEY SK1840
Yeaveley Arms (01335) 330771

On byroad S of Ashbourne; DE6 2DT Comfortable modern open-plan interior with bar, lounge and big airy restaurant, enjoyable food from pub favourites up, friendly efficient service, Marstons Pedigree and three guests; no dogs inside; children welcome, seats out at front and on back terrace with smokers' shelter, closed Sun evenings, Mon. *(Peter Watts)*

YOULGREAVE SK2164
George (01629) 636292

Alport Lane/Church Street; DE45 1WN Handsome 17th-c stone-built inn opposite Norman church, comfortably worn inside, with banquettes running around three sides of main bar, flagstoned tap room (walkers and dogs welcome) and games room, huge helpings of reasonably priced home-made food (all day), John Smiths, Theakstons Mild and a local guest, friendly service; roadside tables, attractive village handy for Lathkill Dale and Haddon Hall, simple bedrooms. *(David and Gill Carrington, Dennis Jones, Ann and Colin Hunt)*

Devon

In one of the country's most popular counties, we've managed to find quite a range of pubs that are new to us this year: the Watermans Arms at Ashprington (rambling rooms and attractive creekside spot), Harbour Inn in Axmouth (thatched and waterside with lots of shipping memorabilia), Lazy Toad at Brampford Speke (a little gem), Anchor at Cockwood (28 recipes for mussels and lots of nautical knick-knacks), Wheelwright in Colyford (sister pub to Harbour Inn at Axmouth and usefully open all day), Culm Valley at Culmstock (gently eccentric but with fantastic food and wines), Fortescue Arms in East Allington (newish licensees and more informal than it was), Turf Hotel near Exminster (lovely remote spot, delightful in summer), Globe in Frogmore (much extended and neatly refurbished), Duke of York in Iddesleigh (unspoilt and friendly with chatty locals), Cleave in Lustleigh (a pretty thatched pub with fairly priced food), Church House in Marldon (welcoming landlord, impressive food and plenty of dining space), London at Molland (a proper Exmoor local), Bell in Parkham (the heart of the community), Lamb in Sandford (super bedrooms, lovely food, plenty of character), Tower in Slapton (inventive food, courteous owners), Cary Arms near Torquay (interesting bar in secluded hotel), Old Church House in Torbryan (13th c and a warm welcome for all), and Kings Arms at Winkleigh (happily unchanging and always hospitable). Our readers also enjoy the Fountain Head in Branscombe (super own-brewed beers), Drake Manor in Buckland Monachorum (welcoming long-standing landlady), Merry Harriers at Clayhidon (so well run, many favourable reports), New Inn at Coleford (a very good all-rounder), Royal Castle Hotel in Dartmouth (two thriving bars in smart hotel), Rock at Haytor Vale (most informal at lunchtime, particularly after a walk, and smashing to stay at), and Rugglestone near Widecombe (delightfully unspoilt and tucked away despite being just up the road from the famous tourist village). For its inventive cooking and charming surroundings, our Devon Dining Pub for 2013 is the Church House, Marldon.

ASHPRINGTON   SX8056   Map 1

Watermans Arms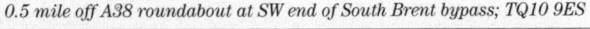

Bow Bridge, on Tuckenhay Road; TQ9 7EG

Bustling pub with plenty of riverside seats, several rambling rooms, lots to look at, friendly staff, real ales, cider, several wines by the glass and enjoyable food; bedrooms

In a quiet spot at the head of Bow Creek, this bustling old pub is just the place to be in fine weather. As well as seats (and a small children's play area) in the garden, there are lots of picnic-sets across the lane beside the stream, where you can watch the ducks (and even swans and kingfishers). Inside, the quarry-tiled main bar area has heavy beams and standing pillars creating a stable-like effect, built-in green-painted and cushioned wall seats and wheelback chairs around stripped wooden tables, a woodburning stove, and stone bottles and copper implements – including a large alembic. A dining room has fishing rods on beams, stuffed fish and lanterns, and steps from here lead down to a comfortable area with leather chesterfields and tub chairs; there's a front bar with a log fire, oars on beams and old sailing blocks. Sizeable mirrors here and there give the feeling of even more space. Palmers Best and Copper on handpump, a farm cider and several wines by the glass served by the charming landlord and his friendly staff; darts, board games, TV and maybe Radio 2. The bedrooms are comfortable.

Using local, free-range and organic produce, the tasty food includes sandwiches, chicken liver pâté with cumberland sauce, baked camembert with an apricot glaze, garlic crust pizzas, omelettes, beer-battered fish, extremely popular meaty or vegetarian burgers, steak in ale pie, red mullet on noodles with oriental vegetables, a huge mixed grill, and puddings such as apple and pear crumble (using home-grown fruit) and treacle sponge; they also offer breakfasts for non-residents, morning coffee and afternoon tea. *Benchmark main dish: organic cheese burger £12.00. Two-course evening meal £19.50.*

Jersey ~ Tenants Rob and Jane Crawford ~ Real ale ~ Bar food (12-2.30(3 Sat and Sun), 6(6.30 in winter)-9) ~ Restaurant ~ (01803) 732214 ~ Children welcome ~ Dogs welcome ~ Open 9-11; 11-11 in winter; closed first three weeks Jan ~ Bedrooms: /£70B ~ www.thewatermansarms.net *Recommended by Roger and Donna Huggins, Rob Oliver, Dave Moorleigh, Richard Marks, David Jackman*

AVONWICK   SX6958   Map 1

Turtley Corn Mill ♀ ⇨

0.5 mile off A38 roundabout at SW end of South Brent bypass; TQ10 9ES

Careful conversion of tall mill house with interestingly furnished areas, local beers, modern bar food and huge garden; bedrooms

The spreading series of linked areas in this carefully converted watermill are decorated with some individuality. There are bookcases, fat church candles and oriental rugs in one area, dark flagstones by the bar, a strategically placed woodburning stove dividing off one area, a side enclave with a modern pew built in around a really big table. Lighting is good, with plenty of big windows looking out over the grounds, and there's a pleasant array of prints, a history of the mill and framed 78rpm discs on pastel-painted walls, elderly wireless sets and house plants dotted about and a mix of comfortable dining chairs around heavy baluster-leg tables. Dartmoor Legend, St Austell Tribute, Sharps Doom Bar and Summerskills Tamar on handpump, nine wines

by the glass and around 30 malt whiskies. The extensive garden has plenty of well spaced picnic-sets, a giant chess set and a small lake with interesting ducks. This is under the same ownership as the Finnygook at Crafthole (in Cornwall). The bedrooms are comfortable and the breakfasts good.

Modern bar food includes sandwiches, eggs benedict, chicken liver pâté with red onion marmalade, steak burger topped with gruyère and bacon, beer-battered haddock, homity pie (potato, onion, leek and cheese), moules frites, pork cutlet with bubble and squeak and cider gravy, pheasant wrapped in bacon with dauphinoise potatoes, and puddings like blueberry sponge pudding with vanilla ice-cream and chocolate mousse with a tuile biscuit; they also offer a two- and three-course set lunch (not Sunday). *Benchmark main dish: slow-cooked pork belly £11.95. Two-course evening meal £16.75.*

Free house ~ Licensees Lesley and Bruce Brunning ~ Real ale ~ Bar food (12-9.30) ~ (01364) 646100 ~ Children welcome ~ Dogs allowed in bar ~ Open 11-11; 12-10.30 Sun ~ Bedrooms: /£89S ~ www.turtleycornmill.com *Recommended by Bruce and Sharon Eden, Ian Malone, P and M Spencer, Helen and Brian Edgeley, Lynda and Trevor Smith, John Evans*

AXMOUTH
SY2591   Map 1

Harbour Inn

B3172 Seaton–Axminster; EX12 4AF

Family-run thatched pub by the Axe estuary with heavily beamed bars, plenty of boating memorabilia, real ales and well liked food

Overlooking the Axe estuary, this thatched pub is family-run and friendly with a bustling atmosphere and plenty of happy customers. There's an entrance hall with seats on huge flagstones that leads into two heavily beamed connected bar rooms with a lot of character: brass-bound cask seats, a high-backed oak settle and one or two smaller ones, leather-topped bar stools and all manner of tables on bare floorboards, fat pots hanging from pot-irons in the huge inglenook fireplace, glass balls in nets, a large turtle shell and lots of model boats and accounts of shipwrecks. There are also two dining rooms with more heavy beams, a little snug alcove leading off, built-in blue cushioned wall-, window- and other seats, and more model yachts, ships in bottles, pulleys and blocks; they hope to instal a big scale model of HMS *Victory* in a large cabinet. Badger Best, First Gold, Pickled Partridge and Tanglefoot on handpump and several wines by the glass; pool, skittle alley. There are contemporary-style seats and tables on the front terrace and plenty of picnic-sets on grass. The handsome church opposite has some fine stone gargoyles. This is sister pub to the Wheelwright in Colyford.

Popular, honest food includes breakfasts (from 9am), sandwiches, salt and pepper calamari with home-made tartare sauce, ham hock terrine with home-made piccalilli, beef burger with cheese and skinny fries, goats cheese and red onion marmalade tart, ham and eggs, steak in ale pie, beer-battered fish with mushy peas, lambs liver and bacon with red onion gravy, fish pie, daily specials, and puddings such as apple and blackberry oat crunch crumble and banana eton mess with butterscotch sauce, meringue and honeycomb ice-cream. *Benchmark main dish: hogs board (using pork from the farm just up the road) £12.00. Two-course evening meal £17.50.*

Badger ~ Lease Gary and Toni Valentine ~ Real ale ~ Bar food (9-9.30) ~ Restaurant ~ (01297) 20371 ~ Children welcome ~ Dogs welcome ~ Open 9-11.30(midnight Sat; 11pm Sun) ~ www.theharbour-inn.co.uk *Recommended by Nigel Fortnam, Joan and Michel Hooper-Immins*

BAMPTON

SS9622 Map 1

Quarrymans Rest

Briton Street; EX16 9LN

Bustling village pub with friendly staff, several real ales, comfortable bars and enjoyable bar food cooked by the landlord; bedrooms

This is a comfortable place to stay (the breakfasts are good) and there's plenty to do and see in the area, too. It's well run and friendly and the licensees and their staff offer a warm welcome to all their customers – regulars or visitors. The beamed and carpeted main bar has leather sofas in front of the inglenook woodburning stove, dining chairs and some housekeepers' chairs around a mix of wooden tables set with church candles. Exe Valley Dobs Best Bitter, Exmoor Fox, Otter Ale and Sharps Doom Bar on handpump, any wine by the glass from their list of around 40 and 15 malt whiskies. A couple of steps lead up to the comfortable stripped-stone dining room with high-backed leather chairs and heavy pine tables. There are daily papers, a shelf of paperbacks, pool and a games machine. The prettily planted back garden has some picnic-sets and there are a few more in front of the building.

Enjoyable food cooked by the landlord might include lunchtime sandwiches, potted salt beef with pear pickle, salmon and crab fishcake with smoked paprika aioli, home-cooked ham with free-range egg, roasted butternut squash risotto with deep-fried brie, beer-battered haddock, steak and kidney in ale pudding, local lamb on red onion tart tatin with thyme and caper jus, slow-cooked smoked pork belly with apple and black pudding crumble and cider jus, and puddings such as white chocolate cheesecake with pecan and maple syrup praline and vanilla panna cotta with strawberry and vanilla gazpacho and ginger parkin. *Benchmark main dish: fillet of bass on bubble and squeak with leek sauce £14.95. Two-course evening meal £19.40.*

Free house ~ Licensees Donna and Paul Berry ~ Real ale ~ Bar food (12-2, 6-9.30; 12-4 Sun; not Sun evening) ~ Restaurant ~ (01398) 331480 ~ Children welcome but must leave bar area by 7pm ~ Dogs allowed in bar ~ Open 11-11 (11.45 Fri and Sat); 12-10.30 Sun ~ Bedrooms: £55S(£65B)/£75S(£85B) ~ www.thequarrymansrest.co.uk
Recommended by M G Hart, Mike and Linda Hudson, Peter Thornton

BEESANDS

SX8140 Map 1

Cricket 🍴 🛏

About 3 miles S of A379, from Chillington; in village turn right along foreshore road; TQ7 2EN

Welcoming pub with enjoyable food (especially fish) and real ales; clean, airy bedrooms

The light and airy new england-style interior is not what you'd expect of this busy inn, given its slightly unassuming exterior. It's a good all-rounder – the sort of place that grows on you the longer you stay – with locals chatting to the cheery landlord and his wife at one end of the counter, enjoyable bedrooms with sea views, and very good food cooked by the landlord's son. It's also on a particularly lovely part of the South Devon Coastal Path – head west for the nicest section which takes you past the remains of a village that was swept away by the sea. Big solid light wood tables with dark wood or leather chairs are well spaced on stripped wooden flooring by the bar and light brown patterned carpet in the restaurant. Big TV screens at either end roll through old local photographs, sport or the news. Otter Ale and Bitter and St

Austell Tribute on handpump, several wines by the glass and local cider; background music. The cheerful black labrador is called Brewster. There are picnic-sets beside the sea wall (a little bleak but essential protection) with pebbly Start Bay beach just over the other side.

🍽 Good food (mainly specialising in fish) includes duck liver and orange parfait with red onion marmalade, a trio of fishcakes with hoisin, coriander and lime dressing, hand-pulled ham hock with a soft poached egg and bacon and rocket salad, a daily vegetarian dish, beer-battered cod and chips, black bream fillet on a sizzling skillet with chinese vegetables, diver-caught scallops with cauliflower purée, shiitake mushrooms and crispy parma ham, lemon sole with with lemon and chive butter, and puddings; you can order crab and lobster in advance. *Benchmark main dish: seafood pancake £11.00. Two-course evening meal £21.50.*

Heavitree ~ Tenant Nigel Heath ~ Real ale ~ Bar food (12-2.30, 6-8.30) ~ Restaurant ~ (01548) 580215 ~ Children welcome ~ Dogs allowed in bar ~ Open 11-11; 11-3, 6-10.30 weekdays in winter ~ Bedrooms: £80S/£100S ~ www.thecricketinn.com *Recommended by Adrian and Dawn Collinge, Sally and John Quinlan, Roy Hoing, DHV, Jane and Rowena Leverington, Ian Roe, R L Borthwick*

BRAMPFORD SPEKE
Lazy Toad 🍽

SX9298   Map 1

Off A377 N of Exeter; EX5 5DP

Well run dining pub in pretty village, delicious food, real ales, friendly service and pretty garden; bedrooms

'A cracking little pub' is how one of our readers describes this 18th-c inn, and we have plenty of enthusiastic reports from other readers, too. It's a carefully restored dining pub with beams, standing timbers and slate floors in the connected rooms, a comfortable armchair and rocking chair (much prized in winter) by the open log fire, and cushioned wall settles and high-backed wooden dining chairs around a mix of tables; the cream-painted brick walls are hung with lots of pictures and there's a rather fine grandfather clock. Otter Ale, Amber and a beer named for the pub from Otter on handpump and nice wines by the glass are served by the friendly, attentive staff; the resident cocker spaniel is called Sam. There are green-painted picnic-sets in the courtyard (once used by the local farrier and wheelwright) and in the walled garden. As we went to press, they were just opening their bedrooms. This is a pretty village of thatched cottages and there are lovely walks along the banks of the River Exe and on the Exe Valley Way and Devonshire Heartland Way.

🍽 Using home-grown fruit and vegetables (which they also make into chutneys, jams and sorbets), their own duck eggs and home-reared lamb and mutton, the inventive food might include sandwiches, home-smoked salmon roulade with basil and mango dressing, potted cornish crab with sourdough toast and crab cappuccino, purple sprouting broccoli with parsley linguine, pine nuts and chilli oil, sausages with wholegrain mustard mash and onion gravy, steak and kidney pie with duck fat roast potatoes, gurnard fillets with a spicy fish stew, clams and aioli, free-range duck breast with beetroot rösti, grilled pear, pancetta and blood orange sauce, and puddings such as gingerbread pudding with treacle and butterscotch sauce and wine poached pears, chocolate chip cookie, crème anglaise and mulled wine sauce. *Benchmark main dish: pigs head three ways with trotter sauce £14.00. Two-course evening meal £19.50.*

~ Licensees Clive and Mo Walker ~ Real ale ~ Bar food (12-2(2.30 Sun), 6.30-9; not Sun evening or Mon) ~ (01392) 841591 ~ Children welcome ~ Dogs allowed in bar ~ Open 11.30-11; 12-3 Sun; 11.30-2.30, 6-11 in winter; closed Sun evening, Mon ~ Bedrooms:

£55S(£65B)/£75S(£95B) ~ www.thelazytoadinn.co.uk *Recommended by John Andrew, Gene and Tony Freemantle, R F Sawbridge, Mary Graham*

BRANSCOMBE

SY1888 Map 1

Fountain Head ◀ £

Upper village, above the robust old church; village signposted off A3052 Sidmouth–Seaton, then from Branscombe Square follow road up hill towards Sidmouth, and after about a mile turn left after the church; OS Sheet 192 map reference SY188889; EX12 3BG

Old-fashioned and friendly stone pub with own-brewed beers and reasonably priced, well liked food

One of our readers describes this friendly and unpretentious 14th-c pub as 'exactly as a real pub should be', and we know exactly what he means. The helpful staff make everyone welcome – whether you're a local or a visitor – and the atmosphere is unchanging and nicely old-fashioned; there are no games machines, background music or TV. The room on the left (formerly a smithy) has forge tools and horseshoes on the high oak beams, and there's a log fire in the original raised firebed with its tall central chimney, cushioned pews and mate's chairs. They brew their own Branscombe Vale Branoc, Summa That and a changing guest beer which they keep on handpump and their annual beer festival is held in June; several wines by the glass and local cider. On the right, an irregularly shaped snug room has another log fire, a white-painted plank ceiling with an unusual carved ceiling rose, brown-varnished panelled walls and rugs on its flagstone and lime-ash floor. Local artists' paintings and greeting cards are for sale; darts and board games. You can sit outside on the front loggia and terrace listening to the little stream gurgling under the flagstoned path; the surrounding walks are very pleasant.

Using own-grown fruit and vegetables, the fairly priced bar food includes lunchtime sandwiches and panini, pheasant, pistachio and smoked bacon terrine, vegetable moussaka, home-cooked honey-roast ham with eggs, a duo of fresh fish with a lime and mango salsa, honey-roast duck with mixed berry sauce, slow-roast pork belly with baked apple and hoisin sauce, and puddings. *Benchmark main dish: beer-battered fish and chips £10.00. Two-course evening meal £15.00.*

Free house ~ Licensees Jon Woodley and Teresa Hoare ~ Real ale ~ Bar food (12-2, 6.30-9) ~ Restaurant ~ (01297) 680359 ~ Children welcome away from main bar area ~ Dogs allowed in bar ~ Live music on summer Sun evenings ~ Open 11-3, 6-11; 12-3, 6-10.30 Sun ~ www.fountainheadinn.com *Recommended by Mrs Sheena and Emily Killick, R and S Bentley, Peter and Giff Bennett, the Didler, C Cooper, Revd R P Tickle, Peter Thornton, C and R Bromage, Chris Johnson, Christine and Neil Townend*

BUCKLAND BREWER

SS4220 Map 1

Coach & Horses

Village signposted off A388 S of Monkleigh; OS Sheet 190 map reference 423206; EX39 5LU

Family run village pub with a mix of customers, open fires, well liked bar food and real ales; good nearby walks

After a walk on the nearby moorland or along the beaches of Westward Ho!, this thatched 13th-c pub is just right for a restorative drink or meal. It's been run by the same friendly family for over 20 years

and the heavily beamed bar (mind your head on some of the beams) has comfortable seats, a handsome antique settle and a woodburning stove in the inglenook; there's also a good log fire in the big stone inglenook of the small lounge. A little back room has darts and pool; the three-legged cat is called Marmite. Forge Litehouse, Otter Ale and Sharps Doom Bar on handpump, Winkleigh cider and quite a few wines by the glass; skittle alley (that doubles as a function room), background music, games machine and occasional TV for sports. There are picnic-sets on the front terrace and in the side garden and some children's play equipment. The RHS garden Rosemoor is about five miles away. They have a holiday cottage to rent next to the pub.

Popular and reasonably priced, the food might include sandwiches, pasties, creamy spiced chicken and mushrooms, beef in Guinness pie with mustard pastry, salmon steak in oatmeal with home-made chilli jam, lamb shank in honey and mint, cod fillet with roasted pepper and tomato sauce, and puddings like sticky pineapple and syrup sponge and lemon polenta cake with lemon syrup. *Benchmark main dish: steak and stilton pie £9.50. Two-course evening meal £16.20.*

Free house ~ Licensees Oliver and Nicola Wolfe ~ Real ale ~ Bar food (12-2, 6.30-9.30) ~ Restaurant ~ (01237) 451395 ~ Well behaved children welcome ~ Open 12-3, 5.30-midnight *Recommended by John Marsh, the Didler, Pat and Tony Martin, Christopher Turner, M and GR, Mark Flynn*

BUCKLAND MONACHORUM
Drake Manor ● £ ⇌   SX4968   Map 1
Off A386 via Crapstone, just S of Yelverton roundabout; PL20 7NA

Nice little village pub with snug rooms, popular food, quite a choice of drinks and pretty back garden; bedrooms

Our readers enjoy staying in the comfortable bedrooms of this delightful little village pub which also has an attractive self-catering apartment. It's run by a welcoming landlady who has now been here for 22 years and loves the place as much as she did when she arrived. The heavily beamed public bar on the left has brocade-cushioned wall seats, prints of the village from 1905 onwards, some horse tack and a few ship badges on the wall and a woodburning stove in a really big stone fireplace; a small door leads to a low-beamed cubbyhole. The snug Drakes Bar has beams hung with tiny cups and big brass keys, a woodburning stove in another stone fireplace, horsebrasses and stirrups and a mix of seats and tables (note the fine stripped pine high-backed settle with its hood). On the right is a small, beamed dining room with settles and tables on flagstones. Shove-ha'penny, darts, euchre and board games. Dartmoor Jail Ale, Otter Bitter, St Austell Tribute and Sharps Doom Bar on handpump, ten wines by the glass and 20 malt whiskies. There are picnic-sets in the prettily planted and sheltered back garden and the front floral displays are much admired.

Fairly priced and enjoyable food using their own home-reared pork and other local produce might include lunchtime filled baguettes, pâté of the day, tempura prawns with sweet chilli, brie, bramley and beetroot tart, gammon with pineapple and cheese, steak and kidney pie, chicken wrapped in bacon with red wine, button onions and sweet pepper sauce, specials like fresh crab salad, rabbit with redcurrants and wine and lamb shank with rosemary and port, and puddings. *Benchmark main dish: beef in ale pie £8.95. Two-course evening meal £14.25.*

Punch ~ Lease Mandy Robinson ~ Real ale ~ Bar food (12-2(2.30 weekends), 7-10(9.30 Sun)) ~ Restaurant ~ (01822) 853892 ~ Children in restaurant and area off main bar ~

Dogs allowed in bar ~ Open 11.30-2.30, 6.30-11; 11.30-11.30 Sat; 12-11 Sun ~ Bedrooms: /£90B ~ www.drakemanorinn.co.uk *Recommended by Maureen Wood, John and Gloria Isaacs*

CLAYHIDON   ST1817   Map 1

Merry Harriers 🍽 ♟ ◑

3 miles from M5 junction 26: head towards Wellington; turn left at first roundabout signposted Ford Street and Hemyock, then after a mile turn left signposted Ford Street; at hilltop T-junction, turn left towards Chard – pub is 1.5 miles on right; at Forches Corner NE of the village itself; EX15 3TR

Bustling and friendly dining pub with imaginative food, several real ales and quite a few wines by the glass; sizeable garden

Always deservedly busy, this is a particularly well run and friendly pub and our readers love it. The hands-on, hard-working licensees and their staff will always make you welcome – even when rushed off their feet. Several small linked newly carpeted areas have a cheerful, bustling atmosphere, comfortably cushioned pews and farmhouse chairs, a sofa beside the woodburning stove, candles in bottles, horsey and hunting prints and local wildlife pictures. Two dining areas have a brighter feel with quarry tiles and lightly timbered white walls. Cotleigh Golden Seahawk, Exmoor Ale and Otter Head on handpump, 14 wines by the glass, two local ciders, 25 malt whiskies, six rums and a good range of other spirits; skittle alley (newly refurbished this year), chess and solitaire. There are plenty of tables and chairs in the sizeable garden and on the terrace, and they have a wendy house and other play equipment for children; there are good surrounding walks.

🍽 Growing some of their own vegetables, keeping their own hens and using seasonal local produce from named suppliers, the imaginative bar food might include lunchtime filled baguettes, partridge breasts on spicy red cabbage with rosemary jus, mussels in a cider cream sauce, wild mushroom and spinach risotto, steak and kidney pie, beer-battered cornish cod, chicken on roasted vegetables with crispy sage and rich gravy, specials like venison steak on garlic mash with red wine gravy and rib-eye steak, and puddings such as dark chocolate terrine with ice-cream and honeycomb pieces and sticky toffee pudding with rich caramel sauce. *Benchmark main dish: scallops with crispy parma ham salad £10.50. Two-course evening meal £15.50.*

Free house ~ Licensees Peter and Angela Gatling ~ Real ale ~ Bar food (12-2(2.15 Sun), 6.30-9; not Sun evening or Mon) ~ Restaurant ~ (01823) 421270 ~ Children welcome ~ Dogs allowed in bar ~ Open 12-3, 6.30-11; 12-3.30 Sun; closed Sun evening, all day Mon ~ www.merryharriers.co.uk *Recommended by Brian Glozier, David Saunders, PLC, Katherine Bright, Ted and Charlotte Routley, Geoff and Linda Payne, John Prescott, Patrick and Daphne Darley, Christine and Neil Townend, Mike Gorton, Bob and Margaret Holder, Peter Thornton, Michael and Maggie Betton, Richard Fox, John and Susan Miln, Bruce and Sharon Eden, Gerry and Rosemary Dobson*

CLYST HYDON   ST0201   Map 1

Five Bells

West of the village and just off B3176 not far from M5 junction 28; EX15 2NT

Attractive thatched pub with several different areas, well liked food and drink, and carefully planted cottagey garden

The immaculate cottagey garden in front of this lovely thatched pub is quite a sight in spring and summer when the thousands of flowers and the big window boxes and hanging baskets are at their prettiest. To the

side and up some steps there are plenty of seats on a sizeable flat lawn and pleasant country views. The friendly licensees are sure to make you welcome and there's a good mix of customers. The bar is divided at one end into different seating areas by brick and timber pillars: there's quite a bit of copper and brass, china jugs hang from big horsebrass-studded beams, lots of plates line delft shelves, and a nice mix of dining chairs surround small tables, with some comfortable pink plush banquettes in a little raised area. Past the inglenook fireplace is another big (but narrower) room they call the Long Barn, which has a series of prints on the walls, a pine dresser at one end and similar furnishings. Cotleigh Tawny, O'Hanlons Stormstay and Otter Bitter on handpump, 11 wines by the glass, three local farm ciders and a wide range of soft drinks; background music, board games and books and toys for children.

Popular food might include filled baguettes and ciabatta sandwiches, tiger prawns with a whisky, lime and chilli glaze, chicken liver pâté, fish pie, vegetarian lasagne, pheasant casserole, chicken with sherry, chorizo and onion sauce, specials like mussels in white wine and cream, lancashire hotpot and pork belly with mustard mash and cider gravy, and puddings like orange almond cake with caramelised orange and ice-cream and chocolate brownie. *Benchmark main dish: steak and kidney suet pudding £10.95. Two-course evening meal £16.50.*

Free house ~ Licensees Mr and Mrs R Shenton ~ Real ale ~ Bar food (not Mon lunchtime) ~ (01884) 277288 ~ Children welcome away from bar area ~ Open 11.30-3, 6.30-11; 12-3, 6.30-10.30 Sun; closed Mon lunchtime ~ www.fivebellsclysthydon.co.uk
Recommended by Bruce and Sharon Eden, Mr and Mrs W Mills, Ryta Lyndley, Mr and Mrs Richard Osborne, R T and J C Moggridge, John and Gloria Isaacs, Peter Thornton, Roger and Donna Huggins, Dr A J and Mrs Tompsett

COCKWOOD
Anchor ♀ 🍺
SX9780   Map 1

Off, but visible from, A379 Exeter–Torbay road, after Starcross; EX6 8RA

Busy dining pub specialising in seafood (other choices available), with five real ales, too

To be sure of a table in this extremely popular pub it's best to book in advance as there are often queues to get in at peak times. As well as an extension made up of mainly reclaimed timber and decorated with over 300 ship emblems, brass and copper lamps and nautical knick-knacks, there are several small, low-ceilinged, rambling rooms with black panelling and good-sized tables in various alcoves; the snug has a cheerful winter coal fire. Otter Ale and St Austell Tribute with guests like Dartmoor Jail Ale, Gales Seafarers Ale and O'Hanlons Yellowhammer on handpump, eight wines by the glass and 80 malt whiskies; background music, darts, cards and shove-ha'penny. From the tables on the sheltered verandah you can look across the road to the inlet (which is a pleasant spot to wander around).

A huge range of fish dishes includes 28 different ways of serving River Exe mussels, six ways of serving local scallops and five ways of serving oysters, as well as crab and brandy soup and various platters to share. Non-fishy dishes also, such as sandwiches, ploughman's, pork, apple and cider sausages with onion gravy, wild mushroom and spinach tagliatelle, steak in ale pie, specials such as skate wing with black butter and monkfish and prawns in a cheese and white wine sauce, and puddings like treacle sponge and custard and apple and cinnamon tart with clotted cream. *Benchmark main dish: shellfish selection £24.95. Two-course evening meal £21.00.*

Heavitree ~ Lease Malcolm and Katherine Protheroe, Scott Hellier ~ Real ale ~ Bar food (all day) ~ Restaurant ~ (01626) 890203 ~ Children welcome if seated and away from bar; no facilities for them ~ Dogs allowed in bar ~ Open 11-11; 11.30-10.30 Sun ~ www.anchorinncockwood.com *Recommended by Mike Gorton, Peter and Giff Bennett, the Didler, Mr and Mrs A H Young, Col and Mrs Patrick Kaye, Dr A J and Mrs Tompsett*

COLEFORD
New Inn

SS7701 Map 1

Just off A377 Crediton–Barnstaple; EX17 5BZ

Ancient thatched inn with interestingly furnished areas, well liked food and real ales, and welcoming licensees; bedrooms

As well as being an enjoyable place to stay (and the breakfasts are particularly good), our readers love dropping into this 800-year-old inn for either a drink and a chat or a leisurely meal – and Mr and Mrs Cowie are always warmly welcoming. It's a U-shaped building with the servery in the 'angle' and interestingly furnished areas leading off it: ancient and modern settles, cushioned stone wall seats, some character tables – a pheasant worked into the grain of one – and carved dressers and chests. Also, paraffin lamps, antique prints on the white walls and landscape plates on one of the beams, with pewter tankards on another. Captain, the chatty parrot, may greet you with a 'hello' or even a 'goodbye'. Otter Ale, Sharps Doom Bar and a guest like Hunters Pheasant Plucker or Skinners Betty Stogs on handpump, local cider, 14 wines by the glass and a dozen malt whiskies; background music, darts and board games. There are chairs and tables on decking under a pruned willow tree by the babbling stream and more in a covered dining area.

Extremely good and using local produce where possible, the changing bar food might include filled baguettes, smoked pigeon breast and bacon salad, seared scallops and roasted red pepper with an asian-style dressing, field mushrooms stuffed with courgette, celery, tomato, peppers and feta cheese, home-made chicken kiev, pork fillet and black pudding with cider sauce, line-caught bass with lemon thyme and chive breadcrumb topping and a lime butter sauce with prawns, and puddings like marmalade bread and butter pudding and meringues with cream, maple syrup and walnuts. *Benchmark main dish: beer-battered fresh cod and chips £12.50. Two-course evening meal £18.00.*

Free house ~ Licensees Carole and George Cowie ~ Real ale ~ Bar food (12-2, 6.30-9.39) ~ Restaurant ~ (01363) 84242 ~ Children welcome ~ Dogs allowed in bar ~ Open 12-3, 6-11(10.30 Sun) ~ Bedrooms: £65B/£85B ~ www.thenewinncoleford.co.uk *Recommended by Simon and Philippa Hughes, S G N Bennett, John and Bryony Coles, Mr Yeldahn, Michael Coleman, Pat and Tony Martin, Mrs P Sumner, Jan and Alan Summers, M A Borthwick*

COLYFORD
Wheelwright

SY2592 Map 1

Swan Hill Road (A3052 Sidmouth–Lyme Regis); EX24 6QQ

Thatched dining pub with plenty of room, real ales and friendly staff, quite a choice of popular food and seats outside

Usefully open all day and serving some kind of food from midday until 9.30pm, this is an attractive thatched dining pub with friendly staff and an easy-going atmosphere. The bar has red leather armchairs and a chesterfield at one end, cushioned wall seating, farmhouse chairs and chunky wooden tables on the stripped floorboards, a pair of giant bellows, a big cartwheel and all sorts of interesting knick-knacks, and

a warming woodburning stove. From the ornate bar counter under its thatched roof, helpful staff serve Badger Bitter and First Gold and a guest beer on handpump and nice wines by the glass. The two dining rooms have high rafters and high-backed black dining chairs around a mix of tables and there's a snug room that's just right for a private party. On the way to a large, further dining room with a chandelier made of wine glasses is their charming gift shop selling all sorts of soaps, candles, pot pourri and so forth; it's rather fun to find this in a pub. Outside on the front terrace are plenty of seats. This is sister pub to the Harbour at Axmouth.

🍴 Popular food using seasonal local produce might include sandwiches, crab cakes with pineapple and chilli salsa, mushrooms with leeks, garlic, blue cheese and cream topped with honey-roasted walnuts, moroccan lamb tagine with orange-infused couscous, steak in ale pie, beef burger with a choice of toppings, slow-roast pork belly on bubble and squeak with an apple and cider sauce, specials like mussels with bacon, thyme and cream, rabbit with wild mushrooms, leeks and pancetta and trio of duck with braised cabbage, and puddings such as vanilla and ginger panna cotta with poached rhubarb and caramel tart with toffee apple sauce. *Benchmark main dish: haddock with mustard sauce, a poached egg and cheddar mash £13.50. Two-course evening meal £18.00.*

Badger ~ Lease Gary and Toni Valentine ~ Real ale ~ Bar food (12-3, 6-9.30; light lunches 3-6) ~ Restaurant ~ (01297) 552585 ~ Children welcome ~ Dogs allowed in bar ~ Open 10.30am-11pm ~ www.wheelwright-inn co.uk *Recommended by Bart Leonard, B D Jones, Patrick and Daphne Darley*

CULMSTOCK
ST1013 Map 1
Culm Valley 🍴 ♗ 🍺

B3391, off A38 E of M5 junction 27; EX15 3JJ

Quirky, friendly dining pub with imaginative food, interesting real ales and wines, lively atmosphere and outside seats overlooking River Culm

A touch eccentric but all the better for that, this is a genuine country pub with a knowledgeable and charming – if slightly offbeat – landlord, and our readers enjoy their visits very much. The atmosphere is lively and informal, there's a good mix of chatty locals and visitors and the bar has a hotch-potch of modern and unrenovated furnishings, horse racing paintings and knick-knacks on the walls and a big fireplace. Further along is a dining room with a chalkboard menu, a small front conservatory and, leading off here, a little oak-floored room with views into the kitchen. A larger back room has paintings by local artists for sale. Board games and a small portable TV for occasional rugby, rowing and racing events; the dogs are called Lady and Spoof. Six quickly changing real ales tapped from the cask (they often have 10 beers at the weekend) might include Bays Best, Branscombe Vale Branoc, Butcombe Mendip Spring Bitter, Exeter County Best, and O'Hanlons Stormstay and Yellowhammer, and the landlord and his brother import wines from smaller french vineyards so you can count on a few of those as well as some unusual french fruit liqueurs, somerset cider brandies, vintage rum, good sherries and madeira and local farm ciders. Outside, tables are very attractively positioned overlooking the bridge and the River Culm. The gents' is in an outside yard.

🍴 They butcher their own meat and use local game and fish for the imaginative (fairly priced for the quality) dishes: sandwiches, home-smoked cold salmon with creamy horseradish, moules marinière, spinach and ricotta pasta, a proper

malaysian chicken curry, line-caught bass with rosemary and garlic, venison pie, chickpea stew with pork and chorizo, portuguese fish stew, smashing seafood platters, and puddings such as spanish orange and caramel cream and chocolate brownies. *Benchmark main dish: beer-battered fish and chips £12.00. Two-course evening meal £18.00.*

Free house ~ Licensee Richard Hartley ~ Real ale ~ Bar food (12-2, 7-9; not Sun evening) ~ Restaurant ~ (01884) 840354 ~ Children allowed away from main bar ~ Dogs welcome ~ Impromptu piano or folk ~ Open 12-3, 6-11; 12-11 Fri and Sat; 12-10.30 Sun ~ Bedrooms: $40B/$70B ~ www.culmvalleyinn.co.uk *Recommended by John Prescott, John Branston, David Saunders, MLR, Sarah Townsend, John and Hilary Penny, M E and F J Thomasson, Patrick and Daphne Darley, Steven King and Barbara Cameron, R T and J C Moggridge, J D O Carter, David and Sharon Collison*

DALWOOD ST2400 Map 1
Tuckers Arms ⓘ

Village signposted off A35 Axminster–Honiton; keep on past village; EX13 7EG

13th-c thatched inn with friendly, hard-working young licensees, real ales and interesting bar food

'What an excellent pub,' say several of our readers – and with its smart new thatched roof, it looks picture-postcard pretty. You can be sure of a warm welcome from the enthusiastic, hands-on licensees who make all their many customers, locals or visitors, feel at home. The beamed and flagstoned bar has a relaxed atmosphere, traditional furnishings including various dining chairs, window seats and wall settles, and a log fire in the inglenook fireplace with lots of horsebrasses on the wall above it. The back bar has an enormous collection of miniature bottles and there's also a more formal dining room; lots of copper implements and platters. Branscombe Vale Branoc, Otter Bitter and a changing local guest beer on handpump, several wines by the glass and up to 20 malt whiskies; background music and a double skittle alley. In summer, the hanging baskets are pretty and there are seats in the garden. Apart from the church, this is the oldest building in the parish.

Enterprising and highly thought of, the food might include sandwiches, coarse fish pâté with crusty bread, slow-roast pork belly wrapped in puff pastry and stuffed with pancetta and apricot and cider chutney on pine nuts and green cabbage, spinach, roast garlic, goats cheese and sundried tomato muffin on a sweet potato purée with a creamy leek and sage sauce, sausage and mash with ale gravy and caramelised onions, local crab and shrimps on a warm noodle salad with a thai broth, home-cooked ham with free-range eggs, sticky mustard and orange chicken with a medley of orange segments, green beans and radishes, slow-cooked persian-style lamb with a feta salad, and puddings such as apricot bakewell pudding and crème brûlée with home-made shortbread. *Benchmark main dish: local pork tenderloin with crispy crackling, bacon and kale mash and leek, apple and sage sauce £15.95. Two-course evening meal £19.00.*

Free house ~ Licensee Tracey Pearson ~ Real ale ~ Bar food (12-2, 6.30-9) ~ Restaurant ~ (01404) 881342 ~ Children in restaurant but must be well behaved ~ Dogs allowed in bar ~ Open 11.30-3, 6.30(6 Sat)-11.30; 12-4, 7-10.30 Sun ~ Bedrooms: $45S/$70S ~ www.tuckersarms.com *Recommended by Fiona Loram, David and Julie Glover, Peter Salmon, Dave Braisted, Mike and Jayne Bastin, Guy Vowles, Stephen and Jean Curtis*

There are report forms at the back of the book.

DARTMOUTH
SX8751   Map 1

Floating Bridge

Opposite Upper Ferry, use Dart Marina Hotel car park; Coombe Road (A379); TQ6 9PQ

Quayside pub with seats by the water and on roof-top terrace, some boating memorabilia, and friendly staff

A s we went to press, new licensees had just taken over this bustling quayside pub. Obviously some refurbishment will take place but what can't change is the position right by the River Dart and the little car ferry; prized seats include picnic-sets by the water and tables and chairs up on the large roof terrace. The bar has lots of stools by the windows to make the most of the view, oak chairs and tables, a few model boats and black and white photographs of local boating scenes on the walls, St Austell Tribute and Sharps Doom Bar on handpump, and several wines by the glass; background music. The dining room on the left is lighter with leather-backed dining chairs around a mix of wooden tables on bare boards and more black and white photographs. They've opened up a back family room with access to the roof terrace. The window boxes are pretty against the white-painted building.

Bar food includes chicken livers, camembert with whole roasted garlic (to share), ham and free-range eggs, steak and kidney pie, apricot chicken, fresh fish such as megrin or whole lemon sole, and puddings like chocolate brownie and sticky toffee pudding. *Benchmark main dish: fresh fish dishes £14.00. Two-course evening meal £18.00.*

Enterprise ~ Lease Alison Hogben ~ Real ale ~ Bar food (12-9.30) ~ Restaurant ~ (01803) 832354 ~ Children welcome away from main bar ~ Dogs allowed in bar ~ Open 11-11 *Recommended by Phil and Sally Gorton, John and Fiona McIlwain, Alun and Jennifer Evans, Dave Webster, Sue Holland*

DARTMOUTH
SX8751   Map 1

Royal Castle Hotel ⇐

The Quay; TQ6 9PS

17th-c hotel with a lot of character in two quite different bars, a genuine mix of customers, real ales and good food served all day; comfortable bedrooms

A t the heart of a lovely old town, this 17th-c hotel has a thriving atmosphere and is busy all day with a really good mix of customers; the staff come in for special praise from many of our readers. There are two ground floor bars, each with its own identity. On the right is the traditional Galleon bar with lots of character, a Tudor fireplace, some fine antiques and maritime pieces and quite a bit of copper and brass. To the left of the flagstoned entrance hall is the Harbour Bar, which is contemporary and rather smart with a big screen TV and regular live acoustic music on Thursday evenings. The more formal restaurant looks over the river. Dartmoor Jail Ale, Otter Amber and Sharps Doom Bar on handpump and several wines by the glass. The inn was originally two Tudor merchant houses (but has a Regency façade) and overlooks the inner harbour; they have their own secure parking.

Naming their local suppliers for the seasonal produce, the enjoyable bar food might include sandwiches and filled baked potatoes, crab bisque, ham hock and black pudding terrine with spicy orange chutney, hand-made burger with

mozzarella, bacon and red onion chutney, a trio of sausages with crispy onions and gravy, butternut squash and parmesan risotto with sage butter, game pie with wild mushroom sauce, steak, kidney and Guinness pie, big helping of mussels in wine and cream, and puddings such as sticky toffee pudding with butterscotch sauce and vanilla bean crème brûlée with home-made walnut shortbread. *Benchmark main dish: whole local cracked crab £12.95. Two-course evening meal £20.50.*

Free house ~ Licensees Nigel and Anne Way ~ Real ale ~ Bar food (all day) ~ Restaurant ~ (01803) 833033 ~ Children welcome but not after 7pm in bar (can eat in restaurant then) ~ Dogs welcome ~ Live acoustic music Thurs evening ~ Open 8am-11pm ~ Bedrooms: £110B/£160B ~ www.royalcastle.co.uk *Recommended by Peter and Giff Bennett, Sandy Butcher, George Atkinson, Dave Webster, Sue Holland, Patrick and Daphne Darley*

DODDISCOMBSLEIGH   SX8586 Map 1
Nobody Inn ♀
Off B3193; EX6 7PS

Busy old pub with plenty of character, a fine range of drinks, friendly staff, and well liked bar food; bedrooms

This 17th-c inn is full of character and run by the welcoming licensees and their friendly staff. The two rooms of the beamed lounge bar have handsomely carved antique settles, windsor and wheelback chairs, a mix of wooden tables, guns and hunting prints in a snug area by one of the big inglenook fireplaces and fresh flowers. The restaurant is more formal. A beer named for the pub from Branscombe Vale and two changing guests such as Branscombe Vale Branoc and Exe Valley Bitter on handpump, 250 whiskies, 29 wines by the glass and local cider. There are picnic-sets in the pretty garden with views of the surrounding wooded hill pastures. The medieval stained glass in the local church is some of the best in the west country.

Using local produce from named suppliers, the popular bar food includes chicken liver pâté, home-smoked salmon with horseradish cream, home-cooked ham and free-range eggs, calves liver with bacon and onion gravy, vegetarian lasagne, fish pie, more restauranty dishes such as crab cake with hollandaise and basil sauce, local venison steak with red wine and sloe gin reduction and free-range duck breast in honey and ginger with confit duck potato cake and orange sauce, and puddings like sticky ginger pudding with toffee sauce and clotted cream and apple crumble and custard. *Benchmark main dish: steak in ale pie £10.95. Two-course evening meal £17.00.*

Free house ~ Licensee Susan Burdge ~ Real ale ~ Bar food (12-2(3 Sun), 6.30(7 Sun)-9(9.30 Fri and Sat)) ~ Restaurant ~ (01647) 252394 ~ Children welcome away from main bar ~ Dogs allowed in bar ~ Open 11-11; 12-10.30 Sun ~ Bedrooms: £65S/£90S ~ www.nobodyinn.co.uk *Recommended by Michael Cooper, Barry Steele-Perkins, Roger and Kathy Elkin, the Didler, Hugh Roberts, Mike Bartram, W K Wood, Chris and Jan Swanwick*

EAST ALLINGTON   SX7648 Map 1
Fortescue Arms
Village signed off A381 Totnes–Kingsbridge, S of A3122 junction; TQ9 7RA

Pretty village pub, gently refurbished recently, good real ales, enjoyable food and outside seating; bedrooms

The licensees of this pretty pub are making some gentle changes to create a more informal and friendly atmosphere. A bar is to be installed in the restaurant, they aim to introduce more real ales and there

are now comfortable armchairs by the open fire. The main part of the two-room bar has a nice mix of wooden tables and cushioned dining chairs on the black slate floor, a dark green dado under cream walls, church candles, some brewery memorabilia, Dartmoor Legend, Sharps Doom Bar and a changing guest such as RCH Pitchfork on handpump and several wines by the glass. The second room now has cream paintwork and is similarly furnished, and there's a dining room, too; background music. There are some seats at the front with more on the sheltered terrace.

🍴 Enjoyable food includes lunchtime sandwiches, pigeon with a bubble and squeak cake and port sauce, seared local hand-dived scallops with cauliflower purée and a raisin and apple salad, ham and eggs, beer-battered fish and chips, a home-made burger with bacon and cheese, a pie of the week, home-made tagliatelle with wild mushrooms and spinach, slow-roasted pork belly with a sweet red onion creamy mash and rhubarb gravy, and puddings such as sticky toffee pudding with butterscotch sauce. *Benchmark main dish: slow-cooked shoulder of lamb £16.00. Two-course evening meal £20.00.*

Free house ~ Licensees Jacqui Clifford and Gerald Smith ~ Real ale ~ Bar food (12-2.30(2 in winter), 6-9) ~ (01548) 521215 ~ Children welcome ~ Dogs welcome ~ Open 11.30-3, 5.30-11; 12-2.30, 6-11 in winter; closed Mon lunchtime ~ Bedrooms: £40S/£60S ~ www.fortescue-arms.co.uk *Recommended by M G Hart, B J Harding, Lynda and Trevor Smith, Anna Kirton*

EXMINSTER
Turf Hotel
SX9686 Map 1

Follow the signs to the Swan's Nest, signed from A379 S of village, then continue to end of track, by gates; park and walk right along canal towpath – nearly a mile; EX6 8EE

Remote but very popular waterside pub with fine choice of drinks, super summer barbecues and lots of space in big garden

Although this family-run pub is pretty remote, it's extremely popular – particularly in fine weather. You can't actually get here by car – you must either walk (which takes about 20 minutes along the ship canal) or cycle or catch a 60-seater boat which brings people down the Exe estuary from Topsham quay (15-minute trip, adult £4.50, child £2); there's also a canal boat from Countess Wear Swing Bridge every lunchtime. Best to phone the pub to check all sailing times. For those arriving in their own boat there's a large pontoon as well as several moorings. Inside, the end room has a slate floor, pine walls, built-in seats, lots of photographs of the pub and a woodburning stove; along a corridor (with a dining room to one side) is a simply furnished room with wood-plank seats around tables on the stripped wooden floor. Exeter Avocet or Ferryman, Otter Ale and Bitter and O'Hanlons Yellowhammer on handpump, local cider and juices, ten wines by the glass (and local wines too) and jugs of Pimms. There are plenty of picnic-sets spread around the big garden; the sea and estuary birds are fun to watch at low tide.

🍴 Growing their own vegetables and salads and using other local produce, the good bar food includes sandwiches and toasties, crispy baby squid with a sweet chilli sauce, smoked mackerel pâté with red onion marmalade, chilli beef nachos, jalapenos and sour cream and tortilla chips, beer-battered fish of the day with home-made tartare sauce, meat or veggie burgers, goan seafood curry, daily specials, and puddings. Their summer barbecues are very good. *Benchmark main dish: moules frites £10.50. Two-course evening meal £16.50.*

Free house ~ Licensees Clive and Ginny Redfern ~ Real ale ~ Bar food (12-3, 6.30-9(9.30 Fri and Sat); not Sun evening) ~ (01392) 833128 ~ Children welcome ~ Dogs welcome ~ Open 11-11(10.30 Sun); open only weekends Oct, Nov, Feb, March in winter; closed Jan and Feb ~ Bedrooms: /$80B ~ www.turfpub.net *Recommended by Richard Tilbrook, Dr and Mrs A K Clarke, Mike Gorton, the Didler, Comus and Sarah Elliott, J D O Carter, W K Wood, Rich Frith*

FROGMORE
SX7742   Map 1
Globe 🛏
A379 E of Kingsbridge; TQ7 2NR

Extended and neatly decorated inn with a bar and several seating and dining areas, real ales and nice wines by the glass, helpful staff, popular food and seats outside; comfortable bedrooms

Much enlarged and refurbished since our last visit some years ago, this is a white-painted inn with lovely summer-flowering window boxes. The neatly kept bar has a double-sided woodburner with horsebrass-decorated stone pillars on either side, another fireplace filled with logs, cushioned settles, chunky farmhouse chairs and built-in wall seating around a mix of tables on the wooden floor – and a copper diving helmet. Attentive staff serve Otter Bitter, Skinners Betty Stogs and South Hams Eddystone from handpump, and several wines by the glass. The slate-floored games room has a pool table and darts and there's also a comfortable lounge with an open fire, cushioned dining chairs and tables on red carpeting, a big leather sofa, a model yacht and a large yacht painting; spot the clever mural of a log pile. The back terrace has teak tables and chairs and steps lead up to another level with picnic-sets. The bedrooms are comfortable and well equipped.

Well liked food might include filled baguettes and baked potatoes, locally made pasty, various pizzas with lots of toppings, beer-battered mushrooms with garlic mayonnaise, smoked haddock fishcakes with sweet chilli sauce, various pizzas with lots of toppings, home-made steak burger with red onion marmalade, vegetable lasagne, honey-glazed home-cooked ham with egg, chicken curry, steak and mushroom pie, swordfish with tomato, basil butter and chive potato cake, slow-roast pork belly with chorizo apple sauce, and puddings. *Benchmark main dish: lasagne £8.95. Two-course evening meal £15.00.*

Free house ~ Licensees John and Lynda Horsley ~ Real ale ~ Bar food (12-2, 6(6.30 Sun)-9) ~ Restaurant ~ (01548) 531351 ~ Children in family room ~ Dogs allowed in bar ~ Open 12-2.30(3 Sun), 6-11.30; 12-3, 6(6.30 in winter)-10.30 Sun; closed Mon lunchtime 1 Oct-end June (except bank holldays) ~ Bedrooms: £50S/£80S ~ www.theglobeinn.eclipse.co.uk *Recommended by Geoff and Carol Thorp, Roxanne Chamberlain, Dennis Jenkin, DHV, Keith Sale*

GEORGEHAM
SS4639   Map 1
Rock 🍴 ☗
Rock Hill, above village; EX33 1JW

Beamed family pub, good food cooked by the landlord, up to six real ales on handpump, plenty of room inside and out, and a relaxed atmosphere

Always busy and cheerful with a good mix of both chatty drinkers and diners, this is a neatly kept pub with a 17th-c heart. There are plenty of heavy beams and the sizeable bar is separated into two areas by a step. The pubby top part has a half-planked walls, an open woodburning

stove in a stone fireplace and captain's and farmhouse chairs around wooden tables on quarry tiles, and the lower bar has panelled wall seats, some built-in settles forming a cosy booth, old local photographs and ancient flatirons. Leading off here is a red-carpeted dining room with attractive black and white photographs of people from North Devon. Friendly young staff serve Exmoor Ale, Fullers London Pride, St Austell Tribute, Sharps Doom Bar and Timothy Taylors Landlord on handpump and around a dozen wines by the glass; background music and board games. The light and airy back dining conservatory has high-backed wooden or modern dining chairs around tables under the growing vine, and beyond that, there's a little terrace. They have wheelchair access. Beside the pretty hanging baskets and tubs in front of the pub are some picnic-sets.

Enterprising food might include sandwiches, salt and pepper chilli squid with asian coleslaw, burgundy-style snails with rouille and gruyère, various sharing deli boards, honey-glazed ham and free-range eggs with home-made piccalilli, chicken curry, home-made beef burger with tomato and chilli jam, cheese or bacon, tagliatelle topped with salmon and crayfish in tarragon cream or mediterranean vegetables in tomato and basil, and specials such as bouillabaisse with cod, salmon, sole, bass and king prawns, venison casserole with dumplings and tournedos rossini. *Benchmark main dish: beer-battered cod and chips £9.50. Two-course evening meal £21.00.*

Punch ~ Lease Darren Stocker and Daniel Craddock ~ Real ale ~ Bar food (all day Jun-Sept (and all day Sun); 12-2.30, 6-9.30 Oct-May) ~ Restaurant ~ (01271) 890322 ~ Children welcome ~ Dogs welcome ~ Open 11am-11.30pm; 12-11 Sun ~ www.therockgeorgeham.co.uk *Recommended by Peter and Josie Fawcett, John and Joan Nash, Bob and Margaret Holder, Ian Herdman, Paul and Penny Dawson, M and GR, Andrew Scott, Vanessa McGlade*

HAYTOR VALE   SX7777   Map 1

Rock ★

Haytor signposted off B3387 just W of Bovey Tracey, on good moorland road to Widecombe; TQ13 9XP

Civilised Dartmoor inn at its most informal at lunchtime; smashing food, real ales, and seats in pretty garden; comfortable bedrooms

Our readers love staying at this particularly well run, civilised inn – the bedrooms are comfortable with good facilities (some are up steep stairs), the breakfasts are excellent and you can be sure of a warm welcome from the friendly staff. But at lunchtime (when they offer a fine value two- and three-course set menu) it's much more informal and appeals to walkers from Dartmoor National Park. The two neatly kept, partly panelled bar rooms have lots of dark wood and red plush, polished antique tables with candles and fresh flowers, old-fashioned prints and decorative plates on the walls and warming winter log fires (the main fireplace has a fine Stuart fireback). Dartmoor IPA and Jail Ale on handpump, 15 wines (plus champagne and sparkling rosé) by the glass and 16 malt whiskies. There's a light and spacious dining room in the lower part of the inn and a residents' lounge. The large, pretty garden opposite has some seats, with more on the little terrace next to the pub itself. You can park at the back of the building.

From named local suppliers, the highly thought of food might include sandwiches, chicken liver parfait with red onion marmalade, mussels in cream, garlic and white wine, sausages with onion gravy, battered haddock with

home-made tartare sauce, squash thai green vegetable curry, saddle of venison with truffle mash, balsamic poached beetroot and red wine sauce, wild bass on chorizo risotto with tomato pesto, and puddings such as steamed chocolate pudding and blueberry bakewell tart. *Benchmark main dish: steak in ale pie £9.95. Two-course evening meal £22.00.*

Free house ~ Licensee Christopher Graves ~ Real ale ~ Bar food (12-2, 7-9) ~ (01364) 661305 ~ Children welcome away from main bar ~ Dogs allowed in bedrooms ~ Open 11-11; 12-10.30 Sun ~ Bedrooms: $79B/$89S($110B) ~ www.rock-inn.co.uk
Recommended by Hugh Roberts, Revd R P Tickle, Paul and Mary Walmsley, W K Wood, Mike and Mary Carter, Barry Steele-Perkins, John and Gloria Isaacs, Hugh Tattersall, Mark O'Sullivan, Mr and Mrs M Stratton, Steve Whalley, Robert Watt, Andrea Rampley

HONITON
SY1198   Map 1

Holt 🍴 ☕
High Street, W end; EX14 1LA

Friendly, informal pub run by two brothers with super tapas and other interesting food, and a fine range of Otter beers

After a gentle refurbishment, this charming little pub is even more appealing. There's just one room downstairs with elm tables surrounded by chunky pine chairs on the slate floor, a bar with high stools where you can enjoy the delicious tapas, a couple of brown leather sofas at one end facing each other across a circular table. and a coal-effect woodburner in the brick fireplace with a shelf of books to one side; the windows are shuttered (and one looks down on to a small stream). Brewing has been in the McCaig family for three generations and indeed they founded the Otter Brewery, so it's not surprising that the full range of Otter beers are kept on handpump: Ale, Amber, Bitter, Bright and Head. Upstairs, a bigger, brighter room now has elegant, high-backed elm tables and chairs on pale floorboards and small, very attractive musician prints, much larger contemporary pictures and an old Chamonix travel poster on the pale grey or maroon walls; background music and friendly staff. It's all very relaxed and informal. The black cat is called Dangermouse. They also run a café and pâtisserie almost next door, called Post.

Interesting and extremely enjoyable, with local growers and producers listed on a blackboard by the open kitchen, the short choice of food includes lunchtime sandwiches and daily-changing tapas, escabeche of mackerel with pickled vegetables and fresh herb pastry, fig and walnut tarte tatin, balsamic reduction and blue cheese, smoked chicken and confit duck terrine with spiced apple compote, vegetable risotto with mushrooms, asparagus and parmesan, slow-roast pork belly with black pudding, pea purée and cider jus, seared lamb rump with colcannon mash, maple-glazed onions, sweetbreads and mint jus, and puddings like marbled milk and white chocolate brownie with vanilla ice-cream and hazelnut and caramel parfait with spiced walnut shortbread. *Benchmark main dish: shin of beef casserole £8.50. Two-course evening meal £18.00.*

Free house ~ Licensees Joe and Angus McCaig ~ Real ale ~ Bar food (12-2, 6.30-9; not Sun or Mon) ~ Restaurant ~ (01404) 47707 ~ Well behaved children welcome ~ Dogs allowed in bar ~ Music festival four times a year ~ Open 11-3, 5.30-11; closed Sun and Mon ~ www.theholt-honiton.com *Recommended by Alan Clark, Tim Gray, John Gould, Derek and Sylvia Stephenson, Guy Vowles, M G Hart, Comus and Sarah Elliott, Richard Wyld, Chris Johnson*

If we know a pub has an outdoor play area for children, we mention it.

HORNDON   SX5280   Map 1
Elephants Nest

*If coming from Okehampton on A386, turn left at Mary Tavy Inn, then left
after about 0.5 miles; pub signposted beside Mary Tavy Inn, then Horndon signposted;
on the Ordnance Survey Outdoor Leisure Map it's named as the New Inn; PL19 9NQ*

**Isolated old inn surrounded by Dartmoor walks, some interesting
original features, real ales and food using seasonal local produce;
comfortable bedrooms**

Our readers enjoy staying in the comfortable and attractively furnished
bedrooms of this cosy old inn, and it's not often that you're offered
fresh scallops, devilled kidneys and kedgeree for breakfast in a pub. The
main bar has lots of beer pump clips on the beams, high bar chairs by the
bar counter, Dartmoor Jail Ale, Palmers Best, Sharps Doom Bar and a
guest beer such as Palmers Dorset Gold on handpump, a couple of farm
ciders, several wines by the glass and 15 malt whiskies. There are two
other rooms with nice modern dark wood dining chairs around a mix of
tables, and throughout there are bare stone walls, flagstones and three
woodburning stoves. The spreading, attractive garden (which has an area
reserved for adults only) has plenty of picnic-sets under parasols and
looks over dry-stone walls to the pastures of Dartmoor's lower slopes
and the rougher moorland above, where there are plenty of walks.

As well as filled baguettes and wraps, the changing food might include pork
terrine, smoked duck and asparagus spring roll, caramelised shallot and goats
cheese tarte tatin, beef burger with red onion marmalade, smoked haddock topped
with rarebit with creamy mash and spinach, slow-roasted pork belly with mustard
mash, lamb curry, duck breast with spiced cherry sauce, and puddings like treacle
tart with clotted cream and lemon posset with blueberry compote. *Benchmark
main dish: escalope of pork with parma ham, sage and marsala wine £13.95.
Two-course evening meal £19.50.*

Free house ~ Licensee Hugh Cook ~ Real ale ~ Bar food (12-2.15, 6.30-9) ~ (01822)
810273 ~ Children welcome ~ Dogs welcome ~ Open 12-3, 6.30-11(10.30 Sun) ~
Bedrooms: £77.50B/£87.50B ~ www.elephantsnest.co.uk *Recommended by Bruce Adams,
John and Bernadette Elliott, D P and M A Miles, Maurice Ricketts*

HORNS CROSS   SS3823   Map 1
Hoops

A39 Clovelly–Bideford, W of village; EX39 5DL

**Striking thatched inn with plenty of character, real ales, good bar and
restaurant food, and a spacious garden; comfortable bedrooms**

As this pretty, thatched former smugglers' haunt is open all day
and serves food from 8am (non-residents are more than welcome
for the wide choice of breakfast), there's always a good, bustling
atmosphere and a cheerful mix of customers. The bar has solid mates'
and other kitchen chairs around wooden tables, china hanging from the
beams, log fires in sizeable fireplaces, and some standing timbers and
partitioning creating separate areas. The more formal restaurant has an
attractive mix of chairs and tables, some panelling and exposed stone
and another open fire. Hoops Bitter (from Country Life) and Hoops Best
and Light (from Forge) on handpump and over a dozen wines by the
glass; occasional background music, and board games. The two black
labradors are called Sky and Scout. There are picnic-sets under parasols
in the enclosed courtyard and plenty more seats on the terrace and in the

two acres of surrounding gardens; the summer window boxes are lovely. The bedrooms are well equipped and comfortable and the Coach House (where dogs are allowed) has family rooms; lots to do and see nearby.

From named local producers, the enjoyable food includes lunchtime sandwiches, pigeon breast with quince jelly and a celery and candied walnut salad, moules mariniere, red bean and potato moussaka and their own foccacia, fish and shellfish stew, pheasant breast with carrots and swede and wilted spinach, aged fillet of beer with rösti potato, wild mushrooms and dark red wine jus, and puddings such as orange and passion fruit cheesecake with coulis and spiced apple pie with clotted cream; in winter they offer an early bird menu (Friday and Saturday 4-7pm) and hold a fish and chip supper (Tuesday), a curry evening (Wednesday) and pie and a pint deal (Thursday). *Benchmark main dish: crisp pork belly, black pudding, dauphinoise potatoes and cider and apple jus £15.75. Two-course evening meal £21.00.*

Free house ~ Licensees Gerry and Dee Goodwin ~ Real ale ~ Bar food (8am-9.30pm) ~ Restaurant ~ (01237) 451222 ~ Children welcome ~ Dogs allowed in bar and bedrooms ~ Open 8am-11pm(10.30pm Sun) ~ Bedrooms: /£105B ~ www.hoopsinn.co.uk
Recommended by Richard Gibbs

IDDESLEIGH   SS5608   Map 1

Duke of York 🛏

B3217 Exbourne–Dolton; EX19 8BG

Unfussy and exceptionally friendly pub with simply furnished bars, popular food and a fair choice of drinks; charming bedrooms

Originally four cottages built for craftsmen rebuilding the church, this long thatched pub dates from the 15th c. It's as friendly and informal as it has always been and both the licensees and the chatty locals are sure to make you welcome. The enjoyably unspoilt bar has a lot of homely character: rocking chairs, cushioned benches built into the wall's black-painted wooden dado, stripped tables and other simple country furnishings, banknotes pinned to beams, and a large open fireplace. Adnams Broadside, Cotleigh Tawny and a changing guest beer tapped from the cask and quite a few wines by the glass. It can get pretty cramped at peak times. The dining room has a huge inglenook fireplace. Through a small coach arch is a little back garden with some picnic-sets. The timbered bedrooms are charming.

Good, honest, fairly priced bar food includes sandwiches, ploughman's, soup, sausage or ham with eggs, liver and bacon, leek and parsnip cakes with minted yoghurt, local sausages, steak and kidney pudding, fish and chips, liver and bacon, red thai prawn curry, lamb shank with mint and rosemary, and puddings like sticky toffee pudding with toffee sauce and Mars Bar cheesecake; there's a three-course evening menu in the dining room. *Benchmark main dish: steak and kidney pudding £12.50. Two-course evening meal £15.00.*

Free house ~ Licensee John Pittam ~ Real ale ~ Bar food (all day) ~ Restaurant ~ (01837) 810253 ~ Children welcome ~ Dogs allowed in bar and bedrooms ~ Open 11-midnight; 12-10.30 Sun ~ Bedrooms: £40B/£70B ~ www.dukeofyorkdevon.co.uk
Recommended by Mark Flynn, Anthony Longden, Ron and Sheila Corbett, Peter Thornton, David Cheetham, Susan Manley

---

Real ale to us means beer which has matured naturally in its cask – not pressurised or filtered.

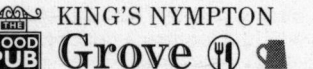

KING'S NYMPTON
SS6819 Map 1

Grove 🍴 🍺

Off B3226 SW of South Molton; EX37 9ST

Thatched 17th-c pub in remote village, local beers, interesting bar food, and cheerful licensees

In a lovely conservation village, this thatched 17th-c pub is much enjoyed by our readers for its local beers and excellent food. It's run by friendly, cheerful licensees and the low-beamed bar has lots of bookmarks hanging from the ceiling, simple pubby furnishings on the flagstoned floor, bare stone walls, a winter log fire and Clearwater Proper Ansome, Cotleigh Barn Owl Premium Ale, and Exmoor Ale on handpump; also, 26 wines (and champagne) by the glass, 60 malt whiskies, local cider, darts, shove-ha'penny and dominoes. They have a self-catering cottage to rent and the pub is surrounded by quiet rolling and wooded countryside.

 Using local, seasonal produce (and maybe trading with regulars for their own-grown surplus vegetables and fruit), the highly thought of food includes sandwiches, chicken liver pâté with toasted brioche, a duo of trout, rabbit stew, rare-breed sausages and mash with onion gravy, chickpea, spinach and cauliflower curry with mango chutney, all-day breakfast, fish pie, chicken breast stuffed with blue cheese, sage and parma ham, an individual beef wellington, and puddings such as hot chocolate pudding and warm cranberry and almond tart with clotted cream. *Benchmark main dish: chicken breast stuffed with parma ham and asparagus £10.50. Two-course evening meal £17.80.*

Free house ~ Licensees Robert and Deborah Smallbone ~ Real ale ~ Bar food (not Sun evening or winter Mon lunchtime) ~ Restaurant ~ (01769) 580406 ~ Children welcome but must be well behaved ~ Dogs welcome ~ Open 12-3, 6-11; 12-4 Sun; closed Sun evening, Mon lunchtime (except bank hols) ~ www.thegroveinn.co.uk *Recommended by Mark Flynn, Mrs Lorna Walsingham, Robert Coleshill*

KINGSBRIDGE
SX7344 Map 1

Dodbrooke Inn 🍺 £

Church Street, Dodbrooke (parking some way off); TQ7 1DB

Chatty, bustling local, genuinely welcoming licensees, good mix of customers and honest food and drink

In warm weather, the attractive covered eating area in the courtyard of this quaint little local is very popular – especially at night when it's candlelit. The long-serving and friendly licensees are sure to make you welcome and there's always a mix of locals (and visitors) of all ages. The atmosphere is comfortably traditional and the bar has plush stools and straightforward built-in cushioned stall seats around pubby tables, ceiling joists, some horse harness, old local photographs and china jugs, and a log fire. Bass, Bath Ales Gem Bitter, and Sharps Cornish Coaster and Doom Bar on handpump and local farm cider. There's also a small, simply furnished dining room.

🍴 Honest bar food includes sandwiches, a changing pâté, garlic mushrooms, home-cooked ham and egg and specials such as scallops with bacon, bass with red onions, and steaks topped with stilton; they offer take-away fish and chips, too. *Benchmark main dish: charcoal-grilled steaks £12.50. Two-course evening meal £18.00.*

Free house ~ Licensees Michael and Jill Dyson ~ Real ale ~ Bar food (12-1.30, 5.30

(7 Sun)-8.30(9 Fri and Sat); not Mon or Tues lunchtime) ~ (01548) 852068 ~ Children welcome if over 5 ~ Dogs welcome ~ Open 12-2, 5-11; 12-2(2.30 Sun), 7-10.30 Sun; closed Mon and Tues lunchtimes *Recommended by MP, DHV, John and Gloria Isaacs*

LUSTLEIGH
SX7881 Map 1
Cleave

Off A382 Bovey Tracey–Moretonhampstead; TQ13 9TJ

In a popular beauty spot – so it's best to arrive early – this thatched pub has a roaring log fire and well liked food and drink; pretty summer garden

Picture-postcard pretty, this thatched 15th-c pub has a lovely sheltered summer garden with plenty of seats and lots of hanging baskets and flower beds. Inside, you can be sure of a genuinely warm welcome from the landlord and his friendly staff – our readers often describe the place as a 'gem'. The low-ceilinged lounge bar has a roaring log fire, attractive antique high-backed settles, cushioned wall seats and wheelback chairs around the tables on its patterned carpet and granite walls. A second bar has similar furnishings, a large dresser, a harmonium, an HMV gramophone and prints, and there's a family room with toys for children. Otter Ale and Bitter and a couple of guests such as Dartmoor Jail Ale and Skinners Betty Stogs on handpump, quite a few malt whiskies, several wines by the glass and local organic soft drinks.

Usefully served all day, the well presented, fairly priced food might include sandwiches, szechuan-style home-cured salmon, lambs kidneys on rösti potato with a piquant sauce, local mussels, sausages in ale gravy with bubble and squeak, pumpkin ravioli with sage butter and balsamic onions, martinique-style fruity chicken curry, a rack of pork ribs, haddock and chips with mushy peas, venison with sweet potato mash, and puddings such as banana cheesecake with toffee sauce and vanilla panna cotta with rhubarb compote. *Benchmark main dish: ligurian fish stew £10.95. Two-course evening meal £16.00.*

Heavitree ~ Tenant Ben Whitton ~ Real ale ~ Bar food (11-9; 12-8.30 Sun) ~ Restaurant ~ (01647) 277223 ~ Children welcome ~ Dogs allowed in bar ~ Open 11-11 ~ www.thecleavelustleigh.com *Recommended by Suzy Miller, Barry Steele-Perkins, Geoffrey Medcalf, Jadzia Denselow, Mrs C Sleight*

MARLDON
SX8663 Map 1
Church House

Off A380 NW of Paignton; TQ3 1SL
Devon Dining Pub of the Year

Spreading bar plus several other rooms in this pleasant inn, well liked drinks and bar food, and seats on three terraces

Very popular locally – always a good sign – this bustling pub is neatly kept and run by a friendly landlord and his helpful staff. The attractively furnished spreading bar with its woodburning stove has several different areas that radiate off the big semicircular bar counter: unusual windows, some beams, dark pine and other nice old dining chairs around solid tables and yellow leather bar chairs. Leading off here is a cosy little candlelit room with just four tables on the bare-boarded floor, a dark wood dado and stone fireplace. There's also a restaurant with a large stone fireplace and, at the other end of the building, a similarly interesting room is split into two parts with a stone floor in one and a wooden floor in the other (which has a big woodburning

stove). The old barn holds yet another restaurant with displays by local artists. Bays Gold, Otter Ale and St Austell Dartmoor Best and Tribute on handpump, 15 wines by the glass and several malt whiskies; background music. There are picnic-sets on three carefully maintained grassy terraces behind the pub.

Using some of their own-grown vegetables, the highly thought of food might include lunchtime sandwiches, spanish fish soup, coarse pork pâté with spiced nectarine chutney, pork, tomato and basil sausages with leek mash and red wine gravy, aubergine and lentil moussaka, tiger prawns in lemon, garlic and rosemary oil, cord-fed chicken filled with mushroom stuffing with a roast garlic sauce, chargrilled pork loin with noodles and a sweet and sour sauce, turbot with sun-blush tomato butter and soused fennel, and puddings such as chocolate and hazelnut meringue gateau with crème fraîche and chocolate drizzle and roasted fig and frangipane tart, mulled wine syrup and vanilla mascarpone cream. *Benchmark main dish: slow-roast lamb shoulder £15.50. Two-course evening meal £20.50.*

Enterprise ~ Lease Julian Cook ~ Real ale ~ Bar food (12-2(2.30 Sun), 6.30-9.30(9 Sun)) ~ Restaurant ~ (01803) 558279 ~ Children welcome ~ Dogs allowed in bar ~ Open 11.30-2.30, 5-11(5.30-11.30 Sat); 12-3, 5.30-10.30 Sun ~ www.churchhousemarldon. com *Recommended by Pat and Tony Martin, Eryl and Keith Dykes, Martin and Judith Tomlinson, Geoff and Linda Payne, Derek and Maggie Washington, Jane Woodhull, Damian and Lucy Buxton*

MOLLAND
London

SS8028   Map 1

Village signed off B3227 E of South Molton; EX36 3NG

A proper Exmoor inn with customers and their dogs to match, a warm welcome, honest food and real ales; bedrooms

Tucked away down narrow lanes, this is a proper Exmoor inn with plenty of chatty locals and a welcoming landlord. The two small linked rooms by the old-fashioned central servery have hardly changed in 50 years and have lots of local stag-hunting pictures, tough carpeting or rugs on flagstones, cushioned benches and plain chairs around rough stripped trestle tables and Exmoor Ale on handpump. On the left an attractive beamed room has accounts of the rescued stag which lived a long life at the pub many years ago and. on the right, a panelled dining room with a great curved settle by its fireplace has particularly good hunting and game bird prints, including ones by McPhail and Hester Lloyd. A small hall has stuffed birds and animals. The low-ceilinged lavatories are worth a look with their Victorian mahogany and tiling (and in the gents' a testament to the prodigious thirst of the village cricket team). There are picnic-sets in the cottagey garden. Don't miss the next-door church, with its untouched early 18th-c box pews – and, in spring, a carpet of tenby daffodils in the graveyard.

Tasty food now includes sandwiches, chicken liver parfait, mussels, goats cheese and tomato tart, faggots with bubble and squeak, home-cooked ham and free-range eggs, fish dishes such as whole black bream and herb-crusted cod, rib-eye steak and chips, and puddings like glazed lemon tart and sticky toffee pudding. *Benchmark main dish: daily-changing fresh fish £11.95. Two-course evening meal £20.00.*

Free house ~ Licensee Stuart Mallen ~ Real ale ~ Bar food (12-2, 6-9; not winter Sun evening or winter Mon) ~ Restaurant ~ No credit cards ~ (01769) 550269 ~ Children welcome ~ Dogs allowed in bar and bedrooms ~ Open 12-3, 6-11; 12-4, 7-11 Sun; closed winter Sun evening and all day winter Mon ~ Bedrooms: /£75B ~ www.londoninnmolland.co.uk *Recommended by Caroline Cornelisse*

PARKHAM
Bell ◀

SS3821   Map 1

Rectory Lane; EX39 5PL

An honest village pub with chatty locals, welcoming landlord, neatly kept bars, four real ales and well liked food

This is a cheerful 13th-c thatched village pub and very much the heart of the community. The three connected rooms are spotlessly kept and full of chatty locals and you can be sure of a first-rate welcome from the landlord and his staff. There are beams and standing timbers hung with horsebrasses, a woodburning stove in the main bar and a small coal fire in the lower one, brass and copper jugs here and there, nice old photos of the pub and the village, a grandfather clock and pubby tables and seats (mates' and other straightforward chairs and burgundy or green plush stools) on the red-patterned carpet. There are some model ships and lanterns above the bar, where Cotleigh Barn Owl, Jollyboat Mainbrace, Sharps Doom Bar and Skinners Betty Stogs are on handpump; there are some model ships and lanterns above the bar. Darts. The covered and fairy-lit back terrace has some picnic-sets.

🍴 Fair value food includes sandwiches, chicken liver pâté with cumberland sauce, creamy garlic mushrooms, ham and eggs, local sausages with onion gravy, hake with a cheese and herb topping, aubergine parmigiana, chicken curry, fresh beer-battered cod, steak and kidney pie, slow-roast pork belly with cider, and puddings such as fresh fruit crumble and knickerbocker glory. *Benchmark main dish: chicken fillet with smoked bacon and mushroom sauce £10.95. Two-course evening meal £16.75.*

Free house ~ Licensees Michael and Rachel Sanders ~ Real ale ~ Bar food (12-1.30, 6-8.30) ~ Restaurant ~ (01237) 451201 ~ Children welcome ~ Dogs allowed in bar ~ Open 12-2.30(3 Sun), 5.30(5 Fri and Sat, 6 Sun)-11 ~ www.thebellinnparkham.co.uk
Recommended by Michael Snaith, Richard Tilbrook, Peter Thornton, M and GR

PORTGATE
Harris Arms ♀

SX4185   Map 1

Leave A30 E of Launceston at Broadwoodwidger turn-off (with brown Dingle Steam Village sign) and head S; Launceston Road (old A30 between Lewdown and Lifton); EX20 4PZ

Enthusiastic, well travelled licensees in roadside pub with exceptional wine list and interesting food

The wines are chosen very carefully here as both Mr and Mrs Whiteman are qualified, award-winning wine-makers (they are growing their own vines). There are detailed, helpful notes with each wine and around 22 of their favourites are served by the glass; you can buy them to take home, too. The bar has a woodburning stove, some rather fine photographs, burgundy end walls and cream ones in between, and afghan saddle-bag cushions scattered around a mixture of dining chairs and along a red plush built-in wall banquette. On the left, steps lead down to the dining room with elegant beech dining chairs (and more afghan cushions) around stripped-wood tables, and there are some unusual paintings on the walls. Bays Topsail and Otter Bitter on handpump, local cider and Luscombe organic soft drinks; there may be a pile of country magazines. On a heated decked area there are seats among pots of lavender and in the sloping back garden plenty of picnic-sets look out over rolling hills.

🍴 Using local farmers, seasonal produce, artisan cheeses, home-grown vegetables and eggs from their own hens, the inventive food might include sandwiches, slow-cooked pork cheeks, sweet potato and mushroom hash with sage and cider sauce, home-cooked ham and eggs, a trio of sausages with onion gravy, crispy confit of duck with haricot bean and chorizo ragout with red wine sauce, specials such as pheasant casserole, beef, venison and mushroom in ale pie and spicy moroccan-style vegetables with cumin and raisin couscous, and puddings like warm treacle sponge with butterscotch sauce and white chocolate cheesecake with home-made shortbread and a fruit compote. *Benchmark main dish: 24-hour roast pork £11.95. Two-course evening meal £19.70.*

Free house ~ Licensees Andy and Rowena Whiteman ~ Real ale ~ Bar food (12-2, 6-9; not Sun evening or Mon) ~ Restaurant ~ (01566) 783331 ~ Well behaved children welcome ~ Dogs allowed in bar ~ Open 12-3, 6-11; 12-3 Sun; closed Sun evening, Mon ~ www.harrisarms.co.uk *Recommended by John Wooll, David Jackman, Di and Mike Gillam*

POSTBRIDGE   SX6780 Map 1
Warren House

B3212 0.75 miles NE of Postbridge; PL20 6TA

Straightforward old pub, relaxing for a drink or meal after a Dartmoor hike

Remote on Dartmoor (and a valuable refuge after a walk), this friendly place has a lot of local character and is something of a focus for the scattered moorland community. The cosy bar is straightforward with simple furnishings such as easy chairs and settles under the beamed ochre ceiling, old pictures of the inn on the partly panelled stone walls and dim lighting (powered by the pub's own generator); one of the fireplaces is said to have been kept alight almost continuously since 1845. There's also a family room. Adnams Broadside, Otter Ale and Sharps Doom Bar and one or two guest beers on handpump, local farm cider and malt whiskies; background music, darts and board games. The picnic-sets on both sides of the road have moorland views.

🍴 Decent bar food includes filled baguettes, mushroom stroganoff, good rabbit or steak in ale pies, gammon and pineapple, breaded king prawns with a garlic dip, cajun chicken, and lamb shank in red wine and rosemary. *Benchmark main dish: rabbit pie £11.50. Two-course evening meal £16.50.*

Free house ~ Licensee Peter Parsons ~ Real ale ~ Bar food (12-9(8.30 Sun); winter Mon and Tues 12-4.30) ~ (01822) 880208 ~ Children in family room ~ Dogs allowed in bar ~ Open 11-11; 11-5 Mon and Tues during Nov-Feb; 12-10.30 Sun ~ www.warrenhouseinn.co.uk *Recommended by Reg Fowle, Helen Rickwood*

RATTERY   SX7461 Map 1
Church House

Village signposted from A385 W of Totnes, and A38 S of Buckfastleigh; TQ10 9LD

One of Britain's oldest pubs with plenty to look at, a friendly landlord, a good range of drinks and popular bar food; peaceful views

The original building here probably housed the craftsmen who built the Norman church, and may then have served as a hostel for passing monks. There are some fine original features – notably the spiral stone steps behind a little stone doorway, on your left as you come in, which date from about 1030. It's a charming place with particularly helpful, friendly staff and plenty of character: massive oak beams and standing

timbers in the homely open-plan bar, large fireplaces (one with a little cosy nook partitioned off around it), traditional pubby chairs and tables on the patterned carpet, some window seats and prints and horsebrasses on the plain white walls. The dining room is separated from this room by heavy curtains and there's a lounge area, too. Dartmoor Jail Ale and Legend, Exmoor Ale and Fullers/Gales Seafarers on handpump, 15 malt whiskies and ten wines by the glass. The garden has picnic-sets on the large hedged-in lawn and peaceful views of the partly wooded surrounding hills.

A wide choice of popular food might include sandwiches, devilled whitebait, lasagne, cider and honey baked ham and egg, stilton and vegetable crumble, battered cod and chips, chicken wrapped in smoked bacon in a cheese and leek sauce, a special grill, specials such as duck and orange pâté, steak and kidney pudding, venison sausages with spicy mash and gravy, guinea fowl with a cherry and port sauce, monkfish with a brandy, cream and mushroom sauce, and puddings like raspberry and blackberry crème brûlée and bread and butter pudding. *Benchmark main dish: Steak in ale pie £9.95. Two-course evening meal £18.50.*

Free house ~ Licensee Ray Hardy ~ Real ale ~ Bar food (11.30-2, 7-9) ~ Restaurant ~ (01364) 642220 ~ Children welcome ~ Dogs allowed in bar ~ Open 11-2.30, 6-11; 12-3, 6-10.30 Sun ~ www.thechurchhouseinn.co.uk *Recommended by Geoff and Carol Thorp, David Jackman, Michael and Lynne Gittins, B J Harding, Hugh Roberts, David Eberlin*

SANDFORD
SS8202 Map 1

Lamb 🍺 ⛉
The Square; EX17 4LW

Bustling, friendly 16th-c inn with much genuine character, beams and standing timbers, cheerful, helpful service, very good food and seats in garden; well equipped bedrooms

Not only is this delightful 16th-c pub the heart of the village and full of cheerful locals who drop in at any time of day for a morning coffee, a chatty pint or a good meal, but there's a genuinely warm welcome for visitors, too. The bustling beamed main bar and dining area are linked and the atmosphere throughout is one of informality and friendliness. On a cold day the red leather sofas by the log fire in its stone fireplace are highly prized and there are a couple of tables with cushioned window seats, a cushioned settle and various dining chairs around them on the patterned carpet; there's also a handsome carved chest, a table of newspapers and magazines, a noticeboard full of local news and adverts and high chairs by the counter where they keep Dartmoor Friggins, Otter Bitter, Red Fox Hunters Gold and Teignworthy Beachcomber on handpump, lots of wines by the glass and 20 malt whiskies. The dining side has a woodburning stove, a cushioned wall pew, all manner of nice old wooden dining chairs and tables (each with a church candle) and the same heavy beams; the landlord's wife does the large animal paintings (which are also in the bedrooms). There's also a simpler public bar and a skittle alley that also functions as a cinema. The jack russell is called Tiny and the collie, Bob. The informal cobbled garden has fairy lights and simple seats and tables and there are picnic-sets on grass beyond the hedge. The bedrooms are comfortable, modern and well equipped. Nearby parking is at a premium but you can use the village car park, which is just a few minutes' walk up the small lane to the right.

From a sensibly short menu and using home-grown and local produce and home-made bread and pasta, there's some sort of enjoyable food all day: lunchtime sandwiches (not Sun), smoked mackerel rillettes with crème fraîche,

jelly and pickled beetroot, duck liver parfait with onion marmalade, local sausages with onion gravy, vegetable parcel with bubble and squeak, tasty guinea fowl breast with brussel sprouts, bacon and cream, sea bream on bourguignon risotto with wild mushrooms and crispy leeks and puddings such as apple crumble and chocolate fondant. *Benchmark main dish: roast haunch of venison with fig tarte, roast celeriac and jus £14.50. Two-course evening meal £19.00.*

Free house ~ Licensee Mark Hildyard ~ Real ale ~ Bar food (12.30-2.15, 6.30-9.15) ~ (01363) 773676 ~ Children welcome ~ Dogs welcome ~ open mike night last Fri of month; Zumba Weds evening, cinema weekends; music festival 2nd weekend Sept ~ Open 9am(10.30 weekends)-midnight ~ Bedrooms: £65S/£85S(£120B) ~ www.lambinnsandford.co.uk *Recommended by Elaine Lee, Peter Thornton, Michael Coleman, Charles Meade-King*

SIDBURY SY1496 Map 1
Hare & Hounds 🍺
3 miles N of Sidbury, at Putts Corner; A375 towards Honiton, crossroads with B3174; EX10 0QQ

Large, well run roadside pub with log fires, beams and attractive layout, popular daily carvery, efficient staff, and a big garden

As we went to press, a new dining extension was being built on to this sizeable roadside pub . It will have a central open fire surrounded by dining chairs and tables, and doors opening out on to a decked area; seats from here and picnic-sets in the big garden have marvellous views down the Sid Valley to the sea at Sidmouth. It's a large place with two log fires (and rather unusual wood-framed leather sofas complete with pouffes), heavy beams and fresh flowers, plenty of tables with red plush-cushioned dining chairs, window seats and leather sofas, and is mostly carpeted, with bare boards and stripped-stone walls at one end. From a long bar with high bar chairs they offer Otter Bitter and Ale and St Austell Tribute tapped from the cask and several wines by the glass.

As well as a very popular carvery (all day on Sunday), the extensive choice of food includes sandwiches, filled baguettes and toasties, chicken liver pâté, natural smoked haddock, prawn and chive mousse wrapped in smoked scottish salmon, beef or lamb and mint burger, cottage pie topped with colcannon mash, vegetable and lentil casserole with herb dumplings, a hot prawn curry, steak and kidney pudding, chicken in a bacon, mushroom, garlic, cream and sherry sauce, and puddings. *Benchmark main dish: lasagne £8.95. Two-course evening meal £15.50.*

Heartstone Inns ~ Managers Graham Cole and Lindsey Chun ~ Real ale ~ Bar food (all day) ~ (01404) 41760 ~ Children welcome away from bar ~ Dogs allowed in bar ~ Open 10am-11pm(10.30pm Sun) ~ www.hareandhounds-devon.co.uk *Recommended by Derek and Maggie Washington, Richard Wyld, George Atkinson*

SIDFORD SY1389 Map 1
Blue Ball 🍺
A3052 just N of Sidmouth; EX10 9QL

Big, popular inn with friendly staff, four real ales, well liked food and a neat garden; bedrooms

With coastal walks just ten minutes away, it's useful that this handsome thatched pub is open all day for food. There's a good bustling atmosphere and the friendly family (who have been here for 100 years now) offer a warm welcome to all their customers. The central bar

covers three main areas and has light beams, bar stools and a nice mix of wooden dining chairs around circular tables on patterned carpet, three log fires, prints, horsebrasses and plenty of bric-a-brac on the walls, and Bass, Otter Bitter, St Austell Tribute and Sharps Doom Bar on handpump; cheerful service. The public bar has darts, games machine and board games; skittle alley and background music. There are seats on a terrace and in the flower-filled garden and a well designed wooden smokers' gazebo.

🍴 As well as opening early for breakfasts, they serve well liked bar food including sandwiches, chicken liver pâté with red onion marmalade, beef or vegetable lasagne, local beer-battered fish with mushy peas and tartare sauce, honey-glazed ham with eggs, sausages with onion and grain mustard gravy, specials like prawn toast with chinese spice dipping sauce, cod wrapped in parma ham with a mixed bean and chorizo stew and thai green chicken curry, and puddings; their roasts are served on Wednesdays as well as Sundays. *Benchmark main dish: steak and kidney pudding £10.95. Two-course evening meal £15.50.*

Punch ~ Lease Roger Newton ~ Real ale ~ Bar food (8-10 for breakfast, 12-2.30, 6-9; 12-3, 5.30-8.30 Sun) ~ Restaurant ~ (01395) 514062 ~ Children welcome away from bar ~ Dogs allowed in bar ~ Open 8am-11pm ~ Bedrooms: £60B/£95B ~ www.blueballinn.net
Recommended by Michael Mellers, Sara Fulton, Roger Baker, Pat and Roger Davies, M G Hart, Dave Braisted

🏠 SLAPTON   SX8245   Map 1

Tower 🍴

Off A379 Dartmouth–Kingsbridge; TQ7 2PN

Bustling inn with friendly young owners, beams and log fires, impressive food, good beers and wines, and pretty back garden; refurbished bedrooms

This fine old inn was built around 1347 to house the workers building the chantry next door – now an ivy-covered ruin that overlooks the picnic-sets on the lawn in the pretty garden. It's a friendly place with a good mix of customers (including a genuine core of chatty locals) and the atmosphere is relaxed and informal. The low-ceilinged beamed bar has armchairs, low-backed settles and scrubbed oak tables on the flagstones or bare boards, open log fires, Butcombe Bitter, Otter Bitter, St Austell Proper Job and Sharps Doom Bar on handpump and several wines by the glass; background music. Our readers have enjoyed staying in the refurbished bedrooms recently. The lane up to the pub is very narrow and parking can be tricky at peak times.

🍴 Imaginative food includes lunchtime sandwiches, diver-caught scallops with jerusalem artichoke purée, chorizo, crispy pancetta and herbs, potted confit duck with fish relish and walnut toast, moules frites, wild mushroom tortellini with a white wine, cream and herb sauce, home-made burger with local bacon or blue cheese, rabbit pie, bass in vodka batter with tartare sauce, a trio of lamb (slow cooked mini casserole, sweetbreads and best end cutlet), and puddings like chocolate and chestnut parfait with a chestnut purée and crème brûlée with a shortbread biscuit. *Benchmark main dish: moules frites £11.95. Two-course evening meal £21.00.*

Free house ~ Licensee Dan Cheshire ~ Real ale ~ Bar food (12-2.30, 6-9.30; not winter Sun evening) ~ (01548) 580216 ~ Children not allowed in bar ~ Dogs allowed in bar and bedrooms ~ Open 12-3, 6-11; 12-3, 7-10.30 Sun; closed Sun evening in winter ~ Bedrooms: £50S/£70S ~ www.thetowerinn.com *Recommended by Mr and Mrs John Clifford, Nick Lawless*

STAVERTON
Sea Trout 🍴 🛏

SX7964   Map 1

Village signposted from A384 NW of Totnes; TQ9 6PA

Hard-working, enthusiastic licensees in bustling village inn, real ales, enjoyable food and seats in garden; comfortable bedrooms

'An excellent all-rounder' and 'a gem' are just two of the comments from enthusiastic readers about this particularly well run, partly 15th-c inn – and the hard-working, hands-on landlord and his staff make all their customers feel genuinely welcomed, even when the place is packed. The neatly kept and rambling beamed lounge bar has sea trout and salmon flies and stuffed fish on the walls and elegant armed wheelback chairs around a mix of wooden tables on the part-carpeted, part-wooden floor. The locals' bar is simpler with wooden wall and other seats, a stag's head, a gun and horsebrasses on the walls, a large stuffed fish in a cabinet above the woodburning stove and a cheerful mix of locals and visitors. Palmers 200, Best and Copper Ale on handpump and nine wines by the glass. The panelled restaurant and conservatory are both furnished with smart high-backed fabric-covered dining chairs around more wooden tables. There are seats in the terraced garden and the bedrooms (our readers love staying here) overlook either this or the country lane; lots to do and see nearby. They are kind to dogs with treats and water bowls dotted about the garden. You can fish on the nearby River Dart and the inn offers packages to fishermen that include accommodation and daily tickets.

Enjoyable food might include lunchtime sandwiches, seared scallops with lemon and cauliflower purée and wild mushrooms, chicken liver pâté with red onion marmalade, thick cut ham and egg, crispy battered fish and chips, wild mushroom tortelli with a mushroom and tarragon cream sauce, massaman curry with monkfish, butternut squash, peanuts and coriander, venison steak with a light juniper jus, daily specials, and puddings such as sticky toffee pudding with pecan sauce and home-made vanilla fudge ice-cream and passion fruit crème brûlée. *Benchmark main dish: slow-roast pork belly with chorizo bubble and squeak £13.85. Two-course evening meal £20.00.*

Palmers ~ Tenants Jason and Samantha Price ~ Real ale ~ Bar food (12-2(3 Sun), 6(7 Sun)-9) ~ Restaurant ~ (01803) 762274 ~ Children welcome away from the bar ~ Dogs allowed in bar and bedrooms ~ Open 9am-11pm(midnight Sat, 10.30 Sun) ~ Bedrooms: £65S/£102S ~ www.seatroutinn.co.uk *Recommended by George Price, Karen Skinner, Michael Coleman, Lynda and Trevor Smith, Sara Fulton, Roger Baker, Richard and Patricia Jefferson, Will Palmer, David Jackman*

TIPTON ST JOHN
Golden Lion

SY0991   Map 1

Pub signed off B3176 Sidmouth–Ottery St Mary; EX10 0AA

Friendly village pub with three real ales, well liked bar food, a good mix of customers and plenty of seats in the attractive garden

Deservedly popular, this is a bustling village pub with a good mix of locals and diners from further afield. The main bar – which is split into two – has a comfortable, relaxed atmosphere, as does the back snug, and throughout the building there are paintings from west country artists, art deco prints, tiffany lamps and hops, copper pots and kettles hanging from the beams. They try to keep a few tables for those just wanting a pint and a chat and have Bass and Otter Ale and Bitter on

handpump and a dozen wines by the glass; maybe background music and cards. There's a verandah for dog walkers and smokers, seats on the terracotta-walled terrace with outside heaters and grapevines and more seats on the grass edged by pretty flowering borders; summer Sunday evening jazz out here.

🍴 As well as lunchtime sandwiches and their popular chunky fish soup, the well liked bar food includes home-smoked duck salad with onion marmalade, crevettes in garlic butter, vegetable lasagne, ham and egg, liver and bacon, steak and kidney pudding, specials like moules frites, chicken with a light creamy sherry sauce and venison pie, and puddings. *Benchmark main dish: bass with tomatoes and pesto £16.00. Two-course evening meal £19.00.*

Heavitree ~ Tenants François and Michelle Teissier ~ Real ale ~ Bar food (12-2, 6.30-8.30; not winter Sun evening) ~ (01404) 812881 ~ Children welcome ~ Jazz summer Sun evenings ~ Open 12-2.30(3 weekends), 6-10.30; 12-3, 6.30-10 Sun; closed winter Sun evening Oct-Mar ~ www.goldenliontipton.co.uk *Recommended by Mrs C Roe, Mr and Mrs W Mills, George Atkinson, Gene and Tony Freemantle*

TORBRYAN
SX8266 Map 1

🏠 GOOD PUB GUIDE Old Church House
Off A381; TQ12 5UR

Ancient inn with original features in neat rooms, friendly service and popular food and beer

Quietly set next to the part-Saxon church with its battlemented Norman tower, this Grade II* listed 13th-c inn is a friendly place with a welcome for all. The particularly attractive bar on the right of the door is neatly kept and bustling and has benches built into the fine old panelling as well as a cushioned high-backed settle and leather-backed small seats around its big log fire. On the left, there's a series of comfortable and discreetly lit lounges, one with a splendid deep Tudor inglenook fireplace with a side bread oven; background music. Hunters Pheasant Plucker, Skinners Betty Stogs, St Austell Tribute and changing guest on handpump, several wines by the glass and around 35 malt whiskies; good service. Plenty of nearby walks.

🍴 Using meat from local farms and other local seasonal produce, the fairly priced food might include filled baguettes, chicken liver pâté with red onion marmalade, salmon and prawn fishcakes with sweet chilli sauce, haddock mornay, lasagne, chicken breast with bacon, port and stilton cream sauce, pork escalope with onions and mushrooms and a brandy and masala cream sauce, beef medallions with pickled dill cucumber, Pernod, cream and french fried onion rings, daily specials, and puddings; curry night is Tuesday. *Benchmark main dish: beef in ale pie £8.95. Two-course evening meal £19.20.*

Free house ~ Licensees Kane and Carolynne Clarke ~ Real ale ~ Bar food (12-2, 7-9) ~ Restaurant ~ (01803) 812372 ~ Children welcome ~ Occasional live music evenings – see website ~ Open 11-11 ~ Bedrooms: £54B/£89B ~ www.oldchurchhouseinn.co.uk *Recommended by Gene and Tony Freemantle, Malcolm and Barbara Southwell*

Bedroom prices normally include full english breakfast, VAT and any inclusive service charge that we know of. Prices before the '/' are for single rooms, after for two people in double or twin (B includes a private bath, S a private shower). If there is no '/', the prices are only for twin or double rooms (as far as we know there are no singles). If there is no B or S, as far as we know no rooms have private facilities.

TORQUAY   SX9265   Map 1

Cary Arms ♀ 🛏

Beach Road: off B3199 Babbacombe Road, via Babbacombe Downs Road; turn steeply down near Babbacombe Theatre; TQ1 3LX

Interesting bar in secluded hotel with lovely sea views, plenty of outside seating, enjoyable if not cheap food, real ales and friendly service; sea-view bedrooms

At the bottom of a tortuously steep lane, this is a rather charming and unusual higgledy-piggledy place in Babbacombe Bay. The fine sea and cliff views can be enjoyed from picnic-sets on the terraces, from good quality teak chairs and tables on gravel, and from the big windows in the bar; there are steps leading down to the quay below, a little raised platform with just one table and a few chairs (much prized in good weather), an outside bar, a barbecue and a pizza oven. Inside, the beamed, grotto-effect bar has rough pinky granite walls, various alcoves, rustic, hobbit-style red leather cushioned chairs around carved wooden tables on slate or bare boards, an open woodburning stove with a ship's wheel above it, and some high bar chairs beside the stone bar counter where they serve Bays Topsail, Devon Coast and Otter Ale on handpump, local cider and decent wines by the glass; cheerful young staff. There's also a small, glass-enclosed entrance room with large ship lanterns and cleats; darts and board games. The civilised boutique-style hotel is a special place to stay; they also have four self-catering properties. There are six mooring spaces and they can arrange a water taxi for guests arriving by boat.

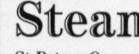 Enjoyable food includes sandwiches, pork, chicken and bacon terrine with fig and plum compote, mussels in white wine, cream and shallots, local fish and chips with tartare sauce and crushed peas, steak in ale pie with pan haggerty, dressed local crab salad, wild mushroom and pistachio nut roast with a port and cranberry sauce, lamb loin with red wine and rosemary gravy, duck breast on champ mash with smoked bacon and shallot sauce, hake fillet with anchovy and tomato butter, and puddings like warm orange and almond tart and warm chocolate brownie and chocolate sauce. *Benchmark main dish: beer-battered fish and chips £13.95. Two-course evening meal £22.50.*

Free house ~ Licensee Jen Podmore ~ Real ale ~ Bar food (12-3, 6.30-9) ~ (01803) 327110 ~ Children welcome ~ Dogs allowed in bar and bedrooms ~ Weekly summer Sun jazz; monthly in winter ~ Open 12-11(10.30 Sun) ~ Bedrooms: £180S/£270S ~ www.caryarms.co.uk *Recommended by Mrs M B Gregg, Comus and Sarah Elliott, Len Beattie, Dr and Mrs A K Clarke*

TOTNES   SX8059   Map 1

Steam Packet

St Peters Quay, on W bank (ie not on Steam Packet Quay); TQ9 5EW

Seats outside overlooking quay, interesting layout and décor inside, popular food and drink; bedrooms

On a fine day, it's best to get to this busy pub early if you're hoping to bag one of the seats and tables on the front terrace overlooking the River Dart; there are walks along the river bank from here. Inside, it's interestingly laid out with bare stone walls and wooden flooring and one end has an open log fire, a squashy leather sofa with lots of cushions against a wall of books, a similar seat built into a small curved brick wall (which breaks up the room) and a TV. The main bar has built-in wall

benches and plenty of stools and chairs around traditional pub tables and a further area has a coal fire and dark wood furniture. Dartmoor Jail Ale, Sharps Doom Bar and a guest from Hunters named for the pub on handpump and several wines by the glass. The conservatory restaurant has high-backed leather dining chairs around wooden tables, and smart window blinds.

🍴 Tasty bar food includes lunchtime sandwiches, chicken caesar salad, salmon and dill fishcakes with tomato salsa, halloumi, roasted pepper and sunblush tomato tagliatelle, beer-battered fish of the day with minted mushy peas, a pie of the day, moroccan-style chicken, and puddings. *Benchmark main dish: slow-roast pork belly with bubble and squeak and onion gravy £9.95. Two-course evening meal £17.95.*

Buccaneer Holdings ~ Manager Richard Cockburn ~ Real ale ~ Bar food (12-2.30, 6-9) ~ Restaurant ~ (01803) 863880 ~ Children welcome ~ Dogs welcome ~ Open 11-11; 12-10.30 Sun ~ Bedrooms: £59.50B/£79.50B ~ www.steampacketinn.co.uk
Recommended by P Dawn, Mike Gorton, Malcolm and Barbara Southwell, Gary Bloyce, Roger and Donna Huggins

WIDECOMBE   SX7276 Map 1
Rugglestone 🍺

Village at end of B3387; pub just S – turn left at church and NT church house, OS Sheet 191 map reference 720765; TQ13 7TF

Unspoilt local near busy tourist village, with a couple of bars, cheerful customers, friendly staff, four real ales and traditional pub food

Just a walk from the busy tourist village, this is a charming, cottagey pub with a warm welcome for both locals and visitors. The unspoilt bar has only four tables, a few window and wall seats, a one-person pew built into the corner by the nice old stone fireplace (where there's a woodburner), and a good mix of customers. The rudimentary bar counter dispenses Butcombe Bitter and Dartmoor Legend and a couple of guests like Otter Bright and Teignworthy Gun Dog tapped from the cask; local farm cider and a decent small wine list. The room on the right is a bit bigger and lighter-feeling with another stone fireplace, a beamed ceiling, stripped-pine tables and a built-in wall bench, and there's also a small dining room. There are seats in the field across the little moorland stream and tables and chairs in the garden. They have a holiday cottage for rent.

🍴 Honest bar food includes sandwiches, a large pasty, chicken liver pâté, ham and eggs, cheese and spinach cannelloni, spicy meatballs with potato wedges, beef in ale pie, lambs liver with bacon and onion gravy and beer-battered fresh haddock. *Benchmark main dish: luxury fish pie £10.50. Two-course evening meal £16.45.*

Free house ~ Licensees Richard and Vicki Palmer ~ Real ale ~ Bar food (12-2, 6-9) ~ Restaurant ~ (01364) 621327 ~ Children allowed but must be away from bar area ~ Dogs welcome ~ Open 11.30-3, 6-11.30(5-midnight Fri); 11.30am-midnight Sat; 12-11 Sun ~ www.rugglestoneinn.co.uk *Recommended by Tim Maddison, Mike Gorton, Michael Coleman, Andrea Rampley*

If a service charge is mentioned prominently on a menu or accommodation terms, you must pay it if service was satisfactory. If service is really bad you are legally entitled to refuse to pay some or all of the service charge as compensation for not getting the service you might reasonably have expected.

GOOD PUB GUIDE WINKLEIGH   SS6308   Map 1

Kings Arms

Fore Street; off B3220 Crediton–Torrington; EX19 8HQ

Friendly pub with woodburning stoves in beamed main bar, west country beers and popular food

With friendly licensees and chatty locals, this thatched village pub hasn't changed much – which is just how our readers like it. The most character can be found in the cosy beamed main bar with old-fashioned built-in wall settles and benches around scrubbed pine tables on flagstones and a woodburning stove in a cavernous fireplace; another woodburning stove separates the bar from the green- or red-painted dining rooms (one has military memorabilia and a glass-covered old mine shaft). Butcombe Bitter, Otter Bitter and Sharps Doom Bar on handpump and two local ciders; board games. There are seats in the garden.

Traditional bar food includes sandwiches, soup, ham and eggs, vegetarian shepherd's pie, a curry of the day, meatballs in bolognaise sauce, seasonal crab salad, fish and chips and lambs liver and bacon. *Benchmark main dish: steak and kidney parcel £11.95. Two-course evening meal £17.50.*

Enterprise ~ Lease Cheryl and Denis MacDonald ~ Real ale ~ Bar food (all day) ~ Restaurant ~ (01837) 83384 ~ Children welcome ~ Dogs allowed in bar ~ Open 11-11; 12-10.30 Sun ~ www.thekingsarmswinkleigh.co.uk *Recommended by Mark Flynn, Mrs P Sumner, Jeremy Whitehorn, John and Judy Phillips, Michael Coleman*

GOOD PUB GUIDE WOODBURY SALTERTON   SY0189   Map 1

Diggers Rest

3.5 miles from M5 junction 30: A3052 towards Sidmouth, village signposted on right about 0.5 miles after Clyst St Mary; also signposted from B3179 SE of Exeter; EX5 1PQ

Bustling village pub with real ales, well liked food and lovely views from the terraced garden

This thatched village pub is 500 years old and very much the heart of the village. The main bar has antique furniture, local art on the walls and a cosy seating area by the open fire with its extra large sofa and armchair. The modern extension is light and airy and opens on to the garden, which has contemporary garden furniture under canvas parasols on the terrace and lovely countryside views. Bays Topsail and Otter Ale and Bitter on handpump, 13 wines by the glass and Weston's cider; background music, darts, TV and board games. The window boxes and flowering baskets are pretty.

Using seasonal produce from named local suppliers, the interesting bar food includes sandwiches, potted pork with pickles and home-made bread, beetroot-cured gravadlax with horseradish cream and crispy capers, thai beef salad, moroccan vegetable and chickpea tagine with apricots and couscous, beer-battered fish and chips, steak and mushroom pie, venison bangers and mash with parsnip crisps and red wine gravy, and puddings like rhubarb crème brûlée with home-made shortbread and sticky toffee pudding with butterscotch sauce and a brandy snap basket. *Benchmark main dish: steak in ale pie £9.95. Two-course evening meal £17.00.*

Heartstone Inns ~ Licensee Ben Thomas ~ Real ale ~ Bar food (12-2(2.15 Sun), 6-9(8.30 Sun)) ~ Restaurant ~ (01395) 232375 ~ Well behaved children welcome ~ Dogs allowed in bar ~ Open 11-3, 5.30-11; 12-3.30, 5.30-10.30 Sun ~ www.diggersrest.co.uk
Recommended by Ian and Joan Blackwell, Douglas and Ann Hare, John Evans

Also Worth a Visit in Devon

Besides the fully inspected pubs, you might like to try these pubs that have been recommended to us and described by readers. Do tell us what you think of them: feedback@goodguides.com

---

ABBOTSKERSWELL　　　　SX8568

☀ **Court Farm** (01626) 361866

Wilton Way; look for the church tower; TQ12 5NY Attractive neatly extended 17th-c longhouse tucked away in picturesque hamlet, various rooms off long crazy-paved main beamed bar, good mix of furnishings, good well priced food from sandwiches to steaks, friendly helpful staff, several ales including Otter, farm cider and decent wines, woodburners; background music; children welcome, picnic-sets in pretty lawned garden, open all day. *(Tom and Ruth Rees)*

APPLEDORE　　　　SS4630

☀ **Beaver** (01237) 474822

Irsha Street; EX39 1RY Relaxed harbourside pub with good well priced food especially fresh local fish, nice home-made puddings too, friendly helpful staff, good choice of west country ales, farm cider, decent house wines and great range of whiskies, lovely estuary view from popular raised dining area, some live music including jazz; pool in smaller games room, TV; children and dogs welcome, disabled access (but no nearby parking), tables on small sheltered water-view terrace. *(Ryta Lyndley, Richard Tilbrook, Derek and Sylvia Stephenson)*

APPLEDORE　　　　SS4630

Royal George (01237) 474335

Irsha Street; EX39 1RY Good local beers such as Clearwater Proper Ansome, thriving beamed bar (dogs allowed) with attractive pictures, simple fresh food including local fish, decent wines, dining room with superb estuary views, family room, regular live acoustic music; disabled access (but no nearby parking), picnic-sets outside, picturesque street sloping to sea, open all day. *(Richard Tilbrook)*

ASHBURTON　　　　SX7569

Exeter Inn (01364) 52478

West Street; TQ13 7DU Welcoming pleasantly old-fashioned low-beamed pub, bar serving two areas (one with a service bell), dark wood and brass, varnished tables on patterned carpet, log fire, enjoyable straightforward food from shortish low-priced menu, well kept Dartmoor IPA and a guest, local cider and decent wines; background music; children welcome, attractive little suntrap courtyard behind. *(Clive and Fran Dutson, Jeremy King)*

ASHWATER　　　　SX3895

Village Inn (01409) 211200

Overlooking village green; EX21 5EY
Roomy and well decorated slate-floored pub with relaxed friendly atmosphere, wide choice of good generous food from sandwiches up, efficient service, well kept Dartmoor and a guest, good sensibly priced wine, dining room, conservatory with venerable grapevine, pool room; background music; children welcome, terrace tables. *(JJW, CMW, Reg Fowle, Helen Rickwood, Garry Talbot, John and Bernadette Elliott)*

BAMPTON　　　　SS9520

☀ **Exeter Inn** (01398) 331345

A396 some way S, at B3227 roundabout; EX16 9DY Long low roadside pub, stone-built with several updated linked rooms, mainly flagstoned, two log fires and wood-burner, large restaurant, wide choice of good generous food at sensible prices including plenty of fresh fish, friendly helpful staff, up to six well kept ales tapped from the cask, decent coffee, newspapers; children and dogs welcome, disabled facilities, tables out in front, ten revamped bedrooms, fairly handy for Knightshayes, open all day. *(David and Julie Glover)*

BANTHAM　　　　SX6643

☀ **Sloop** (01548) 560489

Off A379/B3197 NW of Kingsbridge; TQ7 3AJ Friendly 14th-c pub close to fine beach and walks, good mix of customers in black-beamed bar with stripped-stone walls and flagstones, country chairs and tables, woodburner, well kept St Austell and a guest ale, well liked reasonably priced food from good sandwiches to fresh fish, restaurant; background music; children and dogs welcome, seats out at back, five bedrooms, open all day in summer. *(Geoff and Carol Thorp, David Eberlin, Theocsbrian, Roy Hoing, B J Harding and others)*

BARNSTAPLE　　　　SS5533

Panniers (01271) 329720

Boutport Street; EX31 1RX Centrally placed Wetherspoons, busy and reliable, with good value beers and food served by swift pleasant staff. *(MLR)*

BEER　　　　ST2289

Anchor (01297) 20386

Fore Street; EX12 3ET Friendly sea-view dining pub with wide choice of enjoyable food including good local fish, Greene King and Otter, good value wines, coffee, rambling open-plan layout with old local photographs, large eating area; sports TV, background music; children well looked after, lots of tables in attractive clifftop garden over road, delightful seaside village, reasonably priced bedrooms. *(Peter and Giff Bennett, Simon Pyle)*

BEER　　　　　　　　　　SY2289

✷ **Dolphin**　(01297) 20068

Fore Street; EX12 3EQ　Hotel's comfortable old-fashioned lounge bar with oak panelling and interesting nooks, wonderful old distorting mirrors, nautical bric-a-brac and antique boxing prints, long public bar (open all day) with darts, pool and machines, well kept ales such as Bays, Cotleigh, Fullers and Skinners, decent wine and coffee, enjoyable food including fresh local fish (scallops and bacon the signature dish), friendly service, large back restaurant; background and some live music; children and dogs welcome, sunny back terrace, 22 bedrooms. *(Derek and Maggie Washington, Joan and Michel Hooper-Immins)*

BELSTONE　　　　　　　SX61293

Tors　(01837) 840689

A mile off A30; EX20 1QZ　Small family-run Victorian granite pub/hotel in peaceful Dartmoor-edge village, long carpeted bar divided by settles, changing well kept ales such as Sharps, Otter and Palmers, over 50 malt whiskies, good choice of wines, enjoyable well presented food from sandwiches to specials, cheerful prompt service, restaurant; children and dogs welcome, disabled access, seats out on nearby grassy area overlooking valley, good walks, bedrooms, open all day in summer. *(Chris and Angela Buckell, Jon Wort)*

BERE FERRERS　　　　　SX4563

Old Plough　(01822) 840358

Long dead-end Road off B3257 S of Tavistock; PL20 7JL　16th-c pub with stripped stone and panelling, low beam-and-plank ceilings, slate flagstones and open fires, good value food, well kept Sharps Doom Bar and a couple of guests, farm cider, warm local atmosphere, steps down to cosy restaurant; garden overlooking estuary, secluded village. *(Michael Coleman)*

BERRYNARBOR　　　　　SS5546

Olde Globe　(01271) 882465

Off A399 E of Ilfracombe; EX34 9SG　Rambling dimly lit rooms geared to family visitors (cutlasses, swords, shields and rustic oddments), good choice of reasonably priced straightforward food, real ales, friendly service, games area – and genuine age behind the trimmings, with ancient walls and flagstones, high-backed oak settles and antique tables, lots of old pictures; background music; children looked after well, dogs welcome, crazy-paved front terrace, play area, pretty village. *(Adrian Johnson)*

BICKLEIGH　　　　　　SS9307

Fishermans Cot　(01884) 855237

A3072; EX16 8RW　Greatly extended thatched riverside pub with wide choice of good local food and well kept Marstons ales, reasonable prices, friendly helpful service, lots of round tables on stone and carpet, pillars, plants and some panelled parts, fishing bric-a-brac, raised dining area, charming view over shallow rocky race below 1640 Exe bridge; background music, can get busy especially weekends and with coach parties; dogs welcome, terrace and waterside lawn, 19 good bedrooms, open all day. *(Marianne and Peter Stevens, R J and D S Courtney)*

BIDEFORD　　　　　　SS4526

Kings Arms　(01237) 475196

The Quay; EX39 2HW　Cheerful old-fashioned 16th-c pub with Victorian harlequin floor tiles in alcovey front bar, friendly staff, well kept west country ales and reasonably priced pubby food (not Fri or Sat evenings), back raised family area; background music; dogs welcome, tables out on pavement, three bedrooms, handy for Lundy ferry, open all day. *(Derek and Sylvia Stephenson)*

BISHOP'S TAWTON　　　SS5629

✷ **Chichester Arms**　(01271) 343945

Signed off A377 outside Barnstaple; East Street; EX32 0DQ　Friendly 15th-c cob and thatch pub, good generous well priced food from home-made soup and sandwiches to fresh local fish and seasonal game (all meat from named farms), quick obliging service even when crowded, well kept Exmoor ales, decent wines, heavy low beams, large stone fireplace, restaurant; children welcome, disabled access not good but staff very helpful, picnic-sets on front terrace and in back garden, open all day. *(David Fletcher)*

BLACKAWTON　　　　　SX8050

George　(01803) 712342

Signed off A3122 and A381; TQ9 7BG　Friendly bow-windowed village local with enjoyable reasonably priced pubby food (not Sun evening, Mon lunchtime) from baguettes up, well kept Dartmoor, Teignworthy and guests, chatty traditional bar, lounge with leather-backed dining chairs, woodburners, Mon quiz; children and dogs welcome, good views from garden behind, play area, four bedrooms. *(MP, Mike Hoare)*

BRANSCOMBE　　　　　SY2088

✷ **Masons Arms**　(01297) 680300

Main Street; signed off A3052 Sidmouth–Seaton, then bear left into village; EX12 3DJ　New licensee for this picturesque old longhouse, rambling main bar with a mix of locals and visitors, ancient ships' beams, slate floors, log fire in massive hearth, second bar with stripped-back woodwork and double-sided woodburner, two dining rooms, St Austell ales plus a guest like Branscombe, several wines by the glass, enjoyable generous food; children welcome (not in restaurant), dogs in bar, seats by thatched-roof tables on front terrace with more in side garden, bedrooms in pub and converted cottages, just a stroll from the

sea, open all day. *(Mrs C Roe, Alan Clark, Chris Clark, Barry Steele-Perkins, Tim Gray, the Didler and others)*

BRAYFORD   SS7235

✳ Poltimore Arms (01598) 710381

Yarde Down; 3 miles towards Simonsbath; EX36 3HA Unspoilt 17th-c beamed local – so remote it generates its own electricity – freshened up under present licensees, popular home-made food from local produce (best to book), well kept Skinners Betty Stogs and a guest tapped from the cask, basic traditional furnishings, fine woodburner in inglenook, interesting ornaments and murals, two attractive restaurant areas separated by another woodburner; children and dogs welcome (pub has two labradors), picnic-sets in side garden, closed Sun evening, Mon. *(Tony and Gill Powell, B M Eldridge, Andrew Scott)*

BRENDON   SS7547

✳ Rockford Inn (01598) 741214

Rockford; Lynton--Simonsbath Road, off B3223; EX35 6PT Welcoming unspoilt and interesting 17th-c beamed inn by East Lyn River (pub has fishing permits), enjoyable home-made food including popular Sun roasts, Cotleigh and Exmoor ales, Thatcher's farm cider, interesting wines; small linked rooms with mix of padded settles and chairs around sturdy tables, open fire and three woodburners, fishing books, board games; background music; children and dogs welcome, good walks, five bedrooms (some sharing bathrooms), open all day but closed Mon lunchtime (and evening in winter). *(Richard, Anne and Kate Ansell, Sheila Topham)*

BRENDON   SS7648

Staghunters (01598) 741222

Leedford Lane; EX35 6PS Idyllically set hotel with gardens by East Lyn river, good choice of reasonably priced food, well kept Cotleigh and Exmoor ales, friendly efficient service, bar with woodburner, restaurant; can get very busy; walkers and dogs welcome, riverside tables, 12 good value bedrooms. *(Hugh Roberts, Peter Farman)*

BRIDESTOWE   SX5189

White Hart (01837) 861318

Fore Street (old A38, off A30/A386); EX20 4EL Partly flagstoned beamed main bar, some nice old furnishings in lounge, panelled dining room, ample helpings of tasty food, well kept local ales and decent wines, friendly welcoming staff; informal streamside back garden, peaceful Dartmoor village, two comfortable bedrooms. *(Anon)*

BRIXHAM   SX9256

✳ Maritime (01803) 853535

King Street (up steps from harbour – nearby parking virtually non-existent); TQ5 9TH Single bar packed with bric-a-

brac, chamber-pots hanging from beams, hundreds of key fobs, cigarette cards, pre-war ensigns, toby jugs, mannequins, astronomical charts, even a binnacle by the door, friendly long-serving landlady, Bays Best and Hunters Pheasant Plucker, over 80 malt whiskies, no food or credit cards, lively terrier called George and Mr Tibbs the parrot (watch your fingers); background music, small TV, darts and board games; well behaved children and dogs allowed, fine views over harbour, six bedrooms sharing bathroom, closed lunchtime. *(the Didler)*

BROADHEMBURY   ST1004

Drewe Arms (01404) 841267

Off A373 Cullompton--Honiton; EX14 3NF Under new management as we went to press – reports please; extended partly thatched pub dating from the 16th c, carved beams and handsome stone-mullioned windows, log fire, furniture perhaps not matching age of building, modernised dining room; terrace seats, more on lawn under trees, nice setting near church in pretty village, has been open all day weekends, closed Mon. *(Anon)*

BUCKFAST   SX7467

Abbey Inn (01364) 642343

Buckfast Road off B3380; TQ11 0EA On a sunny day best to arrive early to get a terrace table overlooking the River Dart; partly panelled bar with woodburner and local paintings, St Austell ales and local cider, decent reasonably priced food from sandwiches and baguettes to blackboard specials, big dining room with more panelling and river views; background music; children and dogs welcome, bedrooms, open all day. *(Dr and Mrs A K Clarke, Edward Mirzoeff, Pat and Tony Martin, Mike Gorton, B J Harding)*

BURGH ISLAND   SX6444

Pilchard (01548) 810514

300 yards across tidal sands from Bigbury-on-Sea; walk, or summer Sea Tractor (unique bus on stilts) if tide's in; TQ7 4BG Sadly, the splendid beamed and flagstoned upper bar with its lanterns and roaring log fire is now reserved for locals and guests at the associated flamboyantly art deco hotel, but the more utilitarian lower bar is still worth a visit for the unbeatable setting high above the sea swarming below this tidal island; well kept Sharps, Thwaites Lancaster Bomber and an ale brewed for the pub, local farm cider, good local oysters and lunchtime baguettes, Fri curry night; dogs welcome, tables outside, some down by beach. *(Mike and Eleanor Anderson, J F M and M West)*

BUTTERLEIGH   SS9708

Butterleigh Inn (01884) 855407

Off A396 in Bickleigh; EX15 1PN Small-roomed heavy-beamed country pub, friendly and relaxed, with enjoyable reasonably priced food including Sun carvery, four

real ales and good choice of wines, two big fireplaces, back dining room; children welcome, picnic-sets in large garden, four comfortable bedrooms. *(Jeremy Whitehorn, John and Alison Hamilton)*

CADELEIGH   SS9107

★**Cadeleigh Arms**   (01884) 855238

Village signed off A3072 W of junction with A396 Tiverton--Exeter at Bickleigh; EX16 8HP This attractive civilised old pub closed at the end of 2011 – news, please.

CALIFORNIA CROSS   SX7053

★**California**   (01548) 821449

Brown sign to pub off A3121 S of A38 junction; PL21 0SG Neatly modernised 18th-c or older dining pub with beams, panelling, stripped stone and log fire, wide choice of sensibly priced food from good crab baguettes to steaks in dining bar and family area, restaurant menu, popular Sun lunch (best to book), sofa in small separate snug, Coach House, Fullers and Greene King ales, decent wines, local farm cider; background music; dogs welcome, attractive garden, back terrace, open all day. *(S Holder, B J Harding)*

CHAGFORD   SX7087

Ring o' Bells   (01647) 432466

Off A382; TQ13 8AH Welcoming old pub with beamed and panelled bar, four well kept ales including Dartmoor, traditional fairly priced home-made food, good friendly service, woodburner in big fireplace, some live music; dogs and well behaved children welcome, sunny walled garden, nearby moorland walks, four bedrooms, open all day. *(Anon)*

CHAGFORD   SX7087

Three Crowns   (01647) 433444

High Street; TQ13 8AJ Comfortably refurbished 13th-c stone inn, big dimly lit bar with hunting pictures and big fireplace, separate dining room, well kept St Austell ales, enjoyable food from sandwiches and good ploughman's using local cheeses to game pie, efficient pleasant service, games room with pool. *(Mark Flynn, Pat and Tony Martin)*

CHALLACOMBE   SS6941

Black Venus   (01598) 763251

B3358 Blackmoor Gate--Simonsbath; EX31 4TT Low-beamed 16th-c pub with friendly helpful staff, two well kept changing ales, Thatcher's farm cider, enjoyable fairly priced food from sandwiches to popular Sun lunch, pews and comfortable chairs, woodburner and big fireplace, roomy and attractive dining area, games room with pool and darts; children welcome, garden tables, play area, grand countryside. *(Alan A Newman, B M Eldridge, Andrew Scott, Mrs P Abell)*

CHITTLEHAMHOLT   SS6420

★**Exeter Inn**   (01769) 540281

Off A377 Barnstaple–Crediton, and B3226 SW of South Molton; EX37 9NS Spotless 16th-c thatched coaching inn with friendly staff and long-serving licensees, wide range of good food (should book weekends) from sandwiches up including speciality hog pudding, ales such as Exmoor, Otter and Sharps, farm ciders, good wine choice, open stove in huge fireplace, beams spotted with hundreds of matchboxes, shelves of old bottles, traditional games, lounge with comfortable seating; background music; children and dogs welcome, terrace, bedrooms and self-catering. *(Mark Flynn)*

CHUDLEIGH   SX8679

Bishop Lacey   (01626) 854585

Fore St, just off A38; TQ13 0HY Unpretentious and interesting partly 14th-c low-beamed church house, cheerful obliging staff and character locals, well kept St Austell Dartmoor and changing west country microbrews, farm cider, home-made food including good curries, log fires, dark décor, two bars and dining room; live bands in next-door offshoot; children welcome, garden tables, good value bedrooms, open all day. *(the Didler)*

CHULMLEIGH   SS6814

Globe   (01769) 580252

Church Street; EX18 7BU Attractive little pub by large church, log-fire bar and adjoining panelled restaurant (former public reading room), really good country cooking using seasonal ingredients, friendly staff, well kept Otter and plenty of wines by the glass; five good bedrooms, closed Sun evening, plus Mon and Tues in winter. *(Mark Flynn)*

CHURCHSTOW   SX7145

Church House   (01548) 852237

A379 NW of Kingsbridge; TQ7 3QW Well cared for refurbished pub dating from the 13th c under friendly licensees, heavy black beams and stripped stone, wide choice of enjoyable home-made food including popular evening carvery (Weds-Sat, booking advised), well kept local ales, decent wines, back conservatory with floodlit well; children welcome, dogs in certain areas, tables on big terrace. *(David Eberlin, Tim and Joan Wright)*

CLAYHIDON   ST1615

Half Moon   (01823) 680291

On main road through village; EX15 3TJ Attractive old village pub with pleasant staff and warm friendly atmosphere, wide choice of good home-made food including imaginative snacks, well kept Cotleigh and a guest such as Otter, farm cider, good wine list, comfortable bar with inglenook log fire; children and dogs welcome, picnic-sets in tiered garden over road, valley views. *(Derek and Karin Churchman)*

CLOVELLY   SS3225
New Inn (01237) 431303
High Street; car-free village, visitors charged £5.95 (£3.75 children) to park and enter; EX39 5TQ Quaint peaceful 17th-c inn halfway down the steep cobbled street, Arts & Crafts décor, simple lower bar with flagstones and bric-a-brac (narrow front part has more character than back eating room), well kept Sharps Cornish Coaster and a beer brewed for the pub by local Country Life, short choice of good value bar food, upstairs restaurant; great views, small garden behind, good bedrooms. *(Michael Tack)*

CLOVELLY   SS3124
Red Lion (01237) 431237
The Quay; EX39 5TF Rambling 18th-c building in lovely position on curving quay below spectacular cliffs, beams, flagstones and interesting local photographs in character back bar (dogs on leads allowed here), well kept Sharps Doom Bar and a beer from local Country Life, bar food and upstairs restaurant, efficient service; great views, 11 simple attractive bedrooms. *(David and Gill Carrington)*

COCKINGTON   SX8963
Drum (01803) 690264
Cockington Lane; TQ2 6XA Cheerfully bustling Vintage Inn in thatched and beamed tavern (designed by Lutyens to match the quaintly touristy Torquay-edge medieval village), Butcombe and St Austell, good choice of wines by the glass, roomy well divided wood-floor bar with open fires and family eating areas, decent food, good service; tables on terrace and in attractive back garden by 500-acre park, open all day. *(Roger and Donna Huggins, Richard Hale)*

COCKWOOD   SX9780
⋆ Ship (01626) 890373
Off A379 N of Dawlish; EX6 8NU Comfortable traditional 17th-c pub overlooking estuary and harbour, good value generous food including good fish dishes and puddings (freshly made by landlady so takes time), Butcombe and Sharps Doom Bar, friendly helpful staff, partitioned beamed bar with big log fire and ancient oven, decorative plates and seafaring memorabilia, small restaurant; background music; children and dogs welcome, nice steep-sided garden. *(J D O Carter)*

COLYTON   SY2494
Gerrard Arms (01297) 552588
St Andrews Square; EX24 6JN Friendly unpretentious open-plan local, Bass, Branscombe Vale Branoc, Otter and a guest, good value home-made food (Fri-Sun only), skittle alley; children and dogs welcome, courtyard and garden. *(the Didler)*

COMBE MARTIN   SS5846
Pack o' Cards (01271) 882300
High Street; EX34 0ET Unusual 'house of cards' building originally constructed in the late 17th c to celebrate a big gambling win, with four floors, 13 rooms and 52 windows; snug bar area and various side rooms, St Austell, Sharps and Timothy Taylors kept well, enjoyable inexpensive pub food including children's choices and good Sun roast, restaurant; pretty riverside garden with play area, six comfortable bedrooms, generous breakfast. *(Ian Herdman)*

COMBEINTEIGNHEAD   SX9071
⋆ Wild Goose (01626) 872241
Off unclassified coast road Newton Abbot–Shaldon, up hill in village; TQ12 4RA Rambling pub with good choice of up to seven real ales in spacious back beamed lounge, wheelbacks and red plush dining chairs, agricultural artefacts, pubby food, front bar with beams, standing timbers and some flagstones, step down to area with big old fireplace and another cosy room with comfortable sofa and armchairs, bar billiards, darts and board games, recently opened delicatessen; background music (live on Fri), games machine, TV; children in dining area only, dogs in bar, garden with nice country views. *(Patrick and Daphne Darley, Comus and Sarah Elliott)*

COUNTISBURY   SS7449
Blue Ball 01598 741263
A39, E of Lynton; EX35 6NE Beautifully set rambling heavy-beamed pub, friendly licensees, good range of generous local food in bar and restaurant, three ales including one brewed for the pub, decent wines, farm ciders, handsome log fires; background music; children, dogs and walkers welcome, views from terrace tables, good nearby cliff walks (pub provides handouts of four circular routes), comfortable bedrooms, open all day. *(Lynda and Trevor Smith, Mr and Mrs D J Nash)*

CREDITON   SS8300
Crediton Inn (01363) 772882
Mill Street (follow Tiverton sign); EX17 1EZ Small friendly local with long-serving landlady, well kept St Austell and lots of quickly changing guests (Nov beer festival), cheap well prepared weekend food, back games room; free bookable skittle alley, open all day Mon-Sat. *(the Didler)*

DARTINGTON   SX7861
Cott (01803) 863777
Cott signed off A385 W of Totnes, opposite A384 turn-off; TQ9 6HE Long 14th-c thatched pub back under licensee from ten or so years ago; heavy beams, flagstones, nice mix of old furniture, two inglenooks (one with big woodburner), good home-made locally sourced food from

traditional things up in bar and restaurant, Cottswallop ale brewed for them by local Hunters, also Butcombe and Greene King Old Speckled Hen, Ashridge cider, nice wines by the glass, live music Sat evening; children and dogs welcome, wheelchair access (with help into restaurant), picnic-sets in garden and on pretty terrace, refurbished bedrooms, open all day Sun. *(David Jackman, Charles Trevor-Roper)*

DARTMOUTH   SX8751
✳Cherub (01803) 832571
Higher Street; walk along river front, right into Hauley Road and up steps at end; TQ6 9RB Handsome timbered building (Dartmouth's oldest) with two heavily timbered upper floors jutting over the street and many original interior features, oak beams, leaded lights, tapestried seats, big stone fireplace, Otter, St Austell, Sharps Doom Bar and one or two guests in bustling bar, low-ceilinged upstairs restaurant, good food from pubby favourites to more imaginative dishes (not Mon or Tues evenings in winter), efficient friendly service; background music, no children; dogs in bar, open all day in summer, closed winter afternoons Mon-Thurs. *(P Dawn, M G Hart, Peter and Giff Bennett, M E and F J Thomasson, the Didler, Phil and Sally Gorton and others)*

DARTMOUTH   SX8751
Dartmouth Arms (01803) 832903
Lower St, Bayard's Cove; TQ6 9AN Friendly local with tables out in prime harbour-wall spot overlooking estuary – Pilgrim Fathers set sail from here, well kept beer, enjoyable bar food, panelling and boating memorabilia, log fire. *(Simon Cohen, Dave Webster, Sue Holland)*

DARTMOUTH   SX8751
Dolphin
Market Street; TQ6 9QE Interesting building in picturesque part of town, quirky and laid back, with well kept Bridgetown ales, good food including well priced fish platters, friendly staff; children welcome. *(Mrs Jo Rees)*

DAWLISH   SX9676
Exeter Inn (01626) 865677
Beach Street; EX7 9PN Tucked down narrow street close to the station and getting good reports under present management, decent choice of enjoyable reasonably priced food including well cooked fresh fish, several west country ales, cosy linked beamed bars, live music weekends. *(Paul Welburn)*

DITTISHAM   SX8654
Ferry Boat (01803) 722368
Manor Street; best to park in village carpark and walk down; TQ6 0EX Cheerful riverside pub with lively mix of customers, beamed bar with log fires and straightforward pubby furniture, lots of

boating bits and pieces, tide times chalked on wall, Otter, St Austell, Sharps and Wells & Youngs, a dozen wines by the glass, pubby food; background music; children and dogs welcome, moorings for visiting boats on adjacent pontoon and bell to summon ferry, good walks, open all day. *(Peter and Giff Bennett, Sandy Butcher, Phil and Sally Gorton, Lynda and Trevor Smith, Tim and Joan Wright, David and Sue Atkinson)*

DREWSTEIGNTON   SX7390
✳Drewe Arms (01647) 281224
Off A30 NW of Moretonhampstead; EX6 6QN Pretty thatched pub in lovely village, unspoilt room on left with basic wooden wall benches, stools and tables, original serving hatch, Hop Back, Otter and Sharps from tap room casks, local cider, enjoyable bar food in three dining areas, one with Rayburn and history of Britain's longest serving and oldest landlady, another with woodburner, back room with lots of prints, pictures and copper saucepans, friendly helpful staff; children and dogs welcome, seats under umbrellas on front terrace and in garden, pretty flowering tubs and baskets, bedrooms and bunk rooms, handy for Castle Drogo (NT), open all day in summer. *(Guy Vowles, Michael Cooper, Andrew Hodgkinson, Roger and Donna Huggins, John and Bernadette Elliott, Michael Coleman and others)*

DUNSFORD   SX8189
✳Royal Oak (01647) 252256
Signed from Moretonhampstead; EX6 7DA Comfortably worn-in village inn, good generous food cooked to order, changing ales such as Dartmoor and Sharps, local cider, friendly landlord, airy lounge with woodburner and view from sunny dining bay, simple dining room, steps down to pool room; background music, quiz nights; children well looked after, sheltered tiered garden, good value bedrooms in converted barn. *(the Didler)*

EAST PRAWLE   SX7836
Pigs Nose (01548) 511209
Prawle Green; TQ7 2BY Relaxed and quirky three-room 16th-c pub with low beams and flagstones, local ales tapped from the cask, farm ciders, enjoyable simple pubby food, lots of interesting bric-a-brac and pictures, mix of old furniture, jars of wild flowers and candles on tables, open fire, small family area with unusual toys, pool and darts, friendly dogs (others welcome – even a menu for them); unobtrusive background music, hall for live bands (friendly landlord was 1960s tour manager); tables outside, pleasant spot on village green. *(Sally and John Quinlan, the Didler)*

EXETER   SX9292
Chaucers (01392) 422365
Basement of Tesco Metro, High Street; EX4 3LR Large dimly lit olde-worlde-style

pub/bistro/wine bar down lots of steps, beamed low ceiling and timber-framed walls, several levels with booths and alcoves, comfortable furnishings, candles in bottles, Marstons-related ales, well priced wines, enjoyable good value food from snacks to specials, quick friendly service; background music, no children. *(George Atkinson)*

EXETER SX9390
Double Locks (01392) 256947
Canal Banks, Alphington, via Marsh Barton Industrial Estate; OS Sheet 192 map reference 933901; EX2 6LT Unchanging, unsmart and individual, by ship canal, remote yet busy, Wells & Youngs and guest ales, Gray's farm cider in summer, hearty home-made bar food all day including Sun roast, friendly service but can get swamped; background music, live at weekends; children and dogs welcome, seats out on grass or decking with distant view to city and cathedral (nice towpath walk out – or hire a canoe at the Quay), big play area, summer barbecues, camping, open all day. *(John Prescott, Mr and Mrs Alesbrook, Phil and Sally Gorton, the Didler, Richard Mason)*

EXETER SX9192
Fat Pig (01392) 437217
John Street; EX1 1BL Refurbished Victorian pub, welcoming and relaxed, with several local ales including Exeter, good wine choice, imaginative blackboard food, nice fire; tables in heated courtyard.
(M J Winterton, Mike Gorton)

EXETER SX9193
Great Western (01392) 274039
St David's Hill; EX4 4NU Regulars enjoy up to a dozen or so well kept changing ales, including some rarities, in this large commercial hotel's comfortably worn-in plush-seated bar, friendly efficient staff, fresh good value pubby food all day from sandwiches up (kitchen also supplies hotel's restaurant), daily papers; may be background music, sports TV, pay parking; children welcome, 35 bedrooms, open all day. *(Phil and Sally Gorton, the Didler, Peter Thornton)*

EXETER SX9292
★ Hour Glass (01392) 258722
Melbourne Street; off B3015 Topsham Road; EX2 4AU Old-fashioned corner local with enjoyable surprisingly inventive food including vegetarian, ales such as Adnams, Exeter and St Austell, good range of wines by the glass, comfortable atmosphere (fine either for meeting friends or a lone visit), beams and nice mix of furnishings, dark red walls, open fire in small brick fireplace, resident cats; background music; children away from bar and dogs welcome (resident cats), open all day Fri-Sun, closed Mon lunchtime. *(the Didler, Mike Gorton)*

EXETER SX9193
★ Imperial (01392) 434050
New North Road (above St David's Station); EX4 4AH Impressive 19th-c mansion in own six-acre hillside park with sweeping drive, various different areas including two clubby little side bars, fine former ballroom with elaborate plasterwork and gilding, light and airy former orangery with unusual mirrored end wall, interesting pictures, up to 14 real ales, standard good value Wetherspoons' menu; can get very busy and popular with students; plenty of picnic-sets in grounds and elegant garden furniture in attractive cobbled courtyard. *(Giles and Annie Francis, Ian Phillips, the Didler, Roger and Donna Huggins, Dr and Mrs A K Clarke)*

EXETER SX9292
Old Fire House (01392) 277279
New North Road; EX4 4EP Compact relaxed city-centre pub in Georgian building behind high arched wrought-iron gates, up to eight ales including Otter (regular beer festivals), several real ciders and good choice of bottled beers and wines, bargain food including late evening pizzas, friendly efficient staff, dimly lit beamed rooms with simple furniture; background music, live folk and jazz weekends, popular with young crowd in evenings; picnic-sets in front courtyard, open all day till late. *(P Dawn, L Stevens, the Didler)*

EXETER SX9292
Prospect (01392) 273152
The Quay (left bank, near rowing club); EX2 4AN Early 19th-c pub in good quayside position, enjoyable simple all-day food generously served, well kept Otter, St Austell Tribute and Skinners Betty Stogs, friendly efficient young staff, plenty of comfortable tables including raised river-view dining area; gentle background music, live bands Mon, Tues; children welcome, tables out by historic ship-canal basin, open all day. *(David Crook)*

EXETER SX9293
Rusty Bike (01392) 214440
Howell Road; EX4 4LZ Comfortably refurbished backstreet pub with bistro feel (same owners as Fat Pig in John Street), pine tables on stripped boards in large open bar, big black and white photographs, adjoining dining area, four changing ales, farm cider and good wine choice, enjoyable interesting blackboard food; background music, popular with students, limited parking; walled beer garden with projector for live sport and film nights. *(Becky Moore, Mike Gorton)*

EXETER SX9292
Well House (01392) 223611
Cathedral Yard (attached to Royal Clarence Hotel); EX1 1HB Good position with big windows looking across to cathedral in partly divided open-plan bar, good choice

of west country ales, real cider, quick service, enjoyable food from hotel's kitchen, lots of Victorian prints, daily papers, Roman well below (can be viewed when pub not busy), live music (last Sun of month), beer/cider festivals; open all day. *(the Didler)*

GALMPTON   SX8856
Manor (01803) 661101
Village and pub signed off A3022; Stoke Gabriel Road; TQ5 0NL Large friendly open-plan Edwardian local with well kept ales such as Otter, St Austell Dartmoor and Sharps Doom Bar, good choice of sensibly priced food including local fish, two-part bar and family dining area, games room with sports TV, some live music; tables outside, conker tournament and gooseberry pie fair, new bedrooms, open all day. *(Sam Mitchel, Tom Ben)*

HARBERTON   SX7758
★**Church House** (01803) 863707
Off A381 S of Totnes; TQ9 7SF Ancient partly Norman village pub with unusually long bar, well kept ales such as Butcombe, Courage, Skinners and Wadworths, good choice of wines by the glass, farm cider, wide range of good well priced local food, friendly efficient service, blackened beams, medieval latticed glass and oak panelling, attractive 17th- and 18th-c pews and settles, woodburner in big inglenook, family room; bedrooms. *(Mrs Gillian McAllen, Paul and Karen Cornock)*

HATHERLEIGH   SS5404
George (01837) 810454
A386 N of Okehampton; Market Street; EX20 3JN Completely rebuilt after original 15th-c thatched pub burnt down in 2008; old-style interior with lots of reclaimed timbers and other old materials, mix of furniture (some new) on carpet, wood and tiled floors, open fires, good range of enjoyable home-made food, well kept beers and nice coffee, good friendly staff; bedrooms. *(Ryta Lyndley)*

HATHERLEIGH   SS5404
★**Tally Ho** (01837) 810454
Market Street (A386); EX20 3JN Good generous uncomplicated food (not Sun evening) from lunchtime sandwiches up, good value wines, real ales such as local Clearwater and St Austell, quick friendly service, attractive heavy-beamed and timbered linked rooms, sturdy furnishings, big log fire and woodburner, traditional games, restaurant, busy Tues market day (beer slightly cheaper then); background music; dogs welcome, tables in nice sheltered garden, three good value pretty bedrooms, open all day. *(Reg Fowle, Helen Rickwood)*

HOLNE   SX7069
★**Church House** (01364) 631208
Signed off B3357 W of Ashburton; TQ13 7SJ Two-room medieval inn in lovely moorland village; lower bar with stripped-pine panelling and 18th-c curved elm settle, heavy 16th-c oak partitioning separating it from lounge, open log fires, well kept Dartmoor and Teignworthy ales, farm cider, decent traditional food (not Sun evening); background music; children and dogs welcome, good walks, also worth visiting the church with its fine medieval rood screen, bedrooms, open all day in summer. *(Sally and John Quinlan, Michael Coleman)*

HOLSWORTHY   SS3403
Kings Arms (01409) 253517
Fore Street/The Square; EX22 6EB Village pub under enthusiastic new licensees, fresh modern refurbishment but keeping original Victorian features, well prepared food from pub favourites to interesting daily specials, local beers and several wines by the glass, good coffee; one bedroom. *(Peter Thornton)*

HOLSWORTHY   SS3304
Rydon Inn (01409) 259444
Rydon (A3072 W); EX22 7HU Comfortably extended dining pub with good food from bar snacks up (special diets catered for), friendly welcoming staff, well kept ales, decent wines and coffee; children and dogs welcome (there's a friendly pub dog), disabled facilities, fine views from garden and conservatory, closed Sun evening, Mon. *(Garry Talbot)*

HONITON   ST1599
Heathfield (01404) 45321
Walnut Road; EX14 2UG Ancient thatched pub in contrasting residential area, well run and spacious, with Greene King ales and reliable good value food including lunchtime deals, cheerful service; bedrooms. *(Bob and Margaret Holder)*

HONITON   ST1500
Railway (01404) 47976
Queen Street; EX14 1HE Modernised dining pub with good italian food from open kitchen, well kept beers; closed Sun and Mon. *(Richard Wyld)*

HOPE COVE   SX6740
Hope & Anchor (01548) 561294
Tucked away by car park; TQ7 3HQ Bustling unpretentious inn, friendly and comfortably unfussy, in lovely seaside spot, good open fire, quick helpful service, good value straightforward food including lots of fish, well kept St Austell Dartmoor and a beer brewed for the pub, reasonably priced wines, flagstones and bare boards, dining room views to Burgh Island, big separate family room; background music; children and dogs welcome, sea-view tables out on decking, great coast walks, bedrooms, good breakfast, open all day. *(Sally and John Quinlan, Theocsbrian)*

IDE   SX8990
⋆ **Poachers** (01392) 273847
*3 miles from M5 junction 31, via A30;
High Street; EX2 9RW* Nice beamed inn in
quaint village, good home-made food, Bass,
Branscombe Vale Branoc, Otter and guests
from ornate curved wooden bar, non-standard
mix of old chairs and sofas, big log fire,
restaurant; tables in pleasant garden with
barbecue, three comfortable bedrooms.
(the Didler)

IDEFORD   SX8977
⋆ **Royal Oak** (01626) 852274
2 miles off A380; TQ13 0AY
Unpretentious 16th-c thatched and
flagstoned village local, friendly helpful
service, Courage and guests, basic pub
snacks, navy theme including interesting
Nelson and Churchill memorabilia, panelling,
big open fireplace; children and dogs
welcome, tables out at front and by car park
over road. *(the Didler)*

ILFRACOMBE   SS5247
George & Dragon (01271) 863851
Fore Street; EX34 9ED Oldest pub here
(14th c) and handy for harbour, clean and
comfortable with friendly local atmosphere,
ales such as Courage, Shepherd Neame and
Skinners, decent wines, good value food
cooked by amiable landlord including local
fish, attractive décor with stripped stone,
beams, open fireplaces, lots of ornaments,
china etc, no mobile phones; background
music, quiz nights, can get busy at
weekends. *(Roger and Donna Huggins,
B M Eldridge)*

ILSINGTON   SX7876
Carpenters Arms (01364) 661629
Old Town Hill; TQ13 9RG Pretty, unspoilt
18th-c local next to church in quiet village,
beams and flagstones, county-style pine
furniture, brasses, woodburner, enjoyable
home-made food and well kept changing ales,
friendly atmosphere, darts; children and well
behaved dogs welcome, tables out at front,
good walks, open all day weekends. *(Anon)*

INSTOW   SS4730
Boat House (01271) 861292
Marine Parade; EX39 4JJ Airy modern
high-ceilinged place with huge tidal beach
just across lane and views to Appledore, well
kept ales and decent wines, wide choice of
good food including plenty of fish/seafood,
friendly prompt service, lively family bustle;
background music; roof terrace.
(Ryta Lyndley)

INSTOW   SS4730
Wayfarer (01271) 860342
Lane End; EX39 4LB Unpretentious
locals' pub tucked away near dunes and
beach, well kept ales tapped from the cask,
winter mulled wine, good choice of enjoyable
generous home-made food using local fish
and meat, quick cheerful service; children
and dogs welcome, enclosed garden behind,
six well presented bedrooms (some with sea
view), open all day. *(Mrs V A Taylor, Stephen
Haynes)*

KILMINGTON   SY2798
⋆ **Old Inn** (01297) 32096
A35; EX13 7RB Thatched 16th-c pub,
beams and flagstones, welcoming licensees
and nice bustling atmosphere, enjoyable good
value food using local supplies, well kept
ales such as Butcombe, Cotleigh and Otter,
good choice of wines, small character front
bar with traditional games, back lounge with
leather armchairs by inglenook log fire, small
restaurant; children welcome, skittle alley,
beer gardens. *(Geoff and Linda Payne, C and R
Bromage, Robert Watt)*

KINGSBRIDGE   SX7343
Crabshell (01548) 852345
*Embankment Road, edge of town;
TQ7 1JZ* Lovely waterside position,
charming when tide is in, with big windows
and tables outside; popular and improved
under present owners with emphasis on food
including fish/seafood, friendly staff, well
kept local Quercus ales, feature open fire,
good upstairs views; children welcome, open
all day. *(Geoff and Carol Thorp, MP)*

KINGSTON   SX6347
⋆ **Dolphin** (01548) 810314
*Off B3392 S of Modbury (can also be
reached from A379 W of Modbury);
TQ7 4QE* Cosy peaceful old pub with
knocked-through beamed rooms, traditional
furnishings on red patterned carpet, amusing
drawings on stone walls, open fire and
woodburner, Courage, Otter and Sharps
ales, summer farm cider, enjoyable food (not
winter Sun evening) from open kitchen,
friendly staff and chatty locals; gents'
across lane; children and dogs welcome,
seats outside, walks down to the sea,
bedrooms (some in cottages opposite), good
breakfast. *(S Holder, MP, B J Harding, Simon
Rodway, Steve Whalley, Mrs A Taylor)*

KINGSWEAR   SX8851
⋆ **Ship** (01803) 752348
Higher Street; TQ6 0AG Simple and
attractive old beamed local by the church,
plenty of atmosphere and kind friendly
family service, five well kept ales including
Adnams and Otter from horseshoe bar, farm
cider, nice wines, well liked food including
good fresh fish (best views from restaurant
up steps), nautical bric-a-brac and local
photographs, two log fires, occasional live
music; big-screen sports TV; dogs welcome a
couple of river-view tables outside, open all
day weekends and in summer (when it can
get very busy). *(P Dawn, Alun and Jennifer
Evans, the Didler, Nicky Lee and others)*

KNOWLE SY0582
Britannia/Dog & Donkey
(01395) 442021 *B3178 NW of Budleigh Salterton; EX9 6AL* Victorian pub under newish welcoming licensees, interesting local ales tapped from the cask, enjoyable good value food, small public bar with log fire, lounge leading to dining room/skittle alley; picnic-sets out on lawn. *(Gerry and Rosemary Dobson)*

LAKE SX5288
★ Bearslake (01837) 861334
A386 just S of Sourton; EX20 4HQ Rambling low thatched stone pub, leather sofas and high bar chairs on crazy-paved slate floor at one end, three more smallish rooms with woodburners, toby jugs, farm tools and traps, stripped stone, well kept Otter and Teignworthy, good range of spirits and whiskies, decent wines and enjoyable food, beamed restaurant; children allowed, large sheltered streamside garden, Dartmoor walks, six comfortably olde-worlde bedrooms, generous breakfast. *(Paul Smart)*

LEE SS4846
Grampus (01271) 862906
Signed off B3343/A361 W of Ilfracombe; EX34 8LR Attractive unpretentious 14th-c beamed pub, well kept ales such as local Jollyboat, well priced pubby food, friendly efficient service even when busy, nice relaxed atmosphere, pool; dogs very welcome, lots of tables in appealing sheltered garden, short stroll from sea – superb coast walks. *(Sue Addison, M and GR)*

LIFTON SX3885
★ Arundell Arms (01566) 784666
Fore Street; PL16 0AA Good interesting lunchtime food in substantial country-house fishing hotel, warmly welcoming and individual, with rich décor, nice staff and sophisticated service, good choice of wines by the glass, morning coffee with home-made biscuits, afternoon tea, restaurant; also adjacent Courthouse bar (complete with original cells) doing fairly priced pubby food (not Mon evening), well kept St Austell Tribute and Dartmoor Jail; can arrange fishing tuition – also shooting, deer-stalking and riding; pleasant bedrooms, useful A30 stop. *(Clifford Blakemore)*

LOWER ASHTON SX8484
Manor Inn (01647) 252304
Ashton signposted off B3193 N of Chudleigh; EX6 7QL Well run country pub under friendly hard-working licensees, good quality sensibly priced food including lunchtime set menu, well kept ales such as Dartmoor and Teignworthy, good choice of wines, open fires in both bars, back restaurant in converted smithy; dogs welcome, disabled access, garden picnic-sets with nice rural outlook, open all day Sun, closed Mon. *(Mike Gorton)*

LUPPITT ST1606
★ Luppitt Inn
Back roads N of Honiton; EX14 4RT Unspoilt basic farmhouse pub tucked away in lovely countryside, an amazing survivor, with chatty long-serving landlady, tiny room with corner bar and a table, another not much bigger with fireplace, cheap Otter tapped from the cask, intriguing metal puzzles made by a neighbour, no food or music, lavatories across the yard; closed lunchtime and Sun evening. *(Phil and Sally Gorton, the Didler)*

LUTON SX9076
★ Elizabethan (01626) 775425
Haldon Moor; TQ13 0BL Charming low-beamed old-world dining pub once owned by Elizabeth I, welcoming owners and friendly efficient staff, wide choice of good well presented food including popular Sun lunch, five well kept ales, several reasonably priced wines by the glass, thriving atmosphere; pretty front garden. *(Mike Gorton, Richard and Sue Fewkes)*

LYDFORD SX5184
Castle Inn (01822) 820241
Off A386 Okehampton--Tavistock; EX20 4BH Tudor inn owned by St Austell, friendly chatty staff, traditional twin bars with big slate flagstones, bowed low beams and granite walls, four inglenook log fires, notable stained-glass door, popular generous food (all day Thurs-Sun), restaurant; sheltered beer garden, lovely nearby NT river gorge, open all day. *(Edward Leetham, Reg Fowle, Helen Rickwood)*

LYDFORD SX5285
Dartmoor Inn (01822) 820221
Downton, A386; EX20 4AY Attractive restaurant-with-rooms rather than pub, several small civilised and relaxed areas, stylish contemporary décor, interesting imaginatively presented food (not cheap), separate bar menu (not Fri, Sat evenings), good wines by the glass, well kept ales, competent service; children welcome, dogs allowed in small front log-fire bar, terrace tables, three spacious comfortable bedrooms, good breakfast, closed Sun evening, Mon. *(Angela Nicholson, Oli Coryton, R F Sawbridge)*

LYMPSTONE SX9884
Swan (01395) 272644
The Strand; EX8 5ET Pleasant old-fashioned décor, split-level panelled dining area with leather sofas by big fire, good generously served home-made food including fresh local fish and Sun roasts, well kept ales such as Otter, Palmers, St Austell and Wadworths, short interesting wine list, may be winter mulled cider, friendly helpful staff, games room with pool, Sun live music; children welcome, picnic-sets out at front, smokers' area, open all day. *(Richard Tilbrook,*

the Didler, Andrew Abbott, J D O Carter, George Atkinson, Mrs Jo Rees)

LYNMOUTH   SS7249
Village (01598) 752354
Lynmouth Street; EX35 6EH Welcoming and neatly kept, interesting good value bar food, St Austell ales, Addlestone's cider, warm stove; beer garden, bedrooms. *(J A Snell)*

LYNTON   SS6548
Hunters (01598) 763230
Pub well signed off A39 W of Lynton; EX31 4PY Superb Heddon Valley position by NT information centre down very steep hill, great walks including one down to the sea; big spreading bar with plush banquettes and so forth, woodburner, Exmoor and several other ales, wide choice of generous food; background music; picnic-sets on balconied terrace overlooking attractive pond-side garden with peacocks, open all day summer, hours may be restricted when season tails off. *(Bob and Margaret Holder, B M Eldridge, David and Gill Carrington)*

MEAVY   SX5467
★ Royal Oak (01822) 852944
Off B3212 E of Yelverton; PL20 6PJ Partly 15th-c pub taking its name from 800-year-old oak tree on opposite village green; heavy-beamed L-shaped bar with church pews, red plush banquettes, old agricultural prints and church pictures, smaller locals' bar with flagstones and big open-hearth fireplace, separate dining room, well liked food using local beef and lamb, Dartmoor ales and guests, farm ciders, a dozen wines by the glass and several malt whiskies, cribbage and board games; background music; children in lounge bar only, dogs in bar, picnic-sets out in front and on green, pretty Dartmoor-edge village, open all day in summer, all day weekends winter. *(Jacquie Jones, Martin Roberts)*

MODBURY   SX6551
Modbury Inn (01548) 830275
Brownston Street; PL21 0RQ Welcoming local (former 16th-c coaching inn) with traditional bar and evening restaurant, well kept ales including Otter, decent wines, varied choice of enjoyable food (not Sun or Mon), Sun quiz night; children (in family room) and dogs welcome, tables on attractive terrace, four comfortable bedrooms, good breakfast, open all day Sat. *(Tony and Gill Powell)*

MORCHARD BISHOP   SS7607
London Inn (01363) 877222
Signed off A377 Crediton–Barnstaple; EX17 6NW Prettily placed 16th-c village coaching inn, helpful friendly service (mother and daughter licensees), good generous home-made food (best to book weekends), Fullers London Pride and a

guest, low-beamed open-plan carpeted bar with woodburner in large fireplace, thriving local atmosphere, pool, darts and skittles, small dining room; children and dogs welcome. *(Mrs P Sumner)*

MORELEIGH   SX7652
New Inn (01548) 821326
B3207, off A381 Kingsbridge--Totnes in Stanborough; TQ9 7JH Old-fashioned country local with friendly landlady (same family for several decades), limited choice of wholesome generous home cooking, reasonable prices, Palmers tapped from the cask, character old furniture, nice pictures and good inglenook log fire; may be closed Sat lunchtime and on race days. *(Paul and Karen Cornock)*

MORETONHAMPSTEAD   SX7586
White Horse (01647) 440242
George Street; TQ13 8NF Nicely refurbished old pub with mediterranean-influenced food from chef/landlord including home-made pizzas, extensive wine list with good choice by the glass, well kept beers; some live music, courtyard tables, open all day in summer, closed lunchtime in winter. *(Giles and Annie Francis, Dr and Mrs A K Clarke)*

MORTEHOE   SS4545
Chichester Arms (01271) 870411
Off A361 Ilfracombe--Braunton; EX34 7DU Welcoming former 16th-c vicarage, varied choice of enjoyable local food, quick friendly service, well kept St Austell, Sharps and Wizard, reasonably priced wine, plush and leatherette panelled lounge, comfortable dining room, pubby locals' bar with darts and pool, interesting old local photographs; skittle alley and games machines in summer children's room, tables out in front and in shaded pretty garden, good coast walk. *(Stuart Paulley, David and Gill Carrington)*

MUDDIFORD   SS5638
Muddiford Inn (01271) 850243
B3230 Barnstaple--Ilfracombe; EX31 4EY Family pub dating from the 16th c, plenty of character, enjoyable well priced food from landlord/chef (small helpings available), local real ale, open fire, pleasant restaurant with fancier menu, friendly helpful service; pool, car park over road; big garden with terrace, handy for Marwood Gardens. *(Mr and Mrs D Mackenzie, Sue Rowland, Stephen Haynes, M and GR)*

NEWTON ABBOT   SX8571
Dartmouth (01626) 353451
East Street; TQ12 2JP Friendly old place with well kept west country ales and ciders, low ceilings, dark woodwork and log fire; children welcome till 7pm, nice outside area, open all day. *(the Didler)*

NEWTON ABBOT
SX8571
Locomotive (01626) 365249
East Street; TQ12 2JP Cheerful traditional town pub, well kept Adnams and guests, linked rooms including games room with pool; TV, juke box; open all day. *(the Didler)*

NEWTON ABBOT
SX8671
☆ Olde Cider Bar (01626) 354221
East Street; TQ12 2LD Basic old-fashioned cider house, casks of interesting low-priced farm ciders (helpful long-serving landlord may give tasters), a couple of perries, more in bottles, good country wines from the cask too, baguettes and pasties etc, great atmosphere, dark stools made from cask staves, barrel seats and wall benches, flagstones and bare boards; small back games room with machines; terrace tables, open all day. *(Paul Herbert, the Didler)*

NEWTON ABBOT
SX8671
Richard Hopkins (01626) 323930
Queen Street; TQ12 2EH Big partly divided open-plan Wetherspoons, busy and friendly, with ten real ales, proper cider and their usual good value food; covered tables out at front, open all day. *(the Didler)*

NEWTON ABBOT
SX8468
Two Mile Oak (01803) 812411
A381 2 miles S, at Denbury/ Kingskerswell crossroads; TQ12 6DF Appealing beamed coaching inn, log fires, traditional furnishings, black panelling and candlelit alcoves, well kept Bass, Otter and guests tapped from the cask, straightforward bar food including wkdy lunchtime bargains, decent coffee, cheerful staff; background music, TV and games machine; children in lounge, dogs in bar, terrace and lawn, open all day. *(the Didler, George Atkinson)*

NEWTON ST CYRES
SX8798
Beer Engine (01392) 851282
Off A377 towards Thorverton; EX5 5AX Friendly former railway hotel brewing its own beers since the 1980s, wide choice of good home-made food including local fish and popular Sun lunch; children welcome, decked verandah, steps down to garden, open all day. *(the Didler)*

NEWTON TRACEY
SS5226
Hunters (01271) 858339
B3232 Barnstaple--Torrington; EX31 3PL Extended 15th-c pub with massive low beams and two inglenooks, good reasonably priced food from pub standards to more imaginative dishes, two well kept St Austell ales and Jollyboat Mainbrace, decent wines, friendly prompt service; soft background music; children and dogs welcome, disabled access using ramp, skittle alley popular with locals, tables on small terrace behind, open all day. *(Roger and Pauline Pearce)*

NOMANSLAND
SS8313
Mount Pleasant (01884) 860271
B3137 Tiverton--South Molton; EX16 8NN Informal country local, huge fireplaces in long low-beamed main bar, well kept ales such as Cotleigh, Exmoor and Sharps, several wines by the glass, Weston's cider, good freshly cooked food all day from baguettes up, friendly attentive service, nice mix of furniture including comfy old sofa, candles on tables, country pictures, daily papers, cosy dining room (former smithy with original forge), darts in public bar; background music; well behaved children and dogs welcome, picnic-sets in back garden. *(David Saunders, Ron Logie)*

NORTH BOVEY
SX7483
☆ Ring of Bells (01647) 440375
Off A382/B3212 SW of Moretonhampstead; TQ13 8RB Bulgy-walled thatched inn dating from the 13th c, low beams, flagstones, big log fire, sturdy rustic tables and winding staircases, good imaginative local food, well kept Otter, St Austell and guests, friendly staff, carpeted dining room and overspill room; children and dogs welcome, garden by lovely tree-covered village green below Dartmoor, good walks, five big clean bedrooms, open all day. *(Elven Money, Sue Saunders, Adrian Edmondson)*

NOSS MAYO
SX5447
☆ Ship (01752) 872387
Off A379 via B3186, E of Plymouth; PL8 1EW Charming setting overlooking inlet and visiting boats, thick-walled bars with bare boards and log fires, six well kept west country beers, good choice of wines and malt whiskies, popular often interesting food all day, lots of local pictures and charts, books, newspapers and board games, restaurant upstairs; can get crowded in good weather, parking restricted at high tide; children and dogs welcome, plenty of seats on heated waterside terrace.
(Richard Fendick, S Holder, John Andrew, Sally and John Quinlan and others)

PAIGNTON
SX8860
Isaac Merritt (01803) 556066
Torquay Road; TQ3 3AA Spacious well run Wetherspoons conversion of former shopping arcade, particularly good range of west country ales (regular festivals), usual low-priced food all day, friendly welcoming service, cosy alcoves, comfortable family dining area, air conditioning; good disabled access. *(the Didler, Len Beattie)*

PARRACOMBE
SS6644
☆ Fox & Goose (01598) 763239
Off A39 Blackmoor Gate--Lynton; EX31 4PE Popular rambling village pub, hunting and farming memorabilia and interesting photographs, well kept ales such as Cotleigh and Exmoor, good choice

of wines by the glass, farm cider, generous well prepared food from imaginative menu, friendly staff, log fire, separate dining room; children and dogs welcome, small front verandah, terraced garden leading to garden room. *(John Sharpe, B M Eldridge, M and R Ridge, M G Hart, Sheila Topham)*

PETER TAVY   SX5177
✶ **Peter Tavy Inn** (01822) 810348
Off A386 near Mary Tavy, N of Tavistock; PL19 9NN Old stone village inn tucked away at end of little lane, bustling low-beamed bar with high-backed settles on black flagstones, stone-mullioned windows, good log fire in big stone fireplace, snug dining area with carved wooden chairs, hops on beams and plenty of pictures, up to five well kept west country ales, Winkleigh's cider, good wine and malt whisky choice, well liked fairly priced food including vegetarian options, friendly service, separate restaurant; children and dogs welcome, picnic-sets in pretty garden, peaceful moorland views. *(Chris and Libby Allen, Mick and Moira Brummell, Sally and John Quinlan, Mike Gorton, Jacquie Jones and others)*

PLYMOUTH   SX4854
✶ **China House** (01752) 661592
Sutton Harbour, via Sutton Road off Exeter Street (A374); PL4 0DW Attractive Vintage Inns' conversion of Plymouth's oldest warehouse, lovely boaty views, dimly lit and inviting interior with beams and flagstones, bare slate and stone walls, two good log fires, interesting photographs, enjoyable pubby food, Butcombe, St Austell Tribute and a guest, good choice of wines by the glass, friendly attentive staff; background music, no dogs; children welcome, good parking and disabled access/facilities, tables out on waterside balconies, open all day. *(Sally and John Quinlan)*

PLYMOUTH   SX4854
Dolphin (01752) 660876
Barbican; PL1 2LS Basic unchanging chatty local, good range of well kept cask-tapped ales such as Bass, Hop Back, O'Hanlons and St Austell, coal fire, Beryl Cook paintings including one of the friendly landlord; open all day. *(the Didler, Ian Barker)*

PLYMOUTH   SX4555
Lounge (01752) 561330
Stopford Place, Stoke; PL1 4QT Old-fashioned panelled corner local, cheery landlord and chatty regulars, well kept Bass and guest ales, popular lunchtime food (not Mon), busy on match days; open all day weekends, closed Mon lunchtime. *(the Didler)*

PLYMOUTH   SX4853
Thistle Park (01752) 204890
Commercial Road; PL4 0LE Welcoming bare-boards pub near National Maritime Aquarium, full range of well kept South Hams ales (used to be brewed on premises), Thatcher's cider, friendly service, lunchtime bar food, evening upstairs thai restaurant, interesting décor, open fire, back pool room, juke box, live music at wknds; no children; dogs in bar, roof garden, smokers' shelter, open all day till late. *(the Didler)*

PLYMOUTH   SX4753
Waterfront (01752) 226 326
Grand Parade; PL1 3DQ Restaurant/bar (former 19th-c yacht club) in good spot by Plymouth Sound, enjoyable fairly priced food served quickly by friendly staff including Sun roasts, St Austell, Sharps and Skinners from long central bar, dining areas with light wood tables on bare boards, Sun afternoon jazz, Weds quiz; children and dogs welcome, café-style seating on big decked waterside terrace with superb views. *(Steve Whalley)*

PLYMTREE   ST0502
Blacksmiths Arms (01884) 277474
Near church; EX15 2JU Friendly 19th-c beamed and carpeted pub with reasonably priced home-made food (takeaways available), three well kept changing local ales, decent choice of wines by the glass, pool room and skittle alley; children welcome and dogs (theirs is called Jagermeister), garden with boules and play area, open all day Sat, till 4pm Sun and from 6pm weekdays. *(R J and D S Courtney)*

POUNDSGATE   SX7072
✶ **Tavistock Inn** (01364) 631251
B3357 continuation; TQ13 7NY Friendly and picturesque, liked by walkers (plenty of nearby hikes), beams and other original features like narrow-stepped granite spiral staircase, original flagstones, ancient log fireplaces, Courage Best, Otter and Wychwood Hobgoblin, traditional bar food (all day in summer); children and dogs welcome, tables on front terrace and in quiet back garden, pretty flower boxes, open all day in summer. *(Elven Money)*

RACKENFORD   SS8518
Stag (01884) 881369
Pub signed off A361 NW of Tiverton; EX16 8DT 12th-c thatched pub with ancient cobbled 'tunnel' entry passage between massive walls, Cotleigh, Exmoor and occasional guest ales, food from sandwiches up, scrubbed pine tables and country

---

The letters and figures after the name of each town are its Ordnance Survey map reference. *How to use the Guide* at the beginning of the book explains how it helps you find a pub, in road atlases or large-scale maps as well as in our own maps.

furnishings, huge inglenook fireplace, low beams, Jacobean panelling, flagstones, separate oak-floor white-tablecloth restaurant with woodburner, darts, skittle alley, highwayman ghost; children and dogs welcome, disabled facilities, two picnic-sets out in front, decking and enclosed garden behind, open all day, closed Sun evening. *(Sue Addison, Stuart Paulley)*

RINGMORE   SX6545
Journeys End (01548) 810205
Signed off B3392 at Pickwick Inn, St Anns Chapel, near Bigbury; best to park up opposite church; TQ7 4HL Ancient village inn with friendly chatty licensees, character panelled lounge and other linked rooms, changing local ales tapped from the cask, farm cider, decent wines, pubby food from sandwiches up, log fires, bar billiards (for over-16s), family dining conservatory with board games; pleasant big terraced garden with boules, attractive setting near thatched cottages and not far from the sea. *(the Didler, Mike and Eleanor Anderson)*

ROBOROUGH   SS5717
New Inn (01805) 603247
Off B3217 N of Winkleigh; EX19 8SY Tucked-away 16th-c thatched village pub, family-run, with enjoyable freshly prepared blackboard food and well kept local beers, beamed bar with woodburner, tiny back room leading up to dining room; seats on sunny front terrace. *(Ian Walton, Mark Flynn)*

ROCKBEARE   SY0195
☆ Jack in the Green (01404) 822240
Signed from A30 bypass E of Exeter; EX5 2EE Neat welcoming dining pub run well by long-serving owner, tidy bar with comfortable sofas, Butcombe, Otter and Sharps, local cider, a dozen wines by the glass, popular top-notch food and emphasis on larger similarly traditional dining side with old hunting/shooting photographs and leather chesterfields by big woodburner, competent service, live jazz May-Sept; background music; well behaved children allowed in one part only, plenty of seats in courtyard, open all day Sun, closed 25 Dec-6 Jan. *(Mrs P Sumner, Ted and Charlotte Routley, Barry Steele-Perkins, Derek and Maggie Washington, Comus and Sarah Elliott, Tracy Sheedy and others)*

SALCOMBE   SX7438
Ferry Inn (01548) 844000
Off Fore Street near Portlemouth Ferry; TQ8 8JE Splendid location, breathtaking estuary views from three floors of stripped-stone bars rising from sheltered and attractive flagstoned waterside terrace, including top one opening off street (this may be only one open out of season), middle dining bar, classic seaside pub menu, Palmers and farm cider, good house wines,

quick service from friendly young staff; may be loud background music, can get busy, no nearby parking. *(Steve and Liz Tilley)*

SALCOMBE   SX7439
☆ Victoria (01548) 842604
Fore Street; TQ8 8BU Neat and attractive 19th-c family pub opposite harbour car park, nautical décor, comfortable furnishings and big open fires, enjoyable reasonably priced food from open sandwiches up, well kept St Austell ales, decent wines, friendly enthusiastic service, separate family area; busy at weekends, background music; large sheltered tiered garden behind with good play area and chickens, bedrooms. *(Pat and Tony Martin, Sally and John Quinlan, Simon Rodway, David and Sue Atkinson)*

SAMPFORD PEVERELL   ST0314
☆ Globe (01884) 821214
1 mile from M5 junction 27, village signed from Tiverton turn-off; Lower Town; EX16 7BJ Spacious comfortable village pub backing on to Grand Western Canal, popular with walkers and locals, enjoyable good value home-made food from sandwiches to massive mixed grill and popular carvery (Fri, Sat evenings, all day Sun, Mon lunch), breakfast (8-11am), coffee and cream teas, seven well kept ales including Cotleigh, Exmoor and Otter (Nov beer festival), good wine choice, friendly efficient staff, cosy beamed lounge with boothed eating area, back restaurant; big-screen sports TV in bar, background music; children and dogs welcome, disabled facilities, courtyard and enclosed garden with play equipment, six bedrooms, open all day. *(Andrew Bosi)*

SANDY PARK   SX7189
☆ Sandy Park Inn (01647) 433267
A382 Whiddon Down–Moretonhampstead; TQ13 8JW Welcoming little thatched inn under newish licensees, beams, flagstones, varnished built-in wall settles around nice tables, high stools by counter, Dartmoor, Otter and a guest ale, good food from sensibly short menu including pizzas and vegetarian choices, small dining room on left, inner snug; open mike nights (third Sun of month); children and dogs welcome, big garden with fine views and smokers' shelter, five bedrooms, open all day. *(Barry Steele-Perkins, Roger and Donna Huggins)*

SCORRITON   SX7068
Tradesmans Arms (01364) 631206
Main road through village; TQ11 0JB Welcoming open-plan Dartmoor-edge pub, enjoyable locally sourced food, Dartmoor, Otter and guests, friendly service, wonderful rolling hill views from conservatory and garden; bedrooms, open all day Sun. *(Elven Money)*

SHALDON
SX9372
Clifford Arms (01626) 872311
Fore Street; TQ14 ODE Attractive, open-plan extended 18th-c pub on two levels, clean and bright, with good range of home-made blackboard food (not mid Jan), up to five mainly local ales including Ringmore, eight wines by the glass, low beams and stone walls, wood or carpeted floors, log fire, live jazz Mon evening; front terrace and decked area at back with palms, pleasant seaside village. *(Comus and Sarah Elliott)*

SHALDON
SX9372
Ferryboat (01626) 872340
Fore Street; TQ14 ODL Cosy and quaint little waterside local, basic but comfortable, long low-ceilinged bar overlooking estuary with Teignmouth ferry and lots of boats, welcoming helpful staff, good choice of real ales and interesting wines, enjoyable varied home-made food, open fires, seafaring artefacts, restauarant; children and dogs welcome, tables on sunny terrace across narrow road by sandy beach, summer barbecues. *(Comus and Sarah Elliott, George Atkinson)*

SHALDON
SX9371
Ness House (01626) 873480
Ness Drive; TQ14 0HP Updated Georgian hotel on Ness headland overlooking Teign estuary, comfortable nautical-theme bar, mixed furniture on bare boards, log fire, Badger ales and decent wines by the glass, young friendly well trained staff, pricy food in narrow beamed restaurant or small conservatory, afternoon tea; no dogs; children welcome, disabled facilities, terrace with lovely views, back garden picnic-sets, nine bedrooms, open all day. *(Ian and Jane Irving)*

SHEBBEAR
SS4309
★ Devils Stone Inn (01409) 281210
Off A3072 or A388 NE of Holsworthy; EX21 5RU Still up for sale so this neatly kept beamed village pub may change; brown leather armchairs in front of open woodburner, long L-shaped pew and second smaller one, old photographs of pupils from Shebbear school, bar counter with high-backed leather chairs, four changing west country beers, dining room across corridor, plain back games room with pool, darts, juke box and fruit machine; picnic-sets on front terrace and in garden behind, right by actual Devils Stone, eight bedrooms, open all day weekends. *(Reg Fowle, Helen Rickwood, Ryta Lyndley)*

SHEEPWASH
SS4806
★ Half Moon (01409) 231376
Off A3072 Holsworthy--Hatherleigh at Highampton; EX21 5NE Ancient inn loved by anglers for its 12 miles of River Torridge fishing (salmon, sea trout and brown trout), small tackle shop and rod room with drying facilities; simply furnished main bar, lots of beams, log fire in big fireplace, well kept Nottingham, St Austell and Sharps, several wines by the glass, wide choice of enjoyable blackboard food, friendly service, separate extended dining room, bar billiards; children and dogs welcome, 13 bedrooms (some in converted stables), tiny Dartmoor village off the beaten track. *(Stephen Bennett, David Saunders, Reg Fowle, Helen Rickwood, Ryta Lyndley, Roy Hoing, S G N Bennett and others)*

SIDMOUTH
SY1090
Bowd (01395) 513328
Junction B3176/A3052; EX10 0ND Big thatched and beamed pub improved under present licensees, flagstoned bar with standing timbers and alcoves, well kept ales such as Otter and Sharps Doom Bar from central servery, enjoyable sensibly priced food including Sun carvery, good attentive service, monthly live jazz; children welcome, plenty of seats in big garden with good play area. *(George Atkinson)*

SIDMOUTH
SY1287
★ Dukes (01395) 513320
Esplanade; EX10 8AR More brasserie than pub, but long bar on left has Branscombe Vale, Otter and a guest beer like Bays or Sharps, good food all day specialising in local fish (best to book in the evening), efficient young staff, daily papers, linked areas including conservatory and flagstoned eating area (once a chapel), smart contemporary décor; big-screen TV, may be summer queues; children welcome, disabled facilities, prom-view terrace tables, bedrooms in adjoining Elizabeth Hotel, open all day. *(Joan and Michel Hooper-Immins, Dave Braisted)*

SIDMOUTH
SY1287
Swan (01395) 512849
York Street; EX10 8BY Cheerful old-fashioned town-centre local, well kept Wells & Youngs, good value food from splendid sandwiches up, helpful long-serving licensees, lounge bar with interesting pictures and memorabilia, darts and warm coal fire in bigger light and airy public bar with boarded walls and ceilings, separate dining area; no credit cards; dogs welcome, nice little flower-filled garden with smokers' area. *(Mike Gorton)*

SILVERTON
SS950
Lamb (01392) 860272
Fore Street; EX5 4HZ Flagstoned local run well by friendly landlord, Dartmoor, Exe Valley, Otter and guests tapped from casks, inexpensive home-made pubby food, separate eating area; handy for Killerton (NT), open all day weekends. *(the Didler)*

SLAPTON
SX8245
★ Queens Arms (01548) 580216
Sands Road corner, before church; TQ7 2PN Neatly modernised one-room

village local with welcoming landlady, good straightforward inexpensive food, well kept Dartmoor, Otter and Teignworthy, snug comfortable corners, fascinating World War II photos and scrapbooks, dominoes and draughts; parking needs skill; children and dogs welcome, lots of tables in lovely suntrap stepped garden. *(MP, Dave Webster, Sue Holland)*

SOURTON   SX5390

✶**Highwayman** (01837) 861243

A386, S of junction with A30; EX20 4HN A fantasy of dimly lit stonework and flagstone-floored burrows and alcoves, all sorts of things to look at, one room a make-believe sailing galleon; local farm cider (perhaps a real ale in summer), organic wines, good proper sandwiches or home-made pasties, friendly chatty service, nostalgic background music; outside fairy-tale pumpkin house and an old-lady-who-lived-in-the-shoe house – children allowed to look around pub but can't stay inside; period bedrooms with four-posters and half-testers, bunkrooms for walkers/cyclists. *(the Didler, M J Winterton)*

SOUTH BRENT   SX6960
Royal Oak (01364) 72133

Station Road; TQ10 9BE Friendly village pub with well priced traditional and modern food, three well kept local ales, good choice of wines by the glass, welcoming helpful service, comfortable open-plan bar with some leather sofas, restaurant, Weds folk night; children and dogs welcome, small courtyard, five bedrooms. *(Geoff and Carol Thorp)*

SOUTH POOL   SX7740
Millbrook (01548) 531581

Off A379 E of Kingsbridge; TQ7 2RW Charming little creekside pub with more of a bistro flavour at night, dining area off cheerful compact bar, good french-influenced country cooking from well priced bar menu (pheasant casserole, bath chaps etc) to more expensive restaurant-style food (nice local fish), well kept Red Rock (including an IPA brewed for the pub) and a guest like Otter, local farm cider, log fires, newspapers, live music with emphasis on jazz; children welcome, covered seating and heaters for front courtyard and waterside terrace, summer barbecues. *(Nick Lawless)*

SOUTH ZEAL   SX6593
✶**Oxenham Arms** (01837) 840244

Off A30/A382; EX20 2JT Following the tragic death of the landlord, this stately 12th-c inn was closed as we went to press

---

SPREYTON   SX6996
✶**Tom Cobley** (01647) 231314

Dragdown Hill; W out of village; EX17 5AL Fourteen real ales (some tapped from the cask) and up to 20 ciders at this busy village pub; welcoming landlord

and staff, well priced hearty bar food, straightforward pubby furnishings in small bar, surprisingly large back restaurant with beams and background music; children welcome, dogs in the bar, seats out in front by quiet street, more in tree-shaded garden, six bedrooms, open till 1am Fri, Sat, closed Mon lunchtime. *(D P and M A Miles, David Saunders, Peter Hill, Peter Thornton, Michael Coleman, Mrs P Sumner and others)*

STICKLEPATH   SX6494
✶**Devonshire** (01837) 840626

Off A30 at Whiddon Down or Okehampton; EX20 2NW Warmly welcoming licensees in old-fashioned 16th-c thatched village local next to foundry museum (NT), low-beamed slate-floor bar with big log fire, longcase clock and easy-going old furnishings, key collection, sofa in small snug, well kept low-priced ales tapped from the cask, farm cider, good value sandwiches and home-made pasties from the Aga, games room, lively folk music night first Sun of month; dogs welcome (pub has its own), good walks, bedrooms, open all day Fri, Sat. *(Reg Fowle, Helen Rickwood, the Didler)*

STOKE FLEMING   SX8648
Green Dragon (01803) 770238

Church Street; TQ6 0PX Popular and friendly village pub with yachtsman landlord, well worn-in interior with beams and flagstones, boat pictures, sleepy dogs and cats, snug with sofas and armchairs, grandfather clock and open fire, well kept Otter ales, Addlestone's and Aspall's ciders, good choice of wines by the glass, bargain food; tables out on partly covered heated terrace, lovely garden, handy for coast path. *(Sally and John Quinlan, Nick Lawless, Richard Tilbrook, Dave Webster, Sue Holland)*

STOKE GABRIEL   SX8457
✶**Church House** (01803) 782384

Off A385 just W of junction with A3022; Church Walk; TQ9 6SD Friendly early 14th-c pub, lounge bar with fine medieval beam-and-plank ceiling, black oak partition wall, window seats cut into thick butter-coloured walls, huge log fireplace and ancient mummified cat, Bass, Hancocks HB and a guest, enjoyable good value food, little locals' bar; background music, no children; dogs welcome in bar, picnic-sets on small front terrace, limited parking, open all day. *(Malcolm and Barbara Southwell, Barbarrick)*

STOKEINTEIGNHEAD   SX9170
Church House (01626) 872475

Signed from Combeinteignhead, or off A379 N of Torquay; TQ12 4QA Relaxed 13th-c thatched pub in unspoilt village, heavy beams, antique furnishings, ancient spiral stairs and inglenook fireplace, three well kept west country ales and decent wines, enjoyable food served by friendly helpful staff, smart extended dining room, simple public bar with darts; background music; children welcome in eating area, back garden. *(Anon)*

STOKENHAM   SX8042
⋆ **Church House** (01548) 580253
Opposite church, N of A379 towards Torcross; TQ7 2SZ Attractive extended old pub overlooking common, three spotless open-plan areas, low beams, mix of seating on flagstones and lots of knick-knacks, Greene King, Otter and guests, local organic cider, several wines by the glass, well liked food from good sandwiches up using local produce, pleasant helpful service, dining conservatory, jazz Weds evening; children and dogs welcome, picnic-sets on lawn with play area, interesting church next door.
(Richard Fendick, David Jackman, Damian and Lucy Buxton)

STRETE   SX8446
Kings Arms (01803) 770377
A379 SW of Dartmouth; TQ6 0RW Unusual cross between village local and seafood restaurant, same good generous food in country-kitchen bar and more contemporary restaurant up steps, prompt friendly service, well kept ales such as Otter, good wines by the glass; background music; children and dogs welcome, back terrace and garden with lovely views over Start Bay, open all day, closed Sun evening. *(Jonathan Tate, V Brogden)*

TALATON   SY0699
Talaton Inn (01404) 822214
Former B3176 N of Ottery Street Mary; EX5 2RQ Simply modernised country pub dating from the 16th c, roomy and comfortable timbered lounge bar and restaurant, good inexpensive home-made food including blackboard specials, friendly service, well kept Otter and guests, fresh flowers and candles, large carpeted public bar with pool, skittle alley; picnic-sets out in front. *(Revd R P Tickle)*

TOPSHAM   SX9688
⋆ **Bridge Inn** (01392) 873862
2.5 miles from M5 junction 30: Topsham signposted from exit roundabout; in Topsham follow signpost (A376) Exmouth, on the Elmgrove Road, into Bridge Hill; EX3 0QQ Very special old drinkers' pub (16th-c former maltings) with up to eight real ales and in landlady's family for five generations; quite unchanging and completely unspoilt with friendly staff and locals, character small rooms and snugs, traditional furniture

including a nice high-backed settle, woodburner, the 'bar' is landlady's front parlour (as notice on the door politely reminds customers), simple lunchtime food, live folk and blues; no background music, mobile phones or credit cards; children and dogs welcome, picnic-sets overlooking weir. *(Phil and Sally Gorton, Richard Tilbrook, Mike Gorton, Douglas and Ann Hare, the Didler, Peter Thornton and others)*

TOPSHAM   SX9687
⋆ **Globe** (01392) 873471
Fore Street; 2 miles from M5 junction 30;· EX3 0HR This substantial 16th-c inn has been bought by St Austell and was closed for refurbishment as we went to press – reports please. *(Anon)*

TOPSHAM   SX9687
⋆ **Lighter** (01392) 875439
Fore Street; EX3 0HZ Big, busy well run pub looking out over quay, quickly served food from good sandwiches and light dishes to fresh fish, three Badger ales, nautical décor, old local photographs, panelling and large central log fire, friendly staff, good children's area; games machines, background music; lots of waterside tables – good bird views at half tide, handy for antiques centre but little nearby parking. *(the Didler, George Atkinson, Dr A J and Mrs Tompsett)*

TORCROSS   SX8242
⋆ **Start Bay** (01548) 580553
A379 S of Dartmouth; TQ7 2TQ More fish and chip restaurant than pub but does sell Bass, Otter, local wine and cider; very much set out for eating and exceptionally busy at peak times with staff coping well, wheelback chairs around dark tables, country pictures, some photographs of storms buffeting the pub, winter coal fire, small drinking area by counter, large family room; no dogs during food times; seats outside (highly prized) looking over pebble beach and wildlife lagoon, open all day. *(Bruce and Sharon Eden, Mike Gorton, Barbarrick, Ian Barker, Damian and Lucy Buxton, John and Gloria Isaacs and others)*

TORQUAY   SX9166
Crown & Sceptre (01803) 328290
Petitor Road, St Marychurch; TQ1 4QA Friendly two-bar local in 18th-c stone-built beamed coaching inn, St Austell, Otter, Wells & Youngs and three guests, interesting naval memorabilia and chamber-pot collection (150 at last count), friendly long-serving licensees, basic good value lunchtime food (not Sun), snacks any time, live jazz Tues, folk Fri; dogs and children welcome, two gardens, open all day Fri-Sun. *(the Didler)*

People named as recommenders after the Main Entries have told us that the pub should be included. But they have not written the report – we have, after anonymous on-the-spot inspection.

TORQUAY SX9163
Hole in the Wall (01803) 200755
Park Lane, opposite clock tower;
TQ1 2AU Ancient two-bar local near
harbour, reasonably priced usual food
including good fresh fish, several well
kept ales such as Bays, Butcombe and
Sharps, Blackawton cider, smooth cobbled
floors, low beams and alcoves, lots of
nautical brassware, ship models, old local
photographs, chamber-pots, restaurant/
function room (band nights); can get very
busy weekends; some seats out at front, open
all day. *(Roger and Donna Huggins, the Didler,
Ian Barker, Dr and Mrs A K Clarke)*

TOTNES SX8060
Albert (01803) 863214
Bridgetown; TQ9 5AD Unpretentious
roadside pub with small bar and two other
rooms, low beams, flagstones, panelling,
some old settles and lots of knick-knacks,
friendly landlord brewing own Bridgetown
ales, good local atmosphere; neat garden.
*(the Didler, Roger and Donna Huggins,
Sean Finnegan)*

TOTNES SX7960
Bay Horse (01803) 862088
Cistern Street; TQ9 5SP Popular
traditional two-bar inn dating from the
15th c, friendly landlord, well kept changing
local ales (regular beer festivals), may be
winter mulled cider, good value home-made
food; background and live music including
good Sun jazz; children and dogs welcome,
garden, two nice bedrooms, open all
day. *(Celia Minoughan, the Didler, Roger and
Donna Huggins)*

TOTNES SX8060
King William IV (01803) 866689
Fore Street; TQ9 5HN Roomy and
comfortable town-centre pub popular for its
enjoyable bargain food, friendly landlord and
staff, jolly locals, real ales such as Exeter
and Otter from dark wood bar, stained-
glass windows; children and dogs welcome,
bedrooms. *(Joan and Michel Hooper-Immins)*

TOTNES SX8060
⋆ Royal Seven Stars (01803) 862125
Fore Street, The Plains; TQ9 5DD
Exemplary town-centre bar and coffee bar
in well run civilised old hotel, friendly and
easy-going, with well kept ales and enjoyable
good value food all day from breakfast on,
separate brasserie/grill room with adjoining
champagne bar; heated tables out in front,
river across busy main road, bedrooms, open
all day. *(Michael and Lynne Gittins, the Didler)*

TUCKENHAY SX8156
⋆ Maltsters Arms (01803) 732350
Ashprington Road, off A381 from Totnes;
TQ9 7EQ Old pub in lovely quiet spot by
wooded creek, ongoing improvements by

hard-working landlord, good food from bar
snacks up, well kept west country ales and
farm ciders, great range of wines by the
glass, friendly service; children and dogs
welcome, waterside terrace with open-air bar
and summer barbecues, individually styled
bedrooms, open all day. *(Tim Maddison, MP,
Ian Barker, David and Sue Atkinson)*

TWO BRIDGES SX6175
Two Bridges Hotel (01822) 890581
B3357/B3212 across Dartmoor;
PL20 6SW Rambling 18th-c hotel in
protected central Dartmoor hollow, popular
with walkers – boots and sticks left in porch,
good choice of beers and wines, good food in
bar and striking dining room. *(Rod Stoneman)*

UGBOROUGH SX6755
Ship (01752) 892565
Off A3121 SE of Ivybridge; PL21 0NS
Quietly chatty well run dining pub extended
from cosy 16th-c flagstoned core, nicely
divided open-plan eating areas a step down
from neat bar, wide choice of good home-
made food including fresh fish, willing
pleasant service, well kept Palmers and St
Austell ales, good house wines; background
music; tables out in front. *(S Holder, MP, Neil
and Anita Christopher)*

UMBERLEIGH SS6024
Rising Sun (01769) 560447
A377 S of Barnstaple; EX37 9DU
Old fishing inn under newish management,
three west country beers and a couple of
real ciders, traditional filling food, partly
divided bar with woodburner, flagstones and,
fishing memorabilia, five River Taw salmon
and sea trout beats; darts; children and dogs
welcome, tables outside, bedrooms (some
refurbishment), open all day. *(Jay Master,
Mark Flynn)*

UPOTTERY ST2007
Sidmouth Arms (01404) 861252
Near the church; EX14 9PN Atractive
18th-c pub in pleasant village setting,
roomy and comfortable, with helpful staff,
well kept Otter and good value traditional
food. *(Patrick and Daphne Darley)*

WEARE GIFFARD SS4722
Cyder Press (01237) 475640
Tavern Gardens; EX39 4QR Welcoming
modernised local in pretty village overlooking
River Torridge, friendly licensees, real
ales such as Clearwater, Dartmoor and St
Austell, local ciders, decent food including
Sun roasts, darts in public bar, separate
dining area; handy for Tarka Trail, beautiful
countryside. *(Anon)*

WEMBWORTHY SS6609
⋆ Lymington Arms (01837) 83572
Lama Cross; EX18 7SA Large early
19th-c beamed dining pub, clean and
bright, with wide choice of reliably good

food (not Sun evening or Mon) including some interesting specials, good service from character landlady and friendly staff, well kept Sharps Doom Bar and Skinners Betty Stogs, Winkleigh farm cider, decent wines, comfortably plush seating and red tablecloths in partly stripped-stone bar, big back evening restaurant (not Sun, Mon); children welcome, picnic-sets outside, pleasant country setting, bedrooms. *(Mark Flynn, Mrs P Sumner, Ron and Sheila Corbett)*

WESTLEIGH SS4728
Westleigh Inn (01271) 860867
0.5 mile off A39 Bideford--Instow; EX39 4NL Popular and comfortable beamed pub, well kept ales such as Sharps Doom Bar, enjoyable usual food from sandwiches and baguettes up, friendly prompt service, inglenook log fire, brass and knick-knacks, sleepy pub cat, darts; well behaved children and dogs welcome, play area in big garden overlooking Torridge estuary, Tarka Trail walks. *(Eamonn and Natasha Skyrme)*

WESTON ST1400
★ Otter (01404) 42594
Off A373, or A30 at W end of Honiton bypass; EX14 3NZ Big busy family pub with heavy low beams, enjoyable food from light dishes up including lots of vegetarian options, good Sun carvery, OAP specials and perhaps other deals, cheerful helpful staff, Cotleigh and Otter ales, good log fire; background music; disabled access, picnic-sets on big lawn leading to River Otter, play area. *(Bob and Margaret Holder, Alison Smith)*

WHIMPLE SY0497
New Fountain (01404) 822350
Off A30 Exeter--Honiton; Church Road; EX5 2TA Attractive two-bar beamed pub with friendly local atmosphere, good inexpensive food (not Mon lunchtime), well kept changing beers including O'Hanlons brewed in the village, woodburner; well behaved dogs welcome. *(Anon)*

WIDECOMBE SX7176
Old Inn (01364) 621207
B3387 W of Bovey Tracey; TQ13 7TA Busy comfortably refurbished dining pub, large eating area and roomy side conservatory with central fire – get there before about 12.30pm in summer to miss the coach-loads, enjoyable standard food served promptly by friendly staff, well kept beers; children and dogs welcome, nice garden with water features and pleasant terrace, great walks from this pretty moorland village. *(J F Stackhouse)*

WONSON SX6789
★ Northmore Arms (01647) 231428
Between Throwleigh and Gidleigh; EX20 2JA Far from smart and a favourite with those who take to its idiosyncratic style (not everyone does); two simple old-fashioned rooms, log fire and woodburner, low beams and stripped stone, well kept Adnams, Cotleigh and Exe Valley tapped from the cask, good house wines, cheap plain food (all day Mon-Sat), darts and board games; children and dogs welcome, picnic-sets outside, bedrooms, beautiful remote walking country, normally open all day. *(Anthony Longden, the Didler)*

YEALMPTON SX5851
Rose & Crown (01752) 880223
A379 Kingsbridge--Plymouth; PL8 2EB Central bar counter, all dark wood and heavy brass, solid leather-seated stools, mix of furnishings, stripped-wood floor and open fire, carpeted dining areas, emphasis on good nicely presented food including local fish and vegetarian choices, good value lunchtime and early evening set menu, a couple of west country ales, quite a few wines by the glass; children welcome, dogs in bar, tables in walled garden with pond, also a lawned area, open all day. *(M E and F J Thomasson, R F Sawbridge, Hugh Roberts, John Evans)*

LUNDY SS1344
★ Marisco (01271) 870870
Get there by ferry (Bideford and Ilfracombe) or helicopter (Harland Point); EX39 2LY One of England's most isolated pubs (yet busy most nights), great setting, steep trudge up from landing stage, galleried interior with lifebelts and shipwreck salvage, two St Austell ales labelled for the island, its spring water on tap, good value house wines, welcoming staff, good basic food (all day from breakfast on) using Lundy produce and lots of fresh seafood, open fire; children welcome, tables outside, souvenir shop, and doubles as general store for the island's few residents. *(B M Eldridge, Chas Bayfield)*

Dorset

This year we're happy to welcome four pubs back to this chapter: the Spyway at Askerswell (unspoilt and pubby with good value food), the Anchor in Chideock (great sea views and good value food, too), West Bay at West Bay (fantastic range of fish and seafood) and the Ship in West Stour (a good all-rounder with summer beer festival). The Red Lion in Weymouth (fun and pubby with an impressive range of spirits) is brand new to us this year. Places that stand out for good food are the Brace of Pheasants at Plush (also a nice place to stay), Greyhound at Sydling St Nicholas (top quality produce in relaxed surroundings) and the Langton Arms at Tarrant Monkton (charming thatched inn using home-grown produce), which is Dorset Dining Pub 2013. The lovely old New Inn at Cerne Abbas (three awards and terrific on all counts) has been sympathetically refurbished and is well worth a visit. In contrast, two pubs that have remained almost completely unchanged over the years are the Digby Tap in Sherborne (simple backstreet pub with good beer) and the Square & Compass in Worth Matravers (country tavern with unusual local beers).

ASKERSWELL   SY5393   Map 2
Spyway £
Off A35 Bridport–Dorchester; DT2 9EP

Family-run country inn with friendly welcome, unspoilt décor, real ales, well liked food and fine garden views; bedrooms

---

The unspoilt little rooms at this simple, family-run country inn are cosily filled with old-fashioned high-backed settles, cushioned wall and window seats and some tub chairs. Old photos of the pub and rustic scenes are on the walls and jugs hang from the beams; the warm Rayburn is a bonus on chilly days. Otter Ale and Bitter and a guest such as Butcombe on handpump are served by friendly staff. The dining area has old oak beams and timber uprights, red cushioned dining chairs around dark tables on the patterned carpet, horse tack and horsebrasses on the walls, and a woodburning stove, with two smaller rooms leading off. Eggardon Hill, up which the pub's steep lane continues, is one of the highest in the region, but there are marvellous views of the downs and to the coast from the seats on back terrace and gardens; small children's play area.

Prepared using local produce, good value bar food includes chicken liver, orange and tarragon pâté, grilled goats cheese with beetroot and apple relish, prawn cocktail, vegetable lasagne, scampi, cottage pie, mixed bean chilli, chicken breast stuffed with haggis with whisky cream sauce, roast pork belly with black pudding, and puddings such as eton mess, treacle sponge pudding and white chocolate cheesecake; you can buy their home-made preserves. *Benchmark main dish: pie of the day £9.00. Two-course evening meal £16.00.*

Free house ~ Licensee Tim Wilkes ~ Real ale ~ Bar food (12-3, 6.30-9) ~ Restaurant ~ (01308) 485250 ~ Children welcome ~ Open 12-3, 6-11 ~ Bedrooms: £45S/£80B ~ www.spyway-inn.co.uk *Recommended by Roger Scammell, Pete Flower, Joan and Michel Hooper-Immins, Lois Dyer, Ragged Robin*

CERNE ABBAS
ST6601   Map 2

New Inn 🍴 ♟ 🛏

Long Street; DT2 7JF

Newly refurbished former coaching inn with character bar and two dining rooms, friendly licensees, local ales and inventive food; lovely bedrooms

Just reopening as we went to press after an extensive and sympathetic refurbishment, this is at its heart, still a charming 16th-c former coaching inn with friendly, hands-on licensees. The bar now has a new solid oak counter, an attractive mix of nice old dining tables and chairs on the slate or polished wooden floors, settles built into various nooks and crannies, and a woodburner in the opened-up yorkstone fireplace; throughout the lovely mullioned windows and the heavy oak beams remain untouched. Palmers Copper, Dorset Gold and IPA on handpump, a dozen wines by the glass, several malt whiskies and local cider. The two dining rooms are furnished in similar style. There are seats on the terrace and picnic-sets under mature fruit trees or parasols in the back garden. The newly furnished bedrooms are smart, well equipped and comfortable – some in the inn itself and some in converted stables. You can walk from the attractive stone-built village up and around the prehistoric Cerne Abbas Giant chalk carving and on to other nearby villages.

Using the best local produce, the imaginative food might include lunchtime sandwiches, chicken liver parfait with carrot chutney, smoked salmon cannelloni with ricotta, basil, tomato and wild garlic pesto, home-made beef burger with bacon and cheese, battered fresh haddock with peas and chips, a daily fresh pasta or risotto, pork and toulouse sausage cassoulet, goats cheese and red onion tart, mullet with a cockle and ham risotto and tomato dressing, and puddings such as strawberry crème brûlée with strawberry ice-cream and mint chocolate cheesecake with mint chocolate truffles. *Benchmark main dish: roast pork belly with creamed leeks and glazed apples £12.95. Two-course evening meal £19.00.*

Palmers ~ Tenant Jeremy Lee ~ Real ale ~ Bar food (12-2.15, 6.30-8.45) ~ Restaurant ~ (01300) 341274 ~ Children welcome ~ Dogs welcome ~ Open 11-3, 6-11; 11-11 Sun and Sat ~ Bedrooms: £75S/£110S ~ www.thenewinncerneabbas.co.uk *Recommended by Tony and Gill Powell, T G Shaw, Alan Johnson*

'Children welcome' means the pub says it lets children inside without any special restriction. If it allows them in, but to restricted areas such as an eating area or family room, we specify this. Some pubs may impose an evening time limit. We do not mention limits after 9pm as we assume children are home by then.

CHIDEOCK

SY4191   Map 1

Anchor £

Off A35 from Chideock; DT6 6JU

Dramatically set pub offering lovely sea and cliff views from large terrace, simple snug bars

This strikingly sited pub nestles dramatically beneath the 188-metre Golden Cap pinnacle, just a few steps from the cove beach and very near the Dorset Coast Path. It's ideally placed for the lovely sea and cliff views, so get here early in summer for a table on the spacious front terrace (and a parking space). In winter, when the sometimes overwhelming crowds have gone, the little bars feel especially snug, with low white-planked ceilings, roaring winter fires, some sea pictures, lots of interesting local photographs, a few fossils and shells, and simple but comfortable seats around neat tables. Friendly, efficient staff serve well kept Palmers 200, IPA and Copper on handpump (kept under light blanket pressure in winter), and there's a decent little wine list; background, mainly classical, music.

Good value bar food includes sandwiches and baguettes, crispy whitebait, tempura vegetables, sausage and mash, pie of the day, ham, egg and chips, thai vegetable and noodle broth, seafood chowder, and daily specials such as smoked salmon and prawn salad, roast skate with prawn and caper butter, honey glazed duck breast with port sauce and lobster. *Benchmark main dish: fish and chips £10.25. Two-course evening meal £16.60.*

Palmers ~ Tenant Paul Wiscombe ~ Real ale ~ Bar food (12-9; 12-2.30(5.30 Sun), 6-9(not Sun evening) Nov-March) ~ (01297) 489215 ~ Children welcome ~ Dogs welcome ~ Open 11-11; 11.30-10.30 Sun ~ www.theanchorinnseatown.co.uk
Recommended by Jonathan Weedon, Guy Vowles, MLR, David Bizzell, Joan and Michel Hooper-Immins, B and M Kendall

CHIDEOCK

SY4292   Map 1

George

A35 Bridport–Lyme Regis; DT6 6JD

Comfortably traditional local with well liked food

While working for Hugh Fearnley-Whittingstall, the young couple who own this thatched village pub developed a love for the area and decided to stay. The interior is still nicely traditional and the cosy low-ceilinged carpeted bar is just as you'd hope, with four Palmers beers on handpump, warm log fires, brassware and pewter tankards hanging from dark beams. There are wooden pews and long built-in tongue and groove banquettes, tools on the cream walls and high shelves of bottles, plates and mugs; background music, TV, bar billiards, table skittles and board games. The garden room opens on to a pretty walled garden with a terrace and wood-fired oven.

Using local seasonal and home-smoked produce, the short but popular menu might include sandwiches, leek rarebit, roast beetroot and goats cheese, crispy pigs ear salad with poached egg, ploughman's, burger, ham, egg and chips, rabbit, cider and thyme stew, cod and crab fishcake with lemon mayonnaise and mushroom, leek and spinach gratin. Readers tell us the pizzas from the wood-fired oven are delicious (Thursday nights). *Benchmark main dish: fish and chips £10.50. Two-course evening meal £16.00.*

Palmers ~ Tenants Mr and Mrs Steve Smith ~ Real ale ~ Bar food (12-2.30, 6-9.30) ~ Restaurant ~ (01297) 489419 ~ Children welcome ~ Dogs allowed in bar ~ Live music Weds, Sat evenings in summer ~ Open 12-3, 6-11 ~ www.georgeinnchideock.co.uk
Recommended by Dennis Jenkin, B and M Kendall, David and Sally Frost

MIDDLEMARSH   ST6607   Map 2
Hunters Moon 🛏

A352 Sherborne–Dorchester; DT9 5QN

Plenty of bric-a-brac in several linked areas, reasonably priced food and a good choice of drinks; comfortable bedrooms

You can be sure of a genuinely friendly welcome from the hands-on licensees and their helpful staff at this cheerfully run former coaching inn. There's a properly pubby atmosphere in the comfortably traditional beamed bar rooms which are cosily filled with a great variety of tables and chairs on red patterned carpets, an array of ornamentation from horsebrasses up and lighting in the form of converted oil lamps. Booths are formed by some attractively cushioned settles, walls comprise exposed brick, stone and some panelling and there are three log fires (one in a capacious inglenook); background music, children's books and toys and board games. Butcombe Bitter and a couple of guests such as Brains Reverend James and Ringwood Best on handpump and farm cider, 14 wines available by bottle or glass. A neat lawn has picnic-sets, some circular.

Good bar food includes lunchtime filled baguettes and ciabattas, a popular pie of the day, slow-roasted lamb shank in a rosemary and wine sauce, sharing platters, vegetable lasagne, cajun spiced salmon with mushroom linguine, chicken breast wrapped in bacon and stuffed with smoked cheese, and puddings such as dorset apple and blueberry cake, crème brûlée and chocolate fudge cake. *Benchmark main dish: beer-battered cod £10.25. Two-course evening meal £16.20.*

Enterprise ~ Lease Dean and Emma Mortimer ~ Real ale ~ Bar food (12-2, 6-9(9.30 summer)) ~ (01963) 210966 ~ Children welcome ~ Dogs allowed in bar and bedrooms ~ Open 10.30-2.30, 6-11; 10-11 Sat, Sun; closes 10.30 in winter ~ Bedrooms: £65S/£75S ~ www.hunters-moon.org.uk *Recommended by Ann and Colin Hunt, Mr and Mrs W Mills, Sandra Baldwin, David Jackman*

MUDEFORD   SZ1792   Map 2
Ship in Distress
Stanpit; off B3059 at roundabout; BH23 3NA

Wide choice of fish dishes, quirky nautical décor and friendly staff in a cheerful cottage

The light-hearted interior of this former smugglers' pub is full of amusing seaside themed paraphernalia, the most eye-catching of which are the brightly painted fish cut-outs swimming across the walls. There's everything from rope fancywork and brassware through to lanterns and oars, an aquarium, model boats and the odd piratical figurine; darts, games machine, board games, big screen TV, background music and a winter woodburning stove. Besides a good few boat pictures, the room on the right has tables with masses of snapshots of locals caught up in various waterside japes under the glass tabletops. Ringwood Best and a guest or two such as Sharps Doom Bar are on handpump alongside several wines by the glass. A spreading two-room restaurant area, as cheerful in its way as the bar, has a fish tank, contemporary works by local artists for sale and a light-hearted mural sketching out the impression of a window opening on to a sunny boating scene. There are seats and tables out on the suntrap back terrace and a covered heated area for chillier evenings. The pub is near to Mudeford Quay and Stanpit Nature Reserve is close by.

 As well as sandwiches, a good value two-course set lunch menu and a couple of pubby dishes, the menu might include scallops in garlic butter, duck and orange pâté, roast cod with chorizo, sauté potatoes, rocket and pesto, fillet of black bream with scallops and mustard cream sauce, steaks, and puddings such as lemon posset with raspberry coulis and crème brûlée. *Benchmark main dish: bass in saffron cream sauce £16.50. Two-course evening meal £22.00.*

Punch ~ Lease Maggie Wheeler ~ Real ale ~ Bar food (12-2, 7-9) ~ Restaurant ~ (01202) 485123 ~ Children welcome ~ Dogs allowed in bar ~ Open 11am-midnight(11pm Sun) ~ www.ship-in-distress.co.uk *Recommended by I D Barnett*

NETTLECOMBE

SY5195 Map 2

Marquis of Lorne

Off A3066 Bridport–Beaminster, via West Milton; DT6 3SY

Attractive country pub with enjoyable food and drink, friendly licensees and seats in the large mature garden; bedrooms

The comfortably traditional bars and dining rooms at this attractive pub are named after local hills – Nettlecombe is in an area of lovely unspoilt countryside, within walking distance of Eggardon Hill, one of Dorset's most spectacular Iron Age forts. The comfortable, bustling main bar has a log fire, mahogany panelling and old prints and photographs around its neatly matching chairs and tables. Two dining areas lead off, the smaller of which has another log fire. The wooden-floored snug (liked by locals) has board games, table skittles and background music. Palmers Best, Copper and 200 are on handpump with a dozen wines by the glass from a decent list. A lovely big mature garden has an array of pretty herbaceous borders, picnic-sets under apple trees, and a rustic-style play area.

 Tasty changing bar food, where possible using local produce, includes sandwiches, ham, bean and spinach soup, roast butternut, parsnip and parmesan risotto, crab mayonnaise with pink grapefruit and green apple salad, roast scallops and black pudding with garlic and parsley cream, battered haddock and mushy peas, cottage pie, stuffed roast butternut, roast pork belly with apple purée and beef, Guinness and vegetable suet pie. *Benchmark main dish: lambs liver and bacon £11.25. Two-course evening meal £19.35.*

Palmers ~ Tenants Stephen and Tracey Brady ~ Real ale ~ Bar food (12-2, 6-9) ~ Restaurant ~ (01308) 485236 ~ Children welcome ~ Dogs allowed in bar ~ Open 12-2.30, 6-11(10 Sun) ~ Bedrooms: £65S/£90S(£90B) ~ www.themarquisoflorne.co.uk
Recommended by Mr and Mrs P R Thomas, Matthew Beard, David and Jane Hill, B and M Kendall, Michael Bayne, Paul Goldman

PLUSH

ST7102 Map 2

Brace of Pheasants

Village signposted from B3143 N of Dorchester at Piddletrenthide; DT2 7RQ

16th-c thatched pub with friendly service, three real ales, lots of wines by the glass, well liked food and decent garden; good nearby walks; comfortable bedrooms

Charmingly tucked away in a pretty hamlet in a fold of hills surrounding the Piddle Valley, this handsome thatched place was once the village smithy and two cottages. The welcoming beamed bar has a mix of locals (and maybe their dogs) and visitors, windsor chairs around good solid tables on the patterned carpet, a few standing timbers, a huge heavy-beamed inglenook at one end with cosy seating inside and a good warming log fire at the other. Flack Manor Double Drop, Sharps Doom Bar and a guest such as Palmers Gold are tapped from the cask by the friendly licensees, and they offer a fine choice of wines with 18 by the glass, and two proper farm ciders; A decent-sized garden includes a terrace and a lawn sloping up towards a rockery. The pub is well placed for walks – an attractive bridleway behind goes to the left of the woods and over to Church Hill. The bedrooms are nicely fitted out and comfortable.

Generous helpings of good food from a shortish menu that includes sandwiches, cheesy mushrooms and bacon, lambs kidneys with a mustard cream sauce, scallops with black pudding and sweet chilli sauce, battered fish of the day, local faggots with onion gravy, portabella mushrooms with cream cheese and herb stuffing and red pepper yoghurt dressing, baked hake in tomatoes, white wine and paprika, and puddings such as chocolate and almond tart and apricot bread and butter pudding. *Benchmark main dish: garlic and herb marinated venison steak £17.00. Two-course evening meal £19.00.*

Free house ~ Licensees Phil and Carol Bennett ~ Real ale ~ Bar food (12-2, 7-9) ~ (01300) 348357 ~ Children welcome ~ Dogs allowed in bar ~ Open 12-3, 7-11(10.30 Sun) ~ Bedrooms: £105B/£115B ~ www.braceofpheasants.co.uk *Recommended by John Ecklin, Barry Collett, Mike and Sue Loseby, the Didler, A B Atkinson, Ron and Sheila Corbett, PLC*

SHERBORNE   ST6316   Map 2

Digby Tap

Cooks Lane; park in Digby Road and walk round corner; DT9 3NS

Regularly changing ales in simple alehouse, open all day with very inexpensive beer and food

One couple told us that this simple back street tavern was the sort of pub they thought had died out. It's the lively local atmosphere, friendly welcome and unspoilt interior, with little changing from one year the next, that makes this old-fashioned alehouse special. The simple flagstoned bar, with its cosy corners, is full of understated character, the small games room has pool and a quiz machine, and there's a TV room. Bass, Otter Bitter, Teignworthy Neap Tide and a local guest are on handpump, with several wines by the glass and a choice of malt whiskies. There are some seats outside, and Sherborne Abbey is just a stroll away.

Generous helpings of good value, straightforward lunchtime food includes sandwiches, toasties, ploughman's, ham, egg and chips, breaded plaice, chilli, pasta carbonara, burger, yorkshire pudding filled with pork cooked in cider, apples and cream or chilli, and mixed grill. *Benchmark main dish: ham, egg and chips £4.80.*

Free house ~ Licensees Oliver Wilson and Nick Whigham ~ Real ale ~ Bar food (12-1.45, not Sun) ~ No credit cards ~ (01935) 813148 ~ Children welcome ~ Dogs allowed in bar ~ Open 11-11; 12-11 Sun ~ www.digbytap.co.uk *Recommended by Phil and Sally Gorton, Ann and Colin Hunt, Tim and Sue Halstead, Mike and Sue Loseby, Roger Fox, Mr and Mrs P Wildman*

With the iPhone Good Pub Guide App, you can use the iPhone's camera to send us pictures of pubs you visit – outside or inside.

SHROTON   ST8512   Map 2

Cricketers £

Off A350 N of Blandford (village also called Iwerne Courtney); follow signs;
DT11 8QD

Country pub with four real ales and pretty garden; nice views
and walks nearby

This red brick country pub sits right on the Wessex Ridgeway and
is overlooked by the formidable grassy Iron Age ramparts of
Hambledon Hill, which gradually descends down to become the village
cricket pitch in front of the pub. Walkers are welcome if they leave their
boots outside. The bright, divided bar has a mix of furniture, a big stone
fireplace, alcoves and cricketing memorabilia and is kept pubby with
Butcombe Bitter, St Austell Tribute, Sharps Doom Bar and guest beer
from Isle of Purbeck on handpump. The comfortable back restaurant
overlooks the garden and has fresh neutral décor; background music.
The garden is secluded and pretty with big sturdy tables under cocktail
parasols, well tended shrubs and a well stocked (and well used) herb
garden by the kitchen door.

Bar food includes lunchtime sandwiches, ploughman's, ham hock terrine,
five-spiced seared scallops, whitebait, tempura vegetables with dipping sauce,
liver and bacon, beef or chicken fajitas, curry and pie of the day, chicken stuffed
with haggis and wrapped in bacon with whisky and mushroom sauce, and king
prawn fettucini. *Benchmark main dish: fish and chips £9.50. Two-course evening
meal £16.00.*

Heartstone Inns ~ Licensees Joe and Sally Grieves ~ Real ale ~ Bar food (12-2.30,
6-9.30; 12-3 Sun, 6-8 Sun in summer) ~ Restaurant ~ (01258) 860421 ~ Children
welcome ~ Open 12-3, 6-11; 12-11 Sun ~ www.thecricketersshroton.co.uk
Recommended by Mrs C Roe, Dr and Mrs A K Clarke, Paul Goldman, Robert Watt

SYDLING ST NICHOLAS   SY6399   Map 2

Greyhound

Off A37 N of Dorchester; High Street; DT2 9PD

Former coaching inn in pretty streamside village with good balance of
imaginative food, regular locals and country décor; bedrooms

Though the food at this charming place is quite upmarket, there's still
a good local atmosphere in the beamed and flagstoned serving area,
with drinkers gathered for a pint and a chat. There are plenty of bar
stools by the counter, and the the carpeted bar has a comfortable mix of
straightforward tables and chairs, some country decorations and a warm
fire in a handsome Portland stone fireplace. Butcombe Bitter, St Austell
Dartmoor Best and a changing guest such as Dorset Hardy Pool are on
handpump and they keep a farm cider. The cosy dining room is a little
smarter, with fresh cream walls, white tablecloths and a glass-covered
well set into the floor from which coachmen once pulled up buckets
of water for their horses. A conservatory has attractive rustic furniture
around scrubbed wooden tables and a green leather chesterfield. The
small front garden has picnic-sets and a children's play area.

The changing menu might include starters such as beetroot carpaccio
with blue cheese and red onion marmalade, seared scallops, wild rocket
and celeriac purée, mushroom risotto, crayfish and celeriac remoulade, and
main courses such as mussels steamed with tarragon, samphire, white wine and

shallots, roast cod fillet with red chard, parma ham and aioli, roast pork belly with smoked ham hock rissole, parsnip purée and spiced apple sauce, salmon and dill fishcakes, sweet potato, spinach and chestnut wellington, butternut purée, warm courgette and fennel salad, and battered catch of the day with pea and mint purée. *Benchmark main dish: fish pie £12.50. Two-course evening meal £26.00.*

Free house ~ Licensees Alice Draper and Helena Boot ~ Real ale ~ Bar food (12-2, 6.30-9) ~ Restaurant ~ (01300) 341303 ~ Children welcome ~ Dogs allowed in bar ~ Open 12-3, 6-11; 12-3 Sun; closed Sun evening ~ Bedrooms: £80B/£90B ~ www.thegreyhound.net *Recommended by Brian Glozier, Mr and Mrs John Clifford, John Branston, Tracey and Stephen Groves, Lois Dyer, Martin Roberts, Bruce Jamieson, David and Ruth Shillitoe, Phil and Jane Hodson*

TARRANT MONKTON
ST9408   Map 2

Langton Arms

Village signposted from A354, then head for church; DT11 8RX

Dorset Dining Pub of the Year

Charming thatched pub in pretty village, with real ales in airy bars, good, popular food, friendly staff and seats outside; comfortable bedrooms

A delightful setting, friendly licensees and terrific food all combine to make this 17th-c thatched inn a real winner. The beamed bar has wooden tables and chairs on flagstones, plenty of old black and white photos, a light oak counter with recessed lighting, and three local real ales from brewers such as Flack Manor, Ringwood and Sixpenny on handpump; TV in the public bar. The restaurant and conservatory are in an attractively reworked stable and the skittle alley doubles as a family room during the day; background music. Dogs are allowed only in the Carpenters Bar and in the comfortable bedrooms (in a modern block at the back). In fine weather, you can sit out in front or at teak tables in the back garden; there's also a wood-chip children's play area. The pub is next to the church in a charming village with a ford.

Plenty of effort goes into the carefully prepared food here – they grow lots of their own vegetables, and make their own bread, ice-cream and petits fours. The interesting menu might include seared scallops with jerusalem artichoke purée, gravadlax with caper berries and horseradish cream, blue vinny panna cotta, game burger on toasted onion brioche, bass fillet with prawn and white wine velouté, baked aubergine filled with ratatouille and topped with mozzarella, battered haddock, game pie, and puddings such as coffee crème brûlée and almond meringue with cream, fruit coulis and berries. *Benchmark main dish: steak pie £14.95. Two-course evening meal £21.00.*

Free house ~ Licensees Barbara and James Cossins ~ Real ale ~ Bar food (12-2.30, 6-9(10 Fri); all day weekends) ~ Restaurant ~ (01258) 830225 ~ Children welcome ~ Dogs allowed in bar and bedrooms ~ Open 11am-midnight; 12-11 Sun ~ Bedrooms: £70B/£90B ~ www.thelangtonarms.co.uk *Recommended by Michael Doswell, Mrs C Roe, V A C Turnbull, James A Waller, Robert Watt, David Jackman*

Real ale to us means beer which has matured naturally in its cask – not pressurised or filtered. We name all real ales stocked. We usually name ales preserved under a light blanket of carbon dioxide too, though purists - pointing out that this stops the natural yeasts developing - would disagree (most people, including us, can't tell the difference!).

WEST BAY

SY4690   Map 1

West Bay ♈ ⇋

Station Road; DT6 4EW

Relaxed seaside inn with emphasis on seafood

If you like fish you should be delighted by the extensive choice at this well run seaside pub where you can enjoy a relaxing meal in an informal, welcoming atmosphere. An island servery separates the fairly simple bare-boards front part (with coal-effect gas fire and a mix of sea and nostalgic prints) from a cosier carpeted dining area with more of a country kitchen feel; background music. Though its spaciousness means it never feels crowded, booking is generally essential in season. Palmers 200, Best, Copper Ale and Dorset Gold are served on handpump alongside good house wines (with ten by the glass) and several malt whiskies. There are tables in the small side garden, with more in a large garden. Several local teams meet to play in the pub's 100-year-old skittle alley. The bedrooms are quiet and comfortable.

Fresh fish and seafood, caught from local boats, is listed on blackboards and the main menu (not cheap), with starters such as grilled langoustines or Fowey mussels and main courses such as deep-fried pollack and skate wing with capers and shrimp. Other dishes include roast duck breast with hoisin sauce, beef stroganoff, roast stuffed red peppers and rib-eye steak topped with scallops. At lunchtime they also offer a few traditional favourites such as filled baguettes, ham, egg and chips and roast pork belly topped with apple with cider jus; daily changing puddings. *Benchmark main dish: crab salad £13.95. Two-course evening meal £22.00.*

Palmers ~ Tenants Paul Crisp and Tracy McCulloch ~ Real ale ~ Bar food (12-2(3 Sun); 6-9) ~ Restaurant ~ (01308) 422157 ~ Children welcome till 8pm ~ Dogs allowed in bar ~ Open 12-11; 12-3, 6-11 (Mon-Thurs) in winter in winter ~ Bedrooms: /£85(£100B) ~ www.thewestbayhotel.co.uk *Recommended by David and Julie Glover, B and M Kendall, Matthew Beard, Mr and Mrs Gordon Turner*

WEST STOUR

ST7822   Map 2

Ship ♉ ⇋

A30 W of Shaftesbury; SP8 5RP

Civilised and pleasantly updated roadside dining inn, offering a wide range of food

During his summer beer festival, the landlord at this well cared for roadside inn puts a stage up in the garden and showcases a dozen beers and ten ciders, all from the West Country. At other times you'll find Dartmoor IPA and three guests from brewers such as Butcombe, Fullers and Sharps on handpump, good wines by the glass, a farm cider, elderflower pressé and organic apple juices. The smallish bar on the left is airy with big sash windows looking beyond the road and car park to rolling pastures, cream décor and a mix of chunky farmhouse furniture on dark boards. The smaller flagstoned public bar has a good log fire and low ceilings. On the right, two carpeted dining rooms with stripped pine dado, stone walls and shutters are similarly furnished in a pleasantly informal style, and have some attractive contemporary prints of cows; TV, darts, lots of board games and background music. The bedlington terriers are called Douglas and Toby. The five bedrooms have just been refurbished.

Served in generous helpings, jolly decent food might include interestingly filled ciabattas, scallops with pancetta and pea purée, devilled kidneys on toasted brioche, spicy crab cakes, venison burger, fried pork tenderloin with sloe gin cream sauce, rabbit, smoked bacon and leek hotpot with grain mustard and cider gravy, battered haddock, mushroom, spinach and blue cheese wellington, fried calves liver and bacon with red wine and onion gravy, and puddings such as lemon and lime syllabub with gingernut crumble, mississippi pie and chocolate and brandy torte. *Benchmark main dish: poached haddock with poached egg and mornay sauce £11.95. Two-course evening meal £20.00.*

Free house ~ Licensee Gavin Griggs ~ Real ale ~ Bar food (12-2.30, 6-9; not Sun evening) ~ Restaurant ~ (01747) 838640 ~ Children welcome ~ Dogs allowed in bar ~ Open 12-3, 6-11; 12-11 Sun ~ Bedrooms: £60B/£90B ~ www.shipinn-dorset.com
Recommended by Mrs C Roe, Dr Nigel Bowles, Mr and Mrs J J A Davis, Comus and Sarah Elliott, Lois Dyer, Steve Jackson, Dennis Jenkin, S G N Bennett

WEYMOUTH SY6878 Map 2
Red Lion 🍺 £
Hope Square; DT4 8TR

Cheery place with sunny terrace, great range of drinks including an impressive range of whiskies and rums, and good value pubby food

Opposite the redeveloped brewery (now shops and so forth) in Weymouth's pedestrianised Old Harbour, and sharing its Victorian architecture, this lively place has an outside seating area that enjoys all the local bustle and is warmed by the sun well into the evening – during the summer months it turns one of Weymouth's smallest pubs into one of its biggest. You can warm up here nicely in winter, too, as they stock an impressive range of over 60 rums, well over 100 whiskies and whiskeys displayed behind the bar. Real ales (with helpful tasting notes), pulled by the cheery irish landlord, include Tring Lifeboat, Dorset Red Lion Pride and three guests from brewers such as Dorset, Hop Back and Sharps. The refurbished bare-boards interior is kept cosy with candles, has just enough bric-a-brac to add interest, and some nice contemporary touches like the woven timber wall and loads of mirrors wittily overlapping on stripped brick walls; board games, background music.

 Much enjoyed good value bar food includes filled baps, crispy whitebait, smoked mackerel pâté, seafood chowder, battered haddock, scampi, sausage and mash, aberdeen angus burger, ginger and lime fishcake with chilli dressing, pie of the day, fish pie, and puddings such as black forest chocolate brownies, dorset apple cake and eton mess. *Benchmark main dish: mixed seafood plate £9.95. Two-course evening meal £14.80.*

Free house ~ Licensee Brian McLaughlin ~ Real ale ~ Bar food (12-9; 12-3, 6-8.30 in winter) ~ (01305) 786940 ~ Children welcome ~ Dogs allowed in bar ~ Live music Fri evenings, summer Sun afternoons ~ Open 12-11(midnight Sat, 10.30 Sun) ~ www.theredlionweymouth.co.uk *Recommended by Matthew Beard, Rob Winstanley, Robin Manners*

WIMBORNE MINSTER SZ0199 Map 2
Green Man 🍺 £
Victoria Road at junction with West Street (B3082/B3073); BH21 1EN

Cosy, warm-hearted town pub with simple food at bargain prices

This cheerful local is a proper community pub with regulars popping in and out throughout the day, but as a visitor you'll get just as warm a welcome from the friendly landlord. The four small linked areas have maroon plush banquettes and polished dark pub tables, copper and brass ornaments, red walls and Wadworths IPA, 6X and Bishops Tipple on handpump. One room has a log fire in a biggish brick fireplace, another has a coal-effect gas fire, and they have two dart boards, a silenced games machine, background music and TV; in summer, the Barn houses a pool table. The award-winning window boxes, flowering tubs and hanging baskets at the front are a fantastic sight in summer – there are more on the heated back terrace. Their little border terrier is called Cooper.

 As well as a popular breakfast, the bargain-priced traditional food includes sandwiches, jumbo rolls, whitebait, thai style fishcakes, lasagne, vegetable burger, lamb shank, and a well liked Sunday roast. *Benchmark main dish: fish and chips £6.25. Two-course evening meal £11.00.*

Wadworths ~ Tenant Andrew Kiff ~ Real ale ~ Bar food (10-2; not evenings) ~ Restaurant ~ (01202) 881021 ~ Children welcome until 7.30pm ~ Dogs allowed in bar ~ Open 10am-11.30pm(12.30 Sat) ~ www.greenmanwimborne.com *Recommended by Mrs Blethyn Elliott, Dr and Mrs A K Clarke, B and M Kendall*

WORTH MATRAVERS   SY9777   Map 2

Square & Compass ★ ◖

At fork of both roads signposted to village from B3069; BH19 3LF

Unchanging country tavern with masses of character, in the same family for many years; lovely sea views and fine nearby walks

For most of our readers this 'blissfully eccentric place' is 'worth a huge detour', though its simple offerings are not to everyone's taste, and it can get very busy. The Newman family first took on this fine old pub over 100 years ago and to this day, there's no bar counter. Palmers Copper and guests from brewers such as Bowmans, Otley and Wessex and up to 13 ciders are tapped from a row of casks and passed to you in a drinking corridor through two serving hatches; also about 20 malt whiskies. A couple of basic unspoilt rooms have simple furniture on the flagstones, a woodburning stove and a loyal crowd of friendly locals; darts and shove-ha'penny. From benches (made from local stone) out in front there's a fantastic view down over the village rooftops to the sea around St Aldhelm's Head and there may be free-roaming hens, chickens and other birds clucking around your feet. A little museum (free) exhibits local fossils and artefacts, mostly collected by the current friendly landlord and his father. There are wonderful walks from here to some exciting switchback sections of the coast path above St Aldhelm's Head and Chapman's Pool – you will need to park in the public car park 100 metres along the Corfe Castle road (which has a £1 honesty box).

 Bar food is limited to tasty home-made pasties and pies, which are served till stocks run out. *Benchmark main dish: pasties £3.20.*

Free house ~ Licensee Charlie Newman ~ Real ale ~ Bar food (all day) ~ No credit cards ~ (01929) 439229 ~ Children welcome ~ Dogs welcome ~ Live music some Fri and Sat evenings and Sun lunchtime ~ Open 12-11; 12-3, 6-11 Mon-Thurs in winter ~ www.squareandcompasspub.co.uk *Recommended by Ewan and Moira McCall, P Dawn, Tony and Wendy Hobden, Steve and Sue Griffiths, Mike and Sue Loseby, David Lamb, the Didler, Mr Yeldahn, Michael Sargent, Tich Critchlow, Martin and Sue Day*

If you stay overnight in an inn or hotel, they are allowed to serve you an alcoholic drink at any hour of the day or night.

Also Worth a Visit in Dorset

Besides the fully inspected pubs, you might like to try these pubs that have been recommended to us and described by readers. Do tell us what you think of them: feedback@goodguides.com

---

ALMER　　　　　　　　　SY9098
Worlds End　(01929) 459671
B3075, just off A31 towards Wareham; DT11 9EW Handsome thatched family dining pub, plenty of individuality in long busy beamed and flagstoned bar with panelled alcoves, wide choice of enjoyable reasonably priced food all day, Badger ales, pleasant helpful staff; picnic-sets out in front and behind, play area. *(Richard Stanfield)*

BLANDFORD FORUM　　　　　ST8806
Crown　(01258) 456626
West Street; DT11 7AJ Civilised red-brick Georgian hotel on edge of town, spacious bar area with Badger ales from nearby brewery, good choice of wines, teas and coffee, appetising food from sandwiches to daily specials, restaurant; children welcome, sturdy tables on big terrace with formal garden beyond, 32 bedrooms. *(Michael Doswell)*

BLANDFORD ST MARY　　　　ST8805
Hall & Woodhouse　(01258) 455481
Bournemouth Road; DT11 9LS Visitor centre for Badger brewery, their full beer range in top condition including interesting bottled beers, traditional lunchtime food from well filled baguettes up, friendly staff; spectacular chandelier made of beer bottles, lots of memorabilia in centre and upper gallery; popular brewery tours, open lunchtimes only, closed Sun. *(Joan and Michel Hooper-Immins)*

BOURNEMOUTH
Cricketers Arms　(01202) 551589
Windham Road; BH1 4RN Well preserved Victorian pub near station, separate public and lounge bars, lots of dark wood, etched windows and stained glass, tiled fireplace, Fullers London Pride with guests like Harviestoun Schiehallion and Wharfebank Tether Blond, no food apart from popular Sun lunch. *(Joan and Michel Hooper-Immins)*

BOURTON　　　　　　　　ST7731
⋆White Lion　(01747) 840866
High Street, off old A303 E of Wincanton; SP8 5AT Lively 18th-c low-beamed and stripped-stone dining pub with welcoming energetic landlord, appealing place with fine inglenook fire in pubby bar, two cosy rooms off and decent-sized restaurant, good well priced food from bar snacks up, beers such as Otter and Sharps Doom Bar, Thatcher's cider, nice wines; picnic-sets on back paved area and raised lawn, two neat bedrooms. *(Mrs C Roe)*

BRIDPORT　　　　　　　　SY4692
Ropemakers　(01308) 421255
West Street; DT6 3QP Warm friendly local with well kept Palmers ales and very good value food. *(Comus and Sarah Elliott)*

BRIDPORT　　　　　　　　SY4692
Tiger　(01308) 427543
Barrack Street, off South Street; DT6 3LY Cheerful open-plan Victorian beamed pub with well kept range of changing ales and real cider, enjoyable food, skittle alley; two outside areas, open all day. *(Bill Stanley, Roger Scammell)*

BRIDPORT　　　　　　　　SY4692
Woodman　(01308) 456455
South Street; DT6 3NZ Welcoming traditional little local with well kept Branscombe Vale and interesting guests, decent straightforward home-made food, skittle alley, live music, Sun quiz; seats out on pavement, attractive garden behind, open all day. *(Roger Scammell, the Didler)*

BUCKHORN WESTON　　　　ST7524
⋆Stapleton Arms　(01963) 370396
Church Hill; off A30 Shaftesbury–Sherborne via Kington Magna; SP8 5HS Upmarket dining pub in handsome Georgian building, sizeable bar divided by glazed-in entrance lobby, farmhouse and pew chairs around scrubbed table on slate flagstones, comfortable sofas, log fire in fine stone fireplace, four real ales including Butcombe, Cheddar Valley cider, imaginative daily-changing seasonal menu using locally sourced produce, dining room with mahogany tables on coir, church candles in fireplace; children welcome, dogs in bar, elegant metal tables and chairs out on York flagstones and gravel, good comfortable bedrooms, open all day weekends. *(Joan and Michel Hooper-Immins, Ian Malone, Mr and Mrs B E Lynn)*

BUCKLAND NEWTON　　　　ST6804
⋆Gaggle of Geese　(01300) 345249
Locketts Lane; E end of village; DT2 7BS 19th-c country pub with relaxed atmosphere, sofas and armchairs next to log fire, books and games, enjoyable locally sourced modern pub food, Sun roasts, Ringwood, St Austell and two west country guests, good wine choice, nice coffee, red candlelit dining room with persian rugs and mix of old and new furniture, skittle alley; children welcome and dogs (pub has its own), garden with terrace, orchard and pond, paddock with chickens and goats, charity poultry auction May and Sept, open all day weekends. *(Tim Carron-Brown, Peter Salmon)*

BURTON   SZ1793
Manor Arms (01202) 477189
*The one on B3347 just N of
Christchurch; BH23 7JG* Extensively
refurbished 19th-c hotel, contemporary bar/
restaurant area with open kitchen, good food
including carvery, real ales such as Sharps
Doom Bar, efficient friendly service, snug
side room with easy chairs and TV; seats out
on split-level terrace, ten bedrooms. *(Clare
Mills and Graham Bowman, David Cannings)*

BURTON BRADSTOCK   SY4889
Three Horseshoes (01308) 897259
Mill Street; DT6 4QZ Busy old thatched
place 400 metres from Chesil Beach and
coastal path; array of pictures and local
photographs in pleasant low-ceilinged
carpeted bar, inglenook woodburner, full
range of Palmers beers (under light blanket
pressure in winter), generous food including
local fish and game (booking advised at peak
times), efficient polite service, dining room;
background music; children welcome, dogs
in bar, suntrap back garden with heaters
on large partly covered terrace, open all
day. *(Phil and Jane Hodson, B and M Kendall,
Comus and Sarah Elliott, Adrian Johnson, C and
R Bromage, R J and D S Courtney)*

CERNE ABBAS   ST6601
Royal Oak (01300) 341797
Long Street; DT2 7JG Popular thatched
village-centre pub with low beams, flagstones
and all sorts of rustic memorabilia, friendly
irish landlord and efficient staff, well kept
Badger ales, changing lunchtime and evening
menus may include Portland crab and
local game; children welcome, small back
garden. *(John and Gloria Isaacs, Ann and Colin
Hunt, Joan and Michel Hooper-Immins,
Mrs R Smith)*

CHEDINGTON   ST4805
Winyards Gap (01935) 891244
A356 Dorchester–Crewkerne; DT8 3HY
Attractive dining pub surrounded by NT land
with spectacular view over Parrett Valley
and into Somerset, enjoyable good value food
from sandwiches to some unusual choices,
bargain two-course OAP weekday lunch,
four well kept beers including St Austell
and Sharps Doom Bar, friendly staff and St
Bernard called Daisy, stylish dining room,
skittle alley; children and dogs welcome,
tables on front lawn under parasols, good
walks, open all day weekends. *(Robert Watt,
B and M Kendall)*

CHETNOLE   ST6008
⋆ Chetnole Inn (01935) 872337
*Village signed off A37 S of Yeovil;
DT9 6NU* Attractive inn with beams, huge
flagstones and country kitchen décor, Otter,
Sharps Doom Bar and a guest such as Dorset
Piddle, 16 malt whiskies, central woodburner
and modern leather seats in minimalist snug,

open fire and pale wood tables on stripped
boards in attractive dining room with fresh
flowers, candles and linen napkins, generally
well liked food using local produce including
own duck eggs, deli with small tearoom in
one corner; dogs welcome in bar, picnic-sets
out in front and in delightful back garden,
three bedrooms overlooking old church, good
breakfast, closed Sun evening and Mon in
winter. *(Ian Malone)*

CHIDEOCK   SY4192
Clockhouse (01297) 489423
A35 W of Bridport; DT6 6JW Friendly
family-run thatched village local, well kept
Otter and Palmers, enjoyable straightforward
food including bargain deals, huge collection
of clocks, skittle alley/games room; children
welcome, dogs in bar. *(Terry and
Nickie Williams)*

CHILD OKEFORD   ST8213
⋆ Saxon (01258) 860310
*Signed off A350 Blandford–Shaftesbury
and A357 Blandford–Sherborne; Gold
Hill; DT11 8HD* Welcoming 17th-c village
pub, quietly clubby snug bar with log fire,
two dining rooms, Butcombe, Ringwood
and guests, good choice of wines, enjoyable
reasonably priced home-made food, good
service; children welcome, dogs in bar,
attractive back garden with wooden shelter,
good walks on neolithic Hambledon Hill, four
comfortable bedrooms. *(Robert Watt)*

CHRISTCHURCH   SZ1592
⋆ Olde George (01202) 479383
Castle Street; BH23 1DT Bustling and
cheerfully old-fashioned two-bar low-beamed
pub dating from the 15th c, Dorset Piddle
ales and a guest, real ciders and nice wine,
enjoyable sensibly priced food all day using
local suppliers, Sun carvery and different
evening menu, friendly staff; dogs welcome
(even provide food), lots of teak seats and
tables in heated character coachyard, open
all day. *(A D Lealan)*

CHRISTCHURCH   SZ1593
Rising Sun (01202) 486122
Purewell; BH23 1EJ Sympathetically
updated old pub specialising in authentic
thai food, real ales such as Flack Manor from
L-shaped bar, good choice of wines by the
glass, pleasant helpful young staff; terrace
with palms and black rattan-style furniture
under large umbrellas. *(Joe Gunn, Mr and
Mrs P D Titcomb)*

CHURCH KNOWLE   SY9381
⋆ New Inn (01929) 480357
*Village signed off A351 N of Corfe Castle;
BH20 5NQ* Pleasantly furnished 16th-c
stone and partly thatched dining room, good
food with emphasis on fresh fish, choose
your own wine from walk-in cellar, three real
ales including Greene King Old Speckled
Hen, entertaining mix of bric-a-brac, old

tables and chairs on red patterned carpet in two stone-walled areas, open fires; children welcome, disabled facilities, fine surrounding walks and views from nice garden, camping. *(Ewan and Moira McCall, Mrs Sheena and Emily Killick, R and S Bentley, Dr A J and Mrs Tompsett, Mike and Sue Loseby and others)*

COLEHILL SU0302
Barley Mow (01202) 882140
Colehill signed from A31/B3073 roundabout; Long Lane; BH21 7AH Welcoming part-thatched, part-tiled family-managed 17th-c pub, enjoyable food and well kept Badger ales, low-beamed main bar, open fire in brick inglenook, attractive oak panelling, carpeted restaurant; background music; children and dogs welcome, tethering for horses, seats out at front and in pleasant enclosed lawn behind with terrace, open all day in summer. *(Anon)*

CORFE CASTLE SY9681
Castle Inn (01929) 480208
East Street; BH20 5EE Welcoming little two-room pub mentioned in Hardy's Hand of Ethelberta, enjoyable fairly priced food using local supplies including popular Fri fish night, Dorset and Ringwood ales, heavy black beams, exposed stone walls, flagstones and open fire; children welcome, back terrace and big sunny garden with mature trees. *(Dawn Viner, Richard Stanfield, Mike and Sue Loseby, the Didler, John and Joan Calvert, Malcolm and Maralyn Hinxman and others)*

CORFE CASTLE SY9681
Fox (01929) 480449
West Street; BH20 5HD Old-fashioned take-us-as-you-find us stone-built local, real ales such as Greene King Abbot and Wadworths 6X tapped from the cask, good log fire in early medieval stone fireplace, glassed-over well in second bar; dogs but not children allowed, informal castle-view garden. *(Mike and Sue Loseby, Tich Critchlow)*

CORFE CASTLE SY9682
★**Greyhound** (01929) 480205
A351; The Square; BH20 5EZ Bustling picturesque old pub in centre of this tourist village, three small low-ceilinged panelled rooms, steps and corridors, well kept ales such as Ringwood and Sharps, local cider, wide choice of fairly priced food from sandwiches and light dishes to good local seafood, friendly helpful staff, traditional games including Purbeck long board shove-ha'penny, family room; background music – live on Fri; garden with large decked area, great views of castle and countryside, pretty courtyard opening on to castle bridge, open all day weekends and in summer. *(Richard Stanfield, Mike and Sue Loseby, the Didler, Mr Yeldahn, Lesley and Peter Barrett, Dr and Mrs R E S Tanner)*

CORFE MULLEN SY9798
★**Coventry Arms** (01258) 857284
Mill Street (A31 W of Wimborne); BH21 3RH 15th-c pub with bar and four dining rooms, low ceilings, eclectic mix of furniture on flagstones or parquet flooring, large central open fire, good choice of beers tapped from cooled casks, well liked reasonably priced food from open kitchen, friendly helpful staff; stuffed fish and a mummified cat (to ward off evil spirits); background and occasional live music; children and dogs welcome, big waterside garden with terrace, open all day. *(Roger and Kathy Elkin, Louise Goodison, Fran Lane, John Dorricott, Richard Stanfield)*

DORCHESTER SY6990
★**Blue Raddle** (01305) 267762
Church Street, near central short stay car park; DT1 1JN Cheery pubby atmosphere in long carpeted and partly panelled bar, well kept ales including one brewed for them, Weston's cider, good wines and coffee, enjoyable simple home-made food at reasonable prices, open fire; background music; disabled access (but one step), closed Mon lunchtime. *(John Ecklin, Rob and Catherine Dunster, B and M Kendall, the Didler, Peter Thornton, David and Ruth Shillitoe)*

DORCHESTER SY6790
★**Poet Laureate** (01305) 251511
Pummery Square, Poundbury; DT1 3GW Substantial building in the Prince of Wales's Poundbury development, enjoyable if not particularly cheap food including some interesting dishes, ales such as Fullers, Butcombe and Ringwood, decent wines by the glass, proper coffee, light and airy L-shaped bar with good décor, lots of chandeliers, good solid tables and chairs, flame-effect stove, nice restaurant area, daily papers; unobtrusive background music; wheelchair access (step up at entrance), a few picnic-sets on side terrace. *(Paul Goldman, Joan and Michel Hooper-Immins)*

DRIMPTON ST4105
Royal Oak (01308) 867930
Bridport Road; DT8 3RD Welcoming family-run village pub with enjoyable traditional food from lunchtime baguettes up, reasonable prices, well kept ales and decent selection of wines, skittle alley, some live music, quiz first Sun of month; beer garden, closed Mon. *(Leslie Bedborough)*

EAST CHALDON SY7983
Sailors Return (01305) 854571
Village signposted from A352 Wareham–Dorchester; from village green, follow Dorchester, Weymouth signpost; note that the village is also known as Chaldon Herring; OS sheet 194 map reference 790834; DT2 8DN Friendly thatched village pub with flagstoned bar keeping much of its original rural-tavern character, newer part with open beams showing roof, well kept Palmers

and Ringwood, local cider in summer, enjoyable food from bar snacks up served promptly by courteous staff; children and dogs welcome, garden picnic-sets, useful for coast path, open all day in season. *(Gareth Lewis, David Lamb)*

EAST LULWORTH SY8581
Weld Arms (01929) 400211
B3070 SW of Wareham; BH20 5QQ Thatched 17th-c pub under newish management, civilised log-fire bar, three ales including Palmers and Wells & Youngs, food from lunchtime sandwiches and baguettes up, friendly helpful service, two dining rooms; children and dogs welcome, picnic-sets out in big garden with play area. *(Lawrence Pearse, Miles and Maxine Wadeley)*

EAST MORDEN SY9194
★ **Cock & Bottle** (01929) 459238
B3075 W of Poole; BH20 7DL Popular dining pub with wide choice of good if not cheap food (best to book), well kept Badger ales, nice selection of wines by the glass, efficient cheerful service, two dining areas with heavy rough beams; children and dogs allowed in certain areas, garden and adjoining field, pleasant pastoral outlook. *(Howard and Margaret Buchanan)*

EAST STOUR ST8123
Kings Arms (01747) 838325
A30, 2 miles E of village; The Common; SP8 5NB Extended dining pub with enjoyable food from scottish landlord/chef including bargain lunch menu and all-day Sun carvery (best to book), ales such as Palmers Copper, St Austell Tribute and Wadworths 6X, decent wines and good selection of malt whiskies, friendly efficient staff, open fire in bar, light airy dining area with light wood furniture, scottish pictures and Burns quotes; gentle background music; children welcome, dogs in bar, good disabled access, picnic-sets in big garden, bluebell walks nearby, three bedrooms, open all day weekends. *(Paul Goldman, Jeremy King, Roy Hoing, D M and B K Moores, Anne de Gruchy and others)*

EVERSHOT ST5704
Acorn (01935) 83228
Off A37 S of Yeovil; DT2 0JW 16th-c coaching inn (Sow & Acorn in *Tess of the d'Urbevilles*), two well kept changing ales, real ciders, good choice of wines by the glass including champagne, decent food in restaurant/front part with up-to-date décor as well as log fires and oak panelling, bar snacks from good open sandwiches to salads and pubby hot dishes in beamed and flagstoned back bar with darts and pool, skittle alley; background music; children allowed in eating areas, dogs in bar, terrace with dark oak furniture, ten bedrooms, pretty village, good walks, open all day. *(Bruce Jamieson, Alan Johnson, A B Atkinson)*

FARNHAM ST9515
Museum (01725) 516261
Village signposted off A354 Blandford Forum–Salisbury; DT11 8DE Rather smart 17th-c inn with emphasis on good inventive modern food (not cheap), good comfortably cushioned furnishings in bustling beamed and flagstoned little bar with inglenook, fine antique dresser in dining room, and another room like a contemporary baronial hall with dozens of antlers and a stag's head looking down on a long refectory table, ales such as Flack Manor and Waylands, excellent choice of wines with 15 by the glass and some 30 malt whiskies; children and dogs welcome, terrace tables, good comfortable bedrooms. *(Clare Mills and Graham Bowman, Phyl and Jack Street, A B Atkinson, Bruce Jamieson)*

FIDDLEFORD ST8013
Fiddleford Inn (01258) 475612
A357 Sturminster Newton–Blandford Forum; DT10 2BX Beamed roadside pub with three linked areas, old flagstones, carpets and some stripped stone, enjoyable pubby food, well kept Butcombe and guests; background and occasional live music; children and dogs welcome, picnic-sets in big fenced garden, three bedrooms, open all day. *(Anon)*

GUSSAGE ALL SAINTS SU0010
★ **Drovers** (01258) 840084
8 miles N of Wimborne; BH21 5ET Partly thatched pub with good proper home-made food using local ingredients (some home-grown), friendly service, Ringwood ales and guests kept well, good wines by the glass, log fire and pleasantly simple country furnishings, public bar with piano and darts; well behaved children and dogs welcome, tables on pretty front lawn with views across the Dorset hills, adjoining farm shop, peaceful village. *(Michael Doswell, Howard and Margaret Buchanan)*

HIGHCLIFFE SZ2193
Galleon (01425) 279855
Lymington Road; BH23 5EA Fresh contemporary refurbishment with leather sofas, light wood floors and open fires, well prepared food from snacks and pub favourites up, local ales including Ringwood, good service, conservatory opening on to terrace and sunny garden; background music – live weekends; children welcome, summer barbecues, play area, open all day (till midnight Fri, Sat). *(David M Cundy, Susan Donkin)*

HURN SZ1397
Avon Causeway (01202) 482714
Village signed off A338, then follow Avon, Sopley, Mutchams sign; BH23 6AS Roomy, civilised and comfortable hotel/dining pub, food from well filled baguettes

and pub favourites up, Sun carvery, well kept Wadworths ales, helpful welcoming staff, interesting railway decorations, good disabled access; Pullman-coach restaurant (breakfast served here) by former 1870s station platform; nice garden (some road noise), 12 bedrooms, near Bournemouth Airport (2 weeks free parking if you stay the night before you fly), open all day. *(Val and Alan Green)*

IBBERTON ST7807
Crown (01258) 817448
Village W of Blandford Forum; DT11 0EN Updated traditional village dining pub, flagstones, toby jugs and comfortable seats by inglenook woodburner, back eating area, ales such as Butcombe, Dorset Piddle and Palmers from brick-faced bar, local cider, enjoyable pubby food plus interesting dishes and good value set deals, friendly helpful staff; dogs on leads in bar and in lovely garden, beautiful spot under Bulbarrow Hill, good walks, closed Mon. *(Peter Salmon)*

KINGSTON SY9579
⚹ **Scott Arms** (01929) 480270
West Street (B3069); BH20 5LH Extensively modernised pub rambling through several levels, some sofas and easy chairs, beams, stripped stone, bare boards and log fires, good reasonably priced local food including fresh fish, well kept Dorset and Ringwood ales, decent wines, family dining area; dogs welcome, big attractive garden with outstanding views of Corfe Castle and the Purbeck Hills, summer barbecues, two well equipped bedrooms, good walks, open all day. *(Ewan and Moira McCall, William Henderson, Peter Ellis, Betsy and Peter Little, Mike and Sue Loseby, Lucy Johnstone and others)*

LODERS SY4994
Loders Arms (01308) 422431
Off A3066 just N of Bridport; DT6 3SA Unspoilt 17th-c stone-built pub in pretty thatched village, well kept Palmers ales, Thatcher's cider, good choice of wines by the glass, home-made food from varied menu, log fire, dining room, skittle alley; children and dogs welcome, pleasant views from picnic-sets in small garden behind, good surrounding walks, closed Sun evenings winter. *(Tony and Gill Powell)*

LYME REGIS SY3391
Cobb Arms (01297) 443242
Marine Parade, Monmouth Beach; DT7 3JF Spacious place with well kept Palmers ales and decent wines, good choice of reasonably priced freshly cooked food (gluten-free options), cream teas, quick service, a couple of sofas, ship pictures and marine fish tank, open fire; pool, juke box, TVs; children and dogs welcome, disabled access (one step up from road), tables on

small back terrace, next to harbour, beach and coastal walk, three bedrooms, open all day. *(Michael Tack, Ian Cheal)*

LYME REGIS SY3391
⚹ **Harbour Inn** (01297) 442299
Marine Parade; DT7 3JF More eating than pubby with thriving family atmosphere, attentive young staff, good food from lunchtime sandwiches to local fish (not cheap), good choice of wines by the glass, well kept Otter and local Town Mill, tea and coffee, clean-cut modern décor keeping original flagstones and stone walls (lively acoustic), paintings for sale, sea views from front windows; background music; disabled access from street, verandah tables.
(P Dawn, Nick Birtley, Guy Vowles, Roger Fox, P Houldsworth, Michael Cooper and others)

LYME REGIS SY3492
⚹ **Pilot Boat** (01297) 443157
Bridge Street; DT7 3QA Popular modern all-day family food place near waterfront, neatly cared for by long-serving licensees, friendly service even when busy, good sensibly priced food including local fish, well kept Palmers ales, good choice of wines by the glass, plenty of tables in cheery nautically themed areas, skittle alley; quiet background radio; dogs welcome, tables out on terrace (watch for greedy seagulls). *(Joan and Michel Hooper-Immins, David and Julie Glover)*

LYME REGIS SY3391
⚹ **Royal Standard** (01297) 442637
Marine Parade, The Cobb; DT7 3JF Right on broadest part of beach, properly pubby bar with log fire, fine built-in stripped high settles, local photographs and even old-fashioned ring-up tills, quieter eating area with stripped-brick and pine, four well kept Palmers ales and good choice of wines by the glass, food from massive crab sandwiches up including local fish and good vegetarian choices, friendly helpful service; darts, prominent pool table, free wi-fi, background and some live music, gets very busy in season – may be long waits then; children and dogs welcome, good-sized suntrap courtyard with own servery and harbour views, open all day. *(Joan and Michel Hooper-Immins, Mrs P Abell, Henry Paulinski)*

LYME REGIS SY3492
Volunteer (01297) 442214
Top of Broad Street (A3052 towards Exeter); DT7 3QE Cosy old-fashioned pub with long low-ceilinged bar, nice mix of customers (can get crowded), well kept changing west country ales – some tapped from the cask, farm cider, enjoyable modestly priced food in dining lounge (children allowed here), friendly young staff, roaring fires; dogs welcome, open all day. *(Roger Fox)*

LYTCHETT MINSTER   SY9593
Bakers Arms   (01202) 622900
Dorchester Road; BH16 6JF Large, popular partly thatched Vintage Inn, modernised rambling interior with beams, timbers and log fires, extensive choice of enjoyable all-day food including lunchtime deals and good Sun roasts, well kept changing ales such as Brains, Ringwood and Sharps, efficient chatty staff; no dogs; children welcome, garden picnic-sets, open all day. *(Sue and Mike Todd, Clive Connor)*

LYTCHETT MINSTER   SY9693
★St Peters Finger   (01202) 622275
Dorchester Road; BH16 6JE Well run two-part beamed roadhouse with cheerful efficient staff, popular sensibly priced food from sandwiches and baguettes up, small helpings available, Badger ales and several wines by the glass, welcoming end log fire, cottagey mix of furnishings in different sections giving a cosy feel despite its size; good skittle alley, tables on big terrace, part covered and heated. *(Anon)*

MARNHULL   ST7818
Crown   (01258) 820224
About 3 miles N of Sturminster Newton; Crown Road; DT10 1LN Part-thatched inn dating from the 16th c, linked rooms with oak beams, huge flagstones or bare boards, log fire in big stone hearth in oldest part, more modern furnishings and carpet elsewhere, Badger ales, restaurant; peaceful enclosed garden, bedrooms. *(Anon)*

MELPLASH   SY4897
★Half Moon   (01308) 488321
A3066 Bridport–Beaminster; DT6 3UD Thatched and shuttered roadside dining pub doing well under newish licensees, very good food with emphasis on organic and local produce, Palmers ales, competent service, beams and log fire; children welcome, picnic-sets in front, more in well maintained back garden. *(B and M Kendall, Bruce Jamieson)*

MILTON ABBAS   ST8001
Hambro Arms   (01258) 880233
Signed off A354 SW of Blandford; DT11 0BP Recently refurbished pub in beautiful late 18th-c thatched landscaped village, two beamed bars and restaurant, well kept ales such as Dorset Piddle, Ringwood and Sharps Doom Bar, good food from ciabattas and panini up, prompt friendly service; children welcome, dogs in bar, tables on front terrace, four bedrooms, open all day weekends. *(David and Ruth Shillitoe)*

MOTCOMBE   ST8426
Coppleridge   (01747) 851980
Signed from The Street, follow to Mere/ Gillingham; SP7 9HW Good food from sandwiches to speciality steaks and fresh fish, real ales including Butcombe, decent wines and welcoming service in former 18th-c farmhouse's bar and various dining rooms, some live music; children welcome, ten spacious courtyard bedrooms, 15-acre grounds, play area. *(Mr and Mrs A Curry)*

MUDEFORD   SZ1792
Nelson   (01202) 485105
75 Mudeford; BH23 3NJ Friendly well run local, good service, four well kept ales, wide range of food from bar meals to authentic thai dishes (takeaways available – delivered locally on a tuk-tuk), bright modern back dining area; Thurs quiz, some live music including jazz, sports TV; pleasant back terrace, open all day. *(Malcolm Derrick)*

NORDEN HEATH   SY94834
★Halfway   (01929) 480402
A351 Wareham–Corfe Castle; BH20 5DU Cosily laid out partly thatched pub with friendly staff, Badger beers, good wines by the glass, enjoyable food all day including children's choices, pitched-ceiling back serving bar where the locals congregate, front rooms with flagstones, log fires, stripped stonework, snug little side area; picnic-tables outside with play area, good nearby walks. *(Mike and Sue Loseby, W Bowler)*

OSMINGTON   SY7282
Sunray   (01305) 832148
A353 Weymouth–Wareham; DT3 6EU Light and airy extended pub under new family management, enjoyable food all day from open kitchen including daily carvery, good friendly service, well kept Palmers and maybe a guest, Weston's cider; children and dogs welcome, large garden with terrace and play area. *(Joan and Michel Hooper-Immins, Adrian Johnson, David Eberlin)*

OSMINGTON MILLS   SY7381
★Smugglers   (01305) 833125
Off A353 NE of Weymouth; DT3 6HF Bustling old partly thatched family-oriented inn, well extended, with cosy timber divided areas, woodburners, old local pictures, Badger ales and guests, good choice of wines by the glass, all-day food from varied well priced menu, friendly efficient service; picnic sets on crazy paving by little stream, thatched summer bar, play area, useful for coastal path, four bedrooms, open all day. *(Joan and Michel Hooper-Immins, Mrs Joyce Robson, Ann Salmon, Michael Coleman)*

PAMPHILL   ST9900
★Vine   (01202) 882259
Off B3082 on NW edge of Wimborne: turn on to Cowgrove Hill at Cowgrove sign, then left up Vine Hill; BH21 4EE Simple old-fashioned place run by same family for three generations and part of Kingston Lacy estate (NT); two tiny bars with coal-effect gas fire, handful of tables and seats on lino floor, some under narrow wooden stairs up to games room (darts and

board games), local photographs and notices on painted panelling, two real ales (usually Fullers London Pride), local cider and bottled beers, lunchtime bar snacks; quiet background music, no credit cards, outside lavatories; children (away from bar) and dogs welcome, heated verandah with fairy lights and grapevine, sheltered gravel terrace, grassy area with climbing frame. *(Richard, Anne and Kate Ansell, the Didler)*

PARKSTONE SZ0491
Grasshopper (01202) 741463
Bournemouth Road; BH14 9HT Modern Bistro-type place with enjoyable food from varied menu, Badger ales; children welcome, popular terrace tables. *(Joan and Michel Hooper-Immins, Roger and Donna Huggins)*

PIDDLETRENTHIDE ST7000
Poachers (01300) 348358
B3143 N of Dorchester; DT2 7QX Bright up-to-date décor, comfortable lounge end, well kept Butcombe, St Austell and Sharps, good wines in three glass sizes, generous food from good ciabattas up, smiling service, three linked beamed dining areas; background music; dogs welcome in bar, garden with tables on decking and stream at bottom, 21 comfortable good value motel-style bedrooms around residents' heated swimming pool, good breakfast, open all day. *(Dennis Jenkin)*

PIMPERNE ST9009
★ Anvil (01258) 453431
Well back from A354; DT11 8UQ Attractive 16th-c thatched family pub with wide choice of food from generous lunchtime baguettes to substantial main dishes, well kept ales such as Fullers and local Waylands, cheerful efficient young staff, bays of plush seating in bright spacious bar, neat black-beamed dining areas; fruit machine, background music; good garden with fish pond and big weeping willow, 12 bedrooms, nice surroundings. *(George Atkinson)*

POOLE SZ0391
Bermuda Triangle (01202) 748087
Parr Street, Lower Parkstone (just off A35 at Ashley Cross; BH14 0JY Old-fashioned bare-boards local with four interesting and particularly well kept changing ales, two or three good continental lagers on tap and many other beers from around the world, friendly landlady and staff, no food, dark panelling, snug old corners and lots of nautical and other bric-a-brac, cloudscape ceiling, back room with sports TV; a bit too steppy for disabled access; pavement picnic-sets, open all day weekends. *(Anon)*

POOLE SZ0391
Cow (01202) 749569
Station Road, Ashley Cross, Parkstone; beside Parkstone Station; BH14 8UD Interesting open-plan pub with airy bistro bar, squashy sofas, leather seating cubes and low tables on stripped-wood floors, open fire in exposed brick fireplace, good modern food (not Sun evening) from sensibly short menu, up to four real ales and a dozen wines by the glass from extensive list, friendly welcoming staff, evening dining room, board games and newspapers; background music, discreet TV; children welcome till 7.30pm, dogs in bar, enclosed heated terrace area, open all day. *(Ian Herdman)*

POOLE SZ0190
Poole Arms (01202) 673450
Town Quay; BH15 1HJ 17th-c waterfront pub looking across harbour to Brownsea Island, good fresh fish at reasonable prices, well kept Ringwood, one comfortably old-fashioned room with boarded ceiling and nautical prints, pleasant staff; outside gents'; picnic-sets in front of the handsome green-tiled façade. *(D M and B K Moores, Pat and Tony Martin, Tich Critchlow)*

PORTLAND SY6873
Cove House (01305) 820895
Follow Chiswell signposts – is at NW corner of Portland; DT5 1AW Low-beamed 18th-c pub in superb position effectively built into the sea defences just above the end of Chesil beach, great views from three-room bar's bay windows, enjoyable reasonably priced pubby food (all-day weekends), well kept beers, friendly efficient service; background music, steep steps down to gents'; picnic-sets out by seawall, open all day. *(Russell and Alison Hunt, Pete Flower)*

PORTLAND SY6872
George (01305) 820011
Reforne; DT5 2AP Cheery 17th-c stone-built local mentioned by Thomas Hardy, low doorways and beams, flagstones, small rooms, reputed smugglers' tunnels, scrubbed tables carved with names of generations of sailors and quarrymen, interesting prints and mementoes, well kept ales including Courage and Greene King , Addlestone's cider, basic bargain lunches, family room, newer end bar, events most nights; nice garden, open all day. *(Joan and Michel Hooper-Immins, the Didler)*

PORTLAND SY6873
Royal Portland Arms
(01305) 862255 *Fortuneswell; DT5 1LZ* Friendly stone-built character local, homely and unfussy, with fine range of quickly changing ales tapped from the cask (many west country microbrews), farm cider, live bands; open all day, till late Fri, Sat. *(the Didler)*

PORTLAND BILL SY6768
Pulpit (01305) 821237
Portland Bill Road; DT5 2JT Extended touristy 1950s pub in great spot near Pulpit Rock, well run by cheery long-serving landlord, popular food from landlady including good steak and kidney pie and plenty of local fish (nice crab salad), well kept Fullers and

Ringwood, picture-window views, dark beams and stripped stone; may be background music; dogs welcome, disabled access, tiered sea-view terrace, play area, short stroll to lighthouse and cliffs. *(Joan and Michel Hooper-Immins, Adrian Johnson)*

POWERSTOCK   SY5196
✳ **Three Horseshoes** (01308) 485328
Off A3066 Beaminster–Bridport via West Milton; DT6 3TF Friendly well cared for village inn with stripped panelling, country furniture and good log fires, Palmers ales in traditional bar, good imaginative food from landlord/chef, restaurant; children and dogs welcome, fine uninterrupted valley view from back terrace and big sloping garden, nice walks, comfortable bedrooms (two with view). *(Roger and Donna Huggins, Ken and Barbara Turner, Ben Pump)*

PUDDLETOWN   SY7594
Blue Vinney (01305) 848228
The Moor; DT2 8TE Popular well modernised village pub with beamed oak-floor bar and restaurant, enjoyable nicely presented food (not Sun evening) from lunchtime baguettes and traditional choices to more elaborate dishes, good selection of well kept beers, ciders and wines, friendly service; children welcome, terrace overlooking garden. *(Douglas and Ann Hare, Tim and Rosemary Wells, John and Sylvia Harrop)*

PYMORE   SY4794
Pymore Inn (01308) 422625
Off A3066 N of Bridport; DT6 5PN Attractive Georgian beamed and stone-built pub with good atmosphere, chef/landlord doing enjoyable food including good fish choice (most tables laid for eating), friendly prompt service, St Austell ales, good choice of wines by the glass, prints on panelled walls, old settles and woodburner, small pretty dining room; wheelchair access, large pleasant garden. *(Bob and Margaret Holder)*

SANDFORD ORCAS   ST6220
✳ **Mitre** (01963) 220271
Off B3148 and B3145 N of Sherborne; DT9 4RU Thriving tucked-away country local with welcoming long-serving licensees, three well kept ales such as Ringwood, Sharps and Yeovil, wholesome home-made food (not Mon) from good soup and sandwiches up, flagstones, log fires and fresh flowers, small bar and larger pleasantly homely dining area; occasional open-mike and quiz nights; children and dogs welcome, pretty back garden with terrace, closed Mon lunchtime. *(David Hudd)*

SHAFTESBURY   ST8722
Half Moon (01747) 852456
Salisbury Road, Ludwell (A30 E, by roundabout); SP7 8BS Comfortable and pleasantly extended Badger family dining pub, their usual variety of food from

good lunchtime baguettes up, well kept ales, quick helpful service and spotless housekeeping, low ceilings, tiled and wood floors on different levels, mixed tables and chairs, old local photographs, newspapers; garden with adventure playground, disabled parking. *(Michael and Jenny Back, Mrs C Roe, Edward Mirzoeff)*

SHAFTESBURY   ST8622
Mitre (01747) 853002
High Street; SP7 8JE Imposing ancient building, unpretentious inside, with friendly efficient service, well kept Wells & Youngs ales, good range of wines, decent pub food served all day (till 6pm Sun) including good burgers, fine log fire, daily papers, varied mix of tables, Blackmore Vale views from back dining room and three-tier suntrap back decking; background music; children and dogs welcome, open all day. *(Jonathan Weedon)*

SHAPWICK   ST9301
Anchor (01258) 857269
Off A350 Blandford–Poole; West Street; DT11 9LB Welcoming red-brick Victorian pub now owned by village consortium, popular freshly made food including set deals (booking advised), ales such as Palmers, Ringwood and Sharps, real cider, scrubbed pine tables on wood floors, pastel walls and open fires; children welcome, tables out in front, more in attractive garden with terrace behind, handy for Kingston Lacy (NT). *(Debs Kelly, Robert Watt)*

SHAVE CROSS   SY4198
Shave Cross Inn (01308) 868358
On back lane Bridport–Marshwood, signposted locally; OS Sheet 193 map reference 415980; DT6 6HW Former medieval monks' lodging, small character timbered and flagstoned bar with huge inglenook, Branscombe Vale Branoc, Dorset Marshwood Vale and pub's own-label 4Ms, farm ciders, vintage rums, attractive restaurant with grandfather clock, pricey caribbean influenced food, pleasant staff, ancient skittle alley with bar billiards, pool, darts and a juke box; background music; children and dogs welcome, sheltered pretty garden with thatched wishing-well, carp pool and play area, seven comfortable but boutique bedrooms, helipad, closed Mon. *(Guy Vowles, Matthew Beard, the Didler, Kerry Law, Peter Thornton, Anita McCullough)*

STOBOROUGH   SY9286
Kings Arms (01929) 552705
B3075 S of Wareham; Corfe Road; BH20 5AB Up to four well kept changing ales, Thatcher's farm cider, good choice of enjoyable reasonably priced food in bar and restaurant, live music Sat; children and dogs welcome, disabled access, views over marshes to River Frome from big terrace tables, open all day weekends. *(John Dorricott)*

STOKE ABBOTT   ST4500
★ **New Inn** (01308) 868333
Off B3162 and B3163 2 miles W of Beaminster; DT8 3JW Spotless 17th-c thatched pub with friendly helpful licensees and pleasant efficient service, well kept Palmers ales, good fairly priced food, woodburner in big inglenook, beams, brasses and copper, some handsome panelling, paintings for sale, flagstoned dining room, fresh flowers on tables; occasional background music; children welcome, wheelchair access, two lovely gardens, unspoilt quiet thatched village, good walks, bedrooms, closed Sun evening, Mon. *(Michael David Doyle, Rupert Dick, Patricia and Anthony Daley)*

STOURPAINE   ST8609
White Horse (01258) 453535
Shaston Road; A350 NW of Blandford; DT11 8TA Traditional country local carefully extended from original core, landlord/chef doing good choice of food from lunchtime sandwiches and bar meals to ambitious dishes (particularly evenings), bargain deals mid-week lunchtime, friendly prompt service, well kept Badger ales, sensible wine list, nice layout and décor, scrubbed tables; pool; bedrooms. *(Robert Watt)*

STOURTON CAUNDLE   ST7115
★ **Trooper** (01963) 362405
Village signed off A30 E of Milborne Port; DT10 2JW Pretty little stone-built pub in lovely village setting, friendly staff and atmosphere, good simple food and well kept changing beers, reasonable prices, spotless tiny low-ceilinged bar, stripped stone dining room, darts, dominoes and shove-ha'penny, skittle alley; background music, TV, outside gents'; children and dogs welcome, a few picnic-sets out in front, pleasant side garden with play area, camping, closed Mon lunchtime. *(Ann and Colin Hunt)*

STRATTON   SY6593
Saxon Arms (01305) 260020
Off A37 NW of Dorchester; The Square; DT2 9WG Traditional but recently built flint-and-thatch local, open-plan, bright and spacious with light oak tables and comfortable settles on flagstones or carpet, open fire, well kept Otter, Ringwood and Timothy Taylors Landlord, good value wines, tasty generous food including good choice of specials and lunchtime set deal (Mon-Fri), large comfortable dining section on right, traditional games; background music; children and dogs welcome, terrace tables overlooking village green, open all day weekends. *(M G Hart)*

STUDLAND   SZ0382
Bankes Arms (01929) 450225
Off B3351, Isle of Purbeck; Manor Road; BH19 3AU Very popular spot above fine beach, outstanding country, sea and cliff views from huge garden over road with lots of seating; comfortably basic big bar with raised drinking area, beams, flagstones and good log fire, well kept changing ales including own Isle of Purbeck, local cider, good wines by the glass, all-day food (they ask to keep a credit card while you eat), darts and pool in side area; background music, machines, sports TV, can get very busy with trippers on summer weekends and parking complicated (NT car park); over-8s and dogs welcome, just off Coast Path, big comfortable bedrooms. *(John Faircloth, Mike and Sue Loseby, Lucy Johnstone, Lawrence Pearse)*

STURMINSTER MARSHALL   SY9499
Black Horse (01258) 857217
A350; BH21 4AQ Welcoming and clean with enjoyable good value food from nice sandwiches up, Badger ales, comfortable long bar. *(Anon)*

STURMINSTER MARSHALL   SY9500
Red Lion (01258) 857319
Opposite church; off A350 Blandford–Poole; BH21 4BU Attractive village pub opposite handsome church, welcoming bustling local atmosphere, wide variety of good home-made food including set menu deal, efficient service, well kept Badger ales and nice wines, old-fashioned roomy U-shaped bar with log fire, good-sized dining room in former skittle alley; background music; children and dogs welcome, disabled access, back garden with wicker furniture and picnic-sets, open all day Sun. *(Robert Watt)*

STURMINSTER NEWTON   ST7813
★ **Bull** (01258) 472435
A357, S of centre; DT10 2BS Friendly thatched 16th-c country pub by River Stour, low beams and plenty of character, enjoyable home-made food, Badger ales, soft lighting; children welcome in compact eating area, roadside picnic-sets, more in secluded back garden. *(Ann and Colin Hunt)*

STURMINSTER NEWTON   ST7814
Swan (01258) 472208
Off A357 Blandford–Sherborne, via B3092; Market Place; DT10 1AR Comfortable market-town inn with panelled and stripped-brick bar, fireside sofa, well kept Badger ales, pleasant all-day dining area, good choice of usual food, decent coffee, friendly service; background music, sports TV; terrace and garden, bedrooms, open all day. *(Ian Jones, Ann and Colin Hunt)*

SWANAGE   SZ0278
Red Lion (01929) 423533
High Street; BH19 2LY Busy 17th-c low-beamed local, wonderful choice of ciders and up to six well kept ales including Palmers, Ringwood, Sharps and Timothy Taylors, good value food from sandwiches and baked potatoes up; background music, some live;

children welcome, picnic-sets in garden with partly covered terrace, bedrooms in former back coach house, open all day. *(Tich Critchlow)*

SYMONDSBURY   SY4493
Ilchester Arms (01308) 422600
Signed off A35 just W of Bridport; DT6 6HD Welcoming 16th-c thatched pub with rustic open-plan bar, low beams and a high-backed settle built in by inglenook, three well kept Palmers ales, enjoyable traditional food from lunchtime sandwiches to fresh fish, pretty restaurant with another fire, pub games, skittle alley doubling as family room; dogs welcome in bar, level entrance (steps from car park), tables in nice brookside back garden with play area, peaceful village with good walks, three bedrooms, open all day weekends if busy. *(Martin and Sue Radcliffe)*

TRENT   ST5818
Rose & Crown (01935) 850776
Opposite the church; DT9 4SL Thatched former farmhouse with good variety of enjoyable food including some unusual choices, well kept Wadworths and guests, welcoming helpful service, log fires, mix of old furniture including oak settles and pews, grandfather clock, dining conservatory; children welcome, picnic-sets behind – lovely peaceful surroundings, good walks, open all day weekends. *(Adrian Lawrence, Edward Mirzoeff)*

UPLODERS   SY5093
✶Crown (01308) 485356
Signed off A35 E of Bridport; DT6 4NU Inviting homely village pub under new licensees, log fires, dark low beams, flagstones and lots of bric-a-brac, traditional food and Palmers ales; background music; children and dogs welcome, tables in attractive two-tier garden. *(Anon)*

WAREHAM   SY9287
Duke of Wellington (01929) 553015
East Street; BH20 4NN Small traditional 18th-c beamed pub, half a dozen mainly local ales kept well, wide choice of reasonably priced food especially fish, some original features including panelling, open fire, copper ornaments and old local photographs; background music; back courtyard tables, bedrooms, open all day. *(Robert W Buckle, the Didler)*

WAREHAM   SY9287
Old Granary (01929) 552010
The Quay; BH20 4LP Fine old brick building with riverside terrace, emphasis on food but two small beamed rooms by main door for drinkers, well kept Badger ales, good wines by the glass, neat efficient young staff, airy dining room with leather high-backed chairs and pews around pale wood tables, brick walls and new oak standing timbers, two further rooms with big photographs of the pub, woodburners, nice relaxed atmosphere;

quiet background jazz; boats for hire over bridge. *(Michael Mellers, Sue and Mike Todd, Hugh Roberts)*

WAREHAM   SY9287
Quay Inn (01929) 552735
The Quay; BH20 4LP Comfortable 18th-c inn in great spot by the water, enjoyable food including pubby favourites and cook your own meat on a hot stone, attentive service, well kept Otter, Isle of Purbeck and Ringwood, reasonably priced wine list, flagstones and open fires; children welcome, terrace area and picnic-sets out on quay, boat trips, bedrooms, parking nearby can be difficult, open all day in summer. *(Carol Robertson, Richard Stanfield)*

WAREHAM FOREST   SY9089
✶Silent Woman (01929) 552909
Wareham–Bere Regis road; BH20 7PA Long neatly kept Badger dining pub divided by doorways and standing timbers, enjoyable home-made food, their ales kept well including a seasonal one, country wines, traditional furnishings, farm tools and stripped masonry on left; background music, no children inside; dogs welcome, wheelchair access, plenty of picnic-sets outside including a covered area, walks nearby. *(Richard Stanfield)*

WEST BEXINGTON   SY5386
Manor Hotel (01308) 897660
Off B3157 SE of Bridport; Beach Road; DT2 9DF Relaxing quietly set hotel with long history and fine sea views, recent refurbishment under new owners and good choice of food in beamed cellar bar, flagstoned restaurant and Victorian-style conservatory, well kept Otter, Thatcher's cider and several wines by the glass; dogs on leads allowed (not in restaurant), charming well kept garden, seven bedrooms. *(Pete Flower)*

WEST LULWORTH   SY8280
Castle Inn (01929) 400311
B3070 SW of Wareham; BH20 5RN Pretty 16th-c thatched inn in lovely spot near Lulworth Cove, good walks and lots of summer visitors; beamed flagstoned bar concentrating on wide choice of popular generously served food, well kept changing local ales, 12 ciders/perries, maze of booth seating divided by ledges, cosy more modern-feeling lounge bar, pleasant restaurant; background music; children and dogs welcome, front terrace, long attractive garden behind on several levels, boules and barbecues, 12 bedrooms. *(David Bizzell, Lawrence Pearse)*

WEST PARLEY   SZ0898
Curlew (01202) 594811
Christchurch Road; BH22 8SQ Vintage Inn in early 19th-c farmhouse, informal beamed areas around central bar,

mixed furnishings, candles on tables, two log fires, wide choice of enjoyable food with plenty for vegetarians, three well kept ales including Ringwood and plenty of good value wines, friendly staff; picnic-sets in front garden. *(David and Sally Frost, M J Potts)*

WEST STAFFORD   SY7289
Wise Man   (01305) 261970
Signed off A352 Dorchester–Wareham; DT2 8AG 16th-c thatched and beamed pub near Hardy's cottage, open-plan interior with flagstone and wood floors, enjoyable well priced food from lunchtime ciabattas up, Sun carvery, Butcombe Bitter, Dorset Jurassic, Ringwood Best and St Austell Proper Job from central bar, good choice of wines by the glass, friendly attentive staff; children and dogs welcome, disabled facilities, plenty of seats outside, lovely walks nearby, open all day weekends. *(Michael Coleman, Simon Rodway, Brian Boyland)*

WEYMOUTH   SY6778
Boot   (01305) 770327
High West Street; DT4 8JH Friendly unspoilt local dating from 1600s near harbour, well worn comfort with beams, bare boards, panelling, hooded stone-mullioned windows and coal fires, cosy gently sloping snug, well kept Ringwood ales and guests from fine brass handpumps, real cider, no food or music; disabled access, pavement tables, open all day. *(the Didler)*

WEYMOUTH   SY6878
✳ Nothe Tavern   (01305) 770935
Barrack Road; DT4 8TZ Roomy and comfortable early 19th-c pub near Northe Fort, wide range of good food including fresh local fish and good value Sun carvery, weekday deals too, friendly staff coping at busy times, well kept ales such as Ringwood, decent wines and good choice of malts, lots of dark wood, whisky-water jugs on ceiling, interesting prints and photographs, restaurant with distant harbour glimpses; may be quiet background music; children welcome, more views from terrace. *(Rob Winstanley, Joan and Michel Hooper-Immins, Robin Manners)*

WEYMOUTH   SY6778
Wellington Arms   (01305) 786963
St Alban Street; DT4 8PY Backstreet pub with handsome 19th-c tiled façade, panelled and carpeted interior with banquettes, mirrors and lots of old local photographs, well kept Ringwood and other Marstons-related beers, good value pubby food including a daily roast, friendly landlord and family, some live music; children welcome in

back dining room, disabled access, open all day. *(Joan and Michel Hooper-Immins, MLR)*

WIMBORNE MINSTER   SU0100
✳ Olive Branch   (01202) 884686
East Borough, just off Hanham Road (B3073, just E of its junction with B3078); has good car park; BH21 1PF Handsome opened-up townhouse, contemporary décor throughout but bar area more traditional with Jacobean panelling and log fire, squashy sofas and butcher's block with daily papers, Badger beers, enjoyable bistro-style food in spreading dining areas divided by standing timbers, modern furniture on wood-strip floors, framed Penguin book covers and lots of dog latin mottoes, friendly staff; teak tables and chairs on terrace. *(Joan and Michel Hooper-Immins, Paul Goldman)*

WIMBORNE ST GILES   SU0212
Bull   (01725) 517300
Off B3078 N of Wimborne; BH21 5NF Nicely done open-plan Edwardian dining pub, good original restaurant food using fresh local ingredients (organic where possible), fine choice of wines by the glass, Badger ales, friendly staff, garden room, daily papers; children and dogs welcome, picnic-sets in neat garden, five stylish bedrooms, open all day summer weekends. *(Robert Watt, Michael Doswell)*

WINKTON   SZ1696
Fishermans Haunt   (01202) 477283
B3347 N of Christchurch; BH23 7AS Comfortable big-windowed riverside inn on fringes of New Forest, four well kept Fullers/Gales beers, decent choice of food using local produce such as venison, two log fires, restaurant views of River Avon; background music; children welcome, dogs in bar (may be biscuits), disabled facilities, tables among shrubs in quiet back garden, heaters in covered area, 12 comfortable bedrooms, good breakfast, open all day. *(Stuart Price, Sara Fulton, Roger Baker, Comus and Sarah Elliott, Sue and Mike Todd, Joan and Michel Hooper-Immins)*

WINTERBORNE ZELSTON   SY8997
Botany Bay   (01929) 459227
A31 Wimborne–Dorchester; DT11 9ET Spreading open-plan roadside dining pub, front part divided into areas by partly glazed partitions, back more restauranty, reliable food from sandwiches and panini through usual pubby dishes to grills, sensible prices and good friendly service, well kept Badger ales, decent house wines and coffee; children welcome, tables on back terrace. *(R J and D S Courtney)*

The letters and figures after the name of each town are its Ordnance Survey map reference. *How to use the Guide* at the beginning of the book explains how it helps you find a pub, in road atlases or large-scale maps as well as in our own maps.

Essex

This year two pubs have found their way back into this chapter – the Axe & Compasses at Aythorpe Roding (nicely cared for with good balance between drinkers and diners) and Sun at Feering (handsome and relaxing with enjoyable food). Places we'd pick out as doing particularly well and having some individuality are the Axe & Compasses in Arkesden (reassuringly traditional and welcoming), Queens Head at Fyfield (beautifully maintained with good food), White Hart at Margaretting Tye (cheery country pub), Viper at Mill Green (lovely and unspoilt) and that stalwart of high standards the Bell at Horndon-on-the-Hill (lovely old interior), which is Essex Dining Pub 2013. It's worth noting that pubs in this county host more than the usual number of beer festivals, with one or more taking place each year at the Sun at Feering, White Hart at Margaretting Tye, Viper at Mill Green and Hoop at Stock.

ARKESDEN   TL4834   Map 5

Axe & Compasses ♀

Off B1038; CB11 4EX

Comfortably traditional pub with Greene King beers and decent food

The gleaming brasses and patterned carpets at this thatched village pub are reassuringly unchanged from one year to the next. The atmosphere is relaxed and welcoming with friendly service from the pleasant staff and licensees. The oldest part, which dates back to the 17th c, is the traditionally carpeted lounge bar, which has low-slung ceilings, polished upholstered oak and elm seats and sofas and a blazing fire. A smaller quirky public bar is uncarpeted, with built-in settles and darts. You'll find a very good wine list (with 15 by the glass) and around two dozen malt whiskies, along with changing beers such as Belhaven Robbie Burns and Greene King IPA, Speckled Hen and H&H Olde Trip, kept under light blanket pressure. There are seats out on a side terrace with pretty hanging baskets. Parking is at the back.

They grow their own herbs on a farm in the village. The tasty bar food includes lunchtime sandwiches, chicken liver pâté, whitebait, crunchy squid with lime and chilli mayonnaise, grilled or battered haddock, good breaded scampi, roast pork belly, thai chicken, lamb kebabs, fish pie, sirloin steak, and puddings such as hazelnut and raspberry cheesecakes, crème caramel. There is also a more elaborate, pricier restaurant menu. *Benchmark main dish: steak and kidney pie £12.95. Two-course evening meal £20.75.*

Greene King ~ Tenants Themis and Diane Christou ~ Real ale ~ Bar food (12-2, 7-9) ~ Restaurant ~ (01799) 550272 ~ Children welcome ~ Open 11.30-2.30, 6-11; 12-3, 7-10.30 Sun ~ www.axeandcompasses.co.uk *Recommended by Ian Wilson, David Jackson, Simon Watkins, David and Sue Smith, Alan Bulley*

 AYTHORPE RODING   TL5915   Map 5
Axe & Compasses
B184 S of Dunmow; CM6 1PP

Appealing free house, nice balance of eating and drinking and friendly welcome

Attention to detail goes into all aspects of this lovely old weatherboard pub. Although popular with diners, locals do pop in for a pint of the Sharps Doom Bar or three guests from local brewers such as Colchester, Nethergate and Wibblers which are on handpump or racked behind the counter in temperature-stabilised casks; also up to three Weston's farm ciders on handpump. Everything is neatly kept and warm and cosy with bent old beams and timbers in stripped red brick walls, comfortable bar chairs at the counter, leatherette settles and stools and dark country chairs around a few pub tables on pale boards and turkish carpet. The original part on the left has a two-way fireplace marking off a snug little raftered dining area which has sentimental prints on dark masonry and a big open-faced clock; background music. The small garden behind has stylish modern tables and chairs.

Tasty well presented food from different lunchtime and evening menus might include prawn cocktail, scallops with pickled vegetables and saffron cream sauce, soused herrings with a vodka shot, chicken liver and brandy parfait with spiced chutney, lamb burger, ploughman's, gnocchi with mushroom, sage and chestnut sauce, teriyaki salad, honey glazed duck breast with noodles, oriental vegetables and plum sauce, salmon fillet with crab linguine and parsley fish sauce, beef short ribs with oxtail pudding and parsnip purée, lamb rump topped with chickpea crust with spiced carrot and courgette rösti and lemon purée, and puddings such as pear and frangipane tart with mascarpone ice-cream, chocolate brownie with cherry compote and hazelnut ice-cream, and plum clafoutis. *Benchmark main dish: fish and chips £11.95. Two-course evening meal £21.40.*

Free house ~ Licensee David Hunt ~ Real ale ~ Bar food (12-2.30, 6-9.30; 12-8 Sun) ~ Restaurant ~ (01279) 876648 ~ Children welcome ~ Dogs allowed in bar ~ Open 11-11(12 Fri, Sat); 12-10.30 Sun ~ www.theaxeandcompasses.co.uk *Recommended by George Atkinson, Mrs Lorna Walsingham, R E Munn*

 BURNHAM-ON-CROUCH   TQ9495   Map 5
White Harte
The Quay; CM0 8AS

Lovely waterside position with aptly nautical décor, and waterside tables

You can enjoy your drink at picnic-sets on a small jetty by the River Crouch, across the road from this comfortably old-fashioned hotel. The relaxed, partly carpeted bars have a timeless down-to-earth charm and are filled with assorted nautical bric-a-brac and hardware – anything from models of Royal Navy ships to a compass set into the hearth. Other traditionally furnished high-ceilinged rooms have sea pictures on brown panelled or stripped-brick walls, with cushioned seats around oak tables, and an enormous winter log fire. In summer they open the doors and windows, giving the place a nice airy feel. Charming staff serve Adnams and Crouch Vale Brewers Gold from handpump.

🍴 Bar food includes lunchtime sandwiches, baked potatoes, a choice of three local fish such as cod, plaice and skate, ham and stilton salad and lasagne. *Benchmark main dish: steak and kidney pie £8.20.*

Free house ~ Licensee G John Lewis ~ Real ale ~ Bar food (12-2, 7-9) ~ Restaurant ~ (01621) 782106 ~ Children welcome ~ Dogs allowed in bar and bedrooms ~ Open 11-11; 12-10.30 Sun ~ Bedrooms: £28(£75B)/£50(£89B) ~ www.whiteharteburnham.co.uk
Recommended by LM

CLAVERING
Cricketers 🍴 ♀ ⇋
TL4832   Map 5

B1038 Newport–Buntingford; CB11 4QT

Busy dining pub with inventive food, real ales, a carefully chosen wine list and a friendly welcome; individually decorated bedrooms

You can see where Jamie Oliver gets it all from when you visit this bustling dining pub that's been owned by his parents for a good many years now. Though much emphasis is on the well presented, imaginative food, there's always a warm welcome if it's just a pint and a chat that you're after. Drinks include Adnams Southwold and a couple of guests such as Nethergate Jamies Tipple and Lord of the Rings on handpump, Aspall's cider, well over a dozen wines by the glass, dandelion and burdock, cloudy lemonade and pink cola. The main area with its very low beams and big open fireplace has been gently bought up to date with bays of deep purple button-backed banquettes and neat, padded leather dining chairs on dark floorboards. Back on the left is more obviously an eating part – two fairly compact carpeted areas, a step between them. The right side is similar; set more formally for dining, but still traditional with some big copper and brass pans on its dark beams and timbers; background music. Signed books by Jamie are on sale. The attractive front terrace has wicker-look seats around teak tables among colourful flowering shrubs. The pub is handy for Stansted Airport.

🍴 They make their own bread and pasta and use properly hung meat, as well as produce supplied by Jamie's nearby organic garden. Bar food might include thai-style mussels, potted crab and shrimps, antipasti, smoked mackerel, potato and beetroot salad, spicy meatball spaghetti, braised lamb shank with root vegetable and redcurrant sauce, sautéed lambs liver and bacon with red wine jus, pie of the day, roast squash and spinach lasagne and fresh fish. *Benchmark main dish: home-made pasta dishes £10.95. Two-course evening meal £21.80.*

Free house ~ Licensee Trevor Oliver ~ Real ale ~ Bar food (12-2(2.30 Sun), 6.30-9.30; home-made cakes and tea all afternoon) ~ (01799) 550442 ~ Children welcome ~ Open 7am-11pm ~ Bedrooms: £67.50B/£95B ~ www.thecricketers.co.uk *Recommended by Alan and Jill Bull, Dr Kevan Tucker, David Glynne-Jones, Tina and David Woods-Taylor*

Bedroom prices are for high summer. Even then you may get reductions for more than one night, or (outside tourist areas) weekends. Winter special rates are common, and many inns cut bedroom prices if you have a full evening meal.

FEERING

TL8720 Map 5

Sun  £

Just off A12 Kelvedon bypass; Feering Hill (B1024 just W of Feering proper); CO5 9NH

Striking 16th-c timbered and jettied pub with good beer and pleasant garden

So handsome outside, the Sun lives up to its promise inside, with handsomely carved black beams and timbers galore, and attractive wildflower murals in a frieze above the central timber divider. The spreading carpeted bar is relaxed, unpretentious and civilised, with two big woodburning stoves, one in the huge central inglenook fireplace, another by an antique winged settle on the left. They have half a dozen Shepherd Neame ales in fine condition on handpump – on our most recent visit, Bitter, Kents Best, Spitfire, Early Bird, Amber and Bishops Finger, and hold summer and winter beer festivals; cheerful service, daily papers, board games. A brick-paved back courtyard has tables, heaters and a shelter, and the garden beyond has tall trees shading green picnic-sets.

Enjoyable food from sandwiches up includes pizzas from a wood-fired oven (weekends only), pubby favourites and monthly changing specials. There might be ploughman's, baked potatoes, whitebait, watercress, spinach and stilton soup, ham, egg and chips, chilli, battered haddock, roast pork belly with cider and wholegrain mustard cream, spinach, mascarpone and parmesan tagliatelle, malaysian beef and potato curry, sea trout with herb crust, and puddings such as macadamia, apricot and white chocolate cheesecake and chocolate and raspberry brownie. *Benchmark main dish: beef, mushroom and stilton pie £9.95. Two-course evening meal £14.90.*

Shepherd Neame ~ Tenant Andy Howard ~ Real ale ~ Bar food (12-2.30, 6-9.30; 12-8 Sun) ~ (01376) 570442 ~ Children welcome ~ Dogs allowed in bar ~ Open 12-3, 5.30-11; 12-11.30 Sat; 12-10.30 Sun ~ www.suninnfeering.co.uk *Recommended by the Didler, Mark Price*

FYFIELD

TL5706 Map 5

Queens Head ♀

Corner of B184 and Queen Street; CM5 0RY

Friendly 16th-c pub with good wine list and accent on elaborate food (booking advised at weekends)

The main focus at this beautifully maintained 16th-c pub is the good food, but a pubby balance is maintained by their good range of half a dozen real ales: Adnams Southwold and Broadside and a guest or two from brewers such as Crouch Vale and Timothy Taylors. They also keep Weston's Old Rosie farm cider, over a dozen wines by the glass (including champagne) and some very decent malts. The low-beamed, compact L-shaped bar has some exposed timbers in cream and brown walls, fresh flowers and pretty lamps on nice sturdy elm tables, and comfortable

Real ale to us means beer which has matured naturally in its cask – not pressurised or filtered. We name all real ales stocked. We usually name ales preserved under a light blanket of carbon dioxide too, though purists – pointing out that this stops the natural yeasts developing – would disagree (most people, including us, can't tell the difference!).

seating, from button-back wall banquettes to attractive and unusual high-backed chairs, some in a snug little side booth. In summer, two facing fireplaces have lighted church candles instead of a fire; background music. The same menu is offered throughout the pub, but you can go for a more formal white linen experience upstairs in the smart restaurant. Readers particularly enjoy sitting out in the prettily planted little back garden with its weeping willows trailing in the sleepy River Roding.

🍴 Besides good lunchtime sandwiches, ploughman's and filled huffers (local bread rolls), dishes from the daily changing menu (not cheap) might include seared pigeon breast with butternut glazed plums and five-spice jus, crisp pork belly with scallops, apple purée, pea foam and pancetta, honey and soy roast salmon with thai-style vegetables and crab consommé and fried parmesan gnocchi with confit tomatoes, wilted spinach and balsamic and beurre noisette; reasonably priced set menus and Sunday roasts. *Benchmark main dish: toad in the hole £9.95. Two-course evening meal £22.40.*

Free house ~ Licensee Daniel Lamprecht ~ Real ale ~ Bar food (12-2.30(4 Sat), 6.30-9.30; 12-6 Sun) ~ Restaurant ~ (01277) 899231 ~ Children welcome ~ Open 11-11; 6-11 Mon; 11-11 Sat; 12-10.30 Sun; closed Mon lunchtime ~ www.thequeensheadfyfield.co.uk
Recommended by Mrs Margo Finlay, Jörg Kasprowski, John Saville, Rachel Heatley

GOSFIELD   TL7829   Map 5

Kings Head £

The Street (A1017 Braintree–Halstead); CO9 1TP

Comfortable dining pub with proper public bar and good value food

A well supported whisky club meets four times a year for tastings and to choose the impressive list of 70 internationally sourced single malts that are on offer at this ancient pub. Adnams Southwold, Timothy Taylors Landlord and Sharps Doom Bar on handpump, around a dozen wines by the glass and organic soft drinks are also served. Bright splashes of warm contemporary colour brighten the modernised interior of the softly lit beamed main bar, which has red panelled dado and ceiling, neat modern black leather armchairs, bucket chairs and a sofa, as well as sturdy pale wood dining chairs and tables on dark boards, and a log fire in a handsome old brick fireplace with big bellows. Black timbers mark off a red carpeted and walled dining area with red furnishings that opens into a carpeted conservatory; background music, daily papers. The good-sized quite separate public bar, with a purple pool table, games machine, darts and TV, has its own partly covered terrace; the main terrace has round picnic-sets.

🍴 Neat black-clad young staff serve fairly priced food such as tuna melt foccacia, lemon and chive crayfish tails on fennel, beef carpaccio with redcurrant dressing, lancashire hot pot, home-made burger, fried skate with caper and lemon butter, duck breast with black bean sauce, stir-fried vegetables and noodles, roast pepper stuffed with vegetable cous cous topped with Boursin cheese, and puddings such as Baileys and toffee cheesecake with raspberry coulis and chocolate bread and butter pudding with Cointreau sauce. They serve Sunday roast, including table joints, for which they need four days' notice. *Benchmark main dish: pork belly with cider jus £9.95. Two-course evening meal £16.20.*

Enterprise ~ Lease Mark Bloomfield ~ Real ale ~ Bar food (12-2, 7-9; 12-6 Sun) ~ Restaurant ~ (01787) 474016 ~ Children welcome ~ Dogs allowed in bar ~ Open 12-11(1am Sat, 10.30 Sun) ~ www.thekingsheadgosfield.co.uk *Recommended by Richard Gibbs*

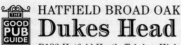

HATFIELD BROAD OAK

TL5416   Map 5

Dukes Head

B183 Hatfield Heath–Takeley; High Street; CM22 7HH

Relaxed, well run dining pub with enjoyable food; attractive layout of nicely linked separate areas

Various intimate seating areas ramble pleasantly around the central feature woodburner and side servery at this comfortable village pub. Seating is mainly good solid wooden dining chairs around a variety of more or less chunky stripped and sealed tables, with a comfortable group of armchairs and a sofa down one end, and a slightly more formal area at the back on the right. Cheerful prints on the wall and occasional magenta panels in the mainly cream décor make for quite a buoyant mood, as does the lively attitude of the friendly, helpful staff; well kept Fulllers London Pride, Greene King IPA and St Austell Tribute on handpump and over a dozen wines by the glass from a good list; background music. Sam the dog welcomes other canines and there are always dog biscuits behind the bar. The back garden, with a sheltered terrace and an end wendy house, has comfortable chairs around teak tables under cocktail parasols; there are also some picnic-sets in the front angle of the building, which has some nice pargeting.

 Good imaginative bar food might include potted brown shrimps, mushroom and spinach stack with red onion marmalade, crispy parmesan and poached egg, chicken liver pâté with fig jam, sausage and mash, battered cod and pea purée, king prawn spaghetti with chilli oil, pumpkin and chestnut gnocchi, pork belly with three-cheese crust, chorizo, cannellini beans and tomato ragout and roast skate wing with parmentier potatoes, samphire, clam and chorizo butter. *Benchmark main dish: bubble and squeak £11.75. Two-course evening meal £21.40.*

Enterprise ~ Lease Liz Flodman ~ Real ale ~ Restaurant ~ (01279) 718598 ~ Children welcome ~ Dogs allowed in bar ~ Open 12-3, 6-11.30; 12-11.30 Sat; 12-10.30 Sun ~ www.thedukeshead.co.uk *Recommended by Brian Adams, Tony Adams, Grahame Brooks*

HORNDON-ON-THE-HILL

TQ6783   Map 3

Bell 🍴 🍷 🗄 🛏

M25 junction 30 into A13, then left on to B1007 after 7 miles, village signposted from here; SS17 8LD

Essex Dining Pub of the Year

Lovely old historic pub with great food and very good range of drinks; attractive bedrooms

Although in the same family for over 70 years this beautiful Tudor inn is definitely not resting on its well deserved laurels – high standards are always a watchword here. Although emphasis is on the good food, the heavily beamed bar maintains a strongly pubby appearance and stocks a great range of drinks. It's furnished with lovely high-backed antique settles and benches, with rugs on the flagstones and highly polished oak floorboards. Look out for the curious collection of ossified hot cross buns hanging along a beam in the saloon bar. The first was put there some 90 years ago to mark the day that Jack Turnell became licensee (it was a Good Friday). The hanging tradition continues to this day, but now the oldest available person in the village hangs the bun each year. During the war, privations demanded that they hang a concrete bun. The impressive range of drinks includes Bass (tapped straight from the cask), Crouch Vale Brewers Gold, Greene King IPA, Sharps Doom

Bar and guests such as Batemans Hooker and Exmoor Antler and over a hundred well chosen wines (16 by the glass). You do need to get here early or book as tables are often all taken soon after opening time. Two giant umbrellas cover the courtyard, which is very pretty is summer with hanging baskets.

The terrific food here does generally take precedence. The daily changing menu includes dishes such as venison carpaccio with venison ravioli, white onion sauce and onion seed tuile, sauté scallops on poached rhubarb and rocket with maple poached pancetta, fried pork fillet with confit pork shoulder, piccalilli and vanilla swede purée, grilled hake with parsnip chips and gherkin and dill mayonnaise, and puddings such as baked passion fruit cheesecake with pineapple and yoghurt compote, potted stilton with roast figs and oatcake and mango and white chocolate mousse with meringue and popping candy. *Benchmark main dish: fillet of beef with braised brisket and spring onion and saffron ravioli £22.95. Two-course evening meal £25.60.*

Free house ~ Licensee John Vereker ~ Real ale ~ Bar food (12-1.45, 6.30(7 Sun)-9.45; not bank holiday Mondays) ~ Restaurant ~ (01375) 642463 ~ Children welcome in restaurant and eating area of bar ~ Dogs allowed in bar and bedrooms ~ Open 11-3, 5.30(6 Sat)-11; 12-4, 7-10.30 Sun ~ Bedrooms: £59.50B/£104B ~ www.bell-inn.co.uk
Recommended by Steve Aluzzi, Phil Clarke, Clifford Blakemore, Roxanne Chamberlain, Bob and Tanya Ekers

LITTLE WALDEN   TL5441   Map 5
Crown ◖ £
B1052 N of Saffron Walden; CB10 1XA

Bustling 18th-c cottage pub with a warming log fire, hearty food and bedrooms

This homely low-ceilinged local looks fairly unassuming from the exterior – it's the particularly warm and cheery welcome from the licensees and their staff that make it so appealing, plus they serve tasty food and a good pint, too. Four changing beers are tapped straight from casks racked up behind the bar – normally Adnams Best, Greene King IPA, Woodfordes Wherry and a guest such as Nethergate. The interior is traditional, with bookroom-red walls, floral curtains, bare boards, navy carpeting, cosy warm fires and an unusual walk-through fireplace. A higgledy-piggledy mix of chairs ranges from high-backed pews to little cushioned armchairs spaced around a good variety of closely arranged tables, mostly big, some stripped. The small red-tiled room on the right has two small tables; TV, disabled access. Tables out on the terrace take in views of surrounding tranquil countryside.

The traditional bar food is good value and popular – you may need to book at weekends: sandwiches, including a delicious hot pork baguette (not Sunday), devilled whitebait, crayfish cocktail, scampi, caribbean king prawn curry, liver and bacon, lasagne, nut loaf, pork fillet in cajun sauce, steak, and puddings such as chocolate gateau and rhubarb crumble. *Benchmark main dish: steak and mushroom pie £9.75. Two-course evening meal £12.70.*

Free house ~ Licensee Colin Hayling ~ Real ale ~ Bar food (11.30-3, 6-11; 12-8 Sun) ~ Restaurant ~ (01799) 522475 ~ Children welcome ~ Dogs allowed in bar and bedrooms ~ Open 11.30-3, 6-12; 12-11 Sun ~ Bedrooms: £65S/£65S ~ www.thecrownlittlewalden.co.uk *Recommended by Marion and Bill Cross, Alec and Joan Laurence, the Didler*

MARGARETTING TYE   TL6801   Map 5

White Hart 🍺 £ 🛏

From B1002 (just S of A12/A414 junction) follow Maldon Road for 1.3 miles, then turn right immediately after river bridge, into Swan Lane, keeping on for 0.7 miles; The Tye; CM4 9JX

Fine choice of ales tapped from the cask in cheery country pub with good family garden

The cottagey interior of this unpretentious weatherboard pub is as fresh and neatly kept as its pristine cream exterior suggests. Walls and wainscoting are painted in chalky traditional colours that look well with its dark old timbers and mix of old wooden chairs and tables, mostly ready for diners to arrive. A stuffed deer head is mounted on the chimneybreast above the woodburning stove. The neat carpeted back conservatory is similar in style, and the front lobby has a charity paperback table; darts, quiz machine, skittles, board games and background music. Friendly, informative staff serve an impressive range of eight real ales tapped straight from the cask. Besides Adnams Best and Broadside, Mighty Oak IPA and Oscar Wilde and Red Fox Hunters Gold, they bring on a constant stream of nationwide guest beers, available to take away, and have interesting bottled beers, too. During their popular June and October beer festivals might have up to 60 kinds a day; winter mulled wine. There are plenty of picnic-sets out on grass and terracing around the pub, with a sturdy play area, a safely fenced duck pond and pens of rabbits, guinea-pigs and a pygmy goat.

As well as good well filled sandwiches, bar food might include roast vegetable crostini topped with creamy goats cheese, chicken liver pâté, trio of crab, king prawns and smoked salmon, lamb shank with rosemary and red wine, fish pie, roast chicken breast stuffed with cream cheese and tomato wrapped in pancetta with sweet tomato and red pepper sauce, pork chops cooked in cider, winter vegetable stew and thyme dumplings, and puddings such as lemon and mascarpone cheesecake and steamed treacle pudding. *Benchmark main dish: steak and ale pie £9.50. Two-course evening meal £15.50.*

Free house ~ Licensee Elizabeth Haines ~ Real ale ~ Bar food (12-2(2.30 Sat, 4.30 Sun), 6.30(6 Fri, Sat)-9(8.30 Sun); not Mon evening) ~ (01277) 840478 ~ Well behaved children welcome ~ Dogs allowed in bar ~ Open 11.30-3, 6-midnight; 11.30-midnight Sat; 12-midnight Sun ~ Bedrooms: /£80B ~ www.whitehartmargarettingtye.com
Recommended by N R White, Roxanne Chamberlain, Rob and Catherine Dunster, Paul Humphreys

MILL GREEN   TL6401   Map 5

Viper 🍺 £

The Common; from Fryerning (which is signposted off N-bound A12 Ingatestone bypass) follow Writtle signposts; CM4 0PT

Delightfully unpretentious with local ales, simple pub food and no modern intrusions

The cosy little lounge rooms of this unspoilt old local have a charmingly timeless atmosphere, spindleback and armed country kitchen chairs and tapestried wall seats around neat little old tables, and a log fire. Booted walkers, dogs and children are directed towards the fairly basic parquet-floored tap room, which is more simply furnished with shiny wooden traditional wall seats and a coal fire. Beyond, another room has country kitchen chairs and sensibly placed darts, also dominoes and cribbage; the pub cat is Millie and the west highland terrier is Jimmy. They have Nethergate Viper Vipa and Mighty Oak Jake the Snake (both brewed for the pub) and Oscar Wilde, and a couple of quickly changing guests from brewers such as Crouch Vale and Cottage on handpump and Weston's Scrumpy and Perry. Live bands play during their Easter and August beer festivals and morris men sometimes dance outside. Tables on the lawn overlook a beautifully tended cottage garden – a dazzling mass of colour in summer, further enhanced at the front by overflowing hanging baskets and window boxes.

Simple but tasty lunchtime bar snacks might include sandwiches, pâtés, ploughman's, baked potatoes, sausage and mash, curry, cottage pie and lasagne, puddings such as spotted dick and apple crumble, and Sunday roasts. The tasty bread comes from a local baker a mile or so down the road. *Benchmark main dish: steak and ale pie £6.95.*

Free house ~ Licensees Peter White and Donna Torris ~ Real ale ~ Bar food (12-2(3 Sat, Sun); not evenings) ~ (01277) 352010 ~ Children and dogs in public and tap bar ~ Open 12-3, 6-11; 12-11 Sat(10.30 Sun) *Recommended by John Saville, Roxanne Chamberlain, the Didler, Tina and David Woods-Taylor*

SOUTH HANNINGFIELD   TQ7497   Map 5
Old Windmill ♀
Off A130 S of Chelmsford; CM3 8HT

Extensive but invitingly converted Brunning & Price pub with interesting food and good range of drinks

The rambling interior of this knocked-through place contains a forest of stripped standing timbers, making it feel at once open-plan and intimate. Décor is comfortably inviting, with an agreeable mix of highly polished old tables and chairs, frame-to-frame pictures on cream walls, woodburning stoves and homely pot plants. Deep green or dark red dado and one or two old rugs dotted on the glowing wood floors provide splashes of colour; other areas are more subdued with beige carpeting. Phoenix Brunning & Price Original and five guests from brewers such as Crouch Vale, Mighty Oak, Timothy Taylor and Wibblers are on handpump, with 20 wines by the glass, farm cider, 70 malts and a good range of spirits; background music. A back terrace has tables and chairs and there are picnic-sets on the lawn here and a few out in front.

As well as interesting sandwiches, bar food might include breaded brie with pear and mustard seed purée, chicken satay thighs with asian salad, tempura coconut king prawns with mango and chilli salsa, crab linguine, ploughman's, pea and broad bean risotto, chick pea, lentil and sweet potato dhal with onion bhajis, chicken, ham and leek pie, fried bass with chorizo, lemon, herb and tomato dressing, venison haunch with bacon lardons and red wine jus, honey and rosemary spatchcock poussin, and puddings such as apple and pear crumble, bakewell tart and banana and butterscotch eton mess. *Benchmark main dish: battered haddock £11.95. Two-course evening meal £19.25.*

Brunning & Price ~ Manager Julia Palmer ~ Real ale ~ Bar food (12-10(9.30 Sun)) ~ (01268) 712280 ~ Children welcome ~ Dogs allowed in bar ~ Open 11.30-11; 12-10.30 Sun ~ www.oldwindmillpub.co.uk *Recommended by Richard Gibbs*

Please tell us if the décor, atmosphere, food or drink at a pub is different from our description. We rely on readers' reports to keep us up to date: feedback@goodguides.com, or (no stamp needed) The Good Pub Guide, FREEPOST TN1569, Wadhurst, E Sussex TN5 7BR.

STOCK

TQ6999   Map 5

Hoop ◖ £

B1007; from A12 Chelmsford bypass take Galleywood, Billericay turn-off; CM4 9BD

Happy weatherboarded pub with interesting beers and a large garden

Simple wood fixtures and fittings, including stripped floors, wooden tables and brocaded wooden settles, keep the interior of this old weatherboard pub feeling appropriately down to earth and pubby – just the right setting for the cheery locals and visitors enjoying the happy bustle and real ales here. Adnams is kept alongside three guests from brewers such as Bishop Nick, Crouch Vale and Mighty Oak, and during the eight days of their late May beer festival (when they open all day) they can get through over 200 real ales and 80 ciders and perries. Standing timbers and beams in the open-plan bar hint at the building's great age and its original layout as a row of three weavers' cottages. In winter, a warming fire burns in a big brick-walled fireplace. A restaurant up in the timbered eaves – very different in style, with a separate à la carte menu – is light and airy with pale timbers set in white walls and more wood flooring. Prettily bordered with flowers, the large sheltered back garden has picnic-sets and a covered seating area. Parking is limited, so it's worth getting here early.

Bar food includes sandwiches, game terrine, curried scallops with lentil dhal, sautéed lambs kidneys on brioche with quince jelly and redcurrant sauce, battered fish of the day, beef, mushroom and ale pie, home-made burger, squash, sage and pine nut risotto with crème fraîche and toasted almonds, rabbit stew, steaks, and puddings such as crumble of the day and gingerbread crème brûlée. *Benchmark main dish: toad in the hole £9.50. Two-course evening meal £19.70.*

Free house ~ Licensee Michelle Corrigan ~ Real ale ~ Bar food (12-3(5 Sun) 6-9; 12-9 Sat; not Sun evening) ~ Restaurant ~ (01277) 841137 ~ Children welcome if eating ~ Dogs allowed in bar ~ Open 11-11; 12-10.30 Sun ~ www.thehoop.co.uk
Recommended by Jim and Frances Gowers, John Saville

Also Worth a Visit in Essex

Besides the fully inspected pubs, you might like to try these pubs that have been recommended to us and described by readers. Do tell us what you think of them: feedback@goodguides.com

BELCHAMP ST PAUL   TL7942
Half Moon (01787) 277402
Cole Green; CO10 7DP Thatched 16th-c pub overlooking green, well kept Greene King IPA and guests, enjoyable good value home-made food (not Sun evening, Mon or Tues), take-away fish and chips Wed-Fri evenings, hospitable staff, snug beamed lounge with log fire, cheerful locals' bar, restaurant, Aug beer/music festival; children welcome, tables out in front and in back garden, closed Mon lunchtime. *(Mr and Mrs T B Staples)*

BIRCHANGER   TL5122
Three Willows (01279) 815913
Under a mile from M11 junction 8:

A120 towards Bishop's Stortford, then almost immediately right to Birchanger Village; don't be waylaid earlier by the Birchanger Services signpost; CM23 5QR This civilised dining pub - handy for M11 but feeling nicely tucked away - is under new management; spacious carpeted bar with lots of cricketing memorabilia, Greene King Abbot, IPA and a guest, well furnished smaller lounge bar, wide range of generously served pubby standards (no starters) including lots fresh fish dishes, cheery service; no children inside; dogs allowed in bar, picnic-sets on heated terrace and on lawn behind (some motorway and Stansted Airport noise), good play area, closed Sun evening. *(Anon)*

BRENTWOOD   TQ5993
Nags Head   (01277) 260 005
A1023, just off M25 junction 28; CM14 5ND Popular open-plan dining pub with good food and wine choice, several real ales, Aspall's cider, prompt friendly service; pleasant garden, open all day. *(John Saville)*

BULMER TYE   TL8438
★ Bulmer Fox   (01787) 312277/377505
A131 S of Sudbury; CO10 7EB Thriving dining pub with enjoyable fairly priced food, neatly laid tables with forms on which to write your order (or order at the bar), Adnams and Greene King IPA, help-yourself water fountain, friendly service from bustling staff, pastel colours and lively acoustics, bare boards (look out for one or two 'rugs' painted on them), quieter side room and intimate central snug, home-made chutneys, preserves etc for sale; children welcome, sheltered back terrace with arbour. *(Anon)*

CASTLE HEDINGHAM   TL7835
Bell   (01787) 460350
B1058; CO9 3EJ Beamed and timbered three-bar pub dating from the 15th c, unpretentious and unspoilt (well run by same family for over 40 years), Adnams, Mighty Oak and guests (July/Nov beer festivals), popular pubby food and turkish specials; background and some live music (lunchtime jazz last Sun of month); dogs welcome, children away from public bar, garden, handy for Hedingham Castle, open all day Fri-Sun. *(Eddie Edwards, Charles Gysin, Roderic Martin, Peter Thornton)*

CHAPPEL   TL8928
Swan   (01787) 222353
Wakes Colne; off A1124 Colchester–Halstead; CO6 2DD Ancient oak-beamed dining pub with restauranty atmosphere but welcoming drinkers, enjoyable food including good value Sun lunch, well kept Adnams and local ales, friendly attentive service, cosy rustic-style refurbishment, soft lighting, inglenook log fire; cobbled courtyard, view of Victorian viaduct from spreading garden by the River Colne, open all day weekends. *(Anon)*

CHELMSFORD   TL7107
★ Alma   (01245) 256783
Arbour Lane, off B1137; CM1 7RG Upscale pub/restaurant with well liked food from lunchtime sandwiches and good value set menu up, friendly service, leather sofas, contemporary artwork and attractive tiling in stylish bar, real ales such as Adnams Broadside and Greene King IPA, good choice of wines by the glass, smart dining area with big open fire; background music, live some evenings; children welcome in restaurant, pretty terraces, comfortable smokers' shelter. *(Michael Holdsworth, Mrs Margo Finlay, Jörg Kasprowski)*

CHELMSFORD   TL7006
Orange Tree   (01245) 262664
Lower Anchor Street; CM2 0AS Bargain lunchtime bar food in spacious local with good cheerful service, well kept Dark Star, Mighty Oak, Wibblers and up to half a dozen changing guests (some tapped from the cask), Tues quiz, some live music; back terrace, open all day. *(Tony Hobden, Andrew Bosi)*

CHELMSFORD   TL7006
★ Queens Head   (01245) 265181
Lower Anchor Street; CM2 0AS Lively, well run Victorian side-street local with very well kept Crouch Vale ales and interesting guests, summer farm cider, good value wines, friendly staff, winter log fires, bargain lunchtime food from doorstep sandwiches up (not Sun); children welcome, colourful courtyard, open all day. *(Andrew Bosi, the Didler)*

CHRISHALL   TL4439
Red Cow   (01763) 838792
High Street; off B1039 Wendens Ambo–Great Chishill; SG8 8RN Popular refurbished 14th-c thatched pub with lots of atmosphere, timbers, low beams, wood floors and log fires, one half laid for dining, decent choice of food from simple bar meals up including weekday set deals, well kept beers and interesting wine list; children welcome, nice garden, handy for Icknield Way walkers, open all day weekends, closed Mon. *(Mrs Margo Finlay, Jörg Kasprowski)*

COGGESHALL   TL8224
★ Compasses   (01376) 561322
Pattiswick, signed off A120 W; CM77 8BG Attractively reworked as more country restaurant than pub, enjoyable well presented food using local produce from light lunches up, also weekday set deals and children's meals, well kept Adnams and Woodfordes Wherry, good wine choice, cheerful attentive staff, neatly comfortable spacious beamed bars, barn restaurant; plenty of lawn and orchard tables, rolling farmland beyond. *(RS, ES, Charles Gysin)*

COLCHESTER   TM9824
Hospital Arms   (01206) 542398
Crouch Street (opposite hospital); CO3 3HA Friendly pub with several small linked areas, wide range of well kept Adnams ales plus guests, enjoyable inexpensive home-made food from sandwiches and panini up, quick cheerful service; games machines; beer garden, open all day. *(Pat and Tony Martin)*

COOPERSALE STREET   TL4701
★ Theydon Oak   (01992) 572618
Off B172 E of Theydon Bois; or follow Hobbs Cross Open Farm brown sign off B1393 at N end of Epping; CM16 7QJ Attractive old weatherboarded dining

pub, very popular especially with older lunchers for ample straightforward food (all day Sun) from sandwiches up including good value specials, Sun roasts and puddings' cabinet, Courage Best, Greene King IPA and John Smiths, friendly prompt service, beams and masses of brass, copper and old brewery mirrors, two woodburners; background music, no dogs; children welcome, tables on side terrace and in fenced garden with small stream, lots of hanging baskets, separate play area, open all day. *(LM)*

DEDHAM   TM0533
⋆ **Sun** (01206) 323351
High Street (B2109); CO7 6DF Stylish old Tudor coaching inn with good italian-influenced food using seasonal local produce, also cheaper set menu (not Fri, Sat, Sun lunchtime), impressive wine selection (lots of bin ends, over 20 by the glass), well kept Adnams, Crouch Vale and two guests, friendly efficient young staff, historic panelled interior with high carved beams, handsome furnishings and splendid fireplaces; background music, TV; children welcome, dogs in bar, picnic-sets on quiet back lawn with mature trees, characterful panelled bedrooms, good Flatford Mill walk, open all day. *(Mrs Margo Finlay, Jörg Kasprowski, Colin McKerrow, Bob and Tanya Ekers, Marion and Bill Cross, Roy Hoing, Keir Halliday)*

DUTON HILL   TL6026
Three Horseshoes (01371) 870681
Off B184 Dunmow–Thaxted, 3 miles N of Dunmow; CM6 2DX Popular friendly traditional village local, well kept Mighty Oak and guests, late spring bank holiday beer festival, central fire, aged armchairs by fireplace in homely left-hand parlour, lots of interesting memorabilia, darts and pool in small public bar, no food; dogs welcome, old enamel signs out at front, pleasant views and pond in garden, closed lunchtimes Mon-Weds. *(the Didler)*

EDNEY COMMON   TL6504
Green Man (01245) 248076
Highwood Road; CM1 3QE Comfortable pub/restaurant with good well presented food cooked by chef-owners including some unusual choices, extensive wine list (several by the glass), a couple of real ales, friendly staff, carpeted interior with black beams and timbers; tables out at front and in garden, closed Sun evening, Mon. *(Mrs Margo Finlay, Jörg Kasprowski, J B and M E Benson)*

ELMDON   TL4639
⋆ **Elmdon Dial** (01763) 837386
Village signposted off B1039 Royston–Saffron Walden; Heydon Lane; CB11 4NH Partly timbered bar with oriental rugs on bare boards, carefully collected furniture including beautifully carved early 18th-c pew (said to come from Norwich Cathedral), framed Flying covers (landlord ex-RAF), bar

skittles and board games, smarter brightly up-to-date lounge with leather tub chairs, modern tables and a decanter collection on handsome mantelpiece, Adnams, Mighty Oak and Timothy Taylors appealing bar food (not Sun evening) from good baguettes up, charming efficient service, back dining extension with pitched ceiling; sports TV; children welcome, dogs in bar, neat terrace with picnic-sets under parasols, big weeping willow on peaceful lawn, chimes from church opposite (pub named after its unusual stained-glass sundial), open all day Sun, closed Mon. *(Brian Glozier, Martyn Postle, Simon Watkins)*

EPPING FOREST   TL4501
Forest Gate (01992) 572312
Bell Common; CM16 4DZ Large friendly open-plan pub dating from 17th c, beams and panelling, good mix of customers, well kept Adnams, Nethergate and guests, enjoyable home-made bar food; tables on front lawn. *(the Didler)*

FINCHINGFIELD   TL6832
Fox (01371) 810151 *The Green; CM7 4JX* Splendidly pargeted old building with spacious beamed bar, exposed brickwork and central fireplace, ales from Adnams and Nethergate, good choice of wines by the glass, traditional home-made food including Sun roasts, evening take-away fish and chips; background and monthly live music; children and dogs welcome, picnic-sets in front overlooking village duck pond, open all day. *(George Atkinson, S Holder)*

FINGRINGHOE   TM0220
Whalebone (01206) 729307
Off A134 just S of Colchester centre, or B1025; CO5 7BG Old pub geared for dining, airy country-chic rooms with cream-painted tables on oak floors, above-average local food (not Sun evening) with some interesting choices, good sandwiches too, well kept beers, friendly chatty staff, barn function room; background music; children welcome, charming back garden with peaceful valley view, front terrace, handy for Fingringhoe nature reserve, open all day weekends. *(N R White, Stephanie Gray)*

FULLER STREET   TL7416
⋆ **Square & Compasses**
(01245) 361477 *Back road Great Leighs–Hatfield Peverel; CM3 2BB* Small well looked after traditional country pub, welcoming and popular, with wide choice of good interesting fresh food from sandwiches up, a beer brewed locally for them and three guests tapped from the cask, Weston's cider and perry, lots of wines by the glass, two woodburners in L-shaped beamed bar, thoughtful staff and attention to detail such as linen napkins, small extension for muddy walkers and dogs; soft background jazz; tables out at front with gentle country views,

open all day weekends. *(Mrs Margo Finlay, Jörg Kasprowski, David Jackson)*

GESTINGTHORPE   TL8138
Pheasant (01787) 461196
Off B1058; CO9 3AU Enjoyable seasonal food including local game and home-grown produce, they also smoke their own fish, friendly service, Adnams, a house beer brewed by Mauldons and a guest, good value wines by the glass, neat simple décor, log fires; children welcome, picnic-sets in garden with far reaching Stour Valley views, five good bedrooms, open all day. *(Anon)*

GOLDHANGER   TL9008
☆ **Chequers** (01621) 788203
Church Street; off B1026 E of Heybridge; CM9 8AS Six rambling miscellaneously furnished rooms including spacious lounge bar with dark beams, black panelling and huge sash window overlooking church and graveyard, functional games room with bar billiards, traditional dining room, carpets and bare boards, real fires and woodburner, up to nine real ales (beer festivals), wide choice of popular fairly priced blackboard food (not evenings Sun and bank holiday Mon), fresh fish on Fri, friendly staff; background music, TV; children welcome (not in tap room), dogs in bar, little courtyard with grape vine, open all day. *(Marion and Bill Cross, Evelyn and Derek Walter, N R White, David Jackson)*

GREAT CHESTERFORD   TL5142
Crown & Thistle (01799) 530278
1.5 miles from M11 junction 9A; pub signposted off B184, in High Street; CB10 1PL Substantial old pub with good fire in 16th-c inglenook, attractive decorative plasterwork and lovely old wooden benches, three changing ales such as Adnams, Buntingford and Fullers, mainly pubby food (not Sun evening), friendly helpful service, long handsomely proportioned dining room with striking photographic mural of the village; they ask to keep a credit card while you eat; children welcome, dogs in bar, picnic-sets in suntrap back courtyard, toddlers' slide on side grass. *(Anon)*

GREAT HENNY   TL8738
Henny Swan (01787) 269238
Henny Street; CO10 7LS Welcoming smartly refurbished dining pub in great location on the River Stour – summer boat trips; bar with open fire, more formal dining room, well-kept regularly changing ales, good variety of food from bar snacks and pubby choices to restaurant-style dishes,

special diets and vegetarians catered for too; children welcome, terrace and waterside garden, play area. *(Anon)*

HASTINGWOOD   TL4807
☆ **Rainbow & Dove** (01279) 415419
0.5 miles from M11 J7; CM17 9JX Pleasantly traditional 16th-c pub with three low-beamed homely rooms, stripped stone, golfing memorabilia, woodburner, Adnams Broadside, Greene King IPA and a guest, popular reasonably priced pubby food in generous helpings, friendly prompt service; background music; children welcome, covered picnic-sets on stretch of grass hedged off from car park, closed Sun evening. *(Ed Hayden, Charles and Pauline Stride, Roger and Pauline Pearce, John Saville)*

HATFIELD HEATH   TL5115
Thatchers (01279) 730270
Stortford Road (A1005); CM22 7DU 16th-c thatched and weatherboarded dining pub at end of large green, popular food (best to book weekends) from varied menu including set lunch deal Mon-Fri, well kept St Austell Tribute, Sharps Doom Bar and two guests from long counter, several wines by the glass, woodburners, beams, some copper and brass and old local photographs; background music, no dogs; children in back dining area, tables in front under parasols, open all day weekends. *(Anon)*

HEMPSTEAD   TL6337
Bluebell (01799) 599199
B1054 E of Saffron Walden; CB10 2PD Comfortable and attractive beamed bar with two rooms off and a restaurant, enjoyable generous food including popular Sun roasts, Adnams, Woodfordes and guests, Aspall's cider, friendly service, log fires, folk music Tues evening, classic car meetings (first Sat of month); children welcome, terrace and garden seating, play area. *(Mrs Margo Finlay, Jörg Kasprowski)*

HENHAM   TL5428
Cock (01279) 850347
Church End; CM22 6AN Welcoming old timbered place striking good balance between community local and dining pub, wide choice of good value home-made food from local suppliers, ales including Adnams and Saffron (brewed in the village), decent wines, good open fires, restaurant with leather-backed chairs on wood floor, sports TV in snug, live music last Sun of month; children welcome, dogs in bar, seats out at front and in tree-shaded garden. *(Charles Gysin, David and Gill Carrington)*

If a service charge is mentioned prominently on a menu or accommodation terms, you must pay it if service was satisfactory. If service is really bad you are legally entitled to refuse to pay some or all of the service charge as compensation for not getting the service you might reasonably have expected.

HERONGATE
TQ6491
⋆ Old Dog (01277) 810337
*Billericay Road, off A128 Brentwood–
Grays at big sign for Boars Head;
CM13 3SD* Welcoming country pub dating
from the 16th c, cask-tapped local ales and
enjoyable food, long attractive dark-beamed
bar, comfortable back lounge area, appealing
raftered restaurant upstairs; pleasant
front terrace and neat sheltered side
garden. *(John Murphy)*

HOWE STREET
TL6914
Green Man (01245) 360203
*Just off A130 N of Chelmsford; CM3
1BG* Friendly new management for this
spacious heavily beamed and timbered
14th-c pub, enjoyable reasonably priced food,
Greene King ales, log fire, some live music;
children welcome, garden with decked
area and adjoining paddock with small
river. *(Anon)*

HOWLETT END
TL5834
White Hart (01799) 599030
*Thaxted Road (B184 SE of Saffron
Walden); CB10 2UZ* Comfortable pub/
restaurant, two smartly set modern dining
rooms either side of small tiled-floor bar
with leather armchairs, enjoyable food from
generous sandwiches and light dishes up,
Greene King IPA and local guests, nice choice
of wines, helpful service, friendly retriever;
children welcome, terrace and big garden,
quiet spot. *(David Jackman)*

KELVEDON HATCH
TQ5798
Eagle (01277) 373472
Ongar Road (A128); CM15 0AA Friendly
family local set back from the road, low-
ceilinged bar area, good choice of food from
sandwiches and baguettes to specials and
Sun roasts, well kept Adnams and Marstons,
efficient service; background music, TV,
quiz night Mon; children welcome, covered
seating area out at front, plenty of nearby
walks. *(Roxanne Chamberlain)*

LEIGH-ON-SEA
TQ8385
⋆ Crooked Billet (01702) 480289
High Street; SS9 2EP Homely old pub
with waterfront views from big bay windows,
packed on busy summer days when service
can be frantic but friendly, well kept
Adnams, Fullers London Pride and changing
guests including seasonal ales, enjoyable
basic pub food (some bargain prices), log
fires, beams, panelled dado and bare boards,
local fishing pictures and bric-a-brac;
background music, Fri night jazz in winter,
no under-21s after 6pm; side garden and
terrace, seawall seating over road shared

with Osborne's good shellfish stall (plastic
glasses for outside), pay-and-display parking
by flyover, open all day. *(George Atkinson, LM,
David Jackson)*

LITTLE BRAXTED
TL8413
⋆ Green Man (01621) 891659
*Kelvedon Road; signed off B1389;
OS Sheet 168 map reference 848133;
CM8 3LB* Homely place with cottagey
feel, windsor chairs on patterned carpets,
mugs hanging from beams and some 200
horsebrasses, open fire in traditional little
lounge, tiled public bar with darts and
cribbage, Greene King ales and a guest, big
helpings of good sensibly priced food, friendly
helpful staff and nice chatty atmosphere;
children till 8pm, dogs in bar, picnic-sets
in pleasant sheltered garden, closed Sun
evening. *(Maria Taylor, Philip Smith, N R White,
Charles and Pauline Stride, Claudia Ives)*

LITTLE TOTHAM
TL8811
⋆ Swan (01621) 892689
School Road; CM9 8LB Welcoming country
local with good changing cask-tapped
ales from the area, farm ciders and perry,
enjoyable good value straightforward food
(not Sun evening, Mon) including basket
meals, low 17th-c beams, log fire, back dining
area, tiled games bar with darts, June beer
festival; children and dogs welcome, disabled
facilities, small terrace and informal front
garden, camping, open all day. *(the Didler)*

LITTLEY GREEN
TL6917
Compasses (01245) 362308
*Off A130 and B1417 SE of Felsted;
CM3 1BU* Unpretentiously quaint and old-
fashioned country pub, isolated but thriving,
with Adnams and guest ales tapped from
cellar casks, farm cider and perry, good range
of whiskies, basic wholesome food (they may
ask to keep a credit card while you eat),
roaring log fire; tables in big back garden,
benches at front, good walks, open all day
Thurs-Sun. *(Dave Lowe, Mitchell Humphreys, the
Didler, H Grace)*

LOUGHTON
TQ4296
Last Post (020) 8532 0751
High Road; IG10 1BB Wetherspoons
post office conversion, Fullers, Greene King
and four guests, usual good value food all
day, friendly helpful staff; TVs; children
welcome. *(Mr and Mrs C F Turner)*

LOUGHTON
TQ4296
Victoria (020) 8508 1779
Smarts Lane; IG10 4BP Welcoming
traditional local with enjoyable home-made
food and good range of beers, chatty panelled
bar with small raised end dining area;

Half pints: by law, a pub should not charge more for half a pint than half the price of
a full pint, unless it shows that half-pint price on its price list.

plenty of picnic-sets in pleasant neatly kept garden, views towards Epping Forest, good walks. *(Darren Scates)*

MALDON   TL8407
⋆**Blue Boar** (01621) 855888
Silver Street; car park round behind; CM9 4QE Quirky cross between coaching inn and antiques or auction showroom, most showy in the main building's lounge and dining room, interesting antique furnishings and pictures also in the separate smallish dark-timbered bar and its spectacular raftered upper room, good Farmers ales brewed at the back, Adnams and Crouch Vale too, enjoyable bar food including daily specials, friendly helpful staff; tables outside, bedrooms (some with four-posters), good breakfast, open all day. *(Ian Scott-Thompson, Peter Thornton)*

MISTLEY   TM1131
⋆**Thorn** (01206) 392821
High Street (B1352 E of Manningtree); CO11 1HE American chef/landlady's good food (especially seafood) is central here, but there's also a friendly all-day welcome if you just want a drink or a good coffee; high black beams give a clue to the building's age (Matthew Hopkins, the notorious 17th-c witchfinder general, based himself here), décor, though, is crisply up to date - comfortable basket-weave chairs and mixed dining tables on terracotta tiles around the horseshoe bar, cream walls above sage dado, colourful modern artwork, end brick fireplace with woodburner, good range of wines by the glass, newspapers and magazines, cookery classes; front terrace tables look across to Robert Adam's swan fountain, interesting waterside village, seven comfortable bedrooms. *(Anon)*

MONK STREET   TL6128
Farmhouse (01371) 830864
Just off B184 S of Thaxted; CM6 2NR Partly 16th-c country pub, good value food in carpeted bar and restaurant including weekday OAP lunchtime deal, Greene King and Mighty Oak ales; children welcome, good-sized attractive garden with terrace and play area, 11 bedrooms, open all day. *(N R White)*

MORETON   TL5307
White Hart (01277) 890890
Off B184, just N of A414; CM5 0LF Traditional old village pub, spacious bar with leather sofas by woodburner, two other areas, well kept Adnams Bitter and Broadside and a guest (bank holiday weekend beer festivals), decent house wines, popular food from bar snacks up including good value weekday set lunch, attractive small timbered dining room, quiz night first Weds of month; background music; children and dogs welcome, picnic-sets on smart decked terrace, garden, six refurbished bedrooms, open all day. *(Mrs Margo Finlay, Jörg Kasprowski)*

MOUNT BURES   TL9031
⋆**Thatchers Arms** (01787) 227460
Off B1508; CO8 5AT Well run modernised pub with good local food (freshly prepared so may be a wait), mid-week meal deals, well kept ales such as Adnams Mild and Bitter and Crouch Vale Brewers Gold, cheerful efficient staff; background music; dogs welcome, plenty of picnic-sets out behind, peaceful Stour Valley views, open all day weekends, closed Mon. *(James Cracknell)*

NEWNEY GREEN   TL6506
⋆**Duck** (01245) 421894
W of Chelmsford; CM1 3SF Tucked-away 18th-c pub with attractive rambling dining bar, dark beams and timbering, panelling, interesting bric-a-brac, comfortable furnishings and nice log fire, enjoyable good value food, well kept ales such as Batemans, decent wines by the glass, friendly service; pleasant terrace, open all day, closed Mon. *(Anon)*

PAGLESHAM   TQ9492
Plough & Sail (01702) 258242
East End; SS4 2EQ Relaxed 17th-c weatherboarded dining pub in pretty spot, popular fairly traditional food from sandwiches up, friendly service, well kept changing ales, decent house wines, low beams and big log fires, pine tables, lots of brasses and pictures, traditional games; background music; children welcome, front picnic-sets and attractive side garden, open all day Sun. *(Bob and Tanya Ekers)*

PAGLESHAM   TQ9293
⋆**Punchbowl** (01702) 258376
Church End; SS4 2DP 16th-c former sailmaker's loft with low beams and stripped brickwork, pews, barrel chairs and lots of brass, lower room laid for dining, Adnams Bitter and changing guests, straightforward fairly priced food including good OAP menu, prompt friendly service, cribbage and darts; background music (mostly 60s and 70s); children usually welcome but check first, lovely rural view from sunny front garden. *(George Atkinson, Bob and Tanya Ekers)*

PELDON   TL9916
Plough (01206) 735808
Lower Road; CO5 7QR Good blackboard food in small traditional tiled and white-boarded village pub, quick friendly service, Greene King and a guest ale, well spaced stripped pine tables and coastal paintings in restaurant, public bar. *(David Jackson)*

PELDON   TM0015
⋆**Rose** (01206) 735248
B1025 Colchester–Mersea (do not turn left to Peldon village); CO5 7QJ Attractive dining pub with elegant interior, dark bowed 17th-c beams, standing timbers, little leaded-light windows, gothic arched

brick fireplace, good antique furniture, also spacious modern conservatory (disabled access), enjoyable sensibly priced changing food (all day Sun in summer, booking advised), good wines from wine merchant owners Lay & Wheeler (many by the glass), well kept Adnams, Greene King and interesting guests, cheerful efficient staff; children welcome away from bar, teak furniture in sizeable garden with duck pond, bedrooms (one over kitchen can be noisy), open all day, closed Sun evening in winter. *(Ryta Lyndley)*

RIDGEWELL   TL7340
White Horse (01440) 785532
Mill Road (A1017 Haverhill–Halstead); CO9 4SG Comfortable beamed village pub with good range of well kept ales tapped from the cask, Weston's cider, good generous food from weekly changing bar and restaurant menus, friendly service; background music, no dogs; children welcome, tables out on terrace, modern bedroom block with good disabled access, closed lunchtimes Mon and Tues, otherwise open all day. *(Simon Watkins)*

SAFFRON WALDEN   TL5438
Old English Gentleman
(01799) 523595 *Gold Street; CB10 1EJ* Busy 19th-c red-brick town pub with bare boards, panelling and log fires, well kept Adnams, Woodfordes Wherry and guests, plenty of wines by the glass, decent choice of lunchtime food from sandwiches up; background music; terrace tables, open all day (till 1am weekends). *(David Hawkes)*

STANFORD RIVERS   TL5300
Woodman (01277) 362019
Little End, London Road (A113 S of Ongar); CM5 9QF Weatherboarded 17th-c roadside dining pub, well extended to ramble around central bar, with beams, log fire in big inglenook, lots of pictures, brasses and bric-a-brac, four well kept Shepherd Neame ales, generous food and friendly service; background music; children welcome, big garden with country views, play area, open all day. *(Mr and Mrs C F Turner)*

STANSTED   TL5024
Cock (01279) 812964
Silver Street; CM24 8HD Friendly little pub with good choice of enjoyable generously served food, reasonable prices, real ales, bar and dining area with half-panelled walls and wood floors, mix of dark wood furniture, some leather sofas; children welcome, tables on decked terrace, garden with play area, open all day Sun (no evening food then). *(Mrs Margo Finlay, Jörg Kasprowski)*

STAPLEFORD TAWNEY   TL5001
★ Mole Trap (01992) 522394
Tawney Common; signed off A113 N of M25 overpass - keep on; OS Sheet 167 map reference 500013; CM16 7PU Popular unpretentious little country pub, carpeted beamed bar (mind your head as you go in) with brocaded wall seats and plain pub tables, steps down to similar area, warming fires, well kept Fullers London Pride and changing guests, pubby food (not Sun or Mon evenings); no credit cards, quiet background radio; plastic tables and chairs outside along with various animals from rabbits and hens to goats and horses. *(David Jackson, LM, the Didler)*

STISTED   TL7923
★ Dolphin (01376) 321143
A120 E of Braintree, by village turn; CM77 8EU Cheerful heavily beamed and timbered bar, good value straightforward fresh food (all day) cooked to order, Greene King and guest ales tapped from the cask, brasses, antlers and lots of small prints, newspapers, log fire, bright extended eating area on left; background music; children and dogs welcome, pretty back garden with heated covered area, nice hanging baskets, views over fields. *(the Didler)*

STOW MARIES   TQ8399
★ Prince of Wales (01621) 828971
B1012 between South Woodham Ferrers and Cold Norton Posters; CM3 6SA Cheery atmosphere in several little low-ceilinged unspoilt rooms, bare boards and log fires, conservatory dining area, half a dozen widely sourced ales, bottled and draught belgian beers including fruit ones, enjoyable food (all day Sun) with some interesting specials, home-made pizzas (Thurs) from Victorian baker's oven, live jazz (third Fri of month); children in family room, terrace and garden tables, summer Sun barbecues, converted stable bedrooms, open all day. *(David Jackson)*

TENDRING   TM1523
Cherry Tree (01255) 830340
Off A120 E of Colchester; B1035 junction with Crow Lane, E of village centre; CO16 9AP Warm-hearted, heavy-beamed, red-brick pub with good sensibly priced country cooking (not Sun evening), professional friendly staff, high-backed black leather chairs around compact pub tables on broad polished boards, open fire, comfortable chairs by counter with Shalford Braintree Market and Sharps Doom Bar, good value wines by the glass, two areas set with white

---

'Children welcome' means the pubs says it lets children inside without any special restriction; some may impose an evening time limit earlier than 9pm – please tell us if you find this.

linen; disabled facilities, teak tables under parasols on sheltered back terrace, more tables on lawn behind tall hedge, closed Mon. *(Ryta Lyndley, R T and J C Moggridge)*

THAXTED   TL6031
⋆**Swan** (01371) 830321
Bull Ring; CM6 2PL Attractively renovated dark-beamed Tudor inn, Adnams and Greene King, good choice of whiskies, enjoyable food served by friendly staff, plenty of well spaced tables in long open bar, leather sofas and log fire, restaurant; roadside picnic-sets overlooking lovely church (Holst was organist here), windmill nearby, 20 bedrooms (back ones quieter), open all day. *(Giles and Annie Francis)*

THEYDON BOIS   TQ4599
Queen Victoria (01992) 812392
Coppice Row (B172); CM16 7ES Nice spot on edge of green, cosy beamed and carpeted traditional lounge, roaring log fire, local pictures and mug collection, two further bars, popular good value food including children's menu, friendly efficient young staff, McMullens ales and decent house wines, end restaurant; background music; dogs welcome, picnic-sets on well laid out front terrace, open all day. *(Robert Lester, Giles and Annie Francis, John and Penelope Massey Stewart)*

WENDENS AMBO   TL5136
⋆**Bell** (01799) 540382
B1039 W of village; CB11 4JY Small cottagey local well run by cheery landlady, brasses on ancient timbers in low-ceilinged pubby rooms, wheelback chairs at neat tables, open fire, Adnams, Woodfordes Wherry and three changing guests (Aug bank hol beer/music festival), tasty pubby food (not Sun evening, Mon) including good Sun lunch; background music; children and dogs welcome, big tree-sheltered lawn with timber play area, open all day (closed Mon lunchtime in winter). *(Anon)*

WEST BERGHOLT   TL9528
White Hart (01206) 240331
2 miles from Colchester on Sudbury Road; CO6 3DD Welcoming old village pub, former coaching inn, with good choice of reasonably priced food including plenty of fish, set lunch deals and children's menu too, Adnams and Greene King, comfortable dining area; big garden, four bedrooms, closed Sun evening. *(Marion and Bill Cross)*

WICKHAM ST PAUL   TL8336
⋆**Victory** (01787) 269364
SW of Sudbury; The Green; CO9 2PT Attractive and spacious old dining pub, interesting choice of good fresh food, friendly efficient service, Adnams and Woodfordes Wherry from brick-fronted bar, beams and timbers, leather sofas and armchairs, inglenook woodburner; background music; children welcome, neat garden overlooking village cricket green, open all day. *(Anon)*

WIDDINGTON   TL5331
⋆**Fleur de Lys** (01799) 540659
Sgned off B1383 N of Stansted; CB11 3SG Welcoming unpretentious low-beamed and timbered village local, well prepared food (not Mon) in bar and restaurant from sandwiches to Sun roasts, children's helpings, well kept Adnams, Hook Norton and guests, decent wines, dim lighting and inglenook log fire, pool and other games in back bar, friendly black labrador (other dogs welcome); picnic-sets in pretty garden, handy for Mole Hall wildlife park, open all day Fri-Sun. *(N R White, David and Gill Carrington)*

WRITTLE   TL6706
Wheatsheaf (01245) 420695
The Green; CM1 3DU Popular traditional two-room 19th-c local, friendly and chatty, with well kept Adnams, Greene King, Mighty Oak and guests, folk nights third Fri of month; terrace tables, open all day weekends. *(the Didler)*

Gloucestershire

In a county full of splendid pubs, we've chosen as our new entries the Bowl at Almondsbury (handy for the M5), Horse & Groom in Bourton-on-the-Hill (run by two brothers and loved by readers), Bakers Arms at Broad Campden (bustling village pub with five ales), Puesdown Inn in Compton Abdale (stylish modern dining, good bedrooms), Gloucester Old Spot at Coombe Hill (really rather special, great food, charming licensees), Green Dragon in Cowley (nicely old-fashioned with open fires and flagstones), Café René in Gloucester (lively bar, interesting food and drink), Royal Oak in Leighterton (elegantly refurbished country pub, kind staff), Kilcot Inn at Kilcot (owned by the cider people Weston's), and Feathered Nest in Nether Westcote (beautifully prepared food, companionable bar, lovely bedrooms). Other entries that are doing well are the Queens Arms in Ashleworth (caring South African licensees, quality food), Kings Head in Bledington (a civilised all-rounder), Old Spot in Dursley (11 real ales and smashing landlord), Plough in Ford (lots of character, very well run), Fossebridge Inn in Fossebridge (imaginative food, smart bedrooms, lovely gardens), Weighbridge at Nailsworth (try their famous 'two-in-one' pies), Bell in Sapperton (devoted licensees, beautiful terrace, special place), Swan at Southrop (much loved by readers, good mix of drinkers and diners), and Horse & Groom at Upper Oddington (enticing food, genuinely welcoming landlord). Particularly well run by two brothers, our Gloucestershire Dining Pub 2013 is the Horse & Groom, Bourton-on-the-Hill.

 ALMONDSBURY   ST6084 Map 2

Bowl £

*Church Road; 1.25 miles from M5 J16; from A38 towards Thornbury, turn
left signed Lower Almondsbury, then right down Sundays Hill, then right; BS32 4DT*

**Busy pub, handy for M5, with popular food, fine range of real ales and
pretty setting**

Considering its proximity to Bristol and the M5, this friendly pub is
in a surprisingly rural spot next to the village church. The main bar
has the most character and is long and beamed with traditional settles,
cushioned stools and mate's chairs around elm tables, horsebrasses on
stripped stone walls, a big winter log fire at one end and a woodburning
stove at the other. There's also a restaurant extension. Butcombe Bitter
and Brains Rev James with guests like Bakehouse Bakers Dozen, Brains
Milkwood, Greene King Morlands Old Speckled Hen and Timothy Taylors
Golden Best on handpump, a dozen wines by the glass and farm cider;
background music. There are seats in front of the pub and on the back
terrace, and the flowering tubs, hanging baskets and window boxes are
lovely in summer.

As well as their popular Tuesday evening steak night, the well thought of
food might include smoked mackerel pâté, home-made scotch egg with sweet
mustard pickle, warm goats cheese and mediterranean vegetable tart, shepherd's
pie, shredded moroccan lamb with beetroot, feta and mint, deep-fried haddock with
mushy peas and tartare sauce, and puddings such as lemon posset with shortbread
and berry and apple crumble. *Benchmark main dish: steaks £12.95. Two-course
evening meal £14.00.*

Brains ~ Manager Kevin Lole ~ Real ale ~ Bar food (12-2.30, 6-9.30 Mon-Thurs; 12-
9.30(8 Sun) Fri and Sat) ~ (01454) 612757 ~ Children allowed during food service times
~ Open 12-11(10.30 Sun) ~ Bedrooms: /£69S ~ www.thebowlinn.co.uk *Recommended
by John Redfern, Kevin Thomas, Nina Randall, John Wooll, Roger and Donna Huggins, Mike and
Jayne Bastin*

 ASHLEWORTH   SO8125 Map 4

Queens Arms ⑪ ♈ ◖

Village signposted off A417 at Hartpury; GL19 4HT

**Neatly kept pub with friendly licensees, a civilised bar, highly thought
of food, thoughtful wines, and sunny courtyard**

Over the 15 years that the friendly, hard-working south african
licensees have been here, we've always had warmly enthusiastic
reports from our readers. It's spic and span throughout and the civilised
main bar has a nice mix of farmhouse and brocaded dining chairs
around big oak and mahogany tables on the green carpet, and all sorts
of pictures and paintings on the faintly patterned wallpaper and washed
red ochre walls; at night it's softly lit by fringed wall lamps and candles.
They also have a little art gallery displaying work by local artists. Brains
Rev James and guests like Adnams Bitter and Timothy Taylors Landlord
on handpump, 15 wines by the glass including south african ones, 22
malt whiskies, winter mulled wine and summer home-made lemonade;
background music, board games and (on request) a skittle alley. There's
a new kitten called Talulah. The sunny courtyard has cast-iron chairs and
tables and the flower beds are lovely in summer; two perfectly clipped
mushroom-shaped yews dominate the front of the building.

¶¶ Imaginative food using top quality local produce might include filled baguettes, deep-fried brie and stilton croquettes with cranberry sauce, lambs kidneys in a rich sherry gravy, smoked natural haddock on chive mash with a poached egg and wholegrain mustard sauce, chicken with a mushroom, bacon and cheese stuffing with port and cream, rack of spare ribs with their own honey and barbecue sauce, bobotie (a popular south african dish with spicy minced beef topped with a savoury egg custard, almonds and raisins with turmeric rice), and puddings like pecan meringue with coffee cream and a brandy snap basket filled with vanilla ice-cream and hot black cherries. *Benchmark main dish: steak and kidney pie £11.75. Two-course evening meal £18.75.*

Free house ~ Licensees Tony and Gill Burreddu ~ Real ale ~ Bar food (12-2, 7-9; not Sun evening or Mon) ~ Restaurant ~ (01452) 700395 ~ Well behaved children allowed ~ Open 12-3, 7-11; 12-3 Sun; closed Sun evening, Mon ~ www.queensarmsashleworth.co.uk
Recommended by J J Hatton, Mr Richard Sleep, Dave and Jackie Kenward, Wayne Davis, Bernard Stradling

BARNSLEY
SP0705   Map 4

Village Pub ¶¶ ♗ ⇌

B4425 Cirencester–Burford; GL7 5EF

Enjoyable modern food in civilised communicating rooms, candles and open fires, good choice of drinks and seats in the back courtyard; individually decorated bedrooms

One of the things our readers enjoy about this smart and civilised country pub is that despite the emphasis on the delicious food, there's a real mix of customers – including regulars (and their dogs) who drop in for a drink and a chat. It's all very contemporary, and the low-ceilinged, communicating rooms have pale paintwork, oil paintings, flagstones and oak floorboards, plush chairs, stools and window settles around polished candlelit tables, three open fireplaces and country magazines and newspapers to read. Butcombe Bitter, Hook Norton Old Hooky and a guest beer on handpump and an extensive wine list with several by the glass. The sheltered back courtyard has good solid wooden furniture under parasols, outdoor heaters and its own outside servery.

¶¶ Inventive and extremely good, the food might include a charcuterie board with pickles, cornish fish soup with saffron mayonnaise and garlic croutons, crispy duck salad with chilli and soy, beer-battered haddock with tartare sauce, rare beef in ale pie, chicken with cabbage, bacon and dauphinoise potatoes, scottish salmon steak with middle eastern slaw, pine nuts and raisin dressing, venison haunch with cavolo nero, anna potato and pepper sauce, and puddings such as chestnut and chocolate torte and baked spiced cheesecake with poached apricots. *Benchmark main dish: slow-roast crispy pork belly with sage and apple £14.75. Two-course evening meal £21.00.*

Free house ~ Licensee Michael Mella ~ Real ale ~ Bar food (12-2.30(3 Sat), 6-9.30(10 Fri and Sat; 9 Sun)) ~ (01285) 740421 ~ Children welcome ~ Dogs welcome ~ Open 11-11(10.30 Sun) ~ Bedrooms: /£125B ~ www.thevillagepub.co.uk
Recommended by Graham Oddey, John Holroyd, Michael Sargent, Caroline de Ville, Ellie Weld, David London

---

Bedroom prices normally include full english breakfast, VAT and any inclusive service charge that we know of. Prices before the '/' are for single rooms, after for two people in double or twin (B includes a private bath, S a private shower).

BLAISDON   SO7016   Map 4

Red Hart

Village signposted off A4136 just SW of junction with A40 W of Gloucester;
OS Sheet 162 map reference 703169; GL17 0AH

Busy pub with cheerful landlord, bustling atmosphere, some interesting bric-a-brac in attractive rooms, popular bar food and several real ales

Run by an enthusiastic, cheerful landlord and his attentive staff, this village pub has a bustling atmosphere and a happy mix of both locals and visitors. The flagstoned main bar has cushioned wall and window seats, traditional pub tables, a big sailing ship painting above the log fire, Hook Norton Bitter and guests from Bath Ales, Malvern Hills and RCH on handpump, several wines by the glass and local cider; background music and bar billiards. Spotty the jack russell is now 15 years old and makes the occasional appearance. On the right, there's an attractive beamed restaurant with interesting prints and bric-a-brac, and on the left, you'll find additional dining space for families. There are some picnic-sets in the garden and a children's play area, and at the back of the building is a terrace for popular summer barbecues. The little church above the village is worth a visit.

Well liked bar food includes open ciabatta sandwiches, home-made soup, pork pâté with red onion chutney, ham, egg and bubble and squeak, chicken curry, liver and bacon with red onion gravy, local trout topped with almonds, chicken in a creamy mustard and sherry sauce, specials such as steak and mushroom in ale pie, goats cheese tart with sun-dried tomatoes and oriental duck stir-fry with vegetables and noodles, and puddings. *Benchmark main dish: slow roasted pork belly with black pudding and celeriac mash £12.75. Two-course evening meal £19.00.*

Free house ~ Licensee Guy Wilkins ~ Real ale ~ Bar food (12-2, 7-9) ~ Restaurant ~ (01452) 830477 ~ Well behaved children welcome ~ Dogs welcome ~ Open 11.30-3(4 Sun), 6(7 Sun)-11(midnight Sat) *Recommended by Ken and Barbara Turner, Lucien Perring, Pete Flower, Paul and Sue Merrick*

BLEDINGTON   SP2422   Map 4

Kings Head

B4450; OX7 6XQ

Beams and atmospheric furnishings in 16th-c former cider house, super wines by the glass, real ales and delicious food; smart bedrooms

Our readers love this well run and civilised old inn and for many it's an absolute favourite. You can be sure of a genuine welcome, the food and beer are first rate and the courtyard bedrooms are smart and comfortable. The main bar is full of ancient beams and other atmospheric furnishings (high-backed wooden settles, gateleg or pedestal tables) and there's a warming log fire in the stone inglenook with its bellows and big black kettle; sporting memorabilia of rugby, racing, cricket and hunting. To the left of the bar, a drinking area for locals has built-in wall benches, stools and dining chairs around wooden tables, rugs on bare boards and a woodburning stove. Hook Norton Best and guests from breweries such as Butcombe, Purity and Wye Valley on handpump, an excellent wine list with ten by the glass and 25 malt whiskies; background music and darts. There are seats in front of the inn and in the back courtyard garden, and resident ducks and chickens.

It's prettily set in a tranquil village, just back from the green, which has a brook running through it. The first class licensees also run the Swan at Swinbrook (Oxfordshire).

🍴 Using carefully sourced meat, game from the nearby estates and seasonal local vegetables, the excellent, interesting food might include lunchtime sandwiches, game terrine with piccalilli and warm brioche, goats cheese, beetroot and pear salad, wild mushroom and leek risotto, chilli cheeseburger with harissa mayonnaise, cornish plaice with capers and brown shrimp butter, corn-fed chicken breast with pancetta and cep mushrooms, aberdeen angus steak with garlic and parsley butter, and puddings like lemon posset with berry compote and warm chocolate brownie with vanilla ice-cream. *Benchmark main dish: devilled lambs kidneys on toast £12.00. Two-course evening meal £21.00.*

Free house ~ Licensees Nicola and Archie Orr-Ewing ~ Real ale ~ Bar food (12-2, 7-9) ~ Restaurant ~ (01608) 658365 ~ Children welcome ~ Dogs allowed in bar ~ Open 11(12 Sun)-11 ~ Bedrooms: £75B/£95B ~ www.kingsheadinn.net *Recommended by Jeff and Wendy Williams, Richard Greaves, John and Jackie Chalcraft, Bruce and Sharon Eden, M and J White, Anthony and Pam Stamer, Christian Mole, Jamie and Sue May, Bernard Stradling, Ann Gray, Walter and Susan Rinaldi-Butcher, Jenny Smith, Jane McKenzie, Alun and Jennifer Evans, Maria Oakley, Sue Callard*

BOURTON-ON-THE-HILL   SP1732   Map 4

Horse & Groom 🍴 ♀ 🛏

A44 W of Moreton-in-Marsh; GL56 9AQ

Gloucestershire Dining Pub of the Year

Handsome Georgian inn with a fine range of drinks, excellent food, friendly staff and lovely views from seats outside; smart bedrooms

'This lovely pub never fails to delight' and 'what a gem of a place' are just two comments from our many enthusiastic readers about this particularly well run honey-coloured stone inn. The licensee brothers and their staff are unfailingly polite and friendly and you are made just as welcome if it's only a drink and a chat that you want rather than a leisurely meal (though it would be a pity to miss out on the delicious food). The pubby bar is light and airy with a nice mix of wooden chairs and tables on bare boards, stripped-stone walls, a good log fire, Goffs Jouster and guests like Cotswold Wheat Beer and Premium Lager, Festival Gold or Wye Valley Ruby Ale on handpump, local cider, and 20 wines by the glass. There are plenty of original features throughout. The large back garden has lots of seats under smart umbrellas and fine views over the surrounding countryside. It's best to get here early to be sure of a space in the smallish car park. This is a lovely place to stay. Batsford Arboretum is not far away.

🍴 Enticing meals might include parmesan and rosemary-crumbed sardine fillets with devilled aioli, rillettes of confit duck with home-made piccalilli, wild mushroom and thyme risotto cakes with smashed roasted squash and parmesan, home-cured glazed tamworth ham with egg, skate wing with cornish mussels and café de paris butter, middlewhite pork and chorizo meatballs with slow-cooked tomato and rosemary sauce and polenta, and puddings such as sticky chocolate pudding with chocolate toffee sauce and spiced apple and pear flapjack crumble. *Benchmark main dish: beer-battered cod with minted pea purée and tartare sauce £12.75. Two-course evening meal £20.00.*

Free house ~ Licensee Tom Greenstock ~ Real ale ~ Bar food (12-2.30, 7-9.30; not Sun evening) ~ (01386) 700413 ~ Children welcome ~ Open 11-2.30, 6-11; 12-3.30 Sun; closed Sun evening ~ Bedrooms: £80B/£120B ~ www.horseandgroom.info

BROAD CAMPDEN
Bakers Arms  £

SP1537 Map 4

Village signed from B4081 in Chipping Campden; GL55 6UR

Friendly village pub with five real ales, traditional food and a good mix of customers

Bustling and traditional, this is a friendly village pub (first licensed in 1724) that attracts both locals and visitors. The tiny beamed bar has perhaps the most character and there's a mix of seats and tables around the walls (which are stripped back to bare stone), an inglenook fireplace and one end, and, at the attractive oak counter, Donnington BB, Wickwar Coopers Bob and WPA and a couple of changing guest beers on handpump; darts and board games. The simply furnished dining room is beamed, with exposed stone walls and a little open fire. There are seats under parasols on a terraced area, with more by flower tubs on other terraces and in the back garden. Plenty of nearby walks.

Fair value honest food includes sandwiches, home-made soup, breaded mushrooms with a garlic dip, chilli con carne, cottage pie, stilton and vegetable crumble, chicken curry, steak and kidney pudding, and puddings like apple pie and spotted dick with custard. *Benchmark main dish: smoked haddock bake £8.50. Two-course evening meal £13.00.*

Free house ~ Licensees Ray and Sally Mayo ~ Real ale ~ Bar food (12-2, 6-9(8.30 in winter); all day Fri-Sun) ~ Restaurant ~ (01386) 840515 ~ Children welcome away from bar ~ Folk music third Tues evening of month ~ Open 11.30-2.30, 5.30-11; 11.30-11 Fri and Sat; 12-10.30 Sun ~ www.bakersarmscampden.co.uk *Recommended by Ian and Nita Cooper, Dennis and Doreen Haward, Sue Kinder, Theocsbrian, Paul Humphreys, Andy and Jill Kassube*

BROCKHAMPTON
Craven Arms

SP0322 Map 4

Village signposted off A436 Andoversford–Naunton – look out for inn sign at head of lane in village; can also be reached from A40 Andoversford–Cheltenham via Whittington and Syreford; GL54 5XQ

Tasty bar food, real ales, seats in a big garden and nice surrounding walks

After enjoying one of the fine surrounding walks, this attractive 17th-c village pub is just the place to head for – and it's in a pretty spot with plenty of seats in the large garden and lovely views. Inside, the bars have low beams, thick roughly coursed stone walls and some tiled flooring, and though much of it has been opened out to give a sizeable eating area off the smaller bar servery, it's been done well to give a feeling of several communicating rooms. The furniture is mainly pine with some comfortable leather sofas, wall settles and tub chairs, and there are gin traps and various stuffed animal trophies, and a warm log fire. Otter Bitter and a couple of changing guests from breweries like Butcombe and Cotswold Spring on handpump and several wines by the glass; board games. The dog is called Max and the cat Polly.

Well liked bar food includes warm goats cheese and fig salad, portobella mushrooms filled with bacon and stilton, ham and free-range eggs, spinach and ricotta cannelloni, sausages with onion gravy, steak in ale pie, duck breast with a green peppercorn sauce, bass with pesto-crushed new potatoes and chargrilled vegetables dressed with red pepper and garlic oil, daily specials, and puddings. *Benchmark main dish: lamb cooked overnight with mint and rosemary jus £16.95. Two-course evening meal £18.50.*

Free house ~ Licensees Barbara and Bob Price ~ Real ale ~ Bar food (not Sun evening or Mon) ~ Restaurant ~ (01242) 820410 ~ Children welcome ~ Dogs allowed in bar ~ Open 12-3, 6-11; 12-11 Sat; 12-6 Sun; closed Sun evening and winter Mon ~ www.thecravenarms.co.uk *Recommended by Neil and Anita Christopher, Richard Tilbrook, Guy Vowles, Geoffrey and Penny Hughes*

CHEDWORTH
SP0512   Map 4

Seven Tuns ♀

Village signposted off A429 NE of Cirencester; then take second signposted right turn and bear left towards church; GL54 4AE

Enjoyable little pub with several open fires, lots of wines by the glass, popular bar food and plenty of outside seats

In a charming village and handy for the famous Roman villa nearby, this is a friendly little 17th-c pub with a bustling atmosphere. The small snug lounge on the right has comfortable seats and decent tables, sizeable antique prints, tankards hanging from the beam over the serving bar, a partly boarded ceiling and a good winter log fire in a big stone fireplace. Down a couple of steps, the public bar on the left has an open fire and this leads into a dining room with yet another open fire. Wells & Youngs Bitter and guests like Otter Ale and Sharps Doom Bar on handpump, up to 14 wines by the glass and 19 malt whiskies; background music and skittle alley. One sunny terrace has a boules pitch and across the road there's another little walled, raised terrace with a waterwheel and a stream; plenty of tables and seats. There are nice walks through the valley.

Popular food might include seared scallops with roasted tomato salsa, crispy confit duck salad with spring onion, cucumber and sweet plum dressing, home-cured ham and eggs, beefburger with onion jam and relish, toad in the hole with rich onion gravy, beer-battered fish with home-made chips and crushed peas, mediterranean vegetable and tomato tagliatelle, rosemary and garlic pork steak with black pudding and a creamy cider sauce, rump of lamb with dauphinoise potatoes and mint jus, and puddings. *Benchmark main dish: trio of local sausages with mash and onion gravy £9.95. Two-course evening meal £18.50.*

Youngs ~ Tenant Alex Davenport-Jones ~ Real ale ~ Bar food (12-2.30(3 Sat and Sun), 6.30-9.30(9 Sun)) ~ Restaurant ~ (01285) 720242 ~ Children welcome ~ Dogs allowed in bar ~ Open 12-3, 6-11; all day in July and Aug; 12-midnight(10.30 Sun) Sat ~ www.seventuns.co.uk *Recommended by Ian and Nita Cooper, Richard Tilbrook, Ken and Barbara Turner, Neil and Anita Christopher*

CHELTENHAM
SO9624   Map 4

Royal Oak ♀ 🍺

Off B4348 just N; The Burgage, Prestbury; GL52 3DL

Bustling and friendly with popular food, several real ales and wine by the glass, and seats in the sheltered garden

There's always something going on at this 16th-c inn – comedy evenings, beer and cider festivals, fish and seafood weekends and, being on the edge of the town (and the pub closest to Cheltenham racecourse), there's a consistently busy, cheerful mood. The congenial low-beamed bar has fresh flowers and polished brasses, a comfortable mix of seating including chapel chairs on the parquet flooring, some interesting pictures on the ochre walls and a woodburning stove in the stone fireplace. Dark Star Hophead, Harveys Best, Otley 01, Timothy Taylors Landlord and Wye Valley Bitter on handpump and several wines by the glass; efficient and friendly service. Dining room tables are nicely spaced so that you don't feel crowded; the skittle alley can also be used as a function room. There are seats and tables under canopies on the heated terrace and in a sheltered garden.

🍴 Usefully served all day at weekends, the good, popular food includes lunchtime ciabatta, ham, tomato and free-range egg, tempura king prawns and squid with spicy bloody mary sauce, aubergine, sunblush tomato, halloumi and cream cheese tart with pesto and chunky tomato sauce, specials like seared king prawns with pak choi, ginger, lemon grass and chilli, chicken breast stuffed with thyme and chicken livers and a pea and bacon stock sauce, gressingham duck breast with sweet wine and berry sauce, and puddings. *Benchmark main dish: braised rare breed blade of beef £14.95. Two-course evening meal £20.25.*

Free house ~ Licensees Simon and Kate Daws ~ Real ale ~ Bar food (12-2, 6-9; all day Sun) ~ Restaurant ~ (01242) 522344 ~ Children welcome ~ Open 11-11 ~ www.royal-oak-prestbury.co.uk *Recommended by R T and J C Moggridge, Guy Vowles, Michael Sargent*

CHIPPING CAMPDEN
Eight Bells 🍺

SP1539 Map 4

Church Street (which is one way – entrance off B4035); GL55 6JG

Handsome inn with massive timbers and beams, log fires, quite a choice of bar food, real ales and large terraced garden; handy for the Cotswold Way; bedrooms

This handsome old inn has been serving customers since it was built as a hostel for workmen building the nearby church. The bars have heavy oak beams, massive timber supports and stripped-stone walls with cushioned pews, sofas and solid dark wood furniture on the broad flagstones and log fires in up to three restored stone fireplaces. Inset into the floor of the dining room is a glass panel showing part of the passage from the church by which Roman Catholic priests could escape from the Roundheads. Hook Norton Best, Goffs Jouster, Purity Mad Goose and a guest such as Wye Valley HPA on handpump from the fine oak bar counter, quite a few wines by the glass and Weston's Old Rosie cider; background music and board games. There's a large terraced garden with plenty of seats, and striking views of the almshouses and church. The pub is handy for the Cotswold Way, which takes you to Bath.

🍴 As well as lunchtime sandwiches and a good value two- and three-course set menu (not Friday evening or weekends), the popular food might include breaded whitebait with garlic and saffron aioli, chicken liver parfait with chutney, roast butternut squash and tomato risotto topped with a soft poached egg, toad in the hole with grain mustard and cider sauce, chicken supreme wrapped in parma ham with a mushroom and tarragon cream sauce, salmon with red and yellow pepper essence, and puddings like dark chocolate crème brûlée and apple and cinnamon sponge pudding with home-made custard. *Benchmark main dish: beer-battered fish and chips with tartare sauce £13.50. Two-course evening meal £20.00.*

Free house ~ Licensee Neil Hargreaves ~ Real ale ~ Bar food (12-2(2.30 Fri and Sat, 2.15-Sun), 6.30-9(9.30 Fri and Sat, 8.45 Sun)) ~ Restaurant ~ (01386) 840371 ~ Well behaved children welcome but only in dining room after 6pm ~ Dogs allowed in bar ~ Open 12(11 Sat)-11(10.30 Sun) ~ Bedrooms: £65B/£100B ~ www.eightbellsinn.co.uk
Recommended by Peter Smith and Judith Brown, Peter Dandy, M G Hart, Paul and Penny Dawson, Mr and Mrs M Stratton, Dennis Jones, Brian and Ruth Young, Michael Carpenter, Jim Wolstenholme

CLIFFORD'S MESNE   SO6922   Map 4

Yew Tree 🍴 ♀ 🍺

From A40 W of Huntley turn off at May Hill 1, Clifford's Mesne 2.5 signpost, then pub eventually signed up steep narrow lane on left; Clifford's Mesne also signposted off B4216 S of Newent, pub then signed on right; GL18 1JS

Unusual dining pub nicely tucked away on slopes of May Hill; wine bargains

The provincial french wines from small producers served in this well run dining pub come in three glass sizes, in a 500-ml jug and of course, by the bottle. They have a seating area in their small informal wine shop making it a sort of wine bar with nibbles and if you buy a bottle with your meal, they charge just the shop price plus £6, which represents excellent value especially at the top end. They also have Battledown Natural Selection, Sharps Own and a guest like Cotswold Spring Ambler on handpump, local farm cider and perry and good value winter mulled wine; service is prompt and genial. The smallish two-room beamed bar has an attractive mix of small settles, a pew and character chairs around interesting tables including antiques, rugs on an unusual stone floor, and a warm woodburning stove. You can eat more formally up a few steps, in a carpeted dining room beyond a sofa by a big log fire; newspapers and unobtrusive nostalgic pop music. Teak tables on a side terrace are best placed for the views and there are steps down to a sturdy play area. Plenty of nearby walks.

Using their own rare-breed pigs, home-grown vegetables and other seasonal local produce, the enjoyable food includes rustic pork terrine with sloe and crab-apple jelly, devilled kidneys in dijon cream sauce on a garlic croûte, sausages and mash with mustard gravy, venison pasty with redcurrant gravy, steak and kidney pudding, broccoli, beetroot and cream cheese roulade, bass fillet with lime and ginger crushed new potatoes and a lime beurre blanc, and puddings such as ginger pudding with chocolate fudge sauce and lemon posset. *Benchmark main dish: gloucester old spot loin steaks £14.50. Two-course evening meal £20.25.*

Free house ~ Licensees Mr and Mrs Philip Todd ~ Real ale ~ Bar food (12-2, 6-9; 12-4 Sun; not Mon or Tues lunchtime) ~ (01531) 820719 ~ Children welcome ~ Dogs welcome ~ Open 12-2.30, 6-11; 12-5 Sun; closed Sun evening, Mon and Tuesday lunchtimes ~ www.yewtreeinn.com *Recommended by Mike and Mary Carter, TB, Guy Vowles, John and Sylvia Harrop*

COATES   SO9600   Map 4

Tunnel House 🍺

Follow Tarlton signs (right then left) from village, pub up rough track on right after railway bridge; OS Sheet 163 map reference 965005; GL7 6PW

Friendly pub with interesting décor, lots of character, popular food and drink, and seats in the sizeable garden; at entrance to derelict canal tunnel

The stretch of the old Thames and Severn Canal nearby is known as the Kings Reach to commemorate a visit by King George III in 1788; the big garden slopes down to the derelict entrance tunnel and there are seats and tables on the terrace in front of this eccentric bow-fronted stone house with a fine views. The atmosphere inside is cheerful and easy-going and there's always a good mix of customers – the place is especially popular with students from the Royal Agricultural College. The rambling rooms have beams, flagstones, a mix of furnishings including massive rustic benches and seats built into the sunny windows, lots of enamel advertising signs, racing tickets and air travel labels, a stuffed wild boar's head and owl, plenty of copper and brass and an upside-down card table complete with cards and drinks fixed to the beams; there's a winter log fire with sofas in front (but you have to arrive early to grab them). The more conventional dining extension and back conservatory fill up quickly at mealtimes. Otter Bright, Prescott Hill Climb, Sharps Doom Bar and Uley Bitter on handpump, several wines by the glass and two draught ciders; background music. Good walks nearby; disabled lavatories.

Quite a choice of food might include sandwiches, potted salt beef with pickled onions and gherkins, baked camembert infused with rosemary with olive flatbread, beef burger with bacon and cheese, gloucester old spot sausages with red onion marmalade gravy, beer-battered cod and chips with home-made tartare sauce, wild mushroom, leek and blue cheese open puff pastry pie, chicken breast stuffed with goats cheese and thyme wrapped in bacon on creamy red pesto linguine, and puddings like cherry and almond tart and banoffi cheesecake. *Benchmark main dish: venison medallions and portabello mushroom stack with redcurrant jus £12.25. Two-course evening meal £17.00.*

Free house ~ Licensee Michael Hughes ~ Real ale ~ Bar food (12-9.30) ~ Restaurant ~ (01285) 770280 ~ Children welcome ~ Dogs welcome ~ Open 12-midnight ~ www.tunnelhouse.com *Recommended by Alan Bulley, Jean and Douglas Troup, Guy Vowles, M G Hart*

COMPTON ABDALE   SP0717   Map 4

Puesdown Inn 🛏

A40 outside village; GL54 4DN

Stylishly refurbished Cotswold stone inn with plenty of room, bold colours throughout, friendly staff, enjoyable food and seats in pretty back garden; bedrooms

From the outside this is a traditional cotswold-stone inn – inside it's been renovated into a contemporary dining pub with a friendly, relaxed atmosphere. There's a spacious series of interconnected stylish bars and extensive eating areas with big art posters and other interesting pictures, prints and photographs all over the mainly stripped stone walls (others are painted orange or cream), rafter-effect or beamed ceilings, bright rugs and bare boards, and both a woodburning stove and a log fire. As well as stools by the counter, the seating ranges from leather or orange-fabric covered sofas and armchairs and high-backed dining chairs (in the same colours or elegant wooden ones) around a happy mix of tables; they've recently opened a pizza restaurant next door. Fullers London Pride and Hook Norton Old Hooky on handpump, good wines by the glass and quite a few coffees; staff are friendly and helpful and you may catch a glimpse of the two resident chocolate labradors; background music. There are plenty of seats and tables in the pretty back garden. The ground-floor bedrooms are comfortable and well equipped.

🍴 Good, enjoyable food might include lunchtime sandwiches, a changing pâté, moules frites, a tian of crab and avocado, ham and eggs with caramelised onion chutney, beer-battered fish and chips, herb pancake filled with confit duck, black bream with crab sauce, slow-cooked pork belly with olive mash, chicken pie, and puddings such as brioche bread and butter pudding with crème anglaise and a trio of chocolate puddings. *Benchmark main dish: slow-cooked shoulder of lamb with lambs kidney and sweetbread £13.50. Two-course evening meal £21.00.*

Free house ~ Licensees John and Maggie Armstrong ~ Real ale ~ Bar food (10-3, 6-11) ~ Restaurant ~ (01451) 860262 ~ Children welcome ~ Dogs welcome ~ Occasional live jazz ~ Open 10-3, 6-11; 10am-11pm Sat; 10-4 Sun; closed Sun evening ~ Bedrooms: £50S/£85S ~ www.puesdown.cotswoldinns.com *Recommended by Ian Herdman, Rod Stoneman, Guy Vowles*

COOMBE HILL
SO8926 Map 4

Gloucester Old Spot ★ 🍺

A mile from M5 junction 10 (access from southbound and to northbound carriageways only); A4019 towards A38 Gloucester–Tewkesbury; GL51 9SY

The country local comes of age – a model for today's country pubs

Carefully restored while keeping its essential simplicity – and avoiding the all too common trap of a surfeit of cheap leather furniture – this country local has a companionable quarry-tiled beamed bar, softly lit, with chapel chairs and other seats around mixed tables, one in a bow-windowed alcove, and opens into a lighter partly panelled area with cushioned settles and stripped kitchen tables. They sometimes have their own-brewed cider or perry (Black Rat if not), as well as well kept ales such as Gwynt y Ddraig Happy Daze, Hop Back GFB, Purity Mad Goose and Skinners Betty Stogs on handpump, and seven decent wines by the glass; the young staff are friendly without being pushy and decoration is in unobtrusive good taste, with winter log fires. A separate dark-flagstoned dining room, handsome with its tall stripped brick walls and candlelight, has similar country furniture. There are picnic-sets under cocktail parasols on the terrace behind. The pub is owned by the same people as the Royal Oak in Cheltenham.

🍴 They make a particular feature of rare-breed pork and sausages here, and other food – strong on local seasonal produce – includes filled cobs, confit duck leg and leek terrine with apple and fig chutney, seared pigeon breast and breaded ox tongue and black pudding salad with hazelnut dressing, honey-glazed ham with a free-range egg, spinach, goats cheese and nutmeg filo parcel with mint and cucumber yoghurt, beer-battered plaice with pea purée and tartare sauce, gloucester old spot pork chop with prune and redcurrant jus, 28-day matured rump steak with green peppercorn butter, specials like venison and game pudding with juniper and rosemary jus and bass fillets with lemongrass, coriander, lime and basil butter, and puddings such as lemon and ginger cheesecake with raspberry coulis and chocolate and orange brownie with walnut and maple syrup ice-cream; they also offer a two-course lunch deal Mon-Sat. *Benchmark main dish: rare breed pork belly £14.95. Two-course evening meal £20.00.*

Free house ~ Licensees Simon Daws and Hayley Cribb ~ Real ale ~ Bar food (12-2, 6-9; all day Sat; 12-6 Sun; not Sun evening) ~ Restaurant ~ (01242) 680321 ~ Children welcome ~ Dogs allowed in bar ~ Open 10.30am-11pm ~ www.thegloucesteroldspot.co.uk *Recommended by Andy and Claire Barker, Guy Vowles, Mrs C G Powell-Tuck, Di and Mike Gillam*

It's very helpful if you let us know up-to-date food prices when you report on pubs.

COWLEY SO9714 Map 4

Green Dragon 🛏

Off A435 S of Cheltenham at Elkstone, Cockleford sign; OS Sheet 163 map reference 970142; GL53 9NW

17th-c stone-fronted inn with plenty of character in beamed bars, two restaurants, popular food, real ales and seats on terraces; well appointed bedrooms

When it opened in 1643 this attractive stone-fronted pub was a cider house, with its own orchard on the site of what's now the car park. Today, it's a smart yet characterful dining pub with a warm welcome for all from the well trained staff. The two beamed bars have a cosy and genuinely old-fashioned feel with big flagstones and wooden floorboards, candlelit tables and winter log fires in two stone fireplaces. Hook Norton Old Hooky, Sharps Doom Bar and a guest beer on handpump and ten wines by the glass. The furniture and the bar itself in the upper Mouse Bar were made by Robert Thompson, and little mice run over the hand-carved tables, chairs and mantelpiece; there's also a small upstairs restaurant. The bedrooms are comfortable and well appointed and the breakfasts are generous. There are seats outside on terraces and this is good walking country.

 Good bar food includes sandwiches, game and chicken liver terrine with prune chutney, pigeon, bacon and quail egg salad, curried parsnip and cranberry risotto with lime yoghurt and macadamia nuts, beef stroganoff with tagliatelle, slow-braised lamb shank with rosemary and redcurrant gravy, monkfish wrapped in parma ham with a white wine, cheese and parsley sauce, daily specials, and puddings. *Benchmark main dish: ham hock with english mustard and cider sauce £14.75. Two-course evening meal £21.50.*

Buccaneer Holdings ~ Managers Simon and Nicky Haly ~ Real ale ~ Bar food (12-2.15, 6-9.30) ~ Restaurant ~ (01242) 870271 ~ Children welcome ~ Dogs allowed in bar and bedrooms ~ Open 11-11; 12-10.30 Sun ~ Bedrooms: £70B/£95B ~ www.green-dragon-inn.co.uk *Recommended by Bruce and Sharon Eden, Andy and Claire Barker, Mike and Mary Carter, Ian Herdman, Dr A J and Mrs Tompsett, Russell Grimshaw, S G N Bennett, B D Jones, Dave Braisted, Richard Tilbrook*

DIDMARTON ST8187 Map 2

Kings Arms ♀ 🛏

A433 Tetbury road; GL9 1DT

Bustling pub with knocked-through rooms, several real ales, tasty bar food and pleasant back garden; bedrooms and self-catering cottages

If you stay in the comfortable bedrooms of this 17th-c former coaching inn, the breakfasts are very good; they also have self-catering cottages in a converted barn and stable block. The several knocked-through beamed bar rooms work their way around a big central counter, with deep terracotta walls above a dark green dado in some, yellow and cream paintwork in others, an attractive mix of wooden tables and chairs on bare boards, quarry tiles and carpet, fresh flowers, and a big stone fireplace. There's also a smart restaurant. Brakspears Bitter, Butcombe Gold and Uley Bitter on handpump and several wines by the glass; darts. There are seats out in the pleasant back garden and boules. The pub is handy for Westonbirt Arboretum.

🍴 Quite a choice of food might include sandwiches, fried pigeon with beetroot and a balsamic dressing, chicken and bacon caesar salad with crispy croutons and olives, home-baked ham with free-range eggs, aubergine, courgette, peppers and red onions in fresh tomato sauce on tagliatelle, a trio of faggots with onion gravy, local rabbit and venison pie, pork and parsley stuffed chicken wrapped in bacon with a creamy white wine and wholegrain mustard sauce, and specials such as chilli and garlic tiger prawns and ham hock with parsley sauce. *Benchmark main dish: beer-battered haddock and chips with home-made tartare sauce £11.25. Two-course evening meal £16.50*

Free house ~ Licensee Steve Payne ~ Real ale ~ Bar food (12-2, 6-9; 12-7.45 Sun) ~ Restaurant ~ (01454) 238245 ~ Children welcome ~ Dogs allowed in bar ~ Open 11-11; 12-10.30 Sun ~ Bedrooms: £65S/£90S ~ www.kingsarmsdidmarton.co.uk
Recommended by Heather and Dick Martin, Barry and Anne, KC, Phil and Gill Wass, Pat Bunting, Brian Boyland, Guy Vowles

DURSLEY   ST7598   Map 4

Old Spot 🍺 £

Hill Road; by bus station; GL11 4JQ

Unassuming and cheery town pub with up to 11 real ales and regular beer festivals

Enthusiasm never wanes for this particularly well run town local – our readers enjoy their every visit. Mr Herbert is a genuinely friendly landlord who welcomes visitors alongside plenty of good-humoured locals and keeps a fantastic range of up to 11 real ales on handpump. This always includes Uley Old Rick plus guests from breweries such as Bath Ales, Butcombe, Moles, Otter, Sawbridgeworth, Severn Vale, Springhead, Wickwar and Wye Valley; they also hold four annual beer festivals and stock quite a few malt whiskies, too. The front door opens into a deep pink small room with stools on shiny quarry tiles along its pine-boarded bar counter and old enamel beer advertisements on the walls and ceiling; there's a profusion of porcine paraphernalia. A small room on the left leads off from here and the little dark wood-floored room to the right has a stone fireplace. A step takes you down to a cosy Victorian tiled snug and (to the right) the meeting room. There are seats in the heated and covered garden.

🍴 Good value bar food at lunchtime and on Monday evenings includes doorstep sandwiches, a grazing board of meat, fish and cheese, sausage and mash, chicken fajitas, pork and apple burger, salmon fillet with a white wine and cream sauce, cottage pie, and puddings like white chocolate cheesecake and blackberry and apple crumble. *Benchmark main dish: pork belly with a pork and plum reduction £9.85. Two-course evening meal £12.00.*

Free house ~ Licensee Steve Herbert ~ Real ale ~ Bar food (12-3; no evening meals except Monday (6.30-9)) ~ (01453) 542870 ~ Children in family room only (best to book) ~ Dogs welcome ~ Open 11(12 Sun)-11 ~ www.oldspotinn.co.uk *Recommended by Dr and Mrs A K Clarke, the Didler, Mrs P Sumner, PL, Jim and Frances Gowers, Chris and Angela Buckell*

FORD   SP0829   Map 4

Plough 🛏

B4077 Stow–Alderton; GL54 5RU

16th-c inn in horse racing country, with lots of horse talk, a bustling atmosphere, first class service, good food and well kept beer; bedrooms

Even when this lively, enjoyable pub is packed to the gunnels (which it always is on race meeting days), the friendly hands-on landlord and his helpful staff remain courteous and efficient; it's certainly worth booking ahead to be sure of a table. There's always a chatty atmosphere and the beamed and stripped-stone bar has racing prints and photos on the walls (many of the customers here are from the racing fraternity and a well known racehorse trainer's yard is opposite), old settles and benches around the big tables on uneven flagstones, oak tables in a snug alcove and open fires and woodburning stoves (a couple are the real thing). Darts, TV (for the races) and background music. Donnington BB and SBA on handpump. There are some picnic-sets under parasols and pretty hanging baskets at the front of the stone building and a large back garden with a play fort for children. The Cotswold Farm Park is nearby. The comfortable bedrooms away from the pub are the quietest and there are views of the gallops.

As well as serving breakfast from 9am, the enjoyable food (using free-range meat and seasonal game) includes lunchtime filled baguettes, chicken, smoked bacon and black pudding terrine with apricot and tarragon chutney, king scallops with chorizo, a vegetarian pasta dish, creamy fish pie topped with cheesy mash, gammon with a free-range egg or pineapple, steak in ale pie, slow-cooked lamb shoulder with mint jelly, local game casserole, half a roast duck with bubble and squeak and orange sauce, daily specials, and puddings. *Benchmark main dish: steak in ale pie £12.95. Two-course evening meal £19.50.*

Donnington ~ Tenant Craig Brown ~ Real ale ~ Bar food (12-2, 6-9; all day Fri-Sun) ~ Restaurant ~ (01386) 584215 ~ Children welcome ~ Dogs allowed in bar ~ Open 9am-11pm ~ Bedrooms: £60S/£80S ~ www.theploughinnatford.co.uk *Recommended by Peter Smith and Judith Brown, Terry Buckland, Giles and Annie Francis, Ian Herdman, KC, Michael Sargent, Jamie and Sue May, Keith and Ann Arnold*

FOSSEBRIDGE
Fossebridge Inn 🍴 🛏
A429 Cirencester–Stow-on-the-Wold; GL54 3JS

SP0711   Map 4

Handsome old inn with a proper bar, a good mix of customers, real ales, interesting food and seats in four acres of grounds; smart bedrooms

Partly Tudor and partly Georgian, this well run and welcoming inn is especially popular in summer, when there are picnic-sets and other seats and tables under parasols on the terrace and in four acres of lawned riverside gardens. The original 15th-c heart is the bustling bar, which has a relaxed and informal atmosphere, plenty of chatty regulars, North Cotswold Best, Otter Ale and St Austell Tribute on handpump, several wines by the glass and Stowford Press cider. The two rooms have beams and arches, stripped-stone walls and fine old flagstones, a happy mix of dining chairs, stools and wooden tables, copper implements, open fires, candles and fresh flowers. Two other dining rooms are rather grand. The bedrooms are comfortable and they have a self-catering cottage. The National Trust Roman villa at Chedworth is nearby.

As well as sandwiches, the reliably good food might include a duck scotch egg, pressed ham hock and confit potato terrine with red onion marmalade, home-made burger with bacon, cheese and triple-cooked chips, sausages of the day with onion gravy, aubergine with confit potato, spinach and goats cheese gratin and jerusalem artichoke velouté, clam, mussel and cockle linguine with chilli and garlic, chicken kiev, rack of lamb (for two) with shallot purée and rosemary jus, and puddings such as chocolate pot and lavender crème brûlée with shortbread biscuits. *Benchmark main dish: 10-oz aberdeen angus onglet with horseradish cream and triple cooked chips £18.00. Two-course evening meal £19.00.*

Free house ~ Licensee Samantha Jenkins ~ Real ale ~ Bar food (12-2.30(3 Sat, 3.30 Sun), 6-9.30(9 in winter)) ~ Restaurant ~ (01285) 720721 ~ Children welcome ~ Dogs welcome ~ Open 12-12(11.30 Sun) ~ Bedrooms: £65S(£75B)/£75S(£85B) ~ www.fossebridgeinn.co.uk *Recommended by Guy Vowles, Rob and Catherine Dunster, Mr and Mrs M J Girdler, Barry and Anne, Richard Tilbrook, Robert Wivell*

GLOUCESTER SO8318 Map 4
Café René ◀

Southgate Street; best to park in Blackfriars carpark (Ladybellegate Street) and walk through passageway – pub entryway then just across road; GL1 1TP

Interesting and interestingly placed bar with good value food all day, wide choice of drinks

Down a flagstoned passageway beside the partly Norman church of St Mary de Crypt, Café René dates back to the 17th c, with some stripped brick and timbering. It has an internal floodlit well, with water trickling down into its depths, and a very subterranean feel – no windows, black beams (with loads of beermats), dim lighting. The long bar counter is made of dozens of big casks, and they have four changing real ales tapped from the cask from breweries like Blindmans, Freeminster, Stroud and Wickwar, farm ciders and a good choice of wines by the glass – decoration consists largely of great banks of empty wine bottles. An antique panelled high-backed settle, typical pub tables and wheelback chairs stand on carpeted floor, and there's a sizeable dining area on the right. Staff are helpful, background music well reproduced, and the games machine silenced; big-screen TV. There are plenty of picnic-sets under cocktail parasols out by the churchyard.

Their chargrilled food is exceptionally popular and includes whole rack of baby back ribs with barbecue sauce, sausages with onion gravy, burgers, gammon with egg and pineapple, duck with orange sauce and quite a choice of steaks; also, chicken liver pâté with cranberry sauce, garlic mushrooms, caesar salad with chicken and bacon, beer-battered cod and chips with home-made tartare sauce, fresh tagliatelle with pesto, pine nuts and spring onion, steak in ale pie, caribbean lamb curry, and puddings like lemon tart with raspberries and a changing cheesecake. *Benchmark main dish: chargrilled steaks £15.95. Two-course evening meal £19.50.*

Free house ~ Licensee Paul Soden ~ Real ale ~ Bar food (11-10; 12-9.30 Sun) ~ Restaurant ~ (01452) 309340 ~ Well behaved children welcome ~ Frequent live music; phone for details ~ Open 11-midnight (later Fri and Sat) ~ www.caferene.co.uk *Recommended by Alan and Eve Harding, Jeremy King*

GREAT RISSINGTON SP1917 Map 4
Lamb ♀ ⇌

Turn off A40 W of Burford to the Barringtons; keep straight on past Great Barrington until Great Rissington is signed on left; GL54 2LN

Busy inn with civilised bar, well liked bar food, changing real ales and seats in the sheltered garden; bedrooms

Overlooking the Windrush Valley, this is a 17th-c inn of cotswold stone. The two-roomed bar has high-backed leather and farmhouse chairs grouped around polished tables on the red carpet, a woodburning stove in the stone fireplace and bar chairs at the counter where they serve Brakspears Bitter, Wychwood Hobgoblin and a guest such as Jennings Cumberland on handpump; also, several wines by the glass and quite a few malt whiskies. Some interesting things to look out for are parts of a propeller, artefacts in display cases and pictures of the canadian crew from the Wellington bomber that crashed in the garden in October 1943. The restaurant has another woodburning stove and various old agricultural tools on the walls; background music, TV, board games and books for sale (the money goes towards guide dogs for the blind). You can sit outside on the front terrace or in the sheltered, well kept hillside garden. There's a local circular walk which takes in part of the idyllic village, church, River Windrush and stunning countryside surrounding the pub.

Sourcing most of their produce from a 25-mile radius and getting their Brixham fish delivered to the door, the food might include sandwiches (the soup and sandwich deal is popular), salmon, celeriac and dill fishcake with hollandaise, blue cheese and walnut salad with a poached pear and honey dressing, line-caught bass with beans, samphire and a lemon butter cream, duck breast with vegetable ribbons and a port and smoked garlic jus, lamb shank, shepherd's pie and rosemary and pan jus, and puddings like lemon panna cotta with citrus crunch and vanilla bean ice-cream and white chocolate mousse with honeycomb and raspberry compote. *Benchmark main dish: beer-battered haddock with twice-cooked fat chips and tartare sauce £12.95. Two-course evening meal £19.00.*

Free house ~ Licensees Paul and Jacqueline Gabriel ~ Real ale ~ Bar food (12-2.30, 6.30-9) ~ Restaurant ~ (01451) 820388 ~ Children welcome ~ Dogs allowed in bar and bedrooms ~ Open 12-11.30(midnight Sat, 11 Sun) ~ Bedrooms: $55B/$80B ~ www.thelambinn.com *Recommended by Tim Maddison, Andrew Scott, Andrea Hughes*

GUITING POWER
SP0924 Map 4

Hollow Bottom
Village signposted off B4068 SW of Stow-on-the-Wold (still called A436 on many maps); GL54 5UX

Popular old inn with lots of racing memorabilia, a good bustling atmosphere, real ales and enjoyable food

Although there are lots of racing folk here and live horse racing is shown on the TV, our non-horsey readers tell us they always enjoy their visits to this snug old stone cottage very much and are warmly welcomed by the helpful, friendly staff. The comfortable beamed bar has plenty of atmosphere, lots of racing memorabilia including racing silks, tunics, photographs, race badges, framed newspaper cuttings and horseshoes (their local horse won the Cheltenham Gold Cup in 2010 and they have dedicated an area in the bar to him); there's a winter log fire in an unusual pillar-supported stone fireplace. The public bar has flagstones and stripped-stone masonry; newspapers to read, darts, board games and background music. Battledown Tipster, Donnington SBA and a beer named for the pub on handpump, several wines (including champagne) by the glass and a dozen malt whiskies. From the pleasant garden behind the pub there are views towards the sloping fields; decent nearby walks.

Fair value, tasty food includes filled baguettes and baked potatoes, home-made pâté with cumberland sauce, four-egg cheese omelette, home-made burger, sausages with mash and gravy, gammon with free-range eggs, a roast of the day, specials like garlic and chilli tiger prawns, spaghetti with wild mushroom sauce, local venison with red wine and shallots and smoked haddock in a chive and cheese sauce and puddings such as banoffi pie and chocolate fudge brownie with chocolate sauce. *Benchmark main dish: pie of the day £11.95. Two-course evening meal £17.00.*

Free house ~ Licensees Hugh Kelly and Charles Pettigrew ~ Real ale ~ Bar food (all day) ~ Restaurant ~ (01451) 850392 ~ Children welcome ~ Dogs allowed in bar ~ Open 9am-midnight ~ Bedrooms: $75B/$90B ~ www.hollowbottom.com *Recommended by Michael and Jenny Back, T Harrison, Ian Herdman, Tracey and Stephen Groves, Michael Sargent, Chris and Val Ramstedt, Andrew Scott, Mrs S Watkins*

 KILCOT   SO6925   Map 4

Kilcot Inn

2.3 miles from M50 junction 3; B4221 towards Newent; GL18 1NG

Attractively reworked small country inn, kind staff, enjoyable local food and drink

Reopened in summer 2011 after sympathetic renovation by Weston's the cider people, this has their Old Rosie, The Governor and Perry on handpump, with more by the bottle, as well as Marstons Pedigree and EPA and Wye Valley Butty Bach, and local wine and organic fruit juice. It's open plan, with stripped beams, bare boards and dark flagstones, sunny bay-window seats, homely armchairs by one of the two warm woodburning stoves, tables with padded dining chairs, and daily papers; big-screen TV, may be background music. The front terrace has picnic sets under cocktail parasols, with more out behind. We have not yet heard from readers using the four new bedrooms, but would expect this to be a nice place to stay – and there's a smart new bicycle shed.

From an immaculate new kitchen, popular food from local suppliers is served all day from 7am (for breakfast): sandwiches, confit duck samosas with sweet chilli dressing, poached pear and goats cheese tartlet, home-made beef burger with skinny fries, fish and chips with home-made tartare sauce, roast vegetables with a pesto cream sauce on tagliatelle, lasagne, chicken with a wild mushroom and tomato compote and dauphinoise potatoes, pork shank with apple mash and cider gravy, bass with a chive cream sauce and parmentier potatoes, daily specials, and puddings. It's best to book evenings. *Benchmark main dish: calves liver and bacon £11.95. Two-course evening meal £19.00.*

Free house ~ Licensee Mark Lawrence ~ Real ale ~ Bar food (12-3, 6-9; breakfast 7-11.30am; afternoon tea 3-5) ~ Restaurant ~ (01989) 720707 ~ Children welcome ~ Dogs allowed in bar ~ Occasional live music – best to phone ~ Open 11-11 ~ Bedrooms: /$80S ~ www.kilcotinn.com *Recommended by TB, P G Topp, Mike and Mary Carter*

 LEIGHTERTON   ST8290   Map 2

Royal Oak ♀

Village signposted off A46 S of Nailsworth; GL8 8UN

Handsome country pub elegantly refurbished, good choice of drinks, imaginative food and kind staff

The rambling bar has plenty of nice touches, from the pair of log fireplaces facing each other (you have to look twice to be sure it's not a mirror) to the splendid antique trolley with the daily papers – including the *Racing Post*. Part parquet, part broad boards, with some stripped stone and pastel paintwork, it has carefully chosen furniture from stylish strung-seat dining chairs to soft sofas. They have some interesting wines by the glass and local farm cider, as well as O'Hanlons Royal Oak Best, Wadworths IPA and Wye Valley O'er the Sticks on handpump, and helpful smartly dressed staff. There's good disabled access. A sheltered side courtyard has mainly teak and metal tables and chairs, and there are good walks near the quiet village, with Westonbirt Arboretum not far off.

Making their own bread, ketchup and pickles and using the best local produce, the interesting food might include sandwiches, quail and pistachio salad with watercress shoots, game chips and raisin jus, honey and sesame glazed pork loin ribs, beer-battered fish with tartare sauce, gammon with chargrilled pineapple, a baked egg and rosemary straw chips, beef burger with cheese and ketchup, herb-crused whiting with wild garlic velouté, jersey royal and sweet roasted shallot tatin with black olive tapenade, lamb breast, seared cutlet, sweetbread pie and lemon thyme potato fondant, 31-day aged local beef with triple-cooked chips, and puddings like white chocolate and honey truffle with pecan nougat and passion fruit crème brûlée with saffron macaroons; they also offer a set two- and three-course lunch menu. *Benchmark main dish: pie of the week £13.25. Two-course evening meal £19.50.*

Free house ~ Licensees Paul and Antonia Whitbread ~ Real ale ~ Bar food (12-2.30, 6-9.30; not Sun evening) ~ Restaurant ~ (01666) 890250 ~ Children welcome ~ Dogs allowed in bar ~ Open 11-3, 5.30-11; 11-11 Sat; 12-10.30 Sun ~ www.royaloakleighterton.co.uk *Recommended by David Shaw, Les Halpin, David and Jill Wyatt, Devereaux Harry-Barnwell, Guy Vowles, Chris and Angela Buckell*

NAILSWORTH
Weighbridge 🍴 🍷

ST8699   Map 4

B4014 towards Tetbury; GL6 9AL

Super 'two-in-one' pies served in cosy old-fashioned bar rooms, a fine choice of drinks, friendly service and a sheltered garden

Dating in part from the 17th c, this neatly kept place was once run by a landlord who also operated the nearby weighbridge – hence the pub's name. The relaxed bar has three cosily old-fashioned rooms with open fires, stripped-stone walls and antique settles, country chairs and window seats. The black beamed ceiling of the lounge bar is thickly festooned with black ironware – sheep shears, gin traps, lamps and a large collection of keys, many from the old Longfords Mill opposite the pub. Upstairs is a raftered hayloft with an engaging mix of rustic tables. No noisy games machines or background music. Uley Old Spot and Wadworths 6X and a couple of guest beers like Great Western Maiden Voyage and Timothy Taylors Landlord on handpump, 18 wines (and champagne and prosecco) by the glass, Weston's cider and 14 malt whiskies; staff are welcoming and helpful. A sheltered landscaped garden at the back has picnic-sets under umbrellas. Good disabled access and facilities.

The extremely popular 'two-in-one' pies (you can now buy them for home baking) come in a divided bowl, half of which contains the filling of your choice, with a pastry topping, and the other half home-made cauliflower cheese (or broccoli mornay or root vegetables); fillings include steak and mushroom, root vegetables with various pulses in a spicy tomato sauce, chicken, ham and leek in a creamy tarragon sauce, salmon in a creamy sauce, and turkey and trimmings. They also serve filled baguettes, thai-style mussels, sticky spare ribs, bangers with mustard mash and red onion gravy, ham and egg, cottage pie, a popular burger with cheese and bacon, and puddings like chocolate torte and bread and butter pudding with custard. *Benchmark main dish: 'two-in-one pie' £11.40. Two-course evening meal £18.00.*

Free house ~ Licensee Howard Parker ~ Real ale ~ Bar food (12-9.30) ~ Restaurant ~ (01453) 832520 ~ Children allowed away from the bars ~ Dogs welcome ~ Open 12-11(10.30 Sun) ~ www.2in1pub.co.uk *Recommended by Tom and Ruth Rees, Dr and Mrs C W Thomas, Howard Moorey, Mrs P Sumner, Jack and Sandra Clarfelt*

 NETHER WESTCOTE   SP2220 Map 4

Feathered Nest ★

Off A424 Burford–Stow-on-the-Wold; OX7 6SD

First rate service, happy atmosphere, attractive surroundings, good food and drink, nice bedrooms

We rather liked this place when we first knew it, as the New Inn and then the Westcote Inn, but since its refurbishment and reopening under new management in 2010 it's become really special. Service is top-notch – friendly and individual, making sure that everyone's enjoying themselves. The softly lit largely stripped-stone bar is a companionable place, with real saddles as bar stools (some of the country's best racehorse trainers live around here), a carved settle among other carefully chosen seats, dark flagstones and low beams. They have 25 wines by the glass from an impressive list, and a couple of guest beers on handpump as well as Hook Norton. The bar opens into an inner ochre-walled high-raftered room with deep, comfortable sofas by a vast log fire. Two attractively decorated dining rooms, both on two levels, have a pleasing mix of antique tables in varying sizes, but a lively, up-to-date atmosphere. A flagstoned terrace and heated shelter have teak tables and wicker armchairs, and a spreading lawn bounded by floodlit trees has groups of rustic seats, with the Evenlode Valley beyond. If you stay, you get a very good breakfast.

Prepared with good ingredients and real imagination (try their slow-cooked egg in a clever edible 'nest'), the food is beautifully presented: home-smoked mackerel and salmon terrine with gherkin caviar and sea purslane, pigeon salad with golden and ruby beetroot, watercress and hazelnuts, tagliatelle of vegetables with an orange and lavender dressing, croûton and seeds, sea bream with salt cod brandade, provençal vegetables, rouille and red papper sauce, suckling pig, pie, loin, head terrine and shoulder with quinoa, carrots and calvados sauce, a 14-oz T-bone veal steak with sage and lemon butter and sauté potatoes, and puddings such as chocolate and mint torte with caramelised custard and mint oil and blood orange and fennel soufflé; their two- and three-course set lunch menu is very fair value given the quality. They also serve afternoon teas on Friday and Saturday. *Benchmark main dish: suckling pig, pie, loin, head terrine and shoulder with calvados sauce £24.95. Two-course evening meal £32.00.*

Free house ~ Licensee Amanda Timmer ~ Real ale ~ Bar food (12-2.30, 6.30-9; 12-3.30 Sun; not Sun evening, not Mon) ~ Restaurant ~ (01993) 833030 ~ Children welcome ~ Dogs allowed in bar ~ Occasional live jazz ~ Open 11-11(9 Sun); closed Mon (except bank holidays) ~ Bedrooms: £90S(£105B)/£130(£180S)(£165B) ~ www.thefeatherednestinn.co.uk *Recommended by Richard Greaves, Christian Mole, Liz Bell*

Stars after the name of a pub show exceptional character and appeal.
They don't mean extra comfort. And they are nothing to do with food quality,
for which there's a separate knife-and-fork symbol. Even quite a basic pub
can win stars, if it's individual enough.

NEWLAND

SO5509   Map 4

Ostrich 🍴 🍷 🍺

Off B4228 in Coleford; or can be reached from the A466 in Redbrook, by turning off at the England–Wales border – keep bearing right; GL16 8NP

Liked by walkers and their dogs, with a friendly feel in spacious bar, great choice of beers, open fire, daily papers and smashing food

In a charmingly picturesque village close to the River Wye, this is a fine old pub with a warmly welcoming landlady; it's much enjoyed by walkers and their dogs. The atmosphere is chatty and relaxed and the low-ceilinged bar is spacious but cosily traditional with creaky floors, window shutters, candles in bottles on the tables, miners' lamps on the uneven walls and comfortable furnishings such as cushioned window seats, wall settles and rod-backed country-kitchen chairs. There's a big fireplace, newspapers to read, perhaps quiet background jazz, and board games. There are between four and eight real ales on handpump: Archers Best Bitter, Badger Bitter, Gales Seafarers, Greene King Abbot, Otter Bitter, RCH Pitchfork, Uley Pigs Ear and Wye Valley Butty Bach. They also have several wines by the glass and Old Rosie cider. The pub lurcher is called Alfie. There are picnic-sets in a walled garden behind and more out in front; the village church, known as the Cathedral of the Forest, is worth a visit.

 Interesting and highly thought of, the food might include potted prawns in coconut and chilli butter, chicken liver parfait topped with duck mousse with crab apple and sloe jelly, three-cheese tart with sun-dried tomatoes and basil, sausages with dauphinoise potatoes and onion gravy, smoked haddock baked in cream, egg and horseradish topped with mozzarella cheese and potatoes, steak in ale pie, sizzling pork ribs in tangy sauce, and puddings. *Benchmark main dish: steak in ale pie £11.00. Two-course evening meal £19.00.*

Free house ~ Licensee Kathryn Horton ~ Real ale ~ Bar food (12-2.30, 6.30(6 Sat)-9.30) ~ Restaurant ~ (01594) 833260 ~ Children welcome ~ Dogs welcome ~ Open 12-3, 6.30-11; 12-3, 6-midnight Sat; 12-4, 6.30-10.30 Sun ~ www.theostrichinn.com
Recommended by LM, M G Hart, Peter and Celia Gregory, Paul J Robinshaw, Christine Shewell, Tom and Ruth Rees, Carol Wilson

NORTH CERNEY

SP0208   Map 4

Bathurst Arms 🍷 🛏

A435 Cirencester–Cheltenham; GL7 7BZ

Bustling inn with beamed bar, open fires, fine wines, real ales and good food; comfortable bedrooms

The original beamed and panelled bar is the heart of this handsome, 17th-c inn, and there's always a good mix of both locals and visitors – and a friendly welcome for all. There's a fireplace at each end of the flagstoned room (one quite huge and housing an open woodburner), a good mix of old tables and nicely faded chairs and old-fashioned window seats. An oak-floored room off here has country tables, winged high-backed settles forming a few booths and background music; TV and board games. The restaurant has leather sofas and another woodburning stove. Hook Norton Hooky Bitter and guests like Box Steam Golden Bolt, Gloucester Mariner, Severn Vale Severn Bells, and a seasonal ale from Prescott on handpump and also a wine room where you can choose your own wines or one of the 20 by the glass; local soft drinks and juices, too. The pleasant riverside garden has picnic-sets sheltered by trees and shrubs, and plenty of surrounding walks. Cerney House Gardens are worth a visit.

🍴 As well as lunchtime filled baguettes, the enjoyable food might include ham hock terrine with home-made chutney, black-peppered mackerel with asian slaw and ginger dressing, chargrilled burger with cheese and bacon, beer-battered cod with home-made tartare sauce, caramelised red onion and brie tart, roasted salmon fillet with parsley mash, brown shrimps and a fish velouté, duck with puy lentil casserole, roasted salsify and cherry jus, and puddings such as warm chocolate fudge cake with chocolate sauce and toasted cardamom cheesecake with vanilla-poached apricots and berries. *Benchmark main dish: old spot pork belly with mustard and cider sauce, five bean casserole and parsnip crisps £15.00. Two-course evening meal £18.50.*

Free house ~ Licensee James Walker ~ Real ale ~ Bar food (12-2(2.30 Fri and Sat), 6-9(9.30 Fri and Sat); 12-2.30, 6-9 Sun) ~ Restaurant ~ (01285) 831281 ~ Children welcome ~ Dogs allowed in bar and bedrooms ~ Open 12-11 ~ Bedrooms: £65B/£85B ~ www.bathurstarms.com *Recommended by E McCall, T McLean, D Irving, Guy Vowles, Andy and Claire Barker, David Gunn, Comus and Sarah Elliott, Brian and Carol Gold, Tom and Ruth Rees*

🏡 NORTHLEACH   SP1114   Map 4

Wheatsheaf 🍴 ⍭ 🛏

West End; the inn is on your left as you come in following the sign off A429, just SW of its junction with A40; GL54 3EZ

17th-c stone inn with contemporary food, real ales, candles and fresh flowers, and a relaxed atmosphere; stylish bedrooms

In a lovely little Cotswold town with a fine old market square, this is a smart and handsome former coaching inn. The big-windowed, airy linked rooms have high ceilings, antique and contemporary artwork, church candles and fresh flowers, an attractive mix of dining chairs and stools around wooden tables, flagstones in the central bar, wooden floors in the airy dining rooms and three open fires. Bath Ales Barnstormer and Gem Bitter, Fullers London Pride and Severn Vale Session on handpump, several wines by the glass from a fantastic list of around 300 and local cider. There are seats in the pretty back garden, and they can arrange fishing on the River Coln. If you are staying, the breakfasts are excellent. Dogs are genuinely welcomed and they even keep a jar of pigs' ears behind the bar for them.

🍴 Highly thought of food might include devilled kidneys, smoked haddock chowder with a poached egg, soft herb polenta with jerusalem artichokes, wild mushrooms and parmesan, beer-battered whiting with frites, pasta with braised hare, red wine and root vegetables, chicken and mushroom pie, venison sausages with creamed lentils and salsa verde, bass with braised snails, herb gnocchi and chorizo, and puddings such as pear and almond tart with crème fraîche and popcorn, pecan and salted caramel sundae. *Benchmark main dish: calves liver with bacon, sherry, shallots and mash £12.00. Two-course evening meal £21.00.*

Free house ~ Licensees Sam and Georgina Pearman ~ Real ale ~ Bar food (12-3, 6-10(10.30 Sat; 9.30 Sun); afternoon tea 4-6 daily) ~ Restaurant ~ (01451) 860244 ~ Children welcome ~ Dogs welcome ~ Summer parties and monthly quiz ~ Open 12-midnight ~ Bedrooms: /£130B ~ www.cotswoldswheatsheaf.com *Recommended by Richard Tilbrook, Peter Smith and Judith Brown, Guy Vowles, Andy and Claire Barker, R and S Bentley, Susan Lang, Graham Oddey, Martin and Pauline Jennings*

OLDBURY-ON-SEVERN

ST6092   Map 2

Anchor ♀ ◀ £

Village signposted from B4061; BS35 1QA

Friendly country pub with tasty bar food, a fine choice of drinks and a pretty garden with hanging baskets

Always deservedly busy with a good mix of drinkers and diners, this is an enjoyable pub with friendly, cheerful staff. The neatly kept lounge has a big winter log fire, modern beams and stonework, a variety of tables including an attractive oval oak gateleg, cushioned window seats, winged seats against the wall and oil paintings by a local artist. The bar has old photographs and farming and fishing bric-a-brac on the walls. Diners can eat in the lounge or bar area or in the dining room at the back (good for larger groups); the menu is the same in all rooms. Bass, Butcombe Bitter, Otter Bitter and a changing guest like Great Western Maiden Voyage on handpump well priced for the area; 85 malt whiskies (the tasting notes are really helpful) and a dozen wines by the glass. In summer, you can eat outside in the pretty garden, whose hanging baskets and window boxes are lovely; boules. They have wheelchair access and a disabled lavatory. Plenty of walks to the River Severn and along the many footpaths and bridleways, and St Arilda's church nearby is interesting on its odd little knoll with wildflowers among the gravestones (the primroses and daffodils in spring are quite a show).

 As well as their good value set two- and three-course menu (not Sunday), the well liked food includes ciabatta sandwiches, queenie scallops with garlic oil and gruyère, warm goats cheese and chorizo salad, herb pancakes filled with goats cheese, spinach and pine nuts with a mustard and cheese sauce, smoked haddock and salmon fish pie, chicken in mushroom and brandy sauce, lamb rump with rösti potato and red wine jus, and puddings such as chocolate tart and crème brûlée with home-made shortbread. *Benchmark main dish: beef in ale pie £9.95. Two-course evening meal £16.00.*

Free house ~ Licensees Michael Dowdeswell and Mark Sorrell ~ Real ale ~ Bar food (12-2(2.30 Sat, 3 Sun), 6-9) ~ Restaurant ~ (01454) 413331 ~ Children in dining room only ~ Dogs allowed in bar ~ Open 11.30-3, 6-11; 11-midnight Sat; 12-11 Sun ~ www.anchorinnoldbury.co.uk *Recommended by Charles and Pauline Stride, Jim and Frances Gowers, Richard and Judy Winn, Dr and Mrs C W Thomas, Chris and Angela Buckell, James Morrell, Roger and Donna Huggins*

SAPPERTON

SO9403   Map 4

Bell ⊕♀ ◀

Village signposted from A419 Stroud–Cirencester; OS Sheet 163 map reference 948033; GL7 6LE

Super pub with beamed cosy rooms, a really good mix of customers, delicious food, local ales, and a very pretty outside dining areas

'A treasure – we love it,' says one of our enthusiastic readers – and many agree with her. It's a fine old pub with a good mix of both locals and visitors, and the hands-on, hard-working licensees continue to tweak things here and there to keep it all running as smoothly as ever. Harry's Bar has big cushion-strewn sofas, benches and armchairs where you can read the daily papers with a pint in front of the woodburning stove – or simply have a pre-dinner drink. The two other cosy rooms have beams, a nice mix of wooden tables and chairs, country prints and modern art on stripped-stone walls, one or two attractive rugs on the flagstones, fresh flowers and open fires. Bath Ales Gem, Otter Bitter, St Austell Tribute and Uley Old Spot on handpump, 22 wines by the glass and carafe from a large and diverse wine list (with very helpful notes; they now have more organic and bio dynamic wines), 20 malt whiskies, farm cider and local soft drinks. The gents' has schoolboy-humour cartoons on the walls. Their young springer spaniel is called William and welcomes other dogs (who get their own little bowl of goodies). There are armchairs and tables out on a small front terrace, with more in a mediterranean-style back courtyard garden with an olive tree, herb-filled pots and a colourful, heated loggia. Horses have their own tethering rail (and bucket of water) and there are plenty of surrounding hacking trails and walks.

As well as their new and very popular two- and three-course set meals (Monday-Thursday), the imaginative food, using rare-breed meat and the best locally sourced produce, might include lunchtime sandwiches, potted crab, pressed ham hock with soft herbs and home-made piccalilli, home-cooked ham with eggs and beef dripping chips, potato risotto with blue cheese and pea shoots, chicken with confit tomato, field mushrooms and garlic butter, crisp breaded flounder fillets with chive aioli and lemon, duckling with honey-roasted vegetables and a red wine jus, and puddings such as chocolate marquise with chantilly cream and pecan pie with banana and peanut butter ice-cream. *Benchmark main dish: home-made burger £13.65. Two-course evening meal £21.00.*

Free house ~ Licensees Paul Davidson and Pat LeJeune ~ Real ale ~ Bar food (12-2.15(2.30 Sun), 7-9.30(9 Sun)) ~ (01285) 760298 ~ Children allowed but must be over 10 in evening ~ Dogs welcome ~ Open 11-3, 6.30-11; 12-10.30 Sun; closed Sun evenings in Jan and Feb ~ www.foodatthebell.co.uk *Recommended by Mike Buckingham, Peter and Audrey Dowsett, R and S Bentley, Neil and Anita Christopher, Jennifer and Patrick O'Dell, Bernard Stradling, Mrs P Bishop, Jack and Sandra Clarfelt, Mrs P Sumner, Betsy and Peter Little*

SHEEPSCOMBE   SO8910   Map 4

Butchers Arms

Village signed off B4070 NE of Stroud; or A46 N of Painswick (but narrow lanes); GL6 7RH

Bustling country pub with enjoyable bar food, real ales, friendly young licensees and fine views

This is the sort of friendly, relaxed pub where a wide mix of customers mingle happily in the chatty atmosphere. The bustling lounge bar has beams, wheelback chairs, cushioned stools and other comfortable seats around simple wooden tables, built-in cushioned seats in the big bay windows, interesting oddments like assorted blow lamps, irons and plates, and a woodburning stove. The restaurant has an open log fire. Butcombe Rare Breed, Otter Bitter and a guest like Wye Valley Butty Bach on handpump, several wines by the glass and Weston's cider or perry; darts, chess, cribbage and draughts. The view over the lovely steep beechwood valley is terrific and there are seats outside to make the most of it. It's thought that this area was once a royal hunting ground for Henry VIII. Walkers and cyclists can pre-book their food orders.

Using as much local produce as possible, the reliably good food might include lunchtime sandwiches, baked camembert with pickles and relishes (for two to share), salmon, cod, lemon and dill fishcakes, pork, ale and sage sausages with honey-roast parsnips and cranberry and port gravy, mushroom and sun-dried tomato risotto, tuna loin on black olive mash with a caper and prawn butter, chicken stuffed with apricots and thyme with toasted cashews and plum chutney, and puddings; they also offer a pie and pint deal (weekday lunchtimes and Sunday-Friday evenings). *Benchmark main dish: home-made burger with lots of toppings £8.95. Two-course evening meal £15.30.*

Free house ~ Licensees Mark and Sharon Tallents ~ Real ale ~ Bar food (12-2.30, 6.30-9.30; all day weekends; no food after 6pm Sun Jan-Feb) ~ Restaurant ~ (01452) 812113 ~ Children welcome ~ Dogs allowed in bar ~ Open 11.30-3, 6.30-11; 11.30-11.30 Sat; 12-10.30 Sun ~ www.butchers-arms.co.uk *Recommended by Ken and Barbara Turner, Mike and Mary Carter, Sue Wilson Roberts, Mr and Mrs W Mills*

 SOUTHROP   SP2003   Map 4

Swan

Off A361 Lechlade–Burford; GL7 3NU

Pretty 17-c pub with proper village bar, two dining rooms, imaginative food and a fine choice of drinks

The first class food in this 17th-c creeper-covered inn is extremely highly thought of by our readers, and you can be sure of a warm welcome, too. The chatty public bar is very much for those wanting a pint and a natter: it's got stools against the counter, simple tables and chairs, Hook Norton Hooky Bitter, Sharps Doom Bar and a beer named for the pub on handpump, 16 wines by the glass from a carefully chosen list and daily non-alcoholic cocktails. The low-ceilinged front dining rooms have open fires, all manner of leather dining chairs around a nice mix of old tables, cushions on settles, rugs on flagstones, nightlights, candles and lots of fresh flowers. There's a skittle alley and tables in the sheltered back garden. They have self-catering cottages to let.

Particularly good and using local, seasonal produce, the inventive food might include sandwiches, a skillet of foie gras and fried egg with brioche and balsamic reduction, crab, grapefruit, avocado and pumpkin seed salad, moules marinière, beef burger with fries, honey-roast ham with free range eggs and mustard sauce, lamb, barley and leek pie with caramelised vegetables, brochette of tiger prawns and Loch Duart salmon with oriental vegetables, spaghetti and a sweet chilli dip, braised shin of beef with horseradish dumplings, carrots and chestnuts, and puddings like baked alaska and chocolate fondant with malt and Baileys ice-cream. *Benchmark main dish: slow-roast pork belly £16.00. Two-course evening meal £23.50.*

Free house ~ Licensees Sebastian and Lana Snow ~ Real ale ~ Bar food (12-3, 6-10; not Sun evening) ~ Restaurant ~ (01367) 850205 ~ Children welcome ~ Dogs welcome ~ Open 12-3, 6-11; 12-11 Sat; 12-3 Sun; closed Sun evenings ~ www.theswanatsouthrop.co.uk *Recommended by Guy Vowles, Graham Oddey, Stephanie Gray, Alan Bulley, Bernard Stradling, Elizabeth Stedman, Mr and Mrs A H Young, Richard Tilbrook*

 TETBURY   ST8494   Map 4

Gumstool

Part of Calcot Manor Hotel; A4135 W of town, just E of junction with A46; GL8 8YJ

Civilised bar with relaxed atmosphere, super choice of drinks and enjoyable food

By no stretch of the imagination is this a proper pub – it's attached to the very smart Calcot Manor Hotel – but they do keep up to four real ales on handpump and as a bar/brasserie it has an informal and relaxed atmosphere; our readers enjoy their visits very much. The stylish space is well divided to give a feeling of intimacy without losing the overall sense of contented bustle: flagstones, elegant wooden dining chairs and tables, well chosen pictures and drawings on mushroom-coloured walls, and leather tub armchairs and stools in front of the big log fire. Butcombe Bitter, Blond, Gold and maybe Rare Breed, lots of interesting wines by the glass and quite a few malt whiskies; background music. Westonbirt Arboretum is not far away.

🍴 Prices are reasonable for such a civilised setting and the food is excellent: sandwiches, devilled lambs kidneys, eggs benedict, a charcuterie platter, cornish crab and leek tart, steak and kidney pudding, confit free-range chicken with dauphinoise potatoes, bread sauce and bacon, lamb hot pot with pickled red cabbage, specials like moules marinière, spinach and ricotta ravioli and bass with caponata, and puddings such as chocolate and cherry cake with crème fraîche and vanilla and clementine panna cotta. *Benchmark main dish: chargrilled aged scottish sirloin steak £18.75. Two-course evening meal £22.50.*

Free house ~ Licensees Paul Sadler and Richard Ball ~ Real ale ~ Bar food (12-2.30(4 Sun), 5.30-9.30(9 Sun)) ~ (01666) 890391 ~ Children welcome ~ Open 10am-11pm(10.30 Sun) ~ Bedrooms: £248B/£275B ~ www.calcotmanor.co.uk
Recommended by Roger and Donna Huggins, Dr and Mrs C W Thomas, Mrs P Sumner, Bernard Stradling, Mr and Mrs P R Thomas, Rod Stoneman, Gordon and Margaret Ormondroyd, Graham Lovis, Tom and Ruth Rees

UPPER ODDINGTON   SP2225   Map 4

Horse & Groom 🍴 ♀

Village signposted from A436 E of Stow-on-the-Wold; GL56 0XH

Pretty 16th-c Cotswold inn with imaginative food, lots of wines by the glass, local beers and other local drinks and comfortable, characterful bars; lovely bedrooms

We get enthusiastic reports on every aspect of this particularly well run and attractive stone pub. It's a lovely place to stay (and the breakfasts are very good), there's a fine choice of wines by the glass and well kept real ales, the food is first class and Mr Jackson is genuinely welcoming and helpful landlord. The bar has pale polished flagstones, a handsome antique oak box settle among other more modern seats, some nice armchairs at one end, oak beams in the ochre ceiling, stripped-stone walls and a log fire in the inglenook fireplace; the comfortable lounge is similarly furnished. Box Steam Piston Broke, Prescott Hill Climb and Wye Valley Bitter on handpump, 25 wines (including champagne and sweet wines) by the glass, 20 malt whiskies, local apple juice and elderflower pressé, and cider and lager brewed by Cotswold. There are seats and tables under green parasols on the terrace and in the pretty garden.

🍴 Making their own bread, pickles and chutneys and using the best local produce, the enticing food might include sandwiches, home-smoked duck breast salad with red wine marinated beetroot and orange syrup, warm potato pancake with smoked salmon, chive crème fraîche and avruga caviar, goats cheese and red onion tart with tapenade dressing, kedgeree and spinach risotto with parsley cream and a poached egg, gloucester old spot sausages with chive mash and red onion marmalade, daily specials such as potted trout pâté with lemon mayonnaise and paprika flatbread, duck breast with ginger and rhubarb sauce and shin of beef with spring onion mash and tarragon-glazed chantennay carrots, and puddings like triple chocolate tart with raspberry sorbet and vanilla crème anglaise and sticky date pudding with butterscotch sauce. *Benchmark main dish: pie of the day £12.50. Two-course evening meal £21.00.*

Free house ~ Licensees Simon and Sally Jackson ~ Real ale ~ Bar food (12-2, 6.30 (7 Sun)-9) ~ Restaurant ~ (01451) 830584 ~ Children welcome ~ Dogs allowed in bar ~ Open 12-3, 5.30-11; 12-3, 6-10.30 Sun ~ Bedrooms: £79S/£99S(£105B) ~ www.horseandgroom.uk.com *Recommended by Richard Greaves, K H Frostick, Michael Doswell, Bernard Stradling, Simon and Polly Alvin, Andy and Jill Kassube, Ian Wilson, M G Hart*

Also Worth a Visit in Gloucestershire

Besides the fully inspected pubs, you might like to try these pubs that have been recommended to us and described by readers. Do tell us what you think of them: feedback@goodguides.com

ALDERTON SP9933
Gardeners Arms (01242) 620257
Beckford Road, off B4077 Tewkesbury–Stow; GL20 8NL Attractive thatched Tudor pub, well kept Greene King and guests, decent wines by the glass, good choice of food from bar snacks up including lunchtime/early evening deal, breakfast from 9am, hospitable landlady and good service, informal restaurant, log fire; may be background music; children welcome, dogs in some areas, tables on sheltered terrace, good-sized well kept garden with boules. *(Dr A J and Mrs Tompsett, Paul and Claudia Dickinson)*

ALDSWORTH SP1510
Sherborne Arms (01451) 844346
B4425 Burford–Cirencester; GL54 3RB Family-run pub with good choice of enjoyable food (not Sun evening, Mon), three real ales, farm cider, beams, stripped stone and log fire, smallish bar and big dining area, conservatory, games/function room; background music; children and dogs welcome, disabled access, pleasant front garden with smokers' shelter, closed Sun evening, Mon lunchtime. *(Helene Grygar)*

AMBERLEY SO8401
Amberley Inn (01453) 872565
Steeply off A46 Stroud–Nailsworth - gentler approach from N Nailsworth; GL5 5AF Old stone inn with two comfortable bars and a snug, well kept Stroud and Uley ales, enjoyable food including bargain OAP Mon roast, friendly helpful staff, beautiful views; children and dogs welcome, side terrace and back garden, good local walks, 11 comfortable bedrooms. *(Neil and Anita Christopher)*

AMBERLEY SO8401
Black Horse (01453) 872556
Off A46 Stroud–Nailsworth to Amberley; left after Amberley Inn, left at war memorial; Littleworth; best to park by war memorial and walk down;

GL5 5AL Relaxed local with spectacular valley views from conservatory and terrace, enjoyable varied food from baguettes to specials, friendly helpful young staff (can be a wait for food though), changing ales, wood and flagstone floors, high-backed settles, woodburner, cheerful sporting pictures, brasses and bells, large family area, games room, live music; they keep your credit card in a locked box if running a tab, big TV; walkers and wet dogs welcome, plenty of tables outside, barbecues. *(Guy Vowles, Neil and Anita Christopher, Pete Flower, Jenny, Paul Goldman)*

AMPNEY CRUCIS SP0701
Crown of Crucis (01285) 851806
A417 E of Cirencester; GL7 5RS Refurbished roadside inn with spacious split-level bar, beams and log fires, good choice of food all day and well kept ales including one brewed for them by Wickwar, decent house wines, efficient service; children and dogs welcome, disabled facilities, lots of tables out on grass by car park, quiet modern bedrooms around courtyard, good breakfast, cricket pitch over stream, open all day. *(Jennifer and Patrick O'Dell, Giles and Annie Francis, Neil and Anita Christopher)*

AMPNEY ST PETER SP0801
☆**Red Lion** (01285) 851596
A417, E of village; GL7 5SL This unspoilt and unchanging country pub has long been a monument to traditional hospitality under its welcoming veteran landlord - only the third in over a century; just two simple chatty little rooms, log fires, well kept Timothy Taylors Landlord and Golden Best and maybe Hook Norton from the hatch, no food, outside lavatories; currently open evenings Fri, Sat and Mon plus Sun lunchtime. *(E McCall, T McLean, D Irving, Michael Hovard, Peter and Giff Bennett, the Didler)*

ANDOVERSFORD SP0219
Royal Oak (01242) 820335
Sgned just off A40; Gloucester Road; GL54 4HR Cosy and attractive beamed

---

Post Office address codings confusingly give the impression that some pubs are in Gloucestershire, when they're really in Warwickshire (which is where we list them).

village pub, lots of stripped stone, nice galleried raised dining room beyond big central open fire, well kept ales including Otter, friendly staff; tables in garden. *(Neil and Anita Christopher)*

ASHLEWORTH QUAY SO8125

✳ **Boat** (01452) 700272

Ashleworth signposted off A417 N of Gloucester; quay signed from village; GL19 4HZ Now run by a tenant though early feedback suggests no changes - reports please; unpretentious tiny alehouse with unique character, little front parlour with built-in settle by scrubbed-deal table, old-fashioned open kitchen range, elderly fireside chairs, rush mats on flagstones, maybe old magazines to read, cribbage and dominoes, back room with two antique settles facing each other, Church End, Otley, RCH, Stonehenge and Wye Valley tapped from casks, along with Weston's ciders, lunchtime rolls; no credit cards; children welcome, sunny crazy-paved front courtyard, more seats at side of building, closed Mon and Weds. *(Ken and Barbara Turner, MLR, Theocsbrian, the Didler)*

AUST ST5788

Boars Head (01454) 632278

0.5 miles from M48 junction 1, off Avonmouth Road; BS35 4AX Marstons pub handy for the 'old' Severn bridge, their ales and Bath Gem, good house wines, decent choice of well priced food from good sandwiches up including weekday deals, friendly service, linked rooms and alcoves, beams and some stripped stone, huge log fire; background music; wheelchair access possible, children in eating area away from bar, dogs on the lead in bar, pretty sheltered garden. *(Barry and Anne, Jim and Frances Gowers, Roger and Donna Huggins)*

BIBURY SP1006

Catherine Wheel (01285) 740250

Arlington; B4425 NE of Cirencester; GL7 5ND Bright cheerful dining pub, enjoyable fresh food from sandwiches up including good value weekday set lunch, well kept ales such as Hook Norton, Sharps and Wickwar, friendly attentive service, open-plan main bar and smaller back rooms, low beams, stripped stone, log fires, raftered dining room; children welcome, picnic-sets out behind in good-sized garden, famously beautiful village, handy for country and riverside walks, four bedrooms. *(Guy Vowles, R K Phillips, Bernard Stradling, Neil and Anita Christopher, George Atkinson)*

BIRDLIP SO9316

Air Balloon (01452) 862541

A417/A436 roundabout; GL4 8JY Loftily placed busy chain dining pub, good range of food from sandwiches, wraps and baguettes up all day, meal deals, friendly helpful service, changing ales such as Hook Norton

Old Hooky, good wine and soft drinks choice, many levels and alcoves including restaurant and brasserie, pubbier front corner with open fire, beams and stripped stone; unobtrusive background music; tables, some covered, on heated terrace and in garden with play area, open all day. *(Neil and Anita Christopher)*

BISLEY SO9006

✳ **Bear** (01452) 770265

Village signed off A419 E of Stroud; GL6 7BD Elegantly gothic 16th-c inn with bustling L-shaped bar, old oak settles, brass and copper implements around extremely wide stone fireplace, low ochre ceiling, well kept ales such as St Austell, Tetleys and Wells & Youngs, enjoyable pubby food, friendly staff, separate stripped-stone family area; dogs welcome, small flagstoned courtyard, stone mounting blocks in garden across quiet road, bedrooms, open all day Sun. *(Neil and Anita Christopher, Derek Hunt, Roger Smith)*

BISLEY SO9006

Stirrup Cup (01452) 770280

Cheltenham Road; GL6 7BL Spacious opened-up local with roaring fire and friendly welcome, two or three well kept ales such as Sharps Doom Bar and Wickwar, Weston's cider, uncomplicated generous food at reasonable prices (regular special offers including OAP discount weekday lunchtime), themed evenings, good service; walkers and dogs welcome, interesting village. *(Guy Vowles, Neil and Anita Christopher)*

BLOCKLEY SP1635

Great Western Arms

(01386) 700362 *Station Road (B4479); GL56 9DT* Nicely updated beamed pub doing well under new landlady, well kept Hook Norton ales and decent wines by the glass, enjoyable good value home-made food, dining room and public bar (dogs welcome here) with darts and TV; terrace seating, lovely valley view, attractive village, closed Mon lunchtime. *(B M Eldridge, Paul Humphreys)*

BOURTON-ON-THE-WATER SP1620

Old Manse (01451) 820082

Victoria Street; GL54 2BX River Windrush view from front garden and end of long beamed bar, good choice of enjoyable food from all-day sandwiches up, friendly young staff, Greene King ales, mixed furniture on carpet or boards, big log fire, attractive old prints, bookshelves, some stripped stone, pretty restaurant (children allowed here); soft background music, TV; 15 good bedrooms. *(Ann Gray)*

BOX SO8500

✳ **Halfway House** (01453) 832631

By Minchinhampton Common; GL6 9AE 300-year-old dining pub with light airy open-plan areas around central servery, simple sturdy furniture on stripped-wood floors, downstairs restaurant, food from traditional favourites to more imaginative specials, ales such as Butcombe, Sharps and Wickwar, decent wines by the glass, friendly efficient young staff; background and some live music; children and dogs welcome, seats in landscaped garden, open all day Fri-Sun, closed Mon lunchtime. *(Tom and Ruth Rees, Richard Tilbrook)*

BRIMPSFIELD   SO9413
Golden Heart (01242) 870261
Nettleton Bottom (not shown on road maps, so we list the pub instead under the name of the nearby village); on A417 N of the Brimpsfield turning northbound; GL4 8LA Traditional inn with low-ceilinged bar divided into five cosy areas, log fire in huge inglenook, well worn built-in settles and other old-fashioned furnishings, exposed stone walls and wood panelling, brass items, typewriters and banknotes, parlour on right with decorative fireplace leading into further room, well kept Brakspears, Jennings, Otter and Ringwood, several wines by glass, popular food from fairly extensive menu, friendly attentive staff; children and dogs welcome, seats and tables on suntrap terrace with pleasant valley views, nearby walks, bedrooms, open all day weekends and school holidays. *(Prof H G Allen, Tom and Ruth Rees, Andy and Claire Barker, Guy Vowles, Graham Oddey, Jeremy King and others)*

BROADOAK   SO6912
White Hart (01594) 516319
A48 Gloucester–Chepstow; GL14 1JB Overlooking tidal Severn, plenty of tables out on high terrace by quay, enjoyable sensibly priced pubby food from sandwiches up, Greene King ales, friendly staff, carpeted bar and dining area, low beams, nautical décor; background music; children and dogs welcome, wheelchair access. *(Dr A Y Drummond)*

BROADWELL   SP2027
★ Fox (01451) 870909
Off A429 2 miles N of Stow-on-the-Wold; GL56 0UF Golden stone pub above broad village green, traditional furnishings on flagstones in log-fire bar, stripped-stone walls, jugs hanging from beams, Donnington BB and SBA, lots of rums, winter mulled wine, honest pubby food (not Sun evening) served by friendly staff, two carpeted dining areas, maybe George the cat; background music, darts, board games; children welcome, dogs allowed in bar, picnic-sets on gravel in sizeable family-friendly back garden, paddock with horse called Herman. *(Andy Dolan, Eddie Edwards, Alun and Jennifer Evans, John and Sarah Webb)*

CAMBRIDGE   SO7403
George (01453) 890270
3 miles from M5 junction 13–A38 towards Bristol; GL2 7AL Brick-built roadside pub with opened-up linked areas,

pubby furniture, some cushioned pews and window seats, lots of bric-a-brac, two woodburners back-to-back, contrasting modern restaurant with light wood-strip floor, enjoyable sensibly priced food from baguettes and pub favourites to grills and specials, well kept Fullers, Wickwar and Moles, Thatcher's cider, helpful well organised service; background music, no dogs inside; children welcome, picnic-sets in fenced streamside garden with play area, one bedroom, pleasant campsite, handy for Slimbridge wildfowl centre, open all day from 8am for breakfast. *(Steve and Liz Tilley, Chris and Angela Buckell)*

CAMP   SO9111
★ Fostons Ash (01452) 863262
B4070 Birdlip–Stroud, junction with Calf Way; GL6 7ES Popular open-plan dining pub, light and airy, with good food including interesting lunchtime sandwiches and imaginative light dishes, real ales such as Goffs, Greene King and Stroud, decent wines by the glass, neat welcoming staff, daily newspapers, one end with easy chairs and woodburner; background music; rustic tables in attractive garden with heated terrace and play area, good walks. *(Neil and Anita Christopher, Guy Vowles)*

CERNEY WICK   SU0796
Crown (01793) 750369
Village signed from A419; GL7 5QH Friendly old village inn with roomy modern lounge bar and comfortable conservatory dining extension, popular inexpensive food, well kept Wadworths 6X, Wells & Youngs Bombardier and a guest, good service, coal-effect gas fires, games in public bar; children welcome, good-sized garden with swings, ten bedrooms in motel-style extension. *(Ian Herdman, Neil and Anita Christopher)*

CHARLTON KINGS   SO9620
Royal George (01242) 228937
Horsefair, opposite church; GL53 8JH Big 19th-c pub with clean modern décor including new dining conservatory, good real ale and food choice, prompt service; children and dogs welcome, picnic-sets in garden overlooking church, open all day (no food Sun evening). *(Guy Vowles)*

CHELTENHAM   SO9422
Beehive (01242) 579443
Montpellier Villas; GL50 2XE Welcoming down-to-earth bare-boards pub with good atmosphere, open fire, two or three real ales and a couple of proper ciders, interesting wines, popular food in bar and upstairs restaurant; back courtyard. *(John Clancy, Guy Vowles)*

CHELTENHAM   SO9421
Jolly Brewmaster (01242) 512176
Painswick Road; GL50 2EZ Popular lively local with open-plan linked areas around big

semicircular counter, fine range of changing ales and farm ciders, perhaps a perry, friendly obliging young staff, newspapers, log fires; dogs welcome, coachyard tables, open all day. *(Theocsbrian)*

CHELTENHAM   SO9624

⋆ **Plough** (01242) 222180

Mill Street, Prestbury; GL52 3BG
Thatched village local opposite church, comfortable front lounge, service from corner corridor hatch in flagstoned back tap room, grandfather clock and big log fire, well kept Adnams Broadside, Wells & Youngs Bombardier and three guests tapped from the cask, real ciders and perry, good traditional home-made food including blackboard specials; lovely big flower-filled back garden (dogs on leads), some summer weekend barbecues, immaculate boules pitch, open all day. *(B M Eldridge, Ian and Jane Irving)*

CHELTENHAM   SO9321
Royal Union (01242) 224686

Hatherley Street; GL50 2TT Backstreet local with large bar and cosy snug up steps, half a dozen well kept ales, reasonably priced wines, enjoyable good value food - landlord cooks nice steaks, skittle alley; courtyard behind, open all day. *(Guy Vowles)*

CHELTENHAM   SO9421
Tivoli (01242) 285799

Andover Road; GL50 2TJ Recently refurbished bar/restaurant, stylish and comfortable, with spacious eating areas on two floors, good food including fixed price menu, good value house wine, ales such as Bath, Otter and St Austell, friendly efficient staff; children welcome, open all day. *(Mrs Jo Rees)*

CHIPPING CAMPDEN   SP1539

⋆ **Kings** (01386) 840256

High Street; GL55 6AW Fresh eclectic décor in 18th-c hotel's bar/brasserie and separate restaurant, cheery helpful service, good food from lunchtime sandwiches and baguettes to pubby dishes and more elaborate meals, well kept Hook Norton and a guest, good choice of wines by the glass, decent coffee, nice log fire, daily newspapers; secluded back garden with picnic-sets and terrace tables, 12 comfortable bedrooms, open all day Sat. *(Peter Dandy, Eithne Dandy, Ryta Lyndley)*

CHIPPING CAMPDEN   SP1539

⋆ **Lygon Arms** (01386) 840318

High Street; GL55 6HB Low-beamed bar in 16th-c coaching inn, ales such as Hook Norton, Wadworths and Wye Valley, generous traditional food including daily roasts, good service, new furniture on stone floor, stripped-stone walls and open fires, small back restaurant; children welcome, tables in shady cobbled courtyard, comfortable

beamed bedrooms, good breakfast, open all day weekends and summer. *(Anon)*

CHIPPING CAMPDEN   SP1539
Noel Arms (01386) 840317

High Street; GL55 6AT Handsome 16th-c inn with refurbished beamed and stripped-stone bar, modern furniture, open fire, decent food from sandwiches to steaks, some good curries too from sri lanken chef, Hook Norton and local guests, good choice of wines by the glass, coffee bar (from 9am), conservatory, restaurant; children and dogs welcome, sunny courtyard tables, 27 well appointed bedrooms, good breakfast, open all day. *(Eleanor Dandy, Eithne Dandy)*

CIRENCESTER   SP0202
Fleece (01285) 658507

Market Place; GL7 2NZ Civilised comfortable old hotel with good value enterprising food, friendly effective largely hispanic staff, good choice of wines by the glass, well kept Hook Norton and a guest beer, bay window looking up market place to parish church, roomy lounge and restaurant; terrace tables, bedrooms. *(Comus and Sarah Elliott)*

CIRENCESTER   SP0201
Waggon & Horses (01285) 652022

London Road; GL7 2PU 18th-c stone-built coaching inn with modernised bar and restaurant, six well kept changing ales, Thatcher's cider and good choice of malt whiskies, nice thai food, log fires; closed Sun, otherwise open all day. *(Russell Blackaller, Roger and Donna Huggins)*

COBERLEY   SO9616
Seven Springs (01242) 870219

Andoversford, just SW of junction with A435 Cheltenham–Cirencester; GL53 9NG Spacious and airy Hungry Horse family dining pub, big helpings of competitively priced straightforward food, Greene King IPA, pleasant efficient service, very high ceiling, big windows, snugger side areas; background music; decking and sloping pond-side garden. *(Neil and Anita Christopher)*

COOMBE HILL   SO8827
Swan (01242) 680227

A38/A4019; GL19 4BA Light airy dining pub with several rooms, popular generous fresh food from sandwiches up including deals, good friendly service, ales such as Battledown, Butcombe and Goffs, decent house wine, polished boards and panelling, red leather sofas; background music; large garden and own vineyard, nature reserve nearby, open all day Sun till 9pm. *(John and Gloria Isaacs, Dave Braisted)*

CRANHAM   SO8912

⋆ **Black Horse** (01452) 812217

Village signposted off A46 and B4070 N of Stroud; GL4 8HP Popular down-to-earth 17th-c local, cosy lounge, main bar with traditional furniture, window seats and log fire, well kept Hancocks HB, Sharps Doom Bar and a guest, real ciders, home-made blackboard food (not Sun evening - pub open from 8.30pm then), two upstairs dining rooms (one with log fire); well behaved children and dogs welcome, tables out in front and to the side, good country views and walks, closed Mon. *(Andy and Claire Barker, Neil and Anita Christopher, Guy Vowles)*

DOYNTON
ST7174

⋆ **Cross House** (0117) 937 2261

High Street; signed off A420 Bristol–Chippenham E of Wick; BS30 5TF
Easy-going 18th-c village pub near fine walking country and Dyrham Park, convivial landlord and staff, honest reasonably priced food, Bass, Bath, Courage, Sharps and Timothy Taylors, around 18 wines by the glass, softly lit carpeted bar with beams, some stripped stone, simple pub furniture and woodburner, cottagey candlelit dining room; background music, games machine, TV; children welcome, dogs in bar, picnic-sets out by the road, open all day Sun. *(Jim and Frances Gowers, Colin and Peggy Wilshire, Dr and Mrs C W Thomas, Paul Humphreys, Mr and Mrs P R Thomas and others)*

DUNTISBOURNE ABBOTS
SO9709

⋆ **Five Mile House** (01285) 821432

E of A417 on parallel old Main Road; GL7 7JR Cheerful father and son team at this characterful village pub, nice old traditional rooms, roaring fire, three well kept changing ales tapped from the cask, but sadly no longer serving food; newspapers, darts and cribbage; children and dogs welcome, garden with nice views, closed lunchtimes Mon-Thurs, currently up for sale. *(Guy Vowles, Andy and Claire Barker, Neil and Anita Christopher, Jennifer and Patrick O'Dell, R K Phillips, the Didler and others)*

DYMOCK
SO6931

Beauchamp Arms (01531) 890266

B4215; GL18 2AQ Friendly parish-owned pub with good licensees, well kept ales such as Brakspears, good value home-made pubby food (not Sun evening); disabled facilities, small pleasant garden with pond, very little parking, closed Mon lunchtime. *(David and Sue Atkinson)*

EASTLEACH TURVILLE
SP1905

⋆ **Victoria** (01367) 850277

Off A361 S of Burford; GL7 3NQ Open-plan low-ceilinged rooms around central servery, attractive seats built in by log fire, unusual Queen Victoria pictures, Arkells and several good value wines by the glass, shortish choice of sensibly priced pub food (not Sun evening) including baguettes; background music; children and dogs welcome, small pleasant front garden with picnic-sets overlooking picturesque village (famous for its spring daffodils), good walks, open all day Sat. *(Chris Glasson)*

EBRINGTON
SP1839

⋆ **Ebrington Arms** (01386) 593223

Off B4035 E of Chipping Campden or A429 N of Moreton-in-Marsh; GL55 6NH
Old Cotswold-stone pub in attractive village, plenty of character, beamed bar with ladder-back chairs and tables on flagstones, fine inglenook, some seats built into airy bow window, ales such as Severn Vale, Stanway, Stroud and Uley, several wines by glass, good interesting food (best to book), friendly young staff, beamed dining room, similarly furnished, with original iron work in inglenook, folk music first Mon of month; darts, TV; children welcome, dogs on lead in bar, arched stone wall sheltering terrace picnic-sets, more seats on lawn, handy for Hidcote and Kiftsgate Court gardens, bedrooms, open all day, closed Sun evening. *(Ewan and Moira McCall, Peter Dandy, Di and Mike Gillam, Guy Vowles, Tim Maddison, David Gunn and others)*

EDGE
SO8409

⋆ **Edgemoor** (01452) 813576

Gloucester Road (A4173); GL6 6ND
Tidy, modernised and spacious 19th-c dining pub with panoramic valley view across to Painswick from picture windows and pretty terrace, good food, friendly efficient service, up to four well kept ales including Stroud, Uley and Wickwar, nice coffee, restaurant; no dogs inside; children welcome, good walks nearby, closed Sun evening in winter. *(Neil and Anita Christopher, Lesley and Peter Barrett)*

ELKSTONE
SO9610

⋆ **Highwayman** (01285) 821221

Beechpike; A417 6 miles N of Cirencester; GL53 9PL Interesting rambling 16th-c building, low beams, stripped stone, log fires, cosy alcoves, bric-a-brac, antique settles, armchairs and sofa among more usual furnishings, good value home-made food, full Arkells range, good house wines, family room and big back eating area; disabled access, outside play area. *(Guy Vowles, Mrs Y Ebdon)*

EWEN
SU0097

⋆ **Wild Duck** (01285) 770310

Off A429 S of Cirencester; GL7 6BY
Unchanging 16th-century inn with stylishly old-fashioned furnishings and pictures in high-beamed log-fire main bar, lounge with handsome Elizabethan fireplace and antique furnishings, some interesting if not cheap food, six real ales including Duck Pond brewed for the pub, very good choice of wines by the glass; background music; children welcome, tables in neatly kept heated courtyard (if you eat here they may ask to keep your credit card behind the bar), garden, 12 bedrooms, open all day. *(D Crook, Andy and Claire Barker, Mr and Mrs A Curry, Jennifer and Patrick O'Dell, Dave Snowden, Ross Balaam)*

FAIRFORD
SP1501
⋆**Bull** (01285) 712535
Market Place; GL7 4AA Rather smart old timbered hotel with bustling chatty atmosphere, comfortable pubby furnishings in relaxed bar including dark pews and settles, aircraft pictures and photographs of actors (previous guests) on ochre walls, coal-effect gas fire, Arkells 2B, 3B and Kingsdown, reasonably priced, traditional bar food, friendly service; children welcome, dogs in bar, disabled facilities, charming village and church with intact set of medieval stained-glass windows, bedrooms, open all day. *(David and Gill Carrington, Jennifer and Patrick O'Dell)*

FOREST OF DEAN
SO6212
Speech House (01594) 822607
B4226 nearly a mile E of junction with B4234; GL16 7EL Superbly placed hotel in centre of Forest (former 17th-c hunting lodge), refurbished interior with oak panelling and huge log fire, all-day bar food from nice sandwiches up, real ales such as Wye Valley, afternoon teas, big conservatory, restaurant; tables outside, comfortable bedrooms. *(John and Gloria Isaacs, Dr A Y Drummond)*

FORTHAMPTON
SO8731
Lower Lode Inn (01684) 293224
At the end of Bishop's Walk by river; GL19 4RE Brick-built 15th-c coaching inn with River Severn moorings and plenty of waterside tables (prone to winter flooding), beams, flagstones, enormous log fire and traditional seating, enjoyable pubby food, friendly helpful staff, half a dozen well kept interesting beers, restaurant, back pool room; children and dogs welcome (lots of summer holiday families), disabled facilities, caravan site, four bedrooms, open all day. *(Ian Kirkwood)*

FRAMPTON COTTERELL
ST6681
Globe (01454) 778286
Church Road; BS36 2AB Large knocked-through bar/dining area with black beams and some stripped stone, usual furniture on parquet or carpet, woodburner in old fireplace, half a dozen well kept changing ales such as Butcombe, Sharps and Uley, real ciders, interesting wine list, enjoyable well presented pubby food, attentive friendly young staff, flowers on tables, newspapers; background music; children welcome, wheelchair access via side door, garden with play area and smokers' gazebo, church next door. *(Chris and Angela Buckell, Roger and Donna Huggins)*

FRAMPTON COTTERELL
ST6681
Live & Let Live (01454) 772254
Off A432; Clyde Road; BS36 2EF Attractive pub owned by Bath Brewery, their ales and good value food (not Sun evening) from sandwiches to popular Sun lunch, decent wines by the glass, helpful staff, linked rooms with carpeted bar and bare-boards dining

areas, pastel walls with panelled dado, daily newspapers, darts; background music, no dogs; children welcome, disabled facilities, picnic-sets in big garden, open all day. *(Chris and Angela Buckell)*

FRAMPTON MANSELL
SO9202
⋆**Crown** (01285) 760601
Bown sign to pub off A491 Cirencester–Stroud; GL6 8JG Welcoming licensees doing good choice of enjoyable home-made food from baguettes up at reasonable prices, well kept Butcombe Stroud, Uley and a guest, efficient charming service, heavy 17th-c beams, stripped stone and rugs on bare boards, two log fires and woodburner, restaurant; children and dogs welcome, disabled access, picnic-sets in sunny front garden, pretty outlook, 12 decent bedrooms in separate block, open all day from midday. *(Paul Humphreys, Mrs P Sumner, Ian and Melanie Henry, Stella and Geoffrey Harrison, Giles and Annie Francis and others)*

FRAMPTON ON SEVERN
SO7408
Bell (01452) 740346
The Green (B4071, handy for M5 junction 13, via A38); GL2 7EP Handsome creeper-covered Georgian inn attractively opened up, enjoyable good value food in extensive all-day family dining area, proper locals' bar with quarry tiles and flagstones, Bath Gem, Moles and Sharps Doom Bar, real cider, steps up to restaurant, rebuilt skittle alley; background music; dogs welcome, plenty of seats outside (front and back), good play area and children's farm, stabling, village cricket green opposite, open all day. *(Mrs Jo Rees, Chris and Angela Buckell, W K Wood, Dr A J and Mrs Tompsett, Neil and Anita Christopher)*

GLASSHOUSE
SO7121
⋆**Glasshouse Inn** (01452) 830529
Off A40 just W of A4136; GL17 0NN Much-extended red-brick beamed pub with appealing old-fashioned and antique furnishings, cavernous black hearth, big flagstoned conservatory, well kept ales including Butcombe tapped from the cask, Stowford Press cider, reasonably priced wines, decent home-made food from sandwiches and basket meals to interesting specials, good friendly service; background music, no under-14s in bars, no bookings except Sun lunch, and they may try to keep your credit card while you eat; good disabled access, neat garden with rustic furniture, interesting topiary, flower-decked cider presses and lovely hanging baskets, nearby paths up wooded May Hill, closed Sun evening. *(Neil and Anita Christopher, Paul and Sue Merrick, Carol Wilson)*

GLOUCESTER
SO8318
Fountain (01452) 522562
Westgate Street; GL1 2NW Tucked-away 17th-c pub off pedestrianised street,

well kept St Austell Tribute, Greene King Abbot and four mainly local guests, good choice of reasonably priced pubby food from sandwiches up, quick helpful service, handsome stone fireplace, plush seats and built-in wall benches; background music; children welcome, disabled access, flower-filled courtyard, handy for cathedral, open all day. *(Joe Green, Theocsbrian, Dave Braisted, David Uren)*

GREAT BARRINGTON   SP2013
✶**Fox** (01451) 844385

Off A40 Burford–Northleach; pub towards Little Barrington; OX18 4TB 17th-c inn with stripped stone, simple country furnishings and low ceiling, well kept Donnington BB and SBA, farm cider and good apple juice, wide choice of quickly served food (all day Sun and summer Sat, not Mon night in winter) from sandwiches through oysters to local meats, big bare-boards river-view dining room with riverbank mural, traditional games, Aug 'Foxstock' folk festival; can get very busy, games machine, TV; children and dogs welcome, heated terraces by the Windrush (swans and private fishing), informal orchard with pond, four bedrooms, open all day. *(David Glynne-Jones, Ian Herdman)*

GUITING POWER   SP0924
✶**Farmers Arms** (01451) 850358

Fosseway (A429); GL54 5TZ Stripped stone and flagstones, well kept cheap Donnington BB and SBA, wide blackboard range of enjoyable food cooked by landlord including good rabbit pie, welcoming prompt service, nice log fire, lots of pictures, carpeted back dining part, games area with darts, dominoes, cribbage and pool, skittle alley; background music, games machine; children welcome, garden with quoits, lovely village, good walks, bedrooms. *(Mr and Mrs A J Hudson, Richard Tilbrook)*

HAM   ST6898
Salutation (01453) 810284

On main road through village; GL13 9QH Unpretentious two-bar carpeted local, brasses on beams, horse and hunt pictures on artex walls, pubby furniture including high-backed settles and bench seats, panelling, four well kept changing ales, ciders and perries tapped from casks, simple low-priced food lunchtime and early evening, friendly helpful landlord and staff, skittle alley; no credit cards; wheelchair accessible, beer garden with views over the Severn. *(John and Gloria Isaacs, Chris and Angela Buckell)*

HAWKESBURY UPTON   ST7786
✶**Beaufort Arms** (01454) 238217

High Street; GL9 1AU Unpretentious 17th-c pub in historic village, welcoming landlord and friendly local atmosphere, well kept Wickwar ales and cider, guest beers, popular no-nonsense food (no starters, small helpings available), extended uncluttered dining lounge on right, darts in more spartan stripped-brick bare-boards bar, interesting local and brewery memorabilia, lots of pictures (some for sale), skittle alley; well behaved children allowed, dogs in bar, disabled access throughout and facilities, picnic-sets in smallish enclosed garden, on Cotswold Way, open all day. *(Neil and Anita Christopher, Jim and Frances Gowers, Dr and Mrs A K Clarke, Les Halpin, Chris and Angela Buckell)*

HORSLEY   ST8497
✶**Tipputs** (01453) 832466

Just off A46 2 miles S of Nailsworth; Tiltups End; GL6 0QE Light and airy L-shaped bar with tall mullioned windows and raftered ceiling, panelling with arched bookshelves, boar's head above woodburner, interesting mix of good solid tables on broad boards, armchairs and chesterfield plus variety of dining chairs, enjoyable food all day from good value lunches to interesting evening meals, Stroud Organic and Tom Long, efficient continental staff, big back galleried restaurant with comfortable anteroom; muffled background music; teak tables out behind on grass and decking, attractive countryside, open all day. *(Tom and Ruth Rees)*

IRON ACTON   ST6883
Lamb (01454) 228265

B4058/9 Bristol–Chipping Sodbury; BS37 9UZ Half a dozen well kept changing ales like Butcombe, St Georges and Wickwar, farm ciders, good competitively priced wines including some interesting country ones, wide choice of well presented food, helpful cheerful staff and chatty locals, huge fireplace in low-ceilinged carpeted bar, panelling and stripped stone, pool upstairs; background music, no dogs; wheelchair accessible, big garden with front terrace, bedrooms, open all day. *(Chris and Angela Buckell)*

KEMBLE   ST9899
✶**Thames Head** (01285) 770259

A433 Cirencester–Tetbury; GL7 6NZ Stripped stone, timberwork, intriguing little front alcove, pews in cottagey back area with log-effect gas fire in big fireplace, country-look dining room with another fire, wide choice of enjoyable food, good value wines and well kept Arkells, friendly obliging staff, skittle alley; TV; children welcome, tables outside, four bedrooms in converted barn, good breakfast, walk to nearby Thames source (crossing railway line), open all day. *(Neil and Anita Christopher, Mike Buckingham)*

KINETON   SP0926
Halfway House (01451) 850344

Signed from B4068 and B4077 W of Stow-on-the-Wold; GL54 5UG Simple and welcoming 17th-c beamed village pub, good nicely presented food (not Sun evening) from sandwiches up, well kept Donnington

BB and SBA, farm cider and decent wines, restaurant, log fire; pool and darts; children welcome, picnic-sets in sheltered back garden, good walks, bedrooms, open all day weekends. *(John and Helen Rushton, Eleanor Dandy, Martin and Pauline Jennings)*

KINGSCOTE ST8196
★ **Hunters Hall** (01453) 860393
A4135 Dursley–Tetbury; GL8 8XZ Tudor beams, stripped stone, big log fires and plenty of character in individually furnished spotless linked rooms, some sofas and easy chairs, wide choice of good home-made food at reasonable prices, well kept Greene King and Uley, friendly attentive service, flagstoned back bar with darts, pool and TV; children and dogs welcome, big garden with good play area, 13 bedrooms, open all day. *(Roger and Donna Huggins, Laurence Davis, Peter and Margaret, Tom and Ruth Rees, Julian Cox)*

LECHLADE SU2199
Crown (01367) 252198
High Street; GL7 3AE Friendly old pub brewing its own Halfpenny ales (six on offer), busy bar with fire each end, back games room with pool and table football, no evening food; children welcome, beer garden, three bedrooms in separate block, open all day. *(Graham Oddey)*

LITTLE BARRINGTON SP2012
Inn For All Seasons (01451) 844324
A40 3 miles W of Burford; OX18 4TN Handsome old coaching inn with attractive comfortable lounge bar, low beams, stripped stone and flagstones, old prints, log fire, good food including fresh fish, Sharps Doom Bar and Wadworths 6X, lots of wines by the glass and malt whiskies, friendly service, restaurant and conservatory; background music; dogs welcome, garden with aunt sally, walks from door, open all day. *(Anthony Longden, Graham Oddey, Mr and Mrs J Mandeville, Mark and Ruth Brock, Rhiannon Stevenson)*

LITTLETON-UPON-SEVERN ST5989
★ **White Hart** (01454) 412275
3.5 miles from M48 junction 1; BS35 1NR Former farmhouse under newish management, three main rooms, log fires, nice mix of country furnishings, loveseat in inglenook, flagstones at front, huge tiles at back, fine old White Hart Inn Simonds Ale sign, family room and back snug, Wells & Youngs, Bath Gem and a guest, maybe cider from own apples, good range of enjoyable food (all day Sun) including specials; dogs welcome, wheelchair access with help, tables on front lawn, more behind by orchard, roaming chickens, walks from door, open all day. *(Chris and Angela Buckell, Chris and Jenny Howland-Harris, Nigel and Sue Foster)*

LONGBOROUGH SP1729
Coach & Horses (01451) 830325
Ganborough Road; GL56 0QU Small friendly 17th-c stone-built local, Donnington ales, Weston's cider, enjoyable wholesome food (not Sun evening or Mon-Weds), friendly staff, leather armchairs on flagstones, inglenook stove, darts, dominoes and cribbage; some background music; well behaved children and dogs welcome, tables out at front looking down on stone cross and village, two simple clean bedrooms. *(Liam and Sue McGreevy, Eddie Edwards)*

LOWER ODDINGTON SP2326
★ **Fox** (01451) 870555
Signed off A436; GL56 0UR Smart 16th-c creeper-covered inn with very good modern food served by efficient friendly staff, well kept Hook Norton, St Austell Tribute and a guest, little country-style flagstoned rooms with mix of chairs around pine tables, fresh flowers, hunting figures and pictures, inglenook fireplace, elegant red-walled dining room; children welcome, dogs in bar, white tables and chairs on heated terrace in cottagey garden, pretty village, three bedrooms. *(John and Enid Morris, Jeff and Wendy Williams, Dennis and Doreen Haward, Richard Greaves, Peter Smith and Judith Brown, Barry Collett and others)*

MARSHFIELD ST7773
★ **Catherine Wheel** (01225) 892220
High Street; signed off A420 Bristol–Chippenham; SN14 8LR High-ceilinged stripped-stone front part with medley of settles, chairs and stripped tables, charming Georgian dining room with open fire in impressive fireplace, cottagey beamed back area warmed by woodburners, friendly staff and chatty locals, well kept ales such as Cotswold and Sharps, interesting wines and other drinks, enjoyable sensibly priced food (not Sun evening) from pub favourites up, darts, dominoes; dogs on leads and children welcome, wheelchair access with help, flower-decked back yard, unspoilt village, four bedrooms, open all day. *(John and Gloria Isaacs)*

MINSTERWORTH SO7716
Apple Tree (01452) 750345
A48 S of Gloucester; GL2 8JQ Refurbished dining pub extended around oak-beamed 17th-c farmhouse, wide choice of well priced generous food from snacks to daily specials and Sun carvery, good service from friendly young staff, well kept ales, various eating areas including large barn-like room, inglenook log fires; children welcome, big garden with play area, lane beside pub leads down to the Severn. *(Christine and Neil Townend)*

If we know a pub has an outdoor play area for children, we mention it.

MINSTERWORTH SO7515
Severn Bore (01452) 750318
A48 2 miles SW; GL2 8JX In splendid Severn-side position, spotlessly clean open layout with central fireplace, usual pubby furniture, welcoming staff, ales such as Wickwar Severn Bore, Ashton's and Weston's cider, pubby food, skittle alley with pool table and darts; fruit machine, TV; wheelchair access (low step into bar), big riverside garden with superb views to the Cotswolds, play area, board giving times/heights of Severn Bore (open for breakfast on Bore days), handy for Westbury Court Gardens (NT). *(Chris and Angela Buckell)*

MISERDEN SO9308
Carpenters Arms (01285) 821283
Off B4070 NE of Stroud; GL6 7JA Country pub with open-plan low-beamed bar, stripped-stone walls, log fire and woodburner, friendly licensees, Wye Valley and a guest ale, good wine list, enjoyable reasonably priced food using local and home-grown produce including good vegetarian choices, charity quiz nights; children and dogs welcome, garden tables, popular with walkers and handy for Miserden Park, open all day. *(Neil and Anita Christopher, Dr A J and Mrs Tompsett, Giles and Annie Francis, Guy Vowles)*

MORETON-IN-MARSH SP2032
✳ Redesdale Arms (01608) 650308
High Street; GL56 0AW Relaxed old coaching inn with prettily lit alcoves, sofas and big stone fireplace in solidly furnished comfortable panelled bar on right, darts in flagstoned public bar, log fires, stripped stone, Bath, Hook Norton and Wickwar ales, decent wines and coffee, enjoyable good value food, courteous helpful service, spacious back child-friendly brasserie and dining conservatory; background music, TVs, games machine; heated floodlit courtyard decking, 24 comfortable bedrooms beyond, open all day from 8am. *(Jason Caulkin, Tom and Ruth Rees, George Atkinson)*

MORETON-IN-MARSH SP2032
White Hart Royal (01608) 650731
High Street; GL56 0BA Refurbished 17th-c coaching inn, cosy beamed quarry-tiled bar with fine inglenook, adjacent smarter panelled room with Georgian feel, separate lounge and restaurant, Hook Norton and a guest ale, good choice of wines, food from sandwiches and pub favourites up, friendly attentive service from smart staff; background music; courtyard tables, bedrooms. *(Eddie Edwards)*

NAILSWORTH ST8499
✳ Egypt Mill (01453) 833449
Off A46; heading N towards Stroud, first right after roundabout, then left; GL6 0AE Stylishly converted 16th-c stone-built mill on three-floors, millstream flowing through and good views of working waterwheels from brick-and-stone-floored split-level bar, emphasis on enjoyable all-day bar food, Nailsworth and Stroud ales, cheerful helpful staff, comfortable carpeted lounge with beams and hefty ironwork from the old machinery; background music and TV; children welcome, floodlit terraced garden overlooking millpond, 28 bedrooms. *(Dr and Mrs A K Clarke, Mr and Mrs W Mills)*

NAUNTON SP1123
✳ Black Horse (01451) 850565
Off B4068 W of Stow-on-the-Wold; GL54 3AD Friendly stripped-stone proper pub with well kept/priced Donnington BB and SBA, good fresh food from generously filled sandwiches and traditional favourites to specials including seasonal game, good service, plain tables, flagstones, black beams and log fire, darts, cribbage, dominoes, dining room; background music; children and dogs welcome (resident labrador), some nice seating outside, charming village, fine Cotswold walks. *(Richard Tilbrook, Charlie Keitch, Dr A Y Drummond, Ann Gray, Di and Mike Gillam and others)*

NEWENT SO7225
George (01531) 820203
Church Street; GL18 1PU Redecorated former coaching inn, friendly locals, three or four well kept changing ales, decent home-made food, carpeted open-plan bar with log fire, evening restaurant; children and dogs welcome, nice location, bedrooms, open all day. *(TB)*

NIBLEY ST6982
Swan (01454) 312290
Badminton Road; BS37 5JF Light fresh refurbishment by small local pub group, good generous food including lunchtime fixed price menu (Mon-Thurs), changing real ales and over a dozen wines by the glass, fireside leather sofas one side, dining tables the other; children welcome, open all day. *(James Morrell)*

NORTH NIBLEY ST7495
Black Horse (01453) 543777
Barrs Lane; GL11 6DT Beamed bar and two dining areas, good popular well cooked food, three local ales and decent selection of wines, log fires; a few tables in pretty garden, near Cotswold Way, six bedrooms. *(Bob and Linda Richardson)*

NORTH NIBLEY ST7596
New Inn (01453) 543659
E of village itself; Waterley Bottom; GL11 6EF Former cider house in secluded rural setting popular with walkers, well kept ales such as Cotleigh, Goffs, Wickwar and Wye Valley from antique pumps, five ciders (plenty more in bottles), basic bar food including good ploughman's, lounge bar with cushioned windsor chairs and high-backed

settles, partly stripped-stone walls, simple cosy public bar with darts, beer and cider festivals; children and dogs welcome, tables on lawn and covered decked area with pool table, bedrooms, open all day weekends, closed Mon lunchtime. *(Guy Vowles)*

NORTHLEACH   SP1114
Red Lion (01451) 860251
Market Place; GL54 3EJ Handsome renovated old pub with welcoming landlady and friendly locals, enjoyable home-made food, well kept changing ales and good choice of other drinks including organic wines and cider, nice log fire, restaurant; sunny garden behind, attractive village. *(Gene and Kitty Rankin)*

OAKRIDGE LYNCH   SO9103
Butchers Arms (01285) 760371
Off Eastcombe–Bisley Road E of Stroud; GL6 7NZ Welcoming beamed pub with enjoyable food (not Sun evening) from landlord/chef, well kept Wadworths ales, rambling partly stripped-stone bar with open fire and woodburner, dining room; children and dogs welcome, picnic-sets on lawn overlooking valley, good walks, closed Mon. *(David and Stella Martin)*

OLD DOWN   ST6187
★**Fox** (01454) 412507
3.9 miles from M5 junction 15/16; A38 towards Gloucester, then Old Down signposted; turn left into Inner Down; BS32 4PR Popular low-beamed cottagey pub, pleasantly unassuming, with warm local atmosphere, seven real ales including Bath and Butcombe, farm cider and good choice of wines by the glass, good reasonably priced hearty food with some interesting specials (best to book), friendly efficient staff, mainly red-carpeted bar with log fire, chunky pine tables and traditional pub seating, snug stone-tiled family room; good disabled access, long verandah with grapevine, front and back gardens, play area. *(Chris and Angela Buckell, Nigel and Sue Foster)*

OLD SODBURY   ST7581
★**Dog** (01454) 312006
3 miles from M4 junction 18, via A46 and A432; The Hill (a busy road); BS37 6LZ Welcoming and popular two-level bar with low beams and stripped stone, wide range of enjoyable food cooked to order (so can be a wait) including reasonably priced fish specials, friendly young staff, three well kept changing ales, good wine and soft drinks choice; games machine, juke box; children and dogs welcome, big garden with barbecue and good play area, bedrooms, open

all day. *(Jim and Frances Gowers, Jonathan Holloway, Roy Hoing, Tom and Ruth Rees)*

PAINSWICK   SO8609
Falcon (01452) 814222
New Street; GL6 6UN Sizeable old open-plan stone-built inn sympathetically refurbished by present owner, popular food and well kept beers, welcoming efficient staff; children and dogs welcome, 12 bedrooms, opposite churchyard famous for its 99 yews. *(Mark Sykes)*

PARKEND   SO6308
Rising Sun (01594) 562008
Off B4431; GL15 4HN Perched on wooded hillside and approached by roughish single-track drive, popular with walkers and cyclists, open-plan carpeted bar with modern pub furniture, Butcombe and a guest, straightforward well priced generous food from sandwiches and baked potatoes up, friendly service, lounge/games area with pool and machines; children and dogs welcome, wheelchair access with help, balcony and terrace tables under umbrellas, big woodside garden with play area and pond, self-catering bedroom, open all day weekends in summer. *(Neil and Anita Christopher, Chris and Angela Buckell)*

PARKEND   SO6107
Woodman (01594) 563273
Folly Road, Whitecroft; GL15 4JF Roomy and relaxed stripped-stone carpeted bar, heavy beams, forest pictures and old tools, smaller back bar and dining room, stone fireplaces (one with woodburner), wide choice of enjoyable fresh food, ales such as Greene King, Fullers and Sharps, friendly landlord and pleasant service; wheelchair access from car park, picnic-sets on front terrace facing green, sheltered back courtyard and garden, bedrooms, good Forest of Dean walks, open all day weekends. *(Chris and Angela Buckell, Neil and Anita Christopher)*

PAXFORD   SP1837
★**Churchill Arms** (01386) 594000
B4479, SE of Chipping Campden; GL55 6XH Smart dining pub with good well presented food from snacks up, Hook Norton Bitter, Sharps Doom Bar and Wadworths 6X, good blackboard wine list, pleasant staff, low ceilings and some timbering, flagstones, log fire, dining extension; children welcome, seats out on small front terrace and gravelled back area, four bedrooms, good breakfast. *(Peter Smith and Judith Brown, Angela Nicholson, Brian and Ruth Young, Caroline and Michael Abbey)*

We can always use photos of pubs on our website – why not e-mail us one –
feedback@thegoodpubguide.co.uk

POULTON SP1001

Falcon (01285) 850878

London Road; GL7 5HN Good food from landlord/chef and well kept local ales such as Cotswold Spring, decent wines, friendly unobtrusive service; well behaved children welcome. *(Guy Vowles)*

PURTON SO6904

Berkeley Arms (01453) 811262

Just upstream from Sharpness village, Severn left bank; GL13 9HU Basic rustic Severn-side local only a short walk from canal bridge, wonderful estuary view, flagstones, high-backed settles and open fire, well kept Uley, long-serving landlady; garden, closed Mon, Tues. *(Giles and Annie Francis)*

QUENINGTON SP1404

Keepers Arms (01285) 750349

Church Road; GL7 5BL Comfortable, cosy village local with stripped stone, low beams and log fires, amiable landlord, value for money food in bar and restaurant, good range of beers; dogs welcome, picnic-sets outside, bedrooms. *(Neil and Anita Christopher)*

REDBROOK SO5309

✳ **Boat** (01600) 712615

Car park signed on A466 Chepstow–Monmouth, then 100-yard footbridge over Wye; or very narrow steep car access from Penallt in Wales; NP25 4AJ Beautifully set riverside pub with well kept Wye Valley and guests tapped from the cask, lots of ciders, perries and country wines, enjoyable good value simple food from baguettes and baked potatoes up (nothing fried), helpful staff, unchanging interior with stripped-stone walls, flagstones and roaring woodburner; children and dogs welcome, rough home-built seats in informal tiered suntrap garden with stream spilling down waterfall cliffs into duck pond, open all day. *(LM, B M Eldridge, MLR)*

SAPPERTON SO9303

Daneway Inn (01285) 760297

Daneway; off A419 Stroud–Cirencester; GL7 6LN Quiet tucked-away local in charming wooded countryside, flagstones and bare boards, woodburner in amazing floor-to-ceiling carved-oak dutch fireplace, sporting prints, well kept Wadworths ales, farm ciders, generous simple food from filled baps up, long-serving landlord and friendly staff, small family room, traditional games in inglenook public bar, folk night Tues; no dogs, tricky wheelchair access; terrace tables and lovely sloping lawn, camping possible, good walks by disused canal with tunnel to Coates. *(Russell Blackaller, Dr A Y Drummond, Neil and Anita Christopher)*

SHIPTON MOYNE ST8989

Cat & Custard Pot (01666) 880249

Off B4040 Malmesbury–Bristol;

The Street; GL8 8PN Popular pub in picturesque village, good food from sandwiches to restaurant dishes (booking recommended), helpful friendly service even when busy, well kept Flowers, Timothy Taylors and Wadworths, Thatcher's cider, well priced wines, several dining areas, beams and bric-a-brac, hunting prints, cosy back snug, chatty locals; walkers and dogs welcome, wheelchair access. *(Guy Vowles, Chris and Angela Buckell, Penny and Peter Keevil, Alan Bulley, Neil and Anita Christopher)*

SIDDINGTON SU0399

✳ **Greyhound** (01285) 653573

Ashton Road; village signed from A419 roundabout at Tesco; GL7 6HR Popular village local, two linked rooms with big log fires, enjoyable good value pubby food from landlord/chef, Sun carvery and Tues thai curry night (landlady is from Thailand), well kept Wadworths, darts and cribbage, Sun folk evening; background music; children welcome, garden tables, open all day. *(Roger and Donna Huggins, D Crook)*

SLAD SO8707

Woolpack (01452) 813429

B4070 Stroud–Birdlip; GL6 7QA Friendly and unpretentiously old-fashioned hillside village local with lovely valley views, four little connecting rooms with Laurie Lee and other interesting photographs, some of his books for sale, log fire and nice tables, enjoyable pub food (not Sun evening) from sandwiches and baguettes up including generous Sun roast, home-baked bread, well kept Uley and guests, local farm ciders and perry, decent wines by the glass, good young staff, games and cards; children and dogs welcome, nice garden. *(Neil and Anita Christopher, Pete Flower)*

SLIMBRIDGE SO7204

Tudor Arms (01453) 890306

Shepherds Patch; off A38 towards Wildfowl & Wetlands Trust; GL2 7BP Much-extended canalside pub, welcoming and popular, with several interesting changing ales, good wines by the glass, eight ciders/perries, food (all day weekends) from baguettes and baked potatoes up, linked areas with parquet floor, flagstones or carpet, some leather chairs and settles, comfortable dining room, conservatory, darts, pool and skittle alley; children and dogs welcome, disabled facilities, picnic-sets outside, boat trips, caravan site off car park, 12 bedrooms, open all day. *(Ewan and Moira McCall, Neil and Anita Christopher, Chris and Angela Buckell)*

SOMERFORD KEYNES SU0195

Bakers Arms (01285) 861298

On main street through village; GL7 6DN Pretty little 17th-c stone-built pub with catslide roof, four real ales including Butcombe and Stroud, Addlestone's cider, good house wine, traditional food and specials, friendly service, lots of pine tables in two linked stripped-stone areas, two log fires; children and dogs welcome, nice garden with play area, lovely village, handy for Cotswold Water Park. *(Mike Buckingham)*

ST BRIAVELS   SO5504
★ George (01594) 530228

High Street; GL15 6TA Comfortable Wadworths pub, their beers and wide choice of good sensibly priced food inc OAP deals, friendly service, spotless rambling linked black-beamed rooms with attractive old-fashioned décor and big stone fireplace, restaurant; can get very busy weekends (booking advised Sun); children and dogs welcome, flagstoned terrace over former moat of neighbouring Norman fortress, four refurbished bedrooms. *(Bob and Margaret Holder, Mike and Mary Carter, MLR)*

STANTON   SP0634
★ Mount (01386) 584316

Village signposted off B4632 SW of Broadway; keep on past village on no-through road up hill, bear left; WR12 7NE 17th-c pub is in lovely spot with fantastic views over the Vale of Evesham on to the welsh mountains; bars with low ceilings, heavy beams and flagstones, inglenook log fire, picture-window restaurant overlooking village, good choice of popular food, well kept/priced Donnington BB and SBA, decent wines by the glass, helpful efficient service, darts and board games; children and dogs welcome, seats on terrace with more in peaceful garden, boules, good walks - on the Cotswold Way National Trail. *(Alan Bulley, M G Hart, Karl Baston, Phil and Helen Holt, David and Jane Hill, Julia and Richard Tredgett and others)*

STOW-ON-THE-WOLD   SP1729
Coach & Horses (01451) 830208

Ganborough (on A424 about 2.5 miles N); GL56 0QZ Beamed and flagstoned country pub, bright and clean, with enjoyable reasonably priced local food from well filled baguettes up, special walkers' menu too, friendly prompt service, well kept Donnington ales and farm cider, decent wines by the glass, cheerful log fire, step up to compact dining area with high-backed settles on wood floor, cat and black labrador (Molly and Pennell); children welcome, skittle alley, big garden with boules. *(Richard and Mary Marsden, Paul Humphreys, Guy Vowles and others)*

STOW-ON-THE-WOLD   SP1925
★ Queens Head (01451) 830563

The Square; GL54 1AB Splendidly unpretentious for this upmarket town, well kept low-priced Donnington BB and SBA, good wines by the glass, good value sandwiches and basic pub meals including proper steak and kidney pudding, cheerful helpful service, bustling and chatty stripped-stone front lounge, heavily beamed and flagstoned back bar with high-backed settles, horse prints and

coal-effect fire; children and dogs welcome, tables in attractive sunny back courtyard, open all day. *(Eleanor Dandy, R K Phillips, Keith McCartney, CFR)*

STOW-ON-THE-WOLD   SP1925
★ Talbot (01451) 870934

The Square; GL54 1BQ Light and airy modern décor, relaxed café-bar feel, food from sandwiches and baguettes up including some interesting blackboard specials, good friendly service even when busy, Wadworths ales, lots of good value wines by the glass, nice coffee, huge mirror over big log fire, plain tables and chairs on wood block floor, modern artwork, daily newspapers, upstairs room (and lavatories); no children inside; open all day. *(Martin and Pauline Jennings)*

STOW-ON-THE-WOLD   SP1925
Unicorn (01451) 830257

Sheep Street (A429 edge of centre); GL54 1HQ Handsome hotel with comfortably traditional low-beamed upmarket bar, nice mix of tables, chairs and settles on wood or flagstones, some panelling, big log fire, Hook Norton and Wye Valley ales, well presented food including good value two-course lunch, attentive service from east european staff, formal modern restaurant; background music, car park with barrier across busy road; 20 bedrooms. *(George Atkinson, Richard Tilbrook)*

STOW-ON-THE-WOLD   SP1925
White Hart (01451) 830674

The Square; GL54 1AF Old coaching inn with updated interior, two-room bare-boards bar with big shuttered windows on to market square, winged armchair by huge log fireplace, mix of pews and café chairs around scrubbed kitchen tables, Arkells ales, good coffee, carpeted lower inner bar with soft sofa, plump leather stools and other comfortable seats, sizeable restaurant, efficient young staff; unobtrusive background music; back yard with a couple of picnic-sets, bedrooms, decent breakfast. *(Anon)*

SWINEFORD   ST6969
★ Swan (0117) 9323101

A431, right on the Somerset border; BS30 6LN Stone-built pub with well kept Bath Ales and a guest, decent ciders and carefully chosen wines, enjoyable food using locally raised meat from bar snacks and pub favourites up, helpful friendly staff, plain furniture on bare boards or tiles, pastel paintwork and panelled dado, big open fire; children welcome, wheelchair access, large garden with play area, open all day. *(Colin and Peggy Wilshire, Andy Cox, Chris and Angela Buckell)*

TETBURY   ST8893
Priory (01666) 502251

London Road; GL8 8JJ More civilised eating house than pub, with central log fire in comfortable if somewhat sombre high-raftered stone-built former stables, enjoyable food with emphasis on interesting local produce, even a local slant to their good wood-fired pizzas, cheerful service, Courage Best and Uley, decent wines by the glass; comfortable coffee lounge, live music Sun; children very welcome, wheelchair access (staff helpful), roadside terrace picnic-sets, 14 good bedrooms. *(Tom Price, Alan Edwards)*

TETBURY ST8993
☀ **Snooty Fox** (01666) 502436
Market Place; GL8 8DD High-ceilinged stripped-stone hotel lounge, unstuffy with well kept ales such as Butcombe, Moles and Wickwar, good house wines, friendly young staff, enjoyable all-day bar food from sandwiches up, leather sofas, brass ceiling fans and elegant fireplace, nice side room and anteroom, restaurant; unobtrusive background music, bar can get very busy weekend evenings; children and dogs welcome, large sheltered front terrace, 12 comfortable bedrooms. *(Ian Herdman, Martin and Pauline Jennings)*

TETBURY ST9195
☀ **Trouble House** (01666) 502206
A433 towards Cirencester, near Cherington turn; GL8 8SG Pretty 17th-c dining pub doing well under current regime, highly-rated food including good value weekday set lunch, Wadworths ales from small saggy-beamed middle room, pleasant staff, big log fire; picnic-sets in back gravel courtyard. *(A Helme, Graham Oddey, Mrs P Sumner and others)*

TEWKESBURY SO8832
Bell (01684) 293293
Church Street; GL20 5SA Hotel bar interesting for its black oak beams and timbers, 17th-c oak panelling and medieval leaf-and-fruit frescoes; big log fire, tapestries and armchairs, good food, house wines and coffee, well kept Greene King, good service; children and dogs welcome, garden above Severnside walk, opposite Abbey, bedrooms. *(Rob and Catherine Dunster)*

TEWKESBURY SO8931
☀ **Gupshill Manor** (01684) 292278
Gloucester Road (off A38 S edge of town); GL20 5SG Quaint old timbered building with Tardis-like series of lounge and dining areas, plenty of easy chairs and sofas on wood floors, beams and open fires, enjoyable well priced food (all day Sun) from pubby dishes up including lunchtime deals, friendly efficient staff, three well kept Greene King ales and a guest, decent wine list, good coffees; background music; children welcome, disabled access, teak tables on

extensive heated terrace, open all day. *(Scott Mitchell, Jeremy King, J Chilver, Rod Stoneman)*

TEWKESBURY SO8933
☀ **Olde Black Bear** (01684) 292202
High Street; GL20 5BJ County's oldest pub (early 14th c), well worth a look for its intricately rambling rooms with ancient tiles, heavy timbering and low beams; up to five real ales, reasonably priced wines, cheap but decent pubby food, well worn furnishings, open fire; background music; children welcome, terrace and play area in nice riverside garden, open all day. *(P Dawn, Paul Goldman)*

TEWKESBURY SO8932
Royal Hop Pole (01684) 278670
Church Street; GL20 5RT Well managed Wetherspoons conversion of old inn, original features, their usual value-minded all-day food and drink, good service; lovely garden leading down to river, bedrooms. *(Theocsbrian)*

THORNBURY ST6491
Anchor (01454) 289376
Gloucester Road (B4061); BS35 1JY Old flower-decked roadside pub with hard-working landlord, carpets and pubby furniture, comfortable wall seats, faux black beams covered in pump clips, pictures and posters including photos of old Thornbury, well kept Bass with guests like Everards, Jennings and Ringwood, some tap-dispensed wine, very good value food (not Sun evening) served by cheerful efficient staff, occasional events such as brass band and country music; big screen sports TV; children and dogs welcome, play area and boules in tidy beer garden, open all day (from 9am for coffee). *(Chris and Angela Buckell)*

TODDINGTON SP0432
Pheasant (01242) 621271
A46 Broadway–Winchcombe, junction with A438 and B4077; GL54 5DT Extended stone-built roadside pub with enjoyable low-priced food from massive baguettes up, friendly helpful staff, well kept good value Stanway (brewed nearby), lots of railway prints - handy for preserved Gloucestershire Warwickshire Railway Station; no dogs while food being served; bedrooms. *(Guy Vowles, Mrs Jo Rees, B M Eldridge, R C Vincent)*

TODENHAM SP2436
☀ **Farriers Arms** (01608) 650901
Between A3400 and A429 N of Moreton-in-Marsh; GL56 9PF Unspoilt old pub with exposed stone and plastered walls in bar, hop-hung beams, polished flagstones by counter, woodburner in big inglenook, cosy

---

We accept no free drinks or meals and inspections are anonymous.

room off with old books and photos, neat restaurant, Hook Norton and a couple of guests, several wines by glass, food generally well liked, darts, board games; background music; children welcome, dogs in bar, country views from walled garden, terrace overlooking quite village road and church, aunt sally, good surrounding walks. *(Trevor and Sheila Sharman, M G Hart, John Holroyd, Alun and Jennifer Evans, M and GR, Clive and Fran Dutson and others)*

TWYNING   SO9036
Village Inn (01684) 293500
Twyning Green; GL20 6DF Warmly welcoming whitewashed pub facing green, traditional low-beamed interior with open fire, good range of ales from local and more distant brewers such as Rudgate, Stowford Press cider, enjoyable generously served pubby food, skittle alley; picnic-sets out at front, peaceful enclosed garden behind, small picturesque village. *(Roger and Marion Brown, Dennis Harvey)*

ULEY   ST7998
Old Crown (01453) 860502
The Green; GL11 5SN Rustic 17th-c pub prettily set by village green just off Cotswold Way, long narrow room with settles and pews on bare boards, step up to partitioned-off lounge area, good range of well kept changing ales and of wines by the glass, nice home-made pubby food from sandwiches up, friendly service, log fire, small games room up spiral stairs; attractive garden behind, four bedrooms. *(Jim and Frances Gowers)*

UPTON CHEYNEY   ST6969
Upton Inn (0117) 932 4489
Signed off A431 at Bitton; BS30 6LY 18th-c stone-built village pub, bar with old prints on stone and dark panelled walls, old tables and captain's chairs, step up to carpeted/bare-boards dining area with woodburner, good choice of home-made pubby food from sandwiches up, Sun carvery, well kept Badger ales, modern opulent mock-regency restaurant with pictures of Bath, friendly helpful service; background music; children and dogs welcome, picnic-sets on terrace, picturesque spot with Avon valley views, open all day. *(Tom and Ruth Rees, Guy Vowles)*

WANSWELL GREEN   SO6801
Salmon (01453) 811194
Station Road; GL13 9SE Reopened after major refit by Quality Inns, linked rooms with wood or carpeted floors, some half-panelling, old earthenware jugs, jars etc on shelves and window sills, modern furniture, stone fireplaces, changing ales and Thatcher's cider from wood panelled bar, good choice of wines and of sensibly priced food, afternoon cream teas, helpful hard-working staff; children welcome away from bar, tables in partially shaded garden,

animals in back paddock, open all day Thurs-Sun. *(Chris and Angela Buckell)*

WESTBURY-ON-SEVERN   SO7114
Red Lion (01452) 760221
A48, corner of Bell Lane; GL14 1PA Beamed and half-timbered traditional pub on busy road but by quiet church-side lane to river, cheerful obliging landlord, wide choice of enjoyable fairly priced local food, well kept ales such as Wye Valley, farm cider, decent wine, comfortable carpeted bar with wall seats, velvet curtains, open fire, snug off to the right, dining room to the left with log fire; children and dogs welcome, some seats out at front, more in back garden, three comfortable clean bedrooms, handy for Westbury Court Gardens (NT). *(Mr and Mrs J R Shrimpton, T E Duncan, B M Eldridge)*

WESTON SUBEDGE   SP1241
Seagrave Arms (01386) 840192
B4632; GL55 6QH Nicely refurbished Georgian country inn/restaurant, small log-fire bar, two dining rooms with mix of furniture on wood floors, good imaginative seasonal food using local suppliers, Hook Norton and Purity ales, Hogan's cider, friendly efficient staff; large seating area outside, eight bedrooms, open all day weekends (food all day then too), closed Mon. *(David Gunn)*

WHITECROFT   SO6005
Miners Arms (01594) 562483
B4234 N of Lydney; GL15 4PE Friendly unpretentious local with up to five changing ales, farm ciders and perries, generous good value food including some greek dishes, attentive helpful service, two rooms on either side of bar, slate and parquet floors, pastel walls with old photographs, conservatory, skittle alley; background and some live music; children and dogs welcome, disabled access, good gardens front and back, one with stream, quoits and boules, good local walks, handy for steam railway, self-catering accommodation, open all day. *(Chris and Angela Buckell, Fred Burt)*

WILLERSEY   SP1039
✶ Bell (01386) 858405
B4632 Cheltenham–Stratford, near Broadway; WR12 7PJ Well run neatly modernised stone-built pub, comfortable front dining area with popular home-made food, Aston Villa memorabilia and huge collection of model cars in back area past big L-shaped bar counter, Flowers, Hook Norton and Wadworths 6X, relaxed atmosphere, quick friendly service, darts; children welcome, overlooks village green and duck pond, lots of tables in big garden (dogs allowed here only), five bedrooms in outbuildings. *(Keith and Margaret Kettell, Dr A J and Mrs Tompsett)*

WINCHCOMBE   SP0228
⋆ Old Corner Cupboard
(01242) 602303 *Gloucester Street;*
GL54 5LX Attractive old golden-stone pub
doing well under present landlord, good
generous fairly priced food in nice back dining
room, well kept Fullers, Hook Norton and
local Stanway, decent wines by the glass, good
service, comfortable stripped-stone lounge
bar with heavy-beamed Tudor core, traditional
hatch-service lobby, small side room with
woodburner in massive stone fireplace,
traditional games; children welcome, tables
in back garden, open all day. *(Dr A J and Mrs
Tompsett, Ellie Weld,David London)*

WINCHCOMBE   SP0228
⋆ White Hart (01242) 602359
High Street (B4632); GL54 5LJ 16th-c
inn with big windows looking out over
village street, mix of chairs and small settles
around pine tables, bare boards, grey/green
paintwork, cricket memorabilia, well kept
Goffs, Otter and Wickwar, wine shop at back
(they add corkage if you buy to drink on
the premises), wide choice by the glass too,
specialist sausage menu plus other enjoyable
food, separate restaurant; children welcome,
dogs in bar and bedrooms, open all day from
9am (10am Sun). *(Derek and Sylvia Stephenson,
Steve Whalley, Dr A J and Mrs Tompsett, Ellie Weld,
David London)*

WINTERBOURNE   ST6678
Willy Wicket (0117) 9567308
*Wick Wick Close, handy for M4 junction
19 via M32, A4174 E; BS36 1DP* Popular
Vintage Inn family dining pub on roundabout,
good all-day food including deals, ales such
as Butcombe, St Austell and Sharps, friendly
courteous service, two eating areas off big
central bar, beams, timbers and stripped
stone, picture windows, two log fires; open all
day. *(Peter Grant, Roger and Donna Huggins)*

WINTERBOURNE DOWN   ST6679
Golden Hart (01454) 774392
*Just off A432 Bristol–Yate, towards
Winterbourne; BS36 1AU* Chef & Brewer
converted from row of 16th-c cottages, low
beamed main bar with series of higher
ceilinged linked rooms (including two further
bars), Fullers London Pride, Wadworths 6X
and guests, plenty of wines by the glass, usual
food, pleasant helpful staff, huge fireplaces,
bare boards or carpet, some stone walls and
panelling, cushioned wall/window seats, old
pictures and photographs, big conservatory;
background music, machines; children
welcome, wheelchair access (two low steps at
front), gardens, play area.
(Christopher Stan Stratton)

WITHINGTON   SP0315
Mill Inn (01242) 890204
Off A436 or A40; GL54 4BE Idyllic
streamside setting for mossy-roofed old stone
inn, recent refurbishment but keeping
character with nice nooks and corners,
beams, wood/flagstone floors and inglenooks,
reasonably priced varied food, friendly
service, dining room, games room with
pool and darts; only Sam Smiths keg beer
(but decent wine list); children and dogs
welcome, big garden, splendid walks, open all
day Fri-Sun. *(Neil and Anita Christopher)*

WOODCHESTER   SO8403
⋆ Old Fleece (01453) 872582
*Rooksmoor; A46 a mile S of Stroud;
GL5 5NB* Old wisteria-clad roadside pub -
part of the small Cotswold Food Club chain;
good choice of well presented interesting
food, friendly accommodating staff, well kept
mostly local ale such as Box Stream, Stroud
and Great Western, good wines by the glass,
bar, dining room and snug, big windows, bare
boards and panelling, stripped-stone or dark
salmon pink walls, modern paintings, large
log fire, daily newspapers; children welcome,
wheelchair access (except dining area - you
can also eat in bar), two front terraces, open
all day. *(Tom and Ruth Rees, Chris and Angela
Buckell, Mike Burkinshaw)*

WOODCHESTER   SO8302
⋆ Ram (01453) 873329
*High Street, South Woodchester; off
A46 S of Stroud; GL5 5EL* Bustling
country pub with up to half a dozen
interesting changing ales (tasting notes
and samples of three available in third-of-
a-pint glasses), friendly helpful landlord,
homely bar food (not Sun) including small
choice of bargain main courses, relaxed
L-shaped beamed bar with bare boards and
stripped stonework, nice mix of traditional
furnishings including several cushioned
antique panelled settles, open fires, live
music; children and dogs welcome,
spectacular valley views from terrace,
open-air theatre in summer, open all day.
*(Chris and Angela Buckell, Tom and Ruth Rees,
Martin Smith and others)*

YATE   ST6983
Cross Keys (01454) 228314
*Sgned off B4059 Yate bypass at the Fox;
North Road; BS37 7LQ* Unpretentious
two-bar beamed village local, good honest
reasonably priced food (5-8pm and Sat
lunchtime, not Sun, Mon) from sandwiches
up including nice old-fashioned puddings,
well kept Bass, Courage, Sharps Doom Bar
and a guest like Cotswold Spring, cheerful
chatty landlord, fires in both rooms, stripped
stone and panelling, flagstones and carpet,
mixed pubby furniture including pews and
old dining tables, brasses and prints; fruit
machine and darts in public bar, Weds quiz;
disabled access (perhaps a bit tricky for some
wheelchairs), open all day Fri-Sun. *(Roger
and Donna Huggins and others)*

Hampshire

Real ales play a strong part in pubs here with nearly half the Main Entries holding one of our Beer Awards – and there are plenty of charmingly individual places worth seeking out. New entries this year include the Red Lion in Boldre (friendly licensees and lots of bygones), Master Builders House in Bucklers Hard (character bar in a smart hotel), Fox & Hounds in Crawley (new licensees for striking looking pub), Bakers Arms in Droxford (bustling and cheerful with interesting food), Star in East Tytherley (hard-working licensees in neat country pub and a nice place to stay at), Golden Pot at Eversley (beers from smaller breweries, tasty food and a bustling atmosphere), Royal Oak near Fritham (very popular country tavern and part of a working farm), Mill at Gordleton near Hordle (very special gardens, informal little bar and excellent food), Plough in Longparish (spic and span upmarket dining pub and handy for the A303), Old Customs House in Portsmouth (a fine old building and part of the interesting waterfront development), and the Rising Sun in Swanmore (a proper country pub and now with a take-away menu). Other pubs doing well include the Sun in Bentworth (long-serving landlady in charming country pub with fine choice of ales), Hurdles in Droxford (delicious food and a warm welcome), Hogget in Hook (friendly landlord, honest food and handy for the M3 and A30), Yew Tree in Lower Wield (charming, enthusiastic and hands-on landlord, a well chosen wine list and good value food), Peat Spade in Longstock and Anchor at Lower Froyle (both in the well run small Millers Collection group and with the same civilised feel and enjoyable food), and the Harrow in Steep (quite unchanging and in the same family for 83 years). Not easy to choose the top dining pub with so much competition, but our Hampshire Dining Pub 2013 is the Purefoy Arms in Preston Candover.

BANK
SU2806 Map 2

Oak

Signposted just off A35 SW of Lyndhurst; SO43 7FE

New Forest pub with a good mix of customers, well liked food and interesting décor

Tucked away in the heart of the New Forest, this well run pub is popular with walkers and cyclists; it's best to book in advance to be sure of a table. On either side of the door in the bay windows of the L-shaped bar are built-in red-cushioned seats, and on the right there are two or three little pine-panelled booths with small built-in tables and bench seats. The rest of the bare-boarded bar has some low beams and joists, a line of stripped old and newer blond tables set against the wall with candles in individual brass holders and all manner of bric-a-brac: fishing rods, spears, a boomerang, old ski poles, brass platters, heavy knives and guns. There are cushioned milk churns along the bar counter and little red lanterns among hop bines above the bar. Fullers London Pride and Gales HSB and Seafarers on handpump and a dozen wines by the glass; background music. The pleasant side garden has picnic-sets and long tables and benches by the big yew trees.

Popular bar food includes doorstep sandwiches, home-cured salmon in citrus and dill, garlic mushrooms, beef and red onion burger with a spiced fruit salsa, five-cheese pasta parcels with a creamy pear sauce and roasted walnuts, maple-syrup roasted ham with free-range eggs and pineapple, beef casserole, scampi with home-made tartare sauce, a pie of the day, and slow-roasted pork belly with caramelised baked apple sauce. *Benchmark main dish: jumbo haddock and chips £14.50. Two-course evening meal £17.45.*

Fullers ~ Manager Martin Sliva ~ Real ale ~ Bar food (12-2.30, 6-9.30; all day weekends) ~ (023) 8028 2350 ~ Children welcome but under-10s must leave by 6pm ~ Dogs welcome ~ Open 11.30-3, 6-11; 11.30-11 Sat; 12-10.30 Sun; 11.30-3, 6-11 weekdays in winter *Recommended by Ian and Rose Lock, Mr and Mrs P D Titcomb, Phil and Jane Villiers, N R White, Steven King and Barbara Cameron, Adrian Johnson, Katharine Cowherd, Jane and Rowena Leverington*

BENTWORTH
SU6740 Map 2

Sun

Sun Hill; from the A339 coming from Alton, the first turning takes you there direct; or in village follow Shalden 2¼, Alton 4¼ signpost; GU34 5JT

Smashing choice of real ales and welcoming landlady in popular country pub; nearby walks

Many of our readers describe this bustling 17th-c place as the perfect country pub. The long-serving landlady and her helpful staff make all their customers welcome and the atmosphere is chatty and easy-going. The two little traditional communicating rooms have high-backed antique settles, pews and schoolroom chairs, old prints and blacksmith's tools on the walls, and bare boards and scrubbed deal tables on the left; three big fireplaces with log fires make it especially snug in winter. An arch leads to a brick-floored room with another open fire. There's a fine choice of half a dozen real ales on handpump: Andwell Resolute Bitter, Bowman Swift One, Fullers London Pride, Hook Norton Old Hooky, Itchen Valley Hampshire Rose and Sharps Doom Bar. There are seats out in front and in the back garden; pleasant walks nearby.

🍴 Generous helpings of carefully cooked, good food might include sandwiches, pork liver pâté, field mushrooms topped with brie, ham and eggs, avocado and stilton bake, beer-battered cod and chips, pheasant casserole, calves liver and bacon with onion gravy, game pie, brill with lemon butter, and puddings like a seasonal crumble and banoffi pie. *Benchmark main dish: home-made pies £13.95. Two-course evening meal £19.00.*

Free house ~ Licensee Mary Holmes ~ Real ale ~ Bar food (12-2, 7-9.30) ~ (01420) 562338 ~ Children welcome ~ Dogs welcome ~ Open 12-3, 6-11; 12-11 Sun ~ www.thesuninnbentworth.co.uk *Recommended by Mr and Mrs H J Langley, Martin and Karen Wake, Tony and Jill Radnor, Stephen Saunders, the Didler, Margaret Grimwood, Ann and Colin Hunt*

BOLDRE
SZ3198 Map 2

Red Lion 🍴 🍺

Off A337 N of Lymington; SO41 8NE

Friendly pub on the edge of the New Forest, lots of bygones in five beamed rooms, four real ales, interesting food and seats outside

Our readers love this well run pub – there's a warm welcome for all from the friendly licensees, the beers are well kept and the food is extremely good. The five black-beamed rooms reveal an entertaining collection of bygones, with heavy-horse harness, gin traps, ferocious-looking man traps, copper and brass pans and rural landscapes, as well as a dainty collection of old bottles and glasses in the window by the counter. Seating is on pews, sturdy cushioned dining chairs and tapestried stools. There's a fine old cooking range in the cosy little bar, and three good log fires. Banks's Bitter, Brakspears Oxford Gold and Ringwood Best and Fortyniner on handpump and 16 wines by the glass. The pub is opposite the village green and on the edge of the New Forest, and in summer there are seats outside among the flowering tubs and hanging baskets with more in the back garden. They have a sunny self-catering apartment for rent.

🍴 Highly thought of and interesting, the good food might include sandwiches, venison pâté with organic bread, mushrooms in a creamy stilton sauce on a crouton, filo parcel of spinach and asparagus with a blue cheese sauce, home-breaded cod cheeks with pea purée and home-made tartare sauce, home-made sausages with onion gravy, their very popular pork duo (slow-roasted pork belly with a black pudding, apricot and herb stuffing on home-made horseradish mash plus sliced pork fillet on cabbage and bacon with a red wine and garlic sauce), salmon and king prawn risotto, and puddings. *Benchmark main dish: duo of local pork £13.95. Two-course evening meal £16.25.*

Eldridge Pope ~ Lease Alan and Amanda Pountney ~ Real ale ~ Bar food (12-2.30, 6-9.30; all day Sun and summer Sat) ~ Restaurant ~ (01590) 673177 ~ Children welcome ~ Dogs allowed in bar ~ Open 11-3, 5.30-11; 11-11 Sat (5.30-11 in winter); 12-10.30 Sun ~ www.theredlionboldre.co.uk *Recommended by Phyl and Jack Street, Steve Kent, Jane Young, Jules Seifert, Adrian Ballard, John and Hilary Murphy, Guy Vowles, Tim Rye*

BRANSGORE
SZ1997 Map 2

Three Tuns 🍴 🍺

Village signposted off A35 and off B3347 N of Christchurch; Ringwood Road, opposite church; BH23 8JH

Interesting food in pretty thatched pub with proper old-fashioned bar and good beers, as well as a civilised main dining area

On the edge of the New Forest Country Park, this 17th-c thatched pub is full of cheerful customers – all welcomed by the friendly landlord and his staff. The roomy low-ceilinged and carpeted main area has a fireside 'codgers' corner', as well as a good mix of comfortably cushioned low chairs around a variety of dining tables. On the right is a separate traditional regulars' bar that seems almost taller than it is wide, with an impressive log-effect stove in a stripped brick hearth, some shiny black panelling and individualistic pubby furnishings. Ringwood Best and Fortyniner and Timothy Taylors Landlord and guests like Otter Bitter and St Austell Tribute on handpump, and nine wines by the glass. The Grade II-listed barn is popular for parties. In summer, the hanging baskets are lovely and there's an attractive, extensive shrub-sheltered terrace with picnic-sets on its brick paving; beyond that are more tables out on the grass looking over pony paddocks.

 Good, popular food made in-house usuing local produce might include sandwiches, dorset snails with smoked garlic butter and halloumi, soft shell crab with a garlic and saffron dip, puy lentil moussaka with feta cheese, rabbit pie with prunes, calves liver and bacon, slow-roast pork with a cider, mustard and pork reduction, king prawns and red mullet in miso broth with enoki mushrooms and a lemon verbena froth, and puddings like strawberry and elderflower trifle and bread and butter pudding with apricots and custard. *Benchmark main dish: burger with bacon, cheese and a pineapple salsa £10.95. Two-course evening meal £21.45.*

Enterprise ~ Lease Nigel Glenister ~ Real ale ~ Bar food (12-2.15, 6-9.15; all day weekends) ~ Restaurant ~ (01425) 672232 ~ No children in lounge bar after 6pm (can use bar and restaurant) ~ Dogs allowed in bar ~ Open 11-11; 12-10.30 Sun ~ www.threetunsinn.com *Recommended by Henry Fryer, Caz Brant, Roger Baynes, David Pollard, Phyl and Jack Street*

BUCKLERS HARD   SU4000   Map 2

Master Builders House

M27 junction 2 follow signs to Beaulieu, turn left on to B3056, then left to Bucklers Hard; SO42 7XB

Sizeable hotel with character bar in lovely spot overlooking the river in charming village; real ales, pubby food, popular outdoor barbecue and seats in waterside garden; bedrooms

In fine weather especially, this is a lovely spot with picnic-sets on the lawn overlooking the river with its boating activity; the summer barbecues are popular. A small gate at the bottom leads to a walkway beside the water. This is a smart, sizeable hotel, but the two-level bar is the original yachtsman's bar and has a lot of character. The main part has heavy beams, a warm winter log fire in an old brick fireplace (have a look at the list of all the ship builders dating from the 18th c on a wooden plaque to one side of it), benches and cushioned wall seats around long tables, rugs on the wooden floor and mullioned windows. There are some bar stools on quarry tiles by the counter, where they serve Ringwood Best and a couple of guest beers on handpump and decent wines by the glass. Stairs lead down to a lower room with a fireplace at each end. This is a lovely and carefully preserved waterside village.

 Some sort of food is served all day from noon (afternoon teas, too) and from the bar this might include lunchtime sandwiches, pork pie or scotch egg, chargrilled king prawns with garlic and chilli, a plate of smoked salmon, chicken caesar salad, steak burger with skinny chips plus bacon and cheese, battered haddock and chips with mushy peas, a vegetarian pasta dish, a pie of the day, and puddings such as warm treacle tart and crème brûlée; the restaurant menu is more elaborate. *Benchmark main dish: beer-battered fish and chips £12.50. Two-course evening meal £21.00.*

Free house ~ Licensee Damir Terzic ~ Real ale ~ Bar food (12-3, 6.30-9.30; afternoon teas, too) ~ Restaurant ~ (01590) 616253 ~ Children welcome ~ Dogs welcome ~ Open 11-11 ~ Bedrooms: £99B/£109B ~ www.themasterbuilders.co.uk *Recommended by Steven King and Barbara Cameron, Martin and Karen Wake, Guy Vowles*

CRAWLEY
Fox & Hounds
Village signed from A272 and B3420 NW of Winchester; SO21 2PR

SU4234 Map 2

Handsome building, three roaring winter log fires, several real ales and interesting food; bedrooms

This is a solidly constructed mock-Tudor building where each timbered upper storey successively juts further out, with lots of pegged structural timbers in the neat brickwork and elaborately carved steep gable-ends. New licensees took over just as we went to press but don't plan any major changes. The neat and attractive linked rooms have a mix of attractive wooden tables and chairs on polished floors, lots of bottles along a delft shelf and three log fires. The traditional little bar has built-in wall seats and Ringwood Best and Fortyniner, Wadworths 6X and Wychwood Hobgoblin on handpump, and several wines by the glass. There are picnic-sets in the gardens, and the bedrooms, in converted outbuildings, are named after the ducks on the village pond (this may change). The inn is one of the most striking buildings in a village of fine old houses.

Good, interesting food includes lunchtime sandwiches (not Sunday), scallops with black pudding, cauliflower, pine nuts and buttermilk, chicken liver parfait with fruit chutney, home-made cheeseburger with fries and ketchup, pork and leek sausages with onion gravy, smoked haddock fishcake with leeks, salsify and champagne cream, soft polenta with a poached egg, asparagus and lemon butter sauce, free-range chicken with truffles and creamed potato, rib-eye steak with triple-cooked chips and béarnaise sauce, and puddings like bitter chocolate mousse with coffee sponge and pistachio custard and vanilla crème brûlée. *Benchmark main dish: pork belly with cabbage, bacon and sage fondant £10.95. Two-course evening meal £17.50.*

Enterprise ~ Lease Alex and Sally Wood ~ Real ale ~ Bar food (12-2.30, 7-9.30; 12-4; not Sun evening) ~ Restaurant ~ (01962) 776006 ~ Children welcome ~ Dogs allowed in bar ~ Open 11-3, 6-11; 11-11 Sat; 12-8(4 in winter) Sun; 11-3, 6-11 Sat in winter; closed Sun evening ~ Bedrooms: /£72.50B ~ www.foxandhoundscrawley.co.uk *Recommended by Peter and Andrea Jacobs, Phyl and Jack Street, Clare Tharme, W A Evershed, P and J Shapley, David and Ruth Hollands, Mike and Lynn Robinson*

DROXFORD
Bakers Arms 🍴 🍺
High Street; A32 5 miles N of Wickham; SO32 3PA

SU6018 Map 2

Attractively opened-up and friendly pub with well kept beers, good, interesting cooking and cosy corners

In a pretty village at the heart of the Meon Valley, this is a bustling pub with friendly licensees. It's attractively laid-out and although the interesting food does play a big part, the central bar is kept as the main focus: Bowman Swift One and Wallops Wood on handpump, Stowford Press cider and a short, careful choice of wines by the glass. Well spaced mixed tables on carpet or neat bare boards spread around the airy L-shaped open-plan bar, with low leather chesterfields and an assortment of comfortably cushioned chairs down at one end; a dark panelled dado, dark beams and joists and a modicum of country oddments emphasise the freshness of the crisp white paintwork. There's a good log fire and board games. To one side, with a separate entrance, is the village post office. There are picnic-sets outside.

Popular food might include filled baguettes, ham hock terrine with piccalilli, pigeon breast salad with pancetta and walnut dressing, sausages and mash with onion gravy, gnocchi with radicchio, parmesan and smoked tomatoes, chicken breast with bacon and red wine sauce, fillet of gurnard with saffron and lemon risotto, slow-cooked duck leg with crushed squash and juniper juice, local hare loin in rich game sauce, and puddings like chocolate fudge brownie with butterscotch ice-cream and blackberry and apple crumble. *Benchmark main dish: local rib-eye steak £17.95. Two-course evening meal £21.50.*

Free house ~ Licensees Adam and Anna Cordery ~ Real ale ~ Bar food (12-2, 7-9; not Sun evening or Mon) ~ (01489) 877533 ~ Well behaved children welcome ~ Dogs welcome ~ Open 11.45-2.30, 6-11; 12-3 Sun; closed Sun evening and Mon ~ www.thebakersarmsdroxford.com *Recommended by Phyl and Jack Street, W A Eversted*

DROXFORD
Hurdles 🍴 🍷

SU6118 Map 2

Brockbridge, just outside Soberton; from A32 just N of Droxford take B2150 towards Denmead; SO32 3QT

Roomy smartly updated country dining pub, food interesting and good value

On the edge of the Meon Valley, this handsome Victorian brick building is always deservedly busy and our readers are full of praise for the genuinely warm welcome from the attentive young staff and the reliably delicious meals. It's been brought very suitably up to date inside, from the dark grey leather chesterfield and armchairs by the log fire in one room with elegant column lamps in its big windows to the dining areas on the right, with their stylish figured wallpaper, toning striped chairs around shiny modern tables and glittering mirrors. There are high ceilings and stripped boards throughout. Bowmans Wallops Wood and Swift One and a changing guest on handpump, decent wines by the glass and good coffee; unobtrusive background pop music. It's a peaceful spot, with wood and metal tables on neat terraces (one covered and heated), and a long flight of steps up to picnic-sets on a sloping lawn by tall trees.

Attractively presented and swiftly served, the good, interesting food includes filled baguettes, goats cheese mousse, black pepper biscotti, waldorf salad and cider dressing, crab, spring onion and parmesan tart, steak and vegetable suet pudding, root vegetable, spinach, chestnut and smoked applewood cheese crumble, rabbit loin, rabbit croquette, mushroom tagliatelle, truffle oil and carrot purée, salmon fillet with lobster ravioli, roast fennel and crab bisque, and puddings like Baileys profiteroles and lemon meringue pie; they also offer a two- and three-course set menu (Monday-Friday lunchtimes and Monday to Thursday evenings 6-7pm) and cream teas. *Benchmark main dish: pork belly with black pudding scallops and creamed cauliflower £14.95. Two-course evening meal £19.45.*

Enterprise ~ Lease Gareth and Sarah Cole ~ Real ale ~ Bar food (12-3, 6-9.30; 12-7.30 Sun) ~ Restaurant ~ (01489) 877451 ~ Children welcome ~ Dogs allowed in bar ~ Open 11-11; 12-10.30 Sun ~ www.thehurdlesdroxford.co.uk *Recommended by Susan Robinson, Ian Herdman*

 EAST TYTHERLEY   SU2927   Map 2

Star 🛏

B3084 N of Romsey; turn off by railway crossing opposite Mill Arms, Dundridge; SO51 0LW

Warm welcome for drinkers and diners in pretty pub, inventive food and real ales; comfortable bedrooms

This is a nice place to stay with bedrooms overlooking the cricket pitch and good breakfasts. It's a spic and span country pub with friendly, hard-working licensees. The bar has comfortable sofas and tub armchairs, pubby dining tables and chairs, bar stools and chairs, an overflowing bookcase to one side of the log fire and rich red walls. The restaurant is attractively set with proper linen napkins and tablecloths. Downton Honey Blonde and Flack Manor Double Drop on handpump, several wines by the glass including fizz, malt whiskies and Thatcher's rose cider; background music and board games. There are picnic-set in front of the building and tables and chairs on the back terrace by a giant chess board. Good nearby walks.

Reasonably priced and cooked by the licensees' son, the popular food might include sandwiches, fish medley of home-cured gin salmon, crayfish tails and smoked mackerel with crème fraîche and dill dressing, oxtail and roast butternut squash ravioli with vegetable consommé, chicken, mushroom and smoked bacon casserole, cumberland sausages with apple mash and thyme jus, wild mushroom and blue cheese tagliatelle with herb olive oil, salmon, cod and prawn fish pie with bubble and squeak topping, grey mullet fillets with salsa verde, and puddings like white chocolate crème brûlée and steamed apricot and almond sponge with custard. *Benchmark main dish: pork tenderloin with herb polenta and haricot bean, smoked bacon and roast garlic casserole £13.50. Two-course evening meal £17.25.*

Free house ~ Licensees Alan and Lesley Newitt ~ Real ale ~ Bar food (12-2, 7-9; not Sun evening or Mon) ~ Restaurant ~ (01794) 340225 ~ Children welcome ~ Dogs allowed in bar and bedrooms ~ Open 11-2.30(3 Sat), 6-10.30; 11-3.30 Sun; closed Sun evening, Mon ~ Bedrooms: £55S/£80S ~ www.starinn.co.uk *Recommended by Phyl and Jack Street, P J Checksfield, JES, David Jackman, Anna and David Abell*

 EASTON   SU5132   Map 2

Chestnut Horse 🍴 🍷

3.6 miles from M3 junction 9: A33 towards Kings Worthy, then B3047 towards Itchen Abbas; Easton then signposted on right – bear left in village; SO21 1EG

Cosy dining pub with log fires, fresh flowers and candles, deservedly popular food and friendly staff; Itchen Valley walks nearby

In a pretty village of thatched cottages, this smart 16th-c dining pub is just the place to head for after a walk in the nearby Itchen Valley. The open-plan interior manages to have a pleasantly rustic and intimate feel with a series of cosily separate areas, and the snug décor takes in candles and fresh flowers on the tables, log fires in cottagey fireplaces and comfortable furnishings. The black beams and joists are hung with all sorts of jugs, mugs and chamber-pots, and there are lots of attractive pictures of wildlife and the local area. Badger K&B and Hopping Hare on handpump, several wines by the glass and 30 malt whiskies; the landlady and her staff are friendly and efficient. There are seats and tables out on a smallish sheltered decked area with colourful flower tubs and baskets, and some picnic-sets in front.

Good, interesting food includes lunchtime sandwiches, crab and crayfish tian, confit rabbit and rice paper parcel with fine red coleslaw, coq au vin, globe artichoke, potato and salsify tarte tatin with tomato fondue, red wine poached salmon with butternut and watercress cream tagliatelle, duck breast with sweet anna potato and a honey and balsamic glaze, lamb rump with apricot and tarragon crushed potato and red wine jus, and puddings like banoffi tower and chocolate brownie; they also offer a good value two-course set menu (not Saturday evening or Sunday). *Benchmark main dish: fish and chips £13.00. Two-course evening meal £21.00.*

Badger ~ Tenant Karen Wells ~ Real ale ~ Bar food (12-2.30, 6-9.30; 12-8 Sun) ~ Restaurant ~ (01962) 779257 ~ Children welcome ~ Dogs allowed in bar ~ Open 12-4, 5.30-11.30; 12-11.30 Fri and Sat ~ www.thechestnuthorse.com *Recommended by Phyl and Jack Street, A M Falconer, Helen and Brian Edgeley, David and Sheila Pearcey, Anita McCullough*

EVERSLEY
SU7861 Map 2
Golden Pot
B3272; RG27 0NB

Bustling and friendly village pub with comfortable interlinked rooms, woodburning stoves, beers from smaller breweries, good food and seats outside

Dating back to the 1700s and at the heart of a village, this is a busy little brick pub with a friendly landlord. There's a comfortable atmosphere in the different spreading areas, a couple of woodburning stoves, sofas, cushioned settles, mates' and farmhouse kitchen chairs around wooden tables on carpeting, brass implements, sizeable mirrors and fresh flowers. High chairs line the counter, where they keep three quickly changing real ales only from small local breweries such as Andwell, Bowman, Rebellion and Windsor & Eton on handpump; several wines by the glass. Monday evenings are fun with live music and a rösti menu. There are seats and tables at the front of the building under the colourful hanging baskets, with more seats among flowering tubs and a view over fields at the back.

Good food might include sandwiches, smoked mackerel and horseradish pâté, prawn and crab cakes with cajun remoulade, wild mushroom ravioli, home-made venison burger with melted brie, aioli and cajun potato wedges, calves liver and bacon, free-range chicken stuffed with goats cheese with chorizo, puy lentils and roasted beetroot purée, specials like fillet of bass with seared scallop, crab and spring onion risotto and loin of lamb with braised faggot and celeriac foam, and puddings such as their popular eversley mess (their own take on eton mess). *Benchmark main dish: steak bavette with chunky chips, beer-battered onion rings and roasted vine tomatoes £13.95. Two-course evening meal £19.50.*

Free house ~ Licensee John Calder ~ Real ale ~ Bar food (12-2(3 Sun), 6-9; not Sun evening) ~ Restaurant ~ (0118) 973 2104 ~ Pianist/vocalist/guitarist Mon evening ~ Dogs allowed in bar ~ Open 11-3, 6-10.30; 12-3.30 Sun; closed Sun evening ~ www.golden-pot.co.uk *Recommended by KC, G Ridgway, Caz Brant, Ray Carter, Joan and Tony Walker*

FRITHAM
Royal Oak 🍺

SU2314 Map 2

Village signed from M27 J1; SO43 7HJ

Rural New Forest spot and part of a working farm; traditional rooms, log fires, seven real ales and simple lunchtime food

'This lovely country pub never fails to disappoint' is just one of the enthusiastic comments from our readers about this charming brick and cob thatched pub. It's part of a working farm so there are ponies and pigs out on the green and plenty of livestock nearby. Three neatly kept black-beamed rooms are straightforward but full of proper traditional character, with prints and pictures involving local characters on the white walls, restored panelling, antique wheelback, spindleback and other old chairs and stools with colourful seats around solid tables on the oak flooring and two roaring log fires; both the chatty locals and the hard-working staff are genuinely friendly. The back bar has quite a few books. Up to seven real ales are tapped from the cask: Bowman Wallops Wood, Flack Manor Double Drop, Hop Back Summer Lightning, Ringwood Best and Fortyniner, and Stonehenge Sign of Spring. Also, ten wines by the glass (mulled wine in winter) and a September beer festival. Summer barbecues may be held in the neatly kept big garden, which has a marquee for poor weather and a pétanque pitch. It's always busy whatever the season but is especially popular at weekends with walkers, cyclists and families.

🍴 The much liked simple lunchtime food is limited to winter soups, ploughman's, pies and quiches, sausages and maybe summer local crab. *Benchmark main dish: ham and cheese ploughman's £7.50.*

Free house ~ Licensees Neil and Pauline McCulloch ~ Real ale ~ Bar food (12-2.30(3 weekends); not evenings) ~ No credit cards ~ (023) 8081 2606 ~ Children welcome if well behaved ~ Dogs welcome ~ Open 11-11; 12-10.30 Sun; 11-3, 6-11 weekdays in winter
Recommended by Richard, Anne and Kate Ansell, Tony Stevens, Phil and Jane Villiers, R and S Bentley, N R White, the Didler, John and Annabel Hampshire, Terry and Nickie Williams, David and Judy Robison, Henry Paulinski

HOOK
Hogget 🍺

SU7153 Map 2

1.1 miles from M3 junction 5; A287 N, at junction with A30 (car park just before traffic lights); RG27 9JJ

Well run and accommodating, a proper pub moving with the times and giving good value

This bustling pub is just the place to escape the boredom of both the M3 and A30 and they are usefully open all day at weekends. As well as attracting plenty of visitors, it's popular locally too, and the rooms ramble right round the central server so there's plenty of room for all. The lighting, wallpaper and patterned carpet, and the leather sofas and tub chairs over on the right at the back, give a friendly and homely feel,

---

If a service charge is mentioned prominently on a menu or accommodation terms, you must pay it if service was satisfactory. If service is really bad you are legally entitled to refuse to pay some or all of the service charge as compensation for not getting the service you might reasonably have expected.

as do the several smallish distinct areas. Ringwood Best, Wychwood Hobgoblin and a guest beer on handpump, decent wines by the glass, and plenty of staff in neat but informal black uniforms. A sizeable terrace has sturdy tables and chairs, with some in a heated covered area.

🍴 Honest food using local ingredients and including fair value lunchtime deals includes sandwiches, meze grazing boards for sharing, mushrooms on toast with a poached egg, home-cured salmon with celeriac remoulade, crispy calamari with garlic mayonnaise, ham and free-range eggs, wild mushroom macaroni, beer-battered hake with home-made tartare sauce, crayfish salad, chicken in north african spices with chilli and cucumber and a grilled lemon and coriander couscous, and puddings like warm treacle tart with salted caramel ice-cream and sticky toffee pudding with warm toffee sauce. *Benchmark main dish: pork belly with celeriac mash and roast parsnips £13.95. Two-course evening meal £19.50.*

Marstons ~ Lease Tom Faulkner ~ Real ale ~ Bar food (12-2.30, 6.30-9; all day Sat; 12-6 Sun; not Sun evening) ~ Restaurant ~ (01256) 763009 ~ Children welcome but not after 7pm Fri and Sat evening ~ Dogs allowed in bar ~ Open 12-3, 5.30-11; 12-11(10.30 Sun) Sat ~ www.hogget.co.uk *Recommended by Mike and Jayne Bastin, Mark and Lia Chance*

HORDLE
SZ2996   Map 2
Mill at Gordleton 🍴 ☐ 🛏
Silver Street; SO41 6DJ

Charming tucked-away country inn with friendly bar, good food and drink and delightful waterside gardens; comfortable bedrooms

The gardens here are very special, an extensive series of interestingly planted areas looping about pools and a placid winding stream, dotted with intriguing art objects (and an entertaining duck family). There are plenty of places to sit, from intimate pairs of seats to the nicely lit teak or wrought iron tables of the main waterside terraces close by the inn. Inside, the small main panelled bar on the right is informal and relaxed: casually dressed local regulars perhaps with their dogs, friendly helpful staff, well kept Ringwood Best and a guest like Oakleaf Quercus Folium on handpump, good wines by the glass, a rack of daily papers, leather armchairs and Victorian-style mahogany dining chairs on the parquet floor, a little feature stove and a pretty corner china cupboard. This overflows into a cosy lounge, and there's a roomy second bar by the sizeable beamed restaurant extension – an attractive room with contemporary art and garden outlook. The bedrooms are comfortable and individual, with excellent breakfasts. Good walks here; they also offer tours to local breweries.

🍴 Everything is made here in the kitchen, including all the breads and preserves, and very good it is: lunchtime sandwiches, venison pâté with chutney, crab and prawn cocktail, twice-baked smoked haddock and cheese soufflé with a curry cream, home-cooked ham with free-range eggs, provençale vegetables with a basil cream and herby couscous, moules frites, whole local lemon sole with potted shrimps, a trio of duck (breast, mousseline of liver and leg) with a light plum jus, and puddings such as their very popular strawberry eton mess cheesecake and dark chocolate torte with espresso ice-cream. *Benchmark main dish: salmon and prawn thai curry £11.95. Two-course evening meal £24.00.*

Free house ~ Licensee Liz Cottingham ~ Real ale ~ Bar food (12-2, 7-9; 12-3, 6.30-8.30) ~ Restaurant ~ (01590) 682219 ~ Children welcome ~ Dogs allowed in bar ~ Open 11-11; 12-10.30 Sun ~ Bedrooms: £95S/£150S ~ www.themillatgordleton.co.uk *Recommended by Richard Gibbs*

LISS
Jolly Drover

SU7826 Map 2

London Road, Hill Brow; B2070 S of town, near B3006 junction; GU33 7QL

Friendly, comfortable pub with plenty of both locals and visitors, real ales, popular food and seats outside; good bedrooms

A traditional pub with friendly, quick service and plenty of regular customers, well run by the hands-on landlord. The neatly carpeted low-beamed bar contains leather tub chairs and a couple of sofas in front of the inglenook log fire. Black Sheep Best Bitter, Fullers London Pride and Sharps Doom Bar on handpump; daily papers, a silenced games machine in one alcove and board games. Several areas, with a gentle colour scheme mainly of muted terracotta or pale ochre, include two back dining areas, one of which opens on to a sheltered terrace with teak furniture, and a lawn with picnic-sets beyond. The neat bedrooms are in a barn conversion.

Generous helpings of well liked pubby food include baps and sandwiches, deep-fried whitebait, feta and cranberry tart, ham and eggs, vegetable lasagne, a roast of the day, sausages with onion gravy, chicken curry, rainbow trout and almonds, a mixed grill, and puddings like treacle tart and chocolate and orange cake. *Benchmark main dish: turkey, bacon and stilton pie £11.50. Two-course evening meal £17.50.*

Enterprise ~ Lease Barry and Anne Coe ~ Real ale ~ Bar food (12-2.15(2.30 Sun), 6.30-9.30; not Sun evening) ~ Restaurant ~ (01730) 893137 ~ Children welcome ~ Open 10.30-3, 5.30(6 Sat)-11; 12-4 Sun; closed Sun evening ~ Bedrooms: £70S/£80S ~ www.thejollydrover.co.uk *Recommended by Tony and Wendy Hobden, Tony and Jill Radnor, Peter and Jean Hoare*

LONGPARISH
Plough

SU4244 Map 2

B3048, off A303 just E of Andover; SP11 6PB

Bustling, upmarket dining pub with friendly staff, real ales, attractive bars, popular food and seats in garden

Although many customers are here to enjoy the good food, there's a comfortable little area for drinkers and you can be sure of a genuinely friendly welcome from the helpful staff. The various rooms are kept spic and span and have flagstones and oak flooring, elegant high-backed wooden dining chairs and pews around a mix of tables, some beams and standing timbers, contemporary paintwork and open fireplaces. The cosy snug has black leather bar chairs against the counter where they serve Ringwood Best and Boondoggle and Timothy Taylors Landlord on handpump, and they have a walk-in wine cellar (and several wines by the glass). On the decking outside are lots of seats, with more under parasols in the garden. The pub makes a good break from the A303.

Good, popular food includes sandwiches, duck egg, asparagus and burnt butter vinaigrette, chicken liver and foie gras parfait with spiced apple jelly, pea risotto with cheese, beer-battered pollack with triple-cooked chips and mushy peas, rack of lamb, braised shoulder and onion purée, 28-day aged fillet steak, salmon with smoked mussel and brown bread velouté, and puddings like hot chocolate fondant and salted caramel ice-cream and vanilla rice pudding with raspberry jam and raspberry ripple ice-cream. *Benchmark main dish: slow-cooked pig cheeks,*

pickled cabbage, potato skins and smoked mash £15.00. Two-course evening
meal £21.00.

Enterprise ~ Lease James Durrant ~ Real ale ~ Bar food (12-2.30(4.30 Sun), 6-9.30; not
Sun evening) ~ (01264) 720358 ~ Children welcome ~ Dogs allowed in bar ~ Open 12-
11(10.30 Sun) ~ www.theploughinn.info *Recommended by Evelyn and Derek Walter,*
Paul, Edward Mirzoeff, Anna and David Abell, Phyl and Jack Street, Ann and Colin Hunt

LONGSTOCK   SU3537 Map 2
Peat Spade
Off A30 on W edge of Stockbridge; SO20 6DR

Former coaching inn with boldly painted rooms, shooting and fishing
themed décor, imaginative food and real ales; stylish bedrooms

With a friendly welcome from the hard-working landlady and diligent
young staff who serve with a smile, this is a well run pub just 100
metres from the River Test. The terrace and garden have plenty of seats
for warm weather and there are lots of surrounding walks. Inside, there's
a nice bustling atmosphere created by locals, diners and residents all
mixing easily together and quite a sporting feel – they arrange fishing
and shooting – with stuffed fish, lots of hunting pictures and prints on
the dark red or green walls and even a little fishing shop at the end
of the garden. Both the bar and dining room have pretty windows, an
interesting mix of dining chairs around miscellaneous tables on bare
boards, standard lamps and candlelight, wine bottles, old stone bottles
and soda siphons, a nice show of toby jugs and shelves of books. There's
also an upstairs room with comfortable sofas and armchairs. Andwell
Ruddy Darter, Flowerpots Bitter and Ringwood Best on handpump
and several wines by the glass; background music. The contemporary
bedrooms are stylish and comfortable.

Enjoyable food includes lunchtime sandwiches, ham hock and caper terrine
with piccalilli, cured venison with roasted red peppers and parmesan, ham
with free-range eggs and triple-cooked chips, steak in ale or pork and mustard pies,
whole lemon sole with braised fennel and butter sauce, crispy pork belly and black
pudding croquette with a honey and mustard dressing, rack and rump of lamb with
minted mash and pea purée, and puddings. *Benchmark main dish: beer-battered*
haddock with triple-cooked chips, minted pea purée and home-made tartare
sauce £13.00. Two-course evening meal £21.00.

Free house ~ Licensee Tracy Levett ~ Real ale ~ Bar food (12-2.30, 6.30-9.30; 12-4, 7-9
Sun) ~ (01264) 810612 ~ Well behaved children welcome ~ Dogs allowed in bar and
bedrooms ~ Open 11-11; 12-4, 7-9 Sun ~ Bedrooms: /£95S ~ www.peatspadeinn.co.uk
Recommended by Phyl and Jack Street, David and Nicola Stout, Ann and Colin Hunt, Graham and
Toni Sanders

LOWER FROYLE   SU7643 Map 2
Anchor
Village signposted N of A31 W of Bentley; GU34 4NA

Civilised pub, lots to look at, real ales, good wines and imaginative
bar food; comfortable bedrooms

Even on wet, miserable days there's always a good bustle of cheerful
customers and blazing fires in this civilised but informal old pub. The
staff are welcoming and helpful even when really pushed and as well as
offering extremely good food, this is a comfortable and stylish place to

stay and the breakfasts are first class. The various rooms have low beams and standing timbers, flagstones in the bar and wood stripped floors elsewhere, sofas and armchairs dotted here and there, a mix of nice old tables and dining chairs, lit candles in candlesticks, an open fire and bar chairs at the counter. Throughout there are all sorts of interesting knick-knacks, books, lots of copper, horsebrasses, photographs (several of Charterhouse School) and all manner of pictures and prints; paint colours are fashionable, values are traditional and they keep Andwells Spring Twist, Bowmans Quiver and Triple fff Altons Pride on handpump, 11 wines by the glass (including fizz) and interesting pressés.

Excellent food might include lunchtime sandwiches, chicken liver parfait with red onion marmalade, crab mayonnaise with chilli and lime, avocado purée and brown crab pâté on toast, honey-roast ham, eggs and triple-cooked chips, roast beetroot and goats cheese salad with pine nuts and balsamic, lamb and rosemary pie, pork shoulder with bacon and cabbage, pan haggerty and meat juices, cod fillet with chorizo, tomato and butter bean casserole and parmesan breadcrumbs, longhorn sirloin steak with pepper sauce, and puddings. *Benchmark main dish: beer-battered haddock with triple-cooked chips £13.00. Two-course evening meal £21.50.*

Free house ~ Licensee Tracy Levett ~ Real ale ~ Bar food (12-2.30, 6.30-9.30; 12-4, 7-9 Sun) ~ Restaurant ~ (01420) 23261 ~ Children welcome ~ Dogs allowed in bar and bedrooms: £100S/£120S ~ www.anchorinnatlowerfroyle.co.uk *Recommended by Tony and Jill Radnor, Martin and Karen Wake, Dave Braisted, John Branston, Neil Hardwick*

LOWER WIELD

SU6339   Map 2

Yew Tree 🍴 ♀ £

Turn off A339 NW of Alton at Medstead, Bentworth 1 signpost, then follow village signposts; or off B3046 S of Basingstoke, signposted from Preston Candover; SO24 9RX

Bustling country pub with a hard-working, hands-on landlord, relaxed atmosphere and super choice of wines and food; sizeable garden and nearby walks

This is a smashing little pub run by a first-class (and always enthusiastic) landlord and his friendly, helpful staff. There's a small flagstoned bar area on the left with pictures above its stripped-brick dado, a steadily ticking clock and a log fire. Around to the right of the serving counter – which has a couple of stylish wrought-iron bar chairs – it's carpeted; throughout there's a mix of tables, including some quite small ones for two, and miscellaneous chairs. Twelve wines by the glass from a well chosen list which may include summer rosé and Louis Jadot burgundies from a shipper based just along the lane and Longdog Bunny Chaser and a beer from Triple fff named after the pub on handpump (and very reasonably priced for the area). There are solid tables and chunky seats out on the front terrace, picnic-sets in a sizeable side garden, pleasant views and a cricket field across the quiet lane; nearby walks.

As well as sandwiches, the fairly priced, interesting food menu might include grilled goats cheese bruschetta with home-made roasted cashew and basil pesto, smoked duck breast and pear salad with a beetroot and apricot compote, sausages with parsley mash and onion gravy, roasted courgette with a tomato, mushroom and leek ragout topped with feta, braised faggots with a potato cake and chilli plum gravy, salmon fillet in chinese spices on oriental noodles, guinea fowl with balsamic roast potatoes and shallots with creamed pan juices, and puddings such as brandy and honey-roasted pineapple with stem ginger ice-cream and chocolate and orange truffle cake. *Benchmark main dish: beef casserole with bacon, mushrooms and thyme £11.50. Two-course evening meal £17.00.*

Free house ~ Licensee Tim Gray ~ Real ale ~ Bar food (12-2, 6.30-9(8.30 Sun); not Mon) ~ Restaurant ~ (01256) 389224 ~ Children welcome ~ Dogs allowed in bar ~ Open 11-3, 6-11; 12-10.30 Sun; closed Mon; first two weeks Jan ~ www.the-yewtree.org.uk
Recommended by Tony and Jill Radnor, Richard and Stephanie Foskett, Martin and Karen Wake, John Walker, Philip and June Caunt, Ian Herdman, Stevie Joy, Glen and Nola Armstrong, Margaret Grimwood, David and Sheila Pearcey, Alan and Liz Haffenden, Phyl and Jack Street, Liz and Brian Barnard, Henry Paulinski, Ann and Colin Hunt

NORTH WALTHAM
SU5645   Map 2

Fox 🍺 £

3 miles from M3 junction 7: A30 southwards, then turn right at second North Waltham turn, just after Wheatsheaf; pub also signed from village centre; RG25 2BE

Traditional flint country pub, very well run, with good food and drink, nice garden

This is a proper pub with a traditional bar for locals and those wanting a drink and a chat, and a separate restaurant, too. This bar on the left is low-ceilinged with a relaxed, conversational atmosphere and Brakspears Bitter, Sharps Doom Bar, West Berkshire Good Old Boy and a guest beer on handpump and lots of bottled ciders as well as Aspell's cider on draught; ten wines by the glass, 22 malt whiskies and quite a collection of miniatures. The big woodburning stove, parquet floor, simple padded country-kitchen chairs, and poultry and 'Beer is Best' prints above the dark dado all give a comfortably old-fashioned feel – in which perhaps the vital ingredient is the polite and friendly efficiency of the hands-on landlord. There may be very faint background music. The separate dining room, with high-backed leather chairs on a blue tartan carpet, is rather larger. The garden, colourful in summer with its pergola walkway up from the gate on the lane, and with immaculate flower boxes and baskets, has picnic-sets under cocktail parasols in three separate areas, and overlooks rolling farmland (with a glimpse of the distant M3). Walks include a nice one to Jane Austen's church at Steventon.

Good home-made food includes sandwiches, chicken liver pâté with home-made chutney, smoked haddock crumble, butternut squash risotto topped with a poached egg, sausages and mash with onion gravy, venison and beef pie, chicken schnitzel (with a topping of napolitana sauce and cheese), halibut fillet stuffed with salmon mousseline on a crayfish sauce, gressingham duck breast with a morello cherry and wine sauce, and puddings such as passion fruit roulade with mango coulis and Mars Bar cheesecake with butterscotch sauce. *Benchmark main dish: twice-baked cheese soufflé £13.50. Two-course evening meal £21.00.*

Free house ~ Licensees Rob and Izzy MacKenzie ~ Real ale ~ Bar food (12-3, 6.30-9) ~ Restaurant ~ (01256) 397288 ~ Children welcome ~ Dogs allowed in bar ~ Open 11-11(midnight Sat, 10.30 Sun) ~ www.thefox.org *Recommended by John Branston*

Real ale to us means beer which has matured naturally in its cask – not pressurised or filtered. We name all real ales stocked. We usually name ales preserved under a light blanket of carbon dioxide too, though purists – pointing out that this stops the natural yeasts developing - would disagree (most people, including us, can't tell the difference!).

NORTH WARNBOROUGH

SU7352 Map 2

Mill House 🍴 ♈ ◖

A mile from M3 junction 5: A287 towards Farnham, then right (brown sign to pub) on to B3349 Hook Road; RG29 1ET

Converted mill with an attractive layout, good food and drink, and lovely waterside terraces

There are several linked areas on the main upper floor of this old heavy-beamed and raftered mill building: lots of well spaced tables in a variety of sizes and styles, rugs on polished boards or beige carpet, coal-effect gas fires in pretty fireplaces, and a profusion of often interesting pictures. A section of glass floor shows the rushing water and mill wheel below, and a galleried part on the left looks down into a dining room on that level, given a more formal feel by its panelling. The well stocked bar has an interesting changing range of malt whiskies, a good choice of wines and well kept B&P Original (the house beer, brewed by Phoenix), Andwells King John, Hook Norton Double Stout, Stonehenge Sign of Spring and Three Castles Saxon Archer on handpump; the young staff are cheerful and effective, and the atmosphere is relaxed and comfortable. In warm weather a very big plus is the extensive garden, attractively landscaped around a sizeable millpond, with plenty of solid tables and chairs on various terraces; there are swings on a neatly kept stretch of grass.

As well as sandwiches, the good modern food might include roast butternut squash with feta cheese and pomegranate salad with a saffron and tahini dressing, moules marinière, sausage and mash with onion gravy, steak burger topped with grilled bacon and cheese, steak in ale pie, sweet potato, spinach and aubergine lasagne, red snapper with stir-fried vegetables, egg noodles and a sesame, soy and honey dressing, orange and rosemary poussin with red wine sauce, and puddings like apple and raspberry crumble and sticky toffee pudding with toffee sauce. *Benchmark main dish: steak burger with bacon and cheese £10.95. Two-course evening meal £17.25.*

Brunning & Price ~ Lease Ashley Harlow ~ Real ale ~ Bar food (all day) ~ Restaurant ~ (01256) 702953 ~ Children welcome ~ Dogs allowed in bar ~ Open 11.30-11(10.30 Sun) ~ www.millhouse-hook.co.uk *Recommended by Richard Gibbs, David Jackman*

PETERSFIELD

SU7227 Map 2

Trooper 🍴 ◖ 🛏

From A32 (look for staggered crossroads) take turning to Froxfield and Steep; pub 3 miles down on left in big dip; GU32 1BD

Charming landlord, popular food, decent drinks, little persian knick-knacks and local artists' work; comfortable bedrooms

There's always a good mix of customers in this well run, popular pub, and the friendly Mr Matini offers a warm welcome to all. The bar has all sorts of cushioned dining chairs around dark wooden tables, old film star photos and paintings by local artists (for sale) on the walls, little persian knick-knacks here and there, quite a few ogival mirrors, lots of lit candles, fresh flowers and a log fire in the stone fireplace; there's a sun room with lovely downland views, carefully chosen background music and newspapers and magazines to read. Bowman Swift One and Ringwood Best on handpump and several wines by the glass or carafe. The attractive raftered restaurant has french windows to a paved terrace with views across the open countryside, and there are lots of picnic-sets on an upper lawn. The horse rail in the car park is reserved 'for horses, camels and local livestock'. Our readers like the comfortable bedrooms.

Good, popular food includes filled baguettes, duck, venison and caramelised kumquat with orange and apricot chutney, spicy king prawn skewers, home-made cumberland sausage with blue cheese sauce and onion rings, parsnip, potato and wild rice cake with wild mushrooms in a cider and sage cream, pork medallions with sweet potato cake and calvados sauce, moroccan cod tagine with lemon and herb couscous, and puddings like dark chocolate crème brûlée and spiced orange and treacle sponge pudding. *Benchmark main dish: slow-roast lamb shoulder £16.00. Two-course evening meal £19.50.*

Free house ~ Licensee Hassan Matini ~ Real ale ~ Bar food (12-3(3.30 Sun), 6-9.30; not Sun evening or Mon lunchtime) ~ Restaurant ~ (01730) 827293 ~ Children must be seated and supervised by an adult ~ Dogs allowed in bar ~ Open 12-3, 6-11; 12-3.30 Sun; closed Sun evening, Mon lunchtime ~ Bedrooms: £69B/£89B ~ www.trooperinn.com
Recommended by Henry Fryer, Mike and Mary Carter, John and Jackie Chalcraft, Richard Mason, Martin and Karen Wake, Doug Kennedy

PETERSFIELD   SU7129   Map 2
White Horse 🍺

Up on an old downs road about halfway between Steep and East Tisted, near Priors Dean – OS Sheet 186 or 197 map reference 715290; GU32 1DA

Unchanging and much-loved old place with a great deal of simple character, friendly licensees and up to ten real ales

Happily unchanging for many years and with up to ten real ales, it's not surprising that this remote 17th-c country pub is so loved by its many customers. The two charming and idiosyncratic parlour rooms (candlelit at night) have open fires, oak settles and a mix of dark wooden dining chairs, nice old tables (including some drop-leaf ones), various pictures, farm tools, rugs, a longcase clock, a couple of fireside rocking chairs and so forth. The beamed dining room is smarter with lots more pictures on the white or pink walls. On handpump, the ales might include two named for the pub, plus Butcombe Bitter, Fullers London Pride, Ringwood Best and Fortyniner and guests such as Adnams Bitter, Gales Spring Sprinter, Holt IPA, and Ringwood Boondoggle, and lots of country wines. They hold a beer festival in June and a cider festival in September. There are some rustic seats outside and they have camping facilities. If trying to find it for the first time, keep your eyes skinned – not for nothing is this known as the Pub With No Name.

Using local produce and free-range meat, the well liked food includes sandwiches, pork terrine with apricot compote, breaded brie with rhubarb chutney, all sorts of sausages with caramelised onions, honey glazed ham with free-range eggs, steak in ale or fish pie, roast butternut squash moussaka, chicken curry with pineapple salsa, salmon with lemon, pea and parmesan risotto, and puddings like white chocolate tart and fruit crumble. *Benchmark main dish: smoked fish pie £12.95. Two-course evening meal £17.50.*

Gales (Fullers) ~ Managers Georgie and Paul Stuart ~ Real ale ~ Bar food (12-2.30, 6-9.30; some cold food all day weekdays) ~ Restaurant ~ (01420) 588387 ~ Children welcome ~ Dogs allowed in bar ~ Open 12-11 ~ www.pubwithnoname.co.uk
Recommended by Jenny and Peter Lowater, Mike and Eleanor Anderson, the Didler, W A Evershed, Ann and Colin Hunt

There are report forms at the back of the book.

PORTSMOUTH   SZ6399 Map 2

Old Customs House ◗ £

Vernon Buildings, Gunwharf Quays; follow brown signs to Gunwharf Quays car park; PO1 3TY

Handsome and well converted historic building in a prime waterfront development with real ales and popular bar food

Once an 18th-c customs house, this fine brick building is part of the extensive modern waterside shopping complex; it can get pretty busy at peak times but is usefully open all day. There are several big-windowed high-ceilinged rooms – refurbished this year – with bare boards, nautical prints and photographs on pastel walls, coal-effect gas fires, nice unobtrusive lighting and well padded chairs around sturdy tables in varying sizes; the sunny entrance area has leather sofas. Broad stairs take you up to a carpeted restaurant with similar décor. Fullers Discovery, ESB, HSB, London Pride, and Seafarers on handpump, a decent range of wines by the glass and good coffees and teas. Staff are efficient, housekeeping is good, the background music well reproduced and the games machines silenced. Picnic-sets out in front are just metres from the water. Around the corner is the graceful Spinnaker Tower (165 metres tall with staggering views from its viewing decks). The bar has disabled access and facilities.

They usefully serve food all day starting with a proper breakfast; also, sandwiches, farmhouse pâté with apricot and ginger chutney, sardines with gooseberry sauce, various sharing boards, cheddar and caramelised onion flan, beefburger with chips and real ale relish, garlic chicken and thyme salad, moules frites, sausages with mash and onion gravy, and rump steak with mushrooms and peppercorn sauce. *Benchmark main dish: steak in ale pie £9.95. Two-course evening meal £16.00.*

Fullers ~ Manager David Hughes ~ Real ale ~ Bar food (all day from 9am) ~ Restaurant ~ (023) 9283 2333 ~ Children allowed until 8pm but must go to upstairs restaurant after that ~ Open 9am–midnight(1.30am Sat, 11 Sun) ~ www.theoldcustomshouse.com
Recommended by Ann and Colin Hunt, Sue and Mike Todd, Phil Bryant, John and Alison Hamilton, Peter Meister

PRESTON CANDOVER   SU6041 Map 2

Purefoy Arms ⑪ ♀

B3046 Basingstoke–Alresford; RG25 2EJ

Hampshire Dining Pub of the Year

First-class food and wines in gently upmarket village pub

If you love wine and chocolates, then this friendly and civilised pub is just the place for you. Every Tuesday they hold a Wine Club evening where for just £5 corkage you can bring a special wine of your own to eat with your meal and talk about with other interested customers; they also hold regular wine tasting events. The delicious truffles and chocolates that they sell are made by the landlord's father. There are two pairs of smallish linked rooms, all with an easy-going country pub feel. On the left, the airy front bar has chunky tables, including ones so tall as to need bar stools, and a corner counter serving a fine changing choice of wines, as well as Andwell Spring Twist and Flack Manor Double Drop on handpump; this opens into a jute-floored back area with four dining tables and characterful mixed seats including old settles. The right-hand front room has red leather sofas and armchairs by a log fire, and goes back into a bare-boards area with three or four sturdy pale pine tables. An understated contemporary décor in grey and puce goes nicely with the informal friendliness of the service; there may be unobtrusive background pop music. The sizeable sloping garden has well spaced picnic-sets, a wendy house and perhaps a big hammock slung between two of its trees; there are teak tables on a terrace sheltered by the pub. This is an attractive village, with nearby snowdrop walks in February.

Inventive and excellent, the food might include ballotine of quail and foie gras with madeira jelly, seared hand-dived scallops with masala sauce, spiced apples and young spinach, beef burger with dripping-cooked chips, beer-battered haddock with mushy peas and tartare sauce, risotto of goats cheese, muscat pears and chives, spiced iberico pork cheeks with judion white beans and pata negra sauce, oxtail and longhorn pie with roasted bone marrow, ray wing with sea kale, brown shrimps and black butter, and puddings like churros con chocolate and sticky toffee soufflé with clotted cream ice-cream and toffee sauce. *Benchmark main dish: cider-cooked ham with two goose eggs and dripping-fried chips £11.50. Two-course evening meal £20.00.*

Free house ~ Licensees Andres and Marie-Louise Alemany ~ Real ale ~ Bar food (12-3, 6-10; not Sun evening or Mon) ~ Restaurant ~ (01256) 389777 ~ Well behaved children welcome ~ Dogs allowed in bar ~ Open 12-3, 6-11; 12-4 Sun; closed Sun evening, all day Mon ~ www.thepurefoyarms.co.uk *Recommended by Jill Hurley*

ROCKBOURNE
Rose & Thistle 🍴 ♀

SU1118 Map 2

Signed off B3078 Fordingbridge–Cranborne; SP6 3NL

Pretty pub with hands-on landlady and friendly staff, informal bars, real ales, good food, and seats in garden

Even on a cold wet day, this 16th-c thatched pub is buzzing with customers; it's best to book in advance to be sure of a table. It's run with friendliness and efficiency by a first-class, hands-on landlady, and the bar has homely dining chairs, stools and benches around a mix of old pubby tables, Fullers London Pride, Palmers Copper Ale and Timothy Taylors Landlord on handpump, a dozen wines (and prosecco) by the glass and Weston's cider. The restaurant has a log fire in each of its two rooms (one is a big brick inglenook), old engravings and cricket prints and an informal and relaxed atmosphere. There are benches and tables under the pretty hanging baskets at the front of the building, with picnic-sets under parasols on the grass; good nearby walks. This is a pretty village on the edge of the New Forest.

The seasonally changing menu uses local produce and the reliably good food might include ploughman's, rillettes of duck and pork with a spiced cucumber pickle, a smoked fish platter, local sausages with horseradish mash, red onion marmalade and red wine gravy, roasted vegetable and feta strudel with mint pesto, corn-fed chicken on parsnip and rosemary mash with sausage and leek stuffing wrapped in smoked bacon with a red wine jus, slow-cooked pork belly with a shallot and apple purée, herb crusted black pudding and wholegrain mustard sauce, daily specials, and puddings like spiced hot chocolate and orange fondant and sticky toffee and date pudding. *Benchmark main dish: steak and kidney pudding £14.00. Two-course evening meal £20.75.*

Free house ~ Licensee Kerry Dutton ~ Real ale ~ Bar food (12-2.30, 7-9.30; not Sun evening) ~ Restaurant ~ (01725) 518236 ~ Children welcome ~ Dogs allowed in bar ~ Open 11-3, 6-11; 11-11 Sat; 12-10.30(8 in winter) Sun ~ www.roseandthistle.co.uk *Recommended by Mrs J Butler, Mr and Mrs P R Thomas, Ian Herdman, Richard and Sue Fewkes, David and Judy Robison*

SPARSHOLT

SU4331   Map 2

Plough 🍴 ♀

Village signposted off B3049 (Winchester–Stockbridge), a little W of Winchester; SO21 2NW

Neat, well run dining pub with interesting furnishings, an extensive wine list and popular bar food; garden with children's play fort

Our readers enjoy their visits to this particularly well run country pub very much indeed – and it's the sort of place customers tend to return to again and again. It's always deservedly busy (you must book a table in advance) but you can be sure of a friendly welcome from the courteous licensees and their staff. The main bar has an interesting mix of wooden tables and chairs with farm tools, scythes and pitchforks attached to the ceiling, and they keep Wadworths IPA, 6X, Bishops Tipple, Horizon and Swordfish on handpump and quite a few wines and champagne by the glass from an extensive list. Outside, there are plenty of seats on the terrace and lawn and a children's play fort; disabled access and facilities.

🍴 Highly thought of food includes lunchtime sandwiches, chicken liver parfait with cumberland sauce, sautéed kidneys in a smoked bacon, mushroom and port sauce, home-made steak burgers with pepper sauce and dauphinoise potatoes, wild mushroom and courgette tagliatelle with parmesan, chicken breast with roasted pepper mousse, pak choi and basil sauce, slow-cooked pork belly with bubble and squeak and five-spice sauce, changing fish specials, and puddings like treacle tart with clotted cream and apple and plum crumble. *Benchmark main dish: home-made salmon and crab fishcakes £12.95. Two-course evening meal £20.00.*

Wadworths ~ Tenants Richard and Kathryn Crawford ~ Real ale ~ Bar food (12-2, 6-9(9.30 Fri and Sat, 8.30 Sun)) ~ (01962) 776353 ~ Children welcome ~ Dogs welcome ~ Open 10-3, 6-11; 10-11 Sun *Recommended by Tony and Jill Radnor, Henry Fryer, Phyl and Jack Street, Jill and Julian Tasker, John and Annabel Hampshire, Tim Gray, John and Joan Calvert*

STEEP

SU7525   Map 2

Harrow 🍺 £

Take Midhurst exit from Petersfield bypass, at exit roundabout take first left towards Midhurst, then first turning on left opposite garage, and left again at Sheet church; follow over dual carriageway bridge to pub; GU32 2DA

Unchanging, simple place with long-serving landladies, beers tapped from the cask, unfussy food and a big free-flowering garden; no children inside

Our readers love this tiny, unspoilt and quite unchanging pub and many of them have been coming here for years. It's been in the same family for 83 years and there's no pandering to modern methods – no credit cards, no waitress service, no restaurant, no music, and outside lavatories. Everything revolves around village chat between the friendly customers, who will probably draw you into light-hearted conversation. There are adverts for logs next to calendars of views being sold in support of local charities and news of various quirky competitions. The little public bar has hops and dried flowers hanging from the beams, built-in wall benches on the tiled floor, stripped-pine wallboards, a good log fire in the big inglenook and wild flowers on the scrubbed deal tables; board games. Ringwood Best and Bowman Swift One are tapped straight from casks behind the counter, and they have Hampshire wine and apple juice; staff are polite and friendly, even when under pressure. The big garden is left free-flowering so that goldfinches can collect thistle seeds from the grass, but there are some seats on paved areas. The Petersfield bypass doesn't intrude on this idyll, though you will need to follow the directions above to find the pub. No children inside and dogs must be on leads.

 Generous helpings of bar food include sandwiches, home-made scotch eggs, hearty ham, split pea and vegetable soup, ploughman's, quiches, and puddings such as treacle tart or seasonal fruit pies. *Benchmark main dish: hearty ham, split pea and vegetable soup £5.50.*

Free house ~ Licensees Claire and Denise McCutcheon ~ Real ale ~ Bar food (not summer Sun evening) ~ No credit cards ~ (01730) 262685 ~ Dogs welcome ~ Open 12-2.30, 6-11; 11-3, 6-11 Sat; 12-3, 7-10.30 Sun ~ www.harrow-inn.co.uk *Recommended by W A Evershed, Prof James Stevens Curl, Tony and Jill Radnor, John and Anne Mackinnon, John and Jackie Chalcraft, the Didler, Greg Gregory*

SWANMORE   SU5815   Map 2
Rising Sun ♀ ◀

Droxford Road; signed off A32 N of Wickham and B2177 S of Bishops Waltham, at Hillpound E of village centre; SO32 2PS

Proper country pub with friendly staff, good beers and popular food

They now offer a takeaway menu in this 17th-c coaching inn on Sunday-Thursday evenings and it's proving very popular. The low-beamed carpeted bar has some easy chairs and a sofa by its good log fire and a few tables with pubby seats. Beyond the fireplace on the right is a pleasant much roomier dining area (with similarly unpretentious furnishings) running back in an L past the bar; one part of this has stripped brick barrel vaulting. Jennings Tizzie Wizzie, Ringwood Best, Sharps Doom Bar and Timothy Taylors Landlord on handpump and 13 wines by the glass. There are picnic-sets out on the side grass with a play area; the Kings Way long-distance path is close by.

 Quite a choice of bar food might include sandwiches and filled baguettes, soup, vegetable lasagne, home-made faggots with mushy peas and gravy, beer-battered fish and chips, lambs liver with bacon and onion gravy, smoked haddock and spring onion fishcakes, specials such as corned beef hash with an egg, chicken curry and mixed fish platter, and puddings like raspberry crème brûlée and spotted dick and custard. *Benchmark main dish: steak in ale pie £10.95. Two-course evening meal £16.50.*

Free house ~ Licensees Mark and Sue Watts ~ Real ale ~ Bar food (12-2(2.30 Sun), 6-9(8.30 Sun)) ~ Restaurant ~ (01489) 896663 ~ Children welcome ~ Dogs allowed in bar ~ Open 11.30-3, 5.30-11; 12-4, 5.30-10.30 Sun ~ www.risingsunswanmore.co.uk *Recommended by Phyl and Jack Street, Jane and Rowena Leverington, mark watts*

WINCHESTER   SU4829   Map 2
Wykeham Arms ♀

Kingsgate Street (Kingsgate Arch and College Street are now closed to traffic; there is access via Canon Street); SO23 9PE

Tucked-away pub with lots to look at, several real ales, plenty of wines by the glass and highly though of food; lovely bedrooms

This is a lovely old pub and our readers enjoy their visits here very much. The series of bustling rooms have all sorts of interesting collections dotted about and three log fires – as well as 19th-c oak desks retired from nearby Winchester College, a redundant pew from the same source, kitchen chairs and candlelit deal tables and big windows with swagged curtains. A snug room at the back, known as the Jameson Room (after the late landlord Graeme Jameson), is decorated with a set of Ronald Searle 'Winespeak' prints and a second one is panelled. Fullers HSB, London Pride, a seasonal guest and Gales Seafarers plus a guest such as Flowerpots Goodens Gold on handpump, lots of wines by the glass and several malt whiskies. There are tables on a covered back terrace with more on a small courtyard. Some of the individually styled bedrooms have four-posters and the two-level suite has its own sitting room.

🍴 Good food includes sandwiches, moules marinière, chicken liver and foie gras parfait with poached rhubarb and caramelised onion and thyme brioche, beer-battered cod with triple-cooked chips, crushed peas and tartare sauce, a pie of the day, salt-baked beetroot, honey roast parsnips and ginger and orange spiced lentils, bream with chorizo confit potatoes and paprika glazed peppers, corn-fed chicken with seared king oyster mushroom, sweetcorn and madeira jus, and puddings like toffee chocolate mousse with warm glazed banana and set lavender cream with honeycomb and caramel ice-cream. *Benchmark main dish: beer-battered chips with triple-cooked chips and tartare sauce £13.50. Two-course evening meal £22.00.*

Fullers ~ Manager Jon Howard ~ Real ale ~ Bar food (12-3, 6-9.30) ~ Restaurant ~ (01962) 853834 ~ Children lunchtime only in restaurant ~ Dogs allowed in bar and bedrooms ~ Open 11-11(10.30 Sun) ~ Bedrooms: £72S/£135S(£145B) ~ www.wykehamarmswinchester.co.uk *Recommended by Franzi Florack, Ann and Colin Hunt, the Didler, Martin and Karen Wake, John and Annabel Hampshire, Mark Sykes, Richard and Sissel Harris, Jane and Rowena Leverington*

Also Worth a Visit in Hampshire

Besides the fully inspected pubs, you might like to try these pubs that have been recommended to us and described by readers. Do tell us what you think of them: feedback@goodguides.com

---

ALRESFORD SU5832
Bell (01962) 732429
West Street; SO24 9AT Comfortable and welcoming Georgian coaching inn (originally the Market Inn), good popular food including weekday fixed-price menu, friendly efficient service, well kept local beer and good choice of wines, spic-and-span interior with bare boards, scrubbed tables, bric-a-brac and log fire, daily newspapers, smallish dining room, may be jazz on Sun in summer; attractive sunny back courtyard, six bedrooms, open all day, closed Sun evening. *(Val and Alan Green, Phyl and Jack Street, Neil Hardwick)*

ALRESFORD SU5832
Swan (01962) 732302
West Street; SO24 9AD Long narrow oak-panelled red-carpeted bar in 18th-c hotel (former coaching inn), three well kept ales including Courage Best, decent wines, tea and coffee, good choice of popular reasonably priced food, good Sun carvery, two dining rooms; children welcome, 23 bedrooms. *(Ann and Colin Hunt, Val and Alan Green)*

ALTON SU7138
French Horn (01420) 83269
The Butts (A339 S of centre, by railway bridge); GU34 1RT Popular and cheery catslide-roof local with well kept Butcombe, Ringwood, Sharps, Triple fff, Wells & Youngs and a guest, plenty of wines by the glass, wide choice of enjoyable food including blackboard specials, nice coffee, good service, tankards and whisky-water jugs on beams, bowler hats and french horn above inglenook log fire, newspapers, partly stripped-brick dining room, separate skittle alley; background music; children welcome, covered heated smokers' terrace, picnic-sets in two garden areas, play area, bedrooms in adjacent building, next to Watercress Line with occasional steam trains, open all day. *(LM, Phil and Sally Gorton)*

AMPFIELD SU4023
★**White Horse** (01794) 368356
A3090 Winchester–Romsey; SO51 9BQ Snug low-beamed front bar with candles and soft lighting, inglenook log fire and

comfortable country furnishings, far-spreading beamed dining area behind, well kept Greene King ales and guests, good food including all-day snacks, several nice wines by the glass, efficient friendly service, locals' bar with another inglenook; background music; children and dogs welcome, high-hedged garden with plenty of picnic-sets, cricket green beyond, good walks in Ampfield Woods, handy for Hillier Gardens, open all day. *(Phyl and Jack Street, Matt Cutting)*

AMPORT   SU2944
Hawk Inn (01264) 710371
Off A303 at Thruxton interchange; Sarson Lane; SP11 8AE Recently refurbished village inn with lots of linked areas, good variety of food from sharing boards up, ales such as Fullers London Pride, Ramsbury and Upham, decent wines by the glass; children and dogs welcome, front terrace, nine bedrooms, open all day. *(Phyl and Jack Street)*

BALL HILL   SU4263
Furze Bush (01635) 253228
leaving Newbury on A343 turn right towards East Woodhay; RG20 0NQ Clean airy décor, pews and pine tables, log fire, wide choice of good generous food promptly served by friendly staff, several well kept ales including Fullers London Pride, decent wines, reasonable prices, restaurant; children welcome, tables on terrace by good-sized sheltered lawn with fenced play area. *(Mr and Mrs H J Langley, Ian Herdman, J V Dadswell)*

BARTON STACEY   SU4341
Swan (01962) 760470
Village signed off A303; SO21 3RL Warm friendly atmosphere in beamed former coaching inn, enjoyable food from pubby things up, well kept ales such as Bowman, Fullers and Otter, good choice of wines, little lounge area between front log-fire bar and cosy dining part, back restaurant; background music; children and dogs welcome, tables on front lawn and back terrace, open all day Fri, Sat, closed Sun evening. *(Russell Traynor, Sarah Flynn)*

BASING   SU6653
★Millstone (01256) 331153
Bartons Lane, Old Basing; follow brown signs to Basing House; RG24 8AE Well run busy pub with lots of picnic-sets out by River Loddon (ducks and swans) looking across to former viaduct through scrubland, enjoyable freshly cooked food, full Wadworths range kept well, Weston's farm cider, good choice of wines by the glass, dark panelling, old prints and etchings, sturdy pub furnishings; may be faint background music;

children and dogs welcome, by ruins of Basing House, open all day. *(Karen Sloan)*

BEAUWORTH   SU5624
Milburys (01962) 771248
Off A272 Winchester/Petersfield; SO24 0PB Attractive old tile-hung pub, beams, panelling and stripped stone, massive 17th-c treadmill for much older incredibly deep well, galleried area, good choice of real ales, straightforward reasonably priced food, efficient service, skittle alley; children in eating areas, garden with fine downland views, good walks. *(Ann and Colin Hunt, Michael and Maggie Betton, the Didler)*

BISHOP'S WALTHAM   SU5517
Barleycorn (01489) 892712
Lower Basingwell Street; SO32 1AJ Buoyant 18th-c two-bar local, enjoyable generously served pub food at sensible prices, friendly efficient service, well kept Greene King ales and a guest, decent wine, beams and some low ceiling panelling, open fires; children and dogs welcome, large garden with back smokers' area, open all day. *(Henry Fryer, Bob Hodges, Stephen and Jean Curtis, Ann and Colin Hunt)*

BISHOP'S WALTHAM   SU5517
★Bunch of Grapes (01489) 892935
St Peter`s Street - just along from entrance to central car park; SO32 1AD Neat civilised little pub in quiet medieval street, smartly furnished keeping individuality and unspoilt feel (run by same family for a century), good chatty landlord and regulars, Courage Best, Goddards and a guest tapped from the cask, no food; charming back terrace garden with own bar, opening times may vary. *(Henry Fryer, Phil and Jane Villiers, the Didler, Stephen and Jean Curtis)*

BRAISHFIELD   SU3725
Newport Inn (01794) 368225
Newport Lane - from centre follow Michelmersh, Timsbury signpost; SO51 0PL Plain old-fashioned two-bar brick local, unchanging and in same family for 70 years, well kept Fullers/Gales ales, bargain sandwiches or ploughman's, cribbage, piano singsongs Sat night and maybe folk music Thurs; informal and relaxing tree-shaded garden. *(the Didler, Andrea Rampley)*

BRAISHFIELD   SU3724
Wheatsheaf (01794) 367737
Village signposted off A3090 on NW edge of Romsey; SO51 0QE Doing well under friendly hard-working licensees, good food, well kept Flack Manor, Timothy Taylors Landlord and a guest, good choice of wines by the glass including champagne, log fire;

We say if we know a pub allows dogs.

background music; children and dogs welcome, garden with nice views, boules, woodland walks nearby, close to Hillier Gardens, open all day Fri-Sun. *(John Chambers, Stuart Harvey)*

BRAMBRIDGE — SU4721
✶Dog & Crook (01962) 712129
Near M3 junction 12, via B3335; SO50 6HZ Cheerful bustling 18th-c pub, good food from traditional favourites to more adventurous à la carte choices, good service, cosy dining room, beamed bar with friendly drinking end, Fullers and Ringwood ales, lots of wines by the glass; background music, TV, regular events and summer music nights; dogs welcome, garden with heated decking and arbour, Itchen Way walks nearby. *(Mr and Mrs D G Waller)*

BRAMDEAN — SU6127
✶Fox (01962) 771363
A272 Winchester–Petersfield; SO24 0LP The long-serving licensees at this pleasant 17th-c weatherboarded dining pub were due to retire as we went to press - news please; old-fashioned open-plan bar, black beams, cushioned wall pews and wheelbacks, tall stools with backrests at counter, Greene King Morland Original; walled-in terraced area and spacious lawn under fruit trees, good surrounding walks, has been closed Sun evening. *(Colin McKerrow, Helen and Brian Edgeley)*

BROOK — SU2714
Bell (023) 8081 2214
B3079/B3078, handy for M27 junction 1; SO43 7HE Really a hotel with golf club and plush restaurant, but has neatly kept bar with lovely inglenook fire, good choice of well kept ales including Ringwood and good bar food from sandwiches to steak, helpful friendly uniformed staff; big garden, delightful village, 25 comfortable bedrooms. *(Phyl and Jack Street)*

BROOK — SU2713
✶Green Dragon (023) 8081 2214
B3078 NW of Cadnam, just off M27 junction 1; SO43 7HE Immaculate thatched New Forest dining pub dating from 15th c, welcoming helpful staff, good fresh food including plenty of seasonal game and fish as well as pubby favourites, well kept Fullers and Ringwood, daily newspapers, bright linked areas with stripped pine and other pubby furnishings; disabled access from car park, attractive small terrace, garden with paddocks beyond, picturesque village, self-catering apartment. *(R and M Thomas, Mr and Mrs P D Titcomb, PL, Janet de Lange, David and Sally Frost, Jennifer Bugg)*

BURGHCLERE — SU4660
Carpenters Arms (01635) 278251
Harts Lane, off A34; RG20 9JY Small unpretentious pub run well by energetic landlady, Arkells and an occasional guest, sensibly priced home-made food (not Sun evening), good country views (Watership Down) from dining extension and terrace picnic-sets, log fire; background music; children and dogs welcome, handy for Sandham Memorial Chapel (NT) and Highclere Castle, six comfortable annexe bedrooms, open all day. *(Mr and Mrs H J Langley, Pat and Graham Williamson)*

BURITON — SU7320
✶Five Bells (01730) 263584
Off A3 S of Petersfield; GU31 5RX Low-beamed 17th-c pub, popular fresh pubby food (not Sun evening) from baguettes up, Badger ales and good wines by the glass, pleasant staff, big log fire, daily newspapers, flowers and church candles, some ancient stripped masonry and woodburner on public side; background music; children and dogs welcome, nice garden and sheltered terraces, pretty village, good walks, self-catering in converted stables, open all day. *(W A Evershed, Terry and Eileen Stott, Ann and Colin Hunt)*

BURLEY — SU2103
Queens Head (01425) 403423
The Cross; back Road Ringwood–Lymington; BH24 4AB Large pub dating partly from 17th c and probably earlier, several rambling rooms, good friendly atmosphere, some flagstones, beams, timbering and panelling, wide choice of food all day including deals, Ringwood and a guest ale, nice coffee; pub and New Forest village can get packed in summer; children welcome, open all day. *(Paul Ward)*

BURLEY — SU2202
White Buck (01425) 402264
Bisterne Close; 0.7 miles E, OS Sheet 195 map reference 223028; BH24 4AZ Popular 19th-c mock-Tudor hotel owned by Fullers, their ales and a guest in long comfortably divided bar, lots of pictures, log fires each end, enjoyable sensibly priced food, pleasant dining room with tables out on decking, helpful friendly young staff; children and dogs welcome, front terrace and spacious lawn, lovely New Forest setting with superb walks towards Burley itself and over Mill Lawn, seven bedrooms, open all day. *(John and Joan Calvert, Sara Fulton, Roger Baker, Ian Herdman and others)*

BURSLEDON — SU4809
✶Fox & Hounds (023) 8040 2784
Hungerford Bottom; 2 miles from M27 junction 8; SO31 8DE Popular rambling 16th-c Chef & Brewer of unusual character, ancient beams, flagstones and big log fires, linked by pleasant family conservatory area to ancient back barn with buoyant rustic atmosphere, lantern-lit side stalls, lots of interesting farm equipment, well kept ales including Ringwood, good choice of wines, decent coffee, enjoyable reasonably

priced food from sandwiches up with vegetarian choices, cheerful obliging staff, daily newspapers; children allowed, tables outside. *(Phyl and Jack Street, Ann and Colin Hunt, Phil and Jane Villiers)*

BURSLEDON
SU4909

✶ **Jolly Sailor** (023) 8040 5557

Off A27 towards Bursledon Station, Lands End Road; handy for M27 junction 8; SO31 8DN Popular Badger dining pub in prime spot overlooking yachting inlet, food cooked to order (may be a wait), their usual ales and good wine choice, log fires; open all day. *(Ann and Colin Hunt, Louisa Fleming)*

CADNAM
SU2913

Sir John Barleycorn

(023) 8081 2236 *Off Southampton Road; by M27, junction 1; SO40 2NP* Picturesque low-slung thatched dining pub extended from cosy beamed and timbered medieval core, fairly standard food including good value weekday two-course menu (till 6pm), good service, Ringwood and a guest ale, two log fires, modern décor and stripped wood flooring; background music; children welcome, suntrap benches in front and out in colourful garden, open all day. *(Phyl and Jack Street, R Aitken-Sykes)*

CADNAM
SU2913

White Hart (023) 8081 2277

Old Romsey Road, handy for M27 junction 1; SO40 2NP Big rambling Home Counties family pub/restaurant, enjoyable food all day, ales from Flack Manor and Ringwood, plenty of wines by the glass, cheerful efficient service, mix of old table and chairs including pews on parquet, quarry tiles or bare boards, painted half-pannelling, some stripped brickwork, lots of old prints, books and photographs, woodburner; background music, no dogs; disabled facilities, picnic-sets in garden with play area. *(Dr Elizabeth Fellows)*

CHALTON
SU7316

✶ **Red Lion** (023) 9259 2246

Off A3 Petersfield–Horndean; PO8 0BG Largely extended thatched all-day dining pub with interesting 16th-c core around ancient inglenook fireplace, wide range of popular food from sandwiches up, well kept Fullers/ Gales ales and lots of country wines, helpful smart staff; children and dogs allowed, good disabled access and facilities, nice views from neat rows of picnic-sets on rectangular lawn by large car park, good walks, handy for Queen Elizabeth Country Park. *(Ann and Colin Hunt)*

CHARLTON DOWN
SU3549

Hare & Hounds (01264) 735672

Hungerford Lane, off A343 N of Andover; SP11 0JA Tucked-away extended brick-and-flint country pub, neat and airy, with enjoyable food including fresh fish, vegetarian dishes and popular Sun roasts, real ales, friendly staff, log fires; tables on pleasant terrace, good local walks, closed Sun evening, Mon. *(Ann and Colin Hunt, Phyl and Jack Street)*

CHARTER ALLEY
SU5957

White Hart (01256) 850049

White Hart Lane, off A340 N of Basingstoke; RG26 5QA Handsome beamed pub with ales such as Bowman, Palmers and Triple fff, continental beers, summer farm cider, decent wines including country ones, good choice of well presented food from interesting menu (not Sun evening), comfortable lounge bar with woodburner in big fireplace, dining area, simple public bar, skittle alley; small garden and sheltered water-feature terrace, nine bedrooms, open all day Sun. *(Joan and Michel Hooper-Immins, J V Dadswell)*

CHAWTON
SU7037

✶ **Greyfriar** (01420) 83841

Off A31/A32 S of Alton; Winchester Road; GU34 1SB Popular flower-decked beamed dining pub opposite Jane Austen's house, enjoyable food (till 7pm Sun) from lunchtime sandwiches and bar snacks up, Fullers ales, decent wines by the glass, good coffees, welcoming relaxed atmosphere and quite a few older midweek lunchers, comfortable seating and sturdy pine tables in neat linked areas, open fire in restaurant end; background music; children welcome till 9pm, dogs in bar, small garden with terrace, good nearby walks, open all day. *(B and F A Hannam, B M Eldridge)*

CHERITON
SU5828

✶ **Flower Pots** (01962) 771318

Off B3046 towards Beauworth and Winchester; OS Sheet 185 map reference 581282; SO24 0QQ Unspoilt country local in same family for over 40 years, own-brewed good value beers (brewery tours by arrangement) along with Flowerpots ales tapped from casks, standard food (not Sun evening or bank holiday evenings, and possible restrictions during busy times), popular curry night Weds, extended plain public bar with covered well, another straightforward but homely room with country pictures on striped wallpaper and ornaments over small log fire; no credit cards or children; dogs welcome, seats on pretty front and back lawns, summer marquee, bedrooms. *(John Coatsworth, Tony and Jill Radnor, Geoff and Linda Payne, Ann and Colin Hunt, the Didler and others)*

CHILWORTH
SU4118

✶ **Chilworth Arms** (023) 8076 6247

Chilworth Road (A27 Southampton–Romsey); SO16 7JZ Stylish, well run modern dining pub, popular food from sharing plates and home-made pizzas up, weekday fixed-price menu till 7pm, good wine choice, ales such as Greene King, Sharps and Wells & Youngs, neat efficient young staff, chunky furniture including quite a lot of leather, log fires, conservatory-style back restaurant, chattier areas too; background music; children welcome, disabled facilities, large neat garden with terrace, open all day. *(Phil and Jane Villiers, Phyl and Jack Street, Mel Poole, Jill and Julian Tasker and others)*

COLDEN COMMON   SU4821
Fishers Pond (023) 8069 2209
Junction B3354/B2177 (Main Road), at Fishers Pond just S; SO50 7HG
Big Vintage Inn in appealing position by peaceful woodside lake, various different areas and alcoves making most of waterside views, some painted brickwork, carpet or rugs on aged terracotta, dark leather built-in banquettes, heavy beams and log fires, brighter modern end section, ales such as Ringwood and Sharps Doom Bar, Aspall's cider, all-day bar food, mixed reports on service; background music, machines; children welcome, solid teak furniture on heated partly covered lakeside terrace, handy for Marwell Zoo. *(Joan and Michel Hooper-Immins, Phyl and Jack Street, Preston Willson)*

CRONDALL   SU7948
Plume of Feathers (01252) 850245
The Borough; GU10 5NT Attractive smallish 15th-c village pub popular for good range of home-made food from standards to more innovative dishes, friendly helpful staff, well kept Greene King and some unusual guests, good wines by the glass, beams and dark wood, red carpet, prints on cream walls, restaurant with log fire in big brick fireplace (not usually lit lunchtimes); children welcome, picturesque village, three bedrooms. *(KC)*

CROOKHAM   SU7952
Exchequer (01252) 615336
Crondall Road; GU51 5SU Welcoming refurbished pub with enjoyable home-made food in flagstoned bar and restaurant (gluten-free and vegetarian choices), three local ales tapped from the cask, good choice of wines by the glass, daily newspapers, woodburner; background music; terrace tables, near Basingstoke Canal and popular with walkers, open all day weekends, closed Mon. *(Jessica Courtney)*

CURDRIDGE   SU5314
Cricketers (023) 8078 4420
Curdridge Lane, off B3035 just under a mile NE of A334 junction; SO32 2BH
Open-plan low-ceilinged Victorian village pub with cheery welcoming landlady, enjoyable well presented food, well kept Greene King ales, good attentive service, lounge part with banquettes, traditional public area, dining section with large Beryl Cook inspired mural of the locals, cricketing memorabilia; soft background music; tables on front lawn, pleasant walks. *(Henry Fryer, David M Smith)*

DAMERHAM   SU1016
Compasses (01725) 518231
Signed off B3078 in Fordingbridge, or off A354 via Martin; East End; SP6 3HQ
Appealing old country inn, well kept ales including Ringwood, good choice of wines by the glass, lots of malt whiskies, enjoyable food from sandwiches up, small neat lounge bar divided by log fire from pleasant dining area with booth seating, pale wood tables and kitchen chairs, conservatory, separate bar with pool, friendly locals; children and dogs welcome, long pretty garden by attractive village's cricket ground, high downland walks, six bedrooms, open all day weekends. *(Anon)*

DENMEAD   SU6211
Chairmakers Arms (023) 9225 5990
Forest Road; PO7 4QX Roomy country pub surrounded by paddocks and farmland, good value quickly served food from bar snacks up, Sun carvery, Fullers ales, log fires; can get busy; tables in spacious garden with pergola, nice walks. *(W A Evershed)*

DIBDEN PURLIEU   SU4106
Heath (023) 8084 2275 *Beaulieu Road; B3054/A326 roundabout; SO45 4PU* Comfortable and welcoming family dining pub, popular and spacious, with bright clean contemporary linked areas, good choice of enjoyable food all day, friendly efficient young staff, beers such as Ringwood, Shepherd Neame Spitfire and Wadworths 6X. *(Phyl and Jack Street, Barrie and Mary Crees and others)*

DUMMER   SU5846
Queen (01256) 397367
Under a mile from M3 junction 7; take Dummer slip road; RG25 2AD
Comfortable beamed pub well divided with lots of softly lit alcoves, Courage Best, Fullers London Pride, John Smiths and a guest, decent choice of wines by the glass, popular food from lunchtime sandwiches and light dishes up, friendly service, big log fire, Queen and steeplechase prints, no mobile phones, restaurant allowing children; background music; picnic-sets under parasols on terrace and in extended back garden, attractive

village with ancient church. *(Michael and Margaret Cross)*

DUNBRIDGE SU3126
★**Mill Arms** (01794) 340401
Barley Hill; SO51 0LF Much extended 18th-c coaching inn opposite station, friendly informal atmosphere in spacious high-ceilinged rooms, scrubbed pine tables and farmhouse chairs on oak or flagstone floors, several sofas, two log fires, well kept Ringwood and guests, food (all day Sat) including grills and wood-fired pizzas, dinning conservatory, two skittle alleys; background music; children welcome, dogs in bar, big pretty garden, plenty of walks in surrounding Test valley, six comfortable bedrooms, open till 4.30pm Sun, closed Mon. *(Glenwys and Alan Lawrence, Phyl and Jack Street, George Harrison)*

DUNDRIDGE SU5718
★**Hampshire Bowman**
(01489) 892940 *Off B3035 towards Droxford, Swanmore, then right at Bishops W signpost; SO32 1GD* Good chatty mix at this friendly relaxed country tavern, five well kept local ales tapped from casks, summer farm cider, well liked food (all day Fri-Sun) from hearty pub dishes to specials using local produce including own vegetables and herbs, smart stable bar sitting comfortably alongside cosy and unassuming original one, some colourful paintings, Archie the pub dog, no mobile phones (£1 fine in charity box); children (under-14s in stable bar) and dogs welcome, hitching post for horses, heated terrace, peaceful lawn, play equipment, open all day. *(Henry Fryer, Ann and Colin Hunt, the Didler, Stephen and Jean Curtis)*

DURLEY SU5116
Farmers Home (01489) 860457
B3354 and B2177; Heathen Street/Curdridge Road; SO32 2BT Helpful long-serving landlord in comfortable beamed pub with two-bay dining area and big restaurant, generous reasonably priced food including fresh fish and lovely puddings, good friendly service, well kept Fullers/Gales and Ringwood, decent wine, log fire; children welcome, big garden with good play area, nice walks. *(Phyl and Jack Street, Ann and Colin Hunt, Stephen and Jean Curtis)*

DURLEY SU5217
Robin Hood (01489) 860229
Durley Street, just off B2177 Bishops Waltham–Winchester - brown signs to pub; SO32 2AA Popular open-plan beamed pub with good food from varied blackboard menu (order at bar), Greene King and a guest ale, log fire and leather sofas in bare-boards bar, dining area with stone floors and mix of old pine tables and chairs, bookcase door to lavatories; background music; children and dogs welcome, disabled

facilities, decked terrace with barbecue, garden with play area and nice country views, open all day Sun. *(Graham, Phyl and Jack Street, Graham Giles-Payne)*

EAST MEON SU6822
★**Olde George** (01730) 823481
Church Street; signed off A272 W of Petersfield, and off A32 in West Meon; GU32 1NH Relaxing heavy-beamed rustic pub with enjoyable if not cheap bar and restaurant food, Badger ales, cosy areas around central bar counter, inglenook log fires; children and dogs welcome, nice back terrace, five comfortable bedrooms, pretty village with fine church, good walks, open all day Sun. *(W A Evershed, Ann and Colin Hunt)*

EAST STRATTON SU5339
★**Northbrook Arms** (01962) 774150
Brown sign to pub off A33 4 miles S of A303 junction; SO21 3DU Charming landlord has left this pleasantly unassuming pub - news please; traditional tiled-floor bar on right with pubby chairs around sturdy stripped-top tables, bric-a-brac, log fire, rather more formal part to the left ending in a proper dining room, ales have included Flower Pots and Otter, skittle alley; picnic-sets out on green, more in good-sized back courtyard, fine walks nearby, bedrooms, has closed Sun evening (in winter) and Mon. *(Ann and Colin Hunt, Phyl and Jack Street, James and Steph Price)*

EASTON SU5132
Cricketers (01962) 779353
Off B3047; SO21 1EJ Pleasantly smartened-up traditional local, home-made food with some modern touches in bar and smallish restaurant, friendly accommodating landlord, well kept Marstons-related ales including Ringwood, good choice of wines by the glass, dark tables and chairs on carpet, bare-boards area with darts, shove-ha'penny and other games; background and some live music, sports TV; children and dogs welcome, front terrace with heated smokers' shelter, handy for Itchen Way walks, three bedrooms, open all day summer. *(Tony and Jill Radnor, John Jenkins)*

ELLISFIELD SU6345
★**Fox** (01256) 381210
Green Lane; S of village off Northgate Lane; RG25 2QW Simple tucked-away place spruced up by present owners; mixed collection of stripped tables, country chairs and cushioned wall benches on bare boards and old floor tiles, some stripped masonry, open fires in plain brick fireplaces, Sharps Doom Bar, Fullers London Pride and a guest or two, sensibly priced home-made food; outside gents'; children and dogs welcome, picnic-sets in nice garden, good walking country near snowdrop and bluebell woods, open all day. *(Ann and Colin Hunt)*

EMERY DOWN SU2808
⋆**New Forest** (023) 8028 4690
*Village signed off A35 just W of
Lyndhurst; SO43 7DY* In one of the best
bits of the Forest for walking, well run and
popular, with good reasonably priced food
(all day weekends) including local venison,
good Sun roast too (best to book), friendly
attentive uniformed staff, ales such as
Fullers, Ringwood and Shepherd Neame,
real cider, good choice of wines by the glass,
coffee and tea all day, attractive softly lit
separate areas on varying levels, each with
its own character, hunting prints, two log
fires; background music; children and dogs
welcome, covered heated terrace, small
pleasant three-level garden, bedrooms, open
all day. *(Laurie Scott)*

EMSWORTH SU7405
Blue Bell (01243) 373394
South Street; PO10 7EG Small timeless
quayside pub with memorabilia everywhere,
friendly busy atmosphere, good choice of
popular no-nonsense food (not Sun evening)
including local fish, should book weekends,
Sharps Doom Bar and guest, live music; dogs
welcome, terrace, Sun market in adjacent car
park, open all day. *(Terry and Nickie Williams)*

EVERTON SZ2994
Crown (01590) 642655
*Old Christchurch Road; pub signed just
off A337 W of Lymington; SO41 0JJ*
Quietly set New Forest-edge restaurant/pub
with enjoyable range of food, good service,
Ringwood and guests, reliable wine choice,
two attractive dining rooms off tiled-floor bar,
log fires; picnic-sets on front terrace and in
garden behind. *(Steve Green, David Sizer)*

EXTON SU6120
⋆**Shoe** (01489) 877526
*Village signposted from A32 NE of
Bishop's Waltham; SO32 3NT* Popular
brick-built country pub on South Downs
Way, three linked rooms with log fires, good
food from traditional favourites to more
imaginative restaurant-style dishes using
own produce, Wadworths ales and a seasonal
guest, good friendly service; children and
dogs welcome, disabled facilities, seats under
parasols at front, more in garden across
lane overlooking River Meon. *(Henry Fryer,
Glenwys and Alan Lawrence, Geoff and Linda
Payne, Nigel and Sue Foster)*

FACCOMBE SU3958
⋆**Jack Russell** (01264) 737315
*Signed from A343 Newbury–Andover;
SP11 0DS* Light and airy creeper-covered
pub in village-green setting opposite pond
by flint church, enjoyable fairly priced
traditional food (not Sun evening) from
snacks to Sun roasts, well kept ales including
Greene King IPA and one brewed for the
pub, good service, carpeted bar with some
old farming tools and other bric-a-brac, log
fire, darts, conservatory restaurant (children
welcome here); background music; disabled
facilities, lawn by beech trees, good walks,
three bedrooms, open all day Wed-Sat,
closed Tues evening. *(Mr and Mrs H J Langley,
David and Judy Robison)*

FAIR OAK SU4919
Fox (023) 8060 0024
Winchester Road (A3051); SO50 7HB
Clean modern décor in lounge, restaurant,
coffee room and conservatory, well liked
food (all day weekends) and ales such as
Ringwood and St Austell, nice wines, friendly
helpful young staff, children welcome, big
garden, path to nearby Bishopstoke woods,
open all day. *(Phyl and Jack Street)*

FAIR OAK SU4917
Lapstone (023) 80601659
Botley Road; SO50 7AP Traditional pub
atmosphere, well kept ales such as Sharps
Doom Bar and good value food including
curry and steak nights, OAP lunch deal Mon-
Thurs, friendly staff, regular events including
live music; children and dogs welcome, nice
back garden with play area, open all day
Fri-Sat, Sun 12-9pm, closed Mon. *(Ann and
Colin Hunt)*

FAREHAM SU5806
Golden Lion (01329) 234061
High Street; PO16 7AE Fullers town
local, clean and welcoming, with their well
kept ales and enjoyable fresh food from nice
baguettes up; open all day (till 9pm Mon,
closed Sun evening). *(Val and Alan Green,
Peter Meister)*

FAREHAM SU5206
Sir Joseph Paxton (01489) 572125
Hunts Pond Road; PO14 4PF Sizable
friendly local on edge of estate, cosy beamed
part with larger plainer area off, well kept
ales including Otter, straightforward cheap
bar food (all day Sun), darts; children
welcome, garden picnic-sets, open all
day. *(Ann and Colin Hunt)*

FARNBOROUGH SU8756
⋆**Prince of Wales** (01252)
545578 *Rectory Road, near station;
GU14 8AL* Up to ten good quickly changing
ales in friendly Victorian local, exposed
brickwork, carpet or wood floors, open fire,
antiquey touches in its three small linked
areas, popular lunchtime pubby food (not
Sun) including deals, good friendly service;
smokers' gazebo, open all day Fri-Sun. *(Joan
and Michel Hooper-Immins, Tim Gallagher)*

FAWLEY SU4603
Jolly Sailor (023) 8089 1305
Ashlett Creek; SO45 1DT Cottagey
waterside pub near small boatyard and
sailing club, straightforward good value bar
food, Marstons Pedigree and Ringwood Best,

cheerful service, raised log fire, mixed pubby furnishings on bare boards, second bar with darts and pool; children welcome, tables outside looking past creek's yachts and boats to busy shipping channel, good shore walks, handy for Rothschild rhododendron gardens at Exbury. *(Ann and Colin Hunt, Phil and Jane Villiers)*

FINCHDEAN SU7312

George (023) 9241 2257

Centre of village; PO8 0AU Red-brick pub dating from the 18th c, beamed front bar, separate dining area with conservatory, food (all day weekends - till 7pm Sun) from good value bar menu up, well kept ales such as Fullers, Sharps and Wells & Youngs, live music; children welcome if eating, dogs in bar, picnic-sets out in front and in garden behind, good nearby walks, open all day weekends (till 9pm Sun). *(W A Evershed, Martin and Karen Wake, Ann and Colin Hunt)*

FLEET SU8053

Oatsheaf (01252) 819508

Crookham Road/Reading Road; GU51 5DR Smartly refurbished M&B dining pub with plenty of contemporary touches, usual good choice of enjoyable food, ales such as Timothy Taylors Landlord; tables on front terrace, garden behind, open all day. *(Mike and Jayne Bastin)*

FROGHAM SU1712

⋇**Foresters Arms** (01425) 652294

Abbotswell Road; SP6 2JA Friendly chatty New Forest pub, chef/landlord doing good value blackboard food from sandwiches to very popular Sun lunch (compact dining room fills quickly - they ask to keep a credit card while you eat), welcoming attentive young staff, well kept Wadworths ales, good wines by the glass, cosy rustic refurbishment with frog-theme bar; children and dogs welcome, pleasant garden with pretty front verandah and good play area, small campsite adjacent, nearby ponies, deer and good walks, closed Tues. *(J Buckby)*

GOSPORT SU6101

⋇**Jolly Roger** (023) 9258 2584

Priory Road, Hardway; PO12 4LQ Popular old beamed harbour-view pub with enjoyable fairly priced food, real ales such as Adnams, Greene King and Shepherd Neame, decent house wines, lots of bric-a-brac, log fire, attractive eating area including conservatory; open all day. *(Ann and Colin Hunt, Peter and Audrey Dowsett)*

GOSPORT SZ6100

Queens (023) 9258 2645

Queens Road; PO12 1LG Classic bare-boards local, long-serving landlady keeps Ringwood Fortyniner, Roosters, Wells & Youngs Special and two guests in top condition, beer festivals, quick service, three areas off bar with good log fire in interesting

carved fireplace, sensibly placed darts, pub dog called Stanley; TV room - children welcome here daytime; closed lunchtimes Mon-Thurs, open all day Sat. *(Ann and Colin Hunt, Peter and Audrey Dowsett)*

GREYWELL SU7151

Fox & Goose (01256) 702062

Near M3 junction 5; A287 towards Odiham then first right to village; RG29 1BY Traditional two-bar village pub popular with locals and walkers, country-kitchen furniture, open fire, home-made pubby food from good lunchtime sandwiches up, Sun roast till 4pm, well kept Courage Best and a couple of guests, friendly helpful service; children and dogs welcome, good-sized garden behind, attractive village, Basingstoke Canal walks, open all day. *(Ann and Colin Hunt, Peter Farman)*

HAMBLE SU4806

⋇**Bugle** (023) 8045 3000

3 miles from M27 J8; SO31 4HA Chatty and bustling little 16th-c village pub by River Hamble, beamed and timbered rooms with flagstones and polished boards, church chairs, woodburner in fine brick fireplace, bar stools along herringbone-brick and timbered counter, ales such as Bowman and Ringwood, popular food (all day weekends); background music, TV; children welcome, dogs in bar, seats on the terrace with view of boats, open all day. *(Ann and Colin Hunt)*

HAMBLE SU4806

Olde Whyte Harte (023) 8045 2108

High Street; 3 miles from M27 junction 8; SO31 4JF Proper village pub, locally popular, with big inglenook log fire and low dark 17th-c beams, small restaurant area, generous fresh pubby food all day along with specials, Fullers/Gales ales and a guest, good wines by the glass, friendly staff; background music; children and dogs welcome, small walled garden, handy for nature reserve, open all day. *(Ann and Colin Hunt)*

HAMBLE SU4806

Victory (023) 8045 3105

High Street; SO31 4HA Well kept ales and enjoyable reasonably priced bar food, cheerful welcoming staff, nautical theme; open all day. *(Ann and Colin Hunt)*

HAMBLEDON SU6716

⋇**Bat & Ball** (023) 9263 2692

Broadhalfpenny Down; about 2 miles E towards Clanfield; PO8 0UB Extended dining pub opposite historic cricket pitch and with plenty of cricketing memorabilia (the game's rules are said to have been written here), log fires and comfortable modern furnishings in three linked rooms, Fullers ales, enjoyable food from well priced snacks up, good friendly service, panelled restaurant; children and dogs welcome, tables on front terrace, garden behind with lovely downs views, good walks, open all day. *(W A Evershed, N R White)*

HAMBLEDON SU6211
Horse & Jockey (023) 9263 2728
Hipley, pub signed well off B2150; PO7 4QY Biggish pub with good sensibly priced food, well kept ales such as Ringwood Best, friendly helpful service; children welcome, large garden by stream, play area. *(W A Evershed)*

HAWKLEY SU7429
Hawkley Inn (01730) 827205
Off B3006 near A3 junction; Pococks Lane; GU33 6NE Small pubby village local with splendid range of well kept ales from central bar, farm ciders too (may be a blackberry one), home made food from short changing menu, good mix of customers, open fires (large moose head above one), bare boards, flagstones and well used carpet, old pine tables and assorted chairs; some live music; children and dogs welcome, covered seating area at front, big back garden, useful for walkers (on Hangers Way), five bedrooms, open all day weekends. *(Tim Maddison, Ann and Colin Hunt, Geoff and Linda Payne, Stephen Sorby)*

HAYLING ISLAND SU7201
Maypole (023) 924 63670
Havant Road; PO11 0PS Sizeable two-bar 1930s roadside local well run by friendly couple, parquet floors and polished panelling, plenty of good seating, well kept Fullers/Gales beers, good choice of generous reasonably priced pub food including fish on Fri; garden, closed Sun evening. *(Val and Alan Green, Ann and Colin Hunt, Dave Jennings)*

HOLYBOURNE SU7341
White Hart (01420) 87654
London Road; GU34 4EY Light and clean with enjoyable nicely presented food including good fresh fish, friendly efficient service, well kept ales. *(Betty Laker)*

HORSEBRIDGE SU3430
John o' Gaunt (01794) 388394
Off A3057 Romsey–Andover, just SW of Kings Somborne; SO20 6PU Traditional pub in River Test village reopened under friendly new management; enjoyable good value home-cooked food, ales such as Ringwood and Palmers, real cider, L-shaped log-fire bar and small back dining area; seats outside, popular with walkers. *(Dawn Harrison)*

HOUGHTON SU3432
★Boot (01794) 388310
Village signposted off A30 in Stockbridge; SO20 6LH Bustling country local with lots of stuffed creatures in cheery dimly lit log-fire bar, good local Andwell ales, food from well filled baguettes up, amiable helpful staff, roomy more decorous lounge/

dining room; well behaved children and dogs welcome, spacious tranquil garden with half a dozen picnic-sets down by lovely (unfenced) stretch of River Test where they have fishing rights, good walks, and opposite Test Way cycle path. *(Edward Mirzoeff, N R White)*

HURSLEY SU4225
Kings Head (01962) 775208
A3090 Winchester–Romsey; SO21 2JW Substantial early 19th-c coaching inn, good local home-made food, five well kept changing ales such as Ringwood and Sharps Doom Bar, good choice of ciders, friendly staff, restaurant, skittle alley; children and dogs welcome, garden tables, eight comfortable bedrooms, open all day. *(Terry Buckland)*

KEYHAVEN SZ3091
★Gun (01590) 642391
Keyhaven Road; SO41 0TP Busy rambling 17th-c pub looking over boatyard and sea to Isle of Wight, low-beamed bar with nautical bric-a-brac and plenty of character (less in family rooms and conservatory), good reasonably priced local food including crab, Ringwood, Sharps, Timothy Taylors and Wells & Youngs tapped from the cask, Weston's cider, lots of malt whiskies, helpful young staff, bar billiards; background music; tables out in front and in big back garden with swings and fish pond, you can stroll down to small harbour and walk to Hurst Castle, open all day Sat, closed Sun evening. *(Joshua Fancett, Barrie and Mary Crees, Neil and Angela Huxter, Stephen and Jean Curtis, David and Judy Robison)*

KING'S SOMBORNE SU3531
Crown (01794) 388360
Romsey Road (A3057); SO20 6PW Long low thatched pub opposite village church, friendly relaxed local atmosphere, good simple reasonably priced home-made food (not Sun evening), well kept Greene King Abbot, Ringwood Best, Wadworths 6X and Wychwood Hobgoblin, real ciders, good wines and decent coffee, several linked rooms, panelling, comfortable sofas, fresh flowers; seats out at front and in garden behind, Test Way and Clarendon Way footpaths nearby, open all day Sun. *(Ian and Rose Lock, Mr and Mrs H J Langley, David and Judy Robison, Mike, Ann and Colin Hunt)*

KINGSCLERE SU5258
Crown (01635) 299541
Newbury Road; RG20 5QU Reworked former school under new welcoming landlady, long comfortable partly panelled lounge with central log fire, Fullers London Pride, Greene King IPA and a guest, enjoyable reasonably priced home-made food (all day Sun till 7pm, not Mon evening), simpler public bar, live music and quiz nights; children and dogs welcome, nice setting opposite village church

with nearby downs walks, two bedrooms, open all day Fri-Sun. *(Ann and Colin Hunt)*

KINGSCLERE SU5258
Swan (01635) 298314
Swan Street; RG20 5PP 15th-c beamed village inn under welcoming long serving licensees, Theakstons XB and four guests, enjoyable reasonably priced home-made food (not Sun evening), friendly helpful staff, log-fire bar and adjoining restaurant; children and dogs welcome, tables on back terrace, good walks, nine refurbished bedrooms. *(Steven Paine)*

LANGSTONE SU7104
⋆**Royal Oak** (023) 9248 3125
Off A3023 just before Hayling Island bridge; Langstone High Street; PO9 1RY Charmingly placed waterside dining pub overlooking tidal inlet and ancient wadeway to Hayling Island, boats at high tide, wading birds when it goes out; Greene King ales and good choice of wines by the glass, reasonably priced food with all-day sandwiches and snacks, spacious flagstoned bar and linked dining areas, log fire; children in eating areas, nice garden, good coastal paths nearby, open all day. *(W A Evershed, Roger and Donna Huggins, David and Judy Robison)*

LANGSTONE SU7104
Ship (023) 9247 1719
A3023; PO9 1RD Busy waterside 18th-c former grain store, lovely views to Hayling Island from roomy softly lit nautical bar and upstairs dining room (order downstairs), Fullers ales, good choice of wines by the glass, log fire, wide range of generous food including local fish; children welcome, plenty of tables on heated terrace by quiet quay, good coast walks, open all day. *(W A Evershed)*

LINWOOD SU1910
High Corner (01425) 473973
Signed from A338 via Moyles Court, and from A31; keep on; BH24 3QY Big rambling pub very popular for its splendid New Forest position up a track, with extensive neatly kept wooded garden and lots for children to do; some character in original upper bar with log fire, big back extensions for the summer crowds, nicely partitioned restaurant, verandah lounge, interesting family rooms, wide choice of generous bar snacks and restaurant-style food, well kept Wadworths; welcomes dogs and horses (stables and paddock available), seven bedrooms, open all day in summer and at weekends. *(J Buckby)*

LINWOOD SU1809
Red Shoot (01425) 475792
Signed from A338 via Moyles Court, and from A31; go on up heath to junction with Toms Lane; BH24 3QT Edwardian pub in nice New Forest setting, big picture-window bar with attractive old tables, mixed chairs and rugs on bare boards, country pictures on puce walls, log fire, large back dining area, generous honest good value food (all day weekends), friendly helpful staff, well kept Wadworths and two or three ales brewed at the pub (beer festivals Apr and Oct); children, dogs and muddy boots welcome, some disabled access, sheltered side terrace, open all day summer - very touristy then (by big campsite and caravan park). *(Carey Tyler)*

LITTLE LONDON SU6259
Plough (01256) 850628
Silchester Road, off A340 N of Basingstoke; RG26 5EP Tucked-away local, cosy and unspoilt, with log fires, low beams and mixed furnishings on brick and tiled floors (watch the step), well kept Palmers, Ringwood and interesting guests tapped from the cask, large good value baguettes with lots of different fillings, bar billiards and darts; dogs welcome, attractive garden, handy for Pamber Forest and Calleva Roman remains. *(D Johnson)*

LITTLETON SU4532
⋆**Running Horse** (01962) 880218
Main Road; village signed off B3049 NW of Winchester; SO22 6QS Popular dining pub refurbished in up-to-date style, enjoyable food from pubby to more elaborate dishes, good service, cushioned metal and wicker chairs at modern tables on polished boards, also some deep leather chairs, good colour photographs of Hampshire scenes, ales such as Itchen Valley and Greene King from marble and hardwood counter with swish bar stools, log fire, flagstoned back restaurant; background music; children welcome, dogs in bar, good disabled facilities, nice front and back terraces and garden, nine bedrooms, open all day. *(Phyl and Jack Street, David and Nicola Stout and others)*

LOCKERLEY SU3025
Kings Arms (01794) 340332
The Street; SO51 0JF Fully refurbished village pub with enjoyable food from bar snacks to more inventive restaurant dishes, interesting wine list, well kept ales, good service and thriving local atmosphere; landscaped back garden with heated

---

'Children welcome' means the pub says it lets children inside without any special restriction. If it allows them in, but to restricted areas such as an eating area or family room, we specify this. Some pubs may impose an evening time limit. We do not mention limits after 9pm as we assume children are home by then.

dining cabins, summer barbecues, open all day. *(John Chambers, Phyl and Jack Street)*

LOCKS HEATH   SU5006
★ Jolly Farmer (01489) 572500

Fleet End Road, not far from M27 junction 9; SO31 9JH Popular flower-decked pub with relaxing series of softly lit linked rooms, nice old scrubbed tables and masses of bric-a-brac and prints, emphasis on wide choice of enjoyable food (all day weekends) including good value Sun lunch (two-sittings), interesting long-serving landlord and good friendly service, Fullers/Gales ales, decent wines including country ones, coal-effect gas fires; two sheltered terraces (one with play area and children's lavatories), dogs allowed in some parts, nearby walks, five nice bedrooms, good breakfast, open all day. *(Ann and Colin Hunt, David and Gill Carrington)*

LONGPARISH   SU4344
Cricketers (01264) 720335

B3048, off A303 just E of Andover; SP11 6PZ Cheerful homely village pub with good chatty landlady, connecting rooms and cosy corners, woodburner, wide choice of carefully cooked food from light snacks to popular Sun lunch, prompt service, good range of real ales; sizeable back garden; closed Mon. *(Mr and Mrs A Curry)*

LYMINGTON   SZ3295
Kings Head (01590) 672709

Quay Hill; SO41 3AR In steep cobbled lane of smart small shops, friendly dimly lit old local with Fullers London Pride, Ringwood, Timothy Taylors Landlord and a couple of guests, several wines by the glass, enjoyable home-made food including specials, pleasant helpful staff, nicely mixed old-fashioned furnishings in rambling beamed and bare-boarded rooms (some recent refurbishment), log fire and woodburner, good classic yacht photographs, daily newspapers; background music, can get very busy; children and dogs welcome, nice little sunny courtyard behind, open all day. *(Guy Vowles)*

LYMINGTON   SZ3295
★ Ship (01590) 676903

Quay Road; SO41 3AY Lively well run pub with popular quayside deck overlooking harbour, light modern interior, lots of nautical bric-a-brac including huge flags, blue gingham and leather sofas, raised log fire, Adnams Broadside, Fullers London Pride and Hook Norton Old Hooky (plenty of standing room by counter), enjoyable fair value interesting food (all day), attractive wall-planked restaurant with blue and cream paintwork and driftwood decorations; children and dogs welcome, showers for visiting sailors. *(John Voos, Georgina Blake, David Whitehead)*

MAPLEDURWELL   SU6851
Gamekeepers (01256) 322038

Off A30, not far from M3 junction 6; RG25 2LU Dark-beamed dining pub with good upmarket food (not cheap) from interesting baguettes up, welcoming landlord and friendly staff, well kept Badger ales, good coffee, a few sofas by flagstoned and panelled core, well spaced tables in large dining room; background music, TV; children welcome, terrace and garden, lovely thatched village with duck pond, good walks, open all day. *(Edward Mirzoeff, David Feldman)*

MARCHWOOD   SU3809
Pilgrim (023) 8086 7752

Hythe Road, off A326 at Twiggs Lane; SO40 4WU Popular picturesque thatched pub (originally three cottages), well managed, with good choice of enjoyable sensibly priced food, well kept Fullers ales, decent wine, open fires; tree-lined garden with round picnic-sets, 14 stylish bedrooms in building across car park, open all day. *(Ian and Rose Lock, Phyl and Jack Street, Terry and Nickie Williams)*

MEONSTOKE   SU6120
Bucks Head (01489) 877313

Village signed just off A32 N of Droxford; SO32 3NA Unassuming little pub with partly panelled L-shaped dining lounge looking over road to water meadows, log fire, plush banquettes and bare boards, popular food including Sun roasts, well kept Greene King ales, friendly public bar (dogs welcome) with another fire; small garden, lovely village setting with ducks on pretty little River Meon, good walks, five bedrooms, open all day weekends. *(Phyl and Jack Street, A and R MacDowall, Ann and Colin Hunt)*

MICHELDEVER   SU5142
Dove (01962) 774288

Micheldever Station, off A33 or A303; SO21 3AU Large square pub with several interconnecting rooms around central bar, enjoyable food from ciabattas and pub favourites up, real ales from Itchen Valley and Longdog, efficient service, beams, exposed brickwork and two woodburners, pool and darts; small side terrace, five bedrooms, open all day weekends. *(Edward Mirzoeff, Diana Brumfit)*

MINLEY MANOR   SU8357
Crown & Cushion (01252) 545253

A327, just N of M3 junction 4A; GU17 9UA Attractive little traditional pub with enjoyable fairly priced food including some unusual choices, well kept Shepherd Neame ales, coal-effect gas fire; big separate raftered and flagstoned rustic 'meade hall' with huge log fire, very popular weekends (evenings more a young people's meeting place), friendly staff cope well when busy;

children in eating area, heated terrace overlooking own cricket pitch. *(David and Sue Smith)*

MINSTEAD   SU2810
✶**Trusty Servant** (023) 8081 2137
Just off A31, not far from M27 junction 1; SO43 7FY Attractive 19th-c building in pretty New Forest hamlet with interesting church (Sir Arthur Conan Doyle buried here), wandering cattle and ponies, and plenty of easy walks; refurbished and doing well under present licensees, two-room bar and big dining room, nice range of well kept real ales and good reasonably priced pubby food, friendly helpful staff; big sloping garden, open all day. *(Henry Fryer, John Redfern, Graham, Martin Gough, Revd Michael Vockins)*

MORTIMER WEST END   SU6364
✶**Red Lion** (0118) 970 0169
Church Road; Silchester turn off Mortimer–Aldermaston Road; RG7 2HU Country dining pub with good varied menu including some unusual dishes, well kept Badger ales and good range of wines by the glass, welcoming helpful staff, beams, stripped masonry, timbers and panelling, log fires, proper locals' bar; children welcome and dogs (jar of biscuits on the bar), seats in pleasant garden and on small front terrace, handy for Roman Silchester, open all day. *(Sam Weedon, Shirley Mackenzie, Dr and Mrs R E S Tanner, J V Dadswell)*

NEW CHERITON   SU5827
✶**Hinton Arms** (01962) 771252
A272 near B3046 junction; SO24 0NH Neatly kept popular country pub with cheerful accommodating landlord, three or four real ales including Bowman Wallops Wood and one brewed for them by Hampshire, decent wines by the glass, enjoyable generous food from good sandwiches to game specials, sporting pictures and memorabilia, relaxing atmosphere; TV lounge; terrace, big garden, very handy for Hinton Ampner House (NT). *(Phil and Jane Villiers, Ann and Colin Hunt, P J Checksfield)*

NEWTOWN   SU4763
Swan (01635) 40313
A339 2 miles S of Newbury, by junction with old A34; RG20 9BH Ancient black and white pub refitted in modern style, good nicely presented food, well kept Badger ales, friendly young staff, flagstones and open fires; children welcome, terrace and lovely streamside garden. *(Keith and Margaret Kettell)*

ODIHAM   SU7450
Bell (01256) 702282
The Bury; RG29 1LY Simple unspoilt two-bar local in pretty square opposite church and stocks, three well kept changing ales, good value straightforward food, log fire; plenty of seats outside. *(Ann and Colin Hunt, Peter Farman)*

ODIHAM   SU7451
Water Witch (01256) 808778
Colt Hill - quiet no through road signed off main street; RG29 1AL Olde-worlde décor in nicely kept Chef & Brewer near picturesque stretch of Basingstoke Canal (boat hire), big but cosily divided with more formal dining area at back, wide choice of food and three mainstream ales, friendly staff; no dogs inside; disabled access and parking, pretty hanging baskets in front, terrace with awning and dark raffia furniture, garden with children's facilities. *(Jim and Frances Gowers, Simon and Mandy King)*

OTTERBOURNE   SU4623
Old Forge (01962) 717191
Main Road; SO21 2EE Popular old bistro-style chain pub, welcoming and comfortable, with wide choice of enjoyable food all day, friendly well organised staff, ales such as Everards, Sharps and Timothy Taylors, good choice of wines by the glass, tables spread through linked rooms, cosy nooks and rather individual décor, log fires; children welcome. *(Phyl and Jack Street and others)*

OTTERBOURNE   SU4522
Otter (023) 8025 2685
Boyatt Lane, off Winchester Road; SO21 2HW Unpretentious dining pub opposite village green, enjoyable food from sandwiches and snacks up, Ringwood ales and Otter, good service, three-sided bar (one side set for dining), dark oak tables and chairs, banquettes; seats in garden. *(Val and Alan Green)*

OVINGTON   SU5631
✶**Bush** (01962) 732764
Off A31 W of Alresford; SO24 0RE Charming spot with streamside garden and pergola dining terrace, appealing low-ceilinged bar high-backed settles, pews and masses of old pictures, blazing fire, well kept Wadworths ales, good choice of wines by the glass, good if pricy food (not Sun evening); children and dogs welcome, nice walks, open all day summer holidays and can get very busy. *(Martin and Karen Wake, W A Evershed, Malcolm Derrick)*

PETERSFIELD   SU7423
Good Intent (01730) 263838
College Street; GU31 4AF Former 16th-c coaching inn, friendly and chatty, with well kept Fullers/Gales beers and enjoyable fresh pubby food, low beams, pine tables and built-in upholstered benches, log fires; background music - live Sun; children and dogs welcome, front terrace, three bedrooms. *(N R White, Val and Alan Green)*

PETERSFIELD   SU7423
Red Lion (01730) 235160
College Street; GU31 4AE Refurbished
Wetherspoons in former coaching inn, usual
good value food and beers; open all day from
7am. *(Dom Humphries, Val and Alan Green, Ann
and Colin Hunt)*

PILLEY   SZ3298
Fleur de Lys (01590) 672158
*Off A337 Brockenhurst–Lymington;
Pilley St; SO41 5QG* Welcoming old
thatched and beamed pub under new
family management, well kept Ringwood
ales, Weston's cider, good value pubby food
including pizzas, dining room with inglenook
log fire; children welcome, garden, fine forest
and heathland walks, open all day.
(Ben Corbridge)

PORTSMOUTH   SZ6399
Bridge Tavern (023) 9275 2992
East Street, Camber Dock; PO1 2JJ
Flagstones, bare boards and lots of dark
wood, comfortable furnishings, maritime
theme with good harbour views, Fullers
ales, plenty of fish dishes; nice waterside
terrace. *(W A Evershed, Ann and Colin Hunt)*

PORTSMOUTH   SU6402
Fountain (023) 9266 1636
London Road, North End; PO2 9AA
Unchanging tiled pub with large bar and
family room off, nicely polished brass,
interesting pictures of local pubs, mirrors
each end, unusual ceiling lights, well kept
beer including Gales HSB, no food; seats
outside. *(Ann and Colin Hunt)*

PORTSMOUTH   SZ6399
Pembroke (023) 9282 3961
Pembroke Road; PO1 2NR Traditional well
run corner local, comfortable and unspoilt
under long-serving licensees, Bass, Fullers
London Pride and Greene King Abbot from
L-shaped bar, fresh rolls, coal-effect gas fire;
open all day (closed 5-7pm Sun). *(Ann and
Colin Hunt, Ole Ponpey)*

PORTSMOUTH   SU6300
Ship & Castle (023) 9283 2009
*The Hard, opposite dockyard entrance;
PO1 3PU* Nicely old-fashioned unchanging
town pub, well kept Fullers/Gales beers,
no-nonsense bargain food; children welcome,
handy for HMS Victory etc. *(Ann and
Colin Hunt)*

PORTSMOUTH   SZ6299
Still & West (023) 9282 1567
Bath Square, Old Portsmouth; PO1 2JL
Great location with superb views of narrow
harbour mouth and across to Isle of Wight,
especially from glazed-in panoramic upper
family area and waterfront terrace with lots
of picnic-sets; nautical bar with fireside
sofas and cosy colour scheme, Fullers ales,

good choice of wines by the glass, food all
day including signature fish and chips;
background music may be loud, nearby pay &
display; children welcome, handy for Historic
Dockyard. *(W A Evershed, J A Snell,
B M Eldridge)*

ROMSEY   SU3523
★Dukes Head (01794) 514450
*A3057 out towards Stockbridge;
SO51 0HB* Attractive 16th-c dining pub
with small comfortable linked rooms, big log
fire, good range of enjoyable food, well kept
ales such as Fullers/Gales, Sharps and Wells
& Youngs, decent wines and coffee, friendly
staff; children welcome, colourful hanging
baskets, sheltered back terrace and pleasant
garden, open all day. *(Ann and Colin Hunt,
Phyl and Jack Street, J V Dadswell, Martin and
Karen Wake)*

ROMSEY   SU3521
Old House At Home (01794) 513175
Love Lane; SO51 8DE Attractive
16th-c thatched pub surrounded by new
development, friendly and bustling, with
appealingly individual and old-fashioned
décor, wide choice of freshly made sensibly
priced bar food including popular Sun lunch,
well kept Fullers/Gales ales and guests,
decent coffee, cheerful efficient service,
good pubby atmosphere; children's play
area. *(Ann and Colin Hunt, Colin and
Peggy Wilshire)*

ROMSEY   SU3520
Three Tuns (01794) 512639
*Middlebridge Street (but car park signed
straight off A27 bypass); SO51 8HL*
Old beamed and bow-windowed pub
refurbished by newish owners, friendly
buoyant atmosphere, well kept ales such
Flack Manor, Ringwood and Sharps,
traditional pub food; children welcome, open
all day. *(Phil and Jane Villiers)*

ROTHERWICK   SU7156
Coach & Horses (01256) 768976
*Signed from B3349 N of Hook; also quite
handy for M3, junction 5; RG27 9BG*
17th-c pub with traditional beamed front
rooms, good value locally sourced pubby
food, well kept Badger ales, log fire and
woodburners, newer back dining area;
children, dogs and muddy boots welcome,
tables out at front and on terrace behind,
pretty flower tubs and baskets, good walks,
open all day Sat, closed Sun evening,
Mon. *(David and Judy Robison)*

ROWLAND'S CASTLE   SU7310
★Castle Inn (023) 9241 2494
*Off B2148/B2149 N of Havant;
Finchdean Road; PO9 6DA* Cheerful
proper country pub with friendly hands-on
tenants, comfortable bar with enormous
log fire and good choice of Fullers/Gales
ales, nice coffee, neat staff, two appealing

little dining rooms on left, attractively priced pubby food with more exotic evening choices; children and dogs welcome, disabled facilities, pony paddock by good-sized garden, open all day. *(W A Evershed, Ann and Colin Hunt)*

ROWLAND'S CASTLE SU7310
Robin Hood (023) 9241 2268
The Green; PO9 6AB Nicely refurbished inn on village green, light and airy stone-tiled bar with log fire, good choice of enjoyable food, Badger ales and a guest, efficient service, restaurant; children and dogs welcome, disabled facilities, tables out on front terrace, six bedrooms, good breakfast, open all day. *(Tony and Gill Powell)*

SARISBURY SU5008
Bold Forester (01489) 576400
Handy for M27 junction 9; Bridge Road (A27), Sarisbury Green; SO31 7EL Roomy and well run with good choice of popular food from baguettes and sharing plates up, decent vegetarian options too, cheerful polite service, four real ales including Ringwood, pictures of this increasingly built-up area in its strawberry-fields days; children welcome, pretty hanging baskets and tubs in front, large recently redone garden behind, open all day. *(Christine Whitehead, Ann and Colin Hunt)*

SELBORNE SU7433
Queens (01420) 511454
High Street; GU34 3JJ Comfortably refurbished and welcoming, open fires, interesting local memorabilia, well kept Hogs Back TEA and Triple fff Alton Pride, food (not Sun evening) from sandwiches and pubby things to french country dishes, cream teas and nice coffee, cheerful smartly dressed staff, occasional jazz; children and dogs welcome, garden picnic-sets, eight bedrooms, very handy for Gilbert White's house, open all day. *(Ann and Colin Hunt)*

SELBORNE SU7433
Selborne Arms (01420) 511247
High Street; GU34 3JR Character tables, pews and deep settles made from casks on antique boards, good range of changing largely local ales, ten wines by the glass, popular food from standards up using locally sourced ingredients, big log fire, daily newspapers, carpeted dining room with lots of local photographs; no dogs inside; plenty of garden tables, arbour and terrace heated by logburner, orchard and good play area, zig-zag path up Hanger, convenient for Gilbert White's house, open all day weekends. *(Ann and Colin Hunt)*

SHEDFIELD SU5513
Wheatsheaf (01329) 833024
A334 Wickham–Botley; SO32 2JG Busy friendly no-fuss local, Flowerpots ales tapped from the cask, farm cider, short sensible choice of bargain bar lunches (evening food Tues and Weds), regular live music; dogs welcome, garden, handy for Wickham Vineyard, open all day. *(Ann and Colin Hunt, Joan and Michel Hooper-Immins)*

SILCHESTER SU6262
Calleva Arms (01734) 9700305
The Common; RG7 2PH Friendly bay-windowed pub facing the common, Fullers/Gales and a guest beer, decent wines by the glass, wide range of food from baguettes up, roomy bar with lots of bric-a-brac, dining conservatory, pool area; handy for the Roman site, sizeable attractive garden, open all day Fri-Sun. *(J V Dadswell)*

SMANNELL SU3849
Oak (01264) 363075
SP11 6JJ Snug brick-and-flint country pub, beams and oak panelling, rugs on bare-boards, log fires, enjoyable food including good value Sun roasts, Wadworths ales, raftered garden room, bar billiards; fortnightly quiz (Weds) and monthly live music; closed Sun evening, Mon. *(Anon)*

SOBERTON SU6116
White Lion (01489) 877346
School Hill; signed off A32 S of Droxford; SO32 3PF Georgian-fronted 16th-c village pub, enjoyable home-made food from bar and restaurant menus, Bowman Swift One and Wallops Wood plus two guests, good house wines, friendly staff, comfortable dining lounge, rambling restaurant and unspoilt little bare-boards low-ceilinged bar with pews and built-in wall seats; children in eating areas, small sheltered garden with suntrap terrace and covered tables, nice spot by green, good walks nearby, closed Mon. *(Tony and Wendy Hobden)*

SOPLEY SZ1596
★Woolpack (01425) 672252
B3347 N of Christchurch; BH23 7AX Pretty thatched dining pub with rambling open-plan low-beamed bar, welcoming helpful staff, generous helpings of enjoyable traditional food, real ales such as Ringwood Best and Fortyniner, good choice of wines by the glass, modern dining conservatory; they ask to keep a credit card if you run a tab; children in eating areas, dogs in certain parts, terrace and charming garden with weeping willows, duck stream and footbridges, open all day. *(David Cannings)*

SOUTHAMPTON SU4111
★Duke of Wellington (023) 8033 9222
Bugle Street (or walk along city wall from Bar Gate); SO14 2AH Striking ancient timber-framed building dating from 14th c, cellars even older, heavy beams, great log fire, well kept Wadworths ales, good choice of wines by the glass, good value traditional pub food (not Sun evening) from baguettes to nursery puddings, friendly

helpful service; background music in cheery front bar, staider back area welcoming children; handy for Tudor House Museum, sunny streetside picnic-sets, open all day. *(Stephen and Jean Curtis, David Ellis, Val and Alan Green)*

SOUTHAMPTON   SU4112
Giddy Bridge (023) 8033 6346
London Road; SO15 2AF Busy Wetherspoons with half a dozen well kept beers including Ringwood, partly divided and not too big, upstairs area with balcony terrace, good staff, enjoyable cheap food; popular with young people and open all day. *(Ross Balaam)*

SOUTHAMPTON   SU4213
White Star (023) 8082 1990
Oxford Street; SO14 3DJ Smart modern bar, banquettes and open fire, comfortable sofas and armchairs in secluded alcoves by south-facing dining area, good up-to-date food from interesting baguettes and light dishes up, efficient attentive service, Itchen Valley and Sharps, nice wines by the glass and lots of cocktails; they may try to keep your credit card while you eat; sunny pavement tables on pedestrianised street, 13 boutique bedrooms, open all day. *(Tracey and Stephen Groves)*

SOUTHSEA   SZ6499
Eldon Arms (0239) 229 6374
Eldon Street/Norfolk Street; PO5 4BS Rambling backstreet tavern under good welcoming licensees, Fullers London Pride and four changing guests, Thatcher's cider, simple cheap lunchtime food (not Mon), Sun carvery, flowers on tables, old pictures and advertisements, attractive mirrors, bric-a-brac and shelves of books; background music, sensibly placed darts, bar billiards, pool, games machine; dogs on leads and children welcome, tables in back garden, open all day. *(Ann and Colin Hunt)*

SOUTHSEA   SZ6499
★Hole in the Wall (023) 9229 8085
Great Southsea Street; PO5 3BY Friendly unspoilt little local in old part of town, up to six well priced changing ales in good condition, Wheal Maiden alcoholic ginger beer, Thatcher's cider, simple good value food including speciality local sausages and meat puddings, nicely worn boards, dark pews and panelling, old photographs and prints, over 700 pump clips on ceiling, little snug behind the bar, daily newspapers, quiz night Thurs, Oct beer festival; small outside tiled area at front with benches, side garden, closed till 4pm weekdays, open all day Fri-Sun. *(Joan and Michel Hooper-Immins, Ann and Colin Hunt)*

SOUTHSEA   SZ6499
King Street Tavern (023) 92873307
King Street; PO5 4EH Sympathetically refurbished corner pub in attractive conservation area, spectacular Victorian tiled façade, bare boards and original fittings, four well kept Wadworths ales and guests, real ciders, good value straightforward home-made food; background and live music including fortnightly Sat jazz; dogs welcome, courtyard tables, closed Mon-Weds lunchtimes. *(Nick Birtley)*

SOUTHSEA   SZ6698
Sir Loin of Beef (023) 9282 0115
Highland Road, Eastney; PO4 9NH Simple spic-and-span corner pub with up to eight well kept frequently changing ales (tasters offered), bottled belgian beers, reasonably priced bar food, helpful friendly staff and buoyant atmosphere, interesting ship photographs. *(Ann and Colin Hunt)*

SOUTHSEA   SZ6499
Wine Vaults (023) 9286 4712
Albert Road, opposite King's Theatre; PO5 2SF Bustling pub with eight changing ales including Fullers London Pride, ESB and London Porter, several chatty rooms on different floors, main panelled bar with long plain counter and pubby furniture, smarter restaurant area, limited choice of bar food but something available all day; background music, sports TV; children welcome, dogs in bar, smokers' roof terrace, open till 1am Fri, Sat. *(Ann and Colin Hunt, the Didler, Jane and Rowena Leverington, Peter Meister)*

SOUTHWICK   SU6208
Red Lion (023) 9237 7223
High Street; PO17 6EF Neatly kept low-beamed village dining pub, popular generous food including vegetarian options, good choice of wines by the glass, Fullers/Gales and a guest ale, good service from smartly dressed staff even though busy; nice walks. *(W A Evershed, Ann and Colin Hunt)*

STOCKBRIDGE   SU3535
Three Cups (01264) 810527
High Street; SO20 6HB Lovely low-beamed building dating from 1500, some emphasis on dining with lots of smartly set pine tables, but still high-backed settles, country bric-a-brac and four well kept ales such as Wells & Youngs, good interesting food along with more pubby choices, amiable service, nice wines by the glass, extended 'orangery' restaurant; children and dogs welcome, vine-covered verandah and charming cottage garden with streamside terrace, eight bedrooms, open all day. *(Geoffrey Kemp, Conor McGaughey)*

STOCKBRIDGE   SU3535
★White Hart (01264) 810663
High Street; A272/A3057 roundabout; SO20 6HF Thriving divided beamed bar, attractive décor with antique prints, oak pews and other seats, friendly helpful staff, enjoyable food from snacks to substantial daily specials, well kept Fullers/Gales beers,

comfortable restaurant with blazing log fire (children allowed); dogs in bar, disabled facilities, terrace tables and nice garden, 14 good bedrooms, open all day. *(Paul Goldman, Edward Mirzoeff, Robert Watt, Ian Herdman, John and Joan Calvert, Val and Alan Green and others)*

STRATFIELD TURGIS   SU6960
Wellington Arms   (01256) 882214
Off A33 Reading-Basingstoke; RG27 0AS
Handsome old country hotel dating from the 17th c, restful and surprisingly pubby tall-windowed two-room bar, part flagstoned, part carpeted, with leather chesterfields by open fire, well kept Badger Best, good food and service; children and dogs welcome, garden, 27 comfortable bedrooms, open all day. *(Richard and Stephanie Foskett)*

STUBBINGTON   SU5402
Crofton   (01329) 314222
Crofton Lane; PO14 3QF Modern two-bar estate local, neat and airy, with friendly efficient staff, five well kept ales including Sharps Doom Bar, good value wines, very popular food from nicely varied menu including weekday OAP deals; children and dogs welcome. *(Sally Matson, Ann and Colin Hunt)*

SWAY   SZ2898
Hare & Hounds   (01590) 682404
Durns Town, just off B3055 SW of Brockenhurst; SO41 6AL Bright, airy and comfortable New Forest family dining pub, popular generously served food, ales such as Itchen Valley, Ringwood, St Austell and Timothy Taylors, good helpful service even at busy times, low beams and central log fire; background music; dogs welcome, picnic-sets and play frame in neatly kept garden, open all day. *(D J and P M Taylor)*

TICHBORNE   SU5730
⋆**Tichborne Arms**   (01962) 733760
Signed off B3047; SO24 0NA Traditional thatched pub with latticed windows, panelling, antiques and stuffed animals, open fire, Palmers and guests tapped from the cask, local cider, food (not Sun evening) from baguettes up, locals' bar, darts, board games and shove-ha'penny; children and dogs welcome, big garden in rolling countryside, Wayfarers Walk and Itchen Way pass close by, closed Sun evening. *(Tony and Jill Radnor, Martin and Karen Wake, Matthew Beard, the Didler)*

TIMSBURY   SU3325
⋆**Bear & Ragged Staff**
(01794) 368602   *A3057 towards Stockbridge; pub marked on OS Sheet 185 map reference 334254; SO51 0LB*

Reliable roadside dining pub with good choice of popular food including blackboard specials, friendly efficient service, lots of wines by the glass, Fullers, Hampshire, Ringwood and Timothy Taylors, log fire, good-sized beamed interior; children welcome in eating part, tables in extended garden with play area, handy for Mottisfont, good walks, open all day. *(Rich Best, Phil and Jane Villiers, Phyl and Jack Street)*

TITCHFIELD   SU5305
Bugle   (01329) 841888
The Square, off A27 near Fareham; PO14 4AF Roomy and comfortable 18th-c coaching inn, popular good value food from light meals up in bar or old barn restaurant behind, friendly attentive service, four well kept ales including Timothy Taylors Landlord, log fires; no dogs; children welcome, attractive village handy for Titchfield Haven nature reserve, fine walk by former canal to coast, eight bedrooms. *(Val and Alan Green, Ann and Colin Hunt)*

TITCHFIELD   SU5406
Fishermans Rest   (01329) 845065
Mill Lane, off A27 at Titchfield Mill pub; PO15 5RA Refurbished dining pub with good value popular food, well kept Greene King ales; fine riverside position opposite Titchfield Abbey, tables out behind overlooking water. *(Ann and Colin Hunt)*

TITCHFIELD   SU5406
Titchfield Mill   (01329) 840931
A27, junction with Mill Lane; PO15 5RF Open airy Vintage Inn family dining pub in neatly kept converted River Meon watermill, olde-worlde room off main bar, smarter dining room, upstairs gallery, stripped beams and interesting old machinery, their usual food served by efficient friendly staff, good value wines by the glass, Ringwood Best and guests; background music; sunny terrace by mill stream with two waterwheels (food not served here), open all day. *(Ann and Colin Hunt, Phyl and Jack Street)*

TOTFORD   SU5737
Woolpack   (08450) 2938066
B3046 Basingstoke–Alresford; SO24 9TJ Nicely refurbished roadside inn, clean and comfortable, with good food from bar snacks to restaurant dishes, Palmers, an ale brewed for the pub and a guest such as Bowman, several wines by the glass including champagne, nice italian coffee, efficient service, raised open fire in bar, smart split-level dining room; pool; round picnic-sets outside on gravel, lovely setting in good walking country, seven bedrooms, open all day. *(John and Anne Mackinnon)*

All *Guide* inspections are anonymous. Anyone claiming to be a *Good Pub Guide* inspector is a fraud. Please let us know.

TWYFORD   SU4824

★**Bugle** (01962) 714888

B3355/Park Lane; SO21 1QT Nicely done modern pub with good enterprising food served by attentive friendly young staff, well kept ales from Bowman, Flowerpots and Upham, woodburner; background music; attractive verandah seating area, good walks nearby, open all day. *(Henry Fryer, Phyl and Jack Street, M and R Ridge)*

TWYFORD   SU4824

Phoenix (01962) 713322

High Street (B3335); SO21 1RF Cheerful open-plan local with lots of prints, bric-a-brac and big end inglenook log fire, friendly long-serving landlord) and attentive staff, Greene King ales, good coffee, good value wines, raised dining area, pool, side skittle alley; unobtrusive background music; children allowed at one end lunchtime, garden with smokers' area. *(Ann and Colin Hunt)*

UPHAM   SU5320

★**Brushmakers Arms** (01489) 860231

Shoe Lane; village signed from Winchester–Bishops Waltham downs road, and from B2177; SO32 1JJ Plenty of regulars and weekend dog walkers at this cheery low-beamed village pub, L-shaped bar divided by central woodburner, cushioned settles and chairs around mix of tables, lots of brushes and related paraphernalia, little back snug with games machine and background music, enjoyable bar food, Fullers, Ringwood, Upham and a guest, decent coffee, pub cats (Luna and Baxter); children and dogs welcome, big garden with picnic-sets on sheltered terrace and tree-shaded lawn, open all day Sun. *(Val and Alan Green, Tony and Jill Radnor, Henry Fryer, Ann and Colin Hunt, W A Evershed and others)*

UPPER CLATFORD   SU3543

Crook & Shears (01264) 361543

Off A343 S of Andover, via Foundry Road; SP11 7QL Cosy 17th-c thatched pub under welcoming licensees, several homely olde-worlde seating areas, bare boards and panelling, three good changing ales, decent reasonably priced food from doorstep sandwiches up, open fires and woodburner, small dining room, back skittle alley with own bar; pleasant secluded garden behind. *(the Didler, Ann and Colin Hunt)*

UPPER FARRINGDON   SU7135

★**Rose & Crown** (01420) 588231

Off A32 S of Alton; Crows Lane - follow Church, Selborne, Liss signpost;

GU34 3ED Airy 19th-c village pub with L-shaped log-fire bar, comfortable and well run, several well kept ales including Triple fff, good reasonably priced food (all day Sun) with some interesting choices including vegetarian options, efficient friendly young staff, formal back dining room, jazz nights (last Mon of month); well behaved children and dogs welcome, wide views from attractive back garden, open all day weekends. *(Tony and Jill Radnor, Ann and Colin Hunt)*

UPTON   SU3555

Crown (01264) 736638

N of Hurstbourne Tarrant, off A343; SP11 OJS Attractive old pub with helpful landlord and staff, enjoyable reasonably priced pubby food including OAP weekday lunch deal, well kept beers such as West Berkshire, good log fire, back conservatory extension; small garden and terrace. *(Alan Wright)*

WALHAMPTON   SZ3396

Walhampton Arms (01590) 673113

B3054 NE of Lymington; aka Walhampton Inn; SO41 5RE Large comfortable Georgian-style family roadhouse, popular food including good carvery in raftered former stables and two adjoining areas, pleasant lounge, Ringwood ales, cheerful helpful staff; attractive courtyard, good walks, open all day. *(Phyl and Jack Street and others)*

WALTHAM CHASE   SU5614

Black Dog (01329) 832316

Winchester Road; SO32 2LX Old brick-built pub under new management, low-ceilinged front bar, three well kept Greene King ales and guest, over a dozen wines by the glass, good choice of enjoyable home-made food, back restaurant; children and dogs welcome, colourful hanging baskets, tables in good-sized neatly kept garden, open all day weekends in summer. *(Ann and Colin Hunt)*

WARSASH   SU4806

Rising Sun (023) 8057 6898

Shore Road; OS Sheet 196 map ref 489061; SO31 9FT Picture-window waterside pub with boating atmosphere, nautical charts and D-Day naval memorabilia, popular food including seafood, Greene King and Ringwood ales, long bar part tiled-floor and part boards, fine Hamble estuary views especially from summer restaurant up spiral stairs; estuary walks, handy for Hook nature reserve. *(Ann and Colin Hunt, Phyl and Jack Street)*

We mention bottled beers and spirits only if there is something unusual about them – imported belgian real ales, say, or dozens of malt whiskies; so do please let us know about them in your reports.

WELL   SU7646
⋆**Chequers** (01256) 862605
*Off A287 via Crondall, or A31 via Froyle
and Lower Froyle; RG29 1TL* Appealing
low-beamed and panelled country pub with
cheerful bustling atmosphere, enjoyable
usual food from sandwiches up, well kept
Badger ales, decent wines by the glass, pews
and brocaded stools, 18th-c country-life
prints and old sepia photographs, a few
GWR carriage lamps, log fire; picnic-sets
on vine-covered terrace and in spacious
back garden. *(Tony and Jill Radnor, Angus
Macfarlane, Martin and Karen Wake, Richard and
Stephanie Foskett)*

WEST END   SU4514
White Swan (023) 8047 3322
Mansbridge Road; SO18 3HW Pleasantly
refurbished family food pub in nice spot,
Itchen Valley and Wells & Youngs ales, busy
carvery restaurant, conservatory; attractive
terrace by River Itchen. *(Phyl and Jack Street
and others)*

WEST MEON   SU6424
⋆**Thomas Lord** (01730) 829244
High Street; GU32 1LN Village pub
named for founder of Lord's cricket ground,
individual rustic style with interesting mix
of chairs around wooden tables, old leather
sofa, stuffed animals in display cabinets, bare
boards and log fires, back room lined with
books for sale, imaginative if not cheap food,
Bowman ales tapped from the cask; children
and dogs welcome, attractive formal garden
with outdoor bar, wood-fired pizza oven,
chicken run and neat vegetable patch, open
all day weekends, closed Mon. *(Val and Alan
Green, Martin and Karen Wake, Ann and Colin
Hunt, Phyl and Jack Street)*

WEST TYTHERLEY   SU2730
Black Horse (01794) 340308
North Lane; SP5 1NF Compact unspoilt
village local, welcoming licensees and chatty
regulars, traditional bar with a couple of long
tables and big fireplace, nicely set dining
area off, three real ales, enjoyable reasonably
priced food including good Sun roasts,
takeaway fish and chips Thurs, skittle alley;
dogs welcome. *(Phyl and Jack Street, Graham
Horder, Ann and Colin Hunt)*

WEST WELLOW   SU2817
Rockingham (01794) 322473
*Pub signed off A36 Romsey–Over at
Canada roundabout; SO51 6DE*
Modernised beamed pub/restaurant down
Forest-edge no through road, enjoyable
food, three well kept changing local ales and
decent choice of wines by the glass; dogs
welcome, disabled access, tables out on
front deck, more behind, opens on to pretty
heathland with roaming horses, may close
Mon out of season. *(Will and Delia Stevens)*

WHERWELL   SU3839
⋆**Mayfly** (01264) 860283
*Testcombe (over by Fullerton, and
not in Wherwell itself); A3057 SE of
Andover, between B3420 turn-off and
Leckford where road crosses River Test;
OS Sheet 185 map reference 382390;
SO20 6AX* Well run busy pub with decking
and conservatory overlooking River Test,
spacious beamed and carpeted bar with
fishing paraphernalia, rustic pub furnishings
and woodburner, ales such as Adnams,
Gales, Hop Back, Palmers and Wadworths,
lots of wines by the glass, wide range of
good popular bar food all day (order from
separate counter), helpful courteous
service; background music; well behaved
children and dogs welcome. *(Ian Herdman,
Helen and Brian Edgeley, Conor McGaughey,
Martin and Karen Wake, Alan Wright, Mr and
Mrs A Curry)*

WHERWELL   SU3840
White Lion (01264) 860317
B3420; SP11 7JF Refurbished early
17th-c multi-level beamed village inn,
good choice of enjoyable food including
speciality pies, Harveys, Ringwood, Sharps
and a couple of guests, several wines by the
glass, very friendly helpful staff, open fire,
comfy leather sofas and armchairs, dining
rooms either side of bar; background music;
dogs on leads and well behaved children
welcome, sunny courtyard with good quality
furniture, Test Way walks, six bedrooms,
open all day from 7.30am (breakfast for
non-residents). *(Michael and Jenny Back, Mike
Gorton, N R White and others)*

WICKHAM   SU5711
⋆**Greens** (01329) 833197
*The Square, at junction with A334;
PO17 5JQ* Civilised dining place with clean-
cut modern furnishings and décor, small bar
with leather sofa and armchairs as well as
bar stools, wide wine choice, Bowmans Swift
One and another ale, efficient obliging young
staff, step down to split-level balustraded
dining areas, enjoyable food from typical bar
lunches to imaginative specials; pleasant
lawn overlooking water meadows, closed Sun
evening and Mon. *(Phyl and Jack Street)*

WINCHESTER   SU4728
Bell (01962) 865284
*St Cross Road (B3335 off M3
junction 11); SO23 9RE* Old two-bar
whitewashed pub handy for St Cross
Hospital (ancient monument, not a
hospital), short choice of good value fresh
food including nice sandwiches, friendly
helpful staff, well kept Greene King ales
and usually a guest, decent wines by the
glass, polished boards and half-panelling,
leather sofas and plush modern chairs and
pine tables, cricket memorabilia; quiet
background music; nice walled garden with

swing and slide, lovely water-meadows walk from centre, open all day. *(John and Annabel Hampshire)*

WINCHESTER   SU4829
Bishop on the Bridge
(01962) 855111 *High Street/Bridge St; SO23 9JX* Neat efficiently run Fullers pub with well kept beers and varied choice of food, leather sofas, old local prints; nice riverside back terrace. *(Val and Alan Green)*

WINCHESTER   SU4828
⋆ Black Boy (01962) 861754
B3403 off M3 J10 towards city then left into Wharf Hill; no nearby daytime parking – 220 metres from car park on B3403; SO23 9NQ Splendidly eccentric décor at this chatty old-fashioned pub, floor-to-ceiling books, lots of big clocks, mobiles made of wine bottles or spectacles, stuffed animals including a baboon and dachshund, two log fires, orange-painted room with big oriental rugs on red floorboards, barn room with open hayloft, half a dozen often local beers, straightforward food (not Sun evening, Mon, Tues lunchtime), friendly service, table football and board games; background music; supervised children and dogs welcome, slate tables out in front and seats on attractive secluded terrace, open all day. *(Henry Fryer, Ann and Colin Hunt, John and Annabel Hampshire, Mark Sykes and others)*

WINCHESTER   SU4829
⋆ Eclipse (01962) 865676
The Square, between High Street and cathedral; SO23 9EX Chatty licensees in picturesque unspoilt 14th-c local with massive beams and timbers in its two small cheerful rooms, chilled ales such as Fullers and Ringwood, decent choice of wines by the glass, good value lunchtime food from ciabattas to popular Sun roasts, open fire, oak settles, friendly burmese cat; children in back area, seats outside, very handy for cathedral. *(Ann and Colin Hunt)*

WINCHESTER   SU4829
Old Gaol House (01962) 850095
Jewry Street; SO23 8RZ Traditional Wetherspoons attracting good mix of customers, ten real ales, decent sensibly priced food all day, nice coffee, walls of books; children welcome. *(Ann and Colin Hunt)*

WINCHESTER   SU4829
⋆ Old Vine (01962) 854616
Great Minster Street; SO23 9HA Lively big-windowed town bar with well kept ales such as Bowman, Flowerpots, Ringwood and Timothy Taylors, high beams, worn oak boards, smarter and larger dining side with good choice of up-to-date food

plus sandwiches and pub staples, modern conservatory; faint background music; by cathedral, with sheltered terrace, partly covered and heated, charming bedrooms, open all day. *(Glenwys and Alan Lawrence, David and Judy Robison, Richard Mason, Neil and Anita Christopher)*

WINCHESTER   SU4728
Queen (01962) 890542
Kingsgate Road; SO23 9PG Roomy two-bar flower-decked pub in attractive setting opposite College cricket ground, enjoyable home-made food including generous sandwiches, well kept Greene King ales and guests such as Black Sheep and Wadworths 6X, friendly competent staff, low ceilings, panelling, central fireplace, dining room; disabled facilities, front terrace and big garden, open all day. *(R T and J C Moggridge, Sue and Mike Todd)*

WINCHFIELD   SU7753
Barley Mow (01252) 617490
The Hurst; RG27 8DE Friendly two-bar local with airy dining extension, enjoyable home-made food and nice selection of beers; dogs welcome, pleasant seats out by cricket ground, near Basingstoke canal - lots of good walks. *(D J and P M Taylor)*

WOLVERTON   SU5658
George & Dragon (01635) 298292
Towns End; just N of A339 Newbury–Basingstoke; RG26 5ST Low-beamed and flagstoned pub in remote rolling country, long-serving licensees, linked cosy areas, log fire, wide choice of enjoyable unpretentious food, attentive service, several beers including Greene King and Wadworths, decent wines, pleasant dining area, skittle alley; children welcome, big garden with small terrace, separate bedroom block, good breakfast. *(J V Dadswell)*

WOODLANDS   SU3211
Gamekeeper (023) 8029 3093
Woodlands Road, just N of A336 Totton–Cadnam; SO40 7GH Unspoilt traditional village local by New Forest, friendly landlord, reasonably priced food and beers including Wadworths 6X and one brewed for the pub, good coffee, dining room with conservatory; terrace tables. *(Phil and Jane Villiers)*

YATELEY   SU8161
White Lion (01252) 890840
Reading Road; GU46 7RX Popular refurbished Vintage inn, enjoyable food all day including fixed-price menu (Mon-Sat till 5pm), three changing ales and plenty of wines by the glass, opened-up old rooms, log fire in raised hearth; background music, children welcome. *(Richard and Stephanie Foskett)*

Herefordshire

Some handsome old buildings, delicious food and fine ciders (this is the home of great ciders, after all) can all be found in this lovely county. New to the Guide are the Tram in Eardisley (plenty of warm local character and organic ciders), Kilpeck Inn, Kilpeck (sensitively reworked and in a pretty village), Kings Head in Ross-on-Wye (welcoming bar in well run small hotel), Lough Pool at Sellack (beautiful building surrounded by fine gardens), Bell in Tillington (cosy bar and civilised dining areas), Chase at Upper Colwall (a cheerful country tavern), and Crown in Woolhope (fantastic ciders and perries and enthusiastic landlord). Top class food can be found at the Cottage of Content in Carey (popular food in medieval inn), the Feathers in Ledbury (brasserie and restaurant menus and easy-going bar in smart hotel), Stagg at Titley (exceptional food, carefully chosen wines and charming bedrooms), Mill Race in Walford (an airy, stylish dining pub), and Butchers Arms in Woolhope (interesting food using carefully sourced produce). As a first class all-rounder and much enjoyed by our readers, Herefordshire Dining Pub 2013 is the exceptional Stagg at Titley.

BODENHAM   SO5454   Map 4

Englands Gate

On A417 at Bodenham turn-off, about 6 miles S of Leominster; HR1 3HU

Some fine original features in a comfortable 16th-c inn, four real ales and pleasant garden

The rambling, open-plan interior of this half-timbered 1540s coaching inn looks every year of its great age. There are heavy brown beams and joists in low ochre ceilings around a vast central stone chimneypiece, well worn flagstones, sturdy timber props, one or two steps, and lantern-style lighting. One corner has a high-backed settle with scatter cushions, a cosy partly stripped-stone room has a long stripped table (just right for a party of eight) and a lighter upper area with flowers on its tables has winged settles painted a soft eau de nil. Hobsons Twisted Spire, Wye Valley Bitter and HPA and a guest such as Hereford Best on handpump, and the pub holds a beer and sausage festival in July; background pop music, board games and TV. There are tables with sun umbrellas out in the garden and on the terrace. The smart, modern bedrooms and suites are in a converted coach house next door.

At lunchtime, food includes hot and cold baguettes, cumberland sausage and mustard mash, scampi, lasagne, battered cod, roast mediterranean vegetable linguini and ploughmans. The evening menu has starters such as spiced pear and stilton with crushed hazelnuts, ginger and star anise syrup and chicken livers, bacon and mushroom in flaky pastry, and main courses such as baked trout filled with spinach, prawns and lobster with dill cream, roast chicken breast wrapped in bacon with apple, chorizo and black pudding, mixed grill, and steaks. *Benchmark main dish: steak and ale pie £14.50. Two-course evening meal £20.00.*

Free house ~ Licensee Evelyn McNeil ~ Real ale ~ Bar food (12-2.30, 6-9.30; 12-3, 6-8.30 Sun) ~ (01568) 797286 ~ Children welcome until 9pm ~ Dogs allowed in bar and bedrooms ~ Open 12-11(midnight Sat, 10 Sun) ~ Bedrooms: /S82S ~ www.englandsgate.co.uk *Recommended by Paul Humphreys, Peter and Heather Elliott*

CAREY

SO5631   Map 4

Cottage of Content 🍴 🛏

Village signposted from good back road betweeen Ross-on-Wye and Hereford E of A49, through Hoarwithy; HR2 6NG

Country furnishings in a friendly rustic cottage, interesting food, real ales and seats on terraces; quiet bedrooms

This cosy medieval inn is in a lovely peaceful spot and was originally three labourers' cottages with its own integral cider and ale parlour. The building has kept much of its old character, with a multitude of beams and country furnishings such as stripped-pine kitchen chairs, long pews by one big table and various old-fashioned tables on flagstones or bare boards. Hobsons Best and Wye Valley Butty Bach on handpump and a local cider, and the friendly landlady serves a local cider during the summer months; background music. There are picnic-sets on the flower-filled front terrace and in the rural-feeling garden at the back. This is a nice place to stay.

 Highly thought of food might include baked goats cheese with roast beetroot, charcuterie, prawn cocktail, roast sea bream with sesame crust and teriyaki glaze, lamb crumble, roast curried vegetables, confit duck leg with honey glaze and mulled wine jus, and puddings such as banoffi meringue, chocolate cheesecake and cinnamon buttermilk pancakes with honey spiced ice-cream and chilli syrup. *Benchmark main dish: local pork plate £13.75. Two-course evening meal £20.00.*

Free house ~ Licensees Richard and Helen Moore ~ Real ale ~ Bar food (12-2, 6.30-9) ~ Restaurant ~ (01432) 840242 ~ Children welcome ~ Dogs allowed in bar ~ Open 12-2, 6-11; 12-3 Sun; closed Sun evening, Mon, also Tues lunchtime Jan-March, two weeks Oct ~ Bedrooms: £55(£65B)/£65(£75B) ~ www.cottageofcontent.co.uk *Recommended by Mike and Mary Carter, Dr and Mrs Michael Smith, Phil Bryant, the Didler, Barry Collett*

EARDISLEY

SO3149   Map 6

Tram £

Corner of A4111 and Woodseaves Road; HR3 6PG

Food a growing focus in character village pub – the village itself is a big draw, too

Since the arrival of the present young couple, the pink-walled hatch-served room on the right has been turned into a small dining room and the pool table has gone. The beamed bar on the left happily keeps its warmly local character, especially in the cosy back enclave behind sturdy standing timbers, where regulars congregate on the bare boards by the counter – which has well kept Hobsons Best, Ludlow Gold and Wye Valley Butty Bach on handpump, and local organic ciders. The rest of it has antique red and ochre floor tiles, a handful of nicely worn tables and chairs, a pair of long cushioned pews enclosing one much longer table, a high-backed settle, old country pictures and a couple of pictorial Wye maps; background music. The outside gents' is one of the most stylish we have ever seen; the sizeable neatly planted garden has picnic-sets on its lawn and a very comfortable shelter complete with sofas. The handsome old building suits this famous black and white village well.

🍴 Bar food includes sweet potato and butternut soup, honey glazed goats cheese with roasted red peppers, local peat-smoked salmon, baked ham, egg and chips, chill con carne, steak and ale pie, battered hake and chips, beetroot and carrot tart, well hung sirloin steak, and puddings such as eccles cake, tiramisu and sticky toffee pudding. *Benchmark main dish: rump steak £10.00. Two-course evening meal £14.20.*

Free house ~ Licensees Mark and Kerry Vernon ~ Real ale ~ Bar food (12-3, 6-9; not Sun evening) ~ Restaurant ~ (01544) 327251 ~ Children welcome ~ Dogs allowed in bar ~ Open 12-3, 6-midnight(7-11 Sun); closed Mon except spring and summer bank holidays ~ www.thetraminn.co.uk *Recommended by John and Bryony Coles, MLR*

KILPECK   SO4430   Map 6
Kilpeck Inn ♀
Village and church signposted off A465 SW of Hereford; HR2 9DN

Imaginatively extended country inn in fascinating and peaceful village

The nearby castle ruins are interesting, the romanesque church even more so. In its way the inn itself is rather special, too, sensitively reworked and reopened a couple of years ago. The softly lit dark-beamed bar, with dark slate flagstones, rambles happily around to give several tempting corners, for instance one with an antique high-backed settle, one with high stools around a matching chest-high table, one with a sheepskin thrown casually and invitingly over a seat. This opens into three cosily linked dining rooms on the left, with high panelled wainscoting. Throughout, the mood is thoroughly up to date, with clean-cut décor and furnishings; well reproduced background music. They have a good choice of wines by the glass, well kept Wye Valley Butty Bach on handpump, and Weston's cider. The neat back grass has picnic-sets (and there's a bicycle rack). We haven't yet heard from readers staying here, but the four bedrooms look nice – they're very eco-minded, with a biomass boiler and rainwater recycling system.

🍴 Extremely good food might include sandwiches, antipasti with celeriac and pear salad, mushroom stuffed with goats cheese and red pepper, trio of sausages with red onion gravy and herb mash, cheese and sun-blush tomato omelette, beer-battered hake and chips, gammon with pineapple or egg, streak frites, free-range chicken with diver-caught scallops with lemon butter sauce, lambs liver and bacon with red wine jus, gressingham duck breast with port wine sauce, and puddings like sticky toffee pudding with toffee sauce. *Benchmark main dish: herefordshire steak frites £10.95. Two-course evening meal £20.95.*

Free House ~ Licensee Catherine Carleton-Smith ~ Real ale ~ Bar food (12-2, 7-9) ~ Restaurant ~ (01981) 570464 ~ Children welcome ~ Dogs allowed in bar ~ Open 12-2.30, 5.30-11; 12-11 Sun; closed Sun evening in in winter ~ www.kilpeckinn.com
Recommended by Neil Hogg, Reg Fowle, Helen Rickwood, Martin and Pauline Jennings, Mr and Mrs M J Girdler, R and S Bentley, R K Phillips

LEDBURY   SO7137   Map 4

Feathers

High Street (A417); HR8 1DS

Handsome old hotel with chatty relaxed bar, more decorous lounge, good food and friendly staff; comfortable bedrooms

Like many readers, we have for years really enjoyed the civilised old-world atmosphere, well prepared food and unfailingly good staff at this strikingly timbered 16th-c hotel. The convivial carpeted back bar/brasserie has a chatty mix of drinkers at one end, with cosy leather easy chairs and sofas by the fire, and contented diners in its main part, with flowers and oil lamps on stripped kitchen and other tables, and comfortable bays of banquettes and other seats. The long beams are a mass of hop bines, and small prints and antique sale notices decorate the stripped panelling. They have Fullers London Pride and a couple of guests such as Prescott Hill Climb and Sharps Doom Bar on handpump, good wines by the glass from an extensive list, and three dozen malt whiskies. The sedate lounge is just right for afternoon teas, with high-sided armchairs and sofas in front of a big log fire, and daily papers. In summer, the sheltered back terrace has abundant pots and hanging baskets.

 Enjoyable bar/brasserie food includes sandwiches, moules marinière, beef and thyme burger, fishcakes with lemon and chervil mayonnaise, fried chicken livers with sherry-roasted baby onions, smoked bacon and croutons, and sharing platters. There's also a formal restaurant – residents get good breakfasts. *Benchmark main dish: beef and ale casserole £10.95. Two-course evening meal £21.50.*

Free house ~ Licensee David Elliston ~ Real ale ~ Bar food (12-2(2.30 Sat, Sun), 6.30-9.30(10 Fri, Sat)) ~ Restaurant ~ (01531) 635266 ~ Children welcome ~ Dogs allowed in bar and bedrooms ~ Open 10-11 (10.30 Sun) ~ Bedrooms: £95B/£140B ~ www.feathers-ledbury.co.uk *Recommended by Pete Coxon, Neil Kellett, P J and R D Greaves, Joan and Tony Walker, Guy Vowles, GSB, Mrs F Smith*

LITTLE COWARNE   SO6050   Map 4

Three Horseshoes

Pub signposted off A465 SW of Bromyard; towards Ullingswick; HR7 4RQ

Long-serving licensees and friendly staff in bustling country pub with well liked food using home-grown produce; bedrooms

Mr and Mrs Whittall, the licensees at this neatly kept pub, genuinely care about all their customers, extending a warm and friendly welcome to regulars and visitors alike, and there's always a good mix of chatty drinkers and those out for a special meal. The quarry-tiled L-shaped middle bar has leather-seated bar stools, upholstered settles and dark brown kitchen chairs around sturdy tables, old local photographs above the corner log fire and hop-draped beams. Opening off one side is a sun room with a wicker armchairs around more tables, and at the other end there's a games room with darts, pool, juke box, games machine and cribbage. Greene King Old Speckled Hen and Wye Valley Bitter and Butty Bach on handpump, local Oliver's cider and perry, a dozen wines by the glass and a dozen malt whiskies. A popular Sunday lunchtime carvery is offered in the roomy and attractive, stripped-stone, raftered restaurant extension. There are well sited tables and chairs on the terrace and on the neat, prettily planted lawn. They have disabled access.

Cooked by Mrs Whittall and son Philip using their own-grown and other local produce and local game, the highly thought of food includes devilled kidneys, prawn and haddock smokies, smoked salmon with beetroot and horseradish relish, fried chicken breast with cider sauce, cheese, leek, celery, walnut and filo pastry, grilled cod fillet with roasted red peppers and capers, braised shoulder of lamb with red wine gravy, lasagne, roasted pork belly with cider gravy and apple purée, and puddings. *Benchmark main dish: steak and ale pie £11.00. Two-course evening meal £18.20.*

Free house ~ Licensees Norman and Janet Whittall ~ Real ale ~ Bar food (12-2, 7-9) ~ Restaurant ~ (01885) 400276 ~ Children welcome ~ Open 11-3(3.30 Sat), 6.30-11.30(midnight Sat); 12-4, 7-10.30 Sun; closed Tuesday, Sun evening in winter ~ Bedrooms: £40S/£70S ~ www.threehorseshoes.co.uk *Recommended by Denys Gueroult, David and Julie Glover, Guy Vowles, David and Stella Martin, Mike and Eileen Vokins*

ROSS-ON-WYE
Kings Head £ 🛏

SO5924   Map 6

High Street (B4260); HR9 5HL

Welcoming bar in well run market-town hotel dating from 14th c, good bedrooms

The little beamed and panelled bar on the right has traditional pub furnishings on its stripped boards, including comfortably padded bar seats and an antique cushioned box settle, and a couple of black leather armchairs by the log-effect fire; well kept Wye Valley Butty Bach and a guest beer such as Sharps Doom Bar on handpump, a farm cider, local apple juice, and sensibly priced wines by the glass. The beamed lounge bar on the left, also bare-boards, has some timbering, soft leather armchairs and padded wicker bucket seats, with shelves of books. Friendly and effective service, TV, unobtrusive background music. There's a big carpeted dining room, and the sheltered back courtyard has contemporary tables and chairs. They do a good breakfast for residents.

Enjoyable food includes good local lamb and beef, with sandwiches and toasties served through the afternoon. The Bargain award is for the pubby lunchtime menu (they also do a good value two-course lunch), which includes mushroom lasagne, shepherd's pie, liver and bacon, fishcakes, battered fish, chicken breast with mushroom and chive sauce. The evening menu is slightly more elaborate with starters such as smoked duck breast with parmesan shavings and cassis dressing and thai-style mussels, crab, main courses such as breast of chicken with ham hock and grain mustard and parsley sauce, hake fillet with samphire and lemon butter, pheasant breast with bacon and madeira jus, cauliflower and salsify tart with blue cheese and spinach and walnut pesto, and puddings such as crème brûlée with candied ginger and cinnamon biscuit and dark chocolate truffle with marinated clementines. *Benchmark main dish: steak and ale pie £9.95. Two-course evening meal £17.50.*

Free house ~ Licensee James Vidler ~ Real ale ~ Bar food (12-2.15, 6.30-9) ~ Restaurant ~ (01989) 763174 ~ Children welcome ~ Dogs allowed in bar and bedrooms ~ Open 10-11(10.30 Sun) ~ Bedrooms: £56B/£80B ~ www.kingshead.co.uk *Recommended by Pete Coxon, Lucien Perring, Neil and Anita Christopher*

> Cribbage is a card game using a block of wood with holes for matchsticks or special pins to score with; regulars in cribbage pubs are usually happy to teach strangers how to play.

SELLACK

SO5526 Map 4

Lough Pool ♀

Off A49; HR9 6LX

Charming cottage pub with individual furnishings in beamed bars, a good choice of food and drinks, and lots of seats outside in the pretty garden

---

The garden in front of this lovely 17th-c black and white cottage is peacefully rural, and if you're lucky you'll catch sight of local jockeys out training on their race horses. The charmingly simple and timeless interior is complete with cheery locals, beams, standing timbers, flagstones, rustic furniture and fires burning in the two woodburners at either end of the bar on all but the warmest days. Wye Valley Bitter and Butty Bach and a guest such as Butcombe are on handpump alongside local farm ciders and perries and several wines by the glass from a thoughtful wine list. The restaurant enjoys views over the lovely garden.

 Heartily enjoyable bar food, with plenty of game in season, might include cream of parsnip soup, game terrine with spicy apple and tomato chutney, smoked salmon, steak and kidney pudding, braised ox cheek, rabbit cooked in mushroom and mustard cream sauce, braised partridge, goats cheese tart, roast vegetable lasagne, faggots and mushy peas, and puddings such as apricot and pear crumble and bread and butter pudding. *Benchmark main dish: steak and kidney pie £10.95. Two-course evening meal £17.15.*

Free house ~ Licensees Jim Watson and Jo Morgan ~ Real ale ~ Bar food (12-3, 6.30-9) ~ Restaurant ~ (01989) 730888 ~ Children welcome ~ Dogs allowed in bar ~ Open 12-3, 6-11; closed Sun evening, Mon ~ www.theloughpoolinn.co.uk *Recommended by Dr and Mrs R E S Tanner, Lucien Perring, Peter Martin, Guy Vowles*

SYMONDS YAT

SO5616 Map 4

Saracens Head ⇐

Symonds Yat E, by ferry, ie over on the Gloucestershire bank; HR9 6JL

Lovely riverside spot with a fine range of drinks in friendly inn, interesting food and seats on waterside terraces; comfortable bedrooms

---

Steps lead up from the River Wye to picnic-sets on the waterside terrace at this friendly pub, which is in a stunning position at the epicentre of the most scenic stretch of the Wye gorge, far below the celebrated Symonds Yat viewpoint. An entertaining riverside walk crosses the Wye a little downstream by a bouncy wire bridge at Biblins and recrosses at the pub by the long-extant hand-hauled chain ferry that one of the pub staff operates. Even when the weather is inclement, the bustling bar tends to be packed with happy customers enjoying the buoyant, welcoming atmosphere. Cheerful staff serve Theakstons Old Peculier, Wye Valley Butty Bach and HPA from handpump, a couple of local guests such as Kingstone Gold, Mayfields Copper Fox and Otley 01, a dozen wines by the glass and a local cider; TV, background music and board games. There's also a cosy lounge and a modernised bare-boards dining room. As well as bedrooms in the main building, there are two contemporary ones in the boathouse annexe.

 As well as lunchtime sandwiches, the popular food might include beef carpaccio, mussels in a thai green sauce, smoked local salmon and crab roulade, braised lamb shank with rosemary jus, fried salmon on creamy seafood chowder, confit duck leg cassoulet, bass fillet with vanilla butter sauce, steak, kidney and ale pie, and rib-eye steak and puddings. *Benchmark main dish: sirloin steak £15.95. Two-course evening meal £19.00.*

Free house ~ Licensees P K and C J Rollinson ~ Real ale ~ Bar food (12-2.30, 6.30-9) ~ Restaurant ~ (01600) 890435 ~ Children welcome ~ Dogs allowed in bar ~ Open 11-11 ~ Bedrooms: £59B/£89B ~ www.saracensheadinn.co.uk *Recommended by N R White, Phil Bryant, MLR, Guy Vowles*

TILLINGTON
SO4645   Map 6
Bell 🍺
Off A4110 NW of Hereford; HR4 8LE

Friendly and relaxed, with snug character bar opening into civilised dining areas – good value

The snug parquet-floor bar on the left has a variety of bucket armchairs around low chunky mahogany-coloured tables, brightly cushioned wall benches, team photographs and shelves of books – and on our visit, its black beams were strung with Six Nations flags as well as their usual dried hops, and there was a big roll-down screen for the rugby. They have Sharps Doom Bar, Wye Valley and a guest such as Worthington Red Shield on handpump, and staff are notably cheerful and welcoming; daily papers, unobtrusive background music. The bar opens into a comfortable bare-boards dining lounge with stripey plush banquettes and a coal fire; beyond that is a pitched-ceiling restaurant area with more banquettes and big country prints; its slatted blinds look out on to a sunken terrace with contemporary tables and a garden with teak tables, picnic-sets and a play area.

Good value food includes sandwiches, smoked mackerel and cream cheese mousse, field mushrooms filled with goats cheese, artichokes and tomato pesto, home-baked honey roast ham with free-range eggs, local sausages with chips, butternut squash bake with gnocchi, parmesan and tapenade, beer-battered cod with mushy peas, steak in ale pie, chicken curry, slow-cooked pork belly with bramley apple glaze and celeriac mash, and puddings like kirsch cherry panettone with custard and apricot and almond tart with orange and honey crème fraîche *Benchmark main dish: seafood chowder £12.50. Two-course evening meal £17.75.*

Free house ~ Licensee Glenn Williams ~ Real ale ~ Bar food (12-2.15(2.45 Sun), 6-9.15; not Sun evening) ~ Restaurant ~ (01432) 760395 ~ Children welcome ~ Dogs welcome ~ Open 11-11; 12-10.30 Sun ~ www.thebellinntillington.co.uk *Recommended by Alistair Stanier, John and Jennifer Spinks, Revd Michael Vockins, Peter Cole*

TITLEY
SO3359   Map 6
Stagg 🍴 🍷 🛏
B4355 N of Kington; HR5 3RL
Herefordshire Dining Pub of the Year

Terrific food using tip-top ingredients served in extensive dining rooms; real ales and a fine choice of other drinks; two-acre garden and comfortable bedrooms

Our readers love this charming place and while the excellent food remains the main draw (this is one of Britain's top dining pubs, after all), it's still very much a pub rather than a pure restaurant and the staff are genuinely welcoming and courteous. The little bar (they hope to enlarge it at some point soon) is comfortably hospitable with a civilised atmosphere, a fine collection of 200 jugs attached to the ceiling, Wye Valley Bitter, Ludlow Gold and a guest such as Wye Valley Butty Bach on handpump, nine house wines by the glass (there's also a carefully chosen 100-strong bin list), local potato and apple vodkas, local gins, farm cider and quite a choice of spirits. The two-acre garden has seats on the terrace and a croquet lawn. The accommodation is in bedrooms above the pub and in a Georgian vicarage four minutes' walk away; super breakfasts.

🍴 Using their own-grown vegetables (they keep free-range chickens as well), the excellent inventive food includes some pubby dishes (not Saturday evenings or Sunday lunch) such as open sandwiches, three-cheese ploughman's, steak sandwich and crispy duck leg with dauphinoise potato and cider. The more elaborate dishes might include fried foie gras with cider and apple jelly, seared scallops with celeriac, artichoke and cauliflower purée, spicy red mullet fillet with mussels, couscous, roast partridge with poached pear, leeks and noisette potatoes, and puddings such as ginger panna cotta with lime jelly and mango sorbet and bread and butter pudding with marmalade ice cream. *Benchmark main dish: beef fillet with béarnaise sauce £22.00. Two-course evening meal £24.00.*

Free house ~ Licensees Steve and Nicola Reynolds ~ Real ale ~ Bar food (12-2, 6.30-9(9.30 Sat)) ~ Restaurant ~ (01544) 230221 ~ Children welcome ~ Dogs allowed in bar and bedrooms ~ Open 11-3, 6.30-11; 12-3 Sun; closed Sun evening, all day Mon, two weeks Nov and two weeks Jan/Feb ~ Bedrooms: £70B/£100B ~ www.thestagg.co.uk
Recommended by Karen Eliot, R and S Bentley, P J and R D Greaves, Guy Vowles, Gaynor Gregory, Chris Flynn, Wendy Jones, Steven King and Barbara Cameron, Peter Harrison, Jonathan Niccol, John Holroyd, Dr Kevan Tucker

UPPER COLWALL
Chase

SO7643   Map 4

Chase Road, brown sign to pub off B4218 Malvern–Colwall, first left after hilltop on bend going W; WR13 6DJ

Gorgeous sunset views from cheerful country tavern's garden, good drinks and cost-conscious food

Tables out on the steep series of small, pretty terraces behind the pub have sweeping views from this western slope of the Malvern Hills, right out over Herefordshire and on a clear day as far as the Black Mountain and even the Brecon Beacons; there are good walks all around. Inside is chatty and companionable, with quite a pack of gilt cast-iron framed and treadle sewing tables, seats in great variety from a wooden-legged tractor seat to a carved pew, an old black kitchen range and plenty of decorations – china mugs, blue glass flasks, lots of small pictures. They have half a dozen changing well kept ales on handpump, such as Bathams Best, Hobsons Mild, Jennings Cocker Hoop, Sharps Doom Bar and Woods Shropshire Lad, and several wines by the glass; friendly, helpful staff. There may be free sandwiches in the early evening.

🍴 Tasty good value food includes lunchtime sandwiches, deep-fried whitebait, ciabatta topped with goats cheese and red onion, hot chicken and bacon salad, beef burger and chips, battered cod and chips, steak and St Georges ale pie, and puddings. *Benchmark main dish: steak and ale pie £9.90. Two-course evening meal £14.00.*

Free house ~ Licensee Andy Lannie ~ Real ale ~ Bar food (12-2(2.30 weekends), 6.30-9) ~ Restaurant ~ (01684) 540276 ~ Children welcome ~ Dogs welcome ~ Open 12-3, 5-11; 12-11 Sat; 12-10.30 Sun ~ www.thechaseinnuppercolwall.co.uk *Recommended by Dr A J and Mrs Tompsett, Tim and Joan Wright, Chris Flynn, Wendy Jones*

WALFORD
SO5820 Map 4

Mill Race 🍴 ♀
B4234 Ross-on-Wye–Lydney; HR9 5QS

Contemporary furnishings in uncluttered rooms, emphasis on good quality food ingredients, attentive staff, terrace tables and nearby walks

This airy, stylish dining pub is fresh and contemporary, with a row of strikingly tall arched windows, comfortable leather armchairs and sofas on flagstones, and smaller chairs around broad pedestal tables. The walls are mainly cream or dark pink, with photographs of the local countryside, and there's good unobtrusive lighting. One wall, stripped back to the stonework, has a woodburning stove, which is open to the comfortable and compact dining area on the other side. The granite-topped modern bar counter has Butcombe and Wye Valley Bitter and Butty Bach on handpump, local ciders, 20 fairly priced wines by the glass, around 120 by the bottle and a dozen malt whiskies; background music. A terrace enjoys views towards Goodrich Castle, and the garden has plenty more dining space. They offer leaflets detailing pleasant nearby walks of an hour or so.

 The pub owns a 1,000-acre farm and woodland close by which supply them with game, rabbits, poultry, beef, fruit and vegetables. As well as sandwiches and imaginative pizzas from their outside oven (Tuesdays and Thursdays evenings only), dishes might include fried squid with parsley salad, grilled black pudding and english mustard cream, game terrine with fried quail egg and green tomato chutney, pie of the day, venison faggot with minted mushy peas and wilted greens, root vegetable tagine with pomegranate salsa, cod with chorizo and butter bean stew, and puddings such as lemon posset and caramelised rice pudding with cinnamon tuile and mulled prunes. *Benchmark main dish: fish and chips £10.50. Two-course evening meal £18.45.*

Free house ~ Licensee Luke Freeman ~ Real ale ~ Bar food (12-2(2.30 Sat), 6-9(9.30 Sat); 12-9 Sun) ~ (01989) 562891 ~ Children welcome ~ Open 11-3, 5-11; 11-11 Sat; 12-10.30 Sun ~ www.millrace.info *Recommended by Guy Vowles, Mike and Mary Carter, Dr A J and Mrs Tompsett, Nick and Meriel Cox, Lucien Perring, Andy and Jill Kassube, GSB, R T and J C Moggridge*

WALTERSTONE
SO3424 Map 6

Carpenters Arms
Follow Walterstone signs off A465; HR2 0DX

Unchanging country tavern in the same family for many years

The lovely Vera has been at this charming, old-fashioned pub for around 70 years, taking over the reins from her mother. Happily, little in its timelessly traditional rooms changes from year to year. Pewter mugs hang from beams, the fire roars in a gleaming black range (complete with hot-water tap, bread oven and salt cupboard), warming ancient settles flank stripped-stone walls, the broad polished flagstones are scattered with pieces of carpet, and Breconshire Golden Valley, Wadworths 6X and a guest such as Breconshire County are tapped straight from the cask. The snug main dining room has mahogany tables and oak corner cupboards and maybe a big vase of flowers on the dresser. Another little dining area has old oak tables and church pews on flagstones. The outside lavatories are cold but in character.

Straightforward food includes sandwiches, soup, a vegetarian choice, curry of the day, gammon and egg, lamb cutlet with redcurrant and rosemary sauce, daily specials such as chicken with stilton. *Benchmark main dish: beef and Guinness pie £9.00. Two-course evening meal £13.40.*

Free house ~ Licensee Vera Watkins ~ Real ale ~ Bar food (12-2, 7-9) ~ Restaurant ~ No credit cards ~ (01873) 890353 ~ Children welcome ~ Open 12-11 ~ www.thecarpentersarmswalterstone.com *Recommended by Terry Davis, MLR*

WOOLHOPE
SO6135 Map 4

Butchers Arms ⊕ ♀ ◧

Off B4224 in Fownhope; HR1 4RF

Pleasant country inn in peaceful setting, with an inviting garden, excellent food and a fine choice of real ales

Standards are consistently high and attention is paid to every detail at this welcoming 16th-c timber-framed pub. It's down a country lane in lovely countryside, surrounded by a pretty garden with picnic-sets beside a stream. Inside, the bar has very low beams (some with hops), built-in, red-cushioned wall seats, farmhouse chairs and red-topped stools around a mix of old tables (some set for dining) on the red patterned carpet, hunting and horse pictures on the cream walls and an open fire in the big fireplace; there's also a little beamed dining room, similarly furnished. Wye Valley Bitter and Butty Bach are kept alongside a couple of guests from brewers such as Breconshire on handpump and there's a well-annotated wine list with several by the glass. To enjoy some of the best of the surroundings, turn left as you come out of the pub and take the tiny left-hand road at the end of the car park; this turns into a track and then into a path, and the view from the top of the hill is quite something.

 Using rare-breed meat and other carefully sourced produce, the first-rate food cooked by the professional landlord includes sandwiches using home-made bread, ploughman's, haggis fritters with beetroot relish, spinach, caerphilly and almond tart, battered whiting, hake fillet with salsa verde, roast pork tenderloin with confit pork belly and squash purée, roast pigeon with mushroom ravioli and red wine sauce, and puddings such as orange and frangipane tart, marmalade brioche and butter pudding and iced damson parfait with puff pastry biscuits. *Benchmark main dish: liver and bacon £11.00. Two-course evening meal £20.00.*

Free house ~ Licensee Stephen Bull ~ Real ale ~ Bar food (12-2, 7-9) ~ (01432) 860281 ~ Children welcome ~ Dogs welcome ~ Open 12-3, 6-11(midnight Sat); 12-3 Sun; closed Sun evening, Mon, one week in Jan ~ www.butchersarmswoolhope.com *Recommended by K and B Barker, John and Jennifer Spinks, Victoria Sanders, Barry Collett*

WOOLHOPE
SO6135 Map 4

Crown

Village signposted off B4224 in Fownhope; HR1 4QP

Cheery local with fine range of local ciders and perries, and tasty food

This busy, cheerful pub, run by an enthusiastic landlord, is the heart of the local community. They keep four draught ciders (two they make themselves) and 20 bottled ciders and perries all from within a 15-mile radius; also Hobsons Best Bitter, Wye Valley HPA and a changing guest on handpump. The bar is straightforwardly traditional with cream walls, some standing timbers, patterned carpets, dark wood pubby furniture, plush built-in banquettes, cottagey curtained windows and a couple of woodburners; background music, darts and TV for sports events. There are terrific views from the lovely big garden, which also has darts, quoits, and cushions in the particularly comfortable smoking shelter, and the garden bar is open in summer; disabled access.

Good food includes lunchtime sandwiches, twice-baked cheese soufflé with creamy garlic mushrooms, pigeon with red onion marmalade and thyme jus, cider-baked ham with free-range eggs, goats cheese and mushroom stack with sunblush tomatoes, beer-battered cod with mushy peas and tartare sauce, rack of local lamb with dauphinoise potatoes and mint jus, local steaks with peppercorn or blue cheese sauce, and puddings. *Benchmark main dish: slow-braised local pork belly with red wine and thyme sauce, crackling and apple £13.00. Two-course evening meal £16.00.*

Free house ~ Licensees Matt and Annalisa Slocombe ~ Real ale ~ Bar food (12-2.30(3 Sat, 3.30 Sun), 6-9(9.30 Sat)) ~ Restaurant ~ (01432) 860468 ~ Children welcome ~ Open 12-3, 6-11; 12-midnight Fri and Sat ~ www.crowninnwoolhope.co.uk
Recommended by Adrian Johnson, Tim and Joan Wright, T M Griffiths

Also Worth a Visit in Herefordshire

Besides the fully inspected pubs, you might like to try these pubs that have been recommended to us and described by readers. Do tell us what you think of them: feedback@goodguides.com

AYMESTREY   SO4265
★**Riverside Inn** (01568) 708440
A4110, at N end of village, W of Leominster; HR6 9ST Terrace and tree-sheltered garden making most of lovely waterside spot by ancient stone bridge over the Lugg; cosy rambling beamed interior with some antique furniture alongside stripped country kitchen tables, fresh flowers, hops strung from a ceiling wagon-wheel, horse tack, open fires, chatty landlord, well kept Hobsons, Wye Valley and a guest, local ciders, good lunchtime bar food and more expensive evening menu using local venison and rare-breed meat, own-grown fruit and vegetables; quiet background music; children welcome, dogs in bar, bedrooms (fly-fishing for residents), closed Sun evening, Mon lunchtime (all day Mon in winter). *(Alan and Eve Harding, Steve Whalley, Paul Humphreys, R T and J C Moggridge and others)*

BISHOPS FROME   SO6648
★**Green Dragon** (01885) 490607
Just off B4214 Bromyard–Ledbury; WR6 5BP Half a dozen well kept ales such as Purple Moose, Timothy Taylors and Wye Valley, farm ciders, friendly licensees, traditional food (not Sun) including good steaks, four linked rooms with nice unspoilt rustic feel, beams, flagstones and log fires including fine inglenook; children and dogs welcome, tiered garden with smokers' shelter, on Herefordshire Trail, closed weekday lunchtimes, open all day Sat.
(Reg Fowle, Helen Rickwood, Roger and Diana Morgan, Guy Vowles)

BRINGSTY COMMON   SO6954
★**Live & Let Live** (01886) 821462
Off A44 Knightwick–Bromyard 1.5 miles W of Whitbourne turn; take track southwards at black cat inn sign, bearing right at fork; WR6 5UW Bustling timbered and thatched 17th-c cottage; cosy flagstoned bar with scrubbed or polished tables, comfortably cushioned little chairs, long stripped pew and high-backed winged settle by log fire in cavernous stone fireplace, earthenware jugs hanging from low beams, old casks built into hop-hung bar counter, Ludlow, Malvern Hills and Wye Valley, local ciders and apple juice, well liked pubby food, two dining rooms upstairs under steep rafters; children and dogs welcome, glass-topped well and big wooden hogshead as terrace tables, peaceful views from picnic-sets in former orchard, handy for Brockhampton Estate (NT), open all day in summer, closed Mon and winter afternoons Tues-Thurs *(Guy Vowles, Chris Flynn, Wendy Jones, the Didler, Susan Cook and others)*

BROMYARD DOWNS   SO6755
★**Royal Oak** (01885) 482585
Just NE of Bromyard; pub signed off A44; HR7 4QP Beautifully placed low-beamed 18th-c pub with wide views, open-plan carpeted and flagstoned bar with log fire and woodburner, dining room with huge bay window, enjoyable good value home-made food from varied menu, well kept Malvern Hills, Purity and Woods, real cider, friendly service, pool and darts; background music; children, walkers and dogs welcome,

picnic-sets on nice front terrace, swings, open all day weekends in Aug. *(P J and R D Greaves, R K Phillips)*

CLIFFORD SO2445
Castlefields (01497) 831554
B4350 N of Hay-on-Wye; HR3 5HB Newly rebuilt family pub, some old features including a well, good helpings of enjoyable fairly priced food, Sharps Doom Bar, friendly helpful staff, woodburner in two-way fireplace, restaurant; good country views, camping. *(Reg Fowle, Helen Rickwood)*

COLWALL SO7440
⋆**Wellington** (01684) 540269
A449 Malvern–Ledbury; WR13 6HW Welcoming landlord and friendly staff, wide choice of generous food from good standards to more imaginative dishes, set price lunch weekdays, well kept ales such as Goffs, good wines by the glass, neat two-level beamed bar with red patterned carpet and nice fire, spacious relaxed back dining area, newspapers and magazines; children welcome, picnic-sets on neat grass above car park, closed Sun evening, Mon. *(Rev Michael Vockins, Mrs B H Adams)*

DORSTONE SO3141
⋆**Pandy** (01981) 550273
Pub signed off B4348 E of Hay-on-Wye; HR3 6AN Ancient timbered inn by village green, homely traditional rooms with low hop-strung beams, stout timbers, upright chairs on worn flagstones and in various alcoves, vast open fireplace, locals by bar with good range of beers including Wye Valley Butty Bach, summer farm cider, quite a few malts and irish whiskeys, good food from baguettes and pubby things to interesting specials, friendly competent staff, board games; background music; children welcome, dogs in bar (resident red setter called Apache), neat side garden with picnic-sets and play area, good bedrooms in purpose-built annexe, open all day Sat, closed Mon lunchtime (except summer and bank hols). *(Jason Caulkin, Mike and Eileen Vokins, the Didler, Simon Le Fort, Mark Sykes, Martin and Sue Day)*

EARDISLAND SO4258
Cross (01544) 388249
A44; HR6 9BW Friendly two-room local in lovely village, quick service, good value honest food (not Tues) from decent sandwiches up, Hobsons and Wye Valley ales, events including fortnightly Thurs quiz, small antiques centre in function room; TV; children and dogs welcome, seats in front and in back garden, next to restored 1920s AA box, open all day. *(Paul Humphreys, MLR)*

FOWNHOPE SO5734
Green Man (01432) 860243
B4224; HR1 4PE Striking 15th-c black and white inn, wall settles, window seats and leather chairs in one beamed bar, standing timbers dividing another, warm woodburners in old fireplaces, good food in bar and restaurant, friendly helpful service, three changing ales and Weston's cider, good wines, nice coffee; background music, no dogs; children welcome, redesigned quiet garden, 11 revamped bedrooms, open all day. *(Trevor Swindells, John and Mary Ling)*

FOWNHOPE SO5734
New Inn (01432) 860350
B4224; HR1 4PE Welcoming little village local with enjoyable lunchtime food (not weekends) cooked by landlady, well kept Hobsons and Wye Valley, small dining area; garden, picturesque village with unusual church and nice views, open all day weekends. *(Lucien Perring)*

GORSLEY SO6726
⋆**Roadmaker** (01989) 720352
0.5 miles from M50 junction 3; village signposted from exit - B4221; HR9 7SW Popular 19th-c village pub run well by group of retired Gurkhas, large carpeted lounge bar with central log fire, very good nepalese food here and in evening restaurant, also Sun roasts, well kept Brains and Butcombe, efficient courteous service; no dogs; children welcome, terrace with water feature, open all day. *(Joe Green, Gerry and Ruth Lowth, Neil and Anita Christopher, LM)*

HAREWOOD END SO5227
Harewood End Inn (01989) 730637
A49 Hereford–Ross; HR2 8JT Comfortable panelled dining lounge in interesting old building, good choice of enjoyable well priced food, helpful friendly staff, well kept ales such as Brains and Flowers, good sensibly priced wines; nice garden and walks, five bedrooms. *(Dennis and Doreen Haward)*

HEREFORD SO5139
Barrels (01432) 274968
St Owen Street; HR1 2JQ Friendly 18th-c coaching inn and former home to the Wye Valley brewery, seven of their very well kept ales from barrel-built counter (beer festival end Aug), Thatcher's cider, no food, cheerful efficient staff; pool room, big-screen sports TV, background and some live music; partly covered courtyard behind, open all day. *(Rick Shallcross, MLR, Reg Fowle, Helen Rickwood, the Didler)*

Post Office address codings confusingly give the impression that a few pubs are in Herefordshire when they're really in Gloucestershire or even Wales (which is where we list them).

HEREFORD   SO4940
Britannia (01432) 341095
Cotterell Street; HR4 0HH Victorian pub refurbished and extended by Wye Valley, their full range and guest ales, no food, pool; round picnic-sets on paved terrace with pond, open all day from midday (5pm Mon). *(Reg Fowle, Helen Rickwood)*

HEREFORD   SO5140
Kings Fee (01432) 373240
Commercial Road; HR1 2BP Big Wetherspoons with good value well kept ales including one brewed for it, good coffee, their usual food, cheerful attentive service, raised back section; terrace seats, open all day from breakfast on. *(George Atkinson, Pat and Tony Martin)*

HEREFORD   SO5039
☆Lichfield Vaults (01432) 266821
Church Street; HR1 2LR A pub since the 18th c (the Dog, then) in picturesque pedestrianised area near cathedral; dark panelling, some stripped brick and exposed joists, impressive plasterwork in big-windowed front room, traditionally furnished with dark pews, padded pub chairs and a couple of heavily padded benches, hot coal stove, charming greek landlord and friendly staff, well kept Adnams, Bass, Caledonian and Sharps, enjoyable food from sandwiches up including selection of greek dishes, good Sun roasts, daily newspapers; faint background music - live blues/rock last Sun of month, games machines; children welcome, no dogs, picnic-sets in pleasant back courtyard. *(Dennis Jones, Martin Ferries, Michael Carpenter)*

HEREFORD   SO5039
Stagecoach (01432) 265894
West Street; HR4 0BX 16th-c black and white building, comfortable unpretentious lounge with dark oak panelling, well kept/priced Wye Valley ales and a guest, cheerful efficient service, bargain food including Sun carvery, low-beamed upstairs restaurant; machines and TV in bar; children welcome, open all day. *(Alan and Eve Harding)*

HEREFORD   SO5139
☆Victory (01432) 342125
St Owen Street, opposite fire station; HR1 2QD Home of the Hereford Brewery - they may show you round if not busy, five of their beers plus farm ciders and a perry, humorous nautical interior including a miniature galleon as the counter complete with cannon, back room decked out as a man o' war with rigging and netting, curved walls, a crow's nest and appropriate lamps, curry and quiz Tues, no other food, skittle alley and back pool table; background music (live Sat), TV, no credit cards; children and dogs welcome, garden seats, closed weekdays until 3pm, open all day weekends. *(Richard Gibbs,*

Shane, Jill and family, Reg Fowle, Helen Rickwood)

HOARWITHY   SO5429
New Harp (01432) 840900
Off A49 Hereford–Ross-on-Wye; HR2 6QH Recently refurbished open-plan dining pub with good local food from chef/landlord, friendly helpful service, four well kept changing ales (usually one from Wye Valley), flagstones and two woodburners; background music - maybe live Fri; children, walkers and dogs welcome, pretty tree-sheltered garden with stream, picnic-sets and decked area, unusual italianate Victorian church, open all day Fri-Sun. *(Barry Collett)*

KENTCHURCH   SO4125
Bridge Inn (01981) 240408
B4347 Pontrilas–Grosmont; HR2 0BY Ancient attractively refurbished rustic pub, big log fire, popular home-made food including set deals, changing ales such as Otter, small pretty back restaurant overlooking River Monnow (two miles of trout fishing), playful collie called Freddie; waterside tables, bedrooms, handy for Herefordshire Trail. *(Reg Fowle, Helen Rickwood)*

KINGSLAND   SO4461
Angel (01568) 709195
B4360; HR6 9QS 17th-c traditional beamed and timbered dining pub, enjoyable home-made food from lunchtime ciabattas and pizzas up, four well kept ales including one brewed for them, a dozen wines by the glass, helpful friendly staff, comfortable open-plan interior with two woodburners, upstair function/overspill area, summer live music (Fri); picnic-sets on front grass, garden behind, closed Sun evening in winter. *(Frankie Owens)*

KINGSLAND   SO4461
☆Corners (01568) 708385
B4360 NW of Leominster, corner of Lugg Green Road; HR6 9RY Comfortably updated partly black-and-white 16th-c village inn with snug nooks and corners, log fires, low beams, dark red plasterwork and some stripped brick, comfortable bow-window seat, and group of dark leather armchairs in softly-lit carpeted bar, Hobsons and a guest such as Wye Valley Butty Bach, airier big raftered side dining room in converted hay loft with huge window, good reasonably priced food from pubby things up, cheerful attentive service; children welcome, no garden, comfortable bedrooms in new block behind. *(Alan and Eve Harding, Paul Humphreys, Mel and May Mackie)*

KINGTON   SO3056
☆Olde Tavern (01544) 230122
Victoria Road, just off A44 opposite B4355 – follow sign to Town Centre, Hospital, Cattle Market; pub on right

*opposite Elizabeth Road, no inn sign but
Estd 1767 notice; HR5 3BX* Gloriously
old-fashioned with hatch-served side room
opening off small plain parlour and public
bar, plenty of dark brown woodwork, big
windows, settles and other antique furniture
on bare floors, gas fire, old local pictures,
china, pewter and curios, four well kept
mainly local beers, Weston's cider, beer
festivals, no food - may have rolls and
chocolate bars, friendly atmosphere; children
and dogs welcome, little yard at back, outside
gents', closed weekday lunchtimes.
(the Didler, MLR)

KINGTON   SO2956
Oxford Arms (01544) 230322
Duke Street; HR5 3DR Well worn in (not to
everyone's taste) with woodburners in main
bar on left and dining area on right, smaller
lounge with sofas and armchairs, well kept
local ales such as Hereford and Mayfields,
enjoyable reasonably priced food, good
friendly service, pool; closed lunchtimes Mon
and Tues. *(Alan and Eve Harding, Carol White,
Reg Fowle, Helen Rickwood, MLR, Dave Braisted)*

KINNERSLEY   SO3449
Kinnersley Arms (01544) 327778
Off A4112 Hay–Leominster; HR3 6QA
Country pub with good choice of food (all day
weekends) using local meat and home-grown
vegetables, well kept Hereford Owd Bull,
separate games bar with pool, restaurant;
children welcome, good-sized garden
with play area, nice walks, self-catering
cottage. *(Reg Fowle, Helen Rickwood, Pat and
Tony Martin)*

LEDBURY   SO7137
★Prince of Wales (01531) 632250
*Church Lane; narrow passage from
Town Hall; HR8 1DL* Friendly busy local
tucked prettily down narrow cobbled alley,
well kept Hereford, Hobsons, Wye Valley and
guests such as Otter and Robinsons Enigma,
Weston's Bounds cider and foreign bottled
beers, knowledgeable staff, bargain simple
home-made food from sandwiches up, low
beams, shelves of books, long back room;
faint background music; a couple of tables in
flower-filled yard. *(Brian and Anna Marsden)*

LEINTWARDINE   SO4073
Lion (01547) 540203
High Street; SY7 0JZ Nicely restored
inn in beautiful spot by packhorse bridge
over River Teme, helpful efficient staff and
friendly atmosphere, good well presented
food from varied menu including some
imaginative choices, popular two-room
restaurant, well kept beer; children welcome,
safely fenced riverside garden with play area,
eight attractive bedrooms. *(Neil Kellett, Donald
Beattie, Lucy Hill, Dr and Mrs James Harris,
Warren Marsh)*

LEINTWARDINE   SO4073
★Sun (01547) 540705
Rosemary Lane, just off A4113; SY7 0LP
Fascinating time-warp run by local
consortium, bare benches and farmhouse
tables by coal fire in wallpapered brick-
floored front bar (dogs welcome here), well
kept Hobsons tapped from the cask and an
occasional guest (Aug beer festival), another
fire in snug carpeted parlour, no food unless
prearranged, friendly staff; new pavilion-style
building with bar and garden room, closed
Mon lunchtime. *(Brian and Jacky Wilson, Reg
Fowle, Helen Rickwood, the Didler, Alun Jones)*

LEOMINSTER   SO4959
Bell (01568) 612818
Etnam Street; HR6 8AE Old pub under
enthusiastic licensees, opened-up beamed
interior with light décor, bare boards and
big log fire, well kept Wye Valley ales and a
guest like Purple Moose from central servery,
simple lunchtime food including sandwiches
and baguettes, good mix of customers,
regular live music; tables in sheltered back
courtyard, garden, open all day. *(Paul
Humphreys, MLR, Reg Fowle, Helen Rickwood,
Alan and Eve Harding and others)*

LINTON   SO6525
Alma (01989) 720355
On main road through village; HR9 7RY
Cheerful unspoilt local in small village,
four well kept/priced changing ales such as
Butcombe and Malvern Hills, no food (may
be free Sun nibbles), homely carpeted front
room with sleepy cats by good fire, small
back room with pool, summer charity music
festival; children very welcome, good-sized
garden behind with nice view, closed
weekday lunchtimes. *(TB, Reg Fowle,
Helen Rickwood)*

LONGTOWN   SO3228
Crown (01873) 860217
South of the village; HR2 0LT Welcoming
place in nice scenic spot, well kept changing
ales such as Golden Valley and Wye Valley,
enjoyable food from sandwiches to good value
Sun lunch, woodburner in main beamed
bar, restaurant, games room with pool;
children welcome, garden, good walks, seven
bedrooms, open all day Fri-Sun. *(MLR)*

LUGWARDINE   SO5441
Crown & Anchor (01432) 851303
*Just off A438 E of Hereford; Cotts
Lane; HR1 4AB* Cottagey timbered
pub refurbished under new management,
traditional lunchtime food with more
ambitious evening dishes, Wye Valley and
a guest beer, various smallish rooms, some
interesting furnishings, fresh flowers and
daily newspapers, inglenook log fire; children
welcome and dogs (resident terriers), seats
in front and back gardens, open all day (but
no food Sun evening, Mon). *(Denys Gueroult)*

MICHAELCHURCH ESCLEY
SO3133
Bridge Inn (01981) 510646
Off back Road SE of Hay-on-Wye, along Escley Brook valley; HR2 0JW Remote black-beamed riverside inn delightfully tucked away in attractive valley, well kept Wye Valley beers and local farm cider, enjoyable food; seats out on waterside terrace, field for camping, good walks. *(Simon Daws)*

MUCH DEWCHURCH
SO4831
Black Swan (01981) 540295
B4348 Ross–Hay; HR2 8DJ Roomy and attractive beamed and timbered local, partly 14th-c, with log fires in cosy well worn bar and lounge with eating area, well kept Hook Norton ales, decent wines, inexpensive wholesome food, friendly atmosphere; pool room with darts, TV, juke box, no credit cards; dogs welcome. *(A Helme)*

MUCH MARCLE
SO6634
Royal Oak (01531) 660300
On A449 Ross-on-Wye–Ledbury; HR8 2ND Superb rural spot with magnificent views, pleasant lounge with open fire, enjoyable reasonably priced food using meat from local farms, efficient friendly service, well kept ales such as Jennings, Marstons and Wye Valley, large back dining area; garden, two bedrooms. *(Alan and Eve Harding, Dr A Y Drummond)*

MUCH MARCLE
SO6533
✶Slip Tavern (01531) 660246
Off A449 SW of Ledbury; HR8 2NG Country pub with splendidly colourful gardens overlooking cider orchards (Weston's Cider Centre close by), welcoming landlady from Trinidad and friendly informal service, good food (not Sun evening) from pub standards to caribbean dishes, reasonable prices, Butcombe and two guests, log fire, conservatory restaurant, folk night first Thurs of month; children welcome, dogs on leads, closed Mon. *(Andrew Gardner)*

NORTON CANON
SO3748
Three Horseshoes (01544) 318375
A480 Yazor–Eccles Green; HR4 7BH Basic two-bar rustic pub brewing its own good Shoes ales, including fearsomely strong Farriers, friendly long-serving landlord, woodburner and log fire, skittle alley with shooting gallery and pool; may be home-pickled eggs; children and dogs welcome, garden tables, lovely countryside near Davies Meadows wildflower reserve, closed lunchtimes except Weds and weekends. *(Reg Fowle, Helen Rickwood)*

ORLETON
SO4967
✶Boot (01568) 780228
Off B4362 W of Woofferton; SY8 4HN Popular pub with beams, timbering, even

some 16th-c wattle and daub, inglenook fireplace in charming cosy traditional bar, steps up to further bar area, good-sized two-room dining part, varied choice of interesting well presented food, friendly quick service, Hobsons, Wye Valley and a local guest (July beer festival), real ciders; children and dogs welcome, seats in garden under huge ash tree, fenced-in play area, open all day weekends. *(Michael and Jenny Back, A N Bance, Dr P Brown)*

PEMBRIDGE
SO3958
New Inn (01544) 388427
Market Square (A44); HR6 9DZ Timeless ancient inn overlooking small black and white town's church, unpretentious lived-in three-room bar with antique settles, beams, worn flagstones and impressive inglenook log fire, one room with sofas, pine furniture, books and family photographs, several well kept changing ales (usually a local one), farm cider, big helpings of enjoyable good value plain food (booking advised), friendly service, traditional games, quiet little family dining room; downstairs lavatories; simple bedrooms. *(Phil Bryant, Simon Velate, Steve Whalley)*

PRESTON
SO3841
Yew Tree (01981) 500359
Village W of Hereford; HR2 9JT Small tucked-away pub handy for River Wye, simple and welcoming, with two quickly changing real ales tapped from the cask, proper cider, no food; children welcome, closed lunchtime except Sun. *(MLR)*

ROSS-ON-WYE
SO6024
White Lion (01989) 562785
Wilton Lane; HR9 6AQ Friendly riverside pub dating from 1650, well kept Otter and Wye Valley, enjoyable traditional food plus specials at reasonable prices, good service, big fireplace in carpeted bar, stone-walled gaol restaurant (building once a police station), games room with pool and darts, Sun quiz; children welcome, lots of tables in garden and on covered terrace overlooking the Wye and historic bridge, bedrooms. *(Neil and Anita Christopher, Reg Fowle, Helen Rickwood)*

SHOBDON
SO4061
✶Bateman Arms (01568) 708374
B4362 NE of village; HR6 9LX Striking 18th-c inn with enjoyable good value food freshly made from local supplies, Sun roasts, well kept Wychwood and a guest ale, good wines by the glass, cheerful service, inglenook woodburner in smallish comfortable beamed bar with relaxed local feel, well decorated restaurant, games room with pool and darts; children welcome, resident dogs (ask before bringing yours), picnic-sets on small lawn behind, nine bedrooms, good walks, open all day. *(Phil Bryant)*

ST OWEN'S CROSS   SO5424
New Inn (01989) 730274
Junction A4137 and B4521, W of Ross-on-Wye; HR2 8LQ Half-timbered 16th-c dining pub with huge inglenook fireplaces, dark beams and timbers, various nooks and crannies, mix of furniture including old pews, Brakspears and Wychwood, several malt whiskies and wines by the glass, food all day in bar and restaurant; background music; children welcome, dogs in bar, spacious sheltered garden with play things, views to Black Mountains. *(Dave Braisted)*

STAPLOW   SO6941
Oak (01531) 640954
Bromyard Road (B4214); HR8 1NP Popular roadside village pub, friendly bustle in comfortable beamed bar, restaurant with open kitchen producing enjoyable good value food, ales such as Bathams, Marstons and Wye Valley, Weston's cider, reasonably priced wines, cheerful quick service; bedrooms. *(John Allman, John and Mary Ling, Mel Poole)*

STIFFORDS BRIDGE   SO7348
Red Lion (01886) 880318
A4103 3 miles W of Great Malvern; WR13 5NN Refurbished beamed roadside pub, wide choice of good value home-made food including popular Sun lunch, Greene King and some interesting guest ales, farm ciders; children and dogs welcome, tables in nicely kept garden. *(Tim and Joan Wright, Denis Kavanagh, Reg Fowle, Helen Rickwood)*

STOCKTON CROSS   SO5161
⋆Stockton Cross Inn (01568) 612509
Kimbolton; A4112, off A49 just N of Leominster; HR6 0HD Cosy half-timbered coaching inn with heavily beamed spotless interior, huge log fire, woodburner, handsome antique settle, old leather chairs and brocaded stools, cast-iron-framed tables, old-time prints, copper and brass, Wye Valley ales and a guest, Robinson's Flagon cider, reasonably priced food cooked by landlord; background music, open mike night (second Weds of month); children welcome, pretty garden, handy for Berrington Hall (NT), closed Sun evening, Mon (except bank hols). *(John Fredericks, Paul Humphreys, Ian and Rose Lock and others)*

SUTTON ST NICHOLAS   SO5345
Golden Cross (01432) 880274
On corner of Ridgeway Road; HR1 3AZ Thriving modernised pub with enjoyable food including meal deals, weekly changing ales from stone-fronted counter, good service, clean décor, some breweriana, relaxed upstairs restaurant, pool and darts, live music Fri, quiz Sun; dogs welcome, pretty village and good walks. *(Reg Fowle, Helen Rickwood)*

WELLINGTON   SO4948
⋆Wellington (01432) 830367
Village signed off A49 N of Hereford; HR4 8AT Welcoming red-brick Victorian pub under new management, comfortably civilised atmosphere, big high-backed settles, antique farm and garden tools, historical photographs of the village, woodburner in brick fireplace, Hobsons, Wye Valley and guests (summer beer festival), bar and restaurant food, charming candlelit stable dining room and conservatory, darts and cribbage; background music - maybe live Sun; children welcome, dogs in bar, nice back garden, closed Mon lunchtime. *(Anon)*

WEOBLEY   SO4051
Salutation (01544) 318443
Off A4112 SW of Leominster; HR4 8SJ Old beamed and timbered inn at top of delightful village green, reopened 2011 under new management, good food cooked by chef/landlord from bar snacks up including set lunch, well kept ales such as Otter, Thwaites and Wye Valley, pleasant service, two bars and restaurant; children welcome, sheltered back terrace, three bedrooms. *(R T and J C Moggridge, Reg Fowle, Helen Rickwood, R K Phillips)*

WHITNEY-ON-WYE   SO2447
⋆Rhydspence (01497) 831262
A438 Hereford–Brecon; HR3 6EU Splendid half-timbered inn (part dates from 1380) on the border with Wales, rambling rooms with heavy beams and timbers, attractive old-fashioned furnishings, log fire in fine big stone fireplace in central bar, a beer from Golden Valley, no food (except breakfast for residents); no dogs inside; children welcome, garden with Wye valley views, six bedrooms. *(the Didler, John Mikadoson)*

YARPOLE   SO4664
⋆Bell (01568) 780359
Just off B4361 N of Leominster; HR6 0BD Pleasant old black and white pub with basic tap room, comfortable beamed lounge with log fire, traditional furniture and some modern art, brass taps embedded in stone counter serving Hook Norton Old Hooky, Timothy Taylors Landlord and a guest, large high-raftered restaurant in former cider mill (the press and wheel remain), good well priced food from pub standards to more enterprising dishes, friendly atmosphere; background music; children welcome, dogs in bar, picnic-sets under green parasols in pretty gardens, handy for Croft Castle, closed Sun evening, Mon. *(Phil Bryant, Dr P Brown, Dr and Mrs James Harris, Philip Walker, Neil and Anita Christopher, R K Phillips)*

Hertfordshire

Pubs new to the *Guide* this year are the Valiant Trooper in Aldbury (friendly staff and six changing ales), Duke of York in Barnet (part of the thriving Brunning & Price stable), College Arms at Hertford Heath (light and airy with contemporary interior, run with care and attention to detail), Cricketers at Sarratt (another Brunning & Price pub, over 50 whiskies, five ales, and good food), and Bull in Watton-at-Stone (informal and friendly, lots of character, imaginative food). Other pubs to look out for include the Bricklayers Arms in Flaunden (restaurant-style food and 20 wines by the glass), Alford Arms in Frithsden (super food and around 24 wines by the glass), Red Lion in Preston (community-owned village pub with cheerful atmosphere), Cock in Sarratt (gently old-fashioned and good value OAP lunches) and Robin Hood in Tring (half a dozen Fullers ales and cheap meals). Our Hertfordshire Dining Pub 2013 is the Alford Arms in Frithsden.

ALDBURY   SP9612   Map 4
Valiant Trooper

Trooper Road (towards Aldbury Common); off B4506 N of Berkhamsted; HP23 5RW

Cheery, traditional all-rounder with appealing interior, six real ales, generous helpings of pubby food, and garden

Readers praise the friendly welcome and attentive, helpful staff at this pleasant old country pub. It's a relaxing place with an easy-going atmosphere throughout its series of unpretentiously appealing old rooms. The first is beamed and tiled in red and black, with built-in wall benches, a pew and small dining chairs around attractive country tables, and an inglenook fireplace. Further in, the middle bar has spindleback chairs around tables on a wooden floor, and some exposed brickwork. The far room has nice country kitchen chairs around a mix of tables, and a woodburning stove, and the back barn has been converted to house a restaurant; dominoes, cribbage and bridge on Monday evenings. They keep a decent range of half a dozen well kept changing beers on handpump from brewers such as Hook Norton, Red Squirrel and Tring, alongside local Millwhite's cider. The enclosed garden has a wooden adventure playground, and the pub is well placed for walks through the glorious beechwoods of the National Trust's Ashridge Estate.

Enjoyable quickly served food includes sandwiches, pâté, quiche, burgers, sausage and mash, fish and chips and smoked haddock fishcakes. *Benchmark main dish: burger £10.50. Two-course evening meal £15.80.*

Free house ~ Licensee Wendy Greenall ~ Real ale ~ Bar food (12-3, 6-9; 12-9 Sat; 12-4 Sun; not Mon evening) ~ Restaurant ~ (01442) 851203 ~ Children in restaurant ~ Dogs allowed in bar ~ Open 11-11; 12-10.30 Sun ~ www.valianttrooper.co.uk
Recommended by Ross Balaam

BARNET   TQ2599   Map 5

Duke of York ♀

Barnet Road (A1000); EN5 4SG

Big place with reasonably priced bistro-style food and nice garden

This Brunning & Price pub opened just as went to press but we had no qualms about including it as we know you can depend on this thriving group to get things just right. The garden is particularly nice, with plenty of tables on a tree-surrounded terrace and lawn, and a tractor in the good children's play area. Though big, the interior is nicely sectioned, giving some intimate areas, with big windows and plenty of mirrors keeping it all light and airy. An eclectic mix of furniture creates a relaxed atmopshere and nice touches such as table lamps, fire places, books, rugs and pot plants keep it all homely. There are stools at the impressive counter, where friendly staff serve Phoenix Brunning & Price Original (brewed for them by Phoenix) and Tring Side Pocket on handpump alongside three guests from brewers such as Adnams, Dark Star and Red Squirrel, 25 wines by the glass and about 80 whiskies; background music.

As well as lunchtime sandwiches, bar food includes minestrone soup with parmesan straws, smoked salmon and bloody mary jelly with ciabatta crostini, duck liver parfait with plum chutney, fried scallops with crispy pork belly, pickled fennel and apple salad and rhubarb dressing, shredded duck salad, fish pie, baked hake fillet with coconut and lemongrass, egg noodles and thai mussel sauce, steak and kidney pudding, braised rabbit broth, battered haddock, and puddings such as raspberry bakewell tart and meringue with lemon curd cream. *Benchmark main dish: braised shoulder of lamb £16.95. Two-course evening meal £19.00.*

Brunning & Price ~ Manager Kit Lett ~ Real ale ~ Bar food (12-10(9.30 Sun)) ~ (020) 8449 0297 ~ Children welcome ~ Dogs allowed in bar ~ Open 11.30-11; 12-10.30 Sun ~ www.brunningandprice.co.uk/dukeofyork *Recommended by Richard Gibbs*

BATFORD   TL1415   Map 5

Gibraltar Castle

Lower Luton Road; B653, S of B652 junction; AL5 5AH

Pleasantly traditional pub with interesting militaria displays, some emphasis on food (booking advised); pretty terrace

Seats on the front terrace of this neatly kept pub look over a nature reserve and there are more tables on a large pretty decked back area with lots of flowers and in a tree-lined garden to one side. Inside, the traditional long carpeted bar is decked out with an impressive collection of military memorabilia – everything from rifles to swords, medals, uniforms and bullets (with plenty of captions to read) and pictures depicting various moments in Gibraltar's history. In one area the low beams give way to soaring rafters and there are comfortably cushioned wall benches and a couple of snugly intimate window alcoves, one with a fine old clock, several board games are piled on top of the piano, and a pleasant old fireplace. Fullers London Pride, ESB and a guest beer on handpump; background music.

🍽 Bar food includes a good range of lunchtime sandwiches, moules marinière, game terrine with onion confit and fig and pear coulis, beef or mushroom stroganoff, beer-battered fish and chips with minted peas and chunky chips, chicken pie, guinea fowl with chorizo and butternut squash risotto, slow-braised lamb shank, and puddings such as mango and blueberry cheesecake and sticky toffee pudding. *Benchmark main dish: chicken pie £9.85. Two-course evening meal £16.95.*

Fullers ~ Tenant Hamish Miller ~ Real ale ~ Bar food (12-2.30, 6-9; 12-9(8 Sun) Sat) ~ Restaurant ~ (01582) 460005 ~ Children welcome ~ Dogs allowed in bar ~ Open 11.30-11(12 Fri, Sat); 12-10.30 Sun ~ www.gibraltarcastle.co.uk *Recommended by Mr R A Buckler*

EPPING GREEN   TL2906   Map 5
Beehive
Off B158 SW of Hertford, via Little Berkhamsted; back road towards Newgate Street and Cheshunt; SG13 8NB

Cheerful bustling country pub, popular for its good value food

The traditional and slightly old-fashioned bar at this weatherboarded pub has low ceilings, wheelback chairs and brocaded benches around tables on a patterned carpet. During the winter months, a woodburning stove in a panelled corner keeps it cosy and warm. Greene King IPA and Old Speckled Hen and a monthly changing guest such as Adnams are on handpump alongside a good range of wines by the glass; service is prompt and pleasant; background music. Between the low building and quiet country road is a neat lawn and a decked area with plenty of tables to take in the summer sunshine; good woodland walks nearby.

🍽 Fresh fish is delivered daily from Billingsgate, and main courses might include baked cod with bacon, mushroom and thyme sauce, baked skate with caper butter, scampi, steak, mushroom and ale pudding, and snacks such as sandwiches, ploughman's, crab and mango salad, tuna and mozzarella fishcake, roast red pepper and courgette lasagne, and puddings such as jam sponge, apple pie and spotted dick. *Benchmark main dish: battered cod and chips £10.95. Two-course evening meal £17.90.*

Free house ~ Licensee Martin Squirrell ~ Real ale ~ Bar food (12-2.30(4 Sun), 6-9.30(8.30 Sun)) ~ Restaurant ~ (01707) 875959 ~ Children welcome ~ Open 11.30-3, 5.30-11; 12-10.30 Sun *Recommended by Grahame and Myra Williams*

FLAUNDEN   TL0101   Map 5
Bricklayers Arms 🍽 ♀
4 miles from M25 junction 18; village signposted off A41 – from village centre follow Boxmoor, Bovingdon road and turn right at Belsize, Watford signpost into Hogpits Bottom; HP3 0PH

Cosy country restaurant with relatively elaborate food; very good wine list

Carefully prepared food is served in a calmly civilised atmosphere and not overblown surroundings at this neatly kept virginia creeper-covered dining pub. Meals tend to be a considered affair (with prices to match) so it's not really the place for a quick bargain lunch. Stubs of knocked-through oak-timbered wall indicate the layout of the original rooms in its fairly open-plan interior. The well refurbished low-beamed bar is snug and comfortable, with a roaring log fire in winter. The extensive wine list includes about 20 by the glass, and they have Rebellion IPA, Fullers London Pride, a beer from Tring and a guest or two such as Sharps Doom Bar on handpump. This is a lovely peaceful spot in summer, when the terrace and beautifully kept old-fashioned garden with its foxgloves against sheltering hedges comes into its own. Just up the Belsize road there's a path on the left which goes through delightful woods to a forested area around Hollow Hedge.

They smoke their own meat and fish, and attractively presented dishes might include battered scallops with pea purée and spicy tomato, olive and crayfish salad, selection of home smoked fish with lemon coriander butter and tomato chutney, mushrooms in calvados cream with julienne vegetables and puff pastry top, ox cheek cooked in ale with honey drizzle and spring onion mash, braised lamb shank, chickens stuffed with provençale vegetables with herb cream and lardons, and puddings such as chocolate fondant with pistachio ice-cream and orange and mandarin baked cheesecake with lemon sorbet. *Benchmark main dish: pork fillet with apple and black pudding crumble with sage and cider jus £17.45. Two-course evening meal £30.00.*

Free house ~ Licensee Alvin Michaels ~ Real ale ~ Bar food (12-2.30(3.30 Sun); 6.30-9.30(8.30 Sun)) ~ Restaurant ~ (01442) 833322 ~ Children welcome ~ Dogs allowed in bar ~ Open 12-11.30(12.30 Sat, 10.30 Sun) ~ www.bricklayersarms.com *Recommended by Peter and Giff Bennett, N J Roberts, Brian Glozier, Mrs Margo Finlay, Jörg Kasprowski*

FRITHSDEN
TL0109   Map 5

Alford Arms 🍴 ♀

A4146 from Hemel Hempstead to Water End, then second left (after Red Lion) signed Frithsden, then left at T junction, then right after 0.25 miles; HP1 3DD

Hertfordshire Dining Pub of the Year

Thriving dining pub with a chic interior, good food from an imaginative menu and a thoughtful wine list

This pretty Victorian pub stands by a village green and is surrounded by lovely National Trust woodland. It's usually full to the brim with cheerful diners – though you might still find a few locals chatting at the bar. The fashionably elegant but understated interior has simple prints on pale cream walls, with blocks picked out in rich Victorian green or dark red, and an appealing mix of good antique furniture (from Georgian chairs to old commode stands) on bare boards and patterned quarry tiles. It's all pulled together by luxuriously opulent curtains; darts and piped jazz. All the wines on their list are european, with most of them available by the glass, and they have Sharps Doom Bar, Rebellion Smuggler and a guest brewer such as Tring on handpump. There are plenty of tables outside.

The seasonally changing menu might include pigeon breast with cauliflower rösti and beetroot with juniper purée, warm ricotta and swiss chard tart with gremolata salad, crab croquettes with chorizo cream, parmesan-crusted lamb shoulder with sautéed liver, soft polenta and roast tomato jus, roast hake with clam, mussel and ham hock chowder and smoked chilli onion rings, creamy leeks and mushrooms with with gruyère scone, and puddings such as hazelnut and caramel mousse, steamed chocolate sponge pudding with treacle ice-cream and apple and clove tarte tatin with apple sorbet. *Benchmark main dish: chicken fricassée with sage dumplings £14.25. Two-course evening meal £24.60.*

Salisbury Pubs ~ Lease Darren Johnston ~ Real ale ~ Bar food (12-2.30(3 Sat, 4 Sun),
6.30(7 Sun)-9.30(10 Fri, Sat)) ~ Restaurant ~ (01442) 864480 ~ Children welcome ~
Dogs allowed in bar ~ Open 11-11; 12-10.30 Sun ~ www.alfordarmsfrithsden.co.uk
Recommended by John and Joyce Snell, Peter and Giff Bennett, Mrs Margo Finlay, Jörg Kasprowski

HERTFORD HEATH
TL3510 Map 5
College Arms ♀
London Road; B1197; SG13 7PW

**Light and airy rooms with contemporary furnishings, friendly service,
good, interesting food and real ales; seats outside**

Very popular locally but with a warm welcome for visitors too, this
nicely refurbished pub is on the edge of a village and backed by
woodland – handy for walks. Clearly run with care and attention to
detail, it's light and airy throughout with comfortable contemporary
furnishings. The bar has some high chairs around equally high tables,
long cushioned wall seating and pale leather dining chairs around tables
on rugs or wooden floorboards, and a modern bar counter where they
serve Sharps Doom Bar and Woodfordes Wherry on handpump and 16
wines by the glass; background jazz. There's an area with long button-
back wall seating, an open fireplace piled up with logs and a doorway
that leads to a charming little room with brown leather armchairs and
a couple of cushioned pews, a small woodburning stove in an old brick
fireplace, another rug on more wooden boards and hunting-themed
wallpaper. The elegant partly carpeted dining room has a real mix of
antique dining chairs and tables and a couple of large house plants. There
are seats and tables and a long wooden bench among flowering pots on
the back terrace, and a children's play house.

As well as stone-baked pizzas and lunchtime sandwiches, the enjoyable food,
using local game and other local seasonal produce, might include devilled
chicken livers with black pudding and rhubarb compote, cauliflower and nutmeg
soup with cumin dumplings, mushroom tagliatelle, confit duck leg with cointreau
jus, goats cheese and red onion tart, braised shin of beef with pickled walnuts,
crispy pork belly with black pudding purée and red wine jus, thai salmon fishcakes
with tomato chilli jam, and puddings such as treacle tart with poached pear and
hazelnut ice-cream, raspberry crème brûlée with white chocolate ice-cream and
cherry bakewell tart. *Benchmark main dish: beer-battered fish and chips £10.95.
Two-course evening meal £21.50.*

Punch ~ Lease Tim Lightfoot ~ Real ale ~ Bar food (12-3(5 Sat, 7 Sun), 6-10; not Sun
evening) ~ Restaurant ~ (01992) 558856 ~ Children welcome ~ Dogs allowed in bar
~ Open 12-11(10.30 Sun) ~ www.thecollegearmshertfordheath.com *Recommended by
Christopher Middleton, Tim Lightfoot*

POTTERS CROUCH
TL1105 Map 5
Holly Bush ◀ £
*2.25 miles from M25 junction 21A: A405 towards St Albans, then first left,
then after a mile turn left (ie away from Chiswell Green), then at T junction turn
right into Blunts Lane; can also be reached fairly quickly, with a good map, from M1
exits 6 and 8 (and even M10); AL2 3NN*

**Well tended cottage with gleaming furniture, fresh flowers and china,
well kept Fullers beers, good value food and an attractive garden**

With no children allowed, this immaculately kept pub, with its
highly polished dark wood furnishings, has a particularly grown-up

atmosphere. There are quite a few antique dressers (several filled with plates), a number of comfortably cushioned settles, a fox mask, some antlers, a fine old clock with a lovely chime, daily papers, and, on the right as you go in, a big fireplace. In the evening, neatly placed candles cast glimmering light over darkly varnished tables, all sporting fresh flowers. The long, stepped bar has particularly well kept Fullers Chiswick, ESB, London Pride and a Fullers seasonal beer on handpump. Service is calm, friendly and sincere, even when they're busy. Behind the pub, the very pleasant fenced-off garden has a nice lawn, handsome trees and sturdy picnic-sets. Though the pub seems to stand alone on a quiet little road, it's only a few minutes' drive from the centre of St Albans (or a pleasant 45-minute walk).

As well as a good choice of sandwiches and burgers, the very fairly priced menu might include smoked mackerel fillet with horseradish sauce, cornish pasty with red onion confit, ploughman's, burgers, beef bourguignon, cod and pancetta fishcakes, lamb kofta and fish pie. *Benchmark main dish: chilli £7.70. Two-course evening meal £17.80.*

Fullers ~ Tenants Steven and Vanessa Williams ~ Real ale ~ Bar food (12-2(2.30 Sun), 6-9; not Sun-Tues evenings) ~ (01727) 851792 ~ Open 12-2.30, 6-11(7-10 Sun) ~ www.thehollybushpub.co.uk *Recommended by Tina and David Woods-Taylor, Chris and Jeanne Downing, Jo Wilson, Peter and Giff Bennett, David Uren*

PRESTON
Red Lion 🍺

TL1824 Map 5

Village signposted off B656 S of Hitchin; The Green; SG4 7UD

Homely village local with changing beers and neat colourful garden

This welcoming place (one of the first community-owned pubs in the country) is pubbily simple but cheery. The grey wainscoted main room on the left has sturdy well varnished pub furnishings including padded country-kitchen chairs and cast-iron framed tables on a patterned carpet, a generous window seat, a log fire in a brick fireplace and foxhunting prints. The somewhat smaller room on the right has steeplechasing prints, some varnished plank panelling and brocaded bar stools on flagstones around the servery; darts and dominoes. As well as Fullers London Pride and Wells & Youngs, three regularly changing interesting guests might be from brewers such as Brewsters, Marston Moor and Red Squirrel. They also tap farm cider from the cask, have several wines by the glass (including an english house wine), a perry and mulled wine in winter. A few picnic-sets out on the front grass face across to lime trees on a peaceful village green. At the back, a pergola-covered terrace gives way to many more picnic-sets (with some shade from a tall ash tree) and, beyond, a good-sized sheltered garden with a colourful herbaceous border.

Reasonably priced bar food might include sandwiches and ploughman's, stilton stuffed mushrooms, fish pie, chilli, chicken curry, ham, egg and chips, grilled plaice with caper butter, roast pumpkin and goats cheese tart and steaks, and puddings such as eton mess and bakewell tart. *Benchmark main dish: fish pie £9.95. Two-course evening meal £13.00.*

Free house ~ Licensee Raymond Lamb ~ Real ale ~ Bar food (12-2, 7-8.30; not Sun evening or Tues) ~ (01462) 459585 ~ Children welcome ~ Dogs welcome ~ Open 12-2.30(3.30 Sat), 5.30-11(12 Sat); 12-3.30, 7-10.30 Sun ~ www.theredlionpreston.co.uk *Recommended by Stuart Gideon, Mrs Catherine Simmonds, Simon and Mandy King, Peter and Jean Hoare, M J Daly, Andrew Jeeves, Carole Smart, George Atkinson*

REDBOURN

TL1011   Map 5

Cricketers

3.2 miles from M1 junction 9; A5183 towards St Albans, bear right on to B487, first right into Chequer Lane, then third right into East Common; AL3 7ND

Good food and beer in a nicely placed attractively updated pub

This nicely refurbished place is appropriately situated opposite the cricket ground. The front bar, which was knocked into quite an unusual shape during restyling of the building, is snugly civilised with leather tub armchairs, plush banquettes and some leather cube stools on its pale carpet. It leads back into an attractive and comfortably modern dining room, also gaining from the unusual shape of the building. Friendly efficient staff serve four thoughtfully sourced guests, alongside Greene King IPA, which might come from brewers such as Aylesbury, Church End, Tring and Sharps. They also serve local Millwhite's Rum Cask cider and about two dozen wines by the glass along with decent coffees; well reproduced background music. There are picnic-sets out on the side grass and sheltered benches by the front door, and a map board by the next-door local museum describes some interesting nearby walks.

As well as lunchtime sandwiches and ploughman's, bar food includes duck and sage terrine with apricot and ginger chutney, salmon gravadlax, devilled chicken livers and mushrooms on toast, sausage and mash, red onion tart, fish and chips, pork tenderloin with sweet potato mash and cider jus, steak burger, steak and mushroom pie, sage and garlic roast rabbit loin on broad bean and pine nut risotto, baked sole with salsa verde, and puddings such as raspberry crème brûlée, glazed lemon tart and crumble-topped stuffed apple. *Benchmark main dish: fish and chips £10.75. Two-course evening meal £20.40.*

Free house ~ Licensees Colin Baxter and Andy Stuart ~ Real ale ~ Bar food (12-3, 6-9 (10 Fri, Sat); 12-5 Sun; not Sun evening) ~ Restaurant ~ (01582) 620612 ~ Children welcome ~ Dogs allowed in bar ~ Open 12-11(midnight Sat, 10.30 Sun) ~ www.thecricketersofredbourn.com *Recommended by Anthony and Marie Lewis, Ross Balaam*

SARRATT

TQ0499   Map 5

Cock

Church End: a very pretty approach is via North Hill, a lane N off A404, just under a mile W of A405; WD3 6HH

Plush pub popular with older dining set at lunchtime and families outside during summer weekends; Badger beers

At lunchtime you're likely to find an older set making the most of the good value OAP meals on offer at this comfortably traditional place. The latched front door opens straight into the homely tiled snug with a cluster of bar stools, vaulted ceiling and original bread oven. Through an archway, the partly oak-panelled cream-walled lounge has a lovely log fire in an inglenook, pretty Liberty-style curtains, red plush chairs at dark oak tables, lots of interesting artefacts, and several namesake pictures of cockerels. Badger Best, Sussex, Tanglefoot and a seasonal Badger guest are on handpump; background music. The restaurant is in a nicely converted barn. In summer, children can play in the bouncy castle and play area, leaving parents to take in the open country views from picnic-sets on the pretty, sheltered lawn and terrace. There are more picnic-sets in front that look out across a quiet lane towards the churchyard.

🍴 Pubby food includes sandwiches, crab cakes, prawn cocktail, ploughman's, battered haddock, curry of the day, scampi, cajun chicken salad, steak and ale pie, creamed leek, mushrooms and tarragon in a filo basket, and sirloin steak. *Benchmark main dish: steak and ale pie £10.95. Two-course evening meal £18.60.*

Badger ~ Tenants Brian and Marion Eccles ~ Real ale ~ Bar food (12-2.30, 6-9; 12-6 Sun) ~ Restaurant ~ (01923) 282908 ~ Children welcome ~ Dogs allowed in bar ~ Open 12-11(11.30 Sat, 9 Sun) ~ www.cockinn.net *Recommended by Peter and Giff Bennett, N J Roberts, David Jackson, Roy Hoing*

SARRATT   TQ0499 Map 5

Cricketers 🍷 🍺

The Green; WD3 6AS

Charming pub by village green with rambling, interconnected rooms, lots to look at, six real ales, good wines, helpful staff and enjoyable food; seats outside

Made up of three charming old cottages by the village green and duckpond, this is another fine pub from the Brunning & Price stable. The interlinked rooms have been refurbished with much character and it's certainly worth wandering around before you decide where you want to sit – you can choose from little snugs and alcoves that are perfect for a quiet drink or several dining areas, connected or more private. Throughout, there's plenty of cricketing memorabilia, fresh flowers, large plants and church candles, all manner of antique dining chairs and tables on rugs or stripped floorboards, comfortable armchairs or tub seats, cushioned pews and wall seats and two open fires in raised fireplaces. Phoenix Brunning & Price is on handpump alongside five guests from brewers such as Batemans, Fullers, Mauldens and Tring, good wines by the glass and 50 whiskies; background music and board games. Several sets of french windows open on to the terrace where there are tables and chairs, with picnic-sets on grass next to a colourfully painted tractor.

🍴 Good enjoyable food includes sandwiches, soup, lime and chilli cured salmon, cauliflower, chick pea and almond tagine with apricot and date couscous, cumberland sausages with rich red onion gravy, oriental crispy beef salad with pickled vegetables and cashew nuts, chicken, ham hock and leek pie, braised lamb shoulder with rosemary and redcurrant gravy, and puddings such as apple and rhubarb crumble and white and dark chocolate terrine with pink grapefruit sorbet; they also offer a two- and three-course set menu. *Benchmark main dish: pork tenderloin with caramelised sweet potato and pear with cider jus £11.95. Two-course evening meal £22.00.*

Brunning & Price ~ Licensee David Stowell ~ Real ale ~ Bar food (12-3, 5.30-10; 12-4, 5-9.30 Sun) ~ Restaurant ~ (01923) 270877 ~ Children welcome ~ Dogs allowed in bar ~ Open 12-11(10.30 Sun) ~ www.cricketers-sarratt.co.uk *Recommended by Peter and Giff Bennett, Martin and Karen Wake, John and Joyce Snell*

'Children welcome' means the pub says it lets children inside without any special restriction. If it allows them in, but to restricted areas such as an eating area or family room, we specify this. Places with separate restaurants often let children use them, hotels usually let them into public areas such as lounges. Some pubs impose an evening time limit – let us know if you find one earlier than 9pm.

TRING   SP9211   Map 5

Robin Hood £

Brook Street (B486); HP23 5ED

Really welcoming pub with good beer and popular pubby food

The pubby menu at this pleasingly traditional place is particularly good value – it's the sort of place where diners who are in for a good value meal happily coexist with regulars on stools along the counter enjoying the half a dozen Fullers ales. It's a carefully run place with a homely atmosphere and genial service in its several immaculately kept smallish linked areas. The main bar has banquettes and standard pub chairs on spotless bare boards or carpets. Towards the back, you'll find a conservatory with a vaulted ceiling and woodburner. The licensees' two yorkshire terriers are called Buddy and Sugar; background music. There are tables out on the small pleasant back terrace.

Enjoyable food includes sandwiches, filled baguettes, battered cod, chilli, shepherd's pie, curry of the day, lamb shank in red wine and rosemary sauce, fishcakes, spicy cajun burger, vegetable curry, steak and kidney pudding, and puddings such as warm chocolate fudge cake and chocolate pot. *Benchmark main dish: scampi £9.50. Two-course evening meal £15.60.*

Fullers ~ Tenants Terry Johnson and Stewart Canham ~ Real ale ~ Bar food (12-2. 15, 7-9; 12-9.15 Sat; not Sun evening) ~ (01442) 824912 ~ Children welcome ~ Dogs welcome ~ Open 11.30-3, 5.30-11(11.30-11 Fri); 12-11.30 Sat; 12-11 Sun ~ www.therobinhoodtring.co.uk *Recommended by D and M T Ayres-Regan, John Branston, Taff Thomas*

WATTON-AT-STONE   TL3019   Map 5

Bull

High Street; SG14 3SB

Bustling old pub, open all day, with much character in several rooms, candlelight and fresh flowers, real ales served by friendly staff and enjoyable food; seats outside

As it's open all day and in a pretty village, this well run old pub has a good mix of customers dropping in and out; on our visit there were a couple of cyclists in one corner and a group of chatty ladies enjoying morning coffee and pastries on the leather button-back chesterfield and armchairs by the inglenook log fire. This main bar has fresh flowers and a relaxed, friendly atmosphere, with interesting landscape-patterned wallpaper on one wall with a button-back leather banquette beside it and solid dark wooden dining chairs and plush-topped stools around a mix of tables on bare boards. Sharps Doom Bar and Woodfordes Wherry on handpump, good wines by the glass and helpful service. By the entrance door there are some high bar chairs along counters by the windows; from here, it's a step up to a charming little room with just four tables, brown-cushioned wooden dining chairs and a wall banquette, decorative logs in the fireplace, books on shelves, board games and an old typewriter. At the other end of the building is an elegantly furnished, part-carpeted and part-slate-floored dining room. Paintwork throughout is contemporary. The covered terrace has some church chairs and tables, there are picnic-sets on grass, and a small, equipped children's play area.

Using seasonal produce, the food includes a duo of salmon (smoked salmon tartare, hot smoked salmon rillette, wasabi crème fraîche and caviar), salad lyonnaise (smoked pancetta, garlic croûtons, a soft poached egg and frisée salad), a pie of the week, vegetable risotto with beetroot crisps and parmesan, beer-battered fish and chips, stuffed breast of lamb with herby couscous, harissa jus and minted yoghurt, cod with chunky caponata and black olive tapenade, and puddings such as Kahlua crème brûlée with chocolate macaroons and caramelised lemon tart with pistachio praline, chantilly cream and raspberry sorbet. *Benchmark main dish: grilled gammon and duck egg with caper dressing £9.95. Two-course evening meal £20.00*

Licensee Alastair and Anna Bramley ~ Real ale ~ Bar food (12-3(5 Sat, 4 Sun), 6-10) ~ Restaurant ~ (01920) 831032 ~ Children welcome ~ Open 9.30am-11pm; 12-6 Sun; closed Sun evening, Mon ~ www.thebullwatton.co.uk *Recommended by Jason Campbell, Adam Jones, Alastair Bramley*

Also Worth a Visit in Hertfordshire

Besides the fully inspected pubs, you might like to try these pubs that have been recommended to us and described by readers. Do tell us what you think of them: feedback@goodguides.com

ALDBURY SP9612

⋆ **Greyhound** (01442) 851228
Stocks Road; village signed from A4251 Tring–Berkhamsted, and from B4506; HP23 5RT Picturesque village pub with some signs of real age inside, copper-hooded inglenook in cosy traditional beamed bar, more contemporary area with leather chairs, airy oak-floored back restaurant with wicker chairs at big new tables, Badger ales, traditional food (all day weekends) from sandwiches up; children welcome, dogs in bar, front benches facing green with whipping post, stocks and duck pond, suntrap gravel courtyard, eight bedrooms (some in newer building behind), open all day. *(Taff Thomas, John Branston)*

ALDENHAM TQ1498
Round Bush (01923) 855532
Roundbush Lane; WD25 8BG Cheery 19th-c village pub with plenty of atmosphere, two front rooms and back restaurant, popular generously served food, five well kept ales including St Austell Tribute, friendly efficient staff; big garden. *(David M Smith, Ross Balaam)*

ASHWELL TL2639
Rose & Crown (01462) 742420
High Street; SG7 5NP Friendly traditional local, Greene King ales and a seasonal guest, enjoyable food (not Sun evening) from changing menu, L-shaped bar with 16th-c beams and lovely log fire, candlelit restaurant; children welcome, big garden with play area and pétanque, open all day weekends. *(Simon Watkins)*

ASHWELL TL2739
Three Tuns (01462) 742107
Off A505 NE of Baldock; High Street; SG7 5NL Comfortable gently old-fashioned red brick hotel in charming village; cosy opulently Victorian lounge with panelling and dark green walls, lots of pictures, stuffed animals and antiques, relaxing chairs and big tables, classical music, more modern public bar with leather sofas on reclaimed oak flooring, good choice of wines, Greene King IPA, St Edmunds and three or four guests, sensibly priced bar food (all day weekends); cribbage, dominoes, games machine and TV; children and dogs welcome, terrace and substantial garden with boules under apple trees, bedrooms. *(Mike and Lynn Robinson, John Wooll, Simon Watkins, Dennis Jones)*

AYOT GREEN TL2213
Waggoners (01707) 324241
Off B197 S of Welwyn; AL6 9AA Former 17th-c coaching inn under french owners, snacks and pubby food in cosy low-beamed bar, more upmarket french cooking in comfortable good-sized restaurant extension, friendly attentive staff, good wine list, real ales; attractive and spacious suntrap back garden with sheltered terrace – some A1(M) noise, wooded walks nearby. *(Hans Liesner, Huw Thomas)*

AYOT ST LAWRENCE TL1916
Brocket Arms (01438) 820250
Off B651 N of St Albans; AL6 9BT Attractive low-beamed 14th-c inn under new management, enjoyable interesting food (not

Post Office address codings confusingly give the impression that some pubs are in Hertfordshire, when they're really in Bedfordshire, Buckinghamshire or Cambridgeshire (which is where we list them).

Sun evening) in bar or restaurant, six real
ales including Black Sheep, Greene King and
one badged for the pub from Nethergate,
wide choice of wines by the glass, inglenook
log fires; children welcome, dogs in bar, nice
sun-trap walled garden with play area, handy
for George Bernard Shaw's house (NT), six
refurbished bedrooms, open all day. *(Anthony
and Marie Lewis)*

BARKWAY   TL3834

✶ **Tally Ho** (01763) 848389

London Road (B1368); SG8 8EX
Quirky little local with inviting old sofa,
armchairs, horsebrasses and log fire in
relaxed cottagey bar, extraordinary range of
drinks including 60 malt whiskies and over
200 other spirits, Buntingford, Rebellion
and a guest ale (apparently tapped from
big casks behind bar, but actually gently
pumped), Aspall's cider, fresh flowers and
silver candelabra, old-fashioned prints on
brown ply panelling, another log fire in old-
world dining area serving fairly traditional
food; children welcome, dogs in bar, well
spaced picnic-sets, weeping willow in
garden behind car park, open all day, but
closed Sun evening. *(Simon Watkins,
Jeremy Donaldson)*

BELSIZE   TL0300

Plough (01923) 262261

Dunny Lane; WD3 4NP Small friendly
local, central bar and barn-like beamed
lounge with open fire, Tring beers, enjoyable
good value home-made food; picnic-sets in
nice garden, good walks. *(Roy Hoing)*

BERKHAMSTED   SP9907

Old Mill (01442) 879590

A4251, Hemel end; HP4 2NB Sizeable
Peach dining pub with attractive rambling
layout, extensive choice of enjoyable food all
day, well kept Greene King ales and a guest
like Tring, friendly efficient staff, two good
fires; children welcome, tables outside by
mill race, some overlooking unspectacular
stretch of Grand Union Canal. *(John
Branston, Dennis Jones)*

BERKHAMSTED   SP9907

Rising Sun (01442) 864913

George Street; HP4 2EG Victorian
canalside pub with five well kept ales
including one brewed for them by Tring,
good range of ciders (three beer/cider
festivals a year), interesting range of spirits,
two very small traditional rooms with a
few basic chairs and tables, coal fire, snuff
and cigars for sale, no food apart from
ploughman's, friendly service; background
music; children and dogs welcome, chairs
out by canal and well worn seating in
covered side beer garden, colourful hanging
baskets, open all day in summer, closed
lunchtimes Mon-Thurs in winter.
(Rick Nunn, Graeme Urwin)

BISHOP'S STORTFORD   TL5021

Nags Head (01279) 654553

Dunmow Road; CM23 5HP Well restored
1930s art deco pub (Grade II listed),
McMullens ales from island servery and
plenty of wines by the glass, wide choice of
popular pubby food, good service; children
welcome, open all day. *(Charles Gysin)*

BOURNE END   TL0206

✶ **Three Horseshoes** (01442) 862585

*Winkwell; just off A4251 Hemel–
Berkhamsted; HP1 2RZ* Renovated 16th-c
pub in charming setting by unusual swing
bridge over Grand Union Canal, low-beamed
three-room core with inglenooks, traditional
furniture including settles, a few sofas, three
well kept changing ales, straightforward
reasonably priced food all day (they may ask
to keep a credit card while you eat), efficient
uniformed staff, bay-windowed extension
overlooking canal; comedy and quiz nights;
children welcome, picnic-sets out by
water. *(Clive and Fran Dutson, Gill and Keith
Croxton, Peter Martin, Dennis Jones)*

BRAUGHING   TL3925

Axe & Compass (01920) 821610

Just off B1368; The Street; SG11 2QR
Pleasant country pub in pretty village
with ford, enjoyable home-prepared food
from traditional to more creative dishes,
own-baked bread, well kept ales and several
wines by the glass, friendly uniformed
staff, mix of furnishings on wood floors in
two roomy bars, log fires, restaurant; well
behaved children and dogs welcome, garden
overlooking playing field, outside bar.
*(Simon Watkins, Kevin McPheat, Mrs Margo
Finlay, Jörg Kasprowski)*

BRAUGHING   TL3925

Golden Fleece (01920) 823555

Green End (B1368); SG11 2PE
Refurbished 17th-c dining pub with good
freshly made food (all day Sun till 6pm)
including some imaginative choices, special
diets catered for, Adnams and guests, plenty
of wines by the glass including champagne,
cheerful service, bare-boards bar and two
dining rooms, beams and timbers, open
fire; back garden with metal furniture on
paved terrace, round picnic-sets out at
front. *(Charles Gysin, Jeremy Donaldson)*

CHANDLERS CROSS   TQ0698

✶ **Clarendon** (01923) 270009

*M25 junction 20; A41 towards Watford,
right at first traffic lights signed Sarratt,
then into Redhall Lane; WD3 4LU*
Stylish modern bar with tall swivelling
chrome and leather chairs at long high
dark wood counter, colourful contemporary
artwork, side area with log fire and leather
chesterfields, dining part with open kitchen,
grand upstairs restaurant, cheerful well
drilled young staff, Tring ales, good choice

of wines by the glass, elaborate pricy food but cheaper lunctime set menu (not Sun); background music; children welcome, square-cut metal benches and tables on neatly landscaped terrace, open fire in substantial brick-built smokers' shelter, open all day. *(Peter and Giff Bennett)*

CHAPMORE END TL3216

⋆**Woodman** (01920) 463143

Off B158 Wadesmill–Bengeo; pub signed 300 metres W of A602 roundabout; OS Sheet 166, map reference 328164; SG12 0HF Peaceful early Victorian country local, plain seats around stripped pub tables, floor tiles or broad bare boards, working period fireplaces, well kept Greene King beers poured from the cask, minimal lunchtime food (also a winter Sun roast and summer barbecues), friendly staff, backgammon, shove ha'penny and cribbage; dogs welcome, children till 8pm, picnic-sets out in front under a couple of walnut trees, bigger back garden with fenced play area and boules, open all day Sat, closed Mon lunchtime. *(Thomas Lane)*

CHORLEYWOOD TQ0395

⋆**Black Horse** (01923) 282252

Dog Kennel Lane, the Common; WD3 5EG Welcoming old country pub popular for its good value generous food (smaller helpings available) from good sandwiches up, OAP lunch some days, well kept ales including Wadworths and Wells & Youngs, decent wines, tea and coffee, good cheery service even when busy, low dark beams and two log fires in thoroughly traditional rambling bar, daily newspapers; big-screen TV; children, walkers and dogs welcome, picnic-sets overlooking common, open all day. *(Peter and Giff Bennett, Peter Collins, Roy Hoing)*

CHORLEYWOOD TQ0294

⋆**Land of Liberty Peace & Plenty** (01923) 282226 *Long Lane, Heronsgate, just off M25 junction 17; WD3 5BS* Well kept local Red Squirrel, Tring and interesting guest beers, Millwhite's and Weston's ciders and perry, bottled belgians, decent coffee, enjoyable lunches with some imaginative dishes, all-day snacks, good friendly service, simple traditional layout, darts, skittles and board games; TV, no children inside; dogs welcome, covered decking, more picnic-sets in garden, open all day. *(LM)*

FLAUNDEN TL0100

Green Dragon (01442) 832269

Flaunden Hill; HP3 0PP Comfortable 17th-c beamed pub with partly panelled extended lounge, back restaurant and traditional little tap bar, good value thai food as well as pubby choices, Fullers, St Austell and Wells & Youngs; background music; children and dogs welcome, well kept

garden with smokers' shelter, pretty village, only a short diversion from Chess Valley Walk. *(Charles Harvey)*

FURNEUX PELHAM TL4327

Brewery Tap (01279) 777280

Bealey Croft End; SG9 0LL Generous and enjoyable home-made food, well kept Greene King IPA and Abbot, cheerful staff, pleasant dining room; background music, pool; children welcome, back garden room and terrace overlooking neat attractive garden. *(Simon Watkins)*

GREAT AMWELL TL3712

George IV (01920) 870039

St Johns Lane; SG12 9SW Pleasant 19th-c pub in pretty spot by church, good well presented fresh food (not Sun or Mon evenings) in coal-fire bar or back restaurant, Adnams Bitter, friendly attentive staff, flowers on tables and candles throughout; beer garden, popular with walkers, River Lea nearby. *(Mrs Margo Finlay, Jörg Kasprowski)*

GREAT HORMEAD TL4030

Three Tuns (01763) 289409

B1038/Horseshoe Hill; SG9 0NT Welcoming old thatched and timbered country pub in lovely surroundings, enjoyable home-made food including local sausages with choice of mash and good Sun roasts, ales such as Butcombe and Greene King, Aspall's cider, small linked areas, huge inglenook with another great hearth behind, big back conservatory extension, friendly cat; children welcome, nice quiet garden. *(Paul Sollohub)*

HARPENDEN TL1116

Fox (01582) 713817

Luton Road, Kinsbourne Green; 2.2 miles from M1 junction 10; A1081 towards town; AL5 3QE Contemporary dining pub with several linked rooms, tiled floor bar area, leather armchairs and sofas, lots of modern dining tables in alcoves on stripped wood floors, enjoyably up-to-date pubby food including weekday fixed-price lunch/early evening menu, friendly helpful service, interesting wines by the glass, well kept Brakspears Oxford Gold and Sharps Doom Bar, open fire; background music; terrace with café-style tables and chairs, open all day. *(Clifford Blakemore)*

HARPENDEN TL1312

⋆**White Horse** (01582) 469290

Redbourn Lane, Hatching Green (B487 just W of A1081 roundabout); AL5 2JP Thriving Peach dining pub with good range of enjoyable modern food from deli boards up, also breakfast (from 9.30am) and a daily roast, friendly young staff, Purity UBU, Timothy Taylors Landlord and a guest, a dozen wines by the glass, L-shaped flagstoned bar with logs either side of little brick fireplace, leather cushioned window seats, room off with armchairs and tub seats on stripped boards, attractive airy dining room, morning coffee and daily newspapers; children welcome, tables on large terrace, more on lawn, open all day. *(John and Joyce Snell)*

HEMEL HEMPSTEAD　　TL0411

✳ **Crown & Sceptre** (01442) 234660

Bridens Camp; leaving on A4146, right at Flamstead/Markyate sign opposite Red Lion; HP2 6EY Traditional, neatly refurbished rambling pub, welcoming and relaxed, with well kept Greene King ales and up to four guests such as Tring and Vale, local cider, good generous reasonably priced pubby food (not Sun evening), friendly efficient staff, dining room with woodburner, quiz nights and beer festivals; children welcome, outside bar/games room (dogs welcome here), picnic-sets out at front and in pleasant garden, good walks, open all day weekends. *(Peter and Jan Humphreys, Ross Balaam, Val and Alan Green, Dennis Jones)*

HEMEL HEMPSTEAD　　TL0508

Marchmont Arms (01442) 254320

By roundabout on new northerly route of A4147; HP1 3AT Large 18th-c pub/brasserie with lots of linked rooms on different levels; huge windows, animal skins on wooden floors in one room, slate and wood-patterned flooring in another, furniture ranging from sofas and armchairs through chunky tables and chairs to sheepskin-covered benches, lots of mirrors, big modern chandeliers, ornate urns, flower paintings on wooden slats, open fires, Adnams, Sharps Doom Bar and plenty of wines by the glass in dimly lit bar, ambitious modern food including weekday fixed-price menu, friendly staff, orangery-style dining room; heated verandah overlooking spreading lawn, open all day. *(Dennis Jones)*

HERTFORD　　TL3212

White Horse (01992) 503911

Castle Street; SG14 1HH Chattily unpretentious little pub tucked away in side street, two small homely rooms separated by warming open fire, one more basic with bare boards, some brewery memorabilia and well worn furniture, the other more comfortable with winged leather armchair and red-tiled floor, eight Fullers beers and perhaps a guest (May and August bank holiday festivals), inexpensive pubby lunchtime food, three cosy upstairs family rooms with timber-framed Tudor brickwork, bar billiards; dogs welcome, pavement benches facing the castle, tables on back terrace, open all day; changing hands as we went to press. *(Anon)*

HIGH WYCH　　TL4714

Hand & Crown (01279) 725892

Signed off A1184 Harlow–Sawbridgeworth; CM21 0AY Nice interior with some interesting features including huge central fireplace dividing off restaurant

area, good reasonably priced and generously served food (popular so best to book), well kept Adnams and Greene King, plenty of whiskies, attentive service; background music. *(Stephen and Jean Curtis)*

HIGH WYCH　　TL4614

Rising Sun (01279) 724099

Signed off A1184 Harlo–Sawbridgeworth; CM21 0HZ Recently refurbished and opened up 19th-c red-brick local, well kept Courage Best, Oakham and up to four guests tapped from the cask, friendly staff and locals, woodburner, quiz night second Tues of month; well behaved children and dogs welcome, small side garden. *(the Didler)*

HITCHIN　　TL1828

Half Moon (01462) 452448

Queen Street; SG4 9TZ Tucked-away open-plan local, friendly and welcoming, with well kept Adnams, Wells & Youngs and interesting guests, real cider and perry, good choice of wines by the glass, traditional food (some themed nights), beer festivals; open all day Fri-Sat. *(Stuart Gideon, Mrs Catherine Simmonds, Nicola Ridding, Ian Dunbar)*

ICKLEFORD　　TL1831

Plume of Feathers (01462) 432729

Upper Green; SG5 3YD Old beamed pub with good choice of real ales, friendly staff and regulars, well appointed dining area; nice quiet spot overlooking green. *(Simon Watkins)*

LEY GREEN　　TL1624

Plough (01438) 871394

Plough Lane; SG4 8LA Small brick-built rural local, plain and old-fashioned, with well kept Greene King ales, maybe simple cheap food like bangers and mash, folk music Tues evening (not 2nd of month); lovely big informal garden with verandah and tall trees (kites and green woodpeckers), peaceful views. *(Conor McGaughey)*

LONG MARSTON　　SP8915

Queens Head (01296) 668368

Tring Road; HP23 4QL Refurnished beamed village local with well kept Fullers beers, Weston's cider and enjoyable traditional food including bargain two-course set lunch (Mon-Fri); dogs welcome, terrace seats, good walks nearby, two bedrooms in separate annexe, open all day. *(Mr R A Buckler)*

MUCH HADHAM　　TL4219

✳ **Bull** (01279) 842668

High Street; SG10 6BU Neatly kept dining pub with good home-made food changing daily, good choice of wines by the glass including champagne, well kept Hancocks HB, cheerful efficient service even at busy times, inglenook log fire in unspoilt bar, attractive pastel décor in roomy civilised dining lounge and back dining room; children welcome, good-sized garden. *(James Hill, MDN, Simon Watkins*

NORTHAW   TL2802
Two Brewers (01707) 655557
Northaw Road W (B156); EN6 4NW
Several traditional snug areas, nice dining room and garden with view of ancient parish church, well kept Wells & Youngs, enjoyable generous food at reasonable prices, friendly efficient staff. *(David Jackson, Ross Balaam)*

NUTHAMPSTEAD   TL4134
★**Woodman** (01763) 848328
Off B1368 S of Barkway; SG8 8NB
Tucked-away thatched and weatherboarded village pub now run by my long-serving licensees' son; comfortable unspoilt core with nice inglenook log fire, 17th-c low beams/ timbers, plainer dining extension, enjoyable home-made food (not Sun evening, Mon) from traditional things up, home-baked bread, ales such as Adnams, Buntingford and Greene King tapped from the cask, friendly service, interesting USAF memorabilia and outside memorial (near World War II airfield); benches out overlooking tranquil lane, two comfortable bedrooms, open all day (Mon 5-8pm). *(Marion and Bill Cross, M R D Foot, David Jackson, Mark Farrington)*

PERRY GREEN   TL4317
Hoops (01279) 843568
Off B1004 Widford–Much Hadham; SG10 6EF Refurbished 19th-c pub/ restaurant in grounds of the Henry Moore Foundation (the sculptor in evidence through posters, photographs, prints and even the cushion covers), airy open-plan interior with beams and standing timbers, spindleback chairs around rustic tables on tiled floor, green banquettes, inglenook woodburner, good reasonably priced locally sourced food including some unusual choices, Adnams Best; no dogs inside; children welcome, garden with large covered terrace, open all day Thur-Sat, till 5pm Tues, Weds and Sun, closed Mon and in winter. *(Mrs Margo Finlay, Jörg Kasprowski)*

RADLETT   TL1600
Cat & Fiddle (01923) 469523
Cobden Hill; A5183, opposite Tabard RUFC; WD7 7JR Welcoming 18th-c local, three small carpeted rooms with fires, traditional furniture including some old settles, ales such as Adnams, Black Sheep and Sharps, good value enjoyable pubby food; children welcome, picnic-sets on terrace and in tree-sheltered garden with barbecue and play area. *(Anon)*

RICKMANSWORTH   TQ0594
Feathers (01923) 770081
Church Street; WD3 1DJ Quietly set off the high street, beams, panelling and soft lighting, well kept Fullers London Pride, Tring and two guests, good wine list, varied choice of freshly prepared food all day from sandwiches up including lunchtime deal, good friendly young staff coping well when busy; children till 5pm, picnic-sets out behind. *(Brian Glozier)*

RICKMANSWORTH   TQ0592
Rose & Crown (01923) 897680
Woodcock Hill/Harefield Road, off A404 E of Rickmansworth at Batchworth; WD3 1PP Friendly low-beamed character pub with warm open fires, Caledonian Deuchars IPA, Fullers London Pride and a guest in traditional country bar, enjoyable food from sharing plates through local steaks to more contemporary dishes, airy restaurant extension; children welcome, large peaceful garden with play area, wide views, open all day. *(Mark Douglas)*

RIDGE   TL2100
Old Guinea (01707) 660894
Crossoaks Lane; EN6 3LH Welcoming country pub extensively refurbished by new owners, pizzeria alongside traditional bar with open fire, enjoyable food all day at reasonable prices, St Austell Tribute; children welcome, dogs in bar, large garden with far reaching views. *(Anon)*

SARRATT   TQ0499
Boot (01923) 262247
The Green; WD3 6BL Refurbished early 18th-c pub geared for dining, young friendly staff, selection of real ales, rambling bar with unusual inglenook, more modern dining room; good-sized garden, pleasant spot facing green, handy for Chess Valley walks, open all day. *(N R White)*

ST ALBANS   TL1407
Farriers Arms (01727) 851025
Lower Dagnall Street; AL3 4PT Plain friendly two-bar backstreet local, McMullens and guests, bar food weekdays, lots of old pictures of the pub (Campaign for Real Ale started here in the early 1970s). *(P Dawn, the Didler)*

ST ALBANS   TL1406
Goat (01727) 833934
Sopwell Lane, off Holywell Hill; AL1 1RN Former coaching inn dating to the 15th c, rambling beamed areas around central servery, traditional furnishings, open fire

---

Most pubs with any outside space now have some kind of smokers' shelter. There are regulations about these – for instance they have to be substantially open to the outside air. The best have heating and lighting and are really quite comfortable.

(and old range in one part), decent low-priced traditional food, four well kept ales including St Austell and Wells & Youngs, Weston's cider, over a dozen wines by the glass, bar billiards, darts and board games, quiz and live music nights; children in eating area, tables in back garden, bedrooms, open all day. *(Dave Braisted)*

ST ALBANS TL1407
Lower Red Lion (01727) 855669
Fishpool Street; AL3 4RX Hospitable beamed local dating from the 17th c (right-hand bar has most character), good choice of well kept changing ales (regular beer festivals), imported beers and proper cider, enjoyable inexpensive lunchtime food including sandwiches, speciality sausages and popular Sun roast, red plush seats and carpet, board games; no nearby parking; tables in good-sized back garden, bedrooms (some sharing bath), open all day Fri-Sun. *(P Dawn, the Didler, Stephen and Jean Curtis, Andrew Jeeves, Carole Smart)*

ST ALBANS TL1805
⋆**Plough** (01727) 857777
Tyttenhanger Green, off A414 E; AL4 0RW 18th-c village pub with well kept Fullers and five changing guests, friendly efficient staff, low-priced straightforward lunchtime food, good log fire and wood-burner, interesting old beer bottles and mats, longcase clock, back conservatory; tables on raised front terrace, big garden with play area, open all day Fri-Sun. *(the Didler)*

ST ALBANS TL1307
⋆**Six Bells** (01727) 856945
St Michaels Street; AL3 4SH Well cared-for rambling old pub popular for its good reasonably priced generous food, cheerful attentive service, five well kept beers including Fullers London Pride and Timothy Taylors Landlord, low beams and timbers, log fire, quieter panelled dining room, some live music; children welcome, occasional barbecues in small back garden, handy for Verulamium Museum, open all day. *(LM, Mike and Jennifer Marsh, Stephen and Jean Curtis)*

ST ALBANS TL1406
White Lion (01727) 850540
Sopwell Lane; AL1 1RN Good atmosphere in small friendly front bar and roomy linked lounge areas, enjoyable fairly priced food (not Sat or Sun evenings) from snacks to daily blackboard specials, up to eight well kept ales, Weston's cider, darts, live music Tues; no children inside; dogs welcome, big enclosed garden with pétanque and chickens, open all day. *(the Didler, Stephen and Jean Curtis, Tony and Wendy Hobden)*

TRING SP9211
Akeman (01442) 826027
Akeman Street; HP23 6AA Popular Oakman Inn (their first – opened 2007),

good choice of interesting food with some mediterranean influences from bar snacks and sharing plates up, open kitchen, three well kept ales including Tring, cocktails, good coffee, open-plan layout with leather sofas by log fire; children welcome, nice garden area, open all day from 8am (breakfast till noon). *(Taff and Gilly Thomas)*

TRING SP9211
⋆**Kings Arms** (01442) 823318
King Street; by junction with Queen Street (which is off B4635 Western Road – continuation of High Street); HP23 6BE Delightful spic-and-span backstreet pub with lots of cheerful customers and relaxed atmosphere, well kept Wadworths 6X and four quickly changing guests, Rosie's cider, hearty helpings of good value food including several spicy dishes, cushioned pews and wooden tables and stools around cast-iron tables on carpet, old brewery advertisements on green painted or pine panelled walls, and two warm winter coal fires; dogs welcome, children till 8.30pm, tables and heaters in attractive side wagon yard. *(Taff Thomas, Roy Hoing)*

WARESIDE TL3915
Chequers (01920) 467010
B1004; SG12 7QY Proper old-fashioned country local with down-to-earth landlady, well kept ales including local Buntingford, good straightforward home-made food at reasonable prices, friendly staff, log fire; children, dogs and walkers welcome. *(Chris Allen)*

WATER END TL0410
Red Lion (01442) 213594
Leighton Buzzard Road (A4146); HP1 3BD Large modernised Oakman Inn extended from 18th-c core, beams and timbers mixing with contemporary furnishings, enjoyable food (some italian influenced including fresh pizzas) from open kitchen, friendly service, real ales and plenty of wines by the glass; garden and terrace tables. *(Simon Scott)*

WATTON-AT-STONE TL3019
George & Dragon (01920) 830285
High Street (B1001); SG14 3TA Appealing candlelit country dining pub, enjoyable food from sandwiches up using local produce (gluten-free diets catered for), Greene King IPA and Abbot plus guest beers, interesting mix of antique and modern prints on partly timbered walls, big inglenook fireplace, daily newspapers; no dogs; children in eating areas, pretty shrub-screened garden with heaters, boules, open all day. *(N R White)*

WELWYN TL2316
Wellington (01438) 714036
High Street, old village – not the Garden City; AL6 9EE Café-like rather than pub with cushioned church and other dining

chairs, window seats and copper-topped or wooden tables, lots of mirrors, standing timbers and open doorways, Greene King ales and several wines by the glass, good coffee and teas, daily newspapers, light airy restaurant with stripped beams and central fire, glass wall looking onto High Street, popular bistro-type food (no booking); background jazz; terrace with modern wicker chairs, bedrooms. *(Jane Plaza)*

WHEATHAMPSTEAD   TL1712
⋆**Wicked Lady** (01582) 832128

Nomansland Common; B651 0.5 mile S; AL4 8EL Unpretentious chain dining pub with clean contemporary décor, wide range of good well presented food including some unusual dishes, good value set lunch, well kept Adnams, Fullers London Pride and Timothy Taylors Landlord, plenty of wines by the glass, reasonable prices, friendly attentive young staff, various rooms and alcoves, low beams and log fires, lots of stainless steel, conservatory; garden with nice terrace. *(Mike and Jennifer Marsh, David and Ruth Shillitoe)*

WILDHILL   TL2606
Woodman (01707) 642618

Off B158 Brookmans Park–Essendon; AL9 6EA Simple tucked-away country local with friendly staff and regulars, well kept Greene King and three guest ales, open-plan bar with log fire, two smaller back rooms (one with TV), enjoyable straightforward weekday bar lunches, darts; picnic-sets in big garden. *(David Hill)*

WILLIAN   TL2230
⋆**Fox** (01462) 480233

A1(M) J9; A6141 W towards Letchworth then first left; SG6 2AE Restauranty dining pub with fresh contemporary décor, light wood furniture on stripped boards or big ceramic tiles, modern pictures on white and pastel walls, pale blue-fronted counter with modern bar stools, Adnams, Brancaster, Fullers, Woodfordes and a guest, good wine list with over a dozen by the glass, creative food (not cheap) from changing menu (not Sun evening, service added automatically), helpful young uniformed staff; background music, TV; children welcome, dogs in bar, disabled access and parking, smart tables on side terrace, picnic-sets in good-sized garden below handsome 14th-c church, open all day. *(Alison and Pete, Stuart Gideon, Mrs Catherine Simmonds, Andy Lickfold, M and J White, David and Ruth Shillitoe, Derek Thomas)*

WILLIAN   TL2230
Three Horseshoes (01462) 685713

Baldock Lane, off Willian Rd; SG6 2AE Welcoming traditional village pub with enjoyable home-made pubby food at reasonable prices, well kept Greene King ales, log fires; lots of colourful hanging baskets outside, handy for A1(M), open all day, closed Mon lunchtime. *(Mrs Margo Finlay, Jörg Kasprowski)*

Stars before the name of a pub show exceptional character and appeal. They don't mean extra comfort. And they are nothing to do with food quality, for which there's a separate knife-and-fork symbol. Even quite a basic pub can win stars, if it's individual enough.

Isle of Wight

Five new entries added this year for this holiday island are the Fishbourne Inn at Fishbourne (attractively refurbished bars in contemporary style and serving all-day food), Horse & Groom in Ningwood (a smashing pub for families and with fair-priced food served all day), Buddle in Niton (a former smugglers' haunt with some character), Boathouse at Seaview (just across the road from the beach and the double bedrooms overlook the water) and Spyglass in Ventnor (good value food and in a fine seaside spot). Our other Main Entries between them offer reasonable prices, plenty of seafood and good real ales. The starred small entries in the Also Worth a Visit section at the end of the chapter are also recommended. The Isle of Wight Dining Pub 2013 is the New Inn at Shalfleet.

ARRETON   SZ5386   Map 2

White Lion £

A3056 Newport–Sandown; PO30 3AA

Friendly local with good value pubby food

The neatly kept beamed lounge at this unchanging white-painted village house is comfortably old fashioned and cosy, with a genuinely warm welcome, dark pink walls or stripped brick above a stained pine dado, gleaming brass and horse tack and lots of cushioned wheelback chairs on the patterned red carpet. The background music tends to be very quiet, and the public bar has a TV, games machine, darts and board games. Three changing real ales on handpump might be Wells & Youngs Eagle, Sharps Doom Bar and Timothy Taylors Landlord; also a farm cider and draught pear cider. There's also a restaurant (no children in here) and family room. The pleasant garden has a small play area.

Traditional tasty food, served in generous helpings, runs from sandwiches and ploughman's to prawn cocktail, grilled black pudding with redcurrant jelly, whitebait, cauliflower and broccoli cheese, scampi, cod steak with creamy white wine sauce, pie of the day, faggots and peas, and puddings such as pork ribs, cod and pancetta fishcakes and roast pork hock with creamy sage and onion sauce. *Benchmark main dish: chicken breast topped with bacon and brie £10.45. Two-course evening meal £16.40.*

Enterprise ~ Lease Chris and Kate Cole ~ Real ale ~ Bar food (12-9) ~ (01983) 528479 ~ Children welcome except in restaurant ~ Dogs allowed in bar ~ Open 11(12 Sun)-11 ~ www.white-lion-arreton.com *Recommended by Terry and Nickie Williams, A N Bance, Tom Evans*

BEMBRIDGE
SZ6587 Map 2
Crab & Lobster

*Foreland Fields Road, off Howgate Road (which is off B3395 via
Hillway Road); PO35 5TR*

Clifftop views from terrace and some bedrooms

There can't be much that's more summery than a seafood meal out
on the terrace of this coastal pub, with its terrific Solent views; the
dining area and some of the bedrooms share the same aspect. Perched
on low cliffs within yards of the shore it's not surprising that it's such
a popular summer destination (picnic-sets outside fill up quickly and
service can slow down) so do arrive early for a table. Inside it's roomier
than you might expect and is done out not unlike a parlour with lots of
yachting memorabilia, old local photographs and a blazing winter fire;
darts, dominoes and cribbage. Goddards Fuggle-Dee-Dum, Greene King
IPA and Sharps Doom Bar are on handpump, with a dozen wines by the
glass, 16 malt whiskies and good coffee.

Heavily weighted towards seafood – particularly crab and lobster – the
menu includes sandwiches and baguettes, crab and lobster soup, crab ramekin,
whitebait, battered calamari, crab salad, crab cakes, seafood tagliatelle, mixed
grill, penne with pesto and chicken breast, chicken or vegetable curry; they may
keep your credit card if you run a tab. *Benchmark main dish: crab cakes £10.95.
Two-course evening meal £20.00.*

Enterprise ~ Lease Caroline and Ian Quekett ~ Real ale ~ Bar food (12-2.30, 6-9(9.30
Fri, Sat) with limited menu 2.30-5.30 weekends and holidays) ~ Restaurant ~ (01983)
872244 ~ Children welcome ~ Dogs allowed in bar ~ Open 11-11; 12-10.30 Sun ~
Bedrooms: £50S(£55B)/£85S(£90B) ~ www.crabandlobsterinn.co.uk *Recommended by
Anne and Jeff Peel, Mark Seymour, Jackie Roberts, Tom Evans*

FISHBOURNE
SZ5592 Map 2
Fishbourne Inn

*From Portsmouth car ferry turn left into Fishbourne Lane (no through
road); PO33 4EU*

Attractively refurbished pub with a contemporary feel, several interconnected rooms, real ales, a good number of wines by the glass and all-day food; bedrooms

This half-timbered pub is handy for the Wightlink ferry terminal. It's
been give an attractive contemporary makeover inside and the open-
plan rooms are connected by knocked-through doorways. There's a mix
of wooden and high-backed dining chairs around square tables on the
slate floor, a red-painted area off the bar with a big model yacht and two
leather sofas facing each other, a woodburning stove in a brick fireplace
with an ornate mirror above it, and a smart dining room with leather
high-backed chairs around circular tables on the new wood flooring and
another model yacht on the window sill; one comfortable room has huge
brown leather sofas, and throughout there are country pictures on the
partly panelled walls.

As well as serving breakfast from 9am (to non-residents, too), the all-day
food includes lunchtime sandwiches, deli boards to share, half a pint of
prawns with aioli, home-made tagliatelle with wild mushroom, walnut and
truffle sauce, ham and free-range egg, chicken caesar salad, a trio of sausages
with mash and gravy, a home-made pie of the day, and seasonal lobster and crab

salads. *Benchmark main dish: beer-battered fish and chips £10.95. Two-course evening meal £16.50.*

Enterprise ~ Lease Richard Morey ~ Real ale ~ Bar food (12-9.30; 12-2.30, 6-9.30 winter weekdays) ~ (01983) 882823 ~ Children welcome ~ Dogs allowed in bar ~ Open 9am-11pm(10.30 Sun) ~ Bedrooms: /£90S ~ www.thefishbourne.co.uk
Recommended by Richard Gibbs

FRESHWATER SZ3487 Map 2
Red Lion ♀

Church Place; from A3055 at E end of village by Freshwater Garage mini-roundabout follow Yarmouth signpost, then take first real right turn signed to Parish Church; PO40 9BP

Good mix of locals and visiting diners, good food and composed atmosphere

Although the food is quite a draw at this civilised place, you're likely to find a row of chatty locals occupying stools along the counter, enjoying the Flowers Original, Goddards Best and Fuggle-Dee-Dum and Sharps Doom Bar. Steady and reliable, this is a longstanding stalwart of the *Guide* , with a nicely grown-up pubby atmosphere. The comfortably furnished open-plan bar has fires, low grey sofas and sturdy country-kitchen-style furnishings on mainly flagstoned floors and bare boards. Outside, there are tables (some under cover) in a carefully tended garden beside the kitchen's herb and vegetable patch. A couple of picnic-sets in a quiet square at the front have pleasant views of the church. The pub is virtually on the Freshwater Way footpath that connects Yarmouth with the southern coast at Freshwater Bay.

 Food, listed on blackboards behind the bar, includes a sensible cross-section of dishes such as whitebait, smoked haddock pâté, scambled egg and smoked salmon, herring roes on toast, sausage and mash, beef madras, steak and ale pie, chicken breast stuffed with brie, roast pork belly with apple sauce, braised lamb shank with minted gravy, mushroom stroganoff, and puddings such as jam roly poly, sherry trifle and chocolate roulade. *Benchmark main dish: steak in ale pie £10.50. Two-course evening meal £18.80.*

Enterprise ~ Lease Michael Mence ~ Real ale ~ Bar food (12-2, 6-9) ~ (01983) 754925 ~ Children over 10 at the landlord's discretion ~ Dogs allowed in bar ~ Open 11.30-3, 5.30-11; 11.30-4, 6-11 Sat; 12-3, 7-10.30 Sun *Recommended by Denise Bowes, D M and B K Moores, Tom Evans*

NINGWOOD SZ3989 Map 2
Horse & Groom

A3054 Newport–Yarmouth, a mile W of Shalfleet; PO30 4NW

Spacious family dining pub with fairly priced all-day food, excellent play area and crazy golf

This is a neatly kept and carefully extended pub with a friendly, helpful licensee and an easy-going atmosphere. The roomy interior has been thoughtfully arranged with comfortable leather sofas grouped around low tables and a nice mix of sturdy tables and chairs, well spaced for a relaxing meal. Walls are pale pink, which works nicely with the old flagstone flooring. Greene King IPA, Ringwood Best and a guest like Adnams Lighthouse on handpump and a dozen wines by the glass; background music, games machine and board games. Children and families will find plenty to keep them occupied outside where there are ample tables in the garden, a bouncy castle, crazy golf and a fully equipped play area.

 Reasonably priced food includes sandwiches, king prawns with garlic mayonnaise, chilli nachos with melted cheese and sour cream, local beefburgers topped with cheese and bacon, home-cooked honey-roast ham with free range eggs and chutney, a rack of barbecue ribs, steak in ale pie, fresh dover sole and puddings like belgian waffle stack with fudge ice-cream and sticky toffee pudding with butterscotch sauce. *Benchmark main dish: steak in ale pie £9.95. Two-course evening meal £16.50.*

Enterprise ~ Lease Steve Gilbert ~ Real ale ~ Bar food (12-9) ~ (01983) 760672 ~ Children welcome ~ Dogs welcome ~ Open 11-11(midnight Fri-Sun) ~ www.horse-and-groom.com *Recommended by Tom Evans*

NITON
SZ5075   Map 2

Buddle

St Catherines Road, Undercliff; off A3055 just S of village, towards St Catherines Point; PO38 2NE

Stone pub with sea views from seats in clifftop garden, six real ales and tasty food

The views from the many picnic-sets on both the stone terraces and on the grass in the neatly kept garden here look down to the sea, as the pub is on a southerly cliff near St Catherine's Lighthouse. It's an attractive stone cottage and a former smugglers' haunt and there's plenty of character in the traditional bar rooms: heavy black beams, captain's chairs and wheelbacks or cushioned wall seating around solid wooden tables on big flagstones or carpet, and an open fire in the broad stone fireplace with its massive black oak mantelbeam. A fine choice of six real ales on handpump might include Fullers London Pride, Gales HSB, Goddards Ale of Wight, Hambleton Bitter, Island Yachtmans Ale and Yates Golden Ale; background music and bar billiards. The pub is surrounded by National Trust land and is handy for the coast path.

Using local produce, the food includes sandwiches or filled panini, pâté of the day, nachos with melted cheese, peppers, tomato salsa and sour cream, spicy bean, chicken or beef burgers, lasagne, a trio of sausages with onion gravy, home-roasted ham with free-range eggs, chicken with bacon and cheese in barbecue sauce, beer-battered fish and chips, and puddings such as treacle sponge and warm chocolate fudge cake. *Benchmark main dish: steak in ale pie £10.95. Two-course evening meal £17.00.*

Enterprise ~ Lease John and Fiona Page ~ Real ale ~ Bar food (12-9) ~ (01983) 730243 ~ Children in Old Barn ~ Dogs welcome ~ Regular live music ~ Open 11-11(12 Fri and Sat); 12-10.30 Sun ~ www.buddleinn.co.uk *Recommended by Bruce and Sharon Eden, George and Linda Ozols, David Glynne-Jones, Tom Evans*

SEAVIEW
SZ5992   Map 2

Boathouse

On B3330 Ryde–Seaview; PO34 5BW

Contemporary décor in well run pub by the beach, real ales, quite a choice of food, a friendly welcome and seats outside; bedrooms

Just across the road from the beach, this extended, blue-painted Victorian pub usefully serves food all day at weekends and all day on weekdays too from April to October. The décor is appealing and contemporary, with light, fresh paintwork and a mix of polished bare boards, flagstones and carpet, and you can be sure of a warm welcome from the friendly staff. The bar has sturdy leather stools and blue, tub-like chairs around circular wooden tables, a large model yacht on the mantelpiece above the open fire with a huge neat stack of logs beside it, fresh flowers and candles, and Ringwood Best and Sharps Doom Bar on handpump from the pale wooden counter; another room has a dinghy with oars in it leaning against the wall. The dining room has a mix of elegant dining chairs, more wooden tables, some portraits on pale blue walls and an ornate mirror over another open fire; background music. There are picnic-sets and white tables and chairs outside, some under parasols, that look across to the sea. The double bedrooms overlook the water.

As well as lunchtime sandwiches, the all-day food includes half a pint of prawns, broccoli and tomato tagliatelle with a blue cheese sauce, ham and free-range eggs, battered fish and chips, a trio of local sausages with a mash of the day, smoked salmon salad with tartare dressing and crème fraîche, rump or sirloin steaks, and seasonal lobster and crab salads. *Benchmark main dish: fish pie £10.25. Two-course evening meal £16.50.*

Punch ~ Tenant Martin Bullock ~ Real ale ~ Bar food (12-9.30; limited between 2.30-6) ~ (01983) 810616 ~ Children welcome ~ Dogs allowed in bar ~ Open 9am-11pm(10.30 Sun) ~ Bedrooms: /£110S ~ www.theboathouseiow.co.uk *Recommended by Richard Gibbs*

SHALLFLEET
New Inn

SZ4089 Map 2

A3054 Newport–Yarmouth; PO30 4NS
Isle of Wight Dining Pub of the Year

Happy pub with seafood specialities, good beers and wines, too

Readers enjoy the genuinely cheerful atmosphere at this nice old 18th-c former fishermen's haunt, and we think it gets better and better, with more attention to detail, from one year to the next. Its rambling rooms have plenty of character with warm fires, yachting photographs and pictures, boarded ceilings and scrubbed-pine tables on flagstone, carpet and slate floors. Sharps Doom Bar and a couple of guests such as Goddards Ale of Wight and Yates Golden are on handpump, and they stock over 60 wines; background music. As it's popular, you will need to book and there may be double sittings in summer; dogs are only allowed in areas with stone floors

They take plenty of care over their food here, using local produce where possible. The seafood is particularly good, though readers have enjoyed the island-reared beef just as much. As well as lunchtime sandwiches, there might be mushroom and blue cheese risotto, crab and lobster cocktail, ploughman's, battered fish of the day, steak and ale pie, gnocchi with roast butternut, parmesan and cream, braised lamb shank with mint gravy, seared swordfish with tagliatelle and their prawn broth, lobster or crab salad puddings such as white chocolate and raspberry cheesecake, banana sticky toffee pudding with toffee sauce and chocolate brownies. *Benchmark main dish: pork belly with apple and sage £13.95. Two-course evening meal £19.30.*

Enterprise ~ Lease Mr Bullock and Mr McDonald ~ Real ale ~ Bar food (9-11, 12-2.30, snacks 2.30-5 Fri, Sat, 6-9.30) ~ (01983) 531314 ~ Children welcome ~ Dogs allowed in bar ~ Open 9-11(10.30 Sun) ~ www.thenew-inn.co.uk *Recommended by Bruce and Sharon Eden, Mr and Mrs P D Titcomb, Joshua Fancett, Penny and Peter Keevil, Mrs Joyce Robson, David Glynne-Jones, Tom Evans*

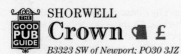

SHORWELL
Crown 🍺 £

SZ4582   Map 2

B3323 SW of Newport; PO30 3JZ

Popular pub with appealing streamside garden and play area

In summer, the tree-sheltered garden around this pretty pub is very appealing with its little stream that broadens into a small trout-filled pool. There are plenty of closely spaced picnic-sets and white garden chairs and tables on grass, and a decent children's play area. Inside, four pleasant opened-up rooms spread around a central bar, with either carpet, tiles or flagstones, and chatty regulars lending some local character. Adnams Broadside and Explorer, Goddards Fuggle-Dee-Dum, St Austell Tribute and Sharps Doom Bar on handpump. The beamed knocked-through lounge has blue and white china on an attractive carved dresser, old country prints on stripped-stone walls and a winter log fire with a fancy tile-work surround. Black pews form bays around tables in a stripped-stone room off to the left with another log fire; background music and board games.

🍴 Pubby bar food includes sandwiches and filled baguettes, garlic mushrooms, a pâté of the day, sausage and mash, beer-battered fish and chips, lasagne, chicken curry, various pizzas (that you can also take away), pumpkin and squash risotto, fisherman's platter or summer tapas plate (to share), butterflied chicken breast, steaks, and puddings. *Benchmark main dish: pie of the day £11.95. Two-course evening meal £16.00.*

Enterprise ~ Lease Nigel and Pam Wynn ~ Real ale ~ Bar food (12-9.30) ~ (01983) 740293 ~ Children welcome ~ Dogs welcome ~ Open 10.30(11.30 Sun)-11 ~ www.crowninnshorwell.co.uk *Recommended by Terry and Nickie Williams, Tom Evans*

VENTNOR
Spyglass £

SZ5677   Map 2

Esplanade, SW end; road down is very steep and twisty, and parking nearby can be difficult – best to use the pay-and-display (free in winter) about 100 metres up the road; PO38 1JX

Interesting waterside pub with appealing seafaring bric-a-brac, four well kept beers and enjoyable food

The terrific seaside location of this cheery, bubbling place seems to draw the crowds whatever the season. It's perched just above the beach, and tables in the bar and outside on a terrace have lovely views over the sea. Inside, the snug quarry-tiled old interior is charmingly done out with a fascinating jumble of seafaring memorabilia (anything from ship's wheels to stuffed seagulls); background music. Ringwood Best and Fortyniner are well kept alongside a couple of guests from brewers such as Banks and Yates. There are strolls westwards from here along the coast towards the Botanic Garden, as well as heftier hikes up on to St Boniface Down and towards the eerie shell of Appuldurcombe House. No children in the bedrooms.

🍴 Generous helpings of good value food from the pubby menu includes sandwiches, baked potatoes, ploughman's, spinach and ricotta cannelloni, macaroni cheese, salads, cottage pie, half a roast chicken, chilli, sausage and chips, burgers and steaks; they may ask to hold your credit card if you run a tab. *Benchmark main dish: fisherman's pie £10.50. Two-course evening meal £13.25.*

Free house ~ Licensees Neil and Stephanie Gibbs ~ Real ale ~ Bar food (12-9.30) ~ (01983) 855338 ~ Children welcome ~ Dogs allowed in bar ~ Live bands every day in summer and Weds-Sun in winter ~ Open 10.30am-11pm ~ Bedrooms: /£80B ~ www.thespyglass.com *Recommended by Penny and Peter Keevil, Francis and Lyn Genever, Tom Evans*

Also Worth a Visit on the Isle of Wight

Besides the fully inspected pubs, you might like to try these pubs that have been recommended to us and described by readers. Do tell us what you think of them: feedback@goodguides.com

BEMBRIDGE   SZ6488
Pilot Boat (01983) 872077
Station Road/Kings Road; PO35 5NN
Welcoming little harbourside pub with smart ship-like interior, good food from sandwiches to local seafood, well kept Goddards and guests; tables out overlooking water or in pleasant courtyard behind, well placed for coast walks, open all day. *(George and Linda Ozols, Stuart Williams, S Holder)*

BINSTEAD   SZ5792
Fleming Arms (01983) 563415
Binstead Road; PO33 3RD Family friendly pub with wide choice of good reasonably priced food, Flowers and Ringwood Best, attentive service; children and dogs welcome, garden. *(Paul Baines, Tom Evans)*

BONCHURCH   SZ5778
✶**Bonchurch Inn** (01983) 852611
Bonchurch Shute; from A3055 E of Ventnor turn down to Old Bonchurch; opposite Leconfield Hotel; PO38 1NU
Quirky former stables with restaurant; fairly basic family room and congenial bar with narrow-planked ship's decking and old-fashioned steamer-style seats, Courage ales tapped from the cask, bar food and good italian dishes (the owners are from Italy), charming helpful staff, darts, shove-ha'penny and other games; background music; dogs welcome, delightful continental-feeling central courtyard (parking here can be tricky), holiday flat. *(George and Linda Ozols, Guy Vowles, Mr and Mrs P D Titcomb, Mark Seymour, Jackie Roberts, Dr D Jeary, S Holder and others)*

CALBOURNE   SZ4286
Sun (01983) 531231
Sun Hill; PO30 4JA Family-friendly old roadside pub with enjoyable sensibly priced food and quick cheerful service even when busy, varying real ales, cosy no-frills bar and plain lower-level extension; extensive views across Brighstone Forest. *(Mrs Joyce Robson)*

CARISBROOKE   SZ4687
✶**Blacksmiths Arms** (01983) 529263
B3401 1.5 miles W; PO30 5SS Quiet hillside pub with friendly landlord and staff, Fullers, Shepherd Neame and Yates, decent wines and cider, food can be good including fresh fish, scrubbed tables in neat beamed and flagstoned front bars, superb Solent views from airy bare-boards family dining extension; dogs and walkers welcome, terrace tables and smallish back garden with same view, play area, open all day. *(Peter Meister, Tom Evans)*

CHALE   SZ4877
✶**Wight Mouse** (01983) 730431
Off A3055/B3399; PO38 2HA Big efficient family dining inn rambling around with flagstones there, carpet there, modern-look woody extension around attractive traditional core with log fire, well kept Badger ales from long bar, enjoyable standard food from baguettes up, fast friendly service; extensive outdoor seating and bar, good play area (inside one too), great views out over cliffs, good bedrooms (some with sea views). *(Karen Eliot, David Jackman)*

COWES   SZ5092
✶**Folly** (01983) 297171
Folly Lane signed off A3021 just S of Whippingham; PO32 6NB Glorious Medina estuary views from bar and waterside terrace of this cheery laid-back place, timbered ship-like interior with simple wood furnishings, wide range of sensibly priced hearty food from breakfast on, speedy service, Greene King, Goddards and possibly a guest; background and live music, TV, games machine and pool – can get very lively at weekends; children and dogs welcome, showers, long-term parking and weather forecasts for sailors, water taxi, open all day. *(Bruce and Sharon Eden, George and Linda Ozols, Terry and Nickie Williams, Matt and Cathy Fancett, Mrs Joyce Robson, Francis and Lyn Genever and others)*

All *Guide* inspections are anonymous. Anyone claiming to be a *Good Pub Guide* inspector is a fraud. Please let us know.

GODSHILL SZ5281

✶ **Taverners** (01983) 840707

High Street; PO38 3HZ Welcoming 17th-c pub with landlord/chef doing good seasonal food with emphasis on fresh local produce, children's menu and Sun roasts too, very popular weekends when booking advised, well kept Fullers London Pride, a house beer from Yates and a guest, good friendly service, spacious bar and two front dining areas, beams, bare boards and slate floors, woodburner; dogs welcome, garden with terrace and play area, own shop, limited parking, open all day, closed Sun evening (except bank/school summer holidays). *(George and Linda Ozols, Alan Clark, Andy Hogben, the Farmers, Tom Evans)*

GURNARD SZ4796

Woodvale (01983) 292037

Princes Esplanade; PO31 8LE Large 1930s inn with picture-window Solent views, friendly staff, good choice of real ales and plenty of wines by the glass, enjoyable food including good fish/seafood specials, weekend live music; children welcome, garden with terrace and summer barbecues, refurbished bedrooms, open all day. *(Anon)*

HAVENSTREET SZ5590

White Hart (01983) 883485

Off A3054 Newport–Ryde; Main Road; PO33 4DP Updated old red-brick village pub, good popular food (all day Sun) including daily specials, Ringwood and Goddards ales, cosy log-fire bar with locomotive prints, carpeted dining area; children and dogs welcome, tables in secluded garden behind, open all day. *(Stuart Williams)*

HULVERSTONE SZ3984

✶ **Sun** (01983) 741124

B3399; PO30 4EH Picture-book thatched country pub in charming peaceful setting with lovely views over the Channel, low-ceilinged bar, ales such as Adnams, Goddards, Ringwood and Timothy Taylors, nice mix of old furniture on flagstones and floorboards, brick and stone walls, horsebrasses and ironwork around fireplace, large windows in traditionally decorated newer dining area, all-day pubby food including local meat, darts and board games; background music – live Sat evening; children welcome away from bar area, dogs in bar, secluded split-level cottagey garden, open all day. *(Geraldine and James Fradgley, Mrs Joyce Robson, Tom Evans)*

NEWCHURCH SZ5685

✶ **Pointer** (01983) 865202

High Street; PO36 0NN Well run two-room pub by Norman church, enjoyable fairly priced food using local produce (booking advised in season), well kept Fullers and a guest ale, friendly service; children and dogs welcome, pleasant back garden, boules. *(Guy Vowles, S Holder, Tom Evans)*

NORTHWOOD SZ4983

Travellers Joy (01983) 298024

Off B3325 S of Cowes; PO31 8LS Friendly real-ale pub with eight well kept beers including local brews (tasters offered), enjoyable reasonably priced pubby food from sandwiches up, long bar with over 200 pump clips on the walls, conservatory, old pinball machine in games room, Sun quiz; background radio; children and dogs welcome, garden with pétanque and play area, open all day Fri, Sat. *(Joan and Michel Hooper-Immins, Tom Evans, Barrie and Mary Crees)*

SEAVIEW SZ6291

✶ **Seaview Hotel** (01983) 612711

High Street; off B3330 Ryde–Bembridge; PO34 5EX Small gently civilised but relaxed hotel, traditional wood furnishings, seafaring paraphernalia and log fire in pubby bare-boards bar, comfortable more refined front bar, Goddards, Yates and a guest, good wine list including some local ones, good well presented pub food (smaller helpings available) and more elaborate restaurant menu using produce from their farm; may ask for a credit card if you run a tab, background music, TV; children welcome, dogs in bar, sea glimpses from tables on tiny front terrace, six nice bedrooms (some with sea views), open all day. *(Mr and Mrs P D Titcomb, Karen Eliot, David Glynne-Jones, Tom Evans)*

SHANKLIN SZ5881

✶ **Fishermans Cottage**

(01983) 863882 *Bottom of Shanklin Chine; PO37 6BN* Unchanging thatched cottage in terrific setting tucked into the cliffs on Appley beach, steep zigzag walk down beautiful chine; low-beamed little flagstoned rooms with stripped-stone walls, old local pictures and bric-a-brac, Goddards Fuggle-Dee-Dum and Yates Undercliff on handpump, simple pubby food, live entertainment Tues, Fri and Sat evenings; background music; wheelchair access, children and dogs welcome, sun-soaked terrace, lovely seaside walk to Luccombe,

---

Please keep sending us reports. We rely on readers for news of new discoveries, and particularly for news of changes – however slight – at the fully described pubs: feedback@goodguides.com, or (no stamp needed) The Good Pub Guide, FREEPOST TN1569, Wadhurst, E Sussex TN5 7BR.

open all day, closed end of Oct–early
Mar. *(Tom Evans)*

SHANKLIN SZ5881
Steamer (01983) 862641
Esplanade; PO37 6BS Nautical-theme
bar, fun for holiday families, with good range
of real ales, enjoyable fresh food including
local seafood, cheery staff, live music most
weekends; fine sea views from covered
floodlit terrace, eight bedrooms, open all
day. *(A N Bance)*

ST HELENS SZ6289
Vine (01983) 872337
Upper Green Road; PO33 1UJ Enjoyable
range of food including stone-baked pizzas,
themed evenings, good choice of well kept
beers, friendly staff, live music Fri, quiz Sun;
children welcome. *(A N Bance, N Jervis)*

WHITWELL SZ5277
✳ **White Horse** (01983) 730375
High Street; PO38 2PY Popular
sympathetically restored old thatched pub,
extensive range of good value generous food
from pub staples to more innovative dishes
and good Sun roasts, several well kept ales
including Goddards, good friendly service,
large cheery high-ceilinged family dining
area with small beamed bar and second area
off; may be background music; picnic-sets in
big garden. *(Terry and Nickie Williams,
Tom Evans)*

WOOTTON BRIDGE SZ5492
Sloop (01983) 882544
*Mill Square (A3054 Ryde–Newport);
PO33 4HS* Comfortable well laid out
Vintage Inn, good choice of sensibly priced
food, friendly quick service, plenty of wines
by the glass, proper cider and real ale; nice
setting with fine views over tidal yacht
moorings. *(Mrs Joyce Robson)*

YARMOUTH SZ3589
Kings Head (01983) 760351
Quay Street; PO41 0PB Cosy low-ceilinged
traditional pub opposite car ferry, rather dark
and quaint, with well kept Otter and Yates,
good popular food from sandwiches to well
prepared local fish, friendly quick service,
plush seats, log fires; background music; good
for families, dogs welcome, courtyard seats,
bedrooms. *(Sally Matson)*

YARMOUTH SZ3589
Wheatsheaf (01983) 760456
Bridge Road, near ferry; PO41 0PH
Opened-up Victorian pub with enjoyable
generous food, cheerful service, Ringwood
and a local ale, glazed extension, pool; handy
for the harbour, open all day. *(D J and
P M Taylor)*

Kent

Right on the *Guide's* doorstep, this county has a lot of well run, friendly pubs with good food and beer. New finds (or pubs back in these pages after a break) include the Unicorn at Bekesbourne (simple bars in friendly little pub), Green Cross in Goudhurst (delicious fish in down-to-earth bar and more formal restaurant), Plough at Ivy Hatch (super food cooked by the landlord), George in Newnham (old-world village pub with well liked food), and George & Dragon at Speldhurst (plenty of character in medieval manor house, enjoyable food and wines). Doing particularly well and worth a special visit are the Three Chimneys at Biddenden (imaginative food in character building), Royal Oak at Brookland (civilised place with lovely food and bedrooms), Hare at Langton Green (Brunning & Price so with bistro-style food and 24 wines by the glass), Bottle House at Penshurst (a pleasing and attractive dining pub), Dering Arms in Pluckley (excellent fish and seafood), White Hart near Sevenoaks (another popular Brunning & Price pub), Plough at Stalisfield Green (local beers and tasty food using seasonal produce) and Sankeys in Tunbridge Wells (bustling ground floor pubby bar and downstairs dining room with top class seafood). Our Kent Dining Pub 2013 is the Three Chimneys at Biddenden.

 BEKESBOURNE   TR1856   Map 3
Unicorn
Bekesbourne Hill, off Station Road; village E of Canterbury; CT4 5ED

Small, friendly pub, simply furnished bars, local beer and pubby food

The licensees at this friendly little pub are particularly welcoming and clearly enjoy their work. It's a simple place with just a few scrubbed old pine tables and wooden pubby chairs on worn floorboards, a nice old leather sofa beside the open fire, a canary yellow ceiling and walls above a dark green dado, minimal décor and a handful of bar stools against the neat counter; background music and board games. They make a point of serving only Kentish beers from brewers such as Ramsgate and Westerham on handpump, alongside Biddenden cider. A side terrace is prettily planted and there's a garden with benches and bat and trap in summer. Parking in front is tricky but there's a large car park at the back reached from the small track at the end of the adjacent terrace of cottages. More reports please.

🍴 Bar food includes filled rolls, fried pigeon breast, garlic mushrooms, fish in beer batter, rabbit and bean casserole, Yorkshire pudding filled with herb sausages, fig, blue cheese and walnut salad, mushroom stroganoff, duck breast on rösti potatoes with caramelised fennel and carrot with blackberry sauce, shepherd's pie, and chicken breast with mushroom, garlic and white wine sauce, and puddings. *Benchmark main dish: shortcrust pie of the day £9.50. Two-course evening meal £15.25.*

Free house ~ Licensee Martin Short ~ Real ale ~ Bar food (12-2.30, 6.30-9; 12-5 Sun; not Mon) ~ (01227) 830210 ~ Well behaved children welcome ~ Dogs welcome ~ Folk or acoustic music Sun ~ Open 12-3, 6-11; 12-10.30 Sun; closed Mon ~ www.pubunicorn.com *Recommended by Ian Coles, Richard Gibbs*

BIDDENDEN   TQ8238 Map 3
Three Chimneys 🍴 ♟

A262, a mileW of village; TN27 8LW
Kent Dining Pub of the Year

Pubby beamed rooms of considerable individuality, log fires, imaginative food and pretty garden

The simple huddled down exterior of this appealingly civilised place, with its low-slung roof and little windows, is absolutely delightful, and its little low-beamed rooms have exactly the charmingly timeless feel you'd hope for. They are simply done out with plain wooden furniture and old settles on flagstones and coir matting, some harness and sporting prints on the stripped-brick walls and good log fires. The public bar on the left is quite down to earth, with darts, dominoes and cribbage. Adnams Best and Old and a guest from a brewer such as Franklins tapped straight from casks racked behind the counter, several wines by the glass, local Biddenden cider and apple juice and several malt whiskies. But don't be misled into thinking this place is in any way old fashioned. In fact, the candlelit bare-boards restaurant though rustic in its décor is chatty and alive with customers and the style of dining is completely up to date. French windows open from the restaurant to a conservatory and garden. Sissinghurst Gardens (National Trust) are nearby.

🍴 Excellent (if not cheap) food changes daily but might include salmon and smoked haddock fishcake, poached pear on goats cheese and walnut salad, baked mushrooms topped with caramelised red onions and goats cheese, duck leg confit, herb couscous with balsamic roasted vegetables, sweet chilli glazed salmon with courgette and aubergine ragout, sausage and mash with port and red onion gravy, and puddings such as blueberry and almond tart and sticky toffee pudding. *Benchmark main dish: rack of lamb £19.95. Two-course evening meal £25.00.*

Free house ~ Licensee Craig Smith ~ Real ale ~ Bar food (12-2(2.30 Sat, Sun), 6.30-9(9.30 Fri, Sat)) ~ Restaurant ~ (01580) 291472 ~ Children welcome ~ Dogs allowed in bar ~ Open 11.30-3.30, 5.30-11; 12-4, 6-10.30 Sun ~ www.thethreechimneys.co.uk *Recommended by Mrs J Ekins-Daukes, Bill Adie, Anthony Longden, Gordon and Margaret Ormondroyd, Malcolm and Barbara Southwell, Derek Thomas, the Didler, Bob and Margaret Holder, Jonathan and Ann Tross, Tony Swanson, Peter Chapman, M P Mackenzie, John Evans*

BOUGH BEECH
Wheatsheaf ♀

TQ4846 Map 3

B2027, S of reservoir; TN8 7NU

Former hunting lodge with lots to look at, fine range of local drinks, popular food, and plenty of seats in appealing garden

This ancient ivy-clad building is thought to have originated as a 15th-c royal hunting lodge, and is full of characterful historic detail. Its neat central bar and long front bar (which has an attractive old settle carved with wheatsheaves) have unusually high ceilings with lofty oak timbers, a screen of standing timbers and a revealed king post. Divided from the central bar by two more rows of standing timbers – one formerly an exterior wall – are the snug and another bar. On the walls and above the massive stone fireplaces, there are quite a few horns and heads as well as african masks, a sword from Fiji, crocodiles, stuffed birds, swordfish spears and a matapee. Look out, too, for the piece of 1607 graffiti, 'Foxy Holamby', who is thought to have been a whimsical local squire. Thoughtful touches include piles of smart magazines, board games, tasty nibbles and winter chestnuts to roast. Harveys Best, Westerham Brewery Grasshopper and a guest are on handpump and they've three ciders (including one from local Biddenden), a decent wine list, several malt whiskies, summer Pimms and winter mulled wine. Outside is appealing, too, with plenty of seats, flowerbeds and fruit trees in the sheltered side and back gardens. Shrubs help divide the garden into various areas, so it doesn't feel too crowded even when it's full.

Bar food (there may be a wait at busy times) might include king prawns wrapped in filo, duck and port pâté, eggs benedict, omelettes, salads, sausages and bubble and squeak, mexican bean burger, poached smoked haddock with parsley cheese sauce and poached egg, beef burger, and puddings such as panna cotta, bread and butter pudding and cheesecake. *Benchmark main dish: toad in the hole £9.75. Two-course evening meal £19.00.*

Enterprise ~ Lease Liz and David Currie ~ Real ale ~ Bar food (12-10) ~ (01732) 700254 ~ Dogs welcome ~ Open 12-11.30(midnight Sat, 11 Sun) *Recommended by John Branston, Nigel and Jean Eames, Kevin Thomas, Nina Randall, Bob and Margaret Holder, John Saville, Conor McGaughey, Pat and Tony Martin, Linda and Pauline, Martin and Sue Day*

BROOKLAND
Royal Oak 🍴 🛏

TQ9825 Map 3

Just off A259 Rye–New Romney; High Street; TN29 9QR

Lovely old building with gently modernised rooms, delicious food and seats in garden; comfortable bedrooms

It's so rewarding to find such a haven of civilisation tucked away like this on Romney Marsh. It's the sort of place where every detail is given careful attention, while at the same time sensitive alterations to the 17th-c building have ensured that it retains an attractive timeless feel. The bar is light and airy with big windows, one nice old pew and leather upholstered chairs around oak tables on flagstones, oak boards and bricks. Locals pop in to sit on the high bar chairs by the granite-topped counter for a chat and a pint: Adnams Best, Harveys and Woodfordes Wherry on handpump and 17 wines by the glass. The friendly landlord knows a lot about the local area and his equestrian interests are manifest in a lovely set of racing watercolours and a couple of signed photographs on the lime white wall panelling in the bar, and in a rather special set of Cecil Aldin prints displayed in the beamed restaurant (with its well spaced tables and big inglenook fireplace). From here, french windows open on to a terrace with metal chairs and there are picnic-sets in the narrow garden beyond and quaint views of the ancient church and graveyard next door; background music and a woodburning stove.

Lovingly sourced and prepared food (often local) might include coquilles st jacques, three scotch quail eggs, baked goats cheese on a croûton with sweet chilli sauce, roast lamb, roast scallops with chilli, ginger, garlic and soy butter, braised shoulder of vension with smoked bacon lardons, chestnuts and wild mushrooms in madeira sauce, spiced tomato and lentil moussaka; they do spit roasts in the inglenook on Wednesday evenings, which readers tell us are delicious. *Benchmark main dish: roast pork belly and crackling with apple sauce and red wine gravy £14.50. Two-course evening meal £20.35.*

Enterprise ~ Lease David Rhys Jones ~ Real ale ~ Bar food (12-2(2.30 Sat, Sun), 6.30-9(9.30 Fri, Sat)) ~ Restaurant ~ (01797) 344215 ~ No children under 14 in evening restaurant or bedrooms ~ Dogs allowed in bar and bedrooms ~ Open 12-3, 6-11; closed Sun evening and Mon ~ Bedrooms: /£95B ~ www.royaloakbrookland.co.uk
Recommended by B and M Kendall, John Peppitt, Sara Fulton, Roger Baker, Colin and Louise English, Kevin Thomas, Nina Randall, Stephen and Jean Curtis, Alec and Joan Laurence, Mike Gorton, M P Mackenzie

BROOKLAND
TQ9724   Map 3

Woolpack £

On A259 from Rye, about a mile before Brookland, take the first right turn signposted Midley where the main road bends sharp left, just after the expanse of Walland Marsh; OS Sheet 189 map reference 977244; TN29 9TJ

15th-c pub with simple furnishings, massive inglenook fireplace, big helpings of tasty food and large garden

Being fairly near Camber Sands, this aged place can get busy at weekends and during the school holidays with families looking for a good value meal. Steeped in the atmosphere of days gone by, it's said to have been the haunt of local smugglers. Its ancient entrance lobby has a lovely uneven brick floor and black-painted pine-panelled walls and, to the right, the simple quarry-tiled main bar has basic cushioned plank seats in the massive inglenook fireplace and a painted wood-effect bar counter hung with lots of water jugs. Low-beamed ceilings incorporate some very early ships' timbers (maybe 12th c) thought to be from local shipwrecks. A long elm table has shove-ha'penny carved into one end and there are other old and newer wall benches, chairs at mixed tables with flowers and candles and photographs of locals on the walls. The two pub cats, Liquorice and Charlie Girl, are often toasting themselves around the log fire. The dining room to the left is traditional with carpets and dark wheelback chairs; background music and games machine. Shepherd Neame Master Brew and Spitfire and a seasonal brew on handpump. There are plenty of picnic-sets under parasols in the garden, and it's all nicely lit up in the evenings.

Generous helpings of pubby food include sandwiches and baguettes, filled baked potatoes, ploughman's, local scallops, dressed crab, half a pint of prawns, mussels, brie and hazelnut wellington, spare ribs, local lamb, battered cod, generous moules marinière, mixed grill, and puddings such as eton mess, cinnamon and honey steamed pudding and chocolate brownies. *Benchmark main dish: steak and ale pie £10.95. Two-course evening meal £24.45.*

Shepherd Neame ~ Tenant Scott Balcomb ~ Real ale ~ Bar food (12-2.30, 6-9; all day
Sat, Sun, bank holidays, school holidays) ~ Restaurant ~ (01797) 344321 ~ Children
welcome ~ Dogs welcome ~ Open 11-3, 6-11; 12-11 Sat, Sun, bank holidays, school
holidays *Recommended by John Prescott, Colin and Louise English, Mr and Mrs Price, Pat and
Tony Martin, B and M Kendall*

GOUDHURST   TQ7037   Map 3
Green Cross
East off A21 on to A262 (Station Road); TN17 1HA

**Down-to-earth bar and more formal restaurant specialising in fresh
seafood and fish**

The little two-roomed front bar here is relaxed and pubby with
stripped wooden floors, dark wood furnishings, wine bottles on
windowsills, hop-draped beams, brass jugs on the mantelshelf above
the fire, and a few plush bar stools by the counter where they serve
Harveys Best on handpump; background music. Attractive in an old-
fashioned sort of way, the back dining room is a little more formal, with
flowers on tables that are set for dining, dark beams in cream walls and
country paintings for sale. You can sit out on a small terrace at the side
of the pub.

The emphasis here is on fresh seafood and fish but there are pubby dishes too.
You can eat from the restaurant menu in the bar: filled baguettes, potted pork,
fish soup with rouille and gruyère cheese, smoked salmon carved to order, cornish
cock crab, oysters, smoked eel, sausage and mash, steak, kidney and mushroom
pie, moules frites, fish pie, linguine with queen scallops, duck cassoulet, halibut
with cheese sauce, paella, dover sole, skate, lobster thermidor, and puddings such
as mulberry crème brûlée, raspberry meringue roulade, zabaglione and a tempting
range of ice-creams. *Benchmark main dish: cod and chips £13.10. Two-course
evening meal £29.00.*

Free house ~ Licensees Lou and Caroline Lizzi ~ Real ale ~ Bar food (12-2.30, 7-9.30) ~
Restaurant ~ (01580) 211200 ~ Children welcome ~ Open 11-3, 6-11; 11-3 Sun ~
www.greencrossinn.co.uk *Recommended by Anthony Longden*

ICKHAM   TR2258   Map 3
Duke William
Off A257 E of Canterbury; The Street; CT3 1QP

**Relaxing family-owned village pub with airy bar, dining conservatory,
enjoyable bar food and plenty of seats outside; bedrooms**

There's a very enjoyable pubby atmosphere in the big spreading bar
of this friendly village pub. It has huge new oak beams and stripped
joists, a fine mix of seats from settles to high-backed cushioned dining
chairs, dark wheelback and bentwood chairs around all sorts of wooden
tables on the stripped wooden floor, a log fire with a couple of settles and
a low barrel table in front of it, a central bar counter with high stools and
brass coat hooks and a snug little area with one long table, black leather
high-backed dining chairs, a flat-screen TV and a computer if you need
it; daily papers, quiet background music, cheerful modern paintings and
large hop bines. Brains IPA and a guest such as Shepherd Neame Master
Brew on handpump alongside some decent wines. Staff are chatty and
attentive. A low-ceilinged dining room leads off to the left with dark
wood chairs, tables and more cushioned settles and paintings and
mirrors on the walls. At the back of the pub, there's a light-filled dining

conservatory with all manner of interesting paintings, prints and heraldry on the walls and similar furniture on the stone floor. Doors lead from here to a big terrace with a covered area to one side, plenty of wooden and metal tables and chairs, and a lawn with picnic-table sets, some swings and a slide.

Tasty bar food includes filled baguettes, chicken liver pâté, whitebait, garlic prawns and scallops with chorizo, steak and ale pie, calves liver and bacon, slow-roasted belly of pork with cider and apple sauce, and chicken with tarragon and mushrooms, and puddings such as chocolate fondant; there's also a good value two-course lunch menu and Sunday roasts (booking advised). *Benchmark main dish: beef and ale pie £10.95. Two-course evening meal £13.00.*

Free house ~ Licensees Louise and Nicola White ~ Real ale ~ Bar food (12-3, 6-9.30) ~ Restaurant ~ (01227) 721308 ~ Children welcome ~ Dogs allowed in bar ~ Open 11-11(midnight Sat, 10 Sun) ~ Bedrooms: /£70S ~ www.dukewilliam.biz
Recommended by David Heath, Dr Kevan Tucker, Sarah Flynn, Paul Goldman

IVY HATCH
TQ5854   Map 3
Plough ♀
High Cross Road; village signed off A227 N of Tonbridge; TN15 0NL

Country pub with landlord-cooked food, real ales and seats in landscaped garden

Close to Ightham Mote, this is a tile-hung village pub with a friendly, relaxed atmosphere. The various rooms have light wooden flooring, leather chesterfields grouped around an open fire, quite a mix of cushioned dining chairs around various tables, and high bar chairs by the wooden-topped bar counter where they keep Royal Tunbridge Wells Dipper, Royal and Sovereign on handpump and quite a few wines by the glass. There's also a conservatory; background music and board games. Seats in the landscaped garden are surrounded by cob trees; there are some very rewarding nearby walks through orchards and woodlands and along the greensand escarpment around One Tree Hill.

Using seasonal local produce, the highly thought of food might include sandwiches, honey-roast ham hock and chicken terrine with celeriac remoulade, mussels in white wine, cream, garlic, shallots and herbs, cheese and ham omelette, sausages with wholegrain mustard mash and red onion marmalade, roast butternut squash, spinach and confit garlic risotto with parmesan, bass fillet with puy lentils, garlic creamed spinach and toasted almonds, roast rack of pork with baked apple and red wine jus, and puddings such as vanilla rice pudding with berry compote and chocolate fondant with chocolate sauce and clotted cream. *Benchmark main dish: herefordshire rump steak £14.50. Two-course evening meal £20.00.*

Free house ~ Licensee Miles Medes ~ Real ale ~ Bar food (12-3), 6-9, also weekday coffee and cakes and brunch from 9am; 12-5.30 Sun) ~ Restaurant ~ (01732) 810100 ~ Children welcome ~ Open 9-3, 6-11; 10am-11pm Sat; 10am-6pm Sun ~ www.theploughivyhatch.co.uk *Recommended by LM, Gordon and Margaret Ormondroyd, R and S Bentley, B and M Kendall, Bob and Margaret Holder, Derek Thomas*

The letters and figures after the name of each town are its Ordnance Survey map reference. *How to use the Guide* at the beginning of the book explains how it helps you find a pub, in road atlases or large-scale maps, as well as in our own maps.

LANGTON GREEN
TQ5439 Map 3

Hare ♀

A264 W of Tunbridge Wells; TN3 0JA

Interestingly decorated Edwardian pub with a fine choice of drinks and popular food

The décor at this roomy mock-Tudor former hotel is more or less in period with the building, which is dated at 1901. Its high-ceilinged rooms have plenty of light flooding through large windows (especially in the front bar where drinkers tend to gather) dark-painted dados below light walls that are covered in old photographs and prints, 1930s oak furniture, light brown carpet and turkish-style rugs on stained wooden floors, old romantic pastels and a huge collection of chamber-pots hanging from beams. Greene King IPA, Abbot alongside a couple of guests from brewers such as Titanic are on handpump alongside two dozen wines by the glass, over 60 whiskies and a fine choice of vodkas and other spirits; board games. French windows open on to a big terrace with pleasant views of the tree-ringed village green. Parking is limited and on the road so best to arrive early.

From a frequently changing menu, interesting bistro-style food might include trout pâté with pickled vegetable salad, goats cheese, mango and pine nut filo pastry with red pepper and hazelnut salad, soy-marinated salmon fillet with pea shoot, radish and stem ginger salad and crispy noodles, crab linguine, ploughman's, braised lamb shoulder with goats cheese and herb mash and ratatouille, fried chicken breast with tuscan bean salad, battered haddock, thai red vegetable curry, chicken, leek and ham pie, and puddings such as sherry trifle, rhubarb and strawberry crumble and glazed lemon tart with raspberry sorbet. *Benchmark main dish: malaysian fish stew with coconut rice £12.95. Two-course evening meal £19.00.*

Brunning & Price ~ Manager Rob Broadbent ~ Real ale ~ Bar food (12-9.30(10 Fri, Sat; 9 Sun)) ~ Restaurant ~ (01892) 862419 ~ Children welcome (away from bar after 6pm) ~ Dogs allowed in bar ~ Open 12-11(midnight Sat, 10.30 Sun) ~ www.hare-tunbridgewells.co.uk *Recommended by William Ruxton, Chris Flynn, Wendy Jones*

NEWNHAM
TQ9557 Map 3

George

The Street; village signed from A2 W of Ospringe, outside Faversham; ME9 0LL

Village pub with open-plan rooms, a fair choice of drinks and food, and seats in spacious garden; pleasant walks nearby

This traditional village pub is very usefully located for walks in this remote-feeling part of the North Downs. The series of spreading open-plan rooms have hop-strung beams, polished floorboards, stripped brickwork, candles and lamps on handsome tables, a mix of dining chairs and settles, and two inglenook fireplaces (one with a woodburning stove). Shepherd Neame Master Brew and a seasonal beer on handpump and several wines by the glass. There are picnic-sets in the spacious tree-sheltered garden.

With the iPhone Good Pub Guide App, you can use the iPhone's camera to send us pictures of pubs you visit – outside or inside.

🍴 Well liked food includes sandwiches, chicken liver parfait with home-made chutney, thai-spiced mussels with coconut and coriander, steak in ale pudding, mushrooms with thyme and slow-roasted tomatoes on toast, steak burger with bacon or cheese topping in a buttermilk bun, slow-braised and shredded lamb shoulder in a puff pastry box, rosemary-scented whole trout, and puddings such as warm chocolate brownie with vanilla ice-cream and fresh berries and meringue. *Benchmark main dish: roast cod loin with a herb crust on pea purée £12.95. Two-course evening meal £17.50.*

Shepherd Neame ~ Tenants Paul and Lisa Burton ~ Real ale ~ Bar food (12.30-2.30, 7-9.30; 12-4.30 Sun; not Sun evening) ~ Restaurant ~ (01795) 890237 ~ Children welcome ~ Open 11.30-3.30, 6.30-11.30; 11.30-6.30 Sun; closed Sun evening ~ www.georgeinnnewnham.co.uk *Recommended by Richard Gibbs*

PENSHURST   TQ5142   Map 3

Bottle House 🍴 ♀

GOOD PUB GUIDE

Coldharbour Lane; leaving Penshurst SW on B2188 turn right at Smarts Hill signpost, then bear right towards Chiddingstone and Cowden; keep straight on; TN11 8ET

Low-beamed, connected bars in country pub, friendly service, chatty atmosphere, real ales and decent wines, popular bar food and sunny terrace; nearby walks

'Everything pleases,' says one reader about his visit to this cottagey dining pub, which seems to have cosy woodwork everywhere. There are standing timbers separating the open-plan rooms into intimate areas, all sorts of beams and joists (one or two of the especially low ones are leather padded), pine wall boards, and bar stools ranged along the timber clad copper-topped counter – Harveys Best and Larkins Traditional on handpump, a local bottled ale, local apple juice and nearly a dozen wines by the glass from a good list. A nice hotchpotch of wooden tables (most with fresh flowers and candles) and chairs are fairly closely spaced on dark boards or coir and warmed by a woodburning stove; background music. There are photographs of the pub and local scenes on the walls (some of which are stripped stone). The sunny, brick-paved terrace has green-painted picnic-sets under parasols and some olive trees in white pots; parking is limited. Good surrounding walks in this charming area of rolling country.

🍴 From a monthly changing seasonal menu featuring local produce and a daily changing specials board, popular bar food might include fried scallops with pea purée, black pudding and red pepper coulis, smoked mackerel and cream cheese pâté, beef carpaccio with goats cheese and pecan salad with cardamom vinaigrette, black bream fillet with salsa verde, roast cherry tomatoes and lemon mash, grilled duck breast with port and thyme jus with spinach and dauphinoise potatoes, steak and kidney pudding, butternut squash, spinach and goats cheese lasagne, and puddings such as vanilla baked yoghurt with winter berry jelly and honeycomb and chocolate chip and Baileys brioche bread and butter pudding. *Benchmark main dish: belly of pork £12.95. Two-course evening meal £19.50.*

Free house ~ Licensee Paul Hammond ~ Real ale ~ Bar food (12-10(9 Sun)) ~ Restaurant ~ (01892) 870306 ~ Children welcome ~ Dogs allowed in bar ~ Open 11-11(10.30 Sun) ~ www.thebottlehouseinnpenshurst.co.uk *Recommended by Sue and Mike Todd, Heather and Dick Martin, R and S Bentley, Christian Mole, Derek Thomas, Bob and Margaret Holder, Martin and Sue Day, Richard Tilbrook, Tina and David Woods-Taylor*

PLUCKLEY

Dering Arms ⑪ ♀ ⇢

Pluckley station, which is signposted from B2077; or follow Station Road (left turn off Smarden Road in centre of Pluckley) for about 1.3 miles S, through Pluckley Thorne; TN27 0RR

Fine fish dishes plus other good food in handsome building, with a stylish main bar, carefully chosen wines, and roaring log fire; comfortable bedrooms

James Buss, the long-standing landlord here, injects individuality and maintains sound traditional standards at this striking pub. Formerly a hunting lodge and part of the Dering Estate, it was built in the 1840s as a mini replica of the manor house. Hence its imposing frontage, mullioned arched windows and dutch gables. The high-ceilinged and stylishly plain main bar has a solid country feel with a variety of wooden furniture on the flagstone floors, a roaring log fire in the great fireplace, country prints and some fishing rods. The smaller half-panelled back bar has similar dark wood furnishings, and an extension to this area has a woodburning stove, comfortable armchairs, sofas and a grand piano; board games. Though emphasis tends to be on the food here, the bar is characterful and comfortable and they do keep a beer named for the pub from Goachers on handpump as well as a very good wine list of around 100 wines; 50 malt whiskies, 20 brandies and an occasional local cider. Classic car meetings (James has a couple of classics) are held here on the second Sunday of the month. Readers very much enjoy staying here – and the breakfasts are excellent.

Beautifully prepared fish is the thing here – the landlord buys straight from the boats in Folkestone, and oversees the kitchen. Dishes might include half a pint of prawns, oysters, provençale fish soup, whole crab salad, fried scallops with basil spaghetti and saffron sauce, fillet of black bream with marsh samphire and beurre blanc and a seafood platter for two (24 hours' notice). There's also a short bar menu that includes ploughman's, coq au vin and sausages and mash. Puddings might include orange in caramel and Grand Marnier, raspberry and apple sherry trifle and tarte tatin. *Benchmark main dish: bass fillet with minted leeks and bacon and red wine sauce £14.95. Two-course evening meal £22.00.*

Free house ~ Licensee James Buss ~ Real ale ~ Bar food (12-2.30, 7-9; 12-3 Sun) ~ Restaurant ~ (01233) 840371 ~ Children welcome ~ Dogs allowed in bar ~ Open 11.30-3, 6-11; 12-4 Sun; closed Sun evening ~ Bedrooms: £60(£80S)/£70(£90S) ~ www.deringarms.com *Recommended by John Prescott, Simon Collett-Jones, Colin and Louise English, Stephen and Jean Curtis, Richard Balkwill, Lee and Liz Potter*

SEVENOAKS

White Hart ♀

Tonbridge Road (A225 S, past Knole); TN13 1SG

Well run and bustling old coaching inn with a civilised atmosphere in many bar rooms, a thoughtful choice of drinks, enjoyable modern food and friendly, helpful staff

This seemingly endless early 18th-c coaching inn is popular with both drinkers and diners. Its many rooms are interconnected by open doorways and steps and there are several open fires and woodburning stoves. All manner of nice wooden dining chairs around tables of every size sit on warming rugs or varnished bare floorboards, the cream walls are hung with lots of prints and old photographs (many of local scenes or schools) and there are fresh flowers and plants, daily papers to read, board games and a bustling, chatty atmosphere. Friendly, efficient staff serve Brunning & Price Original (brewed for the pub by Phoenix), Fullers London Pride, Harveys Best, Old Dairy Blue Top and three guests from brewers such as Belhaven, Sharps and Westerham, and they keep over 25 good wines by the glass, a fair choice of ciders and over 75 whiskies. It's all very civilised. At the front of the building there are picnic-sets under parasols.

Interesting and enjoyable modern bar food includes stuffed mushroom with marinated figs, soy-marinated chicken skewer with bulgar wheat salad, ham and black pudding bubble and squeak cakes with mandarin salad, ploughman's, sausage and mash, sage-crusted pork escalope with parmentier potatoes and apple and watercress salad, guinea fowl with wild mushroom sauce, gorgonzola, courgette and lemon tagliatelle with walnut and fig bruschetta, fried bass fillet with piri piri sauce, harissa couscous and fennel salad, battered haddock, venison, rabbit and pheasant casserole with herb dumplings, and puddings such as rhubarb fool with rhubarb lemonade and chocolate biscotti, chocolate and macadamia tart with orange mascarpone and sticky toffee pudding. *Benchmark main dish: featherblade of beef with bacon dumplings £12.95. Two-course evening meal £19.00.*

Brunning & Price ~ Manager Chris Little ~ Real ale ~ Bar food (12-10(9.30 Sun)) ~ (01732) 452022 ~ Children welcome away from bar ~ Dogs allowed in bar ~ Open 12-11; 12-10.30 Sun ~ www.bandp.co.uk/whitehart *Recommended by Richard Green, Tracy Collins, Martin and Sue Day, Gordon and Margaret Ormondroyd, Mrs G Marlow*

SPELDHURST   TQ5541 Map 3

George & Dragon ♀

Village signed from A264 W of Tunbridge Wells; TN3 0NN

Fine old pub, beams, flagstones and huge fireplaces, local beers, good food and attractive outside seating areas

The rambling interior of this half-timbered building, which is based around a medieval manorial hall, conjures up a great sense of antiquity with its ancient beams and winter log fire burning in a huge sandstone fireplace in the main room. To the right of the rather splendid entrance hall (where there's a water bowl for thirsty dogs), the half-panelled room is set for dining with a mix of old wheelback and other dining chairs and a cushioned wall pew, a few little pictures on the walls, horsebrasses on one huge beam and a sizeable bar counter with Harveys Best, Larkins Traditional Ale and an ale from Westerham Brewery on handpump, 16 wines by the glass and local organic cordials; friendly, efficient staff. A doorway leads through to another dining room with similar furnishings and another big inglenook. Those wanting a drink and a chat tend to head to the room on the left of the entrance (though people do eat in here too), where there's a woodburning stove in a small fireplace, high-winged cushioned settles and various wooden tables and dining chairs on the wood-strip floor; background music. There's also an aged-feeling upstairs restaurant. In front of the pub are teak tables, chairs and benches on a nicely planted gravel terrace, while at the back a covered area has big church candles on more wooden tables and a lower terrace with seats around a 300-year-old olive tree; more attractive planting here, and some modern sculpture.

Enjoyable – if not cheap – bar food might include starters such as seared pigeon breast with puy lentil and smoked bacon, game terrine, salmon gravadlax, main courses such as sausage and mash, steak sandwich, venison stew with herb dumplings, mushroom risotto, confit duck leg with orange marmalade, fried bass fillet with poached fennel, roast tomatoes and clams, and puddings such as plum crumble with cinnamon ice-cream, crème brûlée and chocolate brownie with honeycomb ice-cream. As a 12.5% service charge is added to all bills it's best to pay for your drinks at the bar. *Benchmark main dish: roast belly of pork £13.50. Two-course evening meal £25.60.*

Free house ~ Licensee Julian Leefe-Griffiths ~ Real ale ~ Bar food (12-2.30(3 Sat, 3.30 Sun), 7-9.30; not Sun evening) ~ Restaurant ~ (01892) 863125 ~ Children welcome ~ Dogs allowed in bar ~ Open 12-11(11.30 Sat, 10.30 Sun) ~ www.speldhurst.com
Recommended by John Redfern, Christian Mole, Jamie and Sue May, Gordon and Margaret Ormondroyd, Derek Thomas

---

STALISFIELD GREEN
TQ9552   Map 3

Plough 🍺
Off A252 in Charing; ME13 0HY

Ancient country pub with rambling rooms, open fires, interesting local ales, smashing bar food and friendly licensees

The genuinely cheerful licensees at this ancient country pub – said to date back to 1350 – put in plenty of loving care to make it a winner, and it's the combination of terrific food and local beers served in a lovely cosy atmosphere that makes it so appealing. Its several hop-draped rooms, relaxed and easy-going, ramble around, up and down, with open fires in brick fireplaces, interesting pictures on green- or maroon-painted walls, books on shelves, farmhouse and other nice old dining chairs around a mix of pine or dark wood tables on bare boards and the odd milk churn dotted about. Dixie, the pub cat, likes to find a cosy lap to lie on. Beers come from kentish brewers such as Gadds, Goachers, Old Dairy and Whitstable and they stock kentish lagers, wines, water, fruit juices and cider. The pub appears to perch up on its own on the downs amid farmland, and picnic-sets on a simple terrace overlook the village green below. They have a site for caravans.

Using seasonal fruit and vegetables direct from local farms, local meat and game (they hang their own) and making their own sausages, ketchup, bread and ice-creams, very good food from a daily changing menu might include curried parsnip soup with sesame straws, mussels steamed in cider, jerusalem artichoke and hazelnut faggot with crushed squash, sausage and mash with sage crumb, fish and chips, mutton pie, roast pork belly with bramley sauce, smoked haddock with poached egg and mustard sauce, and puddings such as treacle tart with orange ice-cream and rhubarb and ginger trifle. *Benchmark main dish: shin of beef pie £13.50. Two-course evening meal £21.25.*

Free house ~ Licensees Robert and Amy Lloyd ~ Real ale ~ Bar food (12-2.30(3 Sun), 6-9; 12-9 Sat) ~ Restaurant ~ (01795) 890256 ~ Children welcome away from main bar ~ Dogs allowed in bar ~ Live music Fri monthly ~ Open 12-3, 6-11; 12-12 Sat(6 Sun) Sat; closed Mon, Tues lunchtime, Sun evening ~ www.stalisfieldgreen.com
Recommended by N R White

STOWTING
TR1241   Map 3

Tiger 🍺
3.7 miles from M20 junction 11; B2068 N, then left at Stowting signpost, straight across crossroads, then fork left after 0.25 miles and pub is on right; coming from N, follow Brabourne, Wye, Ashford signpost to right at fork, then turn left towards Posting and Lyminge at T junction; TN25 6BA

Peaceful pub with helpful staff, traditional furnishings, well liked food, several real ales and open fires; good walking country

Nicely down-to-earth and cheerily friendly, this 17th-c inn is cosily traditional with a relaxed mix of wooden tables and chairs and built-in cushioned wall seats on wooden floorboards and woodburning stoves at each end of the bar. There's an unpretentious array of books, board games, candles in bottles, brewery memorabilia and paintings, lots of hops and some faded rugs on the stone floor towards the back of the pub. As well as Shepherd Neame Master Brew three or four guests from local brewers such as Hot Fuzz, Old Dairy Brewery and lots of malt whiskies, several wines by the glass, local Biddenden cider and local fruit juice. On warmer days you can sit out on the front terrace, and there are plenty of nearby walks along the Wye Downs and North Downs Way.

Enjoyable bar food from a daily changing menu, using seasonal local produce, might include seared king scallops with white onion purée, crab with chilli crème fraîche and mango salsa, caramelised goats cheese with grilled strawberries, red onion, mushroom and gorgonzola tart, lemon and caper dover sole, chicken, ham and leek pie, tuna steak niçoise and sausage and mash. *Benchmark main dish: pork belly with caramelisd apple £14.95. Two-course evening meal £20.60.*

Free house ~ Licensees Emma Oliver and Benn Jarvis ~ Real ale ~ Bar food (12(4 Mon)-9(9.30 Fri, Sat, 8 Sun)) ~ Restaurant ~ (01303) 862130 ~ Children welcome ~ Dogs allowed in bar ~ Open 12(4 Mon)-11; closed Mon lunchtime, Tues ~ www.tigerinn.co.uk *Recommended by Matthew Lonergan, Michael Butler, Julie and Bill Ryan, Rob Jones, N R White, Rob and Catherine Dunster, Olly Tolhurst, Paul Goldman*

TUNBRIDGE WELLS   TQ5839   Map 3
Sankeys
Mount Ephraim (A26 just N of junction with A267); TN4 8AA

Pubby street-level bar, informal downstairs brasserie, real ales and good wines, chatty atmosphere and super fish dishes

If it's the fantastic fish menu you're after at this well known place, head down the steps by the entrance to the chatty and informal restaurant, which has an oyster bar and lobster tank on display. Unfussy bistro-style décor includes big mirrors on rustic stripped brick walls and pews or chairs around sturdy tables on rustic flagstones. French windows open on to an inviting suntrap deck with wicker and chrome chairs and wooden tables. The laid-back street-level bar is light and airy with comfortably worn, informal leather sofas and pews around all sorts of tables on bare wooden boards. The walls are covered with a fine collection of rare enamel signs and antique brewery mirrors as well as old prints, framed cigarette cards and lots of old wine bottles and soda siphons. Goachers, Westerham Brewery Joeys Bite and a guest from a brewery such as Meantime are on handpump, alongside fruit beers, american and british craft beers and several wines by the glass from a good list; big flat-screen TV for sports (not football, and it's very busy here when there's a major rugby match) and background music.

Very good value pubby food at lunchtime in the street-level bar includes sandwiches, fish and chips, sausage and mash, malaysian fish stew, fish sharing platter, goats cheese salad and thai beef salad, and puddings such as treacle tart and sticky toffee pudding. Downstairs, the emphasis is on fish: oysters, pickled cockles, fresh anchovies, potted shrimps, local lemon sole, plaice, john dory, black bream, lobster and huge cornish cock crabs. Sunday roasts and summer barbecues. *Benchmark main dish: mussels £10.00. Two-course evening meal £21.00.*

Free house ~ Licensee Matthew Sankey ~ Real ale ~ Bar food (12-3(4 Sun), 6-10(8 Sun, Mon)) ~ Restaurant ~ (01892) 511422 ~ Children welcome ~ Dogs allowed in bar ~ Open 12-1am(3am Sat) ~ www.sankeys.co.uk *Recommended by Laurence Smith, Alan Franck, Gerry and Rosemary Dobson, Chris Flynn, Wendy Jones, Jamie and Sue May*

ULCOMBE TQ8550 Map 3
Pepper Box

Fairbourne Heath; signposted from A20 in Harrietsham, or follow Ulcombe signpost from A20, then turn left at crossroads with sign to pub, then right at next minor crossroads; ME17 1LP

Friendly country pub with lovely log fire, well liked food, fair choice of drinks, and seats in a pretty garden

Nicely placed on high ground above the Weald, this cosy and traditional country inn is a friendly place with helpful licensees. The homely bar has standing timbers and a few low beams (some hung with hops), copper kettles and pans on window sills and two leather sofas by the splendid inglenook fireplace (nice horsebrasses on the bressumer beam) with its lovely log fire. A side area, furnished more functionally for eating, extends into the opened-up beamed dining room with a range in another inglenook and more horsebrasses. Shepherd Neame Master Brew and Spitfire and a seasonal beer on handpump, with local apple juice and several wines by the glass; background music. The two cats are called Murphy and Jim. There's a hop-covered terrace and a garden with shrubs and fine views. The name of the pub refers to the pepperbox pistol – an early type of revolver with numerous barrels; the village church is worth a look and the Greensand Way footpath runs close by.

Enjoyable food might include sandwiches and filled baguettes, duck liver parfait with red onion chutney, scallops with black pudding and apple purée, ham with tomato, mushrooms and an egg, local sausages with mash and onion gravy, chilli con carne, potato gnocchi with asparagus, peas, parmesan and sage butter, herby poussin with rosemary-sautéed potatoes, lamb chops with wild garlic, sauce verde and celeriac and potato gratin, peppered duck breast with a smoked bacon, wild mushroom and masala ragout, and puddings like white chocolate and raspberry cheesecake and vanilla pannacotta with plum compote. *Benchmark main dish: steak and kidney pudding £11.50. Two-course evening meal £19.00.*

Shepherd Neame ~ Tenant Sarah Pemble ~ Real ale ~ Bar food (12-2.15(3 Sun), 6.30-9.30; not Sun evening) ~ Restaurant ~ (01622) 842558 ~ Dogs allowed in bar ~ Open 11-3, 6-midnight; 11-11 Sat; 12-5 Sun; 11-3, 6-midnight Sat in in winter; closed Sun evening ~ www.thepepperboxinn.co.uk *Recommended by Alec and Joan Laurence, Malcolm and Barbara Southwell, Kevin Thomas, Nina Randall, Martin and Sue Day*

WHITSTABLE TR1066 Map 3
Pearsons Arms

Sea Wall off Oxford Street after road splits into one-way system; public parking on left as road divides; CT5 1BT

Seaside pub with an emphasis on interesting food, several local ales and good mix of customers

Always busy with a good mix of both locals and visitors, this weatherboarded pub overlooks a pebble beach and the sea. The two front bars are divided by a central chimney and have cushioned settles, captain's chairs and leather armchairs on the stripped-wood floor, driftwood walls and big flower arrangements on the bar counter where they serve Harveys Best, Hop Back Summer Lightning, Ramsgate Gadds No 3, and Whitstable East India Pale Ale on handpump; background music. A cosy lower room has trompe l'oeil bookshelves and a couple of big chesterfields and dining chairs around plain tables on the stone floor. Up a couple of flights of stairs, the restaurant has sea views, mushroom paintwork, contemporary wallpaper, more driftwood, and church chairs and pine tables on nice wide floorboards.

Quite a choice of interesting food might include nibbles such as deep-fried pigs ears with gribiche sauce and calamari with saffron aioli, marinated mackerel fillet with apple purée and seaweed dressing, ham hock ballotine with piccalilli, beer-battered cod with triple-cooked chips, mushy peas and tartare sauce, shepherd's pie, free-range chicken, crayfish and tarragon stargazy pie, salmon fishcake with sorrel sauce, slow-cooked venison in red wine, smoked bacon and juniper, local lamb shoulder with orange, capers and sultanas, and pudding such as steamed lemon sponge with berry compote and vanilla custard and crème brûlée. *Benchmark main dish: fish and chips £14.95. Two-course evening meal £27.00.*

Enterprise ~ Lease Richard Phillips ~ Real ale ~ Bar food (12-3.30, 6.30-10; not Mon, not Tues evening) ~ Restaurant ~ (01227) 272005 ~ Children welcome ~ Dogs allowed in bar ~ live music Tues and Sun ~ Open 12-midnight ~ www.pearsonsarmsbyrichardphillips.co.uk *Recommended by Richard Mason, Adrian Johnson, John Coatsworth*

Also Worth a Visit in Kent

Besides the fully inspected pubs, you might like to try these pubs that have been recommended to us and described by readers. Do tell us what you think of them: feedback@goodguides.com

ADDINGTON TQ6559
Angel (01732) 842117
Just off M20, junction 4; Addington Green; ME19 5BB 14th-c pub in classic village-green setting, olde-worlde décor with beams, scrubbed tables and big fireplaces, enjoyable food from sandwiches/ wraps and traditional things up including weekday set menus, fair choice of beers from barrel-fronted counter, lots of wines by the glass, good friendly service, stables restaurant, live music Fri; tables out at front and back, two bedrooms. *(Gill and Keith Croxton, A N Bance)*

APPLEDORE TQ9529
Black Lion (01233) 758206
The Street; TN26 2BU Compact 1930s village pub with bustling atmosphere, very welcoming helpful staff, good generous food all day from simple sandwiches to imaginative dishes, lamb from Romney Marsh and local fish, three or four well kept changing ales, Biddenden farm cider, log fire, partitioned back eating area; background music; tables out on green, attractive village, good Military Canal walks. *(Colin and Louise English, Peter Meister, Greg Lawton, Mrs K Sansom)*

BARHAM TR2050
Duke of Cumberland
(01227) 831396 *The Street; CT4 6NY* Open-plan country pub with friendly staff, enjoyable home cooking including good Sun roasts, well kept ales such as Adnams, Greene King, Ringwood and St Austell, bare boards or flagstones, plain tables and chairs, hops and log fire; bedrooms. *(Peter Meister)*

BEARSTED TQ7956
Bell (01622) 738021
Ware Street; by railway bridge, W of centre; ME14 4PA Friendly local with well kept Greene King IPA and a guest, good range of enjoyable competitively priced food including blackboard specials; can get busy; garden and heated terrace. *(Michael Tack)*

BENENDEN TQ8032
★Bull (01580) 240054
The Street; by village green; TN17 4DE Relaxed informal atmosphere in bare-boards or dark terracotta tiled rooms, pleasing mix of furniture, church candles on tables, hops, fire in brick inglenook, friendly hands-on licensees, Dark Star, Harveys, Larkins and a guest from carved wooden counter, local cider too, smarter dining room with burgundy brocade dining chairs, tasty

generously served food (not Sun evening) including various offers and popular Sun roasts; background jazz (live music most Sun afternoons), unobtrusive TV; children welcome, dogs in bar, picnic sets by road, open all day except Mon lunchtime. *(Kevin Thomas, Nina Randall)*

BENOVER   TQ7048
Woolpack (01892) 730356
Benover Road; ME18 6AS Pretty tile-hung and timber-framed pub with well kept Shepherd Neame ales, good choice of generous pubby food, flagstones and stripped brickwork, simple country furnishings, beamed and partly panelled smaller bar; children welcome, tables on front terrace and big back lawn with play equipment. *(Steve and Claire Harvey)*

BODSHAM   TR1045
★ Timber Batts (01233) 750237
Following Bodsham, Wye sign off B2068 keep right at unsigned fork after about 1.5 miles; TN25 5JQ Charming french owner/chef in cottagey country pub, traditional carpeted bar with Adnams Bitter, Woodfordes Wherry and a guest, good french wines by the glass (some from cousin's vineyard), informally rustic beamed dining area with happy mix of stripped-pine tables, pews, dark tables and dining chairs on carpet, french food including set lunch menu, some pubby dishes too; children and dogs welcome (resident labrador called Bounty), lovely views over wide-spreading valley from back garden, closed Sun evening, Mon. *(Peter Heaton, Justin and Emma King, Heather and Dick Martin, Dave Braisted, Julie and Bill Ryan, Derek Thomas)*

BOYDEN GATE   TR2265
★ Gate Inn (01227) 860498
Off A299 Herne Bay–Ramsgate – follow Chislet, Upstreet sign opposite Roman Gallery; Chislet also signed off A28 Canterbury–Margate at Upstreet – after turning right into Chislet main street keep right on to Boyden; CT3 4EB Delightfully unpretentious rustic pub with comfortably worn traditional quarry-tiled rooms, flowery-cushioned pews around tables of considerable character, hop-strung beams, attractively etched windows, inglenook log fire, Shepherd Neame Master Brew, Spitfire and a couple of guests from tap room casks, interesting bottled beers, pubby food lunchtime and evening; children and dogs welcome, sheltered garden bounded by two streams with tame ducks and geese. *(Colin and Louise English)*

BRENCHLEY   TQ6841
Halfway House (01892) 722526
Horsmonden Road; TN12 7AX Beamed 18th-c coaching inn with attractive mix of rustic and traditional furnishings on bare boards, old farm tools, two log fires,

particularly friendly landlord and efficient staff, enjoyable home-made food including good fish and popular Sun roasts, two eating areas, good range of well kept changing ales tapped from the cask such as Goachers; children and dogs welcome, picnic-sets and play area in big garden, summer barbecues and beer festivals, bedrooms, open all day. *(N R White, Alan Franck, Peter Meister)*

BROADSTAIRS   TR3967
Royal Albion (01843) 868071
Albion Street; CT10 1AN Comfortable, smartly refurbished 18th-c seafront hotel reputedly used by Dickens; Shepherd Neame ales, reasonably priced food from sandwiches up, efficient uniformed staff, pleasant conservatory-style area with modern wicker-backed dining chairs and lovely sea views, restaurant; stepped mediterranean-theme front terrace, 21 bedrooms, open all day from 8am. *(John Wooll)*

BURMARSH   TR1032
Shepherd & Crook (01303) 872336
Shear Way; TN29 0JJ Friendly traditional 16th-c marshside local with smuggling history, well kept Adnams and a guest beer, Weston's cider, good straightforward home-made food at low prices, prompt service, interesting photographs and blow lamp collection, open fire; children and dogs welcome, closed Tues and Sun evenings, otherwise open all day. *(N R White, Peter Meister)*

CANTERBURY   TR1458
Dolphin (01227) 455963
St Radigunds Street; CT1 2AA Modernised dining pub with enjoyable home-made pubby food from baguettes up, Sharps Doom Bar, Timothy Taylors Landlord and a couple of guests such as Gadds and Old Dairy, country wines, friendly staff, bric-a-brac on delft shelf, board games, flagstoned conservatory, pianist Sun evening, quiz first Mon of month; no dogs; children welcome, disabled access, good-sized back garden with heaters, open all day. *(Rob and Catherine Dunster, John Baker)*

CANTERBURY
Foundry (01227) 455899
White Horse Lane; Newly opened pub in former 19th-c iron foundry, light and airy interior on two floors, six Canterbury Brewers beers from on-site microbrewery plus guests, enjoyable well presented pubby food from good sandwiches up, helpful cheerful staff; disabled access, small courtyard area. *(John Coatsworth, Sue and Mike Todd)*

CANTERBURY   TR1458
Millers Arms (01227) 456057
St Radigunds Street/Mill Lane; CT1 2AA Shepherd Neame pub in quiet street near river, enjoyable well priced food, changing guest beers and good wine choice, friendly

attentive staff, flagstoned front bar, bare-boards back area, traditional solid furniture, small conservatory, unobtrusive background music; good seating in attractive part-covered courtyard, handy for Marlowe Theatre and cathedral, 11 comfortable bedrooms, ample breakfast, open all day. *(John Coatsworth)*

CANTERBURY — TR1457
★Parrot (01227) 762355
Church Lane – the one off St Radigunds Street, 100 metres E of St Radigunds car park; CT1 2AG Civilised sympathetically updated Youngs pub with their ales and guests, heavy beams, wood and flagstone floors, stripped masonry, dark panelling, big open fire, good value bar food with more extensive traditional menu in upstairs vaulted restaurant, decent wine choice, friendly efficient staff; nicely laid out courtyard with central wood-burning barbecue, open all day. *(Charles Gysin)*

CAPEL — TQ6444
Dovecote (01892) 835966
Alders Road; SE of Tonbridge; TN12 6SU Cosy beamed pub with some stripped brickwork and open fire, pitched-ceiling dining end, enjoyable food (not Sun evening, Mon) from sandwiches to Sun roasts, up to six ales tapped from the cask including Gales and Harveys, farm ciders, friendly staff; lots of picnic-sets in back garden with terrace and play area, nice country surroundings, open all day Sun. *(N R White)*

CHIDDINGSTONE — TQ5045
Castle Inn (01892) 870247
Off B2027 Tonbridge–Edenbridge; TN8 7AH Rambling old pub in pretty NT village, handsome beamed bar, settles and sturdy wall benches, attractive mullioned window seat, woodburners, brick-floor snug, Harveys Best and Larkins including winter Porter (brewed in village), good choice of food with blackboard specials, friendly staff; children and dogs welcome, tables out in front and in nice secluded garden with own bar, circular walks from village, open all day. *(LM, N R White)*

CHILHAM — TR0653
★White Horse (01227) 730355
The Square; CT4 8BY Popular 15th-c pub in picturesque village square, fresh modern décor, handsomely carved ceiling beams and massive fireplace with Lancastrian rose carved on mantel beam, chunky light oak furniture on pale wooden flooring and more traditional pubby furniture on quarry tiles, bright paintings, horsebrasses and a couple of stained-glass panels, well kept changing ales, good popular freshly cooked food (not Sun evening) using local organic produce, home-made cakes and coffee all day; background music and TV; children welcome, dogs in bar, handy for the castle, open all day. *(I A and D J Mullins, N R White, Ron and Sheila Corbett)*

CHILHAM — TR0753
Woolpack (01227) 730351
Off A28/A252; The Street; CT4 8DL Friendly old inn dating from 15th c, traditional beamed bar with pews and good inglenook, well kept Shepherd Neame ales, enjoyable food including weekday set menu, bay-windowed red-carpeted restaurant; children welcome, courtyard tables, delightful village, 14 bedrooms, open all day. *(John Baker, I A and D J Mullins)*

CHILLENDEN — TR2653
★Griffins Head (01304) 840325
SE end of village; 2 miles E of Aylesham; CT3 1PS Attractive beamed, timbered and flagstoned 14th-c pub with two bar rooms and back flagstoned dining room, gently upscale local atmosphere, big log fire, full range of Shepherd Neame ales, good choice of popular home-made food, good wine list, friendly attentive service; dogs welcome in some parts, pretty garden surrounded by wild roses, Sun barbecues, nice countryside. *(Stephen Burke, N R White)*

CHIPSTEAD — TQ4956
Bricklayers Arms (01732) 743424
Chevening Road; TN13 2RZ Attractive pub overlooking lake and green, popular good value food (not Sun evening) served by cheerful helpful staff, full range of Harveys beers kept well and tapped from casks behind long counter, relaxed chatty atmosphere, heavily beamed bar with open fire and fine racehorse painting, unpretentious larger back restaurant; seats out front, open all day Fri-Sun. *(Alan Cowell, N R White)*

CHIPSTEAD — TQ5056
★George & Dragon (01732) 779019
Near M25 junction 5; TN13 2RW Attractive country dining pub under same owners as the George and Dragon at Speldhurst; heavy black beams and standing timbers, grey-green panelling, old tables and chapel chairs on bare boards, log fires, very good food from daily changing menu using organic local produce, Westerham ales including George's Marvellous Medicine brewed for the pub, good choice of wines by the glass, good helpful service, upstairs restaurant; background music; children and dogs welcome, terrace and garden with vegetables and herbs, play area, open all day. *(John Evans, Derek Thomas, Martin and Sue Day, Adrian Taylor)*

We accept no free drinks or meals and inspections are anonymous.

COWDEN   TQ4640
Fountain (01342) 850528
Off A264 and B2026; High Street;
TN8 7JG Good sensibly priced blackboard
food in attractive tile-hung beamed village
pub, steep steps up to unpretentious dark-
panelled corner bar, well kept Harveys,
decent wines, old photographs on cream
walls, good log fire, mix of tables in adjoining
room, woodburner in small back dining
room with one big table; background music;
walkers and dogs welcome, picnic-sets on
small terrace and lawn, pretty village.
(R and S Bentley)

COWDEN   TQ4642
★ Queens Arms
Cowden Pound; junction B2026 with
Markbeech Road; TN8 5NP Friendly
two-room country pub like something
from the 1930s, splendid veteran landlady
still in attendance (pub known locally as
Elsie's), well kept Adnams, coal fire, darts,
occasional folk music or morris dancers; dogs
welcome, closed lunchtimes Mon-Sat, Sun
evening. *(the Didler)*

CROCKHAM HILL   TQ4450
Royal Oak (01732) 866335
Main Road; TN8 6RD Cosy and chatty old
village pub owned by Westerham brewery,
their ales kept well, popular good value
home-made food (best to book), friendly
efficient staff, mix of furniture including
comfy leather sofas on stripped-wood floor,
painted panelling, original Tottering-by-
Gently cartoons and old local photographs,
quiz nights and live folk; walkers (remove
muddy boots) and dogs welcome, small
garden, handy for Chartwell (NT). *(Stephen*
Bennett, N R White, Neil Hardwick, William
Ruxton, Gwyn Jones)

DEAL   TR3751
Berry (01304) 362411
Canada Road; CT14 7EQ Small no frills
local opposite old Royal Marine barracks,
welcoming enthusiastic landlord, well kept
Harveys Best and several changing microbrews
(tasting notes on slates, beer festivals), farm
cider and perry, no food, L-shaped carpeted
bar with coal fire, newspapers, quiz and darts
teams, pool, live music Thurs; small vine-
covered back terrace, open all day weekends,
closed Tues-Thurs lunchtimes. *(N R White,*
Dr Kevan Tucker)

DEAL   TR3753
Deal Hoy (01304) 363972
Duke Street; CT14 6DU Corner local in
Victorian terrace, comfortable bar with local
artwork, old books, sheet music and LPs, well
kept Shepherd Neame and occasional guests
from central servery, good choice of wines by
the glass, enjoyable food including grills and
tapas, live music Weds and Sun; children and
dogs welcome, beach-theme decked garden,

outside kitchen, summer weekend barbecues,
open all day. *(Anon)*

DEAL   TR3752
Kings Head (01304) 368194
Beach Street; CT14 7AH Handsome
three-storey Georgian inn just across from
promenade, good landlord and atmosphere,
interesting maritime décor and cricket
memorabilia in comfortable dimly lit areas
around central servery, flame-effect gas fires,
Shepherd Neame ales and a guest, usual
food from sandwiches up, darts; background
music, TV, can get busy – popular with young
locals weekend evenings; good front terrace
area, bedrooms, open all day. *(John and*
Annabel Hampshire)

DEAL   TR3752
Royal (01304) 375555
Beach Street; CT14 6JD Popular seafront
hotel dating from the early 18th c, light and
comfortable with plenty of casual drinkers,
Shepherd Neame ales, good choice of decent
bar food including fish, friendly uniformed
staff, restaurant, dogs welcome (resident
labrador), sea-view deck and balcony, 18
bedrooms, open all day from 8am.
(Olly Tolhurst, John Wooll, Michael Tack)

DEAL   TR3753
Ship (01304) 372222
Middle Street; CT14 6JZ Dimly lit
traditional local in historic maritime quarter,
Ramsgate Gadds and changing guest ales,
friendly landlord, lots of dark woodwork,
stripped brick and local ship and wreck
pictures, evening candles, woodburner, cosy
back bar; dogs welcome, small pretty walled
garden, open all day. *(N R White,*
Dr Kevan Tucker)

DENTON   TR2147
Jackdaw (01303) 844663
A260 Canterbury–Folkestone; CT4 6QZ
Imposing old brick-and-flint open-plan pub
with enjoyable generously served food all
day, well kept ales such as Harveys and
Shepherd Neame Spitfire, cheerful efficient
young staff, RAF memorabilia in front area,
big back restaurant extension; background
music; children welcome, charming garden
and picturesque village, handy for Battle of
Britain museum at Hawkinge. *(Michael and*
Judy Buckley)

DETLING   TQ7958
Cock Horse (01622) 737092
The Street; ME14 3JT Popular tiled and
weatherboarded village pub with enjoyable
all-day food in bars and back dining room
from baguettes to good value set menu (Mon-
Thurs), well kept Greene King IPA, Thurs
quiz; sports TV; children welcome, tables out
behind, handy for North Downs Way and Kent
Showground. *(Michael Tack)*

DUNKS GREEN   TQ6152
✶**Kentish Rifleman** (01732) 810727
Dunks Green Road; TN11 9RU Tudor pub restored in modern rustic style, welcoming helpful staff, well kept ales such as Harveys and Westerham, enjoyable reasonably priced food (not Sun evening), bar and two dining areas, rifles on low beams, cosy log fire; children and dogs welcome, tables in pretty garden with well, good walks, open all day weekends. *(B and M Kendall, Bob and Margaret Holder, Christian Mole)*

DUNTON GREEN   TQ5156
✶**Bullfinch** (01732) 455107
London Road, Riverhead; TN13 2DR Huge spreading place with modern décor in linked rooms, pubbier part to left with contemporary built-in wall benches, dining chairs and wooden tables, bare-boards area with sofas and brick fireplace, dining rooms with two-way log fire in glass enclosure, upholstered banquettes and wide mix of tables and chairs, popular slightly upmarket traditional fare, pleasant staff, well kept McMullens ales, good choice of wines, newspapers; TV, fruit machine; children welcome, attractive garden with heated terrace, open all day. *(Anon)*

DUNTON GREEN   TQ5157
Rose & Crown (01732) 462343
By turning to Donnington Manor Hotel; TN13 2TH Refurbished Vintage Inn in early 19th century, ales such as Fullers London Pride and Sharps Doom Bar, their usual food including good value set menu (till 5pm, not Sun); children welcome, terrace and garden tables, open all day from 12pm. *(Derek Thomas)*

EYNSFORD   TQ5365
Malt Shovel (01322) 862164
Station Road; DA4 0ER Traditional dark-panelled pub near church, black beams, patterned carpet and copper kettles, well kept interesting changing ales, good choice of wines by the glass, reasonably priced well presented food (all day weekends) including plenty of daily specials, popular Sun lunch, prompt friendly service, restaurant; background radio, silent sports TV, no dogs; children welcome, a few tables out by the pavement, car park across busy road, handy for castles and Roman villa. *(Jeremy King, Adrian Johnson, D P and M A Miles)*

FARNINGHAM   TQ5467
Chequers (01322) 865222
High Street/Dartford Road, just off A20; DA4 0DT Traditional one-bar corner local, up to ten real ales with Fullers, Harveys and Timothy Taylors Landlord as regulars, unpretentious lunchtime food (not Sun), friendly staff; benches outside, picturesque village, open all day. *(N R White)*

FAVERSHAM   TR0161
Anchor (01795) 536471
Abbey Street; ME13 7BP Two-bar character pub, good reasonably priced food from baguettes up, well kept Shepherd Neame range, simple dimly lit bare-boards bar with log fire, ancient beams and dark panelling, frosted windows, boat pictures and models, small side room with pub games and books, restaurant; some live music; dogs welcome, tables in pretty enclosed garden with bat and trap, attractive 17th-c street near historic quay, open all day. *(Nick Lawless, the Didler)*

FAVERSHAM   TR0161
Bear (01795) 532668
Market Place; ME13 7AG Late Victorian (back part from 16th c), locals' front bar, snug hung with chamber pots and back dining lounge all off side corridor, four well kept Shepherd Neame ales, basic good value lunchtime home cooking, friendly service and relaxed atmosphere; couple of pavement tables, lively musical following, open all day Fri-Sun. *(the Didler)*

FAVERSHAM   TR0160
Elephant (01795) 590157
The Mall; ME13 8JN Well run dimly lit traditional town pub, friendly and chatty, with four or five well kept changing ales, belgian beers, Weston's cider, no food (can bring your own), central log fire; juke box and some live music, games machine; children and dogs welcome, suntrap back garden with pond, open all day weekends, from 3pm weekdays. *(the Didler, Graham Warner)*

FAVERSHAM   TR0161
Phoenix (01795) 591462
Abbey Street; ME13 7BH Historic town pub with heavy low beams and stripped stone, well kept beers such as Greene King, Harveys, Fullers and Timothy Taylors, food from pubby choices up (all day Fri and Sat, not Sun evening), afternoon teas, friendly service, leather chesterfields by inglenook log fire, restaurant, various events including live music and poetry reading; children and dogs welcome, back garden, open all day. *(LM)*

FAVERSHAM   TR0161
Sun (01795) 535098
West Street; ME13 7JE Rambling old-world 15th-c pub in pedestrianised street, good unpretentious atmosphere with small low-ceilinged partly panelled rooms, scrubbed tables and big inglenook, well kept Shepherd Neame beers from nearby brewery, enjoyable bar food, smart restaurant attached, friendly efficient staff; unobtrusive background music; wheelchair access possible (small step), pleasant back courtyard, eight bedrooms, open all day. *(LM, Neil Hardwick, Dr and Mrs A Pollock)*

FAWKHAM GREEN   TQ5865
Rising Sun (01474) 872291
Sun Hill; DA3 8NL Pleasant old tile-
hung pub overlooking green, ales such as
Courage, Fullers, Harveys and Westerham,
enjoyable food, courteous service,
beams and inglenook, restaurant; five
bedrooms. *(Simon Jeffs, N R White)*

FINGLESHAM   TR3353
⋆**Crown** (01304) 612555
*Just off A258 Sandwich–Deal; The
Street; CT14 0NA* Popular neatly kept
low-beamed country local dating from 16th
c, good value generous home-made food from
usual pub dishes to interesting specials,
friendly helpful service, well kept local ales
such as Ramsgate, Biddenden cider, daily
newspapers, softly lit carpeted split-level bar
with stripped stone and inglenook log fire,
two other attractive dining rooms; lovely big
garden with play area, bat and trap, field for
caravans, open all Fri-Sun. *(Ian Coles)*

FRITTENDEN   TQ8141
Bell & Jorrocks (01580) 852415
*Corner of Biddenden Road/The Street;
TN17 2EJ* Welcoming simple 18th-c tile-
hung and beamed local, well kept Harveys,
Woodfords and guests (Apr beer festival),
Weston's and Thatcher's ciders, good
traditional home-made food (not Sun evening
or lunchtimes Mon, Tues), open fire with
propeller from crashed plane above, kentish
darts, some live music; sports TV; children
and dogs welcome, open all day. *(N R White,
Donald Bremner)*

GOODNESTONE   TR2554
⋆**Fitzwalter Arms** (01304) 840303
*The Street; NB this is in east Kent NOT
the other Goodnestone; CT3 1PJ* Old
dimly lit beamed village pub with two little
rustic bars, Shepherd Neame ales, good
locally sourced food (not particularly cheap)
including seasonal game, friendly chatty
service, dining room, log fires; children and
dogs welcome, lovely church next door and
close to Goodnestone Park Gardens, open all
day Fri-Sun, closed Mon lunchtime.
*(Dr Kevan Tucker, Rob and Catherine Dunster,
Alan Cowell, Keir Halliday)*

GROOMBRIDGE   TQ5337
⋆**Crown** (01892) 864742
B2110; TN3 9QH Charming tile-hung
wealden inn with snug low-beamed bar,
old tables on worn flagstones, panelling,
bric-a-brac, fire in sizeable brick inglenook,
Harveys, Larkins and a guest, traditional food
(not Sun evening), roughly plastered dining
area with dark wood pubby tables; children
welcome, dogs in bar, narrow old brick
terrace overlooking steep green, bedrooms,
open all day summer Fri-Sun, closed winter
Sun evening. *(Alan Franck)*

HALSTEAD   TQ4861
Rose & Crown (01959) 533120
Otford Lane; TN14 7EA Friendly
19th-c flint village local, well kept Larkins,
Whitstable and four guest beers (always
a mild), enjoyable good value home-made
food all day including popular Sun roasts,
welcoming staff, log fire, two bars with lots of
village photographs, darts, stables tearoom/
restaurant; children and dogs welcome,
wheelchair access, garden behind with
play area, summer bat and trap, open all
day. *(Donna Rogers)*

HARVEL   TQ6563
Amazon & Tiger (01474) 814705
Harvel Street; DA13 0DE Popular village
local (built in 1914) backing on to cricket
ground, traditional pubby interior, bar and
separate dining area, three good changing
ales such as Royal Tunbridge Wells, standard
food from good sandwiches up, friendly
service, bar billiards; children and dogs
welcome, beautiful walking country, open all
day Fri-Sun, closed Mon lunchtime.
(N R White, Richard Mason)

HAWKHURST   TQ7529
⋆**Black Pig** (01580) 752306
Moor Hill (A229); TN18 4PF Bustling
pleasantly refurbished open plan pub,
L-shaped bar and eating areas on different
levels, all manner of nice old dining chairs
and tables, church candles, interesting
old stove, lots of pictures on bare brick or
painted walls, well kept ales such as Larkins,
decent wines by the glass, good food from
lunchtime sandwiches up, friendly attentive
service; plenty of seats in surprisingly big
garden. *(Anon)*

HAWKHURST   TQ7531
⋆**Great House** (01580) 753119
*Gills Green; pub signed off A229 N;
TN18 5EJ* Busy stylish white-
weatherboarded dining pub, well liked food
(not cheap, all day weekends), Harveys Best
and a seasonal brew from marble counter,
sofas, armchairs and bright scatter cushions
in chatty bar, moving into dark wood dining
tables and smartly upholstered chairs on
slate floor, gilt-framed pictures on red or
green walls, steps down to light airy dining
room with big picture windows, colourful
cushions on carved built-in shabby chic
seating, plenty of modern art; background
music, TV; children welcome, dogs in bar,
modern blue furniture on side terrace, open
all day, closed Mon in Jan and Feb. *(Sue and
Mike Todd, Jamie and Sue May, Derek Thomas,
Steve Holloway)*

HEADCORN   TQ8344
George & Dragon (01622) 890239
High Street; TN27 9NL Mock-Tudor pub
with welcoming landlady and nice staff, wide
range of enjoyable home-made food, local

ales and cider, extensive wine list, open fires, separate dining room; children well looked after with colouring sheets and toys. *(Bill Adie, Alec and Joan Laurence)*

HEAVERHAM   TQ5758
Chequers (01732) 763968
Watery Lane; TN15 6NP Attractive 16th-c beamed pub with friendly locals' bar, decent food (not Sun evening), Shepherd Neame ales, dining room with inglenook, raftered barn restaurant with resident ghost; children and dogs welcome, big pretty garden, open all day, closed Mon. *(Gordon and Margaret Ormondroyd, Mark Waters, Howard and Margaret Buchanan)*

HERNE BAY   TR1768
Old Ship (01227) 366636
Central Parade; CT6 5HT Old white weatherboarded pub with window tables looking across road to sea, well kept beers such as Bass and Timothy Taylors, popular choice of food including good Sun roasts; children welcome till 6pm, sea-view deck. *(John Wooll, Michael Tack)*

HERNHILL   TR0660
Red Lion (01227) 751207
Off A299 via Dargate, or A2 via Boughton Street and Staplestreet; ME13 9JR Pretty Tudor inn by church and attractive village green, densely beamed and flagstoned, log fires, pine tables, friendly helpful staff, enjoyable usual food including OAP lunch deal Weds, well kept ales such as Greene King and Shepherd Neame, decent house wines, upstairs restaurant; children welcome, big garden with play area, bedrooms, open all day Fri-Sun. *(Christian Mole)*

HEVER   TQ4744
Henry VIII (01732) 862457
By gates of Hever Castle; TN8 7NH Predominantly 17th-c with some fine oak panelling, wide floorboards and heavy beams, inglenook fireplace, Henry VIII décor, well kept Shepherd Neame ales, traditional food from well filled baguettes up, friendly efficient staff, small dining room; no dogs even in garden; tables out on terrace and pond-side lawn, handy for Hever Castle, bedrooms, open all day. *(LM)*

HODSOLL STREET   TQ6263
⋆Green Man (01732) 823575
Signed off A227 S of Meopham; turn right in village; TN15 7LE Bustling village pub with neatly arranged traditional furnishings in big airy carpeted rooms, friendly atmosphere, Greene King Old Speckled Hen, Harveys Best, Timothy Taylors Landlord and a guest, decent choice of enjoyable generously served food (all day Sun) including good baguettes and popular two-course weekday lunch deal; background music – live second Thurs of month, quiz

Mon; children and dogs welcome, tables and climbing frame on well tended lawn, open all day Fri-Sun. *(A N Bance, Martin and Karen Wake, Gordon and Margaret Ormondroyd, N R White, B and M Kendall, Martin and Sue Day)*

IDE HILL   TQ4851
Cock (01732) 750310
Off B2042 SW of Sevenoaks; TN14 6JN Pretty village-green local dating from the 15th-c, chatty and friendly and under new management, two dimly lit bars with steps between, Greene King ales, enjoyable traditional food (not Sun or Mon or Tues evenings), cosy in winter with good inglenook log fire; well behaved children and dogs welcome, picnic-sets out at front, handy for Chartwell (NT) and nearby walks. *(N R White)*

IDEN GREEN   TQ7437
Peacock (01580) 211233
A262 E of Goudhurst; TN17 2PB Dating from the 14th-c with blazing inglenook log fire in low-beamed main bar, quarry tiles and old sepia photographs, well priced enjoyable pubby food (all day Sat) from sandwiches up, very helpful service, well kept Shepherd Neame ales, pinky-red dining room and public bar with fire; well behaved children and dogs welcome, no muddy boots, attractive good-sized garden, closed Sun evening. *(Nigel and Jean Eames)*

IDEN GREEN   TQ8031
⋆Woodcock (01580) 240009
Not the Iden Green near Goudhurst; village signed off A268 E of Hawkhurst and B2086 at W edge of Benenden; in village follow Standen Street sign, then fork left into Woodcock Lane; TN17 4HT Informal friendly little local with a couple of big standing timbers supporting very low-ceilings, chatty regulars on high stools near corner counter, a comfortable squashy sofa and low table by inglenook woodburner, concrete floor, brick walls hung with horsebrasses, Greene King Abbot, IPA, Morlands Original and XX Mild plus seasonal guests, well liked pubby food (not Sun evening), small panelled dining area with pine tables and chairs; children welcome, dogs in bar, back garden, open all day, closed Mon evening. *(Gordon and Margaret Ormondroyd)*

IGHTHAM   TQ5956
⋆George & Dragon (01732) 882440
A227; TN15 9HH Ancient timbered pub, popular and stylish, with good reasonably priced food from generous snacks up (all day till 6.30pm, not Sun), plenty of friendly smartly dressed staff, well kept Shepherd Neame ales, decent wines, sofas among other furnishings in long sociable main bar, heavy-beamed end room, woodburner and open fires, restaurant; children and dogs welcome, back terrace, handy for Ightham Mote (NT), good walks, open all day. *(Bob and Margaret Holder, Martin and Sue Day)*

IGHTHAM COMMON TQ5855
✳ **Harrow** (01732) 885912
*Signposted off A25 just W of Ightham;
pub sign may be hard to spot; TN15 9EB*
Smart yet comfortably genial pub with
emphasis on particularly good imaginative
food, Sunday roasts, relaxed cheerful bar
area to the right with candles and fresh
flowers, dining chairs on herringbone wood
floor, winter fire, charming little antiquated
conservatory and more formal dining
room, ales such as Gravesend Shrimpers
and Loddon Hoppit; background music;
children welcome (not in dining room on
Sat evening), pretty little pergola-enclosed
back terrace, handy for Ightham Mote (NT),
closed Sun evening, Mon. *(Derek Thomas,
Ian Scott-Thompson, Michael and Maggie Betton,
Andrea Rampley)*

IGHTHAM COMMON TQ5955
Old House (01732) 882383
*Redwell, S of village; OS Sheet 188 map
reference 591559; TN15 9EE* Basic
two-room country pub tucked down narrow
lane, no inn sign, bare bricks and beams,
huge inglenook, half a dozen interesting
changing ales from tap room casks, retired
cash register and small TV in side room,
darts; no food, closed weekday lunchtimes,
opens at 7pm and may shut early if
quiet. *(the Didler)*

KILNDOWN TQ7035
Globe & Rainbow (01892) 890803
*Signed off A21 S of Lamberhurst;
TN17 2SG* Welcoming well cared for pub
with small cheerful bar, Harveys and guests
such as Westerham Finchcocks, decent
wines, simple bare-boards dining room with
good imaginative food (shorter lunchtime
menu), some themed evenings, friendly
young staff; background music; nice country
views from decking out by cricket pitch, open
all day (till 7pm Sun). *(Tom and Rosemary
Hall, Conrad Freezer, J Graveling)*

KINGSDOWN TR3748
Kings Head (01304) 373915
Upper Street; CT14 8BJ Chatty tucked-
away local with four small split-level rooms,
black timbers, lots of old local photographs
on faded cream walls, a few vintage
amusement machines, woodburner, Greene
King IPA and two mainly local guests, popular
reasonably priced food, friendly landlord and
staff, darts; soft background music; children
(in family room) and dogs welcome, garden
with skittle alley, open all day Sun, closed
weekdays till 5pm. *(N R White)*

KNOCKHOLT TQ4658
Three Horseshoes (01959) 532102
Main Road; TN14 7LD Popular village
pub with large open-plan bar and separate
dining room, good range of moderately priced
standard food, changing real ales, friendly

staff; children and dogs welcome, pretty back
garden, classic car meetings, North Downs
Way footpath nearby (shelf for boots in
porch). *(N R White)*

LADDINGFORD TQ6848
Chequers (01622) 871266
The Street; ME18 6BP Friendly old
beamed and weatherboarded village pub with
good sensibly priced food from sandwiches
and sharing boards up (restricted choice Mon
lunchtime), well kept Adnams Bitter and
three guests (April beer festival); children
and dogs welcome, big garden with play
area, shetland ponies in paddock, Medway
walks nearby, one bedroom, open all day
weekends. *(Roy Russell)*

LENHAM TQ8952
Dog & Bear (01622) 858219
The Square; ME17 2PG Early 17th-c
coaching inn, attractive and spacious,
with rare authentic Queen Anne coat of
arms (she visited 1704), timbers and open
fire, enjoyable sensibly priced food from
sandwiches up, friendly attentive service,
Shepherd Neame ales and good choice of
wines, restaurant; sports TV, pool; courtyard
tables, 24 comfortable bedrooms, good
breakfast, pretty village, open all day.
(Simon Le Fort, Mrs Cathy Lintott)

LITTLE CHART TQ9446
Swan (01233) 840702
The Street; TN27 0QB New licensees for
this attractive 15th-c beamed village pub
with its notable rounded Dering windows,
open fires in simple unspoilt front bar and
good-sized dining area, enjoyable fairly
traditional food including children's and
OAP's menus, three well kept beers and
decent wines, friendly staff, pool; nice
riverside garden, open all day from noon
till late, closed Mon lunchtime, Tues.
(Richard Mason)

LOWER HARDRES TR1453
✳ **Granville** (01227) 700402
*Faussett Hill, Street End; B2068 S of
Canterbury; CT4 7AL* Spacious airy
interior with contemporary furnishings,
unusual central fire with large conical hood
and glimpses of kitchen, proper public
bar with farmhouse chairs, settles and
woodburner, deservedly popular food (not
Sun evening – booking advised), fine choice
of wines from blackboard, Shepherd Neame
Master Brew and a seasonal beer, good
service, daily newspapers; background music;
children and dogs welcome, french windows
to garden with large spreading tree and
small sunny terrace, open all day Sun, closed
Mon. *(Anon)*

LUDDESDOWN TQ6667
✳ **Cock** (01474) 814208
*Henley Street, N of village – OS Sheet
177 map reference 664672; off A227 in*

Meopham, or A228 in Cuxton;
DA13 0XB Early 18th-c country pub with
friendly long-serving no-nonsense landlord,
at least six ales including Adnams, Goachers,
Harveys and Shepherd Neame, sensibly
priced all-day pubby food (not Sun evening)
from sandwiches up, rugs on polished
boards in pleasant bay-windowed lounge,
quarry-tiled locals' bar, woodburners, pews
and other miscellaneous furnishings, aircraft
pictures, masses of beer mats and bric-a-brac
such as stuffed animals, model cars and
beer can collections, bar billiards and darts,
back dining conservatory; no children in bar
or part-covered heated back terrace; dogs
welcome, big secure garden, good walks.
(N R White)

MAIDSTONE   TQ7655
Rifle Volunteers (01622) 758891
Wyatt Street/Church Street; ME14 1EU
Relaxed unspoilt backstreet pub tied to local
Goachers, three of their ales including Mild,
good value simple home-made food, friendly
long-serving landlord, two gas fires, darts;
tables outside. (the Didler)

MARDEN   TQ7547
Stile Bridge (01622) 831236
Staplehurst Road (A229); TN12 9BH
Friendly roadside pub/restaurant with five
well kept ales including Adnams Lighthouse,
bottled belgian beers and real ciders, good
choice of enjoyable food, beer and music
festivals (May and Aug bank holidays), live
music Fri evening; pétanque, open all day
(till 7pm Sun). (Steve and Claire Harvey)

NEWENDEN   TQ8327
White Hart (01797) 252166
Rye Road (A268); TN18 5PN Popular
16th-c local, long low-beamed bar with big
stone fireplace, dining areas off with decent
good value food, well kept Harveys and
guests, friendly staff; back games area, sports
TV, background music; children welcome,
boules in large garden, near river (boat trips
to Bodiam Castle). (Peter Meister)

NORTHBOURNE   TR3350
Hare & Hounds (01304) 365429
Off A256 or A258 near Dover; The Street;
CT14 0LG Chatty village pub with several
well kept ales including Harveys, good choice
of generous popular food (lamb from nearby
farm), friendly efficient service, spacious
modernised brick and wood interior, log fires;
dogs welcome, terrace tables. (N R White)

OARE   TR0163
⋆Shipwrights Arms (01795) 590088
S shore of Oare Creek, E of village;
signed from Oare Road/Ham Road

junction in Faversham; ME13 7TU
Remote and ancient marshland tavern with
plenty of character, up to five kentish beers
tapped from the cask (pewter tankards over
counter), enjoyable traditional food (not Sun
evening or Mon), three dark simple little
bars separated by standing timbers, wood
partitions and narrow door arches, medley of
seats from tapestry-cushioned stools to black
panelled built-in settles forming booths,
flags or boating pennants on ceiling, wind
gauge above main door (takes reading from
chimney); background local radio; children
(away from bar area) and dogs welcome,
large garden, path along Oare Creek to Swale
estuary, lots of surrounding bird life, closed
Mon. (Mrs Margo Finlay, Jörg Kasprowski, Colin
McKerrow, Kevin Ball, the Didler, Peter Chapman,
Mrs G Marlow)

OARE   TR0063
Three Mariners (01795) 533 633
Church Road; ME13 0QA Comfortable
simply restored old pub with good reputation
for food including fresh fish, weekday set
lunch deals, Shepherd Neame ales, log fire;
attractive garden overlooking Faversham
Creek, open all day weekends, Mon morning
post office. (Ken and Lynda Taylor)

OLD ROMNEY   TR0325
Rose & Crown (01797) 367500
A259 opposite church; TN29 9SQ Simple
friendly village pub with good value tasty
food from sandwiches up, well kept Courage,
Greene King, Rother Valley and guests,
Biddenden cider, helpful staff, old local
photographs, dining conservatory; TV;
children welcome, pretty garden with boules,
chalet bedrooms, open all day.
(Colin McKerrow)

OTFORD   TQ5259
Bull (01959) 523198
High Street; TN14 5PG Attractively laid
out 15th-c Chef & Brewer, wide food choice
from sandwiches up all day, good Sun lunch,
friendly attentive staff, four well kept ales,
decent wines, several quietly spacious
rooms, two huge log fires, panelling, soft
lighting and candles; nice garden, good walks
nearby. (Conor McGaughey, Martin and
Sue Day)

OTFORD   TQ5259
Crown (01959) 522847
High Street, pond end; TN14 5PQ 16th-c
two-bar local opposite village duck pond,
pleasantly chatty beamed lounge with
woodburner in old fireplace, well kept ales
such as Harveys, Tonbridge and Westerham,
cheerful landlord and staff, locally sourced
food including bargain OAP lunch and good

For those of you that use Sat Nav devices, we include a postcode for
every entry in the Guide.

Sun roasts, darts, frequent interesting events; sports TV; back garden, walkers and dogs welcome, open all day. *(N R White, B and M Kendall)*

PENSHURST   TQ5243
Leicester Arms (01892) 870551
High Street; TN11 8BT Country hotel feel with comfortable old bars and meadowland-view dining room up steps, well kept Fullers London Pride, Harveys and Greene King Old Speckled Hen, enjoyable food all day from bar and main menus, friendly polite service; lavatories down steps (disabled one in car park opposite); children and dogs welcome, pretty back garden, seven bedrooms. *(Paul Rampton, Julie Harding, Martin and Sue Day)*

PENSHURST   TQ4943
★Rock (01892) 870296
Hoath Corner, Chiddingstone Hoath, on back road Chiddingstone–Cowden; OS Sheet 188 map reference 497431; TN8 7BS Tiny welcoming cottage under new licensee, undulating brick floor, simple furnishings and woodburner in fine brick inglenook, well kept Larkins and enjoyable pub food, large stuffed bull's head for ring the bull, up a step to smaller room with long wooden settle by nice table; walkers and dogs welcome, picnic-sets out in front and on back lawn. *(LM, Grahame Brooks, Anthony Bradbury, Gwyn Jones, Tina and David Woods-Taylor)*

PENSHURST   TQ5241
★Spotted Dog (01892) 870253
Smarts Hill, off B2188 S; TN11 8EP Quaint old weatherboarded pub under welcoming family, heavy low beams and timbers, attractive moulded panelling, rugs and tiles, antique settles, inglenook log fire, Harveys, Larkins and two guests, local cider, good mostly traditional food (all day weekends) including weekday lunch deals, friendly caring service; children and dogs welcome, tiered back terrace (they may ask to keep your credit card while you eat here), open all day. *(John Redfern, Andy Surman, Alan Franck, Heather and Dick Martin)*

PETTERIDGE   TQ6640
Hopbine (01892) 722561
Petteridge Lane; NE of village; TN12 7NE Small unspoilt cottage in quiet little hamlet, two small rooms with open fire between, traditional pubby furniture on red-patterned carpet, hops and horsebrasses, well kept Badger ales, enjoyable good value home-made food, friendly staff, steps up to simple back part with piano and darts, flagons in brick fireplace; seats in side garden. *(Anon)*

PLAXTOL   TQ6054
★Golding Hop (01732) 882150
Sheet Hill (0.5 miles S of Ightham, between A25 and A227); TN15 0PT Secluded traditional country local, simple

dimly lit two-level bar with hands-on landlord who can be very welcoming, cask-tapped Adnams and guests kept well, local farm ciders (sometimes their own), short choice of basic good value bar food (not Mon or Tues evenings), old photographs of the pub, woodburners, bar billiards; portable TV for big sports events; no children inside; suntrap streamside lawn and well fenced play area over lane, good walks, open all day Sat. *(Bob and Margaret Holder, Alan Franck, the Didler, Gwyn Jones)*

RINGLESTONE   TQ8755
Ringlestone Inn (01622) 859900
Ringlestone Road, signed Doddington off B2163 NE of Hollingbourne; ME17 1NX Tucked-away former monks' hospice, an inn by 1615, furnished to match the antiquity of its worn brick floor, stripped masonry, sturdy beams and inglenook log fire, good if pricy food including range of pies, friendly helpful service, Shepherd Neame ales, farm cider, country wines and liqueurs, can get very busy in summer; children and well behaved dogs welcome, big attractive garden with play area, open all day weekends, closed Tues evening. *(N R White)*

ROCHESTER   TQ7468
Coopers Arms (01634) 404298
St Margarets Street; ME1 1TL Jettied Tudor building behind cathedral, cosily unpretentious and quaint with good local atmosphere, two comfortable beamed bars, fairly priced pub food and well kept beers such as Wells & Youngs, helpful cheery staff; tables in attractive courtyard. *(David Sizer, Richard Mason, Colin Boocock)*

ROLVENDEN   TQ8431
Bull (01580) 241212
Regent Street; TN17 4PB Small tile-hung cottage with woodburner in fine brick inglenook, high-backed leather dining chairs around rustic tables on stripped boards, built-in panelled wall seats, fresh flowers, Fullers London Pride, Harveys and Larkins, bar food (not Sun evening), pale oak tables in dining room, friendly helpful service; background music, TV; children welcome, dogs allowed in bar, a few picnic-sets in front, more seats in back garden, open all day *(Richard Gibbs)*

ROMNEY STREET   TQ5561
Fox & Hounds (01959) 525428
Back road Eynsford–Heaverham; TN15 6XR Tucked-away open-plan country pub under new landlord, four well kept ales including one brewed for them by Goachers, fairly priced mainly traditional home-made food (not Sun evening), low beams, flagstones and woodburner; background music; children, walkers and dogs welcome, tables out in front and in back garden, open all day. *(Anon)*

SANDWICH   TR3358
Fleur de Lis (01304) 611131
Delf Street; CT13 9BZ Well managed
18th-c coaching inn, long bar with
comfortable split-level lounge end, open fire,
food (all day weekends) from sandwiches
up, real ales, friendly staff and pleasant
chatty atmosphere, panelled back restaurant;
background music, TV and games; dogs
welcome, 11 bedrooms, open all day.
(N R White)

SANDWICH   TR3358
George & Dragon (01304) 613106
Fisher Street; CT13 9EJ Open-plan 15th-c
beamed pub with enjoyable often interesting
food from open kitchen, Wantsum, Shepherd
Neame and a guest ale, good choice of wines
by the glass, friendly obliging staff; children
and dogs allowed, pretty back terrace, open
all day Sat, closed Sun evening. *(Anon)*

SEASALTER   TR0864
✳Sportsman (01227) 273370
Faversham Road, off B2040; CT5 4BP
Restauranty dining pub just inside seawall
and rather unprepossessing from outside;
good imaginative contemporary cooking
with plenty of seafood (not Sun evening
or Mon, must book and not cheap), home-
baked breads, good wine choice including
english, well kept Shepherd Neame ales,
friendly staff; two plain linked rooms and
long conservatory, wooden floor, pine
tables, wheelback and basket-weave dining
chairs, big film star photographs; plastic
glasses for outside; children welcome,
open all day Sun. *(N R White, Jonathan and
Ann Tross)*

SELLING   TR0455
✳Rose & Crown (01227) 752214
Follow Perry Wood signs; ME13 9RY
Tucked-away 16th-c country pub, hops
strung from beams, two inglenook log fires,
friendly service, well kept Adnams and
Harveys, several ciders, generous food from
sandwiches up; background music; children
welcome, dogs on leads in bar, cottagey
back garden with play area, closed Sun
evening. *(Jenny Titford, the Didler)*

SELLING   TR0356
White Lion (01227) 752211
*Off A251 S of Faversham (or exit
roundabout, M2 junction 7); The Street;
ME13 9RQ* 17th-c pub refurbished under
new licensees, Shepherd Neame ales from
unusual semicircular bar counter, locally
sourced food cooked by landlord, main bar
with log fire (working spit), another fire in
small lower lounge, back restaurant; children
and dogs welcome, tables out at front and in
attractive side garden. *(Anon)*

SEVENOAKS   TQ5555
✳Bucks Head (01732) 761330
Godden Green, just E; TN15 0JJ
Welcoming and relaxed flower-decked
pub with neatly kept bar and restaurant
area, freshly cooked blackboard food from
sandwiches up, roast on Sun, well kept
Shepherd Neame and a guest, beams,
panelling and splendid inglenooks; children
and dogs welcome, front terrace overlooking
informal green and duck pond, pretty back
garden with mature trees, pergola and
views over quiet country behind Knole (NT),
popular with walkers. *(N R White)*

SEVENOAKS   TQ5055
Kings Head (01732) 452081
*Bessels Green; A25 W, just off A21;
TN13 2QA* Village-green pub under new
management, french brasserie-style food
including mussels cooked in seven different
ways, Sun carvery, ales such as Harveys,
Sharps Doom Bar and Wells & Youngs,
Stowford Press cider, good wines by the glass
from french list, two log fires, restaurant;
children and dogs welcome, spacious back
garden with play area, open all day, closed
Sun evening. *(Anon)*

SHIPBOURNE   TQ5952
✳Chaser (01732) 810360
*Stumble Hill (A227 N of Tonbridge);
TN11 9PE* Comfortably opened-up with
civilised linked rooms converging on large
central island, stripped-wood floors, frame-
to-frame pictures on deep red and cream
walls, pine wainscoting, candles on mix of
old solid-wood tables, shelves of books, open
fires, well kept Greene King ales, good wine
and malt whisky choice, good popular food all
day (breakfast Thurs, Sat and Sun), friendly
well trained staff, dark panelling and high
timber-vaulted ceiling in striking chapel-like
restaurant; background music; children
welcome, dogs in bar, courtyard and small
side garden, Thurs morning farmers' market,
open all day. *(Tina and David Woods-Taylor,
Gordon and Margaret Ormondroyd, Alan Franck,
Derek Thomas and others)*

SHOREHAM   TQ5261
Olde George (01959) 522017
Church Street; TN14 7RY Refurbished
16th-c pub with low beams, uneven floors
and a cosy fire, friendly staff, changing real
ales, dining area; children and dogs welcome,
picnic-sets by road with view of church,
picturesque village. *(N R White)*

The letters and figures after the name of each town are its Ordnance Survey map
reference. *How to use the Guide* at the beginning of the book explains how it helps you
find a pub, in road atlases or large-scale maps as well as in our own maps.

SNARGATE   TQ9928
⋆**Red Lion** (01797) 344648

B2080 Appledore–Brenzett; TN29 9UQ
Little changed since 1890 and in the same
family for over 100 years, simple old-
fashioned charm in three timeless little
rooms with original cream wall panelling,
heavy beams in sagging ceilings, dark pine
Victorian farmhouse chairs on bare boards,
an old piano stacked with books, coal fire,
local cider and four or five ales including
Goachers tapped from casks behind unusual
free-standing marble-topped counter, no
food, traditional games like toad in the
hole, nine men's morris and table skittles;
children in family room, dogs in bar, outdoor
lavatories, cottage garden. *(Phil and Sally
Gorton, B and M Kendall, the Didler, Mike and
Eleanor Anderson)*

ST MARGARET'S BAY   TR3744
⋆**Coastguard** (01304) 853176

*Off A256 NE of Dover; keep on down
through the village to the bottom of
the bay, pub off on right by the beach;
CT15 6DY* Sea views from prettily planted
balcony and beachside seating, nautical
décor in carpeted wood-clad bar, Gadds No 5,
Goachers Dark and a couple of guests such
as Fyne and Orkney, over 40 whiskies and
carefully chosen wine list with some from
Kent vineyards, good well presented food
and more fine views from wood-strip floored
restaurant; background music; children
and dogs allowed in certain areas, open all
day. *(Richard Mason, N R White, Michael Tack,
Alastair Knowles)*

STAPLE   TR2756
Black Pig (01304) 813000

*Off B2046 in Wingham, passing through
Staple; CT3 1LE* 16th-c half-timbered
beamed inn, three well kept changing beers,
enjoyable sensibly priced bar food, modern
restaurant, some live music; children and
dogs welcome, garden, five bedrooms, closed
Mon, otherwise open all day. *(David Dixon)*

STAPLEHURST   TQ7846
⋆**Lord Raglan** (01622) 843747

*About 1.5 miles from town centre
towards Maidstone, turn right off A229
into Chart Hill Road opposite Chart
Cars; OS Sheet 188 map reference
785472; TN12 0DE* Well run country
pub, cosy chatty area around narrow bar
counter, hop-covered low beams, big winter
log fire, mixed comfortably worn dark wood
furniture, enjoyable food from sandwiches
up, Goachers, Harveys and a guest, farm cider
and perry, good wine list; children and dogs
welcome, reasonable wheelchair access,

high-hedged terrace, picnic-sets in side
orchard, closed Sun. *(Malcolm and Barbara
Southwell, Ken and Marion Watson)*

STODMARSH   TR2160
⋆**Red Lion** (01227) 721339

*High Street; off A257 just E of
Canterbury; CT3 4BA* Quirky country
pub with idiosyncratic landlord, all manner
of bric-a-brac from life-size Tintin and
Snowy to a tiger's head in hop-hung rooms,
one wall covered in sheet music, empty
wine bottles everywhere, green-painted,
cushioned mate's chairs around nice pine
tables, candles, big log fire, good interesting
food using prime local meat and seasonal
produce, Greene King IPA and Harveys
Best tapped from casks, nice wine, good
summer Pimms and winter mulled wine/
cider, dining conservatory; background jazz;
children welcome, dogs in bar, pretty garden
with roaming chickens and ducks, bat and
trap, handy for Stodmarsh National Nature
Reserve, bedrooms (not ensuite). *(Jacqueline
France-McNeill, David Heath, Dave Braisted,
Adrian Johnson)*

STONE IN OXNEY   TQ9327
⋆**Crown** (01233) 758302

Off B2082 Iden–Tenterden; TN30 7JN
Smart country pub with friendly landlord and
staff, well kept Shepherd Neame and Larkins
tapped from the cask, very good food from
landlady/chef including some imaginative
cooking, also wood-fired pizzas Fri evenings
and Sat (takeaways available), light airy
open feel with lots of wood, red walls, and
big inglenook log fire; no under-12s in the
evening, rustic furniture on terrace, two
bedrooms. *(Peter Meister)*

STONE IN OXNEY   TQ9428
⋆**Ferry** (01233) 758246

*Appledore Road; N of Stone-cum-Ebony;
TN30 7JY* Attractive 17th-c smugglers'
haunt, consistently good popular food
including local fish (Rye scallops), welcoming
landlord and friendly efficient staff, well kept
changing ales and a beer brewed for them by
Westerham, small plain bar with woodburner
and inglenook, bare boards, hops and old
maps, steps up to pleasant dining area,
games room; seats in garden and sunny front
courtyard, lovely setting by marshes. *(Peter
Meister, Colin and Louise English, Conrad Freezer,
Paul Brown)*

THURNHAM   TQ8057
⋆**Black Horse** (01622) 737185

*Not far from M20 junction 7; off A249
at Detling; ME14 3LD* Large olde-
worlde dining pub with enjoyable food all
day, children's menu, three well kept ales

Half pints: by law, a pub should not charge more for half a pint than half the price of
a full pint, unless it shows that half-pint price on its price list.

KENT | 463

including Westerham Grasshopper, farm ciders and country wines, friendly efficient uniformed staff, timbers, bare boards and log fires, back restauarant area; dogs and walkers welcome, pleasant garden with partly covered terrace, nice views, by Pilgrims Way, comfortable modern bedroom block, good breakfast. *(Alec and Joan Laurence, Martin and Sue Day)*

TOYS HILL   TQ4752
★**Fox & Hounds** (01732) 750328
Off A25 in Brasted, via Brasted Chart and The Chart; TN16 1QG Traditional country pub with plain tables and chairs on dark boards, leather sofa and easy chair by log fire, hunting prints, old photographs, plates and copper jugs, modern carpeted dining extension with big windows overlooking tree-sheltered garden, enjoyable well presented food (not Sun evening) including some interesting choices like venison cooked three ways, well kept Greene King ales, several wines by the glass, traditional games, no mobile phones; background music; children and dogs welcome, roadside verandah used by smokers, good local walks and views, handy for Chartwell and Emmetts Garden (both NT), open all day weekends, closed Mon in winter. *(C and R Bromage, Jennie George, B and M Kendall, Christian Mole)*

TUDELEY   TQ6145
★**Poacher** (01732) 358934
Hartlake Road; TN11 0PH Smart modern bar and restaurant, light and airy, with wide range of good food including daily specials, ales such as Sharps, Shepherd Neame and one brewed for the pub by Kings, good choice of wines by the glass, friendly attentive staff, live music Thurs evening; terrace tables, near interesting church with Chagall stained glass. *(Peter Eyles, Kellie Williams, Nigel and Jean Eames)*

TUNBRIDGE WELLS   TQ5638
Beacon (01892) 524252
Tea Garden Lane, Rusthall Common; TN3 9JH Cheery Victorian pub with Harveys, Timothy Taylors and Wells & Youngs, lots of wines by the glass, good coffee, airy interior with fireside sofas, stripped panelling, bare boards and ornate wall units, linked dining areas; children welcome, tables on decking with fine view, paths between lakes and springs, three bedrooms, open all day. *(Alan Franck)*

TUNBRIDGE WELLS   TQ5839
Opera House (01892) 511770
Mount Pleasant Road; TN1 1RT Large Wetherspoons restoration of 1900s opera house (still do one or two operas a year), original circle, boxes, stage lighting and ornate ceiling; real ales including more or less local guests, usual cheap Wetherspoons food, friendly service; can get crowded weekend evenings, no dogs; children welcome, open all day. *(Tony Hobden)*

UNDERRIVER   TQ5552
White Rock (01732) 833112
SE of Sevenoaks, off B245; TN15 0SB Welcoming village pub, attractive and relaxed, with good food from pubby fare up (all day weekends, best to book), well kept Harveys, Westerham and a guest, decent wines, beams, bare boards and stripped brickwork in cosy original part with adjacent dining area, another bar in modern extension with woodburner; background and some live music; children welcome, dogs may be allowed (ask first), small front garden, back terrace and large lawn with boules and bat and trap, pretty churchyard and walks nearby, open all day in summer and at weekends. *(P M Dodd, Martin and Sue Day)*

WAREHORNE   TQ9832
Woolpack (01233) 733888
Off B2067 near Hamstreet; TN26 2LL Friendly new landlord for this neatly kept 16th-c pub/restaurant in lovely spot, good traditional food including carvery Weds evening and Sun lunchtime, well kept/priced local ales (one brewed for them by Old Dairy), rambling bar with heavy beams and inglenook woodburner, modern pine furniture in spacious candlelit restaurant, snug with sofas, armchairs and board games; background music; children and dogs welcome, picnic-sets out overlooking quiet lane and meadow with lovely beech trees, flower tubs and little fountain, 15th-c church, closed Mon lunchtime, open all day Fri-Sun. *(Peter Meister)*

WEST PECKHAM   TQ6452
Swan on the Green (01622) 812271
Off A26/B2016 W of Maidstone; ME18 5JW Own-brewed Swan ales and Biddenden cider in relaxed open-plan beamed bar, bare boards, stripped brickwork and mixed furnishings, good home-made food (not Sun evening) such as local venison, friendly efficient service; well behaved children and dogs welcome, charming village green (great for a summer drink), interesting part-Saxon church, open all day summer weekends. *(William Ruxton, Veronica Chrisp, Christian Mole, Martin and Sue Day)*

WESTWELL   TQ9847
Wheel (01233) 712430
The Street; TN25 4LQ Good interesting food from landlady, including fresh fish and good value set lunches, also some pubby choices, well kept Shepherd Neame ales and nice choice of wines, efficient cheery service, dining areas around bar with stripped-pine tables and chairs; children welcome, good-sized garden with metal furniture, closed Sun evening, Mon. *(Jan and Alan Summers)*

WHITSTABLE · TR1066
Old Neptune · (01227) 272262
Marine Terrace; CT5 1EJ Great view over Swale estuary from this unpretentious weatherboarded pub set right on the beach (rebuilt after being washed away in 1897 storm), enjoyable lunchtime food with seafood specials, real ales, weekend live music; children and dogs welcome, picnic-sets on the shingle (plastic glasses out here and occasional barbecues), fine sunsets. *(Adrian Johnson, Mrs G Marlow, Andrea Rampley)*

WINGHAM · TR2457
★Dog · (01227) 720339
Canterbury Road; CT3 1BB Pub/restaurant in Grade IIH-listed medieval building, log fires, uneven walls, heavy beams, old brickwork and panelling, leather sofas and armchairs on wood floors, conservatory restaurant, enjoyable food including good value weekday set lunch, three well kept real ales and good wines by the glass; eight bedrooms. *(Julie and Bill Ryan)*

WORTH · TR3356
★St Crispin · (01304) 612081
Signed off A258 S of Sandwich; CT14 0DF Dating from 16th-c with low beams, stripped brickwork and bare boards, welcoming landlady and friendly attentive staff, popular home-made food from good baguettes and pub staples to more adventurous choices in bar, restaurant and back conservatory (dogs allowed here), three changing real ales, belgian beers, local farm cider and well chosen wines, central log fire; children welcome away from bar, good bedrooms (including motel-style extension), charming big garden behind with terrace, bat and trap and play area, lovely village position. *(Dr Kevan Tucker)*

YALDING · TQ6950
★Walnut Tree · (01622) 814266
B2010 SW of Maidstone; ME18 6JB Timbered village pub with split-level main bar, fine old settles, a long cushioned mahogany bench and mix of dining chairs on brick or worn carpeted floors, chunky wooden tables with church candles, interesting old photographs on mustard walls, hops, big inglenook, Black Sheep, Harveys, Moorhouses and Skinners, good bar food and more inventive restaurant menu, attractive raftered dining room with high-backed leather dining chairs on parquet flooring, lots of local events; background and occasional live music, TV; a few picnic-sets out at front by road. *(Anon)*

Lancashire

with Greater Manchester and Merseyside

Good value food and beers from local breweries feature strongly in the pubs here – and you can be sure of a warm welcome from the licensees, too. New entries include the Ring o' Bells in Lathom (part of the fine Ainscough's small group and with an emphasis on family facilities), Cartford in Little Eccleston (a lovely place to stay overnight), Dukes 92 in Manchester (carefully converted canalside place with three dozen cheeses), Spread Eagle in Sawley (attractive riverside inn with enjoyable food and drink) and Swan at Whalley (17th-c town inn with friendly staff and fair value food and drink). Pubs doing especially well are the Eagle & Child at Bispham Green (top class food in civilised country pub), Three Fishes in Great Mitton (individually furnished bars and imaginative food), Derby Arms in Longridge (run by the same hard-working, friendly family for nearly 30 years), Highwayman at Nether Burrow (extremely popular for real ales and highly thought of meals), Church Inn at Uppermill (own brewed beers and honest food), Waddington Arms in Waddington (20 wines by the glass and well liked country cooking), and Inn at Whitewell at Whitewell (a special place to stay and in a lovely spot). Our Lancashire Dining Pub 2013 is the Eagle & Child at Bispham Green.

BASHALL EAVES   SD6943   Map 7

Red Pump ◀

NW of Clitheroe, off B6478 or B6243; BB7 3DA

Cosy bar, good food in more contemporary dining rooms and changing beers in a beautifully placed country inn; bedrooms

The friendly landlord at this rewarding 18th-c pub is happy to chat, and particularly about his quickly changing range of three usually regional beers on handpump that might be from brewers such as Bass, Cairngorm, Hawkshead and Moorhouses. He also stocks ten wines by the glass, small bottles of champagne and a good range of malt whiskies. As well as two pleasantly up-to-date dining rooms, there's a traditional, cosy central bar with bookshelves, cushioned settles and wheelbacks on green carpet, and a log fire; board games. The pub is in lovely country where the River Hodder carves a course beneath Longridge Fell just south of the moors of the Forest of Bowland and there are splendid views from the terraced gardens and bedrooms; residents can fish in the nearby river.

🍴 Using locally sourced meat, game from local shoots and herbs from pub's own garden, robust country food might include goats cheese tart, rabbit ragu with linguini, mini fish pot, faggots with parsley mash, tempura-battered haddock, nut and mushroom roast, lamb leg confit with lamb haggis and redcurrant and rosemary gravy, and puddings such as chocolate and cherry mousse, blackcurrant sponge with liquorice ice-cream and treacle tart. *Benchmark main dish: roast pork belly £13.50. Two-course evening meal £19.10.*

Free house ~ Licensees Jonathan and Martina Myerscough ~ Real ale ~ Bar food (12-2, 6-9(7 Sun)) ~ Restaurant ~ (01254) 826227 ~ Children welcome ~ Open 12-2.30, 5.45-11; 12-3, 5.30-11 Sat; 12-9 Sun; closed Mon, Tues in winter, two weeks in Jan ~ Bedrooms: £65S(£85B)/£95B ~ www.theredpumpinn.co.uk *Recommended by Steve Whalley, John and Eleanor Holdsworth*

 BISPHAM GREEN   SD4813   Map 7

Eagle & Child 🍴 � 🍺

Maltkiln Lane (Parbold–Croston road), off B5246); L40 3SG

Lancashire Dining Pub of the Year

Successful all-rounder with antiques in stylishly simple interior, great food, interesting range of beers, appealing rustic garden

Charming and stylish, this is a carefully run country pub with a friendly, civilised atmosphere. It's largely open-plan and discerningly furnished with a lovely mix of small old oak chairs, an attractive oak coffer, several handsomely carved antique oak settles (the finest apparently made partly from a 16th-c wedding bed-head), old hunting prints and engravings, and low hop-draped beams. There are red walls and coir matting up a step and oriental rugs on ancient flagstones in front of the fine old stone fireplace and counter; the pub's dogs are called Betty and Doris. Friendly young staff serve Thwaites Original alongside five guests from brewers such as Copper Dragon, George Wright and Phoenix, a farm cider, decent wines and around 30 malt whiskies. They hold a popular beer festival over the first May bank holiday weekend. The gently rustic, spacious garden has a well tended but unconventional bowling green, and beyond this, a wild area that is home to crested newts and moorhens. Selling interesting wines and pottery, the excellent shop housed in the handsome side barn includes a proper butcher and a deli.

🍴 Imaginative and highly thought of food might include sandwiches, pork and sage pâté with rhubarb chutney, steamed mussels with white wine, garlic, herbs and cream, corn-fed chicken liver pâté with tomato relish, mushroom rosemary risotto, steak in ale pie, beer-battered fresh haddock with hand-cut chips and mushy peas, lancashire hotpot with pickles and red cabbage, slow-braised pig cheeks with leeks, peas and bacon mash, free-range chicken wrapped in parma ham and sage with sauteed livers, harissa and red wine sauce, salmon with a toasted fennel and pine nut crust and caper, lemon and chilli butter sauce, and puddings. *Benchmark main dish: steak in ale pie £10.00. Two-course evening meal £19.60.*

Free house ~ Licensee David Anderson ~ Real ale ~ Bar food (12-2, 5.30-8.30(9 Fri, Sat); 12-8.30 Sun) ~ (01257) 462297 ~ Children welcome ~ Dogs welcome ~ Open 12-3, 5.30-11; 12-11 Sat; 12-10.30 Sun ~ www.ainscoughs.co.uk *Recommended by John and Helen Rushton, Jack Clark, Ed and Anna Fraser, Margaret Dickinson, Jane Green, Karen Eliot*

GREAT MITTON SD7139 Map 7

Three Fishes

Mitton Road (B6246, off A59 NW of Whalley); BB7 9PQ

Stylish modern revamp, tremendous attention to detail, excellent regional food with contemporary twist, interesting drinks

Readers have high praise for all aspects of this particularly attractive and imaginatively converted pub. Despite its size it's cleverly laid out with plenty of intimate corners; the areas closest to the bar are elegantly traditional with a couple of big stone fireplaces, rugs on polished floors and upholstered stools. Then there's a series of individually furnished and painted rooms with exposed stone walls, careful spotlighting and wooden slatted blinds, ending with another impressive fireplace. Staff are young and friendly and there's a good chatty atmosphere. The long bar counter (with elaborate floral displays) serves Thwaites Nutty Black, Original and Wainwright, a dozen wines by the glass and unusual soft drinks such as locally made sarsaparilla and dandelion and burdock. Overlooking the Ribble Valley, the garden and terrace have tables and perhaps their own summer menu. You write your name on a blackboard when you arrive and they find you when a table becomes free – the system works surprisingly well.

Food products are carefully sourced from small local suppliers, many of whom are pictured in black and white photographs on the walls and located on a map on the back of the menu – the beef is exclusive to here. As well as imaginative lunchtime sandwiches, there might be dishes such as twice-baked cheese soufflé, baked snails with streaky bacon, creamed mushrooms on toast, fish pie, fish and chips, cheese and onion pie, veal kidneys with mushroom sauce, duck pie, toad in the hole, puddings such as marmalade and orange tart and chocolate mousse, and a local cheeseboard. The afternoon snack menu includes hot or cold sandwiches, dips and salads. *Benchmark main dish: lancashire hotpot £11.00. Two-course evening meal £19.00.*

Free house ~ Licensee Andy Morris ~ Real ale ~ Bar food (12-8.30(9 Fri, Sat, 8 Sun)) ~ (01254) 826888 ~ Children welcome ~ Dogs allowed in bar ~ Open 12-11(10.30 Sun) ~ www.thethreefishes.com *Recommended by Hilary Forrest, Dr Kevan Tucker, John and Sylvia Harrop, Ed and Anna Fraser, Gordon and Margaret Ormondroyd, Rachel and Ross Gavin*

LATHOM SD4510 Map 7

Ring o' Bells £

In Lathom, turn right into Ring o' Bells Lane; L40 5TE

Bustling family-friendly canalside pub, interconnected rooms with antique furniture, six real ales, some sort of food all day and children's inside and outside play areas

Handy for the M6, this red brick Victorian pub is usefully open for some sort of food all day – starting with morning coffee and cakes – and there's a good mix of customers, with an emphasis on families. Several interconnected rooms of all sizes lead from the handsome central bar counter with its pretty inlaid tiles, and throughout there's a real miscellany of antique dining chairs and carved settles around some lovely old tables, comfortable sofas, rugs on flagstones, lots of paintings and prints of the local area, of sporting activities and of plants, and large mirrors, brass lanterns and standard lamps; staffordshire dogs and decorative plates sit on mantelpieces above open fires. Cumbrian Legendary, Thwaites Nutty Black and Wainwright and guests from brewers such as George Wright, Liverpool Organic and Prospect on handpump, good wines by the glass and over 25 whiskies; background music, TV, darts, board games. Downstairs, there's a more plainly furnished room and indoor and outdoor children's play areas. As we went to press, they had all sorts of plans for their four acres of land such as a football pitch, a vegetable garden, a cider orchard – and of course seats and tables by the Liverpool to Leeds Canal.

Using beef from their own organic farm and other local produce, the good value food includes lunchtime baguettes, crayfish cocktail with bloody mary dressing, mushroom rarebit on grilled ciabatta, smoked haddock with poached egg, spinach muffin and hollandaise sauce, fish and chips, pea risotto, tagliatelle with roast aubergine, tomatoes, spinach and goats cheese, steak, ale and mushroom pie, lambs liver with black pudding mash, fish board, cod with hollandaise sauce and fried pigeon breast with truffle mash. *Benchmark main dish: organic beef burger £8.95. Two-course evening meal £17.30.*

Free house ~ Licensee Anna Gervasoni ~ Real ale ~ Bar food (12-2, 5-9; 12-9 Sat; 12-8 Sun) ~ Restaurant ~ (01704) 893157 ~ Children welcome ~ Dogs allowed in bar ~ Open 11-11(10 Sun) ~ www.ainscoughs.co.uk *Recommended by Richard Gibbs*

LITTLE ECCLESTON   SD4240   Map 7
Cartford 🛏

Cartford Lane, off A586 Garstang–Blackpool, by toll bridge; PR3 0YP

Prettily placed 17th-c coaching inn on riverbanks, popular and attractively refurbished

It's advisable to book or arrive early for a table at this 17th-c coaching inn on the banks of the River Wyre on Lancashire's Fylde Coast. Its unusual four-level layout has been given a very sympathetic, fresh makeover that combines traditional and contemporary elements, with pinks and reds, and light wood floors and banquettes alongside oak beams and a log fire; background music, TV and board games. Hawkshead Lakeland Gold, Moorhouse Pride of Pendle, Theakston Old Peculier and a guest, perhaps from Bowland, are on handpump alongside speciality bottled beers and Weston's cider; several wines by the glass. Tables in the garden look out over the River Wyre (crossed by its toll bridge), the Trough of Bowland and Beacon Fell.

Good, interesting food includes a trio of ham hock terrine, scotch quail egg and shot of bloody mary, curried leek and lancashire cheese tartlet, scallops on saffron risotto with fried black pudding and crsipy pancetta, antipasti and seafood platters, beef, oxtail and ale pudding, fish pie, fish and chips, lamb hotpot, cheese swiss roll, duck breast with black cherry and cherry brandy sauce, grilled tuna on paella, steaks, and puddings such as passion fruit tart and raspberry sorbet and brioche and apricot jam pudding. *Benchmark main dish: oxtail pudding £13.50. Two-course evening meal £18.60.*

Free house ~ Licensees Patrick and Julie Beaume ~ Real ale ~ Bar food (12-2, 5.30-9(10 Fri, Sat); 12-8.30 Sun) ~ Restaurant ~ (01995) 670166 ~ Children welcome ~ Open 12-11(10 Sun) ~ Bedrooms: £65B/£100B ~ www.thecartfordinn.co.uk *Recommended by Nik Maguire, Phil and Helen Holt, P M Dodd*

Stars after the name of a pub show exceptional character and appeal. They don't mean extra comfort. And they are nothing to do with food quality, for which there's a separate knife-and-fork symbol. Even quite a basic pub can win stars, if it's individual enough.

LIVERPOOL
Philharmonic Dining Rooms ★ ◧ £

SJ3589 Map 7

36 Hope Street; corner of Hardman Street; L1 9BX

Beautifully preserved Victorian pub with superb period interior, up to ten real ales and sensibly priced food

Originally a gentlemen's club, this magnificent marble-fronted late Victorian building is filled with astonishing period details. The centrepiece is the mosaic-faced serving counter, from which heavily carved and polished mahogany partitions radiate under the intricately plasterworked high ceiling. The echoing main hall has stained glass depicting Boer War heroes Baden-Powell and Lord Roberts, rich panelling, a huge mosaic floor and copper panels depicting musicians in an alcove above the fireplace. More stained glass in one of the little lounges declares 'Music is the universal language of mankind' and backs this up with illustrations of musical instruments. Two side rooms are called Brahms and Liszt, and there are a couple of plushly comfortable sitting rooms. However, this is no museum piece and it can be very busy. There are ten real ales on handpump: Cains Finest Bitter and Jennings Cumberland with guests such as Adnams Bitter, Caledonian Deuchars and Flying Dutchman, fff Pressed Rat & Warthog, Fullers London Pride, Kelham Island Best Bitter, Sharps Doom Bar and Thwaites Original. Also, several malt whiskies and quite a few wines by the glass; quiz machine, fruit machine and background music. Don't miss the original 1890s Adamant gents' lavatory (all pink marble and mosaics); ladies are allowed a look if they ask first.

🍴 As well as breakfast (served till noon), the fairly priced food (available in the bar or from table service in the grand lounge dining room) includes sandwiches, deep-fried brie with caramelised onion chutney, sticky pork ribs in barbecue sauce, roasted vegetable tart, wild boar and chorizo burger with apple and celeriac slaw, thai green chicken curry, gammon and free-range eggs, slow-braised lamb shoulder with redcurrant sauce, and puddings like warm chocolate brownie with vanilla ice-cream and eton mess. *Benchmark main dish: beer-battered haddock and chips £8.45. Two-course evening meal £14.90.*

Mitchells & Butlers ~ Manager Nicola Hamilton-Coburn ~ Real ale ~ Bar food (11-10) ~ Restaurant ~ (0151) 707 2837 ~ Children welcome until 7pm ~ Open 11am-midnight ~ www.nicholsonspubs.co.uk *Recommended by Edward Mirzoeff, David Crook, the Didler, Andrew Bosi, Ed and Anna Fraser, Rob and Catherine Dunster*

LONGRIDGE
Derby Arms ♀

SD6038 Map 7

Chipping Road, Thornley; 1.5 miles N of Longridge on back road to Chipping; PR3 2NB

Welcoming, traditional country pub with hunting and fishing paraphernalia, good food, real ales and very decent wine list

The same warmly friendly family have been running this old stone-built country pub in a lovely spot in the Forest of Bowland for nearly 30 years. Among hunting and fishing bric-a-brac in the main bar, with its comfortable red plush seats, old photographs commemorate notable catches, and there's some nicely mounted bait together with a stuffed pheasant that seems to be flying in through the wall. To the right, a smaller room has sporting trophies and mementoes, and a regimental tie collection; background music and darts. The gents' has dozens of riddles on the wall – you can buy a sheet of them in the bar , with the money going to charity. Black Sheep and a guest such as Moorhouses Pride of Pendle on handpump and a good range of wines, including several by the glass or half bottle; TV, darts and board games. A few tables out in front, and another two behind the car park, have fine views; boules.

🍴 Quite a choice of enjoyable food includes sandwiches, black pudding with fried queenie and king scallops, bacon, and tarragon cream, free-range egg mayonnaise, various platters, ham and egg, an all-day breakfast, vegetable curry, chicken breast in a cream, wine and mushroom sauce, fresh haddock fillet mornay, venison cutlet on a venison cottage pie, good steaks with pepper, creamy mustard or port wine sauce, and puddings such as crème brûlée and a fruit pie of the day; they also offer two- and three-course set menus. *Benchmark main dish: home-made steak and kidney in ale suet pudding £10.95. Two-course evening meal £14.95.*

Punch ~ Lease Will and Carole Walne ~ Real ale ~ Bar food (12-2.15, 6-9.30; 12-9.45(9.15 Sun) Sat) ~ Restaurant ~ (01772) 782623 ~ Children welcome ~ Open 12-3.30, 6-12; 12-12 Sat; 12-11.30 Sun ~ www.derbyarmslongridge.com *Recommended by Ed and Anna Fraser, Margaret Dickinson, Sarah Flynn*

LYTHAM   SD3627   Map 7

Taps 🍺 £

A584 S of Blackpool; Henry Street – in centre, one street in from West Beach; FY8 5LE

Thriving seaside pub with down-to-earth atmosphere, spirited landlord, eight real ales and straightforward lunchtime snacks; open all day

Unassuming and friendly, this down-to-earth town pub carries an impressive range of eight beers, taking in Taps Best, which is brewed exclusively for them by Titanic, Greene King IPA and half a dozen ever-changing guests from smaller brewers such as Hopback, Pendle, Wentworth and York – you can see them all lined up in the view-in cellar; also country wines and a farm cider. A good mix of customers enjoy the bustling pubby atmosphere in the open-plan Victorian-style bare-boarded bar, which has ample standing room, stripped brick walls, nice old farm chairs and captain's chairs in bays around the sides, open fires, and a coal-effect gas fire between two built-in bookcases at one end. There's plenty of stained-glass decoration in the windows, depictions of fish and gulls reflecting the pub's proximity to the beach (it's a couple of minutes' walk away). The landlord is a rugby fan and his expanding collection of rugby memorabilia, old photographs and portraits of rugby stars is on display throughout; TV, shove-ha'penny, dominoes, quiz machine and fruit machine. There are a few seats and a heated canopied area outside. Parking is difficult near the pub so it's probably best to park at the West Beach car park on the seafront (free on Sunday) and walk.

🍴 A handful of cheap bar snacks includes hearty sandwiches, baked potatoes, burgers, chilli, curry, lasagne, and puddings such as chocolate fudge cake, and apple pie. *Benchmark main dish: soup and roast sandwich £4.95.*

Greene King ~ Manager Ian Rigg ~ Real ale ~ Bar food (12-2, not Sun) ~ No credit cards ~ (01253) 736226 ~ Children welcome till 7.30pm ~ Open 11-11(midnight Fri, Sat) ~ www.thetaps.net *Recommended by the Didler, Michael Butler, Dr Kevan Tucker*

MANCHESTER

SJ8397   Map 7

Dukes 92

Castle Street, below the bottom end of Deansgate; M3 4LZ

Waterside conversion with spacious interior, great range of cheeses and pizzas all day

The ultra modern conversion of this old stable block is a great success. It's named after the Duke's Lock, the 92nd and final one on the Rochdale Canal, which runs directly outside at a point where fine Victorian warehouses line the canal basin. The atmosphere is relaxed and informal, with well spaced old and modern furnishings, including comfortable chaises-longues and deep armchairs, throughout the ground floor and boldly bare whitewashed or red walls. Its stylish gallery bar, accessed by an elegant spiral staircase, overlooks the canal. The handsome granite-topped counter serves three real ales, two usually from Moorhouses, as well as decent wines and a wide choice of spirits; background music. Tables outside on a big terrace enjoy good waterside views.

 The menu is short but includes an excellent range of over three dozen cheeses and pâtés with generous helpings of granary bread; also hot and cold sandwiches, soup, salads, chicken wings, a good range of pizzas, caramel pecan brownie and ice-cream sundae. *Benchmark main dish: cheese and pâté £7.95. Two-course evening meal £12.50.*

Free house ~ Licensee James Ramsbottom ~ Real ale ~ Bar food (12-10.30(11 weekends)) ~ Restaurant ~ (0161) 839 8642 ~ Children welcome ~ Open 11.30-11 (1am Sat); 12-11 Sun ~ www.Dukes92.com *Recommended by Tracey and Stephen Groves*

NETHER BURROW

SD6175   Map 7

Highwayman 🍽 ♟

A683 S of Kirkby Lonsdale; LA6 2RJ

Substantial and skilfully refurbished old stone house with country interior serving carefully sourced food; lovely gardens

Our readers enjoy their visits to this friendly pub very much and tend to go back again and again. Although large, the stylishly simple flagstoned 17th-c interior is nicely divided into intimate corners, with a couple of big log fires and informal wooden furnishings. Black and white wall prints and placemats feature the local farmers and producers who supply the kitchen and a map on the menu even locates these 'regional food heroes'. Bowland Hen Harrier, Moorhouses Black Cat and Thwaites Bitter and Wainwright on handpump, several wines by the glass, around a dozen whiskies and a particularly good range of soft drinks. They don't take bookings at the weekend (except for groups of six or more), but write your name on a blackboard when you arrive, and they'll find you when a table is free. Service is busy, welcoming and efficient. French windows open to a big terrace and lovely gardens.

Some sort of reliably good food is available all day: bar nibbles, sandwiches, avocado, prawns and pickled celeriac salad with grain mustard mayonnaise, baked snails with bacon, garlic and herb butter, lancashire hotpot, battered haddock with marrowfat peas and dripping chips, rump burger with battered onion rings, tomato relish and pickles, toad in the hole with onion gravy, lambs liver with bacon, onions and herb sauce, duck pie, and puddings like double chocolate mousse and rhubarb and orange trifle with chocolate crumble. *Benchmark main dish: fish and chips £10.75. Two-course evening meal £18.75.*

Thwaites ~ Lease Andy Morris and Craig Bancroft ~ Real ale ~ Bar food (12-2, 5.30-8.30(8 Sun); reduced menu 2-5.30) ~ (01254) 826888 ~ Children welcome ~ Dogs allowed in bar ~ Open 12-11(10.30 Sun) ~ www.highwaymaninn.co.uk *Recommended by Karen Eliot, Brian and Janet Ainscough, Margaret Dickinson, J F M and M West, Ray and Winifred Halliday, Christine and Neil Townend*

 PLEASINGTON   SD6528   Map 7

Clog & Billycock 🍴 ♀

Village signposted off A677 Preston New Road on W edge of Blackburn; Billinge End Road; BB2 6QB

Carefully sourced local food in appealingly modernised stone-built village pub

Even when this skilfully refurbished and extended village pub is busy (which it often deservedly is) staff remain friendly and efficient and the atmosphere is chatty and easy-going. It has the feel of an upmarket barn conversion and is light and airy with flagstoned floors and pale grey walls; a cosier room has high-backed settles and a fireplace at the end. The whole pub is packed with light wooden tables, and although you may find them all full on arrival, such is the size of the place that you probably won't have to wait long in the little bar area for one to come free. Thwaites Lancaster Bomber, Original, Wainwright and a seasonal guest on handpump and a good choice of wines. There are some tables outside, beside a small garden.

 Reliably good food includes sandwiches, corn-fed chicken liver pâté with cumberland sauce, treacle-baked saddleback pork ribs, toad in the hole, cheese and onion or fish pie, rump burger with dripping chips, pickles and english mustard mayonnaise, beer-battered haddock and chips with marrowfat peas, slow-cooked beef with mushrooms, bacon and red wine sauce, and puddings such as pancakes with chocolate and hazelnut or lemon and sugar with home-made ice-cream and apple crumble with cinnamon custard. *Benchmark main dish: lancashire hotpot £11.50. Two-course evening meal £17.30.*

Thwaites ~ Lease Andy Morris and Craig Bancroft ~ Real ale ~ Bar food (12-8.30(9 Fri and Sat, 8 Sun)) ~ (01254) 201163 ~ Children welcome ~ Dogs allowed in bar ~ Open 12-11(10.30 Sun) ~ www.theclogandbillycock.com *Recommended by W K Wood, Bruce and Penny Wilkie, Ed and Anna Fraser, Rachel and Ross Gavin*

SAWLEY   SD7746   Map 7

Spread Eagle

Village signed just off A59 NE of Clitheroe; BB7 4NH

Nicely refurbished pub with imaginative food and riverside location

At the heart of the Ribble Valley and just across a country lane from the river, this is an attractive coaching inn and a lovely place for a drink or a meal. The interior has a lot of character and a pleasing mix of nice old and quirky modern furniture – anything from an old settle and pine tables to new low chairs upholstered in animal print fabric, all set off well by the grey rustic stone floor. Low ceilings, cosy sectioning, a warming fire and cottagey windows keep it all feeling intimate. The dining areas are more formal, with modern stripes, and, as a bit of a quip on the decorative trend for walls of unread books, a bookshelf mural – much easier to keep dust free; background music. Moorhouses Pride of Pendle, Theakstons Lightfoot Bitter, Thwaites Wainwright and a beer named for the pub on handpump and several wines by the glass. They have two smokers' porches, and individually furnished, comfortable bedrooms. The pub is handy for exhilarating walks in the Forest of Bowland and close to the substantial ruins of a 12th-c cistercian abbey.

Enjoyable food includes sandwiches, chicken liver and orange pâté with red onion marmalade, potted shrimps, honey-roast ham and egg, moules frites, home-made beefburger with blue cheese and bacon, smoked natural haddock with crisp ham, a poached egg and pea cream, steak and stilton pudding, lambs liver with onion, bacon and red wine gravy, griddled rib-eye steak with pepper sauce and hand-cut chips, and puddings. *Benchmark main dish: pork belly with black pudding mash £12.95. Two-course evening meal £20.00.*

Free house ~ Licensee Kate Peill ~ Real ale ~ Bar food (12-2, 6-9.30; 12-7.30 Sun) ~ Restaurant ~ (01200) 441202 ~ Children welcome ~ Dogs allowed in bar ~ Singer Fri nights ~ Open 11-11(10.30 Sun) ~ www.spreadeaglesawley.co.uk *Recommended by Steve Whalley, Brian and Anna Marsden, Gordon and Margaret Ormondroyd, John and Sylvia Harrop, Brian and Janet Ainscough, Margaret Dickinson*

TUNSTALL   SD6073   Map 7
Lunesdale Arms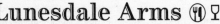
A683 S of Kirkby Lonsdale; LA6 2QN

Emphasis on good imaginative food and a separate area with traditional games

Bare boards and lively acoustics give the opened-up interior of this bustling dining pub a cheerful atmosphere. A white-walled area has a good mix of stripped dining tables and blue sofas facing each other across a low table (with daily papers) by a woodburning stove in a solid stone fireplace. Another area has pews and armchairs (some of the big unframed oil paintings are for sale) and, to one end, an airy games section with pool, table football, board games and TV. A snugger little flagstoned back part has another woodburning stove. Black Sheep and a guest such as Lancaster Blonde on handpump alongside a farm cider. The church in this Lune Valley village has Brontë associations.

Real care goes into the food here, which uses local ingredients and home-grown herbs and vegetables – and they make their own bread, too: pea and mint soup, shallot tatin with glazed goats cheese, meze to share, roast butternut, spinach, thyme and blue cheese tart, dressed crab, caesar salad, smoked haddock fishcakes with seaweed mayonnaise, rib-eye steak with béarnaise sauce, and puddings such as marmalade pudding and damson crème brûlée. *Benchmark main dish: steak and Guinness pie £13.95. Two-course evening meal £17.50.*

Free house ~ Licensee Emma Gillibrand ~ Real ale ~ Bar food (12-2(2.30 weekends), 6-9) ~ (01524) 274203 ~ Children welcome ~ Dogs welcome ~ Open 11-3, 6-midnight; 11-3.30, 6-1am Sat; 12-4, 6-midnight Sun; closed Mon except bank hols ~ www.thelunesdale.co.uk *Recommended by Dr Kevan Tucker, Karen Eliot, Dr and Mrs Leach, Michael Doswell*

UPPERMILL   SD0006   Map 7
Church Inn ⬤ £
From the main street (A607), look out for the sign for Saddleworth Church, and turn off up this steep narrow lane – keep on up!; OL3 6LW

Lively, good value community pub with big range of own-brew beers at unbeatable bargain prices, lots of pets and good food; children very welcome

Next to an isolated church on a steep slope high up on the moors, this enjoyably quirky pub with fine views down the valley has plenty of individual character. The horse collar on the wall of the bar is worn by the winner of their annual gurning (face-pulling) championship, which is held during the lively Rush Cart Festival, which is usually over the August bank holiday. Local bell-ringers arrive on Wednesdays to practise with a set of handbells that is kept here, while anyone is invited to join the morris dancers who meet here on Thursdays. When the springwater levels are too low for brewing, they bring in guest beers such as Black Sheep and Timothy Taylors Landlord. At other times, you might find up to 11 of their own-brew Saddleworth beers, usually starting at just £1.20 a pint. Some of the seasonal ones (look out for Ruebens, Ayrtons, Robyns and Indya) are named after the licensee's children, only appearing around their birthdays; dark lager on tap, too. The big unspoilt L-shaped main bar has high beams and some stripped stone, settles, pews, a good individual mix of chairs and lots of attractive prints and staffordshire and other china on a high delft shelf, jugs, brasses and so forth; TV (when there's sport on) and unobtrusive background music; the conservatory opens on to a terrace. Children will enjoy the burgeoning menagerie of animals, which includes rabbits, chickens, dogs, ducks, geese, alpacas, horses, 14 peacocks in the next-door field and some cats resident in an adjacent barn; dogs are made to feel very welcome.

🍴 Very reasonably priced bar food includes soup, black pudding fritter with spiced fruit chutney, whitebait, chicken goujons, steak and kidney pie, scampi, stuffed vegetable crêpe, rabbit pie, chicken wrapped in bacon with creamy mushroom sauce, lamb shank with red wine and rosemary sauce, fish pie, vegetable wellington with cheese sauce and duck breast with orange and Grand Marnier sauce. *Benchmark main dish: cod and chips £10.50. Two-course evening meal £14.50.*

Own brew ~ Licensee Christine Taylor ~ Real ale ~ Bar food (12-2.30, 5.30-9; 12-9 Fri-Sun and bank hols) ~ Restaurant ~ (01457) 820902 ~ Children welcome ~ Dogs allowed in bar ~ Open 12-12(1am Sat) ~ www.thechurchinn.co.uk *Recommended by Roger and Lesley Everett, the Didler, Bob Broadhurst, John Fiander, Yvonne Hosker*

WADDINGTON   SD7243   Map 7
Lower Buck £
Edisford Road; BB7 3HU

Hospitable village pub with reasonably priced, tasty food and five real ales

This pretty 18th-c village pub has a chatty, friendly atmosphere and is tucked away behind the church. There are several small, neatly kept cream-painted bars and dining rooms, each with a warming coal fire and good solid wood furnishings on stripped boards. Staff and customers are chatty and welcoming and they keep up to five real ales such as Bowland Hen Harrier and Sawley Tempted, Moorhouses Premier Bitter and Blond Witch, and Timothy Taylors Landlord on handpump, around a dozen malt whiskies and several wines by the glass; darts and pool. There are picnic-sets out on cobbles at the front and in the sunny back garden, and the pub is handily placed for walks in the Ribble Valley.

🍴 Using local meat and vegetables, the popular food might include lunchtime sandwiches, Morecambe Bay shrimps, black pudding with apple and wholegrain mustard sauce, fish and chips with mushy peas, gammon and egg, lasagne, chargrilled chicken breast with garlic mayonnaise, specials such as hake with an olive and mediterranean vegetable sauce, 16-oz steak and kidney pudding and duck breast with braised red cabbage and champ mash, and puddings like ice-cream sundae and sticky toffee pudding with toffee sauce. *Benchmark main dish: steak and mushroom pie £10.45. Two-course evening meal £17.50.*

Free house ~ Licensee Andrew Warburton ~ Real ale ~ Bar food (12-2.30, 6-9; 12-9 Sat, Sun and bank holidays) ~ (01200) 423342 ~ Children welcome ~ Dogs welcome ~ Open 11(12 Sun)-11(midnight Sat) ~ www.lowerbuckinn.co.uk *Recommended by Lucien Perring, Ed and Anna Fraser, Rachel and Ross Gavin*

 WADDINGTON   SD7243   Map 7

Waddington Arms ★ ♀ ◧ ⇌

Clitheroe Road (B6478 N of Clitheroe); BB7 3HP

Classic *Guide* pub, good all round, with plenty of character, good value bedrooms – and open all day

Everything at this lovely place runs beautifully, and the friendly easy-going atmosphere makes for a relaxing visit. Of its four linked rooms, the one on the left is snuggest in winter with its blazing woodburning stove in a monumental fireplace putting real warmth into the ancient flagstones. There's plenty to look at in the various low-beamed rooms, from antique prints through an interesting series of vintage motor-racing posters to the contemporary Laurie Williamson prints over on the right, an enlarged 19th-c sporting print here and leather-bound book wallpaper there. The furniture too gives the feeling that it's all been carefully chosen and thought through, with some fine antique oak settles as well as chunky stripped-pine tables. They have a good choice of wines by the glass a dozen malts, an ale Moorhouses brew for them (The Waddy), and four guests on handpump from brewers such as Bowland, Grays and Thwaites. Wicker chairs on a sunny flagstoned front terrace look across to this attractive village's church (it's just on the edge of the Forest of Bowland, too), and there are more tables on a two-level back terrace, with picnic-sets on a neat tree-sheltered lawn.

 Besides generous sandwiches, enjoyable country cooking here includes soups, duck confit or black pudding and poached egg, sausage and mash, lamb shank, steak and ale pie, fried bass with spring vegetables, hotpot, and steaks. *Benchmark main dish: beer-battered fish and chips £10.95. Two-course evening meal £17.50.*

Free house ~ Licensee Phil Glynn ~ Real ale ~ Bar food (12-2.30, 6-9.30; 12-9.30(9 Sun) Sat) ~ Restaurant ~ (01200) 423262 ~ Children welcome ~ Dogs allowed in bar and bedrooms ~ Open 11-11(12 Sat) ~ Bedrooms: £50B/£75B ~ www.waddingtonarms.co.uk *Recommended by Steve Whalley, Rachel and Ross Gavin, Gerry and Rosemary Dobson, David Heath*

WHALLEY   SD7336   Map 7

Swan

King Street; BB7 9SN

Bustling old town inn with cheerful bar, lots of customers, and good value food and drink; bedrooms

There's always a good mix of customers in this friendly 17th-c former coaching inn, and good value food and beer, too. The cheerful bar is big and nicely decorated in mushroom, beige and cream with colourful blinds, some modern artwork, simple dark leather dining chairs around deco-look pedestal tables, Bowland Hen Harrier and Sawley Tempted and Timothy Taylors Landlord on handpump and several wines by the glass. A quieter room leads off here with leather sofas and armchairs on neat bare floorboards; unobtrusive background music, games machine, and maybe a Wednesday quiz night; service is helpful and efficient. There are picnic-sets on a back terrace and on grass strips by the car park. The bedrooms are named after nearby rivers and attractions.

As well as serving breakfasts (for non-residents, too), the popular food might include sandwiches, mushrooms in stilton and cream sauce, black pudding and bacon salad, vegetarian lasagne, gammon and egg, piri-piri chicken kebabs, steak and mushroom pie, and puddings like lemon cheesecake and sticky toffee pudding. *Benchmark main dish: haddock and chips £8.45. Two-course evening meal £14.50.*

Enterprise ~ Lease Louise Clough ~ Real ale ~ Bar food (12-8.45) ~ Restaurant ~ (01254) 822195 ~ Children welcome ~ Dogs allowed in bar ~ Occasional live music weekends ~ Open 12-11 ~ Bedrooms: £50S/£78S ~ www.swanhotelwhalley.co.uk
Recommended by Roger and Donna Huggins

WHITEWELL   SD6546   Map 7
Inn at Whitewell ★ ♀ ⇌

Most easily reached by B6246 from Whalley; road through Dunsop Bridge from B6478 is also good; BB7 3AT

Elegant manor house with smartly pubby atmosphere, good bar food and luxury bedrooms

There's an idyllic view from the riverside bar and adjacent terrace of this ancient hotel, which is fabulously positioned deep among the hills and moors that rise to the high points of the Forest of Bowland. It's a stylish place to stay, dine or just enjoy a drink, with courteous friendly staff. Handsome old wood furnishings, including antique settles, oak gateleg tables and sonorous clocks, are set off beautifully against powder blue walls that are neatly hung with big attractive prints. The pubby main bar has roaring log fires in attractive stone fireplaces and heavy curtains on sturdy wooden rails; one area has a selection of newspapers and magazines, local maps and guidebooks; there's a piano for anyone who wants to play; board games. Early evening sees a cheerful bustle that later settles to a more tranquil and relaxing atmosphere. Drinks include a knowledgeable wine list of around 230 wines with over a dozen by the glass (there's a good wine shop in the reception area), organic ginger beer, lemonade and fruit juices and up to five real ales on handpump that might be from Bowland, Copper Dragon, Lakeland, Moorhouses and Timothy Taylor. They own several miles of trout, salmon and sea-trout fishing on the Hodder, and can arrange shooting and make up a picnic hamper.

Besides lunchtime sandwiches, well presented bar food might include baked goats cheese in filo pastry, spicy fried squid, duck terrine with poached pear and apple jelly, fish and chips, roast chicken breast with sage and onion stuffing and smoked bacon and onion jus, cheese and onion pie, salmon fillet with basil and olive mash and ratatouille, pork belly with braised lentils and shallots and apple puree; they also have a separate dining room menu. *Benchmark main dish: fish pie £11.00. Two-course evening meal £20.00.*

Free house ~ Licensee Charles Bowman ~ Real ale ~ Bar food (12-2, 7.30-9.30) ~ Restaurant ~ (01200) 448222 ~ Children welcome ~ Dogs allowed in bar and bedrooms ~ Open 11-midnight ~ Bedrooms: £85B/£115B ~ www.innatwhitewell.com
Recommended by John Taylor, John and Sylvia Harrop, Karen Eliot, Rachel and Ross Gavin, Steve Whalley

Also Worth a Visit in Lancashire

Besides the fully inspected pubs, you might like to try these pubs that have been recommended to us and described by readers. Do tell us what you think of them: feedback@goodguides.com

APPLEY BRIDGE SD5210
Dicconson Arms (01257) 252733
*B5375 (Appley Lane North)/A5209,
handy for M6 junction 27; WN6
9DY* Well run and civilised, with good nicely presented food (all day Sun) including weekday set menu, friendly attentive service, two or three well kept Marstons-related ales, uncluttered bar area with clubby chairs, dining room beyond, pine floors, woodburner; some seats outside, open all day. *(Norma and Noel Thomas)*

BARLEY SD8240
Pendle (01282) 614808
Barley Lane; BB12 9JX Friendly 1930s stone pub in shadow of Pendle Hill, three cosy rooms, two log fires, simple substantial food (all day weekends) using local produce, five well kept regional ales, conservatory; garden, lovely village and good walking country, self-catering cottages, open all day Fri-Sun. *(Dr Kevan Tucker)*

BARNSTON SJ2783
⋆**Fox & Hounds** (0151) 648 1323
3 miles from M53 junction 3: A552 towards Woodchurch, then left on A551; CH61 1BW Spotless well run pub with cheerful welcome, six real ales including Theakstons, 60 malt whiskies, good value traditional lunchtime food, roomy carpeted bay-windowed lounge with built-in banquettes and plush-cushioned captain's chairs around solid tables, old local prints and collection of police and other headgear, charming old quarry-tiled corner with antique range, copper kettles, built-in pine kitchen cupboards, enamel food bins and earthenware, small locals' bar (worth a look for its highly traditional layout and collection of horsebrasses and metal ashtrays), snug where children allowed; dogs welcome in bar, picnic-sets out at back among colourful tubs and hanging baskets, open all day.
(Clive Watkin, David Jackman)

BARROW SD7337
⋆**Eagle** (01254) 825285
*Village signed off A59; Clitheroe Road
(A671 N of Whalley); BB7 9AQ* Stylish dining pub with modern light leather chairs, sofas and big low tables in bar, brasserie-style dining room with busy open kitchen and cabinet displaying their 35-day dry-aged steaks, good food (all day Sun) including sandwiches, excellent home-made sausages and imaginative main choices, five real ales, good wines, young uniformed staff, back area with chandeliers and big mirrors, clubby panelled piano bar; children welcome, tables outside overlooking big car park, open all day. *(Mr and Mrs John Taylor, Rachel and Ross Gavin)*

BAY HORSE SD4952
⋆**Bay Horse** (01524) 791204
1.2 miles from M6 J33: A6 southwards, then off on left; LA2 0HR Civilised redecorated country dining pub – a useful motorway stop; cosily pubby bar with good log fire, cushioned wall banquettes and fresh flowers, ales such as Black Sheep, Lancaster and Moorhouses, 15 wines by the glass, smarter restaurant with cosy corners, another log fire and carefully presented innovative food (not Sun evening), friendly service; children welcome, garden tables, two bedrooms in converted barn over road, closed Mon. *(Steve Whalley, Karen Eliot, Dave Braisted, Mrs Anne Henley)*

BEBINGTON SJ3385
Travellers Rest (0151) 608 2988
*B5151, not far from M53 junction 4;
New Ferry Road, Higher Bebington;
CH62 1BQ* Friendly semi-rural pub with several areas around central bar, good value food from lunchtime sandwiches and snacks to more substantial evening meals (Thurs-Sat till 7pm), no food Sun, up to eight well kept real ales including some from small breweries, efficient staff, alcoves, beams, brasses etc; no children; open all day. *(MLR)*

BELMONT SD6715
⋆**Black Dog** (01204) 811218
Church Street (A675); BL7 8AB Nicely set Holts pub with their usual good value food (all day Fri-Sun, not Tues evening), bargain beers, friendly prompt staff, cheery small-roomed traditional core, coal fires, picture-window extension; children welcome, seats outside with moorland views above village, attractive part-covered smokers' area, good walks, decent well priced bedrooms (breakfast from 9am), open all day. *(Norma and Noel Thomas, the Didler, Ben Williams, Len Beattie)*

BIRKENHEAD SJ3289
Stork (0151) 647 7506
Price Street; CH41 6JN Mid-Victorian pub with tiled façade, four well restored civilised rooms around island bar, fine polished mosaic floors and art nouveau tilework, old photographs, four changing ales, bargain basic food weekday lunchtime and early evening; open all day. *(the Didler)*

BLACKO   SD8641
Rising Sun (01282) 612173
A682 towards Gisburn; BB9 6LS
Welcoming traditional village pub tied to
Moorhouses, four of their ales plus guests,
enjoyable low-priced pubby food including
local dish stew-and-hard, tiled entry, open
fires in three rooms off main bar; dogs
welcome, tables out on front terrace with
Pendle Hill view, open all day Fri-Sat, closed
lunchtimes Mon-Weds. *(Dr Kevan Tucker)*

BLACKSTONE EDGE   SD9617
✶White House (01706) 378456
*A58 Ripponden–Littleborough, just W
of B6138; OL15 0LG* Beautifully placed
moorland dining pub with remote views,
emphasis on good value hearty food from
sandwiches up (all day Sun), prompt friendly
service, Black Sheep, Theakstons and a
couple of regional beers, belgian bottled
beers, cheerful atmosphere, carpeted main
bar with hot fire, other areas off, most tables
used for food; children welcome. *(Clive Flynn,
Brian and Anna Marsden)*

BOLTON   SD7112
Brewery Tap (01204) 302837
Belmont Road; BL1 7AN Tap for Bank
Top, a well kept guest ale too, no food; dogs
welcome. *(Ben Williams)*

BOLTON   SD6809
Victoria (01204) 849944
Markland Hill; BL1 5AG Refurbished
and extended pub known locally as Fannys,
enjoyable food with a regional slant and well
kept local beers, good service; seats outside,
open all day. *(W K Wood, David Heath)*

BOLTON   SD6913
Wilton Arms (01204) 303307
Belmont Road, Horrocks Fold; BL1 7BT
Friendly roadside pub on edge of W Pennine
Moors, consistently good well priced fresh
food, four well kept regional ales including
Bank Top Flat Cap, open fires, conservatory;
children welcome, valley views and good
walks, open all day. *(W K Wood, Rob and
Gill Wood)*

BOLTON BY BOWLAND   SD7849
Coach & Horses (01200) 447202
Main Street; BB7 4NW Stone-built beamed
pub/restaurant, strikingly modernised, with
black chandeliers, bold fabric wall hangings
and big mirrors, food from pub favourites to
more unusual choices, a couple of ales such
as Bowland and Moorhouses, good choice of
wines, open fires; children welcome, tables
out at back, lovely streamside village with
interesting church, three bedrooms, open all
day weekends, closed Mon, Tues. *(Mary Hill,
Steve Whalley)*

BRINDLE   SD5924
✶Cavendish Arms (01254) 852912
*3 miles from M6 junction 29, by A6 and
B5256 (Sandy Lane); PR6 8NG*
Traditional village pub dating from 15th
c, welcoming and popular, with good
inexpensive home-made food (all day
weekends) from sandwiches up, Banks's,
Marstons and two guest ales, beams, cosy
snugs with open fires, stained-glass windows,
carpets throughout; children welcome, dogs
in tap room, heated canopied terrace with
water feature, more tables in side garden,
good walks, open all day. *(Margaret Dickinson)*

BROUGHTON   SD4838
✶Plough at Eaves (01772) 690233
*A6 N through Broughton, first left into
Station Lane under a mile after traffic
lights, then left after 1.5 miles, Eaves
Lane; PR4 0BJ* Pleasantly unpretentious
old country tavern with two beamed homely
bars, well kept Thwaites ales, straightforward
enjoyable food (all day Sun) including OAP
lunch deal, friendly service, lattice windows
and traditional furnishings, old guns over
woodburner in one room, Royal Doulton
figurines above log fire in dining bar with
conservatory; quiet background music,
games machine; children welcome, front
terrace and spacious side/back garden, well
equipped play area, open all day weekends
(till 1am Sat), closed Mon (except bank
holidays). *(Michael Butler, Pauline and
Derek Hodgkiss)*

BURNLEY   SD8432
Bridge (01282) 411304
Bank Parade; BB11 1UH Open-plan town-
centre pub with well kept Hydes Original
and several changing guests (hundreds each
year), continental beers on tap and many
dozen by the bottle, farm ciders too, bargain
lunchtime food, friendly atmosphere and
good young staff, simple chairs and tables on
left, small snug and leather settees on right,
some live music; open all day (till 1am Fri,
Sat), closed Mon, Tues. *(Dr Kevan Tucker)*

BURY   SD8313
Trackside (0161) 764 6461
*East Lancashire Railway Station,
Bolton St; BL9 0EY* Welcoming busy
station bar by East Lancs steam railway,
bright, airy and clean with eight changing
ales, bottled imports, farm cider and great

Please tell us if the décor, atmosphere, food or drink at a pub is different from
our description. We rely on readers' reports to keep us up to date:
feedback@goodguides.com, or (no stamp needed) The Good Pub Guide, FREEPOST
TN1569, Wadhurst, E Sussex TN5 7BR.

range of whiskies, enjoyable home-made food (not Mon, Tues), fine display of beer labels on ceiling; children welcome till 7.30pm, platform tables, open all day. *(the Didler, Don Bryan, Ben Williams)*

CARNFORTH SD5173
Longlands (01524) 781256

Tewitfield, about 2 miles N; A6070, off A6; LA6 1JH Bustling family-run village inn with four good local beers, friendly helpful staff, well liked interesting food in bar and restaurant (worth booking), pizzas and pub favourites too, live music Mon; children welcome, bedrooms and self-catering cottages, Lancaster Canal nearby, open all day. *(Becky Mason)*

CHEADLE HULME SJ8785
Church Inn (0161) 485 1897

Ravenoak Road (A5149 SE); SK8 7EG Popular old family-run local with good traditional food, well kept Robinsons beers, coal fire, restaurant, friendly atmosphere. *(Stuart Paulley, Andy and Jill Kassube, G D K Fraser)*

CHIPPING SD6141
⋆ **Dog & Partridge** (01995) 61201

Hesketh Lane; crossroads Chipping–Longridge with Inglewhite–Clitheroe; PR3 2TH Comfortable old-fashioned and much altered 16th-c dining pub in grand countryside, enjoyable food (all day Sun) served by friendly staff, Tetleys ales, beams, exposed stone walls and good log fire, small armchairs around close-set tables in main lounge, smart casual dress for evening restaurant; children welcome, open all day Sun, closed Mon. *(Anon)*

CHORLEY SD5817
Yew Tree (01257) 480344

Dill Hall Brow, Heath Charnock – out past Limbrick towards the reservoirs; PR6 9HA Attractive tucked-away restaurant pub refurbished under new management, good food all day including lunchtime bar menu, open kitchen, two ales from Prospect and a dozen wines by the glass, friendly helpful staff; background music, no dogs inside; children welcome, picnic-sets out on decked area, open all day. *(Simon Stott, W K Wood)*

CHORLTON CUM HARDY SJ8193
Horse & Jockey (0161) 860 7794

Chorlton Green; M21 9HS Refurbished low-beamed pub with mock-Tudor façade, own-brewed Bootleg ales and beers, knowledgeable chatty staff, all-day bar food, more restauranty choices in high-ceilinged evening/weekend dining room (part of former Victorian brewery), good mix of customers; children allowed till 9pm, dogs very welcome (even a non-alcoholic beer for them), picnic-sets on front terrace looking across to green, open all day. *(Malcolm and Pauline Pelliatt)*

COLNE SD8940
Black Lane Ends (01282) 864235

Skipton Old Road, Foulridge; BB8 7EP Country pub with good food cooked with some finesse, cheerful landlord and staff, well kept Copper Dragon and Timothy Taylors Landlord, small restaurant; children welcome, garden with play area, good Pennine views, handy for canal and reservoir walks. *(M S Catling)*

COMPSTALL SJ9690
Andrew Arms (0161) 484 5392

George Street (B6104); SK6 5JD Refurbished and new chef producing some good food (more upscale evening menu), friendly welcoming staff, well kept Robinsons ales; garden, handy for Etherow Country Park, open all day. *(Dennis Jones)*

CONDER GREEN SD4556
Stork (01524) 751234

Just off A588; LA2 0AN Fine spot where River Conder joins the Lune estuary among bleak marshes, two blazing log fires in rambling dark-panelled rooms, good reasonably priced food with south african influences, friendly efficient staff, real ales such as Black Sheep and Lancaster; children welcome, handy for Glasson Dock, bedrooms, open all day. *(Michael Butler)*

CROSBY SJ3100
Crows Nest (0151) 924 6953

Victoria Road, Great Crosby; L23 7XY Unspoilt character roadside local with cosy bar, snug and Victorian-style lounge, all neatly looked after by welcoming landlady, well kept Cains, Theakstons and guests; tables outside, open all day. *(the Didler, Brian Conrad)*

DENSHAW SD9710
Printers Arms (01457) 874248

Oldham Road; OL3 5SN Above Oldham in shadow of Saddleworth Moor, modernised interior with small log-fire bar and three other rooms, popular good value food including OAP midweek deal, Timothy Taylors Golden Best and a beer brewed for them by Bazens, several wines by the glass, friendly efficient young staff. *(Michael Butler, Stuart Paulley)*

DENSHAW SD9711
⋆ **Rams Head** (01457) 874802

2 miles from M62 junction 22; A672 towards Oldham, pub N of village; OL3 5UN Sweeping moorland views from inviting dining pub with four thick-walled traditional little rooms, good variety of food (all day Sun) including seasonal game and seafood, well kept Black Sheep and Timothy Taylors, efficient friendly service, beam-and-plank ceilings, panelling, oak settles and built-in benches, log fires, tearoom and adjacent delicatessen selling local produce;

soft background music; children welcome (not Sat evening), open all day Sun, closed Mon (except bank holidays). *(Gill and Malcolm Stott, Clive Flynn, Brian and Anna Marsden, Gerard Dyson, John and Sylvia Harrop, Stuart and Sarah Barrie and others)*

DENTON   SJ9395
Lowes Arms   (0161) 336 3064
Hyde Road (A57); M34 3FF For now no longer brewing their own LAB ales but serving good local Hornbeam and Phoenix, jovial landlord and helpful friendly staff, wide choice of good bargain food including offers, bar with games, restaurant; tables outside, smoking shelter, open all day weekends. *(Stuart Paulley, Dennis Jones)*

DOBCROSS   SD9906
Swan   (01457) 873451
The Square; OL3 5AA Unspoilt low-beamed pub with three areas off small central bar, open fires, flagstones and traditional settles, friendly atmosphere, four Marstons-related beers, enjoyable home-made food including specials; children welcome, tables outside, attractive village below moors. *(Edward Atkinson)*

DOWNHAM   SD7844
⋆Assheton Arms   (01200) 441227
Off A59 NE of Clitheroe, via Chatburn; BB7 4BJ Neatly kept 18th-c pub in lovely village location with Pendle Hill view, cosy low-beamed L-shaped bar with pews, big oak tables and massive stone fireplace, good range of food (all day Sun) including seafood menu, quick service, lots of wines by the glass, two real ales; background music; children and dogs welcome, picnic-sets outside, open all day weekends. *(C A Bryson, Rachel and Ross Gavin)*

DUNHAM TOWN   SJ7288
Rope & Anchor   (01619) 277901
Paddock Lane, Dunham Massey; WA14 5RP Popular refurbished dining pub on two floors, good food from light lunches up, first-rate service, well kept Holts, garden room for families; plenty of room outside with smokers' shelter and play area, open all day. *(Hilary Forrest, David Heath, David M Smith)*

ECCLES   SJ7798
Albert Edward   (0161) 7071045
Church Street; M30 0LS Cheery unpretentious local with main bar and three other rooms, flagstones and old tiles, fire, old local photographs, bargain Sam Smiths; small back terrace, open all day. *(the Didler)*

ECCLES   SJ7798
Lamb   (0161) 7893882
Regent Street (A57); M30 0BP Full-blooded Edwardian three-room local, splendid etched windows, fine woodwork and furnishings, extravagantly tiled stairway, trophies in display case, bargain Holts and lunchtime sandwiches, full-size snooker table in original billiards room, friendly atmosphere with many older regulars; open all day. *(the Didler)*

ECCLES   SJ7698
Stanley Arms
Eliza Ann Street/Liverpool Road (A57), Patricroft; M30 0QN Unspoilt mid-Victorian corner local with bargain Holts, popular front bar, hatch serving lobby and tiled corridor to small back rooms, one with cast-iron range, lunchtime cobs, friendly licensees; open all day. *(the Didler)*

EUXTON   SD5318
Travellers Rest   (01257) 451184
Dawbers Lane (A581 W); PR7 6EG Refurbished old dining pub (most here to eat) with good varied range of popular food including daily specials, organised friendly staff, well kept Black Sheep and four quests; children welcome, dogs allowed in part of back bar, nice side garden, open all day, food all day weekends (till 6pm Sun). *(Margaret Dickinson, Sandie and Andrew Geddes)*

FENCE   SD8237
⋆Fence Gate   (01282) 618101
2.6 miles from M65 junction 13; Wheatley Lane Road, just off A6068 W; BB12 9EE Imposing 17th-c building refurbished into smart pub/brasserie, Caledonian Deuchars IPA, Courage Directors, Theakstons Best and two changing guests, plenty of wines by the glass, teas and coffees, bar food and more expensive restaurant menu, carpeted bar divided into distinct areas with polished panelling, timbers, big fire, mix of wooden tables and chairs, sofas, sporting prints, contemporary brasserie with topiary; background music, TV; children welcome, open all day (till 1am Fri, Sat). *(Rachel and Ross Gavin)*

FENCE   SD8338
Old Sparrow Hawk   (01282) 603034
Wheatley Lane Road; BB12 9QG Big rambling black and white timbered pub, good selection of real ales, enjoyable popular food, good service. *(Guy Vowles, Ken and Lynda Taylor, Dr Kevan Tucker, Rachel and Ross Gavin)*

FORTON   SD4950
New Holly   (01524) 793500
Lancaster Road (A6); PR3 0BL Well run spacious roadside pub, wide choice of good generous food using local supplies, Thwaites ales, young efficient staff, games room; children welcome, tables out under cover, lovely hanging baskets, play area, bedrooms. *(Margaret Dickinson)*

GARSTANG   SD4945
⋆Th'Owd Tithebarn   (01995) 604486
Off Church Street; PR3 1PA Large barn with flagstoned terrace overlooking

Lancaster Canal marina, Victorian country life theme with long refectory table, old kitchen range, masses of farm tools, stuffed animals and birds, flagstones and high rafters, generous simple food all day from filled baguettes up, Black Sheep and York ales, good value wine by the glass, quieter parlour welcoming children; background music; open all day summer. *(Francesca Salvini, Roger and Donna Huggins, Ben Williams)*

GOOSNARGH   SD5738
⋆ **Horns** (01772) 865230
Pub signed off B5269, towards Chipping; PR3 2FJ Plush early 18th-c inn with relaxed atmosphere, neatly kept carpeted rooms with log fires, popular food from pub standards to local duck and pheasant, Bowland ales, plenty of wines by the glass and good choice of malts, friendly service; background music; children welcome, garden, six bedrooms (some with road noise), caravan park, not far from M6. *(Mark Woods Diabs, Rachel and Ross Gavin, Ray and Winifred Halliday)*

GREAT HARWOOD   SD7332
Royal (01254) 883541
Station Road; BB6 7BA Substantial Victorian pub with good changing range of beers from small breweries (May festival), great selection of bottled beers too, no food, simple traditional fittings, friendly atmosphere, pub games including pool and darts, occasional live music; partly covered terrace, three bedrooms, closed lunchtime Mon-Thurs, open all day Fri-Sun. *(the Didler)*

GREAT MITTON   SD7138
Aspinall Arms (01254) 826223
B6246 NW of Whalley; BB7 9PQ Nicely situated pub dating from the 17th-c, roomy bar with red plush wall banquettes, comfortable chairs and sofa by open fire, well kept ales such as Boland, Lancaster, Three B's and Tirril, enjoyable fairly traditional food from good cold or hot sandwiches to specials, newspapers, books and magazines to read, small separate dining room; background and live music including July Cloudspotting festival; children and dogs welcome, picnic-sets on flagstoned terrace and in big garden with play area, summer barbecues, just above River Ribble (fishing permits available), six bedrooms, open all day in summer. *(Richard and Karen Holt)*

GRINDLETON   SD7545
⋆ **Duke of York** (01200) 441266
Off A59 NE of Clitheroe, either via Chatburn, or off A671 in W Bradford; Brow Top; BB7 4QR Welcoming chef/landlord and neat helpful staff in comfortable civilised dining pub, really good imaginative food with plenty of attention to detail, good value set deals too, nice wines and coffee, well kept Black Sheep and Copper Dragon,

various areas- one with open fire, views over Ribble Valley to Pendle Hill; tables on raised decking and in garden behind, closed Mon. *(Peter and Josie Fawcett, Steve Whalley, Margaret Dickinson, Peter Abbott and others)*

HAWKSHAW   SD7515
Red Lion (01204) 856600
Ramsbottom Road; BL8 4JS Refurbished pub/hotel owned by Lees, their ales, enjoyable good value food; children welcome, bedrooms, quiet spot by River Irwell. *(Ben Williams, Norma and Noel Thomas, John and Sylvia Harrop, Rachel and Ross Gavin and others)*

HAWKSHAW   SD7514
Waggon & Horses (01204) 882221
Bolton Road; BL8 4JL Good well priced home-made food (not Mon, Tues) using fresh local ingredients in bar and small restaurant, good service, ales such as Adnams, Banks's and Greene King. *(Norma and Noel Thomas, Rachel and Ross Gavin)*

HESKIN GREEN   SD5315
⋆ **Farmers Arms** (01257) 451276
Wood Lane (B5250, N of M6 junction 27); PR7 5NP Popular family-run country pub, good choice of well priced home-made food in two-level dining area, cheerful helpful staff, Black Sheep, Jennings, Prospect and Timothy Taylors Landlord, heavy black beams, sparkling brasses, china and stuffed animals, darts in public bar, Thurs quiz; background and some live music, Sky TV; children welcome, picnic-sets in big colourful garden, play area, more tables front and side, good value bedrooms, open all day weekends. *(Norma and Noel Thomas)*

HEST BANK   SD4766
⋆ **Hest Bank Inn** (01524) 824339
Hest Bank Lane; off A6 just N of Lancaster; LA2 6DN Good choice of enjoyable food in picturesque three-bar coaching inn, nice setting close to Morecambe Bay, well kept ales, decent wines, friendly helpful young staff, separate restaurant area with pleasant conservatory; children welcome, plenty of tables out by Lancaster Canal, open all day. *(Tony and Maggie Harwood)*

HURST GREEN   SD6837
⋆ **Shireburn Arms** (01254) 826678
Whalley Road (B6243 Clitheroe–Goosnargh); BB7 9QJ Refurbished 17th-c hotel, peaceful Ribble Valley views from big light and airy restaurant and lovely neatly kept garden with attractive terrace, friendly helpful staff, enjoyable food (all day weekends) from sandwiches to traditional dishes with a modern twist, armchairs, sofas and log fire in beamed and flagstoned lounge bar with linked dining area, well kept Bowland, Moorhouses and Tirril, several wines by the glass, daily newspapers; children and dogs welcome, pretty Tolkien

walk from here, 22 comfortable bedrooms, open all day (from 9am for coffee). *(Steve Whalley)*

HYDE   SJ9495
Cheshire Ring (0161) 366 1840
Manchester Road (A57, between M67 junctions 2 and 3); SK14 2BJ Welcoming pub tied to Beartown brewery, their good value ales kept well, guest beers and imports on tap, farm ciders and perries, good house wines, nice home-made pies, Thurs curries and bargain Sun roasts; background music – live upstairs at weekends; open all day Sat and Sun, from 4pm Mon, Tues, 1pm Weds-Fri. *(Dennis Jones, the Didler)*

HYDE   SJ9493
Joshua Bradley (0161) 406 6776
Stockport Road, Gee Cross; SK14 5EZ Former mansion handsomely converted to pub/restaurant keeping panelling, moulded ceilings and imposing fireplaces, good range of well priced popular food, Hydes and a couple of guest beers in great condition, friendly efficient staff; children welcome, heated terrace, play area. *(Dennis Jones)*

HYDE   SJ9595
Sportsman (0161) 368 5000
Mottram Road; SK14 2NN Bright cheerful Victorian local, Rossendale Pennine ales and lots of changing guests (frequent beer festivals), welcoming licensees, bargain bar food, upstairs cuban restaurant, bare boards and open fires, pub games, full-size snooker table upstairs; children and dogs welcome, open all day. *(Dennis Jones, the Didler)*

IRBY   SJ2586
Irby Mill (0151) 604 0194
Mill Lane, off Greasby Road; CH49 3NT Converted miller's cottage (original windmill demolished 1898) doing well under present management, eight well kept ales, good choice of wines by the glass, popular reasonably priced food all day (till 6pm Sun) from generous sandwiches up, friendly service, two low-beamed traditional flagstoned rooms and comfortable carpeted lounge, log fire, interesting old photographs and history; tables on terraces and side grass, open all day. *(Clive Watkin, Tony Tollitt, Martyn Smith, Philip and Jane Hastain)*

LANCASTER   SD4761
★ Borough (01524) 64170
Dalton Square; LA1 1PP Popular city-centre pub, stylishly civilised, with chandeliers, dark leather sofas and armchairs, lamps on antique tables, high stools and elbow tables, seven real ales such as Bowland, Hawkshead, Lancaster and Kirkby Lonsdale, lots of bottled beers, big dining room with central tables and booths along one side, enjoyable all-day food with much emphasis on local suppliers, good value two-course deal till 6.30pm (not Sun), jams

and local produce for sale, upstairs comedy night Sun; children and dogs welcome, lovely tree-sheltered garden, open all day. *(Colin Woodward, Roger and Donna Huggins)*

LANCASTER   SD4761
★ Water Witch (01524) 63828
Parking in Aldcliffe Road behind Royal Lancaster Infirmary, off A6; LA1 1SU Attractive conversion of 18th-c canalside barge-horse stabling, flagstones, stripped stone, rafters and pitch-pine panelling, seven well kept ales including local Cross Bay (third-of-a-pint glasses available) from mirrored bar, enjoyable food all day including specials, prompt pleasant service, upstairs restaurant; children in eating areas, tables outside. *(Brian and Anna Marsden)*

LANESHAW BRIDGE   SD9141
Alma (01282) 863447
Emmott Lane, off A6068 E of Colne; BB8 7EG Renovated and extended pub with extensive choice of good well priced food, real ales and several wines by the glass, friendly efficient service; background music; clean comfortable bedrooms. *(Trevor Waddington, John and Eleanor Holdsworth)*

LEIGH   SJ6599
Waterside (01942) 605005
Twist Lane; WN7 4DB Civilised pub in tall converted 19th-c warehouses by Bridgewater Canal, handy for indoor and outdoor markets, wide choice of enjoyable bargain food all day including deals, Greene King ales, good friendly service, chatty lunchtime atmosphere; younger evening crowd when live music and DJs; children welcome, disabled access and facilities, plenty of waterside tables, ducks and swans, open all day (till 3am Fri, Sat). *(Ben Williams)*

LIVERPOOL   SJ3489
★ Baltic Fleet (0151) 709 3116
Wapping, near Albert Dock; L1 8DQ Unusual bow-fronted pub with convivial local atmosphere, wide range of interesting beers including own good Wapping brews, several wines by the glass, enjoyable straightforward well priced food (not Sat lunchtime) such as traditional scouse, weekend breakfasts, bare boards, big arched windows, simple mix of furnishings and nautical paraphernalia, newspapers, upstairs lounge; background music, TV; children welcome in eating areas, dogs in bar, back terrace, open all day. *(Peter Smith and Judith Brown, Andy and Jill Kassube, the Didler, Claes Mauroy)*

LIVERPOOL   SJ3589
Belvedere (0151) 709 0303
Sugnall Street; L7 7EB Unspoilt little two-room Victorian pub with friendly chatty atmosphere, original fittings including etched glass, coal fires, four changing ales, good pizzas, darts and other games; open all day. *(the Didler)*

LIVERPOOL   SJ3588
✱ Brewery Tap (0151) 709 2129
Cains Brewery, Stanhope Street; L8 5XJ
Victorian pub with full Cains range at
reasonable prices, guest beers too, friendly
efficient staff, good value food weekday
lunchtimes, nicely understated clean
décor, wooden floors, handsome bar, plush
raised side snug, interesting old prints and
breweriana, gas fire, daily newspapers;
sports TV, no dogs; children welcome till
8pm, disabled access, brewery tours, open all
day. *(the Didler, Claes Mauroy)*

LIVERPOOL   SJ3589
Cracke (0151) 709 4171
Rice Street; L1 9BB Friendly unsmart local
popular with students, Liverpool Organic,
Thwaites, and several guests, farm cider,
sandwiches till 6pm, small unspoilt bar with
bare boards and bench seats, snug and bigger
back room with unusual Beatles diorama, lots
of posters for local events; juke box, sports
TV; picnic-sets in sizeable back garden, open
all day. *(the Didler)*

LIVERPOOL   SJ3589
✱ Dispensary (0151) 709 2160
Renshaw Street; L1 2SP Small busy
central pub with up to ten well kept ales
including Cains and other local brews,
bottled imports, no food, bare boards and
polished panelling, wonderful etched
windows, comfortable raised back bar
with coal fire, Victorian medical artefacts;
background music, silent TVs; open all
day. *(Andy and Jill Kassube, the Didler, Don
Bryan, Jeremy King, Claes Mauroy)*

LIVERPOOL   SJ3490
✱ Doctor Duncan (0151) 709 5100
St Johns Lane; L1 1HF Friendly Victorian
pub with several rooms including impressive
back area with pillared and vaulted tiled
ceiling, full Cains range and guests kept
well, belgians beers on tap, enjoyable good
value food, pleasant helpful service, daily
newspapers; may be background music, can
get lively evenings and busy weekends; family
room, open all day. *(the Didler, Claes Mauroy)*

LIVERPOOL   SJ3589
Fly in the Loaf (0151) 708 0817
Hardman Street; L1 9AS Former bakery
with smart gleaming bar serving Okells
and up to seven ales from smaller brewers,
foreign beers too, simple low-priced home-
made food (not Mon), friendly service, long
room with panelling, some raised sections,
even a pulpit; background music, sports TV,
upstairs lavatories, open all day, till midnight
weekends. *(Rachel Platonov, Nigel Schaay,
the Didler, Jeremy King, Claes Mauroy,
Nicky McDowell)*

LIVERPOOL   SJ3490
Globe (0151) 707 0067
Cases Street, opposite station; L1 1HW
Chatty traditional little local in busy
shopping area (can get packed), friendly
staff, good selection of well kept ales,
lunchtime filled cobs, sloping floor to quieter
cosy back room, prints of old Liverpool; 60s
background music; open all day. *(the Didler)*

LIVERPOOL   SJ3490
Hole In Ye Wall (0151) 227 3809
Off Dale Street; L2 2AW Well restored
18th-c pub with thriving local atmosphere in
high-beamed panelled bar, seven changing
ales fed by gravity from upstairs (no cellar
as pub is on Quaker burial site), sandwiches
and basic food till 5pm, free chip butties Sun
when there's a traditional sing-along, friendly
staff, plenty of woodwork, stained glass and
old Liverpool photographs, coal-effect gas fire
in unusual brass-canopied fireplace; no dogs;
children allowed till 5pm, open all day. *(the
Didler, Claes Mauroy)*

LIVERPOOL   SJ3490
Hub (0151) 709 2401
Hanover Street; L1 4AA Recently
opened busy bow-fronted alehouse/bistro,
light modern bare-boards interior with
big windows, decent choice of food from
sandwiches and stone-baked pizzas up,
reasonably priced wines, five local ales
including Liverpool Craft and Liverpool
Organic; children welcome, open all
day. *(Robert W Buckle)*

LIVERPOOL   SJ3490
Lion (0151) 236 1734
Moorfields, off Tithebarn Street; L2 2BP
Beautifully preserved ornate Victorian
tavern, great changing beer choice, over 80
malt whiskies, friendly landlord interested
in pub's history, good value simple lunchtime
food including good home-made pork pies,
sparkling etched glass and serving hatches in
central bar, unusual wallpaper and matching
curtains, big mirrors, panelling and tilework,
two small back lounges one with fine glass
dome, coal fire; silent fruit machine; open
all day. *(Andy and Jill Kassube, the Didler, Claes
Mauroy)*

LIVERPOOL   SJ3489
Monro (0151) 7079933
Duke Street; L1 5AG Stylish gastropub,
popular comfortable and well run, with
good choice of interesting food including
vegetarian menu, early evening deals (not
Sun), well kept Marstons and guests from
small bar, good friendly service; courtyard
tables, open all day (till 1am Fri, Sat).
*(Peter Smith and Judith Brown, the Didler,
Colin Nicolson)*

If we know a pub has an outdoor play area for children, we mention it.

LIVERPOOL SJ3589

Peter Kavanaghs (0151) 709 3443

*Egerton Street, off Catherine Street;
L8 7LY* Shuttered Victorian pub with
interesting décor in several small rooms
including old-world murals, stained glass
and lots of bric-a-brac (bicycle hanging from
ceiling), piano, wooden settles and real fires,
well kept Greene King Abbot and guests,
friendly licensees, popular with locals and
students; open all day (till 1am Fri, Sat).
(the Didler, Claes Mauroy)

LIVERPOOL SJ3490

Richmond (0151) 709 2614

Williamson Street; L1 1EB Popular small
corner pub in pedestrianised area, nice old
interior and fittings including original Bass
mirror, Bass still served along with five other
ales and over 50 malt whiskies; sports TV;
tables out in front, bedrooms, open all day
from 10am. *(the Didler)*

LIVERPOOL SJ3589

Roscoe Head (0151) 709 4365

Roscoe Street; L1 2SX Unassuming old
local with cosy bar, snug and two other
spotless unspoilt little rooms, friendly
long-serving landlady, well kept Jennings,
Tetleys and four guests, inexpensive home-
made lunches (not weekends), interesting
memorabilia, traditional games including
crib, quiz Tues and Thurs; open all day till
midnight. *(Sean Brophy, Andy and Jill Kassube,
the Didler, Claes Mauroy)*

LIVERPOOL SJ3490

Ship & Mitre (0151) 236 0859

Dale Street; L2 2JH Friendly local with
fine art deco exterior and ship-like interior,
popular with university people, up to 12
changing unusual ales (many beer festivals),
over 70 bottled continentals, farm ciders,
good value basic food (all day Fri -Sun),
upstairs function room with original 1930s
décor; well behaved children till 7pm, dogs
welcome, open all day. *(Andy and Jill Kassube,
the Didler, Kerry Law)*

LIVERPOOL SJ3589

Swan (0151) 709 5281

Wood Street; L1 4DQ Neon sign for this
busy unsmart three-floor pub, bare boards
and dim lighting, up to eight beers including
good value Hydes, bottled belgian beers,
Weston's cider, well priced cobs and weekday
lunches, friendly staff; loud juke box draws
younger crowd, silent fruit machine; open
all day (till 2am Thurs-Sat). *(the Didler,
Jeremy King)*

LIVERPOOL SJ3490

★Thomas Rigbys (0151) 236 3269

Dale Street; L2 2EZ Spacious beamed and
panelled Victorian pub with mosaic flooring,
old tiles and etched glass, Okells and five
changing guests, lots of bottled imports,
impressively long bar, steps up to main area,
table service from attentive staff, reasonably
priced hearty home-made food (such as
scouse) all day till 7pm; disabled access,
seats in big courtyard, open all day. *(Frank
Blanchard, Matt Haycox, David Crook, the Didler,
Claes Mauroy)*

LIVERPOOL SJ3197

Volunteer Canteen (01519) 284676

East Street; L22 8QR Classic friendly old
local with superb etched glass and wood
panelling, busy bar, comfortable lounge
(table service here), well kept Black Sheep,
Courage and guests, newspapers; open all
day. *(the Didler*

LIVERPOOL SJ3490

White Star (0151) 231 6861

*Rainford Gardens, off Matthew Street;
L2 6PT* Lively traditional local dating to
the 18th c, cosy bar, lots of woodwork, boxing
photographs, White Star shipping line and
Beatles memorabilia (they used to rehearse
in back room), well kept ales including Bass,
Bowland and Caledonian Deuchars IPA, basic
lunchtime food, friendly staff; sports TVs;
open all day. *(Andy and Jill Kassube, the Didler,
Claes Mauroy)*

LONGRIDGE SD6137

Corporation Arms (01772) 782644

Lower Road (B6243); PR3 2YJ
Comfortably refurbished 18th-c pub next to
reservoir, wide range of largely traditional
food all day, small helpings available, three
well kept changing ales such as Copper
Dragon, Moorhouses and George Wrights,
lots of malt whiskies, good atmosphere in
three small linked rooms and restaurant;
good bed and breakfast (five rooms), open all
day. *(Ron Neville)*

LYDGATE SD9704

★White Hart (01457) 872566

*Stockport Road; Lydgate not marked
on some maps and not the one near
Todmorden; take A669 Oldham–
Saddleworth, right at brow of hill to
A6050 after almost 2.5 miles; OL4 4JJ*
Smart up-to-date dining pub overlooking
Pennine moors, mix of locals in bar or
simpler end rooms and diners in elegant
brasserie with smartly dressed staff, high

Please keep sending us reports. We rely on readers for news of new discoveries,
and particularly for news of changes – however slight – at the fully described pubs:
feedback@goodguides.com, or (no stamp needed) The Good Pub Guide, FREEPOST
TN1569, Wadhurst, E Sussex TN5 7BR.

quality (not cheap) food, Lees, Timothy Taylors and a guest beer, 16 wines by the glass, old beams and exposed stonework contrasting with deep red or purple walls and modern artwork, open fires, newspapers; TV in lounge; children welcome, dogs in bar, picnic-sets on back lawn making most of position, bedrooms, open all day. *(Gill and Malcolm Stott, P J and R D Greaves, Ed and Anna Fraser, W K Wood)*

LYDIATE   SD3604
Scotch Piper (0151) 5260503
Southport Road; A4157; L31 4HD
Medieval thatched pub, well worn-in, with heavy low beams, flagstones, thick stone walls and dogs sprawled in front of roaring fires, Black Sheep and a guest from tiny counter in main room, corridor to middle room with darts and back snug, no food; bikers' night Weds, outside lavatories; big garden, open all day. *(Mike Leadbetter)*

MANCHESTER   SJ8498
Angel (0161) 833 4786
Angel Street, off Rochdale Road; M4 4BR
Good value home-made food from pub standards to more upscale dishes, eight well kept changing ales including Bobs, bottled beers, farm cider and perry, bare boards bar with piano, smaller upstairs restaurant with log fire and paintings by local artist; children and dogs welcome, back beer garden, open all day, closed Sun. *(the Didler)*

MANCHESTER   SJ8398
Ape & Apple (0161) 8399624
John Dalton Street; M2 6HQ Big no-frills open-plan pub, well kept bargain Holts, hearty bar food, comfortable seats in bare-boards bar with lots of old prints and posters, armchairs in upstairs lounge, friendly atmosphere; background music, TV area, games machines, Thurs quiz; beer garden, bedrooms, open all day (till 9pm Sun). *(the Didler)*

MANCHESTER   SJ8498
Bar Fringe (0161) 8353815
Swan Street; M4 5JN Long bare-boards bar specialising in continental beers, also five changing ales from small local breweries and farm cider, friendly staff, basic snacks till 4pm (no food weekends), daily newspapers, shelves of empty beer bottles, cartoons, posters, motorcycle hung above door, rock juke box; no children or dogs; tables out behind, open all day, till late Sat, Sun. *(the Didler)*

MANCHESTER   SJ8397
★ **Britons Protection** (0161) 236 5895
Great Bridgewater Street, corner of Lower Mosley Street; M1 5LE Lively unpretentious city pub with five well kept ales, 235 malt whiskies and cheap lunchtime snacks (range of pies), unspoilt little rooms including two cosy inner lounges with hatch

service, solidly comfortable furnishings, attractive brass, tiled murals of 1819 Peterloo Massacre (took place nearby), massive bar counter with heated footrails, coal-effect gas fire, may have storytelling, silent film shows and acoustic music; gets very busy lunchtime and weekends; tables in back garden, open all day. *(Dennis Jones, Dave Webster, Sue Holland, Mike and Eleanor Anderson, the Didler, Tracey and Stephen Groves)*

MANCHESTER   SJ8498
Castle (0161) 2379485
Oldham Street, about 200 metres from Piccadilly, on right; M4 1LE Restored 18th-c pub well run by former Coronation Street actor, simple traditional front bar, small snug, full Robinsons range plus guests from fine bank of handpumps, Weston's Old Rosie cider, back room for live music and other events, nice tilework outside; open all day till late. *(the Didler, Dr and Mrs A K Clarke)*

MANCHESTER   SJ8497
Circus (0161) 2365818
Portland Street; M1 4GX Traditional little bare-boards local with particularly well kept Tetleys from minute corridor bar (or may be table service), friendly landlord and staff, walls covered with photos of regulars and local celebrities, football memorabilia, leatherette banquettes in panelled back room; often looks closed but normally open all day (you may have to knock), can get very busy. *(Mike and Eleanor Anderson, the Didler)*

MANCHESTER   SJ8398
City Arms (0161) 2364610
Kennedy Street, off Street Peters Square; M2 4BQ Busy little pub with eight quickly changing real ales, belgian bottled beers and bargain bar lunches, quick friendly service, coal fires, bare boards and banquettes, prints, panelling and masses of pump clips, handsome tiled façade and corridor; background music, TV, games machine; wheelchair access but steps down to back lounge, open all day. *(Dean Johnson, Jamie Price, the Didler)*

MANCHESTER   SD8104
Coach & Horses
Old Bury Road, Whitefield; A665 near Besses o' the Barn Station; M45 6TB Thriving early 19th-c Holts pub with traditional bar and lounge, their well kept ales at bargain prices, table service, darts and cards; open all day. *(the Didler)*

MANCHESTER   SJ8298
Crescent (0161) 7365600
Crescent (A6) – opposite Salford University; M5 4PF Three areas off central servery with ten changing ales (regular beer festivals), many continental bottled beers and real cider, buoyant local atmosphere (popular with university), low-priced lunchtime food, Weds curry night, bare

boards and open fire, plenty of character, pool room, juke box; small enclosed terrace, open all day. *(the Didler, Ben Williams)*

MANCHESTER SJ8497
Grey Horse (0161) 236 1874
Portland Street, near Piccadilly; M1 4QX
Tiny one-bar Hydes local, their Bitter and Mild kept well, some unusual malt whiskies, friendly licensees, panelled servery with colourful gantry, lots of prints, photographs and plates; background music, TV; can bring good sandwiches from next door, open all day. *(the Didler)*

MANCHESTER SJ8498
Hare & Hounds (0161) 8324737
Shudehill, behind Arndale; M4 4AA
Old-fashioned 18th-c local with long narrow bar linking front snug and comfortable back lounge, notable tilework, panelling and stained glass, cheap Holts beer, friendly staff; background music, TV; open all day. *(Douglas Wren, the Didler)*

MANCHESTER SJ8398
Kings Arms (0161) 832 3605
Bloom Street, Salford; M3 6AN Plain tables, bare boards and flagstones contrasting with opulent maroon/purple décor and stained glass, Bazens and changing guests, no food; music, poetry and theatre nights upstairs, knitting in snug Mon evening; children welcome till 7pm, open all day, closed Sun. *(the Didler)*

MANCHESTER SJ8397
Knott Fringe (0161) 839 9229
Deansgate; M3 4LY Friendly modern glass-fronted café-bar under railway arch by Castlefield heritage site; Marble organic ales and guests, lots of continental imports, good value all-day food with emphasis on greek dishes, upstairs smokers' balcony overlooking Rochdale Canal; open all day. *(the Didler, Andy and Jill Kassube)*

MANCHESTER SJ8497
Lass o' Gowrie (0161) 273 6932
36 Charles Street; off Oxford Street at BBC; M1 7DB Unspoilt tiled Victorian sidestreet local, welcoming big-windowed long bar with cosy room off, stripped brickwork, up to ten well kept ales including Greene King, Wadworths and a good house beer (Betty's Bitter) brewed by Outstanding, bargain food (good home-made pies), friendly service; terrace overlooking river, open all day. *(the Didler)*

MANCHESTER SJ8499
★ Marble Arch (0161) 832 5914
Rochdale Road (A664), Ancoats; centre of Gould Street, just E of Victoria Station; M4 4HY Cheery own-brew pub with fine Victorian interior, magnificently restored lightly barrel-vaulted high ceiling, extensive marble and tiling, look out for

---

sloping mosaic floor and frieze advertising various spirits, rustic furniture, their own five beers plus guests (brewery visible from windows in back dining room – tours by arrangement), sandwiches and simple bar food; background music, Laurel and Hardy Preservation Society meetings showing old films (third Weds of month); children welcome, small garden, open all day (till midnight Fri, Sat). *(the Didler, Ben Williams, Pat and Tony Martin, Dr and Mrs A K Clarke)*

MANCHESTER SJ8398
Mark Addy (0161) 832 4080
Stanley Street, off New Bailey Street, Salford; M3 5EJ Unusual converted waiting rooms for boat passengers, barrel-vaulted red sandstone bays with wide glassed-in brick arches, cast-iron pillars and flagstones, views over river, signature cheese and pâté board plus some good regionally influenced cooking, several real ales including local microbrews, lots of wines by the glass, brisk friendly service; background music, sports TV facing bar; flower-filled waterside courtyard. *(Dennis Jones, J F M and M West)*

MANCHESTER SJ8492
Metropolitan (0161) 438 2332
Lapwing Lane, Didsbury; M20 2WS Large gabled dining pub (former railway hotel) with good imaginative food, well kept Bass, Caledonian Deuchars IPA and Timothy Taylors Landlord, extensive wine list, efficient service, numerous airy rooms, impressive period décor, open fires; children welcome, tables out on decking, open all day. *(Malcolm and Pauline Pellatt)*

MANCHESTER SJ8298
New Oxford (0161) 8327082
Bexley Square, Salford; M3 6DB Up to 16 well kept changing ales (regular beer festivals), plus a good range of draught and bottled continental beers, a couple of farm ciders too, friendly staff, light and airy café-style feel in small front bar and back room, coal fire, low-priced basic food till 6pm; seats outside, open all day. *(the Didler, Ben Williams)*

MANCHESTER SJ8397
Paramount (0161) 233 1820
Oxford Street; M1 4BH Well run Wetherspoons with their usual good value, particularly friendly service, interesting range of real ales. *(Ben Williams)*

MANCHESTER SJ8397
★ Peveril of the Peak (0161) 2366364
Great Bridgewater Street; M1 5JQ Vivid art nouveau external tilework and three sturdily furnished old-fashioned bare-boards rooms, interesting pictures, lots of mahogany, mirrors and stained or frosted glass, log fire, welcoming long-serving landlady, Caledonian Deuchars IPA, Copper Dragon, Everards and Jennings from central servery, cheap basic lunchtime food; pool, table football, TV;

children welcome, pavement tables, closed weekend lunchtimes. *(the Didler, Dr and Mrs A K Clarke)*

MANCHESTER ☆ Rain Bar (0161) 2356500
SJ8397

Great Bridgewater Street; M1 5JG Bare boards and lots of woodwork in former umbrella works, well kept Lees ales, plenty of wines by the glass, enjoyable good value pubby food all day, friendly efficient staff, relaxed atmosphere, nooks and corners, coal fire in small snug, large upstairs bar/function room, Weds quiz; background music may be loud and can be busy with young crowd in evenings; good back terrace overlooking spruced-up Rochdale Canal, handy for Bridgewater Hall, open all day. *(the Didler, Giles and Annie Francis)*

MANCHESTER Royal Oak (0161) 434 4788
SJ8591

Wilmslow Road, Didsbury; M20 6WF Suburban pub with very well kept Marstons-related ales, huge cheese and pâté ploughman's (not weekends), interesting old music hall posters; tables outside, open all day. *(G D K Fraser)*

MANCHESTER Sams Chop House (0161) 8343210
SJ8398

Back Pool Fold, Chapel Walks; M2 1HN Small thriving dining pub, offshoot from Mr Thomas Chop House, with original Victorian décor, huge helpings of good plain english food including weekend brunch, formal waiters, well kept beers and good wine choice; open all day. *(Ian Leadbetter)*

MANCHESTER ☆ Sinclairs (0161) 8340430
SJ8398

Cathedral Gates, off Exchange Square; M3 1SW Charming low-beamed and timbered 18th-c Sam Smiths pub (rebuilt here in redevelopment), all-day food including fresh oysters, brisk friendly service, bustling atmosphere, quieter upstairs bar with snugs and Jacobean fireplace; tables out in Shambles Square (plastic glasses), open all day. *(the Didler, Ben Williams)*

MANCHESTER Smithfield (0161) 8394424
SJ8498

Swan Street; M4 5JZ Welcoming pub with long bar and a couple of rooms off, eight interesting ales including a house beer brewed by Facers (regular festivals), plenty of bottled beers and good selection of spirits; pool, darts and sports TV; nine good value bedrooms, open all day. *(the Didler)*

MARPLE Hare & Hounds (0161) 4270293
SJ9389

Dooley Lane (A627 W); SK6 7EJ Dining pub above River Goyt, modern layout and décor, decent choice of all-day food at realistic prices, Hydes ales from stainless servery, prompt friendly service; sports

TV, no dogs; well behaved children welcome. *(Dennis Jones, Peter Wilde)*

MARPLE Ring o' Bells (0161) 427 1354
SJ9588

Church Lane; by Macclesfield Canal, Bridge 2; SK6 7AY Popular old-fashioned local with canal and other local memorabilia in four linked rooms, well kept Robinsons ales, decent food at reasonable prices, darts, quiz nights and some live music; canalside garden, own narrowboat, open all day. *(Dennis Jones, David Hoult)*

MARPLE BRIDGE Hare & Hounds (01614) 274042
SJ9889

Mill Brow: from end of Town Street in centre turn left up Hollins Lane and keep on uphill; SK6 5LW Comfortable and civilised stone-built country pub in lovely spot, smallish and can get crowded, good interesting local food (not Mon, Tues) from short menu, well kept Robinsons, log fires; garden behind. *(Gary Wilkinson, David Hoult)*

MELLOR ☆ Devonshire Arms (0161) 4272563
SJ9888

This is the Mellor near Marple, S of Manchester; heading out of Marple on the A626 towards Glossop, Mellor is the next road after the B6102, signposted off on the right at Marple Bridge; Longhurst Lane; SK6 5PP Cheerful, cosy and well run, front bar with old leather-seated settles and open fire, two small back rooms with Victorian fireplaces, well kept Robinsons ales, enjoyable food, alternating live jazz/quiz night Tues; children welcome, garden with waterfall tumbling into fish pond crossed by japanese bridge, large pergola, play area on small tree-sheltered lawn. *(David Hoult)*

MELLOR ☆ Millstone (01254) 813333
SD6530

The Mellor near Blackburn; Mellor Lane; BB2 7JR Restauranty stone-built village dining pub, smart and well run, panelled bar with comfortable lounge one side, modern dining extension the other, good enterprising cooking as well as all-day bar meals and popular substantial Sun lunch, obliging friendly staff, well kept Thwaites, good choice of wines by the glass, big log fire, mementoes of former landlord and England cricketer Big Jim Smith; good bedrooms and breakfast, open all day. *(P M Dodd, Ben Williams, W K Wood)*

MORECAMBE Midland Grand Plaza
SD4264

(01524) 424000 *Marine Road W; LA4 4BZ* Classic art deco hotel in splendid seafront position, comfortable if unorthodox contemporary furnishings in spacious seaview Rotunda Bar, rather pricy but enjoyable food from interesting lancashire tapas to restaurant meals, good service; children welcome, 44 bedrooms, open all day. *(Peter and Eleanor Kenyon)*

MORECAMBE   SD4364

Palatine (01524) 410503

The Crescent; LA4 5BZ Comfortable Edwardian seafront pub, enjoyable reasonably priced food including deli boards, pizzas and pubby standards, four Lancaster ales and guests, friendly helpful staff, leather armchairs and some high tables with stools on wood floor, upstairs panelled sea-view dining lounge; seats out in front, open all day (till 1am Fri, Sat). *(Revd Mike Peatman)*

NEWTON   SD6950

Parkers Arms (01200) 446236

B6478 7 miles N of Clitheroe; BB7 3DY Friendly welcome from chatty landlord, good locally sourced food (suppliers listed) from lunchtime sandwiches up, you can eat in bar or restaurant, four real ales including Bowland, good range of wines, nice coffee and afternoon tea, log fires; children welcome, garden with lovely views, four bedrooms, pretty spot. *(Steve Whalley, Peter G Jenkins)*

PRESTON   SD5329

Black Horse (01772) 204855

Friargate; PR1 2EJ Friendly unspoilt pub in pedestrianised street, good Robinsons ales, inexpensive lunchtime food, unusual ornate curved and mosaic-tiled Victorian main bar, panelling, stained glass and old local photographs, two quiet cosy snugs, mirrored back area, upstairs 1920s-style bar, good juke box; no children, open all day from 10.30am. *(the Didler, Barbarrick)*

RABY   SJ3179

★ Wheatsheaf (0151) 336 3416

Raby Mere Road, The Green; from A540 heading S from Heswall, turn left into Upper Raby Road, village about a mile further; CH63 4JH Up to nine real ales in pretty thatched black and white pub, simply furnished rambling rooms with homely feel, cosy central bar and nice snug formed by antique settles around fine old fireplace, small coal fire in more spacious room, reasonably priced bar food (not Sun, Mon evenings), à la carte menu in large restaurant (Tues-Sat evenings) in former cowshed leading to conservatory; children welcome, dogs in bar, picnic-sets on terrace and in pleasant back garden, open all day. *(Clive Watkin, David Jackman)*

RADCLIFFE   SD7608

Sparking Clog (0161) 723 5690

Radcliffe Moor Road; M26 3WY Bright and clean with welcoming friendly staff, wide choice of good value enjoyable food, three Marstons ales. *(Ben Williams)*

RAMSBOTTOM   SD8017

★ Fishermans Retreat

(01706) 825314 *Twine Valley Park/ Fishery signed off A56 N of Bury at Shuttleworth; Bye Road; BL0 0HH* Remote yet busy pub/restaurant, generous food all day using produce from surrounding estate and trout lakes (they can arrange fishing), also have own land where they raise cattle, mountain-lodge-feel bar with beams and bare-stone walls, five well kept ales including Copper Dragon, Moorhouses, Timothy Taylors and Thwaites, over 500 malt whiskies (some sold in shop), good wine list, small family dining room and new restaurant/function room extension, helpful friendly staff; a few picnic-sets with lovely valley views, closed Mon, otherwise open all day. *(Brian and Anna Marsden, Simon Bessell, Stuart and Sarah Barrie, R T and J C Moggridge)*

RAMSBOTTOM   SD7816

Shoulder of Mutton (01706) 822001

Lumb Carr Road (B6214), Holcombe; BL8 4LZ Refurbished 18th-c village dining pub with good well presented food (all day Sun) in bar or more formal restaurant, three well kept local beers, some live music; children, walkers and dogs welcome, open all day. *(W K Wood)*

RILEY GREEN   SD6225

★ Royal Oak (01254) 201445

A675/A6061; PR5 0SL Cosy low-beamed three-room former coaching inn, good generous home cooking including notable steaks and game, four well kept Thwaites ales from long back bar, friendly efficient service, ancient stripped stone, open fires, seats from high-backed settles to red plush armchairs on carpet, lots of nooks and crannies, soft lighting, impressive woodwork and plenty of bric-a-brac, two comfortable dining rooms; can get packed weekends; tables outside, short walk from Leeds & Liverpool Canal, footpath to Hoghton Tower, open all day Sun. *(Norma and Noel Thomas, Mrs Cooper)*

ROCHDALE   SD8913

Baum (01706) 352186

Toad Lane; OL12 0NU Plenty of old-fashioned charm, five changing ales and lots of bottled beers, food from tapas and good sandwiches to home-made casseroles etc, bare boards, old advertisements, conservatory; garden with pétanque, handy for Co-op Museum, open all day. *(Henry Paulinski)*

Post Office address codings confusingly give the impression that some pubs are in Lancashire when they're really in Cumbria or Yorkshire (which is where we list them).

ROMILEY SJ9390
Duke of York (0161) 4302806
Stockport Road; SK6 3AN Popular old pub refurbished by new licences but keeping character, five well kept beers including Thwaites and Wells & Youngs (Oct beer festival), good food at reasonable prices in bar and upstairs restaurant. *(Dennis Jones, Alan Smith)*

SLAIDBURN SD7152
✴ Hark to Bounty (01200) 446246
B6478 N of Clitheroe; BB7 3EP Attractive old stone-built pub with homely linked rooms, some gentle refurbishment, wide choice of enjoyable fresh food from sandwiches and light dishes up, friendly hard-working young staff, four real ales, decent wines and whiskies, comfortable chairs by open fire, games room one end, restaurant the other; pleasant back garden, charming Forest of Bowland village, good walks, nine bedrooms, open all day. *(Michael Lamm, Norma and Noel Thomas)*

SOUTHPORT SD3317
Sir Henry Segrave (01704) 530217
Lord Street; PR8 1RH Well placed comfortable Wetherspoons, good choice of food all day and well kept cheap beer, efficient service even when busy; children welcome, pavement tables, open all day from 8am. *(Ben Williams)*

STALYBRIDGE SJ9598
✴ Station Buffet (0161) 303 0007
The Station, Rassbottom Street; SK15 1RF Eight quickly changing ales, foreign bottled beers and farm cider in classic Victorian station buffet bar, cheap basic meals (including all day breakfast and pots of tea), cheerful and bustling with period advertisements, station photographs and other railway memorabilia on wood panelled and red walls, newspapers and magazines, cards and board games, newish conservatory, an extension into what was ladies' waiting room and part of station-master's quarters featuring original ornate ceilings and Victorian-style wallpaper; no credit cards; children till 8pm, dogs welcome, picnic-sets on sunny Platform One by the Manchester to Huddersfield line, open all day. *(Dennis Jones, the Didler, John Fiander)*

STALYBRIDGE SJ9896
Waggon & Horses (01457) 764837
Mottram Road; SK15 2SU Popular family-run pub/restaurant with good choice of enjoyable generously served food, Robinsons ales, plenty of wines by the glass, Thurs quiz; children welcome. *(JCW)*

STOCKPORT SJ8990
✴ Arden Arms (0161) 4802185
Millgate Street/Corporation Street, opposite pay car park; SK1 2LX Cheerful Victorian pub in handsome dark-brick building, several well preserved high-ceilinged rooms off island bar (one tiny old-fashioned snug accessed through servery), good reasonably priced daytime food, half a dozen well kept Robinsons ales, friendly efficient service, tiling and panelling, two coal fires; background music may obtrude; tables in sheltered courtyard with much-used smokers' shelter, open all day. *(Dennis Jones, Mr and Mrs Butler, the Didler)*

STOCKPORT SJ8990
Crown (0161) 4290549
Heaton Lane, Heaton Norris; SK4 1AR Partly open-plan Victorian pub popular for its 16 well kept changing ales, also bottled beers and real cider, three cosy lounge areas off bar, spotless stylish décor, wholesome bargain lunches, darts; frequent live music; tables in cobbled courtyard, huge viaduct above. *(Dennis Jones, the Didler, G D K Fraser)*

STOCKPORT SJ8991
Navigation (0161) 480 6626
Manchester Road (B6167, former A626); SK4 1TY Friendly refurbished red-brick local, well kept Beartown ales and a guest, farm ciders, good pies; open all day. *(the Didler, Simon Bessell)*

STOCKPORT SJ8890
Nursery (0161) 4322044
Green Lane, Heaton Norris; off A6; SK4 2NA Popular 1930s pub on narrow cobbled lane (E end of N part of Green Lane), enjoyable straightforward lunchtime food from kitchen servery on right, friendly efficient service, well kept Hydes, big bays of banquettes in panelled stained-glass front lounge, brocaded wall banquettes in back one; children welcome if eating, immaculate bowling green behind, open all day. *(the Didler)*

STOCKPORT SJ8990
Queens Head (0161) 4800725
Little Underbank (can be reached by steps from St Petersgate); SK1 1JT Splendid Victorian restoration, long and narrow, with charming separate snug and back dining area, rare brass cordials fountain, double bank of spirits taps and old spirit lamps, old posters and adverts, reasonably priced lunchtime snacks, bargain Sam Smiths, daily newspapers, good friendly bustle, bench seating and bare boards; famous tiny gents' upstairs; open all day, till 7pm Sun. *(the Didler)*

STOCKPORT SJ8990
Railway (0161) 429 6062
Avenue Street (just off M63 junction 13, via A560); SK1 2BZ Bright and airy L-shaped bar with up to 15 real ales (always a mild), lots of foreign beers, farm cider, friendly staff, no food, old Stockport and railway photographs, bar billiards; tables out behind, open all day. *(Dennis Jones, the Didler)*

STOCKPORT   SJ8990
⋆ **Red Bull** (0161) 480 1286
Middle Hillgate; SK1 3AY Steps up to
friendly well run local, impressive beamed
and flagstoned bar with dark panelling,
substantial settles and seats, lots of pictures
and mirrors, open fires, well kept Robinsons
ales from traditional island servery, good
value home-cooked food; background music;
has expanded into adjoining building, four
bedrooms, open all day. *(the Didler)*

STOCKPORT   SJ8990
Swan With Two Necks
(0161) 480 2341 *Princes Street; SK1 1RY*
Traditional welcoming local with comfortable
panelled bar, back lounge with skylighting
and drinking corridor, bargain pub lunches
from sandwiches up, teas with home-made
scones, Robinsons ales; open all day (till 6pm
Sun). *(M J Winterton, the Didler)*

STRINES   SJ9686
Sportsmans Arms (0161) 427 2888
B6101 Marple–New Mills; SK6 7GE
Pleasant well kept roadside local with
panoramic Goyt Valley view from picture-
window lounge bar, good changing ale range,
enjoyable well priced home-made food
including specials board, small separate bar,
log fire, some live music; children welcome,
tables out on side decking, heated smokers'
shelter, open all day weekends.
(Frank Blanchard, David Hoult)

TYLDESLEY   SD6902
Mort Arms (01942) 883481
Elliott Street; M29 8DG Bargain Holts
ales in two-room 1930s pub, etched glass
and polished panelling, comfortable lounge
with old local photographs, friendly staff
and regulars, darts and dominoes; nice back
terrace, open all day. *(the Didler,
Simon Minshall)*

WEST KIRBY   SJ2186
White Lion (0151) 625 9037
Grange Road (A540); CH48 4EE
Friendly proper pub in interesting 18th-c
sandstone building, several small beamed
areas on different levels, Black Sheep,
Courage Director and a couple of quickly
changing guests, good value simple bar
lunches (not Sun), coal stove; no children;
attractive secluded back garden up steep
stone steps, fish pond, open all day.
(Calvin Morton, MLR)

WHEATLEY LANE   SD8338
⋆ **Sparrowhawk** (01282) 603034
*Wheatley Lane Road; towards E end of
village road which runs N of and parallel
to A6068; one way of reaching it is to
follow Fence, Newchurch 1¾ signpost,
then turn off at Barrowford signpost;
BB12 9QG* Comfortably civilised 1930s feel
in imposing black and white pub with quirky

domed stained-glass skylight, oak panelling,
parquet flooring and leather tub chairs,
Bass, Greene King, Thwaites and a couple
of guests, draught Fransizkaner wheat beer
and nice wines by the glass from cushioned
leatherette counter, good imaginative
bar food (all day weekends), smart young
waitresses, daily newspapers and board
games; background music, TV; children
welcome, dogs in bar, heavy wooden tables
on spacious front terrace with good views to
the moors beyond Nelson and Colne, open all
day. *(John and Eleanor Holdsworth)*

WHEELTON   SD6021
⋆ **Dressers Arms** (01254) 830041
*Briers Brow; off A674, 2.1 miles from
M61 junction 8; PR6 8HD* Traditional
pub in converted cottage, eight real ales,
pubby food (all day weekends, Sun carvery),
snug low-beamed rooms with simple
furnishings on patterned carpets, handsome
woodburner, newspapers and magazines,
restaurant; background music, games
machine, TV and pool; children welcome
(not in bar after 9.30pm), dogs allowed
in bar, picnic-sets under large umbrella
on heated front terrace, open all day till
12.30am. *(Norma and Noel Thomas, Peter
Heaton, Ben Williams, Ed and Anna Fraser)*

WHEELTON   SD5921
Top Lock (01257) 263376
Copthurst Lane; PR6 8LS Picturesque
spot on Leeds & Liverpool Canal, nine well
kept ales (beer festivals) and enjoyable
inexpensive food, prompt friendly service,
canal-related décor, upstairs dining room;
picnic-sets outside. *(Peter Heaton, Brian and
Anna Marsden)*

WISWELL   SD7437
⋆ **Freemasons Arms** (01254) 822218
*Village signposted off A671 and A59
NE of Whalley; pub on Vicarage Fold, a
gravelled pedestrian passage between
Pendleton Road and Old Back Lane in
village centre (don't expect to park very
close); BB7 9DF* Civilised dining place
with the informal feel of an upmarket pub,
rugs on polished flagstones, carved oak
settles and attractive mix of chairs around
handsome stripped or salvaged tables (all
beautifully laid), lots of sporting antique
prints on cream or pastel walls, open fires
and woodburner, more rooms upstairs,
really good food from lunchtime sandwiches
to restauranty dishes (not Sun evening,
Mon), meticulous courteous service from
neatly uniformed young staff, well kept ales
such as Bank Top, Moorhouses and Tirril,
excellent choice of wines by the glass from
good list; dogs allowed in bar, candlelit
tables under awning on heated front
terrace, open all day weekends, closed first
two weeks of Jan. *(Steve Whalley, W K Wood,
Dr Kevan Tucker)*

WORSLEY   SD7500
Barton Arms (0161) 728 6157
Stablefold; just off Barton Road (B5211, handy for M60 junction 13); M28 2ED
Bright clean Ember Inn, popular and friendly, with good value food, Black Sheep, Timothy Taylors Landlord and guests; children welcome in dining areas, open all day.
(Ben Williams)

WORSLEY   SD7400
John Gilbert (0161) 703 7733
Worsley Brow, just off M60 junction 13; M28 2YA Big reworked Greene King family dining pub, small linked areas on several levels, good choice of reasonably priced food from sandwiches up, their ales and guests kept well. *(Gerry and Rosemary Dobson)*

WORSTON   SD7642
Calfs Head (01200) 441218
Village signed off A59 NW of Clitheroe; BB7 1QA Large old stone-built coaching inn, very busy with mostly older people eating wide choice of moderately priced food including popular Sun carvery in bar and spacious conservatory looking towards Pendle Hill, well kept ales such as Black Sheep and Jennings, friendly attentive service, snug with coal fire; lovely big garden with summerhouse and stream, 11 comfortable bedrooms, open all day.
(E A Eaves)

WRAY   SD6067
⋆Inn at Wray (01524) 221722
2 miles E of Hornby off A683 Kirkby Lonsdale–Lancaster; LA2 8QN
Comfortable family-run dining pub, snug sitting room with soft leather sofas and easy chairs, further rooms with oriental rugs on

polished boards or flagstones, open fires and woodburner, larger end room with cabinet of home-made preserves, food from sandwiches to restaurant-style meals, Thwaites and Tirril ales, good cheerful service, two elegant upstairs carpeted dining rooms with upholstered chairs around smart table; background music; children welcome, dogs in bar, bedrooms, open all day weekends, closed Mon. *(Walter and Susan Rinaldi-Butcher, Ray and Winifred Halliday)*

WRIGHTINGTON   SD5011
Rigbye Arms (01257) 462354
3 miles from M6 junction 27; off A5209 via Robin Hood Lane and left into High Moor Lane; WN6 9QB 17th-c dining pub in attractive moorland setting, welcoming and relaxed, with good choice of enjoyable sensibly priced food (all day Sun) including game menu, friendly prompt service even when busy, well kept Black Sheep, Tetleys and Timothy Taylors, decent wines, several carpeted rooms including cosy tap room, open fires; children welcome, garden, bowling green, regular car club meetings, open all day Sun. *(Jack Clark, David Heath)*

YEALAND CONYERS   SD5074
New Inn (01524) 732938
3 miles from M6 J35; village signed off A6; LA5 9SJ Welcoming ivy-covered 17th-c village pub under newish management, traditionally furnished cosy beamed bar, log fire, Robinsons ales and a guest, good choice of malt whiskies, two communicating dining rooms, pubby food; children welcome, dogs in bar, picnic-sets on sheltered lawn, smokers' shelter, usefully positioned for walks through Leighton Moss RSPB reserve and up Warton Crag, open all day. *(Don Bryan, Brian and Anna Marsden)*

Leicestershire
and Rutland

This is a strong area for top class food with many of our Main Entries holding one of our Food Awards. For a special meal head to the Three Horse Shoes at Breedon on the Hill (a former farrier's with much character in several rooms, real ales and enjoyable food), Olive Branch in Clipsham (a very special place to drink, eat or stay), Marquess of Exeter in Lyddington (a handsome, historic inn with excellent food), Red Lion in Stathern (sister pub to the Olive Branch decorated in a charming, rustic style), and Kings Arms in Wing (civilised, with their own smokehouse contributing to the interesting menu). Also doing well this year are the Sun in Cottesmore (back in these pages after a break), Fox & Hounds in Exton (handsome former coaching inn – though new to us – with good food cooked by the landlord), Rutland & Derbys Arms in Leicester (neatly kept modern town bar and another new entry), Grainstore in Oakham (ten of their own-brewed ales and a cheerful atmosphere), Jackson Stops at Stretton (a lot of character, a charming landlady and well liked food), and Wheatsheaf in Woodhouse Eaves (friendly and unchanging with lots to look at). Our Leicestershire Dining Pub 2013 is the Olive Branch in Clipsham.

BREEDON ON THE HILL   SK4022   Map 7

Three Horse Shoes 🍴

Main Street (A453); DE73 8AN

Comfortable, good-looking pub with friendly licensees and emphasis on popular food

We particularly enjoyed the interior of this agreeable 18th-c pub. It's been nicely restored and decorated to make the best of its attractive structure. The clean-cut central bar has a stylishly simple feel with heavy worn flagstones, green walls and ceilings, a log fire, pubby tables and a dark wood counter; Marstons Pedigree on handpump, 30 malt whiskies and decent house wines. Beyond here, a dining room has maroon walls, dark pews and cherry-stained tables. The two-room dining area on the right has a comfortably civilised chatty feel, with big antique tables set quite closely together on seagrass matting, and colourful modern country prints and antique engravings on canary yellow walls. Even at lunchtime there are lighted candles in elegant modern holders. Look out for the quaint conical village lock-up opposite.

🍴 Enjoyable – if not cheap – food includes sandwiches, ploughman's, salads, fish and spinach pancake, smoked salmon, salmon and sweet potato curry, cod with caper butter, roast vegetable casserole, sausages and mash, a changing hot pot, beef and mushroom pudding, duck breast with cabbage and whisky, lamb shank with parsnip mash, and puddings such as treacle oat tart, chocolate whisky trifle and lemon cheesecake. *Benchmark main dish: fish and chips £10.75. Two-course evening meal £21.20.*

Free house ~ Licensees Ian Davison, Jennie Ison, Stuart Marson ~ Real ale ~
Bar food (12-2, 5.30-9) ~ Restaurant ~ (01332) 695129 ~ Dogs allowed in bar ~
Open 11.30-2.30, 5.30-11; 12-3 Sun; closed Sun evening ~ www.thehorseshoes.com
Recommended by David and Sue Atkinson

BUCKMINSTER   SK8822   Map 7
Tollemache Arms 🍴 £
B676 Colsterworth–Melton Mowbray; Main Street; NG33 5SA

Good food to the fore in stylishly updated pub recently reopened by two enthusiastic young couples

Not many pubs in the Guide can boast both a Food and Bargain Award, as does this well run place with its quick and attentive service. The stone and brick building is surprisingly stately for a village pub, and the refurbishments suit it well. One rather elegant corner room has comfortable easy chairs around its log fire, and quite a library of books. The series of other linked areas contain a dark leather chesterfield by a low table of magazines and newspapers in another fireside corner, and otherwise a mix of wheelback, dining and stripped kitchen chairs, and some rather nice specially made small pews, around tables set on floorboards; table lamps and standard lamps, big bunches of flowers, and a shelf of board games add a homely touch, and they don't turn up their noses at dogs or muddy boots. There's a good choice of wines by the glass and changing ales from local brewers such as Belvoir, Grainstore and Oakham on handpump, and perhaps discreet nostalgic background music. There are teak tables out on the back grass, by a clump of sycamores; beyond is a small herb and salad garden, and a swing.

🍴 As well as bar snacks such as calamari, scampi, charcuterie and chilli, the menu includes starters such as mushroom, garlic and raclette on puff pastry, confit duck with hazelnut and pickled rhubarb terrine, potted shrimps with pickled cucumber, main courses such as goats cheese and tomato tatin, duck breast with wild garlic, grilled salmon with wok-fried vegetables, fish and chips, and puddings such as rhubarb crème brûlée, chocolate brownie and toffee banana ice-cream and cherry clafoutis. *Benchmark main dish: chicken, leek and mushroom pie £9.50. Two-course evening meal £17.10.*

Free house ~ Licensees Matt and Amanda Wrisdale ~ Real ale ~ Bar food (12-2 (2.30 Sun), 6.30-9) ~ Restaurant ~ (01476) 860477 ~ Children welcome ~ Dogs allowed in bar ~ Open 12-3, 5-11; 12-4 Sun; closed Sun evening, Mon, 1st week in Jan ~ www.tollemache-arms.co.uk *Recommended by Pat and Stewart Gordon*

The letters and figures after the name of each town are its Ordnance Survey map reference. *How to use the Guide* at the beginning of the book explains how it helps you find a pub, in road atlases or large-scale maps as well as in our own maps.

CLIPSHAM

SK9716   Map 8

Olive Branch ★ ⑪ ☍ ◧ ⇌

Take B668/Stretton exit off A1 N of Stamford; Clipsham signposted E from exit roundabout; LE15 7SH

Leicestershire Dining Pub of the Year

A special place for an exceptional meal in comfortable surroundings, fine choice of drinks, and luxury bedrooms

The various small but charmingly attractive bars at this very thoughtfully run place have a relaxed country cottage atmosphere, with dark joists and beams, rustic furniture, an interesting mix of pictures (some by local artists), candles on tables, and a cosy log fire in the stone inglenook fireplace. Many of the books dotted around were bought at antiques fairs by one of the partners and are sometimes for sale; background music. A carefully chosen range of drinks includes Grainstore Olive Ale and a guest such as Timothy Taylor on handpump, an enticing wine list (with about a dozen by the glass), a fine choice of malt whiskies, armagnacs and cognacs, and quite a few different british and continental bottled beers. Outside, there are tables, chairs and big plant pots on a pretty little terrace, with more on the neat lawn, sheltered in the L of its two low buildings. This is a great place to make a weekend of it as their bedrooms (just opposite in Beech House with delicious breakfasts) are lovely. It can get pretty busy at peak times, so if you're not staying it's worth getting here early.

Extremely highly thought of (if not cheap) food might include sandwiches, a smashing tapas board, roast pigeon breast with date purée, devilled whitebait, seared scallops with caper and raisin vinaigrette, confit duck leg with bean and chorizo cassoulet, paprika and smoked bacon jus, tempura tiger prawns with chilli sauce, fish and chips, and puddings such as dark chocolate and hazelnut pavlova, rhubarb custard tart and sticky toffee pudding. *Benchmark main dish: honey roast pork belly £15.50. Two-course evening meal £25.50.*

Free house ~ Licensees Sean Hope and Ben Jones ~ Real ale ~ Bar food (12-2 (3 Sun), 7-9.30(9 Sun); 12-2, 2.30-5.30, 7-9.30 Sat) ~ Restaurant ~ (01780) 410355 ~ Children welcome ~ Dogs allowed in bar and bedrooms ~ Open 12-3, 6-11; 12-11 Sat; 12-10.30 Sun; may close first week of Jan ~ Bedrooms: £112.50S(£130B)/£130S(£160B) ~ www.theolivebranchpub.com *Recommended by P Dawn, P and J Shapley, Pam and John Smith, Pat and Stewart Gordon, Bruce and Sharon Eden, Roy Bromell, Di and Mike Gillam, Sandy Butcher, David and Ruth Shillitoe, Tony and Maggie Harwood, Mike and Sue Loseby, Bob and Tanya Ekers, Barry Collett, Michael Sargent, Jamie and Sue May, Gordon and Margaret Ormondroyd*

COLEORTON

SK4117   Map 7

George

Loughborough Road (A512 E); LE67 8HF

Attractively traditional homely pub with dining area and large garden

The welcoming atmosphere at this unassumingly comfortable pub is generated by the hands-on friendly licensees here, a couple. The bar on the right is nicely laid out to give the feel of varied and fairly small separate areas: dark leather sofa and tub chairs by a woodburning stove in front, scatter-cushioned pews and mixed chairs below shelves of books in one corner, and other mixed seating elsewhere. This room has lots of local photographs on its ochre or dove-grey walls, black beams and joists, and a dark-panelled dado. A bigger room on the left, broadly similar and again with plenty to look at, has another woodburning stove, and more of a dining-room feel. Burton Bridge XL, Marstons Pedigree and Timothy Taylors Landlord are on handpump. The spreading garden behind has sturdy wooden furniture among sizeable trees, and a children's play area.

 Honest pub food prepared using local produce includes lunchtime filled panini, devilled whitebait, lamb kofta, pork tenderloin with almond and apple stuffing and brandy and apple jus, smoked haddock with whole grain mustard sauce, brie, asparagus and parmesan tart with poached egg, lasagne, beef and ale pie, scampi, liver and bacon, mushroom risotto, and rib-eye steak . *Benchmark main dish: steak in ale pie £10.75. Two-course evening meal £16.30.*

Free house ~ Licensees Mark and Janice Wilkinson ~ Real ale ~ Bar food (12-2.30 (3 Sun), 6-9(9.30 Fri, Sat)) ~ Restaurant ~ (01530) 834639 ~ Well behaved supervised children welcome ~ Dogs allowed in bar ~ Open 12-3.30, 5.30-11; 12-11 Sat; 12-4 Sun; closed Sun evening, Mon ~ www.georgeinncoleorton.co.uk *Recommended by Henry Paulinski*

COTTESMORE
Sun
SK9013   Map 7

B668 NE of Oakham; LE15 7DH

Nice village pub with friendly staff and reasonably priced food

This attractive 17th-c thatched and white-painted village pub is run by friendly licensees. Décor is simple and homely, with stripped pine and plush stools on flagstones, an inglenook fire and lots of pictures and ornaments. The carpeted back restaurant has white walls and dark wheelback chairs. Friendly staff serve Everards Tiger, a seasonal Everards beer, a guest from a brewer such as Oakham and a farm cider; background music. There are picnic-sets in front of the building with more in the large garden.

 As well as lunchtime baguettes, bar food might include brie wedges, smoked chicken and bacon salad, cottage pie, chicken breast in stilton sauce, pie of the day, fish and chips, braised lamb shank with port, rosemary and redcurrant sauce, and puddings such as white chocolate cheesecake and chocolate brownie with walnut and vanilla ice-cream. *Benchmark main dish: steak, ale and mushroom pie £8.95. Two-course evening meal £17.00.*

Everards ~ Tenants Neil and Karen Hornsby ~ Real ale ~ Bar food (12-2, 6-9; 12-4 Sun) ~ Restaurant ~ (01572) 812321 ~ Children welcome ~ Dogs allowed in bar ~ Open 11.30-11(10 Sun) ~ www.everards.co.uk *Recommended by Barry Collett*

EXTON
Fox & Hounds 🍴 🛏
SK9211   Map 7

The Green; signed off A606 Stamford–Oakham; LE15 8AP

Well run, friendly inn with comfortable lounge bar, real ales, popular food cooked by the landlord and quiet garden; bedrooms

Though the road outside is now usually quiet, the size of this handsome building is a reminder of the days when it was the main coach route to Oakham. The comfortable high-ceilinged lounge bar is traditionally civilised with some dark red plush easy chairs and wheelback seats around lots of pine tables, maps and hunting prints on the walls, fresh flowers and a winter log fire in a large stone fireplace. Grainstore Ten Fifty, Greene King IPA and a changing guest beer on handpump served by friendly staff and several wines by the glass; TV and background music. The lovely sheltered walled garden has seats among large rose beds overlooking pretty paddocks. If you stay in the spotlessly clean bedrooms, the breakfasts very good. The inn is handy for Rutland Water and the gardens at Barnsdale.

Attractively presented and cooked by the landlord, the food might include lunchtime sandwiches, home-made salmon fishcake with aioli dip, chicken liver pâté with caramelised red onion chutney, sharing deli boards such as an antipasti or smokehouse plate, ravioli filled with ricotta and parmesan with sage butter, lots of different pizzas, sausages with creamy mash and onion gravy, pork belly with wholegrain mustard mash and red cabbage, gammon with pineapple and egg, beer-battered cod with hand-cut chips, bass with mixed peppers and chorizo, and puddings. *Benchmark main dish: coq au vin £13.25. Two-course evening meal £18.50.*

Free house ~ Licensees Valter and Sandra Floris ~ Real ale ~ Bar food (12-2, 6.30-9; all day weekends) ~ Restaurant ~ (01572) 812403 ~ Children welcome ~ Dogs allowed in bar and bedrooms ~ Open 11-3, 6-11; 11-11 Sat and Sun ~ Bedrooms: £55B/£70B ~ www.foxandhoundsrutland.co.uk *Recommended by P and J Shapley, Alan and Jill Bull, Jim Farmer, Pam and John Smith, Chris Kay, Roy Bromell, David and Ruth Shillitoe, Marcus Mann, Barry Collett, Mike Proctor*

LEICESTER   SK5804   Map 4

Rutland & Derby Arms £

Millstone Lane; nearby metered parking; LE1 5JN

Neatly kept modern town bar with interesting food from deli counter, impressive drinks range, sheltered courtyard

The neat cream-walled courtyard at this city tavern shelters some sunny picnic-sets and there are more on an upper terrace. It's fairly staid on the outside, but the open-plan interior has a pleasing clean-cut modernity. There are comfortable bar chairs by the long counter, padded high seats including one unusual high banquette by chunky tall tables, a few small prints of classic film posters and the like; apart from some stripped brick, décor is in shades of ochre and coffee. Cocktails (they have an impressive array of spirits), and soft drink cocktails are offered, and there are various foreign beers on tap alongside Adnams Broadside, four Everards beers and a guest such as Charles Wells Bombardier on handpump, a farm cider, 20 wines by the glass and 20 whiskies; bright pleasant service, well reproduced background music, games machine.

Bar food includes nachos, salads, hot and spicy prawns, cream cheese jalapenos, toasties, chicken wings served in various ways, deli boards and a good range of pizzas. *Benchmark main dish: pizza £6.95. Two-course evening meal £12.90.*

Everards ~ Tenant Samuel Hagger ~ Real ale ~ Bar food (12-8) ~ (0116) 2623299 ~ Children welcome ~ Dogs welcome ~ Open 12-11 (2am Sat); closed Sun ~ www.everards.co.uk/pubs/rutland_derby_122 *Recommended by Dave Braisted*

Real ale to us means beer which has matured naturally in its cask – not pressurised or filtered. We name all real ales stocked. We usually name ales preserved under a light blanket of carbon dioxide too, though purists – pointing out that this stops the natural yeasts developing – would disagree (most people, including us, can't tell the difference!)

LYDDINGTON
SP8797 Map 4

Marquess of Exeter ⊗

Main Street; LE15 9LT

Stone inn with contemporary décor, real ales and excellent food cooked by the landlord

The interior of this rather handsome inn has been lightly reworked to emphasise its simple but attractive historic features. Its fine flagged floors, thick walls, beams and exposed stonework are left to speak for themselves, and its open-plan areas are spacious and laid out with understated but stylish furnishings – a mix of old tables and chairs, stylish fabrics, leather sofas, pine chests and old barrels that might always have been here. In winter, it's all warmed by several open fires – one a quite striking work in dark iron. Marstons Pedigree and a guest like Jennings Cumberland are on handpump and they offer about a dozen wines by the glass. Friendly service is top notch and accommodating. There are seats out on the terrace and picnic sets in tree-sheltered gardens that seem to merge with the countryside beyond. The pub is named after the Burghley family, which as long owned this charming village. (Burghley house is about 15 miles away.)

Excellent food (you must book ahead to be sure of a table) might include sandwiches, french onion soup, crispy salt and chilli squid, smoked mackerel with marinated cucumber and horseradish crème fraîche, pork and chorizo terrine with piccalilli, roast cod fillet with mushroom salsa and wilted spinach, linguine with king prawns, tomato, chilli and garlic oil, fried calves liver with onion marmalade and crispy parma ham, tarragon chicken on puff pastry with crispy shallots, sweet potato, spinach and parmesan risotto, and puddings such as cinnamon panna cotta with poached winter fruits and ginger biscuit, chocolate marmalade brioche bread, and butter pudding with orange ice-cream. *Benchmark main dish: steak with Café de Paris butter £14.25. Two-course evening meal £23.00.*

Marstons ~ Lease Brian Baker ~ Real ale ~ Bar food (12-2.30 (3 Sun), 6.30-9.30(9 Sun)) ~ Restaurant ~ (01572) 822477 ~ Children welcome but must be supervised by parents ~ Dogs allowed in bar and bedrooms ~ Open 10-11(10.30 Sun) ~ Bedrooms: $69.50B/$89.50B ~ www.marquessexeter.co.uk *Recommended by Robin Constable, Michael Goodden, Malcolm Lee, R L Borthwick, Mike and Sue Loseby*

OAKHAM
SK8509 Map 4

Grainstore ⊲ £

Station Road, off A606; LE15 6RE

Super own-brewed beers in a converted railway grain warehouse, friendly staff, cheerful customers and pubby food

Most of this former Victorian grain store's customers are here to try the own-brewed beers, and the friendly staff will happily let them taste a sample or two before they decide. There are ten real ales, which are served traditionally at the left end of the bar counter and through swan necks with sparklers on the right. As per the traditional tower system of production, the beer is brewed on the upper floors of the building, directly above the down-to-earth bar. During working hours you'll hear the busy noises of the brewery workings rumbling above your head. The décor is plain and functional with wide well worn floorboards, bare ceiling boards above massive joists supported by red metal pillars, a long brick-built bar counter with cast-iron bar stools, tall cask tables and simple elm chairs; games machine, darts, board games, giant Jenga and bottle-walking. In summer they pull back the huge glass doors, opening the bar up to a terrace with picnic-sets, often stacked with barrels. You can tour the brewery by arrangement, they do takeaways, and hold a real ale festival with over 80 real ales and live music during the August bank holiday weekend; disabled access.

Straightforward lunchtime food includes sandwiches, garlic mushrooms, ham, egg and chips and burgers. *Benchmark main dish: steak mushroom and ale pie £8.50.*

Own brew ~ Licensee Peter Atkinson ~ Real ale ~ Bar food (11.30-3; no evening food except Weds pie and pint night; breakfast 9-11.30 Sat, Sun ~ (01572) 770065 ~ Children welcome till 8pm ~ Dogs allowed in bar ~ Open 11-11(midnight Fri); 9am-midnight Sat; 9am-10.30pm Sun ~ www.grainstorebrewery.com *Recommended by P Dawn, Ryta Lyndley, Dr J Barrie Jones, Tony and Maggie Harwood, Barry Collett, the Didler, Jim Farmer*

 OAKHAM   SK8608   Map 4

Lord Nelson ★ ♀ ◀

Market Place; LE15 6DT

Splendidly restored as proper relaxed grown-up pub, full of interest; open all day from 9am

Taken deftly in hand by Michael Thurlby, who redeveloped the Tobie Norris in Stamford so successfully that it won our Newcomer of the Year Award in 2012, this handsome old building now has over half a dozen rooms spread over two floors, giving plenty of companionable places for chatty relaxation. It's worth having a good look round before you decide where to sit: you can choose from cushioned church pews, leather elbow chairs, long oak settles, sofas, armchairs – or, to watch the passing scene, a big bow window seat; carpet, bare boards, or ancient red and black tiles; paintwork in soft shades of ochre, canary yellow, sage or pink, or William Morris wallpaper. There's plenty to look at, too, from intriguing antique Police News and other prints – plenty of Nelson, of course – to the collections of mullers, copper kettles and other homely bric-a-brac in the heavy-beamed former kitchen with its Aga. But the main thing is simply the easy-going good-natured atmosphere. They have well kept Adnams Southwold and Castle Rock Harvest Pale on handpump, with three good guests on our visit – Exmoor Fox, Gales Spring Sprinter and Newby Wyke HM Queen Elizabeth; also Weston's farm cider, and a good changing choice of wines by the glass. Staff are helpful and efficient, and clearly love working here. The resident king charles spaniel is called Buzz.

Proper stone-cooked pizzas are the main event – as you can choose your own toppings, it's all too easy to overcrowd the flavours. Other offerings include indian spiced burgers, tomato, basil and parmesan pasta, home-made meatballs in a chorizo and spicy tomato sauce, wasabi chicken, bass niçoise with lime chilli dressing, belly pork and chickpea cassoulet, and puddings such as banoffi millefeuille and belgian chocolate melting pot. *Benchmark main dish: stone-baked pizza £6.95. Two-course evening meal £17.95.*

Free house ~ Licensee Adam Dale ~ Real ale ~ Bar food (12-2.30,6-9; not Sun evening) ~ (01572) 868340 ~ Over-4s allowed till 8pm away from bar; no pushchairs ~ Dogs welcome ~ Open 9am-11pm(midnight Fri and Sat); 12-11 Sun ~ www.thelordnelsonoakham.com *Recommended by G Jennings*

PEGGS GREEN
New Inn £

Signposted off A512 Ashby–Shepshed at roundabout, then turn immediately left down Zion Hill towards Newbold; pub is 100 metres down on the right, with car park on opposite side of road; LE67 8JE

Intriguing bric-a-brac in unspoilt pub, friendly welcome, good value food and drinks; cottagey garden

With its genial irish licensees and chatty locals, this simple and unspoilt little pub is a real gem – one reader tells us it's 'probably the most friendly pub we've ever been in'. Quirky and quite unique-feeling, the two cosy tiled front rooms are filled with a diverting collection of old bric-a-brac that covers almost every inch of the walls and ceilings. The little room on the left, a bit like an old kitchen parlour (they call it the Cabin), has china on the mantelpiece, lots of prints and photographs and little collections of this and that, three old cast-iron tables, wooden stools and a small stripped kitchen table. The room to the right has nice stripped panelling and some more appealing bric-a-brac. The small back Best room, with a stripped-wood floor, has a touching display of old local photographs including some colliery ones. Bass, Caledonian Deuchars IPA and Marstons Pedigree on handpump; background music and board games. There are plenty of seats in front of the pub, with more in the peaceful back garden. Do check their unusual opening times below carefully.

Unbelievably cheap food includes filled rolls and baked potatoes, soup, ham and eggs, corned beef hash, sausages in onion gravy, and a few daily specials. When they are not serving food, you can order in takeaways (they will provide the crockery and do the washing up), and on summer evenings and Sunday lunchtimes you can bring your own picnic and they will provide rugs. *Benchmark main dish: steak pie £4.95.*

Enterprise ~ Lease Maria Christina Kell ~ Real ale ~ Bar food (12-2, Mon, Fri and Sat, 6-8 Mon; filled rolls might be available at other times) ~ (01530) 222293 ~ Children welcome ~ Dogs welcome ~ Quiz Thurs, folk club monthly second Mon ~ Open 12-2.30, 5.30-11; 12-3, 6.30-11 Sat; 12-3, 7-10.30 Sun; closed Tues-Thurs lunchtimes ~ www.thenewinnpeggsgreen.co.uk *Recommended by Richard and Jean Green, the Didler*

SILEBY
White Swan £

Off A6 or A607 N of Leicester; in centre turn into King Street (opposite church), then after mini-roundabout turn right at Post Office signpost into Swan Street; LE12 7NW

Exemplary town local, a boon to its chatty regulars, its good honest home cooking luring others from further afield

In the same hands for nearly 30 years now, this solidly built red-brick pub has all the touches that marked the best of between-the-wars estate pub design, such as its deco-tiled lobby, the polychrome-tiled fireplaces, the shiny red anaglypta ceiling and the comfortable layout of linked but separate areas including a small restaurant (now lined with books). It's packed with bric-a-brac from bizarre hats to decorative plates and lots of prints, and quickly draws you in with its genuinely bright and cheerful welcome; this, along with its food and the can-do attitude of the helpful staff, is what sets it above the thousands of other worthwhile locals. Fullers London Pride is on handpump, and they stock good value house wines.

🍴 Very popular, homely bar food includes filled rolls (they bake their own bread), duck and vegetable pancake rolls, crispy brie with cranberry sauce, breaded mushrooms with garlic mayonnaise, salmon fillet with prawns and garlic butter, cheese and beetroot tart, pork fillet with mustard, white wine and cream, steaks, and puddings such as hot treacle tart and lemon tart with lemon curd ice-cream. *Benchmark main dish: chicken parmesan £10.95. Two-course evening meal £14.00.*

Free house ~ Licensee Theresa Miller ~ Real ale ~ Bar food (12-1.30, 6-8.30) ~ (01509) 814832 ~ Children welcome ~ Dogs welcome ~ Open 12-2, 6-11; 12-3 Sun; closed Sat lunchtime, Sun evening and Mon and 1-6 Jan ~ www.whiteswansileby.co.uk
Recommended by Rob and Catherine Dunster

STATHERN   SK7731 Map 7
Red Lion 🍴 ♑ 🍺

Off A52 W of Grantham via the brown-signed Belvoir road (keep on towards Harby–Stathern signposted on left); or off A606 Nottingham–Melton Mowbray via Long Clawson and Harby; LE14 4HS

Fine range of drinks and popular food in country-style dining pub with open fires and good garden with a play area; own shop, too

You'll find the same high standards at this rather civilised dining pub as you will at its sister pub, the Olive Branch in Clipsham. It's decorated in a charming rustic style, staff are welcoming and the atmosphere throughout is relaxed and informal. The yellow room on the right, with its collection of wooden spoons and lambing chairs, has a simple country-pub feel. The lounge bar has sofas, an open fire and a big table with books, newspapers and magazines. It leads off the smaller, more traditional flagstoned bar with terracotta walls, another fireplace with a pile of logs beside it and lots of beams and hops. A little room with tables set for eating leads to the long, narrow, main dining room, and out to a nicely arranged suntrap lawn and terrace with good hardwood furnishings; background music. Red Lion Ale (from Grainstore) and a couple of guests such as Batemans XB and Caledonian Deuchars IPA are on handpump, with draught belgian and continental bottled beers, several ciders and a varied wine list (several by the glass). There's an unusually big play area behind the car park with swings, climbing frames and so on.

🍴 As well as a popular two- and three-course set lunch, the carefully sourced and prepared food includes attractively presented sandwiches, ham hock and foie gras terrine with piccalilli, devilled whitebait with garlic aioli, mushroom and tarragon risotto, vegetable curry, fish and chips, steak burger, sausage and mash and roast chicken breast with sherry and mushroom sauce. *Benchmark main dish: fish and chips £11.50. Two-course evening meal £22.40.*

Free house ~ Licensees Sean Hope and Ben Jones ~ Real ale ~ Bar food (12-2(4 Sun), 7-9) ~ Restaurant ~ (01949) 860868 ~ Children welcome ~ Dogs allowed in bar ~ Open 12-3, 6-11; 12-11 Sat; 12-8 Sun; closed Mon ~ www.theredlioninn.co.uk *Recommended by P Dawn, Gwyn and Anne Wake, Derek and Sylvia Stephenson, David Glynne-Jones, Bruce and Sharon Eden, Daz Smith, Vivienne Stott, Comus and Sarah Elliott*

Please keep sending us reports. We rely on readers for news of new discoveries, and particularly for news of changes – however slight – at the fully described pubs: feedback@goodguides.com, or (no stamp needed) The Good Pub Guide, FREEPOST TN1569, Wadhurst, E Sussex TN5 7BR.

STRETTON
SK9415   Map 8

Jackson Stops

*Rookery Lane; a mile or less off A1, at B668 (Oakham) exit; follow village
sign, turning off Clipsham Road into Manor Road, pub on left; LE15 7RA*

Attractive thatched former farmhouse with good food, just off A1

This 16th-c stone inn has one of the only two nurdling bench games
left in Britain. It's a place of great character and the rooms meander
around filled with lots of lovely period features. The black-beamed
country bar down on the left has wall timbering, a couple of bar stools, a
cushioned wall pew and an elderly settle on the worn tile and brick floor,
and a coal fire in one corner. Phipps IPA made for them by Grainstore
and Oakham JHB on handpump alongside several wines by the glass.
The smarter main room on the right is light and airy with a nice mix of
ancient and modern tables on dark blue carpet, and another coal fire in a
stone corner fireplace. Just past the bar is the dining room with stripped-
stone walls, a tiled floor and an old open cooking range, and there's a
second smaller dining room; background music.

As well as good value two- and three-course set lunch and dinner menus, the
well liked food might include baguettes, duck and chicken liver pâté with
cumberland jelly, sardines on toast with sauce vièrge, home-made burgers with
various toppings, beer-battered haddock with french-style peas and tartare sauce,
pork meatballs with tomato sauce on tagliatelle, tarte tatin of leeks, sweet potato
and fennel topped with cheese, herb-crusted lamb rump with beetroot ratatouille
and redcurrant and thyme jus, salmon with spring onion, courgette and coriander
salad and a lemon and toasted sesame dressing, and puddings such as sticky toffee
pudding with caramel ice-cream and fudge pieces and passionfruit cheesecake with
peach and mango ice-cream and tropical fruit compote. *Benchmark main dish:
burgundy beef pie £15.45. Two-course evening meal £19.50.*

Free house ~ Licensee Robert Reid ~ Real ale ~ Bar food (12-2.30, 6.30-9) ~ Restaurant
~ (01780) 410237 ~ Children welcome ~ Dogs allowed in bar ~ Open 12-3, 6-1.30(11 Fri
and Sat); 12-5 Sun; closed Sun evening and Mon ~ www.thejacksonstops.com
*Recommended by Tony and Glenys Dyer, John Cooper, Barry Collett, Arthur Pickering, Ian Prince,
Pat and Stewart Gordon, Peter and Heather Elliott*

SWITHLAND
SK5512   Map 7

Griffin

*Main Street; between A6 and B5330, between Loughborough and
Leicester; LE12 8TJ*

A good mix of cheerful customers, well liked food in a bustling pub

Readers enjoy the hospitable atmosphere at this busy but comfortable
local. Its three beamed communicating rooms are cosy and
traditional with some panelling, banquettes, a woodburner, a nice mix
of wooden tables and chairs, and stools at the counter where Everards
Original and Tiger, Adnams Southwold and four or so guests from
brewers such as Bass and Greene King are on handpump, a couple of
farm ciders, several malt whiskies and wines by the glass from a good
list; background music and skittle alley. The tidy streamside garden has
seats overlooking open fields. The pub is in a quiet tucked-away village in
the heart of Charnwood Forest and is handy for Bradgate Country Park
and walks in Swithland Woods.

🍴 Well liked bar food includes chicken liver and brandy pâté, smoked salmon, tempura king prawns, battered haddock, lamb tagine, fried bass with sauce vièrge, sausage and mash, ham and eggs, mushroom, spinach and tomato frittata, specials such as fried pork with black pudding and cider jus and baked chicken breast with basil mousse and sweet potato ratatouille, and puddings such as chocolate fudge cake, banana split and passion fruit crème brûlée. *Benchmark main dish: paella £12.95. Two-course evening meal £18.40.*

Everards ~ Tenant John Cooledge ~ Real ale ~ Bar food (12-2, 6-9; 12-9.30(8 Sun) Fri, Sat; breakfast 9-11.30 Sat, Sun) ~ Restaurant ~ (01509) 890535 ~ Children welcome ~ Open 9-11(10.30 Sun) ~ www.griffininnswithland.co.uk *Recommended by Kevin and Maggie Balchin, Rob and Catherine Dunster, Gwyn and Anne Wake, SAB and MJW*

WING   SK8902 Map 4

Kings Arms 🍴 ♀ 🍺

Village signposted off A6003 S of Oakham; Top Street; LE15 8SE

Nicely kept old pub, big log fires, super choice of wines by the glass, good modern cooking and smokehouse

You may need to book to be sure of a table at this civilised 17th-c inn as it can be busy with other customers enjoying the thoughtfully prepared food. Long and narrow, the neatly kept and attractive bar is warm and inviting with two large log fires (one in a copper-canopied central hearth), various nooks and crannies, nice old low beams and stripped stone, and flagstone or wood-strip floors. Friendly, helpful staff serve nearly three dozen wines by the glass, as well as Grainstore Cooking and Rutland Beast, Marstons Pedigree and a guest such as Hobgoblin on handpump, several grappas and malt whiskies and a local cider; board games. There are seats out in front, and more in the sunny yew-sheltered garden; the car park has plenty of space. There's a medieval turf maze just up the road, and we are told that one of England's two osprey hot-spots is just a couple of miles away.

🍴 As well as their own smokehouse producing everything from charcuterie to smoked nuts (you can buy their produce to take away), they bake their own bread and biscuits and make their own ice-creams. Alongside classics such as shepherd's pie, hotpot and home baked ham, more elaborate changing specials might include dishes such as suckling pig, pistachio and foie gras terrine with quince jelly and poached apples, soused and smoked herrings with horseradish potato salad and soft-boiled quails eggs, bass with tempura oysters and bouillabaisse sauce, beef cheeks in red wine with smoked shallot and horseradish mash, roast butternut risotto with goats cheese, pesto and toasted pumpkin seeds, and puddings such as orange tart with orange caramel sauce and chocolate sorbet, and chocolate brownie with chocolate sauce and malted milk ice-cream. *Benchmark main dish: pie and mash £12.50. Two-course evening meal £21.00.*

Free house ~ Licensee David Goss ~ Real ale ~ Bar food (12-2, 6.30-8.30 Tues-Thurs; 6.30-9 Fri, Sat) ~ Restaurant ~ (01572) 737634 ~ Children welcome away from the bar ~ Dogs allowed in bar and bedrooms ~ Open 12-3, 6.30-11; closed Sun evening, Mon lunchtime, all day Mon and Tues lunchtime in winter ~ Bedrooms: £77.50S/$100S ~ www.thekingsarms-wing.co.uk *Recommended by Michael Sargent, P and J Shapley, Barry Collett, O K Smyth, Trevor Single*

Post Office address codings confusingly give the impression that some pubs are in Leicestershire, when they're really in Cambridgeshire (which is where we list them).

WOODHOUSE EAVES

Wheatsheaf 🍴

SK5313   Map 7

Brand Hill; turn right into Main Street, off B591 S of Loughborough; LE12 8SS

Bustling and friendly country pub, interesting things to look at, good bistro-type food and a fair choice of drinks; well equipped bedrooms

Happily not much changes from one year to the next at this properly hospitable, rather smart inn. Nicely maintaining a genuinely pubby atmosphere, it strikes an easy balance between good food, beers and accommodation. The beamed bar areas are traditionally furnished (with wooden pews, log fires, daily papers and the like) and are full of interesting motor-racing and family RAF and flying memorabilia. A cosy dining area called The Mess even has an RAF Hurricane propeller. The atmosphere is cheerful and chatty and the service helpful and welcoming, even when pushed. Adnams Broadside, Timothy Taylors Landlord, Thwaites Wainwright and a couple of guests such as Adnams and Marstons Pedigree are on handpump, with about 17 wines by the glass, including champagne, from a thoughtfully compiled list. The floodlit, heated terrace has plenty of seating.

🍴 Bar food includes sandwiches, ploughman's, spaghetti and meatballs, vegetarian lasagne, salmon and tuna fishcake, fish and chips, ham, egg and chips, half a spit-roast chicken, roast nut loaf, burgers, fresh fish, sirloin steak, and puddings such as fruit crumble, cheesecake and chocolate brownie. *Benchmark main dish: smoked haddock in creamy tomato sauce with breadcrumb cheese topping £10.95. Two-course evening meal £19.90.*

Free house ~ Licensees Richard and Bridget Dimblebee ~ Real ale ~ Bar food (12-2(2.30 Sat, 3 Sun), 6.30-9.15(9.30 Sat)) ~ Restaurant ~ (01509) 890320 ~ Children welcome ~ Dogs allowed in bar and bedrooms ~ Open 11-3, 6-11; 11-11 Sat; 12-11 Sun; 11-3, 6-11 Sat in winter ~ Bedrooms: £60S/£80B ~ www.wheatsheafinn.net *Recommended by Chris and Jeanne Downing, Jim Farmer, Michael and Maggie Betton, Rob and Catherine Dunster, Tim and Joan Wright, Sandy Butcher, Andy and Jill Kassube, Ken Marshall, Dennis and Doreen Haward, Andy Lickfold, Barry and Anne, Dr Martin Owton, Peter Ridley, Roger and Ann King, Phil and Jane Villiers, Phil & Jane Villiers, SAB and MJW*

WYMONDHAM

Berkeley Arms

SK8518   Map 7

Main Street; LE14 2AG

Pleasant village pub with interesting food and sunny terrace

Something of a home from home, this golden stone 16th-c inn has a welcoming, relaxed feel with its knick-knacks, magazines, table lamps and cushions. At one end two wing chairs are set on patterned carpet beside a low coffee table and a cosy log fire. The red-tiled dining area, dense with sripped beams and standing timbers, is furnished kitchen-style with light wood tables and red-cushioned chunky chairs, or you can eat in the smarter dining area with its dark leather chairs. Real ales include Greene King IPA, Marstons Pedigree and a guest such as Hopback Glass Hopper; ten wines are offered by the glass, and they keep a local cider. Outside in front, on small terraces to either side of the entrance, picnic-sets benefit from the sun nearly all day.

🍴 Enjoyable bar food, in quite busy presentations, might include crispy whitebait, mussels and chorizo in white wine, grilled pigeon, fig and pancetta salad, battered haddock and mushy peas, steak, vegetable and ale pie, curried monkfish tail with creamed leeks and mussels, pork fillet with black pudding, braised belly and apple cider sauce, and puddings such as hot chocolate fondant with honeycomb and pistachio ice-cream and vanilla panna cotta with honey roasted pears. *Benchmark main dish: honey-glazed duck breast with ginger sauce £17.00. Two-course evening meal £21.35.*

Free house ~ Licensee Louise Hitchen ~ Real ale ~ Bar food (12-2(3 Sun), 6-9 Tues-Thurs; 6-9.30 Fri, Sat) ~ Restaurant ~ (01572) 787587 ~ Children welcome ~ Dogs allowed in bar ~ Open 12-3(5 Sun), 6-11; closed Sun evening, Mon lunchtime, first two weeks in Jan, one week in summer ~ www.theberkeleyarms.co.uk *Recommended by Andy Miksza, M and GR*

Also Worth a Visit in Leicestershire

Besides the fully inspected pubs, you might like to try these pubs that have been recommended to us and described by readers. Do tell us what you think of them: feedback@goodguides.com

AB KETTLEBY   SK7519
Sugar Loaf (01664) 822473
Nottingham Road (A606 NW of Melton); LE14 3JB Beamed pub with comfortably modernised open-plan carpeted bar, country prints and big photographs of Shipstones brewery dray horses, bare-boards end with coal-effect gas fire, good fairly priced all-day food, well kept Bass, Marstons Pedigree and guests, decent coffee, friendly attentive staff, dining conservatory; quiet juke box, games machine; children welcome if eating, picnic-sets out by road and car park, open all day. *(George Atkinson, Ryta Lyndley)*

BARKBY   SK6309
Malt Shovel (0116) 269 2558
Main Street; LE7 3QG Popular old family-run village pub, enjoyable good value food including OAP lunch and bargain steak night Mon, four Thwaites ales and a couple of guests (beer festivals), good choice of wines by the glass, U-shaped open-plan carpeted bar with fire, small dining room (was the local jail), monthly live music; children and dogs welcome, garden with partly covered heated terrace, open all day weekends. *(Jim Farmer)*

BARROWDEN   SK9400
★**Exeter Arms** (01572) 747247
Main Street, just off A47 Uppingham–Peterborough; LE15 8EQ Former coaching inn popular with locals, open-plan bar with beams, stripped stone and open fire, own-brewed ales from long central counter, enjoyable pubby food and specials, collection of pump clips, beer mats and brewery posters, darts; background music; children and dogs welcome, picnic sets on narrow front terrace with lovely views over village green and Welland Valley, big informal garden behind with boules, red kites in nearby Fineshades woods and nice walks, bedrooms, closed Sun evening, Mon lunchtime. *(Jim Farmer, Becky Randall)*

BILLESDON   SK7102
Queens Head (0116) 259 6352
Church Street; LE7 9AE Beamed and thatched pub near village square, friendly landlord and staff, well kept Everards and good choice of wines by the glass, generous reasonably priced food, carpeted lounge bar with log fire, bare-boards public bar with stripped-pine tables, small conservatory; children welcome, pretty stone village. *(Barry Collett, R L Borthwick)*

BOTCHESTON   SK4804
Greyhound (01455) 822355
Main Street, off B5380 E of Desford; LE9 9FF Beamed village pub popular for its freshly cooked generous food including some unusual dishes (should book), bargain OAP weekday lunch and other deals, pine tables in two light and airy dining rooms, three well kept changing ales; children welcome, garden with play area. *(SAB and MJW)*

BRANSTON   SK8129
★**Wheel** (01476) 870376
Main Street; NG32 1RU Recently refurbished 18th-c stone-built beamed village pub with stylishly simple open-plan décor, friendly attentive licensees and smartly dressed staff, chef/landlord doing good country food such as pheasant, bacon and prune pie, and unusual things like stilton ice-cream, three well kept changing ales from central servery (could be Batemans, Brewsters and Dancing Duck), log fires; background and occasional live music; children welcome, dogs in bar, attractive garden, next to church, splendid countryside near Belvoir Castle, closed Mon. *(Phil and Jane Hodson, Richard and Jean Green, Derek and Sylvia Stephenson, Ian Johnson)*

BRAUNSTON SK8306
Blue Ball (01572) 722135
*Off A606 in Oakham; Cedar Street;
LE15 8QS* Pretty thatched and beamed
dining pub doing well under present
management, good food including fixed-
price lunch menu, competent service from
welcoming staff, well kept Marstons-related
ales, decent wines, log fire, leather furniture
and country pine in linked rooms including
small conservatory; children welcome, tables
outside, attractive village. *(Barry Collett,
Gerry and Rosemary Dobson, R L Borthwick,
Nick and Elaine Hall)*

BRAUNSTON SK8306
Old Plough (01572) 722714
*Off A606 in Oakham; Church Street;
LE15 8QT* Comfortably opened-up
black-beamed village local, big helpings of
enjoyable food, Adnams, Fullers London
Pride and a guest, pleasant attentive service,
log fire, back dining conservatory; tables
in small sheltered garden, open all day
weekends. *(Barry Collett)*

BRUNTINGTHORPE SP6089
⋆ Joiners Arms (0116) 247 8258
*Off A5199 S of Leicester: Church Walk/
Cross Street; LE17 5QH* More restaurant
than pub with most of the two beamed rooms
set for eating, drinkers have area by small light-
oak bar with open fire, an ale such as Greene
King or Sharps, plenty of wines (including
champagne) by the glass, first-class imaginative
food, friendly efficient staff, candles on tables,
elegant dining chairs, big flower arrangements,
civilised but relaxed atmosphere; picnic-sets
in front, closed Sun evening, Mon. *(Jeff and
Wendy Williams, Henry Paulinski, Rob and Catherine
Dunster, SAB and MJW)*

CALDECOTT SP8693
Plough (01536) 770284
Main Street; LE16 8RS Welcoming pub
in attractive ironstone village, carpeted bar
with banquettes and small tables leading
to spacious eating area, well kept Langton
and a guest like Wychwood Hobgoblin, wide
range of enjoyable inexpensive food; children
welcome, back garden. *(Simon Collins, Ian
Roberts and family, Barry Collett)*

CASTLE DONINGTON SK4427
Jolly Potters (01332) 811912
Hillside; DE74 2NH Genuine unspoilt
town local, basic and friendly, with pews
on flagstones, hanging tankards and jugs,
framed beer mats, good coal fire, well kept
Bass, Fullers, Marstons, Timothy Taylors and
guests, back room with darts and juke box;
open all day. *(the Didler)*

COLEORTON SK4016
Kings Arms (01530) 815435
The Moor (off A512); LE67 8GD
Refurbished village pub with its own Tap

House ales along with Bass and a changing
guest, enjoyable reasonably priced food (not
Sun evening, Mon) including daily carvery,
pool room with TV, live music last Sun of
month; children welcome, garden with
pétanque and play area, open all day.
(Ian and Jane Irving)

EAST LANGTON SP7292
Bell (01858) 545278
Off B6047; Main Street; LE16 7TW
Appealing creeper-clad beamed country
inn buzzing with locals and families, well
kept Fullers, Greene King, Langton and a
guest, nice wines, good well presented food
including daily specials and popular Sun
carvery, efficient service, long low-ceilinged
stripped-stone bar, spacious restaurant,
modern pine furniture, log fires; picnic-sets
on sloping front lawn, bedrooms.
*(Jim Farmer, John Saville, Gerry and Rosemary
Dobson)*

FOXTON SP6989
⋆ Foxton Locks (0116) 2791515
*Foxton Locks, off A6 3 miles NW of
Market Harborough (park by bridge
60/62 and walk); LE16 7RA* Nice
setting at foot of long flight of canal locks,
large comfortably reworked L-shaped bar,
popular well priced food including winter
fixed-price menu, converted boathouse does
snacks, friendly service (can slow at busy
times), half a dozen well kept ales such as
Caledonian Deuchars IPA, Fullers London
Pride and Theakstons; children welcome,
large raised terrace and covered decking,
steps down to fenced waterside lawn, good
walks. *(Gerry and Rosemary Dobson,
Martin Smith, Rob and Catherine Dunster,
Veronica Brown)*

GADDESBY SK6813
Cheney Arms (01664) 840260
Rearsby Lane; LE7 4XE Refurbished
red-brick country pub with bare boards/
terracotta tiled bar, open fires including
inglenook in more formal dining room,
Everards ales, fairly pubby food from
lunchtime baguettes up, Wed pie night;
back garden with smokers' shelter, four
bedrooms. *(Clark Thornton)*

GILMORTON SP5787
Grey Goose (01455) 5525555
Lutterworth Road; LE17 5PN
Refurbished bar/restaurant with good
range of enjoyable freshly made food from
lunchtime sandwiches up, Sun carvery,
Sharps Doom Bar and Wells & Youngs
Bombardier, several wines by the glass
including champagne, good friendly service,
light contemporary décor, stylish wood and
metal bar stools mixing with comfortable
sofas and armchairs, woodburner in
stripped-brick fireplace with logs stacked
beside; modern furniture on terrace.
(R L Borthwick, SAB and MJW)

GREETHAM
SK9214

Black Horse (01572) 812305

Main Street; LE15 7NL Refurbished stone-built dining pub with good food from chef/landlord; four bedrooms. *(S Holder)*

GREETHAM
SK9214

Plough (01572) 813613

B668 Stretton–Cottesmore; LE15 7NJ Friendly well patronised village local, four real ales including Timothy Taylors Golden Best, Weston's cider and good wine selection, enjoyable home-made food including substantial sandwiches and baguettes sold by the foot, lunchtime fixed price menu, coal-effect gas fire dividing cosy lounge from eating area, traditional pub games; children welcome, dogs in bar, garden behind with pétanque, good local walks and not far from Rutland Water, open all day summer (all day Thurs-Sun winter). *(Pat and Stewart Gordon)*

GREETHAM
SK9314

★ **Wheatsheaf** (01572) 812325

B668 Stretton–Cottesmore; LE15 7NP Attractive old stone-built pub with linked L-shaped rooms, good popular well prepared food (must book weekends) from regularly changing menu including good sandwiches (home-baked bread) and nice steaks, home-made ice-cream too, friendly welcoming service, well kept ales such as Belvoir, Greene King and Oakham, good choice of wines, log fire and blazing open stove, games room with darts, pool and sports TV; soft background music; children welcome, dogs in bar (resident labradoodle and dachshund), wheelchair access using ramp, front lawn, back terrace by pretty stream with duck house, open all day weekends, closed Mon, no food Sun evening and first two weeks of Jan. *(Michael and Jenny Back and others)*

GRIMSTON
SK6821

Black Horse (01664) 812358

Off A6006 W of Melton Mowbray; Main Street; LE14 3BZ Popular village-green pub with interesting interior, welcoming licensees and friendly locals, well kept ales, fairly priced wholesome food, darts; attractive village with stocks and 13th-c church. *(Phil and Jane Hodson, Robert Holmes, Comus and Sarah Elliott)*

GUMLEY
SP6890

Bell (0116) 2792476

NW of Market Harborough; Main Street; LE16 7RU Neatly kept beamed village pub with wide choice of popular good value food (not Sun or Mon evenings) including bargain OAP lunches (Tues-Sat), well kept Batemans, Greene King, Timothy Taylors and a guest, traditional country décor, lots of hunting prints, small fire, darts, cribbage and dominoes, separate dining room, border collie called Bailey; no mobile phones, muddy boots or children under 10; pond in pretty

terrace garden (not for children or dogs), open all day, closed Sun evening. *(Ken and Barbara Turner, Jim Farmer, Gerry and Rosemary Dobson, Edward Leetham)*

HALLATON
SP7896

Bewicke Arms (01858) 555217

On Eastgate, opposite village sign; LE16 8UB Attractive thatched pub dating from the 16th c, Greene King, Langton and Timothy Taylors, two bar dining areas, restaurant of small linked areas, two log fires, scrubbed pine tables, memorabilia of ancient local Easter Monday inter-village bottle-kicking match, darts; background music; children in eating areas, dogs allowed on leads, disabled facilities, big terrace overlooking paddock and lake with play area, tearoom and three bedrooms in converted stables, open all day weekends (no food Sun evening). *(Jim Farmer)*

HATHERN
SK5021

Dew Drop (01509) 842438

Loughborough Road (A6); LE12 5HY Unspoilt two-room beamed local, welcoming landlord, well kept Greene King and guests, lots of malt whiskies, coal fire, good lunchtime cobs, darts and dominoes; tables outside. *(the Didler)*

HEMINGTON
SK4527

Jolly Sailor (01332) 810448

Main Street; DE74 2RB Picturesque three-room village pub, eight real ales (Greene King and guests), friendly staff, food in bar and separate restaurant, log fire, big country pictures, bric-a-brac on heavy beams and shelves, daily newspapers; children and dogs welcome, picnic-sets out in front, open all day Fri-Sun. *(the Didler, Johnston and Maureen Anderson)*

HOBY
SK6717

Blue Bell (01664) 434247

Main Street; LE14 3DT Attractive rebuilt thatched pub, well run, with good range of enjoyable realistically priced food (all day weekends – best to book), small helpings available, friendly attentive uniformed staff, up to six well kept ales, good choice of wines by the glass and of teas/coffees, open-plan and airy with beams, comfortable traditional furniture, old local photographs, skittle alley, darts; background music; children and dogs welcome, valley view garden with picnic-sets and boules, open all day. *(Phil and Jane Hodson)*

HOTON
SK5722

Packe Arms (01509) 889106

A60; LE12 5SJ Spacious old Vintage Inn with sturdy beams and open fires, good choice of enjoyable well priced food, well kept ales such as Batemans, Black Sheep and Everards, prompt service from young uniformed staff; children welcome, tables outside, open all day. *(Maurice and Janet Thorpe, Phil and Jane Hodson)*

HUNGARTON
SK6907

Black Boy
(0116) 259 5410

Main Street; LE7 9JR Large open-plan partly divided restauranty bar, good well priced food cooked to order (weekend booking advised), changing ales such as Greene King, Fullers and Wells & Youngs, cheerful welcoming staff, minimal decoration, open fire; background music; picnic-sets out on deck, closed Sun evening, Mon. *(Jim Farmer, R L Borthwick)*

ILLSTON ON THE HILL
SP7099

★Fox & Goose
(0116) 2596340

Main Street, off B6047 Market Harborough –Melton Mowbray; LE7 9EG Individual two-bar local, simple, comfortable and friendly, with hunting pictures and assorted oddments including stuffed animals, woodburner and good coal fire, well kept Everards and a guest, home-made food (Wed-Sat); children and dogs welcome, closed weekday lunchtimes, open all day weekends. *(Jim Farmer, the Didler)*

KEGWORTH
SK4826

★Cap & Stocking
(01509) 674814

Handy for M1 junction 24, via A6; Borough Street; DE74 2FF Nicely old-fashioned unchanging three-room pub, brown paint, etched glass, coal fires, big cases of stuffed birds and locally caught fish, Bass (from the jug) and well kept guests such as Jennings and Wells & Youngs, home-made food (not Weds evening) from fresh sandwiches to bargain Sun lunch, dominoes, back room opening to secluded garden with decking; background music/radio, no credit cards; children welcome. *(Roger and Donna Huggins)*

KIBWORTH BEAUCHAMP
SP6894

Coach & Horses
(0116) 2792247

A6 S of Leicester; LE8 0NN Friendly and snug 16th-c beamed local, carpeted bar area and refurbished candlelit restaurant, wide choice of home-made food including popular all-day Sun roasts, well kept Bass, Fullers London Pride, Greene King IPA and Wadworths 6X, regular events; background music, TV; children welcome, dogs in bar, disabled access, some outside seating at front and on side terrace, open all day weekends, closed Mon lunchtime. *(Henry Paulinski)*

KIRBY MUXLOE
SK5104

Royal Oak
(0116) 2393166

Main Street; LE9 2AN Comfortable modernish pub (don't be put off by the plain exterior) doing good food from sandwiches and snacks through pub favourites to more inventive things, early-bird deals, pleasant prompt service, Adnams, Everards and a guest ale, good wine choice, sizeable restaurant, some live jazz, Mon quiz; disabled facilities, picnic-sets outside, nearby 15th-c castle ruins, open all day weekends. *(Ian and Joan Blackwell)*

KNIPTON
SK8231

Manners Arms
(01476) 879222

Signed off A607 Grantham–Melton Mowbray; Croxton Road; NG32 1RH Handsome Georgian hunting lodge beautifully renovated by Duke and Duchess of Rutland as upscale country inn, hunting prints and furniture from Belvoir Castle, log fire, well kept Belvoir and other ales, good choice of wines by the glass, enjoyable food, sizeable restaurant with attractive conservatory, sumptuous lounge; background music; terrace with ornamental pool, lovely views over pretty village, ten comfortable individually furnished bedrooms, open all day. *(Jonathan Peel)*

KNOSSINGTON
SK8008

Fox & Hounds
(01664) 452129

Off A606 W of Oakham; Somerby Road; LE15 8LY Attractive 18th-c ivy-covered village dining pub refurbished by present landlady, beamed bar with log fire, cosy dining areas, good food from traditional choices to blackboard specials, Fullers London Pride; no children under 8; dogs welcome, big back garden, closed Mon, Tues-Thurs lunchtimes and Sun evening. *(R L Borthwick, SAB and MJW)*

LEICESTER
SK5804

Ale Wagon
(0116) 2623330

Rutland Street/Charles Street; LE1 1RE Basic 1930s two-room local with great beer choice including own Hoskins ales, Weston's cider and perry, coal fire, events such as comedy nights; juke box, sports TV; handy for station, open all day (Sun afternoon break). *(Dave Braisted, the Didler)*

LEICESTER
SK5804

Cradock Arms
(01162) 706680

Knighton Road/Newmarket Street; LE2 3TT Substantial, recently refurbished beamed and partly thatched Everards pub, good choice of enjoyable well priced food all day (till 4pm Sun) from open kitchen including weekday lunch deal, Tues quiz; children welcome, disabled facilities, beer garden with terrace, open all day. *(Veronica Brown, Nigel Siesage)*

LEICESTER
SK5804

Criterion
(0116) 262 5418

Millstone Lane; LE1 5JN Modern building with dark wood and burgundy décor in carpeted main room, Oakham ales and up to ten guests at weekends, 100 bottled beers, decent wines by the glass, good value stone-baked pizzas, tapas and more traditional pub food (not Sun evening, Mon), relaxed room on left with games, old-fashioned juke box, music, comedy and quiz nights; wheelchair access (small front step), picnic-sets outside, open all day. *(Jim Farmer, the Didler)*

LEICESTER SK5804

⋆**Globe** (0116) 2629819

Silver Street; LE1 5EU Lots of woodwork in cheerfully well worn partitioned areas off central bar, mirrors and wrought-iron gas lamps, good choice of Everards ales and guests, friendly staff, bargain straightforward food 12-7pm (5pm Sun) from snacks up including a good vegetarian choice, charming more peaceful upstairs dining/function room; background music (not in snug) and live, very popular with young people weekend evenings; children welcome, open all day. *(the Didler)*

LEICESTER SK5804

Shakespeares Head (01162) 624378

Southgates; LE1 5SH Welcoming chatty 1960s local with good low-priced Oakwell beers, basic bar, lounge popular with older regulars, pool and darts; open all day (till 1am Fri, Sat). *(the Didler)*

LEICESTER SK5803

⋆**Swan & Rushes** (0116) 2339167

Oxford Street/Infirmary Square; LE1 5WR Triangular-shaped pub with nine well kept ales including Batemans and Oakham, bottled beers, farm cider, welcoming staff and thriving atmosphere in two rooms with big oak tables, enjoyable home-made lunchtime food (not Sun) including stone-baked pizzas, fish and chips Fri evening, live music Sat; open all day Thurs-Sun. *(the Didler)*

LOUGHBOROUGH SK5319

⋆**Swan in the Rushes** (01509) 217014

The Rushes (A6); LE11 5BE Bare-boards town local with three smallish high-ceilinged rooms, open fire, good value Castle Rock and interesting changing guests, foreign bottled beers, farm cider, well priced chip-free food (not Sat or Sun evenings), good service, daily newspapers, traditional games; good juke box – live music nights Thurs-Sat; children welcome in eating areas, tables outside, four bedrooms, open all day. *(Steven Paine, Frank Swann, the Didler)*

LOUGHBOROUGH SK5319

Tap & Mallet (01509) 210028

Nottingham Road; LE11 1EU Basic friendly pub with well kept Abbeydale, Oakham and interesting microbrews, also foreign beers and Weston's cider, nice cobs, coal fire, darts and pool, juke box; children welcome, walled back garden with play area and pets corner, open all day. *(the Didler)*

LYDDINGTON SP8796

⋆**Old White Hart** (01572) 821703

Village signed off A6003 N of Corby; LE15 9LR Popular welcoming old pub, softly lit front bar with heavy beams in low ceiling, just a few tables, glass-shielded log fire, Greene King and Timothy Taylors Landlord, good food (not Sun evening in winter) including own sausages and cured meats (landlord is a butcher), attractive restaurant, further tiled-floor room with rugs, lots of fine hunting prints and woodburner; children welcome, seats by heaters in pretty walled garden, eight floodlit boules pitches, handy for Bede House and good nearby walks, bedrooms. *(Mike and Sue Loseby, John and Sylvia Harrop)*

MANTON SK8704

Horse & Jockey (01572) 737335

St Mary's Road; LE15 8SU Welcoming early 19th-c refurbished stone pub, well kept Grainstore ales and a guest, decent inexpensive food (all day weekends) from baguettes to blackboard specials, good service, low beams, stone or wood floors, woodburner; background music; children and dogs welcome, pretty terrace, nice location – on Rutland Water cycle route (bike racks provided), open all day summer, all day Fri-Sun winter. *(Adam Freckingham, Gill and Keith Croxton, R L Borthwick)*

MARKET HARBOROUGH SP7387

Angel (01858) 462702

High Street; LE16 7AF Popular former coaching inn with good range of reasonably priced food in bar and restaurant including fixed-price menu, friendly efficient uniformed staff, well kept Marstons and a guest, good coffee, daily newspapers; discreet sports TV; 24 bedrooms. *(Gerry and Rosemary Dobson)*

MARKET HARBOROUGH SP7387

Sugar Loaf (01858) 469231

High Street; LE16 7NJ Popular Wetherspoons, smaller than many, with half a dozen sensibly priced real ales (frequent beer festivals), usual good value food all day; children welcome. *(Gerry and Rosemary Dobson)*

MARKET HARBOROUGH SP7387

⋆**Three Swans** (01858) 466644

High Street; LE16 7NJ Comfortable banquettes and plush-cushioned library chairs in traditional bay-windowed front bar of Best Western conference hotel, four real ales including local Grainstore and Langton, decent wines, good spread of enjoyable well presented pubby food from sandwiches up, set deals, friendly uniformed staff, flame-effect fires (one in grand coaching-era inglenook), flagstoned back area, corridor to popular conservatory bistro (evenings Mon-Sat), more formal upstairs restaurant; background music; attractive suntrap courtyard, useful parking, good bedrooms, open all day from 9.30am. *(George Atkinson, Gerry and Rosemary Dobson)*

MARKET OVERTON SK8816

Black Bull (01572) 767677

Off B668 in Cottesmore; LE15 7PW Attractive thatched and low-beamed stone-built pub in pretty village well placed for Rutland Water, welcoming licensees and staff, good interesting home-made food in long red-carpeted bar and two separate dining areas, well kept Batemans, Black Sheep, Greene King and Theakstons, banquettes and sofas, newspapers; some background and live music; children and dogs welcome, tables out in front by small carp pool, bedrooms, open all day Fri-Sun. *(Mike and Ann Pepper, Barry Collett, D and D G Humpherson)*

MEDBOURNE SP7992

⋆ **Nevill Arms** (01858) 565288

B664 Market Harborough–Uppingham; LE16 8EE Handsome stone-built Victorian inn nicely located by stream and footbridge, wide range of good bar and restaurant food including vegetarian choices, pleasant helpful uniformed staff, well kept ales such as Bass, Fullers London Pride and Sharps Doom Bar, beams and mullion windows, log fires, modern artwork, stylish restaurant; no dogs; back terrace with stable-conversion café (8am-4pm), streamside picnic-sets, 11 refurbished bedrooms, good breakfast, open all day. *(Jim Farmer, George Atkinson, Carl Stasiak, Mike and Sue Loseby, Barry Collet and others)*

MOUNTSORREL SK5715

Swan (0116) 230 2340

Loughborough Road, off A6; LE12 7AT Log fires, old flagstones and stripped stone, friendly staff and locals, enjoyable well priced food from baguettes and light dishes to generous full meals (best to book evenings), well kept Theakstons and guest ales, good choice of wines, pine tables and gingham cloths in neat dining area and restaurant; dogs welcome in bar, pretty walled back garden down to canalised River Soar, self-contained accommodation, open all day Sat. *(Mick and Moira Brummell, Jim Farmer)*

MOWSLEY SP6488

Staff of Life (0116) 240 2359

Village signposted off A5199 S of Leicester; Main Street; LE17 6NT High-gabled little village pub, well run and spotlessly kept, with roomy fairly traditional bar, high-backed settles on flagstones, wicker chairs on shiny wood floor and stools lined up along unusual circular counter, woodburner, Banks's Bitter and guests such as Langton, up to 20 wines by the glass including champagne, well liked imaginative food (not Sun or Mon evenings), good service; background music; children welcome (no under 12s Fri and Sat evenings), seats out in front and on nice

leaf-shaded deck, open all day Sun, closed Mon and Tues lunchtimes. *(Mike and Margaret Banks, Veronica Brown, Michael Sargent, Rob and Catherine Dunster, Mark Bernstein, SAB and MJW)*

NETHER BROUGHTON SK6925

Red House (01664) 822429

A606 N of Melton Mowbray; LE14 3HB Substantial and elegant extended Georgian roadside inn, emphasis on good popular restaurant, also more reasonably priced bar food including sandwiches and light dishes, good service, two local Belvoir ales, comfortable lounge bar with red leather fireside sofas and armchairs, another bar on right with TV (dogs allowed here); children welcome, courtyard and garden with picnic-sets, seven well equipped stylish bedrooms, open all day Fri and Sat, closed Sun evening. *(Alex Boyles, John and Sylvia Harrop)*

NEWBOLD SK4018

Gelsmoor (01530) 222507

Rempstone Road, Griffydam; LE67 8HP Busy pub/restaurant with enjoyable traditional food from baguettes up, stone-baked pizzas too, Greene King Abbot, Tollgate and a guest, good service; children welcome, disabled facilities, summer classic car meetings second Tuesday of the month, open all day weekends. *(Ian and Jane Irving)*

OADBY SK6202

⋆ **Cow & Plough** (0116) 272 0852

Gartree Road (B667 N of centre); LE2 2FB Former farm and dairy (converted about 20 years ago), fantastic collection of brewery memorabilia (interesting enamel signs and mirrors), up to eight well kept ales including local Steamin' Billy, six ciders, bar food (not Sun evening) from sandwiches up, a couple of individual original rooms, long front extension and conservatory with real mix of furniture, hop-draped beams, darts; TV, background music, Booze & Blues festival May; children and dogs welcome, picnic-set in yard, open all day. *(Tony and Wendy Hobden, Jim Farmer, Rob and Catherine Dunster, Barry Collett, the Didler and others)*

OADBY SP6399

Grange Farm (0116) 281 5600

Off Glen Road (A6); LE2 4RH Popular roomy Vintage Inn based on early 19th-c farmhouse, smart welcoming young staff, wide choice of generous reasonably priced food, Batemans, Black Sheep and Everards, good range of wines and spirits, log fires, old local photographs, daily newspapers; no dogs; well behaved children welcome, tables out in front, open all day. *(Phil and Jane Hodson)*

Most pubs with any outside space now have some kind of smokers' shelter. There are regulations about these – for instance they have to be substantially open to the outside air. The best have heating and lighting and are really quite comfortable.

OAKHAM   SK8508
Horseshoe (01572) 722564
Braunston Road; LE15 6LE 1960s pub
with well kept Everards and guests, enjoyable
pubby food, comfortable lounge bar leading
to games room with pool, dining room; front
picnic-sets, garden behind. *(Barry Collett)*

OAKHAM   SK8508
Wheatsheaf (01572) 723458
Northgate; LE15 6QS Attractive 17th-c
local near church, friendly helpful staff, well
kept Adnams, Everards and guests, good
lunchtime pub food, a couple of rocking
chairs by open fire, plenty of bric-a-brac,
books and posters, cheerful bar, comfortable
quieter lounge and conservatory (children
welcome here), some live jazz and acoustic
music; pretty suntrap back courtyard. *(Tony
and Maggie Harwood, Barry Collett)*

OLD DALBY   SK6723
Crown (01664) 823134
Debdale Hill; LE14 3LF Early 16th-c pub
under new management, intimate farmhouse
rooms up and down steps, black beams,
antique oak settles among other seats, rustic
prints, open fires, ales from Adnams, Belvoir
and St Austell, plenty of wines by the glass,
traditional home-made food (not Sun or Mon
evenings), extended dining room opening
on to terrace; background music; children
and dogs welcome, disabled facilities,
attractive garden with boules, open all day
weekends. *(Anon)*

ROTHLEY   SK5812
Woodmans Stroke (0116) 230 2785
Church Street; LE7 7PD Immaculate
family-run pub with good value weekday
lunchtime bar food from sandwiches up,
well kept changing ales, good wines by the
glass including champagne, friendly service,
beams and settles in front rooms, open fire,
old local photographs plus rugby and cricket
memorabilia; sports TV; pretty front hanging
baskets, cast-iron tables in attractive garden
with heaters, open all day. *(John Martin)*

SHAWELL   SP5480
White Swan (01788) 860357
*Main Street; village signed down
declassified road (ex A427) off A5/A426
roundabout – turn right in village; not
far from M6 junction 1; LE17 6AG*
Attractive little 17th-c pub, beams, panelling
and open fire, enjoyable food including steaks
cooked on a hot stone, friendly service, a
couple of Brakspears ales, restaurant; no

dogs inside; children welcome, tables out in
front, four bedrooms, closed Sun evening,
Mon, and lunchtime Tues-Sat. *(Anon)*

SHEARSBY   SP6290
Chandlers Arms (0116) 247 8384
*Fenny Lane, off A50 Leicester–
Northampton; LE17 6PL* Comfortable
old creeper-clad village pub, four well kept
ales (July beer festival), good choice of food
(not Sun evening) including some lunchtime
bargains, wall seats and wheelback chairs;
background music, pool, Weds quiz night;
tables in secluded raised garden, nice
hanging baskets, attractive village.
(Jim Farmer)

SIBSON   SK3500
Cock (01827) 880357
*A444 N of Nuneaton; Twycross Road;
CV13 6LB* Picturesque old black and white
thatched pub with Dick Turpin connection,
Bass and Hook Norton, a dozen wines by
the glass, decent if pricy food, cheerful
quick service, low doorways, heavy black
beams and genuine latticed windows,
immense inglenook; background music,
games machine; children welcome, tables
in courtyard and small garden, handy for
Bosworth Field. *(Joan and Tony Walker)*

SOMERBY   SK7710
☆ Stilton Cheese (01664) 454394
*High Street; off A606 Oakham–Melton
Mowbray, via Cold Overton, or
Leesthorpe and Pickwell; LE14 2QB*
Friendly staff in enjoyable ironstone pub
with comfortable beamed and hop-strung
bar/lounge, comfortable furnishings on red
patterned carpets, country prints, copper
pots and a stuffed badger, Grainstore,
Marstons, Tetleys and guests, 30 malt
whiskies, reasonably priced pubby food and
some interesting daily specials, restaurant;
children welcome, seats on terrace,
peaceful setting on edge of pretty village,
bedrooms. *(Mike and Margaret Banks, Jim
Farmer, George Atkinson)*

SOUTH LUFFENHAM   SK9401
☆ Coach House (01780) 720166
Stamford Road (A6121); LE15 8NT
Nicely reworked old inn with flagstoned bar,
stripped stone or terracotta walls, bright
scatter cushions on small pews, church
candles, log fire, Adnams, Greene King and
Timothy Taylors, decent wines by the glass,
good well priced food using some own-grown
produce, friendly efficient staff, neat built-in
seating in separate red-walled snug, smarter

'Children welcome' means the pub says it lets children inside without any special
restriction. If it allows them in, but to restricted areas such as an eating area or
family room, we specify this. Places with separate restaurants often let children use
them, hotels usually let them into public areas such as lounges. Some pubs impose an
evening time limit – let us know if you find one earlier than 9pm.

more modern feeling back dining room with brown suede seating; children welcome, dogs in bar, small deck behind, bedrooms, closed Sun evening, Mon lunchtime. *(Sandy Butcher, Mike and Mary Carter)*

SPROXTON   SK8524
Crown (01476) 860035
Coston Road; LE14 4QB Friendly 19th-c stone-built inn with spotless well laid-out interior, good reasonably priced food from bar snacks to restaurant dishes, well kept Greene King ales, good wines and coffee, light airy bar with woodburner, restaurant with big glassed-off wine store; children welcome, dogs in bar, lovely sunny courtyard, attractive village and nice local walks, three bedrooms, closed Sun evening, Mon. *(Phil and Jane Hodson)*

STRETTON   SK9415
Ram Jam Inn (01780) 410776
Just off A1 by B668 Oakham turn-off; LE15 7QX Useful A1 stop serving food from 7am, big open-plan bar/dining area with bucket chairs, sofas and mix of tables, two back rooms one with fire, daily newspapers, changing beer, good house wines and coffee; children welcome away from bar, garden tables, comfortable bedrooms, open all day. *(John Coatsworth)*

THORPE LANGTON   SP7492
⋆ Bakers Arms (01858) 545201
Off B6047 N of Market Harborough; LE16 7TS Civilised restaurant with bar rather than pub, consistently good imaginative food from regularly changing menu (must book), cottagey beamed linked areas and stylishly simple country décor, well kept local Langton ale, good choice of wines by the glass, friendly efficient staff, maybe a pianist; no under-12s; garden picnic-sets, closed weekday lunchtimes, Sun evening and Mon. *(Jim Farmer, R L Borthwick, SAB and MJW, Phil and Jane Hodson)*

THORPE SATCHVILLE   SK7311
Fox (01664) 840257
Main Street (B6047); LE14 2DQ 1930s pub/restaurant with french chef/landlord doing good food from interesting snacks to full french meals, nice choice of wines and some unusual beers, good service, carpeted front bars and more formal back restaurant with open fire; tables out at front and in garden behind, closed all day Sun, Mon lunchtime. *(O K Smyth, SAB and MJW)*

THRUSSINGTON   SK6415
Star (01664) 424220
The Green; LE7 4UH Refurbished 18th-c beamed pub, enjoyable home-made food in bar or more modern dining area, three changing ales, Sun quiz; children welcome till 8pm, bedrooms, open all day. *(Paul Mcqueen, U Dunton)*

TILTON ON THE HILL   SK7405
Rose & Crown (0116) 259 7234
B6047; LE7 9LF Friendly old beamed place with three rooms, reasonably priced locally sourced food including lunchtime/early evening deal, Sun carvery till 5pm, well kept Greene King, Tolly Cobbold and a local guest like Grainstore, Aspall's cider, inglenook log fire, acoustic music first Sun of month, June 'Tiltonbury' music festival; children and dogs welcome, beer garden at back, open all day weekends, closed Mon lunchtime. *(Anon)*

TUR LANGTON   SP7194
Crown (01858) 545264
Off B6047; Main Street (follow Kibworth signpost from centre); LE8 0PJ Attractive pub with enjoyable competitively priced food from standards up, prompt friendly service, well kept Adnams a guest, bar with central log fire, side room, back restaurant with own bar; children and dogs welcome (resident black labrador called Grace), terrace tables, open all day Fri-Sun. *(Jim Farmer)*

TWYFORD   SK7210
Saddle (01664) 841108
Main Street; off B6047 E of Leicester; LE14 2HU Friendly beamed country pub refurbished and under new management, four real ales, enjoyable food including freshly baked pizzas, interesting pop memorabilia in snug; children welcome. *(Andy Howe, Richard Lowe)*

UPPER HAMBLETON   SK8907
⋆ Finchs Arms (01572) 756575
Off A606; Oakham Road; LE15 8TL 17th-c stone inn with outstanding views over Rutland Water, four log fires, beamed and flagstoned bar, Black Sheep, Timothy Taylors Landlord and a guest, several wines by the glass including champagne, afternoon teas, elegant restaurant with decorative bay trees and modern seating, second newly built dining room, well liked food including set menus, good cheerful service; no dogs; children welcome, suntrap hillside terrace, good surrounding walks, ten bedrooms, open all day. *(Malcolm Lee, John and Sylvia Harrop, Tony and Maggie Harwood, Bruce and Sharon Eden, Jim Farmer, Nichola Hanman and others)*

UPPINGHAM   SP8699
Falcon (01572) 823535
High Street East; LE15 9PY Old coaching inn under newish management, oak-panelled bar and comfortable lounge with big windows overlooking market square, enjoyable food (not Sun evening) from bar snacks up, three Grainstore ales, open fire and woodburner; children welcome, dogs in bar, back garden with terrace, bedrooms, open all day. *(R C Vincent)*

WHITWELL SK9208
Noel at Whitwell (01780) 460334
Main Road (A606); LE15 8BW Smart
spacious bistro/pub handy for Rutland Water,
wide choice of food including good value set
lunches, friendly young staff, local real ales,
decent wines by the glass and good coffee,
live music; children welcome, suntrap tables
outside, play area, bedrooms. *(Roy Bromell)*

WHITWICK SK4316
Three Horseshoes (01530) 837311
Leicester Road; LE67 5GN Unpretentious
unchanging two-room local with tiny snug;
long quarry-tiled bar with old wooden
benches and open fires, well kept Bass and
Marstons Pedigree, piano, darts, dominoes
and cards, newspapers, no food; outdoor
lavatories, no proper pub sign so easy to
miss. *(the Didler)*

WILSON SK4024
Bulls Head (01332) 863921
*Side road Melbourne–Breedon on the
Hill; DE73 8AE* Small, welcoming and
well cared-for village pub, low-beams and
cosy alcoves, good choice of enjoyable fairly
traditional food from panini up, well kept
Marstons Pedigree and Timothy Taylors
Landlord, friendly staff, log fire, monthly
quiz; children and dogs welcome, tables out
on decking. *(Nick Humphreys)*

WITHERLEY SP3297
Blue Lion (01827) 714954
Church Road; CV9 3NA Refurbished
under newish management, good food
at reasonable prices, four well kept ales
including Greene King Abbot, nice wines,
restaurant; bedrooms. *(Ian and Joan Blackwell)*

WOODHOUSE EAVES SK5214
Curzon Arms (01509) 890377
Maplewell Road; LE12 8QZ Welcoming
old beamed pub with enjoyable food (not Sun
evening) from lunchtime sandwiches and
pub favourites up, also good value weekday
set menu, Adnams Bitter, Marstons EPA,
Sharps Doom Bar and a guest, good service,
attractive up-to-date décor, interesting
collection of wall clocks, carpeted dining
room; background music; children and dogs
welcome, ramp for disabled access, good-
sized front lawn and terrace, open all day
weekends. *(Ken and Barbara Turner, Barry
and Anne)*

WOODHOUSE EAVES SK5214
Old Bulls Head (01509) 890255
Main Street; LE12 8RZ Big open-plan
contemporary M&B dining pub, good choice
of food including pizzas, pasta and grills,
fixed-price menu (lunchtime till 7pm
weekdays), good wine list, well kept ales such
as Timothy Taylors Landlord, friendly staff
in black; well behaved children welcome,
outside tables, nice village setting, open all
day. *(Peter and Josie Fawcett)*

WYMESWOLD SK6023
Three Crowns (01509) 880153
Far Street (A6006); LE12 6TZ Snug
chatty 18th-c local in attractive village, good
friendly staff, four real ales including Adnams
and Marstons, good soft drinks choice,
reasonably priced pubby food, pleasant
character furnishings in beamed bar and
lounge, lots of atmosphere; picnic-sets out
on decking, open all day. *(P Dawn, the Didler,
Comus and Sarah Elliott)*

WYMESWOLD SK6023
Windmill (01509) 881313
Brook Street; LE12 6TT Sidestreet village
pub refurbished under new owners, good
value home-made food from lunchtime
snacks up, ales such as Castle Rock, Langton
and Sharps Doom Bar; children welcome,
dogs in bar, back garden, open all day
weekends. *(Anon)*

By law, pubs must show a price list of their drinks. Let us know if you are
inconvenienced by any breach of this law.

Lincolnshire

The Butcher & Beast at Heighington (homely and welcoming) is new to the *Guide* this year with a Bargain Award (over a dozen dishes under £10) and Beer Award (half a dozen real ales). Back in the *Guide* after a break are the Wheatsheaf at Dry Doddington (enthusiastically run and with a happy atmosphere) and Brownlow Arms at Hough-on-the-Hill (terrific food in a civilised restaurant). Highlighting a tremendous improvement in standards over the last few years, almost half the pubs in this county now have Food Awards, with the Ship at Barnoldby le Beck (charmingly eccentric) gaining a new one. However, the George at Stamford (not cheap but pleases universally) remains unrivalled in the county for top notch food in lovely surrounds, and it is Lincolnshire Dining Pub 2013.

BARNOLDBY LE BECK   TA2303   Map 8
Ship 🍴 ♑
Village signposted off A18 Louth–Grimsby; DN37 0BG

Tranquil, refined dining pub with new Food Award this year

There is something quite different about this delightful little dining pub. It's home to a rather charming collection of Edwardian and Victorian bric-a-brac that makes it feel almost demure. The neatly kept bar houses stand-up telephones, violins, a horn gramophone, bowler and top hats, old racquets, crops and hockey sticks. Heavy dark-ringed drapes swathe the windows, with plants in ornate china bowls on the sills. Furnishings include comfortable dark green plush wall benches with lots of pretty propped-up cushions, heavily stuffed green Victorian-looking chairs on a green fleur de lys carpet and a welcoming winter coal fire; background music. A fenced-off sunny area behind has hanging baskets and a few picnic-sets under parasols. Most customers are here for the very good food but drinkers do pop in too – helpful staff serve Black Sheep and Tom Woods from handpump, up to a dozen malt whiskies and wines from a good list.

🍴 Not over elaborate but nicely prepared food might include prawn cocktail, hot and cold smoked salmon with capers, chicken liver, port and brandy pâté with redcurrant and mint jelly, cod cheeks with chorizo, smoked mackerel pâté, tempura king prawns with soy and chilli dip, roast lamb shank with rosemary jus, beef and ale pie, monkfish and smoked salmon risotto, crispy pork belly with apple mash, salt-crusted bass and stir fry, and puddings such as bakewell tart, berry pavlova and cheesecake. *Benchmark main dish: fish pie £9.50. Two-course evening meal £16.00.*

Free house ~ Licensee Michele Hancock ~ Real ale ~ Bar food (12-2(5 Sun), 6-9) ~ Restaurant ~ (01472) 822308 ~ Children welcome ~ Open 12-2, 6-11(midnight Sat); 12-5 Sun; closed Sun evening ~ www.the-shipinn.com *Recommended by David and Jenny Reed, C A Hall, Kay and Alistair Butler, J F M and M West*

DRY DODDINGTON   SK8546   Map 8
Wheatsheaf
Main Street; 1.5 miles off A1 N of Grantham; NG23 5HU

Happy, bustling pub with good food cooked by chef/patron; handy for A1

The welcome at this 16th-c colour-washed village pub is consistently warm and friendly. It's well run by an enthusiastic young couple – the landlord is the chef. Popular with visitors and locals alike, the front bar is basically two rooms, with a woodburning stove, a variety of settles and chairs, and tables in the windows facing across to the green and the lovely 14th-c church with its crooked tower. The serving bar on the right has Batemans XB, Greene King Abbot, Timothy Taylors Landlord and a guest on handpump, and a nice choice of over a dozen wines by the glass. A slight slope takes you down to the extended dining room, comfortable with its thick carpet and relaxing red and cream décor. Once a cow byre, this part is even more ancient than the rest of the building, perhaps dating from the 13th c; background music. The front terrace has neat dark green tables under cocktail parasols among tubs of flowers; disabled access at the side.

Good food, made using own-grown vegetables and herbs and supporting small local rare-breed producers, includes open sandwiches, croques monsieur, macaroni cheese, twice-baked cheese soufflé with apple salad, smoked salmon blinis, scotch quails egg with beetroot coleslaw, roast chicken breast with sweetcorn croquettes and thyme jus, braised blade of beef, asparagus and goats curd tart, and puddings such as strawberry and raspberry cheesecake and panna cotta. *Benchmark main dish: fillet of pollock with braised oxtail £13.25. Two-course evening meal £18.60.*

Free house ~ Licensees Dan and Kate Bland ~ Real ale ~ Bar food (12-2.30(4 Sun), 6-9 (5-7 Sun)) ~ Restaurant ~ (01400) 281458 ~ Children welcome ~ Dogs allowed in bar ~ Open 12-3, 5-11; 12-11 Sat, Sun; closed Mon except bank holidays ~ www.wheatsheaf-pub.co.uk *Recommended by Michael and Jenny Back, William Goodhart, Mike and Margaret Banks, Grahame Brooks, Jeremy King, B and M Kendall, M Mossman, Jim McRobert*

GREAT CASTERTON   SK9909   Map 8
Plough
B1081, just off A1 N of Stamford (coming from the S or returning to A1 southbound, use A606 junction instead); Main Street; PE9 4AA

Cheerful atmosphere and good food in well run comfortably modernised pub, handy for A1

New licensees took over this homely pub just as we went to press and we're keeping our fingers crossed that things don't change too much. Currently there's good service and tasty food the details work well too: quality coffee, for instance, and unusual bar nibbles such as warmed chorizo. A good choice of wines by the glass and Greene King IPA and a guest such as Wychwood Hobgoblin on handpump are served from a counter with comfortable leather and chrome bar stools. The unassuming carpeted bar on the left is small and quite brightly decorated with colourful scatter cushions on seats built into the wall, and light and airy with its big bow window. There may be unobtrusive background music (Peggy Lee and the like) and board games. The main lounge bar, also carpeted, has a mix of dark pub tables and some banquette seating as well as dining chairs. The good-sized garden, like the pub itself kept very neatly, has well spaced picnic-sets by a big weeping willow, with swings and a rabbit hutch; there are also tables on a small wood-screened terrace.

As well as a wide choice of sandwiches, carefully done food (they bake their own bread) might include whitebait, seared scallops with black pudding and roast pork belly, pheasant and wild boar terrine with red onion marmalade, crab and prawn cocktail, sausage and mash, lasagne, burger, roast pork belly, mediterranean vegetable and goats cheese pie, braised shin of beef with horseradish mash and burgundy jus, mushroom and parmesan risotto, roast rack of lamb with herb crust and rosemary jus, and puddings such as apple and blackberry crumble, caramelised lemon tart with orange syrup and eton mess. *Benchmark main dish: venison stew with thyme dumplings £9.95. Two-course evening meal £17.30.*

Punch ~ Real ale ~ Bar food (12-2.30(3 Sun), 6-9.30) ~ Restaurant ~ (01780) 762178 ~ Children welcome ~ Dogs allowed in bar ~ Open 12-3, 6-11(11.30 Sat); closed Sun evening, Mon, one week in Jan ~ www.theplough-greatcasterton.co.uk *Recommended by Richard Gibbs*

HEIGHINGTON   TF0369   Map 8
Butcher & Beast ▇ £
High Street; LN4 1JS

Traditional village pub with terrific range of drinks and pretty garden by steam

It's the friendly, hard-working licensees that make this homely pub so enjoyable. You can be sure of a warm welcome, and there's always something going on here, with events ranging from beer festivals and quizes to themed food evenings. The simply furnished bar has button-back wall banquettes, pubby furnishings and stools along the counter where they keep half a dozen real ales including Batemans XB, XXXB, Victory and three guests from brewers such as Blue Monkey, Castle Rock and Everards, a dozen bottled beers, four ciders, two dozen malt whiskies and 20 gins; occasional TV. The Snug now has red-cushioned wall settles and high-backed wooden dining chairs, and the refurbished, beamed dining room is neatly set with proper tablecloths and napkins; throughout, the cream walls are hung with old village photos and country pictures. There are picnic-sets on a lawn that runs down to a stream, and the award-winning hanging baskets and tubs are very pretty in summer.

Bar food includes salt and pepper squid chunks, creamy garlic mushrooms, thai cod and prawn fishcakes, steak and ale pie, mushroom and pepper stroganoff, vegetable and stilton crumble, scampi, liver and gammon casserole, battered haddock, and steaks. *Benchmark main dish: steak and ale pie £9.25. Two-course evening meal £14.00.*

Batemans ~ Tenants Mal and Diane Gray ~ Real ale ~ Bar food (12-2, 5.30-8; 12-4 Sun, not Sun evening) ~ Restaurant ~ (01522) 790386 ~ Children welcome away from bar area ~ Dogs allowed in bar ~ Quiz Thurs ~ Open 12-11(10.30 Sun) ~ www.butcherandbeast.co.uk *Recommended by Chris Johnson*

HOUGH-ON-THE-HILL

SK9246 Map 8

Brownlow Arms

High Road; NG32 2AZ

Refined country house with beamed bar, real ales, imaginative food and graceful terrace; bedrooms

Although there is a bar at this charmingly run old stone inn, most people are here for a meal in the civilised upmarket restaurant. Do check the limited opening times, and book ahead. The beamed bar is comfortable and welcoming with plenty of panelling, some exposed brickwork, local prints and scenes, a large mirror and a pile of logs beside the big fireplace. Seating is on elegant stylishly mismatched armchairs; the carefully arranged furnishings give the impression of several separate and cosy areas. Impeccably polite staff serve Timothy Taylors Landlord and a guest such as Black Sheep from handpump, several wines by the glass and a good choice of malt whiskies; background easy-listening music. The well equipped bedrooms are attractive and breakfasts are hearty.

 First-class (though not cheap) food might include beer-battered thai prawns, crab thermidor, seared scallops with jerusalem artichoke, braised ox tongue and celeriac remoulade, mushroom risotto with parmesan crisps, beer-battered cod, roast bass with beurre blanc, seared calves liver with leek mash, bacon and shallot gravy, steak and kidney pudding, sausage and mash, and puddings such as treacle sponge pudding with syrup ice-cream, cherry bakewell tart with pistachio mascarpone and rhubarb crumble with rhubarb sorbet. *Benchmark main dish: pork loin steak with black pudding and pickled apple purée pan jus £17.95.* Two-course evening meal £25.40.

Free house ~ Licensee Paul L Willoughby ~ Real ale ~ Bar food (6.30-9(9.30 Fri, Sat) Tues-Thurs; 12-2.30 Sun; not Mon, Sun evening) ~ Restaurant ~ (01400) 250234 ~ Children over 10 welcome ~ Open 6-11; 12-4 Sun; closed Mon, Sun evening ~ Bedrooms: £65B/£98B ~ www.thebrownlowarms.com *Recommended by P and J Shapley, Alan Clark, Kay and Alistair Butler*

INGHAM

SK9483 Map 8

Inn on the Green

The Green; LN1 2XT

Nicely modernised place serving thoughtfully prepared food; chatty atmosphere

The locals' bar at this friendly dining pub has recently been opened up to give attractive views across the village green, and although most tables are occupied by people here for the tasty, good value food, it can still have quite a pubby feel. The beamed and timbered dining room is spread over two floors with lots of exposed brickwork, a mix of brasses and copper, local prints, bric-a-brac and a warm winter fire. The brick bar counter has home-made jams, marmalade and chutney for sale alongside Black Sheep, a couple of guests such as Caldedonian Deuchars IPA and Timothy Taylors Landlord and nine wines by the glass. Opposite is a comfortably laid-back area with two red leather sofas; background music; good service; more reports please.

 Using some home-grown produce, good food might include sandwiches, smoked haddock and halibut pâté, lentil thai curry soup with beetroot salsa, crab, leek and coriander tart, pork wellington, fried monkfish with herb risotto, curried parsnip and sweet potato pasty, chicken and leek pie, sausage and mash, battered haddock, fried chicken breast stuffed with spicy sausage and grilled venison steak with port jus. *Benchmark main dish: shoulder of lamb £12.95. Two-course evening meal £18.20.*

Free house ~ Licensees Andrew Cafferkey and Sarah Sharpe ~ Real ale ~ Bar food (12-1.45, 6-9; 12-4.45 Sun; not Sun evening, not Mon) ~ Restaurant ~ (01522) 730354 ~ Open 11.30-3, 6(5 Fri)-11; 11.30-11 summer Sat; 12-10.30 Sun; closed Mon ~ www.innonthegreeningham.co.uk *Recommended by Geoffrey and Tina Robinson, Tony and Maggie Harwood*

KIRKBY LA THORPE   TF0945   Map 8
Queens Head

Village and pub signposted off A17, just E of Sleaford, then turn right into Boston Road cul-de-sac; NG34 9NU

Reliable dining pub very popular for its enjoyable food and good service

Neatly comfortable and gently traditional, this extended pub is well organised, with plenty of neat dark-waistcoated staff, open woodburning stoves and huge elaborate flower arrangements. You can choose almost any degree of formality (and fresh air), from teak tables and chairs in a lantern-lit back arbour with a glazed canopy, through a sizeable brightly carpeted bar with stools along the counter, button-back banquettes and sofas and dining chairs around its shiny dark tables, to a verdant light and airy conservatory with informal dining tables, or – beyond heavily swagged curtains – a smartly linen-set beamed restaurant. Nice decorative touches take in thoughtful lighting, big prints and five handsome longcase clocks (it's quite something when they all chime at midday). Batemans XB and a guest or two, perhaps from Bass and local Windmill, are on handpump, and in summer they serve home-made lemonade; easy disabled access; background music.

Thoughtfully sourced food covers a broad range as you can choose from pubby bar fare, a more elaborate restaurant menu or the specials board. As well as sandwiches, there might be potted crayfish tails, twice-baked smoked haddock and local cheese soufflé, scampi, moussaka, sausage and mash, red pepper stuffed with goats cheese, grilled bass with pesto and basil mash, roast tomatoes and chorizo, twice-cooked pork belly with bramley apple mash, black pudding fritters and crackling with calvados and cider sauce, and puddings such as Baileys crème brûlée, baked banana and toffee cheesecake and raspberry jam roly poly with cinnamon ice-cream. *Benchmark main dish: steak and kidney pudding £13.95. Two-course evening meal £24.00.*

Free house ~ Licensee John Clark ~ Real ale ~ Bar food (12-2.30, 6-9.30(10 Sat); 12-8.30 Sun) ~ Restaurant ~ (01529) 305743 ~ Children welcome ~ Open 12-3, 6-11; 12-10.30 Sun ~ www.thequeensheadinn.com *Recommended by Dr and Mrs R G J Telfer, Maurice and Janet Thorpe, Mark, Amanda, Luke and Jake Sheard, Mrs P Bishop*

STAMFORD   TF0306   Map 8
George of Stamford ★ ⑪ ♀ ⇌

High Street, St Martins (B1081 S of centre, not the quite different central pedestrianised High Street); PE9 2LB

Lincolnshire Dining Pub of the Year

Handsome coaching inn, beautifully relaxed and civilised, with very good (though pricey) food and wines, and lovely courtyard and garden; bedrooms

Y ou can choose from any number of places to settle down (and you probably won't want to leave) at this carefully preserved and rather grand old coaching inn, which is an exceptional place on all counts. Very civilised but not in the least stuffy, its various lovely areas are furnished with all manner of seats from leather, cane and antique wicker to soft sofas and easy chairs – there's a room to suit all occasions. The central lounge is particularly striking with sturdy timbers, broad flagstones, heavy beams and massive stonework. Though the York Bar is nicely pubby with a relaxed, local mood, you might not feel comfortable turning up in walking gear. There's an oak-panelled restaurant (jacket or tie required) and a less formal Garden Room Restaurant, which has well spaced furniture on herringbone glazed bricks around a central tropical planting. The staff are professional and friendly, with table drinks service in the charming cobbled courtyard at the back, with comfortable chairs and tables among attractive plant tubs and colourful hanging baskets on the ancient stone buildings. A fine range of drinks includes Adnams Broadside, Grainstore Triple B and a guest on handpump, an excellent choice of wines (many of which are italian), with about 17 by the glass, and freshly squeezed orange juice. The immaculately kept walled garden is beautifully planted and there's a sunken lawn where croquet is often played.

🍴 Quality as high as this does come at a price. The simplest option is the York Bar snack menu, which includes sandwiches and toasties, ploughman's and chicken liver pâté with cumberland sauce. In the restaurants (you may need to book), there might be oysters, tuscan ham with figs, pear and parmesan, tempura prawns, seared lambs liver with fried sage polenta, pancetta and red wine sauce, lobster, rack of lamb with garlic and herb crust and redcurrant and rosemary jus, fish and chips, spaghetti with half a lobster, tomato and chilli, roast red pepper risotto with grilled goats cheese and bass with fennel and saffron and tomato vinaigrette. Their morning coffee and afternoon teas are popular. *Benchmark main dish: fish and chips £17.85. Two-course evening meal £25.50.*

Free house ~ Licensees Chris Pitman and Ivo Vannocci ~ Real ale ~ Bar food (12-11) ~ Restaurant ~ (01780) 750750 ~ Children must be over 8 in oak panelled dining room ~ Dogs allowed in bar and bedrooms ~ Open 11-11; 12-10.30 Sun ~ Bedrooms: £100B/£150B ~ www.georgehotelofstamford.com *Recommended by J F M and M West, Alan and Jill Bull, Val and Alan Green, Roy Bromell, Graham Oddey, C Cooper, Clifford Blakemore, Mike and Sue Loseby, Pete Coxon, Roy Hoing, the Didler, Michael Sargent, Andy Lickfold, Mrs P Bishop, Colin Chambers, Tom Carver*

STAMFORD   TF0307   Map 8

Tobie Norris ★ ♀ ☕

St Pauls Street; PE9 2BE

Great period atmosphere in a warren of ancient rooms, splendid drinks' choice, nice pub food, pleasant courtyard

C enturies old, beautifully restored and full of character, this lovely place is a quite charming series of little rooms. Add careful attention by friendly staff, a fine changing range of wines, well kept Adnams and (from the owner's microbrewery) Ufford White Hart on handpump, three guest beers including ones from Adnams and Ufford, and Weston's organic farm cider, and you get a most enjoyable, relaxed and easy-going atmosphere – particularly liked by the two labradoodles Fraggle and Sprocket, it appears. Refurbishments really have made the made the most of the building's age – worn flagstones, meticulously stripped stonework, huge hearth for one room's woodburning stove and steeply pitched rafters in one of the two upstairs rooms. Furnishings here run from pews and heavy leatherette wall settles to comfortable armchairs, with flickering church candles and abundant books and antique prints. Downstairs, several linked rooms include a handsomely panelled shrine to Nelson and the Battle of Trafalgar on the left. These open off a spinal corridor, glass-roofed at the far end to make a snug conservatory that opens to a narrow but sunny two-level courtyard with cast-iron tables, hanging baskets and plant tubs.

Besides their much admired 'compile your own' pizzas (and the signature peking duck pizza), which are cooked in a stone oven, the menu includes antipasti, warm goats cheese and beetroot salad, belly pork and chickpea cassoulet, penne pomodoro and mixed grill. *Benchmark main dish: indian spiced burger £12.95. Two-course evening meal £15.60.*

Free house ~ Licensee William Fry ~ Real ale ~ Bar food (12-2.30, 6-9; not Sun evening) ~ (01780) 753800 ~ Children over 10 at lunchtimes ~ Dogs welcome ~ Open 11-11(midnight Fri, Sat); 12-10.30 Sun ~ www.tobienorris.com *Recommended by Simon and Amanda Southwell, Dr J Barrie Jones, Tony and Maggie Harwood, Andy Lickfold, Roy Bromell*

WOOLSTHORPE   SK8334   Map 8
Chequers ⚓ ♈
The Woolsthorpe near Belvoir, signposted off A52 or A607 W of Grantham; NG32 1LU

Interesting food at comfortably relaxed inn with good drinks and appealing castle views from outside tables

This 17th-c coaching inn is run with great care by friendly licensees offering cheery and welcoming service. As the emphasis tends to be on the food, it's worth booking. The heavy-beamed main bar has two big tables (one a massive oak construction), a comfortable mix of seating including some handsome leather chairs and banquettes, and a huge boar's head above a good log fire in the big brick fireplace. Among cartoons on the wall are some of the illustrated claret bottle labels from the series commissioned from famous artists. There are more leather seats in a dining area on the left in what was once the village bakery. A corridor leads off to the light and airy main restaurant, with contemporary pictures, and another bar; background music and board games. Greene King IPA and Old Speckled Hen and a guest such as Batemans XB are on handpump, with around 35 wines by the glass, 50 malt whiskies, and local fruit pressé. There are good quality teak tables, chairs and benches outside and, beyond these, some picnic-sets on the edge of the pub's cricket field, with views of Belvoir Castle.

Good, often interesting bar food might include sandwiches, spiced parsip soup with honey and greek yoghurt, confit of duck cassoulet, seared scallops with carrot purée, tempura squid with garlic mayonnaise and lime, mozzarella, olive and basil tart with artichokes, roast chicken breast with madeira sauce, pork tenderloin with caramelised apples and red wine jus, baked mackerel with almond and shallot crust, sausage and mash, pie of the day, and puddings such as pear tatin, rice pudding and blackberry and apple crumble. *Benchmark main dish: rib of beef with peppercorn sauce £20.00. Two-course evening meal £23.60.*

Free house ~ Licensee Justin Chad ~ Real ale ~ Bar food (12-2.30(4 Sun), 6-9.30(8.30 Sun)) ~ Restaurant ~ (01476) 870701 ~ Children welcome ~ Dogs allowed in bar and bedrooms ~ Open 12-11; 12-midnight Sat; 12-10.30 Sun ~ Bedrooms: £50B/£70S ~ www.chequersinn.net *Recommended by Alan and Jill Bull, Simon Hatton, Philip and Susan Philcox, M Mossman, Howard and Margaret Buchanan*

Also Worth a Visit in Lincolnshire

Besides the fully inspected pubs, you might like to try these pubs that have been recommended to us and described by readers. Do tell us what you think of them: feedback@goodguides.com

---

ALLINGTON SK8540

★**Welby Arms** (01400) 281361

The Green; off A1 at N end of Grantham bypass; NG32 2EA Friendly, well run and well liked inn with helpful staff, large simply furnished bar divided by stone archway, beams and joists, log fires (one in an attractive arched brick fireplace), comfortable plush wall banquettes and stools, up to six changing ales, over 20 wines by the glass and plenty of malt whiskies, good popular bar food including blackboard specials, civilised back dining lounge; background music; children welcome, tables in walled courtyard with pretty flower baskets, picnic-sets on front lawn, comfortable bedrooms, open all day Sun. *(Michael and Jenny Back and others)*

ASLACKBY TF0830

Robin Hood & Little John

(01778) 440681 *A15 Bourne–Sleaford; NG34 0HL* Nicely renovated timbered village pub, split-level bar with woodburners, mix of seating including a chesterfield in former inglenook fireplace, good choice of well coooked food (not Sun evening) from pub favourites up, ales such as Batemans, Greene King and Oldershaws, friendly staff, separate more modern oak-floored restaurant; discreet background music; three-level terrace with pergola and smokers' shelter, closed Mon. *(Andy Leighton, Tony and Maggie Harwood)*

BELCHFORD TF2975

★**Blue Bell** (01507) 533602

Village signed off A153 Horncastle–Louth; LN9 6LQ Smart 18th-c dining pub with cosy comfortable bar, relaxing pastel décor, mix of chairs and armchairs, Black Sheep and Greene King ales, good fair-priced lunchtime dishes with more inventive (and pricier) restaurant choices, efficient friendly service even when busy; children welcome, picnic-sets in neat terraced back garden, good base for Wolds walks and Viking Way (remove muddy boots), closed Sun evening, Mon and second and third weeks in Jan. *(Ian Robinson, Richard and Mary Bailey, Mrs Denise Dowd, Mr and Mrs D Mackenzie)*

BILLINGBOROUGH TF1134

★**Fortescue Arms** (01529) 240228

B1177, off A52 Grantham–Boston; NG34 0QB Popular country local with old stonework, exposed brick, wood panelling, beams and big see-through fireplace in carpeted rooms, well kept Adnams, Everards, Greene King and Timothy Taylors, pubby

food (all day Sun), good friendly service, Victorian prints, brass and copper, a stuffed badger and pheasant, fresh flowers and pot plants, attractive flagstoned dining rooms each end and another fire; children welcome, picnic-sets on side lawn, more in sheltered courtyard with flowering tubs, open all day weekends. *(Dr and Mrs R G J Telfer, Ian and Helen Stafford)*

BRANDY WHARF TF0196

★**Cider Centre** (01652) 678364

B1205 SE of Scunthorpe (off A15 about 16 miles N of Lincoln); DN21 4RU Up to 15 draught ciders, many more in bottles, also country wines and meads; plain take-us-as-you-find-us bright main bar and dimmer lounge with lots of cider memorabilia and jokey bric-a-brac, reasonably priced straightforward food (all day Sun); background music; children in eating area, simple glazed verandah, tables in meadows or by river with moorings and slipway, play area, closed Mon-Weds in winter. *(Mike and Lynn Robinson, the Didler)*

BURTON COGGLES SK9725

Cholmeley Arms (01476) 550225

Village Street; NG33 4JS Well kept ales such as Fullers London Pride, Greene King Abbot and Grainstore in small beamed pubby bar with warm fire, good reasonably priced home-made food (not Sun evening), friendly efficient service, restaurant; farm shop, handy for A1, open all day weekends, closed lunchtimes Mon, Tues. *(Angela Nicholson, Maurice and Janet Thorpe)*

CLEETHORPES TA3009

No 2 Refreshment Room

(01472) 691707 *Station Approach; DN35 8AX* Comfortably refurbished, carpeted platform bar, friendly staff, well kept Greene King, Worthington and guests, no food, Thurs quiz; tables out under heaters, open all day from 7.30am. *(P Dawn, the Didler)*

CLEETHORPES TA3108

★**Willys** (01472) 602145

Highcliff Road; south promenade; DN35 8RQ Popular open-plan bistro-style seafront pub with panoramic Humber views, café tables, tiled floor and painted brick walls; visibly brews its own good ales, also changing guests and belgian beers, good home-made bargain bar lunches (evening food Mon, Tues and Thurs), friendly fast service, nice mix of customers from young and trendy to weather-beaten fishermen; quiet juke box; a few tables out on the promenade, open all day. *(P Dawn, Chris Johnson, the Didler, John Honnor)*

CONINGSBY   TF2458
Lea Gate Inn (01526) 342370

Leagate Road (B1192 southwards, off A153 E); LN4 4RS Heavy-beamed 16th-c Fenland pub with three cosy linked rooms, medley of furnishings including great high-backed settles around the biggest of the three log fires, dim lighting, ancient oak panelling, attractive dining room, even a priest hole, food (all day Sun) from extensive menu, Adnams, Batemans and Wells & Youngs; children welcome, dogs in bar, pleasant garden, site of old gallows at front, eight motel bedrooms, open all day Sun. *(Roy Bromell, Mrs P Bishop)*

DENTON   SK8632
Welby Arms (01476) 870304

Church Street; NG32 1LG Welcoming local, clean and comfortable, with enjoyable attractively served food at reasonable prices, well kept Greene King ales; background music turned down on request; pretty village nestling in Vale of Belvoir. *(Mrs B H Adams, John Honnor)*

DYKE   TF1022
Wishing Well (01778) 422970

Village signed off A15 N of Bourne; Main Street; PE10 0AF Long heavily beamed stripped-stone front bar with huge fireplace, friendly helpful staff, Greene King Abbot, Shepherd Neame Spitfire and three guests, enjoyable reasonably priced food from sandwiches to steaks, OAP lunchtime deal, big restaurant, small conservatory, darts, pool, TV and so forth in public bar, live music and quiz nights; children and dogs welcome, garden with terrace seating and play area, 12 bedrooms, caravan park, open all day. *(Mr and Mrs M Norris, Tony and Maggie Harwood)*

EWERBY   TF1247
Finch Hatton Arms (01529) 460363

Main Street; NG34 9PH Former 1875 hunting lodge with mock-Tudor carpeted interior, lots of beams and timbers, farming tools, brass and plates, fair choice of generously served food, three real ales and several wines by the glass, coal fire, two bars and two dining rooms; background music; bedrooms. *(JJW, CMW)*

FOSDYKE   TF3132
Ship (01205) 260764

Moulton Washway; A17; PE12 6LH Refurbished roadside pub, simple pine and quarry-tile decor, woodburner, reasonably priced food including good fish, Adnams and Batemans. *(John Honnor)*

GAINSBOROUGH   SK8189
Eight Jolly Brewers (01427) 677128

Ship Court, Silver Street; DN21 2DW Small comfortable pub with up to eight

changing real ales, low prices, also farm cider and country wines, simple lunchtime food (not Sun), friendly staff and locals, beams, bare bricks and brewery posters, quieter areas upstairs, live music Thurs; terrace, open all day. *(the Didler)*

GRANTHAM   SK9136
⋆**Blue Pig** (01476) 563704

Vine Street; NG31 6RQ Cosy three-bar Tudor pub, well kept Timothy Taylors Landlord and changing guests, Weston's cider and perry, cheerful staff, low beams, panelling, stripped stone and flagstones, open fire, daily newspapers, lots of pig ornaments, prints and bric-a-brac, no food; juke box, games machines; dogs welcome; tables out behind, open all day (till 1.30am Fri and Sat). *(Ian and Nita Cooper, the Didler)*

GREAT GONERBY   SK8938
Recruiting Sergeant

(01476) 562238 *High Street; NG31 8JP* Pleasant local with enjoyable food including popular Sun lunch, back dining area, welcoming staff. *(Kay and Alistair Butler, Andy Leighton)*

GRIMSTHORPE   TF0423
Black Horse (01778) 591093

A151 W of Bourne; PE10 0LY Extensive handsome grey-stone coaching inn, light and airy long narrowish bar, eclectic mix of furniture, open fires, well kept Batemans and a guest, good food including weekend carvery, friendly local atmosphere; children welcome lunchtime only; garden picnic-sets, three bedrooms, closed Sun evening, Mon. *(Tony and Maggie Harwood)*

IRNHAM   TF0226
Griffin (01476) 550201

Bulby Road; NG33 4JG Welcoming old stone-built pub with good value generous home-made food, ales such as Batemans and Oakham, three rooms (two for dining), log fires, warm friendly atmosphere; background music; children welcome, nice village setting. *(Tony and Maggie Harwood)*

KIRKBY ON BAIN   TF2462
⋆**Ebrington Arms** (01526) 354560

Main Street; LN10 6YT Popular good value generous food (booking advised), five or more well kept changing ales (festivals Easter and Aug bank holidays), prompt friendly service, low 16th-c beams, two open fires, nicely set out dining areas each side, copper-topped tables, banquettes, jet fighter and racing car pictures, daily newspapers, games area with darts, back restaurant; may be background music; children welcome, wheelchair access, tables out in front, swings on side lawn, campsite behind, open all day. *(Andy Beveridge, Kay and Alistair Butler)*

LINCOLN   SK9871
Green Dragon (01522) 567155
Waterside North/Broadgate; LN2 5DH
Revamped waterside Tudor building on
three floors with handsome carved façade;
downstairs bar with character timbers,
beams, flagstones and stripped brickwork,
lounge bar above and restaurant on top
floor with fine canal views, enjoyable food
including good value Sun carvery, interesting
ales such as Milestone and Welbeck
Abbey, good service; plenty of terrace
seating. *(George Atkinson)*

LINCOLN   SK9771
Jolly Brewer (01522) 528583
Broadgate; LN2 5AQ Popular pub (good
mix of customers) with art deco interior,
good range of well kept ales and real ciders,
open fire, regular live music; can be crowded
weekend evenings; tables outside, open all
day (till 1am Fri, Sat). *(Chris Johnson)*

LINCOLN   SK9871
Morning Star (01522) 527079
Greetwell Gate; LN2 4AW Friendly
traditional local handy for the cathedral,
enjoyable good value lunches, well kept
reasonably priced mainstream ales, helpful
service, two bar areas and comfortable snug,
aircraft paintings, coal fire, some live music
(piano often played); nice covered outside
area, open all day. *(the Didler)*

LINCOLN   SK9771
Strugglers (01522) 535023
Westgate; LN1 3BG Cosily worn-in beer
lovers' haunt, well kept ales such as Bass,
Black Sheep, Greene King, Oldershaws,
Northumberland, Rudgate and Timothy
Taylors Landlord, bargain pub lunches (not
Sun), coal-effect fire in back snug, some live
music; no children inside; dogs welcome after
3pm, steps down to sunny back courtyard
with heated back canopy, open all day (till
1am Thurs-Sat). *(the Didler, Richard Stanfield)*

LINCOLN   SK9771
Tap & Spile (01522) 534015
Hungate; LN1 1ES Friendly lived-in pub
with several well kept changing ales, farm
cider and country wines, small choice of
reasonably priced pubby food, central bar,
linked areas with flagstones, bare boards
and brickwork, breweriana; open all day.
(Chris Johnson)

LINCOLN   SK9771
★Victoria (01522) 541000
Union Road; LN1 3BJ Main draw to this
old-fashioned backstreet local are the eight
changing real ales, foreign draught and
bottled beers and farm cider (beer festivals
end June, Aug bank holiday and Halloween);
simply furnished tiled front lounge with
pictures of Queen Victoria, coal fire, basic
lunchtime food, friendly staff and good mix

of customers (gets especially busy lunchtime
and later in evening); children and dogs
welcome, small conservatory and seats on
heated terrace, castle views, open all day
till midnight (1am Fri, Sat). *(P Dawn, Colin
Bettany, Chris Johnson, Simon Pyle, Pete Coxon,
the Didler and others)*

LINCOLN   SK9771
Widow Cullens Well (01522) 523020
Steep Hill; LN2 1LU Ancient simply
revamped building on two floors, cheap
Sam Smiths beers and bar food, chatty
mix of customers, good service; back
terrace. *(Susan and Nigel Brookes, Pete Coxon,
Michael Butler, Tony and Maggie Harwood)*

LINCOLN   SK9771
★Wig & Mitre (01522) 535190
Steep Hill; just below cathedral; LN2 1LU
Civilised café-style dining pub with plenty
of character and attractive period features
over two floors; big-windowed downstairs bar,
beams and exposed stone walls, pews and
Gothic furniture on oak boards, comfortable
sofas in carpeted back area, quieter
upstairs dining room with views of castle
walls and cathedral, antique prints and
caricatures of lawyers/clerics, all-day food
from breakfast on including good value set
menus and some interesting seasonal dishes,
extensive choice of wines by the glass from
good list, Batemans XB, Black Sheep and
a guest; children and dogs welcome, open
8am-midnight. *(Mike and Lynn Robinson, Pam
and John Smith, Simon Pyle, Susan and Nigel
Brookes, Tom and Ruth Rees and others)*

LONG BENNINGTON   SK8344
★Reindeer (01400) 281382
*Just off A1 N of Grantham – S end of
village, opposite school; NG23 5DJ*
Thriving atmosphere in attractively
traditional low-beamed pub with popular
long-serving landlady, good home-made
food from sandwiches up in bar and more
formal restaurant, well kept ales such as
Black Sheep, John Smiths, and Timothy
Taylors Landlord, nice wines, good friendly
service, coal-effect stove in stone fireplace;
background music not too obtrusive;
picnic-sets under parasols in small front
courtyard. *(Gordon and Margaret Ormondroyd,
Tony and Maggie Harwood)*

LOUTH   TF3287
Wheatsheaf (01507) 606262
Westgate; LN11 9YD Cheerful 17th-c low-
beamed pub near interesting church, coal
fires in all three bars, old photographs, good
changing ales and inexpensive food, spring
'Beer & Bangers' festival; can get busy; tables
outside, open all day Sat. *(Liz Bell)*

MOULTON SEAS END   TF3227
Golden Lion (01406) 370767
Seas End Road; PE12 6LD Busy well run
village pub with good value home-made food,

carvery Weds and Sun, Batemans, Elgoods and Wells & Youngs; no dogs; children welcome, open all day Weds-Sun, closed Mon and lunchtimes Tues and Fri. *(John Honnor)*

NORTH THORESBY   TF2998
New Inn (01472) 840270
Station Road; DN36 5QS Popular and friendly with good reliable pub food, well kept Marstons Pedigree, Theakstons and guests, nice fire in bar, roomy restaurant; disabled facilities, terrace. *(Steven King and Barbara Cameron)*

OASBY   TF0039
Houblon Arms (01529) 455215
Village signed off A52; NG32 3NB Large rambling 17th-c inn under new management, low beams, panelling, stonework and open fire, enjoyable food from tapas to blackboard specials cooked by landlord/chef including early evening deal (Mon-Thurs), ales such as Black Sheep, Greene King, Oldershaws and Timothy Taylors; background music, no dogs; well behaved children welcome, garden area behind with small tables on gravel, boules, four bedrooms, closed Sun evening in winter, Mon lunchtime. *(Anon)*

REDBOURNE   SK9799
Red Lion (01652) 648900
Main Road (B1206 SE of Scunthorpe); DN21 4QR Welcoming and comfortable 17th-c coaching inn with thriving atmosphere, good home-made food (fish in particular) from lunchtime sandwiches up, helpful staff, three or four well kept ales, open fire, flagstones and polished panelling, darts end, garden room restaurant; dogs welcome, attractive village, 11 bedrooms, open all day. *(Kay and Alistair Butler)*

SOUTH ORMSBY   TF3675
⋆**Massingberd Arms** (01507) 480492
Off A16 S of Louth; LN11 8QS Small brick-built village local with unusual arched windows, welcoming landlord, three well kept changing ales, short choice of good fresh food, restaurant; no credit cards or dogs; pleasant garden, good Wolds walks, open all day Sun, closed Mon, Tues lunchtime. *(the Didler)*

SOUTH RAUCEBY   TF0245
Bustard (01529) 488250
Main Street; NG34 8QG Much modernised beamed stone-built pub, well kept ales, bar food can be good including some unusual dishes, welcoming staff, comfortable plush seating, log fire, pictures of bustards and other birds, small dining area; children welcome, attractive sheltered garden. *(Sarah Flynn)*

STAMFORD   TF0306
Bull & Swan (01780) 766412
High Street, St Martins; PE9 2LJ Traditional inn refurbished under newish management, three low-beamed connecting rooms, log fires, enjoyable food from sandwiches and sharing plates up, Adnams, Grainstore and Oakham, plenty of wines by the glass; children and dogs welcome, tables out in former back coachyard, seven individually styled bedrooms named after animals, open all day. *(John Coatsworth)*

STAMFORD   TF0207
⋆**Crown** (01780) 763136
All Saints Place; PE9 2AG Substantial well modernised stone-built hotel with emphasis on good seasonal country cooking using local produce (some from their own farm), friendly helpful staff, well kept ales such as Adnams, decent wines, whiskies and coffee, spacious main bar, long leather-cushioned bar counter, substantial pillars, step up to more traditional flagstoned area with stripped stone and lots of leather sofas and armchairs, civilised dining room; back courtyard, 28 comfortable bedrooms, good breakfast, open all day. *(Gerry and Rosemary Dobson)*

STAMFORD   TF0207
Jolly Brewer (01780) 755141
Foundry Road; PE9 2PP Welcoming 19th-c stone-built pub with at least five well kept ales and good choice of ciders/perries, reasonably priced food including lunchtime baguettes, nice open fire, regular beer festivals and quiz-and-curry nights, pub games; sports TV, open all day. *(Dave Robbo, Simon and Amanda Southwell)*

STAMFORD   TF0303
Mama Liz's (01780) 765888
9a North St; PE9 1EL New Orleans themed bar in former warehouse, real ales and US bottled beers, cocktails, upstairs cajun/creole restaurant (other food available too), regular live music in Voodoo Lounge cellar bar; decked terrace, closed Tues, otherwise open all day (till 2am Fri, Sat). *(Tony and Maggie Harwood)*

STAMFORD   TF0207
St Marys Vaults (01780) 764305
19 St Marys Street; PE9 2DG Late medieval timber-framed pub in centre of conservation area, cheap well kept Sam Smiths beers, decent reasonably priced food in cosy back dining part; wheelchair access but lavatories (and games room) upstairs, terrace seating. *(Michael Tack)*

Post Office address codings confusingly give the impression that a few pubs are in Lincolnshire, when they're really in Cambridgeshire (which is where we list them).

STOW   SK8881
✶**Cross Keys** (01427) 788314
Stow Park Road; B1241 NW of Lincoln;
LN1 2DD Cosy carpeted bar in traditional
pub with big woodburner, straightforward
furnishings, some wood panelling, decorative
china and country prints, five changing ales
such Castle Rock, Batemans and Theakstons,
quite a range of bar food in neatly laid dining
areas; background music; no dogs inside;
children welcome, near interesting Saxon
minster church, open all day Sun till 8.30pm,
closed Mon lunchtime. *(Anon)*

SURFLEET SEAS END   TF2729
✶**Ship** (01775) 680547
Reservoir Road; off A16 N of Spalding;
PE11 4DH Immaculately rebuilt pub just
below seawall, woodburner, chesterfields
and handsomely made seating in good-sized
civilised bar with old scrubbed tables in
open bays, enjoyable reasonably priced food
including OAP deal, changing well kept ales
such as Elgoods and Slaters, helpful friendly
service, upstairs overflow restaurant; tables
on front terrace, boating-view benching and
picnic-sets on embankment across lane, four
good value bedrooms. *(F and M Pryor, Tony*
and Maggie Harwood)

TATTERSHALL THORPE   TF2159
Blue Bell (01526) 342206
Thorpe Road; B1192 Coningsby–
Woodhall Spa; LN4 4PE Ancient
low-beamed pub (said to date from the
13th c) and used by the Dambusters, RAF
memorabilia including airmen's signatures
on the ceiling, big open fire, four real ales,
well priced pubby bar food, small dining
room; garden tables, bedrooms. *(the Didler)*

TEALBY   TF1590
Kings Head (01673) 838347
Kingsway, off B1203 towards bottom
of village; LN8 3YA Thatched medieval
beamed dining pub under new management,
good choice of fresh food from pubby things up
including set menu choices, three Marstons
related beers; children and dogs welcome,
wheelchair access, picnic-sets in side garden,
quiet Wolds village handy for Viking Way walk,
open all day, till 9pm Sun. *(Richard Guy)*

THEDDLETHORPE
ALL SAINTS   TF4787
✶**Kings Head** (01507) 339798
Pub signposted off A1031 N of
Maplethorpe; Mill Road; LN12 1PB
Long, low 16th-c thatched building, carpeted
two-room front lounge with lowest ceiling
we've found in any pub, brass platters on
timbered walls, antique dining chairs and
tables, easy chairs by log fire, central bar

(more low beams) with well kept Batemans
XB, a seasonal ale and Skidbrooke local cider,
shelves of books, coal fire with side oven,
stuffed owls and country pictures, long dining
room with colourful mugs and jugs hanging
from black joists, good local food including
steaks and fresh Grimsby fish, Sun carvery,
cheerful helpful landlord; one or two picnic-
sets in prettily planted front area, more on
lawn, open all day Sat, closed Sun evening,
Mon. *(Anon)*

THREEKINGHAM   TF0836
Three Kings (01529) 240249
Just off A52 12 miles E of Grantham;
Saltersway; NG34 0AU Big entrance
hall (former coaching inn), beamed and
dark panelled bar with coal fire and pubby
furniture including banquettes, compact
restaurant plus bigger dining/function room,
good choice of enjoyable home-made food
from baguettes up, Bass, Timothy Taylors
Landlord and guests such as Cottage and
Tom Woods, friendly staff; children and dogs
welcome, terrace with covered smokers' area,
closed Mon. *(D H Bennett)*

WAINFLEET   TF5058
✶**Batemans Brewery** (01754) 882009
Mill Lane, off A52 via B1195; PE24 4JE
Circular bar in brewery's ivy-covered
windmill tower, Batemans ales in top
condition, czech and belgian beers on tap,
ground-floor dining area with cheap food
including baguettes and a few pubby dishes,
plenty of old pub games (more outside),
lots of brewery memorabilia and plenty for
families to enjoy; entertaining brewery tours
and shop, tables on terrace and grass, open
11.30am-4pm (2.30pm in winter), closed Mon
and Tues. *(the Didler, J F M and M West)*

WELBY   SK9738
Crown & Anchor (01400) 230307
Main Street; NG32 3LP Attractive
refurbished village pub, friendly local
atmosphere in spacious bar, enjoyable varied
choice of food here and in small dining room
including vegetarian options, good service,
three real ales, nice log fire. *(Richard Taylor,*
Heidi Peskett)

WEST DEEPING   TF1009
Red Lion (01778) 347190
King Street; PE6 9HP Stone-built family-
run pub with long low-beamed bar, half a
dozen well kept interesting beers, popular
food including OAP weekday lunch and early-
bird deal, back dining extension, stripped
stone and open fire, live music including
monthly folk club; children welcome, tables
in back garden with fenced play area. *(Phil*
and Jane Hodson)

Norfolk

One of the things that stands out about pubs in this popular county is how friendly the landlords and landladies are and how this in turn helps create a genuinely easy-going and cheerful atmosphere. We've added some excellent new entries this year, which include the Ostrich in Castle Acre (a welcoming landlady in handsome old coaching inn), Saracens Head in Erpingham (obliging new licensees and a comfortable place to stay), Swan at Ingham (a clever blend of old and new décor and inventive food), Anchor at Morston (hard-working young landlords, traditional bars and good food), Jolly Farmers in North Creake (a warm welcome and enjoyable food cooked by landlady), King William IV in Sedgeford (well run and close to beaches and bird-watching), Dun Cow at Salthouse (a super all-rounder), Duck in Stanhoe (sister pub to the Bell in Wiveton; charming landlord, relaxed atmosphere), Lifeboat in Thornham (close to salt-flat walks, six ales, reliable food), Gunton Arms near Thorpe Market (stately manor and with much character), Globe in Wells-next-the-Sea (handsome Georgian inn with contemporary décor and highly thought of meals), Wheatsheaf in West Beckham (warmly friendly and traditional with proper home cooking), and Bell in Wiveton (cordial landlord, relaxed atmosphere and popular food; sister pub to the Duck in Stanhoe). Other good pubs worth visiting are the Hoste Arms in Burnham Market (a civilised hotel but with proper pubby bar; excellent food), Crown at East Rudham (along with the White Hart in Hingham and Kings Head at Letheringsett, which are all part of the thriving Flying Kiwi Inns group), Dabbling Duck at Great Massingham (busy village-green pub popular with both locals and visitors), Angel in Larling (long-serving licensees in traditional local), Fat Cat in Norwich (a beer lovers' paradise), Hare Arms in Stow Bardolph (our readers tend to return again and again) and Orange Tree in Thornham (inventive food and warmly friendly landlord). The Orange Tree in Thornham is Norfolk Dining Pub 2013.

BLAKENEY
White Horse ♀

Off A149 W of Sheringham; High Street; NR25 7AL

Cheerful small hotel with popular dining conservatory, interesting food and drinks and helpful staff; bedrooms

The new landlord has given this bustling former coaching inn a stylish make-over and made some other gentle changes, too. The informal long bar has cream-coloured walls above a pale grey dado hung with equestrian fine-art prints and paintings from a local gallery, high-backed brown leather dining and other chairs around light oak tables on new black and white striped carpet and natural coloured linen window blinds; Adnams Bitter, Broadside, Ghost Ship and a seasonal guest on handpump and a dozen wines by the glass. There's also an airy conservatory. The suntrap courtyard and pleasant paved garden both have plenty of tables, and the inn is just a stroll from the small tidal harbour. This area is a haven for bird-watchers and sailors.

As well as lunchtime bagels and filled baguettes, the food includes mussels with smoked haddock, celery and whisky cream, chargrilled halloumi with shaved fennel and carrot salad and toasted mixed seeds, a pie of the day, home-made beer burger with blue cheese, bacon or mushroom toppings, 'grown up' macaroni cheese with roasted shallots and crispy sage, osso bucco with gremolata dumplings, skate wing with brown shrimp vièrge, and puddings like white chocolate panna cotta with pistachio crème fraîche and honeycomb and steamed rhubarb and ginger pudding with rhubarb and honey pie and pastry cream. *Benchmark main dish: portuguese seafood stew £14.50. Two-course evening meal £20.00.*

Free house ~ Licensee Francis Guildea ~ Real ale ~ Bar food (12-2.15, 6-9) ~ Restaurant ~ (01263) 740574 ~ Children welcome ~ Dogs allowed in bar ~ Open 11-11 ~ Bedrooms: /$100S ~ www.blakeneywhitehorse.co.uk *Recommended by MDN, Michael and Maggie Betton, Sandy Butcher, Tracey and Stephen Groves, David Eberlin, David Carr, W K Wood*

BURNHAM MARKET
Hoste Arms

The Green (B1155); PE31 8HD

Civilised and stylish with excellent food and drinks, a proper bar plus several lounge areas and dining rooms, and a lovely garden; elaborately decorated bedrooms

The emphasis at this civilised 17th-c coaching inn is on the smart restaurant and hotel side, so it's quite a surprise to find that the front bar has the feeling of a proper village pub, with a bustling atmosphere and a good mix of chatty drinkers. This room is panelled, with a log fire, a series of watercolours showing scenes from local walks and Adnams Broadside, Woodfordes Wherry and a changing guest beer on handpump. The extensive and carefully chosen wine list has helpful notes and around 19 (including champagne and sparkling wine) by the glass; lots of whiskies and liqueurs. There's a conservatory with leather armchairs and sofas, a lounge for afternoon tea and several restaurants (for which it's best to book to be sure of a table). The lovely walled garden has plenty of seats, and a big awning covers the moroccan-style dining area.

As well as lunchtime sandwiches, the delicious modern food might include rabbit rillettes with roasted beetroot, red onion and red chard salad, pigeon breasts with poached rhubarb, toasted brioche and black peppercorn ice-cream and a rhubarb and vanilla syrup, steak and kidney pudding, wild mushroom and baby spinach risotto with a poached duck egg and truffle oil, beer-battered cod with minted crushed peas, piri piri chicken with cajun-spiced potatoes, guacamole, crème fraîche and hot chilli sauce, bass fillets with caramelised fennel, mangetouts and fine beans and a mussel, cockle, saffron and chive broth, and puddings like dark chocolate fondant, crushed praline, chocolate popping candy and white chocolate sorbet and french apple tart with apple and vanilla purée, clotted cream ice-cream and cinnamon sugar. *Benchmark main dish: halibut with thai butter crust and oriental vegetables and noodle stri-fry £17.95. Two-course evening meal £22.25.*

Free house ~ Licensee Emma Tagg ~ Real ale ~ Bar food (12-2, 6-9) ~ Restaurant ~ (01328) 738777 ~ Children welcome ~ Dogs allowed in bar and bedrooms ~ Open 11-11(10.30 Sun) ~ Bedrooms: £122S/£149B ~ www.hostearms.co.uk *Recommended by Jeremy and Ruth Preston-Hoar, Peter and Giff Bennett, Sandy Butcher, Roy Hoing, Michael Sargent, Simon Rodway, Michael and Maggie Betton, Mike and Linda Hudson, Derek Thomas*

BURSTON
Crown ◀

TM1383 Map 8

Village signposted off A140 N of Scole; Mill Road; IP22 5TW

Friendly, relaxed village pub usefully open all day, with a warm welcome, real ales and well liked bar food

As this village pub is open all day, there are always customers dropping in and out and the atmosphere is easy-going and friendly. Locals tend to gather in an area by the bar counter, with its high bar chairs, where they serve Adnams Bitter, Greene King Abbot and guests such as Elmtree Norfolks 80 Shilling Ale and Nethergate Britains Best on handpump, two farm ciders and several wines by the glass. In cold weather, the best place to sit in this heavy-beamed, quarry-tiled room is on the comfortably cushioned sofas in front of the big log fire in its huge brick fireplace, and there are also some stools by the low chunky wooden table, and newspapers and magazines to read. The public bar on the left has a nice long table and panelled settle on an old brick floor in one alcove, another sofa, straightforward tables and chairs on the carpet by the pool table, games machine and juke box and, up a step, more tables and chairs. Both of these cream-painted rooms are hung with cheerful naive local character paintings; background music and board games. The simply furnished, beamed dining room has another big brick fireplace. Outside, there's a smokers' shelter, a couple of picnic-sets in front of the old brick building and more seats in a hedged-off area with a barbecue.

Quite a choice of popular food using local produce might include sandwiches, deep-fried crispy beef with sweet chilli sauce, prawns with satay sauce and cucumber salad, sausage and mash with onion gravy, home-made beef burger, ham and free-range eggs, aubergine with indian spices with sweet potato sag aloo and raita, lamb shanks in a red wine and redcurrant sauce, blackened salmon with mango salsa and braised local rabbit in a dijon mustard, bacon and white wine cream sauce. *Benchmark main dish: rib-eye steak with Café de Paris butter £16.50. Two-course evening meal £19.00.*

Free house ~ Licensees Bev and Steve Kembery and Jonathan Piers-Hall ~ Real ale ~ Bar food (12-2(4 Sun), 6.30-9; not Sun evening) ~ Restaurant ~ (01379) 741257 ~ Children welcome ~ Dogs allowed in bar ~ Open 12-11(10.30 Sun) ~ www.burstoncrown.com *Recommended by R C Vincent*

CASTLE ACRE

Ostrich

TF8115 Map 8

Stocks Green; PE32 2AE

Handsome village pub with original 16th-c features, fine old fireplaces, real ales and tasty food

Wandering around the various rooms of this handsome 16th-c former coaching inn, you can still see some of the original masonry along with beams and trusses in the lofty ceilings, although the place was largely rebuilt in the 18th-c. The L-shaped low-ceilinged front bar (on two levels) has a woodburning stove in a huge old fireplace, lots of wheelback chairs and cushioned pews around pubby tables on the wood-strip floor and gold patterned wallpaper; a step leads up to an area in front of the bar counter, where there are similar seats and tables and a log fire in a brick fireplace. Greene King IPA, Abbot and Old Speckled Hen and a seasonal guest beer on handpump, a dozen wines (including fizz) by the glass and several malt whiskies. There's a separate dining room with another brick fireplace. The sheltered garden has picnic-sets under parasols and the inn faces the tree-lined village green. There are some remains of a Norman castle in the village, and a Cluniac monastery.

 Using seasonal local produce, the bar food might include lunchtime sandwiches, fresh crab and leek tart, chicken and bacon terrine with sunblush tomatoes and roasted peppers, beer-battered cod, chips, mushy peas and tartare sauce, gammon and egg with honey and mustard sauce, roasted vegetable and parmesan tagliatelle, beef goulash with bacon dumpling, salmon fillet with vermouth and chive sauce, and puddings. *Benchmark main dish: home-made steak burger with crispy bacon, gruyère, onions and fat chips £12.50. Two-course evening meal £18.00.*

Greene King ~ Tenant Tiffany Turner ~ Real ale ~ Bar food (12-3, 6-9; 12-3 Sun; not Sun evening) ~ Restaurant ~ (01760) 755398 ~ Children welcome ~ Dogs allowed in bar ~ Open 10-11; 10-12.30am(11.30 Sun) Sat ~ Bedrooms: /£80B ~ www.ostrichcastleacre.com *Recommended by Phil Revell, Peter and Jean Hoare, Colin and Louise English*

CLEY NEXT THE SEA

George ♀ 🛏

TG0443 Map 8

Off A149 W of Sheringham; High Street; NR25 7RN

Pubby bar and two dining rooms in sizeable inn, real ales, super choice of wines and bar and restaurant food; bedrooms

This bustling place is in a quiet brick and flint village overlooking the salt marshes – fantastic for bird-watching. The little public bar has photographs of norfolk wherries and other local scenes on the cream walls, a long leather settle and sturdy dark wooden chairs by a couple of green-topped tables on carpet, a huge candle in a big glass jar on one window sill, a table of newspapers and a stained-glass window showing St George and the dragon. Adnams Broadside, Woodfordes Wherry and Yetmans Red on handpump and lots of wines by the glass. The dining rooms are similarly furnished with pale wooden cushioned dining chairs around a mix of tables; the end room has prints of Leonardo drawings on the fleur-de-lys wallpaper, brown blinds on the windows, an ornamental woodburning stove in the end room with nightlights along the mantelbeam and some rather nice old-fashioned glass wall lamps. You can sit in the garden just across the small lane.

🍴 Good bar food includes sandwiches, a plate of smoked mackerel, prawns and home-made salmon gravadlax, chicken liver parfait with spiced apple chutney and home-made bread, roast pumpkin, ginger and chilli risotto, confit duck leg with parsley and olive oil mash and honey-roasted carrots, chicken breast with wild mushrooms and broccoli, black bream with chorizo, olives and sautéed potatoes, and puddings such as star anise panna cotta with rhubarb and ginger sorbet and apple and mixed berry crumble. *Benchmark main dish: beer-battered fish and chips £12.00. Two-course evening meal £20.00.*

Free house ~ Licensee Martin Panter ~ Real ale ~ Bar food (12-2, 6.30-9) ~ Restaurant ~ (01263) 740652 ~ Children welcome ~ Dogs allowed in bar and bedrooms ~ Live music monthly in winter ~ Open 10-11 ~ Bedrooms: /£90S ~ www.thegeorgehotelatcley.co.uk
Recommended by Jim Farmer, MDN, David Carr, Simon and Amanda Southwell, Philip Lane, David and Judy Robison, Pauline Fellows and Simon Robbins, R C Vincent

EAST RUDHAM

TF8228 Map 8

Crown 🍴 ⏻ ⇐

A148 W of Fakenham; The Green; PE31 8RD

Stylish open-plan seating areas, cosy back sitting room, first class contemporary cooking and a friendly atmosphere; bedrooms

The contemporary open-plan bar in this friendly and rather civilised place has several distinct seating areas with brown leather and wood dining chairs around a mix of tables (including a huge round one), a log fire in a modern brick fireplace (with a grandfather clock and bookshelves on either side) and rugs on the stripped floorboards. High bar chairs beside the handsomely slate-topped counter are popular and they keep their own-brewed JoCs Norfolk Kiwi plus Adnams Bitter and Broadside on handpump and several wines by the glass. The other end of the room is slightly more informal with a mix of leather-seated dining chairs around all sorts of tables, a couple of built-in wall seats, another bookshelf beside a second fireplace and 1950s and 1960s prints of actors in Shakespearean costume on the walls. There's also a more pubby part with cushioned white-painted built-in seats and nice photographs on the pink walls, and a cosy lower area to the back of the building with comfortable leather sofas and armchairs and a flat-screen TV; newspapers to read. Upstairs is yet another dining room with a high-pitched ceiling. There are neat picnic-sets under parasols on the front gravel. This pub is part of the Flying Kiwi Inns group.

🍴 Beautifully presented and inventive, the food might include lunchtime sandwiches, smoked haddock brandade with a coriander and lime salsa, chargrilled local quail with beetroot coleslaw and quince jelly, mozzarella and pesto gnocchi with roasted cherry tomatoes, seared bass and crab linguine, lambs liver with champ mash, smoked bacon and red onion gravy, slow-cooked brisket with garlic and parmesan mash, and puddings such as warm chocolate brownie with honeycomb ice-cream and kiwi pavlova with passion fruit, pistachio and ice-cream. *Benchmark main dish: trio of duck, breast, crispy egg and confit leg, plum sauce £15.95. Two-course evening meal £21.00.*

Flying Kiwi Inns ~ Licensee Chris Coubrough ~ Real ale ~ Bar food (12-2.30, 6.30-9.30) ~ (01485) 528530 ~ Children welcome ~ Dogs welcome ~ Open 11-11.30 ~ Bedrooms: £100B/£110B ~ www.crowninnnorfolk.co.uk *Recommended by Jeff and Wendy Williams, Mike and Margaret Banks, Derek Thomas*

It's very helpful if you let us know up-to-date food prices when you report on pubs.

ERPINGHAM
Saracens Head 🛏

TG1732   Map 8

Wolterton; Erpingham signed off A140 N of Aylsham, on through
Calthorpe; NR11 7LZ

New licensees for this remote inn with stylish bars and dining room
and seats in courtyard; good bedrooms

Our readers enjoy staying in the comfortable modern bedrooms here, and the new licensees are friendly and welcoming. It's a rather civilised place with an easy-going atmosphere. The two-room bar is simple but stylish with high ceilings, light terracotta walls and cream and gold curtains at its tall windows – all lending a feeling of space, though it's not actually large. There's a mix of seats from built-in wall settles to wicker fireside chairs as well as log fires and flowers, and the windows look out on to a charming old-fashioned gravel stableyard with plenty of chairs, benches and tables. A pretty six-table parlour on the right has another big log fire. Woodfordes Wherry on handpump, several wines by the glass and local soft drinks.

Popular food includes fresh Cromer crab salad, a deli platter (for sharing), mediterranean vegetable tartlet with a tomato and herb sauce, chicken with black pudding, chorizo, peppers and sautéed potatoes, a trio of herb-crusted lamb cutlets with dauphinoise potatoes and a rosemary and mint jus, slip soles with brown shrimp and caper butter, slow-cooked pork belly with apple mash and calvados sauce, and puddings like raspberry crème brûlée and treacle tart. *Benchmark main dish: slow-cooked pork belly with apple mash and calvados sauce £13.50. Two-course evening meal £20.00.*

Free house ~ Licensees Tim and Janie Elwes ~ Real ale ~ Bar food (12-2(2.30 summer), 6.30-8.30 (9 summer); not Mon, not winter Tues lunchtime) ~ Restaurant ~ (01263) 768909 ~ Children welcome ~ Dogs allowed in bar and bedrooms ~ Open 11.30-2.30, 6-11; 12-10 Sun; closed Mon except bank holidays, Tues lunchtime Oct-June ~ Bedrooms: £70B/£100B ~ www.saracenshead-norfolk.co.uk *Recommended by Canon Michael Bourdeaux, John Cook, Diana Owen, W K Wood*

GREAT MASSINGHAM
Dabbling Duck

TF7922   Map 8

Off A148 King's Lynn–Fakenham; Abbey Road; PE32 2HN

Unassuming from the outside but with a friendly atmosphere,
character bars and warm fires, real ales and imaginative food;
comfortable bedrooms

Even when it's really busy – which it deservedly often is – you can be sure of a friendly welcome and efficient service; our readers enjoy their visits here very much. The bars are relaxed and informal and there are leather sofas and armchairs by the roaring log fire in the raised inglenook, a mix of antique wooden dining tables and chairs on flagstones or stripped wooden floors, a very high-backed settle, quirky 18th- and 19th-c prints and cartoons, and plenty of beams and standing timbers. At the back of the pub is the Blenheim room, just right for a private group; there's also a candlelit dining room. They hold a library on the last Sunday of the month. Adnams Broadside, Beestons Worth the Wait, Greene King IPA, Woodfordes Wherry and a guest beer like Timothy Taylors Landlord on handpump from a bar counter made of great slabs of polished tree trunk; background music, darts and board games. There are tables and chairs on a front terrace looking over the sizeable village green with its big duck ponds, and more seats in the enclosed back garden with a play area. The bedrooms are named after famous local sportsmen and airmen from the World War II air base in Massingham. The village church is opposite.

🍴 Enjoyable food using produce from within a 20-mile radius might include sandwiches, a sharing charcuterie platter, chicken liver and port pâté with apple chutney, toasted focaccia with hummus, goats cheese and balsamic-roasted tomatoes, lager and lime battered haddock with crushed minted peas and tartare sauce, pea, feta and courgette frittata with chive oil and dill potatoes, ground rump burger with smoked bacon and gruyère and tomato relish, beef bourguignon, lemon chicken caesar salad with crispy serrano ham, anchovies and croûtons, and paprika and garlic marinated lamb steak with patatas bravas, greek salad and tzatziki. *Benchmark main dish: duck, maple syrup and tarragon pie with truffle oil mash £11.50. Two-course evening meal £16.75.*

Free house ~ Licensee Dominic Symington ~ Real ale ~ Bar food (12-3, 6-9) ~ Restaurant ~ (01485) 520827 ~ Children welcome ~ Dogs welcome ~ Open 12-11.30 ~ Bedrooms: £65S/£85B ~ www.thedabblingduck.co.uk *Recommended by Philip and Susan Philcox, Tracey and Stephen Groves, John Cook, Brian Glozier, John Wooll, R C Vincent, Anthony Barnes, George Atkinson, F and M Pryor*

HINGHAM
White Hart 🍴 ♈
Market Place, just off B1108 W of Norwich; NR9 4AF

TG0202   Map 5

Carefully and interestingly furnished pub with thoughtful furnishings in attractive town square, a good choice of drinks and imaginative modern cooking

Bustling and friendly, this is a well run place with a civilised but informal atmosphere. The rooms, arranged over two floors, have a great deal of character: stripped floorboards, a few oriental and other colourful rugs, an attractive variety of chairs and tables (some rather fine), a few beams and standing timbers, lots of prints and photographs and objects such as antique hanging scales on walls painted in mushroom and cream, several woodburning stoves and quiet corners with comfortable sofas. Good lighting runs from ceiling spots to interesting lanterns and even – in one rather grand room with a barrel-vaulted ceiling – antler chandeliers. The galleried long room up steps from the main bar with its egyptian frieze is just right for a sizeable party. Their own JoCs Norfolk Kiwi beer and Adnams Bitter on handpump and up to 20 wines by the glass. There are some modern benches and seats in the gravelled courtyard. This is part of the Flying Kiwi Inns group.

🍴 From a sensibly short menu, the extremely good food might include lunchtime sandwiches, chicken liver parfait with red onion, sherry vinegar and thyme chutney, tempura prawns with saffron aioli, chicken caesar salad, sicilian-style cauliflower with crispy polenta and chilli sauce, chargrilled burger with crispy bacon and cheese, beer-battered haddock with tartare sauce, slow-cooked duck leg with a red wine poached pear, moroccan-style lamb with red lentils and dried fruit, and puddings. *Benchmark main dish: fillet of bass with crab risotto and a fennel, orange and watercress salad £15.95. Two-course evening meal £20.50.*

Flying Kiwi Inns ~ Manager Chris Coubrough ~ Real ale ~ Bar food (12-2.30, 6.30-9.30(9 Sun)) ~ (01953) 850214 ~ Children welcome ~ Dogs welcome ~ Open 11-11.30 ~ www.whitehartnorfolk.co.uk *Recommended by Richard Gibbs, Emma Jay*

INGHAM
Swan ♨ ⬤ ⇐
TG3926 Map 8

Off A149 SE of North Walsham; signed from Stalham; NR12 9AB

**Nicely placed and warmly welcoming ancient thatched pub
tied to Woodfordes; their good beers and enjoyable food;
comfortable bedrooms**

A clever blend of old and new, this quietly set country pub dates back
in part to the 14th c. There's plenty of stripped flint and ancient
masonry, and the rustic atmosphere is underlined by low beams,
hefty standing timbers, dim lighting, a few farm tools and the two big
woodburning stoves either side of the massive chimneybreast. This
divides the main area into two more intimate spaces – the further side,
with parquet rather than bare boards, has a quieter atmosphere than the
cheery part by the bar, as does a small brick-floored area up by the back
entrance, with leather sofas by a Plexiglass table. Woodfordes Wherry
and guests like Nelsons Revenge and Sundew on handpump, decent
wines by the glass, and charming efficient staff. A sheltered sunny back
terrace has picnic-sets, some under cocktail parasols, with more round
the side. The simple, comfortable bedrooms are in converted stabling.
The inn is dwarfed by the soaring flint tower of the church beside it and
is in easy reach of both Broads and coast.

As well as good value two- and three-course set menus, the inventive food
might include white crab meat and crispy crab cake with avocado salsa, twice
baked montgomery soufflé with spinach and herb cream, dijon and herb baked
lamb rump with fondant potato, baby leeks, chargrilled aubergine fritter and
rich olive jus, honey roast gressingham duck with roast squash, chinese cabbage,
pancetta, mushrooms and red wine jus, halibut with chive risotto, line-caught
scallops, samphire and brown shrimp sauce, and puddings like strawberry eton
mess with raspberry parfait and macaroons, dark chocolate nemisis with blood
orange ice-cream and marinated strawberries. *Benchmark main dish: wild bass
with brown shrimp beurre blanc and charred asparagus £17.95. Two-course
evening meal £23.50.*

Woodfordes ~ Manager Daniel Smith ~ Real ale ~ Bar food (12-2, 7-9; 12-3 Sun; best to
check for Sun evening and Mon (may be closed))~ (01692) 581099 ~ Children welcome
~ Open 12-3.30, 6.30-11 ~ Bedrooms: /£80B ~ www.theinghamswan.co.uk
Recommended by Roy Hoing, Tony Middis, Sandy Butcher, Sue Kinder, N R White

LARLING
Angel ⬤ ⇐
TL9889 Map 5

*From A11 Thetford–Attleborough, take B1111 turn-off and follow
pub signs; NR16 2QU*

**Good-natured chatty atmosphere in busy pub, several real ales and
tasty bar food; bedrooms**

This genuinely friendly pub makes a fine base from which to explore
the surrounding area, with its endless walks and bird-watching
opportunities. They offer secure cycle storage and can supply packed
lunches and picnics, and food is usefully served all day. The comfortable
1930s-style lounge on the right has square panelling, cushioned
wheelback chairs, a nice long cushioned and panelled corner settle,
some good solid tables for eating, a collection of whisky-water jugs on
the delft shelf over the big brick fireplace, a woodburning stove, a couple
of copper kettles and some hunting prints. The same friendly family have

run the inn since 1913 and they still have the original visitors' books with guests from 1897 to 1909. Adnams Bitter and four guests from breweries such as Elmtree, Hop Back, Orkney and Woodfordes on handpump, 110 malt whiskies and ten wines by the glass. They hold an August beer festival with over 100 real ales and ciders, live music and barbecues. The quarry-tiled black-beamed public bar has a good local feel with darts, juke box (a rarity nowadays), a games machine, board games and background music. A neat grass area behind the car park has picnic-sets around a big fairy-lit apple tree and there's a safely fenced play area. They also have a four-acre meadow and offer caravan and camping sites from March to October.

As well as sandwiches and toasties, the good, traditional food includes a pot of mushrooms and bacon with garlic and cream, crispy coated whitebait, burgers with various toppings, ham and egg, omelettes, sweet pepper lasagne, smoked haddock mornay, chicken korma, a mixed grill, specials like sweet and sour pork, beer-battered cod and coq au vin, and puddings such as raspberry cheesecake and treacle tart. *Benchmark main dish: steak and kidney pie £9.95. Two-course evening meal £16.45.*

Free house ~ Licensee Andrew Stammers ~ Real ale ~ Bar food (all day) ~ Restaurant ~ (01953) 717963 ~ Children welcome ~ Open 10am-midnight ~ Bedrooms: £50B/£80S ~ www.angel-larling.co.uk *Recommended by John Cook, Dave Braisted*

LETHERINGSETT
Kings Head 🍴 ♈
TG0638 Map 8

A148 (Holt Road) W of Holt; NR25 7AR

Neat country house pub with comfortably contemporary drinking areas, friendly young staff, real ales, good wines by the glass, bistro-type food and plenty of outside seating

Our readers enjoy their visits to this large, country-house style pub very much – it's certainly wise to book a table in advance as it gets busy at peak times. The atmosphere is informal and civilised. To the right of the main door, a small room has dining chairs around scrubbed wooden tables, bookshelves beside a black fireplace, a flatscreen TV and apple-green paintwork. The main bar, to the left, is comfortable, with daily papers and an open fire, big leather armchairs and sofas, stools and various dining chairs, reproduction hunting and coaching prints on the mushroom paintwork, rugs on quarry tiles and their own-brewed JoCs Norfolk Kiwi and Adnams Best on handpump; quite a choice of wines by the glass and good coffee. The partly skylit dining room has built-in white-painted wall seating with maroon cushions and a mix of dining chairs around wooden tables, rugs on stripped floorboards, and a few farm tools and cabinets of taps and spiles on the cream-painted flint and cob walls. A back area, under a partly pitched ceiling with painted rafters, has more comfortable leather sofas and armchairs in front of another big flatscreen TV; Scrabble and background music. Outside, there are lots of picnic-sets under parasols on the front gravel with many more on a grass side lawn (where there's also a play fort under tenting).

Top-class, bistro-style food might include lunchtime sandwiches, potted brown shrimps with spiced butter and a radish and pea shoot, duck, pistachio and apricot terrine with beetroot remoulade, risotto with sugar snaps, peas, broad beans and soft herbs, beer-battered haddock with tartare sauce, lambs liver with grilled smoked bacon and creamy mash, confit duck leg with spring onion and pancetta crush, roasted vine tomatoes and truffle oil, fillet of bass with lemon and herb crush, baby fennel and chive butter sauce, and puddings. *Benchmark main dish: crispy slow-cooked pork belly with apple purée, smoked paprika potatoes and romesco sauce £15.95. Two-course evening meal £19.50.*

Flying Kiwi Inns ~ Licensee Chris Coubrough ~ Real ale ~ Bar food (12-2.30, 6.30-9.30; cake and coffee 8-12, 3-6 daily) ~ (01263) 712691 ~ Children welcome ~ Dogs welcome ~ Open 11-11.30 ~ www.letheringsettkingshead.co.uk *Recommended by Judy Buckley, Philip and Susan Philcox, R L Borthwick, R C Vincent, Derek Thomas*

 MORSTON   TG0043   Map 8
Anchor
A149 Salthouse–Stiffkey; The Street; NR2 7AA

Several rooms filled with bric-a-brac and prints, real ales and some sort of food all day

In a small seaside village, this is a bustling pub with an easy-going atmosphere and friendly young licensees. On the right, there are three traditional rooms with pubby seating and tables on original wooden floors, coal fires, local 1950s beach photographs and lots of prints and bric-a-brac. Adnams Bitter, local Winters Golden and Woodfordes Wherry on handpump and several wines by the glass. The contemporary airy extension on the left has groups of deep leather sofas around low tables, grey-painted country dining furniture, fresh flowers and fish pictures. There are tables and benches out in front of the building. You can book seal-spotting trips from here and the surrounding area is wonderful for bird-watching and walking.

Cooked by one of the landlords, the popular food includes sandwiches, mackerel pâté with pickles, crispy goats cheese beignet with fig and red chilli chutney, lots of local fresh fish dishes, honey-glazed smoked ham with free-range eggs, beer-battered haddock with home-made tartare sauce, wild mushroom, sweet onion and blue cheese tagliatelle, aberdeen angus rib burger with smoked bacon, cheese and home-made sauce, chargrilled rare-breed pork chop with salsa verde, free-range chicken breast with crispy pancetta, sautéed potatoes and a light jus, and puddings like baked blood orange cheesecake with mango coulis and mandarin sorbet. *Benchmark main dish: local seafood £11.00. Two-course evening meal £17.50.*

Free house ~ Licensee Harry Farrow and Rowan Glennie ~ Real ale ~ Bar food (12-3, 6-9; light snacks all afternoon) ~ Restaurant ~ (01263) 741392 ~ Children welcome ~ Dogs allowed in bar ~ Open 9-11 ~ www.morstonanchor.co.uk *Recommended by David Carr, Sandy Butcher, David and Judy Robison*

NORTH CREAKE   TF8538   Map 8
Jolly Farmers
Burnham Road; NR21 9JW

Friendly village local with three cosy rooms, open fires and woodburners, well liked food and several real ales

Even when this yellow-painted pub is really busy, you can be sure of a friendly welcome from the cheerful licensees. There are three cosy and relaxed rooms and the main bar has a large open fire in a brick fireplace, pale yellow walls and a mix of pine farmhouse and high-backed leather dining chairs around scrubbed pine tables on the quarry-tiled floor. Beside the wooden bar counter are some high bar chairs. They keep Woodfordes Nelsons Revenge and Wherry and a guest like Adnams Southwold on handpump or tapped from the cask, 11 wines by the glass and a dozen malt whiskies. There's also a cabinet of model cars. A smaller bar has pews and a woodburning stove and the red-walled dining room has similar furniture to the bar and another woodburning stove. There are seats outside on the terrace. This is a charming flintstone village.

Cooked by the landlady, the tasty bar food includes sandwiches, pigeon and bacon salad, crab pot topped with cheese, mushroom, brie and hazelnut en croûte with a wild mushroom sauce, honey-roast ham and egg, lasagne, prawn and coconut curry, lambs liver and bacon in red wine gravy, steak and stilton pie, black bream with sesame and soy, and puddings like dark chocolate, cherry and cherry wine tart and orange and Cointreau bread and butter pudding. *Benchmark main dish: breast of lamb with dauphinoise potatoes £12.00. Two-course evening meal £16.00.*

Free house ~ Licensees Adrian and Heather Sanders ~ Real ale ~ Bar food (12-2, 7-9; not Mon or Tues) ~ (01328) 738188 ~ Children welcome ~ Dogs allowed in bar ~ Open 12-2.30, 7-11; 12-3, 7-10.30 Sun; closed Mon and Tues ~ www.jollyfarmersnorfolk.co.uk
Recommended by Linda Miller and Derek Greentree, Revd John E Cooper, R L Borthwick

NORWICH
Eagle

TG2207   Map 5

Newmarket Road (A11, between A140 and A147 ring roads); NR2 2HN

Popular pub with a variety of seating areas for both drinking and dining, real ales, lots of coffees, wines by the glass and quite a choice of fairly priced food

At peak times, this well run pub is extremely busy, so it's just as well that there are lots of different seating areas both downstairs and upstairs. As well as comfortable sofas and armchairs by the open fire in its ornate fireplace, there are white-painted chairs around pine tables on tiled or stripped-wood flooring, cream paintwork above a red dado and more sofas and straightforward pubby seating in a cosy end room. There's also a low-ceilinged dining room. Another dining room, with high-backed brown leather chairs around various tables on pale floorboards, is accessed from a spiral staircase in the bar. Greene King IPA, Sharps Doom Bar and a house beer from Bass called Eagles Nest on handpump, and decent wines; background music. A covered terrace with chrome and bentwood chairs and wooden tables leads on to a sunny terrace with picnic-sets and a smart barbecue, and there are more seats on grass.

Popular food includes sandwiches, whole baked camembert with thyme and orange, creamy garlic mushrooms on toast, salmon and caper fishcakes, ham with duck eggs and chips, a tart of the day, beer-battered haddock and chips, steak and mushroom pie, aubergine, courgette and gorgonzola in a filo case, chicken with a cider and wholegrain mustard sauce on tagliatelle, calves liver and bacon, a mixed grill, and puddings. *Benchmark main dish: slow roast pork belly £11.95. Two-course evening meal £1675.00.*

Free house ~ Licensee Nigel Booty ~ Real ale ~ Bar food (12-2.30(4 Sun), 6-9) ~ Restaurant ~ (01603) 624173 ~ Children welcome ~ Dogs allowed in bar ~ Open 11-11 ~ www.theeaglepub.co.uk *Recommended by David Carr*

It's very helpful if you let us know up-to-date food prices when you report on pubs.

NORWICH   TG2109   Map 5

Fat Cat

West End Street; NR2 4NA

A place of pilgrimage for beer lovers, and open all day

A visit to this enormously popular and friendly pub is a bit like coming to a private beer festival, as the knowledgeable landlord and his helpful staff keep an amazing range of up to 30 quickly changing real ales. On handpump or tapped from the cask in a stillroom behind the bar – big windows reveal all – are their own beers, the Fat Cat Brewery Tap Bitter, Cougar, Hell Cat, Honey Ale, Marmalade Cat and Wild Cat, as well as Adnams Bitter, Batemans Salem Porter, Burton Bridge Festival Ale, Crouch Vale Yakima Gold, Dark Star American Pale Ale, Elgoods Black Dog Mild, Epping (Pitfield) Pale Ale, Fullers ESB, Grain Redwood, Greene King Abbot, Milestone Dark Galleon, Oakham Bishops Farewell, St Peters Golden Ale, Stonehenge Old Smokey, Thornbridge Jaipur, Timothy Taylors Landlord and Woodfordes Wherry. You'll also find imported draught beers and lagers, over 50 bottled beers from around the world plus ciders and perries. There's a lively atmosphere at busy times, maybe with tranquil lulls in the middle of the afternoon, and a good mix of cheerful customers. The no-nonsense furnishings include plain scrubbed pine tables and simple solid seats, lots of brewery memorabilia, bric-a-brac and stained-glass. There are tables outside.

Bar food consists of rolls and good pies at lunchtime (not Sunday). *Benchmark main dish: pork pies £1.60*

Own brew ~ Licensee Colin Keatley ~ Real ale ~ Bar food (filled rolls available until sold out; not Sun) ~ No credit cards ~ (01603) 624364 ~ Children allowed until 6pm ~ Dogs allowed in bar ~ Open 12-11; 11-midnight Sat ~ www.fatcatpub.co.uk
Recommended by Andy and Claire Barker, Sue Rowland, David Carr, the Didler

SALTHOUSE   TG0743   Map 8

Dun Cow

A149 Blakeney–Sheringham (Purdy Street, junction with Bard Hill); NR25 7XA

Relaxed seaside pub, a good all-rounder

Picnic-table sets out on the front grass look across the bird-filled salt marshes towards the sea, and there are more tables in a sheltered back courtyard, with yet more in an orchard garden beyond. The flint-walled bar consists of a pair of high-raftered rooms opened up into one area, stone tiles in the back half where regulars congregate by the serving counter, carpet matting at the front. There are log fireplaces at each end, scrubbed tables, one very high-backed settle as well as country kitchen chairs and elegant little red-padded dining chairs, with big sailing-ship and other prints on the walls. With well kept Adnams Southwold, Greene King IPA and Woodfordes Wherry on handpump, and quick service by friendly helpful staff, it has a good relaxed atmosphere. There's a pool table in a separate games room. We have not yet heard from readers who have stayed in their self-catering bedrooms.

Interesting food might include sandwiches, crab and avocado mousse, grilled halloumi with watercress, pine nuts and croûtons, cottage pie, deep-fried breaded scallops in a basket with home-made tartare sauce, sticky back ribs with smoked barbecue sauce, whole sole with wild garlic pesto, braised lamb shank with chickpeas and chorizo, and puddings such as lemon posset with shortbread and treacle tart with vanilla ice-cream. *Benchmark main dish: smoked collar of local bacon with cauliflower cheese and fried duck egg £3.40. Two-course evening meal £17.50.*

Punch ~ Lease Daniel Goff ~ Real ale ~ Bar food (12-9) ~ (01263) 740467 ~ Children welcome ~ Dogs welcome ~ Open 11-11 ~ Bedrooms: /£65B ~ www.salthouseduncow.com *Recommended by Philip and Susan Philcox, DF and NF, Carolyn Newman, Fren Ewing, Brian Glozier*

SEDGEFORD
TF7036   Map 8
King William IV ♀ ⇑
B1454, off A149 Kings Lynn–Hunstanton; PE36 5LU

Carefully run inn with enthusiastic owners, plenty of space, a wide choice of bar food, four real ales, good wines by the glass and attractive covered outdoor dining area; bedrooms

With several nearby beaches, fantastic bird-watching and lots to do only a few miles away, this well run inn is just the place to stay for a few days – the bedrooms are comfortable and the breakfasts rather special. The bar is relaxed and homely and there are several intimate dining areas decorated with paintings of the north Norfolk coast, high-backed dark leather dining chairs around a mix of pine tables on the slate tiles, log fires, Adnams Bitter, Greene King Abbot and Old Speckled Hen, and Woodfordes Nelsons Revenge or Wherry on handpump and nine good wines by the glass; friendly obliging staff. The Gallery Restaurant has been refurbished this year, and as well as seats on the terrace and picnic-sets under parasols on the grass there's an attractive covered dining area surrounded by flowering tubs.

Along with filled baguettes and baps, the popular food might include garlic mushrooms, pâté with red onion marmalade, moules marinière, wild mushroom tagliatelle, gammon and pineapple, tuna loin salad, venison with a whisky and pepper sauce, parmesan-crusted bass in pesto sauce, daily specials like seafood linguine, liver and bacon and beef bourguignon, and puddings such as apple, mascarpone and cinnamon puff with butterscotch sauce and chocolate tart. *Benchmark main dish: steak in ale pie £11.50. Two-course evening meal £17.50.*

Free house ~ Licensee Nick Skerritt ~ Real ale ~ Bar food (12-2(2.30 Sun), 6.30-9(8.30 Sun); not Mon lunchtime except bank hols) ~ Restaurant ~ (01485) 571765 ~ Children allowed but not after 6.30pm ~ Dogs allowed in bar and bedrooms ~ Open 11-11(6-11 Mon); 12-10.30 Sun; closed Mon lunchtime except bank holidays ~ Bedrooms: £60B/£105B ~ www.thekingwilliamsedgeford.co.uk *Recommended by Tracey and Stephen Groves, Simon and Amanda Southwell, R C Vincent*

SNETTISHAM
TF6834   Map 8
Rose & Crown ⑪ ♀ ⇑
Village signposted from A149 King's Lynn–Hunstanton just N of Sandringham; coming in on the B1440 from the roundabout just N of village, take first left turn into Old Church Road; PE31 7LX

Particularly well run old pub, log fires and interesting furnishings, imaginative food, a fine range of drinks and stylish seating on heated terrace; well equipped bedrooms

In warm weather, the garden here is a lovely place for a drink or a meal. There are stylish blue café-style chairs and tables under cream parasols on the terrace, outdoor heaters and colourful herbaceous borders; there's also a wooden galleon-shaped climbing fort for children. Inside, the smallest of the three bars is a pale grey colour with coir flooring and old prints of King's Lynn and Sandringham. The other two bars each have their own character: an old-fashioned beamed front bar with black settles on a tiled floor and a big log fire, and a back bar with another large log fire and the landlord's sporting trophies and old sports equipment (which are being slowly edged out to make way for photos of the pub cricket team). There's also the Garden Room, with inviting wicker-based wooden chairs, careful lighting and a quote by Dr Johnson in old-fashioned rolling script on a huge wall board, and a residents' lounge (liked by non-residents, too) with squashy armchairs and sofas, rugs on the floor, newspapers, magazines, jigsaws and board games. Adnams Bitter, Fullers London Pride and Woodfordes Wherry on handpump, ten wines by the glass and cider and perry; staff are neatly dressed and courteous. Two of the comfortable bedrooms are downstairs and there are disabled lavatories and wheelchair ramps. The Bank House in King's Lynn is under the same management and also worth a visit.

🍴 Using carefully sourced local produce, the interesting, highly thought of food might include sandwiches, oxtail terrine with carrot purée and garlic crostini, seared scallops with crispy pork belly, wasabi cream and chilli and lime sherbert, butternut squash and toasted pine nut risotto, chilli con carne with nachos, sour cream, jalapeno and tomato salsa, bangers and mash with onion gravy, steak burger with bacon, cheese and red pepper ketchup, moules marinière, chicken breast with pancetta and little gem stew, beef onglet with confit shallot and wild garlic butter, and puddings like lavender crème brûlée with lemon shortbread and chocolate fondant with pear bombe. *Benchmark main dish: fish and chips with minted mushy peas £10.50. Two-course evening meal £17.45.*

Free house ~ Licensee Anthony Goodrich ~ Real ale ~ Bar food (12-2(2.30 weekends), 7-9) ~ Restaurant ~ (01485) 541382 ~ Children welcome ~ Dogs welcome ~ Open 11-11; 12-10.30 Sun ~ Bedrooms: £70B/£90B ~ www.roseandcrownsnettisham.co.uk
Recommended by Jeff and Wendy Williams, Henry Fryer, J F M and M West, John Wooll, Lesley and Peter Barrett, Mark, Amanda, Luke and Jake Sheard, Peter and Jean Hoare, Pat and Graham Williamson, Tracey and Stephen Groves, David Eberlin, R C Vincent, Pauline Fellows and Simon Robbins

STANHOE
Duck 🍴 🛏

TF8037 Map 8

B1155 Docking–Burnham Market; PE31 8QD

Smart candlelit country dining pub, good food (especially fish), appealing layout and attentive staff; bedrooms

Past the village duckpond and surrounded by quiet farmland, this smart and neatly kept dining pub is close to the beaches of Brancaster and Holkham. The original bar is charming and atmospheric and now forms three cosy dining areas with beams, country-kitchen chairs and pews around wooden tables on bare boards or black slate flooring, a couple of woodburning stoves and original oil paintings by local artists. Elgoods Cambridge and Pageant on handpump from a fine slab-topped counter and several wines by the glass; good service. There's also a garden room and seats under apple trees in the pretty garden. As well as well appointed bedrooms they have a site for touring caravans. This is sister pub to the Bell in Wiveton.

Using local game and with some emphasis on fresh fish, the fairly priced food includes lunchtime bruschette, game terrine with piccalilli, goats cheese and red onion en croûte, beer-battered haddock, chicken and bacon linguine, butternut squash risotto, crispy pork belly with caramelised apple, black pudding and potato purée, fillet of bream with white wine velouté and dill mash, 28-day-aged rib-eye beef with garlic butter and pepper sauce, venison casserole with red wine and port, and puddings. *Benchmark main dish: local mussels £11.45. Two-course evening meal £20.25.*

Elgoods ~ Tenant Berni Morritt ~ Bar food (12-2.15, 6-9.15; not Sun evening, not Mon) ~ (01485) 518330 ~ Children welcome ~ Dogs allowed in bar ~ Open 12-11 ~ Bedrooms: /£95S ~ www.duckinn.co.uk *Recommended by Tracey and Stephen Groves, Paul Clarke-Scholes*

STIFFKEY

TF9643 Map 8

Red Lion ♀ £ ⇔

A149 Wells–Blakeney; NR23 1AJ

Appealing layout, perky atmosphere, good staff, comfortable bedrooms and heated courtyard

Cheerful and friendly, the tiled-floor front bar has a big log fireplace, cushioned pews and other pubby seats, local landscape photographs and shelves of books. A room off has some high-backed stripped settles brightened up with scatter cushions as well as more conventional chairs around its informal candlelit tables, and on the right, another room with dark panelling, maroon paintwork and lots more photographs contains a splendid curved and winged settle. On our most recent inspection visit, some of the loudest laughter came from the pair of back dining rooms, one of them almost a flint-walled conservatory. They have good wines by the glass, a couple of dozen malt whiskies and Woodfordes Wherry, Nelsons Revenge and a beer brewed for them on handpump, served by staff who obviously get on really well with each other, which contributes a lot to the atmosphere. A big gravelled courtyard, sheltered and partly canopied, has heaters for its picnic-table sets, with more tables on a covered heated deck. The bedrooms have their own balconies or terraces, and there are scenic coastal walks nearby.

Good food might include sandwiches, chicken liver pâté with onion jam, wild mushrooms in garlic butter with parmesan, vegetarian lasagne, beefburger with blue cheese and bacon, local mussels in garlic, white wine and cream, steak and Guinness pie, fresh crab salad, spicy lamb meatballs in rich tomato sauce on pasta, rib-eye steak with garlic and mustard butter, and puddings like warm chocolate brownie and apple and blackberry crumble. *Benchmark main dish: beer-battered cod and chips £11.95. Two-course evening meal £17.25.*

Free house ~ Licensee Stephen Franklin ~ Real ale ~ Bar food (12-2.30, 6-9; all day Sun) ~ (01328) 830552 ~ Children welcome ~ Dogs welcome ~ Open 11am-midnight ~ Bedrooms: £90B/£110B ~ www.stiffkey.com *Recommended by Jeremy and Ruth Preston-Hoar, Anthony Longden, Peter and Giff Bennett, David Carr, Neil Shaw, Sandy Butcher, Roy Hoing, Chris Johnson, Jim Farmer, David and Judy Robison, W K Wood, Pauline Fellows and Simon Robbins*

Bedroom prices normally include full english breakfast, VAT and any inclusive service charge that we know of. Prices before the '/' are for single rooms, after two people in double or twin (B includes a private bath, S a private shower). If there is no '/', the prices are only for twin or double rooms (as far as we know there are no singles).

STOW BARDOLPH
Hare Arms ♀

TF6205 Map 5

Just off A10 N of Downham Market; PE34 3HT

Long-serving licensees in this bustling village pub, real ales, good mix of customers, tasty bar food and a big back garden

The hands-on and warmly friendly licensees have now been running this neatly kept village pub for 36 years – and it's as good as ever, our enthusiastic readers tell us. The bar has some interesting bric-a-brac such as old advertising signs and golf clubs suspended from the ceiling, as well as dark pubby furniture and comfortable built-in wall seats, a good log fire and a cheerful, bustling atmosphere. There's also a well planted conservatory where families are allowed. From the central bar they serve Greene King IPA, Abbot and Old Speckled Hen and a couple of guests like Belhaven Robbie Burns and Robinsons Unicorn on handpump, nine wines by the glass and several malt whiskies. There are plenty of seats in the large garden behind, with more in the pretty front garden; you might see a peacock or two, some chickens wandering around and perhaps the plump, elderly pub cat. Church Farm Rare Breeds Centre is a five-minute walk away and is open all year.

Using their own eggs and other local produce, the well liked bar food includes lunchtime sandwiches, a curry of the day, sausages with caramelised onion mash and red wine gravy, barbecue spare ribs, interesting salad bowls with paprika chicken and a thyme and garlic dressing and red mullet fillets in tempura batter with a lime and curry flavoured mayonnaise dip, specials such as nut cutlets with a spicy chilli dip, pork steak with an apricot and tarragon sauce, lamb shank with cider, apple, rosemary and cannellini beans and smoked haddock fillet with a wholegrain mustard and cheese topping, and puddings. *Benchmark main dish: steak and peppercorn pie £11.00. Two-course evening meal £18.00.*

Greene King ~ Tenants David and Trish McManus ~ Real ale ~ Bar food (12-2, 6-10; all day Sun) ~ Restaurant ~ (01366) 382229 ~ Children allowed away from main bar ~ Open 11-2.30, 6-11; 12-10.30 Sun ~ www.theharearms.co.uk *Recommended by John Saville, Henry Fryer, Lesley and Peter Barrett, Phil and Jane Hodson, John Wooll, Malcolm and Barbara Southwell, R C Vincent, Tracey and Stephen Groves, Peter and Jean Hoare, David and Sharon Collison, John Honnor*

SWANTON MORLEY
Darbys ◀

TG0217 Map 8

B1147 NE of Dereham; NR20 4NY

Unspoilt country local with six real ales, old farming equipment, tasty bar food and children's play area

Once a pair of 18th-c cottages, this creeper-covered brick pub has a fine choice of changing real ales and a friendly atmosphere. The long bare-boarded country-style bar has a comfortable lived-in feel with big stripped-pine tables and chairs, lots of gin traps and farming memorabilia, a good log fire (with the original bread oven alongside) and tractor seats with folded sacks lining the long, attractive serving counter. Adnams Bitter and Broadside, Beeston Afternoon Delight, Woodfordes Wherry and two guests like Beeston Squirrels Nuts and Woodfordes Nelsons Revenge tapped from the cask, several wines by the glass and quite a few coffees; good, efficient service. A step up through a little doorway by the fireplace takes you through to the attractive dining room with neat, dark tables and chairs on the wooden floor; the children's room has a toy box and a glassed-over well, floodlit from inside. Background music, TV and board games. There are picnic-sets and a children's play area in the back garden. Plenty to do locally (B&B is available in carefully converted farm buildings a few minutes away) and the family also own the adjoining 720-acre estate. They also have a well equipped camping site.

🍴 Good food at reasonable prices might include sandwiches (there's a soup and a sandwich deal), smoked trout with gooseberry relish, country pâté with melba toast, lamb or beef burger with chips, mushroom and sweet potato risotto, pasta with shrimps, mussels, cockles and calamari, chicken marinated in lemon and thyme with bacon, lamb cutlets with shallots and a red wine jus, daily specials, and puddings like chocolate and almond torte with amaretto cream and panna cotta with roasted rhubarb and ginger shortbread. *Benchmark main dish: chicken and mozzarella bake £10.75. Two-course evening meal £16.00.*

Free house ~ Licensees John Carrick and Louise Battle ~ Real ale ~ Bar food (12-2.15, 6.30-9.45; all day weekends) ~ Restaurant ~ (01362) 637647 ~ Children welcome ~ Dogs allowed in bar ~ monthly live music ~ Open 11.30-3, 6-11; 11.30-11 Fri and Sat; 12-10.30 Sun ~ Bedrooms: £35S(£40B)/£60(£70S)(£75B) ~ www.darbysfreehouse.com
Recommended by Roy Hoing, Richard Gibbs

THORNHAM   TF7343   Map 8

Lifeboat 🍺 🛏

A149 by Kings Head, then first left; PE36 6LT

Good mix of customers and lots of character in traditional inn, real ales and super surrounding walks; bedrooms

This neatly whitewashed inn faces half a mile of coastal sea flats, and there are lots of surrounding walks. Inside, the rambling rooms have a great deal of character, with heavy beams, a mix of seating ranging from low settles and pews to more ornate dining chairs and cushioned window seats on rugs or tiles, and open fires and woodburning stoves. Throughout there are reed-slashers and other antique farm tools, an array of traps and yokes, oars and paddles, lighting by antique paraffin lamps, and fresh flowers and candles. Adnams Bitter, Greene King Abbot and IPA, Woodfordes Wherry and a couple of guest beers on handpump, ten wines by the glass and several malt whiskies; one bench has an antique penny-in-the-hole game. Up some steps from the conservatory with its ancient vine there are seats on a sunny terrace and at the front of the building are some modern grey seats and tables and picnic-sets under parasols.

🍴 Highly thought of food using seasonal local produce includes sandwiches, salt and pepper calamari with lemon mayonnaise, corned beef hash with a poached duck egg and béarnaise sauce, caesar salad with or without chicken, beef burger with melted cheese, gherkin and tomato relish, beer-battered haddock with tartare sauce, hickory pork ribs with barbecue sauce and coleslaw, dijonnaise lamb rump with rosemary potatoes, a cold fish platter, and puddings such as dark chocolate torte and knickerbocker glory. *Benchmark main dish: seasonal mussels £10.50. Two-course evening meal £19.00.*

Free house ~ Licensee Helen Stafford ~ Real ale ~ Bar food (12-2.30, 6.30-9.30; lighter meals 3-5.30) ~ Restaurant ~ (01485) 512236 ~ Children welcome ~ Dogs allowed in bar and bedrooms ~ Open 11-11(midnight Sat) ~ Bedrooms: £90S/£130S ~ www.lifeboatinnthornham.com *Recommended by Tracey and Stephen Groves, Mike and Sue Loseby, the Didler, David Brown, David and Ruth Hollands*

THORNHAM
TF7343   Map 8

Orange Tree 🍴 ♀ ⇌

Church Street/A149; PE36 6LY

Norfolk Dining Pub of the Year

Nice combination of friendly bar and good contemporary dining

With a genuinely warm welcome, excellent food and a relaxed, chatty bar, it's no wonder that this well run pub is so popular. There are stripped beams and a low ceiling, a log fire, a labrador called Poppy, comfortable leather and basket-weave chairs on the tiled floor, Adnams, Woodfordes Wherry and a guest like Crouch Vale Brewers Gold on handpump, 24 wines by the glass and good courteous service. Much the same relaxed feel runs through the more extensive two-part dining area, which is cheerfully contemporary in style, partly carpeted, with colourful neat modern seating around plain tables, and artworks above a dark grey dado; this part may have background music. The main garden, shaded by tall sycamores, has picnic-sets under white canvas parasols and a round smokers' shelter in one discreet corner; a second area has safely enclosed play things. The courtyard bedrooms make a good base for the lovely north Norfolk coast.

 Inventive and extremely good, the food, which uses local seafood and seasonal produce, might include lunchtime sandwiches (not Sunday), scampi and a scallop in an edible basket with a crab and lime sherbert curd, seared pigeon salad with grilled chorizo, green beans, hazelnuts and basil pesto, chicken, prawn or vegetable lime leaf and coconut curry, black treacle-roasted ham with fried eggs and handcut chips, rare-breed burger with cheddar and smoked onion and pepper jus, moroccan-spiced lamb with sweet potato fondant and spiced chickpeas, corn-fed chicken and wild mushroom pie with smoked pancetta mash, and puddings such as an assiette of chocolate and 'the fairground' (bubblegum panna cotta, baby toffee apples, candyfloss, butterscotch popcorn and chocolate covered honeycomb). *Benchmark main dish: bass on mixed seafood risotto £18.50.* Two-course evening meal £20.00.

Punch ~ Lease Mark Goode ~ Real ale ~ Bar food (12-9.30) ~ Restaurant ~ (01485) 512213 ~ Children welcome ~ Dogs allowed in bar and bedrooms ~ Open 11-11(midnight Sat); 12-10.30 Sun ~ Bedrooms: /£85B ~ www.theorangetreethornham.co.uk
Recommended by Emma Beacham, Tracey and Stephen Groves, John F Knutton

THORPE MARKET
TG2434   Map 8

Gunton Arms

Cromer Road; NR11 8TZ

Impressive place with an easy-going atmosphere, open fires and antiques in bar and dining rooms, real ales, interesting food and friendly staff; bedrooms

Surrounded by a 1,000-acre deer park, this rather stately place was rescued from ruin by an art dealer and his artist wife and opened up a couple of years ago. They describe it as a 'traditional pub with bedrooms' – but it's far more grand and interesting than that. The large entrance hall sets the scene, and throughout the atmosphere is informal and relaxed but definitely gently upmarket. The simply furnished bar has dark pubby chairs and tables on the wooden floor, a log fire, a long settle beside the pool table and high stools against the mahogany counter, where they serve Adnams Bitter and Broadside, Woodfordes Nelsons Revenge and Wherry and Yetmans Red on handpump, several wines by the glass and apple juice made on the estate; staff are chatty and friendly. Heavy curtains on a pole line the open doorway that leads into a dining room with vast antlers on the wall above the big log fire (they often cook over this) and straightforward chairs around scrubbed tables on stone tiles. There's also a lounge with comfortable old leather armchairs and a sofa on a fine rug in front of yet another log fire, some genuine antiques, big house plants and standard lamps, a more formal restaurant with candles and napery, and two homely sitting rooms for residents. Many of the walls are painted dark red and hung with all manner of artwork and big mirrors. The bedrooms have many original fittings but no TV or tea-making facilities.

Robust food using their own venison, local fish, shellfish and foraged plants and seashore vegetables might include deep-fried cod cheeks with caper mayonnaise, local crab on toast, smoked salmon with irish soda bread, duck hash with a fried duck egg, whiting fish fingers with chips and mushy peas, chicken, bacon and leek pie, wild mushroom risotto, linguine with mussels and chilli, venison sausages with onion gravy, mixed grill of fallow deer with rowanberry jelly, and puddings like chocolate tart with honeycomb and plum bakewell pudding. *Benchmark main dish: venison mixed grill £15.50. Two-course evening meal £22.00.*

Free house ~ Licensee Simone Baker ~ Real ale ~ Bar food (all day) ~ Restaurant ~ (01263) 832010 ~ Children welcome ~ Dogs allowed in bar and bedrooms ~ Open 12-11(10.30 Sun) ~ Bedrooms: /£120S ~ www.theguntonarms.co.uk *Recommended by Richard Gibbs*

WELLS-NEXT-THE-SEA   TF9143   Map 8
Globe
The Buttlands; NR23 1EU

Attractive contemporary layout, good food and drink and nice back courtyard; bedrooms

Just a short walk from the quay, this is a handsome Georgian inn with a friendly, bustling atmosphere. There's plenty of space and the opened-up rooms are relaxed and contemporary and spread spaciously back from the front bar with its comfortable sofas and armchairs. Three big bow windows look over to a green lined by tall lime trees, there are tables on oak boards, walls in grey and cream hung with drawings on driftwood of quirky fish and shellfish and well judged modern lighting. Adnams Bitter, Broadside and Ghost Ship on handpump, a thoughtful choice of wines and nice coffee; background music, board games and TV. An attractive heated back courtyard has colourful hanging baskets and dark green cast-iron furniture on pale flagstones among terracotta tubs with box balls.

Enjoyable bar food includes lunchtime sandwiches, local mussels, squid and prawn stew, terrine of confit chicken with quince jelly, game pie with celeriac mash, risotto of wild mushrooms and truffle oil with blackberry and pear salad, breast of pheasant, mushroom duxelles and spiced parsnips, king prawn and monkfish curry, 28-day-aged rump steak with triple cooked chips, onion rings and peppercorn sauce, and puddings like passion fruit crème brûlée and chocolate brownie with pistachio ice-cream. *Benchmark main dish: beer-battered fish and chips £12.50. Two-course evening meal £20.00.*

Free house ~ Licensee Viscount Coke ~ Real ale ~ Bar food (12-2.30, 6.30-9) ~ Restaurant ~ (01328) 710206 ~ Children welcome ~ Dogs welcome ~ Jazz every 3rd Sun evening ~ Open 11-11 ~ Bedrooms: /£120S ~ www.holkham.co.uk/globe
Recommended by Jeremy and Ruth Preston-Hoar, David Carr, Chris Johnson, W K Wood

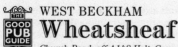

WEST BECKHAM   TG1439   Map 8

Wheatsheaf

Church Road; off A148 Holt–Cromer; NR25 6NX

Traditional pub with several real ales, proper home cooking, and seats in the garden

This is a warmly friendly brick-built pub in a quiet village. There's a genuine welcome for all – dogs included – and the newish landlord works hard at making all his customers feel at home. The bars have beams, standing timbers, cottagey doors, lots of horsebrasses and a couple of roaring winter log fires, and the furnishings are pleasantly traditional with plenty of wheelback chairs, settles and comfortably cushioned wall seats around dark wood pubby tables. Greene King IPA and Old Speckled Hen and Woodfordes Wherry on handpump and quite a few wines by the glass. The charming garden has a covered terrace and seats both here and on the grass.

Well liked food includes filled baguettes, breaded whitebait with home-made tartare sauce, mushrooms in a creamy tarragon sauce, beer-battered haddock, home-made beef burger with their own relish, slow-roasted pork belly with bubble and squeak, apple purée and cider jus, chicken carbonara, sausages of the week, and puddings such as warm chocolate brownie with white chocolate sauce and mixed berry eton mess. *Benchmark main dish: steak in ale pie £11.95. Two-course evening meal £17.00.*

Free house ~ Licensee Matt Lock ~ Real ale ~ Bar food (12-2,6-9(8 Sun)) ~ (01263) 822110 ~ Children welcome ~ Dogs welcome ~ Open 12-3, 6-11(may open all day in summer); 12-10.30 Sun ~ www.thewheatsheafwestbeckham.co.uk *Recommended by Jim Farmer, John Cook, Tony Middis, Philip and Susan Philcox*

WIVETON   TG0442   Map 8

Bell 🍴 🛏

Blakeney Road; NR25 7TL

Busy, open-plan dining pub, drinkers welcomed too, local beers, fine food, and seats outside; bedrooms

Even when this well run dining pub is really busy – which it deservedly usually is – you can be sure of a warm welcome from the helpful landlord and his friendly staff. It's mainly open plan throughout and there are some fine old beams, an attractive mix of dining chairs around wooden tables on the stripped wooden floor, a log fire and prints on the yellow walls. The sizeable conservatory has smart beige dining chairs around wooden tables on coir flooring and the atmosphere is chatty and relaxed. Elgoods Cambridge Bitter, Woodfordes Wherry and Yetmans Red on handpump, and several wines by the glass. Outside, there are picnic-sets on grass in front of the building looking across to the church, and at the back, stylish wicker tables and chairs on several decked areas are set among decorative box hedging. The bedrooms are comfortable and they also have a self-catering cottage to let.

Well presented and enjoyable, the food might include terrine of chicken, guineafowl and wild mushrooms with celeriac remoulade, truffle oil and toasted brioche, local rabbit and pancetta salad with marinated pears and toasted chestnuts, steak burger topped with smoked cheese, beer-battered haddock with home-made tartare sauce, slow-cooked pork belly with black pudding mash and an apple and cider jus, chicken and cashew nut korma, cod with salmon, local mussels, parsley mash and a white wine velouté and venison casserole with pork and thyme sausage balls. *Benchmark main dish: local mussels £11.95. Two-course evening meal £20.45.*

Free house ~ Licensee Berni Morritt ~ Real ale ~ Bar food (12-2.15, 6-9) ~ Restaurant ~ (01263) 740101 ~ Children welcome ~ Dogs allowed in bar ~ Open 12-11 ~ Bedrooms: /£95S ~ www.wivetonbell.co.uk *Recommended by Michael and Maggie Betton, Peter and Giff Bennett, Phil Revell, David Carr, Sandy Butcher, Alan Sutton, Jeremy King, Michael Sargent, Roy Hoing, Peter and Eleanor Kenyon, Simon Rodway, Revd Michael Vockins, Roger and Gillian Holmes, John Wooll*

WOODBASTWICK   TG3214 Map 8

Fur & Feather

Off B1140 E of Norwich; NR13 6HQ

Full range of first-class beers from next-door Woodfordes brewery, friendly service and popular bar food

The beers in this thatched cottagey pub are in tip-top condition as the Woodfordes brewery is right next door. Tapped from the cask by friendly, efficient staff, they include Admirals Reserve, Headcracker, Mardlers, Nelsons Revenge, Norfolk Nip, Norfolk Nog, Once Bittern, Sundew, and Wherry; you can also visit the brewery shop. Also a dozen wines by the glass and around the same number of malt whiskies. The style and atmosphere are not what you'd expect of a brewery tap as it's set out more like a comfortable and roomy dining pub; background music. There are seats and tables out in a pleasant garden. This is a lovely estate village.

As well as serving breakfast from 10-11.30am, the reliably good bar food includes sandwiches, chicken liver pâté with red onion chutney, butterfly king prawns with garlic and lemon mayonnaise, their popular pies like rabbit, bacon and thyme, venison and stilton and lamb, mint, rosemary and garlic, speciality burgers, root vegetable and chestnut crumble, honey-roasted ham with a duck egg, steak and kidney pudding, beer-battered haddock, slow-cooked pork belly with wholegrain mustard mash and red wine gravy, and puddings like Baileys crème brûlée and jam sponge with custard. *Benchmark main dish: home-made pies £11.75. Two-course evening meal £18.00.*

Woodfordes ~ Tenant Tim Ridley ~ Real ale ~ Bar food (10-9) ~ Restaurant ~ (01603) 720003 ~ Children welcome but must be well behaved ~ Open 9-11(10.30 Sun); 10-10 in winter ~ www.thefurandfeatherinn.co.uk *Recommended by Andy and Claire Barker, David Carr, Roy Hoing*

Also Worth a Visit in Norfolk

Besides the fully inspected pubs, you might like to try these pubs that have been recommended to us and described by readers. Do tell us what you think of them: feedback@goodguides.com

AYLMERTON   TG1840
Roman Camp (01263) 838291
Holt Road (A148); NR11 8QD Large late Victorian inn with comfortable panelled bar, cosy sitting room off with warm fire, and light airy dining room, good choice of enjoyable fairly priced food, well kept mainstream ales, helpful staff; children welcome, attractive

sheltered garden behind with terrace and pond, 15 bedrooms. *(David Carr, Judith and David Salter)*

AYLSHAM   TG1926
★ **Black Boys** (01263) 732122
Market Place; off B1145; NR11 6EH Small hotel with imposing Georgian façade and informal open-plan bar, good generously

served food (all day) from snacks up, Adnams and guests such as Timothy Taylors Landlord, Woodfordes Wherry and Wychwood Hobgoblin, decent wines in three glass sizes, comfortable seats and plenty of tables, high beams, part carpet, part bare boards, helpful young uniformed staff; children and dogs welcome, modern seats in front by market place, more behind, bedrooms, open all day. *(Judy Buckley, John Wooll, John Cook, Dr and Mrs R G J Telfer, David Carr and others)*

BANNINGHAM TG2129
Crown (01263) 733534
Colby Road; NR11 7DY Welcoming 17th-c beamed pub, good choice of enjoyable sensibly priced food, well kept Greene King and local guests, decent wines; children and dogs welcome, garden jazz festival Aug, open all day Sun. *(Anon)*

BAWBURGH TG1508
✶ **Kings Head** (01603) 744977
Harts Lane; A47 just W of Norwich then B1108; NR9 3LS Bustling 17th-c pub with small low-beamed rooms, leather sofas and nice mix of old tables on wood-strip floors, knocked through open fire and woodburners, interesting food (not Sun evening, winter Mon) from listed suppliers, Adnams, Woodfordes Wherry and a guest, several wines by the glass, helpful friendly staff; background music; children welcome, dogs in bar, garden tables, little green opposite, open all day. *(Alan Bulley, Anthony Barnes)*

BINHAM TF9839
Chequers (01328) 830297
B1388 SW of Blakeney; NR21 0AL Long low-beamed 17th-c local with coal fires at each end, sturdy plush seats, nice old local prints and photographs, own-brewed Front Street beers and changing guests, lots of bottled imports, decent house wines, pubby food; children welcome, picnic-sets in front and on back grass, interesting village with huge priory church. *(Chris Johnson, Tracey and Stephen Groves, David Carr, Sandy Butcher)*

BLICKLING TG1728
✶ **Buckinghamshire Arms**
(01263) 732133 *B1354 NW of Aylsham; NR11 6NF* Handsome well run Jacobean inn much visited for its enviable spot by gates to Blickling Hall (NT), small and appealing proper unpretentious bar, lounge set for eating with woodburner, smarter more formal dining room with another woodburner, enjoyable fairly priced food, ales such as Adnams, Fullers, Wolf and Woodfordes kept well, good choice of wines by the glass, attentive cheery young staff; soft background music; children welcome, lots of lawn tables, lovely walks nearby, bedrooms. *(Mrs and Mrs J G Telfer, Dr and Mrs R G J Telfer, David Carr, Simon Elwood, Chris Flynn, Wendy Jones and others)*

BRANCASTER TF7743
✶ **Ship** (01485) 210333
A149; PE31 8AP 18th-c inn (part of the small Flying Kiwi chain) in traditional fishing village, elegant bar with contemporary paintwork and built-in cushioned and planked wall seats, dining area with woodburner, pale settles and nice mix of other furniture on rugs and bare boards, restaurant has unusual Norfolk map wallpaper, plates on a dresser, bookcases, shipping memorabilia and lots of prints, good modern food, Adnams Bitter and Jo C's Norfolk Ale, nice wines by the glass, daily newspapers; background music, TV; children and dogs welcome, seats outside, attractive well equipped bedrooms, open all day. *(Tracey and Stephen Groves, Jeremy and Ruth Preston-Hoar, R C Vincent, Michael and Maggie Betton, Derek Thomas)*

BRANCASTER STAITHE TF7944
✶ **Jolly Sailors** (01485) 210314
Main Road (A149); PE31 8BJ Bustling village pub with own-brewed Brancaster ales (brewery not on site) and guests like Adnams and Woodfordes, Aspall's cider, main bar has traditional pubby furniture on quarry tiles, stripped-stone walls and log fire in brick fireplace, two further snugs with local books and harbour views, comfortably old-fashioned dining lounge, straightforward food (all day in summer), pool room with TV, some live music; children welcome, dogs in bar, serving hatch to terrace, play area, open all day in summer, all day Fri-Sun in winter; they may ask to keep your credit card behind the bar. *(Chris Johnson, John Wooll, David Carr, Revd Michael Vockins, Mike and Linda Hudson)*

BRANCASTER STAITHE TF8044
✶ **White Horse** (01485) 210262
A149 E of Hunstanton; PE31 8BY Very popular well run place – not a pub but does have proper informal front locals' bar; three Brancaster ales and Woodfordes, lots of wines by the glass, stripped furniture, good photographs, bar billiards; middle area with comfortable sofas and newspapers, big airy dining conservatory overlooking tidal marshes, enjoyable all-day bar and restaurant food including plenty of fish, cheerful staff; children welcome, dogs in bar, seats on sun deck with fine views, more under cover on heated terrace, nice seasidey bedrooms, coast path at bottom of garden. *(Jeff and Wendy Williams, Chris Johnson, Tracey and Stephen Groves, Jeremy and Ruth Preston-Hoar, W K Wood, David Carr and others)*

BRESSINGHAM TM0781
Chequers (01379) 687472
Low Road; IP22 2AG Welcoming 16th-c thatched and beamed pub restored after devastating 2009 fire; fresh contemporary refurbishment with informal relaxed atmosphere, good sensibly priced food

from chef/landlord, Adnams beers, friendly efficient service. *(Chris and Tony, S Hyland)*

BRISLEY TF9521
Bell (01362) 668686
B1145; The Green; NR20 5DW 16th-c pub in good spot on edge of sheep-grazed common (England's biggest),long beamed bar with massive log fireplace and some stripped brick, four well kept ales from Greene King stable, decent choice of good home-made food including OAP lunches, separate restaurant; tables out on green; children and dogs welcome; bedrooms. *(Rob Holgate, R C Vincent)*

BROOME TM3591
Artichoke (01986) 893325
Yarmouth Road; NR35 2NZ Eight well kept ales including Adnams and Elgoods, belgian fruit beers and excellent selection of whiskies in properly unpretentious split-level roadside pub, enjoyable traditional home-made food in bar or dining room, friendly helpful staff, wood or flagstone floors, inglenook log fire; dogs welcome, garden picnic-sets, smokers' shelter, closed Mon otherwise open all day. *(Martin Crisp)*

BURNHAM MARKET TF8342
Nelson (01328) 738321
Creake Road; PE31 8EN Restyled dining pub under newish management, good well priced food including interesting vegetarian dishes in bar and restaurant, pleasant efficient service, Greene King IPA, Woodfordes Wherry and a guest, extensive wine list, artwork for sale; children welcome, four attractive bedrooms, two in former outbuilding. *(Mike and Linda Hudson, John Wooll)*

BURNHAM OVERY STAITHE TF8444
Hero (01328) 738334
A149; PE31 8JE Modernised spacious pub welcoming locals and walkers alike, wide choice of interesting up-to-date food from good baguettes up, well priced wines by the glass, Adnams and Woodfordes, good coffee, comfortable pastel décor, woodburner, two dining areas; children and dogs welcome, tables in garden. *(N R White, Mike and Linda Hudson)*

BURNHAM THORPE TF8541
★ Lord Nelson (01328) 738241
Off B1155 or B1355, near Burnham Market; PE31 8HL Neatly kept 17th-c pub with lots of Nelson memorabilia (he was born in this sleepy village), antique high-backed settles on worn red tiles in small bar, smoke ovens in original fireplace, little snug leading off, two dining rooms one with flagstones and open fire, good bar food, Greene King, Woodfordes and a guest tapped from the cask, several wines by the glass, secret rum-based recipes (Nelson's Blood and Lady

Hamilton's Nip); children and dogs welcome, good-sized play area and pétanque in big garden, open all day in summer, closed Mon evening (except school/bank holidays). *(Pam and John Smith, Anthony Barnes, Terry Mizen, Anthony Longden, David Carr, Malcolm and Barbara Southwell and others)*

CASTLE RISING TF6624
Black Horse (01553) 631225
Lynn Road; PE31 6AG All-day dining pub with plenty of tables in two front areas and back dining room, tasty well cooked food including bargain lunchtime offer (Mon-Thurs), friendly efficient staff, real ales such as Adnams, Greene King and Woodfordes, decent choice of wines by the glass, warm winter fire; background music, no dogs; children particularly welcome, close-set tables out under parasols, by church and almshouses in unspoilt pretty village. *(John Wooll, Susan and Nigel Brookes)*

CATFIELD TG3821
Crown (01692) 580128
The Street; NR29 5AA Immaculate archetypal village inn with warmly welcoming landlady, good choice of changing ales, real ciders, enjoyable food from italian chef/landlord; bedrooms, not far from Hickling Broad, closed Mon (except bank holidays when closed Tues). *(Roy Hoing)*

CAWSTON TG1422
Ratcatchers (01603) 871430
Off B1145; Eastgate, S of village; NR10 4HA Popular beamed dining pub with old chairs and fine mix of walnut, beech, elm and oak tables, nooks and crannies, quieter candlelit dining room on right, good well priced food cooked to order, Adnams and Woodfordes, quite a few malt whiskies, friendly attentive service, conservatory; background and some live music, no dogs; children welcome, tables on heated terrace, open all day Sun. *(Dr and Mrs R G J Telfer, David Carr, R C Vincent)*

COCKLEY CLEY TF7904
Twenty Churchwardens
(01760) 721439 *Off A1065 S of Swaffham; PE37 8AN* Friendly nicely informal pub in converted former school next to church, three linked beamed rooms, good open fire, popular home-made food, well kept Adnams; may not take credit cards; tiny unspoilt village. *(Peter and Jean Hoare)*

COLKIRK TF9226
★ Crown (01328) 862172
Village signposted off B1146 S of Fakenham, and off A1065; Crown Road; NR21 7AA Unpretentious bustling local with chatty bar and left-hand dining room, comfortable, cosy and neatly kept with solid furniture on rugs and tiling, lots to look at, open fires, Greene King IPA and Abbot plus a guest, good choice of wines by the

glass, popular food, quick service; children welcome, dogs in bar, picnic-sets on suntrap terrace and in pleasant garden. *(Jim Farmer, Anthony Barnes, John Cook, R C Vincent, R L Borthwick and others)*

COLTISHALL   TG2719
☆ **Kings Head** (01603) 737426
Wroxham Road (B1354); NR12 7EA Welcoming reliable dining pub close to river, good imaginative food especially fish, generous bar snacks and good value lunch deals, friendly helpful service, well kept Adnams, nice wines by the glass, open fire, fishing nets and stuffed fish including a monster pike (personable chef/landlord a keen fisherman); background music; seats outside (noisy road), bedrooms, moorings nearby. *(Julie and Bill Ryan, David and Sue Atkinson, Philip and Susan Philcox)*

COLTON   TG1009
Ugly Bug (01603) 880794
Signed once off A47; NR9 5DG Comfortable country pub with plenty of beamery, plush banquettes and some old enamel signs in extensive carpeted bar, enthusiastic friendly staff, enjoyable food including changing blackboard choice in bar and restaurant, ales from Humpty Dumpty and Theakstons, good value wines, friendly pub dog called Alfie, jazz nights; terrace and big garden with koi carp lake, eight bedrooms, closed Tues lunchtime.
(Peter Hallinan, Robert Watt)

CROMER   TG2242
Red Lion (01263) 514964
Off A149; Tucker Street/Brook Street; NR27 9HD Substantial refurbished Victorian hotel with elevated sea views, original features including panelling and open fires, five well kept ales in bare-boards flint-walled bar, enjoyable food from sandwiches and ciabattas up, good service, restaurant and conservatory; background music; children welcome, disabled facilities, back courtyard tables, 12 bedrooms, open all day. *(David Carr, Tony Middis, N R White, Anna Parrott, Anthony Barnes)*

DERSINGHAM   TF6930
Feathers (01485) 540207
B1440 towards Sandringham; Manor Road; PE31 6LN Solid Jacobean sandstone inn with relaxed modernised dark-panelled bar, well kept Adnams, Bass and a guest, friendly obliging service, log fires, back eating room, more contemporary restaurant, converted stables with pool, darts and machines (live music here Sat fortnightly); background music; children and dogs welcome, large garden with play area, attractive secluded adults' garden with pond, six bedrooms, open all day. *(Tracey and Stephen Groves)*

DOWNHAM MARKET   TF6103
Crown (01366) 382322
Bridge Street; PE38 9DH Popular rambling 17th-c coaching inn, all steps, nooks and crannies, with good log fire in oak-panelled bar, 635 Pathfinder bomber squadron photographs, Adnams, Greene King and guests, reasonably priced food (not Mon lunchtime) from snacks to specials; seats in coachyard, 18 bedrooms, open all day. *(John Wooll, David and Sue Atkinson)*

DOWNHAM MARKET   TF6003
Railway Arms (01366) 386636
At railway station, Railway Road; PE38 9EN Small station bar with tiny adjoining rooms, one with glowing coal fire, another with second-hand bookshop, real ales tapped from the cask, tea, coffee and some snacky food, model train sometimes running around; best to check opening times. *(David and Sue Atkinson, John Wooll)*

EAST BARSHAM   TF9133
White Horse (01328) 820645
B1105 3 miles N of Fakenham; NR21 0LH Extended pub under new management, big log fire in long beamed main bar, steps to other areas, well kept Adnams, enjoyable home-made food including bargain two-course lunch, two small attractive dining rooms; children welcome, bedrooms. *(R C Vincent)*

EDGEFIELD   TG0934
☆ **Pigs** (01263) 587634
Norwich Road; B1149 S of Holt; NR24 2RL Friendly bustling pub with carpeted bar, Adnams, Woodfordes and guests tapped from casks, arches through to simply furnished area with mixed chairs and pews on broad pine boards, airy dining extension in similar style split into stall areas by standing timbers and low brick walls, good enterprising food (all day Sun), games room with bar billiards, also children's playroom; background music; dogs allowed in bar, good wheelchair access, rustic seats and tables on big covered terrace, adventure playground, boules, bedrooms, open all day Sun. *(Anthony Barnes, Jim Farmer, Stuart Phillips, Jeremy King, Roy Hoing, Dr and Mrs R G J Telfer and others)*

ERPINGHAM   TG1931
Erpingham Arms (01263) 761591
Eagle Road; NR11 7QA Refurbished 18th-c brick-built pub with good choice of local beers including Woodfordes, enjoyable food from bar and restaurant menus including lunchtime set deal (not Sun, OAP discount); children and dogs welcome, disabled facilities, front terrace and garden behind with play area, bedrooms planned, open all day weekends, closed Mon.
(Anthony Barnes)

FAKENHAM

TF9129

Oak (01328) 855077

Oak Street; NR21 9DX Pub/restaurant with enjoyable good value food from traditional choices up cooked by landlord/chef, ales such as Winters and Woodfordes, plenty of wines by the glass, modernised open plan bar with leather sofas by gas woodburner, upstairs dining room and evening cellar restaurant; no dogs inside, children welcome, disabled facilities, a few pavement tables, more under parasols on back terrace, open all day summer weekends, closed Sun evening in winter. *(John Wooll)*

GAYTON

TF7219

Crown (01553) 636252

Lynn Road (B1145/B1153); PE32 1PA Low-beamed country pub with plenty of character, unusual old features and charming snug as well as three main areas, good choice of popular sensibly priced food from sandwiches up, Greene King ales, friendly service, sofas and good log fire, games room; dogs welcome in bar, tables in attractive sheltered garden, four bedrooms. *(John Wooll)*

GELDESTON

TM3990

⋆ Locks (01508) 518414

Off A143/A146 NW of Beccles; off Station Road S of village, obscurely signed down long rough track; NR34 0HW Remote candlelit pub at navigable head of River Waveney, ancient tiled-floor core with beams and big log fire, Green Jack and guest ales tapped from casks, good choice of enjoyable food including vegetarian, large extension for summer crowds, weekend live music; riverside garden, moorings, open all day weekends and in summer; in winter closed Mon, Tues and lunchtimes Weds-Fri. *(Richard Martin, the Didler)*

GREAT BIRCHAM

TF7632

⋆ Kings Head (01366) 382229

B1155, S end of village (called and signed Bircham locally); PE31 6RJ More hotel/restaurant than pub, yet with plenty of regulars and four real ales in small attractively contemporary bar with log fire and comfortable sofas, good innovative food including deals in light and airy modern restaurant, friendly helpful staff; TV in bar; tables and chairs out front and back with rustic view, 12 comfortable bedrooms, good breakfast. *(Tracey and Stephen Groves, R C Vincent)*

GREAT CRESSINGHAM

TF8401

⋆ Windmill (01760) 756232

Village signed off A1065 S of Swaffham; Water End; IP25 6NN Interesting pictures and bric-a-brac in warren of rambling linked rooms, plenty of cosy corners, good value fresh bar food from baguettes to steak, Sun roasts, good changing beer range including

Windy Miller Quixote (brewed for the pub), decent wines, plenty of malt whiskies and good coffee, cheery staff, well lit pool room, pub games; background music, big sports TV in side snug; children and dogs welcome, large garden with picnic-sets and good play area, caravan parking, bedroom extension. *(Gordon Smale, Anthony Barnes)*

GREAT YARMOUTH

TG5207

St Johns Head (01493) 843443

North Quay; NR30 1JB Friendly traditional flintstone pub, real ales including bargain Elgoods; pool, sports TV; open all day. *(the Didler)*

HAINFORD

TG2219

Chequers (01603) 891657

Stratton Road; NR10 3AY Comfortable thatched and beamed dining pub in charming setting, wide choice of popular food from baguettes up, four or five well kept ales including Woodfordes and Greene King, polite service; children welcome, well arranged gardens with play area. *(R C Vincent, C Galloway)*

HARLESTON

TM2483

J D Young (01379) 852822

Market Place; IP20 9AD Refurbished hotel/pub (former coaching inn), convivial bar with three local ales, comfortable spacious library-feel dining room with lamps on well spaced tables, open fire, enjoyable good value fresh food all day from breakfast on, friendly efficient staff; sports TV; children welcome, disabled facilities, 11 bedrooms. *(Martin and Pauline Jennings)*

HEACHAM

TF6737

Fox & Hounds (01485) 570345

Station Road; PE31 7EX Unpretentious open-plan pub brewing its own good Fox beers, also well kept guests and Saxon farm cider (regular beer festivals), cheery chatty service, good generous home-made food (not Sun evening) in comfortable bar and spotless light and airy dining area; live music Tues, pool; small garden, open all day. *(Alan Weedon, Tracey and Stephen Groves)*

HEYDON

TG1127

Earle Arms (01263) 587376

Off B1149; NR11 6AD Nice little pub in delightfully unspoilt estate village, well kept Adnams, Woodfordes and a guest, enjoyable food using local fish and meat, racing prints and good log fire in old-fashioned candlelit bar, more formal dining room, attentive service; children welcome, dogs on leads in bar, picnic-sets in small cottagey back garden. *(John Beeken)*

HICKLING

TG4123

Greyhound (01692) 598306

The Green; NR12 0YA Small busy pub with welcoming open fire, enjoyable food including nice crab salad and good Sun roasts in bar and neat restaurant, well kept Woodfordes Wherry, friendly long-serving landlord; well behaved children welcome, pretty garden with terrace tables, bedroom annexe. *(J F M and M West, Roy Hoing, Simon Watkins)*

★Victoria (01328) 711008 HOLKHAM TF8943

A149 near Holkham Hall; NR23 1RG Upmarket but informal small hotel (owned by Holkham Estate), eclectic mix of furnishings including deep low sofas, lighted candles in heavy sticks, big log fire, well kept Adnams Bitter, Woodfordes Wherry and a guest, nice wines and coffee, good local seasonal food, friendly if not speedy service, anglo-indian décor in linked dining rooms (best to book); background music; children welcome, dogs in bar, sheltered courtyard with retractable awning, walks to nature-reserve salt marshes and sea, ten stylish bedrooms, open all day. *(Tony Middis, David Carr, Tracey and Stephen Groves, Mike and Sue Loseby, Michael Sargent, John Honnor and others)*

White Horse (01485) 525512 HOLME NEXT THE SEA TF7043

Kirkgate Street; PE36 6LH Attractive old-fashioned place, cosy and rambling, with warm log fire, ample choice of good generous food including local fish and Sun roasts, reasonable prices, friendly helpful service, Adnams beers and decent wine, two friendly pub dogs and cat; children welcome, small back garden, seats out in front and on lawn opposite. *(John Wooll, Tracey and Stephen Groves, Linda Miller and Derek Greentree)*

Feathers (01263) 712318 HOLT TG0738

Market Place; NR25 6BW Unpretentious hotel with popular locals' bar comfortably extended around original panelled area, open fire, antiques in attractive entrance/reception area, good choice of enjoyable fairly priced food, quick friendly service, Greene King ales and decent wines, good coffee, restaurant and dining conservatory; background music, no dogs; children welcome, 15 comfortable bedrooms, open all day. *(David Carr, D and M T Ayres-Regan)*

Kings Head (01263) 712543 HOLT TG0738

High Street/Bull Street; NR25 6BN Reworked inn with bustling rustic public bar, two roomy back bars and conservatory, enjoyable food including charcoal grilled steaks, prompt friendly service, beers such as Adnams, Humpty Dumpty and Woodfordes, fair choice of wines; some live music, sports TV, pool; children welcome, back terrace with heated smokers' shelter, good-sized garden, three stylish bedrooms, open all day. *(Tracey and Stephen Groves, Jeremy King, Simon Watkins, N R White)*

Recruiting Sergeant (01603) 737077 HORSTEAD TG2619

B1150 just S of Coltishall; NR12 7EE Light, airy and roomily set out roadside pub, enjoyable generously served food from fresh baguettes up including good fish choice, efficient friendly service even though busy, real ales including one brewed for them, impressive choice of reasonably priced wines by the glass, big open fire, brasses and muskets, music-free smaller room; children welcome. *(John Wooll)*

Waterside (01485) 535810 HUNSTANTON TF6740

Beach Terrace Road; PE36 5BQ Former station buffet just above prom, now bar/restaurant with great sea views from conservatory (children welcome here), Adnams and Greene King Abbot, good value wines, straightforward inexpensive tasty food all day from sandwiches up, quick service by friendly uniformed staff, Fri quiz; dogs on leads allowed. *(John Wooll, John Honnor)*

★Hunny Bell (01263) 712300 HUNWORTH TG0735

Signed off B roads S of Holt; NR24 2AA Welcoming carefully furnished 18th-c pub, neat bar with nice mix of cushioned dining chairs around wooden tables, stone floor and woodburner, cosy snug with homely furniture on old tiles, some original stripped-brick walls throughout, another woodburner in high-raftered dining room, good variety of popular well presented food, Adnams Bitter, Greene King Abbot, Woodfordes Wherry and a guest, good informal service from young staff; children and dogs welcome, picnic-sets on terrace overlooking village green, more seats in garden among fruit trees. *(D and M T Ayres-Regan, Roger and Lesley Everett, Jeremy King, Richard and Margaret McPhee, Robert Watt, Brian Glozier and others)*

Walpole Arms (01263) 587258 ITTERINGHAM TG1430

Village signposted off B1354 NW of Aylsham; NR11 7AR Unpretentious 18th-c brick pub close to Blickling Hall, sizeable open-plan beamed bar with stripped-brick walls and mix of dining tables, quietly chatty atmosphere, well kept Adnams Bitter and Broadside, Woodfordes Wherry and guest on handpump, good wines by the glass, ambitious and generally very well liked food, light airy dining room with beamery; children welcome, dogs in bar, two-acre landscaped garden with vine-covered terrace, closed Sun evening. *(Julie and Bill Ryan, Tracey and Stephen Groves, Anthony Barnes, Mike Proctor)*

★Bank House (01553) 660492 KING'S LYNN TF6119

Kings Staithe Square; PE30 1RD Attractive and civilised big-windowed bar/brasserie under same management as Rose

& Crown at Snettisham; contemporary conversion of handsome Georgian building in splendid quiet quayside spot, sofas, armchairs and pastel colours, Fullers London Pride and Greene King Abbot kept well, enjoyable food from sandwiches to steaks including light dishes all day, may be weekday lunch deals too, good unhurried service, daily newspapers; children welcome, 11 good bedrooms. *(Sophie de Winton, John Wooll, R C Vincent)*

KING'S LYNN   TF6119
Bradleys (01553) 819888
South Quay; PE30 5DT Stylishly simple bar/restaurant with good sensibly priced food, nice wines by the glass, Adnams, more expensive upstairs restaurant with river views, ornate mirrors, elegant curtains and plenty of flowers, pleasant helpful service; quayside tables and small courtyard garden, open all day. *(John Wooll)*

KING'S LYNN   TF6120
Crown & Mitre (01553) 774669
Ferry Street; PE30 1LJ Old-fashioned pub in great riverside spot, lots of interesting naval and nautical memorabilia, six well kept beers such as Cambridge and Humpty Dumpty, own brews still planned by no-nonsense long-serving landlord, good value straightforward home-made food, river-view back conservatory; no credit cards; well behaved children and dogs welcome, quayside tables. *(John Wooll)*

KING'S LYNN   TF6120
Dukes Head (01553) 774996
Tuesday Market Place; PE30 1JS Imposing refurbished early 18th-c hotel with comfortable bar and elegant restaurant, enjoyable range of food including excellent value lunchtime and evening buffet in smaller front bistro, Adnams, good choice of wines, cheerful attentive service; children welcome, good bedrooms, open all day. *(John Wooll)*

KING'S LYNN   TF6220
Lattice House (01553) 769585
Corner of Market Lane, off Tuesday Market Place; PE30 1EG Old beamed and raftered Wetherspoons with good choice of ales, reasonably priced food and friendly speedy service, several well divided areas including upstairs bar; children welcome, open all day from 9am (till 1am Fri, Sat). *(R C Vincent)*

LITTLE FRANSHAM   TF8911
Canary & Linnet (01362) 687027
Maid Road (A47 Swaffham–Dereham); NR19 2JW 16th-c former blacksmith's cottage, good value food (small helpings avaialable) in redecorated beamed bar and back dining room, well kept ales such as Wolf, inglenook woodburner; children welcome, garden. *(Anon)*

MARLINGFORD   TG1309
Bell (01603) 880263
Bawburgh Road off Mill Road; NR9 5HX Friendly and neatly kept country dining pub, enjoyable well priced standard food (including Sun evening), ales such as Beeston and Woodfordes, nicely furnished half-panelled bar with woodburner, carpeted lounge/dining extension; background music; children welcome, terrace picnic-sets. *(Chris Flynn, Wendy Jones)*

MUNDFORD   TL8093
Crown (01842) 878233
Off A1065 Thetford–Swaffham; Crown Road; IP26 5HQ Unassuming old pub, warmly welcoming, with heavy beams and huge fireplace, interesting local memorabilia, good range of real ales, enjoyable generously served food at sensible prices, spiral iron stairs to large restaurant, games and TV in locals' bar; children and dogs welcome, back terrace and garden with wishing well, Harley-Davidson meeting first Sun of month, bedrooms, open all day. *(Peter and Jean Hoare)*

NEWTON   TF8315
George & Dragon (01760) 755046
A1065 4 miles N of Swaffham; PE32 2BX Useful refurbished roadside pub with several small dining areas, enjoyable home-made food from good rare beef sandwiches up, well kept local ales including one brewed for them, warming winter fire, live folk and jazz nights; children welcome, pleasant garden with play area, great views to Castle Acre Priory, closed Sun evening. *(Brian Glozier)*

NORTHREPPS   TG2439
Foundry Arms (01263) 579256
Church Street; NR27 0AA Welcoming village pub with enjoyable traditional food including bargain Sun lunch, well kept Adnams and Woodfordes, decent choice of wines, woodburner; children and dogs welcome, garden picnic-sets, open all day. *(David and Gill Carrington)*

NORWICH   TG2309
⁎ **Adam & Eve** (01603) 667423
Bishopgate; follow Palace Street from Tombland, N of cathedral; NR3 1RZ Ancient pub dating from at least 1249 when used by workmen building the cathedral, has Saxon well beneath the lower bar floor and striking dutch gables (added in 14th and 15th c); old-fashioned small bars with tiled or parquet floors, cushioned benches built into partly panelled walls and some antique high-backed settles, Adnams Bitter, Theakstons Old Peculier, Wells & Youngs Bombardier and a guest, Aspall's cider and 40 malt whiskies, traditional pubby food (not Sun evening); background music; children allowed in snug till 7pm, outside

seating with award-winning tubs and hanging baskets, open all day, closed 25 and 26 Dec, 1 Jan. *(John Cook, Mike and Eleanor Anderson, David Carr, Jane and Alan Bush, the Didler, John Honnor and others)*

NORWICH TG2408
Coach & Horses (01603) 477077
Thorpe Road; NR1 1BA Light and airy tap for Chalk Hill brewery, friendly staff, generous inexpensive home-made food 12-9pm (8pm Sun) including all-day breakfast, bare-boards L-shaped bar with open fire, dark wood, posters and prints, pleasant back dining area; sports TVs, gets very busy on home match days; disabled access possible (not to lavatories), front terrace, open all day. *(David Carr, Jeremy King, the Didler)*

NORWICH TG2210
Duke of Wellington (01603) 441182
Waterloo Road; NR3 1EG Friendly rambling local with over a dozen well kept changing ales (Aug beer festival), foreign bottled beers, no food but can bring your own, real fire, traditional games, folk music Tues evening; nice back terrace, open all day. *(the Didler)*

NORWICH TG2310
Fat Cat Brewery Tap
(01603) 413153 *Lawson Road; NR3 4LF* This 1970s shed-like building is home to the Fat Cat brewery, their beers and guests (up to 18), local ciders, no food apart from rolls and pork pies, live music Fri night and Sun afternoon; children (till 6pm) and dogs welcome, seats out in front and behind, open all day. *(the Didler)*

NORWICH TG2307
Kings Arms (01603) 766361
Hall Road; NR1 3HQ Busy Batemans local with several changing guest beers, good whisky and wine choice, friendly atmosphere, may be lunchtime food (can bring your own – plates, cutlery provided), airy garden room; unobtrusive sports TV; vines in courtyard, open all day. *(the Didler)*

NORWICH TG2309
★ Kings Head (01603) 620468
Magdalen Street; NR3 1JE Well run traditional Victorian local, friendly licensees and good atmosphere in two bare-boards bars, ten or so very well kept changing regional ales, good choice of imported beers, local ciders, no food except pork pies, bar billiards; open all day. *(Ralph Holland, Mike and Eleanor Anderson, David Carr, the Didler)*

NORWICH TG2208
Plough (01603) 661384
St Benedicts Street; NR2 4AR Friendly little city-centre pub owned by Grain, their ales and guests kept well, good wines, knowledgeable staff, comfortable seating and open fire; good beer garden behind, open all day. *(Ralph Holland)*

NORWICH TG2308
Ribs of Beef (01603) 619517
Wensum Street, S side of Fye Bridge; NR3 1HY Welcoming and comfortable with good range of real ales including local brews, farm cider, good wine choice, deep leather sofas and small tables upstairs, attractive smaller downstairs room with river view, generous low-priced food (till 5pm Sun), quick cheerful service, Tues quiz; tables out on narrow waterside walkway. *(John Wooll, the Didler)*

NORWICH TG2207
Trafford Arms (01603) 628466
Grove Road, off A11/A140 Ipswich Road; NR1 3RL Large estate-type local with great choice of well kept ales, decent freshly made food (not Sun evening); pool, sports TV; open all day. *(the Didler)*

NORWICH TG2207
Unthank Arms (01603) 631557
Newmarket Street; NR2 2DR Relaxed Victorian corner pub, spaciously refurbished, with well priced often ambitious food (all day Sun), good choice of wines by the glass, real ales, friendly service, bentwood furniture on bare boards, open fires, upstairs dining room and lounge, annual comedy festival; children welcome, garden behind with covered area, summer barbecues, open all day. *(Anthony Barnes)*

NORWICH TG2309
Wig & Pen (01603) 625891
St Martins Palace Plain; NR3 1RN Friendly and relaxed beamed bar opposite cathedral close, lawyer and judge prints, roaring stove, prompt generous food, six ales including Adnams, Fullers and local brews, good value wines; background music, sports TV; tables out at front, open all day, closed Sun evening. *(the Didler)*

OLD BUCKENHAM TM0691
★ Gamekeeper (01953) 860397
B1077 S of Attleborough; The Green; NR17 1RE Pretty 16th-c pub with civilised beamed bar, leather armchairs and sofa in front of big inglenook woodburner, nice mix of old wooden seats and tables on fine flagstones or wood floor, local watercolours and unusual interior bow window, well kept Adnams Bitter and Woodfordes Wherry, quite a few wines by glass and several malt whiskies, well liked food, comfortable main back dining area plus a small room for private dining; children welcome away from bar, dogs allowed, sunny back garden with terrace, closed Sun evening. *(John Cook, Helena Reis, Sheila Topham)*

OVERSTRAND TG2440

White Horse (01263) 579237

High Street; NR27 0AB Light fresh refurbishment, comfortable and stylish, with good choice of enjoyable food in bar, dining room or barn restaurant, at least three well kept local ales, friendly staff, pool room; background music, silent sports TV; children and dogs welcome, picnic-sets in front, more in garden behind with play equipment, eight bedrooms, open all day from 8am. *(MDN, Jeremy King, David and Gill Carrington)*

OXBOROUGH TF7401

Bedingfeld Arms (01366) 328300

Opposite church; PE33 9PS Late 18th-c coaching inn refurbished under new management and in peaceful setting opposite Oxburgh Hall (NT), enjoyable food (not Mon) from bar and restaurant menus, Wells & Youngs and a guest such as Adnams, Weston's and Aspall's ciders, friendly helpful staff; background music, TV for major sporting events; children welcome, dogs on leads in bar, garden with terrace, nine bedrooms (five in separate coach house), open all day. *(Anon)*

RINGSTEAD TF7040

★ Gin Trap (01485) 525264

Village signed off A149 near Hunstanton; OS Sheet 132 map reference 707403; PE36 5JU Attractive well run 17th-c coaching inn with friendly helpful licensees, two bar areas, original part with beams, woodburner and pubby furniture, Adnams and Woodfordes ales, generous helpings of home-made food, airy dining conservatory; background and monthly live acoustic music; children and dogs welcome, tables in walled garden, art gallery next-door, Peddar's Way walks, open all day in summer. *(Jeff and Wendy Williams, Anthony Barnes, Alan Sutton, R C Vincent, David Jackman and others)*

SCULTHORPE TF8930

Hourglass (01328) 856744

The Street; NR21 9QD Restauranty place with long open room combining light modern style with some dark beams, good choice of enjoyable fairly priced food including OAP lunch deal (Mon, Tues), Wells & Youngs Bombardier and Woodfordes Wherry, quick friendly service. *(M and J White, John Wooll)*

SCULTHORPE TF8930

Sculthorpe Mill (01328) 856161

Inn signed off A148 W of Fakenham, opposite village; NR21 9QG Welcoming dining pub in rebuilt 18th-c mill, appealing riverside setting, seats out under weeping willows and in attractive garden behind; light, airy and relaxed with leather sofas and sturdy tables in bar/dining area, generally well liked food from sandwiches up, Greene King ales, good house wines,

upstairs restaurant; background music; six comfortable bedrooms, open all day weekends and in summer. *(John Wooll, Roy Hoing)*

SHERINGHAM TG1543

Lobster (01263) 822716

High Street; NR26 8JP Almost on seafront, seafaring décor in friendly panelled bar with old sewing-machine treadle tables and warm fire, wide range of well kept changing ales (bank holiday festivals), bottled belgian beers and real ciders, decent well priced wines by the glass, good value quickly served generous bar meals (helpful with special diets), restaurant with seafood including fresh lobster (get there early) and good crab, games in public bar including pool; dogs on leads, two courtyards, heated marquee, open all day. *(Tracey and Stephen Groves, N R White, Barry Collett)*

SHERINGHAM TG1543

Windham Arms (01263) 822609

Wyndham Street; NR26 8BA Dutch-gabled brick and cobble pub with well kept Woodfordes and other ales, enjoyable sensibly priced food with greek influences (chef is greek), friendly efficient service, woodburner in carpeted beamed lounge with tightly packed dining tables, separate public bar with pool; picnic-sets outside, sizeable car park (useful here), open all day. *(Brian Glozier)*

SMALLBURGH TG3324

★ Crown (01692) 536314

A149 Yarmouth Road; NR12 9AD 15th-c thatched and beamed village inn with friendly proper landlord, old-fashioned pub atmosphere, well kept Adnams and Black Sheep, good choice of wines by the glass, enjoyable straightforward home-made food in bar and upstairs dining room, prompt service, daily newspapers, darts; no dogs or children inside; picnic-sets in pretty back garden, bedrooms, closed Sun evening, Mon lunchtime. *(Roy Hoing)*

SOUTH CREAKE TF8635

★ Ostrich (01328) 823320

B1355 Burnham Market–Fakenham; NR21 9PB Well kept ales including Adnams and Woodfordes Wherry in airy village pub, polished boards, local paintings and shelves of books, plenty of tables, food from sandwiches to ostrich fillet, helpful young staff, woodburner; children and dogs welcome, stylish back terrace, bedrooms, open all day weekends. *(Linda Miller and Derek Greentree)*

SOUTH WOOTTON TF6622

Farmers Arms (01553) 675566

Part of Knights Hill Hotel, Grimston Road (off A148/A149); PE30 3HQ Hotel complex's olde-worlde barn and stables conversion, food all day including good value lunchtime carvery (not Sat), Adnams and guests, good wines and abundant coffee, friendly service, stripped brick and timbers, quiet snugs and corners, hayloft with snooker; may be background music, machines, no dogs; children welcome, tables and play area outside, 79 comfortable bedrooms, open all day. *(John Wooll, R C Vincent)*

SOUTH WOOTTON   TF6422
Swan (01553) 672084
Nursery Lane; PE30 3NG Friendly local overlooking village green, duck pond and bowling green, popular reasonably priced food (not Sun or Mon evenings – booking advised) in bar and conservatory restaurant, Thurs curry night, well kept Greene King and a couple of guests; children welcome, small enclosed garden. *(R C Vincent)*

SOUTHREPPS   TG2536
⋆ Vernon Arms (01263) 833355
Church Street; NR11 8NP Popular old-fashioned village pub, welcoming and relaxed, with good food (not Mon evening) running up to steaks and well priced crab and lobster specials (must book weekend evenings), friendly helpful young staff, well kept ales such as Adnams, Black Sheep, Timothy Taylors and Wells & Youngs, good choice of wines and malt whiskies, big log fire; darts and pool; tables outside, children, dogs and muddy walkers welcome. *(Conrad Freezer, M J Winterton, Jim Farmer, Mrs A S Crisp and others)*

SPOONER ROW   TM0997
Boars (01953) 605851
Just off A11 SW of Wymondham; NR18 9LL 1920s pub/restaurant in tiny village, enjoyable locally sourced food from light meals to more expensive (though not pretentious) choices including good vegetarian options, well kept Adnams and nice range of wines (three glass sizes), friendly service, amazing collection of food/wine books; tables in well tended garden. *(Anon)*

STOKE HOLY CROSS   TG2302
⋆ Wildebeest Arms (01508) 492497
Village signposted off A140 S of Norwich; turn left in village; NR14 8QJ More restaurant than pub with all tables set for diners, but several stools by sleek bar for just a drink; long room with understated african theme, carefully placed carvings and hangings on dark sandy walls, unusual dark leather chairs grouped around striking tables, neatly dressed staff, good contemporary food including fixed-price menus, fine range of wines by the glass, Woodfordes Wherry and guest; children welcome, subtly lit front terrace with comfortable wicker armchairs or cushioned benches around glass-topped tables, garden behind. *(Anon)*

TACOLNESTON   TM1495
⋆ Pelican (01508) 489521
Norwich Road (B1113 SW of city); NR16 1AL Chatty timbered bar with relaxed, comfortable atmosphere, good log fire, sofas, armchairs and old stripped settle, candles and flowers on tables, some booth seating, four well kept ales including one brewed for them by Brandon, Aspall's cider and 36 malt whiskies, restaurant area with high-backed leather chairs around oak tables, good choice of food (not weekday lunchtimes) from pub favourites up, friendly service, shop selling local produce and bottled Norfolk/Suffolk ales; background music; plenty of tables on decking behind, sheltered lawn beyond, three bedrooms, open all day weekends in summer. *(Anthony Barnes)*

THOMPSON   TL9296
Chequers (01953) 483360
Griston Road, off A1075 S of Watton; IP24 1PX Long, low and picturesque 16th-c thatched dining pub tucked away in attractive spot, enjoyable food including bargain weekday lunch offer, real ales, helpful staff and friendly atmosphere, series of quaint rooms with low beams, inglenooks and some stripped brickwork; children welcome, dogs allowed in bar, good-sized garden with play equipment, bedroom block. *(Paul Kemp)*

WALSINGHAM   TF9336
Bull (01328) 820333
Common Place/Shire Hall Plain; NR22 6BP Unpretentious and rather quirky pub in pilgrimage village; bar's darkly ancient walls covered with clerical visiting cards and pictures of archbishops, various odds and ends including a half-size statue of Charlie Chaplin, welcoming landlord and good-humoured staff, three well kept changing ales, food (not Sat, Sun evenings) from good value sandwiches up, log fire, old-fashioned cash register in gents'; dovecote above entrance stuffed with plastic lobsters and crabs, picnic-sets out in courtyard and on attractive flowery terrace by village square, outside games room with pool, open all day. *(Pam and John Smith, Giles Smith and Sandra Kiely)*

WARHAM   TF9441
⋆ Three Horseshoes (01328) 710547
Warham All Saints; village signed from A149 Wells-next-the-Sea–Blakeney, and from B1105 S of Wells; NR23 1NL Old-fashioned pub with gas lighting in simple rooms looking unchanged since the 1920s (parts date from 1720); stripped-deal or mahogany tables (one marked for shove-ha'penny) on stone floor, red leatherette settles built around partly panelled walls of public bar, royalist photographs, old working American one-arm bandit, longcase clock with clear piping strike, twister on ceiling

to show who gets the next round, open fires in Victorian fireplaces, Greene King, Woodfordes and guests (some cask tapped), local cider, generous helpings of pubby food (may be game), gramophone museum opened on request; children away from bar and dogs welcome, seats in courtyard garden with flower tubs and well, bedrooms. *(Roy Hoing, Chris Johnson, Jim Farmer, Tracey and Stephen Groves, David Jackman, Terry Mizen and others)*

WEASENHAM ST PETER   TF8522
Fox & Hounds (01328) 838868
A1065 Fakenham–Swaffham; The Green; PE32 2TD Traditional 18th-c beamed local with bar and two dining areas (one with inglenook woodburner), spotless and well run by friendly family, three changing ales, good honest home-made food at reasonable prices including Sun roasts, pubby furniture and carpets throughout, lots of military prints; children welcome, big well kept garden and terrace. *(Tony Middis)*

WELLS-NEXT-THE-SEA   xx00
Albatros 07979087228
The Quay; NR23 1AT Bar on 1899 quayside clipper, Woodfordes beers served from the cask, speciality pancakes, charts and other nautical memorabilia, good views of harbour and tidal marshes, live music weekends; children and dogs welcome, not good for disabled, cabin accommodation with shared showers, open all day. *(Chris Johnson)*

WELLS-NEXT-THE-SEA   TF9143
★ **Crown** (01328) 710209
The Buttlands; NR23 1EX Smart old coaching inn (part of Flying Kiwi group) overlooking tree-lined green; rambling bar on several levels with beams and standing timbers, burnt-orange walls hung with local photos, grey-painted planked wall seats and high-backed brown leather dining chairs on stripped floorboards, Jo C's Norfolk Ale along with Adnams and Woodfordes, several wines by the glass, contemporary food served by helpful staff, airy dining room and elegant more formal restaurant; background music; children welcome, dogs in bar, 12 bedrooms, open all day. *(John Wooll, David Carr, Jeremy King, Chris Johnson, Peter and Eleanor Kenyon, Colin and Louise English and others)*

WELLS-NEXT-THE-SEA   TF9143
Edinburgh (01328) 710120
Station Road/Church Street; NR23 1AE Traditional 19th-c pub near main shopping area, good home-made food, well kept Fullers, Woodfordes and a guest, open fire, local photographs for sale, sizeable restaurant (check winter opening times); background and occasional live music, sports TV; children and dogs welcome, disabled access, courtyard with heated smokers' shelter, three bedrooms, open all day. *(David Carr, Chris Johnson, John Beeken)*

WEST ACRE   TF7815
Stag (01760) 755395
Low Road; PE32 1TR Good choice of well kept changing ales in appealing local's unpretentious small bar, obliging cheerful staff, good value food, neat dining room; attractive spot in quiet village, closed Mon. *(Dr and Mrs R G J Telfer)*

WEST RUNTON   TG1842
Village Inn (01263) 838000
Water Lane; NR27 9QP Roomy comfortable flint pub with nice community feel, popular food including good Sun roast, decent ales, ales such as Adnams, Woodfordes and Wolf, restaurant, pool room; lots of tables in large attractive garden, pleasant village with good beach and nice circular walk to East Runton, closed Mon. *(Jenny and Brian Seller, Mike Buckingham)*

WEYBOURNE   TG1143
Ship (01263) 588721
A149 W of Sheringham; The Street; NR25 7SZ Popular village pub with up to six local ales such as Grain, Humpty Dumpty and Woodfordes, big straightforward bar with pubby furniture and woodburner, two dining rooms, good reasonably priced home-made food, pleasant service; background music; well behaved children welcome, dogs in bar, nice garden and pretty hanging baskets, handy for Muckleburgh Military Vehicle Museum, open all day weekends. *(Tom Ambrose, David Field, Alan Sutton)*

WYMONDHAM   TG1001
★ **Green Dragon** (01953) 607907
Church Street; NR18 0PH Picturesque heavily timbered 14th-c inn, simple beamed back bar with log fire under Tudor mantelpiece, interesting pictures, bigger dining area, friendly helpful staff, four well kept ales including Adnams; children and dogs welcome, modest bedrooms, near glorious 12th-c abbey church, open all day. *(Rita Scarratt)*

Post Office address codings confusingly give the impression that a few pubs are in Norfolk, when they're really in Cambridgeshire or Suffolk (which is where we list them).

Northamptonshire

Fair prices for food and beer play quite a part in several of our Main Entry pubs in this region, with four of them holding one of our Value Awards. Pubs that readers are enjoying this year include the Kings Arms at Farthingstone (lots of character and with a terrific wildlife garden) and the Olde Sun in Nether Heyford (lively, friendly place with interesting bric-a-brac). The Queens Head in Bulwick has been transformed by newish owners and is now certainly worth a special trip. Our Northamptonshire Dining Pub 2013 is the Falcon in Fotheringhay.

BULWICK

Queens Head ◖

SP9694   Map 4

Off A43 Kettering–Duddington; NN17 3DY

Honey-coloured 17th-c stone pub with five ales, good food and friendly licensees

This pretty 600-year-old stone cottage has been carefully refurbished by its newish owners. The beamed bar has exposed stone walls, contemporary paintwork, cushioned walls seats and wooden dining chairs, stone floors and a woodburning stove – and still has the feel of a traditional village pub; the bellringers continue to pop in after their Wednesday practice. The dining room has high-backed black or brown leather dining chairs around light wooden tables on floor tiles, another fireplace and quite a few interesting little knick-knacks. Digfield Barnwell, Oakham JHB, Shepherd Neame Spitfire and a couple of guest beers from local breweries such as Brewsters, Great Oakley and Potbelly on handpump. Outside, there are rattan tables and chairs under a pergola and on the terrace, and a pizza oven; this is a lovely spot, with the summer sounds of swallows and house martins, sheep in the adjacent field and bells ringing in the nearby church.

Good, interesting food includes sandwiches, stilton, pear and walnut salad, ham hock and pickled quail egg salad with Guinness mustard, sausage medley with mash and buttered cabbage, beefburger with dill pickle, beetroot relish and hand-cut chips, cauliflower and macaroni cheese gratin, pork cutlet with crispy caper potatoes and pear salsa verde, pollack and dill fishcakes with home-made tartare sauce, fillet of sea trout with mussel gnocchi and samphire cream fish sauce, and puddings like summer pudding with raspberry coulis and dark chocolate crumble tart with candied oranges and caramel sauce. *Benchmark main dish: ribe-eye steak with a changing sauce £16.95. Two-course evening meal £20.50.*

Free house ~ Licensees Julie Barclay and Robert Windeler ~ Real ale ~ Bar food (12-2, 6-9; 12-3 Sun; not Sun evening or Mon) ~ Restaurant ~ (01780) 450272 ~ Children welcome ~ Dogs allowed in bar ~ Open 12-3, 6-11; 12-7 Sun; closed Sun evening; Mon ~

www.thequeensheadbulwick.co.uk *Recommended by Mike and Sue Loseby, Maurice and Janet Thorpe, Michael and Jenny Back, Howard and Margaret Buchanan*

FARTHINGHOE
Fox

SP5339   Map 4

Just off A422 Brackley–Banbury; Baker Street; NN13 5PH

Sprucely refurbished, with enjoyable food and well kept ales

As well as a striking triptych of a prowling fox, this lichened golden stone building also has small landscapes, old country photographs and framed period advertisements well spaced on its pastel walls. It's been carefully restored, with seating ranging from dark leather tub chairs, green-padded seats, wall banquettes and neatly built-in traditional wall seats to well cushioned ladder-back and other dining chairs in the eating area, which has quite a low plank-panelled ceiling in one part. The dark-beamed front bar has a log fire in a great stripped-stone fireplace with a side salt cupboard. Lighting is sympathetic, and good new flooring includes some attractively coloured slate tiling. They have Wells & Youngs Bitter, Eagle IPA and Courage Directors on handpump, and there are several wines by the glass; maybe background music. Behind is a sheltered terrace with teak tables, with picnic-sets under cocktail parasols in the neatly kept garden beyond. The comfortable bedrooms are in the adjoining barn conversion.

As well as a takeaway menu, the well liked food includes lunchtime sandwiches, seafood pâté with smoked salmon, hot chicken and bacon salad with caesar salad, various sharing platters, home-baked ham with fried eggs, local butcher's sausages with onion marmalade, mushroom and cream tagliatelle, herb-crused loin of pork on a soft cheese and roasted garlic potato cake and wholegrain mustard sauce, local lamb chops with dauphinoise potatoes and red wine jus, aberdeen angus sirloin steak with peppercorn or stilton sauce, and puddings; they hold popular weekday themed food evenings. *Benchmark main dish: fish and chips £10.50. Two-course evening meal £15.50.*

Charles Wells ~ Lease Mark Higgs ~ Real ale ~ Bar food (12-2.30, 6-9.30; 12-4, 6-8 Sun) ~ Restaurant ~ (01295) 713965 ~ Children welcome ~ Open 12-3, 6-11; 12-11(10.30) Sat ~ Bedrooms: /£60S ~ www.foxatfarthinghoe.co.uk *Recommended by P and J Shapley, Phil and Jane Hodson, Donna Burton-Wilcock, M G Hart, Martin and Karen Wake*

FARTHINGSTONE
Kings Arms £

SP6155   Map 4

Off A5 SE of Daventry; village signed from Litchborough; NN12 8EZ

Individual place with cosy traditional interior and lovely gardens

The licensees at this quirky gargoyle-embellished 18th-c stone country pub give wildlife talks here and are passionate about their wildlife-friendly garden. With a surprise around every corner, it's laid out in a series of tucked away little nooks, and the tranquil terrace is charmingly decorated with hanging baskets, flower and herb pots, plant-filled painted tractor tyres and recycled art. Inside, the intimate flagstoned bar has a huge log fire, comfortable homely sofas and armchairs near the entrance, whisky-water jugs hanging from oak beams, and lots of pictures and decorative plates on the walls. A games room at the far end has darts, dominoes, cribbage, table skittles and board games. Three changing beers might be from brewers such as Black Sheep, Charles Wells and St Austell Tribute, they have a short but decent wine list and quite a few country wines. Look out for the interesting newspaper-influenced décor in the outside gents'. This is a picturesque village and there are good walks near here including the Knightley Way. It's worth ringing ahead to check the opening and food serving times, and do note that they don't take credit cards.

🍴 Food is carefully prepared, and they grow their own salad vegetables and herbs. As well as filled baguettes, dishes might include smoked duck and black pudding salad, salmon terrine, fish and meat platters, game casserole, yorkshire pudding filled with steak and kidney, salmon fishcakes with dill and mustard sauce, pork in ginger, garlic and tomato sauce, and puddings such as sticky toffee pudding, apple and strawberry slice and lemon pudding. *Benchmark main dish: british cheese platter £8.25. Two-course evening meal £14.25.*

Free house ~ Licensees Paul and Denise Egerton ~ Real ale ~ Bar food (12-2.30 Sat, Sun only; 7.15-9.30 last Fri evening of month) ~ (01327) 361604 ~ Children welcome ~ Dogs welcome ~ Open 7-11.30; 6.30-midnight Fri; 12-4, 7-midnight Sat; 12-4, 9-11 Sun; closed Mon and weekday lunchtimes *Recommended by Richard Gibbs*

FOTHERINGHAY   TL0593   Map 5
Falcon 🍴 ♀
Village signposted off A605 on Peterborough side of Oundle; PE8 5HZ
Northamptonshire Dining Pub of the Year

Upmarket dining pub, good range of drinks and food from snacks up, and attractive garden

Readers have only praise for this beautifully kept, civilised pub. Staff here are exceptionally friendly and polite, creating a delightful atmosphere for the good inventive food they serve – not cheap, but the consensus is that it's worth it. Everything is neatly turned out, with fresh flower arrangements and sedate cushioned slatback arm and bucket chairs, and good winter log fires in stone fireplaces. The pretty conservatory restaurant and charming lavender-surrounded terrace have lovely views of the vast church behind, and an attractively planted garden. Surprisingly, given the emphasis on dining, it does have a thriving little locals' tap bar and a darts team. The very good range of drinks includes three changing beers from brewers such as Fullers and Nene Valley on handpump, good wines (most available by the glass), Aspall's cider, organic cordials and fresh orange juice. The village is lovely, with mooring on the Nene, and the ruins of Fotheringhay Castle, where Mary Queen of Scots was executed, not far away.

🍴 As well as imaginative sandwiches, thoughtful food, all prepared from scratch (except the ketchup), might include chorizo niçoise, linguine with crab, chilli and dill, baked goats cheese with roast peppers, crayfish and saffron tart with gruyère and rocket salad, salmon fillet with sauce vièrge, mushroom and tarragon risotto, rack of lamb with dauphinoise potatoes and red wine jus, chicken breast with chorizo mash and thyme jus, and puddings such as white chocolate mousse with milk chocolate parfait and macaroon, baked cheesecake with raspberries and sticky toffee pudding. *Benchmark main dish: salmon and crab fishcakes £9.50. Two-course evening meal £22.70.*

Free house ~ Licensee Sally Facer ~ Real ale ~ Bar food (12-2.15(3 Sun), 6.15-9.15(8.30 Sun)) ~ Restaurant ~ (01832) 226254 ~ Children welcome ~ Dogs allowed in bar ~ Open 12-11(10.30 Sun) ~ www.thefalcon-inn.co.uk *Recommended by P and J Shapley, Michael Doswell, Alan Sutton, Robert Wivell, Michael Sargent, Clive Flynn, Clive and Fran Dutson, Phil and Jane Hodson, Ryta Lyndley, James Stretton*

GREAT BRINGTON
SP6664   Map 4

Althorp Coaching Inn

Off A428 NW of Northampton, near Althorp Hall; until recently known as the Fox & Hounds; NN7 4JA

Friendly golden stone thatched pub with great choice of real ales, tasty food, and sheltered garden

Cheerful staff serve around nine real ales at this lovely old coaching inn. On handpump, these might include Fullers London Pride, Greene King IPA and Abbot, St Austell Tribute, Sadlers Worcester Sorcerer, Warwickshire Shakespeares County, and guests from breweries such as Abbeydale, Goffs, Quartz and Saltaire. The extended dining area gives views of the 30 or so casks racked in the cellar; also, eight wines by the glass and a decent range of malt whiskies. The ancient bar has all the traditional features you'd wish for, from a dog or two sprawled by the huge log fire to old beams, sagging joists and an attractive mix of country chairs and tables (maybe with fresh flowers) on its broad flagstones and bare boards. There are plenty of snug alcoves and nooks and crannies with some stripped-pine shutters and panelling, two fine log fires and an eclectic medley of bric-a-brac from farming implements to an old clocking-in machine and country pictures. One of the bars is used for pub games, and a garden cottage adjoins the lovely little paved courtyard (also accessible by the former coaching entrance), which has sheltered tables and tubs of flowers; more seating in the side garden.

 Food here is popular so it's advisable to book: sandwiches, smoked mackerel pâté, mushrooms and smoked bacon in stilton sauce, macaroni and leeks in a creamy cheese sauce, chicken with goats cheese and sun-dried tomatoes, lasagne, bass fillet on garlic-roasted fennel, slow-braised local venison in red wine sauce, gloucester old spot pork fillet in cider and apple sauce, and puddings such as cherry crumble with custard and warm chocolate brownie with vanilla ice-cream. *Benchmark main dish: chicken fillet with goats cheese and sun-dried tomatoes £13.25. Two-course evening meal £18.00.*

Free house ~ Licensee Michael Krempels ~ Real ale ~ Bar food (12-3, 6.30-9.30 (10 Fri, Sat); 12-5, 6-8 Sun) ~ Restaurant ~ (01604) 770651 ~ Children welcome ~ Dogs allowed in bar ~ Live music Tues evening ~ Open 11-11.30; 12-10.30 Sun ~ www.althorp-coaching-inn.co.uk *Recommended by George Atkinson, Gerry and Rosemary Dobson, Tim and Ann Newell, Michael Butler, Clive and Fran Dutson, Patrick and Daphne Darley*

NETHER HEYFORD
SP6658   Map 4

Olde Sun £

1.75 miles from M1 junction 16: village signposted left off A45 westbound; Middle Street; NN7 3LL

Unpretentious place handy for M1 with diverting bric-a-brac, reasonably priced food and garden with play area

All manner of entertaining bric-a-brac hangs from the ceilings and is packed into nooks and crannies in the several small linked rooms of this lively 18th-c golden stone pub. It includes brassware (one fireplace is a grotto of large brass animals), colourful relief plates, 1930s cigarette cards, railway memorabilia and advertising signs, World War II posters and rope fancywork. The nice old cash till on one of the two counters where the friendly landlord and staff serve well kept Banks's, Greene King Ruddles, Marstons Pedigree and a guest such as Charles Wells Eagle is wishfully stuck at one and a ha'penny. Most of the furnishings are properly pubby, with the odd easy chair. There are beams and low ceilings (one painted with a fine sunburst), partly glazed dividing panels, steps between some areas, rugs on parquet, red tiles or flagstones, a big inglenook log fire and, up on the left, a room with full-sized hood skittles, a games machine, darts, Sky TV, cribbage and dominoes; background music. In the garden you'll find antiquated hand-operated farm machines, some with plants in their hoppers, and the first thing that will catch your eye when you arrive will probably be a row of bright blue grain kibblers along the edge of the fairy-lit front terrace (with picnic-sets).

Pubby bar food includes prawn cocktail, farmhouse pâté, fried brie wedges, battered spicy prawns, ploughman's, steak pie, chicken breast wrapped in bacon topped with stilton sauce, pork fillet in mushroom sauce, mixed grill, battered cod, breaded scampi, and salmon steak in hollandaise sauce. *Benchmark main dish: ham, egg and chips £7.25. Two-course evening meal £16.70.*

Free house ~ Licensees P Yates and A Ford ~ Real ale ~ Bar food (12-2(4 Sun), 7-9; not Sun evening) ~ Restaurant ~ (01327) 340164 ~ Children welcome ~ Dogs allowed in bar ~ Open 12-2.30, 5-11; 12-midnight Sat; 12-11 Sun *Recommended by George Atkinson, Andy Dolan, Nigel and Sue Foster*

NORTHAMPTON
Malt Shovel 🍺 £

SP7559 Map 4

Bridge Street (approach road from M1 junction 15); no parking in nearby street, best to park in Morrisons central car park, far end – passage past Europcar straight to back entrance; NN1 1QF

Well run friendly real ale pub with bargain lunches and over a dozen varied beers

Beer lovers will be in heaven at this pubby place, where they serve an impressive 13 real ales from a battery of handpumps lined up on the long counter, with even more during beer festivals. As well as their three Great Oakley house beers, Frog Island Natterjack and Fullers London Pride, they run through quickly changing guests from the likes of Bridestones, Elland, Mallinsons, Millstone, Oakham and Ruddles. They also have belgian draft and bottled beers, over 40 malt whiskies, english country wines and Rich's farm cider. There's quite an extensive collection of carefully chosen brewing memorabilia, some from Phipps Northampton Brewery Company, which was once across the road – the site is now occupied by Carlsberg Brewery. Look out for the rare Phipps Northampton Brewery Company star, displayed outside the pub, and some high-mounted ancient beer engines from the Carlsberg Brewery. Staff are cheery and helpful; darts, daily papers, disabled facilities, maybe background music. The secluded back yard has tables and chairs, a smokers' shelter and occasional barbecues.

Bargain lunchtime food includes baguettes, wraps, baked potatoes, ploughman's, spinach and ricotta cannelloni, and daily specials such as plaice goujons, gammon, egg and chips, and sausage casserole. *Benchmark main dish: steak and ale pie £6.00.*

Free house ~ Licensee Mike Evans ~ Real ale ~ Bar food (12-2; not evenings or Sun) ~ (01604) 234212 ~ Well behaved children welcome ~ Dogs allowed in bar ~ Blues Weds evening ~ Open 11.30-3, 5-11.30; 11.30-11 Fri, Sat; 12-10.30 Sun ~ www.maltshoveltavern.com *Recommended by George Atkinson, Dr J Barrie Jones*

If you know a pub's ever open all day, please tell us.

OUNDLE

TL0388 Map 5

Ship 🍺 £

West Street; PE8 4EF

Bustling down-to-earth town pub with interesting beers and good value pubby food

This is very much a proper pub, with a lounge and public bar. Off to the left of the central corridor, the heavily beamed lounge (watch your head if you're tall) is made up of three cosy areas with a mix of leather and other seats, sturdy tables and a warming log fire in a stone inglenook. Down one end a charming little panelled snug has button-back leather seats built in around its walls. The wood-floored public bar has a TV, games machine, and board games and you can play poker here on Wednesdays; background music. Friendly staff serve Brewsters Hophead, Oakham Bishops Farewell, Phipps IPA and a guest such as Nene Valley NVB and they've a good range of malt whiskies. Midnight, the sleepy black and white pub cat, seems oblivious to all the cheery chatter and bustle here. The wooden tables and chairs out on the series of small sunny, covered terraces are lit at night.

🍴 Enjoyable bar food served in generous helpings includes sandwiches, breaded whitebait, chilli, haddock and chips, sausage and mash, chicken nuggets, steak, and specials such as thai chicken curry, and spicy tomato and red pepper spaghetti. *Benchmark main dish: ham, egg and chips £9.00. Two-course evening meal £17.40.*

Free house ~ Licensees Andrew and Robert Langridge ~ Real ale ~ Bar food (12-3, 6-9; 12-9 Sat, Sun) ~ (01832) 273918 ~ Children welcome ~ Dogs allowed in bar and bedrooms ~ Folk 2nd Mon of month ~ Open 11-midnight ~ Bedrooms: £30(£39S)/£69B ~ www.theshipinn-oundle.co.uk *Recommended by Ryta Lyndley*

Also Worth a Visit in Northamptonshire

Besides the fully inspected pubs, you might like to try these pubs that have been recommended to us and described by readers. Do tell us what you think of them: feedback@goodguides.com

ABTHORPE SP6446

⋆ **New Inn** (01327) 857306

Signed from A43 at first roundabout S of A5; Silver Street; NN12 8QR Traditional partly thatched country local run by cheery farming family, fairly basic rambling bar with four well kept Hook Norton beers and Stowford Press cider, good pubby food (not Sun evening) using their own meat and home-grown herbs, beams, stripped stone and inglenook log fire, darts and table skittles; juke box, TV; children and dogs welcome, garden tables, bedrooms in converted barn (short walk across fields), open all day Sun, closed Mon, Tues lunchtime. *(David Uren, Ray Fowler, Dr D J and Mrs S C Walker)*

ASHBY ST LEDGERS SP5768

⋆ **Olde Coach House** (01788) 890349

Main Street; 4 miles from M1 J18;

A5 S to Kilsby, then A361 S towards Daventry; village also signed off A5 N of Weedon; CV23 8UN Handsome creeper-clad stone inn, modernised but retaining some original character, bar and several dining areas, flooring from stripped boards and carpet to red and white tiles, high-backed leather dining chairs, comfortable sofas and armchairs, hunting pictures, large mirrors, log fire and old stove, Wells & Youngs ales and a guest, decent wines, enjoyable food (all day Sun) including weekday set lunch deal, friendly helpful young staff; background music, TV; children and dogs welcome, back garden picnic-sets, modern seating in front under hanging baskets, boules, interesting church nearby, six bedrooms, open all day weekends. *(C and R Bromage, Dennis Jones, Gerard Dyson, Michael Butler, Rob and Catherine Dunster, George Atkinson and others)*

AYNHO SP5133

★**Cartwright** (01869) 811885

Croughton Road (B4100); OX17 3BE Carefully refurbished 16th-c coaching inn, linked areas with smart contemporary furniture on wood or tiled floors, cream, maroon and exposed stone walls, well chosen artwork, leather sofas by big log fire in small bar, Adnams and Hook Norton, nice wines and coffee, good well presented food including set deals, friendly helpful uniformed staff, daily newspapers; background music, TV; children welcome, a few seats in pretty corner of former coachyard, pleasant village with apricot trees growing against old cottage walls, 21 bedrooms, good breakfast, open all day. *(C and R Bromage, Sir Nigel Foulkes, George Atkinson, M G Hart)*

AYNHO SP4932

★**Great Western Arms**

(01869) 338288 *Aynho Wharf, Station Road; off B4031 W; OX17 3BP* Attractive old pub with series of linked cosy rooms, fine solid country tables on broad flagstones, golden stripped-stone walls, warm cream and deep red plasterwork, fresh flowers and candles, log fires, well kept Hook Norton and other ales, good wines by the glass, enjoyable pubby food all day, friendly attentive service, elegant dining area on right, magazines and daily newspapers, extensive GWR collection including lots of steam locomotive photographs, pool, skittle alley; background music; children and dogs welcome, white cast-iron furniture in back former stable courtyard, moorings on Oxford Canal and nearby marina, bedrooms (may ask for payment on arrival). *(Meg and Colin Hamilton, Sir Nigel Foulkes, Dave Braisted, Alan Sutton, Malcolm and Jo Hart, Ian Herdman and others)*

BADBY SP5659

Maltsters (01327) 702905

The Green; NN11 3AF Refurbished stone-built pub, long beamed carpeted room with a fire at each end, pine tables and chairs, good choice of enjoyable well priced food including some interesting specials, well kept ales such as Black Sheep, Greene King, St Austell and Wells & Youngs, good friendly service; a couple of picnic-sets out at front, more in side garden and courtyard, well placed for walks on nearby Knightley Way, bedrooms, open all day. *(Brian and Anna Marsden, M Walker, Gerry and Rosemary Dobson)*

BADBY SP5558

Windmill (01327) 311070

Village signposted off A361 Daventry–Banbury; NN11 3AN Attractive refurbished 18th-c thatched and beamed pub, flagstoned bar area with woodburner in huge inglenook, four ales such as Bass, Hoggleys, St Austell and Timothy Taylors, enjoyable varied choice of good value home-made food from lunchtime sandwiches up, friendly welcoming staff, restaurant extension; background and occasional live music; children and dogs welcome, terrace out by pretty village green, nice walks, eight good bedrooms, open all day. *(Roger and Kathy Elkin, George Atkinson, M Walker)*

BARNWELL TL0584

Montagu Arms (01832) 273726

Off A605 S of Oundle, then fork right at Thurning, Hemington sign; PE8 5PH Attractive stone-built pub with Adnams, Digfield (brewed in village) and guests, decent ciders, good range of well priced food, cheerful staff, log fire, low beams, flagstones or tile and brick floors, back dining room and conservatory; children welcome, big garden with play area, pleasant streamside village, nice walks. *(J Buckby)*

BRACKLEY SP5836

Crown (01280) 702210

Market Place; NN13 7DP Smartly refurbished Georgian inn with open fire and stripped masonry in comfortable carpeted bar overlooking market square, lots of motor-racing memorabilia, well kept beers such as Bass and Hook Norton, friendly competent service, reasonably priced food including good Sun carvery, more formal dining room and small lounge; children welcome, dogs in bar (not at eating times), back courtyard leading to popular antiques centre, 26 bedrooms, open all day. *(George Atkinson, Michael Tack)*

BRAYBROOKE SP7684

Swan (01858) 462754

Griffin Road; LE16 8LH Nicely kept thatched pub with good drinks choice including Everards ales, good value generous food (all day Sat), friendly helpful service, fireside sofas, soft lighting, exposed brickwork, stone-ceilinged alcoves, restaurant; quiet background music, silent fruit machine; children and dogs welcome, disabled facilities, attractive hedged garden with covered terrace, open all day weekends. *(Carl Stasiak)*

BRIXWORTH SP7470

Coach & Horses (01604) 880329

Harborough Road, just off A508 N of Northampton; NN6 9BX Welcoming 17th-c stone-built beamed pub, enjoyable good value food, three ales including Greene King, log fire, small restaurant; tables on back terrace, attractive village with famous Saxon church. *(Justin Maeers)*

BUCKBY WHARF SP6066

★**New Inn** (01327) 844747

A5 N of Weedon; NN6 7PW Decent range of tasty straightforward pubby food from baguettes and baked potatoes up, friendly chatty staff, well kept ales such as Hook Norton, St Austell and Sharps, good short choice of wines, several rooms radiating from central servery including a small dining room with nice fire, games area with table skittles; TV, games machine; children welcome, dogs outside only, pleasant terrace by busy Grand Union Canal lock, popular with boaters, open all day. (George Atkinson)

BUGBROOKE — SP6756
Wharf Inn (01604) 832585

The Wharf; off A5 S of Weedon; NN7 3QB Super spot by Grand Union Canal, plenty of tables on big lawn with moorings, large water-view restaurant, bar/lounge with small informal raised eating area either side, lots of stripped brickwork, good food using local organic produce including Sun roasts, prompt cheerful service, well kept local Frog Island and Greene King IPA, lots of wines by the glass, woodburner; background music; children welcome, dogs in garden only, disabled facilities, heated smokers' shelter, open all day. (Gerry and Rosemary Dobson, R K Phillips)

CHACOMBE — SP4943
George & Dragon (01295) 711500

Handy for M40 junction 11, via A361; Silver Street; OX17 2JR Welcoming 17th-c pub with beams, flagstones, panelling and bare stone walls, two inglenook woodburners, even a glass-covered well, good popular food (not Sun evening) in two dining areas from lunchtime sandwiches and traditional choices up including vegetarian options, good service, Everards and a guest ale, several wines by the glass, decent coffee, darts; background music, no dogs; children welcome, picnic-sets on suntrap terrace, pretty village with interesting church, open all day. (William Ruxton, George Atkinson)

CHAPEL BRAMPTON — SP7366
⋆ Brampton Halt (01604) 842676

Pitsford Road, off A5199 N of Northampton; NN6 8BA Well laid out pub on Northampton & Lamport Railway (which is open at weekends), large restaurant, railway memorabilia and train theme throughout, wide choice of enjoyable generous food (smaller helpings available) from sandwiches up, meal deals Mon-Fri, well kept Adnams, Fullers London Pride, Sharps Doom Bar and a guest, good wine choice, cheerful service, games and TV in bar; background music; children welcome, lots of tables in big garden with awnings and heaters, summer barbecues and maybe marquee, pretty views over small lake, Nene Valley Way walks. (George Atkinson, Revd R P Tickle, Gerry and Rosemary Dobson)

CHAPEL BRAMPTON — SP7366
Spencer Arms (01604) 805822

Northampton Road; NN6 8AE Comfortable Chef & Brewer family dining pub, plenty of stripped tables in long timber-divided L-shaped bar, good choice of sensibly priced food all day, Adnams, Fullers, Greene King and a guest ale, several wines by the glass, friendly service, beams, two log fires, knick-knacks, daily newspapers; soft background music; tables outside. (R L Mobbs, S Holder)

CHARLTON — SP5235
Rose & Crown (01295) 811317

Main Street; OX17 3DP Cosy well run 17th-c thatched pub in nice village, enjoyable home-made food using local suppliers, changing ales, friendly prompt service, beams and stripped stone, well spaced pale wood tables and chairs, inglenook log fire; well behaved children welcome, back garden with picnic-sets and wisteria arbour, closed Mon lunchtime. (Sir Nigel Foulkes, M J Winterton)

CLIPSTON — SP7181
Bulls Head (01858) 525268

B4036 S of Market Harboro; LE16 9RT Village pub under welcoming newish management, enjoyable good value food including tapas, Everards and several guest beers, log fire and heavy beams – coins in the cracks put there by World War II airmen who never made it back for their next drink; background music, TV, Tues quiz; children and dogs welcome, terrace tables, three comfortable bedrooms, open all day weekends. (Peter Hallinan)

CLIPSTON — SP7181
Old Red Lion (01858) 525257

The Green; LE16 9RS Unpretentious little village-green pub with locals' bar and log-fire lounge, well kept Wells & Youngs ales and a guest from central servery, decent home-made bar food including sandwiches and snacks, small back dining room; children welcome. (R T and J C Moggridge)

COLLYWESTON — SK9902
⋆ Collyweston Slater (01780) 444288

The Drove (A43); PE9 3PQ Roomy main-road dining pub with enjoyable bar and restaurant food (not Sun evening), surprisingly contemporary with brown leather easy chairs and sofas, smart modern two-part formal dining room (log fire) and two or three more informal areas, one with a raised stove in dividing wall, beams, stripped stone and mix of dark flagstones, bare boards and carpeting, well kept Everards ales and decent wines, friendly service; background music; children welcome, teak seats on flagstoned terrace, bedrooms, open all day; may be recent change of tenancy. (Roy Bromell, Jeremy King, R T and J C Moggridge)

COSGROVE — SP7942
Barley Mow (01908) 562957

The Stocks; MK19 7JD Old village pub by Grand Union Canal, up to four well kept Everards ales, reasonably priced pubby food and blackboard specials, cheerful efficient service, lounge/dining area with dark furniture, small public bar, table football, pool and skittles; children welcome, tables on terrace and on lawn down to canal, open all day. *(Gerry and Rosemary Dobson, Stuart and Jasmine Kelly)*

COSGROVE   SP7843
Navigation (01908) 543156
Castlethorpe Road; MK19 7BE Lovely canalside setting, attractive open-plan bar up steps with open fire, lots of canal prints and memorabilia, friendly helpful service, good choice of beers and wines, popular well presented food including some interesting choices and good value Sun roasts, live music Fri; can be very busy weekends and school holidays; children welcome, lots of tables out by water, moorings. *(Dennis and Doreen Haward)*

CRICK   SP5872
✳ **Red Lion** (01788) 822342
A mile from M1 junction 18; in centre of village off A428; NN6 7TX Jovial landlord at this nicely worn-in stone-and-thatch coaching inn, traditional low-ceilinged bar with lots of old horsebrasses (some rare) and tiny log stove in big inglenook, generous helpings of straightforward good value lunchtime food and pricier more elaborate evening menu (not Sun), bargain Sun roast, well kept Caledonian Deuchars IPA, Greene King Old Speckled Hen, Wells & Youngs Bombardier and an interesting guest; children allowed (under-12s lunchtime only), dogs welcome, picnic-sets on terrace and in Perspex-covered coachyard with pretty hanging baskets. *(John and Joyce Snell, Roger and Pauline Pearce, George Atkinson, Stuart and Jasmine Kelly, Gerard Dyson, Andrew Jeeves, Carole Smart and others)*

DENFORD   SP9976
Cock Inn (01832) 732565
High Street, S of Thrapston; NN14 4EQ Refurbished 16th-c pub under friendly newish management, four well kept ales including Sharps Doom Bar and Greene King IPA, enjoyable pubby food, cosy L-shaped bar with beam-and-plank ceiling, bare boards and log fire, another fire in long restaurant; background music - live last Sun of month; children and dogs welcome, picnic-sets in front and back gardens, handy for River Nene boaters/walkers, open all day weekends. *(Jacky Bright)*

DENTON   SP8358
Red Lion (01604) 890510
Main Street; village off A428; NN7 1DQ Old refurbished pub up steps opposite small green, good well priced pubby food (not Sun evening) and blackboard specials, Wells & Youngs ales, good choice of wines; tables out at front under parasols. *(Alan Sutton)*

EAST HADDON   SP6668
✳ **Red Lion** (01604) 770223
High Street; village signposted off A428

(turn right in village) and off A50 N of Northampton; NN6 8BU Substantial and elegant golden-stone thatched hotel with sizeable dining room, log fire lounge and bar, emphasis on well presented imaginative food and most tables set for dining, but they do have well kept Wells & Youngs ales and over a dozen wines by the glass, efficient service; background music; children welcome, attractive grounds including side walled garden, cookery school, seven bedrooms and two-bed cottage, closed Sun evening. *(Alan Sutton, George Atkinson, Mrs J Plante Cleall, Clifford Blakemore, David and Sue Atkinson)*

EASTON ON THE HILL   TF0104
Exeter Arms (01780) 756321
Stamford Road (A43); PE9 3NS Renovated 18th-c pub with country-feel bar, traditional furniture on stone floor, well kept ales and Aspall's cider from panelled bar, plenty of wines by the glass, wide choice of good food (must book weekends) including pizzas and pub favourites, friendly service, restaurant and new orangery dining area; background music; split level terrace, paddock, six bedrooms, open all day, closed Sun evening. *(G Jennings, Michael and Jenny Back and others)*

EYDON   SP5450
✳ **Royal Oak** (01327) 263167
Lime Avenue; village signed off A361 Daventry–Banbury, and from B4525; NN11 3PG Interestingly laid-out 300-year-old ironstone inn, some lovely period features including fine flagstone floors and leaded windows, cosy snug on right with cushioned benches built into alcoves, seats in bow window, cottagey pictures and inglenook log fire, long corridor-like central bar linking three other small characterful rooms, four real ales including Fullers, Hook Norton and Timothy Taylors Landlord, good food (takeaway only Mon evening), friendly staff, table skittles in old stable; background music; children and dogs welcome, terrace seating (some under cover), open all day weekends, closed Mon lunchtime. *(Alan Sutton, Jenny and Peter Lowater)*

FLORE   SP6460
White Hart (01327) 341748
A45 W of M1 junction 16; NN7 4LW Welcoming recently modernised dining pub with good well presented food (not Sun evening, Mon) including set deals (Tues-Thurs), three changing ales; open all day weekends, closed Mon lunchtime. *(George Atkinson)*

GAYTON   SP7054
Queen Victoria (01604) 858878
High Street; NN7 3HD Four comfortable neat areas off central bar, Wells & Youngs and a guest like Wadworths 6X, good wine choice, enjoyable food (not Sun evening) from snacks to blackboard specials, light panelling, beams, lots of pictures, books and shelves of china,

inglenook woodburner; background music, pool, games machines, Tues quiz night; bedrooms, closed Mon. *(Alan Sutton, Gerry and Rosemary Dobson)*

GRAFTON REGIS SP7546
⋆ White Hart (01908) 542123
A508 S of Northampton; NN12 7SR Thatched dining pub with several linked rooms, good pubby food (not Sun evening) including range of home-made soups and popular well priced Sun roasts (local meat), Greene King ales, good wines by the glass, friendly helpful staff coping well when busy; african grey parrot (can be very vocal), restaurant with open fire and separate menu; background music; good-sized garden with terrace tables and new gazebo-like building, closed Mon. *(George Atkinson, Howard and Margaret Buchanan)*

GREAT BILLING SP8162
Elwes Arms (01604) 407521
High Street; NN3 9DT Thatched stone-built 16th-c village pub, two bars (steps between rooms), wide choice of good value tasty food (all day Fri-Sat, not Sun evening), Black Sheep, Wadworths 6X and Shepherd Neame Spitfire, pleasant dining room (children allowed), darts, quiz Thurs and Sun; background music, TVs, no dogs; garden tables and nice covered decked terrace, play area, open all day Wed-Sun. *(Anon)*

GREAT DODDINGTON SP8864
Stags Head (01933) 222316
High Street (B573 S of Wellingborough); NN29 7TQ Old stone-built pub with pleasant bar and split-level lounge/dining room, Black Sheep and a house beer brewed for them by Caledonian, nice wines and good soft drinks range, varied choice of fairly priced food from sandwiches up, special diets catered for, smart cheery service, also separate barn restaurant extension, public bar with pool and games; background music; picnic-sets out in front and in garden, open all day Sun. *(Anon)*

GREAT HOUGHTON SP7959
Old Cherry Tree (01604) 761399
Cherry Tree Lane; No Through Road off A428 just before White Hart; NN4 7AT Thatched village pub with low beams, stripped stone, panelling and open fires, enjoyable food from lunchtime snacks up, prompt friendly service, well kept Wells & Youngs and a couple of guests, steps up to restaurant; garden tables, closed evenings Sun and Mon, otherwise open all day. *(Gerry and Rosemary Dobson)*

GREAT OXENDON SP7383
⋆ George (01858) 465205
A508 S of Market Harborough; LE16 8NA Elegant 16th-c inn with emphasis on dining but with a convivial bar, well kept Adnams, Timothy Taylors and a guest, lots of wines by the glass, food can be good including cheaper fixed-price menus, friendly staff, green leatherette bucket chairs around small tables, brown panelled dado with wallpaper or dark painted walls above, big log fire, tiled-floor entrance lobby with easy chairs and former inn sign, carpeted conservatory; piped easy-listening music; children welcome, big shrub-sheltered garden, bedrooms, closed Sun evening. *(George Atkinson, Gerry and Rosemary Dobson, Jamie and Sue May, Fergus Munro and others)*

GREENS NORTON SP6649
Butchers Arms (01327) 350488
High Street; NN12 8BA Comfortable welcoming village pub, four well kept mainstream ales, enjoyable straightforward food from sandwiches and pizzas up, Sun carvery, reasonable prices, separate bar and games room with pool, darts and skittles, Sun quiz; piped and some live music; children (till 9pm) and dogs allowed, disabled access, picnic-sets outside, play area, pretty village near Grafton Way walks, closed lunchtimes Mon, Tues. *(George Atkinson, David Uren)*

GUILSBOROUGH SP6772
Ward Arms (01604) 740265
High Street; NN6 8PY Small 17th-c thatched pub in historic village, well kept Nobbys ales (brewed here) and guests, hearty good value food, friendly chatty staff, pool, darts and table skittles; tables outside, open all day Fri-Sun, closed Mon lunchtime. *(Gerry and Rosemary Dobson)*

HACKLETON SP8054
White Hart (01604) 870271
B526 SE of Northampton; NN7 2AD Comfortably traditional 18th-c country pub, wide choice of enjoyable generous food (smaller helpings available) from sandwiches up including early evening bargains, good friendly staff, Fullers London Pride, Greene King IPA and a guest, decent choice of other drinks, nice coffee, dining area up steps with flame-effect fire, stripped stone, beamery and brickwork, illuminated well, brasses and artefacts, split-level flagstoned bar with log fire, pool and hood skittles, curry/quiz night Tues; quiet background music; children (not in bar after 5pm) and dogs welcome, disabled access, sunny garden with picnic-sets and goal posts, open all day. *(Gerry and Rosemary Dobson, George Atkinson)*

HARRINGTON SP7780
⋆ Tollemache Arms (01536) 710469
High Street; off A508 S of Market Harborough; NN6 9NU Pretty thatched Tudor pub in lovely quiet ironstone village, very low ceilings in compact bar with log fire and in pleasant partly stripped-stone dining room, enjoyable food from generous sandwiches up, well kept ales such as Elgoods, Grainstore, Great Oakley and

Wells & Youngs, friendly staff, table skittles; children welcome, nice back garden with country views. *(R T and J C Moggridge, Simon Chandler)*

HARRINGWORTH   SP9197
⋆ **White Swan**   (01572) 747543

Seaton Road; village SE of Uppingham, signed from A6003, A47 and A43; NN17 3AF Handsome former coaching inn with imposing central gable, traditional furnishings, open fire dividing bar and two cosy dining areas, pictures of World War II aircraft at nearby Spanhoe Airfield, old village photos, nice hand-crafted oak counter (sweets in old-fashioned jars behind), Adnams and a couple of guests, enjoyable food, good smiling service, darts and board games; background music; children welcome, tables on partly covered terrace, pretty hanging baskets, not far from magnificent 82-arch viaduct spanning the Welland, bedrooms, closed Sun evening, Mon lunchtime. *(Tracey and Stephen Groves)*

HELLIDON   SP5158
Red Lion   (01327) 261200

Stockwell Lane, off A425 W of Daventry; NN11 6LG Welcoming wisteria-covered inn, bar with woodburner, cosy lounge, softly lit low-ceilinged stripped-stone dining area with lots of hunting prints, ales such as Hook Norton, Shepherd Neame and Timothy Taylors, good home-made food served by helpful friendly staff, hood skittles and pool in back games room; children and dogs welcome, picnic-sets out in front, beautiful setting by unspoilt village's green, windmill vineyard and pleasant walks nearby, four bedrooms, open all day weekends. *(Mark Englert)*

HIGHAM FERRERS   SP9668
Griffin   (01933) 312612

High Street; NN10 8BW 17th-c pub/restaurant with good food including fresh fish and popular Sun carvery (till 5pm), ales such as Adnams Broadside and Wells & Youngs, good wine and whisky choice, back restaurant and dining conservatory; terrace tables, open all day Fri-Sun. *(Howard and Margaret Buchanan)*

HINTON-IN-THE-HEDGES   SP5536
Crewe Arms   (01280) 705801

Off A43 W of Brackley; NN13 5NF 17th-c extended stone-built village pub, well kept Hook Norton and guests, enjoyable home-made food; bedrooms, closed weekday lunchtimes, open all day weekends. *(Mick Furn)*

KETTERING   SP8778
Alexandra Arms   (01536) 522730

Victoria Street; NN16 0BU Friendly real ale pub, with up to 14 changing quickly, hundreds each year, also Julian Church ales brewed in cellar, may be sandwiches, games bar with darts and hood skittles;

back terrace, open all day (from 2pm weekdays). *(P Dawn)*

KILSBY   SP5671
⋆ **George**   (01788) 822229

2.5 miles from M1 J18: A428 towards Daventry, left on to A5 – pub off on right at roundabout; CV23 8YE Popular pub, handy for motorway, with friendly hard-working landlady, proper old-fashioned public bar, wood-panelled lounge with plush banquettes and coal-effect gas stove opening into smarter area with solidly comfortable furnishings, well kept Adnams, Fullers, Greene King and a guest, splendid range of malt whiskies, enjoyable good value pubby food, speedy service; darts, free-play pool tables, TV, quiz nights; children welcome if dining, dogs in bar, garden picnic-sets, bedrooms. *(Rob and Catherine Dunster, G Jennings, Gene and Kitty Rankin, Ted George, Clare Tagg)*

KISLINGBURY   SP6959
⋆ **Cromwell Cottage**   (01604) 830288

High Street; NN7 4AG Sizeable low-ceilinged M&B family dining pub, informal lounge seating, open fire, separate smart bistro dining area with candles on tables, wide choice of good popular food including set choices and specials (booking advised), well kept ales such as Orkney, Roosters and Wells & Youngs, good service from neat cheerful staff. *(Alan Sutton, George Atkinson, G Jennings, Gerry and Rosemary Dobson)*

KISLINGBURY   SP6959
Olde Red Lion   (01604) 830219

High Street, off A45 W of Northampton; NN7 4AQ Roomy renovated 19th-c stone-fronted pub, good freshly cooked bar and restaurant food, well kept Timothy Taylors ales and a guest, friendly helpful service, beams, woodburners and open fire, events including summer beer festival; background music and some live, TV, no dogs; suntrap back terrace with marquee, barbecues, two bedrooms, closed Sun evening, Mon and lunchtime Tues. *(Rose Howell)*

LAMPORT   SP7574
Lamport Swan   (01604) 686555

A508 Harborough Road; NN6 9EZ Modern pub/bistro in imposing stone building, decent-sized front bar with good choice of wines by the glass and one or two mainstream real ales, emphasis on large side dining area with some pubby as well as more restauranty dishes (no food Sun evening); background music; outside tables with good views, open all day. *(Robin and Jasmine Marson)*

LITTLE BRINGTON   SP6663
⋆ **Saracens Head**   (01604) 770640

4.5 miles from M1 junction 16, first right off A45 to Daventry; also signed off A428; Main Street; NN7 4HS Friendly old pub with enjoyable reasonably priced food from interesting baguettes and wraps up, well kept real ales such as Batemans, Greene King and Timothy Taylors, roomy U-shaped lounge with good log fire, flagstones, chesterfields and lots of old prints, book-lined dining room; plenty of tables in neat back garden, handy for Althorp House and Holdenby House. *(Gerry and Rosemary Dobson, D Broughton)*

LITTLE HARROWDEN   SP8671
Lamb (01933) 673300
Orlingbury Road/Kings Lane - off A509 or A43 S of Kettering; NN9 5BH Popular pub in delightful village, split-level lounge with log fire and brasses on 17th-c beams, dining area, good promptly served bargain food, well kept changing ales and short sensibly priced wine list, good coffee, games bar with darts, hood skittles and machines; background music; children welcome, small raised terrace and garden. *(Howard and Margaret Buchanan)*

LITTLE HOUGHTON   SP8059
Four Pears (01604) 890900
Bedford Road, off A428 E of Northampton; NN7 1AB Popular pub refurbished in contemporary style (was the Red Lion), three well kept local ales, several wines by the glass, fresh coffee, enjoyable food (not Sun evening) from open ciabattas and light dishes up, prompt friendly service, good-sized bar, comfortable lounge with woodburner and separate restaurant; spacious outside area, open all day. *(Gerry and Rosemary Dobson)*

LOWICK   SP9780
⋆ Snooty Fox (01832) 733434
Off A6116 Corby–Raunds; NN14 3BH Spacious and attractively reworked 16th-c stone-built pub, leather sofas and chairs, beams and stripped stonework, log fire in huge fireplace, good food from open kitchen including set lunch deal and blackboard specials, well kept ales, lots of wines by the glass and nice coffee, good friendly service, board games; background music; children and dogs welcome, picnic-sets on front grass, play area, closed Mon, otherwise open all day. *(Michael Sargent, Alan Sutton, Cam Smith)*

MAIDWELL   SP7477
⋆ Stags Head (01604) 686700
Harborough Road (A508 N of Northampton); NN6 9JA Comfortable dining pub with log fire in pubby part by bar, extensive eating areas, enjoyable good value traditional food including OAP two-course lunch, helpful friendly staff and cheery locals, well kept Black Sheep and guests, good choice of other drinks; quiet background music; disabled facilities, picnic-sets on back terrace (dogs on leads allowed here), good-sized sheltered sloping garden

beyond, bedrooms, not far from splendid Palladian Kelmarsh Hall and park. *(Jeff and Wendy Williams, George Atkinson, Gerry and Rosemary Dobson, Michael Tack)*

NASSINGTON   TL0696
Queens Head (01780) 784006
Station Road; PE8 6QB Smartly refurbished dining inn, softly-lit beamed bar with mix of old tables and chairs, large oriental rug in front of roaring fire, good reasonably priced food from traditional choices to imaginative restaurant dishes using local ingredients, lunchtimes and Tues evening set meals, pleasant helpful uniformed staff, nice choice of wines by the glass, ales such as Greene King IPA and Oakham, good coffee, separate restaurant; pretty garden by River Nene, delightful village, nine chalet bedrooms. *(Phil and Jane Hodson, Michael Doswell)*

NORTHAMPTON   SP7560
Eastgate (01604) 633535
Abington Street; NN1 2BP Wetherspoons conversion with eight real ales from central servery, their usual good value food, lots of local photos around the walls, upstairs bar with smokers' balcony; open all day from 9am. *(George Atkinson)*

NORTHAMPTON   SP7560
Wig & Pen (01604) 622178
St Giles Street; NN1 1JA L-shaped beamed pub with well kept Greene King IPA, Fullers London Pride and eight interesting guest ales, good choice of bottled beers too, enjoyable food (not weekend evenings) from sandwiches and deli boards up, live music; sports TV; attractive split-level walled garden, open all day. *(Paul Humphreys)*

RINGSTEAD   SP9875
Axe & Compass (01933) 622227
Carlow Road; NN14 4DW Extended stone-built village pub with popular good value food, four Marstons-related ales, open fire in lounge; garden, open all day weekends, closed Mon lunchtime. *(Ryta Lyndley)*

RUSHDEN   SP9566
Station Bar (01933) 318988
Station Approach; NN10 0AW Not a pub, part of station HQ of Rushden Historical Transport Society (non-members can sign in), restored in 1940s/60s style, with Fullers, Oakham and guests, tea and coffee, friendly staff, filled rolls (perhaps some hot dishes), gas lighting, enamel signs, old-fangled furnishings; authentic waiting room with piano, also museum and summer steam-ups; open all day Sat, closed weekday lunchtimes. *(P Dawn)*

RUSHTON   SP8483
Thornhill Arms (01536) 710251
Station Road; NN14 1RL Rambling dining pub opposite attractive village's cricket green, popular keenly priced food, carvery Sun

and Mon evening, friendly helpful service, Fullers, Hook Norton, Shepherd Neame and Wychwood Hobgoblin, several neatly laid out dining areas including smart high-beamed back restaurant, open fire; garden tables, bedrooms, open all day Sun. *(Gerry and Rosemary Dobson)*

SLIPTON SP9579
⋆ **Samuel Pepys** (01832) 731739
Off A6116 at first roundabout N of A14 junction, towards Twywell and Slipton; NN14 3AR Old reworked stone pub with long gently modern bar, heavy low beams and log fire, great central pillar, area with squashy leather seats around low tables, six changing ales including local Digfield, interesting reasonably priced wines, enjoyable food from sandwiches and tapas up, friendly efficient service, dining room extending into roomy conservatory with country views; background music; children welcome, dogs in bar, wheelchair access, well laid-out sheltered garden with heated terrace, open all day weekends. *(P and J Shapley, Peter Travis, Ryta Lyndley)*

STAVERTON SP5461
Countryman (01327) 311815
Daventry Road (A425); NN11 6JH Beamed and carpeted dining pub under enthusiastic landlord, good choice of enjoyable reasonably priced food from sandwiches and baguettes up, Fullers London Pride and two changing guests such as local Hoggleys, friendly attentive staff; background music; children welcome, disabled access, some tables outside and in small garden. *(George Atkinson)*

STOKE BRUERNE SP7449
Boat (01604) 862428
3.5 miles from M1 junction 15 - A508 towards Stony Stratford, then signed on right; Bridge Road; NN12 7SB Old-world flagstoned bar in picturesque canalside spot by restored lock, more modern central-pillared back bar and bistro, half a dozen Marstons-related ales and local Frog Island, Thatcher's cider, fairly standard food from baguettes up including OAP lunch deal, friendly efficient young staff, comfortable upstairs bookable restaurant with more upmarket menu, shop for boaters (nice ice-creams); background music, can get busy in summer especially weekends and parking nearby difficult; welcomes dogs and children (local school in for lunch from midday), disabled facilities, tables out by towpath opposite British Waterways Museum, boat trips, open all day. *(Brian and Anna Marsden, George Atkinson, Peter Lee)*

STOKE BRUERNE SP7449
Navigation (01604) 864988
E side of bridge; NN12 7SD Large Marstons canalside pub with changing selection of their well kept beers, quite a few

wines by the glass, wide choice of good fairly priced pubby food, friendly busy young staff, several levels and cosy corners, sturdy wood furniture, separate family room, pub games; background music (outside too) and some live jazz; wheelchair access, plenty of tables out overlooking the water, big play area, open all day. *(Michael Tack, Ross Balaam)*

STOKE DOYLE TL0286
⋆ **Shuckburgh Arms** (01832) 272339
Village signed (down Stoke Hill) from SW edge of Oundle; PE8 5TG Attractively reworked relaxed 17th-c pub in quiet hamlet, four traditional rooms with some modern touches, low black beams in bowed ceilings, pictures on pastel walls, lots of pale tables on wood or carpeted floors, stylish art deco seats and elegant dining chairs, stove in inglenook, Digfield and Timothy Taylors from granite-top bar, well selected wines, good food served by competent staff; faint background music; children welcome, garden with decked area and play frame, bedrooms in separate modern block, closed Sun evening. *(Howard and Margaret Buchanan)*

SUDBOROUGH SP9682
Vane Arms (01832) 730033
Off A6116; Main Street; NN14 3BX Refurbished thatched pub under newish landlord, low beams, stripped stonework, and inglenook fires, enjoyable freshly cooked food, well kept Everards and guests, friendly staff, restaurant; tables out on terrace, pretty village. *(Ryta Lyndley)*

SULGRAVE SP5545
⋆ **Star** (01295) 760389
Manor Road; E of Banbury, signed off B4525; OX17 2SA Creeper-clad farmhouse, small bar with pews, cushioned window seats and wall benches, flagstones by inglenook (red carpet elsewhere), Hook Norton ales, enjoyable pubby food (best to book Sun lunch), separate dining room with motor-racing theme, friendly staff; children and dogs welcome, seats out at front and in back garden, short walk to Sulgrave Manor (ancestral home of George Washington), four bedrooms, closed Sun evening, Mon. *(Peter Martin, Alan Sutton, Philip and Susan Philcox)*

THORNBY SP6675
Red Lion (01604) 740238
Welford Road; A5199 Northampton– Leicester; NN6 8SJ Friendly old country pub with well kept changing ales, good well priced home-made food (not Mon), beams and log fire, back dining area; children and dogs welcome, garden picnic-sets, open all day weekends when can be busy. *(Gerry and Rosemary Dobson)*

THORPE MANDEVILLE SP5344
⋆ **Three Conies** (01295) 711025
Off B4525 E of Banbury; OX17 2EX Attractive and welcoming 17th-c pub

with wide choice of food from good value sandwiches up, well kept Hook Norton ales and a guest, beamed bare-boards bar with some stripped stone, mix of old dining tables, three good log fires, large dining room, pub cat called Pepper; background and some live music; children and dogs welcome, disabled facilities, tables out in front and behind on decking and lawn, open all day (from 10am for breakfast). *(George Atkinson)*

THORPE WATERVILLE   TL0281
Fox   (01832) 720274
A605 Thrapston–Oundle; NN14 3ED Extended stone-built pub with emphasis on chef/landlord's enjoyable food, well kept Wells & Youngs ales from central bar, several wines by the glass, friendly attentive staff, nice fire, light modern dining area; background music; children welcome, small garden with play area, open all day. *(Iain Akhurst, Guy and Caroline Howard)*

TURWESTON   SP6037
Stratton Arms   (01280) 704956
E of crossroads in village; pub itself just inside Buckinghamshire; NN13 5JX Friendly chatty local in picturesque village, well kept Courage, Shepherd Neame, John Smiths, Timothy Taylors and a guest, good choice of other drinks, enjoyable reasonably priced traditional food (not Sun evening, Mon or Tues), low ceilings and two log fires, small restaurant; background music, sports TV; children and dogs welcome, big garden by the Great Ouse with barbecue and play area, camping, open all day. *(Michael Tack)*

WADENHOE   TL0183
Kings Head   (01832) 720024
Church Street; village signposted (in small print) off A605 S of Oundle; PE8 5ST Beautifully placed 17th-c country pub with picnic-sets on sun terrace and among trees on grassy stretch by River Nene (moorings), uncluttered partly stripped-stone bar with pale pine furniture, a couple of cushioned wall seats, woodburner in fine inglenook, also simple bare-boards public bar, games room with darts, dominoes and table skittles, and attractive little beamed dining room with more pine furniture, beers from Digfield and perhaps three changing guests from other local brewers, good well presented food (all day Sat), friendly efficient service; children and dogs welcome, open all day weekends (closed Sun evening in winter). *(Mike and Margaret Banks, Rob and Catherine Dunster, Di and Mike Gillam, Gerry and Rosemary Dobson, Ryta Lyndley and others)*

WALGRAVE   SP8072
Royal Oak   (01604) 781248
Zion Hill, off A43 Northampton–Kettering; NN6 9PN Welcoming old stone-built village local, up to five well kept changing ales, decent wines, good value food (not Sun evening) including some unusual choices and lunchtime deals, friendly prompt service, long three-part carpeted beamed bar, small lounge, restaurant extension behind; children welcome, small garden with play area, open all day Sun. *(Gerry and Rosemary Dobson)*

WEEDON   SP6359
Crossroads   (01327) 340354
3 miles from M1 junction 16; A45 towards Daventry; High Stret, on A5 junction; NN7 4PX Refurbished spacious Chef & Brewer with beamed bar and dining area, lots of nooks and crannies, comfy sofas, log fires, changing ales such as Courage Best and Wadworths 6X, decent all-day food including set deals, friendly attentive staff; children welcome, disabled facilities, tables on terrace and in attractive gardens down to river (no food outside), comfortable Premier Lodge bedroom block, open all day. *(George Atkinson)*

WEEDON   SP6458
Narrow Boat   (01327) 340333
Stowe Hill (A5 S); NN7 4RZ Canalside pub reopened after expensive refit, decent choice of food from pub favourites and stone-baked pizzas up, Wells & Youngs ales; children welcome, big revamped garden sloping down to water, outside bar, five refurbished bedrooms, open all day. *(Anon)*

WOODNEWTON   TL0394
White Swan   (01780) 470944
Main Street; PE8 5EB Modernised village pub/restaurant with good food including competitively priced set lunch, pleasant service, Digfield beers; open all day weekends in summer. *(Roy Bromell)*

YARDLEY HASTINGS   SP8656
Red Lion   (01604) 696210
High Street, just off A428 Bedford–Northampton; NN7 1ER Pretty thatched pub, refurbished and under same ownership as the village's Rose & Crown, enjoyable italian-influenced food (not Sun evening), Fullers, Wells & Youngs and nice wines by the glass, prompt cheerful service, linked rooms with beams and stripped stone; sloping garden, open all day Sun, closed Mon. *(Alan Sutton)*

YARDLEY HASTINGS   SP8656
★ **Rose & Crown**   (01604) 696276
Just off A428 Bedford–Northampton; NN7 1EX Spacious 18th-c pub in this pretty village, flagstones, beams, stripped stonework and quiet corners, step up to big comfortable family dining room, flowers on tables, good popular food served by friendly staff, six real ales, four ciders, decent range of wines and soft drinks, newspapers; piped and some live music; dogs welcome, picnic-sets in small courtyard and good-sized garden, open from 5pm Mon-Thurs, all day Fri, Sat, closed Sun evening. *(James Meikle, S Holder, Alan Sutton)*

Northumbria
(County Durham, Northumberland and Tyneside)

The North East has a fine range of pubs right across the spectrum but if it's a special meal you want, head for the area's top food pubs: the Rat at Anick (relaxed country pub with emphasis on top quality local produce), County in Aycliffe (genuinely friendly and very popular for its interesting dishes), Feathers at Hedley on the Hill (quaint tavern with imaginative food, beers from micro-breweries and knowledgeable staff) and Rose & Crown at Romaldkirk (civilised inn with excellent food and lovely bedrooms). Our Northumbria Dining Pub 2013 is the Feathers, Hedly on the Hill. Other pubs much enjoyed by readers over this last year are the Red Lion in Alnmouth (a new entry with enjoyable all-day food), Crown at Catton (another new Main Entry with good value food and a friendly landlady), Angel in Corbridge (an imposing coaching inn – another new one for us – with interesting food and drink), Fox & Hounds at Cotherstone (warmly friendly and a popular place to stay), Dipton Mill Inn at Diptonmill (back after a break, with own-brewed beers and good value food), Coach in Lesbury (comfortable and welcoming and new to us), Keelman in Newburn (eight own brews and honest food and another new entry), Ship at Newton-by-the-Sea (a cosy waterside place back in the Main Entries), and Shiremoor Farm at New York (very well run and exceptionally popular).

ALNMOUTH   NU2410   Map 10

Red Lion 🍴 🛏

Northumberland Street; NE66 2RJ

Enjoyable food all day in traditional character bar and restaurant, comfortable bedrooms with estuary views – a fine all-rounder

Go through the coach entry on the left to find this 18th-c inn's black-beamed bar, relaxed and cosy with cheerful fires, scatter cushions brightening up the comfortably worn leather wall banquettes and window seats, and attractively framed old local photographs on the brown panelling. The friendly young landlord has well kept regional ales such as Allendale North Sheep, Black Sheep Best and Tempest Long White Cloud on handpump, mainly New World wines by the glass, and nicely served coffee; background music is unobtrusive. The unpretentious stripped-brick restaurant has comfortable contemporary leather dining chairs around polished tables on its stone-tiled floor. An ancient stone arch at the back of the yard leads into a neat and peaceful sheltered garden – swifts calling overhead, and a raised deck giving a wide view out over the anchorage of the Aln estuary.

Besides good baguettes and cheese platters, a wide choice of locally sourced meat and fish dishes includes Craster kipper pâté, yorkshire blue with a walnut and pear salad, fresh tagliatelle with a three cheese and mushrooms sauce, venison sausages with mash and onion gravy, chicken breast with asparagus, peas and bacon in a shallot cream, lamb rump with roasted garlic mash and red wine sauce, good specials such as starters of curried vegetable soup or pigeon breast with stilton and red onion salad, pork loin with garlic mash, and puddings such as lemon posset, sticky toffee, treacle tart or chocolate brownie. *Benchmark main dish: slow-cooked pork belly with colcannon mash, parsnip purée and roasted root vegetables £13.95. Two-course evening meal £19.00.*

Free house ~ Licensees Jane and Mac McHugh ~ Real ale ~ Bar food (12-9(8 Sun); coffee and breakfasts from 9.30am) ~ Restaurant ~ (01665) 830584 ~ Children welcome ~ Open 9.30-11.30(10.30 Sun) ~ Bedrooms: /£95S ~ www.redlionalnmouth.com
Recommended by Ann and Tony Bennett-Hughes, John Beeken, Dr and Mrs P Truelove, Celia Minoughan, Comus and Sarah Elliott, Dr Kevan Tucker

ANICK NY9565 Map 10
Rat 🍴 🍺
Village signposted NE of A69/A695 Hexham junction; NE46 4LN

Views over North Tyne Valley from terrace and garden, refurbished bar and lounge, lots of diverting knick-knacks, half a dozen mainly local real ales and interesting bar food

The hard-working and enthusiastic licensees at this relaxed country pub are quite rightly proud of the successful business they've built up here. They have a real sense of the local area, which can be seen in the range of both their food and drinks. The traditional bar is snug and welcoming with a coal fire in a blackened kitchen range, lots of cottagey knick-knacks from antique floral chamber-pots hanging from the beams to china and glassware on a delft shelf, and little curtained windows that allow in a soft and gentle light. A conservatory has pleasant views and the garden is quite charming with its dovecote, statues, pretty flower beds and North Tyne Valley views from seats on the terrace; background music, daily papers and magazines. Drinks include Cumberland Corby, Timothy Taylors Landlord, four changing guests on handpump from mostly local brewers such as Harviestoun, Hexhamshire, High House Farm and Wylam, a dozen wines by the glass (including champagne), a local gin and farm cider. Parking is limited, but you can park around the village green.

Using carefully sourced local meat and game and own-grown or local seasonal produce, the good, interesting bar food is all cooked from scratch. A predominantly british menu includes sandwiches, terrine of local game, charcuterie, beef braised in ale, sausage with leek and potato cake and gravy, coley with creamed samphire, lemon and capers, popular roast rib of beef with béarnaise sauce (for two people), and puddings such as apple and blueberry crème brûlée, ginger sponge and ice-cream, chocolate brownie with fudge ice-cream, and local cheeses; booking is advised. *Benchmark main dish: rump steak £13.50. Two-course evening meal £18.40.*

Free house ~ Licensees Phil Mason and Karen Errington ~ Real ale ~ Bar food (12-2(3 Sun), 6-9; not Sun eve or Mon except bank holidays) ~ Restaurant ~ (01434) 602814 ~ Children welcome ~ Open 12-3, 6-11 Mon; 12-11 Tues-Sat; 12-10.30 Sun ~ www.theratinn.com *Recommended by W K Wood, Denis Newton, Comus and Sarah Elliott, Michael Doswell*

AYCLIFFE NZ2822 Map 10
County 🍴 🍺

The Green, Aycliffe; just off A1(M) junction 59, by A167; DL5 6LX

Friendly, well run pub with four real ales, good wines and popular, interesting food; bedrooms

One reader describes this popular pub as 'a shining beacon' when it comes to food. More or less open plan throughout, it's warmly decorated with pastel blue, green and yellow paintwork, some bright red carpeting, local art and careful lighting. The wood-floored bar has attractive solid pine dining chairs and cushioned settles around a mix of pine tables, and some high bar chairs by the counter from which genuinely friendly staff serve Black Sheep and Marstons EPA and a couple of guests such as Hawkshead Gold and Mithril Flower Power on handpump. The carpeted lounge has a woodburning stove in a brick fireplace with candles in brass candlesticks on either side, a second fireplace with nightlights, similar furniture to the bar and painted ceiling joists. The wood-floored restaurant is minimalist with high-backed black leather dining chairs and dark window blinds. Metal tables and chairs in front overlook the pretty village green.

🍴 As well as sandwiches, the interesting changing menu might include mushroom tortellini with parmesan and truffle oil, breaded goats cheese with beetroot salad, jumbo garlic prawns, crispy pork belly with salad of black pudding, chorizo, roast apple and brandy cream, battered cod and mushy peas, roast vegetables with tomato and black olive sauce, baked halloumi and vegetable crisps, rolled fillet of lemon sole filled with smoked salmon mousse with lime and lemon butter, and puddings such as warm raspberry and almond tart and baked ginger parkin with spiced treacle and raspberry ice-cream. *Benchmark main dish: steak in ale pie £10.50. Two-course evening meal £22.00.*

Free house ~ Licensee Colette Farrell ~ Real ale ~ Bar food (12-2, 6-9; 12-9 Sun) ~ Restaurant ~ (01325) 312273 ~ Children welcome ~ Open 11.30-3, 5-11; 11.30-11 Sun ~ Bedrooms: $49S/$70S($89B) ~ www.thecountyaycliffevillage.com *Recommended by Dave and Jenny Hughes, Rob and Catherine Dunster, Michael Doswell*

CARTERWAY HEADS NZ0452 Map 10
Manor House Inn 🍺

A68 just N of B6278, near Derwent reservoir; DH8 9LX

Handy after a walk with a simple bar and more comfortable lounge, bar food and five real ales; bedrooms

There are stunning views over the Derwent reservoir and beyond from picnic-sets on the terrace of this simple slate-roofed stone inn, and the plain but heartwarming locals' bar is a relaxing place if you've worked up a thirst enjoying the nearby Derwent Valley. Homely and old-fashioned, it has an original boarded ceiling, pine tables, chairs and stools, old oak pews and a mahogany counter. The carpeted lounge bar (warmed by a woodburning stove) and restaurant are comfortably pubby with wheelback chairs, stripped stone walls and picture windows that make the most of the lovely setting. Greene King Old Speckled Hen, Timothy Taylors Landlord and a couple of guests such as Black Sheep and Ruddles County are on handpump alongside 15 wines by the glass, 20 malt whiskies and Weston's Old Rosie cider; TV, darts, board games and background music.

Featuring a lot of locally caught game, local meats and exotic cuts such as camel and kangaroo, and usefully served all day, bar food includes tempura king prawns, chicken liver pâté, roast pork belly, sausage and mash, chicken caesar salad, mushroom risotto, fish and chips, fish pie and steaks, with daily specials such as game pie, pheasant stuffed with haggis with pepper sauce, hawk-caught rabbit tagliatelle with white wine and tarragon sauce. *Benchmark main dish: venison wellington £12.95. Two-course evening meal £17.45.*

Enterprise ~ Licensees Barrie and Eileen Wray ~ Real ale ~ Bar food (12-9) ~ Restaurant ~ (01207) 255268 ~ Children welcome ~ Dogs allowed in bar and bedrooms ~ Open 11-11; 12-10.30 Sun ~ Bedrooms: £45B/£65B ~ www.themanorhouseinn.com
Recommended by Mr and Mrs M Hargrave, GSB, Henry Paulinski, Simon Le Fort

 CATTON   NY8257   Map 10
Crown £
B6295, off A686 S of Haydon Bridge; NE47 9QS

Good value food and good drinks in attractive and welcoming pub, usefully open all day

With charming and efficient service, local Allendale Golden Plover and Wagtail on handpump, and a decent choice of wines by the glass, this is a friendly pub liked by our readers. The stripped-stone bare-boards inner bar feels relaxed and civilised, with soft lighting from coloured lanterns and comfortable mate's chairs, dining chairs and a sturdy traditional wall settle around dark polished tables. A partly carpeted extension is rather lighter in décor, and both rooms have interesting local photographs including one of the Allendale Wolf, shot nearby in 1905 and a key ingredient in some hair-raising folk tales. Charming and efficient service, picnic-sets on a side terrace and neat small lawn, plenty of good nearby walks.

They do good generous sandwiches, chicken liver and cognac pâté with onion chutney, locally cured bacon and black pudding salad, well flavoured home-made burgers, pasta with olives, cherry tomatoes, rocket and sun-dried tomato pesto, beer-battered haddock, chicken in a mushroom, cream and tarragon sauce, honey-glazed salmon, juicy lamb chops, and puddings like strawberry eton mess and sticky toffee pudding. *Benchmark main dish: local steak with garlic and parsley butter £13.95. Two-course evening meal £16.00.*

Free house ~ Licensee Emma Carrick-Thomson ~ Real ale ~ Bar food (12-2, 6-9; 12-3 Sun; not Sun evening or Mon) ~ (01434) 683447 ~ Children welcome ~ Dogs allowed in bar ~ Open 12-2, 6-11; 12-11 Fri, Sat and Sun; closed Mon except bank holidays ~ www.crownatcatton.co.uk *Recommended by Comus and Sarah Elliott, S Jackson, B Thompson, Philip Huddleston, Marcus Byron, John Coatsworth, Michael Doswell*

Please tell us if the décor, atmosphere, food or drink at a pub is different from our description. We rely on readers' reports to keep us up to date: feedback@goodguides.com, or (no stamp needed) The Good Pub Guide, FREEPOST TN1569, Wadhurst, E Sussex TN5 7BR.

CORBRIDGE
NY9964 Map 10

Angel 🍺 🛏

Main Street; NE45 5LA

Enterprising food and fine range of drinks in crisply modernised coaching inn; comfortable bedrooms

Deservedly popular, this is a well run, imposing coaching inn in an attractive town. The sizeable main bar is functional in a briskly modern style – light and airy with just a few prints on its pastel walls, plain light wood tables and chairs, overhead spotlighting and a big-screen TV. The carpeted lounge bar has quite a modern feel, too, with its strongly patterned wallpaper and some tall metal-framed café-bar seats as well as more homely leather bucket armchairs. The best sense of the building's age is in a separate lounge, with button-back wing armchairs, sofa, oak panelling and big stone fireplace; and look out for the fine 17th-c arched doorway in the left-hand porch. A smart raftered restaurant has local artwork and some stripped masonry; background music. Hadrian & Border Centurion Best and Tyneside Blonde, Timothy Taylors Landlord and Wylam Gold Tankard on handpump, a dozen wines by the glass, 30 malt whiskies and Weston's cider; daily papers. You can sit out in front on the cobbles below a wall sundial; the building is nicely set at the end of a broad street, facing the handsome bridge over the River Tyne.

Using meat from their own farm, the inventive food might include sandwiches, thai salmon and crab cakes with mango, star fruit, chilli, coriander and vermicelli salad with a sweet chilli dip, twice baked gruyère cheese soufflé with parmesan cream, wild mushroom stroganoff, home-made beefburger with hand-cut chips and relish, chunky cod with brown shrimp and cucumber and slow-roast tomatoes, cajun chicken with celeriac remoulade and wild red camargue rice salad, fillet steak with Café de Paris butter and triple-cooked chips, and puddings such as iced white chocolate parfait with blueberry and thyme soup and vanilla panna cotta with a liquid raspberry centre. *Benchmark main dish: fish and chips and mushy peas £11.95. Two-course evening meal £19.50.*

Free house ~ Licensee Kevin Laing ~ Real ale ~ Bar food (12-9(9.30 Fri and Sat; 5 Sun); not Sun evening) ~ Restaurant ~ (01434) 632119 ~ Children welcome ~ Open 11-11 (midnight Sat); 12-10.30 Sun ~ Bedrooms: £75S/£125S ~ www.theangelofcorbridge.com
Recommended by Pete Coxon, Dr Peter D Smart, Eric Larkham, Comus and Sarah Elliott

COTHERSTONE
NZ0119 Map 10

Fox & Hounds 🛏

B6277; DL12 9PF

Bustling 18th-c inn with cheerful beamed bar, good bar food and quite a few wines by the glass; bedrooms

This Georgian country inn occupies an attractive spot by the village green and is a popular place to stay. There's a cheerful, simply furnished beamed bar with a partly wooden floor (elsewhere it's carpeted), a good winter log fire, thickly cushioned wall seats and local photographs and country pictures on the walls of its various alcoves and recesses. Black Sheep Best and Ale and York Yorkshire Terrier on handpump alongside several malt whiskies from smaller distilleries; efficient service from the friendly staff. Don't be surprised by the unusual lavatory attendant – an african grey parrot called Reva. Seats outside on a terrace and quoits. The inn makes an excellent focal point for walks along the dramatic wooded Tees Valley from Barnard Castle.

Well liked bar food includes sandwiches, bacon, red apple, wensleydale cheese and cranberry salad, a pot of prawns with mushrooms, leeks, local cheese and herbs, french vegetable stew, beer-battered haddock with minty mushy peas (Tuesday and Friday are fish and chip evenings), lambs liver with rich roast gravy and mustard mash, pork tenderloin in an italian marsala cream sauce, salmon, prawns and smoked mackerel fishcakes with home-made tartare sauce, and puddings such as chocolate cream crunch and tipsy raspberry meringues. *Benchmark main dish: chicken stuffed with cotherstone cheese, wrapped in bacon, in a creamy leek sauce £10.50. Two-course evening meal £17.00.*

Free house ~ Licensee Ian Swinburn ~ Real ale ~ Bar food (12-2, 6(5 Tues)-8.30; all day Fri, Sat and Sun) ~ Restaurant ~ (01833) 650241 ~ Children welcome ~ Open 12-3, 6(5 Tues)-11; 12-11 Fri, Sat; 12-10.30 Sun; 12-3, 6-11 Fri, Sat and Sun in in winter ~ Bedrooms: £47.50B/£75B ~ www.cotherstonefox.co.uk *Recommended by John H Smith, Lucien Perring, Michael Doswell*

DIPTONMILL
NY9261 Map 10
Dipton Mill Inn ♀ ◀ £
S of Hexham; off B6306 at Slaley; NE46 1YA

Own-brew beers, good value bar food and waterside terrace

Readers are fond of the genuine character of this hospitable little two-roomed pub, which is charmingly tucked away in a little hamlet by steep hills in a peaceful wooded valley – it's not easy to find, but it's worth making the effort. All six of the nicely named beers from the family-owned Hexhamshire Brewery are well kept here on handpump: Devils Elbow, Devils Water, Old Humbug, Shire Bitter and Whapweasel; also over a dozen wines by the glass, over 20 malt whiskies, Weston's Old Rosie and a guest cider. The neatly kept snug bar has dark ply panelling, low ceilings, red furnishings, a dark red carpet and newspapers to read by two welcoming open fires. The garden is peaceful and pretty with its sunken crazy-paved terrace by the restored millstream and attractive planting; Hexham race course is not far away.

 Good value, homely bar food includes sandwiches, salads, ploughman's with nearly a dozen cheeses to choose from, carrot and celery soup, steak and kidney pie, ratatouille and couscous, dressed crab salad, chicken in sherry sauce, haddock baked with tomato and basil, and puddings such as bread and butter pudding and syrup sponge and custard. *Benchmark main dish: mince and dumplings £7.15. Two-course evening meal £9.75.*

Own brew ~ Licensee Geoff Brooker ~ Real ale ~ Bar food (12-2, 6.30-8) ~ No credit cards ~ (01434) 606577 ~ Children welcome ~ Open 12-2.30, 6-11; 12-3 Sun; closed Sun evening ~ www.diptonmill.co.uk *Recommended by Lawrence Pearse, Eric Larkham, Claes Mauroy, the Didler, LC*

 ## DURHAM
NZ2742 Map 10
Victoria ◀
Hallgarth Street (A177, near Dunelm House); DH1 3AS

Unchanging and neatly kept Victorian pub with royal memorabilia, cheerful locals and well kept regional ales; bedrooms

Virtually unaltered since it was built, this lovingly preserved 19th-c local has been in the same friendly family for well over 30 years. It consists of three little rooms leading off a central bar, with typical Victorian décor that takes in mahogany, etched and cut glass and mirrors, colourful William Morris wallpaper over a high panelled dado, some maroon plush seats in little booths, leatherette wall seats and long narrow drinkers' tables. There are also coal fires in handsome iron and tile fireplaces, photographs and articles showing a real pride in the pub, lots of period prints and engravings of Queen Victoria, and staffordshire figurines of her and the Prince Consort. Big Lamp Bitter and Wylam Gold Tankard and up to three usually local guests from brewers such as Copper Dragon, Durham and York are on handpump, they've over 40 irish whiskeys and cheap house wines; dominoes. You can use a credit card for accomodation (only); the bedrooms have recently been refurbished in period style.

❦❦ Bar food is limited to toasties. *Benchmark main dish: toasties £1.70.*

Free house ~ Licensee Michael Webster ~ Real ale ~ Bar food ~ No credit cards ~ (0191) 386 5269 ~ Children welcome ~ Dogs welcome ~ Open 11.45-3, 6-11; 12-2, 7-10.30 Sun ~ Bedrooms: £49B/£68B ~ www.victoriainn-durhamcity.co.uk *Recommended by Phil and Sally Gorton, Dr and Mrs P Truelove, Eric Larkham, Peter Smith and Judith Brown, the Didler, Comus and Sarah Elliott, Peter F Marshall*

HALTWHISTLE
NY7166 Map 10

Milecastle Inn £

Military Road; B6318 NE – OS Sheet 86 map reference 715660; NE49 9NN

Close to Hadrian's Wall and some wild scenery, with cosy little rooms warmed by winter log fires; fine views and walled garden

As it's open all day in summer, this sturdy stone-built pub, just 500 metres from Hadrian's Wall and some of its most celebrated sites, is a handy refreshment stop, and in winter you can warm-up nicely by the two log fires. The snug little rooms of the beamed bar are decorated with brasses, horsey and local landscape prints and attractive fresh flowers; at lunchtime, the small, comfortable restaurant is used as an overflow. Three Big Lamp beers are on handpump and they stock several malt whiskies. There are tables and benches in the big sheltered walled garden, with a dovecote and rather stunning views; two self-catering cottages and a large car park.

❦❦ Straightforward bar food includes sandwiches, filo duck rolls, potato skins with garlic dip, game pâté, battered haddock, scampi, shepherd's pie, chicken and vegetable curry, belly of pork, chilli, various pies, honey roast duck with orange or redcurrant gravy, and steaks. *Benchmark main dish: venison casserole £10.25. Two-course evening meal £15.60.*

Free house ~ Licensees Clare and Kevin Hind ~ Real ale ~ Bar food (12-8.45; 12-2.30, 6-8.30 in winter) ~ Restaurant ~ (01434) 321372 ~ Children welcome ~ Dogs welcome ~ Open 12-11(midnight Sat); 12-3, 6-11 in winter ~ www.milecastle-inn.co.uk *Recommended by Clive Watkin, Bruce and Sharon Eden, Jean and Douglas Troup*

HAYDON BRIDGE
NY8364 Map 10

General Havelock

A69 Corbridge–Haltwhistle; NE47 6ER

Bustling, chatty riverside dining pub with local beers and interesting food

Just a short stroll downstream from Haydon Bridge itself, this old stone terraced house is well run and friendly. The attractively lit L-shaped bar is imaginatively decorated in shades of green. It's at its best in the back part with a stripped-pine chest of drawers topped with bric-a-brac, colourful cushions on long pine benches and a sturdy stripped settle, interestingly shaped mahogany-topped tables and good wildlife photographs. Mordue Five Bridge Bitter and a local guest such as Geltsdale Tarn on handpump, ten wines by the glass and a fair choice of juices; board games and boules. Both the stripped-stone barn dining room and the terrace enjoy fine South Tyne river views.

🍴 Cooked by the landlord (who makes his own bread and ice-cream) using local produce, the well liked bar food includes lunchtime sandwiches, their famous cullen skink, chicken liver pâté with onion marmalade, lager-battered cod with home-made chips, chicken, bacon and leek pie, local cumberland sausages with onion gravy, brill fillet on fine ratatouille, calves liver with pancetta and chive gravy, and puddings like new season's rhubarb sundae and bread and butter pudding with fresh orange and apricots. *Benchmark main dish: slow-cooked lamb shank in redcurrant jelly and red wine £15.00. Two-course evening meal £20.00.*

Free house ~ Licensees Gary and Joanna Thompson ~ Real ale ~ Bar food (12-2.30, 7-9; not Sun evening, not Mon) ~ Restaurant ~ (01434) 684376 ~ Children welcome ~ Dogs allowed in bar ~ Open 12-3, 7-midnight; 12-5, 7.30-10.30 Sun; closed Mon lunchtime ~ www.generalhavelock.co.uk *Recommended by Alan Sutton, Marcus Byron*

HEDLEY ON THE HILL   NZ0759   Map 10
Feathers 🍴 ♟ 🍺

Village signposted from New Ridley, which is signposted from B6309 N of Consett; OS Sheet 88 map reference 078592; NE43 7SW

Northumbria Dining Pub of the Year

Imaginative food, interesting beers from small breweries and friendly welcome in quaint tavern

This 200-year-old hilltop tavern is run with complete dedication to quality and a passion for local produce. They arrange lots of events, from foraging to a farmers' market and cider and food festivals. Though emphasis is on the food, the three neat, homely bars are properly pubby with their open fires, tankard-hung beams, stripped stonework, solid furniture including settles, and old black and white photographs of local places and farm and country workers. Friendly, knowledgeable staff serve four quickly changing local beers from brewers such as Allendale, Consett, Mordue and Wylam from handpumps, as well as farm ciders, 28 wines by the glass, 34 malt whiskies and several bourbons. They hold a beer and food festival at Easter with over two dozen real ales, a barrel race on Easter Monday and other traditional events; darts and dominoes. Picnic-sets in front are a nice place to sit and watch the world drift by.

🍴 Cooking tends to British in style, with a focus on traditional North Eastern dishes. They use home-butchered game from local shoots and rare-breed beef and are very strict in their fish buying policy – their carefully chosen suppliers are listed on the daily-changing menu: ploughman's, creamy celeriac soup with pickled mushrooms, pickled herring with beetroot salad, rarebit with salted ox tongue and pickled onions, battered fish and mushy peas, leek and cheese pie, roast partridge with smoked sausage, cabbage and bacon, squash, potato and celeriac gratin with glazed chestnut and rocket and parmesan salad, and puddings such as perry-poached pear and almond tart and steamed gingerbread pudding. *Benchmark main dish: grilled rump steak with béarnaise £14.00. Two-course evening meal £21.50.*

Free house ~ Licensees Rhian Cradock and Helen Greer ~ Real ale ~ Bar food (12-2(2.30 Sun), 6-8 Tues-Sat, not Mon) ~ (01661) 843607 ~ Children welcome ~ Open 12-

11(10.30 Sun); closed Mon lunchtime except bank holidays, lunchtimes first two weeks Jan ~ www.thefeathers.net *Recommended by Mike and Lynn Robinson, Peter and Eleanor Kenyon, Eric Larkham, Graham Oddey, Dr and Mrs P Truelove, GSB, Comus and Sarah Elliott*

LESBURY
NU2311   Map 10

Coach
B1339; NE66 3PP

Well run stone inn with enjoyable food and local ales and attractively refurbished bar

The carefully refurbished low beamed interior of this picturesque stone pub is comfortably cosy with a warm welcome for all and a nice balance between the bar and food sides. The paintwork throughout is cream, sage green and soft gray and the bar has dark leather stools by the wooden counter, a row of pubby tables and stools along one wall on the tartan carpet and Black Sheep Best and Golden Sheep on handpump; background music and TV. Leading off to the left is a small area with comfortable sofas and armchairs around low tables, and to the other side is a little dining room with high-backed cane and leather chairs around light wooden tables; another seating area has a woodburning stove in a small brick fireplace and tub-like wicker and leather chairs. The neat terrace has rustic furniture under parasols (there are more seats in front, too) and lovely flowering tubs and baskets among lavender beds. It's at the heart of a pretty village and handy for Alnwick Castle Gardens.

 Generous helpings of good bar food include king prawns with garlic butter, kipper pâté, stilton and mushroom rarebit, braised steak with leek pudding, crispy pork belly with apple and cider reduction, duck breast with strawberry, Cointreau and pepper sauce, chicken jalfrezi, fish and chips with mushy peas, pasta with roast mediterranean vegetables and goats cheese, mushroom and tarragon risotto, bass fillet with lemon butter dressing, and puddings such as lime mousse with raspberries, dutch apple pie, and chocolate pudding. *Benchmark main dish: roast local lamb with mint salsa £16.90. Two-course evening meal £22.60.*

Punch ~ Tenant Susan Packard ~ Real ale ~ Bar food (12-8.30(7 Sun)) ~ Restaurant ~ (01665) 830865 ~ Children welcome in dining areas till 7.30pm ~ Open 11(12 Sun)-11
Recommended by J B Case, Mrs A Nicholls, John Beeken, Comus and Sarah Elliott, Dr Peter D Smart, Clive Flynn, Trevor and Judith Pearson, Ian Townsend

NEW YORK
NZ3269   Map 10

Shiremoor Farm 🏮
Middle Engine Lane; at W end of New York A191 bypass turn S into Norham Road, then first right (pub signed); NE29 8DZ

Large dining pub with interesting furnishings and décor, popular food all day, decent drinks and covered, heated terrace

This very busy dining pub is a successful transformation of some derelict agricultural buildings. The several well divided, spacious areas have beams and joists (the conical rafters of a former gin-gan are in one part), broad flagstones, several kelims, a mix of interesting and comfortable furniture, and farm tools, shields, swords, and country pictures on the walls. The bar is quieter and more relaxed and up to six quickly changing real ales are kept on handpump from breweries like Black Sheep, Greene King, Mordue and Timothy Taylors, with several wines by the glass. There's always a wide mix of customers of all ages, and the efficient serving and waiting staff don't keep anyone waiting.

There are seats outside on the covered, heated terrace.

 Extremely popular, the reasonably priced food might include sandwiches, stir-fried mussels with black beans, ginger and noodles, black pudding, apple and roasted onion salad and honey mustard dressing, asparagus, pea and ricotta filo parcel, chicken caesar salad with parmesan croutons, fish and chips with tartare sauce, beef burger with tomato chilli relish and french fries, lambs liver with crispy pancetta and red onion gravy, steaks with various sauces, and puddings such as rich chocolate cake and vanilla cheesecake with berry compote. *Benchmark main dish: steak in ale pie £8.45. Two-course evening meal £15.00.*

Sir John Fitzgerald ~ Manager C W Kerridge ~ Real ale ~ Bar food (10-10(9 Sun)) ~ (0191) 257 6302 ~ Children welcome ~ Open 10-11(10.30 Sun) ~ www.sjf.co.uk
Recommended by GSB

 NEWBURN   NZ1665   Map 10

Keelman  £ 🛏

Grange Road: follow Riverside Country Park brown signs off A6085; NE15 8ND

Impressive range of own-brewed beers in converted pumping station, easy-going atmosphere, excellent service and straightforward food; bedrooms

The impressive array of eight handpumps in this neatly kept and sizeable pub usually dispenses the full range of their own-brewed Big Lamp beers. Very reasonably priced and kept in tip-top condition, these include Bitter, Keelman Brown, Lamp Light, One Hop, Premium, Prince Bishop Ale, Summerhill Stout and Sunny Daze; the neatly dressed staff will happily let you sample a couple before ordering. There's a relaxed atmosphere and a good mix of customers in the high-ceilinged bar, which is light and airy with lofty arched windows and well spaced tables and chairs. There are more tables in an upper gallery, and the modern dining conservatory (pleasant at sunset) contrasts stylishly with the original old building; background music. You'll find plenty of picnic-sets, tables and benches out on the spacious terraces, among flower tubs and beds of shrubs, and there's a good play area.

 Reasonably priced, straightforward food includes sandwiches, deep-fried brie with cumberland sauce, black pudding stack with peppercorn sauce, beer-battered fish and chips, toad in the hole, honey and nut roast with rice, chicken with cheese and bacon, a king-size grill, and puddings such as a changing home-made sponge with custard, and crunchy chocolate sundae. *Benchmark main dish: steak in their own ale pie £7.95. Two-course evening meal £13.00.*

Own brew ~ Licensee George Story ~ Real ale ~ Bar food (12-9) ~ Restaurant ~ (0191) 267 0772 ~ Children welcome ~ Open 11-11; 12-10.30 Sun ~ Bedrooms: £55.45S/£79.50S ~ www.keelmanslodge.co.uk *Recommended by Eric Larkham, Geoff and Sue Bloxsom*

 NEWTON-BY-THE-SEA   NU2424   Map 10

Ship

Village signed off B1339 N of Alnwick; NE66 3EL

In a charming square of fishermen's cottages close to the beach, good simple food and a fine spread of drinks; best to check winter opening times

Tables outside this row of converted fishermen's cottages look across the sloping village green to the sandy beach – not surprisingly given this idyllic location it can get extremely busy at peak times, so it's best to book in advance – and be aware that there might be a queue for the bar. Inside, the plainly furnished but cosy bare-boards bar on the right has nautical charts on dark pink walls, and another simple room on the left has beams, hop bines, some bright modern pictures on stripped-stone walls and a woodburning stove in the stone fireplace; darts, dominoes. They started making their own beers here four years ago and if the brewer is in he will happily chat about the five or so they usually have on. There's no nearby parking, but there's a car park up the hill.

🍴 At lunchtime, the tasty bar food includes sandwiches (including excellent crab ones), stotties, toasted ciabattas and ploughman's, with more elaborate evening choices such as kipper or mushroom and chicken liver pâté, a roast butternut squash with feta, almonds and puy lentils, chicken breast with cream and tarragon sauce, crab linguine, crab, sirloin steak with onion marmalade, and puddings such as chocolate brownie and lemon posset. *Benchmark main dish: crab stottie £8.75. Two-course evening meal £18.30.*

Own brew ~ Licensee Christine Forsyth ~ Real ale ~ Bar food (12-2.30, 7-8 (check in winter)) ~ No credit cards ~ (01665) 576262 ~ Children welcome ~ Dogs welcome ~ Open 11-11; 12-10.30 Sun; phone for opening hours in winter ~ www.shipinnnewton.co.uk *Recommended by P Dawn, Peter Smith and Judith Brown, Iain and Joanna MacLeod, J F M and M West, Simon Watkins, Colin and Louise English, Graham Oddey, Mike Gerrard, Mike and Sue Loseby, the Didler, Comus and Sarah Elliott, Pat and Tony Martin*

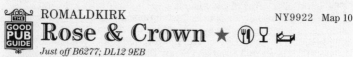

ROMALDKIRK   NY9922   Map 10
Rose & Crown ★ 🍴 ♀ 🛏
Just off B6277; DL12 9EB

A civilised base for the area, with accomplished cooking, attentive service and a fine choice of drinks; lovely bedrooms

Absolutely top notch in all respects, this handsome 18th-c country coaching inn is run with keen attention to detail, resulting in a charming environment, superbly cooked food (you do need to book) and a first class place to stay. The cosily traditional beamed bar has lots of brass and copper, old-fashioned seats facing a warming log fire, a Jacobean oak settle, a grandfather clock, and gin traps, old farm tools and black and white pictures of Romaldkirk on the walls. Allendale, Black Sheep and Theakstons are on handpump, and there are 14 wines by the glass, organic fruit juices and pressed vegetable juices. The smart brasserie-style Crown Room (bar food is served in here, too) has large cartoons of french waiters, big old wine bottles and high-backed dining chairs. The hall has farm tools, wine maps and other interesting prints, along with a photograph (taken by a customer) of the Hale Bopp comet over the interesting old village church. There's also an oak-panelled restaurant. Tables outside look out over the village green with its original stocks and water pump. The exceptional Bowes Museum and High Force waterfall are close by, and the owners can provide an in-house guide for days out in the area, and a Walking in Teesdale book.

🍴 As well as making their own ice-creams, jams, chutneys and marmalade, using seasonal local produce (they list their suppliers on the menu) and eggs from their own hens (whose names are on a board in the brasserie), the imaginative bar food might include smoked haddock soufflé with gazpacho, fried pork belly salad with black pudding and apple, mushroom, spinach and mascarpone risotto with basil pesto, steak, kidney and mushroom pie, fried salmon with samphire, roast tomatoes and sorrel sauce, fried pigeon with carrot and parsnip rösti and wild mushrooms, grilled goats cheese crostini with roasted baby tomatoes, and puddings such as almond and sherry trifle and panna cotta with spiced apricots. *Benchmark main dish: confit of belly pork with baby bean cassoulet £14.95. Two-course evening meal £20.50.*

Free house ~ Licensees Christopher and Alison Davy ~ Real ale ~ Bar food (12-1.45, 6.30-9.30) ~ Restaurant ~ (01833) 650213 ~ Children welcome, must be over 6 in restaurant ~ Dogs allowed in bar and bedrooms ~ Open 11(12 Sun)-11 ~ Bedrooms: £95S(£95B)/£150S(£175B) ~ www.rose-and-crown.co.uk
Recommended by Roxanne Chamberlain, Richard Cole, Mike and Sue Loseby, Peter and Josie Fawcett, Ben and Ruth Levy, Ian Malone

SEAHOUSES   NU2232   Map 10
Olde Ship ★ ◀ £ ⇦
Just off B1340, towards harbour; NE68 7RD

Lots of atmosphere and maritime memorabilia in busy little hotel; views across harbour to Farne Islands; bedrooms

Often bustling with locals and guests, the snugly old-fashioned bar at this homely little hotel – it's been run by the same friendly family for over 100 years – is packed with a rich assemblage of nautical bits and pieces. Even the floor is made of scrubbed ship's decking. As well as lots of other shiny brass fittings, ship's instruments and equipment, and a knotted anchor made by local fishermen, there are sea pictures and model ships, including fine ones of the North Sunderland lifeboat, and the Seahouses' Grace Darling lifeboat. There's also a model of the Forfarshire, the paddle steamer that local heroine Grace Darling went to rescue in 1838 (you can read more of the story in the pub), and even the ship's nameboard. If it's working, an anemometer takes wind speed readings from the top of the chimney. It's all gently lit by stained-glass sea-picture windows, lantern lights and a winter open fire. Simple furnishings include built in leatherette pews around one end and stools and cast-iron tables. Black Sheep Best, Courage Directors, Greene King Old Speckled Hen and Ruddles and Hadrian & Border Farne Island Pale are on handpump, with more at busy times, and they've a good wine list and quite a few malt whiskies; background music and TV. The battlemented side terrace (you'll find fishing memorabilia out here, too) and one window in the sun lounge look out across the harbour to the Farne Islands, and if you find yourself here as dusk falls, the light of the Longstones lighthouse shining across the fading evening sky is a charming sight. It's not really suitable for children, though there is a little family room, and along with walkers, they are welcome on the terrace. You can book boat trips to the Farne Islands Bird Sanctuary at the harbour, and there are bracing coastal walks, particularly to Bamburgh, Grace Darling's birthplace.

A short choice of reasonably priced bar food might include sandwiches, ploughman's, meatloaf, scampi, crab salad, moroccan vegetable casserole, steak in ale pie and sirloin steak, and puddings such as apple and cinnamon tart and apricot crumble. *Benchmark main dish: fish stew £9.75. Two-course evening meal £15.70.*

Free house ~ Licensees Judith Glen and David Swan ~ Real ale ~ Bar food (12-2, 7-9; no evening food Dec to late Jan) ~ Restaurant ~ (01665) 720200 ~ Children allowed in lounge and dining room if eating and must be over 10 if staying ~ Open 11(12 Sun)-11 ~ Bedrooms: £59S/£130S(£130B) ~ www.seahouses.co.uk *Recommended by Dave and Shirley Shaw, P Dawn, Lawrence Pearse, Simon Watkins, J F M and M West, Pat and Graham Williamson,*

Colin and Louise English, Comus and Sarah Elliott, Graham Oddey, Andrew Todd, Mike and Sue
Loseby, the Didler, D Crook

STANNERSBURN   NY7286   Map 10

Pheasant £ 🛏

Kielder Water road signposted off B6320 in Bellingham; NE48 1DD

**Friendly village local close to Kielder Water with quite a mix of
customers and homely bar food; streamside garden; bedrooms**

Warmly traditional and unchanging, the comfortable low-beamed
lounge at this nice former farmhouse has ranks of old local
photographs on stripped stone and panelling, brightly polished surfaces,
shiny brasses on stripped stone walls, dark wood pubby tables and
chairs on red patterned carpets and upholstered stools ranged along the
counter. A separate public bar is simpler and opens into a further cosy
seating area with beams and panelling; background music. The friendly
licensees and courteous staff serve Timothy Taylors Landlord and Wylam
Locomotion No 1, Northern Kite and Rocket on handpump and 36 malt
whiskies. The pub is in a restful valley amid quiet forests, not far from
Kielder Water, with picnic-sets in its streamside garden and a pony
paddock behind. More reports please.

🍴 Good bar food includes feta cheese salad, garlic mushrooms in puff pastry,
melon with passion fruit sorbet, steak and kidney pie, baked haddock fillets,
crab salad, mushroom and spinach lasagne, cider-baked gammon with cumberland
sausage, duck breast with raspberry jus, and puddings such as lemon and lime
cheesecake, bread and butter marmalade pudding and crème brûlée. *Benchmark
main dish: roast lamb with rosemary and redcurrant jus £12.95. Two-course
evening meal £17.70.*

Free house ~ Licensees Walter and Robin Kershaw ~ Real ale ~ Bar food (12-2.30, 6.30-
8.30) ~ Restaurant ~ (01434) 240382 ~ Children welcome ~ Dogs allowed in bedrooms
~ Open 12-3, 6-11; 12-3, 6.30-11 Sun; closed Mon, Tues Nov-Mar ~ Bedrooms: £55S/£90S
~ www.thepheasantinn.com   *Recommended by Claes Mauroy*

WARK   NY8676   Map 10

Battlesteads ◧ 🛏

B6320 N of Hexham; NE48 3LS

**Eco pub with good local ales, fair value interesting food and a relaxed
atmosphere; comfortable bedrooms**

The welcoming owners of this popular stone hotel are conscientious
about the environment and gently weave their beliefs into the
business. They run a biomass boiler, have a charging point in the car
park for electric cars and grow all their own produce, and encouraging
birds into the garden is a priority when they do any planting. This last
is clearly a success, as they tell us there is good birdwatching from
their conservatory, and they've laid out binoculars on the windowsills
so that you can enjoy it. The pub is an enjoyable all-rounder with a
relaxed unhurried atmosphere. The nicely restored carpeted bar has
a woodburning stove with a traditional oak surround, low beams,
comfortable seats including some comfy deep leather sofas and easy
chairs, and old *Punch* country life cartoons on the terracotta walls above
its dark dado. As well as a dozen or so wines by the glass, four good
changing local ales such as Black Sheep Best, Durham Magus, High
House Farm Nel's Best and beers from guest brewers such as Hadrian

& Border Secret Kingdom are on handpump on the heavily carved dark oak bar counter. This leads through to the restaurant and spacious conservatory; good coffee, cheerful service and background music. There are tables on a terrace in the beautifully maintained walled garden. Disabled access to some of the ground-floor bedrooms, and they are licensed to hold civil marriages.

Using home-grown vegetables and other local produce, the well liked food might include chicken liver parfait, grilled goats cheese, battered hake and chips, fried calves liver, burger, mushroom stroganoff, salmon baked in cajun spices with sweet chilli sauce, gammon, egg and chips, fillet steak topped with blue cheese, puddings such as vanilla panna cotta, butterscotch sundae and mixed berry pavlova, and a local cheeseboard. *Benchmark main dish: lamb shank with rosemary and redcurrant jus £13.50. Two-course evening meal £21.30.*

Free house ~ Licensees Richard and Dee Slade ~ Real ale ~ Bar food (12-3, 6.30-9) ~ (01434) 230209 ~ Children welcome ~ Dogs allowed in bar ~ Open 11-11 ~ Bedrooms: £60S/£105B ~ www.battlesteads.com *Recommended by Bruce and Sharon Eden, Kevin Appleby, Michael Doswell, R L Borthwick, LC*

WELDON BRIDGE   NZ1398   Map 10
Anglers Arms ⇨
B6344, just off A697; village signposted with Rothbury off A1 N of Morpeth; NE65 8AX

Large helpings of food in appealing bar or converted railway dining car, real ales and a friendly welcome; fishing on River Coquet; bedrooms

The hotel bar at the heart of this sizeable place has a comfortable early 20th-c appeal. It's divided into two parts: cream walls on the right, and oak panelling, some shiny black beams hung with copper pans and a mantelpiece with staffordshire cats on the left. There's also a grandfather clock, a sofa by the coal fire, old fishing and other country prints and a profusion of fishing memorabilia and some taxidermy. Some of the tables are lower than you'd expect for eating, but their chairs have short legs to match – different and rather engaging; background music. Four constantly changing real ales from brewers such as Adnams, Courage, Greene King and Timothy Taylors are on handpump, with around 30 malt whiskies and decent wines. You can feel very Agatha Christie in the restaurant, which is set out with crisp white linen and a red carpet in a former railway dining car. There are tables in the attractive garden, which has a good play area that includes an assault course. The pub is beside a bridge over the River Coquet and they have rights to fishing along a mile of the riverbank.

Generously served bar food includes sandwiches, scallops with black pudding and minted pea purée, chicken liver pâté, ploughman's, goats cheese and pea risotto, fried chicken with pepper sauce, mushroom stroganoff and gammon steak with brie and pineapple. *Benchmark main dish: cod and chips £10.95. Two-course evening meal £16.90.*

Enterprise ~ Lease John Young ~ Real ale ~ Bar food (12-9.30) ~ Restaurant ~ (01665) 570271 ~ Children welcome ~ Dogs welcome ~ Open 11-11; 12-10.30 Sun ~ Bedrooms: £49.50S/£90S ~ www.anglersarms.com *Recommended by Ann and Tony Bennett-Hughes, Colin McKerrow, Dr Peter D Smart, Jean and Douglas Troup, Dave Braisted, Rob and Catherine Dunster, J F M and M West, Lee and Liz Potter, Gordon and Margaret Ormondroyd*

Also Worth a Visit in Northumbria

Besides the fully inspected pubs, you might like to try these pubs that have been recommended to us and described by readers. Do tell us what you think of them: feedback@goodguides.com

ACKLINGTON   NU2302

Railway (01670) 760320

Just S of village; NE65 9BP Neatly refurbished former 1800s farmhouse with friendly landlady, spotless part-tiled/carpeted bar with brown button-back banquette and dark tables and chairs, horseracing and other photos, brick fireplace with woodburner, pretty restaurant, enjoyable pubby food from substantial lunchtime baguettes up, well kept Hadrian & Border; self-catering cottages. *(Michael Doswell)*

ALLENDALE   NY8355

Golden Lion (01434) 683225

Market Place; NE47 9BD 18th-c two-room village inn with fairly priced enjoyable food, several mainly local well kept ales, good choice of other drinks including reasonably priced wines, chatty Yorkshire landlord, games area with pool and darts, upstairs restaurant, occasional live music; children and dogs welcome (pub dogs), bedrooms. *(Comus and Sarah Elliott)*

ALNMOUTH   NU2511

Hope & Anchor (01665) 830363

Northumberland Street; NE66 2RA Old pub with cheery bar and long beamed dining room, well kept local ales such as Hadrian & Border Farne Island Pale and Northumberland Sheepdog, hearty home-made food including good fish dishes, china and brass, local art for sale; children and dogs welcome, quietly appealing coastal village, attractive beaches and good walks, seven bedrooms, open all day. *(John Beeken, Penny and Peter Keevil, Dr Kevan Tucker)*

ALNMOUTH   NU2410

Sun (01665) 830983

Northumberland Street; NE66 2RA Comfortable banquettes in long low-beamed bar with open fire one end and woodburner the other, carpet or bare boards, decorations made from driftwood, good value traditional food from sandwiches and hot baguettes up, ales such as Black Sheep and Mordue, good coffee, friendly chatty staff, small contemporary dining area; background music; children welcome, attractive seaside village, four bedrooms. *(Colin and Louise English)*

ALNWICK   NU1813

Blackmores (01665) 602395

Bondgate Without; NE66 1PN Smart contemporary pub/boutique hotel in Victorian stone building, well kept Black Sheep and Caledonian Deuchars IPA in lively front bar, several wines by the glass, consistently good food all day from snacky things up in bar, bistro or upstairs restaurant, bargain OAP weekday lunch, friendly efficient service; pleasant street-side raised terrace, 13 bedrooms. *(Richard and Stephanie Foskett, Rosemary and Mike Fielder, Ian Phillips, Lee and Liz Potter)*

ALNWICK   NU1813

John Bull (01665) 602055

Howick Street; NE66 1UY Popular chatty drinkers' pub, essentially front room of early 19th-c terraced house, four changing ales, real cider, bottled belgian beers and over 100 malt whiskies; closed weekday lunchtimes. *(the Didler, Laura Greenaway)*

AMBLE   NU2604

Wellwood Arms (01665) 714646

High Street off A1068; NE65 0LD Refurbished dining pub with pleasant welcoming staff, enjoyable food from traditional choices up including set menu, well kept real ales, extensive wine and cocktail list, separate nicely laid-out restaurant area with own bar. *(Dr Peter D Smart, Jane Dargue, Michael Doswell)*

BAMBURGH   NU1834

Castle (01668) 214616

Front Street; NE69 7BW Clean comfortably old-fashioned pub with friendly landlord and staff, well kept Black Sheep and a local guest, decent house wines, winter mulled wine, wide choice of food all day including good Craster kippers, recently expanded dining area to cope with summer visitors, open fires; big courtyard, garden. *(Comus and Sarah Elliott, Clifford Blakemore, Robin Constable)*

BAMBURGH   NU1834

Lord Crewe Arms (01668) 214243

Front Street; NE69 7BL Small early 17th-c hotel prettily set in charming coastal village dominated by Norman castle, refurbished bar and restaurant (Wynding Inn) with painted joists and panelling, bare-stone walls and light wood floor, woodburner, beers from Northumberland and Wells & Youngs, good interesting food; sheltered garden with castle view, short walk from splendid sandy beach, 17 comfortable bedrooms, good breakfast. *(Barry Collett)*

BAMBURGH   NU1734

Mizen Head (01668) 214254

Lucker Road; NE69 7BS Refurbished hotel (sister inn to the nearby Castle), light airy bar with open fire, enjoyable locally sourced food, ales such as Black Sheep, good reasonably priced house wines, friendly staff; children and dogs welcome, nice bedrooms. *(Comus and Sarah Elliott, Clifford Blakemore)*

BAMBURGH NU1834
⋆Victoria (01668) 214431
Front Street; NE69 7BP Substantial Victorian hotel with sofas with mildly contemporary partly divided bar, chunky tables and chairs in dining area, good food all day from sandwiches up, Black Sheep and two guests, good wines by the glass, recently refurbished restaurant; children welcome, nice setting with seats out in front, more in garden behind with play area, 36 comfortable bedrooms, open all day. *(Colin and Louise English, Gordon and Margaret Ormondroyd, W K Wood)*

BARDON MILL NY7566
Twice Brewed (01434) 344534
Military Road (B6318 NE of Hexham); NE47 7AN Large busy inn well placed for fell-walkers and major Wall sites, half a dozen ales including local microbrews and two brewed for them by Yates, 50 rums and 20 malt whiskies, reasonably priced wines, good value hearty pub food from baguettes up, quick friendly staff, local photographs and art for sale; quiet background music, no dogs; children welcome, picnic-sets in back garden, 14 bedrooms, open all day. *(Pete Coxon, John and Sylvia Harrop)*

BARNINGHAM NZ0810
Milbank Arms (01833) 621213
On main road into village from Newsham; DL11 7DW Cosy little one-room village local, simple and unspoilt with welcoming landlord (in same family for over 70 years), no bar counter, kitchen or real ales, but unusually a full cocktail menu, interesting collection of miniatures; outside gents'; open from 7pm (noon Sun). *(Anon)*

BARRASFORD NY9173
⋆Barrasford Arms (01434) 681237
Village signposted off A6079 N of Hexham; NE48 4AA Good country cooking at this bustling sandstone inn using carefully sourced local ingredients, nice staff and genuinely local atmosphere, traditional log-fire bar with old local photographs and bric-a-brac from horsebrasses to antlers, ales such as Caledonian, Hadrian & Border and Wylam, two dining rooms, one with wheelback chairs around neat tables and stone chimneybreast hung with guns and copper pans, the second with comfortably upholstered dining chairs; background music, TV, darts; children welcome, plenty of nearby walks and handy for Hadrian's Wall, 11 bedrooms plus a well equipped bunkhouse, open all day weekends, closed Mon lunchtime. *(M A Borthwick, Bruce and Sharon Eden, LC)*

BEADNELL NU2229
Beadnell Towers (01665) 721211
The Wynding off B1340; NE67 5AY Large slightly old-fashioned pub/hotel with unusual mix of furnishings, good food in bar or restaurant including local game and fish, well kept ales such as Hadrian & Border, reasonably priced wines by the glass, nice coffee, pleasant obliging service, some live music; can get more touristy in summer; seats outside, ten bedrooms. *(Michael Doswell, Comus and Sarah Elliott, W K Wood)*

BEADNELL NU2229
Craster Arms (01665) 720272
The Wynding off B1340; NE67 5AX Roomy neatly kept old building with modern fittings, red banquettes, stripped-brick and stone walls, popular pubby food and blackboard specials including local fish, well kept Black Sheep and a local guest, friendly efficient staff, pictures for sale, live music including Aug 'Crastonbury' festival, July beer festival; background music, TV; children welcome, dogs in one area, picnic-sets and decking in big enclosed garden, three good bedrooms, open all day in summer. *(Michael Doswell)*

BEAMISH NZ2154
Beamish Hall (01207) 233733
NE of Stanley, off A6076; DH9 0YB Converted stone-built stables in courtyard at back of hotel, popular and family friendly (can get crowded), five or six good beers from own microbrewery, decent wines, good food all day including some interesting choices, efficient service from friendly uniformed staff; plenty of seats outside, big play area, open all day. *(Peter Smith and Judith Brown, GSB, Mr and Mrs Maurice Thompson, Rob Weeks, Gerry and Rosemary Dobson)*

BEAMISH NZ2153
⋆Beamish Mary (0191) 370 0237
Off A693 signed No Place and Cooperative Villas, S of museum; DH9 0QH Friendly down-to-earth former pit village inn, eight well kept mainly local ales (May beer festival), farm cider, good home-made pubby food at bargain prices, coal fires, two bars with 1960s-feel mix of furnishings, bric-a-brac, 1920s/30s memorabilia and Aga with pots and pans, regular live music in converted stables; sports TV; children allowed until early evening, updated bedrooms. *(Peter Smith and Judith Brown)*

BERWICK-UPON-TWEED NT9952
Barrels (01289) 308013
Bridge Street; TD15 1ES Small friendly pub with interesting collection of pop memorabilia and other bric-a-brac, eccentric furniture including dentist's chair in bare-boards bar, red banquettes in back room, well kept Pentland IPA and four guests,

foreign bottled beers, live music (Fri) and DJs (Sat) in basement bar, good quality background music; open all day, from 2pm in winter. *(Dave and Shirley Shaw)*

BERWICK-UPON-TWEED NT9952
Leaping Salmon (01289) 303184
Golden Square; TD15 1BG Wetherspoons in late 18th-c former school, very reasonably priced beer and usual food choices; modern conservatory extension. *(Ian Phillips)*

BERWICK-UPON-TWEED NU9953
Pilot (01289) 304214
Low Greens; TD15 1LZ Small welcoming beamed and panelled backstreet local, old nautical photographs and knick-knacks, comfortable back lounge, well kept Caledonian Deuchars IPA and regional guests, summer lunchtime food, darts and quoits, fiddle music Thurs; children and dogs welcome, garden tables, two bedrooms, open all day. *(the Didler)*

BLANCHLAND NY9650
★Lord Crewe Arms (01434) 675251
B6306 S of Hexham; DH8 9SP This historic hotel with its unusual barrel-vaulted crypt bar was closed for major refurbishment as we went to press – news please. *(M and J White, Claes Mauroy, Liz Bell)*

BOULMER NU2614
Fishing Boat (01665) 577750
Beach View; NE66 3BP Worth knowing for its position, with conservatory dining room and decking overlooking sea; light and airy inside with interesting nautical memorabilia, good value food, real ales such as Black Sheep and Tetleys; dogs welcome. *(John Beeken)*

CORBRIDGE NY9864
★Black Bull (01434) 632261
Middle Street; NE45 5AT Rambling linked old rooms with neat comfortable seating including traditional settles on flagstones in softly lit low-ceilinged core, roaring fire, reasonably priced food all day from sandwiches and light lunches up, good friendly service, Black Sheep and Greene King ales, good well priced wines; open all day. *(Comus and Sarah Elliott, W K Wood)*

CORBRIDGE NY9863
Dyvels (01434) 633633
Station Road; NE45 5AY Refurbished traditional stone inn, friendly and well run, with good value pub food from duck egg sandwiches up, well kept ales such as Black Sheep, Mordue and Shepherd Neame, decent wines by the glass; children welcome, picnic-sets on side terrace and lawn, three bedrooms, open all day. *(Comus and Sarah Elliott)*

CORBRIDGE NY9868
★Errington Arms (01434) 672250
About 3 miles N of town; B6318, on A68 roundabout; NE45 5QB Popular 18th-c stone-built roadside pub by Hadrian's Wall, good mix of diners and walkers, beamed bars with pine panelling, stone and burgundy walls, farmhouse and other chairs around pine tables on strip-wood flooring, log fire and woodburner, well liked home-made food, Jennings and Wylam ales, friendly obliging staff; background music; children welcome, tables out in front, closed Sun evening, Mon. *(Pat and Stewart Gordon)*

CRAMLINGTON NZ2373
★Snowy Owl (01670) 736111
Just off A1/A19 junction via A1068; Blagdon Lane; NE23 8AU Large Vintage Inn, relaxed and comfortable, with reasonable prices, good choice of well-liked food all day including popular Sun lunch, friendly efficient young staff, Black Sheep and a couple of guests, nice wines, beams, flagstones, stripped stone, soft lighting and an interesting mix of furnishings and decorations, three log fires; background music; disabled access, bedrooms in adjoining Innkeepers Lodge, open all day. *(Guy and Caroline Howard, Dr Peter D Smart, Comus and Sarah Elliott, Paul and Sue Merrick, Michael Doswell)*

CRASTER NU2519
★Jolly Fisherman (01665) 576461
Off B1339, NE of Alnwick; NE66 3TR Recently refurbished and under welcoming new management; great spot, long a favourite for its lovely sea and coast views from picture window and grass behind, good food with emphasis on fish/seafood including local crab, Lindisfarne oysters and produce from smokehouse opposite, well kept Black Sheep and Mordue, good wine list, friendly efficient service, front snug leading to bar area with nice open fire, steps up to restaurant, local art for sale; children and dogs welcome, open all day in summer. *(John and Sylvia Harrop, Comus and Sarah Elliott, GSB, Barry Collett, Michael Doswell)*

DARLINGTON NZ2814
Number Twenty 2 (01325) 354590
Coniscliffe Road; DL3 7RG Long bistro-feel Victorian pub with high ceiling, bare boards and exposed brickwork, 14 quickly changing ales including own Village ales (brewed by Hambleton), draught continentals, decent food (not Fri, Sat evenings) in compact panelled back room, good friendly service; open all day, closed Sun. *(Julian Pigg, Peter Abbott)*

We include some hotels with a good bar that offers facilities comparable to those of a pub.

DURHAM NZ2642

Colpitts (0191) 3869913

*Colpitts Terrace/Hawthorn Terrace;
DH1 4EG* Comfortable two-bar traditional
backstreet pub, friendly landlady and locals,
cheap well kept Sam Smiths, open fires and
original Victorian fittings, back pool room;
seats in yard, open all day (from 2pm Mon-
Wed). *(Phil and Sally Gorton, Mr and
Mrs Maurice Thompson, the Didler)*

DURHAM NZ2742

Court (0191) 3847350

Court Lane; DH1 3AW Comfortable
19th-c town pub with good home-made food
all day (till 10.20pm) from sandwiches and
sharing plates to steaks and blackboard
specials, two changing ales from smaller
local brewers, friendly helpful staff, extensive
stripped-brick eating area, no mobile phones;
background music; seats outside, open all
day. *(P and D Carpenter)*

DURHAM NZ2742

✶ Dun Cow (0191) 3869219

Old Elvet; DH1 3HN Unchanging
backstreet pub in pretty 16th-c black-and-
white timbered cottage, cheerful licensees,
tiny chatty front bar with wall benches,
corridor to long narrow back lounge with
banquettes, machines etc (can be packed
with students), particularly well kept
Camerons and other ales such as Black
Sheep and Caledonian Deuchars IPA, good
value basic lunchtime snacks, decent coffee;
background music; children welcome, open
all day except Sun in winter. *(Phil and Sally
Gorton, Eric Larkham, the Didler)*

DURHAM NZ2642

Old Elm Tree (0191) 3864621

Crossgate; DH1 4PS Comfortable friendly
old pub on steep hill across from castle,
two-room main bar and small lounge, four
well kept ales (occasional beer festivals),
reasonably priced home-made food, open
fires, folk and quiz nights; dogs welcome,
small back terrace, open all day. *(Phil and
Sally Gorton, Mr and Mrs Maurice Thompson)*

DURHAM NZ2742

Swan & Three Cygnets

(0191) 3840242 *Elvet Bridge; DH1 3AG*
Victorian pub in good bridge-end spot high
above river, city views from big windows and
picnic-sets out on terrace, bargain lunchtime
food and Sam Smiths OB, helpful friendly
young staff; open all day. *(Phil and Sally
Gorton, Peter Smith and Judith Brown)*

EGGLESCLIFFE NZ4213

Pot & Glass

Church Road; TS16 9DQ Friendly
little village pub with Bass, Black Sheep,
Caledonian Deuchars IPA and a couple of
guests kept well by enthusiastic landlord,
good value straightforward food, folk club

and quiz nights; tables on terrace, lovely
setting behind church. *(Simon Turner, Taff
and Gilly Thomas, Craig Buckingham)*

EGLINGHAM NU1019

✶ Tankerville Arms (01665) 578444

B6346 Alnwick–Wooler; NE66 2TX
Traditional pub with contemporary touches,
cosy friendly atmosphere, beams, bare
boards, some stripped stone, banquettes,
warm fires, well kept local ales like
Hadrian & Border and Mordue, nice wines,
good imaginative well presented food
from changing menu, raftered split-level
restaurant; children and dogs welcome,
nice views from garden, three bedrooms,
attractive village. *(John and Sylvia Harrop,
Trevor and Judith Pearson, Comus and Sarah
Elliott, Dr and Mrs P Truelove)*

EMBLETON NU2322

Greys (01665) 576983

*Stanley Terrace off W T Stead Road,
turn at the Blue Bell; NE66 3UY* Carpeted
main front bar with pubby furniture, more
lived-in part with old photographs and
cuttings, cottagey back dining room, open
fires, well priced home-made food from
sandwiches and pizzas to good specials
including local fish, four well kept local ales,
afternoon teas; small walled back garden,
raised decking with village views, open
all day. *(Michael Doswell)*

FALSTONE NY7287

Blackcock Country Inn

(01434) 240200 *E of Yarrow and Kielder
Water; NE48 1AA* Cosy, clean and friendly
17th-c inn, homely bar with beams and open
fires, well kept ales including one brewed
for them, Weston's cider, bottled beers and
50 malt whiskies, enjoyable food in bar and
restaurant with good vegetarian choice,
pool room; quiet juke box; children allowed,
dogs very welcome (own menu), garden
with covered smokers' area, six bedrooms,
handy for Kielder Water, closed Wed evening,
weekday lunchtimes in winter. *(Alan Sutton)*

FRAMWELLGATE MOOR NZ2644

Tap & Spile (0191) 386 5451

*Front Street; B6532 just N of Durham;
DH1 5EE* Thriving two-bar pub with fine
range of well kept changing local ales,
farm ciders, good friendly staff, warm
and comfortable atmosphere, pub and
board games, weekly folk night; children
welcome. *(Jeff Brunton)*

FROSTERLEY NZ0236

✶ Black Bull (01388) 527784

Just off A689 W of centre; DL13 2SL
The only pub to have its own peal of
bells (licensee is a campanologist); great
atmosphere in three interesting traditional
beamed and flagstoned rooms with coal fires,
landlord's own fine photographs and three
grandfather clocks, four well kept local ales,

farm cider and perry, carefully chosen wines and malt whiskies, good food using local and organic ingredients (best to book evenings), popular Sun lunch, occasional acoustic live music; well behaved children and dogs welcome, attractive no smoking terrace with wood-fired bread oven and old railway furnishings (opposite steam station), closed Sun evening, Mon and Tues, otherwise open all day. *(Dr Peter D Smart, Duncan Walker)*

GATESHEAD   NZ2563
Central (0191) 478 2543
Half Moon Lane; NE8 2AN Large multi-room pub renovated by the Head of Steam chain, great choice of changing local ales, lots of bottled beers, real ciders, low-priced food including themed evenings, roof terrace, live music; open all day (till 1am Fri, Sat). *(Eric Larkham, Peter Smith and Judith Brown)*

GREAT WHITTINGTON   NZ0070
★Queens Head (01434) 672267
Village signed off A68 and B6018 N of Corbridge; NE19 2HP Handsome golden-stone pub with dark leather chairs around sturdy tables, one or two good pictures on stripped-stone or grey/green walls, soft lighting, Caledonian Deuchars IPA, Hadrian & Border and Jennings, several malt whiskies, nice hunting mural above old fireplace in long narrow bar, much emphasis on popular food (not Sun evening) in tartan-carpeted dining areas with modern furnishings, friendly efficient staff; background music; children and dogs welcome, picnic-sets under parasols on little front lawn, open all day Fri-Sun, closed Mon. *(GSB, Graham Oddey, John Prescott, LC)*

GRETA BRIDGE   NZ0813
★Morritt Arms (01833) 627232
Hotel signposted off A66 W of Scotch Corner; DL12 9SE Striking 17th-c country house hotel popular for weddings and the like; properly pubby bar with big windsor armchairs and sturdy oak settles around traditional cast-iron-framed tables, open fires and remarkable 1946 mural of Dickensian characters by J T Y Gilroy (known for Guinness advertisements), big windows looking on to extensive lawn, Thwaites Major Morritt (brewed for them) and Timothy Taylors Landlord, 19 wines by the glass from extensive list, good tasty food, friendly knowledgeable staff, restaurant; background music; children welcome, dogs allowed in bar and bedrooms, attractively laid-out garden with teak tables and play area, open all day. *(Dr and Mrs R G J Telfer, Barry Collett, Comus and Sarah Elliott)*

HART   NZ4634
White Hart (01429) 265468
Just off A179 W of Hartlepool; Front Street; TS27 3AW Interesting nautical-theme pub with old ship's figurehead outside, fires in both bars, traditional food cooked by landlady, ales such as Cameron Strongarm; children welcome, no dogs inside, open all day. *(JHBS)*

HARTLEPOOL   NZ5132
Rat Race
Hartlepool Station; TS24 7ED Former station newsagents, one small room (no bar), four well kept changing ales, real cider and perry, you can bring your own food, newspapers; open all day Sat till 9pm, closed Sun. *(JHBS)*

HAWTHORN   NZ4145
Stapylton Arms (0191) 5270778
Off B1432 S of A19 Murton exit; SR7 8SD Under new management and some redecoration; enjoyable thai food as well as standard pub menu, Black Sheep; children welcome, no dogs inside, nice wooded walk to sea (joins Durham Coastal Path), closed Mon, otherwise open all day. *(JHBS)*

HIGH HESLEDEN   NZ4538
Ship (01429) 836453
Off A19 via B1281; TS27 4QD Half a dozen good value changing ales from the region, log fire, sailing ship models including big one hanging with lanterns from boarded ceiling, enjoyable bar food cooked by landlady along with some interesting restaurant dishes; yacht and shipping views from car park, six bedrooms in new block, closed Mon. *(JHBS)*

HOLY ISLAND   NU1241
Crown & Anchor (01289) 389215
Causeway passable only at low tide, check times (01289) 330733; TD15 2RX Comfortably unpretentious pub/restaurant by the priory, enjoyable fairly traditional home-made food including vegetarian choices, Wells & Youngs Bombardier and Caledonian Deuchars IPA, welcoming helpful staff, compact bar with open fire, roomy modern back dining room; children and dogs welcome, garden with lovely views (may ask to keep a credit card while you eat here), four bedrooms. *(Jean and Douglas Troup, John and Sylvia Harrop, Barry Collett)*

HURWORTH-ON-TEES   NZ2814
★Bay Horse (01325) 720663
Church Row; DL2 2AQ Popular dining pub (best to book - particularly weekends) with top-notch imaginative food, quite pricey but they do a fixed-price lunch menu, children's choices too, three changing ales, smiling efficient young staff, sizeable bar with good open fire, restaurant; seats on back terrace and in well tended walled garden beyond, charming village by River Tees, open all day. *(Michael Doswell, Jill and Julian Tasker, Rory Hutchison)*

KNARSDALE   NY6754
Kirkstyle (01434) 381559
A689 Alston–Brampton, just N of Slaggyford; CA8 7PB Friendly pub in lovely setting, enjoyable food and well kept local ales; good walks along nearby South Tyne Trail. *(Marcus Byron)*

LANGDON BECK   NY8531
Langdon Beck Hotel
(01833) 622267 *B6277 Middleton–Alston; DL12 0XP* Isolated unpretentious inn with two cosy bars and spacious lounge, well placed for walks and Pennine Way, Black Sheep, Jarrow and a guest ale (late May beer festival), good choice of enjoyable generous food including good local teesdale beef and lamb, decent coffee, friendly helpful staff; garden with wonderful fell views, bedrooms, open all day, closed Mon in winter. *(Roxanne Chamberlain, M and J White, John H Smith)*

LANGLEY ON TYNE   NY8160
Carts Bog Inn (01434) 684338
A686 S, junction B6305; NE47 5NW Isolated moorside pub with heavy beams and stripped stone walls, old photographs, lovely open fire, good range of reasonably priced generous food from sandwiches up including popular Sun lunch (best to book), two or three well kept local ales, friendly efficient young staff, games room with pool and darts; children and dogs welcome, picnic-sets in big garden with views, quoits, open all day weekends. *(Lucien Perring, Sara Fulton, Roger Baker)*

LONGFRAMLINGTON   NU1301
Granby (01665) 570362
Front Street; NE65 8DP Attractive and comfortably modernised two-room bar, wide choice of enjoyable food including good value set meals, good range of malt whiskies, decent wines, small restaurant; bedrooms. *(Paul and Sue Merrick)*

LONGHORSLEY   NZ1494
Shoulder of Mutton (01670) 788236
East Road; A697 N of Morpeth; NE65 8SY Comfortable bar and restaurant with welcoming landlady and helpful friendly staff, good choice of generously served food from lunchtime baguettes through pub favourites to some imaginative dishes, popular Sun lunch (must book), Courage Directors, Caledonian Deuchars IPA and Everards Tiger, good selection of other drinks, Tues quiz night; background music; children welcome, tables outside. *(Robert Wivell, Michael Doswell)*

MARSDEN   NZ3964
Marsden Grotto (0191) 455 6060
Coast Road; passage to lift in A183 car park, just before Marsden from Whitburn; NE34 7BS Great location uniquely built into seaside cliff caverns, with lift (or 132 steps) down from car park; on two floors (upper for functions), decent food with emphasis on fish/seafood, good service, bottled beers only; no dogs inside; children welcome, disabled facilities, large terrace with steps on to beach, Marsden Rock close by, open till 9pm, closed evenings in winter. *(John Coatsworth)*

MILFIELD   NT9333
Red Lion (01668) 216 224
Main Road (A697 Wooler–Cornhill); NE71 6JD Welcoming 17th-c coaching inn with good sensibly priced food (may be local game) from chef/landlord, well kept Black Sheep and Wylam, organic wine, good service; pretty garden by car park at back. *(Michael Doswell, M Mossman, Comus and Sarah Elliott)*

MORPETH   NZ1986
★Tap & Spile (01670) 513894
Manchester Street; NE61 1BH Consistently welcoming, cosy and easy-going two-room pub, up to seven ales such as Caledonian, Everards, Hadrian & Border and Mordue, Weston's Old Rosie cider and country wines, limited choice of good value lunchtime food Fri and Sat, traditional pub furniture and interesting old photographs, quieter back lounge (children allowed here) with coal-effect gas fire, board and other games, good local folk music Sun afternoon, Mon quiz night; unobtrusive background music, sports TV and quiz machine; dogs welcome in front bar, open all day Fri-Sun. *(Anon)*

NETHERTON   NT9807
Star (01669) 630238
Off B6341 at Thropton, or A697 via Whittingham; NE65 7HD Simple unchanging village local under charming long-serving landlady (licence has been in her family since 1917), welcoming regulars, Camerons Strongarm tapped from cellar casks and served from hatch in small entrance lobby, large high-ceilinged room with wall benches, many original features; no food, music, children or dogs; open evenings only from 7pm, closed Mon and Thurs. *(Eric Larkham, the Didler)*

NEWBIGGIN-BY-THE-SEA   NZ3188
Queens Head (01670) 817293
High Street; NE64 6AT Unchanging Edwardian pub with good friendly landlord and thriving local atmosphere, high-ceilinged rooms and cosy back snug, well kept low-priced ales such as Marstons Burton Bitter, original features including curved bar, mosaic floors and etched windows, lots of old local photographs; dogs allowed in some parts, open all day from 9.45am to midnight. *(the Didler)*

NEWBROUGH   NY8768
Red Lion (01283) 575785
Stanegate Road; NE47 5AR Light airy refurbishment and buoyant atmosphere, log

fire, flagstones and half-panelling, old local photographs plus some large paintings, good locally sourced food (not Sun evening) in bar and two dining areas, bargain OAP meals and popular Sun roasts, well kept ales such as Hadrian & Border and Mordue, friendly staff, games room with pool and darts, some live music; children welcome, dogs too outside of food times, garden with play area, good local walks (leaflets provided), on NCN cycle route 72, four bedrooms, open all day. *(Marcus Byron, Comus and Sarah Elliott)*

NEWCASTLE UPON TYNE NZ2464
* **Bacchus** (0191) 232 6451

High Bridge E, between Pilgrim Street and Grey Street; NE1 6BX Smart, spacious and comfortable with ocean liner look, ship and shipbuilding photographs, good value lunchtime food from filled baps and focaccia to a few pubby main meals, Sun roasts, splendid choice of well kept changing ales, plenty of bottled imports, farm cider and decent coffee, relaxed atmosphere (but busy on match days), pleasant efficient staff; background music; disabled facilities, handy for Theatre Royal, open all day. *(Peter Smith and Judith Brown, Henry Paulinski, Eric Larkham, Derek Wason, the Didler and others)*

NEWCASTLE UPON TYNE NZ2464
Bodega (0191) 2211552

Westgate Road; NE1 4AG Majestic Edwardian drinking hall next to Tyne Theatre; Big Lamp, Durham and six guest ales, farm cider, friendly service, colourful walls and ceiling, bare boards, snug front cubicles, spacious back area with two magnificent stained-glass cupolas; background music, machines, big-screen TV, very busy on match days; open all day. *(Eric Larkham)*

NEWCASTLE UPON TYNE NZ2563
* **Bridge Hotel** (0191) 2326400

Castle Square, next to high-level bridge; NE1 1RQ Big, well divided, high-ceilinged bar around servery with replica slatted snob screens, Black Sheep, Caledonian Deuchars IPA and seven guests kept well, real cider, friendly staff, bargain generous lunchtime food (not weekends), magnificent fireplace, great river and bridge views from raised back area, live music upstairs including long-standing Mon folk club; background music, sports TV, games machines; flagstoned back terrace overlooking part of old town wall, open all day. *(Eric Larkham, Graham Oddey, the Didler)*

NEWCASTLE UPON TYNE NZ2563
Broad Chare (0191) 2112144

Broad Chare; NE1 3DQ Traditional feel although only recently converted to a pub (was a café), british leaning food (not Sun evening) from bar snacks such as pigs ears and Lindisfarne Oysters to treacle-cured salmon and steaks, four real ales including Writer's Block brewed for

them by Wylam, good choice of wines and whiskies, ground floor bare-boards bar and snug, old local photographs, upstairs dining room; background music, no dogs; children welcome in bar till 7pm (later upstairs), theatre next door, open all day. *(Comus and Sarah Elliott, Peter Smith and Judith Brown, Michael Doswell)*

NEWCASTLE UPON TYNE NZ2464
Centurion (0191) 261 6611

Central Station, Neville Street; NE1 5HL Glorious high-ceilinged Victorian décor with tilework and columns in former first-class waiting room, well restored with comfortable leather seats giving club-like feel, Black Sheep, Jarrow Rivet Catcher, Theakstons Mild and a couple of guests, farm cider, friendly staff; background music, big-screen sports TV; useful deli next-door. *(Eric Larkham, Tony and Wendy Hobden)*

NEWCASTLE UPON TYNE NZ2664
* **Cluny** (0191) 230 4474

Lime Street; NE1 2PQ Trendy bar/café in interesting 19th-c mill/warehouse, striking setting below Metro bridge, good value home-made food all day from massive sandwiches up, cheerful staff, up to eight well kept real ales, some exotic beers and rums, settees in comfortable raised area with daily newspapers and art magazines, back gallery with artwork from studios in same complex; background and regular live music; children welcome till 7pm, picnic-sets out on green, parking nearby can be difficult, open all day. *(Eric Larkham, Comus and Sarah Elliott)*

NEWCASTLE UPON TYNE NZ2563
* **Crown Posada** (0191) 232 1269

The Side; off Dean Street, between and below the two high central bridges (A6125 and A6127); NE1 3JE Popular unchanging city-centre pub with grand architecture, long narrow room with elaborate coffered ceiling, stained glass in counter screens, line of gilt mirrors each with tulip lamp on curly brass mount (matching the great ceiling candelabra), long built-in green leather wall seat flanked by narrow tables, fat low-level heating pipes, old working record player in wooden cabinet, six well kept ales, lunchtime sandwiches, helpful staff and good mix of regular customers (packed at peak times); background music; only a stroll to the castle, open all day, but closed Sun lunchtime. *(P Dawn, Phil and Sally Gorton, Peter Smith and Judith Brown, Eric Larkham, Andy and Jill Kassube, GSB and others)*

NEWCASTLE UPON TYNE NZ2664
* **Cumberland Arms** (0191) 2656151

Byker Buildings; NE6 1LD Friendly unspoilt traditional local, seven particularly well kept mainly local ales (straight from the cask if you wish) including a house beer from Wylam, six farm ciders/perries, two annual beer festivals, limited choice of good value pubby food all day, obliging staff, open fires, events most nights including live music (regular ukulele band); dogs welcome, tables out overlooking Ouseburn Valley, four bedrooms, closed Mon lunchtime otherwise open all day. *(Mike and Lynn Robinson, Eric Larkham, the Didler, R T and J C Moggridge)*

NEWCASTLE UPON TYNE NZ2470
Falcons Nest (0191) 236 7078
Rotary Way, Gosforth - handy for racecourse; NE3 5EH Roomy Vintage Inn with comfortably olde-worlde linked rooms, good value food, pleasant staff, good choice of wines by the glass, well kept Black Sheep and two guests; children welcome, tables out on terrace and lawn, open all day.
(Dr Peter D Smart)

NEWCASTLE UPON TYNE NZ2664
Free Trade (0191) 2655764
St Lawrence Road, off Walker Road (A186); NE6 1AP Splendidly basic proper pub with outstanding views up river from big windows, terrace tables and seats on grass, real ales such as High House, Jarrow and Mordue, good sandwiches, warmly friendly atmosphere, real fire, original Formica tables; steps down to back room and lavatories; open all day. *(Eric Larkham)*

NEWCASTLE UPON TYNE NZ2464
Newcastle Arms (0191) 2212519
St Andrews Street; NE1 5SE Open-plan drinkers' pub on fringe of Chinatown, Caledonian Deuchars IPA and five quickly changing guests including a porter or stout, farm ciders and perries, beer festivals, friendly staff, interesting old local photographs; background music, big-screen sports TV, can get very busy especially on match days; open all day. *(Eric Larkham, Mr and Mrs Maurice Thompson)*

NEWCASTLE UPON TYNE NZ2463
Town Wall (0191) 232 3000
Pink Lane; across from Central Station; NE1 5HX Recently opened pub in handsome listed building, warm friendly welcome, spacious bare-boards interior with dark walls, button-back banquettes and mix of well spaced tables and chairs, pictures in heavy gilt frames, up to 12 ales including one brewed for them, good choice of bottled beers and wines by the glass, fairly simple well priced food including burgers and pub favourites, all day brunch, overspill basement dining area; background music; well behaved children and dogs welcome, open all day (till 1am Fri, Sat). *(Denise McGuire)*

NEWTON NZ0364
Duke of Wellington (01661) 844446
Off A69 E of Corbridge; NE43 7UL Extensively refurbished old stone inn in attractive farming hamlet, good nicely presented interesting food, well kept local ales and comprehensive wine list, good service from friendly uniformed young staff, large L-shaped bar/dining area with wood or flagstone floors, comfortable mix of modern and traditional furnishings, sofas and armchairs in one corner, woodburner, daily newspapers, darts; dogs welcome in bar area, back terrace with lovely views, seven bedrooms. *(Mourveen Scott, W K Wood, Graham Oddey, GSB, Michael Doswell)*

NEWTON ON THE MOOR NU1705
⋆**Cook & Barker Arms**
(01665) 575234 *Village signed from A1 Alnwick–Felton; NE65 9JY* Nicely traditional stone-built country inn, beamed bar with stripped-stone and partly panelled walls, broad-seated settles around oak-topped tables, horsebrasses, coal fires, Black Sheep, Timothy Taylors and a guest beer, extensive wine list, popular food using meat from own farm (set deals Mon, Tues lunchtime and early evenings Weds and Thurs), friendly staff, separate restaurant with french windows opening on to terrace; background music, TV, no dogs; children welcome, 18 comfortably refurbished bedrooms, open all day. *(Ann and Tony Bennett-Hughes, Tony Baldwin, P A Rowe, GSB, Johnston and Maureen Anderson, Comus and Sarah Elliott and others)*

NEWTON-BY-THE-SEA NU2325
Joiners Arms (01665) 576112
In village by turning to Linkhouse; NE66 3EA Stylishly refurbished open-plan pub/restaurant, good imaginative well presented food all day from interesting sandwiches and sharing plates up, takeaway fish and chips too, real ales such as Hadrian & Border and Mordue plus some carefully chosen wines; children welcome, sturdy furniture on terrace overlooking village green, bedrooms. *(John Woodman, Michael Doswell)*

NORTH SHIELDS NZ
Quay Tap House (0191) 2592023
Bell Street; NE30 1HF Recently refurbished quayside pub, clean and airy, with good value tapas, sandwiches and home-made cakes, nice coffee, ales such as Daleside Alnwick IPA and Maxim Wards, good service; children welcome, open all day.
(Comus and Sarah Elliott)

PIERCEBRIDGE NZ2115
George (01325) 374576
B6275 just S of village, over bridge; DL2 3SW Old refurbished riverside pub/hotel, bar food from good sandwiches up, well kept Captain Cook beers, efficient service, river-view dining room; children welcome, decked terrace and attractive garden with bridge to small island (not easy for disabled people), 36 bedrooms, open all day. *(John H Smith)*

PONTELAND NZ1771

Badger (01661) 867931

*Street Houses; A696 SE, by garden
centre; NE20 9BT* Popular Vintage
Inn with relaxing rooms and alcoves, old
furnishings and olde-worlde décor, good log
fire, five well kept beers such as Black Sheep,
Leeds and Timothy Taylors, decent range of
wines by the glass, their usual all-day food,
prompt friendly service; background music;
children welcome. *(Dr Peter D Smart, Peter and
Eleanor Kenyon, Gerry and Rosemary Dobson,
Michael Doswell)*

RENNINGTON NU2118

⋆**Horseshoes** (01665) 577665

B1340; NE66 3RS Comfortable family-run
flagstoned pub with nice local feel (may be
horses in car park), well kept ales such as
Hadrian & Border and John Smiths, good
value generous food including two-course
lunch deals, good local fish and meat,
decent wines by the glass, friendly efficient
unrushed service, simple neat bar with
woodburner, spotless compact restaurant;
children welcome, tables outside, attractive
quiet village near coast, closed Mon.
*(Dr Peter D Smart, Guy and Caroline Howard,
Peter Veness)*

RENNINGTON NU2118

⋆**Masons Arms** (01665) 577275

Stamford Cott; B1340 N; NE66 3RX
Comfortable beamed bar with neat pubby
furniture on tartan carpet, well kept ales
such as Hadrian & Border, High House Farm
and Northumberland, good malt whisky
range, enjoyable straightforward food,
smiling relaxed service, brassware, flintlock
pistols etc, woodburner between bar and
family room; roadside terrace, more picnic-
sets behind, 14 comfortable bedrooms in
converted outbuildings. *(the Dutchman, Ann
and Tony Bennett-Hughes, John Beeken,
W K Wood)*

ROOKHOPE NY9342

Rookhope Inn (01388) 517215

Off A689 W of Stanhope; DL13 2BG
Friendly old inn on coast-to-coast bike route,
real ales such as Black Sheep and Timothy
Taylors Landlord, enjoyable home-made food
from fresh sandwiches to good Sun roasts,
black beams and open fires, small dining
room; sports TV; seats outside, spectacular
views, five bedrooms. *(Claes Mauroy)*

SEDGEFIELD NZ3528

Dun Cow (01740) 620894

Front Street; TS21 3AT Popular
refurbished village inn with low-beamed bar,
back tap room and dining room, above-
average food including good Sun roast,
cheerful efficient staff, well kept ales such
as Black Sheep and Camerons; children
welcome, reasonably priced comfortable
bedrooms, good breakfast. *(Andy Cole)*

SHINCLIFFE NZ2940

⋆**Seven Stars** (0191) 384 8454

*High Street N (A177 S of Durham);
DH1 2NU* Comfortable old-fashioned 18th-c
village inn, varied choice of good food from
pub favourites to gently upmarket dishes,
good value set menus, three well kept ales,
coal fire and plenty of atmosphere in lounge
bar, candlelit panelled dining room, caring
service from licensees; children in eating
areas, dogs in bar, some picnic-sets outside,
eight bedrooms, open all day. *(Bruce and
Sharon Eden, Richard and Stephanie Foskett,
Tim Tomlinson)*

SLALEY NY9658

⋆**Travellers Rest** (01434) 673231

*B6306 S of Hexham (and N of village);
NE46 1TT* Attractive and busy stone-built
country pub, spaciously opened up, with
farmhouse-style décor, beams, flagstones
and polished wood floors, huge fireplace,
comfortable high-backed settles forming
self-contained areas, friendly uniformed staff,
popular generously served food (not Sun
evening) in bar and appealingly up-to-date
dining room, good children's menu, real
ales such as Allendale, Black Sheep and
Wylam; dogs welcome, tables outside with
well equipped adventure play area on grass
behind, three good value bedrooms, open all
day. *(GSB)*

SOUTH SHIELDS NZ3567

Alum Ale House (0191) 427 7245

Ferry Street (B1344); NE33 1JR
Welcoming 18th-c pub handy for ferry, good
choice of well kept ales, bare boards, coal
fire in old inglenook range, no food; open all
day. *(R T and J C Moggridge)*

SOUTH SHIELDS NZ3666

Maltings (0191) 427 7147

Claypath Road; NE33 4PG Former dairy
now home to Jarrow brewery, their full range
and guest ales from upstairs bar (showpiece
staircase), authentic thai food (not Mon);
open all day. *(Eric Larkham)*

STANLEY NZ2054

South Causey (01207) 235555

South Causey Farm; DH9 0LS Stone-
built inn by riding school in 100-acre
grounds, beams, oak floors, open fires and
eclectic mix of old furniture, wide choice of
food all day from sandwiches to local game
using some home-grown produce, good
weekday lunchtime carvery, Wells & Youngs
Bombardier and two local ales kept well,
good service; children welcome, dogs allowed
in one area, picnic-sets outside, small farm
with alpacas, goats etc. *(John Coatsworth)*

STANNINGTON NZ2179

⋆**Ridley Arms** (01670) 789216

*Village signed off A1 S of Morpeth;
NE61 6EL* Attractive extended 18th-c

stone pub with several linked rooms, each with slightly different mood and style, proper front bar with log fire and stools along counter, Black Sheep, Caledonian and two guests, beamed dining areas with comfortable bucket armchairs around dark tables on bare boards or carpet, cartoons and portraits on cream, panelled or stripped-stone walls, pubby food (not Sun evening) from sandwiches up; background music, fruit machine; children welcome, no dogs, good disabled access, front picnic-sets by road, more on back terrace, open all day. *(Dr Peter D Smart, Denis Newton, Robert Wivell, Trevor and Judith Pearson, Comus and Sarah Elliott and others)*

TYNEMOUTH   NZ3669
Hugos at the Coast   (0191) 257 8956
Front Street; NE30 4DZ Well refurbished chain pub, open-plan split-level interior, four real ales and good choice of wines, bar food from wraps and sandwiches up, modest prices; open all day. *(Comus and Sarah Elliott)*

WARDEN   NY9166
Boatside   (01434) 602233
0.5 miles N of A69; NE46 4SQ Comfortably modernised old stone-built pub with enjoyable pubby food, well kept ales and good friendly service; children and muddy walkers welcome, small neat enclosed garden, attractive spot by Tyne bridge, bedrooms in adjoining cottages, open all day. *(Anon)*

WARENFORD   NU1429
White Swan   (01668) 213453
Off A1 S of Belford; NE70 7HY Simply decorated friendly bar with changing ales such as Adnams and Black Sheep, steps down to cosy restaurant with well liked imaginative food (good value set lunch), efficient helpful service, warm fires; dogs welcome. *(Mr and Mrs J P Syner, Michael Doswell, Nick Pickard)*

WARKWORTH   NU2406
Hermitage   (01665) 711258
Castle Street; NE65 0UL Rambling former coaching inn doing tasty home-made food all day (afternoon break Sun), carvery Fri and Sat evenings and Sun lunchtime, Jennings ales and a guest, friendly staff, quaint décor with old range for heating, small upstairs restaurant; background music; children welcome, benches out in front, attractive setting, five bedrooms. *(Ann and Tony Bennett-Hughes, Clive Flynn)*

WARKWORTH   NU2406
Masons Arms   (01665) 711398
Dial Place; NE65 0UR Welcoming village pub in shadow of castle, enjoyable food including daily specials and Sun carvery in

comfortable bar or separate dining area, local beers, friendly staff, Tues night quiz; children and dogs welcome, disabled facilities, back flagstoned courtyard, appealing village not far from the sea, open all day. *(Clive Flynn, Michael Doswell)*

WEST BOLDON   NZ3460
Red Lion   (0191) 5364197
Redcar Terrace; NE36 0PZ Bow-windowed and flower-decked family-run pub, hop-strung beamed bar with open fire, ales such as Mordue Workie Ticket from ornate wood counter, separate snug and conservatory dining room, good choice of well priced pubby food; seats out on back decking, open all day. *(Roger and Donna Huggins)*

WHITLEY BAY   NZ3473
Briar Dene   (0191) 252 0926
The Links; NE26 1UE Smart brightly decorated two-room pub, fine sea-view spot, with up to eight interesting changing ales, good value pubby food till 3pm (4pm weekends) from sandwiches up, friendly efficient staff; children welcome, seats outside, open all day. *(Dr Peter D Smart, Henry Paulinski, Eric Larkham, Guy and Caroline Howard, Adrian Johnson)*

WOLVISTON   NZ4525
Ship   (01740) 644420
High Street; TS22 5JX Gabled red-brick Victorian pub in centre of bypassed village, open-plan multi-level carpeted bar, decent choice of competitively priced food, changing real ales from northern breweries, quiz nights; garden. *(JHBS)*

WOOLER   NT9928
Tankerville Arms   (01668) 281581
A697 N; NE71 6AD Pleasant hotel bar in modernised early 17th-c coaching inn, relaxed and friendly, with reasonably priced food including local meat and fish, ales such as Hadrian & Border, good wines by the glass, small restaurant and larger airy one overlooking nice garden, big log fire; disabled facilities, 16 bedrooms, good local walks. *(Dr Peter D Smart, Peter Veness)*

WYLAM   NZ1164
⋆**Boathouse**   (01661) 853431
Station Road, handy for Newcastle–Carlisle rail line; across Tyne from village (and Stephenson's birthplace); NE41 8HR Thriving convivial pub with splendid ale range including local Wylam, keen prices, good choice of malt whiskies, bargain weekend lunches, polite helpful young staff, open stove in bright low-beamed bar, dining room; children and dogs welcome, seats outside, close to station and river, open all day. *(Eric Larkham, the Didler)*

You can send reports directly to us at feedback@goodguides.com

Nottinghamshire

The pubs here offer both good value and top notch dining. Doing well are the Black Horse in Caythorpe (quaintly old-fashioned with lots of tasty dishes under £10), Martins Arms in Colston Bassett (civilised and very special for a meal out, imaginative food and six real ales), Dovecote at Laxton (back in these pages after a break and carefully refurbished, with good, home-made food) and Cross Keys in Upton (a new entry for this friendly 17th c pub serving tasty, honest meals). Our Nottinghamshire Dining Pub 2013 is the Martins Arms in Colston Bassett.

CAYTHORPE   SK6845   Map 7

Black Horse £

Turn off A6097 0.25 miles SE of roundabout junction with A612, NE of Nottingham; into Gunthorpe Road, then right into Caythorpe Road and keep on; NG14 7ED

Quaintly old-fashioned little pub brewing its own beer, simple interior and enjoyable homely food; no children, no credit cards

Peacefully free of games machines, children and swearing, this timeless 300-year-old country local has been run by the same friendly family for three generations. Its uncluttered carpeted bar has just five tables, decorative plates on a delft shelf, a few horsebrasses on the ceiling joists, brocaded wall banquettes and settles, and a coal fire. Cheerful regulars might occupy the few bar stools to enjoy the Caythorpe Dover Beck (named after the stream that runs past the pub) and One Swallow that are brewed in outbuildings here and served alongside a couple of guests from Adnams or Greene King Abbot. Off the front corridor is a partly panelled inner room with a wall bench running right the way around three unusual long copper-topped tables, and there are quite a few old local photographs; darts and board games. Down on the left, an end room has just one huge round table. There are some plastic tables outside, and the River Trent is fairly close for waterside walks.

Cooked by the landlady, the good value meals attract an older lunchtime set and you will need to book. Simple freshly cooked traditional food from a shortish menu includes sandwiches, celery and blue cheese soup, lambs kidneys in cream, whitebait, grilled grapefruit, cod loin with cheese sauce, pork fillet with mustard and cream sauce, chicken, mushroom and leek pie, steak and kidney pie, sausage and mash, and puddings such as treacle sponge and apple pie. *Benchmark main dish: fried cod £9.00. Two-course evening meal £13.00.*

Own brew ~ Licensee Sharron Andrews ~ Real ale ~ Bar food (12-2, 7-9; not Sat evening or Sun) ~ Restaurant ~ No credit cards ~ (0115) 966 3520 ~ Dogs welcome ~ Open

12-2.30, 6-11.30; 12-5, 8-11.30 Sun; closed Mon except bank holidays and Tues lunchtime after the third Mon of month and bank holidays *Recommended by P Dawn, David Eberlin, Chris Johnson, the Didler, David and Sue Atkinson*

 COLSTON BASSETT   SK6933   Map 7

Martins Arms

Village signposted off A46 E of Nottingham; School Lane, near market cross in village centre; NG12 3FD

Nottinghamshire Dining Pub of the Year

Smart dining pub with imaginative food, good range of drinks including six real ales, and attractive grounds

Top notch in every respect, this lovely country pub is smartly decorated with period fabrics and colours, antique furniture and hunting prints. There are warm log fires in Jacobean fireplaces and the atmosphere is peaceful and comfortably civilised. If you are dining in the elegant restaurant, you may be welcomed by Salvatore, the friendly front of house man, and neatly uniformed staff serve Bass, Greene King IPA, Marstons Pedigree, Timothy Taylors Landlord and a couple of guests from brewers such as Castle Rock and Sharps, as well as Belvoir organic ginger beer, a good range of malt whiskies and cognacs and interesting wines; cribbage, dominoes and board games. The lovely lawned garden (summer croquet here) backs on to National Trust parkland and readers recommend visiting the church opposite and Colston Bassett Dairy, which sells its own stilton cheese, and is just outside the village.

 They use seasonal carefully sourced ingredients so the bar (more reasonable) and restaurant menus change frequently. Exquisitely presented dishes might include sandwiches, eggs benedict, pear, walnut and stilton salad, crab cocktail, pork croque monsieur, fried foie gras with pear and cinnamon chutney, toasted brioche and quails eggs, fish and chips, sausage and new potatoes, ploughman's, brie risotto cake with mushrooms and truffle, blade of beef, guinea fowl with game chips and bread sauce, and puddings such as cinnamon nut millefeuille and baked rice pudding with plum jam. Their well hung sirloin is particularly popular on Sundays. *Benchmark main dish: local venison £24.50. Two-course evening meal £30.70.*

Free house ~ Licensees Lynne Strafford Bryan and Salvatore Inguanta ~ Real ale ~ Bar food (12-2(3 Sun), 6-10; not Sun evening) ~ Restaurant ~ (01949) 81361 ~ Children welcome ~ Open 12-3, 6-11; 12-4, 6.30-10.30 Sun ~ www.themartinsarms.co.uk
Recommended by P Dawn, Dennis and Doreen Haward, the Didler, David Glynne-Jones, O K Smyth, Mike Proctor, Jack and Sandra Clarfelt

 LAXTON   SK7266   Map 7

Dovecote

Off A6075 E of Ollerton; NG22 0NU

Village pub handy for A1; good bar food and garden

This red-brick free house has recently been refurbished without spoiling its cosy country atmosphere. Friendly staff serve a farm cider, several wines by the glass, and Batemans XB, Timothy Taylors Landlord and a couple of guests such as Charles Wells Bombardier and Fullers London Pride; darts and background music. Wooden tables and chairs on a small front terrace and sloping garden have views towards the village church. Laxton is famously home to three huge medieval open fields – it's one of the few places in the country still farmed using this system. Every year, in the third week of June, the grass is auctioned for haymaking, and anyone who lives in the parish is entitled to a bid and a drink. You can get more information from the visitor centre behind the pub.

Good, enjoyable food includes filled baguettes, twice-baked crab and cheddar soufflé, creamed wild mushrooms on home-made sourdough toast with parmesan, honey-roast gammon with free-range eggs, cottage pie, mushroom risotto, hand-made beef burger with home-made coleslaw and fat chips, steak, mushroom and bacon pie, beer-battered fish and chips with minted mushy peas and tartare sauce, and puddings such as raspberry and mascarpone crème brûlée with cinnamon swirl shortbread and iced peanut butter parfait with caramel sauce. *Benchmark main dish: steak in ale pie £10.25. Two-course evening meal £17.80.*

Free house ~ Licensees David and Linda Brown ~ Real ale ~ Bar food (12-2, 5(6 Sat)-9; 12-6 Sun) ~ Restaurant ~ (01777) 871586 ~ Children welcome ~ Open 11.30-3, 5-11; 12-10.30 Sun ~ Bedrooms: £65B/£75B ~ www.dovecoteinnlaxton.co.uk *Recommended by Terry Davis, Michele Summers, Chris Lowe*

UPTON
Cross Keys
A612; NG23 5SY

SK7354   Map 7

17th-c pub with welcoming licensees and well liked food and drink

Friendly, hard-working new licensees took over this bustling 17th-c pub as we went to press, but early reports from readers suggest that things are going well. The rambling, heavy-beamed bar has lots of alcoves, a log fire in the brick fireplace, some brass and copper implements, dark wooden cushioned dining chairs around a mix of tables on traditional red and white floor tiles and Greene King Ruddles H&H Bitter, Wells & Youngs Bombardier and a guest beer on handpump and several wines by the glass. A back extension has a long carved pew, and there's a room for private hire upstairs. The decked terrace outside has plenty of seats, and the pub is opposite the British Horological Institute.

Tasty bar food includes sandwiches, smoked mackerel pâté, deep-fried camembert, ham and eggs, chicken in a basket, lasagne, lambs liver and bacon, a pie of the day, slow-roast pork belly, and puddings such as chocolate brownie and lemon tart. *Benchmark main dish: home-made pie of the day £7.95. Two-course evening meal £14.50.*

Free house ~ Licensees Roy and Laura Wood ~ Bar food (12-2.30, 6-8 (maybe earlier); not Mon evening) ~ Restaurant ~ (01636) 813269 ~ Children welcome ~ Dogs allowed in bar ~ Live music Sun and Mon evenings ~ Open 12-3, 5.30(6 Sat)-11(midnight Sat); 12-10.30 Sun ~ www.crosskeysupton.co.uk *Recommended by Derek and Sylvia Stephenson, R and M Tait*

'Children welcome' means the pub says it lets children inside without any special restriction. If it allows them in, but to restricted areas such as an eating area or family room, we specify this. Places with separate restaurants often let children use them, hotels usually let them into public areas such as lounges. Some pubs impose an evening time limit – let us know if you find one earlier than 9pm.

Also Worth a Visit in Nottinghamshire

Besides the fully inspected pubs, you might like to try these pubs that have been recommended to us and described by readers. Do tell us what you think of them: feedback@goodguides.com

AWSWORTH   SK4844
Gate (0115) 932 9821
Main Street, via A6096 off A610 Nuthall–Eastwood bypass; NG16 2RN Friendly Victorian free house with six well kept ales (usually Blue Monkey and Burton Bridge), cosy bar, coal fire in lounge, small pool room, and a fourth room being added as we went to press, some snacks, refurbished skittle alley; children welcome till 8pm, dogs in bar, disabled facilities, picnic-sets out in front, near site of once-famous railway viaduct, open all day (till 1am Fri, Sat). *(the Didler, Yvonne and Rob Warhurst, Fiona Coupland)*

BAGTHORPE   SK4751
Dixies Arms (01773) 810505
A608 towards Eastwood off M1 J27, right on B600 via Sandhill Road, left into School Road; Lower Bagthorpe; NG16 5HF Friendly unspoilt 18th-c beamed and tiled-floor local with D H Lawrence connections, well kept Greene King Abbot, Theakstons Best and a guest, no food, good fire in small part-panelled parlour's fine fireplace, entrance bar with tiny snug, longer narrow room with toby jugs, darts and dominoes, live music Sat, quiz Sun; children and dogs (on leads) welcome, good big garden with play area and football pitch, open all day. *(the Didler)*

BEESTON   SK5236
Crown (0115) 925 4738
Church Street; NG9 1FY Owned and sensitively restored by Everards, real ale enthusiast landlord serving up to 14 (some keenly priced), also real ciders, perry and good choice of bottled beers (regular beer festivals), no hot food but fresh cobs and other snacks; front snug and bar with quarry-tiled floor, carpeted parlour with padded wall seats, Victorian décor and new polished bar in lounge, beams, panelling, bric-a-brac, old red telephone box; terrace tables, open all day. *(the Didler, MP, Steve Bakewell, Andrew Abbott, Johnston and Maureen Anderson)*

BEESTON   SK5336
⋆**Victoria** (0115) 925 4049
Dovecote Lane, backing on to railway station; NG9 1JG Genuine down-to-earth all-rounder attracting good mix of customers, up to 15 real ales (regular beer festivals), two farm ciders, 120 malt whiskies and 30 wines by the glass, good value interesting food (half the menu is vegetarian), friendly efficient service, three fairly simple unfussy rooms with original long narrow layout, solid furnishings, bare boards and stripped woodwork, stained-glass windows, open fires, newspapers and board games, live music (Sun, Mon evening Oct–May); children welcome till 8pm, dogs in bar, seats out on covered heated area overlooking railway platform (trains pass just a few feet away), limited parking, open all day. *(P Dawn, Ian and Helen Stafford, the Didler, MP, Johnston and Maureen Anderson and others)*

BINGHAM   SK7039
⋆**Horse & Plough** (01949) 839313
Off A52; Long Acre; NG13 8AF Former 1818 Methodist chapel with low beams, flagstones and stripped brick, prints and old brewery memorabilia, comfortable open-plan seating including pews, well kept Caledonian Deuchars IPA, Theakstons XB and four guests (tasters offered), real cider, good wine choice, enjoyable reasonably priced home-made weekday bar food, popular upstairs grill room (Tues-Sat evenings and Sun lunch) with polished boards, hand-painted murals and open kitchen; background music; children and dogs welcome, disabled facilities, open all day. *(P Dawn, Jack Matthew, the Didler, MP, Dr Matt Burleigh)*

BRAMCOTE   SK5037
White Lion (0115) 925 5413
Just off A52 W of Nottingham; Town Street; NG9 3HH Small homely open-plan pub with well kept Greene King ales from bar serving two split-level adjoining rooms, reasonably priced pubby food including Wed curry and Sun roasts, darts and dominoes, quiz nights; tables in attractive garden behind, open all day. *(MP)*

BUNNY   SK5829
Rancliffe Arms (0115) 984 4727
Loughborough Road (A60 S of Nottingham); NG11 6QT Substantial early 18th-c former coaching inn reworked with emphasis on linked dining areas, upscale food from enterprising sandwich range to adventurous dishes, popular carvery (Mon evening, Weds, Sat and Sun), chunky country chairs around mixed tables on flagstones or carpet, well kept Marstons-related ales in comfortable log-fire bar with sofas and armchairs; children welcome, decking outside, open all Fri-Sun. *(P Dawn, Gerry and Rosemary Dobson)*

CAR COLSTON   SK7242
Royal Oak (01949) 20247
The Green, off Tenman Lane (off A46 not far from A6097 junction); NG13 8JE Helpful licensees doing good, well priced,

traditional food (not Sun evening) in biggish 19th-c pub opposite one of England's largest village greens, three or more well kept Marstons-related ales, decent choice of wines by the glass, woodburner in lounge bar with tables set for eating, public bar with unusual barrel-vaulted brick ceiling, spotless housekeeping; children welcome, picnic-sets on spacious back lawn, heated smokers' den, camping, open all day weekends, closed Mon lunchtime. *(P Dawn, David Glynne-Jones, Richard and Jean Green)*

CAUNTON   SK7459
★Caunton Beck (01636) 636793
Newark Road; NG23 6AE Cleverly reconstructed low-beamed dining pub made to look old using original timbers and reclaimed oak, scrubbed pine tables and country-kitchen chairs, rag-finished paintwork, some clever lighting, open fire, Batemans, Black Sheep and Marstons, over two dozen wines by the glass, enjoyable popular food from breakfast on, decent coffee and daily newspapers, helpful friendly staff; children welcome, dogs in bar, seats on flowery terrace, open all day from 8.30am, handy for A1. *(Ian and Nita Cooper, Richard Cole, Pat and Stewart Gordon, John Prescott, Ian Prince and others)*

COLLINGHAM   SK8361
Kings Head (01636) 892341
High Street; NG23 7LA Gently upscale modern pub/restaurant behind unpretentious Georgian façade, two well kept changing ales from long steel bar, courteous helpful staff, food from baguettes to good restaurant dishes with unusual touches, light and airy dining area with pine furniture on polished boards; children welcome, no dogs, disabled access, garden tables, open all day Sun. *(David and Ruth Hollands, Tom Carver)*

COTGRAVE   SK6435
Rose & Crown (0115) 989 2245
Main Road, off A46 SE of Nottingham; NG12 3HQ Friendly and comfortable village pub, good value generous food all day including midweek and early evening bargains, more elaborate evening and weekend dishes, helpful young staff, three changing ales, good wine and soft drinks choice, log fires, newspapers, back eating area with fresh flowers and candles; background music, Sun quiz; children welcome, garden picnic-sets. *(JJW, CMW, P Dawn, David Glynne-Jones)*

EDINGLEY   SK6655
Old Reindeer (01623) 882252
Off A617 Newark–Mansfield at Kirklington; Main Street; NG22 8BE Refurbished roadside pub dating from the 18th c, well liked food (all day weekends) including good fish and chips and bargain carvery, efficient service, well kept Jennings ales, front lounge bar with pool in side area,

comfortable back restaurant; background music, children and dogs welcome, attractive garden, four bedrooms, open all day. *(David Errington, D S Thrall, R and M Tait)*

EDWINSTOWE   SK6266
Forest Lodge (01623) 8244443
Church Street; NG21 9QA Friendly 17th-c inn with enjoyable home-made food in pubby bar or restaurant, good service, well kept Wells & Youngs Bombardier and four regularly changing guests; log fire; children welcome, 13 comfortable bedrooms, handy for Sherwood Forest. *(Derek and Sylvia Stephenson)*

FARNDON   SK7652
★Boathouse (01636) 676578
Off A46 SW of Newark; keep on towards river – pub off Wyke lane, just past the Riverside pub; NG24 3SX Big-windowed contemporary bar-restaurant overlooking the Trent, emphasis on food but Greene King IPA and a guest served from stylish counter, good choice of wines, main area indeed reminiscent of a boathouse with high ceiling trusses supporting bare ducting and scant modern decoration, second dining area broadly similar, modern cooking along with some pubby dishes, neat young staff; background and live music (Sun); children welcome, wicker chairs around teak tables on terrace, own moorings, open all day. *(Michael and Maggie Betton)*

GRANBY   SK7436
★Marquis of Granby (01949) 859517
Off A52 E of Nottingham; Dragon Street; NG13 9PN Popular, stylish and friendly 18th-c pub in attractive Vale of Belvoir village, tap for Brewsters with their ales and interesting guests from chunky yew bar counter, decent home-made food Fri evening (fish and chips) to Sun lunchtime, two small comfortable rooms with broad flagstones, some low beams and striking wallpaper, open fire; children and dogs welcome, open from 4pm Mon- Fri, all day weekends. *(the Didler)*

HARBY   SK8870
★Bottle & Glass (01522) 703438
High Street; village signed off A57 W of Lincoln; NG23 7EB Civilised dining pub with pair of bay-windowed front bars, attractive pubby furnishings, lots of bright cushions on built-in wall benches, arts and crafts chairs, dark flagstones and red walls, log fire, splendid range of wines (big vineyard map of Côte de Beaune in left-hand bar), Black Sheep and Titanic beers, good country cooking all day including set menu, friendly attentive service, small area with squashy sofas and armchairs and more formal restaurant; children welcome, dogs allowed in bar, modern wrought-iron furniture on back terrace, picnic-sets on grass beyond. *(Sue Kinder, Pauline Fellows and Simon Robbins)*

HOVERINGHAM SK6946
⋆**Reindeer** (01159) 663629
Main Street; NG14 7GR Beamed pub with intimate bar and busy restaurant (best to book), good home-made food (not Sun evening) from pubby things to more enterprising dishes, good value lunchtime set menu, Castle Rock and three guest ales, good wines by the glass, log fire; children welcome, seats outside overlooking cricket pitch, open all day weekends, closed lunchtimes Mon and Tues. *(David and Sue Atkinson, the Didler)*

JACKSDALE
Corner Pin (01773) 528781
Palmerston Street, Westwood; off B6016; NG16 5HY Traditional old side-street local, two rooms with coal fires, old-fashioned simple furnishings, half a dozen ales including own-brew beers (microbrewery in former skittle alley), real cider, pool and table skittles, friendly relaxed atmosphere; sports TV, not much street parking; open all day weekends, from 1pm Mon-Fri. *(the Didler)*

KIMBERLEY SK4944
⋆**Nelson & Railway** (0115) 938 2177
Station Road; handy for M1 junction 26 via A610; NG16 2NR Comfortable beamed Victorian pub with well kept Greene King ales and guests, mix of Edwardian-looking furniture, brewery prints (was tap for defunct H&H Brewery) and railway signs, dining extension, traditional games including alley and table skittles; juke box, games machine; children and dogs allowed, nice front and back gardens, good value bedrooms, open all day. *(the Didler, Comus and Sarah Elliott)*

KIMBERLEY SK5044
Stag (0115) 9383151
Nottingham Road; NG16 2NB Friendly 18th-c traditional pub spotlessly kept by devoted landlady, two cosy rooms, small central counter and corridor, low beams, dark panelling and settles, vintage working slot machines, old Shipstones Brewery photographs, good range of ales including Adnams, Black Sheep, Marstons and Timothy Taylors (May beer festival), no food; attractive back garden with play area, opens 5pm (1.30 Sat, 12 Sun). *(the Didler)*

LAMBLEY SK6345
Woodlark (0115) 931 2535
Church Street; NG4 4QB Welcoming and interestingly laid-out village local, neatly furnished bare-brick beamed bar, careful extension into next house giving comfortable lounge/dining area, popular good value freshly made food, downstairs steak bar (Fri, Sat evenings), well kept Castle Rock, Sam Smiths, Timothy Taylors Landlord and a guest, open fire; children and dogs welcome, tables on side terrace, open all day Fri, short afternoon break Sat and Sun. *(the Didler)*

LINBY SK5351
Horse & Groom (0115) 9632219
Main Street; NG15 8AE Picturesque four-room village pub with welcoming enthusiastic landlord, well kept Caledonian (including one badged for them), Greene King Old Speckled Hen, Wells & Youngs and changing guests, enjoyable nicely presented pub food (not Sun-Thurs evenings) from shortish menu, prompt friendly service, inglenook log fire, conservatory; no mobile phones; quiet background music, big-screen TV, games machines in lobby; children welcome, tables outside, big play area, attractive village near Newstead Abbey, good walks, open all day. *(P Dawn, the Didler, David Glynne-Jones)*

MANSFIELD SK5561
Il Rosso (01623) 623031
Nottingham Road (A60); NG18 4AF Refurbished restaurarnty pub with enjoyable italian-influenced food including good fresh fish, takeaway pizza too, up to five well kept changing ales, good service, live acoustic music (Mon Jazz); no dogs inside; children welcome, terraces front and back, open all day from 8.30am for breakfast. *(Derek and Sylvia Stephenson)*

MANSFIELD SK5363
Railway Inn (01623) 623086
Station Street; best approached by viaduct from near Market Place; NG18 1EF Friendly traditional local with long-serving landlady, three changing ales, real cider and good bottled beer choice, bargain home-made food (till 5pm Sun), two little front rooms leading to main bar, another cosy room at back, new laminate flooring throughout; children and dogs welcome, small courtyard and beer garden, handy for Robin Hood Line station, open all day. *(P Dawn, the Didler)*

MANSFIELD WOODHOUSE SK5463
Greyhound (01623) 464403
High Street; NG19 8BD Friendly family-run 17th-c village local with up to half a dozen well kept ales including Adnams and Caledonian Deuchars IPA (beer festivals), cosy lounge, darts, dominoes and pool in busy bar, no food; open all day. *(P Dawn, the Didler)*

MAPLEBECK SK7160
⋆**Beehive**
Signed down pretty country lanes from A616 Newark–Ollerton and from A617 Newark–Mansfield; NG22 0BS Relaxing beamed country tavern in nice spot, chatty landlady, tiny front bar, slightly bigger side room, traditional furnishings and antiques, open fire, well kept Maypole and guests, no food; tables on small terrace with flower tubs and grassy bank running down to a stream, summer barbecues, play area, may be closed weekday lunchtimes in winter, very busy weekends and bank holidays. *(the Didler)*

MORTON   SK7251

⋆**Full Moon** (01636) 830251

Pub and village signed off Bleasby–Fiskerton back road, SE of Southwell; NG25 0UT Attractive, smartly updated village pub, good well presented food including weekday set deals, friendly helpful service, Bass, Greene King IPA and three mainly local guests, decent choice of wines by the glass and nice coffee, restaurant; background music, TV; children and dogs welcome, picnic-sets on peaceful back terrace and sizeable lawn, sturdy play equipment, open all day weekends. *(P Dawn, the Didler, David Glynne-Jones, Derek and Sylvia Stephenson, M Mossman)*

NEWARK   SK7954

Castle (01636) 605856

Castle Gate; NG24 1AZ Spotless old low-ceilinged pub, five or so well kept ales including Sharps Doom Bar and a house brew from Oldershaws, bare-boards front room, long panelled and carpeted back room, old wooden furniture, lots of mirrors and prints; piped and live music, no children; open all day. *(the Didler)*

NEWARK   SK8053

⋆**Fox & Crown** (01636) 605820

Appleton Gate; NG24 1JY Convivial bare-boards open-plan Castle Rock pub with their keenly priced ales and several interesting guests from central servery, Stowford Press cider, dozens of whiskies, vodkas and other spirits, good tea, coffee and decent wines by the glass, friendly obliging staff, inexpensive food from rolls and baked potatoes up, several side areas; piped and weekly live music; children welcome in dining room, good wheelchair access, open all day. *(Simon Elvidge, Richard Martin, the Didler, David and Ruth Hollands, Andy Lickfold)*

NEWARK   SK7953

Just Beer (07983) 993747

Swan & Salmon Yard, off Castle Gate (B6166); NG24 1BG Small welcoming one-room pub (opened 2010), four or five interesting quickly changing microbrewery ales from brick bar, real cider and perry served from cellar, no other alcoholic drinks or food, bright airy minimalist décor with some brewery memorabilia, half a dozen tables on stone floor, eclectic mix of customers; open all day (from 1pm weekdays). *(the Didler, Eric, Tony and Maggie Harwood)*

NEWARK   SK7953

Prince Rupert (01636) 918121

Stodman Street, off Castlegate; NG24 1AW Ancient renovated timber-framed pub near market, several small rooms on two floors, beams, exposed brickwork and many original features (some previously covered up), nice old furniture including high-backed settles, conservatory, five real ales such as Blue Monkey, Oakham and Thornbridge, Weston's cider, blackboard choice of wines by the glass, speciality pizzas with some unusual toppings and other imaginative food, friendly staff, live music; courtyard with old enamel signs, open all day (till 1am Fri, Sat). *(Mr and Mrs Beardsley, the Didler, Richard Martin, G Jennings, Jennie Roberts, Tony and Maggie Harwood)*

NORTH MUSKHAM   SK7958

Muskham Ferry (01636) 704943

Ferry Lane, handy for A1 (which has small sign to pub); NG23 6HB Traditional well furnished panelled pub in splendid location on River Trent, relaxing views from bar/restaurant, fairly priced food including children's meals and Sun roast, three well kept real ales, good wine and soft drinks choice, friendly chatty staff; piped radio, games machine, pool; dogs welcome, waterside terrace, moorings, open all day. *(John and Alison Hamilton)*

NOTTINGHAM   SK5739

⋆**Bell** (0115) 947 5241

Angel Row; off Market Square; NG1 6HL Deceptively large pub with late Georgian frontage concealing two 500-year-old timber-framed buildings; front Tudor Bar with café feel in summer when french windows open to pavement tables, bright blue walls with glass panels protecting patches of 300-year-old wallpaper; larger low-beamed Elizabethan Bar with half-panelled walls, maple parquet flooring and upstairs Belfry with more heavy panelling and 15th-c crown post; up to a dozen real ales from remarkable deep sandstone cellar, ten wines by the glass, reasonably priced straightforward bar food, welcoming staff; piped and regular live music including trad jazz, TV, silent fruit machine; children welcome in some parts, open all day (till 1am Sat). *(P Dawn, Barry Collett, the Didler, Richard Tilbrook)*

NOTTINGHAM   SK5843

Bread & Bitter (0115) 9607 541

Woodthorpe Drive; NG3 5JL In former suburban bakery still showing ovens, three bright and airy bare-boarded rooms, around a dozen well kept ales including Castle Rock, farm cider, decent wine choice, good value home-made food all day from cobs up, defunct brewery memorabilia; dogs welcome in bar. *(P Dawn, the Didler, Tony and Maggie Harwood)*

NOTTINGHAM   SK5739

⋆**Canal House** (0115) 9555060

Canal Street; NG1 7EH Converted wharf building, bridge over indoors canal spur complete with narrowboat, lots of bare brick and varnished wood, huge joists on steel beams, long bar with well kept Castle Rock and three guests, 80 or so bottled beers and good choice of wines, sensibly priced pubby food (not Sun evening), efficient service; background music; masses of tables out on attractive waterside terrace, open all day. *(P Dawn, the Didler)*

NOTTINGHAM   SK5739
Cock & Hoop (0115) 8523231
High Pavement; NG1 1HF Tiny bareboards front bar with fireside armchairs and flagstoned cellar bar attached to decent hotel, characterful décor, reasonably priced fairly traditional food including good Sun roasts, well kept ales such as Amber, Blue Monkey, Flipside and Magpie, attentive friendly service; background music, live jazz last Thurs of month; children and dogs welcome, disabled facilities, smart bedrooms (ones by the street can be noisy at weekends), open all day. *(P Dawn, the Didler)*

NOTTINGHAM   SK5739
✶Cross Keys (0115) 9417898
Byard Lane; NG1 2GJ Restored Victorian city-centre pub on two levels, lower carpeted part with leather banquettes, panelling and chandeliers, upper area with old wooden chairs and tables on polished boards, interesting prints and pictures and more chandeliers, well kept ales such as Batemans, Falstaff, Full Mash and Wychwood, good home-made food from breakfast on, friendly service; sports TV; seats outside, open 8am (9am Sun) to 12.30am. *(P Dawn, the Didler, George Atkinson)*

NOTTINGHAM   SK5542
Fox & Crown (0115) 9422002
Church Street/Lincoln Street, Old Basford; NG6 0GA Good range of Alcazar beers brewed behind refurbished open-plan pub (window shows the brewery, tours Sat, next-door beer shop), also guest ales, continentals and good choice of wines, enjoyable thai food; good background music, games machines, big-screen sports TV; disabled access, terrace tables behind, open all day. *(P Dawn)*

NOTTINGHAM   SK5642
Gladstone (0115) 9129994
Loscoe Road, Carrington; NG5 2AW Welcoming backstreet local with half a dozen well kept ales including Castle Rock, Fullers, Nottingham, Oakham and Timothy Taylors, good range of malt whiskies, comfortable lounge with reading matter, basic bar with old sports memorabilia and darts, upstairs folk club Weds, quiz Thurs; background music and sports TV; tables in back garden among colourful tubs and hanging baskets, closed weekday lunchtimes, open all day weekends. *(P Dawn, the Didler)*

NOTTINGHAM   SK5738
Globe (0115) 9866881
London Road; NG2 3BQ Light and airy roadside pub with six well kept ales including two from Nottingham, good value food, coal fire; sports TVs; handy for cricket and football grounds, open all day. *(P Dawn)*

NOTTINGHAM   SK5542
Horse & Groom (0115) 9703777
Radford Road, New Basford; NG7 7EA Nine good changing ales in well run unpretentious open-plan local by former Shipstones Brewery, still with their name and other memorabilia, good value fresh straightforward food from sandwiches to Sun lunch, daily newspapers, nice snug; music and regular beer festivals in stable block behind, open all day (from 4pm Mon). *(P Dawn, the Didler)*

NOTTINGHAM   SK5739
✶Kean's Head (0115) 947 4052
St Mary's Gate; NG1 1QA Cheery Tynemill pub in attractive Lace Market area; fairly functional single room with something of a continental bar atmosphere, simple wooden café furnishings on wooden boards, some exposed brickwork and red tiling, low sofa by big windows overlooking street, stools by wood counter and small fireplace, Castle Rock and three guests, draught belgian and interesting bottled beers, 20 wines by the glass, 39 malt whiskies and lots of teas/coffees, tasty traditional english and some italian food (not Sun, Mon evenings), friendly if not speedy service, daily newspapers; background music; children welcome till 7pm, church next door worth a look, open all day. *(P Dawn, the Didler, Tony and Wendy Hobden, Andrew Abbott)*

NOTTINGHAM   SK5539
King William IV (0115) 9589864
Manvers Street/Eyre Street, Sneinton; NG2 4PB Two-room Victorian corner local, plenty of character, Oakham and six guests from circular bar, Weston's Old Rosie cider, good fresh cobs, friendly staff, fine tankard collection, pool upstairs, irish music Thurs; silenced sports TV; heated smokers' shelter, handy for cricket, football and rugby grounds, open all day. *(P Dawn, the Didler)*

NOTTINGHAM   SK5838
Larwood & Voce (0115) 9819960
Fox Road, West Bridgford; NG2 6AJ Well run open-plan dining pub mixing modern and traditional, good locally sourced home-made food all day from lunchtime bar meals to more extensive and imaginative evening menu, good choice of wines by the glass

---

Post Office address codings confusingly give the impression that a few pubs are in Nottinghamshire, when they're really in Derbyshire (which is where we list them).

including champagne, cocktail menu, three real ales, cheerful staff; sports TV; children welcome away from bar, on the edge of the cricket ground and handy for Nottingham Forest FC, open all day, from 9am weekends for breakfast. *(P Dawn, Ajay Sethi, David Glynne-Jones)*

NOTTINGHAM   SK5740
⋆**Lincolnshire Poacher**
(0115) 941 1584 *Mansfield Road; up hill from Victoria Centre; NG1 3FR* Impressive range of drinks at this popular down-to-earth pub (attracting younger evening crowd), ten or so real ales, continental draught and bottled beers, farm cider and over 70 malt whiskies, good value all-day food; big simple traditional front bar with wall settles, wooden tables and breweriana, plain but lively room on left and corridor to chatty panelled back snug with newspapers and board games, conservatory overlooking tables on large heated back area, live music Sun evening; children (till 8pm) and dogs welcome, open all day (till midnight Sat). *(P Dawn, the Didler, MP, David Hunt)*

NOTTINGHAM   SK5541
⋆**Lion** (0115) 9703506
Lower Mosley Street, New Basford; NG7 7FQ Ten ales including regulars Batemans and Mallards from one of the city's deepest cellars (glass viewing panel – can be visited at quiet times), farm ciders, ten wines by the glass, good value home-made food all day including doorstep sandwiches; well fabricated feel of separate areas, bare bricks and polished dark oak boards, old brewery pictures and posters, open fires, daily newspapers, weekend live music including Sun lunchtime jazz, beer festivals; children welcome till 8pm, disabled facilities, garden with terrace and smokers' shelter, summer barbecues, open all day. *(P Dawn, the Didler, David Hunt)*

NOTTINGHAM   SK5739
News House (0115) 952 3061
Canal Street; NG1 7HB Friendly two-room 1950s Castle Rock pub with notable blue exterior tiling, their ales and half a dozen changing guests, belgian and czech imports, decent fresh lunchtime food (Mon-Sat), mix of bare boards and carpet, local newspaper/ radio memorabilia, darts, table skittles and bar billiards, Thurs quiz; big-screen sports TV; a few tables out at front, open all day. *(P Dawn, the Didler)*

NOTTINGHAM   SK5739
⋆**Olde Trip to Jerusalem**
(0115) 9473171 *Brewhouse Yard; from inner ring road follow The North, A6005 Long Eaton signpost until in Castle Boulevard, then right into Castle Road; pub is on the left; NG1 6AD* Unusual rambling pub seemingly clinging to sandstone rock face (and some rooms

actually burrowed into it), largely 17th c and a former brewhouse supplying the hilltop castle; downstairs bar carved into the rock with leatherette-cushioned settles built into dark panelling, tables on flagstones, rocky alcoves, Greene King, Nottingham and guests, good value food all day, efficient staff dealing well with busy mix of customers; little tourist shop with panelled walls soaring up into a dark stone cleft, cellar tours (must book); children welcome till 7pm, seats in snug courtyard, open all day (till midnight Fri, Sat). *(P Dawn, Barry Collett, David Glynne-Jones, Andy Dolan, Andy Lickfold, John Honnor)*

NOTTINGHAM   SK5540
Plough (0115) 942 2649
St Peters Street, Radford; NG7 3EN Friendly 19th-c local brewing its own good value Nottingham ales at the back, also guest beers and farm cider, decent cheap food including fresh cobs and popular Sun lunch, mosaic floors, old tables and chairs, two coal fires, traditional games and skittle alley, Thurs quiz; sports TV; dogs welcome (may get a chew), covered smokers' area, open all day Fri-Sun. *(P Dawn, the Didler)*

NOTTINGHAM   SK5739
Salutation (0115) 958 9432
Hounds Gate/Maid Marian Way; NG1 7AA Proper pub, low beams, flagstones, ochre walls and cosy corners including two small quiet rooms in ancient lower back part, plusher modern front lounge, half a dozen real ales and good choice of draught/bottled ciders, quickly served food till 8pm (6pm Sun), helpful staff (ask them to show you the haunted caves below the pub); background music (occasional live rock upstairs); open all day (till 2am Fri, Sat). *(P Dawn)*

NOTTINGHAM   SK5640
Sir John Borlase Warren
(0115) 947 4247 *Ilkeston Road/Canning Circus (A52 towards Derby); NG7 3GD* Roadside pub with four comfortable linked rooms, interesting Victorian decorations, enjoyable good value food all day, friendly staff, Everards and three or four guests, Weston's cider, good mix of customers including students; children welcome, tables in nicely lit back garden with raised deck, open all day. *(John Fredericks)*

NOTTINGHAM   SK5744
Vale (0115) 926 8864
Mansfield Road; NG5 3GG Friendly 1930s local with original layout, panelling and woodwork, Adnams, Castle Rock and four guests, low-priced food, Sun quiz night; open all day. *(the Didler)*

NOTTINGHAM   SK5739
⋆**Vat & Fiddle** (0115) 985 0611
Queens Bridge Road; alongside Sheriffs Way (near multi-storey car park);

NG2 1NB Plain open-plan brick pub acting as tap for next door Castle Rock Brewery; unspoilt 1930s feel, varnished pine tables, bentwood chairs and stools on parquet or terrazzo flooring, some brewery memorabilia, interesting photographs of demolished local pubs, a dozen real ales including guests, bottled continentals, farm ciders, 60 malt whiskies, fresh cobs, nice chatty atmosphere; no credit cards; children and dogs welcome, picnic-sets out front by road, open all day (till midnight Fri, Sat). *(P Dawn, the Didler, MP)*

ORSTON   SK7741
Durham Ox (01949) 850059
Church Street; NG13 9NS New licensee for this comfortable village pub opposite church; four well kept mainstream ales and a guest, traditional pub food, open-plan split-level bar, old local photographs, small dining room with coal fire; background and some live music; children and dogs welcome, tables out at front and in big back garden with four heated summer houses, hitching rails for horses and ferrets, pleasant countryside, open all day weekends. *(the Didler)*

RADCLIFFE ON TRENT   SK6439
Horse Chestnut (0115) 933 1994
Main Road; NG12 2BE Smart pub with plenty of Victorian features, seven well kept beers including Adnams, Batemans and Castle Rock, sensibly priced home-made food including good value Sun roasts (12-4pm), competent service, two-level main bar, panelling, parquet, polished brass and woodwork and impressive lamps, handsome leather seating, books by fireplace; background music; disabled access, attractive terrace, open all day (afternoon break Mon). *(P Dawn, MP, M Mossman)*

RADCLIFFE ON TRENT   SK6439
Manvers Arms (0115) 933 2404
Main Road, opposite church; NG12 2AA Early 19th-c village pub with good well presented food (till 7pm Sun) including set menus, prompt friendly service, well kept Caledonian, Jennings, St Austell, Thwaites and two guests, fairly priced wines, spotless opened-up interior keeping original fireplaces and other features, assorted pubby furniture, some cosy areas with banquettes, pictures and ornaments, chandeliers and potted palms, an old harmonium; mellow background music – live jazz Thurs; well behaved children and dogs welcome, plenty of seats in large back garden with trees and shrubs, open all day. *(David Glynne-Jones, M Mossman, Tony and Maggie Harwood)*

RADCLIFFE ON TRENT   SK6439
Royal Oak (0115) 933 5659
Main Road; NG12 2FD Opened-up village-centre pub (part of the small Mole Face chain), enjoyable food from open kitchen including breakfast till noon, sandwiches (home-baked bread) and bar/restaurant

meals, good friendly service, plenty of wines by the glass including champagne, Castle Rock, Sharps Doom Bar and a guest; children welcome, open all day from 10am. *(David Glynne-Jones, M Mossman)*

ROLLESTON   SK7452
Crown (01636) 819000
Staythorpe Road; NG23 5SG Smartly modernised pub with good well priced food including early evening deal, real ales, friendly efficient service; small garden, five bedrooms, handy for Southwell Racecourse, open all day Sun till 9.30pm (food till 5pm). *(Maurice and Janet Thorpe, Barry Morrison)*

RUDDINGTON   SK5733
Three Crowns (0115) 921 3226
Easthorpe Street; NG11 6LB Open-plan village pub with well kept Fullers, Nottingham and guest ales, indian food in evening restaurant at back, June beer festival; open all day weekends, closed Mon and Tues lunchtimes. *(P Dawn, the Didler)*

RUDDINGTON   SK5733
White Horse (0115) 984 4550
Church Street; NG11 6HD Cheerful 1930s local with half a dozen ales including Black Sheep and Wells & Youngs Bombardier (June beer festival), enjoyable home-made food, comfortable lounge, old photographs, bar with darts, pool, juke box and TV, Thurs quiz; spacious sunny courtyard garden, barbecues, open all day. *(P Dawn, the Didler)*

SELSTON   SK4553
★**Horse & Jockey** (01773) 781012
Handy for M1 junctions 27/28; Church Lane; NG16 6FB Dating from the 17th c, intelligently renovated with interesting 18th- and 19th-c survivals and good carving, different levels, low heavy beams, dark flagstones, individual furnishings, good log fire in cast-iron range, friendly staff, mainstream ales such as Timothy Taylors Landlord (poured from jug) and some unusual guests, real cider, no food; games area with darts and pool; dogs welcome, terrace with smart smokers' shelter, pleasant rolling country. *(Derek and Sylvia Stephenson)*

SOUTH LEVERTON   SK7881
Plough (01427) 880323
Town Street; DN22 0BT Tiny village local with basic trestle tables, benches and pews, log fire, helpful welcoming staff, Bass and a changing guest, no food, traditional games; nice garden, open all day Sun (from 3pm Sat, 4pm weekdays), up for sale as we went to press. *(the Didler)*

SOUTHWELL   SK7054
Final Whistle (01636) 814953
Station Road; NG25 0ET Ten ales including Blue Monkey, Everards and Leatherbritches (beer festivals), real ciders

and perries, foreign bottled beers and good range of wines, snacky food, traditional opened-up bar area with tiled or wood floor, settles and armchairs in quieter carpeted room, corridor drinking area, two open fires, panelling, railway memorabilia and other odds and ends; some live music, Tues quiz; children and dogs welcome, back garden with wonderful mock-up of old station platform complete with track, open all day. *(the Didler)*

SOUTHWELL   SK7053
*★***Hearty Goodfellow** (01636) 812365
Church Street (A612); NG25 0HQ
Traditional open-plan pub under friendly landlord, Everards Tiger and seven changing guests including Mallards, good range of house wines, good value lunchtime food from snacks up, lots of polished wood, two brick fireplaces; children and dogs welcome, nice big tree-shaded garden beyond car park, handy for Southwell Workhouse (NT) and Minster, open all day Fri-Sun, closed Mon lunchtime. *(Steven Morris, the Didler, Tony and Rosemary Swainson)*

THURGARTON   SK6949
Red Lion (01636) 830351
Southwell Road (A612); NG14 7GP
Cheery 16th-c pub with split-level beamed bars and restaurant, ales such as Black Sheep and Claythorpe from dark panelled bar, food all day weekends and bank holidays, comfortable banquettes and other seating on patterned carpets, lots of nooks and crannies, grandfather clock, open fires, big windows to attractive, good-sized two-level back garden (dogs on leads allowed here); children welcome. *(JJW, CMW, Derek and Sylvia Stephenson)*

UNDERWOOD   SK4751
*★***Red Lion** (01773) 810482
Off A608/B600, near M1 junction 27; Church Lane, nearly in Bagthorpe; NG16 5HD Welcoming 17th-c split-level beamed village pub, reliable sensibly priced food including set-lunch deals (Mon-Fri), other bargains and good fresh fish (best to book), interesting changing ales, good soft drinks choice, pleasant helpful service, open-plan quarry-tiled bar with dining area, some cushioned settles, open fire; background music, games machine in lobby; no dogs; children till 7pm in areas away from bar, play area in big woodside garden with terrace, barbecues, good nearby walks, open all day Fri-Sun. *(Derek and Sylvia Stephenson, GSB)*

WATNALL CHAWORTH   SK5046
*★***Queens Head** (0115) 9389395
3 miles from M1 junction 26: A610 towards Nottingham, left on B600, then keep right; Main Road; NG16 1HT
Reasonably priced pubby food including good fish and chips (Fri night) in extended 18th-c roadside pub, well kept Adnams, Everards, Greene King, Wells & Youngs and guests, efficient staff, beams and stripped pine, old photographs, grandfather clock, woodburner, intimate snug, plank-ceilinged dining lounge; background and some live music, Mon quiz; children welcome, dogs in bar, flower tubs and a few picnic-sets out at front, more tables on back lawn with marquee and play area, beer festivals and barbecues, open all day. *(JJW, CMW, the Didler, David and Sue Atkinson)*

WEST BRIDGFORD   SK5837
*★***Stratford Haven** (0115) 9825981
Stratford Road, Trent Bridge; NG2 6BA
Good Tynemill pub, bare-boards front bar leading to linked areas including airy skylit back part with relaxed local atmosphere, their well kept Castle Rock ales plus Batemans, Everards and six changing guests (monthly brewery nights), exotic bottled beers, farm ciders, ample whiskies and wines, good value home-made food all day, fast friendly service, daily newspapers, some live music (nothing loud); dogs welcome, terrace, handy for cricket ground and Nottingham Forest FC (busy on match days), tables outside, open all day from 10.30am (midday Sun). *(P Dawn, the Didler, MP, Steve Holden, Ajay Sethi)*

WEST LEAKE   SK5126
Star (01509) 856480
Melton Lane, off A6006; LE12 5RQ
Old village pub reopened after major refurbishment by new owners, opened-up bar, restaurant – reports please. *(Anon)*

WYSALL   SK6027
Plough (01509) 880339
Keyworth Road; off A60 at Costock, or A6006 at Wymeswold; NG12 5QQ
Attractive 17th-c beamed village local, popular good value lunchtime food from shortish menu, cheerful staff, Bass, Greene King Abbot, Timothy Taylors Landlord and three guests, rooms either side of bar with nice mix of furnishings, soft lighting, big log fire; french doors to pretty terrace with flower tubs and baskets, open all day. *(Ajay Sethi, Nigel and Sue Foster)*

Oxfordshire

This county has a fantastic choice of really well run pubs, ranging from unspoilt country taverns through bustling city bars to smart dining places. Pubs our readers particularly recommend this year are the Olde Reindeer in Banbury (back in these pages after a break and popular with shoppers), Lamb in Burford (proper bar in a fine old inn), Chequers in Chipping Norton (first class pre-theatre suppers), Duke of Cumberlands Head in Clifton (new to the *Guide*, with cosy bedrooms and a warm atmosphere), Woodman at Fernham (friendly landlord and enjoyable food), Blowing Stone at Kingston Lisle (charming landlord and super food and wine), Oxford Arms in Kirtlington (easy-going with food cooked by the landlord), Bell in Langford (delicious fish dishes in appealing country pub), Blue Boar in Longworth (pretty thatched village pub), Old Swan & Minster Mill (perky bar in smart hotel), Punter in Oxford (a new entry with shabby-chic décor), Crown in Pishill (new to us, spotless and friendly), Baskerville at Shiplake (hard-working, dedicated landlord), Swan at Swinbrook (a super all-rounder), Trout at Tadpole Bridge (by the Thames and loved by readers), and Kings Arms in Woodstock (stylish town pub, nice food, comfortable bedrooms). Food plays a strong part here with around a third of our Main Entries holding a Food Award, but it is the Trout at Tadpole Bridge that is our Oxfordshire Dining Pub 2013.

 BANBURY   SP4540   Map 4
Olde Reindeer 🍺 £
Parsons Street, off Market Place; OX16 5NA

Plenty of shoppers and regulars in this interesting town pub, fine real ales, simple food and roaring log fires

---

'The best type of town pub' is how one reader describes this well run and unpretentious tavern, and there's a good bustling atmosphere and plenty of customers keen to enjoy the real ales and fair value lunchtime food served by the friendly, helpful staff. The welcoming front bar has heavy 16th-c beams, very broad polished oak floorboards, magnificent carved overmantel on one of the two roaring log fires and traditional solid furnishings. It's worth looking at the handsomely proportioned Globe Room used by Oliver Cromwell as his base during the Civil War, which retains some very fine carved 17th-c dark oak panelling. Hook Norton Bitter, Hooky Dark, Hooky Gold, Old Hooky and a changing guest beer on handpump, wines by the glass, and several malt whiskies; maybe background music. The little back courtyard has tables and benches under parasols, aunt sally and pretty flowering baskets.

🍴 Honest food, generously served, includes sandwiches, home-made pâté, whitebait, venison burger with chips and salad, beer-battered fish, vegetable lasagne, steak in ale pie, cumberland sausages with gravy in a yorkshire pudding, and puddings like knickerbocker glory and summer fruit pudding. *Benchmark main dish: ham, egg and bubble and squeak £8.75. Two-course evening meal £14.00.*

Hook Norton ~ Tenant Marc Sylvester ~ Real ale ~ Bar food (11-4, 6-9) ~ Restaurant ~ (01295) 264031 ~ Children welcome ~ Dogs allowed in bar ~ Open 11-11 ~ www.yeoldereindeer.co.uk *Recommended by George Atkinson, the Didler, Andy Dolan, Clive and Fran Dutson, Andy Lickfold*

BESSELS LEIGH
Greyhound 🍷 🍺
SP4501 Map 4
A420 Faringdon–Botley; OX13 5PX

Handsome 400-year-old stone pub with knocked-through rooms, plenty of character and interest, half a dozen real ales, lots of wines by the glass and enjoyable food

Several of our readers use this handsome former coaching inn as a civilised break on the A420 Oxford to Swindon road, and there are plenty of locals dropping in and out too, creating a bustling and chatty atmosphere. The knocked-through rooms give plenty of space and interest and the half-panelled walls are covered in all manner of old photographs and pictures. The individually chosen cushioned dining chairs, leather-topped stools and dark wooden tables are grouped on carpeting or rug-covered floorboards, and there are books on shelves, glass and stone bottles on windowsills, big gilt mirrors, three fireplaces (one housing a woodburning stove), and sizeable pot plants dotted about. Wooden bar stools sit against the counter where they serve Brunning & Price Original (brewed for the company by Phoenix), Hook Norton Hooky Bitter, White Horse Wayland Smithy and three changing guest beers on handpump, 15 wines by the glass and 80 malt whiskies. By the back dining extension there's a white picket fence-enclosed garden with picnic-sets under green parasols.

🍴 As well as sandwiches and light meals like crab linguine with ginger, chilli and coriander, harissa-spiced chicken salad with chickpeas, apricots, almonds and pomegranate dressing and thai-infused mussels with coconut cream broth, the modern food might include sausages and mash, red wine and onion gravy, chestnut mushroom, leek and red pepper lasagne with goats cheese crust, steak burger with bacon, cheese, coleslaw and salsa, confit duck with roast plums and hoi sin dressing, caramelised pak choi and jasmine rice, steak and kidney pie, trout fillet with a pine nut, lemon and parsley crust and a caper dill dressing, and puddings such as knickerchoca glory and crème brûlée with a shortbread biscuit. *Benchmark main dish: beer-battered fish and chips £11.95. Two-course evening meal £18.00.*

Brunning & Price ~ Manager Emily Waring ~ Real ale ~ Bar food (12-10(9.30 Sun)) ~ (01865) 862110 ~ Children welcome ~ Dogs allowed in bar ~ Open 12-11(10.30 Sun)

~ www.greyhound-besselsleigh.co.uk *Recommended by Jan and Roger Ferris, Derek Goldrei, David Jackman, Taff and Gilly Thomas*

BRIGHTWELL BALDWIN   SU6594 Map 4
Lord Nelson 🍴 �

Off B480 Chalgrove–Watlington, or B4009 Benson–Watlington; OX49 5NP

Attractive inn with several different character bars, real ales, good wines by the glass and enjoyable food; bedrooms

In a quiet village and set opposite the church, this 300-year-old inn is best known as a well run dining pub – but they do keep Black Sheep Best, Brakspears Bitter and Rebellion IPA on handpump, around 14 wines (including champagne) by the glass and winter mulled wine. There are wheelback and other dining chairs around a mix of dark tables, candles and fresh flowers, wine bottles on window sills, horsebrasses on standing timbers, lots of paintings on the white or red walls and a big brick inglenook fireplace. One cosy room has cushions on comfortable sofas, little lamps on dark furniture, ornate mirrors and portraits in gilt frames; background music. The back terrace has seats and tables, with more in the willow-draped garden.

 Enjoyable if not cheap, the well thought of food might include scallops with an avocado and tomato salsa, duck liver and wild mushroom parfait, courgette and potato cake with a mint and feta cheese salad, free-range pork sausages on bubble and squeak with red onion gravy, beer-battered fresh haddock with triple-cooked chips, calves liver and bacon with red wine sauce, chilli king prawns, and puddings like chocolate truffle with salted caramel and chantilly cream and lemon posset with shortbread biscuits. *Benchmark main dish: half a roast duck with spicy plum sauce £18.95. Two-course evening meal £21.50.*

Free house ~ Licensees Roger and Carole Shippey ~ Real ale ~ Bar food (12-2.30 (3 Sun), 6-10(7-9.30 Sun)) ~ Restaurant ~ (01491) 612497 ~ Children welcome ~ Dogs allowed in bar ~ Open 12-3, 6-11; 12-10.30 Sun ~ Bedrooms: £70B/£90B ~ www.lordnelson-inn.co.uk *Recommended by Roy Hoing, Dave Braisted, Richard Endacott*

BURFORD   SP2412 Map 4
Lamb 🍴 ♥ 🛏

Village signposted off A40 W of Oxford; Sheep Street (B4425, off A361); OX18 4LR

Proper pubby bar in civilised inn, real ales and an extensive wine list, interesting bar and restaurant food, and pretty gardens; bedrooms

Of course, many customers come to this lovely 15th-c inn to dine or stay overnight in the comfortable bedrooms, but the cosy bar remains at the heart of the place and the atmosphere is civilised but relaxed and friendly. There are high-backed settles and old chairs on flagstones in front of the log fire, Hook Norton Bitter and Wickwar Cotswold Way on handpump, an extensive wine list with 20 by the glass, and 15 malt whiskies; board games. The roomy beamed main lounge is charmingly traditional, with distinguished old seats including a chintzy high-winged settle, ancient cushioned wooden armchairs and seats built into its stone-mullioned windows; fresh flowers on polished oak and elm tables, rugs on wide flagstones and polished oak floorboards, a winter log fire under its fine mantelpiece and plenty of antiques and other decorations, including a grandfather clock. Service is impeccable. A pretty terrace with teak furniture leads down to small neatly kept lawns surrounded by flowers, shrubs and small trees. The garden is a real suntrap, enclosed as it is by the warm stone of the surrounding buildings.

🍴 Good, enjoyable food might include open sandwiches, deli boards (fish, meat or antipasti), chicken livers with pink peppercorn jus and toasted brioche, smoked salmon with capers, shallots and horseradish cream, sausages and mash with red onion gravy, pasta with garlic mushroom sauce, chicken and sweetcorn risotto, chump of lamb with crushed potatoes and redcurrant jus, surf 'n' turf, and puddings like chocolate tart with banana ice-cream and vanilla panna cotta with kirsch cherries and chocolate syrup; there's a 'two-for-one' pie offer on Wednesday evening. *Benchmark main dish: local game pie £12.95. Two-course evening meal £20.45.*

Cotswold Inns & Hotels ~ Manager Bill Ramsay ~ Real ale ~ Bar food (12-2.30, 6.30-9.30; all day Thurs-Sun) ~ Restaurant ~ (01993) 823155 ~ Children welcome ~ Dogs welcome ~ Open 12-11(midnight Sat) ~ Bedrooms: £120B/£155B ~ www.cotswold-inns-hotels.co.uk/lamb *Recommended by Peter Dandy, Graham Oddey, Malcolm Greening, George Atkinson, David Glynne-Jones, the Didler, Simon Collett-Jones, Alistair Forsyth, D L Frostick*

CAULCOTT   SP5024   Map 4

Horse & Groom 🍺

Lower Heyford Road (B4030); OX25 4ND

Bustling and friendly with an obliging licensee, enjoyable bar food and changing beers

This is a thatched 16th-c cottage pub run by a friendly french chef/patron. It's not a huge place: an L-shaped red-carpeted room angles around the servery, with plush-cushioned settles, chairs and stools around a few dark tables at the low-ceilinged bar end and a blazing fire in the big inglenook, which has brassware under its long bressumer beam. White Horse Brewery Bitter, Wye Valley HPA and York Dark Knight on handpump and decent house wines; shove-ha'penny and board games. The far end, up a shallow step, is set for dining, and has lots of decorative jugs hanging on black joists, some china plates and attractive watercolours and original drawings. There's a small side sun lounge, and picnic-sets under cocktail parasols on a neat lawn.

🍴 Their ten different types of speciality sausage are as popular as ever and they also serve lunchtime filled baguettes, scallops with a tomato dressing and pea sauce, country pâté with onion chutney, cheese, ham or mushroom omelettes using free-range eggs, home-made burgers, game in stout pie, three-cheese risotto, chump of local lamb with red wine and olive sauce, fillet of beef with stilton and port sauce, daily-changing fresh fish dishes, and puddings such as ginger pudding with caramelised bananas and toffee ice-cream and vanilla crème brûlée. *Benchmark main dish: lemon sole with butter and parsley sauce £13.95. Two-course evening meal £20.00.*

Free house ~ Licensee Jerome Prigent ~ Real ale ~ Bar food (12-2, 7-9; not Sun evening or Mon) ~ (01869) 343257 ~ Children must be over 7 and well behaved ~ Open 12-3, 6-11; 12-3, 7-10.30 Sun ~ www.horseandgroomcaulcott.co.uk *Recommended by Ian Herdman, David Lamb, John Taylor, R J Herd*

Stars after the name of a pub show exceptional character and appeal.
They don't mean extra comfort. And they are nothing to do with food quality,
for which there's a separate knife-and-fork symbol. Even quite a basic pub
can win stars, if it's individual enough.

CHIPPING NORTON   SP3127   Map 4

Chequers ★ ♀ ◖

Goddards Lane; OX7 5NP

Busy town pub open all day with several real ales, popular bar food, a cheerful mix of customers and simple furnishings

Tucked away in a quiet part of town, this cheerful pub has a good mix of locals and visitors. The three softly lit beamed rooms have no frills, but are clean and comfortable with low ochre ceilings, lots of character and a blazing log fire. Quick staff serve up to eight real ales on handpump: Fullers Chiswick, Discovery, ESB, HSB, London Pride and Seafarers Ale and a couple of changing guest beers. They also have good house wines – 15 by the glass. The conservatory restaurant is light and airy and used for more formal dining. The theatre is next door.

As well as their efficiently served pre-theatre suppers, the popular bar food includes sandwiches, ham hock and parsley terrine with piccalilli, potted hot smoked salmon and brown shrimps with pickled beetroot and horseradish, various sharing platters, cauliflower, potato and spinach curry with mango chutney and yoghurt, local sausages with rich onion gravy, honey and cider gammon with free-range eggs, a pie of the day, free-range chicken in sweet pepper, tomato and paprika sauce, venison stew with juniper and redcurrant and chestnut mash, and puddings. *Benchmark main dish: homemade pie £10.50. Two-course evening meal £16.00.*

Fullers ~ Lease Jim Hopcroft ~ Real ale ~ Bar food (12-2.30, 6-9.30; 12-4 Sun; not Sun evening) ~ Restaurant ~ (01608) 644717 ~ Children welcome ~ Dogs allowed in bar ~ Live music monthly and Sun evening quiz ~ Open 11(11.30 Sun)-11(midnight Sat) ~ www.chequers-pub.com *Recommended by Steve Whalley, Richard Tilbrook, Barry Collett, the Didler, Guy Vowles*

CLIFTON   SP4931   Map 4

Duke of Cumberlands Head ♀

B4031 Deddington–Aynho; OX15 0PE

Cosy bars with beams and a big log fire, good food and short walk to canal; cosy good value bedrooms

This thatched and golden stone former coaching inn is just a short walk from the canal. It's a friendly place with an easy-going atmosphere, beams in low ceilings, rugs on bare boards, an attractive mix of dining chairs and settles around nice old tables, church candles, paintings on exposed stone walls, and a good log fire in a vast inglenook fireplace. Hook Norton Hooky Bitter and a couple of changing guest beers on handpump and several wines by the glass. There are a couple of picnic-sets out in front with good quality seats and tables under parasols on the sunny back terrace.

 Good, popular food might include sandwiches, game terrine with cumberland sauce, smoked trout salad with caviar and citrus dressing, sausage and mash with red onion gravy, wild mushroom and truffle risotto, steak in ale pie, beer-battered haddock and chips, chicken breast with green vegetable risotto, salmon with red butter sauce, steaks, and puddings like apple strudel with custard and sticky toffee pudding with butterscotch sauce. *Benchmark main dish: pie of the day £12.00. Two-course evening meal £17.50.*

Free house ~ Licensee Ross Westcott ~ Real ale ~ Bar food (12-2.30(3 weekends), 6.30(6 Sun)-9.30(9 Sun)) ~ Restaurant ~ (01869) 338534 ~ Children welcome ~ Dogs allowed in bar and bedrooms ~ Open 12-11 ~ Bedrooms: /$45B ~ www.cliftonduke.com
Recommended by Maurice Ricketts, David Jackman, Roy Hoing

EAST HENDRED
Eyston Arms ⑪

SU4588   Map 2

Village signposted off A417 E of Wantage; High Street; OX12 8JY

Attractive bar areas with low beams, flagstones, log fires and candles, imaginative food, and helpful service

There are a few tables for drinkers and seats at the bar and locals do pop in for a pint and chat, but most customers come to this well run and pleasant dining pub to enjoy the good, interesting food. It's a busy, welcoming place and there are several separate-seeming areas with contemporary paintwork and modern country-style furnishings. Also, low ceilings and beams, stripped timbers, the odd standing timber, an inglenook fireplace, nice tables and chairs on the flagstones and carpet, some cushioned wall seats, candlelight and a piano; background music. Cheerful staff serve Fullers London Pride and Hook Norton Hooky Bitter on handpump and several wines by the glass. Picnic-sets outside overlook the pretty lane and there are seats in the back courtyard garden.

As well as lunchtime sandwiches, the imaginative food includes crispy fried chilli squid with mango and ginger coulis, chicory, walnut and blue cheese salad with honey vinaigrette, butternut and bean stew with tomatoes, thyme and a gruyère crouton, salt and pepper pork belly with pak choi, sticky rice and a spiced orange glaze, jacob's ladder (12-hour braised beef rib) with bourguignon sauce, horseradish mash and braised red cabbage, venison chateaubriand with parmentier potatoes and red wine and juniper jus, and puddings like dark chocolate and caramel tart and apple and cinnamon crumble pie. *Benchmark main dish: fillet of brill with shrimp butter £16.95. Two-course evening meal £21.50.*

Free house ~ Licensees George Dailey and Daisy Barton ~ Real ale ~ Bar food (12-2, 7-9; 12-9 Fri and Sat; 11.30-3; not Sun evening) ~ Restaurant ~ (01235) 833320 ~ Children welcome but must be well behaved ~ Dogs allowed in bar ~ Open 12-3, 6-11; 12-11 Fri and Sat; 11.30-11 Sun; closed Sun evening ~ www.eystonarms.co.uk
Recommended by Barry Jackson, Bob and Margaret Holder, Dan Rooms

FERNHAM
Woodman 🍺

SU2991   Map 4

A420 SW of Oxford, then left into B4508 after about 11 miles; village a further 6 miles on; SN7 7NX

A good choice of real ales and interesting bar food in a charming old-world country pub

This is a smashing pub, particularly well run by the friendly landlord and his attentive staff – and our readers enjoy their visits here very much. The heavily beamed main rooms have the most character and are full of an amazing assortment of old objects like clay pipes, milkmaids' yokes, leather tack, coach horns, an old screw press, some original oil paintings and good black and white photographs of horses. Comfortable seating includes cushioned benches, pews and windsor chairs, and the candlelit tables are simply made from old casks; a big wood fire, too. As well as some comfortable newer areas, there's a large room for Sunday lunches. The four real ales are from breweries such as Greene King, Oakham, Sharps, Timothy Taylors, Wadworths 6X and White Horse and are tapped from the cask and they keep several wines by the glass and 16 malt whiskies; background music. There are seats outside on the terrace. Disabled lavatories.

🍴 Highly thought-of food includes filled baguettes and panini, rosemary-studded baked camembert with home-made chutney, fried pigeon breast with a cider and apple cream sauce, local sausages with caramelised onion and red wine gravy, risotto stuffed pepper topped with truffle oil, a curry of the day, steak, mushroom and ale pie, free-range chicken topped with mozzarella, roasted vegetables and a pesto and tomato sauce, bass fillets with ginger, chilli and spring onions on spicy polenta, and specials like a trio of lamb with redcurrant and mint jus and barbecue pork ribs with a garlic dip. *Benchmark main dish: pheasant stuffed with sausage and cherries, wrapped in bacon with a cranberry/kumquat sauce £15.95. Two-course evening meal £20.00.*

Free house ~ Licensee Steven Whiting ~ Real ale ~ Bar food (12-2(2.30 weekends), 6.30-9.30) ~ Restaurant ~ (01367) 820643 ~ Children welcome ~ Dogs welcome ~ Open 11-11 ~ www.thewoodmaninn.net *Recommended by Mary Rayner, Barry and Anne, M J Daly, Dave Braisted*

HEADINGTON
Black Boy
SP5407 Map 4

Old High Street/St Andrews Road; off A420 at traffic lights opposite B4495; OX3 9HT

Stylish and enterprising dining pub with good, enjoyable food, and useful summer garden

Friendly and with a cool, contemporary look, this modern dining pub is run by a charming landlady and her well-trained, black-aproned staff. There's black leather seating on dark parquet, big mirrors, silvery patterned wallpaper, nightlights in fat opaque cylinders and glittering bottles behind the long bar counter. It's all light and airy, particularly for the two tables in the big bay window; just to the side is an open fire, with lower softer seats by it. Crisp white tablecloths and bold black and white wallpaper lend the area on the left a touch of formality. Changing weekly, the beers might include Belhaven Grand Slam and Brains Milkwood on handpump and they keep a good choice of wines by the glass and several coffees and teas. Behind the building is an appealing terrace, with picnic-sets under alternating black and white parasols on smart pale stone chippings, and a central seat encircling an ash tree.

🍴 Using only local produce and making their own bread and ice-cream, the interesting food might include lunchtime sandwiches (not Sunday), potted trout and shrimp, black pudding with a soft poached egg, pancetta and micro herbs, wild mushroom and spinach cannelloni with wild mushroom sauce, beer-battered fish and chips with pea and mint purée, sausage and mash with ale and onion jus, home-made burger with cheese, onion and gherkins, pork belly with garlic-scented mashed potato and cider jus, specials like seared tuna with niçoise salad and organic rib-eye steak with pepper or béarnaise sauce, and puddings such as iced white chocolate mousse with home-made raspberry sorbet and sticky toffee pudding with caramel sauce. *Benchmark main dish: cod loin on potato rösti with saffron, cream and mussel sauce £13.95. Two-course evening meal £17.95.*

Greene King ~ Lease Abi Rose and Chris Bentham ~ Real ale ~ Bar food (12-2.45, 6-9.15) ~ (01865) 741137 ~ Children welcome ~ Open 12-3, 5-11 ~ www.theblackboy.uk.com *Recommended by Richard Gibbs, Steve Cocking*

HIGHMOOR
SU6984   Map 2

Rising Sun

Witheridge Hill, signposted off B481; OS Sheet 175 map reference 697841; RG9 5PF

Thoughtfully run, pretty pub with a mix of diners and drinkers

You can be sure of a warm welcome from the friendly licensees and their staff in this pretty black and cream village pub whether you're a local or a visitor and looking for a chatty drink or a leisurely meal. On the right by the bar, there are wooden tables and chairs and a sofa on the stripped wooden floors, cream and terracotta walls and an open fire in the big brick inglenook fireplace. The main area spreading back from here has shiny bare boards and a swathe of carpeting with well spaced tables and attractive pictures on the walls. Brakspears Bitter and Oxford Gold on handpump, Weston's cider and ten wines by the glass; background music and board games. There are seats and tables in the pleasant back garden; boules. As this is the heart of the Chilterns, there are plenty of surrounding walks.

Popular food might include sandwiches, various tapas, pigeon salad with bacon, green beans and pine nuts, crab pâté, pork and leek sausages with onion gravy, spiced aubergine fritters with a cucumber and mint dip, slow-cooked lamb shank with tomato and rosemary sauce and pine nut and sultana braised rice, duck breast with plum compote and a red wine jus, bass fillet with lemon and chive potatoes and a green herb dressing, and puddings like pear and ginger sponge pudding and chocolate and walnut brownie sundae. *Benchmark main dish: slow-cooked pork belly with black pudding mash and cider jus £13.50. Two-course evening meal £18.45.*

Brakspears ~ Tenant Simon Duffy ~ Real ale ~ Bar food (12-2, 6.30-9; some sort of food all day Sat; till 7 Sun evening) ~ Restaurant ~ (01491) 640856 ~ Children allowed in dining areas only under strict supervision ~ Dogs allowed in bar ~ Open 12-3, 5.30-11; 12-11(7 Sun) Sat; closed Sun evening ~ www.risingsunwitheridgehill.co.uk
Recommended by Bob and Margaret Holder, Richard Endacott, Simon Rodway, David and Sue Smith

KINGHAM
SP2624   Map 4

Plough 🍴 🍷 🛏

Village signposted off B4450 E of Bledington; or turn S off A436 at staggered crossroads a mile SW of A44 junction; or take signed Daylesford turn off A436 and keep on; The Green; OX7 6YD

Friendly dining pub combining an informal pub atmosphere with upmarket food; bedrooms

Run by helpful, friendly licensees, this is perhaps more of a restaurant-with-rooms than a straightforward pub, but our readers enjoy their visits very much. There is a properly pubby bar despite the food emphasis, with some nice old high-backed settles and brightly cushioned chapel chairs on its broad dark boards, candles on stripped tables and cheerful farmyard animal and country prints; at one end is a big log fire and at the other (by an unusual cricket table), a woodburning stove. There's a piano in one corner and a snug one-table area opposite the servery, which has Hook Norton Hooky Bitter and Wye Valley HPA on handpump, good wines by the glass, home-made cordials and some interesting liqueurs. The fairly spacious and raftered two-part dining room is up a few steps. If you stay in the comfortable bedrooms, you'll be served a good breakfast. There's a heated smokers' shelter at the back.

Impressive and imaginative, the food might include warm duckling salad with chicory and blood orange vinaigrette, warm pink fir apple and leek salad with truffle and curd, chicken and ham pie, pollack with spinach and a devilled brown shrimp sauce, parsley root dumpling with vegetable broth, stuffed saddle and crisp shoulder of rabbit with pumpkin dumplings, foraged mushrooms and truffle, and puddings such as malted chocolate parfait with hot chocolate sauce and rhubarb and custard trifle with ginger honeycomb; the interesting local cheeses are served with crab apple jelly, home-made oatcakes and hazelnut fruit bread. *Benchmark main dish: well-aged hereford beef burger with home-made muffin, home-made ketchup and triple-cooked wedges £14.00. Two-course evening meal £22.50.*

Free house ~ Licensees Emily Watkins and Miles Lampson ~ Real ale ~ Bar food (12–2, 7–9; 12–3.30, 6–8 Sun) ~ Restaurant ~ (01608) 658327 ~ Children welcome ~ Dogs allowed in bar and bedrooms ~ Open 12–11(12 Sat, 10.30 Sun) ~ Bedrooms: $75S/$90S($115B) ~ www.thekinghamplough.co.uk *Recommended by Richard Greaves, Edward Mirzoeff, Anthony and Pam Stamer, Anthony Longden, Michael Doswell, Richard Tilbrook, David Glynne-Jones, Dr Martin Owton, Jenny Smith, William Goodhart, Andy and Jill Kassube*

KINGSTON LISLE SU3287 Map 4

Blowing Stone

Village signposted off B4507 W of Wantage; OX12 9QL

Easy-going chatty country pub with up-to-date blend of simple comfort, good food and drink

The heart of this friendly village pub with its easy country informality is the central bar, where broad tiles floor by the log fire suit the muddy riding boots of the cheerful young drinkers in from nearby training stables. They have the Racing Post and other daily papers, and most of the photographs on the pale sage walls are of racehorses, often spectacularly coming to grief over jumps. Several areas radiate off, most of them carpeted, quite small and snug, though the back dining conservatory is more spacious. Apart from a couple of high-backed winged settles, most of the furniture is an unfussy mix of country dining tables, each with its own set of matching chairs, either padded or generously cushioned. Greene King Morland Original, Ramsbury Gold and West Berkshire Mr Chubbs Lunchtime Bitter on handpump, ten decent wines by the glass, and chilled manzanilla and oloroso sherry; service is attentive and there may be unobtrusive background music. The pretty front terrace has a couple of picnic-sets under cocktail parasols with more on the back lawn by a rockery; the Ridgeway and Uffington White Horse are both nearby.

 Highly thought of and interesting, the food might include lunchtime sandwiches, butterfly tandoori king prawns with a mango, chilli and cucumber salad, a meze platter, home-reared chargrilled pork chop with sage mash and apple sauce, wild mushroom and roast garlic risotto with parmesan crisps, free-range chicken breast filled with pesto butter with a ratatouille dressing, seafood ragout, specials like mussels with white wine, cream and garlic and chicken kiev with greek salad, and puddings such as lemon and lime cheesecake with orange sauce and chocolate mousse with warmed pine nut cookies. *Benchmark main dish: beer-battered fish and chips with fresh tartare sauce £12.50. Two-course evening meal £22.50.*

Free house ~ Licensees Angus and Steph Tucker ~ Real ale ~ Bar food (12–2, 6.30–9; not Sun evening (except summer Sun for freshly made pizzas)) ~ Restaurant ~ (01367) 820288 ~ Children welcome ~ Dogs allowed in bar ~ Open 12–12(11pm Sun) ~ www.theblowingstone.co.uk *Recommended by Mrs J M Robinson*

KIRTLINGTON
SP4919 Map 4

Oxford Arms ⏍ ♟

Troy Lane, junction with A4095 W of Bicester; OX5 3HA

Friendly stripped-stone pub with enjoyable food and good wine choice

The chef/landlord and his charming young staff ensure a genial atmosphere in this neatly kept stone pub with its pretty, geranium-filled window boxes. A long line of linked rooms is divided by a central stone hearth with a great round stove, and by the servery itself, with Brakspears Bitter and St Austell Tribute on handpump, an interesting range of 13 wines, 14 malt whiskies and a good choice of soft drinks. Past the bar area with its cushioned wall pews, creaky beamed ceiling and age-darkened floor tiles, dining tables on parquet leave neat red chairs, and beyond that leather sofas cluster round a log fire at the end; there are church candles, fresh flowers and plenty of stripped stone. A sheltered back terrace has teak tables under giant parasols with heaters, and beyond are picnic-sets on pale gravel.

Enjoyable, well prepared food using local produce might include lunchtime sandwiches, potted shrimps, pâté with toast and chutney, a risotto of the day, endive and walnut salad with roquefort, salmon and prawn fishcakes with sweet chilli sauce, sausages with onion gravy, turkey, bacon and mushroom pie with parsley mash, cornish cod with chorizo and spring onion, and puddings. *Benchmark main dish: venison burger with triple-cooked chips and chutney £12.00. Two-course evening meal £18.00.*

Punch ~ Lease Bryn Jones ~ Real ale ~ Bar food (12-2.30, 6.30-9.30) ~ (01869) 350208 ~ Well behaved children welcome ~ Dogs allowed in bar ~ Open 12-3, 6-11; 12-3 Sun; closed Sun evening ~ www.oxford-arms.co.uk *Recommended by D C T and E A Frewer, Oxana Mishina, Veronica Hall, Jamie and Sue May, Simon Thomas*

LANGFORD
SP2402 Map 4

Bell ♟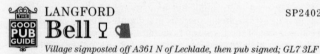

Village signposted off A361 N of Lechlade, then pub signed; GL7 3LF

Civilised pub with beams, flagstones and log fire, friendly service, well chosen wines and beers, and extremely good food

Once they've discovered this enjoyable country dining pub, our readers tend to return again and again. It's a friendly place with an informal country atmosphere, with simple low-key furnishings and décor adding to the appeal. The main bar has just six sanded-down tables on grass matting, a variety of chairs, three nice cushioned window seats, an attractive carved oak settle, polished broad flagstones by a big stone inglenook fireplace with a good log fire, low beams and butter-coloured walls with two or three antique engravings. A second even smaller room on the right is similar in character; daily papers on a little corner table. Hook Norton Hooky Bitter, Sharps Cornish Coaster and St Austell Tribute on handpump and a dozen wines by the glass. The bearded collie is called Madison. There are two or three picnic-sets in the small garden with a play house; aunt sally. The village is quiet and charming.

The fish specials are highly thought of and might include bouillabaisse, arbroath smokie fishcake with a spinach and white wine cream sauce and roasted salmon with a moroccan-style couscous and a mint, coriander and yoghurt dressing; they also have eggs benedict, pigeon breast with spiced lentils, pancetta and game chips, nut roast with a tomato and basil sauce, pork and herb sausages with wholegrain mustard and leek mash and onion gravy, steak and kidney pie, chicken breast with pancetta, tomatoes, mushrooms and red wine jus, saddle of venison with dauphinoise potatoes and a bitter chocolate sauce, and puddings. *Benchmark main dish: king scallops with pancetta, pea purée and micro herbs £16.95. Two-course evening meal £18.60.*

Free house ~ Licensees Paul and Jackie Wynne ~ Real ale ~ Bar food (12-1.45, 7-9; not Sun evening or Mon) ~ Restaurant ~ (01367) 860249 ~ Children welcome but no under-4s after 7pm ~ Dogs allowed in bar ~ Open 12-3, 7-11(midnight Fri, 11.30 Sat); 12-3.30 Sun; closed Sun evening, all day Mon ~ www.bellatlangford.co.uk
Recommended by R K Phillips, Grahame and Myra Williams, Neil and Diane Williams, Graham Oddey, Jennifer and Patrick O'Dell, D C T and E A Frewer, Bernard Stradling, Sue Callard, Chris Fagence, Mrs Dawn Dunleavy

 LONG HANBOROUGH   SP4214   Map 4
George & Dragon
A4095 Bladon–Witney; Main Road; OX29 8JX

Substantial, well organised pub; something for everyone

Busy and very well run by its friendly and efficient hands-on licensees, this is almost best thought of as two separate places. The original two-room bar, 17th c or older, is all stripped stone, low beams and soft lighting, with a thoroughly traditional pubby feel and furnishings to suit, including two stoves (one very elaborate). It forms an L with a roomy thatched restaurant extension, which has comfortably padded dining chairs around sturdy tables on floorboards, plenty of pictures on deep pink walls and decorative plates on the beams. Neat black-uniformed staff are friendly and efficient; they have well kept Courage Directors and Wells & Youngs Bombardier and Eagle IPA on handpump, Weston's farm cider and a good range of wines; there may be soft background music. The peaceful back garden has cream-painted picnic-sets among attractive shrubs, tables beneath a big dark canopy on a separate sheltered terrace, and further areas where you'll find rabbits and guinea-pigs.

Generously served, the wide choice of enjoyable food might include lots of sandwiches, filled baguettes or wraps with fries, salad and coleslaw, duck and orange pâté, mussels with cream, white wine and herbs, mushroom stroganoff, a brunch, chicken, smoked bacon, smoked cheese and avocado bake, half a rack of barbecue ribs, thai fishcakes with chilli dipping sauce, steak in ale pie, braised lamb shank on garlic mash, gressingham duck with dauphinoise potatoes and an apple and calvados sauce, and puddings such as lemon and ginger sponge with custard; they also offer a mid-week two-course lunch menu. *Benchmark main dish: duo of pork £15.95. Two-course evening meal £20.00.*

Charles Wells ~ Lease Mr A and Mrs J Willett ~ Real ale ~ Bar food (12-2(3 Sun), 6.30-9(9.30 Fri and Sat); not Sun evening) ~ Restaurant ~ (01993) 881362 ~ Children welcome ~ Dogs allowed in bar ~ Open 12-3, 6-midnight; 12-4, 6.30-11 Sun ~ www.menublackboard.com *Recommended by Meg and Colin Hamilton*

 LONGWORTH   SU3899   Map 4
Blue Boar ⚟
Tucks Lane; OX13 5ET

Smashing old pub with a friendly welcome for all, good wines and beer, and fairly priced reliable food; Thames-side walks nearby

From outside, this is pretty much the classic image of an english country pub in a charming village. Inside, you can be sure of a warm welcome from the friendly staff and a bustling but easy-going atmosphere – helped by a healthy mix of diners and chatty local drinkers. The three low-beamed, characterful little rooms are properly traditional with well worn fixtures and furnishings and two blazing log fires, one beside a fine old settle. Brasses, hops and assorted knick-knacks like skis and an old clocking-in machine line the ceilings and walls, there are fresh flowers on the bar, and scrubbed wooden tables and faded rugs on the tiled floor; benches are firmly wooden rather than upholstered. The main eating area is the red-painted room at the end, and there's a quieter restaurant extension, too. Brakspears Bitter, Fullers London Pride and a guest like Sharps Doom Bar on handpump, 20 malt whiskies, a dozen wines by the glass, summer Pimms and quite a few brandies and ports. There are tables in front and on the back terrace, and the Thames is a short walk away.

Popular food includes all-day pizzas as well as filled baguettes and ciabatta sandwiches, free-range pork pâté with cranberry and red onion relish, blue cheese panna cotta with powdered walnuts and a poached pear, home-cooked ham and free-range egg, squash, cashew nut and brie lasagne, king prawn malaysian curry, beer-battered fish and chips, partridge with potato purée, red cabbage and smoked bacon sauce, bass fillet with a honey and soy dressing and crushed potatoes, and puddings like dark chocolate tart with confit orange and raspberry sorbet and sticky toffee pudding with toffee sauce. *Benchmark main dish: burger with bacon, home-made aioli and choice of cheese £10.95. Two-course evening meal £20.50.*

Free house ~ Licensee Paul Dailey ~ Real ale ~ Bar food (12-2.30(3 Sun), 6.30-9.30(10 Fri and Sat, 9 Sun); pizzas all day) ~ Restaurant ~ (01865) 820494 ~ Children welcome ~ Dogs allowed in bar ~ Open 11.30-11(midnight Sat) ~ www.blueboarlongworth.co.uk
Recommended by R K Phillips, Jennifer and Patrick O'Dell, Dick and Madeleine Brown, Mark Percy, Lesley Mayoh, Franklyn Roberts, David Fowler

MINSTER LOVELL
SP3211   Map 4
Old Swan & Minster Mill 🍴 ☻ ⇦
Just N of B4047 Witney–Burford; OX29 0RN

Carefully restored ancient inn with old-fashioned bar, lots of antique-filled rooms, real ales, a thoughtful wine list, pubby and more elaborate food and acres of gardens and grounds with fishing; exceptional bedrooms

Although much emphasis is on the hotel and restaurant side of this civilised and rather lovely ancient cotswold inn, its heart is in the unchanging and restful little bar, which has stools at the ancient wooden counter, Brakspears Bitter, Oxford Gold and a guest beer on handpump, several wines by the glass from a fine list, 30 malt whiskies and a good choice of teas and coffees. Leading off here are several attractive low-beamed rooms with big log fires in huge fireplaces, red and green leather tub chairs, all manner of comfortable armchairs, sofas, dining chairs and wooden tables, rugs on bare boards or ancient flagstones, antiques and prints and lots of horsebrasses, bed-warming pans, swords, hunting horns and even a suit of armour; fresh flowers everywhere. Seats are dotted around the 65 acres of grounds (the white metal ones beside the water are much prized) and they have a mile of fishing on the River Windrush, tennis courts, boules and croquet. The bedrooms have a lot of character and at the top end are luxurious.

Using produce from their kitchen garden and other local, seasonal ingredients, the excellent food might include sandwiches, king scallops with pear purée, red amaranth (an edible red leaf) and star anise, rabbit terrine wrapped in prosciutto with quince jelly, a trio of sausages with onion gravy, home-made burger with bacon and cheese, pumpkin and sage risotto with parmesan and truffle oil, beer-battered haddock with triple-cooked chips and mushy peas, a daily-changing fish or game dish, and puddings like warm chocolate fondant with hot chocolate sauce and raspberry coulis and sticky toffee pudding with hot fudge sauce. *Benchmark main dish: steak in ale pie £16.95. Two-course evening meal £22.95.*

Free house ~ Licensee Ian Solkin ~ Real ale ~ Bar food (12-3, 6.30-9) ~ Restaurant ~ (01993) 774441 ~ Children welcome ~ Dogs allowed in bar and bedrooms ~ Live jazz monthly Sun ~ Open 12-10.30 ~ Bedrooms: £165S/£195S ~ www.oldswanandminstermill.com *Recommended by Richard Gibbs*

OXFORD   SP5106   Map 4
Bear 🍺

Alfred Street/Wheatsheaf Alley; OX1 4EH

Delightful pub with friendly staff, two cosy rooms, six real ales and well liked bar food

Tucked away off the tourist trail, this charming little pub is the oldest drinking house in the city. There are two small low-ceilinged, beamed and partly panelled rooms, not over-smart and often packed with students, with a bustling, chatty atmosphere, winter coal fires, thousands of vintage ties on walls and up to six real ales served from handpumps on the fine pewter bar counter: Fullers Chiswick, ESB, Gales HSB and London Pride and a couple of guests beers such as Shotover Prospect and Scholar. Staff are friendly and helpful. There are seats under parasols in the terraced back garden, where summer barbecues are held.

Bar food includes sandwiches, nibbles like olives and hummus with local bread, a proper ploughman's, various burgers including a vegetarian one, smoked haddock and spring onion fishcakes, steak in ale pie, sausage and mash with onion gravy, barbecue chicken, and puddings like treacle sponge and chocolate fudge cake. *Benchmark main dish: beer-battered fish and chips £8.95. Two-course evening meal £15.00.*

Fullers ~ Manager James Verneade ~ Real ale ~ Bar food (all day) ~ (01865) 728164 ~ until 9pm ~ Dogs allowed in bar ~ accoustic night Wed ~ Open 11-11(midnight Fri and Sat); 11-11 Sun *Recommended by Alasdair Mackay, the Didler, Andy Dolan, Simon Watkins*

OXFORD   SP5005   Map 4
Punter

South Street, Osney (off A420 Botley Road via Bridge Street); OX2 0BE

Friendly, relaxed pub overlooking the water; lots of character and enjoyable food

Actually on Osney Island and with views over the Thames, this easy-going pub is run with great enthusiasm by the young landlord. The lower area has attractive rugs on flagstones and an open fire and the upper room has more rugs on floorboards and a single big table surrounded by oil paintings – just right for a private party. Throughout, there are all manner of nice old dining chairs around an interesting mix of tables, affordable art on white-washed walls and one rather fine stained-glass window. Adnams Bitter and Broadside on handpump from the tiled counter, several wines by the glass and friendly service; board games. This is sister pub to the Punter in Cambridge.

 As well as three daily dishes on a £5 lunch board, the good, modern food includes sandwiches, scallops with black pudding, cauliflower purée and caper raisin butter, binham blue with chicory, pear and walnut, chilli con carne, saffron risotto with spring onion and crispy shallots, beef burger with cheese and chips, whole roast plaice with salsa verde, pork belly and cheek with apple purée and potato galette, guinea fowl with truffled pommes purée and pickled mushrooms, and crispy duck leg with asian slaw and peanut dressing. *Benchmark main dish: pork belly and cheek with apple purée £15.00. Two-course evening meal £19.50.*

Greene King ~ Lease Tom Rainey ~ Real ale ~ Bar food (all day) ~ Restaurant ~ (01865) 248832 ~ Children welcome ~ Dogs welcome ~ Open 12-12(11.30 Sun) ~ www.thepunteroxford.com *Recommended by Richard Gibbs*

 OXFORD   SP5107   Map 4

Rose & Crown

North Parade Avenue; very narrow, so best to park in a nearby street; OX2 6LX

Long-serving licensees in a lively friendly local, a good mix of customers, fine choice of drinks and proper home cooking

What could be a fairly ordinary neighbourhood pub is given a great deal of atmosphere and originality by its licensees, who have now been here for nearly 30 years and warmly welcome their mixed clientele of undergraduates and more mature drinkers. The front door opens on to a passage by the bar counter; the panelled back room, with traditional pub furnishings and reference books for crossword buffs, is slightly bigger; no mobile phones, children, dogs, background music or noisy games machines, but they do have board games. Adnams Bitter, Hook Norton Old Hooky, Shotover Scholar and a guest beer on handpump, 26 malt whiskies and 14 wines by the glass (including champagne). The pleasant walled and heated backyard can be covered with a huge awning; at the far end is a 12-seater dining/meeting room. The lavatories are pretty basic.

 Traditional but enjoyable food includes a popular hot dish of the day such as honeyed chicken or beef stew with herb dumplings, as well as sandwiches and filled baguettes, potted shrimps, various dips with pitta bread, egg, bacon, chips and beans, sausages of the day, omelettes, whole trout or battered fish with chips, and puddings like apple pie and chocolate cake. *Benchmark main dish: dish of the day £7.25. Two-course evening meal £12.95.*

Free house ~ Licensees Andrew and Debbie Hall ~ Real ale ~ Bar food (12-2.15(3.15 Sun Sept-June), 6-9) ~ (01865) 510551 ~ Open 11am-midnight; 11-3, 5-11 Aug and early Sept in winter ~ www.rose-n-crown.com *Recommended by Chris Glasson, the Didler*

 PISHILL   SU7190   Map 2

Crown

B480 Nettlebed–Watlington; RG9 6HH

Fine old inn with attractive beamed bars, winter fires, real ales, several wines by the glass and enjoyable food; bedrooms

Kept spotlessly clean, this mainly 15th-c red brick and flint pub is in the heart of the Chilterns. Our readers enjoy their visits here very much and always receive a friendly welcome from the helpful, professional staff. The partly panelled walls in the beamed bars are hung with local photographs and maps, there are nice old chairs around a mix of wooden tables, candles everywhere, Black Sheep Best Bitter, Brakspears Bitter, and Rebellion IPA on handpump and nine wines by the glass. The knocked-through back area has standing oak timbers, and there are three roaring log fires in winter; there's a priest's hole said to be one of the largest in the country. The beautiful thatched barn used for parties and functions is some 500 years old. In warm weather, there are lots of seats and tables under neat blue parasols in the pretty garden; nearby walks. A self-contained cottage can be rented by the night (breakfast provided).

As well as lunchtime sandwiches, the good, hearty food might include chicken liver parfait with pineapple chutney, warm artichoke salad with spiced potatoes, saffron dressing and a poached egg, thai vegetable curry, bouillabaisse (with monkfish, salmon, prawns and mussels), steak burger with cheese, chicken with sage, apricot and onion stuffing and bubble and squeak, pork belly with celeriac mash, caramelised shallots, poached pear and redcurrant jus, lamb rump with confit lamb, couscous and mediterranean vegetables, and puddings such as sticky toffee pudding with toffee sauce and chocolate mousse. *Benchmark main dish: 28-day-aged rib-eye steak with Café de Paris butter £17.00. Two-course evening meal £18.50.*

Free house ~ Licensee Lucas Wood ~ Real ale ~ Bar food (12-2.30(3 Sun), 6.30-9 (9.30 Fri and Sat)) ~ (01491) 638364 ~ Children welcome ~ Dogs allowed in bar ~ Open 12-3, 6-11; 12-10 Sun ~ Bedrooms: /£80B ~ www.thecrowninnpishill.co.uk
Recommended by Paul Humphreys, Mrs Margaret Watson, Tracey and Stephen Groves, the Didler, Nigel Henbest, Robert Polatajko

RAMSDEN
Royal Oak ♀ 🍴
SP3515 Map 4

Village signposted off B4022 Witney–Charlbury; OX7 3AU

Busy pub with long-serving licensees, large helpings of varied food, carefully chosen wines and seats outside; bedrooms

There are no noisy games machines or background music to spoil the relaxed atmosphere in this 17th-c cotswold stone pub. The unpretentious rooms have a mix of wooden tables, chairs and settles, cushioned window seats, exposed stone walls, bookcases with old and new copies of Country Life and, when the weather gets cold, a cheerful log fire. Hook Norton Old Hooky, Stonehenge Heelstone and Wye Valley HPA on handpump, and ten wines by the glass from a carefully chosen list. There are tables and chairs out in front and on the terrace behind the restaurant (folding back doors give easy access). The bedrooms are in separate cottages and there are some fine surrounding walks.

As well as lunchtime sandwiches, the varied food might include chicken liver parfait, devilled lambs kidneys, chargrilled vegetable lasagne, gloucester old spot loin chop with a bean and tomato casserole, crab and smoked salmon fishcakes, steak and kidney pudding, a pie of the week, daily specials such as local partridge with a port and redcurrant glaze and game chips and bass with fennel sauce and leek ribbons, and puddings. *Benchmark main dish: steak and kidney pudding £14.50. Two-course evening meal £19.75.*

Free house ~ Licensee Jon Oldham ~ Real ale ~ Bar food (12-2, 7-9) ~ Restaurant ~ (01993) 868213 ~ Children allowed in restaurant with parents ~ Dogs allowed in bar and bedrooms ~ Open 11.30-3, 6.30-11; 12-3, 7-10.30 Sun ~ Bedrooms: £60S/£80S ~ www.royaloakramsden.com *Recommended by Rob and Catherine Dunster, Mike and Mary Carter, JJW, CMW, Colin McKerrow, Malcolm and Jo Hart, Chris Glasson*

ROTHERFIELD GREYS   SU7282 Map 2

Maltsters Arms ♀

*Can be reached off A4155 in Henley, via Greys Road passing Southfields
long-stay car park; or follow Greys Church signpost off B481 N of Sonning
Common; RG9 4QD*

**Well run, civilised country pub in the Chilterns, nice scenery
and walks**

With Greys Court (National Trust) not far away and two good
footpaths passing close by, this civilised pub is just the place for
lunch; the friendly, helpful staff make you feel quickly at home. The
maroon-carpeted front room has comfortable wall banquettes and lots of
horsebrasses on its black beams, Brakspears Bitter and Oxford Gold and
a guest such as Jennings Cumberland on handpump, a dozen wines by
the glass and decent coffee; there's a warm winter open fire and maybe
soft background music. Beyond the serving area, which has hop bines
and pewter tankards hanging from its joists, a back room has cricketing
prints on dark red walls over a shiny panelled dado, and a mix of
furnishings from pink-cushioned pale wooden dining chairs to a pair of
leatherette banquettes forming a corner booth. The chocolate labradors
have been here as long as the licensees – 14 years. Terrace tables under a
big heated canopy are set with linen for meals, and the grass behind has
picnic-sets under green parasols, looking out over paddocks to rolling
woodland beyond.

 Well liked and fairly priced, the good food includes filled panini, arbroath
smokie and spinach fishcakes in panko breadcrumbs with a sticky tomato and
chilli jam, bacon-wrapped game terrine with pear chutney, mussels with a choice
of three sauces, sage and apricot-stuffed pork tenderloin with apple and mustard
sauce, oyster mushroom and chargrilled pepper risotto, slow-cooked half shoulder
of lamb with red wine jus, and puddings like Mars Bar fondue and sticky toffee
pudding. *Benchmark main dish: chicken and mushroom pancake £9.25. Two-
course evening meal £15.75.*

Brakspears ~ Tenants Peter and Helen Bland ~ Real ale ~ Bar food (12-2.15, 6.15-9.15;
not Sun evening) ~ (01491) 628400 ~ Children welcome ~ Dogs allowed in bar ~ Open
11.45-3, 6-11(midnight Sat); 12-9(5.30pm winter) Sun; closed winter Sun evening ~
www.maltsters.co.uk *Recommended by Simon Collett-Jones, Roy Hoing, David and Sue Smith,
Paul Humphreys*

SHILTON   SP2608 Map 4

Rose & Crown

Just off B4020 SE of Burford; OX18 4AB

**Simple and appealing little village pub with a relaxed, civilised
atmosphere, real ales and good food**

There's a warm welcome from the very nice landlord and his staff for
all their customers, whether visiting or local. It's a pretty and cosy
17th-c stone-built pub with an unassuming feel, in a subtly upmarket way.
The small front bar has low beams and timbers, exposed stone walls,
a log fire in a big fireplace and half a dozen or so kitchen chairs and
tables on the red tiled floor. There are usually a few locals at the planked
counter, where they serve Hook Norton Old Hooky, Wells & Youngs
Bitter and a guest like Stonehenge Heelstone on handpump, along with
10 wines by the glass; big cafetières of coffee. A second room, similar but

bigger, is used mainly for eating, with flowers on the tables and another fireplace. At the side, an attractive garden has picnic-sets.

 Enjoyable food cooked by the landlord includes lunchtime filled ciabattas, potted brawn with black pudding butter and piccalilli, game terrine with red onion marmalade, aubergine parmigiana baked with mozzarella, ham and egg, liver with sweet purée and sage brown butter, steak and mushroom in ale pie, pheasant breast with a leg croquette and bacon, and puddings such as chocolate and walnut brownie with chocolate sauce and prune, armagnac and almond tart. *Benchmark main dish: smoked haddock, salmon and prawn fish pie £12.50. Two-course evening meal £18.00.*

Free house ~ Licensee Martin Coldicott ~ Real ale ~ Bar food (12-2(2.45 weekends and bank holidays), 7-9) ~ Restaurant ~ (01993) 842280 ~ Well behaved children welcome until 7pm ~ Dogs allowed in bar ~ Open 11.30-3, 6-11; 11.30-11 Fri, Sat; 12-10 Sun ~ www.roseandcrownshilton.com *Recommended by Richard Wyld, Glenwys and Alan Lawrence, R K Phillips, T R Austin, Guy Vowles, Andy Dolan, C A Hall, Dennis and Doreen Haward, Richard Willis*

SHIPLAKE

SU7779 Map 2

Baskerville 🍽 ♀ 🛏

Station Road, Lower Shiplake (off A4155 just S of Henley); RG9 3NY

Emphasis on imaginative food though a proper public bar too; real ales, several wines by the glass, interesting sporting memorabilia and a pretty garden; bedrooms

The friendly landlord describes this particularly well run place as a traditional village pub that just happens to have a first-class restaurant and top quality accommodation, and there's always a good mix of customers. There are bar chairs around the light, modern counter (used by the chatty locals), a few beams, pale wooden dining chairs and tables on the light wood or patterned carpeted floors, plush red banquettes around the windows and a couple of log fires in brick fireplaces. A fair amount of sporting memorabilia and pictures, especially old rowing photos (the pub is very close to Henley) and signed rugby shirts and photos (the pub runs its own rugby club), along with maps of the Thames, are hung on the red walls, and there are flowers and large house plants dotted about. It all feels quite homely, but in a smart way, with some chintzy touches such as a shelf of china cow jugs. Well trained, uniformed staff serve Fullers London Pride, Loddon Hoppit and Timothy Taylors Landlord from handpump, 40 malt whiskies and a dozen wines by the glass from a carefully chosen list; they support Wateraid by charging 50p for a jug of iced water and have so far raised £3,000. There's a separate dining room and a small room for private parties. The pretty garden has a covered barbecue area, smart teak furniture under huge parasols and some rather fun statues made out of box hedges. There's a timber play frame for children. The bedrooms are well equipped and comfortable and the breakfasts very good.

From named suppliers and using organic produce and sustainably sourced fish, the impressive food might include sandwiches, chicken liver, veal and pork terrine wrapped in smoked bacon with toasted home-made bread and chunky piccalilli, puff pastry tartlet with brie, olives, sundried tomatoes and baby spinach with a wild garlic pesto, smoked ham with a marmalade and rosemary glaze and free-range eggs, steak and kidney in ale pie, blue swimming crab, tiger prawn and baby squid linguine, marinated and chargrilled tuna with a pineapple and chilli salsa, sesame roasted new potatoes and samphire, lamb rump and black pudding with a parsnip and potato rösti, minted pea purée and redcurrant jus, and puddings like triple chocolate brownie with home-made vanilla ice-cream and rhubarb, apple and ginger crumble with crème anglaise; they also offer a two- and three-course set menu in January, February, October and November. *Benchmark main dish: sustainable cod fillet in crisp beer batter with home-made minted peas and tartare sauce £12.95. Two-course evening meal £21.00.*

Free house ~ Licensee Allan Hannah ~ Real ale ~ Bar food (11-9(10 Fri and Sat); 12-3.30 Sun; not Sun evening (but this may change)) ~ Restaurant ~ (0118) 940 3332 ~ Children welcome but not in restaurant after 7pm Fri, Sat ~ Dogs allowed in bar and bedrooms ~ Open 11-11; 12-10.30 Sun ~ Bedrooms: £82S/£92S ~ www.thebaskerville.com
Recommended by David O'Shaughnessy, Mrs Susan Lines, Ian Herdman, Dr D J and Mrs S C Walker, Paul Humphreys

STANFORD IN THE VALE
SU3393 Map 4
Horse & Jockey ♀ £
A417 Faringdon–Wantage; Faringdon Road; SN7 8NN

Friendly traditional village local with real character, good value food and well chosen wines

Prices are very fair here with main courses (apart from steaks) under £10 – and we've given them one of our Bargain Awards this year. Big Alfred Munnings racecourse prints, card collections of Grand National winners and other horse and jockey pictures reflect not just the pub's name but the fact that this is racehorse training country – which often seems to guarantee the relaxed and welcoming atmosphere found here. Greene King Morlands Original, Old Speckled Hen and Ruddles County on handpump and carefully chosen wines in various glass sizes. The main area, with flagstones, a low ochre ceiling and a woodburning stove in its big fireplace, has several old high-backed settles and a couple of bucket armchairs. On the right is a carpeted area with a lofty raftered ceiling, a lattice-windowed inner gallery and some stripped stone, and at the back a spacious bare-boards dining room. As well as tables out under a heated courtyard canopy, there's a separate enclosed and informal family garden with a play area and picnic-sets on the grass; aunt sally. The bedrooms are comfortable.

Highly thought of and reasonably priced, the food might include sandwiches and filled baguettes, whole baked camembert with red onion marmalade, salt, pepper and chilli battered calamari with dipping sauce, chicken caesar salad, platters for sharing (fish, meat and cheese), vegetable pie, ham and free-range eggs, a burger with home-made onion rings, a curry of the day, beer-battered fish and chips with home-made tartare sauce, specials such as scallops and chorizo with pea purée and rack of lamb with apricot sauce and sweet potato crisps, and puddings. *Benchmark main dish: game pie £9.95. Two-course evening meal £15.80.*

Greene King ~ Lease Charles and Anna Gaunt ~ Real ale ~ Bar food (12-2.15(2.30 Sun), 6.30-9(9.30 Fri and Sat, 8.30 Sun)) ~ Restaurant ~ (01367) 710302 ~ Children welcome ~ Dogs allowed in bar ~ Thurs evening quiz and monthly open mike first Weds evening of month ~ Open 11-3, 5-midnight; 11am-12.30am Fri and Sat; 12-midnight Sun ~ Bedrooms: £50S/£60S ~ www.horseandjockey.org *Recommended by R K Phillips, Valerie Bone*

Post Office address codings confusingly give the impression that some pubs are in Oxfordshire, when they're really in Berkshire, Buckinghamshire, Gloucestershire or Warwickshire (which is where we list them).

 STONESFIELD   SP3917   Map 4

White Horse

Village signposted off B4437 Charlbury–Woodstock; Stonesfield Riding; OX29 8EA

Attractively upgraded small country pub with enjoyable food and a relaxed atmosphere

Handy for the Roman villa (English Heritage) at nearby North Leigh, this is a carefully run pub with quite an emphasis on food. There are contemporary artworks, restful colours (grey or off-white in the snug little bar, dark pink over a grey dado in the dining room) and nicely chosen furniture. One of their best touches is the little inner room with just a pair of sheraton-style chairs around a single mahogany table. Service is cheerful and efficient. The corner bar counter, with padded stools, has Ringwood Best and Boondoggle on handpump; open fire, daily papers, quiet background music. The dining room's french windows open on to a neat walled garden with picnic-sets; there's a skittle alley in the separate stone barn. As the pub is on the Oxfordshire Way there are good walks nearby. Please note the restricted opening times.

Using carefully sourced local produce, the good food cooked by the landlady includes lunchtime sandwiches, guinea fowl and ham hock terrine with game jelly, tian of crab-claw meat and prawns, leek and pesto risotto, hungarian goulash, slow-roast lamb shank in mint and honey with colcannon mash, seared tuna loin with niçoise garnish, rib-eye steak with pepper or blue cheese sauce, and puddings such as cheesecake of the day and chocolate brownie with vanilla ice-cream. *Benchmark main dish: pie of the week £10.00. Two-course evening meal £16.00.*

Free house ~ Licensees John and Angela Lloyd ~ Real ale ~ Bar food (12-2, 6.30-9; not Mon, Tues/Weds lunchtime, Sun evening) ~ Restaurant ~ (01993) 891063 ~ Children welcome ~ Dogs allowed in bar ~ Open 12-3, 5(6 Sat)-11; 12-4 Sun; closed Mon, Tues/Weds lunchtime, Sun evening ~ www.thewhitehorseinnatstonesfield.co.uk
Recommended by Richard Gibbs

 SWERFORD   SP3830   Map 4

Masons Arms 🍴 🍷

A361 Banbury–Chipping Norton; OX7 4AP

Nice-looking dining pub with well liked food, a fair choice of drinks, a relaxed atmosphere, and country views from outside tables

Young, enthusiastic new licensees took over this pretty brick dining pub just as we went to press and have made a few minor changes to the décor. The bar has rugs on pale wooden floors, a big brown leather sofa facing a couple of armchairs in front of the log fire in its stone fireplace, Brakspears Bitter and Wychwood Hobgoblin on handpump and several wines by the glass. The dining extension is light and airy with pastel-painted dining chairs around nice old tables on beige carpet and there are steps down to a cream-painted room with chunky tables and contemporary pictures. Round the other side of the bar is another roomy dining room with great views by day, candles at night and a civilised feel. The neat garden has picnic-sets on the lawn and looks over the Oxfordshire countryside.

As well as a two- and three-course set lunch menu, the food now includes lunchtime sandwiches, a tian of smoked salmon, mackerel and prawns with citrus mayonnaise, filo brie parcels with red onion and cranberry chutney, roasted mediterranean vegetable pancake in a tomato and basil sauce topped with cheese, corn-fed chicken on a sweet potato and parsnip rösti with a burgundy jus, red mullet on a smoked haddock kedgeree with a thai curry sauce, herb-crusted lamb with rosemary fondant potatoes and a redcurrant and red wine jus, and puddings such as chocolate parfait with a raspberry compote and rum and raisin cheesecake with a mocha dressing. *Benchmark main dish: braised beef cobbler £12.95. Two-course evening meal £20.00.*

Free house ~ Licensee Louise Davies ~ Real ale ~ Bar food (12-2, 6-9; 12-8 Sun) ~ Restaurant ~ (01608) 683212 ~ Children welcome ~ Open 11-3, 6-11; 12-10 Sun ~ www.masons-arms.com *Recommended by George Atkinson, Sir Nigel Foulkes, David and Lexi Young, P and J Shapley, Clare Tagg, Richard Tilbrook*

SWINBROOK
Swan 🍴 ♀ 🛏

SP2812   Map 4

Back road a mile N of A40, 2 miles E of Burford; OX18 4DY

Rather smart old pub with handsome oak garden rooms, antique-filled bars, local beers and contemporary food; bedrooms

As this civilised 17th-c pub is owned by the Dowager Duchess of Devonshire (the last of the Mitford sisters, who grew up in the village), there are lots of interesting Mitford family photographs blown up on the walls. There's a little bar with simple antique furnishings, settles and benches, an open fire, and (in an alcove) a stuffed swan; locals still drop in here for a pint and a chat. A small dining room leads off from the bar to the right of the entrance, and there are also two green-oak garden rooms with high-backed beige and green dining chairs around pale wood tables, and views over the garden and orchard. Hook Norton Hooky Bitter and guests from breweries like Brakspear, Butcombe and Wye Valley on handpump, ten wines by the glass and Weston's organic cider. This is a lovely spot by a bridge over the River Windrush and seats by the fuchsia hedge make the best of the view. The bedrooms are in a smartly converted stone barn beside the pub. The Kings Head in Bledington (Gloucestershire) is run by the same first class licensees.

🍴 Using as much free-range, organic and local produce as possible, and beef from the family farm, the inventive food might include cornish sardines with olive oil and lemon, air-dried beef with croutons and parmesan, pasta with olives, spiced almonds, red peppers, grilled radiccio, parmesan and basil oil, chilli cheeseburger, venison sausages with salsa verde, steamed bream fillet with hollandaise, rare breed pork T-bone with garlic roasted potatoes, apple purée and grain mustard jus, barbary duck breast with sweet potato purée and a ginger, honey and soy dressing, and puddings like passion fruit and lime parfait with orange segments and wild berries with meringue and vanilla cream. *Benchmark main dish: devilled lambs kidneys on toast £12.00. Two-course evening meal £22.00.*

Free house ~ Licensees Archie and Nicola Orr-Ewing ~ Real ale ~ Bar food (12-2, 7-9) ~ Restaurant ~ (01993) 823339 ~ Children welcome ~ Dogs allowed in bar ~ Open 11 (12 Sun)-11; 11 (12 Sun)-3, 6-11 in winter ~ Bedrooms: £90B/£120B ~ www.theswanswinbrook.co.uk *Recommended by John and Enid Morris, Richard Wyld, Jeff and Wendy Williams, Richard Greaves, Anthony and Pam Stamer, David and Lexi Young, Tim and Sue Halstead, Graham Oddey, Malcolm Greening, David Glynne-Jones, Andy Dolan, Bernard Stradling, Stuart Turner, Malcolm and Jo Hart, Di and Mike Gillam, C A Hall*

Every entry includes a postcode for use in SatNav devices.

TADPOLE BRIDGE   SP3200   Map 4

Trout 🍴 ♀ 🛏

Back road Bampton–Buckland, 4 miles NE of Faringdon; SN7 8RF

Oxfordshire Dining Pub of the Year

Busy country inn by the River Thames with a fine choice of drinks, popular modern food and seats in the waterside garden; bedrooms

Our readers love this particularly well run inn – as somewhere for a drink or a meal and as an extremely comfortable place to stay overnight. It's all very civilised and friendly and the L-shaped bar has attractive pink and cream checked chairs around a mix of nice wooden tables, some rugs on the flagstones, green paintwork behind a modern wooden bar counter, fresh flowers, two woodburning stoves and a large stuffed trout. The airy restaurant is appealingly candlelit in the evenings. Ramsbury Bitter, Wells & Youngs Bitter and a couple of guests like Loose Cannon Abingdon Bridge and White Horse Wayland Smithy on handpump, 12 wines by the glass from a wide-ranging and carefully chosen list, some fine sherries, several malt whiskies and local cider. This is a peaceful and picturesque spot by the Thames, and there are good quality teak chairs and tables under blue parasols in the pretty garden; it can get pretty packed on a fine day, so it's best to arrive early. You can hire punts with champagne hampers and there are moorings for six boats – if you book in advance.

🍴 As well as themed meals like Sustainable Fish Night, Pie Evening and afternoon tea on Mothers' Day, the inventive and very popular food might include sandwiches, chicken liver and duck foie gras parfait with green fig chutney, chilli and coriander marinated squid with slaw and rocket salad, slow-cooked rabbit with confit red cabbage and rösti potato, a plate of pork with belly, cheek, fillet and black pudding, cider sauce and bubble and squeak, specials such as mussels with garlic and cream, roasted mediterranean vegetable risotto, rillettes of guinea fowl with port and redcurrant jelly and bass fillet with pesto and lyonnaise potatoes, and puddings like Cointreau and orange crème brûlée and chocolate panettone bread and butter pudding with mint cream. *Benchmark main dish: beer-battered haddock and chips £11.95. Two-course evening meal £22.20.*

Free house ~ Licensees Gareth and Helen Pugh ~ Real ale ~ Bar food (12-2, 7-9; some food all day at weekends) ~ (01367) 870382 ~ Children welcome ~ Dogs welcome ~ Open 11.30-11; 11.30-3, 6-11 Mon-Fri in winter; 12-10.30 Sun ~ Bedrooms: £85B/£130B ~ www.troutinn.co.uk *Recommended by Glenwys and Alan Lawrence, Colin McKerrow, David and Diane Young, Eleanor Dandy, Tim Gray, Bob and Margaret Holder, Jennifer and Patrick O'Dell, Mary Rayner, Richard Tilbrook, M and J White, Ross Balaam, Derek Thomas, Charles Gysin*

WOODSTOCK   SP4416   Map 4

Kings Arms £ 🛏

Market Street/Park Lane (A44); OX20 1SU

Stylish hotel in centre of attractive town, well liked food, enjoyable atmosphere and a wide choice of drinks; comfortable bedrooms

You can be sure of excellent service and a warm welcome from the well-trained staff in this stylish town-centre hotel. The unfussy bar has a good mix of customers, creating a relaxed and informal atmosphere, a happy mix of old and new furnishings including brown leather furniture on the stripped-wood floor, smart blinds and black and white photographs; at the front, there's an old wooden settle and an interesting little woodburner. In the bar leading to the brasserie-style dining room there's an unusual stained-glass structure used for newspapers and magazines; the restaurant is attractive, with its hanging lights and fine old fireplace. Brakspear Bitter and Oxford Gold and a guest like Banks's Mansfield Bitter on handpump, good coffees, 15 wines plus champagne by the glass and 21 malt whiskies; background music. The bedrooms are comfortable and the breakfasts very good. There are seats and tables on the street outside.

🍴 Using local produce where possible, interesting food includes breakfasts (available to non-residents, too), lunchtime sandwiches, natural smoked haddock and watercress kedgeree with a poached egg, organic beef burger with blue cheese and bacon, honey and mustard ham with free-range eggs, butternut squash and artichoke tart with thyme and caramelised apple, free-range peppered chicken with a pear and fig salad with toasted hazelnuts, pork belly with cider sauce and black pudding, specials such as pressed guinea fowl, leek and wild mushroom terrine, whisky smoked salmon and fried scallops with pickled cucumber and a potato and dill pancake and whole lemon sole with crayfish butter, and puddings like ginger brûlée with mulled plums and shortbread and chocolate quartet (dark chocolate brûlée, truffle, white chocolate and orange mousse and milk chocolate brownie). *Benchmark main dish: pot-roast leg of lamb with honey and rosemary £11.75. Two-course evening meal £18.00.*

Free house ~ Licensees David and Sara Sykes ~ Real ale ~ Bar food (12-2, 6.30-9; all day Sun) ~ Restaurant ~ (01993) 813636 ~ Children welcome in bar and restaurant but no under-12s in bedrooms ~ Dogs allowed in bar ~ Open 11-11 ~ Bedrooms: £80S/£150B ~ www.kings-hotel-woodstock.co.uk *Recommended by Paul and Mary Walmsley, David and Judy Robison, Graham Oddey, Martin and Pauline Jennings*

Also Worth a Visit in Oxfordshire

Besides the fully inspected pubs, you might like to try these pubs that have been recommended to us and described by readers. Do tell us what you think of them: feedback@goodguides.com

ABINGDON   SU4997
Brewery Tap (01235) 521655
Ock Street; OX14 5BZ Former tap for defunct Morland Brewery (now flats) but still serving Original along with other Greene King ales and guests, proper ciders, good value lunchtime food including popular Sun roasts, stone floors and panelled walls, log fire; background and some live music; children and dogs welcome, three bedrooms, open all day (till 1am Fri, Sat). *(Kenny Moore)*

ADDERBURY   SP4735
⁕ **Red Lion** (01295) 810269
The Green; off A4260 S of Banbury; OX17 3NG Attractive 17th-c coaching inn with good choice of enjoyable well priced food (all day weekends) including deals, helpful friendly staff, Greene King ales, good wine range and coffee, linked bar rooms with high stripped beams, panelling and stonework, big inglenook log fire, old books and Victorian/Edwardian pictures, daily newspapers, games area, more modern back restaurant extension; background music; children in eating areas, picnic-

sets out on roadside terrace, 12 character bedrooms, good breakfast, open all day in summer. *(George Atkinson, M G Hart)*

ALVESCOT   SP2704
Plough (01993) 842281
B4020 Carterton–Clanfield, SW of Witney; OX18 2PU Comfortable neatly kept bar with aircraft prints (Brize Norton close by) and cottagey pictures, china ornaments, big antique case of birds of prey and sundry bric-a-brac, woodburner, Wadworths ales and Weston's cider, straightforward food including good ploughman's, prompt service, proper public bar with TV and darts, skittle alley, pub cats; background music; children welcome, picnic sets on back terrace (lots of hanging baskets), aunt sally and play area in garden (and perhaps ornamental pheasants and japanese quail), nice village, open all day. *(Anon)*

ARDINGTON   SU4388
⁕ **Boars Head** (01235) 833254
Signed off A417 Didcot–Wantage; OX12 8QA Enjoyable restauranty food at one end of this civilised 17th-c pub, cheaper set

menu weekday lunchtime, low-beams and attractively simple country décor, good wine and soft drinks choice, three real ales, locals' end with traditional games; TV, background music and piano; children welcome, peaceful attractive village, three bedrooms, good breakfast, closed Sun evening. *(D C T and E A Frewer)*

ASTON TIRROLD   SU5586

⋆**Sweet Olive** (01235) 851272

Aka Chequers; Fullers Road; village signed off A417 Streatley–Wantage; OX11 9EN Has atmosphere of a rustic french restaurant rather than village pub – but people do pop in for just a drink; main room with wall settles, mate's chairs, a few sturdy tables, grass matting over quarry tiles, small fireplace, good well liked food, nice french wines by the glass (wine box ends decorate the back of the servery), Brakspears and Fullers beers, friendly service, smaller room more formally set as restaurant with restrained décor; background music; children welcome, dogs in bar, picnic-sets under parasols in small cottagey garden, aunt sally, closed Sun evening, Weds, all Feb and two weeks in July. *(Dave Snowden, Rob Winstanley)*

BECKLEY   SP5611

⋆**Abingdon Arms** (01865) 351311

Signed off B4027; High Street; OX3 9UU Old village pub in attractive unspoilt village, comfortably modernised simple lounge, smaller public bar with antique carved settles, open fires, well kept Brakspears and guests, fair range of wines, enjoyable home-made food from pub favourites up including good Sun roasts, friendly service; piped and some live music; children and dogs welcome, big garden dropping away from floodlit terrace to trees, summer house, superb views over RSPB Otmoor reserve – good walks, open all day weekends. *(Martin and Pauline Jennings, Melanie Court, Stephen and Jean Curtis)*

BEGBROKE   SP4713

Royal Sun (01865) 374718

A44 Oxford–Woodstock; OX5 1RZ Welcoming old stone-built pub with modernised bare-boards interior, wide choice of good value food from snacks to Sun carvery, well kept Hook Norton and a guest, good friendly service, free monkey nuts on the bar; may be background music, big screen sports TV; children welcome, tables on terrace and in small garden, open all day from 8.30am for breakfast. *(Brenda Long)*

BINFIELD HEATH   SU7479

⋆**Bottle & Glass** (01491) 575755

Off A4155 at Shiplake; between village and Harpsden; RG9 4JT Chocolate-box thatched black and white Tudor cottage under new licensees, sensibly priced home-made pubby food from lunchtime sandwiches up, two Brakspears ales and

a guest, ten wines by the glass, bleached pine tables, low beams and flagstones, dark squared panelling, old local photographs on pastel walls, old stove (converted to gas) in fine fireplace, board games and dominoes; children and dogs welcome, lovely big garden with picnic-sets (some under little thatched roofs), aunt sally, open all day weekends, closed Mon lunchtime. *(Anon)*

BLOXHAM   SP4235

⋆**Joiners Arms** (01295) 720223

Old Bridge Road, off A361; OX15 4LY Golden stone 16th-c inn with some refurbishment in rambling rooms, white dining chairs around pale tables on wood floor, plenty of exposed stone, open fires, ales such as Braksrears and Marstons, enjoyable traditional food including OAP lunchtime deals, old well in raftered room off bar; children and dogs welcome, pretty window boxes, seats out under parasols on various levels – most popular down steps by stream (play house there too), open all day. *(David Jackman, R T and J C Moggridge, Alan Weedon)*

BRIGHTWELL   SU5890

Red Lion (01491) 837373

Signed off A4130 2 miles W of Wallingford; OX10 0RT Welcoming community-spirited village pub, five well kept local ales, wines from nearby vineyard, enjoyable good value home-made food, two-part bar with snug seating by log fire, unobtrusive dining extension; dogs welcome, tables outside. *(John Pritchard, Franklyn Roberts)*

BRITWELL SALOME   SU6793

⋆**Red Lion** (01491) 613140

B4009 Watlington–Benson; OX49 5LG Recently reopened (former Goose) under new welcoming licensees (previously at the Half Moon in Cuxham), cosy bar with comfortable sofas and traditional pub tables, two dining rooms off, good interesting food from landlord (excellent potted crab) plus standard pub dishes using local produce, well kept Fullers London Pride and West Berkshire Mr Chubbs, 11 wines by the glass, efficient friendly service, log fire; children and dogs welcome, courtyard garden, open all day Sat, closed Sun evening, Mon. *(Jane Taylor and David Dutton, Jackie Martin and Andy Norris)*

BROUGHTON   SP4238

⋆**Saye & Sele Arms** (01295) 263348

B4035 SW of Banbury; OX15 5ED 16th-c pub split into three distinct areas, dining room at one end with over 200 colourful water jugs hanging from beams, tiled area by bar counter with cushioned window seats, a few brasses and dark wooden furnishings, and a carpeted room with red walls and big fireplace, good food cooked by landlord, up to four well kept ales, several wines by the glass, friendly service; children allowed if eating, mix of seats on terrace and lawn, pergola and smokers' shelter, herb garden, aunt sally, handy for Broughton Castle, closed Sun evening. *(R K Phillips, P M Newsome, P and J Shapley)*

BUCKLAND   SU3497
✳ **Lamb** (01367) 870484
Off A420 NE of Faringdon; SN7 8QN
18th-c stone-built dining pub with interesting seasonal food in bar or restaurant, Loose Cannon and a local guest ale, good choice of wines by the glass; well behaved children and dogs welcome (resident cocker called Oats), pleasant tree-shaded garden, good walks nearby, three comfortable bedrooms, closed Sun evening and Mon. *(Jennifer and Patrick O'Dell, the Didler)*

BUCKNELL   SP5525
Trigger Pond (01869) 252817
Handy for M40 junction 10; Bicester Road; OX27 7NE New management for this stone-built beamed pub opposite the pond; small bar with dining areas either side, inglenook woodburner, conservatory, Wadworths ales, standard pub food; children welcome, colourful terrace and garden, open all day Thurs-Sun. *(Anon)*

BURFORD   SP2512
✳ **Angel** (01993) 822714
Witney Street; OX18 4SN Long heavy-beamed dining pub in attractive ancient building, warmly welcoming with good reasonably priced brasserie food, good range of drinks; big secluded garden, three comfortable bedrooms, closed Sun evening, Mon. *(Jennifer and Patrick O'Dell, David Glynne-Jones)*

BURFORD   SP2512
Golden Pheasant (01993) 823223
High Street; OX18 4QA Small early 18th-c hotel's flagstoned split-level bar, civilised yet relaxed and pubby, settees, armchairs, well spaced tables and woodburner, enjoyable food from baguettes to steaks, well kept Greene King ales, good house wines, back dining room down steps; children welcome, pleasant terrace behind, bedrooms, open all day. *(Malcolm Greening)*

BURFORD   SP2512
Highway (01993) 823661
High Street (A361); OX18 4RG Comfortable 15th-c inn with notable float-glass windows in bar, can sit at long cushioned window seat overlooking street, ancient stripped stone mixing with filigree black and pale blue wallpaper, other interesting touches such as stag candlesticks and Cecil Aldin hunting prints, old station clock above simple attractive fireplace,

second bar with another big window seat, Hook Norton and a guest, lots of wines by the glass food from sandwiches up; background music; children welcome, dogs in bar, picnic-sets by pavement, nine bedrooms, open all day but closed first two weeks in Jan. *(N R White, Graham Oddey)*

BURFORD   SP2512
✳ **Mermaid** (01993) 822193
High Street; OX18 4QF Handsome jettied Tudor dining pub with beams, flagstones, panelling, stripped stone and nice log fire, good food at sensible prices including local free-range meat and fresh fish, friendly efficient service, well kept Greene King ales and a guest, bay seating around row of tables on the left, further airy back dining room and upstairs restaurant; background music (live Fri); children welcome, tables out at front and in courtyard behind, open all day. *(Mike Horgan, Di Wright)*

BURFORD   SP2512
✳ **Royal Oak** (01993) 823278
Witney Street; OX18 4SN Relaxed homely 17th-c stripped-stone local, an oasis in this smart village, with long-serving friendly landlord, Wadworths ales and an occasional guest from central servery, simple generous good value food using local produce from filled rolls up, good service, over a thousand beer mugs, steins and jugs hanging from beams, antlers over big log fire (underfloor heating too), light wood tables, chairs and benches on flagstones, more in carpeted back room with bar billiards; well behaved children and dogs welcome, terrace tables, sensibly priced bedrooms by garden behind, good breakfast, open all day Sat, closed Tues lunchtime. *(Pam Service, Guy Vowles)*

CHARLBURY   SP3519
Bull (01608) 810689
Sheep Street; OX7 3RR Comfortable beamed stripped-stone bistro-style dining pub, restaurant on left with inglenook log fire, another in dining bar on right with rattan chairs, interesting food from sandwiches up, a house bitter brewed by Goffs and two guests, good choice of wines by the glass; no dogs; children welcome, attractive sunny back terrace, four bedrooms, closed Sun evening, Mon. *(Geoff Clifford)*

CHARLBURY   SP3519
Rose & Crown (01608) 810103
Market Street; OX7 3PL Welcoming town pub with strong following for its particularly well kept beers (up to seven), real ciders and perry too, simple split-level interior with real pubby feel, no food apart from rolls, regular live music; tables out behind. *(Tony Hobden, Geoff Clifford, Andy and Jill Kassube)*

There are report forms at the back of the book.

CHAZEY HEATH   SU6979
Pack Horse (01189) 722140
*Off A4074 Reading–Wallingford by
B4526; RG4 7UG* Attractive 17th-c beamed
pub (part of Home Counties group), good
choice of enjoyable fairly priced food all
day, real ales and lots of wines by the glass,
friendly staff, polished tables on wood floors,
built-in leatherette banquettes, big log fire
in raised hearth; dogs welcome in main bar,
disabled facilities, back garden.
(Sharon Dooley, David Lamb)

CHECKENDON   SU6684
☆ Black Horse (01491) 680418
*Village signed off A4074 Reading–
Wallingford; RG8 0TE* This charmingly
old-fashioned country tavern (tucked
into woodland away from main village)
has been kept by the same family for 106
years; relaxing and unchanging series of
rooms, back one with Hook Norton and West
Berkshire tapped from the cask, one with
bar counter has tent pegs above fireplace
(a reminder they used to be made here),
homely side lounge with some splendidly
unfashionable 1950s-look armchairs and
another room beyond that, only filled rolls
and pickled eggs; no credit cards; children
allowed but must be well behaved, seats
on verandah and in garden, popular with
walkers and cyclists. *(the Didler)*

CHISLEHAMPTON   SU5998
Coach & Horses (01865) 890255
*B480 Oxford–Watlington, opposite B4015
to Abingdon; OX44 7UX* Extended 16th-c
coaching inn, two homely and civilised
beamed bars, big log fire, sizeable restaurant
with polished oak tables and wall banquettes,
good choice of well prepared food (not Sun
evening), friendly attentive service, well
kept ales such as Hook Norton and Loddon;
background music; neat terraced gardens
overlooking fields by River Thame, some
tables out in front, bedrooms in courtyard
block, open all day, closed 3.30-7 Sun.
(Roy Hoing, Mike and Mary Carter)

CHURCH ENSTONE   SP3725
☆ Crown (01608) 677262
*Mill Lane; from A44 take B4030 turn-off
at Enstone; OX7 4NN* Pleasant uncluttered
bar in beamed country pub, straightforward
furniture, country pictures on stone
walls, some horsebrasses, log fire in large
fireplace, well kept Hook Norton and guests,
consistently good food from pub favourites up,
friendly efficient service, red-walled carpeted
dining room, slate-floored conservatory with
farmhouse furniture; children welcome,
dogs in bar, white metal tables and chairs
on front terrace overlooking lane, picnic-
sets in sheltered back garden, closed Sun
evening. *(JJW, CMW, George Atkinson, Martin
and Pauline Jennings, Barry Collett, Stuart Turner,
Malcolm and Jo Hart and others)*

CHURCHILL   SP2824
☆ Chequers (01608) 659393
*Church Road; B4450 Chipping Norton–
Stow-on-the-Wold (and village signed
off A361 Chipping Norton–Burford);
OX7 6NJ* Great welcome from licensees
Assumpta and Peter Golding at this spic and
span golden-stone village pub, front bar with
modern oak furnishings on light flagstoned
floor, some old timbers and country prints,
exposed stone walls around big inglenook
log fire, Hook Norton and up to three guests,
decent wines and local cider, well liked
food, big back extension with soaring rafters
and cosy upstairs dining area; children
welcome, impressive church opposite, open
all day. *(Richard Greaves, Colin McKerrow, David
and Julie Glover, Jeremy and Ruth Preston-Hoar,
Paul and Mary Walmsley, Dennis and Doreen
Haward and others)*

CLANFIELD   SP2802
☆ Clanfield Tavern (01367) 810223
*Bampton Road (A4095 S of Witney);
OX18 2RG* Newish licensees at this
pleasantly extended pub and emphasis
on traditional food; opened-up beamed
interior keeping feel of separate areas,
mostly carpeted with mix of pubby furniture
including some old settles (built-in one by
log fire), smallish bar with sofas in snug
flagstoned area by woodburner, Banks's
and a couple of guest ales, attractive dining
conservatory; background music; children
welcome, dogs in bar, picnic-sets on small
flower-bordered lawn looking across to village
green, open all day weekends. *(R K Phillips)*

CLIFTON HAMPDEN   SU5495
Barley Mow (01865) 980262
*Towards Long Wittenham, S of A415;
OX14 3EH* Thatched Chef & Brewer dining
pub, plenty of atmosphere with very low
ancient beams, some appropriate furniture
and nice dark corners, log fire, oak-panelled
family room, real ales and good choice of
wines by the glass, decent food all day from
sandwiches up, restaurant; background
music, no dogs inside; tables on pleasant
terrace and in well tended waterside garden,
short stroll from Thames. *(Robert Watt)*

COLESHILL   SU2393
☆ Radnor Arms (01793) 861575
*B4019 Faringdon–Highworth; village
signposted off A417 in Faringdon and
A361 in Highworth; SN6 7PR* Pub and
village owned by NT; bar with cushioned
settles, plush carver chairs and woodburner,
back alcove with more tables, steps down to
main dining area, once a blacksmith's forge
with lofty beamed ceiling, log fire, dozens of
tools and smith's gear on walls, Old Forge
ales brewed on site (tasting trays available),
shortish choice of good well priced home-
made food (not Sun evening), friendly
efficient service; children and dogs welcome,

garden with aunt sally and play area, open all day. *(Graham Oddey, Jennifer and Patrick O'Dell, R K Phillips)*

CRAWLEY
SP3412
Lamb (01993) 703753

Steep Hill; just NW of Witney; OX29 9TW New management taking over at this popular 18th-c stone-built dining pub as we went to press – reports please; simple beamed bar with polished boards and lovely fireplace, steps up to dining room, Brakspears ales; views from tables on back terrace and lawn, pretty village, good walks on Palladian Way, has been closed Sun evening. *(Anon)*

CUMNOR
SP4503
⋆**Bear & Ragged Staff**

(01865) 862329 *Signed from A420; Appleton Road; OX2 9QH* Extensive restaurant/pub dating from 16th c, contemporary décor in linked rooms with wood floors, good food from shared charcuterie and meze plates through pizzas and pub standards up, friendly efficient service, flagstoned bar with log fire, well kept Greene King ales and good wine choice, airy garden room, some events including live music; children welcome, decked terrace, fenced play area, nine new bedrooms, open all day. *(Richard Greaves, Jan and Roger Ferris)*

CUXHAM
SU6695
Half Moon (01491) 614151

4 miles from M40 J6; S on B4009, then right on B480 at Watlington; OX49 5NF Lovely 17th-c thatched restaurant/pub again under new management, good interesting food including cheaper set lunch menu (Tues-Fri), two main eating areas with beams, mirrors and prints, little fireplace in small tiled bar, Brakspears ales, ten wines in three glass sizes; background music; children and dogs welcome, good-sized garden, sleepy village surrounded by fine countryside, open all day Sat, closed Sun evening, Mon. *(Dr A J and Mrs Tompsett)*

DEDDINGTON
SP4631
⋆**Deddington Arms** (01869) 338364

Off A4260 (B4031) Banbury–Oxford; Horse Fair; OX15 0SH Beamed and timbered hotel with emphasis on sizeable contemporary back dining room doing very good food including set lunch deal, comfortable bar with mullioned windows, flagstones and log fire, good food here too, Adnams, Black Sheep and a guest, plenty of wines by the glass, attentive friendly service; unobtrusive background music; children welcome, attractive village with lots of antiques shops and good farmers' market fourth Sat of month, nice walks, comfortable chalet bedrooms around courtyard, good breakfast, open all day. *(John Taylor, Michael Sargent, George Atkinson)*

DEDDINGTON
SP4631
⋆**Unicorn** (01869) 338838

Market Place; OX15 0SE Welcoming refurbished 17th-c inn, beamed L-shaped bar, cosy snug with inglenook log fire, candlelit restaurant, good sensibly priced food (not Mon) from snacks and pub favourites to more imaginative dishes, well kept Hook Norton and Wells & Youngs, good choice of wines by the glass, proper coffee, friendly service, daily newspapers and pub games; background music; well behaved children welcome, cobbled courtyard leading to long walled back garden, good bedrooms and breakfast, open all day weekends (from 9am for good farmers' market – last Sat of month). *(Roxanne Chamberlain)*

DENCHWORTH
SU3891
Fox (01235) 868258

Off A338 or A417 N of Wantage; Hyde Road; OX12 0DX Comfortable 17th-c thatched and beamed pub in pretty village, enjoyable sensibly priced food including good Sun carvery (best to book), friendly efficient staff, well kept Greene King Old Speckled Hen, good choice of reasonably priced wines, two log fires and plush seats in low-ceilinged connecting areas, old prints and paintings, airy dining extension; children welcome, tables under umbrellas in pleasant sheltered garden. *(D C T and E A Frewer, Lesley and Peter Barrett)*

DORCHESTER
SU5794
Fleur de Lys (01865) 340502

High Street; OX10 7HH Former 16th-c coaching inn opposite abbey, traditional two-level interior with interesting old photographs of the pub, open fire and woodburner, some good creative cooking from chef/landlord (more pubby choices lunchtime – no food Sun evening), efficient service, Brakspears, St Austell Tribute and a guest (spring/summer beer festivals); children and dogs welcome, picnic-sets on front terrace and in back garden with play area, four bedrooms. *(John and Hazel Hayward)*

DORCHESTER
SU5794
George (01865) 340404

Just off A4074 Maidenhead–Oxford; High Street; OX10 7HH Handsome 15th-c timbered hotel in lovely village, roaring log fire and charming furnishings in smart beamed bar, enjoyable food from lunchtime baguettes up, ales such as Adnams, Brakspears and Wadworths, cheerful efficient service, restaurant; background music; children welcome, 17 bedrooms, open all day. *(John and Helen Rushton)*

EAST HENDRED
SU4588
Plough (01235) 833213

Off A417 E of Wantage; Orchard Lane; OX12 8JW 16th-c village pub under friendly new landlady, good choice of home-made food (all day weekends) from traditional choices to specials with an emphasis on fish/seafood, Greene King related ales, 11 wines by the glass including champagne, lofty-raftered main room with interesting farming memorabilia, side dining area; background music, sports TV; children and dogs welcome, nice enclosed back garden, attractive village, open all day weekends. *(Anon)*

EWELME   SU6491
Shepherds Hut (01491) 835661
Off B4009 about 6 miles SW of M40 junction 6; High St; OX10 6HQ Cleanly refurbished and extended village pub, beams and bare boards, woodburner, decent home-made food, Greene King ales; children welcome, terrace picnic-sets with steps up to lawn and play area. *(Daniel Wall)*

EXLADE STREET   SU6582
Highwayman (01491) 682020
Just off A4074 Reading–Wallingford; RG8 0UA Two beamed bar rooms, mainly 17th-c (parts older), with interesting rambling layout and mix of furniture, good food (not Sun evening) with plenty of variety, some pricy but also good value deals, friendly efficient service, well kept Fullers London Pride and Loddon, lots of wines by the glass, airy conservatory dining room; soft background music; children and dogs welcome, terrace and garden with fine views, open all day Fri, Sat, and till 8pm Sun, closed Mon. *(Richard Endacott, Mrs R Somers)*

FIFIELD   SP2318
Merrymouth (01993) 831652
A424 Burford–Stow; OX7 6HR Simple but comfortable stone inn dating to 13th c, L-shaped bar with bay-window seats, flagstones and low beams, some walls stripped back to old masonry, warm stove, quite dark in places, generous food from good baguettes to blackboard fish specials, well kept Hook Norton and a couple of other ales, decent choice of wines, friendly landlord and staff; background music; children and dogs welcome, tables on terrace and in back garden, nine stable-block bedrooms. *(Chris Glasson, Noel Grundy, Colin McKerrow, Neil and Anita Christopher)*

FILKINS   SP2304
Five Alls (01367) 860875
Signed off A361 Lechlade–Burford; GL7 3JQ Large 18th-c Cotswold stone inn under newish management; modern pub food (not Sun evening) from landlord chef such as lamb cooked in beer-soaked hay and english tapas, well kept Brakspears and a guest, beams, stripped stone and log fire, settees, armchairs and rugs on polished boards, flagstoned restaurant; background music; well behaved children and dogs welcome, tables on front and back terraces, aunt sally, four refurbished bedrooms, nice village, closed Mon, otherwise open all day. *(Anon)*

FINSTOCK   SP3616
★**Plough** (01993) 868333
Just off B4022 N of Witney; High Street; OX7 3BY Thatched low-beamed village pub nicely split up by partitions and alcoves, long rambling bar with leather sofas by massive stone inglenook, some unusual horsebrasses and historical documents to do with the pub, roomy dining room with candles and fresh flowers on stripped-pine tables, good food cooked by landlord (best to book), well kept Adnams Broadside and two guests, traditional cider, several wines by the glass and 20 malt whiskies, bar billiards, board games; children at discretion of licensees, dogs allowed in bar (pub has two cats), seats in neatly kept garden, aunt sally, woodland walks and along River Evenlode, open all day Sat, closed Sun evening, Mon and two weeks in Feb. *(Ian and Helen Stafford, Dr Nigel Bowles)*

FRILFORD   SU4497
Dog House (01865) 390830
Faringdon Road; OX13 6QJ Comfortable hotel with beamed open-plan log-fire bar, restaurant and conservatory, enjoyable good value traditional food from sandwiches to specials, Greene King ales, friendly attentive young staff; children welcome, garden with heated terrace, 20 bedrooms. *(Ian Herdman)*

FYFIELD   SU4298
★**White Hart** (01865) 390585
Main Road; off A420 8 miles SW of Oxford; OX13 5LW Grand medieval hall with soaring eaves, huge stone-flanked window embrasures and minstrels' gallery, contrasting cosy low-beamed side bar with large inglenook, fresh flowers and evening candles throughout, civilised friendly atmosphere and full of history, good imaginative modern food (best to book) cooked by licensee using home grown produce, Hook Norton, Loddon, Rebellion and Sharps Doom Bar (festivals May and Aug bank holidays), around 16 wines by the glass (including champagne), several malt whiskies and home-made summer elderflower pressé; background music; well behaved children welcome, elegant furniture under umbrellas on spacious heated terrace, lovely gardens, good Thames-side walks, open all day weekends, closed Mon. *(Dick and Madeleine Brown, Malcolm Ward, Ewan Shearer, Taff Thomas, Mrs J P Cleall)*

GODSTOW   SP4809
★**Trout** (01865) 510930
Off A40/A44 roundabout via Wolvercote; OX2 8PN Pretty 17th-c M&B dining pub in lovely riverside location (gets packed in fine weather), good bistro-style food all day (booking essential at busy times), four beamed linked rooms with contemporary furnishings, flagstones and bare boards, log fires in three huge hearths, Adnams and Timothy Taylors Landlord, several wines

by the glass; background music; children welcome till 7pm, plenty of terrace seats under big parasols (dogs allowed here), footbridge to island (may be closed), abbey ruins opposite, open all day. *(Linda Dutton, Martin and Pauline Jennings, Malcolm Greening, P and J Shapley, Simon Watkins)*

GORING   SU5980
⋆**Catherine Wheel** (01491) 872379
Station Road; RG8 9HB Smart and well run with nice informal atmosphere in two neat and cosily traditional bar areas, especially the more individual lower room with its low beams and big inglenook log fire, popular home-made food, Brakspears and several guest ales, good value wines, decent coffee, back restaurant (children welcome here), notable doors to lavatories; nice courtyard and garden behind, handy for Thames Path, attractive village, open all day. *(Rob Winstanley, N R White, the Didler)*

GOZZARD'S FORD   SU4698
⋆**Black Horse** (01865) 390530
Off B4017 NW of Abingdon; N of A415 by Marcham–Cothill Road; OX13 6JH Ancient traditional pub in tiny hamlet, good food (all day Sun) especially fish and seafood, well kept Greene King ales and nice wines, cheerful efficient service, carpeted beamed main bar partly divided by stout timbers and low steps, end woodburner, separate plainer public bar with darts and pool; nice garden, open all day. *(William Goodhart, John Pritchard, T M Griffiths, Karen Aplin)*

GREAT TEW   SP3929
⋆**Falkland Arms** (01608) 683653
The Green; off B4022 about 5 miles E of Chipping Norton; OX7 4DB Golden-stone thatched cottage in lovely village, unspoilt partly panelled bar with high-backed settles, diversity of stools and plain tables on flagstones or bare boards, one-, two- and three-handled mugs hanging from beam-and-boards ceiling, dim converted oil lamps, shutters for stone-mullioned latticed windows and open fire in fine inglenook, Wadworths and guests, Weston's cider, 14 malt whiskies, country wines, straightforward good value food, friendly service, snuff for sale, live folk Sun evening; children and dogs welcome, tables out at front and under parasols in back garden, small fair value bedrooms (no under-16s), open all day. *(David Heath, Mr and Mrs P R Thomas, R J Herd, David and Diane Young, the Didler, JJW, CMW and others)*

HAILEY   SU6485
⋆**King William IV** (01491) 681845
The Hailey near Ipsden, off A4074 or A4130 SE of Wallingford; OX10 6AD Fine old pub in lovely countryside, beamed bar with good sturdy furniture on tiles in front of big log fire, three other cosy seating areas opening off (children allowed in two),

enjoyable food including some interesting specials, Brakspears and guests tapped from the cask, friendly staff, miniature traffic lights on bar (red means bar closed, amber last orders, green open); dogs welcome, terrace and large garden enjoying wide-ranging peaceful views, may be red kites overhead, can tether your horse in the car park, good walking – Chilterns Way and Ridgeway National Trail – leave muddy boots in porch. *(Paul Humphreys, the Didler, Mrs Margo Finlay, Jörg Kasprowski, Linda Fawke, Brian Patterson)*

HAMPTON POYLE   SP5015
⋆**Bell** (01865) 376242
From A34 S, take Kidlington turn and village signed from roundabout; from A34 N, take Kidlington turn, then A4260 to roundabout, third turning signed for Superstore (Bicester Road); village signed from roundabout; OX5 2QD Front bar with three snug rooms, lots of big black and white photoprints, sturdy simple furnishings, scatter cushions and window seats, a stove flanked by bookshelves one end, large fireplace stacked with logs the other, biggish inner room made lively by open kitchen with its wood-fired pizza oven, a couple of fireside leather armchairs, spreading dining room with plenty of tables on pale limestone flagstones, inventive food, good choice of wines by the glass, Hook Norton Old Hooky and Oxfordshire Triple B, efficient uniformed staff, cheerful informal atmosphere; piped jazz; children welcome, dogs in bar, modern seats on sunny front terrace by quiet village lane, nine bedrooms, open all day. *(Rob Hubbard)*

HANWELL   SP4343
Moon & Sixpence (01295) 730544
Main Street; OX17 1HN Good food from pub favourites up in clean comfortable bar and dining area, friendly staff, well kept Hook Norton and decent wines by the glass; pretty garden, nice village setting. *(Martin and Sue Radcliffe)*

HARWELL   SU4988
⋆**Kingswell** (01235) 833043
A417; Reading Road; OX11 0LZ Substantial hotel with dependably good imaginative bar food as well as restaurant meals, plenty of choice, helpful staff; comfortable bedrooms. *(Anon)*

HENLEY   SU7682
Anchor (01491) 574753
Friday Street; RG9 1AH Old-fashioned and homely with two nicely lived-in front rooms, well kept Brakspears, food from lunchtime sandwiches up (not Sun or Mon evenings), simple back dining room; background music; dogs (the pub has its own) and well behaved children welcome, back terrace, open all day. *(the Didler, N R White)*

HENLEY SU7682
Angel on the Bridge (01491) 410678
Thames-side, by the bridge; RG9 1BH
Worth knowing for prime spot by Thames,
with nice waterside deck (plastic glasses for
this), small front bar with log fire, back bar
and adjacent restaurant, Brakspears ales,
good choice of wines by the glass, enjoyable
food from sandwiches and pubby things up,
friendly well organised staff; moorings for two
boats, open all day at least in summer. *(David
and Sue Atkinson, Dr D J and Mrs S C Walker)*

HENLEY SU7582
Argyll (01491) 573400
Market Place; RG9 2AA Smartly
comfortable and efficiently run by friendly
staff, enjoyable pub food all day from
sandwiches up, Greene King ales, decent
wines by the glass, soft lighting, dark
panelling; background music; nice terrace
garden behind, useful parking. *(Sue and Mike
Todd, Paul Humphreys and others)*

HOOK NORTON SP3534
☀ Gate Hangs High (01608) 737387
*N towards Sibford, at Banbury–Rollright
crossroads; OX15 5DF* Snug tucked-
away family-run pub, low-ceilinged bar
with traditional furniture on bare boards,
attractive inglenook, good reasonably
priced home-made food from bar snacks
up, well kept Hook Norton ales and a guest,
decent wines, friendly helpful service,
slightly chintzy side dining extension
(booking advised); background music; pretty
courtyard and country garden, four good
value bedrooms, good breakfast, quite near
Rollright Stones. *(Colin McKerrow, George
Atkinson, K H Frostick)*

HOOK NORTON SP3533
Pear Tree (01608) 737482
Scotland End; OX15 5NU Take-us-as-you-
find-us village pub with new landlady and
character locals, full range from nearby Hook
Norton brewery, kept well, country wines,
enjoyable straightforward food (not Sun
evening) from short menu, knocked-together
bar area with country-kitchen furniture, good
log fire; occasional live music, TV; children
and dogs welcome, attractive garden with
play area, bedrooms, open all day (some
updating planned). *(Gene and Kitty Rankin,
Jennifer and Patrick O'Dell, Barry Collett, Guy
Vowles, K H Frostick)*

HOOK NORTON SP3533
Sun (01608) 737570
High Street; OX15 5NH Beamed and
flagstoned back bar with big fireplace, cosy
carpeted back room leading into attractive
dining room, enjoyable food from bar snacks
to restaurant meals, good service, well kept
Hook Norton and several wines by the glass,
darts and dominoes; children and dogs
welcome, disabled facilities, tables out in

front and on back terrace, six bedrooms, good
breakfast. *(D and M T Ayres-Regan)*

HORNTON SP3945
Dun Cow (01295) 670524
West End; OX15 6DA Traditional 17th-c
thatch and ironstone village pub, friendly
and relaxed, with sensibly short choice of
enjoyable fresh food from good baguettes
up using local suppliers, ales such as Hook
Norton and Purity, a dozen wines by the glass;
children and dogs welcome, attractive small
garden, open all day weekends. *(Guy Vowles)*

KELMSCOTT SU2499
Plough (01367) 253543
*NW of Faringdon, off B4449 between
A417 and A4095; GL7 3HG* Refurbished
interior with ancient flagstones, stripped
stone and log fire, wide choice of good
food (more restauranty in evenings), beers
such as local Halfpenny, Wye Valley and
Wychwood, farm cider, helpful friendly staff;
children, dogs and boots welcome, tables out
in covered area and garden, lovely spot near
upper Thames (good moorings a few minutes
walk away), eight bedrooms, open all day
weekends. *(Meg and Colin Hamilton, Jennifer
and Patrick O'Dell, R K Phillips)*

KIDMORE END SU6979
New Inn (01189) 723115
*Chalkhouse Green Road; signed from
B481 in Sonning Common; RG4 9AU*
Attractive black and white pub by church;
beams and big fire, enjoyable freshly made
food including good value weekday set lunch,
pleasant restaurant; tables in large sheltered
garden with pond, bedrooms. *(Bruce and Trish
Field, Paul Humphreys, Tony and Gill Powell,
Richard Endacott)*

KINGHAM SP2523
Tollgate (01608) 658389
Church Street; OX7 6YA Former 18th-c
farmhouse, flagstoned and bare-boards
bar divided by big stone fireplace with
woodburner, enjoyable food (not Sun evening
or Mon) from pub standards to restaurant
dishes, good traditional Sun lunch, Hook
Norton and guests, back restaurant;
background music; children welcome, dogs
in bar, seats on sunny front terrace, nine
bedrooms, closed Mon till 4pm, otherwise
open all day. *(P and J Shapley)*

LAUNTON SP6022
Bull (01869) 240176
Just E of Bicester; OX26 5DQ Modernised
part-thatched 17th-c village pub, welcoming
and well managed, with enjoyable food (not
Sun evening) including OAP weekday lunch
deals, three well kept Greene King ales and a
guest, Sun quiz; background music; children
allowed away from bar, dogs on leads,
wheelchair access from car park, disabled
facilities, garden with terrace, open all
day. *(Bill Hawkins, Meg and Colin Hamilton)*

LEWKNOR   SU7197
★ **Olde Leathern Bottel**
(01844) 351482 *Under a mile from
M40 junction 6; off B4009 towards
Watlington; OX49 5TH* Popular and
friendly family-run place, two heavy
beamed bars with understated décor and
rustic furnishings, open fires, well kept
Brakspears and Marstons, several wines
by the glass, tasty pub food quickly served,
family room separated by standing timbers;
dogs welcome, splendid garden with plenty
of picnic-sets under parasols, play area
and boules, handy for walks on Chiltern
escarpment. *(Chris Smith, Mike Horgan,
Di Wright, Nigel and Sue Foster, Dr A J and
Mrs Tompsett)*

LONG WITTENHAM   SU5493
Plough (01865) 407738
High Street; OX14 4QH Friendly chatty
local with low beams, inglenook fires and
lots of brass, well kept ales including
Butcombe, good value wines by the glass,
wide choice of generous well priced food
(all day weekends), good friendly service,
dining room, games in public bar; dogs
welcome, Thames moorings at bottom
of nice spacious garden with aunt sally,
bedrooms. *(David Lamb)*

LOWER HEYFORD   SP4824
★ **Bell** (01869) 347176
Market Square; OX25 5NY Charming
creeper-clad building in small thatched
village square, good range of enjoyable fresh
food from baguettes to specials, well kept
interesting beers including one brewed
for them, good coffee, cheerful helpful
staff, uncluttered pleasantly refurbished
rooms around central beamed bar; children
welcome, disabled facilities, nice long walled
garden with aunt sally, Oxford Canal walks
nearby. *(Brian Glozier)*

MAIDENSGROVE   SU7288
Five Horseshoes (01491) 641282
*Off B480 and B481, W of village;
RG9 6EX* 16th-c dining pub set high in the
Chilterns, rambling bar with low ceiling and
log fire, enjoyable food including home-
smoked salmon and local game, weekday
set menu, friendly attentive service, well
kept Brakspears, good choice of wines by
the glass, airy conservatory restaurant;
children and dogs welcome, plenty of garden
tables and lovely views, wood-fired pizzas
on summer weekends (open all day then),
good walks, closed Mon evening. *(Tracey and
Stephen Groves, Sharon Oldham)*

MILTON   SP4535
★ **Black Boy** (01295) 722111
*Off Bloxham Road; the one near
Adderbury; OX15 4HH* 16th-c dining
pub recently taken over by Marco Pierre
White; good comfortable furnishings

alongside plenty of oak beams, exposed
stonework, flagstones and a lovely big
inglenook, enjoyable home-made food
(menu under review as we went to press),
good friendly service, Batemans and Greene
King; background music; children and dogs
welcome, narrow front terrace with heaters,
tables across road in spacious garden beyond
car park, swings and aunt sally, open all day
weekends. *(Anon)*

MINSTER LOVELL   SP3111
New Inn (01993) 708264
Burford Road; OX29 0RZ Reworked
and extended restauranty pub with good
food (not Sun evening) from lunchtime
sandwiches and light dishes up, good
choice of wines by the glass, Hook Norton
and Wadworths 6X, open fire, tremendous
views over pretty Windrush valley; children
welcome, tables on big heated terrace, lovely
setting. *(Paul and Sue Merrick)*

MURCOTT   SP5815
★ **Nut Tree** (01865) 331253
*Off B4027 NE of Oxford, via Islip and
Charlton-on-Otmoor; OX5 2RE*
Refurbished beamed and thatched 15th-c
dining pub, imaginative if not cheap food
using own produce including home-
reared pigs, Vale and two guests, carefully
chosen wines, neat friendly young staff;
background music; children welcome, dogs
allowed in bar, terrace and pretty garden,
unusual gargoyles on front wall (modelled
loosely on local characters), closed Sun
evening, Mon. *(Laurence Smith, Paul Baxter,
Dennis and Doreen Haward, David and
Sue Atkinson)*

NEWBRIDGE   SP4001
Rose Revived (01865) 300221
A415 7 miles S of Witney; OX29 7QD
Roomy comfortably reworked old pub,
beams and standing timbers in flagstoned
and carpeted bar, attractive prints and
photographs, central log-effect fire between
two dining areas, enjoyable food including
deals, good friendly service, well kept Greene
King ales; children welcome, lovely big
Thames-side lawn, prettily lit at night, play
area, moorings, seven bedrooms, open all
day. *(Ross Balaam)*

NORTH MORETON   SU5689
Bear at Home (01235) 811311
*Off A4130 Didcot–Wallingford; High
Street; OX11 9AT* Dating from the 15th c
with traditional beamed bar, cosy fireside
areas and dining part with stripped-pine
furniture, enjoyable reasonably priced food
from baguettes up, friendly service, Timothy
Taylors, a guest ale and a beer brewed for
the pub (July beer festival), Weston's cider,
several wines by the glass; attractive garden
overlooking cricket pitch, pretty village, open
all day Sat. *(Roy Hoing, Franklyn Roberts)*

OXFORD SP5007
Anchor (01865) 510282
Hayfield Road; OX2 6TT Chef/landlord
at this 1930s pub producing good quality
interesting food using local supplies, friendly
efficient service, good value house wine
and well kept Wadworths beers, period
furnishings, log fire, separate dining area;
near Bridge 240 (Aristotle) on Oxford Canal,
open all day. *(Dr Kevan Tucker)*

OXFORD SP5106
Chequers (01865) 727463
Off High Street; OX1 4DH Narrow 16th-c
courtyard pub with several areas on three
floors, interesting architectural features,
beams, panelling and stained glass, wide
choice of rotating ales and of well priced
pubby food (sausage specialities), quick
service, games room with balcony; children
welcome, disabled access, open all day (till
garden. *(George Atkinson, Simon Watkins)*

OXFORD SP5106
⋆ Eagle & Child (01865) 302925
St Giles; OX1 3LU Nicholson's pub with
two charmingly old-fashioned panelled
front rooms, well kept Brakspears, Hook
Norton and interesting guests, wide range
of food all day from sandwiches to Sun
roasts, stripped-brick back dining extension
and conservatory, Tolkien and C S Lewis
connections; games machine; children
allowed in back till 8pm. *(Roger and Donna
Huggins, Chris Glasson, Malcolm Greening, Revd R
P Tickle, the Didler, Stuart Doughty)*

OXFORD SP5106
Far From the Madding Crowd
(01865) 240900 *Friars Entry; OX1 2BY*
Busy open-plan free house, six good changing
ales, regular beer and cider festivals,
straightforward well priced food, quiz
and live music nights; children and dogs
welcome, disabled access, open all day (till
midnight Thurs-Sat). *(the Didler)*

OXFORD SP5007
Harcourt Arms (01865) 310630
Cranham Terrace; OX2 6DG Individual
1930s corner local with proper landlord,
character bare-boards interior with two log
fires, subtle lighting and modern artwork,
Fullers ales including London Porter,
good value snacks, board games, eclectic
background music (perhaps mongolian nose
flute), good mix of customers. *(the Didler)*

OXFORD SP5105
Head of the River (01865) 721600
*Folly Bridge; between St Aldates and
Christchurch Meadow; OX1 4LB* Civilised
well renovated pub by river, boats for hire
and nearby walks; spacious split-level
downstairs bar with dividing brick arches,
flagstones and bare boards, Fullers/Gales
beers, good choice of wines by the glass,
popular pubby food from sandwiches up, good

service, daily newspapers; background music;
tables on stepped heated waterside terrace,
12 bedrooms. *(Dave Braisted)*

OXFORD SP5106
⋆ Kings Arms (01865) 242369
Holywell Street; OX1 3SP Dating from the
early 17th c, convivial, relaxed and popular
with locals and students, quick helpful
service, well kept Wells & Youngs range
and four guests, fine choice of wines by the
glass, eating area with counter servery doing
good variety of reasonably priced food all
day, cosy comfortably worn-in side and back
rooms, interesting pictures and posters, daily
newspapers; a few tables outside, open from
10.30am. *(Mr and Mrs M J Girdler, Revd R P
Tickle, the Didler)*

OXFORD SP5106
Lamb & Flag (01865) 515787
St Giles/Banbury Road; OX1 3JS
Old pub owned by nearby college, modern
airy front room with light wood panelling and
big windows over street, more atmosphere in
back rooms with stripped stonework and low-
boarded ceilings, a beer by Palmers for the
pub (L&F Gold), Shepherd Neame Spitfire,
Skinners Betty Stogs and guests, some
lunchtime food including sandwiches and
tasty home-made pies. *(D W Stokes, the Didler)*

OXFORD SP5006
Old Bookbinders (01865) 553549
Victor Street; OX2 6BT Dark and mellow
local tucked away in Jericho area, friendly
and unpretentious, with old fittings and
lots of interesting bric-a-brac, Greene
King and good choice of guest ales (beer
festivals), enjoyable simple food, reasonable
prices, darts and shove-ha'penny, concealed
bookcase door to lavatories; closed
lunchtimes, open all day Fri-Sun. *(the Didler)*

OXFORD SP5106
⋆ Turf Tavern (01865) 243235
*Tavern Bath Place; via St Helen's
Passage, between Holywell Street and
New College Lane; OX1 3SU* Interesting
character pub hidden away behind high walls
with two small dark-beamed bars, always
packed, but run efficiently by knowledgeable
young staff; up to a dozen constantly
changing real ales (spring and summer
festivals), also Weston's Old Rosie cider and
winter mulled wine, enjoyable reasonably
priced food; children and dogs welcome,
three walled-in courtyards (one with own
bar), coal braziers to roast chestnuts or
toast marshmallows, open all day. *(Roger and
Donna Huggins, LM, Malcolm Greening, Tim and
Ann Newell, Barry Collett, the Didler and others)*

OXFORD SP5106
⋆ White Horse (01865) 728318
Broad Street; OX1 3BB Bustling
and studenty, squeezed between bits of
Blackwells bookshop, small narrow bar with

snug one-table raised back alcove, low beams and timbers, ochre ceiling, beautiful view of the Clarendon building and Sheldonian, good choice of ales including Brakspears, St Austell, Timothy Taylors and White Horse, friendly staff, good value simple lunchtime food (the few tables reserved for this); open all day. *(Paul Humphreys, Nigel and Jean Eames and others)*

PLAY HATCH   SU7477
Shoulder of Mutton (0118) 947 3908
W of Henley Road (A4155) roundabout; RG4 9QU Dining pub with low-ceilinged log-fire bar and large conservatory restaurant, good generous food including signature mutton dishes, well kept Greene King and guests such as Loddon, good service; children welcome, picnic-sets in carefully tended walled garden with well, closed Sun evening. *(Paul Humphreys and others)*

ROTHERFIELD PEPPARD   SU7081
Unicorn (01491) 628674
Colmore Lane; RG9 5LX Attractive country pub in Chilterns, run by same people as Little Angel, Henley, and Cherry Tree, Stoke Row; bustling bar with open fire, real ales and good wines, dining room with high-backed chairs around mix of tables on stripped boards, interesting modern food including lunchtime sandwiches and daily specials; seats out in front and in pretty back garden. *(Anon)*

SHENINGTON   SP3742
★ Bell (01295) 670274
Off A422 NW of Banbury; OX15 6NQ Good wholesome home cooking in hospitable 17th-c two-room pub, nice sandwiches too, well kept Flowers and Hook Norton, good wine choice, friendly informal service and long-serving licensees, heavy beams, some flagstones, stripped stone and pine panelling, two woodburners; children in eating areas and dogs in bar, picnic-sets out in front, charming quiet village with good walks, three simple bedrooms, generous breakfast, closed Sun evening, Mon. *(George Atkinson, Sir Nigel Foulkes)*

SHIPLAKE   SU7476
Flowing Spring (0118) 969 9878
A4155 towards Play Hatch and Reading; RG4 9RB Roadside pub built on bank (all on first floor with slight slope front to back), open fires in small two-room bar, various bric-a-brac, good value home-made food (not Sun or Mon evenings) from sandwiches, wraps and pizzas up, special diets catered for, Fullers ales, Aspall's cider, modern dining room with floor-to-ceiling windows, tables out on covered balcony, various events including astronomy nights and occasional live music; children and dogs welcome, lawned garden bordered by streams, summer marquee and barbecues, open all day. *(Paul Humphreys)*

SHIPLAKE   SU7678
Plowden Arms (0118) 9402794
Reading Road (A4155); RG9 4BX Old Brakspears pub doing well under new landlady, enjoyable home-made food and well kept beers, three linked areas and side dining room, beams and log fire; dogs welcome, floodlit garden (former village bowling green), handy for Thames walk, closed Sun evening, Mon. *(Ross Balaam)*

SHIPTON-UNDER-
WYCHWOOD   SP2717
★ Lamb (01993) 830465
High Street; off A361 to Burford; OX7 6DQ Mother and son team at this handsome stone inn, beamed bar with oak-panelled settle, farmhouse chairs and polished tables on wood-block flooring, stripped-stone walls, church candles and log fire, three changing beers, quite a few wines by the glass, well liked food and usually good friendly service, restaurant area; children welcome, dogs allowed in bar (there are two pub dogs), garden with modern furniture on terrace, themed bedrooms, open all day. *(R K Phillips, Simon Collett-Jones, Andy Dolan, Bernard Stradling, David Jackman and others)*

SHIPTON-UNDER-
WYCHWOOD   SP2717
Shaven Crown (01993) 830330
High Street (A361); OX7 6BA Ancient building with magnificent lofty medieval rafters and imposing double stairway in hotel part's hall, separate more down-to-earth back bar with booth seating, lovely log fires, good helpings of enjoyable food, Hook Norton and a couple of guests, several wines by the glass, helpful service, restaurant; background music; children and dogs welcome, peaceful courtyard with outside heaters, bowling green. *(Christine Murphy)*

SIBFORD GOWER   SP3537
★ Wykham Arms (01295) 788808
Signed off B4035 Banbury–Shipston on Stour; Temple Mill Road; OX15 5RX Cottagey 17th-c thatched and flagstoned dining pub, good food from light lunchtime menu up, friendly attentive staff, two well kept changing ales, plenty of wines by the glass, comfortable open-plan interior with low-beams and stripped stone, glass-covered well, inglenook; children and dogs welcome, country views from big garden, lovely manor house opposite, open all day Sun, closed Mon. *(John Levell, Edward Mirzoeff)*

SONNING COMMON   SU7080
Bird in Hand (0118) 9723230
B481; RG4 9JY Beamed village dining pub under newish licensees, warm friendly atmosphere, good value food from lunchtime sandwiches and baguettes up, well kept local ales, back restaurant; attractive garden behind with pretty

country views. *(Tim Hayward, Barry and Anne, Paul Humphreys)*

SOULDERN SP5231
Fox (01869) 345284

Off B4100; Fox Lane; OX27 7JW Pretty pub set in delightful village, comfortable open-plan beamed layout with settles and chairs around oak tables, big log fire, enjoyable fairly priced food including the Fox Sandwich (roast beef between two yorkshire puddings), well kept Hook Norton and two guests (beer festivals), good choice of wines by the glass, quiz nights; garden and terrace, aunt sally, four bedrooms. *(Andy and Jill Kassube, Andy Dolan)*

SOUTH NEWINGTON SP4033
Duck on the Pond (01295) 721166

A361; OX15 4JE Dining pub with tidy modern-rustic décor in small flagstoned bar and linked carpeted eating areas up a step, enjoyable food from wraps, melts and other light dishes to steak and family Sun lunch, changing ales such as Purity and Wye Valley, range of coffees, cheerful landlord and friendly young staff, woodburner; background music, no dogs; spacious grounds with tables on deck and lawn, aunt sally, pond with waterfowl, walk down to River Swere, open all day weekends. *(Lucien Perring, George Atkinson)*

SOUTH STOKE SU5983
Perch & Pike (01491) 872415

Off B4009 2 miles N of Goring; RG8 0JS Friendly family-run brick and flint pub just a field away from the Thames, cottagey low-beamed bar with open fire, well kept beer, enjoyable home-made food, sizeable timbered restaurant extension where children allowed; may be background music; tables on terrace and flower-bordered lawn, four bedrooms. *(Anon)*

STANDLAKE SP3902
Black Horse (01865) 300307

High Street; OX29 7RH Three-room pub with low ceilings and old brick fireplaces, wide choice of enjoyable food including bargain fixed-price menu and Sun carvery, well kept Hook Norton and three guests, decent wines; children and dogs welcome, garden picnic-sets, open all day weekends. *(Eddie Edwards, DHV, Miss Teresa Evans, Tania Harris)*

STANTON HARCOURT SP4105
Harcourt Arms (01865) 881931

Main Road; OX29 5RJ Roomy and cheerfully informal country dining pub, efficient friendly licensees, Adnams, Fullers and a guest, decent wines, good sensibly priced food, huge fireplaces in attractive simply furnished linked dining areas, beams and stripped-stone walls, flagstone or wood floors, local artwork; children welcome, dogs in bar, adjoining shop and post office. *(Helene Grygar)*

STANTON ST JOHN SP5709
Star (01865) 351277

Pub signed off B4027; village signed off A40 E of Oxford; OX33 1EX Pleasant old Wadworths pub tucked away at end of village; two small low-beamed rooms, one with ancient brick floor, other with close-set tables, up stairs to attractive flagstoned extension (on same level as car park) with old-fashioned dining chairs around dark oak or elm tables, good pewter collection behind bar, bookshelves either side of inglenook log fire, family conservatory; background music; dogs welcome (resident springer called Star), seats in walled garden growing own fruit and vegetables, play area, one bedroom, open all day Thurs-Sat, till 4pm Sun. *(Dave Braisted)*

STANTON ST JOHN SP5709
★ Talk House (01865) 351648

Middle Road/Wheatley Road (B4027 just outside village); OX33 1EX Attractive part-thatched dining pub; older part on left with steeply pitched rafters soaring above stripped-stone walls, mix of old dining chairs and big stripped tables, large rugs on flagstones; rest of building converted more recently but in similar style with massive beams, flagstones or stoneware tiles, and log fires below low mantelbeams, well liked food (all day weekends), three Fullers ales and several wines by the glass, friendly helpful staff, daily newspapers, live jazz first Fri of month; children welcome, dogs in bar, inner courtyard with teak tables and chairs, a few picnic-sets on side grass, affordable bedrooms, good breakfast, open all day from 10am, till 1.30am Fri, Sat. *(Franklyn Roberts, Brenda, V A C Turnbull, Martin and Pauline Jennings)*

STEEPLE ASTON SP4725
★ Red Lion (01869) 340225

Off A4260 12 miles N of Oxford; OX25 4RY Cheerful village pub with neatly kept beamed and partly panelled bar, antique settle and other good furnishings, well kept Hook Norton ales and good choice of wines by the glass, enjoyable food from shortish menu including pizzas served by obliging young staff, back conservatory-style dining extension; well behaved children welcome lunchtime and until 7pm, dogs in bar, suntrap front garden with lovely flowers and shrubs, parking may be awkward, closed Sun evening. *(Robert Watt, William Goodhart, Roy Hoing, Ian Herdman)*

STEVENTON SU4691
North Star (01235) 831309
Stocks Lane, The Causeway, central westward turn off B4017; OX13 6SG
Traditional village pub through yew tree gateway, tiled entrance corridor, main area with ancient high-backed settles around central table, well kept Greene King ales from side tap room, hatch service to another room with plain seating, a couple of tables and good coal fire, simple lunchtime food, friendly staff; background music, sports TV; tables on side grass. *(the Didler)*

STOKE LYNE SP5628
Peyton Arms (01869) 345285
From minor road off B4110 N of Bicester fork left into village; OX27 8SD
Beautifully situated and largely unspoilt stone-built pub, character landlord (Mick the Hat) and loyal regulars, very well kept Hook Norton from casks behind small corner bar in front snug, filled rolls, tiled floor, inglenook fire, memorabilia, games room with darts and pool; no children or dogs in bar; pleasant garden with aunt sally, open all day Sat, closed Sun evening and Mon. *(the Didler)*

STOKE ROW SU6884
Cherry Tree (01491) 680430
Off B481 at Highmoor; RG9 5QA
Recently refurbished pub/restaurant (same owners as Little Angel, Henley, and Unicorn in Rotherfield Peppard) with good up-to-date food, all-day Sun roasts, well kept Brakspears ales, ten wines by the glass, four linked rooms with stripped wood, heavy low beams and some flagstones; background music, TV in bar; well behaved children and dogs welcome, lots of tables in attractive garden, nearby walks, four good bedrooms in converted barn, open all day. *(Anon)*

STOKE ROW SU6884
⋆ Crooked Billet (01491) 681048
Nottwood Lane, off B491 N of Reading – OS Sheet 175 map ref 684844; RG9 5PU
Very nice place, but restaurant not pub (you can't just have a drink); charming rustic pub layout though, with heavy beams, flagstones, antique pubby furnishings and great inglenook log fire, crimsonly Victorian dining room; wide choice of well cooked interesting food using local produce (you can have just a starter), cheaper set lunches Mon-Fri, helpful friendly staff, Brakspears tapped from cask (no counter), good wines, relaxed homely atmosphere – like a french country restaurant; children truly welcome, weekly live music, big garden by Chilterns beechwoods, open all day weekends. *(Judi Sutherland)*

SWINFORD SP4308
Talbot (01865) 881348
B4044 just S of Eynsham; OX29 4BT
Roomy and comfortable 17th-c beamed pub,

well kept Arkells direct from the cask, good choice of wines and soft drinks, reasonably priced pubby food, friendly staff, long attractive bar with some stripped stone, cheerful log-effect gas fire, newspapers, some live jazz; may be background music; children and dogs welcome, garden with decked area overlooking Wharf Stream, pleasant walk along lovely stretch of the Thames towpath, moorings quite nearby, eight bedrooms. *(Meg and Colin Hamilton, Alistair and Joy Hamilton)*

SYDENHAM SP7201
Crown (01844) 351634
Off B4445 Chinnor–Thame; OX39 4NB
Friendly low-beamed pub in picturesque village, good food cooked by landlord, Brakspears, Fullers London Pride and a guest, nice wines, open fires in long narrow bar; children welcome, small garden, views of lovely church, open all day Sat, closed Sun evening, Mon. *(Mr and Mrs E Hughes)*

THAME SP7105
Cross Keys (01844) 212147
Park Street/East Street; OX9 3HP
One-bar 19th-c local with six ales including own good Thame beers (tasting trays available), nice atmosphere, no food; courtyard garden. *(Doug Kennedy)*

THAME SP7005
James Figg (01844) 260166
Cornmarket; OX9 2BL Friendly coaching inn, clean and well furnished, with four ales including Purity and Vale, Addlestone's and Aspall's ciders, ten wines by the glass, enjoyable, straightforward locally sourced food, open fire below portrait of James Figg (local 18th-c boxer), converted stables with own bar for music/functions; busier and noisier evenings; children and dogs welcome, back garden, open all day. *(Richard and Liz Thorne, Tim and Ann Newell)*

THRUPP SP4815
⋆ Boat (01865) 374279
Brown sign to pub off A4260 just N of Kidlington; OX5 1JY Attractive 16th-c stone building, low ceilings, old coal stove, bare boards or ancient tiles, good home-made food from snacks to more upscale dishes, own bread and ice-creams too, friendly landlord and efficient service, Greene King ales, decent wine, restaurant; gets busy in summer; children and dogs welcome, fenced garden behind with plenty of tables, nearby Oxford Canal moorings. *(Ian B, Meg and Colin Hamilton, Phil Lowther)*

TOWERSEY SP7304
Three Horseshoes (01844) 212322
Chinnor Road; OX9 3QY Popular unpretentious country local with well kept ales such as St Austell Tribute and Sharps Doom Bar, decent pubby food from baguettes up, old-fashioned furnishings

in two flagstoned low-beamed bars, good log fire, darts, small restaurant, live music particularly folk; children allowed lunchtime, biggish garden with fruit trees and play area. *(Jenny and Brian Seller, Doug Kennedy)*

UPTON   SU5186
George & Dragon (01235) 850723
A417 Harwell–Blewbury; OX11 9JJ
Welcoming little pub with enjoyable reasonably priced uncomplicated food, Greene King Morland, small end dining area, good service even when very busy; big garden. *(Tim Maddison)*

WANTAGE   SU3988
Lamb (01235) 766768
Mill Street, past square and Bell; down hill then bend to left; OX12 9AB Popular 17th-c thatched pub with low beams, log fire and cosy corners, well kept Fullers London Pride and Greene King, good straightforward food at reasonable prices; children welcome, disabled facilities, garden tables, open all day. *(D C T and E A Frewer)*

WANTAGE   SU3987
★ **Royal Oak** (01235) 763129
Newbury Street; OX12 8DF Popular two-bar corner local with a dozen well kept ales including Wadworths and West Berkshire, good choice of ciders and perries too, friendly knowledgeable landlord, lots of pump clips, old ship photographs, darts; bedrooms, closed weekday lunchtimes. *(the Didler)*

WANTAGE   SU3987
Shoulder of Mutton 07870 577742
Wallingford Street; OX12 8AX Friendly Victorian pub renovated by enthusiastic landlord keeping character in bar, dining lounge and snug, ten well kept changing mainly local ales including own Betjeman brews (beer festivals), good cider/perry choice, vegetarian food, regular folk music and other events (even belly dancing classes); children welcome, dogs allowed in bar, back terrace with hop-covered pergola, four new bedrooms, open all day till midnight. *(the Didler)*

WEST HANNEY   SU4092
★ **Plough** (01235) 868674
Just off A338 N of Wantage; Church Street; OX12 0LN Thatched 16th-c village pub with simply furnished bar, horsebrasses on beams, old photos, wheelbacks and bar stools, log fire, Loddon, Sharps, Vale and West Berkshire, two farm ciders, generous home-made pubby food (not Sun evening), separate dining room, three cats; children and dogs welcome, back terrace overlooking walled garden, aunt sally and trampoline, good walks from the door, open all day Sat, till 7pm Sun. *(D C T and E A Frewer, Dennis and Doreen Haward, Evelyn and Derek Walter)*

WEST HENDRED   SU4489
Hare (01235) 833249
A417 Reading Road, outside village; OX12 8RH Big welcoming open-plan village pub popular for its generous mainly traditional food (not Sun evening), Greene King and a guest, efficient friendly staff, low-ceilinged main bar with bare boards and terracotta tiles, timber dividers, comfortable parquet-floor dining area; background music; children welcome, colonnaded verandah, picnic-sets in side garden with covered deck, open all day. *(D C T and E A Frewer, R K Phillips)*

WESTON-ON-THE-GREEN   SP5318
Ben Jonson (01869) 351153
B430 near M40 junction 9; OX25 3RA Ancient stone-and-thatch country pub, beamed bar with oak furniture, restaurant, open log fire and inglenook woodburner, well kept changing ales such as Brakspears, Hook Norton and Wychwood, good choice of wines including local Brightwell, enjoyable food all day using local produce (some home grown), good helpful service; children and dogs welcome, picnic-sets out in front, rustic smokers' shelter. *(Laura Jones)*

WESTON-ON-THE-GREEN   SP5318
Chequers (01869) 351743
Handy for M40 junction 9, via A34; Northampton Road (B430); OX25 3QH Extended thatched village pub with three homely areas off large semicircular raftered bar, fair choice of food from traditional favourites to some unusual things like home-cured maple salmon, well kept Fullers and a guest, nice wines by the glass; children welcome, tables under parasols in attractive garden, open all day Sat, till 6pm Sun. *(Martin and Alison Stainsby)*

WHITCHURCH   SU6377
Greyhound (0118) 984 4800
High Street, just over toll bridge from Pangbourne; RG8 7EL Pretty former ferryman's cottage run by welcoming enthusiastic licensees, cosy low-beamed bar with fire, well kept ales such as Black Sheep and Shepherd Neame Spitfire, good value tasty pub food; small sheltered back garden, attractive village on Thames Path, open all day weekends. *(N R White, Ross Balaam, Paul Humphreys)*

WHITCHURCH HILL   SU6378
Sun (01189) 842260
Hill Bottom; signed from B471; RG8 7PG Friendly unassuming brick-built pub in sleepy village, L-shaped bar with carpet and bare boards, white textured walls, dark woodwork, plush chairs and wall benches, enjoyable reasonably priced food including vegetarian choices, Brakspears, Hook Norton Ringwood and a guest; children and dogs welcome, couple of picnic-sets out at front,

small side terrace, back lawn with play area, open all day Fri-Sun. *(Phil Bryant, Richard Endacott, Paul Humphreys)*

WITNEY SP3509
Angel (01993) 703238
Market Square; OX28 6AL Wide choice of well priced food from good sandwiches up in unpretentious 17th-c town local, real ales such as Brakspears, Hook Norton, Marstons and Wells & Youngs Bombardier, quick friendly service even when packed, daily newspapers, hot coal fire; background music, big-screen sports TV, pool room; lovely hanging baskets, smokers' shelter, parking nearby can be difficult. *(George Atkinson)*

WITNEY SP3509
Fleece (01993) 892270
Church Green; OX28 4AZ Smart civilised town pub on green, popular for its wide choice of good often imaginative food from sandwiches and deli boards up, friendly attentive service, Greene King ales, leather armchairs on wood floors, daily newspapers, restaurant; background music; children welcome, tables out at front, ten affordable bedrooms, open all day. *(R K Phillips, J A Snell)*

WITNEY SP3510
∗Three Horseshoes (01993) 703086
Corn Street, junction with Holloway Road; OX28 6BS Welcoming and accommodating staff in attractive 16th-c modernised stone-built pub, wide choice of good home-made food from pubby lunchtime things to more imaginative restaurant dishes, Wychwood Hobgoblin and two guests, decent house wines, heavy beams, flagstones, well polished comfortable old furniture, log fires, separate back dining room; sunny terrace, open all day. *(Sally Simon, Peter Lee, Ian Herdman)*

WOLVERCOTE SP4909
Plough (01865) 556969
First Turn/Wolvercote Green; OX2 8AH Comfortably well worn-in pubby linked areas, friendly helpful service, bustling atmosphere, armchairs and Victorian-style carpeted bays in main lounge, well kept Greene King ales, farm cider, decent wines, enjoyable good value usual food in flagstoned former stables dining room and library (children allowed here), traditional snug, woodburner; picnic-sets on front decking looking over rough meadow to canal and woods, open all day weekends. *(Paul Humphreys)*

WOODSTOCK SP4417
Black Prince (01993) 811530
Manor Road (A44 N); OX20 1XJ Old pub with one modernised low-ceilinged bar, timbers and stripped stone, suit of armour, log fire one end, good value home-made food from sandwiches to specials, four well kept ales including St Austell, friendly service, some live music; outside lavatories; children

and dogs welcome, tables in attractive garden by small River Gylme, nearby right of way into Blenheim parkland, open all day in summer. *(Geoff Clifford, Andy and Jill Kassube)*

WOODSTOCK SP4416
Star (01993) 811373
Market Place; OX20 1TA Sizeable old inn with light and airy front part, big windows, high ceiling and bare boards, tall black chairs around high tables, lower ceilinged area with pale stripped stone and comfortable seats on mulberry carpet, back part has a profusion of beams, coal-effect stove and unusually wide antique settle; interesting food (cheaper lunchtime), good variety of wines by the glass, Courage Directors and three Wells & Youngs ales, proficient service; background music; sheltered flagstoned courtyard behind with stylish metal furniture and one or two cask tables, more seats in front, bedrooms, open all day from 8am. *(Anon)*

WOODSTOCK SP4416
Woodstock Arms (01993) 811251
Market Street; OX20 1SX Welcoming 16th-c heavy-beamed stripped-stone pub, lively and stylishly modernised, with prompt helpful service by young staff, enjoyable food from shortish menu including good sandwiches, well kept Greene King IPA and Old Speckled Hen, good wine choice, daily newspapers, log-effect gas fire in splendid stone fireplace, long narrow bar, end eating area; background music; dogs welcome, tables out in attractive yard, bedrooms, open all day. *(Tony and Glenys Dyer, John and Sarah Webb)*

WOOLSTONE SU2987
White Horse (01367) 820726
Off B4507; SN7 7QL Appealing old partly thatched pub with Victorian gables and latticed windows, plush furnishings, spacious beamed and part-panelled bar, two big open fires, Arkells ales, enjoyable food from lunchtime sandwiches up served promptly by friendly staff, restaurant; well behaved children allowed, plenty of seats in front and back gardens, secluded interesting village handy for White Horse and Ridgeway, six bedrooms, open all day. *(David Knowles, Jim and Frances Gowers, Jennifer and Patrick O'Dell, Guy Vowles)*

WYTHAM SP4708
White Hart (01865) 244372
Off A34 Oxford ring Road; OX2 8QA Refurbished 15th-c country pub, several areas with log fires including converted stables, some settles, handsome panelling and flagstones, fairly traditional sensibly priced food, cosy bar with well kept Wadworths ales and lots of wines by the glass, conservatory; children and dogs welcome, courtyard tables, unspoilt preserved village, open all day. *(Franklyn Roberts)*

Shropshire

A couple of good new entries here this year are the Jolly Frog in Leintwardine (smart bistro restaurant specialising in fish dishes but with a cheerful, friendly bar, too) and the Navigation at Maesbury Marsh (well run canalside pub with a cosy bar, friendly landlords, local beers and inventive food). Other pubs doing well include the Old Castle in Bridgnorth (reasonably priced food and ales in particularly nice pub), Royal Oak in Cardington (lovely old place in attractive rural spot), Fox at Chetwynd Aston (civilised Brunning & Price dining pub with interesting and enjoyable food and attentive staff), and Church Inn in Ludlow (lively town pub with genuine character, ten real ales and good value food). Our Shropshire Dining Pub 2013 is the Fox at Chetwynd Aston.

BRIDGNORTH   SO7192   Map 4
Old Castle £
West Castle Street; WV16 4AB

Traditional town pub, relaxed and friendly, with well kept ales and good-sized suntrap terrace

It's so nice to hear from a reader that this pretty little town pub consisting of two knocked-together cottages (you can really see this in its external appearance) is still 'bustling on market day [Saturday] with families and all sorts'. The low-beamed open-plan bar is properly pubby and genuinely characterful with tiles and bare boards, cushioned wall banquettes and settles around cast-iron-framed tables. Bar stools are arranged alongside the counter where the friendly landlord and his cheery staff serve well kept Hobsons Town Crier, Marstons EPA, Sharps Doom Bar and a guest such as Davenports Englands Glory on handpump. A back conservatory extension has darts and pool; background music and big-screen TV for sports events. A big plus here is the sunny back terrace, with shrub borders, big pots of flowers and children's playthings. The decking at the far end gives an elevated view over the west side of town. Do take a walk up the street to see the ruined castle, best viewed before rather than after a drink: its 20-metre Norman tower tilts at such an extraordinary angle that it makes the leaning tower of Pisa look like a model of rectitude.

Generous helpings of good value pubby food include sandwiches and baguettes, burgers, salads, spicy meatballs on linguine, pea and asparagus risotto, fishcakes, chicken breast stuffed with cream cheese and watercress, fish pie, steak in ale pie, chilli, scampi, steaks, and puddings such as fruits of the forest pie, lemon meringue cake and rhubarb and custard cheesecake; Sunday carvery. *Benchmark main dish: lasagne £7.50. Two-course evening meal £12.50.*

Punch ~ Tenants Bryn Charles Masterman and Kerry Senior ~ Real ale ~ Bar food (12-3, 6.30-8.30; not Sun evening except bank holidays) ~ (01746) 711420 ~ Children welcome ~ Dogs welcome ~ Open 11.30-11 ~ www.oldcastlebridgnorth.co.uk *Recommended by George Atkinson, Chris and Angela Buckell, Ian Herdman, Jim and Frances Gowers*

CARDINGTON
SO5095   Map 4

Royal Oak

Village signposted off B4371 Church Stretton–Much Wenlock, pub behind church; also reached via narrow lanes from A49; SY6 7JZ

Lovely rural position, heaps of character inside, too

Dating from the 15th c, this ancient place (it's reputedly Shropshire's oldest continuously licensed pub) is packed with character and historical atmosphere. Gently frayed around the edges, its rambling low-beamed bar has a roaring winter log fire, a cauldron, black kettle and pewter jugs in its vast inglenook fireplace, the aged standing timbers of a knocked-through wall, and red and green tapestry seats solidly capped in elm; shove-ha'penny and dominoes; Hobsons Best, Marstons Pedigree and a couple of guests such as Three Tuns XXX and Salopian Hop Twister are on handpump. A comfortable dining area has exposed old beams and studwork. This is glorious country for walks, such as the one to the summit of Caer Caradoc a couple of miles to the west (ask for directions at the pub), and the front courtyard makes the most of its beautiful position.

 Seasonal bar food includes lunchtime baguettes and ploughman's, creamy garlic mushroom crostini, grilled goats cheese, steak and mushroom pie, lamb shank with mint gravy, battered cod, grilled trout with almonds, pork loin and black pudding with creamy leek and bacon sauce, vegetable tagine with chickpeas, and game pie. *Benchmark main dish: fidget pie £10.65. Two-course evening meal £17.00.*

Free house ~ Licensees Steve and Eira Oldham ~ Real ale ~ Bar food (12-2(2.30 Sun), 6.30(7 Sun)-9) ~ Restaurant ~ (01694) 771266 ~ Children welcome ~ Dogs allowed in bar ~ Open 12-2.30, 6.30-11(midnight Fri, Sat); 12-3.30; 7-midnight Sun; closed Mon ~ www.at-the-oak.com *Recommended by Mike Proctor, Tracey and Stephen Groves, Mark O'Sullivan*

CHETWYND ASTON
SJ7517   Map 7

Fox 🍴 � ⬛

Village signposted off A41 and A518 just S of Newport; TF10 9LQ
Shropshire Dining Pub of the Year

Civilised dining pub with generous helpings of food and a fine array of drinks served by ever-attentive staff

The style of this handsome 1920s Brunning & Price pub, done up a few years ago, will be familiar to anyone who has visited other outposts in this successful chain. Though big and usually busy, it's intimate and friendly, with a welcoming atmosphere helped along by kindly, capable staff. A series of linked areas, one with a broad arched ceiling, has plenty of tables in all shapes and sizes, some quite elegant, and a loosely matching diversity of comfortable chairs, all laid out in a way that's fine for eating but serves equally well for just drinking and chatting. There are masses of attractive prints, three open fires and a few oriental rugs on polished parquet, boards or attractive floor tiling; big windows and careful lighting contribute to the relaxed atmosphere; board games. The handsome bar counter, with a decent complement of bar stools, serves an excellent changing range of about 18 wines by the glass and 50 malt whiskies; Phoenix Brunning & Price Original, Three Tuns XXX, Woods Shropshire Lad and three guests from brewers such as Newmans, Slaters and Titanic are on handpump. Although highchairs are provided, pushchairs and baby buggies are not allowed; good disabled access. The spreading garden is quite lovely, with a sunny terrace, picnic-sets tucked into the shade of mature trees and extensive views across quiet country fields.

As well as sandwiches, well liked food served in generous helpings from a changing menu, might include carrot and coriander soup, grilled mackerel with sundried tomato and basil crème fraîche, grilled trout fillet with confit garlic and sorrel and hazelnut risotto, beef stir fry, mushroom cannelloni, kedgeree, beer-braised ox cheek with parsley and horseradish dumplings, lambs liver and onions, pork belly with apple and sage sauce, battered haddock, and puddings such as chocolate brownie, passion fruit cheesecake, and ginger and rhubarb steamed pudding. *Benchmark main dish: lemon and thyme chicken breast on lentils braised with bacon, leek and stilton cream £11.75. Two-course evening meal £17.80.*

Brunning & Price ~ Manager Samantha Forrest ~ Real ale ~ Bar food (12-10(9.30 Sun)) ~ (01952) 815940 ~ Children welcome ~ Dogs allowed in bar ~ Open 12-11(10.30 Sun) ~ www.fox-newport.co.uk *Recommended by C A Bryson, Bruce and Sharon Eden, Steve Whalley, Henry Pursehouse-Tranter, M G Hart, Brian and Anna Marsden, Ian Herdman*

CLUN
SO3080   Map 6
White Horse ● £
The Square; SY7 8JA

Cheery local with seven real ales and good value traditional food

Drinkers and diners rub along nicely in the cheery low-beamed front bar of this refurbished 18th-c pub. Cosy and friendly, it's warmed in winter by a inglenook woodburning stove. From the bar, a door leads into a separate little dining room with a rare plank and muntin screen. In the games room at the back you'll find a TV, games machine, darts, pool, juke box and board games. As well as two or three of their own Clun beers that are brewed behind the pub, attentive staff serve four or five changing guests, usually local, from brewers such as Hobsons, Salopian, Three Tuns and Wye Valley, as well as Weston's farm cider and a good range of bottled beers; small garden.

Traditional, very good value pubby bar food, served in generous helpings, includes sandwiches and baguettes, ploughman's, battered brie, smoked salmon with prawns and horseradish cream, several salads including scampi and mackerel, macaroni cheese, mushroom stroganoff, lamb cutlets, beer-battered haddock, sausage and mash, and cajun chicken. *Benchmark main dish: suet pudding £9.25. Two-course evening meal £12.50.*

Own brew ~ Licensee Jack Limond ~ Real ale ~ Bar food (12-2(12.30-2.30 Sun), 6.30-8.30) ~ No credit cards ~ (01588) 640305 ~ Children welcome ~ Dogs allowed in bar and bedrooms ~ Live music Fri fortnightly ~ Open 12-12 ~ Bedrooms: £35S/£60S ~ www.whi-clun.co.uk *Recommended by Guy Vowles, Alan and Eve Harding, MLR, Brian and Anna Marsden*

LEINTWARDINE
SO4175 Map 6

Jolly Frog ♨ ⚕

A4113 Ludlow–Knighton, E edge of village; The Toddings; SY7 0LX

Friendly, cheerful bar and good bistro restaurant specialising in fish

The front bar has just a few tables on its light oak boards, with red- or blue-check american-cloth covers, and red leatherette dining chairs with lion's head knobs. Besides good wines by the glass, including two champagnes and a prosecco, or in 50-cl pitchers, they have Hobsons Town Crier and a beer brewed for the pub on handpump, and do good coffees; unobtrusive well reproduced jazz. There's a woodburning stove at each end, and light-heartedly frenchified décor – kepis and other hats hanging from stripped beams, street signs from Paris, a metro map. The dining room, up a few steps, is similarly decorated, and staff are friendly and professional. There are one or two tables under a sail canopy in an inner courtyard, and more wicker chairs and tables on an upper deck with wide and peaceful pastoral views.

They bake good breads here and use only the best seasonal produce: sandwiches, twice-baked blue cheese and chive soufflé, chicken liver parfait with spiced apple and raisin chutney, pizzas from their woodburning oven, local sausages with wholegrain mustard mash and caramelised onion gravy, butternut squash ravioli with sage butter sauce, beer-battered hake with pea purée, chicken chasseur with tarragon mash, spiced braised belly pork with confit onions and braising juices, skate wing in brown butter and capers, duck breast with celeriac rösti and dark cherry and chocolate sauce, and puddings like dark chocolate and beetroot cake, and rhubarb and almond crumble with home-made vanilla ice-cream; they also offer a two- or three-course set menu and a bistro menu. *Benchmark main dish: daily fresh fish such as sole in Pernod and garlic £17.00. Two-course evening meal £24.00.*

Free house ~ Licensee Kelvin Woodfield ~ Real ale ~ Bar food (12-2, 6-9; not Mon) ~ Restaurant ~ (01547) 540298 ~ Children welcome ~ Open 12-3, 6-11; closed Mon ~ www.jollyfrogpub.com *Recommended by Roger White*

LUDLOW
SO5174 Map 4

Church Inn ⬤ £

Church Street, behind Butter Cross; SY8 1AW

Characterful town-centre inn with great range of real ales and good value food

The cheery landlord of this lively pub stocks an impressive ten real ales on handpump, including Hobsons Town Crier and Mild, Ludlow Boiling Well and Gold, and Wye Valley Bitter, with guests from brewers such as Clun, Marstons, Sarah Hughes and Three Tuns. They also serve several malt whiskies and mulled cider. Bustling with happy customers, the ground floor is divided into three appealingly decorated areas, with hops hanging from heavy beams, comfortable banquettes in cosy alcoves off the island counter (part of it is a pulpit), and pews and stripped stonework from the nearby church. There are displays of old photographic equipment, plants on window sills and church prints in the side room. A long central area has a fine stone fireplace (good winter fires), and there are some old black and white photos of the town; daily papers and background music. The civilised upstairs lounge bar has good views of the church and surrounding countryside, vaulted ceilings, a display case of glass, china and old bottles, and musical instruments on the walls. The bedrooms are simple but comfortable, breakfasts are good, and one reader told us their dog was welcomed with dog treats and a bowl of water.

🍴 Straightforward but wholesome and tasty food includes lunchtime sandwiches, battered brie wedges with cranberry sauce, cajun chicken, ploughman's, their speciality home-made pies, scampi, battered cod, ham, egg and chips, vegetable lasagne, pork pie platter, steaks, and puddings such as apple pie and lemon meringue pie. *Benchmark main dish: home-made pie £7.95. Two-course evening meal £14.00.*

Free house ~ Licensee Graham Willson-Lloyd ~ Real ale ~ Bar food (12-2.30, 6.30-9 (8.30 Sun)) ~ (01584) 872174 ~ Children welcome ~ Dogs allowed in bar and bedrooms ~ Open 10(11 Sun)-midnight (1am Fri, Sat) ~ Bedrooms: £50B/£80B ~ www.thechurchinn.com *Recommended by P Dawn, Pete Coxon, P J and R D Greaves, Alan and Eve Harding, Brian and Anna Marsden, Tracey and Stephen Groves, MLR, Derek and Sylvia Stephenson, Theocsbrian, Michelle and Graeme Voss, Edward Leetham*

MAESBURY MARSH

SJ3125 Map 6

Navigation

Follow Maesbury Road off A483 S of Oswestry; by canal bridge; SY10 8JB

Versatile and friendly canalside pub with cosy bar and enjoyable food in a choice of dining areas

Dozens of watches, wrist and pocket, hang from the beams of the left-hand quarry-tiled bar, which has squishy brown leather sofas by the traditional black range blazing in its big red fireplace, and little upholstered cask seats around three small tables. A couple of steps lead up to a carpeted area beyond a balustrade, with dining chairs around a few more tables, and a piano; off to the left is a further dining room with cheerful prints. The main beamed dining room, with some stripped stone, is beyond another small bar with a coal fire – and an amazing row of cushioned carved choir stalls complete with misericord seats. They have Stonehouse Station and a guest beer on handpump, ten wines by the glass and Weston's cider; very quiet background music. The terrace has picnic-table sets under cocktail parasols, safely fenced off from a restored stretch of the Montgomery Canal.

🍴 Using local, seasonal produce and free-range chicken and pork, the good, interesting food might include lunchtime sandwiches, chicken and pistachio terrine with butternut squash jam, tiger prawns with a thai green curry sauce, a meze platter, chestnut mushroom risotto with truffle oil, ham with parsley sauce and sautéed potatoes, beef burger with hand-cut chips, a fish dish and a pie of the day, rabbit ragout with pasta, pork shank in milanese sauce with apple and potato rösti, a trio of beef (steak and kidney suet pudding, strips of fillet steak with wild mushroom gratin, and slow-braised sticky strip of silverside with shallot purée), and puddings such as chocolate and orange panna cotta with orange fruit compote and jellied raspberry, and vodka terrine with lime syrup and lemon meringue ice-cream; they also offer a very good value three-course set menu, an early-bird evening deal and fish and chips on Friday. *Benchmark main dish: local sausages with a bubble and squeak cake and onion gravy £9.75. Two-course evening meal £17.50.*

Free house ~ Licensees Brent Ellis and Mark Baggett ~ Real ale ~ Bar food (12-2, 6-8.30; not Sun evening or Mon, Tues lunchtime) ~ Restaurant ~ (01691) 672958 ~ Well behaved children welcome ~ Dogs allowed in bar ~ folk open night last Fri of month ~ Open 12-2.30, 6-11; 12-6 Sun; closed Sun evening and Mon, Tues lunchtime ~ www.thenavigation.co.uk *Recommended by Nigel Hemsted, Tony Hobden, Stephen Thomas, Julia and Richard Tredgett*

MUCH WENLOCK

SO6299   Map 4

George & Dragon 🍺 £

High Street (A458); TF13 6AA

Bustling and atmospheric with plenty to look at, reasonably priced food and good beer selection; usefully open all day

In the centre of a charming town, this is a friendly and accommodating old place that's popular with both locals and visitors. It's filled with a fascinating collection of pub paraphernalia such as old brewery and cigarette advertisements, bottle labels, beer trays and George and the Dragon pictures, as well as a 200 jugs hanging from the beams. The front door takes you straight into a beamed and quarry-tiled room with wooden chairs and tables and antique settles all the way around the walls, and there are a couple of open fires in attractive Victorian fireplaces. At the back is a timbered dining room. As well as a wide choice of wines by the glass and a dozen decent malts, they keep five real ales like Black Sheep, Greene King Abbot, St Austell Tribute, Sharps Doom Bar, Wadworths 6X and Woodfordes Wherry on handpump; background music, dominoes, cards, board games and daily newspapers. There's a pay and display car park behind the pub.

🍴 Good value lunchtime food includes sandwiches, local faggots, a pie of the day, home-baked ham with free-range eggs, battered cod, daily specials such as lamb braised with rosemary, garlic and tomato and beef wellington; a few additional evening dishes such as duck breast with black cherry and port sauce; also various special offers including pie and a pint on Tuesday for £7.95 and two meals for £10 on Thursdays. *Benchmark main dish: beef in ale pie £7.95. Two-course evening meal £12.50.*

Punch ~ Tenant James Scott ~ Real ale ~ Bar food (12-2.30, 6-9 (not Weds evening all year or Sun evening Oct-June)) ~ Restaurant ~ (01952) 727312 ~ Children welcome ~ Dogs allowed in bar ~ Open 12-11 *Recommended by Reg Fowle, Helen Rickwood, Tim Maddison, Peter Salmon, Pat and Tony Martin, Pete Yearsley, Tracey and Stephen Groves, Mike Proctor*

SHREWSBURY

SJ4812   Map 6

Armoury 🍴 🍷 🍺

Victoria Quay, Victoria Avenue; SY1 1HH

Vibrant riverside warehouse, interestingly converted, enthusiastic young staff, good food all day, excellent drinks selection

An impressively long run of big arched windows at this warehouse conversion gives views across the broad River Severn. Light and fresh, the spacious open-plan interior combines eclectic décor with nicely intimate furniture settings, creating a personal feel despite the vast space. Mixed wood tables and chairs are grouped on stripped-wood floors, huge brick walls display floor-to-ceiling books or masses of old prints mounted edge to edge, and there's a grand stone fireplace at one end. Colonial-style fans whirr away on the ceilings, which are supported by occasional green-painted columns, and small wall-mounted glass cabinets display smoking pipes. The long bar counter has a terrific choice of drinks including Bathams Best, Phoenix Brunning & Price, Salopian Shropshire Gold, Three Tuns XXX, Woods Shropshire Lad and four guests from brewers such as Goffs, Hobsons, Purple Moose and Six Bells on handpump, a great wine list (with 16 by the glass), around 50 malt whiskies, a dozen gins, lots of rums and vodkas, a variety of brandies, some unusual liqueurs and a good range of soft drinks. Hanging baskets and smart coach lights decorate the massive red brick frontage. The crowd is lively and there may be queues at the weekend. The pub doesn't have its own parking, but there are plenty of places nearby.

As well as interesting sandwiches, tempting food, from a daily-changing menu, could include ploughman's, mushrooms in creamy garlic sauce, beetroot and vodka cured salmon, beef, pepper and chilli salad, smoked haddock and salmon fishcakes, braised shoulder of lamb, moroccan spiced lamb with apricot and date couscous, fried bass with spiced mussel broth, sausage and mash, steak and kidney pudding, and puddings such as white chocolate cheesecake and belgian waffle. *Benchmark main dish: fish and chips £11.95. Two-course evening meal £18.80.*

Brunning & Price ~ Manager John Astle-Rowe ~ Real ale ~ Bar food (12-10 (9.30 Sun)) ~ (01743) 340525 ~ Dogs allowed in bar ~ Open 12-11(10.30 Sun) ~ www.armoury-shrewsbury.co.uk *Recommended by P Dawn, C A Bryson, Steve Whalley, Barry Collett, Geraldine and James Fradgley, Mike and Mary Carter, Bruce and Sharon Eden, Jane Woodhull, Richard J Holloway*

Also Worth a Visit in Shropshire

Besides the fully inspected pubs, you might like to try these pubs that have been recommended to us and described by readers. Do tell us what you think of them: feedback@goodguides.com

BASCHURCH   SJ4221
New Inn (01939) 260335
Church Road; SY4 2EF Welcoming pub with good freshly cooked food in bar and restaurant, three well kept ales including Salopian, good choice of wines by the glass, decent coffee; terrace, open all day weekends. *(J S Burn)*

BISHOP'S CASTLE   SO3288
Boars Head (01588) 638521
Church Street; SY9 5AE Comfortable beamed and stripped-stone bar with mix of furniture including pews, settles and sofas, log fire in big inglenook, welcoming efficient young staff, well kept Courage, Joules and Theakstons, enjoyable good value pub food served all day; no dogs inside, children welcome, picnic-sets on back terrace, three good roomy high-raftered bedrooms in converted barn. *(Alan and Eve Harding)*

BISHOP'S CASTLE   SO3288
⁎ **Castle Hotel** (01588) 638403
Market Square, just off B4385; SY9 5BN Imposing early 18th-c panelled coaching inn with three neatly kept bar areas, fire in each, warm welcome, good food including lunchtime meal deal, more restaurant evening menu, well kept beers such as Hobsons, Six Bells and Three Tuns, decent wines and malt whiskies, bar billiards and other games; children and dogs welcome, disabled access, tables in front and in back garden with nice views, eight bedrooms, good breakfast, open all day.

(P J and R D Greaves, Theocsbrian, Pat and Tony Martin, David Field, the Didler)

BISHOP'S CASTLE   SO3288
⁎ **Six Bells** (01588) 630144
Church Street; SY9 5AA 17th-c pub with own-brew beers the main draw – you can tour the brewery; smallish no-frills bar with mix of well worn furniture, old local photographs and prints, bigger room with stripped-stone walls, benches around plain tables on bare boards and inglenook woodburner, country wines and summer farm cider, July beer festival, basic food (not Sun, Mon, Tues evenings); no credit cards; children and dogs welcome, open all day Sat, closed Mon lunchtime. *(Alan Cowell, Guy Vowles, Theocsbrian, Pat and Tony Martin, the Didler, MLR and others)*

BISHOP'S CASTLE   SO3288
⁎ **Three Tuns** (01588) 638797
Salop Street; SY9 5BW Extended and updated old pub adjacent to unique four-storey Victorian brewhouse (a brewery said to have existed here since 1642), busy chatty atmosphere in public, lounge and snug bars, Three Tuns beers (including 1642) from old-fashioned handpumps (cheaper Fri 5-7pm), several wines by the glass, tasty good value food (not Sun evening), friendly young staff, modernised dining room done out in smart oak and glass; lots going on including film club, live jazz, local rugby club events, July beer festival and may be morris dancers or a brass band in the garden; children and dogs welcome, open all day. *(N R White, Guy Vowles,*

Tracey and Stephen Groves, the Didler, Mike and Eleanor Anderson and others)

BONINGALE   SJ8102
Horns (01902) 372347
A464 S of Albrighton; WV7 3DA
Welcoming 18th-c Marstons pub, three of
their ales and good variety of enjoyable
well presented food, two bars and a
panelled dining room, log fires; children
welcome, dogs in public bar, open all day
weekends. *(Brian and Pat Wardrobe)*

BRIDGES   SO3996
Bridges (01588) 650260
Near Ratlinghope; SY5 0ST Old beamed
country pub (former Horseshoe) bought by
Three Tuns as their brewery tap and returned
to its pre-1860 name, four of their well kept
ales, home-made pizzas and other food (not
Mon evening – may be live music then);
tables out by the little River Onny, bedrooms,
open all day. *(Dave Braisted,
Dr Peter Crawshaw)*

BRIDGNORTH   SO7193
Falcon (01746) 763134
St Johns Street; WV15 6AG Refurbished
coaching inn with comfortable open-plan
beamed interior, reasonably priced food
including good Sun carvery, ales such
as Holdens; disabled access (couple of
steps at entrance), 12 bedrooms.
(Henry Pursehouse-Tranter)

BRIDGNORTH   SO7193
Jewel of the Severn (01746) 71198
High Street; WV16 4DS Relatively new
Wetherspoons, five well kept ales, usual
good value food (order and pre-pay at bar),
relaxing modern décor, good friendly service;
sports TV; children welcome, disabled
facilities, open all day till late. *(Alan and Eve
Harding, Henry Pursehouse-Tranter)*

BRIDGNORTH   SO7193
Kings Head (01746) 762141
Whitburn Street; WV16 4QN Well restored
17th-c timbered coaching inn with high-
raftered back stable bar, food here from 5pm
(all day weekends) or in all-day restaurant
with separate menu, Hobsons, Wye Valley and
several changing guests, log fires, beams and
flagstones, pretty leaded windows; children
and dogs welcome, courtyard picnic-sets,
open all day. *(the Didler)*

BRIDGNORTH   SO7192
✶**Railwaymans Arms** (01746) 764361
*Severn Valley Station, Hollybush Road
(off A458 towards Stourbridge);
WV16 5DT* Bathams, Hobsons and other
good value local ales kept well in chatty old-
fashioned converted waiting-room at Severn
Valley steam railway terminus, bustling on
summer days, with coal fire, old station signs
and train nameplates, superb mirror over
fireplace, may be simple summer snacks,

annual beer festival; children welcome,
wheelchair access with help, tables out
on platform – the train to Kidderminster
(station bar there too) has an all-day bar
and bookable Sun lunches, open all day
weekends. *(Pat and Tony Martin, Chris and
Angela Buckell, Theocsbrian, the Didler, Henry
Pursehouse-Tranter)*

BRIDGNORTH   SO7192
White Lion (01746) 763962
West Castle Street; WV16 4AB Fairly
compact two-bar pub with smart flower hung
exterior, seven well kept ales, Thatcher's cider,
reasonably priced home-made lunchtime food
(till 4pm weekends), comfortable carpeted
lounge with open fire, some live music
including folk club (first Tues of month); TV;
children welcome, lawned garden with fenced
play area and chickens, three bedrooms, open
all day. *(Tony Hobden)*

BROCKTON   SO5793
✶**Feathers** (01746) 785202
B4378; TF13 6JR Stylish restauranty
country dining pub with good interesting food
including lunchtime and early evening deals,
good efficient service, well kept changing
ales such as Hobsons and Three Tuns,
comfortable seats in attractively decorated
beamed rooms, conservatory gift shop;
children allowed, closed Mon. *(Alan and
Eve Harding)*

BROMFIELD   SO4877
✶**Clive** (01584) 856565
A49 2 miles NW of Ludlow; SY8 2JR
Sophisticated minimalist bar/restaurant
taking its name from Clive of India who once
lived here; emphasis mainly on imaginative
modern food but they do serve Hobsons and
Ludlow ales, several wines by the glass and
various teas and coffees, also lunchtime
sandwiches, efficient welcoming staff, dining
room with light wood tables, door to sparsely
furnished bar with metal chairs, glass-topped
tables and sleek counter, step down to room
with woodburner in huge fireplace, soaring
beams and rafters, exposed stonework and
well worn sofas, fresh flowers, daily papers;
piped jazz; children welcome, tables under
parasols on secluded terrace, fish pond, 15
stylish bedrooms, good breakfast, open all
day. *(Alan and Eve Harding, David Heath, Mr
and Mrs M Stratton, Michael Rugman and others)*

BURLTON   SJ4526
✶**Burlton Inn** (01939) 270284
*A528 Shrewsbury–Ellesmere, near
B4397 junction; SY4 5TB* Attractively
refurbished old pub with friendly helpful
licensees and staff, wide choice of good
popular food, well kept Robinsons ales,
sporting prints, log fires, comfortable snug,
restaurant with garden dining room; children
welcome, disabled facilities, pleasant terrace,
comfortable well equipped bedrooms, good
breakfast. *(Neville and Julia Lear, J S Burn)*

BURWARTON SO6185

⋆ **Boyne Arms** (01746) 787214

B4364 Bridgnorth–Ludlow; WV16 6QH
Handsome Georgian coaching inn with
welcoming cheerful staff, enjoyable
generous food (not Mon evening) including
good value deals, three Hobsons ales and
a guest, Robinson's cider, decent coffee,
separate restaurant and public bar (dogs
allowed here), function room with pool
and other games; children welcome, good
timber adventure playground in large
garden, hitching rail for horses, open all day
weekends. *(Alan and Eve Harding)*

CHELMARSH SO7287

Bulls Head (01746) 861469

B4555; WV16 6BA Restored group of
18th-c buildings, beams, bare-stone walls
and log fires, well kept ales and good value
interesting food including vegetarian choices,
friendly helpful staff, live jazz and folk music;
terrace and garden tables under parasols,
lovely views, good walking country, bedrooms
and self catering cottages. *(Jennifer Banks)*

CHURCH STRETTON SO4593

Bucks Head (01694) 722898

High Street; SY6 6BX Old town pub
with several good-sized modernised areas
including restaurant, four well kept Marstons
ales, good value pubby food plus
vegetarian options, friendly attentive staff,
black beams and timbers, mixed dark wood
tables and chairs; four bedrooms, open all
day. *(Pat and Tony Martin)*

CLAVERLEY SO8095

Woodman (01746) 710553

*Corner B4176 and Danford Lane;
WV5 7DG* Small 19th-c pub well run by
brother and sister team, contemporary
interior, good fairly priced bistro-style
food using local produce (some from farm
opposite) as well as fresh fish/shellfish, well
kept Black Sheep and Enville, lots of wines
by the glass, friendly service; garden, closed
Sun evening. *(John Fessey)*

CLEE HILL SO5975

Kremlin (01584) 890950

*Track up hill off A4117 Bewdley–
Cleobury, by Victoria Inn; SY8 3NB*
Shropshire's highest pub (former
quarrymaster's house), enjoyable good value
straightforward food including children's
menu, friendly service, well kept ales such
as Hobsons and Ludlow Gold, farm cider;
splendid view from garden and terrace,
play area, open all day weekends (till 9pm
Sun), closed Mon (till 8pm in summer), also
closed Tues lunchtime in winter. *(Alan and
Eve Harding)*

CLEOBURY MORTIMER SO6775

Kings Arms (01299) 271954

A4117 Bewdley–Ludlow; DY14 8BS

Refurbished 15th-c beamed inn, open-plan
bar with good log fire, four well kept Hobsons
ales, good value straightforward food, friendly
staff; four well fitted bedrooms, open all
day. *(Alan and Eve Harding)*

CLUNTON SO3381

Crown (01588) 660265

B4368; SY7 0HU Cosy old country local,
welcoming and friendly, with good choice of
well kept changing ales and of generously
served food at reasonable prices, log fire
in small flagstoned bar, dining room, small
games room. *(A N Bance)*

COALBROOKDALE SJ6604

Coalbrookdale Inn (01952) 432166

*Wellington Road, opposite Museum
of Iron; TF8 7DX* Handsome dark brick
18th-c pub under new management (some
refurbishment), half a dozen changing ales
from square counter in tiled-floor bar, fairly
simple food, former dining room converted
into second bar, two woodburners; long flight
of steps to entrance; dogs welcome, a few
tables outside, open all day. *(Anon)*

COALPORT SJ6902

Shakespeare (01952) 580675

High Street; TF8 7HT Relaxing early
19th-c pub by pretty Severn gorge park,
timbering, bare stone walls and tiled
floors, well kept Everards, Hobsons,
Ludlow and guests, good value food from
sandwiches through pub standards to
mexican specialities; children welcome,
picnic-sets in tiered garden with play area,
handy for china museum, four bedrooms,
open all day weekends, closed weekday
lunchtimes. *(Robert W Buckle)*

CORFTON SO4985

⋆ **Sun** (01584) 861239

*B4368 Much Wenlock–Craven Arms;
SY7 9DF* Lived-in unchanging three-room
country local, own good Corvedale ales
(including an unfined beer) and guest, long-
serving jolly landlord (if not busy in back
brewery), decent well presented pubby food
from baguettes up, lots of breweriana, basic
quarry-tiled public bar with darts and pool,
quieter carpeted lounge, dining room with
covered well, tourist information; background
music; children welcome, dogs in bar, good
wheelchair access throughout and disabled
lavatories, tables on terrace and in large
garden with good play area. *(MLR)*

CRESSAGE SJ5704

⋆ **Riverside** (01952) 510900

A458 NW, near Cound; SY5 6AF Spacious
pub/hotel, neat, light and airy, with good
well presented food from snacks up, efficient
cheerful staff, well kept ales including a
house beer brewed by Coors, lovely Severn
views from roomy conservatory, bar with
central woodburner (dogs welcome here);
big terraced garden, seven comfortable

bedrooms, good breakfast, open all day weekends in summer. *(Mr and Mrs D Hammond)*

DORRINGTON   SJ4703
Bridge Inn (01743) 718209

A49 N; SY5 7ED Busy, attractively refurbished, streamside dining pub, well prepared food including good value set deals, Sun roasts, well kept Jennings Bitter, cheerful helpful staff, roomy bar/dining area with wood floor, conservatory restaurant; piped jazz, no dogs; children welcome, garden tables, open all day. *(Paul and Mary Walmsley, Alan and Eve Harding, T M Griffiths)*

ELLESMERE   SJ3934
⋆Black Lion (01691) 622418

Scotland Street; back car park on A495; SY12 0EG Welcoming former coaching inn, good simple substantial food at bargain prices (pay at bar in advance), friendly helpful staff, two well kept Marstons-related ales, relaxed beamed bar with interesting décor and some unusual features such as the traditional wood-and-glass screen along its tiled entrance corridor, comfortable roomy dining room; background music; children welcome, some covered tables outside, handy car park, not far from canal wharf, bedrooms. *(Dave Braisted, Andrew Jeeves, Carole Smart)*

GRINDLEY BROOK   SJ5242
Horse & Jockey (01948) 662723

A41; SY13 4QJ Enjoyable good value food all day from varied menu, friendly helpful service, four well kept ales including Stonehouse and Three Tuns, teas and coffees; sports TV, pool; children and dogs welcome, big play area, handy for Sandstone Trail and Llangollen Canal. *(Kedren Elliott)*

GRINSHILL   SJ5223
⋆Inn at Grinshill (01939) 220410

Off A49 N of Shrewsbury; SY4 3BL Civilised early Georgian country inn with comfortable 19th-c log-fire bar, Greene King and a local guest such as Six Bells, spacious modern restaurant with view into open kitchen, good well coked food including set-menu choices, cafetière coffee, friendly competent young staff; background music, TV; children and dogs welcome, pleasant back garden with plenty of tables and chairs, comfortable clean bedrooms, closed Sun evening, Mon. *(Paul Sayers, Brian and Anna Marsden, Steve Whalley, Mrs Debbie Tether, R T and J C Moggridge)*

HIGHLEY   SO7483
Ship (01746) 861219

Severnside; WV16 6NU Refurbished 18th-c inn in lovely riverside location, good choice of food, Sun carvery, real ales including one brewed for the pub; children welcome, tables on raised front deck, handy for Severn Way walks (and Severn Valley Railway), fishing rights, bedrooms. *(John Coatsworth)*

HINDFORD   SJ3333
Jack Mytton (01691) 679861

Village and pub signed from A495; SY11 4NL Pleasant rustic bar with log fire, four changing ales kept well by character landlord, food from bar snacks up, airy raftered dining room; children and dogs welcome, picnic-sets in attractive canalside garden, good-sized courtyard with summer bar and carved bear (pub named after eccentric squire who rode a bear), moorings. *(C A Bryson, Roger and Anne Newbury)*

HOPE   SJ3401
Stables (01743) 891344

Just off A488 3 miles S of Minsterley; SY5 0EP Hidden away little 17th-c beamed country pub, regularly changing local ales, enjoyable inexpensive pub food, newspapers, log fires; fine views from garden. *(Gerry Price)*

IRONBRIDGE   SJ6703
Golden Ball (01952) 432179

Brown sign to pub off Madeley Road (B4373) above village centre – pub behind Horse & Jockey, car park beyond on left; TF8 7BA Unassuming partly Elizabethan pub tucked away in steep little hamlet of ancient buildings; some low black beams, red-cushioned pews on worn boards, a dresser of decorative china, woodburner, well kept Everards, Greene King and a guest such as Raw Hop Pole, Weston's Old Rosie cider, generous fairly priced food including sandwiches, friendly efficient staff; background music and TV; children welcome, tables in sheltered side courtyard, pleasant but steep walk down to river, bedrooms, open all day weekends. *(Alan and Eve Harding, Paul Colley, Mrs Blethyn Elliott)*

IRONBRIDGE   SJ6603
⋆Malthouse (01952) 433712

The Wharfage (bottom road alongside Severn); TF8 7NH Converted 18th-c malthouse wonderfully located in historic gorge, spacious bar with iron pillars supporting heavy pine beams, lounge/dining area, up to three well kept changing ales, good reasonably priced food all day from baguettes up, live music Fri, Sat; children and dogs welcome, terrace tables, 11 individually styled bedrooms, self-catering cottage. *(Berwyn Owen, Peter and Jean Hoare)*

LEEBOTWOOD   SO4798
⋆Pound (01694) 751477

A49 Church Stretton–Shrewsbury; SY6 6ND Ancient thatched cruck-framed building – thought to be oldest in village and dating from 1458; bar rooms are stylishly modern with minimalist fixtures and wooden furnishings, Fullers and changing guest such as Salopian Shropshire Gold, decent wines by the glass, good bar food including deals, friendly service; background music; seats on flagstoned terrace; disabled parking spaces, closed Sun evening, Mon. *(Donald Thompson, Alan and Eve Harding, Tracey and Stephen Groves, Mr and Mrs A H Young)*

LITTLE STRETTON   SO4491
Green Dragon (01694) 722925
Village well signed off A49; SY6 6RE
Refurbished village pub under welcoming new management, Wye Valley ales with a guest like Sharps Doom Bar, enjoyable food in bar or adjacent dining area, warm woodburner; tables outside, handy for Cardingmill Valley (NT) and Long Mynd. *(T M Griffiths, Susan and Neil McLean)*

LITTLE STRETTON   SO4492
✳ Ragleth (01694) 722711
Village signposted off A49 S of Church Stretton; Ludlow Road; SY6 6RB
Characterful attractively opened-up 17th-c dining pub, light and airy bay-windowed front bar with eclectic mix of old tables and chairs, some exposed brick and timber work, huge inglenook in heavily beamed brick-and-tile-floored public bar, four mainly local beers, good generous reasonably priced bar food, cheerful attentive owners and staff; background music, TV, darts and board games; children welcome, dogs in bar, lovely garden with tulip tree shaded lawn, good play area, thatched and timbered church and fine hill walks nearby, open all day Sat (summer) and Sun. *(Simon and Mandy King, Alan and Eve Harding, Dr P Brown, Tracey and Stephen Groves, Michael Rugman, Ray and Winifred Halliday)*

LOPPINGTON   SJ4729
Dickin Arms (01939) 233471
B4397; SY4 5SR Cheerful two-bar country local, comfortably plush banquettes, open fire, shallow steps to neat back dining room with good value generous food including landlady's speciality curries, lunchtime OAP deals, well kept Bass and an interesting guests such as Gertie Sweet and Wem Hanby, good service; pool; children welcome, play area, pretty village. *(Alan and Eve Harding, Tim Williams)*

LUDLOW   SO5174
Bull (01584) 879339
Bull Ring; SY8 1AD Welcoming medieval timbered inn with low-beamed traditional bar and comfortable lounge, Jennings ales, enjoyable reasonably priced food including tapas, refurbished restaurant, live music; courtyard through side arch, four bedrooms, open all day. *(Alan and Eve Harding, Roy Payne)*

LUDLOW   SO5174
✳ Charlton Arms (01584) 872813
Ludford Bridge, B4361 Overton Road; SY8 1PJ Big comfortably extended inn in superb position by massive medieval bridge over the Teme; open-plan red-carpeted lounge overlooking the water some 10 metres below with the interesting town spreading uphill on far side, high-backed dining chairs around polished dark tables, some leather armchairs and sofas, adjoining dining room with same view, more pubby back area with two-way woodburner, Hobsons, Ludlow and Wye Valley, good food, cheerfully old-fashioned service; seats on three or four terraces and decks on varying levels, comfortable bedrooms. *(Joe Green, George Atkinson, Roy Payne, T M Griffiths)*

LUDLOW   SO5174
Queens (01584) 879177
Lower Galdeford; SY8 1RU Family-run 19th-c pub with good food concentrating heavily on fresh local produce, five well kept ales including Ludlow, Hobsons and bargain Three Tuns 1642, long narrow oak-floor bar, pine tables in vaulted-ceiling dining area, good friendly service and nice pub dog, popular monthly charity quiz, some live music; children welcome (not in bar after 6pm), no dogs inside at food times, open all day. *(Mr and Mrs A Curry, Roy Payne, N Pitt, Dave Braisted)*

LUDLOW   SO5174
Rose & Crown (01584) 872098
Off Church Street, behind Buttercross; SY8 1AP Small unpretentious pub with 13th-c origins, enjoyable bargain food all day, ales such as Bass, Greene King Abbot and Hobsons, clean comfortably lived-in L-shaped bar with hop-strung beams and open brick fireplace, separate dining area; approached through archway with a few courtyard seats at front, more on terrace behind, pretty spot, bedrooms. *(Phil Bryant, Mr and Mrs A H Young)*

LUDLOW   SO5174
Wheatsheaf (01584) 872980
Lower Broad Street; SY8 1PQ Traditional 17th-c beamed pub spectacularly built into medieval town gate, good value generous pubby food, Sun carvery, efficient cheerful staff, well kept Marstons and related ales; children welcome, no dogs inside, a few seats out in front, five comfortable bedrooms, open all day. *(Alan and Eve Harding, Roy Payne)*

MARTON   SJ2802
✳ Sun (01938) 561211
B4386 NE of Chirbury; SY21 8JP Warmly inclusive family-run pub with well liked food cooked by father and son including seasonal game and good fresh fish, light and airy black-beamed bar with comfortable sofa and traditional pub furnishings, big stone feature fireplace, Hobsons Best and a guest such as Six Bells, chunky pale tables and tall ladder-back chairs in restaurant; front terrace. *(Pete Yearsley, Peter and Sheila Longland, Mike Walker)*

MELVERLEY   SJ3316
Tontine (01691) 682258
Off B4393 W of Shrewsbury; SY10 8PJ Small refurbished pub run by welcoming family, inexpensive straightforward food, a couple of well kept ales and good pint of

Guinness too, comfortable lounge, restaurant; background music, TV, pool; garden, near interesting half-timbered church. *(Anthony Barnes, Dianne Moran)*

MUCH WENLOCK   SO6299
Gaskell Arms (01952) 727212
High Street (A458); TF13 6AQ 17th-c coaching inn with comfortable old-fashioned lounge divided by brass-canopied log fire, enjoyable straightforward bar food at fair prices, friendly attentive service, three well kept ales such as Stonehouse, Woods and Wye Valley, brasses and prints, civilised beamed restaurant, locals' public bar; subdued background music; no dogs; well behaved children allowed, disabled facilities, roomy neat back garden with terrace, 16 bedrooms, open all day. *(N R White)*

MUCH WENLOCK   SO6299
Raven (01952) 727251
Barrow Street; TF13 6EN Small friendly family-run hotel (17th-c coaching inn), bar with dining room off, good well priced food here and in more upmarket restaurant, may have set lunch deal, two ales including one brewed for them by Woods, interesting 1894 Olympic Games memorabilia; no dogs; children welcome, bedrooms around courtyard and in forge annexe, open all day. *(Alan and Eve Harding)*

MUCH WENLOCK   SO6299
⋆**Talbot** (01952) 727077
High Street (A458); TF13 6AA Friendly unspoilt medieval inn, several cosy traditional areas, low ceilings, red tapestry button-back wall banquettes, local pictures and cottagey plates on walls, art deco-style lamps, gleaming brasses, well kept Bass and a guest, several wines and whiskies, enjoyable fair-priced bar food and more elaborate evening choices including good value set menu, cheerful prompt service; background music, TV; seats in courtyard; children welcome, characterful bedrooms, open all day (till 2am if busy). *(Anthony Bradbury, Mark, Amanda, Luke and Jake Sheard, Tracey and Stephen Groves, A N Bance, Mrs Blethyn Elliott, T M Griffiths and others)*

MUNSLOW   SO5287
⋆**Crown** (01584) 841205
B4368 Much Wenlock–Craven Arms; SY7 9ET Former court house with imposing exterior and pretty back façade showing Tudor origins; lots of nooks and crannies, split-level lounge bar with old-fashioned mix of furnishings on broad flagstones, old bottles, country pictures, bread oven by log fire, traditional snug with another fire, eating area with tables around central

oven chimney, more beams, flagstones and stripped-stone, enjoyable imaginative food (local suppliers listed), ales such as Holdens, Ludlow, Salopian and Six Bells, local bottled cider, good wines, helpful efficient staff and friendly bustling atmosphere, Jenna the boxer may wander around; background music; children welcome, level wheelchair access to bar only, bedrooms, closed Sun evening, Mon. *(Glenwys and Alan Lawrence, Alan Cowell, Roger White, Simon and Mandy King, Alan and Eve Harding, Tracey and Stephen Groves)*

NESSCLIFFE   SJ3819
Old Three Pigeons (01743) 741279
Off A5 Shrewsbury–Oswestry (now bypassed); SY4 1DB Friendly 16th-c pub with quaint and appealing dining area, good reasonably priced food, well kept ales such as Salopian and Stonehouse, good choice of wines by the glass, warm log fires, two bar areas; children welcome, some tables outside, opposite Kynaston Cave, good cliff walks. *(Julia and Richard Tredgett)*

NORTON   SJ7200
⋆**Hundred House** (01952) 730353
A442 Telford–Bridgnorth; TF11 9EE Neatly kept pubby hotel bar with appealing gothic décor, Highgate and three guests, good wine choice, very good locally sourced food in bar and two tucked-away dining areas including Sun set lunch deal, woodburners and working Coalbrookdale ranges in handsome old fireplaces, prompt pleasant service, spotless quirky ladies'; occasional background music; lovely garden with herbs (seeds sold for charity), ten comfortable individual bedrooms (some with swings), open all day. *(Brian and Ruth Young, Adrian Ballard, Titia Ketelaar)*

QUEENS HEAD   SJ3326
⋆**Queens Head** (01691) 610255
Just off A5 SE of Oswestry, towards Nesscliffe; SY11 4EB Emphasis on wide choice of generous good value food (all day) from speciality sandwiches and other snacks to steaks and lots of fish, good vegetarian options too, well kept Theakstons and a couple of guests, decent wines by the glass, two well refurbished dining areas with hot coal fires, nice roomy conservatory overlooking restored section of Montgomery Canal; children welcome, picnic-sets under parasols in suntrap waterside garden, country walks. *(Ken Marshall, Deanna Hughes)*

RUYTON XI TOWNS   SJ3922
Talbot (01939) 262882
Church Street; SY4 1LA Old refurbished black and white pub with good choice of local

---

Post Office address codings confusingly give the impression that some pubs are in Shropshire, when they're really in Cheshire (which is where we list them).

beers and enjoyable fresh food from lunchtime sandwiches up, friendly service, bar and separate eating areas with well spaced tables, open fires, live music Sun; dogs welcome, three bedrooms, open all day Fri-Sun. *(Bruce and Sharon Eden, Sarah Farrington)*

SHIFNAL   SJ74508

White Hart   (01952) 461161

High Street; TF11 8BH Half a dozen or more interesting changing ales in chatty 17th-c timbered pub, quaint and old-fashioned with separate bar and lounge, enjoyable home-made lunchtime food (not Sun), good choice of wines by the glass, welcoming staff; couple of steep steps at front door, open all day. *(the Didler)*

SHREWSBURY   SJ4912

Admiral Benbow   (01743) 244423

Swan Hill; SY1 1NF Great choice of mainly local ales including one for them from Six Bells, bottled belgians, also real ciders and perry; no children; closed lunchtimes apart from Sat. *(the Didler)*

SHREWSBURY   SJ4812

Boat House Inn   (01743) 231658

New Street/Quarry Park; leaving centre via Welsh Bridge/A488 turn into Port Hill Road; SY3 8JQ Comfortably modernised pub in lovely position by footbridge to Severn park, river views from long lounge bar and terrace tables, well kept ales such as Salopian and Woods, enjoyable straightforward food including Sun carvery, friendly staff; background music; children welcome; open all day. *(Duncan Kirkby)*

SHREWSBURY   SO4912

Coach & Horses   (01743) 365661

Swan Hill/Cross Hill; SY1 1NF Friendly and relaxed Victorian local with panelled main bar, cosy little side room and back dining lounge, enjoyable fresh food, Salopian Shropshire Gold, Stonehouse and guests, real cider, prompt helpful service, interesting Guinness prints; background music – may be live Sun; children allowed in dining room, dogs in bar, disabled facilities, smokers' roof terrace, open all day. *(Alan and Eve Harding, the Didler)*

SHREWSBURY   SJ4912

Lion   (01743) 353107

Follow City Centre signposts across the English Bridge; SY1 1UY Grand largely 18th-c coaching inn (some parts dating from 16th c) with cosy oak-panelled bar and sedate series of high-ceilinged rooms opening off, enjoyable good value food, tea, coffee and cakes, three local ales, civilised service, restaurant; children welcome, 50 bedrooms, open all day. *(C A Bryson, Giles and Annie Francis)*

SHREWSBURY   SO4812

Old Bucks Head   (01743) 369392

Frankwell; SY3 8JR Quietly placed old

inn with traditional bar and restaurant, cheerful staff, enjoyable inexpensive pubby food, Salopian and a couple of other well kept ales; dogs welcome, flower-decked raised terrace and nice secluded little garden, ten good value bedrooms, open all day Sat. *(Ian Phillips, Alan and Eve Harding)*

SHREWSBURY   SJ4912

Salopian Bar   (01743) 351505

Smithfield Road; SY1 1PW Comfortable modern refurbishment, eight well kept ales such as Bathams, Dark Star, Oakham, Salopian and Stonehouse, good choice of belgian beers and real ciders, cheap sandwiches and pies, friendly staff, local artwork for sale; sports TV; open all day. *(Alan and Eve Harding)*

SHREWSBURY   SJ4912

⋆ **Three Fishes**   (01743) 344793

Fish Street; SY1 1UR Well run timbered and heavily beamed 16th-c pub in quiet cobbled street, small tables around three sides of central bar, flagstones, old pictures, half a dozen changing beers from mainstream and smaller breweries like Stonehouse, good value wines, fairly priced food including blackboard specials ordered from separate servery, good friendly service even if busy, no mobiles; open all day Fri and Sat. *(Alan and Eve Harding, the Didler)*

SHREWSBURY   SJ4912

Wheatsheaf   (01743) 272702

High Street; SY1 1ST Comfortable open-plan beamed lounge, enjoyable good value home-made food (not Sun), eight well kept Marstons-related ales, several wines by the glass, cheerful efficient staff, live music nights; open all day. *(Alan and Eve Harding)*

STIPERSTONES   SJ3600

⋆ **Stiperstones Inn**   (01743) 791327

Village signed off A488 S of Minsterley; SY5 0LZ Cosy traditional pub useful for a drink after walking – some stunning hikes on Long Mynd or up dramatic quartzite ridge of the Stiperstones; small modernised lounge with comfortable leatherette wall banquettes and lots of brassware on ply-panelled walls, plainer public bar with TV, games machine and darts, Hobsons and Three Tuns, good value bar food usefully served all day, friendly service; background music; children and dogs welcome, two comfortable bedrooms, open all day (till 2am Fri, Sat). *(Martin Smith, MLR, Rob and Catherine Dunster)*

TELFORD   SJ6910

Crown   (01952) 610888

Market Street, Oakengates (off A442, handy for M54 junction 5); TF2 6EA Bright 19th-c local (list of licensees to 1835), Hobsons Best and many changing guests, May and Oct beer festivals with up to 60 ales, draught continentals and lots of foreign bottled beers, a real cider or perry, helpful knowledgeable staff, simple snacky food (can bring your own), bustling bare-boards front bar with woodburner, small sky-lit side room, quarry-tiled back room; live music Thurs, mid-Sept folk festival, comedy nights; sun-trap courtyard, handy for station, open all day. *(the Didler)*

UCKINGTON   SJ5709
Horseshoe Inn (01952) 740238
B5061 E of Atcham; SY4 4UL Large low-beamed pub with reasonably priced tasty food (all day Sat, not Sun evening), well kept local ales, good service, inglenook woodburner; picnic-sets outside, open all day. *(Michael Rugman)*

UPTON MAGNA   SJ5512
Corbet Arms (01743) 709422
Pelham Road; SY4 4TZ Refurbished village pub under newish management, Banks's ales and a guest like Salopian Shropshire Gold, food from Weds evening to Sun lunchtime, big L-shaped carpeted lounge with black beams, panelling and log fire, darts and pool in smaller public bar (dogs allowed here); children welcome, great view to the Wrekin from attractive garden, handy for Haughmond Hill walks and Attingham Park (NT), closed weekday lunchtimes, open all day Sat, till 8pm Sun (5pm winter). *(Robert W Buckle)*

WELLINGTON   SJ6511
Cock (01952) 244954
Holyhead Road (B5061 – former A5); TF1 2DL Former 18th-c coaching inn popular for its friendly real ale bar, Hobsons and five well kept quickly changing guests usually from small breweries, farm cider, separate belgian beer bar, knowledgeable staff, big fireplace; bedrooms, closed lunchtime Mon-Weds, open all day Thurs-Sat. *(Nick Jenkins, the Didler)*

WELLINGTON   SJ6410
Wickets (01952) 246991
Holyhead Road (B5061); TF1 2EB Light and modern but keeping some interesting early 20th-c memorabilia, good value well cooked food from snacks up, well kept Greene King IPA and two guests, good seating in open-plan bar, separate dining room; no dogs; children welcome, tables in back garden, handy for Sunnycroft (NT), open all day. *(Mrs R Smith)*

WELLINGTON   SJ6511
William Withering (01952) 642800
43-45 New Street; TF1 1LU Comfortable new Wetherspoons named after 18th-c local physician, half a dozen real ales, usual good value food till 10pm, friendly landlord and staff. *(Nick Jenkins, J F M and M West)*

WENLOCK EDGE   SO5696
Wenlock Edge Inn (01746) 785678
B4371 Much Wenlock–Church Stretton; TF13 6DJ Renovated stone-built country pun in lovely spot, public bar, lounge and more modern dining extension, enjoyable home-made food all day from good sandwiches up, Adnams, Greene King and Hobsons, good wines by the glass, decent coffee, friendly staff, open fire and inglenook woodburner; children welcome in eating areas, dogs in bar, terrace tables front and back, lots of walks, five bedrooms, open all day. *(Mike Proctor)*

WHITCHURCH   SJ5441
Old Town Hall Vaults
(01948) 662251 *St Marys Street; SY13 1QU* Simple cosy 18th-c local (birthplace of composer Sir Edward German), L-shaped front bar with secluded snug behind, seven real ales including Joules, good value straightforward food; dogs welcome, garden. *(Anon)*

WHITCHURCH   SJ5345
Willey Moor Lock (01948) 663274
Tarporley Road; signed off A49 just under 2 miles N; SY13 4HF Large opened-up pub in picturesque spot by Llangollen Canal, low beams, countless teapots, two log fires, cheerful chatty atmosphere, half a dozen changing ales from local breweries, around 30 malt whiskies, enjoyable good value quickly served pub food from sandwiches up; background music, games machine, no credit cards (debit cards accepted), no dogs inside; children welcome away from bar, terrace tables, secure garden with big play area. *(Dr Kevan Tucker)*

WHITTINGTON   SJ3231
White Lion (01691) 662361
Castle Street; SY11 4DF Sizeable nicely refurbished pub just below castle, tasty good value food served by cheerful attentive young staff, two well kept ales, decent wines by the glass, light wood tables in front bar, smaller area with leather sofas, dining room and conservatory beyond; plenty of tables in good outdoor space. *(Alan and Eve Harding)*

YORTON   SJ5023
Railway (01939) 220240
Station Road; SY4 3EP Same family for over 70 years, friendly and chatty mother and daughter, unchanging atmosphere, plain tiled bar with hot coal fire, old settles and a modicum of railway memorabilia, big back lounge (not always open) with fishing trophies, well kept Salopian, Woods and guests, farm ciders, may be sandwiches on request, darts and dominoes; seats out in yard. *(the Didler)*

Somerset

An interesting crop of new entries here includes the Square & Compass at Ashill (family-run, honest food), Candlelight in Bishopswood (friendly, attractively reworked dining pub), Farmers Arms in Combe Florey (mother and daughter team, well liked food, cottagey gardens), Wheatsheaf at Combe Hay (smart, civilised dining pub, especially good modern cooking), Old Station at Hallatrow (extraordinary bric-a-brac and Pullman dining car), Queen Victoria in Priddy (character rooms and reasonably good value food), and Plough at Wrington (neatly kept and home-made food). Other pubs doing well are the Ring o' Bells in Ashcott (long-serving owners in traditional village pub), Red Lion in Babcary (super new bedrooms and fine mix of customers), Highbury Vaults in Bristol (friendly and unpretentious with eight real ales), Crown in Churchill (unspoilt and unchanging), Queens Arms in Corton Denham (an all-round winner), Lord Poulett Arms in Hinton St George (loved by our readers), Rose & Crown in Huish Episcopi (in the same family for 140 years), Royal Oak at Luxborough (character bar, good food and bedrooms), Halfway House in Pitney (smashing pub with ten ales and five ciders), Carpenters Arms at Stanton Wick (warmly friendly, cosy bedrooms), and Rock at Waterrow (mother and son team and produce from own farm). Food, whether honest or inventive, plays an important role in pubs here. Our Somerset Dining Pub 2013 is the Wheatsheaf at Combe Hay.

APPLEY
Globe

ST0721   Map 1

Hamlet signposted from the network of back roads between A361 and A38, W of B3187 and W of Milverton and Wellington; OS Sheet 181 map reference 072215; TA21 0HJ

Unspoilt country pub with small rooms, tasty food, real ales and seats in the garden

---

There's plenty of honest character in this unspoilt 15th-c pub, and it's popular with walkers and cyclists exploring the surrounding countryside. The simple beamed front room has a built-in settle and bare wood tables on the brick floor, and another room has a Great Western Railway bench and 1930s railway posters; there's a further room with traditional and easy chairs, open fires, a growing collection of musical instruments and posters, art deco items and pictures of the *Titanic*; skittle alley. A brick entry corridor leads to a serving hatch with Sharps Doom Bar and a beer named for the pub on handpump, and local cider. There are seats outside in the garden; the path opposite leads eventually to the River Tone.

🍴 Cooked by the landlady, there's quite a choice of food: filled baguettes, chicken liver pâté with red onion marmalade, field mushroom stuffed with blue cheese and parmesan, home-baked ham and egg, four-cheese and mushroom pasta bake, chicken or cheese burgers, spanish-style fish and chorizo stew, lamb tagine with dates, squash and almonds, chicken and fennel in tomato sauce, and puddings like chocolate and walnut brownie and apple and cinnamon crumble. *Benchmark main dish: smoked haddock and bacon £13.95. Two-course evening meal £17.45.*

Free house ~ Licensee LeBurn Maddox ~ Real ale ~ Bar food (not winter Sun evening, not Mon) ~ Restaurant ~ (01823) 672327 ~ Children welcome ~ Open 11-3, 6.30-11.30; 12-3, 7-10.30 Sun; closed Mon, Sun evening November-April ~ www.theglobeinnappley.co.uk *Recommended by Stephen Bennett, Barry Collett, Derek Goldrei, the Didler, Bob and Margaret Holder, Peter Thornton*

ASHCOTT   ST4337 Map 1

Ring o' Bells 🍺

High Street; pub well signed off A39 W of Street; TA7 9PZ

Friendly village pub with traditional décor in several bars, separate restaurant, tasty bar food and changing local ales

This is a fine place for a warming lunch before a visit to Ham Wall Nature Reserve. It's been run by the same friendly family for some years now and the three main bars are on different levels but all are comfortable. There are maroon plush-topped stools, cushioned mate's chairs and dark wooden pubby tables on patterned carpet, horse-brasses along the bressumer beam above the big stone fireplace and a growing collection of handbells. Butcombe Bitter, RCH Pitchfork and Teignworthy Maltsters Ale on handpump, eight wines by the glass and local farm and bottled cider. There's also a separate restaurant and a skittle alley/function room. The terrace and garden have plenty of picnic-sets.

🍴 Using local, seasonal produce, the good, popular food includes sandwiches, crab cakes with a sweet chilli dip, smoked chicken, bacon and mushrooms au gratin, celery, almond and cashew nut roast with cheese sauce, lasagne, home-cooked ham and egg, hake florentine (with spinach, tomato and cheese sauce), specials such as thai-style chicken soup with ginger and coconut, chicken breast stuffed with bacon and cheese in a cider sauce and liver and onion, and puddings such as chocolate fudge pudding and fresh lemon soufflé; Thursday is fresh, beer-battered fish day. *Benchmark main dish: pork escalope in apricot and brandy sauce £10.95. Two-course evening meal £15.50.*

Free house ~ Licensees John and Elaine Foreman and John Sharman ~ Real ale ~ Bar food (12-2, 7-10) ~ Restaurant ~ (01458) 210232 ~ Children welcome ~ Dogs welcome ~ Live folk music first Sat and third Weds of month ~ Open 12-3, 7-11(10.30 Sun) ~ www.ringobells.com *Recommended by Frank Willy, Ian and Nita Cooper, Warren Marsh, Chris and Angela Buckell, R L Borthwick*

ASHILL

Square & Compass 🛏

*Windmill Hill; off A358 between Ilminster and Taunton; up Wood
Road for a mile behind Stewley Cross service station; OS Sheet 193 map
reference 310166; TA19 9NX*

**Simple, welcoming pub with local ales, tasty food and good regular
live music in separate sound-proofed barn; comfortable bedrooms**

A lways friendly and welcoming with long-serving, helpful owners,
this is a traditional pub tucked away in the Blackdown Hills. The
little beamed bar has a nice mix of chatty customers, upholstered
window seats that take in the fine view over the rolling pastures, heavy
hand-made furniture, an open winter fire – and perhaps the pub cat,
Lily. Exmoor Ale and St Austell Tribute and a guest like St Austell
Trelawny on handpump, and good house wines by the glass. The
background music is often classical. There's a garden with picnic-sets
and a large glass-covered walled terrace. The bedrooms are spacious
and comfortable and two have full disabled facilities. The barn, rural-
theme in style, is popular for venues (and live music events) and is
soundproofed.

🍴 Well liked and generously served, the food might include sandwiches, filled
baked potatoes, mushroom stroganoff, sausages and mash with onion gravy,
pork in cider sauce, fresh trout with almonds, turkey and ham pie, fish and chips,
chicken with stilton and bacon, whole cornish plaice, and puddings like eton mess
and fruit crumble. *Benchmark main dish: steak in ale pie £9.95. Two-course
evening meal £13.25.*

Free house ~ Licensees Chris, Janet and Beth Slow ~ Real ale ~ Bar food (12-2, 7-9.30;
not Tues-Thurs lunchtime) ~ (01823) 480467 ~ Children welcome ~ Dogs welcome
~ Open 12-2.30, 6.30-11.30; 12-3, 7-11.30 Sun; closed Tues, Weds, Thurs lunchtimes ~
Bedrooms: £65B/£85B ~ www.squareandcompasspub.com *Recommended by Adrian and
Dawn Collinge, Max Benson, Glenwys and Alan Lawrence, Wendy Boast, Roy Hoing*

BABCARY

Red Lion 🍽 ♀ 🛏

*Off A37 S of Shepton Mallett; 2 miles or so N of roundabout where A37 meets
A303 and A372; TA11 7ED*

**Thatched pub with informal atmosphere in comfortable rambling
rooms, interesting daily-changing food, and local beers; bedrooms**

T hey've now opened up smart bedrooms in this well run stone-built
thatched inn – we'd expect this to be a very enjoyable place to stay
and would love news from readers. It remains as popular as ever with
a relaxed, comfortable atmosphere and a good bustle of both drinkers
and diners, and the landlord and his staff make everyone feel welcome.
Several distinct areas work their way around the carefully refurbished
bar. To the left of the entrance is a longish room with dark pink walls, a
squashy leather sofa and two housekeeper's chairs around a low table by
a woodburning stove, and a few well spaced tables and captain's chairs.
There are elegant rustic wall lights, some clay pipes in a cabinet, local
papers or magazines to read and board games. Leading off here, with
lovely dark flagstones, is a more dimly lit public bar area with a panelled
dado, a high-backed old settle and other more straightforward chairs;
table skittles and background music. The good-sized dining room has a
large stone lion's head on a plinth above the open fire (with a huge stack

of logs to one side), a big rug on polished boards and formally set tables. Otter Bright, Teignworthy Reel Ale and a guest like Cheddar Ales Gorge Best on handpump, around ten wines by the glass and two farm ciders. The long, informal garden has picnic-sets and a play area for children. The pub is handy for the A303 and for shopping at Clarks Village in Street.

🍴 Good, popular food might include sandwiches, pressed chicken and tarragon terrine with red onion chutney, smoked salmon with a poached egg, hollandaise and a toasted muffin, beef burger with cheese or bacon, beer-battered haddock and chips, artichoke, leek and smoked cheese crêpes with a red pepper coulis, pollack fillet with pak choi, spring onion, confit potato and an oriental dressing, slow-cooked duck leg with fondant potatoes and a red wine jus, and puddings such as dark and white chocolate terrine with a berry compote and sticky toffee pudding with ginger ice-cream. *Benchmark main dish: steak in ale pie £11.00. Two-course evening meal £18.75.*

Free house ~ Licensee Charles Garrard ~ Real ale ~ Bar food (12-2.30, 7-9.30(8.30 Sun)) ~ Restaurant ~ (01458) 223230 ~ Children welcome ~ Dogs allowed in bar ~ Open 12-3, 6-midnight ~ Bedrooms: /£104S ~ www.redlionbabcary.co.uk *Recommended by Ian Herdman, Peter and Giff Bennett, Steve Collett, Bob and Margaret Holder, John and Fiona McIlwain, Guy Vowles, John and Philippa Cadge*

BATCOMBE
Three Horseshoes 🛏

ST6839   Map 2

Village signposted off A359 Bruton–Frome; BA4 6HE

Handsome old inn with smart bar rooms, enjoyable food, local ales and friendly owners; comfortable bedrooms

Reached down winding lanes in a quiet village – just head for the church with its striking tower – this inn is 400 years old and built of honey-coloured stone. The friendly landlord and his staff make all their customers welcome and comfortable. The long, rather narrow main room is smartly traditional: beams, local pictures, built-in cushioned window seats, solid chairs around a nice mix of old tables and a woodburning stove at one end with a big open fire at the other. There's also a pretty stripped-stone dining room; best to book to be sure of a table, especially at weekends. Blindmans Golden Spire, Butcombe Bitter and Devilfish Best on handpump, around a dozen wines by the glass and several malt whiskies. This is a nice place to stay and the bedrooms are delightful; local honey for sale.

🍴 Well presented food using seasonal local produce might include sandwiches, chicken liver pâté with spicy tomato chutney, home-cured beetroot salmon gravadlax with dill vodka, sun-blush tomato, red onion and goats cheese tart, ham and free-range eggs, pork and leek sausages with red wine gravy, slow-cooked beef casserole, line-caught pollack fillet with dill cream sauce, and puddings like white chocolate, champagne and ricotta cheesecake with lavender shortbread and sticky toffee pudding with butterscotch sauce. *Benchmark main dish: slow-roasted pork belly with savoy cabbage and crispy bacon, apple sauce, crackling £14.30. Two-course evening meal £20.00.*

Free house ~ Licensee Kav Javvi ~ Real ale ~ Bar food (12-2.30, 6-9.30(9 Sun)) ~ Restaurant ~ (01749) 850359 ~ Children welcome ~ Dogs allowed in bar ~ Open 11-3, 6-11; 11-11 Sat; 12-10.30 Sun ~ Bedrooms: £60B/£85B ~ www.thethreehorseshoesinn.co.uk *Recommended by Richard Oake, Claire Denyer, Jeremy Davis, Chris and Angela Buckell*

BISHOPSWOOD   ST2512   Map 1
Candlelight 🍴 🍺
Off A303/B3170 S of Taunton; TA20 3RS

Friendly, hard-working licensees in neatly refurbished dining pub with granite walls and pale wooden floors, candlelight and fresh flowers, imaginative food and seats in garden

Run by warmly friendly, hands-on licensees, this is a neatly refurbished pub in the Blackdown Hills. It's more or less open-plan inside but separated into different areas by standing stone pillars and open doorways, and the atmosphere throughout is relaxed and informal. The beamed bar has high chairs by the counter where they serve Bass, Branscombe Best, Otter Bitter and RCH East Street Cream tapped from the cask, nice wines by the glass, a couple of farm ciders and winter drinks like hot Pimms, whisky toddies and hot chocolate; also, captain's chairs, pews and cushioned window seats around a mix of wooden tables on newly sanded boards, and a small ornate fireplace. To the left is a comfortable area with a button-back sofa beside a big woodburner, and then wheelback chairs and cushioned settles around wooden tables set for dining, and country pictures and photos, a hunting horn and bugles on the granite walls; background music and shove-ha'penny. To the other side of the bar is a similarly furnished dining room. Outside, there's a decked area with picnic-sets and a neatly landscaped garden with a paved path winding through low walls set with plants.

Highly enjoyable food using seasonal ingredients might include duck liver parfait with crab apple jelly, baked ewes cheese, onion marmalade and pine nuts in a cheddar basket, vegetable tikka masala, marinated pork loin with damson sauce and sage mash, cod with a squid and olive ragoût, duck breast with a blackberry sauce, and puddings like warm chocolate, pecan and prune cake with clotted cream and hazelnut meringues with raspberries and blackberries; they also offer a two- or three-course set lunch. *Benchmark main dish: pork wellington £16.00. Two-course evening meal £20.00.*

Free house ~ Licensees Tom Warren and Debbie Lush ~ Real ale ~ Bar food (12-2(2.30 weekends), 7-9(9.30 weekends)) ~ Restaurant ~ (01460) 234476 ~ Well behaved children welcome ~ Dogs allowed in bar ~ Open 12-3, 6-11; 12-11 Sun; closed Mon ~ www.candlelight-inn.co.uk *Recommended by Patrick and Daphne Darley, Bob and Margaret Holder, Cath Hine*

BRISTOL   ST5873   Map 2
Highbury Vaults 🍺 £
St Michael's Hill, Cotham; BS2 8DE

Cheerful town pub with up to eight real ales, good value tasty bar food and friendly atmosphere

A warm welcome, a fine range of real ales and proper home cooking are the mainstays of this extremely popular, unpretentious pub. The little front bar, with the corridor beside it, leads through to a series of small rooms – wooden floors, green and cream paintwork and old-fashioned furniture and prints, including lots of period Royal Family engravings and lithographs in the front room. There's a model railway running on a shelf the full length of the pub, including tunnels through the walls. Bath Ales Gem Bitter, St Austell Tribute and Wells & Youngs Bitter and London Porter, and guests such as Dorset Durdle Door and Teignworthy Reel Ale on handpump and several malt whiskies. The attractive back terrace has tables built into a partly covered flower arbour. In early Georgian times, this was used as the gaol where condemned men ate their last meal – the bars can still be seen on some windows.

🍴 Good value, hearty bar food includes filled rolls, a free-range pork pie ploughman's, burgers such as beef or stilton, sausages with onion gravy, fish pie, various curries and winter casseroles, and puddings like sticky toffee pudding and chocolate puddle pudding. *Benchmark main dish: chilli con carne with cheese £5.95. Two-course evening meal £11.00.*

Youngs ~ Manager Bradd Francis ~ Real ale ~ Bar food (12-2, 7-9) ~ No credit cards ~ (0117) 973 3203 ~ Children welcome ~ Dogs allowed in bar ~ Open 12-12(11 Sun) ~ www.highburyvaults.co.uk *Recommended by Jenny and Peter Lowater, Chris and Angela Buckell, the Didler, Warren Marsh, Roger and Donna Huggins, Barry Collett*

CHARLTON HORETHORNE
Kings Arms 🛏
ST6623 Map 2

B3145 Wincanton–Sherborne; DT9 4NL

Bustling inn with relaxed bars and more formal restaurant, plenty of drinkers and diners, a good choice of ales and wines, and enjoyable food; comfortable bedrooms

Imposing and rather smart, this carefully furnished Edwardian inn has a really good mix of chatty drinkers and those here to eat the first rate food or to stay in the comfortable contemporary bedrooms; there's a friendly welcome for all. The main bar has all manner of local modern art (all for sale) on the dark mulberry or cream walls, nice old carved wooden dining chairs and pine pews around a mix of tables on the slate floor and a woodburning stove. Leading off here is a cosy room with sofas, and newspapers on low tables. Butcombe Bitter, Sharps Doom Bar and a changing guest on handpump are served from the rather fine granite bar counter and they keep 13 wines by the glass, ten malt whiskies and local draught cider. To the left of the main door is an informal dining room with Jacobean-style chairs and tables on the pale wooden floor and more local artwork. The back restaurant (you have to walk past the open kitchen, which is quite fun to peek into) has decorative wood and glass mirrors, wicker or black leather high-backed dining chairs around chunky polished pale wooden tables on coir carpet and handsome striped curtains. At the back of the building, the attractive courtyard has chrome and wicker chairs around teak tables under green parasols and there's a good smokers' shelter overlooking the croquet lawn.

🍴 Using carefully sourced local produce and own-made breads, pasta and ice-cream, the very good modern food might include a cured meat or antipasti platter with caponata, seafood lasagne, ham and eggs, cauliflower risotto and cumin arancini (an italian rice ball), lamb and mint hotpot, chicken fillet burger with tomato chutney, cod with borlotti beans, fennel confit and black olive salad, and puddings such as coconut panna cotta with pineapple and a coconut tuile and treacle tart with vanilla ice-cream. *Benchmark main dish: loin of pork with sweet potatoes, sherry vinegar, redcurrant jus and watercress salad £14.95. Two-course evening meal £21.00.*

Free house ~ Licensee Tony Lethbridge ~ Real ale ~ Bar food (12-2.30, 7-9.30(9 Sun, 10 Fri and Sat)) ~ Restaurant ~ (01963) 220281 ~ Children welcome ~ Dogs allowed in bar ~ Open 10-11; 10.30-10.30 Sun ~ Bedrooms: /£110S ~ www.thekingsarms.co.uk
Recommended by Edward Mirzoeff, John Branston, Mrs C Roe, Tim and Sue Halstead

CHURCHILL   ST4459 Map 1
Crown ◗ £

The Batch; in village, turn off A368 into Skinners Lane at Nelson Arms; BS25 5PP

Unspoilt and unchanging small cottage pub with friendly customers and staff, super range of real ales and homely lunchtime food

'One of my all-time favourites' is how one of our readers describes this simple pub with its untouched interior. As well as a fine choice of real ales, a roaring log fire and a genuinely warm welcome, the small and rather local-feeling stone-floored and cross-beamed room on the right has a wooden window seat, an unusually sturdy settle, built-in wall benches and chatty, friendly customers. The left-hand room has a slate floor and some steps past the big log fire in its large stone fireplace that lead to more sitting space. No noise from music or games (except perhaps dominoes) and up to ten real ales tapped from the cask: Bath Ales Gem Bitter, Bass, Butcombe Bitter, Glastonbury Thriller, Palmers Best, RCH Hewish IPA and PG Steam, St Austell Tribute and changing guest beers. Several wines by the glass, and local ciders. Lavatories are outdoors, and basic. There are garden tables at the front, a smallish back lawn and hill views; the Mendip morris men visit in summer. There's no pub sign outside but no one ever seems to have a problem finding the place. Some of the best walking on the Mendips is close by.

Using beef from cattle grazed in the field next door, the straightforward and reasonably priced lunchtime bar food includes sandwiches (the rare roast beef is popular), good soup, cauliflower cheese, chilli con carne and tasty beef casserole. *Benchmark main dish: home-made chilli £6.40*

Free house ~ Licensee Tim Rogers ~ Real ale ~ Bar food (12-2.30; not evenings) ~ No credit cards ~ (01934) 852995 ~ Children welcome away from bar ~ Dogs welcome ~ Open 11-11(midnight Fri and Sat); 12-10.30 Sun *Recommended by Barry and Anne, Michael Doswell, Dr and Mrs A K Clarke, John and Joan Nash, the Didler, Bob and Margaret Holder, Taff and Gilly Thomas*

CLAPTON-IN-GORDANO   ST4773 Map 1
Black Horse ◗ £

4 miles from M5 junction 19; A369 towards Portishead, then B3124 towards Clevedon; in north Weston opposite school, turn left signposted Clapton, then in village take second right, may be signed Clevedon, Clapton Wick; BS20 7RH

Old-fashioned pub with lots of cheerful customers, friendly service, real ales and cider, and simple lunchtime food; pretty garden

Very pretty in summer with its hanging baskets and tubs, this unspoilt local is popular with locals, farmers and dog walkers – but visitors are made equally welcome. The partly flagstoned and partly red-tiled main room has winged settles and built-in wall benches around narrow, dark wooden tables, window seats, a big log fire with stirrups and bits on the mantelbeam, and amusing cartoons and photographs of the pub. A window in an inner snug is still barred from the days when this room was the petty-sessions gaol; high-backed settles – one a marvellous carved and canopied creature, another with an art nouveau copper insert bearing the leged 'East, West, Hame's Best' – lots of mugs hanging from black beams and plenty of little prints and photographs. There's also a simply furnished room which is the only place families are allowed; darts. Butcombe Bitter, Courage Best, Exmoor Gold, Otter Ale, St Austell

Tribute and Wadworths 6X on handpump or tapped from the cask, several wines by the glass and farm ciders. There are some old rustic tables and benches in the garden, with more to one side of the car park, whose summer flowers are quite a sight. Paths from the pub lead up Naish Hill or to Cadbury Camp.

 Straightforward lunchtime bar food includes good filled baguettes and hot dishes like home-made soup, cauliflower and broccoli cheese, beef stew and paprika chicken. *Benchmark main dish: home-made soup £3.75.*

Enterprise ~ Lease Nicholas Evans ~ Real ale ~ Bar food (12-2; not evenings, not Sun) ~ (01275) 842105 ~ Children in plain family room only ~ Dogs welcome ~ Open 11-11; 12-10 Sun ~ www.thekicker.co.uk *Recommended by Barry and Anne, Chris and Angela Buckell, the Didler, Roy Hoing, Bob and Margaret Holder, Tom Evans, Pat Bunting, Taff and Gilly Thomas*

COMBE FLOREY   ST1531   Map 1
Farmers Arms
Off A358 Taunton–Williton, just N of main village turn-off; TA4 3HZ

Pretty pub with delightful garden, open fire and real ales in cosy bar, popular food in little dining room and friendly landladies

Run by a mother and daughter team, this is a friendly and pretty thatched pub in attractive countryside that's popular with our readers. The charming cottagey garden is a big draw in warm weather with picnic-sets under white parasols and lovely flowering tubs and beds – you may hear the whistle of a steam train as the Taunton–Minehead line runs close by. Inside, it's a small place so you would be wise to book at peak times. The bar has a log fire in a big stone fireplace with lanterns on either side, cushioned pubby chairs and a settle around wooden tables on the flagstone floor and stools at the bar, where they serve Cotleigh Tawny, Exmoor Ale and Gold and St Austell HSD on handpump, and several wines by the glass. The cosy dining room leads off here with traditional seats and tables on the red patterned carpet and heavy beams. Evelyn Waugh lived in the village, as did his son Auberon.

 Using local produce, the well liked food might include sandwiches, creamy garlic mushrooms, crab cakes with lime mayonnaise, omelettes, nut roast with a tomato and basil sauce, gammon with pineapple salsa or a fried egg, faggots with onion gravy and mash, chicken breast stuffed with cheese and wholegrain mustard and wrapped in pancetta, lamb shank on spring greens and bacon, king prawns in garlic and white wine butter with pasta, daily specials, and puddings such as caramel chocolate pot and apple crumble. *Benchmark main dish: home-made pies £9.95. Two-course evening meal £20.00.*

Free house ~ Licensee Patricia Vincent ~ Real ale ~ Bar food (12-2.30, 6.30-9; only curry or chilli on Sun quiz evening) ~ Restaurant ~ (01823) 432267 ~ Children welcome ~ Dogs allowed in bar ~ Open 12-11 ~ www.farmersarmsatcombeflorey.co.uk *Recommended by John Gould, Christine and Neil Townend, Bob and Margaret Holder*

COMBE HAY   ST7359   Map 2
Wheatsheaf 🍴 ♀ 🛏
Village signposted off A367 or B3110 S of Bath; BA2 7EG
Somerset Dining Pub of the Year

Smart and cheerful country dining pub perched prettily above steep wooded valley; attractice bedrooms

As befits a pub so highly rated for its food, most of the space here is devoted to dining; the exception is one central area by a big fireplace, which has sofas on dark flagstones, with daily papers and current issues of magazines such as *The Field* and *Country Life* on a low table. All the other parts have stylish high-backed grey wicker dining chairs around chunky modern dining tables, on parquet or coir matting. It's all fresh and bright, with block-mounted photoprints, contemporary artwork and mirrors framed in colourful ceramic mosaics (many for sale) on white-painted stonework or robin's-egg blue plaster walls. The sills of the many shuttered windows house anything from old soda siphons to a stuffed kingfisher and a model tugboat, and glinting glass wall chandeliers and nightlights in entertaining holders supplement the ceiling spotlights. They have a very good if not cheap choice of wines, Butcombe Bitter and Adam Hensons Rare Breed on handpump, and Cheddar Valley cider; staff are friendly and informal, the background music faint enough and the cheerful springer is called Brie. Picnic-sets in the two-level front garden have a fine view down over the church and valley; you can walk from the pub. The bedrooms are stylishly simple and spacious.

 Using game and fish caught by the landlord and locally foraged produce (wild mushrooms, damsons, watercress and so forth), the first class food might include lunchtime sandwiches, local crayfish with udon noodles, chilli and cashew nuts, goats cheese with their own honey and pickled walnuts, beer-battered cod with crushed peas and skinny chips, butternut squash and sage risotto, hake with roast garlic mash and creamed mussels, home-made beef and blue cheese burger, fish pie with rouille, herb-crusted lamb with niçoise garnish and fondant potatoes, and puddings such as milk chocolate semifreddo with Jaffa Cakes and mango jelly, coconut panna cotta and mango sorbet. *Benchmark main dish: fresh daily fish £13.00. Two-course evening meal £22.00.*

Free house ~ Licensee Ian Barton ~ Real ale ~ Bar food (12-2, 7-9; not Sun evening, not Mon) ~ (01225) 833504 ~ Children welcome ~ Dogs welcome ~ Open 10.30-3, 6-11; closed Sun evening, all day Mon ~ Bedrooms: /$120S ~ www.wheatsheafcombehay.co.uk
Recommended by Dr and Mrs A K Clarke, M P Mackenzie, Taff and Gilly Thomas

---

CORTON DENHAM   ST6322   Map 2

Queens Arms

Village signposted off B3145 N of Sherborne; DT9 4LR

Civilised stone inn, super choice of drinks, interesting food and a sunny garden; comfortable bedrooms

Our readers enjoy their visits to this 18th-c country inn very much. It's a rather civilised place with a warm welcome for all from the helpful and friendly young staff, and a fantastic choice of drinks and food. The plain high-beamed bar has a woodburning stove in the inglenook at one end, with rugs on flagstones in front of the raised fireplace at the other, some old pews, barrel seats and a sofa, church candles and maybe a big bowl of flowers; a little room off here has just one big table – nice for a party of eight or so – and there's also a busy dining room. Cotleigh Snowy, Moor Illusion, Ported Peat Porter and Revival, and Oakham Scarlet Macaw on handpump, 34 wines (including champagne) by the glass from a carefully chosen list, over 60 whiskies, six ciders, unusual bottled beers from all over the world, and eight local apple juices. A south-facing back terrace has teak tables and chairs under parasols (or heaters if it's cool), with colourful flower tubs. The comfortable bedrooms have lovely country views and the breakfasts include fresh bread and home-made preserves; there are some fine surrounding walks.

The enterprising food (with a beer and a wine recommended for each dish on the main menu) uses their own pigs and free-range eggs and other very local produce, and might include sandwiches, red onion marmalade tart with goats cheese and basil mousse with walnut vinaigrette, steak tartare, haggis, neeps and tatties, a burger with cheddar and tomato chutney, ham, egg and chips, spiced aubergine and halloumi pithivier with coriander couscous and harrisa and carrot purée, tuna loin, tomato and chilli tagliatelle with a lime and coriander dressing, lamb rump with cauliflower pancake, roast root vegetables and a roasted lamb and cranberry jus, and puddings like golden syrup and salted caramel crème brûlée with oat and raisin biscuits and poached pear with mandarin and champagne ice-cream; they also offer a winter three-course set lunch menu (not at weekends). *Benchmark main dish: saddle of venison with wild mushrooms and shallots and garlic pommes purée and whisky jus £16.95. Two-course evening meal £22.50.*

Free house ~ Licensees Jeanette and Gordon Reid ~ Real ale ~ Bar food (12-3, 6-10(9.30 Sun)) ~ Restaurant ~ (01963) 220317 ~ Children welcome ~ Dogs allowed in bar and bedrooms ~ Open 10-11; 11-11 Sun ~ Bedrooms: $75S($80B)/$110B ~ www.thequeensarms.com *Recommended by Dr Nigel Bowles, Patrick and Daphne Darley, Will Douglas German, David Hudd, David and Sue Smith, Edward Mirzoeff, Amber Cotton*

CROSCOMBE ST5844 Map 2
George 🍺 🛏️
Long Street (A371 Wells–Shepton Mallet); BA5 3QH

Carefully renovated old coaching inn, warmly welcoming, informative canadian landlord, bar food cooked by landlady, good local beers, attractive garden; bedrooms

This is a thoroughly enjoyable place and a true all-rounder, and we get warm praise from our readers on all aspects – the terrific food, the local beers, the comfortable bedrooms (there are now two) and of course for the interested and genuinely warm welcome from Mr Graham, who is a first-rate landlord. The main bar has some stripped stone, dark wooden tables and chairs and more comfortable seats, winter log fires in inglenook fireplaces and the family grandfather clock; a snug area has recently been added with a stone fireplace and woodburning stove. The attractive dining room has more stripped stone, local artwork and photographs on the burgundy walls and high-backed cushioned dining chairs around a mix of tables. The back bar has canadian timber reclaimed from the local church, and there's a family room with games and books for children. King George the Thirst (brewed exclusively for them by Blindmans), Butcombe Bitter, Cheddar Ales Potholer and Devilfish Stingray on handpump or tapped from the cask, four farm ciders and ten wines by the glass. Darts, shut the box, a canadian wooden table game called crokinole, shove-ha'penny, background music and separate TV room. The friendly pub dog is called Tessa and the slightly more aloof cat DJ. The attractive, sizeable garden has seats on a heated and covered terrace, flower borders and a grassed area; children's swings.

Using home-grown and local, seasonal produce and cooked by the landlady, the highly thought of food includes filled baguettes, scallops with garlic butter and a balsamic reduction, goats cheese tart, bangers and mash with onion gravy, beer-battered cod, vegetable lasagne, specials like pork and apricot pie, coq au vin and salmon fillet with prawn and saffron sauce on spring onion crushed new potatoes, and puddings such as rich chocolate cheesecake and crème brûlée; steak and chips night is every Wednesday and their extremely popular curry night on the last Thursday of the month. *Benchmark main dish: steak in ale pie £10.95. Two-course evening meal £16.45.*

Free house ~ Licensees Peter and Veryan Graham ~ Real ale ~ Bar food (12-2, 6-9) ~ Restaurant ~ (01749) 342306 ~ Children welcome ~ Dogs allowed in bar ~ Open 12-2.30, 6-11 ~ Bedrooms: £35S/£70S ~ www.thegeorgeinn.co.uk *Recommended by David and Sharon Collison, Rupert Handley, Bruce and Sharon Eden, R T and J C Moggridge, Dr J Barrie Jones, David and Sue Atkinson, Michael Butler*

DULVERTON
SS9127   Map 1

Woods ★ ⑪ ♀
Bank Square; TA22 9BU

Smartly informal place with exceptional wines, real ales, first rate food and a good mix of customers

Our readers love this place and since many others do, too, it's best to book a table in advance. It's run by a charming landlord and his helpful, courteous staff and attracts a really good mix of locals and visitors. Many are here for the top class food, but the local beers and, particularly, the exceptional wines draw customers from far and wide. They will open any of their 400 wines on the quite extraordinarily good list to serve just a glass, and there's also an unlisted collection of about 500 well aged new world wines that Mr Groves will happily chat about. St Austell Dartmoor Best, Otter Head and a changing guest beer tapped from the cask, a farm cider, many sherries and some unusual spirits. The pub is on the edge of Exmoor, and there are plenty of good sporting prints on the salmon pink walls, some antlers, other hunting trophies, stuffed birds and a couple of salmon rods. There are bare boards on the left by the bar counter, some tables partly separated by stable-style timbering and masonry dividers, and a carpeted area on the right with a woodburning stove in the big fireplace; daily papers; maybe unobjectionable background music. Big windows look on to the quiet town centre (or you can sit out on the pavement at a couple of metal tables). A small suntrap back courtyard has a few picnic-sets.

They breed their own pigs and chickens to use in the excellent food and, as well as fair value light lunches like filled ciabatta rolls, honey-roast ham and egg, a good cheeseburger and seared steak with crispy bacon, offer more pricey, restauranty choices including home-cured gravadlax with smoked salmon tartare, marinated squid and wasabi mayonnaise, bresaola with mustard ice-cream, tomato, red onion, olive and feta tart, ballotine of chicken stuffed with wild garlic with wild mushrooms, asparagus and poultry sauce, slow-roast lamb shoulder, rack of lamb and fried liver with caramelised onions, confit garlic and thyme sauce, and puddings like rhubarb eton mess with stem ginger ice-cream and sticky toffee pudding with walnut and toffee popcorn sauce and clotted cream. *Benchmark main dish: slow-roast pork with black pudding, crackling and apple jam £16.50. Two-course evening meal £23.00.*

Free house ~ Licensee Patrick Groves ~ Real ale ~ Bar food (12-2, 7-9.30) ~ Restaurant ~ (01398) 324007 ~ Children welcome ~ Dogs welcome ~ Open 11-3, 6-midnight; 12-3, 7-11 Sun ~ www.woodsdulverton.co.uk *Recommended by Richard, Anne and Kate Ansell, M G Hart, Guy Vowles, Jeremy Whitehorn, Sheila Topham, John and Jackie Chalcraft, Mr and Mrs P D Titcomb, Lynda and Trevor Smith, Gerry Price, Mike Gorton, Bob and Margaret Holder*

The knife-and-fork award ⑪ distinguishes pubs where the food is of exceptional quality.

HALLATROW
Old Station

ST6357 Map 2

A39 S of Bristol; BS39 6EN

Friendly former railway hotel with extraordinary knick-knacks, Pullman carriage restaurant and friendly licensees

The forest of bric-a-brac hanging from the ceiling and on the walls in this friendly 1920s former railway hotel will amaze you. It includes anything from musical instruments to half an old Citroën, from china cows to postboxes, from sailing boats to hundreds of beer badges – and so forth. The rather handsome island bar counter has Brains Rev James and Butcombe Bitter on handpump, and a mix of furnishings includes a sofa, high chairs around big cask tables, and small settles and dining or library chairs around more orthodox tables. The more formal (and opulent) dining room is actually a Pullman train carriage and photographs in the bar show the hair-raising difficulty of getting it here. The garden alongside has modern seats and tables on decking and there are picnic-sets on the grass. The bedrooms are in a converted outbuilding (they don't offer breakfast).

 Popular food includes lunchtime filled baguettes, crab and prawn parcel wrapped in smoked salmon, warm goats cheese tart with tomato, chilli chutney and vinaigrette, local sausages in red wine gravy and onions, roasted butternut squash filled with wild mushroom and pine nut risotto, chicken stuffed with smoked cheese and wrapped in parma ham with pesto mash, outdoor-reared gammon with fresh pineapple, and puddings such as a trilogy of chocolate mousse, dark chocolate and Tia Maria, white chocolate and Cointreau and mild chocolate and Amaretti, and a crumble of the day. *Benchmark main dish: pork hock with crackling, cider gravy and apple and sage mash £12.25. Two-course evening meal £18.50.*

Brains ~ Managers Neville and Debbie King ~ Real ale ~ Bar food (12-2.30, 6-9(9.30 Fri and Sat); all day Sun) ~ Restaurant ~ (01761) 452228 ~ Children welcome ~ Dogs allowed in bar ~ Open 12-3, 5-11; 12-12 Fri and Sat; 12-10.30 Sun ~ Bedrooms: /£57B ~ *Recommended by John and Sheena Radnedge, Dave Braisted, Stuart Paulley*

HINTON ST GEORGE
Lord Poulett Arms 🍴 ☍ 🛏

ST4212 Map 1

Off A30 W of Crewkerne and off Merriott road (declassified – former A356, off B3165) N of Crewkerne; TA17 8SE

Thatched 17th-c stone inn with antique-filled rooms, top class food, good choice of drinks and a pretty garden; nice cottagey bedrooms

A great many of our readers use this charming pub as a civilised stop-off from the busy A30 as they know they will get a genuinely friendly welcome and some delicious food. Several attractive cosy linked areas have rugs on bare boards or flagstones, open fires (one in an inglenook and one in a raised fireplace that separates two rooms), walls of honey-coloured stone or painted in bold Farrow & Ball colours, hop-draped beams, antique brass candelabra, fresh flowers and candles,

---

Please tell us if the décor, atmosphere, food or drink at a pub is different from our description. We rely on readers' reports to keep us up to date: feedback@goodguides.com, or (no stamp needed) The Good Pub Guide, FREEPOST TN1569, Wadhurst, E Sussex TN5 7BR.

and some lovely old farmhouse, windsor and ladderback chairs around fine oak or elm tables. Branscombe Branoc, Otter Ale and a guest such as Dorset Tom Browns on handpump, 14 wines by the glass, jugs of Pimms and home-made cordial; the pub cat is called Honey. Outside, under a wisteria-clad pergola, there are white metalwork tables and chairs in a mediterranean-style, lavender-edged gravelled area and picnic-sets in a wildflower meadow; boules. The bedrooms are pretty and cottagey. This is a peaceful village with nice surrounding walks.

Food – using home-grown vegetables and other local organic produce – is excellent and might include sandwiches, smoked haddock and bacon fishcake with sweet chilli, lemon and sesame mayonnaise, game pâté with red onion jam, chickpea, red lentil and coconut dhal, pork loin chop with garlic and rosemary-roasted potatoes, smoked streaky bacon and cider apple cream, gilthead bream fillets with a herb and shallot salad, chorizo and lemon dressing, confit pigeon breast with butternut squash purée, vegetable crisps and port gravy, and puddings like molten chocolate cake and rhubarb and custard crunch. *Benchmark main dish: crispy lager-battered fish, triple-cooked chips and gribiche sauce £12.95. Two-course evening meal £19.50.*

Free house ~ Licensees Steve Hill and Michelle Paynton ~ Real ale ~ Bar food (12-2.30(4 Sun), 7-9.15; pizzas 3(5 Sun)-6.30) ~ (01460) 73149 ~ Children welcome ~ Dogs allowed in bar ~ Live music every other Sun Jun-Sept ~ Open 12-11 ~ Bedrooms: £65B/£95B ~ www.lordpoulettarms.com *Recommended by Simon and Philippa Hughes, John Chambers, R T and J C Moggridge, Simon Pyle, Hilary Kerr*

HUISH EPISCOPI
Rose & Crown 🍺 £
ST4326 Map 1

Off A372 E of Langport; TA10 9QT

Unchanging old place in the same family for over a century, local cider and beers, simple food and a friendly welcome

Known locally as Eli's (after the present licensees' grandfather), this quite unspoilt old place has been in the same friendly family for over 140 years. There's no bar as such, just a central flagstoned still room with casks of Teignworthy Reel Ale and a couple of guests such as Hop Back Crop Circle and and Palmers 200; also local Burrow Hill farm cider and cider brandy. The casual little front parlours, with their unusual pointed-arch windows, have family photographs, books, cribbage, dominoes, shove-ha'penny and bagatelle, and host a good mix of locals and visitors. A much more orthodox big back extension family room has pool, a games machine and a juke box; skittle alley. There are tables in a garden and a second enclosed garden has a children's play area; you can camp (free by arrangement to pub customers) on the adjoining paddock. Summer morris men, and fine walks and the site of the Battle of Langport (1645) are close by.

Reasonably priced, the pubby food might include sandwiches, ploughman's, steak in ale pie, pork, apple and cider cobber, pork sausages with onion gravy, stilton and broccoli tart, and puddings like apple crumble and bread and butter pudding. *Benchmark main dish: steak in ale pie £7.95. Two-course evening meal £11.00.*

Free house ~ Licensees Maureen Pittard, Stephen Pittard, Patricia O'Malley ~ Real ale ~ Bar food (12-2, 5.30-7.30; not Sun evening) ~ No credit cards ~ (01458) 250494 ~ Children welcome ~ Dogs welcome ~ Live folk music third Sat of month, irish music last Thurs of month ~ Open 11.30-3, 5.30-11; 11.30-11.30 Fri and Sat; 12-10.30 Sun
Recommended by the Didler, Paul Humphreys

LUXBOROUGH   SS9837   Map 1

Royal Oak 🍴 🛏

Kingsbridge; S of Dunster on minor roads into Brendon Hills – OS Sheet 181 map reference 983378; TA23 0SH

Smashing place in wonderful countryside, interesting bar and restaurant food, local beers and ciders and attentive, friendly staff; warm, comfortable bedrooms

---

As ever, our readers love this atmospheric inn, deep in Exmoor National Park. The compact bar has bags of character and there's always a really good mix of chatty locals (often with their dogs) and visitors – and you can be sure of a genuinely warm welcome from the landlord and his helpful staff. There's an informal and cheerful feel, lovely ancient flagstones, several rather fine settles (one with a very high back and one still with its book rest), scrubbed kitchen tables, lots of beer mats on beams, a cart horse saddle and a huge brick fireplace with a warm log fire; a simpler back room has an ancient cobbled floor, some quarry tiles and a stone fireplace. A room just off the bar is set for dining, with attractive old pine furniture and horse and hunting prints, and there are two other dining rooms as well. One is green painted and the larger end one has stuffed fish in glass cabinets, fish paintings and fishing rods on dark red walls, leather and brass-stud dining chairs and more formal chairs around a mix of old tables, with turkish-style rugs on the black slate floor. Exmoor Ale and Gold and a couple of guest beers on handpump, 15 wines by the glass and Thatcher's and Rich's farmhouse cider; darts, shove-ha'penny, and board games. There are some seats out in the charming back courtyard. This is an exceptionally enjoyable place to stay for a few days and there are memorable nearby walks in the wonderful surrounding countryside; the Coleridge Way is popular.

As well as lunchtime filled baguettes, the reliably good food, using lamb and beef from nearby farms and seasonal local game, might include potted duck and juniper with cumberland sauce, ceviche of red mullet and scallops, medley of grilled vegetables with sage polenta and tuscan sauce, tuna loin with chilli-roasted corn and shallots, venison casserole with dark chocolate and red wine, braised lamb shanks with roasted garlic mash, daily specials, and puddings. *Benchmark main dish: rump of local lamb with gremolata and merlot sauce £17.95. Two-course evening meal £21.50.*

Free house ~ Licensees James and Sian Waller ~ Real ale ~ Bar food (12-2, 7-9) ~ Restaurant ~ (01984) 640319 ~ Children must be over 10 or allowed in at landlord's discretion ~ Dogs allowed in bar and bedrooms ~ Open 12-2.30, 6-11 (all day school holidays); 12-11 Sun and Sat ~ Bedrooms: £55S(£65B)/£90S(£75B) ~ www.theroyaloakinnluxborough.co.uk *Recommended by Adrian Johnson, David Jackman, Stephen Bennett, S G N Bennett, Walter and Susan Rinaldi-Butcher, the Farmers, John and Joan Nash, the Didler, Peter Crawford, Bob and Margaret Holder, John and Fiona McIlwain, Mr and Mrs P D Titcomb, Lynda and Trevor Smith, John and Alison Hamilton, Anthony Barnes, Guy Vowles, Dr Nigel Bowles, Chris and Jan Swanwick, Michael Butler, Tony and Gene Freemantle*

PITNEY   ST4527   Map 1

Halfway House 🍺

Just off B3153 W of Somerton; TA10 9AB

Bustling, friendly local with up to ten real ales, local ciders and good simple food

---

As delightful and as unchanging as ever, this remains an honest village local with an excellent range of real ales. Tapped from the cask and changing regularly, they might include Butcombe Bitter, Cheddar Totty Pot, Crouch Vale Brewers Gold, Exmoor Fox, Forge Litehouse, Hop Back Summer Lightning, Moor Southern Star, Otter Bright, RCH Pitchfork and Teignworthy Reel Ale. They also keep five local farm ciders, a dozen malt whiskies and several wines by the glass. No music or games machines. A good mix of people are usually found chatting at communal tables in the three old-fashioned rooms, all with roaring log fires, and there's a homely feel underlined by a profusion of books, maps and newspapers; cribbage, dominoes and board games. Tables outside.

As well as lunchtime sandwiches, simple food served in generous helpings includes filled baked potatoes, french onion tart, sausage and mash with onion gravy, lamb, chicken or beef curry, and pork in cider casserole. *Benchmark main dish: fish and chips £9.50. Two-course evening meal £15.00.*

Free house ~ Licensee Mark Phillips ~ Real ale ~ Bar food (12-2.30, 7-9.30; some sort of food all day Sun) ~ (01458) 252513 ~ Children welcome ~ Dogs welcome ~ Open 11.30-3, 5.30-11(midnight Sat); 12-11 Sun ~ www.thehalfwayhouse.co.uk
Recommended by Patrick and Daphne Darley, B and M Kendall, Ted and Charlotte Routley, Liz and Jeremy Baker, Ken and Barbara Turner, the Didler, Edward Mirzoeff, Bob and Margaret Holder

PRIDDY
ST5250   Map 2
Queen Victoria £
Village signed off B3135; Pelting Drove; BA5 3BA

Stone-built country pub with lots of interconnecting rooms, open fires and woodburners, a friendly atmosphere and staff, real ales and honest food; seats outside

There's a lot of character in the various dimly lit rooms and alcoves in this creeper-clad stone pub, and plenty of original features, too. One room leading off the main bar has a log fire in a big old stone fireplace with a huge cauldron to one side, and there are two woodburners as well, one in a raised fireplace. The floors are flagstoned or slate, the walls are bare stone (though the smarter dining room is half panelled and half painted) and hung with Queen Victoria photographs, horse tack and farm tools, and the customers are chatty and cheerful. Furniture is traditional: cushioned wall settles, farmhouse and other solid chairs around all manner of wooden tables, one nice old pew beside a screen settle making a cosy alcove, and high chairs beside the bar counter, where they serve Butcombe Bitter and Gold and Fullers London Pride on handpump, two farm ciders, 20 malt whiskies and ten wines by the glass. There are seats on the front courtyard and more across the lane, where there's a children's playground.

As well as filled baguettes, the honest, reasonably priced food includes chicken liver and bacon pâté, deep-fried brie wedges with plum sauce, beef in ale or fish pie, vegetable and mozzarella burger, a curry of the day, chilli with chips, chicken breast with barbecue sauce, and puddings like lemon meringue cake and treacle sponge. *Benchmark main dish: beef in ale pie £9.75. Two-course evening meal £13.20.*

Butcombe ~ Manager Mark Walton ~ Real ale ~ Bar food (12-3(4 winter Sun), 6-9; all day Sat and from Easter-October; not winter Sun evening) ~ (01749) 676385 ~ Children welcome ~ Dogs welcome ~ Open 12-11(10.30 Sun) ~ www.queenvictoria.butcombe.com
Recommended by Chris and Angela Buckell, Paul Humphreys

STANTON WICK
Carpenters Arms    ST6162 Map 2
Village signposted off A368, just W of junction with A37
S of Bristol; BS39 4BX

Bustling, warm-hearted dining pub in country setting with enjoyable, popular food, friendly staff and a fine choice of drinks; comfortable bedrooms

Once you've found this attractive little stone inn, you will tend to come back again and again. The landlord and his staff are friendly and helpful, the food is highly enjoyable and there are good country walks close by. Coopers Parlour on the right has one or two beams, seats around heavy tables on the tartan carpet and attractive curtains and window plants; on the angle between here and the bar area, there's a fat woodburning stove in an opened-through corner fireplace. The bar has wood-backed wall settles with cushions, stripped-stone walls and a big log fire in an inglenook. There's also a snug inner room (brightened by mirrors in arched recesses) and a restaurant with leather sofas and easy chairs in a comfortable lounge area at one end. Butcombe Bitter, Courage Directors and Sharps Doom Bar on handpump, ten wines by the glass (and some interesting bin ends), and several malt whiskies; TV in the snug. There are picnic-sets on the front terrace and pretty flower beds, hanging baskets and tubs. The bedrooms are comfortable and well equipped.

Interesting and very good food might include sandwiches, duck liver and port pâté with spicy tomato and caramelised onion chutney, cajun chicken skewers with garlic and saffron mayonnaise, puff pastry of wild and field mushrooms with leeks, red onions and chive cream sauce, steak and mushroom in red wine pie, ham and free-range eggs, chicken breast with dauphinoise potatoes and root vegetables, pork loin on fondant potato and spinach with sage and onion stuffing and baby onion and pancetta sauce, and puddings like vanilla panna cotta with prune and apricot compote and treacle tart with clotted cream. *Benchmark main dish: confit duck with green beans, bacon and rosemary sauce £14.95. Two-course evening meal £20.45.*

Free house ~ Licensee Simon Pledge ~ Real ale ~ Bar food (12-2.30, 6-9.30(10 Fri and Sat); sandwiches all afternoon Sat; 12-9 Sun) ~ Restaurant ~ (01761) 490202 ~ Children welcome ~ Dogs allowed in bar ~ Open 11-11; 12-10.30 Sun ~ Bedrooms: £72.50B/£105B ~ www.the-carpenters-arms.co.uk *Recommended by M G Hart, Dick Withington, Dr and Mrs C W Thomas, Chris and Val Ramstedt, Tania Harris, Steve and Liz Tilley, Alan Bowker, Lindsay White, Warren Marsh, David Jackman, Dr and Mrs A K Clarke*

STOKE ST GREGORY
Rose & Crown    ST3527 Map 1
Woodhill; follow North Curry signpost off A378 by junction with A358 –
keep on to Stoke, bearing right in centre, passing church and follow lane for
0.5 miles; TA3 6EW

Friendly, family-run pub with an extensive menu of popular food and a fine choice of drinks; comfortable bedrooms

With lots of events happening throughout the year, this bustling pub is always fun to visit. It's been run by the same hands-on, welcoming family for well over 30 years now. The interior is more or less open plan; the bar area has wooden stools by a curved brick and pale wood topped counter with Exmoor Ale, Otter Ale and a guest like Butcombe

Bitter on handpump, local farm cider and several wines by the glass.
This leads into a long, airy dining room with all manner of light and dark
wooden dining chairs and pews around a mix of tables under a high-
raftered ceiling. There are two other beamed dining rooms as well, with
similar furnishings and photographs on the walls of the village and the
recent fire damage to the pub; one room has a woodburning stove and
another an 18th-c glass-covered well in one corner. Throughout, there
are flagstoned or wooden floors. The sheltered front terrace has plenty
of seats. They have three ensuite bedrooms, two of which can connect to
make a family room.

As well as a winter 'credit munch' menu and a set two-course menu, the
popular food might include specials such as creamed exotic mushrooms on
toast, saddle of venison and peppered pear salad, and pork tenderloin marinated in
local brandy with grain mustard sauce, plus sandwiches, mussels in local cider with
cream and garlic, a boxed baked camembert (to share), vegetable stroganoff, beef
burger topped with cheese, tandoori chicken with onions and bell peppers, lamb
rump with redcurrant sauce, and puddings like white chocolate panna cotta with
praline and croissant and butter pudding. *Benchmark main dish: liver, bacon and
caramelised red onion gravy £9.75. Two-course evening meal £18.95.*

Free house ~ Licensees Stephen, Sally, Richard and Leonie Browning ~ Real ale ~
Bar food (12-2, 7-9) ~ Restaurant ~ (01823) 490296 ~ Children welcome ~ Dogs
allowed in bar ~ Open 11-3, 6-11; 12-3, 6.30-10.30 Sun ~ Bedrooms: £55B/£85B ~
www.browningpubs.com *Recommended by M G Hart, Sara Fulton, Roger Baker, Richard Cole,
Dr Brian and Mrs Anne Hamilton, Dr and Mrs C W Thomas, Richard and Judy Winn, R T and
J C Moggridge, Derek Goldrei, Bob and Margaret Holder, Damian and Lucy Buxton, Richard and
Liz Thorne*

WATERROW
Rock 🍴 🍷 🛏

ST0525   Map 1

A361 Wiveliscombe–Bampton; TA4 2AX

**Welcoming timbered inn, local ales, interesting food and a nice mix of
customers; comfortable bedrooms**

Although there's quite an emphasis on the imaginative food and
attractive bedrooms in this striking timbered inn, locals drop
in regularly for a pint and a chat and the atmosphere is relaxed and
friendly. The bar area has a dark brown leather sofa and low table with
newspapers and books in front of the stone fireplace with its log fire, and
big blackboard menus. There's a mix of dining chairs and wooden tables
on the partly wood and partly red-carpeted floor, a few high-backed
bar chairs, hunting paintings and photographs and a couple of built-in
cushioned window seats. Cotleigh Tawny, Exmoor Ale and Otter Ale on
handpump, several wines by the glass and farm cider. A back room has
a pool table; darts and background music. Up some steps from the bar is
the heavily beamed restaurant. The welsh collie is called Meg. There are
a few seats under umbrellas by the road.

Using beef from their own farm and other top quality local produce, the
particularly good bar food might include lunchtime sandwiches, pigeon breast
with black pudding and salad, chicken liver parfait with basil jam, home-cooked
ham with free-range eggs, leek, cheddar, shallot and potato croquettes with tomato
and thyme sauce, fresh haddock in home-made batter, free-range chicken breast in
bacon stuffed with wild mushrooms with a madeira and cream sauce and cranberry
compote, slow-roasted outdoor-reared belly of pork with cider gravy and onion
mash, venison steak with dauphinoise potatoes and port and redcurrant sauce,

and puddings. *Benchmark main dish: local rib-eye steak with home-made chips £16.50. Two-course evening meal £19.50.*

Free house ~ Licensees Matt Harvey and Joanna Oldman ~ Real ale ~ Bar food (12-2.30, 6-9.30) ~ Restaurant ~ (01984) 623293 ~ Children welcome ~ Dogs allowed in bar and bedrooms ~ Open 12-3, 6-11 ~ Bedrooms: £60B/£85B ~ www.rockinn.co.uk
Recommended by M G Hart, John Urquhart, David Saunders, Mike and Mary Carter, Liz and Jeremy Baker, Guy Vowles, John and Fiona McIlwain, Patrick and Daphne Darley, Bob and Margaret Holder

 **WELLS** ST5546   Map 2

Fountain
St Thomas Street; BA5 2UU

Friendly and attractive small pub in town centre, with a bustling atmosphere and upstairs restaurant

Popular locally but with a welcome for visitors, too, this is an attractive little pub with blue shutters and pretty window boxes; it was built in the 18th c to house builders working on the nearby cathedral. There are always lots of customers popping in and out but the big, comfortable bar has plenty of room, along with a large open fire, some interesting bric-a-brac, Butcombe Bitter and Sharps Doom Bar on handpump and several wines by the glass; unobtrusive background music and board games. There's an upstairs restaurant, too, called Boxers.

Well liked food includes soup, pork and apricot terrine with a red onion, apple and balsamic jam, ham and eggs, salad niçoise, sausages with onion gravy, a quiche of the day, mediterranean ratatouille pasta topped with goats cheese, cod steak with lemon and dill butter, duck breast with orange and honey jus, and puddings; they have a good value two-course set menu on Monday evening and an over-60s lunch club. *Benchmark main dish: chargrilled steak topped with peppercorn sauce with beer-battered onion rings £15.50. Two-course evening meal £20.50.*

Punch ~ Tenants Adrian and Sarah Lawrence ~ Real ale ~ Bar food (12-2, 7-9.30) ~ Restaurant ~ (01749) 672317 ~ Children welcome ~ Open 12-2.30, 6-11; 12-2.30, 7-10.30 Sun ~ www.fountaininn.co.uk   *Recommended by N R White, Paul Humphreys, R K Phillips*

 **WRINGTON** ST4762   Map 2

Plough
2.5 miles off A370 Bristol–Weston, from bottom of Rhodiate Hill; BS40 5QA

Welcoming, popular pub with bustling bar and two dining rooms, good food and well kept beer, and seats outside

Only a 10-minute drive from Cheddar Gorge and handy for Bristol Airport, this is a neatly kept and friendly pub in a picturesque village, and our readers enjoy their visits here very much. There's a chatty bar with stools against the counter where they serve Butcombe Bitter (the brewery is in the village), St Austell Tribute and Wells & Youngs Bitter on handpump and 18 wines by the glass, and two distinct dining rooms – one at the back with lots of big windows that overlook the gazebo and garden. The rooms are linked by open doorways and throughout there are three winter fires, slate or wooden floors, beams and standing timbers, plenty of pictures on the planked, red or yellow walls and all manner of high-backed leather and wooden dining and farmhouse chairs around many different sizes of table; fresh flowers, a games chest, table skittles and helpful service. There are picnic-sets at the front and on the back grass; boules. They hold a farmers' market on the second Friday of the month. This is sister pub to the Rattlebone at Sherston (Wiltshire).

Using local, seasonal produce, 'country bistro'-style food might include lunchtime sandwiches, crab, spring onion and chilli parcels with mango salsa, coarse game terrine with home-made spiced apple chutney, home-cooked ham with free-range eggs, smoked salmon and prawns with tagliatelle, bangers and grain mustard mash with onion gravy, home-made burger with chips and coleslaw, specials such as whole plaice with home-made tartare sauce and cod fillet with parmesan mash and a tomato pesto, and puddings like white chocolate and cranberry cheesecake with berry compote and black cherry and frangipane tart. *Benchmark main dish: smoked haddock with spinach, poached egg, cheddar and cream £11.00. Two-course evening meal £19.45.*

Youngs ~ Tenant Jason Read ~ Real ale ~ Bar food (12-2.30, 6-9.30; 12-5 Sun; not Sun evening) ~ Restaurant ~ (01934) 862871 ~ Children welcome ~ Dogs allowed in bar ~ Open 12-3, 5-11; 12-12 Fri and Sat; 12-11 Sun ~ www.theploughatwrington.co.uk
Recommended by Hugh Roberts, Bruce and Sharon Eden, Bob and Margaret Holder, Robin Manners

Also Worth a Visit in Somerset

Besides the fully inspected pubs, you might like to try these pubs that have been recommended to us and described by readers. Do tell us what you think of them: feedback@goodguides.com

AXBRIDGE ST4354
★ **Lamb** (01934) 732253
The Square; off A371 Cheddar–Winscombe; BS26 2AP Big rambling carpeted pub with heavy 15th-c beams and timbers, stone and roughcast walls, large stone fireplaces, old settles, unusual bar front with old bottles set in plaster, Butcombe and guests, well chosen wine and good coffee, enjoyable food including vegetarian and children's, OAP lunch deals (Tues, Thurs), friendly service, board games, table skittles and skittle alley; they may try to keep your credit card while you eat; dogs allowed, pretty and sheltered small back garden, medieval King John's Hunting Lodge (NT) opposite, open all day Thurs-Sun. *(M G Hart, Paul Humphreys, Steve and Claire Harvey)*

BACKWELL ST4767
New Inn (01275) 462199
West Town Road (A370 W of Bristol); BS48 3BE Restaur

ury pub with imaginative, well presented modern food (not Sun evening) from owner/chef including good value lunchtime set menu (Wed-Fri), well kept Bath Gem, Butcombe and St Austell Tribute, good wines, friendly willing staff; disabled access with help, big back garden, open all day (till 6pm Sun). *(Steve and Liz Tilley, Tom Evans, Mike Burkinshaw, M G Hart)*

BARROW GURNEY ST5367
Princes Motto (01458) 850451
B3130, just off A370/A38; BS48 3RY Cosy and welcoming, with unpretentious

local feel in traditional tap room, long lounge/dining area up behind, ales such as Butcombe and Wadworths, good value weekday lunchtime food, log fire, some panelling, cricket team photographs, jugs and china; pleasant garden with terrace, open all day. *(Taff and Gilly Thomas)*

BARTON ST DAVID ST5432
Barton Inn (01458) 850451
Main Street; TA11 6BZ Unpretentious lived-in and locally well loved brick pub, open plan bar with bare boards and quarry tiles, old pews and battered tables, rough pine panelling, well kept constantly changing cask-tapped ales, real ciders, simple food such as pizzas and baguettes (no menu), lots of pictures, posters and bric-a-brac; big screen TV for rugby; wet dogs and muddy walkers welcome, wheelchair accessible (friendly locals may also lend a hand), pub sign in mirror writing, events such as frog racing and worm charming. *(the Didler)*

BATH ST7165
Boathouse (01225) 482584
Newbridge Road; BA1 3NB Large, light and airy family-friendly pub in nice riverside spot near Kennet & Avon marina, good value food from club sandwiches and sharing boards up, efficient courteous young staff, well kept Brains and guests, decent house wines, rugs on wooden floor, conservatory on lower level, newspapers; children very welcome, boat views from garden tables and deck, nine bedrooms some with balconies overlooking the river. *(Ian Phillips)*

BATH   ST7465
Chequers (01225) 360017
Rivers Street; BA1 2QA Renovated pub
with enjoyable food including set deals, real
ales and decent wines by the glass, upstairs
restaurant, friendly service. *(Taff Thomas,
S Chaudhuri)*

BATH   ST7564
✶Coeur de Lion (01225) 463568
*Northumberland Place; off High Street
by W H Smith; BA1 5AR* Tiny stained-
glass fronted single-room pub, perhaps Bath's
prettiest, simple, cosy and jolly, with candles
and log-effect gas fire, well kept Abbey ales
and guests, good well priced food from huge
baps to roasts (vegetarian options too), good
Christmas mulled wine; may be background
music, stairs to lavatories; tables out in
charming flower-filled flagstoned pedestrian
alley, open all day. *(Roger and Donna Huggins,
Colin and Peggy Wilshire, David Crook, TB, Taff
Thomas and others)*

BATH   ST7564
Crystal Palace (01225) 482666
Abbey Green; BA1 1NW Spacious two-room
pub with something of a wine bar feel, dark
panelling and tiled floors, freshly prepared
sensibly priced food (not Sun evening) from
snacks up, speedy friendly service, well
kept Marstons-related ales, log fire, family
room and conservatory; background music;
sheltered heated courtyard with lovely
hanging baskets, handy for Roman Baths and
main shopping areas. *(Dr and Mrs A K Clarke,
Roger and Donna Huggins)*

BATH   ST7464
✶Garricks Head (01225) 318368
*St Johns Place/Westgate, beside Theatre
Royal; BA1 1ET* Civilised relaxed place
with high-windowed bar, gingham-covered
wooden armchairs by gas-effect coal fire,
church candles on mantelpiece and fine
silver meat domes on wall above, wheelback
and other dining chairs around wooden
tables on bare boards, big black squashy
sofa and more armchairs at far end, sizeable
brass chandeliers, ales such as Palmers,
Otter and Stonehenge, real ciders and
decent wines by the glass, proper cocktails,
good food including pre-theatre set meals,
separate smartly set dining room; may be soft
background jazz; children welcome, dogs in
bar, pavement tables, open all day. *(David
Crook, S Chaudhuri, Mr and Mrs A H Young)*

BATH   ST7465
✶Hop Pole (01225) 446327
*Albion Buildings, Upper Bristol Road;
BA1 3AR* Bustling family-friendly Bath Ales
pub, well kept guest beers and decent wines
by the glass, good food (not Sun evening or
Mon lunchtime) from traditional favourites
up in bar and former skittle alley restaurant,
settles and other pub furniture on bare
boards in four tastefully reworked linked
areas, lots of black woodwork, ochre walls,
some bric-a-brac, board games and daily
newspapers; Mon quiz night, background
music, discreet sports TV; wheelchair
accessible, attractive two-level back
courtyard with boules, fairy-lit vine arbour
and heated summer houses, opposite Victoria
Park with its great play area, open all
day. *(the Didler, Phil Bryant, Chris and Angela
Buckell, Taff and Gilly Thomas)*

BATH   ST7465
Marlborough (01225) 423731
*Marlborough Buildings; BA1
2LY* Interesting well cooked local food
including good value weekday set lunch
(limited menu Sun evening), nice wines, real
ales, cocktails, attentive pleasant service,
busy at weekends; tables in courtyard
garden. *(Bernard Sulzmann)*

BATH   ST7564
✶Old Green Tree (01225) 448259
Green Street; BA1 2JZ Much loved
atmospheric tavern, unchanging and always
packed; three cosy low-ceilinged oak-
panelled rooms including comfortable lounge
with wartime aircraft pictures (local artwork
in summer), back bar with big skylight, up
to six interesting changing ales including
one for the pub from Blindmans, a dozen
wines by the glass (helpful notes on list) and
35 malt whiskies, lunchtime bar food (good
fresh sandwiches), lots of board games; basic
gents' down steep steps, no credit cards
or children; open all day but closed Sun
lunchtime in summer. *(Malcolm Ward,
Roger and Donna Huggins, Jenny and Peter
Lowater, David Crook, Meg and Colin Hamilton,
TB and others)*

BATH   ST7565
Pig & Fiddle (01225) 460868
Saracen Street; BA1 5BR Lively, not
smart, with half a dozen good sensibly priced
local ales, friendly staff, two big open fires,
bare boards and bright paintwork, clocks
on different time zones, steps up to darker
bustling servery and little dining area,
games part and several TVs for sport; lots of
students at night; picnic-sets on big heated
front terrace, open all day. *(Roger and Donna
Huggins, the Didler, Taff and Gilly Thomas)*

BATH   ST7565
Pulteney Arms (01225) 463923
Daniel Street/Sutton Street; BA2 6ND
Cosy and cheerful 18th-c pub, with Fullers
London Pride, Timothy Taylors Landlord,
Wells & Youngs and guests, Thatcher's cider,
enjoyable well priced fresh food including
Fri fish night, lots of Bath RFC memorabilia,
traditional furniture on wooden floors, gas
lamps, woodburner; background music,
sports TV; pavement tables and small back
terrace, handy for Holbourne Museum, open
all day Fri-Sun. *(Taff and Gilly Thomas)*

BATH ST7464
Raven (01225) 425045
Queen Street; BA1 1HE Small buoyant city-centre local, two well kept ales for the pub from Blindmans and local guests, a changing farm cider, limited food including good reasonably priced pies, quick friendly service, bare boards, some stripped stone and an open fire, newspapers, upstairs area, live acoustic music; open all day. *(TB, PaulS, Nick Barber, the Didler, Andy Lickfold and others)*

BATH ST7364
Royal Oak (01225) 481409
Lower Bristol Road; BA2 3BW Friendly bare-boards pub with Butts ales and guests, four ciders, local artwork, regular live music including Weds folk night; open all day Fri-Sun, from 4pm other days. *(Taff and Gilly Thomas)*

BATH ST7464
Salamander (01225) 428889
John Street; BA1 2JL Busy city local tied to Bath Ales, their full range and guests kept well, good choice of wines by the glass, bare boards, black woodwork and dark ochre walls, popular food including some unusual choices, friendly young staff, two rooms downstairs, open-kitchen restaurant upstairs, daily newspapers, Sun quiz; background music, no dogs; children till 8pm, open all day. *(the Didler, Steve Jackson, Taff and Gilly Thomas)*

BATH ST7565
★ **Star** (01225) 425072
Vineyards; The Paragon (A4), junction with Guinea Lane; BA1 5NA Unspoilt city-centre pub with a real sense of its past, now tap for Abbey Ales with guests including Bass poured from a jug, four small linked rooms served from single bar, many original features including traditional wall benches (one hard one known as Death Row), panelling, dim lighting and open fires, no food apart from rolls and Sun bar nibbles, free snuff, shove-ha'penny and cribbage, live folk nights; children and dogs welcome, open all day weekends when it gets packed. *(the Didler, Andy Lickfold, Taff and Gilly Thomas, Roger and Donna Huggins)*

BATH ST7564
Volunteer Riflemans Arms
(01225) 425210 *New Bond Street Place; BA1 1BH* Compact café/pub conversion, leather sofas and close-set tables, wartime posters, open fires, well kept ales such as Abbey Bellringer, a couple of draught ciders, upstairs restaurant and rood terrace; pavement tables. *(Taff and Gilly Thomas, Roger and Donna Huggins)*

BATH ST7564
White Hart (01225) 313985
Widcombe Hill; BA2 6AA Bare-boards bistro-style pub popular for its food, quick

friendly service even when busy, well kept Butcombe from attractive panelled bar, farm cider, helpful staff, fresh flowers; pretty beer garden, bedrooms and self-catering hostel. *(Dr and Mrs A K Clarke)*

BATHFORD ST7866
Crown (01225) 852297
Bathford Hill, towards Bradford-on-Avon, by Batheaston roundabout and bridge; BA1 7SL Bistro pub with good blackboard food including weekday set deals, ales such as Bath and Fullers London Pride, nice wines, charming french landlady; children and dogs welcome, tables out in front and in back garden with pétanque, open all day. *(John and Gloria Isaacs, Dr and Mrs A K Clarke)*

BECKINGTON ST8051
★ **Woolpack** (01373) 831244
Warminster Road, off A36 bypass; BA11 6SP Well refurbished civilised old inn with welcoming helpful staff, enjoyable home-made food from sandwiches up, Greene King ales and a guest like Butcombe, decent wines, farm cider, big log fire and chunky candlelit tables in flagstoned bar, attractive oak-panelled dining room (separate menu), conservatory; can get very busy Sat night; children and dogs welcome, terrace tables, 11 appealing period bedrooms, open all day. *(Carole Tagg, Taff and Gilly Thomas)*

BLAGDON ST5058
★ **New Inn** (01761) 462475
Signed off A368; Park Lane/Church Street; BS40 7SB Lovely view over Blagdon Lake (where they get their trout) from seats in front of this friendly pub; well kept Wadworths ales and decent wines, tasty fairly priced bar food, cheerful service, bustling bars with two inglenook log fires, heavy beams hung with horsebrasses and tankards, comfortable antique settles and mate's chairs among more modern furnishings, old prints and photographs, plainer side bar; children (over 10) and dogs welcome, wheelchair access (best from front). *(Dennis Jenkin, Jim and Frances Gowers, Chris and Angela Buckell, Jennifer Norie, R T and J C Moggridge and others)*

BLAGDON ST5059
Queen Adelaide (01761) 462573
High Street; BS40 7RA Cosy unpretentious pub in lovely spot overlooking Blagdon Lake, chunky tables and settles, local real ales, traditional pub food plus some interesting additions from smallish blackboard menu, enjoyable and reasonably priced. *(Jane and Alan Bush)*

BLAGDON HILL ST2118
Lamb & Flag (01823) 421736
4 miles S of Taunton; TA3 7SL Atmospheric country pub with 16th-c beams, mixed traditional furniture, woodburner in double-sided fireplace and unusual red and

green colour scheme, four well kept west country ales, good value traditional food (not Mon lunchtime), small helpings available, games room/skittle alley, some live music; children and dogs welcome, picnic-sets in nice garden with Taunton Vale views, open all day Fri-Sun, closed Sun evening in winter. *(Patrick and Daphne Darley)*

BLEADON   ST3457
⋆ **Queens Arms**   (01934) 812080
Just off A370 S of Weston; Celtic Way; BS24 0NF Popular 16th-c village pub with informal chatty atmosphere in carefully divided areas, candles on sturdy tables flanked by winged settles, solid fuel stove, old hunting prints, generous reasonably priced food (not Sun evening) from lunchtime baguettes to steaks, friendly service, well kept Butcombe and guests tapped from the cask, local cider, several wines by the glass, flagstoned restaurant and stripped-stone back bar with woodburner, darts, clean lavatories (mind the steps); children (away from bar) and dogs (away from dining area) welcome, picnic-sets on pretty heated terrace, open all day. *(Ian and Nita Cooper, Michael Doswell, Michael Mellers)*

BLUE ANCHOR   ST0243
Smugglers   (01984) 640385
End of B3191, off A39 E of Minehead; TA24 6JS Mellow building in spectacular setting overlooking bay, beamed and flagstoned cellar with good range of enjoyable food including Sun carvery, a beer from Otter brewed for the pub, pleasant staff, log fire, upstairs dining/function room; background music; children and dogs welcome, big sheltered garden with bouncy castle, self-catering cottage, open all day weekends in summer, closed Sun evening, Mon and Tues in winter. *(Mr and Mrs D J Nash)*

BRADFORD-ON-TONE   ST1722
⋆ **White Horse**   (01823) 461239
Fairly near M5 junction 26, off A38 towards Taunton; TA4 1HF 17th-c stone-built local in centre of quiet village, good reasonably priced food in bar and dining room, competent friendly staff, well kept Cotleigh, Exmoor and Otter, decent wines, sofas by open fire, skittle alley; background music; back garden with arbour and boules, unusual glass pub sign. *(Bob and Margaret Holder)*

BRADLEY GREEN   ST2438
Malt Shovel   (01278) 653432
Off A39 W of Bridgwater, near Cannington; TA5 2NE Low-beamed pub with interconnecting rooms, mix of old and new furniture on quarry-tiles and carpet, some stripped stone, old hunting prints, woodburner, enjoyable food from snacks up including good value lunchtime carvery, weekend breakfast till 10.30am, helpful staff, well kept Butcombe, real cider and decent wines by the glass, sizeable

skittle alley; background music; children in eating areas, dogs in bar, disabled access (highish door sills into restaurant) and facilities, picnic-sets on paved laneside area, bedrooms. *(Chris and Angela Buckell)*

BRIDGETOWN   SS9233
Badgers Holt   (01643) 851204
A396; TA22 9JL Friendly 18th-c roadside pub with good-sized timbered bar, Exmoor ales from brick-fronted servery, decent generously served food including daily specials; old local photographs, antlers, log fire; children and dogs welcome, tables on small sunny terrace, self-catering cottage, good walks nearby. *(Rosemary Budgell, Guy Vowles)*

BRISTOL   ST5773
⋆ **Albion**   (0117) 973 3522
Boyce's Avenue, Clifton; BS8 4AA Bustling 18th-c pub down cobbled alley in Clifton village; entrance with open kitchen, jars of pickles/chutneys on dresser for sale, L-shaped bar with chapel chairs around oak tables on wood floor, leather armchairs in front of woodburner, end room up a step with long high-backed settle, well kept Bath, Otter and two guests, decent wines by the glass, 30 whiskies, all-day tapas and other imaginative if not cheap food, friendly service; children welcome till 9pm, dogs allowed in bar, picnic-sets under fairy lights on covered and heated front terrace, open all day, closed Mon till 5pm. *(Jenny and Peter Lowater, Pamela Rogers)*

BRISTOL   ST5872
Apple   (0117) 925 3500
Welsh Back; BS1 4SB Barge specialising in ciders, cheap comfort food – popular with students; background music; quayside seating under huge umbrella. *(Jeremy King)*

BRISTOL   ST5972
Bridge Inn   (0117) 9499967
Passage Street; BS2 0JF One-bar city pub doing well under current friendly licensees, Bath and guests (beer cheaper on Mon), weekday lunchtime food; tables outside, near floating harbour and station, open all day. *(the Didler)*

BRISTOL   ST5873
Colston Yard   (0117) 376 3232
Upper Maudlin Street/Colston Street; BS1 5BD Popular Butcombe pub on two floors (site of old Smiles Brewery), their full range and guests kept well, interesting bottled beers, good choice of wines and spirits, enjoyable food from lunchtime sandwiches to grills and evening restaurant menu; disabled facilities, open all day (till 1am Fri, Sat). *(Paul Hillier, Phil Bryant)*

BRISTOL   ST5872
Commercial Rooms   (0117) 9279681
Corn Street; BS1 1HT Spacious Wetherspoons conversion (former merchants'

club) with lofty stained-glass domed ceiling, gas lighting, comfortable quieter back room with ornate balcony; wide changing choice of real ales including local ones, friendly helpful landlord, nice chatty bustle (busiest weekend evenings), usual food all day, cheap prices, ladies' with chesterfields and open fire; no dogs; children welcome, side wheelchair access and disabled facilities, good location, open all day from 9am and till late Fri-Sun. *(Tony Hobden, the Didler)*

BRISTOL ST5872
Cornubia (0117) 9254415
Temple Street; BS1 6EN 18th-c backstreet real ale pub with good range including Hidden and several recherché regional guests, interesting bottled beers, farm cider and perry, limited weekday pubby food till 7.30pm (Sun till 6pm), friendly service, nicely worn-in with small woody seating areas; can be crowded evenings, not for wheelchairs; picnic-sets on cobbles outside. *(John and Gloria Isaacs, Jeremy King, the Didler, Warren Marsh)*

BRISTOL ST5772
Cottage (0117) 921 5256
Baltic Wharf, Cumberland Road; BS1 6XG Converted stone-built panelled harbour master's office near Maritime Heritage Centre, comfortable, roomy and civilised with fine views of Georgian landmarks and Clifton suspension bridge, enjoyable generous pub food from sandwiches up at reasonable prices, well kept Butcombe ales and a guest, nice wines, good friendly service even when busy; background music; portable wheelchair ramps, waterside terrace tables, access through sailing club, on foot along waterfront, or by round-harbour ferry, neighbouring camp/caravan site, open all day. *(Ian Herdman, Phil Bryant, Stuart and Jasmine Kelly)*

BRISTOL ST5772
Grain Barge (0117) 929 9347
Hotwell Road; BS8 4RU Floating 100-foot barge owned by Bristol Beer Factory, their ales kept well, good freshly made food including Sun roasts, friendly staff, seats out on top deck, sofas and tables on wood floor below, art exhibitions, live music Fri night; open all day. *(Steve Price, the Didler, Roger and Donna Huggins, Taff and Gilly Thomas)*

BRISTOL ST5872
Hatchet (0117) 929 4118
Frogmore Street; BS1 5NA Tucked-away old pub with plenty of character, simple reasonably priced bar lunches, friendly young staff, Butcombe Bitter from island servery, beamed rooms with wood or flagstone floors, some stained glass, epigrams and framed cartoons on walls; background music can be loud; popular with local workers. *(Jeremy King)*

BRISTOL ST5772
⋆**Hope & Anchor** (0117) 9292987
Jacobs Wells Road, Clifton; BS8 1DR Friendly refurbished 18th-c pub, half a dozen good changing ales such as Cheddar, Otter, Timothy Taylors and Wadworths from central bar, nice wines and good choice of malts, tables of various sizes (some shaped to fit corners) on bare boards, darker back area, flowers and candles, sensibly priced hearty food all day – very popular lunchtime, friendly staff; soft background music (occasional live), can get crowded late evening; children welcome, disabled access, barbecues in good-sized tiered back garden with interesting niches, parking nearby can be tricky. *(Chris and Angela Buckell, the Didler)*

BRISTOL ST6674
Horseshoe (0117) 967 1435
Siston Common; off A4174; BS15 4PA Large open-plan family-friendly food pub with good value simple menu and specials, well kept Sharps Doom Bar, Wadworths 6X and a guest, good helpful service. *(M G Hart)*

BRISTOL ST5874
⋆**Kensington Arms** (0117) 944 6444
Stanley Road; BS6 6NP Smart dining pub with well liked food from light lunches up, nice relaxed atmosphere and cheerful accommodating bar staff, well kept beers, good if not cheap wine choice; may be background music; children and dogs welcome, disabled facilities and access (not to dining room/upstairs dining room), heated terrace. *(Paul Hillier, Lucy Johnstone)*

BRISTOL ST5972
⋆**Kings Head** (0117) 927 7860
Victoria Street; BS1 6DE Friendly relaxed 17th-c pub with big front window and splendid mirrored bar back, corridor to cosy panelled back snug with serving hatch, well kept Bath Gem, Wadworths 6X and Sharps Doom Bar, toby jugs on joists, old-fashioned local prints and photographs, interesting gas pressure gauge, reasonably priced wholesome food weekday lunchtimes (get there early for a seat); 60s background music, no credit cards; pavement tables, closed Sat lunchtime, open all day Weds-Fri. *(Jeremy King, the Didler)*

BRISTOL ST5976
Lazy Dog (0117) 924 4809
Ashley Down Road; BS7 9JR Popular local with two refurbished bar areas (one upstairs), ales such as Bath, Bristol Beer Factory and Wye Valley, local ciders/perries, good choice of wines, gins and malt whiskies, well priced food all-day from snacks and sharing plates to blackboard specials, bargain weekday lunch deal, dark green interior with wood panelled alcoves, white marble-effect bar counter, leather wall

benches, sofas and armchairs on light wood floors, lots of mirrors, family room with metal furniture (children till 7pm), vintage juke box, Tues quiz; dogs welcome, wheelchair access, seats out at front and in partly decked back garden. *(Chris and Angela Buckell)*

BRISTOL ST5772
Merchants Arms (0117) 9040037
Merchants Road, Hotwells; BS8 4PZ Tiny two-room pub close to historic dockside, welcoming landlord and friendly locals, well kept Bath ales and their Bounders cider, modest choice of well chosen wines, limited food, open fire; popular Thurs quiz, singalongs/karaoke; sports TV; wheelchair access with help (narrow door and steps). *(Chris and Angela Buckell)*

BRISTOL ST5772
Nova Scotia (0117) 929 7994
Baltic Wharf, Cumberland Basin; BS1 6XJ Unreconstructed old local on S side of Floating Harbour, views to Clifton and Avon Gorge; Bass, Courage Best and guest beers, real ciders, bargain hearty food from good doorstep sandwiches to Sun roasts, pubby seats in four linked areas, snob screen, mahogany and mirrors, nautical charts as wallpaper, character locals; wheelchair access (easiest through snug), plenty of tables out by water, bedrooms sharing bathroom. *(Chris and Angela Buckell, Warren Marsh, Taff and Gilly Thomas)*

BRISTOL ST5872
Old Duke (0117) 9277137
King Street; BS1 4ER Duke Ellington, that is – inside festooned with jazz posters, besides one or two instruments, good bands nightly and Sun lunchtime, usual pub furnishings, real ales and simple food; in attractive cobbled area between docks and Bristol Old Vic, gets packed evenings, open all day. *(Bob Maskell)*

BRISTOL ST5872
Old Fish Market (0117) 9211515
Baldwin Street; BS1 1QZ Imposing building (former fish market), lots of dark wood including handsome counter, high tables and stools on parquet floor, relaxed friendly atmosphere, well kept Fullers ales and Butcombe as guest, thai food all day (till 7pm Sun); quiet background music, big-screen sports TVs; open all day. *(Jeremy King)*

BRISTOL ST5672
Portcullis (0117) 9085536
Wellington Terrace; BS8 4LE Compact two-storey pub in Georgian building with spectacular views, well kept Dawkins and several changing guests, farm ciders, fine range of wines by the glass and spirits, friendly service, no food as we went to press, flame-effect gas fire, dark wood and usual pubby furniture; tricky wheelchair access,

closed weekday lunchtimes, open all day weekends. *(Roger and Donna Huggins, Phil Bryant)*

BRISTOL ST5772
Pump House (0117) 927 2229
Merchants Road; BS8 4PZ Spacious and attractively converted dockside building (former 19th-c pumping station), charcoal-grey brickwork, tiled floors, high ceilings, good bar and restaurant food, ales such as Bath, Butcombe and St Austell, decent wines from comprehensive list, friendly staff, cheerful atmosphere, smart candlelit mezzanine restaurant; waterside tables. *(Taff and Gilly Thomas)*

BRISTOL ST5972
Seven Stars (0117) 9272845
Thomas Lane; BS1 6JG Unpretentious one-room real ale pub near harbour (and associated with Thomas Clarkson and slave trade abolition), much enjoyed by students and local office workers, up to eight ales including Absolution brewed for them by Sharps, beer, cider and perry festivals, interesting malts and bourbons, dark wood, bare boards, old local prints and photographs, you can bring in takeaways, regular irish music; juke box, pool, games machines, Sky TV; disabled access (but narrow alley with uneven cobbles and cast-iron kerbs). *(Chris and Angela Buckell, Jeremy King)*

BRISTOL ST5872
Three Tuns (0117) 926 8434
St Georges Road; BS1 5UR Owned by local Arbor with their ales and guests, interesting selection of US beers, Thatcher's cider and decent choice of wines, cheerful knowledgeable staff, extended bar area with mix of pubby furniture on bare boards, a couple of armchairs in alcoves, open fire, lunchtime rolls; very busy weekends when live music; garden with smokers' area, near cathedral. *(Chris and Angela Buckell)*

BRISTOL ST5773
Victoria (0117) 9745675
Southleigh Road, Clifton; BS8 2BH Modest little two-room pub, popular and can get crowded, with half a dozen or more changing ales (mostly from small brewers), interesting lagers and belgian beers, local ciders/perries, dozens of malt whiskies, good wines by the glass including organic, cheerful knowledgeable staff, basic snacks, big mirrors and open fire, cards and board games, old silent movies some nights; dogs welcome, disabled access, opens mid-afternoon (all day weekends). *(Chris and Angela Buckell, Barry Collett)*

BRISTOL ST5976
Wellington (0117) 9513022
Gloucester Road, Horfield (A38); BS7 8UR Lively and roomy 1920s pub

refitted in traditional style, well kept Bath Ales and guests, good choice of bottled beers, enjoyable pub food including Sun roasts, large horseshoe bar, sofas and low tables in extended lounge with dining area overlooking sunny terrace; very busy on home match days for Bristol RFC or Rovers; children welcome, disabled facilities, bedrooms, open all day. *(Chris and Angela Buckell)*

BUCKLAND DINHAM   ST7551
✶ **Bell** (01373) 462956

High Street (A362 Frome–Radstock); BA11 2QT Friendly 16th-c pub with great atmosphere and interesting décor in narrow beamed main bar, pine furnishings including booth settles, woodburner in huge inglenook, food from speciality local sausages and pies to a huge 74-ounce steak (free if you can eat it all), Butcombe and two guests, farm ciders, several malt whiskies, two-level dining room (a remote control helicopter may direct you to your table), antiques for sale, dominoes and board games, beer/cider festivals; background and some live music, cinema in attached barn; children and dogs welcome, pet (and human) weddings, walled garden with side terraces, campsite, closed Mon, Tues lunchtimes. *(Alan Bulley, Taff and Gilly Thomas)*

CATCOTT   ST3939
King William (01278) 722374

Signed off A39 Street–Bridgwater; TA7 9HU Grey-stone pub on crossroads in shadow of Polden Hills, rugs on flagstones, traditional furnishings, pictures of old Catcott along with modern local art, big stone fireplaces, good quality pubby food cheerfully served by helpful staff, well kept Palmers ales and decent wines by the glass, big back extension with skittle alley and glass-topped well, pub games; unobtrusive background music; children welcome. *(Shirley and Bob Gibbs, Chris and Angela Buckell)*

CHEDDAR   ST4553
Gardeners Arms (01934) 742235

Silver Street; BS27 3LE Tucked away in the old part (originally four farmworkers' cottages), popular food from generous baguettes to good Sun roasts, well kept ales including Butcombe, friendly service, attractive two-room beamed dining area, interesting old local photographs, woodburner; children welcome, garden behind, open all day weekends, closed Mon. *(Jo Greenman, R T and J C Moggridge)*

CHEW MAGNA   ST5763
✶ **Bear & Swan** (01275) 331100

B3130 (South Parade); BS40 8SL Open-plan Fullers pub with much emphasis on food, their ales and guests, good choice of wines, friendly helpful staff, mix of pine tables, pews and big log fire, L-shaped dining room with stripped stone, bare boards and woodburner; background music, TV; children and dogs welcome, wheelchair access from small car park (street parking not easy), secluded beer garden, smokers' area with big heated parasol, bedrooms, closed Sun evening. *(Chris and Angela Buckell, Mrs Susannah Riley, Hugo Jeune, Meg and Colin Hamilton)*

CHEW MAGNA   ST5763
Pelican (01275) 331777

S Parade; BS40 8SL Refurbished village pub with friendly welcome and buzzy atmosphere, pastel grey/green shades, wood flooring, candles on chunky tables, leather sofas by log fire, Bath, Butcombe and Otter, good choice of wines by the glass, enjoyable food (some served on wooden boards) including daily specials; dogs welcome, courtyard tables, open all day, closed Sun evening. *(Taff and Gilly Thomas)*

CHEW MAGNA   ST5861
✶ **Pony & Trap** (01275) 332627

Knowle Hill, New Town; from B3130 in village, follow Bishop Sutton, Bath signpost; BS40 8TQ Dining pub in nice rural spot near Chew Valley Lake, very good imaginative food from sandwiches through to restaurant dishes (best to book), friendly service, Butcombe, Sharps and a guest, front bar with cushioned wall seats and built-in benches on parquet, snug area on left with old range, dark plank panelling and housekeeper's chair in corner, lovely pasture views from two-level back dining area, rush-seated chairs around white tables on slate flagstones; children welcome, dogs in bar, modern metal and wood furniture on back terrace, picnic-sets on grass with chickens pottering in runs below, front smokers' shelter, good walks, closed Mon (apart from Dec). *(John and Gloria Isaacs, Michael Doswell, A Helme, Dr and Mrs A K Clarke, Gaynor Gregory and others)*

CHILCOMPTON   ST6451
Somerset Wagon (01761) 232732

B3139; Broadway; BA3 4JW Cosy and welcoming Wadworths pub with well liked fairly priced food, good service, pleasant olde-worlde areas off central bar, lots of settles, newspapers, log fire; children welcome, small front garden. *(Ian Phillips, Richard and Judy Winn)*

CHIPPING SODBURY   ST7381
Bell (01454) 325582

Badminton Road; BS37 6LL Light and airy bistro feel in two big open-plan rooms, ales such as Bath Gem, Butcombe and Sharps from ornate wooden bar, decent choice of wines, good food, mix of furniture including tables laid for dining at one end, sofas by blazing fire, popular under present welcoming landlord; background music, TV. *(Roger and Donna Huggins)*

CHISELBOROUGH   ST4614

★ **Cat Head** (01935) 881231

Cat Street; leave A303 on A356 towards Crewkerne; take the third left (at 1.4 miles), signed Chiselborough, then left after 0.2 miles; TA14 6TT Welcoming 16th-c hamstone pub refurbished under newish management, bar and two dining areas, flagstones and mullioned windows, woodburner in fine fireplace, leather tub chairs and traditional light-wood tables, good home-made food (not Sun evening) from lunchtime sandwiches up (more elaborate evening choice), well kept Butcombe and a guest, four real ciders and nice wines by the glass, skittle alley; background music; children and dogs welcome (resident cats), seats on terrace and in pretty garden with play area, open all day. *(Helen and Brian Edgeley, Tony and Gill Powell, Sheila Topham, Bob and Margaret Holder)*

CLEVEDON   ST4071

Moon & Sixpence (01275) 872443

The Beach; BS21 7QU Substantial seafront Victorian family dining pub, large bar area, balconied mezzanine floor with good view of pier and over to Brecon Beacons, enjoyable reasonably priced food with some mediterranean touches including meze, helpful friendly staff, well kept Greene King ales, folk music and quiz nights; limited wheelchair access; terrace seating, comfortable bedrooms, good breakfast. *(Dave Braisted, John Wooll)*

CLEVEDON   ST4071

★ **Old Inn** (01275) 340440

Walton Road (B3124 on outskirts); BS21 6AE Friendly mix of regulars and visitors in neatly extended beamed pub, good value generous pubby food (not Mon lunchtime) from baguettes up, well kept changing ales such as Bath, Cottage and Otter, half a dozen wines by the glass, seating from cushioned settles and stools to sofas, carpeted floors, white german shepherd called Polar Bear; background music, silent TV; children welcome, pleasant secluded back garden with boules, bedrooms. *(Jim and Frances Gowers, R T and J C Moggridge)*

CLEVEDON   ST4071

Royal Oak (01275) 547416

Copse Road; BS21 7QN Friendly local tucked away behind seafront with good real ales and ciders. *(Robin Manners)*

COMPTON MARTIN   ST5457

Ring o' Bells (01761) 221284

A368 Bath–Weston; BS40 6JE Popular country pub in attractive spot; traditional front part with rugs on flagstones, inglenook log fire, steps up to spacious carpeted back area, stripped stone, Butcombe ales and guests, reasonably priced wine, tasty pub food with some south african influences

(licensees from there), cheerful helpful young staff, newspapers; well behaved children and dogs welcome, charming big garden with play area, open all day weekends. *(Stuart Paulley, Warren Marsh)*

CONGRESBURY   ST4363

Old Inn (01934) 832270

Pauls Causeway, down Broad Street opposite The Cross; BS49 5DH Friendly low-beamed and flagstoned 16th-c local, deep-set windows, huge fireplaces, one with ancient stove opening to both bar and dining area, mix of old furniture including pews and upholstered benches, leather ceiling straps, enjoyable reasonably priced pubby food, well kept Wells & Youngs ales and a guest tapped from the cask, Thatcher's cider, decent wines, tea and coffee; children welcome, tables in back garden, open all day (till 1am weekends). *(Robin Manners)*

CONGRESBURY   ST4363

Ship & Castle (01934) 833535

High Street (just off A370 from lights at W end of bypass); BS49 5JA Old family-run inn with series of revamped contemporary rooms, enjoyable food from lunchtime sandwiches and baked potatoes up at solid tables, open fire and soft seats, Greene King ales, helpful staff; children welcome, garden with boules, six individually styled bedrooms. *(M Mossman, Jim and Frances Gowers)*

CONGRESBURY   ST4563

White Hart (01934) 833303

Wrington Road, off A370 Bristol–Weston; BS49 5AR Badger country pub with L-shaped main bar, heavy black beams in bowed ceiling, big stone inglenooks each end, dark wood furniture on timber floors, two areas off, big conservatory, well kept beers and good choice of wines, wide range of food including blackboard specials, prompt service; background and some live music; children (away from bar) and dogs welcome, difficult wheelchair access, picnic-sets on back terrace and in big tree-sheltered garden with paddock, nice walks, open all day weekends. *(Chris and Angela Buckell)*

CRANMORE   ST6643

★ **Strode Arms** (01749) 880450

West Cranmore; signed with pub off A361 Frome–Shepton Mallet; BA4 4QJ Pretty dining pub (former 15th-c farmhouse) with good food (not Sun evening) from traditional to more restauranty choices; rambling rooms with country furnishings, grandfather clock on flagstones, brasses on beams, remarkable old locomotive engineering drawings and big black and white steam train murals in central lobby, log fires in handsome fireplaces, Wadworths ales, several wines by the glass, daily newspapers; children welcome lunchtime/early evening, dogs allowed, pretty tubs and hanging baskets on front terrace, more seats in back garden, may be vintage car meetings first Tues of month, handy for East Somerset Light Railway. *(John Urquhart, R F Sawbridge, Martin and Pauline Jennings, Justin Pumfrey, Pat Crabb)*

CROWCOMBE ST1336
Carew Arms (01984) 618631
Just off A358 Taunton–Minehead; TA4 4AD Interesting 17th-c beamed inn, hunting trophies and inglenook woodburner in small old-fashioned front bar, well kept Cotleigh, Exmoor and Otter, farm cider, fairly traditional home-made food, friendly efficient service, traditional games and skittle alley, dining room allowing children; dogs welcome, garden tables, six bedrooms, open all day summer weekends. *(the Didler)*

CULBONE HILL SS8247
Culbone (01643) 862259
Culbone Hill; A39 W of Porlock, opposite Porlock Weir toll Road; TA24 8JW More restaurant with rooms than pub, set high on the moors and recently refurbished by new owner; good food all day including themed nights, a couple of well kept beers and decent choice of malt whiskies, good service, events such as star gazing, cookery school; children welcome, wonderful views over Lorna Doone valley, five well appointed bedrooms. *(Dave Snowden)*

DINNINGTON ST4013
Dinnington Docks (01460) 52397
Aka Rose & Crown; Fosse Way; TA17 8SX Good cheery atmosphere in large old-fashioned country local, unspoilt and unfussy, with good choice of inexpensive genuine home cooking, well kept Butcombe and guests, farm ciders, log fire, friendly attentive staff, memorabilia to bolster the myth that there was once a railway line and dock here, sofas in family room, skittle alley in adjoining building, live music; large garden behind, good walks. *(Michael Lamm, Peter Thornton)*

DITCHEAT ST6236
✴Manor House (01749) 860276
Signed off A37 and A371 S of Shepton Mallet; BA4 6RB Pretty 17th-c red-brick village inn, buoyant atmosphere and popular with jockeys from nearby racing stables, enjoyable home-made food from sandwiches and pubby bar meals to more sophisticated choices, Butcombe and guests, unusual arched doorways linking big flagstoned bar to comfortable lounge and restaurant, open fires, skittle alley; children welcome, tables on back grass, handy for Royal Bath & West showground, three mews bedrooms, open all day. *(Carey Smith)*

DOWLISH WAKE ST3712
New Inn (01460) 52413
Off A3037 S of Ilminster, via Kingstone; TA19 0NZ Comfortable and welcoming

dark-beamed village pub, decent home-made food using fresh local produce, well kept Butcombe and Otter, local farm cider, woodburners in stone inglenooks, pleasant dining room; attractive garden and village, Perry's cider mill and shop nearby, four bedrooms. *(Tony and Gill Powell)*

DUNSTER SS9943
✴Luttrell Arms (01643) 821555
High Street; A396; TA24 6SG Small hotel in 15th-c timber-framed abbey building, well used high-beamed back bar hung with bottles, clogs and horseshoes, stag's head and rifles on walls above old settles and more modern furniture, big log fires, enjoyable generous food including substantial sandwiches with home-baked bread, small helpings available, friendly attentive staff, well kept Exmoor and guests, good wines in three glass sizes, more formal restaurant; dogs welcome in bar, ancient glazed partition dividing off small galleried and flagstoned courtyard, upstairs access to attractive quiet garden with Civil War cannon emplacements (great views), comfortable if pricey bedrooms – some with four-posters. *(David and Julie Glover, Mr and Mrs P D Titcomb, John and Alison Hamilton)*

DUNSTER SS9843
✴Stags Head (01643) 821229
West Street (A396); TA24 6SN Friendly helpful staff and lively atmosphere in unassuming 15th-c roadside inn, good value food, Exmoor and a guest ale, candles, beams, timbers and inglenook log fire, steps up to small back dining room, games chest; dogs welcome, comfortable simple bedrooms, good breakfast. *(John and Alison Hamilton, Michael Butler)*

EAST COKER ST5412
Helyar Arms (01935) 862332
Village signposted off A37 or A30 SW of Yeovil; Moor Lane; BA22 9JR Old pub in charming village with comfortable big bar, high-backed settles and leather sofas in front of log fire, chairs around candlelit tables, lots of hunting and other country pictures, brass and copper, daily newspapers, steps up to high-raftered back dining room, Butcombe, Dorset and a guest ale, several wines by the glass (cooked by landlord) can be good, skittle alley; background music; children and dogs welcome, picnic-sets on neat lawn, attractive bedrooms, open all day weekends. *(M G Hart)*

EAST HARPTREE ST5453
Castle of Comfort (01761) 221321
B3134, SW; BS40 6DD Chatty former coaching inn set high in the Mendips, three or four changing west country ales and Black Rat cider, good choice of enjoyable promptly served food, hefty timbers and exposed stonework, pubby furniture including cushioned settles on carpet, log fires;

children (away from bar) and dogs welcome, wheelchair access to main bar area only, big garden with raised deck and play area, good walks nearby. *(Richard Blacker, Chris and Angela Buckell)*

EAST HARPTREE ST5655
Waldegrave Arms (01761) 221429
Church Lane; BS40 6BD Welcoming old pub keeping local feel although largely set out for chef/landlord's good food (not Sun evening, Mon), cheerful young staff, well kept Butcombe and guests, log fires in small beamed bar and larger dining area, eclectic mix of furniture and plenty of things to look at; children and dogs welcome, picnic-sets in attractive sheltered garden, delightful village, closed Mon lunchtime. *(Tina Hunt)*

EAST LAMBROOK ST4218
★ **Rose & Crown** (01460) 240433
Silver Street; TA13 5HF Neatly kept stone-built dining pub spreading extensively from compact 17th-c core with inglenook log fire, efficient cheerful staff and relaxed atmosphere, good generous inexpensive food freshly made using local supplies including very popular weekday OAP lunches, full Palmers range kept well, farm cider, decent wines by the glass, restaurant extension with old glass-covered well; picnic-sets on neat lawn, opposite East Lambrook Manor Garden. *(Mrs C Roe, Peter Salmon, Stan Lea)*

EAST WOODLANDS ST7944
★ **Horse & Groom** (01373) 462802
Off A361/B3092 junction; BA11 5LY Small pretty pub tucked away down country lanes, enjoyable well priced fresh food (not Sun evening), friendly service, Butcombe and a couple of quickly changing guests tapped from the cask, pews and settles in flagstoned bar, woodburner in comfortable lounge, big dining conservatory, traditional games; dogs welcome away from restaurant, children in eating areas, disabled access, tables out in nice front garden with more seats behind, handy for Longleat. *(Edward Mirzoeff)*

EMBOROUGH ST6251
Old Down (01761) 232398
B3139; BA3 4SA Sizeable old stone inn with particularly well kept local ales from casks behind bar, good farm cider too, enjoyable inexpensive food, helpful landlady and friendly staff; bedrooms, campsite opposite. *(John Coatsworth)*

ENMORE ST2434
Tynte Arms (01278) 671351
High Street; TA5 2DP Open-plan low-beamed pub with wide choice of good generous food including lots of fish, home-made puddings and good value set menus, friendly service, west country ales from long bar, plenty of dining tables, chesterfields and settles, end inglenook, china collection;

no dogs; car park over road, good walking country. *(B M Eldridge, Bob and Margaret Holder)*

EVERCREECH ST6336
Natterjack (01749) 860253
A371 Shepton Mallet–Castle Cary; BA4 6NA Wide choice of popular generous food at reasonable prices, Butcombe and a couple of guests, real cider and good range of wines, welcoming landlord and cheerful efficient staff, long bar with eating areas off; lots of tables under parasols in big neatly kept garden, bedrooms. *(Col and Mrs Patrick Kaye, Mrs D Lush)*

EXFORD SS8538
Crown (01643) 831554
The Green (B3224); TA24 7PP 17th-c family-run coaching inn, two-room bar with hunting décor, old local photographs and big stone fireplace, Exmoor ales and a guest, farm cider, some interesting food in bar and restaurant, well chosen wines, prompt friendly service; children and dogs welcome, waterside garden behind, smaller terraced side garden overlooking village and green, bedrooms. *(Michael M Cassidy, Guy Vowles)*

EXFORD SS8538
★ **White Horse** (01643) 831229
B3224; TA24 7PY Popular and welcoming three-storey creeper-clad inn, more or less open-plan bar, high-backed antique settle among more conventional seats, scrubbed deal tables, hunting prints and local photographs, good log fire, Exmoor ales and Sharps Doom Bar, over 100 malt whiskies, Thatcher's cider, hearty food from sandwiches to good value Sun carvery, Land Rover Exmoor safaris; children and dogs welcome, play area and outside tables, comfortable bedrooms, pretty village, open all day from 8am. *(Peter and Giff Bennett, Andrew Scott, Lynda and Trevor Smith)*

FAILAND ST5171
Failand Inn (01275) 392220
B3128 Bristol–Clevedon; BS8 3TU Welcoming old coaching inn with wide choice of popular pub food, well kept Butcombe, Courage and Sharps, good wines by the glass, large bright dining areas either side of entrance, two bars, low beams, toby jugs, decorative plates and brasses; gentle background music, may ask to keep a credit card while running a tab; children and dogs welcome, garden with decking and heated smokers' shelter, open all day. *(Dr and Mrs C W Thomas, John and Gloria Isaacs, Tom Evans, Taff and Gilly Thomas)*

FAULKLAND ST7555
★ **Tuckers Grave** (01373) 834230
A366 E of village; BA3 5XF Reopened after brief closure in 2011; unspoilt, unchanging and absolutely tiny cider house with friendly locals and charming licensees,

flagstoned entrance opening into simple room with casks of Butcombe, Fullers London Pride and Thatcher's Cheddar Valley cider in alcove on left, perhaps lunchtime sandwiches, two high-backed settles facing each other across a single table on right, side room with shove-ha'penny, open fires, daily newspapers, skittle alley; children welcome in one area, lots of tables and chairs on attractive back lawn, good views, closed Mon lunchtime (except bank holidays). *(the Didler, Taff and Gilly Thomas, Chris and Angela Buckell)*

FRESHFORD   ST7960
Inn at Freshford   (01225) 722250
Off A36 or B3108; BA2 7WG Roomy beamed stone-built pub in attractive spot near river, enjoyable food from lunchtime sandwiches up, more evening choice, well kept Box Steam ales and guests, real ciders/ perries, decent wines by the glass and good choice of gins and malts, helpful attentive staff; wheelchair access from car park, pretty hillside garden. *(Chris and Angela Buckell)*

FROME   ST7748
Griffin   (01373) 467766
Milk Street; BA11 3DB Unpretentious, civilised bare-boards room, long bar with several good Milk Street beers brewed here by the friendly landlord, etched glass and open fires, easy-going mixed crowd, quiz and live music nights; small garden, closed lunchtime and from 7pm Sun. *(Tessa Clist)*

GLASTONBURY   ST5039
Who'd A Thought It   (01458) 834460
Northload Street; BA6 9JJ High-backed curved settle, coal fire, pine panelling, stripped brick, beams and flagstones, nicely quirky oddments including a red phone box, well kept Palmers ales and decent wines by the glass, fairly traditional food (all day weekends) from ciabattas up, daily newspapers; children and dogs welcome, pleasant garden, five comfortable bedrooms, open all day. *(Dr J Barrie Jones)*

HARDWAY   ST7234
✴ Bull   (01749) 812200
Off B3081 Bruton–Wincanton at brown sign for Stourhead and King Alfred's Tower; Hardway; BA10 0LN Charming beamed 17th-c country dining pub popular locally, especially with older people weekday lunchtimes, good food (not Sun evening) in comfortable bar and character dining rooms, good informal service, well kept Butcombe and Otter, farm cider, nice wines by the glass, log fire; unobtrusive background music; tables and barbecues in garden behind, more in rose garden over road, bedrooms. *(Mrs C Roe, office)*

HINTON CHARTERHOUSE   ST7758
✴ Rose & Crown   (01225) 722153
B3110 about 4 miles S of Bath; BA2 7SN Reliable 18th-c village pub with friendly young licensees, partly divided bar with panelling, blue plush cushioned wall seats and mix of wooden tables and chairs on carpet, candles in bottles, ornate carved stone fireplace (smaller brick one on other side), Butcombe, Fullers and a guest, good straightforward bar food, long dining room with steps to lower area with unusual beamed ceiling; background music, TV; children welcome, dogs in bar (pub dog called Tia Maria), picnic-sets under parasols in terraced garden, pretty window boxes, bedrooms, nice breakfast, open all day weekends. *(Frank Willy, Simon Rodway, Meg and Colin Hamilton, Dave Braisted)*

HINTON CHARTERHOUSE   ST7758
Stag   (01225) 723456
B3110 S of Bath; High Street; BA2 7SW Attractively furnished old family-run pub, good generous food from varied menu in cosy bar and pleasant stripped-stone dining areas, real ales such as Butcombe, helpful staff, coal-effect gas fire; children welcome, tables outside, closed Sun evening, otherwise open all day. *(Meg and Colin Hamilton)*

HOLCOMBE   ST6648
Duke of Cumberland
(01761) 233731 *Edford Hill; BA3 5HQ* Modernised pub with good choice of reasonably priced food including home-made pizzas, local ales such as Bath, Butcombe, Devilfish and Wadworths, Ashton Press and Cheddar Vale ciders, friendly helpful staff, log fires, skittle alley; background music; children and dogs welcome, riverside garden with picnic-sets, open all day. *(Ian Phillips)*

HOLCOMBE   ST6649
Holcombe Inn   (01761) 232478
Off A367; Stratton Road; BA3 5EB Quietly placed 17th-c country inn with several refurbished linked areas including spacious restaurant, log fires, good interesting food alongside pub favourites, Bath, Otter and a guest ale such as Devilfish, local ciders, 30 wines by the glass and 20 malt whiskies; background music; children, dogs and walkers welcome, tables out in front and in garden behind, far-reaching views, eight well appointed bedrooms, open all day Fri-Sun. *(Taff and Gilly Thomas)*

HORTON   ST3214
Five Dials   (01460) 55359
Hanning Road; off A303; TA19 9QH Cleanly refurbished pub run by friendly helpful young couple, popular reasonably priced food including good steaks, Otter, Sharps Doom Bar and a guest, local ciders and good choice of wines by the glass, restaurant; children and dogs welcome, five bedrooms, open all day Fri-Sun, closed Mon. *(Evelyn and Derek Walter, Ted and Charlotte Routley)*

KELSTON   ST7067
✷ **Old Crown** (01225) 423032

Bitton Road; A431 W of Bath; BA1 9AQ
Four small traditional rooms with beams
and polished flagstones, carved settles
and cask tables, logs burning in ancient
open range, two more coal-effect fires,
Bass, Butcombe, Fullers and a guest ale,
Thatcher's cider, good choice of wines by
the glass and whiskies, friendly enthusiastic
staff, good food (not Mon evenings) in bar
and small restaurant; children welcome,
dogs in bar, wheelchair accessible with
help, picnic-sets under apple trees in sunny
sheltered back garden, four bedrooms in
converted outbuildings, open all day. *(Ian
and Rose Lock, Dr and Mrs A K Clarke, Chris and
Angela Buckell, Roger and Donna Huggins)*

KEYNSHAM   ST6669
✷ **Lock-Keeper** (0117) 986 2383

*Keynsham Road (A4175 NE of town);
BS31 2DD* Friendly riverside pub with
plenty of character, bare boards and relaxed
worn-in feel, simple left-hand bar with big
painted settle, cushioned wall benches,
trophy cabinet and old local photographs,
two more little rooms with all manner of
cushioned dining chairs, more photographs
and rustic prints, Wells & Youngs and guests,
good choice of wines and coffees, well
liked reasonably priced bar food, cheerful
young staff, light modern conservatory
(quite different in style), live music Fri,
Sat; children welcome, dogs in bar, disabled
facilities, teak furniture under giant parasols
on big heated decked terrace overlooking
water, steps down to plenty of picnic-sets on
grass, outside bar and barbecue, pétanque
pitch, open all day. *(Dr and Mrs A K Clarke,
Chris and Angela Buckell, Michael Doswell,
Lucy Fey)*

KILMERSDON   ST6952
Jolliffe Arms (01761) 436699

High Street; BA3 5TD Large attractive
stone-built Georgian local overlooking pretty
churchyard, Butcombe and Fullers London
Pride, good wines by the glass, generous
home-made pub food, friendly service,
four linked areas (three mainly for dining)
reminiscent of unpretentious farmhouse
parlour, some huge black flagstones, skittle
alley; background music; front picnic-sets,
Jack & Jill walk close by, open all day Sat, till
4pm Sun. *(Dr and Mrs A K Clarke)*

KILVE   ST1442
Hood Arms (01278) 741210

A39 E of Williton; TA5 1EA Welcoming
neatly kept beamed 18th-c country pub, well
kept Otter, Palmers and guest ales, good
interesting food from bar snacks up including
popular Sun lunch, cosy plush lounge, warm
woodburner in bar, restaurant, skittle alley;
children and dogs welcome, well tended back
garden with tables on sheltered terrace, play

area, 12 bedrooms – two in back lodge.
*(MLR, David Jackman, Steve and Liz Tilley, Ian
Kirkwood, Mrs Jo Rees)*

KINGSDON   ST5126
Kingsdon Inn (01935) 840543

Off B3151; TA11 7LG Pretty 18th-c
thatched dining pub, busy friendly
atmosphere in attractively decorated beamed
rooms, open fires, enjoyable food (more
evening choice), well kept local ales, good
service; children and dogs welcome, picnic-
sets on front grass, three bedrooms and
holiday cottage, handy for Lytes Cary (NT)
and Fleet Air Arm Museum. *(Patric Hosier,
Mr Stan Lea)*

KNAPP   ST3025
Rising Sun (01823) 491027

Village W of North Curry; TA3 6BG This
15th-c longhouse has reopened after ten
years as a private house; handsome beams
and two inglenooks with woodburners,
Exmoor Gold and Sharps Doom Bar, food
from pub staples up in bar or restaurant
including two-course deals (more elaborate
evening choice); children and dogs welcome,
terrace tables, open all day Sat, closed Sun
evening (not first Sun of month when there's
a quiz) and Mon. *(Anon)*

LANGFORD BUDVILLE   ST1122
✷ **Martlet** (01823) 400262

Off B3187 NW of Wellington; TA21 0QZ
Cosy, comfortable cottagey pub with friendly
landlady and staff, good generously served
food popular at lunchtime with older diners,
well kept ales including Exmoor, inglenook,
beams and flagstones, central woodburner,
steps up to carpeted lounge with another
woodburner; skittle alley. *(Stephen Bennett,
Paul Sayers)*

LANSDOWN   ST7268
Blathwayt Arms (01225) 421995

Near Bath Racecourse; BA1 9BT
Interesting old hilltop building with
enjoyable food including some unusual dishes
and popular Sun roasts, well kept local
ales, decent wines, friendly helpful service;
children welcome, racecourse view from
garden, bedrooms, open all day. *(Dr and Mrs
A K Clarke, Brian Glozier)*

LITTON   ST5954
Kings Arms (01761) 241301

*B3114, NW of Chewton Mendip;
BA3 4PW* Refurbished partly 15th-c dining
pub, flagstones, low heavy beams and
open fireplaces, enjoyable food from open
kitchen including home-made pizzas and
pubby dishes plus more upscale/expensive
restaurant choices, well kept Butcombe and
Greene King ales, plenty of wines by the
glass, friendly service; terrace overlooking
River Chew, round picnic-sets on sloping
lawn, good reservoir walks nearby, open all
day. *(Jim and Frances Gowers)*

LONG ASHTON

Bird in Hand (01275) 395222

xx0000

Weston Road; BS41 9LA Recently
refurbished stone-built dining pub, good
locally sourced food from bar meals to
enterprising restaurant dishes, well kept
Bath, Butcombe, St Austell, Sharps and
a guest, Ashton Press cider, nice wines,
spindleback chairs and blue painted
pine tables on wood floors, open fire and
woodburner; children and dogs welcome,
side terrace, parking may be tricky, open all
day. *(John and Gloria Isaacs)*

LONG ASHTON

Dovecote (01275) 392245

ST5570

B3128 Ashton Road; BS41 9LX Roomy
Vintage Inn much extended from original
17th-c beamed core, their usual food from
large reasonably priced menu, Butcombe,
St Austell and guests, cheerful attentive
young staff, conservatory; upstairs gents';
children welcome, wheelchair accessible
(not all parts) from large paved beer garden,
good walks in nearby Ashton Court, open all
day. *(Nigel Higgins, Alan Bulley)*

LONG ASHTON

Miners Rest (01275) 393449

ST5370

Providence Lane; BS41 9DJ Welcoming
three-room country pub, comfortable and
unpretentious, with well kept Butcombe,
Fullers London Pride and a guest tapped
from casks, three or four good farm ciders,
inexpensive simple food, local mining
memorabilia, log fire, darts; no credit cards;
children and dogs welcome, vine-covered
verandah and suntrap terrace picnic-sets,
open all day. *(Taff and Gilly Thomas)*

LONG SUTTON

★**Devonshire Arms** (01458) 241271

ST4625

*B3165 Somerton–Martock, off A372 E
of Langport; TA10 9LP* Handsome gabled
inn (former hunting lodge) with civilised
atmosphere, simple back bar with modern
metal and leather bar stools, rush-seated
high-backed chairs around dark tables on
flagstones, Moor and guest ales tapped from
the cask, local cider brandy and several
wines by the glass, stylish main room with
comfortable leather sofas and glass-topped
log table by fire, scatter cushions on long wall
bench, chunky black church candles, elegant
dining room with brown wicker chairs around
pale wood tables on broad stripped boards,
interesting food (local suppliers listed on
board) from lunchtime sandwiches up,
charming efficient service, evening pianist;
teak furniture out at front, pretty box-
enclosed courtyard with unusual water-ball
feature, more seats on raised terraces, good
bedrooms. *(William and Ann Reid, Comus and
Sarah Elliott, Mr and Mrs P D Titcomb, Chris and
Angela Buckell)*

LOVINGTON

★**Pilgrims** (01963) 240597

ST5831

*B3153 Castle Cary–Keinton Mandeville;
BA7 7PT* Decidedly more restaurant than
pub but does have a pubby corner serving
local Cottage, farm cider and 16 wines by
the glass, good imaginative food (not cheap)
using local produce, efficient friendly service,
cosy flagstoned inner area with modern
prints, bookshelves, china and some sofas
by big fireplace, compact eating area with
candles on tables and more formal carpeted
dining room; children welcome, dogs in bar,
decked terrace in enclosed garden, car park
exit has own traffic lights, bedrooms (no
children), closed Sun evening, Mon and Tues
lunchtime. *(John and Gloria Isaacs)*

LOWER LANGFORD

Langford Inn (01934) 863059

ST4660

Off B3133/A38; BS40 5BL Roomy,
beamed family dining pub, popular good
value food all day, Sun roasts, well kept ales
including Butcombe, decent wines, cheerful
service; background music, Thurs quiz night;
picnic-sets in courtyard and side garden,
seven barn-conversion bedrooms. *(Bruce and
Sharon Eden)*

MELLS

★**Talbot** (01373) 812254

ST7249

W of Frome, off A362 or A361; BA11 3PN
Interesting 15th-c coaching inn, austere
public bar in restored tithe barn, farm tools
on stone walls, big mural behind counter,
dining room/bar in main beamed building
with solid tables and chairs on quarry tiles,
sporting and riding pictures, enjoyable food
including set menu choices, Butcombe
tapped from the cask, helpful pleasant
staff, darts; sports TV; children and dogs
welcome, nice cobbled courtyard leading to
walled suntrap garden, eight comfortable
bedrooms. *(M G Hart, Chris and Angela Buckell)*

MIDFORD

★**Hope & Anchor** (01225) 832296

ST7660

Bath Road (B3110); BA2 7DD Open-
plan roadside dining pub with good
generous home-made food from standards
to more imaginative dishes, civilised bar,
heavy-beamed and flagstoned restaurant
end, new back conservatory, six well kept
changing ales such as Butcombe, Sharps
and Wadworths, good house wines, proper
coffee, relaxed atmosphere, log fire; children
welcome, tables on sheltered back terrace
with upper tier beyond, pleasant walks on
disused Somerset & Dorset rail track, open
all day. *(David Hoult, Michael Doswell)*

MIDSOMER NORTON

White Hart (01761) 418270

ST6654

The Island; BA3 2HQ Well worn chatty
Victorian local with several rooms, Bass,
Butcombe and guests tapped from the cask,
real cider, local coal-mining memorabilia,

bargain simple lunchtime food, cheerful helpful staff; no credit cards; dogs welcome, open all day. *(the Didler, Dr J Barrie Jones)*

MILVERTON ST1225
Globe (01823) 400534
Fore Street; TA4 1JX Popular smartly reworked pub/restaurant (former coaching inn), much liked mainly local food from interesting lunchtime baguettes and ciabattas up, good value Sun roasts, well kept Otter and nice choice of wines by the glass, friendly helpful staff; children welcome, terrace tables, bedrooms. *(David Leyland, Brenda and Stuart Naylor, Bob and Margaret Holder)*

MONKSILVER ST0737
Notley Arms (01984) 656217
B3188; TA4 4JB Beamed village pub on edge of Exmoor National Park revamped by friendly new owners after long closure; initial feedback suggests good food and service – more reports please. *(Anon)*

MONKTON COMBE ST7761
Wheelwrights Arms (01225) 722287
Just off A36 S of Bath; Church Cottages; BA2 7HB Compact old stone-built pub with clean modern uncluttered feel, competently prepared food including sharing plates and good value lunchtime set menu (Mon-Thurs), quick friendly service, well kept Butcombe and Sharps Doom Bar from high green-painted wood counter, good choice of wines, some-stripped stone walls, ladder-back chairs around modern tables, an old settle, wood or carpeted floors, log fire in big stone fireplace; children welcome, attractively expanded garden with valley view, seven good annexe bedrooms. *(Michael Doswell, Hugo Jeune, Mr and Mrs A H Young)*

MONTACUTE ST4916
Phelips Arms (01935) 822557
The Borough; off A3088 W of Yeovil; TA15 6XB 18th-c stone pub in pretty square next to Montacute House (NT), part-carpeted open-plan bar with well kept Palmers, Thatcher's cider and good choice of wines by the glass, reasonably priced home-made food (not Sun evening) including daily specials, nice fireplace with woodburner, homely old-fashioned décor, restaurant area, darts and skittle alley, charity quiz last Tues of month; background music; children and dogs welcome, attractive walled garden behind, six bedrooms. *(Jeremy King)*

MOORLINCH ST3936
Ring o' Bells (01458) 210358
Signed off A39; TA7 9BT Fine old building, carpeted throughout, with black beams, stone and rough plaster walls, modern furniture, grandfather clock, woodburners and open fires, keen chef/landlord doing good value hearty food including good Sun roasts, vegetarian options too, well kept changing ales such as Butcombe, Greene King and St

Austell, local ciders, helpful staff; sports TV in public bar, darts pool and skittles; children welcome, wheelchair access from back, garden tables, open all day weekends, closed Mon and lunchtimes Tues-Thurs. *(Heather Coulson, Neil Cross)*

NAILSEA ST4469
Blue Flame (01275) 856910
West End; BS48 4DE Small well worn 19th-c farmers' local, two rooms with mixed furnishings, well kept RCH and guests from casks behind bar, Thatcher's cider, fresh rolls, coal fire, pub games; plain-speaking landlord, outside lavatories including roofless gents', limited parking (may be filled with Land Rovers and tractors); children's room, sizeable informal garden, best to phone regarding opening times. *(the Didler, Taff and Gilly Thomas)*

NETHER STOWEY ST1939
Rose & Crown (01278) 732265
St Mary Street; TA5 1LJ Friendly former 16th-c posting inn, good value straightforward home-made food, well kept ales such as Jennings, Marstons and Ringwood, Thatcher's cider, decent wines, cosy log-fire bar with interesting old local photographs and memorabilia, back bar with pool, darts and TV, restaurant, folk music and quiz nights; children and dogs welcome, tables in walled garden with play area, comfortable bedrooms, good breakfast, open all day. *(Richard and Liz Thorne, Neil Hardwick)*

NEWTON ST LOE ST7065
Globe (01225) 872891
A4/A36 roundabout; BA2 9BB Popular 17th-c Vintage Inn, large and rambling, with pleasant décor and dark wood partitions, pillars and timbers giving secluded feel, their usual food all day including fixed price menu (Mon-Sat till 5pm), well kept Butcombe, St Austell Tribute and a guest, prompt friendly uniformed staff, good atmosphere; children welcome, nice back terrace. *(Dr and Mrs A K Clarke, Nigel Long, M G Hart, Richard and Judy Winn)*

NORTH CURRY ST3125
Bird in Hand (01823) 490248
Queens Square; off A378 (or A358) E of Taunton; TA3 6LT Friendly village pub, cosy main bar with old pews, settles, benches and yew tables on flagstones, some original beams and timbers, locally woven willow work, cricket memorabilia, good inglenook log fire, well kept real ales and decent wines by the glass, enjoyable food; background music; children, dogs and muddy boots welcome, open all day Sun. *(Richard Tilbrook, Peter and Giff Bennett, Ted and Charlotte Routley, Liz and Jeremy Baker, Bob and Margaret Holder and others)*

NORTON FITZWARREN ST2026
Cross Keys (01823) 333062
A358 roundabout NW of Taunton; TA2 6NR Comfortably extended 19th-c stone-built

beamed pub, up to four well kept changing ales, decent wines by the glass, good value promptly served pubby food (all day) including curries, friendly cheerful staff, stone-tiled bar and carpeted dining area with some plank panelling, log fire in big hearth, skittle alley; children welcome, riverside garden with plenty of seating. *(Ian Phillips, Brenda and Stuart Naylor)*

NORTON ST PHILIP ST7755
Fleur de Lys (01373) 834333
High Street; BA2 7LG Newish licensees at this 13th-c thatched pub, enjoyable home-made food, real ales, log fire in huge fireplace, steps and pillars giving cosy feel of separate rooms in beamed and flagstoned areas around central servery; skittle alley. *(R K Phillips)*

NORTON ST PHILIP ST7755
☆ George (01373) 834224
A366; BA2 7LH Wonderful building full of history and interest – an inn for over 700 years; big heavy beams, timbering, stonework and panelling, vast open fires, distincive furnishings, plenty of 18th-c pictures, fine pewter and heraldic shields, Wadworths ales and 25 wines by the glass, fairly straightforward food; children welcome, dogs in bar, appealing flagstoned courtyard, atmospheric bedrooms (some reached by Norman turret), worth strolling over meadow to attractive churchyard, open all day. *(the Didler, Taff and Gilly Thomas, Andrea Rampley)*

OAKE ST1526
Orchard (01823) 400295
Hillcommon, N; B3227; TA4 1DS Refurbished village pub (was the Royal Oak) with enjoyable food including lunchtime deals (carvery Tues, Thurs), well kept ales such as Exmoor, Otter and Sharps from central servery, friendly service; children welcome, pleasant walled garden with play area. *(Roddy Kane)*

ODCOMBE ST5015
☆ Masons Arms (01935) 862591
Off A3088 or A30 just W of Yeovil; Lower Odcombe; BA22 8TX Pretty thatched cottage with homely small bar, joists and a couple of standing timbers, cushioned dining chairs around wooden tables on patterned carpet, tub chairs and table in former inglenook, steps down to dining room with woodburner, own-brewed Odcombe No 1, Spring, Roly Poly and seasonal beers, good interesting food; dogs welcome, picnic-sets on grass, thatched smokers' shelter, vegetable patch and chickens, comfortable bedrooms, campsite. *(Nigel Fortnam, Dennis Jenkin, Mike and Mary Carter, Michelle Power, Tony & Gene Freemantle)*

PANBOROUGH ST4745
Panborough Inn (01934) 712554
B3139 Wedmore–Wells; BA5 1PN Large

well run 17th-c beamed dining pub, good welcoming staff, enjoyable traditional food, ales such as Boddingtons and Butcombe in cosy bar with wall benches, polished tables and roaring log fire, restaurant, skittle alley; views from tables on front terrace. *(Dr and Mrs C W Thomas, Warren Marsh)*

PITMINSTER ST2219
Queens Arms (01823) 421529
Off B3170 S of Taunton (or reached direct); near church; TA3 7AZ Friendly village pub again under new management; decent generously served pubby food, Otter ales, cosy woodburner. *(Patrick and Daphne Darley, Kerry Law)*

PORLOCK WEIR SS8846
☆ Ship (01643) 863288
Porlock Hill (A39); TA24 8PB Unpretentious thatched bar in wonderful spot by peaceful harbour (so can get packed), long and narrow with dark low beams, flagstones and stripped stone, simple pub furniture, woodburner, Cotleigh, Exmoor, Otter and a guest like Clearwater Proper Ansome, real ciders and a perry, good whisky and soft drinks choice, friendly prompt service, pubby food, games rooms across small back yard, tea room; background music, big-screen TV, little free parking but pay & display opposite; children and dogs welcome, sturdy picnic-sets out at front and side, good coast walks, three decent bedrooms; calls itself the Bottom Ship to distinguish from nearby Ship at Porlock. *(Adrian and Dawn Collinge, Mr and Mrs D J Nash, Neil Hardwick)*

PORTISHEAD ST4576
☆ Windmill (01275) 843677
M5 J19; A369 into town, then follow Sea Front sign and into Nore Road; BS20 6JZ Busy dining pub making most of terrific panorama over Bristol Channel; completely restyled with curving glass frontage rising two storeys (adjacent windmill remains untouched), contemporary furnishings, Bass, Butcombe, Courage and local guests, traditional bar food (may be early evening deal), efficient service; children welcome in lower family floor, dogs allowed in bar, disabled access including lift, picnic-sets on tiered lantern-lit terraces and decking, open all day. *(Michael Lamm, Tom Evans, Ken and Barbara Turner, Steve and Claire Harvey, Pat Bunting and others)*

PRIDDY ST5450
☆ Hunters Lodge (01749) 672275
From Wells on A39 pass hill with TV mast on left, then next left; BA5 3AR Welcoming and unchanging farmers', walkers' and potholers' pub above Ice Age cavern, in same family for generations, well kept local beers tapped from casks behind bar, Thatcher's and Wilkins' ciders, simple cheap food, log fires in huge fireplaces, low beams, flagstones and panelling, old lead mining

photographs, perhaps live folk music; no mobiles or credit cards; children and dogs in family room, wheelchair access, garden picnic-sets. *(Chris and Angela Buckell, MLR, M G Hart, the Didler)*

PRISTON   ST6960
Ring o' Bells   (01761) 471467
Village SW of Bath; BA2 9EE
Unpretentious old stone pub with large knocked through bar, good reasonably priced traditional food cooked by licensees using nearby farm produce, real ales from small local brewers including a house beer from Blindmans, quick friendly service, flagstones, beams and good open fire, skittle alley; children, dogs and muddy boots welcome, benches out at front overlooking little village green (maypole here on May Day), good walks, two bedrooms, closed Mon lunchtime. *(Guy Vowles)*

PURITON   ST3141
Puriton Inn   (01278) 683464
Just off M5 junction 23; Puriton Hill; TA7 8AF Character pub well screened from motorway, clean and tidy, with ample straightforward food and well kept ales, warmly welcoming service even when busy, pool; children welcome, good disabled access, front terrace and back garden with play area. *(Robert Smith)*

RODE   ST8053
Bell   (01373) 830356
Frome Road (A361); BA11 6PW New owners for this quirkily refurbished pub, bare boards or flagstones, oak-panelling, log fires, old club portraits on green flock or fish-print wallpaper, various stuffed animals, mishmash of furniture – scrub-top painted pine tables, chapel chairs and old rescued leather sofas/ armchairs, 1930s standard lamps, a couple of house beers from Blindmans and three regional guests, sensibly priced standard food from sandwiches up; children welcome, big terrace and lawned garden, open all day. *(Taff and Gilly Thomas)*

RODE   ST8054
Mill   (01373) 831100
NW off Rode Hill; BA11 6AG Popular family pub in beautifully set former watermill, smart restauranty layout and up-to-date décor, well liked food, good choice of real ales and of wines by the glass, children's room with impressive games, live music Fri; garden and decks overlooking River Frome, big play area. *(Mr and Mrs A Curry)*

ROWBERROW   ST4458
★ Swan   (01934) 852371
Off A38 S of A368 junction; BS25 1QL Neat and spacious dining pub opposite pond, olde-worlde beamery and so forth, good log fires, friendly atmosphere especially in nicely unsophisticated old bar part, good

reasonably priced food (small helpings available), prompt pleasant service, well kept Butcombe ales, Thatcher's cider and decent choice of wines by the glass, live music (first Sun of month); children welcome, good-sized garden over road, open all day weekends. *(Hugh Roberts)*

RUDGE   ST8251
★ Full Moon   (01373) 830936
Off A36 Bath–Warminster; BA11 2QF Black-beamed 17th-c inn with enjoyable good value food from lunchtime sandwiches and baguettes up, well kept Butcombe, Otter and a guest, local ciders, nice mix of furnishings in cosy front bars, inglenook log fire, flagstoned tap room and back restaurant extension, skittle alley; children and dogs welcome, pretty gardens with plenty of seats and White Horse view, play area, 18 bedroom in modern annexe, three self-catering cottages, swimming pool, open all day. *(Taff and Gilly Thomas)*

RUMWELL   ST1923
Rumwell Inn   (01823) 461662
A38 Taunton–Wellington, just past Stonegallows; TA4 1EL Roomy roadside pub, comfortable and clean, with old beams, cosy corners and roaring log fire, enjoyable reasonably priced food from good lunchtime sandwiches up, well kept changing ales, friendly landlord and staff, family room; tables in nice garden, handy for Sheppy's Cider, closed Sun evening. *(Peter Salmon, Shirley and Bob Gibbs, Christine and Neil Townend)*

SALTFORD   ST6867
Bird in Hand   (01225) 873335
High Street; BS31 3EJ Comfortable and friendly, with lively front bar, good range of beers such as Blindmans, Butcombe, Courage and Sharps, farm cider, attractive back conservatory dining area, good choice of popular fairly priced fresh food from snacks up, friendly staff, pubby furniture including settles, carpets throughout, lots of bird pictures and old plates, small family area; live entertainment, fruit machine; wheelchair access at front (not from car park), picnic-sets down towards river, handy for Bristol–Bath railway path. *(Chris and Angela Buckell, Dr and Mrs A K Clarke, Colin and Peggy Wilshire)*

SALTFORD   ST6968
★ Jolly Sailor   (01225) 873002
Off A4 Bath–Keynsham; Mead Lane; BS31 3ER Great spot by lock and weir on River Avon, with dozens of picnic-sets, garden heaters and own island between lock and pub; enjoyable generous standard food all day, Wadworths ales with guests like Butcombe and Sharps, flagstones, low beams, two roaring log fires, daily newspapers, conservatory dining room; background music; children allowed, disabled facilities, open all

day. *(Dr and Mrs A K Clarke, Colin and Peggy Wilshire, Chris and Angela Buckell, David Crook)*

SHEPTON MONTAGUE ST6731
⋆ Montague Inn (01749) 813213
Village signed off A359 Bruton–Castle Cary; BA9 8JW Simply but tastefully furnished dining pub with welcoming licensees, popular for a civilised meal or just a drink, stripped-wood tables and kitchen chairs, log fire in nice inglenook, good interesting food from lunchtime open sandwiches up, well kept Bath Ales, Wadworths and local guest tapped from the cask, farm ciders, good wine (three glass sizes) and whisky choice, friendly service, bright spacious restaurant extension; children welcome, dogs in bar, garden and terrace with teak furniture, peaceful farmland views, closed Sun evening. *(Mrs C Roe, Mr and Mrs J J A Davis, Edward Mirzoeff, Hugh Stafford)*

SIMONSBATH SS7739
⋆ Exmoor Forest Inn (01643) 831341
B3223/B3358; TA24 7SH Beautifully placed inn under friendly licensees, circular tables by the bar counter, larger area with cushioned settles, upholstered stools and mate's chairs around mix of dark tables, hunting trophies, antlers and horse tack, woodburner, enjoyable local food including game, well kept ales such as Cotleigh, Dartmoor and Exmoor, real cider, good choice of wines by the glass and malt whiskies, residents' lounge, airy dining room; children and dogs welcome, seats in front garden, fine walks along River Barle, own trout and salmon fishing, ten comfortable bedrooms, open all day in full season. *(Sheila Topham, Andrew Scott, Guy Vowles)*

SOMERTON ST4828
Unicorn (01458) 272101
West Street; TA11 7PR Old inn with three interconnecting rooms, one with fine inglenook and bread oven, good choice of home-made food including fresh fish, several well kept ales, wines listed on board, restaurant; courtyard picnic-sets, six bedrooms. *(Comus and Sarah Elliott, Dr J Barrie Jones)*

STAPLE FITZPAINE ST2618
⋆ Greyhound (01823) 480227
Off A358 or B3170 S of Taunton; TA3 5SP Light rambling country pub with wide range of good food (best to book evenings) from long-serving chef, well kept changing ales and nice wines by the glass, welcoming attentive staff, flagstones and inglenooks, pleasant mix of settles and chairs, olde-worlde pictures, farm tools and so forth; children and dogs welcome, well equipped bedrooms, good breakfast. *(Graham Quinn, Geof Cox, Bob and Margaret Holder, Sara Fulton, Roger Baker)*

STOKE ST MARY ST2622
Half Moon (01823) 442271
From M5 junction 25 take A358 towards Ilminster, first right, right in Henlade; TA3 5BY Much-modernised village pub very popular lunchtime for wide choice of hearty good value food, pleasant staff, Butcombe, Fullers London Pride and Greene King Abbot, nice coffee, quite a few malt whiskies, thriving local atmosphere in several comfortable open-plan areas including restaurant; children welcome, well tended garden. *(Ted and Charlotte Routley, Bob and Margaret Holder)*

TARR SS8632
⋆ Tarr Farm (01643) 851507
Tarr Steps – narrow road off B3223 N of Dulverton; deep ford if you approach from the W (inn is on E bank); TA22 9PY Lovely Exmoor setting above River Barle's medieval clapper bridge; compact unpretentious bar rooms with good views, stall seating, wall seats and leather chairs around slabby rustic tables, game bird pictures on wood-clad walls, three woodburners, Exmoor ales and several wines by the glass, good food, residents' end with smart evening restaurant (a mix of bar or restaurant choices using local produce), friendly service, pleasant log-fire lounge with dark leather armchairs and sofas; children and dogs welcome, slate-topped stone tables outside making most of setting, good bedrooms (no under-10s), open all day but closed 1-10 Feb. *(Adrian Johnson, John and Jackie Chalcraft, John and Joan Nash, Lynda and Trevor Smith and others)*

TAUNTON ST2525
⋆ Hankridge Arms (01823) 444405
Hankridge Way, Deane Gate (near Sainsbury); just off M5 junction 25 – A358 towards city, then right at roundabout, right at next roundabout; TA1 2LR Well appointed Badger dining pub based on 16th-c former farmhouse – splendid contrast to the modern shopping complex around it; different-sized linked areas, big log fire, enjoyable generous food from interesting sandwiches through pubby things to restaurant dishes, set lunch deal, well kept ales and decent wines by the glass, quick friendly young staff; background music; dogs welcome, plenty of tables in pleasant outside area. *(Dr and Mrs A K Clarke, Warren Marsh, R T and J C Moggridge, Bob and Margaret Holder)*

TAUNTON ST2225
Plough (01823) 324404
Station Road; TA1 1PB Small, homely and welcoming with up to eight well kept local ales and eight racked ciders, good choice of wines by the glass, simple food all day till 10pm including unusual pies, bare boards, panelling, candles on tables, cosy nooks, open fire, hidden door to lavatories, friendly

pub dog (others welcome), live music Sun night, popular quiz Tues, board games; open all day till late (3am Fri, Sat). *(John and Fiona McIlwain, Kerry Law)*

TAUNTON   ST2223
Vivary Arms (01823) 272563
Wilton Street; across Vivary Park from centre; TA1 3JR Pretty low-beamed 18th-c local (Taunton's oldest), good value fresh food from light lunches up in snug plush lounge and small dining room, friendly helpful young staff, relaxed atmosphere, well kept ales including Butcombe, decent wines, interesting collection of drink-related items; lovely hanging baskets and flowers. *(John Gould, Bob and Margaret Holder)*

THURLOXTON   ST2729
Maypole (01823) 412286
A38 Taunton–Bridgwater, between M5 junctions 24 and 25; TA2 8RF Spacious but cosy beamed pub with several traditional areas, welcoming staff, tasty locally sourced food including good two-course deal and Sun carvery, ales such as Bath, Exmoor and Sharps, local cider, some interesting wines and malt whiskies, pubby furniture on carpet, shelves of jugs and plates, old local photographs, log fire, skittle alley, eggs and preserves for sale at the bar; no dogs; children welcome, wheelchair access (portable ramp to bar), enclosed garden with play area, surrounding paddock, peaceful village, closed Sun evening. *(Chris and Angela Buckell)*

TIMBERSCOMBE   SS9542
Lion (01643) 841243
Church Street; TA24 7TP Refurbished Exmoor-edge coaching inn dating from 15th c, thriving village-pub atmosphere in comfortable flagstoned main bar with rooms off, scrubbed pine tables in dining area, enjoyable pub food from good fresh ciabattas up, friendly service, well kept Exmoor tapped from the cask, nice wines, good log fire; children and dogs welcome, bedrooms. *(Dennis Jenkin)*

TINTINHULL   ST5019
★**Crown & Victoria** (01935) 823341
Farm Street, village signed off A303; BA22 8PZ Handsome golden-stone inn with particularly friendly long-serving licensees; carpeted throughout, with high bar chairs by new oak counter, well kept Butcombe, Cheddar Valley Potholer, Palmers and Sharps Doom Bar, farmhouse furniture and big open woodburner with logs piled up beside, good popular well presented food, dining room with church candles, elegant wicker-seated chairs and a rose on each table, former skittle alley also used for dining, end conservatory; children welcome, disabled facilities, big garden with play area, five bedrooms, handy for Tintinhull House (NT). *(Patrick and Daphne Darley, Charles A Hey, Roger Fox)*

TRISCOMBE   ST1535
★**Blue Ball** (01984) 618242
Village signed off A358 Crowcombe–Bagborough; turn off opposite sign to youth hostel; OS Sheet 181 map reference 155355; TA4 3HE Smartly refurbished old thatched place tucked beneath the Quantocks; first floor of original stables sloping down gently on three levels, each with own fire and cleverly divided by hand-cut beech partitions, Cotleigh and two guests, local farm cider and several wines by the glass, enjoyable imaginative food including local game; background music; children and dogs welcome, chair lift to bar/restaurant area for disabled customers, decking at top of woodside terraced garden making most of views, bedrooms, closed Sun evening, Mon lunchtime. *(John and Sharon Hancock, Kevin Chamberlain, Christine and Neil Townend)*

TRUDOXHILL   ST7443
White Hart (01373) 836324
Off A361 SW of Frome; BA11 5DP Home-made food including good individual pies, real ales such as St Austell, Sharps and a locally brewed house beer, good friendly service, beams and stripped stone, two log fires; children welcome, sheltered side garden, barbecues, nice village, open all day weekends. *(Mike Burkinshaw)*

UPTON   ST0129
Lowtrow Cross Inn (01398) 371220
A3190 E of Upton; TA4 2DB Under new management; character low-beamed bar with log fire and woodburner, bare boards and flagstones, two carpeted country-kitchen dining areas, one with enormous inglenook, traditional home-made food (not Mon, Tues lunchtime), Cotleigh Tawny and two guests, good mix of locals and diners; children and dogs welcome, attractive surroundings, camping nearby, closed Mon lunctime. *(Anon)*

VOBSTER   ST7049
★**Vobster Inn** (01373) 812920
Lower Vobster; BA3 5RJ Roomy old stone-built dining pub with good reasonably priced food including some spanish dishes (chef/landlord is from Spain) and fresh fish daily from Cornwall, good service, Butcombe and a Blindmans seasonal ale, Ashton Press cider, good wines by the glass, three comfortable open-plan areas with antique furniture, plenty of room for just a drink; dogs allowed in bar, side lawn, peaceful views, boules, adventure playground and chickens behind, bedrooms. *(Sophie Holborow)*

WATCHET   ST0643
Star (01984) 631367
Mill Lane (B3191); TA23 0BZ Late 18th-c pub near seafront, main flagstoned bar with other low-beamed side rooms and nooks

and crannies, pubby furniture including oak settles, window seats, lots of bric-a-brac, ornate fireplace with woodburner, enjoyable food cooked to order (seafood a speciality), well kept mainly local ales, Thatcher's cider, some interesting whiskies, cheerful efficient staff; children and dogs welcome, wheelchair access, picnic-sets out in front and in beer garden behind. *(Joan and Michel Hooper-Immins, Chris and Angela Buckell, John and Alison Hamilton, Michael Butler)*

WEDMORE ST4348
✶ **Swan** (01934) 710337
Cheddar Road; BS28 4EQ Newly refurbished 18th-c village dining pub, bare-boards country-chic bar with log fire, airy restaurant, good interesting food using prime local ingredients, own-baked bread, well kept local ales and ciders, nice selection of wines by the glass, polished attentive service; teak furniture on paved terrace, six stylish bedrooms, open all day from 9am. *(Hugo Jeune, John and Gloria Isaacs)*

WELLOW ST7358
✶ **Fox & Badger** (01225) 832293
Signed off A367 SW of Bath; BA2 8QG Opened-up village pub, flagstones one end, bare boards the other, some snug corners, woodburner in massive hearth, Butcombe, Fullers, Greene King and Sharps, four ciders including Thatcher's, wide range of enjoyable bar food from doorstep sandwiches and generous ploughman's up, prompt good-humoured service; children and dogs welcome, picnic-sets in covered courtyard, open all day Fri and Sat. *(Guy Vowles)*

WELLS ST5445
✶ **City Arms** (01749) 673916
High Street; BA5 2AG Bustling town centre pub with up to seven well kept ales, three ciders and decent reasonably priced food from breakfast on; main bar with leather sofas and chairs around assorted tables, plenty of prints and paintings, gas-effect log fire, upstairs restaurant with vaulted-ceiling, red walls and chandeliers; background music; children and dogs welcome, cobbled courtyard and some reminders that the building was once a jail, first floor terrace, open all day from 9am (10am Sun). *(David and Sharon Collison, Mick Dunne, N R White, R T and J C Moggridge, Paul Humphreys and others)*

WELLS ST5445
Crown (01749) 673457
Market Place; BA5 2RF Former 15th-c coaching inn overlooked by cathedral, various bustling areas with light wooden flooring, plenty of matching chairs and cushioned wall benches, Butcombe and Sharps Doom Bar, good value food from sandwiches up

in bar and bistro including early evening deal; background music, TV and games machine; no dogs; children until 8pm, small heated courtyard, 15 bedrooms, open all day. *(Michael Butler)*

WELLS ST5445
Globe (01749) 939137
Priest Row; BA5 2PY Popular unassuming local with welcoming lived-in rooms either side of ancient flagstoned corridor, well kept ales, enjoyable food including good Sun lunch, open fire. *(Anon)*

WELLS ST5445
Kings Head (01749) 672141
High Street; BA5 2SG Interesting old narrow-fronted building, beams and galleries at various levels in high-ceilinged back hall house, flagstoned front bar with log fire and comfortable furniture including unusual swivel bar stools, enjoyable lunchtime pubby food from sandwiches up, Moor, Cheddar and occasional guest beers, Thatcher's cider, cheerful attentive staff; may be live music some evenings; dogs welcome on leads (in courtyard with own bar at food times), wheelchair access with help. *(Paul Humphreys)*

WEST BAGBOROUGH ST1733
✶ **Rising Sun** (01823) 432575
Village signed off A358 NW of Taunton; TA4 3EF Charming village pub lit up with evening candles, small flagstoned bar to right of massive main door with settles and carved dining chairs around polished tables, daily newspapers on old-fashioned child's desk, fresh flowers and some quirky ornaments dotted about, well kept west country ales, good if not cheap food, friendly service, smart cosy dining room with attractive mix of Chippendale and other chairs around a few dark wood tables, big modern photographs and coal-effect gas fire in attractive back snug, upstairs room with trusses in high pitched ceiling, refectory tables and an oriental rug on wood floor, large prints of cathedral cities; children and dogs welcome, teak seats outside by lane, two bedrooms, closed Sun evening and Mon in winter. *(Patrick and Daphne Darley, Bob and Margaret Holder, R T and J C Moggridge, M and R Ridge, Dr Nigel Bowles and others)*

WEST HUNTSPILL ST3145
Crossways (01278) 783756
A38, between M5 exits 22 and 23; TA9 3RA Rambling 17th-c tile-hung pub, six well kept ales, good choice of enjoyable reasonably priced food, friendly efficient staff, split-level carpeted areas with beams and log fires, skittle alley; pool, TV; children and dogs welcome, disabled facilities, garden

---

There are report forms at the back of the book.

with play area and heated smokers' shelter, seven bedrooms, open all day. *(R K Phillips, David Dean, Martin Peters, Richard Tilbrook)*

WEST MONKTON ST2628
⚹ **Monkton** (01823) 412414
Blundells Lane; signed from A3259; TA2 8NP Welcoming village dining pub refurbished under new licensees, good choice of well liked freshly made food including some south african influences (best to book weekends), bare-boards bar with central woodburner, snug off, seperate carpeted restaurant, Exmoor, Otter and Sharps Doom Bar, Aspall's and Thatcher's ciders, wines in three glass sizes, good service; children and dogs welcome, wheelchair access from car park, lots of tables in big garden bounded by stream, play area. *(M G Hart, Bob and Margaret Holder)*

WEST PENNARD ST5438
Lion (01458) 832941
A361 E of Glastonbury; Newtown; BA6 8NH Traditional stone-built village inn, bar and dining areas off small flagstoned black-beamed core, enjoyable pubby food plus daily specials board, Butcombe, Otter and Sharps Doom Bar, inglenook woodburner and open fires; background music; children and dogs welcome, tables on big forecourt, seven bedrooms in converted side barn. *(Alan Todesco-Bond)*

WESTON-SUPER-MARE ST3762
Woolpack (01934) 521670
St George's, just off M5, junction 21; BS22 7XE Opened-up and extended 17th-c coaching inn with full Butcombe range and a guest ale kept well, decent wines, enjoyable pubby food including carvery, friendly local atmosphere (can get packed), pleasant window seats and library-theme area, small attractive restaurant, conservatory, skittle alley; no dogs; children welcome, disabled access, terrace areas with rustic furniture. *(Rod Dykeman, Dave Webster, Sue Holland, Chris and Angela Buckell)*

WINCANTON ST7028
Nog (01963) 32998
South Street; BA9 9DL Welcoming pub with good changing ales such as Plains, Otter and Sharps, real cider, reasonably priced traditional food from lunchtime sandwiches and baked potatoes up, Sun carvery, bare boards, carpet and flagstones, lots of old photographs, open fires, pool and darts, charity quiz (last Thurs); well behaved children and dogs welcome, pleasant back garden with heated smokers' shelter, open all day. *(Joan and Michel Hooper-Immins)*

WINFORD ST5262
Crown (01275) 472388
Crown Hill; BS40 8AY Interesting old pub in deep country, linked rooms with mix of pubby furniture including settles, flagstones

and quarry tiles, musical instruments hanging from black beams, old pictures and photographs on rough walls, lots of copper and brass, leather sofas in front of big open fire, well kept ales including Butcombe and Wadworths 6X, nice wines (selected by locals), enjoyable well presented home-made food (less choice Mon, Tues), helpful friendly landlord and staff, restaurant, live jazz some nights, skittle alley; children welcome, wheelchair access with help, lovely views from terrace. *(Chris and Angela Buckell, David and Bridget Mackwood)*

WINFORD ST5365
Prince of Waterloo (01275) 474930
B3130; BS40 8AR Rambling 16th-c stone pub, large front bar with dining area, slightly smaller back bar/restaurant, lowish black beams, some painted stonework, old cartoons and prints, horse tack, pews and pubby furniture on carpet or flagstones, window seats, well kept ales and enjoyable inexpensive pub food, friendly helpful staff; dogs welcome away from diners, wheelchair access to bars but steps between them, bedrooms in adjacent house, handy for Bristol airport. *(Taff and Gilly Thomas)*

WINSCOMBE ST4257
⚹ **Woodborough** (01934) 844167
Sandford Road; BS25 1HD Big 1930s mock-Tudor village dining pub, smart, comfortable and busy, with wide choice of good generous local food, Butcombe and Sharps Doom Bar, good wine choice, helpful friendly staff, large public bar, skittle alley; disabled access, bedrooms. *(Hugh Roberts, Bruce and Sharon Eden, Susan and Nigel Brookes)*

WINSFORD SS9034
Royal Oak (01643) 851455
Off A396 about 10 miles S of Dunster; TA24 7JE Prettily placed thatched and beamed Exmoor inn, Exmoor ales and Addlestone's cider, lounge bar with big stone fireplace and large bay-window seat looking across towards village green and foot and packhorse bridges over River Winn, more eating space in second bar, several comfortable lounges; children welcome and dogs (they have three), disabled facilities, good bedrooms. *(Sheila Topham)*

WITHAM FRIARY ST7440
⚹ **Seymour Arms** (01749) 850742
Signed from B3092 S of Frome; BA11 5HF Well worn in unchanging flagstoned country tavern, in same friendly family since 1952, two simple rooms off 19th-c hatch-service lobby, one with darts and bar billiards, other with central table skittles, well kept Butcombe and guest ales and Rich's local cider tapped from backroom casks, low prices, open fires, panelled benches, cards and dominoes, no food; dogs welcome, good-sized attractive garden by main rail line. *(the Didler)*

WITHYPOOL
SS8435
✴ Royal Oak (01643) 831506
Village signed off B3233; TA24 7QP Well
run prettily placed country inn – where R
D Blackmore stayed while writing Lorna
Doone; lounge with raised working fireplace,
comfortably cushioned wall seats and slat-
backed chairs, sporting trophies, paintings
and copper/brass ornaments, enjoyable food
here and in restaurant, well kept Exmoor
ales, friendly service, character locals' bar;
children in eating areas, dogs welcome,
wooden benches on terrace, attractive
riverside village with lovely walks, grand
views from Winsford Hill just up the road,
eight bedrooms, open all day. *(John and Joan
Nash, Sheila Topham, Andrew Scott, Mr and Mrs
P D Titcomb, Lynda and Trevor Smith, Guy Vowles
and others)*

WOOKEY
ST5245
✴ Burcott (01749) 673874
B3139 W of Wells; BA5 1NJ Cheerful
beamed roadside pub with two simply
furnished old-fashioned front bar rooms,
flagstones, some exposed stonework and
half-panelling, lantern wall lights, old
prints, woodburner, three changing ales,
Addlestone's cider, enjoyable food (not
evenings Sun, Mon, or Mon lunchtime in
winter) from snacks up in bar and restaurant
(children allowed here), OAP lunch deal,
small games room with built-in wall seats;
soft background music, no dogs; wheelchair
access, front window boxes and tubs, picnic-
sets in sizeable garden with Mendip Hill
views, four self-catering units in converted
stables. *(M G Hart, John Gould, Chris and
Angela Buckell)*

WOOKEY HOLE
ST5347
Wookey Hole Inn (01749) 676677
High Street; BA5 1BP Usefully placed
open-plan family pub, welcoming and
relaxed, with idiosyncratic contemporary
décor, two eating areas and bar, wood floors
and good log fire, three changing local ales,
several belgian beers, ciders and perry,
good generous innovative food using lots of
local ingredients, tables with paper cloths
for drawing on (crayons provided), efficient
friendly staff; background music; dogs
allowed in bar, pleasant garden with various
sculptures, five individually styled bedrooms,
open all day but closed Sun evening.
(N R White, Rich Frith)

WOOLVERTON
ST7954
Red Lion (01373) 830350
*Set back from A36 N of village;
BA2 7QS* Roomy refurbished pub, beams,
panelling and lots of stripped wood, candles

and log-effect fire, well kept Wadworths,
decent wines by the glass, good choice of
enjoyable food all day from baguettes up
including children's meals, friendly staff,
locals' bar with fire (dogs allowed here);
background music; plenty of tables outside, play
area, open all day. *(Meg and Colin Hamilton)*

WRAXALL
ST4971
Battleaxes (01275) 857473
Bristol Road; BS48 1LQ Interesting
stone-built Victorian pub nicely refurbished
by the small Flatcappers group; well kept
local ales including one brewed for them
by Three Castles, good choice of wines and
other drinks, interesting food from snacks
up as well as pub favourites (they ask to
keep a credit card if you run a tab), spacious
interior split into two main areas, polished
boards, painted panelling and good mix of
old furniture; children and dogs welcome,
wheelchair access using ramps, handy for
Tyntesfield (NT). *(Steve and Liz Tilley, Warren
Marsh, Chris and Angela Buckell, Taff and
Gilly Thomas)*

WRAXALL
ST4971
✴ Old Barn (01275) 819011
*Just off Bristol Road (B3130) in
grounds of Wraxall House; BS48 1LQ*
Idiosyncratic gabled barn conversion,
scrubbed tables, school benches and soft
sofas under oak rafters, stripped boards
and flagstones, welcoming atmosphere
and friendly service, well kept Butcombe,
Fullers, Otter, St Austell, Sharps and a guest
tapped from the cask (plans for their own
brews too), farm ciders, good wines by the
glass, simple sandwiches, unusual board
games; occasional background music and
sports TV; children and dogs welcome, nice
garden with terrace barbecue (bring your
own meat), smokers' shelter, closed Mon
lunchtime otherwise open all day. *(Steve and
Liz Tilley, the Didler, Mike Burkinshaw, Taff and
Gilly Thomas)*

YARLINGTON
ST6529
Stags Head (01963) 440393
Pound Lane; BA9 8DG Old low-ceilinged
and flagstoned country pub tucked away
in rustic hamlet, Bass, Greene King IPA
and a local guest from small central bar,
woodburner, chapel chairs and mixed pine
tables on left, carpeted dining area on
right with big log fire, modern landscape
prints and feature cider-press table, second
dining room with doors on to terrace, food
from traditional choices up including OAP
lunchtime menu; background music; well
behaved children welcome, dogs in bar,
picnic-sets in sheltered back garden, three
bedrooms, closed Sun evening. *(Mr Stan Lea)*

We can always use photos of pubs on our website – why not e-mail us one –
feedback@thegoodpubguide.co.uk

Staffordshire

The charming Alan East recently celebrated 50 years of running the eccentric treasure trove that is the Yew Tree at Cauldon – unbelievably cheap beer and an extraordinary collection of curios, the most impressive being the working polyphons and symphonions. Other Main Entries are the Queens at Freehay in Cheadle (neatly kept and family run), the Holly Bush at Salt (charming medieval pub with generously served all-day food), and Hand & Trumpet in Wrinehill (a Brunning & Price pub, light and airy with a good choice of drinks and consistently good, bistro-style food). Our Staffordshire Dining Pub 2013 is the Hand & Trumpet in Wrinehill.

 CAULDON   SK0749 Map 7

Yew Tree ★★ £

Village signposted from A523 and A52 about 8 miles W of Ashbourne; ST10 3EJ

Treasure-trove of fascinating antiques and dusty bric-a-brac, bargain beer; very eccentric

Alan East, the jovial landlord at this uniquely idiosyncratic place, recently celebrated his 50th anniversary here. Much loved for its unusual charm (it's been affectionately described as a junk shop with a bar and it's not exactly what you'd call spic and span), it's filled with a museum's worth of curiosities. The most impressive pieces are perhaps the working polyphons and symphonions – 19th-c developments of the musical box, some taller than a person, each with quite a repertoire of tunes and elaborate sound-effects. But there are also two pairs of Queen Victoria's stockings, ancient guns and pistols, several penny-farthings, an old sit-and-stride boneshaker, a rocking horse, swordfish blades, a little 800 BC greek vase, and even a fine marquetry cabinet crammed with notable early staffordshire pottery. Soggily sprung sofas mingle with 18th-c settles, plenty of little wooden tables and a four-person oak church choir seat with carved heads that came from St Mary's church in Stafford; above the bar is an odd iron dog-carrier. As well as all this, there's a choir of fine, tuneful longcase clocks in the gallery just above the entrance, a collection of six pianolas (one of which plays most nights) with an excellent repertoire of piano rolls, a working vintage valve radio set, a crank-handle telephone, a sinuous medieval wind instrument made of leather and a Jacobean four-poster that was once owned by Josiah Wedgwood and still has his original wig hook on the headboard. Clearly, it would be almost an overwhelming task to keep all this sprucely clean. The drinks here are very reasonably priced so it's no wonder that it's popular with locals. You'll find well kept Bass, Burton Bridge and Rudgate Ruby Mild on handpump or tapped from the cask, along with about a dozen interesting malt whiskies; background music (probably Radio 2), darts, shove-ha'penny, table skittles, dominoes and cribbage. When you arrive, don't be put off by the plain exterior, or the fact that the pub is tucked unpromisingly between enormous cement works and quarries and almost hidden by a towering yew tree.

🍴 Simple good value tasty snacks include pork, meat and potato, chicken and mushroom and steak pies, big hot filled baps and sandwiches, quiche, smoked mackerel or ham salad; no starters. *Benchmark main dish: pork pie £2.80*

Free house ~ Licensee Alan East ~ Real ale ~ Bar food (12-3, 7-12) ~ No credit cards ~ (01538) 308348 ~ Children allowed in polyphon room ~ Dogs welcome ~ Folk music first Tues of month ~ Open 12-3, 7-12 *Recommended by David Austin, Barry Collett, Mr and Mrs N Hall, the Didler*

CHEADLE   SK0342 Map 7
Queens at Freehay
A mile SE of Cheadle; take Rakeway Road off A522 (via Park Avenue or Mills Road), then after a mile turn into Counslow Road; ST10 1RF

Enjoyable dining pub with a couple of local beers and a decent garden

The neatly kept interior of this family-run dining pub has a couple of cottagey touches that soften the modern refurbishments. The comfortable lounge bar has light wood tables on stripped wood floors, small country pictures and curtains with matching cushions. It opens through an arch into a simple light and airy dining area, with neatly spaced new tables and chairs on light blue carpets. Pleasant, welcoming staff serve Charles Wells Bombardier and Peakstones Rock Alton Abbey from handpump; background music. The attractive little back garden with its mature shrubs and neatly arranged picnic-sets is kept in immaculate condition.

🍴 Fairly priced food is carefully cooked and nicely presented. As well as reasonably priced sandwiches and salads, there might be chicken goujons, thai-style prawns, black pudding topped with bacon and melted cheddar cheese, chicken and vegetable crumble, moroccan lamb tagine, fish and chips, fried duck breast with plum and hoi sin sauce, grilled cod loin with parsley hollandaise sauce, and steaks. *Benchmark main dish: beef and merlot pie £10.95. Two-course evening meal £16.70.*

Free house ~ Licensee Adrian Rock ~ Real ale ~ Bar food (12-2(2.30 Sun), 6(6.30 Sun)-9.30) ~ (01538) 722383 ~ Children welcome ~ Open 12-3(4 Sun), 6-11(6.30-10.30 Sun) ~ www.queensatfreehay.co.uk *Recommended by Richard Gibbs*

SALT   SJ9527 Map 7
Holly Bush £
Village signposted off A51 S of Stone (and A518 NE of Stafford); ST18 0BX

Delightful medieval pub, all-day food

Thatched, with a mass of flowering tubs and baskets, this charming white-painted 14th-c house is chocolate-box delightful. It's lovely inside, too, with several cosy areas spreading off from the standing-only serving section, with high-backed cushioned pews, old tables and more conventional seats. The oldest part has a heavy-beamed and planked ceiling (some of the beams are attractively carved), a woodburning stove and a salt cupboard built into the big inglenook, with other nice old-fashioned touches such as an ancient pair of riding boots on the mantelpiece. A modern back extension, with beams, stripped brickwork and a small coal fire, blends in well. Adnams, Marstons Pedigree and a guest such as Lymestone Stone Faced are on handpump, alongside a dozen wines by the glass. The back of the pub is beautifully tended, with rustic picnic-sets on a big lawn. It can get busy so do arrive early for a table. They operate a secure locker system for credit cards, which they will ask to keep if you are running a tab.

Readers enjoy the good value, generously served bar food, which, as well as lunchtime sandwiches, baked potatoes, toasties and ploughman's, might include breaded mushrooms with garlic dip, blue-cheese stuffed pears, staffordshire oatcake stuffed with spiced black pudding with herby tomato sauce, greek lamb, venison casserole, steak and kidney pudding, gammon steak and egg, grilled pork chops with cheese, mustard and beer topping, fried cod and steaks; there's a wood-fired pizza oven in the beer garden *Benchmark main dish: steak in ale pie £9.95. Two-course evening meal £14.80.*

Admiral Taverns ~ Licensees Geoffrey and Joseph Holland ~ Real ale ~ Bar food (12-9.30(9 Sun)) ~ (01889) 508234 ~ Children welcome till 8pm ~ Open 12-11 (11.30 Sat, 10.30 Sun) ~ www.hollybushinn.co.uk *Recommended by Mike Proctor, Charles and Pauline Stride, Paul Humphreys, N R White, R Anderson, Andy Dolan, Henry Pursehouse-Tranter, Brian and Anna Marsden*

WRINEHILL   SJ7547   Map 7

Hand & Trumpet 🍴 🍷 🍺

A531 Newcastle–Nantwich; CW3 9BJ

Staffordshire Dining Pub of the Year

Big attractive dining pub with good food all day, professional service, nice range of real ales and wines; pleasant garden

One of the most liked pubs in the Brunning & Price chain, this substantial dining pub is a relaxing place for an enjoyable meal. It's done out in typical light and airy open-plan style with a gentle mix of dining chairs and sturdy tables on polished tiles or stripped-oak boards and several warming oriental rugs that soften the acoustics. There are lots of nicely lit prints on cream walls between mainly dark dado and deep red ceilings. Original bow windows and, in one area, a large skylight keep it light and airy, and french windows open on to a spacious balustraded deck whose teak tables and chairs look down over ducks swimming on a big pond in the sizeable garden, which has plenty of trees. At the heart of the pub is a long, solidly built counter, where friendly attentive staff serve Caledonian Deuchars IPA, Phoenix Brunning & Price Original, Salopian Oracle and guests from brewers such as Tatton, Wincle and Woodlands as well as a dozen wines by the glass and about 70 whiskies; good disabled access and facilities; board games.

Food is well prepared, and the menu ranges from good traditional dishes to more imaginative ones. As well as interesting sandwiches and ploughman's, there might be whitebait, spiced ham hock and rabbit salad, crab and chorizo linguine, smoked haddock and salmon fishcakes, sausage and mash, roast celeriac, parsnip and spinach with hazelnut crumble, steak and ale pie, roast duck leg and duck faggot with pink peppercorn gravy, thai-style fish casserole, and puddings such as steamed lemon sponge and gooseberry and apple crumble. *Benchmark main dish: fish and chips £11.95. Two-course evening meal £19.00.*

Brunning & Price ~ Manager John Unsworth ~ Real ale ~ Bar food (12-10(9.30 Sun)) ~ (01270) 820048 ~ Children welcome ~ Dogs allowed in bar ~ Open 11.30-11(10.30 Sun) ~ www.handandtrumpet-wrinehill.co.uk *Recommended by C A Bryson, Brian and Anna Marsden, Glenwys and Alan Lawrence, Dave Webster, Sue Holland, Cath, Frank Blanchard, Mike Horgan, Di Wright, Paul and Gail Betteley, Rachel and Ross Gavin*

Also Worth a Visit in Staffordshire

Besides the fully inspected pubs, you might like to try these pubs that have been recommended to us and described by readers. Do tell us what you think of them: feedback@goodguides.com

ABBOTS BROMLEY　　　　SK0824

* **Goats Head** (01283) 840254

Market Place; WS15 3BP Well run beamed and timbered village pub with friendly local atmosphere, Greene King, Marstons, St Austell, Timothy Taylors and two guests (May beer festival), lots of wines by the glass, enjoyable home-made food (not Sun evening) served by attentive helpful staff, opened-up cream-painted interior, unpretentious but comfortable, with oak floors, traditional furnishings and fire in big inglenook; juke box and TV; children and dogs welcome, teak furniture on sheltered lawn looking up to church tower, open all day. *(David Austin, David J Austin, Susan and Nigel Brookes, Richard and Jean Green, Tony W Dickinson, Simon Le Fort)*

ALSTONEFIELD　　　　SK1355

* **George** (01335) 310205

Village signed from A515 Ashbourne–Buxton; DE6 2FX Stone-built pub with friendly landlady, straightforward bar with low beams, old Peak District photographs and pictures, warming fire, Burtons, Marstons and a guest from copper-topped counter, a dozen wines by the glass, farmhouse furniture and woodburner in neat dining room, locally sourced food cooked to order from shortish menu (some prices on the high side); children welcome, dogs in bar, seats out by village green or in big sheltered back stableyard, open all day Fri-Sun (till 9.30pm Sun). *(Clive and Fran Dutson, Mike Proctor, the Didler, Ann and Colin Hunt, Stuart Paulley)*

ALSTONEFIELD　　　　SK1255

Watts Russell Arms (01335) 310126

Hopedale; DE6 2GD Nicely placed 18th-c stone-built beamed pub, well kept Thornbridge ales, fairly short menu including lunchtime wraps and perhaps lobby (a local stew), tapas Fri and Sun evenings, two lived-in carpeted rooms with pubby furniture and banquettes, stone fireplace; children and dogs welcome, picnic-sets on sheltered tiered terrace and in garden, open all day, closed Mon evening. *(Dennis Jones, Ian Phillips)*

ANSLOW　　　　SK2125

Bell (01283) 812101

Main Road; DE13 9QD Friendly flagstoned bar with settles and log fire, Marstons ales, good enterprising food from set menu (choose two or three courses), helpful cheerful service, reasonably priced wine list, restaurant; well behaved children welcome, dogs in bar, garden with heated terrace, open all day weekends, closed Mon. *(Paul Humphreys)*

BARTON-UNDER-NEEDWOOD　　　　SK1818

Shoulder of Mutton (01283) 712568

Main Street; DE13 8AA Modernised 17th-c village pub with low beams, panelling and open fire, pleasant staff, well kept Bass and guests, good range of bar meals and snacks, pool in public bar, live music Fri; seats out at front and on terrace, four bedrooms, open all day. *(Simon Le Fort, B M Eldridge, Dave Braisted)*

BARTON-UNDER-NEEDWOOD　　　　SK2018

Waterfront (01283) 711500

Barton Marina, Barton Turns; DE13 8DZ Huge pub, new but cleverly done to look long-established, part of marina complex; wide choice of enjoyable quickly served food including pubby favourites (light dishes all day), two good value house beers from local Blythe with up to five guests, good friendly service, thriving atmosphere; children welcome until early evening, no dogs inside, seats out overlooking water, open all day. *(John and Helen Rushton, B M Eldridge)*

BLACKBROOK　　　　SJ7638

Swan With Two Necks (01782) 680343 *Nantwich Road (A51); ST5 5EH* Smart contemporary décor in civilised open-plan dining areas, friendly service, quickly served food all day, good value wines by the glass; they aim to keep a credit card while running a tab; comfortable tables out on decking. *(Chris Brammeld)*

BLITHBURY SK0819

Bull & Spectacles (01889) 504201

Uttoxeter Road (B5014 S of Abbots Bromley); WS15 3HY 17th-c pub with obliging friendly service, wide choice of homely food including popular bargain lunchtime Hot Table (half a dozen or so generous main dishes with help-yourself vegetables, and some puddings), an ale from Greene King; children welcome, open all day Sun. *(David Green)*

BOBBINGTON SO8190

Red Lion (01384) 221237

Six Ashes Road, off A458 Stourbridge–Bridgnorth; DY7 5DU Friendly family-run pub popular for its good choice of enjoyable food and well kept ales (Enville, Hereford, Theakstons and Wye Valley), drinking and eating areas well separated, games part with darts, table football and pool; children welcome, good-sized garden with robust play area, 17 comfortable bedrooms in modern block, good breakfast, open all day weekends. *(David Heath)*

BREWOOD SJ8808

Bridge Inn (1902) 851999

High Green; by Shropshire Union Canal Bridge 14; ST19 9BD Buoyant two-bar pub with Marstons-related ales, decent well priced bar food, good friendly service, dining extension; tables outside high over canal. *(Simon Le Fort)*

BURTON UPON TRENT SK2523

★ Burton Bridge Inn (01283) 536596

Bridge Street (A50); DE14 1SY Genuinely friendly down-to-earth local with own good Burton Bridge ales from brewery across old-fashioned brick yard; simple little front area leading into adjacent bar with pews, plain walls hung with notices, awards and brewery memorabilia, 20 malt whiskies and lots of country wines, small beamed and oak-panelled lounge with simple furniture and flame-effect fire, panelled upstairs dining room, simple but hearty food (lunchtimes only, not Sun); no credit cards; children welcome, dogs in bar, skittle alley, open all day Fri, Sat. *(P Dawn, Andy and Claire Barker, Joe Deuter, the Didler, John Honnor)*

BURTON UPON TRENT SK2423

★ Coopers Tavern (01283) 532551

Cross Street; DE14 1EG Old-fashioned no-frills backstreet local, now tied to Joules but was tap for Bass brewery across road and still has some glorious ephemera including mirrors and glazed adverts; homely and warm with coal fire, straightforward front parlour with pleasant jumble of furniture, back bar doubling as tap room, up to half a dozen guest ales including Bass, ciders and perries, friendly landlady, pork pies only but can bring your own food (or take beer to next-door curry house); children

and dogs welcome, small back garden, open all day Fri-Sun, closed Mon and Tues lunchtimes. *(Edward Leetham, the Didler, Andy Dolan, John Honnor)*

BURTON UPON TRENT SK2424

Derby Inn (01283) 543674

Derby Road; DE14 1RU Well worn idiosyncratic local with well kept Greene King Abbot, Marstons Pedigree and two guests, cosy panelled lounge with collection of Burton beer festival glasses, lots of steam railway memorabilia in long narrow bar; outside lavatories, sports TV; well behaved children and dogs welcome, seats out in backyard, open all day Fri, Sat. *(the Didler)*

BURTON UPON TRENT SK2522

Elms (01283) 535505

Stapenhill Road (A444); DE15 9AE Victorian local overlooking the river, well kept Bass, Marstons and changing guests in small character bar with wall benches, larger lounge, friendly staff; open all day. *(the Didler)*

BURTON UPON TRENT SK2423

Old Cottage Tavern (01283) 511615

Rangemoor Street/Byrkley Street; DE14 2EG Friendly local owned by Burton Old Cottage, their well kept ales and guests, two bars, snug and compact back restaurant, upstairs games room with skittle alley; three bedrooms, open all day. *(the Didler)*

BUTTERTON SK0756

Black Lion (01538) 304232

Off B5053; ST13 7SP Nicely placed traditional 18th-c low-beamed stone-built inn, logs blazing in inner room's kitchen range, good-humoured efficient service, enjoyable food from filled rolls up including two-for-one deal on main courses, up to five changing often unusual ales, pool room with darts; background music; no dogs inside; children welcome, terrace tables, three tidy bedrooms, closed weekday lunchtimes in winter, Mon and Tues lunchtimes in summer, open all day Sun. *(the Didler, Phill Robinson, Mike Proctor)*

CHURCH EATON SJ8417

Royal Oak (01785) 823078

Corner of High Street/Wood Eaton Road; ST20 0AJ Community run village pub with four well kept ales (tasting trays available), decent reasonably priced food including specials, prompt friendly service, games room. *(Brian and Anna Marsden)*

CODSALL SJ8603

Codsall Station (01902) 847061

Chapel Lane/Station Road; WV8 1BY Simply restored vintage waiting room and ticket office of working station, comfortable and welcoming, with Holdens beers and basic good value generous food (sandwiches only Sun), lots of railway memorabilia, conservatory; terrace seating, open all day Fri-Sun. *(the Didler, Mrs Margo Finlay, Jörg Kasprowski)*

CONSALL
SK0049

⋆ **Black Lion** (01782) 550294

Consall Forge, OS Sheet 118 map ref 000491; best approach from Nature Park, off A522, using car park 0.5 miles past Nature Centre; ST9 0AJ Traditional take-us-as-you-find-us local tucked away in rustic old-fashioned canalside settlement by restored steam railway station, generous helpings of enjoyable unpretentious food made by landlord (may be only baps mid-week), wide range of well kept mostly local ales (tasting trays available), several ciders, flagstones and good coal fire; background music, can get very busy weekend lunchtimes but staff cope well; seats outside among roaming chickens, good walking area. *(P Dawn, Edward Leetham, the Didler, Mike Proctor, Brian and Anna Marsden)*

ELLASTONE
SK1143

Duncombe Arms (01335) 324275

Main Road; DE6 2GZ Refurbished village dining pub with enjoyable food in bar and restaurant, ales including Marstons Pedigree and one brewed for them by Banks's, friendly staff; garden bar. *(Damian Chase)*

ENVILLE
SO8286

Cat (01384) 872209

A458 W of Stourbridge (Bridgnorth Road); DY7 5HA New management for this ancient beamed pub on Staffordshire Way; two appealingly old-fashioned log-fire rooms on one side of servery, plush banquettes on the other, Enville ales and guests, good choice of well priced food, garden room, upstairs function room; children and dogs welcome, pretty courtyard sheltered by massive estate wall, open all day Sat, closed Sun evening and Mon lunchtime. *(Anon)*

FORTON
SJ7521

Swan (01952) 812169

A519 Newport–Eccleshall; TF10 8BY Former estate manager's house; large open room with mirrors and small wooden bar, separate section with library and sofas, restaurant opening into modern conservatory, enjoyable reasonably priced food from sandwiches up including carvery (weekday lunchtimes, all day Sun), three or four ales including Marstons, good friendly service; background music, no dogs; children welcome, handy for Shropshire Union Canal walks, ten bedrooms (four in converted barn), open all day. *(Alan and Eve Harding)*

FRADLEY
SK1414

⋆ **White Swan** (01283) 790330

Fradley Junction; DE13 7DN Perfect canalside location at Trent & Mersey and Coventry junction, well kept Black Sheep, Greene King Abbot, Marstons Pedigree and a guest like Hydes, bargain food from cobs to Sun carvery, cheery traditional public bar with woodburner, quieter plusher lounge and lower vaulted back bar (where children allowed), cribbage, dominoes; waterside tables, monthly classic car/motorbike meetings, open all day. *(Paul J Robinshaw, B M Eldridge)*

GAILEY
SJ9010

Spread Eagle (01902) 790212

A5/A449; ST19 5PN Spacious Marstons roadhouse, variety of separate areas including relaxing sofas and family part with toys, good value usual food, daily carvery, efficient helpful service; good disabled access and facilities, big terrace, lawn with play area, open all day. *(JCW, Paul Nickson)*

GNOSALL
SJ8120

Navigation (01785) 822327

Newport Road; ST20 0EQ Relaxed two-bar pub with dining conservatory and terrace overlooking Shropshire Union Canal (moorings), good friendly service, popular reasonably priced traditional food and specials, well kept Banks's ales, good value wines, live music Thurs, pool and darts; children welcome, dogs in bar. *(Susan and Nigel Brookes)*

GREAT HAYWOOD
0000

Clifford Arms (01889) 881321

Main Road; ST18 0SR Mock-Tudor pub near Trent & Mersey Canal (Bridge 73) and Shugborough Hall (NT), good-sized bar with restaurant behind, hearty well presented food, well kept Adnams, Bass, Greene King and guests, cheery staff; children allowed if eating, walkers and dogs welcome, beer garden with heated smokers' shelter, open all day Fri-Sun. *(David M Smith)*

HANLEY
SJ8847

Coachmakers Arms (01782) 262158

Lichfield Street; ST1 3EA Chatty traditional town local with four small rooms and drinking corridor, half a dozen or more good changing ales, farm cider, darts, cards and dominoes, original seating and local tilework, open fire; children welcome, open all day (still under threat of demolition). *(Dave Webster, Sue Holland, the Didler)*

Post Office address codings confusingly give the impression that some pubs are in Staffordshire, when they're really in Cheshire or Derbyshire (which is where we list them).

HAUGHTON   SJ8620
Bell (01785) 780301
*A518 Stafford–Newport; ST18
9EX* 19th-c village pub with good value
popular pub food (not Sun or Mon evenings),
well kept Banks's, Marstons, Timothy Taylors
and a guest, good friendly service even when
busy; no dogs inside; children welcome,
picnic-sets in back garden, open all day
Fri-Sun. *(Anon)*

HIGH OFFLEY   SJ7725
Anchor (01785) 284569
*Off A519 Eccleshall–Newport; towards
High Lea, by Shropshire Union Canal
Bridge 42; Peggs Lane; ST20 0NG* Real
boaters' pub on Shropshire Union Canal,
little changed in the century or more this
family have run it, two small simple front
rooms, Marstons Pedigree and Wadworths
6X, Weston's farm cider, may be lunchtime
toasties, owners' sitting room behind bar,
occasional weekend sing-alongs; no children
inside; outbuilding with small shop and
semi-open lavatories, lovely garden with
great hanging baskets and notable topiary
anchor, caravan/campsite, closed Mon-Thurs
in winter. *(the Didler, Richard and Karen Holt,
Peter Stevenson)*

HIMLEY   SO8990
⋆ Crooked House (01384) 238583
*Signed down long lane from B4176
Gornalwood–Himley, OS Sheet
139 map reference 896908; DY3
4DA* Extraordinary sight, building thrown
wildly out of kilter (mining subsidence),
slopes so weird things look as if they roll
up not down them; otherwise a traditional
pub with Marstons-related ales and farm
cider, cheery staff, good choice of enjoyable
locally sourced food from well priced
pubby choices to more creative dishes,
some local antiques in level extension,
conservatory; children in eating areas, big
outside terrace, open all day, closed Mon
lunchtime. *(Dave Braisted, the Didler,
Simon Le Fort)*

HOAR CROSS   SK1323
⋆ Meynell Ingram Arms
(01283) 575202 *Abbots Bromley Road,
off A515 Yoxall–Sudbury; DE13 8RB*
Good interesting food (till 7pm Sun)
from sandwiches to restaurant meals in
comfortably extended country dining pub,
friendly staff, well kept Burton Bridge,
Marstons Pedigree and two guests, several
neat little rooms rambling around central
counter, log fire, some beams and brasses,
hunting pictures and bespectacled fox's head,
dining room with coal-effect fire; children
and dogs welcome, tables on front grass and
in courtyard behind, open all day. *(Clifford
Blakemore, Andy Dolan)*

HOPWAS   SK1704
Tame Otter (01827) 53361
*Hints Road (A51 Tamworth–Lichfield);
B78 3AT* Vintage Inn by Birmingham &
Fazeley Canal (moorings), refurbished
beamed interior on different levels, cosy
corners, their usual fairly priced food
all day, well kept Adnams, Everards and
Marstons, decent choice of wines, efficient
friendly service, nice mixed furnishings,
old photographs and canalia, three fires;
children welcome, large garden with plenty
of seating. *(David Green, Glenwys and Alan
Lawrence, Mike and Mary Carter)*

HULME END   SK1059
Manifold Inn (01298) 84537
B5054 Warslow–Hartington; SK17 0EX
Light and airy 18th-c country dining pub
near river, enjoyable traditional home-made
food in generous helpings, reasonable
prices, ales such as Marstons Pedigree,
Thwaites Wainwright and Whim Hartington,
pleasant staff, lots of brasses and farming
implements, log fire in bar, some stripped
stone, restaurant and conservatory; children
welcome, dogs in certain parts, disabled
facilities, tables outside, ten bedrooms off
secluded back courtyard, campsite, open all
day weekends. *(Malcolm and Pauline Pellatt,
Dennis Jones)*

KIDSGROVE   SJ8354
⋆ Blue Bell (01782) 774052
*Hardings Wood; off A50 NW edge of
town; ST7 1EG* Simple friendly pub
(looks more like a house) with half a dozen
thoughtfully chosen and constantly changing
ales from smaller breweries, around 30
bottled continentals, up to three draught
farm ciders and a perry, filled rolls weekends
only; four small, carpeted rooms, unfussy
and straightforward, with blue upholstered
benches, basic pub furniture, gas-effect coal
fire; may be background music, no credit
cards; dogs and well behaved children
welcome, tables in front and on little back
lawn, open all day Sun, closed Mon and
weekday lunchtimes. *(Mike Proctor, Dave
Webster, Sue Holland, the Didler)*

KING'S BROMLEY   SK1216
Royal Oak (01543) 473980
Manor Road (A515); DE13 7HZ
Welcoming country pub with good food
including stone-baked pizzas and Sun
carvery, Marstons Pedigree and a guest,
friendly helpful staff; open all day. *(Anon)*

KINVER   SO8582
Whittington Inn (01384) 872110
*A449 between Kidderminster and Wall
Heath, by Staffordshire & Worcestershire
Canal; DY7 6NY* Striking half-timbered
house dating from 14th c, genuine Dick
Whittington connection and a priest hole
upstairs, interesting old-fashioned bar,

roaring fire, lots of 18th-c panelling, little nooks and corners, low doorways, passages and wall paintings, conservatory, well kept Banks's, Marstons Pedigree and a guest, decent wines, good value food all day, friendly young staff; background music; attractive garden with fountain. *(Ian and Sharon Shorthouse, Iain Clark)*

LEEK SJ9856
Den Engel (01538) 373751
Stanley Street; ST13 5HG Relaxed belgian-style bar in high-ceilinged Jacobean building, great selection of belgian beers including lots on tap, three dozen genevers, plus three or four changing real ales, knowledgeable landlord, enjoyable food in upstairs restaurant; piped classical music, can get packed weekends; dogs welcome, tables on back terrace, closed lunchtimes, open all day weekends. *(Mike Proctor, the Didler)*

LEEK SJ9856
✳ **Wilkes Head** (01538) 383616
St Edward Street; ST13 5DS Three-room local dating from the 18th c (still has back coaching stables), owned by Whim with their ales and interesting guests, farm cider and good choice of whiskies, filled rolls, gas fire, lots of pump clips, pub games; juke box in back room, Mon music night; children allowed in one room (not really a family pub), dogs welcome but ask first (resident staffy), fair disabled access, tables outside, open all day except Mon lunchtime. *(Mike Proctor, the Didler)*

LICHFIELD SK1109
Acorn (01543) 263400
Tamworth Street; WS13 6JJ Comfortable spacious Wetherspoons, sofas near entrance, cosy drinking nooks opposite bar, dining area at back, usual food and good choice of well kept ales; TVs; children welcome, good disabled access, open all day from 8am (till 1am Fri, Sat). *(George Atkinson, Henry Pursehouse-Tranter)*

LICHFIELD SK0705
✳ **Boat** (01543) 361692
3.8 miles from M6 toll JT6; head E on A5, turn right at first roundabout into B4155, then left on to A461 Walsall Road; leaving pub, keep straight on to rejoin A5 at Muckley Corner roundabout; WS14 0BU Efficiently run dining pub, handy break for a meal off M6 toll; most emphasis on food with huge floor-to-ceiling menu boards, views into kitchen and dishes ranging from lunchtime sandwiches through light snacks to interesting main choices, cheery café atmosphere, bright plastic flooring, striking photoprints, leather club chairs and sofas around coffee tables and potted palms, more conventional and comfortable dining areas with sturdy modern pine furniture on carpet and views

of disused canal, three well kept changing ales, ten wines by the glass, friendly service; background music; children welcome, good wheelchair access, seats on raised decking, open all day Sun (food all day then too). *(David Green, John and Helen Rushton, Gary Law, Keith and Sandra Ross, G Jennings and others)*

LICHFIELD SK1308
Horse & Jockey (01543) 410033
Tamworth Road (A51 Lichfield–Tamworth); WS14 9JE Small old-fashioned pub with half a dozen ales including Fullers, Holdens, Marstons and Timothy Taylors Landlord, pubby food, four linked rooms; Sky sports, darts; open all day. *(David Green)*

LITTLE BRIDGEFORD SJ8727
Mill (01785) 282710
Worston Lane; near M6 junction 14; turn right off A5013 at Little Bridgeford; ST18 9QA Useful sensibly priced dining pub in attractive 1814 watermill, enjoyable food, ales such as Greene King and Marstons, good friendly service, conservatory; children welcome, attractive grounds with adventure playground and nature trail (lakes, islands, etc); open all day. *(Clare Elsby, Stuart Paulley)*

LONGNOR SK0965
Old Cheshire Cheese (01298) 83218
High Street; SK17 0NS Welcoming newish landlady for this 14th-c pub, hearty helpings of good value straightforward food, well kept Robinsons ales, open fire, plenty of bric-a-brac and pictures in traditional main bar and two dining rooms, pool and TV in separate rooms; children, hikers and dogs welcome, tables out in front, four bedrooms in converted stables over road, open all day (may close Mon in winter). *(Michael Butler)*

MILWICH SJ9533
Red Lion (01889) 505310
Dayhills; B5027 towards Stone; ST15 8RU Unpretentious bar at end of working farmhouse, old settles, tiled floor and inglenook fire, Bass, Holdens, Sharps and guests tapped from the cask, Thatcher's cider, good value food, friendly welcoming staff, darts, dominoes and cribbage; lavatories in converted cowshed; open all day weekends, closed lunchtimes Mon-Weds. *(the Didler)*

ONECOTE SK0455
Jervis Arms (01538) 304206
B5053; ST13 7RU Busy country pub, black-beamed main bar with inglenook woodburner, well kept Titanic, Wadworths 6X and three or four changing guests, friendly staff, reasonably priced food, separate dining and family rooms; attractive streamside garden with footbridge to car park, open all day in summer, all day Sun winter. *(the Didler, B M Eldridge, Brian and Anna Marsden)*

PENKRIDGE   SJ9214
Littleton Arms (01785) 716300
St Michaels Square/A449 – M6 detour between junctions 12 and 13; ST19 5AL Busy M&B dining pub/hotel (former coaching inn) with contemporary layout, varied choice of enjoyable good value food including lunchtime deals, several wines by the glass, ales such as Salopian, Wells & Youngs and Wye Valley, friendly young staff; background music; children welcome, ten bedrooms, open all day. *(Stuart Paulley)*

PENKRIDGE   SJ9214
Star (01785) 712513
Market Place; ST19 5DJ Attractive old brick-built pub, well kept and priced Marstons-related ales, good helpings of bargain food served by efficient cheery staff, open-plan interior with lots of low black beams, stripped brick and button-back red plush, open fires; no credit cards; background music, sports TV, darts; a few tables out at front, open all day. *(Jeremy King)*

RANTON   SJ8422
Hand & Cleaver (01785) 822367
Butt Lane, Ranton Green; ST18 9JZ Tastefully extended country pub freshened up under current licensees, enjoyable fairly traditional home-made food, Hook Norton, Marstons Pedigree and a guest, lots of exposed beams and timbers, open fires and woodburners, restaurant; children and dogs welcome, closed Mon. *(John Stallwood)*

ROLLESTON ON DOVE   SK23427
Spread Eagle (01283) 813004
Church Road; DE13 9BE Old gabled Vintage Inn by Alder Brook, enjoyable sensibly priced food all day, great choice of wines by the glass, Bass and Marstons Pedigree, three linked areas and separate dining room, beams and two-way log fire; children welcome, disabled facilities, attractive shrubby garden, open all day. *(Phil Pickstock)*

RUGELEY   SK0220
Wolseley Arms (01889) 883179
Wolseley Bridge, A51/A513 NW; ST17 0XS Modernised Vintage Inn with cosy farmhouse-style interior, wide choice of food all day including lunchtime set deals, changing ales such as Bass, Marstons and Timothy Taylors, friendly helpful staff, log fire; children welcome, disabled access, handy for Shugborough Hall and Cannock Chase. *(Sian Gillham, Henry Pursehouse-Tranter)*

SANDON   SJ9429
Dog & Doublet (01889) 508331
B5066 just off A51; ST18 0DJ Recently refurbished traditional-style pub, enjoyable food, well kept real ales and decent wines, friendly staff; tables outside. *(Susan and Nigel Brookes)*

SHEEN   SK1160
Staffordshire Knot (01298) 84329
Off B5054 at Hulme End; SK17 0ET Welcoming traditional 17th-c stone-built village pub, nice mix of old furniture on flagstones or red and black tiles, stag's head and hunting prints, two log fires in hefty stone fireplaces, good interesting food cooked by landlady including deals, well kept local Whim Hartington, good value wines, friendly helpful staff; closed Mon. *(Nick and Clare Kendall)*

STAFFORD   SJ9223
Chambers (01785) 241752
Victoria Square; ST16 2AQ Light and airy rather grand place opposite the county court, high ceilings, white panelled walls covered in paintings and prints, rugs on wood floors, tiled fireplaces, seven real ales including one brewed for them locally, several wines by the glass, good choice of food all day from sandwiches and sharing plates up, friendly staff; no dogs; children welcome, disabled facilities. *(Richard Tilbrook)*

STAFFORD   SJ9222
Picture House (01785) 222941
Bridge Street/Lichfield Street; ST16 2HL Art deco cinema converted by Wetherspoons keeping ornate ceiling plasterwork and stained-glass name sign, bar on stage with up to six competitively priced ales, farm cider, seating in stalls, circle and upper circle, popular bargain food all day (order and pay in advance at bar), lively atmosphere, film posters, occasional silent movies; good disabled facilities, spacious terrace overlooking river, open all day from 8am. *(Alan and Eve Harding)*

STAFFORD   SJ9321
Radford Bank (01785) 242825
Radford Bank (A34); ST17 4PG Very child-friendly with bargain all-day carvery in large downstairs lounge (easy wheelchair access), well kept Marstons Pedigree and EPA; nice outdoor seating and play area, canal walks nearby, open all day. *(Henry Pursehouse-Tranter)*

Real ale to us means beer which has matured naturally in its cask – not pressurised or filtered. We name all real ales stocked. We usually name ales preserved under a light blanket of carbon dioxide too, though purists – pointing out that this stops the natural yeasts developing – would disagree (most people, including us, can't tell the difference!).

STAFFORD   SJ9126

Shire Horse (01785) 270700

*1 mile from M6 junction 14 via A34 –
junction A34/A513; ST16 1GZ* New Chef
& Brewer built to look old, small secluded
areas and open fires, bric-a-brac, welcoming
staff and good atmosphere, wide choice
of enjoyable food all day, three changing
ales; parking fee refunded against food/
drink; children welcome, disabled facilities,
outside tables by road, bedrooms in next
door Premier Inn. *(Christine and
Neil Townend)*

STONE   SJ8933

Wayfarer (01785) 811023

The Fillybrooks (A34 just N); ST15 0NB
Fresh contemporary refurbishment
(sister pub to the Swan With Two Necks at
Blackbrook), good food from varied menu
including sharing plates and stone-baked
pizzas, beers such as Fullers, Sharps and
Timothy Taylors, lots of wines by the glass;
terrace seating, open all day. *(Susan and
Nigel Brookes)*

STOWE   SK0027

Cock (01889) 270237

Off A518 Stafford–Uttoxeter; ST18 0LF
Popular bistro-style conversion of old village
pub (calls itself Bistro le Coq), competently
cooked french food (not Sun evening)
including set menus, early evening discount
Tues-Fri, some reasonably priced wines,
small bar area serving real ale, friendly
efficient service; well behaved children
welcome, closed Mon lunchtime. *(Susan and
Nigel Brookes)*

TRYSULL   SO8594

Bell (01902) 892871

Bell Road; WV5 7JB Extended 19th-c
village local next to church, cosy bar,
inglenook lounge and large back dining
area, well kept/priced Holdens, Bathams
and a guest like Broughs, popular good value
food from cobs up including meal deals,
friendly service; front terrace, open all
day Fri-Sun. *(John and Helen Rushton, Dave
Braisted, the Didler, Andy Dolan, Tony Hobden)*

WETTON   SK1055

★ **Olde Royal Oak** (01335) 310287

*Village signed off Hulme End–
Alstonefield road, between B5054 and
A515; DE6 2AF* Old stone-built pub in
lovely NT countryside – a popular stop for
walkers; traditional bar with white ceiling
boards above black beams, small dining
chairs around rustic tables, oak corner
cupboard, open fire in stone fireplace, more
modern-feeling area leading to carpeted
sun lounge overlooking small garden, four
changing ales, 30 malt whiskies, reasonably
priced pubby food, darts and shove-ha'penny;
background music, TV; children and dogs
welcome, picnic-sets in shaded garden, self-
catering cottage and paddock for caravans/
tents, closed Mon, Tues. *(Helene Grygar,
Reg Fowle, Helen Rickwood, the Didler, Paul J
Robinshaw, Dennis Jones)*

WHITTINGTON   SK1608

Dog (01543) 432601

*The one near Lichfield; Main Street;
WS14 9JU* Beamed village inn with good
freshly made food from sensibly short menu,
three well kept ales including Black Sheep,
pleasant efficient service; small terrace,
bedrooms. *(John and Helen Rushton, Clive and
Fran Dutson)*

YARLET   SJ9129

Greyhound (01889) 508480

Stone Road; ST18 9SD Popular dining
pub with reasonably priced food including
fresh fish, Wells & Youngs ales and decent
wines, friendly efficient young staff, large
dining conservatory at back. *(Susan and
Nigel Brookes)*

YOXALL   SK1418

Golden Cup (01543) 472295

Main Street (A515); DE13 8NQ Friendly
well run village inn dating from the early
18th c, reasonably priced traditional home-
made food from sandwiches to good value
three-course Sun lunch, well kept Marstons
Pedigree and a guest, lounge bar, games and
sports TV in public bar; cheery window boxes
and hanging baskets, nice garden down to
small river, reasonably priced bedrooms,
open all day weekends. *(Anon)*

Suffolk

W e're delighted with our crop of new entries here, which cover a wide range of pubs: Fleece at Boxford (beautifully done up 15th-c pub, own-brew beers, local cider and enjoyable food), Eels Foot at Eastbridge (simple local, good value food, handy for Minsmere), White Horse in Edwardstone (unpretentious with own-brew ales and honest food), Dog in Grundisburgh (friendly place with ten real ales and especially good food), Fat Cat in Ipswich (a beer lovers' haven and first rate, hands-on landlord), Angel in Lavenham (under Marco Pierre White's umbrella), Anchor at Nayland (carefully updated riverside pub, first class contemporary food and same management as Angel in Stoke-by-Nayland), Harbour Inn in Southwold (interesting, very well run pub down by the boats and same ownership as Bell in Walberswick), Angel in Stoke-by-Nayland (elegant 17th-c inn with enterprising food), and Bell in Walberswick (carefully refurbished 600-year-old inn, lots of charm, enjoyable food and ales). Other places on top form are the Ship in Dunwich (a smashing all-rounder), Red Rose in Lindsey Tye (plenty of contented customers in neatly kept hall house), Bell in Middleton (courteous landlord and very reasonably priced, enjoyable food), White Horse at Sibton (lovely to stay, imaginative meals), Plough & Sail in Snape (run by enthusiastic twin brothers), Crown in Southwold (a beautiful inn – civilised and smart), and Dolphin in Thorpeness (bustling and cheerful). Our Suffolk Dining Pub 2013 is the Crown in Southwold.

ALDEBURGH   TM4656   Map 5

Cross Keys

Crabbe Street; IP15 5BN

16th-c pub near the beach with seats outside, chatty atmosphere, friendly licensee and local beers; bedrooms

I ts position on the seafront makes this cheerful old pub a favourite spot in summer; from seats on the sheltered back terrace there are views across the promenade and shingle to the water. The friendly licensees create a bustling, buoyant atmosphere and the low-ceilinged interconnecting bars have antique and other pubby furniture, the landlord's collection of oils and Victorian watercolours, paintings by local artists and roaring log fires in two inglenook fireplaces. Adnams Bitter, Broadside and Explorer on handpump, Aspall's cider, decent wines by the glass and several malt whiskies; background music, games machine and board games. The bedrooms are attractively furnished.

Tasty, traditional bar food includes sandwiches, pâté with toast, moules marinière, tomato and goats cheese tart, trout stuffed with prawns, steak and kidney pie, mixed grill, and puddings such as sticky toffee pudding and treacle tart. *Benchmark main dish: beer-battered cod and chips £8.95. Two-course evening meal £13.00.*

Adnams ~ Tenants Mike and Janet Clement ~ Real ale ~ Bar food (12-2(3 weekends), 7-9; no food Sun evening) ~ (01728) 452637 ~ Children welcome ~ Dogs welcome ~ Open 11am(midday Sun)-midnight ~ Bedrooms: £55B/£89.50S(£85B) ~ www.aldeburgh-crosskeys.co.uk *Recommended by Terry Mizen, Geoff and Linda Payne, Mike and Sue Loseby, Mr and Mrs A Curry*

BOXFORD
Fleece ★ 🍺

TL9640　Map 5

Broad Street (A1071 Sudbury–Ipswich); CO10 5DX

Attractively restored partly 15th-c pub flourishing under new ownership, splendid beer range

The Star Award is for the Corder Room on the right. The pub's new owners, Mill Green Brewery (at the White Horse, Edwardstone), have done it up beautifully, with dark panelled wainscoting, handsome William Morris wallpaper under a high delft shelf, sweeping heavy red curtains, and a handful of attractive period dining tables with good chairs and a built-in wall settle. With its chatty, companionable atmosphere, this is as nice a room for enjoying a good pub meal as any we have seen this year. The beamed bar on the left has a woodburning stove in the terracotta-tiled front part, a big fireplace under a wall-hanging at the back, a couple of rugs on the boards and a mix of pews, winged settle and other seats around old stripped tables. Centre of attraction is the serving counter, with local farm cider, and well kept changing ales on handpump – on our visit Crouch Vale Golden Nugget, Harwich Town Ganges and their own Mill Green Loveleys Fair, Mawkin Mild, Stella and Red Barn.

Good food includes sandwiches, crispy calamari and chilli tartare sauce, pigeon salad with stilton, walnut and bacon and fig chutney, ham and free-range eggs, asparagus, leek and pea risotto with parmesan, moules frites, beef burger with cheese and crispy bacon, beer-battered haddock with chips, sausages with red wine and onion gravy, lemon sole with prawn and herb butter, and puddings like organic raspberry crème brûlée and sticky toffee pudding with toffee sauce. *Benchmark main dish: slow-roast pork belly with apple chutney and cider jus £11.00. Two-course evening meal £17.00.*

Own brew ~ Licensees Jarred and Clare Harris ~ Real ale ~ Bar food (12-2 (2.30 weekends), 6-9; not Sun evening, not Mon) ~ (01787) 211183 ~ Children welcome ~ Dogs welcome ~ Open 12-3, 5-11; 12-midnight Fri and Sat; 12-11 Sun ~ www.boxfordfleece.com *Recommended by Giles and Annie Francis*

The 🍺 symbol shows pubs which keep their beer unusually well, have a particularly good range or brew their own.

BURY ST EDMUNDS

TL8564 Map 5

Old Cannon 🍺 🛏

Cannon Street, just off A134/A1101 roundabout at N end of town; IP33 1JR

Busy own-brew town pub with local drinks and interesting bar food

With a bustling atmosphere and up to half a dozen real ales (including their own), this Victorian townhouse is popular with both locals and visitors. The bar is dominated by two huge gleaming stainless-steel brewing vessels and has views up to a steel-balustraded open-plan malt floor above the ochre-painted counter with its row of chunky old bar stools. Own-brewed Old Cannon Best, Black Pig and Gunners Daughter and guest beers such as Adnams Bitter, Mauldons Mid Autumn Gold and Nethergate Suffolk County Best Bitter on handpump, Aspall's cider and apple juice, a local lager, continental beers and 20 wines by the glass; a happy mix of old and new chairs and tables and upholstered banquettes on well worn bare boards; background music. Behind, through the old side coach arch, is a good-sized cobbled courtyard with hanging baskets and stylish metal tables and chairs. The bedrooms are in the old brewhouse across the courtyard.

Using only local produce, the interesting food might include lunchtime filled baguettes, home-cured gravadlax, pasta stuffed with spinach and ricotta with a red pepper and tomato sauce, fish- and egg-topped pie with cheddar mash, pork loin steak with a mushroom, apple and brandy sauce and garlic and spinach mash, lambs liver and bacon with bubble and squeak and madeira jus, daily specials, and puddings such as apricot and blueberry sponge and cappuccino mousse with a shortbread biscuit; they hold a thai feast on the first Tuesday of the month. *Benchmark main dish: rare breed sausages with colcannon, onion gravy and beer-batter pudding £11.95. Two-course evening meal £17.70.*

Own brew ~ Licensee Mark Jones ~ Real ale ~ Bar food (12-2(3 Sat, 4 Sun), 6-9; not Sun evening) ~ Restaurant ~ (01284) 768769 ~ Children in restaurant and only if eating ~ Live music last Sun evening of month ~ Open 12-11(10.30 Sun) ~ Bedrooms: £80S/£105S ~ www.oldcannonbrewery.co.uk *Recommended by John Saville, John and Sharon Hancock, Bruce M Drew*

CHELMONDISTON

TM2037 Map 5

Butt & Oyster

Pin Mill – signposted from B1456 SE of Ipswich; IP9 1JW

Chatty old riverside pub with pleasant views, good food and drink and seats on the terrace

Now that some of the old boat hulks have been removed, the views from this simple old bargemen's pub over the bustling River Orwell are even better; to make the most of the water activity try to bag a window seat or one of chairs and tables on the terrace. The half-panelled little smoke room is pleasantly worn and unfussy and has high-backed and other old-fashioned settles on its tiled floor. There's also a two-level dining room with country-kitchen furniture on bare boards, and boating pictures and artefacts on the walls above the dado. Adnams Best, Broadside, Old and a changing guest beer on handpump or tapped from the cask, several wines by the glass and local cider; board games. The annual Thames Barge Race (end June/beginning July) is fun. The car park can fill up pretty quickly.

🍴 As well as lunchtime sandwiches, the good food might include scallops with bacon and a pea and mint purée, baked goats cheese with plum chutney, ham and free-range eggs, wild mushroom risotto, beef burger in a rosemary and rock salt focaccia with home-made relish, skate wing with lemon and caper dressing, chicken with a mushroom and bacon sauce and dauphinoise potatoes, lamb shank with a port and redcurrant gravy, and slow-roast pork belly with a cider sauce. *Benchmark main dish: beer-battered local cod and chips £10.95. Two-course evening meal £18.80.*

Adnams ~ Lease Steve Lomas ~ Real ale ~ Bar food (12-9.30) ~ Restaurant ~ (01473) 780764 ~ Children welcome in dining rooms ~ Dogs allowed in bar ~ Open 11-11 ~ www.debeninns.co.uk/buttandoyster *Recommended by Alistair Mackie, J F M and M West, Jeremy King, the Didler, Mike and Mary Carter*

DUNWICH
Ship 🍺 🛏
St James Street; IP17 3DT

TM4770   Map 5

Friendly, well run and pleasantly traditional pub in a coastal village, tasty bar food and local ales and cider; bedrooms

This is a smashing pub with a warm welcome for both regulars and visitors – and dogs are given a treat and a bowl of water. Our readers always enjoy staying here (and the breakfasts are plentiful) and the atmosphere is informal and relaxed. The traditionally furnished main bar has benches, pews, captain's chairs and wooden tables on its tiled floor, a woodburning stove (left open in cold weather) and lots of sea prints. From the handsomely panelled bar counter they serve Adnams Bitter and Broadside and a couple of guests like Earl Soham Gannet Mild and Humpty Dumpty Norfolk Nectar from antique handpumps, Aspall's cider, a local lager and several wines by the glass; board games. A simple conservatory looks on to a back terrace, and the large garden is very pleasant, with its well spaced picnic-sets, two large anchors and enormous fig tree, and they may have Shakespeare performances here in August. The RSPB reserve at Minsmere and nearby Dunwich Museum are worth visiting and some of Suffolk's best coastal paths are nearby – as well as more walking in Dunwich Forest.

🍴 As well as their famous fish and chips, the very good, generously served food includes chicken liver pâté with fig pickle, smoked haddock and soft quails egg fishcakes with pickled cucumber, home-baked ham with free-range eggs, red onion tart with a warm salad of roast root vegetables, pumpkin seeds and pearl barley, a pie of the day, slow-cooked belly of local pork with black pudding and spiced gravy, calves liver with bacon, bubble and squeak and crispy onion rings, and puddings such as pear and blackberry crumble and steamed treacle pudding. *Benchmark main dish: cod and chips with mushy peas and tartare sauce £11.95. Two-course evening meal £18.75.*

Free house ~ Licensee Matt Goodwin ~ Real ale ~ Bar food (12-3, 6-9) ~ Restaurant (evening only) ~ (01728) 648219 ~ Children welcome away from bar ~ Dogs allowed in bar and bedrooms ~ Open 11-11; 12-10.30 Sun ~ Bedrooms: £75B/£95B ~ www.shipatdunwich.co.uk *Recommended by MJVK, Edward Mirzoeff, DHV, David Edge, Phil and Jane Hodson, Anthony Longden, Norma and Noel Thomas, Geoff and Linda Payne, Sara Fulton, Roger Baker, Andrew and Ruth Triggs, Nigel Long, Ann and Colin Hunt, Derek and Sylvia Stephenson, George Atkinson*

Every entry includes a postcode for use in SatNav devices.

EARL SOHAM

TM2263 Map 5

Victoria  £

A1120 Yoxford–Stowmarket; IP13 7RL

Nice beers from brewery across the road in this friendly, informal local

Unspoilt and easy-going, this simple pub is best known for the ales from the Earl Soham brewery just across the road and for its home-cooking. Fairly basic and definitely well worn, the bar is sparsely furnished with kitchen chairs and pews, plank-topped trestle sewing-machine tables and other simple scrubbed pine country tables, and has stripped panelling, tiled or board floors, an interesting range of pictures of Queen Victoria and her reign, and open fires; board games. Earl Soham Brandeston Gold, Sir Rogers Porter and Victoria Bitter on handpump. There are seats on a raised back lawn, with more out in front. The pub is quite close to a wild fritillary meadow at Framlingham and a working windmill at Saxtead.

Bar food includes sandwiches, salads, casseroles and curries. *Benchmark main dish: corned beef hash £6.50. Two-course evening meal £15.00.*

Earl Soham ~ Licensee Paul Hooper ~ Real ale ~ Bar food (12-2, 7-10) ~ (01728) 685758 ~ Children welcome ~ Dogs welcome ~ Open 11.30-3, 6-11; 12-3, 7-10.30 Sun
Recommended by John Saville, Ian and Nita Cooper, Ann and Colin Hunt

EASTBRIDGE

TM4566 Map 5

Eels Foot 🛏

Off B1122 N of Leiston; IP16 4SN

Country inn with hospitable atmosphere, fair value food, and Thursday evening folk sessions; bedrooms

This is a popular spot with bird-watchers, cyclists and walkers, and the adjacent freshwater marshes offer plenty of opportunity for watching the abundance of birds and butterflies; a footpath leads you directly to the sea. It's a friendly, simple pub on two levels with light modern furnishings on stripped wood floors and a warming fire. Adnams Bitter, Broadside and Ghost Ship and a changing guest on handpump, around a dozen wines by the glass and several malt whiskies; darts in a side area, board games, cribbage and a neat back dining room. There are seats on the terrace and benches out in the lovely big back garden. The bedrooms (one with wheelchair access) in the newish building are comfortable and attractive; they serve their own eggs at breakfast.

Reasonably priced food includes filled baguettes, whitebait, beer-battered cod, local sausages with onion gravy, steak in ale pie, smoked haddock and spring onion fishcakes, three-cheese cannelloni, and puddings such as lemon roulade and chocolate 'lumpy bumpy' pudding. *Benchmark main dish: fish and chips £10.95. Two-course evening meal £15.00.*

Adnams ~ Tenants Julian and Alex Wallis ~ Real ale ~ Bar food (12-2.30, 7-9 (6.30-8.30 Thurs)) ~ Restaurant ~ (01728) 830154 ~ Children welcome ~ Dogs allowed in bar ~ Live folk music Thurs evening and last Sun of month ~ Open 12-3, 6-11(12-11 Fri); 11.30-11(10.30 Sun) Sat ~ Bedrooms: £80B/£99B ~ www.theeelsfootinn.co.uk
Recommended by Roy Hoing, Tim Maddison, Norma and Noel Thomas, Colin McKerrow, Charles and Pauline Stride, Mr and Mrs A Curry, Alan Weedon

EDWARDSTONE

White Horse

Mill Green, just E; village signed off A1071 in Boxford; CO10 5PX

TL9542 Map 5

Own-brew pub, traditional furnishings in simple rooms, hearty food, self-catering and a campsite

This is a thriving and unpretentious village local that always keeps five of their own ales on handpump or tapped from the cask from the on-site Mill Green brewery. These change regularly but might include White Horse Bitter, Citrus Snap, Green Goose, Mawkin Mild and Tess of the Compasses, with a guest such as Adnams Bitter; also, local farm cider and organic fruit juices. There are several bar rooms of various sizes, including a tiny one with just one table and lots of beer mats on the walls. The floors are bare boards throughout, cream walls above a pink dado are hung with rustic prints and photographs. There's a mix of second-hand tables and chairs including an old steamer bench and a panelled settle, a piano, and a woodburning stove as well as a fireplace. Background music, darts, bar billiards, ring the bull, quoits, dominoes, cards and board games. On an end terrace are some sturdy teak tables and seats, an attractive smokers' shelter with green panelled seating and some makeshift picnic-sets on a grassy area. The self-catering 'cottages' are rather scandinavian in style, and there's a campsite with a shower block.

 Tasty food includes filled huffers (local bread rolls), ham hock terrine with piccalilli, tempura chicken strips with chilli dipping sauce, ham and free-range eggs, veggie burger with chips, a trio of sausages with mash and onion gravy, specials like tuna niçoise, slow-roast pork belly with three-bean cassoulet and bass with fennel and orange salad, and puddings such as apple crumble and ginger lemon sponge with ginger compote and chocolate ice-cream. *Benchmark main dish: beef burger with chips £9.95. Two-course evening meal £15.00.*

Own brew ~ Licensee Chantal Weeks ~ Real ale ~ Bar food (12-2.30(3.30 Sun), 6-9; not Sun evening and Mon except bank hols) ~ Restaurant ~ (01787) 211211 ~ Children welcome in bar until 6pm ~ Dogs welcome ~ Open mike night, jazz or blues Weds, live band last Sat of month ~ Open 12-12 (12-11 Sun and Mon); 12-3, 5-11 Mon-Thurs in in winter ~ Bedrooms: /£90B ~ www.edwardstonewhitehorse.co.uk *Recommended by Tim Woodward*

GRUNDISBURGH

Dog 🍴 🍷 🍺

The Green; off A12 via B1079 from Woodbridge bypass; IP13 6TA

TM2250 Map 5

Civilised, friendly pub with enjoyable food, excellent choice of drinks and a log fire; garden with play area

Close to the village green, this pink-washed pub is a cosy place with friendly, cheerful staff. Nicely villagey, the public bar on the left has an open log fire, a tiled floor and oak settles and dark wooden carvers around a mix of tables. The softly lit and relaxing lounge bar is carpeted and has comfortable seating around dark oak tables; it links to a similar bare-boards dining room, with some attractive antique oak settles; darts. The impressive array of ten real ales includes Adnams, Earl Soham and guests from brewers like Cliff Quay, Nethergate and Woodfordes on handpump, half a dozen wines by the glass, ciders, local lager and good espresso coffee. There are several picnic-sets out in front by flowering tubs; the wicker-fenced back garden has a mediterranean feel with herbs for the kitchen, an olive tree and a grapevine and comfortable seats under white parasols; there's also a play area.

🍴 Using game from local estates and meat from local farms – and curing a lot of their own produce – top class food might include sandwiches and filled baguettes, chicken and ham terrine with prune and date chutney, oriental crispy duck salad with ginger, chilli and spring onion, beer-battered haddock with hand-cut chips, home-made beef burger with caramelised onion relish and their own ketchup, bass fillets with pesto mash and roasted red peppers, beef and sweet potato tagine with black beans and couscous, harissa-coated chicken breast with roasted butternut squash risotto, and puddings such as raspberry crème brûlée and chocolate and rum mousse. *Benchmark main dish: seasonal game dishes £12.00. Two-course evening meal £18.00.*

Free house ~ Licensees Charles and Eilir Rogers ~ Real ale ~ Bar food (12-2, 5.30-9) ~ Restaurant ~ (01473) 735267 ~ Children welcome away from bar ~ Dogs allowed in bar ~ Open 12-3, 5.30-11; 12-11 Fri and Sat; 12-10.30 Sun; closed Mon ~ www.grundisburghdog.co.uk *Recommended by J F M and M West, Roger White, Charles and Pauline Stride*

IPSWICH
Fat Cat 🍺
TM1844 Map 5

Spring Road, opposite junction with Nelson Road (best bet for parking); IP4 5NL

Fantastic range of changing real ales in a well run town pub; garden

With up to 20 real ales on handpump or tapped from the cask, this extremely friendly town pub is a favourite with many. Coming from all over the country, there might be Adnams Bitter, Crouch Vale Brewers Gold, Dark Star Espresso Stout and Hophead, Earl Soham Victoria, Elgoods Black Dog Mild, Fat Cat Hell Cat and Honey Cat, Fullers London Pride, Green Jack Trawlerboys, Hop Back Crop Circle and Summer Lightning, Mauldons Black Adder, Oakham JHB, Skinners Cornish Knocker, and Woodfordes Norfolk Nog and Wherry. They also stock quite a few belgian bottled beers, Aspall's cider, and local lager. The bare-boarded bars have a mix of café and bar stools, unpadded wall benches and cushioned seats around cast-iron and wooden pub tables, and lots of enamel brewery signs and posters on canary-yellow walls. Often to be seen perched on a pub stool are the pub cat Dave or the sausage dog, Stanley. There's also a spacious back conservatory, and several picnic-sets on the terrace and lawn. Very little nearby parking.

🍴 They don't have a kitchen but keep a supply of scotch eggs, pasties, pies and sometimes filled baguettes in the fridge and are quite happy for you to bring in takeaways (not Friday or Saturday). *Benchmark main dish: scotch egg £2.90.*

Free house ~ Licensees John and Ann Keatley ~ Real ale ~ Bar food (12-2, 7-9) ~ (01473) 726524 ~ Open 12-11(midnight Fri and Sat) ~ www.fatcatipswich.co.uk *Recommended by the Didler, Richard Gibbs*

LAVENHAM
Angel 🍷 🛏
TL9149 Map 5

Market Place; CO10 9QZ

Handsome old inn with emphasis on dining, good range of drinks, character rooms and sizeable back garden; comfortable bedrooms

Although this Tudor inn places firm emphasis on dining, there is a proper bar and they keep Adnams Bitter, Greene King Abbot and a beer named for Marco Pierre White brewed for them by Lees on handpump; also, quite a few wines by the glass and several malt whiskies. The light and airy long bar area has a big inglenook log fire under a heavy mantelbeam and some attractive 16th-c ceiling plasterwork (even more elaborate pargeting in the residents' sitting room upstairs). Other dining areas have elegant dark wood dining chairs around white-clothed tables, more heavy beams and panelling and cartoons and David Bailey celebrity photographs on the walls. There are seats and tables in a large, sheltered back garden and picnic-sets out in front make the most of the setting in the former market square of this delightful small town, a good base for the area.

🍴 Good – if not cheap – food might include sandwiches, potted duck with green peppercorns and sourdough toast, Morecambe Bay potted shrimps, shepherd's pie, calves liver and bacon, fish and triple-cooked chips with marrowfat peas, grilled cumberland sausages with onion gravy and creamed potatoes, steak in ale pie with swede purée, salmon fishcake with tartare sauce, and puddings like sherry triffle and bitter chocolate mousse; they also offer good value two- and three-course set lunch and evening menus. *Benchmark main dish: fish pie £16.50. Two-course evening meal £26.00.*

Free house ~ Licensee Rob Jackson ~ Real ale ~ Bar food (12-2.30(3.30 Sun), 6-9.30) ~ (01787) 247388 ~ Children welcome ~ Dogs allowed in bar ~ Open 11-11.30 ~ Bedrooms: £70S/£115S ~ www.wheelersangel.com *Recommended by Mike and Shelley Woodroffe*

LEVINGTON
TM2339 Map 5

Ship

Gun Hill; from A14/A12 Bucklesham roundabout take A1156 exit, then first sharp left into Felixstowe Road, then after nearly a mile turn right into Bridge Road at Levington signpost, bearing left into Church Lane; IP10 0LQ

Plenty of nautical trappings and character, in a lovely rural position

It's worth arriving early at this attractively situated pub as ramblers and bird-watchers like coming here at lunchtime. The décor tends towards the nautical, with lots of ship prints and photographs of sailing barges, a marine compass under the serving counter in the middle room and a fishing net slung overhead. As well as benches built into the walls, there are comfortably upholstered small settles (some of them grouped around tables as booths) and a big black round stove. The flagstoned dining room has further nautical bric-a-brac and beams taken from an old barn. Adnams Bitter, Broadside and Sole Star on handpump or tapped from the cask and several wines by the glass. The pub is by a little lime-washed church and has views (if a little obscured) over the River Orwell estuary.

🍴 It's worth noting that they don't take bookings for fewer than six people for food, which includes warm baked goats cheese mousseline with garlic-roasted beetroot, avocado caesar salad with crispy bacon, a free-range boiled egg and shaved parmesan, smoked haddock and salmon fishcake with tartare sauce, escalope of chicken with basil dressing and sautéed potatoes, liver and bacon with madeira jus and lyonnaise potatoes, and puddings such as rich dark chocolate tart with white chocolate ice-cream and eton mess with local strawberries and berry coulis. *Benchmark main dish: liver and bacon £9.95. Two-course evening meal £18.00.*

Adnams ~ Lease Adrian and Susan Searing ~ Real ale ~ Bar food (12-2.30(3 Sun), 6.30-9) ~ (01473) 659573 ~ Children welcome ~ Dogs allowed in bar ~ Open 11.30-3, 6-11; 11.30-11 Sat; 12-10.30 Sun ~ www.theshipinnlevington.co.uk *Recommended by Ian and Nita Cooper, J F M and M West, Mrs Margo Finlay, Jörg Kasprowski*

LINDSEY TYE
Red Rose

TL9846 Map 5

Village signposted off A1141 NW of Hadleigh; IP7 6PP

Handsome 15th-c hall house with a couple of neat bars, enjoyable food, real ales and plenty of outside seating

Our readers enjoy their visits to this neatly kept and well run pub, and there's always a warm and inviting atmosphere and plenty of contented, chatty customers. The main bar has low beams and some standing timbers, a mix of wooden tables and chairs, red-painted walls and dried teasels in glass jugs on the window sills. In front of a splendid log fire in its old brick fireplace are a couple of squashy red leather sofas, a low table and some brass measuring jugs. A second room is furnished in the same way, again with a big brick fireplace, but is much simpler in feel, and perhaps quieter; background music. Adnams Bitter, Mauldons Moletrap Bitter and maybe a guest beer on handpump, and ten wines by the glass. There are flowering tubs and a few picnic-sets in front, with more picnic-sets at the back – where there's also a children's play area, a football pitch and an animal pen with chickens and sheep.

Popular food includes lunchtime sandwiches and filled baguettes, chicken liver parfait with red onion marmalade, bacon, anchovy and shallot salad, tagliatelle with gorgonzola, spinach and roasted pine nuts, chicken kebabs with a sweet red pepper sauce and an aubergine and rice tower, braised pork ribs with red cabbage coleslaw and skinny fries, beer-battered haddock with home-made tartare sauce, and puddings like white chocolate panna cotta with chilli chocolate sauce and sticky toffee pudding with clotted cream. *Benchmark main dish: rare-breed beef burger £14.00. Two-course evening meal £18.50.*

Free house ~ Licensee Peter Miller ~ Real ale ~ Bar food (12-2.30(3 Sun), 6.30-9.30(7-9 Sun)) ~ (01449) 741424 ~ Children welcome ~ Dogs welcome ~ Open 11-3, 5.30-11; 11-11 Sun ~ www.thelindseyrose.co.uk *Recommended by Mrs Margo Finlay, Jörg Kasprowski, John Prescott, MDN, Jeremy King*

MIDDLETON
Bell  £

TM4267 Map 5

Off A12 in Yoxford via B1122 towards Leiston, also signposted off B1125 Leiston–Westleton; The Street; IP17 3NN

Thatch and low beams, friendly chef/landlord, good beer, good value food – a peaceful spot

Our readers love their visits to this well run pub, which always has a cheerful bustle, and the courteous licensees make all their customers, regulars or visitors, feel warmly welcomed. The traditional bar on the left has a log fire in a big hearth, old local photographs, a low plank-panelling ceiling, bar stools and pew seating, Adnams Bitter, Broadside and a seasonal ales tapped from the cask, and darts. On the right an informal two-room carpeted lounge/dining area has padded mate's and library chairs around the dark tables below its low black beams, with pews by a big woodburning stove, and cheery modern seaside brewery prints. Dogs are welcomed with treats and a bowl of water. It's a pretty cream-washed building, with picnic-sets under cocktail parasols out in front, and camping available in the broad meadow behind. Walks on the coast and the RSPB Minsmere bird reserve are nearby.

Good, popular food includes lunchtime sandwiches, chicken and duck liver paté with home-made relish, sausage and mash, bubble and squeak on buttered spinach with stilton cream and a poached egg, lambs liver and bacon with onion gravy, beer-battered fish and chips, and daily specials such as duck on a bed of spinach and kale with roasted pear and redcurrant and ginger sauce, pork fillet with chilli and paprika and a roast lime, beetroot and red onion purée and a changing vegetarian dish. *Benchmark main dish: stuffed pork belly £10.75. Two-course evening meal £17.00.*

Adnams ~ Tenants Nicholas and Trish Musgrove ~ Real ale ~ Bar food (12-2.15, 6-9.15; 12-5 Sun; not Mon evening or winter Mon lunchtime, except bank hols) ~ Restaurant ~ (01728) 648286 ~ Children welcome away from bar ~ Dogs allowed in bar ~ Open 12-3, 6-11; 12-12(11 Sun) Sat; closed winter Mon lunchtime *Recommended by Giles and Annie Francis, Charles and Pauline Stride, B R and M F Arnold, Stephen and Jean Curtis, Paul Humphreys*

NAYLAND
THE GOOD PUB GUIDE
Anchor

TL9734   Map 5

Court Street; just off A134 – turn off S of signposted B1087 main village turn; CO6 4JL

Friendly riverside pub with seats by the water, newly refurbished bar and dining rooms, up to five ales and good food

This is a lovely spot in summer, when you can sit at picnic-sets beside the peaceful River Stour and watch the ducks. Inside, the new landlord has given the pub a careful refurbishment adding contemporary touches to the classic styling. The bare-boards bar has a mix of wooden dining chairs and tables, a big gilt mirror on silvery wallpaper at one end of the room with another mirror above the pretty brick fireplace at the other, fresh flowers on the bar, Adnams Bitter, Greene King IPA, Nethergate Growler and a beer named for them brewed by Hadleigh on handpump and several wines by the glass. Another room behind has individually chosen furniture and an open fire, and leads into the River Room with its elegant tables and chairs. Up some quite steep stairs is a cosy, candlelit restaurant and a small, stylish room for private parties.

Interesting food includes sandwiches, crispy duck egg with asparagus fingers and truffle dressing, crab tian with cucumber, semi-dried tomatoes and avocado, saffron ravioli with lemon and goats cheese and a panache of vegetables, beer-battered fish with mushy peas and tartare sauce, smoked venison burger with emmenthal cheese, triple-cooked chips and burger sauce, bass fillet with samphire, crushed jersey royals and cockle sauce, and puddings like hot chocolate fondant with pistachio ice-cream and apple parfait with marshmallow and honey cress. *Benchmark main dish: fish and chips with fat chips and mushy peas £12.95. Two-course evening meal £18.00.*

Free house ~ Licensee James Haggar ~ Real ale ~ Bar food (12-2.30(3 Sat, 4 Sun), 6-9.30) ~ Restaurant ~ (01206) 262313 ~ Children welcome ~ Dogs allowed in bar ~ Open 10am-11pm ~ www.anchornayland.co.uk *Recommended by Simon and Mandy King*

'Children welcome' means the pub says it lets children inside without any special restriction. If it allows them in, but to restricted areas such as an eating area or family room, we specify this. Places with separate restaurants often let children use them, hotels usually let them into public areas such as lounges. Some pubs impose an evening time limit – let us know if you find one earlier than 9pm.

ORFORD
Kings Head 🛏

TM4249   Map 5

Front Street; IP12 2LW

Enjoyably pubby local with tasty food and Adnams beers

Surrounded by fine walks and a lovely coastline, parts of this likeable old place are 700 years old. It has the character of a traditional harbourside pub with plenty of authentic atmosphere, and the snug main bar has heavy low beams, straightforward furniture on red carpets, Adnams Bitter, Broadside, Ghost Ship and Sole Star on handpump and several wines by the glass. The candlelit dining room has nice old stripped brick walls and rugs on the ancient bare boards; board games, magazines and cards. The pub dogs are called Sam and Teddy.

🍴 Well liked bar food includes sandwiches, ham terrine with courgette pickle, a pint of prawns with mayonnaise, lasagne, cottage pie, pork sausages and mash, fish pie, and puddings like jam roly-poly with cherry ice-cream and chocolate pecan tart with vanilla ice-cream. *Benchmark main dish: beer-battered cod and chips £10.50. Two-course evening meal £16.50.*

Adnams ~ Lease Adrian and Susan Searing ~ Real ale ~ Bar food (12-2.30(3 Sun), 6.30-9) ~ Restaurant ~ (01394) 450271 ~ Children welcome ~ Dogs welcome ~ Open 11.30-3, 6-11; 11.30-11 Sat; 12-10.30 Sun; closed winter Sun evening ~ Bedrooms: /£95S ~ www.thekingsheadorford.co.uk *Recommended by Norma and Noel Thomas, Edward Mirzoeff, Barry Collett, M P Mackenzie, Mr and Mrs A Curry, Lois Dyer, Derek and Sylvia Stephenson*

SIBTON
White Horse 🍴 🍷 🛏

TM3570   Map 5

Halesworth Road; IP17 2JJ

Particularly well run inn, pleasant old-fashioned bar, good mix of customers, real ales and imaginative food; comfortable bedrooms

Our readers really enjoy staying in the comfortable bedrooms here and the breakfasts are excellent. Mr and Mrs Mason are hard-working, hands-on licensees who welcome their guests with genuine friendliness, and they've struck a good balance between village pub and first class restaurant. The comfortable bar has horsebrasses and tack on the walls, old settles and pews, and a large inglenook fireplace with a roaring log fire. Adnams Bitter, Woodfordes Once Bittern and a changing guest beer on handpump (they hold a June beer festival with around 16 ales), several wines by the glass and a dozen malt whiskies are served from the old oak-panelled counter, and there's a viewing panel showing the working cellar and its Roman floor. Steps take you up past an ancient partly knocked-through timbered wall into a carpeted gallery and there's a smart dining room, too. The big garden has plenty of seats.

🍴 The first class food uses produce from their own kitchen garden, free-range meat and poultry from local farms, and seasonal game from the village shoot: lunchtime sandwiches (the soup and sandwich deal is popular), eggs benedict, wild duck and pheasant terrine with a honey and hoi sin glaze, home-cooked ham with free-range eggs and bubble and squeak, twice-baked goats cheese soufflé with artichoke tart and purée and a grape salsa, chicken with haggis, roasted root vegetables and mustard cream, lamb twice (roast rump, rolled and stuffed breast) with pickled beetroot and herb oil, scottish salmon fillet with orange, fennel and a tomato and red onion salsa, and puddings such as hot chocolate fondant with cherry ripple ice-cream and caramelised apple tarte tatin with cinnamon ice-cream. *Benchmark main dish: gressingham duck breast with fondant potatoes, braised red cabbage, parsnip purée and cherry jus £16.50. Two-course evening meal £19.50.*

Free house ~ Licensees Neil and Gill Mason ~ Real ale ~ Bar food (12-2, 7-9) ~ Restaurant ~ (01728) 660337 ~ Well behaved children welcome but must be over 13 for accommodation ~ Dogs allowed in bar ~ Quiz every Mon (not bank holidays) ~ Open 12-2.30, 6.30-11; 12-3.30, 7-10.30 Sun ~ Bedrooms: £70S/£90B ~ www.sibtonwhitehorseinn.co.uk
Recommended by Ian and Nita Cooper, Charles and Pauline Stride, David Rule, Peter Hulland, David Field, Jane and Alan Bush, Lois Dyer, Ann and Colin Hunt

SNAPE
TM4058   Map 5
Golden Key
Priory Lane; IP17 1SA

Traditionally furnished village pub with Adnams beers and changing bar food; walks nearby

This 16th-c pub is a good base for exploring the area, and there are plenty of surrounding walks. The traditional low-beamed lounge bar has an old-fashioned settle curving around a couple of venerable stripped tables on the chequerboard tiled floor, a winter open fire and a mix of pubby tables and chairs; there's also a small snug. The two dining rooms have open fireplaces and are furnished with settles and scrubbed pine tables. Adnams Bitter, Broadside and Ghost Ship on handpump, around a dozen wines by the glass and local cider. Outside are two terraces (one good for early in the day and an evening suntrap) – both with pretty hanging baskets and seats under large parasols.

 Bar food includes sandwiches, potted crab, crispy whitebait with home-made tartare sauce, home-baked ham and egg, sausages and mash, pea and mint risotto, a pie of the day, crispy confit duck leg with curried lentils and stir-fried spinach, a fish dish of the day, and puddings such as summer pudding and warm chocolate brownie. *Benchmark main dish: line-caught cod and chips £12.50. Two-course evening meal £17.50.*

Adnams ~ Tenant Inga Haselmann ~ Real ale ~ Bar food (12-2.45, 6-9) ~ Restaurant ~ (01728) 688510 ~ Children welcome ~ Dogs welcome ~ Open 12-3, 6-11; 12-11 Sun ~ Bedrooms: /£95S *Recommended by Charles and Pauline Stride, Kay and Alistair Butler, John and Eleanor Holdsworth, Evelyn and Derek Walter, Norma and Noel Thomas, Edward Mirzoeff, Hazel Morgan, Bernard Patrick, Simon Rodway*

SNAPE
TM3957   Map 5
Plough & Sail
The Maltings, Snape Bridge (B1069 S); IP17 1SR

Nicely placed dining pub extended around an older bar, real ales, well liked food and seats outside

Twin brothers have taken over this 16th-c former smugglers' haunt and are running it with enthusiasm and friendliness; Alex is front of house and Oliver is head chef. As it's part of Snape Maltings they offer both pre- and post-concert menus. The pub is mostly open-plan and is a clever blend of traditional and modern, with wicker and café-style furnishings around an older heart with a woodburning stove, high bar chairs by the serving counter and rustic pine dining chairs and tables on terracotta tiling; another cosy little room has comfortable sofas and low coffee tables. Most diners head for the simply furnished bar hall and spacious, airy dining room with blue-cushioned chairs around straightforward tables on light, woodstrip flooring, and high ceilings with A-frame beams; motifs illustrating the history of the Maltings decorate the walls. Another restaurant upstairs has similar furnishings; background music. Adnams Bitter, Woodfordes Wherry and a couple of guest beers on handpump and several wines by the glass. The flower-filled terrace has plenty of teak chairs and tables and there are some picnic-sets at the front. The shops and other buildings in the attractive complex are interesting to wander through.

Using local, seasonal produce the popular food might include sandwiches, duck liver parfait with onion jam, home-made potted shrimps, beer-battered fish and chips, wild mushroom, spinach and butternut squash risotto, local sausages with caramelised gravy, corn-fed chicken caesar with crispy pancetta, skate wing with black butter and capers, local duck breast on creamy cabbage and bacon ragoût, rump of lamb with dauphinoise potatoes and red wine jus, and puddings. *Benchmark main dish: crispy pork belly with sweet potato purée and braised red cabbage £13.00. Two-course evening meal £19.00.*

Suffolk Dining Ltd ~ Lease Alex Burnside ~ Real ale ~ Bar food (12-3, 5.30-9) ~ Restaurant ~ (01728) 688413 ~ Children welcome ~ Dogs allowed in bar ~ Open 11-11; 12-10.30 Sun ~ www.theploughandsailsnape.co.uk *Recommended by George Atkinson*

SOUTHWOLD   TM5076 Map 5

Crown 🍴 ♀ 🍺 🛏

High Street; IP18 6DP

Suffolk Dining Pub of the Year

Comfortable hotel with relaxed bars, a fine selection of drinks, newspapers, imaginative food and seats outside; refurbished bedrooms

As this smart and civilised hotel is a favourite with so many of its customers, you really do have to arrive promptly to be sure of a table, as they run a first-come, first-served system. And whether you're popping in for a pint and a chat or a light lunch or staying in the lovely bedrooms you'll be genuinely welcomed by the courteous and extremely efficient staff. Many of our readers are very fond of the cosy, oak-panelled back locals' bar (reserved for drinkers), which has a proper pubby atmosphere, red leatherette wall benches on red carpeting, Adnams Bitter, Broadside and a seasonal guest on handpump, 20 wines by the glass from a splendid list and several hand-crafted spirits. The elegant beamed front bar has a relaxed, informal atmosphere, a stripped curved high-backed settle and other dark varnished settles, kitchen and other chairs, and a carefully restored rather fine carved wooden fireplace; maybe newspapers to read. The tables out in a sunny sheltered corner are very pleasant.

Excellent, inventive – if not cheap – food might include sandwiches, rhubarb and confit duck roulade with sautéed duck livers, scratching, purée and poached rhubarb, local mussels with either cider or beer and frites, beetroot and balsamic tatin with buttered kale, pheasant breast with parsnip purée and fondant and sloe gin jus, bass fillet with cauliflower risotto and a light saffron velouté, roast pork rib with Adnams mustard mash, caramelised apple and roasting jus, and chargrilled 28-day hung sirloin steak with béarnaise or peppercorn sauce. *Benchmark main dish: halibut with crème fraîche mash, broccoli, orange and parma ham with a vermouth butter £21.95. Two-course evening meal £23.00.*

Adnams ~ Manager Francis Guildea ~ Real ale ~ Bar food (12-2, 7-9) ~ (01502) 722275 ~ Children welcome ~ Dogs allowed in bar ~ Open 11-11; 9am-11pm Sun ~ Bedrooms:

£135B/£175B ~ www.adnams.co.uk/stay-with-us/the-crown *Recommended by MJVK, M and GR, Martin Smith, Alan and Jill Bull, Ann and Colin Hunt, Mrs Margo Finlay, Jörg Kasprowski, David Rule, Peter and Giff Bennett, David Carr, J F M and M West, Mike and Sue Loseby, Martin and Pauline Jennings, Andrew and Ruth Triggs, N R White, Stephen Funnell, Sheila Topham, Roger and Lesley Everett, Pat and Tony Martin, Derek Thomas, George Atkinson*

SOUTHWOLD

TM4975 Map 5

Harbour Inn ♀ ◖

Blackshore, by the boats; from A1095, turn right at the Kings Head, and keep on past the golf course and water tower; IP18 6TA

Great spot down by the boats, lots of outside tables – and interesting inside, too

The back bar is nicely nautical, with its dark panelling, built-in wall seats around scrubbed tables, low ceiling draped with ensigns, signal flags, pennants and a line strung with ancient dried fish, quaint old stove, rope fancywork, a plethora of local fishing photographs, even portholes with water bubbling behind them. It's still well used by locals as well as the many visitors, and cheerful staff serve a good choice of wines by the glass along with Adnams Bitter, Southwold, Broadside and Ghost Ship on handpump. They have their own weather station for walkers and sailors. The tiled-floor lower front bar, also panelled, is broadly similar, and the large, elevated dining room has panoramic views of the harbour, lighthouse, brewery and churches beyond the marshes. Teak tables out behind look out over the marshy commons to the town, and green picnic-sets on the front terrace, by a big cannon, face the moored boats of the Blyth estuary. This is under the same good management as the Bell in Walberswick.

As well as daily fresh fish and summer shellfish sharing platters, the little dishes to pick and mix are proving very popular (potted shrimps, squid with chorizo and coriander, ham hock terrine with piccalilli, meatballs with garlicky tomato sauce, home-cured beetroot gravadlax with capers, and so forth). Also, lunchtime sandwiches, courgette, tomato, spinach and red onion quiche, pork, apple and sage burger with chips, spicy chilli con carne, half a roasted and grilled chicken with coleslaw, fish pie, slow-braised lamb shank, and puddings such as baked chocolate cheesecake and strawberry, raspberry and blueberry pavlova. *Benchmark main dish: battered cod and chips with mushy peas £10.00. Two-course evening meal £15.00.*

Adnams ~ Tenant Nick Attfield ~ Real ale ~ Bar food (12-9) ~ (01502) 722381 ~ Children welcome away from top bar ~ Dogs allowed in bar ~ Open 11-11 ~ www.harbourinnsouthwold.co.uk *Recommended by Pat and Tony Martin, Norma and Noel Thomas, David Carr, Theocsbrian, Mike and Sue Loseby, M and GR, Martin and Pauline Jennings, Simon Rodway, Ann and Colin Hunt, N R White*

SOUTHWOLD

TM5076 Map 5

Lord Nelson ◖ £

East Street, off High Street (A1095); IP18 6EJ

Bow-windowed town pub with long-serving owners, well liked pubby food and a good choice of drinks; seats outside

With a happy mix of both locals and visitors, this is a well run pub with a buoyant atmosphere and friendly, helpful staff. The partly panelled traditional bar and its two small side rooms are kept spotless, with good lighting, a small but extremely hot coal fire, light wood furniture on the tiled floor, lamps in nice nooks and corners, and some interesting Nelson memorabilia, including attractive nautical prints and a fine model of HMS *Victory*. They serve the whole range of Adnams beers alongside Aspall's cider and several good wines by the glass; board games. There are seats out in front with a sidelong view down to the sea and more in a sheltered (and heated) back garden, with the Adnams brewery in sight (and often the appetising fragrance of brewing in progress). Disabled access is not perfect but is possible.

Holding one of our Value Awards for fair pricing, the popular traditional bar food includes sandwiches, ham hock and gherkin terrine with home-made piccalilli, barbecue chicken wings, thai green curries, rump burger with bacon and cheese, chilli con carne, scampi, specials such as wild boar sausages with red wine and onion gravy and king scallops with chorizo and spinach purée, and puddings like apple crumble and warm chocolate brownie with chocolate sauce. *Benchmark main dish: beer-battered fish and chips £9.75. Two-course evening meal £14.50.*

Adnams ~ Tenants David and Gemma Sanchez ~ Real ale ~ Bar food (12-2, 7-9) ~ (01502) 722079 ~ Children welcome in snug and family room ~ Dogs welcome ~ Open 10.30am-11pm; 12-10.30 Sun ~ www.thelordnelsonsouthwold.co.uk *Recommended by Rob and Catherine Dunster, Giles and Annie Francis, Martin Smith, DHV, Ann and Colin Hunt, David Edge, Terry Mizen, Peter and Giff Bennett, David Carr, David Field, Mike and Sue Loseby, the Didler, Sheila Topham, Lloyd Johnson, Pat and Tony Martin, Howard and Margaret Buchanan*

STOKE-BY-NAYLAND   TL9836   Map 5
Angel 🍴 🛏
B1068 Sudbury–East Bergholt; CO6 4SA

Elegant, comfortable inn with attractive bars, modern cooking, decent choice of drinks and neat uniformed staff; bedrooms

This elegant place has been offering hospitality to customers since the 17th c and today serves a good mix of both locals and visitors. The lounge area has handsome Elizabethan beams, some stripped brickwork and timbers, leather chesterfields and wing armchairs around low tables by the pile of logs in the non-working fireplace (there are working log fires, too), and paintings and prints of the pub, the village and the surrounding area. The chatty bar has farmhouse pine chairs and tables and high tables and stools on the red-tiled floor, and more stools against the counter, where they keep Greene King IPA, Hellhound Dirty Blond and Nethergate Barfly on handpump and ten wines by the glass (including champagne). The high-beamed and timbered Well Room (which has a glass cover over its 16-metre well) is more formal and carpeted with all sorts of cushioned dining chairs around polished dark tables, and a central lamp-style chandelier; staff are neatly uniformed and friendly. There are seats and tables on a sheltered terrace. The individually styled bedrooms are comfortable and the breakfasts very good.

As well as serving breakfasts to non-residents, morning coffee and afternoon tea (must be booked ahead), the enterprising food might include sandwiches, mussel and cockle marinière with chorizo and chickpeas, confit duck rillettes with rhubarb and vanilla chutney and pistachio dressing, local sausages with onion and thyme gravy, roasted vegetable strudel with a red pepper coulis, home-made beef burger with twice-cooked chips and barbecue sauce, slow-cooked pig cheeks in red wine and rosemary on swede mash with parsnip purée, hake fillet with a beetroot fritter, braised chicory and orange beurre blanc, and puddings like Twix cheesecake and mango and passion-fruit parfait with rump syrup. *Benchmark main dish: beer-battered fish and chips £11.95. Two-course evening meal £17.75.*

Free house ~ Licensee James Haggar ~ Real ale ~ Bar food (12-2.45, 6-9.30; all day
weekends; breakfast from 8am; morning coffee and afternoon tea) ~ Restaurant ~
(01206) 263245 ~ Children welcome ~ Dogs allowed in bar ~ Open 10am-11pm; 12-10.30
Sun; breakfast from 8am ~ Bedrooms: /£95B ~ www.angelinnsuffolk.co.uk
Recommended by Jeremy King, John Prescott

STOKE-BY-NAYLAND   TL9836   Map 5
Crown ★ ⑪ ♀ ⇌
Park Street (B1068); CO6 4SE

**Smart dining pub with attractive modern furnishings, imaginative
food, real ales and a great wine choice; good bedrooms**

This civilised and chatty place is well laid out to give several distinct-
feeling areas in its extensive open-plan dining bar – a sofa and easy
chairs on flagstones near the serving counter, a couple more armchairs
under heavy beams by the big woodburning stove, one sizeable table
tucked nicely into a three-sided built-in seat, a lower side room with
more beams and cheerful floral wallpaper. Tables are mostly stripped
veterans, with high-backed dining chairs, but there are more modern
chunky pine tables at the back; contemporary artworks, mostly for sale,
and daily papers. Friendly, informally dressed staff bustle about, and they
have Aspall's cider as well as Adnams Bitter, Crouch Vale Brewers Gold,
Woodfordes Wherry and a guest beer on handpump. Wine is a strong suit,
with more than three dozen by the glass, and hundreds more from the
glass-walled 'cellar shop' in one corner – you can buy there to take away,
too. Disabled access is good. The sheltered flagstoned back terrace has
comfortable teak furniture, with heaters, big terracotta-coloured parasols
and a peaceful view over rolling, lightly wooded countryside. Beyond is
the very well equipped bedroom block (breakfasts are first class).

Using produce from local farmers and fishermen where possible, the enjoyable
modern food might include sandwiches, pheasant, rabbit and venison terrine
with red onion marmalade, red thai curried mussels, wild mushroom wellington
with buffalo mozzarella, spinach and butternut squash wedges, chargrilled beef
burger with smoked paprika mayonnaise and mango chutney, calves liver, bubble
and squeak mash, crispy onions and red wine sauce, king prawn linguine with chilli
and chorizo, confit duck with new potato hash and a fried egg, skate wing with
smoked bacon, caper and parsley butter, and puddings such as Baileys cheesecake
with crème anglaise and blood orange tart with citrus yoghurt. *Benchmark main
dish: beer-battered haddock with thick-cut chips and home-made tartare sauce
£11.95. Two-course evening meal £19.50.*

Free house ~ Licensee Richard Sunderland ~ Real ale ~ Bar food (12-2.30, 6-9.30(10 Fri
and Sat); all day Sun) ~ (01206) 262001 ~ Children welcome ~ Dogs allowed in bar ~
Open 11-11; 12-10.30 Sun ~ Bedrooms: £90S(£110B)/£120S(£145B) ~ www.crowninn.net
*Recommended by John and Enid Morris, Alan and Jill Bull, Bruce and Sharon Eden, John Prescott,
Patrick Tonkin, J F M and M West, Donna Jenkins, Anthony Barnes*

THORPENESS
Dolphin

TM4759   Map 5

Just off B1353; village signposted from Aldeburgh; IP16 4NB

Neatly kept light and airy extended pub in an interesting village, popular food, local ales, and plenty of outside seating; bedrooms

Our readers really enjoy their visits to this bustling pub whose hands-on landlord keeps everything shipshape and cheerful. The main bar is a light room with a scandinavian feel: little candles in glass vases on each of the well spaced, pale wooden tables and a nice mix of old chairs on modern quarry tiles, a built-in cushioned seat in the sizeable bay window, a winter log fire in its brick fireplace, and fresh flowers on the wooden bar counter. Adnams Bitter and Broadside, Woodfordes Wherry and a couple of guests such as Adnams Sole Star and St Peters Golden Ale on handpump, 18 wines by the glass and a good choice of whiskies and bourbons; darts, TV, background music and board games. The public bar to the left of the door is more traditional, with a mix of pubby furniture on the stripped wooden floor, built-in cushioned wall seats with open 'windows' to the bar and fine old photographs of long-ago sporting teams, villagers and local scenes on the bottle-green plank walls; there's also a small area with a few high bar stools. The large dining room has lots of windows hung with cheerful curtains, wide strips of coir matting on light wooden flooring, similar furniture and seaside prints. French windows lead on to a terrace with teak tables and chairs, and beyond that, there are picnic-sets on an extensive stretch of grass; you can hire electric bikes here; the pub also runs the village stores. Thorpeness is a fascinating early 20th-c curio built as a small-scale upmarket holiday resort.

Good bar food might include sandwiches, potted brown shrimps, wild mushrooms and a duck egg on toast, lamb burger with brie and tomato chutney, gressingham duck egg with sweet potato mash, skate wing with smoked bacon, apple and spring onions, pork chop with buttered potatoes and broccoli, daily specials, and puddings like dark chocolate brownie with chocolate sauce and pistachio ice-cream and blueberry cheesecake. *Benchmark main dish: grilled local cod £10.50. Two-course evening meal £18.00.*

Free house ~ Licensee David James ~ Real ale ~ Bar food (12-2.30(3 Sun), 6-9; not winter Sun evening) ~ Restaurant ~ (01728) 454994 ~ Children welcome ~ Dogs allowed in bar and bedrooms ~ Open 11-3, 6-11; 11-11 Sat; 11-10.30 Sun; closed winter Sun evening (from 6pm) ~ Bedrooms: £65B/£95B ~ www.thorpenessdolphin.com
Recommended by Paul Humphreys, Terry Buckland, Phil and Jane Hodson, Sophie Roberts, Simon Rodway, Mrs Margo Finlay, Jörg Kasprowski, George Atkinson

WALBERSWICK
Bell 🍴 ⏷ 🍺 🛏

TM4974   Map 5

Just off B1387; IP18 6TN

Interesting 16th-c inn thriving under new management, good food, cosy bedrooms, nice garden

The charming rambling bar is practically a chronicle of the history of pub flooring through the centuries, with sagging ancient bricks here, broad boards or flagstones there, black and red tiles in yet another area. The furnishings are similarly diverse, including antique curved settles, cushioned pews and window seats, scrubbed tables and two huge fireplaces, one with an elderly woodburning stove watched over by a pair of staffordshire china dogs. Friendly staff serve a good choice of wines by the glass, and Adnams Southwold, Broadside, Sole Star, Explorer and Ghost Ship from handpump; nostalgic background music. Don't miss the classic *New Yorker* wine cartoons in the lavatories. As we went to press, they had just opened the Barn Café for light snacks, cakes, teas and coffees and takeaways; it will also be used for cookery demonstrations. A big neatly planted sheltered garden behind has blue picnic-sets and solid old teak furniture, with a view over the dunes to the sea, and the rowing-boat ferry to Southwold is nearby (there's a footbridge a bit further away). The newly refurbished bedrooms are well equipped and comfortable. The pub is under the same good management as the Harbour Inn in Southwold.

Using free-range pork and lamb and fish from Lowestoft, the enjoyable food might include sandwiches, smoked mackerel pâté topped with horseradish crème fraîche, camembert baked in the box with rock salt, rosemary and an apricot coulis, mushroom and chickpea tagine with herby couscous, battered cod or plaice with creamed and minted peas and chips, a quiche, a pie and a curry of the week, Cromer crab salad, moussaka with a greek-style salad, confit duck leg with potato, bacon and cream bake and red onion marmalade, and puddings like chocolate and walnut brownie with cinnamon ice-cream and baked lemon cheesecake with raspberry coulis. *Benchmark main dish: fish pie £12.00. Two-course evening meal £16.50.*

Adnams ~ Tenant Nick Attfield ~ Real ale ~ Bar food (12-2.30, 6-9; café open 11-8 weekends and school holidays) ~ (01502) 723109 ~ Children welcome away from bar ~ Dogs allowed in bar and bedrooms ~ Open 11-11 ~ Bedrooms: £90S/£100S(£120B) ~ www.bellinnwalberswick.co.uk *Recommended by Norma and Noel Thomas, Mike and Sue Loseby, Andrew and Ruth Triggs, Lois Dyer*

WALDRINGFIELD   TM2844 Map 5

Maybush £

Off A12 S of Martlesham; The Quay, Cliff Road; IP12 4QL

Busy pub with tables outside by the riverbank; nautical décor and a fair choice of drinks and bar food

In fine weather the many seats outside this popular family pub make the most of the view over the lovely River Deben, and if you arrive early enough, you might be able to bag a window table inside. The spacious knocked-through bar is divided into separate areas by fireplaces or steps. There's a nautical theme, with an elaborate ship's model in a glass case and a few more in a light, high-ceilinged extension – as well as lots of old lanterns, pistols and aerial photographs; background music and board games. Adnams Bitter and Old and a changing guest on handpump and a fair choice of wines by the glass. There are river cruises available nearby but you have to pre-book; this is a haven for bird-watchers and ramblers.

The traditional food is popular and fair value and might include sandwiches, fishcakes with a sweet chilli dip, peking-style shredded duck, spinach and ricotta cannelloni, beef burger with chips, bangers and mash, barbecue chicken with cheese and bacon, steak in Guinness pie, bass topped with garlic butter and prawns, and lamb shank in redcurrant gravy. *Benchmark main dish: beer-battered cod and chips £10.95. Two-course evening meal £15.45.*

Adnams ~ Lease Steve and Louise Lomas ~ Real ale ~ Bar food (12-9.30) ~ Restaurant ~ (01473) 736215 ~ Children welcome ~ Dogs allowed in bar ~ Open 11-11 ~ www.debeninns.co.uk/maybush *Recommended by Alistair Mackie, Neil Brightwell, Charles and Pauline Stride, Colin and Louise English*

WESTLETON

TM4469 Map 5

Crown 🍴 ♈ 🛏

B1125 Blythburgh–Leiston; IP17 3AD

Bustling old inn with a cosy chatty bar, plenty of dining areas, carefully chosen drinks and interesting food; comfortable modern bedrooms

Many customers are here to stay overnight in this comfortably stylish old coaching inn but locals do drop in for a pint and a chat, which keeps the atmosphere informal and relaxed. The attractive little bar is at the heart of the building and has a lovely log fire, plenty of original features, Adnams Bitter, Grain Blonde Ash and Green Jack Excelsior Golden Ale on handpump and a thoughtfully chosen wine list; background music and board games. There's also a parlour, a dining room and conservatory, a happy mix of wooden dining chairs and tables, and old photographs on some fine old bare-brick walls. The charming terraced garden has plenty of seats and the airy, comfortable bedrooms are either in the main inn (some are up steep stairs) or in converted stables and cottages.

🍴 Well thought of – if not cheap – food might include lunchtime sandwiches, pork belly and garlic sausage terrine with sauce gribiche, pigeon breast with butternut squash and sage, suet pudding filled with chicken, mushroom and tarragon, chive potato gnocchi with puy lentils, pumpkin and sesame seeds and sage butter, a trio of pork (slow-cooked belly, tempura of cheek and tenderloin) with pickled vegetables and fondant potato, venison saddle with parsnip and potato dauphinoise, plum tart and a star anise reduction, daily specials, and puddings such as vanilla panna cotta with spiced poached pears and chocolate sauce and syrup pudding with vanilla custard and candied orange. *Benchmark main dish: beer-battered fish and chips with home-made tartare sauce £13.25. Two-course evening meal £20.25.*

Free house ~ Licensee Gareth Clarke ~ Real ale ~ Bar food (12.30-2.30, 7-9.30) ~ Restaurant ~ (01728) 648777 ~ Children welcome ~ Dogs allowed in bar and bedrooms ~ Open 11-11; 12-10.30 Sun ~ Bedrooms: £90B/£120B ~ www.westletoncrown.co.uk
Recommended by Kay and Alistair Butler, Phil and Jane Hodson, Anthony Longden, Andrew and Ruth Triggs, Mr and Mrs A Curry, Paul Humphreys, Derek and Sylvia Stephenson

WHEPSTEAD

TL8258 Map 5

White Horse ♈

Off B1066 S of Bury; Rede Road; IP29 4SS

Charmingly reworked country pub with attractively furnished rooms and well liked food and drink

Although this popular pub was built in the 17th c there are several Victorian additions and plenty of space for a drink or a meal. The dark-beamed bar has a woodburning stove in the low fireplace, little stools around pubby tables on the tiled floor and menu boards. Linked rooms off have sturdy, country kitchen tables and chairs on beige carpet or antique floor tiles, with some attractively cushioned traditional wall seats and rather fine old farmhouse chairs. Landscape paintings (for sale) and old prints decorate walls painted in soft canary yellow or sage; the bookshelves have books that are actually worth reading. Adnams Bitter and Broadside on handpump and eight wines by the glass. A tuck shop sells sweets, chocolates and ice-creams; the resident westie is called Skye. A neat sheltered back terrace is brightened up by colourful oilcloth tablecloths, and at the picnic-sets out on the grass, birdsong emphasises what a peaceful spot this is.

🍴 Good food includes jellied ham hock terrine with home-made piccalilli, mixed hors d'oeuvres to share, sausages with paprika and tomatoes on spring onion mash, warm rocket and blue cheese tart, steak burger with tomato chilli jam, open chicken pie with mushrooms, tarragon and wine, fillet of plaice with pea purée and white wine and cream sauce, and puddings like warm lemon sponge with lemon sauce and chocolate truffle torte. *Benchmark main dish: slow-roast lamb with olives and tomatoes £15.95. Two-course evening meal £18.00.*

Free house ~ Licensees Gary and Di Kingshott ~ Real ale ~ Bar food (12-2, 7-9; not Sun evening) ~ (01284) 735760 ~ Children welcome ~ Dogs allowed in bar ~ Open 11.30-3, 7-11; closed Sun evening ~ www.whitehorsewhepstead.co.uk *Recommended by John Saville, Marianne and Peter Stevens, Jenny Smith, M and GR, Jane and Alan Bush, J F M and M West, George Atkinson*

Also Worth a Visit in Suffolk

Besides the fully inspected pubs, you might like to try these pubs that have been recommended to us and described by readers. Do tell us what you think of them: feedback@goodguides.com

ALDRINGHAM   TM4461
Parrot & Punchbowl   01728 830221
B1122/B1353 S of Leiston; IP16 4PY Attractive and welcoming beamed country pub, good fairly priced food including local fish, good wine choice, well kept Greene King and Woodfordes, decent coffee, two-level restaurant; children welcome; nice sheltered garden, also family garden with adventure play area. *(George Atkinson)*

BARHAM   TM1251
Sorrel Horse   (01473) 830327
Old Norwich Road; IP6 0PG Open-plan country inn with good log fire in central chimneybreast, dark beams and timbers, well kept real ales and popular food; children welcome, disabled facilities, picnic-sets on side grass with big play area, bedrooms in converted barn, open all day Weds-Sun. *(Anon)*

BARTON MILLS   TL72173
Olde Bull   (01638) 711001
Just S of Mildenhall; The Street; IP28 6AA Attractive rambling bars and restaurant, reasonable choice of home-made food all day from lunchtime sandwiches and pubby dishes up, Sun roasts, big log fire, Adnams, Greene King and a local guest, decent wine list and coffee; piped and some live music; well behaved children welcome, no dogs inside, central courtyard, 14 individually styled bedrooms, open all day. *(Jeremy King)*

BILDESTON   TL9949
Crown   (01449) 740510
B1115 SW of Stowmarket; IP7 7EB Good upmarket food (not cheap) in this picturesque and impressively refurbished 15th-c timbered country inn, smart beamed main bar with leather armchairs and inglenook log fire, more intimate back area with contemporary art, ales such as Greene King and Mauldons, good choice of wines by the glass, dining room; children welcome, disabled access and parking, tables laid for dining in attractive central courtyard, more in large beautifully kept garden with decking, quiet comfortable bedrooms. *(Mrs Margo Finlay, Jörg Kasprowski)*

BLAXHALL   TM3656
Ship   (01728) 688316
Off B1069 S of Snape; can be reached from A12 via Little Glemham; IP12 2DY Popular and friendly low-beamed 18th-c pub, good traditional home-made food in bar and restaurant, well kept Adnams Bitter, Woodfordes Wherry and guests, some live music; children in eating areas, dogs in bar, eight chalet bedrooms, good breakfast, attractive country setting; open all day Sun. *(Alistair Bacon, Ken Anderson, Mike Proctor)*

BLYFORD   TM4276
Queens Head   (01502) 478404
B1123 Blythburgh–Halesworth; IP19 9JY 15th-c thatched pub doing well under present licensees, good food, well kept Adnams and cheery staff, very low beams, some antique settles, huge fireplace; tables outside. *(John Lunniss)*

BLYTHBURGH   TM4575
White Hart   (01502) 478217
A12; IP19 9LQ Open-plan roadside family dining pub, a former courthouse dating from the 16th c, with fine ancient beams,

woodwork and staircase, full Adnams range kept well, Aspall's cider and good choice of wines, enjoyable food from huge sandwiches up, friendly service, inglenook log fire; children in eating areas, back terrace and spacious lawns looking down on tidal bird marshes, magnificent church over road, four bedrooms, open all day. *(Giles and Annie Francis, DHV)*

BRAMFIELD   TM3973
✦**Queens Head** (01986) 784214

The Street; A144 S of Halesworth; IP19 9HT High-raftered lounge with scrubbed pine tables, impressive fireplace and some old farm tools, side room with comfortable fireside seats, well kept Adnams, Aspall's cider, decent wines by the glass, seasonal home-made elderflower cordial, good reasonably priced food (emphasis on local organic), home-made bread and ice-creams, friendly service, monthly live music (Fri); children (away from bar) and dogs welcome, cheerful blue-painted picnic-sets in pretty garden with dome-shaped willow bower, nice church next door. *(Neil Powell)*

BRANDESTON   TM2460
Queens Head (01728) 685307

The Street, towards Earl Soham; IP13 7AD Unpretentiously attractive open-plan country pub, good food (not Sun evening) including some interesting dishes, particularly good vegetarian choice and nice puddings, well kept Adnams, good wines by the glass, helpful staff and friendly relaxed atmosphere, two open fires, leather banquettes and old pews, light airy restaurant section; background music; children and dogs welcome, disabled facilities, big neat garden with good play area, campsite. *(Paul Humphreys, M Ross-Thomas)*

BRENT ELEIGH   TL9348
✦**Cock** (01787) 247371

A1141 SE of Lavenham; CO10 9PB Timeless thatched country pub with friendly locals, Adnams, Greene King Abbot and a guest, organic farm cider, some simple food, cosy ochre-walled snug and second small room, antique flooring tiles, lovely coal fire, old photographs of village (church well worth a look), darts and toad in the hole; well behaved children and dogs welcome, picnic-sets up on side grass with summer hatch service, attractive inn sign, one bedroom, open all day Fri-Sun. *(the Didler)*

BROCKLEY GREEN   TL7247
✦**Plough** (01440) 786789

Hundon Road; CO10 8DT Friendly neatly kept knocked-through bar, beams, timbers and stripped brick, scrubbed tables and open fire, good food from lunchtime sandwiches to some enterprising dishes and nice puddings, Tues steak night, cheerful efficient staff, Greene King IPA, Woodfordes Wherry and a guest, good choice of wines by the glass and malt whiskies, restaurant; children

and dogs welcome, extensive attractive grounds, peaceful country views, comfortable bedrooms. *(Muriel Farnden, Adele Summers, Alan Black, G M Hollington)*

BROMESWELL   TM3050
British Larder (01394) 460310

Orford Road, Bromeswell Heath; IP12 2PU Neat beamed restaurny pub with good if not cheap food from chef licensees using local seasonal produce, well kept ales and nice wines by the glass in separate bar, pleasant service, home-made jams etc for sale; children welcome, plenty of tables outside, big play area, open all day weekends. *(J F M and M West)*

BURY ST EDMUNDS   TL8463
Dove (01284) 702787

Hospital Road; IP33 3JU 19th-c alehouse with rustic bare-boards bar and separate parlour, half a dozen or more well kept beers, no food, some folk and blues nights; closed weekday lunchtimes. *(Mo Uchegbu)*

BURY ST EDMUNDS   TL8564
✦**Nutshell** (01284) 764867

The Traverse, central pedestrian link off Abbeygate Street; IP33 1BJ Tiny, simple local with timeless interior (can be quite a crush at busy times), lots of interest such as a mummified cat (found walled up here) hanging from dark brown ceiling (companion rat too), bits of a skeleton, vintage bank notes, cigarette packets, military and other badges, spears and a great metal halberd, one short wooden bench along shop-front corner windows, a cut-down sewing-machine table and an elbow rest running along a rather battered counter, Greene King ales, no food; background music, steep narrow stairs up to lavatories; children (till 7pm) and dogs welcome, open all day. *(Barry Collett, the Didler)*

BURY ST EDMUNDS   TL8563
✦**Rose & Crown** (01284) 755934

Whiting Street; IP33 1NP Cheerful black-beamed corner local with affable helpful licensees, bargain simple lunchtime home cooking (not Sun), particularly well kept Greene King ales (including XX Mild) and guests, pleasant lounge with lots of piggy pictures and bric-a-brac, good games-oriented public bar, rare separate off-sales counter; piped radio, no credit cards or under-14s; pretty back courtyard, open all day weekdays. *(Jeremy King)*

BUTLEY   TM3650
Oyster (01394) 450790

B1084 E of Woodbridge; IP12 3NZ Welcoming old beamed country pub, good daily changing choice of blackboard food, well kept Adnams, stripped pine tables and pews, coal fire; children welcome. *(David Miles-Dinham)*

BUXHALL
TM9957
✶ **Crown** (01449) 736521

*Off B1115 W of Stowmarket; Mill Road;
IP14 3DW* Cosy and welcoming low-beamed
bar with good inglenook log fire, pews and
leather chairs, well kept Greene King ales
and nice choice of wines by the glass, decent
food including good value set menu, airy
dining room; children and dogs welcome,
plenty of tables on heated terrace, pretty
enclosed garden, country views, closed Sun
evening, Mon. *(J F M and M West, Jeremy King)*

CAVENDISH
TL8046
Bull (01787) 280245

*A1092 Long Melford–Clare; CO10
8AX* Spotless old inn with heavy beams,
timbers and fine fireplaces, Adnams ales
and good choice of food, reasonable prices,
attentive friendly service; children in eating
areas, garden tables, car park (useful in this
honeypot village), bedrooms, closed Sun
evening, Mon, Tues. *(Marianne and Peter
Stevens, N R White)*

CAVENDISH
TL8046
✶ **George** (01787) 280248

A1092, The Green; CO10 8BA 16th-c
dining inn with contemporary feel in two
bow-windowed front areas, beams and
timbers, big woodburner in stripped-brick
fireplace, good food from varied menu
including set deals, Nethergate and some
decent wines by the glass, back servery
and further eating area, friendly helpful
staff, daily newspapers; stylish furniture on
sheltered back terrace, tree-shaded garden
with lovely village church behind, five good
bedrooms up rather steep staircase.
*(Penny Lang, Marianne and Peter Stevens, Adele
Summers, Alan Black, Neil and Brenda Skidmore,
P Waterman, Sadie Clayton and others)*

CHELSWORTH
TL9848
Peacock (01449) 740758

*B1115 Sudbury–Needham Market;
IP7 7HU* Attractive and prettily set old
dining pub with lots of Tudor brickwork
and exposed beams, separate pubby bar
with big inglenook log fire, real ales and
fairly standard food, friendly service;
attractive small garden and village.
(MDN, Christopher Sewell)

DENNINGTON
TM2867
✶ **Queens Head** (01728) 638241

A1120; The Square; IP13 8AB Well
refurbished beamed and timbered Tudor pub
prettily placed by church, L-shaped main
bar, Adnams and maybe a guest, local cider,
enjoyable food (best to book weekends)
including some unusual choices, friendly
service; background music; children in family
room, side lawn by noble lime trees, pond
at back with ducks and carp, backs on to
Dennington Park with swings etc. *(Ian and
Nita Cooper, Jeremy Hebblethwaite, Terry Mizen)*

EASTON
TM2858
✶ **White Horse** (01728) 746456

*N of Wickham Market on back road to
Earl Soham and Framlingham; IP13
0ED* Pretty 16th-c pub with new landlord
and refurbishment ongoing as we went to
press; three smartly simple rooms, country
kitchen chairs, good small settles, cushioned
stripped pews and stools, open fires, Adnams
and a guest, eight wines by the glass, good
choice of bar food using local produce,
restaurant; background music; children and
dogs welcome, seats in rustic garden, good
local walks. *(Peter Webb, M Ross-Thomas,
Charles and Pauline Stride, Ann and Colin Hunt,
Hayley Roche)*

FELIXSTOWE FERRY
TM3237
Ferry Boat (01394) 284203

Off Ferry Road, on the green; IP11 9RZ
Much modernised 17th-c pub tucked between
golf links and dunes near harbour, Martello
tower and summer rowing-boat ferry;
enjoyable fair value pub food including good
fish and chips, friendly efficient service,
well kept Adnams, decent coffee, warm log
fire; background music, busy on summer
weekends, and they may ask to keep a credit
card while you eat; dogs welcome, tables out
in front, on green opposite and in fenced
garden, good coast walks. *(Ryta Lyndley,
N R White)*

FORWARD GREEN
TM0959
✶ **Shepherd & Dog** (01449) 711361

A1120 E of Stowmarket; IP14 5HN
Smart dining pub with attractive pastel
décor, comfortable dining tables and some
sofas, good interesting food in contemporary
bar and restaurant including upmarket
burgers from local wagyu herd, well kept
Greene King IPA and Fullers London Pride,
good wines by the glass and coffee, helpful
young staff; disabled access, terrace tables,
closed Sun evening, Mon. *(Ian and Nita
Cooper, J F M and M West)*

FRAMLINGHAM
TM2862
Station Hotel (01728) 723455

Station Road (B1116 S); IP13 9EE
Simple high-ceilinged big-windowed bar with
scrubbed tables on stripped boards, four
well kept Earl Soham ales and a guest, good
choice of house wines, popular reasonably
priced food from varied menu, friendly
service, relaxed atmosphere, plenty of train
pictures, back snug with tiled floor; children
welcome, picnic-sets in pleasant good-sized
garden. *(J F M and M West)*

FRESSINGFIELD
TM2677
✶ **Fox & Goose** (01379) 586247

*Church Street; B1116 N of
Framlingham; IP21 5PB* Relaxed dining
pub in beautifully timbered 16th-c building
next to church, very good food in cosy
informal heavy-beamed rooms with log fire,

upstairs restaurant, good wines by the glass, Adnams and a guest tapped from the cask in side bar; faint background music; children welcome, downstairs disabled facilities, tables out by duck pond, closed Mon. *(Paul Humphreys, Lois Dyer)*

HAUGHLEY TM0262
Kings Arms (01449) 614462
Off A45/B1113 N of Stowmarket; Old Street; IP14 3NT 16th-c extended timbered pub, horsebrasses and other bits and pieces, big brick fireplace, enjoyable fairly traditional pub food cooked to order, well kept Greene King ales and a guest, good choice of wines by the glass, busy public bar with TV and pool; background music, no dogs inside; children welcome, tables in back garden with play area, nice village, open all day weekends. *(Jeremy King)*

HAWKEDON TL7953
★ Queens Head (01284) 789218
Off A143 at Wickham Street, NE of Haverhill; and off B1066; IP29 4NN Flint Tudor pub in pretty setting looking down broad peaceful green to interesting largely Norman village church; quarry-tiled bar with dark beams and ochre walls, plenty of pews and chapel chairs around scrubbed tables, elderly armchairs by antique woodburner in huge fireplace, cheerful young landlady, Adnams, Cottage and Woodfordes ales, farm cider and perry, decent wines, good food using home-reared meat, dining area stretching back with country prints on apple-green walls and a couple of tusky boars' heads; picnic-sets out in front, more on back terrace overlooking rolling country, little shop (Fri and Sat mornings) selling carefully chosen meats as well as their own bacon, pies, casseroles etc, closed Monday to Thursday lunchtimes. *(Gill Janzen, Susan Cook)*

HESSETT TL9361
Five Bells (01359) 270350
Off A14 E of Bury; The Street; IP30 9AX Low-ceilinged open-plan pub near spectacular Norman church, enjoyable food (choose your own steak or seafood from display counter), well kept Greene King ales, caring staff, big log fire; children welcome, large sheltered garden with terrace, closed Mon and lunchtimes Tues, Weds. *(Anon)*

HOXNE TM1877
★ Swan (01379) 668275
Low Street; off B1118, signed off A140 S of Diss; IP21 5AS Timber-framed 15th-c building with pubby bar, two solid oak counters, broad oak floorboards and deep-set inglenook, Adnams, Woodfordes and a guest tapped from the cask (beer festivals May and Nov), Aspall's cider and several wines by the glass, good well presented bar food, friendly staff, restaurant; children and dogs welcome, seats under parasols on two

sheltered terraces or in attractive spacious garden extending to stream, boules, nearby is tree to which King Edmund was tied at his execution, open all day Sun. *(D and J Ashdown, Ian Herdman, KC, Sheila Topham, Pat and Tony Martin, Martin and Pauline Jennings and others)*

ICKLINGHAM TL7772
Plough (01638) 711770
The Street; IP28 6PL Cosy bar area with settles and adjacent good-sized restaurant, wide choice of enjoyable blackboard food, six ales including Greene King IPA and Hook Norton, good choice of wines by the glass, no mobile phones; children welcome at lunchtime, big garden, six bedrooms. *(M and GR, Simon Watkins)*

ICKLINGHAM TL7872
★ Red Lion (01638) 711698
A1101 Mildenhall–Bury St Edmunds; IP28 6PS Welcoming 16th-c thatched pub, beamed bar with cavernous inglenook and attractive mix of furnishings, oriental rugs on wood floor, Earl Soham, Humpty Dumpty and Woodfordes ales, lots of country wines, carpeted dining area behind knocked-through fireplace, short choice of well liked bar food, friendly helpful staff, board games; background music; well behaved children welcome, dogs in bar (the cheery pub dog is Fudge), picnic-sets with colourful parasols on front lawn, West Stow Country Park and the Anglo-Saxon Village near by, closed Sun evening, Mon. *(George Atkinson, Simon Watkins, Dick Vardy, Rita Scarratt, Amy Andrews)*

IPSWICH TM1644
Dove Street (01473) 211270
76 St Helen's Street; IP4 2LA Over 20 well kept quickly changing ales including their own brews, farm ciders, bottled beers and whiskies, cheap hot drinks, friendly staff, simple good value home-made food, regular beer festivals; dogs welcome, two bedrooms in building over the road, open all day. *(Richard Fearn)*

IPSWICH TM1645
Greyhound (01473) 252862
Henley Road/Anglesea Road; IP1 3SE Popular 19th-c pub with aged tables in cosy front bar, corridor to larger lounge, five well kept Adnams ales and a couple of guests, good substantial home cooking including bargain weekday lunch, quick service by well trained young staff; outside lavatories; children welcome, picnic-sets under parasols on quiet back terrace, open all day Fri-Sun (breakfast Sun from 10am). *(Alex Hayton, Jeremy King, the Didler, Giles and Annie Francis)*

KENTFORD TL7066
Cock (01638) 750360
Bury Road, just off A14; CB8 7PR Comfortable and attractive, with inglenook log fire and beautiful carved

beams, good interesting range of food, friendly service, Greene King real ales, airy restaurant; neat garden. *(M and GR)*

KESGRAVE   TM2346
Kesgrave Hall (01473) 333741
Hall Road; IP5 2PU Country hotel with Greene King ales in comfortably contemporary bare-boards bar, popular imaginative food all day in open-kitchen bistro (no booking – so best to arrive early), good service; children and dogs welcome, attractive heated terrace with huge retractable awning, 23 stylish bedrooms. *(J F M and M West)*

LAXFIELD   TM2972
✶**Kings Head** (01986) 798395
Gorams Mill Lane, behind church; IP13 8DW Unspoilt thatched pub with no bar counter – instead, Adnams range and a guest poured in tap room; interesting little chequer-tiled front room dominated by a three-sided booth of high-backed settles in front of old range fire, two other equally unspoilt rooms with pews, old seats and scrubbed deal tables, well liked tasty bar food including good home-made pies served by friendly helpful staff; children and dogs welcome, neatly kept garden with colourful borders, arbour with hops and grape vine, small pavilion for cooler evenings, boules, bedrooms and self-catering apartment, open all day in summer. *(Ian and Nita Cooper, Tim Maddison, Paul and Marion Watts, Jane and Alan Bush, the Didler, Nigel Long and others)*

LITTLE THURLOW   TL6750
Cock (01440) 783224
The Street; CB9 7LA Refurbished 17th-c village pub under new management, enjoyable home-made food (not Sun evening), Greene King IPA and guests, Aspall's cider, decent wines by the glass, attentive friendly service, live music second Fri of month; sports TV; children and dogs welcome, garden with play area, open all day Fri-Sun. *(Matthew Hancock, Adele Summers, Alan Black)*

LONG MELFORD   TL8646
✶**Black Lion** (01787) 312356
Church Walk; CO10 9DN Hotel in striking village street, bar rooms either side of oak servery, one decorated in ochre with deeply cushioned sofas, leather wing armchairs and antique settles, the other in shades of terracotta with leather dining chairs around handsome set tables, good well presented modern food, friendly helpful uniformed staff, Adnams ales, local cider, several wines by the glass and some good whiskies, open fires in both rooms, large racehorse portraits and big windows overlooking green; background music; children welcome, dogs in drinking side, difficult wheelchair accesss, seats under parasols on terrace and in appealing Victorian walled garden, bedrooms, open all

day. *(John and Enid Morris, Ian Wilson, Bob and Tanya Ekers, Annette and John Derbyshire, David Gass)*

LONG MELFORD   TL8645
✶**Bull** (01787) 378494
Hall Street (B1064); CO10 9JG Small 15th-c hotel full of character, beautifully carved beams in old-fashioned timbered front lounge, antique furnishings, log fire in huge fireplace, more spacious back bar with sporting prints, well kept Greene King ales and a guest, Aspall's cider, decent wines, reasonably priced standard Old English Inns menu, cheerful helpful staff, daily newspapers, restaurant; children welcome, tables in attractive courtyard, comfortable bedrooms and substantial breakfast, open all day weekends. *(Paul and Marion Watts, Mrs Margo Finlay, Jörg Kasprowski, Ian Herdman)*

LONG MELFORD   TL8645
Crown (01787) 377666
Hall Street; CO10 9JL Friendly partly 17th-c inn, real ales such as Adnams and Woodfordes from central servery with unusual bar chairs, log fire, some stripped brickwork and nicely placed furnishings, oak-floored restaurant with high-back chairs and vibrant red walls, good variety of food from bar snacks up, efficient service; attractive terrace with big awnings and small pond, 12 well equipped bedrooms. *(Ian Wilson, Simon and Mandy King)*

LONG MELFORD   TL8645
Swan (01787) 464545
Hall Street; CO10 9JQ Smartly updated beamed dining pub run well by brother and sister team, good modern food (not Sun evening) using local seasonal produce, nice choice of wines; background music; tables outside, open all day. *(Marianne and Peter Stevens)*

LOWESTOFT   TM5593
Triangle (01502) 582711
St Peter's Street; NR32 1QA Popular two-bar tap for Green Jack ales, guest beers too and real cider, regular beer festivals, breweriana, open fire; pool and TV in back bar, live music Fri; open all day (till 1am Fri, Sat). *(Mike Mason)*

MONKS ELEIGH   TL9647
✶**Swan** (01449) 741391
A1141 NW of Hadleigh; IP7 7AU Gently upmarket dining pub but has informal side too; long pleasantly bright bar with high-backed leather-seated dining chairs around light wood tables on pale oak floor, red walls hung with Jack Vettriano prints and cheerful country landscapes, good imaginative food including set lunch menu, efficient helpful service, open fire in small brick fireplace in high-ceilinged end room, fresh flowers on cream-painted wooden-topped bar counter, Adnams and a guest, good choice of wines

by the glass; children welcome, village post office in car park, closed Sun evening, winter Mon and two weeks in school holidays (best to ring). *(Mr and Mrs C Prentis, MDN, Alan and Jill Bull, M and GR, Stephen and Jean Curtis, Ian Wilson)*

NEWBOURNE
TM2743

⋆ **Fox** (01473) 736307

Off A12 at roundabout 1.7 miles N of A14 junction; The Street; IP12 4NY Pink-washed 16th-c pub, low-beamed bar with slabby elm and other dark tables on tiled floor, stuffed fox in inglenook, comfortable carpeted dining room with modern artwork and antique mirrors, ales such as Adnams, Brains, Purity and Sharps, decent wines by the glass, good variety of well liked food (all day weekends) including reasonably priced Sun roasts, good service; background music; children welcome, dogs in bar, wheelchair access, attractive grounds with rose garden and pond, open all day. *(Neil Brightwell, Alistair Mackie, George Atkinson)*

ORFORD
TM4249

Crown & Castle (01394) 450205

Castle Terrace; IP12 2LJ Hotel/restaurant rather than pub, enjoyable food from pubby standards up (evening food more upscale and expensive), small smartly minimalist bar (used largely for pre-meal drinks – well kept Greene King and good wines by the glass); children (no under-8s in the evening) and dogs welcome, tables outside, residents' garden, 19 good bedrooms. *(Edward Mirzoeff)*

ORFORD
TM4249

⋆ **Jolly Sailor** (01394) 450243

Quay Street; IP12 2NU Friendly pub liked by walkers and bird-watchers and built mainly from wrecked ships' timbers, several snug rooms with lots of exposed brickwork, boating pictures and shipping charts celebrating the river, four Adnams beers served from counters and hatches in an old-fashioned central cubicle, popular food from doorstep sandwiches up, unusual spiral staircase in corner of flagstoned main bar with horsebrasses, local photographs, two cushioned pews and long antique stripped deal table, open woodburner in big brick fireplace; picnic-sets on back grass with views over marshes, play tower, can camp in the orchard. *(Mrs M E Mills, Neil Powell, Charles and Pauline Stride, Maria Taylor, Philip Smith, Terry Mizen, David Field and others)*

PETTISTREE
TM2954

⋆ **Greyhound** (01728) 746451

The Street; brown sign to pub off B1438 S of Wickham Market, 0.5 miles N of A12; IP13 0HP Two smallish well maintained traditional rooms with polished dark tables on green carpet, matching padding for chairs and heavy settles, pale sage dado, rather low dark brown beams

and open fires, Crouch Vale, Earl Soham, Woodfordes and a guest, several wines by the glass, enjoyable bar and restaurant food, friendly service; children welcome in dining part, picnic-sets in side garden with more in front gravel car park, peaceful setting next to church, closed Mon lunchtime. *(MDN, Roger White)*

POLSTEAD
TL9938

Cock (01206) 263150

Signed off B1068 and A1071 E of Sudbury, then pub signed; Polstead Green; CO6 5AL Beamed and timbered 16th-c local, bar with woodburner and open fire, well kept Adnams, Greene King IPA and a guest, good choice of wines and malt whiskies, enjoyable reasonably priced home-made food from lunchtime sandwiches up, light and airy barn restaurant; background music; children and dogs welcome, disabled facilities, picnic-sets overlooking attractive village's quiet green, side play area, open all day weekends, closed Mon. *(Eddie Edwards, John Prescott)*

RAMSHOLT
TM3041

⋆ **Ramsholt Arms** (01394) 411229

Signed off B1083; Dock Road; IP12 3AB Lovely isolated spot overlooking River Deben, welcoming open-plan nautical bar busy on summer weekends and handy for bird walks and Sutton Hoo; wide choice of good value quickly served food including seafood and game, two sittings for Sun lunch, Adnams and a guest ale kept well, decent wines by the glass, winter mulled wine, good log fire; dogs (pub has two) and children welcome, plenty of tables outside with summer afternoon terrace bar (not Sun), roomy bedrooms with stunning view, open all day. *(David Field, Nigel Long, Simon Rodway)*

RATTLESDEN
TL9758

Brewers Arms (01449) 736377

Lower Road; off B1115 via Buxhall or A45 via Woolpit, W of Stowmarket; IP30 0RJ 16th-c beamed village pub with more emphasis on dining under current management; traditionally furnished bar on right, lounge on left winding back through standing timbers to restaurant area – partly flint-walled with magnificent old bread oven, freshly made daily-changing food from landlord/chef including lunchtime sandwiches, pub favourites and some more ambitious choices, coffee and cakes, Greene King and guests; background music, open mike second Tues of month; walled garden with table tennis, children welcome, dogs in bar, open all day from 10am. *(Jeremy King, Olly Headey)*

REDE
TL8055

⋆ **Plough** (01284) 789208

Village signposted off A143 Bury St Edmunds–Haverhill; IP29 4BE Pretty thatched pub in tucked-away village, traditional low-beamed bar with comfortable seating, solid fuel stove in brick fireplace, popular food (not Sun evening) from quickly changing menu, three real ales; children welcome till 8pm, picnic-sets in sheltered cottage garden and in front near village green. *(Gill Janzen)*

RENDHAM   TM3564
White Horse (01728) 663497
B1119 Framlingham–Saxmundham; IP17 2AF Partly divided open-plan pub with good reasonably priced home-made food using local suppliers, Earl Soham, Mauldons, Timothy Taylors and a guest, two open fires; garden tables, lovely spot opposite 14th-c church, good local walks, closed weekday lunchtimes. *(Martin Smith)*

REYDON   TM4977
☆ Randolph (01502) 723603
Wangford Road (B1126 just NW of Southwold); IP18 6PZ Stylish inn with quite an emphasis on dining and bedroom side; bar with high-backed leather dining chairs around chunky wooden tables on parquet floor, sofa and a couple of comfortable armchairs, prints of pub from 1910 and photographs of Southwold beach, Adnams beers, dining room with more high-backed chairs on red carpet, pretty little Victorian fireplace filled with candles, nicely varied menu including children's choices, pleasant staff; background music, TV, games machine; dogs welcome in little back bar, wheelchair access, picnic-sets on decked area and grass, ten bedrooms, good breakfast, open all day. *(Ann and Colin Hunt, Phil and Jane Hodson)*

ROUGHAM   TL9063
☆ Ravenwood Hall (01359) 270345
Off A14 E of Bury St Edmunds; IP30 9JA Country-house hotel with two compact bar rooms, tall ceilings, patterned wallpaper and big heavily draped windows overlooking sweeping lawn with stately cedar, back area set for eating with upholstered settles and dining chairs, sporting prints and log fire, interesting well presented bar food (own smoked meats and fish), well kept Adnams, good choice of wines and malts, comfortable lounge area with horse pictures, a few moulded beams and good-sized fragment of early Tudor wall decoration above big inglenook, separate more formal restaurant; background music; children and dogs welcome, teak furniture in garden, swimming pool, geese and pygmy goats in big enclosures, croquet, 14 bedrooms, open 9am-midnight. *(Martin Smith, J F M and M West, Ryta Lyndley)*

SAXTEAD GREEN   TM2564
Old Mill House (01728) 685064
B1119; The Green; IP13 9QE Roomy dining pub across green from windmill, beamed carpeted bar, neat country-look flagstoned restaurant extension, wooden tables and chairs, good choice of generous well priced fresh food (all day Sun) including daily carvery, good friendly service, well kept Greene King, decent wines; discreet background music; children very welcome, attractive sizeable garden with terrace and good play area, open all day Sun. *(Ian and Nita Cooper, Jeremy King)*

SHOTLEY GATE   TM2433
Bristol Arms (01473) 787200
End of B1456; Bristol Hill; IP9 1PU Superb estuary views from dining room and picnic-sets outside, good food and service, well kept Adnams. *(Anon)*

SHOTTISHAM   TM3244
Sorrel Horse (01394) 411617
Hollesley Road; IP12 3HD Charming two-bar 15th-c thatched local (now community owned), attentive helpful staff, Adnams, Woodfordes and guests tapped from the cask, decent choice of home-made traditional food including deals, good log fire in tiled-floor bar with games area (bar billiards), attractive dining room with woodburner, fortnightly quiz Weds; children and dogs welcome, tables out on sloping front lawn and in small garden behind, open all day weekends. *(Pat and Tony Martin, the Didler)*

SNAPE   TM3958
Crown (01728) 688324
Bridge Road (B1069); IP17 1SL Small cheery beamed 15th-c pub with brick floors, inglenook log fire and fine double Suffolk settle, well kept Adnams ales, enjoyable fresh food using local ingredients including own meat (reared behind the pub), folk night last Thurs of month, darts; children and dogs welcome, garden. *(John and Eleanor Holdsworth, Edward Mirzoeff, Simon Rodway)*

SOMERLEYTON   TM4797
Dukes Head (01502) 730281
Slugs Lane (B1074); NR32 5QR Nicely positioned red-brick pub (part of the Somerleyton Hall estate), stripped-stone bar, Adnams, Green Jack, Woodfordes and a guest ale, enjoyable seasonal food from estate's own farms, friendly young staff, family dining extension, live music in converted barn; tables out on grass, country views, a stiff walk up from River Waveney, open all day. *(N R White, Peter and Eleanor Kenyon)*

Post Office address codings confusingly give the impression that some pubs are in Suffolk, when they're really in Cambridgeshire, Essex or Norfolk (which is where we list them).

SOUTH COVE   TM4982
Five Bells (01502) 75249
B1127 Southwold–Wrentham; NR34 7JF
Friendly, well run and spacious creeper-
covered pub with stripped pine, three well
kept Adnams ales, Aspall's cider, good pubby
blackboard menu in bar, side room with settles
or back restaurant, good service; tables out
in front, play area, quiet caravan site in back
paddock, bedrooms. *(Andrew and Ruth Triggs)*

SOUTH ELMHAM   TM3385
⋆ St Peters Brewery (01986) 782288
*St Peter South Elmham; off B1062 SW
of Bungay; NR35 1NQ* Beautifully but
simply furnished manor dating from the
13th c (much extended in 1539) with own
St Peters ales and bottled beers, bar and
dining hall with dramatic high-ceiling,
imposing chandelier, elaborate woodwork
and flagstoned floor, antique tapestries, two
further rooms reached up steepish stairs;
outside tables overlooking original moat, has
been open all day Sat, closed Sun evening,
Mon – new licensees taking over as we went
to press. *(Anon)*

SOUTHWOLD   TM5076
⋆ Red Lion (01502) 722385
South Green; IP18 6ET Cheerful pubby
front bar with big windows looking over
green towards the sea, sturdy wall benches
and bentwood bar stools on flagstones, well
kept Adnams ales, quieter back room with
mate's chairs, cushioned pews and polished
dark tables on pale woodstrip flooring,
seaside cartoons by Giles, Mac and the
like, good reasonably priced food including
OAP meals, friendly neatly dressed staff,
three linked dining rooms; maybe nostalgic
background music; tables out in front and
in small sheltered back courtyard, right by
the Adnams retail shop. *(Martin Smith, DHV,
Ann and Colin Hunt, Ryta Lyndley, Mike and Sue
Loseby, Gwyn and Anne Wake and others)*

SOUTHWOLD   TM5076
Sole Bay (01502) 723736
East Green; IP18 6JN Airy pub near
Adnams Brewery, their full range kept well
and good wine choice, cheerful efficient staff,
enjoyable reasonably priced simple food (not
Sun evening) including good fish and chips,
well spaced tables, conservatory; sports
TV; children and dogs welcome, disabled
facilities, picnic-sets outside, moments from
sea and lighthouse, open all day. *(Giles and
Annie Francis, Pat and Tony Martin, Mike and
Sue Loseby, Gwyn and Anne Wake)*

SOUTHWOLD   TM5076
⋆ Swan (01502) 722186
Market Place; IP18 6EG Relaxed
comfortable back bar in smart Adnams-
owned hotel, their full range and bottled
beers, fine wines and malt whiskies, good
bar food including lunchtime set menu
(Mon-Sat), cheerful competent staff, coffee
and teas in luxurious chintzy front lounge,
restaurant; nice garden, 42 bedrooms – some
in separate block where (by arrangement)
dogs can stay too, good breakfast.
(George Atkinson)

STOKE ASH   TM1170
White Horse (01379) 678222
A140; IP23 7ET Popular 17th-c beamed
coaching inn, welcoming helpful young staff,
enjoyable reasonably priced pub food all
day from 8am, well kept Adnams; annexe
bedrooms. *(J F M and M West)*

SUDBURY   TL8741
Brewery Tap
East Street; CO10 2TP Tap for Mauldons
brewery, their full range and guests kept
well, bare boards and scrubbed tables, some
food, darts, cribbage and bar billiards, live
music including jazz; dogs welcome, open all
day. *(John Prescott)*

TOSTOCK   TL9563
Gardeners Arms (01359) 270460
Off A14 or A1088; IP30 9PA Old low-
beamed village pub with enjoyable well
priced traditional food including children's
meals, Greene King and a guest ale,
inglenook log fire, games in tiled separate
bar; picnic-sets in sheltered garden. *(Pat and
Tony Martin)*

TUDDENHAM   TM1948
⋆ Fountain (01473) 785377
*The Street; village signed off B1077 N of
Ipswich; IP6 9BT* Buzzy well run dining
pub in nice village, several linked café-style
rooms (minimal décor) with heavy beams
and timbering, stripped floors, wooden dining
chairs around light tables, open fire, lots
of prints (some by the cartoonist Giles who
spent time here after World War II), good
choice of food (not Sun evening) including
set menus, Adnams, decent coffee, pleasant
helpful service; background music; no under-
10s in bar after 6.30pm, wicker and metal
chairs on covered heated terrace, more seats
under huge parasols on sizeable lawn, closed
Sun evening, first week Jan. *(Ryta Lyndley,
Beckie Harvey, Dickie and Alex Brooks)*

The letters and figures after the name of each town are its Ordnance Survey map
reference. *How to use the Guide* at the beginning of the book explains how it helps you
find a pub, in road atlases or large-scale maps as well as in our own maps.

WALBERSWICK   TM4974
✳ **Anchor** (01502) 722112
*The Street (B1387); village signed off
A12; IP18 6UA* More restaurant with
bar than pub and food highly rated; simply
furnished front bar divided into snug halves
by two-way open fire, big windows, heavy
stripped tables on original oak flooring,
sturdy built-in green leather wall seats and
nicely framed black and white photographs
of fishermen on colourwashed panelling,
Adnams and Meantime, lots of bottled beers,
25 wines by the glass, extensive dining area
stretching back from small more modern-
feeling lounge, good friendly service; young
children (not in bar) and dogs welcome,
garden bar serving flagstoned terrace, coast
path and pleasant walk across to Southwold
– may be summer pedestrian ferry, good
bedrooms (some in chalets), open all
day. *(Giles and Annie Francis, Alan Cowell, Alan
and Jill Bull, Terry Mizen, Mike and Sue Loseby
and others)*

WANGFORD   TM4679
Angel (01502) 578636
*Signed just off A12 by B1126 junction;
High Street; NR34 8RL* Handsome old
village coaching inn with light airy bar, good
value food from sandwiches up, pleasant
efficient service, Adnams, Black Sheep,
Brakspears and Greene King, decent wines,
family dining room; seven comfortable
bedrooms (the church clock sounds on the
quarter), good breakfast. *(Charles and
Pauline Stride)*

WESTLETON   TM4469
White Horse (01728) 648222
*Darsham Road, off B1125 Blythburgh–
Leiston; IP17 3AH* Comfortable and
friendly traditional pub with generous
straightforward food (not Tues) including
good value Sun roasts, four well kept Adnams
ales, unassuming high-ceilinged bar with
central fire, steps down to back dining room;
children welcome, picnic-sets in cottagey
back garden with climbing frame, more out
by village duck pond, three bedrooms, good
breakfast, open all day Fri and Sat, closed
Tues lunchtime. *(Stephen and Jean Curtis,
George Atkinson)*

WOODBRIDGE   TM2648
Cherry Tree (01394) 382513
*Opposite Notcutts Nursery, off A12;
Cumberland Street; IP12 4AG*
Comfortably worn-in open-plan pub with well
kept Adnams and guests, good wines by the
glass, reasonably priced pubby food including

breakfast, friendly service, beams and two log
fires, pine furniture, old local photographs
and aircraft prints; children welcome,
garden with play area, three good bedrooms
in adjoining barn conversion, open all day
weekends. *(MDN, Pat and Tony Martin)*

WOODBRIDGE   TM2748
Crown (01394) 384242
Thoroughfare; IP12 1AD Stylishly
refurbished 17th-c dining inn, well kept
Adnams and Meantime from glass-roofed
bar (boat suspended above counter), lots
of wines by the glass, good imaginative food
including fixed-price menu, pleasant young
staff, various eating areas with contemporary
furnishings, live jazz last Thurs of month;
courtyard tables, ten well appointed
bedrooms. *(J F M and M West)*

WOODBRIDGE   TM2749
Kings Head (01394) 387750
Market Hill; IP12 4LP Handsome
Elizabethan beams, flagstones and timbering
in nicely opened-up town bar, log fire in
massive central chimneybreast, enjoyable
home-made food in bar and dining room
down a couple of steps, Adnams ales, some
nice local pictures; background music;
disabled facilities, picnic-sets outside.
(Pat and Tony Martin)

WOODBRIDGE   TM2749
Olde Bell & Steelyard
(01394) 382933 *New Street, off
Market Square; IP12 1DZ* Ancient and
unpretentious timber-framed pub with
welcoming helpful licensees, two smallish
beamed bars and compact dining room,
lots of brassware, log fire, Greene King
ales and guests from canopied servery, real
ciders, enjoyable home-made food from bar
snacks up, traditional games including bar
billiards, live music; well behaved children
and dogs welcome, back terrace, steelyard
still overhanging street, open till late Fri and
Sat. *(Phil and Jane Hodson, BT)*

WOOLPIT   TL9762
Swan (01359) 240482
The Street; IP30 9QN Welcoming old
coaching inn pleasantly situated in village
square, heavy beams and painted panelling,
mixed tables and chairs on carpet, roaring
log fire one end, promptly served tasty bar
food, well kept Adnams from slate-top bar,
lots of wines by the glass; soft background
music; walled garden behind, four bedrooms
in converted stables. *(Jeremy King, J F M and
M West)*

Surrey

New pubs to look out for in this county are the Jolly Farmers in Buckland (interesting place that's part pub, part restaurant and part deli with carefully sourced ingredients for their inventive food), Crown in Chiddingfold (lovely old building with fine features carefully run by its hands-on owner), White Hart in Chipstead (civilised pub under the Brunning & Price umbrella with a fantastic choice of whiskies, and bistro-style food), and Running Horses at Mickleham (smashing all-rounder doing extremely well). Other places on top form are the Richard Onslow in Cranleigh (smart new bedrooms, a new courtyard garden and all-day food), Marneys in Esher (a surprisingly rural feel and good value meals in charming little pub), Seven Stars in Leigh (traditional and immaculately kept with tasty food), Red Lion at Shamley Green (in a pretty spot by the village green with popular food), and Inn at West End (amazing wine shop to browse around, lots of malt whiskies and enjoyable food). Our Surrey Dining Pub 2013 is the Running Horses in Mickleham.

BRAMLEY   TQ0044   Map 3

Jolly Farmer 🍺

High Street; GU5 0HB

Relaxed village inn near Surrey hills with great selection of beers

The traditional interior of this family-owned free house is filled with a homely miscellany of wooden tables and chairs, with collections of plates, enamel advertising signs, sewing machines, antique bottles, prints and old tools filling the walls and surfaces. Timbered semi-partitions, a mixture of brick and timbering and an open fireplace give it a snug, cosy feel The eight handpumps serve W J King Horsham Best alongside up to seven guests – they can go through up to 20 different ales a week – typically from brewers such as Ballards, Bowman, Langhams, Poachers and Sharps. They also keep six continental lagers, two ciders and up to 20 wines by the glass; background music and board games. There are tables out by the car park and the village is handy for Winkworth Arboretum and walks up St Martha's Hill.

🍴 As well as lunchtime sandwiches, bar food includes whitebait, salt and pepper baby squid with toasted ciabatta, smoked haddock fishcakes, ploughman's, home-made burger, fried cod fillet with citrus and saffron batter, pie of the day, with daily specials such as fried calves liver with red wine jus, fried duck breast with port and redcurrant sauce, mushroom risotto, chicken breast topped with bacon, barbecue sauce and cheese and fried bass with prawn and dill cream. *Benchmark main dish: fish and chips £11.00. Two-course evening meal £18.50.*

Free house ~ Licensees Steve and Chris Hardstone ~ Real ale ~ Bar food (12-2.30, 6 (7 Sun)-9.30) ~ Restaurant ~ (01483) 893355 ~ Children welcome ~ Dogs allowed in bar and bedrooms ~ Open 11-11; 12-11 Sun ~ Bedrooms: £65S/£70S ~ www.jollyfarmer.co.uk *Recommended by John Branston, Tim Chandler*

BUCKLAND   TQ2250   Map 3

Jolly Farmers

Reigate Road (A25 W of Reigate); RH3 7BG

Unusual place that sells and serves a wide range of local produce; fun to eat or shop in and atmospheric, too

Our readers enjoy their visits to this unusual venture, which is part pub, part restaurant and part delicatessen and serves some sort of food all day. The flagstoned bar is beamed and timbered with an informal, relaxed atmosphere, brown leather sofas and armchairs, Dark Star Hophead and Pilgrim Surrey Bitter on handpump, local wines and home-made cordials. A little brick fireplace separates the bar from the small wooden-floored dining room. The shop stretches across three little rooms and stocks fresh vegetables, deli meats, cheeses, cakes, chocolates and their own range of produce; they hold a weekly food market with stalls outside (Saturdays 9am-3pm) and organise several food festivals and events throughout the year. There are tables out on a back terrace overlooking the car park.

Using meticulously sourced local produce, the food starts with pastries and coffees from 9am with full breakfast at weekends. Later, there might be sandwiches, salad of shredded duck and fresh plum with an orange and Grand Marnier dressing and garlic-roasted sweetcorn, steamed mussels with garlic, white wine, sorrel and cream, beef burger with mozzarella and relish (you can add bacon, coleslaw, egg or blue cheese), sausages with mash and red onion and ale gravy, marrow stuffed with oyster mushroom and aubergine with a chive hollandaise and roasted beetroot, chicken with smoked bacon, savoy cabbage and tarragon beurre blanc, and specials such as crispy beef and pigs cheek with a honey and soy dressing and carrot and pak choi salad, and fish pie. *Benchmark main dish: vegetarian wellington £12.50. Two-course evening meal £19.50.*

Free house ~ Licensees Jon and Paula Briscoe ~ Real ale ~ Bar food (12-3, 5.30-9.30; breakfast 9.15-11.15am Sat, Sun; 12-9.30 Sat; 12-8.30 Sun) ~ Restaurant ~ (01737) 221355 ~ Children welcome ~ Dogs allowed in bar ~ Open 9.15am-11.30pm(10.30 Sun) ~ www.thejollyfarmersreigate.co.uk *Recommended by M G Hart, Gordon and Margaret Ormondroyd, Mr and Mrs J M Sennett, Derek Thomas*

CHIDDINGFOLD   SU9635   Map 2

Crown 🍺 🛏

The Green (A283); GU8 4TX

Lovely old inn by village green with several bars and dining rooms, fine old woodwork and stained glass windows, five real ales and enjoyable, fairly priced food; well equipped, comfortable bedrooms

The sense of history is strong here – based on a 13th-c hospice for Winchester monks on the pilgrimage to Canterbury, it's the oldest licensed house in Surrey and one of the oldest in the country. The bar and connected dining rooms (each just the right size for a private party) have massive beams – some over two feet thick – oak panelling, a magnificently carved inglenook fireplace and huge chimneys; do note the lovely stained glass windows. There are mates' and other pubby chairs, comfortable cushioned wall seats, leather dining chairs with wooden barley-twist arms around fine antique tables, and lots of portraits. The simple, two-level back public bar has an open fire. Fullers London Pride, Hogs Back TEA, Ringwood Bitter, Sharps Doom Bar and a guest beer on handpump and several wines by the glass; service is helpful and friendly. Seats outside look across the village green to the interesting church, and there are more tables in a sheltered central courtyard. The well equipped bedrooms have a great deal of character, with sloping floors and heavy beams, and several have four-posters.

Quite a choice of interesting food using the best local produce might include sandwiches, smoked trout and salmon terrine with dill and mustard, grilled tiger prawns on an oriental noodle salad with soy and sesame, sharing platters, home-made beefburger with cheese and bacon, a curry of the day, fishcake with herb crème fraîche, open ravioli of peas, asparagus and feta topped with a minted tomato salsa, rump of lamb with honey-roasted new potatoes and thyme jus, pork tenderloin medallions wrapped in serrano ham on a sun-dried tomato and basil mash with café crème sauce, and puddings such as plum and almond tart with ginger ice-cream and plum coulis and dark chocolate brownie with chocolate sauce. *Benchmark main dish: beer-battered fish and chips £12.00. Two-course evening meal £17.50.*

Free house ~ Licensee Daniel Hall ~ Real ale ~ Bar food (7am-10pm; breakfast is offered to non-residents) ~ Restaurant ~ (01428) 682255 ~ Children welcome ~ Dogs allowed in bar ~ Open 7am-11pm; 8am-11(10.30 Sun) Sat ~ Bedrooms: £100S/£145S ~ www.thecrownchiddingfold.com *Recommended by Richard Gibbs*

CHIPSTEAD

White Hart ♀

Hazelwood Lane; CR5 3QW

TQ2757 Map 3

Neatly kept 18th-c pub with antique tables and chairs in open-plan rooms, lots to look at, real ales and several wines by the glass, bistro-style food and friendly staff

Opposite rugby playing fields and with distant country views, this is a nicely kept pub with an informal, friendly atmosphere. The rooms are open plan with a raftered dining room to the right, elegant metal chandeliers, rough-plastered walls, an open fire in the brick fireplace and a couple of carved metal uprights. The central bar has stools at its panelled counter, where helpful, attentive staff serve Fullers London Pride, Harveys Sussex, Sharps Doom Bar and three guests from brewers such as Hepworth, Hopback and Tring from handpump, around 16 good wines by the glass and up to 80 malt whiskies; board games. The long room to the left is light and airy with lots of windows overlooking the seats on the terrace, some wall panelling at one end, and a woodburning stove. Throughout, there's a fine mix of antique dining chairs and settles around all sorts of tables (each set with a church candle), rugs on bare boards or flagstones, hundreds of interesting cartoons, country pictures, cricketing prints and rugby team photographs, large, ornate mirrors and, on the window sills and mantelpieces, old glass and stone bottles, clocks, books and plants.

🍴 As well as sandwiches, good food includes sweet potato and lentil soup, lobster, crayfish and grapefruit cocktail, fig and gorgonzola tart with chicory and walnut salad, kedgeree, crab, ginger and chilli linguine, shoulder of lamb with redcurrant and rosemary gravy, battered haddock, cajun salmon with citrus couscous, calves liver and bacon, sausage and mash, roast pork belly with roast apples and cider gravy, and puddings such as apple and rhubarb crumble, toffee and hazelnut cheesecake and bread and butter pudding with apricot sauce. *Benchmark main dish: steak burger £11.20. Two-course evening meal £20.00.*

Brunning & Price ~ Manager Damian Mann ~ Real ale ~ Bar food (12-10(9.30 Sun)) ~ Restaurant ~ (01737) 554455 ~ Children welcome ~ Dogs allowed in bar ~ Open 11.30-11; 12-10.30 Sun ~ www.brunningandprice.co.uk/whitehartchipstead *Recommended by C and R Bromage, Rob Hudson, Nick Kounoupias*

CRANLEIGH   TQ0539   Map 3

Richard Onslow 🍺

High Street; GU6 8AU

Busy pub with a good mix of customers in several bar rooms, friendly, efficient staff, real ales and interesting all-day food; bedrooms

Ten smart, well equipped bedrooms have been opened up in this busy town-centre pub, and there's a new terraced garden, too. They open at 7am for breakfasts and serve some kind of food all day, so there are always people popping in and out, which creates a lively atmosphere. The little public bar has stools by the counter, leather tub chairs and a built-in sofa, and a slate-floored drinking area where efficient and friendly staff serve Adnams Lighthouse, Purity Pure Ubu, Sharps Doom Bar and Surrey Hills Shere Drop on handpump, several wines by the glass and home-made summer lemonade and fresh lime soda. Two dining rooms have a mix of tartan tub chairs around wooden tables, a rather fine long leather-cushioned church pew, local photographs on mainly pale paintwork and a couple of open fires, one in a nice brick fireplace. The sizeable restaurant, with pale tables and chairs on the wooden floor and modern flowery wallpaper, has big windows overlooking the street; background music and board games. There are a few tables and chairs on the front pavement.

🍴 A good choice of interesting modern food might include sandwiches and wraps (served with chips or soup), various deli boards, free-range pork and pistachio terrine with pickled beetroot, potted crab with smoked paprika mayonnaise, courgette, pea and broad bean risotto, shredded duck with toasted cashew and roasted fig salad with raspberry vinaigrette, free-range sausages and mash, chilli and lime-spiked fishcake with salsa, cajun free-range chicken breast with sour cream, spicy potato wedges and corn on the cob, a daily roast, 28-day aged steak, and puddings such as Valrhona chocolate tart with orange curd and strawberry parfait with crushed meringue. *Benchmark main dish: beef and cheese burger £10.50. Two-course evening meal £19.00.*

Peach Pub Company ~ Licensee John Taylor ~ Real ale ~ Bar food (7am(7.30am weekends)-10pm) ~ Restaurant ~ (01483) 274922 ~ Children welcome ~ Dogs allowed in bar and bedrooms ~ Open 12-12(11 Sun) ~ www.therichardonslow.co.uk *Recommended by Justin Thomas*

The letters and figures after the name of each town are its Ordnance Survey map reference. *How to use the Guide* at the beginning of the book explains how it helps you find a pub, in road atlases or large-scale maps as well as in our own maps.

ESHER   TQ1566 Map 3

Marneys £

*Alma Road (one-way), Weston Green; heading N on A309 from A307
roundabout, after Lamb & Star pub turn left into Lime Tree Avenue (signposted to All
Saints Parish Church), then left at T junction into Chestnut Avenue; KT10 8JN*

Country-feeling pub with good value food and attractive garden

Cottagey and rather charming, this friendly little pub feels
surprisingly rural for the area and the front terrace has seats and
wooden tables and views over the wooded common, village church and
duck pond; there are more seats on the decked area in the pleasantly
planted sheltered garden. Inside, there are just two rooms. The small
snug bar has a low-beamed ceiling, Fullers London Pride, Sharps Doom
Bar and Wells & Youngs Bitter on handpump, about a dozen wines by
the glass and perhaps horseracing on the unobtrusive corner TV. To the
left, past a little cast-iron woodburning stove, a dining area has big pine
tables, pews, pale country kitchen chairs and cottagey blue-curtained
windows; background music. The pub is only a mile from Hampton
Court Palace.

Very reasonably priced and traditional, the food might include sandwiches and
filled baguettes, deep-fried camembert with redcurrant jelly, thai prawns with
a sweet chilli sauce, vegetable lasagne, sausages and mash with onion gravy, chilli
con carne, liver and bacon, and puddings such as warm chocolate fudge cake and
sticky toffee pudding. *Benchmark main dish: steak in ale pie £8.95. Two-course
evening meal £13.90.*

Free house ~ Licensee Thomas Duxberry ~ Real ale ~ Bar food (12-2.30(3 Sun),
6-9; not Fri-Sun evenings) ~ (020) 8398 4444 ~ Children welcome away from bar ~
Dogs welcome ~ Open 11-11; 12-10.30 Sun ~ www.marneys.com *Recommended by LM,
Ian Phillips, C and R Bromage, Jenny Smith, Simon Rodway*

LEIGH   TQ2147 Map 3

Seven Stars ♀

Dawes Green, South of A25 Dorking–Reigate; RH2 8NP

Popular country dining pub with enjoyable food and good wines

Always beautifully kept and homely, this tile-hung 17th-c tavern has
plenty of traditional atmosphere, and serves well kept beer and jolly
good food. The comfortable saloon bar has fine flagstones, beams, a 1633
inglenook fireback showing a royal coat of arms and dark wheelback
chairs, and there's a plainer public bar. Greene King Old Speckled
Hen, Fullers London Pride and Wells & Youngs Bitter are served from
handpump from the glowing copper counter, alongside decent wines
including about a dozen by the glass. The sympathetic restaurant
extension at the side incorporates 17th-c floor timbers from a granary.
Outside, there's plenty of room in the beer garden at the front, on the
terrace and in the side garden.

Post Office address codings confusingly give the impression that some pubs are in
Surrey when they're really in Hampshire or London (which is where we list them).
And there's further confusion from the way the Post Office still talks about Middlesex –
which disappeared in local government reorganisation nearly 50 years ago.

The nicely varied menu includes lunchtime ciabattas, breaded whitebait with caper and lemon mayonnaise, pâté of the day, chorizo and crayfish tail salad, mushroom, curry and rice, porcini ravioli in creamy parmesan sauce with mushrooms, leeks and peas, sausage and mash, battered cod, grilled monkfish with curried mussel sauce, chicken breast with mushroom and pea sauce, marinated pork chop with sweet potato chips and honey and sherry jus, and puddings such as treacle tart and crème brûlée. They do two sittings for Sunday lunch and tapas on Monday evenings; it's advisable to book at all times. *Benchmark main dish: home made burger £11.95. Two-course evening meal £21.00.*

Punch ~ Lease David and Rebecca Pellen ~ Real ale ~ Bar food (12-2.30(4 Sun), 6-9) ~ Restaurant ~ (01306) 611254 ~ Dogs allowed in bar ~ Open 12-3, 5.30-10.30(10 in winter); 12-11 Sat; 12-7.30 Sun; closed Sun evening ~ www.thesevenstarsleigh.co.uk
Recommended by Nick Lawless, M G Hart, Peter Loader, Mr and Mrs Price, LM, Simon and Mandy King,

MICKLEHAM TQ1753 Map 3
Running Horses
Old London Road (B2209); RH5 6DU
Surrey Dining Pub of the Year

Upmarket pub with elegant restaurant and comfortable bar, and food from sandwiches through to very imaginative smart dining

This terrific place is an accomplished all-rounder that's equally popular as a local drinking haunt, walkers' stop and graceful dining destination. The spacious bar is timelessly stylish with a cheerfully smart atmosphere, hunting pictures, racing cartoons and Hogarth prints, lots of race tickets hanging from a beam, fresh flowers or a fire in an inglenook at one end and cushioned wall settles and other dining chairs around straightforward pubby tables and bar stools. Fullers London Pride, Wells & Youngs Bitter, Sharps Doom Bar and a guest such as Shepherd Neame Spitfire are on handpump alongside good wines by the glass from a serious wine list; background music. The extensive restaurant is quite open to the bar and although set out fairly formally with crisp white cloths and candles on each table, it shares the relaxing atmosphere of the bar. A terrace in front with picnic sets and lovely flowering tubs and hanging baskets takes in a peaceful view of the old church with its strange stubby steeple. You may be asked to leave your credit card if you run a tab, and it's best to get here early, both to secure parking in the narrow lane (though you can park on the main road) and for a table. A notice by the door asks walkers to remove or cover their boots.

There's a tempting choice of food (not cheap but worth the extra) taking in traditional pubby meals and more elaborate dishes: shellfish bisque, smoked trout and salmon pâté with gravadlax dressing, devilled kidneys, welsh rarebit crostini with grilled peppers and ratatouille dressing, tomato, emmenthal and squash risotto, braised lamb shank with balsamic and burgundy, plaice fried in crayfish and lemon butter, roast partridge with red wine and mushroom liquor, seared tuna with seafood and white bean cassoulet, sausage and mash, steak, Guinness and mushroom pudding, fish pie and cottage pie. *Benchmark main dish: mussels £12.95. Two-course evening meal £26.00.*

Free house ~ Licensees Steve and Josie Slayford ~ Real ale ~ Bar food (12-2.30(3 Sat, Sun), 7-9.30; 6.30-9 Sun) ~ Restaurant ~ (01372) 372279 ~ No children under 10 in bar area ~ Dogs allowed in bar ~ Open 12-11.30(10.30 Sun) ~ Bedrooms: £95S(£110B)/£110S(£135B) ~ www.therunninghorses.co.uk *Recommended by LM, Tracey and Stephen Groves, Phil Bryant, N R White, Guy Vowles, Karen Eliot*

MILFORD

SU9542   Map 2

Refectory ♀

Portsmouth Road; GU8 5HJ

Handsome building with plenty of interest inside, beams, timbering, fine stone fireplaces and so forth, lots of room, real ales and well liked food

The interesting interior of this most attractive golden stone and timbered building – thought to have been cattle barn and a tea and antique shop – feels extremely spacious. It's essentially L-shaped and mainly open plan, with strikingly heavy beams, lots of timbering, exposed stone walls, stalling and standing timbers creating separate seating areas and a couple of big log fires in handsome stone fireplaces. A two-tiered and balconied part at one end has a wall covered with huge brass platters; the rest of the walls are hung with some nice old photographs and a variety of paintings. Dining chairs and dark wooden tables are grouped on the wooden, quarry-tiled or carpeted floor and there are rugs, bookshelves, big pot plants, stone bottles on window sills and fresh flowers. High wooden bar stools line the long counter where they serve Hogs Back TEA, Phoenix Brunning & Price and four guests from brewers such as Adnams, Andwell and Hammerpot from handpump, around 16 wines by the glass and around 80 malt whiskies. There are teak tables and chairs in the back courtyard adjacent to the characterful pigeonry.

As well as a good range of sandwiches, the popular food might include celeriac and rosemary soup, seared scallops with parma ham, butternut squash purée and roast pumpkin, indian spiced lentil and bean croquettes with ginger dhal, steamed pheasant pudding with honey roast and cinnamon sauce, prawn and spinach linguine, duck breast with pink peppercorn sauce, jamaican jerk pork belly with baked rice and sweet potato, and puddings such as stem ginger cheesecake with orange cream, bakewell tart and bread and butter pudding. *Benchmark main dish: pie of the day £11.95. Two-course evening meal £19.00.*

Brunning & Price ~ Manager Katie Dallyn ~ Real ale ~ Bar food (12-10(9.30 Sun)) ~ (01483) 413820 ~ Children welcome ~ Dogs welcome ~ Open 11.30-11; 12-10.30 Sun ~ www.brunningandprice.co.uk/refectory *Recommended by Richard Gibbs*

SHAMLEY GREEN

TQ0343   Map 3

Red Lion

The Green; GU5 0UB

Pleasant dining pub with tasty food and nice gardens

In fine weather there's plenty of outside seating both at the back of this friendly pub, where there are hand-made rustic tables and benches on a heated terrace and a lawn, and at the front, which overlooks the village green and cricket pitch. Inside, it's fairly traditional with real fires in its two connected bars, a mix of new and old wooden tables, chairs and cushioned settles on bare boards and red carpet, stripped standing timbers, fresh white walls and deep red ceilings; background music. They serve Youngs, a couple of guests such as Ringwood Fortyniner and Sharps Doom Bar, and over a dozen wines by the glass.

Good, popular food includes sandwiches, crispy duck salad with orange, watercress and hoi sin dressing, chicken liver pâté with onion marmalade, honey-roast ham and eggs, beer-battered fish and chips, wild mushroom lasagne, chicken with cider sauce, asparagus and broad beans, salmon in a white wine sauce topped with caramelised scallops, lamb shank in red wine and redcurrant sauce, and specials such as calves liver with pancetta and lyonnaise potatoes and beef bourguignon. *Benchmark main dish: steak in ale pie £12.95. Two-course evening meal £20.00.*

Punch ~ Lease Debbie Ersser ~ Real ale ~ Bar food (12-2.30(3 Sat, Sun), 6.30-9.30(8.30 Sun); not winter Sun evening) ~ Restaurant ~ (01483) 892202 ~ Children welcome ~ Dogs allowed in bar ~ Open 11.30-11; 12-10.30 Sun ~ www.redlionshamleygreen.com *Recommended by Richard Gibbs*

 THURSLEY   SU9039 Map 2

Three Horseshoes

Dye House Road, just off A3 SW of Godalming; GU8 6QD

Civilised country village pub with a broad range of good food

Well placed for heathland walks – ask at the bar for a walking map – this is a pretty tile-hung pub jointly owned by a consortium of villagers who rescued it from closure. It has the feel of a gently upmarket country local. The convivial beamed front bar has a winter log fire, Hogs Back TEA and a guest such as Sharps Doom Bar or Surrey Hills Shere Drop on handpump, a farm cider and perry; background music. The art on the walls in the dining room is for sale. Tables in the attractive two-acre garden take in pleasant views over Thursley Common and Thursley's 1,000-year-old Saxon church. On the terrace are smart comfortable chairs around tables with parasols. A separate area has a big play fort, a barbecue and a charcoal spit-roast that they use on bank holidays. Visiting dogs and horses might get offered a biscuit or carrot.

 Using produce supplied by customers and other local ingredients, the interesting food might include sandwiches, terrine of rabbit, pigeon, wild mushrooms and bacon with piccalilli, baked brie with smoked chilli jam, a vegetarian risotto, chargrilled chicken caesar salad, gammon with free-range eggs, pork and leek sausages with mash and fried onions, pollack fillet with pea purée and avocado oil, confit duck leg with black pudding and goose fat beans, and puddings like blackberry jelly with vanilla ice-cream and sticky toffee pudding with clotted cream. *Benchmark main dish: lambs liver and bacon £9.50. Two-course evening meal £21.50.*

Free house ~ Licensees David Alders and Sandra Proni ~ Real ale ~ Bar food (12.15-2.15, 7-9; 12-3; no food Sun evening) ~ Restaurant ~ (01252) 703268 ~ Well behaved children welcome ~ Dogs allowed in bar ~ Open 12-3, 5.30-11; 12-11 Sat; 12-8 Sun ~ www.threehorseshoesthursley.com *Recommended by Tony and Jill Radnor, Ellie Weld, David London, Richard Williams, Arthur Snell, Hunter and Christine Wright, John Branston, Martin and Karen Wake, Kate Funnell, Nicky Lee*

WEST END   SU9461 Map 2

Inn at West End

Just under 2.5 miles from M3 junction 3; A322 S, on right; GU24 9PW

Clean-cut dining pub with prompt friendly service, excellent wines, popular food and pretty terrace

Around 500 wines, mostly from Spain and Portugal, are now stocked in the wine shop here, and the landlord holds regular tastings. At least 15 are served in three sizes of glass, and there are quite a few sherries, sweet wines and ports, too. The pub is open plan and café-like with bare boards, attractive modern prints on canary-yellow walls above a red dado, and a line of dining tables with crisp white linen over pale yellow tablecloths on the left. The bar counter, with Fullers London Pride and a guest such as Exmoor Ale on handpump, and around 30 whiskies, is straight ahead as you come in, with chatting regulars perched on the comfortable bar stools. The area on the right has a pleasant relaxed atmosphere, with blue-cushioned wall benches and dining chairs around solid pale wood tables, broadsheet daily papers, magazines and a row of reference books on the brick chimneybreast above an open fire. This leads into a garden room, which in turn opens on to a terrace shaded by a grapevine- and clematis-covered pergola, and a very pleasant garden; boules.

Using village-reared pork, game shot by the landlord and their own vegetables, the inventive food might include sandwiches, potted smoked trout with home-made dill bread, horseradish and crème fraîche, beetroot carpaccio with goats cheese, hazelnuts and honey and lemon dressing, cumberland pork sausages with caramelised onion and red wine sauce, maize-fed chicken with gratin potatoes, cranberry compote and a garlic and herb sauce, malaysian-style prawn and coconut curry with pak choi and sambal, slow-braised game in juniper and red wine with braised red cabbage, and puddings such as dark chocolate brownie with quince poached in red wine and rice pudding with caramelised apples. *Benchmark main dish: kedgeree £10.95. Two-course evening meal £25.25.*

Enterprise ~ Lease Gerry and Ann Price ~ Real ale ~ Bar food (12-2.30, 6-9.30; 12-3, 6-9 Sun) ~ Restaurant ~ (01276) 858652 ~ Children welcome if seated and dining ~ Dogs allowed in bar ~ Open 12-3, 5-11; 11-11 Sat; 12-10.30 Sun ~ www.the-inn.co.uk
Recommended by Ian Phillips, Alan Bowker, Ian Herdman, Sheila Topham, Rosemary and Mike Fielder, Gerald and Gabrielle Culliford, Edward Mirzoeff, Sarah May-Miller, David and Sue Smith, Peter Veness, David and Ruth Shillitoe, David and Katharine Cooke

Also Worth a Visit in Surrey

Besides the fully inspected pubs, you might like to try these pubs that have been recommended to us and described by readers. Do tell us what you think of them: feedback@goodguides.com

ABINGER COMMON   TQ1146
Abinger Hatch (01306) 730737
Off A25 W of Dorking, towards Abinger Hammer; RH5 6HZ Modernised dining pub in beautiful woodland spot, good popular food (not Sun evening) from light dishes up, friendly staff (service charge added), Adnams, Ringwood, Sambrooks and Skinners, heavy beams and flagstones, log fires, pews forming booths around oak tables in carpeted side area, plenty of space; background music, plain family extension; dogs welcome, some disabled access, tables in nice garden, near pretty church and pond, summer barbecues, open all day. *(Ian Phillips, R G Glover, R C Vincent)*

ALBURY HEATH   TQ0646
William IV (01483) 202685
Little London, off A25 Guildford–Dorking – OS Sheet 187 map ref 065468; GU5 9DG Country local with big log fire in rustic low-beamed flagstoned bar, good

straightforward food (not Sun evening) using local produce including landlord's free-range pork, Hogs Back, Surrey Hills and Wells & Youngs, restaurant area up steps; well behaved children welcome, dogs in bar, picnic-sets in front garden, good walks, open all day weekends. *(Phil Bryant)*

ALFOLD   TQ0435
Alfold Barn (01403) 752288
Horsham Road, A281; GU6 8JE Beautifully preserved 16th-c building with bar and restaurant, good locally sourced food including bargain lunchtime deal (Tues-Thurs, noon-1pm), good friendly service, up to three well kept ales from nearby breweries, beams and rafters, mixed furniture on flagstones or carpet, warming log fires; children welcome, garden with play area and animals including a goat called Rosie, closed Sun evening, Mon. *(Shirley Mackenzie, George James, Tony and Wendy Hobden, Lois Dyer)*

ASH VALE   SU8952
Swan (01252) 325212
Hutton Road, off Ash Vale Road (B3411)
via Heathvale Bridge Road; GU12 5HA
Welcoming three-room Chef & Brewer on
Basingstoke Canal, wide choice of generous
well priced food all day including specials,
prompt smiling service, ales such as Fullers
London Pride and Surrey Hills Shere Drop,
good value wines by the glass, mix of furniture
on tiles or carpet, large log fires; background
music; children welcome, attractive garden,
neat heated terraces and window-boxes, open
all day. *(KC)*

BANSTEAD   TQ2659
Mint (01737) 362785
Park Road, off High Street towards
Kingswood; SM7 3DS Rambling Vintage
Inn, low beams and flagstones, dimly lit
cosy areas, friendly helpful staff, good value
food including lunch deals, real ales and
good choice of wines by the glass; children
welcome. *(Maureen and Keith Gimson)*

BETCHWORTH   TQ1950
Arkle Manor (01737) 842110
Reigate Road; RH3 7HB Smart M&B
dining pub with enjoyable gently upscale food,
attractive rambling layout with easy chairs
and so forth, real ales, good choice of wines by
the glass, friendly service; may ask to keep a
credit card while running a tab.
(C and R Bromage, John Evans)

BETCHWORTH   TQ2149
Dolphin (01737) 842288
Off A25 W of Reigate; The Street;
RH3 7DW 16th-c village pub on Greensand
Way, plain tables on ancient flagstones in neat
front bar with inglenook log fire, snug and a
further panelled bar with chiming grandfather
clock, nice old local photographs, well kept
Wells & Youngs ales, traditional fairly priced
food (all day weekends), helpful service,
restaurant; children and dogs welcome, front
and side terraces, back garden, picturesque
village (fine Pre-Raphaelite pulpit in church),
open all day. *(C and R Bromage, M G Hart,*
Conor McGaughey)

BETCHWORTH   TQ2150
Red Lion (01737) 843336
Old Road, Buckland; RH3
7DS Comfortable dining pub with good
sensibly priced home-made food, friendly
helpful staff, Adnams, Fullers London Pride
and Sharps Doom Bar, rather old-fashioned
carpeted bar with dark wood furniture,
restaurant; children welcome, picnic-sets
on lawn with cricket ground beyond, dining
terrace, good bedrooms in separate modern
block, open all day. *(Phil Bryant)*

BLETCHINGLEY   TQ3250
Red Lion (01883) 743342
Castle Street (A25), Redhill side;

RH1 4NU Old beamed village dining pub
with fresh modern décor, well spaced tables,
lots of racing prints, good reasonably priced
mainly traditional food (all day), friendly
helpful staff, well kept Greene King ales,
good choice of wines by the glass, monthly
quiz and some live music; no children after
6pm, tables under umbrellas on heated
terrace, secret garden. *(Geoffrey Kemp, John*
Branston, R K Phillips)

BLINDLEY HEATH   TQ3645
★ Red Barn (01342) 830820
Tandridge Lane, just off B2029, which
is off A22; RH7 6LL Splendid farmhouse/
barn conversion; contemporary furnishings
mixing with 17th-c beams and timbers,
central glass-sided woodburner – chimney
soaring up into roof, large model plane
hanging from rafters, one wall with shelves
of books, another hung with antlers, clever
partitioning creating cosier areas too; red
cooking range and big wooden tables in
farmhouse-style room, adjacent bar with
sofas by large fireplace, bar billiards, one
or two real ales and good wine list, well
liked food efficiently served by smart staff;
background and some live music; children
welcome, dogs in bar, solid granite tables
on lawn, farmer's market first Sat of month,
open all day. *(Colin and Louise English,*
Grahame Brooks, Derek Thomas, N R White, Peter
Loader and others)

BROCKHAM   TQ1949
Inn on the Green (01737) 845101
Brockham Green; RH3 7JS Comfortably
refurbished dining pub facing village green,
enjoyable if not cheap food from traditional
things up including steaks cooked on a hot
stone, well kept Adnams, Black Sheep and
Fullers London Pride, conservatory; children
welcome, picnic-sets out at front, garden
behind. *(C and R Bromage)*

BROCKHAM   TQ1949
Royal Oak (01737) 843241
Brockham Green; RH3 7JS Nice spot
opposite fine church on charming village
green below North Downs, refurbished bare-
boards bar and expanded dining area, well
kept Sharps and Wells & Youngs, enjoyable
standard food, genuinely friendly service;
children and dogs welcome, garden.
(N R White)

BROOK   SU9238
Dog & Pheasant (01428) 682763
Haslemere Road (A286); GU8
5UJ Popular pub looking across busy road
to cricket green, friendly landlord, long bar
divided up by standing timbers, heavy beams,
open fire in brick fireplace, cushioned wall
settles, Adnams Southwold, Sharps Doom
Bar, Ringwood Best and Addlestone's cider
from nice linenfold counter, dining area on
right, room to left with big inglenook log
fire and pubby furniture, well liked fairly

traditional food, tapas and quiz nights; children welcome, picnic-sets on back decking and grass, play equipment, open all day. *(Anon)*

BYFLEET   TQ0661
Plough (01932) 353257
High Road; KT14 7QT Small pub with good range of changing ales, usually simple food from sandwiches to three or four bargain hot dishes lunchtime and Weds evening, friendly service, two log fires, rustic furnishings, farm tools, brass and copper, dominoes, more modern back area, sociable cat, no mobiles; terrace and small shady back garden. *(Ian Phillips)*

CARSHALTON   TQ2764
Hope (020) 8240 1255
West Street; SM5 2PR Community pub saved from closure by local consortium; seven well kept changing ales (regular festivals), real ciders and perry, generous pubby food (limited evening choice), bar billiards, open fire, friendly chatty atmosphere; open all day. *(Mark Franks, Leslie Button)*

CHARLESHILL   SU8844
Donkey (01252) 702124
B3001 Milford–Farnham near Tilford; coming from Elstead, turn left as soon as you see pub sign; GU10 2AU Old-fashioned beamed dining pub with quick friendly service, enjoyable home-made food and good choice of wines by the glass, well kept ales such as Fullers, Greene King and Harveys, traditional games, conservatory restaurant; children and dogs welcome, attractive garden with wendy house, two much-loved donkeys, good walks, open all day Sun. *(Sally Kerr)*

CHERTSEY   TQ0367
Coach & Horses (01932) 563085
St Anns Road; KT16 9DG Unspoilt Fullers local with particularly well kept London Pride, good value home-made weekday food, cheerful barman; three bedrooms, open all day (till 8pm Sun). *(Hunter and Christine Wright)*

CHIPSTEAD   TQ2757
Ramblers Rest (01737) 552661
Outwood Lane (B2032); CR5 3NP M&B country dining pub with contemporary furnishings and cocktail-bar décor in partly 14th-c rambling building, panelling, flagstones, low beams and log fires, enjoyable up-to-date and more traditional food including popular Sun lunch, real ales and interesting continental beers, Aspall's cider, good value wines by the glass, young friendly staff, daily newspapers; children and dogs welcome, disabled access (from front) and facilities, big pleasant garden with terrace, attractive views, good walks, open all day. *(John Branston, C and R Bromage, Sheila Topham, Maureen and Keith Gimson)*

CHIPSTEAD   TQ2555
Well House (01737) 830640
Chipstead signed with Mugswell off A217, N of M25 junction 8; CR5 3SQ Partly 14th-c, cottagey and comfortable with log fires in all three rooms, good choice of well kept ales such as Dorking, Hammerpot and Surrey Hills, food from baguettes up (not Sun evening), bric-a-brac above bar, pewter tankards hanging from ceiling, conservatory; dogs allowed (they have cats), large attractive hillside garden with well reputed to be mentioned in Domesday Book, delightful setting. *(Conor McGaughey)*

CHOBHAM   SU9761
Sun (01276) 857112
High Steet, off A319; GU24 8AF Congenial low-beamed timbered pub, spotless inside with shining brasses, Courage and Timothy Taylors Landlord, pizzas and other bargain food, friendly staff, daily newspapers, woodburner, live jazz. *(Ian Phillips)*

CHURT   SU8538
Crossways (01428) 714323
Corner A287 and Hale House Lane; GU10 2JE Friendly down-to-earth local, quarry-tiled public bar and carpeted saloon with panelling and plush banquettes, busy evenings for great changing beer range at reasonable prices, also four or more real ciders, good well priced home-made pub lunches (not Sun) including nice pies, evening food Weds only (mainly fish and chips), cheerful young staff; TVs and machines; dogs welcome, garden, open all day Fri, Sat. *(Phil Bryant, Emily Murphy)*

CLAYGATE   TQ1663
Griffin (01372) 463799
Common Road; KT10 0HW Properly old-fashioned Victorian village local, well kept ales including Fullers London Pride, some interesting dishes along with usual pub food freshly cooked and reasonably priced. *(Gordon Stevenson)*

CLAYGATE   TQ1563
Hare & Hounds (01372) 465149
The Green; KT10 0JL Renovated flower-decked Victorian/Edwardian village pub with small restaurant, good sensibly priced french food, nice wines and competent service; outside seating at front and in small back garden. *(Tom and Ruth Rees, Nick Stafford)*

COBHAM   TQ1058
Cricketers (01932) 862105
Downside Common; 3.75 miles from M25 J10; A3 towards Cobham, first right on to A245, right at Downside signpost into Downside Bridge Road, follow road into its right fork – away from Cobham Park – at second turn after bridge, then eventually turn into the pub's own lane, immediately before Common

crossroads; *KT11 3NX* Worth visiting
for its idyllic terrace views across village
green; open-plan room areas much in need of
redecoration, though lots of character with
crooked standing timbers, low oak beams
(some with crash pads), wide oak ceiling
boards and ancient plastering laths, log fire,
Fullers, Sharps Doom Bar and Surrey Hills
Shere Drop, bar food (poor recent reports,
and they ask for your credit card if running
a tab); background music; children and dogs
welcome, neatly kept garden (AstroTurf at
front), pretty hanging baskets, open all day
(till 1am Fri, Sat). *(Ian Phillips, Rosemary and
Mike Fielder)*

COLDHARBOUR   TQ1544
Plough (01306) 711793
*Village signposted in the network of
small roads around Leith Hill; RH5 6HD*
Cosy two-bar pub with own-brewed Leith
Hill ales and guests, Biddenden cider,
several wines by the glass, pleasant service,
open fires, light beams and timbering, snug
games room with darts, board games and
cards, food in bar and evening restaurant
(Tues-Sat) specialising in steaks (not cheap);
background music, TV; children welcome if
eating, dogs in bar, front terrace and quiet
back garden overlooking fields, five bedrooms
(ones above bar noisy), open all day.
(N R White)

COMPTON   SU9546
Harrow (01483) 810594
*B3000 towards Godalming off A3;
GU3 1EG* Refurbished 18th-c roadside pub
doing well under present licensees, split level
log-fire bar, beamed dining area, emphasis
on good value-for-money pub food (not Sun
evening), three real ales and good choice
of wines by the glass, friendly attentive
service; children welcome, back terrace and
streamside garden, open all day. *(Anon)*

COMPTON   SU9646
⋆Withies (01483) 421158
*Withies Lane; pub signed from B3000;
GU3 1JA* Carefully altered 16th-c pub,
charmingly civilised and gently old-
fashioned, with low-beamed bar, some 17th-c
carved panels between windows, splendid art
nouveau settle amongst old sewing-machine
tables, log fire in massive inglenook, Adnams,
Greene King and a guest, popular (not
cheap) bar food served by efficient, helpful
bow-tied staff; children welcome, seats on
terrace, under apple trees and creeper-hung
arbour, flower-edged neat front lawn, on edge
of Loseley Park and close to Watts Gallery,
closed Sun evening. *(Gerald and Gabrielle
Culliford, Brian Glozier, Ian Herdman, Helen
and Brian Edgeley, Conor McGaughey, Colin
McKerrow and others)*

DORMANSLAND   TQ4042
Plough (01342) 832933
Plough Road, off B2028 NE; RH7 6PS

Friendly traditional old pub in quiet village,
well kept Fullers, Harveys and Sharps,
Weston's cider, decent wines, good choice
of enjoyable bar food including specials
board, thai restaurant, log fires and original
features; children welcome, disabled
facilities, good-sized garden. *(Richard
Redgrove, David Clarke, Mark Kingsley-Monks)*

DUNSFOLD   TQ0036
Sun (01483) 200242
Off B2130 S of Godalming; GU8 4LE
Elegantly double-fronted pub with four rooms
(brighter at the front), beams and some
exposed brickwork, scrubbed pine furniture,
inglenook log fire, ales such as Adnams,
Harveys and Sharps, decent wines, enjoyable
home-made food at reasonable prices; seats
out on terrace and overlooking quiet village
green. *(Robert A Watson)*

EASHING   SU9543
⋆Stag (01483) 421568
*Lower Eashing, just off A3 southbound;
GU7 2QG* Gently refurbished, civilised
riverside pub with Georgian façade masking
much older interior; attractively opened-up
rooms including charming old-fashioned
locals' bar with armchairs on red and black
quarry tiles, cosy log-fire snug beyond, Hogs
Back, Surrey Hills and a beer brewed for
them by Marstons, good choice of enjoyable
food served by attentive courteous staff,
several linked dining areas including river
room up a couple of steps looking out on to
mature trees by millstream; dogs allowed in
bar, extensive terrace with wicker or wooden
furniture under parasols (some by weir),
picnic-sets on grass, seven bedrooms, open
all day. *(Anon)*

EAST CLANDON   TQ0551
⋆Queens Head (01483) 222332
*Just off A246 Guildford–Leatherhead;
The Street; GU4 7RY* Refurbished
dining pub in same small group as Duke of
Cambridge at Tilford, good food from light
dishes up including set deals (Mon-Thurs),
well kept Hogs Back, Ringwood and Surrey
Hills from fine elm-topped counter, good
friendly service, comfortable linked rooms,
log fire in big inglenook; children welcome,
tables out in front and on new side terrace,
handy for Clandon Park and Hatchlands
(both NT), open all day Fri, Sat and till 9pm
Sun. *(Richard Tilbrook, John Evans,
John Allman)*

EFFINGHAM   TQ1153
⋆Plough (01372) 458121
Orestan Lane; KT24 5SW Popular Youngs
pub with consistently well kept ales from
traditional bar, good choice of enjoyable food
including Sun roasts, plenty of wines by the
glass, nice staff, two coal-effect gas fires,
beamery, panelling, old plates and brassware
in long lounge, carpeted floors; plenty of
tables on forecourt and in attractive garden

with fruit trees, disabled parking, handy for Polesden Lacey (NT). *(Shirley Mackenzie, P G Topp)*

ELLENS GREEN   TQ0936
Wheatsheaf (01403) 822155

B2128 N of Rudgwick; RH12 3AS Dining pub under new spanish couple, good food and service, Badger ales, decent wines by the glass, tiled-floor bar with large fireplace, dining areas either side; seats in front and on back terrace, has been open all day. *(Shirley Mackenzie)*

ELSTEAD   SU9044
Mill at Elstead (01252) 703333

Farnham Road (B3001 just W of village, which is itself between Farnham and Milford); GU8 6LE Fascinating largely 18th-c four-storey mill with internal turning waterwheel, big window views of charming River Wey setting, rambling linked bar areas on spacious ground floor, four Fullers beers, useful all day food including Sun carvery, upstairs restaurant with brown leather armchairs and neat modern furniture on dark woodstrip flooring, also big country tables on broad ceramic tiles, iron pillars and stripped masonry, log fire in huge inglenook; background music; children welcome, dogs in bar, picnic-sets dotted around by lovely millpond, swans and weeping willows, all floodlit at night. *(Peter Scott, Rosemary and Mike Fielder, Gordon Stevenson, Ian Wilson, P G Topp)*

ENGLEFIELD GREEN   SU9771
Sun (01784) 432515

Wick Lane, Bishopsgate; TW20 0UF Well used, beamed local, Courage Best, Sharps Doom Bar and Wells & Youngs Special kept well, good blackboard wine choice, generous inexpensive pubby food from sandwiches up, friendly service, small wooden tables with banquettes and low stools, lots of pub bric-a-brac including interesting beer bottle collection, colourful photographs, daily newspapers, open fire, conservatory; soft background music; children welcome, biscuits and water for dogs, a few tables out at front and in quiet garden, handy for Savill Garden and Windsor Park. *(Ian Phillips)*

EPSOM   TQ2158
Rubbing House (01372) 745050

Langley Vale Road (on Epsom racecourse); KT18 5LJ Popular restauranty dining pub with attractive modern décor, good value food promptly served even when busy, tables perhaps a little close together, Fullers London Pride and Greene King IPA, serious wine list, fantastic racecourse views, upper balcony; background music; tables outside. *(Ian Wilson, Maureen and Keith Gimson)*

ESHER   TQ1264
Prince of Wales (01372) 465483

West End Lane; off A244 towards Hersham, by Princess Alice Hospice; KT10 8LA Busy Chef & Brewer dining pub in lovely village setting by green and duck pond, wide choice of reasonably priced food all day, Fullers London Pride and other well kept ales, good wine choice, friendly efficient staff; background music; children welcome, disabled access, big garden. *(Ian Wilson, Geoffrey Kemp, Tom and Ruth Rees)*

FOREST GREEN   TQ1241
★ Parrot (01306) 621339

B2127 just W of junction with B2126, SW of Dorking; RH5 5RZ Genuinely aged village pub with cheerful atmosphere, heavy beams, timbers, flagstones and nooks and crannies hidden away behind inglenook, generous helpings of well liked food (not Sun evening) using produce from own farm, five well kept changing ales including Ringwood, 16 wines by the glass, local juice, efficient friendly service; shop selling own meat, cheeses, cured hams, pies and so forth; dogs welcome in bar, disabled facilities, attractive gardens with lovely country views, good walks nearby, open all day (till midnight Sat). *(Shirley Mackenzie, Guy Vowles, Alan and Shirley Sawden, Tom and Ruth Rees, K Chard, Chris Jackson and others)*

FRIDAY STREET   TQ1245
Stephan Langton (01306) 730775

Off B2126; RH5 6JR Prettily placed 1930s pub in tucked-away hamlet, enjoyable well presented food (if a little pricey), ales including Fullers and Surrey Hills, log fire in bar, woodburner in large modern dining area; children and dogs welcome, smart seating at front, wooded setting with pond, good nearby walks. *(Ian Phillips, N R White, Jill Hurley, Martin and Karen Wake)*

GODALMING   SU9643
Star (01483) 417717

Church Street; GU7 1EL Friendly 17th-c local in cobbled pedestrian street, cosy low-beamed and panelled L-shaped bar, eight well kept changing ales (four tapped from the cask) including Greene King, farm ciders/perries, lunchtime bar food, more modern function room; heated back terrace, open all day. *(Tony Hobden)*

GODSTONE   TQ3551
Bell (01883) 743216

Under a mile from M25 junction 6, via B2236; RH9 8DX Handsome old M&B family dining pub, comfortably modern furnishings and lighting in heavily beamed open-plan areas including small conservatory, good up-to-date and more traditional food, midweek fixed price menu (till 7pm), well kept ales and decent choice of wines by the glass, good friendly service, three open fires;

terrace and garden seating. *(Grahame Brooks, Mr and Mrs A Curry, Keith Sangster)*

GOMSHALL   TQ0847
Compasses (01483) 202506
A25; GU5 9LA Popular village pub with plain bar and much bigger comfortable dining room, good value home-made food (all day apart from Sun evening), well kept Surrey Hills ales, decent wines by the glass, friendly helpful service; background and Fri live music – also 'Gomstock' festival in Aug; children welcome, pretty garden sloping down to roadside mill stream. *(Alan and Shirley Sawden, Mark Percy, Lesley Mayoh, N R White)*

GRAYSWOOD   SU9134
Wheatsheaf (01428) 644440
Grayswood Road (A286 NE of Haslemere); GU27 2DE Welcoming dining pub with light airy décor, enjoyable food in bar and restaurant, good range of well kept beers, friendly helpful service; front verandah, side terrace, conference/bedroom extension, good breakfast. *(Anon)*

GUILDFORD   SU9949
Kings Head (01483) 575004
Quarry Street; GU1 3XQ Dating from the 16th-c with lots of beams and stripped brickwork, cosy corners with armchairs, stylish oval tables, inglenook log fire, well kept Hogs Back and guests, decent wines, enjoyable reasonably priced food (not Sun evening) including variety of burgers and pizzas, quiz-and-curry night Mon, friendly young staff; background music (live Weds and Sun), fruit machine, sports TV, no dogs inside; picnic-sets in pleasant back courtyard with roof terrace giving castle views, open all day (till 3am Fri and Sat). *(Phil and Jane Villiers)*

GUILDFORD   SU9948
Olde Ship (01483) 575731
Portsmouth Road (St Catherine's, A3100 S); GU2 4EB Three cosy areas around central bar, ancient beams, bare boards and flagstones, roaring log fire in big fireplace, woodburner the other end, comfortable mix of furniture, enjoyable food including good wood-fired pizzas, well kept Greene King ales with a guest such as Hydes, decent wines, friendly service. *(Ian Phillips)*

HAMBLEDON   SU9639
Merry Harriers (01428) 682883
Off A283; just N of village; GU8 4DR Popular beamed country local with huge inglenook log fire and pine tables on bare boards, five real ales and decent wines, enjoyable generous pub food from sandwiches up, friendly staff, beer festivals and live music; children welcome, big garden with boules, llamas and wandering chickens, attractive walking country near Greensand Way, three bedrooms in converted barn, campsite. *(Phil Bryant)*

HASCOMBE   TQ0039
White Horse (01483) 208258
B2130 S of Godalming; GU8 4JA 16th-c origins with beams and small-windowed alcoves, ales from Harveys, Otter and Wychwood, interesting wines by the glass, good variety of food from sandwiches and snacks up, friendly young staff, bar on right with scrubbed tables and pews on wood floor, carpeted lounge on left with dining areas off, woodburner, resident dogs; small front terrace, spacious sloping back lawn, pretty village with good walks, handy for Winkworth Arboretum (NT), open all day. *(Martin and Karen Wake, Mr and Mrs A H Young)*

HOLMBURY ST MARY   TQ1144
✳ Kings Head (01306) 730282
Pitland Street; RH5 6NP Friendly bare-boards pub in walking country (leave muddy boots in porch), enjoyable home-made food including a couple of good vegetarian choices, well kept changing ales such as Arundel, Hammerpot, Surrey Hills and Pilgrim, real cider, good wines by the glass, two-way log fire, small traditional back restaurant, public bar with darts, bar billiards and TV; children and dogs welcome, pretty spot with seats out facing green, more in big sloping back garden, open all day weekends, closed Mon. *(N R White, Save Dore, Phil Bryant, Tom and Ruth Rees)*

HOLMBURY ST MARY   TQ1044
Royal Oak (01306) 730120
Felday Road; RH5 6PF Low-beamed 17th-c coaching inn, enjoyable food from baguettes to some interesting specials, helpful staff, well kept ales and decent wine by the glass, log fire; tables in neat front garden, pleasant spot by green and church, good walks, bedrooms. *(Phil Bryant)*

HORSELL   SU9859
Cricketers (01483) 762363
Horsell Birch; GU21 4XB Country local popular for its good sensibly priced food, Shepherd Neame ales, cheerful efficient service, log fire, quietly comfortable end sections, extended back eating area, carpet and shiny boards, newspapers; no dogs; children welcome, picnic-sets out in front and in big garden, wide views over Horsell Common. *(Ian Phillips)*

HORSELL   SU9959
Plough (01483) 714105
Off South Road; Cheapside; GU21 4JL Small friendly local overlooking wooded heath, relaxed atmosphere, up to six well kept changing ales, three ciders, good choice of wines by the glass and of malt whiskies, reasonably priced fresh food (all day Sat, not Sun evening) including fine range of home-made pies and vegetarian options, quiet dining area one side of L, games machines and TV the other, daily newspapers,

woodburner; children and dogs welcome, tables in pretty garden with play area, open all day. *(David M Smith, Harry Roy, Ian Phillips)*

HORSELL   SU9959
★ Red Lion (01483) 768497
High Street; GU21 4SS Large and very popular with light airy feel, split level bar with comfortable sofas and easy chairs, clusters of pictures on cream-painted walls, Courage Best, Fullers London Pride and a guest from long wooden servery, a dozen wines by the glass, dining room with exposed brick walls, old pews and blackboards listing the good bistro-style food, efficient service; children allowed till early evening, ivy-clad passage to garden and comfortable tree-sheltered terrace, good walks, open all day. *(Ian Phillips, Nigel and Sue Foster, Simon Collett-Jones)*

HORSELL COMMON   TQ0160
★ Sands at Bleak House
(01483) 760717 *Chertsey Road, The Anthonys; A320 Woking–Ottershaw; GU21 5NL* Smart contemporary restauranty pub, grey split sandstone for floor and face of bar counter, brown leather sofas and cushioned stools, two dining rooms with dark wood furniture, good if not cheap food, Andwell, Hogs Back and Surrey Hills, fresh juices, friendly attentive uniformed staff, woodburners, daily newspapers; background jazz, TV, lively acoustics; smokers' marquee in courtyard with picnic-sets, good shortish walks to sandpits which inspired H G Wells's *War of the Worlds*, seven bedrooms, open all day, till 8pm Sun. *(Ian Phillips, Harry Roy)*

IRONS BOTTOM   TQ2546
Three Horseshoes (01293) 862315
Sidlow Bridge, off A217; RH2 8PT Welcoming roadside pub with good home-made food from pub favourites up, Fullers, Harveys, Wells & Youngs and three interesting guests, good friendly service, traditional furnishings including upholstered banquettes, dark wood and patterned carpet, some barrel tables, darts; tables outside, summer barbecues, handy for Gatwick. *(C and R Bromage, LM)*

LALEHAM   TQ0568
★ Three Horseshoes (01784) 455014
Shepperton Road (B376); TW18 1SE Spacious airy bar with white walls and contrasting deep-blue woodwork, easy going mix of furniture on bare boards, well kept Fullers/Gales beers, over a dozen wines by the glass, smarter dining areas with grey woodwork and caramel leather chairs, popular food all day, friendly attentive young staff (they ask to keep a credit card while you eat); background music – live first Fri of month; children welcome in restaurant till 7.00pm, tables on flagstoned terrace, picnic-sets on grass, near pleasant stretch of the Thames. *(Phil Bryant, Geoffrey Kemp,*

M Ross-Thomas, Hunter and Christine Wright, Nigel and Sue Foster and others)

LIMPSFIELD   TQ4053
Bull (01883) 713402
High Street; RH8 0DR Comfortably refurbished village pub dating from the 16th c, welcoming helpful staff, good food including some imaginative choices from regularly changing menu, reasonably priced wines, Westerham and a guest ale, lovely log fire; occasional sports TV; well behaved children welcome, dogs in bar, tables out on back decking, closed Sun evening. *(Grahame Brooks, Christine and Neil Townend, Stella Morris)*

LINGFIELD   TQ3844
★ Hare & Hounds (01342) 832351
Turn off B2029 N at the Crowhurst Street/Edenbridge signpost; RH7 6BZ Smallish open-plan bar, bare boards and flagstones, mixed seating including button-back leather chesterfield, dining area, very good wide-ranging food from french landlord including fixed price lunchtime menu (Mon-Sat), friendly efficient service, well kept ales such as Greene King IPA and Harveys and decent wines by the glass; children and dogs welcome, tables in pleasant split-level garden with decking, good walking country near Haxted Mill – leave boots in porch, open all day, closed Sun evening. *(Chris Parkins, Malcolm Lee, Paul Nash and Colin Rugless, Peter and Michael Lee)*

MARTYRS GREEN   TQ0857
Black Swan (01932) 862364
Handy for M25 junction 10; off A3 S-bound, but return N of junction; KT11 1NG Chunky seating and spacious contemporary restauranty décor (utterly changed from its days as the 'Slaughtered Lamb' in An American Werewolf in London), good freshly made food, grand choice of wines and champagnes, several real ales including Sharps Doom Bar and Surrey Hills Shere Drop, friendly efficient service, log fire and under-floor heating; children welcome, stylish black slate furniture out on extensively landscaped terrace, open all day. *(Sue and Mike Todd)*

MERSHAM   TQ3051
Inn on the Pond (01737) 643000
Nutfield Marsh Road, off A25 W of Godstone; RH1 4EU Popular dining pub with enjoyable interesting food (all day Sun) including children's meals, well kept changing ales such as Hogs Back, Weston's cider, good choice of wines by the glass, comfortable casually contemporary dining room, back conservatory; sheltered terrace behind, views over pond and nearby cricket ground to North Downs. *(Peter Eyles)*

MICKLEHAM   TQ1753
King William IV (01372) 372590
Just off A24 Leatherhead–Dorking;

Byttom Hill; RH5 6EL Steps up to small nicely placed country pub, well kept Hogs Back TEA, Surrey Hills Shere Drop and Triple fff Alton's Pride, wide choice of enjoyable food including blackboard specials and good vegetarian options, friendly service, pleasant outlook from snug plank-panelled front bar; background music, outside gents'; children welcome, plenty of tables (some in heated open-sided timber shelters) in lovely terraced garden with great valley views, closed evenings Sun and Mon.
(LM, Phil Bryant, Jack and Sandra Clarfelt, John Coatsworth)

NEWDIGATE   TQ2043
❋ **Surrey Oaks** (01306) 631200
Off A24 S of Dorking, via Beare Green; Parkgate Road; RH5 5DZ Friendly village pub (known as the Soaks), well kept Harveys, Surrey Hills and three guests from smaller brewers (beer festivals May and Aug), bottled continentals and farm cider/perry, well liked reasonably priced bar food (not Sun or Mon evenings), open fire in snug beamed room, standing area with large flagstones and inglenook woodburner, rustic tables in light airy main lounge, separate games room with pool, skittle alley; piped classical music, TV and machines; children and dogs welcome, garden with terrace, rockery (pools and waterfall), play area and two boules pitches, open all day Sun. *(Donna Huggins, John Branston, Peter Dandy, C and R Bromage, N R White, Graham and Elizabeth Hargreaves and others)*

OCKLEY   TQ1440
Inn on the Green (01306) 711032
Billingshurst Road (A29); RH5 5TD Welcoming 17th-c coaching inn on green of charming village, good fresh traditional food, well kept Greene King and a guest like Kings Horsham, friendly attentive service, slightly dated décor with usual pubby furniture, steps up to quiet eating area and dining conservatory; tables in secluded garden, six comfortable bedrooms, good breakfast.
(Phil Bryant, Steve Tilley)

OCKLEY   TQ1337
❋ **Punchbowl** (01306) 627249
Oakwood Hill, signed off A29 S; RH5 5PU Attractive 16th-c tile-hung country pub with Horsham slab roof, friendly landlord, welcoming relaxed atmosphere, wide choice of good value generously served food (all day weekends) including deals, Badger ales, central bar with huge inglenook, polished flagstones and low beams, collections of brass spiles, horsebrasses and cigarette lighters, restaurant area to left and another bar to right with a couple of sofas and armchairs and TV, daily newspapers; children welcome and dogs (water bowl and biscuits), picnic-sets in pretty garden, smokers' awning, quiet spot with good walks including Sussex Border Path. *(Phil Bryant, Pam Adsley, C and R Bromage)*

OTTERSHAW   TQ0263
❋ **Castle** (01932) 872373
Brox Road, off A320 not far from M25 junction 11; KT16 0LW Friendly two-bar early Victorian local with big crackling log fires, country paraphernalia on black ceiling joists and walls, well kept Greene King, Harveys, Sharps and Timothy Taylors, Addlestone's cider, enjoyable bar food (not Sun evening); background music, TV; children welcome in conservatory till 7pm, dogs in bar, tables on terrace and grass, open all day. *(Ian Phillips)*

OUTWOOD   TQ3246
❋ **Bell** (01342) 842989
Outwood Common, just E of village; off A23 S of Redhill; RH1 5PN Attractive extended 17th-c country pub/restaurant, smartly rustic beamed bar with oak and elm furniture (some in Jacobean style), low beams and vast stone inglenook, Fullers ales, decent wines by the glass and large range of liqueurs, enjoyable generous food (all day Sun) including plenty of fish; background music, Tues quiz; children and dogs welcome, garden with nice country views, play area, handy for windmill, open all day. *(M G Hart, Chris Bell)*

OUTWOOD   TQ3146
Dog & Duck (01342) 842964
Prince of Wales Road; turn off A23 at station sign in Salfords, S of Redhill – OS Sheet 187 map reference 312460; RH1 5QU Unhurried beamed country pub with good home-made food in bar or restaurant, welcoming service, well kept Badger ales from brick-faced bar, decent wines, warm winter fires, monthly quiz and live music nights; children welcome, garden with duck pond and play area. *(Sally Cullen, Richard Tilbrook)*

OXTED   TQ4048
Royal Oak (01883) 722207
Caterfield Lane, Staffhurst Wood, S of town; RH8 0RR Popular well managed pub, cheerful and comfortable, with good range of beers inc Adnams, Harveys and Larkins, Biddenden cider, good value house wines, enjoyable locally sourced food including some imaginative dishes, back dining room; dogs welcome, nice garden with lovely views across fields, open all day weekends. *(William Ruxton, N R White, Simon Rodway)*

PIRBRIGHT   SU9454
Royal Oak (01483) 232466
Aldershot Road; A324S of village; GU24 0DQ Tile-hung Tudor pub with well kept Greene King ales and Hogs Back TEA, good range of wines by the glass, well priced pubby food from sandwiches and sharing boards up, friendly helpful service, three log fires, heavily beamed and timbered rambling side areas, ancient stripped brickwork,

family room; soft background music; disabled facilities, picnic-sets in extensive gardens, good walks, open all day. *(Anon)*

PUTTENHAM   SU9347
Good Intent (01483) 810387
Signed off B3000 just S of A31 junction; The Street/Seale Lane; GU3 1AR Well worn in convivial beamed village local, good choice of well kept changing ales with regulars like Otter, Sharps and Timothy Taylors, popular reasonably priced traditional food (not Sun evening), log fire in cosy front bar with alcove seating, newspapers, old photographs of the pub, simple dining area; children and dogs welcome, small sunny garden, good walks, open all day weekends. *(N R White, John Mitchell)*

PYRFORD LOCK   TQ0559
Anchor (01932) 342507
3 miles from M25 junction 10 – S on A3, then take Wisley slip road and go on past RHS garden; GU23 6QW Light and airy Badger family dining pub (can get very busy), food all day (small helpings available), lunchtime sandwiches too, simple tables on bare boards, quieter more comfortable panelled back area, narrow-boat memorabilia, pleasant oak-framed conservatory, daily newspapers; dogs allowed in part, splendid terrace in lovely spot by bridge and locks on River Wey Navigation, fenced-off play area, handy for RHS Wisley, open all day. *(D Crook, Mervyn Granshaw, C and R Bromage, Ian Phillips)*

REDHILL   TQ2750
Garland (01737) 760377
Brighton Road; RH1 6PP Smartly kept 19th-c Harveys corner local, their full range including seasonals in good condition, well priced simple weekday bar food from doorstep sandwiches up, dim lighting, darts and bar billiards, regular quiz nights; open all day. *(Tony Hobden)*

REDHILL   TQ2850
Home Cottage (01737) 762771
Redstone Hill; RH1 4AW Stylishly refurbished Youngs pub serving food all day – reports please. *(Anon)*

REIGATE   TQ2551
Yew Tree (01737) 244944
0.5 miles from M25 junction 8; Reigate Hill (A217); RH2 9PJ Improved under current management; comfortable oak-panelled bar with log fire, good choice of enjoyable food from lunchtime snacks up, well kept Sharps Doom Bar, Wells & Youngs and a guest, restaurant; children and dogs welcome, split-level paved garden behind, open all day. *(Mike Gorton)*

REIGATE HEATH   TQ2349
Skimmington Castle (01737) 243100
Off A25 Reigate–Dorking via Flanchford

Road and Bonny's Road; RH2 8RL* Nicely located small country pub, emphasis on enjoyable home-made food, ales such as Adnams and St Austell, panelled beamed rooms, big working fireplace; children and dogs welcome. *(C and R Bromage)*

RIPLEY   TQ0455
Jovial Sailor (01483) 224360
Portsmouth Road; GU23 6EZ Large Chef & Brewer, popular and cheerfully run, with decent reasonably priced food, four well kept changing ales and good wine choice, reconstructed well divided interior with standing timbers, beams, stripped brickwork and log fires, country bric-a-brac, daily newspapers; background music; good-sized garden, handy for Wisley. *(Ian Phillips)*

RIPLEY   TQ0456
Seven Stars (01483) 225128
Newark Lane (B367); GU23 6DL Neat family-run traditional 1930s pub, enjoyable food from extensive menu, ales such as Brakspears, Fullers, Hogs Back and Shepherd Neame, good wines and coffee, snug areas, gleaming brasses, open fire; quiet background music; picnic-sets and heated wooden booths in large tidy garden, river and canalside walks, closed Sun evening. *(Ian Phillips, Gordon Stevenson)*

RIPLEY   TQ0556
Ship (01483) 225371
High Street; GU23 6AZ Change to: Compact 16th-c local, two low-beamed front rooms, one with log fire in vast inglenook, nautical-theme carpet, well kept Courage, Fullers, Greene King and Hogs Back, lunchtime food; dogs welcome, small high-walled terrace. *(Hunter and Christine Wright, Ian Phillips)*

SEND MARSH   TQ0455
✳ Saddlers Arms (01483) 224209
Send Marsh Road; GU23 6JQ Genial and attentive licensees in unpretentious low-beamed local, homely and warm, with Fullers London Pride, Sharps Doom Bar, and a couple of guests, good value generous home-made food (Sun till 4pm) from sandwiches to pizzas and pubby favourites, log effect gas fire, sparkling brassware, toby jugs, etc; children and dogs welcome, picnic-sets out in front and behind, open all day. *(Shirley Mackenzie, DWAJ, Ian Phillips)*

SHALFORD   SU9946
Parrot (01483) 561400
Broadford Road; GU4 8DW Big warmly welcoming pub with wide range of popular freshly-made food from interesting menu, Fullers London Pride, Sharps Doom Bar and Surrey Hills Shere Drop, good service, rows of neat pine dining tables, some easy chairs around low tables, pleasant conservatory; children welcome till 8pm, attractive garden, five bedrooms, handy for Loseley Park. *(C and R Bromage, Sue and Mike Todd)*

SHALFORD TQ0047

✳ **Seahorse** (01483) 514350

A281 S of Guildford; The Street;
GU4 8BU Gently upmarket M&B dining pub
with wide range of food from simple to more
sophisticated choices, popular fixed-priced
menu (weekday lunchtimes, early evenings),
friendly well trained young staff, Hogs Back
TEA, good choice of wines and other drinks,
good contemporary furniture and artwork,
smart dining room, comfortable part near
entrance with sofas and huge window; picnic-
sets in big lawned garden, covered terrace,
open all day. *(MDN, Malcolm and Carole Lomax,
Mr and Mrs A H Young)*

SHEPPERTON TQ0765

Thames Court (01932) 221957

Shepperton Lock, Ferry Lane; turn left
off B375 towards Chertsey, 100 metres
from Square; TW17 9LJ Huge Vintage
Inn dining pub well placed by Thames, good
choice of wines by the glass, well kept ales
such as Fullers London Pride, usual well
priced food all day from sandwiches to good
Sun roasts, galleried central atrium with
attractive panelled areas up and down stairs,
two good log fires, daily newspapers; can get
very busy weekends; children welcome, large
attractive tree-shaded terrace with heaters,
open all day. *(Brian Glozier)*

SHERE TQ0747

William Bray (01483) 202044

Shere Lane; GU5 9HS Emphasis on
good well presented locally sourced food,
ales such as Hogs Back, Sharps and Surrey
Hills, decent choice of wines, roomy
contemporary bar with stone floor and
woodburner, more formal airy restaurant
with comfortable leather chairs and large
F1 racing photographs (owner was driver
for Tyrell and Lotus); very busy weekends;
dogs welcome, tables on front split-level
terrace, pretty landscaped garden. *(Tracey*
and Stephen Groves, Terry Buckland, Ian Phillips,
John Allman)

SOUTH GODSTONE TQ3549

Fox & Hounds (01342) 893474

Tilburstow Hill Road/Harts Lane, off
A22; RH9 8LY Pleasant old tile-hung
country pub with woodburner in low-beamed
bar, wholesome good value food, well kept
Greene King ales from tiny bar counter,
inglenook restaurant; children and dogs
welcome, garden (may be bouncy castle),
open all day. *(C and R Bromage)*

STAINES TQ0371

Bells (01784) 454240

Church Street; TW18 4ZB Comfortable
well looked after Youngs pub in old part of
town, their ales in good condition and decent
choice of wines, good food and service,
central fireplace; tables in nice back garden
with heated terrace. *(David M Smith)*

STAINES TQ0371

Swan (01784) 452494

The Hythe; south bank, over Staines
Bridge; TW18 3JB Splendid Thames-
side setting, with moorings, good tables
on riverside verandah and terrace, big
conservatory, several distinctly different
areas including river-view upstairs
restaurant, enjoyable food from sandwiches
up, prompt friendly service, well kept Fullers
ales; can be very busy Sun lunchtime and on
summer evenings; comfortable bedrooms,
open all day. *(Ross Balaam)*

STOKE D'ABERNON TQ1259

Old Plough (01932) 862244

Station Road, off A245; KT11 3BN Nicely
refurbished 300-year-old pub under same
ownership as the Red Lion at Horsell and
Three Horseshoes at Laleham; enjoyable
all-day food, Fullers and a guest like Surrey
Hills, plenty of wines by the glass; children
welcome in restaurant till 7.30pm, dogs in
bar, seats out under pergola and in attractive
garden. *(Lorry Spooner)*

SUNBURY TQ1068

Flower Pot (01932) 780741

1.6 miles from M3 junction 1; follow
Lower Sunbury sign from exit
roundabout, then at Thames Street turn
right; pub on next corner, with Green
Street; TW16 6AA New management for
this popular 18th-c inn near the Thames and
closed for refurbishment as we went to press
– reports please.

SUTTON ABINGER TQ1045

Volunteer (01306) 730798

Water Lane; just off B2126 via Raikes
Lane, 1.5 miles S of Abinger Hammer;
RH5 6PR Picturesque family-run pub in
attractive setting above clear stream, low-
ceilinged linked rooms, log fires, Badger ales,
enjoyable standard food from sandwiches
up, good friendly service, restaurant; terrace
and sun-trap lawns stepped up behind, nice
walks. *(John Ecklin, Gill Hancock)*

SUTTON GREEN TQ0054

✳ **Olive Tree** (01483) 729999

Sutton Green Road; GU4 7QD Big
rambling dining pub in quiet countryside,
good honest fresh food (not Sun or Mon
evenings), cheaper bar menu including
sandwiches, fireside leather sofas, relaxing
back dining room, bare boards and clean-cut
pastel décor, well kept Fullers London Pride,
Ringwood and Timothy Taylors Landlord,
good choice of wines by the glass, pleasant
helpful staff; terrace tables. *(Katherine Tonks,*
Ian Phillips)

TADWORTH TQ2355

Dukes Head (01737) 812173

Dorking Road (B2032 opposite Common
and woods); KT20 5SL Roomy and

comfortably refurbished, popular for its well priced food all day (not Sun evening), five well kept ales including a local microbrew, Aspall's cider, good choice of wines by the glass, helpful jolly staff, two big inglenook log fires; background music; lots of hanging baskets and plenty of tables in well looked after garden, open all day. *(Gwyn Harries, C and R Bromage)*

THAMES DITTON   TQ1567
Albany   (020) 8972 9163

Queens Road, signed off Summer Road; KT7 0QY M&B bar-with-restaurant in lovely Thames-side position, light airy modern feel, with good variety of food from sharing plates and pizzas to more upscale dishes, weekday fixed-price menu lunchtime and early evening, good choice of wines by the glass, cocktails, a couple of beers such as Sharps Doom Bar and Timothy Taylors Landlord, log fire, river pictures, daily newspapers; nice balconies and river-view terrace, moorings, open all day. *(Tom and Ruth Rees, Katherine Tonks, Jennie George)*

THAMES DITTON   TQ1666
Ferry   (020) 8398 1581

Portsmouth Road; KT7 0XY Welcoming and relaxed bistro-style dining pub with good reasonably priced food from chef/landlord, well kept ales; some tables out at front. *(Tim Grey, Tom and Ruth Rees)*

THAMES DITTON   TQ1667
✶ **Olde Swan**   (020) 8398 1814

Summer Road; KT7 0QQ Large refurbished riverside pub (one of very few listed Grade I), enjoyable well priced food, Greene King and three guests, good friendly service, one long bar with three good-sized areas, log fires, upstairs restaurant overlooking quiet Thames backwater; children and dogs welcome, moorings and plenty of waterside tables, outside summer bar, open all day. *(Jacqui Boulton, John Ecklin, Richard and Sissel Harris)*

THORPE   TQ0268
Rose & Crown   (01483) 762363

Sandhills Lane, Thorpe Green; TW20 8QL Part of the small Barons group, spacious with discrete nooks and crannies, Fullers London Pride, St Austell Tribute, Sharps Doom Bar and Wadworths 6X, good choice of fairly priced food, friendly efficient service; children welcome, smart outside eating area, garden play area. *(Ian Phillips, Gerry and Rosemary Dobson)*

TILFORD   SU8743
Barley Mow   (01252) 792205

The Green, off B3001 SE of Farnham; also signed off A287; GU10 2BU Opposite pretty cricket green, with woodburner in snug little low-ceilinged traditional bar, nice scrubbed tables in two small rooms set for food on left, interesting cricketing prints and old photographs, well kept ales and imaginative wine list, pubby food, darts and table skittles; children and dogs welcome, narrow front terrace, picnic-sets in back garden fenced off from Wey tributary, open all day in summer (all day Fri-Sun winter). *(Rosemary and Mike Fielder)*

TILFORD   SU8742
Duke of Cambridge   (01252) 792236

Tilford Road; GU10 2DD Civilised smartly done pub in same small local group as Queens Head at East Clandon, enjoyable food with emphasis on local ingredients from varied interesting menu, children's meals too, good choice of wines, Hogs Back TEA and Surrey Hills Shere Drop, efficient helpful service; terrace and garden with picnic-sets, good play area, open all day weekends. *(Martin and Karen Wake, Mike and Jayne Bastin)*

VIRGINIA WATER   SU9968
Rose & Olive Branch

(01344) 843713   *Callow Hill; GU25 4LH* Small unpretentious pub, with good choice of popular food including speciality pies, gluten-free and children's choices too, three Greene King ales, decent wines, friendly busy staff; background music; tables on front terrace and in garden behind, good walks. *(Ian Phillips, D J and P M Taylor)*

WALLISWOOD   TQ1138
Scarlett Arms   (01306) 627243

Signed from Ewhurst-Rowhook back Road, or off A29 S of Ockley; RH5 5RD Cottagey 16th-c village pub with low beams, flagstones, simple furniture and two log fires (one in big inglenook), Badger ales, well priced traditional food plus some malaysian dishes, back dining room; background music; children and dogs welcome, tables in front, more in garden under parasols, good walks, closed Sun evening, Mon. *(Phil Bryant)*

WALTON ON THE HILL   TQ2255
Blue Ball   (01737) 812168

Not far from M25 junction 8; Deans Lane, off B2220 by pond; KT20 7UE Large cleanly refurbished pub facing common near duck pond, good choice of home-made food served by friendly uniformed staff, several real ales and decent wines, restaurant (open all day Sun) overlooking big garden, pleasant atmosphere, popular with families at weekends; good walking area. *(Pam Adsley, N R White)*

WALTON-ON-THAMES   TQ0966
Anglers   (01932) 223996

Riverside, off Manor Road; KT12 2PF Roomy gastro pub on Thames towpath, peaceful tables outside, good if pricy food, changing real ales, plenty of bare-boards floor area, large first-floor river-view room. *(Martin and Karen Wake)*

WALTON-ON-THAMES   TQ1065
Ashley Park (01932) 220196
*Station Approach/Ashley Park Road;
KT12 1JP* Comfortable well run Ember
Inn with good reasonably priced food all
day, interesting choice of well kept ales,
competent friendly service, good atmosphere;
bedrooms in next door Travelodge.
(Ian Phillips)

WALTON-ON-THAMES   TQ1068
Weir (01932) 784530
*Towpath, Waterside Drive off Sunbury
Lane; KT12 2JB* Edwardian pub in
nice Thames-side spot with big terrace
overlooking river and weir (and steel
walkway), decent choice of food all day
(till 7.30pm Sun) from snacks up, ales such
as Greene King, Sharps and Woodfordes,
traditional décor, river pictures, newspapers;
dogs and children welcome, lovely towpath
walks, six bedrooms. *(Ian Phillips)*

WEST CLANDON   TQ0451
☆ Bulls Head (01483) 222444
A247 SE of Woking; GU4 7ST
Comfortable, spotless and unchanging,
based on 1540s timbered hall house, popular
especially with older people lunchtime for
good value straightforward food including
proper home-made pies (no food Sun
evening), friendly helpful staff, ales such
as Sharps, Surrey Hills and Wells & Youngs,
good coffee, small lantern-lit beamed front
bar with open fire and some stripped brick,
old local prints and bric-a-brac, hops, simple
raised back inglenook dining area, games
room with darts and pool; children and dogs
on leads welcome, disabled access from car
park, good play area in neat garden, good
walks, handy for Clandon Park. *(DWAJ, Ian
Phillips, Ron and Sheila Corbett, Richard and
Sissel Harris)*

WEST CLANDON   TQ0452
Onslow Arms (01483) 222447
A247 SE of Woking; GU4 7TE Fully
refurbished, partly 17th-c beamed country
pub (same owners as Red Lion at Horsell
and Three Horseshoes at Laleham), good
food from traditional choices up, ales such
as Harveys, Hop Back and Ringwood, friendly
efficient service, leather sofas by big log fire,
live music Weds; children (till early evening)
and dogs welcome, terrace and garden
seating, open all day. *(Tim Grey, DWAJ,
M Ross-Thomas, Patrick Spence, Geoffrey Kemp,
Ian Phillips and others)*

WEST HORSLEY   TQ0853
☆ Barley Mow (01483) 282693
*Off A246 Leatherhead–Guildford at
Bell & Colvill garage roundabout; The
Street; KT24 6HR* Welcoming tree-shaded
traditional pub, low beams, mix of flagstones,
bare boards and carpet, leather sofas, two
log fires, well kept ales such as Fullers

London Pride, Greene King IPA, Surrey
Hills and Wells & Youngs, decent wines,
fairly priced food (not Sun evening) from
lunchtime sandwiches up, daily newspapers,
vintage and classic car pictures, comfortable
softly lit barn-like dining room; unobtrusive
background music, TV; children welcome,
dogs on leads, picnic-sets in good-sized
garden, open all day. *(John Branston, Norma
and Noel Thomas)*

WEYBRIDGE   TQ0763
Hand & Spear (01932) 828063
Old Heath Road/Station Road; KT13 8TX
Big popular Youngs pub (former Edwardian
station hotel) with several different areas,
enjoyable generous food including some
unusual choices, their ales and a guest, good
friendly staff; seats outside. *(Anne Rowe,
Ian Phillips)*

WEYBRIDGE   TQ0864
Jolly Farmer (01932) 856873
Princes Road; KT13 9BN Attractive little
low-beamed local opposite picturesque
cricket ground, friendly efficient service,
good value pubby food from sandwiches
up, well kept ales such as St Austell, Hop
Back, Ringwood and Sharps, good choice of
wines by the glass, toby jugs and interesting
old photographs; may be loud live music
weekends; largely covered front terrace, nice
back garden. *(Hunter and Christine Wright,
Ian Phillips)*

WEYBRIDGE   TQ0765
Minnow (01932) 831672
Thames Street/Walton Lane; KT13 8NG
Busy M&B dining pub, contemporary pastel
décor and unusual decorative panels, chunky
tables and chairs on gleaming flagstones,
some sofas and armchairs, two-way log fire in
raised hearth, popular food including pizzas,
pasta and traditional dishes, ales such as
Fullers, Timothy Taylors and Wells & Youngs,
good wines by the glass, friendly service;
children welcome, big front terrace with
heaters, open all day. *(Ian Phillips)*

WEYBRIDGE   TQ0965
Oatlands Chaser (01932) 253277
Oatlands Chase; KT13 9RW Big
attractively modernised building in quiet
residential road, rambling bar with stylish
modern décor, pastels and unusual wallpaper,
glazed panels, flagstones and painted
boards, central feature fireplace, carefully
mismatched furnishings mainly laid out
for the wide range of enjoyable all-day
food from light lunches to Sun roasts and
proper children's meals, good service, three
well kept changing ales, good wine choice,
newspapers; disabled access, lots
of tables out at front (some under trees),
19 bedrooms. *(Katherine Tonks, Minda and
Stanley Alexander, Ian Phillips)*

★ **Old Crown** (01932) 842844
Thames Street; KT13 8LP Comfortably old-fashioned three-bar pub dating from the 16th c, good value traditional food (not Sun-Tues evenings) from sandwiches to fresh fish, well kept Courage, Greene King and Wells & Youngs, good choice of wines by the glass, friendly efficient service, family lounge and conservatory, coal-effect gas fire; may be sports TV in back bar with Lions RFC photographs, silent fruit machine; children welcome, secluded terrace, smokers' shelter, steps down to suntrap garden overlooking Wey/Thames confluence, mooring for small boats. *(DWAJ, Ian Phillips, James Barratt)*

WEYBRIDGE TQ0664
Queens Head (01932) 847103
Bridge Road; KT13 8XS Refurbished 18th-c pub owned by Raymond Blanc's White Brasserie Company, emphasis on dining but also a proper bar serving Fullers and Sharps, friendly staff; children under six eat free, open all day. *(Ian Phillips)*

WINDLESHAM SU9464
Brickmakers (01276) 472267
Chertsey Road (B386, W of B383 roundabout); GU20 6HT Smart bistro-feel dining pub with enjoyable fresh seasonal food, flagstones, pastel colours and different areas, one room with sofas and low tables, Courage Best, Fullers London Pride and Sharps Doom Bar, good choice of wines by the glass and nice coffee, friendly helpful service, log fire, conservatory; well behaved children allowed, attractive courtyard with flower-filled pergola, open all day Fri-Sun. *(Sarah May-Miller)*

WINDLESHAM SU9363
Half Moon (01276) 473329
Church Road; GU20 6BN Much extended and mainly laid for pubby food from sandwiches up, well kept ales such as Fullers, Hogs, Ringwood, Timothy Taylors and Theakstons, Weston's cider, plenty of children's drinks, log fires, World War II pictures and modern furnishings, barn restaurant out along covered flagstoned walkway; background music, silenced games machine; big tidy garden with two terraces and play area. *(Dr Martin Owton, Bertil Nygren, Ian Herdman)*

WOKING TQ0058
Herbert Wells (01483) 722818
Chertsey Road; GU21 5AJ Wetherspoons named after H G Wells, busy with shoppers yet with lots of cosy areas and side snugs, eight well kept ales, three ciders, usual well priced food all day, friendly helpful staff, daily newspapers, old local pictures; open

from 8am. *(Tony Hobden, Harry Roy, Ian Phillips)*

WOKING TQ0158
Inn at Maybury (01483) 722115
Maybury Hill/Old Woking Road (B382); GU22 8AB Popular refurbished Victorian dining pub with wide food range from sharing plates and pizzas up, weekday fixed-price menu till 7pm, good wine choice, Hogs Back TEA and Sharps Doom Bar, helpful friendly uniformed staff, log fire, conservatory; no dogs; children welcome, disabled facilities, plenty of outside tables, open all day. *(Ian Phillips)*

WOOD STREET SU9550
White Hart (01483) 235939
White Hart Lane; off A323 just W of Guildford; GU3 3DZ Smartly modernised 17th-c country dining pub, good if not cheap food from open kitchen, good choice of wines by the glass; a couple of picnic-sets out at front, peaceful spot tucked away off green, open all day. *(Richard Chinn)*

WORPLESDON SU9753
White Lyon & Dragon (01483) 698440 *A322 Guildford–Bagshot; GU3 3RE* Recently refurbished roadside pub, good authentic thai food along with traditional pub choices, well kept Hogs Back and Hook Norton; open all day. *(John Coatsworth)*

WOTTON TQ1247
Wotton Hatch (01306) 732931
A25 Dorking-Guildford; RH5 6QQ Stylish modern M&B roadside dining pub, real ales, continental beers and good choice of wines from imposing zinc-topped bar, popular food including standard and more adventurous dishes, log fire in 17th-c core, daily newspapers, conservatory; no dogs; children welcome, neat garden with impressive views, good local walks, open all day. *(Guy Vowles)*

WRECCLESHAM SU8344
Bat & Ball (01252) 792108
Bat & Ball Lane, South Farnham; approach from Sandrock Hill and Upper Bourne Lane then narrow steep lane to pub; GU10 4SA Neatly refurbished pub tucked away in hidden valley, wide range of pubby and more upmarket food (small helpings available) including good puddings display, well kept Bowman, Hogs Back and four guests (June beer festival), good choice of wines by the glass, friendly efficient staff, some live music; children and dogs allowed, disabled facilities, tables out on attractive heated terrace with vine arbour and in garden with substantial play fort, open all day. *(Anon)*

Sussex

This is where we work and live and so we know many of the best pubs in this popular county rather well. We're pleased to find as new entries or to welcome back places that had dropped out of the *Guide* but are back under new licensees, the Fountain in Ashurst (16th-c pub with smashing food and pretty garden), Six Bells in Chiddingly (busy local, very cheap food), Royal Oak at Chilgrove (an honest country pub with friendly long-serving licensees), Royal Oak at East Lavant (pretty cottage and handy for Goodwood), Star at Heathfield (lots of character in fine old pub), Hollist Arms in Lodsworth (spic and span with good, popular food), George in Robertsbridge (hands-on licensees, local ales and nice to stay at), Ypres Castle in Rye (informal décor and in an interesting spot under the tower ramparts), White Horse at Sutton (handy for Bignor Roman Villa with smart bedrooms and well thought of meals), Horse Guards in Tillington (18th-c inn serving delicious food and thoughtful choice of drinks), and the Half Moon in Warninglid (a good mix of drinkers and diners in bustling village pub). Other places our readers have enjoyed this year are the Rose Cottage in Alciston (fair value food in old-fashioned cottage), George in Alfriston (well run with good food and in a delightful village), Coach & Horses at Danehill (enticing food in country dining pub), Jolly Sportsman near East Chiltington (well trained staff and exceptional food in civilised surroundings), Nevill Crest & Gun at Eridge Green (cleverly and carefully refurbished Brunning & Price pub with bistro-style meals, lots of whiskies and wines by the glass), Cock in Ringmer (friendly and full of character with reasonably priced food), Salehurst Halt in Salehurst (perky little local with pretty back garden), and Cat in West Hoathly (much enjoyed by a wide mix of customers for first class food and service). Our Sussex Dining Pub 2013 is the Horse Guards in Tillington.

ALCISTON

TQ5005   Map 3

Rose Cottage

Village signposted off A27 Polegate–Lewes; BN26 6UW

Old-fashioned cottage with cosy fires and country bric-a-brac, several wines by the glass, well liked food and local beers; bedrooms

It's really worth taking a stroll around this charming small village (and the church, too) and then dropping into this extremely popular pub; get there early on Sunday lunchtimes as it gets packed. There are half a dozen tables with cushioned pews, winter log fires and quite a forest of harness, traps, a thatcher's blade and lots of other black ironware; more bric-a-brac on the shelves above the stripped pine dado and in the etched glass windows and maybe a parrot called Jasper (but only at lunchtimes – he gets too noisy in the evenings). The restaurant area can accommodate a lunchtime overflow from the bar, useful as you can't book bar tables then. Dark Star Hophead, Harveys Best and a guest beer on handpump and several wines by the glass; background music, darts and board games. For cooler evenings, there are heaters outside; a small paddock in the garden has ducks and chickens; boules. Nearby fishing and shooting. They take self-catering bedroom bookings for a minimum of two nights. There are bracing South Downs walks nearby.

 Good food includes potted brown shrimps, pâté of the day with spicy tomato chutney, local sausages with onion gravy and mash, chicken caesar salad, home-cooked honey roast ham with poached eggs, koftas made using home-grown courgettes with spicy tomato and yoghurt sauce, steak in ale or rabbit and bacon pie, scallops with bacon, mushrooms and honey and red wine vinegar, half a crispy ducking with home-grown morello cherry and brandy sauce, and puddings. *Benchmark main dish: fish pie £11.50. Two-course evening meal £17.50.*

Free house ~ Licensee Ian Lewis ~ Real ale ~ Bar food (12-2, 6.30-9.30(9 Sun)) ~ Restaurant ~ (01323) 870377 ~ Children welcome ~ Dogs allowed in bar ~ Open 11.30-3, 6.30-11; 12-3, 6.30-10.30 Sun ~ Bedrooms: /£60S ~ www.therosecottageinn.co.uk
Recommended by Ian and Nita Cooper, Ron and Sheila Corbett, Terry and Nickie Williams, Gene and Tony Freemantle, Simon Watkins, Peter Meister, Phil and Jane Villiers, Alan Franck, R and S Bentley, Mike Gorton, Tracey and Stephen Groves, the Didler

ALFRISTON

TQ5203   Map 3

George ♀

High Street; BN26 5SY

Venerable inn in pretty village with comfortable, heavily beamed bars, good wines and several real ales; fine nearby walks; bedrooms

This well run 14th-c timbered inn is a popular place to drop into after a wander around this lovely village. The busy long bar has massive hop-hung low beams, soft lighting and a log fire (or summer flower arrangement) in a huge stone inglenook fireplace that dominates the room, with lots of copper and brass around it. There are settles and chairs around sturdy stripped tables, Greene King IPA and Abbot, Hardys & Hansons Old Trip and a guest like the local Longman Brewery Best Bitter and Long Blonde on handpump, decent wines including champagne by the glass, board games and background music; good service. The lounge has comfortable sofas, standing timbers, and rugs on the wooden floor, and the restaurant is cosy and candlelit. There are seats in the spacious flint-walled garden. Two long-distance paths, the

South Downs Way and Vanguard Way, cross here; Cuckmere Haven is close by. The beamed bedrooms are comfortable; they don't have a car park but there is parking a couple of minutes away.

🍴 Good, interesting food includes lunchtime sandwiches, crayfish, crab and salmon terrine, ginger-infused scallops with lemon oil, rustic sharing boards, spinach and feta parcels with spicy chickpeas, ham with free-range eggs, pork and leek sausages with red onion gravy, seafood linguine, veal with mushrooms and marsala sauce, duck leg confit with leek and wild mushroom risotto, lamb cutlets with dauphinoise potatoes and mint jus, and puddings such as lemon and lime posset with langue de chat biscuit and chocolate and walnut brownie with chocolate sauce. *Benchmark main dish: chicken breast filled with brie and herbs £14.50. Two-course evening meal £20.00.*

Greene King ~ Lease Roland and Cate Couch ~ Real ale ~ Bar food (12-9) ~ Restaurant ~ (01323) 870319 ~ Children welcome ~ Dogs allowed in bar and bedrooms ~ Open 11-11(midnight Fri and Sat) ~ Bedrooms: £70S/£120S(£100B) ~ www.thegeorge-alfriston.com *Recommended by Ian and Nita Cooper, Phil and Jane Villiers, Brian and Anna Marsden*

ASHURST   TQ1816 Map 3

Fountain ♀

B2135 S of Partridge Green; BN44 3AP

16th-c country pub with beams, flagstones and open fires, good food and drink, and seats outside

'Alway's busy and always good,' commented one of our many contented readers after visiting this welcoming 16th-c country pub. The neatly kept and charmingly rustic tap room on the right has a couple of high-backed wooden, cottagey armchairs by the log fire in its brick inglenook, country dining chairs around polished wooden tables, a few bar stools on the fine old flagstones and horsebrasses on the bressumer beam. The opened-up snug has wonky walls, more flagstones, heavy beams, simple furniture, and its own inglenook fireplace; an oak-beamed skittle alley doubles as a function room. Harveys Best, Courage Directors, Fullers London Pride and Sharps Doom Bar on handpump and 23 wines by the glass; service is friendly and attentive. The garden is prettily planted, there are seats on the front brick terrace, raised herb beds at the back, an orchard and a duck pond.

🍴 Enjoyable food includes sandwiches (the steak or fish baps are much liked), pork and chicken liver terrine with pickled pear chutney and toasted brioche, seared scallops with crispy bacon and sweetcorn purée, sausage and mash with onion gravy, blue cheese and smoky bacon burger and chips, pumpkin risotto, stuffed chicken with a red wine jus, herb-crusted rack of lamb with garlic mash and spinach, sage and onion duck with caramelised orange sauce, luxury fish pie, and puddings like cinnamon and apple crumble tart with vanilla bean sauce and baked white chocolate cheesecake with strawberry sauce. *Benchmark main dish: stuffed salmon fillet with crayfish stuffing £13.00. Two-course evening meal £20.00.*

Free house ~ Licensee Elizabeth Fry ~ Real ale ~ Bar food (12-2.30(3 Sun), 6-9.30(9 Sun)) ~ Restaurant ~ (01403) 710219 ~ Children welcome ~ Dogs allowed in bar ~ Open 11-11(10.30 Sun) ~ www.fountainashurst.co.uk *Recommended by Emma Scofield*

The letters and figures after the name of each town are its Ordnance Survey map reference. *How to use the Guide* at the beginning of the book explains how it helps you find a pub, in road atlases or large-scale maps as well as in our own maps.

CHARLTON
SU8812 Map 2

Fox Goes Free

Village signposted off A286 Chichester–Midhurst in Singleton, also from Chichester–Petworth via East Dean; PO18 0HU

Comfortable old pub with beamed bars, popular food and drink and big garden; bedrooms

Being so close to Goodwood, this friendly, bustling pub can get packed on race days but as it's open all day you can easily avoid peak times; the Weald and Downland Open Air Museum and West Dean Gardens are nearby too. In fine weather, you can sit at one of the picnic-sets under the apple trees in the attractive back garden with the downs as a backdrop or at rustic benches and tables on the gravel front terrace. Inside, the bar is the first of the dark and cosy series of separate rooms: old irish settles, tables and chapel chairs and an open fire. Standing timbers divide a larger beamed bar which has a huge brick fireplace with a woodburning stove and old local photographs on the walls. A dining area with hunting prints looks over the garden. The family extension is a clever conversion from horseboxes and the stables where the 1926 Goodwood winner was housed; darts, games machine, background music and board games. Ballards Best, a beer named for the pub brewed by Arundel and a guest such as Otter Bitter on handpump, several wines by the glass and Addlestone's cider. There are good surrounding walks including one up to the prehistoric earthworks on the Trundle.

 Bar food includes ciabatta sandwiches, sharing plates of italian antipasti and meze, king prawns on toast with garlic and herb butter, chicken liver parfait with apple chutney, home-made sausages with mash and onion marmalade, beer-battered cod with mushy peas and home-made tartare sauce, a pie of the day, spinach and ricotta cannelloni with butternut squash purée, salmon fillet with chorizo and creamed spinach, and puddings. *Benchmark main dish: twice-cooked pork belly with home-made black pudding and apple chutney £15.50. Two-course evening meal £21.00.*

Free house ~ Licensee David Coxon ~ Real ale ~ Bar food (12-2.30, 6.30-9.30; all day weekends) ~ Restaurant ~ (01243) 811461 ~ Children welcome ~ Dogs allowed in bar ~ Live music every second Weds evening ~ Open 11-11(11.30 Sat); 12-10.30 Sun ~ Bedrooms: £65S/£90S ~ www.thefoxgoesfree.com *Recommended by Miss A E Dare, Peter and Jean Hoare, Roy Hoing*

CHIDDINGLY
TQ5414 Map 3

Six Bells £

Village signed off A22 Uckfield–Hailsham; BN8 6HE

Lively, unpretentious village local with good weekend live music, extremely good value bar food and a friendly long-serving landlord

Even when this cheerful village pub is packed out, the hard-working, hands-on landlord keeps everything running smoothly. There's a great deal of unpretentious character in the many small interconnected bars with their interesting bric-a-brac, local pictures, photographs and posters – as well as solid old wood pews, antique chairs and tables and cushioned window seats; log fires, too. A sensitive extension provides some much-needed family space; board games. Courage Directors, Harveys Best and a guest beer on handpump and decent wines by the glass. Outside at the back, there are some tables beyond a big raised goldfish pond and a boules pitch; the church opposite has an interesting monument to local 17-c diarist William Jefferay. Popular weekend live music and vintage and kit car meetings outside the pub every month. This is a pleasant area for walks. Note that dogs are allowed in one bar only.

Exceptionally good value and well liked, the bar food includes sandwiches, filled baked potatoes, ploughman's, meat or vegetarian lasagne, chilli con carne, chicken curry, shepherd's or steak and kidney pie, and puddings like banoffi pie and Malteser crunch. *Benchmark main dish: steak and kidney pie £4.75. Two-course evening meal £8.50.*

Free house ~ Licensee Paul Newman ~ Real ale ~ Bar food (12-2.15, 6-9.30; all day Fri-Sun) ~ (01825) 872227 ~ Children allowed away from main bar ~ Dogs allowed in bar ~ Live music Fri-Sun evenings and Sun lunchtime ~ Open 11-3, 6-11; 11am-midnight Fri and Sat; 12-10.30 Sun *Recommended by B and M Kendall, Nick Lawless, Dr A J and Mrs Tompsett*

CHILGROVE   SU8116   Map 2
Royal Oak £
Off B2141 Petersfield–Chichester, signed Hooksway; PO18 9JZ

Unchanging and peaceful country pub with welcoming licensees and big pretty garden

Down a wooded track in a lovely rural position, this unspoilt country pub has been run by the same friendly licensees for 21 years. The two simple, cosy bars have huge log fires, plain country-kitchen tables and chairs, and Gales HSB, Hammerpot Shooting Star, Sharps Doom Bar and a guest beer on handpump. There's also a cottagey dining room with a woodburning stove and a plainer family room; background music, cribbage, dominoes and shut the box. Twiglet and Amber are the pub staffies and there's a parrot called Gilbert. Outside, the big pretty garden has plenty of picnic-sets under parasols. The South Downs Way is close by.

Honest food includes sandwiches, pâté and toast with cranberry sauce, creamy garlic mushrooms, tuna pasta bake, chilli con carne, sausage and chips, vegetable lasagne, home-made pies, slow-cooked pork hock with apple and cider sauce and venison steak with mulled wine and redcurrant jelly. *Benchmark main dish: venison pie £10.45. Two-course evening meal £16.25.*

Free house ~ Licensee Dave Jeffery ~ Real ale ~ Bar food (12-2, 7-9; not Sun evening or Mon) ~ Restaurant ~ (01243) 535257 ~ Children in family room ~ Dogs allowed in bar ~ Live music last Fri evening of month ~ Open 11.30-2.30, 6-11; 12-3 Sun; closed Sun evening and Mon; last two weeks Oct, first two weeks Nov ~ www.royaloakhooksway.co.uk
Recommended by Ann and Colin Hunt, J A Snell

DANEHILL   TQ4128   Map 3
Coach & Horses ⊕ ♀
Off A275, via School Lane towards Chelwood Common; RH17 7JF

Bustling dining pub with bustling bars, welcoming staff, enjoyable food and ales; downs views from large garden

Our readers enjoy their visits to this well run country pub very much and you can be sure of a warm welcome from the helpful staff. There's a little bar to the right with half-panelled walls, simple furniture on polished floorboards, a small woodburner in the brick fireplace and a big hatch to the bar counter: Harveys Best, Kings Old Ale and a guest such as Sharps Doom Bar on handpump and several wines by the glass including prosecco and champagne. A couple of steps lead down to a half-panelled area with a mix of dining chairs around characterful wooden tables (set with flowers and candles) on the fine brick floor and artwork on the walls that changes every couple of months; cribbage, dominoes and cards. Down another step is a dining area with stone walls, beams, flagstones and a woodburning stove. There's an adults-only terrace under a huge maple tree and picnic-sets and a children's play area in the big garden which has fine views of the South Downs.

Using local produce, the enjoyable food might include, sandwiches, pheasant rillettes with crab apple jelly, ham hock and pistachio terrine with spiced date chutney, moroccan-spiced chickpea fritters with orange and pomegranate salsa and cucumber salad, local sausages with mash and red onion gravy, chargrilled pork loin with apple and black pudding crumble, roast cod fillet with herb gnocchi, roasted peppers and red pesto, specials such as smoked haddock and soft herb risotto and calves liver and bacon with red onion marmalade, and puddings like white chocolate and kirsch panna cotta with chocolate cherry parfait, dark chocolate cherry ganache and amaretti crumb and iced lemon curd parfait with raspberry jelly, raspberry mousse and caramel dust. *Benchmark main dish: local pheasant breast with parma ham and raisin purée £13.50. Two-course evening meal £21.00.*

Free house ~ Licensee Ian Philpots ~ Real ale ~ Bar food (12-2(2.30 Sat, 3 Sun), 7-9(9.30 Fri and Sat); not Sun evening) ~ Restaurant ~ (01825) 740369 ~ Well behaved children welcome but not on adult terrace ~ Dogs allowed in bar ~ Open 12-3, 5-11; 12-11, Sat, Sun; evening opening 6pm in winter ~ www.coachandhorses.danehill.biz
Recommended by Rebecca Gould, Peter Gartrell, David Jackman, N R White

DIAL POST
Crown

TQ1519   Map 3

Worthing Road (off A24 S of Horsham); RH13 8NH

Extended village pub with interesting food, real ales and plenty of space in the bar and two dining rooms; bedrooms

Particularly in the evening, there's a lively, friendly atmosphere here and a good mix of both drinkers and diners. The beamed bar has a couple of standing timbers, brown squashy sofas and pine tables and chairs on a stone floor, a small woodburning stove in the brick fireplace, and Harveys Best and Old and a changing guest beer on handpump from the attractive herringbone brick counter. The pub dog is called Chops. The straightforwardly furnished dining conservatory, facing the village green, is light and airy. To the right of the bar, the restaurant (with more beams) has an ornamental woodburner in a brick fireplace, a few photographs on the walls, chunky pine tables, chairs and a couple of cushioned pews on the patterned carpet, and a shelf of books; steps lead down to a further dining room. The bedrooms are in the converted stables and there are picnic-sets on grass behind the pub.

Using seasonal, local produce, the extremely popular food might include lunchtime sandwiches, chicken liver pâté with beer and apple chutney, rillettes of duck with an orange and watercress salad, home-made steak burger with spicy relish and hand-cut chips, home-roasted ham with a free-range egg, natural smoked haddock baked with cream and cheese on spinach topped with prawns, aubergine rarebit with pesto dressing and crushed potatoes, free-range chicken and leek pie, venison saddle with cherries and red cabbage and port jus, and puddings like passion-fruit and white chocolate mousse in a brandy snap basket and iced lemon meringue pie. *Benchmark main dish: steak and mushroom in ale pie £12.50. Two-course evening meal £21.00.*

Free house ~ Licensees James and Penny Middleton-Burn ~ Real ale ~ Bar food (12-2, 6-9(9.30 Fri and Sat); not winter Sun evening) ~ Restaurant ~ (01403) 710902 ~ Children welcome but after 7pm only for dining ~ Dogs allowed in bar ~ Open 11.30-3, 6-11; 12-10; 12-4 winter Sun; closed winter Sun evening ~ www.floatingcrown.co.uk
Recommended by David and Sharon Collison, Simon and Mandy King, Pat and Stewart Gordon

DUNCTON
SU9517   Map 3

Cricketers

Set back from A285; GU28 0LB

Charming old coaching inn with friendly licensees, real ales, popular food and suntrap back garden

Ideally situated for Goodwood horse-racing and motorsports, this pretty 16th-c coaching inn is also a good option for walkers and families. There are some picnic-sets out in front beneath the flowering window boxes and more on decked areas and under parasols on the grass in the picturesque back garden, which make the most of the pub's position in the Goodwood Hills. The friendly, traditional bar has a few standing timbers, simple seating, cricketing memorabilia and an open woodburning stove in the inglenook fireplace. Steps lead down to the dining room, which is simply furnished with wooden tables and chairs. Gribble Fuzzy Duck, King Horsham Best Bitter and Skinners Betty Stogs on handpump, several wines by the glass and Thatcher's cider.

 Food includes lunchtime sandwiches (not Sunday), chicken liver pâté with chutney, crab, prawn and leek gratin, ham and eggs, home-made burger topped with bacon and brie, chicken caesar salad, cheese risotto topped with a poached egg, toad in the hole with onion gravy, a pie of the day, beer-battered haddock, steamed steak and kidney pudding, and puddings. *Benchmark main dish: steak and mushroom in ale pie £10.95. Two-course evening meal £17.80.*

Inn Company ~ Lease Martin Boult ~ Real ale ~ Bar food (12-2.30, 6-9; 12-9 weekends and summer holidays) ~ Restaurant ~ (01798) 342473 ~ Children welcome ~ Dogs welcome ~ Open 11-11; 12-10.30 Sun ~ www.thecricketersduncton.co.uk
Recommended by Derek and Maggie Washington, Terry and Nickie Williams, John and Anne Mackinnon, Martin and Karen Wake

EAST CHILTINGTON
TQ3715   Map 3

Jolly Sportsman ⑪ ♀

2 miles N of B2116; Chapel Lane – follow sign to 13th-c church; BN7 3BA

Excellent modern food in civilised, rather smart place, small bar for drinkers, contemporary furnishings, noteworthy wine list and huge range of malt whiskies; nice garden

This civilised dining pub has a first class, innovative menu, whether for bar snacks or a three-course meal, and it's a favourite with many of our readers. The bar may be small but it's light and full of character, and has a roaring winter fire, a mixture of furniture on the stripped wood floors and Dark Star Hophead and Harveys Best tapped from the cask. They also have a remarkably good wine list with around a dozen by the glass, over 100 malt whiskies, an extensive list of cognacs, armagnacs and grappas and quite a choice of bottled belgian beers. The pub is extremely well run; the charming staff have evidently had good training. The larger restaurant is smart but cosy and welcoming, with contemporary light wood furniture and modern landscapes on coffee-coloured walls; there's also a new garden room. The cottagey front garden is pretty, with rustic tables and benches under gnarled trees on the terrace and on the front bricked area, and there are more on a large back lawn. There's a children's play area, and views towards the downs, as well as good walks and cycle rides nearby.

Exceptional food includes lunchtime sandwiches, seared king scallops with chorizo and piperade, pigs head and ham hock terrine with piccalilli, calves liver and beef cheek faggot with horseradish mash and savoy cabbage, pigeon breast with pommes anna with chanterelle vinaigrette, roast guinea fowl with parsnip rösti and wild mushrooms, pollack with a bacon and hazelnut crust, confit jerusalem artichokes and cockle beurre noisette, and puddings such as pineapple and coconut sorbet and gypsy tart with frozen yoghurt. *Benchmark main dish: grilled gurnard fillets with caponata £15.85. Two-course evening meal £22.50.*

Free house ~ Licensee Bruce Wass ~ Real ale ~ Bar food (12-2.30(3 Sat, 3.30 Sun),7-9) ~ Restaurant ~ (01273) 890400 ~ Children welcome ~ Dogs allowed in bar ~ Open 12-3, 6-11; 12-11(10.30 Sun) Sat; closed winter Sun evening ~ www.thejollysportsman.com
Recommended by Nick Lawless, John Redfern, Terry and Nickie Williams, David Sizer, Laurence Smith, N R White, Jason Woodford, Kim Turner

EAST DEAN   TV5597   Map 3
Tiger ♀ ⌂
Off A259 Eastbourne–Seaford; BN20 0DA

Charming old pub by cottage-lined village green, two little bars and a dining room, and a chatty, informal atmosphere; bedrooms

This friendly pub can get busy, and, with something of a premium on space, it pays to get here early if you want a seat, but the staff are always welcoming and the service attentive. It's as popular with drinkers as it is with diners, and the atmosphere is always chatty and relaxed. The focal point of the little beamed main bar is the open woodburning stove in its brick inglenook, surrounded by polished horsebrasses, and there are just a few rustic tables with benches, simple wooden chairs, a window seat and a long cushioned wall bench. The walls are hung with fish prints and a stuffed tiger's head, there are a couple of hunting horns above the long bar counter. Harveys Best and Old and their own-brewed Beachy Head Legless Rambler and Original are available on handpump, and several wines by the glass. Down a step on the right is a second small room with an exceptionally fine high-backed curved settle and a couple of other old settles, nice old chairs and wooden tables on coir carpeting, and an ancient map of Eastbourne and Beachy Head and photographs of the pub on the walls; the dining room to the left of the main bar has a cream woodburner and hunting prints. There are picnic-sets on the terrace among the window boxes and flowering climbers, or you can sit on the delightful cottage-lined village green. The South Downs Way is close by and the lane leads on down to a fine stretch of coast culminating in Beachy Head, so the pub is a natural choice for walkers. The bedrooms are comfortable and the breakfasts good.

Using some own-grown salad ingredients and vegetables, the much liked food includes pâté of the day with home-made chutney, bacon, brie and apple salad, sausage and mash with sweet roasted red onion gravy, pasta with three cheeses and spring onion, beer-battered fish of the day, slow-roasted pork belly with cider sauce and onion and herb mash, specials such as pea, rocket and parmesan risotto, pheasant pie, and pork cassoulet, and puddings like chocolate brownie with chocolate ice-cream and a steamed pudding of the day with custard. *Benchmark main dish: home-made beef burger with bacon and cheese £10.50. Two-course evening meal £18.00.*

Free house ~ Licensee Jacques Pienaar ~ Real ale ~ Bar food (12-3, 6-9) ~ Restaurant ~ (01323) 423209 ~ Children welcome ~ Dogs allowed in bar ~ Open 11am-midnight(1am Sat) ~ Bedrooms: /£95S ~ www.beachyhead.org.uk *Recommended by B and M Kendall, MP, David Hill*

EAST LAVANT
SU8608   Map 2

Royal Oak 🍴 ♟ 🛏
Pook Lane, off A286; PO18 0AX

Bustling and friendly dining pub with proper drinking area, excellent food, extensive wine list and real ales; super bedrooms

Very handy for Goodwood and with plenty of nearby walks, this is a pretty little white house that manages to be both a proper village pub and somewhere for a fine meal in relaxed surroundings. It's all open plan, with low beams and exposed brickwork, crooked timbers, winter log fires and church candles. The well used drinking area at the front offers wall seats and sofas, Arundel Gold and Sharps Doom Bar or Skinners Betty Stogs tapped from the cask, 20 wines by the glass from an extensive list, and a friendly welcome from the attentive staff. The neighbouring seating area is focused on dining and sensitively furnished with brown suede and leather dining chairs around scrubbed pine tables, and pictures of local scenes and of motor sport on the walls; background music. Outside, there are cushioned seats and tables under green parasols on the flagstoned front terrace and far-reaching views to the Downs; rambling around the side and back are terraced brick and grass areas with more seats and attractive tubs and baskets. The bedrooms are stylish and well equipped and they also have self-catering cottages. The car park is across the road.

Interesting food includes sandwiches, salt and pepper squid with greek salad and crab mayonnaise, parslied ham terrine with piccalilli, twice-baked watercress soufflé, pork fillet wrapped in serrano ham with dauphinoise potatoes, roast quail on a croûton with cep cream and wild mushrooms, chicken breast with a herb salsa, rösti and vegetables, slow-roasted pork belly with onion velouté, bass fillet with dill-crushed potatoes and a crayfish, ginger and coriander butter, 28-day aged steaks, and puddings such as honey and praline cheesecake with pineapple crush and a trio of chocolate; they also offer a two- and three-course set menu. *Benchmark main dish: beer-battered hake with chips and marrowfat pea purée £14.90. Two-course evening meal £24.00.*

Free house ~ Licensee Charles Ullmann ~ Real ale ~ Bar food (12-2.30, 6-9(9.30 Sat); 12-3, 6.30-9 Sun) ~ Restaurant ~ (01243) 527434 ~ Well behaved children welcome ~ Dogs allowed in bar ~ Open 11-11(midnight Sat); 12-11 Sun ~ Bedrooms: £90S(£99B)/£125S(£140B) ~ www.royaloakeastlavant.co.uk *Recommended by John Chambers*

Bedroom prices normally include full english breakfast, VAT and any inclusive service charge that we know of. Prices before the '/' are for single rooms, after for two people in double or twin (B includes a private bath, S a private shower). If there is no '/', the prices are only for twin or double rooms (as far as we know there are no singles).

ERIDGE GREEN
TQ5535 Map 3

Nevill Crest & Gun ♀

A26 Tunbridge Wells–Crowborough; TN3 9JR

Handsome 500-year-old building with lots of character, beams and standing timbers, hundreds of pictures and photographs, three real ales, enjoyable modern food and friendly, efficient staff

Standing on the estate of the Nevill family (whose crest can be still be seen on the building), this fine 16th-c former farmhouse has plenty of interesting local history. It has been carefully and cleverly opened up inside, with standing timbers and doorways keeping some sense of separate rooms. Throughout there are heavy beams (some carved), panelling, rugs on wooden floors, woodburning stoves and open fires in three fireplaces (the linenfold carved bressumer above one of them is worth seeking out), all manner of individual dining chairs around dark wood or copper-topped tables and lots of pictures, maps and photographs, many of them of local subjects. The window sills are full of toby jugs, stone and glass bottles and plants, there are daily papers, board games and a happy mix of customers of all ages; the atmosphere is civilised but informal. Beers from Tunbridge Wells, Westerham and Phoenix Brunning & Price are on handpump and good wines offered by the glass by efficient, friendly staff. In front of the building are a few picnic-sets with teak furniture on a back terrace, next to the more recent dining extension with its large windows, light oak rafters, beams and coir flooring.

From a bistro-style menu, the popular food might include sandwiches, lamb koftas with tzatziki, chicken liver and thyme parfait with apple and date chutney, mussels with cider, leeks and cream, pork and leek sausages with red wine and onion gravy, cauliflower, chickpea and almond tagine with apricot and date couscous, hake supreme with chorizo and white bean cassoulet, beef burger topped wih grilled bacon and cheese, confit duck with roast plums and hoi sin dressing and caramelised pak choi, and puddings such as black forest cheesecake with boozy cherries and strawberry panna cotta with elderflower syrup and home-made shortbread. *Benchmark main dish: slow-cooked belly pork with cider sauce £13.50. Two-course evening meal £20.00.*

Brunning & Price ~ Manager Adam Holland ~ Real ale ~ Bar food (12-10(9.30 Sun)) ~ (01892) 864209 ~ Children welcome ~ Dogs allowed in bar ~ Open 11.30-11; 12-10.30 Sun ~ www.nevillcrestandgun.co.uk *Recommended by Alan Franck, Richard Gibbs*

EWHURST GREEN
TQ7924 Map 3

White Dog

Turn off A21 to Bodiam at S end of Hurst Green, cross B2244, pass Bodiam Castle, cross river then bear left uphill at Ewhurst Green sign; TN32 5TD

Comfortable pub with a nice little bar, several real ales and popular food

Family-run and dating from the 17th c, this is a bustling village pub with a friendly welcome for all. The bar on the left has a fine inglenook fireplace, hop-draped beams, wood-panelled walls, farm implements and horsebrasses, just a few tables with high-backed, rush-seated dining chairs, and red plush-topped bar stools on the old brick or flagstoned floor. There's also a high-backed cushioned settle by the counter, which serves Caledonian Deuchars IPA, Harveys Best, Sharps Doom Bar and a guest beer from handpump and several wines by the glass. To the right of the door is the dining room, which has murals of the local area and sturdy wooden tables and chairs on more flagstones; background music. There's also a games room with darts, pool and board games. The garden behind has lots of picnic-sets and magnificent views of Bodiam Castle.

🍴 Making the most of local, seasonal produce, the well liked food might include filled baguettes, ham hock terrine with home-made piccalilli, bouillabaisse (served as a starter or main course), a changing vegetable rösti with a duck egg and hollandaise sauce, free-range chicken stuffed with mozzarella, wrapped in pancetta with a spicy carrot and ginger sambal, chargrilled lamb with rosemary pesto, pot-roast rabbit in mustard, cider and cream, and puddings. *Benchmark main dish: grilled local mackerel with chilli £12.95. Two-course evening meal £18.00.*

Free house ~ Licensees Harriet and Dale Skinner and Jack Haytor ~ Real ale ~ Bar food (12-2.30, 6.30-9.30(12-3 Sun); not Sun or Mon evenings) ~ Restaurant ~ (01580) 830264 ~ Children welcome ~ Dogs allowed in bar and bedrooms ~ Live music monthly ~ Open 12-3, 6-11; 12-11.30 Fri, Sat and Sun ~ Bedrooms: /£85B ~ www.thewhitedogewhurst.co.uk
Recommended by Michael Butler, Arthur Pickering, Tom and Rosemary Hall, Conrad Freezer

FLETCHING
THE GOOD PUB GUIDE TQ4223 Map 3
Griffin 🍴 ♈ 🛏
Village signposted off A272 W of Uckfield; TN22 3SS

Busy, gently upmarket inn with a fine wine list, bistro-style bar food, real ales and big garden with far-reaching views; bedrooms

We receive consistently positive reviews from our readers for this civilised, lively and well run inn, which offers a genuinely warm welcome to all – children and dogs included. It also has an appealing and very spacious two-acre back garden with plenty of seats for diners on the sandstone terrace and grass, and lovely views towards Sheffield Park Gardens; regular summer Sunday barbecues. The beamed and quaintly panelled bar rooms have blazing log fires, old photographs and hunting prints, simple close-set furniture including some captain's chairs, and china on a delft shelf. There's a small bare-boarded serving area off to one side and a snug separate bar with sofas and a TV. Harveys Best, Hogs Back TEA, King's Horsham Best and a guest beer on handpump, a fine wine list with 20 (including champagne and sweet wine) by the glass and farm cider. The bright, airy bedrooms are comfortable and the breakfasts are good; the inn is handy for Glyndebourne. There are ramps for wheelchairs.

🍴 Using local produce, the well-rounded menu might include sandwiches, ham hock, mint and pistachio terrine with red onion jam, salt and pepper squid with saffron aioli, rabbit, shallot and leek gnocchi with mascarpone and parmesan, spiced squash, red onion and feta risotto, venison burger with tomato and dill chutney, thai green curry of red mullet and crayfish, chargrilled steak with home-made chips, and puddings such as warm ginger parkin with spiced apple compote and clotted cream and vanilla panna cotta with kirsch cherries. *Benchmark main dish: beer-battered local cod with home-made chips and tartare sauce £13.50. Two-course evening meal £20.50.*

Free house ~ Licensees James Pullan and Samantha Barlow ~ Real ale ~ Bar food (12-2.30, 7-9.30) ~ Restaurant ~ (01825) 722890 ~ Children welcome ~ Dogs allowed in bar ~ Open 12-11(midnight Sat) ~ Bedrooms: £80B/£85S(£95B) ~ www.thegriffininn.co.uk
Recommended by Michael Pelham, Charles Gibbs, Simon and Mandy King, David and Jenny Reed, Grahame Brooks, Alan Franck, Harriet Tarnoy, John Ralph, Nigel and Jean Eames, Tom and Ruth Rees

HEATHFIELD

TQ5920   Map 3

Star 🍺

Church Street, Old Heathfield, off A265/B2096; TN21 9AH

Pleasant old pub with bustling, friendly atmosphere, good mix of locals and visitors, well liked food and decent choice of drinks; pretty garden

Turner thought this 14th-c inn fine enough to paint. These days, it's a smashing and bustling country pub of real character, with a good mix of both locals and visitors. The building has ancient heavy beams, built-in wall settles and window seats, panelling, inglenook fireplaces and a roaring winter log fire; a doorway leads to a similarly decorated room more set up for eating with wooden tables and chairs (one table has high-backed white leather dining chairs) and a woodburning stove. There's also an upstairs dining room. Harveys Best, Shepherd Neame Spitfire and Wells & Youngs Bitter are on handpump and the pub has an extensive wine list, including several by the glass; good food; friendly, helpful staff; background music. The garden is very prettily planted and has rustic furniture under smart umbrellas and lovely views of rolling oak-lined sheep pastures.

Popular food includes devilled kidneys on toast, smoked salmon roulade with dill mustard dressing, local sausages with ale and balsamic onion gravy, home-cooked cold meats with bubble and squeak, mushroom risotto, chicken madras with home-made lime pickle, steak in ale or luxury fish pie, confit duck leg with butternut squash purée, pancetta and herby puy lentils, and puddings such as plum and almond tart and banoffi pie. *Benchmark main dish: wild bass fillet with vegetable and noodle stir fry and a sweet and sour dressing £14.95. Two-course evening meal £19.00.*

Free house ~ Licensees Mike and Sue Chappell ~ Real ale ~ Bar food (12-2.30, 7-9.30; 12-3, 6.30-8.30 Sun) ~ Restaurant ~ (01435) 863570 ~ Children welcome ~ Dogs allowed in bar ~ Open 11.30-11; 12-10.30 Sun ~ www.starinnoldheathfield.co.uk
Recommended by Mike Gorton

HORSHAM

TQ1730   Map 3

Black Jug ♟

North Street; RH12 1RJ

Bustling town pub with wide choice of drinks, efficient staff and good bar food

This well-run old town pub has friendly, knowledgeable and attentive staff and a wide mix of customers. The one large open-plan, turn-of-the-20th-century room has a long central bar, a nice collection of sizeable dark wood tables and comfortable chairs on the stripped-wood floor, board games, bookcases and interesting old prints and photographs above a dark wood-panelled dado on the cream walls. A spacious, bright conservatory has similar furniture and lots of hanging baskets. Caledonian Deuchars IPA and Harveys Best with guests such as Old Mill Old Priory Mild and Sharps Doom Bar on handpump, 20 wines by the glass, around 100 malt whiskies and Weston's cider. The pretty flower-filled back terrace has plenty of garden furniture. The small car park is for staff and deliveries only but there's a council car park next door.

As well as sandwiches, the well liked food may include duck liver pâté with rhubarb chutney, smoked haddock and salmon fishcake, grilled bratwurst with sauerkraut, teriyaki beef linguine, bouillabaisse with saffron mayonnaise, artichoke and israeli-style couscous, steak in ale pie, beer-battered haddock with pea purée and tartare sauce, rump of lamb salad with pomegranate seeds, pickled walnuts and raspberry vinaigrette, slow-roasted five-spice pork belly with noodles, and puddings such as meringue with lemon curd and raspberries and chocolate and Cointreau mousse. *Benchmark main dish: fish and chips £11.95. Two-course evening meal £20.00.*

Brunning & Price ~ Tenant Alastair Craig ~ Real ale ~ Bar food (12-10(9.30 Sun)) ~ (01403) 253526 ~ Children welcome ~ Dogs allowed in bar ~ Open 11.30-11; 12-10.30 Sun ~ www.blackjug-horsham.co.uk *Recommended by Emma Scofield*

HURST GREEN   TQ7326   Map 3
White Horse ♀
Silverhill (A21); TN19 7PU

Friendly, well run pub with relaxed bar, elegant dining room, enjoyable food and seats in garden

In fine weather, the large terrace at the back of this former Georgian farmhouse is a lovely place for a drink or a meal with attractive white metal tables and chairs looking across the lawn and over the Weald. The relaxed bare-boards bar has a few leather armchairs and white-painted dining chairs around various wooden tables (set with nightlights and wooden candlesticks), game trophies, prints and photographs on the walls, fresh flowers and an open fire. Harveys Best on handpump and 14 nice wines by the glass; background music. An open doorway leads through to a second bar room with built-in leather wall seats and similar tables and then it's through again to the dining room. This is an elegant but informal room with similar furniture, oil paintings and ornate mirrors on modern paintwork, chandeliers and some panelling.

Good, popular food includes lunchtime filled ciabatta sandwiches, olive and roast chicken terrine with home-made chutney, crispy duck salad with roasted red peppers and their own eggs, a pie of the day, salmon and cod fishcakes with tartare sauce, beef burger with french fries, grilled chicken breast with creamy tarragon sauce and truffle mash, ostrich fillet with paprika potato wedges and a cherry tomato salsa, and puddings such as dark chocolate truffle and pear tatin with vanilla ice-cream. *Benchmark main dish: confit duck with cranberry jus and dauphinoise potatoes £16.95. Two-course evening meal £23.00.*

Free house ~ Licensee Anthony Panic ~ Real ale ~ Bar food (12-3, 6-10) ~ Restaurant ~ (01580) 860235 ~ Children welcome ~ Dogs allowed in bar ~ Live jazz last Fri of month ~ Open 12-3, 6-11; 12-8 Sun ~ www.thewhitehorsehurstgreen.com *Recommended by David and Jenny Reed, Richard Mason*

LODSWORTH   SU9321   Map 2
Halfway Bridge Inn ⊕ ♀ 🛏
Just before village, on A272 Midhurst–Petworth; GU28 9BP

Restauranty coaching inn with contemporary décor in several dining areas, log fires, local real ales and modern food; lovely bedrooms

This is a nice place to stay, with stylish and comfortable bedrooms in a former stable yard and good breakfasts, too. Much emphasis is on the dining side of things – the tables are mostly set for eating – but regulars still pop in for a pint and chat. The various bar rooms have plenty of intimate little corners and are carefully furnished with good oak chairs and a mix of tables; one of the log fires is a well polished kitchen range. The interconnecting restaurant rooms have beams, wooden floors and a cosy atmosphere. Long Blonde Ale, Langham Hip Hop and Sharps Doom Bar on handpump and 25 wines by the glass; background music. At the back, there are seats on a small terrace.

Using local and foraged produce, the well presented and interesting food includes lunchtime sandwiches, terrine of pork belly and black pudding with shallot jam, beer-battered cod cheeks with tartare sauce, rump burger topped with cheese and smoked bacon, moules marinière, home-made fishcakes with saffron mayonnaise, calves liver with smoked bacon, wholegrain mustard mash and balsamic onion jus, cannon of lamb with braised shoulder hotpot and mead-scented jus, and puddings such as prune and armagnac tart with crème anglaise and profiteroles filled with pistachio cream and glazed with a rich chocolate sauce. *Benchmark main dish: belly of pork with bubble and squeak and creamy cider sauce £15.50. Two-course evening meal £23.00.*

Free house ~ Licensee Sam Bakose ~ Real ale ~ Bar food (12-2.30, 6-9.30; all day weekends) ~ Restaurant ~ (01798) 861281 ~ Children welcome ~ Dogs allowed in bar ~ Open 11-11 ~ Bedrooms: £90B/£130B ~ www.halfwaybridge.co.uk *Recommended by Ian Wilson, Mrs Lorna Walsingham, Martin and Karen Wake, Diana Blake*

LODSWORTH
Hollist Arms
SU9223 Map 2

Off A272 Midhurst–Petworth; GU28 9BZ

Friendly and civilised village pub with local beers, good choice of wines, well liked bar food and seats outside

This smart 200-year-old village pub is just the place to head for after enjoying one of the pretty nearby walks. In fine weather, the cottagey back garden has picnic-sets on the terrace, or you can sit underneath the huge horse chestnut tree on the green. The pub is open all day and you're sure to get a warm welcome from the cheerful landlord and his team. A small snug room on the right has a sofa and two tables by an open fire – just right for a cosy drink. The public bar area on the left has stools against the pale wooden counter, more around a few tables and a comfortable built-in window seat. Langhams Hip Hop, Skinners Betty Stogs and Timothy Taylors Landlord on handpump and a decent choice of wines. The L-shaped dining room has a couple of big, squidgy sofas facing each other in front of the inglenook fireplace and plenty of elegant spoked dining chairs and wheelbacks around tables on the wood-strip floor; the pale blue walls are completely covered with genuinely interesting prints and paintings.

Popular food includes filled ciabatta sandwiches, courgette and roquefort fritters with home-made chutney, smoked salmon, crayfish, prawn, beetroot and avocado medley with pickles, several platters, beef burger with bacon and cheese, steak and wild mushroom pie, seafood tagine, duck leg cassoulet with toulouse sausages, and puddings such as crème brûlée and warm chocolate brownie with crème anglaise. *Benchmark main dish: beer-battered cod and chips £13.50. Two-course evening meal £19.00.*

Free house ~ Licensee Damian Burrowes ~ Real ale ~ Bar food (12-3, 6-9) ~ Restaurant ~ (01798) 861310 ~ Children welcome ~ Dogs welcome ~ Live music every second Sat of month ~ Open 11-11(midnight Sat); 12-10.30 Sun ~ www.thehollistarms.com
Recommended by Neil Ivens, Martin and Karen Wake, Colin McKerrow, Ann and Colin Hunt

 LURGASHALL   SU9327 Map 2

Noahs Ark

Off A283 N of Petworth; GU28 9ET

Busy old pub in nice spot with neatly kept rooms, real ales and pleasing food

This 15th-c tile-hung pub has a lovely setting, overlooked by Blackdown Hill and with views of the village green and cricket pitch; picnic-sets make the most of it, and there are more tables in the large side garden. The simple, traditional bar is popular locally and has leather-topped bar stools by the counter where they serve Greene King IPA and Abbot and a guest such as Thwaites Wainwright on handpump, several wines by the glass, farm cider and a special Bloody Mary. Beams, a mix of wooden chairs and tables on the parquet flooring and an inglenook fireplace are also features. Open right up to its apex, the dining room is spacious and airy with church candles and fresh flowers on light wood tables; a couple of comfortable sofas face each other in front of an open woodburning stove. The pub border terrier is called Gillie; visiting dogs may get a dog biscuit.

From a sensibly short menu, enjoyable food using local produce might include sandwiches (not Sunday), black pudding scotch egg, tempura-battered king prawns with garlic mayonnaise, calves liver with button mushroom sauce and streaky bacon, smoked haddock gratin with emmenthal, spinach and ricotta cannelloni, chargrilled chicken salad with crispy parma ham, a poached egg and honey mustard dressing, specials like seafood linguine and duo of pheasant, and puddings. *Benchmark main dish: home-made beef burger with cheese, bacon and mushroom and chips £10.95. Two-course evening meal £20.00.*

Greene King ~ Lease Henry Coghlan and Amy Whitmore ~ Real ale ~ Bar food (12-2.30, 7-9.30; 12-3.30 Sun; not Sun evening) ~ Restaurant ~ (01428) 707346 ~ Children welcome ~ Dogs allowed in bar ~ Open 11-11(11.30 Sat); 12-10.30(8 in winter) Sun ~ www.noahsarkinn.co.uk *Recommended by Ann and Colin Hunt*

 RINGMER   TQ4313 Map 3

Cock £

Uckfield Road – blocked-off section of road off A26 N of village turn-off; BN8 5RX

16th-c country pub with wide choice of popular bar food, real ales in character bar and plenty of seats in the garden

The roaring log fire in the inglenook fireplace (lit from October to April) makes this family-run place a welcome refuge, particularly on a chilly evening. It's 16th c and weatherboarded and the unspoilt bar is cosy with traditional pubby furniture on flagstones, heavy beams, Harveys Best and a couple of guests from breweries like Hammerpot and Hogs Back on handpump, 11 wines by the glass, 12 malt whiskies and Weston's summer cider. There are also three dining areas; background music. Outside on the terrace and in the garden are lots of picnic-sets with views across open fields to the South Downs; the sunsets are pretty. Visiting dogs are offered a bowl of water and a chew, and the owners' dogs are called Bailey and Tally. Atmosphere and service are good; background music.

A wide choice of popular food using locally sourced produce and seasonal game, with many dishes priced at under £10, might include sandwiches, egg and prawn mayonnaise, deep-fried camembert with cranberry sauce, mixed nut roast with red wine sauce, steak and ale pie, local venison burger with spicy relish, liver and bacon with onion gravy, beer-battered cod with chips, salmon with cream and watercress sauce, pork dijonnaise, chicken breast with a cheese and spinach sauce, and home-made puddings such as sticky toffee and date sponge with butterscotch sauce and rhubarb crumble. *Benchmark main dish: steak and ale pie £10.50. Two-course evening meal £16.50.*

Free house ~ Licensees Ian, Val and Matt Ridley ~ Real ale ~ Bar food (12-2.15(2.30 Sat), 6-9.30; all day Sun) ~ Restaurant ~ (01273) 812040 ~ Well behaved children welcome away from bar ~ Dogs allowed in bar ~ Open 11-3, 6-11.30; 11-11.30 Sun ~ www.cockpub.co.uk *Recommended by Mike and Eleanor Anderson, Alan Franck, Tony and Wendy Hobden, N R White*

ROBERTSBRIDGE

TQ7323   Map 3

George 🛏

High Street; TN32 5AW

Friendly former coaching inn with local beers in bustling bar, good food using seasonal produce in dining room and seats outside; good bedrooms

Popular locally but with a warm welcome for visitors, too, this is a well run former coaching inn. There's a log fire in the handsome brick inglenook fireplace, with a leather sofa and a couple of armchairs in front of it – just right for a quiet pint and a chat. High bar stools line the counter where friendly staff serve Harveys Best, Old Dairy Red Top and Rother Valley Level Best on handpump and several wines by the glass in an easy-going atmosphere; Stanley the basset hounds may appear but please don' t feed him. The adjoining dining area has elegant high-backed pale wooden chairs around a mix of tables (each with fresh flowers and a nightlight) on stripped floorboards, photographs and block paintings of local scenes, and big church candles in the small fireplace; background music. In warm weather there are plenty of seats and tables outside on the back terrace. The bedrooms are comfortable and the breakfasts good.

Using local, seasonal produce, the popular food has some interesting little touches and might include lunchtime filled baguettes, ham hock and herb terrine, home-marinated beef topped with sussex blue crumbles, various platters, home-cooked ham and free-range eggs, tempura cod and chips with home-made tartare sauce (you can take this away too on most evenings), chicken on smoked bacon and cabbage with a cream sauce, specials such as scallops with curried parsnip purée, bacon and toasted pistachios, calves liver with bubble and squeak and roasted onion jus and bass with sizzled ginger, chilli, garlic and spring onions, and puddings. *Benchmark main dish: tempura local cod and chips with home-made tartare sauce £11.00. Two-course evening meal £20.00.*

Free house ~ Licensees John and Jane Turner ~ Real ale ~ Bar food (12-2.30, 6.30-9, 12-3 Sun; not Sun evening or Mon) ~ Restaurant ~ (01580) 880315 ~ Children welcome but must be with adults at all times ~ Dogs allowed in bar ~ Live music last Sun of the month (not summer) ~ Open 11-11; 12-8 Sun; closed Mon; occasionally closed 3-6 winter Weds ~ www.thegeorgerobertsbridge.co.uk *Recommended by Mrs A S Crisp, Nigel and Jean Eames, John and Elspeth Howell*

All *Guide* inspections are anonymous. Anyone claiming to be a *Good Pub Guide* inspector is a fraud. Please let us know.

RYE TQ9120 Map 3

Ship

The Strand, at the foot of Mermaid Street; TN31 7DB

Informal and prettily set old inn with a relaxed atmosphere, straightforward furnishings, local ales and often inventive food; bedrooms

Once a warehouse for confiscating smuggled goods, this is an appealingly quirky 16th-c pub. There's a comfortable, easy-going atmosphere and a friendly welcome from the pleasant staff. The ground floor is all opened up, from the sunny big-windowed front part to a snugger section at the back, with a log fire in the stripped-brick fireplace below a stuffed boar's head. The feeling of distinct areas is enhanced by the varied flooring: composition, stripped boards, flagstones, a bit of carpet in the armchair corner. There are beams and timbers, a mixed bag of rather second-hand-feeling furnishings – a cosy group of overstuffed leather armchairs and sofa, random stripped or Formica-topped tables and various café chairs – that suit it nicely, as do the utilitarian bulkhead wall lamps. Harveys Best and Rother Valley Hoppers Ale on handpump, local farm cider and perry, and eight wines by the glass; background music and board games. Out by the quiet lane are picnic-sets and one or two cheerful oilcloth-covered tables.

A short choice of interesting dishes might include sandwiches (not weekends), fish soup, welsh rarebit with onion marmalade, sweet potato gnocchi with spinach, pine nuts and blue cheese sauce, home-made burger with cheese, bacon, onion rings and tomato relish, chicken and mushroom stroganoff, slow-roasted belly pork with white bean and chorizo stew, scallops with jerusalem artichoke and serrano ham purée and squid ink sauce, and puddings such as white chocolate and passion-fruit brûlée and rhubarb crumble with home-made ginger ice-cream. *Benchmark main dish: fish pie £13.50. Two-course evening meal £20.75.*

Enterprise ~ Lease Karen Northcote ~ Real ale ~ Bar food (12-3(3.30 weekends), 6.30-10; also, breakfast 8.30-11.30am) ~ Restaurant ~ (01797) 222233 ~ Children welcome ~ Dogs welcome ~ Open 10-11; 12-10.30 Sun ~ Bedrooms: /£90S(£100B) ~ www.theshipinnrye.co.uk *Recommended by Barry Collett, Mike Gorton, Mike and Eleanor Anderson, Phil Bryant*

 RYE TQ9220 Map 3

Ypres Castle

Gun Garden; steps up from A259, or down past Ypres Tower; TN31 7HH

Traditional pub with several real ales, quite a choice of bar food and seats in sheltered garden

New licensees took over this pleasant and bustling pub just as we went to press. It's in an interesting spot – perched beneath the ramparts of Ypres Tower and above the river in a quiet corner of the historic town. Conveniently open all day, the bars have various old tables and chairs – the informal, almost scruffy feel adds to the pub's character. There are comfortable seats by the winter log fire, local artwork, quite a mix of customers and a restaurant area serving local seafood apart from on Friday and Sunday nights; background music at other times. Harveys Best, Larkins Best, Old Dairy Copper Top and Timothy Taylors Landlord on handpump. The sheltered garden is a pleasant place to sit or play or watch boules. The resident dog is called Spud.

Using own-make bread, cakes and chutneys, the choice of food might include filled baguettes and sandwiches, crab, prawn and avocado salad, fishcakes with rocket and sun-dried tomatoes, home-baked cider ham with free-range eggs, spiced bean burger with chips, creamy chicken and asparagus tagliatelle, lamb noisettes with roasted mediterranean vegetables and couscous, a large seafood platter, and puddings such as strawberry cheesecake and spotted dick. *Benchmark main dish: home-made fish cakes £10.00. Two-course evening meal £16.00.*

Free house ~ Licensee Jon Laurie ~ Real ale ~ Bar food (12-3, 6-9(8 Fri); all day Sat; best to phone for Sun evening) ~ (01797) 223248 ~ Children welcome ~ Dogs allowed in bar ~ Open 12-11(midnight Fri and Sat; 10.30 Sun) ~ www.yprescastleinn.co.uk
Recommended by Barry Collett, Tony and Wendy Hobden, Colin and Louise English

SALEHURST TQ7424 Map 3
Salehurst Halt
Village signposted from Robertsbridge bypass on A21 Tunbridge Wells–Battle; Church Lane; TN32 5PH

Relaxed small local in quiet hamlet, chatty atmosphere, real ales, well liked bar food, and seats in pretty back garden

Come early to secure a seat at this bustling, friendly and informal little family-run pub, which is very popular with locals and visitors alike. To the right of the door, there's a small stone-floored area with a couple of tables, a piano, a settle, TV and an open fire. To the left, there's a nice long scrubbed-pine table with a couple of sofas, a mix of more ordinary pubby tables and wheelback and mate's chairs on the wood-strip floor. Occasional background music, board games and bookshelves. Dark Star American Pale Ale, Harveys Best and Old Dairy Silver Top on handpump, several malt whiskies and decent wines by the glass. The back terrace has metal chairs and tiled tables and there are more seats in the lovely landscaped garden with stunning views out over the Rother Valley; outdoor table tennis.

 Fairly priced and well liked, the food, using local produce, might include sandwiches and filled baguettes, home-smoked trout, home-glazed ham with egg and chips, tasty fishcakes with tartare sauce, steak in ale pie, venison sausages, beer-battered local fish, and particularly good curries; their specials are really worth trying and the summer pizzas from the wood-fired oven (weather permitting) are extremely popular. *Benchmark main dish: home-made curry £10.00. Two-course evening meal £15.00.*

Free house ~ Licensee Andrew Augarde ~ Real ale ~ Bar food (12-2.30, 7-9; not Mon or winter Tues and not Sun evenings) ~ (01580) 880620 ~ Children welcome ~ Dogs welcome ~ Live music second Sun of month ~ Open 12-11(12-3, 5-11 Tues and Weds); closed Mon ~ www.salehursthalt.co.uk *Recommended by Ellie Weld, David London, Robert Mitchell, Bill Adie, John and Elspeth Howell*

SUTTON SU9715 Map 2
White Horse
The Street; RH20 1PS

Opened-up country inn, contemporary décor, real ales, good wines by the glass and modern food; smart bedrooms

Close to Bignor Roman Villa, this quietly set pub is a friendly place with popular food and real ales. The bar has a couple of little open brick fireplaces at each end, nightlight candles on mantelpieces, cushioned high bar chairs, Harveys Best and a guest such as Timothy Taylors Landlord on handpump, good wines by the glass and helpful service. The wood-topped island servery separates the bar from the two-room barrel-vaulted dining area (coir carpeting here) and throughout, the minimalist décor is a contemporary clotted cream colour, with modern hardwood chairs and tables on stripped wood and a few small photographs; there's another little log fire, church candles and fresh flowers. Outside, steps lead up to a lawn with plenty of picnic-sets, and there are more seats out in front. Good walks in lovely surrounding countryside right from the door.

As well as lunchtime sandwiches, the well thought of food might include mussels with garlic and herb butter, pork terrine with plum chutney, cheddar, tomato, ricotta and spinach cannelloni, sweet chilli, prawn and salmon fishcakes with wasabi mayonnaise, steak burger with blue cheese, bacon and fat chips, pork sausages with shallot gravy, cod fillet wrapped in parma ham with spring onion mash and a tomato and chorizo concassé, lamb rump with roasted vegetables and rosemary jus, confit duck with dauphinoise potatoes and red wine reduction, and puddings like crème brûlée with a mini chocolate and fruit fondue and sticky toffee pudding with butterscotch sauce. *Benchmark main dish: home-made sausages £9.50. Two-course evening meal £17.00.*

Enterprise ~ Lease Nick Georgiou ~ Real ale ~ Bar food (not Sun evening or Mon) ~ Restaurant ~ (01798) 869221 ~ Children welcome ~ Dogs allowed in bar ~ Open 11.30-2.30, 6-11; 12-3 Sun; closed Sun evening, Mon ~ Bedrooms: £65S/£85B ~ www.whitehorse-sutton.co.uk *Recommended by Nick Lawless, Colin and Louise English*

TICEHURST

Bell 🛏

High Street; TN5 7AS

TQ6830   Map 3

Carefully and extensively restored former coaching inn with heavily beamed rooms, real ales and good wines by the glass, popular food and friendly service; bedrooms

After extensive renovations, this former coaching inn is once again the hub of the village. The changes have been sensitively done to preserve the old character, and the two main rooms still have their heavy beams, timbering and bare boards (with rugs). The bar has a couple of armchairs in front of an inglenook fireplace (much prized in winter), tables surrounded by a mix of cushioned wooden dining chairs, some quirky decorations such as a stuffed owl in a niche, a rug in the shape of a tiger skin and fez and top-hat lampshades hanging from the ceiling, sizeable stools beside the wooden counter where they serve Harveys and a couple of guest beers on handpump; good wines by the glass. The dining room is a continuation of the bar and is similarly furnished, with the addition of cushioned wall settles and an eclectic choice of paintings on the red walls; service is helpful and friendly. There's also a separate dining room with comfortable sofas grouped around a low table in front of another open fire, interesting wallpaper, a large globe, an ancient typewriter and various books and pieces of china. The former carriage room has an unusual long, sunken table with benches on either side (perfect for an informal party), and there's an upstairs function room, too. The gents' are well worth a peek for their highly unusual urinals. The comfortable, well equipped bedrooms each have a silver birch tree and other rustic décor. There are solid modern wooden chairs and tables and picnic-sets on the back terrace and on gravel.

🍴 Using local produce, the food includes sandwiches, crab on toast with avocado and chilli, duck breast with hazelnuts and green beans, beef burger with cheese and burger sauce, courgette, thyme and parmesan risotto, chargrilled chicken escalope with tomato dressing, local plaice with soft roes and lemon-buttered shrimps, barnsley chop with vegetable hash and mint gravy, rib-eye steak with béarnaise sauce, and puddings. *Benchmark main dish: deep-fried fish and triple-cooked chips £10.50. Two-course evening meal £20.50.*

Free house ~ Licensee Jhonnie de Oliveira ~ Real ale ~ Bar food (12-3,6-9.30(9 Sun)) ~ Restaurant ~ (01580) 200234 ~ Children welcome ~ Dogs allowed in bar and bedrooms ~ Live music last Sun of the month ~ Open 12-11(11.30 Sat); 12-10.30 Sun ~ Bedrooms: £90S/£120S ~ www.thebellinticehurst.com *Recommended by Jamie and Sue May, Richard Gibbs*

TILLINGTON
SU9621 Map 2

Horse Guards 🍴 � 🛏

Off A272 Midhurst–Petworth; GU28 9AF

Sussex Dining Pub of the Year

18th-c inn by fine church, beams, panelling and open fires in rambling rooms, inventive food and thoughtful choice of drinks; cottagey bedrooms

Formerly called the Old Star, this 300-year-old pub got its name in the 1840s when a squadron of the Royal Horse Guards was billeted in nearby Petworth Park to guard french prisoners of war; the soldiers spent so much time in here that the locals re-christened the place after them. The neatly kept cosy beamed front bar has some good country furniture on bare floorboards, a chesterfield in one corner, a log fire and a lovely view beyond the village to the Rother Valley from a seat in the big black-panelled bow window. High bar chairs line the counter, where they keep Harveys Best and Hammerpot Shooting Star on handpump, 15 wines by the glass, home-made sloe gin and local farm juices. Other rambling beamed rooms have similar furniture on brick floors, rugs, more open fires and original panelling, and throughout there are fresh flowers and a relaxed, gently civilised atmosphere. There's a terrace outside and more tables and chairs in a sheltered garden behind. The cosy country bedrooms are comfortable and our readers enjoy staying here. The 800-year-old church opposite is worth a look.

🍴 Using some of their own vegetables and salads and other local, seasonal produce, the delicious food might include sandwiches, home-cured duck ham with gooseberry compote, venison carpaccio with artichokes and parmesan, corned beef hash with greens, mustard sauce and a duck egg, roast baby chicken with ham hock and egg bread pudding, loin of pork with apple, black pudding and 'trotter goodness', slow-roasted lamb shoulder with dauphinoise potatoes and gravy, venison rack with boston baked beans, rare-breed 28-day hung steaks with peppercorn or wild garlic sauce, and puddings such as chocolate St Emilion torte with amaretti biscuits and mascarpone and lemon polenta cake with home-made seville orange marmalade and crème fraîche. *Benchmark main dish: smoked salmon with a poached egg and hollandaise sauce £9.50. Two-course evening meal £22.00.*

Enterprise ~ Lease Sam Beard ~ Real ale ~ Bar food (12-2.30(3 Sat, 3.30 Sun), 6.30-9) ~ (01798) 342332 ~ Children welcome ~ Dogs welcome ~ Open 12-11.30 ~ Bedrooms: /£85B ~ www.thehorseguardsinn.co.uk *Recommended by Colin McKerrow, Barry Steele-Perkins, Martin Walker, Karen Pearson, Richard Tilbrook*

If we know a pub has an outdoor play area for children, we mention it.

WARNINGLID   TQ2425   Map 3

Half Moon

B2115 off A23 S of Handcross or off B2110 Handcross–Lower Beeding; RH17 5TR

Good modern cooking in simply furnished pub with an informal chatty atmosphere, real ales, lots of wines by the glass and seats in sizeable garden

The friendly staff of this bustling 18th-c village pub work hard to ensure that the emphasis is placed equally on dining and drinking – which suits their many customers very well. The lively locals' bar has straightforward pubby furniture on bare boards and a small Victorian fireplace, and a room just off here has oak beams and flagstones. A couple of steps lead down to the dining areas with a happy mix of wooden chairs, cushioned wall settles and nice old tables on floorboards, plank panelling and bare brick walls, and old photographs of the village; there's also another open fire and a glass-covered well. Dark Star Hophead, Greene King Old Speckled Hen, Harveys Best and a weekend guest beer on handpump and 20 wines by the glass. There are quite a few picnic-sets outside on the lawn in the large, sheltered garden, which has a spectacular avenue of trees, lit by night.

Attractively presented and extremely popular, the carefully sourced bar food might include filled ciabattas, chicken liver parfait with tomato chutney, tempura pork balls with sweet and sour sauce, home-cooked ham with free-range eggs, sausages with onion gravy, home-made basil tagliatelle with goats cheese, leeks, spring onions and red peppers in a spicy tomato sauce, tandoori lamb burger with minty yoghurt, sea trout with chive butter sauce, lamb rump with citrus couscous and date purée, calves liver with smoked bacon, bubble and squeak and onion jus, and puddings such as organic double chocolate brownie with raspberry sorbet and candied fennel and rhubarb crumble, jelly, sorbet and fudge. *Benchmark main dish: beer-battered cod with pea purée £11.50. Two-course evening meal £19.50.*

Free house ~ Licensees Jonny Lea and James Amico ~ Real ale ~ Bar food (12-2, 6-9.30; not Sun evening) ~ Restaurant ~ (01444) 461227 ~ Children welcome but under-4s in own area ~ Dogs allowed in bar ~ Open 11.30-3, 5.30-11; 11.30-11 Sat; 12-10.30 Sun ~ www.thehalfmoonwarninglid.co.uk *Recommended by C and R Bromage, Ian and Barbara Rankin, Geoff and Linda Payne, Conor McGaughey, Michael Rugman, Donna Jenkins*

WEST HOATHLY   TQ3632   Map 3

Cat

Village signposted from A22 and B2028 S of East Grinstead; North Lane; RH19 4PP

Popular 16th-c inn with old-fashioned bar, airy dining rooms, real ales, good food and seats outside; lovely bedrooms

It's worth booking ahead for meals at this attractive and bustling 16th-c tile-hung inn, where hands-on licensees, a genuinely warm welcome for all and very highly thought of food (including first rate vegetarian options) all add to the appeal. There's a lovely old bar with beams, proper pubby tables and chairs on the old wooden floor and a fine log fire in the inglenook fireplace. With a focus on local breweries, Harveys Best and Old and Larkins Traditional Ale are available on handpump, as well as Hertfordshire cider and several wines by the glass; look out for a glass cover over the 23-metre well. The dining rooms are light and airy with a nice mix of wooden dining chairs and tables on pale wood-strip flooring; throughout, there are hops, china platters, brass and copper ornaments and a gently upmarket atmosphere. The contemporary-style garden room has glass doors that open on to a terrace with teak furniture. This is a comfortable and enjoyable place to stay (some of the pleasant rooms overlook the church) and the breakfasts are very good. The Bluebell Railway is near to this lovely hilltop village, as well as a host of appealing walks. Parking is limited.

Cooked by one of the landlords, the enjoyable food, using seasonal local produce, might include sandwiches, crisp salmon fishcake with mint purée, game terrine with chutney, chicken and leek pie, mussels with pancetta and leek cream, broccoli, sunblush tomato and goats cheese tart, pork and veal meatballs with tagliatelle and parmesan, confit leg of free-range duck with cassoulet, lemon sole with brown shrimp and caper butter, daily specials like lamb rump with bubble and squeak, beetroot, chestnut and squash risotto, beer-battered fish and chips, and puddings such as Valrhona chocolate ganache tart and coconut panna cotta with exotic fruit salsa. *Benchmark main dish: beer-battered fish and chips £12.50. Two-course evening meal £21.00.*

Free house ~ Licensee Andrew Russell ~ Real ale ~ Bar food (12-2(2.30 Fri-Sun), 6-9(9.30 Fri and Sat); not Sun evening) ~ (01342) 810369 ~ Children over 7 welcome ~ Dogs allowed in bar ~ Open 12-11.30; 12-4 Sun; closed Sun evening ~ Bedrooms: /£110B ~ www.catinn.co.uk *Recommended by Colin and Louise English, Laurence Evans, Scott Kerr, Chris Bell, Nick Lawless, Simon and Mandy King, B J Harding, Chris Flynn, Wendy Jones, Peter Loader, Keir Halliday*

Also Worth a Visit in Sussex

Besides the fully inspected pubs, you might like to try these pubs that have been recommended to us and described by readers. Do tell us what you think of them: feedback@goodguides.com

ALFOLD BARS   TQ0333
Sir Roger Tichborne
(01403) 751873 *B2133 N of Loxwood; RH14 0QS* Renovated and extended beamed country pub keeping original nooks and crannies, good well presented food (not Sun evening) from varied menu, friendly prompt service, five real ales including Dark Star and Tillingbourne, flagstones and log fires; children and dogs welcome, back terrace and sloping lawn with lovely rural views, good walks, open all day. *(Shirley Mackenzie, Allister Hambly, Ian Phillips)*

ALFRISTON   TQ5203
Olde Smugglers (01323) 870241
Waterloo Square; BN26 5UE Charming 14th-c inn, low beams and panelling, brick floor, sofas by huge inglenook, masses of bric-a-brac and smuggling mementoes, various nooks and crannies, welcoming licensees, wide range of popular bar food from sandwiches to specials, Dark Star, Harveys and a guest like Sharps Doom Bar, real cider, good choice of wines by the glass; background music, can get crowded – lovely village draws many visitors; children in eating area and conservatory, dogs welcome,

tables on well planted back suntrap terrace and lawn, three bedrooms, open all day. *(Phil and Jane Villiers, John Beeken, N R White, Dr A J and Mrs Tompsett)*

ALFRISTON   TQ5203
Star (01323) 870495
High Street; BN26 5TA Fine painted medieval carvings outside, heavy-beamed old-fashioned bar with some interesting features including a sanctuary post, antique furnishings and big log fire in Tudor fireplace, easy chairs in comfortable lounge, more space behind for eating, bar and pricey restaurant food, ales such as Beachy Head; children welcome, 37 good bedrooms in up-to-date part behind, open all day summer. *(the Didler, Brian and Anna Marsden)*

AMBERLEY   TQ0211
Bridge (01798) 831619
B2139; BN18 9LR Popular and welcoming open-plan dining pub, comfortable and relaxed even when busy, pleasant bar and two-room dining area, candles on tables, log fire, wide range of reasonably priced food from good sandwiches up, well kept ales including Harveys, Kings and guests; children and dogs welcome, seats out in front, more

tables in enclosed side garden, handy for station, open all day. *(Michael and Deborah Ethier, N R White, J A Snell, Julie and Bill Ryan)*

AMBERLEY   TQ0313

★ **Sportsmans**   (01798) 831787

Crossgates; Rackham Road, off B2139; BN18 9NR Popular pub with good fairly priced food and well kept ales such as Harveys, Hammerpot, Kings and Langhams (Aug festival), friendly efficient young staff, three bars including brick-floored one with darts, great views over Amberley Wild Brooks from pretty back conservatory restaurant and tables outside; dogs welcome, good walks, neat bedrooms. *(Miss Hazel Orchard, N R White, Bruce Bird, PL, Tony and Wendy Hobden and others)*

ARDINGLY   TQ3430

★ **Gardeners Arms**   (01444) 892328

B2028 2 miles N; RH17 6TJ Reliable food from sandwiches and pub favourites up in old linked rooms, Badger beers, pleasant efficient service, standing timbers and inglenooks, scrubbed pine on flagstones and broad boards, old local photographs, mural in back part, nice relaxed atmosphere; children and dogs welcome, disabled facilities, café-style furniture on pretty terrace and in side garden, opposite South of England showground and handy for Borde Hill and Wakehurst Place, open all day. *(Chris Bell, C and R Bromage)*

ARDINGLY   TQ3429

Oak   (01444) 892244

Street Lane; RH17 6UA 16th-c tile-hung dining pub with enjoyable good value food, Harveys and guests like Dark Star, good range of wines by the glass, efficient staff, brasses on low black beams, magnificent inglenook, simple bright restaurant extension, separate public bar; good-sized garden with swings and slide, handy for show ground and reservoir walks, open all day. *(Anon)*

ARLINGTON   TQ5507

★ **Old Oak**   (01323) 482072

Caneheath; off A22 or A27 NW of Polegate; BN26 6SJ 17th-c former almshouse with open-plan L-shaped bar, beams, log fires and comfortable seating, Harveys and a guest tapped from the cask, traditional bar food (all day weekends), toad in the hole played here; background music; children and dogs welcome, seats in quiet garden, walks in nearby Abbot's Wood nature reserve, open all day. *(Anon)*

ARUNDEL   TQ0208

★ **Black Rabbit**   (01903) 882828

Mill Road, Offham; keep on and don't give up!; BN18 9PB Comfortably refurbished riverside pub well organised for families and can get very busy, lovely spot near wildfowl reserve with timeless views of water meadows and castle; long bar with eating areas at either end, enjoyable fairly priced food all day from baguettes and sharing boards up, well kept Badger ales, several decent wines by the glass, log fires, newspapers; background music; dogs welcome, covered tables and pretty hanging baskets out at front, terrace across road overlooking river, play area, boat trips and good walks. *(Ann and Colin Hunt, Michael Butler, N J Roberts, Meg and Colin Hamilton, Brian and Anna Marsden and others)*

ARUNDEL   TQ0107

★ **Swan**   (01903) 882314

High Street; BN18 9AG Smart but comfortably relaxed open-plan L-shaped bar with attractive woodwork and matching fittings, friendly efficient young staff, well kept Fullers ales, good tea and coffee, good value enjoyable food from baguettes to blackboard specials, sporting bric-a-brac and old photographs, beaten brass former inn sign on wall, fire, restaurant, live jazz (third Sun of month from 5pm); 15 bedrooms, no car park, open all day. *(Jestyn Phillips, Ann and Colin Hunt, Phil and Jane Villiers, Tony and Wendy Hobden, John and Alison Hamilton)*

BALLS CROSS   SU9826

★ **Stag**   (01403) 820241

Village signed off A283 at N edge of Petworth; GU28 9JP Unchanging and cheery 17th-c country pub with friendly staff, fishing rods and country knick-knacks, tiny flagstoned bar with log fire in huge inglenook, a few seats and bar stools, Badger beers, summer cider and several wines by the glass, second tiny room and appealing old-fashioned restaurant with horsey pictures, pubby food (not Sun evening), bar skittles, darts and board games in separate carpeted room; veteran outside lavatories; well behaved children allowed away from main bar, dogs welcome, seats in front under parasols, more in good-sized back garden divided by shrubbery, bedrooms. *(N R White, Gerry and Rosemary Dobson, the Didler)*

BARCOMBE   TQ4416

Anchor   (01273) 400414

Barcombe Mills; BN8 5BS Lots of lawn tables by winding River Ouse (boat hire), two beamed bars, well kept ales including Harveys Best, friendly smartly dressed staff, restaurant and small front conservatory; open all day. *(Ann and Colin Hunt)*

BARNHAM   SU9604

Murrell Arms   (01243) 553320

Yapton Road; PO22 0AS Traditional old-fashioned place freshened-up under welcoming new licensees, but keeping original features and lots of interesting things to look at, well kept Fullers/Gales beers from huge polished half-barrel counter, good reasonably priced pubby food, two open fires; courtyard and cottagey enclosed garden up steps, open all day. *(Axel F Bengsch)*

BARNS GREEN   TQ1227
Queens Head (01403) 730436
Chapel Road; RH13 0PS Welcoming
traditional village pub, extensive blackboard
choice of good generous home-made food,
Kings ales along with Fullers London Pride
and Sharps Doom Bar, a couple of real ciders,
reasonable prices, regular quiz nights;
children welcome, tables out at front, garden
behind with play area. *(Peter Martin, Tony and
Wendy Hobden)*

BEPTON   SU8620
Country Inn (01730) 813466
Severals Road; GU29 0LR Friendly old-
fashioned country local, well kept Ballards,
Fullers, Wells & Youngs and 1648, good value
popular food (not Sun evening) from snacks
up, heavy beams, stripped brickwork and
log fire, darts-playing regulars, quiz nights;
background music, TV; children welcome,
tables out at front and in big garden with
shady trees and play area, quiet spot, open
all day Fri-Sun. *(John Beeken, Tony and Wendy
Hobden, Peter Long, Ann and Colin Hunt)*

BERWICK   TQ5105
★ Cricketers Arms (01323) 870469
Lower Road, S of A27; BN26 6SP
Charming local with three small
unpretentious bars, huge supporting beam in
each low ceiling, simple country furnishings
on quarry tiles, cricketing pastels and bats,
two log fires, Harveys tapped from the
cask, country wines, good coffee, well liked
bar food (all day weekends and summer
weekdays), old Sussex coin game – toad in
the hole; children in family room only, dogs
welcome, delightful cottagey front garden
with picnic-sets among small brick paths,
more seats behind, Bloomsbury Group wall
paintings in nearby church, good South
Downs walks. *(Michael and Margaret Cross,
Mike Gorton, the Didler, Val and Alan Green, MP,
Alec and Joan Laurence and others)*

BEXHILL   TQ7208
Denbigh (01424) 843817
*Little Common Road (A259 towards
Polegate); TN39 4JE* Friendly local
with enjoyable reasonably priced fresh
food, well kept Harveys Best, decent wine,
cheery efficient service; enclosed side
garden. *(Christopher Turner, Sue Addison)*

BILLINGSHURST   TQ0830
Blue Ship (01403) 822709
*The Haven; hamlet signposted off A29
just N of junction with A264, then
follow signpost left towards Garlands
and Okehurst; RH14 9BS* Unspoilt pub in
quiet country spot, beamed and brick-floored
front bar, scrubbed tables and wall benches,
inglenook woodburner, Badger ales served
from hatch, traditional home-made food (not
Sun or Mon evenings), two small carpeted
back rooms, darts, bar billiards, shove-

ha'penny, cribbage and dominoes; children
and dogs welcome, tables out at front and in
side garden with play area, local produce for
sale, open all day Sun. *(the Didler, N R White)*

BILLINGSHURST   TQ0725
Limeburners (01403) 782311
*Lordings Road, Newbridge (B2133/
A272 W); RH14 9JA* Friendly characterful
pub in converted row of cottages, Fullers
ales, enjoyable food (not Sun evening) from
snacks up, good friendly service, open fire; TV
in bar providing background music; children
welcome, pleasant front garden, play area
behind. *(John and Joyce Snell, Richard Luck,
Tony and Wendy Hobden)*

BLACKBOYS   TQ5220
★ Blackboys Inn (01825) 890283
B2192, S edge of village; TN22 5LG
Attractive 14th-c pub under newish
management; beamed locals' bar on left
with bric-a-brac, main bar with timbers and
more knick-knacks on red walls, seats on
parquet, winter log fire, restaurant similarly
furnished, good food (not Sun evening),
Harveys Best, Hadlow and seasonal guests,
15 wines by the glass, darts and board games;
background music; plenty of seats in front,
on terrace, under cover by sizeable pond
and on lawn by gazebo, Vanguard Way passes
the pub, Wealdway is close by and Woodland
Trust is opposite, open all day. *(the Didler)*

BODLE STREET GREEN   TQ6514
White Horse (01323) 833243
Off A271 at Windmill Hill; BN27 4RE
Roomy country pub with friendly landlord,
enjoyable homely food at varnished tables,
well kept Harveys and a guest, open fires, folk
evening every other Mon; children and dogs
welcome, some tables outside, closed Mon
lunchtimes. *(Merul Patel)*

BOGNOR REGIS   SZ9298
Navigator (01243) 864844
Marine Drive W; PO21 2QA Good value
pubby food in picture-window seafront dining
area, Greene King ales, good staff, lively local
atmosphere in carpeted bar; comfortable
bedrooms, some with sea view. *(Terry and
Nickie Williams)*

BOLNEY   TQ2623
Bolney Stage (01444) 881200
*London Road, off old A23 just N of
A272; RH17 5RL* Sizeable well refurbished
16th-c timbered dining pub, enjoyable
varied food all day including sandwiches,
Harveys and quickly changing guests, good
choice of wines by the glass, low beams and
polished flagstones, nice mix of old furniture,
woodburner and big two-way log fire;
children welcome, dogs in main bar, disabled
facilities, tables on terrace and lawn, play
area, handy for Sheffield Park and Bluebell
Railway. *(John Redfern)*

BOLNEY TQ2622
Eight Bells (01444) 881396
The Street; RH17 5QW Welcoming village pub with wide food choice from ciabattas and light dishes to enjoyable specials, bargain OAP lunch Tues and Weds, well kept Harveys and guests such as Kings and Kissingate, local wines from Bookers vineyard, brick-floor bar with eight handbells suspended from ceiling, good log fire, timbered dining extension; tables under big umbrellas on outside decking with neatly lit steps, three bedrooms. *(John Beeken, Tony and Wendy Hobden)*

BOSHAM SU8003
⋆ **Anchor Bleu** (01243) 573956
High Street; PO18 8LS Waterside inn overlooking Chichester Harbour, two simple bars with some beams in low ochre ceilings, worn flagstones and exposed timbered brickwork, lots of nautical bric-a-brac, robust, simple furniture, up to six real ales and popular bar food; children and dogs welcome, seats on back terrace looking out over ducks and boats on sheltered inlet, massive wheel-operated bulkhead door wards off high tides, church up lane figures in Bayeux Tapestry, village and shore are worth exploring, open all day in summer. *(Tony Middis, Malcolm and Barbara Southwell, Tracey and Stephen Groves, Val and Alan Green, Roy Hoing, Shirley King and others)*

BREDE TQ8218
Red Lion (01424) 882188
A28 opposite church; TN31 6EJ Relaxed beamed village pub with plain tables and chairs on bare boards, candles, inglenook log fire, good reasonably priced food including local fish, Sun carvery (should book), well kept Sharps Doom Bar, Wells & Youngs and two local guests, friendly helpful staff, back dining area decorated with sheet music and musical instruments, pub sheepdog called Billy (other dogs welcome); a few picnic-sets out at front, garden behind with roaming chickens (eggs for sale), narrow entrance to car park, open all day weekends. *(Mick B, Carol Wells, Peter Meister, V Brogden)*

BRIGHTON TQ3104
⋆ **Basketmakers Arms**
(01273) 689006 *Gloucester Road – the E end, near Cheltenham Place; off Marlborough Place (A23) via Gloucester Street; BN1 4AD* Cheerful bustling backstreet local with eight pumps serving Fullers/Gales beers and guests, decent wines by the glass, over 100 malt whiskies and quite a choice of other spirits, enjoyable very good value bar food all day (till 6pm weekends), two small low-ceilinged rooms, lots of interesting old tins, cigarette cards on one beam, whisky labels on another, also beer mats, old advertisements, photographs and posters; background music; children welcome till 8pm, dogs on leads, a few pavement tables, open all day (till midnight Fri, Sat). *(Colin Gooch, Peter Meister, Wayne Bartlett, the Didler, Brian and Anna Marsden, Rob and Catherine Dunster)*

BRIGHTON TQ3104
Colonnade (01273) 328728
New Road, off North Street; by Theatre Royal; BN1 1UF Small richly restored Edwardian bar, with red plush banquettes, velvet swags, shining brass and mahogany, gleaming mirrors, interesting pre-war playbills and signed theatrical photographs, well kept Fullers London Pride and Harveys Best, lots of lagers, bar snacks, daily newspapers; tiny front terrace overlooking Pavilion gardens. *(Val and Alan Green, Jeremy King)*

BRIGHTON TQ3104
⋆ **Cricketers** (01273) 329472
Black Lion Street; BN1 1ND Cheerful and genuine town pub, friendly bustle at busy times, good relaxed atmosphere when quieter, cosy and darkly Victorian with lots of interesting bric-a-brac – even a stuffed bear; attentive service, well kept Caledonian, Fullers, Harveys and Wells & Youngs tapped from the cask, good coffee, well priced pubby food (till 7.30pm weekends) from sandwiches up in covered former stables courtyard and upstairs bar, restaurant (where children allowed); background and some live music; tall tables out in front, open all day. *(Dr and Mrs A K Clarke, Michael Butler, Ann and Colin Hunt, Nigel and Jean Eames)*

BRIGHTON TQ3004
⋆ **Evening Star** (01273) 328931
Surrey Street; BN1 3PB Popular chatty drinkers' pub with good mix of customers, simple pale wood furniture on bare boards, up to four well kept Dark Star ales (originally brewed here), lots of changing guest beers including continentals (in bottles too), farm ciders and perries, country wines, lunchtime baguettes, friendly staff coping well when busy; background and some live music; pavement tables, open all day. *(Peter Meister, Paul Davis, the Didler)*

BRIGHTON TQ3105
⋆ **Greys** (01273) 680734
Southover Street, off A270 Lewes Road opposite The Level (public park); BN2 9UA Certainly not a standard pub but does have basic simple furnishings on bare boards and flagstones, some wood panelling and flame-effect stove, bar on right liked by regulars, dining side on left with flowers and candles on tables, Harveys and Timothy Taylors, several belgian bottled beers, carefully chosen wines, good food (not Sun evening, Mon or Fri) using local ingredients, live music Mon evening (tickets only), posters and flyers from previous performers on stair wall; no children; dogs in bar, seats under parasols on heated terrace,

almost no parking on this steep lane or in nearby streets, open from 4pm, all day weekends. *(Anon)*

BRIGHTON
Hand in Hand
TQ3103
(01273) 699595

Upper Street James's Street, Kemptown; BN2 1JN Brighton's smallest pub (can get crowded) brewing its own unusual Kemptown ales, also five weekly changing guests, plenty of bottled beers and Weston's cider, hot pies and sausage rolls, cockles and mussels Fri, cheerful service, dim-lit bar with tie collection and newspaper cuttings all over the walls, photographs including Victorian nudes on ceiling, colourful mix of customers; veteran fruit machine, interesting background music, live jazz Sun; open all day. *(Eddie Edwards)*

BRIGHTON
Lord Nelson
TQ3104
(01273) 695872

Trafalgar Street; BN1 4ED Blue-painted two-room backstreet local, popular and friendly, with full Harveys range kept well along with real cider, good value lunchtime food, log fire, back conservatory, folk night first Mon of month; children and dogs welcome, open all day (till midnight Fri, Sat). *(the Didler)*

BRIGHTON
Prince George
TQ3104
(01273) 681055

Trafalgar Street; BN1 4EQ Three linked rooms (front ones are best) off main bar, mix of furnishings on stripped floor, several big mirrors, six well kept changing local ales, lots of wines by the glass, inexpensive popular organic and vegetarian/vegan food all day, friendly helpful staff; children welcome, small heated back courtyard. *(Rob and Catherine Dunster)*

BRIGHTON
Pub du Vin
TQ3004
(01273) 718588

Ship Street; BN1 1AD Next to Hotel du Vin, long and narrow with comfortable wall seating one end, soft lighting, local photographs, stripped boards, five well kept ales including Dark Star and Harveys from ornate pewter bar counter, good choice of wines by the glass, friendly helpful staff, enjoyable pubby food, modern grey leather-seated bar chairs and light oak tables, flame-effect fire, small cosy coir-carpeted room opposite with squashy black armchairs and sofas; marvellous original marble urinals worth a look; 11 comfortable bedrooms. *(Dr and Mrs A K Clarke, M E and F J Thomasson, Jeremy King)*

BRIGHTON
West Quay
TQ3105
(01273) 645780

Brighton Marina; BN2 5UT Large well run Wetherspoons on two floors, big windows and terraces overlooking the water, their usual good value food and beers; open all day from 8am. *(Tony and Wendy Hobden)*

BUCKS GREEN
Fox
TQ0733
(01403) 822386

Guildford Road (A281 W of Rudgwick); RH12 3JP Ancient open-plan inglenook bar with decent-sized restaurant specialising in good generous fish, Badger beers, decent wines by the glass, efficient service; picnic-sets out on large paved area. *(John Beeken)*

BURPHAM
★ George & Dragon
TQ0308
(01903) 883131

Off A27 near Warningcamp; BN18 9RR Good interesting modern food is the main emphasis at this busy 17th-c pub and the front part is restaurant, small area for drinkers with a couple of real ales, efficient service; they ask to keep a credit card if you run a tab; children welcome, dogs in bar, some picnic-sets out in front, hilltop village and short walk from door gives splendid views down to Arundel Castle and river. *(Tony Middis, Ben Samways, Richard Tilbrook, Phil and Gill Wass, Brian and Anna Marsden, Derek and Marianne Farmer and others)*

BURY
Squire & Horse
TQ0013
(01798) 831343

Bury Common; A29 Fontwell–Pulborough; RH20 1NS Beamed roadside pub with good food and friendly efficient service, well kept Harveys and a guest such as Adnams, good choice of wines, several attractive partly divided areas, plush wall seats, hunting prints and ornaments, log fire; no dogs; children welcome, pleasant garden and pretty terrace (some road noise). *(Terry and Nickie Williams)*

BYWORTH
★ Black Horse
SU9821
(01798) 342424

Off A283; GU28 0HL Popular and chatty country pub with smart simply furnished bar, pews and scrubbed tables on bare boards, pictures and old photographs, daily newspapers and open fires, ales such as Flowerpots, Langhams and Wells & Youngs, decent food (not winter Sun evening) from light lunchtime dishes up, children's menu, nooks and crannies in back restaurant, spiral staircase to a heavily beamed function room, games room with pool; dogs allowed in bar, attractive garden with tables on steep grassy terraces, lovely Downs' views, open all day. *(Tony and Wendy Hobden, Ann and Colin Hunt, the Didler)*

CHAILEY
Horns Lodge
TQ3919
(01273) 400422

A275; BN8 4BD Traditional former coaching inn, heavily timbered inside, with settles, horsebrasses and rural prints, log fires at each end of longish front bar, well kept Harveys and guests, good range of fairly priced bar food (not Tues) from sandwiches up, obliging staff, brick-floored restaurant, games room with darts and bar billiards, cribbage, dominoes and board games too; background music; children and dogs welcome, tables in garden with sandpit, bedrooms, open all day weekends. *(John Beeken, Tony and Wendy Hobden)*

CHELWOOD GATE   TQ4130
Red Lion   (01825) 740265
A275, S of Forest Row junction with A22; RH17 7DE Roomy open-plan dining pub with good choice of enjoyable food, well kept Shepherd Neame ales and nice range of wines, friendly young staff, comfortable sofas by open fire; dogs welcome, big sheltered side garden, handy for Ashdown Forest walks, closed Mon. *(Neil Hardwick)*

CHICHESTER   SU8504
Fountain   (01243) 781352
Southgate; PO19 1ES Attractive two-room front bar, small dining room behind incorporating part of Roman wall, wide choice of enjoyable pubby food, friendly helpful staff, Badger beers, live music; children and dogs welcome, courtyard tables, open all day. *(Dave Braisted, John and Alison Hamilton)*

CLAYTON   TQ2914
Jack & Jill   (01273) 843595
Brighton Road (A273); BN6 9PD Friendly unsmart three-room country pub run by same family since 1970; good interesting food amongst more pubby choices, nice local cheeseboard, well kept changing ales and good wines, dark pubby furniture on patterned carpets, plush wall seats, rural memorabilia and knick-knacks, fresh flowers, log fire in brick fireplace; children and dogs welcome, picnic-sets in big back garden with play area, landmark twin windmills nearby, bedrooms. *(Tamara Pomero)*

CLIMPING   TQ0001
Black Horse   (01903) 715175
Climping Street; BN17 5RL Friendly 18th-c dining pub with good choice of food from traditional choices up, well kept ales including Harveys, decent wines by the glass, log fires, skittle alley; children welcome, tables out in front and on back decking, short walk to the beach. *(Axel F Bengsch)*

COCKING CAUSEWAY   SU8819
Greyhound   (01730) 814425
A286 Cocking–Midhurst; GU29 9QH Pretty 18th-c tile-hung pub, enjoyable good value home-made food (should book weekends), Hop Back Summer Lightning and three guests, friendly prompt service, cosy beamed and panelled bar, log fire, pine furniture in big new dining conservatory; children welcome, grassed area at front with picnic-sets and huge eucalyptus, sizeable garden and play area behind, open all day Sun. *(John Beeken, Ann and Colin Hunt, Tony and Wendy Hobden)*

COLEMANS HATCH   TQ4533
⋆**Hatch**   (01342) 822363
Signed off B2026, or off B2110 opposite church; TN7 4EJ Quaint and attractive little weatherboarded Ashdown Forest pub dating from 1430, big log fire in quickly filling beamed bar, small back dining room with another fire, very wide choice of good generous home-made food, well kept Harveys, Larkins and one or two guest beers, friendly quick young staff, good mix of customers including families and dogs; not much parking, so get there early; picnic-sets on front terrace and in beautifully kept big garden, open all day Sun, and Sat in summer. *(Laurence Smith, Christian Mole, Bruce Bird, the Didler, N R White)*

COMPTON   SU7714
Coach & Horses   (023) 9263 1228
B2146 S of Petersfield; PO18 9HA Welcoming 16th-c two-bar local in pleasant village not far from Uppark (NT), pine shutters, panelling, beams and log fires, up to five changing ales, some interesting food cooked by landlord/chef from lunchtime snacks up, bar billiards; children and dogs welcome, tables out by village square, good surrounding walks. *(Geoff and Linda Payne, John and Alison Hamilton)*

COOLHAM   TQ1423
⋆**George & Dragon**   (01403) 741320
Dragons Green, Dragons Lane; pub signed off A272; RH13 8GE Tile-hung cottage with cosy chatty bar, massive unusually low black beams (see if you can decide whether the date cut into one is 1677 or 1577), timbered walls, simple chairs and rustic stools, roaring log fire in big inglenook, Badger beers and decent pub food served by friendly staff, smaller back bar, separate restaurant; children and dogs welcome, picnic-sets in pretty orchard garden, open all day weekends (till 8pm Sun). *(Ian Phillips, Tony and Wendy Hobden, J V Dadswell)*

COOTHAM   TQ0714
Crown   (01903) 742625
Pulborough Road (A283); RH20 4JN Extended village pub with L-shaped bar on two levels, well kept Bass, Harveys and Wadworths 6X, good choice of hearty reasonably priced food (smaller helping available), friendly efficient service, two open fires, large back dining area, games room with darts and pool; children and dogs welcome, garden with play area and goats, open all day weekends. *(Tony and Wendy Hobden, John Beeken)*

COUSLEY WOOD   TQ6533
⋆**Old Vine**   (01892) 782271
B2100 Wadhurst–Lamberhurst; TN5 6ER 16th-c weather-boarded pub with linked, uncluttered rooms, heavy beams and open timbering, church candles on attractive

old pine tables surrounded by farmhouse chairs, several settles (one by big log fire has an especially high back), bare boards or parquet flooring (restaurant area is carpeted), well kept Harveys Best and a guest from attractively painted servery, several good wines by the glass, tasty food served by friendly helpful staff; dogs welcome, picnic-sets on front terrace, open all day weekends. *(N R White)*

COWBEECH   TQ6114
★ **Merrie Harriers** (01323) 833108
Off A271; BN27 4JQ White clapboarded 16th-c village local, beamed public bar with inglenook log fire, high-backed settle and mixed tables and chairs, old local photographs, carpeted dining lounge, well kept Harveys Best and a guest, winter mulled wine, good food from nice bar snacks up, friendly service, brick-walled back restaurant; rustic seats in terraced garden with country views, open all day Fri-Sun. *(Tobias Sheppard, Gary Neate)*

COWFOLD   TQ2122
Coach House (01403) 864247
Horsham Road; RH13 8BT Comfortable and welcoming, with enjoyable well priced pubby food (not Sun evening), ales including Harveys Best, good coffee and service, attractive traditional main bar, sofas by log fire, roomy neatly laid restaurant area, locals' bar (no children) with darts and pool, quiz and open-mike nights; dogs welcome, lovely garden with terrace and play area, 13 bedrooms (nine in converted stables), open all day from 7.30am. *(Tony and Wendy Hobden)*

CRAWLEY DOWN   TQ3437
Dukes Head (01342) 712431
A264/A2028 by roundabout; RH10 4HH Big refurbished place with emphasis on eating, large lounge bar and three differently styled dining areas, log fires, good choice of well liked food all day including fixed-price menu and popular Sun roasts, decent wines, ales such as Fullers London Pride and Harveys, nice staff; can get very busy weekends; seats out at the front, handy for Gatwick. *(Phil Lowther, Fraser Danbury, Richard Mason)*

CUCKFIELD   TQ3024
Talbot (01444) 455898
High Street; RH17 5JX Thriving pub under same management as the Half Moon at Warninglid (see Main Entries); light airy feel, imaginative food in bar and upstairs restaurant, real ales, good service; open all day. *(Terry Buckland)*

DALLINGTON   TQ6619
★ **Swan** (01424) 838242
Woods Corner, B2096 E; TN21 9LB Popular local with cheerful chatty atmosphere, well kept Harveys, decent wines by the glass, enjoyable pubby food

including deals, takeaway fish and chips (Tues), efficient service, bare-boards bar divided by standing timbers, woodburner, mixed furniture including cushioned settle and high-backed pew, candles in bottles and fresh flowers, simple back restaurant with far-reaching views to the coast; background music; steps down to lavatories and garden. *(Mike and Eleanor Anderson, N R White)*

DELL QUAY   SU8302
Crown & Anchor (01243) 781712
Off A286 S of Chichester – look out for small sign; PO20 7EE Modernised 19th/20th-c beamed pub in splendid spot overlooking Chichester Harbour – best at high tide and quiet times (can be packed on sunny days); comfortable bow-windowed lounge bar, panelled public bar (dogs welcome), two log fires, lots of wines by the glass, well kept Wells & Youngs ales and a guest, enjoyable all-day food served by friendly staff who cope well at busy times; children welcome, large terrace, nice walks. *(Ann and Colin Hunt, Jim and Frances Gowers, Miss A E Dare, N J Roberts, J A Snell, Martin and Karen Wake and others)*

DEVILS DYKE   TQ2511
Devils Dyke (01273) 857256
Devils Dyke Road; BN1 8YJ Vintage Inn set alone on Downs above Brighton and worth visiting for the spectacular views night and day; their usual food, well kept ales such as Harveys Best, Shepherd Neame Spitfire and Timothy Taylors Landlord, helpful friendly staff; children welcome, tables outside, NT pay car park, open all day. *(Colin Gooch, Dave Snowden)*

DITCHLING   TQ3215
★ **Bull** (01273) 843147
High Street (B2112); BN6 8TA Handsome rambling old building, beams, old wooden furniture on bare boards, fire, well kept Harveys, Timothy Taylors Landlord and two guests, home-made food from sandwiches up including good Sun roasts, nicely furnished dining rooms with mellow décor and candles, snug area with chesterfields; background music – live folk last Sun of month; children welcome, dogs in bar, attractive big garden and suntrap terrace, barbecue, four nice bedrooms, good breakfast, open all day. *(Nick Lawless)*

EARTHAM   SU9309
★ **George** (01243) 814340
Signed off A285 Chichester–Petworth, from Fontwell off A27, from Slindon off A29; PO18 0LT Well kept pub with wide range of good blackboard food, friendly helpful staff, local real ales, well listed wines, log fire in comfortable lounge, flagstoned public bar (dogs allowed on leads) with old farm tools and photographs, smart restaurant; background music; children welcome in eating areas, easy disabled

access, large garden, attractive surroundings and lovely walks, open all day summer weekends. *(David H T Dimock)*

EASEBOURNE
White Horse
SU8922
(01730) 813521

Off A272 just NE of Midhurst; GU29 0AL Old-fashioned, unspoilt beamed village pub, comfortably worn fireside armchairs in well divided mainly bare-boards bar with small dining area, short simple menu (not cheap), Greene King ales, efficient friendly service; children and dogs welcome, tables on back grass and in sunny courtyard. *(Ann and Colin Hunt)*

EAST ASHLING
★ Horse & Groom
SU8207
(01243) 575339

B2178; PO18 9AX Busy country pub with well kept Hop Back Summer Lightning, Sharps Doom Bar and Wells & Youngs Bitter, decent choice of wines by the glass, bar food from good sandwiches up, reasonable prices and helpful service, unchanging front drinkers' bar with old pale flagstones and inglenook woodburner, carpeted area with scrubbed trestle tables, fresh and airy extension with solid pale country-kitchen furniture on neat bare boards; children and dogs allowed in some parts, garden with picnic-sets under umbrellas, bedrooms, open all day Sat, closed Sun evening. *(Traudi Wiggins, Ann and Colin Hunt)*

EAST DEAN
Star & Garter
SU9012
(01243) 811318

Village signed with Charlton off A286 in Singleton; also signed off A285; PO18 0JG Newish management at this airy dining pub, attractively furnished bar and restaurant with panelling, exposed brickwork and oak floors, furnishings from sturdy stripped tables and country kitchen chairs through chunky modern to some antique carved settles, Arundel ales tapped from the cask, several wines by the glass, food pricey and can be very good especially the fish; background music; children welcome, dogs in bar, teak furniture on heated terrace, smokers' shelter, steps down to walled lawn with picnic-sets, peaceful village green position and near South Downs Way, bedrooms, open all day weekends (food all day then too). *(Ann and Colin Hunt, Martin and Karen Wake, M and GR)*

EAST GRINSTEAD
★ Old Mill
TQ3936
(01342) 326341

Dunnings Road, S towards Saint Hill; RH19 4AT Interesting 16th-c mill cottage over stream reworked as spacious informal Whiting & Hammond dining pub; lots of panelling, old photographs and pictures, carpeted main dining area with mix of old tables (each with church candle), steps down to ancient very low-ceilinged part with fine timbers and inglenook woodburner, sizeable bar with long curved counter and

bright plush stools, library dining area off, enjoyable hearty fresh food (all day), good choice of wines by the glass, Harveys ales including seasonal, friendly efficient service; background music; children welcome, picnic-sets in front garden, covered deck next to working waterwheel, handy for Standen (NT). *(N J Roberts, Andrew Hughes, Laurence Evans)*

EAST HOATHLY
★ Kings Head
TQ5216
(01825) 840238

High Street/Mill Lane; BN8 6DR Well kept 1648 ales (brewed here) and Harveys Best in long comfortably worn-in open-plan bar, some dark panelling and stripped brick, upholstered settles, old local photographs, log-fire, wide choice of enjoyable sensibly priced hearty food, friendly helpful service, daily newspapers, restaurant; TV; garden up steps behind. *(John Beeken)*

EASTBOURNE
Hurst Arms
TQ5900
(01323) 730385

Willingdon Road; BN21 1TW Popular three-room local with well kept Harveys, friendly chatty staff, darts and pool; big-screen TV, juke box; front terrace and nice back garden, open all day. *(the Didler)*

ELSTED
Elsted Inn
SU8320
(01730) 813662

Elsted Marsh; GU29 0JT Welcoming attractive country pub, enjoyable food from shortish menu, real ales such as Cottage, Ballards and Otter, two log fires, nice country furniture, old Goodwood racing photos (both horses and cars), dining area at back; plenty of seating in lovely enclosed Downs-view garden with big terrace, four bedrooms, open all day summer. *(Geoff and Linda Payne)*

ELSTED
★ Three Horseshoes
SU8119
(01730) 825746

Village signed from B2141 Chichester–Petersfield; from A272 about 2 miles W of Midhurst, turn left heading W; GU29 0JY A congenial bustle at this pretty white-painted old pub, beamed rooms, log fires and candlelight, ancient flooring, antique furnishings, fresh flowers and attractive prints and photographs, four changing ales tapped from the cask, summer cider, home-made food can be good, friendly service but may be a wait on busy summer days; well behaved children allowed, dogs in bar, delightful flowering garden with plenty of seats and fine views of South Downs, good surrounding walks. *(Tony and Jill Radnor, Gael Pawson, Simon and Mandy King, Mr and Mrs W Mills, Miss A E Dare and others)*

ERIDGE STATION
★ Huntsman
TQ5434
(01892) 864258

Signed off A26 S of Eridge Green; TN3 9LE Country local under newish licensees, two opened-up rooms with pubby furniture on bare boards, some tables with carved/painted board games including own 'Eridgeopoly', hunting pictures, three Badger ales, over a dozen wines by the glass, popular bar food (not Sun evening, Mon) including fresh fish, seasonal game and home-grown produce, friendly staff; children and dogs welcome, picnic-sets and heaters on decking, outside bar, more seats on lawn among weeping willows, open all day weekends, closed Mon lunchtime. *(Mrs J Ekins-Daukes, B J Harding, Peter Meister, N R White, Alan Franck and others)*

FERNHURST   SU9028
Red Lion (01428) 643112
The Green, off A286 via Church Lane; GU27 3HY Friendly wisteria-covered 16th-c pub tucked quietly away by green and cricket pitch near church, heavy beams and timbers, attractive furnishings, food from interesting sandwiches and snacks up, well kept Fullers ales and a guest, good wines, cheerful helpful service, restaurant; children welcome, pretty gardens front and back, open all day Sun. *(Chris Harrington, Ann and Colin Hunt, Martin and Karen Wake)*

FERRING   TQ0903
Henty Arms (01903) 241254
Ferring Lane; BN12 6QY Six well kept changing ales, generous attractively priced food (can get busy so best to book), breakfast from 9am Tues-Fri, neat friendly staff, opened-up lounge/dining area, log fire, separate bar with games and TV; garden tables. *(Tony and Wendy Hobden)*

FIRLE   TQ4607
⋆ Ram (01273) 858222
Village signed off A27 Lewes–Polegate; BN8 6NS Refurbished 16th-c village pub geared for dining but welcoming drinkers, locally sourced restaurant food (not particularly cheap) including good Sun roasts, well kept Harveys with guests such as Hop Back and Sharps, real cider and plenty of wines, friendly staff, three main areas with log fires, rustic furniture on wood floors, soft lighting; children and dogs welcome, picnic-sets out in front, big walled garden behind with fruit trees, play area, good walks, four stylish bedrooms, open all day. *(J A Snell, Alan Franck, N R White)*

FISHBOURNE   SU8304
⋆ Bulls Head (01243) 839895
Fishbourne Road (A259 Chichester–Emsworth); PO19 3JP Thoroughly traditional with copper pans on black beams, some stripped brick and panelling, good log fire, well kept Fullers/Gales ales, popular good value food (not Sun evening) changing daily, friendly attentive staff, daily newspapers; unobtrusive background music; children welcome, tables on heated covered deck, four bedrooms in former skittle alley. *(John Beeken, Miss A E Dare, J A Snell, David H T Dimock, Terry and Nickie Williams and others)*

FITTLEWORTH   TQ0118
⋆ Swan (01798) 865429
Lower Street (B2138, off A283 W of Pulborough); RH20 1EL Pretty tile-hung dining inn, comfortable beamed main bar, windsor chairs and bar stools on wood and carpeted floor, big inglenook log fire, Fullers London Pride, Sharps Doom Bar and a guest, wide range of wines, cocktails, good food from pubby choices up in bar and separate panelled restaurant, pleasant attentive staff; children and dogs welcome, big back lawn with plenty of tables, good nearby walks, 15 bedrooms, closed Sun evening, otherwise open all day. *(John Michelson, Colin McKerrow, Tony and Wendy Hobden)*

FULKING   TQ2411
Shepherd & Dog (01273) 857382
Off A281 N of Brighton, via Poynings; BN5 9LU Old bay-windowed pub in beautiful spot below Downs, beams, panelling and inglenook, ales such as Dark Star, enjoyable food from baguettes up, friendly efficient service; terrace and pretty streamside garden with well used picnic-sets, straightforward climb to Devils Dyke. *(John Redfern, Martin and Karen Wake)*

FUNTINGTON   SU7908
Fox & Hounds (01243) 575246
Common Road (B2146); PO18 9LL Old bay-windowed pub with updated beamed rooms in grey/green shades, welcoming log fires, good food from open sandwiches and snacks up, popular Sun carvery, well kept Harveys, Timothy Taylors and guests, lots of wines by the glass and good coffee, comfortable dining extension; children welcome, tables out in front and in walled garden behind, pair of inn signs – one a pack of hounds, the other a family of foxes, open all day from 8am. *(Anon)*

GLYNDE   TQ4508
⋆ Trevor Arms (01273) 858208
Over railway bridge, S of village; BN8 6SS Brick and flint village pub, impressive dining room with mix of high-backed settles, pews and cushioned dining chairs around mixed tables, carpeted middle room with Glyndebourne pictures leading to snug bar with small fireplace and fine downland views, reasonably priced enjoyable home-made food including OAP weekday lunch deal, well kept Harveys ales, cheerful service, locals' bar with parquet flooring, panelled dado, old photographs of the pub, darts and toad in the hole; big garden with rows of picnic-sets and Downs backdrop, popular with walkers, railway station next door, open all day. *(John Beeken, Ann and Colin Hunt)*

GRAFFHAM   SU9218
Foresters Arms (01798) 867202
Off A285; GU28 0QA 16th-c pub under

newish licensees, heavy beams, log fire in huge brick fireplace, pews and pale windsor chairs around light modern tables, two other areas, ales such as Harveys and Dark Star, good food including weekday set lunch menu, monthly live jazz; children and dogs welcome, attractive sunny back garden, good walks, some classic car meetings, three bedrooms. *(Anon)*

GRAFFHAM   SU9217
White Horse (01798) 867331
On road signed to Heyshott/Midhurst; GU28 0NT Spotless local just outside village, good home-made food (best to book weekends), several well kept changing ales (June beer festival), good choice of wines by the glass, welcoming friendly licensees, log fires, small dining room and conservatory restaurant with South Downs views; terrace, lovely big garden, good local walks, new bedroom block, open all day weekends, closed Mon lunchtime. *(John Beeken)*

GUN HILL   TQ5614
★ Gun (01825) 872361
Off A22 NW of Hailsham, or off A267; TN21 0JU Big 15th-c country dining pub, several refurbished rambling areas either side of large central bar, beams and log fires, enjoyable locally sourced food from sandwiches and sharing boards up, Harveys, good wines, efficient friendly service; children welcome, large garden with play area, right on Wealden Way, open all day Sun *(Dr A J and Mrs Tompsett)*

HALNAKER   SU9008
★ Anglesey Arms (01243) 773474
A285 Chichester–Petworth; PO18 0NQ Bare boards, settles and log fire, Black Sheep, Wells & Youngs and a couple of well kept guests like Hop Back Crop Circle and Ringwood Boondoggle, decent wines, good varied if not cheap food including local organic produce and Selsey fish, friendly accommodating service, simple but smart L-shaped dining room (children allowed) with woodburners, stripped pine and some flagstones, traditional games; tables in big tree-lined garden, good nearby walks, may open all day Fri and Sat. *(Howard and Margaret Buchanan)*

HAMMERPOT   TQ0605
★ Woodmans Arms (01903) 871240
On N (eastbound) side of A27; BN16 4EU Well kept pretty thatched pub rebuilt after 2004 fire, beams and timbers, good choice of enjoyable food from sandwiches up (smaller helpings available), Fullers/Gales beers and a guest, efficient service from friendly neat staff, woodburner in inglenook; no dogs inside; children welcome if eating, tables in nice garden, open all day, closed Sun evening. *(Ann and Colin Hunt, Tony and Wendy Hobden, Peter Meister, Val and Alan Green)*

HARTFIELD   TQ4735
Haywaggon (01892) 770252
High Street (A2026); TN7 4AB Sizeable 16th-c dining pub in centre of village, two big log fires, pews and lots of large tables in spacious low-beamed bar, good varied choice of food in former bakehouse restaurant, cheerful helpful staff, well kept Harveys and a guest like Black Cat, reasonably priced wines, live jazz second Mon of month; tables outside, bedrooms in converted stable block, open all day. *(Nigel and Jean Eames)*

HENLEY   SU8925
★ Duke of Cumberland Arms
(01428) 652280 *Off A286 S of Fernhurst; GU27 3HQ* Wisteria-covered 15th-c stone-built pub with log fires in two small rooms, low ceilings, scrubbed oak furniture on brick or flagstoned floors, rustic decorations, well kept Harveys and a couple of guests tapped from the cask such as Langhams, very good food (not Sun or Mon evenings) from well executed pub favourites to interesting restaurant-style dishes, separate tiled-floor dining room with more modern feel, friendly attentive staff; well behaved children and dogs welcome, deck with lovely hill views, charming sloping garden and trout ponds, open all day. *(Chris Harrison, Miss A E Dare, Tracey and Stephen Groves, the Didler, Conor McGaughey, Matthew Cramer)*

HERMITAGE   SU7505
★ Sussex Brewery (01243) 371533
A259 just W of Emsworth; PO10 8AU Bustling, welcoming and interesting, with small boards-and-sawdust bar, good fire in huge brick fireplace, simple furniture, little flagstoned snug, six real ales and several wines by the glass, good value hearty food including wide choice of speciality sausages (even vegetarian ones), small upstairs restaurant; children and dogs welcome, picnic-sets in small back courtyard, open all day. *(Andy Rhodes, Miss J F Reay)*

HOUGHTON   TQ0111
★ George & Dragon (01798) 831559
B2139 W of Storrington; BN18 9LW 13th-c beams and timbers in attractive bar rambling up and down steps, note the elephant photograph above the fireplace, good Arun Valley views from back extension, well liked reasonably priced food served by friendly staff, Marstons-related ales and decent wines; background music; children and dogs welcome, seats on decked terrace and in charming sloping garden, good walks, open all day Fri-Sun. *(Michael and Deborah Ethier, Colin McKerrow, Julie and Bill Ryan)*

HUNSTON   SU8601
Spotted Cow (01243) 786718
B2145 S of Chichester; PO20 1PD Flagstoned pub with friendly staff and locals, wide choice of enjoyable food, chilled Fullers/

Gales beers, big fires and up-to-date décor, small front bar, roomier side lounge with armchairs, sofas and low tables as anteroom for airy high-ceilinged restaurant; may be background music; good disabled access, children welcome if eating, big pretty garden, handy for towpath walkers. *(Ann and Colin Hunt, David H T Dimock)*

HURSTPIERPOINT   TQ2816
✶ **New Inn** (01273) 834608

High Street; BN6 9RQ Popular 16th-c beamed pub under same management as Bull in Ditchling, well kept ales including Harveys, good wines by the glass, enjoyable food with plenty for vegetarians, good friendly young staff, contrasting linked areas including dimly lit oak-panelled back part with bric-a-brac and open fire, and smart apple-green dining room; sports TV; children and dogs welcome, garden tables, open all day. *(Tim Loryman, Conor McGaughey)*

ICKLESHAM   TQ8716
✶ **Queens Head** (01424) 814552

Off A259 Rye–Hastings; TN36 4BL Friendly well run country pub, extremely popular locally (and at weekends with cyclists and walkers), open-plan areas around big counter, high timbered walls, vaulted roof, shelves of bottles, plenty of farming implements and animal traps, pubby furniture on brown pattered carpet, other areas with inglenooks and a back room with old bicycle memorabilia, Greene King, Harveys and a couple of guests, local cider, several wines by the glass, straightforward generous bar food (all day weekends); background jazz or blues (live 4-6pm Sun); well behaved children allowed away from bar till 8.30pm, dogs welcome in bar, picnic-sets, boules and play area in peaceful garden with fine Brede Valley views, you can walk to Winchelsea, open all day. *(Ellie Weld, David London, John Prescott, Mr and Mrs Price, Andrea Rampley)*

ICKLESHAM   TQ8716
✶ **Robin Hood** (01424) 814277

Main Road; TN36 4BD Friendly no-frills beamed pub with enthusiastic landlord and cheerful attentive staff, great local atmosphere, good value unpretentious home-made food including blackboard specials, six well kept changing ales (many from small breweries), two real ciders, hops overhead, lots of copper bric-a-brac, log fire, games area with pool, back dining extension; big garden with Brede Valley views. *(Conrad Freezer, Peter Meister)*

ISFIELD   TQ4417
Laughing Fish (01825) 750349

Station Road; TN22 5XB Nicely old-fashioned opened-up Victorian local, jovial landlord and friendly staff, good value home-made bar food (not Sun evening) including specials board and some good vegetarian dishes, Greene King and guests, extensive wine list, open fire, train pictures, bar billiards and other traditional games, events including entertaining beer race Easter Mon; children and dogs welcome, disabled access, small pleasantly shaded walled garden with enclosed play area, right by Lavender Line (pub was station hotel), open all day. *(John Beeken, Ann and Colin Hunt)*

KINGSTON   TQ3908
✶ **Juggs** (01273) 472523

Village signed off A27 by roundabout W of Lewes; BN7 3NT Popular rose-covered village pub, heavy 15th-c beams and very low front door, lots of neatly stripped masonry, sturdy wooden furniture on bare boards and stone slabs, smaller eating areas including a family room, wide choice of enjoyable food with plenty of fish and good vegetarian options, well kept Shepherd Neame and a beer brewed for the pub, good coffee and wine list, friendly helpful staff, log fires; background music; children and dogs welcome, disabled facilities, nice covered area outside with heaters, lots of hanging baskets, play area, good walks, open all day. *(PL, John Beeken, Richard Mckinstry, Tony and Wendy Hobden)*

LEWES   TQ4210
Gardeners Arms (01273) 474808

Cliffe High Street; BN7 2AN Warmly welcoming, unpretentious small local opposite brewery, light and airy, with plain scrubbed tables on bare boards around three narrow sides of bar, well kept Harveys and interesting changing guests, farm ciders, some lunchtime food including good pies, bar nibbles on Sun, newspapers and magazines, toad in the hole played here; open all day. *(N Wiseman, Ann and Colin Hunt, the Didler)*

LEWES   TQ4210
John Harvey (01273) 479880

Bear Yard, just off Cliffe High Street; BN7 2AN No-nonsense tap for nearby Harveys brewery, four of their beers including seasonals kept perfectly, some tapped from the cask, good well priced food (not Sun evening) from huge lunchtime sandwiches, baked potatoes and ciabattas up, friendly efficient young staff, basic dark flagstoned bar with one great vat halved to make two towering 'snugs' for several people, lighter room on left, newspapers, woodburner; background music and machines; a few tables outside, open all day, breakfast from 10am. *(Ann and Colin Hunt, Gene and Kitty Rankin, the Didler, Martin and Oliver Wright and others)*

LEWES   TQ4110
✶ **Lewes Arms** (01273) 473152

Castle Ditch Lane/Mount Place – tucked behind castle ruins; BN7 1YH Cheerful unpretentious little local with half a dozen well kept ales, 30 malt whiskies and plenty of wines by the glass, very good reasonably priced bar food (all day Sat, not Sun evening), tiny front bar on right with stools along nicely curved counter and bench window seats, two other simple rooms hung with photographs and information about the famous Lewes bonfire night, beer mats pinned over doorways, poetry and folk evenings; children (not in front bar) and dogs welcome, picnic-sets on attractive two-level back terrace, open all day (till midnight Fri, Sat). *(Ann and Colin Hunt, Dominic Morgan, Colin and Louise English, the Didler and others)*

LEWES
TQ4210
✶**Snowdrop** (01273) 471018
South Street; BN7 2BU Welcoming pub tucked below the cliffs, narrowboat theme with brightly painted servery and colourful jugs, lanterns etc hanging from planked ceiling, well kept ales such as Dark Star, Harveys, Hogs Back and Rectory, hearty helpings of enjoyable good value local food including good vegetarian choice, friendly efficient service; background music – live jazz Mon; they may ask to keep your credit card while running a tab; dogs very welcome (menu for them), small garden and terrace, open all day. *(Ann and Colin Hunt, John Beeken, MP, Mrs G Marlow)*

LITTLEHAMPTON
TQ0202
✶**Arun View** (01903) 722335
Wharf Road; W towards Chichester; BN17 5DD Airy attractive 18th-c pub in lovely harbour spot with busy waterway directly below windows, very popular lunchtimes with older people (younger crowd evenings) for its enjoyable interesting food (all day Sun) from sandwiches to good fresh fish, well kept Arundel, Fullers London Pride and Ringwood, 20 wines by the glass, cheerful helpful staff, lots of drawings, caricatures and nautical collectables, flagstoned and panelled back bar with banquettes and dark wood tables, large conservatory; background and some live music, two TVs, pool; disabled facilities, flower-filled terrace, summer barbecues, interesting waterside walkway to coast, four bedrooms, open all day. *(Trevor and Sheila Sharman, Roger Laker, S Holder)*

LITTLEHAMPTON
TQ0202
Crown (01903) 719842
High Street; BN17 5EG Town-centre pub with six well kept changing ales including own Anchor Springs, low-priced pubby food, upstairs Sun carvery, live music weekends; open all day from 9am. *(Tony and Wendy Hobden)*

LOWER BEEDING
TQ2225
Crabtree (01403) 891257
Brighton Road; RH13 6PT Family-run pub with Victorian façade but much older inside with Tudor beams and huge inglenook (dated 1537), dining room in converted barn, good food using genuinely local seasonal produce, swift polite service, well kept Badger beers;

landscaped garden, fine country views. *(R J and D S Courtney)*

LOXWOOD
TQ0331
Onslow Arms (01403) 752452
B2133 NW of Billingshurst; RH14 0RD Comfortable and welcoming with popular food (not Mon evening) from doorstep sandwiches up, three Badger ales, good house wines, coffees and teas, daily newspapers and lovely log fires, quiz and music nights; dogs welcome, picnic-sets in good-sized garden sloping to river and nearby restored Wey & Arun Canal, good walks and boat trips, open all day. *(Ian Phillips, Tony and Wendy Hobden)*

LYMINSTER
TQ0204
Six Bells (01903) 713639
Lyminster Road (A284), Wick; BN17 7PS Unassuming flint pub, enjoyable nicely presented food from weekday soup-and-sandwich and daily roast bargains to some interesting specials, well kept Fullers London Pride and Greene King Abbot, good house wine, low black beams and big inglenook, pubby furnishings; terrace and garden seating. *(Tony and Wendy Hobden)*

MAYFIELD
TQ5826
Middle House (01435) 872146
High Street; TN20 6AB Handsome 16th-c timbered inn, L-shaped beamed bar with massive fireplace, several well kept ales inc Harveys, local cider, decent wines, quiet lounge area with leather chesterfields around log fire in ornate carved fireplace, good choice of food, panelled restaurant; background music; children welcome, terraced back garden with lovely views, five bedrooms, open all day. *(Steve Godfrey)*

MAYFIELD
TQ5927
✶**Rose & Crown** (01435) 872200
Fletching Street; TN20 6TE Pretty 16th-c weatherboarded cottage with two cosy front character bars, low ceiling boards (coins stuck in paintwork), bench seats built into partly panelled walls, stripped floorboards and inglenook log fire, small room behind servery and larger lower room (less character), Harveys and a guest, several by the glass, bar food; children welcome and dogs, picnic-sets under parasols on front terrace, open all day (till midnight Fri, Sat). *(Anon)*

MID LAVANT
SU8508
Earl of March (01243) 533 993
A286; PO18 0BQ Updated and extended with emphasis on eating but seats for drinkers in flagstoned log-fire bar serving well kept ales such as Ballards, Harveys and Hop Back, good if pricey food, much sourced locally, in plush dining area and conservatory with seafood bar, polite efficient staff; nice view up to Goodwood from neatly kept garden with good furniture, local walks. *(Miss A E Dare, Tracey and Stephen Groves, John Ecklin)*

MIDHURST   SU8821
Wheatsheaf (01730) 813450
Wool Lane/A272; GU29 9BX Cosy low-beamed and timbered proper local dating from the 16th c, friendly atmosphere, well kept Badger ales, enjoyable reasonably priced food including huge sandwiches, good staff. *(Geoff and Linda Payne, John and Alison Hamilton, V Brogden)*

MILLAND   SU8328
Rising Sun (01428) 741347
Iping Road junction with main Road through village; GU30 7NA Three linked rooms including cheery log-fire bar and bare-boards restaurant, Fullers/Gales beers, good variety of well cooked nicely presented food including some interesting specials, friendly attentive staff, live music first Mon of month; children welcome (popular with families weekends), garden with heated terrace and smokers' gazebo, good walking area, open all day weekends. *(KC, John Evans, J R Evans)*

MILTON STREET   TQ5304
★ Sussex Ox (01323) 870840
Off A27 just under a mile E of Alfriston roundabout; BN26 5RL Extended country pub (originally a 1900s slaughterhouse) with magnificent Downs views; bar area with a couple of high tables and chairs on bare boards, old local photographs, Dark Star and Harveys, good choice of wines by the glass, lower brick-floored room with farmhouse furniture and woodburner, similarly furnished hop-draped dining room (children allowed here), further two-room front dining area with high-backed rush-seated chairs, popular bistro-style food, friendly service; dogs welcome in bar, teak seating on raised back deck taking in the view, picnic-sets in garden below and more under parasols at front, closed Sun evenings in winter and between Christmas and New Year. *(Laurence Smith, Dr Nigel Bowles)*

NUTBOURNE   TQ0718
Rising Sun (01798) 812191
Off A283 E of Pulborough; The Street; RH20 2HE Unspoilt creeper-clad village pub dating partly from the 16th c, beams, bare boards and scrubbed tables, friendly helpful licensees (same family ownership for 30 years), well kept Fullers London Pride and guests such as Cottage, Hammerpot and Langhams, good range of bar food and blackboard specials, big log fire, daily newspapers, enamel signs and 1920s fashion and dance posters, cosy snug, attractive back family room, some live music; dogs welcome, garden with small back terrace under apple tree, smokers' shelter, listed outside lavatory. *(John Beeken, N R White)*

OFFHAM   TQ3912
★ Blacksmiths Arms (01273) 472971
A275 N of Lewes; BN7 3QD Civilised and comfortable open-plan dining pub with good food from chef/owner including seafood and some nice vegetarian choices, well kept Harveys Best and a seasonal beer, good friendly uniformed staff, huge end inglenook; french windows to terrace with picnic-sets, four bedrooms. *(Tom and Ruth Rees)*

OFFHAM   TQ4011
★ Chalk Pit (01273) 471124
Offham Road (A275 N of Lewes); BN7 3QF Former late 18th-c chalk pit building on three levels, well kept Harveys and a guest, decent wines by the glass, great choice of popular home-made food including OAP bargains, attentive cheerful staff, neat restaurant extension, skittle alley, toad in the hole played Mon nights; children welcome, garden with terrace seating, smokers' shelter with pool table, three bedrooms, open all day Fri-Sun (usually food all day then too). *(PL, Ann and Colin Hunt, John Beeken)*

OVING   SU9005
★ Gribble Inn (01243) 786893
Between A27 and A259 E of Chichester; PO20 2BP 16th-c thatched pub with own-brew beers and guests, lots of heavy beams and timbering in chatty bar, old country-kitchen furnishings and pews, other linked rooms with cottagey feel, huge winter log fires, locally sourced home-made food (not Sun evening) using own ale in some dishes, skittle alley with bar, live jazz first Tues of month; children (in family room) and dogs welcome, seats outside under covered area, more in pretty garden with fruit trees, open all day weekends. *(Ian and Barbara Rankin, the Didler, Jenny Smith, Roy Hoing, David H T Dimock, John Beeken and others)*

PARTRIDGE GREEN   TQ1819
★ Green Man (01403) 710250
Off A24 just under a mile S of A272 junction – take B2135 at West Grinstead signpost; pub at Jolesfield, N of Partridge Green; RH13 8JT Relaxed gently upmarket dining pub with enterprising food, several champagnes by the glass and other good wines, Dark Star and Harveys Best, truly helpful service; unassuming front area by counter with bentwood bar chairs, stools and library chairs around one or two low tables, old curved high-back settle, main eating area opening back and widening into part with pretty enamelled stove and a pitched ceiling on left, more self-contained room on right with stag's head, minimal decoration but plenty of atmosphere; cast-iron seats and picnic-sets under parasols in neat back garden. *(Ron and Sheila Corbett, Philip Stott, N R White)*

PARTRIDGE GREEN   TQ1819
Partridge (01403) 710391
Church Road/High Street; RH13 8JS Spaciously renovated village pub now acting as tap for Dark Star, their full range with

at least one guest, real cider, home-made food; terrace and garden, open from 10am weekends for breakfast. *(Anon)*

PATCHING TQ0705
Fox (01903) 871299
Arundel Road; signed off A27 eastbound just W of Worthing; BN13 3UJ Generous good value home-made food including popular Sun roasts (best to book), quick friendly service even at busy times, well kept Harveys Best and two guests, good wine choice, large dining area off roomy panelled bar, hunting pictures; quiet background music; children and dogs welcome, disabled access, nice tree-shaded garden with play area. *(Tony and Wendy Hobden, John Beeken)*

PETT TQ8713
Royal Oak (01424) 812515
Pett Road; TN35 4HG Refurbished and under same ownership as the Queens Head at Icklesham, roomy main bar with big open fire, Harveys and a couple of changing guests, good popular home-made food (not Sun evening) in two dining areas, efficient friendly service, monthly live music and quiz nights; small garden behind, open all day. *(Peter Meister, Mr and Mrs Price)*

PETT TQ8613
Two Sawyers (01424) 812255
Pett Road; off A259; TN35 4HB Meandering low-beamed rooms including bare-boards bar with stripped tables, tiny snug, passage sloping down to restaurant allowing children, popular good value freshly-made food, friendly service, well kept Harveys with guests like Dark Star and Ringwood, local farm cider and perry, wide range of wines; background music; dogs allowed in bar, suntrap front brick courtyard, back garden with shady trees and well spaced tables, three bedrooms, open all day. *(Ellie Weld, David London, Peter Meister, Kevin Booker, Julia Atkins)*

PETWORTH SU9721
Angel (01798) 342153
Angel Street; GU28 0BG Medieval building with 18th-c façade, under new ownership and fully refurbished, good freshly prepared food; six bedrooms, open all day. *(Nigel Burge, Tim Gray)*

PETWORTH SU9820
Grove (01798) 343659
Grove Lane; GU28 0HY Friendly 17th-c stone pub with black-timbered bar, a couple of sofas by log fire, changing ales tapped from the cask, seven wines by the glass, good food from sandwiches and a sausage menu to more elaborate choices, brick-floored dining conservatory; children and dogs welcome, tables in large garden with downland views, closed Sun evening, Mon. *(Richard Tilbrook)*

PETWORTH SU9721
Star (01798) 342569
Market Square; GU28 0AH Airy open-plan pub in centre, Fullers ales, decent wine, enjoyable reasonably priced food, good coffee, leather armchairs and sofa by open fire, friendly atmosphere. *(Lindsey Hedges, Richard Griffiths, Ann and Colin Hunt)*

PETWORTH SU9722
⁎**Stonemasons** (01798) 342510
North Street; GU28 9NL Attractive old low-beamed pub with good food from sandwiches to enterprising dishes, ales such as Andwell, Hammerpot and Langhams, comfortable eating areas in former adjoining cottages (opposite Petworth House so best to book in summer), good service, monthly live music; children and dogs welcome, picnic-sets in pleasant sheltered back garden, five comfortable bedrooms, good breakfast. *(Terry and Nickie Williams)*

PETWORTH SU9921
⁎**Welldiggers Arms** (01798) 342287
Low Heath; A283 E; GU28 0HG Unassuming L-shaped bar with low beams and log fire, pictures on shiny ochre walls, long rustic settles with tables to match, side room, enjoyable food (not always cheap) including good rib of beef Sun lunchtime, Wells & Youngs kept well, decent wines, cheery landlord; children (in family area) and dogs welcome, plenty of tables on attractive lawns and terrace, nice views, closed Mon, also evenings Tues, Weds and Sun. *(Richard Tilbrook, Colin McKerrow)*

PLUMPTON TQ3613
Half Moon (01273) 890253
Ditchling Road (B2116); BN7 3AF Enlarged beamed and timbered dining pub with interesting home-made food using local produce, also children's menu and traditional Sun roasts, local ales and wines (even an organic Sussex lager), good service, log fire with unusual flint chimneybreast; background music – live Thurs; dogs welcome, tables in wisteria-clad front courtyard and on back terrace, big downs-view garden with picnic area, summer family days (last Sun of July and Aug) with face painting and bouncy castle, good walks, open all day. *(Dominic and Claire Williams)*

POYNINGS TQ2611
Royal Oak (01273) 857389
The Street; BN45 7AQ 19th-c pub with large beamed bar, good food from sandwiches and sharing plates up, helpful efficient service, real ales including Harveys from three-sided servery, leather sofas and traditional furnishing, woodburner; dogs welcome, big attractive garden with country/downs views. *(William Ruxton, Helene Grygar)*

ROGATE   SU8023
✶ White Horse (01730) 821333

*East Street; A272 Midhurst–Petersfield;
GU31 5EA* Rambling heavy-beamed local
in front of village cricket field, civilised
and friendly, with Harveys full range kept
particularly well, relaxed atmosphere,
flagstones, stripped stone, timbers and big
log fire, attractive candlelit sunken dining
area, good range of enjoyable reasonably
priced food (not Sun evening), friendly
helpful staff, traditional games (and quite a
collection of trophy cups), quiz last Sun of
month; some tables on back terrace, open all
day. *(Geoff and Linda Payne)*

ROWHOOK   TQ1234
✶ Chequers (01403) 790480

Off A29 NW of Horsham; RH12 3PY
Attractive, welcoming 16th-c pub, relaxing
beamed and flagstoned front bar with
portraits and inglenook log fire, step up
to low-beamed lounge, well kept Harveys
and guests like Dark Star and Upham,
decent wines by the glass, good cooking
from chef/landlord using local ingredients
including home-grown vegetables, separate
restaurant; background music; children and
dogs welcome, tables out on front terraces
and in pretty garden behind with good
play area, attractive surroundings, closed
Sun evening. *(Ian and Rose Lock, Gerald and
Gabrielle Culliford)*

RUDGWICK   TQ0934
Kings Head (01403) 822200

*Off A281; Church Street (B2128);
RH12 3EB* Beamed 13th-c pub by fine old
church in pretty village, well kept Harveys
and guests such as Hogs Back, good italian
cooking including lots of seafood, reasonable
prices; flower-decked seating area at front,
more seats behind. *(John Beeken)*

RUNCTON   SU8802
Walnut Tree (01243) 785881

*Vinnetrow Road, towards N Mundham;
PO20 1QB* Attractive long building with
friendly efficient staff, good food choice for
baguettes up, Fullers London Pride, Harveys
and Sharps Doom Bar, good choice of wines
in three glass sizes, bare boards, timbers
and open fires, character touches, two steps
up to spacious raftered dining room; good
sized garden with terrace open all day. *(Colin
McKerrow, Tony and Wendy Hobden)*

RUSHLAKE GREEN   TQ6218
✶ Horse & Groom (01435) 830320

Off B2096 Heathfield–Battle; TN21 9QE
Cheerful little village-green pub, L-shaped
low-beamed bar with brick fireplace and
local pictures, small room down a step with
horsey décor, simple beamed restaurant,
enjoyable home-made food, Shepherd Neame
ales and decent wines by the glass; children
and dogs welcome, attractive cottage garden

with pretty country views, nice walks. *(Chris
Saunders, J H Bell)*

RUSPER   TQ1836
✶ Royal Oak (01293) 871393

*Friday Street, towards Warnham – back
road N of Horsham, E of A24 (OS Sheet
187 map reference 185369); RH12 4QA*
Old-fashioned and well worn-in tile-hung
pub in very rural spot on Sussex Border Path,
small carpeted top bar with leather sofas and
armchairs, log fire, steps down to long beamed
main bar with plush wall seats, pine tables
and chairs and homely knick-knacks, well
kept Surrey Hills Ranmore and six changing
guests, farm ciders and perries, short choice of
enjoyable low-priced lunchtime food (evenings
and Sun lunch by pre-arrangement), local
farm produce for sale, plain games/family
room with darts; a few picnic-sets on grass
by road and in streamside garden beyond car
park, roaming chickens, open all day Sat, till
9pm Sun. *(Bruce Bird, the Didler, Ian Barker,
Ian Phillips)*

RUSPER   TQ2037
Star (01293) 871264

*Off A264 S of Crawley; RH12
4RA* Several linked rooms in rambling
beamed coaching inn, friendly helpful
staff, cosy atmosphere, Fullers London
Pride, Greene King Abbot and a guest like
Ringwood, good choice of popular food from
sandwiches and light meals up, open fires;
dogs welcome, picnic-sets on small back
terrace. *(Ian Phillips)*

RYE   TQ9220
George (01797) 222114

High Street; TN31 7JT Sizeable hotel with
lively up-to-date feel in bar and adjoining
dining area, beams, bare boards and log
fire, leather sofa and armchairs, a couple of
quirky sculptures, ales such as Dark Star,
Franklins, Harveys and Old Dairy, continental
beers on tap too, good interesting food with
some mediterranean influences, popular
afternoon tea, good service from pleasant
uniformed young staff; soft background jazz;
nice bedrooms, open all day. *(Colin and Louise
English, M P Mackenzie, Phil Bryant)*

RYE   TQ9220
✶ Mermaid (01797) 223065

Mermaid Street; TN31 7EY Lovely old
timbered hotel on famous cobbled street
with civilised antiques-filled bar, Victorian
gothick carved chairs, older but plainer oak
seats, huge working inglenook with massive
bressumer, Fullers, Greene King and Harveys,
good selection of wines and malt whiskies,
short bar menu, more elaborate and
expensive restaurant choices; background
music; children welcome, seats on small back
terrace, bedrooms, open all day. *(Colin and
Louise English, N J Roberts, Richard Mason, Meg
and Colin Hamilton, the Didler, Mike and Eleanor
Anderson and others)*

RYE TQ9220
Queens Head (01797) 222181
Landgate; TN31 7LH Friendly old two-bar pub refurbished under present licensees, good selection of changing ales and ciders (regular festivals), short choice of enjoyable low-priced home-made food, bar billiards and pool, live acoustic music Sat; small area out at back for smokers, bedrooms. *(Peter Meister, Mike and Eleanor Anderson)*

SCAYNES HILL TQ3824
Sloop (01444) 831219
Freshfield Lock; RH17 7NP Improved under welcoming new owners, good food and well kept Harveys, linked areas, fresh flowers and daily newspapers; sheltered garden. *(Martin and Oliver Wright)*

SELHAM SU9320
Three Moles (01798) 861303
Village signed off A272 Petworth–Midhurst; GU28 0PN Small, quiet and relaxing pub tucked away in woodland village with tiny late Saxon church; steep steps up to bar with well kept ales and farm cider, tasty lunchtime food from short menu, church furniture and blazing coal fires, friendly atmosphere; garden tables, good walks nearby, open all day weekends, closed Thurs. *(Anon)*

SHOREHAM-BY-SEA TQ2105
Red Lion (01273) 453171
Upper Shoreham Road; BN43 5TE Modest dimly lit low-beamed and timbered 16th-c pub with settles in snug alcoves, wide choice of good value pubby food including speciality pies, half a dozen well kept changing ales such as local Adur, Arundel and Hepworths (Easter beer festival), farm cider, decent wines, friendly efficient staff, log fire in unusual fireplace, another open fire in dining room, further bar with covered terrace; pretty sheltered garden behind, old bridge and lovely Norman church opposite, good downs views and walks. *(Tony and Wendy Hobden, Bruce Bird, Terry and Nickie Williams)*

SIDLESHAM SZ8697
★ Crab & Lobster (01243) 641233
Mill Lane; off B2145 S of Chichester; PO20 7NB Restaurant-with-rooms rather than pub but walkers and bird-watchers welcome in small flagstoned bar for light meal, Harveys and Sharps, 17 wines by the glass including champagne (also interesting selection of 50-cl carafes), stylish, upmarket restaurant with good imaginative (and pricey) food including local fish, friendly young staff; background music; children welcome, tables on back terrace overlooking marshes, smart bedrooms, self-catering cottage, open all day (food all day weekends). *(Richard Tilbrook, N R White, Bruce Jamieson, Malcolm and Barbara Southwell, Martin and Karen Wake and others)*

SINGLETON SU8713
★ Partridge (01243) 811251
Just off A286 Midhurst–Chichester; PO18 0EY Pretty 16th-c pub handy for Weald & Downland Open Air Museum; all sorts of light and dark wood tables and dining chairs on polished wooden floors, flagstones or carpet, some country knick-knacks, daily newspapers, open fires and woodburner, Ballards Golden Bine, Fullers London Pride and Harveys Best, several wines by the glass, food from good lunchtime sandwiches up, board games, maybe summer table tennis; background music; children welcome, plenty of seats under parasols on terrace and in walled garden. *(Sue and Mike Todd, Nick Lawless, J A Snell, Tim and Sue Halstead, Peter and Jean Hoare, Martin and Karen Wake)*

SLINDON SU9708
Spur (01243) 814216
Slindon Common; A29 towards Bognor; BN18 0NE Civilised, roomy and attractive 17th-c pub, wide choice of upmarket but good value food changing daily, well kept Courage Directors, welcoming efficient staff, pine tables and two big log fires, large elegant restaurant, games room with darts and pool, friendly dogs; children welcome, pretty garden (traffic noise). *(David H T Dimock)*

SOMPTING TQ1605
Gardeners Arms (01903) 233666
West Street; BN15 0AR Smartened up by friendly licensees, just off main coast road (the famous Saxon church is unfortunately on the far side of the dual carriageway), good choice of tasty food all day including some bargains (railway-carriage restaurant no longer in use), well kept Bass, Harveys, Sharps Doom Bar and a guest, log fire; background music; dogs welcome, smokers' terrace. *(Tony and Wendy Hobden)*

SOUTHWATER TQ1528
Bax Castle (01403) 730369
Two Mile Ash, a mile or so NW; RH13 0LA Popular early 19th-c flagstoned country pub pleasantly extended with former barn restaurant, big log fire in back room, ales such as Ringwood, Jennings and Wychwood, good value generous home-made food including good Sun lunch (best to book); some background music; children and dogs welcome, picnic-sets on two pleasant lawns, play area, near Downs Link Way on former rail track. *(Ian Phillips, Mike Thorne)*

STAPLEFIELD TQ2728
Jolly Tanners (01444) 400335
Handcross Road, just off A23; RH17 6EF Neatly kept split-level local by cricket green, welcoming landlord and pub dogs, two good log fires, padded settles, lots of china, brasses and old photographs, well kept Fullers London Pride, Harveys and guests (always a mild; three beer festivals),

real ciders, pubby food including good Sun roasts, friendly chatty atmosphere; background music, jazz Sun evening, quiz Thurs; children welcome and dogs (may be a treat), attractive suntrap garden with plenty of space for kids, quite handy for Nymans (NT). *(Mike and Eleanor Anderson, Alan Weedon)*

STAPLEFIELD — TQ2728
Victory (01444) 400463
Warninglid Road; RH17 6EU Pretty little shuttered dining pub overlooking cricket green (and Brighton veteran car run, first weekend in Nov), friendly efficient staff, good choice of popular home-made food, smaller helpings for children, well kept Harveys Best from zinc-topped counter, local cider and decent wines, beams and woodburner; nice tree-shaded garden with play area. *(C and R Bromage, N R White, Philip Holloway)*

STEYNING — TQ1711
Chequer (01903) 814437
High Street; BN44 3RE Rambling low-beamed Tudor coaching inn, five or so well kept ales such as Cottage, Dark Star, Gales, Harveys and Timothy Taylors, good choice of wines, enjoyable well priced usual food (not Sun evening) from sandwiches up including breakfast from 10am, log fire, antique snooker table, large painting featuring locals, some live music; smokers' shelter, bedrooms, open all day. *(Tony and Wendy Hobden)*

STOPHAM — TQ0318
★ White Hart (01798) 873321
Off A283 E of village, W of Pulborough; RH20 1DS Fine old pub by medieval River Arun bridge, heavy beams, timbers and panelling, log fire and sofas in one of its three snug rooms, well kept ales such as Arundel Gold, Langhams Hip Hop and Kings Horsham, good generous food (all day weekends) from baguettes and pizzas up, friendly efficient service, some interesting bric-a-brac, Thurs quiz night; children welcome, waterside tables, some under cover, open all day. *(Tony and Wendy Hobden)*

STOUGHTON — SU8011
Hare & Hounds (023) 9263 1433
Signed off B2146 Petersfield–Emsworth; PO18 9JQ Airy pine-clad country dining pub with simple contemporary décor, good reasonably priced fresh food including doorstep sandwiches and Sun roasts (till 4pm), up to six well kept ales such as Harveys, Otter and Timothy Taylors, two real ciders, good helpful service, big open fires, public bar with darts, quiz nights; children in eating areas, dogs welcome, tables on pretty front terrace and on grass behind, lovely setting near Saxon church, good local walks, open all day Fri-Sun. *(Martin and Karen Wake, Paul Smurthwaite, R and R Goodenough)*

THAKEHAM — TQ1017
White Lion (01798) 813141
Off B2139 N of Storrington; The Street; RH20 3EP Tile-hung 16th-c two-bar village pub, good food (not Sun evening) from open kitchen, friendly informal service, real ales such as Arundel, Fullers, Harveys and St Austell, good choice of wines by the glass, heavy beams, panelling, bare boards and traditional furnishings including settles, pleasant dining room with inglenook woodburner, fresh flowers; dogs welcome, sunny terrace tables, more on small lawn, pretty village, open all day. *(Mike and Eleanor Anderson)*

TICEHURST — TQ6831
Bull (01580) 200586
Three Legged Cross; off B2099 towards Wadhurst; TN5 7HH Attractive 14th-c pub with big log fires in two heavy-beamed old-fashioned bars, well kept Harveys, contemporary furnishings and flooring in light airy dining extension; charming front garden (busy in summer), bigger back one with play area. *(Tim Loryman)*

TROTTON — SU8322
★ Keepers Arms (01730) 813724
A272 Midhurst–Petersfield; GU31 5ER Pretty cottage above River Rother with beamed and timbered L-shaped bar, comfortable sofas and old winged-back leather armchairs around big log fire, simple rustic tables on oak flooring, other interesting old furniture, two dining rooms, one with elegant oak tables and woodburner, well liked food, Ballards, Dark Star and a guest, comprehensive wine list, good friendly service; children welcome (no babies or toddlers in evening), dogs allowed in bar, seats on sunny terrace, closed Sun evening, Mon. *(Matthew Cramer)*

TURNERS HILL — TQ3435
★ Red Lion (01342) 715416
Lion Lane, just off B2028; RH10 4NU Old-fashioned, unpretentious country local with snug parquet-floored bar, plush wall benches, homely memorabilia and small open fire, steps up to carpeted area with inglenook log fire, cushioned pews and settles forming booths, Harveys ales, generous home cooking, friendly staff, daily newspapers; background and some live music in summer, fruit machine; children (away from bar) and dogs welcome, picnic-sets on side grass overlooking village, open all day, Sun till 10pm (8pm winter). *(Nick Lawless, Terry Buckland, N J Roberts, Colin and Louise English)*

UDIMORE — TQ8519
Kings Head (01424) 882349
B2089; TN31 6BG Traditional village pub doing well under present management, good quality interesting food cooked by licensees and fairly priced, well kept Harveys

and a guest from long counter, low beams, bare boards and woodburner; background music. *(Peter Meister)*

WALDERTON
SU7910
Barley Mow (02392) 631321
Stoughton Road, just off B2146 Chichester–Petersfield; PO18 9ED
Country pub with good value generous food from lunchtime sandwiches up including Sun carvery, well kept ales such as Arundel, Harveys and Ringwood, good wine choice, friendly service even on busy weekends, two log fires and rustic bric-a-brac in U-shaped bar with roomy dining areas, live jazz suppers (third Tues of month), popular skittle alley; children welcome, big pleasant streamside back garden, good walks (Kingley Vale nearby), handy for Stansted House. *(J A Snell, R and R Goodenough, Ann and Colin Hunt)*

WALDRON
TQ5419
Star (01435) 812495
Blackboys–Horam side road; TN21 0RA
Big inglenook log fire in candlelit, beamed and panelled bar, padded window seat and nice mix of furniture including small settle on bare boards and quarry tiles, old prints and photographs, snug off to left, well kept Harveys and a guest such as 1648 or Bass, locally pressed apple juice, good if not cheap food from lunchtime sandwiches up, friendly prompt service, separate back dining room, quiz last Mon of month; picnic-sets in pleasant garden, a couple more at front overlooking pretty village, wassailing in Jan, small café and shop next door. *(PL, Mike and Eleanor Anderson)*

WARBLETON
TQ6018
⋆ Black Duck (01435) 830636
S of B2096 SE of Heathfield; TN21 9BD
Friendly licensees at this small newly renovated pub tucked down from church; L-shaped main room with pale oak flooring, cushioned leather sofas in front of roaring inglenook, beams and walls hung with horsebrasses, tankards, musical instruments, farm tools, even an old typewriter, high-backed dining chairs around mix of tables, enjoyable pubby food and good daily specials, bar area up a step with stools along counter, Harveys, Sharps Doom Bar and nice wines by the glass, cabinet of books and board games, perky pub dog with 'please don't feed me' sign around his neck; background music; picnic-sets in back garden with sweeping valley views, more on front grass. *(Chris Bell, J H Bell)*

WARTLING
TQ6509
⋆ Lamb (01323) 832116
Village signed with Herstmonceux Castle off A271 Herstmonceux–Battle; BN27 1RY 16th-c country pub refurbished in minimalist style by new owners – reports please; small bare-boards front bar with four plush dining chairs around table, brick

fireplace, opened-up dining area across corridor with painted ceiling joists and new pale oak floorboards, studded leather chairs around pubby tables, brass candlesticks, sizeable old stove in inglenook, back bar with cushioned milk churns along counter, Harveys beers, sizeable back restaurant has limestone tiles and a fine dresser with vast lamp on top; temporary chef as we went to press; terrace up steps with chunky furniture and church view. *(Anon)*

WASHINGTON
TQ1213
Frankland Arms (01903) 892220
Just off A24 Horsham–Worthing; RH20 4AL Popular pub below Chanctonbury Ring, wide choice of generous competitively priced food all day (except Sun evening), helpful welcoming service, three mainstream ales and good value wines, log fires, sizeable dimly lit restaurant, public bar with pool and TV in games area; children welcome, dogs in bar, disabled facilities, neat garden with lots of tables, open all day from 9.30am for breakfast. *(Tony and Wendy Hobden)*

WEST ASHLING
SU8007
Richmond Arms (01243) 572046
Just off B2146; Mill Road; PO18 8EA
Smartened-up village dining pub in quiet pretty setting near big millpond with ducks and geese, good interesting food (quite pricy), Harveys ales and plenty of wines by the glass, competent staff; no dogs; children welcome, two nice bedrooms, closed Sun evening, Mon and Tues. *(Bill Oliver, Ann and Colin Hunt)*

WEST ITCHENOR
SU7901
Ship (01243) 512284
The Street; PO20 7AH Large panelled pub in good spot near Chichester Harbour, tables outside, good long walk to West Wittering or foot ferry to Bosham Hoe; traditional bar one end and two carpeted dining areas, good choice of food from snacks up, efficient friendly service, ales such as Arundel, Ballards, Fullers and Kings, two log fires, pine tables and chairs, a seat made from an old boat, some marine bric-a-brac and pictures; children and dogs welcome, open all day. *(David H T Dimock)*

WEST WITTERING
SZ8099
Lamb (01243) 511105
Chichester Road; B2179/A286 towards Birdham; PO20 8QA Welcoming 18th-c tile-hung country pub, good choice of enjoyable food from light meals to giant fish and chips, Badger ales, good service even during busy summer months, rugs on tiles, blazing fire; children and dogs welcome, tables out in front and in small sheltered back garden. *(David H T Dimock, Tony and Wendy Hobden)*

WILMINGTON   TQ5404
✻ **Giants Rest** (01323) 870207

Just off A27; BN26 5SQ Busy country
pub with affable long-serving landlord,
long wood-floored bar, adjacent open areas
with simple furniture, log fire, well kept
Harveys, Hop Back and Timothy Taylors,
quite a choice of enjoyable bar food (all
day weekends), wooden puzzles and board
games; background music; children and
dogs welcome, lots of seats in front garden,
surrounded by South Downs walks and
village famous for chalk-carved Long Man,
two comfortable bedrooms up narrow
stairs with shared bathroom, open all day
weekends. *(Mark Jiskoot, Anthony Barnes, Ron
and Sheila Corbett)*

WINCHELSEA   TQ9017
New Inn (01797) 226252

German Street; just off A259; TN36 4EN
Attractive pub with L-shaped front bar
mainly laid for dining, good fair-value food
and well kept Greene King ales, friendly
helpful staff, some slate flagstones and
log fire, separate back bar with darts and
TV; background music; children welcome,
pleasant walled garden, delightful
setting opposite church – Spike Milligan
buried here, comfortable bedrooms, good
breakfast. *(Michael Butler, Mr and Mrs Price)*

WINCHELSEA BEACH   TQ9017
Ship (01797) 226767

Sea Road; TN36 4LH Revamped and
extended under new owners, modern airy bar
with café-style furniture, Harveys, a guest
and some continental beers from striking
mosaic counter, good wines and coffee,
enjoyable all day bar food, more upscale
and expensive dishes in restaurant, friendly
relaxed atmosphere, adjoining butchers/deli;
children welcome, coastal-theme garden
with stone paths and seating areas amongst
grasses, lavenders and dwarf pines, open
from 8am. *(Nicola Harold, Alex Sim, Peter
Meister, V Brogden)*

WINEHAM   TQ2320
✻ **Royal Oak** (01444) 881252

*Village signposted from A272 and
B2116; BN5 9AY* Splendidly old-fashioned
local with log fire in enormous inglenook,
Harveys Best and guests tapped from casks
in still room, enjoyable seasonal food (not
Sun evening), jugs and ancient corkscrews on
very low beams, collection of cigarette boxes,
a stuffed stoat and crocodile, more bric-
a-brac in back parlour with views of quiet
countryside; children away from bar and
dogs welcome (resident bearded collie called
Bella), picnic sets outside, closed evenings 25
and 26 Dec and 1 Jan. *(Terry Buckland, John
Redfern, N R White, Kevin and Maggie Balchin, the
Didler, Peter and Heather Elliott and others)*

WISBOROUGH GREEN   TQ0526
Cricketers Arms (01403) 700369

*Loxwood Road, just off A272
Billingshurst–Petworth; RH14 0DG*
Attractive old pub, well kept Fullers and
Harveys, good choice of food including
specials board, cheerful staff, open-plan with
two big woodburners, pleasant mix of country
furniture, stripped brick dining area on left;
live music nights; tables out on terrace and
across lane from green. *(Pam Adsley)*

WISBOROUGH GREEN   TQ0525
Three Crowns (01403) 700207

Billingshurst Road (A272); RH14 0DX
Beamed pub with enjoyable food from varied
menu, prompt friendly service, well kept
Harveys, over a dozen wines by the glass
including champagne; children welcome,
sizeable tree-shaded back garden. *(Gerry
and Rosemary Dobson, John Coatsworth)*

WITHYHAM   TQ4935
✻ **Dorset Arms** (01892) 770278

B2110; TN7 4BD Unpretentious 16th-c
pub handy for Forest Way walks, friendly
service, well kept Harveys ales and decent
wines (including local ones), good choice
of enjoyable fairly priced food, sturdy tables
and simple country seats on wide oak
boards, roaring fire in Tudor fireplace, darts,
dominoes, shove-ha'penny and cribbage,
carpeted restaurant; background music; dogs
welcome, white tables on brick terrace by
small green. *(the Didler, Chris Bell)*

WORTHING   TQ1404
Cricketers (01903) 233369

*Broadwater Street W, Broadwater Green
(A24); BN14 9DE* Extended panelled
local with well kept ales such as Fullers,
Harveys, Ringwood, Sharps and Shepherd
Neame, enjoyable low-priced lunchtime food
(also Fri, Sat evenings), friendly staff, old
photographs, prints and copper knick-knacks,
steps down to small lounge with dining
room beyond, log fires, live music and quiz
evenings, beer festivals; children and dogs
welcome, good-sized garden with play area,
open all day. *(Tony and Wendy Hobden)*

WORTHING   TQ1502
Selden Arms (01903) 234854

*Lyndhurst Road, between Waitrose and
hospital; BN11 2DB* Friendly, chatty
backstreet local opposite the gasworks,
welcoming long-serving licensees, well kept
Dark Star Hophead and several changing
guests, belgian beers and farm cider,
bargain lunchtime food (not Sun) including
doorstep sandwiches, log fire, lots of old pub
photographs, occasional live music; dogs
welcome, open all day. *(Tony and Wendy
Hobden, N R White)*

Warwickshire

with Birmingham and West Midlands

New pubs to look out for here this year are the Golden Cross at Ardens Grafton (country dining pub with contemporary touches and a friendly, relaxed atmosphere), Malt Shovel in Barston (well run, with exciting and inventive food), Inn at Farnborough in Farnborough (snug bar in civilised inn and a wide choice of enjoyable food), Stag at Offchurch (sensitively refurbished thatched village pub with lots of customers, hard-working, keen licensees and imaginative food), Bear in Stratford-upon-Avon (proper pubby bar attached to a riverside hotel with eight real ales and good value food) and Encore, also in Stratford (a good mix of customers of all ages, open all day and wide choice of drinks). Other pubs on top form are the Bell in Alderminster (stylish interior, lovely bedrooms and super food), Malt Shovel in Gaydon (well kept real ales in reliably friendly pub), Red Lion in Hunningham (under the Brunning & Price umbrella with an enthusiastic landlord, lots of fun events and top class food and beer), Crabmill in Preston Bagot (beautifully converted mill extremely popular for its good food and fine choice of drinks), and Bell in Welford-on-Avon (five interesting beers and excellent food in civilised surroundings). Our Warwickshire Dining Pub 2013 is the Malt Shovel in Barston.

THE GOOD PUB GUIDE

ALDERMINSTER — SP2348 Map 4

Bell

A3400 Oxford–Stratford; CV37 8NY

Handsome coaching inn with contemporary décor mixing easily with original features, real ales, a good choice of wines, excellent modern cooking and helpful service; individually decorated bedrooms

Top notch attention to detail marks this stylish Georgian inn – part of the Alscot Estate – as somewhere rather special. Gently refurbished in an attractive, contemporary style, the open-plan layout, beams, standing timbers, flagstone or wooden floors and fresh flowers give an easy-going atmosphere. A small, bustling bar – with Alscot Ale (brewed for them by Warwickshire Beer Co), a couple of guest beers such as Sharps Doom Bar, a good range of wines by the glass, proper cocktails (including a special bloody mary) – has comfortable brown leather armchairs in front of the open fire, high bar chairs by the blue-painted counter and daily papers; background music The restaurant has an eclectic mix of furniture including painted dining chairs and tables, and leads into the conservatory, which shares the same Stour Valley views as the modern chairs and tables in the attractive courtyard. The four boutique-style bedrooms are comfortable and individually decorated.

Using much Estate-grown produce, the interesting food ranges from morning coffees, weekend brunches, sandwiches and filled baguettes to grazing platters and excellent restaurant meals. They might include tomato, apple and celery soup, ham hock, black olive and coriander terrine, baked turbot fillet with samphire and pineapple and citrus cream, roast pepper and brie risotto, braised beef brisket with horseradish mash, maple-roast parsnips, caramelised onion and pancetta jus, and puddings such as baked raspberry-stuffed nectarines with almond crunch topping. *Benchmark main dish: pie of the day £10.95. Two-course evening meal £19.00.*

Free house ~ Licensee Emma Holman-West ~ Real ale ~ Bar food (12-2, 6.30-9; 12-3, 6.30-9.30 Fri, Sat; 12-3 Sun; not Sunday evening) ~ Restaurant ~ (01789) 450414 ~ Children welcome ~ Dogs allowed in bar ~ Open 9.30-3, 6-11; 9.30-11 Fri, Sat; 9.30-4 Sun; closed Sun evening all year and winter Mon (Jan-March) ~ Bedrooms: £75(£100S) (£100B)/£115(£125S)(£135B) ~ www.thebellald.co.uk *Recommended by R J Herd, David and Sue Atkinson*

ARDENS GRAFTON
Golden Cross

SP1153   Map 4

Off A46 or B439 W of Stratford, corner Wixford Road/Grafton Lane; B50 4LG

Friendly relaxed beamed bar and attractive dining room in good country dining pub

Rugs on the ancient dark flagstones, the woodburning stove in the large old fireplace and the warm buff colour of the walls – hung with attractive contemporary photographs – all give a glow to this place, even without the staff's friendly efficiency. They have Wells & Youngs Eagle and Bombardier and a guest such as Purity UBU on handpump, a decent choice of wines by the glass, and – by a fine antique curved-back settle – a table of daily papers including the *Racing Post*. There are other character seats too, among the chapel chairs around the country-kitchen tables. The carpeted dining room has fruit prints, an unusual coffered ceiling and a big mullioned bay window. The good-sized, neatly planted back garden has picnic- sets, with big canopied heaters on the terrace, and a pleasant country outlook.

Pleasing and well thought of, the food might include sandwiches, potted shrimps with a rocket and cucumber salad, bacon and black pudding hash with a poached egg and hollandaise, various sharing boards, sage gnocchi with roasted butternut squash, spinach and cream, beer-battered haddock, gammon with bubble and squeak, roasted root vegetables and parsley sauce, beef burger with red pepper relish and a choice of stilton, cheddar or bacon toppings, and chargrilled tuna with a tomato, avocado and chilli salsa. *Benchmark main dish: faggots with mash and mushy peas £10.95. Two-course evening meal £20.00.*

Charles Wells ~ Lease Debbie Honychurch ~ Real ale ~ Bar food (12-2.30, 5-9; 12-9 Sat; 12-8 Sun) ~ Restaurant ~ (01789) 772420 ~ Children welcome ~ Dogs allowed in bar ~ Live music Thurs evening ~ Open 12-12(1am Fri-Sun) ~ www.thegoldencross.net
Recommended by Stanley and Annie Matthews, Martin and Pauline Jennings, Edward Whittle

BARFORD   SP2660   Map 4

Granville

1.7 miles from M40 junction 15; A429 S (Wellesbourne Road); CV35 8DS

Civilised, attractive respite from the motorway, for fireside comfort or a good meal

With friendly, helpful service and enjoyable food, it's not surprising that so many people leave the M40 to come here. It's an attractive place with a gently up-to-date feel with its sage-green paintwork, berber-pattern hangings on the end walls and contemporary lighting. Soft art-deco-style leather sofas nestle by the fire in the angle of the L-shaped main bar. You can eat here at pale wooden tables and chairs on floorboards or at a mix of simpler tables and chairs in a carpeted section, or you can head through to a more formal raftered and stripped-brick restaurant. Hook Norton Old Hooky and Purity Mad Goose and UBU on handpump, and decent wines by the glass; background music and TV for major events. A floodlit back terrace has smart rattan chairs and loungers under huge retractable awnings, and the grass beyond rises artfully to a hedge of pampas grass and the like, which neatly closes the view. There's a rustic play area tucked away.

 As well as lunchtime sandwiches, the imaginative food might include duck liver parfait with pear chutney, haddock and spring onion fishcakes with tomato salsa, honey-roast ham with free-range eggs, girolle and pea risotto with goats cheese, beef, horseradish and Guinness pie, hake fillet with smoked bacon, boulangère potatoes, roast shallots and a creamy ale sauce, crispy pork belly with a honey, chilli and star anise glaze, sticky rice and pak choi, and puddings such as chocolate nemesis, iced pistachio parfait and orange sauce and banana sticky toffee pudding with butterscotch sauce and honeycomb ice-cream. *Benchmark main dish: beer-battered fish and chips £11.50. Two-course evening meal £18.00.*

Enterprise ~ Lease Val Kersey ~ Real ale ~ Bar food (12-2.30, 6-9.30; 12-9.30 Sat; 12-5 Sun; not Sun evening) ~ Restaurant ~ (01926) 624236 ~ Children welcome ~ Dogs welcome ~ Open 12-3, 5-11(11.30 Fri); 12-11.30 Sat and Sun ~ www.granvillebarford.co.uk *Recommended by Val and Alan Green, Clive and Fran Dutson, Andy Rose, Rob and Catherine Dunster, Ian Herdman, R L Borthwick*

BARSTON   SP1978   Map 4

Malt Shovel ⓘ ♥

3 miles from M42 junction 5; A4141 towards Knowle, then first left into Jacobean Lane/Barston Lane; B92 0JP

Warwickshire Dining Pub of the Year

Well run country dining pub full of happy eaters, attractive layout, good service

The light and airy bar, its big terracotta tiles neatly offset by their dark grouting, rambles extensively around the zinc-topped central counter, which is painted blue to match the dado and other panelling, and has good wines by the glass, and Adnams and Sharps Doom Bar on handpump. It's comfortably furnished, with informal dining chairs and scatter-cushioned pews around stripped-top tables of varying types and sizes. Cheerful fruit and vegetable paintings decorate the cream walls, and at one end brown slatted blinds give a glimpse of the kitchen; efficient service by neat young staff. The sheltered garden behind, with a weeping willow, has picnic-sets, and teak seats for the terrace and verandah tables have cushions in summer.

Delicious food cooked and presented with great care might include smoked ham terrine with home-made piccalilli and crisp sourdough, goats cheese risotto bonbons with beetroot and crème fraîche, butternut squash and sage tortelloni with a white wine cream sauce, beef burger with chips and a mini strawberry milkshake, rack of lamb with gratin dauphinoise, courgette crisps and redcurrant and mint jus, tamarind-marinated pork belly with a coconut and lychee shot, specials like scallops on pea purée with black pudding and crisp bacon, scottish halibut with elderflower roasted parsnips, parma ham and rocket and wild turbot with mussels, crayfish, samphire and saffron broth, and puddings such as rapsberry and hibiscus flower cheesecake with panna cotta ice-cream and dark chocolate meringue pie with pecan honeycomb. *Benchmark main dish: daily changing fresh fish £15.95. Two-course evening meal £20.00.*

Free house ~ Licensee Helen Somerfield ~ Real ale ~ Bar food (12-2, 6-9.30; 12-4 Sun; not Sun evening) ~ Restaurant ~ (01675) 443223 ~ Children welcome ~ Dogs allowed in bar ~ Open 12-12(10 Sun) ~ www.themaltshovelatbarston.com *Recommended by Anthony and Pam Stamer, Susan and John Douglas, Martin Smith*

BIRMINGHAM
Old Joint Stock 🍺 £

SP0686 Map 4

Temple Row West; B2 5NY

Big bustling Fullers pie-and-ale pub with impressive Victorian façade and interior, and a small back terrace

Even when this well run city centre pub is packed out, it effortlessly absorbs what seems like huge numbers of people, and service manages to remain friendly and efficient. The interior is impressively flamboyant: chandeliers hang from the soaring pink and gilt ceiling, gently illuminated busts line the top of the ornately plastered walls and there's a splendid, if well worn, cupola above the centre of the room. Big portraits and smart long curtains create an air of unexpected elegance. Around the walls are plenty of tables and chairs, some in cosy corners, with more on a big dining balcony that overlooks the bar and is reached by a grand staircase. A separate room, with panelling and a fireplace, has a more intimate, clubby feel. As far as we know, this is the northernmost venue to be owned by London-based brewer Fullers and they keep the full range of Fullers beers on handpump alongside up to four local guests, a dozen wines by the glass and a decent range of malt whiskies, all served from a handsome dark wood island bar counter; daily papers, background music and board games. Most nights see something on in the smart purpose-built little theatre on the first floor, and a small back terrace has some cast-iron tables and chairs, and wall-mounted heaters. The cathedral is opposite.

As well as sandwiches, the very reasonably priced menu includes stilton fritters with poached pears, chicken kiev, beef stroganoff, beer-battered fish and chips, steak in ale and sausage, apple and spring onion pies, puy lentil, cumin and red pepper burger, evening sharing plates, and puddings such as chocolate fudge cake and knickerbocker glory. *Benchmark main dish: speciality pies £9.75. Two-course evening meal £15.00.*

Fullers ~ Manager Paul Bancroft ~ Real ale ~ Bar food (12-10; 12-4; not Sun evening) ~ (0121) 200 1892 ~ Children welcome till 7pm away from main bar ~ Jazz in the bar last Weds of month ~ Open 11-11; 12-5 Sun; closed Sun evening ~ www.oldjointstocktheatre.co.uk *Recommended by Ian and Nita Cooper, Martin Smith, Barry Collett, Steve and Liz Tilley, Theocsbrian, Ross Balaam, the Didler, Jeremy King, Andy Dolan, Andy and Jill Kassube, Richard Tilbrook*

FARNBOROUGH

SP4349 Map 4

Inn at Farnborough ⚟ ☒

Off A423 N of Banbury; OX17 1DZ

Snug bar in civilised dining pub with wide choice of enjoyable food

The cosy bar on the right of this popular golden stone house has dark beams and flagstones, some honey-coloured stripped stone, bucket armchairs with scatter cushions and matching window seats, racing car pictures and a log fire in the big stone fireplace. They have Hook Norton Hooky and an occasional guest on handpump, local spirits, about 20 wines by the glass and enterprising bar nibbles – charcuterie, whitebait and crayfish tails, for example; background music. A second fireplace, open on two sides, with a seat built in around it, divides off a compact two-room dining area with sturdy stripped kitchen tables and high-backed leather chairs; the carpeted inner room has wallpaper imitating shelves of books. There are blue picnic-sets and other seats in the neat sloping garden, which has a big yew tree and a canopied deck. Not a lot of nearby parking.

The menu includes both traditionally pubby and more elaborate dishes: thai chicken and tiger prawn soup, duck pâté with rhubarb and ginger chutney, scallops with pancetta, ham, egg and chips, chicken curry, baked aubergine, feta, potatoes and tomatoes, shellfish linguine, bass fillet with minted chickpeas, watercress and celery soup and pepper dressing, goats cheese and artichoke ravioli, and puddings such as lime panna cotta with cassis sorbet and vanilla, honey and prosecco syrup and srawberry and popping candy cheesecake with crushed raspberry and liqueur milkshake. *Benchmark main dish: confit of lamb £16.95. Two-course evening meal £22.50.*

Free house ~ Licensees Anthony and Jo Robinson ~ Real ale ~ Bar food (12-2.30, 6-10; 12-10(9 Sun)) ~ Restaurant ~ (01295) 690615 ~ Children welcome ~ Dogs allowed in bar ~ Open 10-3, 5.30-10.30; 10-midnight Sat; 10-10.30 Sun ~ www.innatfarnborough.co.uk *Recommended by Alison Squance, George Atkinson, Della Young*

GAYDON

SP3654 Map 4

Malt Shovel

Under a mile from M40 junction 12; B4451 into village, then over roundabout and across B4100; Church Road; CV35 0ET

In a quiet village just off the M40; nice mix of pubby bar and smarter restaurant, enjoyable food and four real ales

Spotlessly kept and friendly, this reliable place offers a tasty meal and a range of particularly well kept mainstream beers – Fullers London Pride, Hook Norton Best, Marstons Pedigree, Wadworths 6X – along with a dozen or so wines, most available by the glass. Mahogany-varnished boards through to bright carpeting link the entrance, the bar counter with its line of stools on the right and the woodburning stove on the left at this bustling pub. The central area has a high-pitched ceiling, milk churns and earthenware containers in a loft above the bar. Three steps take you up to a little space with some comfortable sofas overlooked by a big stained-glass window with reproductions of classic posters on the walls. A busy eating area has fresh flowers on a mix of kitchen, pub and dining tables; background music, darts and games machine. They will keep your credit card if you run a tab outside. The springer spaniel is called Rosie and the jack russell is Mollie.

Enjoyable food, cooked by the chef/landlord, includes good lunchtime sandwiches and panini and ploughman's, as well as smoked haddock rarebit, roast duck leg with citrus and honey, steak and kidney pudding, four-cheese ravioli, wild boar and apple sausages, battered haddock, and puddings such as lemon cheesecake and rhubarb crumble. *Benchmark main dish: pie of the day £9.45. Two-course evening meal £17.40.*

Enterprise ~ Lease Richard and Debi Morisot ~ Real ale ~ Bar food (12-2, 6.30-9) ~ Restaurant ~ (01926) 641221 ~ Children welcome ~ Dogs allowed in bar ~ Open 11-3, 5-11; 11-11 Fri, Sat; 12-10.30 Sun ~ www.maltshovelgaydon.co.uk *Recommended by Jean and Douglas Troup, George Atkinson, Ian and Jane Irving, Dr D J and Mrs S C Walker*

 HAMPTON IN ARDEN   SP2080   Map 4
White Lion 🍺
High Street; handy for M42 junction 6; B92 0AA

Useful village local, five real ales; bedrooms

This former farmhouse is nice and relaxed, with a mix of furniture trimly laid out in the carpeted bar with its neatly curtained little windows, low-beamed ceilings and some local memorabilia on the fresh cream walls. Everards M&B Brew XI, Purity Mad Goose, Sharps Doom Bar, St Austell Tribute and a guest such as Hobsons are served on handpump from the timber-planked bar; background music, TV and board games. The modern dining areas are fresh and airy with light wood and cane chairs on stripped floorboards. The pub is in an attractive village, opposite a church mentioned in the Domesday Book, and is handy for the NEC.

🍴 Bar food includes chilli tiger prawns with roasted peppers, smoked salmon salad with poached egg, cream cheese and horseradish, fish and chips, coq au vin, calves liver with bacon and onion and dauphinoise potatoes, smoked haddock and mushroom and pepper risotto. *Benchmark main dish: beef pie £10.50. Two-course evening meal £18.50.*

Punch ~ Tenant Chris Roach ~ Real ale ~ Bar food (12-2.30(4.30 Sun), 6.30-9.30; not Sun evening) ~ Restaurant ~ (01675) 442833 ~ Children welcome ~ Dogs welcome ~ Open 12-11(midnight Sat, 10.30 Sun) ~ Bedrooms: £65S/£75S ~ www.thewhitelioninn.com *Recommended by Comus and Sarah Elliott, Peter and Heather Elliott, Gerard Dyson, Mark, Amanda, Luke and Jake Sheard, Mr and Mrs Graham Prevost, N R White, Martin Smith*

HUNNINGHAM   SP3768   Map 4
Red Lion 🍴 🍷
Village signposted off B4453 Leamington–Rugby just E of Weston, and off B4455 Fosse Way 2.5 miles SW of A423 junction; CV33 9DY

Informal, characterful and civilised, good individual food; fine riverside spot

The enterprising landlord at this spacious pub runs it with imagination and a sense of fun. He employs a house magician, hosts events such as a beer and film festival and is designing a comic book wine list. In fact, vintage comics are a passion and his dazzling collection of 320 brightly coloured examples crammed on the bright white walls leave a lasting impression. His enthusiastic lead imbues the welcoming staff with a positive, interested approach. The light and airy open-plan yet cleverly sectioned layout is an easy-going mix of old and new, with warming red ceilings, a mix of seating from varnished chapel chairs to a variety of dining chairs, various mainly stripped tables, rugs on bare boards and chunky old-fashioned radiators. Windows at one end take in views of the garden with a charmingly arched 14th-c bridge over the gurgling River Leam and a vintage Massey Ferguson tractor that's been converted into a fun children's climbing frame; good coal fires, and the day's *Times*, background music and board games. Drinks include a enterprising changing choice of about 25 wines by the glass, a good range of spirits including 45 single malts, Greene King IPA and Abbot and a couple of guests such as Butcombe Best and Titanic Iceberg on handpump, and home-made elderflower cordial.

Food here is good, fresh, generous and sourced with care. As well as sandwiches, it might include potted crab with sourdough toast, butternut squash risotto and feta cakes, lamb casserole, salmon and crayfish fishcake with spinach, butter sauce and poached egg, lamb shank with scotch broth, battered haddock, mussel and chorizo tagliatelle with cider and thyme cream, and puddings such as raspberry, whisky and almond trifle and strawberry cranachan. *Benchmark main dish: steak burger £10.95. Two-course evening meal £18.60.*

Greene King ~ Lease Sam Cornwall-Jones ~ Real ale ~ Bar food (12-9.30 Sun) ~ (01926) 632715 ~ Children welcome but no prams or pushchairs ~ Dogs welcome ~ Open 12-11(10.30 Sun) ~ www.redlionhunningham.co.uk *Recommended by Ian and Nita Cooper, Ryta Lyndley, Sarah Greenway, Rob and Catherine Dunster, Ian and Joan Blackwell, George Atkinson, Steve Green, Peter and Janet Astbury, Antony Townsend, Katie Carter, Andy Dolan, G Jennings, Martin and Pauline Jennings*

LONG COMPTON
Red Lion 🛏

SP2832 Map 4

A3400 S of Shipston-on-Stour; CV36 5JS

Traditional character and contemporary touches in comfortably refurbished coaching inn; bedrooms

You can be sure of a genuinely warm welcome from the landlady and her attentive staff in this lovely old coaching inn – our readers have enjoyed their visits very much over the last year. There are plenty of original features to look out for. The roomy lounge bar has some exposed stone and beams and nice rambling corners with old-fashioned built-in settles among pleasantly assorted and comfortable seats and leather armchairs; there are tables on flagstones and carpets, and a warming woodburning stove. Hook Norton Hooky Bitter and a couple of guests such as Purity Mad Goose and Wickwar Cotswold Way on handpump and a dozen wines by the glass. The simple public bar has darts, pool, a games machine, juke box (a rarity now) and TV; background music. There are tables out in the big back garden, with a play area.

Good, popular food includes sandwiches, ham hock, mustard and leek terrine with red onion jam, smoked salmon and warm potato cake with sour cream and chives, spinach and parmesan dumplings with a tomato and red pepper coulis, chicken wrapped in parma ham with mascarpone, garlic, thyme and cream, battered cod with mushy peas and tartare sauce, slow-roasted free-range pork belly with chorizo and red wine jus, bass with caramelised fennel and mustard and tarragon butter, and puddings such as steamed treacle sponge with custard and raspberry posset with a chocolate and pistachio biscotti; they also offer a two- and three-course weekday set menu. *Benchmark main dish: steak in ale pie £12.95. Two-course evening meal £20.50.*

Cotswold Inns & Hotels ~ Manager Lisa Phipps ~ Real ale ~ Bar food (12-2.30, 6-9; 12-9.30 Fri-Sun) ~ Restaurant ~ (01608) 684221 ~ Children welcome ~ Dogs welcome ~ Open 10-3, 6-11; 10-11 Fri-Sun ~ Bedrooms: £60B/£90B ~ www.redlion-longcompton.co.uk *Recommended by Chris Glasson, David Gunn, R I Howe, Sara Fulton, Roger Baker, Alun and Jennifer Evans*

OFFCHURCH
SP3665   Map 4

Stag

North of Welsh Road, off A425 at Radford Semele; CV33 9AQ

Characterful refurbishment, good food and lively atmosphere

Sensitive refurbishments have kept the ancient character of this 16th-c thatched village pub intact but added a contemporary spark. Walkers and their dogs enjoy the relaxed atmosphere in the low-beamed oak-floored bar with its warming log fires, or you can be a little more formal in the cosy beamed restaurants which have bold wallpaper, deer antlers, animal heads, big mirrors and striking fabrics. The slightly unusual décor is continued on to the terrace with its black furniture. Lots of customers, enthusiastic licensees and friendly, busy young staff generate a lively atmosphere. Purity Mad Goose and Warwickshire Best and Darling Buds are on handpump and about a dozen wines are offered by the glass.

The good imaginative food is all cooked from scratch (including the bread) and includes filled baguettes, cheddar soufflé, potted crab and brown shrimps, beef carpaccio, herring roes on toast, sharing platters, ploughman's, pork and leek sausages with onion marmalade, chicken and mushroom pie, salmon fishcake with cucumber and dill beurre blanc, confit duck leg with orange sauce, roast pork collar with sage and apple crust, and puddings such as ginger sponge with butterscotch sauce, dark chocolate tart with praline cream and treacle and orange tart. *Benchmark main dish: chicken breast with morel cream sauce £14.50.* Two-course evening meal £19.50.

Free house ~ Licensee Lizzie King ~ Real ale ~ Bar food (12-2.30(3 Sat, 3.30 Sun), 6-9.30(10 Sat, 9 Sun)) ~ Restaurant ~ (01926) 425801 ~ Children welcome ~ Dogs allowed in bar ~ Open 12-11(10.30 Sun) ~ www.thestagatoffchurch.com *Recommended by Peter and Janet Astbury, Clive and Fran Dutson, Ken and Barbara Turner, Anna Field*

PRESTON BAGOT
SP1765   Map 4

Crabmill

A4189 Henley-in-Arden–Warwick; B95 5EE

Cider mill conversion with comfortable décor, relaxed atmosphere, a good choice of drinks and smart food

This rambling old cider mill is a lovely building with an easy-going atmosphere and extremely popular food. It's been attractively decorated with contemporary furnishings and warm colour combinations, and the smart two-level lounge area has comfortable sofas and chairs, low tables, big table lamps and one or two rugs on bare boards. The elegant and roomy low-beamed dining area has caramel leather banquettes and chairs at pine tables and a beamed and flagstoned bar area has some stripped-pine country tables and chairs and snug corners. From the gleaming metal bar they serve Greene King Abbot, the very local Purity Gold and St Austell Tribute on handpump and nine wines by the glass; background music is well chosen and well reproduced. There are lots of tables (some of them under cover) out in a large, attractive, decked garden.

As well as interestingly filled lunchtime (not Sunday) wraps, sandwiches and baguettes and a few good value light meals and baguettes, the imaginative food might include crispy ox tongue with celeriac purée, a poached egg and béarnaise sauce, pheasant, pigeon and partridge terrine with piccalilli, chicken chasseur with roasted carrots and creamed potatoes, hake with toulouse sausage, bean and vegetable cassoulet, sweet potato and feta cannelloni with butternut velouté, slow-cooked shoulder of lamb with mint and lavender jelly, a pork plate (braised belly, cheeks, medallions and roasted apple stuffed with black pudding), and puddings. *Benchmark main dish: bass, sweet potato and spinach curry £16.25. Two-course evening meal £21.50.*

Free house ~ Licensee Sally Coll ~ Real ale ~ Bar food (12-2.30(5 Fri and Sat), 6.30-9.30; 12-3.30 Sun; not Sun evening) ~ Restaurant ~ (01926) 843342 ~ Children welcome ~ Dogs allowed in bar ~ Open 11-11; 12-6 Sun; closed Sun evening ~ www.thecrabmill.co.uk *Recommended by Clive and Fran Dutson, R L Borthwick, Dennis and Doreen Haward, Rob and Catherine Dunster, Martin Smith, Paul and Anita Brannan, S Holder*

STRATFORD-UPON-AVON   SP2055   Map 4

Bear ♀ ◖ ⇌

Swans Nest Hotel, just off A3400 Banbury Road, by bridge; CV37 7LT

Great real ale choice in properly pubby bar of large comfortable riverside hotel

Besides a beer brewed for them by Hook Norton, and Old Hooky, on our last visit the impressive row of handpumps on the pewter-topped counter also dispensed well kept Byatts Coventry, Cheltenham Festive-Ale, Everards Tiger, Silhill 4 Per Cent, Wychwood Dirty Tackle and Wye Valley Butty Bach – a fine choice of wines by the glass, too. They had a big England flag on the ceiling and lots of smaller Six Nations ones (yes, it was that time of year – there was a TV for the matches, though most of the time it's hidden behind a picture frame), and in other ways the two linked rooms are thoroughly traditional: china and other bric-a-brac on the delft shelf above the panelling, a couple of wing armchairs by the fire, a variety of other carefully chosen seats including sofas and scatter-cushioned banquettes, a character settle and a splendid long bench with baluster legs. Big windows look out to the swans on a reach of river between two bridges, and in summer there are teak tables out there on a waterside lawn, beyond the service road. Service is thoroughly professional.

Good value, popular food includes well filled sandwiches, quick bites like devilled lambs kidneys and a sharing platter of nibbles and pâté, deep-fried whitebait with tartare sauce, chicken caesar salad, a curry of the week, beef burger with gruyère, pickles, relish and skinny fries, a changing pasta dish, and puddings such as dark chocolate fondant and eton mess; you can also eat from the menu of the adjoining brasserie – in which case your hotel parking charge is refunded. *Benchmark main dish: pie of the day £7.95. Two-course evening meal £14.00.*

Free house ~ Licensee Simon Taylor ~ Real ale ~ Bar food (12-3, 5-10; all day weekends and school holidays) ~ Restaurant ~ (01789) 265540 ~ Children welcome ~ Dogs welcome ~ Open 10-11 (midnight Fri and Sat) ~ Bedrooms: /£99S ~ www.thebearfreehouse.co.uk *Recommended by JHBS, Val and Alan Green, Alan Johnson*

The knife-and-fork award ⑪ distinguishes pubs where the food is of exceptional quality.

STRATFORD-UPON-AVON
SP2054 Map 4

Encore

Bridge Street; CV37 6AB

Well run relaxed modern bar with enjoyable food all day, good river views from upstairs dining room

The building's old, but the style inside is contemporary – and enjoyed by people of all ages, thanks partly to the efficient, pleasantly informal staff. The main area has well spaced scrubbed-top cast-iron tables with bucket armchairs or fat soft square stools, stripped beams and broad oak boards or polished pale flagstones, big windows on two sides and big charcoal sketches of local sights on its butter-coloured walls. A softly lit dark-walled back area with barrel and other rustic tables has stairs up to the long, comfortable dining room, which looks down over the road to the river. They have good coffees and plenty of wines by the glass, as well as Purity UBU and Sharps Doom Bar on handpump; log fire, well reproduced background music.

Besides interesting sandwiches and sharing plates, the popular food might include crispy pumpkin ravioli with tomato salsa, chicken and chorizo spiedini with chilli jam, stone-baked pizzas, beef burger with cheese, bacon or mushrooms, mustard mayonnaise and frites, salmon and caper fishcake topped with a free-range poached egg and chive hollandaise, cannelloni with spinach, butternut squash, ricotta and tomato sauce, pork fillet wrapped in sage and proscuitto with a blue cheese sauce, calves liver with bacon and tomato dauphinoise, and puddings such as white chocolate crème brûlée and apple and blackcurrant crumble; they offer a two-course lunch and an early evening menu. *Benchmark main dish: linguine with tiger prawns, crab, chorizo, chilli and tomatoes £12.95. Two-course evening meal £16.25.*

Mitchells & Butlers ~ Manager Matthew Skidmore ~ Real ale ~ Bar food (9.30am-10pm) ~ Restaurant ~ (01789) 269462 ~ Children welcome ~ Dogs allowed in bar ~ Open 9am-11pm(midnight Sat, 10.30 Sun) ~ www.theencorestratford.co.uk *Recommended by Val and Alan Green, Eithne Dandy, George Atkinson*

WELFORD-ON-AVON
SP1452 Map 4

Bell 🏠🍴♟🍺

Off B439 W of Stratford; High Street; CV37 8EB

Enjoyably civilised pub with appealing ancient interior, good carefully sourced food, and a great range of drinks including five real ales; terrace

Readers continue to enjoy the kind welcome extended by the charming licensees at this delightful 17th-c place – you can see their attentive hands-on touch in everything from the well kept beer through to the delicious food (most people come to dine so booking is advised). The attractive interior (full of signs of the building's venerable age) is divided into five comfortable areas, each with its own character, from the cosy terracotta-painted bar to a light and airy gallery room with antique wood panelling, solid oak floor and contemporary Lloyd Loom chairs. Flagstone floors, stripped or well polished antique or period-style furniture, and three good fires (one in an inglenook), add warmth and cosiness. Hobsons, Purity Pure Gold and UBU and two or three guests such as Fullers London Pride and Shepherd Neame Spitfire are on handpump, and they've over a dozen wines including champagne and local ones by the glass (though if you are ask nicely they will probably open anything on the list); background music. In summer, the virginia-creeper covered exterior is festooned with colourful hanging baskets. Lots of thought has gone into the garden here with its solid teak furniture, vine-covered terrace, water features and gentle lighting. This riverside village has an appealing church and pretty thatched black and white cottages.

🍴 If you turn to the back of the menu you will see a list of the local food suppliers they use here – the licensees put a lot of effort into sourcing good produce. The menu includes a good choice of sandwiches, fried brie with ginger and apricot compote, crispy whitebait, ploughman's, faggots with sage and onion gravy, smoked salmon and crayfish tail salad, and sirloin steak. Daily specials might take in goats cheesecake with pickled celery, root vegetable tagine with harissa couscous, garlic-roasted plaice and crevettes on paella rice, steak and onion pie, tikka roasted chicken on bombay potatoes with onion bhaji, and puddings such as rhubarb fool and sticky toffee pudding; popular Sunday roast, fish and chips night Tuesday and Spice Night Friday. *Benchmark main dish: steak in Guinness pie £13.25. Two-course evening meal £19.50.*

Laurel (Enterprise) ~ Lease Colin and Teresa Ombler ~ Real ale ~ Bar food (11.45-2.30(3 Sat), 6-9.30(10 Fri, Sat); 11.45-9.30 Sun) ~ (01789) 750353 ~ Children welcome ~ Open 11.30-3, 5.30-11; 11.30-11.30 Sat; 11.45-10.30 Sun ~ www.thebellwelford.co.uk
Recommended by Roger Whittaker, Martin and Pauline Jennings, Mike and Mary Carter, Joan and Tony Walker, R J Herd, Mr and Mrs R L Ham, Mrs A M Sabin, Martin Smith, Theocsbrian, K H Frostick

Also Worth a Visit in Warwickshire

Besides the fully inspected pubs, you might like to try these pubs that have been recommended to us and described by readers. Do tell us what you think of them: feedback@goodguides.com

ALCESTER · SP0957
Holly Bush (01789) 762482
Henley Street (continuation of High Street towards B4089; not much nearby parking); B49 5QX Eight changing ales are the main draw to this unpretentious 17th-c pub; smallish rooms with simple furniture on bare boards or flagstones, stripped masonry and dark board panelling, some antique prints, open fires, restaurant; children and dogs welcome, good disabled access, pretty little garden with seats on sheltered side terrace, open all day. *(Rob and Catherine Dunster, MLR, Ian and Jane Irving, Paul Humphreys)*

ALVESTON · SP2355
Baraset Barn (01789) 295510
Pimlico Lane; CV37 7RJ Stylish barn conversion with popular interesting food from sharing plates up, weekday set menu (lunchtime, early evening), good choice of wines by the glass including champagne, Purity UBU; children welcome, dogs in conservatory, terrace tables under parasols, closed Sun evening, otherwise open all day. *(K H Frostick)*

ALVESTON · SP2356
Ferry (01789) 269883
Ferry Lane; end of village, off B4086 Stratford–Wellesbourne; CV37 7QX Comfortable and stylish beamed dining pub, good imaginative food along with pub favourites, reasonable prices, ales such as Hook Norton, Sharps and Wells & Youngs, friendly staff; nice spot with seats out in front, open all day Sat, closed Sun evening and first Mon of month. *(Mark Sykes)*

ARMSCOTE · SP2444
★ **Fox & Goose** (01608) 682635
Off A3400 Stratford–Shipston; CV37 8DD Popular and nicely modernised – former blacksmith's forge, small flagstoned bar with open fire, woodburner in larger dining area, three changing ales, varied choice of enjoyable food including set deals, good wine list, competent friendly staff; background music, TV; children and dogs welcome, seats on deck overlooking lawn, four brightly painted bedrooms named after Cluedo characters, open all day. *(Eithne Dandy, Dennis and Doreen Haward, K H Frostick)*

ASTON CANTLOW SP1360
⋆ **Kings Head** (01789) 488242
*Village signed off A3400 NW of Stratford;
B95 6HY* Wisteria-covered Tudor pub
with low-beamed bar on right, old settles
on flagstones and log fire in big inglenook,
chatty quarry-tiled main room with attractive
window seats and big country oak tables, ales
such as Greene King and Purity, farm ciders,
wines by the glass from a good list, enjoyable
bar food (not Sun evening) from sandwiches
through to elaborate restaurant-style choices;
background music; children welcome, dogs in
bar, seats in lovely garden with big chestnut
tree and pretty summer hanging baskets,
open all day weekends, till 8.30pm Sun
(7.30pm winter). *(D W Stokes, Anthony and
Pam Stamer, Martin and Pauline Jennings, Philip
Lane, Dave Braisted)*

AVON DASSETT SP4049
Avon Inn (01295) 690270
Off B4100 Banbury–Warwick; CV47 2AS
Traditional double-fronted mellow-stone pub
with pleasant décor and relaxing atmosphere,
welcoming helpful staff, enjoyable good value
pubby food including dozens of varieties of
pies and bargain two-course special, well
kept Fullers London Pride and Timothy
Taylors Landlord, several wines by the
glass, flagstones and bare boards, stools and
cushioned wall benches around simple pub
tables, carpeted area with padded dining
chairs; unobtrusive background music (live
Fri), TV; children and dogs welcome, picnic-
sets out in front by quiet road, small side
garden, attractive village on slopes of Burton
Dassett Hills Country Park, open all day
weekends. *(Guy Vowles, Clive and Fran Dutson,
Martin and Pauline Jennings)*

BAGINTON SP3375
Old Mill (024) 7630 2241
Mill Hill; CV8 3AH Popular Chef & Brewer
watermill conversion near airport, Midland
Air Museum and Lunt Roman fort; heavy
beams, timbers and candlelight, slate and
wood floors, warm rustic-theme bar, leather
seating by open fire, linked dining areas,
decent wine selection and well kept changing
ales, good choice of food including some
unusual specials, friendly uniformed staff;
children welcome, disabled facilities, lovely
terraced gardens down to River Sowe, 26
bedrooms. *(Nigel and Sue Foster)*

BARNT GREEN SP0074
⋆ **Barnt Green Inn** (0121) 445 4949
*3 miles from M42 junction 2; A441
towards Birmingham, then first left
on to B4120; Kendal End Road; B45
8PZ* Large civilised Elizabethan dining
pub with friendly young staff, good choice of
food from shared mezze through wood-fired
pizzas to interesting main dishes, weekday
fixed-price menu too, real ales such as Black
Sheep and Greene King Old Speckled Hen,

log fire, relaxed atmosphere, comfortable
contemporary décor, clubby seating in
panelled front bar, large brasserie area;
can get very busy; tables outside, handy for
Lickey Hills walks, open all day. *(Anon)*

BARSTON SP2078
⋆ **Bulls Head** (01675) 442830
*From M42 junction 5, A4141 towards
Warwick, first left, then signed down
Barston Lane; B92 0JU* Unassuming and
unspoilt partly Tudor village pub, friendly
landlord and helpful staff, well kept Adnams,
Hook Norton and two guests, popular
traditional food from sandwiches to specials,
log fires, comfortable lounge with pictures
and plates, oak-beamed bar with some
Buddy Holly memorabilia, separate dining
room; children and dogs allowed, good-sized
secluded garden alongside, hay barn, open all
day Fri-Sun. *(Don Bryan, Martin Smith, Clive
and Fran Dutson)*

BINLEY WOODS SP3977
Roseycombe (02476) 541022
Rugby Road; CV3 2AY Warm and friendly
1930s pub with wide choice of bargain home-
made food, Bass and Theakstons, Weds quiz
night, some live music; children welcome, big
garden. *(Alan Johnson)*

BIRMINGHAM SP0788
⋆ **Bartons Arms** (0121) 333 5988
High Street, Aston (A34); B6 4UP
Magnificent Edwardian landmark, a
trouble-free oasis in rather a daunting
area, impressive linked richly decorated
rooms from the palatial to the snug, original
tilework murals, stained glass and mahogany,
decorative fireplaces, sweeping stairs to
handsome upstairs rooms, well kept Oakham
and guest ales from ornate island bar with
snob screens in one section, interesting
imported bottled beers and frequent mini-
beer festivals, nice choice of well priced thai
food (not Mon), good young staff; open all
day. *(the Didler)*

BIRMINGHAM SP0686
Brasshouse (0121) 6333383
Broad Street; B1 2HP Handsome bank
conversion with lots of dark oak and brass,
enjoyable reasonably priced food from
sandwiches up, well kept ales including
Marstons and Timothy Taylors, good quick
service, attractive dining area (children
welcome here till 6pm); canalside seats,
handy for National Sea Life Centre and
convention centre, open all day. *(Colin Gooch,
Tony Hobden)*

BIRMINGHAM SP0786
Old Contemptibles (0121) 236 5264
Edmund Street; B3 2HB Spacious well
restored Edwardian corner pub with lofty
ceiling and lots of woodwork, decent choice
of real ales (customers vote for guest beers),
enjoyable well priced food including range

of sausages and pies, friendly efficient young staff; upstairs lavatories, no children; handy central location (popular lunchtime with office workers), open all day (till 6pm Sun). *(the Didler, Tim Green, Andy Dolan, Tony Hobden)*

BIRMINGHAM SP0686
Pennyblacks (0121) 632 1460

Mailbox shopping mall, Wharfside Street; B1 1RQ Good atmosphere and service in well run spacious pub with mix of contemporary and old furnishings on wood or slate floors, appealing up-to-date décor, enjoyable food, up to seven real ales such as Church End, Hook Norton, Slaters and St Austell (third of a pint glasses available), extensive wine range; DJ Thurs-Sat nights, Sky Sports, free Wi-Fi; good spot by the canal, open all day. *(Steve and Liz Tilley)*

BIRMINGHAM SP0586
Prince of Wales (0121) 643 9460

Cambridge Street; B1 2NP Traditional pub behind the repertory theatre and symphony hall; L-shaped bar with friendly mix of customers, half a dozen or more well kept beers such as Everards, Timothy Taylors and Wells & Youngs, bargain straightforward lunchtime food including good baguettes, fast friendly service; may be background music; popular with Grand Union Canal users in summer. *(Chris Evans)*

BIRMINGHAM SP0687
Pub du Vin (0121) 200 0600

Church Street; B3 2NR Their second pub venture (first in Brighton), arched slate-floor cellar bar with island servery, comfortable seating and some unusual artwork, well kept ales such as Kinver, simple food, walk-in humidor/whisky room; sports TV; another bar and 66 good bedrooms in hotel upstairs, open all day, closed Sun. *(the Didler, Tony Hobden)*

BIRMINGHAM SP0686
⋆Wellington (0121) 2003115

Bennetts Hill; B2 5SN Old-fashioned high-ceilinged pub with superb range of changing beers (listed on TV screens – order by number), most from small breweries and always one from Black Country Ales, also farm ciders, experienced landlord and friendly staff, no food but plates and cutlery if you bring your own, regular beer festivals and quiz nights, can get very busy; tables out behind, open all day. *(LM, the Didler, Jeremy King, Tony Hobden)*

BLOXWICH SJ9902
⋆Turf (01922) 407745

Wolverhampton Road, off A34 just S of A4124; WS3 2EZ Utterly uncontrived, unchanging terraced pub in side street and run by the same family for nearly 140 years; entrance hall like a 1930s home, public bar through door on right (reminiscent of a waiting room) with wooden slatted wall

benches and three small tables on fine tiled floor, William Morris curtains and wallpaper and simple fireplace, more comfortable old smoking room and tiny back parlour, friendly landladies and chatty locals, Oakham, Otter, RCH and a couple of guests, no food; no-frills lavatories outside at end of simple garden; best to check opening hours before setting out. *(the Didler)*

BRIERLEY HILL SO9286
⋆Vine (01384) 78293

B4172 between A461 and (nearer) A4100; straight after the turn into Delph Road; DY5 2TN Popular Black Country pub offering a true taste of the West Midlands; down-to-earth welcome and friendly chatty locals in meandering series of rooms, each different in character, traditional front bar with wall benches and simple leatherette-topped oak stools, comfortable extended snug with solidly built red plush seats, tartan-decorated back bar with brass chandeliers, well kept and priced Bathams from brewery next door, a couple of simple very cheap lunchtime dishes; no credit cards, TV, games machine; children and dogs welcome, tables in backyard, open all day. *(P Dawn, Theo, Anne and Jane Gaskin, Ian and Joan Blackwell, Theocsbrian, Dave Braisted, the Didler)*

CHERINGTON SP2836
Cherington Arms (01608) 686233

Off A3400; CV36 5HS Welcoming 17th-c stone-built pub, well kept Hook Norton and guests, decent wines, food from baguettes up, nice beamed bar with log fire, lots of old photographs, separate dining room, some live music; children and dogs welcome, tables on terrace and in big garden bordering the River Stour, good nearby walks, open all day weekends. *(David Gunn, John and Sharon Hancock)*

CHURCHOVER SP5180
Haywaggon (01788) 832307

Handy for M6 junction 1, off A426; The Green; CV23 0EP Good mainly italian food from neapolitan landlord, well kept Purity UBU, nice italian wines and coffee, relaxed atmosphere and friendly staff, two snug eating areas, lots of beams, standing timbers, brasses, nooks and crannies; children welcome, tables outside with play area, on edge of quiet village, beautiful views over Swift Valley, closed Mon. *(Rob and Catherine Dunster, JJW, CMW)*

CLAVERDON SP2064
⋆Red Lion (01926) 842291

Station Road; B4095 towards Warwick; CV35 8PE Beamed Tudor dining pub with good food (all day Sun) from pub favourites up, friendly attentive service, decent wines and well kept Purity Mad Goose, log fires, linked rooms including back dining area with country views over sheltered heated deck and gardens; open all day. *(Martin Smith)*

COVENTRY SP3279
Old Windmill (0247) 625 2183
Spon Street; CV1 3BA Timber-framed
15th-c pub with lots of tiny rooms, exposed
beams in uneven ceilings, carved oak seats
on flagstones, inglenook woodburner, half
a dozen real ales, often farm cider, pubby
lunchtime bar food (Tues evening curry);
popular with students and busy at weekends,
games machines and juke box, darts, no
credit cards; open all day, closed Mon
lunchtime. *(the Didler)*

COVENTRY SP3379
Town Wall (024) 7622 0963
*Bond Street, among car parks behind
Belgrade Theatre; CV1 4AH* Busy
Victorian city-centre local with five real ales
including Adnams, farm cider, nice hot drinks
choice, good generous lunchtime doorstep
sandwiches, filled rolls and cheap hot dishes,
unspoilt basic front bar and tiny snug,
engraved windows, bigger back lounge with
actor/playwright photographs and pictures of
old Coventry, open fires; big-screen sports TV;
open all day. *(Alan Johnson)*

COVENTRY SP3378
★ Whitefriars (024) 7625 1655
Gosford Street; CV1 5DL Pair of well
preserved medieval townhouses, three
old-fashioned rooms on both floors, lots
of ancient beams, timbers and furniture,
flagstones, cobbles and coal fire, nine well
kept changing ales (more during beer
festivals), daily newspapers, bar lunches;
some live music, no children inside unless
eating; smokers' shelter on good-sized
terrace behind, open all day. *(Alan Johnson)*

DUDLEY SO9487
Park (01902) 661279
George Street/Chapel Street; DY1 4LW
Tap for adjacent Holdens brewery, their
beers kept well plus guests, decent simple
lunchtime food, low prices, friendly service,
conservatory, small games room with pool;
sports TV; open all day. *(the Didler)*

DUNCHURCH SP4871
Dun Cow (01788) 810305
*A mile from M45 junction 1: A45/A426;
CV22 6NJ* Handsomely beamed Vintage Inn
with massive log fires and other traditional
features, popular reasonably priced food
all day including specials and deals, good
range of wines by the glass, three well kept
beers from small counter; background music;
children welcome, tables in attractive former
coachyard and on sheltered side lawn,
bedrooms in adjacent Innkeepers Lodge,
open all day. *(George Atkinson)*

EARLSWOOD SP1174
Red Lion (01564) 702325
Lady Lane (past the Lakes); B94 6AQ
Imposing twin-gabled black and white

Georgian pub, good value traditional food
all day (busy weekends) including good Sun
roast, friendly service, several small but high-
ceilinged rooms each with its own character,
sturdy tables and chairs, some wall settles,
back room with open fire, chandeliers and
bigger tables; disabled access. *(Joan and
Tony Walker, Martin Smith)*

EASENHALL SP4679
★ Golden Lion (01788) 833577
Main Street; CV23 0JA Spotless bar in
16th-c part of busy comfortable hotel, low
beams, dark panelling, settles and inglenook
log fire, changing real ales, enjoyable food
including Sun carvery, friendly helpful
service; background music; children
welcome, disabled access, tables out at side
and on spacious lawn, 20 well equipped
bedrooms, decent breakfast, attractive
village, open all day. *(June Holland, Susan and
John Douglas)*

EDGE HILL SP3747
★ Castle (01295) 670255
Off A422; OX15 6DJ Curious crenellated
octagonal tower built 1749 as gothic folly
(marks where Charles I raised his standard
at start of Battle of Edgehill); lots of interest
in museum-like interior, eight-walled
lounge bar decorated with maps, swords,
pistols, photographs of re-enactments
and a collection of Civil War memorabilia,
arched doorways, open fire, decent bar food
including good sandwiches, Hook Norton
ales, 25 malt whiskies, friendly helpful
service; background music, TV; children
and dogs welcome, seats on terrace and in
attractive big garden with outstanding views
(once leaves have fallen), beautiful Compton
Wynyates nearby, four bedrooms, open all
day. *(Susan and John Douglas, Dr A J and
Mrs Tompsett)*

ETTINGTON SP2748
Chequers (01789) 740387
Banbury Road (A422); CV37 7SR Nicely
refurbished and popular locally for its
enterprising well presented food, ales such
as Fullers, Greene King and St Austell, good
wines, efficient friendly service, log fire in
drinkers area at front, steps up to dining
part with painted tables and matching
upholstered chairs; big back garden with
raised section. *(Pat and Graham Williamson,
David Billington)*

FENNY COMPTON SP4352
Wharf Inn (01295) 770332
*A423 Banbury–Southam, near Fenny
Compton; CV47 2FE* Open-plan pub by
Bridge 136 on South Oxford Canal, good
layout with small central flagstoned bar,
four real ales such as Brakspears and Hook
Norton, fairly straightforward food from
breakfast on; background music, games
machine; children welcome, disabled
facilities, waterside garden, moorings

(provisions and laundry for boaters), open all day. *(Clive and Fran Dutson)*

FIVE WAYS   SP2270
★ **Case is Altered**   (01926) 484206
Follow Rowington signs at junction roundabout off A4177/A4141 N of Warwick, then right into Case Lane; CV35 7JD Convivial unspoilt old cottage, licensed for over three centuries, up to five interesting ales served by friendly landlord including one for the pub from local Old Pie Factory, no food, simple small main bar with fine old poster of Lucas Blackwell & Arkwright Brewery (now flats), clock with hours spelling out Thornleys Ale – another defunct brewery, and just a few sturdy old-fashioned tables and couple of stout leather-covered settles facing each other over spotless tiles, modest little back room with old bar billiards table (it takes pre-decimal sixpences); no children, dogs or mobiles; full disabled access, stone table on little brick courtyard. *(the Didler, Martin Smith, Kerry Law)*

FRANKTON   SP4270
Friendly   (01926) 632430
Just over a mile S of B4453 Leamington Spa–Rugby; Main Street; CV23 9NY Old low-ceilinged village dining pub with well cooked food and four real ales, wines in mini-bottles, two heat rooms, open fire, welcoming friendly atmosphere. *(Rob and Catherine Dunster)*

GREAT WOLFORD   SP2434
★ **Fox & Hounds**   (01608) 674220
Village signed on right on A3400, 3 miles S of Shipston-on-Stour; CV36 5NQ Delightful unspoilt 16th-c inn with helpful friendly staff, inglenook log fire with bread oven, low hop-strung beams, appealing collection of old furniture including tall pews on flagstones, motley assortment of antique hunting prints, vintage photographs and so forth, Hook Norton, Purity and a guest from old-fashioned tap room, much enjoyed creative cooking using local ingredients (not Sun evening and two weeks in Jan), home-baked bread; children and dogs welcome, terrace with solid wooden furniture and a well, three bedrooms, open all day Sun, closed Mon. *(Michael Doswell, M Mossman, Clive and Fran Dutson, Jill Hurley, Mrs Ann Revell and others)*

HALESOWEN   SO9683
Hawne Tavern   (0121) 6022601
Attwood Street; B63 3UG Banks's, Bathams and Bobs plus six interesting guests from side-street local's rough-cut central servery, bar with cushioned pews, darts, pool and juke box in games area, lounge with leatherette-backed wall banquettes, good value baguettes (not Sat lunchtime, Sun), friendly staff; small terrace, closed till 4.30pm weekdays, open all day weekends. *(the Didler)*

HALFORD   SP2645
★ **Halford Bridge**   (01789) 748217
A429 Fosse Way; CV36 5BN Cotswold-stone coaching inn with pastel-walled bar on right of cobbled entry, unusual chunky round tables, some seats in bay window and soft leather sofa by woodburner in big fireplace, Hook Norton Hooky and St Austell Tribute from stone counter, good choice of wines by the glass, enjoyable interesting food from bar snacks up, pleasant attentive staff, back room with extraordinary seat (like contorted and time-bleached tree roots – perhaps more fun to look at than to sit in), partly flagstoned restaurant on left; background music; spacious coachyard with teak furniture, modern artwork and water feature, ten bedrooms, open all day. *(Martin Smith, George Atkinson)*

HARBORNE   SP0384
Plough   (0121) 427 3678
High Street; B17 9NT Popular quirky place with enjoyable pubby food including stone-baked pizzas, lots of deals, Purity, Wye valley and a guest ale, quiz Tues, live music Thurs; well behaved children welcome, garden with covered area, open all day. *(Rupert Kenefeck)*

HATTON   SP2367
★ **Falcon**   (01926) 484281
Birmingham Road, Haseley (A4177, not far from M40 junction 15); CV35 7HA Smartly refurbished dining pub with relaxing rooms around island bar, lots of stripped brickwork and low beams, tiled and oak-planked floors, good moderately priced food (not Sun evening) from sandwiches and pub favourites up, good choice of wines by the glass, well kept Marstons-related ales, friendly service, barn-style back restaurant; children welcome, disabled facilities, garden (dogs allowed here) with heated covered terrace, eight bedrooms in converted barn, open all day. *(Paul Goldman, Andy Dolan, Nigel and Sue Foster)*

HENLEY-IN-ARDEN   SP1566
★ **Bluebell**   (01564) 793049
High Street (A3400, M40 J16); B95 5AT Impressive timber-framed dining pub with fine coach entrance, emphasis on imaginative food (not Sun evening) from sandwiches to restaurant-style dishes (not particularly cheap), rambling old beamed and flagstoned interior with contemporary furnishings creating a stylish but relaxed atmosphere, big fireplace, well kept ales such as Church End and Weatheroak, 20 wines by the glass, good coffee and afternoon teas, friendly helpful staff, daily newspapers; may be background music; children welcome if eating, dogs allowed, tables on back decking, closed Mon lunchtime, otherwise open all day. *(John and Sharon Hancock, George Atkinson, Martin Smith, Corienne Reed)*

ILMINGTON
SP2143
☆ Howard Arms (01608) 682226
Village signed with Wimpstone off A3400 S of Stratford; CV36 4LT Attractive golden-stone inn by village green, several rooms with nice mix of furniture ranging from hardwood pews through old church chairs and wheelbacks to leather dining chairs around all sorts of tables, worn flagstones, bare boards and rugs, a good few prints, shelves of books, candles, small basic bar with Hook Norton, Wye Valley and a guest, several wines by the glass from thoughtful list, well liked interesting food in bar and restaurant; background music; children welcome, dogs in bar, some tables on Yorkstone terrace, picnic-sets under parasols in garden with fruit trees, nearby hill walks, bedrooms, open all day. *(Tim Maddison, Mike and Margaret Banks, Jeff and Wendy Williams, Eleanor Dandy, Barry and Anne, Les and Sandra Brown)*

ILMINGTON
SP2143
Red Lion (01608) 682366
Front Street; CV36 4LX Popular stone-built village pub, flagstoned bar with fire on one side of central servery, dining room the other, well kept Hook Norton, enjoyable good value food cooked by landlady; secluded garden. *(K H Frostick)*

KENILWORTH
SP2872
Clarendon Arms (01926) 852017
Castle Hill; CV8 1NB Busy pub opposite castle, good value generous food in several rooms off long bare-boards bustling bar, largish peaceful upstairs dining room, cheerful enthusiastic young staff, a beer for the pub from Slaughterhouse and three changing guests; daytime car park fee deducted from bill; metal tables on small raised terrace, open all day weekends. *(John and Sharon Hancock, Alan Johnson, Ian Herdman)*

KENILWORTH
SP2872
Virgins & Castle (01926) 853737
High Street; CV8 1LY Maze of intimate rooms off inner servery, small snugs by entrance corridor, flagstones, heavy beams, lots of woodwork including booth seating, coal fire, four well kept Everards ales and a couple of guests, good food at reasonable prices, friendly service, games bar upstairs, restaurant; children in eating areas, disabled facilities, tables in sheltered garden, open all day. *(Roger and Donna Huggins, the Didler, R J Herd)*

KNOWLE
SP1876
Black Boy (01564) 772655
Off A4177 about 1.5 miles S; B93 0EB Much-extended open-plan canalside pub, isolated but popular, with wide choice of good food and well kept ales, reasonable prices, attentive staff; fruit machine; outside seating. *(Anthony and Pam Stamer, Martin Smith)*

KNOWLE
SP1875
Herons Nest (01564) 771177
A4110 (Warwick Road) about a mile S; B93 0EE Popular beamed Vintage Inn dining pub, updated but keeping character, enjoyable sensibly priced food all day, plenty of good value wines by the glass, three real ales, open fires, interesting décor, some flagstones and high-backed settles, big dining room overlooking Grand Union Canal; lots of tables out by the water, moorings, Innkeepers Lodge bedrooms, open all day. *(Martin Smith, Rob Bray)*

LAPWORTH
SP1871
☆ Boot (01564) 782464
Old Warwick Road; B4439 Hockley Heath–Warwick – 2.8 miles from M40 junction 1, but from southbound carriageway only, and return only to northbound; B94 6JU Popular upmarket dining pub near Stratford Canal, good contemporary brasserie menu from panini and interesting light dishes up, efficient friendly young staff, upscale wines (big glasses), Purity UBU and St Austell Tribute, stripped beams and dark panelling, big antique hunting prints, cushioned pews and bucket armchairs on ancient quarry tiles and bare boards, warm fire, charming low-raftered upstairs dining room; background music; children and good-natured dogs welcome, teak tables, some under extendible canopy on side terrace, and picnic-sets on grass beyond, nice walks, open all day. *(Martin Smith, Mark Sykes)*

LAPWORTH
SP1872
Punch Bowl (01564) 784564
Not far from M42 junction 4, off old Warwick–Hockley Heath Road; B94 6HR Completely reconstructed in tasteful way with old beams etc, most emphasis on dining with good range of well presented interesting food, stools along bar for drinkers, Greene King IPA and Wells & Youngs Bombardier, friendly efficient staff; garden picnic-sets. *(R L Borthwick)*

LEEK WOOTTON
SP2868
Anchor (01926) 853355
Warwick Road; CV35 7QX Neat and well run dining lounge popular for enjoyable fresh food including good fish specials, well kept Bass, Hook Norton Old Hooky and two guests, good selection of well priced wines and soft drinks, attentive friendly service, lots of close-set tables, smaller overflow dining area; background music, sports TV; children

---

We list pubs that serve food all day on at least some days at the end of the book.

welcome, no dogs inside, long garden behind with play area, open all day Sun. *(Keith and Ann Arnold)*

LIGHTHORNE   SP3455
Antelope (01926) 651188
Old School Lane, Bishops Hill; a mile SW of B4100 N of Banbury; CV35 0AU Attractive 17th-c stone-built pub doing well under friendly newish licensees, pretty village setting, two neatly kept comfortable bars (one old, one newer), separate dining area, well kept local ales and enjoyable food including good sandwiches; little waterfall in banked garden. *(John and Sharon Hancock)*

LITTLE COMPTON   SP2530
✴ Red Lion (01608) 674397
Off A44 Moreton-in-Marsh–Chipping Norton; GL56 0RT Low-beamed 16th-c Cotswold-stone inn, enjoyable good value food cooked by landlady from pubby choices up, Donnington ales, good choice of wines by the glass, snug alcoves, inglenook woodburner; darts and pool in public bar; well behaved children and dogs welcome, pretty side garden with aunt sally, two nice bedrooms. *(Barry and Anne)*

LONG ITCHINGTON   SP4165
Blue Lias (01926) 812249
Stockton Road, off A423; CV47 8LD Pretty flower-decked pub by the Grand Union Canal, spic and span, with well kept ales including Adnams and Greene King (up to six in the summer), pubby food, snug booth seating in eating area, friendly staff; children welcome, disabled facilities, plenty of tables in waterside grounds (dogs allowed here), marquee for functions, may open all day if busy. *(Adrian Johnson, John Clancy)*

LONG ITCHINGTON   SP4165
✴ Buck & Bell (01926) 811177
A423 N of Southam; The Green; CV47 9PH Friendly attractively laid-out dining pub, plenty of character in several charming linked rambling areas, good choice of above average food served by efficient polite staff, decent wines by the glass, well kept ales such as Banks's, Church End, Hook Norton and Marstons, big log fireplaces, hunting prints and interesting variety of seating around cast-iron-framed tables, elegantly furnished flagstoned restaurant, stairs up to carpeted gallery; background music; tables on back verandah, more in front looking across village green and rookery, open all day. *(Rob and Catherine Dunster, Dr Kevan Tucker, Terry Buckland, Andy Dolan, Clive and Fran Dutson)*

LONG ITCHINGTON   SP4164
Two Boats (01926) 812640
A423 N of Southam, by Grand Union Canal; CV47 9QZ Lively canal views from waterfront terrace and alcove window seats in long cheery picture-filled main room,

enjoyable well priced pubby food, well kept Adnams and Wells & Youngs; background music; moorings, open all day. *(Ross Balaam)*

LONGFORD   SP3684
Greyhound (02476) 363046
Sutton Stop, off Black Horse Road/ Grange Road; junction of Coventry and North Oxford canals; CV6 6DF Cosy canalside pub with plenty of character, well kept Marstons Pedigree, John Smiths, Theakstons Mild and three guests, Aspall's cider, enjoyable traditional food including pies, friendly helpful staff, coal-fired stove, unusual tiny snug; children and dogs welcome, tables on attractive waterside terrace, nice spot (if you ignore the pylons), open all day. *(Spencer Davies)*

LOWER BRAILES   SP3139
✴ George (01608) 685223
B4035 Shipston–Banbury; OX15 5HN Handsome old stone-built inn with roomy front bar, dark oak tables on flagstones, inglenook log fire, beamed and panelled back bar, good food cooked by chef/landlord from bar snacks and pub favourites to imaginative restaurant-style dishes, also good value set lunch, well kept Hook Norton ales, country-style flagstoned restaurant, some live music; children and dogs welcome, aunt sally in sizeable neatly kept sheltered garden with terrace and covered area, lovely village and interesting church, good walks, four comfortable bedrooms, open from 9am and all day weekends. *(JHBS, Clive and Fran Dutson)*

LOWER GORNAL   SO9291
Black Bear (01384) 253333
Deepdale Lane; DY3 2AE Simple split-level local based on former 18th-c farmhouse, Kinver ales and microbrewery guests, good choice of whiskies, friendly staff, coal fire; open all day weekends. *(the Didler)*

LOWER GORNAL   SO9191
Fountain (01384) 242777
Temple Street; DY3 2PE Lively two-room local with helpful friendly landlord and staff, nine changing ales (beer festivals), two farm ciders, country wines and imported beers, enjoyable inexpensive food (not Sun evening), back dining area, pigs-and-pen skittles; background music; garden behind, open all day. *(the Didler)*

LYE   SO9284
✴ Windsor Castle (01384) 897809
Stourbridge Road (corner A458/A4036; car park in Pedmore Road just above traffic lights – don't be tempted to use the next-door restaurant's parking!); DY9 7DG Focus on the interesting well kept beers from impressive row of ten handpumps including own Sadlers ales (brewery tours available); central flagstoned part is functionally furnished with bar stools by

counter and by cask table, a tall tripod table and a window-shelf overlooking the road, several snugger rooms off with bare boards or carpet, some brewing memorabilia, enjoyable food (not Sun evening) using free-range and local produce; children welcome, picnic-sets on side terrace plus some verandah seating, handy for Lye station, open all day. *(Pat and Tony Martin, the Didler)*

MONKS KIRBY   SP4682
★ **Bell** (01788) 832352

Just off B4027 W of Pailton; CV23 0QY
Popular pub run by hospitable long-serving spanish landlord, dark beams, timber dividers, flagstones and cobbles, wide choice of good spanish food including starters doubling as tapas and notable zarzuela fish stew, fine range of spanish wines and of brandies and malt whiskies, relaxed informal service, two well kept Greene King ales, appropriate background music; children and dogs welcome, streamside back terrace with country view, closed Mon. *(Susan and John Douglas, Jill and Julian Tasker)*

NETHERTON   SO9488
★ **Old Swan** (01384) 253075

Halesowen Road (A459 just S of centre); DY2 9PY Victorian tavern full of traditional character and known locally as Ma Pardoe's after a former long-serving landlady; wonderfully unspoilt front bar with big swan centrepiece in patterned enamel ceiling, engraved mirrors, traditional furnishings and old-fashioned cylinder stove, other rooms including cosy back snug and more modern lounge, good value own-brewed ales, wholesome bar food (not Sun evening), upstairs restaurant; dogs allowed in bar, open all day (Sun break 4-7pm). *(Pat and Tony Martin, Dave Braisted, the Didler, Tony Hobden)*

NUNEATON   SP3790
Attleborough Arms (024) 7638 3231

Highfield Road, Attleborough; CV11 4PL
Large fairly recently rebuilt pub, attractively open, modern and comfortable, with wide choice of enjoyable low-priced food, good range of Marstons-related beers and a dozen wines by the glass, helpful attentive service; disabled access, open all day. *(David Green, Ian and Joan Blackwell)*

OLD HILL   SO9686
Waterfall (0121) 5613499

Waterfall Lane; B64 6RG Friendly unpretentious two-room local, well kept Bathams, Holdens and guests, low-priced plain home-made food, tankards and jugs hanging from boarded ceiling; background music; children welcome, back garden with play area, open all day Fri-Sun. *(Dave Braisted, the Didler)*

OLDBURY   SO9989
Waggon & Horses (0121) 5525467

Church Street, near Savacentre; B69 3AD

Copper ceiling, original etched windows, open fire and Black Country memorabilia in busy town pub with Enville and guest ales, wide choice of good varied food lunchtime (not weekends) from sandwiches and hot baguettes up including vegetarian, decent wines, friendly efficient service, ornate Victorian tiles in corridor to comfortable back lounge with tie collection, side room with high-backed settles and big old tables, bookable upstairs bistro Weds-Fri nights; open all day. *(the Didler, Tony Hobden)*

OXHILL   SP3149
★ **Peacock** (01295) 688060

Off A422 Stratford–Banbury; CV35 0QU
Popular pleasantly upgraded stone-built country pub, good varied food including two-course deals (Mon-Sat lunchtime, Mon-Thurs evenings), friendly attentive young staff, well kept Timothy Taylors with guests like Brakspears and Wye Valley (May, Aug beer festivals), good selection of wines by the glass, cosy character bar, half-panelled bare-boards dining room; light background music; children welcome, dogs in bar (there a pub dog), nice back garden, pretty village, open all day. *(George Atkinson, JHBS)*

PRINCETHORPE   SP4070
Three Horseshoes (01926) 632345

High Town; junction A423/B4453; CV23 9PR Friendly old beamed village pub with Marstons EPA, Pedigree and Wells & Youngs Bombardier, enjoyable traditional food, decorative plates, pictures, comfortable settles and chairs, two restaurant areas; TV projector; big garden with terrace and play area, five bedrooms, open all day Fri-Sun. *(Alan Johnson)*

PRIORS MARSTON   SP4857
Holly Bush (01327) 260934

Off A361 S of Daventry; Holly Bush Lane; CV47 7RW Clean and smart with beams, flagstones and lots of stripped stone in rambling linked rooms, log fire and woodburners, above-average well presented food, ales such as Hook Norton, friendly efficient young staff; children welcome, terrace and sheltered garden, four bedrooms, open all day weekends. *(Alan Johnson, Di and Mike Gillam)*

RATLEY   SP3847
★ **Rose & Crown** (01295) 678148

Off A422 NW of Banbury; OX15 6DS Ancient golden stone beamed village pub, cosy and charming, well kept Wells & Youngs ales along with Purity Mad Goose, enjoyable good value straightforward food from sandwiches up, friendly helpful staff, daily newspapers, woodburners in flagstoned area on left and in right carpeted part with wall seats, small back restaurant; dogs and children welcome, tables in gravel garden, near lovely church in sleepy village. *(Clive and Fran Dutson)*

RUGBY
SP5075

Merchants (01788) 571119
Little Church Street; CV21 3AN Busy open-plan pub with nine quickly changing ales, real ciders and lots of continental bottled beers (regular beer/cider festivals), pubby food including pizzas, breweriana, live music Tues; sports TVs; open all day, till 1am Fri, Sat. *(Clive and Fran Dutson)*

SALFORD PRIORS
SP0751

Bell (01789) 772112
Evesham Road (B439); WR11 8UU Welcoming smartly refurbished roadside pub, comfortable chairs and sofas in bar, separate dining room, changing choice of enjoyable freshly cooked food including good value lunchtime set menu, special diets catered for and local suppliers listed, Sharps Doom Bar, Wickwar BOB and Wye Valley HPA, real cider and decent wines, friendly service; outside eating and drinking areas, self-catering apartment, open all day. *(Martin and Pauline Jennings)*

SAMBOURNE
SP0561

Green Dragon (01527) 892465
Village signed off A448; B96 6NU Family-run 18th-c pub opposite village green, low-beamed rooms with flagstones and open fires, enjoyable good value food (not Sun evening), well kept Adnams, Hobsons and Purity; children welcome, seats in courtyard, six bedrooms. *(Dave Braisted)*

SEDGLEY
SO9293

⋆Beacon (01902) 883380
Bilston Street; A463, off A4123 Wolverhampton–Dudley; DY3 1JE Plain old brick pub with own highly thought of Sarah Hughes ales from traditional Victorian tower brewery behind; cheery locals in simple quarry-tiled drinking corridor, little snug on left with wall settles, imposing green-tiled marble fireplace and glazed serving hatch, old-fashioned furnishings like velvet and net curtains, mahogany tables, turkey carpeting and small landscape prints, sparse tap room on right with blackened range, dark-panelled lounge with sturdy red leather wall settles and big dramatic sea prints, plant-filled conservatory (no seats), little food apart from cobs; no credit cards; children allowed in some parts including garden with play area. *(Dr and Mrs A K Clarke, the Didler)*

SHIPSTON-ON-STOUR
SP2540

Black Horse (01608) 238489
Station Road (off A3400); CV36 4BT Ancient thatched pub under new management, ales such as Purity and Wye Valley, authentic thai food, low-beamed rooms off central entrance passage, inglenook log fire; enclosed back garden. *(JHBS)*

SHIPSTON-ON-STOUR
SP2540

⋆Horseshoe (01608) 662190
Church Street; CV36 4AP Pretty 17th-c timbered coaching inn, friendly and relaxed, with open-plan carpeted bar, big fireplace, refurbished restaurant, ales such as Bath Gem, Sharps Doom Bar and Wye Valley Butty Bach, Hogan's cider, enjoyable reasonably priced food (not Sun evening), pub games including aunt sally, live folk music (second Tues of month); free wi-fi; children and dogs welcome, sunny back terrace with heated smokers' shelter, open all day. *(JHBS)*

SHUSTOKE
SP2290

⋆Griffin (01675) 481205
Church End a mile E of village; 5 miles from M6 J4; A446 towards Tamworth, then right on to B4114 straight through Coleshill; B46 2LB Unpretentious country local with a dozen real ales including own Griffin (brewed in next-door barn), farm cider and country wines, may be winter mulled wine, standard lunchtime bar food (not Sun), cheery low-beamed L-shaped bar with log fires in two stone fireplaces (one a big inglenook), fairly simple décor, cushioned café seats, elm-topped sewing trestles and a nice old-fashioned settle, beer mats on ceiling, conservatory (children allowed here); no credit cards, games machine; dogs welcome, old-fashioned seats on back grass with distant views of Birmingham, large terrace, play area. *(Martin Smith, Frank Swann, Alan Bulley)*

STRATFORD-UPON-AVON
SP2054

Dirty Duck (01789) 297312
Waterside; CV37 6BA Bustling 16th-c Greene King Wayside Inn near Memorial Theatre, their ales and good choice of wines, well presented fairly priced food all day from sandwiches up, helpful staff, lots of signed RSC photographs, open fire, modern conservatory restaurant (best to book at weekends); children allowed in dining area, attractive small terrace looking over riverside public gardens which tend to act as a summer overflow. *(Paul Humphreys, Edward Mirzoeff)*

STRATFORD-UPON-AVON
SP2054

⋆Garrick (01789) 292186
High Street; CV37 6AU Bustling ancient pub with heavy beams and timbers, odd-shaped rooms and simple furnishings on bare boards or flagstones, good-natured efficient staff, enjoyable fairly priced food all day from sandwiches and light dishes up, well kept Greene King ales, decent wines by the glass, small air-conditioned back restaurant; background music, TV, games machine; children welcome. *(Terry Buckland, Alan Johnson, Paul Humphreys, George Atkinson)*

You can send reports directly to us at feedback@goodguides.com

STRATFORD-UPON-AVON SP1955
Old Thatch (01789) 295216
Rother Street/Greenhill Street; CV37 6LE
Cosy welcoming pub on corner of market
square, well kept ales such as Wye Valley and
Purity, nice wines, popular fairly priced food,
log fire, rustic décor, slate or wood floors,
country-kitchen furniture, old pillar box in
one corner; covered tables outside. *(George
Atkinson, Alan Johnson)*

STRATFORD-UPON-AVON SP1954
Windmill (01789) 297687
Church Street; CV37 6HB Ancient pub
(with town's oldest licence) beyond the
attractive Guild Chapel, very low beams,
panelling, mainly stone floors, big fireplace
(gas fire), enjoyable good value pub food (till
8pm) including deals, friendly efficient staff,
Greene King and guests; background music,
sports TV, games machines; courtyard tables,
open all day. *(George Atkinson)*

STRETTON-ON-FOSSE SP2238
★ Plough (01608) 661053
Just off A429; GL56 9QX Popular
unpretentious 17th-c village local, central
servery separating small bar and snug
candlelit dining area, enjoyable food from
pubby things up including Sun spit roasts in
winter, friendly fast service, Ansells, Hook
Norton and interesting guests, stripped
brick/stone walls and some flagstones, low
oak beams, inglenook log fire, dominoes and
cribbage; no dogs; children welcome, a few
tables outside, smokers' shelter, closed Sun
evening. *(David Gunn)*

TANWORTH-IN-ARDEN SP1170
★ Bell (01564) 742212
The Green; B94 5AL Smartly comfortable
contemporary bar-style décor, good food from
light lunchtime dishes to full meals, also a
fixed price menu, good choice of wines by the
glass, well kept Greene King IPA and Timothy
Taylors Landlord, friendly staff; children
in eating areas, outlook on pretty village's
green and lovely 14th-c church, back terrace
with alloy planters, nine stylish modern
bedrooms – good base for walks, also has a
post office. *(Ross Balaam, Dave Braisted)*

TEMPLE GRAFTON SP1355
Blue Boar (01789) 750010
*A mile E, towards Binton; off A422 W of
Stratford; B49 6NR* Welcoming stone-built
dining pub with good choice of enjoyable
food from bar snacks up, four well kept ales,
beams, stripped stonework and log fires,
glass-covered well with goldfish, smarter
dining room up a couple of steps; big-screen

TVs; children and dogs welcome, picnic-sets
outside, comfortable bedrooms. *(Martin and
Pauline Jennings, Martin Smith)*

UPPER BRAILES SP3039
Gate (01608) 685212
*B4035 Shipston-on-Stour–Banbury;
OX15 5AX* New tenants in this attractively
old-fashioned low-beamed village local which
has been popular for well kept Hook Norton
and a guest such as Batemans XXXB (and for
the previous team's good fresh fish); coal fire,
TV, tables in extensive back garden with play
area, aunt sally, pretty hillside spot, lovely
walks; news please. *(K H Frostick)*

UPPER GORNAL SO9292
★ Britannia (01902) 883253
Kent Street (A459); DY3 1UX Popular
old-fashioned 19th-c local with friendly
chatty atmosphere, particularly well kept
Bathams Best and Mild (bargain prices),
tiled floors, coal fires in front bar and time-
trapped little back room with its wonderful
handpumps, some bar snacks including good
local pork pies; sports TV; nice flower-filled
backyard, open all day. *(the Didler)*

UPPER GORNAL SO9292
Jolly Crispin (01902) 672220
Clarence Street (A459); DY3 1UL
Friendly well run 18th-c local, Titanic Crispy
Nail and eight interesting quickly changing
guests, real ciders (cider/perry festivals),
compact front bar, wall seats and mixed
furniture on tiled floor, beer bottle collection
in larger back room, fresh cobs (hot food
at weekends), open fires; no children; dogs
welcome, beer garden, open all day Fri-Sun,
closed lunchtime Mon-Thurs. *(the Didler)*

WALSALL SP0198
Black Country Arms
(01922) 640588 *High Street; WS1 1QW*
Old restored town pub on three levels,
14 real ales including own Black Country
brews, Mole's and Thatcher's ciders, decent
pub food till 4pm (3pm Sun) from generous
sandwiches up; background music – live
jazz first Mon of month, no dogs; small side
terrace, open all day (till 1am Fri, Sat).
(Tony Hobden)

WARMINGTON SP4147
★ Plough (01295) 690666
Just off B4100 N of Banbury; OX17 1BX
Attractive old stone-built pub, unspoilt
and well cared for by friendly landlord,
good local atmosphere, low heavy beams,
log fire in big fireplace, nice chairs and an
ancient settle, Victorian prints, books to
read, darts, five well kept real ales, varied

choice of good value home-made food (not Mon), extended dining room; tables on back terrace, delightful village with interesting church. *(Roger and Kathy Elkin)*

WARWICK SP2766
Cape of Good Hope (01926) 498138
Lower Cape; CV34 5DP Traditional unsmart two-room pub on Grand Union Canal by Cape Top Lock, friendly atmosphere, half a dozen well kept ales including one brewed for them by Church End, satisfying pub food, darts; hatch service for waterside seats. *(Paul J Robinshaw)*

WARWICK SP2864
✷ Rose & Crown (01926) 411117
Market Place; CV34 4SH Up-to-date uncluttered décor, bustling and friendly, with big leather sofas and low tables by open fire, dining area with large modern photographs, good choice of sensibly priced interesting food all day, well kept Purity and Fullers London Pride, plenty of fancy keg dispensers, good wines and coffee, cheerful efficient service, newspapers; background music; tables out under parasols, comfortable good-sized bedrooms, open all day from 8am for breakfast. *(Dick Vardy, Nigel and Sue Foster, Revd R P Tickle, Alan Johnson, Rob and Catherine Dunster)*

WARWICK SP2967
✷ Saxon Mill (01926) 492255
Guys Cliffe, A429 just N; CV34 5YN Well run M&B dining pub in charmingly set converted mill, beams and log fire, smart contemporary chairs and tables on polished boards and flagstones, cosy corners with leather armchairs and big rugs, mill race and turning wheel behind glass, friendly attentive service, enjoyable good value food in bar and (best to book) upstairs family restaurant, good choice of wines by the glass, M&B and local beers; background music; tables out on terraces by broad willow-flanked river, more over bridge, delightful views across to ruins of Guys Cliffe House, open all day. *(Peter and Janet Astbury, M G Hart, Iain Clark,*

Ian Herdman, Susan and John Douglas, Stephen and Jean Curtis)

WARWICK SP2864
✷ Zetland Arms (01926) 491974
Church Street; CV34 4AB Cosy town pub with good sensibly priced traditional food (not weekend evenings) including nice sandwiches and set-menu deals, friendly quick service even when busy, Adnams, Black Sheep and Marstons, decent wines, small panelled front bar with toby jug collection, comfortable larger L-shaped back eating area with small conservatory, pictures of old Warwick; sports TV; children welcome, sheltered garden, bedrooms sharing bathroom. *(Alan Johnson)*

WHICHFORD SP3134
Norman Knight (01608) 684621
Ascott Road, opp village green; CV36 5PE Sympathetically extended beamed and flagstoned pub, good Patriot ales from own microbrewery and changing guests, real ciders and perry, enjoyable food (not Sun evening, Mon), friendly helpful service, some live music; children and dogs welcome (resident pugs – beer named after them), tables out by attractive village green, aunt sally, small back campsite, good walks, classic car/bike meetings third Thurs of month in summer, open all day. *(P and J Shapley, Clive and Fran Dutson)*

WOLVERHAMPTON SO9298
✷ Great Western (01902) 351090
Corn Hill/Sun Street, behind railway station; WV10 0DG Cheerful pub hidden away in cobbled lane down from station; Holdens and guest beers all in top condition, real cider, bargain home-made food (not Sun – bar nibbles then), helpful friendly staff, traditional front bar, other rooms including neat dining conservatory, interesting railway memorabilia, open fires; background radio, TV; children and dogs welcome, yard with barbecues, open all day. *(P Dawn, Barbarrick, the Didler)*

Wiltshire

Some exceptional dining pubs here, though it's nice to find properly pubby places, too. New finds this year – or back in these pages under new people – are the Talbot in Berwick St John (unspoilt and friendly with honest food), Barbury at Broad Hinton (easy-going roadside pub with rewarding all day food), Red Lion in East Chisenbury (run by two chefs who make everything from scratch; should have bedrooms soon), Rising Sun near Lacock (stunning views and well liked food and drink), Lamb in Marlborough (bustling local with well kept ales and generously served home-cooking), Silver Plough in Pitton (a nice place to stay and lots to look at), Raven in Poulshot (caring, hands-on licensees and good landlord-cooked food), George at Sandy Lane (neatly kept Georgian pub with open fires and a friendly feel), Longs Arms at South Wraxall (plenty of character and a warm welcome for all), Weymouth Arms in Warminster (a surprise in a back street location – civilised and with much character), Bridge Inn at West Lavington (a thoroughly nice pub with enthusiastic licensees), and Pear Tree at Whitley (pretty old farmhouse and under Marco Pierre White's umbrella). It's hard not to have just one long list here as all our Main Entries are doing very well and have so much support from our readers – but picking just a handful, you should head for the Compasses in Chicksgrove (an excellent all-rounder), Red Lion in Cricklade (ten real ales, imaginative food and friendly landlord), Potting Shed at Crudwell (first class food and drinks but still a proper country pub), Beckford Arms in Fonthill Gifford (high praise for every aspect here), Malet Arms in Newton Tony (a smashing place run by a cheerful, hard-working landlord), and Seven Stars in Winsley (west country ales and inventive food in handsome inn). With several places snapping at their heels, our Wiltshire Dining Pub 2013 is the Beckford Arms at Fonthill Gifford.

ALDBOURNE
Blue Boar £

SU2675 Map 2

The Green (off B4192 in centre); SN8 2EN

Bags of character in chatty, low-beamed, traditional pub

This character-filled and quintessential country village pub is a favourite with our readers – and with locals, too. Members of the 506th Parachute Infantry Regiment of the US Army's 101st Airborne Division (made famous in the book and TV series *Band of Brothers*) became Blue Boar regulars when they were stationed in the village during World War II, and the pub had a further moment of glory when it was featured in a 1971 episode of *Doctor Who*. It's right at the heart of a quaint and pretty village, opposite the green, and has an easy-going atmosphere and a friendly welcome for all – dogs included. The left-hand bar is homely, with pubby seats around rustic tables on the bare floorboards or flagstones, lots of low black beams in the ochre ceiling, a boar's head above the bigger of the two log fires, a stuffed pine marten over one table; darts, board games and a corner cupboard of village trophies. Lots of unusual bottled beers line the rail above the dark pine dado. Reasonably priced Wadworths IPA and 6X and a changing guest beer on handpump, and 15 malt whiskies. A separate bare-boards dining bar on the right, stretching back further, has more table space and is rather more modern in style (though with the same pubby atmosphere). There are picnic-sets and a couple of tall hogshead tables under big green canvas parasols in front of the pub.

 Popular, honest food includes sandwiches, garlic mushrooms, pâté and toast, home-cooked ham and egg, beer-battered haddock and chips, ratatouille pancake topped with cheese sauce, cottage pie, chicken breast stuffed with haggis with peppercorn sauce, beef bourguignon, liver and bacon casserole, wild boar with apple, cream and horseradish, and puddings. *Benchmark main dish: steak and kidney pie £9.75. Two-course evening meal £17.00.*

Wadworths ~ Tenants Jez and Mandy Hill ~ Real ale ~ Bar food (12-2, 7-9) ~ Restaurant ~ (01672) 540237 ~ Children welcome ~ Dogs allowed in bar ~ Open 11.30-3, 5.30-11.30; 11.30am-midnight Fri and Sat; 12-11 Sun ~ www.thepubonthegreen.com *Recommended by Richard Tilbrook, Suzy Miller, Mary Rayner, Neil and Anita Christopher, Penny and Peter Keevil, Ian Herdman*

BERWICK ST JOHN
Talbot

ST9422 Map 2

Village signed from A30 E of Shaftesbury; SP7 0HA

Unspoilt and friendly pub with simple furnishings and tasty food, in attractive village

In a pretty and peaceful Ebble Valley village, this is a friendly, unspoilt pub with reasonably priced food. The heavily beamed bar has plenty of character and a huge inglenook fireplace with a good iron fireback and bread ovens and is simply furnished with solid wall and window seats, spindleback chairs and a high-backed built-in settle at one end. Ringwood Best, Wadworths 6X and a guest like Ringwood Fortyniner on handpump and several wines by the glass; darts. There are seats outside and the pub is well placed for choice walks southwards through the deep countryside of Cranborne Chase and towards Tollard Royal.

🍴 Using local produce, the well liked food might include lunchtime sandwiches and filled baguettes, deep-fried brie with redcurrant jelly, butterfly prawns with sweet chilli dip, sausages and mash with onion gravy, pasta vegetable stir-fry in creamy tomato sauce, steak in ale pie, salmon and broccoli mornay, specials like gammon with egg or pineapple, lambs liver and bacon and chicken breast with a mushroom and tarragon sauce, and puddings such as ginger sponge with custard and chocolate nut brownies. *Benchmark main dish: slow-roasted pork belly with apple sauce and sage gravy £12.00. Two-course evening meal £17.00.*

Free house ~ Licensees Pete and Marilyn Hawkins ~ Real ale ~ Bar food (12-2, 7-9; not Sun evening or Mon) ~ Restaurant ~ (01747) 828222 ~ Children welcome ~ Dogs welcome ~ Open 12-2.30, 6.30-11; 12-4 Sun; closed Sun evening, Mon *Recommended by D and J Ashdown, F and D Green, Trevor Watkins*

BRADFORD-ON-AVON ST8261 Map 2
Castle ★ 🍺

Mount Pleasant, by junction with A363, N edge of town; extremely limited pub parking, spaces in nearby streets; BA15 1SJ

Handsome building well reworked in relaxed contemporary style, with enjoyable food all day, good drinks and charming service; comfortable bedrooms

Open all day, this strikingly attractive pub is a popular option whether it be for morning coffee, a full meal, bed and breakfast, or simply a local pint. Efficiently run by a friendly young landlady and her cheerful staff, the imposing building was once a toll house. There's a splendid and highly individual atmosphere and the unspoilt bar, dominated by its long reclaimed mahogany serving counter, has a good log fire, romantic lighting including church candles, anything from armchairs and chapel chairs to a heavy green leather settle, polished dark flagstones, plenty of daily papers and unobtrusive background music; board games. Lightly ragged lime-washed walls have *Vanity Fair* cartoons above a high brown dado, and a couple of rooms on the right, with floorboards and a rather darker décor, are similarly comfortable and relaxed. Abbey Ales Bellringer, Devilfish Bomb Shell, Plain Ales Inspiration, Three Castles Barbury Castle and their own-label Flatcapper Ale (also from Three Castles) and Yeovil Glory on handpump, proper farm cider, and a fine blackboard range of wines by the glass. Beside a lawn, the sunny front terrace has unusual long tables and benches affording sweeping views over the town. Our readers like staying here very much and the attractive rooms also have lovely views over the town's rooftops and the surrounding countryside.

🍴 Some sort of rewarding food is served all day starting with breakfasts: sandwiches, popular tapas-style dishes such as sweetcorn fritters with sweet chilli dip, mini fishcakes with lemon mayonnaise and roasted butternut squash with goats cheese, beef burgers with toppings like cheese, cheddar or stilton, chicken and chorizo salad with sautéed potatoes, thai green vegetable curry, cumberland sausage ring with sweet potato mash and cider sauce, smoked haddock with bubble and squeak, a poached egg and hollandaise sauce, 28-day aged rib-eye steak with peppercorn or béarnaise sauce, and puddings such as chocolate brownie with chocolate sauce and ice-cream and apple and cinnamon crumble. *Benchmark main dish: fish and chips £10.95. Two-course evening meal £16.00.*

Free house ~ Licensee Victoria Hill ~ Real ale ~ Bar food (9am(10am Sun)-10pm(9.30pm Sun)) ~ (01225) 865657 ~ Children welcome ~ Live music most Mon evenings ~ Open 9am-11pm; 10-10.30 Sun ~ Bedrooms: /£100S(£130B) ~

www.flatcappers.co.uk/thecastle *Recommended by Mike Gorton, Taff Thomas, Susan and Nigel Wilson, Dr and Mrs A K Clarke, Mike and Mary Carter*

BRINKWORTH   SU0184   Map 2
Three Crowns
The Street; B4042 Wootton Bassett–Malmesbury; SN15 5AF

Much emphasis on the food but still a proper pub with five good beers and a carefully chosen wine list

Changing hands as we went to press, this has been best known as a dining pub. The bar part of the building is the most traditional with big landscape prints and other pictures, some horsebrasses on dark beams, a log fire in winter, a dresser with a collection of old bottles, big tapestry-upholstered pews, a stripped deal table and a couple more made from gigantic forge bellows. Bath Ales Gem bitter, Greene King IPA, Timothy Taylors Landlord, Weighbridge Best Bitter (from the owner's microbrewery) and a beer named for the village on handpump, 40 wines by the glass from a carefully chosen, extensive list, local cider and several malt whiskies. Most people choose to eat in the conservatory or the light and airy garden room. There's a terrace with outdoor heating to the side of the conservatory and more seats and tables in the garden, which stretches around the side and back and looks across to the church and on to rolling farmland.

The food is at its most informal at lunchtime when there might be sandwiches, beef and venison faggots with garlic mash and rich onion gravy, seafood pancake in a rich creamy sauce topped with cheese, confit duck on black pudding mash with red wine and rosemary, and calves liver with crispy bacon; the more elaborate (and expensive) menu has main course dishes (they don't serve starters) such as steak and kidney pie, chicken filled with smoked bacon lardons and cheese, wrapped in puff pastry with a creamy white wine sauce, slow-roasted pork belly with crispy crackling, caramelised apple mash and cider, rosemary and onion gravy, ostrich, venison and crocodile with a creamy damson sauce and fresh raspberries, and puddings like chocolate caramel sponge with crème anglaise and amaretto and cherry mousse in a brandy snap basket with cherry compote. *Benchmark main dish: pork tenderloin with crispy dumplings £17.50. Two-course evening meal £25.00.*

Enterprise ~ Real ale ~ Bar food (12-2, 6-9.30; 12-8 Sun) ~ Restaurant ~ (01666) 510366 ~ Children welcome before 8pm ~ Dogs allowed in bar ~ Open 11-11(midnight Sat); 12-11 Sun ~ www.threecrowns.co.uk *Recommended by Alan Bulley, Tom and Ruth Rees*

BROAD HINTON   SU1176   Map 2
Barbury ♀
A4361 Swindon–Devizes; SN4 9PF

Refurbished roadside pub with a friendly, informal atmosphere, a mix of comfortable and contemporary furnishings and a good balance between eating and drinking

Not far from M4 junction 16, this well run roadside pub has been saved from dereliction by the professional team that run the Vine Tree at Norton. It's been completely refurbished inside and is welcoming to all its customers (dogs included) whether they are dropping in for a drink and a chat or for a meal. There's a long room with a comfortable sofa and two stumpy armchairs in pale brown leather beside the woodburner at one end, a few high-backed wicker armchairs around a couple of tables on bare boards, some attractive hound paintings and a flat-screen TV on the wall above the fireplace. The bar area has regency-striped modern armchairs and tables opposite the dark-grey painted counter where there are usually cheerful locals sitting at the high chairs enjoying the well kept St Austell Trelawny and Tribute on handpump; good wines by the glass and helpful, willing service. Beside the second woodburner at the other end of the room are leather-cushioned chairs around polished tables (set for dining) – a step leads from here to the carpeted dining room with high-backed black wicker or wooden dining chairs around plain or painted-legged dining tables; throughout there are basket weave lampshades, some ornate mirrors and planked ceilings. Also, newspapers to read and background music; it's all very easy-going and friendly. There are seats and tables on a partly covered back terrace.

Enjoyable food includes sandwiches, home-made scotch eggs, chicken liver parfait with tomato chutney, a tian of crab meat and avocado with sherry dressing and parmesan crisp, free-range chicken caesar salad with crispy bacon, salmon, spring onion and ginger fishcakes with home-made tartare sauce, steak burger with french fries and toppings, pea, broad bean, asparagus and mint risotto, crispy cider-basted pork belly with crackling and caramelised apples with creamed cumin cabbage and cider gravy, salmon fillet on bubble and squeak with basil crème fraîche, and puddings; they hold regular themed evenings such as game, paella and spanish beer and tapas. *Benchmark main dish: paella with fresh seafood £14.95. Two-course evening meal £20.00.*

Free house ~ Licensees Charles Walker and Tiggi Wood ~ Real ale ~ Bar food (12-2.30, 7-9.30(10 Fri and Sat); 12-3, 6.30-9 Sun) ~ Restaurant ~ (01793) 731510 ~ Children welcome ~ Dogs welcome ~ Open 11.30am-midnight; 11-11 Sun ~ www.thebarburyinn.co.uk *Recommended by Tony Baldwin*

BROUGHTON GIFFORD   ST8763 Map 2
Fox 🍴 ♟

Village signposted off A365 to B3107 W of Melksham; The Street; SN12 8PN

Comfortably stylish pub with good, interesting food, real ales and several wines by the glass, and a nice garden

You can be sure of a genuinely warm welcome from the helpful landlord and his courteous staff in this relaxed but civilised pub. Each of the interconnected areas has a chatty atmosphere, and the big bird and plant prints, attractive table lamps and white-painted beams contrast nicely with its broad dark flagstones. You can sink into sofas or armchairs by a table of daily papers or another with magazines and board games, take one of the padded stools by the pink-painted bar counter, or go for the mix of gently old-fashioned dining chairs around the unmatched stripped dining tables, which have candles in brass sticks. Bath Ales Gem Bitter, Butcombe Bitter, Fullers London Pride and Otter Bitter on handpump, lots of wines by the glass, 24 malt whiskies and a good choice of spirits, and a log fire in the stone fireplace. The terrace behind has picnic-sets, and leads out on to a good-sized sheltered lawn. They have biscuits behind the bar for dogs.

People named as recommenders after the Main Entries have told us that the pub should be included. But they have not written the report – we have, after anonymous on-the-spot inspection.

🍴 Growing their own vegetables and rearing their own pigs, they serve enjoyable food that might include sandwiches, home-cured charcuterie with fennel and apple salad, smoked salmon and cucumber bavarois with pea shoots, cheese and herb omelette, ham and free-range eggs, slow-roasted pork belly with black pudding and crackling, whole lemon sole with asparagus and butter sauce, and puddings such as chocolate and orange mousse and custard and honey tart with poached apples. *Benchmark main dish: confit duck leg with sautéed potatoes and olive jus £15.95. Two-course evening meal £22.00.*

Free house ~ Licensee Derek Geneen ~ Real ale ~ Bar food (12-2.30(3 Sat), 6-9.30; 12-5.30 Sun; not Sun evening or Mon lunchtime) ~ Restaurant ~ (01225) 782949 ~ Children welcome ~ Dogs welcome ~ Open 12-midnight; 5-11 Mon; 12-10 Sun; closed Mon lunchtime ~ www.thefox-broughtongifford.co.uk *Recommended by David and Stella Martin, Mrs J P Cleall, Michael Doswell, Guy Vowles, Alan Sutton, Colin and Peggy Wilshire*

CHICKSGROVE   ST9729   Map 2

Compasses ★ 🍴 ♀ 🛏

From A30 5.5 miles W of B3089 junction, take lane on N side signposted Sutton Mandeville, Sutton Row, then first left fork (small signs point the way to the pub, in Lower Chicksgrove; look out for the car park); can also be reached off B3089 W of Dinton, passing the glorious spire of Teffont Evias church; SP3 6NB

An excellent all-rounder with enjoyable food, a genuine welcome, four real ales and seats in the quiet garden; comfortable bedrooms

As this busy pub is very popular with both locals and visitors, it may be worth booking a table in advance. It's the ideal place to retire to for a well earned pint after enjoying one of the nearby walks in the surrounding countryside. It's a 14th-c thatched house whose unchanging bar has plenty of real character: old bottles and jugs hanging from beams above the roughly timbered counter, farm tools and traps on the partly stripped stone walls, high-backed wooden settles forming snug booths around tables on the mainly flagstoned floor, and a log fire. Helpful and friendly young staff serve Box Steam Golden Bolt, Butcombe Bitter and Stonehenge Heelstone on handpump, eight wines by the glass and several malt whiskies. The quiet garden, terraces and flagstoned courtyard are very pleasant places to sit, and our readers have told us that this is also a lovely place to stay overnight – smashing breakfasts, too.

🍴 Good, often interesting food might include sandwiches, spiced crab cake with stewed carrot and fennel salad and hollandaise, deep-fried breaded brie with cranberry sauce, spinach, roasted pepper and cream cheese roulade, pork and apple sausages with mustard mash and shallot jus, beef burger with blue cheese topping, chicken stuffed with tarragon mousse served in a broth, steak and kidney pie, venison steak with red wine and juniper jus, pheasant leg 'shepherd's pie' and roasted breast with pink peppercorn sauce, and puddings such as chocolate tart with orange sorbet and almond and amaretto crème brûlée with biscotti biscuits. *Benchmark main dish: pork belly with black pudding scotch egg £15.00. Two-course evening meal £19.50.*

Free house ~ Licensee Alan Stoneham ~ Real ale ~ Bar food (12-2, 7-9) ~ (01722) 714318 ~ Children welcome ~ Dogs welcome ~ Open 12-3, 6-11; 12-3, 7-10.30 Sun ~ Bedrooms: £65B/£85S ~ www.thecompassesinn.com *Recommended by Mrs C Roe, David and Judy Robison, Mrs Susannah Riley, Andrea Rampley, R and M Thomas, Roxanne Chamberlain, Margaret Grimwood, M and R Ridge, Helen and Brian Edgeley, Dr A McCormick, Martin Warne*

CRICKLADE
Red Lion 🍴 🍺 🛏

SU1093 Map 4

Off A419 Swindon–Cirencester; High Street; SN6 6DD

16th-c inn with imaginative food in two dining rooms, ten real ales, lots of bottled beers, several wines by the glass, a friendly, relaxed atmosphere and big garden; bedrooms

There's a warm welcome for all – children and dogs included – at this popular, attractive and particularly well run former coaching inn. After a walk along the nearby Thames Path or through the pretty historic town, this is just the place to head for. The bar has stools by the nice old counter, wheelbacks and other chairs around dark wooden tables and chairs on the red, patterned carpet, an open fire and all sorts of bric-a-brac, and old street signs on the stone walls. You can eat here or in the slightly more formal dining room, which has pale wooden farmhouse chairs and tables, beige carpeting and a woodburning stove in the brick fireplace. They keep a fine range of ten real ales on handpump (and should have their own brews by the time this book is published): Arbor Single Hop Newport and Nibiru IPA, Bristol Beer Factory Southville Hop, Butcombe Bitter, Festival Oatmeal, Moles Best, Plain Ales Inntrigue, St Austell Tribute, St Georges BDB and Wadworths 6X – all available in half and third pint measures if you want to try several. Around 63 interesting bottled beers, farm cider, nine wines by the glass and their own ginger beer and cordials are also available. There are plenty of picnic-sets in the big back garden. The bedrooms are attractive and comfortable.

🍴 Naming their local suppliers and making their own butter, bread, ice-creams and chutneys and jellies, the popular food might include lunchtime sandwiches, free-range rare-breed pork and rabbit terrine with crab apple jelly, tea-smoked salmon with pickled beetroot and horseradish cream, brie, caramelised onion, spinach and tomato tart, home-made beef burger with relish and bacon or cheese toppings, gloucester old spot pork chop with grain mustard mash, home-made pig quavers (scratchings) and gravy, free-range chicken with red wine sauce and roast new potatoes, haunch of venison with celeriac purée, toasted chestnuts and juniper sauce, and puddings such as chocolate and hazelnut brownie with salted caramel ice-cream and bread and butter pudding with home-made marmalade and clotted cream ice-cream. *Benchmark main dish: beer-battered haddock, mushy peas and triple cooked chips £9.95. Two-course evening meal £18.50.*

Free house ~ Licensee Tom Gee ~ Real ale ~ Bar food (12-2.30, 6-9(9.30 Sat), 12-3 Sun; not Sun evening) ~ Restaurant ~ (01793) 750776 ~ Children welcome ~ Dogs allowed in bar and bedrooms ~ Open 12-11(10.30 Sun); 12-midnight Fri and Sat ~ Bedrooms: /£75B ~ www.theredlioncricklade.co.uk *Recommended by Jenny and Peter Lowater, Robert W Buckle, Sue Bastone, Evelyn and Derek Walter, John Clancy, Dr A J and Mrs Tompsett*

CRUDWELL
Potting Shed 🍴 🍷 🍺

ST9592 Map 4

A429 N of Malmesbury; The Street; SN16 9EW

Appealing variation on the traditional country tavern, a fine choice of drinks, interesting food and friendly staff

Consistently enthusiastic reports from our readers once again for this extremely well run, welcoming Cotswolds inn. Thankfully, it remains very much a proper country pub rather than just another pub/restaurant, with cheerful and efficient young staff and a fine range of drinks such as Bath Ales Gem Bitter, Butcombe Bitter, Woodfordes Wherry and a changing guest beer on handpump, as well as an excellent range of 30 wines and champagne by the glass, home-made seasonal cocktails using local or home-grown fruit, local fruit liqueurs, good coffees and popular winter mulled wine. Low-beamed rooms ramble around the bar with mixed plain tables and chairs on pale flagstones, log fires (one in a big worn stone fireplace), some well worn easy chairs in one corner, and a couple of blacktop daily papers to read. Four steps take you up into a high-raftered area with coir carpeting, and there's a separate smaller room ideal for a lunch or dinner party. The quirky, rustic decorations are not overdone: a garden-fork door handle, garden-tool beer pumps, rather witty big black and white photographs. Visiting dogs may meet Barney and Rubble (the pub dogs) and be offered biscuits. Well chosen background music and board games. They have summer barbecues on fine Saturdays; there are sturdy teak seats around cask tables as well as picnic-sets out on the side grass among weeping willows. The pub's two acres of gardens supply many of the ingredients used in the food. They have also donated ten raised beds to villagers, and these are pleasant to wander through. Good access for those in need of extra assistance. They also own the hotel across the road.

Inventive, very highly thought of food using their own-grown fruit and vegetables might include lunchtime sandwiches, hand-picked crab and pomegranate rillettes with avocado mousse, confit duck and plum boudin with cucumber and coriander salsa, slow-cooked jerusalem artichoke, aubergine and beef tomato casserole, vegetable dumplings with a basil and pine nut crust, salt beef brisket hash, fried duck egg, triple-cooked chips and home-made chutney, game sausages with colcannon and onion gravy, fillet of brill with saffron potatoes and a squid, chilli and spring onion stock, and puddings like chocolate and banana loaf with hot toffee and walnut sauce with vanilla ice-cream and fruit soup with meringue islands. *Benchmark main dish: home-made seasonal burger £13.95. Two-course evening meal £20.00.*

Enterprise ~ Lease Jonathan Barry and Julian Muggridge ~ Real ale ~ Bar food (12-2.30(3 Sun), 7-9.30(9 Sun)) ~ Restaurant ~ (01666) 577833 ~ Children welcome ~ Dogs welcome ~ Open 11am-midnight(11pm Sun) ~ www.thepottingshedpub.com
Recommended by Paul Goldman, David Gunn, R J Herd, Sue Callard, Michael Sargent, Di and Mike Gillam, Malcolm and Jo Hart, M G Hart, Mrs Blethyn Elliott, Mr and Mrs A H Young, KC

THE GOOD PUB GUIDE

EAST CHISENBURY SU1352 Map 2

Red Lion

At S end of village; SN9 6AQ

Thatched country inn run by a hard-working and enthusiastic couple (both are chefs), informal, friendly atmosphere, contemporary décor, delicious food, real ales and home-made cordials; seats in garden

With two top chefs running this thatched inn, the emphasis is of course on the exceptional food. But this not a straightforward dining pub, it's also a proper local selling ales from breweries such as Cottage and Keystone on handpump, and regulars do drop in for a pint and a chat. If you don't fancy a beer, they make a rather special bloody mary (pressing the tomato juice themselves) and their own lime and other seasonal cordials, keep a short, thoughtful wine list and offer unusual choices like brown rice sake and rare Kentucky bourbons. It's basically one long room split into different areas by brick and green-planked pillars. One end has a big woodburner in a brick inglenook and the other a comfortable black leather sofa and armchairs; in between, there are painted and wooden dining chairs around chunky pale oak tables on stone floors or bare boards, and wine bottles and candles on the window sills; drinkers tend to congregate at the high chairs by the bar counter. There's a further dining room, too. Décor includes a huge string of chillis and country and other pictures on the walls; background music, table skittles. Outside, there are picnic-sets on a terrace and tables and chairs on grass above; you can also go into the upper garden, where they keep bantams. Dogs are welcome – they even make their own dog treats. The bedrooms should be opened by the time this guide is published.

They bake their own bread daily, make their own sausages, butter and ketchup and cure and smoke their meat. As well as sandwiches, the imaginative food might include grilled pear and chicory salad with cashel blue, candied walnuts and sweet mustard dressing, crispy pigs head with celeriac purée, pancetta and mustard, aubergine parmigiana with garlic bread, steak in ale pie, bangers and mash with onion gravy, cornish cod with brown shrimps and almond brown butter, rare-breed beef with soy-braised ox cheek, pickled radishes, pak choi, shi-itake mushrooms and crisp spring onion bread, and puddings like white chocolate bavarois with mango and yoghurt sorbet and rhubarb panna cotta. *Benchmark main dish: slow-cooked pork belly with crackling and apple sauce £16.00. Two-course evening meal £22.50.*

Free house ~ Licensees Britt and Guy Manning ~ Real ale ~ Bar food (12-2.30(3.30 Sun), 6.30-9.30(9 Sun)) ~ Restaurant ~ (01980) 671124 ~ Children welcome ~ Dogs welcome ~ Open 12-3, 6-11; 12-12(11 Sun) Sat ~ www.redlionfreehouse.com
Recommended by Agusti Jausas, Michael Doswell

EAST KNOYLE   ST8731   Map 2

Fox & Hounds 🍽 ♟

Village signposted off A350 S of A303; The Green (named on some road atlases), a mile NW at OS Sheet 183 map reference 872313; or follow signpost off B3089, about 0.5 miles E of A303 junction near Little Chef; SP3 6BN

Beautiful thatched village pub with splendid views, welcoming service, good beers and popular food

This lively 15th-c pub, in a pretty spot by the village green, is a reliable choice for a warm welcome, good food and real ale. The three linked areas are on different levels around the central horseshoe-shaped servery and have big log fires, plentiful oak woodwork and flagstones, comfortably padded dining chairs around big scrubbed tables with vases of flowers, and a couple of leather sofas; the furnishings are all very individual and uncluttered. There's also a small light-painted conservatory restaurant. Hop Back Summer Lightning, Plain Ales Sheep Dip and guests like Palmers Copper Ale and St Austell Tribute on handpump, 20 well chosen wines by the glass and farm cider. Background music and skittle alley. The nearby woods are good for a stroll, and the Wiltshire Cycleway passes through the village; there are fine views of Blackmore Vale.

Enjoyable food includes ploughman's (not Sunday), a terrine of the day with chutney, deep-fried rosemary- and garlic-crusted brie wedges with cranberry jelly, chicken caesar salad, aberdeen angus lasagne, pizzas, daily specials like risotto with black tiger and north atlantic prawns, steak and kidney pudding, chickpea, spinach and pumpkin curry, venison casserole with port and chocolate, and duck breast with port and redcurrant sauce, and puddings such as sticky toffee pudding and apple and caramel pancake stack with vanilla ice-cream.

Benchmark main dish: slow-braised lamb shank in red wine £13.00.
Two-course evening meal £17.00.

Free house ~ Licensee Murray Seator ~ Real ale ~ Bar food (12-2.30, 6-9.30) ~ (01747)
830573 ~ Children welcome ~ Dogs welcome ~ Open 11.30-3, 5.30-11(10.30 Sun) ~
www.foxandhounds-eastknoyle.co.uk *Recommended by Michael Doswell, Martin and Karen Wake, Paul Goldman, R and M Thomas, Peter Dandy, David and Judy Robison, Edward Mirzoeff, Roy Hoing*

FONTHILL GIFFORD   ST9231   Map 2

Beckford Arms 🍴 ♀ 🛏

Off B3089 W at Fonthill Bishop; SP3 6PX
Wiltshire Dining Pub of the Year

18th-c coaching inn with refurbished bar and restaurant, interesting food, real ales and an informal but civilised atmosphere; bedrooms

Our readers love every aspect of this elegant and civilised old coaching inn, which is on the edge of the lovely rolling parkland of the Fonthill Estate. The bustling main bar has a huge fireplace, bar stools beside the counter, various old wooden dining chairs and tables on parquet flooring, Butcombe Bitter, Keystone Phoenix (brewed especially for them) and a changing guest on handpump, several wines by the glass, local cider, mulled wine and cider in the winter and cocktails using home-grown ingredients; staff are cheerful and helpful. The stylish but cosy sitting room has comfortable sofas facing each other across a low table of newspapers, a nice built-in window seat and other chairs and tables, and an open fire in a stone fireplace with candles in brass candlesticks and fresh flowers on the mantelpiece. There's also a separate restaurant and charming private dining room. Much of the artwork on the walls is by local artists. They host film nights on occasional Saturdays and will provide water and bones for dogs (the pub dog is called Elsa). The mature, rambling garden has seats on a brick terrace, hammocks under trees, games for children, a dog bath and boules. This is a lovely place to stay: the bedrooms are luxurious and stocked with home-made toiletries, and the breakfasts (featuring home-made jams) are highly enjoyable.

🍴 Using first class ingredients and own-make jams and chutneys, the unfailingly excellent food might include pigeon with bacon, roasted quince, black pudding and hazelnut vinaigrette, seared mackerel fillet with pickled cucumber, dill mayonnaise, capers and shallots, ham with duck and hen eggs and chips, linguine with mushrooms, ceps and parmesan, beef burger with bacon, cheddar and relish, hake with beetroot, a poached egg, crispy breadcrumbs and horseradish, lamb with celeriac purée, greens and spelt, grey mullet with crab broth, braised fennel, butter beans and potatoes, and puddings like white chocolate cheesecake with blackberries and honeycomb and apple and cinnamon crumble with vanilla ice-cream. *Benchmark main dish: cider-battered fish and chips with mushy peas £10.50. Two-course evening meal £21.50.*

Free house ~ Licensees Dan Brod and Charlie Luxton ~ Real ale ~ Bar food
(12-3(3.30 weekends), 6-9.30; breakfast 8-10am) ~ Restaurant ~ (01747) 870385 ~
Children welcome ~ Dogs allowed in bar ~ Open 8am-11pm ~ Bedrooms: /£95B ~
www.beckfordarms.com *Recommended by Michael Doswell, Shirley Mackenzie, Douglas and Ann Hare, Edward Mirzoeff, Alex Talbot, Tony and Caroline Elwood, Anne de Gruchy, Dave Braisted*

If you stay overnight at an inn or hotel, they are allowed to serve you
an alcoholic drink at any hour of the day or night.

GRITTLETON
Neeld Arms
ST8680   Map 2

M4 junction 17, follow A429 to Cirencester and immediately left, signed
Stanton St Quinton and Grittleton; SN14 6AP

Bustling village pub with popular food and beer and friendly staff; comfortable bedrooms

This is a proper village pub with a good, bustling atmosphere and plenty of chatty locals – though visitors are made just as welcome. It dates back to the 17th c and is now largely open plan, with Cotswold stone walls and a pleasant variety of seating ranging from bar stools, a traditional settle, window seats and pale wooden dining chairs around a mix of tables. The little brick fireplace houses a woodburning stove and there's an inglenook fireplace on the right. Wadworths IPA and 6X and guests such as Hook Norton Old Hooky and a seasonal ale from Wickwar on handpump are served from the blue-painted panelled and oak-topped bar counter. The back dining area has another inglenook with a big woodburning stove; even back here, you still feel thoroughly part of the action. There's an outdoor terrace with a pergola. The comfortable bedrooms have a lot of character.

Popular food includes lunchtime ciabatta sandwiches, local wild boar salami and parma ham, moules marinière, ham and egg, a pie of the day, local sausages and mash, goats cheese, tomato and basil pesto tart, calves liver with black pudding on potato rösti, pork medallions with apple and calvados sauce, whole bass with butter and parsley sauce, and puddings like chocolate St Emilion on rum-soaked macaroons and fresh mango crème brûlée. *Benchmark main dish: pie of the day £10.95. Two-course evening meal £17.00.*

Free house ~ Licensees Charlie and Boo West ~ Real ale ~ Bar food (12-2, 6.30-9.30; 12-4, 7-9 Sun) ~ (01249) 782470 ~ Children welcome ~ Dogs allowed in bar ~ Open 12-3, 5.30(7 Sun)-11.30 ~ Bedrooms: £50B/£80B ~ www.neeldarms.co.uk *Recommended by David Jackman, Michael Doswell, Nick Jerman*

LACOCK
Rising Sun
ST9367   Map 2

Bewley Common, Bowden Hill – out towards Sandy Lane, up hill past abbey;
OS Sheet 173 map reference 935679; SN15 2PP

Unassuming stone pub with welcoming atmosphere and great views from garden

The big two-level terrace, where there are plenty of modern steel tables and wood tables and chairs, has a stunning 25-mile view over the Avon Valley, and the sunsets can be glorious. There are plenty of modern steel and from which you can admire them. Inside, three welcoming little rooms have been knocked together to form one simply furnished area with a mix of wooden chairs and tables on stone floors, country pictures and open fires; there's also a conservatory with the same fantastic view as the terrace. Moles Best Bitter, Barleymole and Mole Catcher on handpump, several wines by the glass and maybe farm cider.

Well liked food includes sandwiches, pressing of local ham hock with home-made chutney, bacon and mushroom pepperpot with garlic ciabatta, caesar salad, ham and local eggs, chicken breast with spinach mash and red wine sauce, fish pie, salmon with a balsamic glaze on niçoise salad, rump or rib-eye steaks, and puddings such as chocolate brownie and coconut, lime and mango panna cotta. *Benchmark main dish: risotto of the day £10.95. Two-course evening meal £20.00.*

Moles ~ Managers Adam McGregor and Sarah Delaney ~ Real ale ~ Bar food (12-2.30(2 Sun), 5-9(7 Sun); 12-9 Fri, Sat and bank holidays) ~ Restaurant ~ (01249) 730363 ~ Children welcome ~ Dogs allowed in bar ~ Live entertainment last Weds of month ~ Open 12-3, 5-11; 12-11 Fri, Sat and Sun ~ www.therisingsunlacock.com *Recommended by Martin and Karen Wake, Taff Thomas, Andy Jones, Chris and Angela Buckell, Lois Dyer*

 LOWER CHUTE   SU3153   Map 2

Hatchet

The Chutes well signposted via Appleshaw off A342, 2.5 miles W of Andover; SP11 9DX

Unchanged, neatly kept, 13th-c thatched country pub with a friendly welcome from helpful staff, enjoyable food and real ales; comfortable bedrooms

Huddled in the heart of the villages known as the Chutes, this popular 13th-c thatched pub offers visitors and regulars a warm welcome from the convivial landlord. Its cottagey bedrooms make it a fine place to stay overnight (dogs are welcome in one of them); breakfasts are hearty. The very low-beamed bar has a splendid 16th-c fireback in the huge fireplace (and a roaring winter log fire), a mix of captain's chairs and cushioned wheelbacks around oak tables and a peaceful local feel; there's also an extensive restaurant. Otter Bitter, Sharps Doom Bar, Timothy Taylors Landlord and a guest from fff on handpump, several wines by the glass, 20 malt whiskies and seven farm ciders; board games and cribbage. There are seats out on a terrace by the front car park and on the side grass, as well as a shelter, a thatched children's sandpit and a 41-metre well.

Well liked bar food includes sandwiches, deep-fried whitebait with tartare sauce, chicken liver pâté with apricot chutney, ham and egg, smoked haddock fishcakes with chips, red pepper and spinach lasagne, calves liver with onion gravy, lamb shank in redcurrant and rosemary sauce with chive mash, bass fillet with lemon butter, and puddings. *Benchmark main dish: steak in ale pie £9.50. Two-course evening meal £17.00.*

Free house ~ Licensee Jeremy McKay ~ Real ale ~ Bar food (12-2, 7-9) ~ Restaurant ~ (01264) 730229 ~ Children welcome ~ Dogs allowed in bar and bedrooms ~ Monthly open mike night first Sun of month ~ Open 11.30-3, 6-11; 12-4, 7-10.30 Sun ~ Bedrooms: $70S/$90S ~ www.thehatchetinn.com *Recommended by John Coatsworth, Mr and Mrs H J Langley, John Walker, Ian Herdman*

 MANTON   SU1768   Map 2

Outside Chance ♆

Village (and pub) signposted off A4 just W of Marlborough; High Street; SN8 4HW

Popular dining pub, civilised and traditional, nicely reworked with interesting sporting theme

A new licensee took over this bustling dining pub as we went to press but early reports from our readers suggest things are going well. The three small linked rooms have flagstones or bare boards, hops on beams and mainly plain pub furnishings such as chapel chairs and a long-cushioned pew; one room has a more cosseted feel, with panelling and a comfortable banquette. The décor celebrates unlikely winners, such as 100-1 Grand National winners Coughoo and Foinavon, Mr Spooner's Only Dreams (a 100-1 winner at Leicester in 2007), or the odd-gaited little Seabiscuit who cheered many thousands of Americans with his dogged pursuit of victory during the Depression years. There's a splendid log fire in the big main fireplace and maybe fresh flowers and candlelight; background music and board games. Wadworths IPA, 6X, Bishops Tipple and a guest like Horizon on handpump, quite a few good wines by the glass, nicely served coffees and neatly dressed young staff. A suntrap side terrace has contemporary metal-framed granite-topped tables and the good-sized garden has sturdy rustic tables and benches under ash trees; they have private access to the local playing fields and children's play area.

🍴 Interesting food includes ham hock terrine with home-made piccalilli and a quail's egg, eggs benedict, beer-battered fresh fish with tartare sauce, chicken in a creamy cajun sauce, potato gnocchi with borlotti and flageolet beans, lemon, chives, rocket and parmesan, lamb rump with garlic mash and salsa verde, roasted guinea fowl with potato rösti and red pepper and basil salsa, and puddings such as chocolate and mascarpone cheesecake and meringue with lemon curd and fresh berries. *Benchmark main dish: beef burger with cheese, bacon, gherkins, chips and coleslaw £11.50. Two-course evening meal £18.00.*

Wadworths ~ Tenant Howard Spooner ~ Real ale ~ Bar food (12-2.30(3 weekends), 6(7 Sun)-9) ~ (01672) 512352 ~ Children welcome ~ Dogs welcome ~ Open 12-3, 5.30-11; 12-11 Sat and Sun ~ www.theoutsidechance.co.uk *Recommended by Sheila and Robert Robinson, Guy Vowles, Ian and Rose Lock, Mr and Mrs A Curry, Mr and Mrs P R Thomas*

MARLBOROUGH
Lamb 🍺

SU1869   Map 2

The Parade; SN8 1NE

Friendly former coaching inn with big helpings of popular food, real ales tapped from the cask, plenty of customers and traditional pubby furnishings; comfortable bedrooms

Just off the high street, this is a well run, bustling local with plenty of customers and a friendly atmosphere. The L-shaped bar has lots of hop bines, wall banquette seating and wheelback chairs around cast-iron framed pub tables on the parquet floor, Cecil Aldin prints on the red walls, candles in bottles and a two-way log-effect gas fire; the easy-going pub bulldog may be poddling about. Wadworths 6X and changing guests tapped from the cask and several wines by the glass; games machine, juke box, darts and TV. There are green picnic-sets and modern alloy and wicker seats and tables in the attractive back courtyard. The bedrooms are light and cottagey (some are in the former stable block) and the breakfasts are hearty. The summer window boxes are very pretty.

🍴 Served in large helpings and cooked by the landlady, the very popular food might include sandwiches, eggs benedict, baked goats cheese with honey, walnuts and beetroot, corned beef hash with egg and pickle, chilli con carne, thai coconut, sweet potato, chickpea and spinach curry, battered cod and chips, a giant breakfast (served at lunchtime, too), local free-range pork sausages with bubble and squeak, duck confit with thyme-crushed potatoes and braised red cabbage, and puddings such as gooseberry and elderflower crumble and treacle tart with clotted cream. *Benchmark main dish: steak and kidney in ale pie £9.50. Two-course evening meal £15.00.*

Wadworths ~ Tenant Vyv Scott ~ Real ale ~ Bar food (12-2.30, 6-9 Mon-Thurs; no food
Fri-Sun evenings) ~ (01672) 512668 ~ Children welcome ~ Dogs welcome ~ Occasional
live music Fri and Sat evenings ~ Open 11-11(midnight Sat); 12-10.30 Sun ~
www.thelambinnmarlborough.com *Recommended by Tony Baldwin, Frank Blanchard,
Ian Herdman*

 NEWTON TONY   SU2140   Map 2
Malet Arms
Village signposted off A338 Swindon–Salisbury; SP4 0HF

**Smashing village pub with no pretensions, a good choice of local beers
and highly thought of food**

Nicely situated on the banks of the River Bourne, this 16th-c former
coaching inn receives consistently positive praise from our readers
for its relaxed atmosphere and unpretentious charm – and the cheerful
landlord continues to run it with much friendly enthusiasm. The outside
has been repainted and tidied up, as has the small front terrace, which
has new garden seats; more on grass and in the back garden. Inside,
there have been some changes to the snug, too, which now has an
outstanding collection of photographs and prints celebrating the local
aviation history of Boscombe Down together with archive photographs
of Stonehenge festivals of the seventies and eighties. The other low-
beamed interconnecting room has pleasant furnishings, including a mix
of tables of different sizes with high-winged wall settles, carved pews,
chapel and carver chairs, and lots of pictures, mainly from imperial days.
The main front windows are said to be made from the stern of a ship,
and there's a log and coal fire in a huge fireplace. At the back is a homely
dining room. Four real ales are well kept on handpump from breweries
such as fff, Fullers, Itchen Valley, Palmers, Plain Ales, Ramsbury and
Stonehenge; they also have 31 malt whiskies, 11 wines by the glass and
Weston's Old Rosie cider. Getting to the pub takes you through a ford
and it may be best to use an alternative route in winter, as it can be quite
deep. There's now an all-weather cricket pitch on the village green. The
pub policy of no background music or games machines helps to maintain
the peaceful atmosphere.

Using seasonal game (bagged by the landlord), lamb raised in the surrounding
fields and their own pigs and baking their own bread, the enjoyable and
interesting food might include cornish yarg and stinging nettle tart, pork terrine
with piccalilli, piri piri chicken in pitta bread with yoghurt, cumberland sausages
with mash, goats cheese and honey crostini with wild rocket pesto and sweet potato
ribbons, creamy fish pie, venison burger with cheese and chilli mayonnaise, a fish of
the day with sea salt and fresh lime, oriental spare ribs and trotters, and puddings
such as pear and almond cake with custard and Mars Bar cheesecake. *Benchmark
main dish: beef burger £9.50. Two-course evening meal £16.50.*

Free house ~ Licensees Noel and Annie Cardew ~ Real ale ~ Bar food (12-2.30, 6.30-10
(6-9 Sun)) ~ Restaurant ~ (01980) 629279 ~ Children in restaurant or snug only ~
Dogs allowed in bar ~ Open 11-3, 6-11; 12-3, 7-10.30 Sun ~ www.maletarms.com
*Recommended by B J Harding, Peter Dandy, Ian Herdman, N R White, Richard and Sue Fewkes,
Sarah Odell, Peathey-Johns Andre, Phyl and Jack Street, Pat and Tony Martin, Chris and Jan
Swanwick, James Bedforth, Mr and Mrs P R Thomas*

NORTON
ST8884 Map 2

Vine Tree 🍽 ♀

4 miles from M4 junction 17; A429 towards Malmesbury, then left at Hullavington, Sherston signpost, then follow Norton signposts; in village turn right at Foxley signpost, which takes you into Honey Lane; SN16 0JP

Civilised dining pub, beams and candlelight, big choice of first class seasonal food, super wines (also sold at their deli/farm shop) and a sizeable garden

Once this former mill served drinks through the front windows to passing travellers. Nowadays, it serves thirsty visitors to Westonbirt Arboretum and other fine gardens, houses and race courses in the area – and to riders following the county's official cycle route, too. But there are always lots of loyal locals as well, and with its lovely atmosphere, friendly welcome and delicious food, it's always pretty busy. Three neatly kept small rooms open into each other, with aged beams, some old settles and unvarnished wooden tables on the flagstone floors, big cream church altar candles, a woodburning stove at one end of the restaurant and a large open fireplace in the central bar, and limited edition and sporting prints; look out for Clementine, the friendly and docile black labrador. Butcombe Bitter and St Austell Tribute and a couple of guests like Bath Ales Gem Bitter and Stonehenge Pigswill on handpump, 48 wines by the glass including sparkling wines and champagne (and they have their own wine shop, too), and quite a choice of malt whiskies and armagnacs, as well as mulled wine in the winter and award-winning bloody marys year-round. There are picnic-sets and a children's play area in a two-acre garden, plus a pretty suntrap terrace with teak furniture under big cream umbrellas, and an attractive smokers' shelter. Pets (including horses!) are welcomed and provided for. Look out for the two ghosts that some visitors have spotted. They also run the Barbury at Broad Hinton.

Using local and seasonal produce from farmers and gamekeepers, and seafood that is delivered daily, the excellent, imaginative food might include sandwiches, pigeon and wild mushroom tartlet with leek purée and truffle jus, scallops, puy lentil and bacon salad with warm tomato and tarragon dressing, moroccan-spiced lamb chump with toasted almond and apricot couscous, red pepper and harissa coulis, home-made venison and red wine sausages with colcannon and caramelised shallot gravy, thai red curry of lobster with courgettes, sweet potato, thai basil and ginger, walnut and sage-crusted cutlet of pork with cider fondant potatoes and grain mustard sauce, and puddings such as banana tarte tatin with toffee ripple ice-cream and toffee sauce and rosewater and vanilla panna cotta with pink rhubarb and orange sorbet. *Benchmark main dish: saddle of venison £19.95. Two-course evening meal £23.00.*

Free house ~ Licensees Charles Walker and Tiggi Wood ~ Real ale ~ Bar food (12-2.30(3.30 Sun), 7-9.30(10 Fri and Sat)) ~ Restaurant ~ (01666) 837654 ~ Children welcome ~ Dogs welcome ~ Open 12-3, 6-midnight; 12-midnight Sat and Sun; closed winter Sun evenings ~ www.thevinetree.co.uk *Recommended by Jennifer and Patrick O'Dell, Roger and Anne Mallard, Rod Stoneman, James Morrell*

Bedroom prices are for high summer. Even then you may get reductions for more than one night, or (outside tourist areas) weekends. Winter special rates are common, and many inns cut bedroom prices if you have a full evening meal.

PITTON

SU2131   Map 2

Silver Plough ♀ ⌘

Village signed from A30 E of Salisbury (follow brown tourist signs); SP5 1DU

Bustling country dining pub with popular bar food, good drinks and nearby walks; bedrooms

A farmhouse until World War II, this bustling, friendly place is surrounded by woodland and downland paths and makes a good stop for a pre- or post-walk meal. The comfortable front bar has plenty to look at as the black beams are strung with hundreds of antique boot-warmers and stretchers, pewter and china tankards, copper kettles, toby jugs, earthenware and glass rolling pins, and so forth. Seats include half a dozen cushioned antique oak settles (one elaborately carved, beside a very fine reproduction of an Elizabethan oak table) around rustic pine tables. They serve Badger Bitter, Gold and Tanglefoot on handpump and 13 wines by the glass from a bar made from a hand-carved Elizabethan over-mantle. The back bar is simpler, but still has a big winged high-backed settle, cases of antique guns, and substantial pictures; there are two woodburning stoves for winter warmth; background music. The skittle alley is for private use only. The quiet, south-facing lawn has picnic-sets and other tables under cocktail parasols and there are more seats on the heated terrace; occasional barbecues. They keep dog biscuits on the bar in the snug bar.

 Reasonably priced, the food includes sandwiches, chicken liver pâté with onion marmalade, whitebait and garlic mayonnaise, home-made beef burger with cheese or bacon toppings, beer-battered fish and chips, courgette cake with honey-roasted butternut squash and a roasted red pepper, goats cheese and tomato dressing, marinated rack of ribs with sweetcorn and salad, flounder with caper butter sauce, tikka-marinated rump steak skewers with roasted vegetable couscous, and puddings such as tiramisu. *Benchmark main dish: steak in ale pie £9.95. Two-course evening meal £17.00.*

Badger ~ Tenants Stephen and Susan Keyes ~ Real ale ~ Bar food (12-2, 6-9; 12-8 Sun) ~ Restaurant ~ (01722) 712266 ~ Children welcome ~ Dogs allowed in bar ~ Open 12-3, 6-11; 12-9.30 Sun ~ Bedrooms: £60S/£70S or less if you choose not to take breakfast ~ www.silverplough-pitton.co.uk *Recommended by Ian Herdman, Dave Braisted, Phyl and Jack Street, Conor McGaughey, Malcolm and Maralyn Hinxman*

POULSHOT

ST9760   Map 2

Raven ◄

Off A361; SN10 1RW

Pretty village pub with friendly licensees, enjoyable food and beer and seats in back garden

Just across from village green, this is a pretty half-timbered pub with friendly, welcoming licensees who take great care of both their pub and their customers. The two cosy black-beamed rooms are spotlessly kept and have comfortable banquettes, pubby chairs and tables, an open fire and Wadworths IPA and 6X plus a seasonal guest beer tapped from the cask; background music in the dining room only. The jack russell is called Faith and the doberman, Harvey. There are picnic-sets under parasols in the walled back garden.

Cooked by the landlord, the good, popular food might include filled baguettes, chicken liver pâté with spiced apple chutney, prawn and crayfish cocktail, a mixed cold meat plate with pickles, ham and eggs, beef burger with gherkins, roasted red onion, garlic mayonnaise and toppings such as emmenthal, stilton or bacon (there's a vegetarian option too), fish crumble, chicken piri piri, liver and bacon with red wine gravy and buttery mash, steak and kidney pie, and puddings such as gooseberry flapjack tart and warm chocolate brownie with chocolate sauce. *Benchmark main dish: steak and kidney pie £11.50. Two-course evening meal £18.50.*

Wadworths ~ Tenant Jeremy Edwards ~ Real ale ~ Bar food (12-2(2.30 Sun), 6-9; not winter Mon) ~ Restaurant ~ (01380) 828271 ~ Children welcome ~ Dogs allowed in bar ~ Open 11.30-3, 6.30-11; 12-3, 7-10.30 Sun; closed winter Mon ~ www.ravenpoulshot.co.uk *Recommended by Mr and Mrs P R Thomas, Bridget Scott*

SALISBURY SU1429 Map 2
Haunch of Venison £
Minster Street, opposite Market Cross; SP1 1TB

Ancient pub oozing history, with tiny beamed rooms, unique fittings and a famous mummified hand

A friendly new landlord took over this ancient pub just as we went to press. It's the sort of place that customers return to on a regular basis. Both the tiny downstairs rooms, which date back to 1320 when the place was used by craftsmen working on the cathedral spire, have a great deal of character and atmosphere. There are massive beams in the white ceiling, stout oak benches built into the timbered walls, black and white floor tiles, and an open fire. A tiny snug (popular with locals, but historically said to be where the ladies drank) opens off the entrance lobby. Courage Best, Hop Back Summer Lightning, Ringwood Fortyniner and a changing guest beer on handpump from a unique pewter bar counter with a rare set of antique taps for gravity-fed spirits and liqueurs. They've also up to 100 malt whiskies and several wines by the glass. Halfway up the stairs is a panelled room they call the House of Lords, which has a small-paned window looking down on to the main bar and a splendid fireplace that dates back to the building's early years; behind glass in a small wall slit is the smoke-preserved mummified hand of an 18th-c card sharp still clutching his cards.

 Under the new landlord, the food now includes sandwiches, brown crab cakes with lemon mayonnaise, creamy garlic wild mushrooms on toast, pork and leek sausages with red wine and onion gravy, ham and free-range eggs, chicken in lemon and thyme butter with dauphinoise potatoes, venison and smoky bacon casserole, daily specials like spicy ham hock terrine, beef curry and fish pie, and puddings such as sherry trifle and apple and cinnamon crumble; they also offer a two- and three-course set lunch menu. *Benchmark main dish: venison and smoked bacon casserole £10.95. Two-course evening meal £17.00.*

Scottish Courage ~ Lease Alex Marshall ~ Real ale ~ Bar food (12-2.30, 6-9.30; 12-4 Sun; not Sun evening) ~ Restaurant ~ (01722) 411313 ~ Children welcome ~ Dogs welcome ~ Open 11-11(midnight Sat); 12-6 Sun; closed Sun evening ~ www.haunchofvenison.uk.com *Recommended by Tim Loryman, Val and Alan Green, Andrea Rampley, Ann and Colin Hunt, A D Lealan, Howard and Margaret Buchanan*

All *Guide* inspections are anonymous. Anyone claiming to be a *Good Pub Guide* inspector is a fraud. Please let us know.

SANDY LANE   ST9668   Map 2

George

A342 Devizes–Chippenham; SN15 2PX

Friendly licensees at immaculately kept old pub with open fires, Wadworths ales and well liked food

In a charming thatched village surrounded by the lovely Bowood Estate, this neatly kept and handsome Georgian pub is run by friendly, helpful licensees who have known it since childhood. The cosy bar area has an open fire, plush stools and a mix of chairs around pubby tables on the wooden floor, Wadworths IPA and 6X on handpump and 16 wines by the glass. There's also a back dining room and a wooden-framed conservatory with farmhouse and red-plush dining chairs around dark tables on more pale floorboarding. Outside, the terrace has rattan furniture and picnic-sets, with more on the lawn, and flower beds in the old piggery. The pub overlooks a small green.

 Tasty food includes smoked haddock welsh rarebit with apple and mixed salad, pigeon breast with chestnuts and smoked bacon lardons, home-cooked ham with bubble and squeak with free-range eggs, local faggots with wholegrain mustard mash and roasted shallot gravy, battered fish of the day with tartare sauce, butternut risotto cake with parsley dressing and roasted beetroot, pork belly with prunes and leeks and an apple and brandy sauce, specials like wild bass with bourguignon sauce and sautéed jerusalem artichokes, and puddings. *Benchmark main dish: cornish megrim sole with brown shrimp and herb butter £13.50. Two-course evening meal £20.00.*

Wadworths ~ Tenants Mark and Harriet Jenkinson ~ Real ale ~ Bar food (12-9.30; 12-3 Sun; not Sun evening or Mon) ~ Restaurant ~ (01380) 850403 ~ Children welcome ~ Dogs allowed in bar ~ Open 12-10.30(11 Sat); 12-4 Sun; closed Sun evening, Mon ~ www.georgeinnsandylane.co.uk *Recommended by Neil and Anita Christopher, Mrs Pickwick, Michael Doswell*

SHERSTON   ST8585   Map 2

Rattlebone ⚲

Church Street; B4040 Malmesbury–Chipping Sodbury; SN16 0LR

Village pub with lots of atmosphere in rambling rooms, good bar food and real ales, and friendly staff

There's plenty of bustle and buckets of character in this 17th-c pub, named after the Saxon warrior John Rattlebone – who apparently haunts it to this day. The public bar has a good mix of locals and visitors and the other softly lit rambling rooms – including the long dining room at the back – have beams, standing timbers and flagstones; pews, settles and country-kitchen chairs around a mix of tables; armchairs and sofas; and roaring fires. Butcombe Bitter, St Austell Tribute and Wells & Youngs Bitter on handpump, local cider, home-made lemonade and several wines by the glass on a thoughtful list; background music, board games, TV and games machine. Outside there's a skittle alley, two boules pitches, often in use by one of the many pub teams, a boules festival in July and mangold hurling (similar to boules but using cattle-feed turnips), as well as other events. The two pretty gardens include an extended terrace where barbecues and spit roasts are held. Wheelchair access.

 Using local, free-range produce, the fairly priced food might include sandwiches, wild rabbit, prune and chestnut terrine, crab linguine with chilli, coriander and parmesan, home-made beef burger (or vegetarian burger) with stilton, rocket and skinny fries, ham with free-range eggs, braised chicken with lemon and sea salt and smoked garlic mash, bass with mussels and horseradish velouté, pork steak with pear tarte tatin and stilton sauce, specials like smoked salmon and prawn risotto and slow-braised, spicy lamb shank, and puddings such as white chocolate and pistachio cheesecake with salted caramel and rhubarb and ginger crumble with clotted cream ice-cream. *Benchmark main dish: venison, shallot and red wine pie £10.50. Two-course evening meal £20.25.*

Youngs ~ Tenant Jason Read ~ Real ale ~ Bar food (12-2.30(3 Sun), 6-9.30(8.30 Sun)) ~ Restaurant ~ (01666) 840871 ~ Children welcome ~ Dogs allowed in bar ~ Monthly acoustic music evenings ~ Open 12-3, 5-11(midnight Fri); 12-midnight(11 Sun) Sat ~ www.therattlebone.co.uk *Recommended by Chris and Angela Buckell, Barry and Anne, Tom and Ruth Rees, Michael Doswell, John and Gloria Isaacs*

 SOUTH WRAXALL   ST8364   Map 2

Longs Arms ⑪

Upper South Wraxall, off B3109 N of Bradford-on-Avon; BA15 2SB

Friendly licensees at well run old stone inn, plenty of character, real ales and first class food

Carefully refurbished a year ago by its friendly licensees, this is a handsome and partly 17th-c stone inn by the village church. The bar has windsor and other pubby chairs around wooden tables on flagstones, horsebrasses on beams, a woodburning stove in the fireplace and high chairs by the counter, where they keep Wadworths IPA and 6X and a changing guest beer on handpump and several wines by the glass. Another room has cushioned and other dining chairs, a nice old settle and a wall banquette around a mix of tables on carpet, fresh flowers and lots of prints and paintings, and a further room has nice little boxy settles and other seats on a pale oak floor; the skittle alley is much used during the season; at other times it can be used as extra dining space. There are seats in the pretty little walled back garden. They keep dog biscuits behind the bar.

Using seasonal local produce, baking their own bread and smoking their own salmon, they serve particularly good food that might include lunchtime sandwiches, home-made black pudding with bacon, apple and english mustard, smoked salmon with pickled cucumber, cobnut, cauliflower, broccoli and blue cheese crumble, pigeon cake with fried quails egg, twice-baked cheddar soufflé, shepherd's pie, cumberland sausage with mash and gravy, lamb burger with chips, chicken with pink fir apple potatoes, bacon and corn, venison loin with crab apple jelly and truffle mash, and puddings such as blueberry fool and chocolate blondie with raspberry sorbet. *Benchmark main dish: lobster and truffle risotto £16.50. Two-course evening meal £21.00.*

Wadworths ~ Tenants Rob and Liz Allcock ~ Real ale ~ Bar food (12-3, 5.30-9.30; 12-9.30 Fri-Sun) ~ Restaurant ~ (01225) 864450 ~ Children welcome ~ Dogs welcome ~ Open 12-3, 5.30-11; 12-11 Fri, Sat and Sun ~ www.thelongsarms.com *Recommended by Simon Rodway, Alan Sutton, Gareth Davies*

 WARMINSTER   ST8745   Map 2

Weymouth Arms ♀

Emwell Street; BA12 8JA

Charming backstreet pub with panelled rooms, a roaring winter fire in snug bar, candlelight and fresh flowers, real ales, friendly staff and imaginative food; seats in courtyard; bedrooms

Tucked away down a quiet back street, this handsome old pub comes as quite a surprise. The snug, panelled entrance bar has a roaring log fire in a fine stone fireplace with a copper coal bucket and big log basket to one side and ancient leather books on the mantelpiece. Leather tub chairs around a fine walnut and satinwood table make the most of the fire's warmth, with more seats and tables against the walls and high stools by the counter; on our visit, locals were dropping in for a pint and a chat and to read the daily papers. Butcombe Bitter and Wadworths 6X on handpump and good wines by the glass are served by cheerful, friendly staff. Leading off here is another heavily panelled room with a smaller fireplace and brass candlesticks on the mantelpiece, similar furniture on wide bare floorboards and a chandelier. The dining room (also panelled) on the other side of the bar is on two levels and stretches back to the open kitchen. The lower part has banquette wall seating, spindleback dining chairs and candles on tables and the upper part is more contemporary. There are seats in the flower-filled back courtyard. Bedrooms are well equipped and comfortable.

Good, enjoyable food might include filled baguettes, risotto of crab, baby prawns, parmesan and basil oil, terrine of duck, chicken, ham hock and roasted vegetables with home-made green tomato chutney, sausages with mash, smoked bacon and gravy, gammon with home-made chips and free-range eggs, fishcakes with tartare sauce, roasted peppers filled with feta and herby breadcrumbs, belly of pork, pig cheeks, apple sauce and roast gravy, lamb shoulder and rosemary salty butter pie, and puddings such as dark chocolate mousse with cherry sauce and treacle sponge with home-made custard. *Benchmark main dish: pork belly and pig cheeks with apple sauce and roast gravy £14.95. Two-course evening meal £19.50.*

Free house ~ Licensee Shane Goodway ~ Real ale ~ Bar food (12-2.30, 6-9) ~ Restaurant ~ (01985) 216 995 ~ Children welcome ~ Dogs allowed in bar ~ Open 12-2.30, 6-midnight; closed Mon lunchtime ~ Bedrooms: £65S/£75S ~ www.weymoutharms.co.uk
Recommended by Edward Mirzoeff, Michael Sargent

WEST LAVINGTON   SU0052   Map 2

Bridge Inn 🍴

Church Street (A360); SN10 4LD

Easy-going village pub with good bar food, real ales and a light, comfortable bar

This thoroughly nice pub has been taken over by new enthusiastic licensees. It's quietly civilised and friendly and the comfortable, spacious bar mixes contemporary features with firmly traditional fixtures such as the enormous brick inglenook that may be filled with big logs and candles; at the opposite end is a smaller modern fireplace, in an area mostly set for eating. The cream-painted or exposed brick walls are hung with local pictures of the Lavingtons and there are fresh flowers and evening candlelight; timbers and the occasional step divide the various areas. Sharps Doom Bar and Wadworths IPA on handpump, nine wines by the glass and several malt whiskies; background music. A raised lawn at the back makes a pleasant place to spend a summer's afternoon, with several tables under a big tree; boules.

Cooked by the landlord, the quickly changing seasonal food might include lunchtime filled ciabatta sandwiches, rabbit rillettes, tarragon and quince jelly, black pudding, bacon, cauliflower purée and crispy poached egg, roast vegetable lasagne, home-made beef burger with bacon, cheese and fries, free-range chicken breast with wholegrain mustard sauce, duck breast with port wine sauce and fondant potatoes, bass fillet with saffron potatoes, braised red peppers and salsa verde, and puddings like warm double chocolate brownie with home-made banana and rum ice-cream and buttermilk panna cotta with blackcurrant compote and shortbread; they also offer a set two- and three-course lunch menu (not Sunday). *Benchmark main dish: whole lemon sole £14.50. Two-course evening meal £20.50.*

Enterprise ~ Lease Emily Robinson and James Stewart ~ Real ale ~ Bar food (12-3, 7-9.30; 12-4, 6-8 Sun; not Mon) ~ (01380) 813213 ~ Children welcome ~ Dogs allowed in bar ~ Open 12-3, 6-midnight; 12-4, 6-1am Sat; 12-10 Sun; closed Mon ~ www.the-bridge-inn.co.uk *Recommended by Colin Wood, Mr and Mrs P R Thomas, B and F A Hannam, Mr and Mrs A Curry*

 WHITLEY   ST8866   Map 2

Pear Tree ♀ ⇔

Off B3353 S of Corsham; SN12 8QX

Attractive and civilised dining pub with inventive food, a good choice of drinks, and seats in garden; bedrooms

Now under Marco Pierre White's umbrella of pubs, this is a lovely old former farmhouse with plenty of seating in the carefully maintained gardens. The charming front bar has quite a pubby feel, with cushioned window seats, some stripped shutters, an open fire and stools around pubby tables on the flagstones and against the counter, where they keep a beer named for them brewed by Lees and a changing guest like Moles Bitter on handpump, a cider named for them from Weston's and quite a few good wines by the glass. The big formal restaurant at the back has lots of cartoons on the walls, some interesting stained glass windows, dark wood cushioned dining chairs around quite a mix of tables, fresh flowers and candlelight. A bright spacious garden room opens on to a terrace with good teak furniture and views over the gardens. The bedrooms are well equipped.

Good – if not cheap – food might include sandwiches, potted duck with green peppercorns and toasted sourdough, Morecambe Bay potted shrimps, shepherd's pie, calves liver and bacon, fish and triple-cooked chips with marrowfat peas, grilled cumberland sausages with onion gravy and creamed potatoes, steak in ale pie with swede purée, salmon fishcake with tartare sauce, and puddings like sherry trifle and bitter chocolate mousse; they also offer good value two- and three-course set lunch and evening menus. *Benchmark main dish: fried fish and triple-cooked chips with marrowfat peas £13.50. Two-course evening meal £26.00.*

Free house ~ Licensee Emma Bennett ~ Real ale ~ Bar food (12-2.30(3 Sat), 6-10; 12-4, 6-9 Sun) ~ Restaurant ~ (01225) 709131 ~ Children welcome ~ Dogs allowed in bar and bedrooms ~ Open 12-11 ~ Bedrooms: £95B/£125B ~ www.wheelerspeartree.com *Recommended by Michael Doswell, Dr and Mrs A K Clarke, Mrs Blethyn Elliott, Taff and Gilly Thomas*

 WINSLEY   ST7960   Map 2

Seven Stars ⑪ ◀

Off B3108 bypass W of Bradford-on-Avon (pub just over Wiltshire border); BA15 2LQ

Handsome old stone pub with attractive bars, imaginative food, good real ales and friendly staff; seats outside

On a quiet lane in a pretty village, this early 18th-c stone building has plenty of picnic-sets and tables and chairs under parasols on the terrace or on neat grassy surrounds with flowering borders that look across to the bowling green opposite. Inside, the low-beamed linked areas have stripped stone walls and light pastel paintwork, candlelight, farmhouse chairs and wooden tables on flagstones and carpet and a couple of stone fireplaces – one with a sizeable hearth. Helpful managers and cheerful young staff serve Bath Ales Gem Bitter, Devilfish Bomb Shell (one of the landlords, Mr Metz, also founded and co-owns the Devilfish Brewery), Wadworths 6X and Yeovil Summerset on handpump and several wines by the glass; background music and board games.

Making their own ice-creams and sorbets, chutneys and pickles, salt and corned beef, sausages, black pudding and chorizo (and some of the bread), they serve highly thought of food including sandwiches, crispy brie with caramelised apple and pickled raisin salad and truffled honey, grilled mackerel fillet with spiced rhubarb relish, home-made gnocchi with wild garlic pesto, leeks, walnuts and parmesan, pork tenderloin with smoked pork fritter, bubble and squeak, marinated apple and fennel slaw and honey and mustard sauce, spice-crusted quail with saffron mash, caramelised onion and lemon jus, specials like moules marinière and rare beef fillet with braised ox cheek, mushroom mousse and red wine jus, and puddings such as iced white chocolate and honeycomb parfait with blood oranges, whipped Drambuie mascarpone and salted peanut brittle and warm treacle tart with home-made vanilla ice-cream. *Benchmark main dish: garlic-roast chicken with herb gnocchi, braised gem lettuce, peas, shallots, home-cured bacon £14.20. Two-course evening meal £20.50.*

Free house ~ Licensees Claire Spreadbury and Evan Metz ~ Real ale ~ Bar food (12-2(2.30 Sun), 6-8; not winter Sun evening) ~ Restaurant ~ (01225) 722204 ~ Children welcome ~ Dogs allowed in bar ~ Open 12-2.30(3 Sat), 6-10.30(11 Sat); 12-3.30, 6-10 Sun; closed winter Sun evening ~ www.sevenstarswinsley.co.uk
Recommended by Nigel Long

Also Worth a Visit in Wiltshire

Besides the fully inspected pubs, you might like to try these pubs that have been recommended to us and described by readers. Do tell us what you think of them: feedback@goodguides.com

ALDBOURNE SU2675
Crown (01672) 540214
The Square; SN8 2DU Old local overlooking pretty village's pond, good value straight-forward food, Sharps Doom Bar, Shepherd Neame Spitfire and guests, friendly helpful staff, comfortable two-part beamed lounge with sofas by log fire in huge brick inglenook linking to public bar, old tables and bare boards, small nicely laid out dining room, darts, Tues quiz; background and some live music; children welcome, courtyard tables, Early English church nearby, four bedrooms. *(Jeremy King, Neil and Anita Christopher)*

ALVEDISTON ST9723
Crown (01722) 780335
Off A30 W of Salisbury; SP5 5JY
Refurbished 15th-c thatched inn, three cosy very low-beamed partly panelled rooms, two inglenook fireplaces, good varied choice of fair-priced home-made food, well kept ales, pleasant service; children and dogs welcome, pretty views from attractive garden with terrace, bedrooms, open all day Fri and Sat, till 8.30pm Sun (all week July, Aug).
(Lady Keith)

AMESBURY SU1541
⋆**Antrobus Arms** (01980) 623163
Church Street; SP4 7EU Handsome hotel, quiet, comfortable and relaxed, with good food, friendly helpful staff, four changing real ales, good fires in warmly welcoming smart yet pubby bar and communicating lounge overlooking beautiful walled garden, two dining rooms; children and dogs welcome, 17 attractive bedrooms, open all day. *(Anon)*

AXFORD SU2470
⋆**Red Lion** (01672) 520271
Off A4 E of Marlborough; SN8 2HA
Pretty beamed and panelled pub with big

inglenook, comfortable sofas, cask seats and other solid chairs, good popular food from pub staples to pricier fish etc, welcoming attentive staff, ales such as Ramsbury, good choice of wines by the glass, picture-window restaurant; valley views from nice terrace, children welcome, closed Sun evening. *(John Redfern, Joy and Gordon Kellam, Michael Rowse, Jennifer and Patrick O'Dell, Alec and Mary) MacCaig and others)*

BADBURY   SU1980
✶ **Plough** (01793) 740342

A346 (Marlborough Road) just S of M4 junction 15; SN4 0EP Popular good value pub food all day including Sun carvery, friendly helpful staff, well kept Arkells, decent wines, coffee from 10am, large rambling bar (dogs welcome), light airy dining room (children allowed), log fire and daily newspapers; background music; tree-shaded garden with terrace and play area, open all day. *(JJW, CMW, Mary Rayner, Pat Crabb)*

BARFORD ST MARTIN   SU0531
✶ **Barford Inn** (01722) 742242

B3089 W of Salisbury (Grovely Road), just off A30; SP3 4AB Welcoming 16th-c coaching inn, dark panelled front bar with big log fire, other interlinking rooms, old utensils and farming tools, beamed bare-brick restaurant, wide choice of enjoyable food including deals, prompt friendly service, well kept Badger ales, decent wines by the glass; children welcome, dogs in bar, disabled access (not to bar) and facilities, terrace tables, more in back garden, four comfortable annexe bedrooms, good walks, open all day. *(Dennis Jenkin)*

BECKHAMPTON   SU0868
✶ **Waggon & Horses** (01672) 539418

A4 Marlborough–Calne; SN8 1QJ Handsome stone-and-thatch former coaching inn, generous fair-priced home-made food in open-plan beamed bar or separate dining area, well kept Wadworths ales; background music; children and dogs welcome, pleasant raised garden with play area, handy for Avebury, open all day. *(Sheila and Robert Robinson, Mark and Ruth Brock)*

BERWICK ST JAMES   SU0739
✶ **Boot** (01722) 790243

High Street (B3083); SP3 4TN Welcoming flint and stone pub not far from Stonehenge, good locally sourced food from daily changing blackboard menu, friendly efficient staff, well kept Wadworths ales and a guest, huge log fire in inglenook one end, sporting prints over small brick fireplace at other, lit candles, small back dining room with collection of celebrity boots; children welcome, sheltered side lawn. *(Mark Davies, Fr Robert Marsh, N R White)*

BISHOPSTONE   SU2483
✶ **Royal Oak** (01793) 790481

Cues Lane; near Swindon; at first exit roundabout from A419 N of M4 J15, follow Wanborough sign, then keep on to Bishopstone, at small sign to pub turn right; SN6 8PP Welcoming informal dining pub run by local farmers using good seasonal produce including properly hung home-reared steaks (farm shop too); mainly scrubbed-wood furnishings on bare boards or parquet, animal pictures for sale, log fire on left and little maze of dark pews, well kept Arkells beers, organic wines, over 30 malt whiskies and good choice of gins, maybe home-made elderflower cordial, charity shelves and window sills of paperbacks; children and dogs welcome, picnic-sets on grass and among trees, smarter modern tables on front deck, cheap serviceable bedrooms in back cabins, pretty village below Ridgeway and White Horse. *(John Hickman, Frank Blanchard, Mary Rayner, Dave Snowden, David Jackman, R T and J C Moggridge and others)*

BOX   ST8369
✶ **Quarrymans Arms** (01225) 743569

Box Hill; from Bath on A4 right into Bargates 50 metres before railway bridge, left up Quarry Hill at T junction, left again at grassy triangle; from Corsham, left after Rudloe Park Hotel into Beech Road, third left on to Barnetts Hill, and right at top of hill; OS Sheet 173 map reference 834694; SN13 8HN Enjoyable unpretentious pub with friendly staff and informal relaxed atmosphere, comfortable rather than overly smart (even mildly untidy in parts), plenty of mining-related photographs and memorabilia dotted around (once the local of Bath-stone miners – licensees run interesting guided trips down mine itself), one modernised room with open fire set aside for drinking, Butcombe, Moles, Wadworths and guests, 60 malt whiskies, several wines by the glass, tasty bar food at fair prices; children and dogs welcome, picnic-sets on terrace with sweeping views, popular with walkers and potholers, bedrooms, open all day. *(Guy Vowles, Simon Rodway, Taff Thomas, Ian Herdman, Peter Salmon and others)*

BRADFORD-ON-AVON   ST8260
Barge (01225) 863403

Frome Road; BA15 2EA Large modernised open-plan pub set down from canal, well kept ales such as Brakspears, Fullers, Marstons and Ringwood, good wines by the glass, wide choice of well liked food including children's and vegetarian choices, friendly enthusiastic young staff, stripped stone and flagstones, solid furniture, woodburners; wheelchair access, garden with smokers' pavilion, steps up to canalside picnic-sets, moorings, bedrooms. *(Taff Thomas, Ken and Barbara Turner, Chris and Angela Buckell, Phil Bryant)*

BRADFORD-ON-AVON ST8261
Bunch of Grapes (01225) 863877
Silver Street; BA15 1JY Dim-lit traditional décor, well kept Wells & Youngs and a couple of guests, good range of huge home-made pies (can be shared), cask seats on bare boards in small front room, bigger tables in roomier main bar; children welcome at lunchtime (over-8s till 8pm), open all day Fri-Sun, closed lunchtimes Mon-Weds. *(Charles Harvey, Janina Conrad)*

BRADFORD-ON-AVON ST8060
Cross Guns (01225) 862335
Avoncliff, 2 miles W; OS Sheet 173 map reference 805600; BA15 2HB Congenial bustle on summer days with swarms of people in floodlit partly concreted areas steeply terraced above the bridges, aqueducts and river; appealingly quaint at quieter times, with stripped-stone low-beamed bar, 16th-c inglenook, full Box Steam range kept well and a guest, several ciders, lots of malt whiskies and interesting wines by the glass including country ones, comprehensive choice of enjoyable food, good friendly service, upstairs river-view restaurant; children and dogs welcome, wheelchair accessible, bedrooms, open all day. *(Chris and Angela Buckell, Peter Salmon, Alan Sutton, Paul Humphreys, Don Bryan)*

BRADFORD-ON-AVON ST8261
Dandy Lion (01225) 863433
Market Street; BA15 1LL More continental café bar than typical local, stripped wood floor and panelling, modern furniture, steps to snug bare-boarded back room, restaurant upstairs, Wadworths ales, several wines by glass, enjoyable reasonably priced food, friendly service; children away from bar area and dogs welcome. *(R K Phillips, Martin and Sue Day)*

BREMHILL ST9772
Dumb Post (01249) 813192
Off A4/A3102 just NW of Calne; SN11 9LJ Quirky unspoilt place with mismatched no-frills décor, odds and ends hanging from beams, guns and stuffed animal heads on walls, working model waterwheel, Oscar the parrot, homely armchairs and plush banquettes, big woodburner in brick fireplace and log fire at other end, fine country views from big windows, Wadworths 6X and a changing guest, simple hearty bar food, tap room with pool and darts; background music; children and dogs welcome, couple of picnic-sets outside and some wooden play equipment, may be closed Mon-Weds lunchtimes, open all day weekends. *(Anon)*

BROMHAM ST9665
Greyhound (01380) 850241
Off A342; High Street; SN15 2HA Popular old beamed dining pub with light modern décor, comfortable sofas and log fires, walk-across well in back bar, wide choice of good reasonably priced home-made food (all day) including weekday set lunch, efficient friendly service, particularly well kept Wadworths ales, wide choice of wines, upstairs skittle alley/restaurant; children welcome, pretty hanging baskets in front, big enclosed garden (dogs allowed here) with decking and boules. *(Neil and Anita Christopher, David Coe, Mr and Mrs P R Thomas)*

BROUGHTON GIFFORD ST8764
Bell on the Common
(01225) 782309 *The Common; SN12 8LX* Imposing rose-draped stone local on village common, lounge with well kept Wadworths from handpumps on back wall, big open fire, enjoyable good value food, friendly welcoming staff, dining room full of copper and brass, rustic bar with local photographs, small pool room, live irish music last Sun of month; children welcome, dogs in public bar, charming flower-filled crazy-paved garden, bowls club next door, open all day Fri-Sun. *(Michael Doswell, Taff Thomas, Taff and Gilly Thomas)*

BULKINGTON ST9458
★ Well (01380) 828287
High Street; SN10 1SJ Roomy and attractively modernised open-plan pub, good value competently cooked food from traditional favourites to interesting well presented restaurant-style dishes, good Sun roasts too, efficient friendly service, ales such as Butcombe, Sharps, Timothy Taylors and Wadworths, well priced wines. *(Mrs Blethyn Elliott, Steve Price, Paul Humphreys)*

BURCOMBE SU0631
★ Ship (01722) 743182
Burcombe Lane; brown sign to pub off A30 W of Salisbury, then turn right; SP2 0EJ Busy pub and most customers here for the food – pubby dishes through to elaborate pricey restaurant-style meals; area by entrance with log fire, beams and leather-cushioned wall and window seats on dark slate tiles, steps up to spreading area of pale wood dining chairs around bleached tables on neat dark-brown wood-strip floor, more beams (one supporting a splendid chandelier), small modern pictures and big church candles, Butcombe, Ringwood and Wadworths, good choice of wines by the glass and whiskies; background music; children welcome, dogs in bar, picnic-sets in informal back garden sloping down to willows by safely fenced-off River Nadder. *(Andre Dugas, Col and Mrs Patrick Kaye)*

BURTON ST8179
Old House At Home (01454) 218227
B4039 Chippenham–Chipping Sodbury; SN14 7LT Spacious ivy-clad stone dining pub, popular food including fresh fish and game, friendly efficient service, a couple of

well kept ales and good choice of wines by the glass, log fire. *(Dennis Parnham, Taff and Gilly Thomas, Roger and Donna Huggins)*

CASTLE COMBE ST8477
Castle Inn (01249) 783030
Off A420; SN14 7HN Handsome inn in remarkably preserved Cotswold village, beamed bar with big inglenook, padded bar stools and fine old settle, hunting and vintage motor racing pictures, Butcombe and Great Western, decent wines by the glass, bar food and more restaurANTy evening menu, two snug sitting rooms, formal dining rooms and big upstairs eating area opening on to charming little roof terrace; no dogs; children welcome, tables out at front looking down idyllic main street, fascinating medieval church clock, 11 bedrooms, limited parking, open all day. *(Peter and Giff Bennett)*

CASTLE EATON SU1495
Red Lion (01285) 810280
The Street; SN6 6JZ Thames-side dining pub with cosy linked rooms including sizeable pleasant conservatory, enjoyable home-made food, well kept ales including one named for the pub, good friendly service, log fire, settees and hunting prints, darts in pool room; children welcome, shrubby riverside garden with boules and outdoor chess, popular with Thames Path walkers, pretty village with unusual church, open all day Fri-Sun. *(Ross Balaam)*

CHARLTON ST9688
★ Horse & Groom (01666) 823904
B4040 towards Cricklade; SN16 9DL Smartly refurbished stone-built village inn, appealing and relaxing, keeping flagstones and log fire in proper bar (dogs welcome), interlinked dining areas with stylish understated décor, well liked good value food from pub standards to upscale modern cooking, polished friendly service, well kept Box Steam Golden Bolt and Wadworths 6X, good choice of wines by the glass; tables out under trees, five well appointed bedrooms, good breakfast, open all day. *(Peter and Audrey Dowsett, Michael Doswell)*

CHILMARK ST9732
Black Dog (01722) 716344
B3089 Salisbury–Hindon; SP3 5AH 15th-c beamed village pub under newish landlord, several cosy linked areas, inglenook woodburner, Wadworths ales, enjoyable well priced food including sandwiches and pizzas, prompt courteous service; good-sized roadside garden. *(B and F A Hannam, Muriel and John Hobbs, John and Alison Hamilton)*

CHIRTON SU0757
Wiltshire Yeoman (01380) 840665
Andover Road (A342 SE of Devizes); SN10 3QN Red-brick 19th-c roadside pub under newish management, good variety of food cooked by licensees from light lunch

choices through well aged steaks to some imaginative dishes, three Wadworths ales, a couple of real ciders and good choice of bottled beers, proper bar with log fire, separate carpeted dining room, pool room, skittle alley/function area; children and dogs welcome, background music; back garden with heated gazebo, closed Mon, Sun evening. *(Anon)*

CHITTERNE ST9843
Kings Head (01985) 850004
B390 Heytesbury–Shrewton; BA12 0LJ Attractive traditional pub under friendly newish management, slate-floor bar with wood burner, two dining areas, Flowers and Plain (brewed in the village), pubby food (Tues-Sat evenings, Sun lunchtime); children and dogs welcome, side garden, pretty village, handy for Salisbury Plain walks. *(Edward Mirzoeff)*

COLLINGBOURNE DUCIS SU2453
Shears (01264) 850304
Cadley Road; SN8 3ED Attractive 18th-c flint and brick thatched pub in nice tucked-away setting, enjoyable freshly cooked food in bar and comfortable bare-boards restaurant with open fire, Brakspears ales, friendly service; children and dogs welcome, courtyard garden, six bedrooms, closed Sun from 7pm. *(Mrs J P Cleall, Tony and Caroline Elwood)*

COMPTON BASSETT SU0372
★ White Horse (01249) 813118
At N end of village; SN11 8RG Newly refurbished 18th-c beamed village pub with reliably good food in bar and popular restaurant, fair prices and some adventurous choices, welcoming attentive service, Bath Gem, Wadworths 6X and two guests, real ciders, ten wines by the glass and good range of malt whiskies, two woodburners; children and dogs welcome, large garden with boules pitch, paddock with pot-bellied pigs, sheep and geese, good walks, eight bedrooms in building behind, closed Sun evening, Mon. *(T R and B C Jenkins, Alastair Muir, Bridget Scott, Jan Childe, Mr and Mrs A H Young)*

CORSHAM ST8770
Flemish Weaver (01249) 701929
High Street; SN13 0EZ Welcoming town pub in attractive 17th-c building, three main areas mostly set for good value popular food, ales such as Bath and Bellringer; children and dogs welcome, tables in back courtyard, may be closed Sun evening. *(Matthew Johns, Elizabeth Stedman)*

CORSHAM ST8670
Methuen Arms (01249) 717060
High Street; SN13 0HB Extensively refurbished dining inn (former priory), good if pricey food including set menu choices, local real ales, good service; tables in attractive courtyard, well

appointed bedrooms, open from 7am for breakfast. *(James McAninch, Mr and Mrs P R Thomas, Nicola White, Dr and Mrs A K Clarke)*

CORSHAM   ST8670
✶ **Two Pigs** (01249) 712515
Pickwick (A4); SN13 0HY Friendly and cheerfully eccentric little beer lovers' pub run by individualistic landlord – most lively on Mon evenings when live music; zany collection of bric-a-brac in narrow dimly lit flagstoned bar, enamel advertising signs on wood-clad walls, pig-theme ornaments and old radios, Stonehenge Pigswill and a couple of guests, no food; background blues, no under-21s; covered yard outside called the Sty, closed lunchtimes except Sun. *(Dr and Mrs A K Clarke, Taff Thomas)*

CORSLEY HEATH   ST8145
Royal Oak (01373) 832238
A362 Frome–Warminster; BA12 7PR Good food from bar snacks to daily specials, well kept Wadworths and a guest beer, efficient helpful staff, roomy beamed and panelled bar, good fire, big back family extension with pool, restaurant; dogs welcome in small side bar, disabled facilities, terrace and big garden with valley views, nice walks, handy for Longleat. *(Anon)*

CORTON   ST9340
✶ **Dove** (01985) 850109
Off A36 at Upton Lovell, SE of Warminster; BA12 0SZ Good food from ciabatta and pub favourites to more enterprising dishes, efficient charming service, up to five well kept ales such as Butcombe, Fullers/Gales and Wychwood, good wines by the glass, renovated linked rooms with flagstones and oak boards, woodburner in bar, flowers on dining room tables, conservatory; children welcome, wheelchair access, rustic furniture in garden, lovely valley, five comfortable courtyard bedrooms, open all day Sun. *(Chris and Angela Buckell)*

CROCKERTON   ST8642
✶ **Bath Arms** (01985) 212262
Off A350 Warminster–Blandford; BA12 8AJ Welcoming old dining pub, bar with plush banquettes and matching chairs, well spaced tables on parquet, beams in whitewashed ceiling, crackling log fire, Wessex ales, several wines by the glass and real cider, well liked food including some interesting modern dishes, cheerful staff, two formal dining rooms with chunky pine furniture; background music; children and dogs welcome, several garden areas with plenty of picnic-sets, gets crowded during school holidays (Longleat close by), bedrooms, open all day weekends. *(Mrs C Roe, Edward Mirzoeff, Richard and Judy Winn, Michael Doswell, Mr and Mrs A H Young, Taff and Gilly Thomas and others)*

CRUDWELL   ST9492
Wheatsheaf (01666) 577739
A429; SN16 9ET Small family-run pub with refurbished L-shaped bar, three well kept Marstons ales, good house wines, enjoyable fairly priced food from sandwiches and takeaway pizzas, friendly efficient service; children welcome, doubles as village PO, closed Tues lunchtime. *(Rob and Catherine Dunster)*

DERRY HILL   ST9570
✶ **Lansdowne Arms** (01249) 812422
A342 Chippenham–Calne; SN11 9NS Stately 19th-c stone-built pub opposite one of Bowood's grand gatehouses, roomy, airy and civilised, with good pub food including Sun roasts, well kept Wadworths ales, good value wines by the glass, cheerful service, relaxed period flavour, hearty log fire; children welcome, neat side garden and good play area, fine views, open all day Fri-Sun. *(David Crook)*

DEVIZES   SU0061
Bear (01380) 722444
Market Place; SN10 1HS Comfortable ancient coaching inn with carpeted big main bar, log fires, black winged wall settles and upholstered bucket armchairs, steps up to room named after portrait painter Thomas Lawrence with oak-panelled walls and big open fireplace, well kept Wadworths ales and a guest, up to 15 wines by the glass, several malt whiskies, enjoyable food from sandwiches and light dishes up; wheelchair access, mediterranean-style courtyard, bedrooms. *(Nigel Long, Mary Rayner, Theocsbrian)*

DEVIZES   SU0262
✶ **Hourglass** (01380) 727313
Horton Avenue; follow boat brown sign off A361 roundabout, N edge of town; SN10 2RH Modern pub featuring sturdy beams, broad bare boards, cream and terracotta décor, wall of windows looking across canalside terrace to fields beyond, enjoyable enterprising food at reasonable prices, well kept Marstons-related ales, good coffees and wine list, daily newspapers; unobtrusive background music. *(M J Winterton)*

DONHEAD ST ANDREW   ST9124
✶ **Forester** (01747) 828038
Village signposted off A30 E of Shaftesbury, just E of Ludwell; Lower Street; SP7 9EE Attractive 14th-c thatched dining pub in charming village; relaxed atmosphere in nice bar, stripped tables on wood floors, log fire in inglenook, alcove with sofa and magazines, Butcombe Bitter and a guest, 15 wines by the glass including champagne, very good well presented food from bar tapas up with much emphasis on fresh fish/seafood, comfortable main dining

room with country-kitchen tables, second cosier dining room; children and dogs welcome, seats outside on good-sized terrace with country views, can walk up White Sheet Hill and past the old and 'new' Wardour castles, closed Sun evening. *(Robert Watt, Edward Mirzoeff)*

EBBESBOURNE WAKE   ST9924
★ **Horseshoe**   (01722) 780474

On A354 S of Salisbury, right at signpost at Coombe Bissett; village about 8 miles further; SP5 5JF Unspoilt country pub in pretty village with plenty of regular customers, friendly long-serving licensees and staff, Bowman, Otter, Palmers and guests tapped from the cask, farm cider, good traditional bar food (not Sun evening, Mon), neatly kept and comfortable character bar, collection of farm tools and bric-a-brac on beams, conservatory extension and small restaurant; children welcome (not in bar), dogs allowed, seats in pretty little garden with views over River Ebble valley, chickens and a goat in paddock, good nearby walks, bedrooms closed Sun evening, Mon lunchtime. *(Richard, Anne and Kate Ansell, Marianne and Peter Stevens, Ian Herdman)*

EDINGTON   ST9353
Three Daggers   (01380) 830940

Westbury Road (B3098); BA13 4PG Restored heavily beamed open plan village pub (was the Lamb and briefly the Paulet Arms), welcoming enthusiastic staff, Wadworths and local guests, Weston's cider, good choice of wines by the glass, enjoyable food (not Sun evening) from bar snacks up, takeaways, assorted old pine furniture on slate floor, two open fires, conservatory dining area, upstairs raftered function/overspill room; background and occasional live music; children and dogs welcome, garden tables (access to pretty village's play area beyond), great views and good walks, three new bedrooms, open all day weekends. *(Taff Thomas)*

FARLEIGH WICK   ST8063
Fox & Hounds   (01225) 863122

A363 NW of Bradford-on-Avon; BA15 2PU Rambling low-beamed 18th-c pub, welcoming and clean, with enjoyable food including good value lunchtime set deal (Tues-Sat), six wines by the glass and Bath Gem, log fire in big oak-floored dining area; children welcome, area for dogs, attractive garden, closed Mon. *(Philip and Jan Medcalf)*

FORD   ST8474
White Hart   (01249) 782213

Off A420 Chippenham–Bristol; SN14 8RP Attractive 16th-c stone-built Marstons country inn, their ales and a

guest, wide choice of food all day, service may be slow, heavy black beams and good log fire in ancient fireplace, separate dining room; background music; dogs welcome, plenty of tables outside, attractive stream-side grounds, on the Palladian Way trail, comfortable bedrooms (some in annexe). *(Guy Vowles, Taff Thomas, Dr and Mrs A K Clarke)*

FROXFIELD   SU2968
Pelican   (01488) 682479

Off A4; SN8 3JY Modernised 17th-c coaching inn, good choice of enjoyable food served by helpful friendly staff, local ales, comfortable relaxed atmosphere; pleasant streamside garden with terrace and duck pond, Kennet & Avon Canal walks, bedrooms, open all day. *(Phil Bysh, Penny and Peter Keevil)*

GREAT BEDWYN   SU2764
Cross Keys   (01672) 870678

High Street; SN8 3NU Welcoming 17th-c beamed village pub, enjoyable reasonably priced food including home-made pizzas and vegetarian choices, Wadworths ales, decent wines, comfortable chairs and settles, log fire, two friendly pub dogs, live music in function room; garden with terrace, short walk to Kennet & Avon Canal, two bedrooms. *(N R White)*

GREAT BEDWYN   SU2764
Three Tuns   (01672) 870280

Village signposted off A338 S of Hungerford, or off A4 W of Hungerford via Little Bedwyn; High Street; SN8 3NU This popular traditional country pub was shut as we went to press – news please.

HAMPTWORTH   SU2419
Cuckoo   (01794) 390302

Hamptworth Road; SP5 2DU 17th-c thatched New Forest pub, peaceful and unspoilt, with welcoming landlord, friendly mix of customers from famers to families in four compact rooms around tiny servery, well kept Bowman, Hop Back, Ringwood and guests tapped from the cask (Sept beer festival), real cider, pasties and ploughman's (no evening food), mugs and jugs hanging from ceiling, beer memorabilia, basic wooden furniture, open fire; big garden (adults' area with view of golf course), open all day Fri-Sat. *(Joan and Michel Hooper-Immins)*

HANNINGTON   SU1793
Jolly Tar   (01793) 762245

Off B4019 W of Highworth; Queens Road; SN6 7RP Relaxing beamed bar with big log fire, steps up to flagstoned and stripped-stone dining area, enjoyable straighforward food from baguettes up, well

---

It's very helpful if you let us know up-to-date food prices when you report on pubs.

kept Arkells ales, reasonable prices, friendly helpful service; children welcome, picnic-sets on front terrace and in big garden with play area, bedrooms, pretty village. *(Neil and Anita Christopher)*

HEDDINGTON ST9966
Ivy (01380) 859652
Off A3102 S of Calne; SN11 0PL
Picturesque thatched 15th-c village local under newish management; good inglenook log fire in old-fashioned L-shaped bar, heavy low beams, timbered walls, assorted furnishings on parquet floor, brass and copper, well kept cask-tapped Wadworths ales, pubby food including OAP lunch Tues and Sun carvery, back family dining room; disabled access, front garden, open all day Fri-Sun. *(Anon)*

HEYTESBURY ST9242
Angel (01985) 840330
Just off A36 E of Warminster; High Street; BA12 0ED In quiet village just below Salisbury Plain, spacious and comfortable, with good food from sandwiches up, friendly helpful staff, Greene King ales, log fire, restaurant; children welcome. *(Edward Mirzoeff)*

HINDON ST9032
Angel (01747) 820696
B3089 Wilton–Mere; SP3 6DJ
Smartened-up dining pub with big log fire, flagstones and other coaching-inn survivals, enjoyable food from pub favourites to more unusual dishes, good service, nice choice of wines, ales such as Otter, Sharps and Timothy Taylors; children welcome, dogs in bar, courtyard tables, nine comfortable bedrooms (named after game birds), open all day. *(David Zackheim, Lisa Barratt)*

HINDON ST9132
Lamb (01747) 820573
B3089 Wilton–Mere; SP3 6DP Smart, attractive old hotel with long roomy log-fire bar, two flagstoned lower sections with very long communal table, high-backed pews and settles, up steps to a third, bigger area, well kept Butcombe, St Austell Tribute and Wells & Youngs Best, several wines by the glass and around 100 malt whiskies, cuban cigars, enjoyable bar and restaurant food, polite friendly service from smartly dressed staff; can get very busy, 10% service charge added to bill; children and dogs welcome, tables on roadside terrace and in garden across road with boules, 19 refurbished bedrooms, good breakfast, open all day from 7.30am. *(Edward Mirzoeff)*

HOLT ST8561
⋆ Toll Gate (01225) 782326
Ham Green; B3107 W of Melksham; BA14 6PX Appealing individual décor and furnishings and thriving atmosphere in comfortable bar, good friendly service, three

well kept changing ales, farm cider, some interesting wines and whiskies, popular imaginative food from good lunchtime sandwiches and light meals up, set menus too, daily newspapers, log fire, another in more sedate high-raftered former chapel restaurant up steps; background music; no under-12s, dogs welcome, wheelchair access to main bar only, pretty terrace and fenced garden with gazebo, shop in barn selling local produce, four bedrooms, closed Sun evening, Mon. *(Michael Doswell, Philip and Jan Medcalf, Dr and Mrs A K Clarke, Taff Thomas, Robert P, Chris and Angela Buckell and others)*

HONEYSTREET SU1061
Barge (01672) 851705
Off A345 W of Pewsey; SN9 5PS Early 19th-c community-owned pub in nice setting by Kennet & Avon Canal, good house beers (brewed locally for them) and farm cider, tasty reasonably priced food, friendly attentive service, occasional magic shows, live music Sat; dogs welcome, waterside picnic-sets, good walks. *(Pat and Tony Martin)*

HORNINGSHAM ST8041
Bath Arms (01985) 844308
By entrance to Longleat House; BA12 7LY Handsome old stone-built inn on pretty village's sloping green, stylishly opened up as welcoming dining pub with several linked areas including a proper bar, polished wood floors and open fires, good generous local food, well kept Wessex ales and a guest, local cider, good choice of wines and other drinks, charming efficient staff, side restaurant and conservatory; can get very busy; wheelchair access to bars via side door, attractive garden with neat terraces, smokers' gazebo, 15 bedrooms. *(Chris and Angela Buckell, Lois Dyer)*

HORTON SU0363
Bridge Inn (01380) 860273
Horton Road; village signed off A361 London road, NE of Devizes; SN10 2JS Former flour mill and bakery by Kennet & Avon Canal, carpeted log-fire area on left with tables set for dining, pubby bit to right of bar with some stripped brickwork and country kitchen furniture on reconstituted flagstones, old bargee photographs and country pictures, Wadworths ales; some reader concerns over food, background music, TV; well behaved children welcome, dogs in bar, disabled facilities, safely fenced garden with picnic-sets, original grinding wheel, canal walks and moorings, bedrooms, closed Mon. *(Sheila and Robert Robinson, Taff Thomas)*

KILMINGTON ST7835
Red Lion (01985) 844263
B3092 Mere–Frome, 2.5 miles S of Maiden Bradley; 3 miles from A303 Mere turn-off; BA12 6RP New licensee for this NT-owned country pub; low-beamed

flagstoned bar with cushioned wall and window seats, curved high-backed settle, log fires in big fireplaces (fine iron fireback in one), Butcombe, Butts and a guest, Thatcher's cider, lunchtime bar food and more elaborate evening menu, newer big-windowed dining area with modern country feel; children welcome, dogs in bar, picnic-sets in large attractive garden, smokers' shelter, White Sheet Hill (radio-controlled gliders, hang-gliding) and Stourhead Gardens nearby. *(Edward Mirzoeff)*

LACOCK   ST9268
Bell (01249) 730308
E of village; SN15 2PJ Extended cottagey pub with warm welcome, good changing ales such as Bath, Ramsbury and Palmers (beer festivals), real ciders, decent wines by the glass and lots of malt whiskies, wide choice of enjoyable food, linked rooms off bar including pretty restaurant, conservatory; children welcome away from bar, disabled access, well kept sheltered garden with smokers' shelter, open all day weekends. *(Jean and Douglas Troup, Taff Thomas, Chris and Angela Buckell, MLR)*

LACOCK   ST9168
⋆ George (01249) 730263
West Street; village signed off A350 S of Chippenham; SN15 2LH New management for this rambling inn at centre of busy NT tourist village; low-beamed bar with upright timbers creating cosy corners, armchairs and windsor chairs around close-set tables, seats in stone-mullioned windows, some flagstones, dog treadwheel in outer breast of central fireplace, lots of old pictures and bric-a-brac, souvenirs from filming Cranford and Harry Potter in the village, Wadworths beers and Weston's cider, bar food from snacks up; background music; children and dogs welcome, tricky wheelchair access, picnic-sets on grass and in attractive courtyard with pillory and well, open all day in summer. *(Mr and Mrs A Curry, Roger and Donna Huggins, Chris and Angela Buckell)*

LACOCK   ST9168
⋆ Red Lion (01249) 730456
High Street; SN15 2LQ Busy NT-owned Georgian inn, sizeable bar with log fire, heavy tables and oriental rugs on flagstones, cosy snug with leather armchairs, well kept Wadworths, good choice of enjoyable food (all day weekends) from nice baguettes up, pleasant service; background music; children and dogs welcome, seats outside, bedrooms, open all day. *(Neil and Anita Christopher, Roger and Donna Huggins, Taff Thomas, Ian Phillips, Mr and Mrs A H Young, Paul Humphreys)*

LEA   ST9586
Rose & Crown (01666) 824344
The Street; SN16 9PA Creeper-clad Victorian stone pub next to church, Arkells and guests kept well by friendly landlord, good value pub food, pleasant efficient service and nice atmosphere, daily newspapers, some live music, may be children's films Sun; garden with play equipments, goats and alpacas. *(David and Phillipa Cross, Neil and Anita Christopher)*

LIDDINGTON   SU2081
Village Inn (01793) 790314
Handy for M4 junction 15, via A419 and B4192; Bell Lane; SN4 0HE Some recent refurbishment at this comfortable welcoming pub; enjoyable good value food including early-bird bargains and very popular Sun roasts (must book), well kept Arkells ales, linked bar areas, stripped-stone and raftered back dining extension, conservatory, log fire in splendid fireplace; well behaved children welcome in restaurant area, disabled facilities, terrace tables. *(KC)*

LIMPLEY STOKE   ST7861
Hop Pole (01225) 723134
Off A36 and B3108 S of Bath; BA2 7FS Largely panelled 16th-c stone-built pub, warmly welcoming, with well kept Bath Gem, Sharps Doom Bar and a guest, fairly priced traditional food including OAP weekday lunch, log fire; background music TV; children in eating areas, dogs in bar, disabled access with help, nice enclosed garden behind. *(Anon)*

LOCKERIDGE   SU1467
Who'd A Thought It (01672) 861255
Signed just off A4 Marlborough–Calne just W of Fyfield; SN8 4EL Friendly village pub improved by present licensees, good sensibly priced food including popular Sun lunch, well kept Wadworths and nice house wines; pleasant back garden, lovely bluebell walks. *(Mr and Mrs A Curry)*

LONGBRIDGE DEVERILL   ST8640
George (01985) 840396
A350/B3095; BA12 7DG Friendly extended roadside pub with well kept ales including Deverill Advocate brewed locally for them, reasonably priced usual food, popular Sun carvery, good coffee; children welcome, big riverside garden with play area, bedrooms, open all day. *(Dave Braisted, George Atkinson)*

LOWER WOODFORD   SU1235
⋆ Wheatsheaf (01722) 782203
Signed off A360 just N of Salisbury; SP4 6NQ Refurbished and extended 18th-c Badger dining pub, open airy feel, with good choice of fairly priced traditional food from sharing boards up, well kept beers, good wines and coffee, well trained genial staff, beams, mix of pub furniture, log fire and woodburner; background music; children welcome, dogs in bar, disabled access and parking, tree-lined fenced garden with play area, pretty setting, open all day. *(I D Barnett)*

LUCKINGTON ST8384

⋆ Old Royal Ship (01666) 840222

Off B4040 SW of Malmesbury; SN14 6PA
Friendly pub by village green, opened up
inside with one long bar divided into three
areas, Bass, Stonehenge, Wadworths and
Wickwar from central servery, also farm cider
and several wines by the glass, good range of
well liked food including vegetarian, decent
coffee, neat tables, spindleback chairs and
small cushioned settles on dark boards,
some stripped masonry and small open
fire, skittle alley, live jazz second Weds of
month; background music, games machine;
children welcome, garden (beyond car park)
with boules, play area and plenty of seats,
Badminton House close by, open all day
Sat. *(Michael Doswell, Hugh Thomas, John and
Gloria Isaacs)*

MAIDEN BRADLEY ST8038

Somerset Arms (01985) 844207

Church Street; BA12 7HW Large
welcoming Victorian pub (former railway
hotel), bar with bare boards and black
marble floor, grey/green panelling, unusual
bookshelf wallpaper (write your own title
on a spine), traditional cast-iron tables
and log fire, daily newspapers, well kept
Wadworths ales, good interesting seasonal
food (not Tues) using local and own produce,
restaurant, Tues folk night plus other live
music; children and dogs welcome, nice
garden, skittle alley in barn, five bedrooms,
open all day Fri-Sun. *(Chris Brickell, Michael
Doswell, Chris and Angela Buckell)*

MALMESBURY ST9287

Smoking Dog (01666) 825823

High Street; SN16 9AT Twin-fronted local
with two cosy flagstoned front bars, well kept
ales such as Brains and Castle Rock, good
choice of wines by the glass, tasty generous
food, log fire; children and dogs welcome,
small secluded garden up steep steps,
bedrooms, open all day. *(David Eberlin, MLR)*

MARDEN SU0857

Millstream (01380) 848490

*Village signposted off A342 SE of
Devizes; SN10 3RH* Well liked Wadworths
country pub (former Triple Crown) reopened
under new licensees, appealing layout of
linked cosy areas, beams and log fires,
red-cushioned dark pews and small padded
dining chairs around sturdy oak and other
good tables, more formal dining area, good
smiling service; children and dogs have
been welcome, garden down to tree-lined
stream, 7th-c church worth a visit, closed Sun
evening. *(Anon)*

MARLBOROUGH SU1869

Castle & Ball (01672) 515201

High Street; SN8 1LZ Fully refurbished
Georgian coaching inn with lounge bar and
restaurant, wide choice of food including

deals, Greene King ales, good range of well
listed wines by the glass, enthusiastic staff;
background music; children welcome, dogs
in bar, seats out under projecting colonnade
and in walled garden, 37 bedrooms, open all
day. *(Mary Rayner)*

MARSTON MEYSEY SU1297

⋆ Old Spotted Cow (01285) 810264

Off A419 Swindon–Cirencester; SN6 6LQ
Civilised country pub with interesting home-
made food as well as more traditional dishes,
three well kept ales including Butcombe and
Moles (taster glasses available), welcoming
attentive staff, two open fires, light wood
furniture and cosy sofas, rugs on bare boards
and parquet, plants and cow pictures on
stripped stone walls; well behaved children
and dogs welcome, spacious garden
overlooking fields, play area, open all
day. *(Peter and Audrey Dowsett, Brian Clegg)*

MONKTON FARLEIGH ST8065

Kings Arms (01225) 858705

*Signed off A363 Bradford–Bath;
BA15 2QH* Imposing 17th-c stone building
with sofas, open fire and dining tables in one
bar, huge inglenook and more dining tables
in L-shaped beamed lounge, good if not
cheap food (all day weekends) using local
supplies, efficient friendly service, well kept
changing ales, good wine and whisky choice;
background music; dogs allowed in bar area,
front partly flagstoned courtyard, well tended
two-level back garden, lovely village, three
bedrooms. *(Guy Vowles, Alan Sutton, Taff and
Gilly Thomas)*

NETHERHAMPTON SU1129

⋆ Victoria & Albert (01722) 743174

Just off A3094 W of Salisbury; SP2 8PU
Cosy black-beamed bar in simple thatched
cottage, good generous food from nicely
presented sandwiches up, sensible prices
and local supplies, three well kept changing
ales, farm cider, decent wines, friendly staff,
nicely cushioned old-fashioned wall settles
on ancient floor tiles, restaurant; children
and dogs welcome, hatch service for sizeable
terrace and garden behind, handy for
Wilton House and Nadder Valley walks.
(Peter Salmon)

NOMANSLAND SU2517

Lamb (01794) 390246

*Signed off B3078 and B3079; SP5
2BP* Lovely New Forest village-green setting,
welcoming unpretentious local feel, good
value home-made food including lots of pasta
and fish, popular Sun roasts, four changing
ales and sensibly priced wine list, fast
friendly service, log fire, small dining room,
games room with pool; TV; children and dogs
welcome, tables on terrace, green (with
grazing ponies) and in garden behind, open
all day. *(Sally Matson)*

OGBOURNE ST ANDREW   SU1871
Silks on the Downs   (01672) 841229
A345 N of Marlborough; SN8 1RZ
Civilised restauranty pub with horseracing
theme, good variety of enjoyable food, ales
such as Adnams, Ramsbury and Wadworths,
decent wines by the glass, good service,
stylish décor with mix of dining tables on
polished wood floors, some good prints and
photographs as well as framed racing silks;
well behaved children allowed, small decked
area and garden, closed Sun evening. *(Lesley
York, Jan and Roger Ferris)*

PEWSEY   SU1561
French Horn   (01672) 562443
*A345 towards Marlborough; Pewsey
Wharf; SN9 5NT* Two-part back bar with
steps down to more formal front dining area
(children allowed here), flagstones and log
fires, good choice of enjoyable home-made
food, well kept Wadworths ales, cheery
attentive australian staff; background music;
dogs welcome in bar, picnic-sets out behind,
walks by Kennet & Avon Canal below, closed
Tues. *(Kristin Warry)*

RAMSBURY   SU2771
Bell   (01672) 520230
*Off B4192 NW of Hungerford, or A4 W;
SN8 2PE* Major refurbishment under new
management, light and airy despite lots of
small eating areas, enjoyable reasonably
priced food, Ramsbury Gold and a guest
ale, pleasant understated service, log fires;
bedrooms, open all day Sun. *(Michael
Patterson, Maureen Wood)*

RAMSBURY   SU2771
Crown & Anchor   (01672) 520335
*Crowood Lane/Whittonditch Road;
SN8 2PT* Friendly and relaxed beamed
village pub, popular for good value simple
food, well kept Bass, Wadworths, Ramsbury
and a guest, good house wine, helpful service,
open fires; children welcome, hanging
baskets and small garden with terrace,
two bedrooms, open all day Sun, closed
Mon. *(Mary Rayner)*

ROWDE   ST9762
✶ George & Dragon   (01380) 723053
A342 Devizes–Chippenham; SN10 2PN
Lots of character in this welcoming 16th-c
coaching inn, two low-beamed rooms with
large open fireplaces, wooden dining chairs
around candlelit tables, antique rugs and
walls covered with old pictures and portraits,
Butcombe, Fullers and a guest, generally
well liked if not cheap food including plenty

of fish; background music; children and dogs
welcome, seats in pretty back garden, Kennet
& Avon canal nearby, bedrooms, closed Sun
evening. *(Ari, Richard and Patricia Jefferson)*

SALISBURY   SU1429
Cloisters   (01722) 338102
Catherine Street/Ivy Street; SP1 2DH
Comfortable and rambling city pub with low
beams and bare boards, friendly buoyant
atmosphere, good value food including
generous Sun roasts, well kept ales such
as Sharps Doom Bar, helpful staff; open all
day. *(Ann and Colin Hunt)*

SALISBURY   SU1429
✶ New Inn   (01722) 326662
New Street; SP1 2PH Much extended old
building with massive beams and timbers,
good choice of home-made food from pub
staples up, well kept Badger ales, decent
house wines, cheerful staff, flagstones,
floorboards and carpet, quiet cosy alcoves,
inglenook log fire; children welcome,
attractive walled garden with striking view of
nearby cathedral spire, three bedrooms, open
all day. *(Sue and Mike Todd, Richard Stanfield)*

SALISBURY   SU1329
✶ Old Mill   (01722) 327517
Town Path, West Harnham; SP2 8EU
Charming 17th-c pub/hotel in tranquil
setting, unpretentious beamed bars with
prized window tables, decent good value food
from sandwiches up, local ales, good wines
and malt whiskies, attractive restaurant
showing mill race; children welcome, small
floodlit garden by duck-filled millpond,
delightful stroll across water meadows from
cathedral (classic view of it from bridge
beyond garden), 11 bedrooms, open all
day. *(Tim Loryman, Mr and Mrs P D Titcomb)*

SALISBURY   SU1430
Wyndham Arms   (01722) 331026
Estcourt Road; SP1 3AS Corner local
with unpretentious modern decor, popular
and friendly, with full Hop Back range
(brewery was based here) and a guest such
as Downton, bottled beers and country wines,
no food, small front and side rooms, longer
main bar, darts and board games; children
and dogs welcome, open all day Thurs-Sun,
from 4.30pm other days. *(N R White)*

SEEND   ST9361
✶ Barge   (01380) 828230
*Seend Cleeve; signed off A361 Devizes–
Trowbridge; SN12 6QB* Plenty of seats in
garden making most of boating activity on
Kennet & Avon Canal, unusual seating in bar

The letters and figures after the name of each town are its Ordnance Survey map
reference. *How to use the Guide* at the beginning of the book explains how it helps you
find a pub, in road atlases or large-scale maps as well as in our own maps.

including milk churns, an upturned canoe and high-backed chairs made from old boat parts, small oak settle among the rugs on parquet floor, well stocked aquarium, pretty Victorian fireplace, Wadworths ales and 30 wines by the glass, decent choice of food, good service; background music; children and dogs welcome, summer barbecues, open all day. *(Meg and Colin Hamilton, Robert Watt, Alan Sutton)*

SEEND ST9562
Three Magpies (01380) 828389
Sells Green – A365 towards Melksham; SN12 6RN Unpretentious partly 18th-c pub popular for its good value straightforward home-made food including children's choices and Sun roasts, two warm fires, friendly helpful staff, well kept Wadworths ales, decent choice of wines by the glass; dogs allowed in bar, big garden with play area, campsite next door, open all day Fri-Sun. *(David and Gill Carrington, Alister Borthwick, Mr and Mrs P R Thomas)*

SEMINGTON ST9259
✶ **Lamb** (01380) 870263
The Strand; A361 Devizes–Trowbridge; BA14 6LL Refurbished dining pub under newish landlord, various eating areas including wood-strip-floor bar with log fire, enjoyable food from pub favourites to specials, Wiltshire tapas too, beers from Bath and Box Steam, efficient friendly staff; background music; children and dogs welcome, pleasant garden with views to the Bowood Estate, closed Sun evening. *(Taff Thomas, E Clark, Mark O'Sullivan, Paul Humphreys)*

SHALBOURNE SU3162
Plough (01672) 870295
Off A338; SN8 3QF Low-beamed traditional village pub on green, good choice of enjoyable fairly priced blackboard food including vegetarian options, Butcombe and Wadworths, friendly helpful landlady, neat tiled-floor bar with sofa and armchairs in snug; disabled access, small garden with play area. *(David Gray, E A Sclater)*

STAVERTON ST8560
Old Bear (01225) 782487
B3105 Trowbridge–Bradford-on-Avon; BA14 6PB Bar and two dining areas, nice mix of seats including some high-backed settles, stone fireplaces, good value food including Tues steak-night deal, pleasant efficient service, well kept Marstons Pedigree, Ringwood Best, Sharps Doom Bar and a guest; open all day weekends. *(Neil and Anita Christopher)*

STEEPLE ASHTON ST9056
Longs Arms (01380) 870245
High Street; BA14 6EU 17th-c renovated coaching inn with friendly local atmosphere, well kept Wadworths and guests, food locally sourced and can be good, open fire; children and dogs welcome, big garden with play area, adjoining self-catering cottage, delightful village, open all day weekends if busy. *(Roly Hill, Taff and Gilly Thomas, Paul Humphreys)*

STOURTON ST7733
✶ **Spread Eagle** (01747) 840587
Church Lawn; follow Stourhead brown signs off B3092, N of junction with A303 W of Mere; BA12 6QE Georgian inn, always packed as at entrance to Stourhead Estate; old-fashioned, rather civilised interior with antique panel-back settles, new and old solid tables and chairs, smoky sporting prints, log fires in handsome fireplaces, room by entrance with armchairs, longcase clock and corner china cupboard, well kept Butcombe and a guest, interesting wines by the glass, well liked home-made food (must book), cream teas, restaurant; background music; children welcome, wheelchair access (step down to dining areas), benches in back courtyard, bedrooms (guests can wander freely around famous NT gardens outside normal hours), open all day. *(Guy Vowles, Mr and Mrs A J Hudson, Mr and Mrs A Curry, Chris and Angela Buckell, Sheila Topham, Phyl and Jack Street and others)*

SUTTON BENGER ST9478
Wellesley Arms (01249) 721721
Handy for M4 junction 17, via B4122 and B4069; High Street; SN15 4RD Beamed 15th-c Cotswold stone pub with pleasant bar areas and restaurant, good pubby food (not Sun evening), Wadworths ales, efficient friendly service; background music, TV; children and dogs welcome, revamped garden with play area, paddock, open all day weekends, closed Mon lunchtime. *(David Crook)*

SUTTON VENY ST8941
Woolpack (01985) 840834
High Street; BA12 7AW Small well run village local nicely restored by landlord/chef, good blackboard food including some inventive dishes (best to book), Marstons and Ringwood ales, sensibly priced wines by the glass, charming service, compact side dining area. *(Edward Mirzoeff)*

SWINDON SU1484
Glue Pot (01793) 325993
Emlyn Square; SN1 5BP No-frills alehouse in Brunel's Railway Village, eight or so well kept beers, honest but sometimes very limited pub food, prompt service, pub games and high-backed settles around pine tables; sports TV, can get very busy; terrace tables, open all day. *(Anon)*

SWINDON SU1583
Victoria (01793) 535713
Victoria Road; SN1 3BD Small split-level bare-boards character pub with slight hippie feel (appeals to all ages), three well kept

ales including Shepherd Neame Spitfire and Wadworths 6X, decent freshly made bargain food (not weekday evenings), art for sale, gig posters (frequent live music) and background rock. *(Jeremy King)*

TISBURY ST9429
Boot (01747) 870363
High Street; SP3 6PS Ancient unpretentious village local with welcoming landlord, well kept changing ales tapped from the cask, perry, good range of pizzas and reasonably priced pubby food, notable fireplace; tables in good-sized back garden, closed Sun evening. *(Maureen Wood)*

TOLLARD ROYAL ST9317
⋆ King John (01725) 516207
B3081 Shaftesbury–Sixpenny Handley; SP5 5PS Busy refurbished red-brick Victorian dining pub, well liked interesting food in stylish open-plan country-style interior with old pine tables on terracotta and coir floors, black and white hunting photographs and old etchings, logs stacked by woodburner, Ringwood and two changing guests from long oak counter with wine bottles racked behind (pub also has a wine shop), charming helpful service; well behaved children and clean dogs welcome, solid tables out in front under cream parasols, picnic-sets in terraced garden, eight comfortable bedrooms (three in barn opposite), good breakfast, nice walks. *(Peter Meister, Paul and Marion Watts)*

TROWBRIDGE ST8560
Kings Arms (01225) 751310
Castle Street; BA14 8AN Large refurbished open-plan pub with lots of tables and chairs on stripped boards, well kept ales such as Bath, Sharps and Vale from central bar, Mole's Black Rat cider, enjoyable pubby food served by cheerful staff; children welcome. *(Mike Gorton)*

UPAVON SU1355
Ship (01980) 630313
High Street; SN9 6EA Large thatched pub with enjoyable home-made food including good steak and kidney pie and Sun roasts, friendly helpful staff, welcoming locals, well kept Sharps, Stonehenge and Wadworths, two farm ciders, decent range of wines and whiskies, interesting nautical memorabilia, some gentle live music; parking can be tricky; dogs welcome (may get a treat after Sun lunch), picnic-sets in front and on small side terrace. *(Michael Doswell)*

UPPER CHUTE SU2953
⋆ Cross Keys (01264) 730295
N of Andover; best reached off A343 via Tangley, or off A342 in Weyhill via Clanville; SP11 9ER Country pub run by hospitable landlord, open-plan beamed rooms with pubby tables and chairs, some sofas, a built-in cushioned window seat, log fire and woodburner, Arkells, Fullers and Hop Back, well liked proper pies and other bar food (not Sun evening), shut the box; background music, TV; children welcome and dogs (they have staffies), picnic-sets on grass and terrace with far-reaching rural views, play fort, stables at back for visiting horses, bedrooms, good breakfast, open all day weekends. *(John and Enid Morris, David and Ruth Hollands, Gordon Taylor, Jeff and Wendy Williams, Julia and Richard Tredgett, Matt and Pru Clements)*

UPTON LOVELL ST9441
⋆ Prince Leopold (01985) 850460
Up Street; BA12 0JP Prettily tucked away and freshly modernised Victorian village inn, cheerful staff, good well prepared/presented food from standards up including Wiltshire tapas, Butcombe, Otter and Wadworths 6X in good condition, spacious bar and several smaller rooms, airy newish dining extension with river views from end tables and verandah; attractive little garden beside the clear Wylye trout stream, simple clean bedrooms. *(Chris and Angela Buckell, Michael Levy, Edward Mirzoeff, Richard Zambuni)*

UPTON SCUDAMORE ST8647
⋆ Angel (01985) 213225
Off A350 N of Warminster; BA12 0AG Stylish contemporary dining pub in former 16th-c coaching inn, refurbished airy upper part, a few steps down to bar area with sofas and armchairs by open fire and mixed traditional pine furniture, good choice of enjoyable food from pub favourites up, friendly helpful service, well kept Butcombe, Wadworths 6X and a guest, good value house wines; background music; children welcome, dogs on leads in bar, sheltered flagstoned back terrace, ten bedrooms in house across car park. *(Michael Doswell, Mrs P Bishop)*

WARMINSTER ST8745
Organ (01985) 211777
49 High Street; BA12 9AQ Sympathetic restoration of former 18th-c inn (shut in 1913), front bar, snug, and traditional games room, delightful owners and chatty

---

'Children welcome' means the pub says it lets children inside without any special restriction. If it allows them in, but to restricted areas such as an eating area or family room, we specify this. Some pubs may impose an evening time limit. We do not mention limits after 9pm as we assume children are home by then.

locals, four unusual local beers including one brewed for the pub, real cider, good cheap lunchtime cheeseboard, skittle alley, no music or under 21s; open 4-12, all day Sat. *(Edward Mirzoeff)*

WESTWOOD ST8159
New Inn (01225) 863123
Off B3109 S of Bradford-on-Avon; BA15 2AE Traditional 18th-c country pub with friendly landlord and good staff, several linked rooms, beams and stripped stone, scrubbed tables on slate floor, lots of pictures, imaginative good value food in bar and spacious restaurant, well kept Wadworths, buzzy atmosphere; a few tables out behind, lovely hanging baskets, pretty village with good surrounding walks, Westwood Manor (NT) opposite, closed Mon. *(Taff Thomas, Michael Doswell)*

WINGFIELD ST8256
⋆ Poplars (01225) 752426
B3109 S of Bradford-on-Avon (Shop Lane); BA14 9LN Attractive country pub with beams and log fires, very popular for its good interesting sensibly priced food, especially with older people at lunchtime, Wadworths ales, friendly fast service even when busy, warm atmosphere, light and airy family dining extension; nice garden, own cricket pitch. *(Taff Thomas)*

WINTERBOURNE
BASSETT SU1075
⋆ White Horse (01793) 731257
Off A4361 S of Swindon; SN4 9QB Neatly kept roadside dining pub with gently old-fashioned feel, carpeted bar with plenty of wood, wrought-iron plush-topped stools and cushioned dining chairs, Wadworths ales and quite a few wines by the glass, popular homely food served by friendly helpful staff, dining rooms with country kitchen furniture

on light wood floors, old prints and paintings, assorted plants, woodburner in little brick fireplace, conservatory; background music; children welcome, tables on good-sized lawn, pretty hanging baskets. *(Tony Baldwin, Ian and Julie Campbell, Frank Blanchard)*

WOOTTON BASSETT SU0682
Five Bells (01793) 849422
Wood Street; SN4 7BD Friendly thatched local with great atmosphere, well kept Fullers London Pride and five changing guests, farm cider, good home-made lunchtime food including some interesting choices, also Weds theme night, board games, darts; background music, TV; shaded courtyard behind, open all day Fri-Sun. *(Ric Mason, John Hickman)*

WOOTTON RIVERS SU1963
Royal Oak (01672) 810322
Off A346, A345 or B3087; SN8 4NQ Cosy 16th-c beamed and thatched pub, good food from lunchtime sandwiches to nice fish dishes, ales such as Ramsbury and Wadworths 6X, good choice of wines by the glass, comfortable L-shaped dining lounge with woodburner, timbered bar and small games area; children and dogs welcome, tables out in yard, pleasant village, bedrooms in adjoining house. *(John and Gloria Isaacs, Peter and Audrey Dowsett, David and Judy Robison)*

YATTON KEYNELL ST8676
Bell (01249) 782216
B4039 NW of Chippenham; SN14 7BG Opened-up beamed village pub popular for good value hearty food, friendly staff, well kept Bath Gem and Butcombe, decent wines, dining area with sturdy modern tables and high-backed chairs; well spaced picnic-sets in good-sized fenced garden. *(Ian Herdman)*

Worcestershire

Several of the Main Entry pubs in this county hold one of our Bargain Awards, which means they offer real value meals – with the majority of dishes being under £10. For examples of this, head to the Swan in Birlingham (new to the *Guide* this year; simple and friendly with chatty locals and an immaculate garden), Fleece in Bretforton (quite unspoilt and owned by the National Trust), Crown & Trumpet in Broadway (down to earth and warmly welcoming), and Three Kings at Hanley Castle (timeless gem with five real ales and 75 malt whiskies). Other pubs on top form are the Fountain at Clent (a new entry with 36 wines by the glass and very good, interesting food), Bell & Cross in Holy Cross (terrific all-rounder and a lovely small room layout), Talbot in Knightwick (own-brew beers and super food using own-grown vegetables and home-reared pigs), and Nags Head in Malvern (an exceptional pub with first class landlords, a fantastic atmosphere and fine choice of real ales). Our Worcestershire Dining Pub 2013 is the Bell & Cross in Holy Cross.

BEWDLEY   SO7875   Map 4
Little Pack Horse
High Street; no nearby parking – best to park in main car park, cross A4117 Cleobury road, and keep walking on down narrowing High Street; DY12 2DH

Friendly town pub tucked away in side street with a bustling atmosphere and decent beer and food

Always chatty and with helpful, friendly staff, this 450-year-old town pub is tucked away in a historic street among other similar-looking houses. It's much bigger than its unassuming exterior suggests and is nicely timbered inside with reclaimed oak panelling and floorboards, and has various items of memorabilia on the walls and a warming woodburning stove. Alongside Bewdley Worcestershire Way, they keep a couple of guests from brewers such as St Austells and Timothy Taylors on handpump, a selection of bottled ciders and perries and just under two dozen wines; background music and TV. An area outside has heaters. No parking.

Tasty bar food includes sandwiches, pressed ham hock and duck pâté with piccalilli, mackerel and haddock fishcake with horseradish and lime crème fraîche, mushroom, leek, goats cheese and caramelised red onion quiche, pork, apple and cider pie, sausages with mash and rich gravy, half a free-range crisp roast chicken and chips in a basket, lamb shank in redcurrant and onion gravy, and puddings such as black cherry bakewell tart and whisky and orange bread and butter pudding. *Benchmark main dish: desperate dan cow pie £8.65. Two-course evening meal £15.00.*

Punch ~ Tenant Mark Payne ~ Real ale ~ Bar food (12-2(4 Sat), 6-9(9.30 Sat); 12-4, 5.30-8 Sun) ~ Restaurant ~ No credit cards ~ (01299) 403762 ~ Children welcome ~ Dogs allowed in bar ~ Open 12-3, 6-11; 12-midnight Sat; 12-11 Sun; closed Mon lunchtime ~ www.littlepackhorse.co.uk *Recommended by N R White, Save Dore, Pat Crabb*

BIRLINGHAM   SO9343   Map 4

Swan ⬥ £

Church Street; off A4104 S of Pershore, via B4080 Eckington Road, turn off at sign to Birlingham with integral 'The Swan Inn' brown sign (not the 'Birlingham (village only)' road), then left; WR10 3AQ

Thatched charmer offering interesting beers, enjoyable reasonably priced food and good-sized country garden

A mass of hops hang from the beams in the black-beamed quarry-tiled bar of this pretty black and white timbered cottage. Popular with chatty locals and genuinely welcoming, it's comfortably old-fashioned with copper-topped tables, darts, a woodburning stove in the big stone fireplace and a snug inner carpeted area by the smallish counter. This serves Wye Valley Bitter and three guests from brewers such as Butcombe, Malvern Hills and Woods and three ciders. They also hold beer festivals in May and September; background music, cribbage, dominoes and poker. The back dining conservatory is simple but comfortable, with creepers scrambling overhead. Service is quick and polite. Somebody here loves gardening, as the pub is prettily covered with roses, and the garden behind is beautifully kept. It's divided into two parts by shrubs, with a variety of tables and chairs under parasols; we liked the mini watering can cutlery holders – and the birdsong.

Good value straightforward food includes whitebait, hot chicken and smoked bacon caesar salad, brie wedges in hazelnut crumb with red onion and cranberry relish, ploughman's, gammon and egg, lasagne, tempura-battered haddock, fisherman's pie, crab salad and vegetable and bean chilli. *Benchmark main dish: steak and kidney pie £8.95. Two-course evening meal £13.70.*

Free house ~ Licensees Imogen and Nicholas Carson ~ Real ale ~ Bar food (12-2.30, 6.30-8.30(not Sun evening)) ~ Restaurant ~ (01386) 750485 ~ Children welcome ~ Dogs allowed in bar ~ Open 12-3, 6.30-11(10.30 Sun) ~ www.theswaninn.co.uk
Recommended by Dave Braisted, Theocsbrian, N R White, Roger and Gillian Holmes

BRANSFORD   SO8052   Map 4

Bear & Ragged Staff ♀

Off A4103 SW of Worcester; Station Road; WR6 5JH

Cheerfully run dining pub with pleasant places to sit both inside and out

W elcoming and friendly, this nice country dining pub offers the same menu in the formal restaurant (with its proper tablecloths and linen napkins) and the more relaxed bar. Its interconnecting rooms give fine views of attractive rolling country (as do the pretty garden and terrace) and in winter there's a warming open fire; background music and darts. They carry a good range of wines, with about a dozen by the glass, lots of malt whiskies, quite a few brandies and liqueurs, Hobsons Twisted Spire and a guest such as Sharps Doom Bar on handpump; good disabled access and facilities.

❚❚ Prepared using carefully sourced produce and some vegetables from their own patch, bar food includes lunchtime sandwiches (not Sunday), duck terrine with lemon, thyme and grape chutney, battered fish and chips, seafood and leek risotto, curry of the day, beef braised in coriander and pomegranate, bass fillet with dill crème fraîche and steak and kidney pudding. *Benchmark main dish: pork belly with glazed apple and cider gravy £15.00. Two-course evening meal £21.00.*

Free house ~ Licensee Lynda Williams ~ Real ale ~ Bar food (12-2(2.30 Sun), 6.30-9) ~ Restaurant ~ (01886) 833399 ~ Children welcome ~ Dogs allowed in bar ~ Open 11.30-2, 6(6.30 Sat)-11; 12-3 Sun; closed Sun evening ~ www.bear.uk.com *Recommended by Alan and Eve Harding, R T and J C Moggridge, Vivienne Howard*

BRETFORTON
SP0943   Map 4

Fleece 🍺 £

B4035 E of Evesham: turn S off this road into village; pub is in central square by church; there's a sizeable car park at one side of the church; WR11 7JE

Marvellously unspoilt medieval pub owned by the National Trust

Before becoming a pub in 1848 this lovely old farmhouse was owned by the same family for nearly 500 years, and many of the furnishings, such as the great oak dresser that holds a priceless 48-piece set of Stuart pewter, are heirlooms passed down through the generations. Its almost museum-like little rooms are atmospherically dim, with massive beams, exposed timbers and marks scored on the worn and crazed flagstones to keep out demons. There are two fine grandfather clocks, ancient kitchen chairs, curved high-backed settles, a rocking chair and a rack of heavy pointed iron shafts (probably for spit roasting) in one of the huge inglenook fireplaces, and two more log fires. Plenty of oddities include a great cheese press and set of cheese moulds, and a rare dough-proving table; a leaflet details the more bizarre items. Four or five real ales on handpump are from brewers such as Cannon Royall, Hook Norton, Purity, Uley and Woods, alongside two farm ciders (one made by the landlord), local apple juices, german wheat beer and fruit wines, and ten wines by the glass; darts. At the end of May, as part of the Vale of Evesham Asparagus Festival they hold an asparagus auction, and they host the village fête on August bank holiday Monday. The calendar of events also includes morris dancing, and the village silver band plays here regularly, too. The lawn, with its fruit trees around a beautifully restored thatched and timbered barn, is a lovely place to sit, and there are more picnic-sets and a stone pump trough in the front courtyard. They may want to keep your credit card if you run a tab outside. If you are visiting to enjoy the famous historic interior try and go midweek as it can be very busy at weekends.

❚❚ Bar food includes sandwiches, whitebait, pork and apple terrine, beef madras, steak and kidney pie, fried bass with chorizo and aubergine ragoût, battered cod, pie of the day, game casserole, faggots and mash with red wine gravy and leek, red onion and goats cheese strudel. *Benchmark main dish: sausage and mash £8.75. Two-course evening meal £15.90.*

Free house ~ Licensee Nigel Smith ~ Real ale ~ Bar food (12-2, 7-9) ~ Restaurant ~ (01386) 831173 ~ Children welcome ~ Dogs allowed in bar ~ Open 11-11; 11-3, 6-11 Mon, Tues in winter ~ Bedrooms: /£97.50S ~ www.thefleeceinn.co.uk *Recommended by N R White, Theocsbrian, Dr A J and Mrs Tompsett, Ian and Rose Lock, David Gunn, Dennis Jones, Tom Evans*

BROADWAY

SP0937 Map 4

Crown & Trumpet ◀ £

Church Street; WR12 7AE

Unreconstructed honest local with good real ale and decent food

The friendly staff make visitors so welcome at this genuinely cheerful place that you'll probably feel like a local. The bustling beamed and timbered bar is intimately down to earth and relaxed, with antique dark high-backed settles, large solid tables and a blazing log fire. Four real ales including Cotswold Spring Codrington Codger, a seasonal brew from local Stanway Brewery, Stroud Tom Long and a guest such as Butcombe are on handpump alongside local cider, nine wines by the glass, hot toddies, mulled wine and a good range of soft drinks. They have an assortment of pub games, including darts, shove-ha'penny, cribbage, shut the box, dominoes and ring the bull as well as a quiz machine, TV and background music. The hardwood tables and chairs outside, among flowers on a slightly raised front terrace, are popular with walkers – even in adverse weather.

Straightforward bar food includes baguettes, ploughman's, steak and kidney pie, battered haddock, chilli, lasagne, fried chicken and chorizo, steak, and puddings such as rhubarb crumble and spotted dick. *Benchmark main dish: beef and plum pie £8.95. Two-course evening meal £21.00.*

Laurel (Enterprise) ~ Lease Andrew Scott ~ Real ale ~ Bar food (12-2.30, 6-9.30; 12-9.30 Sat, Sun) ~ (01386) 853202 ~ Children welcome ~ Dogs allowed in bar and bedrooms ~ Live music Thurs, Sat ~ Open 11-3, 5-11; 11-midnight Fri, Sat; 12-11 Sun ~ Bedrooms: /£75S(£85B) ~ www.cotswoldholidays.co.uk *Recommended by Dennis Jones, Derek and Sylvia Stephenson, Theocsbrian, R T and J C Moggridge, Don Bryan, Tracey and Stephen Groves, Roger and Ann King, Canon Michael Bourdeaux*

CLENT

SO9279 Map 4

Fountain ⑪ ♀

Adams Hill/Odnall Lane; off A491 at Holy Cross/Clent exit roundabout, via Violet Lane, then right at T junction; DY9 9PU

Restauranty pub often packed to overflowing, with imaginative dishes and good choice of drinks

The emphasis at this popular place (best to book) is on the interesting food, with tables laid for dining and attentive uniformed staff who lead you to your seat. The long, carpeted dining bar (three knocked-together areas) is fairly traditional, with teak chairs and pedestal tables, with some comfortably cushioned brocade wall seats. There are nicely framed local photographs on the rag-rolled pinkish walls above a dark panelled dado, pretty wall lights and candles on the tables (flowers in summer). Three changing real ales might be from brewers such as Burton Bridge, Marstons and Wychwood, and most of their 36 wines are served by the glass; also speciality teas, good coffees and freshly squeezed orange juice; background music and alley skittles. There are tables out on a deck.

As well as an impressive range of lunchtime sandwiches (anything from chicken and garlic mayonnaise to chips and cheese), meals are served in generous helpings. The daily changing menu might include tiger prawns with garlic butter, chicken liver parfait, mediterranean vegetable wellington, popular lamb pot roast, sweet and sour pork, roast salmon topped with smoked salmon with a prawn and mushroom sauce, breast and confit duck with cucumber, spring onions, sesame soy noodles and oyster sauce, steaks with quite a choice of sauces, and puddings such as home-made chocolate brownies with chocolate sauce and banoffi pie cheesecake; they also offer two- and three-course set menus. *Benchmark main dish: lamb hot pot £14.95. Two-course evening meal £21.00.*

Marstons ~ Lease Richard and Jacque Macey ~ Real ale ~ Bar food (12-2, 6-9(9.30 Fri, Sat); 12-6 Sun) ~ (01562) 883286 ~ Open 11-11; 12-8 Sun ~ www.thefountainatclent.co.uk *Recommended by Emma Scofield*

HANLEY CASTLE
Three Kings 🍺 £
SO8342 Map 4

Church End, off B4211 N of Upton upon Severn; WR8 0BL

Timeless hospitable gem with five real ales and simple snacks

You can take an enjoyable step back in time at this unspoilt country local that's been run by the same characterful family for over a hundred years. It's the cheerful welcome, rather than the housekeeping, that counts in the eyes of those readers who like it, so we've certainly no quibbles with their happy relaxed approach. A homely little tiled-floor tap room on the right is separated from the entrance corridor by the monumental built-in settle that faces its equally vast inglenook fireplace. A hatch serves very well kept Butcombe Bitter, Hobsons and three guests on handpump from smaller brewers such as Church End and St Georges, with around 75 malt whiskies and farm cider. On the left, another room has darts, dominoes, cribbage and other board games. A separate entrance leads to a timbered lounge with another inglenook fireplace and a neatly blacked kitchen range, little leatherette armchairs and spindleback chairs around its tables, and another antique winged and high-backed settle. Bow windows in the three main rooms and old-fashioned wood and iron seats on the front terrace look across to the great cedar that shades the tiny green.

 Food is limited to sandwiches, toasties and ploughman's. *Benchmark main dish: toasted bacon and mushroom sandwich £1.75.*

Free house ~ Licensee Sue Roberts ~ Real ale ~ Bar food (12-2; not weekends or evenings) ~ No credit cards ~ (01684) 592686 ~ Children welcome ~ Dogs welcome ~ Jam sessions Fri lunchtime, Sun evening ~ Open 12-3, 7-11 *Recommended by P Dawn, Guy Vowles, Theocsbrian, MLR, the Didler*

HOLY CROSS
Bell & Cross ★ 🍴 🍷
SO9278 Map 4

4 miles from M5 junction 4: A491 towards Stourbridge, then follow Clent signpost off on left; DY9 9QL
Worcestershire Dining Pub of the Year

Super food, staff with a can-do attitude, delightful old interior and pretty garden

Successful as a dining pub yet still extremely welcoming if you're just popping in for a drink, this charmingly well kept place is run with meticulous attention to every detail to ensure that you have a most enjoyable visit. It has an unspoilt early 19th-c layout with five beautifully decorated little rooms and a kitchen opening off a central corridor with a black and white tiled floor. Rooms offer a choice of carpet, bare boards, lino or nice old quarry tiles, a variety of mood, from snug and chatty to bright and airy, and individual décor: theatrical engravings on red walls, nice sporting prints on pale green walls, and racing and gundog pictures above a black panelled dado. Most of them have coal fires and two have small serving bars, with Enville, Kinver Edge, Wye Valley6 and a guest such as Timothy Taylors Landlord on handpump, around 50 wines (14 by the glass), organic soft drinks and a range of coffees; daily papers; background music. A lovely garden has a spacious lawn, and the terrace offers pleasant views.

Food is quite a draw here so it's worth booking, especially for the popular Sunday lunch. As well as lunchtime baguettes and panini, delicious dishes from a changing seasonal menu might include piri piri king prawn skewer, chicken liver and port parfait with red onion jam, fishcakes with white wine, prawn and chive sauce, sausage and mash, yellow thai curry with chicken, carrot, coriander, jasmine rice and crackers, battered cod and chips, calves liver with smoked bacon and thyme rissole potatoes, spinach, ricotta and gnocchi with rocket, pomodori and pesto cream, sautéed chicken breast with porcini mushroom sauce, and puddings such as bakewell tart with raspberry mascarpone, orange crème brûlée with brandy snap biscuit and chocolate orange ice-cream and white chocolate and passion fruit profiteroles with popping candy. *Benchmark main dish: noisette of lamb shoulder with rosemary glaze £15.50. Two-course evening meal £19.20.*

Enterprise ~ Tenants Roger and Jo Narbett ~ Real ale ~ Bar food (12-2(7 Sun), 6.30-9; not Sun evening) ~ (01562) 730319 ~ Children welcome ~ Dogs allowed in bar ~ Open 12-3, 6-11; 12-10.30 Sun ~ www.bellandcrossclent.co.uk *Recommended by Neil Kellett, Pat and Tony Martin, KC, John and Gloria Isaacs, Dr D J and Mrs S C Walker, Christine and Neil Townend, Brian and Ruth Young, Bernard Stradling, Simon Le Fort, David Jackman, Lynda and Trevor Smith, Brian and Maggie Woodford, Susan and John Douglas, Michael Butler, Dave and Pauline Powers*

KNIGHTWICK SO7355 Map 4

Talbot ♀ 🍺 🛏

Knightsford Bridge; B4197 just off A44 Worcester–Bromyard; WR6 5PH

Interesting old coaching inn with good beer from its own brewery and riverside garden

The long-standing licensees at this rambling country hotel are keen on supporting local suppliers and a farmers' market takes place here on the second Sunday of the month. They also grow some of their own veg, rear their own pigs and even have their own Teme Valley microbrewery, which uses locally grown hops to produce the That, T'other and the seasonal ale that are served alongside Hobsons Bitter, a farm cider, a dozen wines by the glass and a number of malt whiskies. Often lively with locals warming up by the winter log fire, the heavily beamed and extended traditional lounge bar has a variety of seats from small carved or leatherette armchairs to winged settles by the windows, and a vast stove squats in the big central stone hearth. The bar opens on to a terrace and arbour with summer roses and clematis. The well furnished back public bar has pool on a raised side area, a TV, games machine, darts, juke box and cribbage. In contrast, the dining room is a sedate place for a quiet (if not cheap) meal. Across the lane, a lovely lawn has tables by the River Teme (they serve out here, too), or you can sit out in front on old-fashioned seats; dogs may be allowed to stay in the bedrooms by prior arrangement.

Food, including their own breads, pickles and jams, is all home prepared, and the constantly changing menu might include pigs head brawn with pickled egg, pork, orange and cognac pâté, rabbit confit with chilli jam, vegetarian quiche, cottage pie, mushroom, chestnut and spinach spaghetti, chicken biriyani, baked cod with smoked bacon and jerusalem artichokes, pork belly and cheek with creamy mustard sauce, and puddings such as citrus tart, strawberry parfait meringue and white chocolate cheesecake. *Benchmark main dish: venison stew £17.00. Two-course evening meal £20.50.*

Own brew ~ Licensee Annie Clift ~ Real ale ~ Bar food (12-9) ~ Restaurant ~ (01886) 821235 ~ Children welcome ~ Dogs allowed in bar and bedrooms ~ Open 10(12 Sun)-11 ~ Bedrooms: £57.50S/£95B ~ www.the-talbot.co.uk *Recommended by Patrick and Daphne Darley, J R Simmons, Hilary Adams, David Jackman, Pat and Tony Martin, Clare Tagg*

MALVERN SO7845 Map 4
Nags Head
Bottom end of Bank Street, steep turn down off A449; WR14 2JG

Remarkable range of real ales, delightfully eclectic layout and décor, and warmly welcoming atmosphere

Few pubs can have as many real ales as this popular little place. If you struggle to choose from the range of 14, the cheery staff will happily offer you a taster. House beers are Banks's, Bathams, St Georges Charger, Friar Tuck and Dragons Blood, Sharps Doom Bar, Woods Shropshire Lad and Wychwood Hobgoblin, and they've seven changing guests – last year they got through over 500. They also keep two farm ciders, over two dozen malt whiskies and ten gins. A series of snug individually decorated rooms, with one or two steps between and two open fires, have an easy-going chatty atmosphere. Each is characterfully filled with all sorts of chairs including leather armchairs, pews sometimes arranged as booths, a mix of tables with sturdy ones stained different colours, bare boards here, flagstones there, carpet elsewhere, and plenty of interesting pictures and homely touches such as house plants, shelves of well thumbed books and blacktop newspapers; board games. There are picnic-sets and rustic tables and benches on the front terrace (with heaters and umbrellas) and in the garden.

Tasty lunchtime bar food, served in generous helpings, includes good sandwiches, soup, chicken curry, stuffed mushrooms and fish and chips. In the evening, meals are served in the barn extension dining room only and might include scallops with balsamic vinegar, chicken liver pâté, beef bourguignon, fish of the day, and steaks. *Benchmark main dish: beer-battered cod and chips £8.90. Two-course evening meal £18.00.*

Free house ~ Licensees Clare Keane and Alex Whistance ~ Real ale ~ Bar food (12-2(2.30 Sun), 6.30(7 Sun)-8.30) ~ Restaurant ~ (01684) 574373 ~ Children welcome ~ Dogs welcome ~ Open 11-11.15(11.30 Fri, Sat); 12-11 Sun ~ www.nagsheadmalvern.co.uk *Recommended by P Dawn, Pat and Tony Martin, N R White, Mr and Mrs M J Girdler, Don Bryan, Barry Collett, Amanda Kelly, Brian and Anna Marsden, Chris Flynn, Wendy Jones, Steve Tilley, Paul Humphreys*

NEWLAND SO7948 Map 4
Swan
Worcester Road (set well back from A449 just NW of Malvern); WR13 5AY

Popular creeper-clad pub with five real ales and big garden

The dimly lit dark-beamed bar at this attractive old place is quite traditional, with a forest canopy of hops, whisky-water jugs, beakers and tankards. Several of the comfortable and clearly individually chosen seats are worth a close look for their carving, and the wall tapestries are interesting. The carved counter has well kept St Georges Dragons Blood, Friar Tuck and Sharps Doom Bar, Wychwood Hobgoblin and a guest such as Butcombe Best on handpump. On the right is a broadly similar red-carpeted dining room, and beyond it, in complete contrast, an ultra-modern glass cube of a garden room; background music, bar billiards and board games. The garden itself is as individual as the pub, with a cluster of huge casks topped with flowers, even a piano doing flower-tub duty, and a set of stocks on the pretty front terrace.

Lunchtime food includes sandwiches, ham, egg and chips, chilli, spicy vegetable goulash, red thai prawn curry and chicken, ham and leek pie. In the evening there might be smoked salmon and roasted trout roulade, chilli and ginger king prawn cocktail, rabbit casserole with lemon, nutmeg and parsley with herb dumplings in a filo basket, grilled tuna with sweet and spicy pineapple salsa, pork tenderloin with roast apple and black pudding in creamy scrumpy sauce with a cheddar puff biscuit, fidget pie and grilled plaice with leek and caper sauce. *Benchmark main dish: beer-battered cod £10.70. Two-course evening meal £20.25.*

Free house ~ Licensee Nick Taylor ~ Real ale ~ Bar food (12-2.30, 6.30-9; 12-3, 7-9 Sun) ~ Restaurant ~ (01886) 832224 ~ Children welcome ~ Dogs welcome ~ Open 12-11
Recommended by Denys Gueroult, Lynette Willey, Noel Thomas, Paul Humphreys

Also Worth a Visit in Worcestershire

Besides the fully inspected pubs, you might like to try these pubs that have been recommended to us and described by readers. Do tell us what you think of them: feedback@goodguides.com

ABBERLEY SO7567
Manor Arms (01299) 896507
Netherton Lane; WR6 6BN Good value comfortable country inn nicely tucked away in quiet village backwater opposite fine Norman church, façade emblazoned with coats of arms, warm welcome, quick friendly service, six ales including Wye Valley, enjoyable carefully prepared food from baguettes up, lunchtime bargains, two bars and restaurant, interesting toby jug collection; ten bedrooms. *(Brian and Jacky Wilson, Chris Evans, Peter and Jean Hoare)*

ALVECHURCH SP0172
Weighbridge (0121) 4455111
Scarfield Wharf; B48 7SQ Converted little house by Worcester & Birmingham Canal marina, bar and a couple of small rooms, well kept ales such as Kinver Bargee's Bitter and Weatheroaks Tillerman's Tipple, simple low-priced food (not Tues, Weds); tables outside. *(Tony Hobden)*

ASTON FIELDS SO9669
Ladybird Inn (01527) 878014
Finstall Road (B184 just S of Bromsgrove); B60 2DZ Light and airy red-brick Edwardian pub adjoining hotel (next to station), panelled bar and comfortable lounge, reasonably priced pub food along with separate italian restaurant,

well kept local Birds and Wye Valley, good service; children welcome, open all day. *(Tony Hobden)*

BARNARDS GREEN SO7945
Blue Bell (01684) 575031
Junction B4211 to Rhydd Green with B4208 to Malvern Show Ground; WR14 3QP Comfortable panelled dining pub in pleasant setting, good choice of enjoyable well priced food, Marstons-related ales, quiz first Weds of month; children welcome, disabled facilities, nice garden. *(Chris Evans, Paul Humphreys)*

BAUGHTON SO8742
Jockey (01684) 592153
4 miles from M50 junction 1; A38 northwards, then right on to A4104 Upton–Pershore; WR8 9DQ Should have reopened under new management by the time you read this – reports please.

BECKFORD SO9835
Beckford Inn (01386) 881532
A435; GL20 7AN Sizeable 18th-c roadside inn, beams, log fires and some stripped stone, well kept ales and good range of wines by the glass, enjoyable food from traditional choices up, smart dining room, friendly helpful staff; children welcome, wheelchair access, picnic-sets in large garden, eight comfortable bedrooms. *(Roger and Donna Huggins)*

BELBROUGHTON
SO9177
Queens (01562) 730276
Queens Hill (B4188 E of Kidderminster); DY9 0DU Old refurbished red-brick pub by Belne Brook, several linked areas including beamed slate-floor bar, good food with set menu choices, three well kept beers and good selection of wines, efficient staff coping well at busy times, live music Sun; disabled facilities, small roadside terrace, pleasant village. *(Eric Thomas Yarwood)*

BERROW GREEN
SO7458
★Admiral Rodney (01886) 821375
B4197, off A44 W of Worcester; WR6 6PL Light and roomy high-beamed dining pub, big stripped kitchen tables and two woodburners, good generous pubby food including weekend fish (should book Fri, Sat evenings), friendly fast service, well kept Wye Valley and two guests at sensible prices, good choice of wines by the glass, charming end restaurant in rebuilt barn, folk music third Weds of month; surcharge on some credit cards; well behaved children and dogs welcome, disabled facilities, tables outside with pretty view and heated covered terrace, good walks, three bedrooms, closed Mon lunchtime, open all day weekends; up for sale as we went to press. *(Denys Gueroult)*

BEWDLEY
SO7775
Hop Pole (01299) 401295
Hop Pole Lane; DY12 2QH Refurbished family-run pub with good choice of enjoyable food from pub classics up, OAP lunchtime deal (Mon-Sat), changing ales and plenty of wines by the glass, walls decorated with old tools etc, cast-iron range in dining area, live music Weds; children welcome, front garden with scarecrow and vegetable patch, open all day (afternoon break Mon). *(Dave Braisted)*

BEWDLEY
SO7875
Mug House (01299) 402543
Severn Side N; DY12 2EE Pleasantly renovated 18th-c bay-windowed pub in charming spot by River Severn, enjoyable traditional food, five well kept ales including Bewdley, Woods and Wye Valley, friendly helpful service, log fire, restaurant; disabled access, glass-covered terrace behind, seven river-view bedrooms, open all day. *(John Coatsworth, Derek and Sylvia Stephenson, Michael Coleman)*

BIRTSMORTON
SO7936
★Farmers Arms (01684) 833308
Birts Street, off B4208 W; WR13 6AP Timbered village local, pubbily straightforward, with friendly staff and chatty regulars (cribbage and darts teams), well kept Hook Norton and two changing guests, simple cheap bar food, gently old-fashioned room on right with low dark beams and some standing timbers, spindleback chairs and flowery-panelled cushioned settles on big flagstones, large inglenook, lower-beamed room on left (even cosier); children and dogs welcome, seats and swings on lovely big lawn with views over Malvern Hills, plenty of surrounding walks. *(the Didler, Dave Braisted)*

BREDON
SO9236
★Fox & Hounds (01684) 772377
4.5 miles from M5 junction 9; A438 to Northway, left at B4079, in Bredon follow sign to church; GL20 7LA Cottagey 16th-c thatched pub with open-plan carpeted bar, low beams, stone pillars and stripped timbers, central woodburner, traditional furnishings including upholstered settles, a variety of wheelback, tub and kitchen chairs around handsome mahogany and cast-iron-frame tables, elegant wall lamps, smaller side bar, Banks's Bitter, Greene King Old Speckled Hen and a guest, nice wines by the glass, wide choice of enjoyable food, pleasant staff; background music; children welcome, dogs in bar, outside picnic-sets (some under cover), handy M5 break. *(R J Herd, Andy and Claire Barker, J V Dadswell, Dr A J and Mrs Tompsett)*

BROADWAS-ON-TEME
SO7555
Royal Oak (01886) 821353
A44; WR6 5NE Red-brick roadside pub with relaxed lounge bar and dining area, unusual lofty-raftered medieval-style dining hall, and separate public bar with pool, well kept Jennings and Marstons ales, decent wines by the glass, food (all day weekends) from generous lunchtime sandwiches up including OAP weekday deals and popular Sun carvery, good service; they ask for a credit card if running a tab; children welcome, terrace picnic-sets, open all day weekends. *(Nicola Oatway, Jonathan Niccol, Denys Gueroult, Martin and Pauline Jennings)*

BROADWAY
SP0937
Swan (01386) 852278
The Green (B4362); WR12 7AA Sizeable reworked M&B dining pub with several linked areas, imaginative décor, good sensibly priced food, three well kept changing ales, polite friendly young staff; café-style tables on small front terrace looking over road to village green. *(Richard Tilbrook, Steve and Julie Buckingham)*

CALLOW END
SO8349
Old Bush (01905) 830792
Upton Road; WR2 4TE Attractive unfussy local with good range of Marstons-related ales and decent wines, standard bar food

from sandwiches up, some very reasonable prices, attentive friendly staff, cosy small areas around central bar, traditional pleasantly worn furnishings, restaurant; children and dogs welcome, back garden with play area. *(Martin and Pauline Jennings, Caroline and Michael Abbey, Chris Evans)*

CALLOW HILL   SO7473
Royal Forester (01299) 266286
Near Wyre Forest visitors' centre; DY14 9XW Dining pub dating in part from 15th c, good food and friendly helpful service, relaxed lounge bar with two well kept ales such as Greene King Abbot and Wye Valley HPA, Robinson's cider, restaurant; children and dogs welcome, seats outside, seven contemporary bedrooms, open all day. *(Michael Coleman)*

CAUNSALL   SO8480
Anchor (01562) 850254
Off A449; DY11 5YL Traditional unchanging two-room pub (in same family since 1927), friendly atmosphere and can get busy, well kept Enville, Hobsons, Wye Valley and three guests, good filled cobs, efficient service; tables outside, near canal. *(the Didler, Tony Hobden)*

CHADDESLEY CORBETT   SO8973
Talbot (01562) 777388
Off A448 Bromsgrove–Kidderminster; DY10 4SA Comfortably refurbished and neatly kept late medieval timbered pub in quiet village street, well kept Marstons-related ales, enjoyable generous food; comfortable outside area, attractive village and church. *(Alan and Eve Harding, David Lawson)*

CHILDSWICKHAM   SP0738
★ Childswickham Inn (01386) 852461
Off A44 NW of Broadway; WR12 7HP Restauranty dining pub with big rugs on boards or terracotta tiles, contemporary artwork on part-timbered walls, woodburner, good food from pubby choices to more pricy brasserie food, friendly attentive staff, locals' lounge bar with leather sofas and armchairs (dogs allowed here), good choice of wines, beers such as Brakspears, Hook Norton and Greene King; background music, TV; children and dogs welcome, disabled facilities, garden with decked area, barbecue, open all day Sun. *(Anon)*

CLAINES   SO8558
Mug House (01905) 456649
Claines Lane, off A449 3 miles W of M5 junction 3; WR3 7RN Fine views from ancient country tavern in unique churchyard setting by fields below the Malvern Hills; several small rooms around central bar, low doorways and heavy oak beams, well kept Banks's Bitter and other Marstons-related beers, simple lunchtime pub food (not Sun); outside lavatories; children allowed away from servery, open all day weekends. *(Tony Hobden)*

CLOWS TOP   SO7272
Colliers Arms (01299) 832242
A456 Bewdley–Tenbury; DY14 9HA Two-room roadside café/pub reopened 2011 after refurbishment, enjoyable food from breakfast on, pleasant service, two Hobsons ales and plenty of bottled beers, oak table and chairs on wood floors, sofas and armchairs in back room, woodburners, shop selling local produce; children and dogs welcome, disabled facilities, seats on terrace, garden with roaming chickens and vegetable patch, nice countryside, open 9am-6pm (9pm Fri). *(Eric Thomas Yarwood)*

CROWLE   SO9256
Old Chequers (01905) 381275
Crowle Green, not far from M5 jctn 6; WR7 4AA Civilised 17th-c dining pub mixing traditional and contemporary décor; oak beams and log fires, leather sofas, modern tables and chairs in bar and restaurant, friendly prompt service, good choice of enjoyable home-made food from pub favourites up including fixed-price menu, baby grand piano, some live jazz; children welcome, dogs in bar, disabled facilities, picnic-sets in garden behind, open all day, closed Sun evening. *(Alan Weedon)*

DEFFORD   SO9042
★ Monkey House (01386) 750234
A4104, after passing Oak pub on right, it's the last of a small group of cottages; WR8 9BW Tiny black and white cider house, a wonderful time warp and in the same family for 150 years; drinks limited to cider and a perry tapped from barrels into pottery mugs and served by landlady from a hatch, no food (can bring your own); children welcome, no dogs (three resident rottweilers), garden with caravans, sheds and Mandy the horse, small spartan outbuilding with a couple of plain tables, settle and fireplace, open Fri and Sun lunchtimes, Weds and Sat evenings. *(the Didler)*

DEFFORD   SO9042
Oak (01386) 750327
Woodmancote; WR8 9BW Refurbished 17th-c beamed country inn, enjoyable fairly priced food in bar and restaurant, well kept Sharps Doom Bar and Wye Valley ales, Thatcher's cider, friendly staff; children welcome, garden with chickens and orchard, bedrooms. *(Brian and Maggie Woodford, Dave Braisted, Paul Humphreys)*

DROITWICH   SO9063
Hop Pole (01905) 770155
Friar Street; WR9 8ED Heavy-beamed local with panelled rooms on different levels, friendly staff, well kept Wye Valley ales and guests such as Enville and Malvern Hills, bargain home-made lunchtime food including doorstep sandwiches, dominoes, darts and pool, live music first Sun of month; children

welcome, partly canopied back garden, open all day. *(Dave Braisted, Chris Evans, Tony Hobden)*

ECKINGTON   SO9241
Bell (01386) 750033
Church Street (B4080); WR10 3AN Attractively refurbished village dining pub with enjoyable range of food (special diets catered for), can also cook your own on a hot stone, two real ales and good range of wines, friendly efficient staff; children and dogs welcome, garden tables, four bedrooms, open all day weekends. *(Nigel Clifton, John Hammill)*

ELDERSFIELD   SO8131
★ Butchers Arms (01452) 840381
Village signposted from B4211; Lime Street (coming from A417, go past the Eldersfield turn and take the next one), OS Sheet 150 map reference 815314; also signposted from B4208 N of Staunton; GL19 4NX Pretty cottage with deliberately simple unspoilt little locals' bar, ales such as St Austell and Wye Valley tapped from the cask, a farm cider and short but well chosen wine list, just a dozen seats in candlelit dining room, carefully prepared, well presented food using ingredients from named local farms, must book lunchtime and it's advised in the evening; garden picnic-sets, nice surroundings, closed Sun evening, Mon, also for ten days in Jan and the latter part of Aug. *(T Harrison, Rod Stoneman, Chris Marshall)*

ELMLEY CASTLE   SO9841
Queen Elizabeth (01386) 710419
Signed off A44 and A435, not far from Evesham; Main Street; WR10 3HS Old refurbished pub with Fullers, Sharps, Shepherd Neame and Wye Valley, well priced traditional food from generous sandwiches to Sun carvery, flagstone floor in one part with inglenook woodburner, pool room, restaurant; children, dogs and muddy boots welcome, tables out in yard, grassy play area, open all day. *(Dave Braisted, Di and Mike Gillam)*

EVESHAM   SP0344
Evesham Hotel (01386) 765566
Coopers Lane; WR11 1DA Idiosyncratic hotel's busy bar with amazing range of malt whiskies and spirits, good if quirky wine list, no real ales, interesting menu including good value lunchtime buffet (no tips or service charge), redecorated elegant dining room, remarkable lavatories; children welcome, indoor swimming pool, 40 bedrooms. *(Denys Gueroult, Steve Whalley)*

FORHILL   SP0575
★ Peacock (01564) 757307
Handy for M42, junctions 2 and 3; pub at junction Lea End Lane and Icknield Street; B38 0EH Attractive, quietly placed and well run Chef & Brewer with wide range of enjoyable food all day, plenty of tables in

---

comfortably fitted knocked-through beamed rooms, woodburner in big inglenook, Greene King, Highgates, Hobsons, Wells & Youngs and quest ales, friendly prompt helpful service; background music; children and dogs welcome, disabled facilities, picnic-sets on back terrace and front grass, other heated covered areas. *(Anon)*

GRIMLEY   SO8359
Camp House (01905) 640288
A443 5 miles N from Worcester, right to Grimley, right at village T junction; WR2 6LX Unspoilt old character pub in same family for many years, pleasant Severn-side setting with own landing stage, generous bargain food from huge cobs to good scampi and chips, well kept Bathams, farm cider; no credit cards; children and well behaved dogs welcome, attractive lawns. *(Chris Evans)*

GUARLFORD   SO8245
Plough & Harrow (01684) 310453
B4211 E of village; WR13 6NY This well liked, civilised country dining pub was closed as we went to press – news please.

KEMPSEY   SO8548
Walter de Cantelupe
(01905) 820572 *3.7 miles from M5 junction 7: A44 towards Worcester, left on to A4440, then left on A38 at roundabout; Main Road; WR5 3NA* Traditional carpeted bar with inglenook and pleasant mix of well worn furniture, ales such as Blue Bear, Cannon Royall and Timothy Taylors Landlord, summer farm cider and locally pressed apple juice, enjoyable food (till 10pm Fri, Sat), table skittles; background music, sports TV; children in dining area till 8.15pm, dogs in bar and bedrooms, pretty suntrap walled garden, closed Mon. *(P Dawn, Pat and Tony Martin, Martin Smith)*

KIDDERMINSTER   SO8376
★ King & Castle (01562) 747505
Railway Station, Comberton Hill; DY10 1QX Bustling and neatly re-created Edwardian refreshment room suiting its setting in Severn Valley Railway terminus, steam trains outside and railway memorabilia and photographs inside, simple furnishings, Bathams, very good value Wyre Piddle and guests, reasonably priced straightforward food in adjacent dining room (9am-3pm), cheerful staff coping well on busy bank holidays and railway gala days; little museum close by, open all day. *(P Dawn, Ian Shorthouse, George Atkinson, Chris and Angela Buckell, Theocsbrian)*

LOWER MOOR   SO9847
Chestnut Tree (01386) 860380
Manor Road; WR10 2NZ Ancient dark-beamed and flagstoned pub revitalised under present licensees, friendly welcoming staff, good value pub food, three or four well

kept ales, some live music, pool; children welcome. *(Julian Lander)*

MALVERN   SO7746
Foley Arms (01684) 573397
Worcester Road; WR14 4QS Substantial Georgian hotel taken over by Wetherspoons, usual good value; splendid views from sunny terrace and back bedrooms, open all day from 7am. *(S Holder, Dave Braisted)*

MALVERN   SO7640
Malvern Hills Hotel (01684) 540690
Opposite British Camp car park, Wynds Point; junction A449/B4232 S; WR13 6DW Big comfortable dark-panelled lounge bar, very popular weekends, enjoyable bar food, well kept changing ales such as local Malvern Hills and Wye Valley, quite a few malt whiskies, good coffee, friendly service, open fire, downstairs pool room, smart more expensive restaurant; background music; dogs welcome, great views from terrace, bedrooms small but comfortable, open all day. *(David Hawkes)*

MALVERN   SO7745
Unicorn (01684) 574152
Belle Vue Terrace; WR14 4PZ Former 16th-c posting inn with four well kept ales and bargain simple food, friendly efficient young staff; background music, pool. *(A N Bance)*

OMBERSLEY   SO8463
★ **Cross Keys** (01905) 620588
Just off A449; Main Road (A4133, Kidderminster end); WR9 0DS Carpeted bar with easy-going atmosphere, archways opening into several separate areas – nicest on left with attractive Bob Lofthouse animal etchings, hop-strung beams and some horse tack on dark-varnished country panelling, Timothy Taylors Landlord and Wye Valley HPA, good value wines by the glass and decent coffee, comfortable back room with softly upholstered sofas and armchairs leading to dining conservatory, good food including enterprising daily specials, friendly service; unobtrusive background music; children welcome if eating, terrace with alloy furniture under big heated canopy. *(Paul Hanson, Bruce and Sharon Eden, Dave Braisted, Eric Thomas Yarwood)*

OMBERSLEY   SO8463
Crown & Sandys (01905) 620252
A4133; WR9 0EW Big open-plan inn (now part of the small Scoff & Quaff group), good range of food from sandwiches and pubby dishes up, plenty of wines by the glass (including champagne), Wye Valley and a

local guest, friendly uniformed staff, airy modern décor mixing with 17th-c beams and inglenook; background music; children welcome, terrace with fountain, sizeable garden, six bedrooms, open all day. *(Anon)*

OMBERSLEY   SO8463
★ **Kings Arms** (01905) 620142
Main Road (A4133); WR9 0EW Imposing beamed and timbered Tudor pub, rambling rooms with nooks and crannies, three splendid fireplaces, low-ceilinged quarry-tiled bar with dark wood pew and stools around cast-iron tables, three dining areas, one room with Charles II's coat of arms decorating its ceiling, ales such as Jennings and Marstons, well liked food; background music; children and dogs welcome, seats on tree-sheltered courtyard, colourful hanging baskets and tubs, open all day. *(Bruce and Sharon Eden, Roger White, Chris Flynn, Wendy Jones, Stuart Paulley)*

PENSAX   SO7368
★ **Bell** (01299) 896677
B4202 Abberley–Clows Top, Snead Common part of village; WR6 6AE Mock-Tudor roadside pub with buoyant local atmosphere, welcoming landlord, good choice of ales such as Hobsons (festival last weekend of June), also cider and perry, tasty bar food (not Sun evening) including generous sandwiches, L-shaped main bar with traditional décor, cushioned pews and pubby tables on bare boards, vintage beer ads and wartime front pages, open fire and woodburner, dining room with french windows opening on to deck; children welcome, dogs in bar, country-view garden, open all day summer weekends, closed Mon. *(the Didler, R T and J C Moggridge, Kerry Law)*

PEOPLETON   SO9350
Crown (01905) 840222
Village and pub signed off A44 at Allens Hill; WR10 2EE Refurbished cosy village pub with good mix of drinkers and diners, beamed bar with big inglenook fireplace, well laid out dining area, good generous food (must book) from sandwiches up including set deals, Fullers and Hook Norton ales, good wines by the glass, efficient friendly service; surcharge added if paying by card; flower-filled back garden. *(Martin and Pauline Jennings)*

PERSHORE   SO9545
★ **Brandy Cask** (01386) 552602
Bridge Street; WR10 1AJ Plain high-ceilinged bow-windowed bar, own good ales from courtyard brewery and guests, quick friendly helpful service, coal fire, reasonably

---

Post Office address codings confusingly give the impression that some pubs are in Worcestershire, when they're really in Gloucestershire, Herefordshire, Shropshire, or Warwickshire (which is where we list them).

priced food from sandwiches to steaks, quaintly decorated dining room; well behaved children allowed, no dogs inside, terrace and koi pond in long attractive garden down to river (watch the kids). *(the Didler)*

POUND GREEN   SO7578
New Inn (01299) 401271
B4194 NW of Bewdley; DY12 3LF
Attractive pub rambling out from beamed central core, quiet nooks and corners, friendly efficient young staff, good choice of reasonably priced food in bar and well laid out dining room, Timothy Taylors Landlord and two local ales kept well; live music nights, darts, dominoes, pool, fruit machine; pleasant front garden, picturesque area handy for Arley steam railway station, bedrooms. *(Peter and Jean Hoare)*

RYE STREET   SO7835
Duke of York
Tewkesbury Road; WR13 6JQ Recently reopened and refurbished; good monthly changing menu with emphasis on fish (delivered daily). *(Theocsbrian)*

SEVERN STOKE   SO8544
Rose & Crown (01905) 371249
A38 S of Worcester; WR8 9JQ Attractive 16th-c black and white pub, low beams, knick-knacks and good fire in character bar, well kept Marstons-related ales, decent choice of enjoyable sensibly priced food (all day) including vegetarian, friendly staff, back restaurant, music and quiz nights; dogs welcome, picnic-sets in big garden with play area, Malvern Hills views and good walks. *(Brian Yates)*

SHATTERFORD   SO7981
⋆ Bellmans Cross (01299) 861322
Bridgnorth Road (A442); DY12 1RN
Welcoming french-mood dining pub with good well presented food from sandwiches up, smart tasteful restaurant with kitchen view, french chefs and bar staff, pleasant deft service, neat timber-effect bar with Bass, Greene King Old Speckled Hen and a guest beer, good choice of wines by the glass, teas and coffees; picnic-sets outside, handy for Severn Woods walks, open all day weekends. *(Anon)*

SHENSTONE   SO8673
Plough (01562) 777340
Corner Back Lane; DY10 4DL Secluded country local in pleasant surroundings, chatty and comfortable, with two unchanging brown-panelled bars, well kept Bathams, cobs and pork pies, open fire; courtyard. *(Dave Braisted)*

STOKE WORKS   SO9365
Boat & Railway (01527) 831065
Shaw Lane, by Bridge 42 of Worcester & Birmingham Canal; B60 4EQ Friendly pub under newish landlord, enjoyable food, Marstons-related ales, good service; waterside terrace. *(Dave Braisted)*

STOKE WORKS   SO9365
Bowling Green (01527) 861291
A mile from M5 Junction 5, via Stoke Lane; handy for Worcester & Birmingham Canal; B60 4BH Friendly comfortable pub, Banks's and Marstons traditional food, Banks's and Marstons EPA, polished fireplace; big garden with neat bowling green. *(Dave Braisted)*

TIBBERTON   SO9057
Bridge Inn (01905) 345874
Plough Road; WR9 7NQ By Worcester & Birmingham Canal (Bridge 25); two comfortable dining sections with central fireplace, separate public bar, enjoyable reasonably priced traditional food, Banks's ales, friendly staff, some live music; children, dogs and muddy boots welcome, picnic-sets by water and in garden with secure play area, moorings, open all day. *(Tony Hobden)*

UPHAMPTON   SO8464
Fruiterers Arms (01905) 620305
Off A449 N of Ombersley; WR9 0JW
Homely country local (looks like a private house), good value Cannon Royall ales (brewed at back of pub) and guests, farm cider, simple rustic Jacobean panelled bar and lounge with comfortable armchairs, beamery, log fire, lots of photographs and memorabilia, filled rolls (Fri-Sun); back terrace and some seats out in front, open all day. *(the Didler)*

UPTON UPON SEVERN   SO8540
Kings Head (01684) 592621
High Street; WR8 0HF Lovely riverside setting; well kept ales such as Butcombe, Fullers London Pride and St Austell Tribute, popular food served by attentive staff, extended lounge bar and comfortable eating area, live music Fri; outside lavatories; fine Severn-side terrace. *(Reg Fowle, Helen Rickwood)*

WEST MALVERN   SO7645
⋆ Brewers Arms (01684) 568147
The Dingle; WR14 4BQ Attractive and friendly little two-bar beamed country local down steep path, Malvern Hills, Marstons, Wye Valley and up to five guests (Oct beer festival), good value food including bargain

---

Cribbage is a card game using a block of wood with holes for matchsticks or special pins to score with; regulars in cribbage pubs are usually happy to teach strangers how to play.

OAP weekday lunches, neat airy dining room; children, walkers and dogs welcome, glorious view from small garden, smokers' folly, open all day Fri-Sat. *(Jason Caulkin)*

WITHYBED GREEN
SP0172
Crown (0121) 445 2300
By Worcester & Birmingham Canal; B48 7PN Tucked-away pub in row of former canal workers' cottages overlooking fields, simple low-priced food (not Sun evening), Greene King Abbot and a couple of guests, two open fires; no dogs inside; children welcome; picnic-sets out in front and on terrace, near Bridge 61, open all day. *(Tony Hobden)*

WORCESTER
SO8554
Kings Head (01905) 726025
Sidbury; WR1 2HU Stylishly modernised pub/restaurant (part of the small Scoff & Quaff group), enjoyable food in bar and upstairs grill room, Marstons-related beers, helpful quick service; no dogs inside; children till 8pm, canalside terrace, open all day. *(Jeremy Hebblethwaite, Theocsbrian)*

WORCESTER
SO8455
⋆ Marwood (01905) 330460
The Tything (A38); some nearby parking; WR1 1JL Easy to miss this old building; quirky and civilised with a long narrow series of small linked areas, simple cushioned benches and mixed dining chairs, stripped or cast-iron-framed tables, dark flagstones, broad old floorboards, the odd chandelier, a few italian deco posters, open fires, upstairs room looking across to Law Courts, well kept Butcombe, Sharps Doom Bar and guests, enjoyable fair value bar food (not Sun evening), friendly service; background music; children (in bar till 7.30pm) and dogs welcome, rattan seats and tables in sheltered flagstoned backyard, open all day (midnight Sat); some refurbishment planned as we went to press. *(Dave Braisted, R T and J C Moggridge, Peter Smith and Judith Brown)*

WORCESTER
SO8753
Oak Apple (01905) 355121
Spetchley Road; WR5 2NL Comfortable modern pub, popular locally for its well kept Marstons ales and enjoyable very good value food, friendly hard-working staff, bingo and quiz nights; children welcome. *(Chris Evans)*

WORCESTER
SO8555
Plough (01905) 21381
Fish Street; WR1 2HN Traditional corner pub with two simple rooms off entrance lobby, six interesting ales usually including Hobsons and Malvern Hills, farm cider and perry, coal-effect gas fire; outside lavatories; small back terrace, open all day, closed Thurs lunchtime. *(P Dawn, Edward Leetham)*

WORCESTER
SO8455
Postal Order (01905) 22373
Foregate Street; WR1 1DN Popular Wetherspoons in former sorting office, wide range of well kept beers, Weston's cider and their usual good value food; open all day from 8am. *(P Dawn, the Didler, Tony Hobden)*

WORCESTER
SO8554
Swan With Two Nicks
(01905) 28190 *New Street/Friar Street; WR1 2DP* Rambling town pub dating from the 16th c, plenty of character in bare-boards low-ceilinged front rooms, four or five well kept ales and some interesting bottled ciders, simple lunchtime food, friendly atmosphere; other areas including one for live music; open all day (not Sun lunchtime). *(Tracey and Stephen Groves)*

Yorkshire

Provenance Inns pubs here are really rather special and worth seeking out – the Durham Ox in Crayke, Carpenters Arms at Felixkirk, Oak Tree in Helperby and Punch Bowl at Marton Cum Grafton. All are carefully restored interesting buildings and offer first class food – and sometimes bedrooms, too. New entries or pubs back in these pages after a break (often with new licensees) include the Fleece at Addingham (enterprising new management, super food and attached deli and cookery school), Crab & Lobster at Asenby (smart and civilised but with a lively bar), General Tarleton in Ferrensby (real ales and cosy bar area in civilised restaurant-with-rooms), Grantley Arms in Grantley (relaxed dining pub in small village with well presented food), Black Horse at Kirkby Fleetham (attractively reworked country inn with enterprising meals), Fountaine in Linton in Craven (well run and neatly kept place in a pretty hamlet), Nags Head in Pickhill (smashing all-rounder with long-serving licensees), Pipe & Glass at South Dalton (inventive food cooked by chef/patron, four ales and stylish bedrooms) and White Swan at Thornton-le-Clay (in the same family for 25 years, wholesome food and lovely two-acre garden). Our readers are enjoying the Malt Shovel at Brearton (several generations of friendly family running bustling dining pub; occasional opera evenings), Fauconberg Arms in Coxwold (highly enjoyable food and nice to stay at), Blue Lion in East Witton (top notch inn with caring landlord and delicious food), Tempest Arms in Elslack (excellent service, super food and lovely bedrooms), Sandpiper at Leyburn (charming bedrooms, good mix of locals and visitors, excellent food), White Swan in Pickering (bustling little bar at heart of smart hotel), Crown at Roecliffe (smartly updated with hard-working friendly family owners, imaginative meals, plenty of locals and visitors), Buck in Thornton Watlass (an honest village pub, good Sunday jazz and friendly, long-serving licensees) and Wombwell Arms in Wass (consistently enjoyable all round). Our Yorkshire Dining Pub 2013 is the Crown at Roecliffe.

ADDINGHAM

SE0749   Map 7

Fleece 🍴 🍷

Main Street (B6160, off A65); LS29 0LY

Enterprising new management, good food, strong sense of style, attached deli/coffee shop

The smart bar on the right of this creeper-covered stone-built inn has a cool décor of dark flagstones, polished floorboards, crisp cream paintwork and some wallpaper based on antique fish prints above a charcoal-grey high dado. A pair of grey plaid tub armchairs stand by a great arched stone fireplace, and down a few steps is the civilised dining room (occasionally given over to cookery classes). The interesting black-beamed village bar on the left has a good log fire in its high-manteled fireplace, comfortably worn easy chairs as well as cushioned wall benches and window seats, and some most unusual substantial tables on its broad floorboards. Nicely framed local photographs include a series devoted to former landlord 'Heapy', hero survivor of a 1944 torpedoing. A massive choice of wines by the glass includes champagnes and four rosés; Copper Dragon Golden Pippin, Greene King Old Speckled Hen, Ilkley Mary Jane, Saltaire Blonde and Timothy Taylors Landlord are on handpump. The flagstoned front terrace has neat tables under giant parasols, and a further dining terrace looks out over the garden. They have a cookery school and a deli next door.

 Cooked by the landlord and his team, using local, seasonal produce and baking their own bread twice daily, the inventive food might include sandwiches, goats cheese, black olive and roast red pepper bonbons with beetroot purée, honey and wholegrain crème fraîche, pigeon breast with black pudding, hash brown and cauliflower purée, leek and gruyère pasta, fish pie, chicken breast with chorizo, sautéed potatoes and salsa verde, slow-cooked spicy lamb with flatbread, a pig plate (fillet wrapped in pancetta, belly pork, pigs cheek, black pudding) with apple sauce and creamy mash, duck breast with carrot and star anise purée and plum jus, and puddings such as mixed berry panna cotta with vanilla shortbread and bread and butter pudding with crème anglaise; they also offer a two- and three-course early-bird menu (not Fri evening or weekends). *Benchmark main dish: beer-battered haddock and chips £10.00. Two-course evening meal £19.00.*

Punch ~ Lease Craig Minto ~ Real ale ~ Bar food (12-2.15, 5-9; 12-8 Sun) ~ Restaurant ~ (01943) 830491 ~ Children welcome ~ Dogs allowed in bar ~ Open 12-11(midnight weekends) ~ fleeceinnaddingham.co.uk *Recommended by Peter and Judy Frost, Gordon and Margaret Ormondroyd, Jeremy King*

AMPLEFORTH

SE5878   Map 10

White Swan

Off A170 W of Helmsley; East End; YO62 4DA

Quite a choice of seating areas in this attractive pub, attentive service, enjoyable food and real ales; seats on back terrace

This is a first class pub with a choice of seating areas: the beamed lounge with its cream-coloured décor, sporting prints, slate flooring and double-sided woodburning stove; the more conventional beamed front bar, popular with locals, with its blazing log fire, red patterned wall seating, standing timbers and comfortable end seating area with big soft red cushions; or the more formal dining room with its plush furnishings and crisp, white-linen covered tables. There are also seats and tables on the large, attractive back terrace overlooking the valley. It's close to

Ampleforth College and Abbey, so many of its customers are visitors and parents, but there's a warm welcome for all, and it's nearly always busy. Black Sheep Best and Tetleys on handpump, good wines by the glass and ten malt whiskies; background music, pool, darts and dominoes.

Generously served and with quite a choice, the good food might include sandwiches, smoked, fresh and marinated seafood, slow-roasted pork ribs in barbecue sauce, gammon with egg and onion rings, steak in ale pie, mushrooms in a creamy brandy sauce with pasta, beef burger with mozzarella and bacon, cumberland sausage with caramelised onion mash and Guinness gravy, salmon in prawn and chive sauce with lemon and herb-crushed potatoes, pork escalope on a black pudding rösti with smoked bacon and wholegrain mustard sauce, and puddings such as elderflower crème brûlée and warm pecan tart with toffee sauce. *Benchmark main dish: half gressingham duckling with orange sauce £16.65. Two-course evening meal £20.50.*

Free house ~ Licensees Mr and Mrs R Thompson ~ Real ale ~ Bar food (12-2, 6-9) ~ Restaurant ~ (01439) 788239 ~ Children welcome ~ Open 12-3, 6-11; midday-1am Sat; 12-11 Sun ~ www.thewhiteswan-ampleforth.co.uk *Recommended by Margaret Dickinson, Dr and Mrs R G J Telfer, Ed and Anna Fraser*

ASENBY

Crab & Lobster ⑪ ♀ ⇐

SE3975 Map 7

Dishforth Road; village signed off A168 – handy for A1; YO7 3QL

Interesting furnishings and décor in rambling bar, inventive restaurant food, good drinks choice and seats on the attractive terrace; smart bedrooms

Much emphasis at this handsome and civilised place is placed on the hotel and restaurant side, but the rambling L-shaped bar still attracts customers dropping in for a drink and a chat, and they do keep Copper Dragon Golden Pippin and Hambleton Bitter on handpump and quite a few wines by the glass. The bustling bar has an interesting jumble of seats, from antique high-backed and other settles through sofas and wing armchairs heaped with cushions to tall and rather theatrical corner seats; the tables are almost as much of a mix, and the walls and available surfaces are quite a jungle of bric-a-brac including lots of race tickets, with standard and table lamps and candles keeping even the lighting pleasantly informal. There's also a cosy main restaurant and a dining pavilion with big tropical plants, nautical bits and pieces and Edwardian sofas; background music. The gardens have bamboo and palm trees lining the paths, which lead to a gazebo; there are seats on a mediterranean-style terrace. The opulent bedrooms (based on famous hotels around the world) are in the Georgian manor house hotel next door; they also have a few luxury log cabins in the grounds, which include seven acres of mature gardens and a 180-metre golf hole with full practice facilities.

Excellent – though certainly not cheap – food includes a lunchtime fish club sandwich (not Sunday), twice-baked cheese and spinach soufflé with orange-braised carrot ribbons and pine nut salad, terrine of duck confit, ham hock and rabbit with apricot, pear and ginger chutney, free-range chicken breast with prosciutto, basil, creamed cheese and parmesan on pasta, beer-battered fresh haddock with minted mushy peas and tartare sauce, loin of venison with a hazelnut crust, spiced beetroot soufflé, celeriac purée, wild mushrooms and truffled mash, salmon, baby crab cakes, wilted gem lettuce and a leek and sweetcorn chowder, and puddings such as baked rhubarb cheesecake with strawberry ripple ice-cream and a warm stem ginger custard and black forest bocker glory (chocolate cake, boozy black cherries, raspberry jam ice-cream, meringue crunch, whipped cream and chocolate bits). *Benchmark main dish: lobster thermidor with prawns and scallops £21. Two-course evening meal £26.00.*

Vimac Leisure ~ Licensee Mark Spenceley ~ Real ale ~ Bar food (12-2, 7(6.30 Sat)-9) ~ Restaurant ~ (01845) 577286 ~ Children welcome ~ Live jazz Sun lunchtime ~ Open 11am-11.30 pm ~ Bedrooms: /£160B ~ www.crabandlobster.co.uk *Recommended by Dr and Mrs R G J Telfer, Mike and Lynn Robinson, Marcus Mann, Taff and Gilly Thomas*

BLAKEY RIDGE
SE6799   Map 10

Lion 🍷 🛏

From A171 Guisborough–Whitby follow Castleton, Hutton le Hole signposts; from A170 Kirkby Moorside–Pickering follow Keldholm, Hutton le Hole, Castleton signposts; OS Sheet 100 map reference 679996; YO62 7LQ

Sizeable pub in fine scenery and open all day; bedrooms

Situated at the highest point of the North York Moors National Park (404 metres above sea level), this extended pub always has a good crowd of customers, despite being so remote. The views over the valleys of Rosedale and Farndale are breathtaking and there are lots of surrounding hikes; the Coast to Coast path is nearby. The low-beamed and rambling bars have open fires, a few big high-backed rustic settles around cast-iron framed tables, lots of small dining chairs, a nice leather sofa, and stone walls hung with some old engravings and photographs of the pub under snow (it can easily get cut off in winter; 40 days is the record so far). A fine choice of beers might include Black Sheep Best, Copper Dragon Golden Pippin, Greene King Old Speckled Hen, Theakstons Best and Old Peculier, and Thwaites Wainwright on handpump; background music and games machine. If you are thinking of staying, you must book well in advance. This is a regular stop-off for coach parties.

Popular food includes sandwiches, giant yorkshire pudding with gravy, filled baked potatoes, home-cooked ham and egg, mushroom stroganoff, lasagne, beef burger with a choice of sauces, chicken curry, battered cod and chips, duck breast with a port and juniper berry sauce, bass with a smoky bacon and chive butter, pork fillet with a watercress and ginger cream sauce, and puddings such as hot chocolate fudge cake and banana split. *Benchmark main dish: steak and mushroom pie £10.95. Two-course evening meal £21.00.*

Free house ~ Licensees Barry, Diana, Paul and David Crossland ~ Real ale ~ Bar food (12-10) ~ Restaurant ~ (01751) 417320 ~ Children welcome ~ Dogs allowed in bar ~ Open 10am-11pm(midnight Sat) ~ Bedrooms: £23(£44.50B)/£78B ~ www.lionblakey.co.uk *Recommended by Dr J Barrie Jones, G Jennings*

BOROUGHBRIDGE
SE3966   Map 7

Black Bull 🍷 £

St James Square; B6265, just off A1(M); YO51 9AR

Bustling town pub with real ales, several wines by the glass and traditional bar food; bedrooms

This attractive old town pub is said to date from the 13th c and has been looking after travellers between England and Scotland for centuries; these days it makes a good stop-off point from the busy A1. There are lots of separate drinking and eating areas where plenty of cheerful locals drop in regularly for a pint and a chat, and the main bar area has a big stone fireplace and comfortable seats and is served through an old-fashioned hatch; there's also a cosy snug with traditional wall settles and a tap room, lounge bar and restaurant. John Smiths, Timothy Taylors Best and a changing guest beer on handpump, six wines by the glass and 19 malt whiskies; dominoes. The borzoi dog is called Spot and the two cats are named Kia and Mershka. The hanging flower baskets are lovely.

As well as quite a choice of hot and cold sandwiches, the bar food includes a pie of the day, pork and chive sausages with onion gravy, beef curry, large battered haddock with mushy peas, fishcakes with chips, sizzling chicken in chinese spices, pork tenderloin with a pink peppercorn and calvados sauce, specials like vegetable lasagne, haddock in lemon and dill butter and venison steak with a bacon and blue cheese sauce, and puddings like jam sponge with custard and apple pie. *Benchmark main dish: pie of the day £8.50. Two-course evening meal £18.00.*

Free house ~ Licensee Anthony Burgess ~ Real ale ~ Bar food (12-2(2.30 Sun), 6-9(9.30 Fri and Sat) ~ Restaurant ~ (01423) 322413 ~ Children welcome ~ Dogs allowed in bar and bedrooms ~ Open 11-11(midnight Sat); 12-11 Sun ~ Bedrooms: £48S/£72S ~ www.blackbullboroughbridge.co.uk *Recommended by Ian and Nita Cooper, Mike and Lynn Robinson, C J Beresford-Jones, the Didler, Michael Butler, Barry Collett*

BRADFIELD
Strines Inn £ 🛏

SK2290 Map 7

From A57 heading E of junction with A6013 (Ladybower Reservoir) take first left turn (signposted Bradfield) then bear left; with a map can also be reached more circuitously from Strines signpost on A616 at head of Underbank Reservoir, W of Stocksbridge; S6 6JE

Surrounded by fine scenery with quite a mix of customers and traditional beer and bar food; bedrooms

Although a bustling pub since the 18th c, the building is actually five centuries older and it's surrounded by superb scenery and is in the Peak District National Park. Young, friendly and attentive staff offer a warm welcome to walkers and their well-behaved dogs and children, and the atmosphere is pleasant and easy-going. The main bar has black beams liberally decked with copper kettles and so forth, quite a menagerie of stuffed animals, homely red plush-cushioned wooden wall benches and small chairs, and a coal fire in the rather grand stone fireplace. Two other rooms to the right and left are similarly furnished. Bradfield Brown Cow, Jennings Cocker Hoop, Kelham Island Pale Rider and Marstons Pedigree on handpump and several wines by the glass; background music. There are plenty of picnic-sets outside, as well as swings and a play area, and peacocks, geese and chickens. The bedrooms have four-poster beds and a dining table, as the good breakfasts are served in your room – the front room overlooks the reservoir.

The reasonably priced food includes sandwiches, game and port pâté, giant yorkshire pudding with onion gravy, vegetable lasagne, beef burger with chips, liver and onions, a huge mixed grill, specials like pork belly with cider gravy, a fish dish of the day and minted lamb shank, and puddings such as apple pie and chocolate fudge cake. *Benchmark main dish: steak in ale pie £9.25. Two-course evening meal £13.00.*

Free house ~ Licensee Bruce Howarth ~ Real ale ~ Bar food (12-2.30, 5.30-8.30 winter weekdays; all day in summer and winter weekends) ~ (0114) 285 1247 ~ Children

welcome ~ Dogs welcome ~ Open 10.30am-11pm; 10.30-3, 5.30-11 weekdays in winter ~
Bedrooms: £60B/£80B ~ www.thestrinesinn.webs.com *Recommended by the Didler, Brian
and Anna Marsden, Malcolm and Barbara Southwell, Gordon and Margaret Ormondroyd, Brian
and Janet Ainscough*

BREARTON
SE3260 Map 7
Malt Shovel
Village signposted off A61 N of Harrogate; HG3 3BX

**Friendly, family-run dining pub with imaginative food and good choice
of drinks in heavily beamed rooms; airy conservatory**

Run by the friendly Bleiker family, this bustling country dining pub
offers a warm welcome to all. The heavily beamed rooms have a
cosy atmosphere helped by the two fires in original fireplaces and the
woodburning stove, and radiate from the attractive linenfold oak bar
counter (made from old church panelling). There's an attractive mix of
wooden dining chairs around tables on wood or slate floors and some
partitioning that separates several candlelit dining areas. Black Sheep
Best and Timothy Taylors Landlord on handpump, 20 wines by the glass
from a very good list and several malt whiskies. The conservatory is light
and airy with lemon trees and a piano (which is used for Sunday jazz);
they also hold occasional live opera evenings. There are seats and tables
under parasols in the garden and pretty summer hanging baskets. The
family is also associated with Bleiker's Smokehouse near Harrogate.

They bake their own bread and rear their own pigs for the popular food,
which might include sandwiches, a trio of home-smoked and cured salmon,
foie gras and chicken liver parfait, a charcuterie and a fish board to share, spinach
pancake with cheese sauce, chicken with lemon and thyme, calves liver and bacon,
wienerschnitzel with dauphinoise potatoes, half a crispy roast duck with orange
sauce, specials like moules marinière and fillet of bream with brown shimp and
caper butter, and puddings such as chocolate fondant tart with hot chocolate sauce
and lemon posset with lemon ice-cream. *Benchmark main dish: barnsley chop
with sauce vièrge £16.95. Two-course evening meal £23.50.*

Free house ~ Licensee Jurg Bleiker ~ Real ale ~ Bar food (12-2, 5.30-9; 12-4 Sun; not
Sun evening, Mon or Tues) ~ Restaurant ~ (01423) 862929 ~ Children welcome ~ Jazz
pianist Sun, occasional opera evenings with dinner ~ Open 12-3, 5.30-11; 12-3 Sun;
closed Sun evening, all day Mon and Tues ~ www.themaltsshovelbrearton.co.uk
Recommended by Peter Hacker, Michael Butler, Emma Parr, Comus and Sarah Elliott

BROUGHTON
SD9450 Map 7
Bull
A59; BD23 3AE

**Handsome, carefully refurbished inn making good use of pale oak and
contemporary paintwork, good choice of drinks and enjoyable food**

Overlooking the grounds of Broughton Hall, this handsome stone inn
is now under the Ribble Valley Inns umbrella. The various carefully
furnished rooms have lots of pale oak, handsome flagstones, exposed
stone walls, built-in wall seats and a mix of dining chairs around
polished tables, contemporary paintwork hung with photographs of
local suppliers, and open log fires. Bowland Sawley Tempted, Copper
Dragon Scotts 1816, Dark Horse Hetton Pale Ale, and Moorhouses Pride
of Pendle on handpump, several malt whiskies and around a dozen wines
(including champagne) by the glass. Outside, there are solid benches and

tables on the attractive terrace; you can walk through the Hall Estate's 3,000 acres of beautiful countryside and parkland.

Bar food now includes sandwiches, creamed field mushrooms on toast, smoked kipper pâté, toad in the hole, chicken in a mustard and cayenne pepper marinade with piri piri sauce, twice-baked cheese soufflé with pears and toasted walnut salad, rump burger on a toasted muffin with dripping chips, pickles, tomato relish, battered onion rings and english mustard mayonnaise (extra toppings like cheese, bacon and a free-range egg), fish pie, veal kidneys with bacon, onions and mushroom sauce, and puddings such as baked alaska and chocolate cake with salted hazelnuts and milk chocolate ice-cream. *Benchmark main dish: beer-battered fish and chips £12.75. Two-course evening meal £18.00.*

Ribble Valley Inns ~ Manager Leanne Richardson ~ Real ale ~ Bar food (12-2, 5.30-8.30 (9 Fri and Sat); 12-8 Sun) ~ (01756) 792065 ~ Children welcome ~ Dogs allowed in bar ~ Open 12-11(10.30 Sun); closed Mon ~ www.thebullatbroughton.com *Recommended by G Jennings, Hilary Forrest, Margaret and Jeff Graham, Ed and Anna Fraser*

CONSTABLE BURTON   SE1690   Map 10

Wyvill Arms 🍴 🍷 🍺 🛏

A684 E of Leyburn; DL8 5LH

Well run, friendly dining pub with interesting food, a dozen wines by the glass, real ales and efficient, helpful service; comfortable bedrooms

Our readers enjoy their visits to this well run 18th-c former farmhouse – both for the first class food and as somewhere comfortable to stay. There's a small bar area with a mix of seating, a finely worked plaster ceiling with the Wyvill family's coat of arms and an elaborate stone fireplace with a warm winter fire. The second bar has a lower ceiling with fans, leather seating, old oak tables, various alcoves and a model train on a railway track running around the room; the reception area has a huge leather sofa which can seat up to eight people, another carved stone fireplace and an old leaded church stained-glass window partition. Both rooms are hung with pictures of local scenes. The three real ales on handpump come from breweries like Hambleton, Theakstons and Wensleydale, and they have a dozen wines by the glass and ten malt whiskies; chess, backgammon and dominoes. There are several large wooden benches under large white parasols for outdoor dining and picnic-sets by a well. Constable Burton Gardens are opposite and worth a visit.

Imaginative and highly enjoyable, the food – using home-grown produce and game from the estate across the road – might include lunchtime sandwiches, scallops on pea purée with Café de Paris butter and coral dust, pigeon breast with smoked venison, black pudding and bacon lardons, home-made sausages with mash and red wine gravy, parmesan pork with ratatouille and fried new potatoes, chicken stuffed with mozzarella and pancetta with stilton sauce, monkfish wrapped in parma ham with a thai-style risotto, fillet steak rolled in 21 spices with smoked bacon and red wine reduction, and puddings such as caramel panna cotta with home-made gingerbread and home-grown rhubarb parfait with rhubarb spaghetti. *Benchmark main dish: herbed lamb fillet with dauphinoise gratin and parsnip purée £15.50. Two-course evening meal £21.00.*

Free house ~ Licensee Nigel Stevens ~ Real ale ~ Bar food (12-2, 5.30(6 Sun)-9; not Mon) ~ Restaurant ~ (01677) 450581 ~ Children welcome until 8.30 ~ Dogs allowed in bar and bedrooms ~ Open 11-3, 5.30(6 Sun)-11; closed Mon ~ Bedrooms: £60B/£85B ~ www.thewyvillarms.co.uk *Recommended by Ed and Anna Fraser, Noel Thomas, Donna Jenkins, Jill and Julian Tasker, John and Sylvia Harrop*

COXWOLD
SE5377 Map 7

Fauconberg Arms

Off A170 Thirsk–Helmsley, via Kilburn or Wass; easily found off A19, too;
YO61 4AD

**Family-run inn with highly popular food, a good range of drinks and
seats in the back garden; comfortable bedrooms**

Named after Lord Fauconberg, who married Oliver Cromwell's
daughter Mary, this is a family-run, nicely updated 17th-c inn with
a friendly welcome for all – children and dogs included. The heavily
beamed and flagstoned bar has log fires in both linked areas – one in an
unusual arched fireplace in a broad, low inglenook – muted contemporary
colours, some attractive oak chairs by local craftsmen alongside more
usual pub furnishings, nicely chosen old local photographs and other
pictures, and copper implements and china. Theakstons Best and Wold
Top Gold on handpump, a thoughtful choice of wines by the glass and 28
malt whiskies. The pub dogs are called Peggy, Bramble and Phoebe. The
candlelit dining room is quietly elegant with a gently upmarket yet relaxed
atmosphere. The garden behind the inn has seats and tables on the
terrace and views across the fields to Byland Abbey; picnic-sets and teak
benches look out on the front cobbles along this charming village's broad
tree-lined verges, bright with flower tubs. This is a nice place to stay and
the breakfasts are very good. They have a shop selling home-baked bread,
their own cheese and other groceries.

Cooked by the landlord and his daughters using seasonal local produce and
game, the much enjoyed food includes lunchtime sandwiches, black pudding
with a red onion salad and balsamic glaze, prawn cocktail, home-made beef
burgers, chicken with prawns and button mushrooms in Pernod-laced creamy sauce
with wild rice, fresh Whitby scampi, rack of lamb with a herb crust and a lamb
stock, rosemary and red wine gravy, pork medallions with a ginger and apple cider
gravy, half a roast duck with a damson and honey sauce, and puddings. *Benchmark
main dish: beer-battered fish and chips £10.95. Two-course evening meal £20.00.*

Free house ~ Licensee Simon Rheinberg ~ Real ale ~ Bar food (12-2.30(3 weekends),
6.30(6 Sun)-9(8 Sun)) ~ Restaurant ~ (01347) 868214 ~ Children welcome ~ Dogs
welcome ~ Open 11-3, 6-midnight; 11-midnight Sat; 11-11 Sun ~ Bedrooms: /£105S ~
www.fauconbergarms.com *Recommended by Pete Coxon, Tony and Glenys Dyer, Peter Hacker,
Michael Doswell, Janet and Peter Race, Pat and Tony Martin*

CRAYKE
SE5670 Map 7

Durham Ox

Off B1363 at Brandsby, towards Easingwold; West Way; YO61 4TE

**Friendly, well run inn, interesting décor in old-fashioned,
relaxing rooms, fine drinks and smashing food; lovely views
and comfortable bedrooms**

Our readers very much enjoy staying in the comfortable bedrooms in
the converted farm buildings here and the breakfasts are excellent.
Part of Provenance Inns, it's particularly well run by the helpful landlord
and his staff, and there's always a bustling, friendly atmosphere –
particularly in the evening. The old-fashioned lounge bar has an
enormous inglenook fireplace, pictures and photographs on the dark red
walls, interesting satirical carvings in the panelling (Victorian copies of
medieval pew ends), polished copper and brass, and venerable tables,
antique seats and settles on the flagstones. In the bottom bar is a framed

illustrated account of local history (some of it gruesome) dating back to the 12th c, and a large framed print of the original famous Durham Ox which weighed just over a tonne. The Burns Bar has a woodburning stove, exposed brickwork and large french windows that open on to a balcony area. Black Sheep Best, Timothy Taylors Landlord and a changing guest on handpump, 10 wines by the glass and several malt whiskies; background music. There are seats in the courtyard garden and fantastic views over the Vale of York on three sides; on the fourth side there's a charming view up the hill to the medieval church – the tale is that this is the hill up which the Grand Old Duke of York marched his men. They hold interesting regular events such as a Meet the Brewers evening hosted by Timothy Taylors and cookery demonstrations from the head chef. The nearby A19 leads straight to a Park and Ride for York.

Making their own bread and petits fours, the imaginative food includes pubby dishes like sandwiches, beef burger with cheese, bacon, onion rings and chunky chips, fish and chips with mushy peas and tartare sauce and eggs benedict or royale, as well as beetroot-cured organic salmon with a quail egg and rocket salad, carpaccio of fillet of beef, twice-baked blue cheese soufflé with cauliflower purée and walnut dressing, rack of sticky pork ribs with spicy beans, coleslaw and skinny fries, braised lamb shoulder with red wine jus and sweet potato, guinea fowl breast with wild mushroom fricassée and tarragon cream, bass fillets with caper and lemon butter, a seafood platter to share, daily specials, and puddings such as chocolate marquise with coconut ice-cream and sticky toffee pudding with toffee sauce. *Benchmark main dish: rib-eye steak and frites £19.95. Two-course evening meal £22.00.*

Free house ~ Licensee Michael Ibbotson ~ Real ale ~ Bar food (12-2.30(3 Sun), 5.30-9.30(8.30 Sun) ~ Restaurant ~ (01347) 821506 ~ Children welcome ~ Dogs allowed in bedrooms ~ Open 12-11 ~ Bedrooms: £80B/£100B ~ www.thedurhamox.com
Recommended by Pete Coxon, Michael Doswell, Tony and Wendy Hobden, Jeff and Wendy Williams, Peter and Anne Hollindale, Ed and Anna Fraser, Liz Bell, S and D Hunter, Roger and Diana Morgan, Ian Malone, Neil Ingoe, John and Sylvia Harrop

CROPTON

New Inn 🍺

Village signposted off A170 W of Pickering; YO18 8HH

SE7588   Map 10

Genuinely warm welcome in a modernised village pub with own-brew beers, traditional furnishings and brewery tours; bedrooms

The own-brew beers here continue to draw in happy customers and the six on handpump at any one time from their Cropton Brewery might include Blackout, Endeavour, Monkmans Slaughter, North Peak Vicious, Two Pints and Yorkshire Warrior; they also have craft lagers, a dozen malt whiskies and seven wines by the glass. The traditional village bar has wood panelling, plush seating, lots of brass and a small fire. A local artist has designed the historical posters all around the downstairs conservatory that doubles as a visitor centre at busy times. The elegant restaurant has locally made furniture and paintings by local artists. Background music, TV, games machine, darts, pool and a juke box. There's a neat terrace, a garden with a pond and a brewery shop. Brewery tours are available most days at £4.95 per person.

As well as lunchtime sandwiches, the bar food might include ham hock terrine, prawn and crayfish salad, sausage ring with onion gravy, lasagne, broccoli and blue cheese flan, beer-battered cod and chips, chicken wensleydale, steak in ale pie, and puddings such as apple and rhubarb crumble and chocolate brownie sundae. *Benchmark main dish: steak pie £9.50. Two-course evening meal £15.00.*

Own brew ~ Licensee Philip Lee ~ Real ale ~ Bar food (12-2(2.30 Sun), 6-9(8.30 Sun) ~ Restaurant ~ (01751) 417330 ~ Well behaved children welcome ~ Dogs allowed in bar and bedrooms ~ Folk festival four times a year ~ Open 11-11(midnight Sat) ~ Bedrooms: £60B/£85B ~ www.croptonbrewery.com *Recommended by Tony and Wendy Hobden, Mike and Mary Strigenz, Mo and David Trudgill, Derek and Sylvia Stephenson, David and Lin Short*

DOWNHOLME
Bolton Arms
SE1197   Map 10

Village signposted just off A6108 Leyburn–Richmond; DL11 6AE

Enjoyable food in unusual village's cosy country pub, lovely views, garden; bedrooms

This little stone-built pub is one of the last pubs in Britain that belongs to the state – the Ministry of Defence owns the place, along with the village itself, and it's surrounded by MoD land (a largely unspoilt swathe of Swaledale). The friendly and softly lit black-beamed and carpeted bar is down a few steps and has two smallish linked areas off the servery, where they keep Black Sheep Best and Timothy Taylors Landlord on handpump, eight wines by the glass at fair prices, and ten malt whiskies. There are comfortable plush wall banquettes, a log fire in one neat fireplace, quite a lot of gleaming brass, a few small country pictures and drinks advertisements on pinkish rough-plastered walls; service is friendly and efficient. Background music and dominoes. The neat garden, on the same level as the dining room (and up steps from the front), and the back conservatory both offer views; there are also some lower picnic-sets and benches, and quoits.

Cooked by the landlord, the tasty pubby dishes include sandwiches, creamy garlic mushrooms topped with cheese and bacon, spinach and ricotta pancakes, cumberland sausage with onion gravy, gammon and egg with mushrooms and onion rings, lasagne, battered haddock with home-made tartare sauce, lambs liver and bacon, thai king prawn stir fry, and puddings such as vanilla cheesecake with berries and tiramisu. *Benchmark main dish: lamb kleftiko £14.75.* Two-course evening meal £17.00.

Free house ~ Licensees Steve and Nicola Ross ~ Real ale ~ Bar food (12-2, 6-9; not Tues lunchtime) ~ Restaurant ~ (01748) 823716 ~ Children welcome ~ Dogs allowed in bedrooms ~ Open 11-3, 6-midnight; closed Tues lunchtime ~ Bedrooms: £45S/£60S ~ www.boltonarmsdownholme.com *Recommended by Dr D Jeary, Ed and Anna Fraser*

EAST WITTON
Blue Lion 🍴 ☺ ⇔
SE1486   Map 10

A6108 Leyburn–Ripon; DL8 4SN

Civilised dining pub with interesting rooms, daily papers, real ales, delicious food and courteous service; comfortable bedrooms

'One of the best pubs we've been to' and 'faultless' are just two of the warmly enthusiastic reader reports we've had on this 18th-c former coaching inn over the past year. Whether it's just for a drink and a chat, for an excellent meal or for an overnight stay in the very comfortable bedrooms, this place is first class. It's civilised but informal and the proper little bar has a good mix of drinkers and their dogs mingling quite happily with those waiting to eat. This big, squarish room has soft lighting, high-backed antique settles and old windsor chairs on the turkish rugs and flagstones, ham-hooks in the high ceiling decorated with dried wheat, teazles and so forth, a delft shelf filled with bric-a-brac, several prints, sporting caricatures and other pictures, a log fire and daily papers. Black Sheep Best and Golden Sheep and Theakstons Best on handpump, and an impressive list of wines with quite a few (plus champagne) served by the glass; courteous, charming and attentive service. Picnic-sets on the gravel outside look beyond the stone houses on the far side of the village green to Witton Fell, and there's a big, pretty back garden.

Inventive and delicious – if not cheap – food might include sandwiches, home-made pork pie with pickled onions and piccalilli, soft shell crab deep-fried with fennel salad and chilli and ginger jam, local game terrine with kumquat and thyme relish, baked portabello mushroom topped with spinach and a poached egg, rabbit and chicken ballotine, confit leg orzotto (similar to risotto but made with pearl barley), roasted salsify, red wine onions and tarragon velouté, roasted black bream with spinach linguine, parsnip purée, turnips and port, pheasant breast with potato terrine, creamed kale and juniper jus, and puddings such as warm hazelnut cake with hazelnut mousse and filo crisps and dark chocolate marquise with home-made marshmallows, candied banana and salted caramel. *Benchmark main dish: slow-braised pork belly with black pudding and apple and grain mustard cream £15.50. Two-course evening meal £24.00.*

Free house ~ Licensee Paul Klein ~ Real ale ~ Bar food (12-2, 7-9) ~ Restaurant ~ (01969) 624273 ~ Children welcome ~ Dogs allowed in bar and bedrooms ~ Open 11-11 ~ Bedrooms: £67.50S/£94S(£109B) ~ www.thebluelion.co.uk *Recommended by Michael Butler, Susan and Neil McLean, Dr Kevan Tucker, Janet and Peter Race, the Didler, Hunter and Christine Wright, Comus and Sarah Elliott, Mrs W Montague, Rod Stoneman, Lynda and Trevor Smith, Neil and Angela Huxter, John and Dinah Waters, Rob and Catherine Dunster*

ELSLACK

Tempest Arms 🍴 ♀ 🍺 🛏

SD9249   Map 7

Just off A56 Earby–Skipton; BD23 3AY

Friendly inn with three log fires in stylish rooms, six real ales, good wines and extremely popular food; bedrooms

With a good atmosphere, friendly, efficient licensees and staff and a fantastic location close to the Yorkshire Dales, it's no wonder this 18th-c stone dining inn is so popular. There's a wide mix of customers coming and going, from families to diners and walkers with their dogs, but everyone is made to feel welcome and relaxed. It's stylish but understated and cosy with plenty of character in the bar and surrounding dining areas: cushioned armchairs, built-in wall seats with comfortable cushions, stools and lots of tables and three log fires – one greets you at the entrance and divides the bar and restaurant. There's quite a bit of exposed stonework, amusing prints on the cream walls, half a dozen real ales such as Dark Horse Hetton Pale Ale, Ilkley Mary Jane, Theakstons Best, Thwaites Wainwright, and a beer named for the pub on handpump, lots of wines by the glass and up to 14 malt whiskies. There are tables outside largely screened from the road by a raised bank. The comfortable bedrooms are in a newish purpose-built extension and our readers enjoy staying here very much.

Highly enjoyable and generously served, the food includes open sandwiches, baby squid stuffed with chorizo, parsley and shallots on linguine, hand-rolled duck and vegetable spring rolls with sweet chilli and soy dipping sauce, gammon with fried eggs, toad in the hole with wild boar sausages and onion gravy, red thai chicken curry, beer-battered haddock with mushy peas and home-made tartare sauce, steak and mushroom in ale pudding, venison steak on mustard and chive mash with caramelised shallot and smoked bacon sauce, a mixed grill, and puddings. *Benchmark main dish: braised shoulder of lamb £14.95. Two-course evening meal £19.50.*

Free house ~ Licensees Martin and Veronica Clarkson ~ Real ale ~ Bar food (12-2.30, 6-9(9.30 Fri and Sat); 12-7.30 Sun) ~ Restaurant ~ (01282) 842450 ~ Children welcome ~ Dogs allowed in bar and bedrooms ~ Open 11-11; 12-10.30 Sun ~ Bedrooms: £62.50B/ £82.95B ~ www.tempestarms.co.uk *Recommended by John and Eleanor Holdsworth, Brian and Janet Ainscough, Ian Malone, Pat and Tony Martin, Michael Butler, Christopher Mobbs, Janet and Peter Race, Chris Brewster, Tony and Maggie Harwood, Mrs Edna M Jones, Gordon and Margaret Ormondroyd, David and Ruth Shillitoe, Jeremy King, Bruce and Sharon Eden, Steve Whalley, S Holder*

 FELIXKIRK   SE4684   Map 10

Carpenters Arms

Village signed off A170 E of Thirsk; YO7 2DP

Pretty village pub, carefully refurbished, with opened-up rooms, beams and candlelight, friendly service, real ales and highly thought of food; lodge-style bedrooms

With both short and long-distance walks nearby, this refurbished village pub is a friendly place in a quiet setting – and just the place to relax. It's been opened up inside and now has a good, spacious pubby feel with a warm welcome for drinkers, diners and dogs (in the bar). There are dark beams and joists, candlelight and fresh flowers and the bar has a relaxed atmosphere, with stools against the panelled counter where they keep Black Sheep Best and Timothy Taylors Landlord on handpump and 15 wines by the glass, and a mix of chairs and tables on big flagstones; there's also a snug seating area with tartan armchairs in front of the double-sided woodburning stove. The red-walled dining room has a mix of antique and country kitchen chairs around scrubbed tables; throughout, the walls are hung with traditional prints, local pictures and maps. As we went to press, a new extension was being opened, which will house a new dining area, a private dining room and eight lodge-style bedrooms (there are two in the pub itself) overlooking the landscaped garden. The front of the pub enjoys all-day sunshine and is a fine spot in warm weather; large planters shield the outside seating area from the road. The pub is part of Provenance Inns.

Well presented food using local seasonal produce might include sandwiches, eggs benedict, twice-baked goats cheese soufflé, pigeon salad with celeriac and apple salad with a hazelnut dressing, potato gnocchi with butternut squash, wild mushrooms and spinach, beer-battered haddock with mushy peas, rack of spicy and sticky pork ribs, confit shoulder of lamb with garlic-mashed potato and rosemary jus, a fish platter, and puddings like chocolate marquise with candied orange and Cointreau syrup and sticky toffee pudding with toffee sauce; they also offer an early-bird menu before 7pm with seven dishes at £7 each. *Benchmark main dish: baked queen scallops with gruyère and cheddar crust £13.95. Two-course evening meal £20.00.*

Free house ~ Licensee Michael Ibbotson ~ Real ale ~ Bar food (12-2.30(3 Sun), 5.30(6 Sat)-9.30(8.30 Sun)) ~ (01845) 537369 ~ Children welcome ~ Dogs allowed in bar and bedrooms ~ Open 12-11.30(10.30 Sun) ~ Bedrooms: /£145S ~ www.thecarpentersarmsfelixkirk.com *Recommended by Robert Wivell, Ed and Anna Fraser, Jill and Julian Tasker, Ray and Rita Bannon*

FERRENSBY
General Tarleton 🍴 ♟ 🛏

SE3660 Map 7

A655 N of Knaresborough; HG5 0PZ

Stylish coaching inn with enterprising restauranty food, lots of wines by the glass, courteous service and a relaxed atmosphere; comfortable bedrooms

The emphasis at this civilised and smart restaurant-with-rooms is on the exceptional food, but they do keep Black Sheep Best and Timothy Taylors Landlord on handpump and several good wines by the glass, and service is friendly and helpful. You can enjoy a drink in the more informal bar area with its comfortable sofas and woodburning stove; the rest of the rambling open-plan rooms have low beams, brick pillars creating cosy alcoves, some exposed stonework, dark leather high-backed dining chairs grouped around wooden tables and plenty of prints on the cream walls. A door leads out to a pleasant tree-lined garden – seats here as well as in a covered courtyard. The bedrooms are well equipped and individually decorated and the breakfasts excellent.

Beautifully presented and cooked by the chef/patron, the first class food includes their famous little moneybags (seafood in a crisp pastry bag with lobster sauce), braised pig cheek with fennel and shallots, crisp pigs ears and celeriac purée, butternut squash ravioli with butternut purée and herb oil salad, local sausages with red onion marmalade and mash, home-made -angus beef burger with cheddar, pancetta and triple-cooked chips, corn-fed poached and roast breast of duckling with black peas and duck jus, haunch of venison with steak and kidney pie and game jus, bass fillet on a vine tomato and olive tart with basil pesto, and puddings such as chocolate fondant with orange ice-cream and mandarin jelly and sticky toffee pudding with caramel sauce and vanilla ice-cream; they also serve two- and three-course set menus (not Sunday lunchtime). *Benchmark main dish: assiette of rabbit £18.95. Two-course evening meal £26.00.*

Free house ~ Licensee John Topham ~ Real ale ~ Bar food (12-2, 5.30-9.15(8.30 Sun)) ~ (01423) 340284 ~ Children welcome ~ Open 12-3, 6-11 (10.30 Sun) ~ Bedrooms: £85B/£129B ~ www.generaltarleton.co.uk *Recommended by Richard and Mary Bailey, Pat and Graham Williamson, Michael Doswell, Janet and Peter Race, John and Eleanor Holdsworth, Michael Butler, J F M and M West*

GRANTLEY
Grantley Arms 🍴 ♟

SE2369 Map 7

Village signposted off B6265 W of Ripon; HG4 3PJ

Relaxed and interesting dining pub with good food

Dating from the 17th c, this place has a huge fireplace built of massive stone blocks housing the woodburning stove in the front bar, which has brown beams supporting its shiny cream ceiling planks. It's traditionally furnished – green wall banquettes, comfortable dining chairs, nightlights on polished tables (some cast-iron-framed) and flowery carpet, with some of the landlady's own paintings of ponies and dogs above the green dado. The back dining room has crisp linen tablecloths, decorative plates and more paintings, mainly landscapes here. They have well chosen wines and Great Newsome Pricky Back Otchan and Theakstons Best on handpump; attentive friendly service. Teak tables and chairs on the flagstoned front terrace have a pleasant outlook, and Fountains Abbey and Studley Royal are nearby.

🍴 Well presented and very good, the food might include sandwiches, duck egg with scallops and black pudding, chicken liver parfait with shallot marmalade, beer-battered fresh haddock with mushy peas and tartare sauce, cheese and caramelised onion tart, chicken breast with parmesan and leek fondue and rocket and parmesan salad, a fish dish of the day, pork fillet with apple purée and buttered onions, venison haunch steak with parsnip purée, walnut sauce and parsnip crisps, steaks with pepper or red wine sauce, and puddings such as coconut mousse with coconut meringue, pineapple salad and pineapple sorbet and dark chocolate terrine with confit orange, orange segments and orange ice-cream. *Benchmark main dish: pie of the week £13.95. Two-course evening meal £18.95.*

Free house ~ Licensees Valerie and Eric Sails ~ Real ale ~ Bar food (12-2,5.30-9(Sun 12-3.30,5.30-8)) ~ Restaurant ~ (01765) 620227 ~ Well behaved children welcome ~ Open 12-3, 5.30-10.30; may close early if not busy; 12-11 Sat; 12-10.30 Sun; closed Monday (except bank holidays) ~ www.grantleyarms.com *Recommended by John and Eleanor Holdsworth, Grahame Brooks, Ed and Anna Fraser, Mrs Blethyn Elliott*

GRINTON   SE0498 Map 10

Bridge Inn 🍺 🛏

B6270 W of Richmond; DL11 6HH

Bustling pub with traditional, comfortable bars, log fires, several real ales and malt whiskies, and tasty bar food; neat bedrooms

With its lovely surrounding walks in and around this pretty Swaledale village, a warm welcome for dogs and a relaxing, comfortable atmosphere, this former coaching inn is an obvious choice for walkers. There are bow-window seats and a pair of stripped traditional settles among more usual pub seats (all well-cushioned), a good log fire, Jennings Cumberland and Soggy Bottom and a guest like Ringwood Best on handpump, several wines by the glass and 20 malt whiskies. On the right, a few steps take you down into a room with darts and ring the bull. On the left, past leather armchairs and a sofa by a second log fire (and a glass chess set) is an extensive two-part dining room. The décor is in mint green and shades of brown, with a modicum of fishing memorabilia. The bedrooms are neat, simple and comfortable, and breakfasts are good. The inn is right opposite a lovely church known as the Cathedral of the Dales, and has picnic-sets outside.

🍴 Curing their own bacon, making their own black pudding and using their own smokehouse, they serve food all day. It might include filled baguettes, black pudding scotch egg with mustard dressing, smoked salmon and prawns on cucumber salad with beetroot salsa, wild mushroom and chestnut casserole with root vegetable mash and cheese, steak in ale pie, lamb hotpot, free-range chicken breast glazed with honey and thyme on a mushroom ragoût topped with crispy bacon lardons, bass fillet with mussels, garlic and creamy white wine sauce, and puddings such as ginger sponge with sticky toffee sauce and vanilla ice-cream and pear and amaretto cheesecake on a dark chocolate biscuit base. *Benchmark main dish: beer-battered cod and chips £9.95. Two-course evening meal £18.45.*

Jennings (Marstons) ~ Lease Andrew Atkin ~ Real ale ~ Bar food (12-9) ~ Restaurant ~ (01748) 884224 ~ Children welcome ~ Dogs allowed in bar and bedrooms ~ Open 12-11 ~ Bedrooms: $51B/$82B ~ www.bridgeinn-grinton.co.uk *Recommended by JJW, CMW, Sandie and Andrew Geddes, Comus and Sarah Elliott*

The 🍺 symbol shows pubs which keep their beer unusually well, have a particularly good range or brew their own.

HALIFAX
Shibden Mill 🍴 ☐ 🍺
SE1027 Map 7

*Off A58 into Kell Lane at Stump Cross Inn, near A6036 junction; keep on,
pub signposted from Kell Lane on left; HX3 7UL*

**Tucked-away 300-year-old mill with cosy rambling bar, four real ales
and inventive bar food; comfortable bedrooms**

Tucked away at the bottom of a peaceful wooded valley and full of
nooks and crannies, this restored 17th-c mill has the feel of a hidden
treasure. Offering excellent food and friendly service and surrounded by
stunning countryside, it attracts a happy mix of both locals and visitors.
The rambling bar has a bustling atmosphere, cosy side areas with
banquettes heaped with cushions and rugs, well spaced attractive old
tables and chairs, and the candles in elegant iron holders give a feeling of
real intimacy; also, old hunting prints, country landscapes and so forth,
and a couple of big log fires. Cross Bay Nightfall, Little Valley Withens
IPA, Moorhouses's Premier Bitter and a guest beer on handpump and 18
wines by the glass from a long list. There's also an upstairs restaurant;
background music and TV. Outside on the attractive heated terrace, there
are plenty of seats and tables, and the building is prettily floodlit at night.
The bedrooms are well equipped and individually decorated.

Enterprising and highly thought of, the food might include sandwiches, a
plate of local game (venison sausage roll, rabbit pasty and game and mustard
terrine) with brussel sprout coleslaw, home beetroot-cured wild salmon with
horseradish mayonnaise and apple fritters, jerusalem artichoke risotto with red
wine-poached salsify, steak in ale pie with home-made brown sauce, steak burger
with fries, onion rings, cheese and smoked ketchup and mustard, sausages of the
day with mash and onion gravy, grilled line-caught mackerel with hand-made
scallop and coriander ravioli, celeriac and apple remoulade and caper velouté,
guinea fowl breast with pressed rabbit, fondant potato, parsnip purée and garlic
and sage cream sauce, and puddings such as potted chocolate orange soufflé with
kumquat marmalade and roast figs with toasted brioche, vanilla syrup and almond
ice-cream; interesting local cheeses. *Benchmark main dish: venison rump with
macadamia and marrowbone crust, truffle gnocchi and madeira and balsamic
jus £17.95. Two-course evening meal £22.00.*

Free house ~ Licensee Glen Pearson ~ Real ale ~ Bar food (12-2(2.30 Fri and Sat),
6-9.30; 12-7.30 Sun) ~ Restaurant ~ (01422) 365840 ~ Children welcome ~ Dogs
allowed in bar ~ Open 12-2.30, 5.30-11; 12-11(10.30 Sun) Sat ~ Bedrooms: £85B/£105B ~
www.shibdenmillinn.com *Recommended by Ian Malone, Peter Burton, Derek and Sylvia
Stephenson, Michael Butler, Gordon and Margaret Ormondroyd*

HARTSHEAD
Gray Ox 🍴 ☐
SE1822 Map 7

*3.5 miles from M62 junction 25; A644 towards Dewsbury, left on to A62,
next left on to B6119, then first left on to Fall Lane; left into Hartshead Lane; pub on
right; WF15 8AL*

**Attractive dining pub with cosy beamed bars, inventive cooking, real
ales, several wines by the glass and fine views**

With a good value two- and three-course set menu at lunchtime
and in the early evening, and being so handy for the M62, this
attractive stone-built pub is always full of happy customers. The main
bar has beams and flagstones, bentwood chairs, leather stools around
stripped-pine tables and a roaring log fire. Comfortable carpeted dining

areas with bold paintwork and leather dining chairs around polished tables lead off; the hunting-theme wallpaper is interesting and unusual. Jennings Cumberland, Cocker Hoop, Sneck Lifter and a changing guest on handpump, 14 wines by the glass and two champagnes; background music. There are picnic-sets outside, and fine views through the latticed pub windows across the Calder Valley to the distant outskirts of Huddersfield – the lights are pretty at night.

As well as the early-bird menu, the good, popular food includes sandwiches, chicken liver parfait with spiced tomato chutney, king scallops with thai salad and soy dressing, pork sausages with an apple fritter, creamy mash and red wine jus, roast butternut squash gnocchi with toasted pine nuts and pesto dressing, gammon with a poached egg and pineapple pickle, chicken breast on a leek and potato rösti with goats cheese and a red onion spring roll and wholegrain mustard cream, moules marinière and frites, crispy pork belly with black pudding mash and pancetta cream sauce, and puddings like dark chocolate torte with milk sorbet and sticky toffee pudding with butterscotch sauce. *Benchmark main dish: beer-battered haddock and chips with mushy peas £12.00. Two-course evening meal £20.00.*

Banks's (Marstons) ~ Lease Bernadette McCarron ~ Real ale ~ Bar food (12-2, 6-9(9.30 Sat); 12-7 Sun) ~ (01274) 872845 ~ Children welcome ~ Open 12-3, 6-midnight; 12-midnight Sat; 12-11 Sun ~ www.grayoxinn.co.uk *Recommended by Carl Rahn Griffith, Gordon and Margaret Ormondroyd, Tim and Sue Halstead, Sam and Christine Kilburn, Dr Kevan Tucker, Jeremy King, Glenwys and Alan Lawrence*

HEATH
Kings Arms ◀ £

SE3520 Map 7

Village signposted from A655 Wakefield–Normanton – or, more directly, turn off to the left opposite the Horse & Groom; WF1 5SL

Old-fashioned gas-lit pub in interesting location with dark-panelled original bar, up to 11 real ales and well-liked bar food; seats outside

In a lovely spot opposite the village green and the 19th-c stone merchants' houses surrounding it, this remains an old-fashioned and unspoilt pub with a lot of genuine character. The original bar has gas lighting giving it a cosy feel, a fire burning in the old black range (with a long row of smoothing irons on the mantelpiece), plain elm stools, oak settles built into the walls and dark panelling. A more comfortable extension has carefully preserved the original style, down to good wood-pegged oak panelling (two embossed with royal arms) and a high shelf of plates; there are also two other small flagstoned rooms and a conservatory that opens on to the garden. Ossett Silver King, Yorkshire Blonde and a beer named for the pub from Ossett, as well as Fullers London Pride and four guest beers on handpump. There are some sunny benches facing the green, and picnic-sets on a side lawn and in the nice walled garden.

As well as sandwiches, the well liked food includes yorkshire pudding with red onion gravy, chicken liver and brandy parfait, sharing meze or seafood platters, a vegetarian risotto of the day, beer-battered haddock with mushy peas and tartare sauce, moroccan lamp rump with curried chickpeas and red pepper sauce, chicken breast stuffed with pine nuts and spinach with cream sauce, seared salmon with ratatouille, beef medallions with port jus and dauphinoise potatoes, rib-eye steak with peppercorn sauce, and puddings such as chocolate and walnut tart with chantilly cream and mixed berry fool and cinnamon biscuit. *Benchmark main dish: steak in ale pie £10.50. Two-course evening meal £19.75.*

Ossett ~ Manager Angela Cromack ~ Real ale ~ Bar food (12-2, 5-9; 12-8.45 Fri and Sat;
12-5 Sun; not Sun evening) ~ Restaurant ~ (01924) 377527 ~ Children welcome ~ Dogs
allowed in bar ~ Open 12-11(midnight Fri and Sat) ~ www.thekingsarmsheath.co.uk
Recommended by the Didler, Pat and Tony Martin, Malcolm Gillett

HELPERBY

SE4370   Map 7

Oak Tree 🍴 ♆ 🛏

Raskelf Road; YO61 2PH

**Pretty brick pub recently refurbished; real ales in friendly bar, fine
food in elegant dining rooms, bold paintwork and seats on terrace;
comfortable bedrooms**

A fter a major overhaul, this attractive pub is now up and running;
they've been careful to use slate, oak and weathered brick to retain
some of the original character. The informal bar has stools against the
counter where they keep Black Sheep Best and Timothy Taylors Golden
Best and Landlord on handpump and a dozen wines by the glass served
by helpful staff; also, bold red walls, open fires and church chairs and
elegant wooden dining chairs around a mix of wooden tables on old
quarry tiles, flagstones and oak floorboards. The main dining room
has a large woodburner in a huge brick fireplace, a big central flower
arrangement, high-backed burgundy and elegant wooden chairs around
nice old tables on the oak floor, ornate mirrors and some striking
artwork on the turquoise or exposed brick walls. French windows lead
on to the terrace, where there are plenty of seats and tables for summer
dining. Upstairs is a private dining room with a two-way woodburner, a
sitting room and doors to a terrace. The bedrooms are comfortable and
well equipped. The pub is part of Provenance Inns.

🍴 As well as morning menu (served 8am-midday) offering dishes such as a
basket of croissants, pastries and preserves, bacon or sausage butties, and
smoked haddock with a poached egg and hollandaise, the top rate food might
include sandwiches, locally shot game terrine with pear chutney, crispy pork belly
with asian salad, sesame and soy, beer-battered haddock and mushy peas, various
interesting pizzas, a pie of the day, spiced sweet potato and pumpkin crumble
with home-made tomato sauce, rack of sticky and spicy pork ribs, chicken kiev
with dauphinoise potatoes, venison loin with braised red cabbage and redcurrant
sauce, and puddings like vanilla cheesecake with a berry compote and chocolate
fondant with vanilla pod ice-cream; they also serve an early-bird menu before 7pm,
with seven dishes at £7. *Benchmark main dish: fish and chips with mushy peas,
chunky chips and tartare sauce £10.95. Two-course evening meal £20.00.*

Free house ~ Licensee Michael Ibbotson ~ Real ale ~ Bar food (8am-9pm; breakfast
served to non-residents; light snacks in afternoon) ~ Restaurant ~ (01423) 789189
~ Children welcome ~ Dogs allowed in bedrooms ~ Open 8am-midnight ~ Bedrooms:
/£120S ~ www.theoaktreehelperby.com *Recommended by Ed and Anna Fraser*

KIRKBY FLEETHAM

SE2894   Map 10

Black Horse 🍴 ♆ 🍷 🛏

Village signposted off A1 S of Catterick; Lumley Lane; DL7 0SH

**Attractively reworked country inn with enterprising food, cheerful
atmosphere and stylish, comfortable bedrooms**

T he long, softly lit beamed and flagstoned bar on the right has some
cosy little settles and high-backed dining chairs by the log fire at one
end (blazing even for breakfast), and wrought-iron chairs a good deal

more comfortable than they look at the other. They have a good choice of wines by the glass, and well kept Black Sheep Best and All Creatures, Pennine Real Blonde and a beer brewed for them by Moorhouses on handpump; plenty of local regulars congregate at the counter's leather bar stools. The dining room on the right is light and open, with big bow windows on each side, and a casual contemporary look – loose-covered dining chairs or pastel garden settles with scatter cushions around tables painted pale green. There is also a dark and intimate private dining room. Service is friendly and very attentive; background Abba-era music. Teak tables on a flagstoned side terrace include one with a couple of toffs dressed for a country outing – you have to look twice to see that they're models. A neat sheltered back lawn has a guinea pig hutch. Breakfasts are excellent; they don't start till 9, but if you can't wait the bedrooms have appetising continental breakfast hampers.

Good food might include sandwiches, twice-baked blue cheese soufflé with saffron-poached pear, walnuts and rocket salad, home-made black pudding salad with lardons and a soft egg in a light crisp batter, fresh fish and chips with yorkshire caviar and tartare sauce, dry-cured gammon with a duck egg and hand-cut chips, chicken breast with sweet potato, creamed leeks and smoked bacon, a taste of pork (sticky cheek, crisp belly, fillet and black pudding) with vanilla mayonnaise, monkfish wrapped in parma ham with shellfish risotto and langoustine bisque, and puddings such as chocolate fondant with boozy cherries and cherry sorbet and sticky toffee pudding with caramel sauce. *Benchmark main dish: steak and kidney in ale pie £13.50. Two-course evening meal £21.00.*

Free house ~ Licensee Philip Barker ~ Real ale ~ Bar food (12-2.30, 5-9(9.30 Fri and Sat); 12-7 Sun; not Sun evening) ~ Restaurant ~ (01609) 749011 ~ Children welcome ~ Dogs allowed in bar ~ Open 12-11.30(10.30 Sun) ~ Bedrooms: /£100S ~ www.blackhorsekirkbyfleetham.com *Recommended by Jane Taylor and David Dutton, Michael Doswell, John and Eleanor Holdsworth, Jill and Julian Tasker*

LEDSHAM
Chequers ♀

SE4529   Map 7

1.5 miles from A1(M) junction 42: follow Leeds signs, then Ledsham signposted; Claypit Lane; LS25 5LP

Friendly village pub, handy for A1, with hands-on landlord, log fires in several beamed rooms, real ales and interesting food; pretty back terrace

Run by a friendly landlord and his helpful staff, this 16th-c stone inn is much enjoyed by both locals and visitors – it's very handy for the A1. There are several small, individually decorated rooms with low beams, lots of cosy alcoves, toby jugs and all sorts of knick-knacks on the walls and ceilings, and log fires. From the old-fashioned little central panelled-in servery they offer beers from breweries such as Brown Cow, John Smiths, Theakstons and Timothy Taylors, and a dozen wines by the glass. A lovely sheltered two-level terrace at the back has plenty of tables among roses, and the hanging baskets and flowers are very pretty. RSPB Fairburn Ings reserve is close by and the ancient village church is worth a visit. Closed on Sunday.

Interesting and very popular, the food might include sandwiches, a trio of halibut, mackerel and trout, chicken liver pâté, pork, leek and apple sausage with mash and onion gravy, butternut squash, pine nuts and parmesan risotto, gammon steak with a duck egg, swordfish with a garlic and herb crust and a mussel and dill cream sauce, pheasant breast with wild mushrooms, game jus and celeriac chips, duck confit and toulouse sausage cassoulet, specials like corned beef hash layered with caramelised onions and potatoes and braised venison shank with redcurrant jus, and puddings such as chocolate and Baileys cream pots with ginger shortbread and lemon cheesecake. *Benchmark main dish: steak pie £10.45. Two-course evening meal £22.00.*

Free house ~ Licensee Chris Wraith ~ Real ale ~ Bar food (12-9 Mon-Sat; not Sun) ~ Restaurant ~ (01977) 683135 ~ Children until 8pm ~ Dogs welcome ~ Open 11-11; closed Sun ~ www.thechequersinn.f9.co.uk *Recommended by GSB, Jeff and Wendy Williams, Grahame Brooks, Gerard Dyson, Paul Cooper, the Didler, Dr D J and Mrs S C Walker, Piotr Chodzko-Zajko, Paul Goldman, Robert Wivell, M and A H, John and Anne Mackinnon, R C Vincent*

 LEVISHAM   SE8390   Map 10

Horseshoe

Off A169 N of Pickering; YO18 7NL

Friendly village pub run by two brothers, neat rooms, real ales, very good food, and seats on the village green; bedrooms

In a pretty village in the North York Moors National Park, this 19th-c pub is a perfect place to relax after enjoying one of the lovely surrounding walks in gorgeous scenery. It's a busy but friendly traditional pub, run by two jovial brothers, and our readers like staying in the smart, comfortable bedrooms – some with fine views. The bars have beams, blue banquettes, wheelback and captain's chairs around a variety of tables on the polished wooden floors, vibrant landscapes by a local artist on the walls and a log fire in the stone fireplace; an adjoining snug has a woodburning stove, comfortable leather sofas and old photographs of the pub and the village. Black Sheep Best and a couple of guests like Cropton Endeavour Ale and Yorkshire Moors Bitter on handpump, home-made elderflower cordial, 20 malt whiskies and a farm cider; board games and background music. There are seats on the attractive village green, with more in the back garden.

Attractively presented, especially good and cooked by one of the landlords, the food includes sandwiches, grilled black pudding wrapped in bacon with apple sauce and sautéed potatoes, creamy garlic mushrooms on toast, very popular whitby haddock with home-made chips and mushy peas, wild mushroom risotto, duck breast on sweet potato mash with a red wine and port sauce, specials like slow-roasted pork belly with thyme mash and cider gravy, seafood platter and venison suet pudding with sloe gin gravy and puddings such as rum and raisin cheesecake and apple and pear crumble with custard. *Benchmark main dish: steak in ale pie £10.95. Two-course evening meal £19.00.*

Free house ~ Licensees Toby and Charles Wood ~ Real ale ~ Bar food (12-2, 6-8.30) ~ (01751) 460240 ~ Children welcome but bedrooms not ideal for them ~ Dogs welcome ~ Open 10am-11pm(10.30 Sun) ~ Bedrooms: $40/$80S ~ www.horseshoelevisham.co.uk *Recommended by Nick Dalby, P G Wooler, Michael Goodden, Ed and Anna Fraser, Derek and Sylvia Stephenson, Dr Kevan Tucker, B R Merritt, David and Lin Short*

LEYBURN   SE1190   Map 10

Sandpiper

Just off Market Place; DL8 5AT

Appealing food and cosy bar for drinkers in 17th-c cottage; real ales and impressive choice of whiskies; bedrooms

A fine place to stay in charming bedrooms, this attractive 17th-c pub is perfectly located for the Yorkshire Dales. The friendly landlord offers a warm welcome to all, and the cosy bar has an open log fire and is liked by locals for a drink and a chat – which keeps the atmosphere relaxed and informal. It has a couple of black beams in the low ceiling and wooden or cushioned built-in wall seats around a few tables, and a back snug, up three steps, has lovely Dales photographs; get here early to be sure of a seat. Down by the linenfold panelled bar counter there are photographs and a woodburning stove in a stone fireplace; to the left is the attractive restaurant, with dark wooden tables and chairs on bare floorboards, and fresh flowers. Black Sheep Best and a guest from breweries like Copper Dragon, Daleside, Rudgate and Yorkshire Dales on handpump, up to 100 malt whiskies and a decent wine list with several by the glass; background music. In good weather, you can enjoy a drink on the front terrace among the pretty hanging baskets and flowering climbers.

Excellent food cooked by the landlord, who also makes his own bread and ice-cream, might include sandwiches, pork and pheasant sausage with creamed wild garlic, double-baked vintage cheddar soufflé with roasted beetroot, omelette arnold bennett, beer-battered fish and chips, spaghetti of vegetables scented with basil, chicken breast with black bacon and dauphinoise potatoes, pork fillet wrapped in parma ham with roasted provençale vegetables and parmesan macaroni, grilled bass on a crab and spring onion risotto, and puddings such as raspberry and almond tart with mexican chocolate ice-cream and fresh fruit salad with bitter lemon sorbet and caramelised meringue. *Benchmark main dish: free-range pork belly, seared scallops, celeriac purée, apple flavours £9.25. Two-course evening meal £23.50.*

Free house ~ Licensee Jonathan Harrison ~ Real ale ~ Bar food (12-2.30, 6.30-9(9.30 Fri and Sat); not Mon or winter Tues) ~ Restaurant ~ (01969) 622206 ~ Children welcome ~ Dogs allowed in bar and bedrooms ~ Open 11.30-3, 6.30-11(10.30 Sun); closed Mon and some winter Tues ~ Bedrooms: £75S(£80B)/£85S(£90B) ~ www.sandpiperinn.co.uk
Recommended by Gordon Briggs, Pat and Graham Williamson, Sandie and Andrew Geddes, John and Eleanor Holdsworth, Andy Lickfold, M and J White, Comus and Sarah Elliott

LINTON IN CRAVEN
SD9962 Map 7
Fountaine
Off B6265 Skipton–Grassington; BD23 5HJ

Neatly kept pub in charming village, attractive furnishings, open fires, five real ales and popular food; bedrooms

In a pretty hamlet, this is a civilised and neatly kept pub and our readers enjoy their visits here very much; do book a table in advance as it's always deservedly busy. There are beams and white-painted joists in the low ceilings, log fires (one in a beautifully carved heavy wooden fireplace), attractive built-in cushioned wall benches and stools around a mix of copper-topped tables, little wall lamps and quite a few prints on the pale walls. As well as a beer named for the pub from Cuerden, there might be John Smiths, Tetleys Bitter, Theakstons Best and Thwaites Original on handpump and 14 wines by the glass served by friendly, efficient staff; background music, darts, and board games. Outside on the terrace there are teak benches and tables under green parasols and pretty hanging baskets; fine surrounding walks in the lovely Dales countryside. The bedrooms, newly opened as we went to press, are in a converted barn behind the pub.

Good, popular food – usefully served all day – includes sandwiches, pork, rosemary and black pudding terrine with home-made fruit chutney, thai fishcake with a sweet chilli sauce, gammon and eggs, smoked haddock rarebit, slow-cooked lamb shoulder with mint gravy, half a duck with a honey, ginger and spring onion glaze, a fish mixed grill, and puddings. *Benchmark main dish: slow-braised beef with yorkshire pudding £12.25. Two-course evening meal £16.00.*

Individual Inns ~ Manager Christopher Gregson ~ Real ale ~ Bar food (12-9) ~ Restaurant ~ (01756) 752210 ~ Children welcome ~ Dogs allowed in bar and bedrooms ~ Open 11-11; 12-10.30 Sun ~ Bedrooms: /£99S ~ www.individualinns.co.uk
Recommended by Peter Salmon, Tim and Sue Halstead, Tim and Joan Wright, Robert Wivell, Lynda and Trevor Smith, B and M Kendall, Gavin Dingley

LONG PRESTON
Maypole 🍺 🛏
SD8358   Map 7

A65 Settle–Skipton, BD23 4PH

A good base for walkers, with friendly staff, bustling atmosphere, well-liked pubby food and a fair choice of real ales

Named for the maypole on the village green opposite, this comfortingly traditional village pub has been run by the jovial Mr Palmer for 25 years now; there's a list of landlords dating back to 1695 on the butter-coloured walls of the two-room bar. This also has good solid pub furnishings – red leather wall seats, heavy carved wall settles and plush red-topped bar stools around cast-iron-framed pub tables with unusual inset leather tops on a red patterned carpet, and plenty of local photographs. There's a separate dining room. Moorhouses Premier Bitter, Timothy Taylors Landlord and a couple of guests like Dark Horse Best Bitter and Goose Eye Chinook Blonde on handpump, ten wines by the glass, three farm ciders and a dozen malt whiskies. The left-hand tap room has darts, dominoes and TV for important sporting events. On a back terrace, there are a couple of picnic-sets under an ornamental cherry tree, with more tables under umbrellas on another terrace (which has outdoor heaters). The inn makes a good base for walking in the Dales and the bedrooms are quiet and clean, and breakfasts good.

Honest and tasty pubby food includes sandwiches and filled hot baguettes, chicken liver pâté with plum chutney, salmon and tuna fishcakes with lemon and chilli mayonnaise, thai green vegetable curry, ham and eggs, sausages with mash and onion gravy, battered haddock and mushy peas, specials such as pork casserole with red peppers and basil, chicken, orange, watercress and mint salad and hake fillet with a lemon and tarragon butter, and puddings. *Benchmark main dish: steak in ale pie £9.95. Two-course evening meal £16.00.*

Enterprise ~ Lease Robert Palmer ~ Real ale ~ Bar food (12-9(9.30 Fri and Sat)) ~ Restaurant ~ (01729) 840219 ~ Children welcome ~ Dogs allowed in bar and bedrooms ~ Open 12-11 ~ Bedrooms: £42S/£75B ~ www.maypole.co.uk *Recommended by Mrs Judith Kirkham, Dudley and Moira Cockroft, Clive Flynn, Gerard Dyson, Dr Ann Henderson, Dennis Jones, Richard Balkwill, Martin Hickes*

LOW CATTON
Gold Cup
SE7053   Map 7

Village signposted with High Catton off A166 in Stamford Bridge or A1079 at Kexby Bridge; YO41 1EA

Friendly, pleasant pub with attractive bars, real ales, decent food, seats in garden and ponies in paddock

This is a proper village pub with chatty locals, a helpful and informative landlord and spic and span bars – and as it's open all day at weekends (and serves food all day then, too) it's just the place to head for after a walk. The neat, beamed bars have a country feel with coach lights on the rustic-looking walls, smart tables and chairs on the stripped wooden floors, an open fire at one end opposite the woodburning stove and quite a few pictures. The restaurant has solid wooden pews and tables (said to be made from a single oak tree) and pleasant views of the surrounding fields. John Smiths and Theakstons Black Bull on handpump; background music and pool. The garden has a grassed area for children and the back paddock is home to two ponies, Cinderella and Polly. The pub has fishing rights on the adjoining River Derwent.

As well as lunchtime sandwiches (not Sunday), the dependable and reasonably priced food includes chicken liver pâté with onion marmalade, beer-battered mushrooms with garlic mayonnaise, vegetable stroganoff, chicken wrapped in bacon with a creamy stilton sauce, gammon steak topped with pineapple and melted cheese, half a crispy duck with plum and ginger sauce, venison steak braised in red wine on mash, slow-cooked lamb shank with redcurrant gravy, and puddings such as chocolate and brandy torte with vanilla ice-cream and orange and Cointreau cheesecake; they also offer a two- and three-course set evening menu (not weekends). *Benchmark main dish: cajun chicken £9.50. Two-course evening meal £15.50.*

Free house ~ Licensees Pat and Ray Hales ~ Real ale ~ Bar food (12-2, 6-9; all day weekends; not Mon lunchtime) ~ Restaurant ~ (01759) 371354 ~ Children welcome ~ Dogs allowed in bar ~ Open 12-2.30, 6-11; 12-11(10.30 Sun) Sat; closed Mon lunchtime ~ www.goldcuplowcatton.com *Recommended by Gerard Dyson, Pete Coxon, Peter and Anne Hollindale, Gordon and Margaret Ormondroyd*

MARTON CUM GRAFTON
Punch Bowl 🍴 ♈
SE4263 Map 7

Signed off A1 3 miles N of A59; YO51 9QY

Refurbished 16th-c inn in lovely village, with beams and standing timbers, character bar and dining rooms, real ales, interesting food and seats outside

This handsome inn, dating back to the 16th c, has reopened after a recent refurbishment and is under new management. It's been carefully done without stripping away the character and the atmosphere throughout is relaxed and easy-going. The main bar is beamed and timbered with a built-in window seat at one end, lots of red leather-topped stools, cushioned settles and church chairs around pubby tables on the flagstones or bare floorboards, Black Sheep Best and Timothy Taylors Landlord on handpump and lots of wines by the glass served by friendly staff. Open doorways from here lead to five separate dining areas, each with an open fire, heavy beams, red walls covered with photographs of vintage car races and racing drivers (a previous owner was obsessed with vintage cars and the new owners have carried on with the theme), sporting cartoons and old photographs of the pub and village, and an attractive mix of cushioned wall seats and wooden or high-backed red dining chairs around antique tables on the oak flooring. Up a swirling staircase is a coffee loft and a private dining room. There are seats and tables on the back courtyard where they hold summer barbecues. The pub is part of Provenance Inns.

Using only seasonal, local and free-range produce the excellent food might include sandwiches, queen scallops in garlic and parsley butter with gruyère, home-made salmon, haddock and prawn fishcakes with tartare sauce, gnocchi with spinach and wild mushrooms in a parmesan sauce, a pie of the day, beef burger with cheese, bacon and onion rings, beer-battered haddock with mushy peas, bass fillets with a tomato and basil tart and pesto, steak frites with béarnaise sauce, and puddings such as vanilla pod crème brûlée; they also offer an early-bird menu before 7pm with seven dishes at £7 and a two-course set lunch menu. *Benchmark main dish: chicken shawarma kebab with home-made flatbread, yoghurt and dips £9.95. Two-course evening meal £20.00.*

Free house ~ Licensee Michael Ibbotson ~ Real ale ~ Bar food (12-2.30(3 Sun), 5.30-9.30(8.30 Sun)) ~ Restaurant ~ (01423) 322519 ~ Children welcome ~ Dogs allowed in bar ~ Open 12-11 ~ www.thepunchbowlmartoncumgrafton.com *Recommended by Allan Westbury, Gordon and Margaret Ormondroyd, John and Eleanor Holdsworth*

PICKERING

SE7984 Map 10
White Swan 🍴 ☆ 🛏
Market Place, just off A170; YO18 7AA

Relaxed little bar in civilised coaching inn with several smart lounges, an attractive restaurant, real ales, an excellent wine list and first class food; lovely bedrooms

You can expect a welcome and service of the highest order in this smart and civilised 16th-c coaching inn on the edge of the North York Moors National Park. At its heart is a small bar with a relaxed atmosphere, sofas and a few tables, wood panelling, a log fire, Black Sheep Best, Copper Dragon Golden Pippin and a guest from Wold Top on handpump, a dozen wines by the glass from an extensive list that includes fine old St Emilions and pudding wines, and ten malt whiskies. Opposite, a bare-boards room with a few more tables has another fire in a handsome art nouveau iron fireplace, a big bow window and pear prints on its plum-coloured walls. The restaurant has flagstones, yet another open fire, comfortable settles and gothic screens, and the residents' lounge is in a converted beamed barn. The old coach entry to the car park is narrow. This is a fine place to stay in luxurious bedrooms and the breakfasts are delicious.

 Excellent food includes lunchtime sandwiches (their soup and sandwich deal is popular), ham knuckle terrine with potted pork and black pudding, scotch egg and piccalilli, whitby fishcakes with a herb shrimp salad, a smashing ploughman's, beer-battered haddock with mushy peas and tartare sauce, root vegetable risotto, a trio of game (venison haunch, teal and widgeon) with redcurrant jelly, bread sauce and game chips, chargrilled longhorn beef with bourguignon salad, peppercorn sauce and hand-cut chips, specials like halibut with crab butter and white wine sauce and a salad of sautéed squid, salami and rocket with grilled jersey royals and crème fraîche, and puddings. *Benchmark main dish: pork belly with crackling, sweet red cabbage, mustard mash, apple sauce £16.95. Two-course evening meal £23.00.*

Free house ~ Licensees Marion and Victor Buchanan ~ Real ale ~ Bar food (12-2, 7-9) ~ Restaurant ~ (01751) 472288 ~ Children welcome ~ Dogs allowed in bar and bedrooms ~ Open 10am-11pm ~ Bedrooms: £115B/£150B ~ www.white-swan.co.uk *Recommended by Peter Burton, John and Dinah Waters, Mrs G Marlow, Glenwys and Alan Lawrence*

PICKHILL
SE3483 Map 10
Nags Head 🍴 ☆ 🛏
A1 junction 50 (northbound) or junction 51 (southbound), village signed off A6055, Street Lane; YO7 4JG

Neatly kept dining pub with consistently good food, a fine choice of carefully chosen drinks, a tap room, smarter lounge and friendly service; comfortable bedrooms

The enthusiastic and warmly friendly Mr Boynton has now been running this excellent place for 40 years – and our readers love it. It also makes a first class break from the A1. Most of the tables are laid for eating so if it's just a drink you're after, head for the bustling tap room on the left: beams hung with jugs, coach horns, ale-yards and so forth, and masses of ties hanging as a frieze from a rail around the red ceiling. The smarter lounge bar has deep green plush banquettes on the matching carpet, pictures for sale on its neat cream walls and an open fire. There's also a library-themed restaurant. Black Sheep Best, Rudgate Battleaxe, Theakstons Best and a guest beer on handpump, a good choice of malt whiskies, vintage armagnacs and a carefully chosen wine list with several by the glass. One table is inset with a chessboard; darts, TV and background music. There's a front verandah, a boules and quoits pitch and a nine-hole putting green. The bedrooms are comfortable and well equipped.

Using venison shot by the landlord and other local game and seasonal produce, the highly thought of and extremely popular food includes sandwiches, moules marinière, seared pigeon breast with apple and blue cheese salad and mustard seed dressing, pork sausages with onion gravy, beef burger with cheese, onion rings and skinny fries, sautéed potato gnocchi with slow-roasted red peppers and tomatoes, goats cheese and oregano, free-range bacon with fried egg and hand-cut chips, thai chicken, vegetable and noodle stir fry, natural smoked haddock with bubble and squeak potato cake, crispy free-range egg and grain mustard cream, free-range pork and black pudding roulade with slow-roasted and pressed belly pork, crackling and cider reduction, and puddings. *Benchmark main dish: venison haunch, shortcrust pie and liver with fondant potato, white cabbage, jug of game gravy £17.95. Two-course evening meal £19.00.*

Free house ~ Licensee Edward Boynton ~ Real ale ~ Bar food (12-2, 6-9.30; all day weekends (Sat afternoon snacks only)) ~ Restaurant ~ (01845) 567391 ~ Well behaved children welcome until 7.30pm (after that in dining room only) ~ Dogs allowed in bedrooms ~ Open 11-11(10.30 Sun) ~ Bedrooms: £55B/£80B ~ www.nagsheadpickhill.co.uk *Recommended by Ian Malone, David and Ruth Hollands, Oliver Richardson, Edward Atkinson, Jill and Julian Tasker*

RIPLEY   SE2860   Map 7

Boars Head ♀ 🍺 🛏

Off A61 Harrogate–Ripon; HG3 3AY

Smart coaching inn with friendly bar/bistro, several real ales, excellent wine list, good food and helpful service; comfortable bedrooms

Although there is some emphasis on the hotel side in this welcoming old coaching inn, the atmosphere is relaxed and informal and they keep Black Sheep Best, Daleside Crackshot Ale and Theakstons Old Peculier on handpump, 20 wines by the glass and several malt whiskies. The bar/bistro has a nice mix of dining chairs around various wooden tables, warm yellow walls hung with golf clubs, cricket bats and jolly little drawings of cricketers and huntsmen, a boar's head (part of the family coat of arms), and an interesting religious carving. Some of the furnishings in the hotel came from the attic of next-door Ripley Castle, where the Ingilbys have lived for over 650 years. A pleasant little garden has plenty of tables.

Good, popular food using produce from their own kitchen garden (within Ripley Castle) might include open sandwiches, pressed ham hock terrine with home-made piccalilli, deep-fried almond-crusted goats cheese with tomato chutney,

picked whitby crab with fresh tagliatelle and a basil and chilli fondue, potato
gnocchi with spinach, blue cheese and toasted pine kernels, bangers of the day
with spring onion mash and onion gravy, honey-roasted pork chop with cider potato
fondant and apple purée, natural smoked haddock with chive mash, a poached
egg and mustard dressing, and puddings such as a sponge of the day with home-
made custard and dark chocolate fondant with caramelised hazelnuts and orange
cream. *Benchmark main dish: boars head tasting plate £14.00. Two-course
evening meal £20.00.*

Free house ~ Licensee Sir Thomas Ingilby ~ Real ale ~ Bar food (12-2.30, 6.30-9; 12-9
Sun) ~ Restaurant ~ (01423) 771888 ~ Children welcome ~ Dogs allowed in bar and
bedrooms ~ Open 11-11; 11-3, 5-11 weekdays in in winter ~ Bedrooms: /£100S ~
www.boarsheadripley.co.uk *Recommended by Janet and Peter Race, the Didler, Pete Coxon,
Gerry and Rosemary Dobson*

RIPPONDEN
Old Bridge ♀ 🍺

SE0419   Map 7

*From A58, best approach is Elland Road (opposite the Golden Lion),
park opposite the church in pub's car park and walk back over ancient hump-back
bridge; HX6 4DF*

**Pleasant old pub by medieval bridge with relaxed communicating
rooms and well-liked food**

The third generation of the same friendly family are now running this
charming 700-year-old inn; it's by a beautiful medieval pack-horse
bridge over the little River Ryburn and there are seats in the pub garden
overlooking the water. Inside, the three communicating rooms, each
on a slightly different level, all have a relaxed, friendly atmosphere.
Oak settles are built into the window recesses of the thick stone walls,
and there are antique oak tables, rush-seated chairs, a few well chosen
pictures and prints, and a big woodburning stove. Timothy Taylors Best,
Dark Mild, Golden Best and Landlord and a couple of guests such as
Brewsters Decadence and Bridestones Sandstone on handpump, quite
a few foreign bottled beers, a dozen wines by the glass and 30 malt
whiskies. If you have trouble finding the pub (there is no traditional pub
sign outside), just head for the church.

Using meat from local farms and other seasonal local produce, the good
lunchtime food only includes sandwiches and soup or the popular help-
yourself salad carvery; in the evening and at weekends there might be black
pudding fritters with honey and mustard dip, crab and avocado tian with bloody
mary dressing, mediterranean vegetable and goats cheese wraps topped with
cheese and sour cream, corn-fed chicken kiev with yellow tomato and thyme
sauce and fried potatoes, fillet of salmon with soy, chilli, ginger, spring onion
and pak choi noodles, crispy pork belly with sage potatoes and cider sauce, and
puddings. *Benchmark main dish: steak in ale pie £10.00. Two-course evening
meal £17.00.*

Free house ~ Licensees Tim and Lindsay Eaton Walker ~ Real ale ~ Bar food (12-2(2.30
Sun), 6.30-9.30; not Sun evening) ~ (01422) 822595 ~ Children allowed until 8pm but
must be seated away from bar ~ Open 12-3, 5.30-11; 12-11(10.30 Sun) Fri and Sat ~
www.theoldbridgeinn.co.uk *Recommended by Roger and Anne Newbury, Tony Hill, Imscleaners*

Real ale may be served from handpumps, electric pumps (not just the on-off switches
used for keg beer) or – common in Scotland – tall taps called founts (pronounced
'fonts') where a separate pump pushes the beer up under air pressure.

ROBIN HOOD'S BAY

NZ9505 Map 10

Laurel

Bay Bank; village signed off A171 S of Whitby; YO22 4SE

Charming little pub in delightful fishing village, neat friendly bar, and real ales

---

Quite unchanging and unspoilt, this little local has a charming landlord and is at the heart of one of the prettiest and most attractive fishing villages on the north-east coast. The beamed and welcoming main bar is neatly kept and decorated with old local photographs, Victorian prints and brasses, and lager bottles from all over the world. There's an open fire and Adnams Best and Theakstons Best and Old Peculier on handpump; darts, board games and background music. In summer, the hanging baskets and window boxes are lovely. They have a self-contained apartment for two people.

 No food but they do let you bring in sandwiches from the tea shop next door and eat them in the pub.

Free house ~ Licensee Brian Catling ~ Real ale ~ No credit cards ~ (01947) 880400 ~ Children in snug bar only ~ Dogs welcome ~ Open 2-11 Mon-Thurs; 12-11 Fri, Sat and Sun *Recommended by Peter Dearing*

ROECLIFFE

SE3765 Map 7

Crown 🍴 🍷 🍺 🛏

Off A168 just W of Boroughbridge; handy for A1(M) junction 48; YO51 9LY

Yorkshire Dining Pub of the Year

Smartly updated and attractively placed pub with a civilised bar, excellent enterprising food and a fine choice of drinks; lovely bedrooms

---

Under the hard-working and friendly Mainey family, this deservedly popular and attractive pub goes from strength to strength, and there's always a wide mix of both locals and visitors keen to enjoy a chat and a drink, a top class meal or an overnight stay in the cosy, country-style bedrooms. Much emphasis is on the food but they do keep Ilkley Gold and Mary Jane, Theakstons Best and Timothy Taylors Landlord on handpump, a couple of belgian beers on tap, 20 wines by the glass and fruit ciders. The bar has a contemporary colour scheme of dark reds and near-whites with pleasant prints carefully grouped and lit; one area has chunky pine tables on flagstones and another part, with a log fire, has dark tables on plaid carpet. For meals, you have a choice between a small candlelit olive-green bistro with nice tables, a long-case clock and one or two paintings, and a more formal restaurant. The village green is opposite.

 They make their own goats cheese, bread, jams and chutneys, home-smoke their fish and use only small local suppliers and game from local estates for the first-class, imaginative food, which might include lunchtime sandwiches, rabbit pie with sloe gin and cranberry chutney, king scallops over prosciutto crisps and pea purée, goats cheese, shallot and thyme tartlet, salmon fishcakes with twice-cooked fries, steak and mushroom or their popular fish pie, gloucester old spot belly pork with bramley apple and sage mash, cracking and cider sauce, a sharing game plate (pheasant, wild duck wrapped in bacon, pigeon, and venison) with whisky bread sauce and redcurrant jus, and puddings such as melting chocolate fondant with a pistachio tuile and double cream ice-cream and french lemon tart with a caramel glaze and lemon and honeycomb ice-cream; their cheese board is worth investigating. *Benchmark main dish: fish pie £12.95. Two-course evening meal £22.00.*

Free house ~ Licensee Karl Mainey ~ Real ale ~ Bar food (12-2.30, 6-9.15; 12-7 Sun) ~ Restaurant ~ (01423) 322300 ~ Children welcome ~ Dogs allowed in bar ~ Open 12-3, 5-midnight; 12-9 Sun ~ Bedrooms: £82B/£97B ~ www.crowninnroecliffe.com
Recommended by Michael and Maggie Betton, Michael Doswell, Hunter and Christine Wright, Les and Sandra Brown, Peter Hacker, Ian Malone, Donna Jenkins, Martin Cawley, Gordon and Margaret Ormondroyd

---

 SANDHUTTON SE3882 Map 10

Kings Arms

A167, a mile N of A61 Thirsk–Ripon; YO7 4RW

Good chef/landlord in cheerful and appealing pub with friendly service, good food and beer, and comfortable furnishings; bedrooms

While there is a quite a focus on food in this charming village inn, the friendly licensees remain committed to providing a traditional pubby atmosphere. The bustling bar has an unusual circular woodburner in one corner, a high central table with four equally high stools, high-backed brown leather-seated dining chairs around light pine tables, a couple of cushioned wicker armchairs, some attractive modern bar stools, and photographs of the pub in years gone by. Black Sheep Best, Rudgate Viking, Theakstons Best and Village Brewer White Boar Bitter on handpump, several wines by the glass and efficient, friendly service. The two connecting dining rooms have similar furnishings to the bar (though there's also a nice big table with smart high-backed dining chairs), arty flower photographs on the cream walls and a shelf above the small woodburning stove with more knick-knacks and some candles; background music, darts, board games and TV. They have a shop selling their own ready meals as well as cheese, chutneys and local produce.

Cooked by the landlord using local produce, the popular food includes sandwiches, black pudding and sausage stack, apple purée and HP brown sauce, smoked salmon and crayfish roll with crème fraîche, horseradish and lime dressing, chilli con carne, leek, potato and mozzarella sausage in filo pastry with a tomato sauce, a pie of the day, black bean and coriander-marinated chicken with tortillas and soured cream, specials such as potted spicy crab, thai-style curried turkey and tuna with rosemary, thyme and sesame glaze, and puddings. *Benchmark main dish: deep-fried scampi with chunky chips £11.50. Two-course evening meal £16.00.*

Free house ~ Licensees Raymond and Alexander Boynton ~ Real ale ~ Bar food (12-2.30, 5.30-9; 12-5 Sun; not Sun evening) ~ Restaurant ~ (01845) 587887 ~ Children welcome ~ Open 11am-midnight ~ Bedrooms: £45S/£80S ~ www.thekingsarmssandhutton.co.uk
Recommended by Mike and Lynn Robinson

SOUTH DALTON SE9645 Map 8

Pipe & Glass ⑪ ♀ ⌂

West End; brown sign to pub off B1248 NW of Beverley; HU17 7PN

Attractive dining pub with a proper bar area, real ales, interesting modern cooking, good service, peaceful garden and front terrace; stylish bedrooms

Much emphasis in this attractive whitewashed dining pub is placed on the first class food cooked by the chef/landlord, but there is a proper bar area, too. This is beamed and bow-windowed and has copper pans hanging above the log fire in the sizeable fireplace, some old prints, and cushioned window seats, high-backed settles and traditional pubby chairs around a mix of tables (each set with a church candle). Beyond that, all is airy and comfortably contemporary, angling around some soft modern dark leather chesterfields into a light restaurant area overlooking the park, with stylish high-backed dining chairs around well spaced country tables, and bare floorboards. The decorations – a row of serious cookery books and framed big-name restaurant menus – show how high the kitchen aims. Black Sheep Best with guest beers from breweries like Copper Dragon and Wold Top on handpump, ten wines by the glass, over 50 malt whiskies and Weston's Old Rosie cider. Service is friendly and prompt by bright and attentive young staff; background music. There are tables out on the garden's peaceful lawn and picnic-sets on the front terrace; people say the yew tree is some 500 years old. The bedrooms are smart and comfortable and the suites have views over the park. The village is charming and its elegant Victorian church spire, 62 metres tall, is visible for miles around.

Exceptional food using the best local, seasonal produce might include sandwiches, ham hock and guinea fowl ballotine with a scampi fritter, pease pudding and pea shoots, tomato, avocado and mozzarella salad with spiced gazpacho and basil sorbet and olive flatbread, sausages with bubble and squeak and onion and ale gravy, three onion and goats cheese tart with braised baby leeks, roasted beetroot and oregano soubise sauce, free-range chicken breast with peas, morel mushrooms, wild garlic mash and crispy smoked bacon, roast rump of lamb with a vegetable and pearly barley hotchpotch, crispy mutton belly and nettle and mint gravy, fillet of beef with salt beef niçoise salad, hollandaise and hand-cut chips, specials like creamed mussels with cider and sea spinach and fish pie with parsley mash, brown shrimps and pickled fennel salad, and puddings such as ginger burnt cream with poached rhubarb and sugar cakes and hot dark chocolate and cherry pudding with cherry blossom ice-cream. *Benchmark main dish: duck cooked three ways with truffled celeriac purée, thyme and potato rösti and stewed cherries £23.95. Two-course evening meal £24.50.*

Free house ~ Licensees Kate and James Mackenzie ~ Real ale ~ Bar food (12-2, 6-9.30; 12-4 Sun; not Sun evening or Mon (except bank hols)) ~ Restaurant ~ (01430) 810246 ~ Children welcome ~ Open 12-11(10.30 Sun); closed Mon (except bank holidays) ~ Bedrooms: /£160B ~ www.pipeandglass.co.uk *Recommended by Robert Wivell, Huw Jones, G Jennings*

THORNTON WATLASS
SE2385   Map 10
Buck 🍺 ⇌

Village signposted off B6268 Bedale–Masham; HG4 4AH

Honest village pub with five real ales, traditional bars, well-liked food and popular Sunday jazz

Still very much the heart of the community, but with a warm welcome for visitors too, this friendly village pub has now been run by the same hands-on and hard-working licensees for 26 years. The pleasantly traditional bar on the right has upholstered old-fashioned wall settles on the carpet, a fine mahogany bar counter, a high shelf packed with ancient bottles, several mounted fox masks and brushes, and a brick fireplace. The Long Room (which overlooks the cricket green) has large prints of old Thornton Watlass cricket teams, signed bats, cricket balls and so forth. Black Sheep Best, Theakstons Best and guests like Copper Dragon Golden Pippin, Rudgate Ruby Mild and Wold Top Bunnys

Revenge on handpump, a few wines by the glass and over 40 interesting malt whiskies; darts and board games. The sheltered garden has an equipped children's play area and summer barbecues, and they have their own cricket team; quoits. If you stay in the comfortable bedrooms, the breakfasts are especially good.

🍴 Popular bar food using local produce and offering dishes in small or large helpings might include sandwiches, chicken liver parfait with red onion marmalade, rarebit with wensleydale cheese and real ale topped with bacon with home-made pear chutney, beef burgers topped with cheese with home-made chips, spinach and ricotta pasta, beer-battered fish and chips, steak in ale pie, liver and bacon with caramelised onion gravy, specials like king scallops with gruyère and chicken breast with a creamy brandy, almond and sultana curry, and puddings. *Benchmark main dish: fresh whitby cod £9.95. Two-course evening meal £17.00.*

Free house ~ Licensees Michael and Margaret Fox ~ Real ale ~ Bar food (12-2(3 Sun), 6.30-9) ~ Restaurant ~ (01677) 422461 ~ Children welcome ~ Dogs allowed in bedrooms ~ Trad jazz twice monthly on Sun lunchtimes ~ Open 11-11(midnight Sat) ~ Bedrooms: £55(£65S)/£80(£90B) ~ www.thebuckinn.net *Recommended by Richard Gibbs, David and Ruth Hollands*

THORNTON-LE-CLAY   SE6865   Map 7
White Swan
Off A64 SW of Malton, via Foston; Low Street; YO60 7TG

The pub where you feel like a welcome guest in a private home

Ornamental shrubs and fruit trees shelter green picnic-table sets in the neat garden behind the house, and a terrace has more tables, a summer house and penthouse; plantings are entertaining as well as pretty, including a flower-filled wheelbarrow and pair of boots. There's a pond, also a vegetable and herb garden down at the bottom, with a pair of friendly donkeys in the paddock alongside. Inside is just as inviting. The snug L-shaped beamed bar, comfortably cushioned and red-carpeted, has plenty of ornaments, and shelves and arched recesses house books, board games and even toys. They have daily papers as well as decent wines by the glass, changing guest beers such as Copper Dragon Golden Pippin and Moorhouses Broomstick on handpump, and well served coffee; warmly welcoming family service, maybe background music. There's attractive countryside nearby – not to mention Castle Howard.

🍴 Wholesome food using local produce (some of their own) is strong on traditional favourites such as steak and kidney pie, gammon, and succulent sausages served with an enterprising choice of mash; also, sandwiches (their soup and sandwich deal is popular), a changing pâté, chinese spring rolls with a honey and mustard dressing, lasagne, gammon with mustard butter, chicken in a red wine and mushroom sauce, beer-battered fish and chips, venison casserole, and puddings such as toffee nut sponge and ice-cream sundae; they do a pie and pudding evening on Sundays. *Benchmark main dish: home-made pies £8.95. Two-course evening meal £14.00.*

Free house ~ Licensees Susan and Lucy Pilgrim ~ Real ale ~ Bar food (12-2, 6.30-9) ~ (01653) 618286 ~ Children welcome ~ Open 11.45-2.30, 6.30-11 ~ www.tlcwhiteswan.co.uk *Recommended by Matthew Tritton-Hughes, Michael Page, Harry Gordon-Finlayson, Mr and Mrs R W Haste, Mr and Mrs R J Oliver*

> We say if we know a pub allows dogs.

WASS

SE5579 Map 7

Wombwell Arms 🛏

Back road W of Ampleforth; or follow brown tourist-attraction sign for Byland Abbey off A170 Thirsk–Helmsley; YO61 4BE

Consistently enjoyable village pub with a friendly atmosphere, good mix of locals and visitors, interesting bar food and real ales; bedrooms

'Everything a pub should be,' says one of our readers – and many agree with him. It's a bustling 17th-c place and handy for Byland Abbey so it does get busy, at lunchtimes in particular. The two bars are neatly kept with plenty of simple character, pine farmhouse chairs and tables, some exposed stone walls, and log fires; the walls of the Poacher's Bar (in which dogs are welcome) are hung with brewery memorabilia. From the panelled bar counter, the friendly staff serve Theakstons Best, Timothy Taylors Landlord and a guest like Rudgate Viking on handpump, nine wines by the glass (quite a few from the landlady's native South Africa) and several malt whiskies; darts. The two restaurants are in a former granary. Seats outside.

🍴 Using the best local produce, the well thought of food might include sandwiches, a trio of smoked fish (smoked salmon, smoked trout and smoked mackerel pâté), cheese and spinach soufflé with cherry tomato, garlic and chilli jam, pork and apple sausages with creamy mash and gravy, beef burger with cheese and bacon, chicken in a creamy bacon, leek and stilton sauce, mediterranean vegetable open lasagne, king prawn paella, specials like black pudding, bacon, quail's egg and hollandaise on bruschetta and venison steak with a berry and port sauce, and puddings. *Benchmark main dish: bobotie (fruity mince curry) £9.95. Two-course evening meal £19.00.*

Free house ~ Licensees Ian and Eunice Walker ~ Real ale ~ Bar food (12-2(2.30 Sat), 6.30-9(9.30 Fri and Sat); 12-3, 6-8 Sun) ~ Restaurant ~ (01347) 868280 ~ Children welcome ~ Dogs allowed in bar ~ Folk music second Thurs of month ~ Open 12-3, 6-11; 12-11 Sat; 12-10.30 Sun; 12-4 Sun in winter; closed winter Sun evening, Mon ~ Bedrooms: £59S/£79S ~ www.wombwellarms.co.uk *Recommended by Margaret Dickinson, Mr and Mrs D G Hallows, Michael Doswell, Keith Moss, Dr and Mrs R G J Telfer*

WIDDOP

SD9531 Map 7

Pack Horse 🍺 £

The Ridge; from A646 on W side of Hebden Bridge, turn off at Heptonstall signpost (as it's a sharp turn, coming out of Hebden Bridge road signs direct you around a turning circle), then follow Slack and Widdop signposts; can also be reached from Nelson and Colne, on high, pretty road; OS Sheet 103 map reference 952317; HX7 7AT

Friendly pub high up on the moors and liked by walkers for generous, tasty food, five real ales and lots of malt whiskies; bedrooms

Perfect for walkers on the Pennine Way or horse riders on the Mary Townley Loop, this isolated, traditional inn is popular with our readers. The bar has welcoming winter fires, window seats cut into the partly panelled stripped-stone walls that take in the beautiful moorland views, sturdy furnishings and horsey mementoes. Black Sheep Best, Copper Dragon Golden Pippin, Thwaites Bitter and a guest like Cottage Norman Conquest on handpump, around 130 single malt whiskies and some irish ones as well, and a dozen wines by the glass. The friendly golden retrievers are called Padge and Purdey and the alsatian, Holly. There are seats outside in the cobblestone beer garden, and pretty summer hanging baskets. As well as the comfortable bedrooms (the breakfasts are very good), they also offer a smart self-catering apartment.

🍴 Honest food at sensible prices includes sandwiches, garlic mushrooms, prawn cocktail, lasagne, cottage hotpot, mushroom stroganoff, fish pie, gammon and eggs, giant beef burger and chips, lambs liver and bacon with sizzled onions, and puddings. *Benchmark main dish: rack of lamb with mint sauce £13.95. Two-course evening meal £14.00.*

Free house ~ Licensee Andrew Hollinrake ~ Real ale ~ Bar food (12-2, 7-9; 12-8 Sun; not Mon or lunchtimes as below) ~ (01422) 842803 ~ Children allowed in eating area of bar ~ Dogs allowed in bar ~ Open 12-3, 7-11; 12-11 Sun; closed Mon and lunchtimes Tues-Sat Oct-Easter ~ Bedrooms: £43S/£48S(£69B) ~ www.thepackhorse.org/showpage.php?ID=2) *Recommended by Ian and Nita Cooper, Simon Le Fort, Geoff Boswell, Martin Smith*

Also Worth a Visit in Yorkshire

Besides the fully inspected pubs, you might like to try these pubs that have been recommended to us and described by readers. Do tell us what you think of them: feedback@goodguides.com

AINTHORPE   NZ7007
Fox & Hounds   (01287) 660218
Brook Lane; YO21 2LD Traditional beamed moorland inn with wonderful views, nice open fire in unusual stone fireplace, well kept Theakstons ales, generous good value food including some interesting choices, friendly staff, restaurant, games room; great walks from the door, seven bedrooms. *(Dr Kevan Tucker)*

ALDBOROUGH   SE4166
Ship   (01423) 322749
Off B6265 just S of Boroughbridge, close to A1; YO51 9ER Attractive 14th-c beamed village dining pub, good food and service, well kept ales including Theakstons, some old-fashioned seats around cast-iron-framed tables, lots of copper and brass, inglenook fire, restaurant; a few picnic-sets outside, handy for Roman remains and museum, bedrooms, open all day Sun, closed Mon lunchtime. *(Paul Smurthwaite, John and Eleanor Holdsworth)*

ALDWARK   SE4663
Aldwark Arms   (01347) 838324
Opposite church; YO61 1UB Modernised family-owned dining pub with good stylishly presented Yorkshire food from bar snacks to some imaginative restaurant dishes, good value deals too, comprehensive wine list, attentive efficient service; children welcome, outside tables, open all day weekends, closed Mon. *(Mr and Mrs Mike Pearson)*

ALLERTHORPE   SE7847
Plough   (01759) 302349
Main Street; YO42 4RW Airy two-room lounge bar, popular and cheerful, with wide daily-changing choice of good sensibly priced food including local game, well kept Black Sheep, John Smiths and two guests, decent house wines, snug alcoves, hunting prints, World War II RAF and RCAF photographs, open fires, restaurant, games extension with pool; background music; tables out in pleasant garden, handy for Burnby Hall, open all day weekends. *(Roger A Bellingham)*

AMPLEFORTH   SE5878
White Horse   (01439) 788378
West End; YO62 4DX Beamed 18th-c village pub with comfortable relaxed atmosphere, straightforward freshly made food (not Sun evening) including bargain OAP lunch (Tues), friendly helpful service, Black Sheep, Timothy Taylors and Wold Top, flagstones and open fires; children, dogs and muddy boots welcome, sunny terrace, closed Mon, open all day weekends (Sat from 2pm). *(Anon)*

APPLETON-LE-MOORS   SE7388
★ **Moors**   (01751) 417435
N of A170, just under 1.5 miles E of Kirkby Moorside; YO62 6TF Traditional stone-built village pub, beamed bar with built-in high-backed settle next to old kitchen fireplace, plenty of other seating, some sparse decorations (a few copper pans, earthenware mugs, country ironwork), Black Sheep and a two guests, over 50 malt whiskies, generous good value home-made food (something all day) using vegetables from own allotment, darts; background music; children and dogs welcome, tables in lovely walled garden with quiet country views, walks to Rosedale Abbey or Hartoft End, seven bedrooms, open all day. *(Ed and Anna Fraser, Richard and Karen Holt, Shirley and Clive Pickerill)*

APPLETREEWICK   SE0560
⋆**Craven Arms** (01756) 720270

*Off B6160 Burnsall–Bolton Abbey;
BD23 6DA* Character creeper-covered
17th-c beamed pub, comfortably down-to-
earth settles and rugs on flagstones, oak
panelling, fire in old range, good friendly
service, up to eight well kept ales, good
choice of wines by the glass, home-made
food from baguettes up, small dining room
and splendid thatched and raftered barn
extension with gallery; children, dogs and
boots welcome (plenty of surrounding walks),
nice country views from front picnic-sets,
more seats in back garden, open all day
Weds-Sun. *(Dr Kevan Tucker, Jeremy Ward,
Lynda and Trevor Smith)*

APPLETREEWICK   SE0560
New Inn (01756) 720252

W end of main village; BD23 6DA
Unpretentious warmly welcoming country
local with lovely views, six well kept ales
including Black Sheep and Daleside, good
choice of continental bottled beers, generous
tasty home cooking, distinctive décor,
interesting old local photographs; children
and dogs welcome, three garden areas, good
walking, five bedrooms and nearby camping,
open all day. *(Dr Kevan Tucker, John and
Helen Rushton)*

ARNCLIFFE   SD9371
⋆**Falcon** (01756) 770205

Off B6160 N of Grassington; BD23 5QE
Basic no-frills country tavern in same family
for generations (but with new manager);
lovely setting on moorland village green, coal
fire in small bar with elderly furnishings, well
kept Timothy Taylors Landlord tapped from
cask to stoneware jugs in central hatch-style
servery, low-priced simple lunchtime and
early evening food from old family kitchen,
cheerful service, attractive watercolours,
sepia photographs and humorous sporting
prints, back sunroom (dogs allowed here)
overlooking pleasant garden; no credit cards;
children welcome till 9pm, four miles of
trout fishing (free for residents), good walks,
five bedrooms (two with own bathroom),
good breakfast and evening meal. *(B and M
Kendall, the Didler, Claes Mauroy, Neil and
Angela Huxter)*

ASKRIGG   SD9491
Kings Arms (01969) 650113

*Signed from A684 Leyburn–Sedbergh in
Bainbridge; DL8 3HQ* 18th-c coaching
inn now under same ownership as the
Charles Bathurst at Langthwaite; flagstoned
high-ceilinged main bar with good log fire,
traditional furnishings and décor, well kept
Black Sheep, Theakstons, a beer for the pub
from Yorkshire Dales and two guests, 13
wines by the glass, enjoyable food, friendly
helpful staff, restaurant with inglenook,
games room in former barrel-vaulted beer

cellar; background music; children welcome,
pleasant side courtyard, bedrooms run
separately as part of Holiday Property Bond
complex behind. *(Gerry and Rosemary Dobson)*

ASKRIGG   SD9491
White Rose (01969) 650515

Main Street; DL8 3HG Refurbished
19th-c hotel with well presented reasonably
priced food in carpeted bar, dining room or
conservatory, efficient staff, well kept John
Smiths, Theakstons and Yorkshire Dales
(brewed behind), good choice of wines by the
glass, pool room; suntrap back garden,
12 comfortable bedrooms, open all
day. *(Gerry and Rosemary Dobson)*

ASKWITH   SD1648
Black Horse (01943) 461074

Off A65; LS21 2JQ Biggish open-plan
stone-built pub in lovely spot (superb
Wharfedale views from dining conservatory
and good terrace), well kept Timothy Taylors
Landlord, wide choice of enjoyable home-
made food including Sun carvery, welcoming
landlord and good service, woodburner;
children and dogs welcome. *(Robert Wivell,
Gavin Barlow)*

AUSTWICK   SD7668
⋆**Game Cock** (01524) 251226

*Just off A65 Settle–Kirkby Lonsdale;
LA2 8BB* Quaint civilised place in pretty
spot below Three Peaks, good log fire in
old-fashioned beamed bare-boards back
bar, cheerful efficient staff and friendly
locals, good choice of well kept local ales,
winter mulled wine, nice coffee, most space
devoted to the food side, with good fairly
priced choice from french chef/landlord,
pizzas and children's meals as well, two
dining rooms and modern front conservatory-
type extension; walkers and dogs welcome,
tables out in front with play area, three neat
bedrooms, open all day Sun. *(Michael Lamm,
Peter Fryer, David Heath, Martin Smith, John and
Verna Aspinall, Pat and Graham Williamson)*

AYSGARTH   SE0088
George & Dragon (01969) 663358

Just off A684; DL8 3AD Welcoming
17th-c posting inn with emphasis on good
varied food from sandwiches up, two big
dining areas, small beamed and panelled bar
with log fire, well kept Black Sheep Bitter,
Theakstons Best and a beer brewed for the
pub, good choice of wines by the glass; may
be background music; children welcome,
nice paved garden, lovely scenery and walks,
handy for Aysgarth Falls, seven bedrooms,
open all day. *(John and Dinah Waters)*

BAILDON   SE1538
Junction (01274) 582009

Baildon Road; BD17 6AB Wedge-shaped
traditional local with three linked rooms,
friendly atmosphere, good choice of well
kept changing ales, home-made weekday

lunchtime food, live music and sing-alongs Sun evening, games room with pinball and pool; sports TV; open all day. *(the Didler, Andy Barker)*

BARKISLAND   SE0419
Fleece (01422) 820687
B6113 towards Ripponden; HX4 0DJ
Smartened-up 18th-c beamed moorland pub, two rooms laid out for the enjoyable reasonably priced food including a set menu, good service, well kept Black Sheep, stripped stone, woodburner and open fire, mezzanine, brightly painted children's room with games; Pennine views from first-floor terrace and garden, bedrooms, handy for M62.
(Gordon and Margaret Ormondroyd)

BARKSTON ASH   SE4936
Boot & Shoe (01937) 557374
Main Street; LS24 9PR Small refurbished village local, friendly and welcoming, with well kept Leeds, Tetleys, Theakstons, a beer brewed for them by Brown Cow and a guest, enjoyable reasonably priced food, good service, restaurant, beer festival second full weekend July; children and dogs welcome, seats on sunny back deck, open all day Sun, closed Mon and lunchtimes Tues-Sat.
(Les and Sandra Brown)

BARMBY ON THE MARSH   SE6828
Kings Head (01757) 630705
High Street; DN14 7HT Early 19th-c refurbished and extended beamed village pub, enjoyable locally sourced home-made food with some interesting choices, four ales including Black Sheep, good service, large restaurant, deli; children welcome, disabled facilities, open all day weekends, closed Mon and Tues lunchtimes. *(Michael Butler)*

BECK HOLE   NZ8202
✳ **Birch Hall** (01947) 896245
Off A169 SW of Whitby, from top of Sleights Moor; YO22 5LE Tiny pub-cum-village-shop in stunning surroundings, two unchanging rooms (shop sells postcards, sweets and ice-creams), simple furnishings – built-in cushioned wall seats, wooden tables (one embedded with 136 pennies), flagstones or composition flooring, unusual items like french breakfast cereal boxes, tube of toothpaste priced 1/3d and model train running around head-height shelf, well kept ales such as Black Sheep and North Yorkshire, bar snacks including local pies and cakes, exceptionally friendly service, dominoes and quoits; no credit cards; children in small family room, dogs welcome, old painting of river valley outside and benches, streamside garden, self-catering cottage, good walks – one along disused railway, open all day in summer, closed Mon evening in winter, all day Tues Nov-Mar. *(Kevin Thomas, Nina Randall, Matt and Vikki Wharton, the Didler, Eddie Cullen, Dr Kevan Tucker, Roger and Ann King and others)*

BEVERLEY   TA0339
Dog & Duck (01482) 862419
Ladygate; HU17 8BH Cheerful popular two-bar local handy for playhouse and Sat market, good home-made lunchtime food using local produce from sandwiches to bargain Sun lunch, OAP deals too, well kept Caledonian Deuchars IPA, Copper Dragon, John Smiths and guests, good value wines, several malts, helpful friendly staff, coal fires; background music, TV for racing, games machine; cheap basic courtyard bedrooms up iron stairs. *(Mike and Lynn Robinson, the Didler)*

BEVERLEY   TA0339
White Horse (01482) 861973
Hengate, off North Bar; HU17 8BN Carefully preserved Victorian interior with basic little rooms huddled around central bar, brown leatherette seats (high-backed settles in one little snug) and plain chairs and benches on bare boards, antique cartoons and sentimental engravings, gaslit chandelier, open fires, games room, upstairs family room, bargain Sam Smiths and guest beers, basic food; children till 7pm, open all day. *(Huw Jones, the Didler)*

BEVERLEY   TA0239
Woolpack (01482) 867095
Westwood Road, W of centre; HU17 8EN Small welcoming pub with no pretensions in pair of 19th-c cottages, sound traditional food and well kept ales such as Jennings, cosy snug, real fires, simple furnishings, brasses, teapots, prints and maps; beer garden, open all day weekends, closed lunchtimes Mon and Tues. *(Pat and Graham Williamson)*

BILBROUGH   SE5346
Three Hares (01937) 832128
Off A64 York–Tadcaster; YO23 3PH Smart neatly kept village dining pub, ample helpings of enjoyable good value food all day, Sun roasts, well kept real ale, good choice of wines by the glass, leather sofas and log fire. *(Marlene and Jim Godfrey, Mags Houghton)*

BOLSTERSTONE   SK2796
Castle Inn (0114) 288 6300
Off A616; S36 3ZB Stone-built local in small hilltop conservation-area village, spectacular surroundings by Ewden Valley at edge of Peak District National Park, great views from picnic-sets outside; open-plan but with distinct areas including tap room and restaurant, well kept Theakstons Best and two guests, enjoyable good value basic food, unofficial HQ of award-winning male voice choir. *(Michael Butler)*

BRADFIELD   SK2692
Old Horns (0114) 285 1207
High Bradfield; S6 6LG Welcoming old stone-built pub in hill village with stunning views; comfortably divided L-shaped bar,

lots of pictures, good value hearty home-made food, wide choice of ales including Thwaites Lancaster Bomber and Theakstons Old Peculier, also continental beers on tap, friendly knowledgeable staff; children welcome, picnic-sets and play area outside, next to interesting 14th-c church, good walks. *(Roger and Pauline Pearce, Matthew Lidbury)*

BRADFORD   SE1528
Chapel House (01274) 678772
Chapel House Buildings, Low Moor; BD12 0HP Busy stone-built beamed pub in pretty setting opposite church, plenty of atmosphere in L-shaped bare-boards bar, open fires, well kept Greene King, traditional food, helpful friendly staff, restaurant; open all day. *(Clive Flynn)*

BRADFORD   SE1533
Fighting Cock (01274) 726907
Preston Street (off B6145); BD7 1JE Busy bare-boards alehouse by industrial estate, great choice of well kept changing ales, foreign draught and bottled beers, farm ciders, friendly staff and lively atmosphere, all-day doorstep sandwiches and good simple lunchtime hot dishes (not Sun), may be free bread and dripping on the bar, low prices, coal fires; open all day. *(the Didler)*

BRADFORD   SE1533
New Beehive (01274) 721784
Westgate; BD1 3AA Robustly old-fashioned Edwardian inn with several rooms including good pool room, wide range of changing ales, gas lighting, candles and coal fires, friendly atmosphere and welcoming staff; basement music nights; nice back courtyard, bedrooms, open all day (till 2am Fri, Sat). *(the Didler)*

BRADFORD   SE1633
Sparrow Bier Café (01677) 470411
North Parade; BD1 3HZ Bare-boards bar with great selection of bottled beers, draught continentals and local real ales, good deli platters, local artwork, more tables in cellar bar; background music; open all day, closed Sun. *(Pat and Tony Martin)*

BRAMHAM   SE4242
Swan (01937) 843570
Just off A1 2 miles N of A64; LS23 6QA Civilised and unspoilt three-room local with engaging long-serving landlady, good mix of customers, well kept Black Sheep, Hambleton and Leeds Pale.
(Les and Sandra Brown)

BRIGHOUSE   SE1320
Clough House (01484) 512120
Clough Lane; HD6 3QL Well worn-in pub with bar and two dining areas, clean and comfortable, with popular above average food including good steaks (best to book), well kept Bass and two other beers,

efficient chatty service; impressive hanging baskets. *(Gordon and Margaret Ormondroyd, Andy and Jill Kassube and others)*

BRIGHOUSE   SE1421
Globe (01484) 713169
Rastrick Common; HD6 3EL Welcoming local, clean and comfortable, with well kept Camerons, Copper Dragon, Greene King and Tetleys, enjoyable reasonably priced food including cheap two-course light lunch, friendly young staff, restaurant extension; children welcome, open all day Sun (booking advised then). *(Gordon and Margaret Ormondroyd)*

BURN   SE5928
★ Wheatsheaf (01757) 270614
Main Road (A19 Selby–Doncaster); YO8 8LJ Welcoming busy mock-Tudor roadside pub, comfortable seats and tables in partly divided open-plan bar with masses to look at – gleaming copper kettles, black dagging shears, polished buffalo horns, cases of model vans and lorries, decorative mugs above one bow-window seat, a drying rack over the log fire; John Smiths, Timothy Taylors and guests, 20 malt whiskies, good value straightforward food (not Sun-Weds evenings), roast only on Sun; pool table, games machine, TV and may be unobtrusive background music; children and dogs welcome, picnic-sets on heated terrace in small back garden, open all day till midnight. *(Bob and Tanya Ekers, Terry and Nickie Williams, John and Eleanor Holdsworth)*

BURNSALL   SE0361
★ Red Lion (01756) 720204
B6160 S of Grassington; BD23 6BU Family-run 16th-c inn in lovely spot by River Wharfe, looking across village green to Burnsall Fell, tables out on front cobbles and on big back terrace; attractively panelled, sturdily furnished front dining rooms with log fire, more basic back public bar, good imaginative food (all day wknds), well kept ales such as Copper Dragon and Timothy Taylors, nice wines, efficient friendly service, conservatory; children welcome, comfortable bedrooms (dogs allowed in some and in bar), fishing permits available, open all day. *(John and Helen Rushton, Michael Butler, John Urquhart)*

BURTON LEONARD   SE3263
★ Hare & Hounds (01765) 677355
Off A61 Ripon–Harrogate, handy for A1(M) exit 48; HG3 3SG Civilised and welcoming country dining pub, good popular food served promptly, well kept ales such as Black Sheep and Timothy Taylors from long counter, nice coffee, large carpeted main area divided by log fire, traditional furnishings, bright little side room; children in eating areas, pretty back garden.
(Peter Hacker, Phil and Gill Wass, Robert Wivell)

BURYTHORPE   SE7964
Bay Horse (01653) 658302

*Off A64 8.5 miles NE of York ring road,
via Kirkham and Westow; 5 miles S of
Malton, by Welham Road;*
YO17 9LJ Dining pub with linked rooms,
main bar with nice old carved antique
pews and ancient hunting prints, Tetleys,
Theakstons Black Bull and Timothy Taylors
Landlord, 11 wines by the glass, end dining
room with attractive farmyard animal
paintings, also a snug with sofa and log fire
and red-walled room with rugs on flagstones;
children welcome, dogs in bar, contemporary
furniture on terrace under parasols, nice
Wolds-edge village with fine surrounding
walks, open all day Sun, closed Mon. *(C A
Hall, Christopher Turner, Ed and Anna Fraser)*

CARLTON-IN-CLEVELAND NZ5004
Blackwell Ox (01642) 712287
Just off A172 SW of Stokesley; TS9 7DJ
Three linked rooms off big central bar, thai
landlady and helpful friendly staff, good
thai food plus some english dishes, weekday
lunch/early-evening deal, blazing log fires;
children welcome, garden with play area,
picturesque village location, handy for coast-
to-coast and Cleveland Way walkers. *(Graham
Denison, Robert Wivell)*

CARTHORPE   SE3083
★Fox & Hounds (01845) 567433
*Village signed from A1 N of Ripon, via
B6285; DL8 2LG* Welcoming neatly kept
dining pub with emphasis on good well
presented food, attractive high-raftered
restaurant with lots of farm and smithy tools,
Black Sheep and Worthington in L-shaped
bar with two log fires, plush seating, plates
on stripped beams and evocative Victorian
photographs of Whitby, some theatrical
memorabilia in corridors, good friendly
service; background classical music; children
welcome, handy for A1, closed Mon and first
week Jan. *(Janet and Peter Race, Michael and
Maggie Betton, M and J White, P A Rowe)*

CAWOOD   SE5737
Ferry (01757) 268515
*King Street (B1222 NW of Selby), by
Ouse swing bridge; YO8 3TL* Interesting
16th-c inn with several comfortable areas,
enjoyable unpretentious food and well
kept ales, cheerful efficient sevice, log
fire in massive inglenook, low beams,
stripped brickwork and bare boards; nice
flagstone terrace and lawn down to the river,
bedrooms. *(Pat and Graham Williamson)*

CHAPEL LE DALE   SD7477
★Hill Inn (01524) 241256
*B5655 Ingleton–Hawes, 3 miles N of
Ingleton; LA6 3AR* Former farmhouse
with fantastic views to Ingleborough and
Whernside and a haven for weary walkers
(wonderful remote surrounding walks);

relaxed, chatty atmosphere, beams, log fires,
straightforward furniture on stripped wooden
floors, nice pictures, bare-stone recesses,
Black Sheep, Dent and Theakstons, enjoyable
bar food, separate dining room and well
worn-in sun lounge; children welcome, dogs
in bar, bedrooms, open all day Sat, closed
Mon. *(Anon)*

CLIFTON   SE1622
★Black Horse (01484) 713862
*Westgate/Coalpit Lane; signed off
Brighouse Road from M62 junction 25;
HD6 4HJ* Friendly 17th-c inn/restaurant,
pleasant décor, front dining rooms with
good interesting food including a few pubby
dishes, can be pricy, efficient uniformed
service, open fire in back bar with beam-
and-plank ceiling, well kept Timothy Taylors
Landlord and a house beer brewed by Brass
Monkey, decent wines; nice courtyard, 21
comfortable bedrooms, pleasant village, open
all day. *(John and Eleanor Holdsworth, Tim and
Sue Halstead, Michael Butler)*

COLTON   SE5444
★Old Sun (01904) 744261
Off A64 York–Tadcaster; LS24 8EP Some
accomplished cooking at this recently
refurbished and extended 18th-c beamed
dining pub, good wine list with plenty
available by the glass, well kept Black Sheep
and Cropton, competent service; cookery
demonstrations and little shop selling home-
made and local produce; children welcome,
seats out on front terrace, bedrooms in
separate building, open all day Sun (food till
7pm then). *(David and Sue Smith, Tim and
Sue Halstead, Ian Prince, Dunning, Gordon and
Margaret Ormondroyd)*

CONEYTHORPE   SE3958
Tiger (01423) 863632
*2.3 miles from A1(M), junction 47; A59
towards York, then village (and brown
sign to Tiger Inn) signposted; bear left at
brown sign in Flaxby; HG5 0RY*
Spreading red-carpeted bar with hundreds
of pewter tankards hanging from ochre-
painted joists, olde-worlde prints, china
figurines in one arched alcove, padded grey
wall seats, pews and settles around sturdy
scrubbed tables, open fire, more formal
dining area at back, sensibly priced food
from lunchtime sandwiches through pubby
favourites, also set menu deals, Black Sheep,
Ilkley and Timothy Taylors Landlord, friendly
helpful staff; nostalgic background music;
picnic-sets on front gravel terrace and on
small green opposite, open all day. *(Pat and
Graham Williamson, Les and Sandra Brown, Peter
Hardisty, Ed and Anna Fraser, Malcolm Bond)*

CRAY   SD9479
★White Lion (01756) 760262
B6160 N of Kettlewell; BD23 5JB
Highest Wharfedale pub in lovely
countryside and popular with walkers;

welcoming cheerful atmosphere, simple bar with open fire and flagstones, enjoyable well priced food including filled yorkshire puddings and good local trout, Black Sheep, Copper Dragon and Timothy Taylors in good condition, back room, original bull'ook game; children and dogs welcome, picnic-sets above quiet steep lane or can sit on flat limestone slabs in shallow stream opposite, bedrooms. *(Michael Lamm, David M Potts, Lawrence Pearse, Dr Kevan Tucker, the Didler, B and M Kendall and others)*

DACRE BANKS   SE1961
★**Royal Oak**   (01423) 780200
B6451 S of Pateley Bridge; HG3 4EN
Popular solidly comfortable 18th-c pub with Nidderdale views, traditional food done very well, attentive friendly staff, well kept ales including Rudgate, good wine choice, beams and panelling, log-fire dining room, games room with darts, dominoes and pool; TV, background music; children in eating areas, terrace tables, informal back garden, three character bedrooms, good breakfast, open all day. *(Robert Wivell, Angus and Carol Johnson)*

DEWSBURY   SE2622
Huntsman   (01924) 275700
Walker Cottages, Chidswell Lane, Shaw Cross – pub signed; WF12 7SWRevised for hardback Cosy low-beamed converted cottages alongside urban-fringe farm, long-serving landlord and friendly locals, lots of agricultural bric-a-brac, blazing log fire, small front extension, well kept Chidswell (brewed for them), Timothy Taylors Landlord and guests, decent home-made food (not lunchtimes Sun, Mon or evenings except Thurs, Fri). *(Michael Butler, the Didler)*

DEWSBURY   SE2420
Leggers   (01924) 502846
Robinsons Boat Yard, Savile Town Wharf, Mill Street E (SE of B6409); WF12 9BD Good value basic hayloft conversion by Calder & Hebble Navigation marina, low-beamed upstairs bar, well kept Everards Tiger and five guests, bottled belgian beers, farm cider and perry, straightforward food, friendly staff, brewery and pub memorabilia, real fire, daily newspapers, pool; picnic-sets outside, boat trips, open all day. *(the Didler)*

DEWSBURY   SE2421
★**West Riding Licensed Refreshment Rooms**   (01924) 459193
Station, Wellington Road; WF13 1HF
Convivial three-room early Victorian station bar, eight well kept changing ales such as Black Sheep, Oakham, Partners and Timothy Taylors, foreign bottled beers and farm ciders, bargain generous lunchtime food on scrubbed tables, popular pie night Tues, curry night Weds and Yorkshire tapas night Thurs, good weekend breakfast too, friendly staff, lots of steam memorabilia including

paintings by local artists, coal fire, daily newspapers, impressive juke box, some live music; children till 6pm in two end rooms, disabled access, open all day. *(the Didler, Andy Lickfold)*

DONCASTER   SE5702
Corner Pin   (01302) 340670
St Sepulchre Gate West, Cleveland Street; DN1 3AH Plush beamed lounge with old local pub prints, welsh dresser and china, John Smiths and interesting guests kept well (beer festivals), good value traditional food from fine hot sandwiches to Sun roasts, friendly landlady, cheery bar with darts, games machine and TV; open all day. *(the Didler)*

DONCASTER   SK6299
Hare & Tortoise   (01302) 867329
Parrots Corner, Bawtry Road, Bessacarr (A638); DN4 7PB Popular Vintage Inn all-day dining pub, ales such as Adnams, Black Sheep and Everards, friendly young staff, several small rooms off central bar, log fire; background music. *(George Atkinson, Terry and Nickie Williams)*

DONCASTER   SE5703
Plough   (01302) 738310
West Laith Gate, by Frenchgate shopping centre; DN1 1SF Small old-fashioned local with friendly long-serving licensees and chatty regulars, Acorn Barnsley Bitter and guests, bustling front room with darts, dominoes and sports TV, old town maps, quieter back lounge; tiny central courtyard, open all day (Sun afternoon break). *(the Didler)*

EASINGWOLD   SE5270
★**George**   (01347) 821698
Market Place; YO61 3AD Neat, bright and airy market town hotel (former 18th-c coaching inn), quiet corners even when busy, helpful cheerful service, well kept Black Sheep, Moorhouses and a guest, enjoyable food in bar and restaurant, beams and horsebrasses and warm log fires, slightly old-fashioned feel and popular with older customers; pleasant bedrooms, good breakfast. *(Pete Coxon, Ian and Helen Stafford, Tony and Wendy Hobden, Michael Butler, Nick and Alison Dowson, Janet and Peter Race and others)*

EAST MARTON   SD9050
Cross Keys   (01282) 844326
A59 Gisburn–Skipton; BD23 3LP
Comfortable 18th-c pub behind small green near Leeds & Liverpool Canal (and Pennine Way), heavy beams and big open fire, good choice of enjoyable food (all day Sun) from lunchtime sandwiches up, well kept Copper Dragon and Theakstons, friendly service, more restauranty dining room; children and dogs welcome, background music; tables outside; for sale as we went to press. *(Pat and Graham Williamson, John and Hazel Sarkanen)*

EAST WITTON   SE1487
⋆**Cover Bridge Inn** (01969) 623250
A6108 out towards Middleham; DL8 4SQ
Cosy 16th-c flagstoned country local with
friendly accommodating landlord and staff,
good choice of well kept Yorkshire ales,
enjoyable generous pub food, sensible prices,
small restaurant, roaring fires; children
and dogs welcome, riverside garden, three
bedrooms, open all day. *(Jon Forster, the Didler,
Ed and Anna Fraser)*

EGTON   NZ8006
Wheatsheaf (01947) 895271
Village Centre; YO21 1TZ Village pub
of real character, interesting paintings and
prints in small bar with open fire, good
generously served inexpensive food, friendly
service, Black Sheep, John Smiths and
guests, several wines by the glass, restaurant;
six bedrooms, open all day weekends. *(Peter
Dearing, Gordon and Margaret Ormondroyd)*

EGTON BRIDGE   NZ8005
Horseshoe (01947) 895245
*Village signed off A171 W of Whitby;
YO21 1XE* Attractively placed 18th-c stone
inn back under licensees from 13 years
ago – refurbishment ongoing; open fire, high-
backed built-in winged settles, wall seats
and spindleback chairs, various odds and
ends including a big stuffed trout (caught
nearby in 1913), Theakstons, Black Sheep,
Copper Dragon and a guest, traditional food;
background music; children welcome, dogs
in parts, seats on quiet terrace in attractive
mature garden bordering small river Esk,
good walks (on coast-to-coast path), six
bedrooms, open all day weekends. *(Sara
Fulton, Roger Baker, Phil and Jane Villiers)*

EGTON BRIDGE   NZ8005
⋆**Postgate** (01947) 895241
*Village signed off A171 W of Whitby;
YO21 1UX* Moorland village pub with
good imaginative fairly priced food, friendly
staff, well kept Black Sheep and a guest,
traditional quarry-tiled panelled bar with
beams, panelled dado and coal fire in antique
range, elegant restaurant; children and dogs
welcome, garden picnic-sets, three nice
bedrooms. *(Dr and Mrs R G J Telfer,
Mrs Grace Smith)*

FERRENSBY   SE3660
⋆**General Tarleton** (01423) 340284
A655 N of Knaresborough; HG5 0PZ
Smart civilised atmosphere – more
restaurant-with-rooms than pub; excellent
modern cooking and good service from
uniformed staff, nice wines by the glass
(good list), Black Sheep and Timothy Taylors,
beamed bar area divided up by brick pillars,

dark brown leather dining chairs around
wooden tables, more formal restaurant
with exposed stonework; children welcome,
covered courtyard and pleasant tree-lined
garden, white-painted or plain wood furniture
under parasols, comfortable contemporary
bedrooms, good breakfast. *(Richard and Mary
Bailey, Pat and Graham Williamson, Michael
Doswell, Janet and Peter Race, John and Eleanor
Holdsworth, Michael Butler and others)*

FILEY   TA1180
Bonhommes (0172) 3514054
The Crescent; YO14 9JH Friendly bar with
several well kept ales including one brewed
for them locally, live music and quiz nights;
open all day till late. *(Brian Daley)*

FINGHALL   SE1889
⋆**Queens Head** (01677) 450259
Off A684 E of Leyburn; DL8 5ND
Welcoming comfortable dining pub, log fires
either end of tidy low-beamed bar, settles
making stalls around big tables, Black Sheep,
Greene King, John Smiths and Theakstons,
wide choice of good food from traditional
things up, extended back Wensleydale-view
dining room; children and dogs welcome,
disabled facilities, back garden with decking
sharing same view, three bedrooms. *(Ed and
Anna Fraser)*

FIXBY   SE1119
Nags Head (01727) 871100
*New Hey Road, by M62 junction 24
south side, past Hilton; HD2 2EA*
Spacious ivy-covered chain dining pub,
attractive outside and comfortable in, pubby
bar with four well kept ales, decent fairly
priced food including carvery and OAP
deals, friendly efficient service, linked areas
with wood and slate floors; garden tables,
bedrooms in adjoining Premier Inn, open all
day. *(John and Eleanor Holdsworth, Gordon and
Margaret Ormondroyd, Brenda and others)*

FLAXTON   SE6762
Blacksmiths Arms (01904) 468210
Off A64; YO60 7RJ Small welcoming
traditional pub on attractive village green,
enjoyable home-made food, well kept Black
Sheep, Timothy Taylors, Theakstons and York,
good friendly service, carpeted L-shaped bar
and restaurant, open fire; seats out at front
and behind, three bedrooms, closed Sun
evening, Mon, lunchtimes Tues-Sat. *(David
and Ruth Hollands, Roger and Anne Newbury)*

FLOCKTON   SE2314
Sun (01924) 848603
*Off A642 Wakefield–Huddersfield at
Blacksmiths Arms; WF4 4DW* Nicely
refurbished old beamed pub with open fires
in bar and dining area, enjoyable reasonably

If we know a pub has an outdoor play area for children, we mention it.

priced food from shortish menu, real ales, prompt efficient service; children welcome, garden tables with lovely views, open all day. *(John and Eleanor Holdsworth)*

GIGGLESWICK   SD8164
⋆ **Black Horse**   (01729) 822506
Church Street – take care with the car park; BD24 0BE Hospitable licensees in 17th-c village pub prettily set by church, cosy bar with gleaming brass, copper and bric-a-brac, coal-effect fire, good value hearty food, well kept Timothy Taylors, Tetleys and perhaps guests, intimate dining room, good service, piano (often played), monthly quiz; no visiting dogs; children welcome till 9pm, sheltered heated back terrace, smokers' shelter, three reasonably priced comfortable bedrooms, good breakfast, open all day weekends. *(Dudley and Moira Cockroft, Tony and Maggie Harwood, the Didler)*

GIGGLESWICK   SD8164
Craven Arms   (01729) 825627
Just off A65 W of village at junction with Brackenber Lane, opposite station; BD24 0EB Modern refurbishment and interesting well presented food including meat from licensee's organic farm (good vegetarian options too), moderate prices, well kept ales such as Black Sheep, Copper Dragon and Tetleys, attentive friendly service, restaurant; children welcome, disabled access, seven bedrooms, closed Mon. *(John and Susan Miln, Tony and Maggie Harwood, Canon Graham Bettridge)*

GIGGLESWICK   SD8164
Harts Head   (01729) 822 086
Belle Hill; BD24 0BA Cheerful bustling village inn, well kept ales such as Black Sheep, public bar (dogs welcome) with dominoes, good choice of enjoyable reasonably priced food in restaurant, folk night first Fri of month; Sky TV; outside smokers' area, bedrooms.
(Tony and Maggie Harwood)

GILLAMOOR   SE6890
⋆ **Royal Oak**   (01751) 431414
Off A170 in Kirkbymoorside; YO62 7HX Stone-built 18th-c dining pub with interesting food at fair prices (can get busy), friendly staff, ales such as Black Sheep and Copper Dragon, reasonably priced wines, roomy bar with heavy dark beams, log fires in two tall stone fireplaces (one with old kitchen range), overspill dining room (dogs allowed here); children welcome, eight comfortable modern bedrooms, good breakfast, attractive village handy for Barnsdale Moor walks. *(Ed and Anna Fraser, C A Hall, David and Lin Short)*

GILLING EAST   SE6176
⋆ **Fairfax Arms**   (01439) 788212
Main Street (B1363, off A170 via Oswaldkirk); YO62 4JH Smartly refurbished country inn, beamed bar with

bare boards by handsome oak counter, carpeted area with woodburner, Black Sheep, Tetleys and some interesting wines by the glass, daily newspapers, two-part carpeted dining room with big hunting prints on red walls, nicely old-fashioned floral curtains and some padded oak settles, enjoyable modern food plus pub favourites, friendly black-aproned staff; picnic-sets out in front by floodlit roadside stream, pleasant village well placed for Howardian Hills and North York Moors, comfortably up-to-date bedrooms, good breakfast, open all day weekends. *(Michael Butler)*

GLUSBURN   SD9944
Dog & Gun   (01535) 633855
Colne Road (A6068 W) opposite Malsis School; BD20 8DS Comfortably refurbished traditional pub very popular for its wide choice of enjoyable good value food (evening booking advised), attentive friendly service, four well kept Timothy Taylors ales; children welcome, open all day. *(Len Beattie)*

GRASSINGTON   SE0064
⋆ **Devonshire**   (01756) 752525
The Square; BD23 5AD Small handsome reliably run hotel, good window seats and tables outside overlooking sloping village square, decent food from substantial sandwiches up, well kept ales such as Moorhouses Pendle Witches Brew, interesting pictures and ornaments, beams and open fires, pleasant family room, big restaurant, cheerful relaxed atmosphere; seven comfortable bedrooms, open all day Sun. *(Janet and Peter Race, Dr Kevan Tucker, B and M Kendall)*

GRASSINGTON   SE0064
Foresters Arms   (01756) 752349
Main Street; BD23 5AA Comfortable opened-up old coaching inn with friendly bustling atmosphere, good generous well priced food, good choice of ales including Black Sheep and Timothy Taylors, cheerful efficient service, log fires, dining room off on right, pool and sports TV on left, popular Mon quiz; children welcome, outside tables, 14 affordable bedrooms, good walking country, open all day. *(Michael Lamm, Dr Kevan Tucker, B and M Kendall)*

GREAT AYTON   NZ5510
Buck   (01642) 722242
West Terrace, Low Green; TS9 6PA Old inn across road from River Levern, wide choice of good food including daily specials, well kept ales such as Timothy Taylors Landlord, good service. *(Jane Taylor and David Dutton)*

GREAT HABTON   SE7576
⋆ **Grapes**   (01653) 669166
Corner of Habton Lane and Kirby Misperton Lane; YO17 6TU Traditionally refurbished beamed dining pub in small

village, homely and cosy, with good cooking including fresh local fish and game, home-baked bread, Marstons-related ales, open fire, small public bar with darts and TV; background music; a few roadside picnic-sets (water for dogs), nice walks, open all day Sun, closed Tues lunchtime and Mon. *(Chris Paxton)*

GREAT OUSEBURN   SE4461
★**Crown** (01423) 330013
*Off B6265 SE of Boroughbridge;
YO26 9RF* Welcoming, nicely refurbished 18th-c pub, very good locally sourced food from pubby to more restaurants dishes, early-bird deals, well kept Black Sheep, Timothy Taylors Landlord and a house beer from Rudgate, decent wines, various areas including back dining extension; garden with terrace tables, open all day weekends, closed Mon lunchtime, Tues. *(Alison and Pete, David Brown, Ed and Anna Fraser, Judith and Edward Pearson)*

GUISELEY   SE1941
Coopers (01943) 878835
Otley Road; LS20 8AH Light and modern Market Town Taverns bar with good range of food from lunchtime sandwiches up, eight real ales including Black Sheep and Timothy Taylors Landlord, jazz and blues nights in upstairs function/dining room, open all day. *(the Didler)*

GUNNERSIDE   SD9598
Kings Head (01748) 886126
B6270 Swaledale Road; DL11 6LD Small two-room local (former 17th-c blacksmith's) in pretty riverside Dales village, four well kept local ales, plenty of wines by the glass, food from sandwiches up (not Mon), log fire, flagstones and carpet, old village photographs; welcomes children, dogs (menu for them) and muddy boots, some tables out by bridge, good nearby walks, open all day weekends. *(JJW, CMW)*

HALIFAX   SE0924
Three Pigeons (01422) 347001
Sun Fold, South Parade; off Church Street; HX1 2LX Carefully restored, four-room 1930s pub (Grade II listed), art deco fittings, ceiling painting in octagonal main area, original flooring, panelling and tiled fireplaces with log fires, up to six well kept Ossett ales and local guests, friendly chatty staff; tables outside, handy for Eureka! Museum and Shay Stadium, open all day Fri-Sun, from 3pm other days. *(Pat and Tony Martin)*

HARDROW   SD8691
★**Green Dragon** (01969) 667392
Village signed off A684; DL8 3LZ Friendly traditional Dales pub dating from 13th c and full of character; stripped stone, antique settles on flagstones, lots of bric-a-brac, low-beamed snug with log fire in old iron range, another in big main bar,

four well kept ales including one brewed for them by Yorkshire Dales, enjoyable generous food, small neat restaurant, annual brass band competition; children and dogs welcome, bedrooms, next to Hardraw Force – England's highest single-drop waterfall. *(Peter Salmon, Steve Short, Claes Mauroy, David Billington, M and J White, Rob and Catherine Dunster)*

HAROME   SE6482
★**Star** (01439) 770397
High Street; village signed S of A170, E of Helmsley; YO62 5JE Restaurant-with-rooms (need to book for both well in advance) in pretty 14th-c thatched building, but bar does have informal feel, bowed beam-and-plank ceiling, plenty of bric-a-brac, interesting furniture including 'Mousey' Thompson pieces, log fire and well polished tiled kitchen range, three local ales, 18 wines by the glass, home-made fruit liqueurs, snacks served in cocktail bar, popular coffee loft in the eaves, inventive ambitious modern cooking (not cheap); background music; children welcome, seats on sheltered front terrace, more in garden, open all day Sun, closed Mon lunchtime. *(Oliver Richardson, Dr Kevan Tucker, John and Dinah Waters, G Jennings)*

HARPHAM   TA0961
St Quintin Arms (01262) 490329
Main Street; YO25 4QY Comfortable old village pub with enjoyable home-made food including good mixed grill, well kept Tetleys and Wold Top, small dining room; sheltered garden with pond, three bedrooms. *(C A Hall)*

HARROGATE   SE3155
Coach & Horses (01423) 561802
West Park; HG1 1BJ Very friendly bustling pub with speciality pies and other enjoyable reasonably priced food (not every evening), several good Yorkshire ales, obliging service, nice interior with booth seating; open all day. *(Pete Coxon, Adrian Johnson, Tim and Sue Halstead, the Didler, David and Susan Nobbs)*

HARROGATE   SE3157
Gardeners Arms (01423) 506051
Bilton Lane (off A59 either in Bilton itself or on outskirts towards Harrogate – via Bilton Hall Drive); HG1 4DH Stone-built 17th-c house converted into friendly down-to-earth local, tiny bar and three small rooms, flagstone floors, panelling, old prints, big fire in stone fireplace, very cheap Sam Smiths OBB, decent bar lunches (not Tues), dominoes; children welcome, surrounding streamside garden with play area, lovely peaceful setting near Nidd Gorge. *(Alan and Shirley Sawden)*

HARROGATE   SE2955
★**Hales** (01423) 725570
Crescent Road; HG1 2RS Classic Victorian décor in 18th-c gas-lit local close to Pump

Rooms, leather seats in alcoves, stuffed birds, comfortable saloon and tiny snug, seven real ales including Daleside, simple good value lunchtime food, friendly helpful staff; can get lively weekend evenings. *(Michael Butler, David and Ruth Shillitoe, Martin Cawley)*

HARROGATE   SE2955
✶ Old Bell (01423) 507930
Royal Parade; HG1 2SZ Thriving Market Town Taverns pub with eight mainly Yorkshire beers from handsome counter, lots of bottled continentals and impressive choice of wines by the glass, friendly helpful staff, lunchtime snacks including sandwiches (interesting choice of breads), more elaborate evening meals upstairs, newspapers, panelling, old sweet shop ads and breweriana; no children; open all day. *(Tod and Dawn Hannula, the Didler, Roger and Donna Huggins)*

HARROGATE   SE3055
Swan on the Stray (01423) 524587
Corner Devonshire Place and A59; HG1 4AA Refurbished Market Town Tavern, enjoyable reasonably priced food from shortish menu plus a few specials including game, five mostly local ales, ciders and perry, good range of bottled imports, cheerful efficient service, daily newspapers. *(Brian and Janet Ainscough, Pat and Tony Martin)*

HARROGATE   SE3155
Winter Gardens (01423) 877010
Royal Baths, Crescent Road; HG1 2RR Interesting Wetherspoons transformation of former ballroom in landmark building, well kept ales, generous usual good value food, many original features, comfortable sofas in lofty hall, upper gallery; very busy late evening; attractive terrace, open all day. *(S Holder)*

HARTHILL   SK4980
Beehive (01909) 770205
Union Street; S26 7YH Two-bar village pub opposite attractive church, enjoyable generous food from chef/landlord (all day Sun), friendly service, four well kept ales including Timothy Taylors Landlord, good choice of wines, malts and soft drinks, fresh flowers, games room with pool; background music; children welcome till 9pm if eating, outside picnic-sets and attractive hanging baskets, walks nearby, closed Mon. *(JJW, CMW and others)*

HAWNBY   SE5489
Inn at Hawnby (01439) 798202
Aka Hawnby Hotel; off B1257 NW of Helmsley; YO62 5QS Attractively situated inn with good local food including some interesting choices, really welcoming service, real ales such as Black Sheep and Great Newsome, good choice of wines by the glass; children welcome, lovely views from restaurant and garden tables, pretty village in walking country (packed lunches available), nine bedrooms – three in converted stables, open all day Fri-Sun. *(Dr Nigel Bowles)*

HEADINGLEY   SE2736
Arcadia (0113) 274 5599
Arndale Centre; LS6 2UE Small Market Town Tavern in former bank, good choice of changing Yorkshire ales kept well, lots of continental bottled beers, knowledgeable staff, bar food, stairs to mezzanine; open all day. *(Peter Smith and Judith Brown, Daniel Lezcano)*

HEBDEN BRIDGE   SD9827
Stubbings Wharf (01422) 844 107
A mile W; HX7 6LU Warm and friendly pub in good spot by Rochdale Canal with adjacent moorings, enjoyable food (all day weekends) from sandwiches to good value Sun lunch, wide range of ales including local microbrews, usually three real ciders; open all day; dogs welcome. *(Dave Sumpter, Jon Moody, Andy and Jill Kassube, Martin Smith)*

HEBDEN BRIDGE   SD9927
✶ White Lion (01422) 842197
Bridge Gate; HX7 5EX Solid stone-built 17th-c inn with spacious recently refurbished interior, good choice of enjoyable sensibly priced food all day (cooked to order so may be a wait), five well kept ales including Black Sheep and Timothy Taylors, friendly service; children welcome, dogs in snug, disabled facilities, attractive secluded riverside garden, ten good bedrooms – four in courtyard. *(Ian and Nita Cooper, Martin Smith, Brian and Anna Marsden, Michael Butler, David Heath)*

HELMSLEY   SE6183
Feathers (01439) 770275
Market Place; YO62 5BH Substantial stone inn with sensibly priced generous food from sandwiches to good seasonal crab, popular Sun lunch, well kept Black Sheep, Tetleys and a guest, good friendly service, several rooms with comfortable seats, oak and walnut tables (some by Robert 'Mouseman' Thompson – as is the bar counter), flagstones or tartan carpet, heavy medieval beams and huge inglenook log fire, panelled corridors; children welcome in eating area, tables out in front, 22 clean comfortable bedrooms, open all day. *(Philip and Jan Medcalf, Ben and Ruth Levy, Glenwys and Alan Lawrence, David and Lin Short)*

HEPWORTH   SE1606
✶ Butchers Arms (01484) 682857
Village signposted off A616 SE of Holmfirth; Towngate; HD9 1TE Civilised old country dining pub with some nice modern touches; flagstones by counter, dark boards elsewhere, a good log fire, low beams (handsomely carved in dining room on right – one of the nicest beam-and-plank ceilings

we've seen), light-hearted prints on cream or maroon walls, candles on informal mix of stripped-top tables, good choice of wines by the glass, Black Sheep, Copper Dragon Golden Pippin and Little Valley Withens, very good food, not cheap but fairly priced for the quality, cheerful efficient staff; background music; terrace with smart boxy wooden tables and warming pot-bellied stove, open all day. *(David and Cathrine Whiting, John Holt, Gordon and Margaret Ormondroyd, Oliver Richardson)*

HETTON   SD9658
⋆ **Angel** (01756) 730263
Off B6265 Skipton–Grassington; BD23 6LT Busy dining pub with three neatly kept timbered and panelled rooms mainly set for the good imaginative food (all day Sun), main bar with farmhouse range in stone fireplace, well kept Black Sheep, Dark Horse and a guest, 20 wines by the glass, lots of nooks and alcoves, country-kitchen and smart dining chairs, plush seats, all sorts of tables, Ronald Searle wine-snob cartoons, older engravings and photographs, log fires; children welcome, smart furniture on two covered terraces, nice bedrooms, closed Jan. *(Janet and Peter Race, B and M Kendall, Karen Eliot, Margaret and Jeff Graham, Richard and Mary Bailey, Andrew and Ruth Triggs and others)*

HIGH BENTHAM   SD6769
Coach House (01524) 262305
Main Street; LA2 7HE Centrally placed 17th-c coaching inn, low beams, alcoves, nooks and crannies, enjoyable good value food including OAP lunch deal, Robinsons ales; bedrooms. *(Karen Eliot)*

HOLMFIRTH   SD1408
Nook (01484) 681568
Victoria Square/South Lane; HD9 2DN Tucked-away basic 18th-c stone pub brewing its own good ales alongside Timothy Taylors and other guests, home-made pubby food all day and adjoining tapas bar, low beams, flagstones and big open fire, pool, some live music; heated streamside terrace, open all day. *(the Didler)*

HOLYWELL GREEN   SE0919
Rock (01422) 379721
Broad Carr Lane; handy for M62 Junction 24; HX4 9BS Smart comfortable hotel/restaurant rather than pub, very popular for its good food (all day Sun – best to book) including well priced set menu, friendly efficient service, small bar area serving Timothy Taylors Landlord, Churchill-themed restaurant; children welcome, 27 bedrooms, good breakfast. *(Gordon and Margaret Ormondroyd, Simon Le Fort and others)*

HORBURY   SE2918
Boons (01924) 277267
Queen Street; WF4 6LP Lively, chatty and comfortably unpretentious flagstoned local, Clarks, John Smiths, Timothy Taylors Landlord and up to four quickly changing guests, no food, Rugby League memorabilia, warm fire, back tap room with pool; TV, no children; courtyard tables, open all day Fri-Sun. *(Michael Butler, the Didler)*

HORBURY   SE2917
Bulls Head (01924) 265526
Southfield Lane; WF4 5AR Large well divided pub very popular locally for its food, smart attentive staff, Black Sheep and Tetleys, lots of wines by the glass, panelling and wood floors, relaxing linked rooms including snug, library and more formal restaurant; front picnic-sets. *(Michael Butler)*

HORSFORTH   SE2438
Town Street Tavern (0113) 281 9996
Town Street; LS18 4RJ Market Town Tavern with seven well kept ales and lots of continental bottled beers, good generous food including some south african dishes in small bare-boards bar and upstairs evening bistro (closed Sun), good service; small terrace, open all day. *(Pat and Tony Martin)*

HOVINGHAM   SE6675
Malt Shovel (01653) 628264
Main Street (B1257 NW of Castle Howard); YO62 4LF Attractive and comfortably unpretentious, with friendly staff, enjoyable sensibly priced home-made food including substantial specials, well kept Black Sheep and Tetleys, good coffee, cosy dining room; children welcome, appealing village setting. *(Peter and Anne Hollindale)*

HOVINGHAM   SE6675
⋆ **Worsley Arms** (01653) 628234
High Street; YO62 4LA Smart inn in pretty village handy for Castle Howard, good food in friendly and welcoming back bar and separate restaurant (different menu), Hambleton ales, several malts, good wines and coffee, friendly attentive staff, lots of Yorkshire cricketer photographs especially from 1930s and 40s; attractive gardens with tables by stream, 19 pleasant bedrooms, some in cottages across green. *(Michael Butler, George Atkinson)*

HUBBERHOLME   SD9278
⋆ **George** (01756) 760223
Dubbs Lane; BD23 5JE Small beautifully placed ancient Dales inn with River Wharfe fishing rights, heavy beams, flagstones and stripped stone, quick simple enjoyable food, well kept ales including Black Sheep and

---

There are report forms at the back of the book.

Copper Dragon, good log fire, perpetual candle on bar; no dogs, outside lavatories; children allowed in dining area, terrace, six comfortable bedrooms (three in annexe), closed Mon. *(Dr Kevan Tucker, Mark, Amanda, Luke and Jake Sheard)*

HUDDERSFIELD SE1416
Grove (01484) 430113

Spring Grove Street; HD1 4BP Lots of exotic bottled beers, well kept Timothy Taylors, Thornbridge and 16 interesting changing guest ales at sensible prices, 120 malt whiskies and 60 vodkas, also real cider, friendly knowledgeable staff, no food but choice of snacks from dried crickets to biltong, traditional irish music (Thurs evening), art gallery; children and dogs welcome, back terrace, open all day. *(the Didler, Pat and Tony Martin)*

HUDDERSFIELD SE1416
⋆ Head of Steam (01484) 454533

St Georges Square; HD1 1JF Railway memorabilia, model trains, cars, buses and planes for sale, friendly staff, long bar with up to eight changing ales, lots of bottled beers, farm ciders and perry, fruit wines, black leather easy chairs and sofas, hot coal fire, good value enjoyable back buffet, some live jazz and blues nights; unobtrusive background music, can be very busy; open all day. *(Peter Smith and Judith Brown, Ian and Helen Stafford, the Didler, Pat and Tony Martin)*

HUDDERSFIELD SE1416
Kings Head (01484) 511058

Station, St Georges Square; HD1 1JF Handsome Victorian station building housing friendly well run pub, large open-plan room with original tiled floor, two smaller rooms off, Dark Star, Pictish, Timothy Taylors Landlord and six guests, good sandwiches and cobs, live music (Sun, Thurs), Jimi Hendrix pub sign; disabled access via Platform 1, open all day. *(the Didler)*

HUDDERSFIELD SE1416
Rat & Ratchet (01484) 516734

Chapel Hill; HD1 3EB Flagstoned local with Fullers, Fernandes, Ossett and lots of guest beers, farm ciders/perries, cheap lunchtime food (not Sun-Tues), friendly staff, more comfortable seating up steps, brewery memorabilia and music posters; open all day Fri-Sat, from 3pm other days. *(the Didler)*

HUDDERSFIELD SE1417
Sportsman 07766 131 123

St Johns Road; HD1 5AY Same owners as the West Riding Licensed Refreshment Rooms at Dewsbury; Black Sheep, Partners, Timothy Taylors and guests from eight handpumps, regular beer festivals, good value lunchtime bar snacks, comfortable lounge and two cosy side rooms; handy for station, open all day. *(the Didler)*

HUDDERSFIELD SE1415
Star (01484) 545443

Albert Street, Lockwood; HD1 3PJ Unpretentious friendly local with up to 12 competitively priced ales kept well by enthusiastic landlady, continental beers and farm cider, beer festivals in back marquee (food then), bric-a-brac and customers' paintings, open fire; closed Mon, and lunchtimes Tues-Thurs, open all day weekends. *(Andy and Jill Kassube, the Didler)*

HUGGATE SE8855
⋆ Wolds Inn (01377) 288217

Driffield Road; YO42 1YH Traditional 16th-c village pub cheerfully blending locals' bar and games room with civilised and comfortable panelled dining room, wide range of good generous home-made food including excellent local meats, friendly family service, well kept Timothy Taylors, John Smiths and a guest ale, good range of wines; benches out in front, pleasant garden behind with delightful views, lovely village and good walks, handy for Wolds Way, three bedrooms, open all day Sun till 9pm (8pm in winter), closed Mon lunchtime (all day in winter). *(C A Hall)*

HULL TA0929
Hop & Vine 07500 543199

Albion Street; HU1 3TG Small pub with three real ales, bottled belgians, farm ciders and perries, friendly licensees, good sandwiches and bargain basic specials all day, cellar bar; closed Sun, Mon. *(the Didler)*

HULL TA1028
⋆ Olde White Harte (01482) 326363

Passage off Silver Street; HU1 1JG Ancient pub with Civil War history, carved heavy beams, attractive stained glass, two big inglenooks with frieze of delft tiles, well kept Caledonian Deuchars IPA, Theakstons Old Peculier and guests from copper-topped counter, 80 or so malt whiskies, bargain pubby food; children welcome in upstairs restaurant, dogs in bar, heated courtyard, open all day. *(the Didler, G Jennings)*

HULL TA0929
Whalebone (01482) 327980

Wincolmlee; HU2 0PA Friendly local brewing its own good value ales, also Copper Dragon, Tetley, Timothy Taylors Landlord and a guest, real ciders and perry, bar food, old-fashioned décor; open all day. *(the Didler)*

HUTTON-LE-HOLE SE7089
Crown (01751) 417343

The Green; YO62 6UA Spotless pub overlooking pretty village green with wandering sheep in classic coach-trip country; enjoyable unfussy food (all day Sun) from sandwiches up, Black Sheep and Theakstons, decent wines by the glass, cheerful efficient service, opened-up bar with varnished woodwork and whisky-water jugs, dining area; children and dogs welcome, near Folk Museum, handy for Farndale walks. *(Dr and Mrs R G J Telfer, Glenwys and Alan Lawrence)*

ILKLEY SE1147
Ilkley Moor Vaults (01943) 607012
Stockeld Road/Stourton Road, off A65 Leeds–Skipton; LS29 9HD Atmospheric flagstoned pub with log fires in both upstairs and downstairs bars, good food including excellent local steaks, well kept Timothy Taylors Landlord, decent wines by the glass; children welcome, open all day weekends, closed Mon. *(Neil Whitehead, Victoria Anderson, James Stretton)*

ILKLEY SE1048
Riverside (01943) 607338
Nesfield Road; LS29 0BE Friendly family run hotel in good position by River Wharfe, cosy with nice open fire, well kept Copper Dragon, Ilkley, Tetleys and Timothy Taylors Landlord, good home-cooking all day (till early evening in winter); handy for start of Dales Way, 13 bedrooms, open from 10am. *(the Didler)*

ILKLEY SE1347
Wheatley Arms (01943) 816496
Wheatley Lane, Ben Rhydding; LS29 8PP Nice Ilkley Moor location and part of the small Individual Inns group, stylish lounge/dining areas and garden room, open log fires, locals' bar, good food (very popular weekends) from large varied menu, efficient cheerful service; outside tables, 12 good bedrooms. *(Gordon and Margaret Ormondroyd)*

KEIGHLEY SE0641
Boltmakers Arms (01535) 661936
East Parade; BD21 5HX Small open-plan split-level character local, friendly and bustling, with full Timothy Taylors range and a guest beer kept well, keen prices, limited food, nice brewing pictures, coal fire; sports TV; short walk from Worth Valley Railway, open all day. *(Allan Wolf, the Didler)*

KEIGHLEY SE0541
Brown Cow (01535) 602577
Cross Leeds Street; BD21 2LQ Refurbished local, popular and friendly, with good licensee keeping Timothy Taylors ales and guests in top condition, some interesting memorabilia; open from 4pm Mon-Sat, all day Sun. *(the Didler)*

KEIGHLEY SE0641
Cricketers Arms (01535) 669912
Coney Lane; BD21 5JE Yates and guests, selection of bottled beers, downstairs bar open Fri, Sat for live music; sports TV; open all day. *(the Didler)*

KETTLESING SE2257
⋆ **Queens Head** (01423) 770263
Village signposted off A59 W of Harrogate; HG3 2LB Welcoming stone pub with good value food popular with older diners; L-shaped carpeted main bar with lots of close-set cushioned dining chairs and tables, open fires, little heraldic shields on walls, 19th-c song sheet covers and lithographs of Queen Victoria, delft shelf of blue and white china, smaller bar on left with built-in red banquettes and cricketing prints, life-size portrait of Elizabeth I in lobby, Black Sheep, Roosters and Theakstons ales, good service; background radio; children welcome, seats in neatly kept suntrap back garden, benches in front by lane, seven bedrooms, open all day Sun. *(B and M Kendall, Michael Butler, Gerard Dyson)*

KETTLEWELL SD9672
Blue Bell (01756) 760230
Middle Lane; BD23 5QX Roomy knocked-through 17th-c coaching inn, Copper Dragon ales kept well, home-made food all day using local ingredients, low beams and snug simple furnishings, old country photographs, woodburner, restaurant, newspapers; TV, free wi-fi, Sun quiz; children welcome, shaded picnic-sets on cobbles facing bridge over the Wharfe, six annexe bedrooms. *(D W Stokes, John and Helen Rushton)*

KETTLEWELL SD9672
⋆ **Racehorses** (01756) 760233
B6160 N of Skipton; BD23 5QZ Comfortable, civilised and friendly two-bar inn with dining area, generous good value food from pub favourites to local game, well kept Timothy Taylors, good log fire; children welcome, dogs in bar areas, front and back terrace seating, pretty village well placed for Wharfedale walks, parking can be difficult, 13 good bedrooms, open all day. *(Lois Dyer, John and Helen Rushton, B and M Kendall, Jeremy King)*

KILDWICK SE0145
White Lion (01535) 632265
A629 Keighley–Skipton; BD20 9BH Old stone pub by Leeds–Liverpool Canal, enjoyable food (not Sun evening) including good value theme nights, Copper Dragon, Ilkley, Tetleys and Timothy Taylors; children and dogs welcome, next to ancient church in attractive village, two refurbished bedrooms, open all day. *(Pat and Graham Williamson)*

KIRKBY OVERBLOW SE3249
Shoulder of Mutton (01423) 871205
Main Street; HG3 1HD Three linked areas with rugs on bare boards or flagstones, comfortable patterned banquettes, two open fires, well kept local ales and plenty of wines by the glass, good generous fresh food including a daily roast, friendly

attentive service; picnic-sets in back garden, shop. *(Howard and Margaret Buchanan)*

KIRKBYMOORSIDE SE6986
George & Dragon (01751) 433334

Market Place; YO62 6AA 17th-c coaching inn, front bar with beams and panelling, tubs seats around wooden tables on carpet or stripped wood, log fire, good choice of well kept ales, several malt whiskies, enjoyable generous bar food including good value lunchtime set deal and Sun carvery, afternoon teas, also a snug, bistro and more formal restaurant; background music; children welcome, seats and heaters on front and back terraces, 20 bedrooms, Weds market day, open all day. *(Margaret Dickinson, Ed and Anna Fraser, Derek and Sylvia Stephenson, I D Barnett, John and Dinah Waters)*

KNARESBOROUGH SE3556
✶ Blind Jacks (01423) 869148

Market Place; HG5 8AL Simply done multi-floor tavern in 18th-c building (pub since 1990s), old-fashioned traditional character with low beams, bare brick and floorboards, cast-iron-framed tables, pews and stools, brewery mirrors, etc, nine well kept ales including own Village Brewer (made by Hambleton), seven continental draught beers, friendly helpful staff, limited food (cheese and pâté), two small downstairs rooms, quieter upstairs; well behaved children allowed away from bar, dogs welcome, open all day Fri-Sun, closed Mon-Thurs till 4pm; shop next door sells all sorts of rare bottled beers. *(B and M Kendall, Adrian Johnson, the Didler, Paul Smurthwaite)*

KNARESBOROUGH SE3457
Mitre (01423) 868948

Station Road; HG5 9AA Refurbished Market Town Tavern by the station, friendly helpful service, up to eight regional ales including Black Sheep, Copper Dragon, Roosters and Thwaites, interesting continental beers such as Timmermans Strawberry, decent choice of enjoyable sensibly priced food (not Sun evening) in bar and evening brasserie (Fri and Sat); background music – live Sun evening; children and dogs welcome, terrace tables under parasols, four bedrooms, open all day. *(Doug Learmonth, Pat and Tony Martin)*

LANGTHWAITE NY0002
✶ Charles Bathurst (01748) 884567

Arkengarthdale, a mile N towards Tan Hill; DL11 6EN Welcoming busy country inn (worth checking on no corporate events/weddings on your visit) with strong emphasis on dining and bedrooms, but pubby feel in long bar; scrubbed pine tables and country chairs on stripped floors, snug alcoves, open fire, some bar stools by counter, Black Sheep, Theakstons and Timothy Taylors, several wines by the glass, popular often interesting food, dining room with views of Scar House,

Robert 'the Mouseman' Thompson furniture, several other dining areas; background music, TV, pool, darts and other games; children welcome, lovely walks from door and views over village and Arkengarthdale, smart bedrooms (best not above dining room), open all day. *(Bruce and Sharon Eden, Jill and Julian Tasker, Canon Michael Bourdeaux, Anthony Barnes)*

LASTINGHAM SE7290
✶ Blacksmiths Arms (01751) 417247

Off A170 W of Pickering; YO62 6TL Popular old-fashioned beamed pub opposite beautiful Saxon church in attractive village, log fire in open range, traditional furnishings, Theakstons and other regional ales, several wines by the glass, good food including impressive seafood platter, friendly prompt service, darts, board games; background music – live second Sun of month; children and walkers welcome, seats in back garden, nice bedrooms, open all day in summer. *(Dr and Mrs R G J Telfer, Ros Lawler, Michael Butler, Ed and Anna Fraser, W M Hogg, M and A H and others)*

LEALHOLM NZ7607
✶ Board (01947) 897279

Off A171 W of Whitby; YO21 2AJ In wonderful moorland village spot by wide pool of River Esk; homely bare-boards bar on right with squishy old sofa and armchairs by big black stove, local landscape photographs on stripped-stone or maroon walls, china cabinet and piano, left-hand bar with another fire, traditional pub furniture, darts, and a stuffed otter, carpeted dining room, three well kept changing ales, Weston's ciders and dozens of whiskies, good seasonal food using meat from own farm and other local produce, friendly helpful staff; children, dogs and muddy boots welcome, secluded waterside garden with decking, bedrooms and self-catering cottage, open all day. *(Mike and Mary Strigenz, Mo and David Trudgill, James McLean, Susan and Neil McLean)*

LEAVENING SE7863
Jolly Farmers (01653) 658276

Main Street; YO17 9SA Bustling village local, friendly and welcoming, with good choice of changing ales and enjoyable good value pubby food, front bar with eating area behind, separate dining room. *(Anon)*

LEEDS SE3033
Adelphi (0113) 2456377

Hunslet Road; LS10 1JQ Refurbished but keeping handsome mahogany screens, panelling, tiling, cut and etched glass and impressive stairway, Leeds, Timothy Taylors Landlord and guests, foreign draught beers, decent all-day food including fixed-price weekday menu, friendly service, upstairs room with sofas, live music, comedy nights and other events. *(Paul Bromley)*

LEEDS   SE2932
Cross Keys (0113) 243 3711
Water Lane; LS11 5WD Revamped early
19th-c pub; flagstones and bare boards,
stripped brick, original tiling and timbers,
old prints and photographs, a collection of
clocks in one part, good choice of Yorkshire
ales and imported bottled beers, friendly
staff (a bit stretched at busy times),
enjoyable interesting food and good Sun
roasts, winding stairs to upstairs dining room;
children welcome, tables under big parasols
in sheltered courtyard, open all day. *(the
Didler, David and Sue Smith)*

LEEDS   SE3131
Garden Gate (0113) 277 7705
Whitfield Places, Hunslet; LS10 2QB
Impressive early Edwardian pub (Grade II*
listed) owned by Leeds Brewery, their well
kept ales from rare curved ceramic counter,
a wealth of other period features in rooms off
central drinking corridor including intricate
glass and woodwork, art nouveau tiling,
moulded ceilings and mosaic floors, hearty
pub food (not Tues evening); tables out in
front, open all day weekends. *(the Didler)*

LEEDS   SE2932
⋆Grove (0113) 243 9254
Back Row, Holbeck; LS11 5PL Unspoilt
1930s-feel local overshadowed by towering
office blocks, friendly long-serving landlord,
tables and stools in main bar with marble
floor, panelling and original fireplace, large
back room (some live music here) and snug
off drinking corridor, good choice of well kept
ales, Weston's cider; open all day. *(the Didler)*

LEEDS   SE2932
Midnight Bell (0113) 244 5044
Water Lane; LS11 5QN Leeds Brewery
pub on two floors in Holbeck Urban Village,
well kept ales and enjoyable home-made
food, light contemporary décor mixing with
original beams and stripped brickwork; beer
garden, open all day. *(Tim and Sue Halstead,
the Didler)*

LEEDS   SE3037
Mustard Pot (0113) 269 5699
*Strainbeck Lane, Chapel Allerton;
LS7 3QY* Friendly management in relaxed
easy-going dining pub, enjoyable interesting
food (all day Sun till 8pm) including
lunchtime sandwiches, Marstons-related
ales, decent wines by the glass, mix of
furniture from farmhouse tables and chairs
to comfortable banquettes and leather
chesterfields, half-panelling and pastel
paintwork, open fire; background music;
children welcome, pleasant front garden,
open all day. *(Anon)*

LEEDS   SE2236
Palace (0113) 244 5882
Kirkgate; LS2 7DJ Pleasantly uncitified,
with stripped boards and polished panelling,
unusual candelabra lighting, lots of old
prints, friendly helpful staff, good value
lunchtime food till 7pm including popular
Sun roasts in dining area, fine changing
choice of ales; games end with pool, TV,
background music; tables out in front and
in small heated back courtyard, open all
day. *(the Didler)*

LEEDS   SE3033
⋆Victoria (0113) 245 1386
Great George Street; LS1 3DL Opulent
early Victorian pub with grand cut and
etched mirrors, impressive globe lamps
extending from majestic bar, carved beams,
leather-seat booths with working snob-
screens, smaller rooms off, changing ales
such as Cottage, Leeds, Timothy Taylors and
Tetleys, friendly efficient service even when
busy, reasonably priced food 12-6pm from
sandwiches and light dishes up in separate
room with serving hatch; open all day. *(the
Didler, Andy Lickfold)*

LEEDS   SE3033
⋆Whitelocks (0113) 245 3950
Turks Head Yard, off Briggate; LS1 6HB
Classic Victorian pub (unspoilt but some
signs of wear) with long narrow old-fashioned
bar, tiled counter, grand mirrors, mahogany
and glass screens, heavy copper-topped
tables and red leather, well kept Theakstons
ales, enjoyable generous all-day food,
friendly hard-working young staff; crowded
at lunchtime; children welcome, tables in
narrow courtyard, open all day. *(the Didler,
Kay and Alistair Butler)*

LEYBURN   SE1190
Black Swan (01969) 623131
Market Place; DL8 5AS Attractive old
creeper-clad hotel with chatty locals and
character landlord in cheerful open-plan bar,
decent range of food including popular Sun
carvery, quick service, well kept Black Sheep
and other ales, good wines by the glass; no
credit cards; children and dogs welcome,
disabled access, tables on cobbled terrace,
seven bedrooms, open all day. *(the Didler,
Ed and Anna Fraser, M and J White)*

LEYBURN   SE1190
Bolton Arms (01969) 623327
Market Place; DL8 5BW Substantial stone-
built inn at top of market place, varied choice
of well priced home-made food including
good Sun carvery, ales such as Black Sheep,
good mix of customers; bedrooms. *(Mr and
Mrs Ian King, Barry Collett)*

Tipping is not normal for bar meals, and not usually expected.

LEYBURN SE1190
Golden Lion (01969) 622161
Market Place; DL8 5AS Comfortable panelled and bay-windowed hotel bar, two light and airy rooms with log-effect gas fire in eating area, varied good value generous food, well kept Black Sheep, decent coffee, friendly efficient service, paintings for sale, evening restaurant; very busy on Fri market day; dogs allowed, tables out in front, good value bedrooms, open all day. *(Gordon Briggs, Ed and Anna Fraser, M and J White)*

LINTHWAITE SE1014
☀ Sair (01484) 842370
Lane Top, Hoyle Ing, off A62; HD7 5SG Old-fashioned four-room pub brewing its own good value Linfit beers, pews and chairs on rough flagstones or wood floors, log-burning ranges, dominoes, cribbage and shove-ha'penny, vintage rock juke box; no food or credit cards; dogs welcome, children till 8pm, plenty of tables out in front with fine Colne Valley views, restored Huddersfield Narrow Canal nearby, open all day weekends, from 5pm weekdays. *(the Didler)*

LINTON SE3846
☀ Windmill (01937) 582209
Off A661 W of Wetherby; LS22 4HT Welcoming upmarket pub on different levels, beams, stripped stone, antique settles around copper-topped tables, log fires, enjoyable food including lunchtime bargains, more expensive evening menu (not Sun), John Smiths, Theakstons Best and guests, several wines by the glass, friendly service, restaurant and conservatory; background music; children and dogs welcome, sunny back terrace and sheltered garden with pear tree raised from seed brought back from Napoleonic Wars, open all day weekends. *(Peter and Anne Hollindale)*

LITTON SD9074
Queens Arms (01756) 770208
Off B6160 N of Grassington; BD23 5QJ Beautifully placed Dales pub, main bar with coal fire, rough stone walls, beam-and-plank ceiling, stools around cast-iron-framed tables on stone floor, dining room with old photographs, own-brewed Litton ales and guests, hearty home-made food; children and dogs welcome, plenty of seats in two-level garden, good surrounding walks, bedrooms and camping, open all day weekends, closed Mon. *(Claes Mauroy, Robert Wivell)*

LOCKTON SE8488
☀ Fox & Rabbit (01751) 460213
A169 N of Pickering; YO18 7NQ Attractive neatly kept roadside pub with warm inviting atmosphere, good choice of generous well presented food (sandwiches too), quick cheerful service, well kept Black Sheep and Cropton ales, decent coffee, beams, panelling and some exposed stonework, plush banquettes, fresh flowers, brasses, hunting prints and old local photographs, big log fire, busy locals' bar with pool, good views from comfortable restaurant; tables outside and in sun lounge, nice spot on moors' edge, bedrooms, open all day. *(George Atkinson)*

LOFTHOUSE SE1073
Crown (01423) 755206
The one in Nidderdale; HG3 5RZ Prettily placed Dales pub, friendly and relaxed, with hearty simple food from good proper sandwiches up, well kept Black Sheep, good coffee, small public bar, eating extension where children allowed, two well behaved pub dogs; outside gents'; good walks from the door, bedrooms. *(B and M Kendall)*

LOW BRADFIELD SK2691
☀ Plough (0114) 285 1280
Village signposted off B6077 and B6076 NW of Sheffield; New Road; S6 6HW Warm-hearted traditional pub ideally placed for some of South Yorkshire's finest scenery; cosy carpeted L-shaped bar with dark stone walls, comfortable wall banquettes and captain's chairs, lots of gleaming copper and brass, big arched inglenook coal fire, well kept local Bradfield ales with a guest like Hambleton Stallion, enterprising range of very good value food from hearty sandwiches and light dishes to generous honest meals, afternoon cakes too, cheerful, efficient staff; unobtrusive background music; children welcome, seats on fairy-lit back verandah, gravel terrace and lawn with slide, good walks, Damflask and Agden Reservoirs close by. *(Peter F Marshall)*

LOW ROW SD9898
☀ Punch Bowl (01748) 886233
B6270 Reeth–Muker; DL11 6PF Country inn under same ownership as the Charles Bathurst at Langthwaite; long bare-boards bar with peaceful view over Swaledale, stripped kitchen tables and a variety of seats, armchairs and sofa by woodburner at one end, pastel walls, menu written on huge mirror has some interesting choices, good wines by the glass, Black Sheep and Rudgate, cheerful efficient staff, separate dining room similar in style – even an identical giant clock permanently stuck on 12; front terrace set above road, comfortable bedrooms, open all day. *(Walter and Susan Rinaldi-Butcher, Bruce and Sharon Eden, P A Rowe)*

LUND SE9748
☀ Wellington (01377) 217294
Off B1248 SW of Driffield; YO25 9TE Smart busy pub with cosy Farmers Bar, beams, well polished wooden banquettes and square tables, quirky fireplace, plainer side room with flagstones and wine-theme décor, york stone walkway to room with village's Britain in Bloom awards, enjoyable varied choice of food (not Sun evening) in

restaurant and bistro dining area, Copper Dragon, Timothy Taylors Landlord and a guest, good wine list, 25 malt whiskies, friendly efficient staff; background music, TV; children welcome, benches in pretty little back courtyard, open all day Sun, closed Mon lunchtime. *(Adrian Johnson, Pat and Stewart Gordon, Gerard Dyson, Derek and Sylvia Stephenson)*

MALHAM   SD9062
Buck (01729) 830317
Off A65 NW of Skipton; BD23 4DA Superbly set creeper-clad stone inn popular with walkers, enjoyable traditional food, six ales including Timothy Taylors Landlord and Theakstons Old Peculier, log fire in panelled lounge, big basic hikers' bar, dining room; children and dogs welcome, picnic-sets in small heated yard, picture-book village, many good walks from the door, 12 clean bedrooms. *(Chris and Jeanne Downing)*

MALHAM   SD9062
Lister Arms (01729) 830330
Off A65 NW of Skipton; BD23 4DB Friendly creeper-covered stone-built inn tied to Thwaites, their ales kept well (tasting trays available), lots of bottled imports, enjoyable food including lunchtime sandwiches, deli boards and daily specials, steps down to bare-boards dining room with stripped-pine tables, woodburners; children and dogs welcome, seats out overlooking small green, more in back garden, lovely spot by river and good walking country, nine comfortable clean bedrooms, open all day. *(Chris and Jeanne Downing, Barry Collett, Peter Salmon, Comus and Sarah Elliott)*

MANFIELD   NZ2213
Crown (01325) 374243
Vicars Lane; DL2 2RF Traditional unpretentious village local, friendly and welcoming, with eight interesting regularly changing ales, enjoyable simple home-made food, two bars and games room with pool; dogs welcome, garden, good walks nearby. *(Julian Pigg, Mr and Mrs Maurice Thompson, Brian Jones, D G Collinson)*

MARSDEN   SE0411
⋆ **Riverhead Brewery Tap**
(01484) 841270 *Peel Street, next to Co-op; just off A62 Huddersfield– Oldham; HD7 6BR* Owned by Ossett with up to ten well kept ales including Riverhead range (microbrewery visible from bare-boards bar), bustling friendly atmosphere, airy upstairs beamed restaurant with stripped tables (moors view from some) and open kitchen, good value food including interesting specials; unobtrusive background music; dogs welcome, wheelchair access, some riverside tables, open all day. *(Gill and Malcolm Stott, Brian and Anna Marsden)*

MASHAM   SE2381
Bay Horse (01765) 689236
Silver Street, linking A6168 with Market Square; HG4 4DX Two character bare-boards bars with open fires, enjoyable generous food cooked to order (all day weekends), friendly staff, well kept ales including Black Sheep and Theakstons, back room with darts; TV; children and dogs welcome, beer garden, six bedrooms up twisty stairs, open all day. *(John and Eleanor Holdsworth)*

MASHAM   SE2281
Black Bull in Paradise
(01765) 680000 *Theakstons Visitor Centre, off Church Street; signed from market place; HG4 4YD* Converted outhouse of some character attached to Theakstons Visitor Centre with six of their ales; high-vaulted roof and galleried area, thick stone walls hung with portraits of the Theakston family and old photographs of the brewery and Masham itself, traditional furnishings on flagstones, winter open fire; restricted hours, brewery tours. *(Hunter and Christine Wright)*

MASHAM   SE2281
⋆ **Black Sheep Brewery**
(01765) 680100 *Wellgarth, Crosshills; HG4 4EN* Unusual décor in this big warehouse room alongside brewery, more bistro than pub with lively atmosphere and good mix of customers, well kept Black Sheep range and several wines by the glass, enjoyable reasonably priced food, friendly staff, tables with cheery patterned cloths and brightly cushioned green café chairs, pubbier tables by bar, lots of bare wood, some rough stonework, green-painted steel girders and pillars, free-standing partitions and big plants, glass wall with view into brewing exhibition centre; background music; children welcome, picnic-sets out on grass, brewery tours and shop, open all day Thurs-Sat, till 4.30pm other days. *(Ian and Helen Stafford, Janet and Peter Race, Bruce and Sharon Eden, Gerry and Rosemary Dobson)*

MASHAM   SE2280
Kings Head (01765) 689295
Market Place; HG4 4EF Handsome 18th-c stone inn (Chef & Brewer), two modernised linked bars with stone fireplaces, well kept Black Sheep and Theakstons, good wine choice, enjoyable standard food served by friendly helpful staff, part-panelled restaurant; background music, TV; children welcome, tables out at front and in sunny courtyard behind, 27 bedrooms, open all day. *(Mike and Jayne Bastin, Janet and Peter Race, Ed and Anna Fraser, JJW, CMW)*

MASHAM   SE2281
White Bear (01765) 689227
Wellgarth, Crosshills; signed off A6108 opposite turn into town; HG4 4EN

Comfortable stone-built beamed inn, small public bar with full range of Theakstons ales kept well, larger lounge with welcoming coal fire, enjoyable food from sandwiches up (not Sun evening), decent wines by the glass, friendly efficient staff, restaurant extension; background music; children and dogs welcome, terrace tables, 14 bedrooms, open all day. *(Dennis Jones, Ed and Anna Fraser, Mark, Amanda, Luke and Jake Sheard)*

MENSTON
SE1744
Fox (01943) 873024
Bradford Road (A65/A6038); LS29 6EB
Contemporary M&B dining pub in former coaching inn on busy junction, good choice of popular fairly priced food, friendly staff, Black Sheep, Timothy Taylors Landlord and a guest, Aspall's cider, big fireplace, flagstones and polished boards in one part; background music; two terraces looking beyond car park to cricket field, open all day. *(John and Eleanor Holdsworth, Gordon and Margaret Ormondroyd)*

MIDDLEHAM
SE1287
Black Swan (01969) 622221
Market Place; DL8 4NP Popular old inn by the castle, heavy-beamed bar with built-in high-backed settles, big stone fireplace, well kept ales including Theakstons and Black Sheep, bistro-style food, small restaurant; background music, TV; children welcome, dogs in bar, tables on cobbles outside and in back garden, good walking country, eight bedrooms (can be noisy), good breakfast, open all day. *(Michael Butler)*

MIDDLEHAM
SE1287
✳ White Swan (01969) 622093
Market Place; DL8 4PE Extended coaching inn opposite cobbled market town square, beamed and flagstoned entrance bar with built-in window pew and pubby furniture, open woodburner, well kept Theakstons ales, several wines by the glass and malt whiskies, enjoyable bistro-style food, friendly efficient staff, modern spacious dining room, large fireplace and small area with contemporary leather seats and sofa, more dining space in back room; background music; children welcome, comfortable bedrooms. *(Dennis Jones, Ed and Anna Fraser)*

MIDDLETON TYAS
NZ2205
Shoulder of Mutton (01325) 377271
Just E of A1 Scotch Corner roundabout; DL10 6QX Welcoming old pub with three low ceilinged rooms on different levels, good freshly made food from snacks up, well kept ales including Black Sheep, prompt friendly service. *(Gerry and Rosemary Dobson, Lawrence Pearse, M W Graham)*

MIDHOPESTONES
SK2399
Mustard Pot (01226) 761155
Mortimer Road, S off A616; S36 4GW Cosy and friendly character 17th-c country local, three small rooms, flagstones, stripped stone and pine, assorted chairs, tables and settles, two log fires, Black Sheep and Timothy Taylors Landlord, enjoyable home-made food all day including Sun carvery, weekend restaurant; background music; no dogs; children welcome, seats out front and back, three bedrooms, open all day, closed Mon. *(Carl Rahn Griffith)*

MILLINGTON
SE8351
Gait (01759) 302045
Main Street; YO42 1TX Friendly 16th-c beamed village pub, good straightforward food, five well kept ales including York, nice mix of old and newer furnishings, large map of Yorkshire on ceiling, big inglenook log fire; children welcome, garden picnic-sets, appealing village in good Wolds walking country, closed Mon-Thurs lunchtimes, open all day Sun. *(Roger and Anne Newbury)*

MIRFIELD
SE2017
Hare & Hounds (01924) 481021
Liley Lane (B6118 2 miles S); WF14 8EE Popular smartly done Vintage Inn, open-plan interior with several distinct areas, good choice of reasonably priced food all day, well kept Black Sheep and Leeds, cheerful helpful staff, roaring fire; tables outside with good Pennine views. *(Gordon and Margaret Ormondroyd, Michael Butler)*

MOULTON
NZ2303
Black Bull (01325) 377289
Just E of A1, 1 mile E of Scotch Corner; DL10 6QJ Had just shut as we went to press – news please.

MUKER
SD9097
✳ Farmers Arms (01748) 886297
B6270 W of Reeth; DL11 6QG Small unpretentious walkers' pub in beautiful valley village, four well kept ales, wines, teas and coffees, enjoyable straightforward good value food, warm fire, simple modern pine furniture, flagstones and panelling, darts and dominoes; soft background music; children and dogs welcome, hill views from terrace tables, stream across road, open all day. *(the Didler, Arthur Pickering, David Billington, JJW, CMW)*

MYTHOLMROYD
SE0125
Shoulder of Mutton (01422) 883165
New Road (B6138); HX7 5DZ Comfortable fairly basic local with emphasis on popular low-priced home cooking, friendly efficient service, family dining areas and cosy

---

By law, pubs must show a price list of their drinks. Let us know if you are inconvenienced by any breach of this law.

child- and food-free parts, well kept Black Sheep, Timothy Taylors and guests, toby jugs and other china; no credit cards; streamside back terrace. *(Ian and Nita Cooper, Brian and Anna Marsden)*

NEWBIGGIN   SD9985
Street Head (01969) 663282
B6160 W Burton–Cray; DL8 3TE 17th-c coaching inn with three comfortably modernised linked rooms, good well priced food and nice house wines, ales such as Black Sheep and Theakstons; five good bedrooms with Bishopdale views, campsite next door. *(Rod Stoneman)*

NEWLAY   SE2346
Abbey (0113) 2581248
Bridge 221, Leeds & Liverpool Canal; LS13 1EQ Six or so well kept ales, enjoyable generously served food including deals, friendly cat called Smudge. *(Alan and Shirley Sawden, Bharat Dhamrait)*

NEWTON UNDER
ROSEBERRY   NZ5613
Kings Head (01642) 722318
The Green, off A173; TS9 6QR Nicely converted 17th-c cottage row in attractive village below Roseberry Topping (known locally as the Cleveland Matterhorn), emphasis on wide choice of enjoyable well priced food in large restaurant area, good service, real ales including Theakstons; disabled facilities, terrace with water feature, eight bedrooms, good breakfast. *(Ed and Anna Fraser)*

NEWTON-ON-OUSE   SE5160
Blacksmiths Arms (01347) 848249
Cherry Tree Avenue, S off Moor Lane; YO30 2BN Attractive and welcoming village pub, comfortable interior with big fireplace, lots of pump clips and other bits and pieces, well kept Jennings and Ringwood, wide-ranging menu. *(Roger and Lesley Everett)*

NEWTON-ON-OUSE   SE5160
Dawnay Arms (01347) 848345
Off A19 N of York; YO30 2BR 18th-c with two bars and airy river-view dining room, low beams, stripped masonry, open fire and inglenook woodburner, chunky pine tables and old pews on bare boards and flagstones, fishing memorabilia, competently cooked food (till 6pm Sun) from lunchtime sandwiches (home-baked bread) up including vegetarian and children's choices, ales such as Tetleys and Timothy Taylors, good range of wines by the glass, friendly efficient service; terrace tables, lawn running down to Ouse moorings, handy for Beningbrough Hall, closed Mon. *(Roger and Lesley Everett)*

NORLAND   SE0521
Moorcock (01422) 832103
Moor Bottom Lane; HX6 3RP Fairly simple L-shaped bar and beamed restaurant,

wide choice of good blackboard food including competitively priced Sun lunch, children's helpings too, well kept Timothy Taylors and Thwaites, friendly hard-working staff. *(Mike Proctor)*

NORTHALLERTON   SE3794
Tithe Bar (01609) 778482
Friarage Street; DL6 1DP Market Town Tavern with half a dozen good mainly Yorkshire ales changing quickly, plenty of continental beers, friendly staff, tasty food including set deals, three traditional bar areas with tables and chairs, settle and armchairs, bare boards and brewery posters, upstairs evening brasserie; open all day. *(Adrian Johnson, Tony and Wendy Hobden, Ed and Anna Fraser, Pat and Tony Martin)*

NORWOOD GREEN   SE1326
✳ Old White Beare (01274) 676645
Signed off A641 in Wyke, or off A58 Halifax–Leeds just W of Wyke; Village Street; HX3 8QG Nicely renovated and extended 16th-c pub named after ship whose timbers it incorporates, well kept Copper Dragon, Timothy Taylors and a guest, good variety of enjoyable well presented food (all day weekends) including sandwiches, friendly service, bar with steps up to dining area, small character snug, imposing galleried flagstoned barn restaurant, some live music; children and dogs welcome, a few tables out in front and in back garden, Calderdale Way and Brontë Way pass the door, open all day. *(Clive Flynn, John and Eleanor Holdsworth, Michael Butler, Gordon and Margaret Ormondroyd)*

NUNNINGTON   SE6679
✳ Royal Oak (01439) 748271
Church Street; at back of village, which is signposted from A170 and B1257; YO62 5US Reliable neatly kept old pub, bar with high black beams strung with earthenware flagons, copper jugs and lots of antique keys, fine collection of old farm tools on a bare-stone wall, carefully chosen furniture, dining area linked to bar by double-sided woodburner, enjoyable food including local game, Black Sheep and Wold Top, ten wines by the glass and several malt whiskies, friendly service; background music; children and dogs welcome, terrace seating, handy for Nunnington Hall (NT), closed Mon. *(Nick Dalby, John and Eleanor Holdsworth, Michael Butler, Gerard Dyson, Peter Burton)*

OAKWORTH   SE0138
Grouse (01535) 643073
Harehills, Oldfield; 2 miles towards Colne; BD22 0RX Comfortable old Timothy Taylors pub, their ales kept well, enjoyable food all day from baguettes up including weekday set deal, friendly staff; undisturbed hamlet in fine moorland surroundings, picnic-sets on terrace with good Pennine views. *(John and Eleanor Holdsworth)*

OLDSTEAD   SE5380

⋆ **Black Swan** (01347) 868387

Main Street; YO61 4BL Tucked away 16th-c restaurant with rooms in beautiful surroundings; bar with beams, flagstones and 'Mousey' Thompson furniture, log fire, lots of wines by the glass, Black Sheep Best, attractive back dining rooms serving first-class food (not cheap, but bar food and sandwiches available lunchtime), friendly attentive staff; children welcome, picnic-sets out in front, four comfortable well equipped bedrooms with own terrace, good breakfast, fine surrounding walks, closed Mon-Weds lunchtimes, two weeks in Jan. *(John and Verna Aspinall, Andrew and Ruth Triggs)*

OSMOTHERLEY   SE4597

⋆ **Golden Lion** (01609) 883526

The Green, West End; off A19 N of Thirsk; DL6 3AA Busy, attractive old stone pub with friendly welcome, Timothy Taylors and guests, around 50 malt whiskies, roomy beamed bar on left with old pews and a few decorations, similarly unpretentious well worn-in eating area on right, weekend dining room, well liked pubby food and good service; background music; children welcome, dogs in bar, seats in covered courtyard, benches out front looking across village green, 44-mile Lyke Wake walk starts here and Coast to Coast nearby, comfortable bedrooms, closed Mon and Tues lunchtimes, otherwise open all day. *(J F M and M West, Marlene and Jim Godfrey, Ed and Anna Fraser, Mrs J P Cleall, Andy and Jill Kassube, Peter Thompson)*

OSMOTHERLEY   SE4597

Three Tuns (01609) 883301

South End, off A19 N of Thirsk; DL6 3BN Small stylish pub/restaurant, good food in bistro setting mixing local sandstone with pale oak panelling and furniture, friendly efficient service, bar area with built-in cushioned wall benches, stripped-pine tables and light-stone fireplace, a real ale such as Wainstones; charming mediterranean-style terrace, good nearby walks, comfortable bedrooms. *(John Coatsworth)*

OSSETT   SE2719

⋆ **Brewers Pride** (01924) 273865

Low Mill Road/Healey Lane (long cul-de-sac by railway sidings, off B6128); WF5 8ND Friendly local with Bobs White Lion (brewed at back of pub), Rudgate Ruby Mild and seven guests, cosy front rooms and flagstoned bar, open fires, brewery memorabilia, good well priced food (not Sun evening), dining extension and small games room, live music first Sun of month; well behaved children welcome, big back garden, near Calder & Hebble Canal, open all day. *(Michael Butler, the Didler)*

OSSETT   SE2719

Tap (01924) 272215

The Green; WF5 8JS Basic décor with flagstones and open fire, pleasant relaxed atmosphere, Ossett ales and guests (usually Fullers London Pride), decent wines by the glass, friendly service and locals, photos of other Ossett pubs; open all day Thurs-Sun, from 3pm other days. *(Michael Butler, the Didler)*

OTLEY   SE2045

Chevin (01943) 876109

West Chevin Road, off A660; LS29 6BE Well maintained pub largely rebuilt after fire, young enthusiastic staff, good home-made food including some inventive choices and early evening deals, Greene King Old Speckled Hen and Timothy Taylors Landlord; children welcome, garden with splendid Wharfedale views, open all day. *(D W Stokes, John and Eleanor Holdsworth, Gordon and Margaret Ormondroyd)*

OTLEY   SE1945

Fleece (01943) 465034

Westgate (A659); LS21 3DT Refurbished stone-built pub, full range of Wharfebank ales and three changing guests, good choice of enjoyable food; open all day. *(the Didler)*

OTLEY   SE2045

Junction (01943) 463233

Bondgate (A660); LS21 1AD Welcoming family-run beamed pub, single smallish bar with tiled floor, wall benches and fire, 11 well kept ales (cheaper Mon) including Caledonian Deuchars IPA, Timothy Taylors Landlord, Tetleys and Theakstons, a real cider, over 60 malts, no food but can bring your own (good bakery nearby), live music Tues and eclectic DJ night Sun; children (till 9pm) and dogs welcome, covered smokers' area at back, open all day. *(Paul Rowe, the Didler)*

OXENHOPE   SE0434

⋆ **Dog & Gun** (01535) 643159

Off B6141 towards Denholme; BD22 9SN Beautifully placed roomy 17th-c moorland pub, smartly extended and comfortable, with good varied food from sandwiches to lots of fish and Sun roasts (worth booking then), thriving atmosphere, cheery landlord and attentive friendly staff, full Timothy Taylors range kept well, good choice of malts, beamery, copper, brasses, plates and jugs, big log fire each end, padded settles and

---

The letters and figures after the name of each town are its Ordnance Survey map reference. *How to use the Guide* at the beginning of the book explains how it helps you find a pub, in road atlases or large-scale maps as well as in our own maps.

stools, glass-covered well in one dining area, wonderful views; five bedrooms in adjoining hotel. *(Gordon and Margaret Ormondroyd, Michael Butler and others)*

POOL   SE2445
White Hart   (0113) 2037862

Just off A658 S of Harrogate, A659 E of Otley; LS21 1LH Light and airy M&B dining pub (bigger inside than it looks), well liked food all day including sharing plates, pizzas and more restauranty dishes with some mediterranean influences, fixed-price menu too, friendly young staff, good choice of wines by the glass, Greene King and Timothy Taylors, stylishly simple bistro eating areas, armchairs and sofas on bar's flagstones and bare boards; plenty of tables outside. *(Gordon and Margaret Ormondroyd, Michael Butler, Robert Turnham, Jeremy King, Colin Woodward)*

POTTO   NZ4703
Dog & Gun   (01642) 700232

Cooper Lane; DL6 3HQ Tucked-away modern bar/restaurant/hotel, clean contemporary décor, enjoyable food (not Sun evening) from shortish menu including some interesting choices, well kept Captain Cook ales (brewed at sister pub, the White Swan at Stokesley) and guests, friendly attentive staff; tables under parasols on front decking, five bedrooms, open all day. *(David and Sue Smith)*

RAMSGILL   SE1171
⋆ Yorke Arms   (01423) 755243

Nidderdale; HG3 5RL Upmarket 18th-c creeper-clad hotel (not a pub), small smart bar with some heavy Jacobean furniture and log fires, Black Sheep Best, a fine wine list, good choice of spirits and fresh juices, Michelin-starred restaurant; background music, no under-12s; seats outside (snack menu), comfortable bedrooms, good quiet moorland and reservoir walks. *(Robert Wivell)*

REDMIRE   SE0491
Bolton Arms   (01969) 624336

Hargill Lane; DL8 4EA Village pub under friendly newish licensees, popular food, well kept Black Sheep, Wensleydale and a guest, comfortable carpeted bar, attractive dining room; disabled facilities, small garden, handy for Wensleydale Railway and Bolton Castle, good walks, three courtyard bedrooms. *(David Field, Donna Jenkins)*

RIBBLEHEAD   SD7678
Station Inn   (01524) 241274

B6255 Ingleton–Hawes; LA6 3AS Great spot up on the moors by Ribblehead Viaduct (Settle to Carlisle trains), friendly licensees doing varied food from snacks up (all day weekends), half a dozen well kept ales such as Black Sheep, Copper Dragon, Dent and Timothy Taylors, good value wines, tea and coffee, simple public bar with woodburner, dining room with open fire, viaduct and train pictures (some you can buy); background music, TV, darts and pool; children welcome, muddy boots and paws in bar, picnic-sets outside, five bedrooms (some sharing bath), bunkhouse, open all day. *(R C Vincent, Ian and Helen Stafford)*

RIPON   SE3171
⋆ One-Eyed Rat   (01765) 607704

Allhallowgate; HG4 1LQ Friendly little bare-boards pub with numerous well kept real ales (occasional festivals), farm cider, lots of bottled beers and country wines, long narrow bar with warming fire, cigarette cards, framed beer mats, bank notes and old pictures, no food but may be free black pudding, pool; children welcome, pleasant outside area, open all day Sat, closed weekday lunchtimes. *(Nick and Alison Dowson, Tim and Ann Newell)*

RIPON   SE3171
Royal Oak   (01765) 602284

Kirkgate; HG4 1PB Centrally placed coaching inn owned by Timothy Taylors, their ales kept well and good choice of wines, comfortable modernised interior with rooms off L-shaped bar, enjoyable food (all day weekends) from doorstep lunchtime sandwiches to more imaginative dishes using local ingredients; no dogs inside; children welcome, courtyard tables, six bedrooms, open all day. *(Ed and Anna Fraser)*

RIPON   SE3170
Water Rat   (01765) 602251

Bondgate Green, off B6265; HG4 1QW Small pub on two levels, prettily set by footbridge over River Skell and near restored canal basin; three well kept ales, a real cider and keenly priced wines, reliable straightforward food, friendly service, conservatory; charming view of cathedral, ducks and weir from riverside terrace. *(Chris and Jeanne Downing, Liz Bell, Dr Kevan Tucker)*

ROBIN HOOD'S BAY   NZ9504
Bay Hotel   (01947) 880278

The Dock, Bay Town; YO22 4SJ Friendly old village inn at end of the 191-mile Coast to Coast walk, fine sea views from cosy picture-window upstairs bar (Wainwright bar downstairs open too if busy), Caledonian Deuchars IPA, Courage Directors and Theakstons, good value home-made food in bar and separate dining area, young staff coping well, log fires; background music;

We say if we know a pub has background music.

lots of tables outside, cosy bedrooms, steep road down and no parking at bottom. open all day. *(Chris and Jeanne Downing, George Atkinson, the Didler)*

ROSEDALE ABBEY   SE7295
Coach House (01751) 417208
Alder Carr Lane; YO18 8SD Friendly pub with good value generous food, well kept Black Sheep and Theakstons, modern dining room off central bar, games room on right, blazing log fire; children welcome, great dale views from outside tables, 11 bedrooms. *(Glenwys and Alan Lawrence)*

SALTBURN-BY-THE-SEA   NZ6621
Ship (01287) 622361
A174 towards Whitby; TS12 1HF Beautiful setting among beached fishing boats, sea views from nautical-style black-beamed bars and big dining lounge, wide range of inexpensive generous food including fresh fish, Tetleys and good choice of wines by the glass, friendly helpful service, restaurant, family room; busy at holiday times; tables outside, open all day summer. *(Anon)*

SANCTON   SE9039
Star (01430) 827269
King Street (A1034 S of Market Weighton); YO43 4QP Neatly modernised and extended village dining pub, competently cooked food (local produce including own vegetables), extensive wine list, well kept ales such as Black Sheep, good friendly service; lovely surrounding countryside, open all day Sun, closed Mon. *(Marlene and Jim Godfrey, Jonathan Laverack, Eileen and David Webster, John and Eleanor Holdsworth)*

SAWDON   TA9484
★ Anvil (01723) 859896
Main Street; YO13 9DY Pretty high-raftered former smithy with good locally sourced food from chef/landlord, well kept Black Sheep and guests, good range of wines, friendly attentive staff and immaculate housekeeping, feature smith's hearth and woodburner, lower-ceilinged second bar leading through to small neat dining room; two self-catering cottages, closed Mon, Tues. *(Peter Burton, Steve Crosley, Matthew James)*

SAWLEY   SE2467
★ Sawley Arms (01765) 620642
Village signposted off B6265 W of Ripon; HG4 3EQ Spotless dining pub, ultra-civilised in a decorous way, with emphasis on good restauranty food; small carpeted rooms with log fires and comfortable furniture, side snug with daily newspapers and magazines, conservatory (well behaved children allowed here – but phone ahead), nice house wines, no real ales, home-made preserves for sale; quiet background music; pretty garden with lovely flowering tubs and baskets, two stone cottages for rent, close to Fountains Abbey,

closed Mon evenings in winter. *(Ian and Nita Cooper, R J Cowley)*

SCARBOROUGH   TA0488
Leeds Arms (01723) 361699
St Marys Street; YO11 1QW Proper traditional pub, interesting and friendly, with lots of fishing and RNLI memorabilia, well kept ales, great atmosphere, no food or music. *(Alan Burns)*

SCAWTON   SE5483
★ Hare (01845) 597769
Off A170 Thirsk–Helmsley; YO7 2HG Attractive, popular dining pub in quiet spot, really nice well presented food including good fish and seasonal game, enthusiastic hospitable landlord and friendly staff, good wines by the glass, well kept ales such as Black Sheep and Timothy Taylors, stripped-pine tables, heavy beams and some flagstones, open fire and woodburner, William Morris wallpaper, appealing prints and old books, pub ghost called Bob; no dogs; children welcome, wrought-iron garden furniture, closed Sun evening, Mon. *(John and Verna Aspinall, Ed and Anna Fraser, Ben and Ruth Levy, Graham Lovis, Dr Nigel Bowles, M and A H)*

SCORTON   NZ2500
Farmers Arms (01748) 812533
Northside; DL10 6DW Comfortably refurbished little pub in terrace of old cottages overlooking green, well kept Black Sheep, Copper Dragon and Courage Directors, enjoyable good value food, friendly staff, bar with open fire, restaurant, darts and dominoes, fortnightly quiz; background music; dogs welcome, open all day Fri-Sun, closed Mon lunchtime. *(Pat and Stewart Gordon)*

SETTLE   SD8163
★ Lion (01729) 822203
B6480 (main road through town), off A65 bypass; BD24 0HB Refurbished market-town inn with grand staircase sweeping down into baronial-style high-beamed hall bar, lovely log fire, second bar with bare boards and dark half-panelling, lots of old local photographs and another open fire, enjoyable all-day food including deli boards and specials, well kept Thwaites and occasional guests like Fullers, decent wines by the glass, helpful welcoming staff, restaurant; monthly quiz, silent TV and games machine; children and dogs welcome, courtyard tables, 14 bedrooms. *(Peter Salmon, Clive Flynn, Tony and Maggie Harwood, Karen Eliot)*

SHEFFIELD   SK3487
Bath (0114) 2495151
Victoria Street, off Glossop Road; S3 7QL Two small colourfully restored bare-boards 1930s rooms with friendly staff, well kept Abbeydale, Acorn, Tetleys and guests from

central servery, lunchtime bar food (not Sat), nice woodwork, tiles and glass, live jazz/blues most Sun evenings, irish music Mon; open all day, closed Sun lunchtime. *(the Didler)*

SHEFFIELD　　　　　　　SK3687
⋆ **Fat Cat**　(0114) 249 4801
23 Alma Street; S3 8SA Deservedly busy town local with good own-brewed ales and changing guests, draught and bottled belgian beers, real cider/perry and country wines, low-priced mainly vegetarian bar food (not Sun evening), friendly staff, two small downstairs rooms with coal fires, simple wooden tables and cushioned seats, brewery-related prints, jugs, bottles and advertising mirrors, upstairs overspill room; children welcome away from main bar, dogs allowed, picnic-sets in fairylit back courtyard with heated smokers' shelter, brewery visitor centre (book tours on 0114 249 4804), open all day. *(Mike and Eleanor Anderson, Matthew Lidbury, the Didler, Dale Thompson)*

SHEFFIELD　　　　　　　SK3687
Gardeners Rest　(0114) 272 4978
Neepsend Lane; S3 8AT Welcoming beer-enthusiast landlord serving his own good Sheffield ales from light wood counter, also several changing guests tapped from the cask, farm cider and continental beers, no food, old brewery memorabilia, changing local artwork, daily newspapers, games including bar billiards, live music, popular Sun quiz; children welcome (till 9pm) and well behaved dogs, disabled facilities, back conservatory and tables out overlooking River Don, open all day Thurs-Sun, from 3pm other days. *(the Didler)*

SHEFFIELD　　　　　　　SK3588
Harlequin　(0114) 275 8195
Nursery Street; S3 8GG Welcoming open-plan corner pub owned by nearby Brew Company, their well kept ales and great selection of changing guests, also bottled imports and real ciders/perries, straight-forward cheap lunchtime food including Sun roasts, beer festivals, regular live music, Weds quiz; dogs welcome, children till 7pm, outside seating, open all day. *(Peter Monk, the Didler)*

SHEFFIELD　　　　　　　SK3687
⋆ **Hillsborough**　(0114) 232 2100
Langsett Road/Wood Street; by Primrose View tram stop; S6 2UB Chatty and friendly pub-in-hotel, own microbrews along with four quickly changing guests, good choice of wines and soft drinks, generous well priced food including Sun roasts, daily newspapers, open fire, bare-boards bar, lounge, views to ski slope from attractive back conservatory and terrace tables; silent TV; children and dogs welcome, six good value bedrooms, covered parking, open all day. *(JJW, CMW, the Didler)*

SHEFFIELD　　　　　　　SK4086
⋆ **Kelham Island Tavern**
(0114) 272 2482　*Kelham Island; S3 8RY* Busy backstreet local with up to 12 competitively priced ales including a mild and stout/porter, real ciders, knowledgeable helpful staff, cheap well liked bar food (not Sun), traditional pubby furnishings, some nice artwork on yellow walls, live folk Sun evening; children and dogs welcome, plenty of seats and tables in unusual flower-filled back courtyard with woodburner for chilly evenings, award-winning front window boxes, open all day. *(Matthew Lidbury, the Didler)*

SHEFFIELD　　　　　　　SK3290
⋆ **New Barrack**　(0114) 234 9148
601 Penistone Road, Hillsborough; S6 2GA Lively, friendly pub with 11 changing ales and lots of bottled belgians, good choice of whiskies too, tasty good value bar food (Fri, Sat light suppers till midnight), comfortable front lounge with log fire and upholstered seats on old pine floors, tap room with another fire, back room for small functions, daily newspapers, regular events including chess club, live weekend music and comedy nights; TV; children (till 9pm) and dogs welcome, attractive little walled garden, difficult local parking, open all day. *(Matthew Lidbury, the Didler)*

SHEFFIELD　　　　　　　SK3186
Ranmoor　(0114) 230 1325
Fulwood Road; S10 3GD Comfortable open-plan Victorian local with good value home cooking (not Sun, Mon), Abbeydale and guest ales, piano (often played); pleasant garden, open all day. *(the Didler)*

SHEFFIELD　　　　　　　SK3389
Rawson Spring　(0114) 285 6200
Langsett Road; S6 2LN Popular airy Wetherspoons in former swimming baths, their usual value, well kept changing ales, impressive décor with unusual skylights; open all day from 7am. *(the Didler)*

SHEFFIELD　　　　　　　SK3487
Red Deer　(0114) 272 2890
Pitt Street; S1 4DD Thriving backstreet local among University buildings, nine changing ales from central bar, good value food (all day weekends), Tues quiz, live music; tables outside, open all day (till 1am Fri, Sat). *(Sarah Hawley)*

SHEFFIELD　　　　　　　SK3185
Rising Sun　(0114) 230 3855
Fulwood Road; S10 3QA Friendly drinkers' pub with up to 14 ales including full Abbeydale range (many more during summer beer festival), bottled beers, decent food, large lounge with games and reference books, live music and quiz nights; dogs welcome, nice back garden, open all day. *(Mr and Mrs Alesbrook, the Didler)*

SHEFFIELD SK3687
Rutland Arms (0114) 272 9003
Brown Street/Arundel Lane; S1 2BS
Comfortable one-room corner pub with
handsome façade, good range of changing
ales, well priced food all day, photos of old
Sheffield pubs and paintings by local artists;
tables in compact garden, handy for the
Crucible and station. *(the Didler, Tony and
Wendy Hobden)*

SHEFFIELD SK3585
Sheaf View (0114) 249 6455
*Gleadless Road, Heeley Bottom; S2
3AA* Wide range of local and other changing
ales, farm cider and bottled continentals,
good choice of spirits too, spotless unusually
shaped bar, pleasant staff; very busy on
match days; disabled facilities, tables
outside, open all day. *(the Didler, Lliswerrylad)*

SHEFFIELD SK3586
Sheffield Tap (0114) 273 7558
Station, Platform 1B; S1 2BP Busy station
bar in restored Edwardian refreshment room,
popular for its huge choice of world beers
on tap and in bottles, also four Thornbridge
ales and half a dozen guests, knowledgeable
helpful staff may offer tasters, snacky food,
tiled interior with vaulted roof; open all day.
*(Mike and Eleanor Anderson, Adam Gordon, the
Didler, Andy Lickfold, Tony and Wendy Hobden)*

SHEFFIELD SK2786
Three Merry Lads (0114) 2302824
W on Redmires Road; S10 4LJ Enjoyable
food including children's meals and Sun
carvery (they ask for a credit card if running
a tab), four real ales, good wine and soft
drinks choice, chatty bar and dining
extension with uninterrupted views, open
fire; background and live music, TV, games
machine, darts; dogs welcome, garden with
terrace picnic-sets and play area, open all
day weekends. *(JJW, CMW)*

SHEFFIELD SK3687
✫ Wellington (0114) 249 2295
*Henry Street; Shalesmoor tram stop
right outside; S3 7EQ* Unpretentious
relaxed pub with up to ten changing beers
including own bargain Little Ale Cart
brews, bottled imports, real cider, coal fire
in lounge, photographs of old Sheffield,
daily newspapers and pub games, friendly
staff; tables out behind, open all day with
afternoon break on Sun. *(the Didler)*

SHEFFIELD SK3386
York (0114) 2664624
Fulwood Road; S10 3BA Refurbished
popular 19th-c pub, six well kept ales from
heavy oak counter including house beers

from Brew Company, good variety of food
(some from own smokehouse), friendly
helpful service; children welcome, open all
day. *(Anon)*

SHELLEY SE2112
✫ Three Acres (01484) 602606
*Roydhouse (not signed); from B6116
towards Skelmanthorpe, turn left in
Shelley (signposted Flockton, Elmley,
Elmley Moor), go up lane for 2 miles
towards radio mast; HD8 8LR* Civilised
former coaching inn with all emphasis now
on hotel and dining side; roomy lounge
with leather chesterfields, old prints and so
forth, tankards hanging from main beam,
Copper Dragon, 40 malt whiskies and up
to 17 wines by the glass from serious (not
cheap) list, several formal dining rooms,
wide choice of often interesting expensive
food from lunchtime sandwiches up, good
service; conferences, weddings and events;
children welcome, fine moorland setting
and lovely views, smart well equipped
bedrooms. *(Gordon and Margaret Ormondroyd,
Colin McKerrow)*

SHEPLEY SE1809
✫ Farmers Boy (01484) 605355
*Marsh Lane, W of village – off A629 at
Black Bull (leads on past pub to A635);
HD8 8AP* Smart stone-built dining pub,
small traditional beamed public bar on right,
Black Sheep, Bradfield and Copper Dragon,
bare-boards area on left with coal fire and
sturdy country tables, carpeted part rambling
back through plenty of neat linen-set dining
tables, barn restaurant with own terrace,
well liked imaginative food including set
meals, not cheap but good value given
quality, friendly efficient service; unobtrusive
background music; picnic-sets out in front,
open all day. *(Matthew Lidbury, Ian Daines)*

SHIPLEY SE1437
Fannys Ale House (01274) 591419
Saltaire Road; BD18 3JN Cosy and
friendly bare-boards alehouse on two floors,
gas lighting, log fire and woodburner,
brewery memorabilia, up to ten well
kept ales including Timothy Taylors and
Theakstons, bottled beers and farm ciders,
back extension; can be crowded weekend
evenings; dogs welcome, open all day, closed
Mon lunchtime. *(C Cooper, the Didler)*

SINNINGTON SE7485
✫ Fox & Hounds (01751) 431577
Off A170 W of Pickering; YO62 6SQ
Pretty village's popular 18th-c coaching
inn, carpeted beamed bar with woodburner,
various pictures and old artefacts,
comfortable seats, imaginative well
presented food, particularly friendly and

We list pubs that serve food all day on at least some days at the end of the book.

helpful staff, well kept ales such as Black Sheep, Copper Dragon and Wold Top, several wines by the glass, a few rare whiskies, lounge and smart separate restaurant; background music; children and dogs welcome, picnic-sets in front, more in garden, ten comfortable bedrooms. *(Pat and Tony Hinkins, Adrian Johnson, Pat and Stewart Gordon, Jeff and Wendy Williams, Steven King and Barbara Cameron and others)*

SKIPTON   SD9851

★**Narrow Boat** (01756) 797922

Victoria Street; pub signed down alley off Coach Street; BD23 1JE Lively extended pub down cobbled alley, eight real ales, draught and bottled continental beers, farm cider and perry, church pews, dining chairs and stools around wooden tables, old brewery posters, mirrors decorated with beer advertisements, upstairs gallery area with interesting canal mural, decent reasonably priced bar food (not Sun evening) including sausage menu, folk club Mon evening; children allowed if eating, dogs welcome, picnic-sets under front colonnade; Leeds & Liverpool Canal nearby, open all day. *(the Didler, Pat and Tony Martin, John and Dinah Waters)*

SKIPTON   SD9851

Woolly Sheep (01756) 700966

Sheep Street; BD23 1HY Big bustling pub with full Timothy Taylors range kept well, prompt friendly enthusiastic service, two beamed bars off flagstoned passage, exposed brickwork, stone fireplace, lots of sheep prints and bric-a-brac, daily newspapers, attractive and comfortable raised lunchtime dining area, good value enjoyable food (plenty for children); unobtrusive background music; spacious pretty garden, six good value bedrooms, good breakfast. *(Stuart Paulley, John and Hazel Sarkanen, John and Dinah Waters, Gary Simcoe)*

SLEDMERE   SE9364

★**Triton** (01377) 236078

B1252/B1253 junction, NW of Great Driffield; YO25 3XQ Handsome old inn by Sledmere House, open-plan bar with old-fashioned atmosphere, dark wooden furniture on red patterned carpet, 15 clocks ranging from grandfather to cuckoo, lots of willow pattern plates, all manner of paintings and pictures, open fire, John Smiths, Timothy Taylors, Tetleys and Wold Top, 50 different gins, well liked freshly cooked food (only take bookings in separate restaurant), friendly helpful staff; children welcome till 8pm, five good bedrooms, massive breakfast, open all day Sun till 9pm, closed winter Mon lunchtime. *(Gerard Dyson, Pete Coxon, Ed and Anna Fraser, Dennis Jones, Pat Bunting and others)*

SNAINTON   TA9182

Coachman (01723) 859231

Pickering Road W (A170); YO13 9PL More restaurant-with-rooms but also a small bar serving Wold Top ales, good well presented food in smart white-tableclothed dining room, friendly service, comfortable lounge with squashy sofas; well tended gardens, smokers' shelter at front, three bedrooms, good breakfast. *(Ian Malone, Peter Burton)*

SNAITH   SE6422

Brewers Arms (01405) 862404

Pontefract Road; DN14 9JS Georgian inn tied to local Old Mill brewery, their distinctive range of beers kept well, ample helpings of fairly priced home-made food, friendly staff, open-plan bar and conservatory-style dining area, old well, open fireplace; children welcome in eating areas, ten bedrooms. *(John and Eleanor Holdsworth, Pat and Stewart Gordon, Terry and Nickie Williams, Michael Butler)*

SNAPE   SE2684

★**Castle Arms** (01677) 470270

Off B6268 Masham–Bedale; DL8 2TB Neat homely pub in pretty village, flagstoned bar with open fire, horsebrasses on beams, straightforward pubby furniture, Banks's, Jennings and Marstons, well liked bar food, dining room (also flagstoned) with another fire and plenty of dark tables and chairs; children and dogs welcome, picnic-sets out at front and in courtyard, fine walks in Yorkshire Dales and on North York Moors, nine bedrooms. *(Tim and Sue Halstead)*

SOWERBY BRIDGE   SE0623

Jubilee Refreshment Rooms

(01422) 648285 *Sowerby Bridge Station; HX6 3AB* Refurbished station building run by two railway-enthusiast brothers, up to five real ales, bottled continentals, simple food including breakfast and good home-made cakes, railway memorabilia, old enamel signs, art deco ceiling lamps and feature jeweller's clock; open all day from 9.30am (12 Sun). *(Pat and Tony Martin)*

SOWERBY BRIDGE   SE0623

Moorings (01422) 833940

Canal basin; HX6 2AG Spacious multi-level canal warehouse conversion, good choice of popular food (all day Sun till 7pm), up to six real ales including Black Sheep, Timothy Taylors and one brewed for them by Greene King, several wines by the glass, big windows overlooking boat basin, high beams, flagstones and stripped stone, solid booth seating; unobtrusive background music; canopied terrace tables, open all day. *(John and Eleanor Holdsworth)*

We list pubs that serve food all day on at least some days at the end of the book.

SOWERBY BRIDGE SE0523
Works (01422) 835547
Hollins Mill Lane, off A58; HX6 2QG
Big airy two-room bare-boards pub in
converted joinery workshop, seating from
pews to comfortable sofas, eight well kept
real ales and a couple of ciders, good bargain
home-made food from pies and casseroles
to vegetarian choices, Weds curry night,
Sun brunch (10-3pm), poetry readings and
live music in back yard (covered in poor
weather), comedy night in big upstairs
room; children and dogs welcome, disabled
facilities, open all day. *(Pat and Tony Martin,
Herbert and Susan Verity)*

STAINFORTH SD8267
Craven Heifer (01729) 822599
*B6479 Settle–Horton-in-Ribblesdale;
BD24 9PB* Friendly Dales village local, small,
cosy and clean, with well kept Thwaites and
generous helpings of tasty food, roaring log
fire; good walks. *(Tim and Joan Wright)*

STAMFORD BRIDGE SE7055
★ Three Cups (01759) 375901
A166 W of town; YO41 1AX Vintage Inn
family dining pub, clean and spacious, in
cosy, timbered, country style, enjoyable good
value food all day from regularly changing
menu, plenty of wines by the glass, Black
Sheep, Timothy Taylors and a guest, friendly
helpful staff, two blazing fires, glass-topped
well in bar; disabled access, play area
behind. *(Pat and Graham Williamson,
David Carr)*

STANBURY SE0037
Old Silent (01535) 647437
Hob Lane; BD22 0HW Neatly rebuilt
moorland dining pub near Ponden Reservoir,
friendly atmosphere, good reasonably
priced fresh food including specials, real
ales such as Timothy Taylors, attentive
helpful service, character linked rooms
with beams, flagstones, mullioned windows
and open fires, games room, restaurant
and conservatory; children welcome,
bedrooms. *(John and Eleanor Holdsworth)*

STAVELEY SE3662
Royal Oak (01423) 340267
*Signed off A6055 Knaresborough–
Boroughbridge; HG5 9LD* Popular
welcoming pub in village conservation
area; beams and panelling, open fires,
broad bow window overlooking front lawn,
well kept Black Sheep, Timothy Taylors
and a guest, several wines by the glass,
good variety of enjoyable food in bar and
restaurant. *(Michael Coleman)*

STILLINGTON SE5867
★ Bay Tree (01347) 811394
*Main Street; leave York on outer ring
road (A1237) to Scarborough, first exit
on left signposted B1363 to Helmsley;*

YO61 1JU Cottagey pub in pretty village's
main street, contemporary bar areas with
civilised chatty atmosphere, comfortable
cushioned wall seats and leather/bamboo tub
chairs around mix of tables, church candles
and lanterns, basketwork and attractive
prints on cream walls, central gas-effect
coal fire, good bistro-style food including
sandwiches, Black Sheep and Moorhouses,
fair-priced wines, friendly helpful staff, steps
up to cosy dining area, larger conservatory-
style back restaurant; background music;
seats in garden and picnic-sets at in front,
closed Mon. *(Anon)*

STOKESLEY NZ5208
★ White Swan (01642) 710263
West End; TS9 5BL Good Captain Cook
ales brewed in attractive flower-clad pub,
L-shaped bar with three relaxing seating
areas, log fire, lots of brass on elegant
dark panelling, lovely bar counter carving,
assorted memorabilia and unusual clock,
good lunchtime ploughman's (Weds-Sat), live
music, beer festivals; no children; open all
day. *(the Didler)*

SUTTON UPON DERWENT SE7047
★ St Vincent Arms (01904) 608349
*Main Street (B1228 SE of York);
YO41 4BN* Enjoyable consistently cheerful
pub with Fullers and up to seven guests, 14
wines by the glass, good popular bar food
(more elaborate evening meals), bustling
parlour-style front bar with panelling,
traditional high-backed settles, windsor
chairs, cushioned bow-window seat and
gas-effect coal fire, another lounge and
separate dining room open off here; children
welcome, dogs in bar, garden tables, handy
for Yorkshire Air Museum. *(David and Ruth
Hollands, Kay and Alistair Butler, Pat and Tony
Martin, Roger and Anne Newbury, Jonathan
Laverack, Gerard Dyson)*

SUTTON-UNDER-
WHITESTONECLIFFE SE4983
Whitestonecliffe Inn
(01845) 597271 *A170 E of Thirsk;
YO7 2PR* Well located beamed roadside
pub with wide choice of good food from
sandwiches up, well kept ales such as Black
Sheep, John Smiths and Tetleys, friendly staff
and buoyant atmosphere, interesting 17th-c
stone bar, log fire, separate restaurant, games
room; children welcome, six self-catering
cottages. *(Michael Butler, Stanley and Annie
Matthews, Andrew and Ruth Triggs, Terry Stevens)*

TAN HILL NY8906
Tan Hill Inn (01833) 628246
*Arkengarthdale Road Reeth–Brough, at
junction Keld/West Stonesdale Road;
DL11 6ED* Basic old pub in wonderful
bleak setting on Pennine Way – Britain's
highest, full of bric-a-brac and interesting
photographs, simple sturdy furniture,
flagstones, ever-burning big log fire (with

prized stone side seats), chatty atmosphere, five real ales including one for them by Dent, good cheap pubby food, family room, live music weekends, Swaledale sheep show here last Thurs May; can get overcrowded, often snowbound; children and dogs welcome, seven bedrooms, bunk rooms and camping, open all day. *(Claes Mauroy)*

THIRSK   SE4282
Black Lion (01845) 574302
Market Place; YO7 1LB Comfortable well furnished bar/bistro, enjoyable food from snacks up (more restauranty evening choices), good service from uniformed staff, L-shaped bar overlooking the square, Black Sheep Bitter, three dining rooms; small garden behind. *(Ed and Anna Fraser)*

THIRSK   SE4282
Golden Fleece (01845) 523108
Market Place; YO7 1LL Comfortable bustling old coaching inn with enjoyable generous bar food, local real ales, friendly competent service, restaurant, view across market place from bay windows; 23 bedrooms, good breakfast. *(Janet and Peter Race)*

THORNTON   SE0933
⋆ Ring o' Bells (01274) 832296
Hill Top Road, W of village, and N of B6145; BD13 3QL Thoroughly reliable hilltop dining pub with long-serving staff and a friendly chatty atmosphere; cosy series of linked rooms, dark beams and panelling, plush seating for glass-topped tables on red carpet, big flower arrangements, old local photographs one end, elegant more modern linen-set restaurant the other, popular sensibly priced food including set menus, themed and gourmet nights, Black Sheep, Copper Dragon and a guest; faint background music; no dogs; long views towards Shipley and Bingley. *(Keith Moss, John and Eleanor Holdsworth)*

THRESHFIELD   SD9863
Old Hall Inn (01756) 752441
B6160/B6265 just outside Grassington; BD23 5HB Popular place with three old-world linked rooms including smart candlelit dining room, well kept John Smiths, Timothy Taylors and Theakstons, enjoyable food, helpful friendly staff, log fires, high beam-and-plank ceiling, cushioned wall pews, tall well blacked kitchen range; children in eating area, neat garden. *(Anon)*

THUNDER BRIDGE   SE1811
Woodman (01484) 605778
Off A629 Huddersfield–Sheffield; HD8 0PX Stone-built village pub with two roomy spotless bars, low beams and heavy wooden tables, smart fresh décor, welcoming efficient service, good reasonably priced food, well kept Timothy Taylors and Tetleys, upstairs restaurant; tables outside, 12 good bedrooms in adjoining cottages. *(Gordon and Margaret Ormondroyd, Matthew Lidbury)*

TICKTON   TA0742
New Inn (01964) 542371
Just off A1035 NE of Beverley; HU17 9SH Friendly, efficiently run country pub and restaurant, good up-to-date well presented food all day (including sandwiches) using local produce in modern simply decorated dining area (closed Sun evening, Mon), traditional log-fire locals' bar (closed Mon lunchtime) with well kept Black Sheep and Tetleys, Sun quiz night; farm shop in car park. *(Marlene and Jim Godfrey, Pat and Graham Williamson)*

TIMBLE   SE1852
⋆ Timble Inn (01943) 880530
Off Otley–Blubberhouses moors road; LS21 2NN Smartly restored 18th-c inn tucked away in quiet farmland hamlet, good food from pub favourites including well aged Nidderdale beef (not Mon-Weds lunchtime – booking advised), Timothy Taylors Landlord, Theakstons and a guest; children welcome, dogs outside of food times, good walks from the door, seven well appointed bedrooms. *(John and Eleanor Holdsworth, Robert Wivell)*

TOCKWITH   SE4652
Spotted Ox (01423) 358387
Westfield Road, off B1224; YO26 7PY Welcoming traditional beamed village local, three areas off central bar, well kept ales, including Tetleys, carefully served the old-fashioned way, good choice of enjoyable sensibly priced home-made food, attentive staff, relaxed atmosphere, interesting local history; open all day Fri-Sun. *(Les and Sandra Brown)*

TONG   SE2230
Greyhound (0113) 285 2427
Tong Lane; BD4 0RR Traditional stone-built, low-beamed and flagstoned local by village cricket field, distinctive areas including small dining room, enjoyable good value local food, Black Sheep, Greene King Abbot and Tetleys, many wines by the glass, good service; tables outside. *(Frank Dowsland)*

TOTLEY   SK3080
Cricket (0114) 236 5256
Signed from A621; Penny Lane; S17 3AZ Tucked-away stone-built pub opposite rustic cricket field, much focus on dining but still a friendly local atmosphere, pews, mixed chairs and pine tables on bare boards and flagstones, good-quality blackboard food (all day weekends) from sandwiches and pubby staples to some interesting imaginative cooking, friendly service, Thornbridge ales, log fires, good Peak District views, local artwork for sale; children and dogs welcome, tables outside, open all day. *(Matthew Lidbury, W K Wood)*

TOTLEY
SK3079
Cross Scythes (0114) 236 0204
A621 Baslow Road; S17 4AE Refurbished dining pub with good freshly prepared food from sandwiches using home-baked bread up, well kept local ales, attentive helpful staff; children welcome, bedrooms. *(David and Ruth Hollands)*

WAKEFIELD
SE3320
Bull & Fairhouse (01924) 362930
George Street; WF1 1DL Welcoming chatty 19th-c pub, well kept Bobs White Lion, Great Heck Golden Bull and four other changing ales (beer festivals), bare-boards bar with comfortable rooms off, open fire, no music, live music weekends, quiz Thurs; children welcome till 8pm, dogs on leads, open all day Fri-Sun, from 5pm other days. *(the Didler)*

WAKEFIELD
SE3320
Fernandes Brewery Tap
(01924) 291709 *Avison Yard, Kirkgate; WF1 1UA* Owned by Ossett but still brewing Fernandes ales in cellar, interesting guest beers, bottled imports, farm ciders, newish ground-floor bar with flagstones, bare brick and panelling, original raftered top-floor bar with unusual breweriana; closed Mon-Thurs lunchtime, open all day Fri-Sun with some lunchtime food. *(the Didler)*

WAKEFIELD
SE3220
Harrys Bar (01924) 373773
Westgate; WF1 1EL Cheery, well run one-room local, Leeds, Ossett and guests, stripped-brick walls, open fire, live music Wed; small back garden, open all day Sun, closed lunchtimes other days. *(the Didler)*

WALTON
SE4447
Fox & Hounds (01937) 842192
Hall Park Road, off back road Wetherby-Tadcaster; LS23 7DQ Welcoming dining pub with enjoyable food from good sandwiches to specials (should book Sun lunch), well kept ales such as Black Sheep, John Smiths and Timothy Taylors Landlord, thriving atmosphere; handy A1 stop. *(Les and Sandra Brown, Michael Doswell)*

WATH IN NIDDERDALE
SE1467
★Sportsmans Arms (01423) 711306
Nidderdale road off B6265 in Pateley Bridge; village and pub signposted over hump-back bridge on right after a couple of miles; HG3 5PP Civilised, beautifully located restaurant with rooms run by long-serving owner, most emphasis on the excellent food and bedrooms but has proper welcoming bar with open fire, Black Sheep

and Timothy Taylors Landlord, Thatcher's cider, 20 wines by the glass from extensive list and 40 malt whiskies, helpful hospitable staff; background music; children welcome, dogs in bar, benches and tables outside and seats in pretty garden with croquet, own fishing on River Nidd. *(David and Jenny Reed, Derek Thomas, Bruce and Sharon Eden, R and S Bentley, Walter and Susan Rinaldi-Butcher, John and Sharon Hancock and others)*

WELL
SE2682
Milbank Arms (01677) 470411
Bedale Road; DL8 2PX Cosy beamed pub with interesting layout, enjoyable freshly prepared food, well kept Black Sheep, good friendly service; picnic-sets in front. *(Dr D Jeary)*

WEST TANFIELD
SE2678
Bruce Arms (01677) 470325
Main Street (A6108 N of Ripon); HG4 5JJ Comfortable and welcoming with really good freshly made food at reasonable prices, well kept Black Sheep and Copper Dragon, friendly service (can slow at times), flagstones and log fires; two bedrooms, good breakfast, closed Sun evening, Mon. *(Guy, John and Eleanor Holdsworth, Alan English)*

WEST TANFIELD
SE2678
Bull (01677) 470678
Church Street (A6108 N of Ripon); HG4 5JQ Open-plan with slightly raised dining area to the left and flagstoned bar on right, popular blackboard food (all day Sat, not Sun evening) from lunchtime sandwiches up, well kept Theakstons and guests, decent wines, brisk pleasant service; background music; children allowed away from bar, tables on terraces in attractive garden sloping steeply to River Ure and its old bridge, five bedrooms, open all day weekends, closed Tues. *(Dennis Jones, Tim and Sue Halstead)*

WEST WITTON
SE0588
Wensleydale Heifer 01969 622322
A684 W of Leyburn; DL8 4LS Stylish restaurant-with-rooms rather than pub, good fresh fish/seafood and local meat, nice wines, cosy informal upmarket food bar and extensive main formal restaurant, attentive helpful service; saucy seaside postcards in gents'; good bedrooms (back ones quietest), big breakfast. *(P A Rowe)*

WESTOW
SE7565
Blacksmiths Inn (01653) 619606
Off A64 York-Malton; Main Street; YO60 7NE Refurbished 18th-c pub with attractive beamed bar, woodburner in brick inglenook, beers such as Copper Dragon, home-made food from pub favourites up,

---

'Children welcome' means the pubs says it lets children inside without any special restriction; some may impose an evening time limit earlier than 9pm – please tell us if you find this.

restaurant; picnic-sets on side terrace, open all day weekends, closed Mon and lunchtimes Tues and Weds. *(Christopher Turner)*

WETHERBY
SE4048
Muse (01937) 580201
Bank Street; LS22 6NQ Popular single-story bistro-bar (Market Town Tavern) with good brasserie/pub food, friendly helpful young staff, well kept regional ales and good choice of continental beers, decent wines and coffee, simple smart décor; children welcome, dogs allowed in bar and outside seating area, open all day. *(Brian and Janet Ainscough, Stuart Paulley)*

WHITBY
NZ9011
★ Duke of York (01947) 600324
Church Street, Harbour East Side; YO22 4DE Busy pub in fine harbourside position, handy for famous 199 steps leading up to abbey; comfortable beamed lounge bar with fishing memorabilia, Black Sheep, Caledonian and three guests, decent wines and several malt whiskies, straightforward bar food all day; background music, TV, games machine; children welcome, bedrooms overlooking water, no nearby parking. *(Pete Coxon, Adrian Johnson, Pat and Graham Williamson)*

WHITBY
NZ8911
Station Inn (01947) 603937
New Quay Road; YO21 1DH Friendly three-room bare-boards drinkers' pub, clean and comfortable, with good mix of customers, half a dozen well kept changing ales, farm cider and good wines by the glass, traditional games; background and live music; dogs welcome, open all day. *(Tony and Wendy Hobden, Sara Fulton, Roger Baker)*

WIGGLESWORTH
SD8056
Plough (01729) 840243
B6478, off A65 S of Settle; BD23 4RJ Light, airy and comfortable old inn with good elegantly presented food, friendly efficient service, local ales and decent wines by the glass, cosy log fire, panoramic Dales views; bedrooms. *(John and Sylvia Harrop)*

YORK
SE5951
Ackhorne (01904) 671421
St Martins Lane, Micklegate; YO1 6LN Proper unspoilt pub under newish management, friendly and welcoming, with good choice of ales including Caledonian Deuchars IPA and Roosters Yankee, Weston's Old Rosie cider, enjoyable pubby food (weekday lunchtimes, till 7pm weekends), beams, bare boards and panelling, leather wall seats, stained glass, Civil War prints, bottles and jugs, old range and open fire, carpeted snug, traditional games, some live music; suntrap back terrace with smokers' shelter, open all day. *(the Didler, Pete Coxon)*

YORK
SE6051
★ Black Swan (01904) 686910
Peaseholme Green (inner ring road); YO1 7PR Striking timbered and jettied Tudor building, compact panelled front bar, crooked-floored central hall with fine period staircase, black-beamed back bar with vast inglenook, good choice of real ales, decent wines, good value pubby food from sandwiches up; background music; children welcome, useful car park, bedrooms, open all day. *(Pete Coxon, the Didler)*

YORK
SE6051
★ Blue Bell (01904) 654904
Fossgate; YO1 9TF Delightfully old-fashioned little Edwardian pub, very friendly and chatty, with well kept Black Sheep, Roosters, Timothy Taylors Landlord and three guests, a mild always available too, good value lunchtime sandwiches (not Sun), daily newspapers, tiny tiled-floor front bar with roaring fire, panelled ceiling, stained glass, bar pots and decanters, corridor to small back room, hatch service, lamps and candles, pub games; soft background music; no children; dogs welcome, open all day. *(Pete Coxon, Eric Larkham, Dave Webster, Sue Holland, the Didler, Kerry Law)*

YORK
SE5951
★ Brigantes (01904) 675355
Micklegate; YO1 6JX Comfortably traditional Market Town Taverns bar/bistro, eight well kept mainly Yorkshire ales, good range of bottled beers, decent wines and coffee, enjoyable unpretentious brasserie food all day including snacks and sandwiches, quick cheerful service, upstairs dining room, simple pleasant décor. *(Pete Coxon, Brian and Janet Ainscough, Eric Larkham, the Didler, Pat and Tony Martin)*

YORK
SE5853
Dormouse (01904) 640682
Shipton Road, Clifton Park; YO30 5PA Vintage Inn set down leafy driveway (site of former 19th-c paupers' hospital), spacious and comfortable, with friendly efficient staff, three changing ales, wide choice of good value wines, popular competitively priced pubby food and specials (booking advised); children welcome, good disabled access, bedrooms in Premier Inn next door, open all day. *(Paul Goldman)*

YORK
SE6051
Golden Ball (01904) 652211
Cromwell Road/Bishophill; YO1 6DU Friendly well preserved four-room Edwardian corner pub, enjoyable straightforward weekday lunchtime food, six well kept changing ales, bar billiards, cards and dominoes; TV, live music Thurs; lovely small walled garden, open all day weekends, closed weekday lunchtimes. *(the Didler)*

YORK SE6052
Golden Slipper (01904) 651235
Goodramgate; YO1 7LG Dating from
15th c with unpretentious bar and three
comfortably old-fashioned small rooms, one
lined with books, cheerful efficient staff, good
cheap plain lunchtime food from sandwiches
up including an OAP special, John Smiths
and up to three other beers; TV; tables in
back courtyard. *(Pete Coxon, Eric Larkham)*

YORK SE6052
Guy Fawkes (01904) 466674
High Petergate; YO1 7HP Friendly pub
in splendid spot next to the Minster, dark
panelled interior with small bar to the left,
good real ale choice including a house beer
from Great Heck, enjoyable sensibly priced
food (not Sun evening) from shortish menu
plus blackboard specials, dining rooms lit by
gas wall lights and candles, open fires;
13 bedrooms, open all day. *(Eric Larkham,
Dave Webster, Sue Holland, the Didler, Brian and
Janet Ainscough)*

YORK SE6052
Lamb & Lion (01904) 612078
High Petergate; YO1 7EH Sparse
furnishings and low lighting including
candles giving a spartan Georgian feel,
friendly helpful service, four well kept ales
including Black Sheep and one brewed for
the pub locally, enjoyable simple bar food
plus more elaborate evening set menu (Tues-
Sat), no food Sun evening, compact rooms
off dark corridors; steep steps up to small
attractive garden below city wall and looking
up to the Minster, 12 bedrooms, open all
day. *(Eric Larkham)*

YORK SE6051
★ Last Drop (01904) 621951
Colliergate; YO1 8BN Basic traditional
York Brewery pub, their own beers and one
or two well kept guests, samples offered by
friendly knowledgeable young staff, decent
wines and country wines, nice fresh good
value food (12-4pm) including sandwiches
and shared platters, big windows, bare
boards, barrel tables and comfortable seats
(some up a few steps); no children, can
get very busy lunchtime, may ask to keep a
credit card while you eat, attic lavatories;
tables out behind, open all day. *(Derek and
Sylvia Stephenson, Eric Larkham, the Didler,
Pete Coxon)*

YORK SE6051
Lendal Cellars (01904) 623121
Lendal; YO1 8AA Split-level ale house
in broad-vaulted 17th-c cellars, stripped
brickwork, stone floor, linked rooms and
alcoves, good choice of changing ales and
wines by the glass, foreign bottled beers,
farm cider, decent coffee, enjoyable generous
pub food all day, friendly helpful staff;
background music; no dogs; children allowed
if eating. *(the Didler)*

YORK SE5951
★ Maltings (01904) 655387
*Tanners Moat/Wellington Row, below
Lendal Bridge; YO1 6HU* Lively friendly
city pub by the river, cheerful landlord,
well kept Black Sheep and half a dozen
quickly changing interesting guests, several
continental beers, 13 ciders, country wines,
generous tasty bar food (not evenings), old
doors for bar front and ceiling, fine collection
of railway signs and amusing notices, old
chocolate dispensing machine, cigarette
and tobacco advertisements, cough and
chest remedies and even a lavatory pan in
one corner, day's papers framed in gents';
games machine, no credit cards, difficult
nearby parking; children allowed mealtimes
only, dogs welcome, handy for Rail Museum
and station, open all day. *(Pete Coxon, Derek
and Sylvia Stephenson, Eric Larkham, Pat and
Graham Williamson, Tim and Sue Halstead, Leah
Fisher and others)*

YORK SE5952
Minster Inn (01904) 624499
Marygate; YO30 7BH Multi-roomed
Edwardian local, bric-a-brac and dark old
settles, fires and woodburners, corridor
to distinctive back room, friendly staff,
well kept changing Marstons-related ales,
sandwiches, table games; children welcome,
tables out behind, open all day Fri-Sat, from
2pm Mon-Thurs. *(Eric Larkham, the Didler)*

YORK SE6052
Old White Swan (01904) 540911
Goodramgate; YO1 7LF Bustling
spacious pub with Victorian, Georgian and
Tudor-themed bars, popular lunchtime food
including nine types of sausage, Black Sheep
and several other well kept ales, good whisky
choice, central glass-covered courtyard good
for families; background and frequent live
music, big-screen sports TV, games machines,
Mon quiz; open all day. *(Derek and Sylvia
Stephenson, Pete Coxon, R K Phillips)*

YORK SE6051
Phoenix (01904) 656401
George Street; YO1 9PT Friendly, well
restored little pub next to city walls, proper
front public bar and comfortable back
horseshoe-shaped lounge, fresh flowers and
candles, five well kept Yorkshire ales, good
wines, simple food, regular live jazz; beer
garden, handy for Barbican, open all day Sat,

We include some hotels with a good bar that offers facilities comparable
to those of a pub.

closed lunchtimes other days. *(Rick Howell, Stewart Morris, David Gamston, Pat and Tony Martin, Jon Fulton)*

YORK SE6051
Punch Bowl (01904) 615491
Stonegate; YO1 8AN Bustling old black and white fronted pub, friendly helpful service, wide range of generous bargain food all day, small panelled rooms off corridor, TV in beamed one on left of food servery, well kept ales such as Black Sheep Leeds, John Smiths and Thornbridge, good wine choice; background music, games machines, regular quiz nights; open all day. *(Eric Larkham, Mrs Edna M Jones, Pete Coxon)*

YORK SE6151
Rook & Gaskill (01904) 674067
Lawrence Street; YO10 3WP Traditional Castle Rock pub with up to a dozen ales, enjoyable food (not Sun), dark wood tables, banquettes, chairs and high stools, conservatory; open all day. *(Eric Larkham, the Didler, Pete Coxon)*

YORK SE6052
Snickleway (01904) 656138
Goodramgate; YO1 7LS Interesting little open-plan pub behind big shop-front window, lots of antiques, copper and brass, cosy fires, five well kept ales, some lunchtime food including good doorstep sandwiches, prompt friendly service; open all day. *(T Gott, Gerard Dyson, D Walkden)*

YORK SE6051
Swan (01904) 634968
Bishopgate Street, Clementhorpe; YO23 1JH Unspoilt 1930s pub (Grade II listed), hatch service to lobby for two small rooms off main bar, several changing ales and ciders, friendly knowledgeable staff may offer tasters; busy with young people weekends; small pleasant walled garden, near city walls,

open all day weekends, closed weekday lunchtimes. *(the Didler, James Hibbins)*

YORK SE6052
★**Three Legged Mare** (01904) 638246
High Petergate; YO1 7EN Bustling light and airy modern café-bar with York Brewery's full range and guests kept well (12 handpumps), plenty of belgian beers, quick friendly young staff, interesting sandwiches and some basic lunchtime hot food, low prices, back conservatory; no children; disabled facilities (other lavatories down spiral stairs), back garden with replica gallows after which pub is named, open all day till midnight (11pm Sun). *(Eric Larkham, Pete Coxon, Barry Webber, Kerry Law)*

YORK SE5951
★**York Brewery Tap** (01904) 621162
Toft Green, Micklegate; YO1 6JT Members only for York Brewery's upstairs lounge (annual fee unless you go on brewery tour), their own full cask range in top condition, also bottled beers, nice clubby atmosphere with friendly staff happy to talk about the beers, lots of breweriana and view of brewing plant, comfortable sofas and armchairs, magazines and daily newspapers, brewery shop; no food; children allowed during the day, open all day except Sun evening. *(Pete Coxon, Ian and Nita Cooper, Eric Larkham, the Didler)*

YORK SE6052
Yorkshire Terrier (01904) 621162
Stonegate; YO1 8AS York Brewery shop: behind this, a smallish well worn-in bar with their full beer range and guests (tasting trays available), interesting bottled beers, lunchtime pubby food, stair lift for upstairs dining room (children allowed here), small conservatory; handy for the Minster, open all day. *(Pete Coxon, Derek and Sylvia Stephenson, Eric Larkham, the Didler)*

If a service charge is mentioned prominently on a menu or accommodation terms, you must pay it if service was satisfactory. If service is really bad you are legally entitled to refuse to pay some or all of the service charge as compensation for not getting the service you might reasonably have expected.

LONDON

To enjoy Central London pubs at their best you should aim to avoid mid-lunchtime or early evening sessions, when they tend to be packed out, with customers spilling on to the pavements. And, while service copes surprisingly well then, you can't fully appreciate the often remarkable décor. For real character head to the Harp, Old Bank of England, Olde Mitre and Seven Stars (Central London), Grapes (East London), Holly Bush (North London), and Royal Oak (South London; an unusual pub transformed by Harveys, the Sussex brewer, and keeping all their ales). Food is often surprisingly good value but for a special meal aim for the Gun (East London; a top-notch place with modern food and a lovely riverside terrace), Duke of Cambridge (North London; eco-friendly and with organic food and drink), Duke of Sussex (West London; interesting architecture and an imaginative menu) or Old Orchard (Outer London; a Brunning & Price pub with stunning views and interesting bistro-style meals). Our London Dining Pub 2013 is the Gun in East London.

CENTRAL LONDON

Bountiful Cow

Map 13

Eagle Street; ⊖ *Holborn; WC1R 4AP*

Bustling and informal place popular with those wanting either a chat at the bar or a meaty meal

Most customers are here to enjoy the first class steaks and burgers, though Adnams Best and a beer from Dark Star are on handpump and several wines available by the glass. The informal street-level bar in this part pub/part grill house has chrome and white leather bar stools against the counter – grabbed quickly by those wanting a chat and a pint – a raised area by the windows with booth seating and a smallish main room with red wicker dining chairs around wooden tables on stripped floorboards, beef-related prints and posters on the painted brick walls; background jazz, quick service. There's also a basement dining room by the open kitchen, with red-painted walls and cow prints. The licensees run the Seven Stars as well.

Good and popular, the food includes welsh rarebit with Guinness, rilletes of duck with toast, garlic-fried prawns, roast corn-fed chicken with couscous, linguine with artichoke hearts and peas, napoli sausages with mash, a charcuterie plate, their fantastic beef burger and top quality steaks, and puddings like crème brûlée and panna cotta with raspberry coulis. *Benchmark main dish: rare breed beef burger and chips £13.00. Two-course evening meal £18.00.*

Free house ~ Licensee Roxy Beaujolais ~ Real ale ~ Bar food (12-3, 5-10.30) ~ Restaurant ~ (020) 7404 0200 ~ Children welcome ~ Open 11-11; 12-11 Sat; closed Sun ~ www.thebountifulcow.co.uk *Recommended by Richard Gibbs, David Jackman, Ian Phillips*

CENTRAL LONDON

Harp ◀

Map 13

47 Chandos Place; ⊖ ⇌ *Charing Cross, Leicester Square; WC2N 4HS*

Narrow little pub with eight real ales, friendly service, a cheerful atmosphere and nice sausage baguettes

Our readers love this little pub – so handy for the theatres – and the cheerful long-serving landlady and her friendly staff make all their many customers feel warmly welcomed. It pretty much consists of one long narrow, very traditional bar, with lots of high bar stools along the wall counter and around elbow tables, big mirrors on the red walls, some lovely stained glass and loads of interesting, quirkily executed celebrity portraits. If it's not too busy, you may be able to get one of the prized seats looking out through the front windows. A little room upstairs is much quieter, with comfortable furniture and a window looking over the road below. The eight real ales on handpump are particularly well kept and quickly changing. There are usually three from Dark Star, one from Harveys, two from Sambrooks and one or two widely sourced guests – maybe from fff, O'Hanlons, Palmers, Twickenham or Windsor & Eaton; up to nine farm ciders and three perries and quite a few malt whiskies. It gets packed in the early evening, with customers spilling out into the back alley.

Bar food consists of good changing sausages in baps with lots of fried onions: wild boar, duck, venison, pork and ale or pork with garlic, beef and Guinness, and flavours like italian, spanish, mexican and american smoky. These are served until they run out. *Benchmark main dish: sausage in a toasted baguette £3.50.*

Free house ~ Licensee Bridget Walsh ~ Real ale ~ Bar food (12-3; not evenings) ~ (020) 7836 0291 ~ Open 10am-11.30pm; 12-10.30 Sun ~ www.harpcoventgarden.com
Recommended by Tracey and Stephen Groves, Peter F Marshall, Roger and Donna Huggins, Tim Maddison, LM, Taff Thomas, Matt and Vikki Wharton, Phil Bryant, the Didler, Mike and Sue Loseby, Mike Gorton, Richard Endacott, Dr and Mrs A K Clarke, David Jackman

 CENTRAL LONDON   Map 13

Lamb

Lambs Conduit Street; ⊖ Holborn, Russell Square; WC1N 3LZ

Famously unspoilt Victorian pub, full of character, with unique fittings and atmosphere

Victorian London lives on in this quite unchanging pub. There's a great deal of character and plenty to look at, especially the unique original fittings – the highlight being the bank of cut-glass swivelling snob-screens all the way round the U-shaped bar counter. Sepia photographs of 1890s actresses on the ochre panelled walls and traditional cast-iron framed tables with neat brass rails around the rim add to the overall effect. Up to seven real ales on handpump like Wells & Youngs Bitter, Bombardier and Special plus guests such as Adnams Broadside, Otter Bitter, and St Austell Tribute, and a good choice of malt whiskies. No machines or music. There's a snug little room at the back, slatted wooden seats out in front and more in a little courtyard beyond. Like the street, the pub is named for the kentish clothmaker William Lamb, who brought fresh water to Holborn in 1577. No children. The Foundlings Museum is nearby.

 Bar food includes lunchtime sandwiches (not Sunday), platters, salads like niçoise or chicken and bacon, bangers and mash with red onion gravy, sweet potato curry, all-day breakfast, steak in ale pie, gammon and free-range eggs and puddings such as apple and rhubarb crumble and sticky toffee pudding. *Benchmark main dish: steak in ale pie £10.45. Two-course evening meal £15.00.*

Youngs ~ Manager Mr L Tuohy ~ Real ale ~ Bar food (12-9) ~ (020) 7405 0713 ~ Well behaved children allowed until 5pm ~ Open 12-11(midnight Thurs-Sat); 12-10.30 Sun ~ www.youngs.co.uk *Recommended by John and Gloria Isaacs, Andy and Claire Barker, Tracey and Stephen Groves, the Didler, Roy Hoing, David Carr*

CENTRAL LONDON   Map 13

Lamb & Flag £

Rose Street, off Garrick Street; ⊖ Leicester Square, Covent Garden; WC2E 9EB

Historic yet unpretentious, full of character and atmosphere and with six real ales; especially busy in the evening

The eight real ales and friendly efficient service continue to draw huge numbers of cheerful customers to this tucked-away pub. It's an unspoilt and, in places, rather basic old tavern. The more spartan front room leads into a snugly atmospheric low-ceilinged back bar with high-backed black settles and an open fire; in Regency times this was known as the Bucket of Blood, thanks to the bare-knuckle prize-fights held here. As the pub is owned by Fullers they keep many of their beers plus a guest like Adnams Ghost Ship on handpump, as well as ten wines by the glass and 16 malt whiskies. The pub cat is called Beautiful. The upstairs Dryden Room is often less crowded and has more seats (though fewer beers). The pub has a lively and well documented history: the poet John

Dryden was nearly beaten to death by hired thugs outside, and Dickens made fun of the Middle Temple lawyers who frequented it when he was working in nearby Catherine Street.

🍴 The tasty bar food is served upstairs, lunchtimes only: sandwiches, chicken liver parfait with apple chutney, tagliatelle with olives, tomatoes, courgettes, peppers, red pesto and parmesan, chargrilled beef burger with cheese, bacon and tomato relish, cumberland sausages with mash and onion and red wine gravy, a pie of the day and their very popular beer-battered cod with peas and tartare sauce. *Benchmark main dish: fish and chips £8.95. Two-course meal £15.00.*

Free house ~ Licensee Christopher Buckley ~ Real ale ~ Bar food (12-7(Sun 12-5)) ~ Restaurant ~ (020) 7497 9504 ~ Children in upstairs dining room only ~ Dogs allowed in bar ~ Live jazz Sun evening ~ Open 11-11; 12-10.30 Sun ~ www.lambandflagconventgarden.co.uk *Recommended by Anthony Longden, Graham Oddey, Taff Thomas, the Didler, Mike and Sue Loseby, Andrea Rampley*

CENTRAL LONDON   Map 13

Old Bank of England ♀

Fleet Street; ⊖ *Chancery Lane (not Sundays), Temple (not Sundays)* ⇌ *Blackfriars; EC4A 2LT*

Dramatically converted former bank building, with gleaming chandeliers in impressive, soaring bar, well kept Fullers beers, and good pies

This extraordinary Grade I listed italianate building rarely fails to impress first – or even second time visitors. It's a former subsidiary branch of the Bank of England and has a quite astounding interior. The soaring, spacious bar has three gleaming chandeliers hanging from the exquisitely plastered ceiling, high above an unusually tall island bar counter, crowned with a clock. The end wall has huge paintings and murals that look like 18th-c depictions of Justice, but in fact feature members of the Fuller, Smith and Turner families, who run the brewery that owns the pub. There are well polished dark wooden furnishings, luxurious curtains swagging massive windows, plenty of framed prints and, despite the grandeur, some surprisingly cosy corners, with screens between some of the tables creating an unexpectedly intimate feel. A quieter galleried section upstairs offer a bird's-eye view of the action, and some smaller rooms (used mainly for functions) open off. Seven Fullers beers are on handpump alongside a good choice of malt whiskies and a dozen wines by the glass. At lunchtimes the background music is generally classical or easy listening; it's louder and livelier in the evenings. There's also a garden with seats (one of the few pubs in the area to have one).

🍴 Pies have a long if rather dubious pedigree in this area: it was in the vaults and tunnels below the Old Bank and the surrounding buildings that Sweeney Todd butchered the clients destined to provide the fillings in his mistress Mrs Lovett's nearby pie shop. Well, somehow or other, good home-made pies have become a speciality on the menu here, too: smoked fish and leek, sausage, apple and spring onion, chicken, mushroom and tarragon and their speciality steak in venison with redcurrants and leeks in a rich red wine sauce. Other dishes include sandwiches, beef burger with bacon and smoked cheddar, chicken kiev, beer-battered fish and chips and beef stroganoff. *Benchmark main dish: beef and venison in redcurrant pie £10.25. Two-course evening meal £16.00.*

Fullers ~ Manager Jo Farquhar ~ Real ale ~ Bar food (12-9) ~ Restaurant ~ (020) 7430 2255 ~ Children welcome until 5pm ~ Open 11-11; closed weekends and bank holidays ~

www.oldbankofengland.co.uk *Recommended by Chris and Jeanne Downing, Tom and Ruth Rees, Andy and Claire Barker, Barry Collett, the Didler, David Jackman, David Carr, Dr and Mrs A K Clarke*

CENTRAL LONDON   Map 13
Olde Mitre ◧ £

Ely Place; the easiest way to find it is from the narrow passageway beside 8 Hatton Garden; ⊖ Chancery Lane (not Sundays); EC1N 6SJ

Hard to find but well worth it – an unspoilt old pub with lovely atmosphere, unusual guest beers and bargain toasted sandwiches

Run by proper hands-on licensees – rare for London – this is a real refuge from the modern city nearby. The cosy small rooms have antique settles and lots of dark panelling and – particularly in the popular back room – old local pictures and so forth. It gets good-naturedly packed with the city suited and booted between 12.30 and 2.15, filling up again in the early evening, but in the early afternoons and by around 8pm becomes a good deal more tranquil. An upstairs room, mainly used for functions, may double as an overflow at peak periods. Adnams Broadside, Caledonian Deuchars IPA, Fullers London Pride and Gales Seafarer with guests like Fyne Ales Pipers Gold, Caledonian 80/- , Dark Star Over the Moon and Harviestoun Bitter & Twisted are on handpump, and they hold three beer festivals a year. No music, TV or machines – the only games here are board games. There's some space for outside drinking by the pot plants and jasmine in the narrow yard between the pub and St Ethelreda's church (which is worth a look). Note the pub doesn't open at weekends. The iron gates that guard one entrance to Ely Place are a reminder of the days when the law in this district was administered by the Bishops of Ely. The best approach is from Hatton Garden, walking up the right-hand side away from Chancery Lane; an easily missed sign on a lamp post points the way down a narrow alley. No children.

🍴 Served all day, bar snacks are limited to scotch eggs, pork pies and sausage rolls, and really good value toasted sandwiches with cheese, ham, pickle or tomato. *Benchmark main dish: pork pies £1.70*

Fullers ~ Managers Eamon and Kathy Scott ~ Real ale ~ Bar food (11-9.30) ~ (020) 7405 4751 ~ Open 11-11; closed weekends and bank holidays *Recommended by Tom McLean, Chris and Jeanne Downing, Andy and Claire Barker, Anthony Longden, Matt and Vikki Wharton, Taff Thomas, N R White, the Didler, Dr and Mrs A K Clarke*

CENTRAL LONDON   Map 13
Seven Stars ◧

Carey Street; ⊖ Temple (not Sundays), Chancery Lane (not Sundays), Holborn; WC2A 2JB

Quirky pub with cheerful staff, an interesting mix of customers and a good choice of drinks and food

A favourite with lawyers and court reporters, this unchanging small pub has plenty of caricatures of barristers and judges on the red-painted walls of the two main rooms. Also, posters of legal-themed british films, big ceiling fans and a relaxed, intimate atmosphere; checked tablecloths add a quirky, almost continental touch. A third area is in what was formerly a legal wig shop next door – it still retains the original frontage, with a neat display of wigs in the window. It's worth getting here early as they don't take bookings and tables get snapped up quickly. Adnams Best and Broadside and a couple of guests such as Dark Star Hophead and Sambrooks Wandle on handpump, and they do a particularly good dry Martini. On busy evenings there's an overflow of customers on to the quiet road in front; things generally quieten down after 8pm and there can be a nice, sleepy atmosphere some afternoons. The Elizabethan stairs up to the lavatories are rather steep, but there's a good strong handrail. The new pub cat, Ray Brown, wears a ruff. The licensees also run the Bountiful Cow. No children.

🍴 Cooked according to the landlady's fancy, the good, interesting food might include bruschetta with different toppings, goose rillettes with toast, linguine with leeks, wild garlic leaves, peas and butter, tuna kedgeree biriyani, leek and ham risotto, hot smoked german sausages with sautéed potatoes, goose and black pudding pie, and puddings such as posh ice-cream in a Kilner jar (the salt caramel flavour is popular). *Benchmark main dish: homemade poultry pies £10.00. Two-course evening meal £16.00.*

Free house ~ Licensee Roxy Beaujolais ~ Real ale ~ Bar food (all day) ~ (020) 7242 8521 ~ Open 11(noon weekends)-11(10.30 Sun); closed some bank holidays ~ www.thesevenstars1602.co.uk *Recommended by LM, Tracey and Stephen Groves, Tim Maddison, Andy and Claire Barker, the Didler, N R White, Andrea Rampley*

CENTRAL LONDON   Map 13
Star 🍺

Belgrave Mews West, behind the German Embassy, off Belgrave Square;
⊖ *Knightsbridge, Hyde Park Corner; SW1X 8HT*

Bustling local with restful bar, upstairs dining room, Fullers ales, well liked bar food and colourful hanging baskets

Tucked away in cobbled mews in the heart of Belgravia, this classy but friendly pub is covered with an astonishing array of hanging baskets and flowering tubs – a lovely sight in summer. The small bar is a pleasant place with a wooden floor, sash windows, stools by the counter, a restful feel outside peak times and Fullers ESB, Summer Ale and Wild River on handpump, good wines by the glass and 35 malt whiskies. An arch leads to the main seating area, which has well polished tables and chairs, and good lighting; there's also an upstairs dining room. It's said that this is the pub where the Great Train Robbery was planned.

🍴 Likeable bar food includes sandwiches with coleslaw and chips, chicken and chorizo caesar salad, tiger prawns in garlic and herb butter, beef burgers with chips, wild mushroom ravioli with roasted squash in a creamy tomato sauce, sausages with onion gravy, lamb skewers with greek salad and pitta bread, pork stroganoff with basmati rice, chicken, bacon and mushroom pie, and puddings such as lime and ginger cheesecake and iced chocolate terrine. *Benchmark main dish: beer-battered fish and chips £9.80. Two-course evening meal £16.00.*

Fullers ~ Managers Jason and Karen Tinklin ~ Real ale ~ Bar food (12-4, 5-9; 12-7 Sat; 12-5 Sun; not weekend evenings) ~ Restaurant ~ (020) 7235 3019 ~ Children welcome ~ Dogs allowed in bar ~ Open 11(12 Sat and Sun)-11(10.30 Sun) ~ www.star-tavern-belgravia *Recommended by Tracey and Stephen Groves, N R White, the Didler*

The 🍺 symbol shows pubs which keep their beer unusually well, have a particularly good range or brew their own.

EAST LONDON　　　　　　　　　　　　　　　　　　Map 12

Grapes

Narrow Street; ⊖ ⇄ Limehouse (or Westferry DLR); hard to find by car – turn off Commercial Road at signs for Rotherhithe Tunnel, then from the Tunnel Approach slip road, fork left leading into Branch Road, turn left and then left again into Narrow Street; E14 8BP

Relaxed waterside pub with timeless London feel, particularly appealing cosy back room, helpful friendly staff, popular bar food and good upstairs fish restaurant

Full of history, this 16th-c riverside pub is under new owners who are determined to keep it as a proper, traditional tavern. In fact, it's not much changed since Charles Dickens used it as a model for his Six Jolly Fellowship Porters in *Our Mutual Friend*; all the more remarkable considering the ultra-modern buildings that now surround it. There's a good mix of customers and bags of atmosphere, and the chatty, partly panelled bar has lots of prints, mainly of actors, and old local maps, as well as some elaborately etched windows, plates along a shelf and newspapers to read; the cosy back part has a winter open fire. Adnams Best, Marstons Pedigree, Timothy Taylors Landlord and a guest on handpump are served from the long thin bar; board games. The upstairs fish restaurant, with fine views of the river, is highly thought of. In summer, the small balcony at the back is a fine spot for a sheltered waterside drink, with easterly views towards Canary Wharf. You can catch the Canary Wharf ferry and enter the pub via the steps that lead up from the foreshore. No children. A bowl of water is provided for dogs.

Very fairly priced, the popular bar food includes lunchtime sandwiches, devilled crispy whitebait with tartare sauce, hand-made beef burger with chunky chips and cheese, roasted vegetable frittata, bangers and mash, fishcakes with salad, and crispy battered fish with pea mash; the fish restaurant is pricier. *Benchmark main dish: fish and chips £8.95. Two-course evening meal £18.70.*

Free house ~ Licensee Paul Mathias ~ Real ale ~ Bar food (12-3.30(4 Sun), 6.30-9.30) ~ Restaurant ~ (020) 7987 4396 ~ Dogs welcome but must be kept on leads ~ Open 12-11(10.30 Sun) ~ www.thegrapes.co.uk *Recommended by John Saville, Andy and Claire Barker, Mike Gorton, N R White, Claes Mauroy, Ross Balaam, John and Gloria Isaacs*

EAST LONDON　　　　　　　　　　　　　　　　　　Map 12

Gun 🍴 🍷

27 Coldharbour; ⊖ Blackwall DLR; E14 9NS
London Dining Pub of the Year

Top-notch gastropub, pricey but worth it, great views from the riverside terrace, plenty of character and history, well chosen wines

One of the main draws here is the long, narrow terrace behind this busy riverside pub that offers uninterrupted views of the O2 Centre across a broad sweep of the Thames; heaters and huge umbrellas make it welcoming even on cooler days. The two rooms nearest the terrace are the nicest: a busy flagstoned bar for drinkers, with antique guns on the wall and no tables – just a large barrel in the centre of the room – that shares a log fire with the cosy red-painted room next door, with its comfy leather sofas and armchairs, a stuffed boar's head, some modern prints, well stocked bookshelves and views on to the terrace. Crisp white walls and smart white tablecloths and napkins on tables at one end of the main bar contrast strikingly with dark wood floors and the black wood counter at the other. Adnams Bitter and a couple of guests from Dark Star and Sambrooks on handpump and several wines by the glass served by neatly aproned staff; background music. They may occasionally close the pub on Saturdays for weddings, and will keep your credit card if you are sitting on the terrace and want to run a tab.

🍴 You can eat from both the bar and restaurant menu in the bar so there's a good choice of dishes: sausage roll with HP sauce, several different types of oysters, white and brown crab meat with mayonnaise, pork, pigeon, chicken liver and caper terrine with fruit chutney, soft herb and asparagus tagliatelle with parmesan, smoked haddock and salmon fishcake with a poached egg and chive butter sauce, pie, mash and liquor, beef burger with cheese and chips, roast fillet of cod with a chorizo, borlotti bean and confit garlic stew, stuffed rabbit leg with broad beans, peas, mushrooms, gnocchi and a mustard and tarragon sauce, 35-day aged rib-eye steak with béarnaise sauce and hand-cut chips, and puddings such as dark chocolate brownie with salted peanut cream and vanilla ice-cream and apple crumble with vanilla custard. *Benchmark main dish: slow-roast pork belly with red wine jus £16.50. Two-course evening meal £25.00.*

Free house ~ Licensees Ed and Tom Martin ~ Real ale ~ Bar food (12-3(4 Sat, Sun), 6-10.30(9.30 Sun)) ~ Restaurant ~ (020) 7515 5222 ~ children welcome until 8pm ~ Quiz Mon evening ~ Open 11am-midnight(11 Sun) ~ www.thegundocklands.com
Recommended by W T Selwood, Andy and Claire Barker, Stuart Doughty

NORTH LONDON   Map 13
Drapers Arms ♀
Far west end of Barnsbury Street; ⊖ ⇄ Highbury & Islington; N1 1ER

Streamlined place with good mix of drinkers and diners, thoughtful choice of drinks, imaginative modern food and seats in the attractive back garden

It's the good modern cooking that customers are mainly here to enjoy. This is a Georgian townhouse, simply refurbished, and the spreading bar has a mix of elegant dark wooden tables and dining chairs on bare floorboards, an arresting bright-green painted counter contrasting with soft duck-egg walls, gilt mirrors over smart fireplaces, a sofa and some comfortable chairs. Harveys Best and a couple of changing guests are served from handpump and carefully chosen wines by the glass (about 20), carafe or bottle. The stylish upstairs dining room has similar tables and chairs on a striking chequerboard-painted wood floor; background music and board games. The back terrace is most attractive, with white or green benches and chairs around zinc-topped tables, flagstones and large parasols.

🍴 Changing regularly, the interesting food might include sandwiches, clams, cider and tarragon, pork, pickled walnut and prune terrine with chutney, smoked pork chop with a fried duck egg and chips, braised rabbit leg, bacon, spinach, ceps and mustard, whole plaice with brown shrimps, capers and parsley, rump steak with horseradish, and puddings such as vanilla cheesecake with strawberries and elderflower sorbet. *Benchmark main dish: beef and oyster pie £13.50. Two-course evening meal £20.00.*

Free house ~ Licensee Nick Gibson ~ Real ale ~ Bar food (12-2, 7-9(6.30-9.30 Sun)) ~ Restaurant ~ (020) 7619 0348 ~ Children welcome but must be seated and dining after 6pm ~ Open 10-midnight(11 Sun) ~ www.thedrapersarms.com *Recommended by Richard Gibbs*

NORTH LONDON   Map 13
Duke of Cambridge 🍴 ♀ 🍺
St Peters Street; ⊖ Angel, then 15 minutes' walk; N1 8JT

Trailblazing organic pub with carefully sourced, imaginative food, excellent range of organic drinks and a nice, chatty atmosphere

The atmosphere in this busy, friendly pub is warmly inviting: it's the kind of place that somehow encourages conversation, with a steady stream of civilised chat from the varied customers. This was London's first organic pub and they try and re-use and recycle as much as possible and source organic drinks and organic produce for the food. Little Valley Tods Blonde and Withens Pale Ale, St Peters Best Bitter and a guest from Pitfield on handpump, organic draught lagers and cider, organic spirits (including a new ethical whisky list), a wide range of organic wines (many of which are available by the glass), quite a few teas and coffees, and a spicy ginger ale. The big, busy main room is simply decorated and furnished with lots of chunky wooden tables, pews and benches on bare boards. A corridor leads off past a few tables and an open kitchen to a dining room, more formally set for eating, and a conservatory. It's worth arriving early to eat, as they can get very busy.

 Using top quality seasonal food from small organic producers, the good, interesting bar food might include sandwiches, smoked sprats with beetroot, apple, watercress and horseradish, ham hock and mustard terrine with a boiled egg, asparagus and confit summer garlic risotto with ewe's cheese, beer-battered pollack with mushy peas, chips and tartare sauce, game burger with red cabbage coleslaw and pickled cucumber, mutton, mushroom and red wine stew with braised pearl barley, chicken and mushroom pie, and puddings such as cherry tart with vanilla and amaretto ice-cream and warm chocolate and nut brownie with coffee and rum ice-cream. *Benchmark main dish: Sunday roast £19.00. Two-course evening meal £24.00.*

Free house ~ Licensee Geetie Singh ~ Real ale ~ Bar food (12.30-4, 6.30-11(10.30 Sun)) ~ Restaurant ~ (020) 7359 3066 ~ Children welcome ~ Dogs allowed in bar ~ Open 12-11(10.30 Sun) ~ www.dukeorganic.co.uk *Recommended by LM, Mary Shaw*

NORTH LONDON   Map 12
Holly Bush ♀ 🍺
Holly Mount; ⊖ Hampstead; NW3 6SG

Unique village local with good food and drinks, and lovely unspoilt feel

Once the stable block of a nearby house, this is a proper local with a friendly welcome for all from the efficient, helpful staff. The old-fashioned front bar has a dark, sagging ceiling, brown and cream panelled walls (decorated with old advertisements and a few hanging plates), open fires, bare boards, and secretive bays formed by partly glazed partitions. Slightly more intimate, the back room, named after the painter George Romney, has an embossed red ceiling, panelled and etched glass alcoves, and ochre-painted brick walls covered with small prints; lots of board and card games. Fullers London Pride, Discovery and ESB on handpump, as well as 23 whiskies and 16 wines by the glass from a a good wine list. The upstairs dining room has table service at the weekend, as does the rest of the pub on a Sunday. There are benches on the pavement outside.

🍴 Good, popular food includes nibbles like potted shrimps on toast and pork and sage sausage rolls as well as chicken liver parfait with red onion marmalade, gravadlax of salmon with citrus, fennel and wholegrain mustard crème fraîche, bocconcini (little mozzarella balls) and caramelised onion tart with cauliflower purée and blanched cherry tomatoes, beef and wild mushroom in ale pie, seared scallops, brown shrimps and mussels in a mild curry and sauternes sauce on pasta, confit duck leg with red wine jus and dauphinoise potatoes, and puddings like Valrhona chocolate mousse with peppered honeycomb and vanilla ice-cream and apple and mixed berry crumble with crème anglaise. *Benchmark main dish: fish pie £13.95. Two-course evening meal £20.00.*

Fullers ~ Manager Hannah Borkulak ~ Real ale ~ Bar food (12-4, 6-10; 12-5, 6-9 Sun) ~ Restaurant ~ (020) 7435 2892 ~ Children welcome till 7pm ~ Dogs welcome ~ Open 12-11(10.30 Sun) *Recommended by N R White, the Didler*

SOUTH LONDON
Greenwich Union 🍺

Map 12

Royal Hill; ⊖ ⇄ Greenwich; SE10 8RT

Enterprising pub with distinctive beers from small local Meantime Brewery, plus other unusual drinks and good, popular food

This nicely renovated, friendly pub is still one of just two taps for the small Meantime Brewery (which has moved to Greenwich now) and stocks all their distinctive unpasteurised beers. The range includes a traditional pale ale (served cool, under pressure), a mix of proper pilsners, lagers and wheat beers, one a deliciously refreshing raspberry flavour, and a stout. The knowledgeable, helpful staff will generally offer small tasters to help you choose. They also have Adnams Best and Dark Star Hop Head on handpump, and a draught cider, as well as a helpfully annotated list of around 150 bottled beers. The rest of the drinks can be unfamiliar too, as they try to avoid the more common brands. Perhaps feeling a little more like a bar than a pub, the long, narrow stone-flagged room has several different parts: a simple area at the front with a few wooden chairs and tables, a stove and newspapers, then, past the counter with its headings recalling the branding of the brewery's first beers, several brown leather cushioned pews and armchairs under framed editions of *Picture Post* on the yellow walls; background music, TV. Beyond here a much lighter, more modern-feeling conservatory has comfortable brown leather wall benches, a few original pictures and paintings, and white fairy lights under the glass roof; it leads out to an appealing terrace with green picnic-sets and a couple of old-fashioned lamp posts. The fence at the end is painted to resemble a poppy field, and the one at the side a wheat field. Though there are plenty of tables out here, it can get busy in summer (as can the whole pub on weekday evenings). In front are a couple of tables overlooking the street. The pub is slightly removed from Greenwich's many attractions and there's a particularly good traditional cheese shop on the way.

🍴 Seasonally changing and very popular, the food might include lunchtime sandwiches, oysters, smoked mackerel terrine, home-made hummus with garlic bread, watermelon, feta and mint salad with sunflower seeds and a lemon dressing, aubergine and mozzarella lasagne, beef in ale pie, smoked haddock parcel with fennel, red peppers and romesco sauce, 28-day and 35-day aged steaks, and puddings like sticky toffee pudding vanilla ice-cream and caramelised pear with chilled vanilla rice pudding and chocolate sauce. *Benchmark main dish: 28-day aged angus beef burger with tarragon mayonnaise £11.30. Two-course evening meal £18.00.*

Free house ~ Licensee Andrew Ward ~ Real ale ~ Bar food (12-10(9 Sun); 11-10 Sat)
~ (020) 8692 6258 ~ Children welcome ~ Dogs allowed in bar ~ Open 12-11; 11-11 Sat;
12-10.30 Sun ~ www.greenwichunion.com *Recommended by D Crook, N R White*

SOUTH LONDON   Map 12

Royal Oak

Tabard Street/Nebraska Street; ⊖ ⇌ *Borough, London Bridge; SE1 4JU*

**Old-fashioned corner house with particularly well kept beers and
honest food**

When the Sussex brewer Harveys took over this enjoyable corner
house (their only London pub), they transformed it, painstakingly
recreating the look and feel of a traditional London alehouse; you'd
never imagine it wasn't like this all along. The two busy little L-shaped
rooms meander around the central wooden servery, which has a
fine old clock in the middle. They're done out in a cosy, traditional
style with patterned rugs on the wooden floors, plates running along
a delft shelf, black and white scenes and period sheet music on the
red-painted walls, and an assortment of wooden tables and chairs.
They keep the full range of Harveys ales plus a guest from Fullers on
handpump and Thatcher's cider. There's a ramp for disabled customers
at the Nebraska Street entrance.

Reasonably priced food includes impressive doorstep sandwiches, ham, egg
and chips, popular steak and kidney pudding, sausage and mash with onion
gravy, scallops and bacon, game pie, swordfish steak, and puddings. *Benchmark
main dish: steak and kidney pudding £10.25. Two-course evening meal £17.50.*

Harveys ~ Tenants John Porteous and Frank Taylor ~ Real ale ~ Bar food (12-2.30,
5-9.15; 12-8 Sun) ~ (020) 7357 7173 ~ children welcome until 9pm ~ Dogs allowed in bar
~ Open 11-11; 12-9 Sun ~ www.harveys.org.uk/theroyaloaklondon.htm *Recommended by
John Saville, R Anderson, Jeremy King, Comus and Sarah Elliott, the Didler, Mike and Sue Loseby,
Mike Gorton*

WEST LONDON   Map 12

Churchill Arms ♈ ◀ £

Kensington Church Street; ⊖ *Notting Hill Gate, Kensington High
Street; W8 7LN*

**Cheery irish landlord at bustling and friendly local with very well
kept beers and excellent thai food; even at its most crowded, it stays
relaxed and welcoming**

The enthusiastic and friendly irish landlord has now been running
this bustling local for 28 years and there's always a warm welcome
for both locals and visitors. Mr O'Brien is a great collector and loves
butterflies – you'll see a variety of prints and books on the subject dotted
around the bar. He doesn't stop there, though – the pub is also filled
with countless lamps, miners' lights, horse tack, bedpans and brasses
hanging from the ceiling, a couple of interesting carved figures and
statuettes behind the central bar counter, prints of US presidents, and
lots of Winston Churchill memorabilia. Well kept Fullers Chiswick, ESB,
London Pride and Fullers seasonal beers on handpump and two dozen
wines by the glass. The spacious and rather smart plant-filled dining
conservatory may be used for hatching butterflies, but is better known
for its extensive choice of excellent thai food. Look out for special events
and decorations around Christmas, Hallowe'en, St Patrick's Day, St

George's Day, and Churchill's birthday (30 November) – along with more people than you'd ever imagine could feasibly fit inside this place; they have their own cricket and football teams. There can be an overspill on to the street, where there are some chrome tables and chairs. The façade is quite a sight in summer as it almost disappears behind the glorious display of 85 window boxes and 42 hanging baskets.

 Good quality and splendid value, the authentic thai food ranges from a proper thai curry to various rice, noodle and stir-fry dishes. At lunchtime they usually also have a very few traditional pub dishes such as fish and chips or sausage and chips, and there's a good value Sunday roast. *Benchmark main dish: thai dishes £7.00. Two-course evening meal £10.00.*

Fullers ~ Manager Gerry O'Brien ~ Real ale ~ Bar food (12-10(9.30 Sun)) ~ Restaurant ~ (020) 7727 4242 ~ Children welcome ~ Dogs welcome ~ Open 11-11 (midnight Thurs-Sat); 12-10.30 Sun *Recommended by LM, David Uren, Susan and John Douglas, Derek Thomas, the Didler, N R White*

WEST LONDON   Map 12
Colton Arms
Greyhound Road; ⊖ *Barons Court, West Kensington; W14 9SD*

Unspoilt little pub, unchanged thanks to its dedicated landlord; it's peaceful and genuinely old-fashioned with well kept beer

This unspoilt little gem is like an old-fashioned country tavern and is run by a friendly long-serving landlord who has been here since 1963 – though his son now helps out, too. The main U-shaped front bar has a log fire blazing in winter, highly polished brasses, a fox's mask, hunting crops and plates decorated with hunting scenes on the walls and a remarkable collection of handsomely carved antique oak furniture. That room is small enough, but the two back rooms, each with their own little serving counter with a bell to ring for service, are tiny. Fullers London Pride, Sharps Doom Bar and a guest such as Adnams Lighthouse on handpump. When you pay, note the old-fashioned brass-bound till. Pull the curtain aside for the door out to a charming back terrace with a neat rose arbour. The pub is next to the Queens Club tennis courts and gardens. No food.

Enterprise ~ Lease Norman and Jonathan Nunn ~ Real ale ~ No credit cards ~ (020) 7385 6956 ~ Children must be over 4 and are welcome till 7pm ~ Dogs allowed in bar ~ Open 12-3(4 Sat), 6(7 Sat)-11.30; 12-4, 7-11 Sun *Recommended by N R White*

WEST LONDON   Map 12
Duke of Sussex 🍴 ♟ ◖
South Parade; ⊖ *Chiswick Park* ⇌ *South Acton; W4 5LF*

Attractively restored Victorian local with interesting bar food, good choice of drinks and lovely big garden

With a new landlord and some recent refurbishment, this sizeable Victorian pub is extremely popular. Once through the intriguing entrance lobbies with their cut glass, mahogany and mosaics, you enter the classy, simply furnished bar. This has huge windows, some original etched glass, chapel and farmhouse chairs around scrubbed pine and dark wood tables on the new floorboards and a big horseshoe-shaped counter lined with high bar stools where they serve Cottage IPA, Nethergate Essex Border and Trumans Seek and Save on handpump and several wines by the glass. Leading off is a room mainly for eating, again with plenty of simple wooden furnishings on parquet, but also a few little booths, chandeliers and a splendid skylight framed by colourfully painted cherubs; there are a couple of big mirrors, one above a small tiled fireplace. The lighting is mostly modern but a few standard lamps and table lamps create a yellow glow at night that from the street makes the place look warmly inviting. A huge bonus is the most unexpected big back garden. With plenty of tables under parasols, nicely laid out plants, heaters and carefully positioned lighting, it's a real oasis – though it can get packed on sunny days.

Likeable and interesting, the food includes rabbit liver pâté, prawns, chilli and garlic bread, tortilla with courgettes, fennel, tomato and romesco sauce, steak pie for two, ox tongue with mash and onion gravy, pork belly with quince aioli, fish and chips with pea purée and tartare sauce, hake steak with lentils and salsa verde, roast partridge with apples and parsnips, and puddings such as prune and almond tart and sherry trifle. *Benchmark main dish: seafood pie £13.50. Two-course evening meal £20.00.*

Greene King ~ Manager Claude Levi ~ Real ale ~ Bar food (12-10.30(9.30 Sun)) ~ Restaurant ~ (020) 8742 8801 ~ Children welcome ~ Dogs allowed in bar ~ Open 12-11(11.30 Fri and Sat, 10.30 Sun) ~ www.thedukeofsussex.co.uk
Recommended by B and M Kendall, Tracey and Stephen Groves

WEST LONDON Map 12

White Horse 🍴 🍷 ☕

Parsons Green; ✛ *Parsons Green; SW6 4UL*

Cheerfully relaxed local with big terrace, an excellent range of carefully sourced drinks and imaginative food

Even when this easy-going pub is at its busiest, the well trained and friendly staff remain as efficient as ever. The stylishly modernised U-shaped bar has a gently upmarket and chatty atmosphere, plenty of sofas and wooden tables, huge windows with slatted wooden blinds, and winter coal and log fires – one in an elegant marble fireplace. An impressive range of drinks takes in regular real ales like Adnams Broadside, Harveys Best, Oakham JHB, Roosters Yankee and up to four guests from breweries such as Brodies, Fyne Ales, Goddards, Harviestoun, Twickenham and Weltons on handpump, imported keg beers (usually belgian and german but occasionally from further afield), six of the seven trappist beers, around 177 other foreign bottled beers, several malt whiskies and 22 good wines by the glass. They have quarterly beer festivals, often spotlighting regional breweries. The pub overlooks the green and has plenty of seats on the front terrace with something of a continental feel on summer evenings and at weekends; they have barbecues out here most sunny evenings.

Good, interesting bar food includes sandwiches till 6pm (not Sun), a pork plate (scotch egg, sausage roll, pig cheeks, pork belly and scatchlings), smoked eel mousse with potato pancakes, horseradish and celeriac cream, sausages with mash and beer gravy, couscous salad with roast peppers, watercress, red onion, chickpeas and herbs, rabbit and crayfish salad with quail eggs, venison and mushroom pie, 21-day aged dry rib-eye steak for two with triple-cooked chips, roasted bone marrow and béarnaise sauce, and puddings such as rhubarb with sable biscuits and orange and lemon syllabub and custard tart with nutmeg and vanilla ice-cream. *Benchmark main dish: beer-battered fish and chips £12.00. Two-course evening meal £21.00.*

Mitchells & Butlers ~ Manager Jez Manterfield ~ Real ale ~ Bar food (9.30am-10.30pm; brunch 9.30-12) ~ Restaurant ~ (020) 7736 2115 ~ Children welcome ~ Dogs allowed in bar ~ Open 9.30am-11.30pm(midnight Thurs-Sat) ~ www.whitehorsesw6.com
Recommended by B and M Kendall

OUTER LONDON

HAREFIELD

TQ0490   Map 3

Old Orchard 🍴 ♈

Off Park Lane; UB9 6HJ

Wonderful views from the garden in front of this Edwardian house, a good choice of drinks, friendly staff and well liked, interesting food

In fine weather you have to arrive early at this former country house to bag one of the much prized tables on the front terrace – the view is stunning. You look down over the narrowboats on the canal and on to the lakes that make up a conservation area known as the Colne Valley Regional Park; it's a haven for wildlife. Seats on the gazebo and picnic-sets in the garden have the same fantastic view. Inside, the knocked-through open-plan rooms have an attractive mix of cushioned dining chairs around all sizes and shapes of dark wooden tables, lots of prints, maps and pictures covering the walls, books on shelves, old glass bottles on window sills and rugs on wood or parquet flooring. One room is hung with a sizeable rug and some tapestry. There are daily papers to read, three cosy coal fires, big pot plants and fresh flowers. Half a dozen real ales on handpump include Fullers London Pride, Phoenix Brunning & Price and Tring Side Pocket for a Toad, alongside guests from brewers such as Adnams, St Austell and Windsor & Eton; also about two dozen wines by the glass and over 100 whiskies; friendly, helpful staff. The atmosphere is civilised and easy-going. There's a bowl of water for visiting dogs.

Popular brasserie-type food (the orders are sent to the kitchen along an unusual vacuum tube) includes interesting sandwiches, scallops with crisp pork belly and pickled fennel and apple with rhubarb dressing, chicken liver and marsala pâté with red onion chutney, corned beef hash with fried egg and HP sauce, wild mushroom and pea risotto with parmesan and herb oil, beer-battered haddock with mushy peas and tartare sauce, chicken with wild mushrooms, bacon and a crème fraîche broth, lamb shoulder with minted gravy and roast new potatoes, malaysian fish stew with sticky rice, and puddings such as white chocolate cheesecake with raspberry compote and crème brûlée with a shortbread biscuit. *Benchmark main dish: steak and kidney pudding £11.95. Two-course evening meal £20.00.*

Brunning & Price ~ Manager Dan Redfern ~ Real ale ~ Bar food (12-10(9.30 Sun)) ~ (01895) 822631 ~ Children welcome ~ Dogs allowed in bar ~ Open 11.30-11; 12-10.30 Sun ~ www.oldorchard-harefield.co.uk   *Recommended by Richard Gibbs, Dave Hoare, Mark Strathdee, Nicole Strathdee*

Also Worth a Visit in London

Besides the fully inspected pubs, you might like to try these pubs that have been recommended to us and described by readers. Do tell us what you think of them: feedback@goodguides.com

CENTRAL LONDON

EC1

✶**Bishops Finger** (020) 7248 2341
West Smithfield; EC1A 9JR Smartly civilised little pub close to Smithfield Market, friendly welcoming atmosphere, well laid-out bar with cushioned chairs on polished boards, framed market prints on cream walls, big windows, fresh flowers, Shepherd Neame ales including seasonal brews, a fine range of sausages plus other dishes in bar or upstairs restaurant, efficient service; children welcome, outside seating, closed weekends and bank holidays, otherwise open all day. *(Peter Dandy, Colin and Louise English, Derek Thomas, John and Gloria Isaacs, Dr and Mrs A K Clarke)*

Butchers Hook & Cleaver
(020) 7600 9181 *W Smithfield; EC1A 9DY* Fullers bank conversion with friendly helpful staff and pleasant relaxed atmosphere, their full range kept well, all-day pubby food (good choice of pies), breakfast from 7.30am, daily newspapers, nice mix of chairs including some button-back leather armchairs, wrought-iron spiral stairs to mezzanine; background music, big-screen sports TV; open all day, closed weekends. *(Colin and Louise English, Dr and Mrs A K Clarke)*

Craft Beer Company
Leather Lane; EC1N 7TR Old corner pub transformed into a drinking hall with 16 real ales and great selection of other beers including over 300 in bottles (some rarities), good selection of wines and spirits too, high stools and tables on bare-boards, big chandelier hanging from mirrored ceiling, can get very busy but service remains efficient and friendly, food limited to snacks, upstairs room; open all day. *(N R White)*

✶**Eagle** (020) 7837 1353
Farringdon Road; EC1R 3AL Original gastro pub and still popular – arrive early as dishes run out or change quickly; open-plan room dominated by giant range and all too busy, noisy and scruffy for some, basic well worn school chairs, assortment of tables, a couple of sofas on bare boards, modern art (gallery upstairs too), Wells & Youngs and a guest, good wines by glass and decent coffee; background music sometimes loud, not ideal for a quiet dinner (weekends quieter); children and dogs welcome, closed Sun evening, bank holidays and for a week

at Christmas, otherwise open all day. *(Jack Matthew, John and Gloria Isaacs)*

Fox & Anchor (020) 7250 1300
Charterhouse Street; EC1M 6AA Beautifully restored late Victorian pub by Smithfield Market, welcoming staff, long slender bar with unusual pewter-topped counter, lots of mahogany, green leather and etched glass, small back snugs, ales such as Adnams, Harviestoun and Purity served in pewter tankards plus a house beer from Nethergate, oyster bar and good range of freshly cooked food including popular home-made pies and a daily roast carved at your table, tempting traditional puddings too; six individual well appointed bedrooms, open all day from 7am (8.30am weekends). *(Anon)*

Gunmakers (020) 7278 1022
Eyre Street Hill; EC1R 5ET Two-room Victorian pub with four well kept changing ales, friendly knowledgeable landlord, enjoyable food from daily blackboard; dogs welcome, open all day weekdays, closed weekends. *(John and Gloria Isaacs)*

✶**Hand & Shears** (020) 7600 0257
Middle Street; EC1A 7JA Traditional panelled Smithfield pub dating from 16th c, three basic bright rooms and small snug off central servery, bustling at lunchtime, quiet evenings, Adnams and Courage Directors, quick friendly service, interesting bric-a-brac and old photographs, short choice of low-priced pub food; open all day, closed weekends. *(N R White)*

✶**Jerusalem Tavern** (020) 7490 4281
Britton Street; EC1M 5UQ Convincing and atmospheric re-creation of a dark 18th-c tavern (1720 merchant's house with shopfront added 1810), tiny dimly lit bar, simple wood furnishings on bare boards, some remarkable old wall tiles, coal fires and candlelight, stairs to a precarious-feeling (though perfectly secure) balcony, plainer back room, full range of St Peters beers tapped from casks, good lunchtime food, friendly attentive young staff; can get very crowded at peak times, no children; dogs welcome, seats out on pavement, open all day during the week, closed weekends, bank holidays, 24 Dec-2 Jan. *(Tom McLean, Anthony Longden, Mike Gorton, LM, N R White, the Didler and others)*

Sekforde Arms (020) 7253 3251
Sekforde Street; EC1R 0HA Small unspoilt and comfortably simple corner local with

friendly landlord, Wells & Youngs ales and guests, simple good value food, nice pictures including Spy caricatures, upstairs restaurant (not always open), darts, cards and board games; pavement tables, open all day, closed Sun. *(the Didler)*

EC2

★ Dirty Dicks (020) 7283 5888

Bishopsgate; EC2M 4NR Olde-worlde re-creation of traditional City tavern, busy and fun for foreign visitors, booths, barrel tables, exposed brick and low beams, interesting old prints, Wells & Youngs ales, good variety of enjoyable well priced food from sandwiches up, pleasant service, calmer cellar wine bar with wine racks overhead in brick barrel-vaulted ceiling, further upstairs area too; background music, games machines and TV; closed weekends. *(Phil Bryant)*

Fox (020) 7729 5708

Paul Street; EC2A 4LB Relaxed friendly atmosphere in this high ceilinged bare-boards corner pub, well kept Harveys, Sharps Doom Bar and a guest such as Otter from central servery, several wines by the glass, good food from bar snacks up, dining room upstairs with coal-effect gas fire and canopied terrace; gets busy lunchtime and early evening with local office workers; dogs welcome, open all day (till 5pm Sun). *(Jamie and Sue May)*

Hamilton Hall (020) 7247 3579

Bishopsgate; also entrance from Liverpool Street Station; EC2M 7PY Showpiece Wetherspoons with flamboyant Victorian baroque décor, plaster nudes and fruit mouldings, chandeliers, mirrors, good-sized comfortable mezzanine, food all day, lots of real ales including interesting guests, decent wines and coffee, good prices; silenced machines, can get very crowded after work; good disabled access, tables outside, open all day. *(Ian Phillips, Jeremy King)*

Kings Arms (020) 3582 4394

Wormwood Street; EC2M 1RP Popular low-ceilinged bar with good value pubby food and well kept mainstream ales, pool tables downstairs; background music, silent fruit machine; back terrace. *(Robert Lester, Jeremy King)*

EC3

East India Arms (020) 7265 5121

Fenchurch Street; EC3M 4BR Standing-room Victorian corner pub popular with city workers, well kept Shepherd Neame ales, good service, single room with wooden floor, old local photographs and brewery mirrors; tables outside, closed weekends. *(Barbarrick)*

Simpsons Tavern (020) 762 69985

Just off Cornhill; EC3V 9DR Pleasingly old-fashioned place founded in 1757; rather clubby small panelled bar serving Bass, Harveys and a couple of guests, stairs down to another bar with snacks, traditional chop house with upright stall seating (expect to share a table) and similar upstairs restaurant, good value food such as braised oxtail stew, steak and kidney pie and lancashire hotpot; open weekday lunchtimes and from 8am Tues-Fri for breakfast. *(Barbarrick)*

Swan (020) 7929 6550

Ship Tavern Passage, off Gracechurch Street; EC3V 1LY Traditional Fullers pub with bustling narrow flagstoned bar, their ales kept well, friendly chatty service, generous lunchtime sandwiches and snacks, neatly kept Victorian panelled décor, low lighting, larger more ordinary carpeted bar upstairs; silent corner TV; covered alley used by smokers, open all day Mon-Fri (can be closed by 9pm), shut at weekends. *(N R White)*

EC4

★ Black Friar (020) 7236 5474

Queen Victoria Street; EC4V 4EG An architectural gem (some of the best Edwardian bronze and marble art nouveau work to be found anywhere) and built on site of 13th-c Dominican Priory; inner back room (the Grotto) with low vaulted mosaic ceiling, big bas-relief friezes of jolly monks set into richly coloured florentine marble walls, gleaming mirrors, seats built into golden marble recesses and an opulent pillared inglenook, tongue-in-cheek verbal embellishments such as Silence is Golden and Finery is Foolish, and try to spot the opium-smoking hints modelled into the front room's fireplace, Fullers, Sharps and Timothy Taylors, plenty of wines by the glass, traditional all-day food (speciality pies), good friendly service despite crowds; children welcome if quiet, plenty of room on wide forecourt. *(Dr and Mrs A K Clarke, Tom McLean, Roger and Donna Huggins, Ian Phillips, Anthony Longden and others)*

Centre Page (020) 7236 3614

Aka the Horn; Knightrider Street near Millennium Bridge; EC4V 5BH Modernised old pub with window booths or 'traps' in narrow entrance room, more space beyond, traditional style with panelling and subdued lighting, chatty atmosphere, mix of after-work drinkers and tourists, friendly efficient young staff, simple appetising bar menu (from breakfast at 9am), downstairs dining room, well kept Fullers ales, tea and coffee; background music; tables outside with good view of St Pauls. *(N R White)*

Old Bell (020) 7583 0216

Fleet Street, near Ludgate Circus; EC4Y 1DH Dimly lit 17th-c tavern backing on to St Brides, heavy black beams, flagstones, stained-glass bow window, brass-topped tables, half a dozen well kept changing ales from island servery (can try before you buy), friendly efficient young foreign staff, usual food, various seating nooks and coal fire, cheerful atmosphere; background music; covered and heated outside area. *(N R White, the Didler)*

✳ Olde Cheshire Cheese

(020) 7353 6170 *Wine Office Court, off 145 Fleet Street; EC4A 2BU* Best to visit this 17th-c former chophouse outside peak times (early evening especially) when packed and staff can struggle; soaked in history with warmly old-fashioned unpretentious rooms, high beams, bare boards, old built-in black benches, Victorian paintings on dark brown walls, big open fires, tiny snug and steep stone steps down to unexpected series of cosy areas and secluded alcoves, Sam Smiths, all-day pubby food; look out for the famous parrot (now stuffed) who entertained princes and other distinguished guests for over 40 years; children allowed in eating area lunchtime only, closed Sun evening. *(Chris and Jeanne Downing, Roger and Donna Huggins, Peter Dandy, Andy and Claire Barker, Susan and Nigel Wilson, Barry Collett and others)*

Punch (020) 7353 6658

Fleet Street; EC4Y 1DE Enjoyable all-day fresh food including lunchtime buffet, Adnams, Marstons and Timothy Taylors, good choice of wines by the glass, friendly staff, pleasant informal atmosphere, light and airy, with modern tables alongside Victorian features such as superb tiled entrance and mirrored lobby, Punch and Judy paintings; children welcome, open all day. *(Dr and Mrs A K Clarke)*

SW1

✳ Albert (020) 7222 5577

Victoria Street; SW1H 0NP Handsome contrast to the cliffs of dark glass around it; busy open-plan airy bar with cut and etched windows, gleaming mahogany, ornate ceiling, solid comfortable furnishings, enjoyable pubby food all day from sandwiches up, well kept Fullers London Pride, Wells & Youngs Bombardier and guests, 24 wines by the glass, efficient cheerful service, handsome staircase lined with portraits of prime ministers up to carvery/dining room; background music, games machine, lavatories down steep stairs; children welcome if eating, open all day from 8am (breakfast till noon). *(Simon and Mandy King)*

✳ Buckingham Arms (020) 7222 3386

Petty France; SW1H 9EU Welcoming and relaxed bow-windowed 18th-c local, good value pubby food from back open kitchen, Wells & Youngs ales and guests from long curved bar, good wines by the glass, elegant mirrors and woodwork, unusual side corridor fitted out with elbow ledge for drinkers; TVs; dogs welcome, handy for Buckingham Palace, Westminster Abbey and St James's Park, open all day, till 6pm weekends. *(N R White, the Didler, Dr and Mrs A K Clarke)*

Cask & Glass (020) 7834 7630

Palace Street; SW1E 5HN Snug one-room traditional pub with good range of Shepherd Neame ales, friendly staff and atmosphere, good value lunchtime sandwiches, old prints and shiny black panelling; quiet corner TV; hanging baskets and a few tables outside, handy for Queen's Gallery. *(Simon and Mandy King)*

Cask Pub & Kitchen

(020) 7630 7225 *Charlwood Street/ Tachbrook Street; SW1V 2EE* Modern and spacious with simple furnishings, ten well kept frequently changing ales from far and wide, 14 foreign draught beers and over 500 in bottles, decent range of wines too, enjoyable generous food including sharing plates and burgers, friendly efficient staff, chatty atmosphere – can get packed evenings, regular beer related events like 'Meet the Brewer'; downstairs gents'; some outside seating, open all day. *(David Sizer, N R White, Dave Butler, Jack Sutcliffe and others)*

Clarence (020) 7930 4808

Whitehall; SW1A 2HP Civilised beamed corner pub (Geronimo Inn), Wells & Youngs and guests, decent wines by the glass, friendly chatty staff, well spaced tables and varied seating including tub chairs and banquettes, popular food all day from snacks up, upstairs dining area; pavement tables. *(Ian Phillips, Si Young)*

✳ Fox & Hounds (020) 7730 6367

Passmore Street/Graham Terrace; SW1W 8HR Small convivial local, Wells & Youngs ales, warm red décor with big hunting prints, old sepia photographs and toby jugs, wall benches and sofas, book-lined back room, hanging plants under attractive skylight, coal-effect gas fire, some low-priced pubby food; can get crowded with after-work drinkers. *(the Didler)*

✳ Grenadier (020) 7235 3074

Wilton Row; the turning off Wilton Crescent looks prohibitive, but the barrier and watchman are there to keep out cars; SW1X 7NR Steps up to cosy old mews pub with lots of character and

---

You can send reports directly to us at feedback@goodguides.com

military history, but not much space (avoid 5-7pm); simple unfussy panelled bar, stools and wooden benches, changing ales such as Fullers, Timothy Taylors, Wells & Youngs and Woodfordes from rare pewter-topped counter, famous bloody marys, may be bar food, intimate back restaurant (best to book), no mobiles or photography; children (over 8) and dogs allowed, sentry box and single table outside, open all day. *(LM, N R White, Mike and Sue Loseby, Conor McGaughey, Barry and Anne, Richard Tilbrook and others)*

Jugged Hare (020) 7828 1543
Vauxhall Bridge Road/Rochester Row; SW1V 1DX Popular Fullers Ale & Pie pub in former colonnaded bank; pillars, dark wood, balustraded balcony, large chandelier, busts and sepia London photographs, smaller back dining room, six well kept real ales, reasonably priced food from sandwiches up including pie range, good friendly service; background music, TVs, silent fruit machine; open all day. *(Peter Roberts, Roger and Donna Huggins, Jeremy King, the Didler, Nigel and Sue Foster, N R White)*

⋆**Loose Box** (020) 7932 0123
Horseferry Road; SW1P 2AA Modern bar-cum-restaurant, dark tables and chairs on wood flooring, fresh flowers and large plants, relaxed area with comfortable squishy sofas, lots of cartoons on the walls, enjoyable food from breakfast through coffee and pastries to good contemporary dishes, real ales and decent wines by the glass, friendly helpful staff, buzzy atmosphere; seats on front terrace by pavement, open all day. *(Anon)*

⋆**Lord Moon of the Mall**
(020) 7839 7701 *Whitehall; SW1A 2DY* Wetherspoons bank conversion with elegant main room, big arched windows looking over Whitehall, old prints and a large painting of Tim Martin (founder of the chain), through an arch style is more recognisably Wetherspoons with neatly tiled areas, bookshelves opposite long bar, up to nine real ales and their good value food; silenced fruit machines, cash machine; children allowed if eating, dogs welcome, open all day from 9am (till midnight Fri, Sat). *(Andy Lickfold, Dr and Mrs A K Clarke)*

⋆**Morpeth Arms** (020) 7834 6442
Millbank; SW1P 4RW Sparkling clean Victorian pub facing Thames, roomy and comfortable, some etched and cut glass, old books, prints and photographs, earthenware jars and bottles, well kept Wells & Youngs and a guest, decent choice of wines, enjoyable good value food (all day), welcoming service even at busy lunchtimes, upstairs room with fine view across river; background music, may be unobtrusive sports TV (there's also a monitor to check for cellar ghosts), young evening crowd; seats outside (a lot of traffic), handy for Tate Britain and Thames path

walkers, open all day. *(Robert Pattison, the Didler, Pete Coxon, George and Marion Anderson)*

⋆**Nags Head** (020) 7235 1135
Kinnerton Street; SW1X 8ED Unspoilt little mews pub, low-ceilinged panelled front room with unusual sunken counter, log-effect gas fire in old range, narrow passage down to even smaller bar, Adnams from 19th-c handpumps, all-day no-frills food, theatrical mementoes, old what-the-butler-saw machine and one-armed bandit, no mobiles; individual background music; well behaved children and dogs allowed, a few seats outside, open all day. *(N R White, the Didler, Conor McGaughey, John and Gloria Isaacs, Ole Ponpey, Mike Buckingham)*

Orange (020) 7881 9844
Pimlico Road; SW1W 8NE Popular gastropub with good choice of enjoyable food including wood-fired pizzas, friendly attentive staff, real ales such as Adnams, linked light and airy rooms with rustic furniture and relaxed weathered feel; children welcome, four bedrooms, open all day from 8am. *(Richard Tilbrook)*

⋆**Red Lion** (020) 7321 0782
Duke of York Street; SW1Y 6JP Pretty little Victorian pub, remarkably preserved and packed with customers often spilling out on to pavement by mass of foliage and flowers; series of small rooms with lots of polished mahogany, a gleaming profusion of mirrors, cut/etched windows and chandeliers, striking ornamental plaster ceiling, Fullers/Gales beers, simple good value bar food (all day weekdays, snacks evening, diners have priority over a few of the front tables); no children; dogs welcome, closed Sun and bank holidays, otherwise open all day. *(Eleanor Dandy, Peter Dandy, Ian Phillips, Stuart Doughty, James Stretton)*

Red Lion (020) 7930 5826
Parliament Street; SW1A 2NH Congenial pub by Houses of Parliament, used by Foreign Office staff and MPs, soft lighting, parliamentary cartoons and prints, Fullers/Gales beers and decent wines from long bar, good range of food, efficient staff, also cellar bar and small narrow upstairs dining room; outside seating. *(David Pulford, Dr and Mrs A K Clarke)*

Speaker (020) 7222 1749
Great Peter Street; SW1P 2HA Bustling chatty atmosphere in unpretentious smallish corner pub (can get packed at peak times), well kept Shepherd Neame Spitfire, Wells & Youngs and quickly changing guests, lots of whiskies, limited simple food including good sandwiches, friendly helpful staff, panelling, political cartoons and prints, no mobiles or background music; open all day, closed Sat, Sun evening. *(Nigel and Sue Foster)*

White Swan (020) 7821 8568

Vauxhall Bridge Road; SW1V 2SA Roomy corner pub handy for Tate Britain, lots of dark dining tables on three levels in long room, well cooked reasonably priced pubby food, half a dozen ales including Adnams Broadside, Morlands Old Golden Hen and Timothy Taylors Landlord, decent wines by the glass, quick helpful uniformed staff; background music, can get very busy at peak times; open all day. *(John Wooll, Nigel and Sue Foster)*

SW3

Builders Arms (020) 7349 9040

Britten Street; SW3 3TY Trendy dining pub (Geronimo Inn), relaxed, comfortable and chatty, with good food, ales such as Flowers, Sharps and Wells & Youngs from long counter, decent choice of wines; pavement tables under awnings, attractive street, open all day. *(Anon)*

✶Coopers Arms (020) 7376 3120

Flood Street; SW3 5TB Useful bolthole for Kings Road shoppers, dark-walled open-plan bar with mix of good-sized tables on floorboards, pre-war sideboard and dresser, railway clock, moose head, Wells & Youngs ales, decent all-day bar food; well behaved children till 7pm, dogs in bar, seats in courtyard garden. *(Anon)*

Hour Glass (020) 7581 2840

Brompton Road; SW3 2DY Small pub handy for V&A and other nearby museums, welcoming long-serving landlady and friendly young staff, well kept Fullers London Pride with a guest such as Bath Gem, good value pubby food (not Sun evening); sports TV; pavement benches. *(LM)*

Surprise (020) 7351 6954

Christchurch Terrace; SW3 4AJ Late Victorian Chelsea pub revamped by Geronimo Inns – reports please.

W1

Albany (020) 7387 0221

Great Portland Street; W1W 5QU Eclectic mix of furnishings including some big sofas and large tables, bare boards, unusual lamps (quite low lighting), dramatic patterned ceiling, well kept real ales including Fullers London Pride from long bar, good choice of other beers, decent food and pleasant service. *(Jeremy King)*

✶Argyll Arms (020) 7734 6117

Argyll Street; W1F 7TP Popular and unexpectedly individual pub with three interesting little front cubicle rooms (essentially unchanged since 1860s), wooden partitions and impressive frosted and engraved glass, mirrored corridor to spacious back room, Brains, Fullers, St Austell, Sharps and four guests, well liked all-day food in bar or upstairs dining room overlooking pedestrianised street, theatrical photographs; background music, fruit machine; children welcome till 8pm. *(Peter Dandy, Andy and Claire Barker, Ian and Helen Stafford, Barry Collett, the Didler, Mike and Sue Loseby and others)*

✶Audley (020) 7499 1843

Mount Street; W1K 2RX Classic late Victorian Mayfair pub, opulent red plush, mahogany panelling and engraved glass, chandelier and clock hanging in lovely carved wood bracket from ornately corniced ceiling, Fullers London Pride, Greene King IPA, Wells & Youngs Bombardier and guests from long polished bar, good choice of all-day pub food (reasonably priced for the area), friendly efficient service, upstairs panelled dining room; quiet background music, TV, pool; children till 6pm, pavement tables. *(Nigel and Jean Eames)*

De Hems (020) 7437 2494

Macclesfield Street; W1D 5BW Typical London pub recycled as pastiche of a dutch bar (but roomier and less intimate), old dutch engravings, panelled walls, mixed tables on bare boards, big continental founts and good range of interesting bottled beers, dutch-influenced food, friendly service, smaller upstairs area with sofas and armchairs; background music, can get very busy. *(Jeremy King)*

✶Dog & Duck (020) 7494 0697

Bateman Street/Frith Street; W1D 3AJ Tiny Soho pub squeezing in bags of character, unusual old tiles and mosaics (the dog with tongue hanging out in hot pursuit of a duck is notable), heavy old advertising mirrors, open fire, cosy upstairs dining room, good selection of beers including Brains, Fullers and St Austell from unusual little counter, several wines by the glass, food all day, friendly staff, very busy evenings when people spill on to the street; background music; children allowed in dining room, dogs in bar, open all day. *(Mike Gorton, LM, the Didler, Richard Endacott and others)*

✶Grapes (020) 7493 4216

Shepherd Market; W1J 7QQ Genuinely old-fashioned pub with dimly lit bar, plenty of well worn plush red furnishings, stuffed birds and fish in display cases, wood floors, panelling, coal fire and snug back alcove, six ales including Fullers and Sharps, good choice of thai food (not Sun evening) cooked by thai chefs, english food too, lots of customers (especially early evening) often spilling out on to square; children till 6pm weekdays (anytime weekends), open all day. *(Mike Gorton, Ian Phillips, the Didler)*

✱ **Guinea** (020) 7409 1728

Bruton Place; W1J 6NL Lovely hanging
baskets and chatty customers outside this
tiny 17th-c mews pub, standing room only at
peak times, appealingly simple with a few
cushioned wooden seats and tables tucked
to left of entrance, more in snug back area
(most people prop themselves against the
little side shelf), bare boards, old-fashioned
prints, red planked ceiling with raj fans,
famous steak and kidney pie, grills and
some sandwiches (no food weekends),
Wells & Youngs and seasonal brews from
striking counter; very easy to walk into
smart Guinea Grill (uniformed doormen will
politely redirect you); no children; closed Sat
lunchtime, Sun and bank holidays.
(the Didler, Stuart Doughty)

Newman Arms (020) 7636 1127

*Rathbone Street/Newman Passage;
W1T 1NG* 18th-c pub in the same family
for three generations, small panelled bar
with well kept Fullers London Pride and
guests, upstairs dining room serving range of
home-made pies and suet puddings, pictures
and prints reflecting pub's association with
George Orwell and director Michael Powell,
good friendly staff; open all weekdays, closed
weekends. *(Tracey and Stephen Groves)*

Three Tuns (020) 3582 9843

Portman Mews S; W1H 6HP Large bare-
boards front bar and sizeable lounge/dining
area with beams and nooks and crannies,
Greene King Abbot, Timothy Taylors Landlord
and Wells & Youngs London Gold, reasonably
priced pubby food from panini up, good
friendly staff, vibrant atmosphere; benches
out on street. *(Ian Phillips)*

W2
Mad Bishop & Bear

(020) 7402 2441 *Paddington Station;
W2 1HB* Up escalators from concourse, full
Fullers range kept well and a guest beer,
good wine choice, reasonably priced standard
food quickly served including breakfast from
8am (10am Sun), ornate plasterwork, etched
mirrors and fancy lamps, parquet, tiles and
carpet, booths with leather banquettes, lots
of wood and prints, train departures screen;
background music, TVs, games machine;
tables out overlooking station, open all day
till 11pm (10.30pm Sun). *(Roger and Donna
Huggins, Giles and Annie Francis, Susan and
Nigel Wilson, Taff and Gilly Thomas, Dr and
Mrs A K Clarke)*

✱ **Victoria** (020) 7724 1191

Strathearn Place; W2 2NH Well run
pub with lots of Victorian pictures and
memorabilia, cast-iron fireplaces, gilded
mirrors and mahogany panelling, brass
mock-gas lamps above attractive horseshoe
bar, bare boards and banquettes, relaxed
chatty atmosphere, good friendly service, full

Fullers range kept well, several wines by the
glass and good choice of reasonably priced
popular food; upstairs has leather club chairs
in small library/snug, and (mostly for private
functions now) replica of Gaiety Theatre
bar, all gilt and red plush; quiet background
music, TV; pavement picnic-sets, open all
day. *(Dr and Mrs A K Clarke, Conor McGaughey,
Ian Herdman)*

WC1
✱ **Cittie of Yorke** (020) 7242 7670

High Holborn; WC1V 6BN Splendid
back bar rather like a baronial hall with
extraordinarily extended bar counter, 1000-
gallon wine vats resting above gantry, big
bulbous lights hanging from soaring raftered
roof, intimate ornately carved booths,
triangular fireplace with grates on all three
sides, smaller comfortable panelled room
with lots of little prints of York, cheap Sam
Smiths, bar food, lots of students, lawyers
and City types but plenty of space to absorb
crowds; fruit machine; children welcome,
open all day, closed Sun. *(Pete Coxon, Pam
and John Smith, Chris and Jeanne Downing,
Andy and Claire Barker, Anthony Longden,
C Cooper and others)*

Duke (020) 7242 7230

Roger Street; WC1N 2PB 1930s
Bloomsbury corner pub, quietly placed
and unpretentious, with emphasis on good
reasonably priced food including some
interesting choices, real ales and modern
art in front bar, longer back dining room
with booth seating, friendly helpful staff.
(Ian Martin, Aidan Long)

Mabels (020) 7387 7739

*Mabledon Place, just off Euston Road;
WC1H 9AZ* Neat open-plan Shepherd
Neame pub on two levels, well kept ales
and good wine choice, decent reasonably
priced pubby food, friendly staff, bright
décor; big-screen TVs; pavement tables
under awning, open all day. *(Ross Balaam,
Dr and Mrs A K Clarke)*

Museum Tavern (020) 7242 8987

*Museum Street/Great Russell Street;
WC1B 3BA* Traditional high-ceilinged
ornate Victorian pub facing British Museum,
busy lunchtime and early evening, but can be
quite peaceful other times, seven well kept
beers including some unusual ones, Weston's
cider, several wines by the glass, good hot
drinks, straightforward food, friendly helpful
staff; one or two tables out under gas lamps,
open all day. *(Pete Coxon, David and
Sue Atkinson)*

Penderels Oak (020) 7242 5669

High Holborn; WC1V 7HJ Vast
Wetherspoons with attractive décor and
woodwork, lots of books, pew seating around
central tables, their well priced food and

huge choice of good value real ales, efficient friendly staff; open all day. *(Tracey and Stephen Groves)*

Plough (020) 3582 3812

Museum Street/Little Russell Street; WC1A 1LH Popular and welcoming Bloomsbury local, with longish bar and upstairs drinking/dining room, well kept ales such as Greene King Abbot, enjoyable fairly priced food from short menu, quick service; a few tables out in front. *(John Wooll)*

⋆ Princess Louise (020) 7405 8816

High Holborn; WC1V 7EP Splendid Victorian gin palace with extravagant décor – even the gents' has its own preservation order; gloriously opulent main bar with wood and glass partitions, fine etched and gilt mirrors, brightly coloured and fruity-shaped tiles, slender Portland stone columns soaring towards the lofty and deeply moulded plaster ceiling, open fire, cheap Sam Smiths from long counter, pubby bar food (not Fri-Sun); gets crowded early weekday evenings, no children; open all day. *(Pete Coxon, Tim Maddison, Dr and Mrs A K Clarke, Anthony Longden, Giles and Annie Francis, Ian Phillips and others)*

⋆ Skinners Arms (020) 7837 5621

Judd Street; WC1H 9NT Richly decorated, with glorious woodwork, marble pillars, high ceilings and ornate windows, lots of London prints, interesting layout including comfortable back seating area, Greene King Abbot and guests from attractive long bar, decent bar food; unobtrusive background music, muted corner TV; pavement picnic-sets, handy for British Library, open all day, closed Sun. *(Tracey and Stephen Groves, N R White)*

WC2

⋆ Chandos (020) 7836 1401

St Martins Lane; WC2N 4ER Busy bare-boards bar with snug cubicles, lots of theatre memorabilia on stairs up to smarter more comfortable lounge with opera photographs, low wooden tables, panelling, leather sofas, coloured windows; cheap Sam Smiths OBB, prompt cheerful service, bargain food, air conditioning, darts; can get packed early evening, background music and games machines; note the automaton on the roof (working 10am-2pm and 4-9pm); children upstairs till 6pm, open all day from 9am (for breakfast). *(Susan and Nigel Wilson, Taff and Gilly Thomas, G Jennings)*

⋆ Cross Keys (020) 7836 5185

Endell Street/Betterton Street; WC2H 9EB Relaxed and friendly, quick service even at busy times, good lunchtime sandwiches and a few bargain hot dishes, three well kept Brodies ales and couple of guests (usually smaller London brewers), decent wines by the glass, masses of photographs and posters including Beatles memorabilia, brassware and tasteful bric-a-brac; fruit machine, gents' downstairs; sheltered outside cobbled area with flower tubs, open all day. *(John and Gloria Isaacs, Dr and Mrs A K Clarke)*

Edgar Wallace (020) 7353 3120

Essex Street; WC2R 3JE Simple spacious open-plan pub dating from 18th c, eight well kept ales including some unusual ones and a beer for them by Nethergate, enjoyable good value food all day including doorstep sandwiches, friendly efficient service, half-panelled walls and red ceilings, interesting old London and Edgar Wallace memorabilia (pub renamed 1975 to mark his centenary), upstairs dining room; a few high tables in side alleyway, closed weekends. *(LM, Andy and Jill Kassube)*

George (020) 7353 9638

Strand; WC2R 1AP Timbered pub near the law courts, long narrow bare-boards bar, Black Sheep and five guest ales, several wines by the glass , lunchtime food from open sandwiches and ciabattas to weekday carvery in upstairs bar, separate evening menu, comedy club Fri and Sat nights, open all day. *(Pete Coxon, Dr Martin Owton)*

Knights Templar (020) 7831 2660

Chancery Lane; WC2A 1DT Reliable Wetherspoons in big-windowed former bank, marble pillars, handsome fittings and plasterwork, good bustling atmosphere on two levels, some interesting real ales at bargain prices, good wine choice and usual well priced food, friendly staff; remarkably handsome lavatories; open all day Mon-Fri, till 7pm Sat, closed Sun. *(Tracey and Stephen Groves, Andy and Jill Kassube)*

Lyceum (020) 7836 7155

Strand; WC2R 0HS Panelling and pleasantly simple furnishings downstairs, several small discreet booths, steps up to a bigger alcove with darts, food in much larger upstairs panelled lounge with deep button-back leather settees and armchairs, low-priced Sam Smiths beer, civilised atmosphere and efficient service. *(Susan and Nigel Wilson, Taff and Gilly Thomas)*

⋆ Porterhouse (020) 7379 7917

Maiden Lane; WC2E 7NA Good daytime pub (can be packed evenings), London outpost of Dublin's Porterhouse microbrewery, their interesting if pricy beers including porter and stout along with guests (comprehensive tasting tray), lots of bottled imports, good choice of wines by the

---

Tipping is not normal for bar meals, and not usually expected.

glass, reasonably priced food from soup and open sandwiches up with some emphasis on rock oysters, shiny three-level labyrinth of stairs (lifts for disabled), galleries and copper ducting and piping, some nice design touches, sonorous openwork clock, neatly cased bottled beer displays; background and live irish music, big-screen sports TV (repeated in gents'); tables on front terrace, open all day. *(Taff and Gilly Thomas, James Longridge)*

★ **Salisbury** (020) 7836 5863
St Martins Lane; WC2N 4AP Gleaming Victorian pub surviving unchanged in the heart of the West End, a wealth of cut glass and mahogany, curved upholstered wall seat creating impression of several distinct areas, wonderfully ornate bronze light fittings, lots of mirrors, back room popular with diners and separate small side room, some interesting photographs including Dylan Thomas enjoying a drink here in 1941, lots of theatre posters, up to six well kept ales, hot toddies, summer Pimms, good bar food all day, coffees and helpful cheerful staff; children allowed till 5pm, fine details on building exterior, seats in pedestrianised side alley, open till midnight Fri, Sat. *(Roger and Donna Huggins, Mike Gorton, Ian and Helen Stafford, Tracey and Stephen Groves, Jeremy King, the Didler and others)*

Sherlock Holmes (020) 7930 2644
Northumberland Street; aka Northumberland Arms; WC2N 5DB Fine collection of Sherlock Holmes memorabilia, also silent videos of black and white Holmes films; well kept Greene King ales, usual furnishings, quick service at good value lunchtime food counter, quieter upstairs restaurant by replica of his study; background music; roof terrace, more tables out in front, open all day. *(Dr and Mrs A K Clarke)*

★ **Ship & Shovell** 020 7839 1311
Craven Passage, off Craven Street; WC2N 5PH Well kept Badger ales and a guest, good friendly staff, decent reasonably priced food including wide range of baguettes etc; brightly lit with dark wood, etched mirrors and interesting mainly naval pictures, plenty of tables, open fire, compact back section, separate partitioned bar across Underneath the Arches alley; TV; open all day, closed Sun. *(the Didler, Taff and Gilly Thomas, Andy and Jill Kassube)*

Wellington (020) 7836 2789
Strand/Wellington Street; WC2R 0HS Long narrow traditional corner pub, Black Sheep, Fullers London Pride and Timothy Taylors Landlord, several wines by the glass, wide choice of low-priced standard food till 5pm, friendly staff, quiet upstairs bar; tables outside. *(Susan and Nigel Brookes)*

White Lion (020) 7240 1064
James Street; WC2E 8NS Change to: 19th-c Nicholsons corner pub, panelling and bare boards, well kept Fullers London Pride, Timothy Taylors Landlord and guests, their usual menu including evening set deal, dining room upstairs; children welcome, open all day. *(Matt Varey)*

EAST LONDON

E1

Captain Kidd (020) 7480 5759
Wapping High Street; E1W 2NE Great Thames views from large open-plan pub's jutting bay windows in renovated Docklands warehouse stripped back to beams and basics, inexpensive bar food all day, pricier restaurant upstairs, cheap Sam Smiths keg beers, nice wines, obliging bow-tied staff and lively bustle; sports TV; dogs welcome, chunky tables on roomy back waterside terrace. *(Bill Adie, Susan and Nigel Brookes)*

Half Moon (020) 7790 6810
Mile End Road; E1 4AA Wetherspoons conversion of former theatre (was a methodist chapel before that), wide choice of well kept real ales and enjoyable good value food; open all day from 8am. *(Ross Balaam)*

Pride of Spitalfields
(020) 7247 8933 *Heneage Street; E1 5LJ* Nicely worn in little East End local with cheery regulars and friendly cat called Lenny, well kept keenly priced ales such as Crouch Vale Brewers Gold, Fullers London Pride and Sharps Doom Bar from central servery, bargain simple lunchtime food (not Sat) including Sun roasts, friendly prompt service, atmospheric lighting and interesting prints, comfortable banquettes, coal fire, TV in smaller side room; open all day. *(Philip Hollington)*

★ **Prospect of Whitby** (020) 3603 4041
Wapping Wall; E1W 3SH Claims to be oldest pub on Thames dating to 1520 with a colourful history (Pepys and Dickens used it regularly and Turner came for weeks at a time to study the river views) – tourists love it; L-shaped bar has plenty of beams, bare boards, flagstones and panelling, ales such as Adnams, Fullers, Wells & Youngs and Woodfordes from 400-year-old pewter counter, good choice of wines by the glass, bar food from sandwiches up, more formal restaurant upstairs; children welcome (only if eating after 5.30pm), unbeatable views towards Docklands from tables on waterfront courtyard, open all day. *(Paul Rampton, Julie Harding, the Didler, Pete Coxon, Phil Bryant)*

Town of Ramsgate (020) 7481 8000
Wapping High Street; E1W 2PN Interesting old-London Thameside setting, with restricted but evocative river view from

small back floodlit terrace with mock gallows (hanging dock was nearby), long narrow chatty bar with squared oak panelling, ales such as Fullers London Pride and Sharps Doom Bar, friendly helpful service, good choice of generous standard food and daily specials; background music, Mon quiz; open all day. *(Bill Adie, N R White)*

White Swan (020) 7702 0448

Alie Street; E1 8DA Cosy and comfortable Shepherd Neame pub on edge of the City, their ales kept well including seasonal brews, good choice of wines by the glass, reasonably priced pubby food, armchairs and sofas as well as wooden furniture on bare boards, upstairs area; open all day, closed weekends. *(Neil Hardwick)*

E3

⋆ **Crown** (020) 8880 7261

Grove Road/Old Ford Road; E3 5SN Stylish dining pub with relaxed welcoming bar, faux animal hide stools and chunky pine tables on polished boards, big bay window with comfortable scatter-cushion seating area, books etc on open shelves, well kept Wells & Youngs and guests, good choice of wines by the glass, friendly chatty young staff, three individually decorated upstairs dining areas overlooking Victoria Park, imaginative well priced food (all day Sun); background music; children and dogs welcome, open all day. *(Andy and Claire Barker, Georgina Tacagni, Paul Sherfield)*

Palm Tree (020) 8980 2918

Haverfield Road; E3 5BH Lone survivor of blitzed East End terrace, by Regents Canal and beside windmill and ecology centre in futuristic-looking Mile End Park; two Edwardian bars around oval servery, a couple of well kept changing ales, lunchtime sandwiches, long-serving licensees and good local atmosphere, live music weekends; no credit cards. *(Tony Hobden)*

E8

Dove Arms

Broadway Market; E8 4QJ Split-level corner pub with Victorian main bar and other rooms behind, six real ales including Crouch Vale Gold and Timothy Taylors Landlord, lots of continental bottled beers, tasty food from snacks up; pavement tables, open all day. *(Tony Hobden)*

E10

King William IV (020) 8556 2460

High Road Leyton; E10 6AE Imposing flower-decked Victorian building, home to Brodies brewery; up to 20 well kept low-priced ales including guests, beer festivals, enjoyable bargain food, darts and bar billiards; big-screen sports TV; eight bedrooms. *(Andrew Bosi)*

E11

Birkbeck Tavern (020) 8539 2584

Langthorne Road; E11 4HL Down to earth high-ceilinged two-room local, stained-glass and worn-in furnishings, three or four well kept often unusual ales, good value snacks; TV, fruit machine, pool and darts; children allowed in nice garden with plenty of tables. *(Andrew Bosi, Jeremy King)*

George (020) 8989 2921

High Street Wanstead; E11 2RL Large popular Wetherspoons in former 18th-c coaching inn, their usual good value food and real ales, plenty of books to read, pictures of famous Georges down the ages. *(Robert Lester)*

Red Lion (020) 8988 2929

High Road Leytonstone; E11 3AA Large 19th-c corner pub revamped by the Antic group, high-ceilinged open-plan interior, ten changing ales, real ciders, enjoyable sensibly priced food; weekend DJs and live music; back garden, open all day Sat and Sun, from 4pm weekdays. *(John and Annabel Hampshire, Robert Person)*

E14

⋆ **Narrow** (020) 7592 7950

Narrow Street; E14 8DJ Popular stylish dining pub (owned by Gordon Ramsay) with great Thames views from window seats and terrace, simple but smart bar with white walls and dark blue doors, mosaic-tiled fireplaces and colourfully striped armchairs, Adnams, Greene King and a guest, good wines, food from bar snacks to pricier restaurant meals, dining room also white with matching furnishings, local maps and prints, and a boat complete with oars; background music; children welcome, open all day. *(Andy and Claire Barker, Mike Owen, Ian Phillips)*

NORTH LONDON

N1

Albion (020) 7607 7450

Thornhill Road; N1 1HW Front bar and spacious dining area, interesting choice of mid-priced home-made food, a couple of well kept ales such as Caledonian Deuchars IPA and Ringwood Best, helpful cheerful service, Victorian gents'; tables out at front and on back terrace. *(Nigel and Sue Foster)*

Angelic (020) 7278 8433

Liverpool Road; N1 0RJ Spacious high-ceilinged pub popular for its food (should book weekends), good choice of drinks including plenty of wines by the glass, juice bar, good friendly service; background music. *(Matthew Beckitt)*

Charles Lamb (020) 7837 5040

Elia Street; N1 8DE Small friendly backstreet pub with well kept ales including Butcombe and Dark Star, some interesting imports on tap or bottled, decent choice of wines by the glass including own-label, good blackboard food, big windows, polished boards and simple traditional furniture; background jazz; tables outside, closed Mon and Tues lunchtimes. *(Kevin Booker, Julia Atkins, Jim Slattery)*

Compton Arms (020) 7359 6883

Compton Avenue, off Canonbury Road; N1 2XD Tiny villagey local, simply furnished unpretentious low-ceilinged rooms, Greene King and guests; sports TV, can be busy Arsenal match days; dogs welcome, tables under big sycamore tree and glass-covered area, open all day. *(Tim Maddison)*

Eagle (020) 7250 0507

Shepherdess Walk/City Road; N1 7LB On site of the Eagle referred to in Pop Goes the Weasel – 'Up and down the City road in and out the Eagle…'; bare-boards Edwardian pub with original features including tiling and sturdy iron pillars, mix of furniture from leather benches to sofas, some well worn, Fullers London Pride, Sharps Doom Bar and guests from panelled central servery, enjoyable home-made food including sandwiches and blackboard specials, fixed-price menu too; busy at lunchtime; open all day from noon (11am Sun) and till 1am Fri, Sat. *(Simon and Mandy King)*

★ Marquess Tavern (020) 7354 2975

Canonbury Street/Marquess Road; N1 2TB Surprisingly traditional and fairly plain bar in imposing Victorian building, bare boards, a mix of wooden tables around big horseshoe servery, old leather sofa and faded pictures, a couple of fireplaces, Wells & Youngs beers and around 30 malt whiskies, traditional food in bar or back dining room; background music; children and dogs welcome, some picnic-sets out behind front railings, open all day weekends, closed weekday lunchtimes. *(Anon)*

N6
Angel

Highgate High Street; N6 5JT Neat L-shaped panelled bar with well kept ales such as Adnams and Fullers London Pride, decent wines by the glass, fair-priced food from sandwiches up for most of the day, friendly helpful staff, leather settees, dim lighting; open all day. *(Jeremy King)*

Flask (020) 8348 7346

Highgate West Hill; N6 6BU Comfortable Georgian pub now owned by Fullers, intriguing up-and-down layout, sash-windowed bar hatch, panelling and high-backed carved settle in snug lower area with log fire, enjoyable efficiently served food; picnic-sets out in front courtyard, handy for strolls around Highgate village or Hampstead Heath. *(John Wooll)*

Prince of Wales (020) 8340 0445

Highgate High Street; N6 5JX Small unpretentious bare-boards local, said to be haunted, bench seats, stools and old wooden tables, two coal-effect gas fires, well kept Butcombe and up to three guests from horseshoe bar, decent choice of blackboard wines, food from thai dishes to Sun roasts, Tues quiz; background music, TV; tables on small terrace behind, open all day. *(Jeremy King)*

Victoria (020) 8340 4609

North Hill, Highgate; N6 4QA Tucked-away Victorian pub in tree-lined street, Harveys, Timothy Taylors Landlord and Wells & Youngs, good food including popular Sun lunch, themed nights, Mon quiz; children and dogs welcome. *(Jeremy King)*

N14
Cherry Tree (020) 8886 1808

The Green; N14 6EN Roomy beamed Vintage Inn (former coaching inn), comfortable and relaxed, with good value food all day from breakfast on, wide choice of wines by the glass and reasonably priced beers, good cheerful service, mix of big tables, some leather chesterfields; children welcome, tables out behind, bedrooms in adjacent Innkeepers Lodge, open all day. *(Darren Shea, David Jackson)*

N16
Daniel Defoe 020 7254 2906

Stoke Newington Church Street; N16 0LA Fairly recently refurbished two-room pub, friendly and popular with locals, comfortable spacious front bar, smaller back one, six well kept ales (mainly Wells & Youngs), interesting lagers and over 30 malt whiskies, decent food from shortish menu; walled garden. *(Sue and Mike Todd)*

NW1
Betjeman Arms (020) 7923 5440

St Pancras Station; NW1 2QL On upper concourse with outside seating area facing Eurostar trains, good all-rounder with enjoyable food (service charge added to bill), well kept Sambrooks and a house beer from Sharps, friendly efficient service, modern décor; open all day from 9am. *(N R White)*

Bree Louise (020) 7681 4930

Cobourg Street/Euston Street; NW1 2HH Partly divided open-plan bar with half a dozen or more interesting real ales, food emphasising pies (Mon-Thurs bargains), basic décor with prints, UK flags, mixed used furnishings; can get very busy early evening; open all day. *(Jake Lingwood, Jeremy King, Tim Moore)*

Chapel (020) 7402 9220

Chapel Street; NW1 5DP Busy and noisy in the evening (quieter during the day) this dining pub attracts an equal share of drinkers, spacious cream-painted rooms dominated by open kitchen, smart but simple furnishings, sofas at lounge end by big fireplace, Adnams and Greene King ales, good choice of wines by the glass, several coffees and teas, food usually good; children and dogs welcome, picnic-sets in sizeable back garden, more seats on decking under heated parasols, open all day. *(Michael Rugman)*

Crown & Anchor (020) 7383 2681

Drummond Street; NW1 2HL Opened-up, L-shaped bar with ales such as Adnams and Black Sheep, standard good value food, bare-boards or tiled floors, comfortable chairs and mismatched wooden tables; exposed brickwork, one or two quirky touches; background music; can get crowded lunchtime; pavement tables under awnings, open all day. *(Jeremy King)*

Crown & Goose (020) 7485 2342

Corner of Arlington Road/Delancey Street; NW1 7HP Camden pub with plenty of local colour, good food (get there early) including all-day Sun roasts, well kept Adnams from horseshoe bar with stools, tables set for eating at back (front tables are smaller), wood floors, shabby-chic, candles at night; may be background music, open all day (till 2am Fri, Sat). *(Jeremy King)*

☀ Doric Arch (020) 7388 2221

Eversholt Street; NW1 2DN Virtually part of Euston Station, up stairs from bus terminus with raised back part overlooking it, well kept Fullers ales and guests, Weston's cider, friendly prompt service (even when busy), enjoyable well priced pubby food lunchtime and from 4pm weekdays (12-5pm weekends), pleasantly nostalgic atmosphere and some quiet corners, intriguing train and other transport memorabilia including big clock at entrance, downstairs restaurant; discreet sports TV, machines, lavatories on combination lock; open all day. *(Dennis Jones, Dr and Mrs A K Clarke, Jeremy King, the Didler, Tony and Wendy Hobden)*

Euston Flyer (020) 7383 0856

Euston Road, opposite British Library; NW1 2RA Big welcoming open-plan pub, Fullers/Gales beers, good choice of standard food all day, relaxed lunchtime atmosphere, plenty of light wood, mix of furniture on carpet or boarded floors, mirrors, photographs of old London, smaller raised areas and private corners, big doors open to street in warm weather; background music,

Sky TV, silent games machine, can get packed evenings; open all day, till 8.30pm Sun. *(N R White, Brian and Janet Ainscough, the Didler, Dr and Mrs A K Clarke)*

Metropolitan (020) 7486 3489

Baker Street Station, Marylebone Road; NW1 5LA Wetherspoons in impressively ornate Victorian hall, large with lots of tables on one side, very long bar the other, leather sofas and some elbow tables, ten or more real ales, good coffee, their usual inexpensive food; games machines; family area, open all day. *(Tony Hobden, Jeremy King)*

Somerstown Coffee House

(020) 7691 9136 *Chalton Street; NW1 1HS* French-run dining pub with good affordable brasserie food (best to book), well kept Wells & Youngs ales, pubby atmosphere with mixed furniture including old chapel chairs on bare boards, black and white pictures on dark panelling; tables out at front and back, open all day. *(Brian and Janet Ainscough)*

NW3

☀ Flask (020) 7435 4580

Flask Walk; NW3 1HE Bustling local (popular haunt of Hampstead artists, actors, and local characters), unassuming old-fashioned bar, unique Victorian screen dividing it from cosy lounge with smart banquettes, panelling, lots of little prints and attractive fireplace, Wells & Youngs ales, 30 wines by the glass, well liked bar food (all day Fri-Sun), good friendly service; background music, TV; children (till 8pm) and dogs welcome, seats and tables in alley, open all day, till midnight Fri, Sat. *(Charles Harvey, N R White, the Didler, B J Harding)*

☀ Spaniards Inn (020) 8731 8406

Spaniards Lane; NW3 7JJ Busy 16th-c pub right next to Heath with charming big garden split up into areas by careful planting, flagstoned walk among roses, side arbour with climbing plants and plenty of seats on crazy-paved terrace (arrive early weekends as popular with dog walkers and families); attractive and characterful low-ceilinged rooms with oak panelling, antique winged settles, snug alcoves and open fires, up to five real ales, two ciders, continental draught lagers and several wines by glass, enjoyable all-day pubby food with a few twists; car park fills fast and nearby parking is difficult. *(Mike and Lynn Robinson, Nick Lawless, Ross Balaam, Barry and Anne, James White, Phil Bryant and others)*

Washington (020) 7722 8842

Englands Lane; NW3 4UE Ornate Victorian pub with burgundy and gilt ceiling, etched glass and mirrors, stools around central dark-wood servery, mixed furniture including sofas at back, several well kept ales such as Fullers London Pride, good choice of wines by the glass, nice food including fixed-price menu, relaxed atmosphere; soft background music, Tues quiz night, comedy night first Sun of month in cellar bar; well behaved dogs allowed, some street tables. *(R C Vincent)*

NW5

⋆ **Bull & Last** (020) 7267 8955

Highgate Road; NW5 1QS Traditional décor with a stylish twist and liked by customers of all ages; single room with big windows, colonial-style fans in planked ceiling, collection of tankards, faded map of London, stuffed bulls' heads and pheasants, four well kept changing ales, good wines and own sloe gin, imaginative if not cheap food, takeaway tubs of home-made ice-cream and picnic hampers for Hampstead Heath, friendly enthusiastic staff; quiz Sun evening; children (away from bar) and dogs welcome, hanging baskets and picnic-sets by street, open all day. *(Richard Greaves, Tim Maddison)*

Junction Tavern (020) 7485 9400

Fortess Road; NW5 1AG Victorian corner pub with good fresh food (service charge added) including some enterprising dishes in bar, dining room and back conservatory, Caledonian Deuchars IPA and three other well kept ales (beer festivals), good choice of wines by the glass, friendly staff; background music; no children after 7pm, garden tables, open all day Fri-Sun. *(Nick Angel)*

Southampton Arms

Highgate Road; NW5 1LE Nicely restored, well run little pub with impressive range of small-brewery beers, ciders and perries, can get crowded. *(Tim Maddison)*

SOUTH LONDON

SE1

Anchor (020) 7407 1577

Bankside; SE1 9EF In great spot near Thames with river views from upper floors and roof terrace, beams, stripped brickwork and old-world corners, well kept Fullers London Pride and Wells & Youngs, good choice of wines by the glass, popular fish and chip bar including takeaways, other good value all-day food as well as breakfast and tearoom; background music; provision for children, disabled access, more tables under big parasols on raised riverside terrace, bedrooms in friendly quiet Premier Inn behind, open all day. *(Paul Humphreys, Eleanor Dandy, Mike and Sue Loseby, Pete Coxon)*

Anchor & Hope (020) 7928 9898

The Cut; SE1 8LP Busy, informal bare-boards gastropub, food well liked by some readers (prices can be high), well kept Wells & Youngs and guests, wine by tumbler or carafe, plain bar with big windows and mix of furniture including elbow tables, curtained-off dining part with small open kitchen, tight-packed scrubbed tables and contemporary art; children and dogs welcome, closed Sun evening and Mon lunchtime, otherwise open all day. *(Phil Bryant, Mike and Sue Loseby, Tim Maddison)*

Brew Wharf (020) 7378 6601

Stoney Street; SE1 9AD Bright airy place under the railway arches, own-brewed ales plus lots of international bottled beers, good variety of food from sandwiches and sharing plates up; closed Sun evening, otherwise open all day. *(Comus and Sarah Elliott)*

Doggetts Coat & Badge (020) 7633 9081 *By Blackfriars Bridge; SE1 9UD* Well run modern pub on four floors with great Thames views, well kept interesting beers, pleasant service, usual Nicholsons menu including children's choices and fixed-price evening deal; nice outside drinking area by the river, open all day. *(Dave Braisted)*

⋆ **Fire Station** (020) 7620 2226

Waterloo Road; SE1 8SB Unusual fire station conversion, busy and noisy, with two huge knocked-through tiled rooms, lots of wooden tables and mix of chairs, pews and worn leather armchairs, distinctive box-shaped floral lampshades, sizeable plants, back bar with red fire buckets on shelf, smarter dining room, good modern all-day food including breakfast from 9am, Brakspears, Fullers and Ringwood, good choice of wines and spirits; background music; children welcome, tables out in front, picnic-sets in scruffy side alley, handy for Old Vic, open till midnight. *(Rob and Catherine Dunster, Eleanor Dandy, Tom and Ruth Rees, Ian Phillips, N R White and others)*

⋆ **Founders Arms** (020) 7928 1899

Hopton Street; SE1 9JH Modern building with glass walls in superb location – outstanding terrace views along Thames and handy for south bank attractions; plenty of customers (city types, tourists, theatre and gallery goers) spilling on to pavement and river walls, Wells & Youngs and a guest, lots of wines by glass, good well priced bar food all day (weekend breakfasts from 9am), cheerful service; background music; children welcome away from bar, open till midnight Fri, Sat. *(N R White, Phil and Jane Villiers, the Didler, Mike and Sue Loseby, Val and Alan Green, David Carr and others)*

Garrison 020 7089 9355

Bermondsey Street; SE1 3XB Interesting pub with scrubbed tables upstairs, cinema downstairs, good reasonably priced food including breakfast from 8am (9am weekends), more emphasis on wine than beer, buzzy atmosphere and nice staff. *(Mike and Sue Loseby, Ann Bowman)*

⋆**George** (020) 7407 2056
*Off 77 Borough High Street; SE1
1NH* Tucked-away 16th-c coaching inn
(mentioned in Little Dorrit), now owned by
National Trust and beautifully preserved;
lots of tables in bustling cobbled courtyard
with views of the tiered exterior galleries,
series of no-frills ground-floor rooms with
black beams, square-latticed windows and
some panelling, plain oak or elm tables on
bare boards, old-fashioned built-in settles,
dimpled glass lanterns and a 1797 Act
of Parliament clock, impressive central
staircase up to series of dining-rooms and
balcony, well kept Greene King ales plus
a beer brewed for the pub, good value
traditional food all day (not Sun evening),
friendly staff; children welcome away from
bar, open all day. *(Rob and Catherine Dunster,
Andy and Claire Barker, Anthony Longden, the
Didler, Mike and Sue Loseby)*

Goldsmith (020) 7593 1312
Southwark Bridge Road; SE1 0EF Pub/
dining room with well kept Adnams Best,
Wadworths 6X and a guest, imaginative
wine list with many by the glass, enjoyable
food including some thai dishes, friendly
service. *(Oliver Ward, Mike and Sue Loseby)*

⋆**Hole in the Wall** (020) 7928 6196
Mepham Street; SE1 8SQ Quirky
no-frills hideaway in railway arch virtually
underneath Waterloo, rumbles and shakes
with the trains, fine range of well kept
ales, basic bargain food all day, plush red
banquettes in small quieter front bar, well
worn mix of tables set well back from long
bar in larger back room; big-screen sports
TV, machines; open all day, closed weekend
afternoons. *(Jason Pound, Ian Phillips)*

⋆**Horniman** (020) 7407 1991
*Hays Galleria, off Battlebridge Lane;
SE1 2HD* Spacious, bright and airy Thames-
side drinking hall with lots of polished
wood, comfortable seating including a few
sofas, upstairs seating, several real ales with
unusual guests (may offer tasters), lunchtime
bar food from soup and big sandwiches up,
snacks other times, efficient service coping
with large numbers after work; unobtrusive
background music; fine river views from
picnic-sets outside, open all day. *(Phil and
Jane Villiers)*

⋆**Kings Arms** (020) 7207 0784
Roupell Street; SE1 8TB Proper corner
local, bustling and friendly, with curved
servery dividing traditional bar and lounge,
bare boards and attractive local prints,
well kept changing ales, good wine and
malt whisky choice, welcoming efficient
staff, enjoyable food from thai dishes to Sun
roasts, big back extension with conservatory/
courtyard dining area; background music;
open all day. *(Peter Dandy, Eleanor Dandy,
Richard Endacott, Stephen and Jean Curtis)*

⋆**Lord Clyde** (020) 7407 3397
Clennam Street; SE1 1ER Neat panelled
L-shaped local in same friendly family for
over 50 years, five well kept mainstream ales,
simple food from good salt beef sandwiches
up (weekday lunchtimes, early evenings),
darts in small hatch-served public bar;
dogs welcome, outside seating, striking
tiled façade, open all day, till 6pm Sun.
(Mike and Sue Loseby)

⋆**Market Porter** (020) 7407 2495
Stoney Street; SE1 9AA Properly pubby
no-frills place opening at 6am weekdays for
workers at neighbouring market, up to ten
unusual real ales (over 60 guests a week)
often from far-flung brewers, particularly
helpful, friendly service, bare boards and
open fire, beams with beer barrels balanced
on them, simple furnishings, food in bar and
upstairs lunchtime restaurant; background
music; children allowed weekends till 7pm,
dogs welcome, drinkers spill out on to street,
open all day. *(Phil and Jane Villiers, Bruce Bird,
Mike Gorton, Matt and Vikki Wharton, Ian Phillips,
Comus and Sarah Elliott and others)*

Rake (020) 7407 0557
Winchester Walk; SE1 9AG Tiny,
discreetly modern Borough Market bar with
amazing bottled beer range in wall-wide
cooler, also half a dozen continental lagers
on tap and perhaps a couple of rare real ales,
good friendly service; fair-sized terrace with
decking and heated marquee. *(Andrew Hobbs,
the Didler, Mike and Sue Loseby, N R White)*

Wheatsheaf (020) 7407 9934
Southwark Street; SE1 1TY Relocated
Red Car pub in cellars beneath the Hop
Exchange, brick vaulted ceilings and iron
pillars, great range of well kept changing
beers, decent pubby food; sports TV; open
all day. *(Mike and Sue Loseby)*

White Hart (020) 7928 9190
*Cornwall Road/Whittlesey Street;
SE1 8TJ* Backstreet corner local near
Waterloo station, friendly community
bustle, comfortable sofas, stripped boards
and so forth, Fullers London Pride, Sharps
Doom Bar and two guests, several belgian
beers, good range of ciders and wines,
sensibly priced up-to-date blackboard food
including pub standards, helpful efficient
staff; background music; open all day. *(Peter
Dandy, Eleanor Dandy, Phil Bryant)*

SE8
Dog & Bell (020) 8692 5664
Prince Street; SE8 3JD Friendly old-
fashioned tucked-away local on Thames
Path, wood benches around bright cheerfully
decorated L-shaped bar, half a dozen well
kept ales including Fullers, bottled belgians,
prompt friendly service, reasonably priced
pub food including good sandwiches, dining

room, bar billiards; TV; tables in yard, open all day. *(N R White)*

SE9
Park Tavern (020) 8850 8919
Passey Place; SE9 5DA Traditional Victorian corner pub off Eltham High Street, up to eight well kept ales, log fire, friendly easy-going atmosphere; soft background music. *(Michael and Deborah Ethier)*

SE10
☆ Cutty Sark (020) 8858 3146
Ballast Quay, off Lassell Street; SE10 9PD Great Thames views from this early 19th-c Greenwich tavern, genuinely unspoilt old-fashioned bar, dark flagstones, simple furnishings including barrel seats, open fires, narrow openings to tiny side snugs, upstairs room (reached by winding staircase) with ship-deck-feel and prized seat in big bow window, up to five changing ales, organic wines, malt whiskies, all-day bar food; background music; children and dogs welcome, busy riverside terrace across narrow cobbled lane, limited parking (but free if you get a space). *(John Saville, the Didler)*

Kings Arms (020) 8858 4544
King William Walk; SE10 9JH Well placed dark-panelled open-plan pub, shortish choice of enjoyable good value food, Greene King ales, friendly attentive staff; background music; children welcome, pleasant shady back terrace. *(George Atkinson)*

Old Brewery (020) 3327 1280
Pepys Building, Old Royal Naval College; SE10 9LW Modernised 19th-c building with interesting brewing history – now owned by Meantime; front bar with their beers (some brewed here) and guests plus many more in bottles, separate back hall acting as café/evening restaurant complete with gleaming new microbrewery; nice courtyard garden; open all day. *(George Atkinson)*

☆ Richard I (020) 8692 2996
Royal Hill; SE10 8RT Friendly well managed Youngs pub with two bars, carpets and panelling, popular food including enjoyable Sun lunch, good service; children welcome, picnic-sets out in front, lots more in pleasant paved back garden with weekend summer barbecues – busy then. *(D Crook, N R White)*

Yacht (020) 7858 0175
Crane Street; SE10 9NP Neatly modernised with great river views from spacious room up a few steps from bar, four well kept ales and good choice of reasonably priced food, friendly staff, cosy banquettes, light wood panelling, portholes, yacht pictures; cheerful hanging baskets out at front. *(Mike Horgan, Di Wright)*

SE16
☆ Mayflower (020) 7237 4088
Rotherhithe Street; SE16 4NF Unchanging cosy old riverside pub in unusual street with lovely early 18th-c church; good generous bar food including more upmarket daily specials, Greene King and guests, good value wines and decent coffee, obliging service, black beams, panelling, nautical bric-a-brac, high-backed settles and coal fires, good Thames views from upstairs restaurant (closed Sat lunchtime); background music; children welcome, jetty/terrace over water (barbecues), open all day. *(N R White, Phil Bryant)*

SE21
☆ Crown & Greyhound
(020) 8299 4976 *Dulwich Village; SE21 7BJ* Big busy (especially evenings) Victorian pub with cosy period interior, traditional upholstered settles and stripped kitchen tables on bare boards, big back dining room, conservatory, Fullers London Pride, Harveys and a couple of guests (Easter beer festival and summer cider festival), just under two dozen wines by the glass, straightforward bar food (all day), popular Sun carvery; background music; children and dogs welcome, summer barbecues in pleasant back garden. *(John Saville, Giles and Annie Francis, Christine Murphy)*

SE22
Palmerston (020) 86931629
Lordship Lane; SE22 8EP Popular 19th-c panelled dining pub with good enterprising food (not cheap) using prime ingredients, extensive wine list, beers such as Harveys, Sharps Doom Bar and Timothy Taylors Landlord, quick friendly service; children welcome, no dogs at mealtimes, open all day. *(P and D Carpenter)*

SE24
Florence (020) 7326 4987
Dulwich Road; SE24 0NG Handsome Victorian pub visibly brewing its own ales, guest beers and farm cider available too, enjoyable sensibly priced food including Sun roasts, friendly busy atmosphere, contemporary décor with comfortable booth seating, open fire, conservatory; children's play room, a few tables out in front under awning, more on back terrace, open all day. *(Greg Bailey, Mark Stafferton)*

SE26
☆ Dulwich Wood House
(020) 8693 5666 *Sydenham Hill; SE26 6RS* Extended well refurbished Youngs pub in Victorian lodge gatehouse complete with turret, nice local atmosphere, friendly service, good food cooked to order;

steps up to entrance (and stiff walk up from station); children welcome, big pleasant back garden with old-fashioned street lamps, summer barbecues, handy for Dulwich Wood. *(Jake Lingwood, B J Harding)*

SW4
Windmill (020) 8673 4578
Clapham Common South Side; SW4 9DE Big bustling pub by the common, contemporary front bar, quite a few original Victorian features, pillared dining room leading through to conservatory style eating area, good varied choice of food all day, Wells & Youngs ales and decent wines by the glass, background music, Sun quiz; children welcome, bar, tables under red umbrellas along front, also seats in side garden area, good bedrooms, open all day. *(Giles and Annie Francis)*

SW11
Eagle (020) 7228 2328
Chatham Road; SW11 6HG Attractive unpretentious backstreet local, seven changing ales including southern brewers like Harveys, Surrey Hills and Westerham, welcoming prompt service, worn leather chesterfield in fireside corner of L-shaped bar; big-screen sports TV; dogs welcome, back terrace with heated marquee, small front terrace too. *(Mitchell Humphreys)*

Falcon (020) 7228 2076
St John's Hill; SW11 1RU Restored Victorian pub with a dozen or so well kept beers from remarkably long light oak counter, bargain pub food, friendly service, lively front bar, period partitions, cut glass and mirrors, subdued lighting, quieter back dining area, daily newspapers; big-screen TV; handy for Clapham Junction station. *(Mike Gorton, Barbarrick)*

✳ Fox & Hounds (020) 7924 5483
Latchmere Road; SW11 2JU Big Victorian local with particularly good mediterranean cooking (all day Sun, not Mon-Thurs lunchtimes), Fullers, Harveys and a guest, several wines by glass, spacious straightforward bar with big windows overlooking street, bare boards, mismatched tables and chairs, photographs on walls, fresh flowers, daily newspapers, view of kitchen behind, two rooms off; background music, TV; children (till 7pm) and dogs welcome, garden seats under big parasols, open all day Fri-Sun, closed Mon lunchtime. *(Anon)*

SW12
Avalon (020) 8675 8613
Balham Hill; SW12 9EB Part of the growing Renaissance group of S London pubs, good food with some interesting takes on traditional cooking, well kept changing ales such as Fullers London Pride and Sharps Doom Bar, good choice of wines by the glass, plenty of room in split-level bar and dining area, big murals and stuffed animals, coal fires; front terrace and nice sunny back garden. *(Anon)*

✳ Nightingale (020) 8673 1637
Nightingale Lane; SW12 8NX Cosy and civilised early Victorian local, small woody front bar opening into larger back area and attractive family conservatory, well kept Wells & Youngs ales, enjoyable sensibly priced bar food, friendly service, board games; sports TV; small secluded back garden with smokers' shelter. *(Giles and Annie Francis)*

SW13
Brown Dog (020) 8392 2200
Cross Street; SW13 0AP Well renovated with warm relaxed atmosphere, gastropub menu (not cheap), good choice of wines, well kept Sambrooks and Twickenham, friendly helpful staff, subtle lighting and open fires, daily newspapers; children and dogs welcome (resident lab called Willow), garden tables, open all day. *(Jim Jolliffe, C Cooper)*

SW14
Victoria (020) 8876 4238
West Temple Sheen; SW14 7RT Contemporary styling with emphasis on conservatory restaurant, good if not particularly cheap food including breakfast from 8.30am (not Sun), two-course set deal (Mon-Thurs), friendly service, well kept Fullers London Pride and Timothy Taylors Landlord in small wood-floored bar with leather sofas and wood burning stoves; background music, play area in nice garden, comfortable bedrooms, open all day. *(Richard Morris, Simon Rodway, Gerry and Rosemary Dobson)*

SW15
Dukes Head (020) 8788 2552
Lower Richmond Road, near Putney Bridge; SW15 1JN Smart Victorian pub with comfortable furnishings in knocked-together front bars, good range of well presented pubby food all day including sharing plates and snacks, Wells & Youngs ales, lots of wines by the glass, friendly service, light and airy back dining room with great river views, downstairs bar in disused skittle alley; plastic glasses for outside terrace or riverside pavement; children welcome (high chairs and smaller helpings), open all day. *(Peter Dandy)*

Green Man (020) 8788 8096
Wildcroft Road, Putney Heath; SW15 3NG Small friendly old local by Putney Heath, good choice of enjoyable food,

well kept Wells & Youngs ales and guests; TV; attractive good-sized back garden with decking, also seats in front near road, open all day. *(Peter Dandy)*

⋆**Telegraph** (020) 8788 2011
Telegraph Road; SW15 3TU Big pub on Putney Heath, two attractively modernised rooms with bold décor, leather armchairs and sofas, rugs on polished wood, grand dining table, six real ales including house Semaphore brewed by Weltons, bistro-style food all day, newspapers and board games; background music and live blues/jazz nights, sports TV, occasional quiz; children and dogs welcome, great garden with rural feel, busy outside with families and dogs in summer. *(Colin McKerrow, Tracey and Stephen Groves, Peter Dandy, Sophie Holborow)*

SW16
Earl Ferrers (020) 8835 8333
Ellora Road; SW16 6JF Opened-up Streatham corner local, Sambrooks and several other well kept ales (tasters offered), some interesting food as well as pub favourites, good informal service, mixed tables and chairs, sofas, old photographs; background music – live every other Sun, quiz night Weds, pool and darts; children welcome, some tables outside with tractor-seat stools, open all day weekends, from 5pm weekdays. *(LM, Kevin Chamberlain)*

SW18
Ship (020) 8870 9667
Jews Row; SW18 1TB Popular riverside pub by Wandsworth Bridge; light and airy conservatory-style decor, pleasant mix of furnishings on bare boards, basic public bar, well kept Wells & Youngs, Sambrooks and a guest, freshly cooked interesting bistro food in extended restaurant with own garden; children and dogs welcome, barbecue and outside bar in attractive good-sized terrace, open all day. *(Peter Dandy, Mike Bell)*

SW19
Alexandra (020) 8947 7691
Wimbledon Hill Road; SW19 7NE Busy Youngs pub with well kept beers including guests from central bar, good wine choice, enjoyable food from sandwiches to good Sun roasts, friendly alert service, comfortably up-to-date décor in linked rooms; sports TVs; tables out in mews and on attractive roof terrace. *(Colin McKerrow)*

Fox & Grapes (020) 8619 1300
Camp Road; SW19 4UN 18th-c dining pub by Wimbledon common refurbished under french chef/owner, modern bistro feel but keeping some original features in the two dining areas (steps between), some adventurous cooking alongside more

traditional dishes (not cheap and they add a service charge), well chosen wines by the glass, Sharps Doom Bar and guest from central servery, relaxed atmosphere; children and dogs welcome, three bedrooms. *(Paul Bonner, Susan and John Douglas, John Coatsworth)*

⋆**Rose & Crown** (020) 8947 4713
Wimbledon High Street; SW19 5BA Comfortably refurbished 17th-c Youngs pub, alcove seating in roomy bar, old prints including interesting religious texts and drawings, enjoyable pubby food and friendly efficient service, back dining conservatory; partly covered former coachyard, bedrooms. *(Ross Balaam, Colin McKerrow)*

WEST LONDON

SW6
⋆**Atlas** (020) 7385 9129
Seagrave Road; SW6 1RX Busy tucked-away pub with long simple knocked-together bar, plenty of panelling and dark wall benches, school chairs and tables, brick fireplaces, enjoyable generous bar food (all day Sun), well kept Fullers, St Austell, Sharps and a guest, lots of wines by the glass, big mugs of coffee, friendly service; background music and they may ask to keep a credit card while you run a tab; children (till 7pm) and dogs welcome, seats under awning on heated and attractively planted side terrace, open all day. *(Alistair Forsyth, Nick and Elaine Hall, Evelyn and Derek Walter, Fr Robert Marsh)*

Harwood Arms (020) 7386 1847
Walham Grove; SW6 1QP Interesting bare-boards gastropub, good bar snacks as well as enterprising pricy full meals, friendly caring staff, separate eating area, well kept ales such as Fullers London Pride and St Austell Tribute in proper bar area with leather sofas, young lively atmosphere; closed Mon lunchtime. *(Richard Tilbrook)*

Sands End (020) 7731 7823
Stephendale Road; SW6 2PR Enterprising seasonal food including game, real ales such as Black Sheep, Hook Norton and Sharps Doom Bar, simple country furnishings and open fire. *(Sam West, Richard Tilbrook)*

SW7
⋆**Anglesea Arms** (020) 7373 7960
Selwood Terrace; SW7 3QG Very busy Victorian pub run well by friendly landlady, mix of cast-iron tables on wood-strip floor, central elbow tables, panelling and heavy portraits, large brass chandeliers hanging from dark ceilings, big windows with swagged curtains, several booths at one end with partly glazed screens, half a dozen ales including Adnams, Fullers London Pride and Sambrooks, around 20 malt whiskies and 30

wines by the glass, interesting bar food, steps down to refurbished dining room; children welcome, dogs in bar, heated front terrace, open all day. *(the Didler, Phil Bryant, B and M Kendall)*

Queens Arms (020) 7823 9293
Queens Gate Mews; SW7 5QL Victorian corner pub with open-plan bare-boards bar, enjoyable good value home-made pubby food, good wines by the glass, ales including Adnams and Fullers; TV; disabled facilities, handy for Albert Hall, open all day. *(Anon)*

SW10
Chelsea Ram (020) 7351 4008
Burnaby Street; SW10 0PL Refurbished corner Geronimo Inn, mix of furniture on bare boards or stripy carpet including farmhouse tables, padded stools around an old workbench, cushioned wall seats, shelves of books and some striking artwork, Victorian fireplace, Wells & Youngs and guests, enjoayable food including daily specials, friendly service, board games; pavement picnic-sets, open all day. *(Neil Edmundson)*

W4
⋆ ## Bell & Crown (020) 8994 4164
Strand on the Green; W4 3PF Well run Fullers local, good friendly staff, enjoyable sensibly priced food, panelling and log fire, great Thames views from back bar and conservatory, lots of atmosphere, daily newspapers; can get very busy weekends; dogs welcome, terrace and towpath area, good walks, open all day. *(N R White, Ian Phillips)*

⋆ ## Bulls Head (020) 8994 1204
Strand on the Green; W4 3PQ Renovated old Thames-side pub (served as Cromwell's HQ during Civil War), seats by windows overlooking the water in beamed rooms, steps up and down, ales such as Fullers and Wells & Youngs, several wines by the glass, decent all-day pubby food, friendly helpful service; background music, games machine; seats outside by river, pretty hanging baskets, part of Chef & Brewer chain. *(N R White, Tracey and Stephen Groves, Ross Balaam)*

City Barge (020) 8994 2148
Strand on the Green; W4 3PH Small panelled riverside bars with some nice original features in picturesque front part, airy newer back part done out with maritime signs and bird prints, all-day food from sandwiches to popular Sun roasts, Greene King and a guest ale, open fire, back conservatory; well behaved children and dogs welcome, waterside picnic-sets facing

Oliver's Island, nice spot to watch sun set over Kew Bridge. *(N R White)*

Roebuck (020) 8995 4392
Chiswick High Road; W4 1PU Popular relaxed dining pub with high ceilings and bare boards, front bar and roomy back dining area opening into delightful paved garden, enjoyable food from daily-changing menu, open kitchen, four real ales and good choice of wines by the glass; dogs welcome, open all day. *(Simon Rodway)*

Swan (020) 8994 8262
Evershed Walk, Acton Lane; W4 5HH Cosy well supported 19th-c local, good food including some interesting choices, friendly staff, a dozen or so wines by the glass, Sharps Doom Bar and guests such as Hogs Back and Otter, panelled interior with leather sofas by open fire; dogs very welcome, children till 7.30pm, good spacious garden, open all day weekends. *(Seb Royce)*

W6
⋆ ## Anglesea Arms (020) 8749 1291
Wingate Road; W6 0UR Good interesting food including weekday set lunches in homely bustling pub, welcoming staff, good choice of wines by the glass and of real ales, close-set tables in dining room facing kitchen, roaring fire in simply decorated panelled bar; children welcome, tables out by quiet street, open all day. *(Robert Del Maestro, C Cooper, the Didler, Michael Rugman)*

Blue Anchor (020) 8748 5774
Lower Mall; W6 9DJ Refurbished pub right on the Thames (first licensed 1722), two traditional linked areas with oak floors and panelling, good value generous bar lunches, real ales such as Sambrooks Wandle, friendly helpful service, pleasant river-view room upstairs; busy at weekends; disabled facilities, riverside tables. *(N R White)*

Carpenters Arms (020) 8741 8386
Black Lion Lane; W6 9BG Good imaginative cooking at this relaxed corner place, fine for just a drink too with plenty of wines by the glass and Adnams Bitter, friendly staff, simple bare-boards interior with open fire; attractive garden, open all day. *(Simon Rodway)*

⋆ ## Dove (020) 8748 9474
Upper Mall; W6 9TA Lots of history at this 17th-c riverside pub (framed list of writers, actors and artists who have been here), also in Guinness World Records for smallest bar room – front snug is a mere 1.2m by 2.1m, with traditional black panelling, red leatherette built-in wall settles

---

and dimpled copper tables; much bigger similarly furnished room with old framed advertisements and photographs of the pub, Fullers ales, 20 wines by the glass including champagne, pubby food (all day weekends), live band once a month; dogs welcome, seats out on flagstoned area and verandah overlooking Thames reach (much prized so get there early), tiny exclusive area up spiral staircase too (prime spot for watching rowing crews), open all day. *(the Didler, Rob and Catherine Dunster, N R White, Phil Bryant)*

Latymers (020) 8748 3446
Hammersmith Road; W6 7JP Big lively bar with minimal décor, lots of steel and glass including ornate mirrored ceiling, well kept Fullers ales and friendly bar staff; sports TVs, may be background music; good reasonably priced thai food in spacious back restaurant. *(Susan and John Douglas)*

Old Ship (020) 8741 2886
Upper Mall; W6 9TD Spaciously modernised old Thames-side pub, well kept Wells & Youngs ales and good choice of food from 9am breakfast on; children welcome, seats out overlooking river, open all day. *(John Saville)*

Thatched House (020) 8748 6174
Dalling Road; W6 0ET Traditional open-plan Victorian corner pub – Youngs first – their ales and guests such as Sambrooks from large wooden servery, mixed furniture including leather chesterfields on bare boards, old books and photographs, station clocks, stained-glass windows, open fire, good choice of food and wine, efficient friendly service, back conservatory, may be irish music Sun evening; two-tier garden, open all day. *(Dan Stratton)*

W7
Viaduct (020) 8810 0815
Uxbridge Road; W7 3TD Well maintained Fullers pub with railway memorabilia and old photographs of nearby viaduct, decent food from fairly extensive menu, helpful charming service; sports TV in public bar; open all day. *(Sue and Mike Todd, Amanda Kent)*

W8
Britannia (020) 7937 6905
Allen Street, off Kensington High Street; W8 6UX Welcoming refurbished Wells & Youngs pub, decent-sized traditional front bar with pastel shades contrasting the dark panelling, patterned rugs on bare boards, banquettes, leather tub and high-backed chairs, steps down to back area with wall-sized photograph of the old Britannia Brewery (now demolished), dining conservatory beyond, enjoyable pubby food; background music, sports TV; open all day. *(Phil Bryant)*

⋆**Scarsdale** (020) 7937 1811
Edwardes Square; W8 6HE Busy Georgian pub in lovely leafy square, stripped-wood floors, good coal-effect gas fires, various knick-knacks, well kept Fullers/Gales ales from ornate counter, enjoyable good value pubby food, friendly helpful service; nice front terrace, open all day. *(Anon)*

⋆**Uxbridge Arms** (020) 7727 7326
Uxbridge Street; W8 7TQ Friendly and cottagey backstreet local with three brightly furnished linked areas, well kept Fullers and a guest such as Harveys, good choice of bottled beers, china, prints and photographs; sports TV; open all day. *(Giles and Annie Francis, the Didler)*

⋆**Windsor Castle** (020) 7243 8797
Campden Hill Road; W8 7AR One of the city's best pub gardens with high ivy-sheltered walls, summer bar, winter heaters and lots of seats on flagstones; plenty of inside character in three tiny unspoilt rooms (fun trying to navigate the minuscule doors between them), a wealth of dark oak furnishings, high backed sturdy built-in elm benches, time-smoked ceilings and coal-effect fire, cosy pre-war-style dining room, fair-priced enjoyable food (all day Fri-Sun), Timothy Taylors and often interesting guests, summer Pimms and winter mulled wine, friendly staff; children (till 7pm) and dogs welcome, open all day. *(Giles and Annie Francis, the Didler, John Best, Ian Phillips, Phil Bryant, N R White)*

W9
Warwick Castle (020) 7266 0921
Warwick Place; W9 2PX In narrow street near Little Venice, open-fronted with a few pavement tables, darkish rooms inside with traditional décor, a couple of real ales, blackboard menu including sandwiches. *(Robert Lester)*

W11
⋆**Portobello Gold** (020) 7460 4910
Middle of Portobello Road; W11 2QB Cheerful informal atmosphere at this engaging combination of pub, hotel and restaurant; smallish front bar with cushioned banquettes and nice old fireplace, exotic dining room with big tropical plants, sliding roof, impressive wall-to-wall mirror and vocal canaries, wide choice of enjoyable food all day, Harveys Best, a guest ale and several draught belgian beers, bottled imports too, around a dozen wines by the glass from good list, board games, monthly art and photographic exhibition; background music (live Sun evening), sports TV; children till 9pm, street tables, bedrooms and spacious apartment with roof terrace and putting green, open all day. *(Anon)*

W12
★Princess Victoria (020) 8749 5886
Uxbridge Road; W12 9DH Imposing Victorian gin palace with carefully restored rather grand bar, oil paintings on slate-coloured walls, a couple of stuffed animal heads, comfortable leather wall seats, parquet flooring, small fireplace, Fullers and Timothy Taylors, 36 wines by the glass and lots of spirits from handsome marble-topped horseshoe counter, imaginative modern bar food, large dining room with plenty of original features and more paintings, wine and cigar shop; children allowed if eating, dogs in bar, white wrought-iron furniture on pretty terrace, popular Sat artisan market in front, open all day. *(Anon)*

W14
★Havelock Tavern (020) 7603 5374
Masbro Road; W14 0LS Popular gastropub in former shop, light airy L-shaped bar with plain unfussy décor, second small room with pews, good imaginative and often unusual food, home-baked bread, Sambrooks Wandle, Sharps Doom Bar and a couple of guests, 19 wines by the glass, swift friendly service; free wi-fi; children and dogs welcome, picnic-sets on small paved terrace, open all day. *(Martin and Karen Wake, Derek Thomas, John and Annabel Hampshire)*

OUTER LONDON
BECKENHAM   TQ3769
Jolly Woodman (020) 8663 1031
Chancery Lane; BR3 6NR Welcoming old-fashioned local in conservation area, cosy chatty atmosphere in small bar with larger room off, woodburner, five or so good changing ales such as Harveys and Timothy Taylors Landlord, good value home-made food (weekday lunchtimes only) including sandwiches; flower-filled back courtyard and pavement tables, open all day, closed Mon lunchtime. *(N R White)*

BIGGIN HILL   TQ4359
★Old Jail (01959) 572979
Jail Lane; (E off A233 S of airport and industrial estate, towards Berry's Hill and Cudham); TN16 3AX Big family garden with picnic-sets, substantial trees and good play area for this popular country pub (close to the city); traditional beamed and low-ceilinged rooms with RAF memorabilia, two cosy small areas to right divided by timbers, one with big inglenook, other with cabinet of Battle of Britain plates, Fullers, Harveys and Shepherd Neame, standard fairly priced food (not Sun evening) from sandwiches up, friendly service – can slow when busy, step up to dining room with more wartime prints/plates and small

open fire; discreet background music; dogs welcome, nice hanging baskets, open all day weekends. *(B and M Kendall, N R White, Alan Weedon)*

BROMLEY   TQ4069
Red Lion (020) 8460 2691
North Road; BR1 3LG Chatty well managed backstreet local in conservation area, traditional dimly lit interior with wood floor, tiling, green velvet drapes and shelves of books, well kept Greene King, Harveys and guests, lunchtime food, good friendly service; tables out in front, open all day. *(N R White)*

BROMLEY   TQ4265
Two Doves (020) 8462 1627
Oakley Road (A233); BR2 8HD Popular and comfortable unpretentious pub notable for its lovely garden with terrace tables; friendly staff and locals, well kept St Austell Tribute, Wells & Youngs and a guest, no hot food but ploughman's and snacks, modern back conservatory, open all day Fri-Sun. *(N R White)*

CARSHALTON   TQ2764
★Greyhound (020) 8647 1511
High Street; SM5 3PE 18th-c coaching inn opposite duck ponds in picturesque outer London 'village', comfortable panelled front lounge bar with log fire, dining areas, friendly service, Youngs ales, wide choice of enjoyable food from interesting sandwiches and ciabattas up; TV in large public bar; picnic-sets out by road, 21 bedrooms, open all day. *(Mierion Perring)*

CROYDON   TQ3366
Glamorgan (020) 8688 6333
Cherry Orchard Road; CR0 6BE Cleanly refurbished pub with good food including some S African influences (landlord is from there), well kept Harveys Sharps Doom Bar and a guest, reasonable prices; background and some live music, no dogs; children till 7pm, back terrace, open all day weekdays, from 4pm Sat, closed Sun. *(P J Checksfield)*

DOWNE   TQ4464
George & Dragon (01689) 889030
High Street; BR6 7UT Comfortable open-plan beamed pub, fair choice of beers and good reasonably priced food, friendly staff; handy for Charles Darwin's house and Biggin Hill. *(William Ruxton)*

ENFIELD   TQ3599
Pied Bull (01992) 710619
Bulls Cross, Bullsmoor Lane W of A10; handy for M25 junction 25; EN2 9HE Friendly modernised 17th-c pub, low beam-and-plank ceilings, lots of comfortable

little rooms and extensions, well kept ales and decent choice of wines, good well presented food including bargain lunchtime deals, conservatory; dogs welcome, pleasant terrace, open all day. *(Mr R A Buckler)*

GREENFORD TQ1382
Black Horse (020) 8578 1384
Oldfield Lane; UB6 0AS Split-level canalside pub, well kept Fullers ales and enjoyable food from sandwiches up, efficient friendly service. *(Ross Balaam)*

HAMPTON TQ1370
Bell (020) 8941 9799
Thames Street; TW12 2EA Nicely refurbished pub opposite the river and very popular; good food (all day weekends) from sharing boards up, friendly efficient service, beers such as By the Horns, Sambrooks and Sharps Doom Bar, good choice of wines by the glass, monthly comedy night; open all day. *(John Soones, Ian Phillips)*

ISLEWORTH TQ1675
London Apprentice (020) 8560 1915
Church Street; TW7 6BG Large Thames-side Taylor Walker pub, reasonably priced food from sandwiches up, well kept ales such as Adnams, Fullers, Hook Norton, Sharps and Wells & Youngs, good wine choice, log fire, pleasant friendly service, upstairs river-view restaurant; may be background music; children welcome, attractive riverside terrace, open all day. *(Ian Phillips)*

Red Lion (020) 8560 1457
Linkfield Road; TW7 6QJ Friendly unspoilt backstreet local with nine real ales, six farm ciders and good choice of belgian beers, home made food (not Sun evening, Mon lunchtime or Tues) including popular Sun lunch, four annual beer festivals, theatre company, live music including Mon jazz, Thurs quiz; children and dogs welcome, picnic-sets out at front, garden with smokers' shelter, open all day. *(C Cooper, Lori Kelley)*

KESTON TQ4164
Fox (01689) 852053
Heathfield Road; BR2 6BQ Roomy recently refurbished pub with well kept Fullers London Pride and Sharps Doom Bar, good selection of wines, generous nicely presented food at reasonable prices; garden behind. *(Mike Buckingham)*

KEW TQ1977
Botanist (020) 8948 4838
Kew Green; TW9 3AA Own-brew pub handy for Kew Gardens and attracting a good cross-section of customers, ales such as Humulus Lupulus and Kew Green, also

lots of UK and foreign bottled beers, food from sharing plates up, friendly helpful service; children welcome, small back terrace. *(Martin and Karen Wake)*

Coach & Horses (020) 8940 1208
Kew Green; TW9 3BH Modernised former coaching inn overlooking green, decent Wells & Youngs ales and a guest, good coffees, fairly standard bar food from sandwiches up, young friendly staff, relaxed open-plan interior with armchairs, sofas and log fire, small restaurant; background music, sports TV; teak tables on front terrace, nice setting handy for Kew Gardens and National Archive, 31 bedrooms, open all day. *(N R White, Geof Cox, Jeremy King)*

KINGSTON TQ1769
⋆**Bishop Out of Residence**
(020) 8546 4965 *Bishops Hall, down alley off Thames Street; KT1 1PY* Thames-side pub with spacious open-plan bar, sumptuous modern décor, water views from upstairs lounge, Wells & Youngs and a guest, 27 wines by the glass and various cocktails, good modern cooking (all day including sandwiches and stone-baked pizzas); children and dogs welcome (not upstairs), waterside terrace. *(Anon)*

KINGSTON TQ1869
Albert (020) 8546 7669
Kingston Hill; KT2 7PX Sizeable Youngs pub close to Richmond Park, their ales and guest kept well, good choice of wines by the glass, food from sandwiches and light meals up, good helpful service; garden bar and heated courtyard. *(Meg and Colin Hamilton)*

Boaters (020) 8541 4672
Canbury Gardens (park in Lower Ham Road if you can); KT2 5AU Family-friendly pub by Thames, half a dozen real ales, good wines from reasonably priced list, well prepared nicely presented food including weekend breakfast from 10am, efficient staff, comfortable banquettes in charming bar, newspapers, Sun evening jazz; smart riverside terrace, in small park, ideal for children in summer, open all day. *(David and Sally Frost, Sue and Mike Todd)*

Canbury Arms (020) 8255 9129
Canbury Park Road; KT2 6LQ Open-plan pub with simple contemporary décor, bare boards and big windows, relaxed friendly atmosphere, good up-to-date food including breakfast from 9am (10am Sun), attentive young staff, five well kept ales such as Surrey Hills, St Austell and Timothy Taylors, good wine choice, nice coffee, stone-floor side conservatory, regular events; children and dogs welcome, tables out at front under parasols, open all day. *(Keith M Long, Louis Jones, Tom Gardner, Geoffrey and Penny Hughes)*

ORPINGTON
TQ4963

⋆ **Bo-Peep** (01959) 534457

Hewitts Road, Chelsfield; 1.7 miles from M25 J4; BR6 7QL Useful M25 country-feel dining pub, old low beams and enormous inglenook in carpeted bar, two cosy candlelit dining rooms, airy side room overlooking lane, Adnams, Courage and Harveys, cheerful service, pubby food (not Sun evening) as well as some more interesting choices; background music; children welcome, dogs in bar, picnic-sets on big brick terrace, open all day. *(Anon)*

OSTERLEY
TQ1578

⋆ **Hare & Hounds** (020) 8560 5438

Windmill Lane (B454, off A4 – called Syon Lane at that point); TW7 5PR Roomy Fullers dining pub, wide choice of enjoyable food from sandwiches to reasonably priced main dishes, prompt friendly service, pleasant dining extension, local wartime photographs; children and dogs welcome, disabled facilities, spacious terrace and big floodlit mature garden, nice setting opposite beautiful Osterley Park, open all day. *(Ellie Weld, David London, Revd R P Tickle)*

PINNER
TQ1289

Queens Head (020) 8868 4607

High Street; HA5 5PJ Traditional beamed and panelled local dating from the 16th c, welcoming bustle, interesting décor, well kept Adnams, Greene King, Wells & Youngs Bombardier and two guests, simple good value lunchtime bar food; no children inside; dogs welcome (not during lunch), small back terrace for evening sun, open all day. *(Jonathan Peel, Brian Glozier)*

RICHMOND
TQ1877

Princes Head (020) 8940 1572

The Green; TW9 1LX Large unspoilt open-plan pub overlooking cricket green near theatre, clean and well run, with low-ceilinged panelled areas off big island bar, Fullers range in top condition, popular imaginative food, friendly young staff and chatty locals, coal-effect fire; over 21s only, seats outside – fine spot. *(N R White)*

Watermans Arms (020) 8940 2893

Water Lane; TW9 1TJ Friendly old-fashioned Youngs local with well kept ales and enjoyable thai food, traditional layout with open fire, pub games; handy for the Thames. *(N R White, Claes Mauroy)*

⋆ **White Cross** (020) 8940 6844

Water Lane; TW9 1TH Very pleasant garden with terrific Thames views, seats on paved area, outside bar and boats to Kingston and Hampton Court; two chatty main rooms with hotel feel (which it was), local prints and photographs, three log fires (one unusually below a window), well kept Wells & Youngs and guests from old-fashioned island servery, a dozen wines by the glass, decent bar food all day, bright and airy upstairs room (children welcome here till 6pm) with pretty cast-iron balcony for splendid river view, good mix of customers; background music, TV; dogs welcome. *(Paul Humphreys, N R White, the Didler and others)*

White Swan (020) 8940 0959

Old Palace Lane; TW9 1PG Small cottagey pub, civilised and relaxed, with rustic dark-beamed open-plan bar, good friendly service, well kept ales such as Fullers London Pride, St Austell Tribute and Timothy Taylors Landlord, fresh wholesome bar lunches, coal-effect fires, popular upstairs restaurant; background music; children allowed in back conservatory, some seats on narrow paved area at front, more in pretty walled back terrace below railway. *(Jennifer Banks, N R White)*

RICHMOND
TQ1772

New Inn (020) 8940 9444

Petersham Road (A307, Ham Common); TW10 7DB Attractive Georgian pub in good spot on Ham Common, panelling, wood floors and comfortable banquettes, well kept ales including Adnams Broadside, food from good sandwiches through steaks to interesting specials, pleasant dining area, attentive friendly staff, big log fire one side, coal the other; disabled facilities, picnic-sets out among flowers front and back. *(Rob and Catherine Dunster)*

Roebuck (020) 8948 2329

Richmond Hill; TW10 6RN Comfortable and attractive 18th-c bay-windowed pub with friendly helpful staff, well kept changing ales, enjoyable good value food including vegetarian choices, stripped brick alcoves, some substantial bygones, old Thames photographs and prints; children and dogs welcome, terrace over road with fine views of meadows and river, open all day. *(Jennifer Banks, N R White, Theocsbrian)*

TEDDINGTON
TQ1770

Lion (020) 8977 4779

Wick Road; TW11 9DN Refurbished backstreet pub extended to include french restaurant, good food and well kept ales such as Fullers and Sharps. *(Hunter and Christine Wright)*

Tide End Cottage (020) 8977 7762

Broom Road/Ferry Road, near bridge at Teddington Lock; TW11 9NN Low-ceilinged pub in Victorian cottage terrace next to Teddington Studios, two rooms united by big log-effect gas fire, well kept Greene King ales and a guest, decent low-priced bar food to numbered tables from sandwiches up, lots of river, fishing and rowing memorabilia and photographs, interesting Dunkirk evacuation link, back dining extension; background music, TV, minimal parking; children (till 7.30pm) and dogs welcome, small terraces front and back, open all day. *(Chris Evans, LM)*

TWICKENHAM   TQ1673
White Swan 020 88922166
Riverside; TW1 3DN Refurbished 17th-c Thames-side pub up steep anti-flood steps, bare-boards L-shaped bar with log fire, changing ales such as local Twickenham, enjoyable food (all day weekends) including some good value deals; children welcome, tranquil setting opposite Eel Pie Island with waterside terrace across quiet lane, open all day. *(Mrs Barbara Dale, Helen Freeman, N R White, Charles Meade-King)*

TWICKENHAM   TQ1572
Sussex Arms (020) 8894 7468
Staines Road; TW2 5BG Recently reopened traditional bare-boards pub, a dozen real ales and six ciders from long counter, plenty in bottles too, simple food including good home-made pies, open fire, live acoustic music; large back garden with boules, open all day. *(Steve Derbyshire)*

WOODFORD GREEN   TQ4091
Three Jolly Wheelers
(020) 8502 9296 *Chigwell Road (A113); IG8 8AS* Sizeable 19th-c Vintage Inn, carpet, bare boards and flagstones, painted panelling, comfortable seats by open fires, Adnams and a guest ale, popular good value food (all day) from sandwiches up in bar and restaurant, friendly atmosphere; background music, children welcome, front terrace, bedrooms. *(Robert Lester)*

SCOTLAND

Not surprisingly, you'll find some of the world's finest collections of whisky here, with some pubs amassing an extraordinary number: 350 at the Sligachan Hotel, 270 at the Bon Accord in Glasgow, 125 at the Stein Inn on Skye, 100 at the Fox & Hounds in Houston and 80 at Burts Hotel in Melrose. Other pubs our readers are enjoying include the Applecross Inn (an idyllic and remote spot, a no-nonsense bar that gets packed out with both visitors and locals, and lovely seafood), Café Royal in Edinburgh (extraordinarily opulent Victorian interior and good food and drink), Babbity Bowster (a clever blend of pub and café that's always lively) and Bon Accord (ten daily-changing ales and remarkably cheap food) both in Glasgow, Fox & Hounds in Houston (fantastic choice of drinks including their own brews, now run by the second generation of the same family), Border at Kirk Yetholm (hospitable inn with comfortable bedrooms and a friendly welcome), Plockton Hotel (views over the loch and a super place to stay), Sligachan Hotel (basic climbers' bar and plusher hotel side, back in these pages after a break), and Stein Inn on Skye (a terrific all-rounder). Our Scottish Dining Pub 2013 is Burts Hotel in Melrose.

APPLECROSS   NG7144   Map 11

Applecross Inn ★ ⇌

Off A896 S of Shieldaig; IV54 8LR

**Wonderfully remote pub on famously scenic route on west coast;
particularly friendly welcome, real ales and good seafood; bedrooms**

Getting to this waterside inn is quite an experience, with the
exhilarating drive over the pass of the cattle (Beallach na Ba) – one
of the highest in Britain; the sunsets can be stunning. The pub itself
is splendidly remote and tables in the nice shoreside garden enjoy
magnificent views across to the Cuillin Hills on Skye. The no-nonsense,
welcoming bar (extremely busy in high season with a good mix of
locals and visitors) has a woodburning stove, exposed stone walls and
upholstered pine furnishings on the stone floor; Isle of Skye Red Cuillin
and Skye Light on handpump and over 50 malt whiskies; pool (winter
only), TV, and board games; some disabled facilities. The alternative
route here, along the single-track lane winding round the coast from
just south of Shieldaig, has equally glorious sea loch and then sea views
nearly all the way. If you wish to stay here you might have to book well
in advance.

Much emphasis is placed on the top quality local fish and seafood dishes –
squat lobsters in garlic butter, oysters shucked to order, local prawns in hot
lemon, king scallops with crispy bacon, halibut with tarragon beurre blanc and so
forth, but they also offer sandwiches, haggis flamed in Drambuie, fresh haddock in
crispy batter, gammon and eggs, chicken green thai curry, venison casserole, and
puddings such as berry and apple crumble and raspberry cranachan on meringue
topped with praline. *Benchmark main dish: dressed crab salad with smoked
salmon £13.50. Two-course evening meal £22.00.*

Free house ~ Licensee Judith Fish ~ Real ale ~ Bar food (12-9) ~ (01520) 744262
~ Children welcome until 8.30pm ~ Dogs allowed in bar and bedrooms ~ Occasional
live traditional music ~ Open 11am-11.30pm(11.45 Sat); 12-11.30 Sun ~ Bedrooms:
£90B/£130B ~ www.applecross.uk.com *Recommended by Dave and Shirley Shaw, Mr and Mrs
M Stratton, the Dutchman, Kate Vogelsang, Malcolm Cox, Barry Collett*

EDINBURGH   NT2574   Map 11

Abbotsford ◖ £

Rose Street; E end, beside South St David Street; EH2 2PR

**Lively city pub with period features, changing beers, and bar and
restaurant food**

This handsome Edwardian pub was purpose built in 1902 and
remains virtually unaltered since its construction. Perched at its
centre, on a sea of red carpet, is a hefty highly polished Victorian
island bar ornately carved from dark spanish mahogany, serving up to
six changing real ales (on air pressure tall founts) from independent
Scottish brewers such as Fyne Ales, Harviestoun, Highland and
Stewart, and around 50 malt whiskies. At lunchtime you'll usually find
an eclectic mix of business people and locals occupying stools around
the bar and long wooden tables and leatherette benches running the
length of the dark wooden high-panelled walls. Above all this there's
a rather handsome green and gold plaster-moulded high ceiling. The
smarter upstairs restaurant, with its white tablecloths, black walls and
high ornate white ceilings, looks impressive too.

🍴 Bar food includes venison scotch egg, crispy duck salad, crab and salmon cakes, ploughman's, mushroom linguine, lemon grass and green chilli chicken, pork cassoulet, haddock and chips, beef and ale pie, and puddings such as apple and cinnamon filo and cheesecake. *Benchmark main dish: beef and ale pie £9.95. Two-course evening meal £15.50.*

Stewart ~ Licensee Daniel Jackson ~ Real ale ~ Bar food (12-9) ~ Restaurant (12-2.15, 5.30-9.30) ~ (0131) 225 5276 ~ Children in restaurant ~ Dogs allowed in bar ~ Open 11-11(midnight Fri, Sat); 12.30-11 Sun ~ www.theabbotsford.com
Recommended by Trystan Williams, Jeremy King, David and Sue Smith

EDINBURGH
Café Royal
NT2574   Map 11

West Register Street; EH2 2AA

Stunning listed interior, bustling atmosphere and rewarding food

To best appreciate the dazzling Victorian baroque interior of this opulent building, you might be better visiting after the lunchtime crush, when you're more likely to find a free table anyway. It was built in 1863, with no expense spared, by Robert Hume, who was a local plumber – needless to say the plumbing and gas fittings were state of the art. The floors and stairway are laid with marble, chandeliers hang from magnificent plasterwork ceilings, there is elegant stained glass, and the substantial island bar is graced by a carefully recreated gantry. The high-ceilinged viennese café-style rooms have a valuable series of detailed Doulton tilework portraits of historical innovators Watt, Faraday, Stephenson, Caxton, Benjamin Franklin and Robert Peel (forget police – his importance here is as the introducer of calico printing), and the stained glass in the restaurant is well worth a look. First class staff serve Caledonian Deuchars IPA and three guests from brewers such as Harviestoun, Inveralmond and Kelburn from handpumps, nice soft drinks, a decent choice of wines by the glass and 25 malt whiskies; background music and games machine.

🍴 Well liked food includes cullen skink, smoked salmon fishcake, game pâté with redcurrant and ginger chutney, sandwiches, mussels done several ways (and served by the half or whole kilo) and oysters (by the half dozen or dozen), beer-battered fish and chips, fish stew, asparagus and leek risotto, grilled bass, steak burger, and puddings such as crumble of the day, baked vanilla cheesecake with cherry compote and pear, raisin and butterscotch pudding. *Benchmark main dish: beef and ale pie £9.20. Two-course evening meal £14.30.*

Spirit ~ Manager Christine Annan ~ Real ale ~ Bar food (11(12.30 Sun)-10) ~ Restaurant ~ (0131) 556 1884 ~ Children welcome in restaurant till 10pm ~ Open 11-11(midnight Thurs, 1am Fri, Sat); 12.30-11 Sun ~ www.caferoyal.org.uk
Recommended by Dr and Mrs A K Clarke, Comus and Sarah Elliott, Barbarrick, Richard Tingle, Christine and Neil Townend, Barry Collett, Claes Mauroy, Michael Butler

EDINBURGH
Guildford Arms 🍴 £
NT2574   Map 11

West Register Street; EH2 2AA

Busy and friendly, with spectacular Victorian décor, a marvellous range of real ales and good food

The heart of this elaborately façaded, pub, purpose built in 1902, is opulently excessive, with ornate painted plasterwork on the lofty ceiling, heavy swagged velvet curtains, dark mahogany fittings and a busy patterned carpet. Tables and stools are lined up along the towering arched windows opposite the bar, where knowledgeable, efficient staff serve the fine range of ten quickly changing beers including Caledonian Deuchars IPA, Fyne Ales Jarl, Harviestoun Bitter & Twisted, Orkney Dark Gold, a beer from Stewarts and one from Highland, and all sorts of interesting guests from brewers such as Northumberland, Teignworthy and Thornbridge, on handpump; there are regular beer festivals. Also over a dozen wines by the glass, about 40 malt whiskies, a dozen rums and a dozen gins; board games, TV and background music. The snug little upstairs gallery restaurant, with strongly contrasting modern décor, gives a fine dress-circle view of the main bar (note the lovely old mirror decorated with two tigers on the way up).

Tasty food includes lunchtime open sandwiches, fish chowder, mussels, haggis, neeps and tatties, sautéed lambs kidneys and chorizo with onion and port sauce, seared scallops and black pudding and apple, steak pie, sausage and mash, grilled bass with creamed leeks, mushroom and spinach linguine, breaded haddock and chips, steak burger, steaks, mixed vegetable risotto and fillet medallions with tarragon butter. *Benchmark main dish: coq au vin with black pudding £14.80. Two-course evening meal £22.80.*

Stewart ~ Lease Steve Jackson ~ Real ale ~ Bar food (12-9.30(10 Fri, Sat)) ~ Restaurant (12(12.30 Sun)-2.30, 6-9.30(10 Fri, Sat)) ~ (0131) 556 4312 ~ Children welcome in upstairs gallery if dining ~ Live music nightly during Edinburgh Festival ~ Open 11-11(12 Fri and Sat); 12.30-11 Sun ~ www.guildfordarms.com
Recommended by Mrs Margo Finlay, Jörg Kasprowski, Janet and Peter Race, Barbarrick, Richard Tingle, Jeremy King, Claes Mauroy, David Hunt, Roger and Donna Huggins

EDINBURGH
NT2574   Map 11

Kays Bar £
Jamaica Street West; off India Street; EH3 6HF

Cosy, enjoyably chatty backstreet pub with an excellent choice of well kept beers

The interior of this cheery pub is unpretentious but warmly welcoming, with well worn red plush wall banquettes curving around cast-iron tables on red carpets, and red pillars supporting a red ceiling. It's simply decorated with big casks and vats arranged along the walls, old wine and spirits merchant notices and gas-type lamps. A quiet panelled back room (a bit like a library) leads off, with a narrow plank-panelled pitched ceiling and a collection of books ranging from dictionaries to ancient steam-train volumes for boys; there's a lovely coal fire in winter. The seven real ales include Caledonian Deuchars IPA and Theakstons Best, plus guests like Atlas (Orkney) Tempest, Cairngorm Trade Winds, Houston Texas, Summer Wine Apache and Timothy Taylors Landlord on handpump; they also stock more than 70 malt whiskies between eight and 50 years old, and ten blended whiskies. TV and board games. In days past, the pub was owned by John Kay, a whisky and wine merchant; wine barrels were hoisted up to the first floor and dispensed through pipes attached to nipples still visible around the light rose.

Very good value lunchtime food includes sandwiches, herring salad, haggis and neeps, mince and tatties, steak pie, chilli con carne, and beef or chicken curry. *Benchmark main dish: mince and potatoes £4.10. Two-course evening meal £6.20.*

Free house ~ Licensee David Mackenzie ~ Real ale ~ Bar food (12(12.30 Sun)-2.30)
~ (0131) 225 1858 ~ Dogs welcome ~ Open 11am-midnight(1am Sat); 12.30-11 Sun
~ www.kaysbar.co.uk *Recommended by Barbarrick, Peter F Marshall, John and Annabel
Hampshire, Roger and Donna Huggins*

GAIRLOCH   NG8075   Map 11
Old Inn ⚐ ◀

Just off A832/B8021; IV21 2BD

**Quietly positioned old inn specialising local fish and seafood;
good beers**

One of the main draws at this 18th-c inn is the good selection of beers,
which includes their own brews Blind Piper, Erradale, Flowerdale
and Slattadale, in addition to beers from An Teallach Atlas, Cairngorm
and Orkney breweries. Also quite a few fairly priced wines by the glass
and around 20 malt whiskies, too. The relaxed public bar is popular
with chatty locals and is quite traditional, with paintings, murals on
exposed stone walls and stools lined up along the counter and a warming
woodburner; board games, TV, fruit machine and juke box. The pub has
a charming waterside setting at the bottom of Flowerdale Glen, tucked
comfortably away from the road, and there are picnic-sets prettily placed
by the trees that line the stream that flows past under an old stone
bridge. Credit (but not debit) cards incur a surcharge of £1.75.

They have their own smokery producing smoked meats, fish and cheese, and
bake their own bread. As well as fresh local fish and game, such as scallops,
mussels, haddock, crab, lobster, pheasant and venison, the tasty food includes
sandwiches, cullen skink, vegetable tagine, braised pork belly on puy lentil broth,
quite a few pies and pizzas, daily specials such as smoked haddock risotto, grilled
chicken breast with cheese and whisky sauce, and puddings such as vanilla
cheesecake, clootie dumpling and raspberry cranachan crêpe. *Benchmark main
dish: fish and chips £9.95. Two-course evening meal £16.80.*

Own brew ~ Licensees Alastair and Ute Pearson ~ Real ale ~ Bar food (12-3, 5-9) ~
Restaurant ~ (01445) 712006 ~ Children welcome ~ Dogs allowed in bar and bedrooms
~ Live music Fri evening ~ Open 11(12 Sun)-11 ~ Bedrooms: £60B/£104B ~
www.theoldinn.net *Recommended by Richard Gibbs*

GLASGOW   NS5965   Map 11
Babbity Bowster ⊕ ⚐

Blackfriars Street; G1 1PE

**A Glasgow institution: friendly, comfortable and sometimes lively mix
of traditional and modern, with a continental feel; good food**

Genuinely welcoming and often lively, this 18th-c city-centre pub is a
sprightly blend of both scottish and continental, and traditional and
modern. The simply decorated light interior has fine tall windows, well
lit photographs and big pen-and-wash drawings of the city, its people
and musicians, dark grey stools and wall seats around dark grey tables
on stripped wooden floorboards, and a peat fire. The bar opens on to
a pleasant terrace with tables under cocktail parasols, trellised vines
and shrubs; they may have barbecues out here in summer. Caledonian
Deuchars IPA, Kelburn Misty Law and guests such as Fyne Ales Jarl and
Harviestoun Schiehallion on air pressure tall fount, and a remarkably
sound collection of wines and malt whiskies; good tea and coffee, too.
On Saturday evenings, they have live traditional scottish music, while

at other times games of boules are in progress outside. Note that the bedroom price is for the room only.

 Enjoyable food at fair prices from a short bar menu includes sandwiches, west coast oysters, mussels in a creamy curry sauce, haggis, neeps and tatties, mushroom and spinach lasagne, a pie of the day, and daily specials; the more elaborate choices in the airy upstairs restaurant might include wild mushroom risotto, duck breast with a whisky and orange sauce, corn-fed chicken with white pudding and a creamy wild mushroom sauce, and puddings like dark and white chocolate mousse and caramelised lemon tart. They also offer three-course set menus. *Benchmark main dish: cullen skink £5.75. Two-course evening meal £15.75.*

Free house ~ Licensee Fraser Laurie ~ Real ale ~ Bar food (12-10) ~ Restaurant ~ (0141) 552 5055 ~ Children welcome if eating ~ Live traditional music on Sat ~ Open 11am(12.30 Sun)-midnight ~ Bedrooms: £45S/£60S ~ www.babbitybowster.com
Recommended by Peter F Marshall, Theocsbrian, Comus and Sarah Elliott

GLASGOW   NS5765   Map 11
Bon Accord ▩ £
North Street; G3 7DA

Fabulous choice of drinks, with an impressive range of whiskies, ten real ales, a good welcome and bargain food

The friendly landlord at this welcoming pub is rightly proud of the incredible range of drinks he stocks here. Ten daily changing beers (they can get through around 1,000 a year), sourced from breweries around Britain, are served from swan-necked handpumps. They also have continental bottled beers, a farm cider and, in a remarkable display behind the counter, 270 malt whiskies and lots of gins, vodkas and rums. Staff are knowledgeable so do ask for help if you need it. The several linked traditional bars are warmly understated with cream or terracotta walls, a mix of chairs and tables, a leather sofa and plenty of bar stools on polished bare boards or carpet, and a happy mix of customers; TV, background music and board games. There are circular picnic-sets on a small terrace with modern tables and chairs out in front.

 Extremely good value bar food includes soup, cod goujons, peppered mushrooms, fish and chips, scampi, cajun chicken, macaroni cheese, lasagne, all day breakfast, curry, burgers, and puddings such as apple pie and clootie dumpling. *Benchmark main dish: steak pie £4.95. Two-course evening meal £9.50.*

Free house ~ Licensee Paul McDonagh ~ Real ale ~ Bar food (12(12.30 Sun)-8) ~ (0141) 248 4427 ~ Children welcome until 8pm ~ Quiz night Weds, live band Sat ~ Open 11(12.30 Sun)-midnight ~ www.bonaccordweb.co.uk *Recommended by Barry Collett, Ian Barker*

HOUSTON   NS4066   Map 11
Fox & Hounds ♀ ▩
South Street at junction with Main Street (B789, off B790 at Langbank signpost E of Bridge of Weir); PA6 7EN

Village pub with award-winning beers from own brewery and tasty food

This 18th-c pub – now run by the second generation of the same friendly family – is most notable as the home to the Houston Brewery, and their beers are as popular as ever. The six constantly changing ales include a guest beer plus their own Barochan, Killellan, Peters Well and Warlock Stout – you can look through a window in the bar to the little brewery where they are produced. They hold a couple of Best of Scotland beer festivals during the summer. You can try a fantastic choice of other drinks, too, including more than 100 malt whiskies, a dozen wines by the glass, 12 rums and 12 gins. The clean, plush, hunting-theme lounge has beams, comfortable seats by a fire and polished brass and copper; background music. Popular with a younger crowd, the lively downstairs bar has a large-screen TV, pool, juke box and fruit machines. At the back is a covered and heated area with decking.

🍽 Served upstairs (downstairs they only do substantial sandwiches), the food includes scallops with black pudding, streaky bacon and chive cream, mussels in a spicy tomato sauce, chicken liver pâté with cranberry, beef burger with bacon, cheese and onion rings, steak and mushroom in ale pie, sausages of the day with onion gravy, beer-battered fresh scampi tails, haggis, neeps and tatties with whisky cream, slow-braised lamb shoulder with red wine and rosemary, and 28-day hung steaks; they also offer a two-course lunch and early evening menu. *Benchmark main dish: steak frites £11.00. Two-course evening meal £18.00.*

Own brew ~ Licensee Jonathan Wengel ~ Real ale ~ Bar food (12-10(9 Sun)) ~ Restaurant ~ (01505) 612448 ~ Children welcome ~ Dogs allowed in bar ~ Open 11am-midnight(1am Sat); 12-12 Sun ~ www.foxandhoundshouston.co.uk *Recommended by Martin and Sue Day, Barry Collett*

ISLE OF WHITHORN
Steam Packet ♀ 🛏

NX4736 Map 9

Harbour Row; DG8 8LL

Waterside views from this friendly family-run inn with five real ales and tasty pubby food; bedrooms

This modernised inn is enchantingly placed on a quay overlooking a picturesque harbour at the southernmost tip of the Machars peninsula. Big picture windows have fine views out over the busy throng of yachts and fishing boats and then beyond to calmer waters; several bedrooms look over the water, too. It's a welcoming, family-run place. The comfortable low-ceilinged bar is split into two: on the right, plush button-back banquettes and boat pictures, and on the left, green leatherette stools around cast-iron framed tables on big stone floor tiles and a woodburning stove in the bare stone wall. Bar food can be served in the lower beamed dining room, which has excellent colour wildlife photographs, rugs on its wooden floor and a solid fuel stove, and there's also a small eating area off the lounge bar, as well as a conservatory. Timothy Taylors Landlord and guest beers from brewers such as Ayr, Cairngorm and Orkney on handpump, quite a few malt whiskies and a good wine list; TV and pool. There are white tables and chairs in the garden. You can walk from here up to the remains of St Ninian's kirk, on a headland behind the village.

🍽 Quite a choice of bar food might include lunchtime sandwiches, baguettes and baked potatoes, starters such as garlic mushrooms, mussels in cream and white wine sauce, nachos, scampi, chicken stir fry, gammon, egg and chips, aberdeen angus burger, chilli, braised lamb shank, breaded haddock, and puddings such as jam sponge and apple crumble. *Benchmark main dish: beer-battered fish and chips £10.95. Two-course evening meal £17.10.*

Free house ~ Licensee Alastair Scoular ~ Real ale ~ Bar food (12-2, 6.30-9) ~ Restaurant ~ (01988) 500334 ~ Children welcome ~ Dogs allowed in bar and bedrooms

~ Open 11-11(12 Sat); 12-12 Sun; 11-3, 6-11 Tues-Thurs in winter ~ Bedrooms: /£40B ~
www.steampacketinn.biz *Recommended by Dr A McCormick, Norma and Noel Thomas, John and Angie Millar, John and Sylvia Harrop, the Didler*

KIRK YETHOLM

Border

NT8328   Map 10

Village signposted off B6352/B6401 crossroads, SE of Kelso; The Green; TD5 8PQ

Welcoming, comfortable hotel with good interesting food, several real ales, attentive staff and bedrooms – and a renowned objective for walkers

A s well as being a comfortable and enjoyable place to stay, this is a genuinely friendly inn with a warm welcome for all. The cheerfully unpretentious bar (refurbished this year) has beams and flagstones, a log fire, a signed photograph of Wainwright and other souvenirs of the Pennine Way, and appropriate Borders scenery etchings and murals; snug side rooms lead off. A beer named for the pub from Broughton, Scottish Borders Game Bird and a changing guest on handpump, a farm cider (summer only), several malt whiskies and gins, and ten decent wines by the glass. There's also a spacious dining room with fishing themed decor, a comfortable lounge with a second log fire and a neat conservatory (also refurbished this year); background music, TV, and board games. A sheltered back terrace has picnic-sets and a play area, and the colourful window boxes and floral tubs are very pretty. The author of the classic guide to the Pennine Way, Alfred Wainwright, was keen to reward anyone who walked the entire length of the trail with a free drink. He left some money here to cover the cost, but it has long since run out, and the pub now generously foots the bill. There's a water bowl for dogs.

From local suppliers named on the menu, the good, enjoyable food includes lunchtime sandwiches, chicken liver parfait with red onion jam, queen scallops with black pudding and crispy bacon on minted pea purée, wild mushroom, spinach and tarragon en croûte, pork and leek sausages with red onion gravy and mash, beer-battered fish and chips with mushy peas, steak and kidney pudding, specials like field mushrooms stuffed with haggis and topped with whisky sauce and hake fillet with saffron sauce and asparagus, and puddings. *Benchmark main dish: slow-braised lamb shoulder £14.95. Two-course evening meal £16.50.*

Free house ~ Licensees Philip and Margaret Blackburn ~ Real ale ~ Bar food (12-2, 6-9) ~ Restaurant ~ (01573) 420237 ~ Children welcome away from public bar ~ Dogs allowed in bar and bedrooms ~ Open 11.30-11; may close earlier in winter if quiet ~ Bedrooms: £45B/£80B ~ www.theborderhotel.com *Recommended by C A Hall, M Mossman, the Didler, Donna Jenkins, Pat and Stewart Gordon, John and Anne Mackinnon*

MELROSE

Burts Hotel

NT5433   Map 9

B6374, Market Square; TD6 9PL
Scotland Dining Pub of the Year

Nicely kept town-centre hotel with interesting food and lots of malt whiskies

T he bedrooms at this civilised family run hotel, though quite small, are immaculate and comfortably decorated, and the breakfasts are good, too. Neat public areas are maintained with equal attention to detail. The welcoming red-carpeted bar has tidy pub tables between cushioned wall seats and windsor armchairs, a warming fire, scottish prints on pale green walls and a long dark wood counter serving Timothy Taylors Landlord and a guest such as Scottish Borders Game Bird on handpump, several wines by the glass from a good list, a farm cider and around 80 malt whiskies. The elegant restaurant with its swagged curtains, dark blue wallpaper and tables laid with white linen offers a smarter dining experience. Service here is particularly helpful and polite with staff well led by the hands-on licensees. In summer you can sit out in the well tended garden, and the ruins of Melrose Abbey are within strolling distance.

Good food includes lamb meatloaf with redcurrant jelly, crab cakes with pickled cucumber and horseradish cream, smoked haddock, leek, potato and cauliflower crumble, battered haddock, venison burger, moroccan lamb shank, chicken breast stuffed with haggis with grain mustard sauce, pork and apple sausages and mash, chicken caesar salad, crispy duck breast with red onion tart and thyme jus, aubergine and vegetable moussaka, and puddings such as warm spiced pear tart with cinnamon jelly, assiette of chocolate desserts and sticky toffee pudding. *Benchmark main dish: fish and chips £11.35. Two-course evening meal £18.40.*

Free house ~ Licensees Graham and Nick Henderson ~ Real ale ~ Bar food (12-2, 6-9.30) ~ Restaurant ~ (01896) 822285 ~ Children welcome ~ Dogs allowed in bar and bedrooms ~ Open 11(12 Sun)-2.30, 5(6 Sun)-11; closed 3-8 Jan ~ Bedrooms: £72B/£133B ~ www.burtshotel.co.uk *Recommended by Comus and Sarah Elliott, Donna Jenkins, Gordon and Margaret Ormondroyd*

PITLOCHRY
Moulin 🍺 £

NN9459   Map 11

Kirkmichael Road, Moulin; A924 NE of Pitlochry centre; PH16 5EH

Attractive 17th-c inn with own-brewed beers and a nicely pubby bar; comfortable bedrooms

Reasonably priced food and four own-brew beers ensure the popularity of this enjoyably bustling pub. The beers (Ale of Atholl, Braveheart, Light and the stronger Old Remedial) are brewed in the little stables across the street and served on handpump. They also keep around 40 malt whiskies and a good choice of wines by the glass and carafe. Although much extended over the years, the lively bar, in the oldest part of the building, still feels like an entity in itself, nicely down to earth and pubby and with plenty of traditional character. Above the fireplace in the smaller bare boarded room is an interesting painting of the village before the road was built (Moulin used to be a bustling market town, far busier than upstart Pitlochry), while the bigger carpeted area has a good few tables and cushioned banquettes in little booths divided by stained-glass country scenes, another big fireplace, some exposed stonework, fresh flowers, antique golf clubs, and local and sporting prints around the walls; bar billiards, board games and a 1960s one arm bandit; there's also a restaurant. On a gravelled area surrounded by tubs of flowers, picnic-sets outside look across to the village kirk; there are excellent walks nearby.

Well liked traditional food, using local fish and game, includes French onion soup, tomato and aubergine tartlet, fried haggis, venison terrine, fish and chips, haggis, neeps and tatties, chicken breast with mustard cream sauce, salmon steak with lemon and herb butter, seafood pancake, lamb shank with rosemary gravy, game casserole, macaroni cheese, stuffed peppers, and puddings such as apple pie, honey sponge and custard and whisky fudge cake. *Benchmark main dish: steak and ale pie £9.25. Two-course evening meal £17.20.*

Own brew ~ Licensee Heather Reeves ~ Real ale ~ Bar food (12-9.30) ~ Restaurant ~ (01796) 472196 ~ Children welcome till 8pm ~ Dogs allowed in bar ~ Open 11(12 Sun)-11 ~ Bedrooms: £57B/£72B ~ www.moulinhotel.co.uk *Recommended by Pat and Stewart Gordon, Barry Collett, Claes Mauroy, Brian and Anna Marsden*

 PLOCKTON   NG8033   Map 11
Plockton Hotel ★
Village signposted from A87 near Kyle of Lochalsh; IV52 8TN

Lovely views from this family-run lochside hotel with very good food and real ales; bedrooms

This enjoyable family-owned hotel is in the centre of a lovely National Trust for Scotland village and part of a long, low terrace of stone-built houses. It's a great place for a break (it's worth booking well ahead), with most of the comfortable bedrooms in the adjacent building. Half of them have extraordinary views over the loch and the rest, some with balconies, over the hillside garden; good breakfasts. The welcoming comfortably furnished lounge bar has window seats looking out to the boats on the water, as well as antiqued dark red leather seating around neat Regency-style tables on a tartan carpet, three model ships set into the woodwork and partly panelled stone walls. The separate public bar has pool, board games, TV, a games machine and background music. Two real ales might be from breweries like Hebridean, Houston, Orkney or Plockton and are served on handpump, 30 malt whiskies and several wines by the glass. Tables in the front garden look out past the village's trademark palm trees and colourful shrub-lined shore and across the sheltered anchorage to the rugged mountain surrounds of Loch Carron; a stream runs down the hill into a pond in the attractive back garden. There's a hotel nearby called the Plockton, so don't get the two confused.

Especially strong on fresh local seafood, the tasty food includes lunchtime toasted paninis, haggis and a tot of whisky, whisky pâté, cream of smoked fish soup, seafood bake, burger, haggis, neeps and tatties, fish and chips, baked monkfish fillet wrapped in streaky bacon, seafood platter, fried herring in oatmeal, venison casserole, chicken stuffed with smoked ham and cheese with sun-dried tomato, garlic and basil sauce and langoustines. *Benchmark main dish: fish and chips £9.50. Two-course evening meal £15.20.*

Free house ~ Licensee Alan Pearson ~ Real ale ~ Bar food (12-2.15, 6-9) ~ Restaurant ~ (01599) 544274 ~ Children welcome ~ Dogs allowed in bar ~ Local musicians Weds evening ~ Open 11-12(11.30 Sat); 12.30-11 Sun ~ Bedrooms: £55B/£130B ~ www.plocktonhotel.co.uk *Recommended by Joan and Tony Walker, M J Winterton, Peter and Jackie Barnett, T Harrison, Les and Sandra Brown, Dr Peter Crawshaw, Walter and Susan Rinaldi-Butcher,*

 SHIELDAIG   NG8153   Map 11
Tigh an Eilean Hotel
Village signposted just off A896 Lochcarron–Gairloch; IV54 8XN

Separate, contemporary bar of stunningly set hotel with exceptional views, real ales, and enjoyable food; tranquil bedrooms

Tables outside this friendly hotel are in a sheltered little courtyard well placed to enjoy the gorgeous position at the head of Loch

Shieldaig, which is beneath some of the most dramatic of all the highland peaks; if you are lucky, you might spot sea eagles – as well as seals and other bird life. It's all very bright and attractive; the bar, separate from the hotel, is on two storeys with an open staircase; dining on the first floor and a decked balcony with a magnificent loch and village view. It's gently contemporary and nicely relaxed with timbered floors, timber-boarded walls, shiny bolts through exposed timber roof beams, and an open kitchen. An Teallach Saeol Mor and Tachallach on handpump and up to a dozen wines by the glass; board games, pool, TV, darts, wi-fi and background music. Next door, the bedrooms are comfortable and peaceful.

With much emphasis on the delicious local fish and seafood, there might be sandwiches, seafood chowder, mussels roasted in their wood-fired oven, light lunches of crab cakes with lemon mayonnaise or haggis, neeps and tatties, blue cheese and vine tomato tart, venison sausages and mash, hand-made pizzas (again, from the wood-fired oven), specials like local oysters and langoustines grilled with garlic butter, and puddings such as clootie dumpling and vanilla crème brûlée. *Benchmark main dish: seafood stew £16.00. Two-course evening meal £18.50.*

Free house ~ Licensee Cathryn Field ~ Real ale ~ Bar food (12-9; 12-2.30, 6-9 in winter) ~ Restaurant ~ (01520) 755251 ~ Children welcome ~ Dogs allowed in bar and bedrooms ~ Traditional live folk music some weekends and holidays ~ Open 11-11(midnight Fri, 1am Sat) ~ Bedrooms: £75B/£150B ~ www.tighaneilean.co.uk *Recommended by Mr and Mrs M Stratton, the Dutchman, T Harrison*

SLIGACHAN
Sligachan Hotel 🛏 🍺

NG4930 Map 11

A87 Broadford–Portree, junction with A863; IV47 8SW

Summer-opening mountain hotel in the Cuillins with walkers' bar and plusher side, food all day, impressive range of whiskies and useful children's play area

'If I was descending from the Cuillins after an exhausting day of walking I would like to know this place was waiting for me,' says one reader, who thoroughly enjoyed his visit here. The huge modern pine-clad main bar, falling somewhere between a basic climbers' bar and a plusher, more sedate hotel side, is spaciously open to its ceiling rafters and has geometrically laid out dark tables and chairs on neat carpets; pool. The splendid range of 350 malt whiskies makes a most impressive display behind one end of the bar counter, where they keep their own Cuillin Black Face, Eagle, Glamaig, Pinnacle and Skye and a scottish guest beer on handpump. It can get quite lively in here some nights, but there's a more sedate lounge bar with leather bucket armchairs on plush carpets and a coal fire; background highland and islands music. A feature here is the little museum charting the history of the island, and children should be delighted with the big play area, which can be watched from the bar. There are tables out in a garden, and as well as self-catering accommodation there's a campsite with caravan hook-ups across the road. Dogs are only allowed in this main bar and not in the hotel's cocktail bar.

As well as sandwiches, the hearty food might include cullen skink, venison pâté with cranberry jelly, mushroom risotto with sweet potato purée, pies such as chicken and tarragon or beef and mushroom, scampi and chips, bacon-wrapped chicken stuffed with cream cheese and garlic with a creamy thyme sauce, chargrilled rack of lamb with red wine jus, and puddings such as rhubarb and apple crumble with custard and sticky toffee pudding; more elaborate meals in hotel restaurant. *Benchmark main dish: beer-battered haddock with tartare sauce £9.50. Two-course evening meal £16.30.*

Own brew ~ Licensee Sandy Coghill ~ Real ale ~ Bar food (8am-11pm) ~ Restaurant ~ (01478) 650204 ~ Children welcome ~ Dogs allowed in bar ~ Open 8am-midnight; 11-11 Sun; closed Nov-Feb (for the hotel side); the separate attached pubby bar is closed beg Oct-some time in May – best to phone ~ Bedrooms: £55S/£110S ~ www.sligachan.co.uk
Recommended by C A Bryson, Phil Bryant

STEIN

NG2656   Map 11

Stein Inn

End of B886 N of Dunvegan in Waternish, off A850 Dunvegan–Portree; OS Sheet 23 map reference 263564; IV55 8GA

Lovely setting on northern corner of Skye, welcoming 18th-c inn with good, simple food and lots of whiskies; a rewarding place to stay

Standing just above a sheltered inlet on the island's west side with views out to the Hebrides and quite glorious sunsets, this is Skye's oldest inn. All the bedrooms have sea views and breakfasts are good – it's well worth pre-ordering the tasty smoked kippers if you stay. On inclement days, the unpretentious original public bar is cosy, with great character in its sturdy country furnishings, flagstones, beam and plank ceiling, partly panelled stripped-stone walls and warming double-sided stove between the two rooms. There's a games area with pool table, darts, board games, dominoes and cribbage, and there may be background music. Caledonian Deuchars IPA and a couple of local guests such as Isle of Skye Red Cuillin and Caledonian Flying Scotsman on handpump, a dozen wines by the glass and over 125 malt whiskies. Good service from smartly uniformed staff. There's a lively children's inside play area and showers for yachtsmen.

Using local fish and highland meat, the short menu of good, simple and very sensibly priced food might include pumpkin soup, fried scallops, fried camembert with raspberry coulis, peat-smoked salmon, bass fillet with garlic butter, venison pie, pork chop with apple sauce, courgette and mushroom tagliatelli, langoustines, and puddings such as apple and butterscotch crumble and blueberry cranachan. *Benchmark main dish: battered haddock £10.50. Two-course evening meal £16.30.*

Free house ~ Licensees Angus and Teresa Mcghie ~ Real ale ~ Bar food (12(12.30 Sun)-4, 6-9.30(9 in winter)) ~ (01470) 592362 ~ Children welcome ~ Dogs allowed in bar and bedrooms ~ Open 11-midnight; 11.30-11 Sun; 12-11(winter weekdays, till midnight winter Sat); 12.30-11 winter Sun ~ Bedrooms: £43S/£74S(£110B) ~ www.steininn.co.uk
Recommended by C A Bryson, T Harrison, Joan and Tony Walker, Claes Mauroy, Phil Bryant, Walter and Susan Rinaldi-Butcher, Jane and Alan Bush

SWINTON

NT8347   Map 10

Wheatsheaf ⑪ ⑦ 🛏

A6112 N of Coldstream; TD11 3JJ

Civilised restaurant-with-rooms, small bar for drinkers, comfortable lounges, quite a choice of food, good selection of drinks and professional service; comfortable bedrooms

In a pretty Borders village surrounded by rolling countryside, this is a civilised place. Most of the emphasis is on the well equipped and comfortable bedrooms and the highly thought of food, but there is a little bar and informal lounges and they do keep Caledonian Deuchars IPA on handpump, alongside 40 malt whiskies and a dozen wines by the glass. There are comfortable plush armchairs and sofas, several nice old oak settles with cushions, a little open fire, sporting prints and china plates on the bottle-green walls in the bar and small agricultural prints and fishing-theme décor on the stone walls of the lounges. Cushioned bamboo and barley-twist dining chairs surround pale wood tables set with fresh flowers in the carpeted dining room and front conservatory, with its vaulted pine ceiling, and black leather high-backed dining chairs are teamed with linen-dressed tables in the more formal restaurant; background music. The River Tweed is just a few miles away.

As well as a good value two- and three-course set lunch menus (weekends only) and bar dishes such as a club sandwich, beef burger with blue cheese or bacon toppings, steak in ale pie and fish and chips, the more elaborate evening choices might include a warm salad of rabbit stuffed with haggis and confit leg with candied beetroot, crab cakes with sweet chilli sauce, goats cheese gnocchi and wild mushroom fricassée with truffle oil, corn-fed chicken filled with mozzarella and sun-dried tomatoes wrapped in smoked pancetta with a vine cherry tomato sauce, and puddings like glazed lemon tart with raspberry sorbet and Malteser cheesecake with passion fruit coulis. *Benchmark main dish: steak and ale pie £11.95. Two-course evening meal £23.00.*

Free house ~ Licensees Chris and Jan Winson ~ Real ale ~ Bar food (6-9 weekdays; 12-3, 6-9 Sat and Sun, not weekday lunchtimes) ~ Restaurant ~ (01890) 860257 ~ No children under 10 in evenings ~ Open 4-11; 11am-midnight Sat; 11am-10pm Sun; closed weekday lunchtimes ~ Bedrooms: £79B/£119B ~ www.wheatsheaf-swinton.co.uk
Recommended by Ian and Helen Stafford, Mike and Hilary Doupe, Ian Phillips

WEEM
NN8449   Map 11
Ailean Chraggan ☻
B846; PH15 2LD

Changing range of well sourced creative food in homely, family-run hotel

The two acres of ground belonging to this family-run hotel is lovely, and there are great views from the two flower-filled front terraces to the mountains beyond the Tay and up to Ben Lawers – the highest peak in this part of Scotland; the owners can arrange fishing nearby. The simple bar has plenty of chatty locals, a couple of beers from the local Inveralmond Brewery on handpump, over 100 malt whiskies and a very good wine list. There's also an adjoining neatly old-fashioned dining room. Winter darts and board games; homely bedrooms and good breakfasts.

As well as lunchtime sandwiches, the changing menu, served in either the comfortably carpeted modern lounge or the dining room, might include sweet potato and coconut soup, cullen skink, venison, pistachio and prune terrine, asparagus wrapped in parma ham with hollandaise sauce, grilled scallops, lamb shank, chicken schnitzel, roasted pork belly with apple and thyme jus, broad bean and cep risotto, and puddings such as mango mousse with strawberry ice-cream, chocolate baked cheesecake and chocolate baked alaska with Drambuie sauce. *Benchmark main dish: fried bass with pesto £13.45. Two-course evening meal £17.00.*

Free house ~ Licensee Alastair Gillespie ~ Real ale ~ Bar food (12-2, 5.30-8.30(9 Fri and Sat)) ~ Restaurant ~ (01887) 820346 ~ Children welcome ~ Dogs allowed in bar and bedrooms ~ Open 11-11 ~ Bedrooms: £53.75B/£107.50B ~ www.aileanchraggan.co.uk
Recommended by Les and Sandra Brown, Roger and Gill Walker, Susan and John Douglas

Also Worth a Visit in Scotland

Besides the fully inspected pubs, you might like to try these pubs that have been recommended to us and described by readers. Do tell us what you think of them: feedback@goodguides.com

ABERDEENSHIRE

ABERDEEN
Grill (01224) 573530 — NJ9305
Union Street; AB11 6BA Don't be put off by the exterior of this traditional 19th-c local, long bare-boards bar with fine plaster ceiling, mahogany panelling and original leather banquettes, over 500 whiskies (some distilled in the 1930s), five well kept ales including Caledonian 80/- and Harviestoun Bitter & Twisted, basic snacks; no children or dogs; open all day (till 1am Fri, Sat). *(Mike and Lynn Robinson)*

ABERDEEN
Old Blackfriars (01224) 581922 — NJ9406
Castle Street; AB11 5BB Welcoming and cosy ancient building on two levels, several well kept mainly scottish beers, enjoyable interesting food, good service, plenty of character; open all day. *(David Hills)*

ABERDEEN
★**Prince of Wales** (01224) 640597 — NJ9406
St Nicholas Lane; AB10 1HF Eight changing ales from individual and convivial old tavern's very long bar counter, bargain hearty food, painted floorboards, flagstones or carpet, pews and screened booths, original tiled spitoon running length of bar; games machines; children over 5 welcome if eating, open all day from 10am (11am Sun). *(Mike and Lynn Robinson, Christine and Neil Townend)*

ABOYNE
★**Boat** (01339) 886137 — NO5298
Charlestown Road (B968, just off A93); AB34 5EL Friendly country inn with fine views across River Dee, partly carpeted bar with model train chugging its way around just below ceiling height, scottish pictures, brasses and woodburner in stone fireplace, games in public-bar end, spiral stairs up to roomy additional dining area, three well kept ales such as Belhaven, Deeside and Inveralmond, some 30 malts, tasty bar food from sandwiches up, more elaborate seasonal evening menu; background music, games machine; children welcome, dogs in bar, six comfortable well equipped bedrooms, open all day. *(J F M and M West, Christine and Neil Townend, the Dutchman, Michael and Maggie Betton)*

BALLATER
Alexandra (01339) 755376 — NO3795
Bridge Square; AB35 5QJ Simple clean bar popular with locals, well kept Belhaven and decent wine by the glass, enjoyable food including good toasted panini, old photographs; near River Dee, open all day. *(J F M and M West)*

CRATHIE
Inver (01339) 742345 — NO2293
A93 Balmoral–Braemar; AB35 5XN Friendly chatty family-run 18th-c inn by River Dee, comfortable bar areas with log fires, some stripped stone and good solid furnishings including leather sofas, enjoyable fresh home-made food cooked by landlord, decent wines by the glass, lots of whiskies, may be a real ale in summer, restaurant; comfortable bedrooms, closed Mon and Tues lunchtimes. *(J F M and M West)*

OLDMELDRUM
Redgarth (01651) 872353 — NJ8127
Kirk Brae; AB51 0DJ Good-sized comfortable lounge with traditional décor and subdued lighting, three well kept real ales, good range of malt whiskies, popular reasonably priced food, pleasant attentive service, restaurant; gorgeous views to Bennachie, bedrooms (get booked quickly). *(David and Betty Gittins)*

ANGUS

BROUGHTY FERRY
★**Fishermans Tavern** (01382) 775941 — NO4630
Fort Street; turning off shore road; DD5 2AD Once a row of fishermen's cottages, this friendly unchanging pub is just steps from the beach, six well kept changing ales (May beer festival) and good range of malt whiskies, secluded lounge area with coal fire, small carpeted snug with basket-weave wall panels, another fire in back bar popular with diners for the reasonably priced pubby food, fiddle music Thurs night from 10pm, Mon quiz; TV, fruit machine; children and dogs welcome, disabled facilities, tables on front pavement, more in secluded walled garden, bedrooms, open all day (till 1am Thurs-Sat). *(Christine and Neil Townend, Susan and John Douglas)*

ARGYLL

BRIDGE OF ORCHY   NN2939

⋆ Bridge of Orchy Hotel

(01838) 400208 *A82 Tyndrum–Glencoe;
PA36 4AB* Spectacular spot on West
Highland Way, very welcoming with good
fairly priced food in bar and restaurant,
decent choice of well kept ales, house wines
and malt whiskies, interesting mountain
photographs; ten good bedrooms, riverside
bunkhouse. *(Michael and Maggie Betton)*

CONNEL   NM9034

Oyster (01631) 710666

A85, W of Connel Bridge; PA37 1PJ
18th-c pub opposite former ferry slipway,
lovely view across the water (especially
at sunset), decent-sized bar with friendly
Highland atmosphere, log fire in stone
fireplace, enjoyable food including good
local seafood, Caledonian Deuchars IPA,
good range of wines and malts, attentive
service; sports TV, pool and darts; modern
hotel part next door with separate evening
restaurant. *(Richard J Holloway)*

GLENCOE   NN1058

⋆ Clachaig (01855) 811252

*Old Glencoe Road, behind NTS Visitor
Centre; PH49 4HX* In scenic grandeur of
Glencoe and loved by hikers and climbers;
log-fire Boots Bar with half a dozen changing
scottish ales and 180 malt whiskies, pine-
panelled slate-floored snug, lounge (children
allowed here) with mix of dining chairs and
leather sofas, photographs signed by famous
climbers, tasty bar food; background music,
live bands most Sat evenings, TV, games
machine, pool; dogs welcome, bedrooms and
self-catering, open all day. *(Stanley and Annie
Matthews, Brian and Anna Marsden)*

INVERARAY   NN0908

⋆ George (01499) 302111

Main Street east; PA32 8TT Very popular
Georgian hotel (packed during holiday
times) at hub of this appealing small town;
bustling pubby bar with exposed joists, bare
stone walls, old tiles and big flagstones,
antique settles, carved wooden benches
and cushioned stone slabs along the walls,
four log fires, ales such as Belhaven, 100
malt whiskies, nice food in bar and smarter
restaurant, live entertainment Fri, Sat;
children and dogs welcome, well laid-out
terraces with plenty of seats, bedrooms,
Inveraray Castle and walks close by, open all
day till 1am. *(Roger and Gill Walker)*

OTTER FERRY   NR9384

Oystercatcher (01700) 821229

B8000; PA21 2DH Friendly family-run
pub/restaurant in old building in outstanding
spot overlooking Loch Fyne, good locally
sourced food, well kept ales from pine-clad bar
including Fyne, decent wine list; lots of tables
out on spit, free moorings. *(Lindsay White)*

AYRSHIRE

SYMINGTON   NS3831

Wheatsheaf (01563) 830307

*Just off A77 Ayr–Kilmarnock; Main
Street; KA1 5QB* Former 17th-c posting
inn in quiet pretty village, charming and
cosy, two dining rooms with wide choice of
consistently good food served all day (must
book weekends), quick friendly service,
racehorse décor, log fire; keg beers; children
welcome, attractively set tables outside, open
all day. *(Deryn Mitchell, M Rowley)*

BERWICKSHIRE

ALLANTON   NT8654

Allanton Inn (01890) 818260

B6347 S of Chirnside; TD11 3JZ
Pretty stone-built village inn, light and airy,
with welcoming new owners, good fairly
priced food (including fresh fish) from daily
changing menu, a couple of real ales, good
wine list, log fire in small attractive side
dining room; children welcome, sheltered
garden behind, six bedrooms, open all
day. *(Simon Daws, Comus and Sarah Elliott)*

BERWICKSHIRE

AUCHENCROW   NT8560

Craw (01890) 761253

*B6438 NE of Duns; pub signed off A1;
TD14 5LS* Attractive little 18th-c pub in
row of cream-washed slate-roofed cottages,
welcoming courteous landlord, good well
presented food including fresh fish and
seafood, changing ales from smaller brewers,
good wines by the glass, beams decorated
with hundreds of beer mats, pictures on
panelled walls, woodburner, more formal
back restaurant; children welcome, tables
on decking behind and out on village
green, three bedrooms, open all day
weekends. *(Marlene and Jim Godfrey, Robbie
Pennington, GSB)*

LAUDER   NT5347

Black Bull (01578) 722208

Market Place; TD2 6SR Comfortable
17th-c inn with cosy rustic-feel bar, lots
of fishing cartoons and country scenes on
panelled walls, ales such as Caledonian
Deuchars IPA and Timothy Taylors Landlord,
food from good sandwiches up, efficient
service, Weds folk night; children welcome,
bedrooms, open all day. *(the Dutchman)*

There are report forms at the back of the book.

CAITHNESS

MEY   ND2872
Castle Arms (01847) 851244
A836; KW14 8XH 19th-c former coaching
inn with good food and friendly helpful
service, plenty of malt whiskies, lounge with
photographs of the Queen Mother during her
Caithness holidays, views of Dunnet Head
and across Pentland Firth to the Orkneys;
eight bedrooms in back extension, well
placed for N coast of Caithness, Gills Bay
ferry and Castle of Mey. *(Dave Braisted)*

DUMFRIESSHIRE

DUMFRIES   NX9776
★**Cavens Arms** (01387) 252896
Buccleuch Street; DG1 2AH Good home-
made food all day (not Mon) from pubby
standards to imaginative dishes using prime
ingredients, up to eight well kept interesting
ales, Aspall's and Stowford Press cider, fine
choice of malts, friendly landlord and good
helpful staff, civilised front part with lots
of wood, drinkers' area at back with bar
stools, banquettes and traditional cast-iron
tables, recently added lounge areas; can get
very busy, discreet TV, no under-14s or dogs;
disabled facilities, small terrace at back,
open all day. *(Dr J Barrie Jones, the Didler)*

DUMFRIES   NX9775
Globe (01387) 252335
High Street; DG1 2JA Proper town pub
with strong Burns connections, especially
in old-fashioned dark-panelled 17th-century
snug and little museum of a room beyond;
main part more modern in feel, Belhaven,
McEwans and plenty of whiskies, good value
food (evening by arrangement), friendly
service; children welcome in eating areas,
side terrace seating, open all day. *(the Didler)*

DUMFRIES   NX9776
Ship (01387) 255189
St Michael Street; DG1 2PY Small
traditional two-bar pub with interesting
interior, well kept Caledonian Deuchars
IPA, Greene King, and Wells & Youngs
Bombardier; open all day. *(the Didler)*

MOFFAT   NT0805
Buccleuch Arms (01683) 220003
High Street; DG10 9ET Friendly rather
old-fashioned Georgian coaching inn with
roomy carpeted bar and lounge areas,
open fire, good popular food using local
produce (suppliers listed), informal upstairs
restaurant, polite quick service, interesting

wines by the glass, good choice of malts
and bottled beers, cocktails; keg beer, soft
background music, Sky TV; dogs welcome,
garden, 16 bedrooms, open all day. *(Gordon
and Margaret Ormondroyd)*

DUNBARTONSHIRE

ARROCHAR   NN2903
Village Inn (01301) 702279
*A814, just off A83 W of Loch Lomond;
G83 7AX* Friendly, cosy and interesting
with well kept ales such as Caledonian
and Fyne, enjoyable home-made hearty
food in simple all-day dining area (can get
booked up) with heavy beams, bare boards,
some panelling and big open fire, steps
down to unpretentious bar, several dozen
malts, good coffee, fine sea and hill views;
background music, juke box, can be noisy on
busy summer weekends; children welcome
in eating areas till 8pm, tables out on deck
and lawn, comfortable bedrooms including
spacious ones in former back barn, good
breakfast, open all day. *(David Hoult)*

EAST LOTHIAN

ABERLADY   NT4679
Old Aberlady (01875) 870503
Main Street; EH32 0NF Cosy inn in
pretty coastal village, good varied choice
of modestly priced food, decent wines,
Caledonian Deuchars IPA, competent
staff. *(Comus and Sarah Elliott)*

DIRLETON   NT3183
Castle (01620) 850221
*Manse Road opposite village green;
EH39 5EP* Refurbished 19th-c coaching
inn in pretty village overlooking the green
and castle, good bistro food all day with some
emphasis on fish and seasonal game, two
local beers; terrace and garden, children
welcome, five bedrooms. *(Marlene and
Jim Godfrey)*

DUNBAR   NT6779
Rocks (01368) 862287
Marine Road; EH42 1AR Atmospheric
19th-c clifftop hotel with great sea views,
well liked food including local fish, real ales,
welcoming staff; 12 bedrooms. *(Sarah Flynn)*

GULLANE   NT4882
★**Old Clubhouse** (01620) 842008
East Links Road; EH31 2AF Single-story
building with bar and more formal dining
room, Victorian pictures and cartoons,
stuffed birds, pre-war sheet music, golfing

By law, pubs must show a price list of their drinks. Let us know if you are
inconvenienced by any breach of this law.

and other memorabilia, open fires, good choice of enjoyable well priced pubby food, four ales including Belhaven and Caledonian, nice house wines, fast friendly service, views over golf links to Lammermuirs; children and dogs welcome, open all day. *(Comus and Sarah Elliott, GSB)*

HADDINGTON   NT5173
Victoria (01620) 823332
Court Street; EH41 3JD Popular pub/ restaurant with good imaginative local food cooked by chef/landlord at fair prices, good range of real ales, friendly competent service. *(Dr and Mrs R G J Telfer)*

HADDINGTON   NT5173
Waterside (01620) 825674
Waterside; just off A6093, over pedestrian bridge at E end of Town; EH41 4AT Attractively set riverside dining pub next to historic bridge, spacious modernised interior with some stylish touches, enjoyable food including fixed-price lunch menu, a couple of real ales such as Stewart Pentland IPA, good wine choice, friendly staff; children welcome (family room with toys), picnic-sets out overlooking the Tyne. *(Comus and Sarah Elliott)*

FIFE
ELIE   NO4999
⋆**Ship** (01333) 330246
The Toft, off A917 (High Street) towards harbour; KY9 1DT Pleasant seaside inn, very much part of the community, and in good position for enjoying a drink overlooking the sandy bay and on towards the stone pier and old granary; unspoilt beamed nautical-feel bar with old prints and maps on partly panelled walls, coal fires, Caledonian Deuchars IPA, a few malt whiskies, decent bar food, simple carpeted back room with board games (children welcome here); dogs allowed in bar, comfortable bedrooms in next-door guesthouse, open all day (till 1am Fri, Sat). *(John and Alison Hamilton, Susan and John Douglas)*

LOWER LARGO   NO4102
Crusoe (01333) 320759
Harbour; KY8 6BT Popular harbourside hotel with beams, stripped stonework and open fire, comfortable lounge bar with Robinson Crusoe/Alexander Selkirk mementoes, good fish-based menu (fresh daily), well kept beers, cheerful staff; TVs dotted about; pleasant outside seating area, bedrooms with good sea views. *(Susan and John Douglas)*

ST ANDREWS   NO5116
Central (01334) 897581
Market Street; KY16 9NU Traditional Victorian town-centre pub with great choice of english and scottish beers from island

servery, knowledgeable friendly staff, fair-priced pubby food, friendly mix of customers; pavement tables, open all day (till 1am Fri, Sat). *(Pat and Tony Martin, E Dawson)*

HIGHLAND
AULTBEA   NG8689
Aultbea (01445) 731201
Aultbea; IV22 2HX Two-bar hotel (originally a 19th-c hunting lodge) beautifully placed on the shores of Loch Ewe, ales such as Black Isle, Isle of Skye and Orkney, good food in bistro or more formal restaurant; eight bedrooms. *(Johnston and Maureen Anderson)*

INVERNESS-SHIRE
AVIEMORE   NH8612
Cairngorm (01479) 810233
Grampian Road (A9); PH22 1PE Large flagstoned bar in traditional hotel, lively and friendly, with prompt helpful service, good value food from wide-ranging menu using local produce, Cairngorm ales, good choice of other drinks, informal dining lounge/ conservatory; sports TV; children welcome, comfortable bedrooms. *(Christine and Neil Townend)*

CARRBRIDGE   NH9022
Cairn (01479) 841212
Main Road; PH23 3AS Welcoming tartan-carpeted front bar, decent served food, well kept ales such as Black Isle, Cairngorm and Highland, old local pictures, roaring fire, pool, seperate more formal dining room; children and dogs welcome, seven comfortable bedrooms, open all day. *(Johnston and Maureen Anderson, Brian and Anna Marsden)*

DRUMNADROCHIT   NH5029
Fiddlers Elbow (01456) 450678
A82; IV63 6TX Bustling little place with good food from varied menu (best to book evenings in season), friendly atmosphere and good service, well kept Black Isle and Cairngorm, 30 mainly scottish bottled beers, proper ciders and impressive range of some 500 malts (whisky club and tastings); no dogs inside; children welcome, seats out on front terrace, six bedrooms (three across the road), handy for Urquhart Castle, open all day in summer. *(Revd Michael Vockins)*

DRUMNADROCHIT   NH5029
Loch Ness Inn (01456) 450991
Lewiston; IV63 6UW Welcoming roadside inn with good well presented food including a proper vegetarian option, friendly service from young able staff, good beers and whiskies, flagstoned half-panelled bar with darts, restaurant; handy for walkers on Great Glen Way, bedrooms. *(Revd Michael Vockins)*

FORT WILLIAM NN1274

Ben Nevis Inn (01397) 701227

N off A82; Achintee; PH33 6TE Roomy,
well converted, raftered stone barn in
stunning spot by path up to Ben Nevis, good
mainly straightforward food (lots of walkers
so best to book), ales such as Cairngorm
Nessies Monster Mash, prompt cheery
service, bare-boards dining area with steps
up to bar, live music; seats out at front and
back, bunkhouse below, open all day Apr-Oct,
otherwise closed Mon-Weds. *(Michael and
Maggie Betton, Phil Bryant, Michael Peters)*

GLEN SHIEL NH0711

★ Cluanie Inn (01320) 340238

*A87 Invergarry–Kyle of Lochalsh, on
Loch Cluanie; IV63 7YW* Welcoming inn
in lovely isolated setting by Loch Cluanie,
stunning views, friendly table service for
drinks including well kept Isle of Skye, fine
malt range, big helpings of enjoyable food
(good local venison) in three knocked-
together rooms with dining chairs around
polished tables, overspill into restaurant,
warm log fire, chatty parrots in lobby - watch
your fingers; children and dogs welcome,
big comfortable pine-furnished modern
bedrooms, bunkhouse, great breakfasts (for
non-residents too). *(Claes Mauroy,
Dave Braisted)*

GLENUIG NM6576

Glenuig Inn (01687) 470219

*A861 SW of Lochailort, off A830 Fort
William–Mallaig; PH38 4NG* Friendly
refurbished bar on picturesque bay, enjoyable
locally sourced food, well kept ales and a
scottish cider on tap, lots of bottled beers
and good range of whiskies; bedrooms in
adjoining block, also bunkhouse popular with
walkers and divers. *(Ian and Tina Humphrey)*

INVERMORISTON NH4216

Glenmoriston Arms (01320) 51206

A82/A887; IV63 7YA Small civilised hotel
dating in part from 1740 when it was a
drovers' inn, tartan-carpeted bar with open
fire, neatly laid out restaurant, well kept
beer and over 100 malt whiskies; handy for
Loch Ness, 11 bedrooms (three in converted
outbuilding). *(Theocsbrian)*

INVERNESS NH6446

Clachnaharry Inn (01463) 239806

*High Street, Clachnaharry (A862 NW of
city); IV3 8RB* Friendly old beamed bar
with chatty locals, five changing ales and
good well cooked food including fixed-price
lunch deal, log fire, bottom lounge with
woodburner and picture windows looking
over Beauly Firth; children welcome, terrace
overlooking railway, lovely walks by big
flight of Caledonian Canal locks, open all
day. *(Anon)*

INVERNESS NH6645

Number 27 (01463) 241999

Castle Street; IV2 3DU Busy pub opposite
the castle, cheery welcoming staff, plenty
of draught and bottled beers, good choice
of well prepared food at reasonable prices,
restaurant at back. *(the Dutchman)*

ONICH NN0263

Four Seasons (01855) 821393

Inchree; PH33 6SE Wooden building (part
of Inchree holiday complex), smallish bar
with cushioned wall benches, dining area
with unusual central log fire, bare boards,
friendly helpful staff, ales such as Isle of
Skye and local Glen Finnan, generous varied
evening food at reasonable prices, local
maps and guidebooks for sale, daily weather
forecast; children till 8.30, hostel, lodge
and chalet accommodation, handy for the
Corran ferry, closed lunchtime, check winter
opening. *(Tina Wing)*

WHITEBRIDGE NH4815

Whitebridge (01456) 486226

B862 SW of village; IV2 6UN White-
painted 19th-c hotel set in the foothills of the
Monadhliath Mountains, good home-made
food from sandwiches up, friendly service, a
couple of well kept ales such as Cairngorm,
around 50 malts, two bars with woodburners,
summer restaurant; 12 bedrooms, open
all day in summer, all day weekends in
winter. *(Pat and Stewart Gordon)*

KINCARDINESHIRE

FETTERCAIRN NO6573

Ramsay Arms (01561) 340334

Burnside Road; AB30 1XX Hotel with
enjoyable food in tartan-carpeted bar and
smart oak-panelled restaurant, friendly
service, well kept beer, several malts
including the local Fettercairn; children
welcome, garden tables, attractive village
(liked by Queen Victoria who stayed at
the hotel), 12 bedrooms. *(Mike and
Lynn Robinson)*

POTARCH NO6097

Potarch Hotel (01339) 884339

*B993, just off A93 5 miles W of
Banchory; AB31 4BD* Good log fire in
tartan-carpeted bar, a well kept real ale,
enjoyable bar food and restaurant meals
(best to book weekends); six bedrooms,
beautiful spot by River Dee, open all day.
(David and Betty Gittins)

STONEHAVEN NO8785

Marine Hotel (01569) 762155

Shore Head; AB39 2JY Popular
harbourside pub with well kept ales and good
choice of whiskies, nice food especially local
fish, large stripped stone bar with log fire in
cosy side room, upstairs seaview restaurant;

children welcome, pavement tables.
(Stuart Sim)

KINROSS-SHIRE

WESTER BALGEDIE   NO1604
Balgedie Toll   (01592) 840212
*Corner of A911/A919; KY13
9HE* Traditional place with oak beams and
several small rooms, sensibly priced scottish
food including smokies and local venison,
well kept Belhaven and beers from smaller
breweries, good wine and whisky choice,
friendly service; good disabled access.
(M J Winterton)

KIRKCUDBRIGHTSHIRE

CASTLE DOUGLAS   NX7662
Sulwath Brewery   (01556) 504525
King Street; DG7 1DT Bar attached to
this small brewery, four Sulwath ales in top
condition and their bottled beers, Weston's
cider, some food, stools and barrel tables, off-
sales and souvenirs, brewery tours Mon and
Fri at 1pm (unless by prior arrangement);
children and dogs welcome, disabled
facilities, open 10am-5pm Mon-Sat.
(the Didler, J F M and M West)

GATEHOUSE OF FLEET   NX6056
★ **Masonic Arms**   (01557) 814335
Ann Street; off B727; DG7 2HU Spacious
dining pub with comfortable two-room
pubby bar, Caledonian and a guest beer,
good choice of malts, traditional seating,
pictures on timbered walls, blue and white
plates on delft shelf, attractive terracotta-
tiled conservatory with cane furniture,
contemporary restaurant; background
music - live folk Thurs night, games machine
and pool; no children in bar after 9pm, dogs
welcome, picnic-sets under parasols in neatly
kept sheltered garden, more seats in front,
open all day weekends, closed middle two
weeks of Nov. *(Anon)*

HAUGH OF URR   NX8066
★ **Laurie Arms**   (01556) 660246
*B794 N of Dalbeattie; Main Street;
DG7 3YA* Neatly kept and attractively
decorated 19th-c pub, a few tables in log-fire
bar with steps up to similar area, decent food
from bar snacks to steaks, good changing real
ales, decent wines by the glass, welcoming
attentive service, restaurant, games room
with darts, pool and juke box, splendid
Bamforth comic postcards in the gents';
tables out at front and on sheltered terrace
behind, open all day weekends. *(Terry Davis,
Douglas Johnson)*

KIRKCUDBRIGHT   NX6850
★ **Selkirk Arms**   (01557) 330402
High Street; DG6 4JG Comfortable well
run 18th-c hotel in pleasant spot by mouth

of the Dee, simple locals' front bar (own
street entrance), partitioned high-ceilinged
lounge with upholstered armchairs, wall
banquettes and paintings for sale, two beers
specially brewed for them, food ranging
from pub standards to some interesting
dishes in bistro and restaurant, good helpful
service; background music, TV; welcomes
children (not in bar) and dogs, smart wooden
furniture under blue parasols in neat garden
with 15th-c font, 17 bedrooms, open all
day. *(the Didler, J F M and M West, Christine and
Neil Townend)*

LANARKSHIRE

GLASGOW   NS5965
★ **Counting House**   (0141) 225 0160
*St Vincent Place/George Square;
G1 2DH* Impressive Wetherspoons bank
conversion, imposing interior rising into
lofty richly decorated coffered ceiling
culminating in great central dome, big
windows, decorative glasswork, wall-safes,
several areas with solidly comfortable
seating, smaller rooms (once managers'
offices) around perimeter, one like a well
stocked library, a few themed with pictures
and prints of historical characters, half a
dozen ales from far and wide, bottled beers,
35 malt whiskies, wide choice of usual good
value food all day; children welcome if
eating, open 9am-midnight. *(Theocsbrian,
Comus and Sarah Elliott)*

GLASGOW   NS5865
Drum & Monkey   0141 221 6636
St Vincent Street; G2 5TF Nicholsons
bank conversion with ornate ceiling, granite
pillars and lots of carved mahogany, good
range of real ales and wines from island bar,
good value food, quieter back area; open all
day. *(Anon)*

GLASGOW   NS5965
★ **Sloans**   (0141) 2218886
Argyle Arcade; G2 8BG Restored Grade
A listed building over three floors, many
original features including a fine mahogany
staircase, etched glass, ornate woodwork
and moulded ceilings, good choice of food
from sandwiches up in ground-floor bar/
bistro and upstairs restaurant, friendly
staff, events in impressive barrel-vaulted
parquet-floored ballroom; children
welcome, tables in courtyard, Sun
market. *(Comus and Sarah Elliott)*

GLASGOW   NS5865
State   (0141) 332 2159
Holland Street; G2 4NG High-ceilinged
bar with marble pillars, lots of carved wood
including handsome oak island servery, half a
dozen or so well kept changing ales, bargain
basic lunchtime food from sandwiches up,
good atmosphere, friendly staff, armchairs
among other comfortable seats, coal-effect

gas fire in big wooden fireplace, old prints and theatrical posters; background music, silent sports TVs, games machine, weekend live music. *(Ian Barker)*

GLASGOW   NS5666
Three Judges (0141) 337 3055
Dumbarton Road, opposite Byres Road; G11 6PR Traditional corner bar with up to nine quickly changing real ales from small breweries far and wide (they get through several hundred a year), pump clips on walls, friendly staff and locals, live jazz Sun afternoons, no food; dogs welcome, open all day. *(Andy and Jill Kassube)*

MIDLOTHIAN

DALKEITH   NR3264
Sun (0131) 663 2456
A7 S; EH22 4TR Refurbished dining pub/boutique hotel, good-quality local food including some unusual choices and nice puddings, early-bird deals Mon-Thurs, changing real ales; courtyard garden, five individually styled bedrooms, good generous breakfast, open all day. *(David McKinlay)*

EDINBURGH   NT2574
★ Bow Bar (0131) 226 7667
West Bow; EH1 2HH Cheerfully traditional alehouse with eight well kept mostly scottish beers served from tall 1920s founts, 25 international bottled beers and some 200 malts, impressive carved mahogany servery, sturdy leatherette wall seats and heavy narrow tables on wood floor, fine collection of enamel signs and a handsome antique brewery mirror, lunchtime snacks limited to tasty pies (not Sun); free wi-fi; dogs allowed, open all day. *(Barbarrick, Jeremy King, Claes Mauroy, Sophie Holborow)*

EDINBURGH   NT2471
★ Canny Man's (0131) 447 1484
Morningside Road; aka Volunteer Arms; EH10 4QU Utterly individual and distinctive, saloon, lounge and snug with fascinating bric-a-brac, ceiling papered with sheet music, huge range of appetising smorgasbord, very efficient friendly service, lots of whiskies, good wines, well kept ales such as Caledonian and Timothy Taylors Landlord, cheap children's drinks, no credit cards, mobile phones or backpackers; courtyard tables. *(Barbarrick, John and Anne Mackinnon)*

EDINBURGH   NT2573
★ Halfway House (0131) 225 7101
Fleshmarket Close (steps between Cockburn Street and Market Street, opposite Waverley Station); EH1 1BX Tiny one-room pub off steep steps, part carpeted, part tiled, with a few small tables and high-backed settles, lots of prints (some golf and railway themes), four scottish ales

such as Kelburn and Strathaven(third of a pint glasses available), good range of malt whiskies, short choice of decent cheap food all day; 60s/70s juke box, TV turned up for racing; dogs and children welcome. *(Jeremy King, Derek Wason)*

EDINBURGH   NT2676
Kings Wark (0131) 554 9260
The Shore, Leith; EH6 6QU Named to commemorate a visit by George IV, one of several pubs on Leith's restored waterfront; plenty of atmosphere in stripped-stone bare-boards interior, good selection of well kept ales, nice food and good value wines, efficient helpful staff; open all day. *(Peter F Marshall, David Hunt)*

EDINBURGH   NT2473
Oxford (0131) 539 7119
Young Street; EH2 4JB No-frills local with two built-in wall settles in tiny bustling bar, rugby memorabilia, steps up to quieter back room with dominoes, lino floor, well kept Caledonian Deuchars IPA and Belhaven 80/-, a good range of whiskies, cheap filled cobs; links with scottish writers and artists. *(David and Sue Smith)*

EDINBURGH   NT2574
Standing Order (0131) 225 4460
George Street; EH2 2JP Grand Wetherspoons bank conversion in three elegant Georgian houses, imposing columns, enormous main room with elaborate colourful ceiling, lots of tables, smaller side booths, other rooms including two with floor-to-ceiling bookshelves, comfortable clubby seats, Adam fireplace and portraits, some interesting real ales from long counter; sports TV, weekend live music, gets very busy particularly on Sat night; disabled facilities, open all day till 1am. *(Richard Tingle)*

EDINBURGH   NT2574
★ Starbank (0131) 552 4141
Laverockbank Road, off Starbank Road, just off A901 Granton–Leith; EH5 3BZ Cheerful pub in a fine spot with terrific views over the Firth of Forth, long light and airy bare-boards bar, some leather bench seats, up to eight well kept ales, good choice of malt whiskies, reasonably priced food in conservatory restaurant; background music, sports TV; children welcome till 9pm if dining, dogs on leads, sheltered back terrace, parking on adjacent hilly street, open all day. *(David Goodenough, Brian Banks, Richard Tingle, Jeremy King, John and Annabel Hampshire, the Dutchman)*

EDINBURGH   NT2573
White Hart (0131) 226 2688
Grassmarket; EH1 2JU One of Edinburgh's oldest pubs and popular with tourists, small, basic and relaxed with efficient friendly young staff, enjoyable good value food all day, ales such as Belhaven 80/-

and a decent whisky choice, various coffees; background music - live in the evening, Sky TV; pavement tables popular with smokers, open all day. *(Richard Tingle)*

RATHO   NT1470
Bridge (0131) 333 1320
Baird Road; EH28 8RA Extended 18th-c pub with enjoyable food all day from varied menu using local produce including some of their own, daily specials too, good selection of scottish ales such as Fyne and Stewart, friendly staff; children very welcome, garden by Union Canal with wandering ducks, trips on own canal boats, bedrooms. *(Andy and Jill Kassube)*

PEEBLESSHIRE

INNERLEITHEN   NT3336
⋆ **Traquair Arms** (01896) 830229
B709, just off A72 Peebles–Galashiels; follow signs for Traquair House; EH44 6PD Modernised inn at heart of pretty Borders village, only one of three places where you find Traquair ale (produced in original oak vessels in 18th-c brewhouse at nearby Traquair House), also Caledonian Deuchars IPA and Timothy Taylors Landlord, 40 malt whiskies, decent choice of pubby food (all day weekends), main bar with warm open fire, another in relaxed bistro-style restaurant, good mix of customers; background music, TV; children welcome, dogs in bar, picnic-sets on neat back lawn, bedrooms, open all day. *(Jon Stevenson, the Didler)*

PERTHSHIRE

BLAIR ATHOLL   NN8765
⋆ **Atholl Arms** (01796) 481205
B8079; PH18 5SG Sizeable hotel's cosy stable-themed Bothy Bar in lovely setting near the castle, four local Moulin ales, good well priced food all day from sandwiches to interesting dishes, local meat and wild salmon, helpful friendly staff, open fire; 31 good value bedrooms. *(Comus and Sarah Elliott)*

BRIG O' TURK   NN5306
⋆ **Byre** (01877) 376292
A821 Callander–Trossachs, just outside village; FK17 8HT Beautifully placed byre conversion with flagstoned log-fire bar and roomier high-raftered restaurant area, popular food including local trout and some imaginative dishes (best to book), friendly helpful staff; tables out on extensive decking, good walks, open all day, closed Jan.

(Gordon and Margaret Ormondroyd, David and Katharine Cooke)

DUNKELD   NO0243
Atholl Arms (01350) 727219
Bridgehead; PH8 0AQ Comfortably furnished smallish hotel bar, good choice of well kept ales such as Inveralmond Inkie Pinkie, enjoyable food from varied menu including cullen skink and beef stovies, friendly service. *(Pat and Tony Martin)*

DUNKELD   NO0242
Taybank (01350) 727340
Tay Terrace; PH8 0AQ Traditional pub with view over River Tay and Georgian bridge, notable for its regular scottish music including open sessions and workshops (instruments provided), lived-in bare boards interior, big open fire, local Strathbraan Due South and Timothy Taylors, home-made food including stovies. *(Jules Akel, Christine and Neil Townend)*

DUNNING   NO0114
Kirkstyle (01764) 684248
B9141, off A9 S of Perth; Kirkstyle Square; PH2 0RR Unpretentious 18th-c streamside pub with chatty landlady and regulars, log fire in snug bar, up to three real ales and good choice of whiskies, enjoyable home-made food including some interesting specials (book in season), good service, split-level stripped-stone back restaurant; background music; children welcome, dogs allowed in garden only, open all day weekends, closed Mon and Tues lunchtimes. *(Anon)*

INCHTURE   NO2828
Inchture Hotel (01828) 686298
Just off A90 Perth–Dundee; PH14 9RN Small recently refurbished family-owned hotel, contemporary lounge bar with open fire, enjoyable well priced food here or in spacious conservatory restaurant, also bar snacks (try the haggis flavour crisps made in the village), Belhaven Best and good choice of wines by the glass, separate public bar; children welcome, eight bedrooms and self-catering cottage. *(Pat and Stewart Gordon, Susan and John Douglas)*

KENMORE   NN7745
⋆ **Kenmore Hotel** (01887) 830205
A827 W of Aberfeldy; PH15 2NU Civilised small hotel dating from the 16th c in pretty Loch Tay village; comfortable traditional front lounge with warm log fire and poem pencilled by Burns himself on the chimney breast, dozens of malts helpfully arranged alphabetically, polite uniformed staff, modern restaurant with balcony; back public bar and

---

With the iPhone Good Pub Guide App, you can use the iPhone's camera to send us pictures of pubs you visit – outside or inside.

terrace overlooking River Tay with enjoyable food from lunchtime soup and sandwiches up, Inveralmond Ossian, decent wines by the glass; pool and winter darts, juke box, TV, fruit machine; children and dogs welcome, 40 good bedrooms, open all day. *(Comus and Sarah Elliott, Pat and Stewart Gordon)*

KILMAHOG   NN6008
✶Lade (01877) 330152

A84 just NW of Callander, by A821 junction; FK17 8HD Lively place with a strong scottish theme - traditional weekend music, real ale shop with over 130 bottled beers from regional microbreweries and their own-brewed WayLade ales; plenty of character in several cosy beamed areas with red walls, panelling and stripped stone, Highland prints and works by local artists, 40 malt whiskies, pubby bar food, more ambitious dishes in big-windowed restaurant, friendly staff; background music; children welcome, dogs in bar, terrace tables, pleasant garden with three fish ponds and bird-feeding station, open all day (till 1am Fri, Sat). *(Pat and Stewart Gordon)*

LOCH TUMMEL   NN8160
✶Loch Tummel Inn (01882) 634272

B8019 4 miles E of Tummel Bridge; PH16 5RP Beautifully placed traditional lochside inn renovated by present owners, great views over water to Schiehallion, cosy bar area with woodburner, good fresh seasonal food, Inveralmond ales, converted hayloft restaurant; children and dogs welcome, lots of walks and wildlife, six bedrooms, open all day, but closed early Jan to early Feb, and Mon, Tues in Feb and Mar. *(Comus and Sarah Elliott)*

MEIKLEOUR   NO1539
✶Meikleour Hotel (01250) 883206

A984 W of Coupar Angus; PH2 6EB Early 19th-c creeper-covered inn, well run and a good base for rural Perthshire; main lounge bar is basically two rooms (one carpeted, the other with stone floor), comfortable seating, some angling equipment and fishing/shooting pictures, oil-burning fires, Inveralmond ales including one brewed for the pub, good food from lunchtime snacks to local fish and game, attentive friendly service, elegant panelled restaurant; background music; children welcome, seats on small colonnaded verandah, picnic-sets on sloping lawn with distant Highland view, spectacular nearby beech hedge planted over 250 years ago, comfortable bedrooms, good breakfast, open all day weekends. *(Les and Sandra Brown, Sandy Butcher, Christine and Neil Townend, David and Betty Gittins, Susan and John Douglas)*

PITLOCHRY   NN9163
✶Killiecrankie Hotel (01796) 473220

Killiecrankie, off A9 N; PH16 5LG Comfortable splendidly placed country

hotel with attractive panelled bar and airy conservatory, good nicely varied and reasonably priced food, friendly efficient service, well kept ales and good choice of wines, restaurant; children in eating areas, extensive peaceful grounds with dramatic views, ten bedrooms. *(Joan and Tony Walker)*

ROSS-SHIRE

BADACHRO   NG7873
✶Badachro Inn (01445) 741255

2.5 miles S of Gairloch village turn off A832 on to B8056, then after another 3.25 miles turn right in Badachro to the quay and inn; IV21 2AA Superbly positioned by Loch Gairloch with terrific views from decking down to water's edge, popular (especially in summer) with happy mix of sailing visitors (free moorings) and chatty locals; welcoming bar with interesting photographs, An Teallach, Caledonian and a guest ale, about 30 malt whiskies and eight wines by the glass, quieter eating area with big log fire, dining conservatory overlooking bay, good reasonably priced food including locally smoked fish and seafood; background music; children and dogs welcome, one bedroom, open all day. *(Kate Vogelsang)*

FORTROSE   NH7256
✶Anderson (01381) 620236

Union Street, off A832; IV10 8TD Friendly enthusiastic american licensees at this seaside hotel with one of the largest collections of belgian beers in the UK, 200 malt whiskies, quite a few wines and two well kept real ales, good food in homely bar and light airy dining room with open fire, puzzle-type games; background music; children welcome, dogs allowed in bar (there's a pub dog and cat), chickens in garden, bedrooms, open from 4pm (3pm Sun). *(Charles and Pauline Stride, Brian and Anna Marsden)*

PLOCKTON   NG8033
✶Plockton Inn (01599) 544222

Innes Street; unconnected to Plockton Hotel; IV52 8TW Close to the harbour in this lovely village, congenial bustling atmosphere even in winter, good well priced food with emphasis on local fish/seafood (some from back smokery), friendly efficient service, well kept changing beers, good range of malts, lively public bar with regular traditional music; seats out on decking, 14 bedrooms (seven in annexe over road), good breakfast. *(Dave Braisted, Martin and Sue Day, Dr Peter Crawshaw)*

SHIEL BRIDGE   NG9319
Kintail Lodge (01599) 511275

A87; IV40 8HL Lots of varnished wood in large plain bar adjoining hotel, convivial bustle in season, Isle of Skye Black Cuillin and plenty of malt whiskies, particularly good food from same kitchen as attractive conservatory restaurant with magnificent view down Loch Duich to Skye, local game, wild salmon and own smokings, also children's helpings, friendly efficient service, traditional music Thurs night; 12 comfortable bedrooms, bunkhouse, good breakfast. *(Ian and Helen Stafford)*

ULLAPOOL   NH1294

Ferry Boat (01854) 612366

Shore Street; from S, go straight when A835 turns right into Mill Street; IV26 2UJ Neat white-painted 18th-c building with big windows for harbour and Loch Broom views, cosy bar and lounge area, woodburner, Caledonian Deuchars IPA and 80/-, good popular food (booking advised) including bargain lunchtime deal; children till 8pm, nine bedrooms, open all day. *(George Atkinson, Katherine Douglas)*

ROXBURGHSHIRE

KELSO   NT7234

Cobbles (01573) 223548

Bowmont Street; TD5 7JH Small comfortably refurbished 19th-c dining pub just off the main square, friendly and well run with good range of food from pub standards to more enterprising dishes, local Tempest ales, decent wines and malts from end bar, wall banquettes and panelling, welcoming fire, overspill dining room upstairs, folk music Fri till late; children welcome, disabled facilities, open all day. *(Robbie Pennington)*

MELROSE   NT5434

George & Abbotsford

(01896) 822308 *High Street; TD6 9PD* Civilised bar and lounge areas in comfortable hotel, friendly staff, enjoyable freshly made food all day, good changing choice of scottish and english ales (summer beer festival), decent wines and quite a few malt whiskies, restaurant, small shop selling wide range of bottled beers; no dogs; children welcome, 30 bedrooms. *(the Didler)*

ST BOSWELLS   NT5930

Buccleuch Arms (01835) 822243

A68 just S of Newtown St Boswells; TD6 0EW Civilised 19th-c sandstone hotel, good popular food served by prompt friendly staff, real ale, Georgian-style plush bar with light oak panelling, restaurant, open fires; children welcome, tables in attractive garden behind, 19 bedrooms. *(Adele Summers, Alan Black)*

TOWN YETHOLM   NT8128

Plough (01573) 420215

High Street; TD5 8RS Welcoming unpretentious pub facing green, good honest food including local venison and fish from Eyemouth, well kept ales such as Black Sheep and Brains, small dining room; five bedrooms. *(Dr Peter Crawshaw)*

SELKIRKSHIRE

ST MARY'S LOCH   NT2321

Tibbie Shiels (01750) 42231

A708 SW of Selkirk; TD7 5LH In wonderful peaceful setting by beautiful loch, handy for Southern Upland Way and Grey Mares Tail waterfall, good food, well kept Broughton beers and nice wines, interesting literary history; comfortable bedrooms. *(Pat and Stewart Gordon, Maggie Jones)*

STIRLINGSHIRE

KIPPEN   NS6594

★ Cross Keys (01786) 870293

Main Street; village signposted off A811 W of Stirling; FK8 3DN Homely and welcoming 18th-c inn, timelessly stylish bar with attractive dark panelling and subdued lighting, straightforward lounge with good fire, another in attractive family dining room, Harviestoun Bitter & Twisted and a guest, several malts and wines by the glass, well liked bar food (all day weekends) from lunchtime sandwiches up; background music; children (till 9pm) and dogs welcome, garden tables, good views towards the Trossachs, three bedrooms. *(Anon)*

THORNHILL   NS6699

★ Lion & Unicorn (01786) 850204

A873; FK8 3PJ Back pubby-feel bar with exposed stone walls, bare boards and stools lining the counter, carpeted front rooms set for dining, one with log fire in massive 17th-c fireplace, enjoyable home-made food, a couple of changing ales and quite a few malt whiskies, games room with pool, fruit machine and TV; children welcome till 9pm, dogs in public bar, picnic-sets in back garden, four bedrooms, open all day (till 1am Fri, Sat). *(R and S Bentley)*

SUTHERLAND

LAIRG   NC5224

★ Crask Inn (01549) 411 241

A836 13 miles N towards Altnaharra; IV27 4AB Remote homely inn on single-track road through peaceful moorland, good simple food cooked by landlady including their own lamb (the friendly hard-working licensees keep sheep on this working croft), comfortably basic bar with large peat stove to dry the sheepdogs (other dogs welcome), a summer real ale, Black Isle bottled beers in winter, interesting books, piano, pleasant separate dining room; three bedrooms (lights out when generator goes off), simple nearby bunkhouse. *(Les and Sandra Brown, Dr Peter Crawshaw)*

LOCHINVER   NC0922

Caberfeidh (01571) 844321

Culag Road (A837); IV27 4JY Delightful
lochside position with lovely views,
cosy bar, conservatory and more formal
restaurant, shortish menu with emphasis
on local seafood, well kept beers including
Caledonian, charming landlord and staff;
small harbourside garden, open all day in
summer. *(George Atkinson)*

WEST LOTHIAN

LINLITHGOW   NS0077

⋆ **Four Marys** (01506) 842171

*High Street; 2 miles from M9 J3 (and
little further from J4) – town signposted;
EH49 7ED* Evocative 16th-c place - named
after Mary, Queen of Scots' four ladies-in-
waiting - and filled with mementoes of the
ill-fated queen including pictures and written
records, pieces of bed curtain and clothing,
even a facsimile of her death-mask; neatly
kept L-shaped room with mahogany dining
chairs around stripped period and antique
tables, attractive old corner cupboards,
elaborate Victorian dresser serving as part
of the bar, mainly stripped-stone walls with
some remarkable masonry in the inner area,
up to eight real ales (May, Oct beer festivals),
good range of malt whiskies, fair value food
including good cullen skink, cheery landlord
and courteous staff; background music;
children in dining area until 9.30pm, heated
outdoor smoking area, difficult parking, open
all day (till 1am Fri, Sat). *(Peter F Marshall)*

QUEENSFERRY   NT1378

Hawes (031) 331 1990

Newhalls Road; EH30 9TA Vintage Inn
renovation featured famously in Kidnapped,
a great spot for tourists with fine views of the
Forth bridges (one rail bridge support in the
car park); wide choice of enjoyable food all
day including good value set menu (Mon-Sat
till 5pm), roomy separate dining areas,
friendly efficient staff, wide range of wines
by the glass, Caledonian Deuchars IPA and
two other ales; children welcome, tables on
back lawn with play area, 14 bedrooms. *(the
Dutchman, Roger and Donna Huggins)*

WIGTOWNSHIRE

BLADNOCH   NX4254

Bladnoch Inn (01988) 402200

Corner of A714 and B7005; DG8 9AB
Cheerful bar, neat and bright, with eating
area, enjoyable well prepared pubby food
from sandwiches up, friendly obliging service,
restaurant; keg beer, background radio;
children and dogs welcome, picturesque
riverside setting across from Bladnoch
distillery (tours), good value bedrooms, open
all day. *(John and Sylvia Harrop)*

PORTPATRICK   NW9954

Crown (01776) 810261

North Crescent; DG9 8SX Seafront hotel
in delightful harbourside village, enjoyable
reasonably priced food all day including
seafood, friendly prompt service, several dozen
malts, decent wines by the glass, warm fire
in rambling traditional bar with cosy corners,
sewing machine tables, old photographs
and posters, attractively decorated early
20th-c dining room opening through quiet
conservatory into sheltered back garden;
background music, TV; children and dogs
welcome, tables out in front. *(John and
Sylvia Harrop)*

STRANRAER   NX0660

Grapes (01776) 703386

Bridge Street; DG9 7HY Popular 19th-c
local, simple and old-fashioned with 1940s
feel, welcoming landlord, a well kept real ale
and over 40 malts, upstairs lounge; courtyard
seating, open all day. *(the Didler)*

SCOTTISH ISLANDS

BUTE

PORT BANNATYNE   NS0767

Port Royal (01700) 505073

Marine Road; PA20 0LW Cheerful
stone-built inn looking across sea to Argyll,
interior reworked as pre-revolution russian
tavern with bare boards, painted timbers
and tapestries, all-day food including
russian dishes and good seafood, choice
of russian beers and vodkas as well as
real ales tapped from the cask, open fire,
candles and wild flowers; right by beach,
deer on golf course behind, five annexe
bedrooms (some sharing bath), substantial
breakfast. *(Eric Von Willegen)*

COLONSAY

SCALASAIG   NR3893

⋆ **Colonsay** (01951) 200316

W on B8086; PA61 7YP Stylish 18th-c
hotel, a haven for ramblers and birders, with
log fires, interesting old islander pictures,
pastel walls and polished painted boards,
bar with sofas and board games, enjoyable
food from lunchtime doortep sandwiches
to fresh seafood and game, good local
Colonsay ale, lots of malt whiskies, informal
restaurant; children and dogs welcome,
pleasant views from gardens, comfortable
bedrooms. *(David Hoult)*

ISLAY

BOWMORE   NR3159

Lochside Hotel (01496) 810244

Shore Street; PA43 7LB Neatly modernised

family-run hotel, well kept Islay ales along with some mainstream beers, amazing collection of Islay malts (over 300 including some real rarities) and 50 other whiskies, enjoyable food making use of local seafood and lamb, good friendly service, two bars, bright conservatory-style back restaurant with lovely Loch Indaal views, traditional music Sat night; children (till 8pm), dogs in public bar, lochside terrace, ten bedrooms, open all day (till 1am Fri, Sat). *(David Hoult)*

PORT CHARLOTTE   NR2558
✴ **Port Charlotte Hotel**
(01496) 850360 *Main Street; PA48 7TU*
Most beautiful of Islay's Georgian villages and in lovely position with sweeping views over Loch Indaal, exceptional collection of about 140 Islay malts including rare ones, Black Sheep and Islay ales, decent wines by the glass, good food using local meat and seafood, civilised bare-boards pubby bar with padded wall seats and modern art, comfortable back bar, separate restaurant and roomy conservatory, traditional live music weekly; children welcome (not in bar after 10pm), garden tables, near sandy beach, ten bedrooms (nine with sea view), open all day till 1am. *(David Hoult)*

PORTNAHAVEN   NN1652
An Tighe Seinnse (01496) 860224
Queen Street; PA47 7SJ Friendly little end-of-terrace harbourside pub tucked away in this remote attractive fishing village, cosy bar with room off, open fire, good food including local seafood, Belhaven keg beer and bottled Islay ales, good choice of malts; sports TV and occasional live music; can get crowded, open all day. *(Tom and Rosemary Hall, David Hoult)*

JURA
CRAIGHOUSE   NR5266
Jura Hotel (01496) 820243
A846; PA60 7XU Superb setting with view over the Small Isles to the mainland, bar and restaurant; garden down to water's edge, 17 bedrooms, most with sea view. *(David Hoult)*

MULL
DERVAIG   NM4251
✴ **Bellachroy** (01688) 400314
B8073; PA75 6QW Island's oldest inn dating to 1608, enjoyable pub and restaurant food including local seafood and plenty of

other fresh produce, generous helpings, ales such as Belhaven and Fyne, good choice of whiskies and wine, traditional bar with darts, informal dining area and lounge used more by residents; children and dogs welcome, covered outside area, nice spot in sleepy lochside village, six comfortable bedrooms, open all year. *(Mr and Mrs M Stratton, Chris Clark, Michael Butler)*

TOBERMORY   NM5055
Macdonald Arms (01688) 302011
Main Street; PA75 6NT Seafront hotel very popular for its tasty low-priced food, well kept Belhaven Best, basic décor and furnishings. *(Michael Butler)*

ORKNEY
DOUNBY   HY3001
Merkister (01856) 771366
Sout by Harray Loch; KW17 2LF Fishing hotel in great location on the loch shores, bar dominated by prize catches, good food here and in pricy restaurant including hand-dived scallops and local aberdeen angus steaks, Belhaven and McEwans ales; 16 bedrooms. *(Dave Braisted)*

PAPA WESTRAY   HY4905
Beltane House (01857) 644224
Beltane; KW17 2BU Also houses this little island's store and self-catering/hostel accommodation, Highland and Orkney ales, bar food; only open Sat evening. *(Dave Braisted)*

ST MARY'S   HY4700
Commodore (01856) 781788
A961; KW17 2RU Modern single-storey building with stunning views over Scapa Flow, bar with well kept Orkney beers, pool and darts, enjoyable food in popular restaurant; open all day. *(John Winstanley)*

STROMNESS   HY2509
Ferry Inn (01856) 850280
John Street; KW16 3AD Busy place with enjoyable quickly served food and several Orkney ales; bedrooms. *(Brian and Anna Marsden)*

WESTRAY   HY4348
Pierowall Hotel (01857) 677472
Centre of Pierowall village, B9066; KW17 2BZ Comfortable pub/hotel near ferry, friendly main bar largely given over to eating, from sandwiches and light snacks up including good freshly landed fish, bottled Orkney beers

---

Stars before the name of a pub show exceptional character and appeal. They don't mean extra comfort. And they are nothing to do with food quality, for which there's a separate knife-and-fork symbol. Even quite a basic pub can win stars, if it's individual enough.

and good choice of malts, pool room and separate dining area; nine spacious bedrooms with bay or hill views. *(Dave Braisted)*

SKYE

ARDVASAR   NG6303
Ardvasar Hotel (01471) 844223
A851 at S of island, near Armadale pier; IV45 8RS Lovely sea and mountain views from comfortable white stone inn in peaceful very pretty spot, charming owner and friendly efficient staff, good home-made food including local fish and meat (children welcome in eating areas), lots of malt whiskies, real ales including Isle of Skye, two bars and games room; TV, background music; tables outside, bedrooms, good walks, open all day. *(Walter and Susan Rinaldi-Butcher)*

CARBOST   NG3731
⋆ ### Old Inn (01478) 640205
B8009; IV47 8SR Unpretentious simply furnished bare-boards bar in idyllic lochside location (close to Talisker distillery), friendly staff, traditional home-made food

including local seafood, cream teas too, Cullin ales, exposed stone walls and peat fire, darts, pool, cribbage and dominoes; background scottish music, TV; children and dogs welcome, terrace with fine Loch Harport and Cuillin views (bar's at the back though), sea-view bedrooms in annexe (breakfast for non-residents if booked the night before), bunkhouse, moorings and showers for yachtsmen, open all day, closed mid-winter afternoons. *(Phil Bryant, John and Elspeth Howell)*

ISLE ORNSAY   NG7012
⋆ ### Eilean Iarmain (01471) 833332
Off A851 Broadford–Armadale; IV43 8QR Small traditional bar at smartly old-fashioned hotel in beautiful location, friendly locals and staff, bar food most of the day from same kitchen as charming sea-view restaurant, an Isle of Skye real ale, good choice of vatted (blended) malt whiskies including their own Gaelic Whisky Collection, banquettes, open fire; traditional background music; children welcome, outside tables with spectacular views, 16 very comfortable bedrooms, open all day. *(Kate Vogelsang)*

> Cribbage is a card game using a block of wood with holes for matchsticks or special pins to score with; regulars in cribbage pubs are usually happy to teach strangers how to play.

WALES

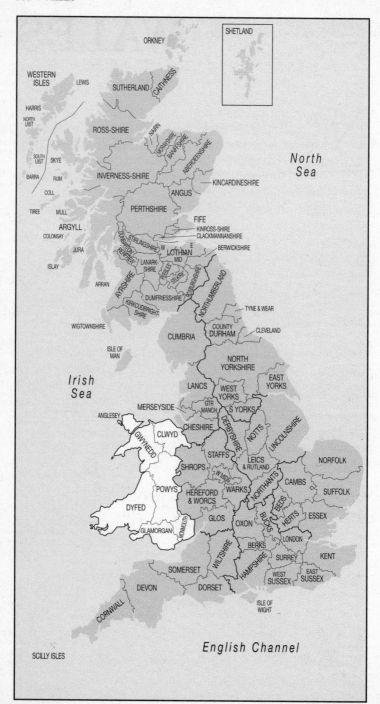

SHETLAND

ORKNEY

WESTERN
ISLES
LEWIS

SUTHERLAND
CAITHNESS

HARRIS

NORTH
UIST

ROSS-SHIRE

NAIRN

MORAYSHIRE

BANFFSHIRE

ABERDEENSHIRE

North
Sea

SOUTH
UIST
SKYE

BARRA
RUM

COLL

INVERNESS-SHIRE

KINCARDINESHIRE

TIREE
MULL

ANGUS

PERTHSHIRE

FIFE

ARGYLL

COLONSAY

DUNBARTON
STIRLINGSHIRE

KINROSS-SHIRE

CLACKMANNANSHIRE

JURA

W

E

RENFREW

LOTHIAN

MID

BERWICKSHIRE

ISLAY

LANARK-
SHIRE

PEEBLES

ARRAN

AYRSHIRE

SELKIRK

ROXBURGHSHIRE

NORTHUMBERLAND

DUMFRIESSHIRE

KIRKCUDBRIGHT-
SHIRE

TYNE & WEAR

WIGTOWNSHIRE

CUMBRIA

COUNTY
DURHAM

CLEVELAND

Irish
Sea

ISLE OF
MAN

NORTH
YORKSHIRE

LANCS

WEST
YORKS

EAST
YORKS

MERSEYSIDE

GTR
MANCH

S YORKS

ANGLESEY

CHESHIRE

DERBYSHIRE

NOTTS

LINCOLNSHIRE

GWYNEDD

CLWYD

STAFFS

LEICS
& RUTLAND

NORFOLK

SHROPS

W MIDS

POWYS

HEREFORD
& WORCS

WARKS

NORTHANTS

CAMBS

SUFFOLK

DYFED

BEDS

ESSEX

MONMOUTH

GLOS

OXON

BUCKS

HERTS

GLAMORGAN

LONDON

WILTSHIRE

BERKS

SURREY

KENT

SOMERSET

HAMPSHIRE

WEST
SUSSEX

EAST
SUSSEX

CORNWALL

DEVON

DORSET

ISLE OF
WIGHT

English Channel

SCILLY ISLES

New among our main entries here are the Hand at Llanarmon Dyffryn Ceiriog (interesting food, pleasant bedrooms, fine walking country), Bunch of Grapes at Pontypridd (very tucked away, sensationally strong for food and drinks) and Stackpole Inn at Stackpole (good food including local fish, very comfortable place to stay). Others that stand out include the Olde Bulls Head at Beaumaris (good all-rounder, much-liked food and drink), Pen-y-Bryn near Colwyn Bay (consistent food and fine views), Bear at Crickhowell (enjoyably unspoilt bar, excellent accommodation), Griffin at Felinfach (attentive service, top class food using own organic produce), Pant-yr-Ochain at Gresford (manor house in splendid gardens, super array of beers and malts), Corn Mill at Llangollen (fascinating old mill building by the river), Golden Lion at Newport in Pembrokeshire (restaurant but with a pubby bar and good accommodation), Harp at Old Radnor (beautifully unspoilt bar and sensibly short, locally sourced menu), Riverside at Pennal (refurbished walker-friendly foody pub in Dovey Valley), Bell at Skenfrith (upmarket with organic kitchen garden and locally sourced produce), Groes at Ty'n-y-groes (much enjoyed as a place to eat and stay), and Nags Head at Usk (where the licensees just get everything right, and make families feel extremely welcome). The Wales Dining Pub 2013 is the Griffin at Felinfach.

ABERDOVEY

SN6196 Map 6

Penhelig Arms

Opposite Penhelig Station; LL35 0LT

Fine harbourside location, enjoyable food, and a nice place to stay

The very special waterside setting draws in quite a few to this fine 18th-c hotel, where a dozen or so customers in the thoughtfully restyled fisherman's bar can make it feel lively enough. There have been no radical modernisations to the interior, just a gentle take on the traditional, with a warm fire in the remaining stud of stone wall, some panelling and a new counter and back display. Efficient and genuinely friendly bar staff serve a couple of brews from the Brains range such as Bitter and Rev James and a guest from a brewery such as Greene King, along with a dozen malt whiskies and a good wine selection with 20 by the glass. The bedrooms are comfortable (some have balconies overlooking the estuary) but the ones nearest the road can be noisy.

Readers have praised the food here, which, in addition to generously filled lunchtime sandwiches, might include cockles with bacon and laver bread or welsh rarebit with beetroot and horseradish relish, whole rainbow trout roasted with lemon and ginger, aubergine gratin, lamb rump, rib-eye steak or sausage and mash with red onion gravy, and puddings such as warm chocolate fondant and sherry trifle. *Benchmark main dish: fish and chips £8.95. Two-course evening meal £15.70.*

Brains ~ Manager Chris Ainsworth ~ Real ale ~ Bar food (12-2, 6-9) ~ Restaurant ~ (01654) 767215 ~ Children welcome ~ Dogs allowed in bar and bedrooms ~ Open 11-11(10.30 Sun) ~ Bedrooms: £45S/£50S(£80B) ~ www.penheligarms.com
Recommended by Bob and Tanya Ekers, David Glynne-Jones, Richard Osborne-Fardon, Michael Butler

ABERGAVENNY

SO3111 Map 6

Hardwick 🍴 ♟ 🛏

Hardwick; B4598 SE, off A40 at A465/A4042 exit – coming from E on A40, go right round the exit system, as B4598 is final road out; NP7 9AA

Noteworthy food in smartly simple restaurant, good beers and wines, too

Really a restaurant with rooms, the emphasis here is pretty much exclusively on the tremendously good (though by no means cheap), imaginative food. You will need to book, and one reader told us they were shown to their table where their drinks order was taken. The bar, with a small functional corner servery (offering a Rhymney beer and a guest such as Wye Valley Butty Bach, local perry and apple juice and about a dozen wines by the glass) is a simple room with spindleback chairs around pub tables and some stripped brickwork around a disused fireplace. The better of the two dining rooms feels more pubby, given its dark beams, one winged high-backed settle by the end serving counter and another facing a small pew across a table tucked in by a huge fireplace, and a nice mix of other tables and chairs on bare floorboards with a big rug (the lack of soft furnishings here can make the acoustics rather lively). The second dining room, in a carpeted extension, is lighter and simpler, more modern in style with big windows; there's some interesting artwork. Service is welcoming and helpful; board games and maybe background music. They have teak tables and chairs out under umbrellas by the car park, and the garden is neatly kept. We'd love to hear from readers about the new bedrooms here.

Owner-chef Stephen Terry uses carefully selected largely local ingredients to create supercharged variations on familiar dishes and more original recipes. Menus might include cannellini soup with chorizo and fried sage, suckling pig terrine, linguini with crab, courgettes and chilli, roast pigeon breast on fried polenta with chorizo and lentils, bass with chorizo, broad beans and peas, roast pork loin with cabbage, sauté potatoes, grilled radicchio and olives, roast cod and spaetzle with brown shrimps, peas, broad beans and capers, and puddings such as panna cotta with rhubarb and ginger shortbread, date loaf with toffee sauce, and home-made ice-creams. *Benchmark main dish: rib-eye steak with béarnaise sauce £23.00. Two-course evening meal £30.20.*

Free house ~ Licensees Stephen and Joanna Terry ~ Real ale ~ Bar food (12-3, 6.30-10; 12-3, 6-9 Sun) ~ Restaurant ~ (01873) 854220 ~ No children under 8 in restaurant after 8pm ~ Open 11-11(midnight Sat); 12-10 Sun; closed Mon in winter and second week in Jan ~ Bedrooms: /£145S(£155B) ~ www.thehardwick.co.uk *Recommended by M E and F J Thomasson, Duncan Cloud*

ANGLE
Old Point House £

SM8703   Map 6

Signed off B4320 in village, along long rough waterside track; SA71 5AS

Simple, welcoming seafarers' inn with quite a choice of food and waterside tables

Remotely situated near a lifeboat station on the south side of Milford Haven, this unpretentious whitewashed pub is right on the Pembrokeshire Coast Path, with walks west around the peninsula to the beach at West Angle Bay. Some of its snug little windows and picnic-sets on the big gravelled terrace give charming views over the water. Run by a friendly landlord and his staff, it's been known in the area as the 'lifeboatman's local' since the neighbouring lifeboat station opened in 1868, and has plenty of seafaring character with all its photographs and charts. Until the 1980s the tiny spartan snug bar was the only public room. It has a short bar at one corner serving Felinfoel Double Dragon and cheap soft drinks, and a concrete floor, two simple wood settles and a warming fire in a lovely old fireplace. There's also a lounge bar and a dining room; outside lavatories. It's reached from Angle by an unmade road, which gets cut off about four times a year for a couple of hours by spring tides.

Likeable pubby food might include sandwiches, fish chowder, half a rack of barbecue pork ribs, lasagne, sausage with egg, chips and beans, sweet potato and mushroom risotto, fresh fish dishes, rib-eye steak with tarragon butter, and puddings like bread and butter pudding with custard and chocolate and orange cheesecake. *Benchmark main dish: beer-battered fish and chips £8.25. Two-course evening meal £15.00.*

Free house ~ Licensee Robert Noble ~ Real ale ~ Bar food (12.30-2.30, 6.30-8.15; food for residents only Mon-Thurs Nov-Feb) ~ Restaurant ~ (01646) 641205 ~ Children welcome ~ Dogs allowed in bar and bedrooms ~ Open 12-10(midnight Sat); 12-3, 6-10 Weds-Sun in winter; closed winter Mon and Tues; closed November, January, February ~ Bedrooms: £43/£75 *Recommended by Louise Mallard, David and Susan Nobbs, Pauline Fellows and Simon Robbins*

You can send reports directly to us at feedback@goodguides.com

BEAUMARIS

SH6076   Map 6

Olde Bulls Head 🍴 ♀ 🛏

Castle Street; LL58 8AP

Interesting historic inn of many faces including a pubby bar, brasserie and restaurant; well equipped bedrooms

At the heart of this relaxed inn is a simple but cosy low-beamed bar that's nicely rambling, with plenty of interesting reminders of the town's past: a rare 17th-c brass water clock, a bloodthirsty crew of cutlasses and even an oak ducking stool tucked among the snug alcoves. There are lots of copper and china jugs, comfortable low-seated settles, leather-cushioned window seats, and a good log fire. Kindly staff serve Bass, Hancocks and a guest such as Brecon Six Beacons on handpump. In contrast, the busy brasserie behind is lively and stylishly modern, with a wine list that includes around 20 by the glass, and the exceptionally good restaurant upstairs is elegantly smart for a more formal meal with a wine list that runs to 120 bottles. The entrance to the pretty courtyard has a huge simple-hinged door that's an astonishing 3.3m wide and 4m high. The inn was built in 1472 and notable visitors have included Samuel Johnson and Charles Dickens, both of whom would find much of it familiar today. Named after characters in Dickens' novels, the bedrooms are very well equipped; some are traditional, and others more contemporary in style, and there are also bedrooms in the Townhouse, an adjacent property with disabled access.

 Soup and sandwiches are served in the bar at lunchtime. The much-enjoyed brasserie menu includes sandwiches, devilled lambs kidneys, mushroom and bacon pasty, cured bass sushi, pork and coriander dumplings, potted brown shrimps, seared calves liver with pink peppercorn sauce, baked hake with mediterranean vegetable lasagne, fish and chips, butternut goulash, and pudding such as hazelnut torte, spotted duck and plum pudding and orange curd and chocolate cappuccino with a garibaldi biscuit. *Benchmark main dish: slow roast lamb £14.00. Two-course evening meal £19.50.*

Free house ~ Licensee David Robertson ~ Real ale ~ Bar food (12-2(3 Sun), 6-9) ~ Restaurant ~ (01248) 810329 ~ Children welcome in China Bar only till 9pm ~ Open 11-11; 12-10.30 Sun ~ Bedrooms: £85B/£105B ~ www.bullsheadinn.co.uk
Recommended by Mike and Mary Carter, Bruce and Sharon Eden, Paul Humphreys, N R White, Martin Smith, Karen Eliot, Jonathan Bamford, Stuart Doughty

COLWYN BAY

SH8478   Map 6

Pen-y-Bryn 🍴 ♀ 🍺

B5113 Llanwrst Road, on southern outskirts; when you see the pub, turn off into Wentworth Avenue for its car park; LL29 6DD

Modern pub in great position overlooking the bay, reliable food all day, good range of drinks, obliging staff

Full of natural light, this carefully revamped spacious open-plan single-storey pub offers sweeping views across the bay and seats outside to appreciate them from: there are two terraces with sturdy tables and chairs and a lawn with picnic-sets. Inside, extending around the three long sides of the bar counter, the mix of seating and well spaced tables, oriental rugs on pale stripped boards, shelves of books, welcoming coal fires, the profusion of pictures, big pot plants, careful lighting and dark green school radiators are all typical of the pubs in this small, well received chain. Friendly, interested young staff serve Phoenix Brunning

& Price, Purple Moose Snowdonia Ale and three or four changing guests from brewers such as Black Sheep, Copper Dragon and Facers from handpump, well chosen good value wines including 20 by the glass and more than 60 malt whiskies; board games and background music.

🍴 Served all day, reliable, much-liked food from a changing menu could typically include substantial sandwiches, cauliflower and goats cheese soup, crab spring roll, bass with noodles and hot and sour sauce, grilled chicken with lemon and coriander couscous and mediterranean vegetables, slow-roast belly pork with dauphinoise potatoes and spiced apple purée, rump steak or haddock and chips, and puddings such as strawberry cheesecake with raspberry coulis and chocolate brownie with chocolate sauce. *Benchmark main dish: steak burger £11.25. Two-course evening meal £19.60.*

Brunning & Price ~ Managers Andrew Grant and Graham Price ~ Real ale ~ Bar food (12-9.30(9 Sun)) ~ (01492) 533360 ~ Children welcome ~ Open 11.30-11; 12-10.30 Sun ~ www.penybryn-colwynbay.co.uk *Recommended by Bruce and Sharon Eden, Dr D A Gidlow*

CRICKHOWELL   SO2118 Map 6

Bear ★ ♀ ⇎

Brecon Road; A40; NP8 1BW

Convivial, interesting inn with splendid, old-fashioned bar area warmed by a log fire, good and sensibly priced food, comfortable bedrooms

Right at the centre of an enchanting small town, this civilised and pleasantly rambling coaching inn has been run by the same welcoming owners for many years and consistently maintains its standards. The heavily beamed lounge has fresh flowers on the tables, lots of little plush-seated bentwood armchairs and handsome cushioned antique settles, and a window seat looking down on the market square. Up by the great roaring log fire, a big sofa and leather easy chairs are on rugs on oak parquet flooring. Other antiques include a fine oak dresser filled with pewter mugs and brassware, a longcase clock and interesting prints. Brains Rev James, Wye Valley Butty Bach and a couple of frequently changing guests such as Rhymney Hobby Horse and Wadsworth 6X are on handpump, as well as 40 malt whiskies, vintage and late-bottled ports, unusual wines (with several by the glass); disabled lavatories. This is a particularly appealing place to stay: older bedrooms in the main building have antiques, while some of the refurbished ones in the converted stables are in a country style, some with jacuzzis and four-poster beds, and breakfast is excellent. Reception rooms, watched over by patient yet efficient staff, are comfortably furnished. There's a small garden.

🍴 Much-liked bar food from a changing menu (with sandwiches and baguettes) might include soup, salmon fishcake, chicken and leek pie, sausages and mash, moroccan lemon chicken with spiced vegetable couscous, slow-braised welsh lamb shank, local steaks or baked salmon marinated in chilli, lime and coriander, and puddings such as saffron parfait with poached peaches and egg custard tart; booking is advised. *Benchmark main dish: fish and chips £11.50. Two-course evening meal £18.60.*

Free house ~ Licensee Judy Hindmarsh ~ Real ale ~ Bar food (12-2.15, 6-10; 12-3, 7-9.30 Sun) ~ Restaurant ~ (01873) 810408 ~ Children welcome ~ Dogs allowed in bar and bedrooms ~ Open 10.30-11; 11-10.30 Sun ~ Bedrooms: /£77S(£118B) ~ www.bearhotel.co.uk *Recommended by Barry and Anne, Ken and Barbara Turner, Michael Mellers, Tony and Maggie Harwood, Anthony Barnes, Terry Davis, Dr and Mrs C W Thomas,*

Taff Thomas, LM, Guy Vowles, Adrian Johnson, David and Sue Atkinson, Tom and Ruth Rees, Michael Carpenter, R T and JC Moggridge, Bob and Margaret Holder

EAST ABERTHAW   ST0366   Map 6

Blue Anchor 🍺 £

B4265; CF62 3DD

Character-laden thatched pub with five real ales

Deeply atmospheric with its cosy collection of low-beamed little rooms, this relaxed medieval tavern makes a memorable spot for a drink, with five real ales on handpump: Brains Bitter, Theakstons Old Peculier, Wadworths 6X and Wye Valley Hereford Pale Ale, alongside a changing guest from a brewer such as Cotleigh, as well as Gwynt y Ddraig farm cider. The building has massive walls, low-beamed rooms and tiny doorways, with open fires everywhere, including one in an inglenook with antique oak seats built into its stripped stonework. Other seats and tables are worked into a series of little alcoves, and the more open front bar still has an ancient lime-ash floor. Outside, rustic seats shelter peacefully among tubs and troughs of flowers, with stone tables on a newer terrace. The pub can get very full in the evenings and on summer weekends, and it's used as a base by a couple of local motorbike clubs. A path from here leads to the shingly flats of the estuary.

Good value bar food includes baguettes, vegetarian antipasti, welsh rarebit, rib-eye steak, haddock and chips, steamed mussels, roast belly pork with crushed parsnip and apple, beetroot and goats cheese risotto, and daily specials such as calves liver on red onion and thyme mash; more elaborate dishes are served in the restaurant. *Benchmark main dish: roast pheasant £10.50. Two-course evening meal £13.90.*

Free house ~ Licensee Jeremy Coleman ~ Real ale ~ Bar food (not Sun evening) ~ Restaurant ~ (01446) 750329 ~ Children welcome ~ Dogs allowed in bar ~ Open 11-11; 12-10.30 Sun ~ www.blueanchoraberthaw.com *Recommended by Roger Fox, Richard Gibbs, Daz Smith*

FELINFACH   SO0933   Map 6

Griffin 🍴 🍷 🍺 🛏

A470 NE of Brecon; LD3 0UB

Wales Dining Pub of the Year

Classy, relaxed dining pub with good, unpretentious cooking featuring lots of home-grown vegetables; upbeat rustic décor, nice bedrooms

Year after year we get confirmation from readers that this splendid dining pub with rooms is doing everything right, with its fine range of drinks, carefully sourced and nicely presented food and delightful accommodation. The back bar is quite pubby in an up-to-date way: four leather sofas sit around a low table on pitted quarry tiles by a high slate hearth with a log fire; behind them are mixed stripped seats around scrubbed kitchen tables on bare floorboards. The colour scheme is bright blue and ochre, with some modern prints. The acoustics are pretty lively, due to so much bare flooring and uncurtained windows; maybe background radio; board games and plenty of books. The two smallish front dining rooms that link through to the back bar are attractive: on the left, mixed dining chairs around mainly stripped tables on flagstones, and white-painted rough stone walls with a cream-coloured Aga in a big stripped-stone embrasure; on the right, similar furniture on bare boards, big modern prints on terracotta walls and smart dark curtains. Efficient staff serve a fine array of drinks, many from smaller, independent suppliers, including a thoughtful choice of wines that varies through the seasons (with 20 by the glass and carafe), welsh spirits, cocktails, an award-winning local bottled cider, locally sourced apple juice, non-alcoholic cocktails made with produce from their garden, unusual continental and local bottled beers, a fine range of sherries, and four real ales from Brecon, Montys, Tomos Watkin, Waen and Wye Valley on handpump. This is a lovely place to stay, with nothing missed. Bedrooms are comfortable and tastefully decorated, and the hearty breakfasts nicely informal: you make your own toast and help yourself to home-made marmalade and jam. Children can play with the landlady's dog and visit the chickens in the henhouse, and dogs may sit with owners at certain tables while dining. Good wheelchair access, and outside tables.

Using carefully sourced seasonal ingredients and organic produce from the pub's own organically certified kitchen garden (from which the surplus is often for sale), as well as game from local shoots and produce from nearby farms, the food may not be cheap but is consistently good. The lunch and evening menus might variously include ploughman's with local cheese and home-made pickles, pressed ham hock with cauliflower velouté and potato or roast squash with goats cheese and pumpkin seeds, venison and mushroom pie, roast monkfish with pearl barley and roast shallots, braised shin of beef, haunch of fallow deer or pollock with new potatoes, spinach and clam broth; puddings could be warm pistachio cake with poached pear and sour cream or dark chocolate brownie with caramelised hazelnuts and malted milk ice-cream. They also do a more reasonably priced set three-course menu. *Benchmark main dish: rib of welsh beef with garlic mushrooms £19.50. Two-course evening meal £19.60.*

Free house ~ Licensees Charles and Edmund Inkin and Julie Bell ~ Real ale ~ Bar food (12-2.30, 6-9(9.30 Fri, Sat)) ~ (01874) 620111 ~ Children welcome ~ Dogs allowed in bar and bedrooms ~ Acoustic session first and third Sun lunchtimes ~ Open 11.30-11(10.30 Sun); closed four days in Jan ~ Bedrooms: $105B/$120B ~ www.eatdrinksleep.ltd.uk *Recommended by David Heath, Mrs P Bishop, Kate Vogelsang, Suzi Clay, MLR, Bernard Stradling, Karen Eliot, B and M Kendall, Taff and Gilly Thomas, David and Susan Nobbs, Warren Marsh*

GRESFORD
Pant-yr-Ochain 🍴 ♟ ▨

SJ3453 Map 6

Off A483 on N edge of Wrexham: at roundabout take A5156 (A534) towards Nantwich, then first left towards the Flash; LL12 8TY

Thoughtfully run, gently refined dining pub in the Brunning & Price chain, good food all day, very wide range of drinks, pretty lakeside garden

This elaborately gabled black and white 16th-c former manor house is an absolute delight, with exemplary service and an enchanting garden with herbaceous borders, mature trees and thriving box-edged herb beds; solid wooden furniture overlooks a lake frequented by waterfowl. The light and airy rooms are stylishly decorated, with a wide range of interesting prints and bric-a-brac, and a good mix of individually chosen country furnishings, including comfortable seats for relaxing as well as more upright ones for eating, and there's a recently rebuilt conservatory and a good open fire; one area is set out as a library, with floor-to-ceiling bookshelves. Their terrific range of drinks includes Flowers Original, Phoenix Brunning & Price Original, and four to six guest ales including Snowdonia and Weetwood, farm cider, a good choice of decent wines (strong on up-front new world ones), with 15 by the glass, and around 100 malt whiskies. Disabled access is good.

The well balanced daily changing menu features thoughtfully prepared food and includes sandwiches and ploughman's, along with changing dishes such as fig and shropshire blue tart with red wine dressing, terrine of pork, prune and pistachio with plum chutney, steak and ale suet pudding, fish and white bean stew, lamb rump with sweet potato mash, pork and black pudding sausages with mash and grain mustard cream sauce, steak burger with grilled bacon and cheddar; puddings might be belgian waffle with butterscotch sauce or chocolate and hazelnut brownie with chocolate sauce; children's menu. *Benchmark main dish: fish and chips £11.95. Two-course evening meal £18.90.*

Brunning & Price ~ Licensee James Meakin ~ Real ale ~ Bar food (12-9.30(9 Sun)) ~ (01978) 853525 ~ Children welcome ~ Dogs allowed in bar ~ Open 11.30-11; 12-10.30 Sun ~ www.brunningandprice.co.uk/pantyrochain/ *Recommended by Clive Watkin, Bruce and Sharon Eden, Dan Guy, Roger and Anne Newbury, Mrs Margo Finlay, Jörg Kasprowski, David Jackman, Dr D A Gidlow*

LLANARMON DYFFRYN CEIRIOG   SJ1532   Map 6
Hand 🛏

B4500 from Chirk; LL20 7LD

Comfortable rural hotel in a remote valley; cosy low-beamed bar area, good bedrooms

Run by welcoming staff, this comfortable inn occupies a supremely rural position tucked away in a peaceful village in the sloping, sheep-grazed pastures of the Upper Ceiriog valley and looking out to the Berwyn Mountains. The black-beamed, carpeted bar on the left of the broad-flagstoned entrance hall has a hearty log fire in its inglenook fireplace, a mixture of chairs and settles, and old prints on its cream walls, with bar stools along the modern bar counter, which has Weetwood Cheshire Cat or Eastgate Ale and a guest from a brewery such as Waen on handpump, several malt whiskies and reasonably priced wines by the glass. Round the corner is the largely stripped-stone dining room, with a woodburning stove and carpeted floor; TV, darts and pool in games room. Bedrooms are attractive and spacious, and breakfasts are very satisfying; the residents' lounge on the right is comfortable and attractive. There are tables out on a crazy-paved front terrace, with more in the garden, which has flowerbeds around another sheltered terrace.

Besides lunchtime sandwiches and ploughman's, dishes from the seasonally changing menu using named local suppliers might include smoked haddock and kipper mousse, cream of curried parsnip and leek soup, sausage and mash, rib-eye steak, roast monkfish tails with leeks and pea shoots, confit of duck leg cooked in white wine with shoulder of venison, home-made lasagne; puddings could be dark chocolate tart or summer berry pudding with cherry coulis. *Benchmark main dish: slow-braised welsh lamb shoulder £17.50. Two-course evening meal £19.50.*

Free house ~ Licensees Gaynor and Martin de Luchi ~ Bar food (12-2.20, 6.30–8.45; 12.30-2.45, 6.30-8.30 Sun) ~ Restaurant ~ (01691) 600666 ~ Children welcome ~ Dogs allowed in bar and bedrooms ~ Open 11(12 Sun)-11(midnight Sat) ~ Bedrooms: £45B/£90B ~ www.thehandhotel.co.uk *Recommended by Clive Watkin*

The price we give for a two-course evening meal in the featured entries
is the mean (average of cheapest and most expensive) price of a starter and
a main course – no drinks.

LLANBERIS SH6655 Map 6

Pen-y-Gwryd

*Nant Gwynant; at junction of A498 and A4086, ie across mountains
from Llanberis – OS Sheet 115 map reference 660558; LL55 4NT*

**Run by the same family since 1947, an illustrious favourite
with the climbing fraternity with a slightly eccentric but cheerily
simple atmosphere**

Much liked by readers for its unchanged character, this inn,
spectacularly sited amid the wilds of Snowdonia, has attracted
generations of climbers, many of whom have contributed to a collection
of memorabilia. The fading signatures of the 1953 Everest team,
who used this as a training base, can still be made out, scrawled on
the ceiling, and on display is the very rope that connected Hillary
and Tenzing at the top of the mountain. One snug little room in the
homely slate-floored log cabin bar has built-in wall benches and
sturdy country chairs. From here you can look out on the surrounding
mountain landscape, including to precipitous Moel Siabod beyond the
lake opposite. A smaller room has a worthy collection of illustrious
boots from famous climbs, and a cosy panelled smoke room has more
fascinating climbing mementoes and equipment; darts, pool, board
games, skittles, bar billiards and table tennis. Purple Moose Glaslyn
and Madogs are on handpump, and they have several malts. Staying
in the comfortable but basic bedrooms can be quite an experience; an
excellent, traditional breakfast is served between 8.30 (or earlier) and
9am; dogs may stay for £2 a night. The inn has its own chapel (built for
the millennium and dedicated by the Archbishop of Wales), sauna and
outdoor natural pool, and the garden overlooks a lake.

The short choice of simple, good value and carefully sourced home-made
lunchtime bar food (you order through a hatch) includes filled rolls,
ploughman's, warm salad of smoked duck and bacon, and quiche of the day, as well
as daily specials like roast beef. The three- or five-course hearty fixed-price meal in
the evening restaurant is signalled by a gong at 7.30pm – if you're late, you'll miss
it. A sample menu might be tomato and basil soup followed by welsh cutlet of lamb
with herby crust or baked salmon in a creamy sauce. *Benchmark main dish: roast
lamb £8.50*

Free house ~ Licensee Jane Pullee ~ Real ale ~ Bar food (12-2, evening meal at 7.30pm)
~ Restaurant (evening) ~ (01286) 870211 ~ Children welcome ~ Dogs allowed in bar
and bedrooms ~ Open 11-11(10.30 Sun); closed all Nov-Dec, and midweek Jan-Feb ~
Bedrooms: £42/£84(£100B) ~ www.pyg.co.uk *Recommended by Tim Maddison, Richard, Anne
and Kate Ansell, Barry and Verina Jones, Doug Kennedy*

LLANELIAN-YN-RHOS SH8676 Map 6

White Lion

*Signed off A5830 (shown as B5383 on some maps) and B5381, S of Colwyn
Bay; LL29 8YA*

**Cosy village pub with friendly staff, pleasantly traditional bar and
roomy dining area**

Tucked away in a knot of lanes in rolling country above Colwyn
Bay, this pleasantly unfussy village local is run by helpful staff. It
comprises two distinct parts, each with its own cheery personality,
linked by a broad flight of steps. Up at the top is a neat and very spacious
dining area, while down at the other end is a traditional old bar, with

antique high-backed settles angling snugly around a big fireplace, and flagstones by the counter, where they serve Marstons Burton and Pedigree, a guest such as Purple Moose and a good wine list; on the left, another dining area has jugs hanging from the beams and teapots above the window. Prompt service; background music. There are tables in an attractive courtyard (also used for parking) next to the church.

Tasty food includes sandwiches, baguettes, ciabatta sandwiches, pâté, mussels poached in creamy garlic and white wine, roast lamb shoulder, steak and kidney pie, pork and leek sausages with smoked bacon and cheddar mash, fish stew, roasted mediterranean vegetables, and daily specials. *Benchmark main dish: roast lamb £9.95. Two-course evening meal £16.40.*

Free house ~ Licensee Simon Cole ~ Real ale ~ Bar food (12-2, 6-9; 12-8.30 Sun) ~ Restaurant ~ (01492) 515807 ~ Children welcome ~ Live jazz Tues evening, bluegrass Weds evening ~ Open 11.30-3.30, 6-11(midnight Sat); 12-10.30 Sun; closed Mon except school and bank holidays ~ www.whitelioninn.co.uk *Recommended by Michael and Jenny Back, Jonjoliz*

LLANFERRES   SJ1860   Map 6
Druid
A494 Mold–Ruthin; CH7 5SN

Friendly inn with fine views and fantastic surrounding walks, a good choice of drinks, and good, hearty food; bedrooms

The views from this friendly extended 17th-c whitewashed inn indicate that it is in choice walking country, with strolls along the Alyn Valley towards Loggerheads Country Park or up through the partly wooded slopes and along Offa's Dyke Path to Moel Fammau, at the top of the Clwydian range. You can savour the scene from the broad bay window in the civilised, smallish plush lounge and from the bigger beamed back bar, with its two handsome antique oak settles, pleasant mix of more modern furnishings, quarry-tiled area by the log fire and three-legged cat, Chu. Marstons Burton, Ringwood Boondoggle and a guest such as Wychwood Hobgoblin are on handpump alongside an array of up to 30 malt whiskies. A games room has darts and pool, along with board games; background music, TV. You can enjoy the setting from tables outside at the front.

Reasonably priced and generously served, the food includes sandwiches, chicken liver pâté, stilton-stuffed mushrooms, ham with free-range eggs and chips, chicken stuffed with asparagus and cheese, lasagne, oriental pork on noodles, salmon fillet with lime, honey and mustard dressing, steaks with sauces like pepper, garlic and béarnaise, and puddings. *Benchmark main dish: steak and mushroom in ale pie £10.65. Two-course evening meal £19.00.*

Marstons ~ Lease James Dolan ~ Real ale ~ Bar food (12-3, 6-9; 12-9 Fri-Sun and bank holidays) ~ Restaurant ~ (01352) 810225 ~ Children welcome ~ Dogs allowed in bar and bedrooms ~ Open 12-3.30, 5-11; 12-11 Fri and Sat; 12-10 Sun ~ Bedrooms: £55S/£78S ~ www.druidinn.com *Recommended by Roger and Diana Morgan, Ian Phillips, Christine and Neil Townend, Mrs Margo Finlay, Jörg Kasprowski, David Jackman, David and Katharine Cooke*

If a service charge is mentioned prominently on a menu or accommodation terms, you must pay it if service was satisfactory. If service is really bad you are legally entitled to refuse to pay some or all of the service charge as compensation for not getting the service you might reasonably have expected.

LLANGOLLEN

SJ2142 Map 6

Corn Mill ⑪ ♈ ◀

Dee Lane, very narrow lane off Castle Street (A539) just S of bridge; nearby parking can be tricky, may be best to use public park on Parade Street/East Street and walk; LL20 8PN

Excellent on all counts, with personable young staff, super food all day, good beers and a fascinating riverside building

Open all day, this converted mill right by the River Dee makes a pleasant spot for watching the world go by, with views of steam trains puffing away at the nearby station across the valley and an assortment of craft on the Llangollen Canal. A long, narrow deck along one side of the building juts out over the water. Quite a bit of working mill machinery remains – most obviously the great waterwheel (sometimes turning), and the interior has been interestingly refitted with pale pine flooring, stout beams, a striking open stairway with gleaming timber and tensioned steel rails, and mainly stripped-stone walls. A bustling, chatty atmosphere greets you, with quick service from plenty of pleasant young staff, good-sized dining tables, big rugs, thoughtfully chosen pictures (many to do with water) and lots of pot plants. One of the two serving bars, away from the water, has a much more local feel, with pews on dark slate flagstones, daily papers and regulars on the bar stools. As well as Phoenix Brunning & Price, they have a great range of drinks, with four guests from brewers such as Facers Flintshire and Plassey, farm cider, around 50 sensibly priced malt whiskies and a decent wine choice with 13 by the glass.

 As the pub can get busy, book if you're planning to eat. In addition to lunchtime sandwiches and ploughman's, good food from a daily changing menu includes dishes such as fried scallops with crisp belly pork, smoked haddock chowder rump steak with hand-cut chips, black pudding, bacon and chorizo salad, sausages and mash, sweet potato and chickpea curry, salmon fillet with lemon parmesan crust, steak burger topped with grilled bacon and cheddar. *Benchmark main dish: haddock and chips £11.95. Two-course evening meal £17.70.*

Brunning & Price ~ Manager Andrew Barker ~ Real ale ~ Bar food (12-9.30(9 Sun)) ~ (01978) 869555 ~ Children welcome but no high chairs available ~ Open 12-11(10.30 Sun) ~ www.brunningandprice.co.uk/cornmill/ *Recommended by Clive Watkin, Dennis Jones, Alastair Stevenson, N R White, Bruce and Sharon Eden, Martin Smith, Mike and Mary Carter, Bob and Margaret Holder*

MAENTWROG

SH6640 Map 6

Grapes

A496; village signed from A470; LL41 4HN

Lively inn with good mix of customers, pleasant garden views; bedrooms

You may well be greeted in Welsh as you enter this welcoming inn in the Vale of Ffestiniog, within sight and tooting distance of the quaint steam trains of the Ffestiniog Railway. Its three bars are each furnished with stripped pitch-pine pews, settles, pillars and carvings, mostly salvaged from chapels; elsewhere are softer furnishings. Warming woodburning stoves are on the go in winter, including one in the great hearth in the restaurant. Four beers on handpump are all from Evan Evans – Best, Cwrw, Warrior and a seasonal guest; background music, TV, darts; disabled lavatories. There are views from the good-sized conservatory, as well as a pleasant back terrace and walled garden.

🍴 Well liked bar food includes sandwiches, creamy garlic mushrooms on granary toast, caramelised onion and cheese tartlet, sausage, bacon and egg, fishcakes with a sweet chilli dip and chips, meaty or mediterranean vegetable lasagne, chicken fajitas with sour cream, local sausages with mash and gravy, beer-battered fish with mushy peas, a curry of the day, moules frites, and puddings like chocolate fudge cake and cheesecake. *Benchmark main dish: spicy spare ribs £10.95. Two-course evening meal £18.00.*

Evan Evans ~ Manager Callisa Smith ~ Real ale ~ Bar food (12-2, 5.30-8.30(6-8 Sun)) ~ Restaurant ~ (01766) 590208 ~ Children welcome ~ Dogs allowed in bar ~ Open 12-11(midnight Sat) ~ Bedrooms: £45B/£80B ~ www.grapeshotelsnowdonia.co.uk
Recommended by Mike and Eleanor Anderson

MOLD
SJ2465   Map 6
Glasfryn 🍴 ♟ 🍺
N of the centre on Raikes Lane (parallel to the A5119), just past the well signposted Theatr Clwyd; CH7 6LR

Lively open-plan bistro-style pub with inventive, upmarket food all day, nice décor, wide choice of drinks

With Theatr Clwyd just over the road, this cheery and enthusiastically run Brunning & Price bistro-style dining pub often buzzes with theatregoers in the evening, while in the day there may be families enjoying a meal. Decorated in this fine chain's trademark style, its attractive open-plan interior is cleverly laid out to create plenty of nice, quiet corners. It has a mix of informal country furnishings, turkish rugs on bare boards, deep red (some high) ceilings, a warming fire and plenty of homely close-hung pictures; board games. Besides 30 wines by the glass, local apple juice, farm cider and around 70 malt whiskies, they've a wide choice of beers on handpump, with Flowers Original, Phoenix Brunning & Price Original and Purple Moose Snowdonia alongside several swiftly changing guests from brewers such as Timothy Taylors and Titanic. On warm days, the large terrace in front of the pub makes an idyllic place to sit out by the wooden tables, from which you get sweeping views of the Clwydian Hills.

🍴 From a daily changing menu, the choice of good, well prepared food might include sandwiches, ploughman's, fried egg with asparagus and hollandaise sauce, grilled mackerel salad with spiced rhubarb relish, corned beef hash with fried egg, fish pie, braised lamb shoulder, aubergine and squash tagine with apricot and deep-fried okra, steak and kidney pudding, sausages and mash; puddings might feature sherry trifle or rice pudding with raspberry jam. *Benchmark main dish: haddock and chips £11.95. Two-course evening meal £18.90.*

Brunning & Price ~ Manager Graham Arathoon ~ Real ale ~ Bar food (12-9.30(9 Sun)) ~ (01352) 750500 ~ Children welcome ~ Dogs allowed in bar ~ Open 11.30-11; 12-10.30 Sun ~ www.glasfryn-mold.co.uk *Recommended by Clive Watkin, C A Bryson, Bruce and Sharon Eden, Andy and Jill Kassube, Chris Flynn, Wendy Jones, David Jackman*

MONKNASH
SS9170   Map 6
Plough & Harrow 🍺 £
Signposted Marcross, Broughton, off B4265 St Brides Major–Llantwit Major – turn left at end of Water Street; OS Sheet 170 map reference 920706; CF71 7QQ

Old building full of history and character, with a good choice of real ales

This is an ancient place that once formed part of a monastic grange. It's the ideal stopping point if you're visiting the spectacular stretch of coastal cliffs nearby; you can walk from here to the lighthouse at Nash Point. The unspoilt main bar, with its massively thick stone walls, used to be the scriptures room and mortuary, and has ancient ham hooks in the heavily beamed ceiling, an intriguing arched doorway to the back, and a comfortably informal mix of furnishings that includes three fine stripped-pine settles on the broad flagstones. There's a log fire in a huge fireplace with a side bread oven large enough to feed a village. The room on the left has background music and darts. Up to eight real ales on handpump or tapped from the cask might include Bank Top Old Slapper, Bass, Brecon Beacon To The Sea, Evan Evans Cwrw, Wye Valley HPA and changing guests; they hold beer festivals in June and September. They also have a good range of local farm ciders and welsh and malt whiskies. There are picnic-sets in the front garden; dogs are welcome in the bar – but not while food is being served.

Under the newish landlady, bar food now includes sandwiches, chicken liver parfait with red onion chutney, salmon and coriander fishcake with sweet chilli sauce, cheese and leek sausages with garlic and herb mayonnaise, italian-style chicken with salsa and tortillas, pork with black pudding mash and creamy cider sauce, rump of lamb on root vegetable mash with red wine and rosemary sauce, and puddings like apple crumble and bread and butter pudding. *Benchmark main dish: beer-battered fish and chips £8.25. Two-course evening meal £16.00.*

Free house ~ Licensee Paula Jones ~ Real ale ~ Bar food (12-2.30(5 Sat, Sun), 6-9; not Sun evening) ~ Restaurant ~ (01656) 890209 ~ Children welcome until 7pm ~ Dogs welcome in bar (except when food served) ~ Live music Sat evening ~ Open 12-11 ~ www.ploughandharrow.org *Recommended by James Morris, Taff Thomas, R T and J C Moggridge, Kevin Thomas, Nina Randall*

NEWPORT
Golden Lion 🛏
SN0539   Map 6

East Street (A487); SA42 0SY

Nicely redone, friendly local, with tasty food, pleasant staff, and well appointed bedrooms

Stylishly refurbished, this welcoming village inn has a nice balance of comfortable dining and pubby character, and readers praise the friendly service. Some of its cosy series of beamed rooms have distinctive old settles. On offer are four changing beers from brewers such as Gwaun Valley, Hook Norton, Sharps and St Austell on handpump, as well as several malt whiskies, wines by the glass and Gwynt y Ddraig cider; pool, juke box, board games, dominoes and games machine. The dining room has elegant blonde wood oak furniture, whitewashed walls and potted plants. There are tables outside at the front and in a side garden; good disabled access and facilities. The bedrooms are very good value.

Enjoyable, carefully presented food includes lunchtime sandwiches, vegetable spring rolls, lemon and garlic free range chicken, italian bean casserole, local lamb chops, steaks, fish specials, and puddings such as white chocolate tart or poached raspberries. *Benchmark main dish: fish platter £16.00. Two-course evening meal £17.90.*

Free house ~ Licensee Daron Paish ~ Real ale ~ Bar food (12-2.30, 6.30-9) ~ Restaurant ~ (01239) 820321 ~ Children welcome ~ Dogs allowed in bar and bedrooms ~ Live music weekends Oct-April ~ Open 12-2am ~ Bedrooms: £70B/£90B ~ www.goldenlionpembrokeshire.co.uk *Recommended by Angela Crum Ewing, M E and F J Thomasson, R T and J C Moggridge*

OLD RADNOR
SO2459   Map 6

Harp ♨ ⇔

Village signposted off A44 Kington–New Radnor in Walton; LD8 2RH

Delightfully placed with cottagey bar, tasty food and comfortable bedrooms

Driving or walking up to this charming hilltop pub you are rewarded with a panoramic view of the welsh borders, across towards the wild heights of Radnor Forest; tables outside make the most of the view. Loved equally by locals and tourists, the warmly welcoming public bar has high-backed settles, an antique reader's chair and other elderly chairs around a log fire; board games, cribbage, darts and quoits. The snug slate-floored lounge has a handsome curved antique settle, a log fire in a fine inglenook, and lots of local books and guides for residents; a quieter dining area is off to the right, extending into another dining room with a wood-burning stove. They have a couple of changing real ales from brewers such as Liverpool Organic Brewery and Three Tuns, as well as Dunkerton's and Ralph's cider, local cassis and several malt whiskies, and they hold a beer and cider festival in June; friendly, helpful service. The impressive village church is worth a look for its early organ case (Britain's oldest), fine rood screen and ancient font.

 The sensibly short menu features produce from the publicans' own garden and other carefully sourced seasonal ingredients; as well as sandwiches, ploughman's, a platter of british cured meats or warm kipper with potato salad, dishes typically include welsh black beef rump steak, grilled bass, slow-roast shoulder of lamb with aromatic spices, and puddings like passion-fruit panna cotta or rhubarb and custard with ginger crumb. *Benchmark main dish: welsh black rump steak £17.00. Two-course evening meal £19.40.*

Free house ~ Licensees Chris Ireland and Angela Lyne ~ Real ale ~ Bar food (12-2.30 Sat, Sun; 6-9(8 Sun); not Sun evening in winter or weekday lunchtimes) ~ (01544) 350655 ~ Children welcome ~ Dogs allowed in bar and bedrooms ~ Open 6-11; 12-3, 6-11 Sat; 12-3, 6-10.30 Sun; closed weekday lunchtimes, all day Mon ~ Bedrooms: £55B/£90B ~ www.harpinnradnor.co.uk *Recommended by Mr and Mrs J Mandeville, John Taylor, Marcus Thorpe, Steve Whalley, Kim Skuse*

OVERTON BRIDGE
SJ3542   Map 6

Cross Foxes ♨ ♀

A539 W of Overton, near Erbistock; LL13 0DR

Terrific river views from well run 18th-c coaching inn with good food and extensive drinks' range

Immediately below this substantial 18th-c coaching inn sweeps the River Dee; big windows all round the walls of an airy dining room give a great view of it. The ancient low-beamed bar, with its red tiled floor, dark timbers, a warm fire in the big inglenook and built-in old pews, is more traditional than most pubs in the Brunning & Price group, though the characteristic turkish rugs and frame-to-frame pictures are present, as they are in the dining areas; board games and newspapers. Friendly, competent staff serve Brakspear Bitter, Jennings Cumberland and a couple of guests from brewers such as Evan Evans and Ringwood from handpumps, a farm cider, 50 malts, an excellent range of armagnacs and a changing choice of around 15 wines by the glass. Good oak chairs and tables on a raised terrace make the most of the riverside position; picnic-sets down on a lawn are even closer to the water.

As well as sandwiches and ploughman's, carefully prepared bar food from a tempting menu might include pressed ham hock terrine, smoked duck salad, indonesian-style vegetable curry, rump steak, steak in ale pie, chicken stuffed with butternut squash and wrapped in bacon, marinated baked aubergine topped with goats cheese, and puddings such as egg custard tart with poached rhubarb or waffle with vanilla ice-cream and chocolate fudge sauce. *Benchmark main dish: haddock and chips £11.95. Two-course evening meal £19.50.*

Brunning & Price ~ Manager Ian Pritchard-Jones ~ Real ale ~ Bar food (12-9.30(9 Sun)) ~ (01978) 780380 ~ Children welcome ~ Dogs allowed in bar ~ Open 12-11(10.30 Sun) ~ www.crossfoxes-erbistock.co.uk *Recommended by Brian and Anna Marsden, Dave Webster, Sue Holland, Bruce and Sharon Eden, Peter and Josie Fawcett*

PANTYGELLI
SO3017 Map 6
Crown ♀ 🍺
Old Hereford Road N of Abergavenny; off A40 by war memorial via Pen Y Pound, passing leisure centre; Pantygelli also signposted from A465; NP7 7HR

Prettily placed country pub, attractive inside and out, with good food and drinks

A lovely place to arrive at after a walk up the nearby Sugar Loaf, this well kept free house is just inside the Brecon Beacons National Park. The neat and efficient staff take their cue from the friendly hands-on owners, giving a warmly welcoming atmosphere. The dark flagstoned bar, with sturdy timber props and beams, has a piano at the back, darts opposite, a log fire in the stone fireplace, and – from its slate-roofed counter – well kept Bass, Rhymney Best, Wye Valley HPA and a guest such as Celt Native Storm on handpump, Stowford Press and Gwatkin's farm cider, good wines by the glass, local organic apple juice, and good coffees. On the left are four smallish, linked, carpeted dining rooms, the front pair separated by a massive stone chimneybreast; thoughtfully chosen individual furnishings and lots of attractive prints by local artists make it all thoroughly civilised; background music, darts and board games. Comfortable wrought-iron and wicker chairs on the flower-filled front terrace look up from this lush valley to the lower slopes of the Black Mountains; a smaller back terrace is surrounded by lavender.

 Bar food includes baguettes and pubby standards like sausages and mash and rib-eye steak, with additional daily specials such as asparagus and cheese tartlet, baked cod on orange lentils with rich tomato sauce, poached chicken breast filled with mango and lemon grass and coconut sauce, or lamb shank. *Benchmark main dish: lamb cutlets with pea and feta salad, grilled new potatoes and rosemary jus £18.50. Two-course evening meal £17.45.*

Free house ~ Licensees Steve and Cherrie Chadwick ~ Real ale ~ Bar food (12-2, 7-9; not Sun evening or Mon) ~ Restaurant ~ (01873) 853314 ~ Children welcome ~ Dogs allowed in bar ~ Open 12-2.30(3 weekends), 6-11(10.30 Sun); closed Mon lunchtime ~ www.thecrownatpantygelli.com *Recommended by Carol Phillips, R T and J C Moggridge*

PENNAL
SH6900 Map 6
Riverside
A493; opposite church; SY20 9DW

Fresh refurbishment with tasty food and local beers

One reader arrived at this cheerfully run dining pub in the Dovey Valley with a group of muddy walkers, and the friendly owners made them feel very welcome. It has been neatly refurbished with fresh green and white walls, slate floor tiles, a woodburning stove, modern light wood dining furniture and some funky fabrics. High-backed stools are lined up along the stone-fronted counter, where they serve three changing beers such as Purple Moose Dark Side of the Moose and Sharps Doom Bar, several malts and around a dozen wines by the glass; background music, TV and garden.

🍴 In addition to lunchtime sandwiches, tasty bar food includes goats cheese or warm duck salad, welsh rarebit, sirloin steak, a pie of the day, haddock and chips, fish stew and three-bean chilli, with puddings such as fruit crumble and sticky toffee pudding. *Benchmark main dish: fish stew with king prawns and chorizo £13.95. Two-course evening meal £18.10.*

Free house ~ Licensees Glyn and Corina Davies ~ Real ale ~ Bar food (12-2.30, 6-9.30) ~ Restaurant ~ (01654) 791285 ~ Children welcome ~ Dogs allowed in bar ~ Open 12-11(midnight Sat); closed two weeks Jan ~ www.riversidehotel-pennal.co.uk
Recommended by Mike and Mary Carter, Mrs F Smith

PONTYPRIDD   ST0790   Map

Bunch of Grapes 🍴 ♀ 🍺

Off A4054; Ynysangharad Road; CF37 4DA

Refurbished pub with a fine choice of drinks in friendly, relaxed bar, delicious food and a warm welcome for all

Our readers love this pub. It's a late 18th-c building, backs on to the remnants of the Glamorganshire Canal and was given a modern refurbishment a couple of years ago. There's a cosy bar with an informal, relaxed atmosphere, comfortable leather sofas, wooden chairs and tables, a roaring log fire, newspapers to read, Otley O1 and two guests plus another five quickly changing guest beers from breweries far and wide on handpump, continental and American ales on draught or in bottles, a couple of local ciders or perrys, seven wines by the glass and good coffee; service is knowledgeable, friendly and efficient. There's also a restaurant with elegant high-backed wooden dining chairs around a mix of tables, and prints on pale contemporary paintwork; some seats outside on decking. They also have a deli selling home-baked bread and chutneys, home-cooked ham, local eggs, quite a choice of welsh cheeses and so forth, and hold cookery classes and regular themed evenings.

🍴 Inventive food from an ever-changing menu and using the best local and seasonal produce might include sandwiches, potted mackerel with horseradish cream, pigeon breast with celeriac purée, pomegranate salsa and black pudding, beef burger with cheese and bacon in a home-made focaccia bun, ham and egg with hand-cut chips, white onion and leek tart with polenta chips and chicory salad, goan beef curry, confit belly of pork with grain mustard mash and caramelised apple sauce, sautéed scampi, cockles, scallops and gurnard risotto with gremolata, oxtail in beer pie, and puddings. *Benchmark main dish: pressed braised ox cheek with tarragon mash, a fresh live oyster and ale jus £15.20. Two-course evening meal £21.00.*

Free house ~ Licensee Nick Otley ~ Real ale ~ Bar food (11.30-2.30(3 Sat), 6.30-9.30; 12-3.30 Sun; not Sun evening) ~ Restaurant ~ (01443) 402934 ~ No children after 8pm unless dining in restaurant ~ Dogs allowed in bar ~ Open 11am-11.30pm; 12-11 Sun ~ www.bunchofgrapes.org.uk *Recommended by Gwyn Jones, James Morris, Taff and Gilly Thomas*

If we know a featured entry pub does sandwiches we always say so – if they're not mentioned, you'll have to assume you can't get one.

RAGLAN

SO3609   Map 6

Clytha Arms

Clytha, off Abergavenny road – former A40, now declassified; NP7 9BW

Beautifully placed in parkland, a relaxing spot for enjoying good food and beer; comfortable bedrooms

Well located for walks along the Usk, this rural inn in spacious grounds has an impressive array of drinks, with well kept Banks Mild, Rhymney Bitter, Wye Valley and four swiftly changing guests, an extensive wine list with about a dozen or so by the glass, over 20 malt whiskies, about three farm ciders and various continental beers; it hosts occasional cider and beer festivals. With long, heated verandahs and diamond-paned windows, it's comfortable, light and airy, with scrubbed wood floors, pine settles, big faux fur cushions on the window seats, a good mix of old country furniture and a couple of warming fires, and there is a contemporary linen-set restaurant; darts, bar skittles, boules, TV for rugby matches and board games. The pub has its own labrador and collie. Bedrooms are comfortable, and residents are offered good welsh breakfasts.

As well as a tapas menu (part welsh, part spanish) and sandwiches, the enjoyable menu typically includes leek and laverbread rissoles, tartare of salmon, pie and mash, stuffed ham with cider sauce, fruit and coconut curry, rump steak, wild boar sausages with potato pancakes and fish specials; puddings could be rhubarb cheesecake with ginger syllabub and chocolate and rum charlotte. *Benchmark main dish: lamb faggots with leek mash £12.90. Two-course evening meal £22.70.*

Free house ~ Licensees Andrew and Beverley Canning ~ Real ale ~ Bar food (12.30-2.15, 7-9.30; not Sun evening) ~ Restaurant ~ (01873) 840206 ~ Children welcome ~ Dogs allowed in bar and bedrooms ~ Open 12-3, 6-12; 12-midnight Fri, Sat; 12-11 Sun; closed Mon lunchtime ~ Bedrooms: £60B/£90B ~ www.clytha-arms.com *Recommended by Guy Vowles, the Didler, R T and J C Moggridge*

ROSEBUSH

SN0729   Map 6

Tafarn Sinc

B4329 Haverfordwest–Cardigan; SA66 7QU

Unique 19th-c curio, a slice of social and industrial history

In a fascinating landscape, by dramatic abandoned slate quarries beneath the Preseli Hills, this maroon-painted corrugated iron shed is a remarkable historic curio both inside and out. It was built in 1876 as a basic hotel on a long-defunct railway serving the quarries. The halt itself has been more or less recreated, even down to life-size dummy passengers waiting out on the platform; the sizeable garden is periodically enlivened by the sounds of steam trains chuffing through – actually broadcast from a replica signal box. Inside, it's like a museum of local history, with sawdust on the floor, hams, washing and goodness knows what else hung from the ceiling, and an appealingly buoyant atmosphere, and you will hear Welsh spoken. The bar has plank panelling, an informal mix of old chairs and pews, a woodburner, and Cwrw Tafarn Sinc (brewed locally for the pub) and Sharps Doom Bar on handpump; background music, darts, games machine, board games and TV.

Basic food includes gammon steak with pineapple, vegetable lasagne, lamb burgers, and steaks; no starters. *Benchmark main dish: faggots and mushy peas £11.50.*

Free house ~ Licensee Hafwen Davies ~ Real ale ~ Bar food (12-2, 6-9) ~ Restaurant ~
(01437) 532214 ~ Children welcome ~ Open 12-11(midnight Sun); closed Mon ~
www.tafarnsinc.co.uk *Recommended by John and Enid Morris, Simon Watkins, Paul Goldman,
the Didler, Pete Flower, Mike and Eleanor Anderson*

SKENFRITH
Bell 🍴 ♀ 🛏

SO4520 Map 6

Just off B4521, NE of Abergavenny and N of Monmouth; NP7 8UH

**Elegant but relaxed, generally much praised for classy food and
excellent accommodation**

An ideal stop if you are visiting the Three Castles country, with
the impressive medieval ruin of Skenfrith Castle just yards away,
this inn puts the accent on carefully prepared food and comfortable
accommodation, but is equally welcoming if you just want to enjoy
a drink. It's the little details, like the set of leaflets detailing walks
from the pub and their immaculate kitchen garden that make all the
difference. For a special occasion, head for the big bare-boards dining
area at the back. It's neat, light and airy, with dark country-kitchen and
rush-seat dining chairs, church candles and flowers on dark tables,
canary-yellow walls and brocaded curtains on sturdy big-ring rails. The
flagstoned bar on the left has rather similar décor, with old local and
school photographs, a couple of pews plus tables and café chairs. From
an attractive bleached oak bar counter, a couple of beers, usually from
Kingstone and Wye Valley, are on handpump, plus bottled local cider.
They have 16 wines by the glass and half bottle from an impressive list,
early landed cognacs and a good range of brandies. The lounge bar on
the right, opening into the dining area, has a nice Jacobean-style carved
settle and a housekeeper's chair by a log fire in the big fireplace. There
are solid round tables out on the terrace, with steps up to a sloping lawn.
Disabled access is good.

🍴 Food here is prepared using carefully chosen fresh ingredients from named
local suppliers, vegetables, soft fruit and herbs from their organic kitchen
garden (you are welcome to look around) and pork from their own-reared
saddleback pigs. As well as lunchtime sandwiches, the changing menus might
include game terrine, beetroot-cured salmon, rib-eye of brecon beef, butternut
squash and caramelised onion tartlet, slow-braised cheek of saddleback pork with
black pudding ravioli and parsnip cake, heather-roasted loin of venison or roast
bass with smoked garlic and lemon purée, and puddings such as marmalade soufflé
and pear crumble. *Benchmark main dish: rack of local lamb with herb and
rosemary crust, confit shoulder and seared kidney, fondant potato and pan juices
£21.50. Two-course evening meal £25.00.*

Free house ~ Licensees William and Janet Hutchings ~ Real ale ~ Bar food (12-2.30,
7-9.30(9 Sun)) ~ Restaurant ~ (01600) 750235 ~ Children over 8 welcome in evening ~
Dogs allowed in bar and bedrooms ~ Open 11-11; 12-10 Sun; closed Tues Nov-March, last
week in Jan and first week in Feb ~ Bedrooms: £75B/£110B ~ www.skenfrith.co.uk
Recommended by R and S Bentley, Mr and Mrs P R Thomas, Lucien Perring

STACKPOLE
Stackpole Inn 🍴 🛏

SR9896 Map 6

Village signed off B4319 S of Pembroke; SA71 5DF

**Enjoyable food, good accommodation, friendly service and usefully
placed for exploring the Stackpole Estate**

Within walking distance of the Pembrokeshire Coast Path and the Bosherston Lily Ponds, this efficiently run pub has attractive gardens, with colourful flowerbeds and mature trees around the car park. One area around the bar has pine tables and chairs, but the major part of the pub, L-shaped on four different levels, is given over to diners, with neat light oak furnishings, ash beams and low ceilings; background music and board games. Brains Rev James, Felinfoel Chwerw Gorau and Double Dragon and a guest from a brewer such as Rhymney are on handpump, with several wines by the glass and farm cider. The spotless bedrooms are comfortable, and readers have enjoyed the breakfast.

The impressive food might include sandwiches, ploughman's, roasted beetroot soup, organic chicken liver and porcini pâté, saddleback pork and leek sausages with caramelised apples and turnip mash, grilled fillet of haddock with chips, local poussin with bacon, welsh sirloin steak, daily fish specials such as whole turbot or locally landed lobster; they also do a good-value Sunday lunch menu at £13.45 for two courses. *Benchmark main dish: grilled haddock with twice-cooked chips £15.00. Two-course evening meal £20.00.*

Free house ~ Licensees Gary and Becky Evans ~ Real ale ~ Bar food (12-2(2.30 Sun), 6.30-9) ~ Restaurant ~ (01646) 672324 ~ Children welcome ~ Dogs allowed in bar ~ Open 12-3, 6-11; 12-11 weekends ~ Bedrooms: £60S/£90S ~ www.stackpoleinn.co.uk
Recommended by John and Enid Morris, Ken and Barbara Turner, Mr and Mrs D Mackenzie, Diane Dallyn, David and Susan Nobbs, Pauline Fellows and Simon Robbins

TRESAITH
SN2751 Map 6

Ship ★ 🛏

Off A487 E of Cardigan; bear right in village and keep on down – pub's car park fills quickly; SA43 2JL

Charming pub in splendid setting overlooking broad sandy surfing beach with enjoyable food, nice terrace and seaview bedrooms

You're about as close to the beach as could be possible at this surfers' and bathers' haunt, with sweeping views of the cliffs on either side. Teak tables and chairs under a glass canopy on heated front decking and unusual picnic-sets on a two-level terrace make the most of the location, and picture windows open the views to the front dining area, too. Behind here is a winter log fire, with some chunky pine tables, tub armchairs and sofas in the carpeted part on the right, and large, attractive local photographs. They have three Brains beers on handpump, and a good choice of wines by the glass and other drinks; the young staff are friendly, cheerful and efficient. Two back rooms, possibly a quieter escape in summer, are appealing, especially the one on the right with its striking blue and red décor, bright floor tiles, old-fashioned range stove and snug alcove with a shelf of board games; background music. As well as watersports, there are good coast walks from this steep little village.

With an accent on fresh fish, the menu here might include whitebait, creamy cockles and bacon, haddock and chips, seafood platter, fish pie, chicken breast in goats cheese sauce, steaks, mushroom and stilton bake, and pizzas. *Benchmark main dish: seafood platter for two £24.95. Two-course evening meal £16.20.*

Brains ~ Manager Carl O'Shaughnessy ~ Real ale ~ Bar food (8-11am, 12-3pm, 5-9pm; 12-9 in summer) ~ Restaurant ~ (01239) 811816 ~ Children welcome ~ Open 11-11(10.30 Sun) ~ Bedrooms: /£59.95B ~ www.shiptresaith.co.uk *Recommended by Rob McGeehan, Mrs H J Pinfield, Roger Jones, Mr and Mrs A Burton, R T and J C Moggridge, D Crook*

TY'N-Y-GROES

Groes

SH7773   Map 6

B5106 N of village; LL32 8TN

Lots of antiques, local beer and lovely garden at this gracious, relaxing Snowdonia hotel

With friendly and efficient service, this delightful hotel has its origins as a 15th-c drovers' inn and is much liked by readers for its abundant character. Past the stove in the entrance area, its rambling, low-beamed and thick-walled rooms are nicely decorated with antique settles and an old sofa, old clocks, portraits, hats and tins hanging from the walls, and fresh flowers. A fine antique fireback is built into one wall, perhaps originally from the formidable fireplace in the back bar, which houses a collection of stone cats as well as cheerful winter log fires. You might find a harpist playing here on certain days. From the family's own Great Orme brewery a couple of miles away come Great Orme and Groes Ale (brewed for the pub), and several bottled Great Orme beers, too, also 15 wines by the glass; background music. Several options for dining include an airy conservatory and a smart white-linened dining restaurant. Well equipped bedroom suites (some have terraces or balconies) have gorgeous views, and the hotel also rents out a well appointed wooden cabin, and a cottage in the historic centre of Conwy. The idyllic back garden has flower-filled hayracks and an enchantingly verdant outlook, and there are more seats on a narrow flower-decked roadside terrace.

Using local lamb, salmon and game, and herbs from the hotel garden, bar food includes sandwiches, garlic prawns, welsh rarebit, seafood pie, root vegetable stew, sausages and mash, chicken curry and steaks, with puddings like chocolate pot and orange syllabub. *Benchmark main dish: home-made pie £12.00. Two-course evening meal £20.50.*

Free house ~ Licensee Dawn Humphreys ~ Real ale ~ Bar food ~ Restaurant ~ (01492) 650545 ~ Children welcome until 7pm if eating ~ Dogs allowed in bar and bedrooms ~ Open 12-3, 6.30-11 ~ Bedrooms: £85B/£115B ~ www.groesinn.com *Recommended by Mike and Jayne Bastin, Margaret and Jeff Graham, Dr and Mrs P Truelove, N R White, Dave Webster, Sue Holland, Alun Jones, Mr and Mrs M Stratton, David and Sue Atkinson, R and S Bentley, Steve Whalley, Mike and Mary Carter, Mr and Mrs J S Heathcote*

USK

Nags Head ♀

SO3700   Map 6

The Square; NP15 1BH

Spotlessly kept by the same family for 45 years, traditional in style with hearty welcome and good food and drinks

'What all pubs should aspire to' is typical of the praise heaped on this supremely well run pub, where families are made to feel very welcome. The beautifully kept traditional main bar is cheerily chatty and cosy, with lots of well polished tables and chairs packed under its beams (some with farming tools), lanterns or horsebrasses and harness attached, as well as leatherette wall benches, and various sets of sporting prints and local pictures – look out for the original deeds to the pub. Tucked away at the front is an intimate little corner with some african masks, while on the other side of the room a passageway leads to a new dining area converted from the old coffee bar; background music. There may be prints for sale. They do ten wines by the glass, along with Brains Rev James and SA, Sharps Doom Bar and a guest such as Brains Arms

Park on handpump. The church here is well worth a look. The pub has no parking and nearby street parking can be limited.

🍴 Huge helpings of reasonably priced popular food include sandwiches, leek and welsh cheddar soup, grilled sardines, faggots and gravy, pheasant in port, white partridge stuffed with apricots or glamorgan sausage; puddings could be sticky toffee pudding or treacle and walnut tart. *Benchmark main dish: rabbit pie £10.00. Two-course evening meal £17.50.*

Free house ~ Licensees the Key family ~ Real ale ~ Bar food (12-2, 5.30-9.30) ~ Restaurant ~ (01291) 672820 ~ Children welcome ~ Dogs welcome ~ Open 10.30-2.30 (3 Sun), 5.30-11(10.30 Sun) *Recommended by GSB, Eryl and Keith Dykes, Harry Williams, Phil and Jane Hodson, Dr and Mrs C W Thomas, M E and F J Thomasson, R T and J C Moggridge, Lucien Perring, Sue and Ken Le Prevost, Maurice Potts*

Also Worth a Visit in Wales

Besides the fully inspected pubs, you might like to try these pubs that have been recommended to us and described by readers. Do tell us what you think of them: feedback@goodguides.com

ANGLESEY

BEAUMARIS   SH6076
White Lion (01248) 810589
Castle Street; LL58 8DA Welcoming and cleanly refurbished 19th-c family-run hotel overlooking Castle Square, two bars, one with open fire, well kept ales including Marstons Pedigree, good locally sourced food from proprietor/chef, restaurant; children welcome, dogs in bar, tables out at front and in sheltered beer garden behind, nine bedrooms with castle or Menai Strait views. *(Philip Hollington, Nick Coleman)*

RED WHARF BAY   SH5281
⋆**Ship** (01248) 852568
Village signed off B5025 N of Pentraeth; LL75 8RJ Whitewashed old pub worth visiting for position right on Anglesey's east coast (get there early for a seat with fantastic views of miles of tidal sands); big old-fashioned rooms either side of bar counter, nautical bric-a-brac, long varnished wall pews, cast-iron-framed tables and open fires, Adnams, Tetleys and a guest, 50 malt whiskies and decent choice of wines, food can be good; if you run a tab they lock your card in a numbered box and hand you the key, background Classic FM in lounge; children welcome in room on left, dogs in bar, disabled access, open all day. *(Mike and Mary Carter, Paul Humphreys, Paul Goldman, Matthew Bradley, Martin Smith, Philip and Jane Hastain and others)*

RHOSCOLYN   SH2675
⋆**White Eagle** (01407) 860267
Off B4545 South of Holyhead; LL65 2NJ Remote place rebuilt almost from scratch on site of an old pub; airy modern feel in neatly kept rooms, relaxed atmosphere, Cobblers Ale (brewed for the pub by Thornbridge), Marstons, Weetwood and a guest from smart oak counter, several wines by the glass, quite a choice of good generously served food (all day Sun, and school holidays), efficient prompt service, restaurant; children welcome, dogs in bar, terrific sea views from decking and picnic-sets in good-sized garden, lane down to beach, open all day. *(Emily Carr, Michael Drury, Mike and Mary Carter, Brian and Anna Marsden, Bruce and Sharon Eden, N R White and others)*

CLWYD

BURTON GREEN   SJ3558
⋆**Golden Groves** (01244) 571006
Llyndir Lane, off B5445 W of Rossett; LL12 0AS Modern revamp for this timbered pub in lovely hidden-away setting, partly knocked-through rooms dating from 13th c, figures carved in beams, open fires, good locally sourced food (all day) from light dishes and sharing plates up, friendly staff, Marstons ales and good wine choice, live acoustic music last Sun afternoon of month; large attractive streamside garden with modern wicker furniture. *(Mr and Mrs J Palmer)*

CARROG   SJ1143
Grouse (01490) 430272
B5436, signed off A5 Llangollen–Corwen; LL21 9AT Small unpretentious pub with superb views over River Dee and beyond from bay window and balcony, Lees ales, enjoyable food all day from sandwiches up, reasonable prices, friendly helpful staff, local pictures, pool in games room; background music; children welcome, wheelchair access (side door a bit narrow), tables in pretty walled garden (covered

terrace for smokers), narrow turn into car park, handy for Llangollen steam railway. *(Myke Crombleholme)*

HAWARDEN   SJ3266
Glynne Arms (01244) 569988
Glynne Way; CH5 3NS Nicely renovated early 19th-c stone coaching inn, all-day food in bar and bistro-style restaurant using own locally farmed produce, four welsh beers; children welcome. *(Anon)*

LLANARMON DYFFRYN CEIRIOG   SJ1532
⋆ West Arms (01691) 600665
End of B4500 W of Chirk; LL20 7LD 16th-c beamed and timbered inn in lovely surroundings, cosy atmosphere in picturesque upmarket lounge bar full of antique settles, sofas, even an elaborately carved confessional stall, good original bar food strong on local produce, friendly staff, good range of wines, malt whiskies and well kept local ales, more sofas in old-fashioned entrance hall, comfortable back bar too, roaring log fires, good restaurant; children welcome, pretty lawn running down to River Ceiriog (fishing for residents), good walks, comfortable character bedrooms. *(Noel Grundy, Peter and Josie Fawcett, Edward Leetham)*

DYFED

ABERAERON   SN4562
Cadwgan Arms (01545) 570149
Market Street; SA46 0AU Small late 18th-c pub opposite harbour, basic with friendly regulars, well kept Hancocks HB and a guest, interesting old photographs, open fire, no food; children and dogs welcome, small back garden, more seats in front overlooking the water, open all day (from 5pm Mon). *(the Didler)*

ABERAERON   SN4562
⋆ Harbourmaster (01545) 570755
Harbour Lane; SA46 0BA Stylish waterside dining pub/hotel overlooking attractive yacht-filled harbour, cleanly decorated bar with leather sofas, a zinc-clad counter and stuffed albatross (reputed to have collided with ship belonging to chatty owner's great-grandfather), Purple Moose and a beer brewed for them, a dozen wines by the glass, good often interesting food (not cheap) including stone-baked pizzas, efficient friendly service, minimalist dining room with modern light wood furniture, four-seater cwtch (or snug) in former porch; background music, TV; children over five welcome if staying, good up-to-date

bedrooms, self-catering cottage, open all day from 8am. *(B and M Kendall, N R White, M E and F J Thomasson, Mr and Mrs P R Thomas, the Didler and others)*

ABERCYCH   SN2539
⋆ Nags Head (01239) 841200
Off B4332 Cenarth–Boncath; SA37 0HJ Tucked-away riverside pub with dimly lit beamed and flagstoned bar, big fireplace, stripped wood tables, clocks showing time around the world, piano, hundreds of beer bottles, photographs of locals and a coracle on brick and stone walls, even a large stuffed rat, own-brewed Old Emrys beers plus guests, two sizable dining areas; background music; children welcome and dogs (pub yorkie called Scrappy), benches in garden overlooking river, play area, three new bedrooms, open all day weekends, closed Mon lunchtime. *(John and Enid Morris)*

ABERGORLECH   SN5833
⋆ Black Lion (01558) 685271
B4310; SA32 7SN Friendly old coaching inn in fine rural position, traditionally furnished stripped-stone bar with flagstones, coal stove, oak furniture and high-backed black settles, copper pans on beams, old jugs on shelves, fresh flowers, local paintings, dining extension with french windows opening on to enclosed garden, one Rhymney ale and a guest, good varied choice of inexpensive food; background music; children and dogs welcome, lovely views of Cothi valley from sloping riverside garden, self-catering cottage, open all day weekends, closed Mon. *(Anon)*

ANGLE   SM8603
Hibernia (01646) 641517
B4320; SA71 5AT Welcoming village pub with helpful friendly licensees, good choice of home-made food and at least one real ale, nautical memorabilia in traditional bar, coal fire in stone fireplace; children welcome, garden tables, one good bedroom (more planned). *(Ian McCrerie and Ann Marsh)*

BROAD HAVEN   SM8614
⋆ Druidstone Hotel (01437) 781221
N on coast road, bear left for about 1.5 miles then follow sign left to Druidstone Haven; SA62 3NE Cheerfully informal, the family's former country house in a grand spot above the sea, individualistic and relaxed, terrific views, inventive cooking with fresh often organic ingredients (best to book), helpful efficient service, folksy cellar bar with local ale tapped from the cask, country wines and other drinks, ceilidhs and folk events, friendly pub dogs (others welcome), all sorts of sporting activities from boules

---

Half pints: by law, a pub should not charge more for half a pint than half the price of a full pint, unless it shows that half-pint price on its price list.

to sand-yachting; attractive high-walled garden, spacious homely bedrooms, even an eco-friendly chalet and an underground apartment built into the hill, closed Nov and Jan, restaurant closed Sun evening. *(John and Enid Morris, Simon Watkins, Mrs H J Pinfield, Pete Flower, John and Fiona McIlwain)*

BURTON   SM9805
Jolly Sailor (01646) 600378
Just off Trinity Terrace; SA73 1NX
Great views of River Cleddau, toll bridge and Milford Haven beyond from lounge and conservatory restaurant, good choice of pubby food at reasonable prices, well kept Bass, Brains and Greene King, friendly staff; children welcome, dogs in bar, waterside garden with lots of picnic-sets and a play area, can moor a small boat at jetty, open all day in school holidays. *(Russell Evans)*

CAIO   SN6739
Brunant Arms (01558) 650483
Off A482 Llanwrda–Lampeter; SA19 8RD Unpretentious and interestingly furnished village pub, comfortable and friendly, with nice log fire, good choice of local ales, enjoyable regularly changing home-made food from baguettes up, stripped-stone public bar with games including pool; juke box, TV; children and dogs welcome, small Perspex-roofed verandah and lower terrace, has been open all day weekends. *(John Crellin)*

CAREW   SN0403
☆ Carew Inn (01646) 651267
A4075 off A477; SA70 8SL Stone-built pub with unpretentious panelled public bar, bentwood stools at counter, mixed tables and chairs on bare boards, neat eating area, dining rooms upstairs with photos of local scenes, sky-blue tongue-and-groove partitions and black leather chairs, well liked bar food, Brains and Worthington ales, open fires; background music, darts and outdoor pool table; children (away from bar) and dogs welcome, seats in front looking down to river (tidal watermill open for summer afternoon visits), back garden with play equipment and view of imposing Carew Castle ruins and remarkable 9th-c Celtic cross, summer barbecues, open all day. *(C A Bryson, the Didler, Andrew and Vanessa Thomas, Michael Rugman, David and Susan Nobbs, Pauline Fellows and Simon Robbins)*

CILGERRAN   SN1942
Pendre Inn (01239) 614223
Off A478 S of Cardigan; High Street; SA43 2SL Friendly local with massive medieval stone walls and broad flagstones, enjoyable home-made pub food (more evening choice), great value Evan Evans and two changing guests; Children and dogs welcome, open all day. *(Ann and Tony Bennett-Hughes, the Didler)*

CILYCWM   SN7540
Neuadd Fawr Arms (01550) 721644
By church entrance; SA20 0ST Former 18th-c drovers' inn, restored by present owners, eclectic mix of old furniture on slate floor, woodburners, one or two changing local ales, enjoyable home-made seasonal food with a modern twist in bar or dining room; children and dogs welcome, good spot by churchyard above river Gwenlas, among lanes to Llyn Brianne, open all day weekends, closed weekday lunchtimes in winter. *(Anon)*

COSHESTON   SN0003
Brewery Inn (01646) 686678
Signed E from village crossroads; SA72 4UD Welcoming village pub with three well kept ales, good reasonably priced food (not Sun evening, Mon) freshly cooked by landlord, helpful friendly service; five self-catering apartments at back. *(Bob Butterworth, David Hughes, R Page, Jon Rowlands)*

CRESSWELL QUAY   SN0506
☆ Cresselly Arms (01646) 651210
Village signed from A4075; SA68 0TE Simple unchanging alehouse overlooking tidal creek, plenty of local customers in two old-fashioned linked rooms, built-in wall benches, kitchen chairs and plain tables on red and black tiles, open fire in one room, Aga in the other with lots of pictorial china hanging from high beam-and-plank ceiling, a third more conventionally furnished red-carpeted room, Worthington and a winter guest ale served from glass jugs, no food apart from rolls on Sat; no children; seats outside making most of view, you can arrive by boat if tide is right, open all day weekends. *(the Didler, David and Susan Nobbs)*

CWM GWAUN   SN0333
☆ Dyffryn Arms (01348) 881305
Cwm Gwaun and Pontfaen signed off B4313 E of Fishguard; SA65 9SE Classic rural time warp, virtually the social centre for this lush green valley, very relaxed, basic and idiosyncratic, with much-loved veteran landlady (her farming family have run it since 1840, and she's been in charge for well over a third of that time); 1920s front parlour with plain deal furniture and draughts boards inlaid into tables, coal fire, well kept Bass served by jug through sliding hatch, low prices, World War I prints and posters, darts, duck eggs for sale; lovely outside view, open more or less all day (may close if no customers). *(Giles and Annie Francis, the Didler, R T and J C Moggridge)*

DALE   SM8105
Griffin (01646) 636227
B4327, by sea on one-way system; SA62 3RB Old waterside pub under enthusiastic couple, two cosy rooms, open woodburner, well kept ales such as Brains,

Evan Evans and Thomos Watkins, nice wines, enjoyable food including good local fish/ seafood specials; children welcome, lovely estuary views – can sit out on seawall. (Ed Cole, Pete Flower)

DINAS   SN0139
Old Sailors (01348) 811491
Pwllgwaelod; from A487 in Dinas Cross follow Bryn-henllan signpost; SA42 OSE Shack-like building in superb position, snugged down into the sand by isolated cove below Dinas Head with its bracing walks; specialising in fresh local seafood including crab and lobster, also good snacks, coffee and summer cream teas, well kept Felinfoel, decent wine, maritime bric-a-brac; children and dogs welcome, picnic-sets on grass overlooking beach, open 11-6ish and all day Fri, Sat Nov-Easter (all day Weds-Sat Easter-Oct). (Ann and Tony Bennett-Hughes, V and E A Bolton)

FISHGUARD   SM9537
★ Fishguard Arms (01348) 872763
Main Street (A487); SA65 9HJ Tiny unspoilt pub; front bar with cask-tapped Bass from unusually high counter, chatty character landlord and friendly atmosphere, open fire, rugby photographs, woodburner and traditional games in back snug, no food; sports TV; smokers' area out at back, open all day, closed Weds evening. (Giles and Annie Francis)

FISHGUARD   SM9637
Ship (01348) 87403
Newport Road, Lower Town; SA65 9ND Cheerful atmosphere and seafaring locals in ancient dim-lit red-painted pub near old harbour, friendly staff, well kept ales including Theakstons tapped from the cask, homely food from sandwiches and cawl up, coal fire, lots of boat pictures, model ships, photos of Richard Burton, piano; children welcome, toys provided. (Giles and Annie Francis)

FRESHWATER EAST   SS0298
Freshwater Inn (01646) 672828
Jason Road; SA71 5LE Welcoming pub built in 1912 as a country club, lovely coastal views, enjoyable reasonably priced home-made food, Felinfoel and guest ales, lounge, dining room and public bar; children and dogs welcome, tables in nice garden, open all day summer. (Louise Harris, Diana Hill and Brian Sturgess)

LITTLE HAVEN   SM8512
★ Castle Inn (01437) 781445
Grove Place; SA62 3UF Welcoming pub well placed by green looking over sandy bay (lovely sunsets), popular food including pizzas and good local fish, Marstons ales, good choice of wines by the glass, tea and cafetière coffee, bare-boards bar and carpeted dining area with big oak tables, beams, some stripped stone, castle prints,

pool in back area; children welcome, front picnic-sets, New Year's day charity swim, open all day. (Bob Butterworth, Pete Flower, John and Fiona McIlwain)

LITTLE HAVEN   SM8512
St Brides Inn (01437) 781266
St Brides Road; SA62 3UN Just 20 metres from Pembrokeshire Coast Path; neat stripped-stone bar and linked carpeted dining area, log fire, interesting well in back corner grotto thought to be partly Roman, Banks's, Marstons and a guest, enjoyable bar food; background music and TV; children welcome, dogs in bar, seats in sheltered suntrap terrace garden across road, two bedrooms, open all day summer. (Jennie George, Pete Flower, Paul and Sue Merrick)

LLANDDAROG   SN5016
★ Butchers Arms (01267) 275330
On back road by church; SA32 8NS Ancient heavily black-beamed local with three intimate eating areas off small central bar, welcoming with charming service, enjoyable generous home-made food at reasonable prices, Felinfoel ales tapped from the cask, good wines by the glass, conventional pub furniture, gleaming brass, candles in bottles, open woodburner in biggish fireplace; background music; children welcome, tables outside, nice window boxes, new bedroom in converted stables, closed Sun and Mon. (Tom Evans, the Didler)

LLANDDAROG   SN5016
White Hart (01267) 275395
Off A48 E of Carmarthen, via B4310; aka Yr Hydd Gwyn; SA32 8NT Ancient thatched pub with own-brew beers using water from 300-foot borehole, comfortable lived-in beamed rooms with lots of engaging bric-a-brac and antiques including a suit of armour, 17th-c carved settles by huge log fire, interestingly furnished high-raftered dining room, generous if not cheap food, Zac the macaw and Bendy the galah; background music, cash or debit cards only, no dogs inside; children welcome, disabled access (ramps provided), picnic-sets on front terrace and in back garden, play area, small farmyard (eggs for sale at the bar), closed Weds. (Chris and Angela Buckell, David and Susan Nobbs)

LLANDEILO   SN6222
White Horse (01558) 822424
Rhosmaen Street; SA19 6EN Friendly well run 16th-c local, several linked bare-boards rooms, fine range of Evan Evans ales, nice chatty mix of customers, woodburner in stone fireplace; background music and occasional live, games machine, TV; tables outside front and back, open all day. (the Didler)

LLANDOVERY   SN7634
Castle (01550) 720343
Kings Road; SA20 0AP Refurbished hotel next to castle ruins, good food and courteous

efficient service, well kept Brains Rev James, Kite Cwrw Haf and Evan Evans May Fly; comfortable bedrooms. *(Brian and Anna Marsden, Gareth Davies)*

LLANDOVERY   SN7634
Kings Head   (01550) 720393
Market Square; SA20 0AB
Sympathetically refurbished early 18th-c coaching inn, enjoyable food from bar and restaurant menus, well kept Evan Evans and a guest, attentive friendly service; bedrooms, open all day. *(Brian and Anna Marsden)*

LLANDOVERY   SN7634
Red Lion   (01550) 720813
Market Square; SA20 0AA One basic welcoming room with no bar, changing ales tapped from the cask, long-serving jovial landlord (pub has been in his family for 100 years), no food; restricted opening – may be just Fri and Sat evenings. *(the Didler)*

LLANFALLTEG   SN1519
Plash   (01437) 563472
Village NE of Whitland; SA34 0UN Small mid-terrace village local with a warm welcome, beamed bar with piano and open fire, well kept Brains, Wye Valley and guests, bar food including pizzas; children and dogs welcome, garden tables, self-catering cottage, closed lunchtimes Mon and Tues, otherwise open all day. *(Brian Yates, C Johnstone, Steve Goymer)*

LLANFIHANGEL-Y-CREUDDYN   00000
Y Ffarmers   (01974) 261275
Village signed of A4120 W of Pisgah; SY23 4LA Nicely refurbished family-run village pub, good locally sourced seasonal food cooked by landlord/chef, well kept welsh beers such as Felinfoel and Purple Moose, friendly service, traditional bar with oak boards and woodburner; closed Mon, Tues lunchtime. *(Anon)*

LLANGADOG   SN7028
Red Lion   (01550) 777357
Church Street; SA19 9AA Striking stone-built coaching inn with a warm welcome, good straightforward food and well kept local ales; comfortable clean bedrooms. *(Taff and Gilly Thomas)*

MARLOES   SM7908
Lobster Pot   (01646) 636233
Gay Lane; SA62 3AZ Village local handy for lovely beach and coast walk; friendly staff, enjoyable fairly priced food from well filled baguettes up, Felinfoel Double Dragon, games area with darts; background music; children welcome, tables out in front and in

back garden with play area,. *(Mike and Jayne Bastin)*

MATHRY   SM8831
Farmers Arms   (01348) 831284
Brynamlwg, off A487 Fishguard–St David's; SA62 5HB Creeper-covered pub with beams, flagstones and dark woodwork in basic homely bar, woodburner, friendly staff and locals, good value pubby food from sandwiches and baked potatoes up including local seafood, Brains Rev James, Felinfoel Double Dragon and a guest, fair range of reasonably priced wines, large vine-covered dining conservatory (simple rather than smart); background music; children welcome, dogs in bar, nearby campsite, open all day in season, closed till 5pm Mon-Thurs in winter. *(Simon Watkins)*

PEMBROKE DOCK   SM9603
Shipwright   (01646) 682090
Front Street; SA72 6JX Little waterfront pub overlooking estuary, good choice of food including authentic thai dishes, well kept beers, friendly efficient service; five minutes from Ireland ferry terminal. *(Pauline Fellows and Simon Robbins)*

PEMBROKE DOCK   SM9603
Station Inn   (01646) 621255
Hawkestone Road; SA72 6JL Converted 19th-c waiting room and booking office in working station, three well kept regularly changing ales, enjoyable good value home-cooked food (not Sun evening, Mon), live music Sat; closed Mon lunchtime. *(David Hughes, R Page)*

PENRHIWLLAN   SN3641
★ Daffodil   (01559) 370343
A475 Newcastle Emlyn–Lampeter; SA44 5NG Smart contemporary open-plan dining pub with comfortable welcoming bar (though most there to eat), scatter-cushion sofas and leather tub chairs on pale limestone floor, woodburner, bar chairs by granite-panelled counter serving well kept Evan Evans and Greene King, two lower-ceilinged end rooms with big oriental rugs, steps down to two airy dining rooms, one with picture windows by open kitchen, good varied menu including interesting evening specials (lots of fresh fish), helpful friendly staff; background music; children welcome, nicely furnished decked area with valley views. *(Anon)*

PONTERWYD   SN7480
George Borrow   (01970) 890230
A44 about quarter-mile W of A4120 junction; SY23 3AD Family-run hotel with well kept Felinfoel Double Dragon, enjoyable

---

We include some hotels with a good bar that offers facilities comparable to those of a pub.

food including good Sun carvery and a warm homely welcome, lounges front and back, restaurant; children welcome, nice views (fine spot by Eagle Falls and gorge, so lots of summer visitors), ten bedrooms. *(Bob Butterworth, Mrs Jean Phillips)*

PONTRHYDFENDIGAID   SN7366
✶ **Black Lion** (01974) 831624
Off B4343 Tregaron–Devils Bridge; SY25 6BE Relaxed country inn, only open evenings, with emphasis on food; smallish main bar set for the sensibly modest choice of well liked meals, Felinfoel Double Dragon and decent wines, helpful service, dark beams and floorboards, lots of stripped stone, woodburner and big pot-irons in vast fireplace, copper, brass and so forth on mantelpiece, tiled back room with pool; unobtrusive background music; children and dogs welcome, picnic-sets out in front, back courtyard and informal tree-shaded garden, bedrooms in separate block, good walking country and not far from Strata Florida Abbey, open 5pm-midnight. *(Anon)*

PONTRHYDFENDIGAID   SN7366
Red Lion (01974) 831232
Bridge Street (B4343 Tregaron–Devils Bridge); SY25 6BH Friendly licensees and appealing simple refurbishment, stripped kitchen tables in comfortable inglenook bar, pubby food, well kept Felinfoel Double Dragon, games bar with pool, darts, juke box and big-screen TV; children welcome, informal streamside garden, play area, good value bedrooms. *(Anon)*

PORTHGAIN   SM8132
Shed (01348) 831518
Opposite village green and carpark; SA62 5BN In what looks to be a seaside former boat shed, not a pub but does sell beer and is well worth knowing for good seafood in upstairs evening bistro (not winter Sun-Weds), daytime tearoom. *(Simon Watkins)*

PORTHGAIN   SM8132
✶ **Sloop** (01348) 831449
Off A487 Street Davids–Fishguard; SA62 5BN Busy tavern (especially holiday times) snuggled down in cove wedged tightly between headlands on Pembrokeshire Coast Path – fine walks in either direction; plank-ceilinged bar with lots of lobster pots and fishing nets, ship clocks and lanterns and even relics from local wrecks, decent-sized eating area with simple furnishings and freezer for kid's ice-creams, well liked bar food from sandwiches to seasonal fish (own fishing business), Brains, Felinfoel and Green King, separate games room with juke box; seats on heated terrace overlooking harbour, self-catering cottage in village, open all day from 9.30 for breakfast, till 1am Fri, Sat. *(Giles and Annie Francis, Pete Flower)*

RHANDIRMWYN   SN7843
Royal Oak (01550) 760201
7 miles N of Llandovery; SA20 0NY Friendly 17th-c stone-built inn in remote and peaceful walking country, comfortable traditional bar with log fire, four well kept local ales, ciders and perries, popular good value food sourced locally, big dining area, pool room; dogs and children welcome, hill views from garden and bedrooms, handy for Brecon Beacons. *(Andy Beveridge)*

WOLFS CASTLE   SM9526
Wolfe (01437) 741662
A40 Haverfordwest–Fishguard; SA62 5LS Good fresh home-made food from varied menu including OAP deals, friendly service, two beers from Brains and nine wines by the glass, comfortable brasserie dining lounge with woodburner, garden room and conservatory, TV and darts in bar (dogs allowed here); background music; children welcome, landscaped garden with picnic-sets, three bedrooms, open all day in summer. *(David and Anne Day)*

GLAMORGAN

BISHOPSTON   SS5789
Joiners Arms (01792) 232658
Bishopston Road, just off B4436 SW of Swansea; SA3 3EJ Thriving local brewing its own good value Swansea ales, usually three of these along with well kept guests, reasonably priced straightforward food, friendly staff, unpretentious quarry-tiled bar with massive solid fuel stove, comfortable lounge; TV for rugby; children welcome, open all day (from 2pm Mon). *(Anon)*

CAERPHILLY   ST1484
✶ **Black Cock** 02920 880534
Watford; Tongwynlais exit from M4 junction 32, then right just after church; CF83 1NF Welcoming beamed country pub with series of interconnecting rooms, large back dining extension, good choice of enjoyable pub food all day (not Sun evening) including children's and OAP menus, well kept ales such as Hancocks HB, Theakstons Old Peculier and Wickwar BOB, cheerful staff, woodburners, newspapers; background and some live music; dogs welcome in bar, disabled access, sizeable terraced garden among trees with barbecue and good play area, up in the hills just below Caerphilly Common, popular with walkers and riders (there's a hitching rail), bedrooms, campsite, open all day. *(R T and J C Moggridge)*

CARDIFF   ST1776
Cayo Arms (029) 2039 1910
Cathedral Road; CF11 9LL Helpful young staff, well kept Marstons and guests, enjoyable competitively priced standard food all day from sandwiches up, pubby front bar

with comfortable side area in Edwardian style, more modern back dining area; background music, big-screen TV in one part, very busy weekends; tables out in front, more in yard behind (with parking), five good value bedrooms, open all day. *(the Didler)*

CARDIFF ST1677
Conway (029) 2023 0323
Conway Road/Mortimer Road, Pontcanno; CF11 9NW Refurbished corner pub in residential area, light bright decor in linked areas around central bar, well kept local ales, good restaurant-style food, pleasant helpful staff; children welcome. *(GSB)*

CARDIFF ST1876
Cottage (029) 2033 7195
St Mary Street, near Howells; CF10 1AA Proper down-to-earth pub with good value generous home-made food including all-day breakfast and other bargains, good cheerful service, full Brains range kept well, decent choice of wines, long bar with narrow frontage and back eating area, lots of polished wood, glass and mirrors, old photographs, relaxed friendly atmosphere even Fri and Sat when crowded (gets packed on rugby international days); open all day. *(Joan and Michel Hooper-Immins, David and Sue Atkinson)*

COWBRIDGE SS9974
✶ Bear (01446) 774814
High Street, with car park behind off North Street; signed off A48; CF71 7AF Busy well run Georgian coaching inn in smart village, well kept Bass, Hancocks HB and two guests, decent house wines, enjoyable usual food from good sandwiches up, friendly young uniformed staff, three attractively furnished bars with flagstones, bare boards or carpet, some stripped stone and panelling, big hot open fires, barrel-vaulted cellar restaurant; children welcome, dogs in one bar, comfortable quiet bedrooms. *(Dennis Jenkin, GSB)*

GWAELOD-Y-GARTH ST1183
Gwaelod y Garth Inn
(029) 20810408 *Main Road; CF15 9HH* Popular for its good well presented home-made food, friendly efficient service, Wye Valley and regional guests from pine-clad bar, log fires, refurbished upstairs restaurant; table skittles, pool, digital juke box; children and dogs welcome, fine valley views, on Taff-Ely Ridgeway path, three bedrooms, open all day. *(Mrs H J Pinfield, Roy Payne)*

KENFIG SS8081
✶ Prince of Wales (01656) 740356
2.2 miles from M4 junction 37; A4229 towards Porthcawl, then right when dual carriageway narrows on bend, signed Maudlam and Kenfig; CF33 4PR Ancient local with plenty of individuality by historic

sand dunes, cheerful welcoming landlord, well kept Bass, Worthington and guests tapped from the cask, good choice of malts, decent wines, enjoyable straightforward generous food at low prices, chatty panelled room off main bar (dogs allowed here), log fires, stripped stone, lots of wreck pictures, restaurant with upstairs overspill room, several ghosts; TV for special rugby events; children till 9pm, handy for nature reserve (June orchids), open all day. *(Kevin Thomas, Nina Randall, the Didler)*

LISVANE ST1883
Ty Mawr Arms (01222) 754456
From B4562 on E edge turn N into Church Road, bear left into Llwyn y Pia Road, keep on along Graig Road; CF14 0UF Large welcoming country pub with good choice of popular food, well kept Brains and guest ales, decent wines by the glass, teas and coffees, friendly service, great views over Cardiff from spacious bay-windowed dining area off traditional log-fire bar; children welcome, disabled access with help to main bar area, big attractive garden. *(Colin McKerrow)*

LLANCARFAN ST0570
Fox & Hounds (01446) 781287
Signed off A4226; can also be reached from A48 from Bonvilston or B4265 via Llancadle; CF62 3AD Good carefully cooked food using local ingredients including fresh fish, welsh black beef and farmhouse cheeses in neat comfortably modernised village pub, friendly open-plan bar rambling through arches, coal fire, Brains Bitter and Rev James kept well, good wine choice, traditional settles and plush banquettes, candlelit bistro with woodburners, simple end family room; unobtrusive background music; tables out behind, pretty streamside setting by interesting church, seven comfortable bedrooms, good breakfast, open all day weekends. *(Guy Masdin, Jillian and Martin Rolls, J D and A P)*

LLANMADOC SS4493
Britannia (01792) 386624
The Gower, near Whiteford Burrows – NT; SA3 1DB Busy summer pub right out on the peninsula, enjoyable locally sourced food and well kept beers, nice coffee, gleaming copper stove in beamed and tiled bar, steps up to stripped stone dining area; children and dogs welcome, tables out in front and in big garden behind, great estuary views, lovely walks. *(Richard Daugherty, Ann and Adrian Bulley, Tom and Ruth Rees)*

LLANTWIT MAJOR SS9668
Old Swan (01446) 792230
Church Street; CF61 1SB Unusual medieval stone building in maze of narrow streets, interesting nooks and crannies, lancet windows, good log fires in big stone fireplaces, enjoyable food from baguettes up,

friendly service, three well kept ales such as Newmans and Wickwar; tables in back garden, open all day. *(R T and J C Moggridge)*

MUMBLES SS6188
Park Inn (01792) 366738
Park Street; SA3 4DA Cosy two-bar Victorian backstreet local with good mix of customers, five interesting well kept beers, lots of photographs of old Mumbles Railway, piano and open fire, back games room; open all day Fri-Sun, from 4pm other days. *(Richard Daugherty)*

OGMORE SS8876
★ Pelican (01656) 880049
Ogmore Road (B4524); CF32 0QP Nice spot above ruined castle, attractive rambling revamp with plenty of beamery and bare boards, welcoming open fire, enjoyable all-day food in generous helpings, good real ale choice, cheerful service; may try to keep your credit card while you eat; dogs allowed in lounge (flagstone floor), tables on side terrace, rather grand smokers' hut, lovely views and quite handy for beaches. *(Chris Smith, Kevin Thomas, Nina Randall, Sue Humphreys)*

OLDWALLS SS4891
Greyhound (01792) 391027
W of Llanrhidian; SA3 1HA 19th-c pub with spacious beamed and dark-panelled carpeted lounge bar, well kept ales including own Gower brews, decent wine and coffee, popular reasonably priced pub food including good Sun roasts, friendly staff, hot coal fires, back dining room and upstairs overspill/function room; children and dogs welcome, picnic-sets in big garden with terrace, play area and good views, open all day. *(Richard Daugherty, M G Hart)*

PENTYRCH ST1081
Kings Arms (029) 2089 0202
Church Road; CF15 9QF 16th-c village pub with snug flagstoned bar, lounge and restaurant, good often interesting food (not Sun evening), Brains and Otley ales; children welcome, tables outside, open all day. *(Lisa Jarman)*

REYNOLDSTON SS4889
★ King Arthur (01792) 390775
Higher Green, off A4118; SA3 1AD Cheerful pub/hotel with timbered main bar and hall, back family summer dining area (games room with pool in winter), good fairly priced food with emphasis on fish, friendly helpful staff coping well when busy, Felinfoel and three guests, country-house bric-a-brac, log fire, lively local atmosphere evenings;

background music; tables out on green, play area, 19 bedrooms, open all day. *(Matt and Vikki Wharton, Mel Lawrence)*

ST HILARY ST0173
★ Bush (01446) 776888
Off A48 E of Cowbridge; CF71 7DP Cosy 16th-c thatched and beamed pub restored after devastating fire; flagstoned main bar with inglenook, snug, bare-boards lounge, good mix of old furniture, Bass, Greene King Abbot, Hancocks HB and a guest, Weston's Old Rosie cider, good choice of wines by the glass, hearty country food including range of home-made pies, gluten-free choices too, carpeted restaurant with open ceiling; children welcome, dogs in bar, some benches out at front, garden behind, open all day Fri-Sun. *(Tony Cheeseman)*

GWENT

ABERGAVENNY SO2914
Hen & Chickens (01873) 853613
Flannel Street; NP7 5EG Popular traditional local with good blackboard choice of well priced food (Sun till 6pm – deals Mon-Thurs), friendly efficient staff, well kept Brains and a guest from bar unusually set against street windows, mugs of tea and coffee, interesting side areas with some nice stripped masonry, pews and wonky tables on wood or tiled floors, darts, cards and dominoes, Sun jazz; TV, very busy on market day, they may ask for a credit card if running a tab; summer pavement tables, open all day. *(Anthony Barnes, Reg Fowle, Helen Rickwood, the Didler)*

CAERLEON ST3490
★ Bell (01633) 420613
Bulmore Road; off M4 J24 via B4237 and B4236; NP18 1QQ Nicely furnished linked beamed areas, good food including some interesting welsh dishes, well kept changing ales and excellent choice of welsh ciders and perries, daily newspapers, big open fireplace, good Weds folk night, jazz Sun afternoon; unobtrusive background music; children welcome, pretty back terrace with koi tank, open all day. *(Dr and Mrs R E S Tanner, M G Hart)*

CHEPSTOW ST5394
Three Tuns (01291) 645797
Bridge Street; NP16 5EY Early 17th c and a pub for much of that time; bare-boards interior with painted farmhouse pine furniture, a couple of mismatched sofas by woodburner, dresser with china plates, local ales and ciders from nice wooden counter at

---

Post Office address codings confusingly give the impression that some pubs are in Gwent or Powys, Wales when they're really in Gloucestershire or Shropshire (which is where we list them).

unusual angle, very reasonably priced home-made bar food, friendly staff; background music – live Sat; open all day (till 10pm Mon-Thurs). *(Anon)*

GROSMONT   SO4024
Angel (01981) 240646
Corner of B4347 and Poorscript Lane;
NP7 8EP Friendly 17th-c local owned by village co-operative, rustic interior with simple wooden furniture, Fullers, Tomos Watkins and Wye Valley ales, real ciders, decent good value straightforward bar food (not Sun or Mon), pool room with darts, live music (instruments provided); no lavatories – public ones close by; a couple of garden tables and boules behind, seats out by ancient market cross on attractive steep single street in sight of castle, open all day Sat, closed Mon lunchtime. *(Guy Vowles, Reg Fowle, Helen Rickwood, the Didler)*

LLANDENNY   SO4103
⋆Raglan Arms (01291) 690800
Centre of village; NP15 1DL Well run dining pub with good interesting fresh food (not Sun evening), Wye Valley Butty Bach and good selection of wines, friendly welcoming young staff, big pine tables and a couple of leather sofas in linked dining rooms leading through to conservatory, log fire in flagstoned bar's handsome stone fireplace, relaxed informal atmosphere; children welcome, garden tables, closed Mon. *(Reg Fowle, Helen Rickwood, LM)*

LLANDEWI SKIRRID   SO3421
Walnut Tree (01873) 852797
B4521; NP7 8AW Appealing and popular dining place with amiable chef/landlord producing some very good if not cheap food, good wines, fireside seats and small tables in little flagstoned bar, airy informal main dining room; children welcome, closed Sun, Mon. *(Dr and Mrs James Harris)*

LLANGATTOCK LINGOED SO3620
Hunters Moon (01873) 821499
Off B4521 just E of Llanvetherine;
NP7 8RR Attractive tucked-away pub dating from 13th c, beams, dark stripped stone and flagstones, friendly licensees and locals, welsh ales tapped from the cask, separate dining room, straightforward food (Thurs and Fri evenings, Sat, Sun lunchtime); children welcome, tables out on deck and in charming dell with ducks, four comfortable bedrooms, glorious country on Offa's Dyke walk, closed Mon and weekday lunchtimes. *(David Harris)*

LLANGYBI   ST3797
White Hart (01633) 450258
On main road; NP15 1NP Friendly village dining pub in delightful 12th-c monastery building, part of Jane Seymour's dowry, pubby bar with roaring log fire, steps up to pleasant light restaurant, good if not cheap food,

several well kept mainly welsh ales; open all day, closed Mon. *(Dr and Mrs C W Thomas)*

LLANOVER   SO2907
⋆Goose & Cuckoo (01873) 880277
Upper Llanover signed up track off A4042 S of Abergavenny; after 0.5 miles take first left; NP7 9ER Unchanging simple pub much loved by walkers (Monmouthshire Canal towpath nearby, or over hilltops towards Blorenge and Blaenavon); essentially one small room with rustic furniture and woodburner, Newmans, Rhymney and a couple of guests, over 80 malt whiskies, wholesome Aga-cooked bar food, friendly landlady, small picture-window extension making most of valley view, daily newspapers, darts and board games; no credit cards; children and dogs welcome, rather ad hoc picnic-sets on gravel below, they keep sheep, goats, geese and chickens, may have honey for sale, bedrooms, open all day Fri-Sun, closed Mon. *(Guy Vowles, Anthony Barnes, LM, Reg Fowle, Helen Rickwood, the Didler)*

LLANTHONY   SO2827
⋆Priory Hotel (01873) 890487
Aka Abbey Hotel, Llanthony Priory;
off A465, back Road Llanvihangel Crucorney–Hay; NP7 7NN Magical setting for plain bar in dim-lit vaulted flagstoned crypt of graceful ruined Norman abbey, lovely in summer, with lawns around and the peaceful border hills beyond; well kept ales such as Brains, Felinfoel and Newmans, summer farm cider, good coffee, simple lunchtime bar food (can be long queue on fine summer days, but number system then works well), evening restaurant, occasional live music; no dogs; children welcome but not in hotel area with four bedrooms in restored parts of abbey walls, open all day Sat and summer Sun, closed winter Mon-Thurs, Sun evening. *(MLR, Reg Fowle, Helen Rickwood, the Didler, David and Sue Atkinson)*

LLANTRISANT FAWR   ST3997
Greyhound (01291) 672505
Off A449 near Usk; NP15 1LE Prettily set 17th-c country inn with relaxed homely feel in three linked beamed rooms, steps between two, nice mix of furnishings and rustic decorations, enjoyable home cooking at sensible prices, efficient service, two or more well kept ales, decent wines by the glass, log fires, pleasant panelled dining room; attractive garden with big fountain, hill views, comfortable bedrooms in small attached motel, closed Sun evening. *(Dr Peter Clinch)*

MONMOUTH   SO5012
Robin Hood (01600) 715423
Monnow Street; NP25 3EQ Ancient pub with low-beamed panelled bar, popular food from sandwiches to specials, well kept ales including Bass and Greene King, friendly

service, restaurant; children welcome, tables and play area outside, open all day. *(B M Eldridge)*

PENALLT   SO5209
Inn at Penallt (01600) 772765
Village signed off B4293; at crossroads in village turn left; NP25 4SE
Refurbished 17th-c stone pub, good home-made bar and restaurant food with emphasis on local produce, also local ales and cider, well priced wine list, courteous efficient service, airy slate-floored bar with woodburner, restaurant and small back conservatory; children and dogs welcome, big garden with terrace and play area, Wye Valley views, four bedrooms, closed Mon, Tues lunchtime, and Weds and Thurs lunchtimes in winter. *(LM, Leo and Susan Horton, Geoff and Linda Payne)*

RAGLAN   SO4107
Beaufort Arms (01291) 690412
High Street; NP15 2DY Pub/hotel (former 16th-c coaching inn) with two character beamed bars, one with big stone fireplace and comfortable seats on slate floor, well kept Fullers London Pride and Wye Valley Butty Bach, good range of locally sourced food including set-price lunchtime/early evening menu, light airy brasserie, attentive friendly staff; background music; children welcome, terrace tables, 17 good bedrooms. *(Reg Fowle, Helen Rickwood, Eryl and Keith Dykes, B M Eldridge, Chris Flynn, Wendy Jones, LM and others)*

SHIRENEWTON   ST4793
Tredegar Arms (01291) 641274
Signed off B4235 just W of Chepstow; NP16 6RQ Popular pub with welcoming landlady and cheery staff, bright and clean, with good choice of well cooked/presented food, real ales in good condition; sheltered courtyard, bedrooms. *(Bob and Margaret Holder)*

TINTERN   SO5300
☆ Anchor (01291) 689582
Off A466 at brown Abbey sign; NP16 6TE Prime spot by the abbey, friendly landlord and staff, wide choice of nicely presented good value food (separate café and restaurant), five well kept ales including Bath, Otter and Wye Valley, Weston's Old Rosie cider, decent wines, great medieval stone cider mill in heavy-beamed main bar, flagstones and stripped stone, children and dogs welcome, paved courtyard with another mill stone, extensive lawn with picnic-sets and sturdy play area, River Wye just behind, open all day. *(K and B Barker, Ian and Rose Lock, Chris and Angela Buckell)*

TINTERN   SO5200
Moon & Sixpence (01291) 689284
A466 Chepstow–Monmouth; NP16 6SG Stripped stone, beams, open fires and woodburners, two dining areas, another room

---

with sofas, natural spring feeding indoor goldfish pool, well kept Wye Valley ales and two ciders from back bar, enjoyable pubby food including good value Sun roasts, friendly staff; background music, sports TV; children welcome, terrace with views along River Wye to abbey, good walks, open all day. *(B M Eldridge, Neil and Anita Christopher)*

TRELLECK   SO5005
Lion (01600) 860322
B4293 6 miles S of Monmouth; NP25 4PA Open-plan bar with one or two low black beams, nice mix of old furniture, two log fires, ales such as Butcombe, Felinfoel and Wye Valley, wide range of good inexpensive food including hungarian and thai specialities, Fri evening fish and chips, traditional games such as shove-ha'penny, ring the bull and table skittles, background music; children and dogs welcome, picnic-sets out on grass, side courtyard overlooking church, self-catering cottage, open all day Fri and Sat, closed Sun evening. *(B M Eldridge)*

TRELLECK GRANGE   SO5001
Fountain (01291) 689303
Minor road Tintern–Llanishen, SE of village; NP16 6QW Traditional 17th-c country pub under friendly newish licensees, some sympathetic refurbishment, enjoyable local food from pub favourites to game specials, three well kept welsh ales, farm cider and perry, roomy low-beamed flagstoned bar with log fire; small walled garden, peaceful spot on small windy road, open all day, closed Mon. *(Ian Barker, LM, Peter Martin)*

USK   SO3700
Cross Keys (01291) 672535
Bridge Street; NP15 1BG Small two-bar stone pub dating from the 14th c, wide choice of popular good value food, well kept Brains Rev James and Hancocks HB, good service and friendly atmosphere, log fire in handsome fireplace, oak beams, wall plaques marking past flood levels; sports TV; children welcome, no dogs during food times, back terrace, disabled access, five comfortable bedrooms, good breakfast, open all day. *(Robert Turnham)*

USK   SO3700
Kings Head (01291) 672963
Old Market Street; NP15 1AL Nice chatty relaxed atmosphere, good food and well kept beers, friendly efficient staff, huge log fire in superb fireplace; sports TV; bedrooms, open all day. *(Anon)*

GWYNEDD
ABERDOVEY   SN6196
Britannia (01654) 767426
Sea View Terrace; LL35 0EF Friendly busting harbourside inn, great estuary

and distant mountain views from upstairs restaurant with balcony, good range of well priced food, downstairs locals' bar with darts and TV, cosy back snug with woodburner; children welcome (not in bar), three bedrooms, open all day. *(Michael Butler)*

ABERGYNOLWYN SH6706
Railway (01654) 782279
Tywyn–Talyllyn pass; LL36 9YW
Traditional 16th-c two-bar village pub in lovely setting (plenty of customers from the splendid Talyllyn railway), friendly staff, enjoyable straightforward food from sandwiches up, three well kept changing ales, big inglenook fire in lounge, small dining room; children welcome, disabled facilities, outside seating and play area, good walks. *(Henry Pursehouse-Tranter)*

BEDDGELERT SH5848
Saracens Head (01766) 890329
Caernarfon Road; LL55 4UY Cheerful village inn with three real ales and enjoyable pubby food, big lounge bar with small dining area, compact back bar; tables on partly covered terrace, small garden opposite river, comfortable bedrooms. *(Ray Tarling)*

BETWS-Y-COED SH7856
Pont y Pair (01690) 710407
Holyhead Road(A5); LL24 0BN Small hotel with enjoyable freshly made food in cosy bar and dining room, good selection of draught beers; bedrooms. *(Martin Cawley)*

BETWS-Y-COED SH7955
✶**Ty Gwyn** (01690) 710383
A5 just S of bridge to village; LL24 0SG
Restaurant with rooms rather than pub (you must eat or stay overnight to be served alcohol – disqualifying it from our main entries), but pubby feel in beamed lounge bar with ancient cooking range, easy chairs, antiques, silver, cut glass, old prints and interesting bric-a-brac, really good interesting food using local produce including own fruit and vegetables, beers such as Adnams, Brains and Great Orme, friendly professional service; background music; children welcome, 12 comfortable bedrooms and holiday cottage, closed Mon-Weds in Jan. *(Ann and Adrian Bulley)*

CAERNARFON SH4762
✶**Black Buoy** (01286) 673604
Northgate Street; LL55 1RW Busy traditional pub by castle walls, renamed losing its historical connection (properly Black Boy, from King Charles II's nickname in its Kings Head days); cheery fire, beams from ships wrecked here in the 16th c, bare floors and thick walls, lots of welsh chat, enjoyable generous food all day from baguettes and doorstep sandwiches to interesting fish and vegetarian dishes, well kept ales such as Brains, Conwy and Purple Moose, good friendly service,

character lounge bar, restaurant, public bar with TV; a few pavement picnic-sets, nice bedrooms. *(Hugh Tattersall, Peter and Anne Hollindale, Jamie Price, John and Gloria Isaacs)*

CAPEL CURIG SH7257
✶**Bryn Tyrch** (01690) 720223
A5 E; LL24 0EL Family-owned inn perfectly placed for the mountains of Snowdonia; bare-stone walkers' bar with big communal tables and amazing picture-windows views, two Great Orme ales and a guest beer, quite a few malt whiskies, good choice of food including sandwiches; second bar with big menu boards, leather sofas and mix of tables on floorboards, coal fire; children and dogs welcome, steep little side garden, more seats on terrace and across road by stream, country-style bedrooms, open all day weekends, from 4.30pm weekdays (midday during holidays). *(N R White, Paul Humphreys, Doug Kennedy)*

CAPEL CURIG SH7357
Tyn y Coed (01690) 720331
A5 SE of village; LL24 0EE Friendly inn across road from River Llugwy, enjoyable good value home-made food using local produce, well kept Purple Moose and three guests, pleasant quick service, log fires, pool room with juke box; nice side terrace, bedrooms, closed weekday lunchtimes out of season, otherwise open all day. *(Peter Harper)*

CONWY SH7777
Albion
Uppergate Street; LL32 8RF Sensitively restored 1920s pub thriving under the collective ownership of four welsh brewers – Bragd'yr, Conwy, Great Orme and Purple Moose, their beers and guests kept well, no hot food, interesting building with plenty of well preserved features. *(Chris and Angela Buckell)*

LLANDUDNO SH7882
Queen Victoria (01492) 860952
Church Walks; LL30 2HD Traditional Victorian pub away from the high street bustle, well kept Banks's, Marstons Pedigree and guests, good choice of enjoyable affordably priced pubby food all-day, eat in bar or upstairs restaurant, congenial atmosphere and good service; children and dogs welcome. *(D W Stokes)*

LLANDUDNO JUNCTION SH8180
✶**Queens Head** (01492) 546570
Glanwydden; heading towards Llandudno on B5115 from Colwyn Bay, turn left into Llanrhos Road at roundabout as you enter the Penrhyn Bay speed limit; Glanwydden is signed as the first left turn; LL31 9JP Comfortable modern dining pub with good well presented bar food (booking advised Sun) and efficient friendly service, spacious lounge partly divided by wall of

broad arches, brown plush wall banquettes and windsor chairs around neat black tables, small public bar with well kept Adnams and guests, decent wines; unobtrusive background music; children welcome, seats outside, can rent pretty stone cottage next door, open all day weekends (food all day then too). *(Paul Humphreys, Mike and Mary Carter, John and Sylvia Harrop and others)*

LLANENGAN SH2826
Sun (01758) 712660
A mile W of Sarn Bach; LL53 7LG Friendly and cosy Robinsons pub in small village near spectacular sandy Hell's Mouth beach, three real ales, enjoyable family food, reasonable prices, lifeboatman landlord; large partly covered terrace and garden (very popular with children), outdoor summer bar and pool table, bedrooms. *(Andy Dolan)*

LLANUWCHLLYN SH8730
Eagles (01678) 540278
Aka Eryrod; A494/B4403; LL23 7UB Family-run and welcoming with good reasonably priced food (bilingual menu) using produce from own farm, opened up slate-floor bar with log fire, beams and some stripped stone, back picture-window view of mountains with Lake Bala in distance, Brains Bitter, limited wine choice in small bottles; picnic-sets under parasols on flower-filled back terrace, open all day summer, closed lunchtime Mon-Weds in winter. *(Anon)*

PENMAENPOOL SH6918
George III (01341) 422525
Just off A493, near Dolgellau; LL40 1YD Attractive inn dating from 1650, lovely views over Mawddach estuary from civilised partly panelled upstairs bar opening into cosy inglenook lounge, more basic beamed and flagstoned downstairs bar for peak times, usual bar food, well kept ale such Black Sheep, Fullers and Purple Moose, restaurant; they ask to keep a credit card if you run a tab; dogs and children welcome, sheltered terrace, 11 good bedrooms including some in converted station (line now a walkway), open all day. *(Norma and Noel Thomas, Michael Butler)*

PORTH DINLLAEN SH2741
⋆ **Ty Coch** (01758) 720498
Beach car park signed from Morfa Nefyn, then 15-minute walk; LL53 6DB Idyllic location right on beach with great view along coast to mountains, far from roads and only reached on foot; bar crammed with nautical paraphernalia, pewter, old miners' and railway lamps, RNLI memorabilia and so forth, simple furnishings and coal fire, a couple of real ales (served in plastic as worried about glass on beach), short lunchtime bar menu; children and dogs welcome, open all day in season (till 4pm Sun), 12-4pm Oct-Easter. *(Richard, Anne and Kate Ansell, Theocsbrian)*

PORTHMADOG SH5639
Royal Sportsman (01766) 512015
High Street; LL49 9HB Extensively refurbished early Victorian hotel with good food from light lunchtime choices to pricier restaurant dishes, popular bar and comfortable lounge with leather armchairs and sofas, restaurant, good friendly staff, a couple of well kept ales from local Purple Moose, ten wines by the glass, cocktails, log fire; children and dogs welcome, pretty terrace, 28 bedrooms. *(Tony Hobden, N Jervis)*

PORTHMADOG SH5738
Spooners (01766) 516032
Harbour Station; LL49 9NF Platform café/bar at steam line terminus, lots of railway memorabilia including a former working engine (Princess) in one corner, eight changing ales (two from Purple Moose), good value pub food including popular Sun lunch, evening meals Tues-Sat (all week in high season); children welcome, platform tables, open all day. *(Tony and Wendy Hobden, Tony Hobden, Mike and Eleanor Anderson, Phil Bryant)*

TREFRIW SH7863
Old Ship (01492) 640013
B5106; LL27 0JH Particularly well kept Marstons-related beers and local guests, good selection of wines, friendly staff, varied choice of enjoyable fresh food from baguettes up including good fish and chips, log fire, cheerful local atmosphere, restaurant with inglenook; children welcome. *(Miles Dobson, Doug Kerr, Martin Cawley)*

TUDWEILIOG SH2336
Lion (01758) 659724
Nefyn Road (B4417), Lleyn Peninsula; LL53 8ND Cheerful village inn with good choice of enjoyable sensibly priced food, lounge bar and two dining rooms (one for families), quick friendly service, real ales such as Purple Moose (up to three in summer), dozens of malt whiskies, decent wines, games in public bar; pleasant front garden, four bedrooms, open all day in season. *(John and Louise Gittins)*

MID GLAMORGAN

MAESTEG SS8689
Cross (01656)732476
A4063; CF34 9LB Friendly roadside pub brewing its own good Cerddin beers using solar power, comfortable interior; pool, sports TV; open all day (till 1am Fri, Sat). *(the Didler)*

PONTYPRIDD ST0790
Llanover Arms (01443) 403215
Bridge Street; CF37 4PE Friendly chatty ale house with three unspoilt rooms, Brains and guests; open all day. *(the Didler)*

POWYS

BERRIEW
SJ1800

Lion (01686) 640452

B4390; village signed off A483 Welshpool–Newtown; SY21 8PQ Black and white beamed 17th-c coaching inn in attractive riverside village (with lively sculpture gallery), friendly welcome from mother and daughter team, old-fashioned inglenook public bar and partly stripped-stone lounge, food here or in restaurant from sandwiches up, helpful cheerful service, well kept Banks's and Jennings, decent house wines, dominoes; quiet background music; children welcome, dogs in bar, seven bedrooms, open all day Fri and Sat. *(Patrick and Daphne Darley, Reg Fowle, Helen Rickwood, David Glynne-Jones)*

BLEDDFA
SO2068

Hundred House (01547) 550441

A488 Knighton–Penybont; LD7 1PA Refurbished 16th-c pub (former court house) opposite village green, friendly new licensees, carpeted lounge bar with woodburner in big inglenook, L-shaped room with lower flagstoned bar, another big fireplace in cosy dining room, enjoyable locally sourced food, Woods and a guest such as Golden Valley or Six Bells; background music; tables in side garden, lovely countryside, closed Mon, otherwise open all day. *(Anon)*

CARNO
SN9696

Aleppo Merchant (01686) 420210

A470 Newtown–Machynlleth; SY17 5LL Good choice of reasonably priced pub food from sandwiches up (open for breakfast too), helpful friendly staff, Boddingtons and Six Bells, plushly modernised stripped stone bar, peaceful lounge on right with open fire, restaurant (well behaved children allowed here), back extension with big-screen TV in games room; background music; disabled access, steps up to tables in back garden, bedrooms, nice countryside, open all day. *(Michael and Jenny Back, Mike and Mary Carter)*

CRICKHOWELL
SO2118

Bridge End (01873) 810338

Bridge Street; NP8 1AR Friendly 16th-c coaching inn by many-arched bridge over the Usk, popular with locals, ales such as Hancocks Hogs Back TEA and Wychwood Hobgoblin, enjoyable food from good value lunchtime baguettes to popular Sun roasts, good service, lots of knick-knacks and fishing photographs, small restaurant; beer garden across road overlooking river, three bedrooms. *(Barry and Anne, Michael Mellers, Tony and Maggie Harwood, Tony and Gill Powell, MLR and others)*

CRICKHOWELL
SO2118

Dragon (01873) 810362

High Street; NP8 1BE Refurbished old inn (more hotel/restaurant than pub but with small bar), good varied choice of enjoyable well presented food from reasonably priced bar meals up including speciality tapas, prompt friendly service, Brains Rev James, log fire; 15 comfortable bedrooms. *(C A Bryson, Eryl and Keith Dykes, Tony and Gill Powell)*

CRICKHOWELL
SO1919

✴Nantyffin Cider Mill

(01873) 810775 *A40/A479 NW; NP8 1LP* Much emphasis on food (booking advised) in this former 16th-c drovers' inn, open-plan grey-stone bar with woodburner in broad fireplace, solid comfortable wooden tables and chairs, ales such as Felinfoel Best and Double Dragon, farm cider, quite a choice of wines and maybe home-made elderflower cordial, attractive high-raftered restaurant with old cider press; children welcome, dogs in bar, disabled access using ramp, seats outside making most of rural River Usk views, closed Mon (except bank holidays) and Sun evening Oct-March. *(Michael Mellers, B and M Kendall, Terry Davis, Mike and Mary Carter and others)*

DERWENLAS
SN7299

✴Black Lion (01654) 703913

A487 just S of Machynlleth; SY20 8TN Cosy 16th-c country pub, good range of enjoyable well priced food including nice children's menu, friendly staff coping well at busy times, Wye Valley Butty Bach and a guest, decent wines, heavy black beams, thick walls and black timbering, attractive pictures, brasses and lion models, tartan carpet over big slate flagstones, good log fire; background music; garden behind with play area and steps up into woods, limited parking, bedrooms, closed Mon. *(B and M Kendall, John Evans)*

DINAS MAWDDWY
SH8514

Red Lion (01650) 531247

Dyfi Road; off A470 (N of A458 junction); SY20 9JA Two small traditional front bars and more modern back extension, changing ales including some from small local brewers, good generous home-made food including specials, reasonable prices and friendly efficient service; pub named in welsh (Llew Coch). *(Keith and Ann Arnold, Peter and Anne Hollindale)*

'Children welcome' means the pubs says it lets children inside without any special restriction; some may impose an evening time limit earlier than 9pm – please tell us if you find this.

GLADESTRY   SO2355
Royal Oak (01544) 370669
B4594; HR5 3NR Village pub on Offa's
Dyke Path with friendly licensees, simple
stripped-stone slate-floor walkers' bar,
beams hung with tankards and lanterns,
piano, darts, carpeted lounge, open fires, two
Golden Valley ales, basic bar food; no credit
cards; children welcome, dogs in bar (and
in bedrooms by arrangement), sheltered
back garden, camping, open all day (may
close if quiet but will reopen if you ring the
bell). *(Reg Fowle, Helen Rickwood)*

GLANGRWYNEY   SO2416
Bell (01873) 811115
A40 Crickhowell–Abergavenny;
NP8 1EH Friendly old beamed pub
comfortably updated by two brothers, three
or four well kept changing ales, enjoyable
generous food mostly using local produce,
live jazz and folk; children welcome, four
bedrooms. *(David Hassall)*

GLASBURY   SO1839
Harp (01497) 847373
B4350 towards Hay, just N of A438;
HR3 5NR Welcoming, relaxed and homely
old place with good value pubby food (not
Mon) cooked by landlady including proper
pies, log-fire lounge with eating areas, airy
bar, well kept local ales, picture windows
over wooded garden sloping to River Wye,
some acoustic music; terrace tables,
campsite and canoeing, river-view bedrooms,
good breakfast. *(Reg Fowle, Helen Rickwood,*
Mike Ashley)

HAY-ON-WYE   SO2242
★ Blue Boar (01497) 820884
Castle Street/Oxford Road; HR3 5DF
Medieval bar in character pub, cosy corners,
dark panelling, pews and country chairs,
open fire in Edwardian fireplace, four ales
including a house beer from Hydes, organic
bottled cider and several wines by the glass,
good food (from breakfast on) in quite
different long open café dining room, bright
light décor, local artwork for sale and another
open fire, good friendly service; background
music; children and dogs welcome, tables
in tree-shaded garden, open all day from
9am. *(R T and J C Moggridge, Mark Sykes, David*
and Sue Atkinson)

HAY-ON-WYE   SO2342
★ Kilverts (01497) 821042
Bell Bank/Bear Street; HR3 5AG High-
beamed bar in friendly hotel, six well kept
ales such as Breconshire, Hobsons, Montys
and Wye Valley, ciders and perries, several
wines by the glass, good food from pubby
choices up; well behaved children welcome
till 8pm if eating, dogs allowed but not in
restaurant or on lawn, front flagstoned
courtyard, pretty back garden with terrace
and fountain, refurbished bedrooms, good

breakfast, open all day. *(John and Bryony*
Coles, Pat and Tony Martin, MLR)

HAY-ON-WYE   SO2342
★ Old Black Lion (01497) 820841
Lion Street; HR3 5AD Comfortable low-
beamed bar with old pine tables and original
fireplace, mostly laid out for dining, bar and
restaurant food available throughout, Wye
Valley (labelled as Old Black Lion) and a
guest, efficient service; no dogs; children over
5 allowed if eating, sheltered back terrace,
ten bedrooms (some above bar), open all
day. *(Pete Coxon, Reg Fowle, Helen Rickwood)*

HAY-ON-WYE   SO2242
★ Three Tuns (01497) 821855
Broad Street; HR3 5DB Enjoyable freshly
prepared food (not Sun evening) including
lovely home-baked bread in big pub with low
black beams and inglenook woodburners,
lighter sofa area, ancient stairs to raftered
restaurant, well kept ales such as Three
Tuns and Wye Valley, good wine choice; no
dogs; children welcome, disabled facilities,
sheltered courtyard, open all day weekends,
closed Mon and Tues out of season. *(C A*
Bryson, Martin and Sue Day)

LLANBEDR   SO2320
Red Lion (01873) 810754
Off A40 at Crickhowell; NP8 1SR Quaint,
welcoming old local in pretty little village
set in dell, heavy beams, antique settles in
lounge and snug, log fires, Rhymney, Wye
Valley and a guest ale, front dining area with
good value home-made food; good walking
country (porch for muddy boots), closed
weekday lunchtime (except 2-5pm Weds),
open all day weekends. *(Anon)*

LLANFRYNACH   SO0725
White Swan (01874) 665276
Village signposted from B4558, off
A40 E of Brecon – take second turn to
village, which is also signed to pub; LD3
7BZ Comfortably upmarket country dining
pub in heart of Brecon Beacons; original part
with stripped stone and flagstones, sturdy
oak tables, leather sofas and armchairs at
low tables, woodburner, Brains, Breconshire
and Rhymney, decent wines and coffees,
good food with plenty of variety (simpler at
lunchtime), more modern high-ceilinged
bare-boards extension; background music;
children welcome, charming back terrace
attractively divided by low privet hedges,
towpath walks along canal, closed Mon, Tues
and first two weeks in Jan. *(David Heath, Taff*
and Gilly Thomas)

LLANGEDWYN   SJ1924
★ Green Inn (01691) 828234
B4396 E of village; SY10 9JW Ancient
country dining pub with various snug alcoves,
nooks and crannies, good mix of furnishings
including oak settles and leather sofas,
blazing log fire, helpful friendly staff, up to

four changing ales such as Stonehouse and Woods, enjoyable well prepared food, plenty of events from music to comedy; children and dogs welcome, attractive garden over road running down towards River Tanat (fishing permits available), camping, open all day weekends, closed Tues. *(Mike Walker)*

LLANIDLOES SN9584

Crown & Anchor (01686) 412398

Long Bridge Street; SY18 6EF Friendly unspoilt town-centre pub known locally as Rubys after landlady who has run it for 47 years, well kept Brains Rev James and Worthington Bitter, chatty locals' bar, lounge, snug, and two other rooms, one with pool and games machine separated by central hallway; open all day. *(the Didler)*

LLOWES SO1941

Radnor Arms (01497) 847460

A438 Brecon–Hereford; HR3 5JA Attractive stone-built country pub doing well under present licensee, well kept Wye Valley Butty Bach and a guest, extensive choice of bottled beers, good blackboard food including fresh fish, children's menu, traditional beamed bar with stripped-stone and log fire, two small dining rooms; dogs welcome, tables in garden looking out over fields to the Black Mountains, small campsite, closed Sun evening, Mon, Tues, and lunchtimes Wed and Thurs. *(Simon Daws, Clare Williams, Reg Fowle, Helen Rickwood)*

MALLWYD SH8612

Brigands (01650) 511999

A470 by roundabout in village; SY20 9HJ Sizeable former 15th-c coaching inn, friendly welcoming uniformed staff, wide choice of good reasonably priced food all day, well kept ales such as Purple Moose and Titanic, Gwynt y Ddraig cider, good selection of wines; children and dogs welcome, extensive lawns with play area, lovely views, fishing on River Dovey, bedrooms, good breakfast. *(Bob and Tanya Ekers, Paul and Sonia Broadgate)*

MIDDLETOWN SJ3012

Breidden (01938) 570880

A458 Welshpool–Shrewsbury; SY21 8EL Run by friendly chinese family with varied choice of food from pubby through to chinese, japanese and thai dishes, two well kept changing ales, takeaway service; children welcome, decent-sized garden with play area, open all day (till 2am Fri, Sat). *(Keith and Ann Arnold, Melvin Spear)*

PAINSCASTLE SO1646

★ Roast Ox (01497) 851398

Off A470 Brecon–Builth Wells, or from A438 at Clyro; LD2 3JL Well restored pub with beams, flagstones, stripped stone, appropriate simple furnishings and some rustic bric-a-brac, well kept ales such as Hook Norton tapped from the cask, good

range of farm ciders, decent roasts as well as other enjoyable hearty food including good lunchtime baps, friendly quick service; dogs welcome, picnic-sets outside, attractive hill country, ten simple comfortable bedrooms. *(Geoffrey and Penny Hughes, MLR, Reg Fowle, Helen Rickwood, T and F Melhuish)*

PENCELLI SO0925

Royal Oak (01874) 665396

B4558 SE of Brecon; LD3 7LX Unpretentious and friendly with two small bars, low beams, assorted pine furniture on polished flagstones, autographed sporting memorabilia, log fires, well kept Brains Rev James and guest such as Breconshire Red Dragon, small blackboard choice of good home-made food (standard times in summer, Thurs-Sat evenings and weekend lunchtimes in winter), simple modern candlelit dining room; children welcome, terraces backing on to Monmouthshire and Brecon Canal, nearby moorings, lovely canalside walks and handy for Taff Trail, closed Mon-Weds out of season. *(Tony and Maggie Harwood, Brian and Anna Marsden)*

PEN-Y-CAE SN8313

Ancient Briton (01639) 730273

Brecon Road (A4067); SA9 1YY Friendly opened-up roadside pub, six or more well kept ales from far and wide, a local cider, reasonably priced food; children welcome, play area, campsite, handy for Dan-yr-Ogof caves, Henrhyd waterfall and Carig-y-Nos country park, open all day. *(MLR, Quentin and Carol Williamson)*

PRESTEIGNE SO3164

Radnorshire Arms (01544) 267406

High Street (B4355 N of centre); LD8 2BE Fine Elizabethan timbered hotel full of rambling individuality and historical charm; relaxed bar, venerable dark oak panelling, latticed windows, elegantly moulded black oak beams, polished copper pans and measures, a handful of armchairs, lovely dining room, friendly efficient staff, enjoyable honest food, a couple of real ales; background music; children welcome, 19 bedrooms (some in garden lodge). *(George Atkinson, James Miller)*

RHAYADER SN9668

★ Triangle (01597) 810537

Cwmdauddwr; B4518 by bridge over Wye, SW of centre; LD6 5AR Interesting mainly 16th-c pub, small and spotless with nice chatty atmosphere and welcoming helpful service, shortish choice of good value home-made pubby food (best to book evenings), well kept Brains Rev James and Hancocks HB, small selection of reasonably priced wines, dining area with nice view over park to Wye, darts and quiz nights; three tables on small front terrace. *(Nigel and Sue Foster, Di and Mike Gillam)*

TALYBONT-ON-USK   SO1122
⋆ **Star** (01874) 676635
B4558; LD3 7YX Old-fashioned canalside
inn unashamedly stronger on character
than creature comforts, fine choice of
changing ales from all over the country
served by enthusiastic landlord, real ciders
too, fair-priced standard bar food, good mix
of customers including walkers with dogs,
several plainly furnished pubby rooms, open
fires (one in splendid stone fireplace), games
room with pool, fruit machine, TV and juke
box, live music last Fri of month, quiz Tues
in winter; children welcome, picnic sets in
sizeable tree-ringed garden with path leading
to river, lovely village surrounded by Brecon
Beacons National Park, bedrooms, open all
day summer. *(Mrs P Bishop, Brian and Anna
Marsden, Taff and Gilly Thomas)*

TALYBONT-ON-USK   SO1122
White Hart (01874) 676227
*B4558, before bridge travelling NE;
LD3 7JD* Comfortable stone-built coaching
inn, big relaxed bar divided by working
fireplace from beamed dining area, good
hearty home-made food including vegetarian
options and all-day Sun roast, half a dozen
well kept changing ales, Thatcher's cider,
Brecon gin and Penderyn whisky, welcoming
knowledgeable landlord; on Taff Trail, some
tables out by Monmouthshire and Brecon
Canal, bunkhouse. *(the Didler, Oliver Bowler,
Taff and Gilly Thomas)*

SOUTH GLAMORGAN

LLANBLETHIAN   SS9873
Cross (01446) 772995
Church Road; CF71 7JF Former staging
inn refurbished under welcoming owners,
well kept Wye Valley and guests (beer
festivals), enjoyable reasonably priced food
from pubby things up in comfortable bar
or light airy restaurant, log fires; children
and dogs welcome, terrace seats, open all
day. *(Phil and Pam Haughton, Tony Prosser,
Colin Taylor, Clive Roberts)*

PENARTH   ST1871
Bears Head (029) 2070 6424
Windsor Road; CF64 1JD Popular well
run Wetherspoons in centre of town (open-
fronted in warm weather), good range of
beers and food, quick friendly service, family
area; open all day from 8am. *(Tony and Gill
Powell, Reg Fowle, Helen Rickwood)*

WEST GLAMORGAN

SWANSEA   SS6592
Queens (01792) 521531
Gloucester Place; SA1 1TY Well kept
Brains, Theakstons and a guest, basic
but very cheap pub food, plenty of local
atmosphere and friendly service, live music
Sat; handy for museums and Dylan Thomas
Centre. *(R T and J C Moggridge)*

A little further afield

CHANNEL ISLANDS

GUERNSEY

ST PETER PORT

Ship & Crown (01481) 728994
*Opposite Crown Pier, Esplanade;
GY1 2NB* Bustling town pub with bay
windows overlooking harbour, very popular
with yachting people and smarter locals;
interesting photographs (especially of World
War II occupation, also boats and local
shipwrecks), good value all-day bar food
from sandwiches up, three changing ales
and a proper cider, welcoming prompt
service even when busy, more modern-feel
Crow's Nest brasserie upstairs with fine
views; sports TVs in bar; open all day from
10am till late. *(MLR)*

VALE

Houmet (01481) 242214
Grand Havre; GY6 8JR Modern building
overlooking Grand Havre Bay, front
restaurant/bar with conservatory, good
choice of reasonably priced popular food
(best to book) including fresh local fish and
seafood, friendly service, a couple of real ales
and several wines by the glass, back public
bar with pool and machines (dogs allowed
here); children welcome, tables out on
decking, open all day (till 6pm Sun). *(MLR)*

KING'S MILLS

⋆**Fleur du Jardin** (01481) 257996
Kings Mills Road; GY5 7JT Lovely
country hotel in attractive walled garden,
relaxing low-beamed flagstoned bar with
good log fire, old prints and subdued
lighting, good food strong on local produce
and seafood, friendly helpful service,
several real ales such as Adnams Broadside
and Liberation, good choice of wines by the
glass, local cider, restaurant; background
music; children and small dogs welcome,
plenty of tables on back terrace, 13 clean
comfortable bedrooms, open all day.
(Mr and Mrs John Clifford)

JERSEY

GRÈVE DE LECQ

⋆**Moulin de Lecq** (01534) 482818
Mont de la Grève de Lecq; JE3 2DT
Cheerful family-friendly converted mill with
massive waterwheel dominating the softly lit
beamed bar, good pubby food, four changing
ales and a couple of real ciders, prompt
friendly service, lots of board games, pool in
upstairs games room, restaurant extension;
dogs welcome in bar, terrace picnic-sets and
good play area, quiet streamside spot with
nice walks, open all day in summer. *(Anon)*

ST AUBIN

Boat House (01534) 747141
North Quay; JE3 8BS Modern steel and
timber clad harbourside building, emphasis
on dining but does have a couple of good
local ales, light and airy with spacious bar/
restaurant and upstairs brasserie (Wed-Sat
evenings, Sun lunchtime), great views
(window tables for diners); balcony and
decked terrace, open all day. *(Anon)*

ST AUBIN

⋆**Old Court House Inn**
(01534) 746433 *Harbour Boulevard; JE3
8AB* Pubby low-beamed downstairs bar with
open fire, other rambling areas including
smarter bar partly built from schooner's gig,
food from pubby snacks to lots of good fresh
fish, well kept real ales and nice wines by the
glass, handsome upstairs restaurant, glorious
views across harbour to St Helier; children
welcome, front deck overlooking harbour,
more seats in floral courtyard behind, ten
comfortable bedrooms, open all day (food all
day in summer). *(Martin Smith)*

ST BRELADE

Old Smugglers (01534) 741510
*Ouaisne Bay; OS map reference
595476; JE3 8AW* Happily unpretentious
black-beamed pub, well kept Bass and two
guests, farm cider, enjoyable reasonably
priced pubby food, friendly service, log fires,
traditional built-in settles, darts, cribbage
and dominoes, restaurant; occasional live
music, sports TV; children and dogs welcome,
sun porch with interesting coast views, just

above Ouaisne beach, open all day.
(Martin Smith)

ST HELIER
★ **Lamplighter** (01534) 723119
Mulcaster Street; JE2 3NJ Small pub
with up to nine well kept ales including
Liberation, local cider, over 40 malt whiskies,
bargain simple food such as crab sandwiches;
heavy timbers, rough panelling and scrubbed
pine tables; sports TV, can get very busy;
interesting façade (with only Union Flag
visible during Nazi occupation), open all
day. *(Joan and Michel Hooper-Immins, Steve and
Claire Harvey, MLR)*

ISLE OF MAN

LAXEY   SC4382
Shore (01624) 861509
Old Laxey Hill; IM4 7DA Friendly
nautically themed village pub brewing
its own Old Laxey Bosuns Bitter, good
value wines by the glass, enjoyable pubby
lunchtime food (also Tues curry and Thurs
steak nights); children welcome till 9pm,
picnic-sets out by lovely stream, nice walk to
Laxey Waterwheel, open all day. *(Anon)*

PEEL   SC2484
Creek (01624) 842216
Station Place/North Quay; IM5 1AT In
lovely setting on the ancient quayside
opposite Manannan Heritage Centre,
welcoming relaxed atmosphere, wide choice
of sensibly priced food all day including fish,
crab and lobsters fresh from the boats, good
local kippers too, well kept Okells and nine
guest ales, nautical theme lounge bar with
etched mirrors and mainly old woodwork,
public bar with TVs and weekend live music;
children welcome, tables outside overlooking
harbour, open all day. *(Anon)*

PORT ERIN
Falcon's Nest (01624) 834077
Station Road; IM9 6AF Friendly family-
run hotel overlooking the bay, good sensibly
priced food including local fish/seafood, five
well kept ales (May beer festival) and some
70 malt whiskies, two bars, one with open
fire and conservatory, restaurant; children
welcome, 39 bedrooms many with sea view,
also eight new self-catering apartmemnts,
handy for steam rail terminus, open all
day. *(Anon)*

Pubs that serve food all day

We list here all the pubs that have told us they plan to serve food all day, even if it's only one day of the week. The individual entries for the pubs themselves show the actual details.

Bedfordshire

Ireland, Black Horse
Oakley, Bedford Arms
Woburn, Birch

Berkshire

Cookham Dean, Chequers
Sonning, Bull
White Waltham, Beehive
Buckinghamshire
Coleshill, Harte & Magpies
Forty Green,
  Royal Standard of England
Grove, Grove Lock
Wooburn Common, Chequers

Cambridgeshire

Bourn, Willow Tree
Cambridge, Punter
Stilton, Bell

Cheshire

Aldford, Grosvenor Arms
Astbury, Egerton Arms
Aston, Bhurtpore
Bickley Moss,
  Cholmondeley Arms
Bunbury, Dysart Arms
Burleydam, Combermere Arms
Burwardsley, Pheasant
Chester, Mill, Old Harkers Arms

Cotebrook, Fox & Barrel
Eaton, Plough
Macclesfield, Sutton Hall
Marton, Davenport Arms
Mobberley, Bulls Head
Peover Heath, Dog
Spurstow, Yew Tree
Tarporley, Rising Sun
Thelwall, Little Manor
Warmingham, Bears Paw
Wrenbury, Dusty Miller

Cornwall

Crafthole, Finnygook
Mitchell, Plume of Feathers
Morwenstow, Bush
Mylor Bridge, Pandora
Porthtowan, Blue

Cumbria

Beetham, Wheatsheaf
Cartmel Fell, Masons Arms
Crosthwaite, Punch Bowl
Elterwater, Britannia
Ings, Watermill
Levens, Strickland Arms
Lupton, Plough
Ravenstonedale, Black Swan
Threlkeld, Horse & Farrier

Derbyshire

Alderwasley, Bear

Beeley, Devonshire Arms

Chelmorton, Church Inn

Fenny Bentley, Coach & Horses

Hathersage, Plough

Hayfield, Lantern Pike

Hope, Cheshire Cheese

Ladybower Reservoir,
  Ladybower Inn

Monyash, Bulls Head

Devon

Avonwick, Turtley Corn Mill

Cockwood, Anchor

Colyford, Wheelwright

Horns Cross, Hoops

Iddesleigh, Duke of York

Postbridge, Warren House

Sidbury, Hare & Hounds

Sidford, Blue Ball

Dorset

Tarrant Monkton, Langton Arms

Weymouth, Red Lion

Worth Matravers,
  Square & Compass

Essex

Aythorpe Roding,
  Axe & Compasses

Feering, Sun

Fyfield, Queens Head

Little Walden, Crown

South Hanningfield, Old Windmill

Gloucestershire

Almondsbury, Bowl

Broad Campden, Bakers Arms

Coates, Tunnel House

Didmarton, Kings Arms

Ford, Plough

Guiting Power, Hollow Bottom

Nailsworth, Weighbridge

Sheepscombe, Butchers Arms

Hampshire

Bransgore, Three Tuns

Bucklers Hard,
  Master Builders House

Portsmouth, Old Customs House

Hertfordshire

Aldbury, Valiant Trooper

Barnet, Duke of York

Batford, Gibraltar Castle

Isle of Wight

Arreton, White Lion

Fishbourne, Fishbourne Inn

Ningwood, Horse & Groom

Niton, Buddle

Seaview, Boathouse

Shorwell, Crown

Ventnor, Spyglass

Kent

Brookland, Woolpack

Langton Green, Hare

Penshurst, Bottle House

Sevenoaks, White Hart

Stalisfield Green, Plough

Stowting, Tiger

Lancashire

Bashall Eaves, Red Pump

Bispham Green, Eagle & Child

Great Mitton, Three Fishes

Liverpool,
  Philharmonic Dining Rooms

Longridge, Derby Arms

Manchester, Dukes 92

Nether Burrow, Highwayman

Pleasington, Clog & Billycock

Uppermill, Church Inn

Waddington, Lower Buck

Whalley, Swan

Leicestershire and Rutland

Coleorton, George

Lyddington, Marquess of Exeter

Swithland, Griffin

Woodhouse Eaves, Wheatsheaf

Lincolnshire

Kirkby la Thorpe, Queens Head

Stamford, George of Stamford

Norfolk

Larling, Angel

Morston, Anchor

Salthouse, Dun Cow

Stiffkey, Red Lion

Stow Bardolph, Hare Arms

Swanton Morley, Darbys

Thorpe Market, Gunton Arms

Woodbastwick, Fur & Feather

Northamptonshire

Oundle, Ship

Northumbria

Alnmouth, Red Lion

Aycliffe, County

Carterway Heads,
  Manor House Inn

Corbridge, Angel

Cotherstone, Fox & Hounds

Lesbury, Coach

New York, Shiremoor Farm

Newburn, Keelman

Weldon Bridge, Anglers Arms

Oxfordshire

Kingham, Plough

Oxford, Bear, Punter

Shropshire

Chetwynd Aston, Fox

Shrewsbury, Armoury

Somerset

Hinton St George,
  Lord Poulett Arms

Stanton Wick, Carpenters Arms

Staffordshire

Salt, Holly Bush

Wrinehill, Hand & Trumpet

Suffolk

Chelmondiston, Butt & Oyster

Snape, Plough & Sail

Southwold, Harbour Inn

Stoke-by-Nayland, Crown

Waldringfield, Maybush

Surrey

Buckland, Jolly Farmers

Milford, Refectory

Sussex

Alfriston, George

Charlton, Fox Goes Free

Chiddingly, Six Bells

East Chiltington, Jolly Sportsman

Eridge Green, Nevill Crest & Gun

Horsham, Black Jug

Ringmer, Cock

Warwickshire

Barford, Granville

Birmingham, Old Joint Stock

Farnborough, Inn at Farnborough

Hunningham, Red Lion

Long Compton, Red Lion

Stratford-upon-Avon, Encore

Welford-on-Avon, Bell

Wiltshire

Bradford-on-Avon, Castle

Brinkworth, Three Crowns

Yorkshire

Blakey Ridge, Lion

Bradfield, Strines Inn

Broughton, Bull

Elslack, Tempest Arms

Grinton, Bridge Inn

Halifax, Shibden Mill

Hartshead, Gray Ox

Ledsham, Chequers

Linton in Craven, Fountaine

Long Preston, Maypole

Widdop, Pack Horse

London

Central London, Bountiful Cow,
Lamb, Old Bank of England,
Olde Mitre, Seven Stars

North London, Holly Bush

Outer London, Old Orchard

South London, Greenwich Union

West London, Churchill Arms,
Duke of Sussex, White Horse

Scotland

Applecross, Applecross Inn

Edinburgh, Abbotsford,
Café Royal

Gairloch, Old Inn

Glasgow, Babbity Bowster,
Bon Accord

Houston, Fox & Hounds

Pitlochry, Moulin

Shieldaig, Tigh an Eilean Hotel

Sligachan, Sligachan Hotel

Wales

Colwyn Bay, Pen-y-Bryn

Gresford, Pant-yr-Ochain

Llanelian-yn-Rhos, White Lion

Llanferres, Druid

Llangollen, Corn Mill

Mold, Glasfryn

Overton Bridge, Cross Foxes

Tresaith, Ship

Pubs near motorway junctions

The number at the start of each line is the number of the junction.

Detailed directions are given in the entry for each pub. In this section, to help you find the pubs quickly before you're past the junction, we give the name of the chapter where you'll find the text.

M1

9: Redbourn, Cricketers (Hertfordshire) 3.2 miles

13: Woburn, Birch (Bedfordshire) 3.5 miles

16: Nether Heyford, Olde Sun (Northamptonshire) 1.8 miles

M3

3: West End, Inn at West End (Surrey) 2.4 miles

5: North Warnborough, Mill House (Hampshire) 1 mile; Hook, Hogget (Hampshire) 1.1 miles

7: North Waltham, Fox (Hampshire) 3 miles

9: Easton, Chestnut Horse (Hampshire) 3.6 miles

M4

9: Bray, Crown (Berkshire) 1.75 miles; Bray, Hinds Head (Berkshire) 1.75 miles

13: Winterbourne, Winterbourne Arms (Berkshire) 3.7 miles

14: East Garston, Queens Arms (Berkshire) 3.5 miles

17: Norton, Vine Tree (Wiltshire) 4 miles

M5

4: Holy Cross, Bell & Cross (Worcestershire) 4 miles

10: Coombe Hill, Gloucester Old Spot (Gloucestershire) 1 mile

16: Almondsbury, Bowl (Gloucestershire) 1.25 miles

19: Clapton-in-Gordano, Black Horse (Somerset) 4 miles

26: Clayhidon, Merry Harriers (Devon) 3.1 miles; Woodbury Salterton, Diggers Rest (Devon) 3.5 miles

M6

17: Sandbach, Old Hall (Cheshire) 1.2 miles

19: Mobberley, Bulls Head (Cheshire) 4 miles

36: Lupton, Plough (Cumbria) 2 miles; Levens, Strickland Arms (Cumbria) 4 miles

39: Shap, Greyhound (Cumbria) 2 miles

40: Yanwath, Gate Inn (Cumbria) 2.25 miles; Tirril, Queens Head (Cumbria) 3.5 miles

M11

9: Hinxton, Red Lion (Cambridgeshire) 2 miles

10: Duxford, John Barleycorn (Cambridgeshire) 1.8 miles; Thriplow, Green Man (Cambridgeshire) 3 miles

M20

11: Stowting, Tiger (Kent) 3.7 miles

M25

16: Denham, Swan (Buckinghamshire) 0.75 miles

18: Chenies, Red Lion (Buckinghamshire) 2 miles; Flaunden, Bricklayers Arms (Hertfordshire) 4 miles

21A: Potters Crouch, Holly Bush (Hertfordshire) 2.3 miles

M27

1: Fritham, Royal Oak (Hampshire) 4 miles

M40

2: Hedgerley, White Horse (Buckinghamshire) 2.4 miles; Forty Green, Royal Standard of England (Buckinghamshire) 3.5 miles

12: Gaydon, Malt Shovel (Warwickshire) 0.9 miles

15: Barford, Granville (Warwickshire) 1.7 miles

M42

5: Barston, Malt Shovel (Warwickshire) 3 miles

6: Hampton in Arden, White Lion (Warwickshire) 1.25 miles

M50

3: Kilcot, Kilcot Inn (Gloucestershire) 2.3 miles

M62

25: Hartshead, Gray Ox (Yorkshire) 3.5 miles

MAPS

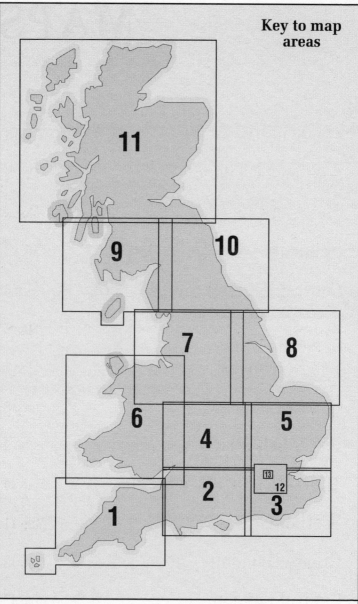

Key to map areas

11

9 **10**

7 **8**

6 **5**

4

2 **13** **12**

1 **3**

Reference to sectional maps

≋≋≋ Motorway		●	Main Entry
≋≋≋ Major road		◉	Main Entry with accommodation
⎯ ⎯ ⎯ County boundary		■	Place name to assist navigation

1

- ● Main Entry
- ⊙ Main Entry with accommodation
- ■ Place name to assist navigation

Channel Islands

ALDERNEY

FRANCE

ST PETER PORT ■
GUERNSEY
SARK

JERSEY

ST HELIER ■

0   10
Miles

— 7
— 6
— 5
— 4
— 3
— 2
— 1

3   4   5   6   7   8   9   1   2   3

The Scilly Isles

ST MARTIN'S
Tresco ■
SV
ST MARY'S

— 1

ST AGNES
9

0   3
MILES

Morwenstow ⊙ — 1

BUDE ■   A3072

A39

Wainhouse Corner ⊙ — 9

Boscastle ●
LAUNCESTO ■

Port Isaac ⊙ — 8

A395

St Merryn ● — 7   Blisland ●

WADEBRIDGE ■   BODMIN ■   CORNWALL

A30   LISKEARD ■

NEWQUAY ■ — 6   Lanlivery ⊙ ⊙ Lostwithiel

A390

SW   Trevaunance Cove ⊙   Mitchell ⊙   A387

Porthtowan ●   ST AUSTELL ■   FOWEY ■ ● Crafth

TRURO ■   Polkerris ● — 5   Polperro ●

Gurnards Head ■ — 4   REDRUTH ■   Devoran ●
Perranwell ■   Philleigh ■

Penzance ●   Mylor Bridge ●
FALMOUTH ■

Mousehole ⊙   Perranuthnoe ⊙   Constantine ⊙ — 3
A394   Helston ■
A3083

Cadgwith ● — 2

— 1

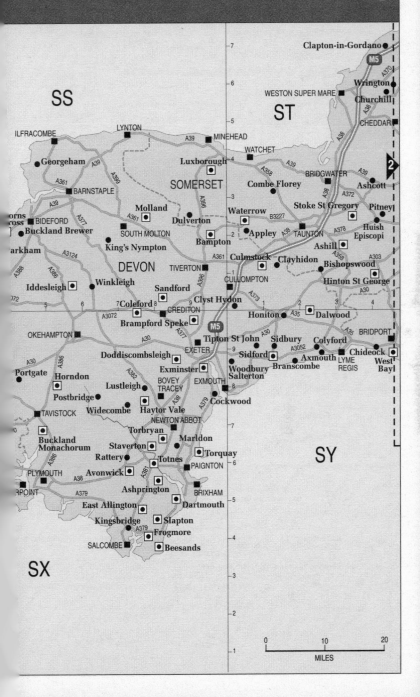

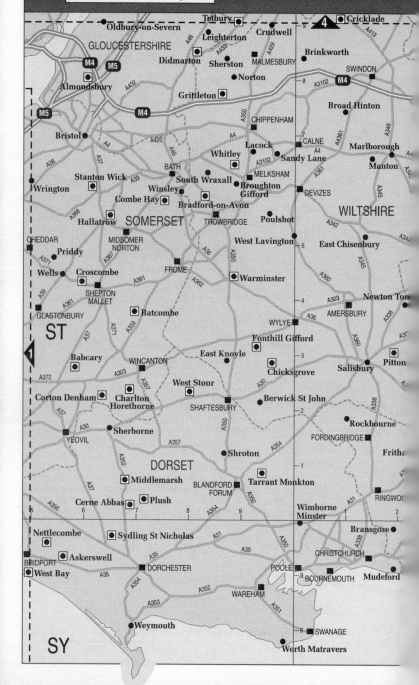

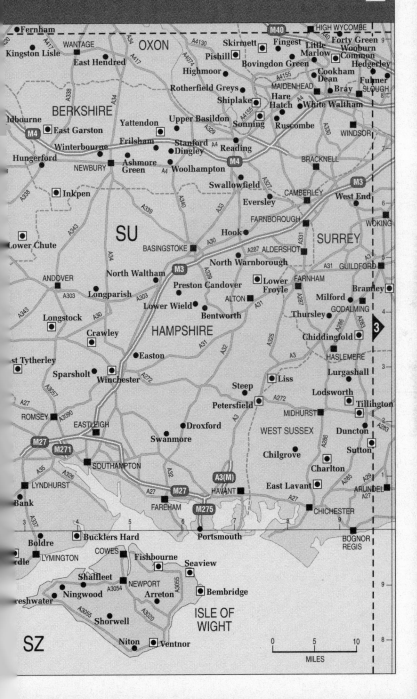

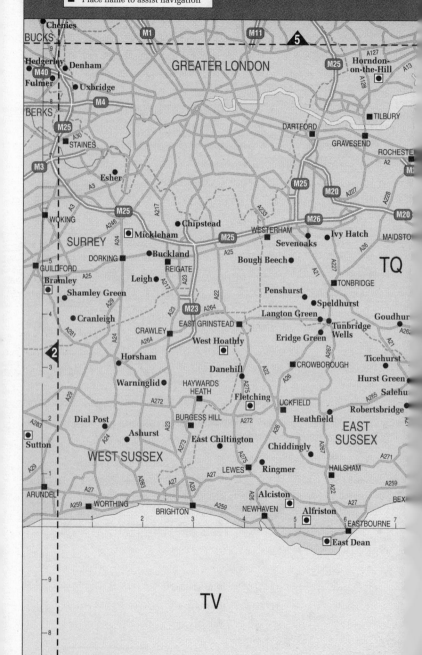

3

- ● Main Entry
- ◉ Main Entry with accommodation
- ■ Place name to assist navigation

BUCKS

● Chenies

M1

M11

▲5

Hedgerley ●
M40
Fulmer ●

Denham ●

Horndon-
on-the-Hill
A127
A13
◉

M25

GREATER LONDON

● Uxbridge

M4

BERKS

9
M25

A30
■ STAINES

M4

DARTFORD ■

TILBURY ■

GRAVESEND ■

ROCHESTE

M3

● Esher

A3

A2

M:

M25

A217

M25

WESTERHAM ■

M26

M20

A227

M20

WOKING ■

A3

A246

● Chipstead

SURREY

◉ Mickleham

M25

A24

DORKING ■

● Buckland

A25

Sevenoaks ●

Ivy Hatch ●

A26

MAIDSTO

TQ

GUILDFORD
5
■

● Shamley Green

A25

Leigh ●

REIGATE
■

A23

Bough Beech ●

A21

A227

TONBRIDGE ■

Bramley
◉

A281

● Cranleigh

A29

A271

M23

A264

EAST GRINSTEAD ■

Penshurst ●

Speldhurst ●

Langton Green ●

Goudhur ●

A26

▲2
4

A24

CRAWLEY ■

A264

● Horsham

● West Hoathly ◉

Eridge Green ●

Tunbridge
Wells ◉

A267

Ticehurst ●

Hurst Green ●

A21

3

● Warninglid

HAYWARDS
HEATH ■

● Danehill

A22

CROWBOROUGH ■

A26

Salehu ●

A265

A23

A272

Fletching ◉

UCKFIELD ■

Robertsbridge ●

● Dial Post

A24

A272

BURGESS HILL ■

A272

Heathfield ●

EAST
SUSSEX

Sutton ◉

A29

● Ashurst

A23

A273

A26

A367

A271

WEST SUSSEX

● East Chiltington

Chiddingly ●

HAILSHAM ■

A283

A27

A259

ARUNDEL ■

A27

LEWES ■

● Ringmer

A275

A26

A22

BEX

A259

A259

WORTHING ■

BRIGHTON ■

A259

● Alciston
◉

NEWHAVEN ■

Alfriston
◉

A27

6
EASTBOURNE ■
7

◉ East Dean

1   2   3   4   5

TV

9

8

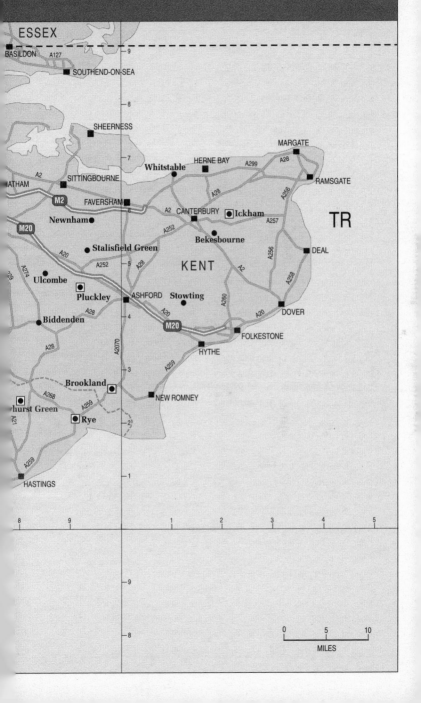

3

ESSEX

BASILDON A127

SOUTHEND-ON-SEA

SHEERNESS

MARGATE

HERNE BAY   A299   A28

Whitstable

SITTINGBOURNE   A2   RAMSGATE

ATHAM   A2   A256

M2

FAVERSHAM   A2   CANTERBURY   ⊙ Ickham

A28

Newnham ●   A257

M20   Bekesbourne   TR

A20   A252   A256

Stalisfield Green   DEAL

A274   A252   A28   KENT   A2   A258

Ulcombe ●   A28

□ Pluckley   ASHFORD   Stowting   A260

Biddenden ●   A28   A20   DOVER

A28   A20   A20

A2070   **M20**   FOLKESTONE

Brookland   A259   HYTHE

A268   A259

hurst Green   A259   □ Rye   NEW ROMNEY

A21

A259

HASTINGS

8   9   1   2   3   4   5

0   5   10

MILES

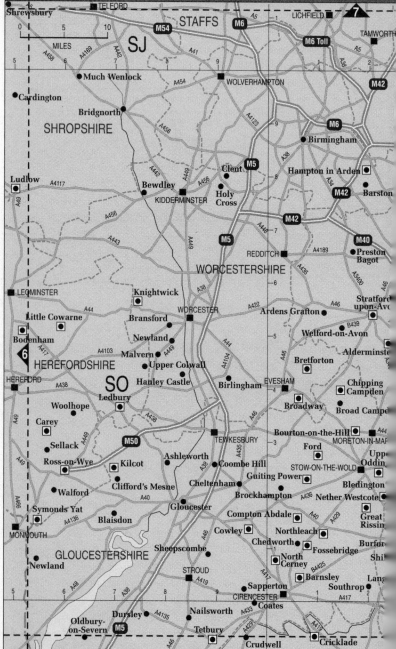

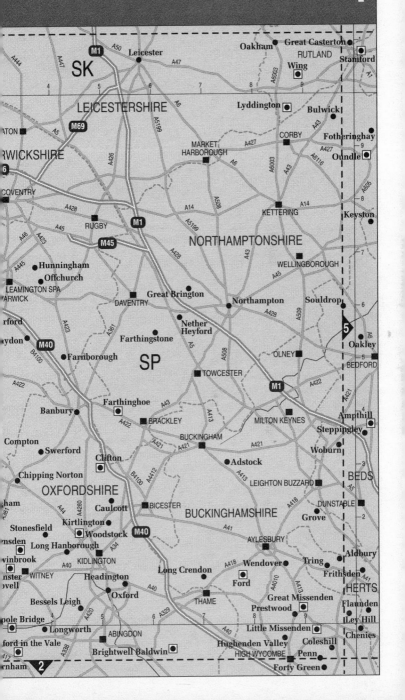

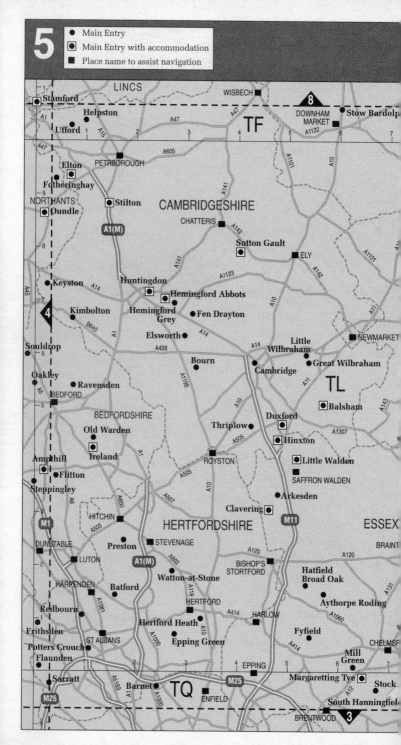

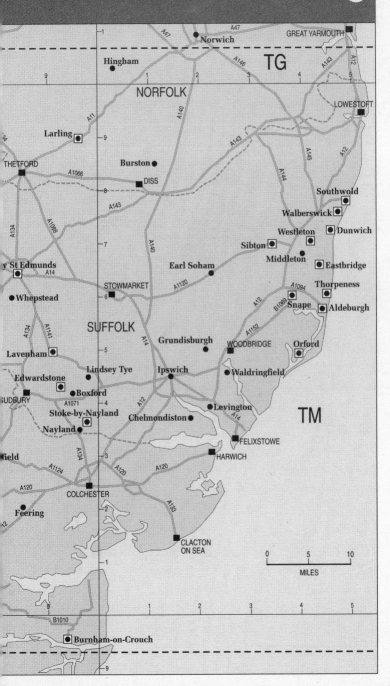

5

GREAT YARMOUTH

Norwich · A47 · A47

Hingham ·

TG

A11

A140 · A146 · A143 · A12

LOWESTOFT

Larling ·

A145 · A12

Burston ·   DISS

THETFORD · A1066 · A143

A149 · A144 · A145

Southwold

Walberswick

Westleton **Dunwich**

Sibton

Middleton

Eastbridge

y St Edmunds · A14 · Earl Soham

STOWMARKET · A1120

· Whepstead

Thorpeness

A1094

A12 B1069 **Snape** **Aldeburgh**

SUFFOLK

A1152

Orford

Lavenham · Grundisburgh

WOODBRIDGE

Lindsey Tye Ipswich

Edwardstone **Waldringfield**

·Boxford

GUDBURY · A1071

Stoke-by-Nayland **Levington**

Chelmondiston·

Nayland

TM

FELIXSTOWE

field · A134

HARWICH

A1124 · A120

COLCHESTER

· Feering

A133

CLACTON ON SEA

0   5   10
MILES

·**Burnham-on-Crouch**

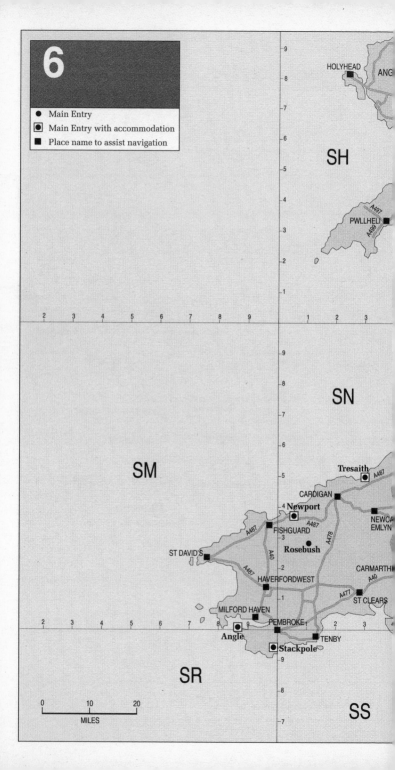

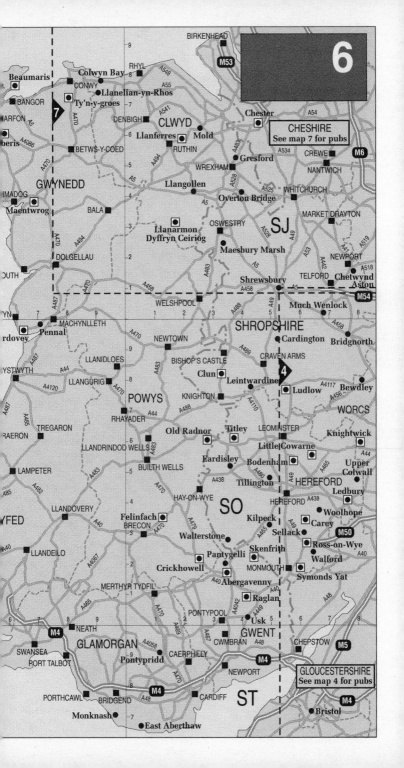

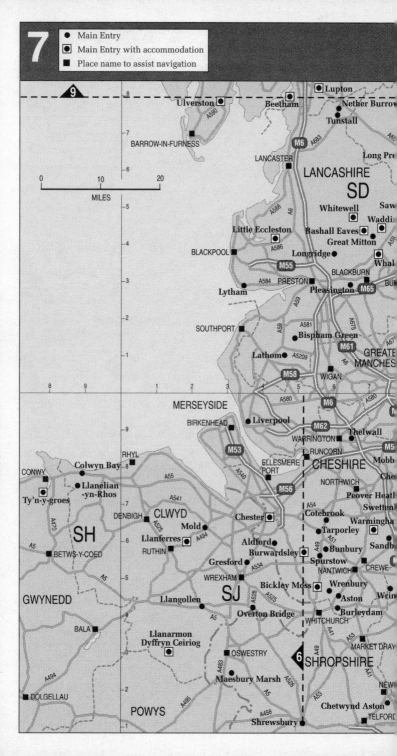

7

● Main Entry
◉ Main Entry with accommodation
■ Place name to assist navigation

9

Ulverston

Beetham

Lupton

Nether Burrow

Tunstall

BARROW-IN-FURNESS

LANCASTER

Long Pre

LANCASHIRE

SD

0   10   20
MILES

Whitewell

Saw

Waddi

Little Eccleston

Bashall Eaves

Great Mitton

Whal

BLACKPOOL

Longridge

M55

BLACKBURN

A584 PRESTON

Pleasington

M65

BU

Lytham

Bispham Green

SOUTHPORT

GREATE

M61

Lathom

A5209

MANCHES

M58

WIGAN

MERSEYSIDE

M6

BIRKENHEAD

Liverpool

M62

Thelwall

WARRINGTON

RHYL

M53

RUNCORN

M5

Colwyn Bay

ELLESMERE
PORT

CHESHIRE

Mobb

CONWY

Llanelian
-yn-Rhos

A55

M56

Che

Ty'n-y-groes

NORTHWICH

Peover Heath

DENBIGH

A541

CLWYD

Cotebrook

Swettin

SH

Mold

Chester

Tarporley

Warmingha

BETWS-Y-COED

Llanferres

RUTHIN

A494

Aldford

Burwardsley

Bunbury

Sandb

Gresford

A534

Spurstow

CREWE

GWYNEDD

WREXHAM

SJ

Bickley Moss

NANTWICH

Llangollen

Wrenbury

Wrin

BALA

Overton Bridge

Aston

Burleydam

WHITCHURCH

Llanarmon
Dyffryn Ceiriog

MARKET DRAY

OSWESTRY

6 SHROPSHIRE

A494

POWYS

Maesbury Marsh

NEW

DOLGELLAU

Chetwynd Aston

TELFOR

Shrewsbury

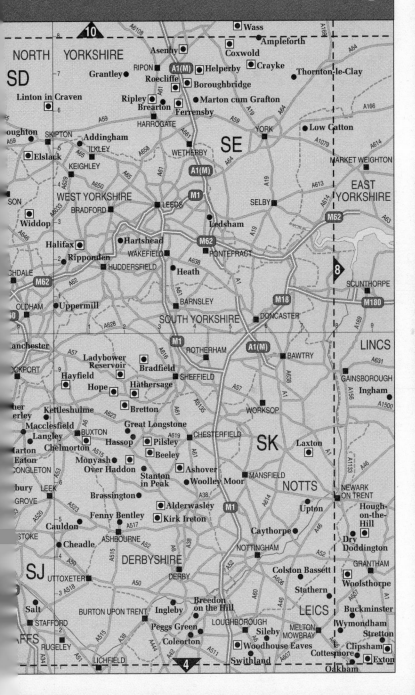

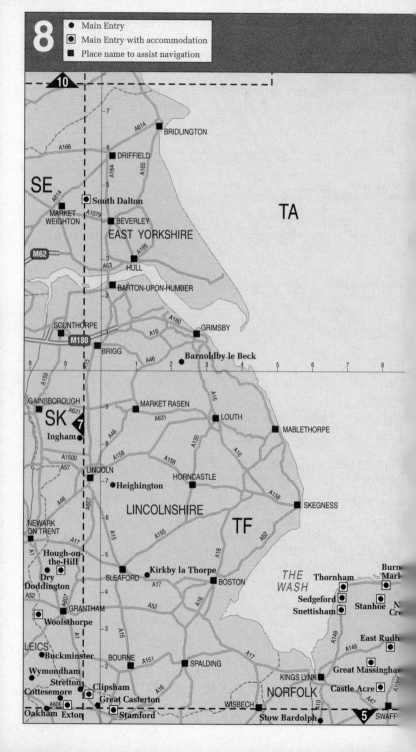

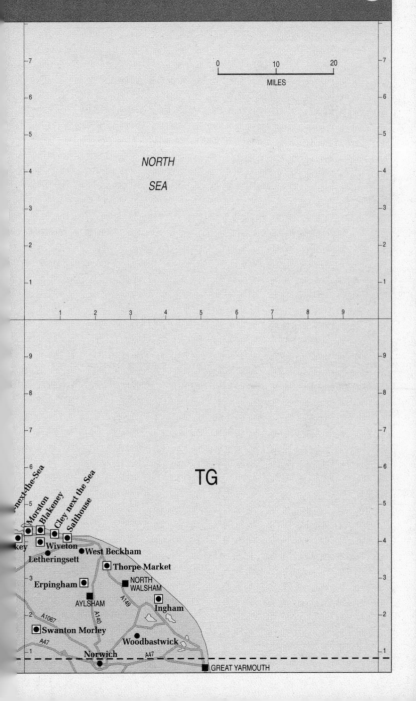

8

NORTH

SEA

TG

...e-next-the-Sea
Morston
Blakeney
Cley next the Sea
Salthouse
...key
Wiveton
West Beckham
Letheringsett
Thorpe Market
Erpingham
NORTH
WALSHAM
AYLSHAM
Ingham
A149
A1067
A140
Swanton Morley
Woodbastwick
A47
Norwich
AA7
GREAT YARMOUTH

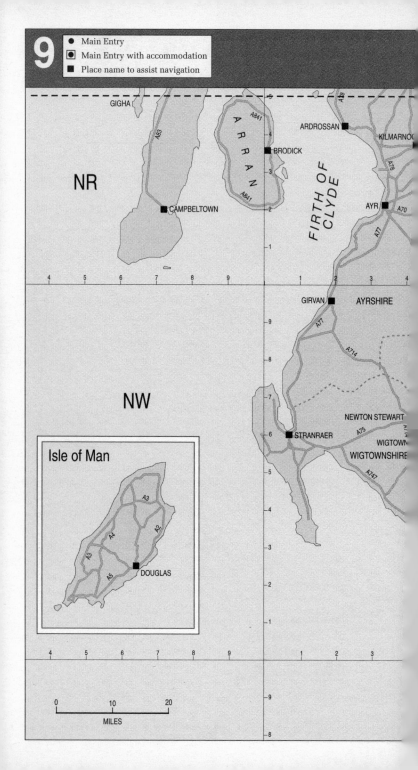

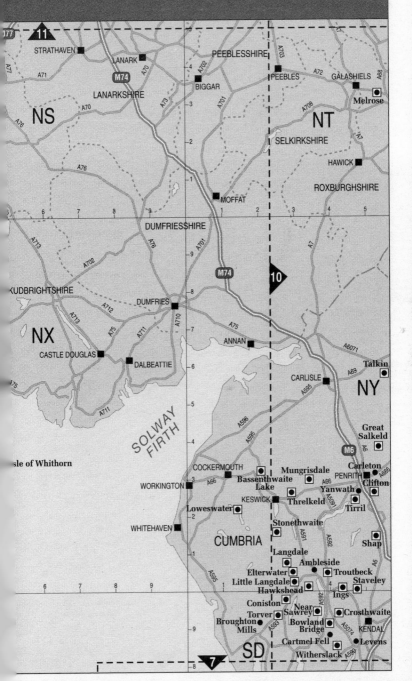

11

M77

STRATHAVEN
A77
A71
A71
LANARK
M74
A70
A70
LANARKSHIRE
A73
BIGGAR
A702
A701
PEEBLESSHIRE
A703
PEEBLES
A72
GALASHIELS
A68
MELROSE

NS

A76

NT
SELKIRKSHIRE
A708
A7

HAWICK
ROXBURGHSHIRE

A76

MOFFAT

4 3 2 1

DUMFRIESSHIRE

6 7 8 9 1 2 3 4 5

A713

A702

KUDBRIGHTSHIRE

A712

DUMFRIES
A701
A76

M74

10

A713
A75
A711

NX

A710
A75

ANNAN

A6071

CASTLE DOUGLAS

DALBEATTIE

Talkin
NY

A711

CARLISLE
A89
A595

SOLWAY
FIRTH

A596
A595

Great
Salkeld

isle of Whithorn

COCKERMOUTH
A66
Bassenthwaite
Lake
Mungrisdale
Carleton
M6
A6
PENRITH
Clifton
A66
A596
WORKINGTON
KESWICK
Threlkeld
Yanwath
Tirril
A66
Loweswater
A591
Stonethwaite
A592
Shap
WHITEHAVEN
CUMBRIA
A6
Langdale
Ambleside
A595
Elterwater
Troutbeck
Little Langdale
Staveley
Hawkshead
Ings
A592
Coniston
Near
Crosthwaite
Torver
Sawrey
Broughton
Bowland
A5074
Mills
Bridge
KENDAL
Cartmel Fell
Levens
Witherslack
A590
SD

6 7 8 9

7

● Main Entry
◉ Main Entry with accommodation
■ Place name to assist navigation

11

BERWICKSHIRE Swinton BERWICK-UPON-TWEED

PEEBLES

GALASHIELS
Melrose KELSO COLDSTREAM

Seahouses

SELKIRKSHIRE Kirk Yetholm WOOLER

NT

JEDBURGH Newton by-the-S

HAWICK ALNWICK Lesbury

ROXBURGHSHIRE Alnmo

Weldon Bridge

DUMFRIESSHIRE OTTERBURN MORPETH

Stannersburn NORTHUMBERLAND

9 Wark

M74 Haltwhistle Haydon Bridge Anick Newburn New Y

BRAMPTON HEXHAM Corbridge NEWCASTLE UPON

CARLISLE Talkin Diptonmill GATESHE

NY Catton Hedley on the Hill CONSETT

M6 ALSTON Carterway Heads

Great Salkeld Durham DURHAM

Mungrisdale PENRITH BISHOP AUCKLAND

Threlkeld Carleton Romaldkirk Aycli

KESWICK Yanwath Clifton

Tirril CUMBRIA Cotherstone

Stonethwaite BARNARD CASTLE DARLINGTON

Shap BROUGH

Langdale SCOTCH CORNER

Elterwater Ambleside

Little Troutbeck M6 Ravenstonedale

Langdale Ings Staveley

Hawkshead Crosthwaite Grinton Downholme NOR

Coniston KENDAL Constable Burton

Torver Near Bowland Bridge Kirk

Sawrey Cartmel Fell Leyburn Fleeth

Witherslack Levens East Witton Pic

SD Beetham Lupton 7 Thornton Watlass

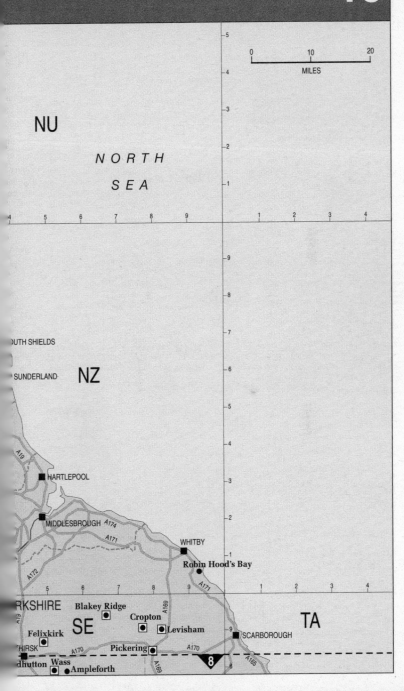

0   10   20

MILES

NU

N O R T H

S E A

—5

—4

—3

—2

—1

4   5   6   7   8   9   1   2   3   4

—9

—8

—7

OUTH SHIELDS

—6

SUNDERLAND   **NZ**

—5

—4

A19

—3

■ HARTLEPOOL

—2

■ MIDDLESBROUGH A174

A171

■ WHITBY   —1

A172   ● **Robin Hood's Bay**

5   6   7   8   9   A171

1   2   3   4

RKSHIRE   **Blakey Ridge**

A169

TA

SE   ◙ ● **Cropton**

◙ **Levisham**   —9

Felixkirk   ◙   ● ■ SCARBOROUGH

HIRSK ● A170   **Pickering** ◙   A170   A165

dhutton **Wass**   ⑧   —8

◙ ● **Ampleforth**   A169

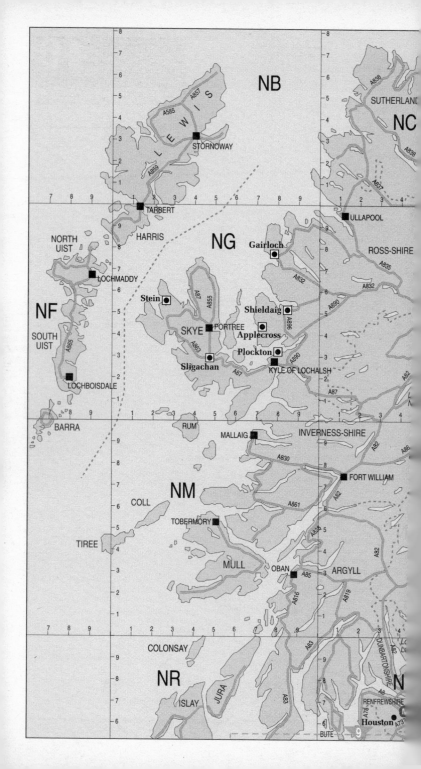

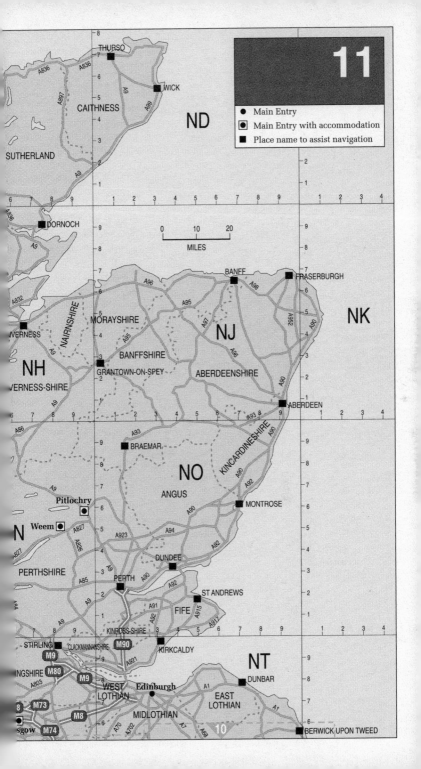

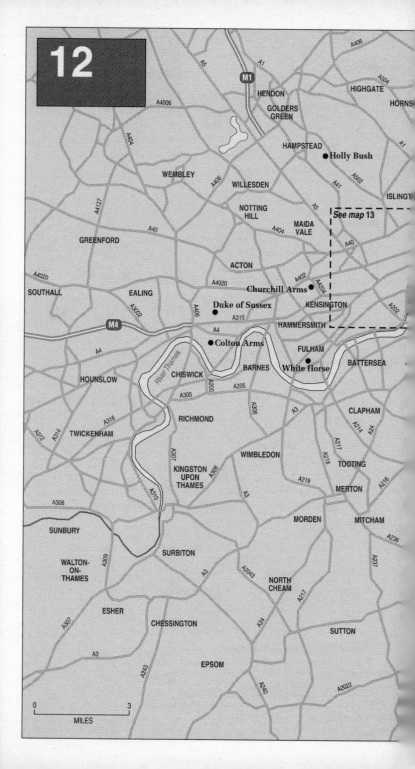

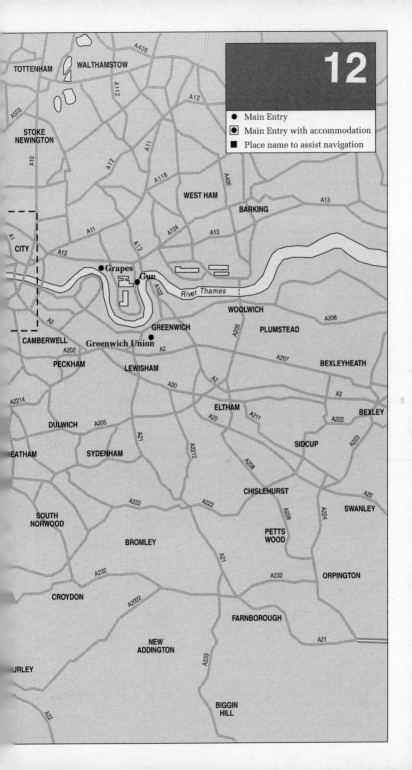

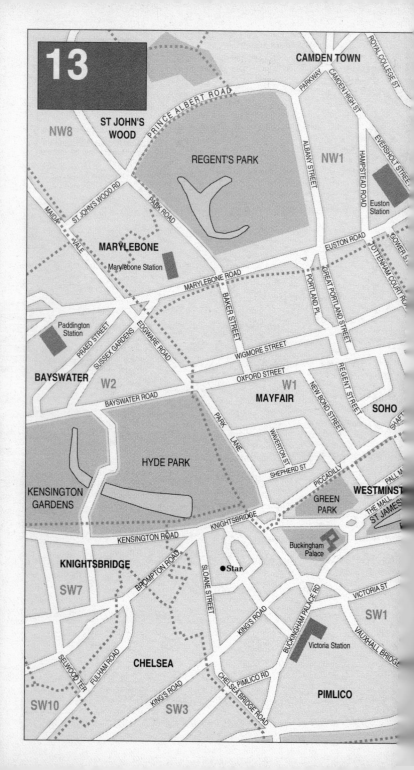

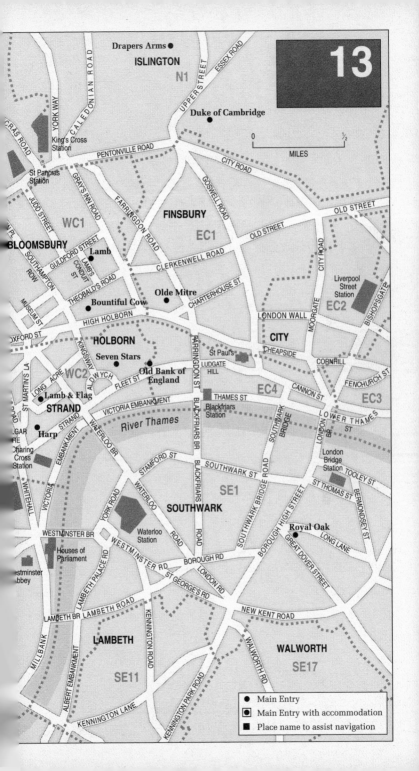

REPORT FORMS

We would very much appreciate hearing about your visits to pubs in this Guide, whether you have found them as described and recommend them for continued inclusion or noticed a fall in standards.

We'd also be glad to hear of any new pubs that you think we should know about. Readers reports are very valuable to us, and sometimes pubs are dropped simply because we have had no up-to-date news on them.

You can use the tear-out forms on the following pages, email us at feedback@goodguides.co.uk or send us comments via our website (www.thegoodpubguide.co.uk) or app. We include two types of forms: one for you to simply list pubs you have visited and confirm that our review is accurate, and the other for you to give us more detailed information on individual pubs. If you would like more forms, please write to us at:

The Good Pub Guide

FREEPOST TN1569

WADHURST

East Sussex TN5 7BR

Though we try to answer all letters, please understand if there's a delay (particularly in summer, our busiest period).

We'll assume we can print your name or initials as a recommender unless you tell us otherwise.

MAIN ENTRY OR 'ALSO WORTH A VISIT'?

Please try to gauge whether a pub should be a Main Entry or go in the Also Worth a Visit section (and tick the relevant box). Main Entries need to have qualities that would make it worth other readers' while to travel some distance to them. If a pub is an entirely new recommendation, the Also Worth a Visit section may be the best place for it to start its career in the *Guide* – to encourage other readers to report on it.

The more detail you can put into your description of a pub, the better. Any information on how good the landlord or landlady is, what it looks like inside, what you like about the atmosphere and character, the quality and type of food, which real ales are available and whether they're well kept, whether bedrooms are available, and how big/attractive the garden is. Other helpful information includes prices for food and bedrooms, food service and opening hours, and if children or dogs are welcome.

If the food or accommodation is outstanding, tick the FOOD AWARD or the STAY AWARD box.

If you're in a position to gauge a pub's suitability or otherwise for disabled people, do please tell us about that.

If you can, give the full address or directions for any pub not currently in the Guide – most of all, please give us its postcode. If we can't find a pub's postcode, we don't include it in the Guide

I have been to the following pubs in *The Good Pub Guide 2013* in the last few months, found them as described, and confirm that they deserve continued inclusion:

continued overleaf

PLEASE GIVE YOUR NAME AND ADDRESS ON THE BACK OF THIS FORM

Pubs visited continued..........

Your own name and address (block capitals please)

....

....

....

Postcode..

Please return to

The Good Pub Guide
FREEPOST TN1569
WADHURST
East Sussex
TN5 7BR

IF YOU PREFER, YOU CAN SEND
US REPORTS BY EMAIL:

feedback@goodguides.com

I have been to the following pubs in *The Good Pub Guide 2013* in the last few months, found them as described, and confirm that they deserve continued inclusion:

continued overleaf

PLEASE GIVE YOUR NAME AND ADDRESS ON THE BACK OF THIS FORM

Pubs visited continued..........

By returning this form, you consent to the collection, recording and use of the information you submit, by The Random House Group Ltd. Any personal details which you provide from which we can identify you are held and processed in accordance with the Data Protection Act 1998 and will not be passed on to any third parties. The Random House Group Ltd may wish to send you further information on their associated products.

Please tick box if you do not wish to receive any such information. ☐

Your own name and address (block capitals please)

....

....

....

Postcode...

In returning this form I confirm my agreement that the information I provide may be used by The Random House Group Ltd, its assignees and/or licensees in any media or medium whatsoever.

Please return to

The Good Pub Guide
FREEPOST TN1569
WADHURST
East Sussex
TN5 7BR

IF YOU PREFER, YOU CAN SEND
US REPORTS BY EMAIL:

feedback@goodguides.com

I have been to the following pubs in *The Good Pub Guide 2013* in the last few months, found them as described, and confirm that they deserve continued inclusion:

continued overleaf

PLEASE GIVE YOUR NAME AND ADDRESS ON THE BACK OF THIS FORM

Pubs visited continued..........

Your own name and address (block capitals please)

....

....

....

Postcode...

Please return to

The Good Pub Guide
FREEPOST TN1569
WADHURST
East Sussex
TN5 7BR

IF YOU PREFER, YOU CAN SEND
US REPORTS BY EMAIL:

feedback@goodguides.com

I have been to the following pubs in *The Good Pub Guide 2013* in the last few months, found them as described, and confirm that they deserve continued inclusion:

continued overleaf

PLEASE GIVE YOUR NAME AND ADDRESS ON THE BACK OF THIS FORM

Pubs visited continued..........

Your own name and address (block capitals please)

....

....

....

Postcode...

Please return to

The Good Pub Guide
FREEPOST TN1569
WADHURST
East Sussex
TN5 7BR

IF YOU PREFER, YOU CAN SEND
US REPORTS BY EMAIL:

feedback@goodguides.com

Report On (pub's name)

....

Pub's address

....

☐ YES MAIN ENTRY ☐ YES WORTH A VISIT ☐ NO don't include

Please tick one of these boxes to show your verdict, and give reasons,
descriptive comments, prices and the date of your visit

☐ Deserves **FOOD Award** ☐ Deserves **STAY Award** 2013:1

PLEASE GIVE YOUR NAME AND ADDRESS ON THE BACK OF THIS FORM

✂ ....

Report On (pub's name)

....

Pub's address

....

☐ YES MAIN ENTRY ☐ YES WORTH A VISIT ☐ NO don't include

Please tick one of these boxes to show your verdict, and give reasons,
descriptive comments, prices and the date of your visit

☐ Deserves **FOOD Award** ☐ Deserves **STAY Award** 2013:2

PLEASE GIVE YOUR NAME AND ADDRESS ON THE BACK OF THIS FORM

Your own name and address *(block capitals please)*

In returning this form I confirm my agreement that the information I provide may be used by The Random House Group Ltd, its assignees and/or licensees in any media or medium whatsoever.

DO NOT USE THIS SIDE OF THE PAGE FOR WRITING ABOUT PUBS

✂ ....

Your own name and address *(block capitals please)*

In returning this form I confirm my agreement that the information I provide may be used by The Random House Group Ltd, its assignees and/or licensees in any media or medium whatsoever.

DO NOT USE THIS SIDE OF THE PAGE FOR WRITING ABOUT PUBS

Report On   (pub's name)

....

Pub's address

....

☐ YES MAIN ENTRY   ☐ YES WORTH A VISIT   ☐ NO don't include

Please tick one of these boxes to show your verdict, and give reasons, descriptive comments, prices and the date of your visit

☐ Deserves **FOOD Award**   ☐ Deserves **STAY Award**   2013:3

PLEASE GIVE YOUR NAME AND ADDRESS ON THE BACK OF THIS FORM

✂ ....

Report On   (pub's name)

....

Pub's address

....

☐ YES MAIN ENTRY   ☐ YES WORTH A VISIT   ☐ NO don't include

Please tick one of these boxes to show your verdict, and give reasons, descriptive comments, prices and the date of your visit

☐ Deserves **FOOD Award**   ☐ Deserves **STAY Award**   2013:4

PLEASE GIVE YOUR NAME AND ADDRESS ON THE BACK OF THIS FORM

Your own name and address *(block capitals please)*

In returning this form I confirm my agreement that the information I provide may be used by The Random House Group Ltd, its assignees and/or licensees in any media or medium whatsoever.

DO NOT USE THIS SIDE OF THE PAGE FOR WRITING ABOUT PUBS

By returning this form, you consent to the collection, recording and use of the information you submit, by The Random House Group Ltd. Any personal details which you provide from which we can identify you are held and processed in accordance with the Data Protection Act 1998 and will not be passed on to any third parties. The Random House Group Ltd may wish to send you further information on their associated products. Please tick box if you do not wish to receive any such information.

✂ ....

Your own name and address *(block capitals please)*

In returning this form I confirm my agreement that the information I provide may be used by The Random House Group Ltd, its assignees and/or licensees in any media or medium whatsoever.

DO NOT USE THIS SIDE OF THE PAGE FOR WRITING ABOUT PUBS

By returning this form, you consent to the collection, recording and use of the information you submit, by The Random House Group Ltd. Any personal details which you provide from which we can identify you are held and processed in accordance with the Data Protection Act 1998 and will not be passed on to any third parties. The Random House Group Ltd may wish to send you further information on their associated products. Please tick box if you do not wish to receive any such information.

Report On (pub's name)

....

Pub's address

....

☐ YES MAIN ENTRY   ☐ YES WORTH A VISIT   ☐ NO don't include

Please tick one of these boxes to show your verdict, and give reasons, descriptive comments, prices and the date of your visit

☐ Deserves **FOOD Award**   ☐ Deserves **STAY Award**   2013:5

PLEASE GIVE YOUR NAME AND ADDRESS ON THE BACK OF THIS FORM

✂ ....

Report On (pub's name)

....

Pub's address

....

☐ YES MAIN ENTRY   ☐ YES WORTH A VISIT   ☐ NO don't include

Please tick one of these boxes to show your verdict, and give reasons, descriptive comments, prices and the date of your visit

☐ Deserves **FOOD Award**   ☐ Deserves **STAY Award**   2013:6

PLEASE GIVE YOUR NAME AND ADDRESS ON THE BACK OF THIS FORM

Your own name and address *(block capitals please)*

In returning this form I confirm my agreement that the information I provide may be used by The Random House Group Ltd, its assignees and/or licensees in any media or medium whatsoever.

DO NOT USE THIS SIDE OF THE PAGE FOR WRITING ABOUT PUBS

By returning this form, you consent to the collection, recording and use of the information you submit, by The Random House Group Ltd. Any personal details which you provide from which we can identify you are held and processed in accordance with the Data Protection Act 1998 and will not be passed on to any third parties. The Random House Group Ltd may wish to send you further information on their associated products. Please tick box if you do not wish to receive any such information.

✂ ....

Your own name and address *(block capitals please)*

In returning this form I confirm my agreement that the information I provide may be used by The Random House Group Ltd, its assignees and/or licensees in any media or medium whatsoever.

DO NOT USE THIS SIDE OF THE PAGE FOR WRITING ABOUT PUBS

By returning this form, you consent to the collection, recording and use of the information you submit, by The Random House Group Ltd. Any personal details which you provide from which we can identify you are held and processed in accordance with the Data Protection Act 1998 and will not be passed on to any third parties. The Random House Group Ltd may wish to send you further information on their associated products. Please tick box if you do not wish to receive any such information.

Report On (pub's name)

....

Pub's address

....

☐ YES MAIN ENTRY ☐ YES WORTH A VISIT ☐ NO don't include

Please tick one of these boxes to show your verdict, and give reasons, descriptive comments, prices and the date of your visit

☐ Deserves **FOOD Award** ☐ Deserves **STAY Award** 2013:7

PLEASE GIVE YOUR NAME AND ADDRESS ON THE BACK OF THIS FORM

✂ ....

Report On (pub's name)

....

Pub's address

....

☐ YES MAIN ENTRY ☐ YES WORTH A VISIT ☐ NO don't include

Please tick one of these boxes to show your verdict, and give reasons, descriptive comments, prices and the date of your visit

☐ Deserves **FOOD Award** ☐ Deserves **STAY Award** 2013:8

PLEASE GIVE YOUR NAME AND ADDRESS ON THE BACK OF THIS FORM

Your own name and address *(block capitals please)*

In returning this form I confirm my agreement that the information I provide may be used by The Random House Group Ltd, its assignees and/or licensees in any media or medium whatsoever.

DO NOT USE THIS SIDE OF THE PAGE FOR WRITING ABOUT PUBS

By returning this form, you consent to the collection, recording and use of the information you submit, by The Random House Group Ltd. Any personal details which you provide from which we can identify you are held and processed in accordance with the Data Protection Act 1998 and will not be passed on to any third parties. The Random House Group Ltd may wish to send you further information on their associated products. Please tick box if you do not wish to receive any such information.

✂ ···

Your own name and address *(block capitals please)*

In returning this form I confirm my agreement that the information I provide may be used by The Random House Group Ltd, its assignees and/or licensees in any media or medium whatsoever.

DO NOT USE THIS SIDE OF THE PAGE FOR WRITING ABOUT PUBS

By returning this form, you consent to the collection, recording and use of the information you submit, by The Random House Group Ltd. Any personal details which you provide from which we can identify you are held and processed in accordance with the Data Protection Act 1998 and will not be passed on to any third parties. The Random House Group Ltd may wish to send you further information on their associated products. Please tick box if you do not wish to receive any such information.

Report On (pub's name)

....

Pub's address

....

☐ YES MAIN ENTRY ☐ YES WORTH A VISIT ☐ NO don't include

Please tick one of these boxes to show your verdict, and give reasons,
descriptive comments, prices and the date of your visit

☐ Deserves **FOOD Award** ☐ Deserves **STAY Award** 2013:9

PLEASE GIVE YOUR NAME AND ADDRESS ON THE BACK OF THIS FORM

✂ ....

Report On (pub's name)

....

Pub's address

....

☐ YES MAIN ENTRY ☐ YES WORTH A VISIT ☐ NO don't include

Please tick one of these boxes to show your verdict, and give reasons,
descriptive comments, prices and the date of your visit

☐ Deserves **FOOD Award** ☐ Deserves **STAY Award** 2013:10

PLEASE GIVE YOUR NAME AND ADDRESS ON THE BACK OF THIS FORM

Your own name and address *(block capitals please)*

In returning this form I confirm my agreement that the information I provide may be used by The Random House Group Ltd, its assignees and/or licensees in any media or medium whatsoever.

✂ ....

Your own name and address *(block capitals please)*

In returning this form I confirm my agreement that the information I provide may be used by The Random House Group Ltd, its assignees and/or licensees in any media or medium whatsoever.

Report On　　　　　　　　　　　　　　　　　　　　　(pub's name)

....

Pub's address

....

☐ YES MAIN ENTRY　　☐ YES WORTH A VISIT　　☐ NO don't include

Please tick one of these boxes to show your verdict, and give reasons,
descriptive comments, prices and the date of your visit

☐ Deserves **FOOD Award**　　☐ Deserves **STAY Award**　　　2013:11

PLEASE GIVE YOUR NAME AND ADDRESS ON THE BACK OF THIS FORM

✂ ....

Report On　　　　　　　　　　　　　　　　　　　　　(pub's name)

....

Pub's address

....

☐ YES MAIN ENTRY　　☐ YES WORTH A VISIT　　☐ NO don't include

Please tick one of these boxes to show your verdict, and give reasons,
descriptive comments, prices and the date of your visit

☐ Deserves **FOOD Award**　　☐ Deserves **STAY Award**　　　2013:12

PLEASE GIVE YOUR NAME AND ADDRESS ON THE BACK OF THIS FORM

Your own name and address *(block capitals please)*

In returning this form I confirm my agreement that the information I provide may be used by The Random House Group Ltd, its assignees and/or licensees in any media or medium whatsoever.

DO NOT USE THIS SIDE OF THE PAGE FOR WRITING ABOUT PUBS

By returning this form, you consent to the collection, recording and use of the information you submit, by The Random House Group Ltd. Any personal details which you provide from which we can identify you are held and processed in accordance with the Data Protection Act 1998 and will not be passed on to any third parties. The Random House Group Ltd may wish to send you further information on their associated products. Please tick box if you do not wish to receive any such information.

✂ ....

Your own name and address *(block capitals please)*

In returning this form I confirm my agreement that the information I provide may be used by The Random House Group Ltd, its assignees and/or licensees in any media or medium whatsoever.

DO NOT USE THIS SIDE OF THE PAGE FOR WRITING ABOUT PUBS

By returning this form, you consent to the collection, recording and use of the information you submit, by The Random House Group Ltd. Any personal details which you provide from which we can identify you are held and processed in accordance with the Data Protection Act 1998 and will not be passed on to any third parties. The Random House Group Ltd may wish to send you further information on their associated products. Please tick box if you do not wish to receive any such information.

Report On (pub's name)

....

Pub's address

....

☐ YES MAIN ENTRY   ☐ YES WORTH A VISIT   ☐ NO don't include

Please tick one of these boxes to show your verdict, and give reasons,
descriptive comments, prices and the date of your visit

☐ Deserves **FOOD Award**   ☐ Deserves **STAY Award**   2013:13

PLEASE GIVE YOUR NAME AND ADDRESS ON THE BACK OF THIS FORM

✂ ....

Report On (pub's name)

....

Pub's address

....

☐ YES MAIN ENTRY   ☐ YES WORTH A VISIT   ☐ NO don't include

Please tick one of these boxes to show your verdict, and give reasons,
descriptive comments, prices and the date of your visit

☐ Deserves **FOOD Award**   ☐ Deserves **STAY Award**   2013:14

PLEASE GIVE YOUR NAME AND ADDRESS ON THE BACK OF THIS FORM

Your own name and address *(block capitals please)*

In returning this form I confirm my agreement that the information I provide may be used by The Random House Group Ltd, its assignees and/or licensees in any media or medium whatsoever.

DO NOT USE THIS SIDE OF THE PAGE FOR WRITING ABOUT PUBS

By returning this form, you consent to the collection, recording and use of the information you submit, by The Random House Group Ltd. Any personal details which you provide from which we can identify you are held and processed in accordance with the Data Protection Act 1998 and will not be passed on to any third parties. The Random House Group Ltd may wish to send you further information on their associated products. Please tick box if you do not wish to receive any such information. ☐

✂ ....

Your own name and address *(block capitals please)*

In returning this form I confirm my agreement that the information I provide may be used by The Random House Group Ltd, its assignees and/or licensees in any media or medium whatsoever.

DO NOT USE THIS SIDE OF THE PAGE FOR WRITING ABOUT PUBS

By returning this form, you consent to the collection, recording and use of the information you submit, by The Random House Group Ltd. Any personal details which you provide from which we can identify you are held and processed in accordance with the Data Protection Act 1998 and will not be passed on to any third parties. The Random House Group Ltd may wish to send you further information on their associated products. Please tick box if you do not wish to receive any such information. ☐